ISBN 978-0-331-94336-8
PIBN 11033459

FB &c Ltd, Dalton House, 60 Windsor Avenue, London, SW19 2RR.
Company number 08720141. Registered in England and Wales.

For support please visit www.forgottenbooks.com

A UNIVERSAL

ENGLISH-GERMAN AND GERMAN-ENGLISH

DICTIONARY

BY

DR. FELIX FLÜGEL.

TWO PARTS IN THREE VOLUMES.

FOURTH, ENTIRELY REMODELLED, EDITION

OF DR. J. G. FLÜGEL'S

COMPLETE DICTIONARY OF THE ENGLISH AND GERMAN LANGUAGES.

Allgemeines

Englisch-Deutsches und Deutsch-Englisches

Wörterbuch

von

Dr. Felix Flügel.

Zwei Theile in drei Bänden.

Zweiter verbesserter und vermehrter Abdruck

der

Vierten gänzlich umgearbeiteten Auflage

von Dr. J. G. Flügel's

Vollständigem Wörterbuch der englischen und deutschen Sprache.

Zweiter Theil:

Deutsch-Englisch.

Braunschweig.

George Westermann.

1894.

Vorwort.

Das vorliegende deutsch-englische Wörterbuch verdankt die Hauptelemente seines Bestandes neben den lexicalischen Sammlungen, welche in ihren Anfängen bereits von Dr. **J. G. Flügel**, dem Vater des Verfassers, sowie vom Verfasser selbst angelegt worden waren und zu großem Theile den deutsch-englischen Wörterbüchern von Dr. **K. W. Meißner** (Vol. II der 3. Aufl. von Dr. J. G. Flügel's Complete Dictionary), sowie dem 2. Theile von Dr. **Felix Flügel's** Practical Dictionary als erste Grundlage dienten, einer Reihe von Werken, welche theils in den Vorreden zu den ebengenannten deutsch-englischen Wörterbüchern aufgezählt werden, theils weiter unten zu nennen sind. Die erwähnten Sammlungen* sind seit dem Abschlusse jener Werke vom Verfasser stetig bis zum Jahre 1878 fortgeführt worden und, soweit es der leider sehr beschränkte Raum zuließ, von einem langjährigen lieben Freunde des Verfassers, dem Prof. **Felix Liebrecht** in Lüttich, mit großem Zeitopfer und Hintansetzung eigener wichtiger Arbeiten diesem deutsch-englischen Theile einverleibt worden; seine genaue Kenntniß der Feinheiten der englischen Sprache befähigte ihn ganz besonders zu dieser Aufgabe, für deren Durchführung (welche ihren Abschluß in dem genannten Jahre erreichte) ihm aufrichtigster Dank zu zollen ist. Diese Vorarbeit wurde vom Verfasser aufs genaueste geprüft, durchgearbeitet und vervollständigt. Benutzt wurden außerdem, obwol in geringerem Maße, der deutsch-englische Theil des Wörterbuches von **Hilpert**, sowie der des **Lucas**. Das Werk des Hilpert oder vielmehr seiner fleißigen Fortsetzer (ich spreche hier immer nur vom II., deutsch-englischen Theile) erschien erst 1845, zwölf Jahre nach Hilpert's Tode, und ist ausgezeichnet in seiner Art, noch vielfach brauchbar, wenn auch von der Zeit in manchen Puncten überholt. Der bereits 1843 als grober Plagiarius überführte Grieb ist nicht auf eine Linie mit dem von ihm ausgeschriebenen Hilpert zu stellen. — Was die Benutzung des Lucas'schen Werkes anlangt, so ist dieselbe stets in den Grenzen des litterarischen Anstandes geblieben, welche umgekehrt Lucas selbst bei der vielfach buchstäblichen Ausschreiberei der beiden oben zuerst genannten Werke nicht einzuhalten verstanden hat; ein Umstand, welchen niemand ahnen kann, der bloß seine Vorrede liest, und welchen auch die sogenannte Kritik in den langen Jahren seit Erscheinen des Lucas'schen Werkes nicht bemerkt oder beachtet hat. Wie beim I. (englisch-deutschen) Theile hat Lucas einige Werke ohne jede Nennung der Namen

---

* Der Hauptsache nach vom Verf. des vorliegenden Buches gemacht; dieselben beziehen sich natürlich in beschränkterem Maße auf die älteren großen Namen der deutschen Litteratur, welche ja in den unten zu nennenden Hauptwerken der deutschen Lexicographie die erste Stelle einnehmen; daher Anführungen aus Luther, Schiller, Göthe rc. zumeist (nicht ausnahmslos) aus diesen lexicalischen Werken entlehnt sind; der Verf. fußt jedoch nicht allein auf diesen Wörterbüchern, sondern hatte Anlaß zu einer bescheidenen Nachlese, welche sich auf die eben genannten Namen, sowie namentlich auf eine Auswahl aus den Werken folgender Schriftsteller bezieht: Hagedorn, Kleist, Gellert, Gleim, Klopstock, Lessing, Wieland, Jean Paul, Schubart, Claudius, Hölty, Voß, Salis, Matthisson, Seume, Körner, Eichendorff, Arndt, Chamisso, Uhland, Rückert, H. Heine, Lenau, J. Mosen, Freiligrath, Geibel, Herwegh, Hartmann, G. Freytag, Auerbach u. s. w.

ausgenutzt: dazu gehören besonders die technologischen Werke, deren jedes allgemeine Wörterbuch allerdings nicht mehr entbehren kann, deren mühselige Arbeit aber doch wol um so mehr wenigstens Namensnennung verdient. Von diesen sind hier besonders zu erwähnen: Technologisches Wörterbuch der deutschen, französischen und englischen Sprache, von Hofrath **J. A. Beil.** Wiesbaden, 1853; sowie: Technisches Taschen-Wörterbuch für Industrie und Handel, 1. Theil (deutsch-englisch-französisch), Wiesbaden, 1873 (bildet einen Auszug aus der 2. Auflage des Beil'schen Werkes); ferner: Dr. **Tolhausen** &c., Technologisches Wörterbuch in deutscher, französischer und englischer Sprache. Paris, 1855 (2. Aufl. Leipzig, 1874/75), ein sehr umfassendes, treffliches Werk; Dr. **Carl Hartmann,** Handwörterbuch der Berg-, Hütten- und Salzwerkskunde, 3. Aufl. Weimar, 1860; Dr. **J. G. Flügel,** Kaufmännisches Wörterbuch in drei Sprachen, 2. Theil (deutsch-englisch-französisch), 2. Aufl. bearbeitet von Dr. Felix Flügel. Leipzig, 1853; Deutsch-englisches Handelscorrespondenz-Lexicon von **Friedrich Noback** und **Thomas John Graham.** Leipzig, 1865, ein besonders Kaufleuten sehr zu empfehlendes, mit großer Umsicht und Genauigkeit gearbeitetes Werkchen, welches ausgiebig zu benutzen der Verfasser um so weniger Anstand genommen hat, als er wiederholt nur seine eigenen Beiträge entlehnt hat; von **Pierer's** bekanntem Universal-Lexicon wurden die neueren Auflagen benutzt; in geringerem Maße wurde **Meyer's** Conversations-Lexicon und eine Anzahl anderer Werke zu Rathe gezogen.

Daß von deutschen Wörterbüchern **Grimm's** Nationalwerk, soweit es erschienen war, sowie **Weigand's** treffliches Wörterbuch benutzt worden ist, wird Jedermann voraussetzen; sie sind oft genug im Werke selbst angeführt. Auch ist hier das einzige Buch, dessen Benutzung Lucas ausdrücklich erwähnt, als beständiger practischer und zuverlässiger Rathgeber zu nennen: **Sanders'** deutsches Wörterbuch, ein Werk außerordentlichen Fleißes und ein fast unerschöpflicher Schatz von Belegen aus der neueren und neuesten Zeit, aus welchen oft überraschende Belehrung in grammatischen und anderen Beziehungen fließt.

Was ein noch mannigfach im Argen liegendes Gebiet aller neueren Lexicographie anlangt, nämlich die naturhistorischen und medicinischen Ausdrücke, so muß ich besonders des thätigen Antheiles dankbar eingedenk sein, welchen mein ältester Sohn, **Alfred Flügel** (Dr. med., † als Arzt zu Siebenlehn 22. Jan. 1890), an der oft sehr mühseligen Prüfung und Zusammentragung dieser Ausdrücke, sowie namentlich an der Berichtigung mancher alten Irrthümer genommen hat, welche in den Wörterbüchern ihr Wesen treiben und aus einem Werke in das andere sich fortpflanzen.

PREFACE.

The present German-English Dictionary is based on the lexical collections begun many years ago by my father, Dr. J. G. Flügel, the author of the Complete Dictionary of the English and German Languages, who intended to add a German-English part to that Dictionary. The working out of the English-German part proved however so laborious, that no time was left for executing the second task, and thus the addition of the German-English part for the first three editions had to be entrusted to other editors, Drs Sporschil and N. W. Meissner. After the lapse of many years the undersigned who had greatly enlarged the original collections, undertook to remodel the inadequate work of the editors mentioned. The result has been before the public since 1852, when the German-English part of "Felix Flügel's Practical Dictionary" appeared, a book of which fifteen editions have since been printed. Besides the solid basis of this work which had cost no common amount of steady labour, ample materials for a larger work had been brought together by the present author up to recent times. These materials were made over to a friend, Prof. Liebrecht, of Lüttich, whose thorough knowledge of the English language and literature fitted him for the task, while the author was busily engaged with the English-German part; but the time Prof. Liebrecht could spare was so limited that he was obliged to give up the labour before 1878, leaving for the present author thorough revision, and in many points a complete re-cast of the work done. The German works consulted in constructing the work are mentioned in the German preface below, where the debt to the great national work of Grimm (as far as it had appeared), the excellent smaller German Dictionary of Weigand, the Technological Dictionaries, and others, are duly acknowledged. The admirable collections of Sanders' "Wörterbuch der Deutschen Sprache", brought together with stupendous diligence, and arranged with critical acumen, offered also an inexhaustible treasury of apt quotations, and the author regrets that the limits prescribed to the German-English part of the present dictionary, prevented him from making a more extensive use of the materials brought together in the storehouses named. In fact the author's own collections could not be embodied to their full extent, although he has ventured to offer a modest after-gleaning of quotations from the works of Luther, Lessing, Schiller, and Göthe, and to call the attention of the reader to many a less familiar name, for example Hagedorn, Kleist, Gellert, Gleim, Klopstock, Wieland, Jean Paul, Schubart, Claudius, Hölty, Voss, Salis, Matthisson, Seume, Körner, de la Motte Fouqué, Eichendorff, Arndt, Chamisso, Uhland, Rückert, H. Heine, Lenau, J. Mosen, Freiligrath, Geibel, Herwegh, Hartmann, G. Freytag, Auerbach.

Leipzig.

Felix Flügel.

PREFACE

to the second reprint of the fourth edition.

It is the constant endeavour of the author, and as well of the publisher, of the present work so to improve it as to keep pace with the progress of the day. As the book is stereotyped, it was necessary to contract or even to omit altogether less important articles in order to give space for a number

Explanation of Abbreviations, Marks of Pronunciation, &c.

I.

English Abbreviations.

abbr. für abbreviated; abbreviation.
Abp. - Archbishop.
Ac. - academical (term, &c.).
Acc. - Accusative.
Acoust. - acoustics.
adj. - adjective.
adv. - adverb; adverbially.
Aer. - aerology.
Agr., Agric. - term used in agriculture.
Alch. - alchemy.
Alg. - algebraical term.
Allem. - Allemannic.
Am. - American; Americanism.
an(al). - analogous(ly).
An., Anon. - Anonymous.
Anat. - anatomical term.
Anc. - ancient.
Angl. - Anglicism.
Annul. - *Annulata (Lat.,* Ringelwürmer).
Ant. - antiquities.
Ar., Arab. - Arabic.
Archit. - architectonical term.
Archæol. - archæology.
Arith., Arithm. - arithmetical term.
Arm. - term used by armorers.
art. - article.
A.-S. - Anglo-Saxon.
Astr., Astron. - astronomical term.
Astrol. - astrological term.
aux. - auxiliary.
b., bk. - book.
Bak. - term used by bakers.
Barb. - term used by barbers.
barb. - barbarous word *or* term.
Bee - term used in the cultivation of bees.
Bell-f. - term used by bell-founders.
Bibl. - Bible; Biblical subjects.
Bill. - billiard.
Bkb., Bks. s. *Bookb., Books.*
Blast-f. für blast-furnace.
Bookb. - term used b. bookbinders.
Books. - term used by booksellers.
Bot. - botanical term.
Bras. - term used by brasiers.
Brew. - term used by brewers.
Brick-m. - term of brickmakers.
Build. - term used in building.
burl. - burlesque.
Butch. - term used by butchers.
Butt. - term used by button-makers.
c. - *caput (Lat.* = chapter, Capitel).
Canall. - term used in canalling.
cant (cant-s.) - cant term (cant terms).
Card-m. - term used by card-makers.
card. numb für cardinal number.
Carp. - term used by carpenters.
cf. - *confer, conferatur (Lat.:* compare).
Ch. - Church; term relating to church-customs.
Chand. - term used by chandlers.
Chem. - chemical term.
Chr. - 1) Christ; 2) Christian.
Chron. - 1) chronological term; 2) Chronicles.
Civ. - civil.
Cloth. - clothiers' expression.
Coach-m. - coach-maker.
Cock(n). - Cockney.
coll. (coll-s.) - colloquial word(s) *or* expression(s).
collect. - collectively.
Comm. - commercial term.
comp., in comp. - in compounds.
comp, compar. - comparative.
Conch. - conchology.
Conf. - term used by confectioners.
conj. - conjunction.
cont. - contemptuously.
contr. - contracted(ly).
Cook. - cookery.
Coop. - cooper's term.
Cor. - Corinthians.
corr. - corrupted, corruptly.
Cott. Man. - Cotton manufactory.
Cryst. - crystallography.
Curr. - term of curriers.
Cust. - term relating to the customs.
Cutl. - term used in cutlery.
Dan. - 1) Danish; 2) Daniel.
Danc. - term used in dancing.
Dat. - Dative.
decl. - declined.
def. - defective.
dem. - demonstrative.
Dent. - term used by dentists.
Deut. - Deuteronomy.
Dial. - dial(l)ing.
Did. - term used in didactics.
diff. - different(ly).
Dik. - term used in diking.
dim., dimin. - diminutive; diminutively.
Diop. - dioptrics.
Dist. - term used in distilling
Dram. - dramatical phrase.
Draw. - term used in drawing.
Dy., Dye. - term used in dyeing.
Eccl. - Ecclesiastical.
Eccles. - Ecclesiastes.
Eccl'us - Ecclesiasticus.
Elec. - electricity.
ellipt. - elliptically.
emph. - emphatically.
Enc. für encyclopedia.
Eng. - engineering.
Engl. - English; England.
Engr. - term used in engraving.
Ent., Entom. - entomology.
Eph. - Ephesians.
Etch. - etching.
Eth. - ethics.
euph. - 1) euphonic, euphonically; 2) euphemism.
Ex. - Exodus.
Ezek. - Ezekiel.
f. - feminine.
Falc. - falconry.
fam. (fam-s.) - familiar word *or* expression(s).
Farr. - farriery.
Fenc. - term used in fencing.
f. i. - for instance (auch *e. g.).*
fig., fig-e. - figuratively, figurative expression.
Fire-w. - term used in fireworks.
Fish. - fishing.
For., Forest. - Forest; term used by foresters.
form. - formerly.
Fort. - term used in fortification.
Found. - term used in foundries.
Fr. - French.
Free-m. - term used by free-masons.
Furr. - term used by furriers *(or* in the fur-trade).
Gal. - Galatians.
Gall. Gallicism.
Gam. - term used in gaming.
Gard. - term used in gardening.
Gen. - 1) Genitive; 2) Genealogy; 3) Genesis.
gener. - generally.
Geogr. - term used in geography.
Geol. - term used in geology.
Germ. - German; Germany; Germanism.
Gild. - term used by gilders.
Glass-gr. - term used by glass-grinders.
Glass-w. - term used in glass-works.
Glaz. - term used by glaziers.
Glov - glover's term.
Gold-b. - term used by gold-beaters.
Gold-sm. - term used by goldsmiths.
Gr. - Greek; Grecism.
Gramm. - grammatical term.
Gunn. - term in gunnery *or* in artillery.
Gun-sm. - term used by gun-smiths.
Gymn. - Gymnastics.
Hab. - Habakkuk.

Hat-m., Hatt. für hat-maker's *or* hatter's term.
Hair-dr. - term used by hair-dressers.
Herald. - term used in heraldry.
Hist. - History.
Histol. - Histology.
Horol. - term in horology.
Hort. - term in horticulture.
Hos. - 1) hosiery; 2) Hosea.
Hunt. - term used by hunters.
Husb. - term in husbandry.
Hydr(aul.). - hydraulic, hydraulics.
Hydrost. - term in hydrostatics.
ib. - *ibidem (Lat.)*, ebenda.
Ichth. - ichthyology.
id. - *idem (Lat)*, derselbe.
i. e. - *id est (Lat.)*, that is (das heißt, das bedeutet).
imp., impers. - impersonal(ly).
imper. - imperative.
imp(e)rf. - imperfect.
impr. - improperly.
incorr. - incorrectly.
inel. - inelegant word *or* expression.
inf(in). - infinitive.
Instr-m. - term used by instrument-makers.
int., interj. - interjection.
interr. - interrogative(ly).
intr. - intransitive.
Introd. - Introduction.
iron. - ironically.
Iron-w. - term used in iron-works.
irr. - irregular, irregularly.
Is. - Isaiah, Jesaias.
It., Ital. - Italian.
Ja., Jas. - James, Jacob(us).
Jerem. - Jeremiah, Jeremias.
Jew. - Jewish.
Jewel(l). - term used by jewellers.
joc. - jocularly.
Join. - term used by joiners.
L. - Linné (Linnaeus).
l. - *liber (Lat.* = book).
Lace-w. - lace-weavers.
Lament. - Lamentations.
Lat. - Latin; Latinism.
Law(-s.) - law term(s).
Law-ph. - law phrase.

Mem. für 1) Memoirs; 2) memorandum.
met. - metaphorically.
Met., Meteor - meteorological term.
Metall. - term used in metallurgy.
Metaph. - metaphysics.
meton. - metonymical(ly).
M. G. - Middle Germany.
MHG. - Middle-High-German.
Mic. - Micah, (Prophet) Micha.
Mid.-Lat. - Middle-Latin.
Midw. - midwifery.
Mil. - military term.
Mill. - term used by millers and mill-wrights.
Min. - miners' term.
Miner. - mineralogical term.
Mint. - term used with minters.
mod. (mod-s.) - modern word *or* phrase(s).
Moh. Rel. - Mohammedan Religion.
Moll. - *(Lat.) Mollusca*, (Classe der) Weichthiere.
m. p. - more properly.
MS. - Manuscript.
MSS. - Manuscripts.
m. u. - more usually.
Mus. - musical term.
Myst. - term used by Mystics.
Myth. - term in Mythology.
n. - neuter, Neutrum.
Nat. - term in Natural History.
Naut., Nav. - nautical term, term in navigation, naval tactics.
NB. - *(Lat.) Nota bene*, bemerke wohl, wohl zu merken.
Needle-m. - needle-makers; needle-mills.
Neh. - Nehemiah.
N. G. - Northern German; North Germany.
NHG. - New-High-German.
n. l. - not legitimate *(or* unauthorised word).
Nom. - Nominative.
North. Myth. - Northern Mythology.
N. T. - New Testament.
n. u. - not used.
Num. - 1) numismatics; 2) numeral.
Numb. - 1) number; 2) Numbers.
Obst. - Obstetrics.

P. N. für proper name.
Poet. - term used in poetry.
Pol. - term used in politics.
Pom., Pomol. - pomology.
Pop. - popular (plant-names, superstition &c.).
Porc. - porcelain-manufactory.
poss. - possessive.
Post. - postal expression.
Pott. - pottery; term used by potters.
Powd.-m. - term used in powder-mills.
p. p., pp. - *participium praeteriti (Lat.)*, participle past.
p. pr. - participle present.
pr. - 1) provincial, provincialism; 2) s. *prov.*
Pref. - preface, Vorwort.
prep. - preposition.
pres. - present tense.
pret. - preterite.
Print. - printer's term *or* phrase.
prob. - probably.
Prol. - prologue, Prolog.
pron. - 1) pronounce; 2) pronoun.
pron. adj. - pronominal adjective.
prop. - properly.
Pros. - prosody.
prov. - 1) *(prov-s.)* proverbial expression(s); 2) Proverbs, die Sprichwörter (Salomonis).
provinc. s. *pr.* 1.
Ps. - Psalms.
pseudon. - pseudonymous.
Pug. - term used with pugilists.
quest. - questionable, *or* a word of which the propriety is rather doubtful.
qv. - *quod vide (Lat.)*, which see, welches siehe.
Railw. - railway-term.
recipr. - reciprocal.
refl. - reflexive.
reg. - regular.
rel., relat. - relative.
Rel. - religion, religious subjects.
Rev. - Revelations, die Offenbarung (St. Johan-

Skin-dr.	für	term used by skin-dressers.
Sl., Slat.	-	term used by slaters.
Sm., Smith.	-	term used by (black-)smiths.
Smelt.	-	term used by smelters.
sol.	-	solemn(ly).
Spinn.	-	spinning.
Sport.	-	sporting; sportsman's expression.
Stat.	-	term used in statistics.
Stone-m.	-	term used by stone-masons.
str.	-	strong (*see* p. IX).
Stuc.	-	stucco(-work).
Stud. slang	-	students' slang.
Sugar-w.	-	term used in sugar-works.
sup., superl.	-	superlative.
Surg.	-	term in surgery.
Surv.	-	term used in surveying.
s. v.	-	*sub verbo (Lat.)*, under the word, unter dem Worte.
Sw.	-	Swedish.
Swab	für	Swabian.
Switz.	-	Switzerland.
Sword-cutl.	-	term used by sword-cutlers.
T. (T-s.)	-	technical term (*or* terms) in general.
Tail.	-	term used by tailors.
Tall.	-	term used by tallow-chandlers.
Tann.	-	term used with tanners.
taut.	-	tautological.
Theat.	-	theatrical term.
Theol.	-	theological term.
Tin.	-	term used by tin-men.
Tin-m.	-	tin-mines.
Tob.	-	term used by tobacconists.
tr.	-	transitive.
Turn.	-	term used by turners.
Typ.	-	typographical term.
Un.	-	University.
v.	-	verb.
v. adj.	-	verbal adjective.
Vet.	für	term of the veterinary art.
vid.	-	*vide (Lat.)*, see (siehe).
Vint.	-	term used by vintagers.
v. s.	-	verbal substantive.
vulg.	-	vulgar word *or* expression; vulgarly.
w	-	weak (*see* p. IX).
w. am Ende e'r Zssetzg	für	works, worker (z. B. *Alum-w., Metal-w.*).
Watch-m.	-	term used by watch-makers.
Wax-ch.	-	term used by wax-chandlers.
Weav.	-	term of weavers.
Wheel-wr.	-	term of wheel-wrights.
Wire-dr.	-	term of wire-drawers.
Wool.	-	term used in preparing *or* dressing wool.
Zech. (Zach.)	-	Zechariah (Zachariah), (der Prophet) Sacharja (Zacharias).
Zool.	-	term in zoology.
Zoot.	-	term in zootomy.

II.

German Abbreviations.

A., a.	für	Andere(s), andere ꝛc.
a. a. O.	-	am angeführten Orte.
abgek.	-	abgekürzt, abbreviated.
Abkrzg	-	Abkürzung, abbreviation.
Abltg	-	Ableitung, derivation.
adj., adv.	-	adjectivisch, adverbialisch (zu unterscheiden von *adj.* u. *adv.*).
afrz.	-	altfranzösisch.
agſ.	-	angelsächsisch, Anglo-Saxon.
ahd.	-	althochdeutsch, Old-High-German.
allgem.	-	allgemein.
altn.	-	altnordisch.
Anf.	-	Anfang.
arab.	-	arabisch, Arabian.
a. S.	-	andere Seite, other, next page.
Ausdr.	-	Ausdruck.
Ausg. (Ausgg.)	-	Ausgabe(n), edition(s).
ausgen.	-	ausgenommen, except(ed).
Ausspr.	-	Aussprache.
Bdtg(n)	-	Bedeutung(en), meaning(s), signification(s).
Bein.	-	Beiname.
bek.	-	bekannt(er ꝛc.), known.
bem., Bem.	-	bemerkt, Bemerkung.
ben., Ben.	-	benannt, Benennung.
bes.	-	besonder(s), particular(ly).
betr.	-	betreffend, relating to.
Bez.; bez.	-	Bezug (Beziehung); bezüglich.
Bindestr.	-	Bindestrich, hyphen.
bzchn., Bzchng	-	bezeichnet(e, er ꝛc.); bezeichnen, Bezeichnung ꝛc.
bzw.	-	beziehungsweise, relatively.
Cap.	-	Capitel, chapter.
Conj.	-	Conjunctiv; Conjunction.
Conj., Conjug.	-	Conjugation.
Cons.	-	Consonant(en).
constr.	-	construiren, construirt ꝛc.
Constr.	-	Construction.
d.	-	der, die, das ꝛc.
D.	-	Deutsch(e, en ꝛc.); Deutschland.
desgl	-	desgleichen, likewise, also.
d. f. A.	-	der folgende (*or* dem, die, den ꝛc. folgenden) Artikel, the following article, &c.
d. f. W.	-	das folgende Wort, the following word.
dſr, dſe, dſs ꝛc.	-	dieser, diese, dieses ꝛc.
d. ü.	für	das üblichere (Wort, word) more in use.
d. v. W.	-	das vorhergehende Wort, the preceding word.
eb.	-	ebenda, in the same place.
ehem.	-	ehemals, formerly.
eig., eig(en)tl.	-	eigentlich, properly.
Ein.	-	Einige(n ꝛc.).
ellipt.	-	elliptisch, elliptically.
E-n.	-	Eigenname, proper name.
entſpr.	-	entsprechend, answering.
entw.	-	1) entweder; 2) entwickelt.
e'r, e's, e'm, ꝛc.	-	einer, eines, einem, ꝛc.
erkl.	-	erklärt, erklaren ꝛc.
Erkl.	-	Erklärung.
et., Et.	-	etymologisch, Etymologie.
etw.	-	etwas.
F.	-	Form.
Fl.	-	Fluß.
F-n	-	Frauenname, woman's proper name.
franz., frz.	-	französisch, French.
freil.	-	freilich.
g in Endungen gekürzt aus …ung (so Endg = Endung ꝛc.)		
gebr.	für	gebräuchlich, gebraucht, usual(ly), used.
Gebr.	-	Gebrauch, use, custom.
gem.	-	gemein, vulgar(ly).
gen.	-	genannt, called.
Gesch.	-	Geschichte, history.
gew.	-	gewöhnlich; gewesen, geworden.
Ggſ.	-	Gegensatz, opposite.
ggw.	-	gegenwärtig.
glchſ.	-	gleichsam.
Glght	-	Gelegenheit.
Gloss.	-	Glossar.
got(h).	-	got(h)isch.
gr., grch.	-	griechisch, Greek.
gram., gramm	-	grammat(ical)isch.
häuf.	-	häufig(er, e, es ꝛc.).
hb.	-	haben
Hdſchr.	-	Handschrift.
hebr.	-	hebräisch, Hebrew.
hrsgeg.	-	herausgegeben, edited.
hybr.	-	hybrid(e ꝛc.), hybrid (von [glchſ. Bastard-]Wörtern, welche aus verschiedenen Sprachen zusammengesetzt sind, wie Supercritical, &c.).
i. g. S.	-	im guten Sinne, in a good sense.
Imp(er).	-	Imperativ.
imperat.	für	imperativisch.
Imperf.	-	Imperfect(um).
ind.	-	indisch, Hindoo, (East-) Indian.
indian.	-	indianisch, Indian.
Inf.	-	Infinitiv.
ir., irl.; Irl.	-	ir(länd)isch, Irish; Irland, Ireland.
irg.	-	irgend.
it., ital.	-	italiänisch.
It., Ital.	-	Italien, Italiener.
i. ü. S.	-	im üblen Sinne, in an ill sense.
j.	-	jetzt.
jdflls	-	jedenfalls.
Jh., Jh's	-	Jahrhundert(s).
Jhrgg	-	Jahrgang.
K.	-	König.
kl., Kl.	-	klein(er, e, es), Klein ꝛc.
…l. in Endungen	-	…lich(er, e, es ꝛc.), so königl., männl., weibl. ꝛc.
lat.	-	lateinisch, Latin.
mal.	-	malayisch.
Med.	-	Medicin.
mgl.	-	möglich.
mhd.	-	mittelhochdeutsch, Middle-High-German.
mlat.	-	mittellateinisch, Middle-Latin.
M-n.	-	Mannsname, man's proper name.
m. r.	-	minder richtig, less proper(ly).
n.	-	nach, after; according to ….
N.	-	1) Name(n); 2) Nord(en).
n. A.	-	nach Andern, according to others.
NAm.	-	Nord-America.
Nachflgg.	-	(die) Nachfolger.
N. D., N-d.; ndd.	-	Norddeutschland, Niederdeutschland, North of Germany, Lower *or* Northern Germany; nord- *or* niederdeutsch.
neufrz.	-	neufranzösisch.
nlat.	-	neulateinisch.
N-ſ.	-	Niedersachsen, Lower Saxony (or Germany).
n-ſ.	-	niedersächsisch, Lower Saxon (Low-German).
n. ü.	-	nicht üblich, not in use, unusual.
ob.	-	oben; obig(er ꝛc.).
Obj.	-	Object.
O. D., O-d.	-	Oberdeutschland, Upper Germany.
od.	-	oder, or.

Or.	für	Original.
orient.	-	orientaliſch, Oriental.
oſt.	-	oſtengliſch.
Paſſ.	-	Paſſiv(um).
perſ.	-	perſiſch, Persian.
phyſ.	-	phyſiſch, physical(ly).
Pl., Plur.	-	Plural.
P-n.	-	Perſonenname, a person's proper name. [ſe(n).
port.; Port.	-	portugieſiſch; Portugie-
präd.	-	prädicativ(iſch).
Präf.	-	Präfix(um), prefix.
Prät.	-	Präteritum, preterite.
Pſeud.	-	Pſeudonym (angenommener Name). [tor(s).
Red.	-	Redacteur.Redaction,edi-
regelm.	-	regelmäßig, regular(ly).
ſ.	-	1) ſiehe, see; 2) ſein.
S.	-	1) Sohn; 2) Subſtantiv; 3) Süd(en).
ſcherzh.	-	ſcherzhaft(er, e, es ꝛc.).
ſchott.; Schottl.	-	ſchottiſch; Schottland.
S. D., S-d.	-	Süddeutſchland, South of Germany. [so-called.
ſ. g, ſog.	-	ſogenannt, denominated,
Sing.	für	Singular.
ſp.	-	ſpät(er) ꝛc.
ſpan.; Span.	-	ſpaniſch; Spanien.
ſp. lat.	-	ſpätlateiniſch.
ſpr.	-	ſprich(t), pronounce(s).
ſ'r, ſ'e, ſ'es ꝛc.	-	ſeiner, ſeine(s) ꝛc.
ſt.	-	ſtatt, anſtatt, instead of.
St.	-	Stadt.
Subſt.	-	Subſtantiv, substantive.
ſ. v. w.	-	ſo viel wie, the same as
ſyr.	-	ſyriſch.
u.	-	und.
übrh.	-	überhaupt.
übrig.	-	übrigens, as for the rest.
übrſ., übrſ.	-	überſetzt, Überſetzung.
übrtr.	-	übertragen.
uneig., uneigentl.	-	uneigentlich.
ungef.	-	ungefähr, about.
ungew.	-	ungewöhnlich,unusual(ly).
unr.	-	unrichtig, incorrect(ly).
unt.	-	unter; unten.
urſpr.	-	urſprünglich, originally.
v.	-	von (vom).
vereinz.	-	vereinzelt.
Verf.	-	Verfaſſer.
verſch.	für	verſchieden(er, e, es ꝛc.).
vgl., vglcht	-	vergleiche, vergleicht ꝛc.
vor., Vor.	-	vorig(e ꝛc.), Vorig(e ꝛc.).
Vrkl.(nrgsform)	-	Verkleinerungsform.
V. St.	-	Vereinigte Staaten.
vwdt	-	verwandt, related.
w.	-	1) werden; 2) w. ſ., welches ſiehe; w. vgl., welches vergleiche. [Wörter
W.	-	1) Weſten; 2) Wort; W-r.,
WB.	-	Wörterbuch (Wbb. Wör-
Wglſſg	-	Weglaſſung. [terbücher).
wlchr,wlche,wlchs	-	welcher ꝛc.
w. ü.	-	wenig üblich, little used.
z. B.	-	zum Beiſpiel, for instance (*f. i.*, or *e. g.*).
zſgſtzt	-	zuſammengeſetzt.
zſgz(n)	-	zuſammengezogen.
Zſhg	-	Zuſammenhang. connexion, &c.
Zſſtzg(n)	-	Zuſammenſetzung(en).
Ztſchr.	-	Zeitſchrift.
Ztw.	-	Zeitwort.
zuw.	-	zuweilen, sometimes.
zw.	-	zwiſchen.

III.

Marks of Pronunciation.

‒ over vowels, denotes the long sound, *f. i* Ad'ler, Täd'ler, Ärt, Ab'ärt (*cf.* Adriat'iſch, Hart, Standar'te), Len'chen (*cf.* Len'de), Ädil' (*cf.* Dil'le), Tön (*cf.* Ton'ne), Rūf (*cf.* Puſ'ſen), Aſȳl' (*cf.* Syl'phe), Bär'tig (*cf.* Hart'lich), Behör'de (*cf.* För'dern), Būb'chen (*cf.* Hübſch). As all the vowels immediately followed by the accent, are long, it is unnecessary to place this sign of length over them; compare, for instance, Ga'be, Re'de, Ädi'le, Mo'deln, Ru'ſen, Wa'gen, Ö'len, Gü'tig, with Ab'gäbe, An'rēde, Ädil', Ab'mōdeln, Ab'rūfen, Ab'wägen, Ab'ölen, Un'gütig. A syllable terminated by an accented consonant, is always short (An'ders, Et'was, = ăn'..., ĕt'... ꝛc.), only excepting the consonant h, which serves to lengthen the preceding vowel: Ah'le, Meh'ren, Ihr, Ohr, Uhr = āle, mēren, īr, ōr, ūr.

˘ over vowels, denotes the short sound; it is generally placed over such vowels which might be expected to have the long sound, compare *f. i.* the derivatives Näch'bar, Höch'zeit, Vŏr'theil, *with* Näch, Höch, Vŏr.

¨ 1) over the vowel e, always marks the broad pronunciation, which is equal to ä; compare *f. i.* Fë'der, Lë'der, Rë'gen (*s.*) with E'del, Le'gen, Re'gen (*v.*). It is, however, to be remarked, that this e is not uniformly pronounced with the same sound in the different parts of Germany; the pronunciation given in this work is that of middle Germany. Here it may be remarked that Ae (ae), Oe (oe), Ue (ue) have not been considered as equivalent to Ä (ä), Ö (ö), Ü (ü), in this work, although they are often erroneously held to be so; thus ae ꝛc. in such words as Laertes, Boetius, Congruent are always to be pronounced separately. — 2) over the vowel i before an e, used as points of diæresis, to denote that these vowels are not to be pronounced as a diphthong, but separately, *f. i.* In'dïen (*pron.* In'djen), different from Dienen (dē'nen); this deviation from the general usage, according to which these points are placed over the e, was rendered necessary, because ë had already been chosen as a natural representative of the a-like pronunciation of the letter e.

IV.

Terms ... used at the construction of Railways 1865.

Hildebrand (Rudolf, Prof. zu Leipzig) * 1824. Bearbeiter des K u. G für das Grimmsche Wörterbuch 1873 u. flgg.

Hilpert (J. L.). Engl.-Deutsches WB., 1828—31: nach seinem Tode: Deutsch-Engl. WB., 1845.

L. für Linné (Karl v.) 1707—78. Ber. Botaniker.

Luc. für Lucas (N. I.). Engl.-Deutsches Wörterbuch, Bremen 1854—56.

Ludwig (M. Christian). A Dict. Engl., Germ., and French, Leipzig (b. Thomas Fritschen) 1706; 4. Aufl. 1791, hrsgeg. v. Rogler, bei Gleditsch.

Meyer's Conversations-Lexicon.

Nemnich (Phil. Andreas). Allgem. Polyglotten-Lexicon der Naturgeschichte, Hamburg 1793—95; Britische Waaren-Encyclopädie 1815.

Pierer's Universal-Lexicon.

Pincas (A.). Ergänzungs-Blätter zu jedem Engl. Handwörterbuch, Hannover 1864.

Röding (Joh. Hinr.). Allgem. Wörterbuch der Marine in allen europäischen Seesprachen 1793.

Röhrig (Ernst). Wörterbuch in Engl. u. Deutscher Sprache für Berg- u. Hüttentechnik 1881 (2 Teile, Kl. Octav).

Sanders (Daniel). Wörterbuch der Deutschen Sprache mit Belegen von Luther bis auf die Gegenwart; I. 1860, II. 1863, III. 1865.

Schade (Oscar). Altdeutsches Wörterbuch (2. Aufl., 1872—82).

Schiebe. Kaufmännische Encyclopädie.

Streit (F. W.). Military Dict., Engl.-Germ. & Germ.-Engl., 1837.

Tolhausen. Technologisches Wörterbuch der Deutschen, Französ. u. Engl. Sprache, in 3 Theilen, 1855 (1874—75 2. Aufl.).

Weigand (Friedr. Ludw. Karl). Deutsches Wörterb. (I. 1857; II. 1860; III. 1871; gänzliche Umarbeitung v. Schmitthenners Wörterbuch).

Wülcker (Ernst, Mitarbeiter an Grimms Wörterbuch), s. Diefenbach.

Lists of strong and irregular verbs and nouns.

Introductory Remarks. According to German grammarians verbs as well as nouns are divided into two large classes, called the strong and the weak; a third class is to be added, viz. those which for some reason or other do not decidedly follow either the strong or the weak conjugation or declension; they are called irregular.

Strong verbs as well as substantives are principally characterised by some change of their radical vowels, exhibited in verbs by the imperfect and participle past, in substantives by the Umlaut of the plural form; take, as examples the verb Singen (the infinitive exhibiting generally the radical vowel), imperfect: sang, participle past: gesungen (sing, sang, sung); and such substantives, as Vater, Sohn, Mutter, the plurals of which change the radical a, o, u, into ä, ö, ü: Väter, Söhne, Mütter.

While this change may be called an internal one, the *weak* forms embracing all the derivative verbs and nouns, are only changed by adding a termination. Thus Fallen, fiel, gefallen (to fall, fell, fallen), and Mann, Männer (man, men) belong to the strong class, while their derivatives fällen, fällte, gefällt (to fell, felled, felled), and Mensch (*originally an adj.:* Männisch), *pl.* Menschen, come under the weak denomination. It is obvious that strong forms, representing the oldest class of words, as it were the marrow of the language, are only a minority, while the long series of derivational forms may be almost increased at will. In order to assist the learner, we here follow a general usage, and give a list of strong and irregular verbs, and a list of irregular substantives.

I.

All the strong verbs may, for practical purposes, be divided into the following eight classes: —

	Radical Vowel — Infinitive	Imperfect	Participle Past
I.	1) i	a	u
	2) i or e (ä, o)	a	o
	3) i (ie, ü) or e (ä, ö, au)	o	o
	4) i or e	a	e
II.	1) ei	i	i
	2) ei	ie	ie
III.	1) a (au, o, u)	i or ie	radical vowel
	2) a	u	radical vowel.

I. 1) embraces the following verbs: Binden (band, gebunden), dingen, bringen, finden, gelingen, klingen, ringen, schinden (*imperf.* schund for schand), schlingen, schwinden, schwingen, singen, sinken, springen, stinken, trinken, winden, zwingen.

I. 2) Befehlen (befahl, befohlen), beginnen, bergen, bersten, brechen, empfehlen, erschrecken, gebären, gelten, gewinnen, helfen, kommen, nehmen, rinnen, schelten, schwimmen, sinnen, spinnen, sprechen, stechen, stehlen, sterben, treffen, verderben, werben, werden, werfen.

I. 3) Bewegen (bewog, bewogen), biegen, bieten, dreschen, fechten, flechten, fliegen, fliehen, fließen, frieren, gähren, genießen, gießen, glimmen, heben, kiesen, klimmen, kriechen, (aus-, er-, ver-)löschen, lügen, melken, pflegen (*gener. w.)*, quellen, riechen, rächen, saufen, saugen, (er-, ver-)schallen, scheren, schieben, schießen, schließen, schmelzen, schnauben, schrauben, schwären, schwellen, schwören, sieden, sprießen, triefen, (be-)trügen, verdrießen, verlieren, wägen, wiegen, weben, ziehen.

I. 4) Bitten (bat, gebeten), essen, fressen, geben, genesen, geschehen, lesen, liegen, messen, sehen, sitzen, treten, vergessen.

II. 1) Befleißen (befliß, beflissen), beißen, erbleichen, gleichen, gleiten, greifen, keifen, kneifen, leiden, pfeifen, reißen, reiten, schleichen, schleifen, schleißen, schmeißen, schneiden, schreiten, streichen, streiten, weichen.

II. 2) Bleiben (blieb, geblieben), gedeihen, leihen, meiden, preisen, reiben, scheiden, scheinen, schreiben, schreien, schweigen, speien, steigen, treiben, weisen, zeihen.

III. 1) Blasen (blies, geblasen), braten, fallen, fangen, halten, hangen, hauen, heißen, lassen, laufen, rathen, rufen, schlafen, stoßen, gehen.

III. 2) Backen (buk, gebacken), fahren, graben, laden, schaffen, schlagen, tragen, wachsen, waschen, stehen.

Irregular verbs have been marked in the list as *irr.*, *i. e.* irregular:

List of strong and irregular verbs.

Infinitive.	*Present Indicative.*	*Imperfect* *Indicative.*	*Imperfect* *Subjunctive.*	*Imperative.*	*Participle past.*
For Ab'backen, Ab'befehlen, Ab'behalten, Ab'beißen, Ab'bekommen, *and similar compounds, vide the simple verbs* Backen, Befehlen ꝛc.					
Bak'en (*w., sometimes str., p. p. always str.*), to bake	ich backe, du bäckst (*w.* backst), er bäckt (*w.* backt) ꝛc	ich buk, (*w.* backte)	ich büke (*w.* backte)	backe	gebacken.
Bedenk'en (*irr.*), to consider	ich bedenke, du bedenkst, er bedenkt	ich bedachte	ich bedächte	bedenke	bedacht.
Beding'en (*str., sometimes w., cf. Dict.*), to stipulate	ich bedinge, du bedingst, er bedingt	ich bedung (*l. w.* bedang)	ich bedünge	bedinge	bedungen.
Bedür'fen (*irr.*), to need	ich bedarf, du bedarfst, er bedarf	ich bedurfte	ich bedürfte	—	bedurft.
Befah'ren, I. (*str.*) to navigate, *see* Fahren; II. (*w.*) † & * to fear	ich befahre ꝛc.	ich befahrte	ich befahrte	befahre	befahrt.
Befal'len, Befang'en ꝛc., *see* Fallen, Fangen ꝛc.					
Befeh'len (*str.*), to command	ich befehle, du befiehlst, er befiehlt	ich befahl	ich beföhle *or* befähle	befiehl	befohlen.
Beflei'ßen (*str.*), to attend to	ich befleiße, du befleißest *or* du befleißt, er befleißt	ich befliß	ich beflisse	befleiße *or* befleiß	beflissen.
Begin'nen (*str.*), to begin	ich beginne, du beginnst, er beginnt ꝛc.	ich begann (begonnte)	ich begönne *or* begänne	beginne	begonnen.
Bei'ßen (*str.*), to bite	ich beiße, du beißest *or* beißt, er beißt	ich biß	ich bisse	beiße *or* beiß	gebissen.
Beklem'men (*gen. w.*, † *str.*), to pinch, &c.*	ich beklemme, du beklemmst ꝛc.	ich beklemmte († beklomm)	ich beklemmte	—	beklemmt († beklommen).
Bel'len (*gen. w.*, † *str.*), to bark	ich belle, † du billst, † er billt	† ich boll	† ich bölle	—	† gebollen.
Ber'gen (*str.*), to hide	ich berge, du birgst, er birgt	ich barg	ich bärge (*l. w.* bürge)	birg	geborgen.
Ber'sten (*str.*), to burst	ich berste, du berstest (*or* birstest), er berstet *or* birst	ich barst *or* borst	ich bärste *or* börste	berste *or* birst	geborsten.
Besin'nen (*str.*), to recollect	ich besinne, du besinnest, er besinnt	ich besann (*provinc. coll.* ich besonn)	ich besänne *or* besönne	besinne	besonnen.
Besit'zen (*str.*), to possess	ich besitze, du besitzest, er besitzt	ich besaß	ich besäße	besitze	besessen.
Betrü'gen (*str.*), to cheat	ich betrüge, du betrügst, er betrügt	ich betrog	ich betröge	betrüge	betrogen.
Bewe'gen (*gen. w., sometimes str., cf. Dict.*), to move	ich bewege, du bewegst, er bewegt	ich bewog	ich bewöge	bewege	bewogen.
Bie'gen (*str.*), to bend	ich biege, du biegst, er biegt	ich bog	ich böge	biege	gebogen.
Bie'ten (*str.*), to offer	ich biete, du bietest (*poet.* beutst), er bietet (*poet.* beut)	ich bot	ich böte	biete	geboten.
Bin'den (*str.*), to bind	ich binde ꝛc.	ich band	ich bände	binde	gebunden.
Bit'ten (*str.*), to beg, ask	ich bitte ꝛc.	ich bat	ich bäte	bitte	gebeten.
Bla'sen (*str.*), to blow	ich blase, du bläsest, er bläset *or* bläs't	ich blies	ich bliese	blase	geblasen.
Blei'ben (*str.*), to remain	ich bleibe ꝛc.	ich blieb	ich bliebe	bleibe	geblieben.
Blei'chen (*gen. w., sometimes str., cf.*	ich bleiche, du bleichst, er bleicht	ich blich	ich bliche	bleiche	geblichen

Infinitive.	Present Indicative.	Imperfect		Imperative.	Participle past.
		Indicative.	Subjunctive.		
Erfrie'ren *(str.)*, to freeze	ich erfriere, du erfrierst, er erfriert	ich erfror	ich erfröre	erfriere	erfroren.
Erkie'sen, *see* Kiesen.					
Erlas'sen *(str.)*, to issue, &c., *see* Lassen.					
Erlösch'en *(str., seldom w. in its tr. sense,* to extinguish), to be extinguished	ich erlösche, du erlischest *or* erlöschest, er erlischt *or* erlöscht	ich erlosch	ich erlösche	erlisch *or* erlösche	erloschen.
Ersau'fen *(str.)*, *coll.* to be drowned	ich ersaufe, du ersäufst, er ersäuft	ich ersoff	ich ersoffe	ersaufe	ersoffen.
Erschal'len *(str., sometimes w.)*, to sound	ich erschalle 2c.	ich erscholl	ich erschölle	erschalle	erschollen.
Erschei'nen *(str.)*, to appear	ich erscheine, du erscheinst, er erscheint	ich erschien	ich erschiene	erscheine	erschienen.
Erschreck'en *(str. as an intr. cf. Dict.)*, to be frightened	ich erschrecke, du erschrickst, er erschrickt	ich erschrak	ich erschräke	erschrick	erschrocken.
Ertrin'ken *(str.)*, to be drowned	ich ertrinke, du ertrinkst, er ertrinkt	ich ertrank	ich ertränke	ertrink	ertrunken.
Erwä'gen *(str.)*, to consider, to reflect upon	ich erwäge, du erwägst, er erwägt	ich erwög	ich erwöge	erwäge	erwogen.
Es'sen *(irr.)*, to eat	ich esse, du issest, er isset *or* ißt	ich aß	ich äße	iß	gegessen.*
† & * **Fah'en** *(str.)*, to catch	ich fahe, du fähst, er fäht	ich fieh	ich fieh	fah	gefahen.
Fah'ren *(str.)*, to pass, to ride (in any vehicle)	ich fahre, du fährst, er fährt	ich fuhr	ich führe	fahre	gefahren.
Fal'len *(str.)*, to fall	ich falle, du fällst, er fällt	ich fiel	ich fiele	falle *or* fall	gefallen.
Fal'ten *(w., formerly str.)*, to fold	ich falte 2c.	ich faltete, † *(str.)* ich fielt	ich faltete, † *(str.)* ich fielt	falte	gefaltet *or* *(str.)* gefalten.
Fang'en *(str.)*, to catch	ich fange, du fängst, er fängt	ich fing	ich finge	fange	gefangen.
Fech'ten *(str.)*, to fight	ich fechte, du fichtst *or* fichst (fechtest), er ficht (fechtet)	ich focht	ich föchte	ficht *or* fechte	gefochten.
Fin'den *(str.)*, to find	ich finde 2c.	ich fand	ich fände	finde	gefunden.
Flech'ten *(str.)*, to plait	ich flechte, du flichtst *or* flichst (flechtest), er flicht (flechtet)	ich flocht	ich flöchte	flicht *or* flechte	geflochten.
Flie'gen *(str.)*, to fly.	ich fliege, du fliegst, er fliegt *(poet.* du fleugst, er fleugt)	ich flög	ich flöge	fliege, *poet.* fleug	geflogen
Flieh'en, *(str.)*, to flee	ich fliehe, du fliehst, er flieht *(poet.* du fleuchst, er fleucht)	ich floh	ich flöhe	fliehe *or* flieh, *poet.* fleuch	geflohen.
Flie'ßen *(str.)*, to flow	ich fließe, du fließest, er fließet *or* fließt *(poet.* du fleußest, er fleußt)	ich floß	ich flösse	fließe *or* fließ, *poet.* fleuß	geflossen.
Fra'gen *(gen. w., sometimes str.)*, to ask	ich frage, du fragst (frägst), er fragt (frägt)	ich fragte (frūg)	ich fragte (früge)	frage	gefragt.
Fres'sen *(str.)*, to devour, feed, eat	ich fresse, du frissest, er frisset *or* frißt	ich fräß	ich fräße	friß	gefressen.
Frie'ren *(str.)*, to be cold, chilly	ich friere 2c.	ich frōr	ich fröre	friere	gefrōren.
Gäh'ren *(str.)*, to ferment	ich gähre, du gährst, er gahrt	ich gohr	ich göhre	gähre	gegohren.
Gebä'ren *(str.)*, to bear, produce	ich gebäre, du gebärst *(or* gebierst), er gebäret *(or* gebiert)	ich gebär	ich gebäre *(l. w.* gebōre)	gebäre *or* gebier	gebōren.
Gē'ben *(str.)*, to give	ich gebe, du giebst *or* gibst, er giebt *or* gibt	ich gāb	ich gābe	gieb *or* gib	gegeben.
Gebie'ten *(str.)*, to order, to command	ich gebiete, du gebietest *(poet.* gebeutst), er gebietet *(poet.* gebeut)	ich gebōt	ich geböte	gebiete *(poet.* gebeut)	gebōten.
Gebrech'en, **Geden'ken** 2c., *see* Brechen, Denken 2c.					
Gedeih'en *(str.)*, to thrive	ich gedeihe 2c.	ich gedieh	ich gediehe	gedeihe	gediehen.
Gefal'len *(str.)*, to please	ich gefalle, du gefällst, er gefällt	ich gefiel	ich gefiele	gefalle	gefallen.
Geh'en *(irr.)*, to go	ich gehe 2c.	ich ging (gieng)	ich ginge (gienge)	geh	gegangen.
Geling'en *(str.)*, to succeed	ich gelinge 2c.	ich gelang	ich gelänge	gelinge	gelungen.
Gel'ten *(str.)*, to be worth	ich gelte, du giltst, er gilt	ich galt († golt)	ich gälte *or* gölte (gülte)	gilt	gegolten.
Gene'sen *(str.)*, to recover	ich genese, du genesest, er geneset	ich genās	ich genāse	genese	genesen.
Genie'ßen *(str.)*, to enjoy	ich genieße, du genießest, er genießt († & *poet.* du geneußt, er geneußt)	ich genoß	ich genösse	genieße *or* genieß *(poet.* geneuß)	genossen.
Gera'then *(str.)*, to come; to turn out, &c.	ich gerathe, du geräthst, er geräth *(l. w.* du gerathest, er gerathet)	ich gerieth	ich geriethe	gerathe	gerathen.
Geschē'hen *(str.)*, to happen	es geschiehet *or* geschieht († & *provinc.* geschicht)	es geschah († & *provinc.* geschach)	es geschähe	geschieh *(gen.* es geschehe)	geschehen.
Gewin'nen *(str.)*, to gain	ich gewinne 2c.	ich gewann	ich gewänne *or* gewönne	gewinne	gewonnen
Gie'ßen *(str.)*, to pour	ich gieße, du gießest, er gießt († & *poet.* du geußest, er geußt)	ich goß	ich gösse	gieße *or* gieß, † & *poet.* geuß	gegossen.
Glei'chen *(str., sometimes w., see Dict.)*, to be like, resemble	ich gleiche 2c.	ich glich	ich gliche	gleiche	geglichen.
Glei'ten *(str., sometimes w.)*, to glide	ich gleite 2c.	ich glitt	ich glitte	gleite	geglitten.
Glim'men *(formerly str., now gen. w.)*, to sparkle	ich glimme, du glimmst, er glimmt	ich glomm	ich glömme	glimme	geglommen.
Gra'ben *(str.)*, to dig	ich grabe, du gräbst, er gräbt	ich grūb	ich grūbe	grabe	gegraben.
Grei'fen *(str.)*, to grasp	ich greife 2c.	ich griff	ich griffe	greife *or* greif	gegriffen.
Ha'ben *(irr.)*, to have	ich habe, du hast, er hat	ich hatte	ich hätte	habe	gehabt.
Hal'ten *(str.)*, to hold, keep	ich halte, du hältst, er hält	ich hielt	ich hielte	halte *or* halt	gehalten.

* *Originally:* geessen, and, *therefore, after an inseparable prefix:* (über)es'sen, (ver)es'sen; *notwithstanding, the forms* übergessen *(Göthe, Faust)*, vergessen *(coll.) are sometimes used.*

Infinitive.	Present Indicative.	Imperfect Indicative.	Imperfect Subjunctive.	Imperative.	Participle past.
Hang'en (str.; Hängen, a weak verb, is often confounded with Hangen), to hang	ich hange, du hängst, er hängt (not du hangst, er hangt)	ich hing (hieng)	ich hinge (hienge)	hange	gehangen.
Hau'en (irr.), to hew, cut, strike	ich haue, du haust, er haut	ich hieb	ich hiebe	haue or hau	gehauen.
He'ben (str.), to lift	ich hebe, du hebst, er hebt	ich hob († & provinc. hub)	ich höbe († & provinc. hübe)	hebe	gehoben.
Hei'ßen (str.), to be called or named	ich heiße, du heißest or heißt, er heißt	ich hieß	ich hieße	heiße	geheißen.
Hel'fen (str.), to help	ich helfe, du hilfst, er hilft	ich half (provinc. ich hulf)	ich hülfe or hälfe	hilf	geholfen.
Kau'fen (w.), to buy	ich kaufe, du kaufst, er kauft (sometimes du käufst, er käuft)	ich kaufte	ich kaufte	kaufe or kauf	gekauft.
Kei'fen (w., sometimes str.), to chide	ich keife ꝛc.	ich keifte (kiff)	ich keifte (kiffe)	keife or keif	gekeift (gekiffen).
Ken'nen (irr.), to know	ich kenne ꝛc.	ich kannte (provinc. [S. G.] ich kennte)	ich kennete	kenne	gekannt (provinc. [S. G.] gekennt).
Kie'sen (cf. Verlieren, the original form of which was Verliesen)	ich kiese ꝛc.	ich kor	ich köre	küre	gekoren.
Klie'ben (str.), † & provinc., to cleave	ich kliebe ꝛc.	ich klob	ich klöbe	kliebe	gekloben.
Klim'men (str. or w.), to climb	ich klimme ꝛc.	ich klomm	ich klömme	klimme	geklommen.
Kling'en (str.), to sound	ich klinge ꝛc.	ich klang	ich klänge	klinge	geklungen.
Knei'fen (str.), to nip	ich kneife ꝛc.	ich kniff	ich kniffe	kneife	gekniffen.
Knei'pen (str.), to pinch	ich kneipe ꝛc.	ich knipp	ich knippe	kneipe or kneip	geknippen.
Kom'men (str.), to come	ich komme, du kommst, er kommt (sometimes du kömmst, er kömmt)	ich kam	ich käme	komm (sometimes komme)	gekommen.
Kön'nen (irr.), can, to be able	ich kann, du kannst, er kann, subj. ich könne	ich konnte	ich könnte	(l. u.) könne	gekonnt.
Krie'chen (str.), to creep	ich krieche, du kriechst, er kriecht (provinc. & poet. du kreuchst, er kreucht)	ich kroch	ich kröche	krieche or kriech, (provinc. & poet. kreuch)	gekrochen.
Kü'ren gener. adopts the strong forms of Kiesen					
La'den (str.), to lade	ich lade, du ladest, er ladet (coll. du lädst, er lädt)	ich lud (sometimes w. ich ladete)	ich lüde (sometimes w. ich ladete)	lade	geladen.
Las'sen (str.), to let	ich lasse, du lässest or läßt, er lässet or läßt	ich ließ	ich ließe	lasse or laß	gelassen.
Lau'fen (str.), to run	ich laufe, du läufst, er läuft	ich lief	ich liefe	laufe or lauf	gelaufen.
Lei'den (str.), to suffer	ich leide ꝛc.	ich litt	ich litte	leide	gelitten.
Leih'en (str.), to lend	ich leihe ꝛc.	ich lieh	ich liehe	leihe	geliehen.
Le'sen (str.), to read	ich lese, du liesest, er lieset or lies't	ich las	ich läse	lies (provinc. lese)	gelesen.
Lie'gen (str.), to lie	ich liege, du liegst, er liegt	ich lag	ich läge	liege	gelegen.

Infinitive.	Present Indicative.	Imperfect Indicative.	Imperfect Subjunctive.	Imperative.	Participle past.
Rei'ßen *(str.)*, to tear	ich reiße ꝛc.	ich riß	ich risse	reiße *or* reiß	gerissen.
Rei'ten *(str.)*, to ride	ich reite ꝛc.	ich ritt	ich ritte	reite	geritten.
Ren'nen *(irr.)*, to run	ich renne ꝛc.	ich rannte *(provinc. [S. G.]* ich rennte)	ich rennete	renne	gerannt *(provinc. [S. G.]* gerennt).
Rie'chen *(str.)*, to smell	ich rieche, du riechst, er riecht *(provinc. [S. G.]* du reuchst, er reucht)	ich roch	ich röche	rieche *or* riech *(provinc. [S.G.]* reuch)	gerochen.
Ring'en *(str.)*, to wrestle, wring	ich ringe ꝛc.	ich rang	ich ränge	ringe	gerungen.
Rin'nen *(str.)*, to run	ich rinne ꝛc.	ich rann	ich rönne *or* ränne	rinne	geronnen.
Ru'fen *(str.)*, to call	ich rufe ꝛc.	ich rief *(coll. w.* ich rufte)	ich riefe	rufe	gerufen.
Sal'zen *(w., p. p. gener. str.)*, to salt	ich salze ꝛc.	ich salzte	ich salzte	salze	gesalzen *(str.; sometimes w.:* gesalzt).
Sau'fen *(str.)*, *coll.* to drink	ich saufe, du säufst, er säuft	ich soff	ich söffe	saufe *or* sauf	gesoffen.
Sau'gen *(str.)*, to suck	ich sauge, du saugst, er saugt *(not* du säugst, er säugt)	ich sög	ich söge	sauge	gesogen.
Schaf'fen *(str. & w., see Dict.)*, to create	ich schaffe, du schaffst, er schafft	ich schuf	ich schüfe	schaffe *or* schaff	geschaffen.
Schei'den *(str.)*, to separate, to depart	ich scheide ꝛc.	ich schied	ich schiede	scheide	geschieden.
Schei'nen *(str.)*, to shine, appear	ich scheine ꝛc.	ich schien	ich schiene	scheine	geschienen.
Schei'ßen *(str.)*, *vulg.* to shite	ich scheiße ꝛc.	ich schiß	ich schisse	scheiße *or* scheiß	geschissen.
Schel'ten *(str.)*, to scold	ich schelte, du schiltst, er schilt	ich schalt	ich schölte *or* schälte	schilt	gescholten.
Sche'ren *(str. & w., see Dict.)*, to shear	ich schere, du scherst, er schert *(provinc.* du schierst, er schiert)	ich schor *(provinc.* ich schur)	ich schöre	schere *(provinc.* schier)	geschoren.
Schie'ben *(str.)*, to shove	ich schiebe, du schiebst, er schiebt	ich schob	ich schöbe	schiebe *or* schieb	geschoben.
Schie'ßen *(str.)*, to shoot	ich schieße, du schießest, er schießt († & *provinc.* du scheußest, er scheußt)	ich schoß	ich schösse	schieße *or* schieß († & *provinc.* scheuß)	geschossen.
Schin'den *(str.)*, to flay	ich schinde ꝛc.	ich schund *(sometimes w.* ich schindete)	ich schünde	schinde	geschunden.
Schla'fen *(str.)*, to sleep	ich schlafe, du schläfst, er schläft	ich schlief	ich schliefe	schlafe *or* schlaf	geschlafen.
Schla'gen *(str.)*, to beat, strike	ich schlage, du schlägst, er schlägt	ich schlug	ich schlüge	schlage	geschlagen.
Schlei'chen *(str.)*, to sneak	ich schleiche ꝛc.	ich schlich	ich schliche	schleiche	geschlichen.
Schlei'fen *(w. & str., see Dict.)*, to grind, whet	ich schleife ꝛc.	ich schliff	ich schliffe	schleife *or* schleif	geschliffen.
Schlei'ßen *(str., sometimes w.)*, to slit, split	ich schleiße ꝛc.	ich schliß	ich schlisse	schleiße *or* schleiß	geschlissen.
Schlie'fen, † & *provinc. (S. G.) (str.)*, to slip, glide	ich schliefe ꝛc.	ich schloff	ich schlöffe	schliefe	geschloffen.
Schlie'ßen *(str.)*, to shut, close	ich schließe, du schließest, er schließt († & *poet.* du schleußest, er schleußt)	ich schloß	ich schlösse	schließe *or* schließ († & *poet.* schleuß)	geschlossen.
Schling'en *(str.)*, to twist, wind	ich schlinge ꝛc.	ich schlang	ich schlänge	schlinge	geschlungen.
Schmei'ßen *(str.)*, to smite, strike	ich schmeiße ꝛc.	ich schmiß	ich schmisse	schmeiße *or* schmeiß	geschmissen.
Schmel'zen *(str. & w., see Dict.)*, to melt	ich schmelze, du schmilzest, er schmilzt	ich schmolz	ich schmölze	schmilz	geschmolzen.
Schnau'ben *(w. & str.)*, to snort	ich schnaube, du schnaubst, er schnaubt	ich schnob	ich schnöbe	schnaube	geschnoben.
Schnei'den *(str.)*, to cut	ich schneide ꝛc.	ich schnitt	ich schnitte	schneide	geschnitten.
Schnei'en *(w. & provinc. [S. G.] str.)*, *impers.* to snow	es schneit ꝛc.	es schneite; *(str.)* es schnie	es schneite; *(str.)* es schnie	schneie	geschneit; *(str.)* geschnieen.
Schnie'ben, † *see* Schnauben.					
Schrau'ben *(w. & str.)*, to screw	ich schraube ꝛc.	*(str.)* ich schrob	*(str.)* ich schröbe	schraube	*(str.)* geschroben.
Schreck'en *(gen. w., sometimes str., see Dict.)*, to fright	ich schrecke, du schrickst, er schrickt	ich schrak *(not* schrack)	ich schräke	schrick	geschrocken.
Schrei'ben *(str.)*, to write	ich schreibe ꝛc.	ich schrieb	ich schriebe	schreibe	geschrieben.
Schrei'en *(str.)*, to cry	ich schreie ꝛc.	ich schrie	ich schrie	schreie *or* schrei	geschrieen.
Schrei'ten *(str.)*, to stride, step	ich schreite ꝛc.	ich schritt	ich schritte	schreite	geschritten.
Schro'ten *(irr.)*, to gnaw; to rough-grind.	ich schrote, du schrotest, er schrotet	*(w.)* ich schrotete, † & *provinc. (str.)* ich schriet	ich schrotete	schrote	*(str.)* geschroten *(rarely w.* geschrotet).
Schwä'ren *(str.)*, to imposthumate	ich schwäre, du schwärest *(provinc.* du schwierst), er schwärt *(provinc.* er schwiert)	ich schwor	ich schwöre	schwäre	geschworen.
Schwei'gen *(str.)*, to be silent	ich schweige ꝛc.	ich schwieg	ich schwiege	schweige *or* schweig	geschwiegen.
Schwel'len *(str., sometimes w., see Dict.)*, to swell	ich schwelle, du schwillst, er schwillt	ich schwoll	ich schwölle	schwill	geschwollen.

Infinitive.	*Present Indicative.*	*Imperfect*		*Imperative.*	*Participle past.*
		Indicative.	*Subjunctive.*		
Schwim'men (*str.*), to swim	ich schwimme ꝛc.	ich schwamm	ich schwämme & schwömme	schwimme *or* schwimm	geschwommen.
Schwin'den (*str.*), to disappear, vanish	ich schwinde ꝛc.	ich schwand	ich schwände	schwinde	geschwunden.
Schwing'en (*str.*), to swing	ich schwinge ꝛc.	ich schwang	ich schwänge	schwing	geschwungen.
Schwö'ren (*str.*), to swear	ich schwöre ꝛc.	ich schwör *or* schwur	ich schwöre *or* schwüre	schwöre	geschworen.
Se'hen (*str.*), to see	ich sehe, du siehst (siehest), er sieht (siehet)	ich sah	ich sähe	siehe *or* sieh	gesehen *or* gesehn.
Sein (*irr.*), to be	ich bin, du bist, er ist, wir sind, ihr seid, sie sind; *subj.* ich sei, du seist, er sei; wir seien, ihr seied, sie seien	ich war, du warest (warst), er war	ich wäre	sei	gewesen.
Sen'den (*w. & irr.*), to send	ich sende ꝛc.	ich sendete *or* sandte	ich sendete	sende	gesendet *or* gesandt.
Sie'den (*str.*), to seeth, to boil	ich siede ꝛc.	ich sott	ich sötte	siede	gesotten.
Sing'en (*str.*), to sing	ich singe ꝛc.	ich sang	ich sänge	singe	gesungen.
Sin'ken (*str.*), to sink	ich sinke ꝛc.	ich sank	ich sänke	sinke	gesunken.
Sin'nen (*str.*), to meditate, reflect	ich sinne ꝛc.	ich sann († ich sonn)	ich sänne *or* sönne	sinne	gesonnen.
Sit'zen (*str.*), to sit	ich sitze ꝛc.	ich saß	ich säße	sitze	gesessen.
Sol'len (*irr.*), shall, to owe, to be obliged	ich soll, du sollst, er soll	ich sollte	ich sollte	—	gesollt.
Spal'ten (*w., p. p. str., sometimes w.*), to split, slit	ich spalte, du spaltest (*provinc.* spältst), er spaltet	ich spaltete	ich spaltete	spalte	(*str.*) gespalten (*rarely w.* gespaltet).
Spei'en (*str.*), to vomit, spew	ich speie ꝛc.	ich spie	ich spie	speie *or* spei	gespieen.
Spin'nen (*str.*), to spin	ich spinne ꝛc.	ich spann (*provinc. coll.* ich sponn)	ich spänne *or* spönne	spinne	gesponnen.
Splei'ßen (*str.*), to slice	ich spleiße ꝛc.	ich spliß	ich splisse	spleiße	gesplissen.
Sprech'en (*str.*), to speak	ich spreche, du sprichst, er spricht	ich sprach	ich spräche	sprich	gesprochen.
Sprie'ßen (*str.*), to sprout	ich sprieße ꝛc.	ich sproß	ich sprösse	sprieße *or* sprieß	gesprossen.
Spring'en (*str.*), to jump, leap, spring	ich springe, du springst, er springt	ich sprang	ich spränge	springe	gesprungen.
Stech'en (*str.*), to sting, pierce	ich steche, du stichst, er sticht	ich stach	ich stäche	stich	gestochen.
Steck'en (*str.*), to stick	ich stecke ꝛc.	ich stak	ich stäke	stecke	gesteckt (*coll.* gestecken).
Steh'en (*irr.*), to stand	ich stehe, du stehest (stehst), er stehet (steht) ꝛc.	ich stand († & *provinc.* stund)	ich stände *or* stünde	stehe *or* steh	gestanden.
Steh'len (*str.*), to steal	ich stehle, du stiehlst, er stiehlt	ich stahl (*provinc. coll.* ich stohl)	ich stähle *or* stöhle	stiehl	gestohlen.
Stei'gen (*str.*), to mount, rise	ich steige ꝛc.	ich stieg	ich stiege	steige *or* steig	gestiegen.
Ster'ben (*str.*), to die	ich sterbe, du stirbst, er stirbt	ich starb (*provinc.* ich sturb)	ich stürbe	stirb	gestorben.
Stie'ben (*str.*), to dust	ich stiebe ꝛc.	ich stob	ich stöbe	stiebe *or* stieb	gestoben.
Stin'ken (*str.*), to stink	ich stinke ꝛc.	ich stank	ich stänke	stinke	gestunken.
Sto'ßen (*str.*), to thrust	ich stoße, du stößest, er stößt	ich stieß	ich stieße	stoße *or* stoß	gestoßen.

Infinitive.	*Present Indicative.*	*Imperfect* *Indicative.*	*Imperfect* *Subjunctive.*	*Imperative.*	*Participle past.*
Verheh'len *(w., p. p. sometimes str.)*, to conceal	*(w.)* ich verhehle ꝛc.	*(w.)* ich verhehlte	*(w.)* ich verhehlete	*(w.)* verhehle	*(w.)* verhehlt, *(str.)* verhohlen.
Verlie'ren *(str.)*, to lose	ich verliere ꝛc.	ich verlor	ich verlöre	verliere	verloren.
Verlösch'en *(str. & w., cf. Dict.)*, to be extinguished	ich verlosche, du verlischest *or* verlöschest, er verlischt *or* verloscht	ich verlosch	ich verlosche	verlisch *or* verlösche	verloschen.
Verschal'len *(str. & w.)*, to cease sounding, to die away (of sounds)	ich verschalle, du verschallst, er verschallt	ich verscholl	ich verschölle	verschalle	verschollen.
Verschrau'ben *(str. & w.)*, to misscrew	ich verschraube ꝛc.	ich verschrob	ich verschröbe	verschraube	verschroben.
Verschwin'den *(str.)*, to disappear	ich verschwinde, du verschwindest, er verschwindet	ich verschwand	ich verschwände	verschwinde	verschwunden.
Verwir'ren *(gen. w., p. p. sometimes str.)*, to complicate, entangle, puzzle	*(w.)* ich verwirre, du verwirrst, er verwirrt	*(w.)* ich verwirrte	*(w.)* ich verwirrte	*(w.)* verwirre	*(w.)* verwirrt, *(str.)* verworren.
Verzeih'en *(str.)*, to forgive	ich verzeihe ꝛc.	ich verzieh	ich verziehe	verzeih	verziehen.
Wach'sen *(str.)*, to grow	ich wachse, du wächsest, er wächst	ich wuchs	ich wüchse	wachse	gewachsen.
Wä'gen *(gen. w.)* *or* **Wie'gen** *(str.)*, to weigh	ich wäge *or* wiege, du wägst *or* wiegst, er wägt *or* wiegt	*(w.)* ich wägte, *(str.)* ich wog	ich wöge	wäge *or* wiege	gewogen.
Wasch'en *(str.)*, to wash	ich wasche, du waschest, er wäscht	ich wusch	ich wüsche	wasche	gewaschen.
We'ben *(w., † & poet. str.)*, to weave	ich webe ꝛc.	ich wob	ich wöbe	webe	gewoben.
Wei'chen *(str., sometimes w., see Dict.)*, to yield, retire	ich weiche ꝛc.	ich wich	ich wiche	weiche	gewichen.
Wei'sen *(str.)*, *coll.* to show	ich weise ꝛc.	ich wies	ich wiese	weise	gewiesen.
Wen'den *(w. & irr.)*, to turn	ich wende ꝛc.	ich wendete *or* wandte	ich wendete	wende	gewendet *or* gewandt.
Wer'ben *(str.)*, to enlist; to woo	ich werbe, du wirbst, er wirbt	ich warb	ich würbe	wirb	geworben.
Wer'den *(irr.)*, to become, grow	ich werde, du wirst, er wird, wir werden, ihr werdet, sie werden	ich wurde *or* ward, du wurdest (wardst), er wurde (ward), wir wurden, ihr wurdet, sie wurden	ich würde	werde	geworden *or* (*as an auxiliary verb*) worden.
Wer'fen *(str.)*, to throw	ich werfe, du wirfst, er wirft	ich warf	ich würfe (*u.* ich wärfe)	wirf	geworfen.
Wie'gen *(str.)*, to weigh; to rock	ich wiege ꝛc.	ich wog	ich wöge	wiege	gewogen.
Win'den *(str.)*, to wind	ich winde ꝛc.	ich wand	ich wände	winde	gewunden.
Wis'sen *(irr.)*, to know	ich weiß, du weißt, er weiß, wir wissen ꝛc.	ich wußte	ich wüßte	wisse	gewußt.
Wol'len *(irr.)*, to will, to be willing, &c.	ich will, du willst, er will, wir wollen, ihr wollt, sie wollen	ich wollte	ich wollte	wolle	gewollt.
Zeih'en *(str.)*, to accuse	ich zeihe ꝛc.	ich zieh	ich ziehe	zeihe	geziehen.
Zerschel'len, *(intr., gen. w., † [& *] str.)*, to split, &c.	ich zerschelle, † du zerschillst, † er zerschillt	† ich zerscholl	† ich zerschölle	—	† zerschollen.
Zieh'en *(str.)*, to draw	ich ziehe, du ziehst, er zieht (*poet.* du zeuchst, er zeucht)	ich zog	ich zöge	ziehe *or* zieh (*poet.* zeuch)	gezogen.
Zwing'en *(str.)*, to force, compel	ich zwinge ꝛc.	ich zwang	ich zwänge	zwinge	gezwungen.

II.

As a list of all the strong substantives would have to embrace many words of foreign origin, and be of considerable length, it is preferable here merely to give the distinctive marks of this as well as of the weak declension.

Nouns of the *strong* declension, which are recognisable by an -s terminating the genitive,* frequently take the modification of vowel in the plural, invariably so, when the plural ends in -er. This modification of vowel has been indicated in the following table by ".

Table of the terminations of the strong and weak declensions: —

Strong declension:			Weak declension:	
Singular	*Plural* (first form)	*Plural* (second form)	*Singular*	*Plural*
Nom. —	(") —e	" —er	*Nom.* —	—en
Gen. —(e)s	(") —e	" —er	*Gen.* —en	—en
Dat. —(e)	(") —en	" —ern	*Dat.* —en	—en
Acc. —	(") —e	" —er	*Acc* —en	—en

Accordingly, it is only necessary for those who make use of this Dictionary to know, whether a substantive is strong (and in this case the form of the plural has always been given when modifying the radical vowel), or whether it is weak, or irregular. — The number of *irregular* substantives being very large and including many words derived from foreign languages (designated in the dictionary by an * preceding the word), merely a limited number of these has been given, with all the irregular words of purely German origin.

* Except in Feminines. No German feminine is declined in the singular.

Irregular Substantives.

A'berglaube, A'bername, A'berwille, Ab'sproß, Ab'strahl &c., *see* Glaube, Name, Wille, Sproß, Strahl &c.
Au'ge, *n.* eye, *sing. str. (Gen.* des Auges), *pl. w.* die Augen.
Bau'er, *m.* peasant, *sing. str. (Gen.* des Bauers), *pl. w.* die Bauern.
Bett, *n* bed, *sing str. (Gen.* des Bettes), *pl. w.* die Betten.
Buch'stabe, *m.* letter, *generally weak; Gen. sing* des Buchstabens.
Diamant', *m.* diamond, *sing. generally str. (sometimes w.), pl. w.*
Dorn, *m.* thorn, *generally str., Gen sing.* des Dornes, *pl.* die Dörner; *the plural is more frequently weak,* die Dornen.
En'de, *n.* end, *sing. str. (Gen.* des Endes), *pl. w.* die Enden.
Forst, *m.* forest, *sing. str. (Gen.* des Forstes), *pl. w.* die Forsten; *the strong forms* Forste *and* Förste *are little used.*
Frie'de, *m* (Frieden *l. u.)* peace, *Gen. sing.* des Friedens, *Dat.* dem Frieden, *Acc.* den Frieden.
Funke, *m.* (Funken *l. u.)* spark, *Gen. sing.* des Funkens, *Dat.* dem Funken, *Acc.* den Funken, *pl.* die Funken.
Gau, *m.* district, *generally str. (Gen. sing.* des Gaues, *pl.* die Gaue); *pl sometimes weak,* die Gauen.
Gedanke, *m.* thought, *Gen. sing.* des Gedankens, *Dat.* dem Gedanken, *Acc.* den Gedanken, *pl.* die Gedanken.
Gevat'ter, *m.* god-father, *sing. str. (Gen.* des Gevatters), *pl. w.* die Gevattern.
Glau'be, *m.* belief, *Gen. sing.* des Glaubens, *Dat.* dem Glauben, *Acc.* den Glauben, *pl. (l. u.)* die Glauben.
Granāt', *m. Ichth.* shrimp, *sing str. (Gen.* des Granates), *pl. w.* die Granaten.
Ha'der, *m.* rag, *sing. str. (Gen* des Haders, *rarely w.* des Hadern), *pl. w.* die Hadern.
Hau'fe *or* **Hau'fen,** *m.* heap, crowd, &c., *Gen. sing.* des Haufens, *Dat.* dem Haufen, *Acc.* den Haufen, *pl.* die Haufen.
Hemd, *n.* shirt, *sing. str. (Gen.* des Hemdes), *pl. w.* die Hemden.
Herz, *n.* heart, *Gen. sing.* des Herzens, *Dat.* dem Herzen, *Acc.* das Herz, *pl.* die Herzen.
Hu'del, *m. provinc. coll.* rag, *sing. str. (Gen.* des Hudels), *pl. w.* die Hudeln.
Hu'hu, *see* Uhu.
Ingredienz', *f. (orig. Lat.:* **Ingre'diens,** *n.)* ingredient, *pl.* Ingredien'zien.
Juwēl', *n.* jewel, *sing str. (Gen.* des Juwels), *pl. w.* die Juwelen.
Kapaun', *m* capon, *generally str., pl. sometimes w.*
Klamp, *m.* clamp, *sing. str. (Gen.* des Klampes), *pl. w.* die Klampen.
Lor'beer, *m.* laurel, *sing. str. (Gen.* des Lorbeers), *pl. w.* die Lorbeeren.
Mars, *n. Mar.* top (of a ship), *sing. str. (Gen.* des Marses), *pl. w.* die Marsen *(sometimes str.* die Marse).
Mast, *m.* mast, *sing. str. (Gen.* des Mastes), *pl. w.* die Masten.
Mus'kel, *m.* muscle, *sing. str (Gen.* des Muskels), *pl. w.* die Muskeln.
Nach'bar, *m.* neighbour, *sing. str. (Gen.* des Nachbars), *pl. w.* die Nachbarn.
Na'me, *m.* name, *Gen. sing.* des Namens, *Dat.* dem Namen, *Acc.* den Namen, *pl.* die Namen.
Ohr, *n.* ear, *sing. str. (Gen.* des Ohres), *pl. w.* die Ohren.
Ost, *m.* east, *the strong forms (Gen.* Ostes) *are rarely used, the Gen., Dat. and Acc. of* Osten (des Ostens, dem Osten, den Osten) *supplying their place.*
Pantof'fel, *m.* slipper, *sing. str. (Gen.* des Pantoffels), *pl. w.* die Pantoffeln.
Pfau, *m.* peacock, *sing str. (Gen.* des Pfaues, † *& provinc. [S. G.] w.* des Pfauen), *pl. w.* die Pfauen *(sometimes str.* die Pfaue).
Prāfect', *m.* prefect, *generally w., sing. sometimes str.*
Psalm, *m.* psalm, *sing. str.* des Psalmes, *pl. w.* die Psalmen *(sometimes str.* die Psalme).
Rubin', *m.* ruby, *generally str., pl. sometimes w.*
Sa'me, *m.* seed, *Gen. sing.* des Samens, *Dat* dem Samen, *Acc.* den Samen, *pl.* die Samen.
Scha'de, *gener.* **Scha'den,** *m.* damage, *Gen. sing.* des Schadens, *Dat.* dem Schaden, *Acc* den Schaden, *pl.* die Schaden.
Schmerz, *m.* pain, *sing. str. (Gen.* des Schmerzes, *formerly* des Schmerzens, *Dat.* dem Schmerze, *formerly* dem Schmerzen), *pl. w.* die Schmerzen.
See, *m.* lake, *sing. str. (Gen.* des Sees), *pl. w.* die Seen.
Sporn, *m.* spur, *sing str. (Gen.* des Spornes); *pl. w.* die Spornen *(or* Sporen), *sometimes str.* die Sporne.
Staat, *m.* state, *sing. str. (Gen.* des Staates), *pl. w.* die Staaten.
Stach'el, *m.* sting, *sing. str. (Gen.* des Stachels), *pl. w.* die Stacheln.
Stie'fel, *m.* boot, *sing str. (Gen.* des Stiefels), *pl. w.* die Stiefeln, *sometimes str.* die Stiefel.
Strahl, *m.* ray, *sing str. (Gen* des Strahl[e]s), *pl. w.* die Strahlen.
Strauß, *m.* ostrich, *generally str., pl.* die Strauße, *sometimes w.* die Straußen.
U'hu, *m.* owl, *str., Gen. sing.* des Uhus, *pl.* die Uhu, *coll. (particularly N. G.)* die Uhus.
Un'terthan, *m.* subject, *sing. str. (Gen.* des Unterthan[e]s; † *& provinc. [S. G.]: w.* des Unterthanen), *pl. w.* die Unterthanen.
Vet'ter, *m.* cousin, *sing. str. (Gen.* des Vetters), *sometimes w. (Gen* des Vettern), *pl. w.* die Vettern.
Wil'le, *m.* will, *Gen. sing.* des Willens, *Dat.* dem Willen, *Acc.* den Willen.
Zie'rath, *m.* ornament, *sing. str. (Gen.* des Zierathes), *pl. w.* die Zierathen *(sometimes str.* die Zierathe).
Zins, *m.* interest on capital, *sing. str. (Gen.* des Zinses), *pl. w.* die Zinsen.

SECOND PART:

GERMAN AND ENGLISH.

A.

A, a, I. *s.* *(str. or not decl.)* *n.* 1) *Gramm.* A, a, the first letter of the Alphabet; ein großes — (A), a great (capital) a; ein kleines — (a), a small (little) a; von — bis Z, from A to Z, from the beginning to the end; er erzählte alles von — bis Z, he detailed the whole affair; wer — sagt, muß auch B sagen, *proverb*, he who begins with a thing, must go on with it; *cf.* in for a penny, in for a pound; ich bin das — und das O, *Script.* I am Alpha and Omega, the beginning and the ending; 2) *Mus.* (the sixth note of the gamut, named *la* in Italy and France); A dur, (the key of) A major; A moll, (the key of) A minor; diese Melodie geht aus A, this tune is in la *or* A; II. a, à (*abbr. from* ana, *see* Vol. I.) *prep. Comm.* used *for* zu, at: à fünf Procent, at (the rate of) five per Cent; à Conto *(à Cto)*, on account; à Conto-Zahlung, payment on account; *Law*, indefinite payment; à uso, *Comm.* at double usance; *a tempo* Stoß, *Fenc.* time-thrust.

A., *abbr. Comm.* 1) (on letters of exchange, *for*:) acceptirt, accepted; 2) (on lists of prices, for the *Fr.* word:) *argent*, money; a. a. O., 1) *for* an andern Orten, in other places; 2) am angeführten Orte, in the place cited; A. *or* Ann. (A. Ann.) *for (Lat.) Anno*, in the year; A. B. *for (Lat.) Artium Baccalaureus*, Baccalaureus der freien Künste; Ab. *or* Abonn. *for* Abonnement, subscription; a. c. *for anni currentis, anno currente (Lat.)*, des laufenden Jahres, im laufenden Jahre, of, in the present year; A. C. *or* Augsb. C. 1) *Comm. for* Augsburger Courant, Augsburg currency; 2) *Eccl. for* Augsburgische Confession, Confession of Augsburg, Augustan Confession; a. D. 1) *Comm. for a Dato (Lat.)*, vom Tage der Ausstellung (eines Wechsels &c.) an, from this day *or* date, after date; 2) *for (Lat.) anno Domini*, im Jahre unsers Herrn, in the year of our Lord; a. D. *for* außer Diensten (said of officers), out of service, on half pay; add. *for (Lat.) adde*, füge hinzu, setze bei, add; Adm. *for* Admiral, admiral; a. b. *for* an der, on the; a. d. Saale, Oder, *or* a/S., a/O., on the Saale, on the Oder; a. f. *for (Lat.) anni futuri, anno futuro*, des künftigen, kommenden Jahres, im kommenden Jahre, next year; a. g. *Comm. for (Ital.) a governo*, zur Richtschnur, for (your) government; A. G. *for* Apostelgeschichte, Acts of the Apostles; a. G. u. b. M. *for* außerordentlicher Gesandter und bevollmächtigter Minister, envoy (ambassador) extraordinary and minister plenipotentiary; Alt. Test. *for* altes Testament, old testament; a. M., a/M. *for* am Main, on the Main(e); A. M. 1) *for (Lat.) anno mundi*, im Jahre der Welt, in the year of the world; 2) *for (Lat.) Artium Magister*, Master of Arts; amtl. *for* amtlich, official; Ank. *for* Anker (a liquid measure), anker; a. O. *see* a. a. O.; a. p. *for (Lat.) anni praecedentis, anno praecedente*, des vorigen Jahres, im vorigen Jahre, (of, in the) last year; a. pr. *for (Lat.) anni praesentis, anno praesente*, des gegenwärtigen Jahres, im gegenwärtigen Jahre, of, in the present year; Apr. *for* April, April; A. R. *for (Lat.) anno regni*, im ... Regierungsjahre, in the ... year of ...; A. St. *for* alter Stil, *Chron.* old style; A. T. *see* Alt. Test.; a U. *Comm. for (Ital.) a uso*, nach hergebrachter Gewohnheit, in the usual way; Aufl., Ausg. *for* Auflage, Ausgabe, edition; Aug. 1) *for* (Monat) August, August; 2) Augustus (*P. N.*); Augm. *for (Lat.) augmentum*, Vermehrung, Zusatz, augmentation, addition; a. u. s. *for (Lat.) actum ut supra*, geschehen wie oben (angegeben), an dem nämlichen Tage, *Law*, done as above, on the same day; ausüb. A. *for* ausübender Arzt, practising physician.

Aa, *(w.)* *f.* flowing water, river, rivulet.

Aa'chen, *(str.)* *n. Geogr.* Aix-la-Chapelle.

Aak, *(str.)* *m.* aak (a kind of flat-bottomed lighter employed on the Rhine).

Aal, I. *(str.)* *m. Ichth.* eel *(Muraena anguilla* L.); der chinesische —, snake-gourd, sword-fish *(Trichiurus lepturus* L.); A-e fangen, *see* Aalen; ein kleiner —, grig; ein Stückchen —, a cut of an eel; 2) *Bak.* a kind of eel-shaped butter-cake; 3) *Cloth.* a wrong fold in cloth, a crumple, crease; er schlüpft wie ein — durch die Finger, he slips through one's fingers like an eel; den — beim Schwanze fassen, to begin a thing at the wrong end; II. *in comp.* —artig, *adj.* anguilliform; —baum, *m. see* Heckenkirsche; —beere, *f.* —beerstrauch, *m.* —besing, *m. see* Johannisbeere, schwarze; —behälter, *m.* eel-trunk; eel-pond; —bock, *m. Ichth.* a species of salmon in the lake of Thun in Switzerland; snipe (Schnäpel, *Salmo Wartmanni*); —butte, —quappe, —raupe, *f. Ichth.* birdbolt, burbot, eell, eel-pout, cony-fish, quab *(Gadus lota* L.); —damm, *m.* —lege, *f.* —wehr, *n.* eel-dam; —eidechse, —schleiche, *f. Zool.* a species of lizard *(Lacerta chalcides* L.; *Seps chalcidica* Ok.); —eisen, *n.* —gabel, *f.* eel-spear; —fang, *m.* 1) eeling, eel-fishing; sniggling; 2) season and place for catching eels; eel-fishery; 3) eel-trunk; —fänger, *m.* eel-fisher, eel-catcher; —fell, *n.* —haut, *f.* eel-skin, skin of an eel; —fellband, —fellseil, *n.* eel-skin band *or* rope; —fett, *n.* eel-grease; —flöße, *f. see* —puppe; —förmig, *adj.* eel-shaped, anguilliform; —frau, *f.* 1) eel-monger; 2) *or* —quappe, *f. see* —mutter; —gabel, *f.* eel-spear, eel-fork; —grube, *f.* eel-pond; —grundel, *f.* —gründling, *m. Ichth.* gudgeon, goby *(Cyprinus gobio* L.); —hälter, —hälter, *see* —behälter; —kirsche, *f. Bot.* 1) *see* Traubenkirsche; 2) *see* Heckenkirsche; 3) *see* Vogelbeere; —köpfchen, *n. Conch.* snake's head coralline *(Sertularia anguinia* L.); —korb, *m.* 1) eel-pot, junket; 2) eel-wear; —krug, *m.* large (earthen) vessel with perforations to keep eels in; —lager, *n.* bed of eels; —lege, *f. see* —wehr; —molch, *m.* a species of lizard; —mutter, *f. Ichth.* the viviparous blenny, guffer *(Blennius viviparus* L.); —natter, *f.* a species of water-snake *(Rhagerrhis coerulea)*; —nest, *n. see* —lege; —netz, *n. see* —wehr; —pricke, *f. see* —gabel; —puppe, —quaste, *f.* a baited bundle of rushes *or* green twigs for eeling, bob; —quappe, —raupe, *f. see* —butte; —reuse, *f.* a basket in which eels are caught, bully, junket, eel-pot; —schlange, *f. Zool.* a snake with scales under the belly and tail *(Anguis* L.); —schleiche, *f. see* —eidechse; A-schorn, *n. see* Holunder; —stachel, *m. see* —gabel; —stecher, *m.* 1) *see* —fänger; 2) *see* —gabel; —streif, —strich, *m.* a black streak on the back of an eel, also of a dun-coloured horse; mit einem —striche, eel-backed; —teich, *m.* eel-pond; —thierchen, *n. Zool.* vibrio *(Vibrio* L.); —wade, *f.* a net for catching eels; —wehr, *n.* 1) eel-wear, eel-dam; 2) *see* —reuse; —welk, *m. see* Bunkel; —wurm, *m. see* —thierchen; —zaun, *m. see* —lager, —wehr.

Aa'len, *(w.)* *v. tr.* 1) to fish for eels in (a pond); also *intr.* to sniggle; 2) *Hydr.* to cleanse by means of an eel; das —, *v. s.* *(str.)* *n.* eel-fishing.

Aam, *f. see* Ahm, 1.

Aap, *(w.)* *m.* (*L. G. for* Affe) *Mar.* mizzen-stay-sail; A-enfall, *m. Mar.* hallard of the mizzen-stay-sail.

Aar, I. *(str., pl.* Aa're*)* *m.* 1) † & *Nat.* any large bird of prey; 2) * eagle, *see* Adler; —beere, —kirsche, *see* Elsebeere; —weihe, *m.* & *f. Ornith. see* Kornweihe; II. *(w.)* *f. Geogr.* Aar, several rivers in Switzerland &c.: —gau, *m. Geogr.* Argovia, Argow; —gauer, *m.* —gauerin, *f.* Argovian; —gauisch, *adj.* Argovian.

Aa'ron, *(str.)* *m.* Aaron; A-sstab, *m. Bot. see* Zehrwurz; *cf.* Aron.

Aas, I. *(str., pl.* A'ser*)* *n.* 1) offal; 2) carrion, (rotten) carcass; 3) *a)* food for animals: *b) Sport.* lure, bait; 4) *Tann.* scrapings *or* parings of hides; 5) *Mill.* groats; *Sport.-s.* ein — legen, to lay a bait *or* lure; ein — an die Angel stecken, to bait a hook; II. *in comp.* —blatter, *f. Med.* putrid carbuncle; —blume, *f. see* —pflanze; —fliege, *f. Entom.* dung-fly *(Musca cadaverina* L.); —fräßig, —fressend, *adj.* feeding on carrion, carnivorous; —geier, *m. Ornith.* 1) horse-kite, carrion-kite *(Vultur percnopterus* L.); 2) carrion-vulture, turkey buzzard *(Vultur aura* L.); —geruch, *m.* cadaverous smell, carrion smell; —grube, *f.* carrion pit; —jäger, *m.* a person that hunts after game in an unsportsmanlike manner; —jägerei, *f.* an unsportsmanlike manner of hunting; —käfer, *m. Ent.* carrion-beetle, dorr-beetle, black-fly *(Silpha* L.); —kopf, *m. Archit.*

an ornament of the Doric order, representing the skinned head of an immolated victim; —krähe, *f. Ornith.* carrion crow (*Corvus corone* L.); —kuhle, *f. see* —grube; —mücke, *f. see* —fliege; —pflanze, *f. Bot.* fritillary coxcomb, stapelia (*Stapelia* L.); —pocke, *f. see* —blatter; —rabe, *m. Ornith.* raven (*Corvus corax* L.); —seite, *f. Skin-dr.* fleshside; —vogel, *m.* any bird that feeds on carrion.

Aa'sen, (*w.*) *v.* I. *tr.* 1) *Tann.* to flesh, to shave off, to curry (skins); 2) *Sport.* to bait a hook *or* snare; II. *intr.* 1) *Sport.* to browse, to graze (of deer); 2) to feed on carrion; 3) *vulg.* to spoil one's work, clothes &c. by dirt, uncleanliness.

Aas'haft, Aa'sig, *adj.* 1) cadaverous, carrion, carrion-like; 2) *fig.* ugly, dirty.

Ab, I. *prep.* († *&*) *provinc.* off (down *or* away), from; II. *adv.* (*generally denoting deviation or separation from*) 1) down; auf und —, up and down; Strom —, down (the) stream (*opp.* Strom auf, up [the] stream); 2) off, away; of, from, fro: — und zu, to and fro; off and on; sie kommt — und zu, she is coming backwards and forwards; — und zu fanden Scharmützel statt, occasional skirmishes took place; auf und — (gehen, to go), up and down; zehn Thaler auf und —, *fam.* ten dollars more or less; Hut —! off with your hat! Hüte —! hats off! er hatte den Hut —, he had his hat off; der Deckel ist —, the cover (lid) is off; *Comm.-s.* — an Unkosten (*or* Auslagen), charges to be deducted; — Leipzig, to be delivered at Leipzig; vom 1. Januar —, from the 1st of January; — (abgezogen), hiervon *or* davon geht —, discount ..., deduct ...; *Mar.* off; weit —, far off; er wohnt weit (von) hier —, he lives a great way off; wie weit ist es von hier —? how far is it off? wir waren ganz vom Wege —, we were quite out of our way; von Jemand — sein, to have done with one; kurz —, abruptly, shortly.

Ab'aasen, (*w.*) *v. tr. see* Aasen.

* **Aba'ca,** *see* Rossfolden [illegible]

Ab'ächzen, *v. refl.* to pine away, to fret, waste by sighing and moaning.

Ab'ackern, (*w.*) *v.* I. *tr.* to separate *or* take off by ploughing; mein Nachbar ackert mir alle Jahre einige Furchen von meinem Eigenthume ab (eignet sie sich zu), my neighbour encroaches several furrows every year on my property; II. *intr.* to finish ploughing.

* **Ab'acus,** *m.* 1) *Ant.* (a kind of writing-table) abacus; 2) *Archit.* (uppermost part of the capital of a column) abacus; 3) *Arith. see* Multiplications-, Rechen- & Zahlentafel.

* **Abaissirt'** [abässirt'], *adj. Herald.* abased.

* **Abar'jouns,** *incorr. see* Abajouns.

* **Abälardisi'ren,** (*w.*) *v. tr. see* Entmannen.

* **Abalienatiōn',** (*w.*) *f.* **Abaliení'ren,** (*w.*) *v. tr. see* Veräußerung, Veräußern & Aufgeben.

Ab'änderlich, *adj.* 1) alterable, modifiable; 2) *Gramm.* declinable.

Ab'änderlichkeit, (*w.*) *f.* alterability, &c.

Ab'ändern, (*w.*) *v. tr.* 1) to alter, to change; to rectify (an account *or* an error of account); to qualify; to modify, diversify; 2) *Gramm.* to decline (a noun), to inflect (a verb); 3) einen Gesetzvorschlag —, to amend a bill.

Ab'änderung, (*w.*) *f.* 1) alteration, (partial) change, modification, variation, diversification; mit *or* nach den nöthigen A-en, after making the necessary changes; 2) *Gramm.* inflection (of a verb), declension (of a noun); 3) amendment; *Orgad.* A-Stöckchen, *f. pl.* secondary, subordinary *or* subordination-faces; A-Formen, *f. pl.* secondary forms.

* **Abandon'** [*pr.* abangdong'], (*str.*) *m.* (*Fr.*), **Abandonni'rung,** (*w.*) *f. Comm. & Law,* abandonment, assignment; *see* Abtrand, 2.

* **Abandonni'ren,** (*w.*) *v. tr. Comm.* to abandon, to relinquish.

Ab'ängsten, Ab'ängstigen, (*w.*) *v.* I. *tr.* 1) to weary with anxiety, to vex, torment, to distress; 2) (*l. u.*) to extort from; II. *refl.* to be in (to weary one's self with) great anxiety, to fret.

Ab'ängstigung, (*w.*) *f.* 1) (the act of) vexing, &c.; 2) fretting, anxiety; anguish, uneasiness. [to put to sea.

Ab'ankern, (*w.*) *v. intr. Mar.* to unmoor,

* **Abannatiōn',** (*w.*) *f. Law,* abannition.

* **Abap'tiston,** (*str.*) *n. Surg. see* Trepan.

Ab'arbeiten, (*w.*) *v.* I. *tr.* 1) to work off; das Gröbste —, to rough-hew; to rough-work; einen Marmorblock —, to chip a block of marble; Steine —, *see* Behauen; 2) *Mar.-s.* to work off, to loosen; ein Schiff vom Strande — (los-, wegarbeiten), to get a ship afloat *or* off from the ground; ein Boot vom Ufer —, to let go a boat from the shore; ein geentertes Schiff — (losmachen, abstoßen), to repulse off the enemy, who attempts to board; 3) *a)* to wear out (an axe, &c.) by frequent use; *b) fig.* to wear out, fatigue, overtire; *vulg.* to fag; 4) eine Schuld —, to clear a debt by work, to work it out; das Sauerkraut —, *Print. slang,* to work for a dead horse; 5) sein Tagewerk —, to work out, finish one's task; II. *refl.* 1) to overlabour one's self, work one's self weary, to toil *or* struggle hard, to strain every nerve, to drudge, to toil and moil; 2) *Mech.* to wear out, to waste (by continued friction); sich (*Dat.*) die Finger —, to work one's fingers to the bone; III. *intr.* to cease fermenting, working (said of wine).

Ab'arbeitung, (*w.*) *f.* 1) the act of working off, &c. *cf.* Abarbeiten; 2) exhaustion.

Ab'ärgern, (*w.*) *v.* I. *tr.* to weary by vexation; II. *refl.* to be mortified *or* vexed.

Ab'ärnten, *see* Abernten.

Ab'art, (*w.*) *f.* 1) *Bot., Zool. & Miner.* variety; 2) *a)* degenerate breed; *b) fig.* degeneracy.

Ab'arten, (*w.*) *v. intr.* (*aux.* sein) 1) to deviate, to vary (von, from); to degenerate; 2) *fig. see* Ausarten.

Ab'artig, *adj.* varying; degenerate.

Ab'artung, (*w.*) *f.* 1) variation, degeneration; 2) deviation, *see* Abart.

* **Abarticulatiōn',** (*w.*) *f. Surg.* 1) abarticulation; 2) *see* Verrenkung.

Ab'äschern, (*w.*) *v.* I. *tr. Cook.* to scour with ashes; II. *refl. fig. fam.* to overheat one's self and get out of breath, to fatigue *or* harass one's self by bodily exertion.

Ab'äsen, Ab'äsen, (*w.*) *v. intr. Sport.* to browse, to bark ([gnaw the bark of] young trees). [(trees).

Ab'ästen, (*w.*) *v. tr.* to lop, poll, detruncate

Ab'äthmen, (*w.*) *v. tr.* (*l. u.*) *Metall. & Chem.* to glow out, to redden (a cupel) in the fire (in order to dry it).

Ab'ätzen, (*w.*) *v. tr.* to eat away, to corrode; *Surg.* to remove by caustics *or* cauterization.

Ab'äugeln, (*w.*) *v. tr.* 1) *a) T.* to ascertain the straightness &c. by sight (Absehen); *b) Sport.* to search (the track) with the eye; 2) (Einem etwas) *fig.* to win *or* get (something) from (one) by ogling *or* insinuating looks.

Ab'äußern, (*w.*) *v. tr. Law,* to eject from a tenement, *see* Abmeiern.

* **Ab'ba,** (*Hebr.*) *Script.* abba (father).

A. **Ab'backen,** (*str. cf.* Backen) *v.* I. *intr.* (*aux.* sein) to separate in baking; das Brod ist abgebacken, the crust of the bread has separated from the crumb; II. *tr.* 1) (*sometimes intr.*) to finish baking; der Bäcker hat abgebacken, the baker has done baking; 2) to dry completely (in an oven, &c.), to dry (fruit, &c.).

B. **Ab'backen,** (*w.*) *v. tr. see* Abbaken.

Ab'baden, (*w.*) *v. tr.* 1) to remove by bathing, to wash off, *sometimes fig., f. i.* die Sünde in der Reue abbaden (*J. Grimm*); 2) to wash thoroughly, to cleanse by bathing; sich tüchtig —, *coll.* to give one's self a good washing; 3) (*also intr.*) to finish bathing.

Ab'bähen, (*w.*) *v. tr.* to foment thoroughly.

Ab'bahren, (*w.*) *v. tr.* to take (a coffin, &c.) down from the bier.

Ab'baken, (*w.*) *v. tr. Mar.* to mark with buoys; *Dik.* to mark (a line) with stakes.

Ab'balgen, *sometimes* **Ab'bälgen,** (*w.*) *v. tr.* 1) to uncase, to strip *or* divest of the skin, to flay, to skin (a hare, &c.); 2) (*usually recipr.* einander [*coll.* sich] abbalgen) to fatigue *or* exhaust (one another) by wrestling, grappling, boxing, thumping, &c.

Ab'bamsen (*corr. from* Abwamsen), (*w.*) *v. tr. Tann.* to beat (skins) duly *or* sufficiently.

Ab'bangen, (*w.*) *v. tr.* (*an unusual word coined by Lessing,* 2, 269: um Geld, [illegible] einem Juden abzubangen) to extort (Einem etwas, something from one) by frightening; to get by intimidating, *cf.* Abängstigen, which is the usual word.

Ab'banfen, (*w.*) *v. tr.* to remove (the sheaves, &c.) from the barn-floor.

Ab'barbieren, (*w.*) *v. tr.* to shave off.

Ab'basten, (*w.*) *v. tr.* to strip (a tree) of the inside bark. [(*for* Ab[illegible]

* **Abbas, Abbat,** (*str.*) *m.* abbot [illegible]

* **Abbatis'sin,** (*w.*) *f.* abbess, *see* [illegible]

Ab'bäuchen, (*w.*) *v. tr.* 1) to [illegible] with lye; 2) to clear of lye, to remove the [illegible] from ... by washing, &c. *cf.* Ablaugen, Ab[illegible]laugen.

Ab'bau, (*str.*) *m. particul. Min.* 1) *a)* the act of working a mine; *b)* exhaustion (of a mine, &c.); in — bringen, to exhaust (the fertility of land, &c.); 2) the vacant space proceeding from the working of a mine, [illegible] excavated working; an exhausted [illegible] (*Cornwall*) a hulk.

Ab'bauen, (*w.*) *v. tr.* 1) (*l. u.*) to [illegible] take down, to demolish (a building, &c.), *see* Abtragen, 1, *c.*; 2) to build *or* erect (a [illegible] etc.) at a certain distance from ...; 3) [illegible] (*intr.*) to finish *or* to complete a building; *a)* to work (a mine, &c.) till it is exhausted; to exhaust (land, &c.); *Min.-s.* *b)* to [illegible] (a mine) on account of its being exhausted; *c) Min.* to pay off (the shares of a mine) [illegible] its produce, to defray (the charges of a [illegible]

Ab'bauern, (*w.*) *v. intr.* to give over farming, to give up agricultural pursuits.

Ab'baumen, (*w.*) *v. intr. Sport.* by [illegible] to light from a tree, to tree (as [illegible] squirrels, &c.); *frequently* to fly off [illegible] tree (*opp.* Aufbaumen).

Ab'bäumen, (*w.*) *v. tr. Weav.* to [illegible] web), to take (the web) from the loom.

Ab'bau..., *in comp.* —ort, *m.* [illegible] *Min.* board, stall, precinct, thirling.

Ab'bausen, (*w.*) *v. tr. F.* to [illegible]

Ab'bauung, (*w.*) *f.* 1) the act of [illegible] down, &c. *cf.* Abbauen; 2) abandonment [illegible] mine, &c.

Ab'bauwürdig, *adj.* (of beds of [illegible] coals, &c.) worth working (*syn.* [illegible] 442: [this] led to the hope that [illegible] deposit of coal worth working would [illegible] on the south side of [illegible]

Ab'beeren, (*w.*) *v. tr.* to pick, [illegible] strip off the berries from (the [illegible] einen Strauch, einen Weinstock, [illegible] to strip a shrub, a vine, a bunch of [illegible] also *fig.* to use every particle of [illegible] enjoy to the utmost, to make use [illegible] breeze jede Minute euers Lebens [illegible] ab (*Jean Paul, Hesperus*).

Ab'befehlen, (*str.*) *v. tr.* to [illegible] to countermand; to recover [illegible] befohlen worden, the chase has [illegible] manded (*cf.* Abbestellen).

Ab'begehren, *(w.)* v. *tr.* (Einem etwas) to ask (something of), *see* Abverlangen.

Ab'behalten, *(str.)* v. *tr.* to keep off; den Hut —, to be *or* to remain uncovered.

Ab'beißen, *(str.)* v. I. *tr.* to bite off, to nip off, to snap off; sich *(Dat.)* die Nägel —, to bite one's nails; sich *(Dat.)* vor Lachen die Zunge —, *fig.* to burst with (suppressed) laughing; den Heiligen die Füße —, *fig.* to bite off the feet of the saints *(said in derision of those who show an excess of zeal in kissing the images of saints)*; er hat aller Schande *(Dat.)* den Kopf abgebissen, *fig.* he is dead to all sense of shame; II. *recipr.* sich *([Acc.] coll. for* einander) —, to fatigue one another by biting, worrying (as dogs).

Ab'beizen, *(w.)* v. *tr.* 1) to take away with corrosives, to consume by corroding, to eat off; 2) T. to macerate, to taw, to dress (skins) in white; abgebeizte (Sterblings- oder Sterbe-) Wolle, mortlings; 3) (Abbrennen, Gelbbrennen) T. to dip, to pickle (tin-plate, metal to be gilt, &c.).

Ab'beizung, *(w.)* *f.* 1) *Med.* abrasion; 2) *Skin-dr.* maceration, (the act of) tawing, &c.

Ab'bekommen, *(str.)* v. *tr.* 1) *fam.* to get off, to get loose, remove; 2) (— von) to partake of *or* in, to (get *or* have a) share in, to take *(or* bear a) part in; Schläge &c. —, to get blows, &c.

Ab'bellen, *(w.)* v. I. *tr.* *vulg.* to bellow forth, to recite with a loud, barking tone of voice; II. *refl.* to exhaust one's self with barking, to cease to bark.

Ab'bengeln, *(w.)* v. *tr.* *vulg.* 1) (Abbel'zen) to beat *or* cudgel soundly; 2) to beat down with a stick (as nuts, apples, &c. from a tree).

Ab'bersten, *(str.)* v. *intr.* *(aux.* sein) to burst off, to crack off, to fly off, to spring off.

Ab'berufen, *(str.)* v. *tr.* 1) to recall, to call home; der König berief seinen Gesandten von Paris ab, the king withdrew his ambassador from Paris; 2) *Law,* to appeal, *see the more usual* Appelliren.

Ab'berufung, *(w.)* *f.* 1) recall, (the act of) calling home (an envoy, &c.); 2) *Law,* appeal *(cf.* Appellation); die von den Klägern eingewandte — an den großen Rath *(Wieland),* the appeal to the great council made by the plaintiffs, *see the more usual* Appellation; A-srecht, *(str.)* n. 1) right of revocation; 2) right of appeal; A-sschreiben, *(str.)* n. avocatory letter, letter (order) of recall *or* revocation; recredentials. [ren, 2.

Ab'beschwören, *(str.)* v. *tr.* † *for* Abschwö-

Ab'bezahlen, *(w.)* v. *tr.* *(not used)* to pay off, *cf.* Abbüßen.

Ab'bestellen, *(w.)* v. *tr.* to countermand (an invitation, &c.), to counterorder.

Ab'bestellung, *(w.)* *f.* (the act of) countermanding, &c. countermand, counterorder; bis [illegible] countermanded, till [illegible].

Ab'beten, *(w.)* v. *tr.* 1) to repeat (prayers), to recount in prayer; *gener. contemptuously,* to speak, to recite *or* to deliver monotonously, to drawl, to drone; den Rosenkranz —, to say one's beads; 2) (Einem etwas) to obtain (something from one) by praying; es müßt ein armer Teufel sein, dem die [illegible] eine Seele — [illegible], he should be a poor devil, from [illegible] like these could rescue a soul; [illegible] (from one's self) by praying, to deprecate [illegible]; 4) to atone for (one's [illegible]).

[illegible] *(w.)* v. *tr.* *coll.* (Einem etwas) to [illegible] (something from one) by begging [illegible] *or* abjectly, to beg (some[illegible]).

[illegible] v. *tr.* usually *refl.* sich ab[illegible] one's bed (from ...), to sleep apart.

Ab'beugen, *(w.)* v. *incorrectly used for* Abbiegen, *although it has the authority of good writers (Voss, &c.) and extensive usage:* I. *tr.* to bend downwards, off *or* aside (vines, twigs, &c.); to lay (plants), *see* Absenken; II. *intr.* to deviate, to turn off, *see* Abbiegen.

Ab'beuten, *(w.)* v. *tr.* (Einem etwas) to take (something from one) as booty, to plunder (one of a thing).

Ab'bezahlen, *(w.)* v. *tr.* 1) to pay *or* to discharge in part, to pay off, *in this sense* Abzahlen *or* Abtragen *is more generally used;* 2) to pay in full, to discharge (a debt, &c.).

Ab'bezahlung, *(w.)* *f.* 1) the act of paying in part, &c. *see the preceding word;* 2) *fig.* repayment; die — lustiger Höflichkeiten *(Zschokke),* the return of gay civilities.

Ab'biegen, *(str.)* v. I. *tr.* to bend downwards, to turn down; to bend *or* turn off *or* aside; II. *intr.* *(aux.* sein) to turn off *or* aside, to deviate.

Ab'bieten, *(str.)* v. *tr.* 1) to proclaim (from the pulpit, &c.), *cf.* Aufbieten; 2) to outbid (at a public sale).

Ab'bild, *(str., pl.* Ab'bilder) n. image, likeness *(of some actual prototype* [Vorbild] *which is or was before the eyes of him who imitates or represents;* Abbild *is more expressive than* Bild, *by the reference to an original which it implies);* effigy; copy, imitation.

Ab'bilden, *(w.)* v. I. *tr.* 1) to portray, to take the likeness of (a person), *cf.* Abmalen; nach dem Leben —, to draw *or* take from (or after) the life; er ist sprechend ähnlich abgebildet, he is drawn to the life; 2) to copy; to represent (in a picture), to delineate; to form, to figure, to model; in Wachs —, to emboss in wax; 3) *fig.* to paint, to describe, to delineate; im Geiste —, to image; II. *refl.* *(l. u.)* to be delineated, to be reflected, to be thrown *or* cast back (as an image from a polished surface, &c.), to mirror itself.

Ab'bildern, *(w.)* v. *tr.* to portray, &c. *(Jean Paul), see* Abbilden.

Ab'bildner, *(str.)* m. **Ab'bildnerin,** *(w.)* *f.* one who portrays, represents, delineates, &c. *cf.* Abbilden.

Ab'bildung, *(w.)* *f.* 1) (das Abbilden) the act of portraying, &c. *(cf.* Abbilden, v.), representation; drawing, delineation, portraiture; 2) das Abgebildete, the thing portrayed, &c.: *a) lit. & fig.* portrait, picture, representation, delineation; *fig.* description, sketch; *b)* cut, illustration; ein Buch mit A-en, an illustrated book; 3) copy, imitation.

Ab'billigen, *(w.)* v. *tr.* *Law,* (Einem etwas) to deprive *or* dispossess (one of a thing, estate, &c.) by judicial sentence, *cf.* Aberkennen, Absprechen.

Ab'bimsen, *(w.)* v. *tr.* to pumicate, to rub (off) with pumice-stone.

Ab'binden, *(str.)* v. *tr.* 1) to unbind, to untie, to unloose, to untruss; to loosen; 2) *Husb.* to wean (a calf) by removing it from its mother *(also* Absetzen, Abspänen); 3) *Surg.* *(also* Unterbinden): *a)* eine Ader —, to tie *or* take up a vein; eine Warze —, to wither a wart, &c. by tying it hard, to string a wart; *b)* to geld, to castrate (as cattle); 4) *Iron-works,* to separate (iron bars) by tying them into bundles of a certain weight; 5) to finish (or to complete the process of) binding, joining, &c.: *a) Coop.* to hoop (ein Faß, a cask); *b) Carp.* to frame (ein Gebäude, a building); to join (die Zulage, the timber-work of a building); den Bären —, *slang,* to pay a debt *(opp.* einen Bären anbinden). [&c. *see* Abbinden.

Ab'bindung, *(w.)* *f.* the act of unbinding,

Ab'biß, *(str.)* m. 1) the act of biting off, *cf.* Abbeißen; 2) the thing bitten off, a bite; des Teufels —, m. —kraut, n. *Bot.* devil's bit *(Scabiosa succisa* L.).

Ab'bitte, *(w.)* *f.* (the act of) begging pardon; apology (for); deprecation; (Einem *or* bei Einem) — thun *or* leisten (für *or* wegen), to ask (crave, beg) (one's) pardon, to apologise (to one — for ...), to make excuse (for); eine öffentliche — thun, to make honourable amend (amende); schriftliche —, written apology.

Ab'bitten, *(str.)* v. *tr.* 1) (Einem etwas) to apologise (to one) for (a thing), to make excuses for, to beg, to ask, to implore (one's) pardon for (an offence, &c.); 2) (Einem etwas) *l. u.* to obtain (something from one) by begging *(cf.* Abbetteln); 3) *(l. u.)* to beg off, to avert by begging, to deprecate (a punishment, &c.); a-d, *p. a.* deprecative, deprecatory.

Ab'bittlich, I. *adj.* 1) pardonable, that for which pardon may be obtained, venial; 2) to be begged off, to be deprecated, averted by begging *(syn.* Erbittlich); die Gerechtigkeit Gottes kann nicht als gütig und — vorgestellt werden *(Kant),* the justice of God cannot be imagined as being mild or capable of being averted by prayer; II. *adv.* *(l. u.) see the next word.*

Ab'bitt(s)weise, *or (less usual)* **Ab'bittungsweise,** *adv.* by way of (an) apology, in the way of excuse *or* apology, apologetically, deprecatorily, entreatingly.

Ab'blänken, v. *tr.* *(l. u.)* to polish off, to make bright *or* glossy by rubbing off *or* scouring (a tin vessel, &c.).

Ab'blasen, *(str.)* v. I. *tr.* 1) to blow off, to blow away, to remove by blowing; 2) *a)* to cleanse by blowing *(maloGermanically,* den Tisch —, *for* den Staub vom Tische —); *b) Gunn.* to scale (the guns) in order to cleanse them, to blow (the pieces) off; 3) *a)* to blow *or* sound (a tune, &c.) on a wind-instrument, as ein Lied — (said of town-musicians, &c.); to sound (the hours, said of watchmen); *b) gener. intr.* *Sport., Mil. &c.* (die Jagd —) to order off, to proclaim the end of (the chase, &c.) by winding a horn, by the sound of a trumpet, &c.; (zum Abzuge blasen) to sound the retreat, return home; *Sport.* to blow a mort (at the death of the game); 4) (die Suppe im Löffel —) to blow (soup) in order to cool (it); II. *intr.* *(aux.* haben) to cease to blow, to sound for the last time.

Ab'blassen, *(w.)* v. *intr.* *(aux.* sein) to grow pale, to fade off, to lose colour.

Ab'blatten, *(w.)* v. I. *tr.* *Husb.* to take, pluck, or strip off the leaves (as) of (tobacco, cabbage, vines, &c.); II. *intr.* *Sport.* to browse, to feed on fresh leaves (as deer, &c.).

Ab'blattern, *(w.)* v. *intr.* to scale off (said of the small-pox in the last stage of convalescence from the disease); to lose the small-pox.

Ab'blättern, *(w.)* v. I. *tr.* 1) to unleave, to strip, divest, *or* deprive of the leaves *(syn.* Entblättern); der Frost blättert die Bäume ab, the frost strips the trees of their leaves; 2) to scale off, to take off in thin laminæ *or* scales, to shiver off; to desquamate (foul bones, &c.); II. *intr. & refl.* 1) to lose *or* drop the leaves; 2) to come off in thin laminæ or scales; to scale *or* to shell off, to flake (like slate); *Surg.* to exfoliate; a-d, *p. a. Surg.* causing exfoliation or the desquamation of a bone, exfoliative.

Ab'blätterung, *(w.)* *f.* 1) the act of unleaving, stripping of the leaves, &c. *cf.* Abblättern; 2) anything stripped off; fragment; *Surg.* exfoliation, desquamation *(the detachment or elimination of dead portions of bones, cartilage, &c.; the term is generally limited to the separation of the bony structure);* 3) anything which has separated or come off in thin scales; lamina, scale.

Ab'blätterungs..., *in comp. Surg.* exfoliative: —mittel, n. exfoliative, any means procuring exfoliation; —trepan', m. desquamatory.

Ab'blauen, *(w.)* v. *intr. Cloth. &c.* to lose the blue colour (said of stuffs).

A. **Ab'bläuen,** *(w.)* v. I. *tr.* 1) to give a sufficient tinge of blue, to make blue (Leinenzeug, linen); II. *intr. see* Abblauen.

B. **Ab'bläuen,** *(w.)* v. *tr.* *(of different derivation from the preceding word, see* Bläuen, *B.)* *coll.* to cudgel, to beat soundly.

Ab'bleiben, *(str.)* v. *intr.* *(aux.* sein) 1) to keep off *or* at a distance (von, from); 2) to remain off *or* separated; dieser Knopf soll —, this button is to remain off, is not to be sewed on again. *(This compound ought to be spelt in two distinct words, ab having retained its original adverbial nature, Grimm.)*

Ab'bleichen, v. I. *(str.)* *intr.* *(aux.* sein) to grow pale, to fade off, to lose colour (of stuffs, &c.); abgeblichene, lose, überzwerch gesprungene Rinde *(Zschokke)*, discoloured, loose bark, cracked across; abgeblichen stehn die Hügel, deprived of their beautiful colours (verdure) stand the hills; doch in der äußersten Ferne fangen die Gegenstände an, wie Nebel, abzubleichen und ungewiß zu werden *(Zschokke,* 1, 358), but in the farthest distance the objects begin, like mist, to fade and to grow indistinct; wie an einem blütenreichen Rosenstock eine a-de Rose *(Zschokke* 3, 18), like a rose, fading away, on a rose-bush full of buds: *(sometimes w.:)* sie kannten kaum die abgebleichte Gestalt *(Jean Paul)*, they scarcely knew (or recognised) the pale, faded form; II. *(w.)* *tr.* to bleach thoroughly *or* duly; to finish bleaching (as linen, cotton stuffs, &c.).

Ab'blicken, *(w.)* v. *intr.* 1) to look away *(syn.* Wegblicken); 2) *Smelt. & Metall.* to cease shining (of silver appearing on the test).

Ab'blitzen, *(w.)* v. *intr.* 1) to cease lightening, glittering; 2) *(aux.* sein) to flash off, to flash in the pan; to miss fire (of guns).

Ab'blöken, *(w.)* v. *tr.* to bawl *or* bellow forth.

Ab'blühen, *(w.)* v. *intr.* *(aux.* haben, *less properly* sein) 1) to go out of flower, to cease blooming, blowing *or* flowering; die Kirschbäume haben abgeblüht, the cherry-trees have ceased to blossom, have shed their blossoms: abgeblüht, p. a. *Bot.* deflorate, past the flowering state; 2) to decay, to fade, to wither.

Ab'blüte, *(w.)* *f.* the season when plants go out of flower, fall of the blossom.

Ab'bluten, *(w.)* v. I. *intr.* to cease bleeding *(syn.* Ausbluten); II. *tr.* * *(l. u.)* to atone for (a crime, &c.), to expiate with one's blood.

Ab'blüten, *(w.)* v. *tr.* to deprive of flowers, to deflower (trees, &c.), to strip of the blossoms, to strip *or* divest of the bloom.

Ab'bohnen, *(w.)* v. *tr.* 1) to strip of the beans; 2) to polish by waxing (as a piece of furniture), to rub down (a floor).

Ab'bohren, *(w.)* v. I. *tr.* to bore sufficiently, to bore through; II. *intr. Min. &c.* to finish the boring (of a hole).

Ab'bohrer, *(str.)* m. *Min.* augur to finish the boring of a hole, *(Bull:)* terrier.

Ab'bören, *see* Abbeeren.

Ab'borgen, *(w.)* v. *tr.* (Einem etwas) to borrow (something from one); *syn.* Entlehnen.

Ab'borsten, *(w.)* v. *intr. Dial.* to burst open through the influence of the wet.

Ab'bossen, Ab'bosseln, Ab'bossiren, *(w.)* v. *tr. T.* to emboss in wax, &c. *see* Bossiren, Modelliren.

Ab'brand, *(str., pl.* Ab'brände) m. *Min.* 1) diminution *or* decrease of silver, &c. on the test *or* in cleansing; 2) loss in the weight of chalk-stone in burning.

Ab'brändler, *(str.)* m. *(l. u.)* one who collects alms for others *or* for himself, having suffered damage by fire.

Ab'brassen, *(w.)* v. *tr. Mar.* 1) to brace (full); 2) to fill (the sails) after they have been braced aback.

Ab'braten, *(w. cf.* Braten) v. *tr.* to roast thoroughly *(syn.* Ausbraten).

Ab'brauchen, *(w.)* v. *tr.* to use up, to wear off, to wear out, *cf.* Abnutzen; abgebraucht, p. a. 1) worn (off), worn out, stale, decayed, *cf.* Abgenutzt; 2) *fig.* trite, hackneyed, *cf.* Abgedroschen.

Ab'brauen, *(w.)* v. *tr. & intr.* to brew (the-[roughly), to finish brewing.

Ab'braunen, *(w.)* v. *intr. Dy.* to lose the brown colour (said of stuffs).

Ab'bräunen, *(w.)* v. *tr.* to give the proper brown colour to ...; to brown sufficiently, to make *(Cook.* to roast) brown.

Ab'brausen, *(w.)* v. *intr.* 1) to cease fermenting, rushing, roaring, &c. *cf.* Brausen; 2) to go off roaring; der Dampfwagen brauste eben ab *(Grimm)*, *coll.* the steam-carriage whizzes off just now.

A. **Ab'brechen,** *(str.)* v. I. *tr.* 1) to break off, to break; to snap, to knock off; kurz (morsch, *or* plötzlich) —, to snap short; ein Messer mit abgebrochener Spitze, a knife with a broken point; eine Blume —, to pluck (off) a flower; Obst —, to break off fruits, to crop *or* gather fruits; abgebrochene Stücke, broken pieces, fragments, *cf.* Abgebrochen; 2) *a)* to break *(or* rip) up (an old vessel); to break down, take away *or* down (a scaffold, &c.), pull down, to demolish, dismantle (a building, a ship, a wall, &c.), to unwall (a house, &c.) *(sometimes syn. with* Abtragen 1, *a.)*; der Sturm brach den Mast ab, the storm carried away the mast; die Zelte —, to strike the tents; das Lager —, to break up, to dislodge *or* to shift the camp, to decamp; die Franzosen hatten alle Brücken abgebrochen, the French had broken *or* taken away all the bridges; *b)* *Typ. (formerly)* to knock off (die Ballen, the balls); *c)* *Farr.* einem Pferde die (Huf-)Eisen —, to unshoe a horse; 3) *Brew.* to stir, turn (the beer) in the cooler *(also* Aufbrechen); 4) *Mil.* die Glieder —, to break off the files, to diminish the front; 5) *Gramm.* to break, separate (syllables); 6) *Sport.* to disengage (dogs which have locked their teeth in fastening upon the game); *fig.-s.* 7) to break off (eine Unterhandlung, a negociation, &c.), to discontinue, (kurz —) to stop *or* cut short, to desist from (a labour, &c.), to put an end to, to interrupt, cut off; eine Rede —, to break off a speech, to close a speech abruptly; eine Verbindung (Heirat) —, to break off a match; mit Einem allen Umgang —, to break off the intercourse with a person, to break with one, to disown an acquaintance, *slang,* to cut one; den diplomatischen Verkehr —, to break off diplomatic relations; 8) *a)* to abate, deduct, abridge, defalcate, *cf.* Abziehen; ich kann mir nichts (in meiner Rechnung) — lassen, I cannot allow any deduction (from my account); den Soldaten wurde an ihrer Löhnung abgebrochen, a deduction was made from the pay of the soldiers *(different from:* den Soldaten wurde ihre Löhnung abgebrochen, the soldiers were cut short of their pay); jeden Augenblick, den ich meinen amtlichen Geschäften — konnte, widmete ich ihm, every moment I could snatch from my official engagements I devoted to him; *b)* *refl.* sich *(Dat.)* etwas —, to pinch one's self in ..., to deprive one's self of ...; er bricht sich nichts ab, he does not stint himself in anything, he denies himself nothing, he indulges every enjoyment; er hat sich den Wein abgebrochen, he has begun to abstain from wine; sich am Schlafe — *(intransitive: elliptically for* sich etwas am Schlafe —), to stint one's self in sleep.

II. *intr.* 1) *(aux.* sein) *lit.* *a)* to break off, to snap; *b)* to break down; to crumble to pieces; *fig.-s.* 2) *(aux.* haben) *a)* to break off, to stop short (in speaking, &c.); sie brachen im Gespräche ab, als ich hereintrat, they broke off talk at my coming in; wir wollen davon — *(i. e.* nicht weiter davon sprechen), [illegible] off, no more of that; das letzte, [illegible] neue Heft bricht mit dem Worte [illegible] last number, which has just been [illegible] breaks off with the word *Frauen*; [illegible] to break down, to decay, to be on [illegible] to be in a declining state.

Ab'brechen, v. *s.* *(str.)* n. 1) the act of breaking off, &c. *cf.* Abbrechen, v. & [illegible] 2) demolition.

B. **Ab'brechen,** *(w.)* v. *tr.* to finish [illegible]

Ab'brechung, *(w.)* *f.* 1) (das [illegible]) the act of breaking off, &c. *cf.* [illegible] *A.*; abruption; 2) *a)* *Rhet.* aposiopesis, [illegible] sion; *b)* *Gramm.* separation (of syllables) syllabication; *c)* *Mus.* a sudden breaking off or stop (Abreißung); 3) cessation (of hostilities, &c.), discontinuance, abrupt termination; (das Abgebrochene) 4) the thing broken off, fragment, *see* Abbruch.

Ab'breiten, *(w.)* v. *tr. T.* to stretch [illegible] to plate, to flatten (as a sheet of copper, [illegible]

Ab'breitung, *(w.)* *f. T.* (the act of) stretching, &c. *see* Abbreiten.

Ab'brennen, v. I. *intr.* *(originally* [illegible] *imperf.* ich brann ab, *pp.* [illegible] *present irregular: imperf.* ich brannte ab, [illegible] gebrannt — *aux.* sein) 1) to burn off *or* down, to be burnt down, to be consumed *or* destroyed by fire; ehe die Lichter zur Hälfte abgebrannt waren, before the candles had burnt half way down; das Kölner Theater ist bis auf den Grund abgebrannt, the theatre of Cologne has been burnt to the ground; 2) to go off [illegible] gun); das Zündkraut ist abgebrannt, the powder has flashed in the pan *(cf.* [illegible] to suffer damage (to lose one's property) by fire; abgebrannte Menschen, burnt-out people; 4) to cease burning; das Feuer ist abgebrannt, the fire has burnt down; *fig.-s.* die [illegible] des eilig abbrennenden Frühlings *(Jean Paul)*, the bonfires of fast waning spring; [illegible] brannte des Lebens *(Jean Paul)*, worn-out [illegible] used up people (of those who have [illegible] life prematurely).

II. *tr.* *(gener. irregular:* ich brannte ab, abgebrannt, *sometimes weak:* ich brennte ab, abgebrennt, *but these latter forms are* [illegible] *obsolete)* 1) to burn off *(or* down), to [illegible] with *(or* consume by) fire; to burn away; [illegible] *Agr.* to burn down (a forest, *also* [illegible] den); 3) to fire, fire off, discharge (a gun, &c.), to let off (fireworks); 4) to cause to wither by heat, to scorch, to burn (grass *or* plants); 5) *Surg.* to extirpate by burning (with [illegible] tics); 6) *a)* to burn sufficiently, thoroughly, to burn off duly (chalk, earthen vessels, &c.); *b)* to finish burning, to heat (a kiln, &c.) [illegible] the last time; *c)* to cleanse by burning, [illegible] to deflagrate; *d)* to calcine with [illegible] fire, to burn (oyster-shells *or* limestone) [illegible] *e)* to temper (steel); *f)* to dip into [illegible] (as iron-plates, at the first process in [illegible]) *g)* to heighten the yellow colour (of [illegible] in aquafortis, to pickle *(cf.* Abbeizen); [illegible] ein Schiff (von außen) —, to grave, to [illegible] a ship.

Ab'brennen, v. *s.* *(str.)* n. [illegible] *(w.)* *f.* 1) the act of burning off *or* down [illegible] *cf.* Abbrennen, v.; 2) *Chem.* deflagration [illegible]

Ab'brennling, *(str.)* m. *see* [illegible]

***Abbreviatur,** *(w.)* *f.* *(Lat.)* abbreviation [illegible] (short-hand) note; —schrift, *f.* short-hand writing.

***Abbreviiren,** *(w.)* v. *tr.* *(Lat.)* to [illegible] [viate, abridge, cut [illegible]

Ab'bringen, *(irr.)* v. *tr.* 1) *a)* to bring off, to remove; *b)* Heu — (einbringen, [illegible] get in hay, &c.; 2) to do away with, [illegible] into disuse; 3) *lit. & fig.* to get away [illegible] to lead astray, to draw *(or* bring) [illegible] off, to divert (from any course, [illegible] intended application); [illegible] to turn from the right way, to mislead; durch Geld —, to dissuade (from); durch Vernunftgründe —, to reason (one) out of (his plan, convictions, &c.); nichts in der Welt soll mich davon —, nothing in the world shall prevent me from doing it, or from going on with it; wenn ihr Papa sich etwas in den Kopf setzte, war er nicht abzubringen, when her papa took a thing into his head, there was no turning him; ein Entschluß, von dem sie niemand — konnte, a resolution from which nobody could move her; er ist von diesem Laster glücklich abgebracht, he has been successfully reclaimed from this vice; sie wollte sich nicht — lassen, she would not be dissuaded; sie waren weder durch Gewalt, noch durch Lockung von ihrem Vorhaben abzubringen, they were not to be either driven or decoyed from their purpose.

Ab'bringung, (w.) f. the act of getting off, &c., removal, cf. Abbringen; eine — von der gegebenen Bahn (Kind), a diversion from the course enjoined.

Ab'bröckeln, (w.) v. I. tr. to crumble off, to detach in small pieces, to break off in minute parts; II. intr. (aux. sein) & refl. to crumble down, to peel off, to scale (or break) off (as varnish, &c.); die Tugend wankt und bröckelt ab (Claudius), fig. virtue wavers and gradually breaks down.

Ab'bröckelung, (w.) f. 1) the (act of) crumbling off, &c. cf. Abbröckeln; 2) a detached piece, (broken) fragment.

Ab'brocken, (w.) v. tr. to break off in small pieces or fragments, almost synonymous with Abbröckeln, from which it merely differs by denoting larger pieces.

Ab'brocken, (w.) v. intr. see Abbüßen.

Ab'bruch, (str., pl. die Ab'brüche) m. 1) the (act of) breaking off, pulling down, &c. cf. Abbrechen & Abbrechung; ein Haus auf (den) Abbruch verkaufen, to sell a house which is to be pulled down; 2) a) the thing broken off, detached piece, (broken) fragment; b) Min. broken off ore; c) T. building-materials of a demolished house; 3) the place where a building has been pulled down; 4) a) the action of the waves by which exposed shores or islands are reduced; b) a piece of land detached or washed off by the floods, land-slip (in marshy countries, &c.); die Insel Wangeroogе liegt schon seit einer Reihe von Jahren in starkem —, the island of Wangeroogе has been for many years past considerably exposed to the encroachment of the sea; 5) a) shiver, piece of metal broken off; b) Min. ore broken off or detached; c) Letter-found. break (of a letter); fig-s. 6) the act of breaking off, rupture (of diplomatic relations, &c.); ein — des diplomatischen Verkehrs zwischen der Türkei und Griechenland, a rupture of diplomatic relations between Turkey and Greece; die türkische Regierung hat eingewilligt, den — des diplomatischen Verkehrs mit Griechenland bis zum 17. d. M. aufzuschieben, ... to suspend the act of breaking off diplomatic relations with Greece to the 17th inst.; 7) a) diminution, abridgment, abatement, deduction, defalcation, cf. Abgang; ohne —, undiminished; b) detriment, loss, damage, hurt, injury, prejudice, harm; c) † abstinence, fasting; 8) a) cessation, &c. see Abbrechung, 2.; b) end, termination; Abbruch thun: 1) Min. to break the stones to advantage; 2) fig. a) (einer Sache (Dat.)) to abridge, curtail; b) (Einem [or an einer Sache (Dat.)]) to injure, damage, hurt; to prejudice, to derogate (or to be derogatory) to ...; die Bürger thaten auf dem Rückzuge in Verbindung mit den [illegible] den Franzosen — (Göthe), the citizens in conjunction with the imperial troops harassed the French on their retreat; dies [illegible], was ihrem Glücke — that, [illegible] the only drawback on their happi-

ness; sich (Dat.) an einer Sache (Dat.) — thun, to pinch one's self in (a thing), to deprive one's self of (a thing), cf. Abbrechen, 8, b.

Ab'brüchig, adj. 1) a) particul. Min. shivering, brittle; b) crumbling; dilapidated; fig-s. (einer Person or Sache (Dat.)) 2) prejudicial, derogatory, detrimental (to); 3) † stinting one's self, continent (Stumpf).

Ab'brühen, (w.) v. tr. 1) to scald (a fowl, &c.), to parboil (as cabbage, &c.); 2) fig. coll. to draw out the essence of (a substance); Schiller's zehnmal abgebrühte Phrase (Platen), Schiller's ten times cooked up phrase.

Ab'brühung, (w.) f. (the act of) scalding, &c.

Ab'brüllen, (w.) v. tr. 1) to roar out (a song), to bawl forth (a song, &c.); 2) (Einem etwas) to bawl (one) out of (a thing), to obtain (something) of (a person) by bawling; 3) sich —, refl. to fatigue one's self by roaring or bawling, to bawl one's fill.

Ab'brummen, (w.) v. I. tr. to hum over (a tune); II. intr. (aux. sein) to go off or away grumblingly.

Ab'brunften, Ab'brunsten, (w.) v. intr. (aux. haben) Sport. to cease rutting; das Wild hat abgebrunftet, the rutting season is over.

Ab'brüten, (w.) v. intr. 1) to cease brooding, hatching; 2) sich —, refl. to tire one's self out by brooding.

Ab'buden, (w.) v. intr. to take away or remove the booths (tr. from ...). [or duly.

Ab'bügeln, (w.) v. tr. to iron sufficiently

Ab'buhlen, (w.) v. I. tr. (Einem etwas) to obtain (something from one) by coquettish tricks, to wheedle (one) out of (a thing); II. refl. sich (Acc.) —, to waste one's strength with women. [load.

Ab'bürden, (w.) v. tr. to disburden, to unload.

Ab'bürsten, (w.) v. tr. to brush off or away (the dust, &c.); to brush duly or sufficiently, to brush (a coat, &c.) clean.

Ab'büßen, (w.) v. tr. 1) to expiate, to atone, to make atonement, to do penance for ...; 2) to pay a fine or penalty for (any transgression); er hat es mit Geld abgebüßt, he has been fined for it; 3) (rarely used) to expiate fully, to make full atonement for ....

Ab'büßung, (w.) f. (eines Verbrechens 2c.) expiation, atonement, the act of doing penance for (a crime, &c.), &c.

Ab'buttern, (w.) v. intr. to finish churning; wir haben abgebuttert, we have done churning.

Abc (pr. ah,beh,tseh'), (indecl.) n. 1) a-b-c, the alphabet; nach dem —, alphabetically (generally used with a tinge of contempt in reference to the very first attempts of children or persons learning to read, in other cases the word Alphabet [which, being less usual, seems to be more refined!] is employed); 2) fig. coll. the (first) rudiments, elements; beginnings; bedenk' in Wohl und Weh | dies goldne Abc (Göthe), always bear in mind this golden rule: —bank, f. the lowest form in a school or class; —bube, m. coll. primer-boy, abecedarian, cf. Abcschüler; —buch, 1) primer, horn-book; 2) Conch. tiger-stamper (also Abcbute); —knabe, m. primer-boy, abecedarian, cf. Abcschüler; —lehrer, m. teacher of the alphabet, abecedarian, teacher of the first elements; —schule, f. coll. elementary school, dame-school; —schüler, —schütz, m. coll. primer-boy, abecedarian, alphabetarian; —tafel, f. a table on which the letters of the alphabet are written for school-children, alphabetical board, abecedary; —trenschütz, m. (Luther) lud. for Abcschütz, abecedarian.

Ab'capiteln, (w.) v. tr. coll. to give (one) a lecture or magisterial reprimand, to rate (one) soundly.

Abceda'r' (ah-be-tse-dār'), I. (str., pl. A-e, Abceda'rien) (from Abc, with a Latin termination, abecedarium, n. abecedarius, m.) n. the alphabet; II. (str., pl. Abceda're, or [str.] Abcedarier (Jean Paul)), m. abecedarian, a teacher or learner of the alphabet.

Abceda'risch, adj. abecedarian.

Abcedi'ren, (w.) v. intr. Mus. to practise the scale (Ital. solfeggiare).

Ab'cirkeln, (w.) v. tr. 1) to measure or gauge with the compasses; 2) fig. a) to define precisely; b) to utter with affected nicety, to mince (one's words).

Ab'complimentiren, (w.) v. tr. 1) (Einen) to divert the attention of (one) in a polite manner; 2) (Einem etwas) to compliment or talk (one) out of (a thing).

Ab'conterfeien, (w.) v. tr. coll. to take the likeness of (a person), to portray, cf. Abbilden & Abmalen.

Ab'copiren, (w.) v. tr. coll. for Copiren, to copy, to take a copy of ....

Ab'dach, (str., pl. Ab'dächer) n. 1) overhanging or sloping roof, penthouse; 2) Archit. larmier, descent of a gutter (Beil).

Ab'dachen, (w.) v. I. tr. 1) to unroof (a building); das Haus wurde (vom Sturme) gänzlich abgedacht, the roof of the house was entirely blown off; 2) to give a sloping form or direction, to make sloping, to build slopingly, to slope; eine Mauer —, to cope a wall (cf. Abböschen, Böschen); II. refl. (sometimes intr.) to be or become declivous, to run out in a slope, to have or assume a sloping direction; ein sich allmählich a—der Hügel, a gently subsiding hill (cf. Abfallen, 3.).

Ab'dachig, adj. sloping, declivous; adv. slopingly, &c., aslope.

Ab'dachung, (w.) f. 1) the (act of) unroofing, &c. cf. Abdachen; 2) sloping or shelving direction; slope, fall, declension, descent, declivity; Fort. (cf. Böschung), Archit. & Geol. talus; Fort-s. A-sgrundlinie, f. base of the talus; A-sverhältniß, n. proportion of the base of the talus to its height; A-swinkel, m. angle of the talus (Beil).

Ab'dämmen, (w.) v. tr. 1) to dam up, to embank; to keep off by a dam, to dam out (the water); 2) to undam, to free from a dam or mound.

Ab'dämmer, (str.) m. one who dams up, &c.

Ab'dämmung, (w.) f. the act of damming up, &c.; embankment (the act of embanking as well as the bank to keep off the water).

Ab'dampfen, (w.) v. I. intr. 1) (aux. sein) to evaporate, to pass off in vapour, to vapour (or to fly) away; 2) (aux. haben) to cease steaming; II. tr. see Abdämpfen.

Ab'dämpfen, (w.) v. tr. 1) to (cause to) evaporate, to make evaporate, to resolve into vapour; 2) Chem. to concentrate by evaporation, to graduate; 3) (sometimes intr., aux. haben) to stew duly, to finish stewing.

Ab'dampfschale, (w.) f. T. evaporating dish.

Ab'dampfung, (w.) f. 1) evaporation; 2) see Abdämpfung; A-sgefäß, n. Chem. evaporating vessel; A-s (or Abdämpfungs-)kessel, m. T. evaporating kettle; A-smaschine, f. T. evaporator; A-sofen, m. Pott. &c. slip kiln.

Ab'dämpfung, (w.) f. evaporation, Chem. graduation.

Ab'danken, (w.) v. I. intr. 1) to resign, abdicate, renounce, withdraw; 2) to dismiss an assembly with thanks; bei einer Leiche —, (of a priest) to thank the attendants of a funeral for their presence in behalf of the family of the deceased, to hold (deliver) a funeral oration; der Nachtwächter dankt ab, the night-watch calls for the last time (at the break of day or at the close of a year); II. tr. 1) (l. u.) to resign; das Reich —, to resign the crown, to abdicate; 2) a) to dismiss, discharge, discard, to divest (of an office, &c.);

to reform (an officer); ein Heer —, to disband an army; zur Strafe — (cassiren), to cashier: *Mar.-s.* das Schiffsvolk —, to pay off, discharge the crew; ein Schiff —, to lay up a vessel: ein abgedankter Beamter, Soldat, a broken officer *or* soldier; *fig.-s.* *b) coll.* to cast off (old clothes, &c.), to dismiss, discard, reject (a lover, &c.); *c)* to leave off, to give up, to part with, to quit (ill habits, &c.); 3) einen Verstorbenen —, to announce the death of a deceased person (at church), *cf. intr.* 2.

Ab'dankung, *(w.) f.* 1) dismission, discharge; *Mil.* cassation; reform: 2) resignation, abdication; 3) A-rede, *(w.) f.* *a)* a rendering of thanks to the attendants of a funeral, funeral oration, funeral sermon; *fig.-s.* *b)* farewell address, valedictory speech, epilogue; 4) last call of a night-watch in the morning.

Ab'darben, *(w.) v. refl.* sich *(Dat.)* etwas —, to pinch *or* stint one's self in ...., to deprive one's self of necessaries, such as food, &c., to starve one's body (for a certain purpose).

Ab'darren, *(w.) v. tr. & intr. Brew.* to (kiln-)dry (malt, corn) thoroughly, to finish drying. [process of kiln-drying.

Ab'darrprocess, *(str.) m. Brew.* the act or

† **Ab'dauben, Ab'däuben,** *(w.) v. tr.* to quench thoroughly, to overwhelm, to master.

† **Ab'dauen,** *(w.) v. tr.* to digest duly *or* thoroughly (Verdauen).

Ab'deckeln, *(w.) v. tr. coll.* to remove the cover of ...., to take off the cover of .....

Ab'decken, *(w.) v. tr.* 1) to uncover; ein Dach —, to untile *(or* unshingle) a roof; ein Haus —, to unroof a house *(cf.* Abdachen, 1.); die Ziegel —, to take off the tiles; den Tisch — *(or* Abdecken, *intr.)*, to clear the table, to draw *or* remove the cloth; 2) to flay, to skin; 3) *coll.* to beat soundly, to cudgel *(also* Zudecken).

Ab'decker, *(str.) m.* flayer, *vulg.* Schinder; —leder, *n. Comm.* morkins, morkins' hides, skin of beasts dead through sickness or mischance.

Abdeckerei', *(w.) f.* 1) (the business of) flaying: 2) flaying-place, flaying-house; the flayer's dwelling-house.

Ab'deichen, *(w.) v. tr.* to separate with dikes, to enclose with dikes, embank; sich —, (of a community) to leave a dike-union in order to construct one's own dikes.

Ab'deichung, *(w.) f.* the act of separating *or* enclosing with dikes, embankment, &c.

Ab'denken, *(irr.) v. intr.* (*with* über *& Acc.)* to prejudicate in one's thoughts: über eine Sache absprechen und — *(Hippel)*.

* **Abderisi'ren,** *(w.) v. intr.* to act in a silly (Abderian) manner, to behave *or* talk foolishly.

Abderit'(e), *(w.) m.* 1) (Abderit'in *(w.) f.)* Abderite, an inhabitant of Abdera, a maritime town in ancient Thrace, the inhabitants of which are said to have been exceedingly stupid; 2) *fig.* a fool: A-englaube, *m.* implicit belief: A-enstreich, *m.*, a piece of folly, foolish trick. [ish, silly.

Abderit'isch, *adj.* 1) Abderian; 2) *fig.* fool-

* **Abdication',** *(w.) f.* abdication *(syn.* Abdankung, [Thron-]Entsagung).

* **Abdici'ren,** *(w.) v. intr.* to abdicate *(syn.* Abdanken, [dem Throne] Entsagen).

Ab'dicken, *(w.) v.* I. *tr.* to make thick by boiling down *(different from* Eindicken, Verdicken); II. *intr. (aux.* sein) to thicken.

Ab'dieben, *(w.) v. tr.* (Einem etwas) *coll. & obsolescent*, to filch (something) from (one), *see* Abstehlen.

Ab'dielen, *(w.) v. tr.* 1) to separate by boards, to board off, to partition off; 2) to board duly, to floor with planks, to plank throughout; to finish flooring.

Ab'dienen, *(w.) v. tr.* 1) to serve for (a debt), to pay off (the wages advanced) by personal service; 2) *(rarely used)* to remove *or* carry off the dishes (particularly in large or courtly establishments), to take away *(opp.* Aufdienen).

Ab'dingen, *(str., sometimes w.) v. tr.* 1) to abate in buying, to beat down (in the price), *cf.* Abhandeln, 1.; er läßt sich *(Dat.)* nichts —, he won't suffer any deduction to be made from his price; *fig.* ein strenges Pflichtgefühl, dem sich nichts — läßt, a stern uncompromising sense of duty; 2) (Einem etwas) to hire (something) from (one); ich wollt' euch nicht gerathen haben, mir vor einem halben Jahre noch abzudingen, was ich jetzt freiwillig mich erbiete *(Schiller)*, I should not have advised you but half a year ago to bargain me out of what I now offer spontaneously; 3) *(often intr.)* to make a final agreement *or* settlement about ...., to settle (a price &c.), to bargain for ....; 4) to dismiss (an apprentice, after his time is out).

Ab'disputiren, *(w.) v. tr. coll.* (Einem etwas) to dispute *or* argue (one) out of (a thing), *see* Abstreiten.

Ab'docken, *(w.) v. tr. Hunt. & Weav.* to unwind (cords, threads, &c.).

* **Abdo'men,** *(Lat.) n. (str., pl.* Abdo'mina) *(l. u.) Anat.* abdomen, lower belly.

* **Abdominal',** *adj. Med.* abdominal.

Ab'donnern, *(w.) v.* I. *tr.* to let (cannons, &c.) thunder *or* roar; *fig.* to thunder forth: II. *intr. (l. u.)* to cease thundering. [stitch.

Ab'doppeln, *(w.) v. tr. Shoe-m.* to double-

Ab'dorren, *(w.) v. intr. (aux.* sein) to dry away, to dry (up), to get dry and fall off (as leaves); to become arid, to wither; to parch, to scorch.

Ab'dörren, *(w.) v. tr.* 1) to dry (up), to make thoroughly dry, to arefy; to roast, to parch duly; 2) *Metall.* to melt out, to extract all (the ore).

Ab'dörrofen, *(str., pl.* A-öfen) *m. Metall.* refining-furnace (Frischherd).

Ab'dörrstein, *(str.) m. Min. (used in the Tyrolian mines)* lead ore containing silver and copper. [&c. *cf.* Abdörren.

Ab'dörrung, *(w.) f.* the act of drying up,

Ab'dossiren, *(w.) v. tr. see* Abböschen & Dossiren.

Ab'draht, *(str., pl.* Ab'drähte) *m. (lit.* that which has been turned off, *from* Abdrehen, 2.) *Pewt.* (tin-)shavings, (pewter-)chips.

Ab'drängen, *(w.) v. tr.* 1) (Einen) to force (one) away, to push off *(syn.* Wegdrängen); 2) (Einem etwas) to force (something from one), *see* Abdringen.

Ab'dräuen, *(w.) v. tr.* (Einem etwas) († &) * to extort (something from one) by threats, *see* Abdrohen.

Ab'drechseln, *(w.) v. tr.* 1) to separate by turning on a lathe, to turn off; 2) to give the last finish in turning; to turn (off), to make round, to round off; 3) *fig.* to mince (one's words), to refine, to speak with affected nicety; abgedrechselt, *p. a.* nicely turned, over-refined, punctilious, formal, stiff, affected.

Ab'dreh..., *in comp.* —eisen, *n. see* —stahl & Drehéisen.

Ab'drehen, *(w.) v. tr.* 1) to twist *or* to wring off; er drehte den Tauben die Hälse ab, he twisted the necks of the pigeons; 2) *see* Abdrechseln.

Ab'dreh..., *in comp.* —maschine, *T.* lathe for turning the trunnions, &c.; —nagel, *m. T.* cutter (instrument for turning iron, &c.); —stahl, *m. T.* turner's chisel.

Ab'dreschen, *(str.) v. tr.* 1) to thrash off: to thrash out, to gain by thrashing: 2) *(sometimes intr.)* to thrash duly *or* thoroughly, to finish thrashing: wir werden bald abgedroschen haben, we shall soon have done thrashing; 3) to pay (a debt) by thrashing; *fig.-s.* 4) *vulg.* to thrash *(i. e.* to beat) soundly, *see* Abprügeln; 5) to practice *or* use frequently [illegible] to wear out, *a sense which is generally confined to the participle past* Abgedroschen [illegible], trite, hackneyed), which *see*; 6) [illegible], to agree privately (on, about), to [illegible] settle beforehand.

Ab'drieseln, *(w.) v. tr. coll.* to [illegible] (threads, &c.) by twisting, to twist off [illegible] thread, &c. [illegible]

Ab'drift, *(w.) f.* [illegible]

Ab'drillen, *(w.) v. tr. vulg.* [illegible] to wring (something from one) by [illegible] (him) incessantly, to worry [illegible] thing), *cf. the next word.*

Ab'dringen, *(str.) v. tr.* [illegible] extort, exact, force *or* wring (a thing [illegible] one). — **Ab'dringung,** *(w.) f.* [illegible] tion, &c.

Ab'drohen, *(w.) v. tr.* [illegible] (something from one) by [illegible] *or* bully (one) out of (a thing). [illegible]

Ab'drüseln, *(w.) v. tr.* to twist off, [illegible]

Ab'druck, *(str., pl.* Ab'drücke, *l. u.* [illegible] *m.* 1) the act of printing or copying [illegible] Abdrucken) and also the object printed [illegible] an original): *(in this sense* [illegible] drucke) *Typ.* impression; (an individual [illegible] &c.) copy, print; *Typ.-s.* [illegible] print; — vor der Schrift, proof-impression [illegible] *lit. & fig.* impress, impression; [illegible] cast (any thing cast *or* formed from a [illegible] 2) *Petr.* typolite, a stone or fossil having [illegible] of animals or vegetables impressed [illegible] Abdrücke von Fischen, Pflanzen, [illegible] ichthyolites, dendrolites, carpolites [illegible] counter-part; transcript, antitype; [illegible] der Natur sind Abdrücke der Gottheit [illegible] works of nature are antitypes of God [illegible] 4) *Gun-sm.* trigger, *see* Drücker, [illegible] act of pulling the trigger; 6) *fig.* [illegible] moment of expiring *(cf.* Abscheiden), [illegible] death.

Ab'drucken, *(w.) v.* I. *tr.* 1) *Typ.* [illegible] to draw off, to strike off, to work off [illegible] (letter-)press; wieder —, to reprint, [illegible] again, to renew the impression of (a book, &c.); 2) *in other senses* Abdrücken [illegible] *used; in the following sentences* [illegible] tene Scene in seinen Thon abgedrucken [illegible] abgedrückten *would have been preferable* [illegible] *in the same way we would at present* [illegible] drücken *in the following examples* [illegible] Pistole auf einen Freund [illegible] ab [illegible] griffe, die sich von den Gegenständen [illegible] Seele abdrucken *(Wieland)*; II. *intr.* [illegible] sich wieder —), to maculate (of fresh [illegible] press).

Ab'drücken, *(w.) v.* I. *tr.* 1) to [illegible] pressing, to squeeze off; to loosen by [illegible] sure; *fig.-s.* Einem das Herz —, to make [illegible] heart burst; die Angst will mir das [illegible] my heart is ready to burst with [illegible] würde ihm das Herz abgedrückt haben, [illegible] schweigen sollen, his heart would have [illegible] if he should have remained silent; [illegible] charge (a gun, &c.), to shoot, to [illegible] off, to let fly (an arrow, &c.); 3) *lit. & fig.* [illegible] imprint, to set or put a stamp [illegible] thing by presswork to impress, to [illegible] mould from an original; 4) *fig. coll.* [illegible] etwas) to press (something) out [illegible] extort *(vulg.* to squeeze), screw out [illegible] thing from one); II. *intr.* 1) *Mar.* [illegible] break adrift from the moorings, [illegible] to break ground, to set sail, [illegible] depart, *cf.* Absegeln; 2) *fig. coll.* to [illegible] life, to expire, to die *(cf.* [illegible]

Ab'druck(s)stange, [illegible] *Gun-sm.* stopper (in fire arms). — [illegible]

* **Abduci'ren,** *(w.) v. tr.* 1) to [illegible] Abführen, Ablenken; 2) *Surg.* to [illegible] draw (off) to a different part. [illegible]

* **Abductiōn'**, *(w.) f.* 1) the act of drawing off, &c. *cf.* Abziehung; 2) *Surg.* abduction, fracture of a joint (Gelenkbruch) in which the broken parts recede from each other; 3) *Log.* abduction, a conclusion from premises of which the minor is doubtful.

* **Abduc'tor**, *(Lat.) (str., pl. (w.)* die Abducto'ren) *m.* *lit.* Abzieher, *ye.; Anat.* abductor, abducent muscle *(opp.* Adductor).

Ab'drusch, *(str., pl.* Ab'drüsche) *m. (from* Abdreschen) *Husb.* a certain quantity of sheaves which are thrashed at once.

Ab'dudeln, *(w.) v. tr.* to sing or play (on a clarionet or similar instrument) (a tune) in a drawling, monotonous way, to hum off.

Ab'duften, *(w.) v. intr.* (of the outlines of a landscape) to vanish into hazy indistinctness; die unendliche Fläche des Effeffes, die sich in immer mehr a-den Landschaftsgründen dem Gesicht entzieht *(Göthe).*

† **Ab'dünkel**, *(str.) m.* perverse opinion, presumption, preposterous pride.

Ab'dunkeln, *(w.) v.* I. *intr.* to grow darker, to assume a darker shade; II. *tr.* to make darker, to give a darker shade to (a colour).

Ab'dunsten, *(w.) v. intr. (aux.* sein) to evaporate, to pass off in vapour (as a fluid), *cf.* Abdampfen.

Ab'dünsten, *(w.) v. tr.* to evaporate, to convert or resolve (a fluid) into vapour, to expel in vapours, *cf.* Abdämpfen.

Ab'dunstung, *(w.) f.* evaporation (the act of flying off in fumes).

Ab'dünstung, *(w.) f.* evaporation (the conversion of a fluid into vapour): A-Bad, *n.* *Chem.* vapour-bath, water-, sand-, or vapour-bath for evaporation; A-Haus, *n. Salt-w. &c.* a building for graduation (Gradirhaus), drying-house.

Ab'dupfen, *(w.) v. tr.* to take away or to remove (Feuchtigkeit, moisture) by tipping, &c.; (eine Wunde) to dry (a sore, &c.) by tipping with lint, &c.

Ab'dursten, *(w.) v. intr. (aux.* sein) & *ref.* (sich —) to be exhausted with thirst.

Ab'ebnen, *(w.) v. tr.* 1) to level, to make even; 2) *Furr.* to slip the edges of (a piece of fur).

Abece, *see* Abc.

Ab'ecken, *(w.) v. tr.* 1) to take off the edges or corners of (a stone, &c.); 2) to give proper edges or corners to ..., to dent, to scallop, to sharpen the corners of ....

Ab'egen, **Ab'eggen**, *(w.) v. tr.* 1) *a)* to harrow off, to remove by harrowing; *b)* to clear (an acre, &c.) by harrowing; 2) *(also intr. with* haben) to finish harrowing.

Ab'eichen, *(w.) v. tr.* to adjust (measures, &c.), to give the proper measure to ..., to gauge duly, *cf.* Eichen.

Ab'eiden, *(w.) v. tr.* (Einem etwas) *(l. u.)* to get or wring (something from one) by swearing an oath or oaths; abgeeidet *(Logau),* extorted by perjury.

Ab'eifern, *(w.) v. ref.* to harass or to exhaust one's self by zeal, eagerness, or anger, to spend one's passions, to pother one's self.

Ab'eilen, *(w.) v.* I. *intr. (aux.* sein) to hurry or hasten away, to hurry off *(syn.* Forteilen); die Bergeleute eilt ab *(Schiller);* the [illegible] *(i. e. from the stage,* a [illegible] *from* Abgehen, *&c.)*; II. *tr.* (Einem etwas) *coll.* to take (something from one) by surprising him, to seize upon in the hurry of the moment; III. *ref.* (sich —) to exhaust one's self by hurrying.

Ab'eisen, *(w.) v.* I. *tr.* to free or clear [illegible]; II. *intr. (aux.* sein & haben) to thaw.

* **A'bele**, *(w.) f.* (originally Albele, Alberbaum), *Ital.* albero, albarello, *Fr.* aubel, *Engl.* abele, *a tree very common in the provinces of Holland and England)* abel-tree, a fine kind of white poplar: nur die Abele bewegt ihr silbernes Laub *(Voss).*

* **A'belmosch**, *(str.) m. Bot.* abel-musk *(Hibiscus abelmoschus);* —same, *m.* musk-seed.

A'bend, *(str.) m.* 1) evening, * even, eve, vesper; close of the day; 2) *a)* (West) west, occident; *b)* (Abendland) western country, occident; 3) *a)* (Lebensabend) * decline or latter part of life; *b)* conclusion, end; das fürchterliche Ungewitter, am A-e *(i. e.* am Ausgang) des vergangenen Jahrhunderts *(Herder),* the terrible thunderstorm *(i. e.* the French revolution) at the close of last century; der heilige — (vor einem Feste), eve (the vigil or fast before a holiday); der Weihnachtsheiligabend, Christmas eve: des A-s (Abends), am —, zu, zum —, den —, in the evening, at night; es ist nicht wahrscheinlich, daß ich mich an diesem warmen — erkälten sollte, it is not likely that I should take cold on this warm night; P. war A-s immer pünktlich um zehn Uhr zu Hause, P. was always home precisely at ten o'clock at night; vom Morgen bis (zum) —, from morning till evening; eines A-s *(less usual:* einen —), one evening, one night; einen — kam ein Priester zum König *(Göthe),* one evening a priest came to the king; auf den —, in the evening; this evening, to-night; auf den — kommt er nach Haus, towards evening he will be home; gegen —, 1) towards evening (night); 2) (nach Westen) westerly; gegen — gelegen, western, occidental; gegen einen —, (towards) one evening; so schritten zween Wanderer zu — da heran *(Schlegel),* thus two travellers walked up there in the evening; diesen —, heute —, this evening, to-night; heute — war es voll, we had a full night; morgen —, to-morrow evening, to-morrow night; gestern —, yesterday evening, last night, * yester-eve, yester-evening, yester-night; vorgestern —, (on) the night before last; alle A-e, every evening, every night; jeden — und jeden Morgen, every night and every morning; (einen) guten —! *(coll.* schönen guten —!) good evening! (good night! *G. P. R. James,* Beauchamp); — werden, to grow night, to grow dark; es wird —, it grows dark, evening draws near, night approaches; bleibe bei uns, denn es will — werden (Luke 24, 29. *Luther),* abide with us, for it is towards evening; es geht gegen den —, auf den —, it draws towards evening; der — bricht an, the evening sets or closes in; der — nahte allmählich heran, (the) evening was gradually advancing; der — beginnt mit dem Untergang der Sonne, (the) evening commences at the setting of the sun; zu — essen, to sup, to take one's supper, to eat the evening-meal; nicht zu — essen, to go supperless; einen — bei einem Freunde zubringen, to spend an evening with a friend; — machen, *fig. intr.* to cease to work, to rest (from the day's toils), *cf.* Feierabend; die Stunde, die mit dem Leben — macht *(Günther),* the hour which puts a stop to the toils of life; *proverbs:* es ist (noch) nicht aller Tage —, *(Lat.* omnium dierum sol nondum occidit) man soll den Tag nicht vor dem — loben, the evening crowns the day; *anal.* never praise a ford till you get over; don't whistle before you are out of the woods; ist der Tag auch noch so lang, dennoch *(or* endlich) kommt der —, the longest day must come to an end, be the day ever so long, at length comes even-song, *anal.* it is a long lane which has no turning.

A'bend..., *in comp. (many compounds are formed with* Abend, *which are to be translated by prefixing either:* 1) evening-, even-; vespertine, *or* 2) west-, western: —andacht, *f.* evening-devotion, evening-prayers, *Church.* evening-service, complotory, *Rom. Cath.* compline; —besuch, *m.* 1) evening-visit; 2) evening-visitor; —betglocke, *f.* evening-bell calling to prayers: —betstunde, *f.* hour of evening-prayers, *cf.* —andacht; —blatt, *n.* evening-paper *(syn.* —zeitung); —arbeit, *f.* work done in the evening, evening-task: —belustigung, *f.* evening-amusement; —beleuchtung, *f. Paint.* evening-lights, the tints by which the setting sun illuminates (tinges) a landscape *(opp.* Morgenbeleuchtung); —blume, *f. Bot.* marvel of Peru *(Mirabilis,* a genus of plants; order, *Nictaginaceae);* —brot, *n.* supper, evening-meal, particularly *(according to the etymology of the word which merely denotes evening-bread)* a simple or frugal one, bread and cheese &c.; *two meals of this kind are popularly denominated by the terms* Abendbrot *and* das kleine Abendbrot *(or* Halbabendbrot), *the latter preceding the former; the following terms are almost synonymous:* Vesperbrot, Abendzehr, Abendimbiß, Unteressen, Nachtbrot, Nachtessen, *Upper-Germ.* Abendjause); —chor, *m.* * evening-song of birds; —cirkel, *m. see* kreis; —dämmerlicht, *n.* *, —dämmerung, *f.* evening-twilight, nightfall; —duft, *m.* evening-vapour, evening-mist; —dunkel, *n.* the dark of the evening, *see* —dämmerung; —ein', *adv.* towards evening, approaching towards night, nightward.

A'benden, *(w.) v. intr. (derived from* Abend, *as* Tagen *from* Tag, to west *[Chaucer],* westering *[Milton] from* west, *&c.) little used, and only in a few tenses,* to grow night; to grow dark; to pass into darkness; laß mit säuselndem West den abenden *(used for the ill-sounding* abendenden) Weltkreis erfrischen *(Eschenburg),* let the darkling globe be refreshed with rustling zephyr.

A'bend..., *in comp.* —essen, *n.* 1) *a)* the act of supping; *b)* evening-meal, evening-repast, supper *(cf.* —brot & Nachtessen); 2) *Luther uses it for* —mahl, eucharist, *in which sense it is now never used;* 3) *sometimes for* —speise: Lachs ist kein gesundes —essen, salmon is not wholesome eating towards evening; —essenszeit, *f.* supper-time; —esser, *m.* one who takes his supper; de Luc, der überhaupt kein großer —esser ist, aß wenig *(Lichtenberg),* de Luc, who is not in the habit of tasting much food in the evening, eat little; —falke, *m. Ornith. falco vespertinus;* —falter, *m. Entom.* hawk-moth, sphinx; —feier, *f.* 1) celebration of an evening-festivity; vigil, *cf.* —andacht; 2) the solemn quiet of evening: so naht die —feier im frischen Kräuterduft *(Tiedge),* thus tranquil eve draws near in the midst of the fresh scent of herbs; —fest, *m.* evening-festival, festivity celebrated at night, *cf. the preceding word,* 1.; —feucht, *adj.* moist with evening-dew; —feuer, *n.* the fiery appearance of the setting sun; große im —feuer stehende Natur *(Jean Paul),* grand nature in the midst of a flaming sun-set; —flur, *f.* a plain or field viewed in the evening; er gleichet dem Entschlummern dieser —flur *(Neubeck),* it (Death) resembles the fading of this evening-landscape; —frist, *f.* evening-time appointed as a term; heut zur —frist *(Gotter),* to-night at the appointed time; —frosch, *m. Zool. Rana vespertina;* —gang, *m.* 1) evening-walk; 2) *Min.* a lode striking in a westerly direction; —gast, *m.* a passing guest who stays only for an evening; auf Erden als einen armen —gast *(B. Ringwaldt),* on earth as a poor transient guest; —gebet, *n.* evening-prayer; —gegend, *f.* western region, west; —geläute, *n.* the ringing of evening-bells; —gemälde, *n.* picture representing an evening *(cf.* —landschaft); —gesang, *m.* evening-song (the act of singing, and a song to be sung at evening); evening-hymn; —gesellschaft, *f.* evening-party; evening-meeting; große —gesellschaft, rout; —gespräch, *n.* evening-discourse; conversation, talk in the evening; —gewölk, *n.* evening-clouds; —glanz, *m.* (der Sonne) * brightness, radiance

come a sloping direction, to incline, subside, see sich Absenken; ein Haus mit steil a-dem Dache, a steeply pitched house; steil a-d, sloping down abruptly, abrupt (cf. Abschüssig & Abschiefern); steil a-e Schultern, sloping shoulders; sich a-e mit Bäumen bepflanzte Anlagen, steeply sloping wooded grounds; 4) a) to fall off, to deviate or depart from a certain direction: der Gang fällt ab, Min. the lead takes another direction; Mar-s. b) to cast (when the anchor is first loosened); c) to pay off, to sag (or fall) to the leeward: fall ab! ease the helm! 5) a) to diminish (in value, &c.), to decrease; b) to decay, to fall away (to lose flesh), to tabefy; c) to diminish in intensity, to decrease (as a sound, a colour, &c.); 6) to fall off (desert from a party, &c.) (cf. Abtrünnig werden); ein Theil dieser Partei wird — und mit den Whigs verschmelzen, a portion of this party will fly off and become incorporated with the Whigs; von Einem —, to fall from one; vom Glauben —, to fall off, to apostatize or to revolt from the faith; von Gott —, to turn recreant to God; 7) (mit einer Sache) coll. to get a rebuff, &c. cf. Abfahren, 2, c.); Einen — lassen, to leave in the lurch, &c., to give one a set-down, &c. see Abfertigen; 8) to contrast strongly; 9) coll. to yield profit: dabei fällt nicht viel ab, it is an unprofitable business; 10) † to slip or escape one's memory, see Entfallen; II. refl. sich (Dat.) etwas —, to break (off) in or by falling (cf. Abstürzen).

Ab'fallen, v. n. (str.) n. the act of falling down, off, &c. (cf. the verb Abfallen); fall.

Ab'fallend, p. a. falling off, &c. cf. Abfallen, v.; Bot-s. leicht —, deciduous; nicht —, indeciduous.

Ab'fällig, adj. 1) falling off; 2) liable to falling off; 3) declivous, sloping, shelving; 4) decaying; 5) (either with von or (less usual) the simple Dat.; syn. Abtrünnig) deserting, revolting (from): der Teufel brachte sie (Eva) zu Fall, daß sie von Gott — ward (Luther), the Devil seduced her that she turned recreant to God; 6) disapproving, denying, dissenting: — bescheiden, to give a refusal to ....

Ab'fälligkeit, (w.) f. 1) declivity, fall; 2) fig. a falling off or away, defection, apostasy (Abtrünnigkeit).

Ab'fall..., in comp. T-s. —kutte, f. waste-board; —röhre, f. waste-pipe, conduit-pipe.

Ab'falzen, (w.) v. tr. 1) Tann. to cleanse with the shaving knife (syn. Abaasen, Abfleischen); 2) Join. to groove.

Ab'fangen, (str.) v. tr. 1) to intercept, (Einem etwas) to catch, snatch (something from one): er fing dem Nachbar die Tauben ab, he caught his neighbour's pigeons; 2) Min. den Schacht or Einsturz drohendes Gestein mit Bolzen —, to support a pit, &c. by beams and props, to prop; 3) Dik. to turn off (a water-course); 4) Sport. to kill, to stab (a stag, &c.) with the hunting-knife.

Ab'färben, (w.) v. I. intr. to lose colour, to stain, not to stand in the grain; ein Mantel entfasert, abgefärbt und ausgerückt (Wieland), a threadbare, discoloured and worn-out cloak; II. tr. 1) to give the proper dye or colour to ..., to dye, to colour (also intr. to finish dyeing); 2) fig. kenn' ihr essen, werd' ich die übrigen Gäste — (Jean Paul), I shall represent the rest of the guests in their true colours, when they dine.

Ab'färbig, adj. liable to lose colour or to stain.

Ab'fasern (**Ab'fäseln**), (w.) v. I. tr. to free from (or to take off the) fibres; Bohnen —, to string beans (cf. Abschnüren); II. intr. (aux. haben) & refl. to lose or part with fibres or filaments, to come off in fibres, to unravel.

Ab'fasen, (w.) v. tr. (according to Heyse and others, from Ab and the Fr. face) Join. to round off (sharp edges) by planing.

Ab'fassen, (w.) v. tr. 1) Sm. to bend (a piece of iron); 2) Sport. to unwind, wind off, uncouple; 3) coll. to intercept, take up, arrest to take hold of; 4) a) to sort, to separate; b) Comm. to weigh out and pack up (articles) for retail; 5) (particul. schriftlich —) to compose, draw up, to put down (in writing), to write (in due form), to word (down), to write, to pen, to indite (an address, &c.); einen (officiellen) Bericht —, to draw up a return; schlecht abgefaßt, indifferently worded; in bündigen Ausdrücken abgefaßt, couched in concise terms.

Ab'fasser, (str.) m. 1) T. a maker up of packages (as in ribbon-factories, &c.), cf. Abfassen; 2) he that draws up any composition in writing, a writer, author, compiler (different from Verfasser, author of any original composition, although both are sometimes used synonymously).

Ab'fassung, (w.) f. 1) the act of composing, drawing up, writing, &c. cf. Abfassen; 2) composition, wording; die — der Evangelien, the composition of the gospels; die — dieses Vertrags, the wording of this treaty.

Ab'fasten, (w.) v. tr. 1) to atone for (a sin, &c.) by fasting; 2) to exhaust (refl. one's self) by fasting. [off, &c.

Ab'faulen, (w.) v. intr. (aux. sein) to rot off, to putrefy and fall off.

Ab'fäumen, (w.) v. tr. (Lessing, &c.) see Abfeimen.

Ab'fechsen, (w.) v. tr. to strip off the sprouts [of (plants).

Ab'fechten, (str.) v. I. tr. to get by fighting; nachdem wir dieses Böhmen den Sachsen abgefochten (Schiller), after we have taken this very Bohemia in battle from the Saxons; II. refl. to exhaust or weary one's self with fighting.

Ab'federn, (w.) v. I. tr. 1) to strip of the feathers (a goose, &c.), to pluck; 2) Sport. to kill (a bird) by driving a quill into its brains; II. intr. to lose or to shed the feathers (cf. Mausen, III.).

Ab'fegen, (w.) v. tr. 1) to sweep (or to wipe) off, to rub off; to cleanse by sweeping; den Staub von ... —, to dust; 2) ein Hirsch fegt den Bast ab, Sport. a deer frays his head; 3) a-de Mittel, (l. u.) Med. cleansing medicines, abluents. [wiern).

Ab'feiern, (w.) v. tr. Mar. to veer (Abwiern).

Ab'feilen, (w.) v. tr. 1) to file off, to cut with a file; einen Nagel —, to file a nail; 2) to give the last finish to (an instrument, &c.) by filing; eine Klinge —, Sword-cutl. to rub a blade; 3) fig. (l. u.) to cut off, to take away; was noch der Reif nicht abgefeilt (Matthisson), what the frost has not yet nipped off.

Ab'feilichte, (str.) n. filings (cf. Feilspäne).

Ab'feilraspel, (w.) f. great rasp (used in filing lead, &c.).

Ab'feilschen, (w.) v. tr. 1) to beat down (a certain sum) from the price, to obtain (a certain reduction) by chaffering and higgling; 2) (Einem etwas) to get (something from one) by bargaining (cf. Abhandeln, 1.).

Ab'feimen, (w.) v. tr. 1) to clear off by skimming, to take off the foam or froth of (molten glass, &c.), to skim (off), to scum; 2) fig. (l. u.) to refine or intensify by removing impurities: gener. used in the participle past: abgefeimt, p. a. arrant, crafty; ein abgefeimter Schelm, an arch-rogue, an arrant knave (cf. ein Schurke vom reinsten Wasser); abgefeimte Bosheit, concocted malice.

Ab'feinen, (w.) v. tr. to clear off, to refine (sugar, &c.).

Ab'fenstern, (w.) v. tr. coll. to chide or scold vehemently, to upbraid, rebuke (cf. Ausschelten).

Ab'fertigen, (w.) v. tr. 1) a) to despatch, to expedite, to clear off; b) to send [illegible] forward; c) to dismiss, to send [illegible] Streitsache —, to dispose of a [illegible] auf den ersten Anblick [illegible] a question not to be disposed of [illegible] 2) (kurz) fig. to take (one) up short [illegible] (one) short, to rebuff, to snub [illegible] a set-down, to set (one) down [illegible] nicht — lassen, he was not to [illegible] not) be rebuffed or put off.

Ab'fertiger, (str.) m. despatcher, &c.

Ab'fertigung, (w.) f. 1) a) the [illegible] despatching, forwarding, &c.; despatch [illegible] tion; b) dismissal; 2) fig. rebuff [illegible] partee, a set-down.

Ab'fertigungsschein, (str.) m. [illegible] claration (entry) at the custom-house [illegible]

Ab'fesseln, (w.) v. tr. to unfetter [illegible] chain, to unshackle.

Ab'fetten, (w.) v. I. tr. 1) to take [illegible] off the fat, the grease of (soup [illegible]) to fatten (victuals); II. intr. to lose fat.

Ab'feuchten, (w.) v. I. tr. 1) to [illegible] moisture, to dry; 2) (& intr.) to [illegible] ture, to moisten; II. intr. to lose moisture.

Ab'feuern, (w.) v. tr. 1) to fire [illegible] to discharge; 2) (gener. intr.) Metall. [illegible] heating (or to cool) the furnace.

Ab'feuerung, (w.) f. the act of [illegible] (cf. Abfeuern), discharge.

Ab'fiedeln, (w.) v. tr. coll. 1) to [illegible] fiddle), to fiddle; 2) to separate or [illegible] out by rubbing; 3) Metall. to scour [illegible]

Ab'fiedern, (w.) v. I. tr. [illegible] break) off the extremities of [illegible] see Abfedern, II.

Ab'filtriren, (w.) v. tr. to pass through a filter, to percolate, to clear off by [illegible] filter (off).

Ab'filzen, (w.) v. tr. vulg. see [illegible]

Ab'finden, (str.) v. I. tr. 1) to [illegible] pay off (creditors, &c.); to portion [illegible] a settlement on (a daughter, &c.) [illegible] dene Kinder, portioned (off) children [illegible] fundene Prinzen, appanaged princes [illegible] times used with a slight degree of [illegible] Einen mit einer Summe &c. —, to pay one off in order to get rid of him, to put [illegible] with a (paltry) sum, &c. (cf. [illegible]) 1) (l. u.) to forego the habit of [illegible] &c.), see sich Abgewöhnen; 2) to [illegible] agree (mit, with), to come to terms, to come to an agreement or understanding, to [illegible] an arrangement or composition, to [illegible] (with); er suchte sich mit seinem Gewissen abzufinden, he tried to make a compromise with his conscience; 3) sich — (bei Jemand) [illegible] to make an acknowledgment for [illegible]

Ab'finden, v. n. (str.) n. agreement [illegible] ment, understanding, composition [illegible] — treffen, to make an agreement [illegible] finden, II. 2. (syn. Abkommen).

Ab'findung, (w.) f. the act of [illegible] (claims of) others, &c. cf. sich Abfinden [illegible] pointment, allowance; composition [illegible] ditors, &c.); agreement, compromise [illegible]

Ab'findungs..., in comp. —[illegible] trag, m. —summe, f. money or [illegible] get clear of all demands, sum of [illegible] sum of indemnity, composition.

Ab'fingern, (w.) v. tr. coll. 1) [illegible] the fingers (syn. an den Fingern [illegible] das läßt sich leicht —, it takes no [illegible] to find that out, it is as clear as [illegible] (used rather contemptuously) to [illegible] tune) with volubility of fingers.

Ab'finnen, (w.) v. tr. 1) Sm. [illegible] edges of (iron, &c.) by beating [illegible] welding; 2) Tin. to beat [illegible] shape with the thin end (finne) [illegible]

Ab'fischen, (w.) v. tr. 1) to [illegible] by fishing; fig-s. 2) see [illegible] boat of a thing; 3) (Einem etwas) coll. to forestall one in obtaining any advantage, &c., to trick (one) out of (a thing).

Ab'fitzen, (w.) v. tr. Mas. to close the seams of (a wall) with mortar and smoothing them over, to smooth (a wall).

Ab'flachen, (w.) v. I. tr. to level, to slope; II. rfl. to subside (into a plain), &c. cf. Abdachen, Flächen.

Ab'flachung, (w.) f. Cryst. bevelment.

Ab'flammen, (w.) v. tr. Skin-dress. to grease or tallow (hides) over a charcoal-fire.

Ab'flattern, (w.) v. I. intr. (aux. sein) to flutter away; II. rfl. to exhaust one's self or to grow wearied by fluttering.

Ab'flauen, Ab'flauern, (w.) v. tr. 1) Min. to wash (ore), to buddle; 2) to rinse (linen).

Ab'flau..., in comp. Min. —faß, n. buddle, a square frame of boards used in washing tin-ore, washing-tub; —herd, m. buddling dish.

Ab'flechen, (w.) v. tr. see Abflauen.

Ab'flechten, (str.) v. tr. to untwist, unbraid.

Ab'flecken, (w.) v. intr. to stain by losing colour.

Ab'fledern, (w.) v. tr. to fan (grain), to separate (the chaff from grain) with a goosewing.

Ab'flegeln, (w.) v. tr. to beat out with a flail.

Ab'flehen, (w.) v. tr. I. see Abflauen; II. i. w. (Einem etwas) to obtain (something from one) by imploring.

Ab'fleisch..., in comp. —eisen, n. —messer, m. Tann. fleshing-knife, scraper.

Ab'fleischen, (w.) v. tr. 1) a) to pick (or tear) the flesh from (a bone); b) fig. to deprive of flesh and blood; 2) Tann. to flesh (Abaasen).

Ab'flensen, (w.) v. tr. Mar. to flinch, to cut up the blubber of (a whale or seal).

Ab'fleihen, (w.) v. tr. see Abflauen.

Ab'fließherd, (str.) m. see Abflauherd.

Ab'fliegen, (str.) v. intr. (aux. sein) 1) lit. & fig. to fly off; 2) T. (of the wood of forest-trees) to wither on the stem.

Ab'fließen, (str.) v. intr. (aux. sein) 1) to flow down, to flow off, to ebb, to run down; 2) to flow or issue out, to discharge or disembogue itself (of rivers sich Ergießen); in das Meer —, to fall into the sea; 3) fig. to emanate, follow or result (from), to be derived (from).

A. Ab'flößen, (w.) v. tr. see Abflauen.

B. Ab'flöhen, (w.) v. tr. vulg. to flea.

Ab'flößen, (w.) v. tr. 1) to cause to float down (the river) or off (Hinabflößen, Wegflößen); Holz —, to float wood or timber down; ein Floß —, to float a raft down the river; 2) to float, skim, cream (milk = Abrahmen, 1.).

Ab'flöten, (w.) v. tr. coll. to play (a tune) on the flute.

Ab'flug, (str., pl. Ab'flüge) m. 1) the (act of) flying away, flight (of migratory birds); 2) digression, excursion turning aside from the main course, cf. Ausflug; 3) T. (of the wood of forest-trees) the withering on the stem.

Ab'flügeln, (w.) v. I. tr. 1) to deprive of the wings; 2) T. (of the winged seeds of firs, &c.) to waft through the air and disperse; II. intr. see Abfliegen, 2.

Ab'fluß, (str., pl. Ab'flüsse) m. 1) a) the (act of) flowing or running down or off; ebb, reflux; b) Med. defluxion, defluxion (of humours); [illegible] (of blood); c) outlet, escape; — [illegible], to drain off; 2) (das Abfließende) [illegible] refuse, ooze; 3) a water-[illegible], gutter, kennel, sewer; 4) lapse [illegible], Verfluß; der gehemmte [illegible] Strom (Schiller), the checked [illegible]; nach — der Gewässer [illegible], after the stream [illegible] had subsided (on leaving [illegible]

[illegible] in comp. —graben, m. drain, see Abzugsgraben; —rinne, f. —röhre, f. drain-pipe, waste-pipe; —schnur, f. Farr. a strap or thread spread with salve, answering to a seton, and inserted into a wound (—wunde, f.) for the discharge of matter.

Ab'flutern, (w.) v. intr. (aux. sein) to flow off, to recede.

Ab'fodern, (w.) v. tr. see Abfordern.

Ab'fohlen, (w.) v. intr. see Abfüllen, II.

Ab'folge, (w.) f. Log. conclusion, inference drawn from certain premises.

Ab'folgen, (w.) v. tr. obsolescent, to deliver, surrender, see Verabfolgen.

Ab'foltern, (w.) v. tr. (l. w.) (Einem etwas) to extort (something from one).

Ab'fordern, (w.) v. tr. 1) to call off or away, see Abrufen; 2) Einem etwas — (syn. Abverlangen), to ask one for a thing, to demand, to require it from one; etwas —, to come for a thing; etwas — lassen, to send for a thing; Einem Rechnung —, to call one to account.

Ab'forderung, (w.) f. the act of calling off or away, &c. cf. Abfordern; demand, request; A-sbrief, m. A-srecht, n. see Abberufungsschreiben, Abberufungsrecht.

Ab'form, (w.) f. a representation or similitude of anything (particul. any figure or form of cubic extent, called die Urform) formed of a material substance, image, effigy; cast; copy, likeness.

Ab'formen, (w.) v. tr. 1) to form a representation of (any figure or prototype of cubic extent), to form, model, mould, shape; to copy, imitate; von einerlei Urbild abgeformt (Wieland), modelled from the same prototype; von ihm abgeformt (id.), moulded in his likeness; 2) Shoe-m. to remove (a shoe, &c.) from the last; 3) see the next word.

Ab'formiren, (w.) v. tr. Bookb. to give the proper shape to (the covers of a book) (Abrichten).

Ab'forschen, (w.) v. tr. (Einem etwas) to elicit (something from one) by inquiry, vulg. to pump (one) out.

Ab'fragen, (w. & irr.) v. tr. 1) (Einem etwas) to get (or draw) out (something from one) by questioning, to elicit (something from one) by inquiry, vulg. to pump (one) out; er läßt sich alle Geheimnisse —, every secret is to be got out of him; doch nicht erkühnt' ich mich was du vor mir | in dieses Dunkel hüllst, dir abzufragen (Schiller), but I did not venture to ask you to reveal what you involve in dark mystery; 2) to examine judicially, to hear, see Abhören, 2.

Ab'fressen, (str.) v. tr. 1) to eat off, to clear off by eating (said of animals), to knap, knapple, to depasture; Sprossen —, to browse; die Spitzen —, to crop; 2) fig. to corrode, consume; der Gram frißt ihm das Herz ab, grief gnaws his heart; a-d, p. a. depascent.

Ab'frieren, (str.) v. I. intr. (aux. sein) to be blasted with cold, to freeze off; II. rfl. sich (Dat.) etwas —, to lose something (a member, &c.) by extreme cold.

Ab'frohnen, Ab'frohnen, (w.) v. tr. Law, 1) to pay off by menial labour or service; 2) to perform (the labour or service) due to the lord of the manor. [to pommel, cf. Fuchteln.

Ab'fuchteln, (w.) v. tr. coll. to beat soundly,

Ab'fügen, (w.) v. tr. 1) Carp. & Join. Bretter —, to smooth with the long plane the edges of planks to be joined; 2) see Abfiedern, I.

Ab'fühlen, (w.) v. tr. to perceive by the touch; (Einem etwas) to become sensible of (the feelings, intentions, &c. of another); der Zuhörer fühlt es dem Redner bald ab, daß er aufrichtig ist, fig. the hearer soon becomes aware (or sensible) of the sincerity of the speaker.

Ab'fuhr(e), (w.) f. the act of carrying off or away by vehicles, removal by wheel-carriage, conveyance or carriage from a place, transportation, exportation (opp. Anfuhr, Zufuhr); zur — des Holzes (Zschokke), for removing or carting off the wood: für An- und —nichts berechnen, to charge nothing for cartage.

Ab'führ..., in comp. (see Abführen) T-s. —arbeit, f. wire-drawing work; —eisen, n. wire-bench, reducing-bench.

Ab'führen, (w.) v. I. tr. 1) to lead off, to lead away: vom rechten Wege —, to lead astray, to mislead; der Polizeidiener führte ihn in Gewahrsam ab, the constable marched him off in custody; sie wurden ins Gefängniß abgeführt, they were marched off to prison; 2) a) to carry off, down, away or out, to convey; b) fig. to carry or lead out of the way; es würde uns zu weit (von unserem Gegenstande) —, it would lead us too far out of our way, it would carry us too far from our subject; 3) to export, see Ausführen; 4) to fetch off, to carry off (by drainage), to drain; sie haben Canäle, um das Wasser abzuführen, they have channels to carry off the water (cf. Ableiten); 5) Anat. to abduce, see Abziehen, 3.; 6) Sport. to break in (dogs), to train (cf. Abrichten); 7) Med. a) to deterge, to cleanse (the vessels or the skin) from offending matter; b) to divert (to another part of the body), to expel (humours); to purge, cleanse, evacuate; abgeführt werden, to be voided or excerned, to pass; 8) a) Wire-draw. Draht — (i. e. verfeinern), to draw wire smaller and smaller; b) Min. to wear out, blunt (the tools); 9) Comm. & Law, a) to pay (off), to discharge, to settle (a debt, &c.); b) to credit or pass to the credit of a person's account; 10) fig-s. to derive (see Ableiten); man führt des Geschlechts Ursprung von Karl dem Großen ab, the origin of the family is traced back to Charlemagne; Irrthum derjenigen, die ihn von den schwäbischen Herzögen — (Hahn), an error of those who assume his descent from the Swabian dukes; 11) † and almost always found as a pp.: abgeführt, p. a. practised, cunning, expert, arrant, crafty, artful; 12) to check, rebuke, coll. to snub, to pay off, to fit (one) with a smart answer (cf. Abfertigen); II. intr. Med. to act as an aperient, to evacuate the bowels; III. rfl. coll. to pack off, to make one's exit, cant. to cut one's stick, to make one's self scarce.

Ab'führend, p. a. 1) Med. a) detergent, excretory, dejectory; b) purgative, cathartical, aperient; gelinde —, lenient; das a-de Mittel, see Abführmittel; 2) Anat-s. der a-e Muskel, abducent muscle, abductor: a-e Wege, m. pl. excretory passages.

Ab'führ..., in comp. —mittel, n. Med. purgative, aperient; —tisch, m. T. a wire-drawer's bench (Ziehbank).

Ab'führung, (w.) f. 1) the (act of) leading off, &c. cf. Abführen; 2) Anat. abduction, the act of drawing back or apart; 3) Med. abstersion, expulsion, purgation.

Ab'führungs..., in comp. —mittel, n. see Abführmittel; —röhre, f. Mech. escape-pipe.

A. Ab'füllen, (w.) v. tr. (from Ab and Füllen, A.) to fill out, to pour out from a cask, &c.; ein Faß —, to empty a cask; Wein —, to draw off wine: see Abziehen, 5, b.

B. Ab'füllen, (w.) v. intr. (from Ab and Füllen, B.) to have done foaling.

Ab'fund, (str.) m. (from Abfinden; — l. w.) agreement, arrangement, see Abfindung.

Ab'furchen, (w.) v. tr. 1) to divide by furrows; 2) see Abackern.

Ab'füttern, Ab'futtern, (w.) v. tr. 1) to feed, to give sufficient provender (as to cattle at night); 2) Einen —, coll. & hod. to give (one) an ample meal (orml. feed).

Ab'fütterung, (w.) f. 1) the feeding (of animals); 2) usu. Stud. (applied to grand banquets or ceremonial dinners) a general entertainment, usu. feeding, feed.

Ab'gabe, (w.) f. (from Abgeben) 1) delivery, deliverance; 2) tribute; duty; tax, custom; impost; die directen A-n, assessed taxes; 3) Comm. draft, bill (of exchange), assignment.

Ab'gabeln, (w.) v. tr. (l. u.) to reach down, to remove, to take away with a fork.

Ab'gaben..., in comp. —frei, adj. duty-free, exempt from taxes, unencumbered; —freiheit, f. exemption from taxes, immunity; —pachter, m. Nation. Econ. farmer of the revenues; —wesen, n. system or state of the imposts or taxes.

Ab'gähren, (str.) v. intr. to ferment sufficiently.

Ab'gang, (str., pl. Ab'gänge) m. (from Abgehen) 1) a) the act of going off, riding off, setting out, departure, starting; b) Theat. exit, the act of going off the stage; fig.-c. c) departure, the going out of office, &c., resignation; — nehmen, among Miners, to leave the pit, to cease to work; der — (eines Schauspielers) von der Bühne, retirement from the stage; d) removal (from the present life), decease, death; extinction (of a family, &c.); hed. exit; 2) a) Med. emission, evacuation; flux, oozing, or loss (of blood, wine, mucus, &c.); b) a passing out, issue; eine Öffnung zum A-e des Rauches, an aperture for the escape of smoke; 3) Comm.-c. sale (of goods), market, draft, run; der gute —, saleableness, run; ein schneller —, a quick (and short) return; — haben, to sell (well, &c.); guten (schnellen) — haben or finden, to meet with a ready sale or market, to have a quick draft, to sell well, coll. to run or go off readily or easily; schlechten or langsamen — haben, to go off heavily, to be (or lie) heavy on hand; keinen — finden, to find no purchasers, to be dull of sale; 4) (particul. pl. Abgänge) a) waste, sheeds; worthless remains; refuse; chips, chippings, clippings, shavings, scrapings, filings (cf. Abfälle); b) spill-water; c) Typ. waste-paper; d) Min. worn out tools; 5) Med. abortion, miscarriage; fig.-c. 6) a) departure; deviation; b) desuetude; in — kommen, to go out of fashion; man hat es in — gebracht, it has been done away with, abolished; 7) a) deduction (see Abzug); b) diminution; decrease, decline; c) want; loss; deficiency (in the weight, &c.), deficit; d) Min. loss of ores or metal in smelting, &c.; in — kommen, (of a mine) to cease to be workable, to be abandoned; in — kommen, to be lost, to cease to exist; in — der Nahrung kommen, to lose customers.

Ab'gängig, adj. 1) going off, departing, &c. cf. Abgehen; 2) Med. excremental; 3) Comm. merchantable, sal(e)able, vendible; fig.-c. 4) deficient, wanting; 5) a) worn out (as clothes, &c.), cast off; b) wasted and worn out with age, decrepit; c) declining; d) provinc. out of fashion.

Ab'gängling, (str.) m. **Ab'gängsel**, (str.) n. 1) waste, refuse, see Abgang (Abgänge) 4.; 2) Med. abortion.

Ab'gangs..., in comp. —dampf, m. Mech. dead steam; —haus, n. in Sugarplantations a house in which the cane-trash is dried in order to serve as fuel; —loch, n. a hole in the bottom of bee-hives, through which the bees remove impurities and dead bees; —rechnung, f. Comm. &c. bare account; —zeit, f. time of departure; —zeugniß, n. testimonial given to a pupil &c. on leaving school; —zinn, n. Min. tin-ore of inferior quality which has separated from the better ores in washing.

Ab'garben, (w.) v. tr. see Abgerben.

Ab'gäschen, (w.) v. intr. to cease foaming or fermenting. [weed (a garden, &c.).

Ab'gäten, (w.) v. tr. to clear of weeds, to

Ab'gattern, (w.) v. tr. (Einem etwas) to get (something) out of ....

Ab'gaukeln, (w.) v. tr. (Einem etwas) to obtain (something from one) by juggling, to deprive (one) of (a thing) by juggling.

Ab'gaunern, (w.) v. tr. (Einem etwas) to swindle (one) out of (a thing).

Ab'gebacken, p. a. see Abbacken.

Ab'geben, (str.) v. I. tr. 1) to give (away); to deliver; to hand; to make over; ich habe ein Packet an ihn abzugeben, I have a packet to deliver to him; er hatte Auftrag das Briefchen blos abzugeben, he had instruction merely to leave the note; das Gedinge —, Min. to submit to a mining officer (for examination) the work which was undertaken by contract (cf. Gedinge); Zölle —, to pay duties; abzugeben bei ..., (on the directions of letters: to the) care of ...; 2) (syn. Aufgeben, Niederlegen) to give up, to hand over, to quit, to part with, to resign (an office, &c.); 3) Comm. a) (eine Summe, einen Wechsel rc. auf Einen) to value (a sum), to draw (a bill), to pass (a draft upon one); b) to sell, to negotiate; 4) Einem etwas —, a) to hit one a blow; b) fig. to give one a cutting reply, &c.; to hit one hard, to give it him, to cut one up, to lash, scold, abuse; Böse gibt ihm immer was ab, wie ers verdient (Göthe), B. every now and then gives him a set-down as he deserves; es wird etwas —, fam. we are likely to have some rain or any sudden, unexpected, particul. disagreeable occurrence, such as vexation, &c.; 5) Gam. (also intr.) to finish dealing, to deal for the last time; fig.-c. 6) to give (an opinion, &c.); eine Erklärung —, to make a declaration or statement; wenn ich ein Urtheil (eine Meinung) über (with Acc.) — soll, if I am to pass judgment (if I may presume to offer an opinion) upon (on); Zeugniß —, to bear witness; 7) a) to be good (or fit) for ...; kann er einen Courier —? is he fit for a courier? er würde einen guten Soldaten —, he would make a good soldier; b) to act or serve as ...; die Mittelsperson —, to act as mediator, to stand between; einen Narren —, to play the fool; einen Beweis —, to establish a proof, to stand in proof; er gab einen Professor zu Leipzig ab, er gab zu Kronweißenburg einen Apotheker ab (&c. — Möser), he was a professor at Leipzig, he was an apothecary at K.; einen Punct —, Min. to determine the situation of a point in or near a mine (sometimes used as an intransitive); II. refl. (with mit) 1) to deal (in or with), to concern or occupy one's self with, to engage one's self in; sich mit Einem —, to have intercourse, to have or keep company (in an ill sense to meddle) with one; er verkennt die Gegenstände, mit denen sich die Philosophie — sollte, he mistakes the objects with which philosophy ought to be concerned; 2) (in this sense [l. u.] syn. with auf ... Ausgehen) to addict one's self to, to aim at, to be bent on ...; (damit is sometimes omitted:) eine Närrin, die sich abgibt gelehrt zu sein (Göthe), a fool who sets up for a learned woman.

Ab'geber, (str.) m. Comm. seller, one who offers for sale.

Ab'gebinde, (str.) n. Carp. frame-work, timber-work (of a wooden &c. building).

Ab'gebissen, p. a. (from Abbeißen) Bot. premorse, end-bitten, truncated.

Ab'geblüht, p. a. (from Abblühen) Bot. deflorate.

Ab'gebogen, p. a. (from Abbiegen) Nat. (particul. Bot.) declined.

Ab'gebot, (str.) n. (from Abbieten) 1) the act of proclaiming from the pulpit, &c. see Aufgebot; 2) a higher bid (at public sales), out bidding.

Ab'gebrannt, p. a. 1) burnt off, &c.; 2) burnt out; der A-e, a. one who [illegible] damage by fire, cf. Abbrennen 2.

Ab'gebrochen, I. p. a. (from [illegible]) lit. & fig. broken, (also Bot.) [illegible] (Bot.) truncate; 2) fig. interrupted, [illegible] ingly; — gefiedert, Bot. abruptly pinnate [illegible] a-e Worte, disjointed or broken [illegible] Seufzer, broken sighs; II. A-heit, [illegible] ruptness.

Ab'gebung, (w.) f. the act of giving [illegible] &c. cf. Abgeben; delivery, &c. [illegible]

Ab'gecirkelt, p. a. fig. punctual or exact to excess, punctilious, precise, [illegible]

Ab'gedroschen, p. a. trite, hackneyed, common-place, trivial; a-e Redensarten, [illegible] phrases; eine a-e Materie, a beaten [illegible]

Ab'gedroschenheit, (w.) f. [illegible] will:) commonplaceness.

Ab'gefeimt, **Ab'ge[illegible]**, I. p. a. [illegible] feimen; II. A-heit, (w.) f. [illegible]

Ab'gehauen, p. a. (from Abhauen) [illegible] couped, cut close (of the heads or [illegible] animals, &c.).

Ab'gehen, (irr.) v. I. intr. [illegible] a) to go down, see Hinabgehen, [illegible] generally used in this sense; b) to [illegible] to walk off, to go out; Theat.-c. [illegible] —, to go off the stage, coll. to [illegible] exit; (Stage-directions:) Faust [illegible] Faust; Faust und Mephistopheles [illegible] exeunt Faust and Mephistopheles; [illegible] ab, exeunt omnes, all go out; c) [illegible] set out, to start, depart; eine Post [illegible] um elf Uhr ab, one post has gone out [illegible] o'clock; der (Dampfwagen-)Zug [illegible] ab, the train starts at twelve; [illegible] the departing train; dd) to go off, [illegible] off, despatched or forwarded (as goods [illegible]) — lassen, to expedite, to forward, [illegible] 2) to branch off (as a road, &c.), to [illegible] aside; 3) to come off (in German [illegible] is not used in this sense, cf. [illegible] to give way, to wear off; das [illegible] the wheel came off; die Farbe [illegible] colour comes off; diese Pflanzen [illegible] vom Kerne ab, these plants do [illegible] themselves from their kernels; ein [illegible] welcher abgegangen war, a hook that [illegible] away; er riß so stark am Klingelzug, [illegible] selbe vom Drahte abging, he gave [illegible] to the bell-rope that it came away [illegible] wire; 4) a) Med. to pass, to be [illegible] evacuated; es gingen ihm [illegible] voided worms; die Leibesfrucht ging [illegible] she miscarried, she had a [illegible] pass off (as vapour, &c.); der a-de [illegible] dead steam, see Abgangsdampf; 5) [illegible] off (as a gun, &c.), see Losgehen, [illegible] usual in this sense; b) to go out, [illegible] extinct (as fire); c) fig. to keep a [illegible] to end, see Ablaufen; 6) Comm. gut [illegible] — rc., (of commodities) to sell (well, [illegible] go or run off readily, to go off [illegible] see Abgang, 3.; gut a-d, [illegible] Comm. &c. to be abated, deducted, [illegible] hiervon geht ab, discount (of ...); [illegible] seiner Forderung rc.) — lassen, [illegible] yield some abatement; die [illegible] sollten —, the odd pennies ought to [illegible] ich lasse keinen Heller davon —, [illegible] bate one farthing of it; b) to be [illegible] gehen mir fünf Thaler ab, I want [illegible] five dollars; ich fühle wenig [illegible] Wenn dieser Art abgeht (Göthe), I [illegible] keenly that a man of this [illegible] ing to me; natürlicher Verstand [illegible] ab, he does not want for natural [illegible] ing; es geht ihm alles Gefühl [illegible] ab, he is lost to every sense of [illegible] ging auch diesesmal der [illegible] again this time the entertainment [illegible] wanting in anything; es [illegible] shall want for nothing: er läßt sich nichts —, he does not deny himself anything; he indulges every enjoyment; *fig-s.* 9) (*formerly often used without any addition, or with the Gen.* Todes, *or* tödtlich, *or* mit Tode: *use has now generally decided for the phrase,* mit Tode —) to depart this life, to decease, to die; G. F. S. geboren Berlin 1712, abgegangen daselbst 1775 (*Göthe*), G. F. S. born at Berlin, 1712, died at the same place, 1775; wenn das innere Mark einer Tanne verdirbt, geht der Baum bald ab (*Zschokke*), when the pith and marrow of a fir decays, the tree soon dies: 9) *a)* to go out of office, to leave school, a situation, &c., to retire (von der Bühne, from the stage, &c.), to resign; *b)* to secede (von, from), to withdraw (from a party), to retire; von … —, to leave …; 10) *a)* (*Wieland, &c.*) to depart, to deviate (from), to differ (from), = Abweichen; *b)* to digress, to go (from one's subject, &c.); Sie gehen von der Sache ab, you turn off from the subject; to swerve, to wander (from the path of duty, &c.); davon kann ich nicht —, I cannot depart from this resolution, I must insist upon it; II. *tr.* 1) *a)* to wear off *or* out by walking; (sich [*Dat.*]) die Absätze von den Schuhen —, to wear off the heels of one's shoes by walking; *b)* *refl.* to exhaust one's self by walking; to grow tired with walking; 2) to measure by steps; einen Kreis —, to walk *or* stalk round in a circle.

Ab'geigen, (*w.*) *v. tr. coll.* to play off (a tune, &c.) on a fiddle, to fiddle away.

Ab'geißeln, (*w.*) *v. tr.* 1) to take off with the scourge; 2) to scourge (whip, flog) soundly.

Ab'geizen, (*w.*) *v. tr. fam.* (Einem etwas) to get by avarice from; sich (*Dat.*) etwas —, to starve one's self by avarice, to pinch or stint one's self in …, *cf.* Abdarben.

Ab'gekartet, *p. a.* collusive, *see* Abkarten.

Ab'gekränkt, *p. a.* (*l. u.*) worn out, exhausted, debilitated by grief *or* mortification

Ab'gekürzt, *p. a.* 1) abbreviated, &c. *see* Abkürzen; compendious; 2) *Bot.* short; 3) *a)* *Geom. & Astr.* curtate; *b)* *Geom.* (*syn.* Abgestumpft) truncated (as a cone, &c.); der a-e Kegel, truncated cone; die a-e Pyramide, truncated pyramid (whose vertex is cut off parallel to the base); 4) *Herald.* couped.

Ab'gelben, (*w.*) *v. intr.* (*aux.* haben) to lose the yellow colour.

Ab'gelebt, *p. a.* 1) *lit. & fig.* decrepit: worn with age; 2) debilitated by excesses; decayed, faded; 3) deceased, *see* Verstorben; 4) *fig.* obsolete, gone out of use.

Ab'gelebtheit, (*w.*) *f.* decrepitude, last stage of decay, old age, infirmity.

Ab'gelediget, *p. a. Herald.* couped, detached so as not to touch the edges of the shield.

Ab'gelegen, I. *p. p. see* Abliegen; II. *adj.* remote, distant, out of the way; sequestered, retired, solitary (*syn.* Entlegen, *&c.*); ein a-es Dorf, a retired village; der a-e Spaziergang, by-walk.

Ab'gelegenheit, (*w.*) *f.* remoteness, distance; sequestered *or* retired situation, solitariness.

† Ab'geleibt, *p. a.* (*seems to be corrupted from the MHG.* abelîp, lifeless, *since a verb* Ableiben *does not occur*) exanimate, inanimate, lifeless, deceased.

Ab'geleitet, *p. a. Gramm., Mus. &c.* derivative, [illegible], secondary; das a-e Wort, [illegible].

Ab'geloben, (*w.*) *v. tr.* to renounce solemnly [illegible].

† Ab'gelten, (*str.*) *v. tr.* (Einem etwas) to [illegible] (something from one), to requite [illegible].

Ab'[illegible], *p. a.* unassociate(d).

Ab'gemessen, I. *adj. fig.* measured, exact, precise; formal, over-nice; II. A-heit, (*w.*) *f.* exactness, preciseness, precision, precise measure, regularity, formality.

Ab'geneigt, *adj.* (*from* Abneigen) 1) (*l. u.*) inclined, tending downwards, sloping; 2) *Math. & Bot.* divergent; 3) *fig.* *a)* (*with Dat., sometimes with* von, *rarely with* vor) disinclined (from), indisposed, averse (to), unwilling, reluctant, loath; nicht — (*as if were* sich nicht scheuend) vor ungerechtem Gewinn (*Schiller, unusual*), not averse to unrighteous lucre; *b)* (*with Dat.*) alienated (from a person), indisposed (towards), disaffectionate, unfavourable, unfriendly (to); — machen, to disincline, indispose, to render averse, to alienate (Einen einer Sache [*Dat.*], one from …); der Stolz und die Selbstsucht der Menschen macht sie religiösen Pflichten —, the pride and selfishness of men indisposes them to religious duties.

Ab'geneigtheit, (*w.*) *f.* 1) aversion, unwillingness; disinclination, indisposedness, indisposition; 2) disaffectedness, alienation (from); die — der Menschen, sich strenger Zucht zu unterwerfen, the indisposition of men to submit to severe discipline.

Ab'genicken, (*w.*) *v. tr. Hunt.* to stab (a stag, &c.) in the nape of the neck, to give the finishing stroke to ….

Ab'genutzt, *p. a.* 1) worn out, stale, decayed; threadbare; 2) *fig.* used up, worn out, trite, hackneyed (Abgedroschen).

Ab'genutztheit, (*w.*) *f.* 1) state of being much worn, *or* worn out, attriteness, threadbareness, staleness; 2) *fig.* triteness.

Ab'geordnete, (*decl. like adj.*) *m.* deputy, legate, delegate, commissary: das preußische A-nhaus, *n.* the Prussian chamber of deputies.

Ab'geordnetenschaft, (*w.*) *f. mod.* deputation, delegation (*syn.* Deputation).

Ab'gerben, (*w.*) *v. tr.* 1) *Tann.* *a)* to take off by tanning; *b)* to tan sufficiently; 2) *fig. vulg.* to cudgel, drub, curry soundly.

Ab'gerechnet, *pp.* (*from* Abrechnen) exclusive (of), without regard to …, setting aside, save, except, *cf.* Abgesehen von …; alles übrige —, deducting *or* setting aside all the rest.

Ab'geredet, *coll.* Ab'geredt (*Rückert, &c.*), *pp. cf.* Abreden, *which see.*

Ab'gerieben, *p. a.* (*from* Abreiben) practised, artful, cunning, *see* Gerieben *&c.*

Ab'gerippt, *p. a. T.* of a certain (fine or bad) construction of ribs; ein gut a-tes Pferd, Blatt *&c.*, a nicely ribbed horse, leaf, &c.

Ab'gerissen, I. *p. a.* 1) torn off, &c. *see* Abreißen; 2) *Herald.* erased; 3) demolished, out of repair; 4) clothed in rags, ragged, &c; 5) abrupt; II. A-heit, (*w.*) *f.* 1) raggedness, &c.; 2) abruptness.

Ab'gesandte, *m. & f.* (*decl. like adj.*) messenger; deputy, delegate; ambassador, *see* Gesandte; der geistliche —, missionary.

Ab'gesang, (*str., pl.* Ab'gesänge) *m.* 1) *among the Master-Singers*, the stanza or verse which follows the strophe and antistrophe (the Stollen), concluding verse; 2) a short, comprehensive prayer chanted together with other parts of the service, collect (Collecte, 2.).

Ab'geschabt, *p. a.* threadbare, shabby.

Ab'geschieden, *p. a.* (*from* Abscheiden) 1) *a)* separate; *b)* retired (von, from), deceased; secluded, secret; 2) expired, departed, dead; ein A-er, a departed one; die A-en, the deceased, the dead; das Gespenst einer lieben A-en (*Wieland*), the ghost of a dear departed friend.

Ab'geschiedenheit, (*w.*) *f.* retirement, seclusion.

Ab'geschlagen, *p. p. & a.* 1) struck or beaten off, &c. *cf.* Abschlagen; 2) knocked up, worn out, fatigued (Zerschlagen); 3) *fig.* practised, cunning, crafty.

Ab'geschlagenheit, (*w.*) *f.* worn out state of the body, utter fatigue of the limbs.

Ab'geschliffen, *p. a.* (*from* Abschleifen) 1) *Vet.* ground off, &c. *cf.* Abschleifen, 2.; having lost the bean *or* mark (of horses which generally lose the black stain on their teeth in the eighth year of their age): 2) *fig.* polished, refined, polite.

Ab'geschliffenheit, (*w.*) *f. fig.* polish, refinement, politeness, elegance of manners.

Ab'geschlossen, *p. a.* 1) shut up, &c. *see* Abschließen; *fig-s.* 2) secluded, unknown: 3) exclusive. [3) exclusiveness.

Ab'geschlossenheit, (*w.*) *f.* 1) seclusion, &c.:

Ab'geschmack, I. *s.* (*str.*) *m.* (*l. u.*) *lit. & fig.* insipid taste, insipidity, *cf.* Abgeschmacktheit; II. *adj.* † insipid, tasteless.

Ab'geschmackt, *adj.* 1) *lit. & fig.* insipid, tasteless: 2) *fig.* *a)* flat, dull, mawkish, absurd; *b)* awkward; preposterous, impertinent.

Ab'geschmacktheit, (*w.*) *f.* 1) *a)* *lit. & fig.* insipidity, tastelessness: 2) *fig.* absurdity, dulness; 3) impertinence.

Ab'geschnitten, *p. a.* (*from* Abschneiden) 1) cut off, cut, &c.: 2) *Herald.* couped, *see* Abgehauen; 3) *fig.* *a)* clearly defined, precise; *b)* detached, disjointed, desultory (mode of writing, &c.).

Ab'geschnittenheit, (*w.*) *f.* state of utter separation *or* seclusion, isolation.

Ab'geschwemmt, *p. a. fig.* (*Auerbach, unusual*) blasé (Blasirt).

Ab'geschwitzt, *p. a. T.* (of leather) depilated by a salt-corrosive.

Ab'gesehen, *p. p. of* Absehen, *which see.*

Ab'gesetzt, *p. a. see in* Absetzen.

Ab'gesinnt, *p. a.* (*l. u.*) (*Schiller: with the Dat.*) indisposed (towards), unfavourable (to), *see* Abgeneigt.

Ab'gesondert, *p. a.* 1) separated, &c. *see* Absondern; 2) *Med. &c.* secretitious; die a-e Feuchtigkeit, der a-e Stoff, secretion; 3) *Bot.* segregate, parted, disunited; 4) sequestered; die a-en Berge in der Nachbarschaft, the sequestered hills in the neighbourhood: eine a-e Lage, a sequestered situation (*cf.* Abgeschieden); 5) *fig.* separate, *adv.* apart, distinctly, separately; wir werden in Übereinstimmung, aber — handeln, we shall act in concert, but apart: der a-e Zustand, *m.* separateness.

Ab'gesondertheit, (*w.*) *f.* separation, isolation, seclusion, &c.; a separate state or thing, &c.

Ab'gespannt, *p. a.* (*cf.* Abspannen) *Med. & fig.* atonic, wanting tone *or* tension; unnerved, debilitated, weakened, tired: low-spirited.

Ab'gespanntheit, (*w.*) *f. Med. & fig.* relaxation, atony, state of exhaustion, languor, apathy, lowness of spirits, &c. (Abspannung).

† Ab'gestalt, I. *adj.* shapeless, deformed: II. *s.* (*w.*) *f.* shapelessness, deformity.

Ab'gestanden, *p. a.* (*cf.* Abstehen) *lit. & fig.* decayed, stale, vapid; dead (said of wood, wine, beer, &c.).

Ab'gestorben, *p. a.* (*cf.* Absterben) 1) dead (of wood, of a limb [= mortified], of colour, &c.); 2) *fig.* dead, lost (für, gegen [*with Acc.*], to a thing).

Ab'gestorbenheit, (*w.*) *f.* deadness, want of vital powers (of a limb, &c.); die — (das Abgestorbensein) für diese (für die Vergnügungen dieser) Welt, deadness to (the pleasures of) this world; *cf.* Abgestumpftheit.

Ab'gestumpft (*cf.* Abstumpfen), *p. a.* 1) blunted, blunt; die a-en Ecken eines Stückchens Papier, the blunt corners of a piece of paper; 2) *a)* stubbed; *b)* *Bot. & Geom.* truncated; der a-e Kegel, die a-e Pyramide, truncated cone, truncated pyramid, *see* Abgekürzt; 3) *fig.* obtuse, dull.

Ab'gestumpftheit, (*w.*) *f.* 1) bluntness, obtuseness (of an edge, &c.); 2) obtuseness (of the senses, &c.), dulness, deadness.

Ab'gestupft, *p. a.* (*cf.* Abstupfen) stabbed, tormented, *see* Abgestumpft, 2.

Ab'gethân, *p. a. see* Abthun.

Ab'getragen, *p. a.* 1) carried off, *&c. see* Abtragen; 2) *a)* (of clothes, &c.) worn out, worn, threadbare, shabby; *b) fig.* worn-out; *aa)* cast off (like an old garment, &c.), discarded, superannuated; *bb)* threadbare, hackneyed, trite; der a–e Gedanke (*Jean Paul*), the worn-out, hackneyed idea; *cc)* tired out, knocked up, fatigued.

Ab'getragenheit, (*w.*) *f.* state of being worn, threadbareness, shabbiness.

Ab'getrieben, *p. a.* (*cf.* Abtreiben) overdriven, overworn, outworn (as a horse, &c.).

Ab'gewähren, (*w.*) *v. tr. Min.* Einem seinen Kux —, to discharge (in the counter-book) and to transfer the amount of a share to another.

Ab'gewältigen, (*w.*) *v. intr. Min.* to remove (refuse, &c.).

Ab'gewettert, *p. a.* (*from* Abwettern) weather-worn, *see* Abgewittert.

Ab'gewichen, *p. a.* passed, &c. *see* Abweichen.

Ab'gewinnen, (*str.*) *v. tr. formerly used with the simple Dat.:* Einem —, to be superior to one, to excel; *now an Accusative, or an Infinitive used as an object, is always added:* Einem etwas —, to win, gain *or* obtain (something from one); to bear away, to carry off (a prize) from one, to gain (ground) on ...; Einem den Vortheil —, to gain the advantage over one; Einem den Vorzug —, to get the better of one; einer Sache Geschmack —, to get a taste for a thing; einem Schiffe den Wind —, *Mar.* to gain (*or* get) the wind (the weather-gage) of a ship; er konnte dem schalsten Gegenstande eine komische Seite —, he knew to extract mirth from the dullest subject; Stunden, welche der Verfolgung weltlicher Interessen abgewonnen waren, hours snatched from the pursuit of worldly interests; sich (*Dat.*) mit Mühe —, etwas zu thun &c., to prevail upon one's self with difficulty to do a thing, &c.

Ab'gewittert, *p. a.* (*from* Abwittern) weather-beaten (*syn.* Verwettert).

Ab'gewogen, *p. a.* (*from* Abwägen) exactly weighed *or* balanced, &c.

Ab'gewöhnen, (*w.*) *v. tr.* 1) to wean (a child, &c.), *see* Entwöhnen; 2) (Einem etwas; *rarely:* Einen von etwas) to disaccustom, disuse, to wean (from), to break of (an ill habit, &c.); einem Kinde seine Unarten —, to break a child of its tricks; sich (*Dat.*) etwas —, *refl.* to divest one's self (of), to unlearn, to forego the habit of ....

Ab'gezehrt, *p. a.* wasted (by disease), emaciated, worn out, tabid.

Ab'gezirkelt, *see* Abgezirkelt.

Ab'gezogen, *p. a.* (*from* Abziehen, *q.v.*) *lit.* drawn off: 1) retired, remote; 2) (*Leibnitz, Fichte, Wieland, &c.*) *Log.* abstract (Abstract).

Ab'gezogenheit, (*w.*) *f.* 1) retirement, seclusion (*syn.* Zurückgezogenheit, Abgeschiedenheit); 2) abstractedness (Abstraction).

Ab'gieren, (*w.*) *v.* I. *intr. Mar.* to sheer or steer off (away), to get sea-room; II. *tr.* (Einem etwas) to obtain (something from one) by importunate desire.

Ab'gießen, (*str.*) *v. tr.* 1) to pour off, clear off; to decant; 2) *Found.* to take a cast of ..., to cast.

Ab'gießer, (*str.*) *m.* 1) moulder, former; 2) ewer.

Ab'gießung, (*w.*) *f.* 1) the act of pouring off, clearing off, decanting; 2) the act of casting; cast.

Ab'gift, (*w.*) *f.* (*from* Abgeben) *obsolescent*, Loan, tribute, tax, duty (*cf.* Abgabe).

Ab'gilben, (*w.*) *v. tr.* to tinge with a yellow colour (*cf.* Abgelben).

Ab'gipfeln, (*w.*) *v. tr.* to top (a tree, &c.).

Ab'girren, (*w.*) *v. tr.* (Einem etwas) to coax (something) out (of one).

Ab'gitschen, (*w.*) *v. intr. see* Abglitschen.

Ab'gittern, (*w.*) *v. tr.* to separate by a railing *or* lattice.

Ab'glanz, (*str.*) *m.* 1) resplendence, reflected splendor *or* brightness, reflection; 2) *fig.* image.

Ab'glänzen, (*w.*) *v.* I. *intr.* (*aux.* sein) to be reflected with splendor *or* brightness; II. *tr.* to reflect brightly *or* with splendor.

Ab'glätten, (*w.*) *v. tr.* 1) to polish off, to make smooth, to levigate; 2) *fig.* to smooth, round *or* finish off, to give the last finish, to polish (duly).

Ab'glättung, (*w.*) *f.* the act of smoothing *or* polishing off, finish.

† Ab'gläubig, *adj.* (*Luther*) incredulous, unbelieving; infidel (*at present* Ungläubig *is more usual*).

Ab'gleichen, (*str., according to Heyse &c. w., cf.* Gleichen) *v. tr.* 1) to equal, equalize; 2) to level, to make even; 3) *Mech. &c.* to justify, to adjust; 4) to settle (accounts), to audit, *cf.* Ausgleichen.

Ab'gleich ..., *in comp. Mech.* —feile, *f.* equalling-file; —stange, *f.* adjusting-tool.

Ab'gleichung, (*w.*) *f.* 1) the act of equalling, &c.; *cf.* Abgleichen; equalization; 2) *Mech.* the act of justifying, adjusting, adjustment; A–swage, *f.* adjusting-scale.

Ab'gleiten, (*str.*) *v. intr.* (*aux.* sein) to slip, slide *or* glide down or off, to glance off.

Ab'gliedern, (*w.*) *v. tr.* 1) to dismember; 2) to unlink.

Ab'glimmen, (*str. & w.*) *v. intr.* (*aux.* sein) to cease glowing *or* glimmering, to die away gradually (of sparks, &c.).

Ab'glitschen, (*w.*) *v. intr.* to slip, slide *or* glide down suddenly, to slip, slide, glide *or* glance off.

Ab'glühen, (*w.*) *v.* I. *intr.* (*sometimes refl.* sich —) to cease glowing, to lose heat gradually; II. *tr.* 1) to heat thoroughly, to anneal, *cf.* Ausglühen; Wein —, to mull wine; 2) to purge by fire.

Ab'glühung, (*w.*) *f.* 1) a ceasing to glow, gradual diminution of heat; 2) the act of heating thoroughly, annealing, &c.

Ab'gott, (*str., pl.* Ab'götter) *m. lit. & fig.* idol; einen — aus Einem machen, to make an idol of one, to idolise one.

Ab'gottdienst, &c. *m. see* Abgötterei.

Ab'götter, (*str.*) *m.* (*Luther, Claudius, Klinger, &c., l. u.*) *see* Abgötterer.

Ab'götterei', (*w.*) *f.* idolatry, idol-worship; — treiben, to worship idols, to idolatrise.

Ab'götterer, (*str.*) *m. obsolescent*, idolater (Abgottanbeter); Ab'götterin, (*w.*) *f.* idolatress.

Ab'götterisch, *adj. obsolescent*, idolatrous.

Ab'göttern, (*w.*) *v. intr.* (*l. u.*) to idolatrise.

Ab'göttin, (*w.*) *f.* (a female) idol.

Ab'göttisch, *adj.* idolatrous: — (*adv.*) verehren, to worship as an idol *or* idolatrously, to idolise.

Ab'gott(s)schlange, (*w.*) *f. Zool.* the boa serpent, anaconda.

Ab'graben, (*str.*) *v. tr.* 1) to dig off (a hill, &c.), to remove by digging; 2) to separate by digging, to cut off by a ditch; to furnish with a trench; 3) to lead off by a ditch; 4) to turn off the course of (a stream, &c.), to drain; 5) to pay (a debt) by digging for it.

Ab'gräben, (*w.*) *v. tr.* to mark with (*or* divide into) degrees, to graduate.

Ab'grämen, *coll.* Ab'grämeln, (*w.*) *v. refl.* to pine away with grief; to wear, waste away with grief, to grieve exceedingly.

Ab'grapfen, Ab'grapschen, (*w.*) *v. tr. coll.* to grasp, to snatch away, to sweep off.

Ab'grasen, (*w.*) *v. tr.* 1) to cut the grass of (a meadow, &c.), to mow; 2) to graze, to eat from the ground, as grazing [illegible] Abweiden).

Ab'greifen, (*str.*) *v. tr.* to [illegible] stant handling *or* touching; [illegible] cher, (well-)thumbed volumes.

Ab'grenzen, (*w.*) *v.* I. *tr.* [illegible] parate or divide by a boundary [illegible] the limits of ...; to define; [illegible] durch hohe Gebirge abgegrenzt [illegible] line of Switzerland is formed [illegible] tains; *fig.* (*cf.* Abschneiden) [illegible] Himmel scharf abgegrenzten [illegible] sharply outlined against the blue [illegible] —, *refl.* to be separated *or* divided [illegible] dary-line.

Ab'grenzung, (*w.*) *f.* demarcation [illegible] (the act of separating by a boundary [illegible] fixed limits, and the boundary-line [illegible]

Ab'grund, (*str., pl.* Ab'gründe) [illegible] precipice, gulf, (bottomless) pit [illegible] abyss (used of a deep mass of water [illegible] depth; 3) abyss, interminable space [illegible] &c.), immense expanse, boundless [illegible] measurable depth; 4) *a)* [illegible] hell, Erebus: die Furien des [illegible] the furies of hell; mag er [illegible] (*Wieland*), may he burn in the infernal [illegible] *b) fig.* an abyss or gulf in which [illegible] lost, gulf (of crimes, &c.); der [illegible] Sünde, the fearful pit of sin; [illegible] du vom — ihn gerettet (*Schiller*), [illegible] cause thou hast saved him from the [illegible] perdition; 5) *fig.* infinity; der — [illegible] (*Heine*), the abyss of time [illegible] ist ein — ewiger Liebe (*Luther*) [illegible] finite source of eternal love.

Ab'gründen, (*w.*) *v. tr.* [illegible] the grooving-plane, to groove.

† Ab'gründig, Ab'gründlich, [illegible] ly deep, profound, unfathomable.

Ab'grundwärts, *adv.* downward [illegible] abyss (*Lenau*).

Ab'grünen, *v. intr.* 1) [illegible] &c.) to lose the green colour [illegible] 2) to cease to be verdant (as the [illegible]

Ab'gucken, (*w.*) *v.* I. *tr.* (Einem [illegible] to learn (a thing from one — [illegible] stealth) by minute observation, [illegible] knack, &c. *cf.* Absehen; wie er [illegible] wie er spuckt, das habt ihr ihm [illegible] guckt, aber sein Genie ... (*Schiller, Wallenstein's* Lager, 6), you have exactly caught [illegible] of clearing his throat and spitting [illegible] his genius ...; II. *refl.* sich (*Dat.*) [illegible] —, to fatigue one's eyes by looking [illegible]

Ab'gunst, *f.* disfavour, discountenance [illegible] propitious regard, dislike.

Ab'günstig, *adj.* unfavourable [illegible] averse (*with Dat.*, to ...); er [illegible] — zu werden (*Lessing*), he begins [illegible] great disfavour to me.

Ab'gurgeln, (*w.*) *v. tr.* 1) [illegible] throat; 2) *coll.* to remove by [illegible] to sing with a full throat *or* in a [illegible] low way; ein Lied —, *coll.* to [illegible]

Ab'gürten, (*w.*) *v. tr.* to ungird [illegible]

Ab'gürtung, (*w.*) *f.* the act of [illegible]

Ab'guß, (*str., pl.* Ab'güsse) *m.* [illegible] gießen) 1) the act of pouring off [illegible] gießen; 2) *Found. &c.* [illegible] pression of any figure taken in [illegible] ter, wax, or other fusible [illegible] (in bronze, &c.), copy; 3) [illegible] tobacco-pipe, called also [illegible] chamber for the preservation of [illegible]

Ab'güten, (*w.*) *v. tr.* to [illegible] &c.) by making a settlement [illegible] finden, 1.).

Ab'haaren, (*w.*) *v.* I. *intr.* [illegible] *tr.* (*cf.* Abhären) *Tann.* to unhair [illegible]

Ab'haben, (*irr.*) *v. tr.* 1) [illegible] &c.) off; 2) to partake of, to [illegible] er will etwas —, he comes in for a share; 3) to receive a punishment for, coll. to get it; 4) Einem etwas —, † for Einem etwas aufhaben.

Ab'hacken, (w.) v. tr. to chop or cut down or off; Einem den Kopf —, to cleave or cut off one's head, to behead one.

Ab'hadern, (w.) v. tr. (l. u.) (Einem etwas) to extort (something from one) by quarrelling or by litigation.

Ab'hageln, (w.) v. (impers.) I. tr. to beat down (the blossoms, &c., said of hail or hailstones); II. intr. to cease hailing: es hat sich abgehagelt, it has done hailing.

Ab'hagen, (w.) v. tr. to separate by enclosure, to enclose, to fence in.

Ab'hagern, (w.) v. intr. (aux. sein) to grow lean or thin, to fall away, to emaciate (syn. Abmagern).

Ab'hagung, (w.) f. 1) the act of separating by enclosure: 2) enclosure, fence.

Ab'häkeln, (w.) v. tr. 1) to unloose what is fixed by little hooks, to unclasp, unhook (different from Abhaken); 2) to imitate or copy (a pattern) in crochet-work.

Ab'haken, (w.) v. tr. 1) a) to draw down with a hook; b) to disengage from a hook, to unhook; 2) to separate or take off by ploughing with the horse-hoe (Haken), to plough off; 3) (also intr.) to finish ploughing; 4) (also intr.) to loose from the plough or horse-hoe, to unyoke (oxen), to unharness (horses), to put out (cf. Ausspannen).

Ab'halftern, (w.) v. tr. to undo the halter of (a horse), to unhalter.

Ab'hallen, (w.) v. intr. (l. u.) to resound, re-echo, reverberate (syn. Wiederhallen).

Ab'halsen, (w.) v. tr. (from Hals) 1) coll. to decollate, to cut (one's) throat; 2) einander (coll. sich) —, vulgr. to embrace (or hug) one another; 3) Sport. to uncouple (dogs).

Ab'halt, (str.) m. detention, hinderance, impediment (cf. Abhaltung).

Ab'halten, (str.) v. I. tr. 1) to hold off, to keep off (away or back); den Regen, die Sonne &c. —, to keep off the rain, the sun, &c.; 2) Mar. to fend off (a boat or vessel, to prevent its running against another, &c.): das Schiff vom Lande —, to keep off, to lay ahold; 3) to ward (fend or bear) off (a blow, &c.); fig.-a. 4) a) to keep back, to detain, hinder, prevent, restrain, withhold: (Einen) vom Bösen —, to keep (one) from doing mischief; das soll mich nicht —, that shall not deter me: b) to disturb, interrupt, cf. Stören; 5) a) to (be able to) endure, to bear (fatigue, &c.), to stand, sustain, to bear up under ... or against ... (syn. Aushalten, Ertragen); b) to endure, to resist without yielding; den ersten Angriff —, to stand the first brunt, see Aushalten; 6) to keep (to the end), to go through with ...; to perform, observe, celebrate (a festival, &c.); eine Predigt, Rede &c. —, to deliver a sermon, a speech; die Schule —, to keep school regularly; er hielt seine Stunden ab, he attended to his lessons, he gave his lessons regularly; der Markt wird diesmal nicht abgehalten werden, the fair will not take place this time; II. refl. sich —: 1) to keep back (von, from); to keep aloof (sich entfernt halten); 2) to refrain, forbear, &c. see sich Enthalten; III. intr. Mar.-a. 1) (vom Lande —) to keep off; 2) (vom Winde —) to sheer; von einer Bank —, to keep aloof from a rock, to take a good birth; auf ein Schiff —, to bear up to a ship, to bear down on a ship; halt ab! bear away, bear up! [illegible] don't fall off!

Ab'halter, (str.) m. 1) he that keeps or holds off, [illegible] see Abhalten; 2) Mar. guy.

Ab'haltung, (w.) f. 1) the act of holding [illegible]; 2) hinderance, detention, [illegible]; [illegible] —, I was otherwise engaged, I had an engagement; er hat sehr viele A-en, he has many things to detain him from his labour; — haben, to be prevented; 3) celebration, &c.

Ab'hämmern, (w.) v. tr. to strike off with a hammer.

Ab'handeln, (w.) v. tr. 1) (Einem etwas) to get (something from one) by bargaining, to cheapen, to beat down from the price; er läßt sich nichts —, there is no abating his price; 2) to settle, to accommodate, cf. Unterhandeln; einen Frieden &c. —, to negociate a peace; 3) to treat of, discuss; to debate on ...; wenn Liebe abgehandelt wird (Schiller), when the subject in question is love; der a-de Theil eines Werkes, the theoretic part of a work.

Abhan'den, adv. not at hand, away; mislaid; lost; — sein, not to be at hand; — kommen, to be lost; es ist ein Löffel — gekommen, there is a spoon missing; es ist ihm alles Gefühl für Ehre und Schicklichkeit — gekommen, he is lost to every sense of honour and of propriety.

† **Ab'händig,** adj. (from the preceding word) missing, lost; — machen, to cause the loss of ..., to remove, lose; to purloin.

† **Ab'händigen,** (w.) v. tr. 1) to take off one's hands (opp. Behändigen, Einhändigen); 2) to remove, to drive (from).

Ab'handler, (str.) m. discusser of a matter.

Ab'handlung, (w.) f. 1) negociation, transaction; 2) a) discourse, discussion; b) essay, memoir, treatise, dissertation, paper (über eine Sache, on a thing): die folgenden A-en wurden vorgelesen, the following papers were read.

Ab'hang, (str., pl. Ab'hänge) m. 1) the act or state of hanging down; 2) the branches of trees borne down by the weight of snow; 3) slope, slopeness, descent, declivity; ein jäher —, a cliff, steep precipice; der — eines Hügels, side, brow or slope of a hill; b) fall of a river, see Fall (Abfall); 4) fig. dependency (von, on), see Abhängigkeit.

Ab'hangen, (str.) v. intr. 1) to hang down, see Herabhangen, which is more usual in this sense; 2) to hang at a distance (von, from), to hang off; 3) to decline, slope; 4) fig. von Einem or einer Sache —, to depend on (or upon) a person or thing, to be dependent on (upon) ...: sie wartete auf seine Worte, als ob die Entscheidung über ihr Leben oder ihren Tod davon abhinge, she waited for his words, as if her sentence of life or of death turned upon them.

Ab'hängen, (w.) v. I. tr. to take off, to take down, to hang off, to unhang; II. intr. less properly, but more usual than Abhangen, qv.

Ab'hängig, adj. 1) a) hanging down, bending downwards: die Natur macht den Menschen — zur Erde (Göthe), nature forms man prone to the earth; b) inclining, sloping, hanging, shelving, steep: die a-e Fläche, Math. inclined plane (die schiefe Ebene); — sein, to shelve, to take an oblique direction, to slope; — machen, to form obliquely, to incline, to slope; 2) fig. depending, dependent (von, on, upon): — sein, to be dependent, to depend (von, on, upon), see Abhangen, 4.; er machte sein Urtheil von dem seines Bruders —, he subjected his judgment to that of his brother; sie war geneigt, sich von dem Urtheil der Vornehmen — zu machen, she was apt to defer to the opinion of the great.

Ab'hängigkeit, (w.) f. 1) inclination downwards, declivity (cf. Abhang); 2) fig. dependence, dependency (von, on, upon), subjection, subservience, subserviency (to): A-sverhältniß, n. state or condition of dependence.

Ab'hänglich, adj. (Wieland) rarely used for Abhängig.

Ab'hänglichkeit, (w.) f. (Wieland, Klinger, &c.) rarely used for Abhängigkeit.

Ab'hängling, (str.) m. (Göthe — l. u.) usual. a dependant, an underling.

Ab'hären, (w.) v. I. tr. to deprive of hair, to take away the hair of (hides, &c.), unhair, depilate; II. intr. to lose hair (Abhaaren).

Ab'harken, (w.) v. tr. 1) to rake off, to remove with a rake; 2) to rake thoroughly, to make even with raking.

Ab'härmen, (w.) v. refl. sich —, to fret, to pine (away), to languish, to grieve; ein abgehärmtes Gesicht, a care-worn face.

Ab'härten, (w.) v. I. tr. 1) a) lit. & fig. to harden; to indurate; b) T. to harden, to temper (iron, steel), see Härten; 2) fig. a) to steel or harden thoroughly (gener. refl.); b) to render obdurate or callous; abgehärtet, p. a. hardened (gegen, to, against), callous (Verhärtet); II. refl. to steel or harden one's self thoroughly (gegen, to, against), to inure one's self (to hard labour or fatigues), to make one's self hardy.

Ab'härtung, (w.) f. induration: 1) the act of hardening, &c. cf. Abhärten; 2) the state of being hardened, hardness.

Ab'harzen, (w.) v. tr. to take away the resin from (trees).

Ab'haschen, (w.) v. I. tr. (Einem etwas) to snatch (something from one); II. refl. to tire one's self by chasing or catching (as at the play of hide and seek).

Ab'haspeln, (w.) v. tr. 1) († Ab'haspen) to reel off, wind off from a reel; 2) coll. a) to reel off (superfluous verbiage, &c.); b) to wind off as from a reel, to repeat in a monotonous, unvarying manner; unbedeutende Tage — (Göthe), to draw out insignificant days in dull, unvaried sameness.

Ab'hauben, (w.) v. tr. Falc. to unhood (a hawk).

Ab'hauchen, (w.) v. tr. (l. u.) 1) to blow away by the breath; 2) to elicit by soft breathing: der Aeolsharfe (Dat.) abgehauchte Töne (Jean Paul), sounds drawn forth from the Æolian harp by the soft breath of zephyr.

Ab'hauen, (irr.) v. tr. 1) to hew down, to cut off, away or down, to chop off, strike off, fell: Gras, Getreide —, to mow; Einem den Kopf —, to strike off one's head, to behead one; ein abgehauener Baum, log, stock, trunk: den Knoten abhauen (used repeatedly by Kant, instead of the more usual Zerhauen), to cut the knot asunder: 2) vulg. to beat soundly.

Ab'häufeln, (w.) v. tr. to divide into small heaps.

Ab'häufen, (w.) v. tr. 1) to separate into heaps: 2) to diminish (a heap).

Ab'häuteln, (w.) v. tr. to strip of a thin skin or cuticle.

Ab'häuten, (w.) v. I. tr. to skin, uncase; to excoriate, to strip of the cuticle; II. intr. Zool. & Anatom. to cast (off) the skin (as snakes, silkworms, &c.).

Ab'häutung, (w.) f. the act of skinning, uncasing; excoriation; desquamation.

Ab'hebeiße, Ab'hebeißse, (w.) f. Min. rake, see Abhubeiße.

Ab'heben, (str.) v. I. tr. 1) to lift off, take off (a cover, &c.): eine Kanone von der Laffette —, Gunn. to dismount a cannon; 2) a) Min. to take off (the top layer); b) Gam. (sometimes intr.) to cut (to divide a pack of cards): um das (Karten-)Geben —, to cut for the deal; 3) fig. to detach, to contrast, to bring into contrast (shades of colours, &c.), cf. II. refl.; 4) to abstract, separate (ideas) by the operation of the mind, see Abziehen; 5) to unwind cat's (scratch-) cradles (a children's play); II. refl. to detach itself, to be contrasted, relieved, to stand or come out (cf. sich Abheben, sich Abziehen, Abstechen) die Schneemassen über uns heben sich deutlicher vom blauen Himmel ab, the snowy masses above us detached themselves more distinctly from the blue sky; eine Klippe, welche sich von dem lichten Himmel dahinter scharf abhebt, a cliff which stands out in strong relief from the clear sky behind.

Ab'hebung, *(w.) f.* 1) the act of lifting off, &c. *cf.* Abheben, *v.*; 2) *Gam.* cut, cutting (the act of dividing a pack of cards).

Ab'hecheln, *(w.) v. tr. & intr. Husb.* to finish hatchelling.

Ab'hefteln, *(w.) v. tr.* to unclasp, to unhook, to loosen (the hooks) from the eyes.

Ab'heften, *(w.) v. tr.* to unpin, to unstitch; to untack, *gener.* to unfasten.

Ab'heilen, *(w.) v.* I. *tr.* to effect a thorough cure, to heal, to cure; II. *intr.* (*aux.* sein) to heal thoroughly, to be healing *or* healed.

Ab'heilung, *(w.) f.* 1) the act of producing a thorough cure, healing, curing; 2) the state of healing *or* being healed.

Ab'heischen, *(w.) v. tr.* (Einem etwas) to demand (something from one), *see* Abfordern.

Ab'helfen, *(str.) v. intr.* 1) (*with Dat.*) to help down (von, from), *see* Herabhelfen; 2) (einer Sache [*Dat.*] —) to remedy (a disease, evils, &c.), to redress (wrongs, injuries, grievances, &c.), to relieve, supply (wants); dem Ding ist leicht abgeholfen, the thing is easily remedied; dem ist nicht abzuhelfen, it cannot be remedied, it cannot be helped; dem Übel war nicht abzuhelfen, the evil was beyond the reach of remedy; Schwierigkeiten —, to remove difficulties; ich habe den Fehlern abgeholfen, I have removed (corrected, amended) the faults; mit der heftigsten Begierde allen Drangsalen seiner Mitgeschöpfe abzuhelfen (*Wieland*), with the most ardent desire to relieve his fellow-creatures of all their hardships; die Hülfsquellen des Reiches sind gänzlich unzureichend diesem Unglücke abzuhelfen, the resources of the empire are utterly inadequate to meet this calamity.

Ab'helflich, I. *adj.* 1) remedial, affording remedy, relieving; einer Sache (*Dat.*) a-e Maße geben, *Law*, to redress a grievance, &c., to remedy, &c. *cf.* (einer Sache) Abhelfen; 2) remediable, relievable, capable of remedy, curable; II. **A-keit**, *(w.) f.* remediableness, &c.

Ab'helfung, *(w.) f.* the act of remedying, redressing, &c. *cf.* Abhelfen; redress; removal (of unfairness, &c.).

Ab'hellen, *(w.) v.* I. *tr.* to clear off, to clarify (*syn.* Abklären); II. *refl.* to clear off, to become clear, to clear up, to brighten (*syn.* sich Aufhellen, Aufklären).

Ab'henken, *(w.) v. tr.* to hang *or* take off, to unhang (*cf.* Abhängen).

† **Abher'**, *adv.* down, downward (Herab).

Ab'herbsten, *(w.) v. tr.* (*l. u.*) to clear off (a crop, &c.) by reaping, to bring *or* get in (the harvest), *see* Abernten (*cf.* Einherbsten).

Ab'herzen, *(w.) v. tr. coll.* to kiss (one) heartily, to kiss to excess; (Jemand) tüchtig —, *coll.* to hug to one's heart's content.

Ab'herzung, *(w.) f. coll.* the act of kissing heartily, hugging, embracing, &c.

Ab'hetzen, *(w.) v.* I. *tr.* 1) (Einen) *a)* to tire *or* fatigue (one) by hunting, to wear out by chasing; einen Hirsch —, *Sport.* to run down a stag; *b)* to weary to death, to jade, to fag out; 2) (Einem etwas) to obtain (something from one) by hunting, pursuing (him); II. *refl.* to fatigue, *or* weary one's self extremely by pursuing an object, to tire one's self out by chasing for a thing.

Ab'heucheln, *(w.) v. tr.* (Einem etwas) to obtain (something from one) by hypocrisy.

Ab'heuern, *(w.) v. tr.* (Einem etwas) to hire (something from one), *see* Abmiethen.

Ab'heulen, *(w.) v. only.* I. *tr.* to howl; (*of persons*) to utter in a howling tone; II. *refl.* to weary one's self with howling.

Ab'hexen, *(w.) v. tr.* (Einem etwas) to obtain (something from one) by witchcraft, to deprive (one of a thing) by juggling.

Abhier', *adv.* (*orig.* ab hier, *cf.* Ab, I.) *Comm.* from this place.

Ab'hilfe, *(w.) f. see* Abhülfe (*cf.* Hilfe).

† **Abhin'**, *adv.* (*transposition for* Hinab, *which see*; *cf.* Abher) down, downward.

Ab'hinken, *(w.) v. intr.* (*aux.* sein) *l. u.* 1) to limp off *or* away; 2) *coll.* to slink off with disgrace. [dannen).

Abhin'nen, *adv.* † (from) hence (*syn.* von

Ab'hobeln, *(w.) v. tr.* 1) *Join.* to plane off; to shoot, to plane, smooth; 2) *Skin-dr.* to rub (hides); 3) *fam. fig.* to polish (off), *see* Abschleifen.

Ab'hocken, **Ab'hucken**, *(w.) v. tr.* to put down (a load) from the back *or* shoulders.

Ab'hold, *adj.* (*see* Abgeneigt, Abgünstig) disinclined, unfavourable, unfriendly, averse (*with Dat.*, to ...); Einem — sein, to bear one ill-will; nicht —, not disinclined (towards).

Ab'holen, *(w.) v. tr.* 1) *Mar.* to haul off, to get off; 2) (*among calico-printers*) to remove the starch from (printed calico) by boiling; 3) *a)* (eine Sache) to fetch off, away, to go to fetch (a thing); *b)* (eine Person) to call for (a person); ich will ihn —, I will go for him; ich will Sie bei Ihrem Vater —, I will come for you to your father's; der Wagen wird mich —, the carriage will come for me; — lassen, to send for ....

Ab'holung, *(w.) f.* 1) the act of hauling off, &c. *cf. the preceding word*; 2) the act of fetching off, calling for, &c.; die — der Briefe, the collection of letters (from letter-boxes by inferior post-officers).

Ab'holz, (*str.*, *without pl.*) *n.* 1) *T.* chips of wood; 2) *For.* dead wood, waste wood, windfallen wood (*cf.* Abraum, 1.).

Ab'holzen, *(w.) v. tr.* to cut down, to root out (a forest); to clear.

Ab'holzig, *adj.* 1) *For. &c.* deficient (weak) in timber (of trees); 2) (*among Hatters*) cracked, chinky (of a hatter's block).

Ab'holzung, *(w.) f.* the act of cutting down the forests of (a country), &c., clearing.

Ab'hoffen, *(w.) v. tr. Brew.* to flavour with hops. [Abhörung.

Ab'hör, *f.* the hearing (of witnesses), *see*

Ab'horchen, *(w.) v. tr.* 1) (Einen) to listen *or* hearken to what another has to say, to draw (one) out (*syn.* Ausforschen); 2) (Einem etwas) to learn (something from one) by listening attentively, to overhear (one).

Ab'hören, *(w.) v. tr.* 1) (Einem etwas) to learn (something from one) by hearing *or* listening; 2) (Einen *or* etwas [*Acc.*]) *a)* to hear (one) say his lesson, *see* Überhören; *b)* *partic. Law*, to hear, try, examine, to question (witnesses, &c.); Zeugen gegen einander —, to confront witnesses; du mußt darüber dein Gewissen —, *fig.* you must examine your conscience on that point, you must hear what your conscience says on the matter; *c)* Rechnungen —, *T.* to audit (*i. e.* to examine and settle *or* adjust) accounts; 3) sein Geld —, to attend a prepaid concert *or* course of lectures (*cf. analogous expressions*: eine Schuld absitzen, &c.).

Ab'hörer, (*str.*) *m.* a hearer (of witnesses), one who conducts a trial, examining judge.

Ab'hörung, *(w.) f.* a hearing (of witnesses), trial, examination.

Ab'hub, (*str.*, *without pl.*) *m.* 1) the act of lifting off, &c. *see* Abhebung, 1. & 2.; 2) *a)* that which is lifted *or* taken off, &c.; remains of a meal, offal; *b)* *Metall.* the light particles of washed ore coming up by the sieving-process (Siebsetzen), which are taken off (abgehoben) by the rake, (*G. Hardmann*) skimpings, skippings; —löffel, —kelle, *f. Metall.* rake.

Ab'huden, *(w.) v. tr. coll.* 1) *see* Abhudeln; 2) to carry off.

Ab'hudeln, *(w.) v. tr. coll.* to [illegible] outrageously.

Ab'hulk, *(w.) f.* (*l. u.*) [illegible] (*see* Abgunst, Abgeneigtheit).

Ab'hülfe, *(w.) f.* relief, [illegible] mildern, lindern, schaffen, to give [illegible] afford relief, redress, remedy, [illegible] ration *or* amends; — suchen bei ..., [illegible] for redress to ...; — suchen für ..., [illegible] redress of (grievances, &c.); — [illegible] take redress; Mittel gegen —, remed[illegible]

Ab'hülsen, *(w.) v. tr.* to pull or [illegible] draw or to take off, to strip (of [illegible]

Ab'hülsen, *(w.) v. tr.* to take [illegible] of ..., to husk (Indian corn, &c.), [illegible] peel, decorticate; Mandeln —, to [illegible] monds; sich —, *Cult.* to come off (of [illegible] vegetable integument).

Ab'humpeln, *(w.) v. coll.* I. *intr.* [illegible] to limp off; II. *refl.* to weary one's [illegible] hobbling or limping about.

Ab'hungern, *(w.) v.* I. *intr.* (*aux.* [illegible] be starved, famished; II. [illegible] *tr.* to afflict with hunger, to famish, [illegible] (*see* Aushungern); III. *refl.* to starve [illegible] one's self. [illegible]

Ab'hüpfen, *(w.) v. intr.* (*aux.* [illegible]

Ab'huschen, *(w.) v. intr.* (*aux.* [illegible] off or away, to slip or pop off [illegible] Abwischen &c.).

Ab'husten, *(w.) v.* I. *tr.* to cough away, [illegible] II. *refl.* to exhaust one's self with [illegible]

Ab'hüten, *(w.) v. tr.* to let cattle [illegible] on (a meadow, &c.), to feed on (grass), [illegible] *see* Abweiden.

Ab'hütten, *(w.) v. tr. Min.* to give up [illegible] neglect (a mine).

Ab'hütung, *(w.) f.* the act of letting [illegible] graze on (pasture-grounds).

A'bicht, *adj. Cloth. &c.* turned, [illegible] a-e Seite, the left side; eine A-e, [illegible] with the back of the hand, *coll.* [illegible] (Verwendte). [illegible]

A'bichten, *(w.) v. tr. Cloth.* to [illegible]

Ab'irren, *(w.) v. intr.* (*aux.* sein) [illegible] one's way, to err, stray, deviate, [illegible] wander.

Ab'irrung, *(w.) f.* deviation, [illegible] (*also Astr. & Phys.*) aberration; — [illegible] *Phys.* aberration of the rays of light, [illegible] tion; A-kreis, *m.* crown of aberration [illegible]

* **Abiturient'**, (*Lat.*) *(w.) m.* [illegible] leaves a gymnasium or learned school [illegible] college or university.

Ab'jachtern, *(w.) v. refl. coll.* to weary [illegible] self by romping, running or capering [illegible]

Ab'jagen, *(w.) v.* I. *tr.* 1) to weary [illegible] pursuing; to over-drive, to overwork, [illegible] jade (a horse, &c.) (*see* Abhetzen, 1) [illegible] all the game of (a hunting-district, &c.) [illegible] (Einem etwas) *a)* to get or wrest (some[illegible] from one) by hunting, pursuing; to [illegible] retrieve, recover (something from [illegible] Strafen, die dem Zuschauer Schauder [illegible] (*Kant*), punishments which force [illegible] the cheeks of the bystanders; Eure [illegible] jagte mir einen Schauder ab (*Schiller*), [illegible] your crime struck a sudden horror [illegible] soul; Einem einen Schrecken — (*Lessing*) [illegible] to strike with a sudden fright, [illegible] II. *refl.* to fatigue one's self by [illegible] exertion; III. *intr. Sport.* to leave off [illegible] to discontinue or to finish the chase, [illegible]

Ab'jammern, *(w.) v.* I. *tr.* [illegible] (*l. u.*) to get or obtain (something [illegible] by lamenting; II. *refl.* to exhaust [illegible] with lamenting.

Ab'jochen, *(w.) v. tr.* to unyoke [illegible]

Ab'justiren, *(w.) v. tr.* to adjust [illegible] (weights, measures, &c.), [illegible]

Ab'kahnen, *(w.) v. tr.* to [illegible] guide) from mould or [illegible]

Ab'kalben, (w.) v. intr. to leave off calving.

Ab'kälken, (w.) v. tr. Tann. to scrape off the lime from (hides).

Ab'kälten, (w.) v. tr. 1) to cool down, to cool sufficiently or to a certain degree; to ice wine; 2) fig. to cool, allay, calm, abate (love, &c.), cf. Abkühlen

Ab'kämmen, (w.) v. tr. 1) to comb down or off, to comb (wool) sufficiently; 2) Fort. to shoot off the crest of (a wall or breast-work).

Ab'kampeln (Bav. Abkämpeln), (w.) v. recipr. einander —, to contend with each other in violent altercation, to wrangle, quarrel.

Ab'kämpfen, (w.) v. tr. 1) (Einem etwas) to get, take or wrest (something from one) by fighting, to deprive (one) of (a thing) in battle: einem Schiffe den Wind —, Mar. to share the wind with some other ship; 2) a) Sport. to drive away by fighting (said of harts at rutting-time); b) fig. to repel, to strive against (death, &c.) with main force.

Ab'kanten, (w.) v. tr. 1) Join. to plane off the corners or edges of (a board, &c.); 2) Cloth. & Weav. to cut off the lists of (cloth, or the selvage of linen cloth).

Ab'kanzeln, (w.) v. tr. 1) Ch. a) to proclaim the bans of (persons about to marry) from the pulpit; b) to preach down, to rebuke; 2) (gener. coll.) to give a severe reprimand, to take (sharply) to task.

A. **Ab'kappen,** (w.) v. tr. Falc. to unhood (the hawk).

B. **Ab'kappen,** (w.) v. tr. 1) to cut or chop off; to lop, to top (a tree, cf. Abköpfen), to crop (a dog, &c.); 2) Mar. see Kappen; 3) coll. to rebuke severely, to fit (one), cf. Abmucken.

Ab'kargen, (w.) v. tr. (Einem etwas) to deprive (one of a thing) by stinginess, to stint, cf. Abdarben, Abgeizen; Bischöfe, denen er so Vieles abgekargt hatte, bishops whom he had curtailed of so many things by his niggardliness.

Ab'karren, (w.) v. tr. (l. u.) to remove with a cart, to cart off, &c. for this and other meanings, cf. Abfahren, tr.

Ab'karten, (w.) v. tr. to concert beforehand, to plan or settle privately, particul. in an ill sense; eine abgekartete Sache, a plan of operations secretly agreed upon: sie hatten es unter sich (Dat.) vorher abgekartet, they had preconcerted it among themselves; ein abgekarteter Handel, a concerted game, a collusive agreement, collusion, coll. a put-up thing.

Ab'kasteien, (w.) v. tr. particul. refl. sich —, to mortify one's flesh, to inflict severe pain on one's self.

Ab'kauen, (w.) v. tr. sich (Dat.) die Nägel —, to bite one's nails (see Abbeißen); die Pferde kauen das Gebiß ab, the horses champ the bit.

Ab'kauf, (str., pl. Ab'käufe) m. the act of buying, purchasing, purchase.

Ab'kaufen, (w.) v. I. tr. 1) (Einem etwas) to buy, purchase (something of or from one); 2) a) to buy off (a punishment, &c.); b) to induce (a person) to desist from a claim &c. by purchasing his acquiescence, to satisfy one's claims by paying a certain sum; II. refl. sich —, to buy one's self off, see sich Loskaufen.

Ab'käufer (str.) m., **Ab'käuferin,** (w.) f. purchaser, buyer (cf. Abnehmer).

Ab'käuflich, adj. purchasable, redeemable.

Ab'kaupeln, (w.) v. tr. (Einem etwas) fam. to get (something from one) by underhand dealing, to obtain (a thing from a person who has no right to dispose of it) by clandestine [illegible].

Ab'kehlen, (w.) v. tr. 1) coll. to cut the throat of (a pig, &c.), to kill; 2) Join. to [illegible] chamfer.

Ab'kehr, (w.) f. 1) the act of turning off or [illegible]; alienation, estrangement (from God, from Men), backsliding; the act of [illegible], desistance (from sin, &c.), recession; 2) (l. u.) aversion, disinclination, see Abneigung.

A. **Ab'kehren,** (w.) v. tr. 1) to brush, to sweep sufficiently, to clean by sweeping or brushing; 2) to wear out by repeated brushing or sweeping; ein abgekehrter Besen, a broom worn to the stump.

B. **Ab'kehren,** (w.) v. I. tr. 1) to turn off or away, &c. see Abwenden; 2) fig. to turn off, withdraw, to divert, to distract (one's attention), cf. Abziehen, Abwenden; II. refl. (& † intr.) 1) a) to turn off or away; b) (von) to turn one's back (upon), to withdraw one's assistance; c) to turn aside (from the cause of God, &c.), cf. sich Abwenden, Abfallen (intr. 6.) &c.; 2) Min. (also intr.) to leave a pit, to cease to work in a mine.

Ab'kehrer (str.) m., **Ab'kehrerin,** (w.) f. sweeper.

Ab'kehricht, Ab'kehrsel, (str.) n. sweepings, rubbish, see Kehricht.

Ab'kehrig, adj. (l. u.) alienated, estranged.

Ab'kehr..., in comp. —schein, —zettel, m. Min. license for a minor to leave the pit.

Ab'kehrung, (w.) f. 1) the act of turning off or away, withdrawal, distraction, cf. Ablenkung, Abziehung; 2) alienation, estrangement (von, from).

Ab'keichen, (w.) v. tr. to cough away or out, to gasp out.

Ab'keifen, (str., sometimes w.) v. I. tr. 1) (Einem etwas) to get or extort (something from one) by scolding; 2) to scold exceedingly; II. refl. to weary or exhaust one's self by scolding.

Ab'keilen, (w.) v. tr. 1) to cleave, separate by means of a wedge; 2) vulg. (Einem etwas) to buy (something of), see Abkaufen.

Ab'keltern, (w.) v. I. tr. to press (wine); II. intr. to finish or leave off pressing.

Ab'ketteln, (w.) v. tr. 1) to loose what has been fastened by a little chain (Kettel) or chains, to unchain, unfasten; 2) Stocking-weav. to fasten (meshes) with a frame-knitter's needle.

Ab'ketten, (w.) v. tr. to unchain.

Ab'keulen, (w.) v. tr. vulg. to give a sound drubbing, to cudgel, see Abprügeln

Ab'kichern, (w.) v. refl. to tire or exhaust one's self by tittering.

Ab'kimmen, (w.) v. tr. Coop. to cut off the crose of (the staves in worn out casks).

A. **Ab'kippen,** (w.) v. I. intr. (aux. sein) to glide off an edge, to tilt or turn over; II. tr. to turn off, to tilt or turn over.

B. **Ab'kippen,** (w.) v. tr. to cut off (the rims of coins, &c.), to crop, cf. Abköpfen.

Ab'kitzeln, (w.) v. tr. to tire (one) with tickling, to tickle very much.

Ab'klaffen, (w.) v. intr. to be ajar (said of a door, &c.), to gape, to stand off.

Ab'klaftern, (w.) v. tr. 1) to divide into fathoms; 2) to measure by the fathom, to cord (wood).

Ab'klagen, (w.) v. tr. (Einem etwas) to get or obtain (something from one) by a lawsuit.

Ab'klammern, (w.) v. tr. to take off or detach what is fastened with clothes-pegs or cramp-irons, cf. Klammer.

Ab'klang, (str., pl. Ab'klänge) m. 1) echo (cf. Wiederhall); 2) sinking sound; 3) dissonance.

Ab'klappen, (w.) v. tr. to let down the leaf of (a table), the flaps of (a hat, &c. cf. Abkrämpen, Herunterklappen).

Ab'klären, (w.) v. I. tr. to clear off, to clarify (wine, &c.), to purge, purify; to decant; to defecate; II. refl. to clear off, become clear, to clarify.

Ab'klärmittel, (str.) n. any ingredient to purge liquors, &c. from lees or foulness.

Ab'klärung, (w.) f. the act of clearing off, clarification; decantation (of liquors); (also fig.:) purification from impurities or foreign matter; the act of purifying from admixture, and the state of being purged of extraneous matter.

Ab'klärungsmittel, (str.) n. any ingredient or (**Ab'klärwasser,** (str.) n.) fluid to purge liquors, &c. from dregs or impurities, cf. Kläre, 3.

Ab'klatsch, (str.) m. cast, impression.

Ab'klatschen, (w.) v. tr. 1) coll. to slap (a child) thoroughly; 2) Typ. &c. to beat off; to take a cast, impression; 3) Danc. to take the partner of the first dancer in certain dances, in order to continue the dance with her, previously giving a kind of signal by clapping one's hands.

Ab'klauben, (w.) v. tr. coll. to pick off, pluck off; das Fleisch von einem Knochen —, to pick a bone; abgeklaubte Phrasen (Thack), worn-out phrases.

Ab'kleckern, (w.) v. coll. I. intr. (aux. sein) 1) to fall down in small particles and blot (as ink from a pen); 2) lud. to drop off, i. e. to die; II. tr. to drop or pour off (from a thick fluid).

Ab'klecksen, (w.) v. tr. to copy in a daubing manner.

Ab'kleiden, (w.) v. tr. 1) a) (l. u.) to undress (opp. Ankleiden), see Auskleiden, Entkleiden; die Toue —, Mar. to take off the service; b) fig. to strip, divest or deprive of necessaries; 2) to partition (off), to separate (a room, &c.) by a partition.

Ab'kleidung, (w.) f. 1) the act of undressing, &c. see Abkleiden; 2) the act of partitioning, erection of a partition-wall; 3) partition; Mar. pl. bulk-heads.

Ab'klemmen, (w.) v. tr. (Einem etwas) to pinch off, to squeeze off; sich (Dat.) die Finger —, to squeeze off one's fingers.

Ab'klimpern, (w.) v. tr. to play badly (on a pianoforte, or any stringed instrument), anal. to strum off (a tune, &c.).

Ab'klingen, (str.) v. intr. to decrease in intensity, to expire, to die off or away (of sounds, sometimes of colours, &c.); cf. Verklingen.

Ab'klitschen, (w.) v. tr. the same with Abklatschen, &c.

Ab'klopfen, (w.) v. tr. 1) to knock, beat off; 2) to beat (eggs, &c.); 3) to remove (the dust, &c. from clothes, &c.) by beating, see Ausklopfen; 4) Typ. to strike off (einen Probebogen, a proof) by the brush, cf. Abklatschen, 2.; 5) coll. to beat soundly (cf. Abprügeln).

Ab'klören, (w.) v. tr. (from Klör, coll. for Couleur) Dy. to boil the faded colour out of (a dyed stuff), in order to dye it anew.

Ab'klötzen, (w.) v. tr. to hew (a piece of wood) into block-shape.

Ab'klügeln, (w.) v. tr. (Einem etwas) to dispute or word (one) out of (a thing) by oversubtle arguments.

Ab'knabbern, Ab'knäbbern, (w.) v. tr. to nibble off.

Ab'knacken, (w.) v. tr. & intr. see Abknicken

Ab'knallen, (w.) v. I. tr. to discharge with a loud report, to crack, fire off; eine Flinte —, to fire a gun (off); II. intr. (aux. sein) 1) to go off with a report (as a gun); 2) Chem. to detonise, fulminate.

Ab'knappen, Ab'knappern, (w.) v. tr. 1) to break off by little bits or with a snapping sound; 2) fig. (Einem etwas) to withhold (something from one) through parsimony, to stint (one in his meals, &c.); am Lohne —, to curtail wages; sich (Dat.) etwas —, to deprive one's self of a thing, to pinch one's self in ..., cf. Abdarben.

Ab'knapsen, (w.) v. tr. 1) to snap or to nibble off (as a bird eating sugar, &c.); 2) to shut or lock with a smart, snapping sound.

Ab'knattern, (w.) v. intr. (aux. sein) to be discharged, or to go off with a crackling sound (as musketry, &c.).

Ab'knaupeln, (w.) v. tr. (diminutive of † Abknaupen) to pick off with the fingers or teeth;

to gnaw off; einen Knochen —, to gnaw or pick a bone.

Ab'knausern, *(w.) v. tr.* (Einem or sich *[Dat.]* etwas) to deprive (one) of (what is due or necessary) through niggardliness, to withhold (something from one), &c. *see* Abknappen.

Ab'kneifen, *(str.) v. tr.* 1) to pinch off, to nip off, *cf.* Abkneipen; 2) *Mar. a)* den Wind —, to haul the wind, to ply, turn or work to windward; *b)* einem Schiffe den Wind —, to gain or get the wind (or the weather-gauge) of a ship.

Ab'kneipen, *(str.) v. tr.* 1) to cut off with a short knife; 2) *see* Abkneifen.

Ab'knicken, *(w.) v.* I. *tr.* 1) to crack off, break off; 2) *Sport.* to kill (game) by cutting the neck *(also* Abnicken); II. *intr. (aux.* sein) 1) to crack or break off; 2) *Hunt.* to fall dead.

Ab'knickern, *(w.) v. tr. see* Abknausern & Abknappen, 2.

Ab'knieen *[pr.* — k-ne'en], *(w.) v. tr.* 1) to wear off or out by kneeling; 2) to expiate (sins) by kneeling.

Ab'knippen, Ab'knipsen, *(w.) v. tr.* 1) to nip off, to cut (or take) off the top of (a pen, &c. *syn.* Abkippen); 2) *(Freytag,* Verl. Handschr.) to discharge (a percussion-cap, &c.) with a smart, snapping sound.

Ab'knirschen, *(w.) v. tr.* to bite off with a gnashing or grating sound, to crush.

Ab'knistern, *(w.) v. tr.* 1) to fly off with a crackling noise; *Chem.* to decrepitate; — lassen, to decrepitate; 2) to cease to crackle; das —, *v. s.* *(str.)* *n.* decrepitation.

Ab'knixen, *(w.) v. intr. (aux.* sein) to go off curtsying, to curtsy off.

Ab'knöpfen, *(w.) v. tr.* to unbutton and take off (a coat, &c.), *dif. from* Aufknöpfen.

Ab'knubbern, Ab'knuppern, *(w.) v. tr. see* Abknabbern. [loosen (a knot).

Ab'knüpfen, *(w.) v. tr.* to unbind, untie,

Ab'knuspern, *(w.) v. tr.* to nibble off.

Ab'knütteln, *(w.) v. tr.* 1) to beat or throw off with a cudgel; 2) to cudgel soundly.

Ab'kochen, *(w.) v.* I. *tr.* 1) to separate by boiling, to boil off; 2) to boil in water, so as to draw the strength or virtue of any thing; 3) to boil (a liquid) till it bubbles, to boil (meat) till it is done, to subject to a boiling heat, to prepare by boiling; to decoct; gelinde —, to soften by the heat of water, to parboil, to coddle; *Pharm.* to elixate; abgekochter Trank, decoction; 4) to separate by boiling; 5) *(gener. intr.)* to cook with all the despatch necessary (as soldiers on their march); II. *intr.* 1) to be separated or to fall off by boiling; 2) to pass into a boiling state, to boil.

Ab'kochung, *(w.) f.* decoction: 1) the operation of boiling, &c.; 2) or **Ab'köchsel,** *(str.) n.* *(l. u.)* the thing boiled or decocted.

Ab'kohlen, *(w.) v. tr. Carp.* to mark off (a line, &c.) with charcoal *(cf.* Abschnüren, 2.).

Ab'köhlen, *(w.) v. tr. Min.* to cease to work or to give up (a mine), *see* Abbütten.

Ab'kollern, *(w.) v. tr.* & *intr. (aux.* sein) to roll down, off, away.

Ab'komme, *(w.) m.* descendant, *see* Abkömmling.

Ab'kommen, *(str.) v. intr. (aux.* sein) 1) to come (down) from; *gener. fig.* to proceed from a source or original, to descend; to be derived *(see* Herkommen, Abstammen); diese Kinder kommen alle von einem Vater ab *(Grimm),* all these children are the issue or offspring of one (common) father; die Hessen kommen von den alten Chatten ab, the Hessians are descendants of the old Catti *(cf.* Abkömmling); 2) *a)* to come or get down from, to get off (a sandbank, &c.); *see* Loskommen; *b)* to come away, to get off (from an engagement, &c.); ich kann heute nicht —, I cannot disengage myself to-day, I am engaged or detained by business; können Sie wol (auf) eine Viertelstunde —? are you disengaged for (or can you spare) a quarter of an hour? in dieser Woche werde ich kaum — können, this week I shall scarcely be able to get away from my business (spare any time to call on you, &c.); *c)* to get off, to go free, *see* Loskommen; mit Ehren —, to come off with flying colours; mit Verlust —, to come off a loser; *d)* von Einem or von einer Sache —, to get rid of a person or thing, to rid one's self of; ich bin vom Tanzen ganz abgekommen, I have given up (oder quitted) dancing entirely *(cf.* Zurückkommen von ...); *e)* mit Einem — *(more usual:* ein — treffen), to come to an agreement, &c.; *f) (l. u.) for* Abhanden kommen, Wegkommen: die Sache ist mir abgekommen, I have lost the thing; er kann — *(i. e.* wir brauchen ihn nicht), we can do without him, let him go, it is a good riddance; *g)* to come or get off; to deviate, to wander or swerve from the common or right way, course or line; vom Wege —, to miss the road, to go out of one's way; vom Winde —, *Mar.* to come by the lee, to fall to leeward; er kommt von der Sache ab, *fig.* he is wandering from the subject or point; *h) fig.* to deviate, swerve (from one's duty, &c.); 3) *fig.* to grow out of use, to fall into disuse or desuetude; dieser (Waaren-)Artikel ist ganz abgekommen, this article is fallen into disuse, is out of fashion; die Parteinamen Whig und Tory sind fast abgekommen, the party-names of Whig and Tory are almost antiquated; 4) to decline in health, to fall off (Abmagern, &c.).

Ab'kommen, *v. s. (str.) n.* 1) (the act of) coming off, &c. *see* Abkommen, *v.*; 2) *Min. a)* deviation of a vein of ore; *b)* a deviating vein; 3) descent; origin *(more usual:* Abkunft, Herkommen); 4) agreement, accommodation, compromise, settlement; ein — mit Einem treffen, to come to an agreement (oder to terms) with one; 5) disuse, discontinuance (of a custom, &c.), desuetude.

Ab'kommenschaft, *(w.) f.* 1) descent; 2) offspring, posterity.

Ab'kömmling, *(str.) m.* 1) descendant, offspring; 2) *Chem.* derivative. [& 4.

Ab'kommniß, *(str.) n. see* Abkommen, *s.* 3,

Ab'köpfen, *(w.) v. tr.* 1) to behead, decapitate (Köpfen *more usual in this sense);* 2) (Abkoppen, *with which it seems to be confounded, preferable in the following sense:)* to top, to lop or to clip off the top of (trees, &c.), to poll.

Ab'koppeln, *(w.) v. tr.* to uncouple (Hunde, Pferde, dogs, horses).

Ab'koppen *(not etymologically related to* Kopf, *see* Koppen; *cf.* Abköpfen), *(w.) v. tr.* to lop or to cut off, to top, clip, poll.

Ab'kosen, *(w.) v. tr.* (Einem etwas) to get (something) from (one) by wheedling, coaxing or fawning, to coax or wheedle (one) out of (a thing). [tasting.

Ab'kosten, *(w.) v. tr.* to take away by

Ab'krachen, *(w.) v. intr.* to go or to break off with a crash.

Ab'krächzen, *(w.) v. tr.* to utter or to recite in a croaking, groaning tone; sich —, *refl.* to wear one's self out with croaking, to croak away, to croak or groan unceasingly.

† **Ab'kraft,** *(str.) f. (Hans Sachs, &c.)* (sudden) loss of strength or power; fainting fit *(in MHG.* unkraft); (Entkräftung; Ohnmacht).

Ab'kräften, *(w.) v. tr.* **Ab'kräftig,** *adj. see* Entkräften, Entkräftet.

Ab'krähen, *(w.) v. tr.* to utter crowing, to crow or screech forth; to proclaim or announce (the hours, &c. as the cock) by crowing; *refl.* to weary one's self with crowing, to crow away or unceasingly.

Ab'krallen, *(w.) v. tr.* to claw off or away.

Ab'krämen, *(w.) v. tr.* (& *intr.)* to clear away or off, to clear (einen Tisch, a table, &c.).

Ab'krämpeln, *(w.) v.* I. *tr.* to [illegible] comb (Wolle, Baumwolle, wool, [illegible] card thoroughly; II. *intr.* to [illegible]

Ab'krämpen, *(w.) v. tr.* [illegible] or off the flap or brim of (a hat), [illegible]

Ab'kränkeln, *(w.) v. refl. ill-[illegible]* to weaken one's self, to be wa[illegible] away with illness.

Ab'kränken, *(w.) v.* I. *tr.* to [illegible] tate by grief; II. *refl.* & *intr.* [illegible] away with grief (or sich [illegible]

Ab'kratzen, *(w.) v.* I. *tr.* 1) [illegible] scratch off, to remove [illegible] scraping; sich *(Dat.)* die Schuhe [illegible] —, to scrape one's shoes upon the [illegible] 2) *coll.* ein Stück auf der Geige [illegible] or scrape a tune on the violin [illegible] way); II. *intr. coll.* 1) to run, [illegible] *see* Auskratzen; 2) *bund.* to pop off, [illegible] *cf.* Abfahren, I. 3, *a.*

Ab'kratzung, *(w.) f.* (the act of) [illegible]

Ab'kraut, *(str.) n. see* [illegible]

Ab'krauten, *(w.) v. tr.* to weed, [illegible] vineyard, &c.) of weeds, (mit der [illegible] *(cf.* Gäten).

Ab'kreischen, *v.* I. *tr.* 1) to [illegible] bawl forth; 2) *(according to* [illegible] cause to produce a hissing sound, [illegible] *in a frying pan) a)* to melt ([illegible] substances), to fry thoroughly; *b)* [illegible] cleanse, to purify ([illegible] II. *refl.* to tire one's self out [illegible] to screech away, to grow hoarse by [illegible]

Ab'kreisen, *(w.) v.* I. *tr.* to [illegible] cular form, to separate by a circle, [illegible] II. *intr. (aux.* sein) to diverge or [illegible] circular motion; a—d, *p. a.* [illegible]

Ab'kriechen, *(str.) v. intr. (aux.* [illegible] creep off or away *(more usual:* [illegible]

Ab'kriegen, *(w.) v. tr.* 1) ([illegible] get (something) from (one) by [illegible] ing war, to snatch (a country, &c.) [illegible] by force of arms; 2) to get off; [illegible] von einer Sache) to get, obtain ([illegible] *particul. in an ill sense, as f. i.* [illegible] was —, *coll.* you'll get it *(i. e.* your [illegible] reprimand, a punishment or injury [illegible] kind); wir werden etwas —, the rain [illegible] &c.) will overtake us, we'll have it [illegible] we'll get our share.

Ab'krippen, *(w.) v. tr.* to dam [illegible]

Ab'kritzeln, *(w.) v. tr.* to copy [illegible] bling manner.

Ab'kröschen, *incorrect* [illegible] word Abkreischen, which see.

Ab'krümeln, *(w.) v. tr., intr.* [illegible] *refl.* to crumble off.

Ab'krümmen, *(w.) v.* I. *tr.* to [illegible] bend off, to form into a crook [illegible] end; II. *refl.* to run crooked or [illegible] line at the end, to curve off.

Ab'krusten, *(w.) v. tr.* to take [illegible] crust of (bread, &c.), to scale off. [illegible]

Ab'kugeln, *(w.) v.* I. *intr.* to [illegible] a ball; II. *tr.* 1) to bowl off; 2) [illegible] to count (the votes, &c.) by [illegible] balloting), to decide by ballot, [illegible] gebetabkugelnd *(Voss),* telling [illegible] beads.

Ab'kugelung, *(w.) f.* decision [illegible] of) voting by ballot, balloting.

Ab'kugel-Apparat, *(str.) m.* [illegible]

Ab'kühlen, *(w.) v.* I. *tr.* to [illegible] to refresh, refrigerate; Gläser —, *Glass-m.* & *Iron-m.* to anneal; [illegible] (desire, zeal, ardour, love, &c.) [illegible] calm, appease, to moderate [illegible] sein Mütchen an Einem —, to [illegible] upon one; II. *refl.* & *intr.* [illegible] to cool (down), to grow cool [illegible] sich etwas abgekühlt, her anger [illegible] (abated) a little.

Ab'kühler, (str.) m. 1) any one or any thing which cools (down), see Abkühlen; 2) or **Ab'kühlfaß**, n. cooling vat, cooler, refrigeratory.

Ab'kühl..., in comp. —ofen, m. Glass-m. & Iron-m. annealing-oven; —rinne, f. Brew. &c. cooling-channel (cf. Silberrinne); —trog, m. cooling-trough, cooler.

Ab'kühlung, (w.) f. (the act of) cooling, &c. see Abkühlen; 2) Chem. refrigeration.

Ab'kühlungsmittel, (str.) n. Med. refrigerant, cooling medicine.

Ab'kümmern, (w.) v. I. intr. to waste, to wear out, to emaciate, see Verkümmern; II. refl. to pine away, to be worn out with grief; to grieve unceasingly.

Ab'künden, **Ab'kündigen**, (w.) v. tr. 1) to proclaim, to make known; to announce, to notify; ein Brautpaar —, to publish (or proclaim) the bans of matrimony; 2) Law, to give up, resign.

Ab'kündigung, (w.) f. 1) (the act of) proclaiming, &c., proclamation; announcement, notification; bidding the bans, &c.; 2) notice, warning of resignation, &c.

Ab'kunft, (str., pl. Ab'künfte) f. 1) descent, family, parentage, birth, origin, pedigree (cf. Abstammung[?]); 2) (of animals) race, breed; von guter —, (of persons) of good family, well descended, well-born; (of animals) thoroughbred; von edler —, nobly extracted, of gentle, noble birth; von gemeiner (niedriger) —, low-born, of humble parentage; 3) (l. u. for Abkommen, v. s. 4.) agreement.

Ab'kuppen, (w.) v. tr. to cut off minute particles of (vines, &c.), to nip off, to prune.

Ab'kuppeln, **Ab'kuppen**, **Ab'kupfen**, (w.) v. tr. to cut (or take) off the top of ...; to nib (a pen); to nip off (cf. Abkneipen).

Ab'kürzen, (w.) v. tr. 1) a) lit. to shorten, to make shorter, to lessen, to clip, curtail; fig-s. b) to abridge, abbreviate, to cut short, to retrench; c) to diminish, lessen (the price of a thing, &c.); 2) Geom. to cut off, truncate, see Abgekürzt; 3) Math. to reduce (einen Bruch, a fraction, &c.); es läßt sich nicht —, it is not reducible; sie wünschte seinen Besuch abzukürzen, she wished to cut short his visit; einen (geschriebenen) Aufsatz —, to abridge, cut down a (written) article; Jemandes Lohn —, to curtail one's wages; abgekürztes [illegible] ([illegible]), Farr. lanette or lancet.

Ab'kürzer, (str.) m. abbreviator, abridger; epitomiser, epitomist.

Ab'kürzung, (w.) f. 1) a) (the act of) shortening, curtailing, &c. see Abkürzen; b) abridgment, (eines Wortes) abbreviation; c) retrenchment; 2) Math. reduction (or abbreviation [of fractions]), diminution; A-strich, m. division; A-stück, n. Geom. frustum, a part of a solid body separated from the rest; A-zeichen, n. abbreviature, (short-hand) note.

Ab'küssen, (w.) v. tr. 1) (Einem etwas) (as much as Wegküssen) to kiss away or off (tears from the cheeks); 2) to kiss heartily.

Ab'kutschen, **Ab'kutschiren**, (w.) v. intr. (aux. sein) to drive away or off in a coach or carriage.

Ab'kütteln, (w.) v. tr. see Abschütteln.

Ab'lachen, (w.) v. refl. coll. to laugh one's self out of breath, to laugh heartily, immoderately, incessantly, to laugh one's fill.

* **Ablactiren** (Lat. ablactare, to wean from the breast), (w.) v. tr. (& intr. [aux. haben] by leaving out the object) Gard. to graft by approach, see Absäugen, 3.

Ab'laden, (str.) v. tr. 1) to unload, to unlade, to disburden; to unpack, to discharge (a cargo, &c.); noch bevor der Schiffer — konnte, even before the master could discharge; sie [illegible] [illegible] Wasserfässer ab, they unloaded the water; das Schiff war im — begriffen, the vessel was unlading; dann wurde das Gepäck abgeladen und jeder Reisende nahm das seinige in Anspruch, then the luggage was unladen, and each passenger claimed his own; beim — zersprang die Kiste, in discharging the case burst; man muß die Gefäße vorsichtig —, the casks must be carefully unpacked; 2) unusual for Verladen, which see.

Ab'lade..., in comp. —ort, m. —platz, m. Comm. place for unloading: landing-place; quay; port of discharge.

Ab'lader, **Ab'läder**, (str.) m. unloader; discharger, heaver; A-lohn, m. fees for unloading.

Ab'ladung, (w.) f. 1) (the act of) unloading; discharging, &c. see Abladen; 2) A-en, cargoes, incorr. for Verladungen.

Ab'lage, (w.) f. 1) (the act of) putting away, laying aside, &c. cf. Ablegen & Ablegung; 2) Law, separation (of property); 3) anything laid aside, deposit; 4) a place of deposit.

Ab'lager, (str.) n. 1) the (act of or [in Feudal Law] the privilege of) turning in or putting up (at an inn, in convents, &c.); 2) a) stopping-place, resting-place, rest; b) cont. den, lurking-place (of thieves, vagabonds, &c.); 3) Min. bed, deposit, see Ablagerung; A-platz, m. (l. u.) place of transmission, destination, see Ablieferort.

Ab'lagern, (w.) v. I. tr. 1) to lay down, to lodge, to deposit; abgelagerte Massen, Geol. matter laid or thrown down after being suspended in or carried along by water, deposits; 2) to remove from a storehouse; II. refl. & intr. 1) (of fluids) to settle, to subside, to fall to the bottom of liquor, as dregs or lees; abgelagerte (or abgelegene) Weine, matured (old) wines; abgelagerte Cigarren, old (well seasoned) cigars (dry and of sufficient age to be fit for use); 2) to separate from and encamp in another place.

Ab'lagerung, (w.) f. 1) the act of laying down, lodging, depositing, &c. see Ablagern; 2) Geol. a) deposition (of mud, &c.), transmission (of boulders, &c.); stratification; b) mineral layer, deposit; 3) separate encampment, &c. [yeaning.

Ab'lammen, (w.) v. intr. to discontinue

Ab'landen, **Ab'länden**, (w.) v. intr. Mar. to lift the anchor, to set sail, to depart (opp. Anlanden).

Ab'ländisch, (l. u.) adj. coming (blowing, &c.) from the land; a-er Wind, land-breeze.

† **Ab'lang**, adj. oblong, see Länglich.

Ab'langen, (w.) v. tr. to reach, to fetch (down).

Ab'längen, (w.) v. tr. 1) Min. to dig lengthwise; 2) Carp. to cut the trunk of (a tree) in proper lengths, to saw lengthwise.

† **Ab'länglich** adj., **Ab'langs**, adv. see Ablang.

Ab'laschen, (w.) v. tr. Forest. (cf. Abplätzen, Anschlagen) 1) to blaze or notch (trees in a forest) either for felling, or for marking out a way; 2) to mark out (einen Weg, a way) by blazing trees, to blaze out (a path).

Ab'laß, (str., pl. Ab'lässe) m. 1) the (act of) letting off, draining, &c. cf. Ablassen; discharge; 2) drain, water-course, see Schleuse; 3) cessation, intermission (Unterlaß); 4) Rom. Cath. a) indulgence, pardon, grant of the Holy Church, remission; b) the ceremonies or festivities on days of indulgence; vollkommener —, plenary indulgence; den — betreffend, indulgential. [indulgence.

Ab'laßbrief, (str.) m. Rom. Cath. letter of

Ab'lassen, (str.) v. I. intr. (syn. Nachlassen) to leave off, to cease, to desist (von, from), wenn Sie nur von Ihrer großen Strenge — wollten, if you would only be a little more yielding; II. tr. 1) a) to let off; einen Brief — (more usual: abgehen lassen), to send off, to forward a letter; ein Schiff — (syn. vom Stapel laufen lassen), to launch a vessel; einen (Eisenbahn-)Zug —, T. to despatch a (railway-)train, to let off, cf. Abgehen, 1, e.; b) to slacken, see Abspannen; 2) a) (Abschlagen) to let or to draw off (water), to drain; b) to rack, to draw off from the lees (wine, &c.); c) aa) Found. to tap, run off, see Abstechen; bb) den Ofen —, to cease smelting; einen Teich —, to let off a pond; ein Faß Wein —, to broach, to tap a cask of wine; 3) Shoe-m. die Sohlen —, to pare, to cut or edge off the soles, to shape or fashion the edges of the soles; 4) T. to temper (steel, &c.), to let down (by heat) (also Anlassen, Nachlassen); 5) fig. a) to give over, to cede; b) (verkäuflich —) to sell, to dispose of; unter dem Preise —, to sell under (below) the cost-price, to under-sell; wohlfeil —, to let one have (an article) cheap, to sell cheap (at a low rate); c) to abate (from the price, to make an allowance); von einer (Preis-)Forderung etwas — (syn. etwas nachlassen), to abate the price, to come down; ich kann davon nicht das Geringste —, I cannot make the least abatement of this price; auf beiden Seiten etwas —, coll. to split the difference (in a bargain).

Ab'laß..., in comp. —geld, n. —pfennig, m. shrove-money; —hahn, m. Steam-eng. delivery-cock; purging-cock, mud-cock; —handel, m. see —kram; —horn, n. a piece of horn used by shoemakers for paring the soles; —jahr, n. year of jubilee; —kanzlei, f. penitentiary (of the pope); —kirche, f. Rom. Cath. station (a church where indulgences are to be had on certain days); —krahn(en), m. see —hahn; —kram, m. —krämerei, f. Rom. Cath. selling of indulgences; —krämer, m. seller or vender of (the Pope's) indulgences, pardonmonger; pardoner; —pfennig, m. see —geld; —prediger, m. preacher (seller) of indulgences; —tage, m. pl. Rom. Cath. days of grace (on which indulgences are granted); —verkauf, m. Rom. Cath. sale of indulgences; —woche, f. Rom. Cath. week of corpus Christi day (Frohnleichnams-Woche, during which indulgences are granted).

Ab'lassung, (w.) f. the (act of) letting off, drawing off, &c. see Ablassen.

Ab'laßbogen, **Ab'lassungsbogen**, (str.) m. Archit. discharging arch (Entlastungsbogen).

Ab'lästern, (w.) v. tr. (Einem etwas) to deprive (one) of (a thing) by calumnies or blasphemy (cf. Abschwatzen, 1, b.).

* **Ablativ'**, (str.) m. (Lat.) Gramm. ablative (case); der unabhängige —, ablative absolute.

Ab'latten, (w.) v. tr. to take away the laths from (a roof, &c.).

Ab'lauben, (w.) v. tr. to pluck off the leaves of (shrubs, &c.), to unleave, strip of the foliage; to prune (vines, &c.).

Ab'laurer, (str.) m. lurker, sculker, waylayer, see Ablauern.

Ab'lauern, (w.) v. tr. 1) to wait or tarry for (one, &c.), particul. in an ill sense, to lurk, to sculk, lie in wait for, to waylay; die Gelegenheit —, to watch for an opportunity, to wait one's chance; 2) (Einem etwas) a) to obtain (something from one) by lying in wait for, by watching a chance; b) fig. to get at or to discover (a secret, &c.) by clandestine observation.

Ab'lauf, (str., pl. Ab'läufe) m. 1) the (act of) running down; running off, flowing off; going off, cf. Ablaufen; — des Meeres, ebb, ebbing of the sea; 2) sink, gutter, kennel, drain, common sewer, outlet, vent; 3) anything sloping off: a) Archit. (cf. Anlauf) aa) hollow congé, upper apophyge (of a column); bb) cymatium, an undulating moulding, generally the upper one of a cornice;

Ab- und Anlauf eines Säulenschaftes, spring of a column; *b)* slope, acclivity, *see* Böschung; *c)* *Found.* (Verjüngung eines Modells) delivery, draw, draft (*Tech.*); *d)* *Ship-b.* rake (of the stem), *see* Ausschießen, *s.*; 4) *a)* expiration (of a term, of a treaty, &c.); (eines Wechsels) *Comm.* expiration, maturity, falling due (of a bill), time (*or* term) of payment; vor — des Semesters, before the half-year *or* term (-time) closes; mit — der Frist, at expiration of the term; — des Jahres, end of the year; *b)* end, event; es wird vom — der Auction abhängen, ob —, it will depend on the result of the sale, whether ....

Ab'laufen, (*str.*) *v.* I. *intr.* (*aux.* sein) 1) to run down *or* off; von dem Geleise — (Entgleisen, Entschienen), to run off the rails; to wriggle off; der Dampfwagen lief von den Schienen ab, the steam-engine went off the rails; ein Schiff — lassen, to launch a ship (vom Stapel laufen lassen); vor dem Winde —, *Mar.* to bring the wind aft; 2) to run *or* flow down, to run off, to flow off; (wieder) —, to ebb; die Gewässer liefen ab, the waters subsided; das a-de Wasser eines Wassertrogs, overflowings; das Licht läuft ab, the candle gutters; 3) to set off, to depart (Abgehen); kein Schiff konnte bei dem Sturme —, no vessel could put to sea in such a storm; ein Schiff — lassen, to despatch a vessel, *see* Abgehen lassen; einen Brief — lassen, to despatch a letter; lassen Sie die Einlage gef. sogleich —, please to have the enclosure forwarded immediately; 4) to run out, to run down, to cease moving; die Uhr ist abgelaufen, the watch is (gone) down; 5) *fig.* *a)* to run out, to expire; *Comm.* to fall *or* become due; abgelaufen, expired, due, payable; der Wechsel ist abgelaufen, the bill falls due; ein abgelaufener Wechsel, a bill which is due; der Termin ist noch nicht abgelaufen, the term has not yet expired; der abgelaufene Monat, last month, ult. (ultimo); *b)* to elapse, pass away; *c)* to end; die Hochzeit lief ab wie andere, the wedding went by as other weddings do; wie lief es ab? how did it speed? das wird übel —, that will turn out a sad affair; das Geschäft ist noch leidlich für Sie abgelaufen, you have after all come off pretty well in this transaction; — lassen, 1) *see above*; 2) *Fenc.* to ward off (a thrust); 3) *Carp.* &c. (Abschärfen, Abschrägen &c.) to rabbet, to chamfer; 4) *fig.* to let (one) go by, to rebuff severely, to give (one) a set-down, *see* Abfertigen.

II. *tr.* 1) *Min.* to run *or* transport (ores) to the shaft; 2) to run off; to wear off *or* out by rubbing *or* attrition; 3) to outrun; (Einem) den Rang —, to get the start (*or* to get the better) of ...., to distance, to beat (one), to cut (one) out; *coll.-e.* sich (*Dat.*) die Beine (*or* Füße, Hacken) nach etwas (*Dat.*) —, to run one's heels for a thing, to run one's feet off, to take the utmost pains to obtain a thing; sich (*Dat.*) die Hörner —, to sow one's wild oats; das habe ich längst an den Schuhen gelaufen, that I have known long ago.

III. *refl.* to tire one's self out by running.

Ab'laufen, *v. s.* (*str.*) *n.* 1) the (act of) running down *or* off, &c. *see* Ablaufen, *v.* & Ablauf; 2) *Weav.* rounding off of the wing transom (*Tech.*).

Ab'läufer, (*str.*) *m.* 1) a person who, *or* a thing which, runs down *or* off, &c. *cf.* Ablaufen; 2) *Mar.* (Speigat) scupper-hole (*pl.* scuppers); 3) *Weav.* *a)* a spool become empty; *b)* a wrong thread, a thread out of its place.

Ab'lauf ..., *in comp.* -loch, *n.* a hole to carry off water, &c.; side-hole (of a pump, &c.); —rinne, *f.* 1) *Print.* &c. gutter; 2) *Found.* (Gußloch, Gerinne), gutter; basin, gate, pouring-hole (*Tech.*); 3) *Mar.* scupper-hole, scupper; —röhre, *f.* waste-pipe, tunnel, scupper; *see also* —rinne; —schleuse, *f.* discharging-sluice, delivery-sluice; A-splanken, *f. pl.* *Ship-b.* launching planks.

Ab'laugen, (*w.*) *v. tr.* 1) to impregnate with lye, to lixiviate; 2) *a)* to clear off, remove the lye from (yarn, &c.) by washing, to wash out, rinse off the lye; *b)* *coll.* to reprimand, *see* Abscheuern; das — des Garnes, the scouring of yarn.

Ab'läugnen, (*w.*) *v. tr. see* Ableugnen.

Ab'lauschen, (*w.*) *v. tr.* (Einem etwas) to get (at) *or* learn by listening *or* eavesdropping; (eine Gelegenheit, einen Vortheil) to lurk *or* watch for (an opportunity, a chance, an advantage), *cf.* Ablauern.

Ab'lausen, (*w.*) *v. tr. vulg.* 1) to louse, to clean from lice; 2) *fig.* (Einem etwas) to cheat *or* do (one) out of (a thing).

Ab'laut, (*str.*) *m.* *Gramm.* (*first introduced by Jacob Grimm, see his* Deutsche Grammatik) change of the radical vowel (of verbs), *as f. i. in* binde, band, gebunden (*different to the* Umlaut, *which see*); das Präteritum starker Zeitwörter wird durch — gebildet (z. B. trinke, trank, getrunken), the preterite of strong verbs is formed by changing the radical vowel (f. i. drink, drank, drunk).

Ab'lauten, (*w.*) *v. intr. Gramm.* to change the radical vowel (as verbs, &c.); starke Zeitwörter lauten ab (z. B. singe, sang, gesungen), strong verbs change their radical vowel (f. i. sing, sang, sung).

Ab'läuter ..., *in comp.* *Metall.* —arbeit, *n.* (the process of) buddling, trunking; —faß, *n.* buddle, washing-tub, (*Devon.*) launder; —kiste, *f.* washing-trunk.

Ab'läutern, (*w.*) *v. tr.* to clarify (syrup, &c.), to filter, to refine (sugar), to purify (liquors *or* metals); *Min.* to wash (ore), to buddle; *cf.* Abspülen.

Ab'läuterung, (*w.*) *f.* 1) the (act of) clarifying, refining, &c. *see* Abläutern; 2) *see* Abspülung; A-sfaß, *see* Abläuterfaß.

Ab'leben, (*w.*) *v.* I. *tr.* (*l. u.*) to live through (many a winter) (*B. Waldis*); to consume (one's life); Einer, der seine Zeit abgelebt, one who has lived out his time; II. *used as a refl. by Tieck:* daß ich so in die Welt hineinkam und daß ich mich nun ablebe, that I thus entered this world, and am now spinning off the thread of life; III. *intr.* (*aux.* sein; *gener. used in the past participle*) 1) to consume one's life, to decay, to wear *or* waste away, to die by degrees, slowly; auf ihrem Siechbette begrüßten wir die a-de Nichte Gleim's (*Göthe*), on her sick-bed we saluted Gleim's niece slowly fading away; 2) to become decrepit; abgelebt, worn with age.

Ab'leben, *v. s.* (*str.*) *n.* decease, death; seit dem — unseres Hrn. N., *Comm.* since the decease of our Mr. N.; (das fig. engl. Wort nur von königlichen oder bedeutenden Personen gebraucht:) demise.

Ab'lecken, (*w.*) *v.* I. *tr.* to lick off; II. *intr.* 1) (*aux.* haben) *provinc.* (*Switzerland*) to flash in the pan; 2) (*aux.* sein) to dry (off) (of evaporating fluids).

† Ab'ledern, (*w.*) *v. tr.* (*Leather*, &c.) (Einem etwas) to obtain *or* get (something from one) by deceit, to wheedle *or* swindle (one out of a thing).

Ab'ledern, (*w.*) *v. tr.* 1) to skin; 2) *Instr.-m.* to remove the leather from (the hammers of a pianoforte); 3) *vulg.* (Einen, Einem den Buckel &c.) to leather one's hide, to drub, thrash, *see* Abprügeln.

Ab'leeren, (*w.*) *v. tr.* I. (*from* Ab & leeren) to empty; to clear (the table, &c.); II. (*from* Ab & Lehre) *Min.* 1) to verify the dimensions of (a thing); 2) *see* Abmessen.

* Ablegat', (*w.*) *m.* (*Lat.*) legate of the [pope.

Ab'legen, (*w.*) *v.* I. *tr.* 1) *a)* to lay aside, down, off, to put *or* take off [illegible] eine Last —, to lay *or* put down [illegible] Kleider —, to put off one's clothes [illegible] (Ausziehen, sich [illegible]) [illegible] Trauer —, to go out of mourning [illegible] aside (as no longer serviceable) [illegible] off, away, by; abgelegte [illegible] away (*or* off) clothes; 2) [illegible] Geweih, the antlers [illegible] lay (plants) (Absenken, [illegible]) *Typ.* (eine Form, die Schrift [illegible]) letters of a form; 4) (*often* [illegible]) Karten —) to lay out [illegible] card; *fig.-s.* 5) to leave off [illegible] bits, &c.), to lay aside, to [illegible] to throw off (formality), [illegible] reserve), to leave off; 7) *Mil.* [illegible] discard (workmen, &c.); 8) *a)* [illegible] Abstatten, Ableisten, [illegible] is due); *b)* (Rechnung —) to give an account, proofs, &c.); [illegible] to give an account, to render [illegible] account for ...; *c)* to make [illegible] to make one's confession [illegible] (an oath); *d)* to bear (witness, [illegible] mony); wenn Sie einmal [illegible] werden Sie sie nie wieder — [illegible] once wear glasses, you will never leave them off; *Script.-s.* [illegible] — (*Ephes.* 4, 22), to put off the [illegible] Lügen — (*Ephes.* 4, 25), to put away [illegible] Laster —, to forsake a vice; die [illegible] ihre Maske ab, hypocrisy puts off [illegible] eine Zurückhaltung ab, welche [illegible] Freundschaft verbüßt, cease a [illegible] sive to friendship; nationale [illegible] den gegenseitig abgelegt werden, [illegible] dices will be reciprocally laid aside [illegible] fürchtungen in Bezug darauf [illegible] werden, all fears on that head may be [illegible] Besuche — (*Göthe, unusual for* [illegible]) pay visits; einen Glückwunsch — ([illegible] *for* einen Gl. abstatten), to offer [illegible] tions; reumüthiges Bekenntniß —, [illegible] repentant confession of sin; [illegible] darauf —, I will take my oath [illegible] kann das Zeugniß —, daß ..., I [illegible] or bear witness that ...; [illegible] richtlich Zeugniß — lassen, he [illegible] upon to give evidence (depose) [illegible] law.

II. *intr.* 1) *a)* (of animals) [illegible] young, to calve, to cub, [illegible] Entbunden werden, to be delivered [illegible] *Mar.* to put off (from shore); 2) [illegible] the eyesight, memory, &c., *cf.* [illegible] grow weak, to decline, to fade [illegible]

Ab'legefehler, (*str.*) *m.* *Typ.* [illegible] mitted in distributing the letters [illegible]

Ab'leger, (*str.*) *m.* 1) *a)* [illegible] sprig, scion (slon) (*syn.* [illegible]) *b)* *fig.* branch, offshoot; 2) [illegible] young one, a cub, a pup; 3) a swarm [illegible] bees; —stock, *m.* hive for a swarm [illegible] bees.

Ab'legespahn (—span), (*str.*, [illegible] —späne) *m.* *Typ.* distributing rule [illegible]

* Ablegi'ren, (*w.*) *v. tr.* [illegible] to send off, abroad on some legation [illegible] *times as a kind of punishment*).

Ab'legung, (*w.*) *f.* (the act of) lay[illegible] &c. *see* Ablegen; — der Rechnung [illegible] ing *or* giving up of accounts; — [illegible] nung der Gerichte, [illegible] — des [illegible] des, *Rom. Cath.* profession of [illegible] tering into a religious order; — [illegible] the act of taking an oath, [illegible] (Abgabe) ihrer Stimme ([illegible]) their vote.

A. Ab'lehnen (*from* [illegible]) *v. tr.* to borrow (rather [illegible])

B. Ab'lehnen (*from* [illegible])

lehnen; ablainen still in the seventeenth century, and even later, see Ableinen; Dutch: afleenen), (w.) v. tr. 1) to lean, turn aside; 2) to decline, to shift off, to waive, to refuse, excuse one's self from, to repel; leider muß ich Ihren Vorschlag —, I regret being obliged to decline your proposal; einen Antrag —, Parl. to throw a motion out.

Ab'lehnung, (w.) f. (the act of) declining, &c. refusal.

Ab'lehren, (w.) v. tr. (unusual) lit.: to unteach; to break of or to wean from (a thing).

† **Ab'leiben**, (w.) v. intr. to depart this life, to decease, die; it is used as a transitive: to kill, by Fleming.

† **Ab'leibig**, adj. dead, defunct.

† **Ab'leibung**, (w.) f. decease, death.

Ab'leiern, (w.) v. tr. fig. to drawl out (a speech, an air).

Ab'leihen, (str.) v. tr. (Einem etwas) to borrow (something) from (one).

Ab'leimen, (w.) v. intr. to unglue.

Ab'leinen, (w.) v. tr. 1) † for Ablehnen, II.: er hofft die Strafe von sich abzuleinen (Wieland), he hopes to divert punishment from himself; 2) to take off from the line (as clothes, &c.), to untie.

Ab'leisten, (w.) v. tr. 1) Shoe-m. to take off from the last; 2) to perform or fulfil duly; einen Eid —, to take an oath in due form.

Ab'leitbar, adj. derivable, deducible (von, from).

Ab'leitbarkeit, (w.) f. derivability, deducibleness, (l. u.) deducibility.

Ab'leiten, (w.) v. tr. 1) to turn off or aside, to divert, to lead off, away or aside: Wasser (durch Gräben &c.) —, to drain, to draw off, to run off water; der kürzere Schenkel des Hebers wird in die abzuleitende Flüssigkeit getaucht, the shorter leg of the siphon is immersed in the liquid to be drawn off; den Dampf —, to let the steam escape; Feuchtigkeiten —, Med. to draw off, to revulse humours; vom (rechten) Wege —, to mislead, misguide; seduce; es hat mich vom Hauptzwecke abgeleitet, it has led me aside from the main purpose; 2) to derive: a) Gramm. to trace back, to deduce or draw (a word from its root, &c.); b) to deduce, draw from (in reasoning), to infer (something from what precedes); aus diesen zwei Ursachen leiteten sie alle Krankheiten ab, from these two causes they derived all diseases; eine (Schluß-)Folgerung aus ... —, to draw an inference from ..., to infer a conclusion from ...; abgeleitet (von Vernunftschlüssen), Log. inferential; ein abgeleitetes Wort, a derivative word, derivative; a-de Gefäße, Anat. deferents, antispastics.

Ab'leiter, (str.) m. 1) one who or that which turns off, &c.; 2) conduit-pipe, channel; 3) Phys. conductor, see Leiter, A.

Ab'leitung, (w.) f. 1) (the act of) turning off or aside, &c. cf. Ableiten, diversion (of water from its channel, &c.); drainage; 2) Med. derivation, antispasis; 3) Gramm. derivation, etymology; durch —, Gramm. derivatively; 4) conduit, channel.

Ab'leitungs..., in comp. pertaining to derivation, &c. cf. Ableiten; —canal, m. T. channel for the passage of water, drain, cf. —graben; —gesetz, n. law of derivation; —graben, m. (Abzugsgraben, Ableitungsröhre, Abzugsröhre) T. trench, drain, outfall, ditch, kennel, culvert; —kunst, f. the art of deriving (words from their origin), etymology; —regel, f. rule of derivation; —rinne, f. gutter, drought; —röhre, f. 1) Hydraul. conduit-pipe, waste-pipe, drain; (für schmutzige Flüssigkeit) [illegible]; 2) Gas-w. conduit-pipe; 3) (in steam-engines) eduction-pipe (Abzugsröhre am Schornstein) (für Rauch &c.) funnel; —silbe, f. [illegible] derivational affix, termination (such as ...heit, ...hood; ...ig, ...y; ...lich, ...ly; ...sam, ...some &c. in Kindheit, Wässerig, Göttlich, Wundersam, &c.).

Ab'lenken, (w.) v. I. tr. lit. & fig. to turn off, aside, away, to divert, avert; vom rechten Wege —, to put out of the right way; einen Stoß — (beim Fechten), to parry, ward off (a thrust, blow); lenke nicht seine Aufmerksamkeit ab, do not distract his attention; das Vergnügen hatte keine Macht, ihn von dieser Beschäftigung abzulenken, pleasure had no power to seduce him from this occupation; lasse nicht zeitliche Vortheile dich von der Bahn der Pflicht —, let not temporal advantages sway you from the line of duty; der König wurde durch seine Räthe von der Bahn abgelenkt, welche er zu verfolgen gedachte, the king was swayed by his council from the course he intended to pursue; II. intr. to turn aside, off oder away; to take another direction, to deviate, depart (von, from), to decline; Mar. to sheer or steer off; von der Sache —, to turn, deviate, digress or ramble from the subject.

Ab'lenkung, (w.) f. 1) the act of turning off, &c. cf. Ablenken; diversion; 2) Phys. deviation (of the magnetic needle), cf. Abweichung; die — der öffentlichen Aufmerksamkeit auf andere Gegenstände, the diversion of public attention to other topics; A-sangriff, m. Mil. diversion.

Ab'lernen, (w.) v. tr. (Einem etwas) to learn (something) from (one) by close observation, to imitate (some one) in ..., to take after (one) in ....

Ab'lerschen, see Ablörschen.

Ab'lese, (w.) f. the second shoot of the vine.

Ab'lesen, (str.) v. tr. 1) to pluck off, pick off, to gather (fruits, &c.); Raupen von den Bäumen —, to rid trees, &c. of caterpillars; Steine von einem Felde —, to clear or take away stones from a field, &c.; 2) to gather duly, to finish gathering (the crop of grapes, &c.); man hat abgelesen, the vintage is over; 3) a) to read (something) from a book, &c., to read aloud; b) to read (as opp. to repeating from memory); ich sah wie er alles aus dem Buche ablas, I saw him cribbing (Sprache der Schulknaben) it all out of the book; to read off (eine Scala, a scale, &c.), to call over (ein Namensverzeichniß, a list of names, &c.); 4) to wear out (a book) by much reading, i. e. by much thumbing.

Ab'leser, (str.) m. 1) gatherer, picker, &c. cf. Ablesen; 2) one who reads from a book, &c., reciter.

* **Ablet'te**, (w.) f. (Fr.) Ichth. bleak (Weißfisch, Cyprinus alburnus).

† **Ab'letzen**, (w.) v. I. tr. 1) to bid (one) farewell; sich —, to bid or say farewell, see Verabschieden (sich); II. refl. (scarcely used) to refresh one's self thoroughly.

Ab'leugnen, (w.) v. tr. to deny, disown, disavow, disclaim; er will mir die Schuld —, he wants to deny the debt he owes me.

Ab'leugner, (str.) m. denier, &c.

Ab'leugnung, (w.) f. (the act of) denying, &c. see Ableugnen; A-seid, m. Law, oath of abnegation.

Ab'lichten, (w.) v. tr. 1) to give a lighter shade to (a colour), to make light or clear; 2) to clear (a forest).

Ab'liebeln, (w.) v. I. tr. 1) (Einem etwas) to fondle or coax (one) out of (a thing), to get by caressing; 2) see Ablieben; II. refl. to enfeeble one's self by too much yielding to the passion of love, by too much caressing.

Ab'lieben, (w.) v. I. tr. Sport. to stop (a hound) in the scent, and by fondling make him understand that he is on the right track; II. refl. see Abliebeln, II.

Ab'lieferer, (str.) m. deliverer, &c. cf. Abliefern.

Ab'liefern, (w.) v. tr. to deliver (over, up), to consign; gleich nachdem die Gebinde abgeliefert waren, immediately on the delivery of the casks (cf. Ausliefern, Ausfolgen, Verabfolgen).

Ab'lieferung, (w.) f. delivery; issue (of rations or provisions from a store, &c.); Comm.-s. nach, bei —, on delivery; nach erfolgter —, when delivered; die — der Dividendenscheine, the issue of the dividend warrants (coupons); A-sprämie, f. Comm. prime, premium paid on delivery; A-sschein, m. certificate of delivery; A-stermin m., A-szeit f., A-stage, m. pl. 1) gener. term (time) of delivery; 2) settling-days (certain days fixed for the transfer of public stock).

† **Ab'liegen**, (str.) v. tr. (Luther, &c.) see Ableugnen.

Ab'liegen, (str.) v. I. intr. 1) (aux. sein) to be or lie at a distance; es liegt weit (zwei Meilen &c.) ab, it lies far (two miles, &c.) off; die Mühle lag nicht weit ab, the mill was not far off; weit —, to lie far out of the common road, far out of one's way, to lie in a sequestered spot; weit (von der Sache) a-de Fragen, questions away from the point; ein von der Tugend nicht weit a-der Fehler, an error not very far removed from virtue; 2) (aux. haben) to lie a sufficient length of time for settling, to clear, &c. see Ablagern; abgelegener Wein, settled wine; II. tr. 1) to wear oder rub off by (long) lying; 2) to lie out (a given time); to pay off (a debt, &c.) by lying in prison (cf. Absitzen); III. refl. to be worn out by long lying (of a bedridden person) (cf. sich wund liegen, sich aufliegen); sich (Dat.) etwas (die Haare &c.) —, to wear or rub off (the hair, &c.) by much lying (of horses, dogs, &c.).

Ab'listen, (w.) v. tr. (Einem etwas) to gain oder get (something) from (one) by cunning, artifice, crafty wiles, &c., to trick (one) out of (a thing); durch einen Eid, den wir ihnen durch Gaukelkunst betrüglich abgelistet (Schiller, Picol. III. 1.), by an oath which we had tricked them into by a juggle (Coleridge).

† **Ab'loben**, (w.) v. tr. to bind one's self by a vow to cease from doing a thing, to renounce; das Trinken —, to forswear drinking.

† **Ab'lobung**, (w.) f. solemn promise or vow to discontinue (drinking, gambling, &c.), abjuration; vow of separation or abstinence.

Ab'locken, (w.) v. tr. 1) to entice away, to draw off by coaxing; 2) (Einem etwas) to get (something) from (one) by flattery, by fair words, raillery, &c., to draw out (a secret, or tears, &c.) from (one), to coax or wheedle out of, to extract (cf. Entlocken).

Ab'lockern, (w.) v. tr. 1) to loosen and detach by repeated efforts (as the earth about the roots of a tree, &c.); 2) sometimes used for Ablocken.

Ab'lohen, (w.) v. tr. Tann. to detach the bark from (a tree), to bark.

Ab'lohnen, (w.) v. tr. to pay off, to discharge (seine Arbeiter, one's workmen, &c.); für die gehabte Müh' mich abzulohnen (Schiller, Wall. II. 4), to pay me off for the trouble undergone by me (and so to be rid of any further claim; das remunerate des Coleridge ist viel zu schwach, um den beleidigten Stolz des Max auszudrücken).

Ab'lörschen, (w.) v. tr. Min. to bore or sink (a pit) to a small depth (by way of preliminary examination), opp. Abteufen, Abschachten.

Ab'lös'bar, adj. see Ablöslich.

Ab'löschen, (w.) v. tr. 1) † to extinguish (fire, lights), see Löschen, Auslöschen; 2) T. to cool; to quench, to slacken (lime); to temper (iron, steel); 3) a) to wipe off, to blot out (what has been written with chalk, slate-pencil, &c.); b) fig. to clear off, discharge (a debt), cf. Löschen, Tilgen.

Ab'lösen, (w.) v. I. tr. 1) a) to loosen,

untie, unbind, detach; to unsing; to unlock (Schloss, Typ. die Forme, the form, &c.); alle Coupons waren abgelöst, Comm. all the coupons were detached: b) fig. to detach (a province, &c.); c) fig. to detach, to contrast (shades of colours, &c.), cf. II. refl. 2., & Abheben, &c.); 2) Surg. a) to cut off, to amputate, to sever (ein Glied, a limb); b) to take off in thin lamina or scales, to scale; 3) Med. to resolve; a-e Mittel, resolvents, pectorals; 4) to fire off, to discharge (a gun), see Losschießen; 5) a) Mil. to relieve (a guard); to set (the watch), Mar. to spell (the watch); die Mannschaft in den Laufgräben —, to relieve the trenches; Abgelöst! relieve! b) gener. to relieve, to discharge (from duty, &c.), to take the place of (something else), to replace; ein neues Jahr löste das alte ab, a new year stepped in in the place of the old one; 6) to pay (off), discharge (a debt); to redeem (buy up an annuity, &c.), cf. Auslösen & Einlösen; 7) Law, to commute (penalties, &c.).

II. refl. 1) to grow loose, to come off, to drop off; Surg. &c. to slough or come off (as the scab from a wound); to scale (off); to peel off; sich in Platten —, to flake; 2) Paint. & fig. to detach itself (as a light figure from a dark background), to stand out or forth (in [bold] relief); 3) coll. for the reciprocal form (which see): to relieve one another; a) sie lösten sich (instead of einander) beim Lesen ab, they relieved each other in reading; b) sich (strictly refl.) mit Einem —, to change places with one, to act alternately; III. recipr. (cf. the preceding) einander —: to relieve one another (or each other), to act alternately, to do a thing by turns; beide Chefs lösen einander im Reisegeschäft ab, the two principals travel by turns; IV. sometimes used as an intransitive: to alternate, to come or succeed by turns (cf. Abwechseln).

Ab'löslich, † Ab'lösig, adj. 1) what may be loosened, untied, detached, &c. cf. Ablösen; 2) redeemable (as debts, &c.).

Ab'lösung, (w.) f. 1) (the act of) loosening, untying, &c. cf. Ablösen; 2) Surg. amputation (eines Gliedes, of a limb); 3) a) the peeling, scaling or sloughing off (of skin, &c.); b) scale, slough; 4) a) relief, relieving (of a guard); — durch frische Arbeiter, relays of fresh hands; b) alternation; 5) Law, redemption; commutation (of a penalty, &c.); 6) — einer Schuld, full discharge of a debt; A-s-recht, n. right of redemption.

Ab'löthen, (w.) v. tr. to unsolder.

Ab'lüdern, (w.) v. tr. T. & vulg. to flay, to skin, see Abledern, Abludern.

* Abluen'tien (pr. Abluĕn'tsĭen), (w.) n. pl. (Lat.) Med. abluents, lotions for cleansing sores, abstergents.

Ab'lugen, (w.) v. tr. (N. G.) (Einem etwas) to learn, to discover, &c. (something) by closely watching (a person), see Absehen.

Ab'lügen, (str.) v. tr. 1) to deny by false assertion; 2) (Einem etwas) to obtain (something) from (one) by lying or by asserting untruths.

Ab'lugsen, rarely Ab'luxen, (w.) v. tr. (Einem etwas) 1) (l. u.) to learn, discover (something) from (one) by sly and close attention, see Absehen, 5.; 2) to get (something) from (one) by roguery, by tricking, to cheat or trick (one) out of (a thing).

* Ablui'ren, (w.) v. tr. (Lat. abluere, to wash off or away) Chem. to lave.

Ab'lungern, (w.) v. tr. (Einem etwas) to obtain (something) from (one) by persevering efforts, to trick (one) out of (a thing).

Ab'lüpfen, (w.) v. tr. to lift off, see Abheben.

* Abluti'ren, (w.) v. tr. (Lat.) Chem. to separate from the cement or luting, to unlute. [len).

Ab'mahlen, (w.) v. tr. to mark off (cf. Mal-

Ab'machen, (w.) v. I. tr. 1) lit. to take, bring or get off, loosen, separate, detach; 2) † to make ready, to give the last finish to (a thing), to prepare; 3) coll. (abstract expression for Abbilden) to copy, to take the likeness of (one, &c.) (cf. Nachahmen); 4) a) to do (a thing) in a certain time, to get through with ...; b) to adjust, regulate, settle (an account, a question, &c.), arrange; eine Schuld —, to discharge or clear a debt; ein Geschäft —, to do or clear off, or wind up a business; womit unsere Rechnung bis auf heutigen Tag abgemacht ist, which balances our transactions up to this day, or received payment in full of all demands up to (this) date; ich hatte diesen Punct (diese Frage &c.) bei mir (selbst) abgemacht, I had settled this point (determined this question, &c.) in my own mind; ich habe es bei mir abgemacht, I have made up my mind about it; es kurz —, to cut the matter short, to make it short; abgemacht, pp. Comm. &c. settled, &c.; paid; in order; interj. done! quits! II. used sometimes intransitively: um endlich mit ihm abzumachen, in order to arrange matters (or to come to an understanding) with him; lassen Sie uns nun —, let us now finish the business (or settle the matter, or come to a conclusion), cf. Abschließen (in the abstract phrases Abmachen is frequently synonymous with Abthun).

Ab'machung, (w.) f. (the act of) settling, adjusting, &c.; settlement, adjustment; discharge; termination; die — der Rechnung eilt nicht, the settlement of the account is not pressing; erkundigen Sie sich vor —, inquire before you settle; — des Schadens (beim Seehandel), T. adjustment of the average.

Ab'mägern, (w.) v. intr. (aux. sein) to grow thin or lean, to emaciate, to fall away or off, to abate in one's flesh, to lose flesh, to waste away; — lassen, Falc. to unfatten (a falcon).

Ab'mägerung, (w.) f. emaciation, wasting of the body, Med. atrophy.

Ab'mähen, (w.) v. tr. 1) to mow, mow off, to cut down; 2) (often intr., aux. haben) to finish mowing.

Ab'mahlen, (irr.) v. tr. 1) to grind off; 2) to grind duly or completely, to finish grinding.

Ab'mahnen, (w.) v. tr. 1) to dissuade, to warn (von einer Sache, from a thing), to advise to the contrary; 2) (Einem etwas) to obtain or get by dunning; a-d, p. a. dissuasive, dehortatory.

Ab'mahnung, (w.) f. dissuasion, remonstrance; A-sschreiben, n. dissuasive (or dehortatory) letter.

Ab'majoriren, (w.) v. tr. see Abmehren.

Ab'malen, (w.) v. tr. 1) (Einen oder etwas) to paint, to draw (or take) a likeness of (a person or thing), to portray; nach dem Leben —, to draw (one) from the life; sich — lassen, to sit for one's portrait; 2) fig. a) to paint, draw, delineate, describe, represent, depict; „ich muß die Mama" [dieselbe ist blind] „hierher bringen und ihr die Aussicht —", "I must bring mamma" [a blind person] "here and paint the view for her" (i. e. describe it to her in vivid words); b) Einen —, coll. to depict a person unsparingly, i. e. to expose his bad qualities or actions, vulg. to show one up.

Ab'malzern, (w.) v. tr. coll. for Abmergeln.

Ab'mangeln, (w.) v. tr. 1) to mangle (linen) duly or thoroughly; 2) (often intr.) to finish mangling.

Ab'märgeln, provinc. Ab'marachen, (w.) v. tr. see Abmergeln.

Ab'marken, (w.) v. tr. to mark out the boundaries of ..., to mark off or out (eine Flur, a field, &c.).

Ab'markten, (w.) v. tr. 1) to beat down from (the price), to effect an abatement in ..., to deduct (cf. Abfeilschen, Abdingen, Abhan-

deln); 2) gener. &c. an [illegible] to bargain (one) out of (a [illegible] (one) to bargain for [illegible]

Ab'markung, (w.) f. (the act of [illegible] off the boundaries (of a field [illegible] marks.

Ab'marsch, (str., pl. Ab'märsche) [illegible] act of) marching off, march, d[illegible] dem Lager) decampment; [illegible] trommeln, to strike up the march.

Ab'marschiren, (w.) v. intr. [illegible] particul. Mil. to march off, to march, part, decamp; Marsch für Marsch [illegible]

Ab'martern, (w.) v. tr. 1) [illegible] torture exceedingly, to [illegible] plague, vex, worry extremely [illegible] life, out of patience, &c.); 2) [illegible] to torture (one) out of (a thing [illegible] (something) from (one).

Ab'marterung, (w.) f. (the act [illegible] ing to excess, excessive torturing [illegible] ment, excruciation.

Ab'maß, (str.) n. the measure [illegible] a thing, measure or dimensions of [illegible]

Ab'matten, (w.) v. I. tr. 1) to [illegible] tire out, to wear (out), weary, [illegible] tigue; to jade (a horse) [illegible] heit geschwächt, weakened by [illegible] von der Arbeit ganz abgemattet, [illegible] with labour, entirely knocked up [illegible] dull (metals), to dim or tarnish [illegible] [gold, silver, &c.] a pale or dim [illegible] either polish or burnish), cf. [illegible] Mattiren; II. refl. to exhaust [illegible] one's self; to be exhausted, worn out [illegible]

Ab'mattung, (w.) f. 1) (the act of [illegible] reasing, tiring or wearing out, [illegible] tion, debilitation; 2) (state of being [illegible] out, exhaustion, &c., weakness, [illegible] fatigue.

Ab'mauern, (w.) v. tr. (lit. to w[illegible] to separate by walling round or by a [illegible]

Ab'mauern, (w.) v. tr. to recite, sing [illegible] deliver, &c. in a bleating voice.

Ab'mehren, (w.) v. tr. (used in [illegible] land) 1) to reject by a majority of [illegible] (Ermehren); 2) (sometimes for [illegible] Majorisiren) to outvote.

† Ab'meien, (w.) v. tr. see [illegible]

Ab'meiern, (w.) v. tr. 1) to turn [illegible] &c.) out of a farm, to expel, eject; [illegible] to settle or finish one's business; ich [illegible] meiert, my business is settled, I am [illegible]

Ab'meischen, (w.) v. tr. Brew. [illegible] mash duly or sufficiently; 2) (often [illegible] finish or to have done mashing.

Ab'meißeln, (w.) v. tr. 1) to chisel [illegible] take off or to smooth with a chisel [illegible] chisel out; 2) Hunt. to take off (the [illegible] the skin.

Ab'melden, (w.) v. tr. to countermand [illegible] give (due) information or notice of [illegible] change or alteration (cf. [illegible] vious engagement, &c.; einen [illegible] notice that an intended visit cannot [illegible] einen Dienstboten (bei der Polizei) — [illegible] (due) information (to the police) of [illegible] missal of a servant, to notify (to [illegible] that a servant is no longer engaged [illegible] melden).

Ab'meldezettel, (str.) m. paper [illegible] written) notice is given of a servant [illegible] &c., written notice of the discontinu[illegible] an engagement, &c.

Ab'meldung, (w.) f. (the act of) [illegible] manding, &c. cf. Abmelden; [illegible] mation of some intended [illegible]

Ab'melken, (w.) v. tr. 1) to [illegible] milking, to milk; 2) (often [illegible] or to have done milking.

Ab'mengeln, (w.) v. tr. [illegible] squeeze excessively; 2) to [illegible] emaciate, harass (to death): to exhaust, debilitate.

Ab'merken, *(w.)* v. I. *tr.* mit Kreide —, to mark off *or* out, to trace with chalk: II. *intr.* (Einem etwas) to learn *or* gather by observing, to mark and learn; to mark, observe, remark, perceive, discover (something) in (one): sie sucht ihm abzumerken was er wünscht, she seeks to anticipate his wishes (*cf.* Absehen).

Ab'meßbar, *adj.* capable of being measured off &c., commensurable.

Ab'meßbarkeit, *(w.) f.* commensurability.

Ab'messen, *(str.)* v. I. *tr.* 1) *a)* to measure off; *b) T.* to take the gauge of, to gauge; nach der Schnur —, to lay out, to trace by a line (*cf.* Abschnüren); *Glas.* to range; mit der Wasserwage —, to take the level of, to level (Nivelliren); to compass (Abzirkeln), to survey (a field); den Zapfen auf das Loch —, *Carp.* to countergage: 2) to measure off (dry-goods, &c.), to cut off; *fig.-s.* 3) *T.* to divide into feet, to measure, to scan (einen Vers, a verse, *see* Scandiren); 4) *a)* to adjust, to regulate, to proportion, to suit (nach, to), to square (our actions by the opinions of others, &c.); *b)* to compare, to judge; er mißt Andere nach sich ab, he judges of others from himself; er maß seine Ausdrücke nicht ab, he did not measure his terms; er maß seine Worte sehr sorgfältig ab, he expressed himself very guardedly; sonst pflegt er seine Worte besser abzumessen, in general he is in the habit of weighing his words more carefully.

Ab'messen, *s. (str.) n.* (the act of) measuring off, &c. *see* Abmessung; das — der Zapfenlöcher, *Carp.* countergage.

Ab'messer, *(str.) m.* measurer, surveyor.

Ab'messung, *(w.) f.* 1) (the act of) measuring off, &c. *cf.* Abmessen, survey; 2) admeasurement, mensuration; 3) dimension: der Raum hat drei A-en *(Kant)*, space has three dimensions; 4) (the act of) scanning *or* measuring verses *or* words, scansion; 5) a proportioning, adjustment.

Ab'metzeln, *(w.)* v. *tr.* to cut off; to cut down.

Ab'metzen, *(w.)* v. *tr. Mill.* to take a peck of grain from ... as payment, to take the multure (*i. e.* the fee for grinding) from.

Ab'miethen, *(w.)* v. *tr.* (Einem etwas) to hire, rent (a room, &c.) from (one); to take in hire, to farm.

Ab'miether *(str.) m.*, **Ab'mietherin,** *(w.) f.* hirer, lessee, tenant.

Ab'miethung, *(w.) f.* (the act of) hiring, renting, &c. *cf.* Abmiethung; hire.

Ab'mildern *(Göthe [l. u.]:* Ab'mildern), *(w.)* v. *tr.* to mitigate, moderate, to soften, soothe; to extenuate, modify.

Ab'milderung, *(w.) f.* moderation, &c. *cf.* Abmildern.

Ab'mindern, *(w.)* v. *tr.* to lessen, to diminish; to abate, to yield some abatement from ....

Ab'minderung, *(w.) f.* (the act of) lessening, &c., diminution, abatement, deduction, reduction.

Ab'misten, *(w.)* v. *tr.* to take off *or* remove dung from ...., to cleanse of dung *or* manure (the cattle, &c., *or* a farmyard, &c.; *in the latter application* Ausmisten *is nearly synonymous).*

Ab'modeln, *(w.)* v. *tr.* to model *or* form according to a plan *or* prototype, to imitate *or* copy in forming.

Ab'moosen, Ab'mosen, *(w.)* v. *tr.* to clear of (*or* to free from) moss.

Ab'mucken, *(w.)* v. *tr. coll.* to fit (one), to give (one) a set-down, to give (one) tit for tat, to punish soundly; ich will ihn tüchtig —, I'll trounce him.

Ab'müden, *(w.)* v. *tr.* to tire *or* weary (*refl.* one's self) out; vollständig abgemüdet, fairly tired out.

Ab'müdung, *(w.) f.* the (act of) tiring out, &c.

Ab'mühen, *(w.)* v. *refl.* to fatigue, to exert, to strain one's self, to moil, to trouble one's self; sie mühten sich ab, einen neuen Weg zu finden, they strained every nerve, they beat about to discover a new path; sie mühten sich mit dieser schwierigen Frage ab, they grappled with the difficulties of this question.

Ab'müßigen, *(w.)* v. *tr.* 1) *a)* to cause (one) to take leisure for a short time, to draw (off) from labour: to detain from occupation, to disturb; *b)* to spare (time) from business; ich darf ihn nicht von der Arbeit — (abziehen), I must not withdraw *or* take him from his labour; wenn Ihr noch einen Augenblick von Euern Geschäften — könnt *(Tieck)*, if you can snatch another moment from your business: *gener. refl.* sich *(Acc.)* —, to find time *or* leisure; sich *(Dat.)* die nöthige Zeit —, to spare the needful time; sich *(Acc.)* von einer Sache (Arbeit &c.) —, to withdraw (for a time) from a thing (occupation, &c.), to spare the time from (labour, &c.): ich kann mich keinen Augenblick —, I cannot spare a moment's time; kannst du dich nicht einen Augenblick von deiner Beschäftigung &c. —? cannot you spare or snatch a moment's time from your occupation (engagement, &c.)? wenn ich mich — kann, if I can find leisure, if my engagements (business, &c.) will permit me; 2) *a) in Law style used for* Abnöthigen, Abdringen, to exact (something) from (one); Einem eine Erklärung —, to oblige one to make a declaration *or* statement; *b) in the same sense, but applied ironically or ludicrously:* ich könnte ihr die Börse ganz ohne Gefahr — *(Platen)*, I could without any danger ease her of her purse.

Ab'müßigung, *(w.) f.* 1) (the act of) causing to take leisure, &c. *cf.* Abmüßigen; 2) enforced leisure (*cf.* Abhaltung).

Ab'mutzen, *(w.)* v. *tr. coll.* to mutilate, truncate, to reduce (wear down) to a stump *or* stub, to crop, lop (off).

Ab'nägeln, *(w.)* v. *tr.* 1) *Ship-b.* to drive the tree-nails into the sides *or* bottom of (a ship); 2) to unnail, to remove *or* take off (away) by drawing out the nail *or* nails.

Ab'nagen, *(w.)* v. *tr.* 1) to gnaw off, to nibble, to pick (a bone); der Hund nagt das Fleisch vom Knochen ab, the dog gnaws the flesh from (off) the bone; 2) *fig.* to gnaw, fret, consume, to wear out *or* away; to torment; der Kummer nagt ihm das Herz ab, sorrow preys upon his heart, his heart is consumed with grief.

Ab'nagung, *(w.) f.* the (act of) gnawing off, &c. *cf.* Abnagen; abrasion, erosion.

Ab'nähen, *(w.)* v. I. *tr.* 1) *a)* to sew duly, thoroughly, to quilt; *b)* to sew round, to partition *or* mark off by sewing; 2) to pay (a debt) by sewing *or* doing needle-work; II. *intr.* (*aux.* haben) to finish *or* have done sewing.

Ab'näher, *(str.) m. Tail.* a seam *or* fold drawn in in sewing.

Ab'nahme, *(w.) f.* 1) the (act of) taking off, away, &c. *cf.* Abnehmen; die — eines Gliedes, *Surg.* the cutting off of a limb, amputation; die — (Christi) vom Kreuze, *Paint.* the descent *or* deposition from the cross; 2) the taking *or* receiving (an account, &c.); (*officially*) audit; — eines Eides, taking an (*i. e.* a person's) oath; 3) diminution, decline, decrease, falling off; der Gebrauch ist in —, the custom goes out of fashion (*cf.* Abgang, 6, *b.*): wane, waste; sinking, decay; seine Augen, sein Gedächtniß erleiden große —, his eye-sight, his memory begin to be greatly impaired; mein Gesicht erleidet —, my eye-sight begins to fail; impairing (of the intrinsic value); abatement; in — gerathen, to fall into decay, to decay: — des Mondes, wane, decrease of the moon; — der Gewässer, the subsiding *or* ebb of the waters; ohne —, undecaying; 4) *T. (Herald., Mus., Astr., &c.)* cadence, decrement; 5) sale, *cf.* Abgang, 3., Absatz, 3., *and* Abnehmer, 1.

Ab'narben, *(w.)* v. *tr.* 1) *Tann.* to cut off the grain of (skins), to grain (skins); 2) *Agric.* to cut, take *or* reap (off), *cf.* Abmähen.

Ab'narren, *(w.)* v. *tr.* (Einem etwas) to fool *or* trick (one) out of (a thing), to obtain (a thing) from (one) by foolery, pranks *or* tricks.

Ab'naschen, *(w.)* v. *tr.* to remove *or* take clandestinely and eat a portion of dainties, sweetmeats, &c., to steal dainties from ...: er naschte den Zucker vom Kuchen ab, he secretly nibbled off the sugar from the cake.

Ab'necken, *(w.)* v. *tr.* (Einem etwas) to tease (one) out of (a thing).

* **Abnegation',** *(w.) f. (Lat. abnegatio)* entire denial, refusal, renunciation.

* **Abnegi'ren,** *(w.)* v. *tr. (Lat. abnegare)* to deny, refuse, renounce altogether.

Ab'nehmen, *(str.)* v. I. *tr.* 1) to take off, away, down: *a)* die Flagge —, *Mar.* to haul down (*or* strike) the colours; den Hut (die Mütze &c.) —, to take off one's hat (cap, &c.); den Hut vor Einem —, to uncover to (*gen.* to bow to) one; die Maske —, to take *or* pull off the mask, to unmask; dem Falken die Kappe —, to unhood a falcon, to strike the hood; von einem Fasse die Reifen —, to unhoop a cask; die Ziegel von einem Dache —, to take off the tiles from *or* to untile a roof; Obst —, to gather or pluck fruit; ein Schloß —, to take off (to unnail, unscrew) a lock; die (gedruckten) Bogen —, *Print.* to take down the sheets; die (Gieß-)Formen —, *Found.* to lift (out) the forms; das Fett von der Brühe — (Abschöpfen), to take off the fat, to skim the broth; den Rahm von der Milch —, to take off the cream from the milk, to cream *or* to skim the milk of its cream; die Ruderpinne —, *Naut.* to unship the tiller; das Bonnet —, *Naut.* to unlace the bonnet (of a sail); die Sohlen von einem Stiefel —, to unsole a boot; die Speisen, das Tischtuch —, to serve off the meats (from a table), to clear the table, to take away, *see* Abräumen; den Verband —, to take off the dressings; einem Pferde das (*or pl.* die) Hufeisen —, to take off the shoe(s) of a horse, to unshoe a horse; einem Pferde den Sattel —, to unsaddle a horse; den Stieren das Joch —, to unyoke the steers; Einem eine Last —, to take a burden from one; die Hunde —, *Sport.* to call off the dogs (from a wrong scent); ein Kalb —, to wean a calf; die Karten —, *Gam.* to cut the cards (Abheben); *b)* ein Glied —, *Surg.* to take *or* cut off, to amputate a limb; Einem den Bart —, to shave one's beard; den Schafen die Wolle —, to shear, to fleece the sheep; die Kruste —, *Tin.* to take off the crust; den Bart (das Rauhe, Ungleiche) —, *T.* to clip uneven edges, the burr, &c.; to take off the edges; die Gießnaht —, *Found.* to take off the seam; (die Maschen) —, *(in knitting)* to narrow, to lessen the width of a stocking *or* other piece of knitting by taking two meshes into one (*opp.* Zugeben); ein Kleid —, to shorten (to make shorter) a dress *or* gown.

Fig.-s. 2) (Einem etwas) *a)* to deprive (one) of (a thing), to take (it) from (him): die Festung wurde den Franzosen durch Sturm abgenommen, the fortress was taken by storm from the French; Einem (sein) Geld —, to gain *or* win a person's money (of gamblers, &c.); Einem sein Amt —, to remove one from his office *or* employment; *b)* to take off one's hands, to purchase, buy; ich möchte ihm gern die ganze Partie —, I would willingly buy the whole parcel (lot) of him; *c)* to relieve (one) of (a thing); ich möchte dir gern die Mühe —, I would willingly take the trouble off your hands; 3) (Einem etwas) to take, receive (one's account, &c.); das Gedinge —, see Gedinge; Einem den Eid —, to take one's oath, to administer an oath to one; to bind by an oath; ich muß dir das Versprechen —, mir nicht von der Seite zu gehen, I must make you (or I must take or have your) promise not to stir from my side; 4) (ein Bild 2c.) a) to transfer (a fresco painting &c. in order to preserve it from decay); b) to take, draw or paint (a likeness): sich — lassen, to have one's likeness taken, to sit for one's picture; er ließ sich photographisch —, he had his photograph taken; 5) etwas aus (more rarely von, an, † bei) einer Sache 2c. — (cf. Entnehmen), to gather (one's opinion, &c.) from (a thing, &c.); to judge from, conclude, conjecture, guess; so viel ich — kann, for aught I perceive; dies ist leicht abzunehmen, this is very plain; hast du das von dir selbst abgenommen? have you drawn this inference from your own case? have you concluded this from your own experience? was sollen wir daraus —? what inference shall we draw from it? die Lehre, welche man sich daraus — muß, ist ..., the lesson to be drawn from it is ...; wie wichtig dieser Handelszweig ist, kann man daraus —, daß ..., the importance of this branch of trade may be estimated from the fact, that ....

II. intr. 1) (opp. Zunehmen) to diminish (an (with Dat.) Größe, Länge, Gewicht 2c., in size, length, &c.), to decrease (in weight, length, wealth, prosperity, &c.); to grow less; to abate; to fall away, decline; to decay, to wane; to waste, to wear away (off, out); der Tag nimmt ab, the day wanes or is on the decline; die Tage nehmen ab, the days decrease in length, grow shorter, begin to decline; der Mond nimmt ab, the moon wanes (cf. Abnehmen, v. s. & Abnehmend, p. a.); an Gewicht —, to decrease or to lose in the weight; die Höhe der Ströme nimmt ab, the level of streams (rivers) is on the decline, the streams subside; an Helligkeit —, to diminish or to be reduced in brightness; an Stärke —, to abate or to lose in intensity; die Nachfrage nimmt eher ab, als zu, the demand is rather on the decrease than on the increase; die Hitze, das Fieber nimmt ab, the heat, the fever abates; die Jugendkraft nimmt (im Alter) ab, the vigour of youth declines (in age); seine (Lebens-) Kräfte nehmen sichtlich ab, his strength visibly declines, his vital powers are (or he is) sinking fast, he is visibly (rapidly) sinking; mein Gesicht nimmt ab, my eye-sight begins to fail (cf. Ablegen); sein Gedächtniß nimmt vom Alter ab, his memory is impaired with age; 2) to unwind cat's cradles (a children's play), cf. Abheben, I. 5.

Ab'nehmen, v. s. (str.) n. 1) the (act of) taking off, &c. cf. Abnehmen, v. & Abnahme; 2) diminution, decrease, &c. cf. Abnahme; das — des Mondes, the decrease or wane of the moon; im — sein, to become or grow less, to decrease, &c. see Abnehmen, v. intr.; to be on the decline; der Mond ist im —, the moon is waning, the moon is on the wane; die Preise sind im —, (the) prices are getting low.

Ab'nehmend, p. a. 1) declining, &c. cf. Abnehmen, v.; (m. K.:) decrescent; 2) Mus. gradually diminishing (in tone and quickness), (Ital.) decrescendo, calando; die a-e Flut, neap tide; a-e Gesundheit, Kräfte 2c., declining, sinking health, strength, &c.; eine a-e Kühlte, Mar. a fainting gale; der a-e Mond, the waning (decrescent) moon; bei a-em Monde, at the fall (wane) of the moon; der Mond ist im a-en Viertel, the moon is on the wane.

Ab'nehmer, (str.) m. 1) one who takes off, &c. cf. Abnehmen; particul. buyer, purchaser; die Häuser in dieser Straße finden sehr bald —, houses are caught up very quickly in this lane; consumer, customer; diese Zeitung hat viele —, this newspaper has many subscribers; 2) T. doffer (of a carding-machine); doffing-cylinder, fillet (Tech.).

† Ab'nehmig, † Ab'nehmlich, adj. decreasing; declining; sinking.

Ab'nehmsel, (str.) n. siftings (of grain).

Ab'nehmung, (w.) f. (l. u.) 1) the (act of) taking off, &c. cf. Abnehmen, v., v. s. & Abnahme; 2) † slaughtering, killing (of animals, victims, &c.).

Ab'neigen, (w.) v. I. tr. 1) a) orig. lit. to incline, decline, bend downwards; b) to avert, to turn away or aside; 2) Math. &c. to diverge, to render averse; II. refl. 1) to incline, slope; 2) to turn aside from.

Ab'neigung, (w.) f. 1) lit. (l. u.) the (act of) turning aside, &c., declination, deviation from a certain line (horizontal, perpendicular, &c.), Math. divergence; slope (of a hill); 2) fig. (gener. followed by gegen before the object; sometimes it admits vor (with Dat.)) disinclination (to), (starke) aversion (to, nur ausnahmsweise from), averseness, dislike; distaste, disrelish, disgust, (natürliche —) antipathy (to, against), cf. Abgeneigtheit.

Ab'nicken, (w.) v. tr. Sport. to kill (a stag) by cutting the neck, see Abgenicken.

Ab'nieseln, (w.) v. tr. Min. to wear out, to blunt (the working tools).

Ab'nießen, (w.) v. tr. Law. to consume by having the use or usufruct of an estate, &c.

Ab'nieten, (w.) v. tr. T. to unrivet, to unclinch. [liquor, &c. cf. Nippen.

Ab'nippen, (w.) v. tr. to sip, to taste of a

* Abnorm', adj. (Lat.) abnormal, irregular; unsere Marktpreise sind völlig —, our market-prices are quite exceptional.

* Abnormität', (w.) f. abnormity; irregularity; sometimes deformity.

Ab'nöthigen, (w.) v. tr. 1) (u. u.) a) to harass or plague to excess, see Abquälen; b) refl. see sich Abmühen; 2) (Einem etwas) to exact (something) from (one), force (out) from, to extort, to wring from; to elicit; man nöthigte ihm eine Entschuldigung ab, they obliged him to make an apology; ihre Hochherzigkeit nöthigt uns Bewunderung ab, their magnanimity commands our admiration.

Ab'nutscheln, Ab'nutschen, v. tr. to take away, to deprive of or to exhaust by (frequent) sucking; to suck the juice from (a sweetmeat).

Ab'nutzen, Ab'nützen, (w.) v. I. tr. 1) to use (up); to waste, wear out, off, away (cf. Abgenutzt); 2) Law, see Abnießen; II. refl. to wear out by long usage, &c.

Ab'nutzung, (w.) f. 1) the (act of) wearing out, wasting, &c., cf. Abnutzen; wear and tear; 2) Law, usufruct.

Ab'öden, (w.) v. tr. to lay waste, to cut down (einen Wald, a forest).

Ab'ödung, (w.) f. the (act of) laying waste, cutting down (eines Waldes, a forest).

Ab'ohrfeigen, (w.) v. tr. (Einen) to box (one's) ears soundly or well.

Ab'ölen, (w.) v. tr. 1) to unoil, to free or cleanse from oil; 2) to oil thoroughly or duly.

* Aboli'ren, (w.) v. tr. (Lat. abolere, to check the growth of, to destroy) (l. u.) to abolish.

* Abolition', (w.) f. (l. u.) abolition; abrogation, annulment (von Gesetzen, of laws).

* Abolitionist', (w.) m. (from the E. word) abolitionist.

* Abolitions'brief, (str.) m. letter or mandate of abolition or amnesty, act of indemnity.

* Abonnement' [pr. —mang'], (str., pl. A-s) n. (Fr.) subscription (with auf & Acc.); das — auf diesen Platz kostet einen Thaler or im — kostet dieser Platz einen Thaler, the subscription-price for this place is one [illegible] (w.) f. subscription-[illegible] of subscribers.

* Abonnent', (w.) m. [illegible]

* Abonni'ren, (w.) v. refl. [illegible] or haben) to subscribe (auf [illegible] to subscribe or to become a [illegible] (a newspaper, work, &c.), to [illegible]

Ab'ordnen, (w.) v. tr. 1) to [illegible] gate, to send; to constitute, [illegible] Abgeordnet; einen andern an [illegible] to appoint another in one's place, [illegible] legate; 2) (rarely used) to [illegible] Abbestellen.

Ab'ordner, (str.) m. constituent.

Ab'ordnung, (w.) f. 1) † [illegible] the usual order, irregularity; [illegible] delegation.

Ab'orgeln, (w.) v. tr. coll. 1) to [illegible] the organ; 2) to recite or deliver [illegible] but monotonous voice, to drawl out [illegible]

Ab'ort, (str., pl. Ab'örter) m. 1) [illegible] spot, remote or out-of-the-way place; [illegible] cessary, privy.

* Abort', (str.) m. (Lat.) abortion, [illegible] ture delivery, miscarriage ([illegible]

Ab'örtern, (w.) v. tr. 1) [illegible] to saw off (a planed piece of wood) [illegible] angles; b) to saw in proper length [illegible] length, to match; 2) to [illegible] on, see Abbestellen.

* Aborti'ren, (w.) v. intr. ([illegible] to bring forth before the time, [illegible] to have an abortion ([illegible] geburt thun); 2) Bot. to develop [illegible] imperfectly, (of flowers) to fall [illegible] ducing fruit.

* Abortiv', adj. abortive, [illegible] procuring abortion ([illegible] —heilmethode, (w.) f. Med. method [illegible] cal treatment by which diseases are [illegible] acted in their very origin; —mittel, [illegible] Med. abortive remedy or medicine, [illegible]

* Abor'tus, m. (Lat.) see Abort.

Ab'paaren, (w.) v. tr. to range in [illegible] to pair; refl. to pair off (of [illegible] posite parties), to agree not to vote [illegible] leave the room in couples.

Ab'pachten, (w.) v. tr. ([illegible] rent or farm (something) from [illegible] tete dem Eigenthümer sein Gut [illegible] ab, he rented the owner's estate [illegible]

Ab'pachter, (str.) m. one who [illegible] estate, a mill, &c. from one, [illegible] (of a farm).

Ab'packen, (w.) v. tr. (sometimes [illegible] haben)) 1) (Packete, Kisten 2c. von [illegible] gen 2c.) to take off or remove ([illegible] &c. from a waggon, &c.); to unpack [illegible] (cf. Abladen); 2) to unload [illegible] burden, &c.), to disburden.

Ab'packer, (str.) m. one who [illegible] packages, &c. cf. Abpacken, unpacker [illegible] Ablader.

Ab'päheln, (w.) v. tr. [illegible]

Ab'pariren, (w.) v. tr. to ward [illegible] or thrust in fencing), cf. Pariren.

Ab'paschen, (w.) v. I. tr. to [illegible] of, overcome, surpass or beat [illegible] in dicing; II. intr. (aux. sein) out [illegible] or away.

Ab'passen, (w.) v. tr. 1) [illegible] to measure off with compasses, [illegible] square, to proportion; 2) fig. to [illegible] watch, stay for; Einem — (cf. [illegible] lauern), to lie in wait or to [illegible] order to seize him or to find him [illegible] er paßte die Gelegenheit ab, he [illegible] opportunity; etwas übel —, to [illegible] one's time ill; sie hätten es [illegible] nen, they could not have [illegible] a better (or more fit) opp[illegible] abgepaßt habe, wo es in Rom hinaus will (*Göthe*), having already ascertained what they are about at Rome (*see* Abwarten).

Ab'patrouilliren, (*w.*) *v. tr.* (einen Strich, eine Gegend, die Straßen) to send patrols over (a tract of country, &c.) *or* through (the streets, &c.) in order to obtain intelligence, &c.

Ab'pauken, (*w.*) *v. tr.* 1) to announce with the kettledrum: 2) *fig. & fam.* to thrash soundly (*cf.* Abprügeln).

Ab'peinigen, (*w.*) *v. tr.* 1) to excruciate (*cf.* Abquälen); 2) (Einem etwas) to extort (something) from (one) by torments.

Ab'peitschen, (*w.*) *v. tr.* 1) to whip off (as a leaf, &c. with the whip); 2) to lash, scourge, whip soundly; 3) *T.* Seidengehäuse —, to undo cocoons with a whipping motion.

Ab'pellen, (*w.*) *v. tr.* to strip of the skin, &c., (gekochte Kartoffeln) to peel (potatoes, *see* Schälen).

Ab'pelzen, (*w.*) *v. tr.* 1) *Skin-dr.* to beat (skins) (*syn.* Abbaumsen); 2) *coll.* to thrash (one) soundly.

Ab'perlen, (*w.*) *v. tr.* to unstring (like pearls).

Ab'pfählen, (*w.*) *v. tr.* to pale off, to pale, inclose with pales, to palisade; to mark out with poles (*cf.* Abstecken), *Min. see* (einen Punkt) Abgeben

Ab'pfählung, (*w.*) *f.* 1) *a)* the (act of) paling, &c.; 2) palisade, empalement.

Ab'pfänden, (*w.*) *v. tr.* (Einem etwas) to take (something) from (one) as a pledge *or* pawn, to seize (something) from (one) by law, to distrain; sie haben ihm das Pferd Schulden halber abgepfändet, they seized (distrained) his horse for debt.

Ab'pfändung, (*w.*) *f.* (einer Sache [*Gen.*]) the (act of) taking (something) from one as a pledge, &c.; distraining, seizure.

Ab'pfarren, (*w.*) *v. tr.* to separate (eine Gemeinde, a community) from one parish, in order to attach it to another.

Ab'pfeifen, (*str.*) *v. tr.* 1) to whistle (off) (a song, a tune); 2) *Mar.* to pipe off (the crew).

Ab'pfetzen, (*w.*) *v. tr.* to tear off.

Ab'pflastern, (*w.*) *v. tr.* to provide *or* cover with pavement, to pave duly.

Ab'pflöcken, **Ab'pflocken**, (*w.*) *v. tr.* 1) to mark off *or* out with pegs, to stake out (a railway-line, &c.); 2) *Bleach.* to take (linen, &c.) from the pegs, to unfasten from the pickets.

Ab'pflücken, (*w.*) *v. tr.* to pluck off, gather (Obst, fruit), to crop: ein Huhn &c. — (*see* Rupfen), to pluck a chicken, &c.

Ab'pflückung, (*w.*) *f.* the (act of) plucking off, &c. *cf.* Abpflücken.

Ab'pflügen, (*w.*) *v.* I. *tr.* 1) *a)* to plough off, to take off *or* separate by ploughing (*cf.* Abackern); *b)* to mark by ploughing; 2) to pay (a debt) by ploughing; 3) (*often intr.*) to finish ploughing (a field); II. *refl.* to tire one's self out by ploughing.

Ab'picken, (*w.*) *v. tr.* 1) to peck off (the berries, as a bird), to snatch off *or* away by pecking; 2) *Min.* to take off with the pick-axe.

Ab'pinnen, (*w.*) *v. tr. see* Abfinnen.

Ab'placken, (*w.*) *v. tr. & refl.* to weary (one's self) out, &c. to jade, harass, to worry to death; *refl.* to drudge, to toil hard, to toil and moil; ich habe mich nun hier seit vier Jahren von früh bis abends abgeplackt, I have been slaving here these four years from morning till night.

Ab'plagen, (*w.*) *v.* I. *tr.* 1) to tire *or* weary out, to plague, tease, fatigue, &c.; die Kinder plagen ihn ab, the children plague his life out of him; 2) (Einem etwas) to extort (something) from (one), to get by importunate solicitations; abgeplagt, *p. a.* tired out, exhausted, weary, jaded; II. *refl.* to tire *or* weary one's self out, to exhaust one's self; sich mit einem (schwerverständlichen &c.) Buche —, to puzzle over a book.

Ab'plaggen, (*w.*) *v. tr.* (*in Westphalia, &c.*) to remove the turf from (heathy ground); to level (a meadow, &c.) by cutting off the turfy hillocks.

Ab'planschen, (*w.*) *v. tr. see* Abflatschen.

Ab'plärren, (*w.*) *v. coll.* I. *tr.* to utter in a bellowing, braying, bleating, &c. voice, to bawl out; II. *refl.* to tire one's self with bellowing, bawling, &c.

Ab'platten, (*w.*) *v.* I. *tr.* (*also* Ab'plätten) to flatten down *or* out, to flatten, laminate (as metal under the rolling-press), to level; II. *refl.* to flatten down, to grow flat.

Ab'plätten, (*w.*) *v. tr.* 1) to smooth down (linen, &c.) with an iron, to iron duly; 2) *see* Abplatten; 3) (*often intr.*) to finish *or* have done ironing.

Ab'plattung, **Ab'plättung**, (*w.*) *f.* 1) the (act of) flattening down, &c. *see* Abplatten; 2) die — der Erde, *Phys.* the flattened, depressed *or* oblate form of the earth.

Ab'platzen, (*w.*) *v. intr.* (*aux.* sein) to crack off: 1) to explode with a crack; 2) to burst off (*cf.* Losplatzen); seine Rockknöpfe platzten mit Gewalt ab, his coat-buttons spirted violently off.

Ab'plätzen, (*w.*) *v. tr.* 1) to make to crack off, to rebound; 2) *T.* to temper (steel, &c. *cf.* Ablöschen); 3) *a)* *Forest.* to mark (trees) that are to be felled, to blaze, *cf.* Ablaschen, Anschlagen; *b)* (*often intr.*) to buy (standing wood); to strike a final bargain in purchasing timber.

Ab'plaudern, (*w.*) *v. tr. see* Abschwatzen.

Ab'plündern, (*w.*) *v. tr.* 1) to plunder *or* rob thoroughly; 2) (Einem etwas) to plunder, rob (one) of (a thing); 3) *Uphol.* to take off the covers, &c. of (chairs, &c.).

Ab'pochen, (*w.*) *v. tr.* 1) to knock off; 2) *T.* to beat flat, to stretch, &c. *cf.* Abtreiben; 3) *coll.* to rap *or* knock about, to beat soundly; 4) *vulg.* (Einem etwas) to gain (money, &c.) from (one) by rapping (alluding to a certain game, das Poch-Spiel *which see*); 5) (Einem etwas) to wring *or* force (something) from (one), to bully (one) out of (a thing).

Ab'pölen, (*w.*) *v. tr. Tann. see* Abhaaren.

Ab'posaunen, (*w.*) *v. tr.* 1) to perform on the trombone; 2) *coll.* to announce with a full or thick voice, to trumpet forth (*cf.* Ausposaunen).

Ab'posten, (*w.*) *v. tr. Forest.* 1) to mark or blaze (trees) that are to be felled (*cf.* Abplätzen &c.); 2) to separate (timber which is to be sold) into lots *or* parcels.

Ab'prägen, (*w.*) *v. tr.* 1) to strike off, to reproduce *or* transfer by coining *or* stamping, to impress; das auf (*or* in) den (*or* in dem) Thon abgeprägte Bildniß, the image impressed on the clay; 2) *fig.* to imitate, represent, to give a (faithful) impression *or* image of...; 3) (*often intr., aux.* haben) to finish coining *or* stamping.

Ab'prägung, (*w.*) *f.* the (act of) striking off, reproducing by coinage or stamping, &c.

Ab'prall, (*str.*) *m.* the (act of) flying off, rebound (*opp.* Anprall).

Ab'prallen, (*w.*) *v. intr.* (*aux.* sein) to fly, spring *or* start off *or* back, to glance off, to rebound, recoil; (of sounds) to reverberate; a-d, *p. a.* rebounding, resilient.

Ab'prallen, *v. s.* (*str.*) *n.*, **Ab'prallung**, (*w.*) *f.* the (act of) flying off, &c.; rebounding, rebound; resiliency; reverberation; das — *or* die Abprallung der Lichtstrahlen, *Phys.* the reflection of rays of light; Abprallungswinkel, *m. Phys.* angle of reflection.

Ab'prasseln, (*w.*) *v. intr.* 1) to leave off crackling; 2) (*aux.* sein) to crackle off.

Ab'predigen, (*w.*) *v. refl.* to weary one's self by preaching.

Ab'prellen, (*w.*) *v.* I. *tr.* to make rebound, to drive off *or* back with violence; II. *intr.* (*aux.* sein) *see* Abprallen.

Ab'preschen, (*w.*) *v. coll.* I. *tr.* to fatigue (*refl.* sich) by chasing, pursuing, to drive with the utmost violence (*cf.* Abjagen); II. *intr.* (*aux.* sein) 1) to run *or* dart off with the utmost speed: das Pferd preschte links ab, the horse dashed off to the left; 2) *see* Abbrausen.

Ab'pressen, (*w.*) *v. tr.* 1) to separate by pressing, to squeeze off, to pinch off (*cf.* Abklemmen); 2) to press duly *or* thoroughly; 3) *fig.* (Einem etwas) to force, exact, extort, wring, wrest (something) from (one).

Ab'pressung, (*w.*) *f.* 1) the (act of) pressing *or* squeezing off, &c.; 2) *fig.* exaction, extortion.

Ab'pritschen, (*w.*) *v. tr.* to slap soundly with a harlequin's wooden dagger *or* bat, to beat soundly.

Ab'processiren, (*w.*) *v. tr.* (Einem etwas) to get, obtain, *or* gain (something) by litigation from (one).

Ab'profilen, (*w.*) *v. tr. see* Abbrassen.

Ab'protzen, (*w.*) *v. tr.* (*sometimes intr., aux.* haben) *Gunn.* to unlimber, to dismount (ein [Stück] Geschütz, a piece of ordnance); to take (a gun) from the limber *or* carriage.

Ab'prügeln, (*w.*) *v. tr.* to beat, cudgel soundly, *coll.* to lick, to bang, to curry one's coat (hide) well, to give (one) a sound drubbing, beating *or* hiding.

Ab'puffen, (*w.*) *v.* I. *tr.* 1) *a)* to buffet *or* beat soundly; *b)* to beat off with the fist; *c)* to flay by beating the inner side of the skin, to skin; 2) *coll.* to pop off (a pistol, &c.); die Brigg puffte auf allen Seiten ein wenig Pulver ab, the brig fizzed off a little gunpowder on all sides; II. *intr.* (*aux.* sein) *particul. Chem.* to explode, detonate, decrepitate.

Ab'purzeln, (*w.*) *v. intr.* (*aux.* sein) to tumble off *or* down. [(*cf.* Abblasen).

Ab'pusten, (*w.*) *v. tr.* to blow off *or* away

Ab'putzen, (*w.*) *v. tr.* 1) *orig.* to cut off, (*particul.* stray ends, &c.) *still preserved in several phrases*: die Taue —, *Rope-m.* to clip off ropes, cables, to cut off the loose strands *or* ends from hempen cables; mit dem Hobel —, *Carp.* to take off with the plane, to smooth, plane; die Schnuppe vom Lichte —, to take off the snuff of a candle; das Licht —, to snuff the candle; 2) *a)* to scrape, rub, scour, &c. off (the dirt, &c.); *b)* to clean (boots, the teeth, &c.), to cleanse; to scrape, to rub, polish, furbish; 3) *Mas.* to rough-cast, to coat, to plaster, to finish down (a wall, &c.); ein Haus —, to smooth, to plaster the walls of a house; 4) *fig. coll.* Einen tüchtig (wacker, vortrefflich) —, to give one a wipe, a (nice) set-down, to give one a severe reprimand, to dispose of one satisfactorily.

Ab'quälen, (*w.*) *v. tr.* 1) to plague to excess, to tire out, to harass (*refl.* sich, one's self) to death, to excruciate; 2) (Einem etwas) to torment (one) out of (a thing), to extort (something) from (one), to wring (something) from (one); von dieser unaufhörlichen Angst abgequält, racked and jaded by this incessant anxiety; der hat sein ganzes Leben lang sich abgequält (*Schiller*), he has, his whole life long, fretted and toiled; er quälte sich länger als eine Stunde ab, um die Geschworenen zu überzeugen, he tortured his faculties for more than an hour to convince the jury.

Ab'quarlen, *see* Abquirlen.

Ab'quetschen, (*w.*) *v. tr.* 1) to squeeze off, to crush off; 2) *fig.* (Einem etwas) to extort *or* wring (something) from (one).

Ab'quicken, (*w.*) *v. tr. Min.-e.* 1) to purify (gold *or* silver-ore) by means of quick-silver; 2) to cool (the silver) after melting; (*Tech.*) abgetriebenes Silber —, to wash the silver-cake.

Ab'quieken, *(w.) v. tr.* to utter *or* sing in squeaking tones, to squeak *or* squeal off (as a song), to squeak out.

Ab'quirlen, *(w.) v. tr.* to beat up with a twirling-stick, to twist, to mill.

* **Abracada'bra,** *(abbr.* **Abra)** *n.* 1) abracadabra, a cabalistic word, written triangularly, and formerly worn as a charm against agues, &c.; 2) *fig. a)* any powerful charm; *b) iron.* unintelligible talk, jargon, nonsense.

Ab'rackern, *(w.) v.* I. *tr. coll.* to fatigue by hard labour, to jade; II. *refl. coll.* to toil hard, to fag one's self, to toil and moil.

Ab'rädeln, *(w.) v. tr.* 1) to cut off by means of a little wheel; *particul. Bak.* to cut (paste) with the jagging-iron; 2) *(opp.* Aufrädeln) *Wire-dr., &c.* to wind off; 3) *or* Ab'räden, *see the next word.*

Ab'rädern, *(w.) v. tr.* 1) to separate or cut off by means of a wheel; 2) to execute by breaking on the wheel; 3) to jolt soundly; ich bin vom Fahren ganz abgerädert, I am almost jolted *or* shaken to death by riding (in a carriage on rough ground &c.); 4) *Husb.* to separate by a coarse sieve (riddle), to riddle, to winnow (seed-corn).

Ab'raffeln, *(w.) v. tr.* to snatch off with a quickly repeated motion

Ab'raff, Ab'rafft, *(str.) n.* anything snatched away in a hurry, *particul. Mill.* corn that is lost between the mill-stones and appropriated by the miller *(also* Rape).

Ab'raffen, *(w.) v. tr.* 1) to snatch (sweep) away from the surface; 2) *Husb.* to take up *or* gather (the reaped corn) in order to make it up into sheaves.

Ab'raffer, *(str.) m. Husb.* one who following closely on the reaper (Schnitter) gathers the reaped corn and makes it up into sheaves.

A'braham, *(str.) m.* Abraham; in A-s Schoße sitzen, *proverb.* to be *(literally* to sit) in Abraham's bosom, *i. e.* to enjoy the good things of this world (wealth and affluence), to live in clover; A-s Schoß, *Mil.* a safe retreat or place secure from the fire of a beleaguered fortress; A-sbaum, *m. Bot.* chaste-tree (Keuschbaum). Abraham's balm *(Vitex agnus castus).* – **Abraha'misch, Abrahamit'isch,** *adj.* Abrahamic, Abrahamitic. – **Abrahamit',** *(w.) m.* Abrahamite (name of several Christian sects).

A. **Ab'rahmen,** *(w.) v. tr. (from* Rahmen, I.) 1) to skim the cream from (milk), to cream (off), to float; die abgerahmte Milch, skimmilk, float-milk; 2) *fig.* to take the best part of ..., to cream (off).

B. **Ab'rahmen,** *(w.) v. tr. (from* Rahmen, III.) to take off the frame from (a picture, &c.), to unframe.

Ab'rainen, *(w.) v. tr. Agr.* to separate or mark off (fields) by balks *or* stripes on which grass is suffered to grow (Raine), to ridge (fields).

Ab'raiten, *(w.) v. tr. provinc. (S. G.) for* Abrechnen.

Ab'raffen, *(w.) v. tr. Mar.* to disengage (a ship) from a bank.

Ab'rammeln, *(w.) v. intr. (aux.* haben) *Sport.* to cease bucking *or* rutting.

Ab'rändeln, Ab'randen, Ab'ränden, *(w.) v. tr.* 1) to take off or away the edge or margin of ..., to emarginate; 2) to clip (coins); 3) *Plum., &c.* to edge (sheet-lead), to edge (a dish, &c.) off; 4) (Ab'rändeln, Ab'rändern) to stamp on the edge, to mill (coins, &c.).

Ab'ranften, *(w.) v. tr.* to take off the edge of ..., to uncrust.

Ab'ranken, *(w.) v. tr.* to divest of the tendrils, to prune.

Ab'ranzen, *(w.) v.* I. *intr. Sport.* to cease to be proud; II. *refl.* to exhaust one's self by roaming about, to run, dance, &c. furiously.

Ab'rappen, *(w.) v. tr.* to pick (the grapes) from the stalk *(see* Abbeeren).

Ab'rascheln, *(w.) v. intr. (aux.* sein) to fall off with a rustling noise, to rustle off.

A. **Ab'räsen,** *(w.) v. tr. (from* Rasen, *s.)* 1) to graze (off), to browse (Abgrasen); 2) to divest of the turf, to take off the green sward *or* turf from (a grass-plot, &c.).

B. **Ab'räsen,** *(w.) v. tr. (from* Rasen, *v.)* (Einem etwas) to get, obtain, extort &c. (something) from (one) by raging.

Ab'raspeln, *(w.) v. tr.* 1) to rasp off, to chip off, to take off *or* away with the scraper; 2) to smooth by rasping.

Ab'rasseln, *(w.) v. intr. (aux.* sein) 1) to rattle off: der Wagen rasselte ab, the carriage drove off with a rattling noise; 2) *(for* Herabrasseln) to rattle down.

Ab'rathen, *(str.) v. intr.* (Einem von etwas) *& tr.* 1) (Einem etwas) to counsel to the contrary, to dissuade (one) from (a thing *or* from doing a thing), to advise *or* exhort one against, to dehort: der Minister rieth dem Fürsten von dieser Maßregel *(or* diese Maßregel) ab, the minister dissuaded the prince from adopting the measure *(Wb.)*; sie rieth ihm von seinem Vorhaben ab, she dissuaded him from his purpose; 2) *(l. u.) a)* to deliberate to the end *i. e.* fully *or* duly, to take due counsel upon (a thing), to take into due consideration; *b)* (Verabreden) to agree upon, determine; 3) † (Einem etwas) to obtain (something) from (one) by crafty counsel *or* speech, to talk (one) out of (a thing), *cf.* Abschwatzen; 4) (Einem etwas) to guess at, divine, learn (things secret or obscure) from (one); der Natur *(Dat.)* ihre Handgriffe – *(Kant)*, to divine nature's ingenious contrivances; a-d, *p. a.* dissuasive.

Ab'räther, *(str.) m.* dissuader, &c. *cf.* Abrathen.

Ab'räthung, *(w.) f.* dissuasion, the (act of) advising *or* counselling against; A-sschreiben, *n.* dissuasive letter.

Ab'rauben, *(w.) v. tr.* (Einem etwas) to snatch (something) from (one) by robbery, to rob *or* plunder (one) of (a thing).

Ab'rauch, *(str.) m. provinc.* rocambole (Rockenbollen).

Ab'rauchen, *(w.) v.* I. *intr. (aux.* sein) to evaporate (Abdampfen); II. *tr.* T. *(Chem., &c.)* to dry off by evaporation; to condense by evaporating the fluid parts *(cf.* Abdampfen); das –, *s. a. (str.) n.* (the act of) evaporating, &c., evaporation.

Ab'räuchern, *(w.) v. tr.* to smoke thoroughly.

Ab'rauchschale, *(w.) f. Chem.* evaporating vessel, evaporator.

Ab'raufen, *(w.) v.* I. *tr.* 1) *(cf.* Abzupfen) to pull off *(cf.* Abrupfen); 2) to crop off (grass, &c. like sheep); II. *recipr.* einander (*or* sich) –, to scuffle, worry, belabour one another excessively by pulling about; sie rauften sich (einander) ab, they thrashed each other soundly.

Ab'raum, *(str.) m.* 1) anything to be removed, rubbish (in mines, &c.), rubble; refuse, trash (Abgang); 2) *a) Forest* dead *or* waste wood, loppings (Abholz, Abfälle, Afterschlag); *b) Forest the same as* Afterholz, *which see c) Min.* shelf (loose stones, &c.); 3) *a)* the act of removing (Abräumung), removal (of the materials of a demolished house (Abbruch, Abtragung); *b) Forest aa)* removal of the loppings from a forest; *bb) (according to Sanders) in the sense of* Abbaum, *which see.*

Ab'räumen, *(w.) v. tr. (& intr.)* 1) *a)* to remove, to take *or* clear away: die Teller, Schüsseln x. –, to remove the plates, dishes, &c.; die Speisen –, to serve off the meats (from the table); *b) subsequently (for* die Teller, die Speisen x. vom Tische, die Bücher vom Gesimse x. –): den Tisch –, to clear the table (Abdecken), to clear *or* take [illegible] Gesimse –, to take down (books [illegible]) shelf; lassen Sie –, call the [illegible] &c.) to clear away; [illegible] table was cleared; 2) *Forest* [illegible] felled trees; to clear [illegible] *Min.* to clear a lode.

Ab'räumer, *(str.) m.* one who [illegible] takes away, &c. *see* Abräumen.

Ab'raupen, *(w.) v. tr.* to pick off [illegible] x., trees, &c.) of caterpillars.

* **Abrag'as,** *m.* *Church-hist.* [illegible] by the heretic Basilidians [illegible] &c., it served as a charm.

Ab'rechen, *(w.) v. tr.* 1) [illegible] *coll.* to remove with a rake [illegible] of corn, broken in threshing [illegible] with a rake, to rake duly.

Ab'rechicht, Ab'rechling, *(str.)* [illegible] the broken ears &c. of corn to [illegible] or away after threshing.

Ab'rechnen, *(w.) v. tr. & intr.* [illegible] rechnen) to count off, to [illegible] abate *(cf.* Abziehen); wir [illegible] von abzurechnen, we are unable [illegible] anything from it *(or* to [illegible] abgerechnet (*with Acc.* either [illegible] *lowing, never with von* ...), [illegible] ing allowance for ..., *cf.* [illegible] man (seine schlechte Erziehung [illegible] allowing *or* making allowance [illegible] of education, &c.); 2) *(intr.)* [illegible] to settle, to balance or close accounts [illegible] count *(or* reckon) with one, [illegible] accounts, to quit (scores) with [illegible] off ...; ich werde sofort mit [illegible] once come to a settlement with [illegible] die mit Gerechtigkeit und [illegible] mehr abzurechnen hatten, [illegible] up all dealings with justice [illegible] 3) to tell *or* count off: [illegible] an den Fingern –, daß ..., it is, [illegible] be foretold by an easy calculation [illegible]

Ab'rechnung, *(w.) f.* 1) [illegible] tion; nach – der Spesen, after [illegible] *(or* deducting) charges; in – [illegible] deduct; 2) the (act of) settling [illegible] reckoning with one, settlement [illegible] gegenseitige Bank-Anweisungen, [illegible] or checks (with city bankers) [illegible] to balance accounts with ...; [illegible] count; bei – ergab sich, on [illegible] it appeared; nach geschehener –, [illegible] accounts; 3) † account given of [illegible] meration, calculation.

Ab'rechnungs..., in *comp.* – [illegible] clearing-house; Eisenbahn– [illegible] way clearing-house; –tag, *m.* [illegible] dation, settling day.

Ab'rechte, *(w.) f. Cloth.* the [illegible] side of cloth; back [illegible]

A. **Ab'rechten,** *(w.) v. tr.* [illegible] *ing word) Cloth.* to dress the [illegible] of (cloth, &c.); das –, [illegible]

B. **Ab'rechten,** *(provinc.* [illegible] Ab & Rechten) *(w.) v. tr.* [illegible] get or obtain (something) from [illegible] gation.

Ab'rechts, *adv.* on or to [illegible] the wrong way, awry, &c. *cf.* [illegible]

Ab'recken, *(w.) v. tr.* 1) to [illegible] iron) the first stretching, to [illegible] stretch (iron) duly or [illegible]

Ab'rede, *(w.) f.* 1) [illegible] agreement, concert, convention [illegible] (bestimmte –) stipulations [illegible] men or treffen (über [illegible] together; to make an agreement [illegible] ment with one; to [illegible] mit einander nehmen [illegible] counsel together, we [illegible] standing; unserer – gemäß [illegible] (our, &c.) agreement, as agreed upon, as concerted; 2) speech or words by which anything is disavowed or disclaimed: a) † (syn. Ausrede, Ausflucht) evasive speech, excuse (cf. the Engl. to say off); b) denial, contradiction; in — sein (originally succeeded by a Genitive, then by an Accusative or daß ...), ich bin es nicht in —, I do not deny or question, I do not disallow; die Wirkung, die Sie selbst nicht ganz in — sind (Lessing), the effect which you yourself do not altogether deny; daß in der Bibel sich Widersprüche finden, wird jetzt Niemand in — sein (Göthe), nobody will at present deny that contradictions are to be found in the Bible; in — stellen (less usual in — nehmen, ziehen), to deny, disaffirm, disallow, to controvert, to (call in) question, dispute, to disclaim; es kann nicht in — gestellt werden, it cannot be denied; er stellte eifrig jede Absicht der Beleidigung in —, he earnestly disclaimed all intention to offend.

Ab'reden, (w.) v. I. tr. 1) (more usual Verabreden) a) to discuss (a matter) finally, fully or to the end; b) to concert, settle, adjust or plan (particul. in private) by mutual consultation, to confer upon; to agree upon; to appoint; abgeredet, p. a. (clandestinely) concerted; 2) (Einem etwas) a) to get (a thing) from (one) by talking him over, to talk (one) out of (a thing); b) fig. to deprive (one) of (a thing), to cause to forego, &c. by talking to him; 3) fig. (Einem etwas) to deny the existence of (a certain quality, &c.) in (a person), to refuse to acknowledge (unusual for Absprechen); es ist thöricht dieser Gesellschaft große Einflüsse — zu wollen (Gervinus), it is foolish to deny the great influence exercised by this society; 4) (Einem [rarely Einen] von etwas or Einem abreden, daß ..., or zu ...) to dissuade (one) from ..., see Abrathen (opp. Zureden); er wollte mich —, daß ich dich nicht mit nach Burg Ringstetten nehmen sollte (De la Motte-Fouqué, Undine, unusual for er wollte mir —, dich mit nach B. R. zu nehmen), he wanted to dissuade me from taking you along with me to B. R.; 5) (l. u., lit. to talk off, i. e. from the mark, at random) to talk incoherently, to wander, see Irre reden; II. refl. to fatigue or tire one's self by talking.

Ab'redig, adj. (l. u.) denying, disclaiming: — sein, see in Abrede sein or stellen.

Ab'redung, (w.) f. discussion, (mutual) conference; concert, agreement, cf. Verabredung, Besprechung.

Ab'reffeln, (w.) v. tr. see Abriffeln.

Ab'regeln, (w.) v. tr. to regulate; to arrange according to rules; abgeregelte Worte, affected or formal words, set speech.

Ab'regnen, (w.) v. I. intr. 1) to rain, drop, or pour down (Herabregnen); wo es —, abschmelzen oder sich selbst verzehren mag (Göthe), whence it may descend as rain or snow, or where it may consume itself; 2) (syn. Ausregnen) often refl. (commonly used impersonally) to discharge its contents (as a cloud); es hat (sich) abgeregnet, der Himmel ist wieder heiter, the rain has spent itself (it has done raining), the sky is again serene; II. tr. 1) to rain, drop, or pour down (volumes of water, &c.); 2) to beat or wash off, to spoil (by raining); die Blüten waren alle abgeregnet, the blossoms had all been beaten off by the rain; die Farbe ist abgeregnet, the colour is washed off by the rain; eine traurige abgeregnete Perücke, a sorry wig, spoiled by many a rain.

Ab'reibe..., in comp. F.-a. —bank, f. firework-bench; —brett, n. board on which the materials of fireworks are pulverised.

Ab'reiben, (str.) v. I. tr. 1) a) to rub off, remove by rubbing; b) to rub off or down, to clean by rubbing; ein Schiff —, Mar. to hog a vessel (to scrub the bottom of a ship with a hog, or flat broom); 2) a) to wear off, away or out, to remove by rubbing or friction, to abrade, to fret and wear by rubbing; die Bewegung reibt das Tau ab, (the) motion chafes the cable; die abgeriebene Stelle im Tuche, Cloth. fray, rub, chafe, fret; die Farben eines Gemäldes —, to efface the colours of a painting by rubbing; b) to rub duly or thoroughly, to smooth or polish by rubbing or scouring; mit Bimsstein —, to smooth with pumice; mit dem Reibebret —, Mas. to smooth (the plastering of a wall, a house, &c.) with the float; mit Tripel —, to rub, to polish with tripoli; Saiten —, to scour catguts; Farben —, to grind colours; Diamanten —, to grind diamonds; c) fig. to smooth down, to free from harshness or roughness; die feinere Welt hatte das Grade, Deutsche von ihm noch nicht abgerieben (Klinger), the polite world had not yet refined away his straightforwardness and German characteristics; abgerieben, p. a. cunning, see Gerieben; II. refl. to wear off, away or out by rubbing, friction, or attrition, to wear, to fret, to be fretted and worn by rubbing: das Tau reibt sich ab, the cable chafes.

Ab'reibung, (w.) f. the (act of) rubbing off, wearing off, &c. cf. Abreiben; detrition, abrasion, attrition.

Ab'reichen, (w.) v. tr. 1) l. u. for Herabreichen, to reach or hand down; 2) to reach, to touch by extending the hand, arm, or holding forth something; so [nahe], daß ich es abreichen kann (daß du es abreichen kannst rc.), within my (your, &c.) reach; so daß dein Stab sie abreicht (Schlegel, Hamlet 1, 2), within his truncheon's length (Sh.); nicht für möglich acht ich's ... | vom Schiff es [das Riff] springend abzureichen (Schiller, Tell 4, 1), impossible I deem it ... to reach it with a bound from the ship; 3) (Einem etwas) to hand, deliver, give, see Verabreichen.

A. **Ab'reifen**, (from Reifen, A.) (w.) v. intr. (aux. sein) to ripen fully, or to perfection, to grow quite ripe.

B. **Ab'reifen**, (from Reifen, C.) (w.) v. tr. 1) to unhoop, take away the hoops of (a cask); 2) Lock-sm. a) to take off the sharp edges of...; b) to break off, to take down (a lock).

Ab'reihen, (w.) v. tr. to unstring (Perlen rc., beads, &c.).

Ab'reise, (w.) f. departure (nach, for), parting, setting out; bei meiner — von hier sage ich meinen Freunden Lebewohl, on leaving this place I bid farewell to my friends.

Ab'reisen, (w.) v. intr. (aux. sein) 1) to depart, part, set out, set off, to take one's departure (nach, for), to set forth (upon a journey); 2) coll. (cf. Abfahren, 2, a) to take one's departure, i. e. to die.

Ab'reißen, (str.) v. I. tr. 1) a) to tear off, rend off, to pull off (with violence), to pluck off, break off; to sunder, detach; Mar. to rip off (planks); to slip off (a twig); der Blitz reißt einen Zweig vom Stamm der Eiche ab, the lightning dissevers a branch from the stem of the oak; einer Taube den Kopf —, to wrench off a pigeon's head; einen Faden —, to break off a thread; b) fig. to sunder, dissever; abgerissen, p. a. (cf. Abgerissen, p. 13) detached, disjointed (sentences, &c.), desultory (thoughts, &c.), abrupt; in abgerissenen Sätzen vortragen, to utter in broken fragments of sentences; 2) to pull or break down, to demolish (ein Gebäude, a building); eine Brücke —, to break or take away a bridge (see Abbrechen); das Gerüste —, to take off or away the scaffolding (cf. Abbrechen); 3) to wear out to rags, to wear away, to wear off, to rend (clothes); er war ganz abgerissen, coll. he was entirely out at elbows; ein abgerissener Mensch, a ragged fellow; 4) to draw, design, delineate, plan, sketch; eine Landschaft —, to trace off a landscape; II. refl. 1) to tear one's self off, away, see Losreißen; 2) fig. to exert one's self to the utmost; III. intr. (aux. sein) 1) to break (off), tear (off), to be broken, to snap asunder, &c.; die Kette riß ab, the chain broke; ein abgerissener Faden, a snapped thread; der zu scharf gespannte Lebensfaden reißt endlich plötzlich ab, the strained thread of life breaks at last with a sudden snap; die Geduld (der Geduldsfaden) reißt mir ab, I lose all patience; meine Geduld ist abgerissen, my patience is gone, at an end; 2) coll. to cease, to be discontinued, gener. in negative sentences: to go on unceasingly; das Geklingel reißt nicht ab (often expressive of a slight degree of indignation), the (door-)bell goes incessantly; seine nicht a—de Polemik, his unceasing polemics or controversies; ohne Abreißen, unceasingly, incessantly, without intermission.

Ab'reißer, (str.) m. 1) one who tears off, &c.; one who designs, &c. cf. Abreißen; 2) T. (Vorreißer, Reißer, Reißstift) an instrument for sketching or tracing lines or figures, cutting-point, (iron) tracer; 3) Mill. gener. pl. corn not yet fully ground.

Ab'reißung, (w.) f. 1) the (act of) tearing off, plucking away, &c.; forcible separation (of parts from a whole); avulsion, divulsion; 2) Mus. a sudden breaking off or stop (Abbrechung).

A. **Ab'reiten**, (str.) v. I. intr. (aux. sein) 1) to ride off or away, to set off or out on horseback; 2) to turn off; II. tr. 1) a) to ride off, to lose in riding; ein Hufeisen —, to cast or throw a shoe; b) to wear out, tear off (one's clothes, &c.) by riding; 2) to measure out (a distance) by riding; to perform on horseback, to travel over, to clear (a certain space) on horseback: ich ritt eine Meile nach der andern ab (Rückert), I did one mile after the other (i. e. on horseback); Damenfenster — (R. Heller), to pass on horseback the windows of fair ladies; 3) a) to harass by riding, to ride down, to override, to founder (a horse); abgeritten, foundered, broken; b) (Zureiten) to break in (a horse); ein auf der Schule abgerittenes Pferd, a managed or broken horse; 4) (Einem etwas) to gain on (one) in riding, to obtain (an advantage, victory, &c.) over (one) in riding; III. refl. 1) to chafe one's self by riding; 2) to fatigue one's self by riding.

B. **Ab'reiten**, see Abreuten.

Ab'rennen, (irr.) v. (syn. Ablaufen) I. intr. (aux. sein) 1) to run off, away, to start (running) from a certain point; 2) to run down, gener. in the phrase auf- und abrennen, to run up and down; II. tr. 1) to run off, to knock off in running (as in the game of running the ring); er rannte mir den Hut ab, he knocked off my hat in running against me; 2) to run or throw off from a horse, to unhorse; 3) (Einem etwas) to get (a thing) from (one) by running, to gain or get (the wind, &c.) of (a hare, &c.) by outrunning him, to outrun, get the start of (cf. Ablaufen); III. refl. to exhaust or to fatigue one's self by running.

† **Ab'rich**, (str.) n. see Abrechlicht.

Ab'richten, (w.) v. tr. 1) to give the proper direction, due shape or necessary proportions, to prepare for any purpose, to fit for ready use; to measure exactly, to level, adjust or regulate (as weights, &c.), limited almost exclusively to technical phrases, such as the following: a) Stabeisen —, to dress, to beat out, to straighten rod-iron; Schienen —, to bend the rails; einen Hammer, Amboß —, to smooth the face of a hammer, or of an anvil by filing; ein Bret —, to plane or dress a board; den Boden —, Coop. to smooth the heads of a cask; die Ecken eines Kistchens glatt —, to smooth the corners of a box; eine Mauer —, *Mas.* to level a wall; *Bookb.* see Abformiren; das Scheermesser —, to sharpen or to set a razor, see Abziehen; die Lauge —, *Soap-boil.* to prepare the lye; b) *Mar.* to make (a ship) ready for sailing, to put to sea; c) *Comm.* to send off, forward, see Absenden; 2) a) to form (animals) to any practice by exercise, to train (up), dress; to teach (birds, dogs, &c.); auf eine Sache or zu einer Sache —, to train for a certain purpose; Hunde —, *Sport.* to teach dogs, to enter hounds; *Falc.-s.* einen Falken —, to man, tame or train a hawk; der abgerichtete Falke, bird of game; *Man.-s.* ein Pferd —, to break in, put in, dress a horse; ein Pferd zum Zuge —, to break in a horse to harness; der Hund ist dazu abgerichtet, the dog has been trained for the purpose; ein gut abgerichteter Hund, *Sport.* a dog under command; einen Hund auf's Apportiren —, to teach a dog to fetch and carry; b) (*of human beings:*) aa) † (*in the better sense of* Unterweisen, unterrichten &c., to instruct, teach, train, &c.; Hamlet wenn er die Schauspieler abrichtet (*Lessing*), Hamlet teaching (*or* instructing) the actors; auf Karten- oder Taschenspielerkünste —, to teach tricks; bb) *contl.* to drill, discipline, train (like an unreasoning being): er ist gut darauf abgerichtet, he has got the knack of it, he understands his part well, he knows his cue; 3) *provinc.* (*S. G.*) den Tisch —, *see* Abräumen, Abdecken; 4) *obsolete meanings:* a) *refl. for* sich Zurichten (*in the sense of* sich Beschmutzen; b) *see* (eine Schuld) Entrichten, (Zahlung, einen Eid &c.) Leisten; c) den Schaden —, *see* Ersetzen, Ausgleichen; d) *see* Ausrichten, Verrichten; Abthun, Abstellen, Ändern; e) (durch richterlichen Spruch) *see* Aberkennen.

Ab'richt..., *in comp.* (*see* Abrichten) —(e)hammer, *m. Iron-w., &c.* straightening-hammer, large dressing- or stretching-hammer (Streckhammer); —(e)peitsche, *f. Man.* horsewhip; —(e)bank, —(e)stock, *m.* anvil to straighten iron bars upon, straightening-anvil; —wagen, *m.* a carriage used for breaking in horses, a break, brake.

Ab'richtung, (*w.*) *f.* 1) (the act of) preparing for a certain purpose, fitting, dressing, &c. *cf.* Abrichten; adjustment; 2) (the act of) training, breaking in (of horses, dogs, &c.) (*syn.* Dressur); die — von Stereotyp-Platten, the planing of stereotype plates; Erziehung ist hierbei nicht so wol erforderlich als —, education is not so much wanted here as mechanical training.

Ab'riebeln, (*w.*) *v. tr.* to rub off with slight, but frequent motion.

Ab'riechen, (*str.*) *v.* I. *tr.* 1) to deprive (eine Blume *or* einer Blume (*Dat.*) den Duft, a flower, &c.) of the odour by frequent smelling (*cf.* Ausriechen); 2) (Einem etwas) a) to perceive or recognise by the smell, to discover (something) in (one &c.) by the smell, *see* Anriechen; b) to obtain, get at (something) from (one or a thing) by the smell, to gain on (an animal) by following its scent; II. *intr.* (*aux.* sein) † to evaporate (Abrauchen).

Ab'riegeln, (*w.*) *v. tr. & intr.* (*aux.* haben) to bolt or shut off, to bolt up, to shut or fasten with a bolt or bar, to render (a door) impassable by bolting it (Verriegeln, Zuriegeln).

Ab'rieseln, (*w.*) *v. intr.* (*aux.* sein) to drizzle or trickle down, to flow down gently (as a rivulet, tears, &c.); to drop, glide gently down, to crumble down (as sand, dry and loose earth, &c.); wie vom hohen Ast abrieseln Laub auf Laub (*Rückert*), as from the high branch leaves on leaves drop down unceasingly (without intermission).

Ab'riffeln, (*w.*) *v. tr.* 1) *Husb.* to pull off or separate by the flax-comb, to top (hemp, &c.); 2) *fam.* *see* Abreffeln.

Ab'rinden, (*w.*) *v. tr.* to bark, rind, decorticate, peel; Bäume —, to take or peel off the rind from trees; ein Brot —, to cut off the crust of a bread; abgerindet, *p. a.* bark-bared, bark-stripped.

Ab'rindig, *adj.* 1) having the crust detached from the crumb; das Brot ist —, the crust of the bread is detached from the crumb, *cf.* Abbacken; 2) *fig.* sich — gehen, to get sore places or blisters by excessive walking.

Ab'rindern, *v. intr. Husb.* (of cows) to cease longing for the bull.

Ab'ringeln, (*w.*) *v.* I. *tr.* to unring; 1) to detach in small rings or ringlets; 2) to detach from the ringlets; II. *refl.* to detach itself or come off in ringlets, as the bark of a tree.

A. **Ab'ringen**, (*w.*) *v. tr.* to unring, to detach in rings, or from a ring or rings.

B. **Ab'ringen**, (*str.*) *v.* I. *tr.* 1) to twist or to squeeze off; 2) (Einem etwas) a) to get or obtain (something) from (one) by wrestling, to wrest (something) from (one); b) *fig.* to wring or wrest (something) from (one); 3) to wring (Wäsche, linen) thoroughly or sufficiently, to finish wringing, *cf.* Auswringen; sich (*Dat.*) die Hände —, to wring one's hands excessively; II. *refl.* to weary or fatigue one's self by wrestling, to struggle to the utmost or painfully.

Ab'rinnen, (*str.*) *v. intr.* (*aux.* sein) to run off, to run, flow, drop, or trickle down.

Ab'rispen, (*w.*) *v. intr.* (*aux.* sein) (of oat-grains, &c.) to detach itself from, or to fall out of the panicles.

Ab'riß, (*str.*) *m.* (*from* Abreißen, *which see*) 1) *rarely used for* das Abreißen (*v. a.*): a) the (act of) tearing off or away; b) the (act of) snatching away, eruption (Entreißung); 2) a) (first or rough) draught (*often syn. with* [Profil-]Zeichnung), drawing, delineation, design, sketch, outline; plan, model; scheme; b) statement; einen — von etwas nehmen, to take a sketch of, to take off a thing (*cf.* Abreißen); — nennen or lesen, *Weav.* to read a design; 3) (kurzer —, brief or compendious) abstract, epitome, compendium, summary, abridgment; ein — der Astronomie, a synopsis of astronomy.

Ab'ritt, (*str.*) *m.* (*from* Abreiten) the riding away or departure on horseback.

Ab'rohren, (*w.*) *v. tr.* 1) to clear, rid or divest of reeds; 2) to cover with reeds (Berohren).

Ab'rollen, (*w.*) *v.* I. *intr.* (*aux.* sein) 1) to roll or run down; ein Tau schnell — lassen, *Mar.* to surge a cable (*cf.* Abschricken); 2) (of carriages, &c.) to roll off, to drive, dash, dart &c. off; 3) (*applied to periods of time*) to run out or down, to roll, hasten or pass away (Verfließen); II. *tr.* 1) a) (abwärts rollen, niederwälzen) to roll or precipitate down, to devolve (as a stream its waters); b) to carry or cart off in a truck (Rollwagen); vom Bahnhof nach der Stadt —, to convey or transport from the station to town; 2) to unroll, to open from being rolled or convolved; 3) *fig.* to unroll (a picture, &c.), to disclose, display, unfold gradually; 4) *huckster.* to roll or rattle off, to repeat or recite in a quick monotonous way (Abschnurren); 5) to suffer to roll off or to run down (*cf. intr.* 3); ein solcher Armer, der mit Plackerei | die Tage abrollt und mit Schlaf die Nächte (*a very apt, but not literal translation by Schlegel of Shaksp. K. Henry V.* 4, 1: such a wretch, | winding up days with toil, and nights with sleep); 6) (*often intr., aux.* haben) to mangle (linen, &c.) sufficiently or duly, to cease mangling; 7) *Bookb.* ein Buch —, to impress flourishes &c. on the back of a book with a back-tool, called Roll-Eisen; III. *refl. gener. fig.* to unroll, unfold itself (*cf. tr.* 2 & 3).

Ab'roffeln, (*w.*) *v. tr. Husb.* *see* Abriffeln (Abreffeln).

Ab'rösten, (*w.*) *v.*
sufficiently, to
Ab'rosten, (*w.*) *v. intr.*
off, to come or drop off
corroded by rust.
Ab'röthen, (*w.*) *v. tr.*
or thoroughly (also
Ab'röthen, (*w.*) *v.* I. *tr.*
redden; II. *intr.* (*aux.*
colour.
Ab'rotten, (*w.*) *v. intr.* (*aux.*
Ab'rücken, (*w.*) *v.* I. *tr.* 1)
move off; 2) *T.* to move (the
shaft, &c.) out of its place
connect it from the rest of
throw out of gear
Zeilen —, to begin with a new
a break (Absetzen); II. *intr.* (*aux.*
move off, remove, withdraw;
bodies) to start, to march off.
Ab'rückwelle, (*w.*) *f.* *T.* a
which can be removed from
to throw any wheel connected
gear.
Ab'rudern, (*w.*) *v. intr.* (*aux.*
Ab'ruf, (*str.*) *m.* 1) the (act
see Abrufung; 2) *provinc.* the
coins), *cf.* Abrufen, 4.
Ab'rufen, (*str.*) *v.* I. *tr.* 1) a)
away; Einem die Kunden —
abspänstig machen), to entice
customers by calling them off;
Sport. to call off the hounds
to recall; von einem Amt —,
—, *for these and similar senses*
c) *fig.* to remove (one) by death,
ruft uns alle ab, death
call for or on (a person) in
with him, *cf.* Abholen;
send for one; 3) (mit der
errufen) to reach by calling;
be within call; so nahe, daß
— konnten (*Forster*), so near that
were within hail of each other;
claim by calling aloud
almost entirely limited to the
die Stunden —, to call or cry the
the streets); b) *intr.* to call
(at the expiration of the watch
(*S. G.; acc. to Adelung*) to call
cf. Verrufen; II. *refl.* to tire or
self by calling.
Ab'rüffeln, (*w.*) *v. tr. coll.* to
reprove or chide severely, to
(one) a good scolding.
Ab'rufschuß, (*str.*, *pl.*
signal gun of recall
Ab'rufung, (*w.*) *f.* 1) a) the
ing off, away, &c. *cf.* Abrufen;
vocation, *see* Abberufung; 2)
berufung, 2; 3) a loud calling
clamation: A-brief *m.*, A-
of recall, *see* Abberufungsschreiben;
see Abrufschuß.
Ab'rühren, (*w.*) *v. tr.* 1) to
about, to beat (up), to stir (with
Eier —, to beat up eggs;
Ei — (Abquirlen), to beat up
broth; 2) to separate by stirring
men —, to stir plums about
the kernels.
Ab'rumpeln, (*w.*) *v.* I.
(*l. u.*) to drive off in a
(*f. i.* in a jolting carriage, &c.)
II. *tr. coll.* to rub off by
Ab'rund, *adj.* (*l. u.*) oval.
Ab'runden, (*w.*) *v.* I. *tr.* 1)
to round; 2) *Carp.* to
edges), to chamfer; 3) *fig.* to
off, finish off; to make
smooth and flowing, to
einen Redesatz —, to round

dete Ecken, circular corners; abgerundete Kanten, bruised edges; eine abgerundete Periode, ein abgerundeter Satz, *Gramm.* a well-rounded period, a well-turned phrase; II. *refl.* to grow or become round, to be rounded off.

Ab'ründen, *(w.) v. tr.* to round off; *Gold-sm. &c.* to cut out (in a circular shape), *see* Abrunden.

Ab'rundung, *(w.) f.* 1) *a)* the (act of) rounding off, rounding, &c. *cf.* Abrunden; *b)* *fig.* the (act of) rounding or finishing off, smoothing, embellishment; 2) rotundity (of a full cheek, &c.).

Ab'rupfen, *(w.) v. tr.* 1) to pull off with a quick, jerking motion, to pluck (off); Blätter —, to pick off leaves; 2) *coll.* to fleece (one), *see* Rupfen. [Abgebrochen).

* **Abrupt',** *adj. (Lat.)* abrupt (Abgerissen,

* **Abruptio'n,** *(w.) f. (Lat.)* abruption, *see* (*also Mus., &c.*) Abbrechung, Abreißung.

Ab'rüsten, *(w.) v.* I. *tr.* 1) to remove (a mill-stone, &c.) from a framing; (*gener. intr.*) to take off or down a scaffold (*opp.* Aufrüsten); die (Schwib-)Bogen —, to strike the centres; das — eines (Schwib-)Bogens, the striking of a centre (removal of a timber framing upon which an arch is built, after its completion); 2) † to train for a certain purpose (Abrichten); II. *intr.* (*aux.* haben) to stop or discontinue warlike preparations, to restore the military establishment to a peace footing, to disarm.

Ab'rüstung, *(w.) f.* 1) removal (of a mill-stone, &c.) from a framing, &c. *cf.* Abrüsten; the taking down of a scaffold; 2) discontinuance of warlike preparations, reduction of the military establishment to a peace footing, disarmament (Entwaffnung).

Ab'rutschen, *(w.) v.* I. *intr.* (*aux.* sein) 1) *a)* to slip, glide, or slide down; *b)* to slip or glide off; to move or scamper away or off (*cf.* Abfahren, 1); *c)* *sometimes coll.* to get off with disgrace; 2) *vulg.* to die, *cf.* Abfahren, 2; II. *tr.* to wear out or off by frequent gliding or slipping.

Ab'rütteln, *(w.) v. tr.* to shake off.

Abruz'zen, *(w.) pl. Geogr.* the Abruzzo mountains.

Ab'säbeln, *(w.) v. tr.* (Einem den Kopf *rc.*) *coll.* to cut off (one's head, &c.) with the sword or sabre &c., to sabre off.

A. **Ab'sacken,** *(w.) v. tr.* 1) *a)* (ein Lastthier or eine Last vom Esel —), to take off the bag or burden from the back of (an ass, &c.), to unload, to disburden (*opp.* Aufsacken); *b)* (Einem sein Geld *rc.*) to take away, carry off (one's money, &c.); 2) to divide by sacks.

B. **Ab'sacken,** *(w.) v. intr.* (*aux.* sein) *Mar.* to drop or fall down (auf einem Flusse, a river) with the tide, to sag (with the stream).

Ab'säen, *(w.) v. tr.* 1) *a)* to sow (a field) thoroughly or duly; *b)* to reduce the quality of ..., to impoverish (a field) by repeated sowing; 2) *Tann.* to besprinkle (hides) with unbolted meal (preparatory to the Anfäen or Gerben).

Ab'sage, *(w.) f.* 1) *a)* the (act of) countermanding, counterorder; *b)* refusal (of an invitation); 2) *Law,* renunciation; 3) a disowning (of friendship); recusancy; defiance, challenge.

Ab'sagebrief, *(str.) m.* 1) *a)* countermanding letter; *b)* *Law,* letter of renunciation; 2) letter of defiance, declaration of enmity (Fehdebrief), challenge.

Ab'sagen, *(w.) v.* I. *tr.* 1) *a)* to countermand; (— lassen) to counterorder; *b)* (*often used intransitively*) to retract, revoke; to refuse, disclaim, decline, resign, renounce; Einem den Frieden —, or *without the object:* Einem —, to renounce one's friendship, to declare hostility, *see intr.;* ein abgesagter Feind, a professed, declared or sworn enemy, an open foe (*cf.* Erklärt, Entschieden); eine Einladung —, to retract, revoke or recall an invitation (gänzlich veraltet ist: to disinvite one); einen Besuch — lassen, to send an excuse; weshalb in aller Welt glaubst du, daß ich sie eingeladen habe, wenn ich es ihnen jetzt — lassen soll? why on earth do you suppose I asked them, if I am to put them off now? sie ging nicht in das Concert, sondern hatte es ihrem Vetter — lassen, she did not go to the concert, but had sent to put her cousin off; ich ließ ihm die heutige Stunde —, I sent word to (or desired) him to omit this day's lesson; falls Sie es mir nicht —, unless I hear from you to the contrary; 2) (Einem etwas) to deny (one) a thing, *see* Absprechen.

II. *intr.* to declare against a person or thing; *a)* Einem — (*orig. transitive, cf.* I. 1, *b:* den Frieden *rc.*) to break with one, to declare off, to renounce one's friendship or allegiance, to declare hostility or war; Jemandes eignes Herz (*Luther*), sein Gewissen sagt ihm ab, a man's own heart, his conscience rejects him, casts him off; Gott sagt uns ab (*Luther*), God casts us off; *b)* einer Sache (*Dat.*) —, to renounce, give up, forsake, abjure a thing (Entsagen).

Ab'sägen, *(w.) v. tr.* to saw off, to saw.

Ab'sagung, *(w.) f.* 1) the (act of) countermanding, &c. *cf.* Absagen & Absage; 2) renunciation; declaration of hostility, &c.

Ab'sägung, *(w.) f.* the (act of) sawing off, sawing.

Ab'sahnen, *(w.) v. tr. provinc.* to skim the cream from (milk), &c. *see* Abrahmen, *B.*

Ab'saigern, *see* Abseigern.

Ab'salzen, *(w.) v. tr.* to salt sufficiently or duly (Durchsalzen).

Ab'sanden, *(w.) v. tr.* 1) *a)* to strew, sprinkle, or mix sufficiently with sand; to sand, to sprinkle (paper newly inked) with sand thoroughly; *b)* to scour with sand; 2) to free from sand, to ungravel.

Ab'satteln, *(w.) v.* I. *tr.* 1) (ein Pferd *rc.*) to unsaddle, to take off the saddle of (a horse, &c.); 2) to throw off (or out of) the saddle, to unhorse, unsaddle; II. *intr.* to dismount (a horse).

Ab'satz, *(str., pl.* Ab'sätze) *m.* 1) the act of putting down, setting off, depositing, &c. *cf.* Absetzen; 2) *(l. u.)* reduction, depreciation, *see* Herabsetzung; 3) the act of disposing of goods, selling, &c. *cf.* Absetzen (Vertrieb von Waaren), *Comm.* sale, vent, market: nur in kleinen Posten — erzielen, to sell only in small quantities; der — beschränkte sich auf den Platz, the sale (business) was confined (limited) to the place; der — war gleich Null, there was no sale at all; bei beschränktem —, with limited sale; viel Angebot bei wenig —, many offers with little sale; keinen — finden, to find no market; guter, schneller —, brisk or ready sale; guten (raschen, leichten) — haben, to have (find) a quick (brisk, ready, easy) sale (prompt dispatch), to sell well, to run off readily, to have a quick draught: das Buch hatte reißenden —, the book met with a rapid sale; schlechter —, heavy sale; schwierigen (schlechten) — finden, to go off sluggishly, to meet with an indifferent (dull) sale; 4) deduction (from an account, &c.), *see* Abzug *which is more usual;* 5) any thing laid or thrown down, left, or lodged, accumulation of something deposited, lodgment; sediment (of a liquid); *particul.* the solid matter left by flowing water, deposit; (*in steam-boilers and other vessels:*) fur, sediment (*calcareous incrustation from hard water,* Kesselstein); 6) anything breaking or interrupting the continuity of a line or surface, place where a straight line is interrupted, break: *a)* break, shelf (of a mountain); *b)* *aa)* *Archit.* off-set, set-off; *bb)* *Fort.* berme; *c)* *Archit.* &c. landing place (of a staircase), landing; stair-head; broad step (of an altar, &c.); *d)* *Min.* *aa)* break in the direction of strata, or of a lode; *bb)* landing-place, stopping-place, resting-place (Ruhebühne); *e)* *Bot.* knot, knee, joint (of or in a plant); articulation (in a vine); mit Absätzen, kneed, knee-jointed, geniculated; *f)* heel (of a shoe, &c.); mit hohen Absätzen, high-heeled; sich auf dem — herumdrehen, to turn upon one's heels; *g)* *Smith., &c.* step (between the wide and pointed side of an anvil, *Tech.*); 7) *a)* *Typ.* break, period; *b)* paragraph, section [§]; *c)* *Mus.* *aa)* section (a complete but not independent musical idea); musical sentence; *bb)* pause; *d)* stanza, staff (of a song); *e)* cadence (of verses); 8) *a)* stop, pause, intermission; *b)* interval; — in einer Periode, break of a period, breathing-place; ein Glas ohne — (or ohne Absätze) austrinken, to empty a glass at one draught; in Absätzen, at intervals, intermittingly, by catches, startingly, snatchingly; 9) *fig.* *(l. u. for* Abstand, Abstich, Abfall) contrast.

Ab'satz ..., *in comp.* —ahle, *f.* *Shoe-m.* pegging-awl; —bohrer, *m.* *Shoe-m.* heel-borer; —canal, *m.* *Comm.* channel of exportation, market, opening (for the sale of goods); —draht, *m.* *Shoe-m.* thread for heels of boots; —ferkel, *n.* a pig newly weaned (Absetzling); —fieber, *n.* intermitting or intermittent fever (Wechselfieber); —gebiet, *n.* *Comm. fig.* a market for the sale of goods; es eröffnet sich ein neues —gebiet für den Hauptfabricationszweig des Platzes, a new market for the staple manufacture of the place is opened; wir haben noch keine neuen —gebiete ausfindig gemacht, we have not yet discovered any new markets; —holz, *n.* *Shoe-m.* wood used for making a sort of heels.

Ab'sätzig, *adj.* intermissive, with stops or breaks, *particul. Min.* not continuing in the same stratum, exhibiting a different stratification.

Ab'satz ..., *in comp.* —kreuz, *n.* *Herald.* a cross with steps at the ends; —flecken, *m.* *Shoe-m.* chips of leather used for making heels; —leder, *n.* *Shoe-m.* 1) heel-band; 2) heel-tap; —macher, *m.* *Shoe-m.* heel-maker; —markt, *m.* *fig.* a market for the sale of goods (*cf.* —gebiet, —ort); —ort, *m.* 1) *Shoe-m.* pegging-awl (—ahle); 2) *Comm. fig.* market or place for the sale of goods; —pflock, *m.* *Shoe-m.* heel-peg; —quelle, *f.* *Comm. fig.* a (good) market, *cf.* —canal; —scheu, *f.* *Man.* over-sensitiveness of a horse to the heels of its rider; —schneider, *m.* heel-maker; —spritze, *f.* *T.* intermittent pump; —stift, *m.* *Shoe-m.* hob-nail; —weg, *m.* channel of exportation, market or opening for the sale of goods; den Fabricaten eines Landes neue —wege eröffnen, to create for a country's manufactures an outlet (into ...); —weise, *adv. & adj.* (happening) at intervals, intermittingly; intermittent; —zwecke, *f.* *Shoe-m.* hob-nail.

Ab'säubern, *(w.) v. tr.* 1) to cleanse off; to absterge, to clean; 2) *Min.* to clear (a mine which is to be relinquished) by the removal of ores, stones, gear, &c.; 3) *fig.* to polish off, to refine away.

Ab'saufen, *(str.) v. vulg.* (*cf. the more refined word,* Abtrinken) I. *tr.* 1) to swill or guzzle off, to drink grossly or greedily from the surface; 2) sich (*Dat.*) das Leben (*Simplic.*), die Gurgel (*Schiller*) —, to deprive one's self of life, of the throat (*i. e.* the capability of drinking any more) by swilling or guzzling, *the latter equal to* sich todt saufen; 3) to obtain or gain by outdrinking another; II. *refl.* to ruin one's health by excessive swilling.

Ab'säugeln, *(w.) v. tr.* (*diminutive of* Absaugen & Absäugen) 1) to suck off by small draughts; 2) *Gard.* *see* Absäugen, 3.

Ab'saugen, *(str.) v.* I. *tr.* 1) to suck off;

2) to weaken by sucking; 3) *fig.* to suck off, to exhaust; II. *intr.* to finish *or* cease sucking (*cf.* Aussaugen).

Ab'säugen, (*w.*) *v. tr.* 1) to give suck, to suckle sufficiently; 2) (Entwöhnen) to wean from the breast (*particul. of animals, cf.* Absetzen, 2, *b*); 3) *Gard.* to inarch, to graft by approach.

Ab'säuseln, (*w.*) *v. tr.* to blow off or down with a buzzing or rustling noise, *cf.* Abwehen.

Ab'sausen, (*w.*) *v.* I. *tr.* to dash, blow off: II. *intr.* (*aux.* sein) to rebound, fly off with a hissing noise.

* **Absceß',** (*str.*) *m. Med.* abscess, imposthume.

Ab'schab, (*str.*) *n.*, **Ab'schabete,** (*w.*) *f.* (†*&*) *provinc., see* Abschabsel.

Ab'schabe-Eisen, (*str.*) *n.* scraper, grater.

Ab'schaben, (*w.*) *v. tr.* 1) to scrape or to shave off, to pare, to abrade: *Mas.* to plane, to grave (a ship); die Rinde vom Brote —, to chip bread: Wurzeln —, to scrape roots: das —, *v. s.* (*str.*) *n.* the act of scraping *or* rubbing off, &c., abrasion; 2) to wear off, to wear out; abgeschabt, *p. a.* (*a strong form:* abgeschaben *l. u.*) shabby, worn-out, threadbare.

Ab'schabsel, (*str.*) *n.* shavings, parings, abrasions; das — von Lammfellen, lambskin paring *or* shreds.

Ab'schach, (*str.*) *n.* (*Lessing,* Nathan 2, 1) *probably* = ein abthuendes Schach, a check making an end of the game.

Ab'schachern, (*w.*) *v tr. coll.* (Einem etwas) to cheapen, barter (something) from (one).

Ab'schachteln, (*w.*) *v. tr. Join.* to rub or polish with shave-grass (Schachtelhalm), to smooth.

Ab'schäkeln, (*w.*) *v. tr. Mar.* to fleet or shift (a tackle), to slack up (a tackle) and draw the blocks apart for another pull; to shift the position of (a block or fall), so as to haul to more advantage.

Ab'schaffen, (*w.*; *the strong form is entirely obsolete*) *v.* I. *tr.* to do away with: 1) (*obsolete — of persons*) to send or turn away, to dismiss, to bid *or* tell to be gone (*Hans Sachs, &c.*); 2) (of persons and things) to discharge (Dienstboten *x.*, servants, &c.), to dismiss, to discard (soldiers, &c.), to remove; to give up keeping, to keep no longer (horses, &c.), to part with; er schaffte seinen Schreiber ab, he dismissed his clerk (*i. e.* in order to do without one); er hat seine Hunde abgeschafft, he has rid himself of his dogs; 3) (of institutions, customs, &c. *cf.* Abstellen) to abolish, abrogate, repeal, annul, nullify (laws); to suppress (an office), do away with (abuses, &c.); to put down, to remedy; II. *intr.* mit Einem —, *provinc.* to settle (accounts) with one, to quit (scores) with one (*cf.* mit Einem Abrechnen); III. *refl. provinc.* (*S. G.*) to work one's self weary, to exhaust one's self with labour (sich Abarbeiten).

Ab'schaffer, (*str.*) *m.* one who discharges, dismisses, &c. *cf.* Abschaffen; abolisher, suppressor.

Ab'schaffung, (*w.*) *f.* 1) the act of discharging, &c. *cf.* Abschaffen; dismission, dismissal, discharge (of servants, &c.); the keeping no longer, selling; 2) abrogation (*of a* law), annulment, disannulment, abolition (of slavery, &c.); die — der Königswürde, the abolition of royalty; von der gänzlichen — der Volksgewalt an kann der Verfall Roms datirt werden, from the total abolition of the popular power, may be dated the ruin of Rome.

Ab'schaften, Ab'schäften, (*w.*) *v. tr.* to deprive of the handle, to unhaft; *Gun-sm.* to unstock (a gun).

Ab'schäkeln, (*w.*) *v. tr. Mar. see* Abschäkeln.

Ab'schäkern, (*w.*) *v. tr.* (Einem etwas) to get (something) from (one) by playing tricks, to cajole (one) out of (a thing).

Ab'schälen, (*w.*) *v. tr. Mas.* to chisel off the soft crust of (a stone).

Ab'schälen, (*w.*) *v.* I. *tr.* 1) to peel off (Rinde, bark), to peel, to pare off, to pare (fruit, &c.); to blanch (Mandeln, almonds), to shell; to decorticate, to strip off, (Abrinden) to bark (a tree); to cut off the crust of (bread, sod, &c.) (Abkrusten); *T.* to flake, to scale; *Surg.* to excoriate (the skin); abgeschälte Zweige, bark-bared or bark-stripped branches; 2) *fig. a*) to strip, denude, lay bare (as a rocky mountain, &c.); *b*) to divest, to free (from the trammels of duty, &c.); II. *refl.* 1) to peel off in scales, to scale off, to peel, to scale, to come off in thin layers or laminæ; 2) *fig.* to detach itself, to fall away.

Ab'schalmen, (*w.*) *v. tr. Forest* to blaze trees.

Ab'schälschaufel, (*w.*) *f.* turf-spade, turf-cutter, paring-shovel.

Ab'schälung, (*w.*) *f.* the act of peeling or stripping off (the bark, &c.), *cf.* Abschälen; the paring, blanching, &c., decortication: — der Haut, *Med.* excoriation, abrasion of the cuticle.

† **Ab'schank,** (*str.*) *m.* (*from* Abschenken) parting-cup, night-cup.

Ab'schärfemesser, (*str.*) *n. T.* (*Bookb., Shoem., Glov.*) paring-knife; *Bookb.* edge-tool.

Ab'schärfen, (*w.*) *v. tr. T.* 1) to take away the sharp edges, to dull the edge *or* point of (an instrument, &c.), to blunt; 2) to sharpen; to cut into a sloping form; to form to an edge; to taper off; *Carp., &c.* to rabbet; to chamfer; der abgeschärfte Brückenpfeiler, *m.* counter-fort; *Bookb.* to pare (off); *Letter-found.* to kern; 3) *Sport.* to cut off; 4) *Cook.* to make (a sauce, &c.) piquant *or* pungent, to render sharp; 5) *provinc.* to scratch off (the skin, &c.).

Ab'schärfung, (*w.*) *f.* the (act of) taking away the edges, &c.

Ab'scharren, (*w.*) *v. tr.* to scrape, scratch *or* grate off, to remove (dirt, &c.; *sometimes* to clean) by scraping (*cf.* Abkratzen).

Ab'scharricht, (*str.*), **Ab'scharrsel,** (*str.*) *n.* shavings, scrapings.

Ab'schatten, (*w.*) *v. tr.* 1) *lit. & fig.* to shade (*or* shadow) off, to shadow out, to take the outline of ..., to sketch, to adumbrate; to take the profile *or* shade of (a person *or* thing — *much employed, in this sense, since the introduction of silhouettes, about* 1760; *Jean Paul particularly has a great predilection for the word, cf. Grimm's W.-B.*); 2) *fig.* to image *or* form: II. *refl.* to be marked *or* projected in dark outlines on a light ground.

Ab'schattiren, (*w.*) *v. tr.* to represent or paint with gradations of colours; to shadow out, to adumbrate, *cf.* Schattiren.

Ab'schattung, Ab'schattirung, (*w.*) *f.* 1) sketch following the outlines of the shadow, adumbration (*also fig.*), delineation, silhouette; 2) (nice) gradation of light or colour, shade, degree.

Ab'schätzbar, *adj.* appreciable.

† **Ab'schatzen,** (*w.*) *v. tr.* (Einem etwas) to deprive (one) of (a thing) by imposing a duty or assessment, to extort.

Ab'schätzen, (*w.*) *v. tr.* 1) to appraise, to tax; to estimate, value; 2) (*l. u.*) to depreciate (coins, &c.).

Ab'schätzer, (*str.*) *m.* appraiser, taxer, &c.

Ab'schätzig, *adj.* (*l. u.*) valueless, worthless, contemptible, *see* Geringschätzig, Verächtlich.

Ab'schätzung, (*w.*) *f.* 1) valuation, taxation; 2) (*l. u.*) depreciation.

Ab'schauen, (*w.*) *v.* I. *tr.* 1) to reach with the eye; 2) (Einem etwas) *see* Absehen; II. *intr.* 1) (*for* Niederschauen) to look down; 2) to avert the look.

Ab'schauern, (*w.*) *v. tr. Carp.* to partition off.

Ab'schaufeln, (*w.*) *v. tr.* to [illegible] clear away with a shovel.

Ab'schaukeln, (*w.*) *v. tr.* to [illegible] (*in conjunction with* Hin[illegible]) [illegible] swing up and down, *fig.* to [illegible] thither.

Ab'schaum, (*str., pl.* Ab'schäume) [illegible] scum, scum (froth or refuse that [illegible] surface of heated liquors), dross, [illegible] refuse (des menschlichen Geschlechts, [illegible] society); an outcast.

Ab'schäumen, (*w.*) *v. tr.* 1) to [illegible] (off); 2) (*Polit.*) *Letter-found.* to [illegible] *sm.* to clean, to wash [illegible]

Ab'schäumung, (*w.*) *f.* the (act [illegible] ming, skimming (off), &c.

Ab'scheeren [*pr.* —schären], (*w.*) [illegible]

† **Ab'scheid,** (*str.*) *m.* departure [illegible] life), decease (*cf.* Abschied).

Ab'scheiden, (*str.*) *v.* I. *intr.* (*aux.* [illegible]) depart; von der Welt —, to depart [illegible] die; ihr Abscheiden (*v. s., str. n.*) [illegible] ture (*i. e.* from this life, decease) [illegible] *a*) to separate (*also Chem., &c.*) [illegible] (*see* Scheiden); Metalle —, to [illegible] to disengage (carbonic acid, [illegible] *Law,* to portion *or* pay off, to give [illegible] &c.) their portion and to exclude [illegible] all future claims, to make a final and [illegible] nite settlement with ...; 3) † to [illegible] III. *refl.* to separate one's self, &c.; [illegible] parated or divided by a boundary-line [illegible] scharf —, to be clearly defined (*of a* [illegible] line, &c.).

Ab'scheider, (*str.*) *m.* refiner (of [illegible]) one who parts gold and silver, [illegible] scheider.

Ab'scheidung, (*w.*) *f.* the (act of) separating, parting, &c. *cf.* Abscheiden; [illegible] departure; A-Thätigkeit, *f. Physiol.* [illegible] tory agency, secreting process.

Ab'schein, (*str.*) *m.* (*l. u.*) reflecting [illegible] dor or brightness (*cf.* Abglanz).

Ab'scheifen, Ab'scheifern, [illegible] (*w.*) *v. tr.* (*& refl.*) to peel off (*refl.* [illegible] off) in thin, small scales, to abrade, [illegible] (*cf.* Abschälen).

Ab'scheifung, Ab'scheiferung, [illegible] rung, (*w.*) *f.* a peeling off, [illegible] rasion (of the cuticle).

Ab'schellen, (*w.*) *v. tr. & intr.* (*aux.* [illegible]) to scale off by violent concussion.

Ab'schelmen, (*w.*) *v. tr.* (Einem etwas) [illegible] deprive (one) of (a thing) by [illegible] roguish tricks, to cheat (one) out of [illegible]

† **Ab'schenke,** (*w.*) *f.* parting-[illegible]

Ab'schenken, (*w.*) *v. tr.* 1) to [illegible] out liquor; 2) to pour out the [illegible] or cup; 3) (ein Kind —, *Bav.*) to [illegible] suckle, *i. e.* to wean (a child).

Ab'scheren [*pr.* —schären], (*str.*) [illegible] to shave (off); 2) to shear off (the [illegible] sheep); 3) *Ship-carp., &c.* to partition [illegible] separate by a partition.

Ab'scherzen, (*w.*) *v. tr.* (Einem etwas) [illegible] get (something) from (one) by [illegible] to joke (one) out of (a thing).

Ab'scheu, (*str.*) *m.* 1) (*followed by* [illegible] *Dat.*) *before the object* [vor, with *Acc.*, or] gegen; *less frequently by* an [*with.* ...] [*with. Acc.*], or, *still more rarely,* [illegible] *Gen.*) abhorrence (of, before for), [illegible] detestation (of), abomination, [illegible] (to), loathing (of), disgust; — vor [illegible] haben, to abhor a thing; 2) object [illegible] tion or abhorrence, abomination, [illegible]

Ab'scheuchen, (*w.*) *v. tr.* to [illegible] to scare off.

Ab'scheuern, (*w.*) *v.* I. *tr.* 1) [illegible] to clear away, to mop; 2) *fig.* [illegible] mand, rebuke severely, [illegible] II. *refl.* to wear off or [illegible]

Ab'ſcheulich, *adj.* 1) † serving to deter or discourage crime (Abſchreckend); Strafe zum e-n Exempel, exemplary punishment; 2) detestable, abominable, horrid, horrible; atrocious, heinous, outrageous, execrable; ein e-es Verbrechen, an atrocious or heinous crime; eine e-e That, an atrocious, horrible, hateful or black deed: ein e-er Böſewicht, a detestable, execrable villain, an abandoned wretch; eine e-e Angewohnheit, an odious habit; 3) *fac. & coll.* *a)* odious, wicked; das war wirklich recht — von Ihnen, that was really very wicked of you; *b)* enormous, vast, prodigious, *particul. adv.* excessively or *usual.* abominably: — reich, enormously rich.

Ab'ſcheulichkeit, *(w.) f.* 1) detestableness; abominableness, horribleness; atrocity, enormity; nefariousness, heinousness; blackness; loathsomeness; 2) detestable deed, heinous crime, atrocity, enormity, abomination.

Ab'ſcheuvoll, *adj.* *(l. u.)* full of horror, horrid, detestable, execrable, atrocious.

Ab'ſchichten, *(w.) v. tr.* 1) to divide into rows, to pile off, to range or partition off: 2) *Law*, to portion or pay off *(see* Abſcheiden, II. *tr.* 2. Abtheilen, Abfinden).

Ab'ſchichtung, *(w.) f.* 1) the (act of) ranging or partitioning off, &c. *cf.* Abſchichten; 2) the portioning or paying off, &c.

Ab'ſchicken, *(w.) v. tr.* to send off, to send away, to despatch, delegate.

Ab'ſchickung, *(w.) f.* the (act of) sending off, despatch, delegation.

Ab'ſchieben, *(str.) v.* I. *tr.* 1) *a)* to shove off, push off, to move off, remove from a certain point; *b)* to separate by shoving or moving; 2) *a)* to knock off (ein Tiſchbein, the leg of a table, &c.) by shoving; *b)* (of animals) to shed (teeth), *see intr.*; 3) *Gam.* (at the game of nine-pins) *a)* (Einem) to knock down or carry more pins than (another); to diminish (points, a debt, &c.) by carrying pins; 4) *fig.* to shift off; er will es von ſich ab und mir zuſchieben, he wishes to clear (exonerate, exculpate) himself and lay it at my door.

II. *intr.* 1) *a)* to lose the young teeth (applied to cattle and sheep); *b)* to finish the teething-process; 2) *(aux.* ſein) *coll.* to pack off, shab off, to retreat meanly or clandestinely *(syn.* ſich drücken).

Ab'ſchied, *(str.) m.* *(cf. the original form* Abſcheid) 1) † *a)* the (act of) going away, departure; *b)* *fig.* departure from this life, decease; 2) farewell, leave, adieu, congé; (das —nehmen) valediction, leave-taking; beim A-e, at parting; zum A-e, by way of leave-taking, on taking leave, at parting: ein Wort zum A-e, a valedictory or parting word: von Einem — nehmen, to take leave of one, to bid one adieu or farewell; ohne — weggehen, hinter der Thüre — nehmen, *coll.* to go away or to depart without bidding farewell, to take French leave, to make off; Einem zum A-e die Hand geben, to give one a parting shake of the hand; ich gab ihm zum A-e meinen Segen, I gave him my parting blessing; 3) *a)* dismission, discharge; liberation from service: den or ſeinen — erhalten or bekommen, to be discharged or dismissed; Einem den — geben, to turn one off, to discard, discharge, dismiss one from (military) service, to break (an officer); einem Regiment den — geben, to disband a regiment; ſeinen (den) — nehmen (or verlangen), to ask one's discharge, to send in one's resignation, *Mil.* to sell out, *coll.* to throw up one's commission; *b)* *coll.* *for* A-ſchein, testimony, certificate granted at the expiration of the time of service; 4) † *a)* final (judicial) decision, decree (richterlicher Beſcheid, Urtheil); *b)* final decree of the old German diet, or similar deliberative assemblies (Reichs—, Reichstags—) recess.

Ab'ſchiedchen, *(str.) n.* *(dimin. of* Abſchied) a little farewell-poem (kleines Abſchiedsgedicht), a few parting lines or verses.

Ab'ſchiedlich, *adj.* pertaining to leave-taking, valedictory; *adv.* by way of leave-taking, *see* zum Abſchied; — grüßen, to salute at parting, to bid farewell.

Ab'ſchieder, *(str.) m.* a discharged soldier *(cf.* Urlauber).

Ab'ſchieds…, *in comp.* —audienz, *f.* audience of leave; —beſuch, *m.* farewell visit; —blick, *m.* parting look, last look; —brief, *m.* 1) farewell letter, valedictory letter; 2) letters testimonial, *see* —zeugniß; 3) letter of discharge, discharge, dimissory letter.

Ab'ſchiedsſchwer, *adj.* heavy or bowed down by the parting-scene; Flügel ſchenk' dem a-en Geiſt *(Chamisso)*, wings give to the soul, so loath to flee *(Baskerville)*.

Ab'ſchieds…, *in comp.* —gedicht, *n.* valedictory poem, farewell or parting verses; —geſchenk, *n.* farewell-present, present at parting, parting-gift; —geſuch, *n.* tender of resignation: er reichte ſein —geſuch ein, he tendered his resignation; —glas, *n.* parting-glass, parting-cup; —gruß, *m.* parting-salutation, farewell, adieu (Scheidegruß); er erſchien am Fenſter, um ihnen bei der Abfahrt den —gruß zuzunicken, he appeared at the window to give his parting nod as they drove away; —hand, *f.* parting hand *(Ld. Byron)*; —kuß, *m.* parting-kiss; —mahl, *n.* farewell-dinner; —predigt, *f.* valedictory or farewell-sermon *(opp.* Antrittspredigt); —rede, *f.* valedictory speech, farewell-address; —ſchmaus, *m.* valedictory or farewell-dinner or supper, parting-treat; —ſtunde, *f.* hour of parting, parting-hour; —tag, *m.* parting-day; —thräne, *f.* tear of (or at) parting, parting-tear; —trunk, *m.* parting-draught, parting-cup, parting-glass, parting-goblet, stirrup-cup; —wort, *n.* parting or valedictory word, farewell, adieu; —zähre, *f.* **for* —thräne; —zeugniß, *n.* letters testimonial, certificate *(cf.* Lehrbrief).

Ab'ſchiefern, *(w.) v.* I. *tr.* & *rfl.* to scale off, to shell off, to peel off (in thin flakes or scales), to split off, *Surg.*, &c. to exfoliate; II. *rfl.* to scale or peel off, to come off in scales or thin laminæ, *Surg.*, *Miner.*, &c. to exfoliate. — **Ab'ſchieferung**, *(w.) f.* the (act of) scaling off, &c.; exfoliation, excoriation.

Ab'ſchielen, *(w.) v. tr.* (Einem etwas) *coll.* to learn, discover, &c. (a thing) from (another) by looking slyly askance.

Ab'ſchienen, *(w.) v. tr.* 1) *Surg.* *a)* to take off the splints from (a broken bone after its having been healed); *b)* to confine duly or properly with splinters (as a broken limb), to splint or splinter properly; 2) *a)* *Rails.* to take off the rails from …; ein Rad —, to take off the tire of a wheel; 3) *Min.* to measure out, to survey (a mine). — **Ab'ſchiener**, *(str.) m.* mine-surveyor, &c.

Ab'ſchießen, *(str.) v.* I. *tr.* 1) to shoot off, to discharge: *a)* to let fly or go, as a missile; eine Kugel, einen Pfeil —, to discharge a ball, an arrow, to shoot, or to let fly an arrow; to let go the charge of (fire-arms, &c.); *b)* ein Gewehr, einen Bogen —, to discharge a musket, a bow, &c.: die beiden Enden eines abgeſchoſſenen Bogens, the two ends of a bow shot off; eine Kanone auf den Feind —, to fire or discharge a gun at the enemy; 2) *a)* to strike off by shooting, to shoot off (ein Glied, a limb); es wurde ihm das Bein abgeſchoſſen, his leg was shot or carried off (by a cannon shot); dem Kinde den Apfel vom Kopfe — (or *simply* ſchießen), to shoot the apple off from the child's head; einen (hölzernen) Vogel — *(a German pastime)*, to shoot at an artificial (or wooden) bird *(cf.* Vogelſchießen); den Vogel —, *lit.* & *fig.* to bring down the bird; *b)* † *with regard to human beings:* dem Feind ward abgeſchoſſen mancher ehrlicher Kriegsmann *(Soltau, Volksl.)*, many an honest soldier of the enemy's was brought down; 3) *Sport.* das Wild —, to shoot all the game preserved in an enclosure; 4) to surpass in shooting, to outshoot (another person); 5) *(l. u.)* to shoot down (as felled wood from mountains), to drive or push off with sudden force *(cf.* Rieſen).

II. *intr.* 1) to cease, to leave off, or to finish shooting *(cf. tr.* 3); *(aux.* ſein:) 2) *a)* (Abſtürzen) to fall, shoot, rush, or sweep down rapidly (as a cascade, &c.); hier ſchießt das Waſſer ſtromweiſe ab, here the water escapes downwards (or rushes down) in torrents; eine Treppe —, to fall headlong down stairs; *b)* to dart or shoot off (as a boat, &c.); 3) to slope down abruptly: die Naſe ſchießt nur wenig von der Stirn ab *(Heinse)*, the nose springs but little from the line of the forehead *(cf.* Abſchüſſig); 4) (of colours) to fade away or off, to grow pale, to pale, to turn gray; III. *rfl.* ſich *(Dat.)* etwas (den Hals &c.) —, to break (off, one's neck, &c.) in or by falling precipitately.

Ab'ſchießen, *v. s.* *(str.) n.*, **Ab'ſchießung**, *(w.) f.* the (act of) shooting off, discharging, &c. *cf.* Abſchießen.

† **Ab'ſchießig**, **Ab'ſchießigkeit**, *(w.) f.* *(Opitz, Kant) see* Abſchüſſig, Abſchüſſigkeit.

Ab'ſchiffen, *(w.) v.* I. *intr.* *(aux.* ſein) to sail off or away, to set sail, to sail; II. *tr.* to ship off, to ship (Waaren, goods); to carry away on board of (or to) transport in a ship.

Ab'ſchildern, *(w.) v. tr.* 1) to depict, to paint, portray, picture; 2) *fig.* *(particul. in an ill sense)* to depict, to represent (in words), to describe, delineate, portray.

Ab'ſchilderung, *(w.) f.* *gener. fig.* the (act of) depicting, &c. *cf.* Abſchildern; portraiture, delineation, representation, description.

Ab'ſchilfern, *v.*, **Ab'ſchilferung**, *(w.) f. see* Abſchelfen &c.

Ab'ſchinden, *(str.) v.* I. *tr.* 1) to strip of the skin, to skin, to flay, to excoriate: einem Thiere die Haut —, to flay an animal; einem Baum die Rinde —, to peel off the bark of a tree; Einem die Haut an (or von) den Fingern —, to strip the skin from one's fingers; ſich *(Dat.)* den Arm —, to tear one's arm; das Geſchirr hat das Pferd abgeſchunden, the harness has galled the horse; die Karren haben im Vorbeifahren dieſen Baum abgeſchunden *(Hülp.)*, the carts in passing have peeled this tree; 2) *(l. u.)* to wear off by scratching or scraping; 3) *coll.* to exhaust by hard labour, to harass to excess, to plague, to tire or to weary out; II. *rfl.* *coll.* to toil and moil.

Ab'ſchirren, *(w.) v. tr.* to unharness, to ungear (horses — *opp.* Anſchirren).

Ab'ſchlachten, *(w.) v.* I. *tr.* 1) to slaughter (animals) for food, for market, to kill duly, to butcher, to stick (ein Schwein, a pig); 2) *fig.* to kill off (human beings), to kill with cruelty or in a brutal way, to butcher; II. *intr.* *(aux.* haben) to finish slaughtering.

Ab'ſchlacken, *(w.) v. tr.* to clean from dross, to rid of slags, to scum (as ore in melting).

Ab'ſchlaffen, *(w.) v.* I. *tr.* to slacken, relax; II. *intr.* *see* Abſchlappen.

Ab'ſchlag, *(str., pl.* Ab'ſchläge) *m.* 1) the act of striking off, &c. *cf.* Abſchlagen & Abſchlagung; 2) any thing beaten or hewn off *(cf.* Abſchlagen): *a)* branches of trees that have been felled, loppings; *b)* chips, fragments; *c)* broken off ore; 3) *a)* *Letter-found.* & *Mint.* matrice; *b)* a set of matrices for founding types; 4) partition, *Archit.* reduct; partition-wall; 5) *a)* the (act of) letting or drawing off (water), draining (Abſchlagung); *b)* (Abſchlagsgraben, Abzug) drain, fall, outlet, vent (of a pond, &c.); over-fall (of a mill-dam); 6) *(opp.* Anſchlag, Aufſchlag) rebound; rebounding; 7) *Mus.* fall:

6) *a)* the (act of) taking away, deduction; die reine Natur ohne Zuſchlag und —, pure nature without adding or taking away; *particul. Comm.* *b)* deduction; an abatement, reduction; decline, falling (of the price), diminution; ein — iſt ſeit geraumer Zeit bemerkbar, a decline (fall, reduction) has for a considerable time been perceptible; mit einem — verkaufen, to sell at a decline; *bb) (for* Abſchlagszahlung) part payment; auf —, in part payment, in part of payment, on account; auf — (abſchläglich) zahlen, to pay on account; auf — nehmen (verkaufen), to take (sell) beforehand, by anticipation; *c) gener.* diminution, &c.; der — der Kälte, the abatement of the cold; ein — der Witterung, a lowering (decrease) of (or a fall in the) temperature; es iſt ein großer —, it differs widely; 7) *(l. u. for* abſchlägige Antwort) refusal, denial, rebuff.

Ab'ſchlagsgraben, *(str., pl.* A-gräben) *m.* drain, trench, outfall, ditch for carrying off superfluous water.

Ab'ſchlageiſen, *(str.)* *n.* 1) *(Tech.)* plane-iron, plane; 2) (Stabeiſen, Schmiedeeiſen) bar-iron, forged iron.

Ab'ſchlagen, *(str.)* *v.* I. *tr.* 1) to separate or to bring down by beating, knocking, hewing, &c.; *a)* to beat, strike or knock off; to cut, hew off; Einem den Kopf, die Hand —, to strike off, to sever one's head, hand; ſchlagt ihm den Kopf ab! strike (or cut) off his head! ein Stück Zucker —, to knock off a lump of sugar; den Gypsbewurf von der Wand —, to knock off the plaster-coating from the wall; *Göthe (metonymically):* ein Saal *(for* der Gypsbewurf des Saales, *Sanders)* iſt wieder abgeſchlagen worden; (Welſche) Nüſſe &c. — (Herabſchlagen), to knock down wall-nuts, &c.; abgeſchlagenes Obſt, fruit beaten off (by hail, &c.), blown down (by wind), windfall; Bäume, einen Wald &c. —, to cut down trees, a wood (Fällen); den Miſt, die Erde &c. —, *Husb.* to draw (remove) manure, earth, &c. from a cart with hooks or forks; die Knochen &c. —, *Sport (in dissecting game)* to break or disjoint the bones *(cf.* Abgeſchlagen, *p. a.)*; er ſchlug dem Manne den Hut ab, he knocked off the man's hat; *b)* to take off or down in a regular way; to break down or off (ein Gerüſt, ein Zelt &c., a scaffold, a tent, &c.), to take to pieces (eine Bettſtelle, eine Maſchine &c., a bedstead, an engine, &c.) *(opp.* Aufſchlagen); die Bude, das Gerüſt wurde abgeſchlagen, the booth, the scaffolding was taken down; ein Zelt —, to strike a tent; ein Lager — (Abbrechen), to break up a camp; ein Schloß —, to take off, unnail, unscrew a lock; *Printer's terms:* die Ballen —, *(formerly)* to knock off the balls (Abbrechen); das Formet —, to unlock the chase; eine Preſſe —, to break down a press; die Segel, ein Reff —, *Mar.* to unbend, unbind (the sails), to unlace (a bonnet) *(opp.* Anſchlagen); Maſchen —, to take off the meshes from the needles; to diminish the number of meshes, *see* Abnehmen; ein Stück Pelzwerk —, *T.* to clip a piece of fur; 2) to force or drive back by beating, to beat or turn off, to strike aside; einen Stoß —, *Fenc.* to parry a thrust; 3) † (Einem etwas) *a)* dem Feinde gewiſſe Perſonen, Fahnen &c. —, to snatch or take prisoners, colours, &c. from the enemy in battle; *b)* to slay or vanquish (the troops of the enemy) in battle; 4) to beat thoroughly, to beat well; das Eiweiß mit dem Quirl —, to beat the white of an egg with a mill; Einen — (Abprügeln), *coll.* to beat one soundly; 5) to strike off a copy of (a coin, &c.), to take an impression, cast of... (Abklatſchen, Abdrücken); eine Münze in Blei —, to impress, to stamp a coin in lead; 6) *(cf.* 8) to turn off (a stream of water, &c.), to let or draw off (water, *cf.* Ablaſſen); to dam off (as the water from a mill-pond, &c. for the purpose of dragging, &c.); einen Teich, den Mühlgraben —, to drain a pond, to shut out the water from the mill-stream; den fließenden Metallſtrom —, *in metal foundries,* to turn off the stream of liquid iron, &c. into new channels and moulds (the old ones being filled); das *(or* ſein) Waſſer —, to make water; 7) to partition off (einen Raum, a room), *cf.* Abſchlag, 4; 8) *fig.* † to abate, deduct, *see* in Abrechnung bringen; 9) (Einem etwas *[gener.* eine Bitte, ein Geſuch] —) to refuse, deny, decline (one's request); Einem etwas rund —, to give one a peremptory negative, a flat denial or refusal; Sie dürfen es mir nicht —, I won't be denied, I won't take a refusal; 10) to reduce, &c. *see intr.* 4, *a;* 11) Abgeſchlagen, *p. a.* practised, cunning, *see* Abgeſchlagen, 2.

II. *refl.* 1) to strike off, to take a different direction, to turn off (suddenly), to deviate *(cf.* Schlagen, *refl.)*; ich ſchlug mich rechts vom Wege ab, I left the road, and turned to the right; das Wild ſchlägt ſich ab, *Sport.* the game flies, runs away (when it separates from its kind); 2) *incorrectly for* einander —, *reciproc.* to beat each other soundly *(cf.* I. *tr.* 5).

III. *intr.* 1) *(aux.* ſein) to rebound, to recoil; die Kugel ſchlägt ab, the ball rebounds; 2) *(aux.* ſein) *obsolescent, lit. & fig.* to turn off suddenly, *see* II. *refl.* 1; 3) *(aux.* ſein) *(for* fehlſchlagen, mißrathen, *opp.* einſchlagen, gerathen) to fail, to miscarry; to lose; 4) *(aux.* ſein *&* haben) to abate, to decline: *a) (particul. of prices, &c.)* to fall, to go down, to experience a depression; to sink (in price, &c. — *opp.* Aufſchlagen); der Preis der Waare ſchlägt ab or die Waare ſchlägt im Preiſe ab, the price of a commodity falls; die Preiſe haben *(or* ſind) noch keineswegs abgeſchlagen, prices have by no means fallen (declined) as yet; das Brot, das Getreide *(for* der Preis des Brotes, des Getreides) ſchlägt ab, the price of bread, of corn falls; der Kaufmann ſchlägt mit ſeiner Waare ab, the merchant reduces the price of his commodity; *for* — mit... *(as used in the last phrase) the simple verb is sometimes used as a transitive:* das Brot —, to diminish or reduce the price of bread; eine Münze — *(for* Abwürdigen), to reduce the value of a coin; *b)* die Kuh ſchlägt ab, the cow gives less milk than formerly; *c)* der Wein ſchlägt ab, the wine loses in taste; *d)* die Hitze, Kälte &c. ſchlägt ab, the heat, the cold, &c. abates; im Verlauf der Morgenſtunden ſchlug das Wetter wieder ab, as the morning-hours wore on, the weather moderated again; kaltes Waſſer, heißen Kaffee ein wenig — laſſen *(cf.* Überſchlagen, Verſchlagen), to let the chill go off, to suffer to grow cooler, to temper extreme cold or heat; 5) *(aux.* haben) *Mil. a)* (das Signal zum Abzug ſchlagen) to beat the retreat; *b)* to give notice (on the march) by beat of drum that the soldiers are allowed to march more at their ease.

Ab'ſchlagen, *v. s. (str.)* *n.* the act of beating off, &c. *cf. the verb; particul.* a falling (of prices, &c.), *see* Abſchlag, 2, *b*, *aa.*

Ab'ſchlagewiſch, *(str.)* *m.* a wisp of straw used in salt-works for cleansing the salt-pans.

Ab'ſchlägig, *adj.* 1) *lit.* (easily) broken, brittle; a-e Stücke, fragments, splinters; 2) containing a refusal, denying, refusing; eine a-e Antwort, a refusal, denial, rebuff; eine a-e Antwort bekommen, to be refused; 3) *(l. u.)* paid on account, *see* Abſchläglich.

Ab'ſchläglich, *adj.* 1) *(l. u.)* containing a refusal, *see* Abſchlägig; 2) *Comm.* given in part-payment, paid on account; a-e Zahlung, payment on account, instalment (Abſchlagszahlung).

Ab'ſchlags..., *in comp.* —anleihe, *f.* a loan of money to be repaid by instalment; —graben, *see* Abſchlagegraben; —zahlung (Abſchlagszahlung), *f.* part-payment, [illegible] account, instalment.

Ab'ſchlagung, *(w.)* *f.* 1) the act [illegible] ing, striking off, &c. *see* Abſchlagen [illegible] (act of) turning, letting or drawing [illegible] 3) refusal (of a request).

Ab'ſchlämmen, **Ab'ſchlammen,** *(w.)* [illegible] 1) to clear of mud, to clean from [illegible] *Min.* to wash (ore), *see* Schlämmen.

Ab'ſchlängeln, *(w.)* *v. refl.* to [illegible] down in windings, to meander off or [illegible] wards.

Ab'ſchlappen, *v. intr.* *(aux.* haben) [illegible] hang down loosely or slovenly.

Ab'ſchlarfen, *(w.)* *v. tr.* *coll.* to [illegible] (ſich) *[Dial.]* die Schuhe, one's boots, by [illegible] ing about slipshod or in a slovenly [illegible]

Ab'ſchlauchen, *(w.)* *v. tr.* *see* [illegible]

Ab'ſchleichen, *(str.)* *v.* I. *tr.* 1) [illegible] steal upon, to take by surprise, [illegible] 2) (Einem etwas) to get, obtain [illegible] insidiously, sneakingly from (one) [illegible] *(aux.* ſein) or *refl.* to sneak or [illegible] steal away (Wegſchleichen).

Ab'ſchleifeiſen, *(str.)* *n.* *T.* [illegible]

A. **Ab'ſchleifen,** *(str.)* *v.* I. *tr.* 1) [illegible] *a)* to take off by grinding, to rub off, [illegible] away, to blunt (a point); die Spitze [illegible] Meſſers (or ein Meſſer) —, to grind [illegible] point of a knife; den Roſt, die [illegible] Klinge —, to do away, to get out, [illegible] the rust from a blade (by grinding) [illegible] *mically:* *b)* to smooth, to polish by [illegible] eine Klinge —, to rub a blade; [illegible] to furbish a sword; eine [illegible] Spiegel —, to polish a marble [illegible] glass; *c)* to whet, to sharpen; 2) [illegible] ficiently; 3) *fig.* to rub off, wear [illegible] (asperities, &c.), to smooth [illegible] refine; *refl. fig.* to improve one's [illegible] II. *intr.* 1) to be ground off, to [illegible] wear off; ein abgeſchliffener [illegible] penny-piece worn smooth; 2) *fig.* [illegible] fined, *see* I. *tr.* 3.

B. **Ab'ſchleifen,** *(w.)* *v. tr.* 1) *a)* [illegible] out by dragging, &c.; *b)* *provinc.* [illegible] (land) out of heart, to impoverish [illegible] Abzergeln); 2) to carry or drag [illegible] away on a sledge.

Ab'ſchleifer, *(str.)* *m.* one who [illegible] &c., grinder; furbisher, polisher.

Ab'ſchleifſel, *(str.)* *n.* the [illegible] settlings of a grindstone from the [illegible] grinding, grindings, (in [illegible]) swarf.

A. **Ab'ſchleifung,** *(w.)* *f.* 1) the [illegible] grinding off, &c.; grinding, wearing [illegible] 2) (the act of) polishing, &c.; [illegible]

B. **Ab'ſchleifung,** *(w.)* *f.* 1) the [illegible] wearing out by dragging, &c. *see* [illegible] *B.*; 2) the (act of) carrying or dragging [illegible] off, &c. (on a sledge).

Ab'ſchleimen, *(w.)* *v. tr.* to [illegible] Zucker —, to clarify sugar [illegible] men); Fiſche &c. —, to soak, water, [illegible] fish, &c.

Ab'ſchleißen, *(str.)* *v. tr.* to [illegible]

Ab'ſchlemmen, *see* Abſchlämmen, [illegible]

Ab'ſchlendern, *(w.)* *v. intr.* [illegible] saunter down or away.

Ab'ſchleudern, *(w.)* *v. tr.* to [illegible]

Ab'ſchleppen, *(w.)* *v.* I. *tr.* 1) [illegible] by dragging, to wear out [illegible] &c.) by constant and [illegible] down; 3) to carry off [illegible] Wegſchleppen); II. *refl.* to [illegible] by carrying heavy loads.

Ab'ſchleſſen, *(w.)* *v. tr.* *see* [illegible]

Ab'ſchleudern, *(w.)* *v.* I. *tr.* [illegible] with a sling or a [illegible] away; II. *intr.* *(aux.* ſein) [illegible]

Ab'ſchlichten, *(w.)* *v. tr.* [illegible]

wings of a bird; Bäume —, to poll trees; 3) *Millin.*, &c. to shape or form by cutting, to cut a pattern of (a cap, &c.) in paper; Muſter —, to cut out (or off) patterns; *T.* (*formerly, among soldiers, &c.*) to settle (accounts) by tallies (to cut off the notches of a score or tally); *fig.*-s. 4) *Geom.* to cut off, truncate, *cf.* Abſtumpfen & Abgeſtutzt; 5) *Gramm.* einen Buchſtaben oder eine Silbe —, to cut off or omit a letter or a syllable, to apocopate; 6) *a)* to cut through (as a thread); den Lebensfaden —, to cut the thread of life (Einem, to kill one); *b)* (Einem etwas) to deprive (one) of (a thing); Einem ſeine Ehre, ſeinen guten Namen, den guten Leumund ꝛc. —, to injure (wound, blast) one's reputation; *c)* to separate from the other parts, *particul. Mil.* to cut off, intercept; das Waſſer —, to dig off the water; *d)* to bring to an abrupt end, to cut short; Einem das Wort —, to stop one's utterance, to cut one short; ein Geſpräch —, to break off a conversation abruptly, to put a sudden stop to a conversation; es ſchneidet mir alle Hoffnung ab, it precludes me from (or deprives me of) all hope; die Möglichkeit übler Nachrede —, to prevent the possibility of slander; der Eintritt in den Staatsdienſt iſt dir abgeſchnitten, the public service is closed to you; wenn uns der Gebrauch dieſer Anlagen abgeſchnitten iſt, if we are debarred from the exercise of these faculties; *e)* *Math.* to cut or take off (a curve, an angle, &c.); *f)* to separate or define by a distinct boundary-line (Abgrenzen).

II. *refl.* 1) to be brought to a sudden stop, to cease, stop, end; die Erze ſchneiden ſich ab, *Min.* the vein of ore discontinues; the vein disappears suddenly, it makes a start or leap; 2) (*or intr.*) *a)* to be sharply defined or outlined, to be traced, to be contrasted; die Umriſſe dieſes Gebirges ſchneiden ſich ſcharf am Himmel ab, the outlines of these hills are sharply defined against the sky; *b)* to form a contrast, to contrast, to differ.

III. *intr.* 1) *see refl.* 1 & 2; 2) *provinc.* to fare badly or ill.

Ab'ſchneideln, (*w.*) *v. tr. see* Abſchnitzeln.

Ab'ſchneider, (*str.*) *m.* one that cuts off, cutter, &c. *cf.* Abſchneiden.

Ab'ſchneide…, *in comp.* —linie, —maſchine, *see* Abſchneide… .

Ab'ſchneidſel, (*str.*) *n. see* Abſchnitzel.

Ab'ſchneidung, (*w.*) *f.* the act of cutting off, recision, &c., *Surg.* abscission, amputation.

Ab'ſchneid…, *in comp.* —werkzeug, *n.* cutting-tool; —winkel, *m.* *Typ.* token, cutting-line (Abſchneidelinie).

Ab'ſchneien, (*w.*) *v. impers.* to cease snowing, *cf.* Abregnen.

Ab'ſchneiteln, (*w.*) *v. tr. Gard.* to lop, prune, trim (tendrils, a hedge, &c.).

Ab'ſchnellen, (*w.*) *v.* I. *tr.* to fling off (as a stone, &c.) with a jerk, to let fly with a jerk, to jerk off, to jerk, to snap; einen Pfeil —, to fling a dart; II. *intr.* (*aux.* ſein) to fly off with a jerk, to jerk, spring, or crack off.

Ab'ſchneuzen, (*w.*) *v. tr. provinc.* (*S. G.* & *Austr. for* Putzen) to snuff (a candle).

Ab'ſchnippeln, Ab'ſchnippern, (*w.*) *v. tr.* to clip, chip, or snip off by repeated little cuts.

Ab'ſchnippen, (*w.*) *v. tr.* to clip, chip, or snip off.

Ab'ſchnipperling, (*str.*) *m.*, **Ab'ſchnipſel,** (*str.*) *n.* (& *m.*) clippings, parings (*cf.* Abſchnitzel).

Ab'ſchnitt, (*str.*) *m.* 1) (Abſchneidung) *a)* (the act of) cutting off, &c.; *b)* (*among soldiers, &c. formerly*) a cutting off of notches, &c.) settling of accounts (by tallies); 2) *a)* cut (a part cut off); *Join.* balement; *b)* *gener.* *pl.* A-e, cuttings, chips, shreds, parings (*cf.* Abſchnitzel); *Carp.* balement (Abfall); 3) *a)* *Geom.* segment; *b)* *Fortif.* ..., *c)* *Fort.* intrenchment, trench, priest's cap; 5) *T.* a pattern cut out; 6) *a)* *Fort.* stop, caesura; *b)* *Gramm.*, &c. rest, breathing place, pause; *c)* section, paragraph, book (as a division of a volume or book); (Einem) A-e aus der Bibel vorleſen, to read to (one) portions of the Bible; *d)* *Mus.* section, musical sentence (*cf.* Abſatz, 7, *a*); *e)* *fig.* period, epoch, stage (des menſchlichen Lebens ꝛc., of human life, &c.); 7) *Comm.* *a)* additional payment, balance paid in addition; *b)* (Staatspapier—) coupon (*cf.* Zins-Coupon); *c)* (Wechſel—) appoint (*cf.* Appoint); die kleinſten A-e lauten auf einen Thaler, the smallest appoints (shares) are to the value of one thaler; eine Rimeſſe in drei A-en, a remittance in three appoints; 8) *fig. rarely used for* Abſtich, contrast.

Ab'ſchnittchen, Ab'ſchnittlein, (*str.*) *n.* 1) small cut or shred chip, &c. *cf.* Abſchnitzel; 2) little section or period, &c.

Ab'ſchnittling, (*str.*) *m.* 1) cutting, shred, chip, &c., *see* Abſchnitzel; 2) *Hortic.* cutting, cut; 3) *Geom.* abscissa (Abſciſſe).

Ab'ſchnitt…, *in comp.* —(s)linie, *f.* *Typ.* cutting-line; —(s)ſchein, *m.* check; —(s)winkel, *m.* *Geom.* angle of a segment; —(s)zeichen, *n.* *Typ.* mark used to denote a division of a subject, section [§].

Ab'ſchnitzel, (*str.*) *n.* shred, chip, cutting, clipping, snipping, paring, *gener. in the pl. collectively* shreds, chips, &c.; *Coin.* sizel.

Ab'ſchnitzeln, (*w.*) *v. tr.* to cut off in little chips, to pare, to whittle.

Ab'ſchnitzen, (*w.*) *v. tr.* 1) to cut off in chips, to chip off; 2) *a)* to carve; *b)* to imitate by carving.

Ab'ſchnüren, (*w.*) *v. tr.* 1) *a)* to unlace, unstring (Losſchnüren); *b)* *Bookb.* to untie; 2) *Carp.*, &c. *a)* to measure out or divide with a line; *b)* to lash, switch, strap, or to lay out by the (chalk-)line; to mark with a line (Abkohlen, if the line is blackened); 3) *a)* to separate with a string; eine Warze —, to tie off or to string a wart (*cf.* Abbinden, 3); *b)* to separate by a deep incision.

Ab'ſchnurren, (*w.*) *v.* I. *intr.* (*aux.* ſein) to run down (as spools, &c.) with a whirring noise, to rattle, whir or whiz, off; II. *tr.* 1) to cause to run down (as machinery, &c.) with a whirring noise; to reel off, *cf.* Abhaſpeln; 2) to utter in a monotonous, mechanical way, to rattle off (prayers, &c.); 3) (Einem etwas) to get or obtain (something) from (one) by begging (Abbetteln).

Ab'ſchocken, (*w.*) *v. tr.* (*l. u.*) to divide into scores.

Ab'ſchöpfen, (*w.*) *v. tr.* to scoop off; to scum (off), to skim (off); die Milch —, to skim or fleet milk; Fett von der Fleiſchbrühe —, to skim off the fat of broth; abgeſchöpfte Milch, skim-milk, fleet-milk.

Ab'ſchoß, (*str.*) *m.* 1) (*rarely used for* Schoß, Schößling) offshoot; 2) *or* —geld, *n.* 1) tax on emigration (Abzugsgeld); 2) (*census hereditarius*) legacy-tax, duty to be paid in certain countries by aliens for an inheritance devolving on them in the said countries; —pflichtig, *adj.* liable to pay the emigration-tax or the legacy-tax (*see* —geld); —pflichtigkeit, (*w.*) *f.* liableness to pay the emigration-tax or the legacy-tax (*see* —geld).

Ab'ſchrägen, (*w.*) *v.* I. *tr.* to make oblique, *particul. Carp.*, &c. to cut into a sloping form, to cut off (to grind off, &c.) aslope or bevelwise; to slope, slant; to bevel, to cut to a bevel angle, to chamfer; II. *refl.* to slope away; ein Wieſenplan ſchrägte ſich vom Herrenhauſe ab, a lawn sloped away from the mansion. — **Ab'ſchrägung,** (*w.*) *f.* 1) the act of making oblique, of sloping, &c.; 2) slope, sloping form.

Ab'ſchrammen, (*w.*) *v.* I. *tr.* to slash or scratch off, to scar; II. *intr.* (*aux.* ſein) *coll.* to slip off in silence (in either [illegible] [illegible]ation).

Ab'ſchranken, (*w.*) *v. tr.* to [illegible] clude by barriers, rails or any [illegible] which prevent common access [illegible] Weideplätze, hedged-off (fenced off) [illegible] lands; ein abgeſchranktes [illegible] being.

Ab'ſchraubemeſſer, (*str.*) *n.* [illegible] knife, counting iron, counting-[illegible]

Ab'ſchrapen, (*w.*) *v. tr.* [illegible] off (*see* Abſcharren, Abſchaben, [illegible]

Ab'ſchrauben, (*w.*) *v. tr.* [illegible] unscrew, to screw off; ganz — [illegible] made to unscrew or to screw off.

Ab'ſchrecken, (*w.*) *v. tr.* 1) [illegible] to scare or fright away (as game [illegible] &c.), to scare up, to start, [illegible] or modify by applying sudden [illegible] bodies, or heat to cold substances [illegible] Metall —, to cool off heated [illegible] (by thrusting it into cold water [illegible] Sandguß ſchreckt die Feuchtigkeit [illegible] des Eiſens ab und macht ſie [illegible] in sand-casting the moisture [illegible] off the surface of iron and [illegible] einen Fiſch —, *Cook.* to sprinkle [illegible] vinegar (in order to turn the [illegible] boiling); abgeſchrecktes Waſſer, [illegible] moderately warm; 3) (Einem etwas [illegible] to deter, discourage (one) [illegible] frighten (fright) (one) from (a [illegible] timidate, dispirit, dishearten, [illegible] Laſter durch eigenes Beiſpiel —, [illegible] vice by direct example; das [illegible] von abzuſchrecken, the best aid of [illegible] ment; er läßt ſich leicht —, he [illegible] spirited; 4) † Einem etwas —, [illegible] one out of a thing; den [illegible] — (*Hans Sachs*), to frighten [illegible] out of their money.

Ab'ſchreckend, *p. a.* 1) deterring [illegible] warning; dies war ein a-es [illegible] a warning example or a [illegible] outward appearance) forbidding [illegible] iſt etwas A-es im Ausſehen der [illegible] something forbidding in the [illegible] eine a-e Terminologie, a [illegible]nology.

Ab'ſchreckung, (*w.*) *f.* (the act [illegible] ring, &c.; discouragement; [illegible] irgendwo, daß — der Zweck [illegible] Macaulay says somewhere that [illegible] end of punishment; A-smittel, [illegible] discouragement, deterrent; A-s[illegible] *Criminal Law*, theory of deterrence [illegible] committal of crimes) by punish[illegible]

Ab'ſchreibegebühr, (*w.*) *f.*, [illegible] geld, (*str.*) *n.* copy-money, [illegible]

Ab'ſchreiben, (*str.*) *v. tr.* 1) [illegible] writing; to dull or blunt (a pen, &c. [illegible] ich ſchreibe mir faſt die Finger ab [illegible] almost wear out my fingers with [illegible] Bleiſtift ganz —, to wear a pencil [illegible] 2) *a)* to copy, transcribe [illegible] gross; *b)* *fig.* (*l. u.*) to copy [illegible] likeness by following a model [illegible] imitate; die Natur (*Schiller*) [illegible] copy nature (said of a painter [illegible] other's writings) [illegible] ein abgeſchriebenes [illegible] another, a pirated book or [illegible] to take out (an amount), to [illegible] to subtract, substract [illegible] charge, to blot out, to efface [illegible] Schuld, a bad debt; *c)* to [illegible] one's credit; *d)* [illegible] transfer (as invested [illegible] article; *e)* die Summe — [illegible] write off, to transfer [illegible] exchange, &c. in [illegible] revoke in writing (an [illegible] previously given, made, &c.), to write off, to put off, to countermand, to cancel; ich muß Ihnen leider wieder —, I regret being obliged to cancel (to countermand or to retract) my order (or to recede from our agreement); er schrieb es ihnen ab, he wrote off refusals to them; 5) (l. u.) eine Schuld —, to pay off a debt by writing (for one's creditor).

Ab'schreiber, (str.) m. 1) copier, copyist, transcriber; 2) cont. piratical writer, plagiary; 3) fig. (slavish) imitator (cf. Abschreiben, 2, b).

Abschreiberei', (w.) f. the act (or the custom) of copying, transcribing, gener. cont. the purloining of another man's writings or of passages of other works, literary theft, plagiarism.

Ab'schreibung, (w.) f. 1) (the act of) copying, transcription, &c. cf. Abschreiben; 2) (the act of) writing off, transferring, crediting (a payment), &c.

Ab'schreien, (str.) v. I. tr. 1) to bawl forth, to roar out (a song, &c.); 2) to cry out, to proclaim with a loud voice; to cry off; 3) Sport., &c. to recall with loud cries, to call off (the hounds); 4) to reach (with the voice) by crying aloud; 5) (Einem etwas) a) to get or obtain (a thing) from (one), to frighten (one) out of (a thing) by dint of crying; b) to contest (a thing, one's right, &c.), to deny (the claims of another, &c.) by loud cries rather than by argument; 6) to outcry, to drown (every thing) with cries; II. refl. 1) sich (Acc.) —, to tire one's self (out) by crying: das Kind hat sich (Acc.) ganz abgeschrieen, the child has quite exhausted itself with crying; 2) sich (Dat.) die Kehle, den Hals —, to bawl till one grows hoarse, to cry one's self to death (nach einem Dinge, for or after a thing); das Kind wird sich (Dat.) die Kehle —, the child will kill itself by crying.

Ab'schreiten, (str.) v. I. intr. (aux. sein) 1) to pass or stride away or down (von, from ...), to step aside; to retire; 2) (rarely used) to alight (from a horse, &c.), see Absteigen; 3) fig. to deviate, to digress, to swerve (from one's duty, &c.); II. tr. to measure (out) by steps, by pacing, to pace, to step; sie haben unsere Schußweite so genau, daß man vermuthen sollte, sie hätten die Entfernung abgeschritten, they have our range so accurately, one would suspect they had stepped the ground; a-d, p. a. (l. u.) digressive; discursive.

Ab'schricken, (w.) v. tr. Mar. to pay out or to ease off a little, to surge (ein Tau, a rope); das (um das Gangspill laufende) Ankertau —, to surge at the windlass or capstern.

Ab'schrift, (w.) f. copy, transcript; duplicate; die zweite —, triplicate; gerichtliche —, exemplification; eine — nehmen, to draw or to take a copy; nehmen Sie — davon, take a copy of it; die beigefügte beglaubigte —, the annexed certified copy; gerichtliche — nehmen, Comm. durch eine beglaubigte — belegen, to exemplify.

Ab'schriftlich, adj. copied (out), transcriptive, by way of copy: wir theilen es Ihnen hierbei — mit, we hereby hand you duplicate (copy); die a-e Beilage, the annexed copy.

Ab'schröpfen, (w.) v. tr. (cf. Schröpfen) 1) a) Surg. (Einem das Blut) to draw off (one's blood) by cupping; b) to weaken (one) by cupping; c) fig. to fleece (one), usual. to make (one) bleed (cf. Anzapfen); 2) Agr. (das Getreide, die Saaten &c.) to cut off the tops of (wheat, &c.) with a reaping-hook; 3) a) Forest. to rough-hew (felled trees), to take off the slabs (see Abschwarten); b) see Abschroten.

Ab'schrot, (str.) m. (dimin. Abschrötlein, Ab'schrötel) 1) remnant, small part, &c.; cutting or clipping off pieces of metal from which blanks for coins have been cut (cf. Abschnitzel); 2) or **Ab'schrote**, (w.) f. —meißel, m. (dimin. Ab'schrötel, [str.] m. small) chisel; (Schrotmeißel, m., Schroteisen, n.) rod-chisel, hot-chisel; 3) ([Sahl-]Leiste, Kante, f.) selvage, list.

Ab'schroten, (w.) v. tr. 1) to gnaw off, devour (as grubs, &c. little roots); 2) to take off the rough, to rough-hew, to cut or clip off, to work, hew, &c. rudely or coarsely, as for first purposes; to give the first form or shape, among different trades: a) Mill. to grind coarsely; b) Carp., &c. to cut, to saw off transversely, to saw off with a large double saw; to rough-plane; c) Smith., &c. to hew (off), to chop off; d) Pin-m. to clip (the wire); 3) a) to turn or lead off (the course of a spring); b) to cut (a ditch, &c.) in a sloping direction, to slope sufficiently; 4) to roll down, to shoot, to lower (a cask, &c.).

Ab'schrubben, (w.) v. tr. 1) Mar. to hog (a vessel); 2) or Ab'schruppen, Join., &c. to clip off the rough of (a piece of wood, &c.).

Ab'schub, (str., pl. Ab'schübe) m. digression from the main route, excursion, see Abstecher.

Ab'schuhen, (w.) v. tr. to pull off the shoes from (one's feet, &c.).

Ab'schulden, (w.) v. tr. (Einem etwas) (l. u.) to discharge or pay a debt owing to some one.

Ab'schülfern, (Ab'schilfern), (w.) v. &c. see Abschelfern.

Ab'schultern, (w.) v. tr. to take (a musket, &c.) from the shoulder (mostly used in a military sense, often as an intransitive); den Mehlsack —, Miller. to remove the meal-sack from the shoulder or shoulders.

Ab'schuppen, (w.) v. I. tr. 1) a) to scale off, to scale, unscale, to strip or clear of scales, to shell; einen Fisch —, to scale a fish; b) particul. Med. to scale off, to desquamate, to take off or remove in thin laminae or scales; sich (Dat.) die Haut —, to scale or scratch off one's dead skin; c) fig. to scale away, to peel off, to remove; 2) coll. to push away; II. refl. or intr. to scale off, to peel off in scales, to come off in thin layers or laminae, to scale, peel, flake, (von der Haut, of the skin) to desquamate.

Ab'schüppen, (w.) v. tr. to shovel off, to take off or to remove with a shovel.

Ab'schuppern, (w.) v. tr. to scale or scratch off with a jerking motion.

Ab'schuppung, (w.) f. (the act or condition of) scaling off, &c. cf. Abschuppen, particul. Med. desquamation, separation of the cuticle in small scales.

Ab'schur, (w.) f. (the act or time of) shearing off, &c., (sheep-)shearing.

Ab'schurfen, **Ab'schürfen**, (w.) v. tr. 1) a) to scratch or take off the scurf from (the skin, &c.); b) sich (Dat.) die Haut —, to scratch, tear or raze one's skin; 2) Sport. to cut off (Abschärfen, 3); 3) Join., &c. to scrape off.

Ab'schurren, (w.) v. I. tr. (suggesting a more obscure sound than Abscharren, which compare) to scrape or to scratch off; II. intr. (aux. sein) 1) (Hinabschurren) to glide or slip down or off with a rumbling noise; 2) burl. to pop off, i. e. to die (cf. Abfahren, 2).

† **Ab'schürzen**, (w.) v. tr. to shorten, abbreviate.

Ab'schuß, (str., pl. Ab'schüsse) m. 1) the act of shooting off, discharging, &c.; der — (l. u. for das Abschießen) der Pfeile, the discharge of arrows; 2) the rushing down (des Wassers, of water), rapid fall; 3) a) abrupt, slope, steep declivity, precipitous descent; b) fig. auf dem — zum Verderben, on the point of rushing into ruin, on the verge of ruin; 4) Carp. (spiral, winding or well-)staircase; 5) among Dyers, alteration, decolouring, fading (of colours), cf. Abschießen, intr. 4.

Ab'schüssig, I. adj. 1) steep, precipitous; declivous, abrupt, sloping, shelving; adv. slopingly, slopewise, aslope; a-es Gewölbe, T. inclined vault; 2) fading (of colours); II. A-keit, (w.) f. declivity, steepness, precipitousness &c.

Ab'schütteln, (w.) v. tr. 1) to shake off, to shake down, to throw down by shaking; Obst —, to shake off fruit (von dem Baume, from the tree; (den Baum —, in the same sense); 2) a) to shake violently, to give (one) a good (sound) shaking; b) fig. to reprimand severely; 3) fig. to shake off, to throw off, to rid one's self of, to put away; Deutschland schüttelte das Joch des Fremdlings ab, Germany shook off the yoke of the foreigner; sie schüttelten ihn ab, they shook him off (coll. gave him the go-by); 4) a) to throw off, to perform, &c. in a careless way; ein Geschäft —, to shuffle off a business; solche Sachen lassen sich nicht — (or aus den Ärmeln schütteln), things of that kind are not arranged or settled in a hurry (Hilp.); b) Verweise &c. —, to be careless or unmindful of reprimands, to make light of reproofs, coll. to shake it off; er schüttelt Vorwürfe ab, he does not heed reproaches.

Ab'schütten, (w.) v. tr. 1) to pour off (as from a liquid); 2) to throw off (as grain from a loft, &c.); to throw down.

Ab'schüttsel, (str.) n. fruit blown, fallen or shaken down from trees before it is ripe, windfall.

Ab'schützen, (w.) v. tr. 1) a) das Schutzbrett (gener. intr.:) —, to draw up, to open the floodgate; b) to let off by opening the floodgate: einen Teich, einen Fluß —, to drain a pond, a river; 2) to shut up (water) by dams, to dam off, to stop by a floodgate; 3) T. to stop.

Ab'schwächen, (w.) v. I. tr. 1) a) to weaken by degrees, to lessen (break) the force of the waves; b) to debilitate, enfeeble: abgeschwächte Augen, debilitated or impaired eyesight; eine abgeschwächte Seele, a soul enfeebled; 2) fig. a) to weaken, to break (einen Eindruck &c., the force of an impression, &c.); b) to attenuate, to tame down, to soften down; das Interesse für den Staat war gänzlich abgeschwächt, the interest in the state had altogether declined; II. refl. (or III. intr., l. u.) to grow gradually weaker; to decline, decrease, fall off; der Wind schwächte mehr ab, the wind diminished in force.

Ab'schwächung, (w.) f. (the act of) weakening by degrees, &c. cf. Abschwächen; debilitation (Entkräftung); attenuation, diminution, decrease, &c. (cf. Abnahme).

Ab'schwämmen, (w.) v. tr. see Abschwemmen.

Ab'schwanken, (w.) v. intr. (aux. sein) to stagger or to walk down, more frequently to move off with a staggering step; ab und zu schwanken, to waver to and fro; to be irresolute (cf. Schwanken, Abwanken).

Ab'schwänzeln, (w.) v. tr. coll. (Einem etwas) to get or obtain (something) from (one) by fawning and coaxing, see Abschmeicheln.

Ab'schwären, (str.) v. intr. 1) (aux. sein) to fall off by ulceration; to be separated by an ulcer; es ist mir ein Nagel abgeschworen, one of my nails is festered away; 2) (aux. haben) to cease festering.

Ab'schwärmen, (w.) v. I. intr. 1) (aux. sein) to fly off in swarms (as bees, &c.), to withdraw swarming; 2) (aux. haben) Bee. to swarm for the last time; II. refl. to weary one's self by revelling and rioting.

Ab'schwarten, (w.) v. tr. 1) to peel off the rind, skin of (a flitch of bacon, &c.); 2) Carp. to saw off the slabs of (a log or an unhewn piece of timber).

Ab'schwärzen, (w.) v. I. tr. 1) a) to blacken thoroughly or sufficiently; b) provinc. (S.G.) for Abschmutzen, to dirty thoroughly, to foul, smut, taint; 2) fig. (scarcely used) to blacken, calumniate, see Anschwärzen, 2; II. intr. to let off (or to part with) the black colour, to stain, as black colour, blacking; dieſes Tuch ſchwärzt ab, the black comes off this cloth (*Hilp.*).

Ab'ſchwatzen, *provinc.* (*S.G.*): **Ab'ſchwätzen**, (*w.*) *v. tr.* 1) (Einem etwas) *a)* to obtain (something) from (one) by talking, to talk (one) out of (a thing); *b)* *fig.* to deprive (one) of (a thing) by idle talk: ſie ſchwatzte ihrem Manne ein Ohr ab, she talked off her husband's ear, *ridiculous exaggeration* (*cf.* Ohr) *for* she assailed her husband's ears by incessant talk or argument, she kept dinning (a certain thing) into his ears: *c)* to contest (a thing, &c.), to deny (one's right, &c.) by idle talk; 2) to talk over, to prattle about (a thing), to discuss fully.

Ab'ſchwelgen, (*w.*) *v. tr. Bookb.* to cleanse by washing, to wash, (*Spiers:*) to ungum.

Ab'ſchwefeln, (*w.*) *v. tr.* 1) to desulphurate, to deprive *or* clear of sulphur: Steinkohlen —, to coke coal: abgeſchwefelte Steinkohlen, coke: 2) to impregnate sufficiently with sulphur.

Ab'ſchwefelung, (*w.*) *f.* (the act or operation of) depriving or clearing of sulphur, &c., desulphuration, &c. *cf.* Abſchwefeln.

Ab'ſchweif, (*str.*) *m.* 1) digression, *see* Abſchweifung; 2) (*l. u.*) deviation; — machen, to commit breach of faith.

Ab'ſchweifen, (*w.*) *v.* I. *intr.* (*aux.* ſein) 1) *lit.* (*l. u.*) to deviate, to go astray, to start (from); 2) *fig.* to digress (from the main design *or* subject): *a)* to deviate, to wander (off), to stray, to swerve (from); *b)* to ramble, to be prolix: von ſeinem Gegenſtande zu weit —, to wander too far from one's subject: ſeine Gedanken ſchweiften vom Buche ab, his thoughts wandered off from the book: ſeine Aufmerkſamkeit ſchweifte alle Augenblicke von ſeiner Arbeit ab, his attention wandered from his work every moment: er ſchweift von ſeinem Vorhaben ab, he swerves from his purpose: wir erlauben uns hier ein wenig von unſerem Hauptgegenſtand abzuſchweifen, we presume here to digress a little from our main subject: ich bin von meinem Gegenſtande abgeſchweift (*Hilp.*), I have launched out of my subject: II. *tr.* 1) *T.* to rinse (cocoons, &c.), to wash (yarn, &c.); 2) *Join.*, &c. to cut off with a sweep, *cf.* Ausſchweifen.

Ab'ſchweifend, *p. a.*, (*l. u.:*) **Ab'ſchweifig**, *adj.* digressive, swerving.

Ab'ſchweifſpule, (*w.*) *f.* *T.* warping-spool (*Tolh.*).

Ab'ſchweifung, (*w.*) *f.* 1) *a)* deviation, *cf.* Abſchweif; *b)* (Abſtecher) ramble, excursion; 2) *fig.* *aa)* digression, wandering (from the main subject, &c.); *bb)* prolixity.

Ab'ſchweißen, (*w.*) *v. tr. Smith.*, *&c.* to separate (a piece of iron, &c.) after bringing it to a welding heat (*opp.* Anſchweißen).

Ab'ſchwelgen, (*w.*) *v.* I. *intr.* to have done revelling and rioting, *see* Ausſchwelgen, *which is more usual in this sense;* II. *refl.* to weaken one's self by debauchery.

Ab'ſchwemmen, (*w.*) *v. tr.* 1) to cause to float down *or* off: 2) to wash away *or* off: ein Platzregen hatte die abhängige Straße zum Theil abgeſchwemmt, a sweeping rain had carried off parts of the sloping road: der Strom ſchwemmt Erde vom Ufer ab, the stream detaches land from the shore (*opp.* Anſchwemmen); 3) *a)* to remove (dirt from wool, &c.) by washing, to wash off; *b)* to purify *or* to clean by washing *or* straining off, *Min.* to elutriate: to clean *or* cleanse (wool, sheep, the street) by washing off (the impurities): die Pferde —, to ride the horses into the water.

Ab'ſchwemmung, (*w.*) *f.* (the act *or* operation of) floating down, &c.: ablution (of a precipitate, &c.)

Ab'ſchwenden, (*w.*) *v. tr.* to lay waste, to destroy: to burn down (a forest): to burn up (a heath), to make (a field) arable by burning the wood or grass. — **Ab'ſchwendung**, (*w.*) *f.* (the act) of laying waste, burning down, &c. *see* Abſchwenden.

Ab'ſchwenken, (*w.*) *v.* I. *tr.* 1) to remove or turn off by swinging: *a)* eine Schiffbrücke —, to swing a pontoon-bridge; *b)* *aa)* to remove by swinging or shaking: *bb)* to clean by swinging or shaking: *cc)* to cleanse by rinsing: II. *refl.* to turn aside, to wheel off *or* aside: rechts (links) abgeſchwenkt! *Mil.* (to the) right (left) wheel!

Ab'ſchwimmen, (*str.*) *v. tr.* (*aux.* ſein) 1) to swim *or* float down; 2) to swim *or* float off *or* away: der Kahn iſt abgeſchwommen (*Hilp.*), the boat has gone adrift: II. *refl.* to tire *or* exhaust one's self by (prolonged) swimming.

Ab'ſchwindeln, (*w.*) *v. tr.* (Einem etwas) to swindle (one) out of (a thing).

Ab'ſchwinden, (*str.*) *v. intr.* (*aux.* ſein) to waste away, *cf.* Abzehren, Auszehren.

Ab'ſchwindung, (*w.*) *f.* a wasting away, consumption (Abzehrung).

Ab'ſchwingen, (*str.*) *v.* I. *tr.* 1) to shake off (the dust from the hat); 2) (*cf.* Abſchwenken) to cleanse (the hat) by shaking; to fan, to winnow (corn, &c.). II. *refl.* to swing one's self down, to leap down (from a moderate height); ſich vom Pferde —, to leap from the horse, to alight, dismount nimbly (*Hilp.*).

Ab'ſchwirren, (*w.*) *v. intr.* (*aux.* ſein) to whiz, buzz off.

Ab'ſchwitzen, (*w.*) *v.* I. *intr.* to have done sweating *or* perspiring: II. *tr.* 1) to remove (impurities, &c.) by sweating, to clear (hides) by sweating: to heat (the hides or skins): 2) *burl.* to expiate, atone (one's sins) by sweating (in purgatory): 3) to exhaust *or* weaken by sweating: III. *refl.* to become weak by sweating (perspiring).

Ab'ſchwören, (*str.*) *v. tr.* 1) *obsolescent*, to swear to (a thing) in due form: einen Eid —, (*in law-style*) to take an oath in due form; 2) (Einem etwas) *a)* to deprive (one) of (a thing) by taking an oath (*particul.* by perjury); *b)* *fig.* to deny the existence of (any and everything) by cursing and swearing (*or else according to the meaning of a*): to go to the most extravagant lengths in blasphemy (*cf.* Abſchwatzen, 1, *b*); 3) (*l. u.*) to free (from ...) by taking an oath: ſich von der Strafe — (loſchwören), to free one's self from (*or* to escape) punishment by taking an oath: 4) to deny by *or* upon oath: *a)* to abjure, to take an oath of not having done, committed, received, &c. a thing: eine Unterſchrift —, to abjure a signature: einen Diebſtahl — (*Hilp.*), to take an oath of not having committed a theft: er ſchwor dieſe ihm anvertrauten Summen ab, he denied upon oath having received (*or* having in his possession) these sums entrusted to him; *b)* to renounce *or* disavow (future intentions, &c.) upon oath, to abjure, forswear, to retract, recant or revoke solemnly; er ſchwur (*or* ſchwor) ſeine Religion ab, he abjured *or* forswore his religion; *c)* to cast off or renounce upon oath *particul. of moral obligations entered into with regard to other persons, &c.; construed with the Dat. of the person and Acc. of the thing renounced:*) ſoll ich dem Kaiſer Eid und Pflicht —? (*Schiller*, Wall. III, 21), shall I forswear my oath and duty to the emperor? einem Fürſten die Lehnstreue —, to abjure allegiance to a prince: (*in many cases either the Dat. or the Acc. is omitted, in others they seem to change places*): wollt ihr dem Kaiſer —? (*Schiller*, Wall. II, 5), will you break your oath to the emperor? (*Coleridge*): du haſt die alten Fahnen abgeſchworen (*ib.* IV, 3), thou hast forsworn the ancient colours: der ganzen Welt (*Dat.*) — (*Rabener*), to renounce the whole world: er ſchwört den Kaiſer (*for* des Kaiſers Sache) ab, he abjures the emperor (*for* the emperor's cause): ſein abgeſchworener Feind, his [illegible] enemy (*cf.* Abgeſagt, *under* [illegible]).

Ab'ſchwörung, (*w.*) *f.* abjuration, [illegible] of abjuring, forswearing, &c.; [illegible] abnegation upon oath; recantation.

Ab'ſchwung, (*str.*, *pl.* Ab'ſchwünge) [illegible] *Gymn.* the act of swinging (one's self) [illegible] (*opp.* Aufſchwung); 2) *Metall.* that [illegible] swung or taken off, *see* Abſtich.

* **Abſciſ'ſe**, (*w.*) *f. Math.* abscissa, [illegible]

* **Abſciſſion'**, (*w.*) *f.* abscission, [illegible] amputation: 2) *Rhet.* aposiopesis.

Ab'ſegeln, (*w.*) *v.* I. *intr.* (*aux.* [illegible] *with* haben) 1) to sail off *or* away [illegible] dem Winde —, to bear off: 2) to [illegible] sail, to clear the port, to put to sea [illegible] part: die Brigg wird nach L. — [illegible] der Wind umſetzt, the brig will [illegible] sail) for L. as soon as the wind [illegible] (*cf.* Ablaufen, Auslaufen, *under* [illegible] Fahren); 3) *coll.* *a)* to go or to be off [illegible] stick, to pack off: *b)* *burl.* [illegible] to launch into eternity, *usual.* to [illegible] Abfahren, I. *intr.* 2.

II. *tr.* 1) die Windmühlenflügel [illegible] —, to take down the sails of a wind[illegible] *Mar.* den Maſt —, to spring *or* to [illegible] mast.

Ab'ſehbar, *adj.* 1) within reach [illegible] within sight; 2) *fig.* imaginable, [illegible] nicht —, beyond the reach of the [illegible] be conceived, inconceivable (*see* [illegible])

Ab'ſehen, (*str.*) *v.* I. *intr.* ([illegible]) to look off *or* away, to turn away [illegible] one's eyes; 2) *fig.* von einer Sache [illegible] aside from a question, to leave [illegible] thing out of the question: wir wollen [illegible] (von dieſer Frage, von dieſer Sache [illegible]) jetzt —, let us turn aside from this [illegible] &c.), let us waive this consideration [illegible] ment: *particul. used in the* [illegible] *ciple with* von *following* (*rarely* [illegible]) abgeſehen des ungeheuren Unterſchied[illegible] apart from the immense difference [illegible] tive of ..., let alone ..., over and [illegible] not to mention *or* without mention[illegible] stractedly, apart *or* aside from ..., [illegible] putting aside ..., in addition *or* [illegible] gard to ..., exclusively *or* independ[illegible] abgeſehen von der Verzögerung, [illegible] delay out of the question; abgeſehen [illegible] von dem Umſtande, daß ..., let alone [illegible] mention, without mentioning that [illegible] what ....

II. *tr.* 1) *a)* *lit.* to reach with the [illegible] Allee, deren Ende nicht abzuſehen [illegible] avenue the end of which is lost [illegible] or is out of sight: was nur dein [illegible] (*Schiller*), as far as your eye reach[illegible] *aa)* to see, to perceive (*as in* [illegible]) Niemand kann das Ende —, [illegible] where (*or* how) it will end [illegible] dem man das Ende nicht — kann [illegible] no one can see the end of [illegible] ſehen, was daraus werden will [illegible] is no knowing what may [illegible] come of it; noch läßt ſich nicht — [illegible] there is no telling if ... [illegible] im Voraus ab, daß ... [illegible] understood beforehand, that [illegible] auch dieſes Ereigniß — [illegible] have foretold this result [illegible] understand: ſo viel ich — [illegible] can see or perceive [illegible] warum er es that (*Hilp.*) [illegible] conceive why he did it [illegible] or to learn by close observation [illegible] Erde ſelbſt läßt ſich [illegible] the motion of the earth [illegible] by observing the [illegible] ſehen es dem Künſtler ab [illegible] carcasses discovered [illegible]

dunkelt, vergrößert ihre Umrisse, that which obscures the distinctive shades of objects enlarges their outlines; 9) a) Law, to eject (farmers, &c.) from a tenement; b) to depose (from office, cf. Entsetzen); (in an ill sense) to degrade: to dismiss (magistrates, professors, &c.), to discharge, remove (from a public office); to cashier (an officer); einen König —, to depose or to dethrone a king; Könige ab- und einsetzen, to remove and to set up kings; vorläufig or einstweilen —, to suspend; 10) Comm. a) to dispose of (goods), to sell, vend (Verkaufen); Zucker ist gut abzusetzen, sugar commands a ready sale; ist nicht abzusetzen (cf. Absetzbar), is not to be sold, is not salable; viel —, to have a good riddance (cf. Loswerden); sich gut, rasch, leicht, gar nicht, schlecht &c. —, (refl.) to sell well, speedily, readily, &c. &c.; b) aa) to put by or aside (Zurücksetzen); abgesetzte Artikel, old stock, goods laid by; bb) also fig. to cast off, reject; abgesetzte Kleider, cast off clothes (cf. Abgelegt); abgesetztes Geld, money put out of circulation (cf. außer Curs setzen); abgesetzte Liebhaber, coll. dismissed or discarded lovers (cf. Abdanken).

II. tr. (impers.) es (Nom.) setzt .. (Acc.) ab, ... will result, follow, &c. (cf. Geben, impers.); es wird Sturm, Regen und Kälte (Acc.) —, we shall have storm, rain, and cold; es wird einen Zank —, there will be a quarrel, a quarrel will be the result or consequence; es setzte einen Zank ab, a quarrel arose or took place; es wird Schläge —, it will come to blows.

III. refl. 1) to branch off, to deviate, &c. see IV. intr. 2, b; 2) to be detached or contrasted, cf. I. tr. 8, IV. intr. 6. & sich Abheben, refl.

IV. intr. 1) Mar. vom Lande —, to put from shore (cf. Abstoßen, II. intr.); 2) Min. a) to deviate from the (direct) course; b) to change (in quality, &c.): der Gang setzt ab, the vein fails or loses its direction, the lode changes; das Erz setzt ab, the ore becomes inferior in quality or it ceases altogether: das Gestein setzt ab, the gangue changes, the rock becomes unsound; 3) Typ. to get through with putting something in type, to finish composing (cf. I tr. 6); 4) to stop, to make (a) short stop or pause; to intermit (cf. tr. 2, c); er mußte oft —, he was obliged to make frequent pauses; ohne abzusetzen, without pause or intermission; 5) to make a break (cf. tr. 7), to be formed into breaks or steps; im Schreiben —, to break off in writing, to make a break; 6) to contrast, to differ (von, from); 7) obsolescent, to turn away, to depart, to fall off (von, from): von Einem —, to desert one

Ab'setzen, v. s. (str.) n. 1) the setting or putting down, &c.; deposition, &c.; 2) Min. deviation, rupture; 3) interruption: — der Stimme, hesitation (hack) in speaking, catching of the voice.

Ab'setzer, (str.) m. 1) one who sets or puts down, &c.; 2) deposer, &c.; 3) Comm. retailer, &c.

Ab'setzling, (str.) m. an animal newly weaned (such as Ab'setzferkel, n., Ab'setzfüllen, n., Ab'setzkalb, n., Ab'setzlamm, n. a pig, a foal, a calf, a lamb newly weaned.

Ab'setz ..., in comp. (see Absetzen) —säge, f. T. tenon-saw; —tisch, m. 1) a sideboard; 2) Cloth. table on which cloth is brushed (cf. Absetzen I. tr. 5, f), (Tech.) shearing-table.

Ab'setzung, (w.) f. 1) (the act of) setting or putting down, &c.; deposition: — von Niederschlag, deposition of sediment: — des Oxyds, Chem. oxidation; 2) interruption (also T. in electric telegraphy, &c.); 3) removal, deduction, &c.; 4) fig. deposition (the act of divesting of office, &c.), deposal, dismission, (w. 2. dismission, ganz unwürdig degradement, nur bei schimpflicher Absetzung gebräuchlich): degradation), removal (of judges from office, &c.); die Ursachen seiner (Jacob des Zweiten) —, the causes of his (James II.) deposition (dethronement); A-en von Königen durch die Gewalt des Papstes, depositions of kings by the authority of the pope; vorläufige or einstweilige —, suspension.

Ab'setzungs ..., in comp. —decret, n., —urtheil, n. Law, sentence of deposition.

Ab'seyn, obsolete orthography for Absein.

Ab'sicheln, (w.) v. tr. to cut off with a sickle or reaping-hook.

Ab'sicht, (w.) f. 1) obsolescent, contrivance to assist the eye in taking sight, see Absehen, v. s. 3); 2) a) intention, aim, view, design, purpose, end, object, point: das war nicht meine —, I did not intend it; [ich konnte] nur selten | mit ihr ganz offen sein, und wenn sie auch | die — hat, den Freunden wohlzuthun, | so fühlt man — und man ist verstimmt (Göthe, Tasso II. 1), (A. Swanwick:) [I can] rarely feel at ease with her; | e'en when she seeks to benefit her friends, | they feel the purpose, and are thence constrained; in der besten —, with the best intentions, without meaning any harm; in der —, Ihnen zu dienen, with a view of serving you; haben Sie ernstlich die —? do you really intend? gewiß, ich habe eine gute —, I am sure I intend well; er hat keine böse —, he does not mean any harm; N. hat schlimme A-en, N. intends serious harm; er verfolgt seine —, he pursues his end (aim, point); ein Schmeichler, der auf seine A-en ausgeht (Kant), i. e. der seine Zwecke im Auge hat, a flatterer who pursues his (selfish) intentions or purposes; aus A-en, for certain purposes or reasons; in der — Kunde zu erlangen, with a design or view to obtain information, for the purpose of obtaining ...., to the end that he might obtain ...; mit —, intentionally, on purpose (absichtlich); ohne —, unintentionally (unabsichtlich); in — haben (etwas zu thun &c.), seine — auf eine Sache haben or richten, to have a design or to design, intend (to do something, &c.), to aim at (doing, &c. or at a thing), to have (a thing) in view: es ist mir lieb, daß Sie ehrliche A-en auf meine Tochter haben, I am happy to find that your intentions as to my daughter are strictly honourable: ich glaube nicht, daß sie dann ihrer — näher rücken wird, I do not think she will be then nearer her point: Frankreichs und Rußlands A-en auf die Türkei, the designs of France and Russia upon Turkey; b) object, design, purpose; end or aim to which the view is directed (in this sense the word Zweck is preferable); 3) obsolescent, view, consideration, regard, respect, relation; in gewisser — (Lessing), in some respect or sort; in mehr als einer — (Wieland), in more than one respect; in dieser — (Kant), in this respect; in aller — (Bürger), in every respect, &c., see Hinsicht; in — auf eine Sache or in — einer Sache (Gen.), with regard to ...., in respect (of) &c., see Hinsicht &c.

Ab'sichern, (w.) v. tr. to sift off.

Ab'sichtlich, adj. intentional, intended, designed, wilful, premeditated; adv. through (or with a) design, on purpose, coll. of set purpose, purposely, intentionally, designedly, &c.; sie scheinen sich — der Abstimmung enthalten zu haben, they seem to have made a point of abstaining from voting: Sie haben es — (mit Vorsatz) gethan, you did it on purpose, indem sie das Gesetz mit Vorbedacht und recht — verletzen, deliberately and of set purpose violating the law.

Ab'sichtlichkeit, (w.) f. design, purpose, (Coleridge:) intentionality.

Ab'sichtslos (less usual Ab'sichtlos), I. adj. unintentional, undesigned, designless, undesigning; dieses a-e [illegible] or casual word; ich [illegible] (Göthe), I wanted my [illegible] purpose; II. A-igkeit, (w.) f. [illegible] want of a set purpose or design [illegible] die anscheinende A-igkeit der [illegible] parent carelessness of nature.

Ab'sichtsvoll, adj. full of [illegible]

Ab'sickern, (w.) v. intr. (aux. [illegible]) down or off.

* Ab'siden, (w.) f. pl. (Lat. [illegible]) siden, the two extreme and [illegible] of the orbit of a planet; —[illegible] standslinie.

Ab'sieben, (w.) v. tr. to sift off [illegible]

Ab'siechen, (w.) v. intr. (aux. [illegible]) or waste away with sickness, to [illegible] (Hinsiechen).

Ab'sieden, (str.) v. tr. 1) to [illegible] duly, to elixate, extract by boiling, [illegible] (Abkochen); einen Trank —, to [illegible] tion; Eier —, to poach eggs; 2) to [illegible] boiling.

Ab'singen, (str.) v. I. tr. to sing [illegible] recite singing, to sing (as in the [illegible] vice, &c.), to chant; II. refl. to [illegible] self by singing; III. intr. to [illegible] to sing to the end: to sing for [illegible] (cf. Abdanken).

Ab'sinken, (str.) v. I. intr. (aux. [illegible]) to sink down, (of the sun) to set [illegible] away (from): die Pfeile sinken [illegible] land), the arrows glance off [illegible] Min. to sink (a shaft, &c.) to a [illegible] das —, v. s. (str.) n. shaft, &c. [illegible] tain depth.

Ab'sintern, (w.) v. intr. (aux. [illegible]) trickle down or off, to leak, see [illegible]

* Ab'sinth, (str.) m. Bot. absinth [illegible] Artemisia absinthium, Wermuth.

* Ab'sis, f. (Lat. (from Gr. [illegible]) sides) 1) Astr. gener. pl. die [illegible] see; 2) Archit. apsis (cf. [illegible]) vault; arched roof; b) a domed [illegible] of the choir or aisles, where the [illegible] placed, apse (Chornische, [illegible]).

Ab'sitzen, (str.) v. I. intr. 1) a) [illegible] or at a distance (from); b) fig. to [illegible] off; 2) (aux. sein) a) (poetical) [illegible] sit down (sich niedersetzen); b) [illegible] a horse, &c.), to dismount, to [illegible] (aux. sein) Min. to slide or [illegible] land undermined by the action of [illegible] syn. Abrutschen); II. tr. 1) to [illegible] sitting; 2) a) to sit out (a given [illegible]) atone for (an offence, &c.) [illegible] by sitting in prison; er hat [illegible] abgesessen, he has endured his [illegible] finement; 3) Cloth. to take off [illegible] ter (Hilp.); 4) † fig. (Slang [illegible]) to extort (something) from [illegible] mitting endeavours; III. refl. to [illegible] self (out) by sitting; ich habe [illegible] sessen, I am quite tired out with [illegible]

A. Ab'socken or Ab'sacken, [illegible] (aux. sein) Sail-or., &c. to [illegible]

B. Ab'socken, v. intr. (aux. [illegible]) trudge away hastily, to trot, [illegible] off, &c.

Ab'sod, (str.) m. see [illegible]

Ab'sohlen, (w.) v. tr. 1) [illegible] (a boot), to rip off the sole [illegible] 2) a) to wear out the soles of [illegible] Ablatern); b) Min. to wear off [illegible]

Ab'sömmern, (w.) v. tr. see [illegible]

Ab'sohren, (w.) v. intr. (aux. [illegible]) to waste away, to fade, wither, [illegible]

Ab'sold, (str.) m. the [illegible] wages of a person [illegible]

Ab'solden, (w.) v. tr. 1) [illegible] full salary to (one); 2) to pay [illegible] Ablohnen.

Ab'ſpiegeln, *(w.) v.* I. *tr.* to reflect (as from a mirror), to mirror; abgeſpiegelt, mirrored; II. *refl.* 1) to be reflected; 2) to look at one's self in the glass.

Ab'ſpiegelung, *(w.) f.* reflection (*i. e.* the act of reflecting as well as that which is reflected) as from a mirror.

Ab'ſpielen, *(w.) v.* I. *tr.* 1) to play off (a tune, &c., *i. e.* from the notes); 2) to play, act, perform to the end, to enact (one's part, &c.); 3) to wear out by playing, to play off *or* away; ſich *(Dat.)* die Finger —, to wear out one's fingers with playing; 4) to diminish or pay off (a debt, &c.) by playing (at cards, &c.); 5) † to pre-arrange (a game) clandestinely (Abkarten); 6) (Einem etwas) to win (something) of (one) at play; to cheat (one) out of (a thing) by false play; II. *intr.* 1) to finish playing; 2) *sometimes in the sense of* ſich —; III. *refl.* 1) to be performed, enacted, *coll.* to come off; 2) to tire one's self by playing.

Ab'ſpießen, *(w.) v. tr.* 1) to take from the spit; 2) to take off *or* fetch down with a spear (fork, or any similar instrument).

Ab'ſpindeln, *(w.) v. tr.* to take from the spindle.

Ab'ſpinnen, *(str.) v.* I. *tr.* 1) *a)* to spin off; *b) fig.* to spin *or* draw out, to reel *or* wind off (interminable yarns of florid verbiage, &c.); 2) to wear out (ſich *[Dat.]* die Finger, one's fingers, &c.) by spinning; 3) to pay off by spinning, to spin off (a debt); II. *intr.* to finish spinning; III. *refl. particul. fig.* to unwind, unfold, develop itself.

Ab'ſpitzen, *(w.) v. tr.* 1) *a)* to sharpen the end of (a thing) to a point, to taper off, to cut, forge, grind, file, &c. to an acute end; *b)* to point duly *or* properly; eine (Schreib-)Feder —, to nib a pen; *c) fig. (obsolescent)* to make pointed, to give a point or epigrammatic force to ..., to (over-)refine; 2) to divest of the point *or* top, to lop, to crop, to take off the top, the point, *or* the upper part of (a thing); to blunt, to dull; 3) to take off *or* to fetch down with a pointed instrument; 4) *fig.* es — auf eine Sache *(Acc.)*, *coll.* to aim sharply at (a thing), to have an especial design upon ....

Ab'ſpleißen, *(str.) v. tr. obsolescent*, to split off, to rive *or* rend off, to tear off with violence.

Ab'ſplittern, *(w.) v.* I. *tr.* to splint, splinter; to break off in splinters; II. *intr.* *(aux.* ſein) & *refl.* to come off in splinters; *Surg.* to desquamate, exfoliate.

Ab'ſplitterung, *(w.) f.* 1) the act of splintering off, &c.; 2) a splintering part, splinter.

Ab'ſpötteln, *(w.) v. tr.* 1) (Einem etwas) to obtain (something) from (one) by jeering or gibing; 2) (Einen) to dissuade (one) by jeering (von, from).

Ab'ſpotten, *(w.) v. tr.* 1) (Einem etwas) to get (a thing) from (one) by deriding; 2) to ridicule (one) to excess.

Ab'ſprache, *(w.) f.* oral agreement (über eine Sache *[Acc.]*, about a thing); *see* Abrede.

Ab'ſprechen, *(str.) v.* I. *tr.* (Einem etwas, *opp.* Zuſprechen) *a) Law*, to take away (something) from (one), to deprive *or* dispossess (one) of (a thing) by judicial sentence, to pronounce, pass, *or* give a sentence *or* verdict against (one); Einem das Leben —, to condemn, to sentence one to death; *fig.-a. b)* to speak despairingly of a sick man's recovery, of a man's chances in life, &c.; die Ärzte haben ihm das Leben abgeſprochen, the physicians have given him up (*or* over); Einem alle Hoffnung —, to bid one give over all hopes, to take all hope from one *(Hilp.)*; *c)* to deprive (one) of (a thing) by (calumnious) talk; er hatte mir den (guten) Ruf abgeſprochen, he had taken away my character; *d)* to refuse to recognize *or* acknowledge (certain qualities, claims, &c.), to deny, to gainsay, contest (the right of somebody, &c.), to dispute, disallow &c. (*cf.* in Abrede ſtellen); einer Sache *(Dat.)* ihren Werth —, to deny the value of a thing; ich ſpreche ihm nicht den (*or* ſeinen) Geiſt ab, I do not deny his genius; wer ſpricht ihm ab, daß er die Menſchen kenne? *(Schiller)*, who denies his knowledge of men? ein Geſchlecht, dem Niemand eine Stelle unter den edelſten — wird *(Wieland)*, a family whose claim to a place among the noblest nobody will gainsay (contest, &c.); 2) *a)* to talk (a matter) over (mit Einem, with one), to discuss to the end, fully, *or* finally; *b)* to settle *or* fix by judicial sentence *(different from* 1 *a)*; die über ihn abgeſprochene Enthauptung *(Pfeffel)*, the sentence of decapitation passed upon him.

II. *intr.* 1) *a)* (*l. u.*) to dissent, object, oppose (in a disputation, &c.); *b)* † einer Sache *(Dat.)* —, to renounce a thing, *cf.* Abſagen, *intr.*; 2) (endgültig) to arbitrate, to pass final sentence, to give final judgment; 3) *fig.* (über eine Sache) to decide hastily (on a matter, &c.), to be decisive (of), to be dogmatical, to dogmatize (on); über ... —, to forejudge ..., prejudge ...; er iſt ſehr geneigt, über Alles abzuſprechen, he is greatly given to lay down the law about every thing.

Ab'ſprechend, *adj.* peremptory, authoritative, positive, dogmatic(al), decisive; asserting opinions with authority *or* with overbearing and arrogance; overbearing, arrogant, *cf.* Abſprechen, *intr.*; er hat etwas ſehr A-es, he has an overbearing way of stating his opinions.

Ab'ſprecherei', *(w.) f.* the act *or* (bad) custom of deciding overhastily, of prejudging, &c. *cf.* Abſprechen, *intr.*; peremptoriness, overbearingness, dogmaticalness.

Ab'ſprecheriſch, *adj.* disposed to assert opinions with authority *or* with overbearing, &c., in the habit of laying down the law, &c., dogmatic; a-es Weſen, *see* Abſprecherei & Abſprechend.

Ab'ſprechung, *(w.) f.* (*l. u.*) the (act of) passing judgment (on ...), &c.; peremptory *or* dogmatical judgment.

Ab'ſpreizen, *(w.) v. tr. T. particul. Min.* to underprop, to prop (with timber, &c.), to provide with props.

Ab'ſprengen, *(w.) v.* I. *tr.* 1) to cause to burst off, fly off, start off, *or* to break off suddenly, to spring, to burst, strike off; das Reh war von der Herde abgeſprengt worden, the doe had been driven away from its herd; 2) to blast, to blow off with gunpowder; 3) to ride off (a horse's shoe); II. *intr.* *(aux.* ſein) to hasten *or* fly off *or* away; to gallop off (Fortſprengen, Wegſprengen).

Ab'ſprießen, *(str.) v. intr.* *(aux.* ſein) to sprout or spring forth (from); Abſproſſen.

Ab'ſpringen, *(str.) v.* I. *intr.* *(aux.* ſein) 1) *a)* to leap *or* jump off *or* away; vom Pferde —, to leap from a horse, to alight (from a horse), to dismount; *b)* to leap *or* jump down; *c)* to start off with a leap *or* bound (from a certain point); 2) *a)* to fly off, rebound; das Schwert ſpringt vom Steine ab, the sword glances off from the stone; *b)* to snap off, to fly in pieces; 3) to break, crack, burst *or* fly off; to chip off (as of potters' ware); to start, gape, warp, disjoint (as wood); to red-sear (said of iron); die Farbe ſpringt ab, the paint comes off; *fig.-a.* 4) *a) aa)* to fall off suddenly; von einer Partei —, to forsake *or* desert a party suddenly *(Hilp.)*; *bb)* to break off, to recede abruptly (from an agreement, &c.); trotz ſeines Verſprechens wollte er wieder —, notwithstanding his promise he wanted to retract; die Haſtigkeit, womit er von dieſem Vorhaben wieder abſprang *(Wieland)*, the hurry with which he again changed his purpose; *b)* von einem Gegenſtande —, [illegible] a subject suddenly (*cf.* [illegible] etwas (ſich) von Gegenſtande [illegible] away from the subject [illegible] *bb)* to shift (from one subject [illegible] ramble, to stray, to launch [illegible] ject; ſpringen Sie nicht ab! [illegible] cate! stick to the point! *(Hilp.)* [illegible] ...) to contrast (strongly with [illegible] to spring, to issue, to proceed [illegible] cestors; II. *refl.* to tire, fatigue [illegible] one's self by leaping *or* jumping [illegible]

Ab'ſpringend, *p. a. Her.* [illegible]

Ab'ſpringer, *(str.) m.* 1) [illegible] off, &c.; 2) anything that [illegible] *particul.* among *foresters*, the [illegible] trees, oaks, &c.) of [illegible] come off in spring (Abſprung).

Ab'ſpritzen, *(w.) v.* I. *tr.* 1) [illegible] to knock off by squirting; 2) [illegible] jet of water (auf [with *Acc.*], at [illegible] remove, clear off (dirt, &c.) by [illegible] to clean by squirting *or* sprinkling [illegible] *(aux.* ſein) to spurt off *or* back, to [illegible] come off in drops.

Ab'ſproß, *(str.) m.* offshoot, [illegible] ſprößling.

Ab'ſproſſen, *(w.) v. intr.* [illegible] sprout, spring forth; to proceed, [illegible] scend (von, from).

Ab'ſprößling, *(str.) m.* offshoot [illegible]

Ab'ſprudeln, *(w.) v.* I. *intr.* [illegible] bubble forth, to issue from, [illegible] bubbling noise; II. *tr.* to [illegible] music) in an overhasty manner.

Ab'ſpruch, *(str., pl.* Ab'ſprüche) *m.* [illegible] final sentence, decision, judicial [illegible] 2) a taking away (des Lebens, [illegible] by judicial sentence.

Ab'ſprung, *(str., pl.* Ab'ſprünge) [illegible] *a)* the (act of) leaping off, &c. [illegible] gen; *b)* downward leap; 2) rebound [illegible] ing off; 3) anything broken or [illegible] *cf.* Abſpringer, 2; 4) *a)* a sudden [illegible] or leaving a place, deviation; *b)* [illegible] which a leap &c. is taken, [illegible] bin auf dem Abſprunge (Landung) [illegible] I am on the point of [illegible] gression from the main route, [illegible] *see* Abſtecher; *b) fig.* digression [illegible] machen, to quit one's subject [illegible] from one subject to another, &c. [illegible] gen, I. 4; 6) interruption of a [illegible] *or* surface, break, *see* Abſatz, [illegible] (of a mountain); off-set; 7) *fig.* [illegible] parity, distance, falling off.

Ab'ſprungswinkel, *(str.) m.* [illegible] of reflection.

Ab'ſpulen, *(w.) v. tr.* 1) to wind [illegible] from the spool, to unwind from [illegible] 2) *(often intr.)* to finish spooling [illegible]

Ab'ſpülen, *(w.) v. tr.* to wash [illegible] 1) *a) lit.* den Schmutz von [illegible] —, to wash off (the dirt from [illegible] cleanse by washing, to rinse [illegible] to wash up (the dishes), to wash [illegible] to wash, to mop (the wheels [illegible] der Regen hat die Straßen [illegible] has washed the streets; 2) [illegible] away, to detach by the action [illegible] wash off *or* away (*opp.* [illegible] ſpült ſeine Ufer ab, the stream [illegible] away its banks.

Ab'ſpuler, *(str.) m.* one that [illegible] from a spool.

Ab'ſpülicht, *(str.) m.* [illegible]

Ab'ſpülung, *(w.) f.* 1) [illegible] ing off *or* away, &c.; 2) [illegible] washing, rinsing, &c.

Ab'ſtäuben, *(w.) v. tr.* [illegible] try (like dye) duly by [illegible] of cloth or tuft of wool [illegible] observing the result; 2) *fig.* to steel *or* harden thoroughly (*cf.* Abhärten).

Ab'stähren, (*w.*) *v. intr. Husb.* to cease longing for the ram (said of ewes).

Ab'stamm, (*str., pl.* Ab'stämme) *m.* 1) race, generation derivable from common ancestors, branch; 2) descent, &c. (Abstammung).

Ab'stammen, (*w.*) *v. intr.* (*aux.* sein) to be descended, to issue, proceed, to descend (from), to come (of, *two.* from); to be derived (from): ich stamme von der älteren Linie ab, I come from the elder branch; das Wort Gift stammt von der Wurzel Geben ab, the word Gift is to be traced to the root Geben.

Ab'stämmen, (*w.*) *v. tr.* 1) *Forest.* to separate from the trunk, to fell; 2) *Surg., &c. see* Abstemmen.

† **Ab'stämmling,** (*str.*) *m.* descendant (Abkömmling).

Ab'stammung, (*w.*) *f.* descent, derivation; parentage, extraction; von adeliger —, of noble extraction; die welche durch Geburt oder — Franzosen waren, those who, by birth or extraction, were French; die Religion gibt den Menschen eine gemeinsame —, religion gives man a common parentage; — der Wörter, derivation of words, etymology; A-Stafel, *f. see* Stammtafel; A-szeugniß, *n. Comm. see* Ursprungszeugniß.

Ab'stämpeln, (*w.*) *v. tr. see* Abstempeln.

Ab'stampfen, (*w.*) *v.* I. *tr.* 1) to stamp off; 2) to stamp *or* pound duly; 3) to wear off *or* out by stamping; II. *intr.* (*aux.* haben) to finish stamping; III. *refl.* to fatigue one's self by stamping.

Ab'stand, (*str., pl.* Ab'stände) *m.* 1) distance (Entfernung), interval, space; interspace; der — der Säulen, *Archit.* the (clear) space between (two) columns, intercolumniation; *Astr.* der geringste — eines Planeten von der Sonne, perihelion; der weiteste — eines Planeten von der Sonne, aphelion; der — vom Scheitel, zenith distance; 2) *Law, &c.* the (act of) desisting from (*or* relinquishing of) claims (an einen Andern, to another), &c. (*cf.* Abstehen, *v.* a.), abandonment, cession; — thun, to abandon *or* relinquish (to insurers) all claim to a ship or goods insured in order to be entitled to indemnification for a total loss (Abandonniren); — leisten *or* zahlen, to give a compensation (for claims relinquished by others); von einer Sache — nehmen, to desist from a thing, &c. *see* Abstehen, I. 4, *a*; 3) contrast, difference; der — der Jahre (with reference to the age of persons), the disparity of years.

Ab'ständer, (*str.*) *m.* 1) any superannuated *or* decrepit domestic animal; 2) *Forest.* a decaying *or* dead tree.

Ab'ständig, *adj.* 1) deteriorated, spoiled, *or* decayed by too long standing (*cf.* Abstehen, I. 3); *Forest.* (of wood) dry, dead; *lit. & fig.* stale, tasteless, insipid; die Eichen fangen an, — zu werden (*Hipp.*), the oaks are beginning to decay, are on the decline; 2) (*l. u.*) desisting, receding; — werden, to desist, &c. *see* Abstehen, I. 4. *a.*

Ab'stands..., *in comp.* —geld, *n.* money (*or* amount) paid in compensation (for claims relinquished by others); als —geld zahlte ich fünf Thaler, by way of indemnification I paid five Thalers; ohne —geld wird man von ihm nicht loskommen (*Eb. & Gr.*), without compensation there will be no satisfying him; —linie, *f. Astr.* line of the apsides (Absidenlinie); —messer, *m.* apsomeometer; —messung, *f.* the [illegible] of measuring things distant, [illegible]; —punkt, *m. Astr.* apsis; —quantum, *n.*, —summe, *f.* sum *or* amount of compensation, *see* —geld; —winkel, *m. Astr.* angle of [illegible].

Ab'stapeln, (*w.*) *v. tr.* 1) to take down from a pile or stack (*opp.* Aufstapeln); der Markt ist aus, du kannst — (*intr.*), the market (the fair, &c.) is over, you may pack up; 2) *cant.* (of professional beggars, &c.) to frequent *or* visit with the object of begging; II. *intr.* (*aux.* sein) 1) to be launched, *see* vom Stapel laufen; 2) to stalk off, to trudge away, to trot *or* make off.

Abstatt', *adv.* † *& provinc. for* von statten, weg, von dannen, *lit.* from the place (*cf.* Statt), away, forward, on, &c.

Ab'statten, (*w.*) *v. tr.* 1) † to give away, to marry (a daughter), to portion out, *see* Ausstatten; 2) *a) obsolescent for* Erstatten, Entrichten *2c.*, to pay, to discharge (a debt, &c.); *b) at present limited to a few phrases, implying a kind of moral obligation:* to render, to give, to make; Bericht —, to return a statement, to give (an) account (Erstatten); (Einem) einen Besuch —, to visit, to make, pay *or* give (one) a visit, to give (one) a call; Dank —, to pay, give, render, return thanks; Einem seine Schuldigkeit —, *a)* † to pay one's debt; *b) fig.* to pay one's respects *or* devoirs to one; seinen Glückwunsch —, to offer one's congratulations; einen Gruß —, to deliver a compliment.

Ab'statter, (*str.*) *m.* one who pays (a visit, &c.), one who returns (a report, &c.) (Berichterstatter).

Ab'stattung, (*w.*) *f.* 1) † *for* Ausstattung, endowment; 2) the (act of) paying (a visit, &c.), return (of thanks, &c.).

Ab'staub, (*str.*) *m.* (einer Blume, *unusual*) fecundating dust or pollen taken from (a flower, for artificial impregnation of another).

Ab'stauben, (*w.*) *v. tr.* (*l. u.*) *see* Abstäuben.

Ab'stäuben, (*w.*) *v.* I. *tr.* 1) *a) or* Ab'stäubern, to remove the dust from (a thing), to free from dust, to dust; *b)* (*unusual*) plötzlich stäubte ich die Gelehrsamkeit ab, at once I shook off the dust of learning; 2) *Nat. a)* (eine männliche Blüte) to remove the (fecundating) dust from (a male flower); *b)* (einen Schmetterlingsflügel *2c.*) to remove the dust from (the wing of a butterfly, &c.); II. *intr.* (*aux.* sein) 1) to fly off as *or* like dust; diese Farbe ist (*sometimes* hat) sehr abgestäubt, this colour has come off to a great degree in dusty particles; 2) *Sport.* to fly off suddenly, to fly hastily from (a tree, &c.).

Ab'stäuber, (*str.*) *m.* duster, &c.

Ab'stäubern, (*w.*) *v. tr. see* Abstäuben.

Ab'stauchen, (*w.*) *v. tr.* to stamp, pound *or* toss against the ground thoroughly.

Ab'stäupen, (*w.*) *v. tr.* to flog *or* scourge soundly.

Ab'stech..., *in comp.* (*see* Abstechen) —eisen, *n.* 1) *or* —messer, *Iron-w.* spade; 2) turfing-iron or spade; 3) *Turn.* (turning) chisel, plane; *Post.* scraper, parer; —grube, *f.*, —herd, *m. Found.* hearthpit *or* receiver of the melted metal, whence it may be made to run into moulds prepared for it; —messer, *n.* butchering-knife; —pflug, *m. Husb.* breast-plough; —rechel, *m.*, —stange, *f. Found.* fire-iron or large poker used in opening the mouth of a melting furnace, (*Tech.*) opening-tool (Abstichspieß).

Ab'stechen, (*str.*) *v.* I. *tr.* 1) to bring down by a thrust, to carry off with a lance *or* other pointed instrument (as in running at the ring); sein Speer stach mich ab, his spear thrust me down (*i. e.* from the horse); Heu —, to pitch down hay (*i. e.* from the waggon), to unload hay; 2) to cut off, to cut (with a turfing-iron, &c.); Rasen —, to cut green sods; 3) to cut slopingly, to slope down, *Mil.* to escarp; 4) to stab, to pierce, to cut, to stick (a pig, &c.); 5) to draw off by making a cut, incision, &c.: *a)* to dig off *or* drain (a pond); *b)* to tap *or* rack off (wine), to draw; *c) Found.* to open (the mouth of a melting-furnace) with a pike-headed iron (for giving vent to the molten metal), to tap, to run off; 6) *a)* to stake out (a road); to mark the place for (a camp, &c.), *see* Abstecken, 3; *b) Forest.* to mark *or* blaze (trees), *see* Abposten, 1; *c) Engr.* to engrave, mark out; *d)* to copy out (a model) by pricks upon paper, to prick (a pattern) upon paper; 7) *fig.* (*cf.* 1) to surpass (*orig.* in thrusting, &c.): *a)* to out-do, to beat, to cut (one) out (*cf.* Ausstechen), &c.; *b) Gam.* to take *or* beat by a superior card, to trump, to ruff; *c) Mar.* einem Schiffe (*sometimes* Einem) den Wind —, to take (gain *or* get) the wind *or* weathergage of a ship; *d)* to deprive (one) of (a thing) by superior skill *or* manoeuvring.

II. *refl.* † *for* sich Abheben *or* Abstechen, *see* III. *intr.* 2.

III. *intr.* 1) (*aux.* sein) to sheer off, to shove off, to set sail; 2) (*aux.* haben) to be contrasted, to contrast; die Farbe wird zu sehr —, the colour will contrast too strongly (will be too glaring or showy); etwas sticht von etwas Anderem *or* gegen etwas Anderes, *less usual* mit etwas Anderem ab, something contrasts with another; Blumen, die auf dem pechschwarzen Haar schön abstachen (*Forster*), flowers which were beautifully set off by the jetty hair; der Glanz der Juwelen stach seltsam gegen die Todtenblässe ihrer Gesichtsfarbe ab, the lustre of the jewels made a strange contrast to the deadly paleness of her complexion; diese Farben stechen gut gegen einander ab, these colours contrast finely (*or* form a fine contrast) with each other *or* contrast each other finely, or are finely contrasted; sie sticht gegen ihn ab, she is a foil to him.

Ab'stecher, (*str.*) *m.* 1) one who *or* the instrument which cuts off, &c. *cf.* Abstechen & Abstecheisen; 2) *Cloth.* contrivance for turning and fixing the warp-beam; 3) *a)* short voyage *or* journey digressing from the main route, digression *or* deviation from the direct *or* regular path, *détour*, excursion, ramble, trip; unser Reisender wird einen — nach X. machen, *Comm.* our traveller will take X. on his way; *b) fig.* digression.

Ab'stechung, (*w.*) *f.* contrast, set-off, (*Lessing, Kant, &c.*) † *for* Abstich, 4.

Ab'steckeisen, (*str.*) *n. Civil Eng.* iron pole used in surveying, laying out grounds, &c., picket.

Ab'stecken, (*w.*) *v. tr.* 1) (*opp.* Aufstecken) *a)* to unpin, to unfasten by removing the pin *or* pins from, to untack, to unpeg; das Haar —, to undo, unfasten the hair; *b) Silk-weav.* to take off from the beam; to remove *or* take out (pins); 2) *Husb.* to wean (pigs, dogs, &c.), *see* Absetzen, I. 3, *b*; 3) to mark off *or* out with sticks *or* poles, to picket; to mark out (the walls of a town, [the place for] a camp, the boundaries, &c.), to stake out (a piece of land, a new road, a railway line, &c.), (eine Curve) to range out (a curve, in railway building), to set out (by boundaries, &c.; *fig.* [the frontier] by metes and bounds); to set out (the plan of a building), to trace out (an encampment by fixing poles); nachdem der Boden geebnet war, steckte man vier und einen halben Fuß breite Beete ab, after the ground had been levelled, they marked it off in beds four feet and a half wide (*cf.* Abstechen, I. 6, *a*).

Ab'steck..., *in comp. Civil Eng.*: —leine, *f.* a line used in laying out ground, measuring-line; —pfahl, *m.* pole used in staking out a piece of land, ranging-pole, stake; —schnur, *f.* measuring-cord (—leine); —stab, *m.* picket used in laying out ground, station-staff; ein langer —stab, —stange, *f.* (ranging-)pole; kleinere —stäbe, pegs.

Ab'stehen, (*str.*) *v.* I. *intr.* 1) (*aux.* haben, *provinc.* sein, *cf.* Stehen) to stand off, to stand *or* to be at a distance *or* distant (von, from); parallele Linien stehen in allen Theilen gleich weit von einander ab, parallel lines are in all parts equally distant (or equidistant) from each other: b) to grow vapid or insipid, to get stale or flat (as beer, &c.); to turn, pall (of wine, &c.). — (aux. ſein, rarely haben) 2) to leave off standing, particul. Sport. a) to leave the stand (of the hunter having unsuccessfully waited for any game to pass), opp. Anſtehen; b) (of game) to alight from a tree, to fly down, cf. Abbaumen; 3) a) (of animals) to lose appetite, to grow averse to food, to waste away; b) to die (away) (of fishes and trees, rarely of human beings), to perish, decay, fade; abgeſtandene Fiſche ꝛc., see Abſtändig; 4) a) (von einer Sache, † with Gen. eines Dinges) —, to desist or abstain (from a thing), to recede (from a demand, &c.); to break off (from), to shrink or retreat (from), to leave off, to quit, abandon, relinquish, to give up or over, to drop, forbear (a bad habit, &c.); b) obsolescent, Einem or von Einem —, to abandon, desert one, to leave one unassisted (Abfallen).

II. tr. 1) to stand out (a given time), cf. Abſitzen, tr.; 2: 2) to cede (gener. in favour of another, and for a certain consideration: Einem etwas, etwas an Einen) to render or give up (a thing to one); ein Amt —, to resign an office.

III. refl. to get (over-)tired with standing: das Pferd hat ſich abgeſtanden, the horse has injured itself by standing too long.

Ab'ſtehen, v. n. (str.) n. 1) the (act of) standing off, &c. see Abſtehen, v. & cf. Abſtand; 2) the abandoning (of claims), desistance, recession, &c.

Ab'ſtehend, p. a. Bot. expanding, patent, spreading, forming an acute angle nearly approaching to a right angle with the stem or branch; ſparrig (horizontal) —, squarrose, spread out at a right angle from the stem.

Ab'ſteher, (str.) m. (l. u.) ceder, assigner, seller.

Ab'ſtehlen, (str.) v. tr. (Einem etwas) 1) to steal or filch (a thing) from (one), to rob (one) of (a thing); dem lieben Gott die Tage —, coll. to kill one's time, to beguile the time with good-for-nothing pursuits: fig.-a. 2) to learn (a thing) of (one) by stealth; 3) to snatch by stealth (moments, &c.) from (engagements, &c.).

Ab'ſteifen, (w.) v. I. tr. 1) Carp. to stiffen: to prop, support, underprop; Mas. to prop or shore up (a wall), einen Schacht —, see Abſpreizen; 2) a) to stiffen (linen) duly with starch, to starch sufficiently; b) to remove the starch from (linen), to unstarch; II. intr. (aux. ſein) to stiffen gradually, to become stiff.

Ab'ſteige ..., in comp. -haus, -quartier, n., -wohnung, f. house of accommodation, house of call, temporary lodging.

Ab'ſteigen, (str.) v. intr. (aux. ſein) 1) to descend, to step or get down: von einem Berge —, to descend a hill; to alight, to light (von einem Pferde, von einem Wagen, from a horse, from a coach); (particul. Mil.) to dismount: der Zug hielt an der Station, wo die Knaben — mußten, the train stopped at the station where the boys had to alight; 2) to alight (at an inn, &c.), to stop (on the road), to put up, to take temporary lodgings: ſie ſtiegen im Bairiſchen Hofe ab, aber wir kehrten bei einem Freunde ein, they put up (stopped, &c.) at the Bavarian Hotel, but we took up our quarters at a friend's; Garibaldi iſt bei Crispi abgeſtiegen, Garibaldi has taken up his quarters at Crispi's.

Ab'ſteigend, p. a. descending (also Med.); Her. descendant: die a-e Linie, the descending line or lineage; Astr.-a. das a-e Zeichen, the descending sign; der a-e Knoten, the descending node.

Ab'ſteigern, (w.) v. tr. to outbid (one, at a public sale).

Ab'ſteigung, (w.) f. 1) the (act of) descending, alighting, &c.; descent (also in fortification); 2) Math. & Astr. (gerade, right, ſchiefe, oblique) descension.

Ab'ſteinen, (w.) v. tr. 1) to provide duly with stones, to mark out (fields, &c.) with boundary-stones; 2) a) to clear of stones, to remove the stones from (a field, &c.); b) to take out the stones from (cherries, &c.), see Ausſteinen.

Ab'ſteinigen, (w.) v. tr. to knock down or [off with stones.

Ab'ſtellbar, adj. 1) that may be put down, &c. cf. Abſtellen; 2) admitting of removal, redress, &c.; remediable.

Ab'ſtellen, (w.) v. tr. 1) a) to put down (gener. temporarily); b) to put off or away; einen Schrank von der Wand —, to remove a press from the wall; ſtelle dich von dieſem Baume ab, place yourself at a distance from this tree; c) fig. to remove (from office, &c.), see Abſetzen, I. 9; 2) a) to stop the running of (water, &c.); b) T. to throw out of gear, to stop (a machine), to disconnect (a wheel, &c.); 3) Brew. to flavour (beer, by infusing it with wort); 4) fig. a) to put off, countermand, see Abbeſtellen; b) to put down, to remove (abuses, nuisances, &c.), to redress (grievances, &c.), to discard, leave off (a bad or an unnecessary custom), to abolish, repeal (a law), see Abſchaffen; to put an end to (daily bathing, &c.); 5) es auf Einen or etwas — (Zschokke, l. u. for Abſehen, II. 3, b), to have some one or an object in view, to aim at ....

Ab'ſteller, (str.) m. one who puts down, &c.; abolisher, &c.

Ab'ſtellung, (w.) f. 1) the (act of) putting down, &c.; 2) the (act of) stopping, &c., stoppage; 3) the (act of) redressing, &c., removal, redress, abolition, &c.: wirkſame Maßregeln zur — des Übels, effectual measures to remedy the evil: A-smittel, n. means of redress; Abſtellvorrichtung, f. T. stop-motion.

Ab'ſtemmen, (w.) v. tr. T. to chisel off (with a mortise-chisel).

Ab'ſtempeln, (w.) v. tr. 1) to provide or mark with the necessary or usual stamp: a) T. to stamp duly (a book, &c. with letters, flourishes, &c.), to flourish, to letter, cf. Abrollen, II. 7; b) to stamp for a certain purpose (railway-tickets, bonds, &c.); Briefmarken —, to deface, obliterate, blacken (postage-)stamps; 2) (often intr. [aux. haben]) to finish stamping; er hat (die Briefe ꝛc.) noch nicht (alle) abgeſtempelt, he has not yet done stamping (all the letters, &c.); 3) see Abprägen.

Ab'ſtempelung, (w.) f. the (act of) duly stamping, &c.; Briefmarken werden durch — entwerthet, (postage-)stamps are cancelled by defacement.

Ab'ſteppen, (w.) v. tr. Tail., &c. to quilt duly; to finish quilting (a coat, &c.).

Ab'ſterben, (str.) v. intr. (aux. ſein) 1) a) to die off or away: meine Eltern ſind mir ſehr früh abgeſtorben, I lost my parents when I was very young; an ihm iſt mir ein ſehr guter Freund abgeſtorben, I have lost a very good friend in him; unſere Hausthiere ſterben uns nach einander ab (Chamisso), our domestic animals die off in (quick) succession; b) to become extinct, see Ausſterben; c) provinc. in a general sense for Sterben, Verſterben, to die; 2) a) (of plants, &c.) to die off, to fade, wither, decay; ein abgeſtorbener Baum, a dead tree; b) to become paralyzed or insensible, to mortify: abgeſtorbene Glieder, dead limbs; meine Hände ſind mir (wie) abgeſtorben, my hands are benumbed; c) fig. to decay, to wither; 3) fig. (einer Sache [Dat.]) —, to become indifferent or insensible (to a thing); der Sünde (Dat.) —, Script. to die to sin; der Sünde abgeſtorben ſein (Rom. 6, [illegible] 2, 24), to be dead to sin.

Ab'ſterben, v. n. (str.) n. 1) [illegible] demise (of a king, &c.); 2) [illegible] ſterben, v.; 3) Surg. [illegible] the passions, &c.) the state of [illegible] lysed or insensible, &c.

Ab'ſterbung, (w.) f. [illegible] of) dying off, dying (to sin), cf. [illegible]

* **Ab'ſtergiren**, (w.) v. tr. [illegible] deterge, to cleanse, &c. see [illegible]

Ab'ſteuer, (w.) f. 1) tax on [illegible] Abzugsgeld; 2) settlement, a [illegible] settled upon one for final adjustment [illegible] &c.; cf. Ausſteuer.

Ab'ſteuern, (w.) v. I. intr. [illegible] steer off or away, to leave the [illegible] 1) to steer off; 2) fig. to turn off or [illegible] Abwenden; 3) to make a final [illegible] (one), to portion out, share off, [illegible] Abfinden ꝛc.

Ab'ſtich, I. (str.) m. 1) the (act of) [illegible] with a pointed instrument, &c. cf. [illegible] 2) Metall. a) the (act of) tapping (for [illegible] the mouth of) the melting-furnace; b) [illegible] tain quantity of metal run off into the [illegible] c) see —loch; 3) anything that is [illegible] off with a pointed instrument: esp. [illegible] sewing) a pattern pricked off (the [illegible] fig. contrast; einen — gegen eine [illegible] Sache machen, less usual than, zu einer [illegible] zwiſchen zwei Dingen (cf. [illegible] and the English to make a contrast [illegible] contrast between two things); [illegible] gegen ... den lächerlichſten — [illegible] a notion forming the most ridiculous [illegible] to ...; Tacitus findet eine [illegible] an dem — barbariſcher Tugend [illegible] ſchwelgenden Weſen römiſcher Damen, [illegible] indulges an honest pleasure in the [illegible] of barbarian virtue with the [illegible] duct of Roman ladies; der — [illegible] und weiß, the contrast between [illegible] white.

Ab'ſtich ..., in comp. [illegible] side of the running; —loch, n., — [illegible] opening, mouth of the furnace; — [illegible] —ſtange, f. opening-tool, rake [illegible]

Ab'ſticken, (w.) v. tr. to imitate [illegible] embroidery.

Ab'ſtieben, (str.) v. intr. see [illegible]

Ab'ſtimmen, (w.) v. I. tr. 1) [illegible] to lower, see Herabſtimmen; [illegible] (lit. & fig.) out of tune; [illegible] tune properly (an instrument, [illegible] (l. u.) to outvote, see Überſtimmen [illegible] 1) obsolescent particul. fig. to be [illegible] to disagree; 2) to vote; to [illegible] vote by division; über eine Sache [illegible] to vote, to divide on (upon) a [illegible] etwas — laſſen, to put a thing to [illegible] see zur Abſtimmung bringen.

Ab'ſtimmig, adj. obsolescent, [illegible] discordant; dissenting, cf. [illegible] Sache (Dat.) —, discordant, at variance [illegible] a thing.

Ab'ſtimmung, (w.) f. 1) (l. u.) [illegible] of) tuning down, &c. cf. [illegible] dissonance, discordance; 2) the [illegible] ing, vote; division; [illegible] Wahlen); dies hängt von [illegible] ſes ab, this depends upon the [illegible] the house; zur — bringen, to [illegible] er wollte ſeinen Antrag zur — [illegible] tended to divide the house upon [illegible] die — fand ſtatt und der [illegible] (the) division took place, and [illegible] was carried; bei der — fand [illegible] viding it was found ...; [illegible] — beſchließen, to vote an [illegible] — enthalten, to abstain from [illegible]

Ab'ſtöbern, (w.) v. tr. 1) [illegible]

doctor (thin plate of steel used in scraping the colour or mordant off copper-plates, in calico-printing), *cf.* Streichmesser; —riemen, *m.* razor-strop (Streichriemen).

Ab'streifbar, *adj.* capable of being stripped off.

Ab'streifeln, (*w.*) *v. tr.* to strip off by short, repeated movements.

Ab'streifen, (*w.*) *v.* I. *intr.* (*aux.* ſein) 1) to roam, rove, wander downwards *or* off (away); 2) to glance off (as a bullet, &c.): der Pfeil traf den Schild und streifte ab, the arrow struck the shield and glanced: die Kugel traf gegen einen Knopf ſeiner Uniform, von welchem ſie abſtreifte, the ball struck against a button of his uniform, from which it glanced off: II. *tr.* 1) *a)* to strip off, to slip off (a twig, &c.): von einem Baume (*or* einem Baume: *Luther*, Dan. 4, 11) das Laub —, to strip a tree of its leaves, to unstring (beans): die Handſchuhe —, to draw off one's gloves; *b)* die Haut —, to cast the skin (von einer Schlange auch the slough): einem Thiere die Haut —, to strip the skin from an animal: *motion.* ein Thier —, to strip an animal of its skin; to skin an eel, to flay, &c. *cf.* Abziehen; *c)* *fig.* to slip off, to slip; to divest (one's self) of (a thing), to disengage (one's self) from, to throw off; 2) to range over (the country) in quest of a person, a piece of game, &c.; 3) to take *or* throw off by a glancing motion; die Kugel ſtreifte ihm den Hut ab, a glancing bullet carried off his hat (*Bilp.*); III. *refl.* to be stripped off *or* divested: to drop off: *gener. fig.* to disclose *or* reveal itself, &c.

Ab'streifer, (*str.*) *m.* 1) one who strips off, &c.; 2) ramble, excursion, &c. digressing from the main route, *see* Abſtecher, 3.

Ab'streiten, (*str.*) *v.* I. *tr.* 1) (Einem etwas) *a)* to take *or* wrest (a thing) from (one) by contest *or* dispute; *particul.* to deprive (one) of (a thing) by a lawsuit, to obtain by litigation; *b)* *fig.* to wrest, to snatch; 2) to deny with vehemence; 3) *gener.* Einem etwas —, *a)* to contest, to impugn, to dispute some one's right *or* claim to a thing, &c.: Einem die Autorſchaft —, to deny, contest, controvert, &c. one's authorship; *b)* to argue (one) out of (an opinion, &c.): dies laſſe ich mir nicht —, I won't be disputed *or* worded out of it, in this I will not yield; II. *refl.* to contend, dispute, fight to exhaustion; ſie hatten ſich endlich abgeſtritten, they had at length ceased to contend, &c.

Ab'strich, (*str.*) *m.* 1) downstroke ([Grundſtrich] of the pen in writing, &c.); 2) the act of striking off, cancelling, &c. *cf.* Abſtreichen; 3) *a)* that which is skimmed *or* taken off, scum; *b)* *or* —blei, *n.* skimmed lead, litharge; 4) a kind of auction (*opp.* Aufſtrich), *see* Abſtreich, 2; —holz, *n.* 1) strickle, *see* Streichholz; 2) skimming-stick; —zinn, *n.* skimmed tin.

Ab'stricken, (*w.*) *v. tr.* 1) to knit off: *a)* eine Nadel —, to knit off a needle; *b)* eine Schuld —, to pay *or* clear off a debt by knitting; *c)* to spend a given time (an hour, &c.) by knitting; *d)* to accomplish a certain task, &c. (by) knitting: einen Roman — (*Auerbach*), *ludicr.* to read *or* get through (*coll.* to do) a novel while knitting; 2) *a)* to loose from a cord (as a dog, &c.), to uncord, untie, unfasten; *b)* *fig.* to release, free from the toils of (snare, &c.); *c)* (Einem etwas) *fig.* (*obsolescent*) to deprive (one) of (a thing), to intercept, &c.: to cheat *or* to swindle (one) out of.

Ab'strickung, (*w.*) *f.* (*obsolescent*) the act of depriving, &c.: robbery, depredation.

Ab'striegeln, (*w.*) *v. tr.* 1) to curry, rub down (a horse); 2) *coll.* to curry, thrash, beat (one) soundly.

Ab'strom, (*str.*, *pl.* Ab'ſtröme) *m.* 1) downflowing stream *or* current; *fig.* ein ewiger Ab- und Zuſtrom, a perpetual ebb and flow: 2) issue, outlet, vent, escape (*cf.* Abfluß).

Ab'strömen, (*w.*) *v.* I. *intr.* (*aux.* ſein) 1) *a)* to be carried down, off, *or* away by the stream, to flow off rapidly: ab- und zuſtrömen, to ebb and flow; *b)* *Mar.* to be carried away by currents; *c)* to flow off in a steady current, to emanate, issue, escape; 2) to crowd away *or* off, to disperse: II. *tr.* 1) to float down a stream; 2) to wash away.

Ab'strossen, (*w.*) *v. tr. Min.* to work (a mine, &c.) by stopes (*i. e.* steps), to cut down (mineral ground) *or* hew away (ore) in a mine, so that the upper or undersurface of the excavation presents the form of a series of steps.

Ab'strüpfen, (*w.*) *v. tr.* to strip off with a quick, jerking motion.

* **Abstrūs',** *adj.* (*Lat.*) abstruse, hid, *or* remote (from apprehension), difficult (to be comprehended or understood).

Ab'stückeln, (*w.*) *v. tr.* to break off, *or* to detach in small particles.

Ab'stücken, (*w.*) *v. tr.* 1) to break off, separate, *or* detach in pieces, to crumble off; 2) to lay (a rope) by interweaving short strands.

Ab'studiren, (*w.*) *refl.* to tire one's self out by severe study, to overstudy one's self.

Ab'stufen, (*w.*) *v.* I. *tr.* 1) to separate *or* form into steps; 2) *Min.* to cut down (mineral ground), to break off (ore) with the pick; 3) to graduate, to mark with degrees, gradations *or* differences of any kind, to shade (off); II. *refl.* & *intr.* (*aux.* ſein) to graduate, to be shaded *or* diversified by gradation, to pass by degrees, to change gradually: ein Klima, das ſich von größter Hitze bis zur äußerſten Kälte abſtuft, a clime which exhibits all the gradations between the extremes of heat and cold.

Ab'stufung, (*w.*) *f.* gradation, degree, shade: in genauſter, feinſter —, graduated to the greatest nicety.

Ab'stülpen, (*w.*) *v. tr.* to let down, turn down *or* over the flap of (a hat, &c.).

Ab'stummeln, Ab'stümpeln, (*w.*) *v. tr.* to cut off so as to leave mere stumps, to detruncate.

Ab'stümpern, (*w.*) *v. tr.* to play off, to perform in a bungling manner.

Ab'stumpfen, (*w.*) *v.* I. *tr.* 1) to truncate, to cut off, to lop, *cf.* Abgeſtumpft; einem Pferde den Schwanz —, to dock the tail of a horse: 2) *a)* *lit.* & *fig.* to blunt, dull (the edge, point, a sword, the senses, &c.); *b)* *Chem.* to neutralise (acids) by alcaline substances: *c)* *fig.* to blunt, to dull, to deaden, to weaken, to stupify: das Gewiſſen —, to blunt the conscience: das ſittliche Gefühl —, to dull, to weaken, &c. the moral sense; II. *refl.* & *intr.* (*aux.* ſein) 1) to get, grow, *or* become blunted, dull, &c.: 2) *fig.* to dull, to become dull *or* stupid, to dolt.

Ab'stümpfen, (*w.*) *v. see* Abſtumpfen.

Ab'stumpfung, (*w.*) *f.* 1) *a)* truncation, the (act of) cutting *or* lopping off &c. (edges, angles, points, &c.); *particul.* *in Geom.* the cutting off of an edge *or* angle, so that it becomes replaced by a plane equally inclined to the adjoining faces: *b)* truncation, the state of being truncated; 2) *lit.* & *fig.* *a)* the (act of) blunting, dulling, &c.; *fig.* hebetation; stupefaction; the state of being blunted, dulled, deadened, &c. (Abgeſtumpftheit).

Ab'stürmen, (*w.*) *v.* I. *intr.* 1) (*aux.* ſein) to hasten *or* rush off in a stormy rage, *see* Fortſtürmen, 1; 2) (*aux.* haben) to leave off storming; II. *tr.* 1) to shake off by a storm: 2) (Einem etwas) to obtain, get, force, wrest, &c. (a thing) from (one) by stormy violence, by violent assault, &c.

Ab'sturz, (*str.*, *pl.* Ab'ſtürze) *m.* 1) rapid *or* violent downfall, &c. *cf.* Sturz, 1; 2) precipice, steep descent, steep.

Ab'stürzen, (*w.*) *v.* I. *intr.* [illegible] to fall, rush *or* dash headlong [illegible] to be precipitated, *cf.* [illegible] Felſen, precipitated rocks; [illegible] ruptly, to descend perpendicular[illegible] so (as a precipice); II. *tr.* 1) [illegible] to throw headlong; 2) to [illegible] by dashing *or* thrusting down [illegible] Genick *or* ſich (Dat.) den [illegible] one's neck; 3) to remove the [illegible] (Stürze) from (a pot, &c.).

Ab'stutzen, (*w.*) *v. tr.* 1) to cut [illegible] end of a thing), to trim off, to [illegible] curtail, to dock; to crop; to [illegible] lop (trees); einem Pferde den [illegible] dock the tail of a horse; [illegible] —, to dock a horse; to crop [illegible] horse or dog); to clip (the wings [illegible] Haar, hair cut close *or* short; [illegible] ped hair; abgeſtutzt, *p. a.* *a)* [illegible] &c.; *b)* presenting an appearance [illegible] end had been cut off square, [illegible] cated (*Bot.*, *Herald.*, &c.); [illegible] a truncated column, &c. *cf.* [illegible] abgeſtutztes Blatt, a truncate(d) [illegible] aufgeſtutzt und abgeſtutzt, the [illegible] and stunted (*or* snubbed); [illegible] (woollen stuffs, cloth, &c.) for [illegible] to give the first shearing.

Ab'stützen, (*w.*) *v. tr.* to [illegible] prop (as a ship on the stocks); [illegible] *see* Abſpreizen).

Ab'suchen, (*w.*) *v. tr.* 1) to [illegible] off, away, &c., to pick off (as [illegible] bush, caterpillars, &c.); 2) to [illegible] roughly, to range *or* scour [illegible] directions in search of (game, [illegible] der Hühnerhund ſucht ein Feld ab, [illegible] quarters a field (*i. e.* ranges over [illegible] search of game (*Milit.*)), *cf.* [illegible]

Ab'sud, (*str.*) *m.* 1) decoction [illegible] decocting or boiling anything, [illegible] virtues, *but particul.* an extract [illegible] made by boiling an organic [illegible] water), extract: apozem ([illegible] *dyers, calico-printers, &c.*) [illegible] beize); 2) *Mint.* blanching (of [illegible] *see* Weißſud).

Ab'sudeln, (*w.*) *v. tr.* to [illegible] ly, to copy in a daubing manner.

Ab'süffern, (*w.*) *v. tr.* [illegible] for Abſäubern, to clean off, [illegible] of stains, to give (one) a [illegible] set-down, reprimand.

Ab'säuern, (*w.*) *v. tr.* to [illegible] thoroughly.

Ab'sumpfen, (*w.*) *v. tr.* 1) to [illegible] by drawing off humidity, to [illegible] (a marshy country); 2) [illegible] down the sepals.

* **Absurd',** *adj.* (*Lat.*) [illegible]

* **Absurdität',** (*w.*) *f.* [illegible] ſchmacktheit).

Ab'surren, (*w.*) *v. intr.* [illegible] or buzz off, to fly *or* hasten away [illegible] ming sound (Abſchwirren, [illegible]

Ab'süßen, (*w.*) *v. tr.* to [illegible] thoroughly, to dulcify; [illegible] to edulcorate, to free from [illegible] or acrimony by copious washing [illegible] *pharmacy* [*Ann Paul*, &c.]); — [illegible]

Ab'süß..., *in comp.* [illegible] *m.* edulcorating vat *or* tub [illegible] ſchale, *f.*, —wanne, *f.* [illegible]

Ab'süßung, (*w.*) *f.* [illegible]

Abt, (*str.*, *pl.* Äbte) [illegible] abbot: *proverb* (*shortly* [illegible] *riotous living of the* [illegible] *cf. Grimm & Sandhagen* [illegible] (*extremes*) bis Willlen [illegible] ben — reiten laſſen [illegible] without restraint, [illegible]

m. abbot's cap; A-Würde, *f.* abbotship, abbacy.

Ab'tafeln, *(w.)* v. I. *tr. Weav.* to take off from the beam; II. *intr.* to finish dining or supping (*cf.* Abspeisen, II.); die Gesellschaft hatte abgetafelt, the company had done dining, had risen from table.

Ab'täfeln, *(w.)* v. *tr.* 1) to (line with) wainscot; 2) *provinc.* to depict (a person's character) minutely and unsparingly, *see* Abmalen, 2, *b.*

Ab'takeln, *(w.)* v. *tr.* 1) *Mar.* to unrig, to dismantle, to lay up (ein Schiff, a ship, eine Flotte, a fleet); die Masten —, to strip the masts; ein abgetakeltes Schiff, a ship laid up (*opp.* Auftakeln); 2) *fig. coll.* to lay by (as persons unnecessary for the time), to put aside or out of use, to shelve. — **Ab'takelung,** *(w.) f.* the (act of) unrigging (a vessel), &c.

Ab'taljen, *(w.)* v. *tr. Mar.* to lower (heavy bodies, parts of the cargo, &c.) by means of a tackle (Talje, *opp.* Auftaljen).

Ab'tändeln, *(w.)* v. *tr.* (Einem *etwas*) to obtain (a thing) from (one) by toying and trifling, to dawdle (one) out of (a thing).

Ab'tanzen, *(w.)* v. I. *intr.* 1) (*aux.* sein) to dance down or off (Forttanzen); von der Bühne —, to dance off the stage; 2) (*aux.* haben) to finish dancing; to leave off dancing; II. *tr.* *a)* to wear off or out by dancing: sich (*Dat.*) die Sohlen (or die Schuhe) —, to wear out one's soles (or shoes) by dancing: sich (*Dat.*) die Beine —, to dance off (to wear out) one's legs (by dancing); *b)* *refl.* to exhaust or tire one's self by dancing; 2) (Einem *etwas*) to deprive (one) of (a thing) by dancing; einer Braut (*Dat.*) den Kranz —, (a usage among German bridesmaids) to obtain or gain the bridal garland through a dance formed round the bride; 3) to dance through (a certain measure, a waltz, &c.).

† **Ab'täuben,** *(w.)* v. *tr.* to make dull, insensible, to mortify (the flesh), *cf.* Betäuben.

Ab'tauchen, *(w.)* v. I. *intr.* (*l. u.*) to dive, submerge (*cf.* Hinabtauchen); II. *tr.* to wash or clean (thoroughly) by submerging.

Ab'taufen, *(w.)* v. *tr. provinc.* (*S. G.*) to baptize out of hand or hastily, *cf.* Nothtaufen.

Ab'taumeln, *(w.)* v. *intr.* (*aux.* sein) 1) (Hinabtaumeln) to tumble down; 2) (Forttaumeln) to stagger or reel off or away, to go off staggering.

Ab'tausch, *(str.)* m. the (act of) obtaining by exchange, exchange.

Ab'tauschen, *(w.)* v. *tr.* (Einem *etwas*) to obtain (something) from (one) by exchange or trafficking, to exchange, barter (eine Sache gegen eine andere or mit einer anderen [*Dat.*], one thing for another).

Ab'tauschung, *(w.) f.* the (act of) obtaining, &c. by exchange, &c. *cf.* Abtauschen.

Äb'tchen, (*provinc.* [*S. G.*] & *poet.*) **Äbt'lein,** *(str.)* n. (*dimin. of* Abt) little abbot.

Abtei', *(w.) f.* 1) abbey (residence of an abbot); 2) abbacy (office, dignity, rights, or possessions of an abbot); abbotship.

Abtei'lich, *adj.* abbatial, relating to an abbey.

Ab'telegraphiren, *(w.)* v. *tr.* to write off, despatch, announce, convey (eine Nachricht &c., a piece of intelligence, a message, &c.) by telegraph, to telegraph off: diese Nachricht konnte erst nach Verlauf von zwei Stunden abtelegraphirt werden, the telegram announcing this news could not be executed before the lapse of two hours. — **Ab'telegraphirung,** *(w.) f.* the (act of) telegraphing off, &c.

Ab'terrorisiren, *(w.)* v. *tr.* (Einem *etwas*) to [illegible] (something) from (one), or to wrest (by terrorism) from (a government, &c.) by means of terrorism.

Ab'teufeln, *(w.)* v. *tr. vulg.* to chase or knock about devilishly, to beat like the deuce.

Ab'teufen, *(w.)* v. *tr. Min.* to sink (einen Schacht, a shaft or pit).

Ab'teufer, *(str.)* m. pit-man, shaft-man.

Ab'thauen, *(w.)* v. I. *intr.* (*aux.* sein) to thaw off; II. *tr.* to cause to thaw off, to make (a thing) thaw off.

Ab'theil, *(str.)* m. (*l. u.*) share, appanage.

Ab'theilbar, *adj.* capable of being divided into distinct parts, or of being partitioned, divisible, separable, *cf.* Abtheilen.

Ab'theilen, *(w.)* v. I. *tr.* 1) *a)* to separate, set apart by division: weit abgetheilte Lichter im finstern Bergwerk (*Jean Paul*), lights in the dark mine, divided by long intervals: *b)* to divide into distinct parts, to divide into shares, to part, partition; to allot or parcel out in parts or portions; to share; to portion off, to parcel, lot (Waaren &c., goods, &c.); Silben — (*grammar:* Wörter in Silben —), to divide syllables (*meton. for* to divide words into syllables); *c)* to partition (the floor of a house, &c.), to story; to trench (the ballast); *d)* *T.* to graduate, to mark with degrees: *e)* to arrange (in Classen, into classes), to [illegible]-order, dispose, set; to classify, distribute; 2) † to sever thoroughly or entirely, so as to exclude from all connection or communication; 3) (*cf. the intr.*) *Law,* to portion or pay off (Erben &c., heirs, &c.); abgetheilte (abgefundene) Prinzen, appanaged princes; II. *intr.* mit Einem —, to come to a settlement or to settle accounts with one: wir haben abgetheilt (*Auerbach*), *fig.* we have settled our accounts, we have done with each other, we have nothing to say to each other any more (*cf.* wir sind geschiedene Leute).

Ab'theilig, *adj. obsolescent,* 1) separated or divided into distinct parts; 2) (*Campe*) portioned off, &c. (Abgetheilt).

Ab'theiligen, *(w.)* v. *tr.* (*Campe, l. u.*) to portion off, *see* Abtheilen, 3.

Ab'theilung, *(w.) f.* 1) the (act of) dividing into distinct parts, &c. *cf.* Abtheilen: *a)* division, partition, allotment; die — von Waaren in Partien, the lotting of goods; die — der (Wörter in) Silben, the division or dividing of (words into) syllables, syllabication; *b)* distribution, disposition, arrangement into classes, classification: *c)* die — in Grade &c., graduation, regular division into degrees, &c. *cf.* Theilung; 2) the part which is separated by dividing, &c.: *a)* division, partition; allotment, share; *b)* *aa)* compartment (eines Eisenbahnwagens &c., of a railway-carriage, &c.), (com)partition: *bb)* set of rooms, accommodation, story; *cc)* crib, stall; box; *c)* section, part, division (einer Armee, of an army, eines Buches, of a book, &c.); *d)* parcel, lot of goods; A-Zeichen, n. 1) mark of division or separation: *sometimes used for* Bindestrich, hyphen; 2) section mark (on railways, &c.).

Ab'thon, *(str.)* m. *a popular name for* Streifenfarren (a plant: maiden's hair).

Ab'thun, *(irr.)* v. I. *tr.* 1) *a)* to put down or off (articles of dress — *literally* to do off, *cf. the English* to doff) to take off, to pull off, to lay aside (*opp.* Anthun, Anthun, *cf.* to don); *b)* (*l. u.*) *lit.* & *fig.* to take off or away, to turn away, to remove; eine Figur &c. —, *T.* to lift a cast figure out of the sand; die Frucht vom Felde —, to remove (gather in) the fruits from the field, & *meton.:* das abgethane Feld (*Rumohr*), the field cleared of grain, the reaped field; die Hand — (abziehen), to withdraw one's hand: *aa)* von einer Sache, einem Werke &c., from a thing, a work &c., to leave off &c. (*cf.* Nehem. 6, 3; 9: 2 Chron. 15, 7); *bb)* von einer Person, from one, *i. e.* to cease to help or support him: laß mich nicht, und thue nicht von mir die Hand ab (*Luther,* Ps. 27, 9), leave me not, neither forsake me; *c)* *fig.* (Ablegen) to put off (false shame, &c.), to do away (imperfections, prejudices, &c.), to lay aside, to divest one's self of (a thing), to discard (prejudices, &c.); da ich aber ein Mann ward, that (that) ich ab, was kindisch war (*Luther,* 1 Corinth. 13, 11), when I became a man, I put away childish things; er hat alle selbstsüchtigen Rücksichten abgethan, he has cast away all selfish considerations; er that den Kaufmann ab, he put off the merchant (*i. e.* the manners and feelings of a merchant); mancher ... Rittersmann hat dort den Trunk sich (*Dat.*) abgethan (abgewöhnt) (*Uhland*), many a knight there weaned himself from the habit of drinking; 2) to take away (from a thing, *opp.* Hinzuthun, to add), to deduct, &c.; 3) to do away with ..., to remove (a person, a thing, &c. so that they should be dead and gone, „ab und todt", (*Sanders*); *a)* (Einen) to make away with (one, *i. e.* to kill him), to dispatch, to put to death (*pecul.* ist to do to death, *Shaksp.* 2. Hen. VI. 3, 2: Why, Warwick, who should do the duke to death?), to execute: Gehülfen des Scharfrichters, die zugleich Verbrecher mit — müssen (*Lessing*), assistants of the executioner, who have likewise to assist in the execution of criminals; mit dem Schwerte —, to put to the sword: ehe sie marternd ihn abthaten (*Stolberg*), before they dispatched him with torments; (*often applied to the killing or slaughtering of animals*) ein Schwein —, to stick a pig: eine Ziege —, to kill a goat; dem Leibe abgethan sein (*Opitz*), to be dead to the flesh; *b)* *fig.* to abolish, put an end to (a thing), to set aside, remove, &c.; Gesetze — (*obsolescent for* abschaffen), to abolish laws; die Zerrissenheit Deutschlands ist eine abgethane Sache, the dismembered state of Germany is a by-gone thing; laßt abgethane Dinge abgethan sein, let by-gones be by-gones; die abgethanen Thorheiten abgethaner Jahrhunderte, the exploded (discarded) follies of by-gone centuries; dies ist eine völlig abgethane Classe von religiösen Begriffen, this is an entirely gone-by order of religious ideas; ein abgethaner Aberglaube, a discarded (worn-out) superstition; Einwürfe —, to obviate, to do away (overthrow) objections (beseitigen); solche Gegenstände (der Unterhaltung &c.) that er mit einem Scherz oder einem Lachen ab, such subjects he dismissed with a joke or a laugh; die Sprachwissenschaft thut die Frage des deutschen Ursprungs der englischen Sprache ab, philology sets at rest the question of the German origin of the English language; diese Frage ist vollständig abgethan, this question has been completely set at rest; er betrachtet es als eine abgethane Sache, he looks upon it as a settled matter; einen Streit —, to put an end to a quarrel, to settle a dispute; eine Schuld —, to clear off a debt; 4) to do or accomplish thoroughly, to finish entirely, to bring to an end or final issue (*this meaning often borders closely on that explained in* 3, *b*): *a)* Wär' es auch abgethan, wenn es gethan ist, | dann wär' es gut, es würde rasch gethan (*Schiller,* Macbeth I, 7), If it were done, when 'tis done, then 't were well | it were done quickly; damit ist's noch nicht abgethan, that does not settle the matter; *b)* to execute, despatch, to do off or to wind up (a business); eine Rechnung —, to close or settle an account, *cf.* Abmachen; *c)* geschwind —, to execute speedily: *aa)* to despatch, to perform with despatch; er that eine Menge dringlicher Geschäfte ab, he cleared off a press of business, of affairs, &c.; *bb)* schnell und obenhin —, to perform in haste and disorder, to huddle up in a hurry; 5) *Comm.* einen (Waaren-)Posten —, to dispose of a lot (of goods) at a certain price, *cf.* Absetzen, 1, *f,* & Absetzen, 10.

II. *rfl.* 1) to turn off *or* away (from association), to withdraw, depart, retire (from ...), *i. e.* to leave: 2) *fig.* sich — von einer Sache, *or more usually* einer Sache (*Gen.*), to divest *or* strip one's self of a thing, to disengage *or* free one's self from ...; to give up, lay aside, throw *or* cast away: to renounce: sich seines Glaubens —, to renounce one's faith: abgethan, *p. a.* released, free (einer Sache [*Gen.*], from ...: Los, ledig).

Ab'thüren, (*w.*) *v. tr.* (& *intr.*) *T. provinc.* to remove the shingle-boards (*see* Thüre) from (the wings of a windmill).

Ab'thürmen, (*w.*) *v. tr.* & *intr.* (*l. u.*) to pull down *or* remove (a tower or anything towering aloft or piled up), *opp.* Aufthürmen.

Ab'thuung, (*w.*) *f.* 1) the (act of) settling, &c. *cf.* Abthun; settlement, adjustment, &c. *see* Abmachung; 2) execution (of a criminal).

Ab'tiefen, (*w.*) *v. tr.* to deepen by digging downwards, to sink (a shaft, &c., Abteufen).

Ab'tilgen, (*w.*) *v. tr. obsolescent,* to remove by extinguishing, to extinguish, blot out, *see* Austilgen; eine Schuld —, to clear off a debt.

Ab'tischen, (*w.*) *v. tr.* (*l. u.*) to remove from the board, to consume (*opp.* Auftischen).

* **Äbtis'sin, Abtis'sin,** *coll.* **Äb'tin,** (*w.*) *f.* abbess.

Äbt'lein, (*str.*) *n. see* Äbtchen.

Äbt'lich, † **Äb'tig,** *adj.* abbatial, belonging *or* relating to an abbot.

Ab'toben, (*w.*) *v.* I. *tr.* (Einem etwas) to get *or* wrest (a thing) from (one) by raging, to bully (one) out of (a thing); II. *rfl.* & III. *intr.* to spend, exhaust *or* vent one's fury *or* rage, *see* Austoben; *fig.* to sow one's wild oats, *cf.* (sich die Hörner) Ablaufen; die Wogen hatten sich abgetobt, the waves had exhausted their rage.

Ab'tödten, (*w.*) *v. tr.* 1) † to put an end to ... by killing, to kill off, to kill: *fig.-s.* 2) to destroy gradually, but entirely: *a)* to annihilate; to mortify, subdue (fleischliche Lüste &c., bodily appetites, &c.); to smother, to blunt (die Gefühle, Neigungen &c., the sensations, desires, &c.): *b)* einem Wilde den Wind — (*Auerbach*), to cut off game from the scent: *c)* (*l. u.*) to annihilate, diminish by payment, to sink (a public debt, &c.: Tilgen, Amortisiren).

Ab'tödtung, (*w.*) *f.* the (act of) killing off, &c. *cf.* Abtödten; a deadening by degrees, *Surg.* mortification (sinnlicher Begierden &c., of sensual appetites, &c.).

Ab'tollen, (*w.*) *v. rfl. see* Abtoben.

* **Ab'tön,** *see* Abthon.

Ab'tönen, (*w.*) *v.* I. *intr.* 1) (*l. u.*) to deviate in sound, to sound differently: 2) (*or* Ab'tönen) & II. *rfl.* to be diversified *or* shaded off by gradation of tints: III. *tr.* to gradate, mark *or* contrast with gradations of tints, to shade off. — **Ab'tönung,** (*w.*) *f.* the (act of) diversifying *or* marking with gradation of tints, &c.

Ab'tosen, (*w.*) *v. see* Austosen.

Ab'trab, (*str.*) *m. Mil.* detachment.

Ab'traben, (*w.*) *v. intr.* (*aux.* sein) 1) to trot off; to march off; 2) *coll.* to move off, to take one's self off, *cf.* Abschleichen.

Ab'trag, (*str.*, *pl.* **Ab'träge**) *m.* 1) *a)* the (act of) carrying off, taking away; digging off, cutting (earth works, &c.); *b)* the quantity of earth, &c. carried off, taken away; cutting (*opp.* Auftrag); *c)* remains of a meal (Abhub); 2) *a)* reduction or diminution (of a debt, &c.) by payment, payment, discharge; *b)* compensation (for injury sustained), indemnification, reimbursement of loss or damage, satisfaction, amends, reparation; — thun, to make reparation, &c., *see* Ersatz leisten; 3) injury done by carrying off, embezzling property, &c.; detriment, damage, &c.; Einem — thun, to injure, damage, prejudice, *see* Eintrag, Abbruch thun; 4) *provinc.* (*Swiss.*) *a)* difference (Unterschied); *b)* (Ertrag) yield (of the soil, &c.), produce, &c.

Ab'tragbar, *adj.* 1) what may be carried off, &c.; 2) redeemable, reducible.

Ab'träge..., *in comp.* —geld, *n.* letter-carrier's fees or dues (Bestellgeld), *cf.* Abtragen, I. *tr.* 1, *a*; —lohn, *m.* fees paid for carrying off or removing burdens, porterage.

Ab'tragen, (*str.*) *v.* I. *tr.* 1) *a)* to carry off, to take away off; das Auftragen und —, the serving and removing: Briefe — lassen, to have letters delivered: den Tisch (*mston. for* die Speisen &c. vom Tische) —, to clear the table (*opp.* Auftragen); *b)* to carry *or* take down; to level *or* lower (an elevation, a hill, &c. by removing the earth — *opp.* Auftragen); *c)* to pull *or* take down (a house, so that the building-materials may still be used, *different from* Abreißen, Abbrechen); *d) Sport.* to carry (a bloodhound) away from the scent (in training); *e) Math.* & *Survey.* to transfer (lines, angles, &c.) in plotting; *f)* † (Einem etwas) to deprive *or* defraud (one) of (a thing), to purloin, embezzle: to occasion loss (to one), to injure, damage, prejudice, *cf.* Abtrag, 3; 2) to make up, to clear, &c.; (Einem etwas) *a) provinc.* † to requite, restore, to make amends for, to make good, &c.; *b) aa)* to discharge, to pay off (a debt, a capital, &c.), to acquit, pay off, liquidate (a debt, &c.), to pay up (a capital, &c.), to sink (a fund); der Pächter trägt seinen Pacht in Naturalien ab, the farmer pays *or* discharges his rent in kind: das Capital soll abgetragen werden, the capital is to be paid off, to a sinking fund; *bb) fig.* wird mein Leben die Verbindlichkeiten —, die Sie auf mich gehäuft haben? will my life pay the obligations you have conferred upon me? du hast gehofft, dein Lohn ist abgetragen (*Schiller*), thou hast had hope, thy reward has been meted out to thee: zum Henker mit seiner Unverschämtheit! wenn ich's ihm je — kann, so soll's an meinem guten Willen nicht fehlen, hang his impudence! if ever I can pay him off, I shall not fail for want of good will; *c)* (*with impersonal subject*) *provinc.* (*Swiss.*) to remunerate (one) for money, time, labour, &c. expended on a thing, to yield (profit, &c.), bring in, &c.; 3) to carry for a (sufficient) length of time: *a) Sport.* to train (a hawk) for the chase: *b)* to wear off, away *or* out (clothes); abgetragen, *p. a.* worn out, *see* Abgetragen.

II. *rfl.* 1) *a)* to exhaust *or* fatigue one's self by carrying (loads), &c. *cf.* Abtragen, *tr.* & Tragen; ich habe mich mit dem Kinde ganz abgetragen, *coll.* I am quite spent with carrying the child; *b)* (applied to fruit-trees) to exhaust itself by bearing, to cease, leave off bearing fruit, *see* Austragen, *intr.*; 2) to wear off *or* out, to become threadbare: das Haar des Pelzwerks hatte sich an vielen Stellen abgetragen, the hair of the fur had been worn off in many places; dieses Tuch trägt sich schnell ab, this cloth wears itself out very soon.

Ab'träger, (*str.*) *m.* one who carries off loads, &c., porter.

Ab'träglich, *adj.* 1) (*obsolescent*) injurious, prejudicial, detrimental (*opp.* Zuträglich); 2) *provinc.* (*Swiss.*) productive, remunerative, profitable (Einträglich).

Ab'tragsböschung, (*w.*) *f. T.* slope of a (railway-)cutting.

Ab'tragung, (*w.*) *f.* 1) the (act of) carrying off, &c. *cf.* Abtragen; 2) the (act of) pulling down, demolition, &c.; 3) the act of discharging, paying off, &c., discharge, payment, liquidation, &c.

Ab'trampeln (**Ab'trämpeln,** *l. u.*), (*w.*) *v.* I. *intr.* (*aux.* sein) *coll.* to tramp off: II. *tr.* 1) to knock *or* wear off by trampling; 2) (*Ab'trampeln*) to [illegible] ing and stamping, *i. e.* in a [illegible] manner; 3) to [illegible] steps: III. *rfl.* to exhaust [illegible] self with tramping about.

Ab'traufen, (*w.*) *v. tr.* 1) [illegible] ficiently with drink; 2) to [illegible]

Ab'trappeln, (*w.*) *v. intr.* [illegible] patter off, to run away with a [illegible] of short clattering steps.

Ab'trappen, (*w.*) *v. intr.* [illegible] tramp *or* trot off with clattering [illegible]

Ab'trauern, (*w.*) *v.* I. *intr.* [illegible] mourn (*gener.* outwardly, *i. e.* [illegible] ing), *see* Austrauern; II. *rfl.* [illegible] pine away with grief.

Ab'träufeln, (*w.*) *v.* I. *intr.* [illegible] trickle off *or* to fall down in a [illegible] cession of small drops; II. *tr.* to [illegible] move in small drops.

Ab'traufen, Ab'träufen, (*w.*) *v. intr.* [illegible] (sein) to trickle off *or* to fall down [illegible] to drop off.

Ab'treibbar, *adj.* to be driven [illegible] treiblich.

Ab'treib(e)..., *in comp.* [illegible] arbeit, *f.* 1) *Min.* the work of [illegible] mine, &c.) with timber; [illegible] work; —herd, *m.* refining hearth [illegible] ing hearth; —holz, *n.*, —[illegible], &c. [illegible] used as fuel for the [illegible] *f.* finery; —lohn, *m.* fee for [illegible] *m.* master-refiner; —mittel, *n.* [illegible] medicine, draught for causing [illegible]

Ab'treiben, (*str.*) *v.* I. *tr.* 1) [illegible] driving, &c., to force away; [illegible] off, to drive away, to drive [illegible] repel, to rebuff; to put to flight; [illegible] schlag —, to turn *or* ward off [illegible] *Mar.* ein Schiff vom Course —, to [illegible] from the right course: *aa)* to [illegible] possess, expel, &c. by legal [illegible] tion-right, &c.) *or* by force; *bb)* [illegible] by argument, to rebuff, refute; [illegible] —, to repel, refute an argument [illegible] dislodge (a swarm of bees); *c)* [illegible] off (intestinal worms, &c.); die [illegible] ein Kind —, to cause a miscarriage [illegible] abortion; abtreibende Mittel, [illegible] cines or draughts; *d) Forest.* to [illegible] forest, &c.), to cut down (woods) [illegible] to break off, to make to [illegible] *Min. aa)* to cut down (das Gebirge [illegible] ground, &c.), (*Tech.*) to [illegible] *bb)* to prop with timberwork; [illegible] Schacht —, to repair a shaft [illegible] *f) Chem.* to separate (water from [illegible] acids); *g) Metall.* to refine [illegible] cupellation (with lead, &c.); *h)* [illegible] remove (rust, &c.); *i) Paper-m.* [illegible] cut off the edges with a [illegible] District &c. —, to graze cattle [illegible] pasturage: *k)* ein Revier &c. —, [illegible] *or* drive all the game out of a [illegible] ing-district (in the direction of [illegible] 3) to overdrive, jade (a horse, [illegible] ben, *p. a.* overdriven, [illegible] worn-out.

II. *intr.* (*aux.* sein) 1) *a)* to [illegible] floated down; *b) aa)* to drift [illegible] off, away (*opp.* Antreiben) [illegible] deflect, to drive, to be driven [illegible] course, *cf.* I. 1, *a*, *bb*, *or* to [illegible] make leeway; stark —, to [illegible] 2) to drive cattle downwards.

Ab'treiber, (*str.*) *m. T.* [illegible]

Ab'treib(e)..., *in comp.* [illegible] *n. see* Abtreibeherd; —[illegible] hütte); —mittel, *m.* [illegible] *n.* almond furnace, [illegible] used in refining metals [illegible] furnace (Treibofen); —[illegible] or vessel in the nature of a cupel, for refining metals.

Ab'treiblich, *adj.* (*like* Abtreibbar, *l. u. except in combination with a negative, cf.* Unabtreiblich) capable of being driven off, (not) to be driven off *or* back, forced away, repelled, &c. *cf.* Abtreiben; to be warded off.

Ab'treibung, (*w.*) *f.* 1) the (act of) driving down, off, &c., repulsion; repulse; niemals griff Alfred an, alle seine Kriege waren A-en der ungerechten Angriffe (*Haller*), never did Alfred attack, all his wars were repulsions of unjust attacks; 2) the refining (of metals), cupellation, &c.; 3) *fig.* repulsion, refutation (eines Einwurfs *rc.*, of an argument, &c.).

Ab'trennbar, *adj.* separable, capable of being separated, disjoined, dismembered, &c. *cf. the next word.*

Ab'trennen, (*w.*) *v.* I. *tr.* 1) *Tail. & Sew.* to rip off (the sleeve of a shirt), to separate *or* remove by ripping off; to unstitch, unseam, unrip; 2) to dissever, separate, disjoin, dismember (von, from); II. *refl.* to separate one's self (*or* itself), to dispart, withdraw (von, from), *cf.* Trennen, *refl.*; Wesley trennte sich von der Kirche ab, Wesley seceded from the church.

Ab'trennlich, *adj.* separable, *see* Abtrennbar.

Ab'trennung, (*w.*) *f.* 1) the (act of) ripping off, &c. *cf.* Abtrennen; 2) disseverance, separation, dismemberment; 3) dismembered piece, detached portion, fragment.

Ab'treppen, (*w.*) *v. tr.* to form (a wall, &c.) into stair-like steps, to build in the form of stairs.

Ab'tretbar, *adj.* capable of being ceded, yielded, made over, &c., transferrible, transferable: eine Wohnung in a-em Stande, a lodging in a state to be made over (to a successor).

Ab'treten, (*w.*) *v.* I. *intr.* (*aux.* sein) 1) to alight, stop, take up one's quarters (in einem Wirthshause, bei Einem *rc.*, at an inn, at a person's house, &c.), *see* Absteigen; in der Pfarre — (*Rabner*), to stop, to take up one's quarters at the parsonage; 2) *a)* to go off *or* away, to recede, retire, withdraw, *particul. in a military sense* (*opp.* Antreten); von der Bühne —, to go off the stage; Faust tritt ab (*as a stage-direction*), *exit* Faust, *see* Abgehen, I. 1, *b*; von der Bühne des Lebens —, *fig.* to pass from the stage of life, to pass away; laßt die beiden einstweilen zusammen —, let the two pair off together for the present: der a-de Bürgermeister, the retiring mayor; *b) fig.* to recede (from a thing), *i. e. aa)* to quit, abandon, *or* leave it: to recede from...., to renounce, depart, resign a thing: *particul. bb)* von einem Amte — (*obsolescent*), to resign an office; *cc)* Einem eines Dinges —, † (*for* zu Gunsten Eines von einem Dinge —) to cede a thing to one.

II. *tr.* 1) *a)* to break off *or* down, to separate by treading, trampling; to tread off *or* down, to trample under foot; *b)* to wear off *or* out by treading, to wear out; die durch Kirchgänger abgetretenen Grabsteine, the tombstones worn (out) by church-goers; ein abgetretenes (abgedroschenes) Gleichniß, a worn-out, hackneyed, trite simile; *c)* to remove (dirt, &c.) from (shoes, &c.) by treading (*i. e.* by wiping them on a mat, &c.): sich (*Dat.*) den Schmutz von den Stiefeln, Füßen *rc.* —, *mostly* sich (*Dat.*) die Stiefeln, Füße *rc.* —, *or refl.* sich — (*cf.* Abstreichen, II. 1, *c*), to scrape, rub, *or* wipe [illegible] off) one's boots (on a doormat); *d)* to mark *or* form by treading; to tread out *or* to beat (a path); *e)* to mark off, separate (paths, parterres, &c. in a garden, [illegible]) to tread sufficiently *or* duly: to work [illegible] together (potter's clay) by treading, [illegible]; 2) *Print.* (*formerly*) to take an impression of (a proofsheet) by a turn of the printing-press; 4) *fig.* (*cf.* I. 2, *b*) to cede, yield (up), to surrender, resign, render up (rights, claims, &c., Einem *or* an Einen, to one); *Law & Comm.* to abandon: to make *or* give over, transfer; seinen Antheil —, to cede, resign or to transfer one's share; einen noch nicht fälligen Wechsel —, to discount a bill; einen Pachtvertrag —, to assign a lease.

Ab'treter, (*str.*) *m.* 1) one who retires, resigns, &c. *cf.* Abtreten; ceder, surrenderor, transferrer, &c.; 2) (Fußabtreter) *coll.* foot-rug, door-mat (Abstreicher).

Ab'tretung, (*w.*) *f.* 1) the (act of) treading off, &c. *cf.* Abtreten; 2) cession (Cession), relinquishment, resignation; der, an den die — geschieht, cessionary (Cessionar), assignee; *Comm., &c.* abandonment; die — der Güter des Fallitén, the surrender (transfer, cession) of the estate (property) of the bankrupt: (A-s-schrift) conveyance, *cf. the next word*; A-s-urkunde, *f.*, A-s-schrift, *f.* deed of cession, deed of conveyance.

Ab'treugen, (*w.*) *v. tr. & intr. provinc.* (*M. G.*) *for* Abtrocknen.

Ab'trieb, (*str.*) *m.* 1) the (act of) driving down, off, &c. *cf.* Abtreiben & Abtreibung; the driving (cattle) down (from the alps), *opp.* Auftrieb; 2) *a)* the (act of) rooting out (a forest); the cutting down *or* felling (of trees); *b)* a district (in a forest) the trees of which have been felled; 3) *Law*, the prior right of purchase (Näherrecht), the refusal, pre-emption-right (Vorkaufsrecht); A-s-hieb, *m.*, A-s-schlag, *m. see above*: 2, *a*.

Ab'triefen, (*str. & w.*) *v. intr.* (*aux.* sein) to drop, drip, trickle down.

Ab'trift, (*w.*) *f.* 1) *Mar.* leeway, drift, deflection: stern-board; 2) *Law*, common of pasture, right of pasturage. [treiben.

Ab'triften, (*w.*) *v. intr.* to drift off, *see* Ab-

Ab'trillern, (*w.*) *v.* I. *tr.* to sing through (a tune) with a trill *or* shake: II. *intr.* (*aux.* sein) to go off, to run away, &c. trilling.

Ab'trinken, (*str.*) *v.* I. *tr.* 1) to drink off, sip off, to drink from the surface; etwas von dem (*& vulg.* den) Becher —, to sip from the cup; 2) *a)* to finish the drinking of (any fluid); *b) fig.* (*Jean Paul, &c.*) to reduce *or* diminish (a debt) by drinking on the debtor's account, *cf.* Abzehren, 1; 3) to beat (one) in drinking, to outdrink (Niedertrinken); 4) to consume by drinking: *a)* Einem sein Geld —, to drink one out of his money; *b)* einem (Bier-)Wirthe *rc.* sein Bier *rc.* —, to drink an alehouse keeper's beer; II. *refl.* to fatigue or exhaust one's self by drinking.

Ab'trippeln, (*w.*) *v.* I. *intr.* (*aux.* sein) to trip off, to run off, *or* to go away with short, quick, light steps; II. *tr.* to wear off *or* out by tripping *or* stepping; III. *refl.* to fatigue *or* exhaust one's self by tripping about, to bustle about.

Ab'tritt, (*str.*) *m.* (*from* Abtreten, *q. v.*; *this word is generally avoided on account of the meaning explained under* 2, *b.*): 1) the (act of) alighting, stopping, taking up one's quarters, &c. (*cf.* Abtreten); 2) *a)* the (act of) going off *or* away, receding: departure, withdrawal, exit, as of an actor from the stage (Abgang); *b)* departure (from the stage of life), decease (Hintritt, Abgang); den *or* seinen — nehmen, to take one's departure, to take leave, to retire, withdraw; um seinen — bitten, to ask for leave of absence; einen — nehmen, withdraw, *particul. in order to obey a call of nature*; *hence c) the place of withdrawal itself*: privy, water-closet: necessary-house, necessary; *d) aa)* place of retirement (in mines), stepping-place, step (Absatz, 6, *d*, *bb*); recess; *bb) fig.* † contrast, difference: 3) retirement (from office, &c.), *opp.* Antritt; 4) *a)* † deviation, digression; *b)* departure (from the right way, &c.); secession, a falling off *or* away; apostasy; 5) *a)* recession, the (act of) receding *or* withdrawing (from a claim, &c.); *b)* cession, &c. *see* Abtretung, 2; 6) *Sport.* blades of grass, corn, &c. trodden down (das Abgetretene) by a stag or deer in passing.

Ab'tritts..., *in comp.* —geld, *n.* money paid in compensation, &c. (*see* Abstandsgeld); —grube, *f.* sink-hole, sink; —predigt, *f.* valedictory sermon (*see* Abschiedspredigt); —räumer, *m.* one who empties privies, night-man; —röhre, *f.* *Fort.*, &c. shaft of a privy.

Ab'trockengefäß, (*str.*) *n.* *Fott.*, &c. angger for plates, dishes, &c.

Ab'trocknen, (*w.*) *v.* I. *intr.* (*aux.* sein) 1) to dry off *or* up (Wegtrocknen), to be consumed (of moisture): *gener. mostly* to grow dry, to dry (of wet things); 2) to wither and fall off (as leaves), to fall off from drought; II. *tr.* 1) *a)* to dry off *or* up; to wipe off; *Surg.* to absterge; sich (*Dat.*) die Thränen —, to dry up one's tears; *b) mostly* to dry, to air, &c.; die Stirne (*for* den Schweiß von der Stirne) —, to wipe (the moisture off) the forehead; sich (*Dat.*) die Hände —, to dry one's hands; der Wind trocknet die Straße schnell ab, the wind dries the road fast; *sometimes used as an intr.* (*aux.* haben) *by leaving out the object*: es hat schnell (*i. e.* den Boden) abgetrocknet (*or* aufgetrocknet), it has dried fast; 2) to drain (a swamp), *see* Austrocknen.

Ab'trocknung, (*w.*) *f.* the (act of) drying off *or* up, &c.

Ab'troddeln, (*w.*) *v. intr.* (*aux.* sein) 1) to come off; 2) *see* Abtrotteln.

Ab'trollen, (*w.*) *v. intr.* (*aux.* sein) *& refl.* (*rare*) 1) to walk off with short and negligent, *sometimes* with quick steps, to trot off; 2) *coll.* to walk off with a rebuff.

Ab'trommeln, (*w.*) *v. tr.* 1) *a)* to perform on the drum, to drum off (a march); *b)* (auf dem Pianoforte) *coll.* to play (a tune, &c.) on the piano with a quick motion and heavy touch; sie trommelt ihre Tonleitern des Abends gehörig ab, she duly pounds away at her scales in the evening; *c) coll.* to consume (a certain time) by drumming; die kurze halbe Stunde der Übung wurde greulich abgetrommelt, the short half hour of practising was horribly strummed through; 2) to announce *or* publish with beat of drum; 3) *Bee*, to dislodge (bees) by beating with a stick on the hive.

Ab'trummen, (*w.*) *v. tr.* *Forest.* to cut off with an axe short pieces or stumps from (the trunk of a tree).

Ab'trompeten, (*w.*) *v. tr.* 1) to perform on the trumpet; 2) to announce, publish *or* make known by sound of trumpet.

Ab'tropf..., *in comp.* (*see* Abtropfen) — —bank, *f.* *Paper-m.*, &c. drainer, dropping-board; —brett, *n.* *Paper-m.*, &c. dropping-board, drainer, (*Tech.*) leaning-board.

Ab'tröpfeln, (*w.*) *v.* I. *intr.* (*aux.* sein) to fall down or off in a quick succession of small drops, to drip or trickle off; II. *tr.* to let fall *or* throw down *or* off in small drops; *fig.* to grant or give in driblets.

Ab'tropfen, **Ab'tröpfen**, (*w.*) *v.* I. *intr.* (*aux.* sein) to drop down *or* off, to drip *or* trickle down; — lassen, *or* II. *tr.* to cause the moisture of (skins, &c.) to trickle off, to drain, to dry.

Ab'tropf..., *in comp.* —korb, *m.* *Salt-w.* dropping-basket, crib; —pfanne, *f.*, —trog, *m.* 1) *Paper-m.* dropping-board; 2) *Metall.* list-pot; —tafel, *f.* *Glass-w.* dropping-board.

Ab'trüseln, (*w.*) *v. tr.* (*Thümmel, &c.*) to twist off, *see* Abdrehen.

Ab'trösten, (*w.*) *v. tr.* to give (one) due or sufficient consolation, to comfort thoroughly, *sometimes iron.* to put off with consolatory speeches.

Ab'trotteln, *(w.) v. intr. (aux.* sein) to trot off with short, quick steps, to tottle off.

Ab'trotten, *(w.) v. intr. (aux.* sein) to trot down or off.

Ab'trotzen, *(w.) v. tr.* (Einem etwas) 1) † to hector or bully (one) out of (a thing, his money, &c.); 2) to obtain, force, wring, wrest, extort (a thing) from (one) by open defiance, by sullen perseverance, &c. *(cf.* Trotz); sie trotzten dem Kaiser ihre Freiheit ab, they wrested their liberty from the emperor by stubborn persistence: er trotzte sich *(Dat.)* den Entschluß ab, he wrung the resolve from himself by obstinate perseverance.

Ab'trügen, *(str.) v. tr.* (Einem etwas) to cheat (one) out of (a thing).

Ab'trümmern, *(w.) v.* I. *intr. (aux.* sein) to fall off *or* down in fragments *or* ruins, to fall *or* crumble off, away: II. *tr.* to strike off in pieces, to dash off *or* down in fragments.

Ab'trümmerung, *(w.) f.* a falling down of fragments: a dashing in pieces.

Ab'trumpfen, *(w.) v. tr.* 1) *Carp.* to cut off the end of (a beam) in order to join it to another beam by a cross-beam *or* traverse; 2) *a) Gam. aa)* to beat by a trump card, to trump, ruff; *bb)* Einem eine Karte —, to take an opponent's trick by a higher trump: *b) coll.* to rebuke (one) with a tart sarcastic reply or remark, to snub, fit (Abfertigen).

Ab'trumpfung, *(w.) f. coll.* a set-down, &c.

Ab'trünnig, *adj.* seceding from, *or* abandoning a cause, &c. to which one before adhered, deserting *or* departing from one's faith or religion, faithless; apostatical; schismatical; recreant: disloyal, rebellious; die *(i. e.* vom Glauben)-e Welt, the apostate world; — werden *(gener. followed by* von, from..., *less frequently by the simple Dat.)*, to depart, to desert (from), to fall off *or* away (from), to turn recreant (to); to revolt; von der Religion — werden, to forsake *or* abandon one's religion, faith, &c., to turn apostate; — von den Deinen *(Schiller)*, a deserter from your party; seinen Versprechungen — werden, *(l. u.)* to break one's promise; — machen, to cause to forsake, &c., to turn (from), to draw off, away, to pervert; vom Christenthum — machen, to turn from Christianity: der A-e, a deserter, forsaker; turncoat, apostate, (o-er Christ) renegade; recreant; ich würde als ein A-er betrachtet werden, I should be regarded as having left my party.

Ab'trünnigkeit, *(w.) f.* a falling off *or* away; defection, desertion; apostasy (= desertion *or* departure from one's faith or religion, in der religiösen Sprache: backsliding), disloyalty, revolt, insurrection.

Ab'truppen, *(w.) v.* I. *intr. (aux.* sein) to march off in troops, to troop off; II. *tr.* to disband, dismiss (soldiers) from duty.

Abts'..., *in comp.* —hut, *m.* abbot's cap, abbot's mitre; —würde, *f.* dignity of an abbot, abbotship, abbacy.

Ab'tummeln, *(w.) v.* I. *tr.* to knock up, to fatigue (a horse) by turning *or* tumbling about; II. *refl.* to fatigue one's self by turning *or* tumbling about.

Ab'tünchen, *(w.) v. tr.* to whitewash duly *or* thoroughly, to finish whitewashing (a wall).

Ab'tupfen, Ab'tüpfen, *(w.) v. tr.* to dry up (moisture, &c.) *and metom.* to dry (a moist body) by dabbing (with a dry sponge, &c.), to desiccate.

Ab'tuschen, *(w.) v. tr.* 1) *Paint.* to copy with indian ink; 2) *coll.* to beat (one) soundly, *see* Abprügeln.

Ab'tuten, *(w.) v. tr. & intr. coll.* to sound (the hours, &c.) on a big horn (Tute); to cease to blow, &c. *cf.* Abblasen.

Ab'urtheilen, Ab'urteln, *(w.) v.* I. *tr.* 1) (Einem etwas *[Acc.]*, *opp.* Zuurtheilen) to deprive *or* dispossess (one) of (a thing) by judicial sentence, &c. *see* Absprechen, 1; 2) *a)* (eine Sache, einen Proceß &c.) to decide finally, to settle *or* fix (a matter, a lawsuit, &c.) by judicial sentence: *b)* (Einen) to pass *or* pronounce final sentence upon (one), *often in an unfavourable sense*, to condemn (hastily) (Verurteilen); II. *intr.* to pronounce *or* give final *(and gener.* unfavourable) judgment (über eine Person oder Sache, on, upon [im ungünstigen Sinne: against] a person or thing), to pass final sentence (on, upon), to adjudicate (on, upon).

Ab'urtheilung, *(w.) f.* the (act of) passing final sentence (on...), &c.; adjudication, final decision, judgment, *or* sentence, *particul. in an unfavourable sense*, (hasty) condemnation.

* **Abusiv',** *adj. (Lat.)* improperly applied, &c. *see* Mißbräuchlich.

Ab'verdienen, *(w.) v. tr.* 1) (Einem etwas) to earn (something) from (one), to obtain *or* get (something) from (one) by rendering services; 2) to clear (a debt, an obligation, &c.) by working for one's creditor, benefactor, &c., to work off (a debt).

Ab'verlangen, *(w.) v. tr.* (Einem etwas) to ask (a thing) from (one): es war unrecht, ihm alle Papiere und Schlüssel abzuverlangen, it was wrong to ask him to give up all his papers and keys *(cf.* Abfordern).

Ab'vieren, *(w.) v. tr.* 1) to square off, to square duly, to form with right angles, to make sufficiently square; to square (a stone, a beam); das — *(v. s.)*, *Carp.* scantling; 2) *Mar.* *(cf.* Vieren) to veer, to ease away (off): — und anholen, to veer and haul. — **Ab'vierung,** *(w.) f.* the (act of) squaring duly, sufficiently, &c.

Ab'visiren, *(w.) v. tr. (see* Visiren) 1) to estimate, rate by ocular survey, to ascertain *or* determine (the height, &c. of an object) by sight (Abäugeln), to measure by the level: *Forest* to estimate the measure of (a tree, before it is felled); 2) to measure (the contents of a vessel, cask, &c.) with a gauge, to gauge.

Ab'votiren, *(w.) v.* I. *intr. (aux.* haben) to vote duly; II. *tr.* to vote against; to outvote (überstimmen; *cf.* Abstimmen).

Ab'wachen, *(w.) v. refl.* to tire *or* wear one's self out by watching.

† **Ab'wachsen,** *(str.) v. intr. (aux.* sein) to decrease.

Ab'wackeln, *(w.) v.* I. *tr.* 1) to separate by shaking, to shake off; 2) to cudgel *or* bang (one) soundly; II. *intr. (aux.* sein) to go off totteringly, to waddle off (Abwatscheln).

Ab'wäge, *(w.) f. (l. u.) Phys.* 1) the mutual difference between a depth and a height; 2) *(Adelung)* the distance between the resistance and the fulcrum or point of suspension in a lever.

Ab'wäge..., *in comp. (cf.* Abwägen) —cirkel, *m. Watch-m.* a pair of compasses used for careful measurement of wheels to be adjusted; —kasten, *m. Glass-m.* chest *or* box for weighing off *(i. e.* the ingredients used in manufacturing glass); —kunst, *f.* *(lit.* the art of weighing off, &c. *cf.* Abwägen) art of levelling (Nivellirkunst).

Ab'wägen, *(str.) v. tr.* 1) *(coll.* Abwiegen, *particul. in the literal sense) a) aa) lit.* to weigh duly, to determine the weight of (a certain quantity) by the balance, to weigh, to balance, to poise; *bb) fig.* to weigh (in the mind) carefully *or* exactly; to balance: die militärischen Hülfsmittel der Römer und Karthager waren sehr verschieden, jedoch in vieler Beziehung nicht ungleich abgewogen *(Mommsen)*, the military resources of the Romans and Carthaginians were very different, but in many respects not unevenly balanced; seine Worte (auf der Goldwage) —, to [illegible] carefully, to be [illegible] one's expressions[illegible] abzuwägen, es ist no [illegible] unter einander [illegible] des Königs Rechte und [illegible] zuwägen wissen *(Hume*[illegible] ourselves we may confess, [illegible] to strike a nice balance [illegible] rights and our own; *b)* to [illegible] &c.) as a merchant [illegible] *a) (in surveying, &c.)* to [illegible] ence of level between [illegible] on the surface of the earth, [illegible] a levelling-instrument; *b)* [illegible] *or* regulate (wheels, &c.) [illegible] passes, to compass: *a) fig.* [illegible] rately, to ascertain by [illegible] Grenzen waren noch nicht abgewogen [illegible] held), the limits had not yet [illegible] 3) *fig.* to compare by the [illegible] to balance in the mind, [illegible] thoughts (gegen etwas [illegible] etwas Anderem &c., against *or* [illegible] jects, &c.); er hatte die [illegible] reiflich gegen die [illegible] gewogen, he had maturely [illegible] vantages of rising higher [illegible] of the fall *(Dryden)*; [illegible] Wege Wahrheit gegen [illegible] Vortheil gegen leeres [illegible] truth with gold she weighs, [illegible] ding against empty praise [illegible] sich immer Eins gegen das [illegible] thus one thing is always [illegible] against the other; er hatte [illegible] Schwäche gegen einander abgewogen [illegible] he had carefully balanced [illegible] strength and his weakness; [illegible] und Sommer abgewogene [illegible] *mann)*, a temperature evenly [illegible] winter and summer.

Ab'wäger, *(str.) m. gener. fig.* [illegible] careful balancer, &c.

Ab'wägung (Ab'wiegung), *(*[illegible] of) weighing duly, exactly, [illegible] weise — seines Beistandes, by [illegible] out his assistance; die — der [illegible] *(Kant)*, the exact balancing of [illegible] of reason. — A.-kunst, *see* [illegible]

Ab'wägbrief, *see* [illegible]

Ab'wählen, *(w.) v. intr.* [illegible] sist from electing at a [illegible]

Ab'walken, *(w.) v. tr.* 1) [illegible] (Tuch, cloth) sufficiently, to [illegible] the last fulling; 2) *coll.* to [illegible] *cond.* to mill (one) soundly.

Ab'wallen, *(w.) v. intr.* [illegible] soar *or* roll down with [illegible] to fall down in ringlets.

Ab'wälken, *(w.) v. tr. see* [illegible]

Ab'walzen, *(w.) v.* I. *tr.* 1) [illegible] *or* off: 2) to smooth down [illegible] roller; den Rasen —, to [illegible] ciently, thoroughly, [illegible] rub off by a roller; II. *refl.* [illegible] self by waltzing; III. *intr.* [illegible] waltz down; 2) to go off [illegible]

Ab'wälzen, † **Ab'walzen,** [illegible] to roll down; *b)* to roll [illegible] *Watch-m.* to give a [illegible] to round off (with a [illegible] off, to cast *or* throw off, [illegible] sich —, to exonerate one's [illegible] to clear one's self of a [illegible] daß er des Angriffs [illegible] von Schweden [illegible] the odium of the [illegible] on to the King of [illegible] *as it were*, to [illegible] ought to bear, [illegible] wolltungen [illegible] or [illegible] tries to shirk *or* evade even the slightest trouble.

Ab'wamsen, Ab'wamschen, *(w.) v. tr. coll.* to beat *or* cudgel (one) soundly, to give (one) a thorough hiding, to dress (one's) hide.

Ab'wandelbar, *adj. Gramm.* capable of being altered by inflection.

Ab'wandeln, *(w.) v.* I. *tr.* 1) † to alter *or* change thoroughly: *a)* to atone for (errors), to expiate (Büßen); *b)* to punish, chastise (Büßen); 2) *Gramm.* to vary (a verb, a noun) in its terminations, to inflect (Flectiren); to conjugate (a verb), to decline (a noun); 3) *gener.* to vary, modify; sich —, *refl.* to be varied, modified, to undergo outward change: II. *intr.* (*aux.* sein) 1) to walk down (Hinab-, Herabwandeln); 2) to walk off (Fortwandeln).

Ab'wand(e)lung, *(w.) f.* 1) † *a)* atonement, expiation; *b)* legal punishment (Buße); 2) *Gramm.* inflection (Flexion): conjugation (of a verb — Conjugation), declension (of a noun — Declination).

Ab'wandern, *(w.) v.* I. *intr.* (*aux.* sein) to wander down, *more frequently* off *or* away, to depart (Fortwandern, Wegwandern); II. *refl.* to wear *or* tire one's self out by walking.

Ab'wanken, *(w.) v. intr.* 1) to waver downwards, *see* Abschwanken; 2) to stagger off; *fig.* to wander, deviate, stray (from the goal).

Ab'wärmen, *(w.) v. tr.* 1) to warm duly *or* sufficiently, to warm through (Durchwärmen), (*also T., particul. Metall.*) to heat *or* to dry gradually, to temper by a gradually increasing heat; 2) *Glass-w.* to suffer the heat of (a furnace, &c.) to decrease gradually, to anneal (Auswärmen).

Ab'wärm(e)ofen, *(str.) m. T. (Metall., &c.)* drying-kiln, drying-furnace.

Ab'warnen, *(w.) v. tr. (l. u.)* to warn impressively, to caution against a thing.

Ab'wart, *(str.) m. provinc. (Switz.)* assistant of a physician, &c., amanuensis (Famulus).

Ab'warten, *(w.) v. tr.* 1) *a)* to wait to the end of (a thing), to await the termination of ...; wir wollen das Gewitter —, let us wait till the storm is over *(Hilp.)*; er wollte den Gottesdienst nicht —, he would not wait till the service should be over; *b)* to expect, to stay for, wait for, to attend the coming of (a person *or* thing); sie wollen es nicht —, they will not wait for the end; *c)* to wait, await (a result, &c.), to (a)bide (one's time): dies wird abzuwarten sein, this remains to be seen; warten wir's ab, let us await the result; ich kann's —, I can bide (abide) my time: du kannst doch nichts —, you can't bide your time, you will always be in a hurry; (*often used intr. or rather without an expressed object:*) wartet ihr ab, ich handle! *(Schiller)* do you bide and wait, I shall act; die a-de Methode, the expectant method (*in Med.*); er beschloß sich a-d zu verhalten, eine a-de Stellung einzunehmen, he resolved to abide the issue, to pursue a neutral course (a course which would enable him to act according to circumstances), *cf.* Zuwarten; *d)* to watch (an opportunity, &c.), *cf.* Abpassen; 2) († & *provinc.*, *with the Gen. & Dat. of the thing attended to:* eines Dinges, einem Dinge —) *a)* to attend to (a business, &c.), to care for; *b)* to take care of, to attend (the sick, &c., *only applied to a nurse, &c., not to a physician*), to nurse, wait upon: sie [illegible] sich [illegible] erkältet und wollte sich —, she had caught a bad cold and wanted to nurse [illegible]; der Patient hielt sich ruhig und wartete sich ab, the patient kept quiet and took care of himself; er war in die Nothwendigkeit versetzt, [illegible] selbst abzuwarten, he was reduced to the necessity of grooming his horse himself.

[illegible], I. *adj.* distant, remote; II. A-heit, *(w.) f.* distance, absence (Abwesenheit).

Ab'wärts, *adv.* 1) down, downward, downwards (*opp.* Aufwärts); (den) Strom —, down (the) stream; geh den Hügel — *(Platen)*, go down the hill; *often in comp.:* berg—, hügel—, fluß—, strom—, rhein— &c., down the mountain, down (the) hill, down the river, down (the) stream, down the Rhine, &c.; der Weg, der — (d. h. zum Verderben) führt, the way that leads downward (*i. e.* to perdition), the downward road; 2) off, aside, *Mar.* aloof, offward; wie er — treibet *(Chamisso)*, as he drives aside; — stehen, sitzen &c., to stand, sit, &c. aloof; das Mädchen lächelte — *(Novalis)*, the girl turned away smiling; — fahren, to go down (with the) stream, to descend a river, &c.; ihm schwärmen — immer die Gedanken | nach seines Vaters Hallen *(Göthe)*, his thoughts are ever roaming off or away to his father's halls; *with a Genitive (instead of the Acc.) following (cf.* Abwärts, 1, & Seitwärts, Vorwärts &c.): — des Einganges *(Humboldt)*, aside from the entrance; — der Brust *(Streckfuss)*, downward from the breast.

Ab'wartung, *(w.) f.* 1) the (act of) waiting for, awaiting, &c. *cf.* Abwarten; 2) attendance (der Kranken *[Gen.]* &c., on the sick, &c.), nursing, &c.; the grooming (of a horse).

Ab'wasch ... *(from* Abwaschen*), in comp.* —becken, *n.* a basin for cleansing anything in by washing or ablution, wash-handbasin; —faß, *n.* wash-tub, washing-tub (Waschfaß); —wasser, *n.* water in which anything is cleansed by washing, dish-water (Aufwaschwasser).

Ab'waschen, *(str.) v.* I. *tr.* 1) *a)* to wash off, away, out, to remove (dirt, &c.) by washing: er suchte von diesem Vergehen den Flecken der Bestechung abzuwaschen, he attempted to wash this proceeding of the stain of bribery; *b) fig.* to wipe off (a stain, &c.) with one's tears, blood, &c.; to cleanse *or* purify by washing, to wash, to bathe, to lave; 2) *a)* (Abspülen) to wash off *or* away, to carry off, away *or* to detach (the banks of a river, &c.) by the action of water; *b)* (Verwaschen, Zerwaschen) to wear out *or* off (a shirt, &c.) by frequent washing; 3) to clear *or* to pay (eine Schuld, a debt) by washing: II. *refl.* 1) to wash one's self thoroughly, to cleanse one's self by washing; 2) to tire *or* wear one's self out by washing.

Ab'waschung, *(w.) f.* 1) the act of washing away, &c. *cf.* Abwaschen; 2) *a)* ablution, act of washing or bathing the body, as a religious rite, &c. (*also in Med. & Chem.*); *b) Med.* lotion; wash.

Ab'wasser, *(str., pl.* Ab'wässer*) n.* water flowing off after having been used, &c., superfluous *or* redundant water.

Ab'wässern, *(w.) v. tr.* 1) to draw off water from (marshy ground, &c.), to free from water, to drain (Entwässern); 2) *a)* (Auswässern, Wässern) to steep in water, to water (as herrings or other salted fish); *b) Chem.* to purify by the affusion of water; 3) *Carp.* to slope off, to cut slanting, to make sloping so as to turn *or* throw off the rain from (the sill of a door or window, &c.) (Abwettern).

Ab'wässerung, *(w.) f.* 1) the (act of) drawing off water, draining, &c.: drainage; 2) *a)* the (act of) watering, washing, &c.; *b) Chem.* ablution, purification by the affusion of water; 3) *Carp., &c.* sloping, slope to turn *or* throw off water, (am Gesimse) weathering.

Ab'watscheln, *(w.) v. intr.* (*aux.* sein) to waddle off.

Ab'weben, *(w.; orig. str., cf.* Weben*) v. tr.* 1) to wind off, to unwind (Abwickeln); 2) to finish weaving, to weave to the end.

Ab'wechsel, *(str.) m. (l. u.)* change, variation, *see* Abwechselung.

† **Ab'wechselig,** *adj.* changeable.

Ab'wechseln, *(w.) v.* I. *intr.* (*aux.* haben) 1) es wechseln auf und ab des Lebens Stunden *(Rook)*, life's hours alternate between elevations, *or* successes and abasement, *or* depressions (nur in der Alltagsrede erlaubt: between ups and downs); 2) *a)* to alternate, to happen, take place, to come, go, follow, &c. by turns *or* alternately: mit a-den Manualen, *Mus.* alternately from the great to the choir organ, &c. *(Hamel.)*; mit *or* in einer Beschäftigung —, to perform, do, &c. by turns, to alternate *or* vary certain objects, to make a change in, with &c.; mit einander &c. —, to alternate with each other, to relieve one another by turns: wir wollen im Vorlesen mit einander —, let us take the reading by turns, let us relieve each other in reading; der Koch wechselt mit den Speisen ab *(Hilp.)*, the cook varies his dishes: — lassen, to alternate: Gott läßt Gutes und Böses —, God alternates good and evil; man ließ (am Bord eines Schiffes) Sauerkraut mit Kohl —, they alternated sauerkraut with cabbage; *b) Med.* to intermit (as a fever); 3) (*sometimes used for* Wechseln) to vary, change; to be changeable, variable.

II. *tr.* 1) (Einem etwas) to change (a piece of money, &c.) from (one), to exchange; 2) *a)* † etwas mit etwas (*Dat.*, *or* gegen, um etwas *[Acc.]*) —, to exchange one thing for another, *see* Vertauschen; *b)* *unusual for* Wechseln: des Königs Leibwache wurde abgewechselt (*i. e.* exchanged for one more trust-worthy: *Schiller; cf.* Sanders); *c) provinc. (S. G.) for the commonly used* Ablösen, to relieve (a sentinel, &c.); 3) to cause *or* make to succeed by turns; to alternate; to relieve (by turns); 4) to vary, to modify (the tone of one's voice, &c.), to give a new form to ....

III. *refl.* † *for the intransitive.*

Ab'wechselnd, *adj.* 1) *a)* alternating, alternative, *Bot., &c.* alternate: *adv.* alternately, by (in) turns: — folgen, to follow in succession, alternate; *b)* reciprocal; *c)* periodic, *Med.* intermitting; 2) changeable, variable, various, fitful; mit (ab)wechselndem Erfolg, with varying *or* various success.

Ab'wechselung, Ab'wechslung, *(w.) f.* 1) † exchange, *see* Austausch; 2) alternation; alternativeness, reciprocal succession, vicissitude, variation (der Jahreszeiten &c., of the seasons, &c.), round; 3) *a)* diversification; *b)* diversity, variety, change: — ermöglichen, — geben, to diversify; — erhalten, to be diversified; angenehme —, agreeable change, relief: eine Ebene, welche dem Auge kaum einen Busch zur — bietet, a plain hardly presenting a bush to relieve the eye; zur —, by way of variety, for a change; *c)* changeableness, &c.; 4) the (act of) relieving (a guard, &c.), *see* Ablösung, 4, *a*; *b)* modification, *Mus.* modulation.

Ab'wedeln, *(w.) v. tr.* to drive off *or* away by fanning, to fan off, to flap off (flies, &c.).

Ab'weg, *(str.) m.* 1) a way departing from the direct or regular road, by-way, by-road, by-path, by-turning; 2) *fig.* devious path *or* track, wrong way, the going wrong *or* astray; auf A-e gerathen, to get off the right path, to fall into *or* to take bad courses.

Ab'wegig, *adj.* 1) having by-roads; 2) departing from the direct or regular road, devious.

Ab'wegs, *adv.* out of the way.

Ab'wegsam, *adj.* 1) out of the way, devious; remote, secluded; 2) leaving the beaten track, *see* Abwegig.

Ab'wehen, *(w.) v.* I. *intr.* (*aux.* haben) 1) to blow or wave down (from ...), *see* Herabwehen; 2) to blow from (a certain direction): der Wind weht vom Lande ab, the breeze comes from the land *(Hilp.)*; 3) to cease to blow: es hat abgeweht, the storm has blown over, the wind has subsided (*cf.* Abwittern); II. *tr.* 1) *a)* to blow down; *b)* to blow off *or* away; 2) to fan, brush away, off, *cf.* Abwedeln.

Ab'wehr, *(w.) f.* any thing that wards off, repels, turns aside, opposes attack *or* danger, &c., guard, safeguard, protection, fence, defence: *particul.* the (act of) warding off, &c. (Abwehrung), *with Gen. of the thing warded off, or with prepositions:* die — eines Stoßes, Schlages &c., the warding off, parrying, &c. of a thrust, blow, &c.; nach jungfräulicher — *(Voss)*, after virgin-(*or* maiden-)like resistance.

Ab'wehren, *(w.) v.* I. *tr.* to ward off, to ward, to stave off, fend off; to avert, keep off, keep back, to repel, to hinder: *differently construed:* (Einen *or* etwas; Einem *or* von Einem *or* von einer Sache) die Mutter wehrt (von) sich und dem schlafenden Kinde die Fliegen ab, the mother drives off the flies from herself and the sleeping child: unter dem Baum, der die Mittagssonne mir abwehrt *(Voss)*, under the tree which protects me from the noonday sun: (Einem *or* einer Sache *[Dat.]* —, *cf.* Wehren; *now limited to the elevated style:*) ist dem nicht abzuwehren, | der mit dem Säbel kommt? *(Opitz)*, is he not to be driven back who comes with the sword? sie sucht den Kindern abzuwehren, she seeks to restrain the children: II. *intr.* *(l. u.)* wer kann —, daß nicht das Gräßlichste geschieht? *(Auerbach)*, who, by any measure of precaution, can prevent the most dreadful thing from happening?

Ab'wehrer, *(str.) m.* one who wards off, parries; defender, guard (against), &c.: Schäferhunde als — der Raubthiere *(Voss)*, shepherd's dogs, as warders-off of animals of prey.

Ab'wehrung, *(w.) f.* the (act of) warding off, parrying, &c.: repulse: Abwehr(ungs)-mittel, *n.* a preventive (of disease, &c.).

A. **Ab'weichen,** *(w.) v.* I. *tr.* 1) to detach, separate, loosen by soaking *or* making soft; 2) to soften thoroughly *or* duly: die Häute —, *Curr.* to soak the skins sufficiently: II. *intr.* *(aux.* sein) to become soft (by being steeped into moisture) and fall off. — **Ab'weichen,** *v. s. (str.) n.* 1) the act of detaching, &c.; 2) *Med.* diarrhœa, looseness (of the bowels).

B. **Ab'weichen,** *(str.) v.* I. *intr.* *(aux.* sein) 1) *a)* to deviate, to turn aside, away, off *or* from ...: *b)* *T.* to depart (from a certain standard), to vary; *Math., &c.* to decline, diverge, deflect (as the [magnetic] needle from the meridian, &c.); (von der horizontalen Richtung der Magnetnadel) to dip, to incline downward; *a)* to warp (as a board, &c.); 2) *fig.* *a)* abandoned, to recede, von Einem —, to leave, forsake one: *b)* vary, differ (in opinion, &c.); in seiner Meinung — von ..., to dissent from ...: *c)* to deviate (von der Regel &c., from the rule, &c.), to decline, depart (from analogy, truth, &c.); to swerve; 3) to digress, to deviate, &c.; *see* Abschweifen, *intr.* 2, *a*; 4) to pass by, *scarcely ever used except in the pp.* Abgewichen, (of time) passed, past, elapsed: die Berichte des abgewichenen Decenniums, the reports of the last ten years (Verwichen, Vergangen *more usual*); II. *tr.* † to turn off, away *or* aside, *see* Abwenden.

Ab'weichend, *p. a.* 1) deviating, &c. *cf.* Abweichen; a-de Sonnenuhr (Declinationsuhr), *T.* declining dial, decliner; *fig.* 2) departing from the rule, &c., anomalous, irregular; 3) varying, different, discrepant: a-der Meinung sein, to dissent.

Ab'weichstein, *(str.) m.* curb-stone (Prellstein), *cf.* Abweisestein.

A. **Ab'weichung,** *(w.) f.* 1) the (act of) detaching, loosening, &c. by soaking, *cf.* Abweichen, *A.*; 2) a thorough soaking *or* softening by steeping into moisture, &c.

B. **Ab'weichung,** *(w.) f.* 1) *a)* deviation; die — eines Schiffes vom geraden Wege, *Mar.* the leeway (deflection) of a vessel; *b)* *Phys., Astr., &c.* deflection, divergence, declination (eines Sternes, der Magnetnadel &c., of a star, of the [magnetic] needle from the true meridian of a place, &c.), variation (of the compass *or* needle, &c.); *c)* *Astr. & Opt.* aberration, *see* Abirrung; 2) *a)* deviation (from a common rule, &c.), departure (from a doctrine, &c.); *b)* variation from analogy, anomaly, irregularity; *c)* difference, variety; 3) digression (Abschweifung).

Ab'weichungs ..., *in comp.* —**compaß**, *m.* declinator (Declinatorium), azimuth-compass; —**finder**, *m.* *see* —**messer**; —**karte**, *f.* *Phys. Geogr.* chart of declinations; —**kreis**, *m.* *Astr.* circle of declination; —**linien**, *f. pl.* *Phys. Geogr.* isogonic lines; —**messer**, *m.* declinator, declinatory; *in dialling*, instrument for taking the angles made by different planes; *Astr.* instrument for taking the declination of stars; —**nadel**, *f.* *Phys.* declining needle; —**tafel**, *f.* table of declinations; —**zeiger**, *m.* *see* —**messer**.

Ab'weiden, *(w.) v. tr.* 1) *a)* to graze on (a meadow, &c.), feed on (grass); Sprossen &c. —, to browse; *b)* *sometimes fig.* to consume entirely; 2) to turn cattle into (a meadow, &c.), to graze cattle over (a tract of pasturage) (Abweiden). [reel off.

Ab'weifen, *(w.) v. tr.* to wind off a reel; to

Ab'weinen, *(w.) v.* I. *tr.* 1) (Einem etwas, *scarcely used*) to obtain *or* force (a thing) from (one) by weeping; 2) to expiate by weeping *or* by tears; II. *refl.* to weep to excess, *coll.* to cry one's eyes out.

Ab'weis, *(str.) m.* (*from* Abweisen) refusal, rejection, &c. *l. u. for* Abweisung.

† **Ab'weise,** *abbr.* **Ab'weis,** *(w.) f.* (*from* Ab & Weise, *cf.* Abart, 2) unsuitable state of things; nonsense, insolence.

Ab'weisen, *(str.) v. tr.* 1) † to point out the wrong way to (one), to lead astray; 2) *lit. & fig.* *a)* to refuse admittance, &c. to, to reject, to put *or* turn (one) off *or* away, to send back, cast off: einen armen Mann von der Thüre —, to turn away a poor man from one's door; eine Bestellung —, to decline an order; einen Anspruch —, to reject *or* deny a claim; kurz —, to dismiss without ceremony, *coll.* to send (one) about his business, to cut short; ein abgewiesener Liebhaber, a rejected lover; abgewiesen werden, to be turned off, &c., to meet with a rebuff: mit seinen Ansprüchen abgewiesen werden, to have one's claims rejected (*Law* to be non-suited); ich lasse mich nicht —, I take no denial *or* refusal; ich verhielt mich a-d, I preserved a cold demeanour, I showed disinclination; diese Frage ist zu feierlich, als daß man sie von sich — könnte, this question is too solemn to be put aside; etwas vornehm, mit Kennermiene, als nicht der Rede werth &c. —, to reject disdainfully, *coll.* to pooh-pooh a thing; *b)* *Mil.* to drive off *or* back (the enemy, &c.); *c)* (von sich) to disavow (an intention, &c.), to disclaim (interference, responsibility, &c.); 3) *Comm.* to protest, dishonour (einen Wechsel, a bill); 4) *Law.* to non-suit, dismiss (a cause).

Ab'weiser, *(str.) m.* *lit. & fig.* a person who, or a thing which turns off, aside, &c.: a breakwater (Buhne); a curb-stone (Abweisestein, Abweisstein, Abweisestock, *m.*) &c. *cf.* Abweichstein.

Ab'weisung, *(w.) f.* 1) *a)* refusal, rejection, putting *or* turning off, &c. *cf.* Abweisen; repulse, rebuff; *b)* disavowal, disclaimer, &c.; 2) *Comm.* the dishonouring, non-acceptance (eines Wechsels, of a bill), protest; 3) *Law, &c.* dismission, non-suit; 4) *Mar.* *a)* — der Magnetnadel, *see* Abweichung, 1, *b*; *b)* — der

[illegible], the variation [illegible] (arising from the motion of the [illegible]

Ab'weißen, *(w.) v.* I. *tr.* [illegible] ly *or* gradually, to bleach [illegible] *intr.* to whiten, to lose the [illegible]

Ab'weite, *(w.) f.* [illegible]

Ab'welken, *(w.) v.* I. *intr.* [illegible] to wither, fade, and fall off [illegible] fade away; II. *tr.* to dry [illegible] open air.

Ab'welle, *(w.) f.* *T.* [illegible] (Anwelle, [illegible]).

Ab'wellen, *(w.) v. tr.* [illegible] sufficiently, to boil *or* [illegible]

Ab'wendbar, I. *adj.* that [illegible] prevented, preventable; II. [illegible] bility of being averted, [illegible] bility.

Ab'wenden, *(w. & str.) v.* I. [illegible] turn off, away, *or* aside, to [illegible] von einem Gegenstande —, [illegible] the eyes from an object [illegible] Ekel von ihm ab, [illegible] him; *b)* *Fenc., &c.* to ward off, [illegible] *a)* (etwas von Einem, [illegible] *cf.* Abwehren) to avert ([illegible] to divert, keep off, [illegible] freundlichen Worten [illegible] cate a quarrel by sweet words [illegible] — ! (Gott behüte! Gott [illegible] God forefend! (Einen von [illegible] Einen einer Sache *[Dat.]*) to [illegible] (from a purpose, &c.); to [illegible] turn away *or* aside, to [illegible] von Einem &c., to turn from, [illegible] abandon one, &c.

Ab'wender, *(str.) m.* one [illegible] &c., averter.

Ab'wendig, *adj.* turned off [illegible] clined, alienated (*usu.* from [illegible] *simple Dat.*); averse, [illegible] (Einen *or* etwas von, [illegible] (one, &c.) away, aside (from), [illegible] to avert, alienate, disincline, [illegible] duce; (Einem etwas) to deprive [illegible] thing), to take away, [illegible] Evangelium — machen, to turn [illegible] the Gospel; Einem die Kunden [illegible] entice away one's customers; [illegible] hass, das Herz eines Mannes [illegible] alten Freunde — zu machen, [illegible] deal to turn a man's heart from [illegible]

Ab'wendung, *(w.) f.* 1) [illegible] ing off, averting, &c. *cf.* [illegible] tion, avoidance; 2) *a)* [illegible] estrangement; *b)* state of being [illegible] *or* disinclined (to), [illegible] mind, contrariety of nature, [illegible] einer Sache, to a thing).

Ab'werben, *(str.) v. tr.* [illegible] (Einem etwas) to deprive [illegible] &c.) by (clandestine) [illegible] ben, Abwendig machen).

Ab'werfen, *(str.) v.* I. *tr.* 1) [illegible] *or* cast down ([illegible] break down, to demolish [illegible] *c)* to throw *or* cast off; [illegible] *or* take out ballast; [illegible] off, throw, dismount, [illegible] Pferd wirft den Reiter ab, [illegible] its rider; sein Pferd [illegible] warf ihn ab, his horse [illegible] and threw him; er [illegible] [illegible] worfen wurde, he held [illegible] away, and how the [illegible] his back; *d)* to cast *or* [illegible] (one's clothes, &c.) [illegible] he threw off his [illegible] cast off (das Joch [illegible] (the distinctions of [illegible] self from; 2) to [illegible]

tear off by the roots; 2) to deprive of the roots, to cut off the roots from (a tree, &c.).

Ab'würzen, *(w.) v. tr.* 1) to season duly or thoroughly; 2) *coll.* to belabour with hard words or blows, to snub off, *cf.* Abfertigen.

Ab'wüthen, *(w.) v.* I. *intr.* (*aux.* haben) to cease to rage; II. *refl.* to tire one's self with raging, to exhaust or spend one's fury.

Abyssi'nien, *(str.) n. Geogr.* Abyssinia.

Abyssi'nier, *(str.) m.,* **Abyssi'nierin,** *(w.) f.* Abyssinian, (male, female) inhabitant of Abyssinia; die A-innen, the Abyssinian women. – **Abyssi'nisch,** *adj.* Abyssinian.

Ab'zacken, *(w.) v. tr.* 1) *see* Abzwacken; 2) to break or cut off into jagged protuberance, to jag, notch, indent.

Ab'zackern, *(w.) v. tr. provinc.* (Einem Land &c.) to deprive (one, a neighbour) of (land) by ploughing (it up), to encroach on (one), to cheat or trick (one) out of....

Ab'zahlen, *(w.) v. tr.* 1) (Etwas) *a) lit.* to pay off or up, to pay, to discharge (debts, &c.); etwas von der Schuld or auf die Schuld –, to pay part of a debt, to pay an instalment; er kann augenblicklich auch nicht einmal einen Theil –, he is unable at the moment to pay even an instalment (part of his debt); zögernd –, to be dilatory in payment: Artigkeiten, an denen ich stets abzuzahlen haben und doch in eurer Schuld bleiben werde (*Tieck,* Shakesp. Cymb. 1, 5), (debtor to you for) courtesies, which I will be ever to pay, and yet pay still; *b) fig.* to pay for, to atone for (misdeeds, &c.): durch edle Thaten wird er die Vermessenheit –, he will expiate the presumption by noble deeds; 2) (Einen) *a)* to pay off (to make compensation and discharge: Miethstruppen, Bootsleute, hired troops, boatsmen, &c.), *syn.* Ablohnen; *b) fig. coll.* to pay (one) off, to punish or to reprimand (one) severely (*syn.* Auszahlen, *cf.* Abtragen, 2).

Ab'zählen, *(w.) v. tr.* 1) (*opp.* Zuzählen) to count or tell off, to detach, separate, deduct by numbering (*cf.* Abrechnen, Abziehen); 2) to count out, enumerate (Auszählen), to fix or determine a certain number or amount; to compute, to count, number, tell, or name exactly, one by one; *Print.* to put in or lay on a heap (the quantity of paper for the pressman to wet); die Garben im Felde –, to count (accurately) the number of sheaves; etwas an den Knöpfen –, to let the even or odd numbers of (coat-)buttons decide whether a thing is to be or not (a kind of popular oracle); *coll.-s.* an den Fingern –, to find out by an easy mode of computation; etwas an den Fingern – (herzählen) können, to have a thing at one's finger's ends; das kannst du dir an den Fingern –, you may easily know or imagine that, you can easily guess as much.

Ab'zahlung, *(w.) f.* the (act of) paying off, &c. *cf.* Abzahlen, payment, liquidation; ratenweise –, payment on account, instalment; gänzliche –, clearing off (an amount).

Ab'zählung, *(w.) f.* 1) the (act of) counting or telling off, &c.; deduction, &c.; 2) enumeration, exact counting, &c.; computation.

Ab'zahnen, *(w.) v.* I. *intr.* (*aux.* haben) 1) (*applied to young animals or children*) to finish the process of teething, to cease cutting teeth (Auszahnen, Verzahnen); 2) *a)* to shed the milk-teeth; *b)* to lose one's teeth, to become toothless; II. *tr. T.* to take off with a toothplane or a similar instrument: to indent, notch, or groove with a toothing-plane.

Ab'zahnung, *(w.) f.* 1) the finishing the teething-process, &c. *cf.* Abzahnen; 2) indentation, &c.

Ab'zanken, *(w.) v.* I. *tr.* 1) (Einem etwas) to obtain (something) from (one) by scolding or quarrelling; 2) (Einen) to scold or rate (one) soundly, to reprimand sharply, *see* Ausganken; II. *refl.* to tire one's self out, to fatigue one's self with scolding or quarrelling.

Ab'zapfen, *(w.) v. tr.* 1) to tap, draw, draw off (Flüssigkeiten, liquors, &c.); *mostw.* ein Faß –, to tap or to broach a cask; *Min.* (*sometimes intr.*) to open a passage for (the waters); 2) *Surg.* to tap (einen Wassersüchtigen, a dropsical person); 3) *fig.* to cheat (one) impudently, to bleed (one).

Ab'zapfer, *(str.) m.* 1) one who taps or draws liquor from a cask, tapster; 2) *coll.* a tapper, instrument for tapping, *particul. Surg.* instrument to draw off urine, catheter (Trokar).

Ab'zapfung, *(w.) f.* 1) the (act of) tapping, drawing off (liquors); 2) *Surg.* tapping, paracentesis.

Ab'zappeln, *(w.) v.* I. *intr.* to move off, to withdraw with a jerking or kicking motion, to tottle off; *coll.* to die, to kick the bucket (*cf.* Abfahren); II. *refl.* to tire or wear one's self out with jerking about, with violent kicking, &c.

Ab'zäsern, *(w.) v.* I. *tr.* to free from fibres, &c. (Abfasern); II. *refl.* & *intr.* to lose or part with fibres, to come off in fibres or filaments.

Ab'zaubern, *(w.) v. tr.* (Einem etwas) 1) to free (some one) of (a thing) by witchcraft or sorcery; 2) to obtain (a thing) from (one) by witchcraft, to deprive (one) of (a thing) by the power of charms (*opp.* Anzaubern).

Ab'zäumen, *(w.) v. tr.* (*sometimes intr.*) to take off the bridle from (a horse), to unbridle, unbit (*syn.* Abschirren), *opp.* Aufzäumen. – **Ab'zäumung,** *(w.) f.* the (act of) unbridling, &c.

Ab'zäunen, *(w.) v. tr.* 1) to fence off, to separate by a hedge; to fence in, to enclose; 2) (Einem ein Stück Land &c.) to deprive (one) of (a piece of land, &c.) by fencing it off, to encroach on (one's estate, &c.) by enclosing or hedging off a part.

Ab'zausen, *frequentative:* **Ab'zauseln,** *(w.) v. tr.* 1) to pull or tear off; 2) to pull or haul about, to worry, to tousle mercilessly.

Ab'zechen, *(w.) v. tr.* 1) to consume by drinking freely, by carousing; 2) *a)* to beat (one) in drinking hard (Niederzechen); *b)* (Einem etwas) to drink (one) out of (a thing), to deprive (one) of (a thing) by outdrinking him.

Ab'zehnten, *(w.) v.* I. *tr.* 1) to tithe, levy the tithes of (a field, &c.); 2) to pay off the tithes to (the parson, &c.); II. *intr.* to make over the tithes, to pay tithe.

Ab'zehren, *(w.) v.* I. *tr.* 1) to reduce (eine Schuld, a debt – owing by another) by living at the debtor's expense, to make one's self paid by eating or drinking for (a debt owing by the landlord, &c.); 2) to consume gradually, to waste away, to waste, spend, to weaken by degrees; to macerate, emaciate, wither; die welche durch langwierige Krankheit abgezehrt werden, those who are wasted away by lingering disease; meine Kleider hingen lose an mir, denn ich war sehr abgezehrt, my clothes hung loose on me, for I was much wasted; tödtliche Krankheit hatte sie zu Schatten abgezehrt, mortal disease had wasted them (their frames) to shadows: eine a-de Krankheit, a wasting, wearing, lingering, consumptive disease; abgezehrte Glieder, wasted limbs; ein abgezehrtes Gesicht, a wasted, worn face.

II. *refl.* & *intr.* (*aux.* sein) to consume (*i. e.* to be consumed), to waste away; to wear off, to fall off; to pine away; to run to waste.

Ab'zehrung, *(w.) f.* 1) the (act of) consuming, wasting, &c.; consumption, waste; 2) *Med.* a wasting (of flesh), gradual decay (of the body), (pulmonic) consumption (*more usual:* Auszehrung).

Ab'zeichen, *(str.) n.* 1) a (light-coloured) spot contrasting with the ground-colour, star, speck, mole (Mahl); 2) *a)* mark or sign of distinction; [illegible] die schönste [illegible] habit of the Quakers [illegible] badge of their religion.

Ab'zeichnen, *(w.) v.* I. [illegible] to mark out, to mark [illegible] of combat; 2) [illegible] design, delineate [illegible] of, to copy [illegible] or draw the plan of [illegible] &c. outlines, to be [illegible] lined, outlined [illegible] the sky.

Ab'zeichner, *(str.) m.* [illegible] an original, designer [illegible]

Ab'zeichnung, *(w.) f.* [illegible] outlines against the sky [illegible] mark, *see* Abzeichen [illegible] from an original [illegible] *cf.* Abzeichnen; [illegible] lineation, sketch [illegible]

Ab'zerren, *(w.) v. tr.* [illegible] off, away (von, from [illegible]) the booty from him.

Ab'zetteln, *(w.) v. tr.* [illegible] ando (ein Gewebe, a woof [illegible])

Ab'zieh..., *in comp.* [illegible] ling apparatus [illegible] graving, &c. to be [illegible] &c.; –blase, *f.* [illegible] (of glass); –bogen, *m.* [illegible] proof-paper; –bürste, *f.* [illegible] –eisen, *n.* 1) [illegible]

Ab'ziehen, *(str.) v.* I. *tr.* [illegible] down [illegible] to take off; to take away [illegible] –, to pull or to take off [illegible] hat off; die Handschuhe [illegible] gloves; die Kleider [illegible] to pull off one's clothes [illegible] from a man's back [illegible] –, to take a ring off [illegible] Maske (Larve) – [illegible] one's mask [illegible] Larven; *b)* † to [illegible] (*Acc.*) –, *refl.* [illegible] (one's self); 3) *a)* [illegible] Thiere die Haut –, to [illegible] a beast [illegible] of his skin [illegible] *b)* to take off (the [illegible]) the strings of beans [illegible] (beans); 4) *a)* [illegible] ment) from the [illegible] skim or take off [illegible] to remove [illegible] –, to draw the [illegible] amount of metal [illegible] to abduce; 5) *a)* [illegible] work off (an [illegible]) Kreislen [illegible] a proof; *b)* to [illegible] porcelain, &c. [illegible] pare (ein [illegible]) skin); *b)* [illegible] shave; to give [illegible] or wood); *d)* [illegible] *d) Letter-found.* [illegible] by rubbing [illegible] stone, to make [illegible]

&c. see –chane; 2) Steam-eng. eduction-pipe, wastewater-pipe: –rösche, f. Min. drain, canal (Rösche); –schach, m. Chess a certain mode of checking the king by withdrawing one chessman before another; –schlacken, f. pl. metallic scoria: –schlackenblei, see –blei; –schleuse, f. drain-sluice, drain-trunk: Roads, &c. culvert, (arched) passage or drain for water beneath a road, canal, or railway: cf. Schleuse; –schmaus, m. parting-treat, see Abschiedsschmaus (opp. Einzugsschmaus); –schnalle, f. Horol. detent (that lifts up the minute wheel), stop, warning: –stein, m. 1) whetstone, see Abziehstein; 2) sink-stone: –tag, m. day of departure, (in den V. St. zur Feier des Abzugs der Engländer:) evacuation-day: –teich, m. see –grube; –walze, see Abzugwalze; –weg, m. channel of exportation, see Absatzweg; –wehr, n. T. waste-weir: –zahl, f. Arith. minuend; subtrahend (Abziehzahl); –zeit, f. time for leaving a residence hitherto inhabited, quarter day; time for leaving service, &c.: in general, time of departure: –ziegel, m. T. draining-tile; –zoll, m. emigration-tax, see –geld.

Ab'zugwalze, (w.) f. Cotton-sp. delivering-roller, delivering-ball.

Ab'zupfen, (w.) v. tr. to pluck off, to pull off.

Ab'zwacken, (w.) v. tr. 1) to pinch off, to nip off; to snap away; (Einem etwas) to stint (one) of (a thing): was man verspricht, das sollst du rein genießen, | dir wird daran nichts abgezwackt (Göthe, Faust), the promised good, therein expressed, shall to a tittle be by you possessed (Swanwick); 2) (Einem etwas) to squeeze (something) out of (one), to extort (something from).

A. Ab'zwecken, (w.) v. tr. to unpeg.

B. Ab'zwecken, (w.) v. intr. to aim at, to tend to (synonymous with, & construed like Abzielen). [(Abzielung).

Ab'zweckung, (w.) f. intention; tendency

Ab'zweigen, (w.) v. I. tr. to deprive of the branches, to lop; II. tr., refl. (sich) & intr. (aux. haben) to branch off.

Ab'zweigung, (w.) f. 1) the (act of) branching off, leaving the mother-stem; 2) branching, branch, offshoot; die verschiedenen A-en der christlichen Kirche, the various denominations of the Christian church.

Ab'zwicken, (w.) v. tr. to nip off, to pinch off (den Draht &c., the wire, &c.).

Ab'zwingen, (str.) v. tr. 1) (Einem etwas) to extort, to wring, wrest, to force (something) out from (one), cf. Abnöthigen; er hat ihnen immer und immer wieder das Bekenntniß abgezwungen, daß ..., he has again and again wrung from them the confession that ...; 2) (Einen von etwas) to force (one) away (from ....) [&c.).

Ab'zwingung, (w.) f. extortion.

Ab'zwirnen, (w.) v. tr. to wind off (thread,

Ab'zwitschern, (w.) v. tr. to sing in a chirping manner, to chirp.

A. C., Lat. abbr. for 1) Anno Christi, im Jahre ... nach Christi Geburt, in the year of our Lord; 2) ante Christum, vor Christo, before Christ; 3) anni currentis, des laufenden Jahres, of the present year; anno currente, im laufenden Jahre, in the present year; 4) Augustana Confessio, Augsburgische Confession.

* Aca'cie [pr. Akâ'tsie], (w.) f. Bot. acacia: echte –, gum-tree; amerikanische –, locust; tamarindartige –, wild tamarind; farnesische –, sweet-scented acacia, sponge-tree; unechte or wilde –, Virginian acacia, false acacia or locust tree; A-nsaft, m. Pharm. juice of acacia.

* Academie', see Akademie.

* Ac'ajou, (str.) m. cashew; –baum, m. cashew-nut tree (Acajoubaum, Elephantenlausbaum, Anacardium occidentale L.); –holz, n. white mahogany; –nuß, f. cashew-nut (Elephantenlaus).

* Acale'phe, see Akalephe.

* Acan'thus, (indecl.) m. 1) Bot. acanthus, brank ursine, bear's foot, bear's claw, bear's breech (Bärenklau); 2) Archit. acanthus, an ornament used for the enrichment of the Corinthian capital, resembling the leaves of acanthus.

* Acatalec'tisch, adj. Prosod. acatalectic, (of verses) having the complete number of syllables, without defect or excess (opp. Catalectisch).

* Accapari'ren, (w.) v. tr. (Fr.) to forestall, to engross.

* Accedi'ren [pr. Aktse–], (w.) v. intr. (aux. sein) to accede, see Beitreten.

* Accent' [pr. Aktsänt'], (str.) m. Gramm., &c. accent, tone: der scharfe – (Acutus), acute accent: der tiefe – (Gravis), grave accent; der schlechte –, bad accent, (Irish) brogue; das Accentsystem der Masoreten, the accentual system of the Masorites; auf einen Punct – (or Gewicht) legen, to lay stress on a point.

* Accent'los, adj. unaccented; soundless, dull.

* Accentuation' [aktsäntuâtsjôn'], (w.) f. accentuation. – Accentui'ren, (w.) v. tr. to accent, accentuate; der accentuirte Tacttheil (Niederschlag), Mus. the accented part of a bar. – Accentui'rung, (w.) f. accentuation.

* Accent'voll, adj. full of (harmonious) sound, rich.

* Accept' [Aktsäpt'], (w.) n. particul. Comm. acceptance (Annahme); mit – versehen, to provide with acceptance: mit Ihrem – versehen, provided with your acceptance; wir erwarten Ihre A-e, we are waiting your acceptance: zum – gesandt, being out for acceptance; (Nob. & Gr.:) Kauf gegen A-e, purchase for acceptance; er ist allzurasch mit seinem – bei der Hand, he is too ready with his acceptance; seine A-e nicht einlösen können, not to be able to take up one's acceptance: seine A-e zurückgehen lassen, to return his drafts, to let them go back; für Einlösung seiner A-e Sorge tragen, to take care to meet one's acceptance: theilweises –, partial acceptance.

* Accepta'bel, adj. acceptable (Annehmbar).

* Acceptant', (w.) m. particul. Comm. acceptor, cf. Annehmer.

* Acceptation', (w.) f. particul. Comm. acceptation, acceptance, cf. Annahme; Nob. & Gr.: zur – vorlegen (präsentiren), to present for acceptance; – per onore (Interventionsannahme), intervention, acceptance upon honour; stillschweigende –, tacit acceptance; Protest Mangels –, protest in default of acceptance or for non-acceptance: A-sblanco, n. blank credit; A-sbuch, n. bills payable or bills receivable-book (Wechselannahme- or Trattenbuch); A-scredit, m. credit in blank, blank-credit: A-sprovision, f. commission (or brokerage) for acceptance: A-sgeschäfte, n. pl. (uncovered) acceptances; A-sfrist, f. time or term of acceptation.

Accept'geschäft, (str.) n. Comm. acceptance-business (gener. in the pl.); A-e machen, to effect acceptances.

* Acceptir'en, (w.) v. tr. to accept (also fig.), see Annehmen; particul. Comm. to accept, to pay, to honour (eine Tratte, a draft); einen Wechsel –, to accept or to honour a bill: eine Tratte unverzüglich – lassen, to get a bill accepted without delay; acceptirt werden, to meet due honour, to be duly honoured; in blanco –, to accept in blank; nicht –, to refuse acceptance, to dishonour; acceptirte Wechsel, bills accepted.

* Accepti'rung, (w.) f. acceptance, see Acceptation & Annahme.

* Access' [pr. Aktsäss'], (str.) m. 1) access, admittance (Zutritt, Beitritt); 2) Med. accession, access, (beginning of a) paroxysm, fit (Anwandlung, Anfall). – Accessi'bel, adj. accessible (Zugänglich) [illegible] f. accessibility [illegible] (w.) f. accession [illegible] tritt). –Accessist', (w.) [illegible] (an expectant for [illegible] office. – Acces'sit, [illegible] best premium. –[illegible] (Hinzukommend, [illegible] accessory nerves. – [illegible] Accesso'rien, Accesso'ria) n. [illegible] age (Zubehör, Beiwerk, [illegible]

* Acciacatu'r [pr. [illegible]] ciacatura (Ital.), a kind of [illegible] note, one semitone below [illegible] prefixed, being, as it were, [illegible]

* Ac'cidens, (indecl. [illegible]) Acciden'tien, Accidentia) [illegible] pl. Acciden'zien), f. perquisite, [illegible] (Nebeneinkünfte); particul. [illegible]

* Accidenzar'beiten, n. pl. [illegible]

* Accidentell', adj. accident[illegible]

* Acciden..., in comp. –[illegible] cidental or casual work, [illegible] sites (Nebenverdienst) [illegible] druckerei arbeiten (in [illegible]) to be on the establishment; –[illegible] position upon the establishment [illegible] by the day.

* Acci'sbar, I. adj. excisable, subject to excise; II. [illegible] to pay excise-duty.

* Acci'se [Aktsî'se], (w.) f. [illegible] nehmen von ... or anlegen [illegible] to levy excise upon, to excise [illegible] auf den Tabak und das Salz [illegible] tobacco and salt were excised [illegible]

* Acci'se..., in comp. –[illegible] fice: –beamter, –[illegible] schreiber, m. exciseman, [illegible] officer; –einnehmer, m. [illegible] excise: –kammer, f. court of [illegible] –frei, adj. free from excise; [illegible] exemption or immunity from [illegible] n. law of excise; –[illegible] excise, see Acciser; –[illegible], f. excise bureau; –[illegible], m. [illegible] the law of excise, [illegible] m. bond; unter –[illegible] –zettel, m. excise-bill, permit [illegible]

* Acclamation', (w.) f. acclaiming, cheer; durch – wählen, [illegible] mation (a vote cast [illegible] fice, &c.).

* Acclami'ren, (w.) v. tr. [illegible]

* Acclimatisation', (w.) [illegible] rung, (w.) f. acclimation [illegible] mation), act of making or becoming [illegible] a climate.

* Acclimatisi'ren, (w.) v. tr. [illegible] acclimatise, to accustom, to [illegible] mate, to habituate (the [illegible]) not native, to inure (plants [illegible]) ferent from that which is [illegible]

* Accola'de, (w.) f. 1) [illegible] neck on the shoulder (conferred [illegible]) in conferring knighthood; 2) [illegible] (in Mus. connecting two [illegible]) pianoforte or harp music, [illegible]

* Accolli'ren, [illegible] to put (Setzen, [illegible])

* Accommodation', (w.) [illegible] modation (Anbequemung) [illegible] plication of one thing to [illegible]

* Accommodi'ren, (w.) [illegible] modate (Anbequemen) [illegible] to make up, to fit or [illegible] (injured) goods [illegible] accommodirte [illegible] (Nolen, I, n.) be [illegible] derstanding (sich [illegible])

* Accompagni'ren [illegible] Fr. accompagner) [illegible]

particul. as a mus. term; einem Singenden —, to play to a person singing, see Begleiten.

• Accompagnement' [pr. ăkŏmpănyĕmăng'; Fr.], (str., pl. A-s) n. particul. Mus. accompaniment (Begleitung).

• Accompagnist' [pr. ăkŏmpănyĭst'], (w.) m. (formed after the analogy of other words in —ist, differing from the Fr. accompagnateur) accompanist.

• Accord', (str.) m. 1) Mus. chord (two or more tones sounded together which harmonize); 2) (l. u.) concord, harmony (of sounds), accord; 3) Law, Comm., &c. a) settlement, agreement, composition; b) among Min., &c. tut-bargain, bargain by the lump; einen — (syn. Vergleich, Übereinkunft) machen, schließen, treffen, to make, conclude an agreement, to come to terms; gerichtlicher —, judicial agreement; außergerichtlicher —, extrajudicial agreement; eine Arbeit in — geben, to contract for a job; auf — unternehmen, in — nehmen, to undertake by contract, coll. to farm a job; in (im) —, auf —, by (the) job; —arbeit, f. (Stück-Arbeit) job-work, task-work, piece-work, jobbing; —summe, f. stipulated sum.

• Accordi'ren, (w.) v. I. intr. 1) Mus. to accord, to agree in pitch and tone; 2) Law, &c. to agree, to make or to come to an agreement, to compound (sich Vergleichen); mit den Gläubigern zu 50% (funfzig Procent) —, to compound with one's creditors at fifty per cent; II. tr. 1) to make to agree, to accord; 2) a) to come to an agreement upon (a certain transaction, &c.); coll. to farm (a job); ich accordirte die Lieferung zu fünf Thalern, aa) (ich machte mich verbindlich die Waare zu fünf Thalern zu liefern) I agreed to furnish the goods at five Thalers; bb) (ich bedang, daß mir die Waare zu fünf Thalern geliefert werde) I bargained (contracted) for the goods at five Thalers; b) to consent to, to grant (Bewilligen).

• Accouchement' [Fr., pr. ăkŏoshmăng'], (str., pl. A-s) n. 1) confinement, delivery, childbirth (Entbindung); 2) midwifery, obstetrics (Entbindungskunst, Geburtshülfe).

• Accoucheur' [Fr., pr. ăkŏoshör'], (str., Gen. A-s, pl. A-e, or A-s) m. accoucheur, man-midwife, obstetrician (Geburtshelfer). — Accoucheu'se [ăkŏoshö'ze], (w.) f. female accoucheur, accoucheuse, midwife (Hebamme). — Accouchi'ren [pr. ăkŏoshi'ren], (w.) v. tr. to deliver, to assist (a woman) at her confinement (Entbinden).

• Accoucheur' [ăkŏoshör']..., in comp. —anstalt, —haus, —instrument, —kunst, —stuhl, —zange &c., see Entbindungsanstalt, -haus &c.

• Accrediti'ren, (w.) v. tr. 1) to accredit (einen Gesandten, an envoy), see Beglaubigen; das Land, in welchem dieser Diplomat accreditirt ist, the country to which this diplomatist is accredited; 2) Comm. to open or lodge a credit in (any one's) favour (bei, with); wir haben Sie bei (den) Herren Gebrüdern B. dort für tausend Thaler (or mit tausend Thalern) accreditirt, we have opened (or lodged) a credit in your favour with Messrs. B. brothers, of that (your, &c.) place, to the amount of one thousand Thalers. [dit (Creditbrief).

• Accreditiv', (str.) n. Comm. letter of cre-

• Accrochi'ren [pr. ăkroshi'ren, from the Fr. accrocher, to hook on], (w.) v. intr. to meet with some impediment (sich an etwas stoßen); Comm. to be at a stand.

• Accroupi'ren, (w.) v. refl. [Fr. s'accroupir] to squat, to cower (down), particul. of horses, to cower. [häufung).

• Accumulation', (w.) f. accumulation (An-

• Accumuli'ren, (w.) v. tr. & intr. (anhäufen) to accumulate (Anhäufen).

• Accurat', adj. accurate, exact, precise, punctual (Genau, Sorgfältig).

• Accurateſſe, (w.) f. (Fr.) accuracy, exactness, nicety, precision (Genauigkeit, Sorgfalt).

• Accusation', (w.) f. accusation (Anklage).

• Accusativ', (str.) m. Gramm. accusative (case), objective (Zielfall).

• Acetat', [pr. ăssetat'], (str.) n. Chem. acetate (essigsaures Salz, Essigsäure). — Ace'tisch, adj. acetic (Essig enthaltend, essigsauer). — Acetome'ter, (str.) n. (m.) Chem. acetometer (an instrument or apparatus for measuring the strength of vinegar and other acids), acidimeter.

Acetyl', (str.) n. Chem. acetyle, hypothetic radical of acetic compounds.

A. Ch., abbr. for (Lat.) Anno Christi & ante Christum, see A. C., 1, 2.

Ach, interj. ah! oh! alas! heigh ho! — Gott! — Himmel! ah me! O dear! O heavens! — ja! yes indeed!

• Acha'ras-Holz, n. a hard kind of wood, from the West Indies, used for making printing-blocks (in cotton-printing).

• Achat' (Agat), (str.) m. Miner. agate; bunter —, mocha-stone; gehackter or Trümmer—, broken agate; isländischer —, obsidian; milchweißer —, chalcedony (Chalcedon); rothaderiger —, red-veined agate; rother —, cornelian; schwarzer —, siliceous schist (Kieselschiefer); violetter —, amethyst (Amethyst).

• Achat'..., in comp. —ähnlich, adj. resembling agate, like agate, agatine, agatized, agaty; —artig, adj. agaty, of the nature of agate; —breccie [brĕk'tshe], f. broken agate (Trümmer-Achat).

• Acha'ten, adj. agaty, agate.

• Achat'..., in comp. —feuerstein, m. agaty flint; —glas, —holz, n. agate-wood, agatized wood; —jaspis, m. Miner. agate jasper (Jaspachat, veraltet ist jaspachate); —kiesel, m. Miner. Egyptian stone or pebble; —muschel, f. Conch. agate-shell; —schnecke, f. achatina, agate snail; —stufe, —walze, f. Conch. agate-stamper, agate-shell. [change into agate.

• Achatisi'ren, (w.) v. tr. to agatize, to

Ach'el, (w.) f. 1) orig. any sharp point, f. i. the sting of bees, &c.; 2) (syn. Hachel, Granne, Ahne) a) awn, spike of corn; b) gener. in the pl. the broken particles of awns, chaff, &c.; 3) provinc. leech (Blut-Igel).

Ach'eln, (w.) v. intr. Jew. Germ. (from Hebrew achal', to eat) to eat, to consume.

Ach'en, sometimes Ächen, (w.) v. intr. (from Ach, interj.) to cry alas! to groan, to moan; achen und krächzen, † to groan and moan; to sigh and cry.

• Ach'eron, (str., Gen. A-(s)) m. Greek Mythol. Acheron (a river in the infernal regions). — Acheron'tisch, adj. relating to Acheron, Acherontian, infernal.

• Achillē'isch, adj. Achillean.

• Achil'lesferse, (w.) f. fig. the most vulnerable part of a person or thing (scheme, &c., so named from the heel of Achilles having been the only vulnerable part of his body), the weak side.

• Achil'lesflechse (w.) f., Achil'lessehne, (w.) f. Anat. Achilles-tendon.

• Achirit', (str.) m. Miner. achirite (green malachite, Kupfersmaragd).

A. Ch. n., abbr. for ante Christum natum (Lat.), before the birth of Christ, vor Christi Geburt (cf. A. C., 2).

• Achroma'tisch, adj. achromatic; a-es Fernrohr, achromatic telescope.

• Achro'nisch, adj. see Akronisch.

Achs' [pr. ăks]... (from Achse), in comp. —büchse, f. T. chair of wheel, bush (of railway-carriages), axle-box, grease-box, oil-box.

Ach'se [pr. ăk'—], Axe, (w.) f. 1) axis, axletree (of a carriage-wheel, &c.); auf der —, per — (i. e. zu Wagen) versenden, (Etwas) zur — fortschaffen, Comm. to send by land(-carriage), to transport by land-carriage; auf einer —, (i. e. ohne unterwegs umzuladen), by one conveyance; 2) Math. (also Bot., Miner., Anat., &c.) axis, Mech. arbor, shaft, spindle (Welle).

Ach'sel [pr. ăk'sel], (w.) f. 1) the angle, (particul. the inner side) formed by the connexion of the arm with the body, different from Schulter (shoulder), which is only the upper part of the joint; 2) upper part of the joint by which the arm is connected with the body, forepart of the shoulder, sometimes syn. with shoulder: Einem auf die — (less usual Einem die —) klopfen, to pat one's shoulder, to clap or slap upon the shoulder (familiarly); ich will das auf meine A-n nehmen, I'll take that on my shoulders, i. e. I'll bear the responsibility; etwas auf die leichte — nehmen, to take a thing lightly, to make light of a thing, to treat with (culpable) levity; er nimmt's auf die leichte —, coll. he takes it easy; auf beiden A-n tragen, to act two different parts in the same business, or at the same time, to serve two masters or (opposed) parties, to be (coll. Jack) of both sides, to trim, temporize, serve the time, to carry two faces under one hood; die A-n or mit den A-n zucken or ziehen, to shrug, to contract or to draw up the shoulders, to give a shrug (gesture of contempt, pity, perplexity, or resignation); Einen über die — (or Schulter) ansehen (in the ancient language without the article über —), to look askance at one, i. e. contemptuously, to look down upon one, to cut one; 3) † for Achse.

Ach'sel [pr. ăk'—]..., in comp. —ader, f. axillary vein; —arterie, f. Anat. axillary artery; —band, n. (shoulder-)strap; —bein, Anat. shoulder-blade; shoulder-bone; —blutader, f. see —ader; —drüse, f. Anat. axillary gland; —fleck, m. (—stück) shoulder-piece (of a shirt); —grube, f. arm-pit, arm-hole; —hemd, n. shirt (among the lower classes, also: shift) without sleeves; —höhle, f. Anat. axillary cavity, arm-pit, arm-hole; —klappe, f. Mil. shoulder-strap, cf. —stück, 2; —kleid, n. amice (oblong square of fine linen, cloth, worn under the alb by Catholic priests); —naht, f. (among sempstresses) a seam upon the shoulder-piece of a gown, &c.; —nerve, f. Anat. axillary nerve; —quaste, f. particul. Mil. shoulder-knot, epaulet; —ranke, f. Bot. axillary clasper or tendril; —schlag, m. shoulder-strap (—band); —schlagader, f. Anat. axillary artery; —schnur, f. shoulder-strap, pl. shoulder-points; —schwenkung, f. see Achsschwenkung; —ständig, adj. Bot. axillary; —stück, n., —streifen, m. 1) shoulder-piece, gusset; 2) Mil. epaulet; —träger, m. doubledealer, equivocator, hypocrite, trimmer, timeserver, shuffler; —trägerei', f. doubledealing, duplicity, hypocrisy, timeserving, shuffling; —trägerisch, adj. doubledealing, timeserving, shuffling, disingenuous; —troddel, f. shoulder-knot (—quaste); —tuch, n. amice, see —kleid; —vene, f. Anat. axillary vein (—ader); —zucken, n. shrug, shrugging; —zucker, m. one who shrugs his shoulders; —zug, m. Mech. block and fall (Flaschenzug), block, polyspast.

Ach'seln [pr. ăk'—], (w.) v. intr. 1) to take or throw upon the shoulder; 2) to serve both sides, to serve the time; see auf beiden Achseln tragen.

Ach'sen, Äch'sen [pr. ăk'—, ĕk'—], (w.) v. tr. to provide with an axletree or with axles.

Ach'sen [pr. ăk'—]..., in comp. —blech, n. Locom., &c. axle-guard, clout of the axletree; —büchse, f. axle-box, wheel-box; —drehung, f. rotation, motion about an axis, rotatory or circular motion; —eisen, n. axle-guard, see —blech; —förmig, adj. axiform; —fügung, f. Anat. trochoid, an articulation in which one bone turns upon another like a wheel upon its axle; —futter, n. axle(tree)-bed, axle-

Journal; —geld, n. wheelage; —lager, n. see —futter; —nagel, m. axle-pin, linch-pin; —neigung, f. Astr. obliquity of the ecliptic; —rahmen, m. carpenter frame of an axletree; —riegel, m. cross-timber; —ring, m. axle-ring, axle-hoop; —runge, f. T. clout of an axletree; —scheibe, f. T. axle-washer; —schemel, m. axle-bench; —schenkel, m. spindle; neutrale —schicht, f. neutral surface, neutral axle; —schiene, f. clout (of the axletree); —schmierbüchse, f. grease-box; —schmiere, f. axle-grease, wheel-grease; —schnitt, m. T. axal section; —schraube, f. axle-nut; —stoß, m. 1) see —blech; 2) (or —stift, m.) see —nagel; 3) axle-washer.

Achs' [pr. Aks] ..., in comp. —schenkel, m. T. gener. pl. axle bearings (of railway-carriages); —schenkelblech, n. see Achsenblech; —schwenkung, f. Mil. a turning or wheeling (of a body of troops) round a pivot; —strich, m. Archit. axis (of a column; Senkstrich).

A. Acht, I. (indecl., excepting the n. Dat. achten used without a subst. following) cardinal number, eight; — Tage, lit. eight days, used for a week, sennight (cf. Vierzehn Tage); in — Tagen, in a week; in a week's time; heute über — Tage, this day week (i. e. a week to come) or this day sennight; heute vor — Tagen, this day week (i. e. a week ago) or this day sennight; ich bin vor — (i. e. Uhr, coll. vor achte, or vor achten) aufgestanden, I rose before eight (o'clock); er wird morgen — (i. e. Jahre alt), he will be eight (years old) to-morrow; mit achten (i. e. mit — Pferden) fahren, to drive with eight horses; II. s. (w.) f. an eight (the figure of eight, &c.); zwei Achten werfen (Hdp.), to throw two eights (at dice).

B. Acht! interj. (L. u.) sound imitating the croaking of frogs (see the more usual Quack).

C. Acht, (w.) f. 1) attention, heed, watch, care: auf Einen or eine Sache — (Achtung) geben or haben, to pay attention to a person or thing, to give heed to ..., to attend to ..., to be on the watch as to ..., to watch, to mark, to mind, to heed: haben or geben Sie —! 1) pay attention, take care, have a care! beware! 2) mark (or bear in mind, &c.) what I say! mark my words! mark me! auf Jemand (Acc.) genau — geben, to eye one closely, to look sharp upon one; — haben, mostly used with auf (& Acc.), more rarely with Gen.: flüchtig hat er des Weges nicht — (Körner), as he flees he does not heed the way: still less usual is the Acc.: er hat sein armes Ländchen nicht — (Körner); eine Sache in guter — haben, to take good care of a thing; aus der or außer — lassen, to lose sight of, to be unmindful or thoughtless of, to overlook, forget, neglect: es war einige Gefahr, daß die Hauptsache aus der — gelassen würde, the main fact was in some danger of being discarded from view; etwas in — nehmen, a) to take care of, to look after or to, to be mindful of; b) sometimes used for wahrnehmen, beachten, to become or be aware of, to mind; c) unusual for sich (etwas) merken, to bear in mind, to note; d) sometimes construed with the Gen.: Tief unter mir nahm ich der Wogen in — (Platen), I saw the waves urging beneath me their flight: sich in — nehmen, to be cautious, careful, to take care, to be or stand on (upon) one's guard (vor [with Dat.], against; to beware of ...); nimm dich in —, wenn du diese Vögel fütterst, take care how you feed these birds: sich in — nehmen, like sich hüten (to be cautious how ..., &c.) and similar verbs, is often followed by a negative: nimm dich in —! dich treibt der böse Geist | der Rache — daß dich Rache nicht verderbe! (Schiller, Wall. Tod, 4, 1), (Coleridge:) Friedland, beware — | the evil spirit of revenge impels thee — beware, then, that revenge destroy thee not; er möge sich in — nehmen, daß er nicht in einem guten Rock nach Billingsgate geht, let him beware how he enters Billingsgate in a good coat.

2) † for a) Erachten, judgment, opinion; nach seiner —, as he deems fit, as he pleases; b) Beachtung, consideration, notice, attention; c) Achtung, Ansehen, regard, esteem; d) character; station.

D. Acht, (w.) f. Med. Law, outlawry, ban (of the law), attainder, proscription; in die — verfallen, to become an outlaw; Einen mit der — belegen, ihn in die — erklären, thun, sprechen, erkennen, to outlaw, to ban, to proscribe: die — ist ausgesprochen über ihn (Schiller), the sentence of attainder is passed on him; er war noch in der —, he was still under the ban of the law; Einen von der — befreien, to inlaw, to reclaim one's outlawry.

Ächt, adj. genuine, see Echt.

Acht' ..., in comp. —äugig, adj. having eight eyes, octonocular; —batzner, m. a Swiss coin of eight batzens.

Acht'bar, I. adj. respectable, estimable, deserving regard, honourable, creditable; Comm. eines unserer a-sten Häuser, one of our most esteemed (most respectable, best, first-rate) houses; II. A-keit, (w.) f. 1) respectability, dignity, estimableness; 2) † a) (Würde, Ansehen) dignity, honour; b) (Achtung) respect; c) used as a title (cf. Achtbar) or mode of addressing men princes: Euer (for Eure) —, your honour.

Acht' ..., in comp. —beinig, adj. eight-legged; —blattig, adj. Weav. eight-leaved (twill); —blätterig, adj. 1) eight-leaved; 2) —blumenblätterig, —blumig, octopetalous, having eight petals or flower-leaves; —brief, m. (from Acht, D) writ of outlawry, letter of outlawry or proscription, warrant of caption; —decht, m. a sort of coarse woollen cloth, used as tapestry.

Ach'te, I. adj. 1) coll. cardinal numeral, see Acht; 2) ordinal numeral, the eighth; zum A-en, in the eighth place, eighthly; II. s. (w.) f. Mus. octave (Octave); —halb or Acht'halb, seven and a half.

Acht' ..., in comp. —eck, n. Geom. octagon, a plane figure having eight sides and eight angles; —eckig, adj. eight-angled, octagonal, octangular.

Ach'tel, (str.) n. 1) eighth, the eighth part; 2) Mus. a) quaver; eighth part of a semibreve (Achtelnote); b) unusual, octave (Octave); 3) the eighth part of any quantity, of an arc (Octant), &c.

Ach'tel ..., in comp. —form, f., —format, n., —größe, f. Print. octavo size; —kreis, m. Geom. eighth part of an arc, octant (Octant).

Ach'teln, (w.) v. tr. to divide into eight parts.

Ach'tel ..., in comp. —note, f. Mus. quaver; —pause, f. Mus. quaver rest; —zoll, m. eighth part of an inch; —zeile, f. Astr. octand.

A. Ach'ten, (w.) v. I. tr. 1) (to express this sense, the verb is now generally used intransitively with auf ... &c.:) a) to attend to, to fix the mind or the thoughts upon, to take notice of, to mind (almost syn. with Beachten); b) to regard with care, interest, sympathy, to mind, heed, care for, to take heed of; nicht —, to take no heed of, to be mindless of; 2) to deem, to judge, to consider, think, to count, to take for ..., to be of a certain opinion as to ... (in modern prose für, als, wie &c. is gener. added); die Krone, der (Gen.) mein Fürst mich würdig achtete (Göthe), the crown of which my prince deemed me worthy; für gut — (or befinden), to deem or judge proper, to think fit; sie achteten es sich (Dat.) zum Ruhme (Novalis), they deemed it an honour to themselves; ich achte es für eine große Ehre, I take it as a great honour, I esteem it a great honour; ich achte es für eine Schande, I deem it a disgrace; ich achte es [illegible] it as loss; [illegible] Luther; ich achte es [illegible] werden (Luther, 2. Petr. 1, [illegible]) meet ... to stir you up [illegible] and and with [illegible] Grimm and Sanders [illegible] which, however, [illegible] Grimm's rules, [illegible] paid to [illegible] estimate, esteem [illegible] on ..., which may be high [illegible] at a certain degree of [illegible] (Göthe: [illegible]) —, to [illegible] to hold in mean [illegible] opinion of, to slight, [illegible] daß sie es nicht für [illegible] ben, ihn, als [illegible] asserted that they would [illegible] shooting him than his [illegible] regard, to make light of [illegible] it were die Mühe nicht [illegible] not to mind any trouble [illegible] no trouble or pains); er [illegible] nicht geachtet, he did not [illegible] achtet weder Ehre noch Schande [illegible] sense of shame ([illegible]) [illegible] disregard, to make no account [illegible] to set or hold at nought; [illegible] gard with reverence or [illegible] respect and affection, to [illegible] to prize, to esteem, [illegible] achtet, p. a. esteemed, respected (cf. Angesehen); ein sehr [illegible] männisches) Haus, a very [illegible] curable, esteemed) house [illegible] achtete Firma, a firm of [illegible]

II. refl. († & provinc. [illegible] Sache; now followed by [illegible] thing), to pay regard to, to [illegible] conform to, to keep, to observe [illegible] keep (precepts, &c.), to obey [illegible] nach (jedermann) sich zu — ([illegible] is to be observed (by every [illegible] to be taken (by every one).

III. intr. (gener. with [illegible] or the Gen., cf. Achten, &c.) to [illegible] to attend to, to mind, [illegible] des Weges —, to mind, [illegible] attention to the road; [illegible] attend to or to observe as [illegible] fluence our conduct; to [illegible] to lay to heart; auf Sitte —, [illegible] morality or good manners.

B. † Ach'ten, (w.) v. tr. [illegible]

Ach'ten, s. (str.) m. see [illegible]

Ach'ten, (w.) v. tr. to [illegible] ban, to put under the ban; [illegible] under the ban, outlaw.

Acht'ender, (str.) m. [illegible] branches or starts ([illegible])

Ach'tens, adv. eighthly, in [illegible]

Ach'tenswerth, [illegible] spectable, worthy of regard [illegible] tungswerth, Achtbar).

A. Ach'ter, s. (str.) m. [illegible] a thing consisting of eight [illegible] &c.: a small silver coin of [illegible] N. G.), Kreuzer ([illegible]) [illegible] eight branches ([illegible]) [illegible] for eight hours ([illegible]) [illegible] die Achtgroschen, the eight, [illegible] (two kinds of [illegible]) Tuch.); 5) a verse consisting [illegible] 6) anything resembling [illegible] an eight; 8) [illegible]

B. Ach'ter, provinc. [illegible] similar sense, f. i. [illegible] entirely superseded [illegible] [After]) I. prep. [illegible] particul. Mar. adj. [illegible] —steven, —schiff [illegible]

or culture of the ground: —bauend, adj. tilling the ground, see —bautreibend; —bauer, m. tiller of the ground, husbandman, farmer; —baugeräth, n. agricultural implements, farming utensils, instruments of husbandry (—geräth); —baugesellschaft, f. agricultural society; —bauinstitut, n. agricultural institution or college; —baukunde, f. theory of agriculture, agriculturism; —baukundig, adj. versed in the science of agriculture, agricultural; der —baukundige, m. agriculturist; —baukunst, f. the art of agriculture; —bauschule, f. agricultural school or college; —bautreibend, adj. engaged in agricultural pursuits, agricultural, rural (opp. Fabrik-, manufacturing [districts, &c.]); —bauwissenschaft, f. the science of agriculture; —beere, see —brombeere; —beet, n. a piece of ground between two furrows, land, ridge; —bemüht, adj. (l. u.) engaged in agriculture (Göthe); —bestellung, f. tillage, cultivation of the ground; —boden, m. soil fit for cultivation (in which anything grows), surface soil; —brame, —breme, f. see —brombeere; —brand, m. the same with —kuhweizen; —breite, f. (lit. breadth of land) a certain extent or quantity of land; —brombeere, f. dew- or wheat berry (Rubus caesius L.); —buch (Kataster), n. (official) register of lands (Grundbuch, Flurbuch); —bürger, m. inhabitant of a town, who practises agriculture; —camille, see Feldcamille.

Äckerchen, (str.) n. (dimin. of Acker) a small piece of ground, a little field.

Acker..., in comp. —cultur, f. cultivation of the land, tillage, culture; —distel, f. common thistle (Felddistel); —doppe, f. Comm. valonia (a corruption from Eckerdoppe); —drossel, f. Ornith. rose-coloured thrush (Turdus roseus); —ehrenpreis, m. Bot. germander-speedwell, chickweed (Veronica agrestis L.).

Ackerei, (w.) f. the operation, practice, or act of cultivating the ground, ploughing, tillage, husbandry.

Acker..., in comp. —eichel, f. Bot. tuber of the vetchling (Lathyrus tuberosus — syn. Erdnuß).

Ackerer, v. a. (from Ackern) (str.) m. tiller of the land, plougher, ploughman.

Acker..., in comp. —erbse, f. wild pea (Felderbse); —erde, f. mould, black earth, upper or surface soil (Dammerde); —fadenkraut, n. Bot. common (or field) cudweed (Filago arvensis L.); —fähig, adj. cultivable; —feld, n. arable field or ground; field under cultivation; —filzkraut, n. see —fadenkraut; —fleischblume, f. see (Acker-)Kuhweizen; —fontanell, m. (or f.) subterraneous ditch, laid out with stones or brushwood, for draining fields; —frauenmantel, m. see —sinau; —frohn or —frohne, m. provinc. field-guard, field-constable, ranger (Flurschütz, Feldhüter); —frohne, f., —frohndienst, m. plough-service, service done in soccage; —frucht, f. gener. in the pl. fruits or produce of the field, crops (Feldfrucht); —fuchsschwanz, m. Bot. field fox-tail grass (Alopecurus agrestis L.); —furche, f. furrow of a field; —galle, f. a marshy or sandy part in otherwise good soil, a slough (Galle); —gaul, m. farm-horse; —gefilde, n. poet. fields, fertile plains; —gehöfte, n. see —hof; —geld, n. 1) land-rent, rent levied on arable land; 2) (—lohn) ploughman's wages; —geräth, —geschirr, n. farming utensils, ploughing-tools, see —baugeräth; —gericht, n. court of agriculture; —gesetz, n. (particul. in reference to the old Roman law about dividing public lands among the people) agrarian law; —gewerte, n. extent of land containing four acres (Voss); —gilde, f. agricultural gild or company; —gras, n. Bot. mouse-ear; —grindkraut, n. Bot. meadow scabious (gemeine or Acker-Scabiose — Scabiosa arvensis L.); —günsel, m. Bot. field-bugle, see Feldcypresse; —gurre, f. farm-jade.

Ackerhaft, adj. unusual for Ackerbar.

Acker..., in comp. —hahnenfuß, m. Bot. corn-crow foot (Ranunculus arvensis L.); —haken, m. T. cultivator; —hauhechel, f. Bot. rest-harrow (Ononis arvensis L.); —hederich, m. Bot. common hedge-mustard (Sisymbrium officinale); —heu, n. hay from a fallow field; —hirtentasche, f. Bot. see —täschelkraut; —hof, m. farm-yard, farm, farm-house; —holder, —holunder, m. Bot. common elder (Sambucus ebulus L.); —holz, n. undergrowth or wood sprung from inferior soil on a field; —huhn, n. Ornith. partridge (Feldhuhn, Rebhuhn); —innung, f. agricultural corporation (—gilde); —junge, f. ploughboy; —kamille, see Feldcamille; —kannenkraut, n. see —schachtelhalm; —klapper, f. Bot. cockscomb, see Hahnenkamm; —klee, m. Bot. 1) harefoot (trefoil), white clover (Trifolium arvense L.); 2) lucerne (Medicago L.); —klette, f. Bot. prickly parsnip (Lappa tomentosa Lam.); —knabe, m. (l. u.) cont. ploughboy, anal. clodhopper; —knecht, m. farmer's servant employed in ploughing, ploughman, ploughboy, hind; —knoblauch, m. Bot. 1) wild garlic, crow garlic (Allium vineale L.); 2) (Feldknoblauch, Rocambole) rocambole (Allium scorodoprasum L.); —knöterich, m. Bot. corn-spurry, see —spergel; —kohl, m. Bot. 1) see Feldkohl, 1; 2) wild raddish; 3) (Rainkohl) dock-cresses, common nipplewort (Lapsana communis L.); —krähe, f. (Saatkrähe) rook (Corvus frugilegus L.); —krebs, m. Zool. earth-crab, mole-cricket (Gryllus gryllotalpa); —krume, f. mould, soil, fine soft earth, fertilizing earth easily pulverised, such as constitutes soil (Fruchterde); —kuhweizen, m. Bot. purple cow-wheat (Melampyrum arvense L.); —kümmel, m. Bot. (schwarzer) corn-cockle, see —rade; —kummet, n. a collar for a farm-horse; —land, n. arable land, plough land, tillage land; (land actually under tillage) ploughed land, cultivated land; schwarzes —land, wood land; —länge, f. the length of an acre, as a kind of measure; —lattich, m. Bot. 1) (Lämmerlattich) corn salad (Feldsalat); 2) (Huflattich) colt's foot (Tussilago farfara L.); 3) prickly lettuce (Lactuca scariola L.); —leben, n. (l. u.) 1) agricultural life (opp. Hirtenleben, nomadic life); 2) country-life (opp. Stadtleben).

Ackerlei, see Aklei.

Äckerlein, (str.) n. (dimin. of Acker) provinc. & poet. for Äckerchen, which see.

Acker..., in comp. —leine, f. cord or line used for guiding plough-horses; —leinkraut, n. Bot. flaxwood (Linaria vulgaris, see Leinkraut); —lerche, f. field lark (Feldlerche); —leute, pl. ploughmen, ploughers, husbandmen; —levkoje, f. see Feldlevkoje, Schaftkraut.

Ackerley, Ackerlei, see Aklei.

Acker..., in comp. —lichtröschen, n. Bot. Lychnis vespertina L.; —lohn, m. money paid for ploughing, ploughman's wages; —mähre, f. plough-mare; —mann, m. 1) obsolescent for Ackersmann, ploughman, plougher, husbandman, tiller (of the ground); 2) popular denomination of several beetles, particul. scarabæus and tenebrio; 3) or —mannswurzel, f. Bot. sweet flag (—wurz, which see); —männchen, n. 1) popular denomination of the (gray) wagtail (Bachstelze); 2) Entom. a species of scarlet spider, tant (Erdmilbe); —mannskraut, n. Bot. ox-tongue, see Ochsenzunge; —maschine, f. see —baumaschine; —maß, n. a measure by which a field is measured, land-measure (Feldmaß); —maus, f. field-mouse (Mus agrarius Pall.); —mauseohr, n. Bot. scorpion-grass, mouse-ear (Vergißmeinnicht); —melisse, f. Bot. calamint (Calamintha officinalis); —mennig, m. & f. (not to be derived from Acker; cf. to [illegible]

one of the many forms [illegible] Lat. agrimonia [illegible] Agrimonie [illegible] (cf. [illegible]) [illegible] Agrimonie; —meier, [illegible] m. Bot. corn-poppy [illegible] —münze, f. Bot. 1) corn [illegible] L.); 2) see —[illegible].

Ackern, (w.) v. tr. 1) [illegible] with Pflügen, to till or [illegible] to cultivate (the lands [illegible]) or incisions in...; 2) fig. to [illegible] boriously.

Acker..., in comp. [illegible] —nägelein, n. [illegible] ged chickweed [illegible] Holosteum umbellatum L.) [illegible] nettle (Galeopsis ladanum [illegible]) hedge-nettle (Lamium [illegible]) L., see [illegible] ground-nut, see [illegible] —sinau; [illegible] management of land, [illegible] tion, tillage; [illegible] see [illegible]; [illegible] instrument used instead of [illegible] making the surface even, [illegible] Bot. yellow vetchling [illegible] [illegible]

—spergel, —spark, —spergel, m. Bot. corn-spurry (Spergula arvensis L.); —steinsamen, m. Bot. gromwell, painting root (Lithospermum arvense); —sternkraut, n. Bot. 1) see —meliffe; 2) woodroof; —steuer, f. land tax, tax assessed on fields (different from Grundsteuer); —tag, m. day on which plough-service is (to be) rendered (Frohntag); —täschelkraut, n. Bot. shepherd's purse (Thlaspi arvense); —theil, m. (vergl. das englische acredale, nach Brockett [Gloss. of North Country Words]: land in a common field, different parts of which are held by different proprietors) among miners, share in a mine (Erbkux); —thymian, m. see —melisse; —trappe, 1) m. & f. Ornith. bustard (Otis tarda); 2) m. †, see —schroll; —trespe, f. Bot. corn-brome-grass (Bromus arvensis); —trolle, m. †, see —schroll; —umsatz, m. the laying out of an estate or farm into parcels; rotation (Ackerumschlag); —vertheilung, f. (equal) division of lands; —vieh, n. farm-cattle serving for tillage; —viole, f. Bot. corn-violet (Specularia speculum D. C.); —vogel, m. Ornith. plover, golden plover (Charadrius pluvialis L.); —vogelmilch, f. Bot. common star of Bethlehem (Ornithogalum arvense Pers.); —vogt, m. field-guard, field-constable; —waage, f. a level (instrument) for measuring the depth of the furrows; —walze, f. land roller, cylinder; —weg, m. field-way (Feldweg); —weiderich, m. Bot. purple loosestrife; —wirbel, Bot. see —treber; —werk, n. †, agricultural concerns, husbandry; —werkzeug, n. ploughing tool, see —baugeräth; —wesen, n. agricultural affairs; —wicke, f. Bot. common vetch (Vicia sativa); —wicke, f. see Feldwicke; —winde, f. corn-bind (Convolvulus arvensis L.); —wintergrün, m. see —schmele; —wirthschaft, f. agriculture (Landwirthschaft); —wurm, m. Entom. grub (Engerling); —wurz, f. Bot. sweet flag (Acorus calamus L.); —zeit, f. ploughing-season; —zeug, n. farming-tools, see —geräth; —zins, m. land-rent; —zwiebel, f. Bot. see —vogelmilch.

* [illegible], see Aglei.

* [illegible], (w.) m. see Afolath.

* Aconit', (str.) m. Bot. aconite, wolfsbane (Aconitum, Eisenhut). — Aconitin', (str.) n. Chem. aconitine. [De'don.

* Acotyledo'ne, (w.) f. (Gr.) Bot. acotyle-

* Acquiri'ren, (w.) v. tr. to acquire.

* Acquisition', (w.) f. acquisition, particul. of valuable things; wir haben daran eine recht gute — gemacht, it has turned out or proved a good bargain.

* Acquit' [pr. akkī'], s. n. (Fr.) 1) Comm. a) discharge; b) receipt; pour (coll. p^r or par) —, (at the foot of a bill, &c.) received (rec^d), received payment; paid (p^d); 2) (at billiards) lead; — geben, to take the lead, to lead.

* Acquittiren, (w.) v. tr. (Fr. acquitter) Comm. (I. u.) 1) to discharge, to clear (accounts); 2) to pay, to discharge or answer (a bill).

* Act, Act, (str.) m. 1) a) act, action, performance; b) Law, (official) deed; — nehmen von einer Sache, to take out or receive an official certificate of a thing; von einem Vorfalle — nehmen, to take note of an occurrence (cf. [illegible]); 2) T. (Aufzug) act (of a dramatic performance).

* Acta, (Lat. pl.) acts, actions, deeds, transactions ([illegible], opp. Agenda), particul. [illegible] (judicial) acts, &c., see Acten; ad — legen, see zu den Acten legen.

* Acte, (w.) f. act, deed, bill; gener. in [illegible], public papers, reports, records, [illegible] documents, (judicial) acts, [illegible] proceedings (at law), registers, [illegible] journals, belonging to courts of [illegible] reports of (adjudged) cases; [illegible] Act, on examining the legal documents (deeds); über etwas (Acc.) — nehmen, see Act; in den A-n nachschlagen, to consult, refer to official documents; zu den A-n (ad acta) legen, to subjoin or to add to the acts; fig. to lay by, to put by, to lay or put on the shelf, to shelve.

* Ac'ten..., in comp. —faszikel, n. Law, a roll or bundle of (legal) documents, acts, &c. (cf. Acten), register; —kammer, f. Law, office of the rolls; —mäßig, adj. documentary, documental, derived from documents or written evidence in law; authentic (urkundlich); —reiter, m. contr. red-tapist; —reiterei, f. contr. red-tapism; —schluß, m. Law, inrotulation of proceedings (at law), &c.; —stoß, m. (ein großer, a large) pile of (legal) documents; —stück, n. (official) document, see Acte.

* Ac'tie [pr. Aktsie], (w.) f. (Fr. action) Comm. share (Antheilschein); pl. funds (in shares), stocks; Inhaber von A-n, shareholder (A-ninhaber); unsichere A-n, fancy-stocks; A-n ausgeben (emittiren), to issue shares; A-n besitzen, to hold shares; voll eingezahlte A-n, shares paid up in full; mit A-n wuchern, to stock-job; die A-n stehen jetzt sehr hoch, the shares are now at a premium.

Ac'tien..., in comp. —abschnitt, m. see —coupon; —antheil, m. share; —ausgabe, f. issue of shares; —bank, f. joint-stock-bank; —bankwesen, n. joint-stock-banking; —besitz, m. share-holding, fund-holding; —besitzer, m. see —inhaber; —(Bier)brauerei, f. joint-stock brewery; —börse, f. railway-market; —capital, n. joint stock; —coupon [pr. kûpong'], m. coupon, dividend-warrant (—abschnitt); —cours, m. price or rate of shares; —dividende, f. dividend; —einzahlung, f. instalment; —emission, f. see —ausgabe; —fonds, m. joint stock; —gesellschaft, f. joint-stock company; —handel, m. stock-dealing; cont. stock-jobbing; —händler, m. dealer in stocks, cont. stock-jobber; —inhaber, m. share-holder, stock-holder; —kapital, see —capital; —makler, m. stock-broker; —promesse, f., —schein, m. scrip; —reiter, m. cont. see —spieler; —schwindel, m. mania of stock-jobbing, stock-jobbery (—spiel); —speculant, m. dealer in stocks, cont. stock-jobber; —speculation, f. speculation in shares, stock-adventure, cont. stock-jobbing; —spiel, n. stock-jobbing (transactions), stock-jobbery, coll. fund-bubbles; —spieler, m. stock-adventurer, stock-jobber; —spinnerei, f. joint-stock cotton mill; —verein, m. see —gesellschaft; —wesen, n. stock-business, fund-business; —zeichnung, f. subscription to shares.

Ac'tig, adj. consisting of (a certain number of) acts; ein zweiactiges Lustspiel, a comedy of two acts.

* Acti'nie, (w.) f. (Lat. Gr.) Zool. actinia.

* Action' [pr. akßion'], (w.) f. action: 1) act or thing done, deed; 2) gesture, gesticulation, acting, by-play (Mienenspiel); 3) engagement, battle, fight, engagement.

* Actionär' [pr. akßionär'], (str.) m. (Fr. actionnaire) shareholder; stockholder; (nur in Bezug auf kaufmänn. Verhältnisse:) actionary.

* Actioni'ren [pr. akßi—], (w.) v. tr. (Fr. actionner) † Law, to bring or to enter an action against (one), to take legal measures against, to sue (for payment, &c.).

* Actionist' [pr. akßi—], (w.) m. † 1) see Actionär; 2) agent, broker.

* Activ' (sometimes accented on the first syllable, ac'tiv, when opposed to passiv), I. adj. 1) active, busy, &c.; 2) actual, effective (of military service, &c.); in a-em Dienst stehend, effective (opp. non-effective); a-e Theilnahme, active participation; 3) Gramm. active, transitive (opp. passiv); die a-e Form (das Activum), the active form; II. s. (str.) n. see Activum.

* Acti'va (Lat. pl. of. activum), Acti'ven, (w.) n. pl. Comm. active property, assets (Activ-Vermögen, Activschulden), active or outstanding debts; — und Passiva, assets and liabilities; seine — sind gleich null (Nob. & Gr.), his assets are next to nothing, there are no assets at all.

* Activ'..., in comp. —handel, m. Comm. active commerce (commerce which a nation carries on in its own ships), export-trade (Ausfuhrhandel); Großbritannien führt einen —, China einen Passiv-Handel (Hilp.), the commerce of Great Britain is active, that of China is passive.

* Activ'isch, adj. Gramm. used in an active signification, active, adv. actively (opp. passivisch). [Wirksamkeit).

* Activität', (w.) f. activity (Thätigkeit,

* Activ'..., in comp. —recest, m. Law, the residue of a claim; —saldo, (pl. (Ital.) A-saldi) m. (in book keeping) balances in my favour, amount of my effects; —schulden, f. pl. Comm. active or outstanding debts, assets; — und Passivschulden, assets and debts, debts due and owing; —stand, m. actual state or position; —vermögen, n. active property, assets.

* Acti'vum, Activ', (Lat. activum, pl. activa) (str.) n. Gramm. active (active form or active verb).

* Ac'tor, (str., pl. [w.] Acto'ren) m. (Lat.) Law, plaintiff; plaintiff's counsel.

* Acto'rium, (str.) n. (Lat.) Law, power of attorney granted to counsel.

* Actri'ce [pr. aktri'ße], (w.) f. (Fr. actrice) actress.

* Actualität', (w.) f. actuality.

* Actuar', (str.), Actua'rius, (Lat., sing. not decl., pl. [w.] Actua'rien) m. actuary, registrar, clerk.

* Ac'tus, (indecl.) m. (Lat.) public act, solemn performance, celebration.

* Acut'il &c., see Ak....

* Acupunctur', (w.) f. (Lat.) Surg. acupuncture.

* Acut', (from Lat. acutus, sharp-pointed, sharp) I. adj. acute: 1) Med. attended with symptoms of severity, and coming speedily to a crisis (opp. Chronisch); a-e Krankheit, acute or inflammatory disease; 2) Gramm. sharp, high; der a-e Accent, acute accent (opp. Gravis); II. (str.) m. or Acu'tus, (Lat.) Gramm. acute accent, see the preceding word.

A d., abbr. for a dato (Lat.), from (this) date (von diesem Tage or Datum).

A. d., abbr. for (Lat.) Anno Domini, in the year of the Lord, im Jahre des Herrn.

Ad absur'dum (Lat.) führen, Log. to convict of absurdity.

Ad ac'ta, (Lat. to the acts) see Acta.

Ada'gio [pr. adâ'dschio], I. adv. (Ital. at leisure) Mus. adagio, slowly: II. s. (str., pl. A-s) n. Mus. adagio.

A'dalbert, see Adelbert.

A'dam, m. Adam (Hebrew P. N.); der alte —, Theol. fig. the old man, i. e. original sin (Erbsünde); den alten — ausziehen, to put off the old man, to amend one's life.

* Adamant', (w.) m. † & poetic. adamant (a very hard stone; diamond).

* Adaman'ten, adj. adamantine, (seltener:) adamantean.

* Adamantin', (str.) m. Miner. adamantine spar (a variety of corundum). [earth.

Ada'mitisch, adj. Adamic; a-e Erde, Adamic

Adamit'en, (w.) m. pl. (sing. Adamit') Church Hist. Adamites, Christian sect (Adamia'ner).

Adamit'isch, adj. Adamitic.

A'dams..., in comp. —apfel, m. 1) Bot. a) (Paradiesapfel) Adam's apple (fruit of the plantain-tree, Musa paradisiaca) see Pardiesapfel; 2) or —bitz, m. Anat. coll. Adam's apple,

Adam's bit, prominent part of the throat (Adamsapfel); —feige, *f. Bot. a) see* —apfel; *b) according to others*, (the fruit of) the Egyptian fig-tree (*Ficus sycomorus*); —holz, *n.* Adam's wood, black, hard, fossile wood, found near Astrachan, and used like ebony; —nadel, *f. Bot.* Adam's needle, yucca.

* Adanſo'nie, *(w.) f.* sour gourd, baobab-tree, monkey's bread (the African tree *Adansonia digitata*).

* Adäquat', *adj.* adequate.

* Ad'(d)aties, Ad'atais, *m. pl.* adatais, adatis, fine Bengal muslin or cotton cloth.

A dato, *see* A d.

Add., *abbr. (on recipes) for addatur (Lat.)*, let there be added, *or* adde, add.

Ad'del, *(str.) m. provinc. (cf.* Addle) filthy water, dung-water (Jauche); *spelled also* Adel.

Ad'der, *(w.) f. provinc. for* Natter, adder.

* Addici'ren, *(w.) v. tr. (Lat.) Law*, to make over by legal sentence (Zuſprechen, Zuerkennen).

* Addi'ren, *(w.) v. tr. (Lat.)* to add up, to cast up, to sum up (Zuſammenzählen, Zuſammenziehen); Sie haben falſch addirt, you have cast up wrong; die Koſten — ſich *(refl.)* zu einer hübſchen Summe, the charges amount to a considerable sum *(Rob. & Gr.)*.

* Addition' *(pr.* addiziōn'), *(w.) f.* addition (Zuſammenzählung); ein A-exempel rechnen, to do an addition sum; A-fehler, *m.* fault of addition, error in casting up.

* Additionäl, *adj.* additional (Zuſätzlich, Ergänzend).

* Additiv', *adj. Math.* that is to be added, additive (Größen, quantities).

* Adduc'tor, *(str., pl. [w.]* Adducto'ren) *m. (Lat.) Anat.* adductor (*opp.* Abductor).

Ade', *interj. & sometimes s. (str., Gen.* A-s, *pl.* A-s) *m. (a corruption from the French* adieu *which see)* adieu, farewell, good-by.

Ad depo'situm, *(Lat.)* in deposit, in a state of pledge, or of trust for safe-keeping: — (in Verwahrung geben (deponiren), to put in trust; to give in charge, to deposit.

A'debār, A'debār, *(str.) m. (MHG.* adebar, *OHG.* odeboro, odebāro, *child(?)bearer) L. G.* name of the stork, who, when a child is born, is popularly said to have carried it into the house.

A. A'del, *(str.) m. see* Addel

B. A'del, *(str.) m.* 1) *a)* nobleness, distinction by birth; von — (*or* adelich), of noble birth, a nobleman by birth, (von gutem —) of a noble extraction; von altem —, of ancient nobility, stock; *b)* nobility; optimacy; peerage; der niedere —, gentry; der geſammte —, the body of nobility; Einer (Eine) vom —, nobleman (noblewoman); 2) *fig.* nobility (of soul), nobleness, dignity (of mind), honourableness, magnanimity; der — des Menſchen, dignity of man, human excellence.

A'del..., *in comp.* —aar, *m.* noble eagle, *original form of* Adler; —bauer, *m.* a peasant who is the vassal of a nobleman; —beere, *f.* service-berry, *see* Elſebeere.

A'delbert, A'dalbert, *m. (P. N. from OHG.* Adalpëraht, *splendid or excellent of race*, Adalbert, *shortened into* Albrëcht, Albert; *A. S.:)* Ethelbert. [midshipman.

A'delburſch, *(w.) m.* young nobleman, page;

Adele *(pr.* adā'lo), *f.* Adela *(P. N. from the Fr.* Adèle, *which again is derived from OHG.* Adala, *a woman of illustrious [noble] race)*

A'deler, † *for* Adler.

A'del..., *in comp.* —eſche, *f. Bot.* (true) service-tree, *see* Adeleſche; —fiſch, *m. Ichth.* lavaret, ulmpu, *see* Schnäpel; —geſchlecht, *n.* noble race or family; —gras, *n. Bot.* a kind of plantain (*Plantago alpina*).

A'delhaft, *adj. (Lavater, unusual)* imbued with nobility, expressive of nobility.

A'del..., *in comp.* —herriſch, —herrlich, *(l. u.)* aristocratic(al); —herrſchaft, *see* Adelsherrſchaft; —herrſcher, *m. (l. u.)* aristocrat.

A'delig, *(usual, but incorrect for* Adel(l)ich, *a spelling which we still find in Wieland, Göthe, Voss) adj.* 1) noble, of noble extraction or birth; belonging to the nobility; 2) *fig.* noble, high-minded; ein Adelicher, *m.* a noble, nobleman; patrician; grandee; eine A-e, *f.* a lady of noble birth, noblewoman.

A'deling, *m.* 1) *or* A'delung, *(Wieland* Adeling) †, one belonging to a noble race or family, nobleman, noble; 2) *cont.* favourer or follower of noblemen, aristocrat, scion of nobility; ultra-nobleman.

† A'deliſch, *adj.* noble, *adv.* after the manner of noblemen or the nobility.

A'dellos, *adj. (Blumberg, l. u.)* destitute of nobility, ignoble.

A'deln, *(w.) v. tr.* to ennoble: 1) to raise to nobility, to make noble (gänzlich veraltet: to nobilitate); das —, *v. s. (str.) n.* ennoblement, act or custom of ennobling, raising to nobility; 2) *fig.* to dignify, to exalt.

A'dels..., *in comp.* —brief, *m.* charter, patent of nobility; er war Einer von denen, welchen die Natur den —brief ausgeſtellt, he was one of Nature's noblemen; —buch, *m.* book of the nobility or peerage, nobiliary.

A'delſchaft, *(w.) f.* 1) † *see* Adelſtand; 2) *(Schiller, l. u.)* nobility (as a body).

A'delſchein, *(str.) m. (Bürger, l. u.)* semblance of nobility.

A'dels..., *in comp.* —diplom, *n. see* —brief; feind, *m.* an enemy to the nobility; —freund, *m.* a friend, favourer, or follower of the nobility, aristocrat; —gewalt, *f.* the power of the nobility; —herrſchaft, *f.* a government of nobles, aristocracy. [nanimity.

A'delſinn, *(str.) m.* nobility of mind, mag-

A'dels..., *in comp.* —kunde, *f.* knowledge of the history and privileges of the nobility; —lexicon, *n.* alphabetical list or dictionary of noble families, nobiliary.

A'del..., *in comp.* —ſtand, *m.* 1) nobility, rank of a nobleman; in den —ſtand erheben, to raise to nobility, to knight; 2) (body of) nobility; —ſtolz, I. *adj.* proud of nobility; II. *s. m.* pride of nobility; —ſucht, *f.* a longing after the rank of nobility; —ſüchtig, *adj.* longing after the rank of nobility, attached to the nobility.

A'delthum, *(str., pl.* A-thümer) *n.* 1) *see* Adelſtand; 2) *see* Adel(s)herrſchaft.

A. A'delung, *(str.) m. see* Adeling. [&c.

B. A'delung, *(w.) f.* the act of ennobling.

* Ademption', *(w.) f. (Lat.) Law, &c.* ademption (of a legacy, &c.).

* Adenographie', Adenologie', Adenotomie' &c., *(w.) f. (Gr.)* description, doctrine, dissection, &c. of the glands.

* Adept', *(w.) m. (term of the alchemists)* adept, one who has attained to the full knowledge of the profoundest mysteries of alchemy.

A'der, *(w.) f.* 1) *a) Anat.* vein, vessel for the conveyance of blood: die unpaarige —, the vein without a pair; die goldne —, *Anat.* hemorrhoidal vein; hemorrhoids, (bloody) piles; Einem die — ſchlagen *or* öffnen, zur — laſſen, to bleed or blood a person, to let one blood, to breathe a vein; ich habe (zur) — gelaſſen, I have let blood; *b)* vein, a passage or anything resembling a vein in appearance, use, or action: Milchadern, lacteal veins; Waſſeradern, lymphatic veins; *by old writers sometimes used syn. with* fibre, sinew, &c.; *c) fig.* vein, tendency or turn (of mind), disposition, cast: eine dichteriſche —, a poetical vein; eine ſatiriſche —, a satirical vein; in *or* an ihm iſt keine gute —, there is no good in or about him; keine falſche — *(Göthe)*, not the least particle of falsehood; er hat keine — von fal-

nem Blute, he is [illegible] 2) *a)* course [illegible] the earth, [illegible] seam, dike; [illegible] A-n, transcholdung [illegible] of different colours [illegible] marble or other [illegible]

A'der..., *in comp.* [illegible] scription of the [illegible] giography; —binde, *f.* [illegible] tie up a vein; —bruch, *m.* [illegible] or rupture of a vein, [illegible] Krampfaderbruch.

A'derchen, *(str.) n.* [illegible] little vein (*cf.* Aderl[illegible]) Fünkchen von ſeinem [illegible] the least vestige of [illegible] a spark of his feeling.

A'der..., *in comp.* [illegible] —hautentzündung; [illegible] monoptera, *see* [illegible] vessel or arterial system [illegible] mahl, *n.* vascular [illegible] *f.* dilatation or swelling of [illegible] —knoten; —haut, *f. (Anat.* [illegible] choroid membrane (of the [illegible]) exterior membrane which [illegible] —hautentzündung, *f. Med.* [illegible] the choroid; —hautſack, [illegible] of the choroid; —holz, [illegible] *(Karm.:)* plankway of the [illegible]

A'dericht, *adj.* resembling [illegible]

A'derig, A'drig, *adj.* [illegible] streaked.

A'der..., *in comp.* [illegible] *Med.* swollen vein, varix [illegible] Adergeſchwulſt); —kreislauf, [illegible] of the veinous circulation, [illegible] or swelling; varix; —laß, [illegible] *m.*, —läſſe, *(w.) f. (Schiller,* [illegible] ting of blood, bleeding, [illegible] botomy; —laßbinde, [illegible] letting compress; —laß[illegible] basin; —(laß)binde, *f.* [illegible] dage; —läſſe, *see* —laß; [illegible] *& Veter.* bleeding-lancet, [illegible] 1) bloodletter, surgeon; 2) [illegible] of the genus [illegible] ſchwänze), the [illegible] —laßgeräth, *n.* bleeding-instr[illegible] ing-case; —laßkunſt, *f.* [illegible] ting, venesection, [illegible] eiſen, *f.*, —laßſchnepper, [illegible] lancet; human lancet; [illegible] band, *m. Surg.* ligature or [illegible] a vein is tied up; —laß[illegible] ing instruments, bleeding-[illegible] season for letting blood; [illegible] or knowledge of the veins, [illegible] giology.

A'derlein, *(str.) n.* [illegible] *utive, & poet. for* Aderchen.

A'derlos, *adj.* [illegible] not veined or nerved.

A'dermennig, *(str.) m.* [illegible] *be derived from* [illegible]

A'dermeſſer, *(str.) m.* [illegible] for measuring the [illegible] beating or throbbing of [illegible]

A'dern, A'dern, *(w.) v.* [illegible] or mark with veins, to [illegible] with veins; to grain [illegible]

A'der..., *in comp.* [illegible] opening of a vein; [illegible] fungus of the [illegible] also [illegible] by [illegible] tightened by [illegible] a strong [illegible] —reich, *adj.* full of [illegible] *adj. Bot.* nerved [illegible] beating or throbbing [illegible] tion, pulse; 2) [illegible] venesection (—öffnung, —laß); —schwamm, m. Bot. 1) see Pfifferling; 2) a species of dry rot (Merulius lacrymans); —haar, m. see —haarhaar; —strang, m. Med. venal plexus (—geflecht); —system, n. venous or arterial system (—gebäude).

Äderung, Äderung, (w.) f. particul. Bot. the veining or venation (of leaves).

Äder ..., in comp. —verrenkung, f. (from Ader, 1, b) a spraining of the sinews of a foot (of animals), producing halting; —wasser, n. Med. the lymph mixed with the blood, serum.

* Adhäri'ren, (w.) v. intr. (Lat. adhaerere, to stick to ...) to adhere. — Adhäsiōn' (w.) f. adhesion (also in Med.). — Adhäsīv', adj. adhesive (also Med.: inflammation, &c.).

* Adhibi'ren, (w.) v. tr. (Lat. adhibere) l. u. for Anwenden, Zulassen, Zuziehen; to apply, to admit (to adhibit). — Adhibitiōn' [pr. —ziōn'], (w.) f. l. u. for Anwendung, Zuziehung &c., application; admission, &c. (adhibition).

* Adiant', (str.) m. Bot. a species of fern, Adiantum L., particul. the Adiantum capillus Veneris (Frauenhaar).

* Adiaphōr', adj. (Gr. adiaphoros, indifferent, neutral) Chem. adiaphorous.

* Adieu' [pr. adiö'], interj. (from the Fr. à Dieu, used elliptically for à Dieu je vous commande, I commend you to God, similar to the German Gott befohlen! for Gott [Dat.] seiest du befohlen! to God, i. e. to the care of God be thou commended, Ital. addio!) adieu, farewell, good-bye (sometimes used as a subst. [str.] n.); Einem — sagen, to bid one farewell, to say good-bye to one, to tender one's adieus (to one); Adieu variously transformed in popular pronunciation: Adjēs' [pr. adjäs', sometimes adjüs'], Adjes', Adjes', Ades, Adie', Adje', † Adē', &c., cf. Grimm and Sanders, and the word Ade. This word "Adieu", introduced into the German, as it was into the English language, centuries ago, is, like all useless foreign terms, looked upon with unfavourable eyes in modern times, and will probably share the fate of other French words, rather senselessly adopted in bygone times, as f. i. Demoiselle, Merci, Plaisir, and a flood of others, for a while assumed to be part and parcel of our language, but at present utterly rejected by educated persons, so that there is no danger, that we "will be reduced", as the great lexicographer Johnson apprehended his countrymen would be, "to babble a dialect of France". A rhyme like the following: Da nahm ich von meinem Kind Adjes | und schweigend blickt' es in die Höh (Göthe), has something very ridiculous in it nowadays.

* Ädil', Ädi'le, (w.) m. Rom. Archaeol. edile,
* Ädilität', (w.) f. edileship, office of edile.
* Adipinsäure, (w.) f. Chem. adipic acid.
* A dirittu'ra, (Ital.) adverbial phrase particul. Comm. in a direct manner, directly; (of goods transported from one place to another): by one conveyance (auf einer Achse); a dirittura (or a drittura) ziehen, to draw directly (without the intervention of a broker).

* Adj., abbr. 1) for Adjectiv; 2) for Adjunct; 3) for Adjutant.

* Adjacent', I. adj. (Lat.) adjacent; II. s. (w.) m. near or close neighbour.

* Adjectiōn', (w.) f. adjection, addition.

* Adjectiv', (str., pl. A-e, sometimes (w.) A-en), (Lat.) Adjecti'vum, (str., pl. [Lat.] Adjectiva) n. Gramm. adjective (Eigenschaftswort).

* Adjectivisch, adj. adjectival; adv. adjectively.

* Adjoint', (w.) m. incorrect for Adjunct, which see.

* Adjudicat', (w.) m. (Lat.) Law, one to whom something (a title, &c.) is adjudged or awarded by judicial decision. — Adjudicatiōn', (w.) f. Law, adjudication, the awarding by judicial sentence (Zuerkennung, Zusprechung). — Adjudici'ren, (w.) v. tr. to adjudicate, adjudge, to give or award by judicial sentence (Zuerkennen, Zusprechen).

* Adjunct', (w.) m. (Lat.) adjunct, assistant (teacher, &c.), associate. — Adjunctiōn', (w.) f. adjunction. — Adjunctūr', (w.) f. office of an adjunct or assistant. — Adjungi'ren, (w.) v. tr. (Lat. adjungere, to add or join to ...) to adjoin, associate, to give as an assistant.

* Adjusti'ren, (w.) v. tr. to adjust, particul. Mint. to size (Justiren, Abgleichen).

* Adjustir' ..., in comp. —amt, n. assaying-office, gauging-office (Eichamt); —bank, f. see —werk; —schraube, f. T. adjusting-screw (Stellschraube); —wage, f. adjusting-balance; —werk, n. Mint. drawing-bench, flatting-mill.

* Adjutant', (w.) m. Mil. adjutant, aid-de-camp. — Adjutantūr', (w.) f. 1) adjutancy, office of an adjutant; 2) corps of officers, acting as adjutants to the commander-in-chief.

A. Ad'ler, (str.) m. (s. a. from Adeln) one who ennobles, raises to nobility, &c.; fem. die Ad'lerin, (w.).

B. Ad'ler, (str.) m. 1) Ornith. eagle (Aquila); der braunfahle, or schwarzbraune (gemeine) —, the cinereous or white-tailed eagle, fawn-killer (Falco melanaëtus); der weibliche —, female or hen eagle, eagless; der kleine or junge —, eaglet; 2) Herald., Numism., &c. eagle; ein — mit ausgebreiteten Flügeln, a spread eagle; ein doppelter (Doppel-) —, eagle with two heads.

Ad'ler ..., in comp. —ähnlich, adj. eagle-like, aquiline: —auge, n. eagle-eye, piercing and discerning eye, acute sight; —äugig, adj. eagle-eyed, eagle-sighted, sharpsighted, as an eagle; —beere, f. service-berry, see Kriechbeere: —blick, m. 1) (Adlersblick) the glance of an eagle; 2) eagle- or keen glance; —blume, f. Bot. culver-key, see Akelei; —bohne, f. Bot. a kind of kidneybean (Hilp.).

Ad'lerchen, (str.) n. (dimin. of Adler) eaglet.

Ad'ler ..., in comp. —eile f. eagle-speed, swiftness like that of an eagle; —eule, f. Ornith. eagle-owl, one of the bubonina, or horned owls (Baird), Strix bubo L.; —farren, m. Bot. brake (Pteris aquilina, a kind of fern, Saumfarren); —fisch, m. Ichth. sea-eagle, eagle-ray (Myliobatis aquila Hill.; Meeradler); —fittig, m. poet. for —flügel; —flug, m. flight of an eagle; mit —flug, eagle-flighted; —flügel, m. eagle-wing; —geier, m. Ornith. bald eagle (Aquila leucocephala, Weißkopf).

Ad'lerhaft, Ad'lermäßig, adj. eagle-like, lofty, sublime.

Ad'ler, ..., in comp. —holz, n. Bot. eagle-wood: 1) the purple-coloured, fragrant wood of Aquilaria Malaccensis, or ovata, an East-Indian tree used by cabinet-makers, for dyeing, &c. (Pierer); 2) satin-wood; 3) aloes-wood; —kraut, n. see —farren; —mennig, m. see Adermennig; —nase, f. aquiline nose, hooked nose: —orden, m. Herald. the order of the (black, red, white) eagle; —rochen, m. see —fisch; —saumfarren, see —farren; —schnelle, f. eagle-speed; —schwinge, f. eagle-pinion; —schwung, m. eagle-flight; —stein, m. eagle-stone (globular clay iron-stone, generally containing a sort of loose kernel), aetites; —vitriol, n. eagle-vitriol, coppery sulphate of iron from Salzburg; —zange, f. Metall. great pincers with beak-shaped limbs, devil's claw.

Ad'ling, see Adeling.

* Adminiculi'ren, (w.) v. tr. (Lat.) Law, &c. to support or substantiate (proof) (Unterstützen).

* Adminic'ulum, (Gen. A-s, pl. [Lat.] Adminic'ula) n. (Lat.) Law, &c. anything tending to substantiate or establish proof (Hülfsmittel, unterstützender Grund), (im schott. Recht:) adminicle.

* Administratiōn', (w.) f. (Lat.) administration (Verwaltung); unter —, under administration, in trust. — Administrativ', adj. administrative (verwaltend); —behörde, see Verwaltungsbehörde. — Administra'tor, (str., pl. (w.) Administrato'ren) m. (Lat.) administrator; trustee (Verwalter, Verweser). — Administrato'rium, (Gen. A-s, pl. A-ien) n. Law, mandate or commission appointing an administrator or trustees. — Administri'ren, (w.) v. tr. to administer (Verwalten).

* Admirāl', (str., pl. A-e or Admirä'le) m. 1) Mar. admiral; 2) Mollusc. admiral-shell, admiral (Conus admirabilis); 3) Entom. admiral (a kind of butterfly, Papilio atalanta); —schiff, n. admiral's ship, admiral, flag-ship; A-sflagge, f. admiral's flag: 1) flag of an admiral; 2) Mollusc. a species of bulla (Bulla ampullacea); A-srath, m. board of admiralty.

* Admiralität', (w.) f. admiralty; navy-office: A-samt, n., A-sbehörde, f. board of admiralty; A-sgericht, n. admiralty court.

Admirālschaft, (w.) f. 1) the office, dignity or power of an admiral, (w. A.:) admiralship; 2) — machen, unter — segeln, Mar. to sail under convoy, in company with other ships.

* Admissiōn', (w.) f. (Lat.) admission (Zulassung); A-sklappe, f. T. steam-valve. — Admitti'ren, (w.) v. tr. to admit (Zulassen, Gestatten); admittatur (Lat.), let (him, her) it be admitted (es werde zugelassen), let it be printed (a license to print, in countries subjected to censorship of the press).

* Admoni'ren, (w.) v. tr. (Lat.) to admonish. — Admonitiōn', (w.) f. admonition.

* Admortisatiōn', (w.) f. Law, admortisation, see Amortisation, 2.

* Admotiōn', (w.) f. (Lat. — l. u.) the act of bringing near to ..., or in contact with (Hinzubringung, Annäherung). — Admovi'ren, (w.) v. tr. to put near, to bring near, or to apply to ..., to bring in contact with ... (†: to admove).

Ad no'tam, (Lat.) eine Sache — nehmen, to notice a thing particularly, to bear in mind (sich etwas [be]merken).

* Annotatiōn', (w.) f. (Lat.) 1) annotation, note (Anmerkung); 2) a rescript of the pope, subscribed with his own hand; 3) Med. a slight attack, approaching fever-fit (Anmeldung). — Annoti'ren, (w.) v. tr. to note down, remark, observe, to write notes on, to annotate (Aufzeichnen, Bemerken, Anmerken).

Ad o'culos, (Lat.) before one's eyes; Einem etwas — demonstriren, to convince one by ocular proof (Einen durch den Augenschein überzeugen).

A'dolf (A'dolph), m. Adolphus (P. N.).

* Ado'nis, (indecl., pl. sometimes str. Ado'nisse, cf. Hercules &c.) m. 1) Greek Mythol. Adonis; 2) a) Bot. a plant, particul. the Adonis autumnalis (—blume, f., —röschen), adonis, pheasant's eye; b) Gard. a fall kind of hyacinth; 3) Entom. a butterfly (Papilio adonis).

Ado'nisch, adj. Adō'nian, Adōn'ic; der a-e Vers, Adonic verse.

* Adonisi'ren, (w.) v. tr. (Fr. adoniser) to dress out or up, to deck out, to make fine; to bedizen.

* Adopti'ren, (w.) v. tr. (Lat.) to assume as one's own, to adopt, affiliate ([an Kindes Statt] annehmen). — Adoptiōn', Adoptatiōn', (w.) f. adoption, affiliation. — Adoptiv', adj. adoptive; Adoptivkind, -sohn, -tochter, -vater, -eltern, adoptive child, son, daughter, &c.

* Ados' [pr. adoh'], (indecl.) n. (Fr.) Hortic. a shelving (garden-)bed, parterre with a southerly direction (schräg auflaufendes [Garten-]Beet).

° Adoucement' [pr. adußmang'], (str., Gen. A-s, pl. A-s) n. (Fr.) (the act of giving) a sloping direction (Abdachung, Böschung). — Adouci'ren, (w.) v. tr. (Fr. adosser, to lean) to slope, to give a sloping direction (Abdachen, [Ab]böschen).

° Adouci'ren [pr. adußi'ren], (w.) v. tr. (Fr. adoucir, to sweeten) 1) Paint., &c. to soften, to sweeten; 2) T. to smooth down (rough edges, &c.), to polish; 3) to temper (steel, &c.).

° Adressant', (w.) m. the person addressing, the writer of a letter ([Brief-]Absender); Comm. the drawer. — Adressat', (w.) m. the person addressed, receiver of a letter ([Brief-]Empfänger); Comm. drawee.

Adreß..., in comp. —berathung, f. debate on a (political) address; —billet, n. address in case of need (Nothadresse); —buch, n. directory; handbook; —bureau, —comptoir, n. register office, office of intelligence or address; office of inquiry, intelligence-office; advertising-office.

° Adres'se, (w.) f. (Fr. adresse) 1) (Aufschrift, less usual Überschrift eines Briefes) direction (of a letter); superscription; address; 2) (Adreßzettel, Begleitadresse) label or letter bearing the address of a person, to accompany a parcel (to be) forwarded by the post to this person (in Germany); 3) Comm. firm; einen Brief, aber nicht von Josef, das sah man schon der Überschrift — auf deutsch „Adresse" — an (Polder, Nummernäffeen, 154), a letter, but not from Joseph, that was evident from the very superscription — in good German "address"; Ihre werthe — verdanke ich Herrn N., I am indebted for, or I owe your (esteemed) address to Mr. N., Mr. N. has favoured me with your address; ausführliche —, full address; — auf den Nothfall, address in case of need; der Brief war an meine — (i. e. an mich gerichtet), the letter was addressed to me; die Güter sind an die — des Herrn N. verladen, the goods are consigned to the address of Mr. N.; an die —, per —, (to the) care of ...; unter — des Herrn N., care of Mr. N.; senden Sie uns die Ballen unter — des Herrn J., send the bales through the medium of Mr. J.; befördern Sie den Brief an seine —, forward the letter to its destination; der Brief ist nie an seine — gelangt, the letter has never reached its destination; er gab mir seine —, he gave me his address; ich werde ihr meine — zurück- or hinterlassen, I shall leave her my direction; er nahm die — des fremden Herrn aus seiner Brieftasche, he took the strange gentleman's direction from his pocket-book; ohne —, (of a letter or parcel) without an address, undirected; 4) (political) address (to a constituted authority, &c.).

° Adressi'ren, (w.) v. I. tr. 1) to direct, to address (a letter), to superscribe; einen Brief richtig (falsch, undeutlich) —, to direct a letter properly (wrongly [to misdirect], illegibly); wenn Sie Gegenwärtiges beantworten, so — (imdr.) Sie: Venedig, poste restante, if you answer this, direct — Venice, poste restante; 2) to introduce by a letter; ich erlaube mir, diesen Freund an Sie zu — (Ihnen zu empfehlen), I take the liberty to recommend this friend to you; 3) Comm. to forward, consign (goods, &c.); wir — sämmtliche Colli an Sie (Rob. & Gr.), we send all the parcels to you; II. refl. (sich) abandonned, to address one's self (an Einen, to one), to apply (to ...).

Adreß..., in comp. —karte, f. address-card; —zettel, m. (auf Waaren rc.) label, ticket, docket; —zettelchen, n. (dimin. of the foregoing word) address in case of need (Nothadresse).

° Adroit', adj. (corrupted fr. the Fr. adroit) abandonned, 1) clever, skilful, adroit; 2) smart, neat, tidy; —machen, Sport. see Hochmachen.

Adria'tisch, adj. Adriatic; das a-e Meer, the Adriatic (Sea).

° Adritta'ra, (Mal.) see A dirittura.

° Adst..., in words fr. the Lat., see Ast ....

° Adstriction', (w.) f. (Lat.) adstriction, (particul. Med.) contraction (of the parts of the body). — Adstringi'ren, (w.) v. tr. to astringe (particul. Med.), to contract; a-d, astringent; a-de Mittel, pl. astringents.

° Adular', (str.) m. (from Mount Adula in Switzerland) Miner. adularia, a semi-transparent variety of feldspar (Kali-Feldspath), moonstone.

° Adulteri'ren, (w.) v. tr. (Lat. — I. m.) to adulterate (Verfälschen).

Ad valorem, (Lat.) according to the value (nach dem Werthe), on the value or price.

° Advent', (str.) m. (Lat. adventus, coming, arrival) advent; A-svogel, m. Ornith. ember diver; ember-goose, ammer-goose (Eistaucher, Colymbus immer).

° Adventiv', adj. adventitious, secondary. Adventuria'stein, see Aventurinstein.

° Adverb', (str., pl. sometimes w. A-en) Adver'bium, (str., pl. [Lat.] Adver'bia, Germ. [w.] Adver'bien) n. Gramm. adverb. — Adverbia'lisch, adj. adverbial; dies Wort ist — gebraucht, this word is used adverbially.

° Adversativ', adj. Gramm. adversative (sentences, particles, &c.).

° Advis', Avisi'ren rc., see Avis rc.

° Advocat', (w.) m. (Lat.) advocate (Sachwalter, Anwalt, Rechtsbeistand, Gerichtsbeistand, [Switz.] Fürsprech) pleader; lawyer, solicitor; counsel, counsellor; barrister(-at-law); defender, attorney; — (Anwalt) beim Handelsgericht, solicitor to the board of trade; einen A-en annehmen, to take a solicitor; ich werde die Klage einem A-en übergeben, I shall place the matter (action) in the hands of a lawyer.

Advocaten..., in comp. —gebühr, f. gener. in the pl. lawyer's fees; —kniff, m. lawyer's trick; —schreiber, m. attorney's or lawyer's clerk; —streich, m. lawyer's trick; —vorschuß, m. amount placed at the disposal of a lawyer by his client in a law case, lawyer's fees paid in advance.

° Advocatur', (w.) f. office, privilege or dignity of an advocate, pleader, lawyer, &c., advocateship.

° Advoci'ren [pr. advoß'—], (w.) v. intr. to practise as an advocate, to follow the law; to plead as an advocate.

A. E., abbr. for Archiepiscopus (Lat.), archbishop (Erzbischof).

° Aerat', (str.) n. Chem. aerated water.

° A'ero..., in comp. —dyna'mik, f. aerodynamics; —graph', (w.) m. aerographer; —graphie', (w.) f. aerography; —lith', (str. & w.) m. aerolite, meteoric stone, or mineral mass; —log', (w.) m. aerologer, one versed in aerology; —logie, (w.) f. aerology; —mantie', (w.) f. aeromancy; —mecha'nik, (w.) f. pneumatics (Pneumatik); —mecha'nisch, adj. pneumatic; —mechanische Presse, see Luftpresse; —me'ter, (str.) m. aerometer (Luftmesser); —metrie', (w.) f. aerometry (Luftmeßkunst); —naut', (w.) m. aeronaut (Luftschiffer); aerial navigator, one who sails or floats in the air (applied to persons who ascend in air-balloons); —nau'tik, (w.) f. aeronautics; —nau'tisch, adj. aeronautic, aeronautical; —phobie', (w.) f. aerophobia (Luftscheu), a dread of air (occasional symptom of hydrophobia); —phyt', (w.) m. Bot. aerophyte: 1) a plant which derives its sustenance from the air (Luftpflanze); 2) see Ektrosphyt; —skopie', (w.) f. aeroscopy, investigation of the air; —sit', (str.) m. Miner. aerosite, a dark, scaly kind of red-silver-ore in

[illegible]mana, the monkey tribe: —gesicht, n. 1) ape's face, monkey-face; 2) Bot. a genus of plants of the order of Sapotaceæ, particul. the *Mimusops elengi* of Ceylon: —haft, adj. apish, monkey-like: —jacke, f. coll. monkey-jacket; —knabenkraut, n. Bot. the *Orchis morio*; —könig, m. a species of Brazilian monkey (mandrill?); —liebe, f. apish, i. e. blind partiality (as of parents for their children), dotage: —mäßig, adj. see —artig; —miene, f. apish features, mien, or face; —musa, f. Bot. a species of plantain (*Musa troglodytarum*); —nase, f. monkey's nose, flat nose; —nasig, adj. flat-nosed; —pisang, m. see —musa; —posse, f. monkey-trick (cf. Narrenspossen); —prediger, m. Zool. a species of Brazilian ape (*Mycetes guariba*); —schädel, m. 1) skull of an ape; 2) Bot. a species of snap-dragon (*Antirrhinum orontium*); —schande, f. coll. a very great shame; —schwanz, m. 1) tail of an ape or monkey; 2) fig. a) einen —schwanz führen, coll. † to cheat, deceive, to bamboozle, to humbug; b) aa) a droll or foolish fellow, trifler, tomfool; bb) an affected person, prig, fop (Zieraffe); —spiel, n. apishness, apish tricks, monkeyism, foolery; —sprung, m. gambol; in gymnastics, a kind of backward-leap; —stein, m. see —bezoar; —topf, Bot. a South American plant, *Lecythis ollaria* (with a fruit as large as a child's head, opening by a lid, like a jar or urn); —weibchen, n. (dimin.) female of the monkey, she-monkey, she-ape; —wurm, m. Entom. Guinea-worm (*Filar.*).

Äfferei', (w.) f. 1) a) the act or habit of aping, cf. äffen; mimicry; b) apish behaviour, monkey-tricks; 2) trickery, delusion, mockery, hoax.

Affholder, see Affolter.

* Affiche [pr. affisch'e], (w.) f. (Fr. affiche) † bill posted up, handbill (Anschlagezettel).

* Affichi'ren [pr. affischi'ren], (w.) v. tr. (Fr. afficher) † 1) to stick up, to post up; to paste up (Ankleben, Anschlagen; Aushängen); 2) fig. to advertise, to make a show of, to expose (zur Schau tragen).

* Affici'ren, (w.) v. tr. (Lat.) to affect (Bewegen, schmerzlich rc.) Berühren, Ergreifen, Angreifen, Rühren rc.). — Afficir'bar, adj. (easily, &c.) to be affected, susceptible (Reizbar, Angreifbar, Empfindlich).

* Affidation', (w.) f. †, a mutual contract or oath of fidelity († affidation).

* Affigi'ren, (w.) v. tr. (Lat.) to affix, to stick up, &c. see Affichiren.

* Affiliation', (w.) f. (Low Lat.) 1) affiliation, adoption; 2) association, union. — Affilii'ren, (w.) v. tr. 1) to affiliate, adopt; 2) to associate, unite (with ...).

Äffin, (w., pl. Äffinnen) f. (from Affe) female of the monkey, she-monkey, she-ape.

* Affineur' [pr. —nör], (str.) m. refiner (of metals), gold-refiner, parter (Goldscheider).

* Affinage [pr. —nahsch], (w.) f., Affinerie', (w.) f. (Fr. affinage, affinerie) the act of fining, refining, &c., particul. the process of refining metals by the cupel (Läuterung rc.).

* Affingi'ren, (w.) v. tr. (Lat.) to devise in addition; to attribute, impute, (falsely) to ascribe (Andichten, Aufbürden rc.).

* Affinir' ..., in comp. Metall. —cement, m. royal cement (used in assay-furnaces); —cirkel, m. refining-compass; —gefäß, n. fining-pot; —wasser, n. aqua fortis (Scheidewasser).

* Affini'ren, (w.) v. tr. (Fr. affiner) to refine (particul. Metall.). — Affinir'er, m. refiner.

* Affinität', (w.) f. affinity (also Chem., [illegible]).

* [illegible], (w.) f. (Lat.) affirmation [illegible].

[illegible], I. adj. affirmative (opp. Negativ) [illegible] affirmative proposition; II. [illegible] affirmative (bejahende Meinung).

Äffisch, adj. apish, monkey-like (Affenartig).

* Affix', (str.) n. (Lat.) Gramm. affix, a syllable or something united to the end of a word, postfix (Suffix).

Äfflich, adj. (unusual) see Affenartig.

* Affluí'ren, (w.) v. intr. (aux. sein) (Lat.) to flow to (Zufließen, Zuströmen). — Affluenz', (w.) f. a flowing to ..., flowing in, afflux (Zufluß, das Zuströmen).

Affner, see Afner.

* Affodill', (str.) m. Bot. (—lilie, —wurz) 1) asphodel-lily (*Asphodelus*); 2) day-lily, daffodill (*hemerocallis*).

Affol'ter (Afhol'der, Apfol'ter), (str.) m. 1) († &) provinc. (in Bavaria) appletree; 2) a) water-elder (Wasserholder), guelder-rose (Gerlderholder, Rosenholder) (*Viburnum opulus*); b) (Affol'le, [w.] f., Mistel) mistletoe (*Viscum album*).

Affrusch, (str.) m. corrupted from abrotanum, see Aberraute.

* Affusion', (w.) f. (Lat.) affusion.

Afhol'der, see Affolter.

Af'ner, (str.) m. 1) (or Affner) Spinn. see Öffner, 2; 2) see After, B.

A'frica, A'frika, n. Africa (P. N.). — Africa'ner, (str.) m., Africa'nerin, (w.) f. an African. — Africa'nisch, adj. African.

Af'rusch, see Affrusch.

A. Af'ter, I. prep. † after, behind (with Dat., and, exceptionally, with Acc.); II. as an adv. in comp. still in use, signifying 1) behind in place or order, as —mind, —bürge, —erbe, —lehen rc.; 2) later in time, following, subsequent, as —geburt, —kind rc.; 3) denoting anything imitated, similar or approaching to some original (—siegel, —kugel rc.), particul. an imperfect imitation, false formation, anything inferior, not genuine, pseudo- (—blatt rc., —poet rc.).

B. Af'ter, s. (str.) I. m. 1) Anat. anus; 2) coll. backside, buttocks; 3) Ornith. part of the body of birds between the legs and the tail (Untersteiß, *crissum*); 4) Saddl. (or Äfter, Efter, Afner, Achter) the protuberant part of a saddle behind, cantle; II. n. (& m.) among workmen of different trades: the inferior parts of a thing, waste matter, refuse, offal; 1) (or —mehl, Afner, Achter) Mill. mill-dust, coarse flour, see —mehl; 2) (or Äfterig, Afterig, Geafter, Achterste) a) Husb. the grain remaining behind in winnowing; b) chaff, dust, litter (Abrechling); 3) Butch. garbage, the bowels of an animal, offal, refuse; 4) Metall. residue, &c., see —erz.

After ..., in comp. —aaskäfer, Entom. the same as Glanzkäfer; —abscess, m. Anat. abscess of the anus; —advocat, m. back (i. e. hired or low) attorney, inferior lawyer, pettifogger; —ahorn, m. Bot. bastard or false sycamore *Acer pseudoplatanus*, a species of maple, the plane-tree of Scotland, called sycamore in England); —alabaster, m. Miner. a kind of inferior, untransparent alabaster; —alaun, m. artificial alum, particul. saccharine alum (Zuckeralaun); —ameise, f. Entom. hymenopterous insect (*Mutilla* Latr., Bastardameise); —anwalt, m. 1) substitute attorney, deputy-attorney; 2) see —advocat; —arzt, m. medicaster, pretender to medicine, quack, charlatan; —belehnte, m. & f. under-feudatory, see —lehnsmann; —belehnung, f. subinfeudation, act of enfeoffing by a tenant or feoffee, who holds lands of the crown; —beredtsamkeit, f. false eloquence, bombast; —biene, f. see Bienenameise; —bier, n. small beer (Dritte swipes); —bildung, f. a formation foreign to the species to which a thing belongs, irregular or anomalous formation or structure of parts, malformation, pseudomorphous or unnatural organization, deformity (particul. with respect to the organization of the human body); —binde, f. Surg. bandage used in anal diseases (Mastdarmbinde); —birkhuhn, n. see Bastardbirkhuhn; —blatt, n., dimin. —blättchen, n. stipula, stipule (a leafy appendage to the proper leaves, or to their footstalks; commonly situated at the base of the latter in pairs); mit —blättchen versehen, stipulaceous; —blattlaus, f. Entom. a genus of minute hemipterous insects (*psylla*), allied to the aphides, or plantlice; —blume, f. see —flaue; —blutfluß, m. Med. discharge of blood from the anus, particul. in hemorrhoidal diseases; hemorrhoids; —blutflüssig, adj. suffering of discharge of blood from the anus, hemorrhoidal; —blutkraut, n. (After, A. II. 3) Bot. common or garden burnet, salad-burnet (gemeine Becherblume, Nagelkraut, Großsterbenkraut, Sperberkraut; *Poterium sanguisorba*); —bockkäfer, m. Entom. wasp-beetle (*Leptura*, Schmalbockkäfer); —bremse, f. Entom. a kind of gadfly (*Oestrus hemorrhoidalis*, —kriecher); —bürde, f. († &) Sport. (of deer) see —geburt; —bürge, m. (After, A. II. 1) second bail, counter-bail (Gegenbürge, Rückbürge); —bürgschaft, f. counter-surety (Gegenbürgschaft); —camille, f. Bot see Feldcamille; —christ, m. false christian, pretended christian, pseudo-christian; —christus, m. (Vans) a poor imitation of Christ, pseudo-Christ; —cicade, f. Entom. see Schaumcicade; —crystall, n. Miner. pseudomorphous crystal (Pseudocrystall); —darm, m. Anat. strait gut (Mastdarm); —deich, m. secondary embankment (cf. Binnendeich); —denker, m. pseudo-thinker, pretender to philosophy (—philosoph); —diamant, m. Miner crystallised hyaline quartz; Bot. —dolde, f. cyma, cyme, tuft, sprout (Trugdolde); —doldenförmig, —doldig, adj. cymoid, cymose, cymous; —doldentragend, adj. cymiferous, bearing cymes; —dotter, m. gold of pleasure, see Dotterkraut; —drohne, f. (After, A. II. 3) small imperfect drone (a drone not having attained to full growth on account of the cold); —einsetzung, f. Law, entail; —entzündung, f. Med. inflammation of the anus (*proctitis*); —erbe, m. substitute-heir; —erz, n. Metall. residue, remains of milled ore, bottom; —falke, m. Ornith. (der große Würger, Neuntödter) the greater shrike or butcher-bird (sometimes trained like a hawk); —falte, f. see —gefälle; —feder, f. Ornith. anal feather; —finne, f. Ichth. anal fin; —fissur, f. Med. fissure of the anus (Schrunde am After); —fistel, f. Med. fistula of the anus (Mastdarmfistel); —flinz, m. Miner. common quartz mixed with lime-clay (Tolh.); —flosse, f. see —finne; —flügel, m. Ornith. bastard wing; —fluß, m. Med. proctorrhœa, (continued) flow (of blood or mucus) from the anus; —fratt, m. Med. intertrigo, excoriation about the anus (attended with inflammation and moisture); —füße, m. pl. Entom. prolegs, spurious legs (assisting various larvæ in walking and other motions, but disappearing in the perfect insect); —gebilde, n. irregular formation or structure, malformation, see —bildung; —geburt, f. Med. 1) (After, A. II. 2) after-birth (Nachgeburt); 2) (After, B. I.) see Steißgeburt; —gefälle, n. Min. rump; —gefinse, n. Metall. 1) or —flut, Herdflut, f. residue of milled or washed ore, bottom; 2) or —graben, m. rump-canal (Tolh.); —gelehrsamkeit, f. pretended learning; —gelehrte, m. & f. pretender to learning; —gemß, (Tolh. —gäms) m. Miner. common quartz mixed with schörl; —geschwulst, f. Med. tumour of the anus; —geschwür, n. Med. ulcer; abscess of the anus; —getreide, n. see —korn; —gewächs, n. Med. anal excrescence; —glaube, m. false, wrong or erroneous belief, superstition (Aberglaube); —glimmer, m. Miner. micaceous schist with garnets; —gold, n. false gold

(gold with an alloy of three fourths of the weight); —granit, m. *Miner.* heap of impalpable powder (*Tölh.*), granitic aggregate; —größe, f. pretended greatness; —gräßling, m. *Miner.* common feldspar mixed with quartz; —hase, m. (*lit.* pseudo-hare, *cf.* After, *A*, II. 3) the guinea-pig; —heu, n. after-grass, second crop of grass, aftermath (Grummet); —holz, n. dead-wood, windfallen wood (Abholz); —holzbock, m. *Entom.* pseudo-cerambyx or capricorn-beetle (*Necydalis*); —horn, n. horn-like excrescence, cornicle; —hüfner, m. *see* —lehnsmann; —hummel, f. *see* —drohne.

Afterricht, Afterig, Afterig, (*obs.*) *m.* see After, *B*, II. 2.

After..., *in comp.* —jucken, n. *Med.* itching or irritation about the *sphincter ani*; *Entom.-s.* —jungfer, f. *Entom.* see Ameisenjungfer; —käfer, m. proscarab, *see* Maiwurm; —kameel, n. *Zool.* alpaca (forming an *aberrant* group of the camel family), *see* Lama, Guanaco; —kamille, *see* —camille; —kaninchen, n. *Zool.* guinea-pig, *see* Meerschweinchen; —kegel, m. *Geom.* conoid (*i. e.* that which resembles a cone); —kegelartig, —kegelförmig, *adj.* *Geom.* conoidic, conoidical, conoidal, approaching to a conic form; —kiel, m. false keel; —kind, n. 1) posthumous child; 2) *a*) bastard child; *b*) *Med.* mole, mooncalf; —klaue, f. the bones or little nails behind a deer's, &c. foot; dewclaws; —knoten, m. (After, *B*, I. 1) *Med.* hemorrhoidal tumour; —kobalt, m. *Miner.* pseudo-cobalt, arsenical nickel; —kohle, f. 1) (erdige —kohle) alumen, alumina, lignitic earth (Alaunerde, Erdkohle); 2) (holzige —kohle) bituminous wood; 3) poor, mean coal, small coals, dust of coals; —könig, m. pseudo-king, pretended king, pretender; —königin, f. pretended queen, pseudo-queen; —korn, n. 1) the grain remaining behind in winnowing; 2) blighted corn, ergot (Mutterkorn); —kräuling, m. *Miner.* see —schörl; —krebs, m. *Med.* cancerous ulcer of the rectum or fundament (Mastdarmkrebs); —kriecher, m. *see* —bremse; —kritiker, m. would-be critic; literary hack; —krystall, *see* —crystall; —kugel, f. (After, *A*, II. 3) spheroid (Sphäroid); —kugelicht, *adj.* spheroidal, spheroidic, spheroidical; —lähmung, f. *Med.* paralysis of the *sphincter ani*; —läufer, m. *Metall.* conveyor at the crushing-machine (*Tölh.*); —lauge, f. *Curr.* lye for ungreasing the leather; —leder, n. 1) heel-piece inside; 2) tawed skin; 3) chips of leather; —lehen, —lehn, n. *Feudal Law*, mesne tenure, mesne fief, arriere fee, rere- (or rear-)fief, under-fief (fief held of a superior feudatory); —lehner, m. *Feudal Law.* 1) tenant of a mesne fief, under-tenant, vavasor; 2) *see* —lehnsherr; —lehnsherr, m. *Feudal Law*, mesne-lord, mean lord; —lehnsmann, —lehnsträger, m. *Feudal Law*, under-feudatory, arriere-(or rear-)vassal, tenant-paravail, under-tenant; —lehnspflichtig, *adj.* *Feudal Law*, subject to a mesne lord, liable to under-tenancy; —lehnsverhältniß, n. *Feudal Law*, subinfeudation, under-tenancy; —lehre, f. erroneous, false, or wrong doctrine, heterodoxy (Irrlehre); —lehrer, m. one who teaches false or wrong doctrine, heterodox teacher (Irrlehrer); —leuchtkäfer, m. *see* Johanniswürmchen; —made, f. *Entom.* ascaris (Springwurm, Mastdarmwurm); —marl, m. *Miner.* common quartz with schörl and garnets; —mehl, n. mill-dust, pollards, coarse flour (remaining behind, after the better parts have been sifted off, termed *seconds* by Shakespeare); —mensch, m. degenerate man or human being; —miethe, f. second-hand hire or renting; —miethsmann, m. after- (or under-)tenant, one who hires, rents or takes (a lodging, &c.) second hand; —milz, f. *Med.* splenoidal tumour; —montag, m. † the day following Monday, Tuesday; —moos, n. *Bot.* *lit.* pseudo-moss, *gener.* in the *pl.* algæ, sea-weeds; —motte, f. a genus of lepidopterous insects: *galleria*; —möwe, f. *Ornith.* sea-swallow, *see* Seeschwalbe; —münze, f. *Bot.* a genus of herbaceous plants, *Monarda didyma*; —muse, f. false muse; —muskel, f. *Anat.* anal muscle; —mutter, f. unnatural mother, stepmother.

Aftern, (*w.*) *f. pl.* *Sport.* see Afterklauen.

After..., *in comp.* —nachtigall, f. *Ornith.* mock-nightingale, *see* Blattmönch; —nymphe, f. *Entom.* imperfect nymph or chrysalis; —organ, n. irregular or anomalous form, unnatural organ; —organisation, f. *see* —bildung; —pacht, m. under-tenancy; in —pacht geben, to underlet, sublet; —pachter, —pächter, m. under-farmer, under-tenant; —pachtländereien, f. subletting lands; —papst, m. pretended pope, anti-pope; —pfand, n. counterpledge; —philosoph, m. pseudo-philosopher; —philosophie, f. pseudo-philosophy (—weisheit); —philosophisch, *adj.* pseudo-philosophic (—weise); —raupe, f. *Entom.* pseudo-caterpillar (caterpillar with more than sixteen feet), *particul.* the larva of *tenthredo* (Blattwespe); —raupentödter, m. *see* —wespe; —rede, f. (*lit.* the act of speaking behind a person, Nachrede) *obsolescent*, slander, backbiting; —reden, *v. intr.* (*lit.* to speak behind a person, Einem [Übles] nachreden; Einem, von Einem, über Einen or etwas, gegen Einen) *obsolescent*, to slander, backbite, to speak or talk ill of (one whose back is turned so as not to be able to hear), to traduce secretly, to calumniate; —reder, —redner, m. (*from* —reden) *obsolescent*, backbiter, slanderer, &c.; —rente, f. under-rent; —sabbath, m. 1) the day after the sabbath (*cf.* —montag); 2) the first sabbath after the second day of the passover; —schabe, f. *see* —motte; —schanze, f. *Fortif.* redoubt (Feldschanze); —schirmherr, m. *see* —lehnsherr; —schlacke, f. *Metall.* twice tried scoria, twice refined slag; —schlag, m. the act of felling underwood, or the loppings of brushwood in a forest where timber is cut or felled (Abraum); —schlich, m. *Metall.* slich prepared from the residue of milled ore; —schmetterling, m. *Entom.* may-fly, *see* Köcherjungfer; —schörl, m. *Miner.* sianite, axinite, violet shorl, yanolite, thumer-stone; —schwarm, m. *T.* the second swarming of bees; —scorpion, m. *Entom.* pseudo-scorpion (Arachnidian); —siedler, m. *see* —lehnsmann; —silber, n. false or impure silver, silver containing dross; —sohn, m. posthumous male child (son), &c., *see* —kind; —sperre, f. *Med.* stricture of the anus (*tenesmus ani*), *cf.* Stuhlzwang; —spiegel, m. *Surg.* *speculum ani*, an instrument for distending and obtaining a view of the anus, dilator of the anus; —spinne, f. *Entom.* shepherd-spider (*Phalangium*, Weberknecht); —sprache, f. 1) †. *see* —rede; 2) spurious language; —stein, m. *Miner.* artificial gem, paste; —stück, n. *Saddl.* cantle, back part of a saddle; —sturmhaube, f. *Mollusc.* leaf-whelk; —theolog(e), m. pseudo-theologian; —thräne, f. *see* —drohne; —topas, m. *Miner.* Bohemian brown topaz; —vasall, m. *see* —lehnsmann; —verhör, n. mock trial; —vermiether, —verpachter, m. under-letter; —vermiethung, f. (the act of) under-letting; —verschließung, f. *see* —sperre; —vorfall, m. (After, *B*, I. 1) *Med.* a prolapse or falling down of the rectum (Mastdarmvorfall); —walze, f. (After, *A*, II. 3) *Geom.* cylindroid (Cylindroid); —wasserwanze, f. *see* Wasserscorpion; —weise, I. *adj.* pretendedly wise; sophistic; II. *s.* (*decl. like adj.*) *m.* & *f.* (After, *A*, II. 3) pretended sage, pseudo-philosopher, philosophaster; sophist; wiseacre; —weisel, m. second queen-bee in a hive; —weisheit, f. pretended or spurious wisdom; over-wiseness; —welt, f. *obsolescent* & *poet.* 1) after-ages, posterity (Nachwelt); 2) degenerate race (*cf.*

[zusammenhäufung]; —zustand, m. condition of aggregation. — Aggregi'ren, (w.) v. tr. 1) to aggregate (Zusammenhäufen); 2) to admit, receive into a public body, to annex to, incorporate with (Beigeben, Zutheilen), particul. Mil. to attach (an officer) to a regiment for the purpose of supplying future vacancies: aggregirt, supernumerary.

* Aggreß', (str.) m., Aggressión', (w.) f. aggression, first attack, or act of hostility (Angriff). — Aggressiv', adj. aggressive (Angreifend, angriffsweise).

* Agi'de, (w.) f. (Greek aigis, Gen. aigidos, a goat skin, and shield) 1) ægis, the shield of Jupiter or Minerva; 2) a breast-plate, coat of mail, or shield of a god, particul. of Minerva; 3) fig. a shield, or means of defence, shelter, protection.

Agi'dius, m. (P. N.) Ægidius, coll. Giles.

Aginet', (w.) m. Æginetan, inhabitant of Ægina (Old Greece).

Agine'tisch, adj. Æginetan.

* Agio [with Fr. pr. a'zhio], (str., Gen. A-s or Agio, pl. A-s) n. (orig. from the Ital. aggio, a differentiated form of agio, Fr. aise, E. ease, comfort; a consideration given in exchange) Comm. agio, sum (premium) given above the nominal value (Aufgeld); ich mußte .. als — (beim Geldwechsel) zahlen, I had to pay ... by way of change; mit hohem — in Cours sein, to be currently saleable at a high premium. — Agiota'ge [azhiotä'zhe], (w.) f. (Fr.) Comm. stock-jobbing, jobbing, gambling in the funds. — Agioteur' [azhiotör'], (str. pl. A-s, A-e) m. (Fr.) stock-jobber, (money-) jobber. — Agioti'ren, (w.) v. intr. (aux. haben) (Fr. agioter) to play (gamble) in the funds, stocks.

* Agi'ren, (w.) v. intr. (aux. sein) & tr. (Lat. agere, to act) 1) (Handeln) to act (also to perform a part on the stage, to mimic (Spielen, Darstellen); 2) Mil. to manoeuvre (Manövriren).

* A'gis, f. see Agide.

* Agitatión', (w.) f. (Lat.) agitation. — Agita'tor, (str., pl. w. Agitato'ren) m. agitator (Aufreger, gener. in a bad sense: Unruhstifter, Aufrührer, Wühler). — Agiti'ren, (w.) v. tr. to agitate (in Bewegung setzen, aufregen, erregen, cont. wühlen).

Ag'leikraut, (str.) n. the same as Ackerhauhechel.

Ag'laster, Ag'elaster, Ag'elster, A'laster, Al'ster, (w.) f. provinc. for Elster (magpie).

Ag'lei, Aglei'(e), (w.) f. & m. (Low Germ. forms: Akelei, Ackelei, Akerlei &c.) Bot. columbine, culverkey (Aquilegia vulgaris).

Ag'lerkraut, n. see Agleikraut.

* Agnat', (w.) m. Germ. Law, agnate, male relation by the father's side (Schwertmage). — Agnatión', (w.) f. kindred or descent by the father's side, or from the same father in the male line. — Agna'tisch, adj. agnatic, related by descent from the father.

Ag'nes, Ag'nese, f. (P. N.) Agnes; sometimes used for a simple girl, simpleton, fr. the part of Agnes in Molière's École des femmes.

* Agnitión', (w.) f. (Lat.) Law, &c. acknowledgment, recognizance.

* Agnosci'ren, (w.) v. tr. (Lat.) to acknowledge, recognize (Anerkennen).

* Ag'nus Dei, (Lat.) Rom. Cath. the Lamb of God (das Lamm Gottes), i. e. Christ (according to St. John's Revelation).

* [illegible], (w.) f. [illegible] alburn, see Fauchen.

* Agonie', (w.) f. (Greek agonia, a struggle) agony, death-struggle, pangs of death (Todeskampf, Todesangst). — Agonisi'ren, (w.) v. intr. (aux. haben) to suffer dying agonies (mit dem Tode ringen).

* Agraf'fe, (w.) f. (Fr.) hook (to some [illegible]) clasp.

* Agra'risch, adj. (Lat.) agrarian; das a-e Gesetz, see Ackergesetz.

* Agrest', (Lat.) I. adj. agrestic; rustic; rude; II. (str.) m. juice of unripe grapes, verjuice.

* Agricultur', (w.) f. agriculture, see Ackerbau.

* Agrimo'nie, (w.) f. (Low Lat., fr. Gr. argemonia) Bot. agrimony (Agrimonia eupatoria).

Agrippi'nisch, adj. Agrippine, relating to Agrippa (i. e. one born with the feet foremost); a-e Geburt, see Fußgeburt.

* Agronom', (w.) m. (Gr.) agricultural theorist, agriculturist. — Agronomie', (w.) f. agronomy, theory of agriculture. — Agrono'misch, adj. agronomic, agricultural.

* Agrypnie', (w.) f. (Gr.) Med. watchfulness, sleeplessness.

Ag'ster, (w.) f. see Aglaster

Ag'ter, see Achter, B.

Agt (contr. from Agat), in comp. —käfer, m. Entom. a coleopterous insect, the lenthyria (Latr.); —stein, m. (MHG. aget-stein, a blackish stone, from agate for gagate, i. e. Greek gagates, bituminous anthracite, the agate, gagate, amber, and magnet being often confounded in the Middle Ages, on account of their power of attraction) amber (Bernstein).

Agur'ke, (w.) f. the obsolete form of Gurke.

* Agu'ti, (str., pl. A-s) n. Zool. agouti (a rodent animal in South Am., &c., Dasyprocta aguti Illig.).

Ägyp'ten, (str.) n. Geogr. Egypt.

Ägyp'ter, Ägyp'tier, (str.) m. (A-in, (w.) f.) Egyptian. — Ägyp'tisch, adj. Egyptian.

A. Ah, (w.) f. see Aa.

B. Ah! interj. I. if pr. short, and approaching to Ach, it expresses contempt and quick, impatient rejection, ah! pooh! poh! pshaw! pish! II. Ah! an exclamation of surprise, real or feigned, ah! less frequently expressive of pain.

A. Aha'! interj. (exclamation of [often ironical] surprise) aha! oho!

B. Aha'! (str., pl. A-s) n. aha, haha, a sunk fence, bank or ditch not seen till close upon it (Haha).

Ah'bele! interj. provinc. (S. G. — Auerbach, see Sanders, who compares Acheli) diminutive of Ah!

Ahi'! (from Ital. & Fr. ahi, although in those languages orig. an exclamation of pain) interj. oh! expressive of joy or happy surprise.

A. Ahl, (str.), Ahln, (sing. & pl. alike) m. provinc. 1) dung-water, see Adel, A; 2) (in the western part of middle Germany) confined space between houses, alley.

B. Ahl, (str.) m. see Ahle.

Ahl'baum, m. (Aalbaum) see Heckenkirsche.

Ahl'beere, (w.) f. see Alantbeere.

Ahl'borste, (w.) f. Bot acicular bristle (Pfriemborste).

Ah'le, (w.) f. awl (syn. Pfriem).

Ah'len..., in comp. —förmig, adj. particul. Bot. (of leaves) awl-shaped, acuminated, tapering to a point; —heft, n. handle of an awl, awl-handle; —käfer, m. (from Ahl, A) Entom. a kind of carrion-beetle (Aaskäfer); —macher, —schmidt, m. awl-maker, awl-smith.

Ahl'kirsche, (w.) f. see Aalkirsche.

Ahl'horn, see Aalshorn.

Ahm, (w.) f. 1) awm, a liquid measure, see Ohm, which is more usual at present; 2) or Ah'ming, (w.) f. Mar. gauge of the draught of a ship (for which purpose the feet are marked on the stem and sternpost from the keel upwards).

Ah'men, (w.) v. tr. 1) provinc. (Bavaria) to gauge (a cask, barrel, &c.), to measure (a cask, &c.) with respect to its contents; 2) fig. († except in the compound nachahmen) to imitate.

Ah'ming, (w.) f. see Ahm, 2.

Ahn, (sing. str., pl. w. Ah'nen), Ah'ne, (w.) m. ancestor, grandsire, progenitor, forefather; A-en, pl. ancestry; adelige A-en, descents; von vierzehn A-en, of fourteen descents; man erwartete, daß der Yankee vor der Zurechtweisung von Adeligen mit sechzehn A-en erzittern würde, the Yankee was expected to quail before the rebuke of nobles with their sixteen quarterings; er hat die meisten A-en, he has the oldest pedigree.

Ähn, Äh'ni, Eh'ni, provinc. (Swiss.) for Ahn.

Ahnd, (w.) m. see And.

Ahn'den, (w.) v. tr. 1) to resent, revenge, visit (with punishment), punish; 2) formerly sometimes used for Ahnen, which see.

Ahn'dung, (w.) f. 1) resentment, revenge, vengeance, visitation, punishment; 2) formerly used for Ahnung, which see.

Ahn'denswürdig, adj. worthy to be punished (Strafwürdig)

Ahn'devoll, adj. (Göthe) for Ahnungsvoll.

A. Ah'ne, I. (w.) m. see Ahn; II. (w.) f. (cf. Ahn) grandmother; ancestress, foremother.

B. Ah'ne, (w.) f. a provinc. contraction of Agen.

C. Ah'ne, prep. † (Luther, &c.) for Ohne, without.

Äh'neln, (w.) v. I. tr. (& refl.) (I. u.) to make similar to a certain degree, to assimilate; II. intr. (aux. haben) to be somewhat similar (Einem or einer Sache [Dat.], to...), to resemble to a certain degree, to bear some resemblance or similitude (to).

Ah'nen, (w.) v. tr. & intr. (impers.) (aux. haben) 1) to feel a secret sense of (something future), to anticipate, to have a presentiment of; to augur, to forebode, to guess, to divine; to surmise; to be prescient of, to presage, to foreknow: es ahnet mir (Klopstock, unusual: mich ahndet), my mind gives me; es ahnet mir ein schweres Unglück, my heart forebodes a sad reverse; es ahnet mir nichts Gutes, my mind misgives me; mir ahnet, daß er es ist, my heart tells me it is he; sein Besuch ließ mich nichts Gutes —, his visit boded me no good; alles das ahnte ich schon dunkel, ich konnte es nur nicht aussprechen, all that floated across me before, only I could not say it; die Stärke seiner Gefühlserregungen wurde von der Welt nicht geahnt, the strength of his emotions was not suspected by the world: und lauter immer wird die Frage, | und a-d fliegt's mit Blitzesschlage | durch alle Herzen (Schiller, Kran. d. Ibycus). (Bulwer) Questions on questions louder press | like lightning flies the inspiring guess | leaps every heart; einen ungünstigen Ausgang —, to suspect (foresee) an unfavourable result: wie konnte ich das auch —! how could I guess (foresee) that! how could I anticipate such a result! — lassen, to foreshadow: der Knabe ließ den Mann —, the boy gave augury of the man; die nichts a-den Commissäre gingen gerade über den Pulverfässern umher, the unconscious commissioners were walking about just over the barrels of gunpowder; 2) (Göthe, unusual) to feel a painful, powerful yearning, cf. And.

Ah'nen, v. s. (str.) n. foreboding, presentiment, see Ahnung.

Äh'nen, (w.) v. intr. L. u. for Ähneln.

Ah'nen..., in comp. —bild, n. image or portrait of an ancestor; —dünkel, m. overbearing, conceited pride of ancestry; —glanz, m. splendour of ancestry or noble descent; —probe, f. proof of noble descent, of nobility or gentility; —recht, n. prerogative founded upon ancestry; —reihe, f. line of ancestors.

Ah'nenschaft, (w.) f. ancestry; noble descent.

Ah'nen..., in comp. —stolz, I. adj. proud of ancestry; II. m. pride of ancestry or pedigree; —tafel, f. table of ancestry, pedigree: —zeit, *f.* time of ancestors, ancestral age (*Wenzel*).

Ahn'..., *in comp.* —frau, *f.* grandmother: ancestress, foremother: —herr, *m.* grandsire, ancestor, forefather, *see* Ahn; —herrlich, *adj.* ancestral, according to the fashion of one's ancestors *or* forefathers.

Äh'nl, *provinc. see* Ahn.

Ahn'lich, *adj.* (*Voss. l. u.*) ancestral.

Ähn'lich, *adj.* like (einer Person oder Sache [*Dat.*], a person or thing), similar (to ...), resembling: agreeing: analogous: *in Geom.* &c. ä-e Figuren, similar (rectilineal) figures; ä-e Körper, similar solids: ä-e Glieder einer Gleichung, *Algebr.* equal terms of an equation: ä-e Begriffe, Ausdrücke, analogical ideas, analogous expressions (terms): einem großen Zelte — eingerichtet, arranged in imitation of a large tent: ä-e Umstände, similar or analogous cases, circumstances: bei ä-en Gelegenheiten, on similar (such) occasions: was würden Sie in einem ä-en Falle thun? (*Hilpert*), what would you do in a like case, or under similar circumstances? der Geist erfaßt bald seinen Gegenstand, indem er die Verschiedenheiten sowol als das Ä-e entdeckt, the mind soon grasps its subject, discovering the points of diversity as well as of similarity; —machen, to make similar (*with Dat.*, to ...), to assimilate: — werden, to grow like (a person or thing), to take after: — sein *or* sehen (Einem &c.), to be *or* look like, to come near, to resemble (one, &c.), to have *or* bear resemblance (*fig.* an analogy to): sich einander — sein, to resemble one another: sieht er nicht seinem Bruder recht —? does he not look very much like his brother? er sieht sich nicht mehr —, he does not look like himself any more, there are no traces left of his former self; er sah sich gar nicht mehr —, (of a person in a rage, &c.) he had entirely altered his looks: das sieht ihm —, this looks or is like him, that was to be expected from him; gestern war er sich (*Dat.*) gar nicht —, he was not himself yesterday, he was unlike his usual self yesterday: dies sieht einem seiner Streiche sehr —, this is very much like one of his tricks.

Ähn'lichen, (*w.*) *v. tr. & intr. obsolescent*, to make or to be similar (to), &c. *see* Ähneln, *which has supplanted this word.*

Ähn'lichgleich, *adj. Geom.* similar.

Ähn'lichkeit, (*w.*) *f.* 1) likeness, resemblance, similitude; similarity; — haben mit ... (*cf.* ähnlich sein), to bear resemblance to ...; to bear an analogy to ...: 2) (Analogie) analogy, agreement: der Ä-sbeweis, analogical proof, the argument by analogy: das Ä-sgesetz, the law of analogy: der Ä-sgrund, analogical reason, analogism: die Ä-sregel, analogy: der Ä-sschluß, reasoning by analogy, analogism: Ä-szeichen, *n. Math.* sign of analogy (*different from* Gleichheitszeichen).

Ähn'lichmachung, **Ähn'lichung**, (*w.*) *f.* the act of making similar, conformation after the likeness of some original, assimilation.

Ah'nung, (*w.*) *f.* (*from* Ahnen, *which see*) 1) presentiment, anticipation, presage: (besonders schlimme, üble:) foreboding, misgiving: sie selbst hatten keine — davon, they themselves had no suspicion of it: sie hatten nicht die geringste — davon, daß sie unrecht thaten, they had no shadow of idea that they were doing wrong: 2) (*Sommer, unusual*) presage, omen, portent.

Ah'nungs..., *in comp.* —drang, *m.* (*Göthe*) prescient yearning (*Swanwick*); —los, *adj.* having no presentiment, foreboding, &c., without any misgiving: die Unglücklichen! Wie —los sie in das aufgethürmte Mordnetz stürzen (*Schiller*), Unhappy men! how free from all foreboding! they rush into the outspread net of murder! (*Coleridge*); (*with Gen.*) so —los des Unglücks (*König*), so unsuspicious of any disaster: —reich, *adj.* full of presentiment, &c. (*cf.* —voll), fraught with anticipation, filled with foreboding, misgiving, &c.: —schauer, *m.* shuddering presentiment, foreboding shiver, presageful dread, awful misgiving: —vermögen, *n.* (*Göthe, l. u.*) faculty of presaging: —voll, *adj.* full of presentiment, anticipation, &c. (*cf.* Ahnung & Ahnungsreich), foreboding; presageful: awe-inspiring: —weise, *adv.* through a kind of presentiment or anticipation, &c. *cf.* Ahnung.

Ahoi! *interj.* (*Anglicism, from* ahoy) *Mar.* ahoy! used in calling to any one (a ship) at a distance.

A'horn, (*str.*, *pl.* A-e, *sometimes w.* A-en, *but gener. unaltered*) *m. Bot.* (—baum, *m.*) maple(-tree) (*Acer*); der gemeine (großblätterige, weiße) — (Ahler—), sycamore maple (*Acer pseudoplatanus*): der spitzblätterige —, *Acer platanoides*; der kleine, deutsche (kleinblätterige) —, (Maßholder—, Feld—, Weißeder), *Acer campestre*; der eschenblätterige —, *Acer negundo*; der rothe —, the red-flowering maple (*Acer rubrum*). [maple, maple.

A'hornen, (*l. u.*: A'hörnen) *adj.* made of

A'horn..., *in comp.* —laus, *f. Entom.* maple aphis: —maser, *f.* gnarled excrescence of maple: —saft, *m.* maple-juice, juice of maple: —säure, *f. Chem.* aceric acid: das —saure Salz, acerate: —zucker, *m.* maple-sugar.

Äh'rchen, (*str.*) *n.* (*dimin. of* Ähre, *B*) little ear, spikelet (*spicula*).

Äh're, (*w.*) *provinc.* 1) *or* Ähre, *for* Ahorn; 2) *for* Ähre, *B.*

A. **Äh're**, (*w.*) *m.* †, *see* Ahorn.

B. **Äh're**, (*w.*) *f.* ear (of corn), spike (of grass or corn): eine Korn—, an ear of corn (in den V. St. gewöhnlich = Mais—); die taube —, tare: in Ä-n schießen, to shoot out into ears; das Korn hat (*or* ist in) Ä-en, the corn is in ear: Ä-n lesen, to glean (ears of corn after the reapers).

A. **Äh'ren**, **Ähre**, (*str.*) *m.* († &) *provinc.* (Hausähren, Hausähre, *Bav.* Ehren, Öhrn, *Swabia*: Öhrn [*Schiller*]) floor, entrance-hall (of a house). *Low Germ.* die Dehle (Diele), *usual HG. expression* Hausflur.

B. **Äh'ren**, (*w.*) *v.* (*from* Ähre, *B*) I. *refl.* to ear, to form ears, to shoot (out) into ears (as corn); II. *tr. & intr.* to glean (ears of corn).

C. **Äh'ren**, (*w.*) *v. tr.* †, to plough and prepare (the ground) for seed.

Äh'ren..., *in comp.* —bekränzt, *adj.* crowned with ears (of corn, wheat, &c.); —farren, *m. Bot.* 1) a species of fern resembling ears or spikes, *Stachyopterides*; 2) a kind of common club-moss (*Lycopodium clavatum*); 3) a kind of adder's tongue (*Ophioglossum vulgatum*): —feld, *n.* corn-field in ears; —fisch, *m.* atherine (*Atherina hepsetus* L.): —flur, *f.* corn-field in ear: —förmig, *adj.* like an ear of corn, like a spike, spiked; —frucht, *f.* cereal grass, grain (*in distinction from* Hülsenfrucht); —graupen, *f.* (—förmiges Graupenerz) *Miner.* granular ore (*Tulh.*); —habend, *adj.* spiked, with ears, eared like corn, *cf.* —tragend; —kranz, *m.* wreath or crown consisting of ears (of corn or wheat, &c.), Erntekranz; —lese, *f.* —lesen, *n.* a gleaning or gathering of the ears (of corn after reaping — Nachlese; —lese as the title of a book (*Lat. spicilegium*), corresponding to the English: Gleaner: —leser, —sammler, *m.*, —leserin, —sammlerin, *f.* gleaner: —meer, *n.* sea of (waving) ears (of corn); —monat, *m.* (*lit.* month of ears) harvest month (Erntemonat), August: —reich, *adj.* full of ears: —reiche Fluren, *pl.* plains rich in fertile corn-fields; —schnitt, *m.* (*Blichert, unusual*) the ears (*i. e.* the corn) cut off; —schwanger, *adj.* (*Brockes*) pregnant with ears, full of ears (*cf.* —reich); —spitze, *f.* point of

of sounds (Schalllehre). — Akus'tisch, adj. acoustic, relating to acoustics: assisting the propagation or production of sound.

* Akut', see Acut.

Al (Ital., combination of the prep. a [from Lat. ad] and the article, before a fem. alla [all', when followed by a vowel]), to the: sometimes by way of, in the style of, &c.; al fine, Mus. to the end; al fresco, on the fresh(-laid plaster), see Al fresco; al loco, to some (previous) place (a term of reference in musical pieces); al segno, Mus. (return) to the sign; commercial terms, &c.: al marco, by the weight: al numero, by the piece; al pari, at par; al piacere, at pleasure (Mus. gener.: a piacere, a piacimento, at the pleasure of the performer, ad libitum); alla capella, Mus. in the church style; alla polacca, in the style of a Polish dance; alla Scozzese, in the Scotch style; all' antica, in the old style; all' Inglese, in the English style; all' improvvisata, extemporaneously, without premeditation; all' ottava, in the octave, &c., &c.

Alaaf! [pr. Alaf'] interj. provinc. (particul. in the Rhine-country) a kind of cheer (hoch auf! hoch! es lebe!) occurring in Freiligrath's poems: Alaaf, Colonia! Cologne for ever!

* Alabas'ter, † Alabast', (str.) m. Miner. alabaster; —bild, n. an alabaster figure; —bruch, m. alabaster quarry; —brust, f., —hals, m., —hand, f. a bosom, a neck, a hand as white as alabaster; —gyps, m. plaster of Paris made of alabaster; —schimmel, m. see Milchschimmel; —tute, f. Conch. wax-stamper (Conus virgo L.). — Alabas'terer, (str.) m. an artist who works in alabaster. — Alabas'tern, adj. 1) made of alabaster, alabaster; 2) as white as alabaster. — Alabastrit', (str.) m. Miner. alabastrite, see Marmoralabaster.

* Alambik', (str.) m. (Italian) see Alembik.

† Alamo'de, adv. (Fr. à la mode) after the fashion, nach der (neuern) Mode. — Alamo'disch, adj. fashionable, according to the fashion or prevailing mode; a-s Gewürz, see Neue Würze; boeuf à la mode, Cook. alamode beef (meat dressed in a peculiar manner); a-er Styl, the alamode style.

Aland, see Alant.

Alan'der, (str.) m. provinc. smelt, see Stint.

A. Alant, (str.) m. Ichth. chub, cheven (Cyprinus cephalus; Klein: Leuciscus jeses).

B. Alant, (str.) m. Bot. elecampane, horseheal (Inula helenium L.); —bier, n. elecampane-beer; —blecke, f. Ichth. a fish of the carp-kind (Cyprinus bipunctatus, Strmlk); —meth, m. see —bier; —öl, n. oil extracted from the root of elecampane; —wein, m. elecampane-wine.

* Alantin', (str.) n. Chem. alantine (an amylaceous powder).

* Alar', adj. (Lat. ala'ris) Anat. wing-like, pterygoid; —arterie, —vene, f. see Schulterarterie, Schultervene; —ligamente, n. pl. pterygoid ligaments (within the knee joint); —processe (Flügelfortsätze), m. pl. pterygoid or wing-like processes.

A latere, (Lat. from the side) Legaten a latere, cardinal legates a latere (the pope's confidants and counsellors in ordinary).

* Alarm', (str.) m. 1) alarm, particul. a signal by which soldiers are suddenly summoned to take arms; 2) tumult, disturbance; — blasen, to sound alarm; — schlagen, to beat to arms (cf. Lärm); es war blinder —, there was a false alarm; —[illegible] [illegible] see Lärm; [illegible] [illegible].

* Alarmi[illegible], (w.) v. tr. (Fr.) to alarm.

* Alaun, (str.) m. Miner. & Chem. alum; [illegible] —, rock-alum; der [illegible] —, burnt alum; der künstliche —, artificial alum, English alum.

Alaun..., in comp. —artig, adj. alumi[illegible] [illegible]; —bad, n., —beize, f. Dy., Tann., &c. bath of alum-water, a solution of alum; alum mordant; in die —beize legen, Tann. to pile (the hides); —bereiter, m. manufacturer of alum, alum-maker (—sieder); —bereitung, f. the manufacturing of alum (—sieden); —bergwerk, n. alum-mine, alum-pit; —bildung, f. formation of alum; —blume, f. (gener. pl. A-n) flowers of alum; —bruch, m. alum quarry, alum pit; —brühe, f. see —bad.

Alau'nen, (w.) v. tr. to alum, or to mix, prepare with alum; to steep in alumwater.

Alau'nen, adj. of alum, alum.

Alaun'..., in comp. —erde, f. Miner. alum-earth; salzsaure —erde, muriatic alumina; —erden-Metalloid, n. Chem. aluminium, aluminum (the metallic base of alumina); —erz, n. Miner. alum-ore; —essigsäure, f. Chem. acetate of alumina; —fabrik, f. alum-works, a manufactory at which alum is made (—werk); —faß, n. alum-vat, cooler (used for crystallizing alum); —federweiß, n. 1) (Tech.) feathered, plumose alum; sulphate of zinc; 2) see Asbest; —fels, m. alum-rock; —gar, adj. dressed with or in alum (as hides, &c.); alumed; —geist, m. watery sulphuric acid obtained in roasting alum-stone; —gerber, m. a tanner who dresses skins with alum and tallow (Weißgerber); —haloid, n. see —stein; —haltig, adj. aluminiferous, containing or affording alum, aluminous; —holz, n. aluminous pit-coal, bituminous wood; —hütte, f. alum-house, alum-work (—werk).

Alau'nig, adj. alumy, aluminous.

Alaun'..., in comp. —kessel, m. alum-boiler; —kies, m. aluminous pyrites; —küpe, f. Dy. balneum of alum (Tech.); —lauge, f. aluminous lye; —läuter, m. refined alum flour; —leder, n. leather dressed in alum (weißgares Leder), alum-leather; —lösung, f. Chem. solution of alum; —mehl, n. powder of alum; alum, the refuse of alum-works; —miner, f. see —mutter; —molken, f. pl. alum-whey, a decoction of milk and alum; —mutter, f. alum-ore; —mutterlauge, f. residue of alum; —pulver, n. see —mehl; —quelle, f. aluminous spring; —salz, n. common alum; —satz, m. aluminous coal (Tech.); —sauer, adj. Chem. aluminous; das —saure Salz, aluminate; —schiefer, m. alum-slate; —sieder, m. alum-boiler; —siederei, f. 1) (or —sieden, v. a., n.) the act of boiling or manufacturing alum; 2) place where alum is boiled, alum-works; —stein, m. Miner. alum-stone (a silicious subsulphate of alumina and potash; —sulphat, n. Chem. sulphate of alumina; —wachs, n. T. precipitate of crystallized alum; —wasser, n. alum-water, water impregnated with alum; —werk, n. alum-work (—fabrik, —hütte); —wurzel, f. the root of Geranium maculatum, a North-American plant, containing tannic acid, and used as a remedy against dysentery; —zucker, m. alum-sugar, saccharine alum.

A. Alb, (str.) m. see Alp.

B. Alb, (w.) f. provinc. (S. G.) see Alpe.

Alba'ner, (indecl.) adj. Albanian.

Alba'nien, n. Geogr. Albania, Albany.

Alba'nier (str.) m., Albane'se, (w.) m. (A-in, Albane'sin, (w.) f., pl. A-innen) Albanian.

Alba'nisch, Albane'sisch, adj. Albanian.

Al'batroß, (str., sometimes (w.) A-en) m. (& n.) Ornith. albatross (syn. Schiffsflügler, Kriegsschiff, man-of-war, Diomedea exulans).

Al'be, (w.) f. I. or Al'ba (Lat. alba) alb, albe, a long white linen vestment worn by Roman Catholic priests; II. 1) (Al'ben, Al'bling, m.) name of several small white fishes, particul. of Cyprinus alburnus L., orig. die Al'bel, bleak, ablen, ablet (Bleihe, Weißfischchen ꝛc.); 2) a white cow; 3) Bot. a) (Al'ble) white poplar (cf. Alber); b) (Elbe, Elbling) a kind of grape with light, thin-skinned berries.

Al'bel, (w.) f. see Albe, II. 1 & Alber, A.

Al'beln, (w.) v. intr. provinc. to grow weak or impotent, to degenerate (said of bees).

Al'ben, (str.) m. I. see Albe, II. 1; II. provinc. (Bavaria, &c.) a kind of calcareous tuff (Kalktuff).

Al'benrausch, (str.) m. (cf. Alm, A) provinc. (Bavaria, &c.) for Alpenrose, 2.

A. Al'ber, (w.) f. (Albel, Aller, Abele ꝛc.) († A) provinc. poplar, gener. the white poplar (according to Weigand from Ital. albero, tree).

B. Al'ber, adj. † for Albern, which see.

Alberei', (w.) f. (from Albern, v.) foolish doings, nonsensical behaviour, silliness.

Al'b(e)rig, adj. foolish, nonsensical, silly.

Al'berkeit, (w.) f. †, see Albernheit.

Al'bern, adj. silly, simple, sottish, dull; foolish, absurd, preposterous; idle-headed, brain-sick; ein a-er Mensch, a foolish fellow, a simpleton; das a-e Zeug, nonsense, absurdities.

Al'bern, (w.) v. intr. (aux. haben) to talk or behave sillily, to play the fool.

Al'bernhaft, adj. (l. u.) silly-like, foolish.

Al'bernheit, (w.) f. simpleness, silliness; foolishness, folly; absurdity, preposterousness; nonsensical behaviour.

Al'berschwärmer, Al'berspinne, see Pappelschwärmer, Pappelspinne.

Al'bertät, (w.) f. (a ludicrous hybrid word) see Albernheit.

Al'bert, m. (P. N.) Albert, shortened from Adelbert.

Albertiner, Alber'tus-(Al'berts)Thaler, (str.) m. Albert's Thaler (orig. Dutch coin, = Mark 4. 37½ Pfennig).

Albi'genser, (str.) m. (A-in, (w.) f.) Albigensian, gener. in the pl. Albigenses (a party of reformers in the 12th cent., in Albigeois, a small territory of France); der Kreuzzug gegen die —, the Albigensian crusade. — Albigen'sisch, adj. Albigensian.

* Albi'no, (str., pl. A-s, sometimes (w.) Albi'nen) m. albino (Weißling).

Al'bion, (str.) n. ancient name of England, still used in poetry.

* Albit', (str.) m. (Lat.) Miner. albite (a species of mineral, of the feldspath family, of a white colour).

Alb'ling, (str.) m., Al'bock, (str.), Al'bule, (w.) f. see Albe, II. 1.

Alb'rausch, see Albenrausch.

Al'brecht, m. (P. N.) Albert (shortened from Adelbrecht, OHG. Adalperaht, see Adelbert).

* Al'bum, (str., Gen. A-s, pl. A-s) n. album: 1) a blank book in which friends insert autographs, short pieces, &c. as memorials (Stammbuch); 2) scrapbook, sketchbook, &c.; ein photographisches —, a photographic album; A-s in Glanzleder, albums wholebound in calf; A-s in Glanzleinwand, albums in glazed cloth.

* Albumin', (str.) n. albumen (Lat., Eiweißstoff). — Albuminös', adj. albuminous.

* Al'bus, (indecl., pl. —) m. formerly a small silver-coin (Weißpfennig) in Hessia, &c. of the value of nine Hessian Pfennigs (three Kreuzers).

Alcä'isch, adj. alcaic, pertaining to Alcæus, an ancient Greek poet; a-e Verse, alcaics.

* Alca'li, see Alkali.

* Alcarra'za [pr. —ſ'ßa], f. (pl. A-s) (Span.) alcarraza, a large (porous) earthen vessel for cooling water, water-cooler (Kühlkrug).

Alcan'na, see Alkanna.

Alce'ste, f. (P. N.) Alcestis.

* Alchemie', (w.) f., Alchemist ꝛc., see Alchymie ꝛc.

Äl'chen, (str.) n. (dimin. of Aal) a small or young eel.

* Alchimie', Alchymie', (w.) f. alchemy (alchymy). — Alchimist', Alchymist', (w.) m. alchemist (alchymist). — Alchymisterei', (w.) f. alchemistic or alchemic science, alchemy. — Alchymis'tisch, adj. alchemistic, alchemic.

—besessen, adj. (Bürger; rare) fully possessed, altogether in (another's) possession; —besitzend, adj. (Bürger; rare) in full possession of an object, all-possessing; —besungen, adj. universally celebrated by song, all-praised, all-sung; —bewältigend, adj. all-overwhelming, all-vanquishing; —bewegend, adj. all-moving, all-shaking; —beweint, adj. wept for or deplored by all; —bewundert, adj. all-admired; —bezaubernd, adj. all-enchanting; —bezwinger, m. he who vanquishes all; der —bezwinger Tod, all-conquering death; —biegsam, adj. flexible or pliable in the highest degree; —buntbesternt, adj. (Göthe) adorned all over with gay stars; —da', (sometimes all'da) adv. obsolescent, although more emphatic than the simple da (opp. —hier): in that very place, in the same place (ebendaselbst), in such a place, there; —dieweil, conj. † (like —dieweilen & Dieweil) because, whereas, see Weil; —dort, adv. obsolescent, like —da, & its opp. —hier, meaning: in yonder very or same place (ebendort, dortselbst), yonder; —durchdringend, adj. all-penetrating, all-pervading, all-piercing; —durchdrungen, adj. wholly penetrated, all-pervaded; —eben, adj. entirely plane; —ecken, adv. (Hans Sachs) † (for in allen Ecken) in all corners.

Allee', (w.) f. (Fr. allée) alley, walk (particul. planted with trees, [Baum-]Gang); avenue: sometimes used for a double row of other objects.

Allegha'nisch, adj. Alleghanean, pertaining to the North American mountains called Alleghany, or Allegheny.

* Allegat', (str.) n. (Lat.) Law, &c. a passage (of a law, &c.) quoted by way of proof, plea, &c.; quotation, citation. — Allegation', (w.) f. Law, 1) allegation: a) an alleging or adducing anything by way of proof, plea, or excuse; b) that which is offered as a plea, excuse, or justification, see Allegat; 2) a rescript, answer to a petition.

* Allegorie', (w.) f. (Gr.) allegory. — Allego'risch, adj. allegoric (sinnbildlich); fictitious. — Allegorisi'ren, (w.) v. intr. to allegorize. — Allegorist', (w.) m. allegorist. — Allegoristerei', (w.) f. inclination to allegorize, allegorizing propensity.

* Alle'gro, adv. & s. n. (Ital.) Mus. allegro (denoting a brisk and vivacious movement: — moderato, lively, but not too fast).

Allei'gen, I. adj. all (one's) own; II. s. (str.) n. (l. u.) a freehold (alleigenes Gut), freehold estate, allodium.

A. Allein', I. adj. (& adv.) (orig. an intensified numeral from All & Ein [cf. Allein, B] like the E. alone from all & one [alone, in its present form as early as in the 13th cent.]; allein never occurs as a declined adj. before the substantive to which it belongs, but is always used predicatively; examples of the str. form alleiner [Göthe, see Grimm] or of an oblique case [allein mit dem alleinen, Nicolai, see Sanders] are quite exceptional; but the weak nom. alleine [quite common in MHG.] is still in popular use).

1) a) alone; single; solitary; b) apart, by himself, herself, itself, &c.; — (as a stage-direction), solus, sola (Lat., wie vom Anbeginn des englischen Dramas die meisten englischen Bühnenweisungen), f. i. Wallenstein —, Wallenstein (solus); Myrrha —, Myrrha (sola); gang —, all alone (absolute loneliness is likewise expressed by a series of familiar expressions, f. i. Mutter—, Mutterseelen—, Seelenallein —, Mutterseel—, Mutterselig—; — sein, 1) to be alone, &c.: es ist unangenehm an einem fremden Orte — zu sein, it is disagreeable to be in a strange place by one's self; 2) (ohne die [störende] Gegenwart Anderer) to be private; ich konnte ihn nicht — sprechen, I could not speak to him in private; er speist —, he takes his dinners in private (nicht mit seiner Familie); es ist ein fremder Herr gekommen; ... ich schäme mich, daß er so lange — gelassen worden ist, there's a strange gentleman come; .... I am ashamed to have him left to himself so long; ich gehe dort oft —, I often walk there by myself; der Ort sichert dem Spaziergänger das —sein, the place secures privacy to the walker; einsam bin ich nicht —, when by myself, I am not alone; die Familie kann so — wohnen, the family may thus have lodgings of its own; er lebt —, he lives by himself, single, or separated; —stehen, 1) to stand alone (in the world); 2) to stand apart, to be isolated; er gehört zu keiner Schule, er steht —, he belongs to no school, he stands by himself; ich stehe nicht — mit meiner Ansicht und meinem Urtheil, I am not alone in thinking and reasoning so; diese beiden Männer standen fast — im Kampfe gegen die kirchlichen Eiferer, these two men were nearly single-handed in combating the ecclesiastical zealots; er will stets die Unterhaltung — führen, he always wants to monopolize the conversation; es würde für Einen — zu schwer sein, it would be too difficult for any one man; er führte es fast — aus, he executed it almost single-handed.

2) adv. (blos, nur) a) alone, only, merely, solely; — Noah blieb über, Noah only remained alive; ich bin — von dieser Rücksicht geleitet worden, I have been led solely by this consideration; nicht —, not only, (... but also ...); b) alone, by himself, &c. (without regard to others, &c.): — die Stadt Bergen brachte jährlich einige tausend Schiffsladungen, the town of Bergen alone brought several thousands of cargoes a-year; schon — das Bellen des Hundes schreckt ihn, even the mere barking of the dog terrifies him; es waren nur — sechs junge deutsche Prinzen dabei (Schiller), there were alone no less than six young German princes present; 3) alone, unaided, without assistance (almost syn. with selbst); das weiß ich —, I know that myself (i. e. without your telling me); das Kind kann schon — gehen, the child can already walk by itself; du mußt die Nelke binden an den Stab, | es rankt der Epheu sich — [= von selbst] empor (Platen, see Sanders), you have to bind the carnation to a stick, the ivy climbs up by itself.

II. conj. but (more emphatic than aber, with which it is sometimes connected in familiar talk); er ist reich, — (er ist) nicht glücklich, he is rich, but he is not happy.

B. All'ein', adj. (different from the preceding by the secondary accent on the first syllable which retains its full etymological meaning) "all-one": der all-eine (all-einige) Geist, the universal spirit uniting every thing in one (i. e. himself), according to the pantheistic doctrine (All-Einheits- [Göthe: All-Einigkeits-] or All-Eins-Lehre), which assumes that the universe is God.

Allein' ..., in comp. —berechtigung, f. exclusive right, title or claim (zu einer Sache, to a thing); —besitz, m. exclusive or absolute possession (opp. Gemeinbesitz); —friede(n), m. see Separatfriede; —gesang, m. (l. u., for Einzel- or Solo-Gesang) an air sung by a single voice, solo (opp. All-Gesang); —gespräch, n., —rede, f. (l. u.) soliloquy, monologue; —gewalt, f. exclusive or independent power, uncontrolled authority; —gültigkeit, f. exclusive validity, lawfulness, or admissibility; —handel, m. monopoly (Monopol); —handel treiben, to monopolize, to engross the trade; mit Tabak —handel treiben, to monopolize the tobacco trade; der Artikel ist im —handel der Regierung (Mil. & Gr.), this article is a monopoly of government; —händler, m. monopolist.

A. Allein... the state of being... (Alleinsein).
B. All'einheit... the being all in one...
Allein'..., in comp. ... monarch, autocrat... dominion or sway... führte im Orkus... der Chaos und... hatten, Linnaeus... where chaos and... reigned supreme.
A. Allei'nig, adj. (alone in dieser...) unique; exclusive;... only) God; Gemein-... one's sole or own... Vertrieb dieses Artikels... of this article; ... deinen a-en Gebrauch... your separate use;... Bürgermeisters, with... the burgomaster.
B. All'ei'nig, adj.
All'ei'nigkeit, (w.)... ness, &c.; see also All...
Allein'..., in comp. ... right, privilege of... —nützig, adj. advantageous... only (opp. Gemein...) owner (of a ship)... singer (Solosänger)... saving; —singer, ... solo (Solo); —spieler... plays a solo (Solo...) adj. standing apart... Baum, stander; —... buildings; —verkauf... sole (power of) vend...
* Allein'ze, † for...
All'emal (l. u. alle...) all times, at any time... once for all; 2) ... wise, certainly, to be... yet, notwithstanding...
All'emalig, adj. ... or at all times, with...
Alleman'n', (w.) m. ... n. Allemannia, ... nisch, adj. Allemanni...
All ..., in comp. ... assiduous, altogether... directions; —endlich... at the very last, at l...
Allenfalls' (lies f...) 1) † in every case, ... see Jedenfalls, to ... limited; 2) in case... haps, by chance; — could afford to admit... and for that matter... tual (allfällig), possi... and therefore uncert... expenses; ein a-er F... tually become a ... sations, a few possi...
Allenthal'ben, ad... places, at every hand... times used for in ... Wieland, &c.) in eve...
Allenthal'benheit... † ubiquity, omnipre...
All'entscheidend,... conclusive or final,...
All'entwegen, ad...
A. Aller, (w.) f. ... alder-tree.
... aller..., ... used to intensify... before which it... variably ...

first of all, the very first, die allergebräuchlichsten Wörter, the words used most of all); —anständigst, adj. most respectable of all; —ärgst, adj. worst of all: die —ärgste Thorheit, the greatest folly imaginable, the height of folly; —ärmst, adj. poorest of all; —aus'schweifendst, adj. most extravagant of all: der —ausschweifendste Geschmack, the most extravagant taste conceivable.

All'..., in comp. —erbarmend, adj. all merciful; —erbarmer, m. the All-merciful.

Al'ler..., in comp. —best', adj. best of all, very best; —christ'lich, —christ'lichst, adj. most or very Christian (particul. an epithet of the kings of France); —dings', adv. 1) obsolescent, by all means, altogether, surely (durchaus, schlechterdings); 2) now gener. used in a concessive sense, of course, surely, sure enough, it must be admitted, it is true, to be sure, certainly (cf. Freilich, Zwar rc.); —durchlauch'tigst, adj. most serene, most high, most illustrious; —edelst, adj. noblest or most precious of all; —entgegengesetzt, adj. diametrically opposed; —erst', adj. (as an adv. l. u. in prose, instead of zu —erst) first of all, first and foremost; die —ersten Bedürfnisse, the prime and immediate necessaries.

All'..., in comp. —erfreuend, adj. all-gladdening, all-cheering; —erfahren, adj. experienced in every thing (Allkundig).

Al'ler..., in comp. —geringst', adj. lowest of all; —getreu'est, adj. most (very) faithful (epithet of the kings of Portugal); —gnä'digst, adj. most gracious; adv. most graciously; —größt, adj. greatest of all.

All'erhalter, m. (All ...) he who sustains all; all-sustainer.

Al'ler..., in comp. —hand, (l. u. allerhand') adv. of all sorts, of all kinds, omnifarious, various, divers, sundry: —hand Blumen, flowers of all kinds, all kinds of flowers: er schwatzte —hand Unsinn, he talked all kinds of nonsense: er hatte —hand mitzutheilen, he had to communicate all and sundry matters; cf. —lei; —heiligen, (orig. Gen. pl.) All-saints' i. e. day, now construed like an indeclinable subst. eine Woche nach —heiligen, auf —heiligen rc. (cf. —seelen), All-saints-day (the first of November on which there is a general celebration of the saints), coll. All-hallows; —heiligenholz, n. log-wood, Brazil wood of All-saints' day; —heiligst, adj. most holy of all: das —heiligste, n. 1) a) Jew. Rel. the holiest of all (Hebr. 9, 3); the holiest place, the holy of holies (Lat. sanctum sanctorum); b) fig. sanctum; 2) Rom. Cath. monstrance (Monstranz).

All'erheiternd, adj. (All-) all-exhilarating, all-cheering.

Al'ler..., in comp. —höchst', adj. highest of all, supreme, sovereign: von der —höchsten Kraft, of sovereign virtue; er war aufs —höchste gereizt, he was irritated to the very last degree: der —höchste, the most High (i. e. God); —höchstderselbe, —höchstdieselbe, obsolescent, a kind of superlative of Hochderselbe rc., which see: His (Her) Majesty; —in'nerst, adj. innermost of all: ihr —innerstes war aufgeregt (Göthe), her very innermost soul was agitated.

Al'lerlei [l. u. allerlei'], I. adv. of all kinds, of all sorts, of all manners or modes, omnifarious, various, divers, sundry; — Leute, people of all kinds, all sorts of people; — Kraut (or Kräuter), all kinds of herbs; — Weine, a variety of wines; II. n. (Gen. [illegible]) 1) [illegible] —, a bird of multifarious [illegible] molecular; 2) a) all [illegible] things; medley, hodge-podge, [illegible] a kind of olio, or mixture made [illegible] of herbs (called also Potage); [illegible] n., —würze, f. allspice. [illegible] in comp. —letzt, adj. last of all, ultimate; zum —letzten Male, for the very last time; zu —letzt, last of all, in conclusion; —liebst, adj. dearest of all; most charming, extremely amiable, most delightful, very engaging; hübsche Frauen mit —liebsten Mützchen, neuster französischer Façon, pretty women, with little darling caps of the last French make; ein —liebstes Muster, a most charming or pretty pattern; —liebst! from. very fine! ooh! very nice, indeed! I like that exceedingly! am —liebsten, adv. best of all; ich habe ihn am —liebsten, I like him best of all; —männiglich, adj. (see Männiglich) gener. used as an indeclinable substantive; obsolescent, every body without exception; —mann, m. provinc. every body's man, one who seeks to please every body (Allmann); gener. cont. like its compositions; —mannsfreund, m. every body's friend, &c.; —mannsharnisch, m. Bot. 1) der lange —mannsharnisch, spotted ramson, long rooted garlic (Allium victorialis, Siegwurz); 2) (or Mannsschild) Androsace, a genus of herbs; —maßen, † I. adv. in every way, quite; II. conj. because, since, whereas; —meist, I. adj. most of all, most part; II. adv. obsolescent (more usual am —meisten) especially, particularly, chiefly; —nächst, adj. next of all, the very next; am —nächsten, adv. nearest of all, close by, hard by, immediately.

All'ernährend, adj. (All-) all-nourishing, all-sustaining.

Al'ler..., in comp. —neuest, adj. newest of all, das —neu(e)ste, the very latest news, information, intelligence, &c.; —neustens, adv. most recently; —niedrigst, adj. lowest or meanest of all; —nothwendigst, adj. most necessary of all; absolutely necessary; —oberst, adj. uppermost, highest of all; die —oberste, the very highest; —ortig, adj. existing, to be found, &c. in every place, everywhere; —orts, adv. (an abbreviation from [the more frequent] Aller Orten formed with the adverbial ... s, cf. Allerseits) in every place, everywhere.

All'erregend, adj. (All-) all-exciting, all-inciting.

Al'ler..., in comp. —reinst, adj. purest of all; —richtigst, adj. most correct of all; —ruhigst, adj. most quiet of all.

All'..., in comp. —erschaffend, adj. all-creating; —erschaffer, m. creator of all things.

Al'ler..., in comp. —schlech'test, —schlimmst', adj. worst of all; —schönst', adj. finest or most beautiful of all; —seelen, orig. Gen. pl., like —heiligen (sc. das Fest —seelen) (often construed like an indeclinable substantive) Rom. Cath. All-souls (day), the second day of November; —seiten, adv. † see —seits; —seitig, adj. existing, occurring, &c. on every side or hand or every part, on all hands; comprising persons all together (cf. —seits); zu —seitigem Untergang (Göthe), to the destruction of all, to universal destruction; zu unserm —seitigen Vergnügen (Schiller), for the enjoyment of all of us; —seits [& allerseits'], adv. 1) lit. † on every side, from all parts; 2) fig. (gener. of persons) all together; es wird —seits zugestanden, it is conceded on all hands; ich empfehle mich Ihnen —seits, I recommend myself to all of you; ich wünsche (Ihnen) —seits wol zu schlafen, I wish a good night to all (of you); —unterthä'nigst, adj. most humble (of all), adv. most humbly, with profoundest submission; —wärts [less usual —wärts'], adv. everywhere, in all places or directions; —wege, adv. l. u. for —wegen, every way, in every respect, at all; always, ever; —wegen [& we'gen], adv. 1) everywhere, in every place, in every direction; so geht die Welt nun, Es giebt —wegen Unglücks genug (Schiller, W. Tell 4, 2), so goes the world, misfortune meets us everywhere; 2) (the notion of place passing into that of condition or time) throughout, everywhere and always, thoroughly, in every respect, always, ever; Weg' hast du —wegen, | an Mitteln fehlt dirs nicht (Paul Gerhard), thou hast ways everywhere and always, thou art never wanting in means; —wegs, † —wegens, adv. l. u. for —wegen; —wei'sest, adj. wisest of all, most wise; —welts' ..., often in compounds, denoting persons or things belonging or in some relation to all the world (cf. —manns...) and gener. with an admixture of contempt, thus an —weltsbürger is one who is too easily at home in every place, arrant cosmopolitan; —welts'bürgerschaft, f. undue cosmopolitism; —welts'freund, m. a friend of any and every body; it may, however, likewise express a mere gradation of the word with which it is compound: —welts'narr (like Erz-Narr), arrant fool; —welts'halunke (Immermann, Münchh. 1, 167), or it may express a familiar kind of admiration: —welts'kerl, —welts'mädchen rc., cf. Hauptkerl, Mordkerl, Blitzmädchen rc.; —we'nigst, adj. (& adv. am —wenigsten) least of all, the very least; —we'nigstens, adv. at the very least; —widersprech'endst, adj. most contradictory of all or conceivable; —wunder'lichst, adj. most wonderful of all.

All'erwünscht, adj. (All ...) wished for or desired by all.

Al'les, I. see All, A, I. 3; II. adv. † & provinc. (mostly contracted into Alls, which see) always, still, evermore, perpetually, continually.

Al'lesammt', adv. altogether, all together (alle zusammen, sämmtlich); — seid unter einander unterthan (1 Pet. 5, 5), yea, all of you be subject one to another (cf. Ps. 19, 10).

Al'les..., in comp. —entdeckend, —erfreuend, —heilend rc., adj. disclosing everything, cheering all, all-healing, &c. not properly compounds (cf. Allentdeckend rc.), and gener. spelt in two words; —fort', adv. provinc. (for allfort, immerfort, in Einem fort, see Fort) continually, still, always; —fresser, m. an all-devouring man or animal, omnivorous beast; —leugner, m. one who denies everything (Nihilist); —thuer, m. a doer of all work, factotum; —wisser, m. one who knows, or who pretends to know, everything.

Al'le..., in comp. —tagsfeld rc., see Alltagsfeld rc.; —wege (All'ewege, All'weg), † —wegen, adv. obsolescent (see the more usual alle Wege & in alle Wege, under Weg) in every way, in every place, everywhere, altogether, throughout, always; —weile, weil, I. adv. 1) obsolescent & provinc. (S. G.) at all times, always; 2) (gener. accentuated differently: allewei'le) coll. just now, presently, immediately; ich will —weile nichts haben, I want nothing at present; II. conj. † 1) as long as, while; 2) because (cf. Alldieweil).

Alle'wig, adj. (All intensifying the word ewig, eternal, everlasting) lasting for ever and ever.

Al'lewilschen, (dir.) n. (dimin. from All & Wille) coll. one (a child) who wants to, and who is permitted to have his way in every thing (allen Willen).

Al'lezeit, All'zeit, adv. at all times, always, (at) everytime, evermore (Stets, Immer).

All'..., in comp. —fähig, adj. unusual, altogether capable or qualified; —fällig, adj. eventual, possibly happening, &c. cf. Allenfallsig, Etwaig; adv. eventually, possibly, &c. (syn. Etwa); bei einer —fälligen Untersuchung, in case of a trial or examination, das Geld, welches er —fällig erhalten könnte, the money which he might eventually (or possibly, perhaps) obtain; —farbig, adj. of all colours; —fort, adv. (l. u. for immerfort) always without intermission, continually, still, evermore; —frei, adj. (l. u.) entirely free, altogether unbounded; —fressend, adj. (l. u.) all-devour-

nig; —gebend, adj. all-giving, all-bestowing, all-dispensing; —gebenedeit, adj. all-blessed; —geber, m. All-giver, the Giver of all things; —gebietend, adj. all-commanding; —gebieter, m., —gebieterin, f. sovereign ruler, all-ruling sovereign: Fortuna, die —gebieterin, Fortune, the all-ruling goddess; —geehrt, adj. all-honoured, honoured by all; —gefallenheit, f. (Lessing, unusual) endeavour to please every body; —gefällig, adj. 1) pleasing all, all-pleasant; 2) endeavouring to please every body; time-serving; —gefälligkeit, f. endeavour to please or oblige every body; —gefürchtet, adj. all-dreaded; —gegenwart, [frequently —ge'genwart], f. omnipresence, ubiquity; —gegenwärtig [frequently —ge'genwärtig], adj. omnipresent, present everywhere at the same time, ubiquitous; —geheim, adj. (Bürger, l. u.) entirely secret; —gelehrt, adj. learned or versed in all knowledge; ein —gelehrter Mann, a universal genius; —geliebt, adj. all-loved, loved by all; —gelobt, adj. all-praised, praised or lauded by all; —gemach (†—gemachsam, —gemächlich), adv. particul. used in poetry and the elevated style, by (slow) degrees, &c. see —mählich.

Allgemein', adj. (all'gemein, with the accent on the first syllable, when the strict etymological meaning, which is "common to all", is to be rendered particularly prominent; this, however, is exceptional, and allgemein' the usual accentuation) 1) a) common to all, universal; a-e or —herrschende Krankheiten, epidemic diseases; ein a-es (Heil-)Mittel, a universal or sovereign remedy; er wird — (adv.) geliebt, he is universally beloved; b) embracing all, catholic (in diesem Sinne gew. cathol'ic betont); die a-e christliche Kirche, the catholic Christian church (zu unterscheiden von dem gew. Gebrauch von Cath'olic gleich Roman Catholic); —christlich, cathol'ic; das —Christliche der Lehre, was unter den verschiedenen Formen des Protestantismus verborgen ist, the catholicity of doctrine that lies hidden under the diverse forms of Protestantism; 2) a) general, common: es geht ein a-es Gerücht, there is a general rumour, it is commonly rumoured; —angenommen, commonly accepted or received, conventional: b) general, common, public; das a-e Beste, the general or public good, the common weal; zur a-en Kunde bringen, to bring into public notice: das a-e Ohr (Wieland — das Ohr des Publicums), the public ear (vergl. Shaksp. the general ear [Hamlet], the common ear [Meas. for Meas.], the common eye [Macbeth], the public eye [Ant. & Cleop.], &c.); 3) a) general (opp. Besonder, Einzeln rc.), generic, &c.: die a-e Weltgeschichte, universal history; eine a-e Regel, eine a-e Ähnlichkeit rc., a general rule, a general resemblance; von Einzelheiten auf A-es zu schließen, ist eine falsche Art der Folgerung, to conclude from particulars to generals is a false way of arguing; einzelne Erfahrungen auf a-e Regeln, Maximen bringen, sich vom Einzelnen zum A-en erheben (im Denken, beim Philosophiren), to generalise; er hält sich im A-en, he deals in generalities: seine Rede hielt sich im A-en, his speech was one of generalities (cf. Allgemeinheit); im A-en, in general, generally (speaking); dies Haus, obgleich es im A-en das Ansehen einer Privat-Wohnung hatte, zeigte die schönsten Verhältnisse, this house, though with the general appearance of a private residence, exhibited the finest proportions; ich glaube, daß die Grundeigenthümer von Irland im A-en sehr herabgesetzt werden, I think the landlords of Ireland are, as a class, much abused; b) general, indefinite, vague; a-e Ausdrücke, general terms; 4) a) general, extensive, wide; Je höher du wirst aufwärts gehn, | dein Blick wird immer a-er (Rückert), the higher thou wilt mount, the more extensive thy view (will become); diese Maßregel ist viel zu — und durchgreifend, this measure is far too wide and sweeping; b) (—ansprechend, verständlich rc.) popular, &c.

Allgemein'..., in comp. —christlich, —gläubig, adj. catholic, pertaining to all Christians, and not to any particular church (cf. Allgemein, 1, b).

All'gemeinde, (w.) f. (l. u.) all-embracing community, universal union.

Allgemein'..., in comp. —geltend, see —gültig; —glaube, m. universality of belief, catholicism (cf. the next word); —gläubig, adj. universal of belief, catholic, adhering to a general Christian belief, not sectarian (cf. Allgemein, 1, b); —gültig, adj. of universal or general validity, catholic; eine —gültige Regel, an established rule; diesen Grundsätzen ist ein axiomatischer und —gültiger Charakter aufgeprägt, these principles have been stamped with an axiomatic and catholic character.

Allgemein'heit, (w.) f. 1) universality; generality; commonness, cf. Allgemein, adj.; 2) a) (Göthe, Allgemeinde, unusual) l. u. all-embracing community; generality (of mankind), mass, main body; b) l. u. for Allmende, which see; 3) general maxim, generalisation, generality.

Allgemein'..., in comp. —schrift, f. a manner or system of writing to be universally understood, pasigraphy; —verständlich, adj. intelligible to the generality, adapted to the popular mind; die Wissenschaft —verständlich machen, to popularise science; —verständlichkeit, f. general intelligibility, adaptability to the popular mind.

All'..., in comp. —genannt, adj. named or mentioned by every one; —genug, —genugsam, adj. all-sufficient; —genugsamkeit, —genügsamkeit, f. all-sufficiency; —gepriesen, adj. all-praised; —gerecht, adj. all-just, all-righteous: der —gerechte, m. the All-righteous (God); —gericht, n. judgment of all, universal judgment, judgment-day; —gesammt, adj. entire, whole, total, joint without exception; —gesang, m. (l. u., cf. —sang, Vollgesang) chorus (opp. Alleingesang); —geschätzt, adj. all-esteemed, valued by every body; —gestaltig, adj. of all kinds of shapes; —gesucht, adj. sought for or desired by all; —getreu, adj. all-faithful; —gewalt, f. all-vanquishing power, supreme power (this word, which is of comparatively recent origin [it is not found f. i. in Luther's writings] is generally applied to that kind of [human or other] power, which conquers or crushes every obstacle, while the syn. Allmacht refers to the highest degree of power, which is manifested in the creation and government of the world); —gewaltig, adj. all-powerful, all-conquering; —glaubend, adj. (Klopstock, l. u.) believing every thing, over-credulous; —gnädig, adj. (l. u.) all-gracious, most gracious; —groß, adj. great beyond every thing, greatest; —götter, m. (l. u. for Pantheist) pantheist; —götterei, f. pantheism (Pantheismus); —göttler, m. (Lenau, l. u.) see Abgötter; —göttertempel, m. (Campe, not used) a temple dedicated to all the gods, pantheon (Pantheon); —gültig, adj. valid in every respect, of universal validity, decisive in every case; —gut, I. adj. (l. u.) all-good; II. s. n. Bot. all-good, good Henry (Chenopodium bonus Henricus, guter Heinrich, cf. Heinrich); —gütig, adj. all-kind, all-good, all-gracious, all-bountiful, all-bounteous; der —gütige, the supreme disposer of all good; —heil, s. n. panacea, a sovereign remedy; —heilig, adj. most sacred or saintly.

All'heit, (w.) f. universality, totality; diese Erziehung muß an der — versucht werden (Fichte), this kind of education has to be attempted with all; [illegible] (Chamisso), the whole, all [illegible] the) foreigners.

All'..., in comp. [illegible] adv. †, hither, to this [illegible] —herrschend, adj. all-[illegible] [illegible] altogether; [illegible] in this very place; [illegible] all) adv. [illegible] style, [illegible] verstorben: Hr. M., [illegible] Mr. M., merchant of [illegible] (intensified [illegible]) † and [illegible] yonder, to that (very) [illegible]

* Allianz', (w.) f. [illegible]

* Alligation', (w.) f. [illegible] schung, [illegible] (arithmetical) rule of allig[illegible] regel), by which questions [illegible] relate to the mixture of [illegible] equal value.

* Alliga'tor, [illegible] m. Zool. alligator ([illegible] amerikanische Krokodil; [illegible] Alligator [crocodilus] [illegible]

* Alligi'ren, (w.) v. tr. [illegible]

* Alliiren, (w.) v. tr. [illegible] unite; sich —, to ally one's[illegible] m. ally confederate.

* Alliteration', (w.) f. [illegible]

* Alliteri'ren, (w.) v. [illegible] (or to exhibit) alliteration [illegible] Silben, alliterative syllab[illegible]

All'..., in comp. [illegible] lich], adj. (happening, [illegible] nual; adv. annually, anniver[illegible] adj. all-knowing; —klar, [illegible] perfectly clear; —klarheit, [illegible] —kraft, f. universal power; [illegible] powerful, (acting) with full [illegible] f. all-powerfulness, univer[illegible] vency; —kundig, adj. all-[illegible] versed (des Streites, in [illegible] (Göthe, unusual) universal[illegible] adj. all-beaming, all-illum[illegible] all-embracing love, infini[illegible] adj. all-loving; [illegible] macher, m. (not used) [illegible] f. almightiness, omnipote[illegible] ver. —mäch'tig], adj. almighty[illegible] powerful; [illegible] mäch'tigkeit, f. all-powerful[illegible]

All'machts..., in comp. [illegible] creation or creature of the [illegible] f. hand of the Almighty, [illegible] werk, n. work of the Almi[illegible]

All'mäh'lich, adj. [illegible] tensified by All, syn. [illegible] mächlich, spelled [illegible] quently, but [illegible] gradual, progressive, [illegible] gradually; by degrees; [illegible] softly, gently; das [illegible] durch Zeitwörter [illegible] den rc. bezeichnen; [illegible] geworden, [illegible] die Landwirthe [illegible] Getreidehandel [illegible] reconciled to free trade [illegible] sie ihn zu einer [illegible] grown to expect him [illegible] Zurückhaltung wird — [illegible] wear off (gradually), [illegible] progressive.

All'mäh'lichkeit, (w.) [illegible] gradualness, gradual [illegible]

All'mannig'faltig, [illegible] extremely diversified [illegible]

All'mende, (w.) f. [illegible] tract of land [illegible] a community, [illegible]

All'..., *in comp.* —mild', *adj.* all-mild; —mögend, *adj.* all-potent, all-powerful; —monatlich, *adj.* done or happening once a month or every month, monthly: *adv.* once a month, monthly: —mor'gens, *adv.* every morning; —mutter, *f.* (*formed like* Allvater) universal mother, allbearing earth, nature; —nächt'lich, *adj.* done or happening every night: *adv.* every night: —nährend, *adj.* all-nourishing.

* Allocation', (*w.*) *f.* (*Lat.*) *Law, &c.* allocation, admission of an article in reckoning, and the addition of it to the account.

* Allochroit', (*str.*) *m.* *Miner.* allochroite (a kind of garnet).

* Allocution', (*w.*) *f.* allocution, address.

* Allod', (*str.*) *n.*, Allo'dium, (*str.*, *pl.* [*w.*] Allo'dien) *n.* *Feud. Law*, allodium (*a word of purely German orig. with a Latin termination*), an estate held in absolute possession, without a feudal superior, freehold-estate, freehold. — Allodial', *adj.* allodial (lehnsfrei, erblich); —erbe, *m.* heir to an allodial estate; —gut, *n.* allodial estate, *see* Allod. — Allodification', (*w.*) *f.* transmutation into an allodium or freehold-estate. — Allodifici'ren, (*w.*) *v. tr.* to transmute into an allodium.

* Allon'ge [*pr.* Allong'zhe], (*w.*) *f.* (*Fr.*) 1) lengthening-piece (Verlängerungs-Stück); 2) a long rein, *see* Longe; 3) an addition attached to a document (Anhängsel, Anhangzettel), *particul. Comm.* rider of a bill of exchange (Wechsel-Anhang); A-perücke, *f.* a full-bottomed wig with very long flowing curls of the time of Louis XIV. of France. — Allongi'ren, [Allongzhe'ren], (*w.*) *v. tr.* (*Fr.*) to lengthen, to add (Verlängern).

* Allopath', Allöopath', (*w.*), *less usual:* Allopath'iker, (*str.*), Allopathist', (*w.*) *m.* *Med.* allopathist, one who adheres to allopathy; one who practises allopathically. — Allopathie', Allöopathie', Allöopathi'e, (*w.*) *f.* allopathy (*opp.* Homöopathie). — Allopath'isch, *adj.* allopathic (*adv.* allopathically).

* Allophan', I. *adj.* allophanic; II. *s.* (*str.*) *m.* *Miner.* allophane, argillaceous mineral.

* Allo'tria, (*indecl.*) *n. pl.* extraneous or incidental matters; things foreign to the main subject (Nebendinge).

* Allotrop', Allotro'pisch, *adj.* *Chem.* allotropic, pertaining to allotropy. — Allotropie', (*w.*) *f.* *Chem.* allotropy, allotropism (change of physical and chemical properties without change of chemical composition).

All'raun, *see* Alraun.

All'..., *in comp.* —recht, *adj.* quite right, *adv.* altogether justly; —rein, *adj.* quite clean, altogether pure; —reinigend, *adj.* all-cleansing, all-purifying.

Alls, *provinc.* I. *s. contracted form of the n.* Alles, *often spelt* als; was als (*Schiller, coll. [illegible]*, &c.) *for* was alles, *cf.* All, *a.* A. II. 6, b); II. *adv.* (*orig. the Acc. of the n. of* All) 1) altogether; 2) a) always, ever; continually, still; b) every now and then.

All'..., *in comp.* —sacht, *adj.* quite soft; *adv.* very softly or gradually; —sammt, *see* Allesammt; —säugend, *adj.* (*Stolberg*) all-suckling, all-nourishing; —schaffend, *adj.* all-creating; der —schaffende, *see* —erschaffer; —schmachtend, *adj.* (*Göthe*) intensely yearning, all-languishing; —schmähend, *adj.* all-reviling; —schöpferisch, *adj.* all-creative, all-creating, all-producing; —schöpfer, *m.* (*scarcely used*) [illegible], [illegible]; —schreckend, *adj.* all-terrifying; —schriftkunst, *f.* pasigraphy; —sehend, *adj.* all-seeing; der —sehende, the All-seeing, All-seer; —seitig, *adj.* *lit.* & *fig.* from or in all directions; in all respects, in every [illegible], universal (*opp.* Einseitig); es ist —seitig [illegible], it is acknowledged on all hands; [illegible] —seitigem Geiste, a man of universal [illegible] genius; der Plan ist —seitig erwogen, the plan has been considered in all its bearings; —seitigkeit, (*w.*) *f.* universality; thoroughness, &c. (*opp.* Einseitigkeit); —seits, *adv.* (*cf.* Allerseits) on every hand, in or from every direction: everywhere: —selig, *adj.* all-blessed, all-happy: —sichtig, *adj.* gifted with universal sight, all-seeing, all-perceiving: —siegreich, *adj.* all-victorious, all-conquering: —stets, *adv.* ever and always: —stündlich, *adj.* happening or occurring every hour; *adv.* every hour, hourly; —süß, *adj.* quite or altogether sweet, most sweet; —tag, *m.* 1) work-day, working-day, week-day; 2) *fig.* commonplace; *particul. in comp. see* Alltags...; —tags, *used adverbially*, on work- or week-days.

All'tägig, *adj.* 1) *lit.* (*cf.* Tägig), *scarcely used*, lasting a whole day and of daily recurrence; 2) occurring every day, daily, &c., *see* Alltäglich, *which is more usual*.

All'täglich, I. *adj.* 1) happening every day, of daily recurrence, daily, quotidian, every day; ein a-es Fieber, a quotidian fever; die a-e Erfahrung, every day's experience; 2) pertaining to, or worn every-day, *i. e.* every week- or working-day (*opp.* sonntäglich, festtäglich); ein a-er Anzug, a-es Kleid *ec.*, *see* Alltagsanzug *ec.*; 3) commonplace, flat, trivial, trite, common; er war kein a-er Schriftsteller, he was no everyday writer: a-e Betrachtungen, everyday or commonplace reflections; ihre Ideen waren durchaus gewöhnlich und —, her ideas were perfectly commonplace and everyday (*Trafford*, George Geith I., 20 C T. R.); II. A-keit, (*w.*) *f.* commonness, (what is) commonplace, triteness, triviality.

All'tags..., *in comp.* —anzug, *m.* everyday suit (of clothes); —bemerkung, *f.* a commonplace observation, an ordinary remark; ein —christ, *m.* a common or ordinary Christian; —gast, *m.* everyday guest; —geschichte, *f.* a tale of everyday occurrence; —geschwätz, —gewäsch, *n.* ordinary tittle-tattle, empty or idle talk; —haube, *f.* everyday or ordinary cap; —kind, *n.* 1) a common, ordinary child; 2) (*Hippel*) a child born on a weekday (*opp.* Sonntagskind); —kleid, *n.* 1) an everyday (ordinary or work-day) coat (—rock, *m.*); undress robe; uniform, &c.; 2) *fig.* undress; —kreis, *m.* (*Bürger*) ordinary sphere of life; —leben, *n.* everyday life, common, ordinary life; —mensch, *m.* a commonplace fellow, votary of commonplace: —rock, *m.* everyday coat, ordinary coat; —sonne, *f.* the sun which we see everyday (in opposition to a supposed larger invisible sun); —tag, *m.* (*a bold combination of Jean Paul's, quoted by Sanders*) a day of the everyday kind, a common, ordinary, commonplace day; —welt, *f.* working-day world; common, ordinary life; —witz, *m.* everyday or commonplace wit.

All'..., *in comp.* —thätig, *adj.* active in all directions, all-efficient; —thätigkeit, *f.* universal activity or efficiency; —tragend, *adj.* all-bearing; —triumphirend, *adj.* all-triumphing; —trotzend, *adj.* all-defying; —umfassend, *adj.* all-embracing, all-comprehending: —umfasser, *m.* (*Göthe*) all-embracer; —umfunkelnd, *adj.* surrounding with sparkling splendour on every side; —umklammernd, *adj.* all-clasping, all-encompassing, all-encircling: —umschattend, *adj.* (*Stolberg*) all-shadowing; —umschließend, *adj.* all-surrounding; —unverändert, *adj.* altogether unaltered.

* Allü're, (*w.*) *f.* (*Fr.*) 1) *a)* gait, carriage: *b)* (of animals) gait, (of horses) pace; 2) *fig.* manner, way.

* Alluvial', *adj.* (*Lat.*) *Geol.* alluvial (angeschwemmt); —gebilde, *n.* alluvial formation. — Alluvion', (*w.*) *f.* alluvion (Anschwemmung). — Allu'vium, (*str.*, *pl.* [*indecl.*] Allu'via) *n.* *Geol.* alluvium.

All'..., *in comp.* —vater, *m.* (*ON.* alfaðir) universal father, father of all; —verbreitet, *adj.* diffused through the universe; —verderber, *m.* all-destroyer; —verderblich, *adj.* all-destructive; —verehrt, *adj.* all-worshipped, all-revered, universally revered or honoured; —verein, *m.* universal or absolute, complete union; —verflucht, *adj.* all-cursed, cursed by all; —verfolgerin, *f.* (*Bürger*) universal persecutrix; —vergänglich, *adj.* altogether perishable; —vergessen, *adj.* all-forgotten; —vergessenheit, *f.* total oblivion; —verheerend, *adj.* all-devastating; —verhindernd, *adj.* (*Göthe*) all-preventing; —verhüllend, *adj.* all-veiling, all-dimming; —verlangen, *n.* (*Bürger, unusual*) all-powerful desire; —verlassen, *adj.* all-abandoned; —vermessen, *adj.* utterly audacious; —vermögen, *n.* *see* —vermögenheit; —vermögend, *adj.* all-efficient, all-powerful; —vermögenheit, *f.* (*Kant*) all-efficiency, all-powerfulness; —vernichtend, *adj.* all-annihilating, all-destroying; —versöhner, *m.* one who reconciles all or every thing, universal mediator; —vertheilt, *adj.* universally distributed; —verzehrend, *adj.* all-consuming, all-devouring; —vollender, *m.* all-perfecter; —vollkommen, *adj.* all-perfect; —vollkommenheit, *f.* all-perfectness; —vorderst, *adj.* (*Wieland, l. u.*) foremost of all (Allervorderst); —wagend, *adj.* all-daring; —waltend, *adj.* all-ruling, all-governing; —wärts, *adv.* in every direction (*cf.* Allerwärts, *which is more usual*); —weise, *adj.* all-wise, infinitely wise; der —weise, the All-wise; —weisheit, *f.* infinite wisdom; —weit, *adv.* (*Herder*) in all expanse, far and wide; —wichtig, *adj.* (*Schiller, l. u.*) all-important; —wissend, *adj.* all-knowing, omniscient (ungebräuchlich ist omniscious); der —wissende, the All-knowing, Omniscient; —wissenheit, (*freq.* —wiss'enheit) *f.* omniscience, unbounded knowledge; —wisserei', *f.* pretension of knowing every thing; —wissenschaft, *f.* 1) universal knowledge, *nearly the same as* —wissenheit; 2) pantology (*in this sense used now and then for* Philosophie); —wo', *adv.* (*we dialectical by all, cf.* —da, —dort, —hier) *obsolescent, lit.* in which same place (*syn.* woselbst), where; —wöchentlich, *adj.* occurring every week, hebdomadary; *adv.* once every (or a) week, every week, weekly; —würgend, *adj.* all-strangling, all-killing, all-destroying; —zeit, *adv.* *obsolescent*, always, evermore (Allezeit); —zerstörend, *adj.* all-destroying.

All'zu, *adv.* far too, too much, over; — klein, far too small; — groß, over-great; ein — milder Herrscher (*Schiller*), much too mild a governor; — straff gespannt zerspringt der Bogen (*Schiller*), if strained to excess, the bow will break.

All'zu..., *in comp.* —ängstlich, *adj.* far too fearful, over-anxious; —freundlich, *adj.* over-friendly; —fruchtbar, *adj.* over-fruitful.

All'zugegen, *adj.* (All...) ubiquitous (Allgegenwärtig).

All'zugenau, *adj.* far too precise, too particular, quaint, &c. *cf.* Genau.

All'zugleich, *adv.* (All...) al-together (verschieden von altogether), all at once.

All'zugroß, *adj.* far too great, over-great; a-e Beschwerde, over-fatigue; a-e Gefälligkeit, over-complaisance.

All'zuhauf, *adv.* (All...) *obsolescent*, altogether.

All'zumal, *adv.* (*from* All- & Zumal) all at once, altogether; ihr seid Götter und — Kinder des Höchsten (Ps. 82, 6), ye are gods, and all of you are children of the most high; ihr seid — leidige Tröster (Job 16, 2), miserable comforters are ye all.

All'zu..., *in comp.* —sehr, *adv.* far too much, over-much; —straff, *see* Allzu; —zärtlich, *adj.* over-fond; —zeitig, *adj.* far too

familiar, over-familiar; —viel, *adv.* (zu) too much, over-much: —viel ist ungesund, *prov.* too much of a (good) thing is injurious to health, *vulg.* too much pudding may choke a dog.

A. **Alm, Al'me,** *(w.) f. provinc.* high grazing land, mountain meadow, *see* Alpe.

B. **Alm,** *(w.) f. see* Alme.

* **Al'manach,** *(str.) m.* almanac (annual publication), calendar.

* **Almandin, Al'mandin,** *(str.) m. Miner.* almandine, precious garnet (edler Granat).

* **Alma'ne,** *see* Almene.

Al'me, *(w.) f.* 1) *obsolescent & provinc.* a cupboard, case, cabinet; 2) *T.* a drying-apparatus, used in the manufacture of playing-cards.

A. **Al'mei,** *(str.) m. see* Galmei.

B. **Al'mei,** *(w.) f. see* Almer, *A.*

Al'mende (*Swab.* Allmende), *see* Allmende.

* **Alme'ne,** almena, an East Indian weight of about two pounds used for weighing saffron.

Al'menrausch, *(str.) m. provinc.* (*Bavaria, &c.*) *for* Alpenrose, 2.

A. **Al'mer,** *(w.) f.* (*Lat. almarium, OFr. armoire, almaire*) († &) *provinc.* almery, ambry, &c.

B. **Al'mer,** *(str.) m.* 1) *provinc. for* Älpler, *which see*; 2) alpine song.

C. **Al'mer,** *(str.) m.* (*according to others n., f.*) *provinc.* black alder, *see* Faulbaum.

Al'merin, *(w.) f. provinc. for* Älplerin.

Al'mosen, a. I. *(str.) n.* alms, relief given to the poor, charitable gift, charity (milde Gabe); um ein — bitten, to ask or beg an alms, to beg a charity; Jemandem ein — geben, to bestow an alms upon one; vom — leben, to live upon alms or charity; II. *in comp.* —amt, *n.* 1) office for the distribution of alms or charity, alms-house, almonry; 2) almonership; —bruder, *m.* member of an alms-house, alms-man (—genosse); —büchse, *f.* alms-box, poor's-box; —einnehmer, *m.* collector of alms; —empfänger, *m.* one who lives upon alms or charity, eleemosynary, beneficiary, pauper.

Al'mosenierer, Al'moser, *(str.) m. obsolescent,* 1) almoner (Almosenpfleger); 2) *see* Almosenempfänger.

Almosenier', *(str.) m.* 1) *see* Almosenpfleger; 2) lord almoner, an ecclesiastical officer of a prince, &c.

Al'mosen..., *in comp.* —geld, *n.* charity-money, poor-money; poor-rate (Armensteuer); —genosse, *m.* alms-man, member of an alms-house, &c. (—empfänger); —kasten, *m.* alms-chest (—büchse); —korb, *m.* alms-basket; —pflege, *f.* care of the poor (Armenpflege), district or office of an almoner, almonry; —pfleger, *m.* almoner, overseer of the poor (Armenpfleger); —sammler, *m.* gatherer or collector of alms; —sammlung, *f.* collection of alms or of money for the poor; subscription; —spende, 1) (*or* —spendung, *f.*) distribution of alms; 2) charitable gift; —stock, *m.* alms-stock, alms-box.

* **Alod', Alodial** &c., *see* Allod, Allodial &c.

* **A'loe,** [*pr. three syllables:* A'loë] a. I. *f.* (*pl.* Aloes & *(w.)* A'loen) 1) *Bot.* aloe (*Aloe* L.); die große or hundertjährige — (*among gardeners*), the great American aloe, *or* century plant (*Aloë americana, Agave americana*), *see* Agave; 2) *Pharm.* (—auszug, —saft &c.) aloe, (*generally pl.*:) aloes; 3) (*Bastard*) *(str.) n. see* —holz; II. *in comp.* —bitter, *n.* 1) *Chem.* aloine, aloetine, aloetic gum; 2) *or* —auszug, *m., &c., see* Aloe, 2; —harz, *n.* aloetic resin; —holz, *n.* (*in Pharm. Lignum aloës, Lignum agallochum,* Paradiesholz) 1) (genuine) aloes-wood, a resinous, aromatic wood (*Xylaloë calambac*), *or rather substance obtained from Aloëxylon agallochum* (*Lour.* [illegible]) or agallochum, *improperly called* aloes-wood, *having no connection with the common aloe*; —saft, *m. see* Aloe, 2; —säure, *f. Chem.* aloetic acid; —stoff, *m. see* —bitter, 1.

* **Aloë'tisch,** *adj.* (aloehaltig) aloetic(al).

* **Alomantie',** *see* Halomantie.

* **Alonge** &c., *see* Allonge &c.

* **Alopecie',** *(w.) f. Med.* alopecy, fox-evil, a falling off of the hair from disease (Fuchsräude).

Alo'se, *shortened* **Al'se,** *(w.) f. Ichth.* shad, chad (Maifisch, Gangfisch — *Clupea alosa*).

A. **Alp,** *(str.) m.* 1) *a)* hobgoblin, demon, sprite; *b)* nightmare (Mahr, Nachtmahr), incubus: der — drückt mich = ich habe —drücken, *which see*; 2) *fig.* incubus, any encumbrance, dead weight.

B. **Alp',** *(w.) f. see* Alpe.

Alp..., *in comp.* —aar, *m.* alpine eagle.

* **Alpac'a, Alpaka,** (*str., pl.* A-s) *n.* 1) *Zool.* alpaca (*Camelus paco, alpagna*); 2) a thin stuff or cloth made of the wool of the alpaca and silk.

Al pari [*pr.* al pä'ri], *Ital. mercantile phrase, denoting*: in a state of equality or equal value, at par; diese Actien stehen — (*often abbr.*: pari), these shares are at par (*i.e.* when they sell for their nominal value).

Alp'..., *in comp.* —balsam, *m. see* Alpenbalsam; —druck, *m.,* —drücken, *n.* oppression of the nightmare, nightmare; er hat oft — drücken, he often suffers from the nightmare.

Al'pe, *(w.) f.* 1) alp, *gener. in the pl.* die A-n, the Alps, mountains whose tops are covered with snow (*hence particularly of the lofty mountains of Switzerland, but applied by geographers to any high snow-covered mountain-ridge*); 2) (*in Switzerland*) pasture-land on the hills or lower parts of the mountains, *cf.* Alm; jenseits der A-n befindlich, transalpine; diesseits der A-n befindlich, cisalpine.

Al'peln, *(w.) v. intr.* (*aux.* haben) 1) to manage a small Alpine dairy; 2) to have a savour of Alpine husbandry.

Al'pelig, *adj.* resembling an Alpine dairy, &c.

Al'pen..., *in comp.* —abfahrt, *(w.) f.* departure from the Alpine dairies on the approach of winter (*opp.* Alpenfahrt); —ampfer, bastard rhubarb, alpine dock (*Rumex alpinus*); —amsel, *f. Ornith.* 1) *see* —dohle; 2) (Schwarze *or* Steindrossel, Steinamsel) rock thrush (*Turdus saxatilis*); —bachstelze, *f.* alpine wagtail, alpine lark (*Motacilla alpina*); —baldrian, *m. Bot. Valeriana celtica*; —balsam, *Bot.* dwarf rosebay (*Rhododendron arboreum*); —bärlapp, *m. Bot.* alpine club-moss (*Lycopodium alpinum* L.); —baum, *m. Bot.* alpine medlar (*Mespilus amelanchier*); —bewohner, *m.* inhabitant of the Alps (Älpler); —birke, *f. Bot.* the smooth dwarf birch (*Betula nana*); —blume, *f.* alpine flower; —bock, *m. Zool.* (Bergbock) male of the wild goat (Alpenziege), *see* Steinbock; —dohle, *f. Ornith.* alpine crow, mountain jackdaw (*Pyrrhocorax alpinus* Vieill., *Corvus pyrrhocorax* L.); —doppelbeere, *f. see* —heckenkirsche; —doppelblume, *f. see* —rebe; —ebenholz, *n.* alpine cytisus (*Cytisus alpinus*); —eis, *n.* alpine ice; —enzian, *m. Bot.* dwarf-gentian, gentianella (*Gentiana acaulis*); —erde, *f.* dingy mould or soil favourable to the growth of alpine shrubs (braune Dammerde); —erle, *f. Bot.* alpine alder (*Alnus alpina*); —fahrt, *f.* departure for the Alpine dairies on the approach of summer (*opp.* —abfahrt); —fettkraut, *n. Bot.* alpine butterwort (*Pinguicula alpina*); —flockenblume, *f. Bot.* alpine centaury (*Centaurea alpina*); —flüevogel, *m. Ornith.* alpine hedge-sparrow (*Accentor alpinus* Bechst., *Motacilla alpina* L.); —föhre, *f. Bot.* mountain-pine (*Pinus montana* L.); —forelle, *f. Ichth.* (case or red) char (*Salmo alpinus* L.); —fuß, *m.* 1) foot or lower part of the Alps; 2) (*of different derivation*) *see* Al-

trian tour through the Alps: —wasser, n. alpine water or flood: —wegebreit, —wegerich, m. Bot. alpine plantain (Plantago alpina): —wiese, f. alpine pasture: —winter, m. alpine winter: —wirthschaft, f. alpine husbandry (Sennerei): —zünsling, m. Bot. see —hecken-kirsche; —ziege, f. wild goat (Bergziege, Steinbock).

Alp' ..., in comp. —fleck, —flecken, m. see under Alpenstich; —fuß, m. see —kreuz; —gegend, f. (Göthe, l. u.) see Alpengegend.

* Alphabet', (str.) n. from Alpha (A) and Beta (B) the first and the second letters of the Greek alphabet: 1) a) alphabet (ABC); b) fig. aa) a full series; bb) the rudiments, see Abc, 2; 2) Typ. a number of twenty-three printed sheets (J, V, & W being omitted, cf. Signatur), quire: eine Schrift, zwei Alphabete und sechs Bogen stark (Rabener), a volume comprising fifty-two sheets: das ganze Werk möchte etwa ein halbes — ausmachen (Rabener), the whole work (publication) might perhaps consist of upwards of eleven sheets: dachfrage —weise zu verlieren, was ich bogenweise gewonnen (Lessing), to lose that by alphabets (i. e. in quantities of twenty-three sheets) which I had gained by sheets: —schloß, n. T. letter-keyed lock (Buchstabenschloß).

* Alphabe'tisch, adj. alphabetic(al): a-e Anordnung, alphabetical arrangement: eine a-e Sprache, an alphabetical language: a-e Schrift, alphabetic writing (opp. f. i. Zeichenschrift); — ordnen, to arrange alphabetically.

* Alphabetisi'ren, (w.) v. tr. to alphabet, to arrange alphabetically, to range in an alphabetical order.

Alp'hahn, (str., pl. A-hähne) m. Ornith. mountain-cock (Auerhahn).

* Al'phamuschel, (w.) f. Conch. alpha-cockle.

* Alphodill', see Asphodel, Affodill.

* Alphonsin', (str.) n. Surg. alphonsin (instrument for extracting balls from wounds).

* Alphonsi'nisch, adj. Alphonsine, see Alfonsinisch.

Alp'horn, (str., pl. A-hörner) m. see Alpenhorn.

* Alpi'nisch, Alpin', (obsolescent:) Al'pisch, adj. Alpine.

* Alpiß'er, (str.) m. (Dutch) Canary seed, see Kanariensamen.

Alp' ..., in comp. —kirsche, f. (probably from Alp, A) Bot. bird-cherry, see Traubenkirsche; —kladde, f. (Mahrenlocke, Elflocke) provinc. (L. G.) see —zopf; —kräuter, f. see Alpenkräuter; —kraut, see Alpenkraut; —kreuz, n. (from Alp, A) (Alpenkreuz &c., Drudenkreuz, Drudenfuß, Pythagorisches Zeichen) a threefold triangle, forming a figure of five lines and five angles, pentagram, considered by the superstitious as of magic virtue against evil spirits, witches, &c.; —land, see Alpenland.

Älpler (L. u.: Älpler, Alpecker], Alpner, Alpner], (str.) m., Alp'lerin, (w.) f. inhabitant of the Alps (also animal or plant indigenous to the Alps, cf. Bündern), alpine mountaineer, highlander, particul. alpine cowherd, cattle-keeper.

Alp' ..., in comp. —männchen, n. (from Alp, A) hobgoblin; —maus, see Alpenmaus; —[illegible] m. farmer on the Alps; —meister, m. [illegible] of an Alpine dairy, or cattle-ground; [illegible] f. Ornith. see Alpendohle; —ranke, f. [illegible] (from Alp, A, cf. —schoß, —zopf) [illegible] Bot. popular name of several twining [illegible] 1) [illegible], see Mistel; 2) bitter-[illegible]; 3) (Ohm) honeysuckle [illegible]; —rauch, m. Bot. fumitory [illegible]; —raute, f. Bot. the [illegible] —rose, see Alpenrose; — [illegible] (from Alp, A) 1) (—ruthe, Druden-busch, Hexenbesen, Donnerbesen) a knot of twigs and branches (of birches, ashes, willows and other trees) grown together, sometimes resembling a bird's nest, supposed to be twisted by elves (cf. elf-lock), or produced by a thunderbolt; 2) (—stein, Donnerstein, Donnerkeil), a name sometimes given to the fossil remains of cephalopods, the echinus, &c. fairy-stone, thunder-stone, &c. Echinit &c.); —see, see Alpensee; —stein, m. see —schoß, 2; —zopf, m. (from Alp, A) elf-locks (hair matted and entangled inextricably, as elves were said to do (—kladde, Drudenzopf, Wichtelzopf, Weichselzopf), see Weichselzopf.

Al'raun, Al'raune [& Alraun', Alrau'ne], (w.) f. 1) alruna (pl. alrunas), prophetess of the ancient Germans, sage woman, weird-sister; sorceress, hag: 2) (gener. str.) m. a) (dimin. Al'räunchen, Al'räunchen, Al'raunmännchen, n.) mandrake, small, omniscient spright, formed of the roots of several plants (see below), which bore a resemblance to the human form: this rootlike diminutive being was generally dug for under the gallows (Galgenmännchen, Erdmännchen), and when torn from the earth, was supposed to emit fearful shrieks fatal to him who dug it out (cf. Sh. 2 Hen. VI. 3, 2: Rom. & Jul. 4, 3; 2 Hen. IV. 1, 2 & 3, 2); it brought riches and luck to its owner (Heckmännchen, Geldmännchen), but endangered his final salvation; b) name of several plants the roots of which were supposed to resemble the human form (as stated above): aa) mandrake, mandragora (Atropa mandragŏra); bb) bryony: cc) long-rooted garlic (Allermannsharnisch).

A. Als, a frequent mode of spelling the contraction Als (for Alles), which is to be preferred in order to avoid confusion with the conjunction Als (B).

B. Als, conj. 1) † in the primary demonstrative sense of also, so, at the head of a conclusive sentence, for the modern so, which is not expressed in English: nachdem unser Feldherr ... sich bewegen lassen, noch bei der Armee zu verbleiben ..., — verpflichten wir uns ... (Schiller, Picc. 4, 1), (Coleridge:) inasmuch as our supreme commander ... has consented to remain still with the army, ... so we ... do hereby oblige ourselves ....

2) In comparisons: a) in connection with a verb, † for our present wie: du sollst deinen Nächsten lieben — (wie) dich selbst (Matth. 22, 39), thou shalt love thy neighbour as thyself: seine Hörer zu bewegen | sprach er — (wie) ein Cicero (Hagedorn), to move his hearers he spoke like a Cicero: in this sense als wie were sometimes combined, a phrase avoided by modern prose: bedarf er nicht der Nacht — wie des Tags? (Göthe), does he not want the night as well as the day? so klug als wie zuvor (the same), no wiser than before: b) in connection with a substantive, also † for wie: in einem Lande — Deutschland (Lessing), in a country like Germany: — wie for wie: die Zeiten sind — wie ein Rad (Logau), time is like a wheel; c) in connection with the positive degree of an adj., † for wie: weiß — Schnee (Matth. 28, 3), white as snow: — wie for wie: weiß und roth — wie ein wächsern Bild (Wieland), as white and red as a waxen image; d) aa) in all the cases mentioned under a, b, & c — († also) was often preceded in the first clause of the sentence by a correlative word, viz. so († — for also) before verbs, adjectives, and adverbs, solch before substantives, &c.; thus als ... als ... was used as late as the 16th cent.: — roth — Scharlach, as red as scarlet, &c.: either of these correlatives or correspondent words is not seldom omitted: a mere so in the modern mode of speech so sufficient to connect the two clauses: — (for the ancient also) viel (omitted als) an uns ist (Luther): modern examples: so viel (—) an uns liegt, as much as in us lies; so gut (—) ich konnte, as well as I could; instances of the second kind (i. e. omission of the first correlative) are very numerous: der Ofen glüht, die Bälge blasen [omitted so, so sehr], | — gält es Felsen zu verglasen (Schiller, Gang zum Eisenhammer), the furnace glows, the bellows blew, as if the task were to melt rocks into glass; bb) in correlative sentences and phrases, such as so viel (so wenig, so gut, so schlecht &c.) — möglich, &c.; so schnell (so langsam, so kurz, so lang &c.) — ... &c., als is still, and perhaps more frequently used than wie: Einer ist so viel werth — (or wie) der Andere, one is as much worth as the other. So likewise in the combinations — wenn (or wie wenn, wie wann), — ob, — daß (never wie ob, wie daß) &c.; er that (stellte sich), — wenn (or — ob) er nichts wüßte, he made (a show) as if he knew nothing; e) aa) after the comparative degree of an adjective. This is the proper province of als in modern High-German: (roth wie Blut, but:) rother — Blut, redder than blood. But even here wie (and — wie) is not only used colloquially, but by good writers. Besides this als the old denn has been retained in the more elevated style and even in common usage, when a collision of two als would have produced a bad sound: — Knabe war er schöner denn (for als) — Jüngling (Grimm), as a boy he was more beautiful than as a youth; lieber frei sterben, denn — Sklaven leben, rather to die free than to live as slaves, &c.; bb) als is also used after words which, though not comparatives as to their outward form, imply a comparison; thus after ein anderer and its derivatives, sonst, negations and interrogations, &c., the latter term of an exclusive comparison is introduced by als, exactly corresponding to the cases which in English require than after other (cf. Ander), otherwise, else, or but (in the sense of besides): er gab keine andere Antwort, — einen barschen Ton der Zustimmung, he gave no other answer than a gruff sound of acquiescence: was wir Fabeln oder Parabeln nennen, sind nichts anderes, — Allegorien, what we call fables or parables are no other than allegories: Stil ist nichts anderes, — die Art des Ausdrucks, welchen &c., style is nothing else than that sort of expression which, &c.: wir urtheilen anders von ihnen — von uns selbst, we judge otherwise of them than of ourselves: sie liebt keinen — ihn (perhaps better: außer ihm), she loves none but him: wer anders kann gemeint sein, — ich? who can be aimed at but I? keiner — ich war zugegen, none but I was present: er ist zu klug, — daß er an Gespenster glauben sollte (Hayne), he is too clever to believe in ghosts: er ist zu klug, — daß ihm dieser Vortheil entgehen sollte, he is too prudent for this advantage to escape him: eine zu fest eingewurzelte Gewohnheit, — daß das mildeste Frühlingswetter sie ändern könnte, a habit too inveterate for the most genial spring-weather to alter.

3) Als identifying: a) before predicative nouns, particularly the nom. & acc., identifying a logical subject and its predicate: ich komme — Bote means I come as a messenger, i. e. although not in general a messenger; er starb — Bettler, he died (as) a beggar: er schrieb mir — Antwort (auf ...), — Erwiederung, he wrote to me in answer (to ...), in return; b) this als rendered by other English turns of phrase: sie läßt die armen Kinder Sackleinwand — Lätzchen und Bindfaden — Strumpfbänder tragen, she lets the poor children wear sackcloth for pinafores, and packthread for garters: er ließ nie Jemand — Minister zu, der ..., he never admitted any person to be his minister, who ...; ich wurde — Ungläubiger angesehen, I was considered (to

ve) an infidel; die gereiften Früchte seiner Arbeiten — Geistlicher und Professor, the matured fruit of his ministerial and professorial labours: er unterzeichnete das Document — Sachwalter, he signed the document in the capacity of an attorney; das Gesuch kam — Denkschrift vor den gesetzgebenden Körper, the application came before the legislature in the shape of a memorial; alles dies, obschon es — Anregung von Werth ist, ist — Beweis nichts werth, all this, valuable as it is in the way of suggestiveness, is worth nothing in the way of proof; *c) the omission of this* als *is frequent in poetry and the elevated style:* bist du ein Knecht berufen, sorge dir nicht (1 Cor. 7, 21) art thou being called a servant? care not for it; daß ich ein Bettler geboren werden durfte! *(Schiller)*, oh, that I might have been born (as) a beggar! (Vgl.: I'll live and die a maid, to live and die her slave, &c.); *d)* als *introducing enumerations, &c., to be explained as representing a shortened sentence: aa)* es gibt drei grammatische Geschlechter, — *(for — da sind, which is likewise used)* Masculinum, Femininum, Neutrum, there are three grammatical genders, viz. masculine, feminine, neuter; diejenigen neueren Sprachen, — [or wie] die französische &c. *(Lessing)*, those modern languages, as, for instance, *(or, such as)* the French, &c.; Weihnachtsgeschenke, — *(or* wie) Bücher, Kleider, Spielzeug, lagen auf dem Tisch, Christmas presents, in the form of books, clothes, playthings, lay on the table; *bb) before* heute, morgen, gestern &c., *similar to the English* as to-day, as to-morrow, &c., *rather colloquial:* er benachrichtigte mich, daß er — *(or* — wie) heute Morgen hatte zu mir kommen wollen, he informed me that he had intended to come to me as this morning *(cf.* As, Vol. I.). *This* als *always serves to put the word or words which it introduces prominently forward, and is seen, though seldom in recent usage, combined with the relative:* ihr habt diesen Menschen zu mir gebracht, — der das Volk abwende (Luke 23, 14), ye have brought this man to me, as one that perverteth the people.

4) Als, *temporal,* when; *always relating to some past event which took place simultaneously with some other event:* — wie in die Stadt fuhren, hörte es auf zu regnen, when we drove into the town, it ceased to rain *(just as the one event took place, so the other took place, i. e. simultaneously);* — ich das Vorgemach durchgehe *(Schiller; the historic present for the imperfect* [durchging] *of common prose),* on passing through the antechamber, I heard, &c.

C. Als, *(w.) f. see* Alse.

Alsbald', *adv.* forthwith, directly, immediately.

Alsbal'dig, *adj.* done, effected, *or* happening forthwith, immediate, instantaneous.

Alsdann', Alsdenn', *adv. obsolescent,* then *(sometimes as much as* not till then, just then, at that very time, *cf.* Sodann).

A. Al'se, *(w.) f. see* Alose. [mut).

B. Al'se, *(w.) f. provinc.* wormwood (Wermut).

C. Al'se, *(w.) f. provinc. (Scotch.)* awl (Ahle).

Al'senach, Al'seneck, *(str.) m. Bot.* popular name of *Athamanta palustre, see* Ölsenich.

Alsfort', *adv.* [† &] *provinc. see* Sofort.

Alsgemach', *adv. (from* Als, II.) gradually.

† Alslang', *conj.* as long as (Solang, *or* so lang[e]).

Al'so, I. *adv.* † & *poet.* thus, so, in this way, in such a manner *(cf.* So); II. *conj.* 1) consequently, accordingly; therefore: so, then; es sind vier, — mehr als drei, there are four, consequently more than three; „—", bemerkte eine alte Dame, indem sie die Brille zurechtlegte, „— dies ist der Kaiser Titus!" "so", observed an old lady, adjusting her spectacles, "so this is the Emperor Titus"; was! Sie haben — nicht gehört, ...? what! you have not heard, then, ...? es ist — keine Hoffnung, Herr Doctor? then there is no hope, Doctor? ach, theuerster Rudolf, du warest — nicht untreu, wie man mich gern überredet hätte! oh, dearest Rudolphus! you were not then, as they would fain have persuaded me, untrue; auf ihren Brief war keine Antwort gekommen, ... der Gläubiger war — geduldig, to their letter no answer had come, the creditor was then a patient one.

Alsobald', *adv.* † & *poet. for* Alsbald.

Alsofort', Alsogleich', *adv.* † & *poet. for* Sofort, Sogleich.

Alsohin', Alsonst', *adv.* † *for* Sohin, Sonst.

Alst, *adv. provinc. for* Als.

Al'ster, *(w.) f.* († &) *provinc. for* Elster, magpie (Aglaster).

A. Alt, *adj.* 1) old: *a) having existed for some time, of any specified duration;* das Kind ist zwei Stunden —, the child is two hours old; sie ist zwanzig Jahre —, she is twenty years old *or* of age; er starb funfzig Jahre —, he died aged fifty years; alt, *in this combination, often omitted, f. i.* sie ist noch nicht sechzehn Jahre, she is not yet sixteen years *(and even* Jahre *is often omitted, as in English);* einen Tag ([† &] *poet. with the Gen.* eines Tages) —, a day old; er ist so — als ich, he is as old as I, *coll.* he is my age: er ist einige Jahre älter als ich, he is a few years my older *or* senior; von zwei Brüdern der ältere, the older one of two brothers (im Engl. oft auch der Superlativ, wo nur von zweien die Rede ist); unter dreien der älteste, the oldest of three; Fortescue der Ältere, nicht F. der Jüngere, (in engl. Schulen) Fortescue-major, not F.-minor *((in German schools, &c., obsolescent:* Flügel senior, Flügel junior): der ältere Zweig einer Dynastie, the older branch of a dynasty *(opp.* der jüngere, the junior *or* younger branch); *b) having existed a long time or many years,* (far) advanced in life, aged, elderly; der alte Mann, die alte Frau *(and substantively* der Alte, die Alte, *which see),* the old man, the old woman; *for* Junge und Alte *the undeclined neuter singular* Jung und Alt *(less usual* Alt und Jung) *is often used:* wir wollen ziehn mit Jung und — (Exod. 10, 9), we will go with our young and our old; dir unterwirft sich Jung und —, to thee the young and the old submit; *proverbs:* jung gewohnt — gethan, as the twig is bent, so is the tree inclined; wie die Alten sungen *(obsolescent for* sangen), so zwitschern (pfeifen, pipen) auch die Jungen, as the old cock crows, so crows the young; like father like son; *c) sometimes of lifeless things (see 2), particul. as opposed to* frisch: alter Wein, old wine; altes Bier, old beer *(opp.* junger *[also* neuer] Wein, junges Bier); alter Wein, altes Bier &c. *may sometimes denote* stale wine, stale beer *(opp.* frischer Wein &c.); alte Butter, alter Schinken, alter Speck, alte Wurst, alte Eier, altes Brot *almost always in an ill sense, and opposed to* frisch, old (rancid) butter, old ham, (rusty) bacon, sausage, old eggs, old (stale) bread; alter Käse *(opp.* frischer Käse), ripe, rotten, *or* decayed cheese.

2) Old: *as opposed to* neu (new, modern, &c.); *a) having existed long time ago or in former ages,* long past, ancient, antique, &c.: die alte Zeit, die alten Zeiten, ancient time, ancient times; in *or* vor alten Zeiten, in ancient, old *(poet.:* olden) times, in times *or* days of old, of old, in times of yore: Rom war in alten Zeiten volkreicher als gegenwärtig, Rome was anciently more populous than at present; die alte Geschichte, ancient history; das alte Deutschland, das alte Athen, das alte Rom, ancient Germany, ancient Athens, ancient Rome: die alten Völker *(or* die Alten, *see* Alte,

s.), the ancient [illegible] *cul.* the ancient [illegible] Vase, an antique vase [illegible] tur, ancient art and [illegible] menschlich-[illegible] unsere Alten, our [illegible] longing to a former time or [illegible] Jahr, the year passed over, [illegible] das neue Jahr, the new year, [illegible] das junge Jahr, *a particul.* [illegible] *opposed to* das alte Jahr [illegible] year far advanced [illegible] *(syn.* der alte Bau, die [illegible] mine or pit filled up [illegible] subsisting, known, or [illegible] thing else; das alte Gesetz [illegible] aufgehoben, the old law is [illegible] new; das alte Testament, the [illegible] die alte Welt, the Old World [illegible] of old; die Venetianer [illegible] Gesetzen und Gebräuchen, the [illegible] tenacious of old laws and [illegible] or long standing; ein alter [illegible] acquaintance; ein altes Übel, [illegible] rate evil; *c) aa)* experienced [illegible] thing by (long) experience; [illegible] old in practice; Rome, jung [illegible] in weisem Rathe —, Rome, you[ng] [illegible] but in sage counsel old ([illegible] bedürft: to have an old head [illegible] dern); — thun, to give oneself [illegible] air, to play the old sage; ein [illegible] an old (experienced) soldier; *bb)* [illegible] tested by long experience; [illegible] Schrot und Korn, of fine weight [illegible] coins); er ist von altem Schlag [illegible] is of the (good) old stamp [illegible] *endearment;* mein alter lieber [illegible] zu einem fünfjährigen Knaben [illegible] fellow! said he to a boy five [illegible] was machst du, altes Haus [illegible] you, old fellow! *d) what has* [illegible] *or formerly: aa) in a good sense* [illegible] die gute alte Zeit, the good old [illegible] Liebe rostet nicht, old affection [illegible] sie waren alte Schulkameraden [illegible] had been old schoolfellows; [illegible] der alte ehrgeizige Politiker [illegible] ambitious politician that he [illegible] ist immer noch der Alte, he is [illegible] he is the same as ever; er [illegible] Alte, he is not the same, [illegible] he used to be, he is not his [illegible] is greatly altered, *coll.* he [illegible] way with him (*at* alles *as* [illegible] *(n.)*, things remain as they [illegible] bleibe beim Alten, I am still [illegible] er ließ Alles beim Alten, he [illegible] he had found them; [illegible] legen, ausziehen (Ephes. 4, [illegible] to put off the old man; [illegible] *land) prefixed to names or* [illegible] *noting that a person has* [illegible] *office, f. i.* Alt-[illegible] Alt-Hauptmann, Alt-[illegible] man, &c. *In his* [illegible] *happily translate the* [illegible] *torius, consortius,* [illegible] ter, Alt-Geselle; *e)* [illegible] by time, superannuated [illegible] an old broken soldier; [illegible] thee; alte Bücher, [illegible] books; altes Eisen, [illegible] busheled iron; *bb)* [illegible] alte Gebräuche, old [illegible] Witzer, old or [illegible] teile; das ist eine [illegible] Geschichte, that [illegible] new; beschäftige mich [illegible] Geschichte, don't [illegible] old affair (thing [illegible] Witze, those [illegible]

B. Alt, *(str.) m. Ichth.* 1) *see* Aland, *A;* 2) *see* Alse.

C. * Alt, *(str.) m. (Ital. alto) Mus.* alto, alt, counter-tenor, high-tenor.

Alt'adelig, *adj.* of old nobility.

Altai'isch, *adj.* Altaic, Altaian, pertaining to the Altai ridge of mountains in Asia.

Alt'ammen, *see* Alt, *A.* 2, *d,* bb.

*** Al'tan** *[sometimes* Altan'*], (str.) m. (& coll. n.),* **Alta'ne,** *(w.) f.* 1) platform, (open) gallery with balustrades on the roof of a (country-)house, or before windows; flat roof (Hochaltan, Söller); 2) balcony (Balcon); —**dach,** *n. T.* flat roof: —**fenster,** *n.* French casement or window (opening to the ground).

Alt'antheil, *(str.) m. see* Altentheil.

Al'tar *[& frequently* Altar'*], s.* I. *(str., pl.* **Altäre** *&* **Altare,** *the accent being mostly on the second syllable) m. (dimin.* **Al'tärchen, Al'tärlein,** *(str.) n.)* 1) altar: *in Christian churches, also* communion-table; das Sacrament des A-s, the sacrament (of the holy communion); 2) *fig.* shrine: II. *in comp.* —**bekleidung,** *f.* decoration of an altar (—decke); —**blatt,** *n.* back-piece of an altar (—bild, *n.*): altar-piece, altar-painting: —**buße,** *f.* expiation before the altar; —**decke,** *f.* altar-cloth; communion-cloth: —**diener,** *m. Rom. Cath.* 1) acolythist, acolyte (church-servant); 2) (Altarist) altarist, the priest that ministers at the altar; —**geld,** *n.* altarage (Altaragium), emolument of priests ministering at the altar: —**gemälde,** *n.* altar-piece (painting placed over or behind the altar); —**geräth(e),** *n.* altar-furniture: —**geschirr(e),** *n.* sacred vessels, altar-plate.

*** Altarist',** *(w.) m.* altarist, altar-chaplain, *see* Altardiener, 2.

Al'tar..., *in comp.* —**kranz,** *f.* (altar-) flagon; —**kelch,** *m.* chalice (the cup in which the wine of the eucharist is administered); —**kerze,** *f.,* —**licht,** *n.* altar-candle: —**lehen,** *n.* altar-fief; —**mann,** *m. (pl.* —leute, —männer) *see* —diener; —**recht,** *n. Canon Law,* patronage, the right of presenting a clergyman to an altarist's benefice; —**rede,** *f.* sermon preached before the altar *(as distinguished from* Kanzelrede); —**stufe,** *f.* step of an altar; —**stück,** *n.* altar-piece (painting or ornamental sculpture, placed over an altar): —**teppich,** *m.* altar-carpet; —**tuch,** *n.* altar-cloth (—decke).

Alt..., *in comp.* —**backen,** *adj.* 1) stale (applied to anything baked that has grown hard or tasteless from age, *opp.* Neubacken, Frischbacken); —**baum,** *m. Bot. see* Traubenkirschenbaum; —**begründet,** *p. a.* established of old: —begründete Rechte, vested rights; —**bekannt,** *adj.* known of old, long-known, well-known; —**binder,** *m.* cooper, repairer of old casks; —**britisch,** *adj.* Old British; —**castilisch,** *n.* Old Castile; —**deutsch,** *adj.* Old German.

Al'te, *s. (weak form of the adj.* Alt, *which* [illegible] *declined like an adj.)* I. *m. & f.* 1) *a)* old man *(dimin.* Altchen *(str.) n.);* [illegible] ich den Alten gern *(Göthe, Faust),* the ancient one! I like sometimes to [illegible]; *b)* old woman; 2) *a) coll. (and* [illegible]*) term used by children, speaking of their parents, by apprentices in reference to their principals, &c.:* the old one; [illegible] governor; der — will nicht blechen, *slang,* [illegible] won't come down with the ready; [illegible]! old man! old one! old fellow! old [illegible] „[illegible], Alter", pflegte mein [illegible] (als einem 14jährigen Knaben) zu sagen, [illegible] die Flasche!" "hallo, old man", [illegible] would say, "go and bring your [illegible]"; ehrlicher Alter! honest veteran; [illegible] *coll.* gaffer, dame, crone; 3) the male [illegible] (of animals); 4) *a) familiar* [illegible] *of the* Wenzel-Ober *(being the highest* [illegible] *word, cf.* Wenzel), [illegible] *of the* Eichel-Ober, *used in* [illegible]

b) an officer (the king's man or counsellor) was likewise so called in an obsolete kind of chess-play; c) see Alt, 2, *a, bb;* II. die Alten, *pl.* the ancients *(particul.* the Greeks and Romans), *see* Alt, 2, *a;* der Rath der Alten, (French Revolution) the council of the Ancients; III. *n.* an old thing (etwas Altes), *see* Alt, 2, *d & e.*

Al'te, *(w.) f. (l. u.)* quality of being old, [age, old age.

Alt'..., *in comp.* —**edel,** *adj.* of old nobility; —**ehrwürdig,** *adj.* time-honoured, age-honoured; —**eisler,** *m. (l. u.)* a vender of old iron.

† **Alteclä're,** *(w.) f. (Old Fr. Hauteclaire)* name of Oliver's battlesword *(Uhland).*

Al'telig, *adj. provinc.* growing stale.

Al'teln, *(w.) v. intr. (dimin. of* Alten) 1) to begin to grow old, to grow oldish, to grow or be elderly: 2) to grow stale, to fade, to wither.

† **Alt'eltern,** *(w.) pl.* ancestors, forefathers [(Voreltern)

Al'ten, *(w.) v. intr. (aux.* haben, *less frequently* sein) *(l. u.)* to grow old, *see* Altern.

Alt'england, *(str.) n.* Old England.

Alt'englisch, *adj.* Old English.

Altenmann'nebrasse, *(w.) f. (Wieland)* (assumed) part of an old man.

Al'tentheil, *(str.) n. Law,* reservation made by an old person in disposing of his *(or* her) property (Ausgedinge, Auszug).

Al'ter, *(str.) n.* 1) age (of a man, a horse, of wine, &c.); sein — ist zwanzig Jahre, his age is twenty years; in seinem —, at his age, at his time of life; er ist in meinem —, he is of my (own) age; die Mama sagt oft, daß sie sehr viele Unarten beging, als sie in meinem — war, mamma often says she did many naughty things when she was my age: das blühende, jugendliche —, the prime of life, youth, flower of age; das zarte —, tender age, tender years: im besten —, in the vigour of life; das hohe —, great, advanced *or* old age, declining age; das mittlere —, middle age: bis in das höchste *or* späteste —, to the latest period of one's existence:

2) *obsolescent for* Zeitalter, Weltalter, Zeit; das goldene —, the golden age: ein besseres — *(Schiller),* a better age; vor A-s, of old (dichterisch: [in days] of yore), anciently, in former times, formerly; von A-s her, from remotest antiquity, from ancient *or* former times; of old: Gott ist mein König von A-s her (Ps. 74, 12), God is my king of old:

3) priority in office: die Beamten werden nach dem — befördert, (the) officers are promoted by seniority; das — vor Einem haben: *aa)* to be older *or* one's senior in office, to have priority of office or appointment over another; *bb)* to have priority of possession: sein — augenscheinlich machen, *among Miners,* to prove priority of possession;

4) long duration, ancientness, (great) age, antiquity; das — des Erdballes, the antiquity of the globe: das — der Erde, the age of the earth; die Stoffe, aus denen dieser Ball besteht, sind von sehr hohem —, the materials of which this globe is composed, are of high antiquity: das — einer Familie, the ancientness *or* antiquity of a family; das — eines Rechts, the ancientness of a right:

5) *a)* old age, decline of life *(opp.* Jugend); er fürchtet ein einsam, hülflos — *(Göthe),* he is afraid of a lonely, helpless age: das — naht, old age approaches: — schützt vor Thorheit nicht, *proverb,* age is not proof against folly, age does not always bring wisdom; *b)* old men *or* persons collectively: das — muß man ehren, we must honour old age: *c) fig.* oldness, staleness, &c. *cf.* Alt, *adj.*

Al'ter, *compar. of* Alt, *adj.: sometimes occurring in compounds denoting ancestral relations:* —**ahn,** *m. (Lessing)* a great grandfather; —**ältern,** *pl.* great grandparents (Ureltern, Voreltern), *cf.* —mutter, —vater.

*** Alteration',** *(w.) f. (Lat.)* 1) alteration (Änderung); 2) *Mus.* †, the doubling the value of a note; 3) *obsolescent,* violent emotion, ont turn (heftige Gemüthsbewegung, Ärger &c.).

Al'terbrüder, *(str.) m. (Herder) unusual for* der ältere Bruder.

Al'terchen, *(str.) n. (dimin. of* Alter, *see* Alte, I. *a)* 1) *a term of endearment,* good old man, dear old fellow, &c.

Alt'erfahren, *adj. (from* Alt) having the experience of a long life, experienced.

Al'tergrau, *adj. (comp. of* Alter) gray with age, hoary (Altersgrau).

Al'terhaft, *adj. (from* Alter) old fashioned, antique *(Voss, l. u.).*

Al't(e)rig, *adj. (only in comp.)* of (a certain) age (Dreialterig, Gleichalterig &c.).

*** Alteri'ren,** *(w.) v. tr.* 1) to alter (Ändern); a-de Mittel, *Med.* alterative remedies, alteratives: 2) to change for the worse, to aggravate: *obsolescent,* sich —, to be violently agitated, to be vexed.

Al'terlich, *adj. l. u. (except in the comp.* Mittel-) antique (Alterthümlich).

Äl'terlich, *see* Elterlich.

Al'termann, *(m., pl.* A-männer, *sometimes* A-leute) *m.* presiding officer of a corporation or guild, elder, senior (Zunft-Vorsteher &c.).

Al'termutter, *(str., pl.* A-mütter) *f. (see* Alter & Altervater) great grandmother, or grandmother (Altmutter, Eltermutter).

Al'tern, *sometimes* **Äl'tern,** *(w.) v.* I. *intr. (aux.* haben, *sometimes* sein) *(from* Alt, *stronger than* Alteln, *expressing less than* Alten, *but having supplanted both these words)* to grow old *or* older; to decay, decline; *coll.* to age: er altert mit jedem Tage, he ages every day *(Dickens);* II. *tr.* to make (prematurely) old, *coll.* to age: Sorgen — mehr als Jahre, sorrows age more than years.

Äl'tern, *pl.* parents, *see* Eltern.

*** Alternat',** *(str.) n. (Lat.)* alternate, alternation. — **Alternation',** *(w.) f.* reciprocal succession of things, alternation (Abwechselung). — **Alternativ',** *adj. (Fr.* alternatif, *from the Lat.)* alternative, alternate, offering the choice of two things (Abwechselnd). — **Alternati've,** *(w.) f.* alternative *(choice given of two things, so that if one is taken, the other must be left);* option; dilemma (das Entweder-Oder, die Zweiwahl). — **Alterni'ren,** *(w.) v. intr.* to alternate (Abwechseln, Umwechseln, Wechseln); a-d, *p. a. Bot.* alternate (of leaves, &c., Wechselständig):

Al'tersallein, *adj. (from* Alter, *in the obsolete meaning of* world) †, alone (in the world), entirely alone (Mutter(seelen)allein).

Al'ter..., *in comp.* —**schwach,** —**schwäche,** *see* Altersschwach, Altersschwäche; —**schwer,** *adj.* heavy with age.

Al'ters..., *in comp.* —**erlaß,** *m. Law,* dispensation in respect of age *(Lat.* venia ætatis, *Hilp.);* —**folge,** *f.* succession of men or things according to their respective ages; nach der —folge (im Amte) verrücken, to advance (in office) by seniority; —**genoß,** *m.* contemporary, one of the same age; —**grau,** *adj.* gray with age, hoary, (dicht.:) time-gray; —**kreis,** *m. Med.* gerontotoxon, a bow-shaped collection of opaque matter in the cornea of old persons; —**präsident,** *m.* (in preliminary parliamentary assemblies) president (chairman) of an assembly on account of his being the oldest member present: —**ring,** *m. see* —kreis; —**schwach,** *adj.* weak from age, worn out *or* decayed with age, decrepit; —**schwäche,** *f.* decrepitude, feebleness of age, decline of life: er starb an —schwäche, he died of old age: —**stufe,** *f.* stage of life, age: Shakespeare spricht von sieben —stufen des Menschen, Shakespeare speaks of the seven ages of man; —tod, m. death from old age: —unterschied, m. difference of age; —vormund, m. Law, guardian of a minor (as distinguished from Abwesenheitsvormund &c.).

Al'terthum, (str., pl. Al'terthümer) n. 1) †, old age, decline of life, see Alter, 5, a; 2) antiquity: 3) a) a piece of ancient art (A-stück); b) the remains of ancient times, antiquities: griechische und römische Alterthümer, Grecian and Roman antiquities.

Al'terthums..., in comp. —forscher, m. student of antiquity, antiquary, antiquarian: —forschung, f. study of antiquity, archæology: —gesellschaft, f. antiquarian society: —kenner, m. one versed in a knowledge of antiquity, antiquary: —krämer, m. one meddling with objects of ancient art, pseudo-antiquary: —kunde, f. archæology: —kundig, adj. versed in antiquity, antiquarian: der —kundige, see —kenner; —stück, n. a piece of ancient art, antique: —verein, m. antiquarian association: —wissenschaft, f. science of archæology.

Alterthümelei', (w.) f. pretension to antiquity, antiquarianism.

Al'terthümeln, (w.) v. intr. to assume the semblance of antiquity: to exhibit an exaggerated or perverse predilection for antiquity.

Al'terthümler, (str.) m. 1) one possessed of undue partiality for antiquity or antiquities, antiquarian: 2) (or Al'terthümer, (str.) m. employed by some to avoid the ill sense, generally attached to the word Alterthümler) antiquary, see Alterthumsforscher.

Al'terthümlich, I. adj. 1) antique, ancient; 2) having the appearance of, or imitating antiquity, antique: II. A-keit, (w.) f. 1) antiqueness: appearance of antiquity: 2) antique or ancient work, piece of antiquity.

Al'tervater, (str., pl. A-väter) m. (from Alter, which see: cf. Altvater) great grandfather: also, for an ancestor.

Alter-Weiber-Sommer. Alte(r)-Wei'ber-Sommer, (Alt decl. like adj.) m. see Altweiber .....

Al'teste, (superl. of Alt) I. adj. 1) oldest, eldest, most ancient: der — Sohn, the eldest son: 2) often used as a substantive: dies ist mein A-r, this is my eldest (son): II. m. (decl. like adj.) elder: senior: alderman: A-amt, n., A-amtswürde, f., A-recht, n. eldership, seniority.

Altes Weib, see Altweib.

Alt..., in comp. —fisch, m. Ichth. see Aland; —flicker, m. mender of old things (shoes, clothes, &c.): cobbler: —flöte, f. (from Alt, C) Mus. counter-tenor flute (flûte à bec): —förmig, adj. old-fashioned: —franke, m. gener. pl. die —franken, the ancient Franks: —fränkisch, adj. †, old-fashioned, antique (—modisch, —väterisch): —fromm, adj. (J. Paul) of old-fashioned piety: —gebacken, see —backen; —gedient, adj. having served a long time, veteran —gegründet, p. a. founded or established of old: —gehabt, p. a. †, had of old, of old standing: —geige, f. (from Alt, C) Mus. tenor-violin (Bratsche); —geschlecht, n (Göthe, l. u.) ancient lineage or descent: —gesell, m. head-journeyman, foreman: —gesittet, adj. of (good) old manners: —gevatter, m. one who has already stood godfather to other children of some one: —gewandflicker, m. †. one who mends old clothes, or a dealer in old clothes, old-clothes-broker (Kleiderhändler); —gewohnt, p. a. accustomed of old: die —gewohnte Ordnung, the old accustomed order; —gläubig, adj. addicted to the old doctrine, orthodox; —gläubigkeit, f. a belief in the old doctrine, orthodoxy: —gothisch, adj. ancient Gothic: —griechenland, n. old or ancient Greece: —griechisch, adj. old Greek, ancient Greek (opp. Neugriechisch); —händler, m. a dealer in old clothes, &c. (Trödler).

* Althee' (popularly accented on the first syllable, as if it were a word compounded with Thee; Lat. althæa, from Gr. althaia, healing-herb, Heilkraut), (w.) f. Bot. althea, marsh-mallow (Eibisch, Althæa L.).

Alt'heit, (w.) f. (l. u.) 1) oldness: 2) (piece of) antiquity.

Alt'..., in comp. —herkömmlich, —hergebracht, adj. customary from old times, traditional: old, ancient (cf. —gewohnt); —herr, m. provinc. & †, alderman: member of the senate (Altermann); —heu, n. the first or crop of grass (opp. Grummet, after-math); —hiebig, adj. Forest. (said of underwood) of more than ten years' standing: —hochdeutsch, adj. Old High German (referring to the remotest period of High German, from the seventh to the beginning of the twelfth century): —holz, n. Forest. old wood, applied to stems two or three years old (opp. Jungholz).

* Altist', (w.) m., Altist'in, (w.) f. see Altsänger, Altsängerin.

Alt'..., in comp. —jagdbar, adj. Sport. (of a stag) having reached the best age for being hunted (which is in the eighth year), full-grown: —klug, adj. knowing or prudent like an old man, or beyond one's years, too early matured for one's age, old-fashioned, precocious, forward: —knecht, m. 1) head-servant (Großknecht); 2) in some trades syn. with —gesell; —krank, adj. having been ill or indisposed for a long time: —landammann, see under Alt, 2, d; —lapper, see —flicker; —lehrig, adj. scarcely used, addicted to the old doctrine, orthodox (cf. —gläubig).

Alt'lich, I. adj. (from Alt, adj.) 1) elderly (of persons), bordering upon old age, somewhat old, oldish: 2) (of the taste of eatables, &c.) stale, oldish: II. A-keit, (w.) f. elderliness, &c.

Alt'..., in comp. —macher, see —flicker; —magd, f. among farmers, &c. the eldest serving-girl (Großmagd); —mann, m. old man, see Alt, A, 1, b; —mannskraut, n. Bot. 1) erigeron; 2) groundsel (senecio, Kreuzkraut); —meister, m. 1) head-master, elder, senior, particul. presiding officer of a corporation or guild (Obermeister, cf. Altermann); 2) fig. senior master: Göthe der —meister der deutschen Dichter, Göthe, the patriarch of German poets: —melk, —melkend (coll. —melken), —milchen(d), adj. Husb. having given milk for some time (opp. Frischmelk, Neumelk); —modisch, adj. old-fashioned: —mutter, f. (cf. —vater) grandmother: —nordisch, adj. Old Norse: —papa, m. (Voss) grandpapa (—vater); —posaune, f. (from Alt, C) Mus. alto-trombone: —reh, n. Sport. the hind or doe after the first rutting: —reis, —reißer, m. see —flicker; —römisch, adj. old or ancient Roman: —sachse, m. Old Saxon: —sächsisch, adj. old Saxon: —sänger, m. (from Alt, C), —sängerin, f. alto-singer: —schön, adj. (l. u.) of antique beauty: —schlüssel, m. (from Alt, C) Mus. counter-tenor clef, alto-clef, the C clef on the third line of the stave: —schuster, m. cobbler (—flicker); —sessen, adj. belonging to the old inhabitants of a place: —gesessene Leute, old settlers: —sitzer, m. former owner of an estate or house, having reserved to himself part of the lodgings, &c. (Ausgedinger Auszügler); —schelleisen, n. old cable iron: —sprochen (for —gesprochen), p. a. obsolescent. long since said, reported of old: —sprochen Wort, for Sprichwort (Spenser: an old-said saw); —stadt, f. old town or city, particul. the old part of a large town or city: —städter, m. inhabitant of the old part of a city: —stimme, f. (from Alt, C) Mus. the counter-tenor, or highest male voice: —testamentlich, adj. relating to the Old Testament, Mosaical: die a-en Heiligen, the Old Testament saints: a-e Bruchstücke, Old Testament fragments (opp. Neu-

lutherisch)'; —thier, ... stag or buck.

Alt'väterisch, ... who appears ...

Al'tung, (w.) f. ...

Alter Mann (Alt ...

Alt..., in comp. ... father, used for gr... Scotland. Dutch ... 2) forefather, ... vater, Stammvater ... unserer neueren Dich... patriarch of our ... der ersten Kirche, th... see Kirchenväter; ... tian; 5) Surg. a ... may be laid in the... —väterlich, adj. old... (väterlich); —väterlich... father, patriarchal; ... herited from one's ... vaterrecht, n. see ... (l. u.) wise like old... traut, adj. familiar ... ance, intimate, an... —vettelisch, adj. † ... an old woman, silly ... a-e Fabeln (1 Timot... —vieh, n. horned-... —thier); —viole, f. ... viola, a small tena... dere, f. & m. (decl. ... existed or was befo... pl. (die —vordere(n)... —wald, m. old or ... forest: —wasser, n. ... branch where once ... weib, n. 1) l. u. ... (prating) old wom... Ichth. name given ... Geweib); b) savan... likewise so named ... papilio, &c.: —weib... women's tittle-tattl... m. T. name of a ... looking horse's 'ba... in this comp. is gen... pendent adj.) m. 1) ... in the latter part ... called Indian Summ... 2) gossamer, see ... adj. (l. u.) of old... zeichen, n. (from ... —schlüssel.

* Alu'min, (dual ... (Alaun-Erde). —Al... alumina, alumine ... earth). — Aluminat... (saures Salz) alumi... m. Miner. alumini... nit', Alu'minium, ... aluminium, alumi... aluminium-bronze... & Chem. aluminum...

* Alumnat', (... pl. w. Alumnat'en) ... nary whose pupils ... and tuition (opp. ... (sing. Alumnus, pl. ... (Lat. alumnus, ... child (Pflegekind) ... boarding, lodging ... college, or seminary ... (Externer).

* Alaun', (str.) ...

* Alveolar', adj... alveolary. — Alve... lus (small cavity ... fach &c.). — Alveoli... lite.

* Alwei'(?), (w.) ... wort (Alphabet, ...

A. M., a/M., *abbr. for* am Main, *see* A, *abbr.*, p. 1.

Am, *contr. of* an dem, *see* An: Sie sind — Spiele, it is your turn (*i. e.* in play); — Leben, in life, alive; Frankfurt — Main, Frankfort on the Main; es liegt — Tage, it is evident or manifest; es steht geschrieben Matthäi — letzten (*i. e.* an [† *for* in, *see* An, 2] dem letzten Kapitel des Matthäus), it is written in the last chapter of Matthew; am *is never dissolved into* an dem, *when it serves to circumscribe the adverb of a superlative*; — ersten, first, in the first place; — letzten, (*Luther, &c.*) † *for* zuletzt, at last, finally; — besten, best; es ist — besten, it is (the) best; ich bin — besten daran, I have the best of it; er singt — besten, he sings best (*different* auf das Beste, *cf.* Auf); er lebt — längsten, he lives longest; es geschieht — leichtesten, it is done most easily; stille Wasser sind — tiefsten, still waters are deepest; als der Tag — heißesten war, when the day was hottest.

A'madis, (*str., pl.* A-e, *sometimes* Amadisse) *m. orig. P. N. of an old French mythical hero, then, used as a general term for a heroic lover.*

* Amalgam', (*str.*), Amal'gama, (*str.*) *n.* (*Arab.-Gr.*) *Chem. & Metall.* amalgam. — Amalgamation', (*w.*), Amalgami'rung, (*w.*) *f. lit. & fig.* amalgamation (Vereinigung). — Amalgami'ren, (*w.*) *v. tr.* to amalgamate (Vereinigen; *also fig.* to mix, unite, blend closely). — Amalgamir'maschine, (*w.*) *f.* amalgamator (amalgamating machine). — Amalgamir'werk, (*str.*) *n.* amalgamating works.

Ama'lie [[illegible]], *f.* Amalia (*P. N.*).

* Amanitin', (*str.*) *n. Chem.* amanitine, mushroom-poison.

* Amanuen'sis, (*Lat., sing. without decl., pl.* A-[illegible]), *m.* amanuensis, copyist, clerk.

* Amarant', Amaranth', (*str., pl.* [*w.*] A-e) *m.* 1) *a) Bot.* amaranth, velvet flower (*Amaranthus* L.); *particul. Amaranthus caudatus*, der rothe —, Fuchsschwanz, flower gentle, a plant of which the flower long retains its colour; *b) in poetry*, an imaginary, unfading flower, an emblem of immortality; *also a proper name*; 2) (—roth) a colour inclining to purple. (scenes).

* Amaranten, *adj.* amaranthine (in all its

* Amarant'holz, (*str., pl.* A-hölzer) *n.* [illegible] *cabinet-makers*, purpled wood (from the West Indies), violet-wood, palisander-wood [illegible], Violet-, or Purpurholz, Palisanderholz, &c.).

* Amarel'le, (*w.*) *f.* 1) *Pomol. a)* (Amarel'lenkirsche) Armenian cherry; *b)* (Morelle) Armenian apricot; 2) *Bot.* (Amarell'kraut, *n.*) bitter gentian (*Gentiana amarella*).

* Amarin', (*str.*) *n. Chem.* amarine.

* Amaryl'lis, (*indecl.*) *f. Bot.* lily asphodel (*Amaryllis*, Narziß-Lilie).

Ama'ta, *f.* (*Lat. amata, beloved one*), Amata, Amy (*P. N.*).

* Amauro'se, (*w.*) *f. Med.* amaurosis, drop serene (der schwarze Staar). — Amauro'tisch, *adj.* amaurotic.

* Amazo'ne, I. (*w.*) *f.* 1) Amazon; 2) *fig.* a [illegible] woman, virago; II. *m. rarely* [illegible] A-nstrom; III. *in comp.* A-nameise, *f.* [illegible], a kind of ant (*Polyergus rufescens* Latreille [illegible]), A-nammer, *f. & m.* [illegible] bunting (*Emberiza amazona*); A-n[illegible], *m.* amazon kingfisher (*Alcedo amazona*) [illegible], *m. see* —strom; A-nkleid, *n.* [illegible] riding-dress, a riding-habit for a [illegible]; A-nland, *n.* Amazonia; A-n[illegible] [illegible] (Amazonischer Stock); A-n[illegible] [illegible] a green parrot, frequent [illegible] Amazon (*Psittacus amazonicus*) [illegible]; A-nstein, *m. Miner.* [illegible] Amazonian feldspar; 2) a beautiful dark-green variety of feldspar, found in Siberia, &c.; A-nstrom, *m.* the river Amazon.

Amazonenhaft, (*l. u.*: Amazo'nisch) *adj.* Amazonian, Amazon-like.

† Am'bacht, *OHG. & MHG. form of the word* Amt; A-lehen &c., *see* Amtslehen &c.

* Ambar're, (*w.*) *f.* (*in Russia*) *Comm.* storehouse, ambar; warehouse; A-nmiethe, *f.* warehouse-rent, storage.

* Ambassa'de, (*w.*) *f.* (*Fr.*) †, embassy, legation (Gesandtschaft).

* Am'be, (*w.*) *f.* (*Ital.*) 1) *Math.* a combination of two and two; 2) two numbers drawn as a prize in the game of lotto, double prize.

* Am'ber, (*str.*) *m.* & (*indecl.*) *f.* 1) *see* Ambra; 2) name of fossil yellow resin (Bernstein); —baum, *m. Bot.* sweet-gum (*Liquidambar styraciflua*), *see* Ambrabaum (—baum); —fisch, *m. Zool.* sperm-whale (Pottfisch); —geruch, *see* Ambraduft; —kraut, *n.*, —strauch, *m.*, —thymian, *see* Ambrakraut &c.

* Amberi'ne, (*w.*) *f.* (*Fr.*) *Chem. see* Ambrastoff; Amberin'säure, *f.* ambreic acid; Amberin'salz, *n.* ambreate.

* Ambiguität', (*w.*) *f.* (*l. u.*) ambiguity (Ungewißheit, Zweideutigkeit &c.).

* Ambi'ren, (*w.*) *v. tr.* (*Lat.*) *unusual*, to endeavour to obtain or gain, to seek (favour or preferment), to sue for, solicit, &c. (sich um ... bewerben).

* Ambition', (*w.*) *f.* (*Lat., l. u.*) ambition (Ehrgeiz; Ehrgefühl).

* Amblygonit', (*str.*) *m.* (*Gr.*) *Miner.* amblygonite, a pale-green mineral found in Saxony, named in allusion to the obtuse angles of its prism.

* Amblyop(s)ie', (*w.*) *f.* (*Gr.*) *Med.* amblyopy, dulness of sight (Stumpfsichtigkeit); incipient amaurosis. — Amblyo'pisch, *adj. Med.* dull of sight (Stumpfsichtig, Kurzsichtig).

Am'boß, (*str.*) *m.* 1) *Smith., &c.* anvil (mundartlich: stithy, stiddy); ein zweispitziger (*or* Horn-) —, beak-iron, bick-iron, bickern; 2) *Anat.* incus (one of the small bones in the tympanum); *T-s.* —bahn, *f.* face of an anvil; —bett, *n.* bed of an anvil; —block, *m.* anvil-block; —fuß, *m.* foot of an anvil; —futter, *n.* anvil-bed; —horn, *n.* beak of an anvil; —klotz, *m. see* —stock; —loch, *n.* hole in an anvil; —pfeiler, *m.* anvil-pillar (*Tech.*); —platte, *f.* plate of an anvil; —rand, *m.* edge of an anvil; —schmidt, *m.* anvil-smith, blacksmith who forges anvils; —stock, *m.* anvil-stock, block of an anvil.

Am'bößchen, (*str.*) *n.* (*dimin. of* Amboß) *Goldsm., &c.* little anvil.

* Am'bra, I. (*str., pl.* A-s) *m. & f.* (*cf.* Amber) 1) (echter grauer —) ambergris (*Lat. Ambra grisea, Fr. Ambre gris*: das englische amber ohne Beisatz wird nur im Sinne von Bernstein gebraucht); 2) (flüssiger —) liquidamber (*Lat. Ambra liquida, liquidambar*); 3) (gelber —) amber (*Lat. Ambra flava*, Bernstein); II. *in comp.* —apfel, *gener. used in the pl., see* —kügelchen; —baum, *m. Bot.* amber-tree: 1) liquid-amber (so named from the amber-like resin it yields — *liquidambar*); 2) anthospermum (*L.*); —birne, *f. see* Amberbirne; —duft, *m.* the fragrant odour of ambergris, sweet scent; —farbig, *adj.* amber-coloured; —fett, —harz, *n.* the fatty matter of ambergris, *see* —stoff; —holz, *n.* a name of yellow sandal-wood; —kraut, *n. Bot.* 1) *Marum verum*; 2) sweet-scented goosefoot (*Chenopodium ambrosioides*); —kugel, *f.* amber-ball, musk-ball, pomander; —kügelchen, *n. gener. in the pl.* amber-seed, musk-seed (Bisamkörner); —öl, *n.* oil of ambergris; —staude, *f. see* —baum, 2; —stoff, *m. Chem.* the (fatty) substance obtained from ambergris, ambreine (—fett).

* Ambrett'e, (*w.*) *f.* (*Fr.*) 1) *Comm. see* Ambrettkörnchen; 2) *Conch. see* Bernsteinschnecke; 3) *Pomol.* a kind of pear.

* Ambri'ren, (*w.*) *v. tr. obsolescent*, to amber, scent with amber.

* Am'brós, *m.*, Ambro'sius, *m.* Ambrose, Ambrosius (*P. N.*).

* Ambro'sia, (*indecl.*) *f.* (*Wieland, unusual as a n.*) *Gr. Myth.* ambrosia (Götterspeise, *opp.* Nectar); —kraut, *n. Bot.* goosefoot (*Chenopodium*); —mandel, *f.* Ambrosine almonds.

* Ambrosia'lisch, *adj. l. u.* ambrosial (Ambrosisch).

* Ambrosia'ner, (*str.*) *m.* 1) Ambrosian, monk of the order of St. Ambrose; 2) ambrosin (an old Milanese gold-coin, bearing the figure of St. Ambrose on horseback).

* Ambrosia'nisch, *adj.* Ambrosian, relating to St. Ambrose: die a-e Liturgie, the Ambrosian ritual or office; der a-e Kirchengesang, the Ambrosian chant; der a-e Lobgesang, the Ambrosian hymn (the Lat. hymn of thanksgiving, beginning with the words *Te Deum laudamus*, still so sung in the Roman Catholic ritual, but rendered into German in the German Protestant church: Herr Gott, dich loben wir &c.).

* Ambro'sienkraut, *see* Ambrosiakraut.

* Ambrosin', (*str.*) *n. unusual*, ambrosial fragrance.

* Ambrosi'ne, (*w.*) *f. see* Ambrosiamandel.

* Ambro'sisch (*l. u.*: Ambrosi'nisch, Ambrosi'ner), *adj.* 1) ambrosial (*w. S.*: ambrosian, ambrosiac); fragrant; delicious; 2) *see* Ambrosianisch.

* Ambulant', *adj.* (*from the Lat.*) ambulating, moving about, itinerant (wandernd, umherziehend). — Ambulanz', (*w.*) *f.* (*from the Fr.* ambulance) *Mil.* ambulance, a moving or flying hospital (fliegendes Lazareth), field hospital, attached to an army, first introduced by the French surgeons in the Napoleonic wars; *particul.* a carriage which serves as a movable hospital for the wounded in battle.

A'meise, (*w.*) *f. Entom.* ant, emmet (*Formica* L.): die braune — (Holz-, Hügel-, Klammer-), red ant (wood-ant, hill-ant — *Formica rufa*); die weiße —, white ant, termite (Termit).

A'meiseln, (*w.*) *v. intr.* (*aux.* sein & haben) (*l. u.*) 1) to move quickly about ant-like; 2) to itch (*cf.* Ameisenschauder).

A'meisen ..., *in comp.* —äther, *m. Chem.* formic ether; —bad, *n. Med.* formic bath or lotion; —bär, *m.* ant-bear, *see* —fresser; —drossel, *f. see* —fänger; —ei, *n.* ant's egg; —fänger, *m. Ornith.* ant-catcher, a species of thrush (*Turdus formicivorus*); *according to others* identical with Fliegenfänger (*Myiothera* Illig.); —fresser, *m. Zool.* ant-eater (*Myrmecophaga*), *particul.* the large ant-eater, ant-bear (*Myrmecophaga jubata*); —geist, *m. Chem.* formic spirit; —haufen, *m.* ant-hill, ant-hillock; —jäger, *m. see* —fresser; —jungfer, *f. see* —löwe; —kriechen, —laufen, *n. see* —schauder; —löwe, *m. Entom.* ant-lion, lion-ant (landschaftl.: groundass), formica-leo (*Myrmeleon*); —naphtha, *n. see* —äther; —nest, *n.* ant's nest, *see* —haufen; —öl, *n. Chem.* formic oil; —sauer, *adj. Chem.* formic: das —saure Salz, formiate; das —saure Ammonium, formiate of ammonia; —säure, *f. Chem.* formic acid; —saft, *m.* ant-juice; —scharrer, *m. Zool.* orycteropus, ground-hog, South African insectivorous animal (*Orycteropus capensis* L.); —schauder, *m.* formication, a sensation like that of ants creeping over the skin; —spiritus, *m.* (*Spiritus formicarum*), *see* —geist.

* Am'el ..., *in comp.* —korn, *n.* amel-corn (old name for a kind of grain of which starch was made); —mehl, *n.* starch (Stärke).

A'men, I. *adv.* 1) amen; — zu Einem

(*Bibl.*) sagen, to say Amen to a thing, *i. e.* to confirm, to consent to, to sanction a thing; 2) done, finished, over; mit Einem aus und — machen, *obsolescent*, to make an end of one: II. *used as a subst.* (*str.*, *Gen.* A-s, *pl.* —) *n.* amen; sein — zu etwas geben, to give one's consent, sanction to a thing.

* **Amendement'** [*pr.* Amängd'mang'], (*Fr.*) (*str.*, *pl.* A-s) *n.* amendment (Verbesserungs-Antrag); ein — stellen, to propose an amendment. — **Amendi'ren**, (*w.*) *v. tr.* (of deliberative assemblies) to amend (a motion, a bill, &c.).

* **Americanis'mus**, (*sing. indecl.*, *pl.* [*w.*] A-men) *m.* (*Lat.*) Americanism. — **Americanisi'ren**, (*w.*) *v. tr.* to Americanise.

Ame'rika (*rarely* America, *for, having become a "household word", in daily use, it is gener. spelt as a German word, with a k, cf.* Afrika), (*str.*) *n.* America (*orig. a Latinised adjective: America, the American, sc. terra (country), so called from Amerigo Vespucci, a Florentine, who accompanied Columbus in his second voyage* (1499), *and published the first description of the newly discovered countries. According to Humboldt, a German professor, M. Waldseemüller, translator of Vespucci's much read account, first proposed the name which occurs on a map, published at Metz, as early as* 1522, *and was soon generally adopted. As to Amerigo, or rather Amerrigo, an assimilation for* Amelrigo, *we find it to be derived from* Amalric (*OHG., MHG.* Amalrich, Amelrich), *a German name of high antiquity, while it was considered by Vespucci and his Florentine contemporaries as a secondary form for* Alberico (*Lat.* Albericus, *from MHG.* Alberich).

Amerika'ner, (*str.*) *m.*, **Amerika'nerin**, (*w.*) *f.* an American. — **Amerika'nisch**, *adj.* American.

* **Amethyst'**, (*str. & w.*) *m.* *Miner.* amethyst, violet quartz; —artig, **Amethyst'en**, *adj.* amethystine.

Amha'risch, *adj.* Amharic, relating to Amhara, a division of Abyssinia; das A-e, *n.* Amharic, the language of Abyssinia.

* **Amiant'**, *less correctly* **Amianth'**, (*str.*) *m.* *Miner.* amianthus, amianth, earth-flax (Erdflachs), the flaxen variety of asbestos.

* **Amid'**, (*str.*) *n.* *Chem.* amide, ammid. — **A'midam**, (*str.*) *n.* (*Fr.* amidon), *Chem.* starch (Stärkemehl). — **Amidin'**, (*str.*) *n.* *Chem.* amidine.

Am'mann, (*str.*, *pl.* Am'männer, *provinc.* sometimes A-e) *m.* *provinc.* (*Switzerland*) bailiff, justice, magistrate.

A. **Am'me**, (*w.*) *f.* nurse, *particul.* wet-nurse (Säug-Amme, *opp.* Trocken-Amme).

B. **Amme**, *provinc. abbrev. of* Ammann.

Am'meister, (*str.*) *m.* †, one of the chief magistrates in several cities of Southern Germany (Strassburg, Basel, Regensburg, &c.).

* **Ammelid'**, (*str.*) *n.* *Chem.* ammelide.

* **Ammelin'**, (*str.*) *n.* *Chem.* ammeline.

Am'meln, (*w.*) *v. tr. & intr.* *provinc.* to suckle, nurse; (of birds) to feed (the young).

Am'men ..., *in comp.* —dienst, *m.* nurse's service; —geschwätz, *n.* nurse's tittle-tattle, idle talk; —lied, *n.* nurse's (gewöhnlicher:) nursery-song; —märchen, *n.* (*rigtl.* nurse's tale, gewöhnlicher:) nursery-tale.

A. **Am'mer**, (*w.*) *f.* *Leather*, &c. †, embers, hot cinders.

B. **Am'mer**, (*w.*) *f.* & (*str.*) *m.* *Ornith.* yellow-hammer, gold-hammer, bunting (*Emberiza citrinella*).

C. **Am'mer**, (*w.*) *f.* *Pomol.* Armenian cherry (Ammerkirsche).

Am'merling, Em'merling (*gener.* **Emmerling**), (*str.*) *m.* *see* Ammer, *B.*

* **Ammoniak'**, (*str.*) *n.* (*& sometimes m.*) *Chem.* ammonia, volatile alcali; arseniksaures —, arseniate of ammonia; eisenblausaures — (Ferrocyan—), ferro-cyanate of ammonia; hydrothionsaures —, hydrosulphate of ammonia; kohlensaures —, carbonate of ammonia; schwefelsaures —, sulphate of ammonia; —alaun, *m.* (schwefelsaure Thonerde, *f.*) sulphate of alumine and ammonia.

* **Ammoniaka'lisch**, *adj.* ammoniacal.

* **Ammo'niak** ..., *in comp.* —auflösung, *f.* solution of an ammoniacal salt; —flüssigkeit, *f.* liquid ammonia; —gas, *n.* ammoniac gas, (alkalische Luft) volatile alkali in a gaseous state; —gummi, *n.* gum ammoniac, ammoniacum (—harz); —haltig, *adj. see* Ammoniakalisch; —salz, *n.* sal ammoniac (*called also* hydrochlorate of ammonia, *and* muriate of ammonia, flüchtiges Laugensalz, Salmiak); —seife, *f.* muriate *or* hydrochlorate of ammonia (Salmiakgeist); —silberoxyd, *n.* ammoniacal oxyde of silver. [snake-stone.

* **Ammonit'**, (*w. & str.*) *m.* *Pal.* ammonite: **Ammonit'er**, (*str.*) *m.* Ammonite; die A-in, (*w.*) *f.* Ammonitess.

* **Ammo'nium**, (*str.*) *n.* *Chem.* ammonium, ammonia. [Ammonit.

Am'monshorn, (*str.*, *pl.* A-hörner), *n.* *see*

* **Ammunition'**, (*w.*) *f.* *Mil.* (*l. u.*) ammunition, *see* Munition.

* **Amnestie'**, (*w.*) *f.* amnesty.

* **Amnesti'ren**, (*w.*) *v. tr.* (Einen) to grant amnesty to (one), to pardon (political offenders).

* **Am'nion**, (*str.*) *n.* 1) *Med.* amnion, amnios (a soft membrane that surrounds the foetus in the womb — Schafhäutchen); —wasser, *n.* *see* Schafwasser; 2) *Bot.* a thin, gelatinous covering of the embryo of a seed (Keimsack).

* **Amnio'tisch**, *adj.* *Med.* amniotic; die a-e Flüssigkeit, amniotic fluid *or* liquor; a-e (*or* Am'nische) Säure, amniotic acid (Allantoin).

* **Amo'me**, (*w.*) *f.*, **Amom'**, (*str.*) *m.* *Bot.* amomum.

* **A'mor**, *m.* (*Lat.*, love) Cupid (m. A.: Amor).

* **Amoret'te, Amori'ne**, (*w.*) *f.* *see* Amourette. [*f.* Amoritess.

Amorit'er, (*str.*) *m.* Amorite; A-in, (*w.*)

* **Amorphie'**, (*w.*) *f.* (*Gr.*) *Nat. Hist.* amorphia, amorphism, shapelessness, irregularity of form. — **Amor'phisch, Amorph'**, *adj.* amorphous, shapeless, devoid of (regular) form, irregular of form.

Amorrä'er, (*str.*) *m.* *see* Amoriter.

A'morshorn, (*str.*, *pl.* A-hörner), *n.* *Mus.* a kind of bugle.

* **Amorti'ren**, (*w.*) *v. tr.* (*Fr.* amortir) to amortise, *see* Amortisiren. [Amortisirbar.

* **Amortisa'bel**, *adj.* (*Fr.* amortissable) *see*

* **Amortisation'**, (*w.*) *f.* 1) *Med.* mortification; 2) *Law*, †, amortisation, transfer of real estate in mortmain; 3) *Fin. & Comm.* redemption (einer Anleihe &c., of a loan, &c.); 4) *Law*, (A-sverfahren, *n.*) legal proceedings by which a bill, &c. (lost or missing) is declared to be extinct; — eines Wechsels, legal extinction of a bill; A-sfond (Tilgungsfond), *m.* sinking fund.

* **Amortisir'bar**, *adj.* (of funds) that may be sunk; (of annuities) that may be redeemed, redeemable (Tilgungsfähig).

* **Amortisi'ren**, (*w.*) *v. tr.* (*Norm. Fr.* amortiser) 1) *Med.* to mortify; 2) *Law*, †, to amortise, to alienate (real estate) in mortmain, to sell to dead hands; 3) *Fin. & Comm.* (eine Schuld tilgen) to redeem (liquidate a debt), to sink (a fund).

* **Amotion'**, (*w.*) *f.* *Law*, amotion (*l. u.*): 1) the act of parcioning (Entwendung); 2) removal from office (Entfernung, Entsetzung).

* **Amouret'te** [*pr.* amur—], (*w.*) *f.* (*Fr.*) 1) a little god of love or Cupid; 2) a passing amour or love intrigue; 3) *Cook.* calf's marrow, fried in a marinade of onions and fine

Amt Amt

to confer a place on one; Einem ein — übertragen, to appoint one to a place *or* office, to admit one into an office: ein — antreten, to enter upon an office; im Amte, in office: in the commission; von Amtswegen, officially, *(Lat.) ex officio;* das geistliche —, the ministerial office; *b) Script.* ministry (ecclesiastical function, Lehramt rc.); .... es sind mancherlei Ämter, aber es ist ein Herr (1 Cor. 12, 5), there are differences of administrations, but the same Lord; *c) Eccl.* sacred ministry, service: *aa) Rom. Cath.* several ecclesiastical function, as the Chor—, Hoch—, Meß—, particularly the latter; das — halten, to celebrate or perform mass; *bb) Protest. church* (Abendmahlsfeier) communion service, the sacrament of the Lord's supper; das — halten, to administer the sacraments; 2) *a)* board, court (of justice), council; *b)* court-house, office, the offices; residence of a magistrate, &c.; 3) *a)* administration of a public domain; *b)* (Kammer—) domain; government-district, &c.; *c)* bailiwick, jurisdiction; 4) corporation, guild, company, *see* Innung; 5) *fig.* business, concern, province, call; was deines Amts nicht ist, (da) laß deinen Vorwitz, *proverb,* meddle not with what does not concern you *(Hilp.),* do not meddle with other people's business; das ist nicht meines Amts, that is not my business: das ist nicht deines Amts, that is no business *or* concern of yours, that is nothing to you.

Ämt'chen, *(str.) n. (dimin. of* Amt) little *or* minor office; — bringt Käppchen, *proverb,* offices yield honours *or* emoluments.

Amtei', *(w.) f.* († *&) provinc.* court of justice; court-house, *&c. see* Amt, 2.

Am'ten, *(w.) v. intr.* 1) to officiate, to act in any office, to discharge the duties of an office; 2) *provinc. (S. G.)* to perform *or* celebrate mass; mit Einem —, to lecture, reprove one *(cf.* die Leviten lesen).

Ämter..., *in comp.* —handel, *m.* barter (purchase and sale) of offices: —sucht, *f.* office-seeking.

Amt'..., *in comp.* —frau, *f. see* Amtsfrau; —frei, *adj.* private, not invested with any office, free from *or* (being) without official employment (—los); seine —freie Stellung, his being free of all public duties; —führend, *adj.* officiating, acting; —geld, *n. Feud. Law,* money paid for certain fiefs; —gericht, *n.* 1) *see* Amtsgericht; 2) *see* Pflegeramt; —haber, *m.* office-bearer, one who holds *or* discharges an office (A-Inhaber); —handeln, *v. intr. (l. u.)* to act officially, to institute *or* commence official proceedings: —haus, *n.,* —hof, *m.* 1) court-house, office, court: official residence of a magistrate, bailiff's house; 2) *see* Innungshaus; —hörig, *adj.* obsolescent, subject *or* belonging to the jurisdiction of a district-court (A-pflichtig, A-angehörig).

Amti'ren, *(w.) v. intr. see* Amten.

Amti'rung, *(w.) f.* the act of officiating, &c., administration of office.

Amt'[illegible], *see* Amts[illegible].

Amt'[illegible], *(str.) n. see* Ämtchen.

Amt'[illegible], *pl. see* [illegible].

Amt'lich *(provinc.* [illegible] *(S. G.):* Amt'lich), I. *adj.* official; nicht der a-en Form gemäß, informal; a. besiegelt, officially sealed; II. A-keit, *(w.)* [illegible] official character *or* authority.

Amt'ling, *(str.) m. gener. cont.* official, [illegible]; red-tapist.

Amt'los, *adj.* (being) without official employment; 1) out of office, place, *or* employment; 2) private, independent. — **Amt'losigkeit,** *(w.) f.* the being without official employment, &c.

Amt'[illegible]..., *in comp.* —[illegible], *adj. (Jean Paul)* [illegible] —mann, *(str., pl.* —leute *&* —männer) *m.* 1) † any one placed in authority over others; 2) justiciary: district-judge, district-magistrate; bailiff; 3) (Verwalter) *a)* superintendent *or* farmer of a crown domain; *b)* warden: steward; 4) *in some parts of Bavaria, &c.* bailiff, beadle (Gerichtsdiener); 5) *provinc. (N. G.)* member of a corporation (Innungsmitglied); —männin, *less frequently* —mannin, *(w.) f.* wife of a justiciary, bailiff, &c.: —mannschaft, *f.* office, jurisdiction *or* dignity of a justiciary, bailiff, &c., bailiwick: —meister, *m. provinc. (N. G.)* chief *or* head of a guild *or* corporation (Innungs-Obermeister).

Amts'..., *in comp.* —actuar, *m.* clerk of a district-court; —adel, *m.* a kind of personal nobility (in Russia) devolving on one on account of his employment as a government officer; —adjunct, *m.* assistant justiciary, &c.; —alter, *n.* seniority in office (Anciennetät); —angehörig, *adj.* belonging to the jurisdiction of a government district; —ansehen, *n.* official authority *or* dignity; —antritt, *m.* entrance *or* the entering upon (the duties of) an office; (eines Geistlichen:) entrance on the ministry; —anzeige, *f.* official notice, notification, information, &c.: —arbeit, *f.* official work *or* duty: —ärger, *m.* vexation occurring during the discharge of office; —arzt, *m.* district physician.

Amt'sasse, *(w.) m. Law,* one *(i. e.* a nobleman in former times) subject (**Amt'sässig,** *adj.)* to the jurisdiction of a district *or* lower court *(opp.* Schriftsasse, Schriftsässig). — **Amt'sässigkeit,** *(w.) f.* the being subject to the jurisdiction, &c. as above.

Amts'..., *in comp.* —aufseher, *m. see* —verweser; —bauer, *m.* peasant belonging to, *or* subject to the jurisdiction of a certain government-district; —befehl, *m.* official order, judicial writ; —beflissenheit, *f. see* —eifer; —befohlen, *p. a. see* —angehörig; —beförderung, *f.* promotion to an office; advancement in station, rise, preferment; —befugniß, *f.* official right, authority, *or* competence; —beisitzer, *m.* judge lateral (assessor) of a court; —bekanntmachung, *f.* official notice *or* notification; —bericht, *m.* official account, report, return, despatch; —beruf, *m.* official calling, vocation, *or* duty; sphere of office; —beschäftigung, *f.* official employment; —bescheid, *m.* official decree *or* sentence: —beschwerde, *f.* onerous official duty; —besetzung, *f.* the filling (up) of an office; appointment to office, nomination: —bewerber, *m.* applicant *or* candidate for an office: —bewerbung, *f.* application *or* canvassing for an office; —bezirk, *m.* jurisdiction: district of a public domain, &c.; —blatt, *n.* official gazette; —bote, *m.* messenger of a district-court; —brauch, *m.* custom in office, official custom: —brief, *m.* 1) official letter; 2) *provinc. (N. G.)* written document containing the statute, privileges, &c. of a guild *or* corporation (Gildebrief); —bruder, *m.* 1) brother in office, colleague, *see* —genosse; von einem Geistlichen: fellow-minister; 2) *provinc. (N. G.)* member of a guild, *see* Innungsmeister; —brüderschaft, *f.* colleagueship, fellowship, association in office; —buch, *n.* court roll; —büttel, *m.* beadle of a district-court (—diener); —casse, *f.* treasury, pay-office of a government-district, a domain, *or in gener.* of a public office; —cassirer, *m.* treasurer *or* cashier of a public office *(cf. the preceding word).*

Amt'schild, *see* Amtsschild.

Amts'chirurg, *(w.) m.* district surgeon.

Amt'schreiber, *preferred by Grimm to* Amtsschreiber, *which see.*

Amts'..., *in comp.* —commissär, *m.* deputy-justiciary *(gener.* the first clerk of a district-court); —copist, *m.* copying clerk; —diener, *m.* beadle; messenger of a district-court; —dorf, *n.* village belonging to a certain government-district *or* jurisdiction; —ehre, *f.* honour due to an office *or* officer; —eid, *m.* oath taken upon entering on an office, oath of office, official oath; oath of fidelity in the discharge of official duties; er hatte seinen —eid abgelegt, he had taken the oath when he entered on his office; —eidlich, *adj.* (declaration, &c.) made on the oath of office; —eifer, *m.* zeal in the discharge of official duties, official zeal; —eifrig, *adj.* zealous in discharging official duties; —eigenschaft, *f.* official quality *or* capacity; —einkünfte, *f. pl.,* —einnahme, *f.* emoluments of an office, official income, revenue; —entlassung, *f.* discharge from an office; —entsetzung, *f.* cessation, cashiering, dismissal; —entziehung, *f.* 1) (temporary) suspension from office; 2) *see the preceding word;* —erfahrung, *f.* professional experience; —erschleichung, *f.* a seeking after, *or* an obtaining of office by surreptitious means *or* underhand dealings; —ertrag, *m.* 1) *see* —einkünfte; 2) the revenues *or* rents of a domain; —exceß, *m.* transgression *or* violation of official duty *(cf.* —mißbrauch); —fähig, *adj.* qualified for office: —fähigkeit, *f.* qualification for office; —fälle, *m. pl.* † *for* —gefälle; —feier, *f.* celebration in honour of one who has been in office for a certain term; —folge, *f.* 1) *Law,* official persecution of a criminal (Nacheile); 2) *Law,* obedience due to the official summons of a district-court; —folge leisten, to obey the orders of (the presiding officer of) a district-court; 3) succession in office *(gener.* —nachfolge); —folger, *m.* successor in office (—nachfolger); —frau, *f.* (in convents) officiating nun, *particul.* a (female) chorister; —frohn, *m. see* —diener; —frohne, *f.* statute labour *or* service due to a district-court or a public domain by the peasantry; —fuhre, *f. Law,* conveyance by carriage due as a socage-service; —führung, *f.* administration of office; —gebäude, *n. see* Amthaus; —geberde, *f. see* —miene; —gebühr, *f.* anything due to an office; *particul. in the pl.* A-en, official fees; —gebührlich, *adj.* official; —gefährte, *m. l. u. for* —genosse; —gefälle, *n. gener. in the pl.* 1) the revenues of a domain; 2) emoluments *or* fees of office; —gefängniß, *n.* prison of a government-district, public jail; —gehalt, *m.* official salary; —geheimniß, *n.* official secret; —gehülfe, *m.* assistant in office, adjunct; —gemäß, *adj.* according to official custom *or* duty, official; —genosse, *m.* official colleague, associate, partner, assistant, joint commissioner; —genossenschaft, *f.* colleagueship, partnership in office; —gericht, *n.* 1) district-court; 2) *see* Pflegeramt; —geschäft, *n.* official duty, business, professional labour; —gesicht, *n.* official, *i. e.* grave, solemn, *or* magisterial air (—miene); er macht ein strenges —gesicht, he looks as grave as a judge: —gewalt, *f.* official authority; gemäß der mir zustehenden —gewalt, *Law style,* pursuant to the power and authority unto me granted; Mißbrauch der —gewalt, abuse of official power: —gewissen, *n.* conscience of one who feels the responsibility of office; bei meinem —gewissen *(Wieland),* upon my conscience as a judge; —gilde, *f. provinc. (N. G.)* guild, corporation, *see* Gilde, Innung (Amt, 4); —grenze, *f.* border *or* frontier of a district; —halben († —halb), —halber, *adv. see* —wegen; —hand, *f.* official custody *or* keeping; —handlung, *f.* official act *or* function; official proceeding; *Theol.* ministration; —hauptmann, *m.* chief officer, prefect, or governor of a district; high constable, upper bailiff; —hauptmannschaft, *f.* district *(sometimes* the dignity) of an Amtshauptmann, prefectship, prefecture; —haus, *n. see* Amthaus; —helfer, *m. see* —gehülfe; —herrlich, *adj. (Göthe,* of a mansion) magnifi-

court as befits an official residence, of dignified proportions: —hoheit, f. seigniory of an Amtmann (Hilp.); —holz, m. 1) wood belonging to a domain; 2) fire-wood granted in part-payment to an official; —inhaber, m. holder of an office, office-holder, functionary, incumbent; —kammer, f. chamber or office for the administration of a domain; —kanzlei, f. chancery or office of a district-court; —kasse, see —casse; —keller, m. 1) cellar belonging to a public office; 2) † a) administrator of (the revenues of) a district or domain; b) see —verwalter; —kellerei, f. †, the office or jurisdiction of an —keller (see No. 2 of the preceding word); —kenntniß, f. knowledge of official business, official knowledge; —kleid, n. official gown, robe, &c.; die —kleider und die heiligen Kleider des Priesters Aarons (Exod. 31, 10), the clothes of service, and the holy garments for Aaron the priest; —kleidung, f. official dress, attire, robe, &c.: die päpstliche (or bischöfliche) —kleidung, pontificals; —knecht, m. see —diener; —kosten, f. pl. 1) official or court expenses; 2) provinc. (see Amt) expenses of a guild or corporation; —kreis, m. district: jurisdiction of a district-court, &c.; —lade, f. see Innungslade; —landrichter, m. judge of a rural district belonging to a court of justice; —last, f. burden of office; —lehen, n. Law, 1) fief granted by a district-court; 2) fief connected with a certain office; —local, n. official room, locality, or place, office; —lust, f. desire of office; —lustig, adj. desirous of office; der —lustige, office-seeker, candidate; —mäßig, adj. official (cf. —gemäß); ministerial; professional; —meister, m. see Amtsmeister; —miene, f. solemn, stern, or severe air (such as fits a grave official, cf. —gesicht); —mißbrauch, m. abuse of official power and authority (Mißbrauch der —gewalt); —mühle, f. mill belonging to a government-district or public domain; —nachfolge, f. succession in office (sometimes —folge); —nachfolger, m. successor in office (sometimes —folger); —name, m. official denomination or title; —niederlegung, f. a laying down or resigning of office, abdication; —ordnung, f. order or succession according to seniority in office; —ort, m. place where a public officer has to reside, official place of residence; see also —sitz; —person, f. a person in office, civil officer, official; —pflege, f. 1) administration of a public office; 2) official district, jurisdiction; —pfleger, m. 1) see Amtmann; 2) see —schösser; —pflicht, f. 1) official duty; 2) (—verpflichtung) see —eid; —pflichtig, adj. subject to the jurisdiction of a government-district or district-court; —physikus, (cf. Physikus) m. see —arzt; —predigt, f. Protest. principal (forenoon) sermon succeeded by the administration of the sacrament (cf. Amt, 1, c); —probe, f. a kind of examination which any (public) officer has to pass in order to prove his qualification for the office to which he may have been nominated; —rang, m. official rank; —rath, m. 1) councillor of a district-court; 2) see Amtmann; 3) council-board; —registratur, f. 1) official record; 2) archive of a district-court; —reise, f. official journey or tour; circuit; —rentenverwalter, m. administrator of the revenues of a domain or government-district; —revisor, m. see —schösser; —richter, m. district-judge; justice of a domain, &c., justiciary; —rock, m. see —kleid; —rolle, f. provinc. (N. G.) roll containing the statutes, privileges, &c. of a guild, &c. (—brief); —sache, f. 1) official affair, business or matter; 2) business or case falling under the jurisdiction of a district-court; —saß, —sässig &c., see Amtsaß &c.; —schaden, m. dues, payable by a town to a district-court for expenses incurred by the latter in the performance of official duties (Luther); —schaffner, m. see —keller, 2; —schild, m. 1) official arms or sign; badge of office (worn by lower officials), messengers, &c.; 2) Jew. Archæol. (Luther, Exod. 28, 15 & 29: Amtschildlein, n. dimin.) the breast-plate of judgment (part of the high-priest's apparel); —schösser, m. auditor or accountant of the revenues of a domain; treasurer of a government-district, &c.; —schreiben, n. official letter; —schreiber, m. clerk of a (district-)court or public office; recorder; —schreiberei, f. recorder's office; —schrift, f. official writ, judicial paper or instrument; —schultheiß, m. see —richter; —schutz, m. official protection; —siegel, n. seal of office, official seal; —sitz, m. place where a public office is located; official place of residence (—ort); —sorge, f. (Luther, &c.) anxiety for the careful discharge of (the ministerial) office; (—pflege) discharge of official duties; —sperre, f. a prohibition of the discharge of official functions; —stab, m. staff of office; —stadt, f. 1) town belonging to a certain government-district or domain; 2) town in which a public officer has to reside (cf. —ort); —statt, f., —stätte, f. see —stelle; —stelle, f. place where a public office is located; court-house (—local); office, court itself; N. wird beschieden, an hiesiger —stelle zu erscheinen, N. is summoned to appear before this court; —stellung, f. official place or position; ein Mann in hoher —stellung, a man high in office; —steuer, f. district-tax; —stube, f. apartment in which official business is transacted (Hilp.), office; audit-office, hall; court; —stübler, m. cont. one employed in a public office, particul. one confined to his office, i. e. to narrow views, anal. red-tapist; —tag, m. court-day; —thätigkeit, f. the performance of official duty; der Kreis seiner —thätigkeit, the sphere of his official activity; außer —thätigkeit setzen, to suspend from office; —thierarzt, m. veterinary surgeon attached to a district (court); —titel, m. official title; —tracht, f. see —kleidung; —treue, f. fidelity or faithfulness in the discharge of official duties; —unterthan, I. or —untergeben, adj. subject to the jurisdiction of a district-court or a domain; II. s. m. one subject to the jurisdiction of a district-court or a domain; —unterwürfigkeit, f. the being subject to the jurisdiction of a district-court or a domain; —verbrechen, n. official crime; criminal practice in public office; malversation; —verfassung, f. constitution of an office, or of public offices in general; —vergehen, n., —vergehung, f. misdemeanour in the discharge of office; —verhältniß, n. office relation or position; —verrichtung, f. official duty, function, or performance; —versammlung, f. assembly of the magistrates of a certain (government-)district; meeting of the quorum; —vertreter, m. substitute in office, deputy; —verwalter, m. 1) justiciary, district-judge, &c. see Amtmann; 2) substitute of a justiciary or district-judge, &c.; bailiff's deputy or substitute; steward of a public domain, &c.; —verwaltung, f. 1) administration of office; [illegible] —verwalterei, f. see —vogtei; —verwandt, [illegible] see —angehörig; —verweisung, f. see —[illegible]ung; —verweser, m. (deputy) administra[illegible] an office, public domain, &c.; —vogt, m. [illegible] justiciary, &c., see Amtmann; 2) see the preceding word; 3) provinc. bailiff's substitute, steward, beadle of a bailiff (—frohn); —vogtei, f. 1) office of an Amtsvogt; stewardship; bailiwick; 2) court-house; —vorfahr, —vorgänger, m. predecessor in office; —wappen, n. coat of arms alluding to a certain office transferred to the bearer; —wechsel, m. rotation in office; —wegen, see von Amtswegen, under Amt; —wirksamkeit, f. official activity, cf. —thätigkeit; —woche, f. week of office; official week (in which it is

…der auf dem…; — den Fersen, am Anfang beinahe, 4, 8, &c.

3) *A remnant of the use of* an *for* in *is to be remarked in combinations like the following:* — dem Orte, Platze, — der Stelle, Statt &c., in the place, &c.; — diesem Orte ist nichts zu finden, there is nothing to be found in this place: — der linken Hand stehen, *less usual than* zur linken Hand *or* auf der linken Seite stehen; er ist Professor der Chemie — der Universität zu Leipzig, he is professor of chemistry in the university of Leipzig: am Hofe, at court.

4) *Common use of* An *(cf.* 1): der Hund liegt — der Kette, the dog lies fastened to the chain; die Kinder saßen am Boden, — der Erde, the children sat on the ground; kein Glied, keine Faser — ihm war unthätig, not a limb, not a fibre about him was idle; er trug viele Briefe — sich verborgen, he carried many letters concealed about his person; zwei Ranken werden — jeder Pflanze gelassen, two tendrils are left on each plant; es stehen viele Sterne am Himmel, there are many stars in the sky; er hatte Sporen — den Stiefeln, he had spurs on his boots; Einem — den Fersen sein *(Göthe)*, — den Fersen folgen *(Göthe)*, *less usual than* Einem auf den Fersen sein, folgen, to be, to follow at one's heels; — der Hand führen, to lead by the hand; Einen — der Nase (herum)führen, *fig.* to lead one by the nose; er muß — Krücken gehen, he is obliged to walk with crutches: der Greis am Stabe, the old man leaning on his staff; er hörte ein Klopfen — der Thür, ahnte aber nicht, wer — die Thür klopfte, he heard a knocking at the door, but did not surmise who it was that knocked at the door: der Zöllner schlug — seine Brust (Luke, 18, 13), the publican smote upon his breast; sie verbarg ihr Gesicht — seiner Brust, she hid her face in his breast; dicht *or* nahe — der Mauer &c., close *or* hard by (next) the wall; — der Quelle saß der Knabe *(Schiller)*, by *(i. e.* beside) the brook sat the boy; das Mägdlein sitzt — Ufers Grün *(Schiller)*, the girl sitteth lonely beside the green shore *(Bulwer)*; der Arzt saß am Bette, the physician sat at the bed-side; der Alte saß am Hügel, the old man sat on the hill-side, near the hill; das Dorf stand am Berge, the village stood on the mountain-side, near the mountain; ein Wirthshaus — der Straße, a road-side inn; die Waare ist am Schiff zu liefern, the goods are to be delivered at the ship's side; — Bord, on board; am Walde, by the side of the wood; wir wollen uns am Flusse halten, we will keep by the river-side; die Kühe gingen — den Fluß, the cows went to the river-side; ihr Kinder, geht nicht ans Wasser! you children, don't go near the water! links am See, to the left of the lake *or* left of the lake; — dem Ufer, upon the shore: er wandelt am Ufer, he walks along the shore; er wandelt — das Ufer, he walks towards (*or* up to, &c.) the shore: — der Mündung des Flusses, at the mouth of the river; die Stadt liegt am nördlichen Ufer der Themse, the town is situated on the northern bank of the Thames; — der Themse, on the Thames; Aberdeen liegt am Dee, Aberdeen is situated on the Dee; Kingston — der Themse, Newcastle am Tyne, Kingston-upon-Thames, Newcastle-upon-Tyne; Frankfurt am Main, Frankfurt — der Oder, Frankfurt on the Main, Frankfort on the Oder.

5) Welle — Welle, wave on wave *(cf.* Auf); Bank — Bank gedränget *(Schiller)*, one bunch [illegible] wedged against another; sie kämpften [illegible] — Brust, they fought breast to breast; [illegible] — Paar und munter drehen *(Bürger)*, [illegible] merrily round, pair joining pair; [illegible] Welle auf Welle zerrinnet, [und Stunde [illegible] *(Schiller)*, — wave on wave succeeds and dies, | and hour on hour [remorseless] flies *(Bulwer)*.

6) — einem Felsen scheitern, to split on (upon) a rock; der Schnee schmilzt — der Sonne, the snow melts in the sun; er wärmte sich — der Sonne, he warmed himself in the sun; — der freien Luft, — freier Luft, in the open air; — die (freie) Luft setzen, to expose to the open air.

7) Nahe — zehn Thaler *(Acc.)*, — die zehn Thaler, near ten Thalers, about ten Thalers; — die dreimalhunderttausend Mann, about (*or* as many as) three times a hundred thousand men; so viel — Macherlohn *(Dat.)*, so much for making; *(in commercial accounts and book-keeping)* Herr F. hier debet (*or* soll) — Spesen, Mr. F. of this place Dr. [d. i. debtor] to charges; S. & Comp. sollen — Waaren-Conto, S. & Co. Drs. [d. i. debtors] to Goods Account; — Wechsel-Conto, to Bill Account; sie hatten genommen, was sie — Kleidern und Lebensmitteln erwischen konnten, they had taken what clothes and food they could lay their hands on; es erschienen ihrer hundert — der Zahl, there appeared a hundred of them in number; ein Ring vier Thaler — Werth, a ring four Thalers in value; sie sind gleich — Größe, they are equal in size; reich — Geistesgaben, rich in mental gifts; arm am Beutel, krank am Herzen *(Göthe)*, poor in purse, and sick at heart; er ist schmutzig — seinem Körper, he is dirty in his person; ein Riese — Gestalt, ein Löwe — Muth, a giant in size, a lion in courage; ein Jüngling — Jahren, a youth in years; sollte er deßwegen kein Mensch — Empfindung sein? *(Herder)*, should he therefore not be a man as to feeling?

8) *The following uses of* an, *expressing relations of order, time, &c. seem to be derivable from those enumerated under* 3: *a)* die Reihe (*or simply* es) ist — mir, dir, ihm *(m. & n.)*, ihr, uns, euch (Ihnen), ihnen, *or, as it may likewise be expressed:* ich bin, du bist, er ist &c. — der Reihe, it is my, your, his (its), her, our, your, their turn *(cf.* Reih); jetzt ist es — mir, zu befehlen, it is now my turn to command; Sie sind am Ziehen, (at draughts, &c.) it is your turn to move, it is your move, you are to play; es ist — der Zeit, — der Stunde zu gehen, it is time to go, the hour of departure is at hand; am Anfang schuf Gott Himmel und Erde, in the beginning God created the heaven and the earth *(here we would now prefer to say* im Anfang); am Anfange seines Buches, towards *or* near the beginning of his book; am Ende des Wörterbuches, at the end of the Dictionary; am Ende (*or* zu Ende) sein, to be at an end *(cf.* Ende); am Tode sein *or* liegen, to be at the point of death, to lie in a dying state; am Abend (*or* des Abends), in the evening; am Morgen (*or* des Morgens), in the morning; am Tage, in the day-time; er mußte die Aufgaben am Abend lernen, welche er am Tage nicht gelernt hatte, he was obliged (*or* he had) to learn the lessons in the evening (*or* at night) which he had not learnt in the day *(but* in der Nacht, *not* an der Nacht); am Nachmittage, in the afternoon; er pflegte — Nachmittagen spazieren zu gehen, he used to walk of afternoons; er bewies, daß er — jenem Abend gar nicht außer dem Hause gewesen war, he proved that he had not been out of his house on that evening; die Schlacht fand am Morgen des dritten Juli statt, the battle took place on the morning of the third of July; es geschah — einem Sonntage, it happened on a Sunday; am ersten Januar, on the first of January; *b)* — einer Sache arbeiten, to be at work on a thing; er arbeitet — zwei Gemälden, he is working on two pictures; er lernte zwei Stunden — dem Verse, he was two hours in getting the verse by heart; *c)* es ist — ihnen, uns zuerst entgegen zu kommen, it is for them to make the first advances to meet us *(cf.* es ist ihre Sache); jetzt ist's — uns, now is the time *or* it is now our duty …; ich thue alles, was — mir ist, *or* so viel — mir ist, I do everything in my power; so viel — ihnen ist, so far as in them lies, to the best of their ability; die Vernunft sucht, so viel — ihr ist, abzuleiten *(Kant)*, reason, to the extent of its powers, seeks to derive (matters from their causes); es ist nichts Gutes *(coll.* kein gutes Haar) — ihm, there is no good in him, he is a worthless *or* good-for-nothing fellow; versuche deine Pflicht zu thun und du weißt gleich, was — dir ist *(Göthe)*, try to do your duty, and you will at once know your own value; da könnt ihr gleich sehn, was — dem Fremden ist *(Göthe)*, thus you may at once find out what kind of man the stranger is; es wird dadurch offenbar, was — unserer Liebe zu Gott ist, by this it becomes manifest, what our love to God is worth; es muß mehr — (*or* in) ihnen gewesen sein, als die Welt glauben wollte, they must have had more in them than the world was inclined to believe; es ist nichts *(i. e.* Wahres, *or* es ist kein wahres Wort) — der ganzen Geschichte, there is not a true word about the whole affaire; es ist — dem, 1) *obsolescent*, matters have come to that point, things are advanced so far; 2) it is so, it is certain, it is true; und wär' es? Theurer Herzog, wär's — dem? *(Schiller*, Wall.), and were it so? dear duke, were it indeed true? es ist nicht — dem, es ist nichts — der Sache, there is no truth in it, there is nothing in it; er fing an zu glauben, daß etwas — der Sache sein könnte, he began to think there might be something in it; ich — meiner Person, ich — meiner Seite, ich — meinem Theile &c., *obsolescent for* ich für meine Person, ich meinerseits, ich meines Theils *or* für meinen Theil &c., I for my part, &c.; der Major — seiner Seite *(Göthe for* seinerseits) …, for his part; *d)* — sich, by himself, herself, itself, apart from others or other things, abstractly; das Spielen — sich ist nicht tadelnswerth, playing in itself is not reprehensible; dies ist — sich unwahrscheinlich, this is intrinsically improbable; *sometimes* für *is added:* die Tugend ist — und für sich begehrenswerth, virtue in itself (independently of other considerations) is a desirable thing; es ist — (und für) sich klar, gewiß, offenbar &c., it is apparent *or* manifest in itself, it is evident in its own nature.

9) An *in connection with other verbs: a)* — einer Krankheit leiden, sterben &c. *(see* Leiden, Sterben &c.), to suffer, to die of a disease, &c.; *b)* du hast viele Fehler — dir, you are subject to many faults; Sie haben nichts vom Advocaten — sich, you have nothing of the lawyer about you; sie fanden keine Schuld — ihm, they found no guilt in him; man bemerkte Spuren des Wahnsinns — ihm, indications of insanity were perceived in him; *c)* wir loben — ihm die Bescheidenheit und Artigkeit, we praise his modesty and politeness; man tadelte — ihm seine Geschwätzigkeit, his garrulity was blamed; *d)* sich — etwas *(Dat.)* freuen, ärgern &c., *for* über etwas *(Acc.)*, *which is more usual;* ich labte mich — den Früchten, I refreshed myself with fruit; sie erquickten sich — dem Wein, they regaled themselves with wine; sich ergötzen —, ein Wohlgefallen haben — einer Sache, *see* Ergötzen &c.; *e)* — ihm habe ich einen rechten Freund, I have a thorough friend in him; — ihr besitze ich einen Schatz, in her I possess a treasure; was für ein Künstler, was für ein Held stirbt — mir! *(Manner)*, what artist, what hero dies with me! ich möchte schwer zu überreden sein, | daß ich — dir ein schuldvoll

Haupt beschirme (*Göthe*), ... that protecting thee I should a guilty hand (*Swanwick*); *f*) etwas *or* Jemand (*Acc.*) sehen, hören, erkennen &c. — einer Sache: *i. e.* by a thing; ich sehe — der Handschrift, von wem der Brief kommt, I see by the handwriting from whom the letter comes: ich würde sie — ihrem Gange erkennen, I should know her by her walk, &c.; *g*) redlich — Einem handeln, to deal fairly by one; handle — Andern, wie du willst, daß man — dir handle, do by others as you would be done by: Sie werden nicht als Freund — mir handeln, you will not act as a friend towards me (*cf.* Handeln); so konntet ihr — einem Manne handeln, — dem sich Gottes Hand sichtbar verkündigt? (*Schiller*, Tell 3, 3), wouldst thou thus treat the man, in whose behalf God's hand hath been so visibly displayed? (*W. Peter*); hat der Tell auch so — euch gehandelt? (*Ib.* 1, 2), did Tell deal likewise so with you? einen Raub, ein Verbrechen — Einem begehen, to commit a robbery, a crime upon one; es war geradezu ein Raub — ihm, it was a dead robbery on him; sich — seinen armen Nebenmenschen versündigen, to sin against one's poor fellowmen; sich vergreifen — &c., *see* Vergreifen &c.; *h*) zweifeln — einer Sache (*Dat.*, *but* glauben — ..., *with Acc.*, *see* 10 *a.* E.), to doubt of a thing (*cf.* Zweifeln); — einer Sache verzweifeln &c., to despair of a thing, &c.; *i*) es mangelt — einer Sache (einem Beweis &c.), a thing (proof, &c.) is wanting; aus Mangel — Beweis (*Dat.*), from (*or* owing to) want of proof (*cf.* Mangeln, Fehlen &c.); *k*) an *in connection with* hin, vorbei &c., by, past, &c.: die Stadt erstreckt sich — den Ufern des Flusses hin, the town extends along the banks of the river; der Zug fuhr — ihm vorbei, the train rushed by him: das Summen des Käfers, indem er im Bogen — Einem vorbeifliegt, klingt ..., the drone of the cockchafer as he wheels by you, sounds ...; der Sturm brach den Stamm (des Rosenbusches) — der Erde weg, the storm broke off the stem level with the ground; sie fuhr — ihm die Treppe hinunter und verschwand (*Göthe*), she glided past him down stairs and vanished.

10) An *with Accusative* (*cf.* 1): *a*) das Wasser reichte (trat, ging) ihm fast (bis) — den Mund, the water reached almost up to his mouth; die Flut stieg (bis) — die Brücke, the flood rose up to the bridge; mit dem Fuße — einen Stein stoßen, to knock one's foot against a stone; er warf das Dintenfaß — die Wand, he threw the inkstand against the wall; sie warf ihm den Stein — den Kopf, she threw the stone at his head; es kommt ans Licht, it comes to the light; — Einen gehen, † *for* to go up to one, in order to address or to attack him, &c., to accost; to aggress, assault (sich — Einen machen, — Einen kommen &c.); *hence elliptical phrases like the following*: Emmerich, komm! — die wollen wir (*Schiller*), Come, Emmerich! let us go up to them, let us address them (*for* — die wollen wir uns machen *or* wenden); wer wollte nicht viel lieber — einen sichtbaren Feind? who would not much rather attack a visible enemy? *b*) *aa*) — Einen schreiben, etwas — Einen berichten &c., to write to one, to report a thing to one, &c.: *the phrases* — Einen reden, etwas — Einen erzählen, *although employed by Göthe, are quite unusual, perhaps mere Gallicisms, for* zu Einem reden, Einem etwas erzählen; etwas — Einen fordern, suchen &c., *see* Fordern &c.; eine Frage &c. — Einen richten, to address a question, &c. to one; sich — Einen wenden, to address one's self to one, to apply to one; *bb*) *substantives of analogous meaning are construed similarly*: ein Schreiben — seinen Vorgesetzten, a letter to one's superior; ein Bericht — den General, a report addressed to the general; der Brief — die Hebräer, the letter to the Hebrews: ein Brief — ihn (*supply* gerichtet &c.) ist angekommen, a letter has arrived for him; hat der Briefträger etwas — mich? has the letter-carrier anything for me? es ist ein Bote — dich da, a messenger for you has arrived; ich habe eine Bitte, ein Gesuch &c. — dich, I have a request, &c. to make to you; eine Frage — das Orakel, a question addressed to the oracle (*cf.* Frage); wir haben noch eine Forderung — ihn, we have still a claim upon him; eine Rede — den König, a speech, oration to the king; Schiller's Lied — die Freude, Schiller's hymn to Joy; ein kleines Gedicht — den Mond, a little poem addressed to the moon; ein Kind kann mancherlei — seinen Vater auf dem Herzen tragen, das nicht für einen Dritten taugt (*Schiller*), a child may have many a thing on its mind it wishes to confide to its father ...; *bb*) — († in) Einen glauben, to believe in one; — Einen denken, to think of one, &c. *see* Glauben, Denken &c.

II. An *as an adverb not often to be met with except in compounds*:

1) *After substantives, either separately or coalescing* (*cf. Grimm*); der Weinstock breitet sich Baum — (*Opitz*), the vine spreads itself up the tree; bindt's Pferd Haus —! (*Göthe*), tie the horse to the house: berg—, himmel—, strom—, *and a few other compounds, expressing a similar meaning, are the only examples now to be found*

2) *After other prepositions or adverbs*: von ... an († aus ... an), beginning from ...; from ... upwards, oben—, unten— &c. *see* Von, Oben—, Unten—, Neben—, Vorn—, Hinten— &c.

3) *Elliptically, some word being understood* (*cf. the English* on! off! down! up! &c. *for* go on! go *or* move off! &c.), *often expressing a short command or exhortation, or some other sense to be known by the construction*: fertig! —! Feuer! *military command*: make ready! present! fire! (*for* macht euch fertig! legt [das Gewehr] —! gebt Feuer!); oben naus und nirgends —! up and out, touching nowhere! *proverbial exclamation of witches on rushing out of a chimney*; hart — mich! (*Göthe*, Faust: *cf. Sanders*), (keep) close to me! muthig —! (*Körner*), (go) on, courageously (*for* rückt muthig —).

An'aasen, An'aaßen, (*w.*) *v. tr. see* Anäsen.

* **Anabaptis'mus**, (*indecl.*) *m.* (*Gr.*) anabaptism (Lehre der Wiedertäufer). — **Anabaptist'**, (*w.*) *m.* anabaptist (Wiedertäufer). — **Anabaptist'isch**, *adj.* anabaptistic(al).

* **An'abas**, (*indecl.*) *m.* (*Gr.*) *Ichth.* anabas (Kletterfisch).

* **Anacar'dienbaum**, *m.* cashew-nut tree, *see* Acajoubaum. — **Anacar'dienholz**, *n.* wood of the cashew-nut tree. — **Anacard'säure**, *f. Chem.* anacardic acid.

* **Anachoret'**, (*w.*) *m.* (*Gr.*) anachorite, anchoret (Einsiedler). — **Anachore'tisch**, *adj.* (anchoretic[al] veraltet), relating to an anchorite or hermit (Einsiedlerisch).

* **Anachronis'mus**, (*sing. indecl.*, *pl. w.* Anachronis'men) *m.* (*Gr.*) anachronism (Zeitrechnungsfehler). — **Anachronist'isch**, *adj.* anachronistic.

An'ackern, (*w.*) *v. tr.* 1) to turn (the clods, &c.) over in ploughing so as to lean them against the elevation of the furrow; 2) to add (a piece of ground, &c.) to a field, &c. by ploughing.

* **Anacon'da**, (*pl.* A-s) *f. Zool.* anaconda, a large snake of the island of Ceylon and tropical America, a species of Boa.

* **Anacreon'tisch**, *see* Anakreontisch.

* **Anadem'**, (*str.*) *n.* (*Gr.*) anadem, a chaplet or crown of flowers, a wreath, a garland; a band or fillet worn on the head (Haarbinde).

* **Anadiplo'sis**, (*sing. indecl.*, *pl.* (*w.*) Ana-

zu analogisieren, to reason from analogy. — Analogis'mus, (indecl., pl. [w.] Analogis'men) m. analogism. — Analogist', (w.) m. analogist (one who reasons from analogy).

* Analy'se, (w.) f. (Gr.) Philos., Math., &c. analysis (a resolution [Auflösung] of a thing into its component parts; opp. Synthese). — Analysi'ren, (w.) v. tr. to analyse (auflösen); Gramm. to parse. — Analysir'bār, adj. analyzable. — Analysi'rung, (w.) f. analyzation. — Analy'tik, (w.) f. analytics, analytical science. — Analy'tiker, (str.) m. analyst, analyzer (opp. Synthetiker). — Analy'tisch, adj. analytical, analytic (opp. Synthetisch); a-e Methode, analytical method.

* Anämie', (w.) f. (Gr.; lit. bloodlessness) Med. anæmia (Blutlosigkeit; Blutarmut). — Anä'misch, adj. Med. anæmic, destitute of blood (blutlos; blutarm).

An'anas, (str., pl. Ananasse, rarely w. Ananassen) f. (introduced from the Span. & Port. ananas, m.) Bot. ananas, a South American plant (Bromelia ananas, Ananassa sativa) that produces the pine-apple (Königsapfel, Ananas); —apfel, m. see Schlotterapfel; —birne, f. pine-apple pear; —erdbeere, f. cone, pine, or pine strawberry (Fragaria grandiflora); —flachs, m. the dried root-fibres of the pine-apple, manufactured into cloth by the South-Americans; —(treib)haus, n. pinery, pine-house; —laus, f. Entom. pine-apple insect (Coccus bromeliæ); —leinen, n. grass-cloth manufactured from the root-fibres of the ananas; —vogel, m. Ornith. humming-bird (Trochilus); —wein, m. pine-apple wine; —zeug, n. grass-cloth, see —leinen.

* Anan'drisch, adj. Bot. anandrous, destitute of stamens; a-e Blumen, anandrous or female flowers.

An'ankern, (w.) v. tr. 1) to fasten (a ship, &c.) by anchors, to anchor; 2) Archit. to fasten (beams to a wall, &c.) by means of iron braces or cramps (Anker).

* Anapäst', (str., pl. A-e, or [w.] A-en) m. Gramm. 1) anapest, anapæst (a metrical foot in Greek and Latin: ⏑⏑—). — Anapäst'isch, adj. anapestic; ein a-er Vers, an anapestic.

* Ana'pher, (w.) f. (Gr.) Rhetor. anaphora.

* Anaphrodisie', (w.) f., Anaphrodisis'mus, (sing. indecl., pl. w. Anaphrodisis'men) m. Med. anaphrodisia, impotence. — Anaphrodi'tisch, Anaphrodisi'isch, adj. Med. anaphrodisiac, anaphroditic; impotent.

* Ana'plasis, (indecl.) f., Anaplas'mus, (indecl.) m. (Gr.) Med. & Surg. anaplasis: 1) a restoration of flesh where it has been lost; 2) the re-uniting of fractured bones. — Anaplas'tik, (w.) f. anaplastic art. — Anaplas'tisch, adj. anaplastic, restoring flesh, &c.

An'arbeiten, (w.) v. I. tr. to join to by means of work, to add (one piece of work) to (another); II. intr. gegen Einen —, to work, or act, in opposition to one, fig. to oppose one by contrary action; to run counter to ..., to counteract (Einem entgegenarbeiten).

* Anarchie', (w.) f. (Gr.) anarchy. — Anar'chisch, adj. anarchical, anarchic. — Anarchist', (w.) m. anarchist.

An'ärgern, (w.) v. tr. Einem (gener. sich [Dat.]) etwas —, to inflict (an illness, &c.) upon one by vexing him; sich (Dat.) die [illegible] —, to vex one's self into a consumption.

[illegible], (w.) v. I. intr. (aux. sein) & refl. 1) to become equal or identical in kind (einer Sache [Dat.], to a thing, &c.); to be assimilated ([illegible]), to be converted into the substance of organized beings; 2) to become [illegible] to or in ..., to grow into a nature; [illegible] sein, to be implanted (by nature), to be innate, inborn; es war [illegible], it had become (their) second nature; mir ist nicht a-d (Voss, Iliad), it is or lies not in my nature (es ist or liegt nicht in meiner Art); II. tr. to assimilate, to make equal or identical to ...: der Körper artet sich (Dat.) die Speise an, the body turns or converts food into its own substance (by digestion). — An'artung, (w.) f. a becoming equal or identical in kind, &c., assimilation.

* Anästhesie', (w.) f. Med. anæsthesis. — Anästhe'tisch, adj. anæsthetic.

Anästhesi'ren, (w.) v. tr. to anæsthetise (to render insensible by means of an anæsthetic).

An'äßen, (w.) v. tr. see Anätzen. — An'äßig, adj. provinc. covetous, eager, desirous, agog. [octahedrite.

* An'atas, (str.) m. & n. Miner. anatase,

* Ana'thema, (str., pl. A-s or [Gr.] Anathe'mata) Anathem', (str.) n. (Gr.) anathema (die von Sheldon u. A. versuchte Anglisirung anatheme ist nicht in Gebrauch, anathem existirt gar nicht): 1) New Test. a person or thing anathematized; 2) an ecclesiastical curse, excommunication (Kirchenbann, Bannfluch). — Anathemat'isch, adj. anathematical (verbannend, verdammend). — Anathematisi'ren, (w.) v. tr. to anathematize (mit dem Bann belegen, verdammen).

An'äthmen, (w.) v. tr. to breathe at, on (upon), against (Anhauchen, more usual). — An'äthmung, (w.) f. a breathing upon, &c.; exhalation.

* Anatom', (str. & w.) m. (Gr.) Med. anatomist, dissector. — Anatomie', (w.) f. 1) anatomy: a) the act or art of dissecting animal bodies, dissection; b) the science which treats of the internal structure of the human body (Zergliederung, Section; Zergliederungskunst); 2) anatomical building or room. — Anatomi'ren, (w.) v. tr. to anatomise, to dissect (Zergliedern, Seciren). — Anatomi'rung, (w.) f. anatomisation. — Anato'miker, (str.) m. (l. u.: Anatomist', [w.] m.) anatomist, one versed in the art of dissection. — Anato'misch, adj. anatomical; ein a-es Theater, an anatomical theatre.

* Anatrop', adj. Bot. anatropous (Gegenläufig).

An'äßen, (w.) v. tr. 1) to bring to the lure, to lure (Anködern, Anlocken); 2) to begin to cauterise or to act upon ... by acids, Engrav. to begin to etch; nach dem — des Gesteins mit Salzsäure, after applying muriatic acid to the mineral.

An'äugeln, (w.) v. tr. (Einen) to look at or upon (one) tenderly or amorously, to ogle, leer at (a person, &c.).

An'backen, (str. & [rarely] w., cf. Backen) v. I. tr. an etwas (Acc. & Dat.) —, to make to stick or to adhere to a thing (Ankleben), orig. by baking or by any similar process; an einander —, to bake, to cake, or to clod together (opp. Abbacken); II. intr. (aux. haben & sein) to cling, to cleave, to stick, or to adhere to a thing by baking, &c.; an einander —, to cleave, to stick, to adhere, &c. together.

An'bahnen, (w.) v. tr. fig. to break a path for (Verbesserungen &c., improvements, &c.), to pave or prepare the way for ..., to open a road or a passage for ..., to open up a favourable way for ...; to facilitate the introduction of ..., to bring ... about, &c., cf. in Gang bringen, Einleiten &c.; eine Geschäftsverbindung —, to open the way for a business-connection.

An'ballen, (w.) v. refl. (sich an etwas [Acc. & Dat.]) to stick or adhere to (a thing) in balls or clods, to ball or clod to .... — An'ballung, (w.) f. the act of gathering or adhering to (a thing in a ball or round mass), conglobation, conglomeration.

An'bannen, (w.) v. tr. 1) Einen an etwas (Acc. & Dat.) —, to fix or bind one to a thing by witchcraft or a spell; er ist wie angebannt an seine Arbeit, an seine Bücher (Mühl.), he is bound to his work, to his books, as it were, by a spell: dem Boden angebannt (Göthe), implanted in the ground as if by a charm; 2) Einem etwas —, to bewitch one with a thing, see Anzaubern.

An'bau, (str.) m. 1) (des Landes &c.) a) the (act of) first preparing (land) for crops, a beginning (see Anbauen, I. 2) to raise (crops, &c.) by tillage, first cultivation (of a field, &c.; of a plant, &c.); culture, tilth: der Flachs, sein — und seine Zubereitung in Irland, flax, its cultivation and preparation in Ireland; b) (first) cultivation (of science, literature, &c.), study, pursuit, improvement by original research; 2) the act of building on new ground, the act of settling, settlement; 3) a) additional building, addition; lean-to; superstructure; b) new part of a building, or of a town (where new buildings have been erected); 4) (rarely used) newly cultivated lands: ein reicher — (Rückert), a rich and fertile tract of land; 5) provinc. alluvial land, alluvion (Anschwemmung). [cultivable.

An'baubār, adj. susceptible of cultivation,

An'bauen, (w.) v. I. tr. 1) to build (a house, &c.) close up to (another building, &c., ein Haus &c. an ein anderes Gebäude &c. —), to add (an [with Acc. & Dat.], to) by building: einen Flügel an das Haus or an dem Hause —, to add a wing to a house; angebaut, p. a. erected near, contiguous; 2) a) to till for the first time, to commence cultivating; b) aa) to bring under cultivation, to till, cultivate (in general); bb) to raise or produce by tillage (on new ground, or such as has lately been untilled, or occupied by different crops); c) fig. to (begin) to cultivate (a certain branch of science, &c.), to undertake, pursue (cf. Anbau, 1, b); 3) to settle (anew) by building houses, &c., to build, to introduce new settlers, &c.; II. refl. to settle (an einem Orte, in a place), to establish one's residence, to establish one's self: sie bauten sich an der Mündung des Po an, they settled at the mouth of the Po.

An'bauer, (str.) m. cultivator; planter; improver; settler, colonist.

An'baulich, adj. cultivable, easy to be cultivated (cf. Anbaubar).

An'bauung, (w.) f. 1) (eines Hauses an ein anderes &c.) the (act of) building (a house, &c.) close up (to another building, &c.), &c. cf. Anbauen; 2) cultivation, culture, &c.; 3) the act of settling, &c., settlement.

An'befehlen, (str.) v. tr. (Einem etwas) 1) to command, order, direct, charge one to do a thing, to bid one do a thing, to give orders to, &c.; 2) (obsolescent for Anempfehlen) to recommend, to give in charge.

An'beginn, (str.) m. obsolescent, the (very) first beginning, commencement, beginning, prime: von —, from the first of time.

An'beginnen, (str.) v. intr. (a rare word and used only in the inseparable forms — Bürger, Göthe) to make a first beginning, to commence. [&c. previously worn).

An'behalten, (str.) v. tr. to keep on (clothes,

Anbei', adv. 1) annexed, inclosed, subjoined, herewith, cf. Hierbei; — folgt, annexed you (will) receive, I adjoin to this; — folgt der bewußte Brief, under this cover we send you the letter in question; — (sende ich) die verlangten Zeuge, accompanying this letter I send you the goods ordered (by you, &c.); 2) l. u. a) for nebenbei, außerdem, & b) for dabei, daneben.

An'beißen, (str.) v. I. tr. to bite at or into, to begin to bite, to bite the first piece or a little of ... (in order to taste, &c.); wer hat diesen Apfel angebissen? who has bitten a piece off this apple? who has bitten into the apple? II. intr. 1) a) † to break one's fast, to touch food (cf. Imbiß, Jmbiß); b) Sport. (of wolves and foxes) to touch or take food, particul. carrion; 2) an einer Sache (Dat.) —, to bite or to nibble at a thing; (of fishes, &c.) to bite or to nibble at the hook (an die Angel [Acc.] beißen), to take the bait (often fig.), to bite: jetzt beißt er an (Göthe), now he swallows the bait: sie mag sich (Dat.) die Mühe sparen ihn anzulocken, denn er wird nie —, she may spare her pains to allure him, for he will never bite; das Publicum war in der Stimmung sich täuschen zu lassen und biß eifrig an, the public were in the mood to be deceived, and caught eagerly at the bait.

An'bekommen, (str.) v. tr. to get on (clothes, boots, &c.).

An'belang, (str.) m. rarely used, concern, regard (Anbetreff).

An'belangen, (w.) v. tr. (Einen) to relate to (one), to concern, &c., see Anlangen, Betreffen: was mich anbelangt, as for me, &c.

An'bellern, (w.) v. tr. coll. to bark at (one) repeatedly or incessantly, to yelp at.

An'bellen, (w., sometimes str., see Bellen) v. I. intr. 1) to begin to bark; 2) angebellt kommen, to approach barking (cf. Kommen); II. tr. to bark or to yelp at: fig. to snarl at (a person or thing).

An'benében, adv. († &) quaint for Anbei or Hierneben, herewith, annexed, &c.

An'bequemen, (w.) v. tr. to accommodate, to adapt, to fit; gener. as a refl. sich (Acc.) einer Sache (Dat.) —, to accommodate one's self to, to conform, submit, or yield to (circumstances, &c.). — An'bequemung, (w.) f. accommodation, adaptation.

An'beraumen, (w.) v. tr. Law, to appoint, set, fix, or state (a certain time or day); die anberaumte Frist, the time or term stated. — An'beraumung, (w.) f. appointment, act of appointing, fixing, &c.

† An'beregen, (w.) v. tr. particul. used in the pp. anberegt, Law Style, (above) mentioned, (afore)said; cf. Beregen.

An'bereiten, (w.) v. tr. (l. u. for Anmachen, Anrühren rc.) to prepare, make up, &c. — An'bereitung, (w.) f. preparation, &c.

An'berg, (str.) m. 1) a slight elevation, a rising (and, as it were, incipient) hill, hillock; 2) less usual (Hilp.), a small hill or hillock, contiguous to and forming part of the foot of a mountain.

† An'berühren, (w.) v. tr. for Anrühren, Berühren (Betreffen, Anbetreffen).

† An'bestellen, (w.) v. tr. for Bestellen, in Auftrag geben.

An'beten, (w.) v. tr. & intr. 1) to adore, to worship; 2) † (Luther, &c.) to pay obeisance to (one) by inclining the body, knees, &c. (also intr. with vor [& Dat.], Klopstock with gegen, Herder with Dat.), to bow in reverence before ...; 3) fig. to adore, to worship, to idolize, to dote upon (one); der (die) Angebetete, the adored one, love, sweetheart (Geliebte). — An'betenswerth, An'betenswürdig, adj. adorable (Anbetungswerth rc.).

An'beter, (str.) m. 1) adorer, worshipper (also fig.); 2) fig. adorer; votary; lover; sie hat viele —, she has many admirers.

An'betracht, (str.) m. (l. u., except with in ..., see below) manner of seeing or understanding a thing, regard, opinion, view, consideration, respect (Betracht); in diesem —, in this respect; in keinem —, in no respect, by no means; in — (Erwägung) einer Sache (Gen.), or daß ..., in consideration of a thing, considering that ....

An'betreff, (str.) m. relation, regard, reference, respect; in — or A-s (or a-s); a-s einer Sache (Gen.), in regard to a thing, as to, respecting, &c. a thing (cf. Betreff rc.).

An'betreffen, (str.) v. tr. to concern, to touch; was mich anbetrifft, as far as I am concerned; a-d, touching, concerning, as for, as to (cf. Angehen, Anbelangen rc.).

An'betteln, (w.) v. I. tr. 1) to address begging, to ask or beg alms of (one), to importune by begging; 2) (Einem etwas) to obtrude (a thing) upon (one) by begging, or by abject, importunate entreaty, &c.; II. refl. (bei Einem) to intrude one's self into a place or business (into one's good graces, &c.) by mean or importunate entreaties, to insinuate one's self in a (mean) begging manner.

An'betten, (w.) v. I. tr. (Einen) to place the bed of (a person) near some place; II. refl. to place one's bed close to another bed, &c. (opp. Abbetten).

An'betung, (w.) f. 1) adoration, worship; 2) fig. adoration, idolatry, admiration: a-strunken, adj. (Rodarits, l. u.) intoxicated with devotional feeling; a-svoll, adj. full of adoration or devotion; a-swerth, a-swürdig, adj. adorable; A-swürdigkeit, f. adorableness.

† An'bezielen, (w.) v. tr. Law, to appoint, to state, to fix (a term, &c.).

An'biegen, (str.) v. tr. 1) an etwas (Acc.) —, to bend to or towards ...; 2) Law & Comm. orig. to fold (a sheet of paper, &c.) to some document, &c., then, in general, to add, to annex, to subjoin; mostly used in the pp. angebogen; die angebogene (inliegende) Rechnung, the annexed or enclosed account; angebogen behändige ich Ihnen Factur, I hand you invoice on the other side; angebogen empfangen Sie ..., annexed you will receive ...; ohne angebogenen Vortheil (Jean Paul), without an additional advantage.

An'bieten, (str.) v. I. tr. to offer, to hold out, to proffer, to tender: Einem seine Dienste —, to offer or proffer one's services to a person, to make an offer or a tender of one's services to one; dem Feinde eine Schlacht —, to offer battle to the enemy; er hat ihr seine Hand angeboten (Hilp.), he offered her his hand (in marriage); die angebotene Gnade annehmen, to receive the overtures of mercy; anzubieten, offerable; II. refl. 1) to offer one's self; to offer; er hat sich selbst angeboten (better erboten) uns zu begleiten, he offered (himself) of his own accord to accompany us; 2) fig. (of abstract notions) to obtrude or force itself upon one's notice, &c.; III. intr. to bid first, to offer the first bid, to start a price (in public sales).

An'bietung, (w.) f. offer, offering.

† An'bild, (str.) n. image, representation, see Abbild.

An'bilden, (w.) v. tr. 1) †, to represent, delineate, portray (Abbilden, Darstellen); 2) (Einem etwas) a) to affix, add, impart, &c. by newly forming, moulding, framing, &c.: Phöbus, ergrimmt, bildete dem Midas Eselsohren an, Phœbus, enraged, fashioned Midas's ears into asinine shape; b) fig. to bestow (something) on (one, &c.) by a new creation; wie er (der Grieche) jeder Idee sogleich einen Leib anbildet (Schiller), as he at once bestows a bodily shape on every idea; (die [illegible] menschliche Gestalt,) welche die [illegible] Göttern anbildet (W. v. Hum[illegible]), with which mytho[illegible] shape) Verfassung, wie die [illegible] die Zeiten sie (Acc.) sich (Dat.) angebildet hat (Schlegel), the constitution, such as the nation in the course of time created for, and adapted to itself; 3) fig. (Einem etwas) to form, to create, to fashion, to model, &c. (something in one) by instruction and discipline; to implant by education, cultivation, &c.; to impart by training, &c.; sich (Dat.) etwas —, to accustom one's self to, to acquire (a knowledge of, in); b) Einen — (better Heranbilden), to bring or lead up to a certain state or standard by education, to accustom.

An'binde..., in comp. —blof, m. Mar.

[illegible], *adj. provinc. (N. G.)* bitterish, [illegible] bitter (Bitterlich).

[illegible], *(w.) v. tr. (l. u.)* to impregnate [illegible] a bitterish taste, to make bitterish *(cf.* [illegible], [illegible]).

[illegible], *(w.) v. tr. provinc. (N. G.)* to [illegible] at (one).

[illegible], *(w.) v. tr. (Luther) see* Anblöfen.

[illegible], *(w.) v. tr.* to blacken with smoke [illegible] of a burning lamp, &c.

[illegible], *provinc. (Saxony) see* Anblecken.

[illegible], *(str.) m.* 1) *or* An'blaſt, †, a [illegible] upon, breath, (pestilential, &c.) [illegible]; 2) *Metall.* the point over the mouth of [illegible]-furnace where the blast strikes.

[illegible], *(str.) v. tr.* 1) to blow at, against, [illegible], to breathe at *or* upon; 2) *lit. & fig.* [illegible] *or* to excite by blowing (Anfachen); [illegible] up (the fire): das Feuer der Leiden[illegible] —, to kindle the flames of passion; das [illegible] der Zwietracht — *(Hilp.)*, to foment [illegible], to sow dissension; Einen — *(seldom.* [illegible] Eines Leidenſchaft ꝛc. —), to incite one [illegible] passion, &c.; er ſcheint höchſt angeblaſen [illegible] *(Arndt)*, he seems in the highest [illegible] excited and indignant; 3) to distend [illegible], to blow up (as a bladder, &c.), *see* [illegible]; 4) *(obsolescent,* to strike with a sudden [illegible] destructive wind, to blast (a mysterious [illegible], ascribed to evil spirits, in opposition [illegible] life-giving breath of holy spirits, *cf.* [illegible] 1, & Anhauchen); *fig.* (Einem etwas) to [illegible] (something) upon (one) as if by witch[illegible], to affect (one) suddenly and unexpect[illegible], to touch, to seize (as a sudden humour, [illegible]); 5) Einen (mit Scheltworten) —, to fly at [illegible] (with chiding words), to snarl at one, [illegible] snap up short (Anſchnauben); 6) *Paint.* to [illegible] (the colours) lightly on, *cf.* Anhauchen; 7) *Metall.* to set the blast of (a furnace) to work for the first time, *syn.* Anlaſſen; 8) *Mus.* [illegible] wind-instruments) *a) aa)* to commence to [illegible], to cause to sound, to sound: *bb)* to sound [illegible] notes, &c.); *b) T.* to blow (newly made [illegible]-instruments) for the first time (in order [illegible] try and to perfect the sound emitted); *c)* [illegible] meet, to receive, to welcome, to excite, [illegible] summon, to announce, &c. by sound of trumpet, &c.: eine Stadt, eine Feſtung ꝛc. —, [illegible], to summon a town, a fortress, &c. by sound of trumpet (to surrender, &c.); den Tag — ([illegible], Volksl.), †, to announce the approach of day with a blast on a horn: die ([illegible]) Feinde —, †, to announce the (approach of the) enemy by sound of trumpet, &c.; *Sport.* to announce by blowing a bugle, by [illegible] a horn, &c.: die Jagd, the commencement of the chase, &c. *(opp.* Abblaſen); den [illegible], the approach of the stag, &c.: *d)* ange[illegible], to approach with sound of trumpet, horn, flute, or other wind-instrument, to [illegible] with flourish of trumpets, &c.

[illegible], *(str., pl.* An'blätter) *n.* 1) † *for* [illegible], name of a leafless, scaly herb, particularly of *Lathraea squamaria (cf.* Zahnwurz [illegible]); 2) *provinc.* wafer, *see* Oblate.

[illegible], *(w.) v. tr. Join. & Carp.* to [illegible] by the square ([illegible]), to join (a piece of [illegible] to (another piece) by laying the two [illegible] together and fastening a third piece [illegible] to both, to clamp.

[illegible], *(w.) v. tr.* to give *or* to impart [illegible] colour *or* tint to, to blue.

[illegible], *(w.) v. tr.* to show [illegible], to put out one's tongue to ....

[illegible], *(str.) v. intr. (aux.* ſein) *see* [illegible]

[illegible], *(w.) v. tr. ([illegible], Sanders)* [illegible] with galling lustre.

[illegible] *(w.) v. tr.) Sport.* to wound with [illegible] (Anſchießen).

[illegible] *m.* 1) *obsolescent,* the act of [illegible]

looking at (a thing, eines Dinges), look, sight *(Göthe with* in *[& Acc.], cf.* Einblick); erſten A-s *or* beim erſten —, *see* auf den erſten Blick; 2) view, aspect, sight; appearance; spectacle: mein — iſt ihr verhaßt, she hates the sight of me.

An'blicken, *(w.) v. tr.* to look at *or* upon, to glance at *or* upon, to cast an eye upon, to give a look; zornig —, to dart angry looks at, to frown upon; Einen ſtarr —, to gaze fixedly upon one, to stare at one.

An'blinken, *(w.) v. tr.* 1) to gleam, glitter, glance, twinkle, *or* shine upon (as the rays of a luminous object); 2) (Anblinzen) to give (one) a quick glance, to glance, blink *or* wink at, &c.

An'blinzeln, *(w.) v. tr.* to blink at (one) with frequent winking, to wink at.

An'blinzen, *(w.) v. tr.* to stare *or* goggle at with unmeaning, &c. eyes; to leer *or* wink at.

An'blitzen, *(w.) v. tr.* to glance *or* flash at (one) like lightning, to dart a rapid look or glance at (one); to dazzle *or* strike with the brilliancy of lightning: mit dem Spiegel — *(Hilp.)*, to dazzle by suddenly throwing on (one) the rays of the sun reflected from a mirror.

An'blöken, *(w.) v. tr.* 1) to bleat *or* low at: 2) *fig.* to bawl at (one) with a loud voice.

An'blühen, *(w.) v. I. intr.* 1) to begin to blossom *or* bloom: 2) to begin to flourish *or* develop itself; II. *tr.* to strike the sense or sight of (one) like a blooming plant.

An'blümen, *(w.) v. tr. (particul. in S. G.)* 1) to sow (newly ploughed ground) with clover or similar herbage for the first time: angeblümte Felder, newly sown clover-fields *(syn.* Beſämen); 2) *fig.* to cover (the cheeks) with the bloom of health or with blushes.

An'bluten, *(w.) v. intr.* to begin to bleed.

An'bohren, *(w.) v. tr.* 1) to bore at the surface, to begin to bore, to bore into *(opp.* Durchbohren); einen Baum —, to bore into (a tree) to a certain depth (not through): *a)* in order to examine the quality of the wood; *b)* to make a hole in a tree in order to obtain the sap, to box, to tap a (coniferous) tree to make the resin flow out; ein Faß —, to pierce, to broach, to tap a cask (in order to draw the liquor); eine Quelle —, to open a well by boring; 2) *fig.* to break *or* run holes through (the law, &c.); 3) *fig.* to make strong *or* importunate attempts on (one, in order to obtain a certain object, such as money *(cf.* Anpumpen], &c.); 4) to fasten (brackets, &c.) by boring the necessary holes to receive the objects intended to be fastened *(cf.* Einbohren, *Sanders)*; ſie bohren ſo das Thier an, thus they fix the animal (by running a pole into it).

An'bohrung, *(w.) f.* 1) the act of boring at the surface, &c.; 2) *Med. see* Abzapfung (Paracenteſe).

An'bolzen, *(w.) v. tr.* to fasten (one piece of timber) to (another) with a bolt, peg, &c. or bolts, &c., to secure with a bolt, to bolt, peg, pin, to treenail. — An'bolzung, *(w.) f.* the (act of) fastening (one piece of timber) to (another) with a bolt, &c.

An'borden, *(w.) v. tr. Mar. see* Entern.

An'borgen, *(w.) v. tr.* 1) to procure *or* obtain by borrowing; angeborgter Schimmer, fictitious lustre *(cf.* Borgen); 2) (Einen) to borrow a sum of money of (one).

An'borſten, *(w.) v. intr. (aux.* haben) *Sport.* to bristle up, to erect the bristles (said of the wild boar).

An'bot, *(str.) n.* 1) first bid *or* offer (at public sales), *gener.* Angebot, *which see*; 2) (Anerbieten) offer, tender; 3) *(sometimes m.)* judicial order, writ.

An'branden, *(w.) v. intr. (aux.* ſein) to strike *or* surge against (gegen, an *(with Acc.)*), to break upon (the rocks, &c. as the surf).

An'braſſen, *(w.) v. tr. Mar.* to brace (the sails) in, to haul in (the weather-braces).

An'braten, *(str.) v. tr.* to begin to roast, to roast superficially.

An'bräunen, *(w.) v. I. intr. (aux.* ſein) to begin to grow brown, to grow brownish; II. *tr.* to imbrown, to make brownish, to darken the colour of.

An'brauſen, *(w.) v. I. intr. (aux.* ſein) to come roaring *or* rushing along; II. *tr.* to rush on (one), or to attack in a blustering manner, to assail with a loud voice.

An'brechen, *(str.) v. I. tr.* 1) to begin to break, to break (off), to cut, *or in gener.* to use for the first time, to open: ein Laib Brot —, to make the first cut in a loaf (Anſchneiden); ein Faß —, to broach *or* tap a cask: eine Flaſche Wein —, *see* Anſtechen; ein Stück Zeug —, to cut into a piece of cloth: die geſtaute Ladung —, to break cargo; die Vorräthe ſind noch nicht angebrochen *(Nob. & Gr.)*, the stock is still untouched: einen Geldſack — *(Hilp.)*, to break in upon a bag of money *(cf.* Angreifen); einen Gang —, *Min.* to open a lode: 2) to break partially (as the boughs of a tree, &c. *syn.* Einknicken, *opp.* Durchbrechen, Abbrechen);

II. *intr. (aux.* ſein) 1) *"according to some,"* *as Grimm says, "used in the present and other tenses of the verb besides the participle past," but it is improbable that phrases like* das Obſt bricht an, das Bier bricht an ꝛc. (the fruit begins to decay, the beer grows stale, &c.), *should ever have been used popularly; on the contrary the participle* angebrochen *seems to belong to the passive voice of the transitive, as explained above:* angebrochenes Obſt, broken, *i. e.* unsound, decaying fruit; angebrochenes Fleiſch, broken, *i. e.* decaying, tainted, putrid meat; angebrochenes Bier, angebrochener Wein, stale, vitiated beer, stale, palled *or* dead wine; 2) *(aux.* ſein) *a) aa)* † *or unusual,* of the approach of the enemy, an avalanche, &c.; *bb)* (of a fountain, &c.) to break forth (anew); *b)* to break, to open (as the morning), to break forth (as the rays of light), to dawn, to approach, to draw near (less frequently of the approach of night or darkness); der Tag bricht an, the day breaks; bei a-dem Tage, at break of day, at day-break; bei a-dem Morgenlicht, at the approach of daylight; mit angebrochenem Tage *(Wieland)*, when day has dawned.

An'brechung, *(w.) f.* 1) the act of beginning to break, &c., *cf.* Anbrechen, I. 1; das Anbrechen *(v. s.) more usual in this sense*; 2) *see* Anbruch.

An'brennen, *(irr.) v. I. intr. (aux.* ſein) 1) to begin to burn: *a)* to burn off partially *(opp.* Abbrennen), to be partly burned or consumed: das Licht iſt angebrannt *(Hilp.)*, the candle is partly burned; *b)* to catch fire, to take fire, to burn up, to kindle, to light; naſſes Holz brennt ſchwer an, wet wood will not take fire easily; Stroh brennt leicht an, straw kindles, or ignites easily; die Katze kann über die Milch gerathen, der Braten kann — u. ſ. w., the cat may get at the milk, the meat may burn, &c.; — laſſen, to burn; *c) fig.* (of anger, &c. — † *for* Entbrennen) to be kindled, to burn; 2) *Cook.* to adhere (to the pot, &c.) on account of excess of heat or want of moisture and thus to be burnt; II. *tr.* 1) to begin to burn, to burn partially, to ignite at one end; 2) to light, to kindle (ein Feuer, a fire), to ignite, to set on fire; ſie brannten die Stadt an vielen Orten an, they set fire to the town in many places; 3) *Cook.* to burn (meat, &c. so as to give the food a disagreeable taste); die Köchin hat den Brei angebrannt *(Hilp.)*, the cook has burnt the pap; angebrannt riechen, to smell of burning. [Verständlich).

An'bringbar, *adj.* salable, marketable (*cf.*

An'bringe . . ., *in comp.* —geld, *n.*, —gebühr, *f. obsolescent*, 1) (*Hilp.*) a premium or bounty given to the person who enlists a recruit; 2) premium or bounty given to informers, &c.

An'bringen, (*str.*) *v. tr.* 1) *a)* to bring (close) to a certain place; ich kann diese Stiefeln nicht — (*coll.* antriegen), I cannot get on these boots (*Hilp.*); Sie empfangen hierbei durch die Post von New York eine Kiste, pr. Dampfer Bremen angebracht, you will receive with this by mail a case from New York, forwarded pr. steamer "Bremen"; *b) Sport.* to set (the blood-hounds) on the game;

2) *lit. & fig. a)* to apply, to contrive, to fix in a certain place, to plant, to place; to construct, to put up; einen Schrank in der Wand —, to fix a cupboard in a wall; eine an der Wand angebrachte Bank, a bench fixed to the wall; ein in einer Mauer angebrachter Altar, an altar constructed in a wall (*Hilp.*); der französische Zuckerbäcker hatte seine Kunst aufgewendet, um geschmackvoll einen Spiegel anzubringen, the French confectioner had exerted his art to introduce a looking-glass; das — eines grünen Abhanges von sammetgleichem Rasen, the introduction of a green slope of velvet turf; eine Vorrichtung —, to contrive an arrangement; eine Verbesserung an einer Maschine —, to introduce *or* effect an improvement in a machine; dies Haus hat zwei Ausgänge, die so angebracht sind, daß sie sich nach verschiedenen Straßen öffnen, to this house there are two exits, contrived to open in different streets; einen Schlag —, to bring home, to hit, or to plant a blow; ein wohl angebrachter Stoß, a home-thrust (*Hilp.*); eine Kugel —, to lodge a ball; Einem einen Schlag —, *see* Beibringen;

3) to dispose of (an den Mann bringen, absetzen); *Comm.* (*cf. Nob. & Gr.*) to sell or vend (commodities); to negociate (bills); to pass off; für voll —, to pass at its full value; leicht —, to sell easily; schwer —, to sell with difficulty; schwer anzubringen (Anbringbar), difficult of sale; gar nicht mehr anzubringen, no longer salable; vortheilhaft —, to place advantageously; der Artikel wird kaum anzubringen sein, it will be difficult to dispose of the article; wir werden die Wechsel anzubringen suchen, we shall try to negociate the bills; nicht anzubringende Briefe, dead letters;

4) *a)* (*syn.* Hinterbringen, Melden) to lay (a case, &c.) before one, to introduce, to exhibit (a charge), to bring before a court, to prefer (an accusation, &c.), to lodge a complaint, information against one; Klage gegen Einen —, to enter an action against one, to inform against one, to denounce one (*sometimes intr.*); mein Geschäftsführer brachte diese Klage bei dem General-Postmeister an, my agent laid this complaint before the Postmaster-General; *b)* to bring *or* put forward, to advance, to offer, to present, to address; eine Bitte —, to prefer a request; ein Wort für seinen Freund —, to put in a word for his friend; was ist dein —? what is your business (*coll.* errand)?

5) (*syn.* Unterbringen, Versorgen) to get a place or to procure an office for (one), to provide for; einen Sohn beim Militär —, to obtain a military appointment for a son; eine Tochter —, to provide for a daughter, to settle a daughter in marriage; einen Lehrling als Gehülfen —, to provide an apprentice with a place as paid clerk; ich werde alle meine Freunde und Verwandte — (*Göthe*), I'll place or provide for all my friends and relations;

6) *fig.* to adapt to the time or occasion (*cf.* 4, *b*); *frequently used in the participle past:* angebracht, wohl angebracht, well applied *or* timed, seasonable; durch eine wohl angebrachte Geldhülfe, by a well-seasoned pecuniary aid; übel angebracht, ill-placed, misplaced, ill-timed; einfältige und übel angebrachte Späße über den Krieg, silly and ill-placed jokes on the subject of war; übel angebrachtes Vertrauen, misplaced confidence; eine Bemerkung —, to put in a remark; er brachte diese Redensart oft an, he often used to introduce this phrase.

An'bringen, (*str.*) *n.*, **An'bringung,** (*w.*) *f.* (*l. u.*) 1) the act of bringing to a certain place, &c. *see* Anbringen, *v.*; 2) information, denouncement, &c.

An'bringer, (*str.*) *m.* 1) *Mech.* supply-hose, &c. (Zubringer); 2) † (**An'bringerin,** [*w.*] *f.* female) informer, accuser, denouncer.

An'bruch, (*str.*, *pl.* An'brüche) *m.* 1) the act or state of beginning to break, &c., *see* Anbrechen, *v.*; breakage: *particul. among miners a)* the first opening of a mine (*Tech.* beginning of the streak); *b)* place where a break or first cut has been made; open lode, opening; edler —, good, rich vein; *c)* (*also in other senses*) the piece first broken off, first cut, *pl.* (Anbrüche) first products (of a mine); ist der — heilig, so ist auch der Teig heilig (Rom. 11, 16), for if the first-fruit be holy, the lump is also holy; *d)* (Bruch) fracture (of a mineral, exhibiting its texture); 2) (*obsolescent*) *a)* a breaking up of land having long lain fallow; neuer —, *see* Neubruch; *b) fig.* attack, first opening, *or* beginning; outbreak; 3) (Tages- —) the break, dawn (of day), day-break; der Tag ist im — (*Wieland*), day is breaking; *less usual* — der Nacht, night-fall; 4) a beginning to spoil, incipient putrescence; decay, rot (rotten state), mould; *also* a distemper of sheep, the rot (Fäule).

An'brüchig, I. *adj.* beginning to spoil *or* turn; decaying, putrescent, tainted; spoiled, rotten, mouldy; (of sheep) affected with the rot; — werden, to turn or to grow rotten *or* mouldy; a-es Obst, unsound, decaying fruit; a-er Wein, tainted *or* turned wine; II. A-keit, (*w.*) *f.* a beginning to spoil *or* turn, decay, incipient putrescence, &c., rottenness.

An'brüdern, (*w.*) *v. refl.*: sich Einem, *unusual*, to join one as a brother, to fraternise with one.

An'brühen, (*w.*) *v. tr.* to prepare (food, &c.) by pouring scalding water at or upon (Aufbrühen), to scald, soak, infuse, steep.

An'brüllen, (*w.*) *v. tr.* to bellow *or* low at, to roar at, to bawl at. [growl at.

An'brummen, (*w.*) *v. tr.* to grumble, *or*

An'brüten, (*w.*) *v. tr.* 1) to begin to hatch, to commence brooding; ein angebrütetes Ei, an egg in which the development of the chick has already begun by the process of brooding; 2) *fig.* to brood, to foster, to cherish.

An'buben, (*w.*) *v. tr.* (*l. u.*) to infect with knavery.

An'bug, (*str.*) *m.* (*l. u.*) any thing (a document, letter, &c.) annexed, subjoined, added, &c., supplement, enclosure; im — erhalten Sie ..., annexed you will receive ... (*cf.* Angebogen, Anlage &c.).

An'bumsen, (*w.*) *v. intr.* to bump at *or* against ....

An'bürgern, (*w.*) *v. tr. gener. refl.* (*l. u.*) to settle at a place as a citizen, to become a resident citizen or naturalised at some place.

An'bürsten, (*w.*) *v. tr.* to make to adhere by close brushing.

An'buschen, (*w.*) *v. intr. Sport.* to sit down near *or* in a bush (of birds).

* **Anscho'vis** [*pr.* antscho'vis], (*w.*) *f.* (*pl. sometimes Ital.* Ancho'vi, *coll.* Ancho'vis) anchovy (*Clupea encrasicholus*, unechte Sardelle).

* **Ancienneté** [*pr.* angsi—], (*w.*) *f.* (*Fr.*

ancienneté) seniority (Dienstalter).

And, (*indecl.*) ...
agreeable emotion...
Ore-mountains, &c.
count of ...), ...
painful yearning ...

An'dacht, (*w.*) *f.* ...
of), thought; 2) ...
verent attention ...
devotional feelings ...
devotion; ich ...
die ich mit — ...
half precious ...
down from ...
(*Seume*); der ...
großer — zu, *fam.* ...
wrapped attention, ...
of devotion, ...
ten, to attend to ...
one's prayers.

An'dacht . . ., ...

Andächtelei, (...
formal or false de...
gotry, hypocrisy.

An'dächteln, (...
outward, ostensi...
the over-pious, to ...
wardly *or* superstiti...
bigoted.

An'dächtig, I. ...
devout; devotional ...
dachtsvoll, which ...
attentive; nach ...
Verzehrung (...
lamb) had been ...
nity; II. A-keit, (...

An'dächtler, (...
f. devotee, devot...
superstitiously de...
bigot, hypocrite, ...

An'dachtlos &c., ...

An'dachtsreich, ...
devotion (Andacht...
prayer.

An'dachts . . ., ...
&c.) devotional ...
devotion, devotion...
m. alliance for ...
nal union, pious ...
fervour of devotion ...
the connection of ...
tional as being ...
duldsieben); —...
—glut, *f.* fervent ...
—haus, *n.* house ...
haus); —...
Dei (Lamm Gottes ...
crated wax, or ...
the figure of the ...
supporting the ...
Agnus ...

An'dachtsvoll, ...
devotion, ...
devout). — An'dac...
of devotion, (...

An'dachts . . ., ...
place of devotion; ...
or exercise; —...
the performance ...
duty, pilgrimage ...
of devotion (—...
set apart for) ...
impulse or ...
übung, *f.* devotio...
voll, *adj.* full of ...
eine —volle ...
frame of mind; ...
account of (religio...
motives.

* **Andal,** ...
wine-...

Andalu'sien, *(str.) n. Geogr.* Andalusia. — **Andalu'sier,** *(str.) m.,* **Andalu'sierin,** *(w.) f.* Andalusian; der Andalusier, *sometimes for* das andalusische Pferd. — **Andalu'sisch,** *adj.* Andalusian.

An'dämmen, *(w.) v. tr.* to force (a river, &c.) up to *or* towards a certain point by raising an embankment; to swell (a river) by damming it up, to dam up.

An'dämmern, *(w.) v.* I. *intr.* *(aux.* sein) 1) to approach *or* draw near dawning (as the day); 2) to begin to dawn; II. *tr.* to shine upon with dawning-light. — **An'dämmerung,** *(w.) f.* approaching dawn.

An'dampfen, *(w.) v.* I. *intr.* to be precipitated (an *[with Acc.]*, against) *or* to subside by evaporation; II. *tr.* to strike the senses of (one) with steam *or* vapour.

Andan'te, *(Ital.) Mus.* I. *adv.* andante (moderately slow; *dimin.:* andantino, less slow); II. *(str.) n.* andante, andantino.

An'dauern, *(w.) v. intr.* to last for a time without intermission *(stronger than* Dauern), to continue uninterruptedly, to last; ein a-des Interesse an seinen Angelegenheiten, a sustained interest in his affairs; im Zustande a-den Grolles, *fig.* in a state of chronic resentment; des Königs Besserung schreitet a-d fort, the king's convalescence proceeds steadily.

An'den, *(w.) pl. Geogr.* Andes (South American chain of mountains).

† **An'denk,** *adj.* *(with Gen.* mindful of …) remembering … (Eingedenk).

An'denken, *(irr.) v.* I. *tr.* 1) *(after the analogy of* Ansehen 3, *often without expressing the object [intr.],* to think of (a thing) with wonder and astonishment; denkt einmal an! only think! denk' mal Einer an! let any one think of such a thing! *(i. e.* it is scarcely possible to conceive such a thing); 2) Einen *or* etwas —, *entirely* †, *for* an Einen *or* etwas denken; *only the participle present is now and then used:* a-d, remembering, mindful of, bearing in mind (past things, &c.); II. *refl.* sich *(Acc.)* Einem —, *unusual,* to adapt one's self to another's mode of thinking *(cf. the refl. of* Anpassen &c.).

An'denken, *(str.) n.* remembrance, reminiscence, recollection, memory *(with* an *[& Acc.], or the Gen. of the person or thing remembered);* zum — an…, in remembrance *or* memory of, in commemoration (and commemorative) of, as a memorial of…; zum — an diese tapfere That, in remembrance of this brave deed; ein Denkmal zum — an die Feuersbrunst, a monument in memory of the conflagration; das — Gellerts wird nie verlöschen, the remembrance of Gellert will never die out; sein —, his memory; Königgrätz ist noch in frischem —, K. is yet fresh in the minds of men, *or* freshly remembered; das — einer Person oder Sache feiern, to commemorate a person or thing; in noch allzu frischem — *(Schiller)*, too green in remembrance; …das — zurückrufen, to revive the memory of …; rühmlichen, [illegible], verhaßten &c. A-s, of glorious, [illegible], hateful, &c. memory; 2) (token of) remembrance, token, memorial; (Geschenk zum —) keepsake; er schenkte es ihr als —, he presented it to her by way of keepsake. — **A-s-würdig,** *adj.* worthy of remembrance, memorable (Denkwürdig).

An'der, *adj.* 1) *orig. used as the second numeral* [illegible] the second (*poetic*); zum A-n, secondly; 2) [illegible], when the usual [illegible] is to be designated: ein a-er [illegible] unserer Bühne aufer[illegible] [illegible], another (*i. e.* not a different, [illegible]) [illegible] ought to arise for our [illegible].

[illegible] *in this sense [illegible] [illegible], like comparatives and several other words (negatives and interrogatives) used in comparative sentences:*

a) dies ist ein a-es Kind, this is another *(i. e.* not the same) child; *(emphatically [cf. below, b]* das ist ein [ganz] a-er Bursche, that is [quite] a different sort of lad); ein A-er *(m.)*, jemand A-es *(or* anders), another (man), some one (somebody) else; eine A-e *(f.)*, another (woman); a-e Leute, other people, others; etwas A-es, another thing, something else; *particul.* something (quite) different; a-er Orten, *adv. phrase, see* Anderwärts; Einer nach dem A-n verließ das Haus, one after another left the house; Einer oder der A-e wird sicher da sein, some one or other is sure to be there; ein Wort gab das a-e, one word led to another; ein Jahr nach dem a-n *(or* ein Jahr um das a-e) verging, one year after another *(or* year after year) passed by; ein Schritt nach dem a-n, step after step; eines in das a-e, adding one thing to another, taking *(or* mixing up) one thing with another; taking things together, without choice *or* order; das Eine in das *(or* eins ins) A-e gerechnet sind sie das vielleicht werth, one with another they may perhaps be worth so much; damit wir nicht eines in das a-e reden, in order not to lose ourselves in random speech; eins zum a-n gerechnet, war's danach angethan, ihr fast das Herz zu brechen, take it for all in all, it was going on well nigh to break her heart; einen Tag um den a-n *(provinc. [S. G.]* jeden a-n Tag), every other *(or* second) day; eine Woche um die a-e, every other week (Umggsspr.: week about); eins um das a-e, by *(or* in) turns, alternately (Umggsspr.: turn and turn about); einmal über das a-e, again and again, repeatedly; unter a-en *(supply* Dingen &c.) *or* unter A-em *(neuter)*, among other things, among the rest; das kann auch ein A-er, any one (else) may do that; kein A-er, niemand A-es, no one else (weniger üblich: no other *or* no others); wer a-s? who else? er hatte keinen a-en Vater als *(or* außer) Gott, he had no other father besides God; dies ist alles A-e eher als vernünftig, this is any thing but reasonable; das ist etwas *(coll.* was) (ganz) A-es, that is (quite) a different (sort of) thing, that alters the case (entirely); dies ist nichts A-es, *(or* a-s) als …, this is nothing but …, *or* than … *or* nothing short of …; *sometimes treated as an indeclinable phrase:* da die Reinigung in nichts a-s beruht *(Lessing)*, *for* in nichts A-em, in nothing else; von was a-s *(Göthe, &c.) (for* von was A-em) of something else; nichts A-es als …, nothing else but *or* than …;

b) other *(syn. with* different); a-e Kleider anziehen, to put on other clothes, to change one's clothes; a-e Zeiten, a-e Sitten, *proverb,* other times, other manners; die a-e Seite, the other side; the reverse; auf der a-en Seite (andrerseits), *fig.* on the other hand; das a-e Ufer, the opposite shore; das a-e Geschlecht *(Schiller, not very usual)*, the other, *i. e.* the female sex; a-er Ansicht sein, to be of a different opinion; a-en Sinnes werden, to change one's mind; seitdem ist er ein a-er Mensch geworden, from that time he has been a different *(or* an altered) man; von etwas A-em (zu sprechen) anfangen, to introduce another subject; ein a-es ist Einem Weihrauch streuen, und ein a-es Einem das Rauchfaß um den Kopf schmeißen *(Lessing)*, it is one thing to honour one with the incense of flattery, and another to beat the censer about his ears; eines A-en *(or* eines Bessern) belehren, to teach differently, to set (one) right; das ist ein a-es Lesen, that is a different way of reading; jetzt ging's aus einem a-en Tone, das steht auf einem a-en Blatte, *see* Ton, Blatt &c.

3) Ander, etwas A-es &c., *sometimes euphemistically for any thing which the speaker is loth to name;* was A-es denken *(Göthe) for* etwas Schlimmes denken; er hat an mir gehandelt wie ein A-er *(Grimm)*, *i. e.* like a scoundrel; sie ist in a-en Umständen, she is in the family way; er kann mir was A-es thun, *vulg.* he may do me a certain unmentionable service.

An'derärtig, *adj.* of another or different kind *(less properly:* Anderwärtig).

Än'derbar, *adj.* alterable, changeable; ä-e Gesetze, laws that may be altered.

Änderei', *(w.) f. fam.* groundless or too frequent change, alteration, useless innovation.

Än'derer, *(str.) m. (Voss)* alterer, one who changes, &c.

An'dererseits, *adv.* on the other side *or* hand *(opp.* Einerseits).

An'dergeschwisterkind, *(str.) n.* cousin twice removed, *pl.* cousins whose grandparents were children of the same parents, *cf.* Geschwisterkind.

An'derhalb, *adj.* one and a half, † *for* Anderthalb.

An'derheit, *(w.) f.* the quality of being other or not the same, non-identity.

Än'd(r)erin, *(w.) f.* one (a female) who alters, alterer, &c.

An'derlei, *adj. indecl.* of another kind.

An'derleute, *(str.) pl. as a compound for* Andere Leute.

Än'derlich, *adj.* (easily) alterable, changeable, &c. *see* Veränderlich.

Än'derling, *(str.) m. provinc. for* Engerling.

An'dermal, *for* (ein) anderes Mal.

An'dermalig, *adj.* taking place, happening, *or* occurring another time: eine a-e Besprechung, a further conversation.

Än'dern, *(w.) v.* I. *tr.* to alter, to change; die Kleider —, *a)* to alter (the make of) one's clothes; ein Schneider ändert Kleider, welche nicht passen, a tailor alters clothes which do not fit; *b) l. u. for* die Kleider wechseln, to change one's clothes; seine Meinung —, to change one's opinion; seine Stellung —, to shift one's position; Ändern *often means* to change for the better, to reform, to mend (one's behaviour, &c.); es läßt sich nicht —, it can't be helped, there is no remedy; ich kann meine Gedanken *(or* ich kann mich) nicht —, I can't help my thoughts; was sich nicht — läßt, muß man ertragen, what cannot be cured, must be endured; der Vertrag ändert nichts an der Streitfrage, the treaty leaves the question, where it found it; es ändert nichts an dem Verfahren, welches er eingeschlagen hat, it makes no difference in the course he is pursuing; II. *intr. & refl.* to alter, to change, to vary (to change from worse to better or from better to worse); das Wetter ändert sich, the weather changes; die Preise werden sich nicht bald —, prices are not likely to alter for some time; es läßt sich daran nichts mehr —, there is no alteration *(or* change) to be made; er hat sich sehr (zu seinem Vortheil) geändert, he has greatly improved.

An'dernfalls, *adv.* else, otherwise.

An'derns, *adv. formed after the analogy, and used (by Lessing) for* Zweitens, secondly *(not in use).*

An'derntheils, *adv.* on the other hand.

An'der(n)orts, *adv.* elsewhere, somewhere else.

An'ders, I. *contr. for* Anderes, *nom. sing. of the neuter of* Ander (Jemand —, Niemand —, Etwas —, Nichts — &c.), *which see;* II. *adv.* 1) otherwise, (in) another way, in another manner, differently; ganz —, far otherwise; — färben, to alter or change the colour of (a thing), to give another colour to …; — werden, to become or grow different, to alter, to change, *see* Ändern, II.; er wurde —, he became a different person; he amended himself; es wurde —, als ich gedacht hatte, it turned out differently from what

I had expected; die Dinge gestalteten sich —, matters took a different turn; nicht —, not otherwise, exactly so, just so; wir können sie nicht — als religiös und ehrenhaft nennen, we cannot call them other than religious and honourable; es war nicht —, als ob ein König einträte, it was exactly, or just as if a king entered; ich kann mich nicht — machen, als ich von Natur bin, I cannot make myself different from what I am by nature; es kann für den Verfasser nicht — als schmeichelhaft sein (*Wieland*), it cannot but be flattering to the author; daß gewisse Sachen — nicht als zur Barbarei leiten müssen (*J. v. Müller*), that certain things cannot but lead to barbarism; sein Benehmen kann nicht — als abscheulich genannt werden, his behaviour cannot be called anything but abominable; was ist es — als Feigheit, what is it but cowardice; 2) *a) in conjunction or composition with adverbs of pronouns:* else (*syn.* sonst): (irgend) wo —, —wo, somewhere else, elsewhere; nirgend(s) —, nowhere else: wo — her, — wo her, from some other place; wo — hin, — wohin, to some other place, &c.; *b) in conditional sentences:* wenn — (*and in the same sense* wo —), if at all, provided that at all; jeder Menschenmaler ... wenn er — eine Copie der wirklichen Welt geliefert haben will (*Schiller*), every painter of men, if at all he pretends to have furnished a copy of real life; und stimmst ihr — ein (*Wieland*, *for* und wenn — ihr einstimmt), and, if you consent withal: dies andere im Englischen oft gar nicht ausgedrückt: wenn — nicht ..., unless; wenn — du nicht verziehst, unless you prefer; 3) *sometimes euphemistically* (*see* Ander, 3) *for another word:* es wird mir — (*i. e.* es wird mir schlimm) zu Muthe &c.; sich — besinnen, to bethink one's self differently, to alter or change one's mind; —denken, to think differently, to differ in opinion, to dissent.

An'dersartig, *adj.* (*perhaps more euphonious than anderartig, which see*) differently constituted (anders geartet), belonging or peculiar to a different kind, of a different kind or nature, heterogeneous (*opp.* Eigenartig).

An'dersdenkend, *p. a.* thinking otherwise, differently-thinking.

An'derseitig, *adj.* being on the other side, hand or party, opposite; ich will die a-en Gründe nicht anführen (*Campe*), I will not adduce the reasons existing on the other hand.

An'derseits, *adv.* (*contr. from* Andererseits) on the other hand.

An'ders..., *in comp.* —gesinnt, *adj.* having a different opinion, dissenting (*cf.* —gläubig); die —gesinnten, the dissenters; —gläubig, *adj.* holding an opinion (other than *or*) different from the established one, heterodox, heretical (*opp.* Rechtgläubig); —hin, *adv. sometimes used for* —wohin, *which see;* —redend, *p. a.* speaking a different language; —wann, *adv. provinc.* at another time; —warum, *adv. obsolescent*, for another reason; —wie, *adv.* in another or different way, otherwise, differently; —wo, *adv.* in another or different place, elsewhere, somewhere else; *rarely used as a subst.* an alibi; —woher, *adv.* from elsewhere, from another place; —wohin, *adv* to another place; er sah —wohin, he looked another way.

An'derst, *adv.* († *&*) *vulg. for* Anders.

An'derthalb, *num. adj.* (*curiously enough designated as indeclinable by Heinsius, Heyse, and others following in their wake; the truth is that it often precedes substantives in the character of a cardinal number without being declined; but it may be declined like a common adjective notwithstanding*) one and a half: a-er Apfel, a-e Stunde (*cf.* — Stunde, *Zelter*), a-es Glas Wasser (*or* — Apfel, — Stunden, — Gläser Wasser), one apple and a half, one hour and a half, one glass of water and a half; — Fuß lang, a foot and a half in length; — mal so groß, one and a half time as big; — Pfund, one (a) pound and a half; — Austern (*Tieck*), one oyster and a half; *it is likewise used as a plural, because according to its nature it represents more than one:* auf einen Schelmen a-e (*Göthe*), against a rogue pit one and a half; (einen Weg gehen) in a-en (*i. e.* Stunden, *Hebel*), (to walk a certain distance) in one and a half (*i. e.* in an hour and a half); hier sind 3 Pfund, du wirst aber wohl mit —(en) auskommen (*Sanders*), here are three pounds, but one and a half will probably do for you; — Ellen kosten *or* a-e Elle kostet eine Mark, one ell (*or* an ell) and a half costs one Mark.

An'derthalbig, *adj. Math.* sesquialteral; ein a-es Verhältniß, sesquialter, a sesquialteral proportion (2 : 3 = 6 : 9); das a-e Verhältniß, *Arith.* sesquiduplicate ratio (*Hilp.*).

Än'derung, (*w.*) *f.* change, alteration (the act of changing or altering, &c. and the state of being changed, &c.); variation, modification; in einem (geschriebenen) Artikel Ä-en machen, to correct, to retouch, to revise a (written) article; Ä-en treffen, to make alterations; der Markt war wenig belebt und ohne — der Preise, the market was in a quiet state without variation in prices; die Preise haben wenig — erfahren, prices have undergone little change; Ä-absatz, (*str.*, *pl.* Ä-sätze) *m. Mus.* section of a musical composition where the dominant chord is introduced (*also* Quint-Absatz, *opp.* Grundabsatz).

An'derwärtig, I. *adj. obsolescent*, existing or happening in (*sometimes* coming from) some other place or at another time; es ist ihm eine a-e Heurath vorgeschlagen worden (*Adelung*), another or a different marriage has been proposed to him; II. *or* **An'derwärts**, *adv.* in another place, elsewhere.

An'derweit, I. *adv.* 1) †, a second time, anew, again; 2) in another place or manner; otherwise, else; at another time; further, in other respects, &c.; ich habe — zu thun, I have other matters to attend to; *Lessing repeatedly uses an adv.* A-s, *almost syn. with* Anderwärts, *f. i.* Ihr Einfall hätte erst müssen a-s aus der Geschichte erwiesen werden, your idea ought to have been previously proved from other events of history; II. *or* **An'derweitig**, *adj.* repeated or done another time, in another manner or place, another, additional, further, ulterior; die a-en hundert Thaler (*Göthe*), the other hundred Thalers; eine a-e öffentliche Feilbietung, another public offering for sale (a former one having proved ineffectual, &c.).

An'deuten, (*w.*) *v. tr.* 1) to indicate, intimate, to signify or declare by signs; to give (one) to understand, to suggest, to hint; das deutet nichts Gutes an, that presages nothing good; eine Sache, die ich nur leicht angedeutet habe, a subject to which I have only slightly alluded; wie gerecht und dennoch wie zart hatte er den Tadel angedeutet, how justly, yet how gently had he conveyed reproof; wüchsen die Kinder in der Art fort, wie sie sich —, if children continued to develop themselves in the way they appear to do temporarily; 2) Einem etwas — (*more usual* Bedeuten), to notify one of a thing (in a judicial sense), to give warning to one, to enjoin something upon one.

An'deutung, (*w.*) *f.* indication, intimation, insinuation, suggestion, hint; allusion, innuendo; eine flüchtige — (*with. Gen.*), a hasty glance, glimpse, &c. (at); Wildpret mit einer kleinen — von Fäulniß, venison with a slight shade of putridity; a-sweise, *adv.* by intimation, by hints, by innuendo, &c.

An'dichten, (*w.*) *v.* I. *tr.* (Einem etwas) 1) to ascribe (something to one) by fiction, *poetical* falsely; to attribute or to impute something to a person; falsely to charge one

[illegible]

einen Kegel rc.) by turning on the lathe: wie angedrechselt sitzen, (of clothes) to fit tight (to the body), to fit exceedingly well; 2) see Andrehen.

An'drehen, *(w.)* v. *tr.* 1) to fit or join by turning on the lathe (Andrechseln); 2) *a)* to fix or fasten by turning or twisting; to screw on; die Wand —, *Mar.* to set up the shrouds of the topmast; den Drath (eine Borste) —, *Shoe-m.* to bristle the thread; die Fäden —, *Weav.* to piece the threads; *b)* Einem eine Nase — (aufheften), *coll.* to impose upon one, to tell one a fib, to humbug one; *c)* *fig.* (*in the sense of* Anspinnen, Einfädeln) to contrive, to bring (a thing) about; 3) sich *(Acc.)* an Einen *or* eine Sache —, to get nearer to ... by turning and twisting *(opp.* sich abdrehen); allmählich hub er an sich näher anzudrehen *(Bürger)*, by degrees he began to turn and twist himself nearer.

An'dreher, *(str.)* m. *Weav.* piecer, *provinc.* piecener.

An'dreschen, *(str.)* v. I. *tr.* (& *intr.*) to begin to thrash; II. *intr.* to beat (an die Wand, against the wall) in threshing with a flail.

An'drillen, *(w.)* v. *tr.* to fix or fasten by twisting (*cf.* Andrehen).

An'dringen, *(str.)* v. *intr.* (*aux.* sein) to press or push on, to press or push forward (auf *[with Acc.]*, gegen, against), to advance impetuously; auf den Feind rc. —, to advance, to rush, to fall, to charge upon the enemy, &c.; auf etwas —, *fig. obsolescent for* auf etwas dringen, to insist upon ... strenuously; sich —, *refl. obsolescent (for* sich aufdringen), to intrude (one's self upon ...); a-d, *p. a.* urgent, impetuous, impressive, moving (eloquence, &c.); das —, *v. n. (str.)* n. impetuous advance, urgent pressing on, &c., urgency; importunacy, earnest solicitation.

An'dringlich, I. *adj. (obsolescent for* Eindringlich, Zudringlich rc.) urgent, pressing; impetuous; impressive; obtrusive; forward, importunate; II. A-keit, *(w.) f.* urgency, pressingness, impressiveness, &c.

An'dringling, *(str.)* m. *contl.* importunate urger, intruder, &c.

* **Androgyn',** *(w.)* m. *(Gr.)* an androgyne, hermaphrodite. — **Androgy'nisch,** *adj. Bot., &c.* androgynous, having the organs of both sexes (Mannweibig).

An'drohen, *(w.)* v. I. *tr.* 1) *(l. u.)* Einen —, to meet one in a threatening manner, to address with threats or menaces; 2) Einem etwas, to threaten or to menace one with ...; II. *intr.* to approach threateningly, to be imminent. — **An'drohung,** *(w.) f.* (einer Sache, *Gen.*) the act of threatening with ..., &c.; *often in the law style:* bei — or unter — von Geldstrafe verbieten, to forbid under penalty of a fine.

An'dröhnen, *(w.)* v. *intr.* (an *[with Acc. or Dat.]*) to strike against ... with dinning, roaring, or thundering noise.

An'druck, *(str.)* m. 1) *(pl.* An'drücke, An'drucke) the act of pressing or squeezing (Andrücken) against some object, close pressure, impact; 2) *(pl.* Andrucke, Andrücke) additional printing (Andrucken) or print.

An'drucken, *(w.)* v. *tr.* 1) † *for* Andrücken; 2) to print (something) in addition (to another sheet of paper, &c.): eine Übersetzung mit angedruckter Urschrift, a translation with the [illegible] original annexed.

An'drücken, *(w.)* v. *tr.* (an *with Acc.*) to press (against), to press, squeeze close to.

An'duseln, *(w.)* v. I. *intr.* (*aux.* sein) to come along (angeduselt kommen) humming, &c. *cf.* Duseln; II. *tr.* sich *(Dat.)* (Einen) —, see Beduseln.

An'duft, *(str., pl.* An'düfte) m. 1) vapour which adheres to objects (particularly in winter, congealed vapour, hoar-frost); 2) *(l. u.)* fragrance striking against (the sense of smell), exhaled fragrance.

An'duften, *(w.)* v. *tr.* to exhale or send fragrance towards ..., to involve or imbue with fragrance, to strike the sense (of smell) with fragrance.

An'düngen, *(w.)* v. *tr.* to apply manure to [(fields, &c.).

An'dunkeln, *(w.)* v. *intr.* (*aux.* sein & haben) to begin to grow or fall dark.

An'dunsten, An'dünsten, *(w.)* v. *intr.* (*aux.* sein) 1) to be precipitated (an *[with Dat. or Acc.]*, against) in the form of vapour, to strike (against), to settle (on) as vapour; 2) *motion.* to be overrun and dimmed by vapour (as glass). — **An'dünstung,** *(w.) f. Chem., &c.* precipitation in the form of vapour.

An'dupfen, *(w.)* v. *tr.* see Antupfen.

An'durch [& andurch'], *adv. obsolescent, Law style,* by this, by the present; hereby (hierdurch); thereby (dadurch).

An'duseln, *(w.)* v. I. *(or* **An'dusseln)** *intr.* (*aux.* sein) to come staggering on (angeduselt kommen), to approach in a dazed manner; II. *tr.* sich *(Dat.)* Einen —, see Beduseln.

An'düten, *(w.)* v. *tr.* to blow at (one) with a horn.

An'ebnen, *(w.)* v. *tr.* to level (something) in proximity to something else, to smooth up.

* **Anecdo'te,** *(w.) f. (Gr.)* anecdote *(dimin.* **Anecdöt'chen,** *[str.]* n. little anecdote); a-n-artig, a-nhaft, **Anecdo'tisch,** *adj.* anecdotical, anecdotal; A-njäger, A-nmann, m. *coll.* anecdotemonger, anecdotist.

An'ecken, *(w.)* v. *intr. Gam.* (*at skittles*) to touch the sideboard (of a skittle alley) with the bowl, so as to hit one or more of the skittles at an angle *(opp.* Stechen).

An'eifern, *(w.)* v. *tr. (l. u.)* to incite, to stimulate, to urge on, to spur on, to animate *(syn.* Anfeuern). — **An'eiferung,** *(w.) f.* incitement, stimulation, &c.

An'eignen, *(w.)* v. *tr.* 1) *a)* (Einem etwas) to appropriate, to assign (a thing) as proper or peculiar to ..., to make the property of ...; *fig.* to impart: mit stiller Hoffnung mich ihrer Gesinnung anzueignen *(Göthe)*, with silent hopes to convert myself to their own state of feeling; *b)* sich *(Acc.)* einer Person *(Dat.)* rc. —, to dedicate or devote one's self to ..., to yield one's self up to ...; seiner Vaterstadt leidenschaftlich angeeignet *(Göthe)*, passionately devoted to his native town; 2) sich *(Dat.)* etwas: *a)* to appropriate to one's self, to make one's own; *b)* *fig.* to adopt; sich *(Dat.)* Gewohnheiten —, to contract habits: wenn der Schüler sich *(Dat.)* diese erste Lection ganz angeeignet hat, wird ihm ... gelehrt, this first lesson being familiarised by practice, the pupil is taught ...; der Schüler muß sich *(Dat.)* dieses Gedicht ganz —, the pupil has to make this piece of poetry thoroughly his own: sie konnte sich *(Dat.)* den Ton der Gesellschaft nicht —, zu der sie zu gehören wünschte, she could not catch the tone of the society to which she wished to belong.

An'eigner, *(str.)* m. appropriator, &c.

An'eignung, *(w.) f.* 1) *a)* appropriation, *i. e.* the act of appropriating or assigning to a particular use, &c.; *b)* *sometimes in the sense of* Hingebung, devotion, &c. (*cf.* Aneignen, 1, *b*); 2) *a)* appropriation to one's own use, the act of taking as one's own by exclusive right; *b)* *Law,* conversion; unrechtmäßige —, usurpation; 3) *Chem., &c.* appropriation, intro-susception: A-skraft, *f. Chem.* appropriating power *(Tieck)*.

Aneinan'der, *adv.* together, see Einander; — hangend (hängend), coherent, contiguous (Zusammenhängend); Aneinander *often coalesces with verbal substantives (cf.* Einander, *f. i.)* —fügung, *(w.) f.* junction, joining (Zusammenfügung); —halten, *(str.)* n. a keeping together (Zusammenhalten); —kettung, —knüpfung, *(w.) f.* the being joined or linked one to another (Verkettung), mutual concatenation (of causes and effects, &c.); —reiben, *(str.)* n. *Phys.* attrition: rubbing friction: —reihung, *(w.) f.* arrangement in successive order; —setzen, *(w.)* v. *tr. Join.* to join, to rabbet; —schließen, —schluß, see Zusammenschließen rc.; das —ziehen der Töne, *Mus.* the playing or singing tones in a continuous manner *(legato)*.

* **Äne'is,** *(indecl.)*, **Änei'de,** *(w.) f. Rom. Lit.* Æneid, Eneid, Virgil's epic poem of which Æneas is the hero.

* **Anekdo'te,** see Anecdote.

An'ekeln, *(w.)* v. I. *tr.* 1) to disgust: ich ekle ihn an, I disgust him, he is disgusted with me: er ekelt mich an, he disgusts me, I am sickening at him; das Leben ekelt mich an, I loathe (*or* am tired of) life: Stutzerei ekelt mich an, I am disgusted at foppery; 2) *obsolescent,* to loathe, to feel disgust at ...; den Becher der Freude so anzuekeln *(Schiller)*, so to loathe the cup of joy; II. *intr.* es ekelt mir an (= es ist mir zuwider), I loathe it.

An'ekelung, *(w.) f. obsolescent, (with Gen.)* a loathing (of ...), aversion (to).

* **Anelek'trisch,** *adj. (Gr.)* anelectric.

* **Anemo'ne,** *(w.) f. (Gr.) Bot.* anemone, windflower (Windrose).

† **An'empfänglich,** *adj.* acceptable (Angenehm).

An'empfehlen, *(str.)* v. *tr.* to recommend (Einem etwas, something to ...) strongly.

An'empfinden, *(str.)* v. *refl.* sich *(Dat.)* etwas, or sich *(Acc.)* einem Andern —, to assume or adopt the feelings, sentiments, &c. of another person, &c.: die Fähigkeit, alle poetischen Stoffe gelten zu lassen, sich *(Dat.)* anzuempfinden rc., the capacity of admitting without dispute all kinds of poetical subjects, of attuning one's sentiments to their state of feeling, &c. — **An'empfinderei,** *(w.) f.* a weak or exaggerated practice of assuming the sentiments of others. — **An'empfindung,** *(w.) f.* the adoption of the sentiments of another.

...(i)a'ner, *(from the Lat. adjectival termination* ...anus, *pertaining to* ...*) a termination (generally limited in German to substantives, f. i.* Dominicaner, Franciscaner, Swedenborgianer, Kantianer, Fichtianer, Lassallianer rc., follower of Dominicus, Franciscus, Swedenborg, Kant, Fichte, Lassalle, &c.: Hannoveraner, Weimaraner, inhabitant of Hanover, Weimar, &c.) *has been used by Blumauer, Bürger, Göthe, and others as an independent substantive:* der Aner, *(str.)* m. a slavish follower, disciple, sectarian, &c.; die ganze Schaar der Aner, Iner, Isten *(Blumauer)*, all die Herren Aner und Iner *(Nicolai, cf. Sanders)* rc.

An'erbe, *s. Law,* I. *(w.)* m. the next heir, or the heir on whom an estate devolves undivided, while his co-heirs (Miterben) have to be portioned off by him; II. *(str.)* n. hereditary portion. — **An'erben,** *(w.)* v. I. *tr.* 1) to impart, to transmit by inheritance; 2) to obtain by inheritance; angeerbt, *p. a.* inherited; hereditary; II. *intr.* Einem († & Einen) —, to devolve upon one by inheritance. — **An'erblich,** *adj.* easily inheritable; inherited, hereditary.

An'erbieten, *(str.)* v. *tr. (a more formal word than* Anbieten) *obsolescent,* to offer (in a formal or solemn way), to tender. — **An'erbieten,** *v. s. (str.)* n. offer (formally made), tender. — **An'erbietung,** *(w.) f.* (formal) offer.

An'erboren, *p. a. obsolescent,* acquired by birth, inborn, innate (Angeboren).

An'erbötig, An'erbietig, *adj.* see Erbötig

An'ererben, *(w.)* v. *tr. l. u. in the sense of* Anerben and Ererben.

Anerbung, (w.) f. the act of transmitting or acquiring by inheritance, cf. Vererbung.

Anerdichten, (str.) v. tr. (einer Sache [Dat.] etwas) to invent with a view of adapting the invention to ...; so konnte Bacon leicht der Mythologie die allegorische Bedeutung — (Jean Paul), thus it was easy for Bacon to invent and assume for mythology the allegorical meaning. Dag.

Anerfüllen, (w.) v. tr. to fill to overflow-

Anerinnerung, (w.) f. 1) reminiscence of a thing, distinct recollection, remembrance, memory; 2) the act of calling to mind (or reminding of) a thing, reminder, admonition.

Anerkannt, I. p. a. (from Anerkennen) acknowledged, &c.; notorious: eine — zweckmäßige Einrichtung, an arrangement acknowledged to be useful; Comm. a. seine a—e Solidität, his well-known respectability; ein — solides Haus, a house of established credit; die anerkanntesten Meister (Maler), the masters most generally acknowledged; anerkannter Maßen, acknowledgedly; II. A-heit, (w.) f. the state or fact of being acknowledged, &c., cf. Anerkennung.

Anerkennbar, adj. that may be acknowledged, recognizable.

Anerkennen, (irr.) v. tr. 1) to acknowledge, to own, to recognize; nicht —, to refuse to acknowledge, to disown, to disavow, to disclaim, to disacknowledge; die Klage —, to plead guilty to a charge: wir erkennen Gott als höchsten Herrscher an, we acknowledge God as the supreme ruler; durch einen Ferman wurde Milosch 1831 als erblicher Fürst von Serbien anerkannt, by a firman, in 1831, Milosch was recognized as hereditary prince of Servia; man wird die Regierung von Spanien — müssen, they will have to recognize the government of Spain; seine Unterschrift, eine Urkunde &c. —, to acknowledge one's signature; er erkannte seinen Namen, seine Unterschrift, das Kind nicht an, he disowned his name, his signature, the child, &c.; eine (Schuld-)Forderung nicht —, not to acknowledge a debt; eine Schuld —, to admit a debt; einen Anspruch —, to acknowledge, allow, admit (and to accede to) a claim; sie erkannten die Unvollkommenheit des Gesetzes bereitwillig an, they readily admitted the imperfectness of the law; 2) to acknowledge with gratitude, praise, or appreciation, to appreciate, to value: man erkennt niemand an, als den, der uns nutzt (Göthe), we appreciate none but him who is useful to us; 3) used by Göthe in a sense nearly synonymous with wieder erkennen, to recognize (under altered circumstances); 4) sometimes used in the sense of Zuerkennen, Zusprechen, to adjudge, adjudicate, to award. [knowledgment.

Anerkennenswerth, adj. worthy of ac-

Anerkenntlich, adj. 1) l. u. for Anerkennbar; 2) (& Anerkenntlichkeit) scarcely used for Erkenntlich, Erkenntlichkeit.

Anerkenntniß, (str.) f. & n. (both genders used without any distinction, cf., on the contrary, Erkenntniß) acknowledgment.

Anerkennung, (w.) f. acknowledgment; recognition; Law, recognisance: ihre Meisterschaft nöthigte selbst den Neidischen — ab, her musical power extorted recognition even from the envious; der König verweigerte diesem Anspruch seine —, the king refused to accede to this claim; sie drückte ihre — dieser Güte aus, she expressed her sense of such kindness; gebührende — finden, to be appreciated; — gefunden haben, zur — gelangt sein, to be fully known and appreciated.

Anerkennungslos, adj. without acknowledgment, unappreciating.

Anermahnen, (w.) v. tr. (l. u.) to exhort and remind (one) of a thing.

* Aneroid, adj. (Gr.) aneroid (barometer).

* Anersitzen, (str.) v. tr. Law, to acquire by one's ancestors or in the course of time (Ersitzen). — Anersitzungsrecht, (w.) f. acquisition (Ersitzungsrecht).

Anerschaffen, (str.) v. tr. to ingenerate. (Einem etwas) to bestow (something) upon (one) or to impart (something) to ... in creating or at the moment of creation; fig. to implant or to instil by birth or nature: dem Menschen war der aufrechte Gang — (Göthe), to man an upright carriage was imparted at his creation; Nichtdankbarkeit ist dem Menschen angeboren, ja — (Göthe), non-gratitude is innate, nay ingenerate in man; — ist ihm der Freund (Schiller, Braut von Messina), a friend was created for him (who has a brother; i. e. he need not seek for a friend). — Anerschaffen, p. a. ingenerate, implanted by nature, &c., inborn, innate. [acquired.

Anerschlichen, p. a. (l. u.) surreptitiously

† Anersterben, (str.) v. intr. (Einem) to devolve upon (one) by the decease of some other person.

† Anerwachsen, (str.) v. intr. (Einem) to accrue, to accede to, to be added to.

Anerwägung, (w.) f. (from an † v. Anerwägen) statement, formal or careful consideration, accurate weighing (of complicated circumstances, &c.). — Anerwogen, pp. † Law, considering, since (in Anbetracht, in Erwägung, daß ...).

Anerwünschung, (w.) f. (obsolescent and pedantic) a formally expressed wish in favour of another.

Anerzählen, (w.) v. tr. to ascribe (f. i. fictitious things to ...) by narration.

Anerzeugen, (w.) v. tr. (Einem etwas) to beget (something) in (one).

Anerziehen, (str.) v. tr. to communicate, to impart, or to instil by education: wir haben angeborene und anerzogene Schwächen (Göthe), we have weaknesses inborn, and weaknesses produced by education.

Anfabeln, (w.) v. tr. (Einem etwas) to ascribe (something) to (one) fictitiously (cf. Andichten).

Anfachbar, adj. (easily) to be kindled.

Anfächeln, (w.) v. tr. to waft the air against (one) with a fan, to fan.

Anfachen, (w.) v. tr. to fan or to blow (zur Flamme, into a flame), to enkindle, to kindle; to inflame; Jemandes Eifer —, to animate one's zeal. — Anfachung, (w.) f. the (act of) fanning or blowing into a flame, &c.

Anfädeln, (w.) v. tr. 1) to add by stringing, to put on a string: wir fädelten die Pilze an, we put mushrooms on strings (or we strung mushrooms together) in G.; 2) fig. to contrive artfully, to manage, &c.: ein Gespräch — (Zschokke), to manage to get into a conversation with some one (Anknüpfen, Einfädeln).

Anfahen, (str.) v. tr. († &) poet. to take in hand, to begin, &c. (Anfangen).

Anfahrbar, adj. 1) that may be brought by carriage to a place, &c. cf. Anfahren; 2) (Naut., of a port) accessible (to large ships), easy of approach.

Anfahren, (str.) v. I. intr. (aux. sein, rarely with haben) 1) gener. with an (& Acc., less frequently with the Dat.) a) to drive close (to), to drive (against), to run, strike, beat, or push (against), to come close (to); b) to come near or up (to), to advance in a carriage, ship, or similar vehicle; to arrive: die Flotte fuhr an die Insel an, the fleet touched at the island, the fleet put in at the island, the fleet came to anchor near the island; die Stadt, vor welche ein Dampfboot bis auf 20 Schritte — kann (Wieland), the town which a steam-boat may approach as near as twenty paces; die Dampfschiffe ... kam ... mit Schiffen angefahren,

begin or commence with ...; bei sich (selbst) den — machen (mit der Besserung rc.), *fig.* to begin at home; 2) *Archit.* springing, spring (lowest part of an arch or vault, or the point from which it springs *or* rises); vom (ersten) — an, from the (very) outset, from the first; vom — bis zum Ende der Gerichtssitzung, from the sitting of the Court to its rising.

An'fangen, *(str.)* v. I. *tr. & intr.* (*aux.* haben) 1) to begin, commence; von vorn —, to begin at the beginning; wieder von vorn *or* von neuem —, to begin again at the beginning, to begin anew; to start again; 2) to originate, start, to undertake, to go *or* to set (one's self) about, to set up (a *[or* in] business, &c.); to enter upon, to betake one's self to; to open (a campaign, &c.); ein Geschäft, einen Handel —, to enter into business, to establish one's self, &c.; es ungeschickt —, to set out unskilfully; übel —, to begin inauspiciously; einen Briefwechsel mit ... —, to enter into correspondence with ...; die lateinische Grammatik —, to begin with the Latin grammar; einen Proceß —, to commence a law-suit, to go to law, to bring an action, to institute a suit (mit *or* gegen, against); einen Hader, Streit rc. —, to begin to quarrel, *coll.* to pick a quarrel; Händel —, to begin *or* stir up brawls, quarrels, &c.; was er auch anfängt, Alles schlägt ihm fehl, he his unsuccessful in whatever he undertakes, all his speculations turn out failures; er fängt zu viel an, he begins too much at once, he has too many irons in the fire; 3) *coll.* to do: was soll ich —? what shall I do? was soll ich mit dem Gelde —? what am I to do with the money? sie wissen nicht, was sie mit ihrer Zeit — sollen, they know not how to dispose of their time; was ist nun anzufangen? what is to be done now (next)? es ist nichts mit ihm anzufangen, there is nothing to be done with him; was kann man mit dem Burschen —? wie kann man ihn zur Vernunft bringen? what can be done to the boy? how can he be brought to hear reason? ich will es anders mit ihm — *(Hilp.)*, I'll go another way to work with him; 4) es — auf *(with Acc.)*, to aim at, to make it one's object (*cf.* Anlegen, Absehen).

II. *refl.* sich —, to be begun, to begin, commence; Manches, was sich leicht anfängt (was leicht angefangen ist), many a thing that is easily to be commenced *or* undertaken; die Nennwörter, die sich mit A —, the nouns that begin with an A; ich werde mich künftig mit einem andern Buchstaben — müssen, I shall have to spell my name with another initial in future.

III. *intr.* to begin, to commence, &c.; to take rise, &c.; mit ... *or* bei ... —, to commence with ...; man hat mit den Erdarbeiten schon angefangen, the ground-work is already begun; er fängt (in dem Buche) mit *or* bei der Erschaffung der Welt an, he begins with *or* at the creation of the world; bei ihm wurde angefangen, they commenced with him; er fing von etwas Anderem an (*sc.* zu sprechen), he introduced another subject; und die Heldenjugend, die Herrscher, an (*Schiller*, Die vier Weltalter), and the age of the hero, the ruler, began *(Bulwer)*; — zu lachen, zu weinen, to begin to laugh, to weep, *coll.* to fall a-laughing, a-crying; klein —, to begin (business) with a small capital; *the verb dependent on* anfangen, *and according to strict rule, expressed by the infinitive preceded by* zu, *is sometimes* [illegible] *by* und, *and transformed* [illegible] *verb coordinate with* anfangen: er [illegible] (Dan. 9, 16; 2, 20; 4, 16, [illegible]), er fing an zu sprechen; sie fingen an [illegible] (Mark 6, 17), they began to [illegible]

[illegible] *(str.)* m. 1) beginner; one who [illegible]; author; originator; der —

(Urheber) eines Streites, the author of a quarrel; 2) beginner, one in his rudiments, a young practitioner, tyro, novice; ein junger —, a young beginner; one who has just set up in business; 3) *Glass-m.* blower; 4) *Archit.* *a)* the lowest step of a stair; *b)* (eines Gewölbes) springer, springing-stone (first or bottom stone of an arch or vault, lying immediately on the impost), *cf.* Anfang, 2.

An'fängerei' (**An'fängerschaft**), *(w.) f.* the state or work of a beginner, tyro, &c.

An'fänglich, I. *adj.* original, incipient, initial; diese Geldopfer sind nur a-e, these pecuniary sacrifices are only connected with the beginning of the undertaking; II. *adv.* in the beginning, at first, primarily.

An'fanglos, *adj. see* Anfangslos.

An'fangs, *adv.* in the beginning, at first; gleich —, at the very beginning, outset; *sometimes followed by a Genitive:* a-s der Schlacht *(Jean Paul)*, in the beginning of the battle.

An'fangs..., *in comp.* —bohrer, *m. Min.* preparatory bore *(Beil)*; —buch, *n.* an elementary book, a primer; —buchstabe, *m. Typ.* initial letter, capital letter, initial, capital; —columne, *f. Typ.* head-page; —eindruck, *m.* first impression; —geschwindigkeit, *f. Phys.* initial *(Tech.:* primitive) velocity *or* speed (bewegter Körper, of bodies in motion); —grund, *m. gener. in the pl.* principles, rudiments, elements, beginnings; in den —gründen unterrichten, to instruct in the rudiments, to initiate; —kraft, *f. Phys.* initial force; —linie, *f. Typ.* head line; (Columnentitel) running title.

An'fangslos, *adj.* without a beginning (*seldom:* beginningless).

An'fangs..., *in comp.* —punct, *m.* the point of beginning, starting-point; —ritornell, *n. Mus.* introductory symphony to an air, &c.; —schule, *f.* primary school (Elementarschule); —terminus, *m.* initial term; —zeile, *f.* initial line; head line (*cf.* —linie); —zustand, *m.* initial, first, *or* primitive state.

An'färben, *(w.)* v. *tr.* 1) *a)* to begin to colour *or* to paint, to colour superficially, to tinge, tincture; *b) coll.* (*for* Anstreichen) to colour, to paint; 2) to give a colour not originally belonging to an object, to give a false colour, to adulterate by colouring (wine, &c.); 3) *fig.* to tincture, to tinge, to imbue.

An'fas, *(str.) m. coll.* handle (Handhabe).

An'fassbar, *adj.* that may be taken hold of, seizable, tangible.

An'fassen, *(w.)* v. I. *tr.* 1) to take, lay, *or* to catch hold of, to seize; to touch, to handle; Einen bei den Haaren, bei dem Kragen —, to get hold of one's hair, one's collar, &c.; faßt das Gewehr an! *Mil.* support arms! sechs Männer, welche sich einander anfaßten, konnten kaum den Baum umspannen, six men, taking hands, could scarcely encompass the tree; 2) *coll.* *a)* (mit —, *mostly intr.*) to give *or* lend a hand; etwas falsch *or* verkehrt —, to take by the wrong end, to mismanage, to go the wrong way to work; *b)* to set about (a thing), to undertake, to manage, *syn.* Angreifen, 7; diesen Geschäftszweig mag ich nicht —, I am not inclined to embark in this line of business; 3) to put *or* place (pearls, &c.) on a string, to string together, to file (Anreihen); 4) *fig.* to attack, to commence an act of hostility upon (one); wir werden ihn gerichtlich — müssen, we shall have to institute judicial proceedings against him; 5) *fig.* to take hold (the mind) of suddenly and forcibly, to seize; to set upon; 6) *fig.* to treat *or* use well or ill, to handle (roughly, tenderly, &c.).

II. *intr. coll.* to lend a hand, to assist (in working, &c.), *see* I. *tr.* 2, a.

III. *refl.* sich *(Acc.)* —, to be soft, rough, &c. to the touch; ihre Hand faßt sich wie Atlas an, her hand feels like silk (*cf.* Anfühlen, *refl.*).

An'fauchen, *(w.)* v. *tr.* (*frequentative:* **An'fauchzen,** *(w.)* v. *tr.*) to blow at *or* upon (one) with a hissing noise (like a cat, &c.).

An'faulen, *(w.)* v. *intr.* (*aux.* sein) to begin to rot, to grow rotten *or* putrid, to be attacked by putridity; a-des Obst, putrescent fruit; angefaulte Leichname, putrid corpses.

† **An'faulen,** *(w.)* v. *tr.* to putrefy, to make rotten *or* putrid.

An'fechtbar, I. *adj.* that may be contested, impugned, *or* called in question, contestable, liable to contest *or* litigation, disputable, controvertible; II. **A-keit,** *(w.) f.* the state of being possibly contested, &c., disputableness, &c.

An'fechten, *(str.)* v. *tr.* 1) *a) lit.* († *& prov.*) to attack, to assault; *b) fig.* to attack *or* assail by arguments *or* by words (Angreifen, 4), to impugn, to combat, to contest, to controvert, to dispute, to call in question; ein Testament —, to contest a will; ein Urtheil, eine Meinung —, to combat *or* oppose an opinion; wegen bescholtenen und angefochtenen Rufes, on account of a reputation open to charges and accusations; 2) *journeymen's slang,* to beg of (one), *cf.* Fechten; 3) *a) Script.*, &c. to assail with temptations, to try, to tempt (Versuchen, in Versuchung führen); *b)* to trouble, to disturb, to concern, touch; was ficht dich an? what possesses you? laßt euch nichts —, es geschehe was wolle, let nothing disturb you, happen what will; was ficht das mich an? what do I care for that? lassen Sie sich das nicht —, never trouble yourself (*or* don't be uneasy) about that, never mind it.

An'fechter, *(str.) m.* 1) one who attacks with arguments, &c. *cf.* Anfechten, opponent; 2) one who assails with temptations, (arch-) tempter (Versucher).

An'fechtung, *(w.) f.* 1) *a)* the act of attacking by arguments, &c. *cf.* Anfechten; opposition (einer Sache *[Gen.]*, to a thing), attack; die — eines Testaments, the contesting of a will; seine Familie hatte nun sechzig Jahre lang ohne — regiert, his family had now reigned undisputed for sixty years; *b) fig.* attack; allen A-en der Zeit Trotz bieten, to resist the brunt of ages; 3) *Script.*, &c. *a)* the act of assailing with temptations, temptation (Versuchung); trial; *b)* disturbance, vexation.

An'feilen, *(w.)* v. *tr.* 1) to begin to file, to cut *or* to abrade with a file; 2) (an eine Sache *[Acc.]*, *& more rarely* an einer Sache *[Dat.]* —) to produce by filing; eine Spitze an einen Draht —, to file a point to a wire.

An'federn, *(w.)* v. *tr. see* Anfiedern.

An'fehden, *(w.)* v. *tr.* to attack, to combat, to stand up against.

An'feilschen, *(w.)* v. *tr.* to begin to bargain for (a commodity), to begin to cheapen (goods, &c.), to ask the price of (a thing), to pretend to buy.

An'feinden, *(w.)* v. *tr.* to pursue *or* treat with enmity, hostility *or* rancour, to bear ill-will towards, to show enmity to, to prosecute, to malign; sie feindeten sich *(Acc.)* einander an, they exchanged hostilities.

An'feindung, *(w.) f.* the (act of) pursuing *or* treating with enmity *or* hostility, &c., prosecution, hostility, enmity shown to ....

An'fexen, *(w.)* v. *tr. coll.* to smirk upon.

An'fertigen, *(w.)* v. *tr.* 1) to make ready for use (Verfertigen), to manufacture; to compose; er ließ eine saubere Abschrift —, he had a neat transcript made; eine Liste — *(Hilp.)*, to draw up a list; 2) *Law style (obsolescent)*, to make over, to transmit, to send (a summons, &c. to ...), *cf.* Zufertigen. — **An'fertigung,** *(w.) f.* the (act of) making ready for use (Verfertigung), manufacture; composition, &c.

[illegible] wooing; 2) to acquire (a right, &c.) by wooing or taking in marriage.

Anfremden, *(w.) v. tr. provinc. (S. G.)* 1) to treat (one) like a stranger, to cut (one); 2) eine Sache (es) fremdet mich an, a thing appears strange to me *(opp.* Anheimeln); a–d, *p. a.* strange, uncommon, odd, particular; 3) for Anfrummen, *provinc.* to cause to be made, to order (Anfertigen lassen, Bestellen).

Anfressen, *(str.) v. tr.* 1) to begin to eat (only applied to animals, or to the immoderate eating of men, *cf.* Fressen), to devour, partially to gnaw or to nibble at ...; angefressen, *p. a.* bitten (as a pear, &c.); von Motten &c. angefressen, moth-eaten, &c.; 2) *fig.* to begin to consume, to eat into ..., to eat away gradually: *Chem.*, &c. to corrode (of acids, &c.); *Med.* to canker, to gangrene: durch Zeit und Witterung sehr angefressen *(Göthe)*, greatly time- and weather-worn: angefressen, *p. a. Med.*, &c. carious, gangrenous, canker-bit; 3) *in a moral sense,* to corrode, to eat into, to prey upon, to wear, to impair, to consume, to canker; II. *refl.* sich *(Acc.)* —, sich *(Dat.)* einen Bauch —, (of animals *or vulg.* of human beings) to eat one's fill, to fill one's belly with food: to grow fat with feeding: der Wolf hatte sich sehr angefressen, the wolf had raised himself a high paunch by voracious feeding *(cf.* Anmästen).

Anfrieren, *(str.) v. intr.* (aux. sein) to become attached (an *[with Acc. or Dat.]*, to some object) by frost, to cling or to stick fast by freezing, to freeze to the ground, &c.

Anfrischen, *(w.) v. tr.* 1) *a)* to refresh: *b) T–s., &c.* das Alaunbad wieder —, *in dyeing,* to refresh the dye with alum *(Hülp)*; die Thonerde —, *Sugar-r.* to wet the clay for the second time *(Hülp.)*; die Pumpen —, *Min.* to moisten the pumps; den Docht —, to moisten the wick with fresh oil: Wunden —, *Surg.* to moisten wounds anew; *Metall.* to reduce the litharge: Kupfer, Blei &c. —, *see* Frischen; *c)* to renew, to replenish, &c.; den Köder — *(Bürger)*, to replace the old bait by a fresh one; 2) *Sport., &c. chiefly used,* to animate (die Hunde, the dogs [Anhetzen, Anfeuern]), to incite, to arouse, to encourage, to enliven, to quicken; 3) *fig.* to refresh, (wieder —) to revive, to renew (the memory of ..., &c.).

Anfrischer, *(str.) m. Metall.* refiner (Frischer).

Anfrischfeuer, Anfrischofen, Anfrischschlacke, *see* Frischfeuer &c. — **Anfrischung,** *(w.) f.* 1) the act of refreshing, &c. *cf.* Anfrischen, refreshment; 2) *Metall.* reduction (of litharge), &c.; 3) *fig.* [illegible], encouragement, animation; 4) renewal (of old recollections, &c.), revival.

Anfröstein, *(w.) v. tr.* to affect with a feeling of slight cold, *gener. fig.* to appear [illegible] to ...

Anfüge, *(w.) f.* 1) *Carp., &c.* a board or piece of wood, &c. joined or bolted to another, [illegible], additional timber; 2) something annexed († annex), addition attached to a manuscript, &c., additional leaf or [illegible], [illegible]: in her — annexed, enclosed, subjoined.

Anfügen, *(w.) v. tr. Join., &c.* an etwas *(Acc.)* —, to join or attach (a board, &c.) to something else by a rabbet or groove (Fuge), to [illegible] in ...

Anfügen, *(w.) v. tr.* 1) *Join., &c.* to fit or to join to; 2) to adjoin, to join or to unite to, to annex, to subjoin; angefügt übersende [illegible], annexed I (beg to) transmit [illegible]; II. *refl.* to fit or to attach one's [illegible], &c.

Anfügung, *(w.) f.* the act of fitting, joining, [illegible], &c. to ..., *cf.* Anfügen, adjunction, [illegible].

[illegible], *adj.* 1) that may be [illegible],

tangible, palpable; 2) *fig.* perceptible; selbst unserem Drama ist es —, it is even perceptible in our drama.

Anfühlen, *(w.) v.* I. *tr.* 1) to feel, to touch, to handle; er fühlte die Schneide der Axt an, he felt the edge of the axe; den Puls —, to feel the pulse; die Haut der Mohren ist weit sanfter anzufühlen, als die unsrige *(Winckelmann)*, the skin of the negroes is much softer to the touch *(cf. refl.)*; 2) Einem *or* einer Sache *(Dat.)* etwas —, to perceive something in ... by the touch *(cf.* Anriechen &c.); der Blinde fühlt es dem Gelde an, was es für ein Gepräge hat, the blind man distinguishes the coinage of money by the sense of touch; möchtest du diesem Blatte recht —, wie lieb du mir bist *(Göthe)*, mightest thou perceive from this leaf, how dear thou art to me; man fühlt Ihrem Briefe die Gereiztheit an *(Nob. & Gr.)*, one feels a degree of irritability pervading your letter; *cf.* Abfühlen; II. *refl.* to cause sensation through the touch, to feel: es fühlt sich weich an, it feels soft: Blinde sagen, schwarz fühlt sich rauh an, und weiß fühlt sich glatt an, blind men say black feels rough, and white feels smooth: Hanfleinwand fühlt sich sehr dicht und derb an, hemp-linen feels very tight and tough.

Anfuhr, *(w.) f.* 1) the act of carrying, transporting or conveying (by land or water) to some place *(opp.* Abfuhr), carriage, transportation, or conveyance to ...; cartage (of building materials, &c.); 2) that which is carried, or conveyed to some place, cargo, shipment; die Preise befestigen sich, da die A–en klein bleiben, prices gain in consistency, the quantities brought to the market remaining small.

Anführbar, *adj.* adducible, allegeable; that may be quoted, quotable.

Anführegespan, *see* Anführgespan.

Anführen, *(w.) v. tr.* (I, *w.*) 1) *a) lit.* (an einen Ort) to lead, conduct, or guide to a place; to bring on or near; *b) fig.* to bring together, to collect, accumulate; 2) *a)* († *&) provinc. for* Anfahren: to carry, transport, or convey to a place, &c.; 3) *Min.* die Bergeisen —, to bring up new miner's tools, to use for the first time; 4) to lead, to command, to head; to bring up (the rear); eine Meute —, *Sport.* to hunt a pack of dogs; den Tanz, den Zug —, to lead the dance, the procession, &c.; den Reihen —, *fig.* to take the lead; ein wohlangeführtes Heer, a well-led army: das Wörtchen Ich führt alles an, was aus Peters Munde kommt *(Lessing)*, the little word *I* heads every sentence that issues from Peter's mouth; 5) *chiefly used,* to guide, to lead up to ..., to initiate, to direct, to point out to (one) the course to be pursued, to instruct (an apprentice, &c.); das Mädchen ist zur schweren Arbeit nicht angeführt, the girl has not been brought up to heavy work; 6) *fig. a)* to allege, to adduce (zum Beweise, in proof, &c.); to assign (reasons, &c.); to plead (in favour of): als Beispiel —, to instance; er wollte seine Beweggründe nicht —, he would not state his motives; *b)* to quote, cite; falsch —, to misquote; *c)* to mention, to say, to assert; 7) *coll. & jocul.* to deceive, to cheat, to trick (one), to impose on (upon), to take in, to delude, to dupe: er wollte uns damit —, his object was to mislead us; sich von ... — lassen, to be a dupe to ..., to be made a dupe of ...; ich lasse mich nicht so leicht —, I am not so easily taken in.

Anführ(e)..., *in comp. Print.* —geld, *n.* money paid to a journey-man printer for instructing an apprentice; —gespan, *m.* a journey-man printer instructing an apprentice, instructor.

Anführer, *(str.) m.* 1) *a) unusual,* one who leads to a place, &c. *(cf.* Anführen), guide, conductor; *b)* †, instructor (Lehrmeister); 2) leader, commander; chief; der oberste — einer großen Armee, the commander-in-chief of a great army.

Anführerei', *(w.) f. coll.* the act or practice of taking in, deceiving, &c., imposition, deception.

Anführerschaft, *(w.) f.* leadership, the state or the office of a leader or commander.

Anfuhrt, *(w.) f. see* Anfurt.

Anführung, *(w.) f.* 1) *chiefly used, a)* the act of leading to a place, direction; *b)* guidance, instruction (Anleitung); 2) the (act of) leading, lead, command; 3) *a)* the (act of) alleging, &c. *cf.* Anführen, 6; allegation, adduction, &c.: statement (Angabe); *b)* quotation, citation (the act of quoting, &c. and the passage or words quoted); 4) *coll.* the (act of) taking in, duping, &c. *cf.* Anführen, 7; deception, imposition, cheat, deceit: A-zeichen, *n.* sign of quotation, *pl.* inverted commas (" " „ ").

Anfüllen, *(w.) v.* I. *tr.* to fill up, to fill; to replenish, to store, to stock; to crowd, to cram, to swell: eine Flasche mit Wasser —, to fill a bottle with water: Fässer — lassen, to have casks filled up, to replenish casks: eine Blase mit Gas —, to fill a bladder with gas; *rarely (in poetry) with a Genitive:* fülle frischer Kräuter die Krippen an *(Rückert)*, fill with fresh herbs (mit frischen Kräutern) the mangers: the *pp.* angefüllt (filled, replete [with]) *sometimes with* von: das Theater war mit *or* von Zuschauern angefüllt, the theatre was filled or crammed with spectators; II. *refl.* to be filled (with): die Stadt füllte sich mit Gesindel an, the town was (beginning to be) crowded with rabble: sich mit Speise —, to fill one's self with food, to cram, to eat to repletion: mit glänzendem Öl fülle die Lampe sich an *(Schiller)*, with bright oil let the lamp be filled. [repletion.

Anfüllung, *(w.) f.* the (act of) filling, &c.,

Anfunkeln, *(w.) v. tr. (sometimes intr.)* to look or glare at (one) with sparkling, fiery eyes.

Anfurchen, *(w.) v. tr.* to draw the first furrows of (a field).

Anfürchten, *(w.) v. tr.* (Einem etwas) *unusual,* to impute (something) to (one) from fear.

Anfurt, *(w.) f.* 1) landing-place, landing, wharf, quay; 2) *unusual for* Anfahrt, Anzug: *a)* the act of coming near, touching at, &c., landing; *b)* approach, procession, arrival.

Anfußen, *(w.) v. intr.* 1) to get a footing; 2) *Sport.* to alight, light (of birds), *cf.* Anfallen, 2; 3) *Gymn.* to touch any part of one's own body with the foot.

Anfüttern, *(w.) v. tr. & refl.* sich *(Acc.)* —, or sich *(Dat.)* ein Bäuchlein &c. —, 1) to feed one's fill, to fill one's stomach with food; to make one's self fat with feeding: to raise one's self a paunch by feeding; 2) *(Göthe) jocul.* sich mit Steinen —, to fill one's self (i. e. one's mineralogical collections) with stones.

Angabe, *(w.) f.* 1) *a)* the (act of) giving or paying on account, instalment; earnest-money: *b)* the giving (of goods) in part-payment, part-payment in goods; 2) *a)* declaration, statement; estimate; specification; account, exhibition; A-n, *pl.* data: unter — des Betrages, stating the amount or value: ohne — des Verfassers, without acknowledgment of the original author; nach seiner —, according to his statement; — der Schulden, enumeration (statement) of the debts; *b)* denunciation, denouncement, information (das Angeben); *c) Comm.* entry (von Waaren beim Zollamt, of goods at the custom-house); 3) suggestion; instruction; design, sketch, plan.

Angäbeln, *(w.) v. tr.* to put on a fork, to

fork up, to pierce and raise with a fork, &c. cf. Aufgabeln.

An'gabezettel, (*str.*) *m. Comm.* declaration, statement, specification: manifest (of goods shipped on board of a vessel, &c.), freight-list.

An'gaffen, (*w.*) *v. tr.* to gape at (a person or thing) with stupid astonishment, &c., to stare at ... — An'gaffung, (*w.*) *f.* astonished or vacant gaping, staring, &c.

An'gähnen, (*w.*) *v. tr.* to gape or yawn at, to stare at (one) yawning.

An'gällen, (*w.*) *v. tr.* to fill or mix with bile or bitterness.

An'gang, (*str., pl.* An'gänge) *m.* 1) *lit.* a going to or up to, meeting with, encountering, *in Germ. Mythol.* the first (accidental) falling in with beasts, birds, or other beings, encountering a person early in the morning, considered to be lucky or unlucky, as the case might be (*called also* Widergang); der — des Hasen, des Schweines bedeutet Unglück, to meet a hare, a hog, the first thing in the morning, forebodes ill: der — des Wolfes war ein gutes Zeichen (*or* der Wolf hatte einen guten —), it augured well, if a wolf was the first object meeting a person of a morning; Kinder sind ein guter — (*Auerbach*), it is a lucky sign, if children should be the first objects encountering a person in the morning: †: 2) ascent (of a mountain, &c., = Aufgang); 3) beginning, start, &c.

An'gänger, (*str.*) *m.* 1) († &) *provinc.* beginner; 2) †, assailant.

An'gängig, An'gänglich, *adj.* (*l. u.*) feasible, possible; admissible; es ist nicht —, *syn.* with es geht nicht an.

An'gebäude, (*str.*) *n.* a building attached to another, adjoining building (Anbau, 3).

An'gebbar, *adj.* that may be stated, specified, declared, mentioned, declarable; gewisse nicht näher a–e Veränderungen, certain changes, not to be specified more distinctly.

An'gebeliste, (*w.*) *f.* see Angabezettel.

An'gebelle, (*str.*) *n.* a barking, yelping at.

An'geben, (*str.*) *v.* I. *tr.* 1) *lit.* (Kleider &c. anzuziehen geben) to give (Einem, to one) to wear; man gab ihm schlechte Kleider an, um ihn unkenntlich zu machen, they gave him bad clothes to wear (they made him wear bad clothes) in order to disguise him:

2) *a)* to begin to give: *b)* (*Comm. aa*) to give (part of an amount) on account, *see* Anzahlen, *which is more usual in this sense; bb)* to give (goods, &c.) in part payment: er mußte einen Theil seines Lagers an Zahlungsstatt — (*Nob. & Gr.*), he was obliged to give part of his stock as payment;

3) *a)* to state, to declare, to specify: den Werth (einer Postsendung) —, to make a declaration of value (of goods sent by the post); einzeln —, to detail; eine Summe —, to specify a sum; *b)* (*Comm.* to enter (goods at the custom-house); beim Zoll zu wenig —, to make an entry at the custom-house short of the value, to enter short; *c)* to denounce, to inform against (one), to lodge information against (one), (bei *or* vor Gericht) to accuse publicly: *often in a bad sense, of persons giving secretly malicious or officious information, different from* Anzeigen, 3, Anklagen; *coll.* to inform on (one), to tell of (*coll.* on) (one); die Zahlungsunfähigkeit eines Schuldners —, *Law*, to strike a docket against a debtor; *d)* *aa)* to state, to mention, to name, to tell, &c.; *bb)* to allege, assign (Gründe &c., reasons, &c.); Bridport ist in Bradshaw's Eisenbahn-Cours-Buch nicht angegeben (aufgeführt), Bridport is not marked in Bradshaw's railway-guide; sein Spiel —, *Cans.* to call one's game; ich kann nicht bestimmt —, I cannot say for certain; das Dienstmädchen fragte den Fremden: „welchen Namen soll ich — (*syn.* ansagen, melden)?" the servant girl asked the stranger, "what name shall I give?" Clarendon gibt in seinem Tagebuche an, daß die Majorität 11 war, aber Tindal u. A. stimmen darin überein, sie zu 14 anzugeben, Clarendon, in his Diary, says that the majority was eleven, but Tindal and others agree in putting it at fourteen; die Quelle, aus welcher solche Artikel entnommen sind, ist angegeben, the source from whence such articles are taken, is acknowledged; das Bild —, *Weav.* to tell the pattern (*Hlp.*); den Cours —, to quote the rate of exchange; zu den angegebenen Preisen, at the prices quoted; Gründe —, to show cause or reason (why, &c.); geben Sie mir einen guten Grund dafür an, yield me a good reason for it (*Hlp.*); (*sometimes in the sense of* Vorgeben); *ee)* *Sport.*, &c. to determine the nature of ..., *see* Ansprechen, I. 2, & *v. a.* 2;

4) *lit. & fig.* to indicate, to define, to mark, &c.; *a)* die Muskeln dieser Figur [in einer Zeichnung] sind zu stark angegeben, the muscles of this figure [in a drawing] are too strongly indicated; *b)* to originate (a plan), to design, to devise, to contrive, to sketch, to plan; *Mar.* to shape (the course); to point out; to appoint (eine Stunde &c., an hour, &c.); eine angegebene (*more usual* gegebene) Linie, *Math.* a given line (*see* Geben); in angegebener Weise, in the manner pointed out or indicated; belieben Sie uns anzugeben, wie wir verfahren sollen, be kind enough to let us know how we are to proceed; ein junges Weibchen gibt einen klugen Einfall an (*Bürger*), a young little wife starts a clever idea: Verbesserungen —, to suggest improvements;

5) *a)* *Mus.* den Ton —, to give the tune or key; eine Melodie —, to touch an air; to pitch or lead off the tune (in singing); to strike a note (on the piano, &c. = Anschlagen); den Tact —, to mark the time; *b)* *fig.* den Ton (*sometimes* die Mode) —, to set the ton, to lead or set the fashion;

6) *coll.* to do (*cf.* Anfangen, 3), to enact, to perform, to achieve, *generally in a bad sense,* to commit, to perpetrate; das närrische Zeug, so sie schwatzten und angaben (*Wieland*), the foolish things they talked and did; von allen den ungereimten Dingen, die er auf dieser Reise angab (*id.*), of all the preposterous things he committed on this journey: sie wußten nicht was sie — sollten, they did not know how to dispose of themselves;

7) *provinc.* Einem etwas —, to put a trick upon one, to make one believe a thing, to talk into ..., to persuade one of ..., &c. (Vormachen, Weismachen).

II. *refl.* 1) to declare one's self, to make a statement, declaration concerning one's self, &c.; sich als fallit —, to declare one's self insolvent; sich zu (*sometimes* in) einem Termine —, *Law phrase,* to announce one's self or to give in one's name at the day of appearance (of persons answering in law); 2) to present one's self as ...: *a)* sich für or als Jemand (*Acc.*) or für etwas (*Acc.*) — (*syn.* Ausgeben), to pretend to be; selbst der Weise erröthet nicht sich für ihren Schüler anzugeben (*Wieland*), even the wise does not blush to own himself her scholar; weil sie sich fälschlich als Geliebte Jupiters angegeben (*Göthe*), because she had falsely given herself out to be the mistress of Jupiter; *b)* obsolescent, sich zu ... —: wenn der Schuldner stirbt und sich Keiner zum Erben angibt, when the debtor dies and nobody offers as an heir; er gibt sich zum Husaren an (*Lessing*), he offers to serve or he enlists as a hussar.

III. (*intr.* 1) (*cf.* I. *tr.* 2, *a*) *Gam.* to deal first (at cards); 2) to answer the purpose; to be efficient, &c.: to mark (of a pen); die Feder will nicht — (*or* ansprechen), the pen

An'gehören, *(w.) v. intr. (with Dat.)* 1) to belong, appertain; 2) to be related (to) *or* connected (with).

An'gehörig, I. *adj. (with Dat.)* 1) belonging (to), attached (to); 2) related (to); 3) *s. (decl. like adj.)* A-e, *m. & f.* relative; meine A-en, my relations, my kinsmen, my parentage; my servants; II. A-keit, *(w.) f.* a belonging to, &c.

An'geifern, *(w.) v. tr.* 1) to slaver at; 2) *fig.* to calumniate.

An'geklagte, *m. & f. (decl. like adj.)* defendant; indictee.

An'gekünstelt, *p. a.* produced by excessive refinement; artificial, extraneous.

A. **Ang'el,** *(w.) f.* 1) hinge (einer Thür, of a door); 2) *Fish. (also [str.] m.)* angle, hook, fishing-hook; 3) *a) Mech.* pivot, pin, spindle; *b)* pole (of the earth); 4) *Cutl.* tang (tongue), tang, spike (of a sword, knife, fork, file, &c.); 5) *Entom. see* Stachel; zwischen Thür und — stecken, *fig.* to be in a sad dilemma *or* at a pinch; mit A-n versehen, to hinge (a door); aus den A-n heben, to unhinge, unhang (a gate, &c.); aus den A-n sein, to be off the hinges; mit der — fischen, *see* Angeln; die — auswerfen nach, *fig.* to angle, fish for; mit einer goldenen — fischen, *coll.* to angle with a golden rod.

Ang'el..., *in comp.* —band, *n.* loop (of a door); *Lock-sm.* butt-hinge; —fischer, *m.* angler; —haken, *m.* fishing-hook; —kork, *m.* float of an angle; —kreis, *m.* polar-circle; —leine, *f. see* —schnur; —punkt, *m.* pole; *fig.* vital, cardinal point, point on which something (the whole question, &c.) turns, *cf.* Angel, 1; —ring, *m. Lock-sm.* pan, socket, sole; —ruthe, *f.* (angling-)rod; fishing-rod, *see* Rachtangel; —schnur, *f.* (angling- *or* fishing-)line; die aufgewickelte —schnur, pirn of a fishing-line; —stern, *m. Astr.* polar-star, north-star; —stift, *m. Lock-sm.* bar of the lintel; —tasche, *f. see* Tiene; —weit, *adv.* wide-open; —zeug, *n.* fishing-tackle.

B. **Ang'el,** *(w.) m. gener. pl.* Angles (name of a German tribe); *in comp.* Anglo: —sachse, *m.*, —sächsisch, *adj.* Anglo-Saxon.

Ang'ela, Angeli'na, Angeli'ne *[pr.* ang'ge—], *f.* Angela, Angelina, Angeline *(P. N.)*.

An'gelangen, *see* Anlangen, Ankommen.

An'geld, *(str., pl.* A-er) *n.* earnest, earnest-money; hand-money, fasting-penny; (Einem) — geben, to pay (one) money in hand.

An'gelegen, *adj.* 1) adjacent, confining; adjoining; 2) important, of consequence; sich *(Dat.)* — sein lassen, to take care of, be (very) careful about, to have at *or* take to heart, to take an interest in, to be solicitous about (for), to make a point of, to use one's utmost endeavours; er läßt es sich — sein, he makes it his business.

An'gelegenheit, *(w.) f.* concern, business, affair, matter; transaction; innere A-en, home-affairs; auswärtige A-en, foreign affairs; ich komme in [illegible] A-en, I come on matters of [illegible].

An'gelegentlich, I. *adj.* of concern, urgent, [illegible], pressing; mein a-er Wunsch ist es, it is my particular wish; II. *adv.* with concern, [illegible], urgently, pressingly; a-st, auf's [illegible], *adv.* most particularly, anxiously (expecting, sich erkundigen &c.).

Ange'lika, *f.* 1) Angelica *(P. N.)*; 2) *Bot.* [illegible] *(Angelica archangelica* L.); wilde —, [illegible] (Waldbrustwurz); 3) *Bot.* angelot.

[illegible], *m. see* Eckerbaum.

Ang'eln, *(w.) v. tr. & intr.* to angle (nach), [illegible]; to fish with a line; to hook; mit Fliegen [illegible], to fly-fish; nach etwas [illegible], to fish for.

An'geloben, *(w.) v. tr.* to vow (to one), to [illegible] solemnly, to plight, stipulate. **An'gelobung,** *(w.) f.*, **An'gelöbniß,** *(str.)* *n.* vow (of obedience, &c.), solemn protestation, stipulation.

Ang'elsachse, *(w.) m. see* Angel ..., *B.*

* **Ang'elus** *[pr.* ang'ge—], *(indecl.) n. (Lat.) Rom. Cath.* prayer of salutation.

An'gemessen, I. *adj. (with Dat.)* conformable, suitable, adapted, fit; adequate (to), appropriate, condign (punishment); due, sufficient, suitable (recompense); consistent, compatible (with); für — halten, to think *or* see fit; — sein, to suit (one), to accommodate (to); II. A-heit, *(w.) f.* conformity, suitableness, fitness; proportionality; expedience; sufficiency.

An'genehm, *adj.* 1) (annehmbar) acceptable; 2) agreeable, pleasant, pleasing, delightful, sweet; (von Personen, Besuchen) welcome; die a-e Empfindung, delight; — machen, to endear; es ist mir — es zu erfahren, I am glad, pleased (auch: it affords me pleasure) to hear it; sich bei Jemand — machen, to approve one's self to one; ein a-es Leben führen, to live a comfortable life; *Comm.* Mittelsorten sind am a-sten, middling qualities are most in demand; der Artikel wird a-er, the article is improving (getting brisker); du wirst mehr davon haben, als dir — ist, *iron.* you will have a benefit of it.

An'genommen, *p. a. (cf.* Annehmen) 1) *Comm.* accepted (auf Wechseln); 2) assumed; affected; mock ...; 3) hypothetical, suppositive.

Ang'er, *(str.) m.* 1) *a)* green, grass-plot, *poet. (for* Wiese) mead; (Weideplatz) pasture ground; *b)* grassy ridge (between two fields, Rain); *unusual:* 2) down (Düne); 3) laystall (Schindanger); *Bot.* a. —blume, *f.* common or perennial daisy; —kraut, *n.* knot-grass *(Polygonum aviculare* L.); —weide, *f.* trailing willow *(Salix incubacea* L.).

Äng'erling, *see* Engerling.

An'geschleppe, *(str.) n. Mar.* sea-drag.

An'geschlossen, *pp. (from* Anschließen) *Comm.* enclosed.

An'gesehen, I. *conj.* seeing, considering (daß, that); II. *adj.* important, esteemed, creditable, considered, looked up to, of consequence, honourable, distinguished; das a-e Handelshaus, *Comm.* house of rank, of high standing; einer unser a-sten Banquiers, one of our first bankers.

An'gesessen, *p. a. (orig. pp. of* Ansitzen) settled, resident; der A-e, *(s. decl. like adj.) m.* householder.

An'gesicht, *(str., pl.* A-er) *n.* face, countenance, visage, air, look, mien; im —, in the face, sight, presence (des Herrn, of the Lord, &c.); von — zu —, face to face; ich will es ihm ins — sagen, I will tell it him to his face; von —, by sight; A-s der Stadt, in the face of the town; im — des Landes, *Mar.* in sight of the land; land to; im Schweiße deines A-s, *Script.* by the sweat of thy brow.

An'gesichts, *adv.* 1) in face (sight) of; 2) †, upon the spot, immediately.

An'gestammt, *p. a.* 1) hereditary, ancestral; 2) innate, natural.

An'gestellt, *p. a. see* Anstellen; der A-e, *m.* official, functionary, *see* Beamte.

An'gestohlen, *adj.* furtively acquired, got by theft.

An'gewachsen, *p. a. (cf.* Anwachsen) *Bot.* adnate; *Anat.* die a-e Haut des Auges, the conjunctive tunica (of the eye); mit a-er Haut *or* Rinde, hide-bound (of horses or trees).

An'gewandt, *p. a.* applied, &c. *from* Anwenden, which *see*.

An'gewelge, An'gewelle, *(str.) n. T.* plummerblock, cushion, bearing.

An'gewöhnen, *(w.) v. tr.* to accustom, inure, use, habituate (one to); sich *(Dat.)* etwas —, to contract (bad habits, &c.), to take to ...; angewöhnt, *p. a.* habitual.

An'gewohnheit, *(w.) f.* habit, custom, usage, habitude, practice; üble —, trick; aus —, habitually.

An'gewöhnung, *(w.) f.* 1) the act of accustoming (one's self, &c.) to ...; contracting, &c.; 2) *see* Angewohnheit.

An'gezeigt, *p. a. (cf.* Anzeigen) dies Verfahren ist —, this proceeding is self-indicated, *or* a matter of course.

An'gieren, *(w.) v. tr.* 1) to stare at greedily; 2) *Mar.* to sheer up.

An'gießen, *(str.) v. tr.* 1) (eine Flüssigkeit an etwas *[Acc.]*) to pour to, against, on; 2) (Begießen) to water (plants, &c.); 3) (Anreißen) to broach (a bottle); 4) *Found.* to cast to, add by casting, founding; 5) *Pott.* to colour (potter's ware) by a coat of coloured clay; 6) †, to calumniate, to denounce; der Rock sitzt wie angegossen, the coat fits tight.

An'gift, *(w.) f. see* Angeld.

* **Angio...,** *in comp.* —graph', —graphie', —logie', —log', *see* Gefäßbeschreiber, Gefäßbeschreibung, Gefäßlehre &c.; —tomie', *(w.) f. Anat.* angiotomy; —sperm'(isch), *adj. Bot.* angiospermous.

An'girren, *(w.) v. tr.* to coo at; *fig.* to allure.

* **Anglai'se** *[pr.* angglä'se], *(w.) f. (Fr.)* country-dance.

An'glänzen, *(w.) v. tr.* to reflect against, glitter on, to irradiate.

An'gleichen, *(str.) v. tr.* to assimilate.

An'gleichung, *(w.) f.* 1) assimilation; 2) symbolization.

An'gleiten, *(str.) v. intr. (aux.* sein) to strike (an *[with Acc.]*, against) in gliding.

Ang'ler, *(str.) m.* angler.

* **Anglica'nisch,** *adj. (Lat.)* Anglican, English; die a-e Kirche, *Eccl.* church of England.

* **Anglicis'mus,** (*pl.* Anglicis'men) *m. (Lat.)* Anglicism.

An'gliedern, *(w.) v. tr.* to join, add (a thing so as to make it a member of another thing).

An'glimmen, *(str. & w.) v. intr. (aux.* sein) to catch fire, to kindle, to begin to glow.

* **Anglisi'ren,** *(w.) v. tr.* 1) to anglicise; 2) *Farr.* to dock, nick, curtail (a horse). — **Anglisir'maschine,** *f. Farr.* docking engine.

An'glotzen, *(w.) v. tr. coll.* to stare, gape at ... with open eyes, to glare upon.

An'glühen, *(w.) v.* I. *tr.* to irradiate; to fire; *pp.* angeglüht, red-hot (of iron); II. *intr. (aux.* sein) to begin to glow.

Ango'raziege, *(w.) f. see* Kameelziege.

Ango'risch, *adj.* a-e Seidenhase, *m.* Angora rabbit *(Lepus cuniculus Angorensis* L.); a-e Ziegenhaar, *n.* Angora goat's hair.

Angostu'rarinde, *see* Angusturarinde.

An'grenzen, *see* Angrenzen.

An'grauen, An'grausen, *(w.) v. tr.* to offer a terrible aspect to, to awe, horrify.

An'greifbar, I. *adj.* 1) assailable; 2) *Phot.* — gemacht, made sensitive; nicht —, un—, unassailable; II. A-keit, *(w.) f.* assailableness, &c.

An'greifen, *(str.) v.* I. *tr.* 1) to handle, to touch, to get, lay, *or* take hold of, to lay hands on, to seize; 2) to attack, assault, to charge upon ...; 3) to invade (a country); *fig.* a. 4) to insult, offend, affront, aggress, strike at; 5) to affect; exhaust; weaken, fatigue, to hurt (the eyes, &c.); seine Gesundheit ist sehr angegriffen, his health is broken, he is in a bad state of health; meine Nerven sind sehr angegriffen, my nerves are dreadfully weakened, unstrung; Brechmittel greifen die Lunge ein wenig an, vomitives are slightly injurious to the lungs; es wird seine Casse stark —, it will be a heavy drain on his capital; die Casse —, to rob the cash; die Ehre (den guten Namen) —, to injure (assail) the good reputation; die Feile greift nicht an, the file does not cut (bite); Meinungen —, to attack, combat opi-

ziehen; Gründe —, to oppose arguments; ein Testament —, to contest a will; fremde Gelder —, to embezzle money entrusted to one; 6) die Ladung —, Mar. to break bulk; den Vorrath —, to broach the provisions; das Capital —, to touch the capital; 7) etwas —, coll. to undertake, attempt; to charge one's self with; to engage (in), set about; verkehrt —, to begin at the wrong end, to go to work in the wrong way; die Erdarbeiten sind bereits angegriffen, the earth works are already begun; 8) coll. see Befehlen, cf. 5.

II. intr. 1) to bear a hand, cf. Anfassen, I. 2; 2) to give battle, to charge.

III. refl. 1) coll. see sich Anfühlen; 2) to strain, strive, to exert one's self; to do one's utmost; 3) coll. to draw the pursestrings, to come down liberally or handsomely; a-d, adj. offensive; weakening, exhausting; der a-de Theil, the aggressive party; aggressor.

An'greifer, (str.) m. aggressor, assailant, attacker, &c.; encounterer, smiter, striker.

An'greiflich, An'greiflich, adj. coll. tempting (of things); thievish (of persons).

An'greifung, (w.) f. see Angriff.

An'greinen, (w.) v. tr. to grin at.

An'grenzen, (w.) v. intr. (with an [& Acc.]) to border upon, to confine on or with, to adjoin; a-d, p. a. adjacent, contiguous, verging on (to), conterminous.

An'grenzung, (w.) f. adjacency, juxtaposition.

An'griff, (str.) m. 1) the act of touching, feeling, handling, &c. cf. Angreifen; 2) attack, aggression; charge, rencounter, invasion; fig. brunt (of ages, &c.); 3) handle (Griff); 4) Weav. the upper end of a web; Lock-sm. frontward; (am Riegel) bolt-toe; bit; beard; verlorener —, movable bit; — am Deckel, Typ. thumb piece; 5) Mil-a. einen — thun, machen, to attack, to charge, to come to the charge; to strike (auf [with Acc.], for); den ersten — aushalten, to stand the first brunt or shock; einen neuen — thun, to charge again; zum — blasen, to sound the charge; 6) undertaking; in — nehmen, to undertake, to take in hand, to commence operations; T. to break ground (on a railway); in — genommen, in course of construction or execution.

An'griffs ..., in comp. —arbeiten, pl. Fort. works of attack; —brunnen, m. Min. shaft à la bonde; —bündniß, n. offensive alliance; —krieg, m. offensive war, invasive war; —punct, m. Mech. working-point; Mec., &c. point of application; —punct paralleler Kräfte, Mech. centre of parallel forces; —waffen, f. pl. arms of offence; —weise, adv. offensively, by way of attack; —weise zu Werke gehen, to act on the offensive.

An'grinsen, (w.) v. tr. to grin at or on; höhnisch or einfältig —, to fleer at ....

An'grollen, (w.) v. tr. to grumble, look angrily (at one).

An'grunzen, (w.) v. tr. to grunt (at one).

Angst, (str., pl. Äng'ste) f. 1) (extreme pain of body or mind) anguish; (Besorgniß) anxiety; in großer — leben, to live in (a) great anxiety (of mind); disquiet, nervous dread, fright; fear, terror; seine — vor tollen Hunden, his fear of mad dogs; agony, pangs of death; — haben, to shrink with apprehension (vor [with Dat.], from); in Ängsten sein, to be seized with anguish, to be in a state of alarm; in tödtlichen Ängsten, in an agony of fear; in — gerathen, to take alarm; II. in comp. —geheul, —geschrei, n., —ruf, m. lamentable outcry, howl, howling; cry of distress, scream; —mann, provinc. for Scharfrichter; —sprung, m. (1 st.) a leap taken in distress or anguish; —schweiß, —tropfen, m. cold sweat; —voll, adj. anxious, fearful; painful.

Angst is used in certain phrases as an adjective predicative, etc. mir ist —, I am in fear, I am uneasy; mir wird (sehr) —, I grow (very) uneasy; Einem — machen, to put one in fear; to alarm, frighten one; — und bange, very uneasy, terribly frightened.

Äng'sten, see Ängstigen. [Angstsprung.

Äng'stesprung, (Göthe, Faust I. 5) for

Äng'stig, adj. full of anxiety, see Ängstlich.

Äng'stigen, (w.) v. tr. to alarm, strike with fear, anguish; to make uneasy, to harass with commotion; sich über etwas (Acc.) —, refl. to be uneasy (with apprehension), to be harassed or in a fright, to fret (about ...).

Ängst'lich, I. adj. 1) anxious, uneasy; nervous; diffident, timid, timorous; 2) scrupulous, careful, solicitous; precise, punctilious; ohne — zu rechnen, Comm. without being too nice (over-anxious) in one's calculations; II. Ä-keit, (w.) f. 1) anxiousness, anxiety; uneasiness; diffidence, timidity, timorousness, fearfulness; perplexity; 2) solicitude, (scrupulous) care, nicety.

An'gucken, (w.) v. tr. coll. to look at.

An'gürten, (w.) v. tr. to gird, gird about.

An'guß, (str., pl. An'güsse) m. what is poured against or added by casting; Mech. runner, runner-stick. [gustura-bark.

Angustu'ra-Rinde, (w.) f. Pharm. an-

An'haben, (irr.) v. tr. 1) (Kleider) to have on, wear; Stiefeln —, to go in boots; 2) fig. coll. (Einem etwas) a) to get or gain the better of, to overcome; b) to do one harm, get at, to get hold on. [out, to hoe.

An'hacken, (w.) v. tr. to begin to hack, to

An'haften, (w.) v. intr. to stick to, to be attached to, to adhere to.

An'häften, (w.) see Anheften.

An'hageln, (w.) v. intr. to strike, beat at (of hail).

An'hägern, (w.) v. tr. 1) to deposit, float on (sand or earth; used of rivers); 2) (also Einhägern) to gain (land) from (a river, &c.).

An'hägerung, (w.) f. land gained by the washing up of sand or soil from a river or the sea, &c.

An'häkeln, (w.) v. tr. to clasp, to hook on, to fix with little hooks; to catch with the claws; fig. refl. to cling to.

An'haken, (w.) v. tr. 1) to hook on (to), to grapple; Mech. to fix by hooks; 2) Kartoffeln —, to go through the potato-lot with the cultivator.

An'halftern, (w.) v. tr. to fix by the halter.

An'hall, (str.) m. sound.

An'hallen, (w.) v. intr. to sound against.

An'halsen, (w.) v. tr. Sport. to tie (the limehound) to the cord.

An'halt, (str.) m. 1) the halting, stopping; 2) (Unterstützung) hold, support.

An'halten, (str.) v. I. tr. 1) (an [with Acc.]) to hold (up) to; 2) to arrest, hold, stop, to stop short, to stay (the progress of a movement); Mech. to pin; 3) a) to rein or draw in, to rein or pull up (a horse); b) fig. to restrain, control; to stay; 4) Med. to astringe; 5) to seize, detain, arrest (a debtor); 6) fig. (with zu) to hold (one) to, to keep (one) to (his work, &c.), to enjoin or to admonish to ...; scharf —, to ply hard; II. intr. 1) to take hold, to keep fast, to stick to; 2) to continue, last, to persevere, hold on, keep on, persist (in), stand; 3) to halt, to stop; weswegen halten wir an? what are we stopping for? (in einem Gespräche) to stop short; to call (at stations, &c.); to pause; 4) to cease, to stop; mit ... — (Einhalten, Aufhören), to discontinue, to delay (the sale, &c.); 5) to apply (um [with Acc.], for), to seek, petition or sue for; to solicit, request, supplicate; um ein Frauenzimmer —, to ask or desire in marriage, to propose for (a lady), to court, to woo; III. refl. (with an & Acc.) to stick (to), to cling (to), lay hold (of), to hold (to), to catch hold (of).

An'halten, n. s. (str.) n. 1) the act of

hen (with Acc.), to), adherence, adhesion; A-s-[illegible], m. Phren. adhesiveness.

Anhängling, (str.) m. cont. (l. u.) hanger-on.

Anhängschloß, (str., pl. A-schlösser) n. padlock.

Anhängsel, (str.) n. 1) appendix, appendage; (eines Vertrags) annexed proviso; conditional clause; 2) amulet; 3) Mar. sea-drag.

Anharken, (w.) v. tr. to rake to, on.

Anhaspen, Anhäspen, (w.) v. tr. to fasten with iron hooks or bands, Min. to cramp.

Anhauch, (str.) m. 1) breathing on, afflation; 2) fig. see Anflug, 3.

Anhauchen, (w.) v. tr. to breathe at or upon; to blow (one's fingers, &c.); pp. & adj. angehaucht, slightly laid on (of colours); ein angehauchtes Roth, a slight tinge of red.

Anhauen, (irr.) v. tr. to whip on, to drive forward by whipping; to cut on, to begin to cut; to cut off the first piece (of butcher's meat, a calf, &c. for sale, or of a cake, &c.); den Fisch mit der Angel —, Sport. to give a jerk with the angling-rod when the fish has taken the bait; Forest. to mark or blaze a tree; Carp. to examine by cutting; Mas. to cut bricks or tiles.

Anhäufeln, (w.) v. tr. to form into small heaps.

Anhäufen, (w.) v. I. tr. to heap up, to pile up, treasure up, to amass, accumulate; II. refl. to increase, accumulate.

Anhäufer, (str.) m. accumulator.

Anhäufung, (w.) f. accumulation; Phys. accretion; Miner. agglomeration; Geol., Phys., Chem. aggregation, aggregate; (fremdartiger Flüssigkeiten im Zellgewebe) Med. infiltration.

Anheben, (str.) v. tr. 1) to lift up, lift close to; eine Pumpe —, Mar. to fetch a pump, to put water into, to light; 2) also intr. to begin, commence.

Anheber, (str.) m. beginner, author.

Anheften, (w.) v. tr. 1) to fasten, affix; 2) (durch Nähen) to stitch or sew on to (slightly or with long stitches); 3) (mit Stecknadeln) to pin to.

Anheftung, (w.) f. the act of fastening, &c.

Anheilen, (w.) v. I. tr. to heal on; II. intr. (aux. sein) to get fixed by healing.

† **Anheim'**, adv. home; in comp. (with Dat.) —fallen, v. intr. 1) to fall to, to devolve; to revert; 2) fig. to be subject to; —geben, v. tr. (Einem etwas) to leave with, to put into one's hand; —stellen, v. tr. (Einem etwas) to commit, to leave, to put, to defer, to submit, to refer to (another's determination or judgment, &c.).

Anheimeln, (w.) v. tr. to put in mind or remind of home; fig. dieses Gebiet heimelt mich mehr an, I feel more at home in this department (of science).

Anheim'..., in comp. —fall, m. devolution; —stellung, f. the act of referring to, &c. see Anheim.

Anheischig, adj. pledged by promise, bound; sich — machen, to promise, to bind, oblige, or pledge one's self; ich mache mich —, I will be bound, I will engage.

Anheizen, (w.) v. tr. & intr. 1) to begin to heat; 2) T. to urge a fire.

Anhelfen, (str.) v. tr. (with Dat. or Acc.) 1) to assist; ich habe ihm den Rock angeholfen, I helped him on with his coat; 2) to obtain an employment for a person.

Anhenkeln, (w.) v. tr. (l. u.) to fasten with a little ring or hook.

Anhenken, (w.) see Anhängen.

Anher († Anher'wärts), adv. hither, to this place; bis —, hitherto; —kunft, (w.) f. arrival.

Anhetzen, (w.) v. tr. 1) Sport. a) to begin hunting, chasing, to start, to unharbour (a stag, &c.); b) einen Hund —, to set on a dog. [illegible] aufhetzen. — **Anhetzer**, (str.) m. [illegible], instigator, abettor, inciter.

Anhetzerei, (w.) f. see Aufhetzerei.

Anheucheln, (w.) v. refl. to assume, to pretend hypocritically; er heuchelte sich (Dat.) ein redliches Bestreben an, he feigned honest intentions; das angeheuchelte Christenthum, false or fictitious christianity.

Anheulen, (w.) v. tr. to howl at.

† **Anheut'**, see Heute.

Anhexen, (w.) v. tr. to inflict by witchcraft.

Anhieb, (str.) m. Forest. 1) the commencement of felling wood; 2) the place where wood is felled.

Anhissen, (w.) v. tr. (l. u.) 1) see Anhetzen; 2) see Aufhissen.

Anhöhe, (w.) f. rising or high ground, height, hill, slight eminence, elevation.

Anholen, (w.) v. tr. Mar. to haul taut (the bowlines, &c.); die Schoten —, to haul aft the sheets; Min. to raise, to heave up.

Anholtau, (str.) n. Mar. hawser, halser.

Anhören, (w.) v. tr. 1) to hearken to, listen to, give ear to, to hear (one), give (one) hearing, to bow the ear to one; Law. to receive an audit; 2) (Einem etwas) to perceive by listening to; das hört sich schön an, this sounds fine, is agreeable to the ear; das läßt sich —, this may be listened to, is worth hearing or consideration; das kann ich nicht mit —, I cannot (bear or stay) to hear this.

Anhörung, (w.) f. (the act of) hearing or listening to, &c.; hearing, audience.

Anhosen, (w.) v. refl. lud. to put on breeches.

Anhüpfen, (w.) v. intr. (aux. sein) to hop to.

Anhusten, (w.) v. tr. to cough at; to make signs by coughing.

* **Änigmatisch**, adj. (Gr.) enigmatic; fig. dark, difficult.

* **Anilin'**, (str.) n. Chem., &c. aniline.

* **Animalien**, (w.) n. pl. (Lat.) animal bodies; animal food. — **Animalisch**, adj. animal (Thierisch), beastly, brutish; der a-e Faserstoff, fibrine.

* **Animiren**, (w.) v. tr. (Lat.) 1) to animate; 2) see Anreizen.

* **Anis**, (str.) m. Bot. anise (Pimpinella anisum L.); in comp. —branntwein, m. aniseed-spirit, or cordial, anisette; —holz, n. aniseed wood; —kerbel, m. Bot. sweet cicely (Myrrhis odorata); —öl, n. aniseed-oil; —zucker, m. sugared anise.

Anjagen, (w.) v. I. tr. 1) see Anhetzen; 2) fig. to impel to greater speed, to drive on; II. intr. (aux. sein) angejagt kommen, to rush on impetuously.

† **Anjetzo, Anjetzt, Anjetzund**, see Jetzt.

Anjochen, (w.) v. tr. to yoke, couple under the yoke.

Ankämmen, (w.) v. tr. to comb smooth (one's hair).

Ankampf, (str.) m. the act of struggling against. — **Ankämpfen**, (w.) v. tr. (gegen) to struggle, or to bear up against; to combat.

Ankarren, (w.) v. tr. to cart up or near.

Ankauf, (str., pl. Ankäufe) m. 1) the act of buying; purchase, acquisition; 2) earnest-money.

Ankaufen, (w.) v. I. tr. to buy, purchase; II. refl. to buy lands, to settle at or in a place.

Ankaufspreis, (str.) m. original cost; zum A-e, at the (first, prime) cost.

A. **Anke**, (w.) f. 1) Goldsm., Engr., &c. thimble (a kind of stamp), puncheon; 2) Husb. a small peg (in a plough).

B. **Anke**, (w.) m. provinc. see Lachsforelle.

C. **Anke**, (w.), **Anken**, (str.) m. butter (in Switzerland); —brunt, f. see Maibutter.

Ankehren, (w.) v. tr. 1) to sweep towards; den Schmutz an die Wand —, to sweep the dirt against the wall; 2) obsolescent, to employ (diligence, &c.); 3) in ein Wirthshaus —, provinc. to put up in an inn, see Einkehren.

Ankeilen, (w.) v. tr. 1) to fasten with wedges, to key (up); 2) see Antreiben.

Ankel, (str.) m. see Enkel, 2.

Ankelblume, (w.) f. provinc. for Wiesen-Ranunkel. [sod (Rasen).

Anken, (w.) v. intr. provinc. to groan, to

Anker, (str.) m. 1) (a liquid measure) anker; 2) Archit. brace, key; Mech. grappling-iron (of a steam-engine); 3) Mar. anchor (also fig. emblem of perseverance and hope); ein blinder —, an anchor which has no buoy; der kleine —, grapnel; der größte —, sheet anchor; der tägliche —, bower anchor; den — vom Bug abhalten, to bear off the anchor; den — aufkatten, to cat the anchor; den — aufwinden, to start the anchor; den — mit dem Boot ausbringen, to boat the anchor; einen Sturm vor — aushalten, to ride out a gale, a storm; dem — mehr Tau ausstechen, to pay out or veer away more cable; den — auswerfen or werfen, to cast (drop) anchor, see Ankern; den — mit der Rustleine befestigen, to seize the anchor with the shank-painter, to stow the anchor on the bow; den — bekleiden, see den — schuhen; den — aufpentern, auf den Bug setzen, kippen, to fish the anchor; den — einholen, zu Hause holen, to heave in the cable; den — fangen or auffangen, to get the anchor up along the bow in order to clean the cables; unter Segel alle — fallen lassen, to let go all the anchors at best advantage; auf den — getrieben werden, to fall over the anchor; einen — fischen, to drag or sweep for an anchor; der — ist zum Fallen klar, the anchor is a-peak; der — greift zu, the anchor bites; der — hält, the anchor has got hold of the bottom; der — hängt, the anchor is a-trip (a-cock-bill); der — hängt vor dem Krahn, ist zum Fallen klar, the anchor is at the cat-head; den — kappen, to cut the cable; sich vor — legen, to anchor, to moor; die — lichten, to weigh anchor, to be under weigh, to trip, hoist the anchors; to break ground; to break adrift from the moorings; der — ist gelichtet, the anchor is a-trip; den — mit dem Tau lichten, to weigh the anchor by the hair; vor — liegen, to ride at anchor; sicher vor — liegend, well anchored; mit geleiten Raaen vor — liegen, to ride a-peak; mit Stangen und Raaen im Holl vor — liegen, to ride a portoise; vor Ebb- und Flut- — liegen, to moor against ebb and flood; vor — reiten, bei hohler See vor — stampfen, to ride hard, to set and heave; den — am Ringe fest machen, to clinch the cable; einen — schuhen, to shoe an anchor; das Schiff schwelt vor seinem —, the ship swings with the tide; um den — schwenken, to trend; das Schiff spielt um seinen —, the ship rides easy; der — setzt nicht durch, see der — hält; den — stocken, to stock an anchor; der — springt aus, the anchor starts; vor — treiben, to run foul of or over the anchor; to drag the anchor; das Schiff treibt vor —, or der — schleppt, ist triftig, setzt durch, the anchor comes home or drives; den — verkatten, to back the anchor; den — versetzen, to change a birth; mit A-n vorn und hinten vertäuen, to moor by the head and stern; vor zwei, drei, vier A-n vertäut liegen, to come to, or to moor with two, three or four anchors a-head; einen — unter Segel zugehen lassen, to drop the anchor while the sails are still abroad; den — werfen, see den — auswerfen & Ankern; der — wacht, see der — ist zum Fallen klar; auf den — zusteuern, to steer the ship to her anchor.

Anker..., in comp. Mar.-s. —achseln, pl. shoulders of an anchor; —arm, m. arm of an anchor; —auge, n. eye of an anchor; —balken, m. anchor-beam; pl. cat-heads; Carp. anchor, tie-beam; —beting, f. the (main) bitt; —bolzen, clinch-bolt; —bekleidung, see —schuhung; —boje, f. buoy (fastened to an anchor); beacon; break-water; die —boje fangen, to hitch the buoy; —fliege, —schaufel, f., —flügel, m. fluke, palm; —floß, n. buoy; —förmig, adj. shaped

An'kratzen, An'kritzeln, *(w.)* v. *tr. & intr.* to scratch at, against.

An'kreiden, *(w.)* v. *tr.* to note with chalk; to score (a reckoning); — lassen, *fam.* to buy on credit, on tick.

An'kreischen, *(w.)* v. *tr.* to scream at.

An'kreuzen, *(w.)* v. *tr.* to mark with a cross.

An'kriechen, *(str.)* v. *intr.* *(aux.* sein) to creep up, to; *and.* to crawl near: angekrochen kommen, to approach crawlingly.

An'kriegen, *(w.)* v. *tr.* 1) see Anbekommen; 2) to get (one) to do something. [on.

An'kritzeln, *(w.)* v. *tr.* to scratch or scribble

An'kucken, *(w.)* see Angucken.

An'künden, An'kündigen, *(w.)* v. *tr.* to announce, give notice, advertise; to declare, proclaim: es wird mir angekündigt, I am informed. — **An'künd(ig)er,** *(str.)* m. announcer, &c. — **An'kündigung,** *(w.)* f. declaration; announcement; (öffentliche) proclamation; (in einem Zeitungsblatte) advertisement.

An'kunft, (w., *pl.* An'künfte) *f.* arrival, coming; advent; nicht erfolgte —, non-arrival.

An'künsteln, *(w.)* v. *tr.* to fix or add to artificially, to introduce or to adopt artificially, *cf.* Angekünstelt; sich *(Dat.)* ... —, to affect....

An'kuppeln, *(w.)* v. *tr.* to couple; to leash; Einem eine Person —, *vulg.* to procure one a person in marriage. [upon.

An'lachen, An'lächeln, *(w.)* v. *tr.* to smile

An'lage, *(w.)* f. 1) (the act of) laying out, &c. *cf.* Anlegung; 2) establishment, plantation, *particul. pl.* A-n, improvements; pleasure grounds; 3) capital, stock; 4) (Gründung eines Geschäfts &c.) beginning, foundation, plan; construction (of a railway); 5) natural disposition (zu, to), capacity, temper, parts, talents (zu, for); predisposition; 6) (eines Tonstücks) design, plan, or outline, (eines Romans) plot; (eines Gemäldes) rough sketch or draught: 7) (zu einem Briefe &c.) any thing annexed; aus der — werden Sie ersehen, by (from) the annexed you will see; 8) tax, duty; eine — machen, to impose a tax; 9) *Horol.* onset; 10) *Arch.* drawing-book; 11) *Mus.* patten, sole; 12) *T.* the cheek-piece of a gun-stock (Anschlag); 13) *Lock-sm.* the staple for a bolt, *see* Klammer, Krampe; 14) *Metall.* ore welded together; 15) *Bot.* germ, ovary, seed-bed (especially of mosses and cryptogamic plants).

An'lage..., *in comp.* —capital, *n.* stock, business-capital; —kosten, *pl.* original costs; —walze, *f.* *T.* roughing roll; puddler's roll.

An'lallen, *(w.)* v. *tr.* to address in infantine language; to lisp at.

An'landbar, *adj.* boardable, approachable.

An'lände, *(w.)* f. *see* Anfurt.

An'landen, *(w.)* v. *intr.* *(aux.* sein) to fall in with the shore; to come to shore, to disembark, to make a descent (on, upon); to touch at, or put into a port; *cf.* Landen. [ship).

An'länden, *(w.)* v. *tr.* to put to shore (a

An'langen, *(w.)* v. I. *intr.* *(aux.* sein) to arrive; II. *tr.* 1) to concern, touch, belong; 2) [illegible] to request, solicit; 3) †, *see* Belangen, [illegible]; a-d, *adj.* concerning, touching: as for, as to, with regard to, in point of...

An'[illegible], *(w.)* f. [illegible] *for* [illegible] [illegible], *n.* [illegible]-piece.

An'[illegible], *(w.)* v. *tr.* to patch to or on.

An'[illegible], *(w.)* v. *tr.* 1) *Forest.* see An[illegible] [illegible] to put a new latchet to.

An'[illegible], [illegible] *m.* 1) occasion, [illegible] *cf.* Veranlassung; [illegible] Berichte, [illegible] report; ohne — zu [illegible] having nothing more [illegible] &c.; auf — des [illegible] of the defend[illegible] commencing; 2) (the act of) [illegible] (Gefäßen) ap-[illegible]

pearance; 3) *Law,* compromise; —brief, *m.* written agreement of the contending parties to have the cause in dispute settled by arbitration.

An'lassen, *(str.)* v. I. *tr.* 1) to let on; 2) *fig.* Einen hart, übel —, to address, treat, receive harshly, ill; scharf —, to snap, to snub, to give a bad reception; *cf.* Anfahren, 2; 3) (Wasser) to let (water) into; einen Teich —, to let water into a pond: eine Mühle —, to set a mill a-going; 4) *ellipt.* a) to keep on; b) Einem ein Kleid —, to allow one to keep on a dress; 5) einen Hund —, *Sport.* to set a dog on; 6) *ellipt. for* Anlaufen (8) lassen; 7) to temper (iron or steel); II. *refl.* sich gut —, to promise or bid fair: es läßt sich zu ... an, there is a likelihood, an appearance of or for (war, &c.); das Wetter läßt sich zum Regen an, it looks as if it would rain; der Knabe läßt sich gut an, he is a hopeful boy; der Weizen läßt sich gut an, the wheat promises a good yield; die Sache läßt sich nicht sonderlich an, the matter is not very promising; wie läßt es sich mit seinem Fieber an? how goes his fever?

An'laßhebel, *(str.)* m. *Mech.* starting-lever (of a locomotive).

An'lauf, *(str., pl.* An'läufe) *m.* 1) start, onset, run; einen — nehmen, to run for a leap, to stand off for an advantage, to take a run; 2) assault, attack; 3) swelling, rising (of water); 4) frequent petition, frequent application, trouble; er hat immer großen — von jungen Leuten, many young people continually flock to him; 5) *Mar.* headway; im A-e sein, to be under headway; *see* Ausbauchung & Einzieher; 6) *Archit.* lower apophyge; cymatium; der — einer Wölbung, the spring or rising of a vault; der — eines Daches, the gradual rise of a roof; der — des Kiels, the forefoot of the keel; der — des Wassers, the swelling, rising of water; *Min.* the gradual rise of a shaft or stulm; *Smelt.* the rise of the furnace; *Sport.* the approach of game within gun-shot (at battues); *Horol.* that part of the works in a clock, by which the striking is effected and the wheels during the stroke are regulated; *T.* touch.

An'laufeisen, *(str.)* n. *Smelt.* the ore which, in passing through the bloomary, adheres to the iron-rod.

An'laufen, *(str.)* v. I. *tr.* to importune, solicit; II. *intr.* *(aux.* sein) 1) to begin to run; to take a run (against, gegen); *see* Anrennen; to run up, to; to rush upon: *Mar.* to put into (a port), to touch at; 2) to rise, swell; 3) (von Schulden &c.) to swell on, to increase; 4) (schräge —) to rise sloping or with a (gentle) slope; 5) *Typ.* to rut; 6) a) *Min.* to work upwards, to be inclined, sloping; b) *Archit.* to shape, to scape; 7) (den Glanz verlieren) a) das Glas läuft an, the glass tarnishes, dims; der Athem macht den Spiegel —, breath tarnishes (dims) the surface of the looking-glass; b) vom Schimmel —, to get mouldy; c) vom Roste —, to get rusty; d) (von Farben) to dull, deaden; e) (von Metall) to oxidise; angelaufen (von Metallen), dim; blaß angelaufen (von Farben), dim; 8) — lassen, to stain (metals) by chemical agents; blau — lassen, a) to make (steel, &c.) blue; Klingen blau — lassen, to damaskeen; b) *fig.* to frighten out of one's wits; 9) *fig.* to run counter to (gegen...); schlecht —, to be disappointed, thwarted; to run a bad chance; er ist schön angelaufen, *iron.* he has met with a fine reception; laß ihn nur —, let him run his head against the wall; 9) *Hunt.* ein wildes Schwein — lassen, in hunting the wild boar, to present the spear in such a manner that the animal runs against it.

An'lauf..., *in comp.* —farbe, *f.* *T.* the tempering-colour (assumed by metal in the bloomary); —feuer, *n.* refining-fire, furnace; —frischen, *n.* the transfusion of raw into refined iron; —kolben, *m.* the iron staff used in the bloomary, the bloom-staff; —rad, *n.* *Horol.* a certain wheel, *see* Anlauf, 6, *Horol.*; —stab, *m.*, —stange, *f.* *see* —kolben; —stift, *m.* *see* —rad.

An'laut, *(str.)* m. *Gramm.* commencing sound of a word or syllable; s im A-e ist im Englischen scharf, s at the beginning of words has its sharp hissing sound in English.

An'lauten, *(w.)* v. *intr.* *(& tr.)* *Gramm.* to commence a word or syllable: Wörter die mit s —, words beginning with an s; s-des s, initial s.

An'läuten, *(w.)* v. *tr.* to ring the bell; to announce by ringing the bell (dinner, the commencement of work, &c.).

An'lecken, *(w.)* v. *tr.* to lick at.

An'legemarken, *f. pl.* *see* Wohlfstmarken.

An'legen, *(w.)* v. I. *tr.* 1) to put, place, apply, or lay to, on, against (the wall, &c.), to fasten, fix (the shrouds, &c.); to leave upon the latch (a door); Kleider —, to put on clothes; Trauer —, to put on (*coll.* to go into) mourning; ein Kind —, to put a child to the breast; ein Gewehr —, *see* Anschlagen, I, 11; Hand —, to set hands to, to take in hand, or begin a work, to be active, *cf.* Hand; 2) a) to place, dispose of, to lay out, to sink (money in a bargain, &c.), to put (capitals, sums) out at interest, to employ (funds), to (invest; sein Capital gut —, to turn one's money to good account; b) to spend, employ; 3) a) to lay out (grounds, &c.), to draw garden-plots; *fig.* b) to found, establish; to set up; (eine Festung &c.) to construct, build; to form (a bank, ein Bankett, *Roche.*); *Carp.* to truss (ein Hängewerk); to practise or lay down (a road); c) to lay, concert, devise (a scheme, &c.), to plan (a conspiracy, &c.); es auf *(with Acc.)* —, to plan, to aim at, to make it one's object; es war darauf angelegt zu ..., it was intended or the plan was to ...; alles ist darauf angelegt mich zu reizen, every thing is calculated to irritate me; Feuer —, to burn another man's house, &c. maliciously, to be guilty of arson; angelegte Feuer, *pl.* incendiary or wilful fires; 4) to hoop (a cask); lassen Sie eiserne Bänder —, have the casks bound with iron hoops; *Mar.* die Marssegel —, to haul home the topsail-sheets; *Typ.* die Stege —, to arrange the form for the press; ein Schiff zum Bau —, to put a ship on the stocks; *Sport.* die Hunde —, to put the dogs upon the scent; 5) a) to assess, determine, fix (taxes); b) to assess (one); wie hoch sind Sie angelegt? how much are you assessed? 6) *Comm.* ein Handlungsbuch —, to form a book; Sie werden höhere Preise — müssen, you will be obliged to consent to pay higher prices; wie viel würden Sie dafür —? how much could you afford to give for it?

II. *intr.* 1) to put to shore, to put in, to moor; to land; bei Einem —, to lay a ship alongside of another; zur Ladung —, to put to shore in order to commence loading (taking in a cargo), to make ready for loading, lading; 2) to take aim (auf *[with Acc.]*, at); 3) to mark (at cards).

III. *refl.* 1) to stick to, settle on: sich an ein feindliches Schiff —, to board, to grapple; sich — mit..., to quarrel with ...; 2) sich —, to dress one's self.

An'lege..., *in comp.* —schloß, *n.* padlock; —span, *m.* *Typ.* scale-board; *Carp.* feather-edge; —stege, *m. pl.* *Typ.* side-sticks, (Capitalstege) head-sides and foot-sticks.

An'leger, *(str.)* m. 1) establisher, &c., *see* Anlegen; 2) *see* Richtscheit.

An'legung, *(w.)* f. 1) the act of putting on, &c., *see* Anlegen & Anlage; 2) employment (of capitals), investment (of funds).

 Anl

An'lehen, *(str.)* n. loan, *see* Anleihe.

An'lehne, *(w.) f.* a thing to lean upon, back of a chair, &c.

An'lehnen, *(w.)* v. I. *tr.* to lean against; to support by; die Thür —, to leave the door upon the latch; den linken (rechten) Flügel einer Armee an ein Gehölz, einen Morast —, *Mil.* to have the left (right) wing of an army supported by a wood, a marsh; II. *refl.* 1) to lean, lie against, to recline; 2) *fig.* to fall back (upon).

An'lehn ..., *in comp.* —punct, *m. Mil.* support or defence afforded to an army by the ground; —wand, *f. Archit.* back-wall.

An'lehren, *(w.)* v. *tr.* 1) *see* Unterweisen; 2) †, to bind apprentice.

An'leihe, *(w.) f.* loan: öffentliche —, government-loan; eine — machen, to raise, contract, negotiate, make, conclude a loan; —papiere, *n. pl.* government bonds.

An'leihen, *(str.)* v. *tr.* to borrow, raise a [loan.]

An'leiher, *(str.)* m. 1) borrower; 2) lender.

An'leimen, *(w.)* v. *tr.* to glue on, to join with glue.

An'leite, *(w.) f. Law,* 1) *a)* personal inspection of a jury; *b)* the decree appointing such an inspection; 2) *provinc. a) see* Lehngeld; *b)* writ putting the plaintiff in possession of the defendant's goods, but not of their enjoyment; —brief, *f. see* Anleite, 2, *b.*

An'leiten, *(w.)* v. *tr.* 1) to guide, lead, conduct; 2) to direct, to instruct.

An'leiter, *(str.)* m. leader, &c., guide.

An'leitung, *(w.) f.* 1) leading, guidance; 2) direction, instruction, method; schooling; André's — zum Gebrauch des Pedals beim Orgelspiel, André's introduction to the use of the pedals in organ-playing; 3) *fig.* opportunity, occasion, inducement; nach — ihrer Vernunft, as reason directs them; nach — von ..., *Comm.* under the direction *or* management of ....

An'lenken, *(w.)* v. *tr.* to link.

An'lernen, *(w.)* v. *tr.* 1) to learn *or* acquire mechanically *or* by habit; 2) to teach (one a thing, Einen zu etwas *or* Einem etwas).

An'leuchten, *(w.)* v. *tr. & intr.* to hold a candle to *or* for ...; to direct light to, to cast light upon; to touch with a burning candle.

An'liebeln, *(w.)* v. *tr.* to look amorously on ..., to ogle; to caress, soothe.

An'liegen, *(str.)* v. *intr.* 1) *a)* to lie near *or* close to; a-d, *p. a.* adjacent *(also Geom.)*; *(anat.)* recumbent; *b) fig.* to be near to one's heart, to interest; 2) to border, to be adjacent *or* contiguous (an *[with Dat.]*, to); 3) to fit well, sit close; eng a-d, straight to the shape; 4) Einem —, to entreat, solicit; to importune; to urge; to ply; 5) sich angelegen sein lassen, to bestow care upon, to treat with earnest attention, to interest one's self in, for; 6) *Mar.-s.* wie liegt das Schiff an? how does the ship head? how winds the ship? ostwärts —, to stand (to head) to the east; seewärts —, to stand off, to stand for the offing.

An'liegen, v. s. *(str.) n.* 1) the lying close to, &c.; 2) *(or [l. u.]* **An'liegenheit,** *[w.] f.)* concern; care, solicitude; wish; request (Gesuch).

An'lispeln, *(w.)* v. *tr.* to address in a lisping manner.

An'loben, *(w.)* v. *tr.* to praise, to extol.

An'locken, *(w.)* v. *tr.* to allure, entice, to decoy, attract; a-d, *p. a.* alluring, &c., attractive. — **An'locker,** *(str.)* m. allurer, enticer.

An'lockung, *(w.) f.* allurement, enticement.

An'lodern, *(w.)* v. *intr. (aux.* sein) to flare up.

An'löthen, *(w.)* v. *tr.* to solder.

An'ludern, *(w.)* v. *tr. Sport.* to allure by means of baits, &c.

An'[illegible], *(w.)* v. *tr. see* [illegible], [illegible].

An'lügen, *(str.)* v. *tr.* to belie; to calumniate; to impute falsely.

An'lüstern, *(w.)* v. *tr. imp.* to excite an appetite, *or* desire in ....

An'luven, *(w.)* v. *intr. Mar.* to go to windward (to the weather-side); luv an! luff!

An'machen, *(w.)* v. *tr.* 1) to fasten, to bind, attach, *or* tie to, to knit on; 2) Feuer —, to make light (up) *or* kindle (a fire); 3) *a)* to mix (with water, &c.), to temper; mit Gewürzen —, to spice; mit Hopfen —, to hop; mit Weinstein —, to tartarise; *b)* to dilute; to slack (lime); to adulterate, to sophisticate; *c)* to dress (salad).

An'mahlen, *see* Anmalen.

An'mahnen, *(w.)* v. *tr. see* Ermahnen. — **An'mahnung,** *(w.) f.* exhortation, admonition; **A-sschreiben,** *n. Law,* letter monitory.

An'malen, *(w.)* v. *tr.* to paint, paint at, over.

An'marsch, *(str., pl.* An'märsche) m. (the act of) marching on, approaching, advance; im — sein, to be approaching, advancing.

An'marschiren, *(w.)* v. *intr. (aux.* sein) to march on, to advance.

An'maßen, *(w.)* v. *refl.* (sich *[Dat.]* etwas) to usurp; to assume, arrogate, presume, to pretend to, to lay claim to, to encroach on; er maßt sich zu viel an, he encroaches too far, he takes too much upon himself; angemaßt, *p. a.* (self-)assumed, &c.; a-d, *p. a.* presumptive, presuming, presumptuous, arrogant; assuming, self-assuming; imperious, domineering; insolent, haughty; das a-de Wesen, arrogance, &c., *see* Anmaßung.

An'maßlich, I. *adj. see* Anmaßend; II. **A-keit,** *(w.) f.* arrogant demeanour, arrogance.

An'maßung, *(w.) f.* usurpation, intrusion; impetuousness; assumption, arrogance; pretension, self-sufficiency; presumption.

An'mästen, *(w.)* v. I. *tr.* to fatten; II. *refl.* sich *(Acc.)* —, to get fat; die Ratte hat sich *(Dat.)* ein Bäuchlein angemästet *(Göthe, Faust)*, the rat had raised himself up a paunch.

An'mauern, *(w.)* v. *tr.* to build against (a wall, &c.).

An'maulen, *(w.)* v. *tr.* to grumble (mutter) against one; to pout at, to sulk at.

An'meckern, *(w.)* v. *tr.* to bleat at.

An'melden, *(w.)* v. *tr. & refl.* to announce, &c., *see* Melden; Appellation —, *Law,* to give notice of appeal.

An'melde ..., *in comp.* —rolle, *f. Theat.* the part of a servant who announces new comers, &c.; —stelle, *f.* a place *or* office where persons or things are registered.

An'melken, *(w.)* v. *tr.* to begin to milk; to milk (a cow that has calved) before letting the calf suck.

An'mengen, *(w.)* v. *tr.* to mix, mingle, blend. — **An'mengsel,** *(str.) n. Husb.* chopped straw, bran, shorts.

An'merkebuch, *(str., pl.* A-bücher) n. note-book, *see* Notizbuch.

An'merken, *(w.)* v. *tr.* 1) to mark, note, to put down, to write down, annotate, to jot, to item; *Comm.* die angemerkten Preise, the prices quoted; *T.* to saw up; 2) (Einem etwas) to remark, perceive (in one); sich *(Dat.)* — lassen, *see* Merken, I. 2; a-swerth, *adj.* noteworthy (Bemerkenswerth).

An'merker, *(str.)* m. marker, annotator, &c.

An'merklich, *adj. (l. u.)* observable, remarkable.

An'merkung, *(w.) f.* 1) remark, observation; 2) note, annotation; A-en zu ... machen, to comment on (an author); *fig.* to comment on, to pass observations (über *[with Acc.]*, on); a-swerth *or* a-swürdig, *see* Anmerkenswerth.

An'messen, *(str.)* v. *tr.* 1) Einem etwas —, to take one's measure for ...; sich *(Dat.)* einen Rock &c. — lassen, to have one's measure taken or to get measured for a coat, &c.; ich habe mir einen Rock — lassen, I have had my measure taken for a coat; laß ihm sogleich einen

An'nehmen, (*str.*) v. I. *tr.* 1) *a)* to take (to one's self); to accept, to receive; *b)* to take in (work); *c)* to take (a direction): daß er den Königstitel angenommen haben würde, ist zweifellos, that he would have taken the title of king there is no doubt; einen Antrag —, to engage, to close with an offer; eine Entschuldigung —, to take, to admit of an excuse; *Sport.* die Fährte —, to take (up) the scent; hier zu Lande wird das Geld nicht angenommen, this money is not current in this country; 2) to take for granted, to suppose; 3) to engage; sich — lassen, to engage; to enlist (as a soldier); 4) to embrace, adopt (an opinion), to espouse (a doctrine, &c.); (als or für wahr) to enter into, to subscribe to, to admit, to approve of; der angenommene Münzfuß, the approved standard; to grant; to consent to; einen Vorschlag —, to agree (accede to) a proposal; ihn nicht —, to decline it; keine Entschuldigungen — wollen, to refuse to listen to, or to accept any excuses (apologies); Rath —, to take advice; 5) (an Kindes Statt) to adopt; 6) *Chem.* to absorb; Farbe —, to imbibe colour; to take the dye; nicht —, not to take colour; 7) *Comm.* to accept, honour (a draft), to protect, to pay (show) due honour or protection; nicht —, to refuse acceptance; nicht angenommen, unaccepted; Besuche —, to receive or to see company; 8) eine Gestalt —, to assume (a shape, &c.); to put on (a scornful air, &c.); to affect (humility, &c.); eine Gewohnheit —, to contract, acquire a habit; 9) *Sport.* die Sau nimmt den Jäger an, the sow assails the huntsman.

II. *refl.* 1) *a)* (sich (*Acc.*) einer Person or Sache (*Gen.*) —) to interest one's self in or for, to take care of (for), to assist; (eifrig) to stickle for; sich Jemandes Sache —, to espouse a person's cause; *b)* to enter into, to attend, to pay attention to (one's business), to ply (one's trade, &c.); 2) sich (*Dat.*) eine Sache —, to take or apply a thing to one's self, to lay a thing to one's own account; annehmbar, supposable; angenommen (or gesetzt), daß..., suppose, *adj.* hypothetical; suppositive.

An'nehmenswerth, *adj.* see Annehmbar.

An'nehmer, (*str.*) m. *Comm.* 1) acceptor, drawee; 2) shipwright (as the contracting party with the ship's husband).

An'nehmlich, I. *adj.* 1) see Annehmbar, acceptable; 2) see Angenehm; II. A-keit, (*w.*) f. 1) see Annehmbarkeit; 2) amenity; charm: cf. Anmuth; pleasure, delight; A-keiten, *pl.* sweets, comforts (of life).

An'neigen, (*w.*) v. I. *tr.* to incline, lean to; II. *refl.* 1) *a)* to lean on, against; *b)* to converge; 2) see sich Anschmeicheln.

An'neigung, (*w.*) f. the (act of) inclining, &c.; A-[illegible], n. *T.* a peculiar process usual with dyers in rendering the colours fixed; A-winkel, m. *Geom.* see Neigungswinkel.

An'nesteln, (*w.*) v. *tr.* to lace, to tie with points or tags. [little.

An'netzen, (*w.*) v. *tr.* to wet, to moisten a

An'netzpinsel, (*str.*) m. *Mas.* brush.

An'nicken, (*w.*) v. *tr.* to nod at.

An'nieten, (*w.*) v. *tr.* to rivet to.

An'nisten, (*w.*) v. *refl.* sich —, to build a nest, to nestle; *fig.* to settle. [niversaries.

* **[illegible],** *pl.* (*Lat.*) *Rom. Cath.* an-

* **[illegible],** *adv.* (*Lat.*) *abbr.* Ao., in the year [illegible].

[illegible], *adv.* as yet, still now.

[illegible], (*w.*) f. (*Fr.*), [illegible] v. *tr.* see Anzeigen, Angeben.

[illegible] f. (*Lat.*) *Comm.* A-en, *pl.* [illegible] annuities; (jährliche Abgaben) [illegible]; consolidirte —, consolidated [illegible].

[illegible] f. (*Lat.*) annulment; [illegible] annulling; [illegible]; defeasance.

* **Annullir'bar,** *adj.* defeasible. — **Annulli'ren,** (*w.*) v. *tr.* to annul, *cf.* Aufheben, 3, *b.* — **Annulli'rung,** (*w.*) f. annulment.

* **Ano'de,** (*w.*) f. (*Gr.*) *Electr.* anode (*opp.* Kathode).

An'öhren, (*w.*) v. *tr.* to furnish with an eye (as a needle, &c.); *fig.* sich (*Dat.*) —, to attach to one's self.

An'ölen, (*w.*) v. *tr.* to oil, paint with oil.

* **Anomalie',** (*w.*) (*Lat.-Gr.*) f. anomaly, irregularity. — **Anoma'lisch,** *adj.* anomalous.

* **Anonym',** **Anony'misch,** *adj.* (*Gr.*) anonymous: a-e Arterie, *Anat.* innominate artery.

* **Ano'nymus,** (*Lat.* [*from the Gr.*], *pl.* Ano'nymi) m. anonymous writer; *cont.* nameless person, fellow.

An'ordnen, (*w.*) v. *tr.* 1) to bespeak, order; institute; to appoint, fix (a certain time); 2) to dispose, regulate, to arrange; to direct, to conduct; to marshal.

An'ordner, (*str.*) m. regulator, disposer, &c.

An'ordnung, (*w.*) f. the (act of) ordering, &c.; direction, disposal, order; disposition, regulation, arrangement, adjustment, preparation; appointment; instruction; injunction; auf — (*Acc.*), by the direction.

* **Anorga'nisch,** *adj.* (*Gr.*) *T.* inorganic.

An'packen, (*w.*) v. *tr.* to lay hold of, to seize, catch, grasp, gripe, to attack, to collar (*also fig.*).

An'pappen, (*w.*) v. *tr.* to paste on, to paste up.

An'passen, (*w.*) v. I. *tr.* 1) to fit, suit, accommodate, adapt, to conform, adjust, square; to fashion; 2) to fit or try on (clothes, &c.); ein Ereigniß der Prophezeiung —, to adjust an event to the prediction; II. *intr.* to be adapted to a thing, to fit (Passen). — **An'passung,** (*w.*) f. the (act of) fitting, accommodation, &c.; A-fläche, f. *Mech.* chipping-piece of the flanch of a pipe (*Tolh.*).

An'patschen, (*w.*) v. *intr.* (*aux.* sein) (*with* an [*& Acc.*]) to splash or fall plashing against.

An'pauken, (*w.*) v. *intr.* (*aux.* haben) (*with* an [*& Acc.*]) to drum at, against.

An'peitschen, (*w.*) v. *tr.* to whip on.

An'pfahl, (*str.*) m. *Min.* upper prop of a drift.

An'pfählen, (*w.*) v. *tr.* 1) to pale up; 2) to empale, to prop.

An'pfeifen, (*str.*) v. I. *tr.* to whistle at; to hiss at; II. *intr.* (angepfiffen kommen) to approach whistling.

An'pflanzen, (*w.*) v. *tr.* to plant, cultivate; to lay out; *refl.* sich —, to settle.

An'pflanzer, (*str.*) m. planter, settler.

An'pflanzung, (*w.*) f. 1) the (act of) planting, &c.; 2) *a)* plantation; settlement; *b)* (von Gesträuch) shrubbery.

An'pflöcken, (*w.*) v. *tr.* to peg, to pin, to fasten with pegs or pins.

An'pflügen, (*w.*) v. I. *tr.* 1) (*also intr.*) to begin ploughing; 2) to join by ploughing; II. *intr.* to drive against something in ploughing.

An'pfropfen, (*w.*) v. *tr.* to inoculate, to insert, to graft; *fig.* sich (*Dat.*) den Magen —, to cram one's stomach.

An'pichen, (*w.*) v. *tr.* to pitch; to pitch to.

An'picken, (*w.*) v. *tr.* to peck (fruits).

An'pinkeln, (*w.*) v. *tr.* see Anpissen.

An'pinseln, (*w.*) v. *tr.* to paint, daub with a brush.

An'pissen, (*w.*) v. *tr.* to piss at, against, on.

An'placken, (*str.*) n. (das Pfropfen durch —) beaked-grafting.

An'plärren, (*w.*) v. *tr.* *coll.* to bawl at.

An'plätzen, **An'platzen,** (*w.*) v. *tr.* see Anschalmen.

An'plappern, (*w.*) v. *tr.* to prattle at.

An'platten, (*w.*) see Anschilden.

An'platzen, (*w.*) v. *intr.* (*aux.* sein) 1) to strike or burst against; 2) to begin to crack; *coll.* mit einer Nachricht angeplatzt kommen, to burst out with a piece of news.

An'pochen, (*w.*) v. *intr.* & *tr.* see Anklopfen.

An'poltern, (*w.*) v. I. *intr.* to knock violently at the door; angepoltert kommen, *coll.* to come or approach boisterously; II. *tr.* to address in a blustering, boisterous manner.

An'poschen, (*w.*) v. *tr.* *Sport.* see Ankörnen.

An'posten, (*w.*) v. *tr.* *Forest.* see Abposten.

An'prägen, (*w.*) v. *tr.* to fix by an impression.

An'prall, (*str.*) m. a bounding against, bounce; *Mil.* see Choci —punct, m. *Hydr.* the point or place against which the principal force of the water is directed; —winkel, m. *Phys.* angle of reflexion.

An'prallen, (*w.*) v. *intr.* (*aux.* sein) to bound or strike against.

An'prasseln, (*w.*) v. *intr.* (*aux.* sein) to crackle against (of fire). [at, to.

An'predigen, (*w.*) v. *tr.* *tnol.* & *cont.* to preach

An'preisen, (*str.*) v. *tr.* (Einem etwas) to praise, commend, recommend, to extol; *cont.* to puff. [bound against.

An'prellen, (*w.*) v. *tr.* to dash, to make to

An'pressen, (*w.*) v. *tr.* (*with* an [*& Acc.*]) to press or squeeze against.

An'prickeln, (*w.*) v. *tr.* to drive on, to impel by prickling; *fig.* to incite, to urge on.

An'proben, **An'probiren,** (*w.*) v. *tr.* see Anversuchen.

An'pudern, (*w.*) v. *tr.* to cover with powder.

An'pumpen, (*w.*) v. *tr.* *coll.* to borrow money of ....

An'purzeln, (*w.*) v. *intr.* angepurzelt kommen, *coll.* to come or approach reeling, rolling.

An'pusten, (*w.*) v. *tr.* to blow (at).

An'putz, (*str.*) m. finery, dress; the act of dressing, &c.; *T.* architectural ornaments.

An'putzen, (*w.*) v. I. *tr.* 1) to dress finely, to adorn; 2) to trick out; II. *refl.* to deck one's self out, put on one's best (or holiday) clothes.

An'quaken, (*w.*) v. *tr.* to croak at.

An'quäken, (*w.*) v. *tr.* to squeak, quack at.

An'qualmen, (*w.*) v. *tr.* *fam.* to blow the smoke (of tobacco) into one's face.

An'quetschen, (*w.*) v. *tr.* to squeeze against.

An'quieken, (*w.*) v. *tr.* to squeak at.

An'quicken, (*w.*) v. *tr.* *Metall.* to amalgamate.

An'quickfaß, n. barrel for amalgamation.

An'quicksilber, n. impure silver.

An'quickung, (*w.*) f. amalgamation.

An'racken, (*w.*) v. *tr.* *Mar.* to fasten (the sails) with a parrel.

An'rahmen, (*w.*) v. *intr.* to border on, upon.

An'rainen, (*w.*) v. *intr.* to border upon.

An'räken, (*w.*) v. *intr.* *Mar.* to run aground.

An'rammen, **An'rammeln,** (*w.*) v. *tr.* to fasten by ramming, to ram down tight.

An'ranken, (*w.*) v. I. *tr.* to fasten by means of tendrils; II. *refl.* to cling to, twine round.

An'raspeln, (*w.*) v. *tr.* to begin to rasp; to rasp a little.

An'rasseln, (*w.*) v. I. *tr.* to rattle at, against; II. *intr.* angerasselt kommen, to approach with a rattling noise.

An'rathen, (*str.*) I. v. *tr.* (Einem etwas) to recommend, to advise; to suggest; II. s. (*str.*) n. or **An'rathung,** (*w.*) f. (*nominale* **An'rath,** m.) advice, recommendation.

An'räthig, *adj.* *with* sein, to advise; *with* machen, to make advisable.

An'rauchen, (*w.*) v. *tr.* 1) to season by smoking; 2) *a)* to smoke (a pipe) for the first time, to begin to smoke (it); *b)* to give a brownish colour to (a meerschaum-bowl) by smoking: angeraucht, *p. a.* smoke-coloured.

An'räuchern, (*w.*) v. *tr.* 1) to drive smoke or perfume against; 2) to smoke a little; 3) *Chem.* to fumigate.

An'rauschen, (*w.*) v. I. *intr.* to rush on, against; (angerauscht kommen) to approach

[illegible] see moderate; in — bringen, to place to account; 7) tendency, disposition; er hat einen — zum Starkwerden, he inclines to corpulency; ein — zur Preissteigerung, a beginning of a rise in prices; II. in comp. —feile, f. Horol. (safe edge) flat-file, hand-file; —größe, f. Math. differential quantity; —preis, m. [illegible] tension; —rechnung, f. differential method, or calculus; —stück, n. see Ansatz, 3.

An'säuern, (w.) v. tr. to sour; to mix with leaven; Chem. to acidify, acidulate.

An'saufen, (str.) v. refl. vulg. to drink immoderately, fam. to drink like a sponge.

An'saugen, (w. & str.) v. I. tr. & intr. to suck; — lassen (eine Pumpe), to fetch (a pump), see Anheben; II. refl. to suck fast; der Blutegel hat sich angesogen, the leech has taken.

An'sauger, (str.) m. Ichth. sucking-fish (Echeneis remora L.).

An'säuseln, (w.) v. tr. to touch, to fan (of the wind); angesäuselt, p. a. slang, half-drunk, half seas-over.

An'sausen, (w.) v. intr. (aux. sein) to rush up, to buzz against. [rub.

An'schaben, (w.) v. tr. to begin to scrape or

An'schaffen, I. v. tr. (str.) see Anerschaffen; II. (w.) (Einem [refl. sich] etwas) to procure, to furnish one's self with, to supply, find, to lay one's self in or with ..., to purvey, provide, buy to get in, lay in, put up (goods, &c.), to purchase, to buy; Comm. to remit, to make, or to provide remittances or provisions; sich (Dat.) zu viel Waare —, to overstock one's self; sie wollen sich (Dat.) eine Equipage —, they are going to set up (keep) their carriage; Lebensmittel —, to cater; Bediente —, to engage; Geld zu etwas —, to find money for; 3) to order, bespeak, see Bestellen; 4) to overlook (as overseer of works).

An'schaffer, (str.) m. purveyor, furnisher, &c.; Comm. remitter, overseer (of works, in factories, &c.).

An'schaffung, (w.) f. purveyance, providing, furnishing with; Comm. -s. remittance, provision; — machen, see Anschaffen, II. (Comm.); [illegible] — machen, to make remittances in first [illegible] bills or paper.

An'schäften, (w.) v. tr. to provide with a shaft; to mount, stock (a gun); Shoe-m. to put new legs (to boots); Carp. see Schäften; [illegible] to put the kill on.

An'schälen, (w.) v. tr. see Abschalmen.

An'schallen, (w.) v. intr. (aux. haben) to strike against (of sound).

An'schalmen, see Anlaschen, Abschalmen.

An'scharen, (w.) v. tr. Min. to dispose [illegible] for working. [one lode.

An'scharen, (w.) v. refl. Min. to unite in

An'scharfen, (w.) v. intr. to graze upon, to touch superficially.

An'scharren, (w.) v. I. tr. (with an [& Acc.]) to scrape close to; to draw near by raking; II. intr. to scratch at; III. refl. see Anscharren.

An'schauen, (w.) v. tr. 1) to look at, to view, behold, contemplate; to gaze at (admiringly, &c.); 2) a) to consider; b) to perceive, [illegible] by intuition.

An'schauen, n. & (str.) n. contemplation, [illegible]; a-swürdig, adj. worthy [illegible]

An'schauend, p. a. intuitive, contemplative; [illegible] Erkenntniß, an intuitive perception; [illegible] Erkenntniß aller Dinge haben, to see [illegible] intuitively. [eyer.

An'schauer, (str.) m. looker on, beholder,

An'schaufeln, (w.) v. tr. to put to with a [illegible] shovel up or against.

An'schaulich, I. adj. 1) perceptible; 2) [illegible] distinct, clear, plain; 3) see An[illegible] [illegible], to render plain or intuiti[illegible] [illegible] II. A-keit, (w.) [illegible] 2) distinctness, clear-ness; 3) the quality of being perceived intuitively.

An'schauung, (w.) f. 1) contemplation, view; inspection; 2) intuitive vision, intuition; 3) (A-sweise) mode of viewing things; A-slehre, f. doctrine of instruction by means of which the intuitive powers of children are awakened; A-sunterricht, m. method followed in the A-slehre, which see, method of intuitive instruction; (a course, &c. of) object-lessons; A-svermögen, n. intuitive power.

An'schäumen, (w.) v. intr. (aux. sein) to foam against.

An'scheeren [pr. an'schēren], see Anscheren.

An'schein, (str.) m. appearance; 1) semblance, outward show; 2) likeliness, likelihood, probability; es ist aller — dazu, there is every appearance of it; allem A-e nach, in all likelihood; auf den ersten —, at first view; nach dem A-e zu urtheilen, to judge from appearances; von gutem —, of good promise, auspicious.

An'scheinen, (str.) v. I. tr. & intr. to shine upon; II. intr. to appear; a-d, p. a. (An'scheinlich, adj.) apparent, seeming (adv. —ly).

An'schellen, (w.) v. tr. & intr. to ring the bell. Doom.

An'schēre, (w.) f. Weav. warp, warping

An'schēren, v. tr. I. (w.) 1) Weav. to warp; 2) Mar. to warp (a rope); 3) Join. to let in, to join with slit and tongue; II. (str.) to begin to shave; to shave or shear a little.

An'schērpfahl, (str., pl. A-pfähle) m. Weav. warping post; Rope-m. rack for warping ropes.

An'schichten, see Aufschichten.

An'schicken, (w.) v. refl. (zu etwas) 1) to prepare, to make arrangements (for); 2) to begin, set (be) about a thing, to set or compose one's self to; to be going (to write, &c.); 3) to be disposed for; er schickt sich gut dazu an, he goes the right way to work.

An'schieben, (str.) v. I. tr. (with an [& Acc.]) 1) to shove on, to push against; 2) to join or connect by moving up to an object; II. intr. Gam. to bowl first (at ninepins).

An'schiebetisch, (str.) m. sliding-frame table.

An'schieber, (str.) m. 1) one who puts something to, &c.; 2) what is put to (leaf of a table, &c.); (An'schiebring, m.) runner (of an umbrella); T. sking-piece.

An'schielen, (w.) v. tr. to squint at, look asquint upon, to leer at or upon, to ogle.

An'schienen, (w.) v. tr. to fix or join by means of a cleat, an iron band, &c.; Surg. to splint; fig. to add.

An'schießen, (str.) v. I. tr. 1) to shoot, wound (by shooting); 2) T. to join; Tail. to sew to; 3) Typ. to print to; 4) eine Flinte —, to try a gun; fig. angeschossen sein, fam. a) to be in love; b) to be tipsy; c) to have a little touch of folly (fam. to have a bee in one's head); II. intr. 1) to shoot first, to have the first shot; (aux. sein:) 2) (anlaufen) to rush or run against; 3) to shoot forth (as water, &c.); 4) to be adjacent; 5) Chem. (in Krystallen —) to crystallise, to shoot into crystals; das —, s. s. (str.) n. (l. u.: An'schießung, [w.] f.) crystallisation.

An'schieß ..., in comp. —kessel, m. Befin. filler; —pinsel, m. T. gilding brush.

An'schiffen, (w.) v. intr. (aux. sein) (with an [& Acc.]) to ship to, approach (with a ship); an eine Insel —, to touch at an island.

An'schiften, (w.) v. tr. to join (together); An'schiftstück, (str.) n. joining piece.

An'schilden, (w.) v. tr. Gard. to scutcheon-graft; Sport. to stalk (a deer, &c.).

An'schimmeln, (w.) v. intr. (aux. sein) to grow mouldy.

An'schimmern, (w.) v. tr. to glimmer, shine faintly upon.

An'schirren, (w.) v. tr. to harness; intr. to put on the harness, cf. Anspannen.

An'schlag, I. (str., pl. An'schläge) m. 1) (the act of) striking at, &c., stroke; 2) a) (the act of) affixing, posting up; b) Tail. (the act of) basting; c) (the act of) aiming; 3) (—zettel) bill set or posted up; posting-bill, placard, advertisement; coll. poster; 4) statement, calculation, computation, estimate; estimation, valuation; 5) plan, project, design, plot, device; (böser —) complot, underplot; einen (bösen) — auf (with Acc.) or gegen ... machen, to conspire against ...; einen — auf Jemands Leben machen, to attempt a person's life; 6) advice, counsel; 7) T. rabbet; 8) a) Horol. (or —stift) warning-piece; b) Typ. see Dummbaum; c) the upper part of a dam; d) the cheek of a saw; 9) Mill. mill-clapper, mill-clack; 10) Mus. a) stop; b) manner of touching an instrument, touch, finger; 11) (A-ort) the place against which something strikes; 12) butt-end of a gun; im A-e (zum Verkaufe), put up for sale; in — bringen, to take into account; to make allowance for; in — kommen, see in Betracht kommen; meinem vorläufigen A-e nach, on a rough estimate I made.

An'schlageisen, (str.) n. T. bolt-chisel, Lock-sm. carp's tongue.

An'schlagen, (str.) v. I. tr. 1) (an etwas) to strike at, upon, or against, to knock at; 2) to clap on, to fasten, to nail to, at (on); Mar. to bend (a sail) to its yard; Cloth. to put on the tenter; Hosiery, to begin (a stocking); 3) Sew. to baste; 4) Mar. to splice; 5) to affix, placard, to post up (bills, placards); Placate wurden an die Thore angeschlagen, placards were posted upon the gates; 6) to set out, to put up (for sale); 7) (den Werth einer Sache abschätzen) to rate, value, estimate (auf [with Acc.], at); zu niedrig —, to underrate, understate; zu hoch —, to overrate, &c.; 8) to toll (the bell); to touch upon (a string, &c.); 9) Feuer, Licht —, to strike fire, a light; 10) Mus. den Ton —, to give the key-note; 11) ein Gewehr —, to level, point, present aim (a musket; auf [with Acc.], at); 12) Forest. to blaze (trees), see Ablaschen.

II. intr. 1) (aux. sein) to fall against, strike, or dash against; 2) (aux. haben) a) (anfangen zu schlagen) to begin to strike; to chime, to toll; (von Thüren) to slam; Gam. to play at span-counter (as boys); b) (von Arzneien) to operate, take effect; c) to prevail; to take; to agree (of food, &c.); to succeed (well), prosper; Alles schlägt ihm wohl an, every thing he undertakes thrives with him; es schlägt nichts mehr bei ihm an, he is past mending; es wird —, it will take; d) to begin to sing, or to chirp (of birds); Sport. to call, to bark, to bay, to cry, to give tongue, to open; zur unrechten Zeit —, to babble.

III. v. s. (str.) n. 1) the (act of) striking at, against, &c. cf. v.; 2) Gam. (an der Mauer) span-counter, span-farthing; 3) Join. boxing; 4) (der See) wash, surf of the sea; 5) Sport. lapping, calling, &c.; 6) cutting (of horses).

An'schläger, (str.) m. 1) he or that which strikes; 2) fig. projector, speculator; 3) Mus. jack (of a pianoforte, &c.) (Fr. sautereau); 4) Min. onsetter, hanger-on.

An'schlägig, An'schläglich, adj. inventive, ingenious, clever, full of devices.

An'schlag ..., in comp. —faden, m. basting-thread; —holz, n. see Anschlag, 9; —lineal, n. T-ruler, T-square; —(s)rad, n. Horol. warning-wheel; —stift, m. T. pin; —winkel, m. T. square, bevel.

An'schlämmen, (w.) v. I. tr. to mire, to fill with mud; to depose mud; Bäume —, to fill with diluted earth the hole into which young trees have been planted; II. refl. to be choked up with mud, to get muddy.

An'ſchlenkern, see Anſchlendern.

An'ſchleichen, *(str.)* v. *intr.* (*aux.* ſein) to creep *or* steal near slowly and gently: angeſchlichen kommen, to come on creepingly, sneakingly.

An'ſchleifen, I. *(str.)* v. *tr.* 1) to begin to grind; to set an edge on; eine Spitze —, to grind to a point; II. *(w.)* v. *tr.* 1) (auf der Schleife) to bring or to transport (on a sledge); 2) to fasten by a slip-knot.

An'ſchlemmen, see Anſchlämmen.

An'ſchlendern, *(w.)* v. *intr.* (*aux.* ſein) (*gener.* angeſchlendert kommen) to come trailing on *or* along, to approach *or* draw near saunteringly.

An'ſchlenkern, *(w.)* v. *tr.* to throw at, to pitch at; to fling against.

An'ſchleppen, *(w.)* v. *tr.* to drag along.

An'ſchleudern, *(w.)* v. *tr.* (*gener. with* an & *Acc.*) to fling at *or* against.

An'ſchlichten, *(w.)* v. *tr.* 1) *T.* to pile up: to lay up smooth and even against a plane; 2) *Weav.* to spread over with weaver's starch.

An'ſchlicken, *(w.)* v. see Anſchlämmen.

An'ſchließen, *(str.)* v. I. *tr.* 1) to chain to, to fix with a lock; to tack; 2) to add, annex, enclose: II. *refl.* (*with* an & *Acc.*) *a)* to join *or* attach one's self to, to follow, to join; der Frühzug ſchließt ſich an den Schnellzug an, the early train connects with the express train; *b) fig.* to conform to, to sympathise with; III. *intr.* 1) to fit close, tight; 2) to sit close *or* closely (on horseback).

An'ſchlingen, *(str.)* v. *tr.* to fasten to with a string *or* noose.

An'ſchlitzen, *(w.)* v. *tr.* to make a slit in a thing, to slit a little.

An'ſchluß, *(str., pl.* An'ſchlüſſe) *m.* 1) fit; 2) thing annexed, enclosed, &c.; 3) joining, accession; 4) connexion; der — von Eiſenbahnzügen, the connexion of railway-trains; der Eilzug hat — in B., the fast train times at B. with other trains (*Rob. & Gr.*); der Perſonenzug hat keinen —, the ordinary train goes no further; Poſt—, connexion with the diligence (mail); 5) enclosure, enclosed letter; —bahn, *f. Railw.* junction railway.

An'ſchmauchen, *(w.)* v. *tr. coll.* to blow the smoke against, to smoke.

An'ſchmauchung, *(w.) f. Min.* slight junction (*Tech.*).

An'ſchmecken, *(w.)* v. *tr.* 1) *a)* to taste; *b)* to know by the taste; 2) *Sport.* to scent.

An'ſchmeicheln, *(w.)* v. I. *tr.* 1) to address with flatteries; 2) to attribute flatteringly; II. *refl.* to insinuate one's self (*with Dat. or* bei).

An'ſchmeißen, *(str.)* v. *vulg.* I. *tr.* 1) see Anwerfen; 2) to soil; II. *intr.* (*aux.* haben) to dash against.

An'ſchmelzen, v. I. *(str.) intr.* (*aux.* ſein) to adhere by melting, to get melted; II. *(w. & str.) tr.* 1) to begin to melt; 2) to fasten by melting.

An'ſchmettern, *(w.)* v. *tr. & intr.* (*aux.* haben & ſein) to peal against (of trumpets); to strike *or* dash against violently.

An'ſchmieden, *(w.)* v. *tr.* 1) to join by forging; to shut together; 2) (einen Verbrecher) to fetter, to chain to, to clap up in irons.

An'ſchmiegen, *(w.)* v. I. *tr.* to bend to, press to, join closely; *fig.* to adapt; II. *refl.* 1) to stick close, to cling, to nestle, *coll.* to snug (an (*with Acc.*), to); 2) *fig.* to accommodate one's self to, to follow closely.

An'ſchmieren, *(w.)* v. *tr.* 1) to daub, to blot, to scribble against, besmear; 2) *vulg.* *a) refl.* see ſich Anbringen; *b) aa)* see Aufſchmieren; *bb)* to cheat (one).

An'ſchminken, *(w.)* v. *tr.* to paint, to rouge; *fig.* ſich (*Dat.*) —, see Anheucheln.

An'ſchmitzen, *(w.)* v. *tr.* to soil.

An'ſchmollen, *(w.)* v. *tr.* to look surly at (one); to pout at, on, *or* upon . . .

An'ſchm[illegible], *(w.)* v. *tr. Angl.* see Schm[illegible].

An'ſchmunzeln, *(w.)* v. *tr.* to smirk at ....

An'ſchmutzen, *(w.)* v. *tr.* to soil.

An'ſchnäbeln, v. s. *(str.) n. Sport.* (der Hähne) beaking.

An'ſchnallen, *(w.)* v. *tr.* to buckle on, to fasten with buckles; ſich (*Dat.*) etwas —, *vulg.* to get hold of a thing.

An'ſchnallſporn, *(str.) m.* jack-boot spur, rough-rider's spur.

An'ſchnappen, *(w.)* v. *tr.* to snap at....

An'ſchnarchen, **An'ſchnauzen**, *(w.)* v. *tr. vulg.* to snarl at, growl at; to snap (one) short.

An'ſchnarcher, *(str.) m. vulg.* snap-short.

An'ſchnarren, *(w.)* v. *tr.* to address in a rattling tone.

An'ſchnattern, *(w.)* v. *tr.* to cackle at....

An'ſchnauben, v. I. *(str.) intr.* (*aux.* ſein) to approach snorting, blowing and puffing; II. *(w. & str.) tr.* 1) to snort at; 2) to address harshly, to snub, to take up short.

An'ſchnauzen, *(w.)* v. see Anſchnarchen.

An'ſchneidemeſſer, *(str.) n.* carving knife.

An'ſchneiden, *(str.)* v. *tr.* 1) to give the first cut to, to cut (into), to carve; Zeug —, to cut stuffs; 2) to fit by cutting; 3) (*l. u.*) auf dem Kerbholz —, to notch, to score; 4) *Min.* to score down (the amount of labour done); 5) *Sport. for* Antreffen, I. 1; das Buch iſt angeſchnitten, *Bookb.* the work bleeds.

An'ſchneidezettel, *m.* see Anſchnittbogen.

An'ſchneien, *(w.)* v. *intr.* (*with* an & *Acc.*) to snow against....

An'ſchnellen, *(w.)* v. I. *tr.* to jerk against; II. *intr.* (*aux.* ſein) to fly against.

An'ſchniegeln, *(w.)* v. *tr. & refl. fam.* to deck out.

An'ſchnitt, *(str.) m.* 1) first cut, cut: das Tuch iſt hart im —, the cloth is a hard cut (*Rob. & Gr.*); 2) nick, notch, scotch; 3) *Min.* statement of labour done; den — halten: *a)* to have such a statement certified by the burgomaster of the district; *b)* to pay miners their wages; —bogen, *m. Min.* list of accounts; —buch, *n. Min.* book of accounts; —regiſter, *n.* see —bogen; —ſchere, *f. Glas.* small scissors.

An'ſchnüffeln, **An'ſchnubbern**, *(w.)* v. *tr.* to smell at (like dogs).

An'ſchnüren, *(w.)* v. *tr.* 1) *a)* to lace, string; to fasten; *b)* to string (one) to the rack, &c.; 2) *fig. vulg.* (Einem etwas) to palm (something) upon (one).

An'ſchnurren, *(w.)* v. *tr.* 1) to purr at; 2) *slang*, to beg, *cf.* Anfechten, 2.

An'ſchnürung, *(w.) f. T.* the act of cording, tying, &c.

An'ſchobern, *(w.)* v. *tr.* to pile up like a stack.

An'ſchönen, *(w.)* v. *refl.* to become clear (of liquids).

* **Anſcho've**, see Anchove.

An'ſchrauben, *(w.)* v. *tr.* to screw, screw on or up; zum — (*p. a.*) (eingerichtet), for screwing on (up), for fastening with a screw.

An'ſchrecken, *(w.)* v. *tr. Sport.* to frighten (by whistling at, &c.).

An'ſchreiben, *(str.)* v. *tr.* 1) to write down, down, set down; (mit Kreide) to chalk put (mit Bleiſtift) to pencil down; 2) *a)* (Einem etwas) to put to one's account, to charge in one's bill; Porto —, to charge postage; wir laſſen nichts —, we do not buy on credit; *b)* to book down: Einen als Schuldner —, to bring some one in one's books; hoch angeſchrieben ſtehen, 1) (of debtors) to stand high in one's books; 2) *or* gut bei Einem angeſchrieben ſtehen, *fig.* to be in favour, to stand well with one; to be in one's good books.

An'ſchreiben, s. s. *(str.) n.* 1) (the act of) writing down, &c.; 2) letter; written application; *Law*, see Reſcript.

An'ſchreiber, *(str.) m.* marker.

An'spießen, *(w.) v. tr.* to spit, broach: to put upon the spit; to pierce with a spear; to empale (a punishment in the East).

An'spinnen, *(str.) v.* I. *tr.* 1) to spin together, spin to; 2) to begin to spin; 3) *a) fig.* to begin (a narrative, correspondence, &c.); *b)* to contrive, lay (a plot, conspiracy), *cf.* Anzetteln; *c)* to cause; II. *refl.* 1) to spin or fasten the web on to; 2) to originate, begin.

An'spitzen, *(w.) v. tr.* to point, to furnish with a point; *T. & Mar.* to splice (a rope); wieder —, to new-point.

An'splissen, *(w.) v. tr. Mar.* to splice (a rope).

An'splittern, *(w.) v.* I. *tr.* to splinter, begin to split; II. *intr.* (*aux.* sein) to splinter, shiver against.

An'spornen, *(w.) v. tr.* 1) to clap (put) spurs to; 2) *fig.* to spur on; to stir up, to incite.

An'spornung, *(w.) f.* (the act of) spurring on, &c.; incitement.

An'spötteln, An'spotten, *(w.) v. tr.* to address mockingly, to mock at, to jeer.

An'sprache, *(w.) f.* 1) address, speech; 2) *Law,* legal claim; 3) *Mus.* intonation, sound; die Geige hat eine gute —, the violin sounds easily; zur — bringen, to intone, to regulate the intonation of…, *cf.* Ansprechen lassen.

An'sprachzimmer, *(str.) n.* (front) parlour.

An'sprechen, *(str.) v.* I. *tr.* 1) to accost, address; 2) *Sport.* to call; 3) *Law,* to indite; 4) *fig.* to please, to interest; to touch; 5) *a)* etwas —, to lay claim to, to claim, to appeal to (one's assistance, &c.), to require; *b)* (Einen) um (*with Acc.*) —, to beg (something) of, ask (one) for; II. *intr.* 1) (bei Einem) to call (on), to look in (upon one); 2) *Mus.* to give (emit) a sound, to sound; gut, leicht —, to have a good, easy touch; 3) *see* Angeben, III. 2; eine Orgelpfeife — lassen, to voice the pipe of an organ; das —, *s. a.* (*str.*) *n.* 1) the act of speaking to, &c.; 2) *Sport.* calling or sporting nomenclature; a-d, *p. a.* pleasing, prepossessing.

An'spreizen, *(w.) v.* I. *tr.* to fix by spreading out; II. *refl.* to sprawl against, to place one's hands and feet firmly against.

An'sprecher, *(str.) m. An. Law,* plaintiff; defendant.

An'sprengen, *(w.) v.* I. *tr.* 1) to begin to burst, blast; 2) to make to strike against; to drive against (by explosion); 3) *a)* to cause to run or to spring forward; to put (a horse) into a gallop; *b)* to ride against in full speed; 4) to besprinkle, to wet, to water; II. *intr.* (*aux.* sein) (*gener.* angesprengt kommen) to approach or sweep along in full gallop.

An'springen, *(str.) v. intr.* I. (*aux.* sein) 1) to begin to spring, to leap, or to jump; 2) (*with* an & *Acc.*) to bounce (against), fly (against); 3) to crack, burst a little; II. (*aux.* haben) to take the first leap, to leap first.

An'spritzen, *(w.) v.* I. *tr.* to besprinkle, splash, dash, or spatter (with a liquid, as dirty water, &c.); II. *intr.* (*aux.* sein) to plash, to be dashed against.

† **An'spruchig,** *adj.* litigious.

An'spruch, *(str., pl.* An'sprüche*) m.* 1) address, act of speaking to; 2) claim, pretension, demand, title (auf, an [*with Acc.*], to); Ansprüche an die Concursmasse, claims on a bankrupt's estate; — auf etwas machen, or etwas in — nehmen, *a)* to claim (a thing; an Einen, from one), to pretend or to lay claim to; to demand; to come in for; *b)* to take up, occupy, tax; es wird geraume Zeit in — nehmen, it will require a considerable time; Jemandes Hülfe in — nehmen, to call in one's assistance; auf etwas — haben, to be entitled to; wir müssen Sie deshalb or dafür in — nehmen, we are obliged to hold you responsible for it.

An'spruch…, *in comp.* —*los, adj.* 1) free from claims; 2) or a-*los,* unpretending, unassuming; A-*losigkeit, (w.) f.* unpretendingness; a-(s)reich, a-(s)voll, *adj.* pretentious; A-*sklage, f. Law,* petition, petitory action.

An'sprudeln, *(w.) v.* I. *tr.* to sputter at or into one's face: II. *intr.* to bubble or spout against.

An'sprühen, *(w.) v. tr.* to fly at in sparks.

An'sprung, *(str., pl.* An'sprünge*) m.* 1) (the act of) leaping at, &c.; 2) *Med.* milk-scab, achor.

An'spucken, *(w.) see* Anspeien.

An'spulen, *(w.) v. tr.* to spin a thread to.

An'spülen, *(w.) v.* I. *intr.* (*with* an & *Acc.*) to ripple against, wash, or touch upon; II. *tr.* to wash earth, &c. ashore, to float or carry to a shore or bank, to deposit.

An'spülung, *(w.) f.* alluvion; wash.

An'stacheln, *(w.) v. tr.* 1) to fix to, or to fasten with a prick; 2) *fig.* to goad on, to instigate.

An'stählen, *(w.) v. tr.* to provide with a steel point or edge, to steel.

An'stalt, *(w.) f.* 1) preparation, regulation, disposition, order, direction; zu … — machen, A-en treffen, to make preparations (arrangements) for …; 2) institution, establishment; 3) contrivance.

An'stammeln, *(w.) v. tr.* to address stammering.

An'stammen, *(w.) v. tr. only used in the pp.* Angestammt, *which see.*

An'stampfen, *(w.) v. tr.* to ram, beat against.

An'stand, *(str., pl.* [*l. u.*] An'stände*) m.* 1) *Sport.* stand; auf dem — sein, to be at a standing, to be in the shooting-stand; 2) *Man.* carriage of a horse; 3) *a)* good grace, gracefulness; deportment, address, behaviour, demeanour; *b)* decency; propriety, decorum; dem geschäftlichen — zuwider, contrary to (at variance with) mercantile usage (*Nob. & Or.*); 4) *a)* delay, pause, demur, suspense, suspension; die rasche Erledigung wird keinen — haben, there will be no delay in bringing this matter to a close; im — lassen, to put off, to delay; im — sein, to be put off; von meiner Seite soll es keinen — haben, I will not be the cause of its being delayed; *b) Law, aa)* vacancies (in some parts of Germany); *bb)* respite (granted by the court to poor creditors); 5) hesitation, doubt; — nehmen or haben, to pause, hesitate; to have doubts, to doubt.

An'ständig, I. *adj.* 1) acceptable, suitable, convenient; ist Ihnen der Preis so —? does this price suit you? do you find this price acceptable? 2) decent, becoming, fit, fitting, suitable, seemly, proper; honest, respectable; mannerly; das a-e Betragen, good manners; (bei Männern) gentlemanly bearing; (bei Frauenzimmern) ladylike behaviour, propriety of conduct; *coll.-s.* ich bot einen sehr a-en Preis, I offered a very fair price; eine recht a-e Forderung, *iron.* a very pretty demand, indeed! II. A-keit, (*w.*) *f.* becomingness, conveniency; decency, propriety, respectability.

An'stands…, *in comp.* —*brief, m. Law,* letter of respite (of grace); —*geld, n. Law,* debts not excluded from official respite; —*lehre, f.* instruction in good manners; —*rollen, f. pl. Theat.* parts requiring a noble deportment; —*schirm, m. Sport.* screen (used in stalking); —*voll, adj.* graceful; —*widrig, adj.* informal.

An'stängeln, *(w.) v. tr.* to prop up with sticks, to stick.

An'stapeln, *(w.) v.* I. *tr.* to pile, store up; II. *intr.* (*aux.* sein) *fam.* angestapelt kommen, to come stalking along.

An'stärken, *(w.) v. tr.* to starch a little.

An'starren, *(w.) v. tr.* to stare at or upon, to glare upon, gaze at.

An'statt, I. *prep. with Gen.* instead, in lieu, in the place (room) of; by way of, for; II. *conj.* instead; — dies zu thun, or — daß er dies that, instead of doing this.

—, a great many, a great deal; in geringer —, few in number; der — (*Dat.*) nach, numerically; nach der — verkaufen, to sell by tale.

An'zahlen, (*w.*) *v. tr.* to pay on account.

An'zählen, (*w.*) *v. tr.* to begin to number, count.

An'zahlung, (*w.*) *f.* instalment; eine — von 25% leisten, to pay twenty-five per cent. on account.

An'zapfen, (*w.*) *v. tr.* 1) to tap, broach, pierce; Ahornbäume —, to box maples; 2) *Med.* to tap; 3) *fig. a)* (ärgern) to smoke, nettle (one); *b)* to borrow money of (one), to bleed; *c)* to worm something out of (one).

An'zaubern, (*w.*) *v. tr.* 1) (Einem etwas) to affect with ... by a charm, to bewitch with; to root to the spot by witchcraft; angezaubert, *adj.* spell-bound.

An'zäumen, (*w.*) *v. tr.* to put the bridle on, to bridle.

An'zechen, (*w.*) *v. tr. & refl.* 1) *see* Antrinken; 2) sich (*Dat.*) eine Schuld —, to run up a score (for drink).

An'zeichen, (*str.*) *n.* 1) sign, mark, indication, symptom, token; alle — sind vorhanden, every thing seems (all appearances seem) to indicate; 2) omen, foreboding, augury.

An'zeichnen, (*w.*) *v. tr.* to mark, note; to distinguish by a sign; Einem etwas —, to put to somebody's account.

An'zeige, (*w.*) *f.* 1) notice, account, announcement, communication, information, intelligence; gerichtliche —, denunciation; warning; 2) advertisement; 3) *see* Anzeichen; eine — machen *or* thun, to inform against; to notify, to give information; —amt, *n. see* Adreßcomptoir; —blatt, *n.* advertiser.

An'zeigen, (*w.*) *v. tr.* (*& intr.*) 1) (Einem etwas) to give information, notice, to send word, to inform, to apprise; to announce; to notify, intimate; den Empfang —, *Comm.* to acknowledge, own (the receipt); to advise (the sale); die angezeigten Preise, the prices quoted; 2) to advertise; 3) vor Gericht —, *see* Angeben, 4; *fig.* to show, point to, *or* out; to indicate, signify; to express, bespeak, prove, to denote, declare; 4) to forebode, augur; Böses —, to portend evil; dies zeigt an, this is a sign; a-d, *p. a. Gramm.* indicative; die a-de Art, the indicative mood; das a-de Fürwort, the demonstrative pronoun; a-de Tage, *Med.* indicant *or* critical days; angezeigt, *p. a.* 1) *Med.* indicated, pointed out as the proper remedy; 2) *fig.* advisable; eligible; necessary.

An'zeiger, (*str.*) *m.* 1) informer; 2) *Typ.* index; 3) advertiser, intelligencer; 4) *Math.* argument; 5) *Railw.* railway-accident-detector.

An'zettel, (*str.*) *m. Weav. see* Anzug, 2.

An'zetteln, (*w.*) *v. tr.* 1) *Weav.* to warp; 2) *fig.* to contrive, project, cause, plan, devise, *coll.* to brew (mischief), *cf.* Anspinnen, 3. — **An'zettelung,** (*w.*) *f.* the (act of) warping, &c.

An'zettler, (*str.*) *m.* contriver, author (of a plot).

An'ziehbar, I. *adj.* attractable; II. A-keit, (*w.*) *f.* attractability, attractableness.

An'ziehen, (*str.*) *v.* I. *tr.* 1) *a) gener.* to draw, pull (on, in, &c.); *b)* to begin to draw; to give a pull at (the bell, &c.); *c) Mar.* to haul home; 2) *Anat.* to adduce; 3) to put on, to dress (*refl.* one's self); to pull on (boots, &c.); sich (*Dat.*) die Strümpfe —, to pull on one's stockings; er half mir den Rock —, he helped me on with my coat; oberflächlich, hastig &c. — (Kleider &c.), to huddle on, to slip on (Überwerfen); andere Kleider —, to change one's dress; 4) *a)* to draw in, imbibe (as a sponge); *b) Phys.* to draw, attract (as the loadstone); 5) to draw tight, to tighten, stretch; to draw closer, to turn (a screw) home; einen Nagel, ein Brett —, to drive a nail, a board (plank) home; (beim Reiten) to gather (zusammenziehen); die Zügel —, to draw in the reins; to rein up; 6) to draw (crowded audiences, &c.), to interest, engage, attract; 7) sich (*Dat.*) etwas —, to take something, to apply something to one's self; 8) to quote, cite, allege, refer to; angezogene Stelle, passage referred to, reference; 9) *Husb.* to breed, bring up (Vieh, cattle); Pflanzen —, *Gard.* to plant, cultivate.

II. *intr.* 1) to draw, take effect, hold well; der Nagel zieht an, the nail draws *or* takes; 2) *Comm.* to rise (in price), to be on the rise, to be looking up; 3) (*aux.* sein) *a)* (angezogen kommen) to draw, march on *or* near, approach; damit komm mir nicht angezogen, *coll.* do not talk to me of this; *b) see* Einziehen; *c)* to enter upon duty, to enter *or* to come into service; 4) to make the first move (at chess); Weiß zieht an und setzt in fünf Zügen matt, white moves, and mates in five moves (*or* white to move and to give checkmate at the fifth move, *or* white to play, and mate in five moves); angezogen, *p. a.* clad, attired; a-d, *p. a. fig.* attractive.

An'zieher, (*str.*) *m.* 1) *in comp.* an instrument for drawing (pulling) on, *see* Schuhanzieher, Stiefelanzieher; 2) attirer, dresser; 3) *Anat.* adducent muscle, adductor.

An'ziehschlüssel, (*str.*) *m. T.* screw-key.

An'ziehung, *s.* I. (*w.*) *f.* 1) *Anat.* adduction; 2) *Phys., &c.* attraction; II. *in comp.* A-kraft, *f. Phys.* attractive power, power of attraction; A-kreis, *m.* sphere of attraction.

An'ziehungslos, *adj.* unattractive.

An'ziehungspunct, (*str.*) *m.* point *or* centre of attraction.

An'zinnen, (*w.*) *v. tr. T.* to cover with a coating of tin, to tin.

An'zischeln, (*w.*) *v. tr.* to wisper at, to address in whispers.

An'zischen, (*w.*) *v. tr.* to hiss at.

An'zittern, (*w.*) *v. intr.* (angezittert kommen) to come on, to approach trembling.

An'zotteln, (*w.*) *v. intr. coll.* (angezottelt kommen) to come sauntering *or* trotting along.

An'zucht, (*w., pl. sometimes* (*str.*) An'züchte) *f.* 1) (the act of) breeding, raising; breed (of horses *or* sheep); *Gard.* nursery, cultivation (of plants, trees, &c.); 2) common sewer; *T.* draft-hole; —schweine, *pl.* store-pigs.

An'zuckern, (*w.*) *v. tr.* to sugar over.

An'zug, *s.* I. (*str., pl.* An'züge) *m.* 1) the act of drawing, &c. *cf.* Anziehen; 2) a drawing near, approach; im A-e, approaching; im A-e sein, to be going to happen; große Ereignisse sind bereits im A-e, the march of great events has already commenced; 3) clothing; dress, array, attire, raiment, accoutrement; vollständiger —, complete suit of clothes; full dress; ein anderer (zweiter) —, a change of dress; 4) an entering into place (of servants); II. *in comp.* A-geld, *n.* reception-money (*opp.* Abzugsgeld); A-geschenk, *n.* entrance-money; A-gut, *n.* removed goods; A-predigt, *f.* entrance-sermon; A-rede, *f.* entrance-speech; A-tag, *m.* day of entering into service or office.

An'züglich, I. *adj.* 1) attractive, *see* Anziehend; 2) poignant, keen, invective, offensive, abusive, satirical, cutting; — reden, to be personal; II. A-keit, (*w.*) *f.* 1) attractiveness, charm; 2) poignancy, invective, offensiveness, abusive language, *pl.* personalities.

An'zünden, (*w.*) *v. tr.* to light, kindle; to set on fire, to fire, to inflame, ignite.

An'zündung, (*w.*) *f.* the act of lighting, &c.; ignition.

An'zupfen, (*w.*) *v. tr.* to begin to pull, to pull, to twitch (by the sleeve, &c.).

An'zwacken, (*w.*) *v. tr. fig.* to assail with abusive language.

An'zwängen, (*w.*) *v. tr.* 1) (with an sich

[illegible], adj. Theol. &c. apocryphal; —cryphische [illegible], n. pl. apocrypha; —dik'tisch, adj. apo[illegible](al); der —diktische Beweis, m. (full) de[illegible]; —logie', (w.) f. apology; —lo[illegible], adj. apologetic; —neuro'se, (w.) f. [illegible] aponeurosis; aponeurosy; —pha'se, (w.) [illegible] Rhet. apophasis; —phtheg'ma, (str., pl. [illegible] —phtheg'mata) n. Rhet. apophthegm; [illegible]tisch, adj. apoplectic; —plexie', (w.) f. [illegible] apoplexy.

* [illegible]rie', (w.) f. (Gr. a & poria) Rhet. & [illegible] aporia, apory.

[illegible], m. Myth. Apollo (P. N.).

* [illegible]s..., in comp. —stasie', (w.) f. Rel. [illegible] Pol. apostasy, apostacy; —stat', (w.) m. [illegible], see Abtrünnige; —stat'isch, adj. apo[illegible], apostatic.

* [illegible]el, (str.) m. apostle; in comp. —[illegible], n. apostleship; —geschichte, f. the Acts of the Apostles; —salbe, f. a salve composed of [illegible] ingredients (Unguentum apostolorum).

* [illegible]', (str.) n. apostema, see Ge[illegible]; —kraut, n. see Ackerscabiose.

* [illegible]lisch, adj. apostolical; der a-e Le[illegible], ablegate.

[illegible]s..., in comp. —stroph', (str.) m. [illegible]. apostrophe; —stro'phe, (w.) f. Rhet. apostrophe; —strophi'ren, (w.) v. tr. 1) to mark with an apostrophe, to apostrophise; 2) a) to address by apostrophe, to apostrophise; b) [illegible], to box a person's ears; —stro'phisch, adj. apostrophic. [shop.

* [illegible]'ke, (w.) f. (Gr.) apothecary's

* [illegible]ker, s. I. (str.) m. apothecary; druggist; pharmaceutist; II. in comp. —birne, [illegible] a species of winter-pear; —buch, n. [illegible]tory, pharmacopœia; —gewicht, n. [illegible] weight; —gras, n. Bot. dog's grass [illegible]; —kunst, f. pharmacy; —ordnung, f. [illegible]atory; —rechnung, f. apothecary's bill; [illegible] an unreasonable bill or account of charges; —topf, m. gallipot; —wage, f. apothecary's scale; —waaren, pl. drugs; —wissenschaft, f. pharmacology.

* [illegible]se, (w.) f. (Gr.) apotheosis.

* [illegible]rat', (str.) m. (Lat.) apparatus; implements; Print. (zum Auftragen) inking-cylinder; Mech. Tel. work-table.

* [illegible]ment' [Fr., pr. apartmang'], (str., pl. A-s) n. 1) chamber; 2) coll. privy; a-[illegible], see Hoftöpfig.

* [illegible]', (str.) m. Mil., &c. call: muster; alarm: der Hund hat den —, the dog is well trained or broken in.

* [illegible]lant', (w.) m. (Lat.) Law, appellant, appellor, appealer. — [illegible]lat', (w.) m. Law, appellee, respondent.

* [illegible]tion', (w.) f. Law, appeal: — an[illegible], to enter an appeal; in comp. A-frist, f. time for appealing; A-sgericht, n., A-shof, m. court of appeals; A-sklage, f. action upon appeal; A-srath, m. counsellor of appeals; A-sschrift, f. appellatory libel; A-sverfahren, n. proceedings of the court of appeals.

* [illegible]i'ren, (w.) v. intr. 1) Law, to appeal (an [with Acc.], to), to interpose an appeal; 2) [illegible] (an das Appellationsgericht in [illegible]) to remit. [m. appendix.

* [illegible], (str., pl. [Lat.] Appen'dices)

* [illegible]tien, pl. (Lat.) see Zubehör.

* [illegible]', (str.) m. (Lat.) appetite; — be[illegible], to get or earn an appetite; den — rei[illegible], [illegible] what is one's appetite; starker —, [illegible] of appetite; a large appetite; fig. [illegible], wish, desire. — [illegible]lich, adj. [illegible] the appetite, appetizing, inviting. [illegible]; Mus. [illegible]. — [illegible]los, adj. [illegible] of appetite. — [illegible]keit, (w.) [illegible] of appetite; Med. dysorexy. — [illegible] adj. see Appetitlich; etwas A-es, [illegible], an appetiser, whetter.

[illegible] (str.) m. Bot. see Eppich.

Ap'pisch, adj. Appian, relating to Appius; a-e Straße, f. the Appian road.

* Applaudi'ren, (w.) v. intr. (Lat.) to applaud. — Applaus', (str.) m. applause, plaudit.

* Applicant', (w.) m. (Lat.) applicant.

* Applications'farben, f. pl. T. chemical or topical colours.

* Applicatur', (w.) f. (Lat.) Mus. fingering.

* Applici'ren, (w.) v. tr. (Lat.) to apply.

* Applombi'ren, Applumbi'ren, (w.) v. tr. (Fr., Lat.) see Ausbleien, Auslöthen.

* Appoint' [Fr., Apoäng'], m. Comm. or —wechsel, balance bill; draught par appoint: per — trassiren, to draw par appoint or for the exact sum due. — Appointi'ren [Apoängti'ren], (w.) v. tr. (Fr.) 1) Comm. to compare (an account) with the books; 2) to summon (the parties) before the court; 3) Gunn. to aim (a cannon); 4) T. to full (the hides) for the last time.

* Apporti'ren, (w.) v. tr. (Fr., Lat.) Sport. to fetch and carry. [sition.

* Appositiōn', (w.) f. (Lat.) Gramm. appo-

* Appreti'ren, (w.) v. tr. (Fr.) Cloth. to prepare, to calender (cloth); Comm. to finish, dress; to accommodate. — Appretūr', (w.) f. finish, dressing: die geschickte —, the superior finish; ohne —, unglazed (linen), undressed (cloth); —papier, n. pressed paper.

* Approbi'ren, (w.) v. tr. (Lat.) to approve.

* Appropriatiōn', (w.) f. (Lat.) 1) appropriation; 2) Chem. the union or combination of two bodies.

* Approsch'en, (w.) f. pl. (Fr. approches) Fort. parallels, approaches, lines of approach.

* Approximatiōn', (w.) f. (Lat.) see Annäherung. — Approximativ', approximative.

* Aprac'tisch, adj. (Gr.) 1) inactive; 2) Med. impotent; a-e Tage, holidays (Feiertage).

* Apragmosie', (w.) f. (Gr.) Med. insufficiency (of drugs and medicine).

* Apragie', (w.) f. (Gr.) 1) inactivity; leisure; 2) Med. impotence.

* Aprico'se, (w.) f. (Lat.) apricot; A-nbaum, m. Bot. apricot tree (Prunus armeniaca L.).

April', (str.) m. April; der erste —, april fool-day; Einen zum (in den) — schicken, to make an April fool of one, to send one upon a fool's errand; —glück, n. fig. good fortune or good luck of short duration; —narr, m. April fool, one easily fooled or made a fool of; —regen, m. April shower, passing rain; —wetter, n. April weather.

* Apropos' [Fr., Apropō'], adv. by the by.

* Apsi'de, (w.) f. (Gr.) Astr., &c. apsis.

Apu'lien, (str.) n. Geogr. Apulia, Puglia.

* Apyrit', (str.) m. Miner. red turmalin, rubellite. [aquaduct, aqueduct.

* Aquaduct, Aquäduct', (str.) m. (Lat.)

* Aquamarin', (str.) m. (Lat.) Miner. aquamarine.

* Aquarell', (str.) n., A-e, (w.) f. (Ital.) aquarelle: 1) water-colour; 2) (—malerei) painting in water-colours; —maler, m. painter in water-colours; —manier, f. Paint. painting in water-colours, aquarelle. — Aquarelli'ren, (w.) v. intr. & tr. to paint in water-colours. [chung).

* Äquatiōn', (Lat.) (w.) f. equation (Glei-

* Äqua'tor, (str., pl. [w.] Äquato'ren) m. (Lat.) Geogr. & Astr. equator (Gleicher).

* Aquavit', (str.) m. (Lat.) Dist. aquavitæ, see Likör & Gewürzbranntwein; —laden, see Branntweinladen.

* Äquivalent', I. adj. (Lat.) equivalent; II. s. (str.) n. 1) equivalent; 2) Comm. consideration; gegen irgend ein —, Law, assumpsit implied.

* Äquinoctial', adj. (Lat.) equinoctial; —linie, f. equinoctial line (Äquator); —uhr, (w.) f. equinoctial dial.

* Äquinoc'tium, (Lat.) s. (str., pl. [w.] Äquinoc'tien) n. Astr. equinox.

Aquita'nien, (str.) n. Geogr. Aquitain.

* A'ra, (str., pl. A-s, or Ara) m. Ornith. arara (Psittacus Macao L.).

* Ä'ra, (pl. [i. w.] Ä'ren) f. Chron. era, aera.

A'raber, (str.) m. 1) (Ara'berin, [w.] f.) Arabian; 2) Arabian horse.

* Arabes'ke, (w.) f. Archit. arabesque, moresk-work: eine Geschichte in A-n, a tale in arabesques.

* Ara'bias, f. pl. arabias (kind of linen).

Ara'bien, (str.) n. Geogr. Arabia.

Ara'bisch, adj. Arabic, Arabian; Arab; der a-e Aussatz, die a-e Krätze, elephantiasis: der a-e Balsam, opobalsamum; das a-e Gummi, gum arabic: der Kenner des A-n, Arabist.

* Ar'ack, (str.) m. Dist. arrack, rack.

Arago'nien &c., see Arragonien.

* Aräome'ter, (str.) n. (& m.) areometer.

* Ärār', (str.) n., Ära'rium, (str., pl. [w.] Ära'rien) n. (Lat.) exchequer, public treasury. — Ärarial'vermögen, n. public fund.

Ar'be, (w.) f. see Arve.

Ar'beit, (w.) f. 1) work, labour (and Freem.), toil, pains, fatigue; char; job; 2) task; 3) composition, performance; workmanship; 4) employment; 5) Dist. fermentation; der Wein ist in —, the wine is working or fermenting; 6) Sport. the training of sporting dogs; — in Stein, stone work; — im Hause, in-door-work; — im Freien, out-door-work; getriebene —, chased work: sich an die — machen, to fall to work or to one's business; bei der — sein, to be at work; von seiner Hände — leben, to live by one's manual labour; — bekommen, to get employment; — geben, to give employment, to supply work; an die — stellen, to set to work: Einem eine — geben, to set a person to task; in die — geben, to give out to be made, to put in hand; in — nehmen, to take in hand; viele — verursachen (machen), to give much trouble; es ist in der —, it is being made; it is in hand (fig. on the anvil); wie die —, so der Lohn, proverb. as the work, so the pay; best service, best pay.

Ar'beiten, (w.) v. I. tr. to work, perform, make, execute; ein Schiff über eine Bank —, to force a vessel over a sand-bank; II. intr. 1) a) to work, labour; to be at work; mit vollem Dampfe — (von der Maschine), to have all the steam on; der König arbeitete mit dem Minister, the king was closeted with the minister; b) Comm. to deal, to do (to transact) business, to have to do, to be connected (with one); 2) Dist. to be working, ferment; 3) Join. to warp, to distort (of wood); 4) fig. to use effort, to struggle (against the stream, &c.); — an (with Dat.), to be busied with ... or employed in ...; — auf (with Acc.) ..., in (with Dat.) ..., to work upon ...; das Schiff arbeitet (stampft), the ship works, labours; bei Jemand — lassen, to employ (a tradesman) regularly; auf Stück — lassen, to have piece work done (in America to stint); in Droguen —, to do business in drugs; ich arbeite bei Hrn. B. als Cassirer, I am employed as Mr. V.'s cashier, I keep the cash at Mr. V.'s; die a-den Classen, the working or labouring classes; fürs Brot —, to labour for one's subsistence; hart —, to toil, drudge; III. refl. sich durch ... —, to work one's way through; sich krank —, to fall ill by hard labour: sich todt —, to work one's self to death.

Ar'beiter, (str.) m. worker, workman, labourer, manufacturer, mech. (Hand- or Fabrik-) operative; — auf Schiffswerften, hay-porter; der — im Schiffsraum, holder; —bank, f. workman's bench; —buch, n. see Arbeitsbuch; —entlassung, —sperre, f. lock-out; —familien, pl. working-class families; —stand, m. working class; —verein, m. workingmen's union or association.

Ar'beiterin, *(w.) f.* workwoman, &c., *cf.* Arbeiter.

Ar'beitgeber, *(str.) m.* employer.

Ar'beitsam, I. *adj.* laborious, active, industrious, diligent; II. **A-keit,** *(w.) f.* laboriousness, activity, industry, diligence.

Ar'beits ..., *in comp.* **—ameise,** *f.* neuter or working ant; **—anstalt,** *f. see* **—haus,** 1; **—bank,** *f.* work-bench; **—beutel,** *m.* (lady's) work-bag, wells, ridicule, reticule; **—biene,** *f. Bee.* worker, working-bee; **—buch,** *n.* workman's book; **—bütte,** *f. Paper-m.* vat; **—celle,** *f.* labour-cell; **—einstellung,** *f.* strike.

† **Ar'beitselig,** *adj.* toilsome (Mühselig).

Ar'beits ..., *in comp.* **—fähig,** *adj.* able to work or labour; able-bodied; **—frau,** *f.* workwoman; **—genoß,** *m. see* Mitarbeiter; **—gesellschaft,** *f.* working party; **—gewölbe,** *n. Metall.* working-arch, tymp-arch, fauld, fold; **—haft,** *f.* imprisonment to hard labour; **—haus,** *n.* 1) (für Freiwillige) house of industry, (für Arme) workhouse; 2) (Zwangsarbeitshaus) house of correction, penitentiary; **—holz,** *T.* timber; **—kammer,** *f. Chem.* laboratory; **—kistchen,** *n.* work-chest, tool-box; work-box; **—korb,** *m.* work-basket; **—kraft,** *f.* power of work, working faculty; **—kräfte,** *pl.* labour; seine riesige **—kraft,** his giant faculty of labour; **—leute,** (*pl. of* **—mann**) work- *or* working men, labouring people, work- *or* working people, operatives; **—loch** (in einem Dampfkessel), *n. Mech.* man-hole; **—löcher,** *pl. Metall.* boccas, working-holes; **—lohn,** *m.* wages, hire, pay, make, *Comm.* porterage.

Ar'beitslos, *adj.* out of work *or* employ, unemployed, wanting employment; **—werden,** to be thrown out of work. — **Ar'beitslosigkeit,** *(w.) f.* want of employment.

Ar'beits ..., *in comp.* **—lustig,** *adj.* labour-loving; **—mann,** *m.* workman, journeyman, labouring man; **—meister,** *m.* task-master; **—nachweisungsanstalt,** *f. see* Versorgungsanstalt; **—preis,** *m.* price of labour; **—raum,** *m.* body (of a furnace); **—saal,** *m.* work-room; **—scheu,** I. *adj.* averse to labour, lazy; II. *s. f.* aversion to labour, laziness; **—schule,** *f.* labour-school; **—seite,** *f. see* **—gewölbe;** **—stärke,** *f.* working power (of a river); **—steuer,** *f. see* Gewerbesteuer; **—stock,** *m.* seal-engraver's vice; **—stube,** *f.* work-room; study; **—stunde,** *f.* hour for working, hour of study; **—tag,** *m.* working-day; day's work; **—tasche,** *f. see* **—beutel;** **—theilung,** *f.* division of labour; **—tisch,** *m.* 1) shop-board; work-bench; 2) work-table (for ladies, &c.); working-desk; **—thür,** *f. Metall.* working-door; **—verein,** *m. see* Arbeiterverein; **—vogt,** *m. see* **—meister;** **—voll,** *adj.* toilsome; **—weisen,** *f. pl. T.* workers; **—zeit,** *f.* time for working; **—zeug,** *n.* 1) working-tools; 2) (der Damen) *see* Strickzeug, Nähzeug; **—zelle,** *see* **—celle;** **—zimmer,** *n. see* **—stube;** studio (of artists).

* **Arbitra'ge** (—trä'she), *(w.) f. (Fr.)* 1) (*or* **Arbitral'spruch,** *(str.) pl.* **A-sprüche,** *m.*) award, decision; 2) (*or* **—rechnung,** *f.*) arbitration (of exchanges).

* **Arbitri'ren,** *(w.) v. tr. & intr. (Lat.) Comm.* 1) to award; 2) to calculate by arbitration. [*into citrullus* L.).

* **Arbu'se,** *(w.) f. Bot.* water-melon (*Cucurbita*

* **Arca'de,** *(w.) f. (Fr., from Lat. arcus, bow)* 1) *Archit.* arcade; 2) *pl. Weav.* neck-twines.

Arca'dien, *n.* 4*n. Geogr.* Arcadia. — **Arca'disch,** *adj.* Arcadian. — **Arca'dier,** *(str.) m.* (**A-rin,** *(w.) f.*) Arcadian.

* **Arca'num,** (*str., pl.* [*Lat.*] **Arca'na**) *n.* (*Lat.*) arcanum, nostrum.

* **Archais'tisch,** *adj. (Lat.-Gr.)* archaic. — **Archais'mus,** (*pl.* **A-'men**) *m.* archaism.

* **Archäologie',** *(w.) f. (Gr.)* archæology. — **Archäolo'gisch,** *adj.* archæologic.

Ar'che, *(w.) f.* 1) ark; 2) (**A-muschel,** *f.*) *Conch.* boat shell (*Arca* L.); 3) *see* Windlade; 4) *see* Gerinne; 5) *Fish.* eel-trunk, eel-pond; 6) *Forest.* a pile or stack of wood for fuel; 7) *Sport.* a net used in sporting; 8) *Glass.* arch; **—muschel,** *f. see* Arche, 2.

* **Ar'chi ...,** *(Gr.) in comp.* **—dia'con(us),** *m. Eccl.* arch-deacon; **—diaconat',** *(str.) m.* archdeaconry; **—mandrit',** *(w.) m.* archimandrite.

Archime'disch, *adj.* Archimedean; **a-e Schraube,** *f. Mech.* Archimedean (*or* Archimedes') screw; *Ship-b.* Archimedean or screw-propeller. [Archipelago.

* **Archipel',** **Archipe'lagus,** *(str.) m. Geogr.*

* **Ar'chitect,** *(w.) m. (Gr.)* architect. — **Architecto'nisch,** *adj.* architectonic(al); architectural. — **Architectur',** *(w.) f.* architecture.

* **Architrav',** *(str. & w.) m. (Gr.) Archit.* architrave, epistyle.

* **Archiv',** *(str.) n. (Lat.-Gr.)* archives: 1) (**—gebäude**) repository of (public) records: muniment-house; muniment-room; record-office, paper-office; 2) records; **—stück,** *n.* record, authentic memorial. — **Archiva'lisch, Archiva'risch,** *adj.* archival. — **Archivar',** *(str.),* **Archiva'rius,** (*str., pl.* [*w.*] **Archiva'rien**) *m.* archivist, recorder, keeper of the archives.

* **Archont',** *(w.) m. Gr. Archæol.* archon.

* **Arc'tisch,** *adj. (Gr.)* Arctic, Northern.

* **Ar'dassin-Seide,** *(w.) f. (Fr.-Ar.) Comm.* ardasine silk.

* **Areal',** *(str.) n. (Lat.)* (**—größe,** *f.* measure of) area.

* **Are'ca ...,** *in comp.* **—nuß,** *f.* faufel; **—palme,** *f. see* Catechupalme.

† **Aren, A'ren,** *(w.) v. tr. see* Ackern.

* **Areopag',** *(str.) m. Gr. Archæol.* areopagus.

Arg, I. *adj.* (*compar.* är'ger, *sup.* ärgst) 1) bad, base; arch; arrant, wicked; mischievous; shrewd, cunning; 2) suspicious, deceitful; 3) severe (treatment, punishment); 4) gross (error, negligence, &c.); *coll.* sad, &c.; ein a-er Schelm, an arch-rogue; an arch-wag; ein a-er Tabacksraucher, an inveterate smoker; eine a-e Verwüstung, a sad havoc; immer ärger und ärger, worse and worse; es ist zu —, it is too bad; ärger konnte es nicht kommen, worse could not befall (happen); II. *s. n.* 1) (*decl. like adj.*) *n.* **A-es** denken, to think ill (von, of); etwas A-es von *or* bei einer Sache denken, to have suspicions about a thing; sie vermutheten sich (*Dat.*) nichts A-es, they suspected no harm; die ganze Welt liegt im A-en, the whole world lieth in wickedness; 2) (*str.*) ich habe (denke mir) kein — dabei, I mean no harm; es ist kein — in ihm, there is no deceit in him; ohne —, undesigning; kein — ahnend, in unwary ignorance.

* **Argentan',** *(str.) n. Metall.* German or nickel-silver, white copper, packfong.

Är'ger, I. *compar.* of **Arg,** *which see;* II. *s. (str.) m.* vexation, fret, anger, chagrin; provocation, spite; dir zum —, to vex you *or* in spite of you; man kann ihn leicht in — bringen, he is easily provoked to anger.

Är'gerlich, I. *adj.* 1) (of things) *a)* vexatious, irksome, afflicting, annoying, provoking, teasing; *b) see* Anstößig; 2) (of persons) fretful, peevish, irritable; angry, vexed (auf *or* über eine Person, über eine Sache, at ...); annoyed (at); crusty; II. **Ä-keit,** *(w.) f.* 1) vexatiousness, &c.; 2) fretfulness, &c.

Är'gern, *(w.) v.* I. *tr.* 1) to vex, fret, chagrin, to spite, to provoke, to irritate, to nettle; 2) to scandalise, to offend. II. *refl.* sich über etwas (*Acc.*) —, to be vexed or angry, to fret, to be offended (at).

Är'gerniß, *(str.) n.* 1) vexation, anger; 2) scandal; offence; Einem ein — geben, to scandalise, offend one; — nehmen, to be irritated (an [*with Dat.*], at).

Arg'gesinnt, *adj.* evil-minded (Arg, 1 & 2).

Arg'heit, *(w.) f.* wickedness, malice.

* **Armesin'**, *(str., pl. A-e) m. (Fr. armoisin) Comm.* (Taffetas) armozine.

Ar'meslänge, *see* Armlänge.

Arm'..., *in comp.* **—feile**, *f.* arm-file, rough file, rubber; **—förmig**, *adj.* brachiate; *Bot.* decussate; **—geige**, *f. see* Bratsche; **—geschmeide**, *n.* bracelets; **—grube**, *f. see* Achselgrube; **—harnisch**, *m.* brace, armlet; **—heber**, *m. Anat.* brachial levator; **—höcker**, *m. Anat.* ancon, olecranon; **—höhle**, *f. see* Achselhöhle; **—holz**, *n.* graining-board, pommel.

Ar'mig, *adj. (in comp.) f. i.* kurz—, having short arms, short-armed. *[(Lat.)* sphere.

* **Armillar'sphäre**, *(w.) f. Astr.* armillary

Arminia'ner, *(str.) m.* Arminian. — **Arminia'nisch**, *adj.* arminian. — **Arminianis'mus**, *m.* Arminianism.

* **Armi'ren**, *(w.) v. tr. (Lat.)* 1) *see* Bewaffnen; 2) *Mar.* to equip (a vessel); 3) *T.* to arm *or* truss (a beam *or* timber), to arm (a load-stone)

Arm'..., *in comp.* **—kissen**, *n. see* **—polster**; **—korb**, *m.* basket with a handle to carry on the arm; **—kraft**, *f.* manual power; **—kraftmesser**, *m. Phys.* dynamometer, dynometer.

Arm'kupfer, *(str.) n.* copper from the so called Armstein (in the Harz mines).

Arm'..., *in comp.* **—lade**, *f. Surg.* capsular sling for the arm in cases of fracture; **—lage**, *f. (in Midwifery)* arm-presentation; **—länge**, A-eslänge, *f.* length of the arm; cubit; **—längs**, *adv.* at arm's length; **—lehne**, *f.* elbow-piece; (eines Cabriolets) elbow-rail; **—leuchter**, *m.* 1) chandelier, branched candle-stick, a pair of branches, sconce; 2) *Bot. chara*, a tribe of aquatic water-plants.

Ärm'lich, I. *adj.* poor, miserable, needy, scanty; die Prosa dieses Taschenbuches ist ä-er, als die Poesie, the prose of this pocket-book is poorer than the verse; — gekleidet, poorly dressed; II. **Ä-keit**, *(w.) f.* poorness, poverty, misery.

Arm'..., *in comp.* **—loch**, *n. Tail.* arm-hole; *Anat.* arm-pit, *see* Sprichenloch.

Arm'los, *adj. & adv.* armless.

Arm'..., *in comp.* **—nerven**, *pl. Anat.* brachial nerves; **—nervengeflecht**, *n. Anat.* brachial plexus; **—polster**, *n.* cushion to support the elbow; **—polyp**, *m. Zool.* hydra *(Hydra L.)*; **—ring**, *m. see* **—band**; **—röhre**, *f. Anat.* radius; **—säule**, *f.* hand-post, finger-post; guide-post; **—schiene**, *f.* armlet, brassard; *Surg.* splint; *Anat.* radius; **—schlagader**, *f. see* **—arterie**; **—schleife**, *f.* sleeve-knot; **—schlinge**, *f. see* **—binde**; **—schloß**, *n.* bracelet-lock; **—schmalz**, *n.* (schwere Arbeit) elbow-grease; **—schützer**, *m. T.* arm-protector.

Arms'dick, *adj.* as big as an arm.

Arm'selig, I. *adj.* poor, needy, poverty-stricken; paltry, wretched; frivolous; pitiable; miserable; a-er Prunk, *m.* shabby finery; die Ernte wird — ausfallen, the crops will prove wretchedly deficient; es ist — im Vergleich zu ..., it is a poor trifle in comparison with ...; a-e Politik, *f.* narrow, contracted, *or* illiberal policy; II. **A-keit**, *(w.) f.* poorness; wretchedness; shabbiness; A-keiten, *pl. coll.* miserable things; niggardly doings.

Arm'..., *in comp.* **—sessel**, *m.* arm-chair, elbow-chair, easy-chair; **—spange**, *f.* solid bracelet, bracelet, buckle; **—spindel**, *f. see* **—röhre**.

Arm'stein, *(str.) m. (from* Arm, *adj.)* a stone in the Harz-mines, so called from the inferior quality of its silver contents. [sessel.

Arm'stuhl, *(str., pl. A-stühle) m. see* Arm-

Ar'muth, *(w.) f.* 1) poverty, want (of, an *(with Dat.)*), penury. — theut weh, *proverb*, poverty is a sharp weapon; 2) *collect.* the poor; **A-schein**, *m.*, **A-zeugniß**, *n.* certificate of poverty; sich *(Dat.)* selbst ein A-zeugniß ausstellen, to prove one's own incapacity; der A-s-zustand, pauperism.

Ärn'te *&c.*, *see* Ernte, *&c.*

† **Ar'nen**, *(w.) v. tr.* to earn, acquire.

* **Aro'be**, *(w.) f. (Span.) Comm.* arobe.

* **Aro'ma**, *(str.) (Gr.) n.* aroma; flavour. — **Aromat'isch**, *adj.* aromatic(al), spicy.

* **Ar'ron**, *(str.) m.* 1) *see* Aaron; 2) *see* Arum.

* **Arquebusa'de**, *(w.) f. Pharm.* (— *(or* Schußwunden-)Wasser, *n.)* arquebusade-water.

* **Arquebu'se** *[pr. ark—]*, *(w.) f (Fr.) Gunn.* arquebuse, arquebuss. — **Arquebusi'ren**, *(w.) v. tr.* to shoot with an arquebuse.

* **Ar'rack**, *see* Arack.

Arrago'nien, *(str.) n. Geogr.* Arragon *(P. N.)*. — **Arrago'nier**, *(str.) m.* (A-in, *(w.) f.)* Arragonese. — **Arrago'nisch**, *adj.* Arragonian.

* **Arragonit'**, *(str.) m. Miner.* arragonite.

* **Arrangi'ren** *[pr. ărangzhē'ren]*, *(w.) v. tr. (& refl.) (Fr.)* to arrange (one's self); to make an arrangement, to compound *or* settle with.

* **Ar'rasgarn**, *(str.) n. Comm.* arras-yarn (for carpets). [the Orinoco)

* **Ar'rau-Schildkröte**, *(w.) f. Zool.* arrau (on

* **Arrera'gen** *[pr. —ā'zhen]*, *f. pl. (Fr.)* outstanding debts; accumulated interest added to the capital.

* **Arrest'**, *(str.) m. (Mid. Lat.)* 1) *see* Beschlag; 2) imprisonment, prison; **—anlage**, *f* legal proceedings of arrest; sequestration.

* **Arrestant'**, *(w.) m.* prisoner. — **Arrestat'**, *(w.) m. Law.* one against whom a warrant of arrest *or* capture is made out. — **Arrestation'**, *(w.) f.* arrestation; arrest; capture. — **Arreti'ren** *(l. u.:* Arresti'ren), *(w.) v. tr.* to arrest (auch *Phys.* die Magnetnadel *&c.*), attach, seize; *Man.* to stop (a horse) running at full gallop.

* **Arriè're**, *(Fr.) in comp.* **—garde**, *f.* rear-guard, rear; **—pasten**, *m. see* Hinterhalt & Nachtrab *(Pierer)*. *[Comm.* alewage.

* **Arrima'ge** *[pr. —ā'zhe]*, *(w.) f. (Fr.)*

* **Arrogant'**, *adj.*, **Arroganz'**, *(w.) f (Lat.) see* Anmaßend, Anmaßung.

* **Arrogation'**, *(w.) f.*, **Arrogi'ren**, *(w.) v. tr. (Lat.) see* Adoption, Adoptiren.

* **Arrondi'ren** *[pr. arrongdi'—]*, *(Fr.) see* Abrunden. — **Arrondir'maschine**, *(w.) f. T.* finishing engine.

* **Arrosement'** *[pr. ărōzmăng']*, *(str., pl. A-s) n. (Fr.) Comm.* payment on account. — **Arrosi'ren**, *(w.) v. intr.* to pay on account; to contribute one's share.

Arsch, *(str., pl.* Ärsche) *m. vulg.* 1) arse; backside, bum; 2) butt-end of a tree-stem; *in comp.* **—backe**, *f.* buttock; **—fuß**, *m.*, **—füßlein**, *n. Ornith.* arse-foot *(Podiceps Latr.)*; der kleine **—fuß**, didapper; dabchick *(Colymbus minor L.)*, *see* Steißfuß; **—leder**, *n. see* Fahrleder; **—lings**, Ärschlings, *adv.* backwards (*cf.* Arse-line), *see* Rücklings; *most vulg.*: **—loch**, *n.* arse-hole; **—pauker**, **—peitscher**, *m.* whip-arse, bum-brusher, flat-bottomist; **—wisch**, *m.* bum-fodder.

* **Arsenal'**, *(str., pl. A-e, l. u.:* Arsena'le) *n. (Ital.)* arsenal (Zeughaus).

Arse'nig, *adj. Chem.* arsenious; a-e Säure, *f.* arsenious acid; **—saures Salz** *n.* arsenite.

Arsenica'lisch, *adj.* arsenical.

Arse'nik, *s.* I. *(str.) m. Miner. & Chem.* arsenic, rat's bane; weißer —, white *or* crystalline arsenic; rother —, red arsenic, realgar; natürlicher —, gediegener —, native arsenic; gelber —, yellow arsenic, orpiment; mit — verbinden, to arseniate; II. *in comp.* **—antimon**, *n.* antimonious arsenic; **—asche**, *f.* a suboxyde of arsenic; **—äther**, *m.* arsenic-ether; **—blei**, *n.* arseniate of lead; **—blüthe**, *f.* arsenic-bloom; **—bromid**, *n.* arseniate of bromide; **—butter**, *f.* butter of arsenic; **—eisen**, *n.* arseniate of iron; **—erz**, *n.* arsenic-ore; **—fahlerz**, *n.* common copper ore; **—glas**, *n.* realgar; red orpiment; **—haltig**, *adj.* arsenical; **—kalk**, *m.* arseniate of lime, pharmacolite; **—kies**, *m.* arse-

Ath'men, I. *(w.) v.* 1) *intr.* to breathe, to draw breath; to respire; schwer —, to breathe thick *or* with difficulty; tief —, to fetch a long and deep breath; er athmete leiser um zu horchen, he hushed his breath to listen; 2) *tr. a)* to breathe, draw in; *b)* (aus—) to breathe (Rache), exhale; *fig.* to breathe (vengeance, &c.); II. *v. s. (str.) n.* the (act of) breathing, respiration.

Ath'mung, *(w.) f. l. u. for* das Athmen; **a-sfähig**, *adj.* capable of breathing, respiring; **A-sgeräusch**, *n. Med.* respiratory murmur, **A-swerkzeuge**, *n. pl. Anat.* organs of respiration, respiratory organs.

* **Ätiologie'**, *(w.) f. (Gr.) Philos. & Med.* etiology. — **Ätiolo'gisch**, *adj.* etiological.

Atlan'ten, *(w.) pl. of* Atlas.

* **Atlanti'den**, *(w.) m. pl. Astr.* Atlantides.

Atlan'tisch, *adj.* Atlantic, Atlantean; das a-e Meer, the Atlantic (ocean).

* **At'las**, I. *(str., pl.* At'lasse & Atlan'ten) *m.* 1) *Gr. Myth.* Atlas, giant who bears up the pillars of heaven; 2) *Geogr.* Atlas; 3) atlas, collection of maps; 4) *Anat.* atlas; 5) *Conch.* atlas (species of shell), *see* —tute; species of rhomb-shell, *see* —rolle *or* —walze; 6) *see* —schmetterling; 7) *Miner. see* —erz; 8) *or* At'laß *(pl.* A-sse), *Comm.* satin; II. *in comp.* —apfel, *m. Pom.* green winter apple; —art, *f.* kind of satin; auf —art weben, to weave in imitation of satin; —artig, —ähnlich, *adj.* satined; —band, *n.* satin-ribbon; —beschlag, *m.* satin-top; —baum, —beerbaum, *m. see* Elsebeerbaum; —birne, *f. Pom. see* Dauphine; —blech, *n. see* Metallmohr; —blume, *f. Bot. see* Mondviole; —boden, *m.* satin-ground (half satin stuff); —erz, *n. Miner.* fibrous malachite; —falter, *m. see* —schmetterling; —federn, *f. pl.* glossy, satin-like feathers *or* plumes; —format, *n.* large square-folio; —grund, *m. see* —boden; —holz, *n.* satin-wood; —kies, *m.* malachite; —kirschbaum, *m. see* Elsebeerbaum; —köper, *m.* satin-twill; —kraut, *n. Bot.* species of satin-flower *(Lunaria biennis)*; —rolle, *f.* species of rhomb-shell *(Voluta ispidula* Lam.); —schmetterling, *m. Entom.* atlas *(Saturnia atlas* L.); —spath, *m. Miner.* satin-spar; —tapete, *f.* satin-paper hangings; —tute, *f.* species of shell *(Conus tenuistriatus)*; —vitriol, *m.* green vitriol, copperas; —walze, *see* —rolle; —weber, —wirker, *m.* satin-weaver.

* **At'lassen**, *adj.* satin, made of satin.

* **Atmidome'ter**, **Atmome'ter**, *(str.) n.* *(m.) (Gr.) Meteor.* atmometer, evaporometer.

* **Atmosphä're**, *(w.) f. (Gr.)* atmosphere.

* **Atmosphä'risch**, *adj.* atmospheric(al).

Ät'na, *(str.) m. Geogr.* (mount) Etna, Ætna; den — betreffend, Etnean.

* **Atom'**, I. *(str.) n. (Gr.)* atom, molecule, (indivisible) particle, corpuscle; element; ein — Metalloxyd, Säure, *Chem.* one equivalent of metallic oxyd, acid; II. *in comp.* a-enähnlich, *adj.* atom-like; A-engewicht, *n. Chem.* atomic weight; A-enlehre, *f.* atomism.

* **Ato'misch**, *adj.* atomic; die a-e Theorie, *Chem.* atomic theory; das a-e Gewicht, *see* Atomengewicht.

* **Atomist'**, *(w.) m.* atomist. — **Atomist'isch**, *adj.* atomistic, atomic; die a-e Theorie, atomistic theory; die a-e Philosophie, atomic *or* corpuscular philosophy.

* **Atramental'stein**, *(str.) m. (Lat.) Chem.* inkstone; der gelbe —, misy.

* **Atresie'**, *(w.) f. (Gr.) Surg.* imperforation.

* **Atschiar'**, *(str.) m. Chem.* achia, achiar *(from the sprouts, &c. of the* Ashoka).

* **Attaque'**, *(w.) f. (Fr. attaque)* attack (Angriff).

* **Attemperi'ren**, *(w.) v. intr. (Lat.)* to accommodate one's self to *or* comply with circumstances.

* **Attentat'**, *(str.) n. (Lat.)* outrage; premeditated attempt on some one's life.

At'ter, *f. Zool. see* Otter.

* **Attest'**, **Attestat'**, *(str.) n. (Lat.)* schriftliches —, certificate, testimonial, attestation. — **Attesti'ren**, *(w.) v. tr.* to testify, certify, test, attest.

At'tich, *(str.) m. Bot.* dane-wort, dwarf-elder, walwort *(Sambucus ebulus* L.); der virginische —, Virginian golden rose; gueldres-rose-leaved spiræa *or* ninebark *(Spiræa opulifolia* L.); —beeren, *f. pl.* dwarf-elder berries; —saft, *m.* inspissated juice of dwarf-elder berries.

* **Atticis'mus**, *(not decl.; pl. [w.]* Atticis'men) *m. (Lat.)* Atticism. — **At'tiker**, *(str.) m.* Attic (Athenian author). — **At'tisch**, *adj.* Attic; die a-e Redensart, atticism.

* **Attribui'ren**, *(w.) v. tr. (Lat.)* to attribute. — **Attribut'**, *(str.) n.* attribute.

† **Atz**, *(w.) m. & f.* food.

At'zel, *provinc. (w.) f.* 1) *Ornith. see* Elster; 2) *Entom. see* Assel.

At'zelspecht, *(str.) m. Ornith. see* Buntspecht.

† **At'zen**, *(w.) v. tr. & intr.* to give food; to feed.

Ätz'bar, I. *adj.* corrodible; corrosive, caustic; II. **Ä-keit**, *(w.) f.* corrodibility; corrosiveness, causticity.

Ät'zen, *(w.) v. tr.* 1) *a)* to feed; *b)* to bait; 2) *Chem.* to corrode, macerate; 3) *Surg.* to cauterize; 4) *Engr.* to etch.

Ät'zend, *p. a. Chem., Med., &c.* caustic, corrodent, corrosive; ä-e salzsaure Quecksilber, ä-e Sublimat, *see* Ätzquecksilber; ä-e Potasche, *see* Kali.

Ätz'..., *in comp.* —beize, *f.* chemical discharge: *Engr.-s.* —bild, *n.* etching; —druck, *m.* discharge-work; —grund, *m.* (etching) varnish; ground; *Chem.-s.* —kali, *n.* caustic potassa; —kalilauge, *f.* caustic lie; —kalk, *m.* unslacked lime, quick-lime; —kraft, *f.* causticity, caustic strength; —kunst, *f. Engr.* art of etching; —mittel, *n. Chem. & Surg.* corrosive, cauter, escharotic, corrodent; —mittel *(pl.)* bei ... anwenden, *fig.* to cauterise; —nadel, *f. Engr.* etching-needle, pointer; *Pharm.-s.* —natron, *n.* caustic soda; —natronlauge, *f.* etching-lie of soda; —paste, *f.* corrosive paste; —platte, *f.* etching-plate; —pulver, *n.* caustic powder, pulverised corrosive, corrosive powder; *Med.* ruptory; *Chem.-s.* —quecksilber, *n.* corrosive sublimate; —silber, *n.* lunar caustic; —stein, *m. Surg.* (Höllenstein) lunar caustic; caustic stone; —stoff, *m.* caustics; —sublimat, *n. see* —quecksilber; —taube, *f.* decoy-pigeon; —wasser, *n. see* Scheidewasser; —zeichnung, *f.* etching.

† **At'zung**, *(w.) f. see* Ätzung.

Ät'zung, *(w.) f.* 1) *a)* feeding, food; *b)* baiting, lure; 2) *Surg.* cauterisation; 3) *Engr.* etching; — auf Kupfer, aquatinta.

Au! *interj. (expressing pain)* oh!

Au, *(w.) f. see* Aue; —hirsch, *m.* stag living in meadows and plains.

Auch, *conj.* also, too, likewise, even; es wäre schändlich — nur davon zu reden, it were a shame even to speak of it; — nicht einer, not so much as one; aber —, but, but yet; sowohl ..., als —, as well ... as, both ... and; nicht allein *or* nicht nur ... sondern —, not only . but; so oft —, so groß — &c., as often as, so great as, &c.; — noch, still; withal; oder —, or else; er mag gehen oder — bleiben, he may go or else remain; ohne — nur zu fragen, without so much as asking; ich —, I too; so am (do, &c.) I; *A.* Ich bin arm, I am poor; *B.* Ich —, so am I; ihr geht gern spazieren, ich —, you like to take walks, so do I; *A.* Du bist ein Narr, you are a fool; *B.* Du —, you are another; ... — nicht, nor ... neither; ich — nicht, nor I (n)either; neither (*or* nor) am

Finger: einen Ring — den Finger thun, to put a ring on the finger; — dem Markte, 1) in the market-place: 2) at (in the) market; ich traf ihn — dem Markte, I met him in the market; — dem Markte gekauft, bought at the market: sie schickt ihr Dienstmädchen — den Markt, she sends her servant-girl to the market; — der Straße herumlaufen, to run about the street; — offener Straße, in the open street: — die Straße laufen, to run into the street; wir ritten — dem Berge (spazieren), we took a ride on the hill; wir ritten — den Berg, we rode up the hill; sie wohnen immer — dem Lande, they live in the country all the time; sie gehen jede Woche — das Land, they go into the country every week; — dem Fechtsaale, — dem Ballsaale, — dem Rathhause, in the fencing-room, in the ball-room, in the town-house; — dem Balle, at the ball; er ging — das Rathhaus, he went to the town-house; — der Börse, on the Exchange, *coll.* on 'Change: sie ist — ihrem Zimmer, she is in her chamber; er war — dem Verdeck, he was on deck; — das Verdeck gehen, to go on deck; viele Leute mußten — dem Felde liegen, many people were obliged to lie in the fields; er starb — dem Schlachtfelde, he died on the battle-field; wir wollen — das Feld gehen, um zu sehen, wie der neue Pflug probirt wird, let us go out into the field to see the new plough tried; — drei Füßen, on three legs; platt — dem Gesicht liegen, to lie flat on one's face; wir fanden diesen Ort nicht — der Karte, we did not find this place in the map; — dem Wege sein, to be on one's road; er schläft nicht gern — der Reise, he does not like to sleep in travelling; — dieser Welt, in this world; — geradem Wege, by the straight road; — der Universität sein, to be at the university, at college; — dem Comptoir, in or at the office; mein Bruder ist — einem Comptoir, my brother is in a counting-house (*i. e.* is clerk to a merchant); — der Flotte dienen, to serve in the navy; — einem Auge blind, blind of one eye; — die Post gehen, to go to the post-office; er ging — das Polizeiamt, he went to the police-office; — die Messe reisen, to go to the fair; — Reisen gehen, to go abroad; — Abenteuer fahren, ausgehen, to go in search of adventures; ein Schlag — die Nase, — das Auge, a blow on the nose, in the eye; er fiel — die Kniee, he fell on his knees; — das Schaffot bringen, to bring to the scaffold; — Einen zugehen, to walk up to (*or* towards) one; es geht — neun, it draws towards (turns on) nine; es ist ein Viertel — zwei, it is a quarter past one; es ist drei Viertel — zwei, it is a quarter to two; eine Steigung von 1 Fuß — jede 100, an acclivity of 1 foot in each 100 feet; ein Druck von 5 Pfund — den Quadratzoll, a pressure of 5 pounds to the square inch; von diesen gehen fünf — das Pfund, of these there go five to a pound; so viel — die Person, so much to each (*or* a-piece, a-head); Geld — Zinsen, money at interest; er war — den Namen M. eingeschrieben, he was booked in the name of M.; er hörte — beide Namen, he answered to both names; — das Evangelium schwören, to swear on the gospel; bis —, bis (weiterm) Befehl, further orders; alle bis — Einen, all except one; — einige Tage, for a few days; nur noch — eine Minute, but for a minute; — drei Monate, *Comm.* at three months' date; — seine eigene Gefahr, at his own risk; — Leben und Tod, for life and death; es kostet — hundert Thaler, it costs about a hundred Thalers; — meine Ehre, upon my honour; — sein Bitten, at his request; — Anfrage, on inquiry; on application; — [illegible] wurde das Buch der Weisen [illegible] des Kaisers gedruckt, the book of [illegible] was printed by order of the emperor; — eine gewisse Entfernung, to a certain distance: wir schoben es — den Abend auf, we put it off for the evening: sich — das Trinken legen, to take to drinking; — das Essen spazieren gehen, to walk after dinner (*or* supper): Briefe — Briefe, letter after letter; Verlust — Verlust, loss upon loss; er war — französische Art gekleidet, he was dressed in *or* after the French manner *or* fashion; das heißt — Deutsch, that is in German; — diese und andere Anklagen (hin) wurde er in den Tower gesperrt, on these and other accusations he was confined in the Tower; — das (*contracted into* aufs) *before the superlative*, in the ... manner, &c.: — das (—s) Beste, in the best manner possible, to the best of one's ability; sie sangen — das Beste (*Uhland*), they sang to the best of their ability, they sang exceedingly well; —s Prächtigste, most splendidly; —s Neue, anew; —s Eheste, as soon as possible; *fig.*-s. es hat Nichts — sich, it is no matter; das hat viel — sich, this is of great moment *or* importance.

II. *adv.* 1) up, upwards; 2) astir; 3) *coll.* *for* Offen, open: — sein, to be up *or* stirring; was soll ich denn so spät —? why am I to stay up so late? was haben Sie so früh — gesollt? why had you to rise so early? wohl — sein, *see* Wohlauf; von (meiner) Jugend —, from my youth upwards; — und ab, up and down, to and fro; *fig.* more *or* less; das — und Ab des Lebens, the ups and downs of life; — und nieder, *Mar.* apeek, right down; die Auf- und Niederbewegung, *Mech.* up and down motion; Treppen —, up stairs; Berg —, up hill; — daß, that, in order to; — daß nicht, lest; *see* Daß; III. *interj.* —! up! about!

Auf'ächzen, (*w.*) *v. intr.* to groan, sigh heavily.

Auf'ackern, (*w.*) *v. tr.* to plough up, to turn up (from the subsoil) in ploughing; to plough up, to break ground; to plough over again.

Auf'angeln, (*w.*) *v. tr.* 1) to draw up (a fish) with the fishing line; 2) *fig.* to fish up (news, &c.).

Auf'arbeiten, (*w.*) *v.* I. *tr.* 1) to break open *or* up; 2) *a)* to spend, to work up *or* consume (the material); *b)* to finish one's task, *also intr.* to clear off arrears of business; II. *refl.* 1) to struggle, *or* get up again; to rise, *cf.* Emporarbeiten; 2) sich (*Dat.*) die Hände —, to bruise one's hands by hard working.

Auf'athmen, (*w.*) *v. intr.* to draw a long breath; to breathe again, to recover.

Auf'ätzen, (*w.*) *v. tr. Surg.* to open by corrosives.

Auf'backen, (*str.*) *v. tr.* 1) to consume by baking; 2) to bake again.

Auf'bähen, (*w.*) *v. tr. Surg.* to open by fomentation.

Auf'bahren, (*w.*) *v. tr.* to put upon a bier.

Auf'ballen, (*w.*) *v. tr. a)* (Waaren) to put *or* pile up in bales; *b)* to unbale (goods).

Auf'bansen, (*w.*) *v. tr.* to pile *or* heap up (sheaves in a barn).

Auf'bau, (*str.*) *m. a)* a building, erection, raising up; *b)* superstructure.

Auf'bauschen, (*w.*) *v. refl. see* Aufbauschen, II.

Auf'bauen, (*w.*) *v.* I. *tr.* to build up, to erect; Luftschlösser —, to build castles in the air; ihr Verdienst besteht mehr im Niederreißen, als im — (*v. a.*), their merit is rather that of demolition than that of construction; II. *refl. Smelt.* to collect in the corners of the furnace (of scoria, &c.).

Auf'bauer, (*str.*) *m.* builder (up) &c.

Auf'bäumeln, (*w.*) *v. refl. Sport.* (*of hares*) to rise upon the hinder legs and look about.

Auf'baumen, (*w.*) *v. intr. Sport.* to climb up, *or* take a tree (*opp.* Abbaumen).

Auf'bäumen, (*w.*) *v.* I. *tr. Weav.* to wind round the weaving staff, (auf den Kettenbaum) to beam, (auf den Zeugbaum) to wind up; II. *refl.* 1) to rear (*also of a horse* = to prance); 2) *Min.* to appear; 3) *provinc. see* Aufschwellen (of rivers).

Auf'bauschen, (*w.*) *v.* I. *tr.* to puff (out one's cheeks, &c.); II. *refl.* to puff, to swell; to bag.

Auf'bauung, (*w.*) *f.* the building up, erecting.

Auf'beben, (*w.*) *v. intr.* to start up; to tremble, shake.

Auf'befinden, (*str.*) *v. refl.* to be up.

Auf'behalten, (*str.*) *v. tr.* 1) to keep on (one's hat); 2) to keep (in store), to lay up, to save; to reserve, to garner up.

Auf'beißen, (*str.*) *v. tr.* 1) to bite open; to crack (nuts); 2) *see* Aufbeizen.

Auf'beizen, (*w.*) *v. tr. see* Aufätzen.

Auf'bekommen, (*str.*) *v. tr.* to get on, up, *or* open.

Auf'bellen, (*w.*) *v.* I. *intr.* to bark, to yelp; II. *tr.* to wake by barking *or* yelping.

Auf'bereiten, (*w.*) *v. tr. Min.* to prepare, to clean, to dress (ores). — **Auf'bereitung**, (*w.*) *f.* mechanical preparation *or* dressing (of ores).

Auf'bergen, (*w.*) *v. tr. Agr.* to heap up, or raise (the furrows) towards the middle to make the water run off the sooner.

Auf'bersten, (*str.*) *v. intr.* to burst (open), to chap, to gape, to chink; to split, to crack.

Auf'bessern, (*w.*) *v. tr.* to ameliorate, to increase (the salaries of officials, &c.). — **Auf'besserung**, (*w.*) *f.* amelioration, &c.

Auf'betten, (*w.*) *v. tr.* 1) to put up, set up (a bed); 2) to make anew (a bed).

Auf'beugen, (*w.*) *v. tr. see* Aufbiegen; *refl.* to bend over.

Auf'bewahren, (*w.*) *v. tr.* 1) to put by, keep, save, to lay up, to store, to preserve; to take charge of; Einem zum — geben, to give in charge of another; 2) *fig. see* Aufbehalten.

Auf'bewahrung, (*w.*) *f.* (the act of) keeping, &c.; preservation; (safe) keeping; A-Sort, *m.* receptacle, depository; A-Fläche, *f. Chem.* barrne-pipe.

Auf'biegen, (*str.*) *v. tr.* to bend upwards.

Auf'bieten, (*str.*) *v. tr.* 1) *a)* to summon (by public order), to summon up; *b)* to call, to call in *or* up, to raise (up); das ganze Land —, to raise the country in a mass; *c)* to ask (a lady) to dance; 2) to exert, muster (up), summon; Alles —, to make *or* use every effort *or* exertion; to strain every nerve; ich werde Alles —, I shall do all I can; sie bot alle ihre Reize auf, she displayed all her charms; 3) *Eccl.* Verlobte —, to proclaim, to bid, to publish the bans; 4) *coll.* to revile, to abuse; 5) to outbid, to overbid (at an auction).

Auf'bilden, (*w.*) *v. refl.* to develop one's faculties.

Auf'binden, (*str.*) *v. tr.* 1) *a)* to tie, truss *or* tuck up; *b)* to fasten *or* bind upon; *Mar.* die Segel —, to hand the sails? 2) to untie, unbind, uncord, loosen; *Surg.* to take off (the dressing); 3) (Einem etwas) *fig.* to impose upon one, to tell one a fib, to hoax *or* humbug one, to put a flam *or* banter upon one.

Auf'blähen, (*w.*) *v.* I. *tr.* to puff (up), swell, bloat (up); II. *refl. see* Aufblasen.

Auf'blähung, (*w.*) *f.* the (act *of*) puffing, swelling, &c., inflation.

Auf'blasen, (*str.*) *v.* I. *tr.* 1) to blow up, inflate; to distend with wind, to puff (a bubble, bladder, &c.); 2) to blow open, to open by blowing (a window, &c.); 3) *a)* to call up *or* forth, to rouse, wake, &c. by blowing a trumpet; (zum Streite, Angriffe, Rückzuge) to sound the battle, charge, retreat; (zum Aufsitzen der Reiterei) to sound to horse; *b)* Eins —, to sound a flourish with trumpets; *c)* to wake *or* call forth by blowing (an instrument); to blow upwards *or* raise (the dust); II. *refl.* to swell, to puff one's self up, to be inflated.

Auf'bläser, (*str.*) *m. Ichth. see* Stachelfisch.

Auf'blatten, (w.) v. tr. see Abblatten.

Auf'blättern, (w.) v. I. tr. to turn over, to open the leaves of (a book); to search (for a passage) by turning over the leaves; II. refl. to open.

Auf'bleiben, (str.) v. intr. 1) to stay up, to sit up; Abends lange —, to sit up late at night; 2) coll. (for offen bleiben) to remain open, to be left open. [Chem. lightning.

Auf'blick, (str.) m. look upwards; glimpse;

Auf'blicken, (w.) v. intr. 1) to look up, to cast one's looks upwards or to heaven; 2) or Aufblinken, Aufblitzen, (w.) to flash or flare up, to emit a transient gleam or glitter; 3) Metall. to appear shining.

Auf'blühen, (w.) v. intr. (aux. sein) 1) to begin to bloom, to blossom; to open; 2) fig. to begin to blossom, to rise, to increase; pp. aufgeblüht, (ganz, full-)blown; das —, v. s. (str.) n. the flourishing, development, growth (of a country, &c.).

Auf'bohren, (w.) v. tr. 1) to bore open, to open by boring; 2) to bore again.

Auf'bojen, (w.) v. tr. Mar. to buoy up.

Auf'borgen, (w.) v. tr. to borrow, to take up (money), to collect by borrowing.

Auf'bot, (str.) n. see Aufgebot.

Auf'brachen, (w.) v. tr. see Aufbrechen.

Auf'branden, (w.) v. intr. (aux. sein) to surge, foam up. [to heave to.

Auf'brassen, (w.) v. tr. Mar. to bring to,

Auf'braten, (str.) v. tr. to roast afresh.

Auf'brauchen, (w.) v. tr. see Verbrauchen.

Auf'brauen, (w.) v. tr. to consume by brewing.

Auf'brausen, (w.) v. intr. 1) to rush up, to (begin to) roar; to chafe; to foam up; to fizz (like champagne, &c.); Chem. to effervesce; to ferment; 2) fig. to effervesce; to fly into a violent passion; coll. to fly out, to flare up; er braust gleich auf, his blood is soon up; das —, v. s. (str.) n. 1) Chem. & fig. effervescence, ebullition; 2) flash (of temper); a-d, adj. 1) Chem. & fig. effervescent; 2) fig. passionate, irascible.

Auf'brechen, (str.) v. I. tr. 1) to break open or up; to open or force (a door, &c.); das Pflaster —, to break or take up the pavement; 2) Brew. to stir, turn (the beer) in the cooler; 3) Agr. to break (ground), see Brechen, Umpflügen; 4) Metall. to dress (ores); 5) Sport. to eviscerate, to gut; II. intr. (aux. sein) 1) to burst open, to open; von der Kälte —, see Aufspringen, Aufreißen; 2) to start, to break up, to set out, to set forth, to depart; Mil. to decamp; Sport. das Wild bricht auf, the deer leaves its usual place of food, and seeks another; das —, v. s. (str.) n. or Auf'brechung, (w.) f. the (act of) breaking up, &c.

Auf'breiten, (w.) v. tr. 1) to spread, to stretch out, to display; 2) Min. see Aufbereiten.

Auf'breitmaschine, (w.) f. T. blower and spreader, lap-machine.

Auf'brennen, (irr.) v. I. tr. 1) to burn up, to consume (wood); 2) see Aufbrühen; 3) (einer Sache oder Person (Dat.) etwas) to brand, to burn (a mark) upon; 3) Coop. to smoke with brimstone; II. intr. (aux. sein) 1) to burn up suddenly; Chem. to take fire; 2) fig. to be excited to sudden anger; 3) see Abbrennen, I. 2.

Auf'bringen, I. (irr.) v. tr. 1) a) to cause to get up, or to rise; b) to restore (a patient) to health; 2) Mil. to levy (men); 3) to rear, bring up (children, &c.); 4) Comm. to house, to warehouse; 5) Mar. to bring up or in a prize, to capture; 6) to get or set up, to bring on; to raise (money), to afford (a sum), to make up or good; 7) a) to produce, allege (Vorbringen); b) to get up, set (up), to introduce (new fashions): eine Mode —, to set, &c. a fashion; wieder —, to bring again into use; c) to start, broach (an opinion, &c.); 8) to provoke, irritate, pique, chafe, exasperate, to put in a passion; coll. to put (one) up; Einen gegen den Andern —, see Aufhetzen, 2; II. v. s. (str.) n. 1) the (act of) getting up, &c.; 2) Mar. capture.

Auf'bringer, (str.) m. Mar. captor.

Auf'brocken, (w.) v. tr. to break into small pieces (as bread). [bubble up.

Auf'brodeln, (w.) v. intr. (aux. sein) to

Auf'bruch, (str., pl. Auf'brüche) m. 1) the (act of) breaking up, move, rising (from table, &c.); setting out, departure; 2) Mil. decampment or move of an army; zum — blasen, to sound the march; 3) Sport. the opening and eviscerating; 4) Agr. breaking up.

Auf'brücken, (w.) v. tr. to bridge over; to erect a bridge (over); to construct in form of a bridge. [water.

Auf'brühen, (w.) v. tr. to soak in boiling

Auf'brüllen, (w.) v. I. intr. to raise a lowing or roaring; II. tr. to wake by roaring.

Auf'brummen, (w.) v. I. tr. Stud. slang, Einem eine Beleidigung, eins &c. —, to put an insult upon one; II. see Aufbrüllen.

Auf'brüsten, (w.) v. I. tr. Butch. to open the breast of (a slaughtered beast); II. refl. fig. to assume a pompous air, to make one's self look big. [back.

Auf'buckeln, (w.) v. tr. coll. to take on one's

Auf'bucht, (w.) f. Ship-b. a rounding up, round up.

Auf'buden, (w.) v. I. intr. to put up booths or stalls; II. tr. to lay out for sale.

Auf'bügeln, (w.) v. tr. Tail. to smooth up with the pressing iron, to iron (over) again; to raise the button holes by means of the iron.

Auf'bühnen, (w.) v. tr. Min. to erect scaffolds in ....

Auf'buhlen, (w.) v. tr. Mar. to plank (a ship).

Auf'bündeln, (w.) v. tr. (Einem etwas) coll. to burden (one) with (a bundle or other heavy object), cf. Aufbürden, Aufpacken &c.

Auf'bürden, (w.) v. tr. 1) (Einem etwas) to burden, or load (one with), to lay or put on one's back or shoulders, to charge; coll. to saddle (one) with; 2) fig. to impose, to put (a fault, the blame, &c.) upon, to charge with, to impute.

Auf'bürsten, (w.) v. tr. 1) to brush up; 2) to brush again; einen Hut —, to dress up or trim a hat; 3) Cloth. to roughen the cloth previous to piling.

Auf'cirkeln, (w.) v. tr. to transfer (the exact dimensions of ..., &c.) with compasses, to fit exactly.

Auf'damen, (w.) v. tr. Gam. to crown or king a man (at draughts).

Auf'dämmen, (w.) v. I. tr. to dam up; see Abdämmen; II. refl. coll. (of the clouds) es dämmt sich nach Süden zu auf, it's banking up to the southward.

Auf'dämmern, I. (w.) v. intr. (aux. sein) to dawn, open; to rise with a faint gleam; II. v. s. (str.) n. or Auf'dämmerung, (w.) f. dawn, first rise; opening; das erste — des Verstandes, the first dawning(s) of intellect.

Auf'dampfen, (w.) v. intr. (aux. sein) to rise in smoke, steam or vapour.

Auf'dauern, (w.) v. intr. to keep up, to stay up (watching).

Auf'decken, (w.) v. tr. 1) a) lit. & fig. to uncover; to bare, to lay bare; sein Spiel —, Gam. to show or let see one's cards; b) T. to uncape (a quarry); c) to detect, disclose, unveil, to discover, to expose (one's shame, a fallacy, &c.); 2) to cover over, to lay (the table cloth).

Auf'deckung, (w.) f. 1) the (act of) uncovering, &c.; 2) fig. discovery, exposure, disclosure. (2) see Abdämmen.

Auf'deichen, (w.) v. tr. 1) to raise a dike;

Auf'dichten, (w.) v. tr. see Andichten.

consecution, succession; —folgend, consecutive, successive; —fügung, *f. Carp.* rabbeting, *see* Aufpfropfen; das —stoßen, conflict; —treiben, *Mar.* to drive or fall aboard a ship, to run foul of each other (said of two ships).

Auf'eisen, *(w.) v.* I. *tr.* to break the ice of (a river); to break up and clear away the ice (from the roads or pavements); to break holes in the ice of (a pond) to let in air for the fish: um ein Schiff herum —, to clear a ship; II. *intr. see* Aufthauen.

Auf'enthalt, *(str.) m.* 1) stay: *a)* stoppage, sojourn; *b)* abode; biding-place; home, dwelling; residence; retirement; haunt; whereabout(s); 2) *fig.* delay, stop, hind(e)rance, detention, stoppage (der Posten, Bahnzüge &c.); hier sind 5 Minuten —, here we stop five minutes; A-e inbegriffen, stoppages included; ohne —, without stopping; *Mar.* demurrage (die Extraliegetage); A-skarte, *f.* certificate (permit) of residence, permission to reside; A-sort, *m.* place of abode or residence; domicile; A-szeit, *f.* time of continuance in a place; sojourn.

Auf'erbauen, *(w.) v. tr.* 1) *see* Aufbauen; 2) *see* Erbauen, 2.

Auf'erbaulich, *adj.* edifying.

Auf'erlegen, *(w.) v. tr.* (Einem etwas) to impose (something on, upon); to enjoin (one) to ...; *cf.* Auflegen. — **Auf'erlegung,** *(w.) f.* imposition (of contributions, &c.).

Auf'erstehen, I. *(irr.) v. intr. (aux.* sein) to rise up, to rise from the dead; II. *v. s. (str.) n. see* Auferstehung.

Auf'erstehung, *(w.) f.* resurrection; A-sfest, *n.* Easter-festival; A-sgarten, *m. fig.* churchyard; A-stag, *m.* day of resurrection.

Auf'erwachen, *(w.) v. intr. (aux.* sein) to awake (especially, from the slumber of death).

Auf'erwecken, *(w.) v. tr.* to resuscitate, to raise (from the dead). — **Auf'erwecker,** *(str.) m.* he that raises from the dead, &c. — **Auf'erweckung,** *(w.) f.* resuscitation, &c.; die — des Lazarus, the raising of Lazarus.

Auf'erziehen, *(str.) v. tr.* to bring up, *see* Aufziehen.

Auf'essen, *(str.) v. tr.* to eat up, to consume.

Auf'faseln, Auf'fasen, *(w.) v. tr. see* Ausfasern.

Auf'fädeln, Auf'fädmen, *(w.) v. tr.* 1) to string, thread; 2) to unweave, to unravel, untwist.

Auf'fahren, *(str.) v.* I. *intr. (aux.* sein) 1) (in die Luft, im Wasser) to ascend, to mount, rise, fly up; 2) to approach driving, to drive up (in a carriage, &c.; Vorfahren); 3) *Mar.* to run or strike upon (the sands, &c.), to run aground; 4) *a)* to start up (aus, from or out of); *b)* to fly open (as windows, &c.); *c) fig.* to fly out in a passion; to fly into a passion; II. *tr.* 1) to drive open; 2) to cut up or break (a road) by driving; 3) to raise (a road, garden, &c.); 4) to place, plant (cannons); 5) *Min.* to open (a mine), to drive (a gallery, &c.).

Auf'fahrend, *p. a.,* **Auf'fahrerisch,** *adj.* and. apt to fly out in a passion, passionate, irritable, vehement, impetuous, snappish; das a-e Wesen, snappishness, &c.

Auf'fahrt, *(w.) f.* 1) ascension, ascent; 2) rising ground; 3) *T.* approach (of a bridge, &c.); rising or height (of a bridge, &c.); 4) the driving up, drawing up (of carriages).

Auf'fallen, *(str.) v.* I. *tr.* 1) to open by falling; 2) to hurt, wound, bruise by falling; sich *(Dat.)* den Kopf —, to break one's head by a fall; II. *intr. (aux.* sein) 1) to fall or alight upon; 2) *fig. (with Dat.) a)* to strike, [illegible], to startle; surprise; es fällt mir auf, it strikes me; das war mir nicht aufgefallen, that had not noticed by me; *Impl.* to make [illegible] or a show; *b)* to startle, offend, [illegible]; 3) *Sport.* to light on (of birds); [illegible] up the scent (of pointers).

Auf'fallend, *p. a.,* **Auf'fällig,** I. *adj. fig.* 1) startling, striking, remarkable, conspicuous; 2) strange; extravagant; offending, flagrant; — gekleidet, extravagantly, showily dressed, dressed out of the usual way; ein zu a-es (zu buntes) Muster, too conspicuous (showy, gay) a pattern; II. **Auf'fälligkeit,** *(w.) f.* strikingness, &c., striking feature, &c.

Auf'fallspiegel, *(str.) m. see* Feldspiegel.

Auf'falten, *(w.) v. tr.* 1) to unfold; 2) to fold up: *Cloth.* to fold or lay in proper plaits.

Auf'fangen, *(str.) v. tr.* 1) to catch or snatch up, to catch; 2) to break (a blow, a fall, &c.); 3) to gather, to collect; ein Tau —, to hang or get up a rope; Briefe &c. —, to intercept letters, &c.; Neuigkeiten —, to fish up news; *Mar.-e.* den Wind —, to catch the gale; einem Schiffe den Wind —, to becalm a ship.

Auf'fange..., *in comp.* —glas, *n. Opt. see* Objectivglas; —stange, *f. Phys.* metallic point of the lightning-rod; —trog, *m. T.* sebilla, wooden-bowl used in mirror-making; —werk, *n. Agr.* reservoir of irrigation.

Auf'färben, *(w.) v. tr.* to dye afresh, to dye again, to new-dye.

Auf'fasen, Auf'fasern, *(w.) v. tr.* 1) *see* Ausfädeln, 2; 2) *Bookb.* die Enden der Schnüre —, to open and scrape the bands.

Auf'fassen, *(w.) v. tr.* 1) eine Masche —, to take up (a stitch, &c.); to catch up; to take in; 2) *fig.* to perceive, to conceive, comprehend, apprehend, grasp; falsch, irrig —, to take a wrong view of (a subject), to mistake, misconceive, misunderstand; to catch (an idea, &c.); schnell or leicht —, to be quick of comprehension, apprehension; schwer —, to be slow or dull of comprehension.

Auf'fassung, *(w.) f.* apprehension, comprehension, perception, conception; A-skraft, *f.,* A-svermögen, *n.* perceptive faculty.

Auf'feilen, *(w.) v. tr.* 1) to polish up by filing, to new-file; 2) to open by filing.

Auf'feuchten, *(w.) v. tr.* to moisten again.

Auf'fiedeln, *(w.) v. tr. vulg.* to scrape (on a violin).

Auf'findebuch, *(str., pl.* A-bücher) *m.* repertory.

Auf'finden, *(str.) v. tr.* 1) to find out; to discover; 2) to find (a person) up, awake or stirring.

Auf'findung, *(w.) f.* discovery, finding out.

Auf'firnissen, *(w.) v. tr.* to new-varnish.

Auf'fischen, *(w.) v. tr.* to fish up or out, to pick up; to intercept (Auffangen).

Auf'fitzen, *(w.) v. tr.* to untangle, to disentangle.

Auf'flackern, *(w.) v. intr. (aux.* sein) to rise with quick and transient flame, to flare up.

Auf'flammen, *(w.) v. intr. (aux.* sein) to flame up or forth, to blaze, to break out into a flame.

Auf'flattern, *(w.) v. intr. (aux.* sein) to flutter upwards.

Auf'flechten, *(str.) v. tr.* 1) to twist up; to plait; to braid up; 2) to tie (a malefactor) down (on the wheel); 3) to untwist, unmat, to unbraid, unplait.

Auf'flecken, *(w.) v. tr. see* Beflecken, Aufflecken.

Auf'flehen, *(w.) v. intr.* to pray up (zu, to); to implore.

Auf'flicken, *(w.) v. tr.* 1) to place, patch or vamp up; 2) to lay or sew on (a patch).

Auf'fliegen, *(str.) v. intr. (aux.* sein) 1) to fly up (also = to explode); *(lit. & fig.)* to start, to soar; 2) *(with* auf *[& Acc.])* to fly down (upon), to perch, light, or settle (on); 3) to fly open; hoch —, to take a high flight; — lassen, *a)* to let fly, to fly (a hawk, a kite, &c.); *b) Mil.* to blow up (with gunpowder), to spring (a mine).

Auf'flimmern, *(w.) v. intr. (aux.* sein) to glimmer up.

Auf'flößen, *(w.) v. tr.* to convey up by floating.

Auf'flöten, *(w.) v. tr.* 1) to play (a tune) on the flute; 2) to awaken by playing on the flute.

Auf'fluchen, *(w.) v. tr.* to rouse from sleep by swearing.

Auf'flug, *(str., pl.* Auf'flüge) *m.* the (act of) flying, soaring up, &c., *cf.* Auffliegen; ascension, rising (of a balloon).

Auf'flügeln, *(w.) v. refl. see* Aufdonnern, III.

Auf'fluten, *(w.) v. intr. see* Aufwallen.

Auf'fordern, *(w.) v. tr.* 1) to summon, to challenge; eine Festung zur Übergabe —, to summon a fortress (to surrender); 2) to invite, ask, call upon, request; zum Tanze —, to ask to dance, to take out; darf ich Sie, mein Fräulein, zum Tanze —, may I have the honour (pleasure) of dancing with you, Miss? dringend wozu —, to urge (a thing, *f. i.* payment).

Auf'fördern, *(w.) v. tr. Min.* to draw up the shaft; die Soole —, *Salt-w.* to raise the brine.

Auf'forderung, *(w.) f.* 1) call, summons, challenge; es erging eine — an das Volk, auseinander zu gehen, a summons was made to the people to disperse; 2) invitation; eine — ergehen lassen, to issue an appeal.

Auf'formen, *(w.) v. tr. Hatt.* to trim up (a hat).

Auf'fragen, *(w.) v. tr.* to find out by asking.

Auf'fressen, *(str.) v. tr.* 1) *a)* to devour, to eat up; to consume; *b) fig. vulg.* Einen —, to eat one out of house and home; 2) *Chem.* to corrode.

Auf'frieren, *(str.) v. intr. see* Aufthauen.

Auf'frischen, *(w.) v. tr.* to refresh, renew, to revive, *coll.* to brush up; to freshen up (the colours of a picture); to touch up, retouch (pictures); *Pewt.* to remove damaged spots in tin by retinning; *Dy.* to fill up; *Comm.* (Waaren künstlich —) to give (goods) a new finish.

Auf'fügen, *(w.) v. tr. see* Auffügen, Einfügen; *T.* to join to the spokes; *Carp* to fit, to dovetail, to clamp.

Auf'führbar, *adj.* what may be raised, built, represented, &c. *cf.* Aufführen.

Auf'führen, *(w.) v.* I. *tr.* 1) to lead up; 2) to raise, to set up, to erect, to build up, to construct; eine Schanze —, to throw up a trench or redoubt; 3) to represent, to perform, to act (plays); Sprichwörter, Charaden —, *Gam.* to play *proverbes (Fr.),* to act charades; 4) *Comm.* to charge, note down, enter; einzeln —, to detail, to specify; 5) *Mil.* to place or plant (cannons); to post (the guard, a sentry); 6) to produce, adduce (Zeugen, witnesses); 7) den Tanz, zum Tanz —, to lead off the dance, to lead out to the dance; *T.* to batten; II. *refl.* to behave or conduct one's self.

Auf'führung, *(w.) f.* 1) the act of leading up, &c.; 2) erection; 3) representation, performance; acting; 4) behaviour, conduct, deportment; manners; gute —, good breeding; rohe —, ill-breeding.

Auf'füllen, *(w.) v. tr.* to fill up again, to cask, to bottle; der Wein ist höchstens zum — tauglich, the wine is at best only fit for mixing.

Auf'funkeln, *(w.) v. intr.* to emit a transient glitter, to throw up sparks.

Auf'furchen, *(w.) v. tr.* to furrow.

Auf'füßen, *(w.) v. intr.* to stand on one's feet.

Auf'futtern, *(w.) v. tr.* 1) *Carp.* to line, to box up, to case.

Auf'füttern, *(w.) v. tr.* 1) to spend, consume (food); 2) *a)* to breed up, bring up, food; to bring up by the hand (children); *b)* to fatten.

Auf'fütterung, *(w.) f. Ship-b.* die A-en eines Schiffes beim Kielholen, the water-boards of a ship laid on a careen.

Auf'gabe, *(w.) f.* 1) delivery (of a telegram at the telegraph-station); posting (of a letter); 2) *a)* task; lesson; (schriftliche) exercise; (zum Rechnen) sum; *b)* proposition; problem, theme; *c) fig.* business (of one's life);

gression (of philosophy, &c.); 3) a) surrender (of a town); b) resignation (of an office); giving up (one's right, &c.); retirement (from business, des Geschäfts); 4) Comm. order, instructions: unter —, with advice; laut —, as per advice, as advised; nach —, according to statement; Ihrer — gemäß, agreeably to your order (instructions); —ort, m. eines Briefes, place where a letter is or was posted, cf. Aufgeben.

Auf'gabeln, (w.) v. tr. 1) to take up with a fork, to pick up; 2) see Aufgattern.

Auf'gaffen, (w.) v. intr. to look (stare) upward.

Auf'gähnen, (w.) v. intr. to yawn aloud; to yawn; fig. to gape.

Auf'gähren, (str.) v. intr. to ferment anew: — lassen, to raise a new fermentation, to stum: der aufgegohrene Wein, stum.

Auf'gällen, (w.) v. intr. see Aufprallen.

Auf'gang, (str., pl. Auf'gänge) m. 1) a) the act of going up, &c. (cf. Aufgehen), rising, ascent; rise (of the sun, &c.); b) rising ground, slope, ascent; c) a flight of steps or stairs on the outside of a building (Freitreppe); 2) east, orient; 3) consumption, spending.

Auf'gattern, (w.) v. tr. 1) coll. to pick up, find out; 2) to keep an animal's mouth open whilst administering physic.

Auf'geben, I. (str.) v. tr. 1) to deliver; to send (a telegram), to post (a letter); 2) to give up: a) to surrender; to yield up; b) to give up (retire from) (business), to vacate (an employment, &c.), lay down, resign; c) to give over (a patient, i. e. to despair of his recovery), to drop (an acquaintance, &c.), abandon (a measure, &c.), relinquish (an opinion, &c.), to quit (a claim), renounce (hope, &c.); den Geist —, to give up the ghost, to expire; 3) (Einem etwas) to set or impose (one a task); to order, direct (one), to propose or put a question, a riddle: Comm. Adressen —, to supply (furnish) with addresses; eine Bestellung —, to give an order: to order; sämmtliche aufgegebene Artikel, all the articles ordered: Waaren zur Versicherung —, to order an insurance to be effected on goods: Metall. to charge, feed, serve the furnace; II. s. (str.) n., or Auf'gebung, (w.) f. surrender, relinquishment, &c.: Metall. charge, feeding of the furnace.

Auf'geber, (str.) m. he that delivers, proposes, &c.; Metall. charger.

Auf'gebig, adj. Law, a fief which the proprietor can at any time inhabit and occupy with soldiers.

Auf'gebirgen, (w.) v. tr. see Aufthürmen.

Auf'geblasen, I. p. a. fig. inflated, puffed up, swelling, big, haughty, elated, huffy, huffish, arrogant, flushed (with ambition); II. A-heit, (w.) f. inflation, haughtiness; insolence, arrogance, huffishness.

Auf'gebot, (str.) n. 1) public call, summons; — der Gläubiger, calling of a meeting of the creditors; 2) the (publication of the) banns; 3) Mil. levy: cf. Aufhebung, 2; 4) — (Aufbietung) aller Mittel, utmost exertion.

Auf'gebracht, p. a. (cf. Aufbringen) irritated, angry, indignant (über [with Acc.], at).

Auf'gebung, (w.) f. the (act of) giving up, &c. see Aufgeben, v. s. & Aufgabe.

Auf'gebeilt, p. a. (cf. Aufbeilen) T. a-es Holz, wood to be used in building after previous examination; squared timber.

Auf'gedinge, (str.) n. the binding and money paid for an apprentice, indenture, cf. Aufdingen & Aufdingegeld.

Auf'gedreht, p. a. (cf. Aufdrehen) das a-e Ende eines Taues, fag-end of a rope.

Auf'gedunsen, I. p. a. 1) Med. bloated; 2) see Aufgeblasen; II. A-heit, (w.) f. bloatedness.

Auf'gehen, (irr.) v. I. intr. (aux. sein) 1) lit. (only in combination with abgehen) to walk up: ein paar mal in der Stube auf- und abgehen, to walk up and down in the room, to take a turn or two about the room; 2) a) to rise, arise, mount; a-des Mauerwerk, masonry above ground: der Vorhang ging auf, the curtain drew up: die Sonne geht auf, the sun rises; die Sonne ist aufgegangen, the sun is up; b) fig. (with the Dat.) to break or dawn (upon one, as the light of truth, &c.); ein Strahl der Hoffnung geht uns auf, a beam (gleam) of hope shines upon us; eine neue Welt schien ihm aufgegangen, a new creation seemed to open on him; 3) to shoot, come up; come forth; to bud, blossom; 4) Bak. & Cook. to heave, swell, rise (said of dough); 5) Mas. to swell, rise, increase (said of slacked lime); 6) a) to open (as a door, &c.), to break up, as ice, &c.; die Wunde ging auf, the wound opened; das Wetter geht auf, it thaws; b) to open, commence: die Jagd geht auf, the shooting-season begins; das — (v. s., [str.] n.) der Schifffahrt, der Flüsse, the opening of the navigation, of the rivers; 7) to get or come loose: to fag out, untwist, unwind, untwine; to uncurl, come out (as curls); 8) a) to be spent; er läßt viel —, he spends a great deal; b) to get consumed; in Feuer, in Rauch —, to be consumed by fire; fig. to end in smoke; c) (with in [with Dat.]) fig. to be merged (in), to be amalgamated or identified (with), to coincide (with); Preußen geht fortan in Deutschland auf, from this day forward Prussia is fused in Germany; ihr Glück geht in dem ihrer Tochter auf, her happiness is bound up in that of her daughter; 9) Arith. to be even (of numbers); es geht auf, there is no rest, nothing left; there remains nought; 6 von 6 geht auf, 6 subtracted from 6 leaves no remainder; 5 geht nicht in 9 auf, 9 cannot be divided by 5 without a remainder; eine Rechnung — lassen, Comm. to strike a balance, to balance; wechselseitige Schulden — lassen, to set off mutual debts; es geht mir ein Licht auf or mir gehen die Augen auf, I begin to see clear

II. tr. fam. sich (Dat.) die Füße —, to walk one's feet sore.

Auf'geien, (w.) v. tr. Mar. to brail up, to clew or haul up (a sail).

Auf'geigen, (w.) v. tr. coll. 1) (Einem etwas) to play (a tune to one) upon the violin, to fiddle; 2) to rouse from sleep by fiddling.

Auf'geklärt, I. p. a. enlightened, (highly) civilised, intelligent, clear(-headed), luminous, bright, liberal; II. A-heit, (w.) f. enlightenment, (high state of) civilisation, instruction; brightness (of intellect).

Auf'geld, (str., pl. A-er) n. 1) Comm. agio, premium, change, exchange, balance; 2) see Angeld.

Auf'gelegt, p. a. (gut or schlecht) disposed (zu, for a thing, to jest, &c.) in a (good or bad) humour; wenn er dazu — gewesen wäre, if he had been so minded.

Auf'geleiten, (w.) v. tr. to lead up.

Auf'geräumt, I. p. a. fig. good-humoured; in high or good spirits, of good cheer; in a merry cue; careless: ein a-er Mann, a good-humoured man; II. A-heit, (w.) f. goodhumouredness, &c.

Auf'geregt, I. p. a. excited, &c. cf. Aufregen; II. A-heit, (w.) f. excitement, &c. (Aufregung).

Auf'gerichtet, p. a. Bot. erect.

Auf'gerollt, p. a. Bot. convolute(d).

Auf'geschürzt, p. a. Vet. shrunk in the flank (of horses).

Auf'geschwemmt, p. a. diluvial, &c. cf. Aufschwemmen.

Auf'geschwollen, I. p. a. Bot., &c. tumid, cf. Aufschwellen; II. A-heit, (w.) f. tumidness, tumidity.

fig.-a. 2) sich bei Kleinigkeiten —, to stand upon (stick at) trifles; sich bei einer Sache —, to dwell, to enlarge upon ..., to linger over ...; 3) sich über (*& Acc.*), to mock, sneer (at), to find fault (with), to criticise, censure.

Auf'halter, (*l. u.:*) **Auf'hälter,** (*str.*) *m.* 1) any instrument for stopping; 2) *Mus.* see Vorhalt; 3) *a) Mar.* relieving-rope; *b) Print.* cords of the carriage; 4) breeching (of horses); 5) *Lock-sm.* tumbler; 6) *Cord-m.* stopping-motion; 7) *Electr. Tel.* stop-work, interruptor.

Auf'halterei', (*w.*) *f. coll.* (*l. u.*) fault-finding, criticism.

Auf'halt..., *in comp.* —haken, see Sperrhaken; —kette, *f.* breeching-chain (of shaft-harness); —riemen, *m. Saddl.* breeching breech.

Auf'haltung, (*w.*) *f.* 1) a stopping, &c., hindrance, *cf.* Aufhalten; 2) *Watch-m.* scotching.

Auf'hämmern, (*w.*) *v.* I. *tr.* 1) to hammer on; to touch up with the hammer *or* on the anvil; 2) to wake (one) by hammering; 3) to open by hammering; II. *intr.* to hammer along, to beat hard.

Auf'hänge, (*w.*) *f. T.* a frame of any description used for hanging things on.

Auf'hänge..., *in comp.* —band, *n.* 1) *Anat.* suspensory, truss; 2) —bänder, *pl.* strong leather straps *or* girths to keep quiet refractory horses, when being shod *or* conveyed on board ship; —boden, *m. Typ.* printer's hanging room, drying-place; drying-loft; —feder, *f. Electr. Tel.* suspension spring; —kreuz, *n.* peel; —muskel des Auges, *m. Anat.* suspensory muscle of the eye; —punkt, *m. Mech.* point of suspension, fulcrum, bearance; —pfeiler, *Archit. m.* see Strebepfeiler; —schnüre, *f. pl. Typ.* drying-ropes; —thurm, *m. Archit.* suspension tower.

Auf'hängen, (*w.*) *v. tr.* 1) to hang up, hang, suspend; ein Bild —, to put up a picture; Wäsche —, to hang out linen to dry; 2) *coll.* (Einem etwas) to palm (a thing) upon ... (*cf.* Aufheften).

Auf'harken, (*w.*) *v. tr.* to rake up.

Auf'härten, (*w.*) *v. tr. Rope-m.* to give the necessary twisting to (the ropes).

Auf'haschen, (*w.*) *v. tr.* to snatch, catch, pick up.

Auf'haspeln, (*w.*) *v. tr.* 1) to reel, to wind, to uncoil off; *Mech.* to wind up, to weigh, to hoist; 2) to finish reeling; 3) to raise up; sich wieder —, to rise slowly from the ground; to recover from an illness; *vulg.* to pick up one's crumbs.

Auf'hauben, (*w.*) *v. tr.* to put a cap on.

Auf'hauchen, (*w.*) *v.* I. *tr.* to breathe, blow open; II. *intr.* to breathe up.

Auf'hauen, (*str.*) *v.* I. *tr.* 1) *a)* to cut, hew, break up, open *or* anew; *b)* to cleave, split (wood); *c)* to strike upon; 2) to finish cutting; 3) *T.* to cut *or* sharpen anew, to re-sharpen (a file); 4) *Tin.* to chase, to draw up by beating; 5) *Lock-sm.* to cut open with the bolt-chisel; 6) *Carp.* to assemble the timber; II. *intr.* 1) to strike (upon), to hit hard; 2) *Gunn.* mit der Lunte —, to cock the match.

Auf'hauer, (*str.*) *m. Lock-sm.* bolt-chisel, carp's tongue.

Auf'häufeln, (*w.*) *v. tr.* 1) *Agr.* to raise (the earth) about plants; to hill, earth up (potatoes, &c.); 2) to gather up and to form into small heaps.

Auf'häufen, (*w.*) *v.* I. *tr.* to heap up; to pile up, accumulate, amass, to store up, hoard up; II. *refl.* to accumulate, increase; to run up (as debts), to drift (as snow, sand, &c.).

Auf'häufung, (*w.*) *f.* accumulation.

Auf'hebe..., *in comp.* —binde, *f. Surg.* [illegible], suspensory, truss; —muskel, *m.* see [illegible], 2.

Auf'heben, (*str.*) *v. tr.* 1) to raise, lift (up), to lift from, to heave (up), take up, pick up; den Anker —, to weigh anchor; eine Masche (ein Auge) —, to take up a stitch; ein Kind —, to take up *or* adopt a child; 2) *Law,* to lay up *or* by, to keep, set aside, save, spare, preserve; 3) *a)* to break (up), raise (a siege, &c.); bei Gelegenheit der Verheiratung des Kaisers wurde der Belagerungszustand in Ungarn und in der Lombardei aufgehoben, on the occasion of the emperor's marriage the state of siege was removed in Hungary and Lombardy; to finish (dinner), end (a quarrel, &c.); ein Lager —, to break up a camp, decamp; die Sitzung &c. —, to break (up) the session, meeting, &c.; einen Ball —, to break up a ball; to dissolve (parliament, &c.); das Stillschweigen —, to break silence; *b)* to do away with, abolish, abrogate, repeal (laws, &c.); to revoke, recall, quash, reverse (a sentence, &c.); to invalidate (a will); cancel, annul, nullify, undo (a treaty, contract, &c.); dissolve, break up (partnership, &c.); to withdraw (an action); den gerichtlichen Beschlag —, to retake *or* replevy a distress; *Mar.* to take off the embargo; der aufgehobene Verkauf, *Comm.* sale annulled; die aufhebende Clausel, *Law,* derogatory clause; *c)* to break (off, a match, &c.); die Freundschaft mit ... —, to break with ...; *d)* to neutralise (the effect, &c.); to level (all distinctions, &c.); sich gegenseitig —, to neutralise *or* to destroy each other (as reasons of equal value, &c.); *e) Math.* to clear, solve, reduce (a fraction); 4) to take up, arrest, seize, to apprehend, capture; einen Pfuscher —, to fine a bungler, &c.; er ist gut aufgehoben, he is in good keeping, well taken care of; schlecht aufgehoben, ill provided for; der ist aufgehoben, *iron.*, we have settled his business, he is done for; aufgeschoben ist nicht aufgehoben, *proverb,* forbearance is not acquittance; durch Reibung aufgehoben, *Mech.* destroyed by friction.

Auf'heben, *v. s.* (*str.*) *n.* 1) the (act of) lifting up, raising, &c., elevation, heave; upheaval; das — der Hände (beim Abstimmen), show of hands; 2) *fig.* viel A—s machen, to make much bustle *or* a great fuss (von, about); viel A—s um nichts, much ado about nothing.

Auf'heber, (*str.*) *m.* 1) *T.* an instrument for lifting up; 2) *Anat.* uplifting, attollent *or* levator muscle (of the scapula &c.); 3) (*or* **Auf'hebezüngelchen,** *n.*) *Surg.* elevator; 4) *Mar.* clab-line; 5) *Weav.* levator, *pl.* neck-twines; 6) *Print.* lifter, layer.

Auf'hebung, (*w.*) *f.* 1) see Aufheben, *v. s.* 1; 2) *Law, &c.* abolition, defeasance, abrogation; repeal, &c.; — der Sclaverei, abolition of slavery; *cf.* Aufheben; — des Vorbehalts, removal of restrictions; — einer Klage, non-suit; *b)* dissolution, suppression (of a convent, of the equilibrium, &c.), suspension (of intercourse, &c.); A—sbefehl, *m. Law,* decision of annulment; A—sgericht, *n. Fr. Law,* court of cassation.

Auf'hefteln, (*w.*) *v. tr.* see Aufhaken.

Auf'heften, (*w.*) *v. tr.* 1) to pin up, to fasten; to fix to; to tie up; (aufnähen) to stitch upon; 2) to undo, unhook, unclasp; 3) *fig.* (Einem etwas) to impose *or* palm (something upon one); Einem eine Lüge —, to tell one a fib; Sie werden sich doch nicht solchen Unsinn — lassen, you surely won't be led to believe such nonsense! 4) *Bookb.* to stitch.

Auf'heißen, (*w.*) *v. tr. coll. for* Aufhissen.

Auf'heitern, (*w.*) *v.* I. *tr.* 1) to make clear *or* serene, to clear up, to brighten; 2) *fig.* to cheer up; II. *refl.* 1) to clear up (of the weather, &c.); 2) *fig.* to brighten, to become cheerful, to clear up the brow; to unbend one's mind, to relax; aufgeheitert, *p. a.* 1) clear, cleared up, serene; 2) *fig.* merry, cheerful, gay, enlivened.

Auf'heiterung, (*w.*) *f.* 1) the (act of) clearing up, &c.; 2) *fig.* relief, recreation.

Auf'helfen, (*str.*) *v.* I. *intr.* (*with Dat.*) 1) to help (one, Einem) up, to give a lift; 2) *fig.* to set up, prop up, to lend a hand, to succour, support, assist; dem Schuldner läßt sich nicht mehr —, there is nothing more to be done for the debtor; II. *refl.* to raise one's self with difficulty, to struggle up; *fig.* to get out of one's difficulties.

Auf'helfer, (*str.*) *m.* 1) he that succours, assists, helper, &c.; 2) a string *or* cord with a tassel, fastened to the tester, used in raising one's self the more easily in bed.

Auf'hellen, (*w.*) *v.* I. *tr.* 1) to brighten *or* clear up, to illuminate (Erhellen); 2) to clarify, purify (liquids); 3) *fig.* to enlighten (the mind, &c.), elucidate (a passage in a book, &c.), to clear up (a doubt, &c.); 4) *Paint.* to brisk up, to enliven (a picture); II. *refl.* 1) to clear up, brighten; 2) to grow clear, to clarify.

Auf'hellung, (*w.*) *f.* 1) the (act of) clearing up, &c.; 2) enlightening, elucidation.

Auf'henken, (*w.*) *v. tr.* see Aufhängen.

Auf'hetzen, (*w.*) *v. tr.* to hunt *or* stir up, to start (game); *fig.* to stir up, incite, instigate; Einen wider den Andern —, to set one against the other. — **Auf'hetzer,** (*str.*) *m.* inciter, &c.

Auf'hetzerei', **Auf'hetzung,** (*w.*) *f.* the act *or* practice of stirring up, &c., instigation.

Auf'heucheln, (*w.*) *v. refl.* to gain favour (bei, with) by flattery *or* dissimulation.

Auf'heulen, (*w.*) *v.* I. *intr.* to set up a howl, begin howling; II. *tr.* to wake by howling.

Auf'hissen, (*w.*) *v. tr. Mar.* to hoist, haul, *or* pull up, to heave out (a sail); eine Flagge —, to heave (a flag) abroad; aufgehißt, *p. a.* a-weigh (as the anchor), a-trip (as the anchor *or* top-sails).

Auf'hocken, (*w.*) *v.* I. *tr.* 1) to take on one's back; 2) (Einem etwas) to put something on one's back; 3) *Agr.* to pile up in sheaves *or* cocks; to put in heaps; II. *intr.* to cling to *or* hang one's self upon one (in order to be carried).

Auf'höhen, (*w.*) *v. tr. Paint.* die Farben (Lichter) —, to heighten *or* increase the effect of the lights (colours), to set off.

Auf'holen, (*w.*) *v. tr.* to fetch *or* draw up; *Weav.* to draw up (the threads of the warp); *Mar.-s.* to haul up (a boat); das Ruder —, to bear up; ein Schiff —, to ground a vessel, to draw up for repairs; das Schiff bei dem Winde —, to haul the wind again, to bring a ship to the wind.

Auf'holer, (*str.*) *m.* 1) *Weav.* see Aufheber, 5; 2) *Mar.-s.* relieving tackle; tracing-line (passing through a block); — des Stagsegels, halliard of a stay-sail; — der Stückpforten, port-tackle; — des Racks, parrel-truss; — des Besansegels, girtline to haul up the mizen-brails; — der Reefen, mart(i)nets.

Auf'holzen, (*w.*) *v. intr. Sport.* see Aufbaumen.

Auf'horchen, **Auf'hören,** (*w.*) *v. intr.* to listen with raised head *or* with roused attention; to prick up one's ears, to hearken attentively *or* with astonishment.

Auf'hören, I. (*w.*) *v. intr.* 1) see Aufhorchen; 2) to cease, discontinue, to desist; to leave off; to end, terminate; to stop; plötzlich —, to break *or* stop short; hör' auf! have done! mit ... —, to put a stop to ..., drop (the conversation, &c.); —zu fließen, to staunch (of blood); —zu zahlen, *Comm.* to stop payment; II. *v. s.* (*str.*) *n.* cessation, intermission; ohne —, incessantly, without intermission.

Auf'hub, (*str.*) *m.* (*l. u.*) that which is kept, reserved, or laid up, see Aufheben; the remnants; refuse, the rest (Abhub, Brocken); *fig.* rise, elevation.

Auf'hucken, *(w.)* v. *tr.* see **Aufhocken**.

Auf'hügeln, *(w.)* v. *tr.* to raise up like a hill, to pile up in hillocks.

Auf'hülfe, *(w.)* *f.* a helping up, aid, *cf.* Aufhelfen.

Auf'hüllen, *(w.)* v. *tr.* to uncover (Enthüllen).

Auf'hüpfen, *(w.)* v. *intr.* *(aux.* sein) to frisk, skip, to hop, jump up, bound (vor Freude *[Dat.]*, with joy).

Auf'husten, *(w.)* v. I. *intr.* to cough loud; II. *tr.* 1) to bring up by coughing; 2) to wake by coughing.

Auf'jagen, *(w.)* v. *tr.* 1) to start, to rouse, scare up; to drive away; *Sport-s.* to unharbour, dislodge (a hart); to rouse (a buck, a deer); to uncouch, rear *or* unslough (a bear); to vent (an otter); to unkennel (a fox); to start (a hare); to bolt out (a rabbit); to spring (partridges); to tree (a squirrel, a marten); 2) *fig.* to hunt up (out) a person.

Auf'jammern, *(w.)* v. I. *intr.* to set up, begin a lamentation, to moan, wail aloud; II. *tr.* to rouse by lamentation, moaning, &c.

Auf'jauchzen, *(w.)* v. I. *intr.* to cry in triumph, to set up an exultation, shouting, to give a great shout; II. *tr.* to rouse by shouting.

Auf'jochen, *(w.)* v. *tr.* (Einem etwas) to put a yoke, burden upon (one).

Auf'jubeln, *(w.)* v. *intr.* see Aufjauchzen.

Auf'kämmen, *(w.)* v. *tr.* 1) to comb upwards; 2) to comb afresh, to repair (a wig, &c.); 3) *a) Carp.* to cog, to join by cogging; *b) Mech.* to indent.

Auf'kappen, *(w.)* v. *tr.* to cap, to put on a cap; *Falc.* to hoodwink (a hawk).

Auf'karren, *(w.)* v. *tr.* 1) to heap up, to raise (as a road, by carting *or* wheeling earth upon it); 2) to break (as a road by too frequent driving over it).

Auf'katten *(L. G.)*, **Auf'katen**, *(w.)* v. *tr.* *Mar.* to cat (the anchor).

Auf'kauen, *(w.)* v. *tr.* to consume in chewing, to chew up.

Auf'kauf, *(str., pl.* Auf'käufe) *m.* the (act of) buying up, engrossment, purchase on speculation.

Auf'kaufen, *(w.)* v. *tr.* to buy up, to engross, forestal; to regrate; *Comm.* alle Posten, die Einem vorkommen, —, to purchase all the lots one meets with.

Auf'käufer, *(str.)* *m.* engrosser, forestaller, &c.; monopoliser; *Comm.* purchaser.

Auf'kegeln, *(w.)* v. *tr.* to pile up, to range into a cone.

Auf'kehren, *(w.)* v. *tr.* 1) to sweep up (together); 2) to turn up; 3) *Gold-sm.* to anneal, to stamp; to work on (a stamp).

Auf'kehricht, *(str.)* *n.* sweepings; *Min.* sweepings.

Auf'keimen, *(w.)* v. *intr.* *(aux.* sein) to shoot up, bud, germinate; a-d, *p. a. fig.* budding, nascent, dawning (love, &c.).

Auf'keltern, *(w.)* v. *tr.* to press all (the grapes).

Auf'kerben, *(w.)* v. *tr.* to mark, note by scoring *or* notching score.

Auf'ketteln, **Auf'ketten**, *(w.)* v. *intr.* to unchain, to unfasten, *or* open the chain of (a door).

Auf'keilen, *(w.)* v. *tr.* *Min.* to cleave with wedges.

Auf'klatschen, *(w.)* v. *intr.* to beat, knock up with a club.

Auf'kippen, *(w.)* v. I. *tr.* to raise up; to tilt up; II. *intr.* to tilt.

Auf'kisten, *(w.)* v. *tr.* to strengthen the head *or* top of (a dam or dyke).

Auf'kitten, *(w.)* v. *tr.* to fasten upon with cement, to cement on.

Auf'kitzeln, *(w.)* v. *tr.* to wake *or* rouse by tickling. [a cart.

Auf'klaffen, *(w.)* v. *intr.* to gape; to get

Auf'klaftern, *(w.)* v. *tr.* to pile up in fathoms, to cord.

Auf'klagen, *(w.)* see Aufjammern.

Auf'klappe, *(w.)* *f.* the flap of a hat *or* coat.

Auf'klappen, *(w.)* v. *tr.* to put up the folds of (a table, &c.); to cock (a hat).

Auf'klären, *(w.)* v. *tr.* & *refl.* see Aufhellen; Jemand über etwas *(Acc.)* —, to give one a clear insight into a matter; sich über etwas *(Acc.)* — wollen, to wish to get a clear insight into, to seek enlightenment on (a matter). — **Auf'klärer**, *(str.)* *m.* enlightener, illuminator, clearer, &c. — **Auf'klärerei'**, *(w.)* *f.* pseudo-enlightenment, false enlightening. — **Auf'klärerisch**, *adj.* *(l. u.)* tending to enlighten by (superficial) knowledge, elucidatory.

Auf'klärung, *(w.)* *f.* 1) clarification; 2) *fig.* *a)* clearing up, elucidation, explanation, *éclaircissement;* er wird uns einige — darüber geben, he will give us some insight into it; *b)* enlightenment; das Fortschreiten der —, the march of mind; A-ssucht, A-swuth, *f.* rage of enlightening, explaining everything, &c. (Aufklärerei).

Auf'klatschen, *(w.)* v. I. *intr.* *(aux.* sein) to fall clashing (auf *[with Acc.]*, upon); II. *tr.* 1) to rouse by cracking (a whip, &c.); 2) *T.* to stencil.

Auf'klauben, *(w.)* v. *tr.* to pick up; to open by picking with the fingers, by clawing.

Auf'kleben (**Auf'kleiben**), *(w.)* v. I. *tr.* to paste up *or* on, to stick up; to mount (a map on cloth, &c.); II. *intr.* to stick to.

Auf'kleistern, *(w.)* v. *tr.* to paste on, to paste up.

Auf'klettern, *(w.)*, **Auf'klimmen**, *(str. & w.)* v. *intr.* *(aux.* sein) to climb up.

Auf'klimpern, *(w.)* v. *tr.* 1) to play in a bungling manner (a piece of music on a piano); 2) to wake *or* rouse by strumming or thrumming.

Auf'klingeln, *(w.)* see Aufschellen.

Auf'klinken, *(w.)* v. *tr.* to unlatch.

Auf'klirren, *(w.)* v. *intr.* *(aux.* sein) to open with a rattling noise.

Auf'klopfen, *(w.)* v. I. *tr.* 1) to open by knocking, to knock open; 2) *Typ.* to knock up (die Ballen, the balls); 3) to wake *or* rouse from sleep by knocking; II. *intr.* to knock upon.

Auf'klotzen, *(w.)* v. *tr.* *Calico-print.* to pad.

Auf'knabbern, *(w.)* v. *tr.* to gnaw up, to crunch, cranch.

Auf'knacken, *(w.)* v. *tr.* to crack (open).

Auf'knallen, *(w.)* v. I. *intr.* *(aux.* sein) to shoot up with a report; II. *tr.* to let go up; to rouse by a report.

Auf'knarren, *(w.)* v. *intr.* *(aux.* sein) to open with a creaking noise.

Auf'knastern, *(w.)* see Aufknarren.

Auf'knattern, *(w.)* v. *intr.* *(aux.* sein) to crepitate, to crackle up, to burst with a small, sharp sound, rapidly repeated.

Auf'knäueln, *(w.)* v. *tr.* to coil *or* wind up into a ball.

Auf'knaupeln, *(w.)* v. *tr.* to pick open, to open with difficulty.

Auf'knebeln, *(w.)* v. *tr.* 1) to fasten on by a gag *or* short piece of wood; 2) to ungag, to undo. — **Auf'knebelung**, *(w.)* *f.* *Mar.* (der Scheren) the shroud-bridles.

Auf'kneipen, *(w.)* v. *tr.* to open with pincers; to pinch open.

Auf'knicken, *(w.)* v. *tr.* to crack, to break open.

Auf'knieen, *(w.)* v. I. *intr.* (with auf *[& Acc. or Dat.]*) to kneel down upon; II. *tr.* to wear holes into (the breeches) by kneeling, to wear out by kneeling.

Auf'knistern, *(w.)* see Aufknattern.

Auf'knöpfen, *(w.)* v. *tr.* 1) to unbutton; 2) to button up.

Auf'knüpfen, *(w.)* v. I. *tr.* to tie up, to

kündigen, without giving previous notice; b) to recall (a capital), cf. Aufsagen; c) to recant, retract (what one has said); 2) to renounce (another's friendship), to break with ....

Auf'kündigung (l. u.: **Auf'kündung**), (w.) f. the giving previous notice, warning, &c. cf. Aufkünden; — eines Capitals, recalling of a capital, re-demand; A-sfrist, f., A-stermin, m., A-szeit, f. warning-time.

Auf'kunft, (str., pl. Auf'künfte) f. (l. u.) recovery (Aufkommen).

A. **Auf'lachen**, (w.) v. I. intr. to break out into a laugh, to laugh out loudly; II. tr. to rouse by loud laughing.

B. **Auf'lachen**, (w.) v. tr. Forest. to make incisions in (a tree to extract the resin).

Auf'laden, (str.) v. tr. 1) to load, lade; 2) to load (something) upon, to burden (one) with: Einem die Mühe —, to put one to the trouble, cf. Aufbürden; Einem eine Tracht Schläge —, to thrash, hide, or cudgel one.

Auf'lader, **Auf'läder**, (str.) m. loader, packer; —lohn, m. fee for loading, packing; Comm. loading charges; (in Speicherrechnungen) loading, packing.

Auf'lage, (w.) f. 1) impost, tax, imposition, assessment, duty; 2) (with handicraftsmen) a) (or —geld) collection (of money); b) also vulg. & coml. meeting, club, conventicle; 3) the money collected in a plate at meetings, charity-sermons, &c., the collection; 4) gerichtliche —, summons; eine — thun, Law, to issue a writ against one; 5) edition, impression; neue —, reimpression; 6) († &) vulg. accusation (especially a false one); 7) Carp. the timbers or balks of a building on which the superstructure is raised; 8) Turn. rest; 9) Gun-sm. cast, cover for the pan.

Auf'lagern, (w.) v. tr. to store up, to lay in a magazine, to lay in stock; to warehouse (goods). — **Auf'lagerung**, (w.) f. 1) the (act of) storing up, &c.; warehousing; 2) Miner. & Geol. aggregate.

Auf'langen, (w.) v. tr. to reach up.

Auf'langer, (str.) m. Mar. futtock; pl. — der Kattpoorten, futtock-riders; verkehrte —, top-timbers.

Auf'lärmen, (w.) v. tr. to wake up by noise.

Auf'laßbrief, (str.) m. the legal document containing the act of resignation called Auflassen, sb. II.

Auf'lassen, I. v. (str.) tr. 1) to let (one) get up; to suffer to rise; 2) coll. (for offen lassen) to leave open; eine Grube —, Min. to abandon a mine; II. v. s. (str.) n. Law, resignation of rights to real estate in favour of another (resignatio judicialis).

Auf'lassung, (w.) f. the abandoning of a mine; — ansagen, to give notice to the proper authorities of the abandonment of a mine.

Auf'lasten, (w.) v. tr. see Aufladen.

Auf'lauerer, (str.) m. one who lies in wait, way-layer, watch, spy.

Auf'lauern, (w.) v. intr. (with Dat.) to way-lay, to lie in wait or ambush for; to lurk for, to watch, espy, dog.

Auf'lauf, (str., pl. Auf'läufe) m. 1) riotous assembly, rout, mob, rabble; uproar, tumult; 2) a) (Mar.) a swelling, &c. cf. Auflaufen; b) tide; b) Cook. see Auflaufer; 3) fig. increase (of expenses); 4) Archit. rising, scaffold-bridge, gangway.

Auf'laufen, (str.) v. I. tr. 1) to make open by running; 2) to make sore by running; II. intr. (aux. sein) 1) to swell; to rise; auflaufende Flut, Mar. young flood; 2) to increase, [illegible] up (auf [with Acc.], to; of costs, interest, &c.); 3) Mar. a) to run aground; b) das [illegible] — lassen, to man the yards; 4) to germinate, [illegible]; das aufgelaufen, pp. & adj. [illegible] swelled, inflated; swollen; 2) Bot. [illegible] distended.

Auf'laufer, (str.) m. Mar. younker.

Auf'läufer, (str.) m. 1) see Auflaufer; 2) Cook. a sort of high raised paste; Spanish paste; puff-paste; 3) Found. smelter.

Auf'lauschen, (w.) v. tr. see Aufhorchen.

Auf'läuten, (w.) v tr. to wake up by ringing the bells.

Auf'lavieren, (w.) v. intr. & tr. Mar. to sail up a river by plying to windward by boards, or by tacking, to board it up.

Auf'leben, (w.) v. I. intr. (aux. sein) to revive, to return to life; II. tr. Paint. to touch, to refresh (the colours of a picture); III. v. s. (str.) n. revival.

Auf'lecken, (w.) v. tr. to lick up, lap (up).

Auf'legegeld, (str., pl. A-er) n. see Auflage, 2, a.

Auf'legen, (w.) v. I. tr. 1) a) to put on, lay on, to apply (a poultice, &c.), to store up (provisions); to exhibit, expose, lay out (wares at the shop-front); den Ellbogen —, to lean one's elbow on or upon; die Hände —, Theol. to impose (the) hands; das Tischtuch —, to spread or lay the table-cloth; ein Geschütz —, Gunn. to mount a cannon; Fett —, vulg. to grow fat; roth, weiß — (sich schminken), to paint one's face with red, white; sie legt auf (intr.), she paints; Farben —, Paint. to lay colours; b) Mar. to lay up (a ship); aufgelegte Schiffe, ships in ordinary; c) coll. (for offen legen) die Karten or sein Spiel —, to spread one's cards upon the table, to show one's cards; 2) fig.-s. to impose, lay on (taxes, duties); Einem eine Geldstrafe —, to fine one; Brandschatzung —, to put under contribution; Einem eine Strafe ꝛc. —, to inflict a punishment (slights, humiliations, &c.) upon one; Einem Stillschweigen —, to impose silence (upon); Einem einen Eid —, to administer or tender an oath to one, to put one on his oath; Jemandem eine Verbindlichkeit —, to lay one under an obligation; eine Buße —, to enjoin a penance (upon...); 3) Print. to put into the press (a sheet); to print, to publish (a book); neu —, to reprint, republish; Bank —, Gam. to hold the bank (at pharo and games of hazard); der Baum legt viel Holz auf, Forest. the tree gets branchy, or full of branches; Einem etwas Schändliches —, to throw disgrace upon a person; II. refl. lit. & fig. see Auflehnen (sich), 1 & 3; der Tabak legt sich auf die Zunge auf, the tobacco bites the tongue; pp. & adj. aufgelegt, q. v.

Auf'leger, (str.) m. 1) Salt-w. the workman who removes the crystallized salt from the pans to the baskets; 2) a spade used in cutting turf or peat; 3) one of a certain class of pilots on the Danube.

Auf'leg(e)..., in comp. —maschine, f. Weav. spreader; —schaufel, f. Salt-w. a flat wooden shovel used by the Aufleger.

Auf'legung, (w.) f. 1) the (act of) laying on, &c. cf. Auflegen & Auflage; Theol. imposition (of hands); 2) Med. application; 3) infliction (of a punishment, &c.).

Auf'lehnen, (w.) v. refl. 1) to lean, rest (auf [with Acc.], upon): sich nachlässig —, to loll (on); 2) Man. to prance; 3) fig. (with gegen) to oppose, resist, withstand (one), to be refractory, to rise, mutiny, or rebel (against one); to set one's mind (against).

Auf'leihen, (str.) v. tr. to borrow up.

Auf'leimen, (w.) v. tr. 1) to glue (upon, on); 2) to unglue.

Auf'lesen, (str.) v. tr. to pick up, to gather.

Auf'leuchten, (w.) v. intr. to shine, to flash up, to rise resplendent.

Auf'lichten, (w.) v. tr. Paint. see Aufleben.

Auf'liegen, (str.) v. I. intr. 1) to lie, lean, rest upon; 2) Man. to bear too heavy on the bridle, to bore, to carry the nose to the ground (of horses); 3) to be out of place or without employment (of servants, &c.); II. refl. to get sore by lying or keeping the bed, to become bed-sore, to contract bed-sores.

Auf'locken, (w.) v. tr. see Aufringeln.

Auf'lockern, (w.) v. tr. to break up (the ground); to loosen (the soil); to shake, to unfix.

Auf'lodern, (w.) v. intr. (aux. sein) 1) to flash, blaze, or flare up; to flame out, to burn up; to leap up; 2) fig. to grow angry, to kindle into wrath.

Auf'löffeln, (w.) v. tr. to take or eat up with the spoon.

Auf'lösbar, **Auf'löslich**, I. adj. 1) dissolvable, (dis)soluble; leicht a-e Salze, Chem. salts readily soluble; 2) Math. solvable; 3) Mus. resolvable; II. A-keit, (w.) f. Chem. (dis)solubility; Math. & Mus. resolvability.

Auf'lösen, (w.) v. I. tr. 1) to loosen, unloose, untie, unfix, open; mit aufgelöstem Haar, with dishevelled hair; to temper, to dilute (as colours in water, &c.); Sport. to eviscerate, to gut; 2) Chem., &c. to dissolve, resolve (in [with Acc.], into); deliquate; melt; absorb (gas); decompose; analyse; fig.-s. 3) to break up (a meeting, a ministry, &c.); to dismiss, disband, break up (an army, &c.), to break (a spell, &c.); 4) to solve (an equation, a problem, doubts, &c.), to decipher, unriddle; to solve, to guess (a riddle), to unravel (the plot or intrigue of a play); to disorganise (government, society, &c.); Comm. to dissolve (partnership, a business, a connexion); Law. to dissolve, break off (a marriage); to reduce (fractions); to cancel, annul (a contract); eine Dissonanz —, Mus. to resolve a discord; II. refl. 1) to get loose; 2) a) to be solved, to dissolve; to resolve (into steam, &c.); to melt (of snow); to deliquate; to be reduced (into, &c.); b) fig. to be broken up, to break up (as a language), &c. cf. tr.; c) to die, to expire; Alles dies wird sich schließlich in nichts —, all this will in the end come to nought; sich — lassen, to be soluble.

Auf'lösend, p. a. (cf. Auflösen) dissolvent, diluent, solvent; a-e Mittel, pl. dissolvents.

Auf'löslich, see Auflösbar.

Auf'lösung, (w.) f. 1) a) the (act of) undoing, loosening; b) Sport. evisceration, disembowelling, gutting; c) the (act of) tempering; diluting; dilution (of colours); fig.-s. 2) solution, guess (of a riddle); Dram. winding up, discovery, unravelling (of a plot), dénouement; dissolving, breaking off (of a marriage); dissolution (of the body, &c.; of partnership, &c.); disorganisation; 3) Chem., &c. a) dissolution, liquefaction; b) analysis; solution, resolution (of a body into its constituents, &c.), decomposition; c) solution (i. e. the liquid obtained by a chemical solution); deliquation; 4) Math. solution, conversion, solving (of equations); — des Unendlichen, analysis; (eines Bruches) reduction (of a fraction); Mech. resolution (of forces); 5) Mus. resolving, resolution (einer Dissonanz, of a discord); 6) Gramm. (eines Doppellautes in einen Grundlaut) diaeresis.

Auf'lösungs..., in comp. —begebenheit, f. (l. u.) catastrophe; —fähig, adj., —fähigkeit, f. see Auflösbar, Auflösbarkeit; —kraft, f. solvent power; —kunst, f. science of analysis, analytical art, analytism; —mittel, n. Chem. & Med. dissolvent, solvent, diluent; menstruum; —wort, n. (des Räthsels) guess; —zeichen, n. Mus. natural, see B-quadrat.

Auf'löthen, (w.) v. tr. 1) to solder upon; 2) to unsolder.

Auf'lüften, **Auf'lüpfen**, (w.) v. tr. to lift up a little, to hang up in the air (to dry).

Auf'lügen, (str.) v. tr. (Einem etwas) 1) to impute falsely; 2) to tell (one) a falsehood.

Auf'machen, (w.) v. I. tr. 1) to put up

(curtains, &c., see Aufziehen); 2) to open (a door, letter, &c.): to open, uncork (a bottle); to crack (nuts); to turn (the cock); to open, put up, or spread (an umbrella); to pick (a lock); to undo (a bundle, a knot, &c.); to uncord (a packet, &c.); (los machen) to unfasten; to unlace (stays); to turn or tuck up (the sleeves, trowsers, &c.); Book-b. die planirten Bogen eines Buches —, to distribute and glaze the sized sheets of a book; 3) fig. to fix, to get ready; aufgemachtes Leinen, dressed linen; Comm-s. die Handelsbücher —, to begin a new set of books; die Haferstoffen —, to settle, to adjust the average; eine Rechnung —, to draw out (to make an extract of) an account; die Kosten —, to charge the costs; II. intr. fam. to watch, to sit up; was machst du noch so spät auf? why do you sit up so late? III. refl. 1) to get up, to rise; der Wind hat sich aufgemacht, the wind has risen high; 2) to prepare (one's self) for a journey; to set out; sich auf und davon machen, to run away, to decamp.

Auf'mahlen, (irr.) v. tr. to grind all.

Auf'malen, (w.) v. tr. 1) to refresh, to touch up a painting, to new-paint; 2) to consume all (the colour).

Auf'mangeln, (w.) v. tr. to mangle again.

Auf'marsch, (str., pl. Auf'märsche) m. Mil. marching up; —linie, f. line of march.

Auf'marschiren, (w.) v. intr. (aux. sein) Mil. to march (up), to draw up in line; to deploy; — lassen, to draw up; das —, v. s. (str.) n. the (act of) marching up, &c., deployment.

Auf'maß, (str.) n. over-measure (Übermaß).

Auf'mauern, (w.) v. tr. to build with brick, to raise (a wall, &c.).

Auf'meißeln, (w.) v. tr. 1) to open with a chisel; 2) to produce (an ornament, &c.) upon stone, &c. with the chisel.

Auf'mengen, (w.) v. tr. to mix the several articles of food for cattle.

Auf'merken, (w.) v. I. tr. to mark, note, or put down; II. intr. gener. with auf (& Acc.) to mind, mark, heed, observe (a thing), to attend, to give heed (to); to give ear, to listen. — **Auf'merker,** (str.) m. marker, &c.; observer, listener.

Auf'merksam, I. adj. 1) attentive (to, auf (with Acc.)), mindful, heedful, heedy (of), intent (upon); watchful, careful; — machen auf etwas, to draw or call one's attention to; to remind (one) of, to put (one) in mind of: der Fall, auf den wir in voriger Woche — machten, the case to which we drew attention last week; wir haben jetzt auf einen wichtigen Abschnitt in Hrn. Bishop's Werk — zu machen, we have now to draw the attention to an important section in Mr. B.'s work; 2) see Zuvorkommend; sie ist zu — gegen andere, she is overthoughtful for others; II. A-keit, (w.) f. attention (auf [with Acc.], to): 1) attentiveness; vigilance; mindfulness; 2) courtesy; civility (cf. Zuvorkommenheit); die — abziehen, to distract the attention; — erregen, to attract attention or notice; das anziehende Werk, auf welches wir jetzt die — der Leser zu lenken wünschen, the interesting work to which we now wish to draw the attention of our readers; — schenken, to pay attention.

Auf'messen, (str.) v. tr. 1) to measure and put up (in the granary); vulg. fig. Einem Schläge —, to serve one out, to thrash him; 2) to survey (land). — **Auf'messung,** (w.) f. the act of measuring, &c.; survey.

Auf'mischen, (w.) v. tr. 1) Gam. to mix or shuffle again (cards); 2) ein Faß Wein —, to fill up a cask of wine with some of a different sort.

Auf'muntern, (w.) v. tr. see Aufwickeln, Entwickeln, Enthüllen, Entlarven.

Auf'munterer, (str.) m. rouser, &c., encourager.

Auf'muntern, (w.) v. I. tr. 1) to awake, rouse; fig-s. 2) to enliven, animate, cheer up; 3) to encourage, incite, stir up, to (zu ..., good or evil, &c.); to urge, spur, goad or egg on (to evil); II. refl. to brisk one's self up, to rouse, to take heart.

Auf'munterung, (w.) f. 1) the (act of) rousing, &c.; animation; 2) encouragement, incitement, spur, excitation, &c., cheering up.

Auf'münzen, (w.) v. tr. 1) to coin all (the gold, &c.), 2) see Umprägen.

Auf'müssen, (irr.) v. intr. coll. 1) for aufstehen müssen, to be forced to get up; er muß auf, he must rise; 2) for aufgemacht werden or aufgehen müssen; die Thür, das Fenster muß auf, the door, window must be opened.

Auf'mutzen, (str.) n. Sport. beating the game out of their lair.

Auf'mutzen, (w.) v. tr. coll. 1) (l. u.) see Aufputzen; 2) (Einem etwas) coll. to take (one) up (with), &c. see Aufstechen, 4.

Auf'nageln, (w.) v. tr. to nail or spike down.

Auf'nagen, (w.) v. tr. 1) to consume by gnawing; 2) to open by gnawing.

Auf'nähen, (w.) v. tr. 1) to sew on; 2) to consume by sewing.

Auf'nahme, (w.) f. 1) the taking or picking up, &c. cf. Aufnehmen; 2) the borrowing, loan, taking up (of a capital); 3) a) accommodation; reception (of visitors, &c.): eine freundliche — ist die beste Bewirthung, welcome is the best cheer; eine herzliche —, a hearty welcome; b) admittance, admission, reception (into a company, &c.); adoption; 4) Chem. (eines Gases &c.) absorption (of carbonic acid, &c.); 5) Geom. survey: flüchtige —, hasty or rough sketch, eye-sketch; 6) registration; the taking stock, &c.; 7) fig. improvement, prosperity: in — sein, to be in favour or in vogue, to be the fashion; in — bringen, to bring into fashion; to introduce, set up (a new fashion); to forward, to promote, to raise (up); to improve; in — kommen, to thrive, to prosper; to gain credit; to come, rise, or get into fashion; — finden, to find favour, protection, to meet with a good reception; Comm-s. — bereiten, to pay due honour: mit der — unseres Lagers (Inventur) beschäftigt, busy in taking stock, making up an inventory; —bedingungen, f. pl. terms of admission.

Auf'nahms ..., in comp. —compaß, m. azimuth-circle, vertical circle; —fähig, adj. qualified for admission; —fähigkeit, f. admissibility, eligibility; —schein, m. ticket or certificate of admission; —schiff, n. surveying-ship; —würdig, adj. worthy of being admitted.

Auf'naschen, (w.) v. tr. 1) to consume (dainties) by nibbling, or stealthily; 2) to spend (one's money) in dainties.

Auf'nehmen, (str.) v. I. tr. 1) to take up (also Weav.), pick up; Mil. das Gewehr —, to advance arms; 2) Geom. to survey, to measure; eine Grube —, Min. to dial, line, survey underground; 3) to shelter, to harbour, to accommodate, to take in; 4) to receive; to entertain; to admit (into a society); 5) to put upon paper; to make a design of...; to draw; nach der Natur —, to draw from nature; nach dem Leben —, to draw (or to copy) from life; 6) to register (the number of a population, &c.); 7) Chem. to absorb; 8) (with für) to take for, as, to look upon or consider as ...; etwas wohl, übel —, to take well, ill, &c.; übel —, to resent; es gut — von ..., to take it kind in ..., to take a thing in good part; 9) es mit Einem —, to make head against one, to cope or compete with one, to be a match for, to match; in die Columne —, Typ. to impage; Knitt. to take up (stitches); die Spur or Fährte —, Sport. to catch the scent or track (said of dogs); der Eber nimmt den Jäger auf, the boar attacks the huntsman; to borrow,

Auf'pflöcken, (w.) v. tr. to plug up; to fasten on with pegs.

Auf'pflügen, (w.) v. tr. to plough up.

Auf'pfropfen, (w.) v. tr. to ingraft, to graft; Carp. to join, to rabbet.

Auf'pichen, (w.) v. tr. to fasten on with pitch.

Auf'picken, (w.) v. tr. to peck, pick up, or open (of birds).

Auf'pinseln, (w.) v. tr. to put on with a (painter's) brush; to new-brush.

Auf'plappern, (w.) v. tr. to awake by chattering.

Auf'plärren, (w.) v. tr. to awake by squalling.

Auf'plätten, (w.) v. tr. see Aufbügeln.

Auf'plattung, (w.) f. (Holzverbindung) rabbeting (Build.).

Auf'platzen, (w.) v. intr. (aux. sein) & tr. to burst open, to crack.

Auf'plustern, (w.) v. tr. die Federn or sich —, refl. to puff up its feathers (of a bird).

Auf'pochen, (w.) v. tr. 1) to knock open; 2) to knock up (to awaken by knocking).

Auf'polieren, (w.) v. tr. to polish (anew), to touch up.

Auf'polstern, (w.) v. tr. to pad anew.

Auf'poltern, (w.) v. tr. to wake with great noise.

Auf'posaunen, (w.) v. tr. to rouse by blowing a trumpet.

Auf'prägen, (w.) v. tr. to imprint, impress.

Auf'prallen, (w.) v. intr. (aux. sein) 1) to bounce upon; 2) to rebound, to burst, fly open.

Auf'prasseln, (w.) v. intr. (aux. sein) to crackle up.

Auf'prassen, (w.) v. tr. see Verprassen.

Auf'prellen, (w.) v. tr. to toss or jerk up.

Auf'pressen, (w.) v. tr. 1) to press open; 2) to press down on or against; 3) to imprint, impress; 4) to press anew.

Auf'probiren, (w.) v. tr. to try on (a hat, &c.).

Auf'protzen, (w.) v. tr. Gunn. to limber up (a piece of ordnance).

Auf'prudeln, (w.) v. intr. see Aufsprudeln, Aufwallen.

Auf'prügeln, (w.) v. tr. to make rise, to cause to get up by cudgelling.

Auf'pudern, (w.) v. tr. to new-powder, to use up in powdering.

Auf'pumpen, (w.) v. tr. 1) to heave or pump up; 2) fig. to borrow.

Auf'pusten, (w.) v. tr. to blow up.

Auf'putz, (str.) m. 1) the (act of) adorning, &c.; 2) a) ornament; b) trimming(s), dress, finery, attire; gaudiness, jewelry, trinkets.

Auf'putzen, (w.) v. tr. to adorn, to fit up; to dress or to trim up, to trick up; to smarten (up); to (make) tidy, to clean, brush up.

Auf'quaken, (w.) v. I. intr. to croak suddenly, to emit a croaking sound; II. tr. to awake by croaking.

Auf'qualmen, (w.) v. I. intr. (aux. sein) to rise up in steam, smoke, vapour; II. tr. coll. to consume by smoking.

Auf'quellen, v. I. (str.) intr. (aux. sein) 1) to spring up, to well, to bubble (of wells, springs, &c.); 2) to swell up, to rise (of things); II. tr. (w.) to swell, soak, steep (peas in water, &c.).

Auf'quetschen, (w.) v. tr. to squeeze open.

Auf'quirlen, (w.) v. tr. to beat up with a twirling-stick; to whisk (eggs); to mill (chocolate).

[illegible], (w.) v. tr. to wind up on a reel or a bobbin.

Auf'raffen, (w.) v. I. tr. 1) to rake, snatch, [illegible], to gather indiscriminately; 2) fig. to [illegible] to get hold of; II. refl. 1) to struggle [illegible] quickly; 2) a) to rouse one's self, [illegible] one's (moral) strength, to make an effort; b) (sich wieder —) to recover one's [illegible] again (after an illness), to rally.

Auf'ragen, (w.) v. intr. to rise high or [illegible] up.

Auf'rahmen, (w.) v. tr. Cloth. to tenter.

Auf'rammeln, Auf'rammen, (w.) v. tr. to open or loosen by ramming.

Auf'ranken, (w.) v. intr. (aux. sein) & refl. to creep, twine, or climb up.

Auf'ränzeln, (w.) v. intr. to fasten or strap on one's knapsack.

Auf'rappeln, (w.) v. I. tr. see Aufschütteln, Aufrütteln; II. refl. coll. for sich Aufraffen.

Auf'rasen, (w.) v. intr. to start up in, or to break out into, a rage.

Auf'raspeln, (w.) v. tr. to open with a rasp or rough-file, to rasp open.

Auf'rasseln, (w.) v. I. tr. to wake up by rattling; II. intr. 1) (aux. sein) to open with a rattling; 2) (aux. haben) to rattle aloud.

Auf'rauchen, (w.) v. I. tr. to consume by smoking; II. intr. (aux. haben & sein) (von Rauch, aufsteigen) to rise like smoke.

Auf'räuchern, (w.) v. tr. to season, dry up in smoke.

Auf'rauheisen, (str.) m. Cloth. teaseling-iron.

Auf'rauhen, (w.) v. tr. 1) to roughen the surface of...; to scratch, scrape; Stone-cutt. to tooth (a stone) with the granulated hammer; Weav. to card; Mill. to nott; Cloth. to tease, teasel, nap, raise the nap of (cloth); 2) to colour (leather) black for mourning gloves.

Auf'räumen, (w.) v. tr. 1) to put in order, arrange, set or place in order; to remove, to clear away; 2) (or intr. mit ... —) a) to rob, plunder; to empty; b) to thin (the population, as a plague, &c.); 3) to clear (a piece of ground, &c.); das ganze Lager —, Comm. to clear a shop, to clear off one's stock; um aufzuräumen, to sell or clear off; 4) fig. see Aufhellen; 5) Vint. see Behacken; 6) T. to widen, to drift (a hole); 7) to pick (the touch-hole); 8) Print. to sort and distribute (pie).

Auf'räumer, (str.) m. 1) T. rimer, pin; chamfering-broach; 2) Mil. see Raumnadel.

Auf'rauschen, (w.) v. I. intr. (aux. sein) 1) to rush up, fly up, or open with a rustling noise; 2) to resound; II. tr. to awake by a rustling noise.

Auf'räuspern, (w.) v. tr. to hawk up, to expectorate.

Auf'rebbeln, (w.) v. tr. Mar. to ravel out.

Auf'rechen, (w.) v. tr. 1) to rake together, up; 2) to loosen with a rake.

Auf'rechnen, (w.) v. tr. 1) to balance (accounts); 2) a) to reckon or count up, to specify, to enumerate; b) Einem etwas —, to charge to one's account.

Auf'recht, I. adj. & adv. 1) upright, Bot. erect; a-right; (stehend) on end; straight; 2) fig. courageous, in good spirits: — halten or erhalten, to maintain, to support, sustain, to keep or hold up, to uphold; sich — halten, to stand upright; fig. to keep up one's courage; — gehen, to go upright, to walk erect; — stellen, to set or place upright or on end; II. in comp. —halter, m. supporter; —haltung, f. maintaining, maintenance; —sitzend, adj. sitting upright; Herald. sejant; —stehend, adj. (standing) upright; Herald. (von Thieren) salient; —stehende Balken, m. T. story post; Mech-s. —stehende conische Röhre, f. or Trichter, m. upright conical tube or hopper; der —stehende Röhrenkessel, m. vertical tubular boiler.

Auf'recken, (w.) v. tr. to lift up, hold up; to prick up (the ears); to reach forth or up.

Auf'reden, (w.) v. tr. 1) to instigate, incite; 2) (Einem etwas) to press upon by persuasion.

Auf'regen, (w.) v. tr. to excite, to rouse, arouse, to stir up; to agitate, disturb, flush, fluster; to alarm; a-d, p. a. exciting, alarming; seditious (as articles of journals, &c.), cf. Aufreizen. — **Auf'reger**, (str.) m. exciter, &c., agitator. — **Auf'regung**, (w.) f. the (act of) stirring, &c.; stir, tumult; emotion, excitement, agitation.

Auf'reiben, (str.) v. I. tr. 1) to rub open, gall, fret (away); 2) to wear away by rubbing; 3) to scrub (a floor); 4) to knead well or thoroughly (the dough); 5) to grind (colours); 6) to grate (sugar, a nutmeg); 7) fig. a) to cut up (a hostile troop); to wear up or away; b) to destroy, sweep away, extirpate, ruin, consume, undo; to exhaust; eine a-de Thätigkeit, an exhausting (wearing) activity; a-e Krankheiten, wasting diseases; 8) Cloth. see Aufrauhen; 9) T. to bore; to broach; II. intr. Clock-m. to be in contact with; III. refl. 1) to run to waste; 2) to wear one's self out; sich gegenseitig —, to destroy one another.

Auf'reiber, (str.) m. 1) T. see Aufräumer; 2) a kind of auger used in boring flutes; 3) the journeyman-baker who has to knead the dough for light cakes.

Auf'reibung, (w.) f. 1) the (act of) rubbing up, &c.; 2) destruction, extirpation, &c. cf. Aufreiben.

Auf'reihen, (w.) v. tr. to string, to make a string of, to file (papers).

Auf'reihung, (w.) f. Mil. evolution.

Auf'reißen, (str.) v. I. tr. 1) to rend, to tear open or up, to rip open or up; 2) Cloth. see Aufrauhen; 3) to burst, wrench, force, or fling open (a door); to rip up, to slit, cut, rend (a seam, a floor, an old sore, &c.); das Pflaster —, to unpave a street; den Erdboden —, to cut or plough up the ground (auch von Kanonenkugeln &c.), to harrow; 2) T. to sketch, draw, design, to plot, to lay out; die Lehrbogen —, to construct, lay out the centres; vulg-s. die Augen weit —, to stare with one's eyes wide open; das Maul —, 1) to open one's mouth wide, to gape; 2) to talk loud, to jaw; alte Wunden wieder —, fig. to harrow up old wounds; II. intr. (aux. sein) to be torn, to gape, chap, burst, split, chink, crack; III. refl. to rise or get up quickly, to struggle up.

Auf'reiten, (str.) v. I. intr. (aux. sein) to ride up (in a line); II. tr. to gall, chafe, or make sore by riding; pp. & adj. aufgeritten, ein aufgerittenes Pferd, a galled horse; III. refl. to gall, to chafe (by riding).

Auf'reizen, (w.) v. tr. to incite, excite, stir up, inflame, spur (to evil); to provoke, rouse; to set on (cf. Aufregen); a-de Reden, inflammatory speeches. — **Auf'reizung**, (w.) f. the (act of) inciting, &c.; provocation, instigation.

Auf'rennen, (irr.) v. I. intr. (aux. sein) see Auflaufen, II. 3; II. tr. see Auflaufen, I.

Auf'richten, (w.) v. I. tr. 1) to raise, to make to stand upright, to erect, set up, rear, to put up; fig-s. 2) to erect, found, to create, to establish, to make; 3) to comfort, console; to support, (ermuthigen) to hearten, to strengthen; ein Schiff (wieder) —, Mar. to right a ship; II. refl. to get up, to rise; to raise one's self; aufgerichtet, p. a. upright; der aufgerichtete Muskel, Auf'richter, (str.), Auf'richtemuskel, (str.) m. Anat. erector.

Auf'richthammer, (str.) m. Lock-sm. double-faced hammer.

Auf'richtig, I. adj. candid, sincere, open, plain, honest, frank, true, genuine; II. A-keit, (w.) f. sincerity, candour, candidness, uprightness, honesty, artlessness, frankness, ingenuousness.

Auf'richtung, (w.) f. the (act of) raising, &c., erection, foundation.

Auf'richtzug, (str.) m. Build. crane; Carp. windlass.

Auf'riegeln, (w.) v. tr. to unbolt, unbar, to unhasp.

Auf'rinden, (w.) v. tr. to make incisions into the bark of (fir-trees, &c. in order to cause the resin to flow out).

Auf'ringeln, (w.) v. I. tr. 1) to turn up in ringlets, to curl; 2) to uncurl; II. refl. 1) to rise in ringlets or curls; 2) to coil up (of

aux. sein)
vel. 2) to
II. tr. to

up, to pile
in heaps.
ufschiebling.
up in stacks
ess or do up
autify anew,
take up with

aux. sein) to

shoot, sprout,
upstart, mush-
aise (the skin).
to scratch, to
o lay crossways

1) to fasten down
with screws; 2)
sich — (lassen), to
[windlass.
T. jack-screw,
tr. to frighten up,
) intr. (aux. sein)

rick, scream.
v. tr. to write or set
ecord; einen Schuld-
ook a debt.
I. intr. to cry aloud,
) scream, to (give a)
with crying.
v. intr. (aux. sein) to
Aufschreiten).
1) direction, superscrip-
sement; 2) Label (on
ription, epigraph (on
ticket, title head (of a
cribed.
) v. tr. 1) to roll up (casks,
; 2) T. to make a hole or
sm. to open with a chisel
p. to widen with a peg;
ely: Forest. see Abtrommen.
(str.) m. 1) see Schroter, 4;
ated peg; rimer.
(str., pl. A-schübe) m. 1) the (act
putting off, &c. cf. Aufschieben;
lay; adjournment; retardation,
t; procrastination; respite; pro-
suspension; suspense; Zahlung
mediate payment; die Sache leidet
the matter (business, &c.) admits
no delay; II. in comp. A-befehl,
eve; A-brief, m. letter of respite.
schultern, (w.) v. tr to take, put upon
oulder.
Aufschippen, (w.) v. tr. to take or throw
with a shovel, to shovel up.

Auf'schüren, (w.) v. tr. 1) to stir up, to
rake, poke; 2) T. to new-pitch (old beer-
casks); 3) Weav. to warp.

Auf'schürfen, (w.) v. tr. Min. to scrape off.

Auf'schürzen, (w.) v. tr. to tuck up, truss
up; Mar. to furl (the sails).

Auf'schüsseln, (w.) v. tr. to dish or serve
up (Auftischen)

Auf'schuß, (str., pl. Auf'schüsse) m. the (act
of) shooting up, &c. cf. Aufschießen.

Auf'schütteln, (w.) v. tr. 1) to shake or stir
up; 2) to rouse from sleep.

Auf'schütten, (w.) v. I. tr. 1) to heap up,
accumulate; to hoard or store up, to lay up
in store; ... put or pour (down) on or into,
Korn— ... corn; Kohlen auf das Feuer
—, to replenish the fire with coals; Pulver
—, to put powder on the pan, to prime (a gun).
auf eine Straße Knack —, or eine Straße mit
Knack —, to put broken stone (or metalling)

... into
fingers.
rk up with
cutting open;
assay of gold;
(cut up into slices).
schnitzen, (w.) v. tr. to
..., (w.) v. tr. to find out by
track by the scent (as dogs).
upfen, (w.) v. tr. to snuff up.
schnüren, (w.) v. tr. 1) to unlace, to
, untwist, uncord, unbrace; 2) to lace,
on down or upon ...; 3) Carp to trace in
full size with strings.

fix by striking; einem Pferde die Hufeisen —, to shoe a horse: 4) *Mar.* to unlay, unstrand, untwist (a rope); 5) to put up, set up (a bedstead, a booth, &c.); to pitch (a tent, a camp); seine Wohnung —, to take up one's lodgings; to establish *or* settle one's self; 6) *Cam.* to turn up (a card); 7) *a)* to truss up; to turn up (a table, a coat, the sleeves, &c.); gelb —, to turn up with yellow; weiß aufgeschlagen, with white facings; *b)* to cock (a hat); *c)* to line, face, border; 8) to open, to fold down (a book); eine Stelle —, to look for a passage in a book; 9) to cast, lift *or* turn up, raise, open (one's eyes); mit aufgeschlagenen Augen, with upcast eyes; ein Gelächter —, to set up a laugh, to break out into a (roar of) laughter; 10) *T.* die Ballen —, *Typ. a)* to put *or* knock up the balls; *b)* *Tann.* to turn (the hides) in the pit; *c)* *Stone-Mas.* to ornament with mouldings; *d)* *Shoe-m.* to put upon the last; *e)* *Hydr.* to throw (water) upon the wheels of a machine; II. *intr.* (*aux.* sein) 1) to spring up, to turn up; in Flammen —, to blaze up; 2) *a)* (auf [*with Acc.*]) to strike, hit, *or* fall violently upon (the ground, &c.); *b)* to beat against (as rain, &c.); 3) *Comm.* to rise (in price), to look up.

Auf'schlag(e)..., *in comp.* —gerinne, *n.* (mill-)race (Ende des —gerinnes, pen-trough); —hammer, *m.* about-sledge; —schaufel, *f.* 1) *Found.* ladle; 2) float-board, flat-board, ladle-board, adle (of a mill-wheel); —tisch, *m.* folding-table; —wasser, *n.* moving-water, water-supply (of a mill, &c.).

Auf'schleifen, *v. tr.* I. (*str.*) 1) to grind *or* cut (figures, &c.) on (glass, &c.); 2) to wound *or* cut (one's fingers, &c.) in grinding: II. (*w.*) to drag on, up (to bring up) on a sledge.

Auf'schlemmen, (*w.*) *v. tr.* 1) to raise by deposit, mud; 2) *see* Aufschwelgen.

Auf'schlendern, *coll.* **Auf'schlenkern,** (*w.*) *v.* I. *tr.* to fling, throw up with a sling: II. *intr.* (*aux.* sein) to strike against, upon, up ward.

Auf'schlichten, (*w.*) *v. tr. see* Aufschichten.

Auf'schlicken, (*w.*) *v. tr. see* Aufschlemmen; Aufspülen.

Auf'schließen, (*str.*) *v.* I. *tr.* 1) to unlock, open: 2) *Hatt.* *see* Filzen; 3) *Chem.* to flux; 4) *Min.* *a)* to open, to begin to work (a mine); *b)* to drain of water; *c)* to open (fresh land); *fig.* *a)* to unfold, disclose: Einem sein Herz —, to open, disclose one's heart to one; *b)* to unriddle; *c)* to make accessible (Erschließen); II. *rfl.* 1) to open, to unfold itself; 2) *Min.* der Gang schließt sich auf, the lode swells. [opener, &c.

Auf'schließer, (*str.*) *m.* he that unlocks,

Auf'schlingen, (*str.*) *v.* I. *tr.* 1) to swallow up; 2) to fasten up with a loop; 3) to untwine, untwist; to untie, undo (a knot, &c.); II. *rfl.* to twine upward, to creep up.

Auf'schlitzen, (*w.*) *v. tr.* 1) to rip up, to unseam; 2) to split, to slit; aufgeschlitzter Sachs, scalloped cutwater.

Auf'schluchzen, (*w.*) *v.* I. *intr.* to sob; II. *tr.* to wake by sobbing.

Auf'schlucken, (*w.*) *v. tr.* to swallow up.

Auf'schlüpfen, (*w.*) *v. intr.* (*aux.* sein) to slip up.

Auf'schlürfen, (*w.*) *v. tr.* to sip up.

Auf'schluß, (*str.*, *pl.* Aufschlüsse) *m.* 1) the (act of) unlocking, opening, &c.; 2) *fig.* [illegible] disclosure; explanation, explication, information; über (*with Acc.*) — geben, to [illegible] (a matter), to give information [illegible] to tell the particulars. [Inbeiß.

Auf'schmausen, (*w.*) *v. tr. vulg. see* Auf-

Auf'schmauchen, (*w.*) *v. tr.* to smoke up all.

Auf'schmausen, (*w.*) *v. tr.* 1) to eat up all, [illegible] 2) to dissipate in banqueting.

Auf'schmeicheln, (*w.*) *v.* I. *tr.* (Einem etwas) [illegible] one into the acceptance of a [illegible] (sich Einem) to insinuate *or*

ingratiate one's self by flattery into a person's good graces.

Auf'schmeißen, (*str.*) *v. vulg. for* Aufwerfen.

Auf'schmelzen, *v.* I. (*str.*) *intr.* (*aux.* sein) 1) to open by melting, to dissolve; 2) to coalesce with, *or* to adhere to another body by melting down upon; II. (*w.* & *str.*) *tr.* 1) to dissolve, separate, *or* open by melting; 2) to fasten down by melting, to melt on; 3) to melt anew; 4) to consume the whole stock (of lead, &c.) by melting.

Auf'schmettern, (*w.*) *v.* I. *tr.* to open with a crash; to dash up; II. *intr.* (*aux.* sein) 1) to dash against, to fall upon with a crash; 2) to yield a mighty sound.

Auf'schmieden, (*w.*) *v. tr.* 1) to forge down (auf [*with Acc.*], upon), to fasten down *or* to ... by forging: die Radschiene —, to rim the wheel, to lay the tire of a wheel: 2) to open, *or* to unfix by forging; 3) to consume by forging.

Auf'schmieren, (*w.*) *v. tr.* 1) to smear *or* spread upon; 2) to consume by smearing; 3) (Einem etwas) *vulg.* to trick *or* palm (something) upon (one).

Auf'schminken, (*w.*) *v. tr.* & *rfl.* to paint up, again, *or* afresh; to put on rouge.

Auf'schmoren, (*w.*) *v. tr.* to stew (up) again.

Auf'schmücken, (*w.*) *v. tr.* & *rfl.* to adorn, to dress up: to embellish, to ornament.

Auf'schnäbeln, (*w.*) *v. tr.* (von Vögeln) to peck up with the beak.

Auf'schnallen, (*w.*) *v. tr.* 1) to buckle up, to tie on: 2) to unbuckle; to unbrace; 3) *coll.* Einem etwas, to put a hoax upon one, to humbug, bamboozle (one).

Auf'schnappen, (*w.*) *v.* I. *tr.* to snap, snatch, *or* catch up; II *intr* (*aux.* sein) to spring up, to fly up.

Auf'schnarchen, (*w.*) *v.* I. *intr.* to snore aloud; II. *tr.* to wake by snoring

Auf'schnauben, (*w.* & *str.*) *v. intr.* 1) to snort aloud; 2) (*aux.* sein) to start up snorting.

Auf'schneidemesser, *n.* cutting-out-knife.

Auf'schneiden, (*str.*) *v.* I. *tr.* 1) *a)* to cut (up), to cut open; to rip up, to unrip, to unseam; *b)* to carve, &c. (Vorlegen); *c)* to notch, to mark by notches; 2) *a)* *Anat.* to dissect, anatomise; *b)* *Surg.* to make an incision: ein Buch —, to cut open the leaves of a book; aufgeschnittene Exemplare, copies with cut edges; II. *intr.* *fig.* to swagger, brag, boast, to talk big, speak broad, to draw the longbow, to rodomontade, vapour; to hector, flourish.

Auf'schneider, (*str.*) *m.* 1) cutter up, &c.; 2) *fig.* swaggerer, boaster, hector, braggart, &c.

Auf'schneiderei', (*w.*) *f.* (the act of) swaggering, bragging, braggardism, gasconade, rodomontade, humbug, *vulg.* blarney.

Auf'schneidung, (*w.*) *f.* the (act of) cutting up, &c.; der Gebärmutter, *Med.* hysterotomy.

Auf'schneiteln, (*w.*) *v. tr.* *T.* to prune, to lop (trees).

Auf'schnellen, (*w.*) *v.* I. *tr.* to throw with a jerk, to jerk up; II. *intr.* (*aux.* sein) to spring, snap, *or* fly up.

Auf'schniegeln, (*w.*) *v. tr.* *coll.* to dress, trick up *or* out, to smarten.

Auf'schnippeln, (*w.*) *v. tr.* to cut up into little pieces. [the fingers.

Auf'schnippen, (*w.*) *v. tr.* to jerk up with

Auf'schnitt, (*str.*) *m.* 1) a cut, cutting open; slit, slash, incision; 2) *Metall.* assay of gold; 3) (*Tailor*) cold (roast) meat (cut up into slices).

Auf'schnitzeln, Auf'schnitzen, (*w.*) *v. tr.* to cut, carve upon.

Auf'schnüffeln, (*w.*) *v. tr.* to find out by the smell, to track by the scent (as dogs).

Auf'schnupfen, (*w.*) *v. tr.* to snuff up.

Auf'schnüren, (*w.*) *v. tr.* 1) to unlace, to untie, untwist, uncord, unbrace; 2) to lace, fasten down *or* upon ...; 3) *Carp.* to trace in full size with strings.

Auf'schnurren, (*w.*) *v.* I. *intr.* (*aux.* sein) 1) to untwist, come undone, to unravel; 2) to fly open with a whizzing noise; II. *tr.* to wake up with a rattle.

Auf'schobern, (*w.*) *v. tr.* to cock up, to pile up, to put up in stacks, to pile up in heaps.

Auf'schößling, (*str.*) *m.* *see* Aufschießling.

Auf'schocken, (*w.*) *v. tr.* to put up in stacks *or* heaps. [to dress *or* do up.

Auf'schönen, (*w.*) *v. tr.* to beautify anew,

Auf'schöpfen, (*w.*) *v. tr.* to take up with a ladle *or* scoop, to scoop up.

Auf'schossen, (*w.*) *v. intr.* (*aux.* sein) to shoot up, to sprout.

Auf'schößling, (*str.*) *m.* 1) shoot, sprout, sprig; 2) *fig.* stripling; 3) *cont.* upstart, mushroom. [raise (the skin).

Auf'schrammen, (*w.*) *v. tr.* to scratch, to

Auf'schränken, (*w.*) *v. tr.* to lay crossways and pile up.

Auf'schrauben, (*w.*) *v. tr.* 1) to fasten down *or* upon (auf [*with Acc.*]) ... with screws; 2) to screw up; 3) to unscrew; sich — (lassen), to unscrew. [windlass.

Auf'schrauber, (*str.*) *m.* *T.* jack-screw,

Auf'schrecken, (*w.*) *v.* I. *tr.* to frighten up, to rouse, to alarm; II. (*str.*) *intr.* (*aux.* sein) to start up with fright.

Auf'schrei, (*str.*) *m.* shriek, scream.

Auf'schreiben, (*str.*) *v. tr.* to write *or* set down, to note, to enter, record; einen Schuldposten —, to charge *or* book a debt.

Auf'schreien, (*str.*) *v.* I. *intr.* to cry aloud, to cry out; to (set up a) scream, to (give a) shriek; II. *tr.* to awake with crying.

Auf'schreiten, (*str.*) *v. intr.* (*aux.* sein) to march steadily along (Zuschreiten).

Auf'schrift, (*w.*) *f.* 1) direction, superscription, address; endorsement; 2) label (on boxes, &c.); 3) inscription, epigraph (on monuments); *Print.* ticket, title head (of a page); ohne —, uninscribed.

Auf'schroten, (*w.*) *v. tr.* 1) to roll up (casks, &c.) from a cellar; 2) *T.* to make a hole or slit into ...; *Lock-sm.* to open with a chisel *or* puncheon; *Carp.* to widen with a peg: *Mill.* to grind coarsely: *Forest. see* Abtrammen.

Auf'schröter, (*str.*) *m.* 1) *see* Schröter, 4; 2) *T.* square-pointed peg, rimer.

Auf'schub, I. (*str.*, *pl.* A-schübe) *m.* 1) the (act of) deferring, putting off, &c. *cf.* Aufschieben; deferment, delay; adjournment; retardation, postponement; procrastination; respite; prolongation; suspension; suspense; Zahlung ohne —, immediate payment; die Sache leidet keinen —, the matter (business, &c.) admits of, *or* bears no delay; II. *in comp.* A-befehl, *m.* reprieve; A-brief, *m.* letter of respite.

Auf'schultern, (*w.*) *v. tr.* to take, put upon the shoulder.

Auf'schüppen, (*w.*) *v. tr.* to take *or* throw up with a shovel, to shovel up.

Auf'schüren, (*w.*) *v. tr.* 1) to stir up, to rake, poke; 2) *T.* to new-pitch (old beer-casks); 3) *Wars.* to warp.

Auf'schürfen, (*w.*) *v. tr.* *Min.* to scrape off.

Auf'schürzen, (*w.*) *v. tr.* to tuck up, truss up; *Mar.* to furl (the sails).

Auf'schüsseln, (*w.*) *v. tr.* to dish *or* serve up (Auftischen).

Auf'schuß, (*str.*, *pl.* Aufschüsse) *m.* the (act of) shooting up, &c. *cf.* Aufschießen.

Auf'schütteln, (*w.*) *v. tr.* 1) to shake or stir up; 2) to rouse from sleep.

Auf'schütten, (*w.*) *v.* I. *tr.* 1) to heap up, accumulate; to hoard *or* store up, to lay up in store; [illegible] put or pour (down) on *or* into: Korn — [illegible] corn; Kohlen auf das Feuer —, to replenish the fire with coals; Pulver —, to put powder on the pan, to prime (a gun); auf eine Straße Knack —, *or* eine Straße mit Knack —, to put broken stone (*or* metalling) on a road, to metal a road (for macadamising); II. *intr. Mill.* to put corn into the mill-hopper.

Auf'schüttern, *(w.) v. intr. (aux.* sein) to start up.

Auf'schütt . . ., *in comp.* –faß, *m.* hopper; –junge, *m. Dy.* vat-boy.

Auf'schüttung, *(w.) f.* 1) the (act of) putting on broken stone, gravel, &c. for macadamising roads, metalling; 2) the stone, gravel, &c. put on a road for macadamising, metalling. [to dam up (the water).

Auf'schützen, *(w.) v. tr. Mill.* to shut off,

Auf'schwänzen, *(w.) v. tr.* to truss up the tail of (a horse); *Cook.* to serve up (fish) with the tail stuck into their mouth.

Auf'schwärmen, *(w.) v. intr. (aux.* sein) to swarm up.

Auf'schwärzen, *(w.) v. tr.* to blacken afresh.

Auf'schwatzen, *(w.) v. tr.* (Einem etwas) to persuade one by much talking to take a thing, to press (something) upon by talking, to humbug into taking a thing.

Auf'schweben, *(w.) v. intr. (aux.* sein) to soar up *or* upwards.

Auf'schwefeln, *(w.) v. tr.* to dip again into sulphur, to sulphur afresh.

Auf'schweifen, *(w.) v. tr. see* Aufschwänzen.

Auf'schweißen, *(w.) v. tr.* to weld on, to fasten down (auf *[with Acc.]*, on) by welding.

Auf'schwelgen, *(w.) v. tr.* to squander, to consume in debauchery, revelry, and rioting.

Auf'schwellen, *v.* I. *(w.) tr.* to swell (up), to puff (up), to distend, to bloat, to tumefy; 2) *fig.* to inflate, flush (with pride, &c.); II. *(str.) intr. (aux.* sein) to swell (up), bloat, distend; to intumesce; to surge (of the sea), to rise (of rivers); to billow (of waves), to heave (of the bosom); der Kamm schwillt ihm auf, *fig.* he gets proud *or* into a passion.

Auf'schwellung, *(w.) f.* 1) the (act of) swelling up, puffing, &c., distension; 2) a swelling, tumefaction, *Med.* turgescence.

Auf'schwemme, *(w.) f.* landing-place for floating wood.

Auf'schwemmer, *(str.) m.* workman employed in landing floating wood.

Auf'schwemmen, *(w.) v. tr.* 1) to bring, carry, *or* throw down (auf *[with Acc.]*, upon) by floating, to float *or* wash down (upon), to deposit; *Agr.* to warp, to inundate by letting in the tide; aufgeschwemmter Schlamm, deposit of warp (as manure); 2) to swell up, to bloat.

Auf'schwenken, *(w.) v. tr.* to flourish, to brandish aloft.

Auf'schwingen, *(str.) v. tr.* to swing up; *refl.* to swing one's self up, to get up *or* rise by a sudden effort; to soar, fly up, tower; to soar, to soar up; sich a–d, soaring.

Auf'schwirren, *(w.) v. intr. (aux.* sein) 1) to buzz up, to whir; 2) to fly open with a whizzing noise.

Auf'schwung, *(str., pl.* Aufschwünge) *m.* 1) *Gymn.* the act of swinging up (*opp.* Abschwung); 2) *a)* the (act of) soaring up, rising, &c.; *b) fig.* a rising, rise; elevation (of mind); (rapid) development, flourishing; advancement (of learning, &c.), impulse, growth; — nehmen, to be rising, &c.; der — der Alterthumsforschung, welchen diese Entdeckung zur Folge hatte, the impulse given to antiquarian research in consequence of this discovery; seine Regierung ist durch den — der Baukunst denkwürdig geworden, his reign is rendered memorable by the growth of architecture; der Handel wird nun einen neuen — nehmen, trade will now revive with a redoubled vigour.

Auf'segeln, *(w.) v. intr.* to [illegible] *or* turn up a river; to sail *or* strike [illegible] sailing; to run aground.

Auf'sehen, I. *(str.) v. intr.* to look up; II. *n. (str.)* the looking up; *fig.* sensation, noise, eclat; — erregen *or* machen, to make a noise, to cause, excite, a sensation; to make a show, to cut a figure, to draw attention, to rise into notoriety; um — zu vermeiden, to avoid notice.

Auf'seher, *(str.) m.* overseer, inspector, superintendent; surveyor; steward; (über Dämme, Gefängnisse, &c.) warden; (über öffentliche Stiftungen) guardian; conservator, keeper (of museums, &c.); *Railw.* platform-master (Inspector); wharfinger (of a quay *or* wharf); controller; A–in, *(w.) f.* overseer, directress, guardianess; first hand; –amt, *n.*, A–schaft, –stelle, *f.* overseer's office, surveyorship, keepership, mastership.

Auf'sein, *(irr.) v. intr. (aux.* sein) 1) to be up *or* out of bed; to sit up; 2) to be open; 3) to be spent, to be consumed; wohl —, to be in good spirits, to be in good health; to be well off.

Auf'seilen, *(w.) v. tr. Mar.* das Ankertau an die Kabelaring —, to nip the cable.

Auf'sellen, *(w.) v. tr. provinc.* to lavish; *see* Vergeuden, Durchbringen.

Auf'senden, *(irr.) v. tr.* to send up.

Auf'sengen, *(w.) v. tr.* to burn a mark upon.

Auf'senkeln, *(w.) v. tr.* 1) *Min.* to fasten with cramp-irons; 2) *Mar.* to remove the cramp-irons from ....

Auf'setzbar, *adj.* what may be put on.

Auf'setzband, *(str., pl.* A–bänder) *n. gener. pl. T.* butt-hinges, butts (of a door); hinge and loop.

Auf'setzen, *(w.) v.* I. *tr.* 1) *a)* to set up, to put up *or* on; to pile (up); Steine —, to set up stones, to stack; *b)* to raise; *c)* to lay on, *cf.* Aufnahme; 2) *Typ.* to set *or* put up (the type); 3) *a)* (of trees) to put out (fresh shoots); *b)* (Gehörn) *Sport.* to get new antlers; 4) *Vet. see* Angtisiren; 5) *Mar. a)* to hoist *or* sway up (die Stengen, the top-masts); *b)* (den Anker) to fish (the anchor); *c)* das Besteck —, to prick the chart; 6) to dress (the hair, a person's head); to turn up (the mustachios); 7) *Game. a)* to crown (einen Stein, a man at draughts); *b)* to stake (money) at play; 8) *fig. a)* to draw up (legal documents, &c.), put *or* set down in writing, to compose; *b)* eine Rechnung —, to cast an account, to draw (up) a bill, to make out one's bill; den Hut —, to put on one's hat; die Kimme —, *Coop.* to fix the chimes *or* staves of a cask; ein aufgesetztes Faß, *Coop.* a finished cask; das Siegel —, to put the seal to, to fix the seal upon; die Speisen —, to serve up (the dishes), to dish up; Waaren —, to land (goods); *T.* die Zähne an einer Säge —, to file out the teeth of a saw; die Zähne —, *Farr.* to bite the crib; den Kopf —, to be obstinate, to make head.

II. *intr.* 1) *see above;* Gehörn *(tr.* 3, *b)* & die Zähne —; 2) *Min.* to rest from work (from 11 to 12); 3) *T.* to ram down the shot *or* bullet (with the rammer); 4) *Dy.* to dye brown (by putting a black colour on red).

III. *refl.* 1) to sit upright; 2) to mount, to get on horseback; 3) *fig.* to be refractory, to rise against one (den Kopf —).

Auf'setzer, *(str.) m.* 1) one who puts up, &c.; 2) *Farr.* crib-biter (of horses; Krippenbeißer); 3) *Mech.* creel-filler; 4) A–in, *(w.) f.* hair-dresser.

Auf'setzholz, *(str.) n. Bak.* long cleft wood used in heating the oven.

Auf'setzig, *adj. see* Aufsässig.

Auf'setz . . ., *in comp.* –röhre, *f.* spout (of a *jet d'eau*), *pl.* ajutage; –stunde, *f. Min.* hour of resting from work (from 11 to 12 at noon; *cf.* Aufsetzen). [a (deep) sigh.

Auf'seufzen, *(w.) v. intr.* to heave *or* fetch

Auf'sicht, *(w.) f.* inspection, survey, supervision, superintendence; care, charge, keep, control; tutelage (of wards, minors); custody (of prisoners); — führen, to superintend, to

Auf'sperrhäken, *(str.) m. Lock-sm.* see Dietrich.

Auf'spielen, *(w.) v.* I. *tr. & intr.* to play to one; to play to the dance; to strike up: wenn das Glück aufspielt, der hat gut tanzen, *proverb,* he dances well, to whom fortune pipes: II. *tr.* 1) to awake by playing on an instrument; 2) sich *(Dat.)* die Finger —, to make one's fingers sore by playing on an instrument; III. *ref. coll.* to behave in a certain way *(gener. in an ill sense:* impudently, &c.).

Auf'spießen, *(w.) v. tr.* 1) to spit, broach; 2) to pierce *or* run through; 3) to empale; 4) *Pin-m.* to head (pins); *Tann.* to stretch (skins) on the frames.

Auf'spindeln, *(w.) v. tr.* to put on the spindle.

Auf'spinnen, *(str.) v.* I. *tr.* 1) to spin up; sich *(Dat.)* die Finger —, to make one's fingers sore by spinning; 2) to consume (a quantity of flax, &c.) by spinning.

Auf'spitzen, *(w.) v. tr. & intr.* to prick up (the ears, *cf.* Spitzen).

Auf'splittern, *(w.) v.* I. *tr.* to open forcibly so that the splinters fly about; II. *intr. (aux.* sein) to fly up in splinters.

Auf'spreiten, Auf'spreizen, *(w.) v. tr.* to stretch *or* spread out; sich aufspreizen, to sprawl one's self out; to stand straddling.

Auf'sprengen, *(w.) v. tr.* 1) to break up, to wrench open; to force *or* burst open; 2) to spring (a mine); to blow up (a ship, &c.); 3) to rouse, to put in motion *(cf.* Auffagen).

Auf'sprießen, *(str.),* **Auf'sprossen,** *(w.) v. intr. (aux.* sein) to sprout, shoot up, spring up.

Auf'springen, *(str.) v.* I. *intr. (aux.* sein) 1) *a)* to jump, leap, spring, *or* bounce up; *b)* to start up; to give a jerk; to start to one's feet; er sprang vor Wuth auf, he bounded with rage; sie springt vor Freuden auf, she leaps with joy; *c)* to jump, leap, &c. down (auf *[with Acc.],* upon); *d)* (of balls, &c.) to strike (against), to rebound: 2) to split asunder, to crack, chink, cleave; to chap (of the skin, &c.); —machen, to chap, cut; von der Kälte springen die Lippen auf, cold weather chaps *or* cuts the lips; aufgesprungene Hände, cracked *or* chapped hands; aufgesprungene Lippen, chapped *or* parched lips; 3) to spring *or* fly open (as doors, &c.); 4) to sparkle (up), mantle, mount (of wine, when poured into the glass); II. *ref.* sich *(Acc.)* —, *or* sich *(Dat.)* die Füße —, to get sore feet by springing; a-d, *p. a.* *a)* *Bot.* dehiscent; *b)* *Herald.* salient, rampant.

Auf'springegeld, *(str.) n.* fee (paid to the owner of a bull) for fecundating a cow.

Auf'spritzen, *(w.) v.* I. *tr.* 1) to blow up (water), to squirt up; 2) *Surg.* to open with a syringe (as an abscess); II. *intr. (aux.* sein) to squirt up, fly up, splash up.

Auf'sprossen, *(w.) v. intr.* to shoot (up, forth, &c.), to sprout. [see Aufschößling.

Auf'sprößling, *(str.) m.* scion, shoot, &c.

Auf'sprudeln, *(w.) v.* I. *intr. (aux.* sein) (of water, &c.) to bubble *or* boil up; er [illegible] auf, *fig.* his blood is soon up; to sparkle, to mount (of wine); II. *tr.* to throw up (water) with a bubbling noise.

Auf'sprühen, *(w.) v.* I. *intr. (aux.* sein) [illegible]; II. *tr.* to make fly up as sparks, to throw up in small particles, &c.

Auf'sprung, *(str., pl.* Auf'sprünge) *m.* the [illegible] up, bound, &c. *cf.* Aufspringen.

[illegible] *(w.) v. tr.* to wind upon a [illegible] reel (yarn).

[illegible] *(w.) v. tr.* 1) see Aufschwemmen; 2) see Aufweichen.

[illegible], **Auf'spunden,** *(w.) v. tr.* to [illegible] to start the bung of (a cask).

[illegible] *(w.) v. tr.* to trace out, spy out; to smell out: *Sport-s.* Wild —, to draw, to cover: den Feind —, to request.

Auf'stäben, *(w.) v. tr. Dy.* to hang upon sticks.

Auf'stacheln, *(w.) v. tr.* 1) to spit, to pierce, and take up with a pointed instrument; 2) (auch *fig.)* to stir, goad up *or* on, to spur on.

Auf'staffiren, *(w.) v. tr.* to equip, accoutre; *T.* to fit *or* brush up (a hat).

Auf'stakern, *(w.) v. tr. Agr.* to stack, pile up (the sheaves).

Auf'stallen, *(w.) v. tr.* to put up (into the stable) for fattening; to stall.

Auf'stämmen, *(w.) v. tr.* 1) to prop up; 2) *T.* to open with a chisel.

Auf'stampfen, *(w.) v.* I. *tr.* 1) to fix by stamping; 2) to head (a pin); 3) to open by stamping; II. *intr.* to stamp upon the ground.

Auf'stand, *(str., pl.* Auf'stände) *m.* 1) *a)* a stirring, rising; *b)* *Fish.* *aa)* the rising of fishes to the surface (or to the ice-holes in winter) for want of air; *bb)* the expiring for want of air; 2) *fig.* *a)* insurrection, &c., see Aufruhr; *b)* the (act of) leaving service (used of journeymen-tailors and such whose work is done in a sitting posture); 3) *Min.* a special report as to the state of a mine.

Auf'stapeln, *(w.) v. tr.* to pile up, to heap up, to stack up.

Auf'starren, *(w.) v. intr.* 1) to rise up, or above; to stand up, to bristle; 2) to stare up.

Auf'stäuben, *(w.) v.* I. *tr.* to make to rise as dust; II. *or* **Auf'stauben,** *(w.) v. intr. (aux.* sein) to rise, fly up as dust. [jagen.

Auf'stäubern, *(w.) v. tr. Sport.* see Auf-

Auf'stäuberer, *(str.) m. Sport.* springer.

Auf'stauchen, *(w.) v. tr.* 1) to knock, push against some hard body; 2) to put (flax) up for drying; 3) see Aufstauen, 2; 4) *T.* to thicken (iron) by welding.

Auf'stauen, *(w.) v. tr.* 1) *Mar.* to stow away in the hold of the ship; 2) *T.* to swell, dam up, stem (the water in a millpond, &c.).

Auf'staunen, *(w.) v. intr.* to look up with astonishment. [banking.

Auf'stauung, *(w.) f. Dik.* dammed water,

Auf'stechen, *(str.) v. tr.* 1) *a)* to pick, pierce open, to cut open; *b)* *Surg.* to open by a puncture; 2) see Aufstacheln, 1; 3) *Engr.* to retouch (a copperplate); 4) *fig.* (Einem etwas) to take (one) up; to cavil at, to find fault with, to taunt, upbraid (for trifling errors), to tease (one about), to mock (at); ein Wort —, to lay hold of a word; Einem den Schwödern —, *coll.* to tell one an unpleasant truth; 5) *Mar-s.* beim Winde —, to ply or work to windward; einen Katzenrücken *or* sich den Rücken —, to become cambered *or* broken-backed; ein Schiff, das einen Katzenrücken aufgestochen hat, a hogged ship; zwei Taue —, to tie two ropes together; Halsen und Schoten —, to give up tacks and sheets; 6) *Shoe-m.* to sew on the latchets *or* heels; 7) *Sport.* to hunt up, run after game (of dogs).

Auf'stecher, *(str.) m. coll.* fault-finder, &c.

Auf'stecken, *(w.) v. tr.* 1) to put *or* fix upon, to set up; 2) to pin up; to truss up, to tuck up; to put up (curtains); ein Licht —, to put (a candle) into a candle-stick; ein Rad —, *Mech.* to ship *or* key (a wheel); die Flagge (ein Schau) —, *Mar.* to hoist the flag (with a waft); mit aufgestecktem Bajonnet, with fixed bayonet; Einem ein Licht —, *fig. coll.* to inform one of the true state of things *or* as to the bearings of a case; 3) *coll.,* to give up.

Auf'stehen, *(irr.) v. intr.* I. *(aux.* haben) 1) *coll. for* offen stehen, to stand open; 2) to stand (firm) upon; II. *(aux.* sein) 1) *a)* to stand up, to get on one's feet, to rise, arise, get up; *b)* to get up (from bed, aus dem Bette), to rise, arise: *Mar.* to turn out (*i. e.* to leave the hammocks); aufgestanden sein, to be up; *c)* (wieder) to recover (from a sickness); 2) *Sport.* to rise, &c.: *a)* der Hirsch steht auf, the stag breaks cover; *b)* to spring, to fly up (of birds); die Vögel stehen auf, the fowls fly up; *c)* (of fish) *aa)* to rise to the surface *(or* in winter: to rush to the ice-holes) for want of air; *bb)* to expire from want of air; 3) *Mar.* to right up (as a ship); 4) *Found.* to swell; 5) *fig.* to arise, to make one's appearance: es ist ein Prophet aufgestanden, a prophet has arisen; 6) to rise up in arms; wider Jemand —, to rise (in insurrection) against, to revolt; 7) to leave service (of journeymen-tailors and shoemakers; *cf.* Aufstand, 2, *b*); das —, *v. s.* *(str.) n.* the (act of) rising, &c.; das späte —, the getting up late, *coll.* fashionable hours.

Auf'steifen, *(w.) v. tr.* to stiffen (up), to (clear-)starch; to cock (a hat).

Auf'steige ..., *in comp.* —block, *m.* horse-block; —klappe, *f. Mech.* suction-valve, up-stroke-valve; —riemen (für Bediente), *pl.* footmen's holders; —seite, *f.* left *(or* off side) (of a horse).

Auf'steigen, I. *(str.) v. intr. (aux.* sein) to mount; to rise; to ascend, get up, arise; auf einen Wagen —, to get into a coach; der Nebel steigt auf, the fog is dispersing; das Blut stieg ihr ins Gesicht auf, the blood mounted *or* flushed up to her face; der Wein steigt in den Kopf auf, wine flies up to one's head; to fly; der Wind steigt auf, the wind *(or* a breeze) springs up; ein Gewitter steigt auf, a storm is coming on; der Gedanke stieg in mir auf, the thought arose in my mind *(or* occurred to me, struck me); — lassen, to fly (a kite, &c.); II. *v. s.* *(str.) n.* 1) the (act of) mounting, rising, rise (of a hawk, &c.), elevation (of vapours); dispersion (of a fog); ascent (of *or* in a balloon); 2) *Astr.* ascension; 3) das — der (or die a-de) Mutter, *Med.* rising of the womb, mother-fit, hysterical passion, 4) the brewing, gathering (of a tempest).

Auf'steigend, *p. a. Bot., Astr., &c.* ascending; die a-e Linie (der Verwandtschaft), ascending line; ein Verwandter der a-en Linie, ascendant.

Auf'steigung, *(w.) f.* 1) see Aufsteigen, II. (*v. s.*); 2) *Astr., &c.* ascension: gerade —, schiefe —, right ascension, oblique ascension; A-sunterschied, *m.* ascensional difference.

Auf'stellen, *(w.) v.* I. *tr.* 1) to set, put up to raise; to erect; eine Armee —, to raise an army; eine Falle —, to (put up a) trap, to lay *or* set a snare; die Lehrbogen —, *Build.* to set the centres; Netze —, to spread nets; Heu in Haufen —, to cock *or* stack hay; to expose (for sale); 2) to place, plant, *or* post (guards, &c.); to draw up, station, range, dispose (troops, &c.); verdeckt —, *Mil.* to place under cover; 3) *fig.* to start, set up (a doctrine, &c.), to lay down (a principle, &c.), to state, to set, *or* carry forth, advance, make (an assertion, &c.), to bring forward, adduce (a proof); *Comm.* to draw up, exhibit (an account); to produce, bring (a witness); to appoint (as arbiter); to put or state (a question); er stellte Alles auf, zu erfahren ..., he did all he could to ascertain ...; II *intr.* to have a care, to pay attention; III. *ref. Mil., &c.* to draw up (in a line, &c.), *(Mil.)* to fall in; to stand up *or* out (to dance); aufgestelltermaßen, *adv.* as it has been set forth *or* advanced.

Auf'stellspiegel, *(str.) m.* see Toiletten-spiegel.

Auf'stellung, *(w.) f.* 1) the act of setting up, &c.; 2) *Comm.* statement; 3) assertion.

Auf'stemmen, *(w.) v.* I. *tr.* 1) to plant firmly; to prop up, to support; to lean upon or against, sich *(or* die Arme auf den Tisch) —, to lean upon the table; 2) to open, to force open with a crow-bar; II. *ref.* to lean upon or against.

Auf'stempeln, (w.) v. tr. 1) to stamp on, upon; 2) to stamp afresh or anew.

Auf'steppen, (w.) v. tr. Tail. to quilt on, to sew on with a quilted seam.

Auf'steuer, (w.) f. (l. u.) longing, desire (nach, for).

Auf'steuern, (w.) v. I. intr. (aux. sein) to steer upward; II. tr. to support with the arm.

Auf'sticheln, (w.) v. tr. 1) to sew on with fine stitches; 2) see Aufstacheln, 2.

Auf'sticken, (w.) v. tr. to embroider upon.

Auf'stieben, (str., rarely w.) v. intr. (aux. sein) 1) see Aufstäuben; 2) Sport. to fly up, to rise in great numbers (of smaller birds).

Auf'stieren, (w.) v. intr. to stare up.

Auf'stiften, (w.) v. tr. see Anstiften.

Auf'stimmen, (w.) v. tr. Mus. to set higher (in tuning).

Auf'stöbern, (w.) v. tr. 1) see Aufstäubern; 2) to find out, to hit upon, to meet with.

Auf'stöhnen, (w.) v. I. intr. to groan (faint, aloud); II. tr. to wake up by groaning.

Auf'stocken, (w.) v. tr. Stone-cutt. to tooth, &c. see Aufrauhen, 1.

Auf'stopfen, (w.) v. tr. 1) to stuff out, anew, or again; to darn up or upon; 2) to unstop. [pick up.

Auf'stoppeln, (w.) v. tr. to scrape together,

Auf'stöpseln, (w.) v. tr. to uncork (a bottle).

Auf'stören, (w.) v. tr. 1) a) to stir or rake up (also fig. = Aufrühren, Aufwühlen); b) Sport. to uprouse, to spring; 2) to disturb (aus dem Schlafe rc., from sleep, &c.), startle.

Auf'stoßen, (str.) v. I. tr. 1) to push up, kick up; to throw up; 2) to push, kick, thrust open: den Boden eines Fasses —, to stave or knock out the head of a cask; 3) Typ. see [illegible], 2; 4) Sport. to start, flush (game); 5) to wound by pushing against; to gall, fret (the skin, &c.); II. intr. (aux. sein) 1) impers. to be pushed upward; a) to rise up; Rettig stößt mir auf, radish rises with me; b) to ferment afresh (of beer in a cask); to become acid (of wine); 2) a) to occur, to come in one's way: impers. es stößt mir auf, I hit, chance, light on, upon; I meet with, come across, &c.; es stößt mir ein Zweifel auf, a doubt arises in (crosses) my mind; b) to strike, startle: es stößt mir auf, it strikes me: 3) Mar. to run aground; das —, s. a. (str.) n. 1) the (act of) pushing open, &c.; 2) a) rising of the stomach; eructation, &c.; — haben, to break wind upward; to vomit up; 3) a meeting, encounter.

Auf'stößig, I. adj. 1) vapid, flat, sour; 2) sick; 3) causing eructations; II. A-keit, (w.) f. (of chickens and geese) indigestion, want of appetite.

Auf'strahlen, (w.) v. intr. to rise in (splendid) rays, to rise with a splendour.

Auf'sträuben, (w.) v. tr. & refl. to bristle up, to stand on end (of hair).

Auf'streben, (w.) v. intr. (aux. sein) 1) a) to strive upwards, to soar up; b) aspiring; 2) to rise high; a-d, p. a. (also fig.) aspiring. — **Auf'strebung**, (w.) f. 1) a striving upwards, &c.; 2) aspiring; effort, exertion.

Auf'strecken, (w.) v. tr. to stretch up

Auf'streich, (str.) m. 1) public auction or sale; 2) Mus. see Aufstrich.

Auf'streicheisen, (str.) n. Cloth-m. napping-comb; Shoe-m. scraper. [wards.

Auf'streicheln, (w.) v. tr. to stroke up-

Auf'streichen, (str.) v. I. tr. to spread (butter upon bread, &c.), to lay on; to draw upwards; to turn up (one's whiskers); to strike up (a tune, &c.); to strike (a colour); II. intr. 1) Cloth. to shear against the grain; 2) to rub the hindlegs together, to cut (of horses); 3) see Aufstreifen; 4) Hunt. to graze the floor (of dogs).

Auf'streichmesser, (str.) n. Shoe-m. scraper.

Auf'streifeln, (w.) v. tr. to fold back, to turn up; to tuck up (the sleeves).

Auf'streifen, (w.) v. I. tr. 1) to draw up, turn, tuck up; 2) to tear or wound, to fret: II. intr. to strike, touch upon the surface, to graze, to sweep the ground (gener. with auf [& Acc. or Dat.]); III. refl. sich (Dat.) die Ärmel —, to tuck up one's sleeves; sich (Dat.) die Haut —, to tear one's skin.

Auf'streuen, (w.) v. tr. to strew upon, sprinkle on.

Auf'strich, (str.) m. 1) a) Mus. an up-bow; b) see Auftakt, 2 (stroke upwards on an instrument); 2) provinc. public auction.

Auf'stricken, (w.) v. tr. 1) to untwist (Seile, ropes); 2) to consume, use up (yarn, &c.) in knitting.

Auf'striegeln, (w.) v. I. tr. to comb or curry upwards: II. refl. fam. see sich Aufschniegeln.

Auf'strömen, (w.) v. tr. to float upwards: to carry up.

Auf'stufen, (w.) v. I. tr. to raise gradually, to bring to a climax: II. intr. (aux. sein) & refl. to rise gradually, by gradation.

Auf'stufung, (w.) f. gradation, climax.

Auf'stülpen, (w.) v. tr. 1) to turn up; to cock (up) (a hat); eine aufgestülpte Nase, a turned up nose, snub-nose; 2) to top (boots); 3) to put or clap on in a hurry.

Auf'stürmen, (w.) v. I. intr. (aux. sein) to rush upwards: II. tr. 1) to open by violence, to burst or bounce open; 2) to wake up by a stormy noise, violence, &c.; 3) to drive upwards.

Auf'stürzen, (w.) v. I. tr. 1) to clap on, put on (a cover); to put on in a hurry; 2) to turn up; II. intr. (aux. sein) to strike, fall (auf [with the Acc., rarely with the Dat.], upon, on).

Auf'stutzen, (w.) v. I. tr. 1) Hatt. to turn up (the rim of a hat); 2) coll. to trim; to prank up; to vamp up; to accommodate, to pinme, &c. cf. Stutzen; II. intr. to look up with surprise, to start.

Auf'stutzer, (str.) m. trimmer, &c.

Auf'stützen, (w.) v. I. tr. to prop up: II. refl. 1) to lean on; 2) to pull hard at the bit (of horses).

Auf'suchen, (w.) v. tr. to seek out, to look or search after, or for, to go in quest of, to inquire after; coll. to look (one) up; 2) fig. a) to trace (God in his works, &c.); b) to court (danger, &c.); die geographische Lage rc. —, Mar. to take the bearings; Einen — lassen, to cause search to be made for one. [for, &c.

Auf'suchung, (w.) f. the search, looking

Auf'summen, (w.) v. I. intr. (aux. sein) to rise, to fly or go up with a humming noise; II. refl. to sum up, to increase; to run up; III. tr. to wake by a humming noise.

Auf'sumsen, (w.) v. I. tr. to rouse by humming; II. intr. (aux. sein) to buzz up.

Auf'süßen, (w.) v. tr. Chem. to sweeten.

Auf'tact, (str.) m. see Aufschlag, 3.

Auf'täfeln, (w.) v. tr. 1) coll. to dish up; 2) Cloth. to fold up (cloth). [next day.

Auf'tagen, (w.) v. tr. to adjourn to the

Auf'takeln, (w.) v. tr. Mar. to rig (out); to new rig: nicht gut aufgetakelt, not rigged shipshape; aufgetakelt, p. a. coll. tricked out, see Aufgedonnert.

Auf'taljen, (w.) v. tr. Mar. to bowse.

Auf'tanzen, (w.) v. I. intr. (Einem) to dance at one's bidding, i. e. to do whatever he may command; II. tr. 1) to wear out (shoes) by dancing; sich (Dat.) die Füße —, to dance one's feet sore.

Auf'tassen, (w.) v. tr. to pile up (corn) in heaps or shocks, to shock, cf. Taß.

Auf'tauchen, (w.) v. intr. (aux. sein) 1) to rise up, to emerge (from the water, &c.); 2) (of distant objects) to come in sight, to begin to appear; 3) fig. to spring up, arise.

tisch, m. scullery; —wasser, n. 1) dish-water; 2) see Spülicht.

Aufweben, (w. & * str.) v. tr. 1) to unweave, unravel; 2) to consume by weaving.

Aufwechsel, (str.) m. obsolescent for Aufgeld.

Aufwechseln, (w.) v. tr. 1) to buy up (and thereby to bring out of circulation); 2) to change, exchange with agio.

Aufwechsler, (str.) m. money-changer; stock-jobber.

Aufwecken, (w.) v. tr. 1) to awake (aus dem Schlafe, from sleep), rouse, wake, (a)waken; to call up; fig.-s. 2) to call to life; 3) to enliven, cheer.

Aufwehen, (w.) v. I. tr. 1) to blow up; 2) to blow open; II. intr. (aux. sein) to rise (of the wind).

Aufweichen, (w.) v. I. tr. 1) to soften, mollify; 2) to soak, moisten, wet, make soft; Häute —, Skin-dr. to soak hides; to temper (colours); 3) to open by mollifying; II. intr. (aux. sein) to soak and dissolve; to open after having soaked; a-d, p. a. Med. emollient; das a-de Mittel, emollient (remedy).

Aufweifen, (w.) v. tr. 1) to reel on; 2) T. to brush up (the set jewels).

Aufweinen, (w.) v. I. tr. to awake by weeping or crying; II. intr. to begin crying, weep aloud.

Aufweisen, (str.) v. tr. to show (forth), produce, exhibit; to present (one's credentials, &c.); die Geschichte hat kein besseres Beispiel aufzuweisen, history has no better example to show. — **Aufweisung**, (w.) f. exhibition, production.

Aufweißen, (w.) v. tr. to whitewash anew.

Aufwelken, (w.) v. tr. to dry (fruit).

Aufwellen, (w.) v. tr. see Aufwallen.

Aufwenden, (w. & irr.) v. tr. to spend, expend, lay out (auf [with Acc.], in, on, in); to bestow, employ (auf, in, on, in); to devote (auf, to, on); die aufgewendete (or aufgewandte) Mühe, the pains one has taken, &c.

Aufwerfen, (str.) v. I. tr. 1) a) to throw up (a stone, entrenchments, &c.), to cast up, to raise (a bank, &c.), to toss up (a ball, &c.), to turn up (the soil, the nose, &c.); Schaum, Blasen —, to rise in scum, in bubbles; die Erde um einen Baum herum —, Gard. to heap up the earth round the roots of a tree; einen Graben —, to dig a ditch; b) Gam-s. to throw up (the cards); die Würfel —, to fling up the dice; die Lippen, den Mund —, to turn up or pout one's lips or mouth; aufgeworfene Lippen, pouting, protuberant lips; eine aufgeworfene Nase, a cocked-up nose; c) fig. einen Zweifel —, to raise a doubt; eine Frage —, to start a question, to put a case; 2) to throw down (auf [with Acc.], upon); 3) a) to open (a net, &c.) by throwing down upon or against, to strike open; b) to throw or fling open (a door, &c.); II. refl. sich — zu ..., to set up for ..., to put one's self forward as ..., to erect one's self into ..., to usurp authority; er warf sich zum Schiedsrichter auf, he assumed the office of an arbitrator; sich gegen Jemand —, to rise up against one (cf. Empören).

Aufwerfhammer, (str., pl. A-hämmer) m. T. lift-hammer.

Aufwettern, (w.) v. tr. coll. to rouse from sleep by noisy and abusive language.

Aufwichsen, (w.) v. tr. 1) to polish up, to brush up (with wax or blacking); 2) vulg.-s. see Aufwiegeln; 3) Einem —, to treat, entertain sumptuously, to give a famous blow-out or spread.

Aufwickeln, (w.) v. tr. 1) to wind up, roll up, take up (yarn, &c.); to turn up (the hair, &c.), to put (one's hair) in (curl-)papers; 2) to wind, &c. (auf [with Acc.], upon); 3) to unfold, unwrap, unwind, untuck, unfurl; 4) to unswaddle, unswathe (a child); aufgewickelt, p. a. unwrapped; aufgewickelte Seide, Comm. sleave silk.

Aufwiegelei', (w.) f. the practice of stirring up, instigating (to rebellion), &c., agitation.

Aufwiegeln, (w.) v. tr. to stir (up), to excite, instigate, to rebellion, to tamper with, to raise up (the people).

Aufwiegelung, (w.) f. the act of stirring up, &c. instigation (to rebellion).

Aufwiegen, (str.) v. tr. 1) to outweigh; to counterbalance, to counterpoise, countervail; to make amends for ...; Fehler durch Tugenden —, to redeem faults by virtues; 2) coll. see Aufwägen.

Aufwiegler, (str.) m., **Aufwieglerei'**, (w.) f., **Aufwieglerisch**, see Aufrührer, 1, Aufwiegelei & Aufrührerisch.

Aufwiehern, (w.) v. I. intr. 1) to burst out neighing; 2) coll. to laugh immoderately; II. tr. to awake by neighing.

Aufwimmern, (w.) v. tr. to wake by moaning.

Aufwindebewegung, (w.) f. winding-on motion (Karm.).

Aufwindeln, (w.) v. tr. to unswathe.

Aufwind(e)..., in comp. Weav-s. —draht, m., —rad, n. faller (pl.), faller-wire, rim; —maschine, f. whim, winding engine.

Aufwinden, (str.) v. I. tr. 1) to wind up; to hoist up, to heave (up), pull up; 2) Mar. to ground (a vessel); den Anker —, to weigh anchor; to start or purchase the anchor; 3) to open by winding; 4) to unwring, untwist, undo; II. refl. to rise in windings.

Aufwinder, (str.) m. 1) a winder-up, &c.; 2) see Aufwinddraht.

Aufwinken, (w.) v. tr. to make or cause to rise by a sign, a beck, or wink.

Aufwippen, (w.) v. tr. 1) see Aufwägen; 2) Mil. to strappado.

Aufwirbeln, (w.) v. I. tr. 1) to open (as a window) by turning the bolt; 2) to raise, whirl up; Staub —, to occasion a great deal of noise, discussion, &c., coll. to kick up a dust; 3) to wake by beating a drum; II. intr. (aux. sein) to rise (with a rotary motion).

Aufwirken, (w.) v. tr. 1) to work (out); den Teig —, Bak. to knead the dough; to form the loaves; ein Wild —, Sport. see Aufweiden; den Huf eines Pferdes —, Farr. see Auswirken; 2) to unweave, unravel; 3) to consume by weaving.

Aufwirren, (w.) v. tr. to disentangle, unravel (Entwirren).

Aufwischen, (w.) v. tr. to wipe away (up).

Aufwischer, (str.) m., **Aufwischlappen**, m., **Aufwischtuch**, n. wiping-clout.

Aufwittern, (w.) v. tr. to find out by smelling, to track by the scent.

Aufwogen, (w.) v. intr. to rise in waves, to swell, to billow.

Aufwölben, (w.) v. tr. Archit. to erect in the shape of a vault, to vault.

Aufwölken, (w.) v. intr. & refl. impers. to rise like (as) clouds, to lower (of the sky).

Aufwollen, (irr.) v. intr. to wish to get up or rise.

Aufwuchern, (w.) v. intr. (aux. sein) to grow up rank or luxuriantly.

Aufwuchten, (w.) v. tr. to raise by a lever.

Aufwühlen, (w.) v. tr. 1) a) to turn, dig, root up; den (Erd-)Boden —, to plough, or rake up the ground (as cannon-balls, &c.); b) to stir up by wallowing about; die Glut (glimmender Kohlen) — (Goethe), to rake up dying embers; c) fig. to rip up (old sores, &c.), to rake up (Aufstören); 2) fig. see Aufwiegeln.

Aufwurf, (str., pl. Aufwürfe) m. earth thrown or dug up, mound, jetty, dam, bank.

Aufwürfling, (str.) m. outcast.

Aufwürgen, (w.) v. tr. to consume with greediness, to devour.

Aufzählen, (w.) v. tr. to count, number,

flecken, m. pl. see —fell; —fluß, m. catarrh, rheum, or watering in the eye; —flüssig, adj. affected with ophthalmic fluxion or a watering of the eye; —förmig, adj. eye-formed, in the form of an eye; oculiform, ocellated; —funken, m. pl. Med. photopsy; —gefäße, n. pl. Anat. the arteries, veins, and lymphatic vessels of the eye; Med-s. —geschwür, n. ulcer of the eye; —geschwulst, f. exophthalmy; —gewölk, n. nebula; —glas, n. eye-glass (a glass to assist the sight); —grube, f. Anat. cavity over the eye-brows; the hollow over the eyes of horses; —halter, m. Surg. instrument to keep the eye-lids open; —haut, f. coat of the eye; —häutchen, n. 1) winking membrane; 2) Vet. white film; —heilanstalt, f. eye-infirmary; —höhle, f. eye-hole, socket, orbit; giena; —holz, n. see Ablerholz; —klappe, f. eye-flap; winker-piece, pl. winkers; —klappenränder, m. pl. winker-frames; —klinik, f. ophthalmic infirmary; —koralle, f. see —coralle; —krampf, m. see —muskelkrampf & Augapfelkrampf; —krankenanstalt, f. see —heilanstalt; —krankheit, f. disease of the eye; —kraut, n. Bot. see —trost; —krebs, m. cancer of the eye; —kreis, m. orbit; —lähmung, f. paralysis of the eye; —leder, n. see —blende; —lehre, f. ophthalmology; —leiden, n. disease of the eye; —licht, n. eye-sight; —lied, lid, (str., pl. A-er, & (L. u.) A-e) n. eye-lid; —liederentzündung, f. inflammation of the eye-lids, blepharitis; —liederknorpel, m. Anat. cartilage of the eye, tarsus; —liederumkehrung, f. Med. eversion of the eye-lid, ectropium; —loch, n. 1) Anat. opening of the iris, pupil; 2) Archit. an eye-formed window, or opening of a roof.

Au'genlos, adj. eyeless; sightless.

Au'gen..., in comp. —lust, f. delight of the eyes; —marmor, m. eye-spotted marble; —maß, n. estimate by the eye, eye-sight; ein gutes —maß haben, to have a correct or just eye; nach dem —maß kaufen, to buy in the lump; —merk, n. object in view, aim, mark; sein —merk richten or gerichtet haben, to have in view, to aim at; —messer, m. 1) eyemeter; 2) Surg. a kind of cataract-knife; —mittel, n. ocular medicine, ophthalmic; (zu äußerem Gebrauch) eye-wash, eye-lotion, collyrium; —muskel, m. ocular muscle; (der abziehende) Abductor oculi; (schräge) oblique muscle, (oberer schiefe) trochleary muscle; —muskelkrampf, m. Med. (klonischer) nystagmus; (tonischer) strabismus spasticus (Lat.); —nadel, f. needle, see Nähnadel; —nagel, m. see —fell; —nebel, m. see —gewölk; —nerv, m. ocular nerve, eye-string; —nicht(e), —nichts, n. Metall. white tutty; —pappel, f. vervain-mallow (Siegmannswurz); —perpendikel, m. Opt. cathetus of reflection; —pflege, f. proper care and attention given to the preservation of the eye; —pulver, n. 1) powder for the eyes, xerocollyrium; 2) fig. very small print; —punkt, m. point of sight, object in view, visual point; —reiz, m. 1) tickling in the eye; 2) see —lust; —ring, m. iris; —salbe, f. eye-salve; —schein, m. autopsy, inspection; evidence, appearance, eye-sight; durch den —schein belehrt, taught by the evidence of senses; in —schein nehmen, to take a view of; to view, to inspect; Archit. to make a survey of; —scheinlich, adj. evident, apparent, manifest, self-evident; visible, conspicuous, obvious; imminent (of danger); ocular (of a proof), palpable (facts, &c.); —scheinlichkeit, f. evidence; apparentness; obviousness; self-evidence; —schirm, m. shade, eye-screen; —schlagader, f. Anat. ophthalmic artery; —schlange, f. see Natter; —schleim, m. see —butter; —schleimfluß, m. ophthalmic fluxion; —schmalz, n. see —butter; —schmaus, m. see —weide; —schmerz, m. pain in the eye(s); —schnupftabak, m. eye-snuff; —schützer, pl. goggles; —schwäche, f. weakness of sight; —schwund, m., —schwinden, n. Med. atrophy of the eye-ball; —sperre, f. Med. synizesis; —spiegel, m. Surg. ophthalmoscope, speculum oculi; —spiel, n. expression of the eye, ogling; —sprache, f. language of the eyes; —sprosse, Augsprosse, m. Sport. brow-antler; —staar, m. cataract. —stechen, n. 1) Med. shooting pains in the eye(s); 2) Surg. couching; —stein, m. Pharm. sulphate of zinc, white copperas; Miner. eye-stone; —stern, m. 1) pupil; 2) fig. pet, favourite (cf. Augapfel); —sternerweiterung, f. Med. mydriasis, enlargement of the eye-ball or pupil; —sternverengerung, f. Med. myosis, contraction of the pupil; —tabak, m. eye-snuff; —täuschung, f. 1) Med. ocular spectrum, spectral deception; 2) ocular deception, illusion of vision; —talg, m. Med. see —butter; —theriak, m. Bot. valerian (Valeriana silvestris); —thierchen, n. pl. Zool. infusoria; —thränen, n. watery eye, epiphora; —träger, m. Bot. bulb through which the germ shoots forth; —treibend, adj. Bot. gemmiparous, producing buds; —triefen, n. lippitude; —triefig, adj. bleared, blear-eyed; —trost, m. (lit. that which cheers the eyes) 1) fig. comfort, consolation; 2) Bot. eye-bright, euphrasy (Euphrasia L.); —trostgras, n. see Sternpflanze; —verdunkelung, f. Med. amblyopia, amaurosis, (schwarze Staar) gutta serena; —vorfall, m. Med. prolapsus oculi, exophthalmia, protrusion of the eyeball; —wasser, n. eye-water, collyrium; —wassersucht, f. Med. hydrophthalmia; —weh, n. pain in the eyes; —weide, f. delight of the eyes; —weite, f. reach of the eye, coll. eye-shot; —welle, f. see —axe; —wimper, f. eye-lash (pl. cilia (Lat.)); —wink, m. eyewink; —winkel, m. (innerer, äußerer, inner, outer) angle or corner of the eye; canthus; —winkelgeschwulst, f. Med. encanthis; —wölkchen, n. Med. nubecula; —wonne, f. see —weide; —zahn, m. eye-tooth, dog-tooth; —zauber, m. fascination; —zeuge, m. eye-(ocular)witness; —zeugniß, n. ocular testimony; —zierde, f. see Ochsenzunge (plant); —zirkel, see —cirkel.

Augi'as, m. Gr. Myth. Augias, Augeas (a king of Elis); den Stall des — reinigen, to cleanse the Augean stable.

Au'gicht, adj. eye-spotted, ocellated.

Au'gig, adj. 1) Miner. see Blasig; 2) in comp. -eyed; trief—, blear-eyed.

* Augit', (str.) m. Miner. augite; petaloner —spath, diopside, pyroxene; der prismatische —spath, tabular spar; wollastonite; prismatoidischer —, epidote.

Äug'lein, (str.) n. (dimin. of Auge) * little eye.

Aug'ler, (str.) m. (lit. observer) Mas. & Carp. head-mason, foreman.

* Augment', (str.) n. (Lat.) Gramm. augment. — Augmenti'ren, (w.) v. tr. to add the augment to.... — Augmenti'rung, (w.) f. placing of the augment.

Augs'burg, n. Geogr. Augsburg(h).

Augs'burgisch, adj. of Augsburg(h), Augustan (confession, &c.).

Aug'splissung, (w.) f. Mar. eye-splice.

* Au'gur, (str., pl. (w.) Au'guren, Augu'ren) m. Rom. Archaeol. augur.

August, m. 1) (as a German personal P. N. with the accent on the first syllable) Au'gust, Augu'stus, Augustus ((Lat.) P. N.); 2) August', (the month of) Au'gust; —hafer, m. hasty oats; —kirsche, f. sour cherry, agriot.

Augustë'isch, Augu'stisch, adj. Augustan (Zeitalter, age, &c.)

Au'gustin, Augusti'nus, m. Augusti'nus, Augus'tin, Austin (P.N.). — Augustiner, (str.) m. Eccl. Austin friar; die A-in, (w.) f. Austin nun. — Augustinisch, adj. Augustinian.

* Au'ra, f. (Lat.) see Prunuswellen (Flower).

* Aurat', (str.) n. (Lat.) Chem. aurate.

Zeit ist —, the time is over, expired, passed, up: es ist —, 'tis past, there is no hope; es ist — mit ihm, it is all over or up with him, he is undone, or quite down: he is gone, a gone, or a dead man; weder — noch ein wissen, coll. to be at a non-plus, to be put to one's last shifts; er weiß weder — noch ein, he does not know how to help or extricate himself, he is at his wits' end: trinke es —, drink it up; mein Geld ist —, my money is gone, I am out of cash; nach dem Tode ist es —, death puts an end to everything; damit ist es —, this affair is off; und damit ist es —, and there is an end of the matter: von dem Tage an, wo Pitt die Leitung der Geschäfte übernahm, war es — mit geheimen Einflüssen, from the day on which Pitt was placed at the head of affairs, there was an end of secret influence.

Aus'ächzen, (w.) v. I. tr. to groan forth, out; II. intr. to leave off groaning.

Aus'ackern, (w.) v. I. tr. to plough up or out; II. intr. to finish, leave off ploughing.

Aus'ädern, (w.) v. tr. to pluck the veins out of ...., to divest of the veins. [mock.

Aus'äffen, (w.) v. tr. to deride, jeer at,

Aus'ähren, (w.) v. tr. to break off the ears of (corn after being thrashed). [ling.

Aus'angeln, (w.) v. tr. to empty by ang-

Aus'antworten, (w.) v. tr. particul. Law, &c. to deliver, surrender (Ausliefern).

Aus'arbeiten, (w.) v. I. tr. 1) to work out; 2) Butch. to skin, flay (slaughtered cattle); 3) a) to perfect, complete, elaborate, to labour, finish; (gut, forgsam) ausgearbeitet, well laboured, finished, elaborate: high-wrought: b) to compose, prepare (a book, &c.); sein Handbuch ist nicht bloß zusammengetragen, sondern ein gut ausgearbeiteter Bericht, his handbook is not a mere compilation, but an elaborately executed account; 4) a) Man. to break in or train (a horse); b) Sport. to break in (a dog); c) Mil. to exercise, drill (a recruit); den Hochofen —, Smelt. to remove or clear away the scoria or slag from the furnace; roh —, Wood-cutt., &c. to boast; II. intr. 1) to leave off working; 2) to cease working or fermenting (of beer and wine).

Aus'arbeiter, (str.) m. 1) elaborator, &c.; 2) T. workman (artist) who gives the last touch to a fabrication or work of art, finishing workman.

Aus'arbeitung, (w.) f. 1) composition, &c.; 2) elaboration, &c., (elaborate, careful, &c.) execution, last finish; 3) workmanship, making.

Aus'ärgern, (w.) v. I. tr. Einem die Seele —, to vex a person's soul out; II. refl. to leave off fretting, vexing. [variety.

Aus'art, (w.) f. degeneration; degenerated

Aus'arten, (w.) v. intr. (aux. sein) to degenerate (in [with Acc.], into); to deteriorate: ausgeartet, p. a. degenerate. — Aus'artung, (w.) f. degeneration; degeneracy: deterioration.

Aus'ästen, (w.) v. tr. to cut or lop off the branches of (a tree), to clear (a tree) of its superfluous branches.

Aus'athmen, (w.) v. I. tr. to breathe out, forth; to exhale; II. intr. to breathe one's last, to expire, to die. [tion.

Aus'athmung, (w.) f. expiration, exhala-

Aus'ätzen, (w.) v. I. tr. 1) to take away by corrosives; Surg. to remove by caustics; 2) to corrode, eat through.

Aus'babbeln, (w.) v. see Ausplaudern.

Aus'baken, (w.) v. tr. Surv. to mark out.

Aus'backen, (str.) v. I. tr. 1) to bake sufficiently; das Brot ist nicht ausgebacken, the bread has not been baking long enough; II. intr. to have done baking.

† Aus'[illegible], (str.) m. baker's-peel (a kind of wooden shovel).

Aus'baden, (w.) v. I. intr. to bathe enough; to have done bathing; II. tr. fig. — müssen, to have to pay, suffer, smart for (another's faults); auszubaden, was Andere eingerührt haben, coll. to be made a cat's paw of.

Aus'baggern, (w.) v. tr. T. 1) to clean, drag, dredge (a harbour); 2) to deepen by dredging (a river).

Aus'bähen, (w.) v. tr. Mar. to dry (a ship).

Aus'balgen, Aus'bälgen, (w.) v. tr. 1) to strip off the skin of (an animal), to flay, skin, uncase; 2) to stuff (animals, &c.)

Aus'ballen, (w.) v. tr. to unbale, unpack.

Aus'balzen, (w.) v. intr. to cease pairing (of grouse).

Aus'bannen, (w.) v. tr. to banish (aus, out of, from); to exorcise (spirits).

Aus'bau, (str.) m. 1) a) the finishing the inside (of a building); im — begriffen, in course of completion; b) Min. tubbing (of a mine); c) T. the breaking-up of a bridge; 2) a) out-building; b) Coach-m. boot; c) Archit. exedra; d) show-front (of a shop); 3) fig. enlargement, cultivation.

Aus'bauchen, Aus'bäuchen, (w.) v. I. tr. 1) to give a belly, to make bulge, to hollow out; to thrust outward; 2) T. to chase, emboss; II. refl. to belly or swell out (like a sail, a wall, &c.), to bulge, to jut out; ausgebaucht, p. a. arched; convex or oval (glasses).

Aus'bauchung, (w.) f. Archit. belly (of a column or pillar), swelling (of the shaft of a column); bulging (of a wall).

Aus'bauen, (w.) v. I. tr. 1) to finish the inside of (a building); 2) Min. to exhaust (a mine); ausgebaute Kohlengruben, exhausted coal-pits: die Grube baut sich frei aus, the mine pays its expenses; 3) to withdraw, break up, dismantle (a bridge); 4) fig. to enlarge, finish, cultivate, improve; II. intr. to finish or to cease building.

Aus'bauer, (str.) m. 1) finisher of a building; 2) coll. a) see Ausbau, 2, d; b) see Treibkasten; 3) one erecting a building in the outskirts of a place, out-settler.

Aus'bedingen, (str. & w.) v. tr. (sich [Dat.] etwas) to condition, reserve (to one's self), to stipulate.

Aus'beeren, (w.) v. I. tr. to pick out the berries of (syringes, &c.), cf. Abbeeren; II. intr. (aux. sein) coll. to run away.

Aus'beichten, (w.) v. I. tr. to confess every particular of ..., to make a full confession of (one's sins, &c.); II. intr. to finish confession.

Aus'beinen, (w.) v. tr. to take out the bones of (meat, &c.), to bone, deprive of bones.

Aus'beißen, (str.) v. I. tr. 1) to bite out; sich (Dat.) einen Zahn —, to break out a tooth in biting; 2) a) to force or drive away by biting (of beasts); b) coll. to work out of favour, to supplant in the favour of, to oust; II. intr. 1) a) to cease to bite; b) coll. to give over quarrelling; 2) Min. to crop out (to appear above the surface), to basset; ausgebissen, p. a. Bot. erose.

Aus'beizen, (w.) v. tr. to take out, remove or purify by caustics or corrosives.

Aus'belfern, (w.) v. intr. 1) to leave off yelping; 2) fig. to leave off scolding. [ing.

Aus'bellen, (w.) v. intr. to leave off bark-

Aus'bersten, (str.) v. intr. (aux. sein) to burst forth or out, to burst and fall out. [&c.

Aus'besserer, (str.) m. mender, repairer,

Aus'bessern, (w.) v. tr. 1) to mend, repair, put in repairs, refit; to touch up, retouch; to piece up, to patch, botch; to trim up, dress (clothes, &c.); to vamp (up) (shoes, &c.); to darn (stockings, see Stopfen); to correct: die Maschine wird ausgebessert, the engine is undergoing repair(s); es ist nicht mehr auszubessern, it is past mending; 2) T. a) auf der Drehbank —, Pott. to finish on the wheel; b) das —, v. s., (str.) n. aa) Mas. the making good, dubbing out (of a wall); bb) T. research (of a roof).

Aus'besserung, (w.) f. the (act of) mending, &c., reparation, repair, refitment, &c.; A-Eisen, n. Potl. finishing tool; A-Kosten, pl. costs of repair, mendings, repairs.

Aus'beten, (w.) v. I. intr. to finish praying; II. tr. to pray to the end.

Aus'betten, (w.) v. tr. 1) to fit or provide with beds; 2) to remove (a person) from a bed; 3) to embank.

Aus'bettung, (w.) f. embankment.

Aus'beuge, (w.) f. T. turn-out.

Aus'beugen, (w.) v. see Ausbiegen.

Aus'beulen, (w.) v. tr. to beat out the bosses or prominences of (metals); Copperem. to adjust the dints of, to planish.

Aus'beute, (w.) f. profit, gain, yield; Min. share, dividend; reichliche — geben, to yield abundantly; in — stehend, (of a mine) productive; — schließen, to determine the amount of dividend of a mine; —grube or —zeche, f. productive mine; —zettel, m. account of a mine, made out quarterly.

Aus'beuteln, (w.) v. tr. 1) Mill. to bolt (flour); 2) fig. to drain (one's) purse, to fleece (one), to clean (one) out.

Aus'beuten, (w.) v. tr. 1) Min. to gain, find (in a mine); to work (a mine) to its full extent; 2) fig. to appropriate to one's self, to make the most (or the best use) of, to turn to the best advantage, to ransack: die Priester haben ihr gewöhnliches Geschick an den Tag gelegt, ein öffentliches Unglück zu ihrem Vortheile auszubeuten, the priests have displayed their accustomed tact in transforming a public calamity into a piece of good fortune for themselves; die besten lexicalischen Werke sind ausgebeutet worden, the best lexicographical works have been laid under contribution.

Aus'bezahlen, (w.) v. tr. 1) to pay in full, to complete or to make up a payment to ...; 2) see Ablohnen.

Aus'biegen, (str.) v. I. tr. 1) to turn out, to bend, bow; 2) Gold-sm. to work on the edges, to godroon; II. intr. vor Einem (l. u.: Einem) —, 1) to turn aside from ..., to turn out of one's way; 2) fig. to evade, elude, avoid (Ausweichen). [bissen.

Aus'biesen, (w.) v. tr. provinc. for Aus-

Aus'bieten, (str.) v. tr. to offer or set up for sale, to put up or set out for (or to) sale; to hawk; ausgebotene Briefe, Comm. offered paper; 2) (Überbieten) to outbid; 3) to give notice to quit (on the part of the landlord).

Aus'bildbar, adj. capable of improvement.

Aus'bilden, (w.) v. I. tr. 1) to form, to mature, to develop; völlig ausgebildet, fully developed (of leaves, &c.); 2) to cultivate; to perfect, improve, to refine; to give a finishing education; to accomplish; II. refl. 1) to be formed, &c.; to improve, to arrive at maturity or perfection; 2) to grow to a head (of an ulcer); ausgebildet, p. a. perfect, finished. — Aus'bildung, (w.) f. formation, development: (a process of) training; maturity: perfection; improvement, cultivation, culture; die — eines Geschwüres, gathering of an ulcer.

Aus'binden, (str.) v. tr. 1) a) to untie and take out; b) Typ. to untie (a column); 2) Build. to frame (a gable, &c.); eine ausgebundene Wand, a partition wall of frame-work.

Aus'bitten, (str.) v. tr. 1) to ask out; ich bin zum Mittagessen ausgebeten, I have been asked out to dinner; 2) to beg, ask for, to request; das bitte ich mir aus, a) I must make that a condition; b) (elliptically for ich bitte mir aus, daß dies nicht geschieht = das verbitte ich mir) I won't suffer that: I must decline that: ich bitte mir aus, daß du artig bist, I must insist on your behaving well; darf ich mir ... —? may I be favoured with ...? may I trouble you for ...? I will thank you for ....

Aus'blaffen, *(w.)* v. *intr. see* Ausbellen.

Aus'blänken, *(w.)* v. *tr.* to polish thoroughly.

Aus'blasen, *(str.)* v. I. *tr.* 1) to blow out: *a)* to empty by blowing (as an egg, &c.); *b)* to extinguish (a candle, &c.); 2) *Iron-w., &c.* *a)* to blow out, to stop *or* to draw (the furnace); *also intr.* to let down the fire; *b)* den Hohofen —, to blow the furnace; *c)* die Schlacke —, to blast the cinders; 3) *a)* to improve the sound of (a flute) by frequent playing; *b)* to blow (a musical piece) to the end; *c)* to proclaim by sound of trumpet: Einem das Lebenslicht —, *coll.* to stop one's wind, *i. e.* to kill him; II. *intr.* 1) to have done blowing; 2) *fam.* *(l. u.)* to die: das —, v. s. *(str.)* n. (des Dampfkessels zu seiner Reinigung) blowing down *or* off (the boiler).

Aus'blas... *(or* **Aus'blase...**), *in comp.* *Steam.* —hahn, m. blow-off cock, delivery cock, purging cock, mudcock: —klappe, *f.*, —ventil, n. blow valve; —röhre, *f.* blow-off pipe.

Aus'blatten, *(w.)* v. *tr.* 1) *T.* to cut off, to take away the sideshoots of (hops, vines, &c.); 2) *Carp.* to notch, jag.

Aus'blättern, *(w.)* v. I. *tr.* 1) to pluck out the leaves of (a plant, &c.), *cf.* Entblättern; 2) to turn (over) all the leaves of (a book); II. *intr.* to finish shedding the leaves.

Aus'bläuen, *(w.)* v. *tr.* to bang, cudgel thoroughly.

Aus'bleiben, *(str.)* v. *intr.* *(aux.* sein) 1) to stay out *or* away; to fail (to come); not to come out, forth, not to be forthcoming, to be absent; die englische Post war dreimal ausgeblieben, the English mail had three times been due; 2) to be left out, to be omitted; 3) *a)* to stop, discontinue, leave off; to intermit (of fever, &c.); not to take place, not to be held; *b)* der Puls bleibt ihm aus, his pulse stops; das Fieber ist ihm ausgeblieben, the fever has left him; das Geld bleibt ihm aus, his money does not come (in); ausgeblieben sein, to be due *or* overdue (of mails).

Aus'bleiben, v. s. *(str.)* n. staying out, &c., non-appearance; non-attendance; non-arrival; das — der Zahlung, the non-payment; das vorsätzliche — vor Gericht, default of appearance; contempt of court.

Aus'bleichen, v. I. *intr.* 1) *(w.)* to finish bleaching; 2) *(str.)* to grow pale, to fade; II. *(w.)* *tr.* to bleach out.

Aus'bleien, *(w.)* v. *tr.* to fill with lead.

Aus'blick, *(str.)* m. look-out, view, prospect *(also fig.)*. — **Aus'blicken**, *(w.)* v. *intr.* to look out *or* into [ning; fulguration.

Aus'blitz, *(str.)* m. sudden flash of light-

Aus'blitzen, *(w.)* v. *intr.* to cease lightening.

Aus'blühen, *(w.)* v. *intr.* 1) to pass through all the stages of florification; 2) to cease flowering, *see* Abblühen; 3) *Miner.* to effloresce.

Aus'bluten, *(w.)* v. I. *intr.* to cease bleeding; II. *tr.* sein Leben —, to shed one's lifeblood.

Aus'böden, *(w.)* v. *tr.* to provide with a bottom; *Coop.* to head (a cask).

Aus'bogen, *(w.)* v. *tr.* 1) *T.* to slope (a piece of cloth, &c.); 2) *Carp., Join., &c.* to channel, to slope out. [the floor.

Aus'bohlen, *(w.)* v. *tr.* to plank, to board,

Aus'bohren, *(w.)* v. I. *tr.* to bore out; *Iron., &c.* to pink; *Herol.* (fingerförmig) to chamfer; *Lock-sm., &c.* (zu einer Schraubenmutter) to tap, to worm *(Tech.)*; II. *intr.* to cease boring.

Aus'bohrer, *(str.)* m. *T. see* Ansleger. — **Aus'bohrmaschine**, *(w.)* *f.* boring machine.

Aus'bölzeln, *(w.)* v. *tr.* *Tann.* to stretch out (the hides).

Aus'borgen, *(w.)* v. *tr.* to lend out.

Aus'bracken, *(w.)* v. *tr.* *T.* to turn out, reject.

Aus'brägen, *(w.)* v. *tr.* *Tann. see* Ausbölzeln.

Aus'braten, *(str.)* v. I. *tr.* 1) to roast out; 2) to roast sufficiently; II. *intr.* *(aux.* sein) 1) to be well roasted; 2) to run out in roasting.

Aus'brauchen, *(w.)* v. *tr.* 1) to consume, to use up; 2) to use no more.

Aus'brauen, *(w.)* v. I. *tr.* to brew to perfection; 2) to extract *or* take out by brewing; II. *intr.* to cease brewing.

Aus'brausen, *(w.)* v. I. *intr.* 1) to cease roaring; 2) to cease to ferment; ausgebrauset haben, *fig.* to be past fermenting, to have subsided, to be cooled down; II. *tr.* seinen Zorn —, to give vent to, to evaporate one's passion. [iron.

Aus'brecheisen', *(str.)* n. *Tann.* softening-

Aus'brechen, *(str.)* v. I. *tr.* 1) *a)* to break out; to force, to take out *or* draw (a tooth, &c.); *b)* to notch (a knife); *c)* to quarry (stones *or* marble); *d)* *Min.* to work (einen Gang, a lode); *e)* *T.* to bore (a tunnel); *Herald-s.* ausgebrochen, *p. a.* voided; die ausgebrochene Raute, *f.* mascle; das ausgebrochene Kreuz, n. cleche, clecheé; 2) *Gard.* to cut *or* take off (the suckers, &c.); to clear of superfluous shoots, branches, &c., to prune, disbud; ausgebrochenes Holz, *Forest.* young wood *or* trees cleared off; &c.; 3) *Bee.* das Gewirk —, *see* Zeideln; 4) to vomit, throw up, bring up; Lunge und Leber —, to spew one's heart up; 5) to shell (peas *or* beans); 6) *Tann.* die gar gemachten Felle —, to soften the skins upon the boards; 7) *Brew.* to pour (beer *or* water) from the boiler into the trough; ein gegossenes Stück —, *Found.* to open the mould.

II. *intr.* *(aux.* sein) 1) to break out, to come off (as a broken piece of a cup, &c.); 2) to break out, forth; to break loose (from a prison, &c.); 3) *fig.* to break out (as a war, an epidemic, &c.); to occur, to take place suddenly, to prevail; es sind mehre Fallimente ausgebrochen, several failures have occurred; 4) to take vent, to become known, to come out; 5) to burst ([out] into [a fit of laughter, into tears; into abusive language, into a merry laugh, &c.]), to break forth (in raptures); er brach in Gelächter aus, he burst out laughing, &c.

Aus'breitemaschine, *(w.)* *f.* *Weav.* spreading-machine.

Aus'breiten, *(w.)* v. I. *tr.* 1) to spread out, spread, extend, expand; to unfold (the sails, &c.); to stretch forth *or* out (the arms, wings, &c.); 2) *a)* *Tann.* to air (hides); *b)* *Print.* to hang up (the sheets); 3) *T.* to flatten (metal-plates); *Gild.* to spread (gold- *or* silver-foils) with the polisher *(Tech.)*; *fig.*-s. 4) to extend, enlarge; 5) *a)* to spread abroad, to divulge; *b)* to diffuse, disseminate (opinions, &c.), propagate, circulate; II. *refl.* 1) to spread (out), to run out, to stretch (over), grow wide, widen, enlarge; to branch, widen (of trees); 2) to unfold itself (to the view); 3) with über (& *Acc.*), to expatiate, enlarge upon ...., to discourse at great length, *cf.* sich Verbreiten, II. 2; 4) *a)* to gain ground; *b)* to come into use; ausgebreitet, *p. a.* *Bot.* 1) spreading; 2) *Herald.* displayed (wings); 3) *fig.* extensive (acquaintance, correspondence, &c.); das —, v. s. *(str.)* n. the (act of) spreading out, &c.; *T.* (der Glasblase zur Tafelform) flashing out.

Aus'breiter, *(str.)* m. disperser, divulger.

Aus'breitung, *(w.)* *f.* 1) the (act of) spreading, &c.; 2) extension, expanse; 3) diffusion, propagation, dissemination (of knowledge, &c.); **A-sfähigkeit**, *f.* diffusibility.

Aus'brennen, *(irr.)* v. I. *intr.* 1) *(aux.* sein) *a)* to be consumed by fire in the interior; to be burnt out; das Haus brannte aus, the house was internally destroyed by fire; die Stube ist gänzlich ausgebrannt, every thing in the room was consumed by the fire; ein ausgebrannter Vulkan, a burnt-out volcano; die [illegible] [illegible] cend, *fig.* the ashes of [illegible] to be consumed [illegible] dry; mein Herz war [illegible] — ich konnte weder [illegible] all else — I could have [illegible] haben) *a)* to cease burning [illegible] kiln, &c. for the last time; [illegible] to burn; 2) to [illegible] bodies) by applying fire, &c. [illegible] ney, &c.; *b)* eine [illegible] —, [illegible] *c)* *Brew.* to cleanse (the [illegible] (or *[Pott.]* to bake) [illegible] 4) *T.* to burn (down) [illegible] *Surg.* to cauterize (a wound) [illegible] drive away by fire or smoke.

Aus'brennmesser, *(w.)* *f.* [illegible]

Aus'bringbar, *adj.* *Min.* [illegible] duced, won, *or* extracted.

Aus'bringen, I. *(irr.)* v. [illegible] out; to get out; to drive out [illegible] off; 2) *T.* to broach, *see* [illegible] to drive out, to keep out [illegible] 4) *Mar.* *a)* to hoist out [illegible] Anker mit dem Boot —, to [illegible] 5) *Min.* *a)* to bring up [illegible] obtain, gain, extract (a metallic [illegible] from the ore); 6) to divulge [illegible] spread, publish, divulge; 8) [illegible] to propose a toast, (with [illegible] (a person), to drink the health [illegible] prosperity to ...; die ausgebrachte [illegible] toast, health; meinen [illegible] sundheit aus, Hr. D.; [illegible] nicht Ihren Trinkspruch? why [illegible] a health, Mr. D.; why don't [illegible] toast? II. das —, v. s. *(str.)* [illegible] brachte, (decl. like adj.) [illegible] every description, the produce [illegible]

Aus'bruchen, *(w.)* v. *tr.* [illegible]

Aus'brüdeln, *(w.)* v. *refl.* [illegible]

Aus'brühemen, [illegible] *Min.* to expose (*intr.* to be [illegible] action of vapours, to bring [illegible] *cf.* Auswittern *&c.*

Aus'bruch, *(str.,* pl. **Aus'brü**[illegible] (act of) breaking out, &c. [illegible] break; 2) (Hungarian) wine [illegible] 3) *Med.* — der Blattern, [illegible] vulcanischer, a volcanic [illegible] ing out (of prison, &c.), [illegible] ment; 6) *fig.* outburst, [illegible] hatred, passion); [illegible] of passion; gust, flash [illegible] &c.); — einer Verschwörung, [illegible] ing out of a conspiracy; [illegible] burst of rapture, ecstasy; [illegible] volly, burst of applause; [illegible] einen — geschehen, [illegible] zum — kommen lassen, to give [illegible] tears.

Aus'bruchig, *adj.* (l. u.) [illegible]

Aus'brühen, *(w.)* v. *tr.* [illegible] purify by scalding, to [illegible]

Aus'brüllen, *(w.)* v. *intr.* [illegible]

Aus'brummen, *(w.)* v. [illegible] humming, murmuring, [illegible] brummt haben, to have [illegible]

Aus'brunsten, *(w.)* v. [illegible]

Aus'brüsten, *(w.)* v. [illegible] pluck off (ploughshare [illegible]

Aus'brüten, *(w.)* v. I. [illegible] hatch, to sit on (eggs) [illegible] tion; 2) *fig.* to [illegible] II. *intr.* 1) to sit, in [illegible] ing, hatching; III. [illegible] tung, *(w.)* *f.* the [illegible] ing, &c. *cf.* [illegible]

Aus'buchten, [illegible] line (as a wooden [illegible]

schen, 1); 2) that which is threshed out, the yield. [hale, evaporate.

Aus'dunsten, (w.) v. intr. (aux. sein) to ex-

Aus'düften, (w.) v. tr. to exhale, to spread (odours). — **Ausduftung**, (w.) f. exhalation.

Aus'dulden, (w.) v. tr. & intr. to endure, suffer to the end; er hat ausgeduldet, his sufferings are ended.

Aus'dunst, (str., pl. (l. u.) Aus'dünste) m. vapour, exhalation, perspiration.

Aus'dunstbar, Aus'dünstbar, I. adj. evaporable; perspirable, transpirable; II. A-keit, (w.) f. evaporability.

Aus'dunsten, (w.) v. intr. (aux. sein) to evaporate, steam or vapour away or out.

Aus'dünsten, (w.) v. tr. to perspire, exhale, transpire.

Aus'dünstung, (w.) f. 1) evaporation; effluvium (pl. effluvia): schädliche A-en, noxious exhalations or vapours, (in mines) damps; ansteckende —, contagion; 2) (Schweiß) perspiration, transpiration; A-maß, n., A-messer, m. Phys. evaporometer, atmidometer, atmometer; A-ofen, m. T. evaporating-furnace.

Aus'dupfen, (w.) v. tr. T. to press down (the gold leaves).

Aus'ecken, (w.) v. tr. to cut out in angles; to cut into angles.

Aus'eggen, (w.) v. I. tr. to harrow out or up; II. intr. to finish harrowing.

Auseinan'der, adv. asunder, apart; separated, divided; weit — fallende Regentropfen, widely scattered raindrops; ihre Geburtsjahre (coll. sie) sind drei Jahre —, they were born within three years of one another; —breiten, v. tr. to unfold (linen, &c.); to (lay) open; —bringen, v. tr. to separate, part; —fahren, v. intr. to part asunder, to break up; to separate; Phys. to diverge; (v. s.) n. Phys. divergence; —fallen, v. intr. to fall asunder or in pieces, to disjoint; —fliegen, v. intr. to fly asunder, scatter; sich —geben, (of parts screwed together, &c.) to recede from each other; —gehen, v. intr. to come undone or asunder; to disunite; disperse (of a crowd), to break up (of a meeting, &c.), to part (company), to separate (of persons); die Ansichten über diesen Gegenstand gehen weit —, the views on this subject diverge considerably, men are widely divided on this subject; —gehen lassen, to dismiss; to break up (an army); —gehend, divergent; —halten, v. tr. to keep apart, separate, distinct; —laufen, v. intr. Math. to diverge; —legen, —machen, —nehmen, v. tr. 1) to dismount, to take to pieces (a watch, machine, &c.); to unfold, to lay, or spread out; 2) fig. to unfold, explain, shew; to analyse; —reißen, v. I. tr. to separate with violence, to tear, rend asunder; II. intr. to sever; —rücken, v. tr. to move, push asunder; —schlagen, v. tr. 1) to break or beat asunder; 2) to take down, to take to pieces (a bed or any frame-work); 3) to unfold, lay open (a sheet, &c.); —setzen, v. I. tr. 1) to put, set, or place asunder; 2) fig. to analyse, to explain; to expound, to set forth (clearly); II. refl. sich —setzen mit ..., 1) to arrange (one's self), to settle, to balance accounts, to compound with ...; to separate, to dissolve partnership; —setzung, f. 1) detailed statement; explanation, declaration; 2) arrangement, settlement; composition; liquidation; —sperren, —spreizen, v. tr. to extend; to divaricate; die Beine —spreizen, to straddle; —strömen, v. intr. to flow asunder, to separate, diverge in flowing; fig. to disperse; —treiben, v. tr. to disperse, scatter (the enemy, crowd, &c.); to drive asunder; —wehen, v. tr. to drive away, scatter, or disperse (clouds, &c.); —wickeln, v. tr. to unroll, unfold; —wirren, v. tr. to disentangle; —ziehen, v. I. tr. 1) to draw, pull asunder; 2) to stretch, lengthen; II. intr. to remove into different quarters, &c.; to part company, &c.

Aus'eisen, (w.) v. tr. 1) to get, dig, &c. out of the ice; 2) to clear of the ice.

Aus'eisen, (str.) n. Found. rake.

Aus'eitern, I. (w.) v. intr. 1) (aux. haben) to cease festering; 2) (aux. sein) to suppurate, to generate pus, to run out in the shape of matter; II. v. s. (str.) n. Surg. depuration.

Aus'erkennen, (irr.) v. tr. to know thoroughly.

† **Aus'erkiesen**, (w.), **Aus'erküren**, (str.) v. tr. to choose (from a number, &c.), see Auserwählen; aus'erkoren, p. a. chosen, selected, elect.

Aus'erlesen, I. (str.) v. tr. to select, choose; II. p. a. chosen, &c.; picked, exquisite, select, choice, excellent; einige A-e, several picked men; III. A-heit, (w.) f. selectness, &c., excellence.

Aus'ersehen, (str.) v. tr. (gener. refl. sich [Dat.] etwas) to mark out, to choose, select, to pick or single out, to fix upon; to destine, doom. [vent, devise.

Aus'ersinnen, (str.) v. tr. to contrive, in-

Aus'erwählen, (w.) v. tr. to elect, choose, make choice of; to foredoom; ein auserwähltes Gefäß (Rüstzeug) Gottes, Script. a chosen vessel; Gottes auserwähltes Volk, God's chosen people; die Auserwählten, pl. the elect, the called; the select.

Aus'erzählen, (w.) v. I. tr. to tell all one knows, to tell to the end, to finish the tale; II. refl. to exhaust one's fund of conversation (cf. sich Aussprechen).

Aus'essen, (irr.) v. I. tr. to eat out, to empty by eating; — was ein Anderer eingebrockt hat, coll. to pay for the faults of another; was man eingebrockt hat, muß man auch —, self do, self have; II. intr. to dine out, to take one's meals out.

Aus'fabeln, (w.) v. intr. to cease telling stories or lies.

Aus'fachen, (w.) v. tr. to lay out, fill up or provide with shelves or drawers; to furnish with compartments.

Aus'fächse(r)n, (w.) v. I. intr. Vint. to provine; II. tr. to propagate (a vine).

Aus'fädeln, (w.) v. I. tr. to ravel out, unravel; to unweave; to unthread (a needle); II. refl. to unweave, unravel, to ravel out.

Aus'fahren, (str.) v. I. intr. (aux. sein) 1) a) to go out, or ride about, or abroad (or take a ride) in a coach; to set out in a carriage, to drive out, to take an airing or the air; b) Mar. to put to sea; aus einer Bucht, einem Canal —, to disembogue; c) Phys. to emerge; d) Min. to get out of the pit, to leave the mine, to ascend the shaft; 2) fig. to set out in a hurry; 3) to slip, slide; 4) a) to break out; b) am Körper —, to have eruptions, pustules on the skin; to grow scurvy; er ist im Gesichte ausgefahren, he has pimples in his face, his face is flown out; b) fig. (l. u.) see Auffahren, I. 4, c; II. tr. 1) to wear out (the road) by too frequent driving of wheel-carriages over it; 2) (l. u.) to carry outward, to export; 3) to drive out, take out for a ride [Min. ascending-shaft.

Aus'fahrschacht, (str., pl. A-schächte) m.

Aus'fahrt, (w.) f. 1) the (act of) riding abroad, &c. cf. Ausfahren; ride, drive; 2) excursion; 3) doorway; gateway, outgate.

Aus'fall, (str., pl. Aus'fälle) m. 1) a) the (act of) falling out; b) Med. see Vorfall, 1, b; 2) Fenc. pass, thrust, lunge; 3) a) Mil. sally, sortie, issue; einen — machen, to make a sally or sortie, to sally out or forth; b) (or —gatter, —thor, n., —pforte, f.) sally-port, postern; c) fig. attack; invective; fig. &c. 4) [illegible]; 5) a falling off (in one's income, &c.), abatement, deficiency; deficit; loss; 6) result, issue.

Aus'fertiger, *(str.) m.* dispatcher, dispenser.

Aus'fertigung, *(w.) f.* 1) dispatch, expedition; 2) the (act of) issuing, making known; 3) drawing up, execution (of a deed); 4) portioning of a child: **A-sgebühren,** *f. pl.* fees for drawing up a deed; **A-stag,** *m.* date of a dispatch: **A-szimmer,** *n.* bureau, office.

Aus'fetten, *(w.) v. tr. T.* to take the fat *or* grease out of, to scour (wool); *Dy.* to ungrease *(Tuch).*

Aus'feuchten, *(w.) v. tr.* to dry out.

Aus'feuern, *(w.) v. I. tr.* 1) to warm thoroughly, to heat in every part, &c.; 2) *Coop.* to burn out: II. *intr.* 1) to cease firing; 2) *coll.* to kick (of horses). [(wedges).

Aus'fiedern, *(w.) v. tr. Min.* to fill up with

Aus'filzen, *(w.) v. tr.* 1) to furnish or to stuff with felt (hair); 2) *coll.* to check, chide, rebuke, *vulg.* to ring (one) a peal, to jobe.

Aus'findbar, *adj.* what can be found out, discoverable.

Aus'finden, *(str.) v. tr. see* **Ausfindig machen.**

Aus'findig, *adj.* (used exclusively with machen) — machen, 1) to find out, make out, seek out, to discover, *coll.* to smell out, hunt out: — machen, wie ein Schiff segelt, to find (out) the trim of a vessel; 2) eine Grube — machen, *Min.* to renovate a mine.

Aus'findlich, *adj. see* **Ausfindbar.**

Aus'fischen, *(w.) v. I. tr.* 1) to fish out; 2) to empty by fishing; 3) *fig.* to find out by cunning: II. *intr.* ausgefischt haben, to have done fishing.

Aus'flackern, *(w.) v. intr.* 1) to cease to flare; 2) *(aux.* sein) to go out flaring.

Aus'flammen, *(w.) v. tr.* 1) to clean by means of a flame; 2) *Gunn.* to scale (a cannon).

Aus'flattern, *(w.) v. intr. (aux.* sein) to flutter out; to go out fluttering: *lit. & fig.* to flutter abroad.

Aus'flechten, *(str.) v. I. tr.* 1) to unplait, untwist; 2) to line with wickerwork; II. *refl.* to extricate or disentangle one's self (von, from).

Aus'fleisch..., *in comp.* —eisen, —messer, *n. Tann.* fleshing iron, fleshing knife, beadknife.

Aus'fleischen, *(w.) v. tr. Tann.* to flesh (out); ein ausgefleischter Bube, an arrant knave.

Aus'flicken, *(w.) v. tr.* to mend, patch, botch, piece, to vamp up; to cobble.

Aus'fliegen, *(str.) v. intr. (aux.* sein) 1) to take wing; fly out; to leave the nest; 2) *fig.* *a)* to leave home for the first time; *b)* to make a trip or excursion; *c)* to escape, bolt, run away. [*for* Entfliehen.

Aus'fliehen, *(str.) v. intr. (aux.* sein) *l. u.*

Aus'fließen, *(str.) v. intr. (aux.* sein) 1) to flow out or off: to issue out from, to emanate; to discharge itself: to be poured out; to leak (of casks); 2) to cease to flow: das —, *s. s. (str.) n.* the (act of) flowing out, &c. (Ausfluß) issuing, efflux: emanation, &c., flow (of the sap, &c.).

Aus'flimmern, *(w.) v. intr. see* **Ausflackern.**

Aus'flöhen, *(w.) v. tr.* 1) to rid of fleas; 2) *fig. vulg.* to fleece, *see* **Ausbeuteln.**

Aus'fluchen, *(w.) v. I. tr.* to curse; II. *intr.* to cease cursing, swearing.

Aus'flucht, *(str., pl.* Aus'flüchte) *f.* 1) *see* Ausflug; 2) *fig.* evasion, escape, shift, subterfuge, loophole, prevarication, *coll.* fetch, back-door: eine bloße —, a thin pretext; eine elende, faule, kahle, lahme —, a miserable, shuffling, paltry, empty, lame excuse or plea; *coll.* a sham-excuse, a blank come-off; Ausflüchte machen or suchen, to shuffle, shift, prevaricate, to flinch; *vulg.* dodge; to turn tail; er weiß immer eine —, *prov.* he always finds a hole to creep out at.

Aus'flug, *(str., pl.* Aus'flüge) *m.* 1) the (act of) flying out, &c. *cf.* Ausfliegen; flight; 2) *a)* the (first) flight of young birds after fledging; *b)* a brood of fledgelings; 3) *a)* excursion, trip, tour, jaunt, ramble: einen — (auf das Land &c.) machen, to make an excursion, to take a trip (into the country, &c.); *b) fig.* (first) setting out, coming abroad; 4) *a)* entrance, egress (in the bee-hive); *b)* pigeon-hole.

Aus'flüstern, *(w.) v. I. tr.* to make known by whispers; II. *intr.* to cease whispering.

Aus'fluß, I. *s. (str., pl.* Aus'flüsse) *m.* 1) *a)* the (act of) flowing out, &c. *cf.* Ausfließen; affluence, efflux; outrun, discharge (of water, &c.); eduction; *b)* the matter discharged, secretion (of an ulcer, &c.); 2) *a)* mouth, estuary; *b)* outgate, passage, outlet; spout (of a gutter); *c)* sluice, (—loch, *n.*) gully-hole; 3) *fig.* emanation; ein unmittelbarer — sein von ..., to flow directly from ...; II. *in comp. T-s.* —loch, *n.* 1) gully-hole; 2) running-hole: —öffnung, *f.* aperture (of a pipe); —rohr, *n.* delivery-pipe; —röhre, *f.* jet-pipe.

Aus'flut, *(w.) f.* the (act of) flowing or streaming out or off: outrun, discharge, &c. *cf.* Ausfluß.

Aus'fluten, *(w.) v. intr. (aux.* sein) to flow or stream out.

Aus'fohlen, *(w.) v. intr.* to leave off foaling.

Aus'folgen, *(w.) v. tr.* to deliver (up): Geld —, to hand over money: — lassen, to deliver up: *Comm.-s.* Ballen — lassen, to transfer bales. — **Aus'folgeschein,** *(str.) m.* bill of delivery.

Aus'foppen, *(w.) v. tr.* to quiz, make a fool of (one).

Aus'forderer, *(str.) m.* challenger; defier.

Aus'fordern, *(w.) v. tr.* to challenge (Herausfordern); to defy, provoke; Trumpf —, *Gam.* to play trump, to trump out.

Aus'fördern, *(w.) v. tr.* 1) †, *see* Bewerkstelligen; 2) *Min.* to get out or up (from a shaft).

Aus'forderung, *(w.) f.* challenge: defiance; **A-sbrief,** *m.* a written challenge.

Aus'formen, *(w.) v. tr.* to form (a thing) in all its parts: to execute in perfection.

Aus'forschen, *(w.) v. tr.* 1) to inquire after: to seek, search, explore, investigate, spy, to find out, trace out, sift out: *coll.* to fish or hunt out; 2) to sound (one), *coll.* to pump (one), to bolt or draw (one) out: ihr wollt mich —, you come to feel me.

Aus'forschung, *(w.) f.* the (act of) inquiring, &c.: exploration, *see* Ausforschen; **A-smethode,** *f. Med.* method of investigation.

Aus'fouragiren [*pr.* —'fûrashî'ren], *(w.) v. I. tr.* to strip (a country) by excessive foraging: II. *intr.* to forage excessively.

Aus'fracht, *(w.) f.* freight out or outwards, outward-freight.

Aus'fragen, *(w.) v. I. tr.* 1) to question, examine, interrogate, to query, *coll.* to pump out, *cf.* Ausforschen; 2) to find out by inquiring: II. *refl.* to tire one's self by questioning. [ing, pumping, &c.

Aus'fragerei', *(w.) f. coll.* much question-

Aus'fransen, *(w.) v. I. tr.* to fringe: II. *refl. see* Ausfasern.

Aus'fräsen, *(w.) v. tr. Turn., &c.* to bead (a border), to curl, to crisp: vertieft —, to countersink; der ausgefräste Rand, **Aus'fräsung,** *(w.) f.* beaded border, curling, crisping.

Aus'fressen, *(str.) v. I. tr.* 1) *(of animals)* to eat up or out all the food, to empty (as a trough) by eating: 2) *fig.* to consume, ruin, impoverish, waste; 3) to corrode, to hollow: 4) etwas —, *vulg.* to be guilty of some misdemeanour: ausgefressen, *p. a. Bot.* eaten through; II. *refl.* (of animals) to fatten by feeding.

Aus'frieren, *(str.) v. I. intr. (aux.* sein) 1) to freeze thoroughly or to the bottom: 2) to lose in goodness of quality by the frost: — lassen, or II. *tr.* to condense or increase the strength of (beer, &c.) by congealing the watery particles.

Aus'frischen, *(w.) v. tr. Sport.* 1) einen Hund —, to purge a dog: 2) eine Büchse —, to renovate the channels in the barrel of a rifle (*cf.* Ausmüffern).

Aus'fuchteln, *(w.) v. tr.* to beat soundly (with the flat side of a sword); to give a sound thrashing.

Aus'fugen, *(w.) v. tr. Mas.* to fill up, flush, point (the joints).

Aus'fühlen, *(w.) v. tr.* to find out by the touch or feeling: *fig.* to feel (out), to sound, pump.

Aus'fuhr, *s. (w.) f.* export, exportation: — und Einfuhr, export and import: *in comp.* —artikel, *m. pl.* export goods, exports, exportable goods or articles: —declaration, *f.* cocket, bill of sufferance: —handel, *m.* export- or outward trade, active commerce: —prämie, *f.* bounty: (auf wieder ausgeführte Güter) drawback: —schein, *m. see* —declaration; —verbot, *n.* prohibition of exportation; —waaren, *pl. see* —artikel; —zoll, *m.* duty on exportation: export-duty; —zollpflichtig, *adj.* liable to export-duty.

Aus'führbar, I. *adj.* 1) exportable; 2) feasible, practicable, performable, achievable, effectible; II. **A-keit,** *(w.) f.* practicability, feasibility.

Aus'führen, *(w.) v. tr.* 1) to lead out; to give an airing; 2) *Comm.* to export (goods): to send abroad, ship off (a superfluous population, &c.); 3) *T.* to clean (a pond); 4) *Med.* to evacuate, purge; 5) *fig. a)* to perform, realize, do, finish, execute, accomplish, to carry through, out, on, or into effect, proceed with; to prosecute: *b)* to fill up (an outline) completely; *c)* to construct, to work out (einen Gedanken, an idea); einen Auftrag —, *Comm.* to effect, carry out an order: genau nach Vorschrift —, to fulfill to the letter: einen Charakter —, to draw a character; eine Schilderung weiter —, to amplify a description; eine Materie —, to follow up, to deduce, to elucidate a subject; einen Entschluß nicht —, to fall back from a resolution; ich kann es nicht —, I cannot carry it through, accomplish it, afford it.

Aus'führer, *(str.) m.* 1) exporter; 2) *a)* accomplisher, &c.; *b) T.* finishing workman (Ausarbeiter).

Aus'führlich [*gener.* pronounced **Ausführ'lich**], I. *adj.* large, ample, full, detailed, complete: prolix; copious: e-e Nachrichten, *Comm.* particulars, ample information, full advices: II. *adv.* largely, &c.: at large, in detail, at full length, fully: III. **A-keit,** *(w.) f.* 1) fulness, &c., completeness; prolixity: 2) exact or detailed account.

Aus'führung, *(w.) f.* 1) the (act of) leading out, &c. *cf.* Ausführen; 2) *Med.* evacuation: excretion: 3) performance, execution, achievement; sorgfältige —, elaboration; 4) deduction: written evidence: in — bringen, to put or bring into practice or execution, *see* Ausführen; **A-sgang, A-sweg,** *m. Anat.* excretory duct: *Mech.-s.* **A-sklappe,** *f.* eduction-valve: **A-sröhre,** *f.* eduction-pipe: **A-stelegramm,** *n.* telegram announcing that an order, &c. is executed.

Aus'füllen, *(w.) v. tr.* 1) *a)* to fill up, to fill (out), to stuff: to plug (a tooth); der ausgefüllte Schanzkorb, gabion; hier war ein stehendes Gewässer auszufüllen, here, a piece of stagnant water was to be filled in: *b)* ein Schema &c. —, to fill up (out) a blank-form, &c.; *c) Typ.* to prick in; 2) to empty, draw off; 3) *fig.* Jemandes Stelle —, to fill one's place (with success, &c.), to supply one's place; a-d, *p. a.* expletive: a-de Wörter, Silben, *Gramm.* expletives: a-de Musik, *Mus.* ritornello: das —, *s. s. (str.) n. see* Ausfül-

Aus'geschnitten, *p. a.* 1) *a)* cut out, &c. *cf.* Ausschneiden; *b)* (of female dresses) low-bosomed, low; 2) *Bot.* notched, scalloped, crenated.

Aus'gestalten, *(w.) v. tr. gener. fig.* to develop duly *or* fully, to mature, to bring to perfection.

Aus'gesucht, *adj.* 1) exquisite, choice; *Comm.* of prime quality, picked; 2) signal (vengeance, &c.); — artig, elaborately courteous.

Aus'gezeichnet, I. *p. a.* 1) distinguished, eminent, signal: excellent, superior; illustrious, conspicuous, egregious; 2) *(l. u. in an ill sense)* egregious, arrant (liar, rogue, &c.); im höchsten Grade —, supreme; transcendent; II. **A-heit**, *(w.) f. (l. u.)* excellence, superiority.

Aus'giebig, *adj. see* Ergiebig.

Aus'gießen, *(str.) v. tr.* 1) to pour out, to fill out, empty, effuse, diffuse, shed; *cf.* Ausschütten; 2) to put out with water; 3) to fill up (with lead): ein (mit Blei &c.) ausgegossener Stock, a loaded cane: seinen Zorn über Jemand —, to vent one's anger upon one.

Aus'gießung, *(w.) f.* 1) the (act of) pouring out, &c., effusion; *Archaeol.* libation; 2) *Theol.* effusion *or* descent (of the Holy Ghost).

Aus'gilling, *(w.) f. Mar.* goring (of a sail).

Aus'gipfeln, *(w.) v. tr. Gard.* to lop (Bäume, trees).

Aus'gipsen, *(w.) v. tr.* to fill with plaster, [&c.

Aus'gischen, *(w.) v. intr. see* Ausgäschen.

Aus'glätten, *(w.) v. tr.* to smooth (out): to take out by smoothing.

Aus'gleich, *(str.) m.* adjustment, agreement, settlement; arrangement, &c. *cf.* Ausgleichung.

Aus'gleichbar, *adj.* compensable.

Aus'gleichen, *(str.) v.* I. *tr.* 1) *a)* to even, equalize, level; *b) Mint.* die Schrötlinge —, to size the planchets for coining; 2) *Comm.* to balance, to adjust: to make up, to clear (an account, a debt), to strike (a balance): 3) to compensate, to make up (a difference, a deficiency, &c.), to adjust, arrange, accommodate, reconcile, redeem: alle Rechnungen mit Jemand ausgeglichen haben, to be upon the square with one; womit Sie meine Rechnung — wollen, balancing thereby my account: womit ich dieses Geschäft ausgeglichen habe, balancing this transaction in (your) conformity: II. *refl.* to come to an agreement *or* settlement, to square *or* balance accounts: das — der Wände, *Mas.* smooth plastering the inner *or* partition walls.

Aus'gleicher, *(str.) m.* 1) *Mint.* controller; 2) *Mech.* compensator; compensation.

Aus'gleichung, *(w.) f.* 1) balance, settlement, clearing (of draughts), compensation, liquidation; 2) adjustment (of differences, &c.), accommodation; arrangement; zur — dieses Gegenstandes, for (the) closing (of) this transaction; zur — dieses Postens, as payment for (or in full of) this item: zur völligen — unserer Rechnung, in full of all demands; 3) *Mech.* compensation; **A-spiel**, *m. Comm.* counter-vailing duty.

Aus'gleichwage, *(w.) f.* adjusting scales, adjusting balance.

Aus'gleiten, *(str.)*, **Aus'glitschen**, *(w.) v. intr.* (aux. sein) to slide, slip, trip; to miss [illegible], to lose one's footing, to lose footing: er glitt aus, his foot slipped.

Aus'glimmen, *(str. & w.) v. intr.* 1) to glimmer, glow to the end; 2) *(aux.* sein) to [illegible], to expire with a glimmer.

[illegible] *(str.) n. T.* glowing-iron.

[illegible] *(w.) v.* I. *tr.* to heat thoroughly; [illegible] —, to anneal (*(foll.* need) metals); [illegible] glow to the end, to cool gradually.

[illegible] *(str.) m.* annealer of metals; [illegible] furnace.

Aus'glühung, *(w.) f.* the (act of) glowing out, &c. *cf.* Ausglühen; *Mint.* ignition.

Aus'graben, *(str.) v. tr.* 1) to dig out (of, aus); to excavate (ruins, &c.); 2) to dig, delve (a wall); to cut out; 3) to disinter, to untomb, unbury, exhume (a corpse); 4) *Sport.* to unearth, dig (a badger, a fox).

Aus'gräber, *(str.) m.* digger out, &c.; excavator.

Aus'grabung, *(w.) f.* 1) the (act of) digging up, &c., effossion; excavation (of ruins, &c.); 2) burning the teeth (of old horses, in order to pass them off for younger).

Aus'grasen, *(w.) v. tr.* to weed out; to mow partially.

Aus'gräten, *(w.) v. tr.* to bone (a fish), to pick out the bones.

Aus'greifen, *(str.) v.* I. *tr.* to take, pick out; 2) to handle: II. *intr.* to stride out (of horses).

Aus'griff, *(str.) m. Sport.* stride (of a horse).

Aus'griebsen, **Aus'gröbsen**, *(w.) v. tr.* to take out the core of (apples).

Aus'grollen, *(w.) v. intr.* to leave off grumbling.

Aus'grübeln, *(w.) v. tr.* to investigate, to find out by poring over, meditating, *or* ruminating, to puzzle out, to dive into.

Aus'gründen, *(w.) v. tr.* 1) *Join., Sculpt.* to cut out, gutter, groove, flute with a plane *or* chisel; to form in rilievo, to raise; 2) *fig. see* Ergründen.

Aus'grünen, *(w.) v. intr.* to break into verdure, to get green.

Aus'guck, *(str.) m. Mar.* look-out, (watch) captain of the fore-top.

Aus'gucken, *(w.) v.* I. *intr.* to look, peep out: II. *refl.* ich habe mir (fast) die Augen ausgeguckt, I have (almost) stared my eyes out.

Aus'gucker, *(str.) m. see* Ausguck.

Aus'güren, *(w.) v. intr. Min.* to branch off, to deviate: to appear on the surface.

Aus'gurgeln, *(w.) v.* I. *tr.* to get out, or to clean by gargling; II. *refl. see* sich Ausspülen.

Aus'guß, *(str., pl.* Aus'güsse) *m.* 1) the (act of) pouring out, &c. *cf.* Ausgießen; effusion; 2) *a)* gutter, sink, outlet, conduit; *b)* gargoyle; 3) lip, spout; **—blech**, *n. Found.* kennel; *Metall.* (**—kelle**, *f.*) ladle: **—bogen**, *m.* angle of discharge; **—kasten**, *m. Min.* water-box; **—mörser**, *m. Pharm.* mortar with a lip: **—pfännchen**, *n. Metall.* ingot-mould; **—rinne**, **—röhre**, *f. T.* drain-pipe, conduit-pipe, waste-pipe; (des Wasserhahnes) jib; **—wasser**, *n.* tail-water.

Aus'güten, **Aus'gütten**, *(w.) v. refl. Law,* to come to an agreement *or* settlement; to come to terms.

Aus'gütern, *(w.) v. tr.* to provide with ample provisions, &c.

Aus'haaren, *(w.) v.* I. *intr.* to loose the hair: II. *tr.* to pull out the hair of ....

Aus'haben, *(irr.) v. tr. coll. for* Ausgetrunken, ausgelesen, ausgezogen &c. haben, to have drunk off, read through, pulled off, &c.

Aus'hacken, *(w.) v. tr.* 1) to grub up; to hoe, to rake up *or* out; *Coop.* to rough-hew (the staves); *Butch.* to cut up (a slaughtered beast); 2) to pick out (the eyes, &c.); 3) *see* Aushauen. — **Aus'hacker**, *(str.) m.* 1) grubber, &c.; 2) *T.* (strap-)punch.

Aus'hadern, *(w.) v. intr.* to give over quarrelling, to cease bearing ill-will.

Aus'hageln, *(w.) v. intr.* to cease hailing.

Aus'haken, **Aus'häkeln**, *(w.) v. tr.* to hook out; to unhook; unpegging.

Aus'halftern, *(w.) v.* I. *tr.* to unhalter: II. *refl. fig.* to slip one's neck out of the collar.

Aus'hallen, *(w.) v. intr.* to sound at a distance; to cease sounding, to die away (as sound).

Aus'halten, *(str.) v.* I. *tr.* 1) *Mus. a)* to sustain, dwell on (a note) for a certain length of time; *b)* to continue (a note *or* rest) beyond the regular time: ausgehalten, *(Ital.)* tenuto; 2) to hold out, endure, bear, suffer, stand, sustain, to abide; to bear up under *or* against: eine Belagerung —, to stand, sustain a siege; *Mar.-s.* einen Sturm —, to weather (out) a storm; einen Sturm vor Anker —, to ride out a storm; die Probe —, to stand the proof *or* test, to stand out, to abide the touch: er kann den Vergleich mit seinem Bruder —, he will bear to be compared with his brother; er kann es nicht —, he cannot stand it; es ist nicht zum — *(v. s.) or* nicht auszuhalten, it is beyond bearing, beyond endurance, &c.; es ist mit ihm nicht auszuhalten, there is no bearing with him; II. *intr.* to hold out; to stay, last, continue; to persevere, persist, to stand fast; to be firm; to stand the brunt; *Sport.* to keep *or* lie close; das —, *v. s. (str.) n.* endurance, sufferance, perseverance, &c. *cf.* above.

Aus'halter, *(str.) m.*, **Aus'haltungszeichen**, *(str.) n. Mus.* a pause (Fermate).

Aus'hämmern, *(w.) v. tr.* to beat out with the hammer.

Aus'handeln, *(w.) v.* I. *tr.* to conclude, strike (a bargain); II. *intr.* to give up business, to retire from business, to shut up shop.

Aus'händigen, *(w.) v. tr.* (Einem etwas) to hand over, to deliver.

Aus'hang, *(str., pl.* Aus'hänge) *m.* 1) placard: 2) — am Gewölbe, show.

Aus'hangen, *(str.) v. intr.* to hang out.

Aus'hängen, *(w.) v.* I. *tr.* 1) to hang out; to display: eine Flagge —, to hang out *or* set up a flag: 2) to unhang *or* unhinge (a door, &c.); 3) *fig.* to make a show of; II. *intr. frequently used for* Aushangen, *which see;* hier hängt nicht viel aus, *fig. coll.* no great profit is to be made here *or* by this.

Aus'hänge..., *in comp.* **—bogen**, *m. Typ.* proof-sheet; **—schild**, *n.* 1) sign-board, firm; (mit Waarenverzeichniß) shop-bill; 2) *fig.* show.

Aus'harken, *(w.) v. tr.* to rake out, to clear with a rake.

Aus'harren, *(w.) v. intr.* to persevere (bei, in), to be constant, to stand fast, to hold out.

Aus'hau, *(str.) m.* 1) the act of hewing, cutting out; 2) opening through a wood, avenue, glade; *Gard.* haw-haw.

Aus'hauch, *(str.) m.* 1) (the act of) breathing out; breath, fume, exhalation; 2) *(Ausathem, &c.)* the expiring breath; last utterance.

Aus'hauchen, *(w.) v.* I. *tr.* 1) to breathe out *or* forth: 2) den Geist —, *or* II. *intr.* to breathe, sigh or gasp out one's last, *or* one's existence, to expire.

Aus'hauen, *(irr. & w.) v. tr.* 1) to hew *or* cut out; 2) to carve, cut out; to cut into figures; to sculpture: in Stein —, to chisel in stone (as a statue, &c.); to engrave (an inscription on stone, brass, &c.); 3) *Butch.* to cut up into pieces (for sale); 4) *a)* to whip, scourge: *b) intr. see* Ausschlagen, *intr.* 1: einen Baum —, to lop a tree; Bäume —, to clear away trees; einen Wald —, to thin a wood; Stöcke —, to grub *or* root out stumps; *Min.-s.* eine Grube —, to work a mine; das ausgehauene Kohlenfeld, exhausted coal-mine.

Aus'hauer, *(str.) m.* 1) carver, &c.; 2) *T.* (hollow) punch; round *or* flat graver; hewing-chisel.

Aus'häuten, *(w.) v. tr.* 1) to skin, uncase (a hare, &c.); 2) to strip *or* divest of skins *or* skinny particles.

Aus'heben, *(str.) v. tr.* 1) to heave off, to lift out, to take out; 2) *Horol.* to lift up, lift (the detents of a clock); also *intr.* to lift the detents, to warn; 3) *a) Jewel.* to unset; *b)* to unhinge, to unhang: 4) to draw out (with the crane, siphon); 5) *Found.* to block out; 6) *fig.* *a)* to pick out, to select; *b)* to levy, raise, draw (men, soldiers); 7) *Typ. a)* to shoot, to empty (the stick) into the galley; *b)* to lift out (the forms); 8) to dislocate, to disjoint.

Aus'heber, *(str.) m.* 1) *Horol.* lifter, wheel

of the clock-work; 2) *Gard.*, &c. (gardener's) trowel used in taking up plants, trees, &c.

Aus'hebespan, *(str., pl. A-späne) m. Typ.* composing rule, setting rule, reglet.

Aus'hebung, *(w.) f.* 1) the (act of) heaving off, &c. *cf.* Ausheben; 2) the (act of) raising soldiers, levying, (compulsory) enrollment; conscription, levy, draft; A-shaken, *m. Naval.* lifter.

Aus'hecheln, *(w.) v. tr.* 1) *Husb.* to hatchel out; 2) *fig. see* Durchhecheln, 2.

Aus'hecken, *(w.) v. tr.* 1) (von Vögeln) to hatch, breed; 2) *fig. coll.* to hatch, contrive, devise, beget, invent, to brew (a plot, &c.).

Aus'hefteln, *(w.) v. tr.* to unclasp, unhook.

Aus'heilen, *(w.) v.* I. *tr.* to heal or cure thoroughly; II. *intr.* (*aux.* sein) to be healed.

Aus'heimisch, *adj.* foreign, alien.

Aus'heischung, *(w.) f. Law*, requisition.

Aus'heitern, *(w.) v. tr.* to clear up (Aufheitern).

Aus'heizen, *(w.) v. tr.* to warm thoroughly.

Aus'helfen, *(str.) v. intr.* to help out, supply, furnish, provide, *or* fit with, to aid, assist, succour; Einem mit Geld —, to accommodate one with money; er hilft mir oft aus, he frequently supplies me.

Aus'hellen, *(w.) v. tr.* to clear up (Aufhellen).

Aus'hemmen, *(w.) v. tr.* to untrig, unskid; (*intr.*) to take away the (drag) chain *or* trigger.

Aus'henken, *(w.) v. tr. see* Aushängen.

Aus'herrschen, *(w.) v. intr.* to rule, reign to the end; sie hatten ausgeherrscht, their reign was at an end. [dogs).

Aus'hetzen, *(w.) v. tr.* to hunt out (with

Aus'heucheln, *(w.) v. intr.* to cease dissembling.

Aus'heuern, *(w.) v. tr. see* Ausmiethen.

Aus'heulen, *(w.) v. intr.* to cease howling.

Aus'hieb, *(str.) m.* 1) first cut, blow, &c. *cf.* Aushauen; 2) that which is hewn *or* cut out: *Mint.* piece of refined silver broken off for an assay; —meißel, *m. T.* hewing-chisel.

Aus'hilfe, *(w.) f. see* Aushülfe.

Aus'hobeln, *(w.) v. tr. Join.* to plane off *or* away. [give up hoping.

Aus'hoffen, *(w.) v. intr.* to cease, *or* to

Aus'höhlen, *(w.) v. tr.* to hollow, *or* scoop out; *Carp.*, &c. to dish out; to make hollow, cave, excavate, to delve; to undermine by hollowing (the banks of a river, &c.); *Engr.* to incise; *Wood.* to carve; *Needle-m.* to ridge: to wear (away) stones; der Länge nach —, to groove; Säulen —, *Archit.* (cannelliren) to rebate, to channel, chamfer, flute columns; Metall, Holz —, to groove, to gutter; ausgehöhlt, *p. a. Bot.* channelled, canaliculated, striated, sinuated.

Aus'höhlung, *(w.) f.* the (act of) hollowing out, &c.; *Engr.* lowering, deepening; *Gun-m.* notch, groove (of a breech); excavation; fret; *Archit.* fluting, channel.

Aus'höhnen, *(w.) v.* I. *intr.* to cease to mock *or* to jeer; II. *tr.* to mock at ..., *see* Verhöhnen.

Aus'höken & Aus'hökern, *(w.) v. tr.* to retail.

Aus'holen, *(w.) v.* I. *tr.* 1) (*l. u.*) *a)* to draw out, *Mar.* to haul, to run out; *b)* to fetch, draw (breath); 2) *coll.* to examine by artful questions in order to draw out secrets, &c., to sound, pump, &c. (one), *cf.* Ausforschen; eine a-de Bemerkung, a fishing observation; II. *intr.* 1) to lift up the arm for striking, flinging, &c.; er holte nach mir aus, he offered to strike me; 2) to run for a leap, &c. *see* einen Anlauf nehmen; to take a run (in leaping); weit —, *fig.* to begin far off, to expatiate, to use prolixity.

Aus'holer, *(str.) m. Mar.-s.* a name for certain ropes; — der Blinde, the sprit-sail hallards; — des Klüvers, the tack of the jib; — des Klüverbaums, the top-rope of the jib-boom; — des Ladebaums, girt-line; — der Schiebblinde, the bowsprit topsails hallards; — des Toppreeps, girt-line of the stay-tackles.

Aus'holzen, *(w.) v. tr.* 1) *Forest.* to thin (a forest); 2) *vulg.* to beat soundly, *see* Ausprügeln. [slope (the heels).

Aus'hölzen, *(w.) v. tr. Shoe-m.* to pare or

Aus'horchen, *(w.) v. tr.* 1) to learn by hearkening, listening; 2) *see* Ausholen, 2.

Aus'hören, *(w.) v. tr. & intr.* to hear to the end.

Aus'horneisen, *(str.) n. Tann.* tool for scraping off the hair from the hides.

Aus'hub, *(str.) m.* 1) *see* Aushebung; 2) *Mint. see* Aushieb; 3) *fig.* (*l. u.*) choice, flower (*see* Kern, 7); —meißel, *m. see* Aushiebmeißel.

Aus'hülfe, *(w.) f.* 1) the (act of) helping out, supply, &c. *see* Aushelfen; assistance, accommodation; 2) shift, *see* Behelf.

Aus'hülsen, *(w.) v.* I. *tr.* to husk, unhusk, hull, peel (barley, &c.), shell (peas, beans); II. *refl.* to shell (*i. e.* to cast the shell, as nuts in falling, *or* to be disengaged from the husk, as wheat or rye in reaping, *Wb.*).

Aus'hungern, *(w.) v. tr.* to famish, to starve; to subdue by hunger; ausgehungert, *p. a.* famished, starved, hunger-bitten; das ausgehungerte Thier, a starveling (animal).

Aus'hunzen, *(w.) v. tr. coll.* to blow up, to scold, chide, rebuke, reprimand, abuse.

Aus'husten, *(w.) v.* I. *intr.* to cease coughing; II. *tr.* to cough up, to expectorate.

Aus'jagen, *(w.) v.* I. *tr.* 1) to chase, hunt, force *or* drive out, to expel; 2) *Mar.* den Wurfanker —, to warp; 3) *fig. see* Auspressen, 2; II. *intr.* to leave off hunting; er hat ausgejagt, he has done hunting, his hunting days are over.

Aus'jammern, *(w.) v.* I. *intr.* to leave off lamenting; II. *tr.* seinen Schmerz —, to give vent to one's sufferings in complaints.

Aus'jäten, *see* Ausgäten.

Aus'jauchzen, *(w.) v.* I. *intr.* to have done shouting; II. *tr.* to proclaim with a loud, exulting tone, in loud shouts.

Aus'jochen, *(w.) v. tr.* to unyoke.

Aus'jubeln, *(w.) v. intr.* to cease exulting, shouting, *or* carousing.

Aus'jungen, *(w.) v. intr.* to cease breeding.

Aus'kabeln, *(w.) v. tr. see* Auslassen.

Aus'kalben, *(w.) v. intr.* to cease calving.

Aus'kälten, *(w.) v. intr.* (*aux.* sein) to cool thoroughly.

Aus'kämmelkamm, *(str., pl. A-kämme) m.* wide tooth comb, hair comb.

Aus'kämmen, *(w.) v. tr.* to comb, comb out; ausgekämmter Wein, juice of the grape freed from the stalks.

Aus'kämpfen, *(w.) v.* I. *intr.* to cease wrestling, fighting; II. *tr.* to fight out.

Aus'karbatschen, *(w.) v. tr. vulg.* to whip soundly, to scourge. [sand.

Aus'karbe, *(w.) f. Mech.* finisher, finishing-

Aus'karren, *(w.) v. tr.* to cart out *or* away; to carry away in a wheel-barrow.

Aus'kauen, *(w.) v.* I. *intr.* to finish chewing; II. *tr.* 1) to champ up, chew; to draw out, extract by chewing; 2) *Mar.* das Werg —, to work out the oakum.

Aus'kauf, *(str., pl. Aus'käufe) m.* 1) the (act of) buying out, outbidding; 2) redemption-money, ransom.

Aus'kaufen, *(w.) v.* I. *tr.* 1) to buy *or* purchase out (an establishment); 2) to anticipate *or* forestall (another purchaser) in buying; to outbid; 3) *fig.* to use, employ well (occasion, time), to make the most of ...; II. *intr.* to cease purchasing.

Aus'kegeln, *(w.) v.* I. *intr.* to finish playing at ninepins; II. *tr.* 1) to play at ninepins for ...; 2) *Vet.* die Köthe —, to dislocate the fetlock-joint.

Aus'kehlen, *(w.) v. tr.* [illegible] chamfer, to flute; [illegible] striate, striated. — [illegible] chamfer, channel (of a [illegible]

Aus'kehren, *(w.) v. tr.* 1) [illegible] sweep up *or* clean; [illegible] *fam.* to brush; ein [illegible]

Aus'kehricht, [illegible]

Aus'keilen, *(w.) v. tr.* [illegible]

Aus'keilen, *(w.) v.* I. *tr.* [illegible] wedges; 2) *fam.* to [illegible] out of the change *or* [illegible] II. *intr. & refl.* to run out [illegible] to dwindle, to terminate, [illegible] ers, &c.).

Aus'keimen, *(w.) v.* I. *intr.* [illegible] to germinate, sprout, shoot [illegible] germinating; II. *tr.* to [illegible] of the shoots.

Aus'[illegible], *(w.) v. tr.* to [illegible]

Aus'keltern, *(w.) v.* I. *tr.* [illegible] to squeeze out *or* press by [illegible] II. *intr.* to finish pressing [illegible]

Aus'kennen, *(irr.) v. refl.* [illegible] to have knowledge *or* [illegible] (a thing), to be fully [illegible] see one's way.

Aus'kerben, *(w.) v. tr.* to [illegible] lop, indent; ausgekerbt, *Bot.* [illegible] rated. — **Aus'kerbung**, *(w.) f.* [illegible]

Aus'kernen, *(w.) v. tr.* 1) [illegible] out of, to stone; 2) *fig.* to [illegible] to choose the best from ..., — [illegible] *(w.) f.* the taking the [illegible] &c.); enucleation, &c.

Aus'kesseln, *(w.) v.* I. *tr.* [illegible] shape of a kettle; II. *intr.* [illegible] and get kettle-shaped (of [illegible]

Aus'[illegible], *(w.) v. tr.* [illegible] clefts in order to apply [illegible]

Aus'keulen, *(w.) v. tr.* to [illegible] mer out.

Aus'kielen, *(w.) v.* I. [illegible] feathers *or* quills (of [illegible] with quills.

Aus'kindern, *(w.) v. intr.* [illegible] bearing children; 2) to [illegible]

Aus'kippen, *(w.) v. tr.* [illegible]

Aus'kiste, *(w.) f. T.* [illegible] stamping-mills for [illegible]

Aus'kitten, *(w.) v. tr.* to [illegible] ment; to cement with [illegible]

Aus'klaftern, *(w.) v.* I. [illegible] measure (a tree) by fathoms, [illegible] II. *intr.* to stretch out [illegible]

Aus'klagbar, *adj. Law*, [illegible] may be sued for.

Aus'klagen, *(w.) v.* I. [illegible] (something); 2) to [illegible] law for ...; II. *refl.* [illegible] 2, 82) to give full vent [illegible] III. *intr.* to cease [illegible]

Aus'klären, *(w.) v. tr.* [illegible] geklärtes Wohl, fine [illegible]

Aus'klatschen, *(w.) v.* [illegible] tering, &c., *cf.* [illegible] off (an actor from the [illegible] condemn (a play) by [illegible] *vulg.* 2) to thrash [illegible]

Aus'klauben, *(w.) v.* [illegible] (with the fingers) [illegible] cull (the best; 2) a) [illegible] &c. *see* [illegible]

Aus'kleben, *(w.)* [illegible] to close by pasting [illegible] —, to fill up with [illegible]

Aus'kleiden, *(w.)* [illegible] clothe, to unclothe [illegible] one's clothes; 2) [illegible] side, *cf.* Bekleidung [illegible] undressing-room [illegible] (the act of) [illegible]

thoughts, to deliver one's self (über (with *Acc.*), on): er hat sich nicht weiter ausgelassen, he did not explain himself any further, or express himself more fully.

Aus'laß ..., *in comp.* *T.-s.* —röhre, *f.* outlet-pipe; discharging-pipe: —ventil, *n.* eduction-valve; (eines Kastengebläses) forcing-valve.

Aus'lassung, *s.* I. (*w.*) *f.* 1) *a)* the (act of) letting out, &c.: *b)* emission: discharge (from prison): 2) *a)* leaving out, omission; *b)* *Gramm.* *aa)* elision; *bb)* ellipsis; 3) *Typ.* the out: II. *in comp.* *Mech.-s.* A-klappe, *f.* exit-valve, discharge-valve, delivery-valve: A-pforte, *f.* eduction-port: eduction-valve; A-röhre, *f.* eduction-pipe: A-zeichen, *n.* *Gramm.* apostrophe, mark of elision; *Typ.* caret.

Aus'lauben, (*w.*) *v.* *tr.* 1) to thin out the foliage of (a tree); 2) to adorn with foliage.

Aus'lauern, (*w.*) *v.* I. *tr.* to spy, lurk: to watch: II. *intr.* to cease lurking.

Aus'lauf, (*str.*, *pl.* Aus'läufe) *m.* 1) the (act of) running out, &c. *cf.* Auslaufen; 2) leakage; 3) *a)* outset; start, starting, &c.: *b)* port-clearing, sailing, setting sail: 4) outlet, issue, mouth; 5) *Archit.* *a)* projection, a jutting out, *see* Ausladung, 3; *b)* haunces or haunches; 6) *Min.* barrow-load; 7) profit of saltworks.

Aus'laufen, (*str.*) *v.* I. *intr.* (*aux.* sein) 1) *a)* to run out (*also of things*: das Ankertau — lassen, to slip the cable); *b)* to leak, run out: das Ausgelaufene, tap-droppings; *c)* to discharge itself (as a river, &c.); *d)* to run out of drawing (of colours), to blot, to sink (*cf.* Durchschlagen, III. 1); 2) *a)* to begin running; to start, set out; to depart: *b)* to clear (*or* run out) of a port, set sail, put to sea; der Befehl zum —, sailing orders: auf Beute —, to cruise; 3) *a)* to issue (*or* to taper) into a point, &c.; *b)* *Archit.* to project, jut out; *c)* to spread (of plants); *d)* to swell out; *e)* to extend, to run or branch out: *f)* to end, come to an end, turn out, *see* Ablaufen, 5, *c*; — lassen, *aa)* *Typ.* to keep out; *bb)* *Mar.* to slip (a cable): II. *refl.* 1) to wear out or to grow wider by friction; 2) *coll.* to take sufficient exercise by running about: III. *tr.* 1) *Mar.* die Weite nicht regelmäßig —, to narrow; 2) *Min.* to remove or convey away (ores, &c.) in wheel-barrows.

Aus'läufer, (*str.*) *m.* 1) runner; errand-boy; porter: 2) *Mil.* deserter; 3) *Bot.* shoot, sprout, sucker, stoloniferous stem, stolon; 4) *fig.* spur (of a mountain), branch: — treibend, stoloniferous.

Aus'läuteln, **Aus'läutern**, (*w.*) *v.* *tr.* to shell (beans, &c.), *cf.* Ausschälen.

Aus'lauf ..., *in comp.* —(e)platz, *m.* starting-place or -point, starting-post; —farren, *m.*, —ofen, *m.* *Glass-m.* flashing-furnace: —röhre, *n.* *T.* drain-pipe, waste-pipe (Ausgußröhre): —stein, *m.* *Archit.* gutter-stone.

Aus'laufung, (*w.*) *f.* the (act of) running out, *cf.* Auslauf.

Aus'laugen, (*w.*) *v.* *tr.* 1) to clear of lye; 2) to get (the salt) out of ashes; 3) to wash in lye; to impregnate or soak with salts from wood-ashes: *Chem.* to lixiviate: ausgelaugte Asche, buck-ashes; 4) *Metal.* to buddle, to wash. [slime-pit.

Aus'laugeäscher, (*str.*, *pl.* A-äscher) *m.*

Aus'lauschen, (*w.*) *v.* *tr.* to find out, discover by watching or listening.

Aus'lausen, (*w.*) *v.* *tr.* 1) to clear of lice, to louse; 2) *Min.* eine Kette —, to disentangle a chain; 3) Einen —, *vulg.* to fleece one, to drain his purse.

Aus'laut, (*str.*) *m.* *Gramm.* final sound of a word or syllable (*opp.* Anlaut); das englische e (so im A-e verstummt wird), *e*, in English, when it terminates a word, is generally vocal.

Aus'lauten, (*w.*) *v.* *intr.* 1) to cease to sound; 2) *Gramm.* to terminate a word or syllable (*opp.* Anlauten); Wörter die mit a —, words ending in *a*; auslautendes r ist im Englischen kaum hörbar, *r* is scarcely heard at the end of English words.

Aus'läuten, (*w.*) *v.* I. *tr.* to proclaim the end of (a thing) by ringing bells; to publish or proclaim by ringing a bell or the bells: einen Todten —, to announce the death of a person by tolling the bell, to ring the passing-bell over or for a person deceased; II. *intr.* to cease to ring the bells.

Aus'läutern, (*w.*) *v.* *tr.* *Forest.* to clear, to thin (a forest).

Aus'leben, (*w.*) *v.* I. *tr.* to live to the end of, to live to see the end (Erleben); II. *intr.* to finish one's life: du hast ausgelebt, you are a dead man.

Aus'lecken, (*w.*) *v.* I. *tr.* to lick up, out, lap up; II. *intr.* (*aux.* sein) to run, ooze, or drop out, to leak.

Aus'ledern, (*w.*) *v.* *tr.* 1) *T.* to line with leather; to leather: 2) *vulg.* to leather, to drub, to thrash (*see* Ausgerben, 2).

Aus'leeren, (*w.*) *v.* *tr.* 1) to empty, to clear (a house, room); 2) *Med.*, &c. to void (excrements), to excrete, evacuate, emit, eject, egest: *Med.-s.* a-de Mittel, evacuants: ausgeleert, *p.* & *a.* excremental; *Vet.* to drench (a horse): einen Teich —, to drain a pond: 3) to empty by drinking, to drink up (off): bis auf die Neige *or* Hefe —, to empty to the very dregs. — **Aus'leerer**, (*str.*) *m.* emptier, &c. — **Aus'leerung**, *s.* I. (*w.*) *f.* 1) the (act of) emptying, &c.; 2) *Med.* evacuation; excretion, voiding (through the anus): gehörige —, *Med.* a normal stool; II. *in comp.* A-smittel, *n.* *Med.* evacuant, purgative; *Mech.-s.* A-spumpe, *f.* exhausting syringe: A-röhre, *f.* evacuation-pipe, waste-pipe (*Rail*).

Aus'lege ..., *in comp.* —fenster, *n.* show-window; —holz, *n.* *Join.* veneers (*pl.*), inlay; —laden, *n.* shop-front.

Aus'legen, (*w.*) *v.* *tr.* 1) to lay out: ein Schiff —, *Mar.* to lay out a vessel upon the road; einen gedruckten Bogen —, *Print.* to lift up a printed sheet: 2) *Join.*, &c. to inlay, to veneer; to tessellate; to damaskeen, to incrust; ausgelegte Arbeit, inlaid (tessellated) work, inlaying, veneering, marquetry; 3) *a)* to lay out for show, to set to show, expose to view, expose, exhibit for sale; to display; *b)* *fig.* (*l. u.*) to exhibit, display (auch später legt sie große Zärtlichkeit gegen Imogen aus, *Gervinus*, *Shaksp.* III, 420); 4) *fig.* to elucidate, explain, expound (a text of scripture, &c.), to interpret (dreams, &c.); to decipher; to construct (als or für, into), to put a (harsh, wrong, &c.) construction on, upon: etwas zum Besten —, to put the best construction on a thing: falsch —, to misinterpret; 5) Geld —, to advance, disburse money: Geld auf Zinsen —, to put out money at interest; 6) Soldaten —, to change the quarters of soldiers (Ausquartieren).

Aus'leger, (*str.*) *m.* 1) *Mar.* *a)* loose bowsprit, boom used for a bow-sprit in small vessels; *b)* (Spiere zum Ausholen des Besanschots) sailing-boom; *c)* guard-ship, revenue-prame (Auslieger); 2) explainer, interpreter, &c.; expounder (of scripture, &c.), commentator.

Aus'legerei', (*w.*) *f.* *cont.* 1) incorrect or loose interpretation; 2) the practice of useless or over-refining interpretation, hair-splitting.

Aus'lege ..., *in comp.* —hölzchen, *n.* *pl.* *see* —holz; —tisch, *m.* stall; shop-counter; table, bench, &c. on which to expose goods for sale.

Aus'legung, (*w.*) *f.* 1) the (act of) laying out, &c. *cf.* Auslegen; 2) explanation, interpretation, exposition, construction. Der heiligen Schrift exegesis: falsche —, misinterpreta-

Aus'löffeln, (w.) v. tr. to empty with a spoon or spoons.

Aus'lohen, (w.) v. tr. T. to bake (a casting-mould), cf. Ausbrennen.

Aus'lohnen, Aus'löhnen, (w.) v. tr. to pay the wages to ....

Aus'loosen, (w.) v. tr. to draw out by lot, &c. see Verloosen; ausgelooste Staatsschuldscheine, released bonds.

Aus'lootsen, (w.) v. tr. Mar. to pilot out of a harbour, to conduct or carry (a vessel) out to sea.

Aus'lösbar, adj. redeemable; repleviable.

Aus'löschen, v. I. (w.) tr. 1) to extinguish, to put out; 2) a) to expunge, to do or put out; to efface, obliterate, to blot or dash out: to paint out, to erase, to work out; to cancel: b) Script. to expiate (one's guilt); II. (str. & w.) intr. (aux. sein) 1) to be extinguished, to go out, to be effaced or erased; 2) fig. to die, to become extinct.

Aus'löschlich, adj. quenchable, extinguishable; that may be erased, obliterated: A-keit, (w.) f. quenchableness.

Aus'löschung, (w.) f. extinguishment; defacement, effacement, deletion, obliteration: extinction.

Aus'lösen, (w.) v. tr. 1) a) to loosen, see Lösen; b) Mech. to free, to disengage: Horol. to lift (up), see Ausheben, 2; 2) a) Butch. to cut out (bones); b) Surg. to extirpate; 3) Sport. Lerchen —, to take out of the net (larks): fig.-a. 4) to pay for (one), to release, ransom, redeem, deliver; 5) to replevy, to redeem, recover (a pawn); 6) Comm. to take up (bills).

Aus'löslich, see Auslösbar.

Aus'löser, (str.) m. 1) one who loosens, &c.; 2) (Auslösung) Horol. lifter, see Ausheber, 1.

Aus'lösung, (w.) f. 1) Horol. lifter, see Ausheber, 1; 2) the (act of) redeeming: a) releasing, deliverance, ransom; b) replevin; 3) Surg. extirpation: A-casse, f. branch-establishment (of a bank); A-schere, f. T. pincers of a pile-engine. [sich —, to take an airing.

Aus'lüften, (w.) v. tr. to air, to ventilate;

Aus'machen, (w.) v. tr. 1) to make out; 2) a) to put out (the fire, &c.); b) to take out, to get out; to shell (chestnuts, peas, &c.), to blanch (almonds); fig.-a. 3) to find out; Wild —, Sport. to draw a cover; 4) to amount or come to, to make up, to compose, to be composed or consist of, to constitute (a whole, &c.); 5) a) to settle, make up, to stipulate; b) to finish, end, terminate; c) to decide; to fix, to determine; 6) to matter, to be of (great, little, &c.) consequence; 7) fam. see Ausschelten; 8) to gut, eviscerate (animals); Geflügel —, to draw poultry; 9) Lace-manuf. to [illegible], border, line, trim; Einem einen Dienst, ein Logis u. s. w. —, to procure one an office, a lodging, &c., on certain conditions: was habt ihr ausgemacht? what have you settled between you? Einem eine Summe —, to settle a sum upon one; er hat es ausgemacht, he is gone (i. e. dead); es macht nichts [illegible], it matters not, it does not matter or signify, [illegible] no matter, never mind (it); es macht nicht viel aus, it is no great matter; call.-a. [illegible] macht das nichts aus, that breaks [illegible] among friends; würde es Ihnen [illegible] —, wenn Sie mir das Buch halten? [illegible] holding this book for me? [illegible] als ausgemacht an, I take it for [illegible]. Ausgemacht, p. a.; a-d, p. a. con[illegible]

[illegible], (w.) f. T. hitchel, hatchel.

[illegible] (w.) f. Law, see Vermächtniß.

[illegible] (w.) v. I. tr. to emaciate; [illegible] become emaciated or lean (Ab-[illegible]

[illegible] (w.) f. Med. emaciation.

Aus'mähen, (w.) v. tr. to mow part of...

Aus'mahlen, (irr.) v. I. tr. to grind out; II. intr. to cease grinding.

Aus'mäkeln, (w.) v. I. tr. 1) to sell by retail; 2) to reject with censure; II. intr. to cease censuring.

Aus'malen, (w.) v. I. tr. to paint, to finish painting; to colour, illuminate; einige Bilder zum Ausmalen, some pictures to colour; (mit Wappenschildern) to emblazon; II. intr. to cease or finish painting.

Aus'mangeln, (w.) v. tr. to mangle properly, sufficiently; II. intr. to cease mangling.

Aus'mann, (str., pl. Aus'männer) m. see Ausbürger.

Aus'marken, (w.) v. tr. 1) to mark out; 2) to set out by marks.

Aus'marsch, (str., pl. Aus'märsche) m. a marching out. [march out.

Aus'marschiren, (w.) v. tr. (aux. sein) to

Aus'martern, (w.) v. tr. to torture out: Einem die Seele —, to plague a person's soul out.

Aus'mästen, (w.) v. tr. to fatten thoroughly.

Aus'matriculiren, see Exmatriculiren.

Aus'mauern, (w.) v. tr. to face with a wall, to case or line with brickwork, stones, or masonry; Mas. to fill up with bricks, to brick or nog (the bays of a bay-work).

Aus'mauerung, (w.) f. a casing, lining (of brickwork, &c.); Min. ginging (the lining of a shaft with stones or bricks for its support.

Aus'meckern, (w.) v. tr. to leave off bleating.

Aus'meißeln, (w.) v. tr. to chisel out; to chisel off; to chase; to gouge; to carve; Gold. to scorp; die ausgemeißelte Arbeit, fretwork, (in Metall) chase-work; fig. elaborate.

Aus'melken, (str.) v. tr. to milk out, to drain by milking.

Aus'mergeln, (w.) v. tr. 1) to enervate, exhaust; to emaciate, make lean, meagre, thin; 2) to wear (land) out of heart, to exhaust, to impoverish; Einen ganz —, to suck one's substance; ausgemergelt, p. a. enervated, &c.; barren, effete. [2) to find out.

Aus'merken, (w.) v. tr. 1) to mark out;

Aus'merzen, (w.) v. tr. 1) to cast off, reject, turn out or away; to cull, weed; 2) Math. to exterminate; 3) Typ. to rough.

Aus'messen, (str.) v. tr. 1) to measure (out); to survey (land); to gauge, to take the measurement of (the contents of a vessel); to find the solid contents of (a piece of timber); 2) to sell by measure; 3) to dispart (a piece of ordnance).

Aus'messer, (str.) m. measurer; surveyor.

Aus'messung, (w.) f. the (act of) measuring, &c., measurement, survey; gauge; Math.-a. a) dimension; b) (körperliche) cubature; — der Körper, stereometry; — der Ebenen, planimetry; die — eines Schiffes nehmen, to take the bearings of a ship.

Aus'metzen, (w.) v. tr. Mill. to take the multure, the lawful quantity of (the flour ground) in lieu of payment.

Aus'meubliren (pr. —'möb—), (w.) v. tr. to furnish (a room).

Aus'miethen, (w.) v. tr. 1) to let out for hire; 2) to eject by raising the rent; 3) to dislodge by offering a higher rent; 4) (Einem einen Dienstboten) to engage (the servant of another person), to take or entice away by offering higher wages, &c.; 5) to find a, or another lodging for ....

Aus'misten, (w.) v. tr. to cast the dung out of (the stable), to cleanse (the stable).

Aus'mitteln, (w.) v. tr. to find out, to discover, to ascertain.

Aus'möbeln, (w.) v. tr. see Ausmeubliren.

Aus'möbler, (str.) m. a furnisher of a house or a room, upholsterer; seller of furniture.

Aus'modeln, (w.) v. tr. to model properly, perfectly. [(soldiers).

Aus'montiren, (w.) v. tr. Mil. to equip

Aus'moosen, (w.) v. tr. to rid of moss.

Aus'münden, (w.) v. intr. & refl. to discharge itself, to disembogue.

Aus'mündung, (w.) f. mouth of a river.

Aus'münzen, (w.) v. tr. to coin, stamp.

Aus'murmeln, (w.) v. intr. to leave off grumbling.

Aus'müssen, (irr.) v. intr. (used elliptically, gehen, &c. being understood) to be obliged to go out; er muß aus, he must go out; der Rock muß aus, the coat must be taken off.

Aus'mustern, (w.) v. tr. 1) to reject, to sort; to discard, turn off, dismiss, to cashier; 2) to purge or clear (a work) from incorrect or offensive passages; call.-a. 3) to dress out, see Ausputzen, 2; 4) to reprimand, see Ausputzen, 5.

Aus'nähen, (w.) v. I. tr. to embroider; to quilt; mit Blumen —, to diaper; ausgenäht, p. a. out-stitched; II. intr. 1) to give over sewing; 2) to go out to sew.

Aus'nahme, v. I. (w.) f. exception (von, to); diese Regel hat keine —, there is no exception to this rule; mit — und Vorbehalt, Law, excepted and foreprised; ich mache mit ihm eine —, I make a distinction or exception in his favour; II. in comp. —fall, m. exceptional case; —gesetz, n. exceptional law.

Aus'nahmslos, adj. admitting of no exception; adv. without exception.

Aus'nahmsweise, I. adv. by way of exception; II. adj. exceptional.

Aus'narren, (w.) v. intr. to leave off acting foolishly or fooling.

Aus'naschen, (w.) v. tr. to sip, eat, or take out by stealth.

Aus'nehmen, (str.) v. I. tr. 1) to take out, cf. Herausnehmen; to draw, extract (a tooth); Honig —, to take part of the honey from the hives (Bienen beschneiden); 2) to choose, take up (commodities); 3) to embowel, dress (a fish); to eviscerate, to gut, to hulk (a hare &c.); to gip (a herring), to draw (poultry); 4. Found. to draw; Weav. to design (the patterns); 5) fig. to except, exempt, exclude; keinen ausgenommen, nobody excepted, cf. Ausgenommen, p. a., &c.; II. refl. coll. to distinguish one's self, to make a figure, to look or show (well, ill); von hier nimmt es sich am besten aus, here it is seen to the best advantage; es nimmt sich nicht sonderlich aus, it makes but a poor figure; sich schlecht a-d, unsightly.

Aus'nehmend, p. a. (orig. exceptional) exceeding, extraordinary; exquisite, surpassing; — theuer, exceedingly, uncommonly dear.

Aus'nehmezange, (w.) f. T. button-maker's pincers.

Aus'neigen, (w.) v. tr. to empty by tilting, by raising the one end.

Aus'nicken, (w.) v. intr. to cease nodding.

Aus'niesen, (w.) v. I. tr. to bring up by sneezing; II. intr. to cease sneezing.

Aus'nippen, (w.) v. tr. to sip up, out.

Aus'nutschen, (w.) v. coll. see Aussaugen.

Aus'nutzen, Aus'nützen, (w.) v. tr. 1) to use up, to wear out (by use); 2) to use, employ well, to turn to the best advantage; to make the most of....

Aus'öden, (w.) v. tr. to desolate, lay waste.

Aus'ösen, (w.) v. tr. to bale (out), to free (a boat) from water.

Aus'ölen, (w.) v. tr. to oil on the inside.

Aus'pachten, (w.) v. tr. 1) to dislodge by offering or asking a higher rent; 2) see Verpachten.

Aus'packen, (w.) v. tr. to unpack, to unbale (goods); to open (a pack); ist die Waare noch nicht ausgepackt? are the goods not yet unpacked? — Aus'packer, (str.) m. unpacker, &c.

Aus'pappen, *(w.) v. tr.* to line with paste-board. [ward off, fend off.

Aus'pariren, *(w.) v. tr. Fenc.* to parry, to

Aus'paschen, *(w.) v. tr. Gam.* to throw first (at dice).

Aus'passen, *(w.) v. tr.* to seek out that which fits *or* suits; to watch (an opportunity).

Aus'passiren, *(w.) v. intr.* to pass through the gate of a town on leaving it.

Aus'patschen, *(w.) v. tr. vulg.* to slap soundly.

Aus'pauken, *(w.) v. I. tr.* 1) to drum out; 2) to drub *or* beat soundly; II. *intr.* to cease drumming.

Aus'pauschen, *(w.) v. tr. Min.* to beat small, to clean of dross, to stamp, to bruise.

Aus'peilen, *(w.) v. tr. Mar.* to sound (den Grund, the bottom).

Aus'peitschen, *(w.) v. tr.* 1) to whip (out), to scourge, to horsewhip; 2) to expel by whipping; ich will ihm seinen Eigensinn —, I'll whip his obstinacy out of him. [shell.

Aus'pellen, *(w.) v. tr. provinc.* to peel,

Aus'pelzen, *(w.) v. tr.* to beat soundly, to dust a person's jacket.

Aus'pfählen, *(w.) v. tr.* to set (out) with piles. *Build.* to pile. — **Aus'pfählung,** *(w.) f.* pile-work.

Aus'pfänden, *(w.) v. tr.* 1) to distrain, seize for debt; 2) to seize the goods of (a person) for debt; — lassen, to levy a distress *or* lodge a detainer against (a person).

Aus'pfänder, *(str.) m.* distrainer, seizor.

Aus'pfändung, *(w.) f.* distress, seizure; execution; distraint; A-befehl, *m. Law,* distress-warrant.

Aus'pfarren, *(w.) v. tr.* to take from one parish (and attach to another).

Aus'pfeifen, *(str.) v. I. intr.* to cease, or to have done whistling; II. *tr.* 1) to hiss, to damn, condemn (a play), to drive off the stage (an actor) by hissing *or* whistling, to hiss off; to catcall; 2) *Min.* (den Brief aus Spreng-löchern herauswerfen) to blow.

Aus'pferchen, *(w.) v. tr.* to unpen.

Aus'pflanzen, *(w.) v. tr. see* Verpflanzen.

Aus'pflastern, *(w.) v. tr.* to pave the inside of (an inclosed place).

Aus'pflöcken, *(w.) v. tr.* to provide (on the inside, &c.) with pegs.

Aus'pflücken, *(w.) v. tr.* to pluck up, out, *or* off; to untwist (die Kabelgarne alter Taue, old ropes).

Aus'pflügen, *(w.) v. I. tr.* to plough up; II. *intr.* to cease ploughing.

Aus'pfützen, *(w.) v. tr. Min.* to draw out *or* off (the low waters).

Aus'pichen, *(w.) v. tr.* to pitch the inside of (a cask, &c.); er ist ausgepicht, *fac.* (of a drinker) he is a seasoned cask.

* **Auspicien,** *n. pl.* (*sing.* [*Lat.*] Auspicium) auspices.

Aus'picken, *(w.) v. tr.* to peck out.

Aus'pinseln, *(w.) v. tr.* 1) to paint *or* brush all over (on the inside); 2) to efface by painting, by a dash of the brush.

Aus'placken, *(w.) v. tr.* to torture, torment, plague, &c. *cf.* Ausquälen.

Aus'plappern, *(w.) v. tr. see* Ausplaudern.

Aus'platten, Aus'plätten, *(w.) v. tr.* to smooth (out) by ironing, to iron thoroughly.

Aus'platzen, *(w.) v. intr.* 1) to burst out *or* asunder; 2) *see* Herausplatzen.

Aus'plaudern, *(w.) v. I. tr.* to blab (out), to let out in secret; II. *refl.* to prattle, talk to one's heart's content; III. *intr.* to have done prattling. — **Aus'plauderer,** *(str.) m.* blabber, &c.

Aus'plumpen, *(w.) v. tr. see* Auspumpen.

Aus'plündern, *(w.) v. tr.* to empty *or* strip by pillage *or* plundering, *see* Plündern; to spoil (a country); to spoliate. — **Aus'plünderung,** *(w.) f.* the (act of) pillaging, ransacking, &c.

Aus'pochen, *(w.) v. tr.* 1) to beat (clothes, skins); 2) *fig.* to explode, *cf.* Austrommeln & Auspfeifen; 3) *Sport.* to dislodge, untree (martens). [inside, to burnish up.

Aus'poliren, *(w.) v. tr.* to polish on the

Aus'polstern, *(w.) v. tr.* 1) to stuff, to pad, quilt on the inside; 2) to provide with stuffed seats, &c. [tobern.

Aus'poltern, *(w.) v. intr. & tr. see* Aus-

Aus'posaunen, *(w.) v. tr. fig.* to trumpet forth, divulge, blazon, to blast abroad, (about), to cry up, sound (one's praise); sein eigenes Lob —, to trumpet one's own merits, to sound one's own trumpet; seine Waaren —, *Comm.* to cry up, to puff one's articles.

Aus'prägen, *(w.) v. tr.* 1) *Mint.* to coin, stamp; 2) to imprint well, to stamp distinctly; ein scharf ausgeprägtes Gesicht, a strongly marked face; ein ausgeprägtes griechisches Gesicht, a decided Greek face.

Aus'prahlen, *(w.) v. I. intr.* to leave off boasting *or* bragging; II. *tr.* to divulge in a boasting way.

Aus'predigen, *(w.) v. I. intr.* to cease preaching; II. *tr.* (*l. u.*) to divulge from the pulpit, &c.

Aus'preisen, *(str.) v. tr.* to praise duly.

Aus'pressen, *(w.) v. tr.* 1) *a)* to press *or* squeeze out (the moisture, &c., aus, from), *cf.* Ausdrücken; *b)* to press out, to squeeze out, crush out (grapes, &c.); to strain, force, *or* wring out; 2) *fig.* to extort, to draw (tears, sighs, Einem, from one).

Aus'pressmaschine, *(w.) f. T.* squeezing-machine, squeezer (*Farm.*).

Aus'probiren, Aus'prüfen, *(w.) v. tr.* 1) to try thoroughly; to select by trying *or* proving; Wein —, to taste wine; 2) *Min.* to put in the ingot-mould.

Aus'prügeln, *(w.) v. tr.* to cudgel soundly, *vulg.* to dust one's coat (jacket), to curry one's coat (hide), to baste.

Aus'pudern, *(w.) v. tr.* to strew all over (on the inside) with powder, &c.

Aus'puffen, *(w.) v. tr.* to thump (out).

Aus'pumpen, *(w.) v. tr.* 1) to pump (out), to empty by pumping; 2) *Phys.* to exhaust, extract by an air-pump.

Aus'punctiren, *(w.) v. tr.* to mark the outline of by puncturing, to trace by pricking, to mark out *or* prick (a pattern for embroidery, &c.). [out (Ausblasen).

Aus'pusten, *(w.) v. tr. provinc.* to blow

Aus'putz, *(str.) m.* 1) articles of dress, dressing; 2) trimming(s), ornaments.

Aus'putzen, *(w.) v. tr.* 1) *a)* to clean out, to clean, cleanse, or polish on the inside; *b)* to sponge (a cannon); *c)* to sweep out (a stove); *d) Paint.* to clear the parts of ...; *e) Manuf.* to pick *or* clean (silk, woollen stuff, cloth); 2) to dress *or* trim out, to fit up; *Hatt.* to iron (an old hat), *cf.* Ausschmücken; 3) *Gard.* to prune (trees), disbud; 4) to snuff out (a candle); 5) *coll.* to reprimand, to blow (one) up. — **Aus'putzer,** *(str.) m.* 1) dresser, &c.; *Letter-found.* trimmer, finisher; 2) *coll.* reprimand, lecture, scolding; *vulg.* wipe, set-down.

Aus'quaken, *(w.) v. intr.* to leave off croaking.

Aus'quälen, *(w.) v. I. tr.* (Einem etwas) to torture (something) out of one; II. *refl.* to cease tormenting one's self. [ing.

Aus'qualmen, *(w.) v. intr.* to cease smok-

Aus'quartieren, *(w.) v. tr.* to dislodge, to change the quarters of (soldiers).

Aus'quetschen, *(w.) v. tr.* to squeeze *or* crush out.

Aus'quiriren, *(w.) v. tr. Typ.* to impose (die Columnen, the columns). [[illegible]

Aus'rädeln, Aus'rädern, *(w.) v. tr. see*

Aus'reibe..., *in comp.* **—holz**, *n.*, **—lappen**, *m.* Shoe-*m.* polisher, burnisher.

Aus'reiben, *(str.)* *v.* I. *tr.* 1) to rub out, off, *or* away; 2) to clean by rubbing: to polish, burnish: to rub up; 3) *Hatt.* to dress, fit up, form (a hat): II. *intr.* to finish rubbing.

Aus'reichen, *(w.)* *v.* I. *intr.* 1) to suffice, &c. *see* Hinreichen; 2) *see* Auslangen, 4; II. *tr.* to issue (dividend-warrants, &c.), *see* Ausgeben.

Aus'reichung, *(w.)* *f.* issue, *cf.* Ausreichen, II. & Ausgabe.

Aus'reihen, *(w.)* *v.* *tr.* 1) to range out, to sort out; 2) to unstring.

Aus'reinigen, *(w.)* *v.* *tr.* to clean, cleanse thoroughly; to purify: *Med.* to purge.

Aus'reisen, *(w.)* *v.* *intr.* 1) *(aux.* ſein) to set out, to depart: 2) ausgereiſt haben, to have done travelling.

Aus'reißen, *(str.)* *v.* I. *tr.* to pull out (the eyes), to tear out (the hair); to extract, to draw out (einen Zahn, einen Nagel aus der Wand, a tooth, a nail from a wall); mit den Wurzeln —, to uproot, to tear up by the roots; to pluck up (weeds), to pluck (a feather); einen Damm —, to break a dam or dike; II. *intr.* *(aux.* ſein) 1) *fig*-*s.* to break loose, to dash or tear off (of horses, &c.): to decamp, scamper off, run away, escape, to take to one's heels, *coll.* to cut one's stick: *Mil.* to desert; 2) to tear, burst; 3) to fail, to be exhausted (as one's patience). — **Aus'reißer**, *(str.)* *m.* 1) *Gard.* instrument, used in removing roots; 2) deserter, &c.: fugitive; renegade; 3) *Min.* side-lode going upwards. — **Aus'reißerei'**, *(w.)* *f.* (frequent) desertion, practice of desertion.

Aus'reiten, *(str.)* *v.* I. *intr.* *(aux.* ſein) to ride out, take a ride, to take the air on horseback; to take to horse; II. *tr.* 1) to air (a horse), to give an airing; 2) einen Raum —, to ride over a space.

Aus'reiter, *(str.)* *m.* out-rider; messenger, attendant; a mounted gendarm.

Aus'renken, *(w.)* *v.* *tr.* to sprain, to wrench out or off, to dislocate, disjoint, to put out of joint; ſich *(Dat.)* das Bein —, to sprain one's leg; einem Pferde die Schulter —, to splay a horse. — **Aus'renkung**, *(w.)* *f.* a spraining, &c., sprain, dislocation.

Aus'rennen, *(irr.)* *v.* I. *intr.* *(aux.* ſein) 1) to run out; 2) to start from; 3) *(aux.* haben) to cease running: II. *tr.* to knock out (ſich *(Dat.)* ein Auge &c., one's eye, &c.) by running against some object.

Aus'reuten, *(w.)* *v.* *tr.* *see* Ausroden.

Aus'rheden, *(w.)* *v.* *tr.* to rig, fit out, equip (a ship). — **Aus'rhedung**, *(w.)* *f.* the rigging, &c.; (A-Koſten, *pl.*) outfit (of a ship).

Aus'richten, *(w.)* *v.* *tr.* 1) *a)* to make straight; *b)* *T.* Beulen in einem Gefäße —, to hammer bruises out of a vessel; 2) *a)* *Min.* to discover (a passage); *b)* *Sport.* to track [illegible] —, to draw a cover; 3) to furnish the expenses of; 4) to do, perform, execute [illegible] eine Hochzeit —, to defray the [illegible] of a wedding, to give a wedding-party; [illegible] —, to give a christening-party; eine Mahlzeit —, to give a dinner- or supper-party; ſoll ich Ihre Botſchaft or Bestellung —? shall I do your errand? shall I [illegible] your message? einen Gruß —, to [illegible] compliments from one; viel —, to prove [illegible], to work well; nichts —, to labour [illegible], to prove ineffectual; mit ihm können [illegible] —, you cannot do anything with [illegible] Wort wird viel bei ihr —, your [illegible] will do much (will go a great way) [illegible] etwas bei ihm —, can you [illegible] upon him? was haſt du ausgerichtet? [illegible] have you done? ich kann gleich nichts —, [illegible] good to it; man kann nichts —, [illegible] to be done; damit iſt nichts ausʒurichten, that will not (won't) do; damit iſt nichts ausgerichtet, that is not sufficient.

Aus'richter, *(str.)* *m.* performer, message-bearer, provider, &c.; *Law*, executor (of a will).

Aus'richtig, **Aus'richtſam**, *adj.* *(l. u.)* adroit, dexterous.

Aus'richtung, *(w.)* *f.* 1) performance, execution, preparation, &c.; 2) *see* Ausſtattung.

Aus'riechen, *(str.)* *v.* I. *tr.* to smell out, find out by the smell; II. *intr.* *(aux.* haben) to cease emitting scent or smell.

Aus'riefen, *(w.)* *v.* *tr.* *Archit.* to flute, chamfer, channel; to rifle the barrel of a gun: ausgeriefelt, *adj.* *Bot.* channelled, striated.

Aus'rindern, *(w.)* *v.* *intr.* (of cows) to cease longing for the bull. [machine.

Aus'ringemaſchine, *(w.)* *f.* wringing-

Aus'ringen, *(str.)* *v.* I. *tr.* 1) to wring out (the water, &c.): to press or squeeze out (a lemon); 2) *see* Auswinden; 3) (Einem etwas) to wrest (something) from (one): II. *intr.* to end one's struggle; er hat ausgerungen, his struggles are over.

Aus'rinnen, *(str.)* *v.* *intr.* *(aux.* ſein) to run, leak, trickle out; das —, *v.* *s.* *(str.)* *n.* leakage.

Aus'rippen, *(w.)* *v.* *tr.* to rid (leaves) of fibres: ausgerippte Blätter, *Bot.* 1) stripped leaves; 2) striated leaves.

Aus'ritt, *(str.)* *m.* ride, excursion on horseback; departure.

Aus'röcheln, *(w.)* *v.* *intr.* *(aux.* ſein) to cease rattling (in the throat).

Aus'roden, *(w.)* *v.* *tr.* 1) *Agr.* to root out or up; to grub (out or up), to dig out, stub (up) (roots); 2) to clear of underwood, thorns, brambles, &c. in order to make arable.

Aus'rohren, *(w.)* *v.* *tr.* *Mas.* to provide (walls) with reed (in order to make the plaster stick). [flute,

Aus'röhren, *(w.)* *v.* *tr.* to channel, to

Aus'rollen, *(w.)* *v.* I. *tr.* 1) *Bak.* to roll out; 2) to unroll, to take out of a roll; 3) to sift, riddle (corn); II. *intr.* to cease rolling.

Aus'roſten, *(w.)* *v.* *intr.* to be rust-eaten on the inside.

Aus'rottbar, *adj.* extirpable, eradicable.

Aus'rotten, *(w.)* *v.* *tr.* 1) to root up, &c. *see* Ausroden; 2) *fig.* to exterminate, to extirpate; to eradicate; to destroy. — **Aus'rottung**, *(w.)* *f.* 1) the (act of) uprooting, &c.; 2) *fig.* extermination, eradication; 3) *Med.* extirpation, excision; A-Krieg, *m.* war of extermination; A-Pocken, *f.* *pl.* *(l. u.)* cow-pox.

Aus'rücken, *(w.)* *v.* I. *intr.* *(aux.* ſein) to march out; to move out; aus dem Lager —, to decamp; II. *tr.* 1) *Mech.* to disengage (ein Rad, a wheel), to ungear (ausgerückt, out of gear): aus- und einrücken, *coll.* to ship and unship (the gear); 2) *Typ.*, &c. eine Zeile —, to commence a new line, to form a break (in composition).

Aus'rück..., *in comp.* *T.*-s. —hebel, *m.* starting-lever; —zeug, *n.* disengaging-gear.

Aus'ruf, *(str.)* *m.* 1) cry, outcry; exclamation: ſie ſtand auf mit dem A-e: „hier iſt er!" she rose, exclaiming: "here he is!" 2) the (act of) crying out, proclamation; 3) auction, public sale: durch öffentlichen — feilbieten, to offer for sale by the public crier.

Aus'rufen, *(str.)* *v.* I. *intr.* to cry out or aloud, to exclaim; II. *tr.* 1) to call out; 2) *a)* to cry (of the crier or bellman); Jemand in den Zeitungen —, to advertise for one in the (news-)papers; *b)* (zum Verkaufe) to call out, to cry (wares, &c., to be sold, as a hawker); 3) to proclaim; zum König —, to proclaim king; (Verlobte) to proclaim, to bid the bans, to ask in church, *cf.* Aufbieten.

Aus'rufer, *(str.)* *m.* 1) crier, proclaimer; bellman; 2) hawker.

Aus'rufung, *(w.)* *f.* 1) the (act of) crying out, &c.; exclamation; 2) proclamation; 3) proclamation, bans of marriage, asking in church, *cf.* Aufgebot; A-szeichen, *n.* *Gramm.* sign or note of admiration or exclamation, exclamation- or admirative point; A-sgebühr, *f.* public crier's fee; A-swort, *n.* *Gramm.* interjection.

Aus'ruhe, *(w.)* *f.* rest, repose.

Aus'ruhen, *(w.)* *v.* *intr.* & *refl.* to rest, repose (sufficiently), to take (a) rest, to rest one's self; haben Sie (ſich) ausgeruht? are you rested?

Aus'rühmen, *(w.)* *v.* *tr.* *see* Ausprei[illegible]

Aus'rühren, *(w.)* *v.* *tr.* to churn (butter).

Aus'runden, **Aus'ründen**, *(w.)* *v.* *tr.* to round (off); to form into a round shape; to round on the inside. [mer.

Aus'rundſchlägel, *(str.)* *m.* *T.* form-ham-

Aus'runzeln, *(w.)* *v.* *tr.* to take out the wrinkles, to smooth (down), unwrinkle.

Aus'rupfen, *(w.)* *v.* *tr.* to pull out, pluck (out); (einem Vogel &c.) die Federn —, to strip (a bird) of its feathers; 2) *fig.* to pluck, plunder, fleece, bleed.

Aus'rüſten, *(w.)* *v.* *tr.* 1) to fit out, equip; to furnish, accoutre; to arm; to man; 2) *fig* to endow. — **Aus'rüſter**, *(str.)* *m.* fitter-out (of a vessel), &c. — **Aus'rüſtung**, *(w.)* *f.* the (act of) equipping, &c., equipment, equipage, preparation; *Mar.*, &c. outfit (of an expedition, &c.). [gleiten.

Aus'rutſchen, *(w.)* *v.* *intr.* *coll.* *for* Aus-

Aus'rütteln, *(w.)* *v.* *tr.* *see* Ausſchütteln.

Aus'ſaat, *(w.)* *f.* 1) the (act of) sowing; 2) seed; 3) seed-corn; —korb, *m.* hopper.

Aus'ſäbeln, *(w.)* *v.* *tr.* to cut out with the sabre; *coll.* to cut out in a rough or clumsy fashion.

Aus'ſacken, *(w.)* *v.* *tr.* to take out of a sack or pocket; to empty bags or sacks of ....

Aus'ſäen, *(w.)* *v.* *tr.* 1) to sow, to seed; to scatter (seed); 2) *fig.* to disseminate (errors, false news, &c.).

Aus'ſage, *(w.)* *f.* 1) verbal statement; declaration; deposition (of a witness), evidence: eine gerichtliche — thun, to make deposition, to give one's evidence; eidliche —, deposition upon oath, affidavit; nach ſeiner —, according to his statement, from what or according to what he says; ſeine — beweiſen, to prove what one says, one's assertion; eine — anhören, *Law*, to receive an audit; 2) *(or* —begriff, *m.)* *Gramm.* predicate.

Aus'ſagen, *(w.)* *v.* I. *tr.* 1) to say, express; to assert, to state, to declare; gerichtlich —, to depose, to give evidence; eidlich —, to give evidence upon oath: es iſt nicht auszuſagen, it is not to be expressed in words; 2) *Gramm.* to affirm or predicate (etwas von einer Perſon or Sache, something of a person or thing); II. *intr.* (of remedies, &c.) to cease to be effectual; to take no effect, to be of no avail, *cf.* Verſagen, *intr.*

Aus'ſägen, *(w.)* *v.* *tr.* 1) to saw out; 2) to fashion or form by sawing; 3) *(also* *intr.)* to finish sawing. [ness.

Aus'ſager, *(str.)* *m.* stator, deponent, wit-

Aus'ſagewort, *(str.*, *pl.* A-wörter) *n.* *Gramm.* a word which affirms or predicates, a verb.

Aus'ſaigern, *(w.)* *v.* *tr.* *see* Ausſeigern.

Aus'ſalben, *(w.)* *v.* *tr.* to smear with ointment on the inside.

Aus'ſanden, *(w.)* *v.* *tr.* 1) to clear of sand; 2) to strew with sand (on the inside, &c.).

Aus'ſatz, *(str.*, *pl.* Aus'ſätze) *m.* 1) a thing set or put out, *cf.* Ausſetzen; 2) *Med.* leprosy; scab, rot (of sheep); tetters (of horses); 3) *Gam.* *a)* lead (at billiards); *b)* stake; 4) *Comm.* show (of articles set out for sale); —bank, *f.* *T.* spoil-bank, a bank formed by the earth taken from an excavation.

Aus'ſätzig, *adj.* leprous, leprosed: ein A-er,

a leper, lazar: das Spital für A-e, leper-house, leprous house or hospital.

Aus'säubern, *(w.)* v. tr. 1) to cleanse, to sweep; 2) *Gard.* to prune, to lop.

Aus'säuern, *(w.)* v. *tr. Chem.* to extract the acidity from ..., to disacidify.

Aus'saufen, *(str.)* v. *(only used of animals, or of immoderate drinking)* I. *tr.* to drink out or up, to swig, swill; II. *intr.* to finish drinking grossly or greedily, to cease to drink.

Aus'saugen, *(str. & w.)* v. I. *tr.* 1) to suck (out); ein Kind — lassen, to let a child suck its fill; 2) *fig.* to exhaust; *coll.* to fleece, bleed, draw, drain; to impoverish; to weaken; bis auf den letzten Heller —, to drain to the last farthing; Einen ganz —, to suck one's marrow, to drain one dry; ein Land —, to eat up a country; II. *intr.* to cease sucking.

Aus'säugen, *(w.)* v. I. *tr.* to suckle sufficiently or the full time; II. *intr.* to leave off suckling.

Aus'sauger, *(str.)* m. 1) *Bot.* parasitical plant *(gener. pl.)*, suckers; 2) *fig.* extortioner, oppressor, blood-sucker.

Aus'saugerei', *(w.)* *f.* oppression, draining, impoverishing.

Aus'säumen, *(w.)* v. I. *tr.* to hem entirely; II. *intr.* to finish hemming.

Aus'säuseln, Aus'sausen, *(w.)* v. *intr.* to cease blowing.

Aus'schaben, *(w.)* v. *tr.* to scrape or scratch out, to erase; to hollow out by scraping.

Aus'schachteln, *(w.)* v. *tr.* 1) to scrape on the inside with shaving-grass; 2) to take out of a box, to unbox.

Aus'schaffen, v. I. *(str.)* *tr.* 1) to complete or perfect (any creation not yet perfect), to finish the creation of ...; to give the finishing touch to; 2) to fulfil, to realize; II. *(w.)* *tr.* to turn out, remove (Hinausschaffen).

Aus'schäften, *(w.)* v. *tr. Mar.* to pierce (a ship) for a given number of guns.

Aus'schäkern, *(w.)* v. *intr.* to have done playing, romping.

Aus'schalen, *(w.)* v. *tr.* 1) *Build.* to line with boards; die Decke eines Zimmers —, to lath a ceiling; 2) to take out of the shell, *cf.* Ausschälen.

Aus'schälen, *(w.)* v. *tr.* 1) to shell, peel; blanch (almonds); to decorticate; to bark, unbark (a tree, &c.); 2) *Surg. see* Auslösen, 2, *b*; 3) *vulg.* to strip, rob, fleece; 4) *Build. see* Ausschalen, 1.

Aus'schallen, *(w.)* v. *intr. see* Ausklingen.

Aus'schalmen, *(w.)* v. *tr. Forest.* to mark (out) or blaze (trees). [apparatus.

Aus'schalter, *(str.)* m. *Electr. Tel.* silent

Aus'schalung, *(w.)* *f.* lining of (with) boards, lathing; *cf.* Ausschalen, 1.

Aus'schämen, *(w.)* v. *refl.* 1) to cease to be ashamed; to be lost to all (sense of) shame; 2) sich *(Dat.)* die Augen —, to be greatly ashamed.

Aus'schänden, *(w.)* v. *tr. see* Ausschimpfen.

Aus'schank, *(str.)* m. retail of liquor.

Aus'schärfen, *(w.)* v. *tr. T.* to cut out.

Aus'scharren, *(w.)* v. I. *tr.* 1) to take or scrape out; to dig up; 2) to insult or drive off by scraping with the feet, to scrape (one) down; II. *intr.* hinten —, *vulg.* to kick, fling out.

Aus'schärten, *(w.)* v. *tr. T.* to notch, jag. — **Aus'schärte-** or **Aus'schärtungs-Eisen**, *(str.)* n. *Saddl.*, &c. jagging-iron, pinking-iron.

Aus'schatten, Aus'schattiren, *(w.)* v. *tr. Paint.* to shade. [(an insolvent debtor).

Aus'schätzen, *(w.)* v. *tr. Law.* to dispossess

Aus'schauen, *(w.)* v. *intr.* to look out.

Aus'schaufeln, *(w.)* v. *tr.* 1) to throw or scoop out with a shovel; 2) to bale (a boat).

Aus'schaukeln, *(w.)* v. I. *intr.* to leave off swinging; II. *tr.* to throw out of a swing.

Aus'schäumen, *(w.)* v. I. *intr.* 1) to cease foaming; 2) to cease raging; II. *tr.* 1) to throw up or out as froth, foam; 2) *fig.* to foam out, to throw out with rage or violence; seinen Geifer wider ... —, to vent one's bitterness or spleen upon ....

Aus'scheiden, *(str.)* v. I. *tr.* 1) *Chem.*, &c. to extract, separate, secrete, secern; *Min.* to pick out: die Erze —, to wash the ore; 2) *fig.* to separate, sift, expunge; to discard, reject; ich wünschte alles Fremdartige von der Frage ausgeschieden, I would have the question cleared of all foreign matter; II. *intr.* *(aux.* sein) to withdraw, to secede; to retire (of a partner); to go out (of a committee-member, &c.), *cf.* Abtreten; der a-de Director, the out-going director; der dritte Theil soll am Schlusse eines jeden Jahres (aus dem Amte &c.) —, the third part (of a representative body, &c.) shall go out of office at the expiration of each year; a-de Gefäße, *Anat.* secretory vessels; ausgeschieden, *p. a. Med.* secretitious.

Aus'scheidung, *(w.)* *f.* 1) separation; 2) a withdrawing; 3) *Med.* secretion.

Aus'scheinen, *(str.)* v. I. *intr.* to cease shining; II. *tr.* to outshine. [dämmen.

Aus'scheitern, *(w.)* v. *tr. Cloth. see* Aus-

Aus'scheller, *(str.)* m. *(L. u.)* bellman.

Aus'schelten, *(str.)* v. I. *tr.* to chide, scold, abuse, upbraid, reprove, rebuke, to rate; II. *intr.* to cease scolding.

Aus'schenken, *(w.)* v. *tr.* 1) to pour out, to fill out; 2) to sell (wine, &c.) by retail, *cf.* Schenken, to keep a tavern or an alehouse; 3) to give the parting cup.

Aus'scheren, v. *tr.* I. *(str.)* 1) *Cloth.* to give the last shearing to; 2) *Carp.* to taper (a beam); II. *(w.)* *Mar.* to unreeve (a rope).

Aus'scherzen, *(w.)* v. *intr.* to leave off joking. [frighten away.

Aus'scheuchen, *(w.)* v. *tr.* to scare, to

Aus'scheuern, *(w.)* v. I. *tr.* 1) to scour out; 2) *fig. see* Ausschelten; II. *intr.* to cease or finish scouring; III. *refl.* to wear out or off by friction.

Aus'schicken, *(w.)* v. *tr.* to send out or forth (mit Aufträgen, Botschaften, on messages, errands); auf Commando —, to detach.

Aus'schieben, *(str.)* v. I. *tr.* 1) to shove, push out; einen Tisch —, to draw out a table; 2) *Bak.* to draw (the bread) out of the oven; 3) *Gam.* *a)* to finish, end (a bowling-game); *b)* *provinc.* to play or bowl for (a prize, &c.); es wird ein Schwein ausgeschoben, a pig is bowled for; 4) sich *(Dat.)* den Arm —, to put out one's arm (in bowling, &c.); II. *intr.* 1) to throw or play first; 2) to cease shoving, bowling, &c.

Aus'schienen, *(w.)* v. *tr.* to furnish with splints; to splint on the inside.

Aus'schießbrett, *(str., pl.* B-er) n. *Typ.* imposing-board.

Aus'schießen, *(str.)* v. I. *tr.* 1) to shoot out; 2) to cast out, sort, reject; 3) *Mar.* to heave out, shoot, discharge (the ballast); 4) *Typ.* to impose (die Columnen, the columns); 5) einen Wald —, to destroy all the game of a forest; 6) to play for by shooting, to shoot for; 7) to improve or wear out (a gun) by shooting; 8) *T.* to smooth or polish (the paper in card-manufacturing); II. *intr.* *(aux.* sein) 1) to shoot up, to bud, to sprout; 2) *Mar.* *a)* to flare (of timbers); das — *(v. a.)* des Vorstevens, the rake of the stem; *b)* to keep pace with the sun (said of the wind).

Aus'schießer, *(str.)* m. one who shoots (out), &c.; sorter; *Paper-m.* gatherer. [stone.

Aus'schießstein, *(str.)* m. *Typ.* imposing-

Aus'schiffen, *(w.)* v. I. *tr.* to disembark, unship, land; to discharge, unload; to ship, to export; II. *intr.* *(aux.* sein) & *refl.* to set sail, leave the land or port, to put to sea;

eruptions on the skin, to be flown out; 6) to break out in flames; 7) a) to turn, to bias (of the scale); b) to turn out, to turn (to one's advantage, ruin, &c.), prove; cf. Ausfallen, 6; der Adler mit ausgeschlagener Zunge, Herald. langued eagle; der A-de or Aus'schläger, (str.) m. 1) a) beater-out, &c.; b) workman who separates the dross from the ore; 2) he who gives the first blow; 3) (of a horse) jerker.

Aus'schlagen, v. s. (str.) n. 1) the (act of) beating out; planishing, &c.; 2) see Ausschlag, 1; 3) refusal, &c.

Aus'schläger, (str.) m. see Ausschlagen, s.

Aus'schlag..., in comp. —fäustel, m. Min. pounding-hammer; —fieber, n. eruptive fever; —maschine, f. T. punching-machine; —punze, f. see —eisen; —schuppen, pl. Bot. ramenta, (Lat.) ramenta; —schuppig, adj. Bot. ramentaceous; —steiger, m. Min. inspector or overseer of the workmen who separate the dross from the metals; A-winkel, m. Astr. angle of elongation. [mud.

Aus'schlämmen, (w.) v. tr. to clear of

Aus'schlampen, Aus'schlappen, (w.) v. tr. vulg. to sip up, to lap up. [(water-pipes).

Aus'schlauchen, (w.) v. tr. to cleanse

Aus'schlecken, (w.) v. tr. to lick out greedily.

Aus'schleichen, (str.) v. I. intr. (aux. ſein) to sneak out, about, off; II. tr. to search out unceasingly.

Aus'schleifen, v. I. (str.) tr. 1) to grind out, whet out, remove or get out by grinding (notches); 2) to grind sufficiently; 3) to grind hollow; II. (w.) tr. to carry or drag out on a sledge; III. intr. to finish grinding; IV. refl. to wear out by friction.

Aus'schleimen, (w.) v. tr. to clear of slime.

Aus'schlemmen, (w.) v. I. tr. see Ausschlämmen; II. intr. to give over feasting, living a disorderly life.

Aus'schlendern, (w.) v. intr. (aux. ſein) to saunter out.

Aus'schleudern, (w.) v. tr. to fling out.

Aus'schleppen, (w.) v. tr. to drag out.

Aus'schleudern, (w.) v. I. tr. 1) to throw (out) with a sling; 2) Einem ein Auge —, to jerk or knock out a person's eye; II. intr. (aux. ſein) to swerve from the path or orbit.

Aus'schlichten, (w.) v. tr. T. to straighten, beat out, flatten by hammering; Mil. to dress.

Aus'schließegeld, (str., pl. A-gelder) n. gaoler's fee on release from prison.

Aus'schließen, (str.) v. I. tr. 1) to lock, bar, shut out; 2) to loosen, unfetter (a prisoner); 3) Typ. to justify; 4) fig. a) to exclude, debar (aus, from); to except, exempt; b) to excommunicate; II. refl. to seclude, separate one's self, secede; a-d, p. a. exclusive; (Grammar a-d) disjunctive; ausgeschlossen, excepted; das —, s. a. (str.) n. justification.

Aus'schließlich, adj. exclusive; die Gesellschaft bestand — aus Männern, the company consisted of men exclusively; with Gen.: — des Theaters, exclusive of fees.

Aus'schließung, s. I. (w.) f. 1) a locking out, &c.; 2) a) exclusion; exemption; seclusion, privation; b) excommunication; 3) A-en, Typ. justifiers; II. in comp. A-sfrist, f. Law, term of exclusion; A-sgesetz, n. law of exclusion; A-srecht, n. the right of exclusion; a-sweise, adv. by way of exclusion; exclusively.

Aus'schlingen, (str.) v. tr. 1) to disengorge; 2) to eat voraciously, to devour.

Aus'schlingern, (w.) v. intr. Mar. to cease rolling. [hailing.

[illegible] (w.) v. intr. impers. to cease

[illegible] (w.) v. I. intr. to cease [illegible] to be sob out. [gulp down.

[illegible] (w.) v. tr. to swallow or

[illegible] (w.) v. intr. to slumber [illegible] slumbering.

Aus'schlumpe(r)n, (w.) v. see Ausschlendern.

Aus'schlüpfen, (w.) v. intr. (aux. ſein) to slip (out); to creep forth (out of); aus dem Ei —, to break the shell.

Aus'schlürfen, (w.) v. tr. to sip up, sup up.

Aus'schluß, (str., pl. [I. u.] Aus'schlüſſe) m. exclusion, exemption; mit — eines Einzigen, except one; —stimme, f. exclusive vote (opp. Wahlstimme); —weise, adv. by way of exclusion. [finish piping.

Aus'schmachten, (w.) v. intr. to cease,

Aus'schmaddern, (w.) v. tr. vulg. see Ausschmieren.

Aus'schmähen, (w.) v. see Ausschelten.

Aus'schmälen, (w.) v. I. intr. to cease to chide; II. tr. to chide, check, scold, reproach.

Aus'schmatzen, (w.) v. tr. coll. to empty with smacking one's lips.

Aus'schmauchen, (w.) v. I. tr. 1) to smoke out or to the end; 2) Sport. to drive out by smoke; 3) to purify by smoke; II. intr. to cease smoking.

Aus'schmausen, (w.) v. I. tr. to consume by banqueting; II. intr. to cease banqueting.

Aus'schmeißen, (w.) v. tr. see Ausstoßen.

Aus'schmeicheln, (w.) v. intr. to cease flattering.

Aus'schmeißen, (str.) v. vulg. (for Auswerfen, Ausschlagen) I. tr. to throw, fling out; II. intr. 1) to throw first, to have the first throw; 2) to kick (of horses).

Aus'schmelzen, v. I. (str.) intr. 1) (aux. ſein) to melt out, run out by melting, dissolve; 2) to cease melting; II. (w. & [less correct] str.) tr. 1) to melt; to clear, purify by melting; Talg —, to try tallow; to fuse (ore); to get out, extract by melting.

Aus'schmettern, (w.) v. tr. to knock out with great force, violence, to dash out.

Aus'schmieden, (w.) v. tr. 1) to forge or hammer sufficiently; 2) to stretch by hammering or forging, to beat out; 3) to unfetter.

Aus'schmieren, (w.) v. tr. 1) to smear the inside of; vulg.-s.: 2) to copy in a slovenly manner; particul. to purloin (another's writings) without acknowledgment, to plagiarise, pirate; 3) to drub, beat, cudgel soundly.

Aus'schmierer, (str.) m. low copyist, plagiarist, compiler, &c. see Ausschreiber.

Aus'schmiererei', (w.) f. cont. miserable compilation, plagiarism. [Zieren.

Aus'schminken, (w.) v. tr. see Schminken,

Aus'schmollen, (w.) v. intr. to cease being sulky or sulking.

Aus'schmoren, (w.) v. I. intr. to run out in stewing; II. tr. to extract by stewing.

Aus'schmücken, (w.) v. tr. to decorate, deck out, ornament (as a room, &c.); to adorn, dress (up), trim (up), embellish. — Aus'schmücker, (str.) m. decorator. — Aus'schmückung, (w.) f. decoration, adorning, embellishment, &c.; — der Wahrheit, improvement on reality.

Aus'schmuggeln, (w.) v. I. tr. to smuggle (out) (opp. Einschmuggeln).

Aus'schnäbeln, (w.) v. I. tr. to peak (out); II. intr. to cease billing; fig. to cease kissing.

Aus'schnallen, (w.) v. tr. to unbuckle, to loose from buckles. [snap off.

Aus'schnappen, (w.) v. intr. (aux. ſein) to

Aus'schnapsen, (w.) v. I. tr. to drink out, off (drams); II. intr. to leave off drinking gin.

Aus'schnarchen, (w.) v. intr. to cease snoring.

Aus'schnattern, (w.) v. tr. see Ausplaudern.

Aus'schnauben, (w.) v. I. tr. 1) sich (Dat.) die Nase or sich (Acc.) —, to blow one's nose; 2) (Schleim, Blut) to bring up by blowing one's nose; II. or Aus'schnaufen, (cf. Verschnaufen) intr. 1) to cease to storm, to cease fuming and fretting; 2) a) to respire, recover breath; b) to snort (of horses); ein Pferd — lassen, to let a horse recover its breath, to breathe a horse.

Aus'schnäuzen, (w.) v. tr. 1) to snuff out (das Licht, the candle); 2) die Nase or sich —, see Ausschnauben.

Aus'schneide ..., in comp. —bilder, n. pl. cut-paper work; —eisen, n. pinking-iron; —meißel, m. Join. carving-gouge; —messer, n. 1) Tann. cutting(-out-)knife; 2) Farr. see Wirkmesser.

Aus'schneiden, (str.) v. I. tr. 1) a) to cut out; to carve; b) to cut into figures; to jag at the edges; Tail. (Ärmel) to cut hollow or sloping; to hollow; 2) Vet. to castrate, see Verschneiden; 3) Surg. to cut out or off, to extirpate; 4) Comm. to sell (cloth, &c.) by retail; 5) Gard. Bäume —, to lop or prune trees; 6) Bee. die Bienenstöcke —, to take part of the honey from the hives, see Zeideln; die Schafsmarke aus der Wolle —, to clack wool.

Aus'schneider, (str.) m. 1) a) cutter out, &c.; b) Vet. gelder; 2) retail dry good merchant.

Aus'schneidung, (w.) f. 1) the (act of) cutting out, &c.; 2) Surg. extirpation, excision; — der (Leibes-)Frucht, embryotomy.

Aus'schneien, (w.) v. intr. impers. to cease snowing (Paul Gerhard also pers. [I. u.]: wenn der Winter ausgeschneiet, tritt der schöne Sommer ein).

Aus'schneiteln, (w.) v. tr. to prune, to lop (trees); to cut out and fashion (bean or hop-poles). [snap off.

Aus'schnellen, (w.) v. intr. (aux. ſein) to

Aus'schnitt, s. I. (str.) m. 1) the (act of) cutting out; cut; 2) a) anything cut out, cut; b) Archit. embrasure, (window-)splay, aperture (of a window); c) scallop, slope; neck (of a barber's basin); 3) retail; 4) Geom. sector; 5) Fort. indent, crenelle (of an embattlement); II. in comp. —handel, m. retail-business or trade, retail; —händler, (coll. Ausschnitter) m. draper, mercer, retailer, retail-shopkeeper; —gewölbe, n., —handlung, f., —laden, m. mercery, retail-shop; —waaren, f. pl. retail-goods, dry goods; —waarengeschäft, n. dry good business.

Aus'schnitzeln, Aus'schnitzen, (w.) v. tr. to cut out, pink, carve. [out, to nose.

Aus'schnüffeln, (w.) v. tr. vulg. to smell

Aus'schnupfen, (w.) v. I. tr. to snuff out, to empty by taking snuff; II. intr. to give over taking snuff. [ſein.

Aus'schnuppern, (w.) v. tr. see Ausschnüf-

Aus'schnüren, (w.) v. tr. to unlace.

Aus'schöpfen, (w.) v. tr. 1) to scoop (out), bale out, to draw (water); 2) to drain (off), to empty; exhaust.

Aus'schöpf ..., in comp. —kelle, f., —löffel, m. T. ladle, scoop, scooper.

Aus'schöpfer, (str.) m. scooper.

Aus'schoren, (w.) v. tr. see Ausrichten.

Aus'schossen, (w.) v. intr. to shoot out, sprout. — Aus'schößling, (str.) m. shoot; sucker.

Aus'schoten, (w.) v. tr. to shell, husk (peas, &c.). [(a window, &c.).

Aus'schrägen, (w.) v. tr. Archit. to splay

Aus'schramm, (str.) m. Geol. partition-rock of metallic veins; extremity.

Aus'schrapen, (w.) v. I. tr. to rub out, scrape out, to erase; die Kabelgarne —, Mar. to untwist the ends of the strands; II. intr. to make (hud. to scrape) a leg, cf. Kratzfuß.

Aus'schrauben, (w.) v. tr. to screw out, (losschrauben) to unscrew.

Aus'schreiben, (str.) v. I. tr. 1) to write out: a) to copy, transcribe; to extract; eine Rechnung —, to draw out or make out an account; Wechsel —, to draw bills of exchange; b) to take by literary theft, to plagiarise, to pirate; 2) a) to finish (in writing); b) to write to the bottom of (a page); 3) to write in full or at full length; ausgeſchrieben, in words at full length: 4) a) to summon to meet (and, to issue the writs for…), to call, assemble, convoke by writing; einen Landtag —, to summon, call in the states; b) to appoint by a special decree, &c.; einen Fasttag —, to appoint a day of fasting; Steuern —, to impose, lay on taxes; to exact (contributions); Comm.-a. einen Concurs —, to issue a statute in bankruptcy; eine Concurrenz —, to advertise a vacancy; einen Preis —, to propose a prize; ausgeſchriebene Rollen, Theat. written parts; eine ausgeſchriebene Hand, a firm hand-writing, a round, running hand; II. intr. to cease writing; III. refl. fig. to write one's self out; das —, v. s. (str.) n. the (act of) writing out, &c.; proclamation, edict, decree.

Aus'ſchreiber, (str.) m. 1) one who writes out, &c.; 2) copyist, copier; 3) plagiarist.

Aus'ſchreiberei', (w.) f. 1) the (practice of) writing out, &c.; 2) plagiarism, literary piracy.

Aus'ſchreibung, (w.) f. 1) the (act of) writing out, &c.; cf. Ausſchreiben; 2) convocation, proclamation, conscription.

Aus'ſchreien, (str.) v. I. tr. 1) to cry out, proclaim; 2) to cry down, to defame; to cry (one) out, report (one) to be…; 3) ſeine Stimme —, to form the voice by much practice; II. intr. 1) to cry aloud, exclaim; to scream; 2) to cease crying; III. refl. 1) to cry one's self out, to exhaust one's self with crying; 2) to cry one's fill; 3) see I. 3.

Aus'ſchreiten, (str.) v. I. intr. (aux. ſein) 1) to step out, to stride; 2) fig. see Ausſchweifen, 2; II. tr. to measure with steps.

Aus'ſchreitung, (w.) f. 1) the (act of) measuring with steps, &c.; 2) fig. excess, transgression.

Aus'ſchrift, (w.) f. see Ausſchreiben, s.

Aus'ſchröpfen, (w.) v. tr. to draw out by the application of cupping glasses.

Aus'ſchroten, (w.) v. tr. 1) to eat out (said of animals, or of a hungry or greedy person); 2) to sell (beer) by the barrel or by barrels; 3) to pull or draw out of a cellar; 4) Turn. to rough-turn, to gouge.

Aus'ſchuhen, (w.) v. tr. to take off the shoes of (a person).

Aus'ſchulen, (w.) v. I. intr. provinc. (Switz.) for Ausſlernen; II. tr. coll. to scold (one), to blow (one) up like a schoolboy.

Aus'ſchuppen, (w.) v. tr. see Ausſchaufeln.

Aus'ſchüren, (w.) v. tr. Min. to draw (the dross or slags) out of the furnace.

Aus'ſchürfen, (w.) v. tr. Min. to uncover (the lode).

Aus'ſchurren, (w.) v. intr. see Ausgleiten.

Aus'ſchuß, (str., pl. Aus'ſchüſſe) m. 1) a) refuse, trash, outcast, garbage, offal; Comm. erſter — eines Waare, second best, first rejections; b) or —hanf, m. hemp shakings; the second sort of hemp, out-shot hemp; 2) committee, board of commissioners; der geſchäftsleitende —, committee of management; 3) Mil. militia, train-bands; 4) Sport. the side of the game through which the ball has passed out of the body; —bogen, m. 1) Paper-m. outside sheet, waste-sheet; 2) Typ. mock-sheet; —cigarren, f. pl. refuse cigars; —mitglied, n. member of a committee, board-officer; —papier, n. waste-paper (cf. —bogen); —tag, m. day appointed for the sessions of a committee; —waare, f. refuse, garbles, out-shot or defective goods; seconds and thirds; —wolle, f. lock-wool.

Aus'ſchütteln, (w.) v. tr. to shake out; to shake (Teppiche &c., carpets, &c.).

Aus'ſchütten, (w.) v. tr. 1) a) to shoot out (grain, &c.); b) to pour out, to empty; to diffuse, shed; 2) to fill up (a ditch, &c.); fig.-s. 3) to shower down (abuse, &c.); to give plentifully; 4) to open, disclose, disburden (ſein Herz gegen…, one's heart to…), to pour out one's heart or break one's mind (to one), to pour out or unbosom one's self; ſeinen Groll, ſeine Galle &c. —, to give vent to one's anger, to vent one's spleen; 5) Comm. die Concursmaſſe —, to divide a bankrupt's estate; das Kind mit dem Bade —, fig. coll. to reject the good together with the bad; ſich vor Lachen —, to split one's sides with laughing.

Aus'ſchwämmen, Aus'ſchwänken, see Ausſchwemmen, Ausſchwenken.

Aus'ſchwären, (str.) v. intr. 1) (aux. ſein) to fester out, to be ejected or come out by suppuration or ulceration; 2) to cease festering.

Aus'ſchwärmen, (w.) v. intr. 1) Bee. to finish swarming; 2) fig. to give over leading a disorderly or vicious life, to sow one's wild oats; 3) (aux. ſein) to swarm out.

Aus'ſchwatzen, (w.) v. I. tr. 1) to blab out, spread out, divulge; unbeſonnen —, to blunder out, to let out (a secret); 2) see Ausreden, II. 2; II. intr. to cease to prattle; III. refl. to talk or prattle one's self out, to have nothing more to say.

Aus'ſchwefeln, (w.) v. tr. to clear or sweeten with sulphur (as a wine cask).

Aus'ſchweif, (str.) m. 1) deviation, digression, see Abſchweifung, 2; 2) T. slope, curvature.

Aus'ſchweifen, (w.) v. I. intr. 1) to deviate; to launch out, &c. see Abſchweifen, I. 1; 2) to commit excesses, to lead a dissolute life; im Spiele —, to gamble; II. tr. to cut into a bend, to slope, to turn, to carve; to scallop; ausgeſchweift, adj. Bot. imbricated; serpentine.

Aus'ſchweifend, p. a. 1) eccentric, extravagant, exorbitant; 2) dissolute, unrestrained, wild, loose, licentious, debauched.

Aus'ſchweiffeile, (w.) f. T. file used in making ornamental slopes, curves, &c.

Aus'ſchweifling, (w.) m. (l. u.) debaucher, debauchee, libertine, rake.

Aus'ſchweifung, (w.) f. 1) curvature, curve, slope, imbrication; fig.-s. 2) (l. u.) deviation, &c. see Abſchweifung, 2, a; 3) a) extravagance, extravagation (of imagination, &c.), eccentricity, exorbitance; b) disorder, dissolution, excess; wildness; licentiousness, debauch, debauchery; zu A-en verleiten, to debauch; große A-en begehen, to indulge in great excesses.

Aus'ſchweißen, (w.) v. tr. T. 1) to purify, to stretch or hammer out (iron) by a welding-heat; 2) Sport. to bleed, let the blood out; 3) Tel. to sweat, cure by sweating (horses).

Aus'ſchwelgen, (w.) v. intr. to cease revelling, rioting.

Aus'ſchwellen, v. (str.) intr. (aux. ſein) & (w.) tr. to swell out.

Aus'ſchwemmen, (w.) v. tr. to water, wash out or away; T. to scour in a river; to wear out or away by continual washing; to rinse, cleanse, wash.

Aus'ſchwenken, (w.) v. tr. 1) to rinse (a glass, &c.); 2) Mil. see Schwenken.

Aus'ſchwingen, (str.) v. I. tr. 1) to swing; 2) to winnow, fan; 3) to swingle, scutch, rough-dress (flax); II. intr. (aux. ſein) to swing out, cease swinging, oscillating, vibrating.

Aus'ſchwirren, (w.) v. intr. 1) to cease flying, swarming; 2) to cease twanging; 3) (aux. ſein) to fly up, whiz up.

Aus'ſchwitzen, (w.) v. I. tr. 1) to exude, exudate; 2) fig. to forget (Verſchwitzen); II. intr. 1) (aux. ſein) to sweat out, perspire; 2) (aux. haben) to cease perspiring; das —, s. (str.) n. or **Aus'ſchwitzung,** (w.) f. exudation.

Aus'ſeckeln, (w.) v. tr. 1) to take out of the purse; to empty (the purse); 2) to drain

to put out of joint, dislocate by leaping; III. *refl.* to leap *or* jump one's fill.

Aus'ſpritzeln, *(w.) v. tr.* to spurt, sputter out in small drops.

Aus'ſpritzen, *(w.) v.* I. *tr.* 1) to spurt, spout, *or* sputter out, to throw out, squirt; 2) to put out (a fire) by an engine; 3) *a) Anat.* to inject (*(i. e.* to fill) the vessels of an animal body) with some coloured substance, &c.) by means of a syringe; *b) Surg.* to wash and cleanse (wounds) by injections from a syringe, to syringe; II. *intr.* (*aux.* ſein) to spout *or* sputter forth: das —, *v. s.* *(str.) n. or* **Aus'ſpritzung,** *(w.) f.* 1) a spurting out, &c., sudden spurting, discharge, ejection; 2) *Anat. & Surg.* injection.

Aus'ſproſſen, *(w.) v. intr.* (*aux.* ſein) to sprout, shoot forth; to finish sprouting.

Aus'ſprößling, *see* Sproßling.

Aus'ſpruch, *(str., pl.* **Aus'ſprüche)** *m.* 1) a saying, speech; remark, comment; declaration, sentence; 2) decision, judgment, sentence, doom: — eines Schiedsrichters, award of an arbitrator, arbitrament; — der Geſchworenen, verdict; den — thun, to give, pass, *or* pronounce sentence (über (*with Acc.*), upon); ſich (*Dat.*) den — eines Schiedsrichters gefallen laſſen, to stand to (*or* to abide by) the award.

Aus'ſprudeln, *(w.) v.* I. *tr.* to sputter forth out; II. *intr.* 1) (*aux.* ſein) to bubble up, sputter out; 2) (*aux.* haben) to cease bubbling (out).

Aus'ſprühen, *(w.) v.* I. *tr.* to emit (sparks), to cast up, vomit forth (fire, flames); II. *intr.* (*aux.* ſein) to be thrown *or* cast up: es ſprühten Funken aus, sparks of fire darted or shot up.

Aus'ſprung, *(str., pl.* **Aus'ſprünge)** *m.* 1) the (act of) leaping out, &c. *cf.* Ausſpringen; 2) projecting part, projection; A-Winkel, *m.* *Opt.* angle of reflection.

Aus'ſpucken, *(w.) v. tr.* *coll.* to spit out, *cf.* Ausſpeien.

Aus'ſpuken, *(w.) v. intr.* to cease haunting (said of spectres); in dieſem Hauſe hat es ausgeſpukt, this house is no longer haunted; es hat ausgeſpukt in ſeinem Kopfe, he has got the better of his (mad) fancies.

Aus'ſpülen, *(w.) v.* I. *tr.* 1) to clean, rinse, wash out; 2) to wash (away); 3) to undermine by frequent washing; II. *refl.* or ſich (*Dat.*) den Mund —, to rinse one's mouth.

Aus'ſpülicht, *(str.) n.* *see* Spülwaſſer.

Aus'ſpülſtock, *(str., pl.* A-ſtöcke) *m.* *T.* 1) scouring-stick; 2) washing-trough.

Aus'ſpültrog, *(str., pl.* A-tröge) *m.* *T.* fulling-trough.

Aus'ſpunden, *(w.) v. tr.* *see* Ausſchalen.

Aus'ſpüren, *(w.) v. tr.* to track (game); *fig.* to trace out, spy, track, find out, to discover; to hunt out, to ferret; to smell out. — **Aus'ſpürer,** *(str.) m.* tracer(-out); emissary, spy. — **Aus'ſpürerei',** *(w.) f.* spying.

Aus'ſtaffiren, *(w.) v. tr.* 1) *a)* to dress (out), equip; (bes. *Mil.*) to accoutre; *b) coll.* to provide *or* furnish with; 2) to decorate, to trim (up), to trick *or* fig out, to rig, dight; to garnish, border, edge, lace (clothes). — **Aus'ſtaffirer,** *(str.) m.* 1) garnisher, decorator; out-fitter, trimming-maker; 2) *Mar.* rigger. — **Aus'ſtaffirung,** *(w.) f.* 1) the (act of) dressing, &c.; 2) equipment; outfit; trimming, garnishing, edging, furbelow.

Aus'ſtäfern, *(w.) v. tr.* *Carp.* to insert crossbeams in ..., to stake (a panel).

Aus'ſtallen, *(w.) v.* I. *tr.* to take out of the stables; II. *intr.* to cease stalling.

Aus'ſtammeln, *(w.) v.* I. *tr.* to stammer out; II. *intr.* to cease stammering.

Aus'ſtampfen, *(w.) v.* I. *tr.* to stamp out, beat out; to pound; II. *intr.* to leave off stamping.

Aus'ſtand, *(str., pl.* **Aus'ſtände)** *m.* 1) the act of striking work, strike (of workmen); 2) arrears; outstanding debt.

Aus'ſtänder, *(str.) m.* a stock of bees that have outlived the winter.

Aus'ſtändig, *adj.* outstanding; in arrears.

Aus'ſtänkern, *(w.) v. tr.* *vulg.* 1) to fill with stink, to stink (out); 2) to ferret (out), to rummage, to smell out (Ausſtöbern).

Aus'ſtapeln, *(w.) v. tr.* to remove from a warehouse. [ing.

Aus'ſtarren, *(w.) v. intr.* to leave off staring.

Aus'ſtatten, *(w.) v. tr.* 1) *see* Ausliefern; 2) to endow, portion (out: mit, with ...), marry (a daughter); to establish (a son); to settle; 3) *Books.* to get up (a book); das Buch iſt ſchön ausgeſtattet, the book is beautifully got up; 4) *fig.* to supply with, to endow, gift. — **Aus'ſtatter,** *(str.) m.* endower, &c., outfitter.

Aus'ſtattung, *(w.) f.* 1) the (act of) endowing, &c., endowment; 2) dotal gift, dowry, portion, dower; endowment, dotation, establishment: ohne —, dowerless; ein (armes) Mädchen ohne —, a dowerless girl; 3) *a)* the fitting (of a shop); *b) Books.* the getting-up, get-up (of a book): die — des Werkes iſt prachtvoll, the work is got up in a most splendid style; 4) *fig.* the being endowed, gifted.

Aus'ſtäuben, *(w.) v. tr.* to beat out the dust, to dust.

Aus'ſtäubern, *(w.) v. tr.* *see* Ausſtöbern.

Aus'ſtäupen, *(w.) v. tr.* to whip, scourge publicly, to flog at the cart's tail.

Aus'ſtechen, *(str.) v. tr.* 1) to dig, prick, cut out; den Raſen im Garten —, to take off the green turf of a garden, to peel the earth with a spade; 2) to carve; to engrave; 3) *Mar.* das Ankertau —, to pay out (*or* away) the cable: ſtich mehr A. aus, veer more cable; 4) to mark out by pricking or pointing, to prick out, to pierce (lace): *fig.*-s. 5) *coll.* to crack (a bottle), to crush, discuss, to drink *or* drain out, dispatch, empty; 6) to get the better of, to overtake, distance, outdo, supplant, *coll.* to cut out, to beat hollow: Einem die Augen —, to put out one's eyes.

Aus'ſtecher, *(str.) m.* *Mar.* *see* Ausleger.

Aus'ſtechmeißel, *(str.) m.* *T.* punch.

Aus'ſtecken, *(w.) v. tr.* 1) *see* Auspflanzen; 2) to set up, to hang, or put out (Herausſtecken); 3) *a)* to mark or set out (a garden, &c.); *b) Engin.* to stake out.

Aus'ſtehen, *(irr.) v.* I. *intr.* (*aux.* ſein) 1) to stand out (Herausſtehen); 2) to stand in an open place: mit Waaren —, to keep a shop or stall; 3) to stand out, to be owing: ich habe Geld or Schulden —, I have money or debts owing me; 4) *provinc.* *a)* to change one's service (of servants); *b)* (of workmen) to strike work; II. *tr.* 1) ſeine Jahre —, *fig.* to serve one's time; ſeine Lehrjahre —, to serve (out) one's apprenticeship; 2) *fig.* to suffer, endure; to stand, bear; to go through, undergo, encounter (hardships, sufferings); a-d, *p. a.* standing out: a-de Gelder, money lent out; a-de Schulden, outstanding debts; a-de Poſt, mail due.

Aus'ſtehlen, *(str.) v.* I. *tr.* to clear by stealing, to plunder; II. *intr.* to leave off stealing. [endurable.

Aus'ſtehlich, *adj.* supportable, bearable.

Aus'ſteifen, *(w.) v. tr.* 1) to stiffen; 2) *T.* to stay, to prop; 3) to line with boards (a wall).

Aus'ſteigen, *(str.) v. intr.* (*aux.* ſein) to step out, get out, alight; to disembark.

Aus'ſteinen, *(w.) v. tr.* 1) *a)* to take out the stones; *b)* to take out the kernels of (cherries, &c.); to unkernel; 2) to line, face, mark with stones; to lay the boundary stones of (a field); 3) to take off, to remove the stones from (arable land).

Aus'ſtellen, *(w.) v. tr.* 1) *a)* to put out or

[illegible]

Aus'stopfen, *(w.)* v. *tr.* 1) to stuff (chaise, birds, &c.): ausgestopfte Vögel in Glaskästen, stuffed *or* mounted birds in glass-cases; 2) *Mech.*, &c. to plug; 3) to fill, to cram (with meat and drink).

Aus'stoppeln, *(w.)* v. *tr.* 1) to remove stubble from (a field); 2) *fig.* to scrape up, pick out, up; to botch up, &c. *cf.* Zusammenstoppeln. [ferret out.

Aus'stören, *(w.)* v. *tr.* to search, rummage,

Aus'stoß, *(str., pl.* **Aus'stöße)** *m.* 1) a thrust (outwards), a push; *Fenc.* pass; 2) first thrust.

Aus'stoßen, *(str.)* v. I. *tr.* 1) to push, thrust, throw out; to throw off, to evacuate; 2) *Join.*, &c. to shoot (eine Nut, a joint); 3) *Hatt.* to fashion *or* block (hats); 4) *Bak.* to knead for the last time; 5) *Mas.* to smooth (the rough edges); 6) *Gard.* die Beete, die Sandgänge —, to trim with a weeding-iron (the edges of) flower-beds, gravel-walks, &c.; 7) *Mar.* to set out (die Marssegel, the topsails): *fig.*-s. 8) to turn out, to expel; to oust, turn off *or* away; to eject, relegate, to ostracise; 9) to utter (*vulg.* rap *or* rip out: oaths, blasphemies); to throw *or* fling out (words of contempt), to sputter out, forth: Schimpfreden gegen Einen —, to abuse one, to call one (all manner of) names; *vulg.* to blow up: böse Reden —, to sputter foul speeches: einen Schrei —, to set up a cry, to yell, scream: einen Seufzer —, to heave a sigh: eine Silbe —, *Gramm.* to elide, cut off a syllable: Einem *or* sich *(Dat.)* die Augen —, to knock out a person's *or* one's eyes: dem Fasse den Boden —, 1. to knock out *or* stave a cask; 2. *fig.* to spoil a thing all at once, to ruin a plan by headlong rashness; II. *intr.* 1) to push *or* thrust first; *Fenc.* to make a pass; 2) *Min.* see Ausgehen.

Aus'stößer, *(str.)* m. 1) (am Mühltrichter) *Mill.* nog; 2) *Hatt.* form. [plane.

Aus'stoßhobel, *(str.)* m. *Join.* grooving-

Aus'stoßung, *(w.)* f. 1) the (act of) thrusting out, &c. *cf.* Ausstoßen; 2) expulsion, ejection; eviction (by judicial process); *Eccl.* excommunication; 3) utterance; 4) *Med.* ejection, a casting out, discharge; 5) *Gramm.* elision, suppression of a vowel at the end of a word, &c.

Aus'stottern, *(w.)* v. I. *tr.* to stammer, stutter out; II. *intr.* to cease stammering.

Aus'strahlen, *(w.)* v. I. *intr.* to beam forth, to emit rays, to radiate; II. *tr.* to send out in rays, radiate, emit (light, heat, &c.): das —, *s.* a. *(str.)* n., *or* **Aus'strahlung,** *(w.)* f. radiation (of heat); irradiation, irradiance.

Aus'strecken, *(w.)* v. *tr.* 1) to stretch, spread out *or* forth, to distend, extend; to reach, hold, put out *or* forth: sich —, to stretch, extend, *cf.* Ausdehnen; 2) *T.* to hammer out or roll (metal, *cf.* Strecken, I. 1, *b)*; das — (v. a.) [illegible] mit allseitiger Anwendung der [illegible], drawing down (*Karm.* 191), drawing out (*Francis*); sich lang —, to sprawl, to loll, to recline at full length, to spread one's [illegible] *Heraldr.* mit ausgestreckter Zunge, languid; die ausgestreckte flache Hand, spanne; [illegible] *Anat.* extensor, tensor.

Aus'strecker, *(str.)* m. *or* **Aus'streckmuskel,** *(str.)* m. *Anat.* extensor, tensor.

Aus'streichelsen, *(str.)* n. see Aufstreicheisen.

Aus'streichen, *(str.)* v. I. *tr.* 1) to cross, [illegible], *or* do out, to strike, *or* score out: to blot out, efface; to erase, expunge (a letter, word, [illegible]); der junge Gott war kaum hinaus, | so [illegible] (*Gellert*), the [illegible] had disappeared | when he [illegible] the God of Battle erased [illegible] *vulg.* scrape (out); 2) *a)* to [illegible], to smoothe (creases, folds, *or* [illegible]) to [illegible] *Hatt.* to brush up (the [illegible]); *b)* *Shoe-&c.* to stretch [illegible] back of the finishing-knife; *c)* *Gard.* to roll, beat, smooth (a walk); *d)* *Agr.* to clean, deepen (the trenches, furrows): *e)* *Mas.* (mit der Kelle) to point (die Fugen, the joints); 4) *a)* to spread: die Farbe —, *Typ.* see Auftragen; *b)* *T.* to fill up, stop: das — mit einer Leimpaste der beim Fourniren durch ausgebrochene Theilchen entstandenen Löcher, (cement-)stopping (*Karm.* 835); *c)* to paint on the inside; 5) *Metall.* see Ausfeilen; 6) *fig.* to cry up, see Herausstreichen; II. *intr.* (*aux.* sein) 1) *a)* to stroll out, to roam about; *Sport-s.* *aa)* to beat the field (for game); *bb)* to follow the track at too great a distance from the sportsman (of dogs); *cc)* das Wild — lassen, to let the game fly at a certain distance, that the shot may spread more; *b)* to run fast; 2) *Min.* see Ausgehen, 1, *b.* *cf.* Ausfeilen, II.

Aus'streichfeile, *(w.)* f. equalling file.

Aus'streifeln, *(w.)* v. *tr.* to draw off the husk, pod, skin, &c. of (beans, &c.), to unhusk, strip.

Aus'streifen, *(w.)* v. *intr.* (*aux.* sein) to make an excursion, to rove, straggle, stroll, to ramble about; to prowl about.

Aus'streiten, *(str.)* v. I. *tr.* to fight out, to terminate (a difference) by disputing it out; Einem etwas —, to argue one out of a thing; II. *intr.* to leave off contending, disputing, wrangling.

Aus'streuen, *(w.)* v. *tr.* to strew, scatter, spread, sow; *fig.* to disseminate, diffuse, disperse, circulate. — **Aus'streuung,** *(w.)* f. diffusion, dissemination, &c., circulation.

Aus'strich, *(str.)* m. 1) *a)* the (act of) blotting out, &c. *cf.* Ausstreichen; *b)* erasure, correction; 2) granular tin, stream-tin; —**feile,** *f.* *T.* see Ausstreichfeile.

Aus'striegeln, *(w.)* v. *tr.* 1) to take out with a horsecomb, to get out by currying; 2) *fig.* (Einen) *a)* to curry a person's hide, to thrash, to hide; *b)* to reprimand severely.

Aus'strömen, *(w.)* v. I. *intr.* 1) (*aux.* sein) to stream *or* pour forth, to gush, rush, *or* flow out; *Phys.* to emanate; 2) to cease streaming, flowing: — lassen, *or* II. *tr.* to pour out, send forth, emit, discharge in copious abundance: das — e, *s.* *(str.)* n. a streaming forth, &c., *cf.* Ausströmung; das — des Dampfes, the flowing out, escape *or* vent of steam.

Aus'strömung, *(w.)* f. (*cf.* Ausströmen, v. *a.)* effluence, efflux, effluxion, effusion; flush, flow; flood: — des Lichts, emission of light: **A-söffnung,** *f.* *T.* exhaustionport: **A-srohr,** *n.* *T.* blast-pipe (für den Dampf); veränderliches A-srohr (an der Locomotive), delivery-pipe, outlet-pipe.

Aus'stückeln, *(w.)* v. *tr.* to cut out in small pieces: *Mint.* to cut to standard-weight.

Aus'stückelungsmaschine, *(w.)* f. *Mint.* blank-cutting machine.

Aus'studiren, *(w.)* v. I. *tr.* to study, meditate; to find out by study; to study thoroughly; II. *intr.* to finish one's studies: ausstudirt, *p. a.* thorough-bred.

Aus'stufen, *(w.)* v. *tr.* to cut into steps.

Aus'stürmen, *(w.)* v. *intr.* 1) (*aux.* sein) to storm out, to rage on; 2) to cease raging: es hat ausgestürmt, the storm is over *or* past.

Aus'sturz, *(str., pl.* **Aus'stürze)** *m.* the rushing out, rush.

Aus'stürzen, *(w.)* v. I. *tr.* 1) to pour out; 2) to swallow; to toss off, to gulp down, to empty; II. *refl.* sich *(Dat.)* den Arm —, to dislocate one's arm by falling.

Aus'stutzen, *(w.)* v. *tr.* see Ausstaffiren.

Aus'stützen, *(w.)* v. *tr.* to stay, prop on the inside, to set out with props.

Aus'suchen, *(w.)* v. *tr.* 1) to select, cull, pick out; to elect, fix upon, choose; to single (out), to sort, assort; 2) to search thoroughly: ausgesucht, *p. a.* picked; II. *intr.* to cease searching: das —, *s. a.* *(str.)* n. selection, &c.: das — von ... haben, to have picking choice of ....

Aus'sühnen, *(w.)* v. *tr.* see Aussöhnen.

Aus'summen, *(w.)* v. *intr.* 1) (*aux.* haben) to leave off humming *or* swarming; 2) (*aux.* sein) to fly, buzz out.

Aus'süßen, *(w.)* v. *tr.* *Chem.*, &c. to edulcorate, *cf.* Absüßen.

Aust, *(str.)* m. *provinc.* (*abbr. from* August, 2) 1) *or* *(w.)* f. (*N. G.*; *S. G.*: Augst) harvest-time; 2) ephemera (Eintagsfliege).

Aus'tafeln, *(w.)* v. *intr.* ausgetafelt haben, to have done dining, banqueting.

Aus'täfeln, *(w.)* v. *tr.* to wainscot.

Aus'tagen, *(w.)* v. *intr.* es hat ausgetagt, the day has waned, the sun has set.

Aus'tändeln, *(w.)* v. *intr.* to leave off toying, trifling.

Aus'tanzen, *(w.)* v. I. *tr.* to dance out, to finish (a dance); II. *intr.* to leave off dancing.

Aus'tapeziren, *(w.)* v. *tr.* to hang (a room) with tapestry: mit Papier —, to paper.

Aus'tappen, *(w.)* v. *tr.* to find out by groping, to grope out. [cover by the touch.

Aus'tasten, *(w.)* v. *tr.* to examine *or* dis-

Aus'tauchen, *(w.)* v. *intr.* 1) (*aux.* sein) to come up after diving; 2) *Phys.* to emerge, appear suddenly; 3) (*aux.* haben) to cease diving.

Aus'taumeln, *(w.)* v. *intr.* 1) (*aux.* sein) to stagger out; 2) (*aux.* haben) to cease staggering.

Aus'tausch, *(str.)* m. exchange; interchange (*also fig.*: of ideas, &c.), barter, commerce. — **Aus'tauschbar,** I. *adj.* exchangeable, interchangeable; II. **A-keit,** *(w.)* f. interchangeableness, exchangeability. — **Aus'tauschen,** *(w.)* v. *tr.* 1) *lit.* & *fig.* to exchange (für, for), to interchange; 2) to barter, to truck, *vulg.* to swap; unter einander —, to reciprocate. — **Aus'tauschung,** *(w.)* f. (the act of) exchanging, &c., *Mec.*, &c. change, interchange.

Aus'teppichen, *(w.)* v. *tr.* to lay out, to spread with carpets, to carpet.

Aust'er, *s.* I. *(w.)* f. *Conch.* oyster (*Ostrea edulis* L.): marinirte A-n, pickled oysters; A-n fangen, to dredge for oysters; II. *in comp.* —**bank,** *f.*, —**lager,** *n.* oyster-bed, bed of oysters, oyster-bank; —**baum,** *m.* *Bot.* common *or* black mangrove, mangle (Mangelbaum); —**brecher,** *m.* oyster-knife; **A-(n)fänger, A-(n)fischer,** *m.* 1) dredger, dredgeman; 2) *or* **A-ndieb, A-nmann,** —**vogel,** *m.* *Ornith.* tirma, sea-pie, oyster-catcher (*Haematopus ostralegus* L.); —**fang,** *m.*, **A-(n)fischerei,** *f.* 1) place where oysters are taken; 2) dredging (for oysters); **A-(n)grus,** *m.* bed of ostracites; **A-(n)händler, A-(n)krämer,** *m.* dealer in oysters; **A-(n)mann,** *m.* oysterman; **A-(n)laich,** *m.* spat; **A-(n)nessel,** *f.* see Seeblume, Seenessel; —**netz,** *n.* dredge; **A-(n)park,** *m.* bed *or* breeding-place of oysters; **A-(n)schale,** *f.* oyster-shell; versteinerte —schalen, *Petr.* ostracites; **A-nschüssel,** *f.* oyster dish; —**schwamm,** *Bot.* edible fungus on certain trees (*Agaricus pleurotus*); —**stein,** *m.* *Petr.* ostracite; —**vogel,** *m.* see —fänger.

Aus'thauen, *(w.)* v. *intr.* 1) (*aux.* sein) to thaw out; 2) (*aux.* haben) to cease thawing.

Aus'theeren [*pr.* —'têren], *(w.)* v. *tr.* to tar the inside of.

Aus'theilen, *(w.)* v. *tr.* 1) to distribute; to spend, dispense, bestow, deal out; to serve, portion, carve, give out; to issue, give out (orders); to share, part, divide; 2) *a)* *Mas.* to lay on; *b)* *Carp.* to saw out; das Abendmahl —, to administer the sacrament; **a-d,** *p. a.* distributive.

Aus'theilung, *(w.)* f. distribution, &c.; administration; **A-swelle,** *f.* *Mech.* distribution-shaft.

Aus'thun, *(str.)* v. *tr.* 1) to put off or out; Geld auf Zinsen —, to put out money at interest; 2) to pull or take off (clothes, &c.); sich —, to undress (one's self); 3) see Ausmachen; 4) to erase, to blot out; *Comm.* (einen begablten Schuldposten im Buche —) to discharge, strike, or score out; ein Kind auf die Ziehe (or Kost) —, to put out a child to nurse (or wet-nurse).

Aus'thüren, *(w.)* v. *tr.* & *intr.* *T.* to take (shingle-boards) out of (the wings of a windmill); to remove the shingles (*opp.* Einthüren).

Aus'tiefen, *(w.)* v. *tr.* 1) to deepen, to dig or make deeper; to sink; 2) *a)* to emboss; to chase; to carve; *b)* to beat out, to hollow by beating; *c)* *Turn.* see Ausdrechen; 3) to fathom, to measure by sounding; ausgetieft, *p. a.* concave.

Aus'tiefungsmaschine, *(w.)* *f.* see Baggermaschine.

Aus'tilgen, *(w.)* v. *tr.* 1) to extirpate, destroy, to exterminate; to efface, extinguish, to obliterate; 2) to expiate (a crime, &c.); 3) to discharge, pay off.

Aus'tilgung, *(w.)* *f.* 1) extirpation, destruction, extermination, obliteration; 2) expiation (of a crime, &c.).

Aus'toben, *(w.)* v. I. *intr.* to cease, leave off raging; to spend one's rage; to become calm, to abate; er hat ausgetobt, his passion is over, his rage is spent; II. *tr.* to vent in a rage, to give vent to: seinen Groll an Einem —, to wreak one's anger on one.

Aus'tollen, *(w.)* v. *intr.* to leave off being wild, disorderly, or riotous; er hat ausgetollt, he has sown his wild oats.

Aus'tönen, *(w.)* v. *intr.* to cease, die away (of sound), *cf.* Ausklingen.

Aus'tonnen, *(w.)* v. *tr.* *Min.* to line with boards.

Aus'torkeln, *(w.)* v. I. *tr.* see Auskeltern, Auspressen; II. *intr.* to cease reeling.

Aus'toßen, *(w.)* v. *tr.* see Austoben.

Aus'traben, *(w.)* v. *intr.* 1) *(aux.* sein) to trot out; ein Pferd — lassen, to let a horse trot out; 2) *(aux.* haben) to cease trotting.

Aus'trag, *(str., pl.* Aus'träge) m. 1) the carrying out, see Austragen; 2) *a)* issue; end, decision; *b)* arbitration; accommodation; settlement (of a dispute, of certain conditions, &c., *cf.* Ausgedinge); vor — der Sache, whilst the cause is pending; bis zu — der Sache, till the matter is decided; A-sgericht, see Austrägalgericht.

Austrägal'..., in *comp.* *Germ. Law,* —gericht, n., —instanz, f. *(formerly)* a court deciding doubtful matters between the sovereigns of the German confederation (anciently between noblemen in general).

Aus'tragen, *(str.)* v. I. *tr.* 1) *a)* to carry out; sich — lassen, to go out in a chair; *b)* to deliver, distribute (letters); 2) to wear out; to wear the proper time; to carry (the fruit in the womb) the full time; ein ausgetragenes Kind, a child born at the right time, a full-borne child; ein nicht ausgetragenes Kind, a child born before its time; *fig.-c.* 3) *a)* to amount to ...; *b)* to matter, see Ausmachen, 4 & 6; 4) *(l. u.)* to arbitrate, decide, to determine; 5) *a)* to blab, report; *b)* to defame, see Afterreden; II. *intr.* to cease, leave off bearing (said of fruit-trees); ein Baum, der ausgetragen hat, a tree past bearing.

Aus'träger, *(str.)* m. 1) (letter) carrier; porter; distributer; 2) *conf.* tell-tale, talebearer; A-in, *(w.)* *f.* 1) a woman carrying newspapers, &c. out; 2) a prattling woman, tell-tale, blab.

Aus'trägerei', *(w.)* *f.* (the practice of) blabbing, tale-telling.

Aus'tragestempel, *(str.)* m. *T.* the third iron pestle of a stamping-mill (*Buil.*).

Aus'trägler, *(str.)* m. *provinc.* for Ausdingner, *cf.* Bedarung, 2, b.

Aus'träglich, *adj.* yielding largely, &c. (Einträglich).

Aus'trägung, *(w.)* *f.* the (act of) carrying out, &c.; delivery (of letters, &c.).

Austra'lien, Australa'sien, n. *Geogr.* Australia, Polynesia, Australasia.

Austra'lisch, *adj.*, **Austra'lier,** *(str.)* m., **Austra'lierin,** *(w.)* *f.* Australian.

Aus'trällern, *(w.)* v. *intr.* to finish humming a tune (*cf.* Austrillern).

* **Austral'...,** *(Lat.)* in *comp.* —land, n. *Min.* Sydney-earth; —schein, m. see Südlicht.

Aus'trampeln, *(w.)* v. *tr.* to stamp out (with the feet).

Aus'tränken, *(w.)* v. *tr.* to empty by watering.

Aus'trauern, *(w.)* v. *intr.* to mourn the due time; to cease mourning; to leave off mourning, to go out of mourning (and out of black).

Aus'träufeln *(dimin. of* Austraufen), *(w.)* v. *intr.* 1) *(aux.* sein) to trickle out in small drops; 2) *(aux.* haben) to cease trickling.

Aus'traufen, *(w.)* v. *intr.* to drop out or down, *cf.* Austräufeln.

Aus'träumen, *(w.)* v. *intr.* 1) to dream out or to the end; 2) to cease dreaming.

Aus'treibbar, *adj.* expellable.

Aus'treibeisen, *(str.)* n. *T.* puncheon; clearing-iron.

Aus'treiben, *(str.)* v. I. *tr.* 1) to drive out (cattle, &c.); 2) to expel, cast out, eject; Teufel —, to cast (out) devils; to exorcise; er hat ihm die Bosheit mit dem Stocke ausgetrieben, he has whipped him out of his malice; Einem den Dünkel —, to take the conceit out of one; den Schweiß —, to cause sweating; 3) *T.* to emboss, chase, carve; II. *intr.* *Found.* to cease smelting; a-d, *p. a.* expulsive. — **Aus'treibung,** *(w.)* *f.* the (act of) driving out, &c. expulsion; *Min.* extraction (of sulphur, &c.).

Aus'trennen, *(w.)* v. *tr.* to rip up, to unsew; das Futter —, to take out the lining.

Aus'treten, *(str.)* v. I. *intr.* *(aux.* sein) 1) to step out, come forth; 2) to leave, quit (a society); to retire (from service, from office, &c.), to resign; 3) *a)* to swell (out); die Mauer tritt aus, the wall bellies or bulges; *b)* to swell; to overflow, to break out of the banks; die Flüsse sind ausgetreten, the rivers have overflowed their banks, the floods are out; *c)* *Med.* to extravasate; 4) to abscond, run off, escape; der Ausgetretene, a fugitive (from the law), outlaw; II. *tr.* 1) to tread out; Trauben —, to tread grapes; 2) to widen, to stretch, to make larger by use (shoes, boots, &c.), to make hollow, to wear (by treading); *fig.-c.* die Kinderschuhe ausgetreten haben, to be past the spoon; Einem die Schuhe —, to cut one out (*cf.* Ausstechen, 6); III. v. *n.* *(str.)* n., or **Aus'tretung,** *(w.)* *f.* 1) the treading out, &c.; 2) see Austritt, 1 & 2; 3) *a)* overflow, inundation; *b)* *Med.* extravasation (of blood).

Aus'trieb, *(str.)* m. 1) see Austreibung; 2) young shoots, sprouts.

Aus'triefen, *(str. & w.)* v. *intr.* *(aux.* sein) to trickle or run out.

Aus'trillern, *(w.)* v. *intr.* to cease trilling, shaking, quavering.

Aus'trinken, *(str.)* v. I. *tr.* to drink off, drink out, drink up; to finish (a bottle, &c.); II. *intr.* to leave off drinking.

Aus'tritt, *(str.)* m. 1) *a)* the (act of) stepping out, &c. *cf.* Austreten; *b)* step; 2) *a)* a leaving, quitting, resigning; retirement (from the cabinet, *Comm.* of a partner); der — aus diesem Leben, departure, demise, death; *b)* a running away; absconding (of a debtor); *c)* secession; 3) *Archit.* step, stepping-place, stair-head; vestibule, fore-hall, porch; balcony; terrace; 4) *Astr.* emersion; A-stagen,

[illegible]schaking: 2) see Ausprügeln; II. intr. (aux. sein) to waddle out.

Aus'wägen, (w. & str. [cf. Auswiegen]) v. tr. 1) to weigh; to weigh out; 2) to sell by weight or retail. [forth.

Aus'wagen, (w.) v. refl. to venture out or

Aus'wahl, (w.) f. 1) the (act of) choosing: choice, selection; 2) a) assortment; b) elite, flower, the best; eine — treffen, to make a choice, to pick out; ohne —, indiscriminately.

Aus'wählen, (w.) v. tr. to choose (out), select, cull, to pick or single out, to seek or sort out; to fix on. cf. Auserwählen; ausgewählt, choice, exquisite, select.

Aus'walken, (w.) v. tr. 1) to remove (spots, &c.) by fulling; 2) to full thoroughly or sufficiently; 3) fig. to drub, thrash, lace, leather.

Aus'wallen, (w.) v. intr. (aux. sein) to set forth on a pilgrimage.

Aus'walten, (w.) v. intr. to cease ruling.

Aus'walzen, (w.) v. I. tr. to roll (out) (metals); ausgewalztes Tafelblei, milled sheet-lead; II. intr. to cease waltzing.

Aus'wälzen, (w.) v. tr. to roll out.

Aus'wandeln, (w.) v. intr. to go, walk out.

Aus'wanderer, (str.) m. emigrant.

Aus'wandern, (w.) v. I. intr. (aux. sein) 1) to set out, depart; 2) to emigrate; der Ausgewanderte, emigrant; 3) (aux. haben) to cease wandering, to finish one's travels; II. tr. to travel over or through (countries).

Aus'wanderung, (w.) f. emigration.

Aus'wanken, (w.) v. intr. (aux. sein) to walk out tottering.

Aus'wannen, (w.) v. tr. to winnow, to cleanse by winnowing.

Aus'wärmen, (w.) v. tr. to warm thoroughly; Metall. to anneal. — Aus'wärmofen, m. Glass-m. leer, annealing-furnace.

Aus'warten, (w.) v. tr. to wait to the end.

Aus'wärtig, adj. foreign; outward; abroad: das a-e Amt, the foreign office; Minister der a-en Angelegenheiten, minister of foreign affairs, foreign secretary; ein a-er Krieg, a foreign war; a-e Staatspapiere, foreign funds; ein a-er Freund, a friend, a correspondent abroad; a-es Erkenntniß, judgment (legal opinion) of a foreign (outward) court of justice (or judicial faculty).

Aus'wärts, adv. outwards; from without; abroad: — (außer dem Hause) essen, schlafen, to dine out, to sleep out; eine Mittheilung von —, a communication from abroad; — gekehrt, Herald. addorsed; — setzen, to turn out: Anat.-s. das — stehende Knie, der — stehende Knöchel, out-knee, out-ankle; das —drehen der Hand, supination; —drehende Muskeln der Hand, supinators; —zieher, m. abductor.

Aus'waschen, (str.) v. I. tr. 1) to wash, wash out or off, &c. see Ausspülen, 1; 2) a) to cleanse by washing, to bathe (a wound); b) Chem. to edulcorate (a precipitate); II. intr. to cease washing; III. refl. to lose the colour by washing; das —, v. n. (str.) n. the washing, &c.; Chem. & Med. lotion, ablution.

Aus'wässern, (w.) v. tr. to water; soak; to freshen, to free from salt by soaking in water; das —, v. n. (str.) n., or Aus'wässerung, (w.) f. the (act of) watering, &c.; Aus'[illegible], f. Mar. water-line, load-water-line.

Aus'wechsel, (str.) m. change, exchange; —blatt, n. Typ. cancel.

Aus'wechseln, (w.) v. tr. 1) to exchange, to change; 2) die Zimmerung —, Min. to renew the [illegible], to change or repair the [illegible].

Aus'wechselung, (w.) f. 1) exchange, [illegible]; 2) Min. renewing of old timber-[illegible] Wechsel, Wechselbalken) [illegible] trimmer (joist); A-svertrag, [illegible] for the exchange of prisoners.

Aus'wedeln, (w.) v. tr. to fan, put out by fanning.

Aus'weg, (str.) m. 1) outlet, way out, outgoing, issue, vent; opening; 2) fig. a) (way of) escape, way, expedient, means; b) shift, evasion, subterfuge.

Aus'wehen, (w.) v. I. tr. & intr. 1) to blow out (the candle, &c.); 2) a) to raise into the air; to carry, waft away (of the wind); b) to fill with air, to swell; II. intr. 1) to cease blowing; 2) to flutter, to fly out, turn in the wind; ein ausgewehtes Segel, a sail blown from the bolt-rope.

Aus'weich(e)bahn, f. coll. Aus'weiche, Wei'che, (w.) f. Railw., &c. turn-out track, turn-out, siding, cf. Ausweichplatz.

Aus'weichen, (w.) v. I. tr. 1) to soak thoroughly; 2) to get out, or to remove by soaking and softening; II. intr. (aux. sein) to fall out from being soaked.

Aus'weichen, (str.) v. intr. (gener. with Dat. or vor [& Dat.]) 1) to give way, step aside, turn out or aside, to make way for, &c. see Ausbiegen, intr. 1; 2) Mus. to modulate, to change or pass from one key to another; 3) fig. to evade, shun, avoid; to elude; to flinch from; coll. to shirk, to fight shy of; listig —, to shuffle off, to shift off; einem Stoß —, Fenc. to break measure; to parry (ward off) a thrust; a-d, p. a. evasive (answers).

Aus'weich(e)..., in comp. Railw.-s. —platz, m. siding or passing place; shunt, turn-out (track), siding; —schiene, f. siding rail, turn-out rail, crossing rail; —zunge, f. switch.

Aus'weichung, (w.) f. 1) the (act of) giving way, &c.; 2) Surg. & Astr. elongation; 3) Phys. see Abweichung; 4) Mus. modulation, a change or passing from one key to another.

Aus'weiden, (w.) v. tr. 1) eine Wiese —, to graze a meadow, to drive cattle on a meadow for grazing; 2) to gut, bowel, embowel, draw, eviscerate, unbowel; to unease (a hart), to undo (a boar), to break up (a deer).

Aus'weinen, (w.) v. I. intr. to cease weeping; II. tr. to weep out, to utter weeping; seinen Schmerz —, to alleviate one's pains (grief) with weeping; III. refl. to weep one's self out; sich (Dat.) die Augen —, to cry one's eyes out.

Aus'weis, (str.) m. statement; tenor, purport, contents, substance; argument; proof; voucher; cf. Nachweis & Beweis; nach — der Gesetze, in conformity with the law(s); der jährliche —, the annual returns (of a bank, &c.).

Aus'weisen, (str.) v. I. tr. 1) to order out (of a place, &c.), to order to quit, to expel; to banish, exile; to turn out; 2) fig. to show; to prove; to decide; die That weiset es aus, the very deed speaks it, proves it; wie es die Gesetze —, according to the tenor of the laws; II. refl. to prove; to turn out; sich vor Einem —, to prove one's claim, to legitimize one's self; das wird sich —, we shall see, the end will show or discover it, time will manifest.

Aus'weisung, (w.) f. 1) the (act of) turning out; banishment, expulsion; removal; A-sbefehl, m. order of removal; 2) see Ausweis.

Aus'weißen, (w.) v. tr. to whiten, whitewash on the inside.

Aus'weiten, (w.) v. tr. to widen, enlarge; to stretch (shoes, &c.).

Aus'weit..., in comp. —eisen, n. Metal. rimer; —holz, n. Glov. stretching-stick.

Aus'wellen, (w.) v. intr. see Ausquellen.

Aus'wellern, (w.) v. tr. see Ausstaken.

Aus'wendig, I. adj. outer, outward; outside; II. adv. fig. —, without book; — lernen, to learn by heart, to commit to memory; — können, wissen &c., to have or know by heart.

Aus'werben, (str.) v. intr. to leave off courting, enlisting, suing.

Aus'werden, (irr.) v. intr. (aux. sein) to end, see Aus.

Aus'werfen, (str.) v. I. tr. 1) a) to throw, cast or fling out; Geld unter das Volk —, to throw or scatter money amongst the people; Mar.-s. to throw overboard, to heave out; Güter —, to cast goods (overboard); den Anker —, to cast or drop anchor, see Ankern; ein Boot —, to hoist out a boat; das Loth —, to heave the lead, to sound; die Boje —, to stream the buoy; die Angel — nach ..., to strike for ...; b) to knock out by throwing a stone or stones; c) to cast out, throw up, expectorate, bring up (flegm, &c.), spit; durch den Stuhlgang —, Med. to egest; d) to vomit (fire), disgorge (streams of lava, &c.); 2) a) to geld (a horse); to gut (a hare); b) to clear of mud (a ditch, &c.); 3) a) to reject (bad money, &c.); b) to eject, expel; 4) Comm., &c. eine Summe —, to draw out, to put aside or set apart a sum; eine Rechnung —, to draw out an account; eine Geldsorte in einer andern —, to reduce one denomination of coin into another (as dollars into pounds sterling, &c.); einen Posten —, a) to put (bring) to account; b) (in die Hauptcolonne bringen) to carry out; der nicht ausgeworfene Posten, deferred entry; Einem ein Gehalt (Jahrgehalt) —, to fix, appoint one a salary; to settle an annuity on one; II. intr. 1) a) to throw out, outward; b) Man. to step; c) Horol. to oscillate or move regularly; 2) Gam., &c. to throw first, to begin; wer wirft aus? who has the first throw (at dice, &c.)? das —, v. n. (str.) n. 1) cast (of the lead), &c.; 2) Med.-s. a) a (sudden) discharge, ejection; b) expectoration; c) eruption (of the skin).

Aus'werk, (str.) n. Salt-w. see Gradirhaus.

Aus'wettern, (w.) v. intr. to cease, to leave off thundering, storming.

Aus'wetzen, (w.) v. tr. 1) a) to whet off or out; b) to hollow or excavate by whetting; 2) to wipe off, away, or out, obliterate (a blot, stain, or spot); to make amends for, repair (a fault); einen Schimpf —, to revenge an affront.

Aus'wichsen, (w.) v. tr. 1) to line with wax on the inside; 2) fig. to thrash soundly.

Aus'wickeln, (w.) v. I. tr. 1) to unfold, unwrap, disentangle, extricate; 2) to unswaddle, unswathe (a child); II. refl. fig. sich —, to extricate one's self from ..., to get out of ....

Aus'wiegen, (str.) v. tr. coll. for Auswägen.

Aus'wimmern, (w.) v. I. intr. to cease moaning, whimpering; II. tr. to moan out.

Aus'windeln, (w.) v. tr. 1) to unswathe; 2) see Ausstaken.

Aus'winden, (str.) v. I. tr. 1) to wring out (Ausringen); 2) to draw out with a windlass; 3) (Einem etwas) to wring or wrest from one; II. refl. fig. see Auswickeln, 2. [wimmern.

Aus'winseln, (w.) v. tr. & intr. see Aus-

Aus'wintern, (w.) v. I. tr. to winter; II. intr. 1) (aux. sein) to perish in winter; 2) to pass the winter (at a place); 3) es hat ausgewintert, the winter is over; das —, v. n. (str.) n. or Aus'winterung, (w.) f. 1) the (act of) wintering, &c.; 2) the passing of a winter without injuries from frost, &c. [(trees).

Aus'wipfeln, (w.) v. tr. to top, poll, lop

Aus'wippen, (w.) v. tr. to cast (whip) out of the scales in weighing (gold-coins, &c.), cf. Wippen.

Aus'wirken, (w.) v. I. tr. 1) a) to work out; b) T. to take out (the salt from the pans); 2) see Ausweiden; 3) fig. to effect, procure, get, obtain (bei Einem, from one); den Huf eines Pferdes —, Farr. to pare a horse's hoof; den Teig —, Bak. to knead the dough; einen Verhaftsbefehl gegen Jemand —, to have a warrant served upon one; einen Pardon —, to sue out a pardon; II. intr. 1) to work, operate sufficiently; 2) to cease working (in general) or weaving, working at the loom.

Aus'wirren, (w.) v. tr. to untwist, unravel, to disentangle, to do out; T. to sort (wool).

Aus'wischen, (w.) v. tr. 1) a) to wipe out: Mil. to sponge (the guns); to blot out, to efface; 2) coll. (Einem etwas) to punish one, to take revenge upon by giving by-wipes.

Aus'wittern, (w.) v. I. intr. (aux. sein) 1) to get decomposed by exposure to the air; 2) to season (as timber): — lassen, see II. 1, b; 3) to expose to the (action of the) air; 4) to cease thundering and lightening: II. tr. 1) a) to decompose, to air; to weather; b) to season (timber); 2) Sport. & fig. to smell, hunt out, to get scent of; III. refl. to swarm round the hive (of bees). — **Aus'witterung,** (w.) f. decomposition, &c.: A-en, pl. Min. vapors promoting decomposition.

Aus'witzeln, (w.) v. intr. to leave off playing the wit, punning, bantering.

Aus'witzen, (w.) v. tr. to make witty, cunning: ein ausgewitzter Bursche, a crafty, cunning fellow or knave.

Aus'wölben, (w.) v. tr. Archit. to vault, arch on the inside. — **Aus'wölbung,** (w.) f. vault, arch-roof; vaulting.

Aus'wölken, (w.) v. I. tr. Paint. to cloud; II. refl. to clear up. [out, &c.

Aus'wollen, (irr.) v. intr. to wish (to go)

Aus'wuchern, (w.) v. intr. 1) to spread out luxuriantly (of plants); 2) to leave off practising usury.

Aus'wuchs [pr. —'wŭx], (str., pl. Aus'wüchse) m. 1) the (act of) sprouting, growth, efflorescence; 2) Med., &c. a growing-out (of the shoulders, &c.), excrescence; protuberance, exuberance; wart; tubercle; — der Knochen, exostosis; (Buckel) hunch, humpback; (of trees, &c.) gnarl, knob.

Aus'wühlen, (w.) v. tr. to grub up; to root; to undermine. [dering.

Aus'wundern, (w.) v. refl. to cease won-

Aus'wünschen, (w.) v. refl. to exhaust one's wishes, to cease to wish (for).

Aus'wurf, (str., pl. Aus'würfe) m. 1) a) the (act of) throwing out, &c. cf. Auswerfen; b) eruption (of a volcano); 2) Gam. first throw, cast; 3) Mech. heaving, oscillation, vibration; 4) Med., &c. a) the (act of) casting out, throwing up, spitting, &c., expectoration: haben Sie einen leichten —? do you expectorate easily? b) spittle, saliva ejected; c) excretion; d) egestion, excrement, dung; 5) Law, flotsam, jetsam; 6) Print. waste-paper: —bogen, m. waste-sheet; 7) fig. outcast; refuse, trash, dregs, scum (of the people).

Aus'würfeln, (w.) v. I. intr. to cease playing with dice; II. tr. to raffle; play for (a thing) with dice.

Aus'würfling, (str.) m. 1) anything thrown out, &c. cf. Auswerfen; eruptive product, rock, &c.; 2) one expelled, outcast.

Aus'wurf..., in comp. —hafen, m. Leak-om. cramp-iron; —münzen, pl. refuse of coin; verschiedene —seide, f. ardass silk, ardasses; —wolle, f. outshot-wool.

Aus'wurzeln, (w.) v. tr. to root out, to stub or grub out, to uproot.

Aus'würzen, (w.) v. intr. see Austaben.

Aus'zacken (**Aus'zackern**), (w.) v. tr. 1) to indent, notch, jag, scallop: Herald. to engrail; aus'gezackt, p. a. dented, jagged, notched, denticulate(d), laciniate(d); vandyked (as lawn, &c.); das Ausgezackte, see Auszackung, 2.

Aus'zackeisen, (str.) n. Saddl., &c. jagging-iron; pinking-iron.

Aus'zackung, (w.) f. 1) indentation; 2) indenture, denticulation, jaggedness; 3) Sport. advancer (of a buck's horn).

Aus'zahlen, (w.) v. tr. 1) to pay down (out, away, or over, Einem, to ...), to tense; 2) to pay off; seine Gläubiger vollständig —, to satisfy one's creditors in full; übel ausgezahlt werden, to be badly served; iron. ich habe ihn ausgezahlt! I paid him out or off for it.

Aus'zählen, (w.) v. I. tr. 1) to count out; enumerate; 2) to sell by the number (by retail); einen Holzbestand —, Forest. to tax, appraise the standing trees singly; II. intr. to count to the end; to cease counting, telling.

Aus'zahler, (str.) m. paymaster, cashier, disburser. [pay-sheet.

Aus'zahlung, (w.) f. payment: A-sliste, f.

Aus'zahnen, (w.) v. I. intr. to cease cutting teeth; II. tr. 1) to tooth (a comb); 2) or **Aus'zähneln, Aus'zähnen,** (w.) v. tr. to indent, jag, scotch; to notch, emarginate.

Aus'zanken, (w.) v. I. tr. to scold, rate; II. intr. to leave off scolding.

Aus'zapfen, (w.) v. tr. 1) to draw, tap out; 2) to sell by retail from the barrel (liquor).

Aus'zappeln, (w.) v. intr. to cease kicking, writhing, sprawling.

Aus'zaudern, (w.) v. intr. to cease loitering or hesitating.

Aus'zäunen, (w.) v. tr. to hedge, furnish with a hedge; to fence in.

Aus'zausen, (w.) v. tr. to pull, tear, pluck out; to pull about, to tousle.

Aus'zechen, (w.) v. I. intr. to finish carousing; II. tr. to empty by drinking; to quaff off. [2) to tithe (a field).

Aus'zehnten, (w.) v. tr. 1) to decimate;

Aus'zehren, (w.) v. I. tr. lit. & fig. to consume, emaciate, exhaust, drain; II. intr. (aux. sein) & refl. to pine away, languish, waste, to become emaciated, &c.: a-d, p. a. consumptive. [sumption; decline, phthisis.

Aus'zehrung, (w.) f. particul. Med. con-

Aus'zeichnen, (w.) v. I. tr. 1) to mark out, note out, discriminate; to blaze (trees): Waaren —, Comm. to mark out, ticket, label (goods); die Prime im Manuscripte —, Typ. to mark out the prime; 2) to distinguish, signalise; to show respect to ...; 3) to finish a draught or design; II. refl. 1) to be (rendered) conspicuous; 2) fig. to distinguish one's self or signalise one's self, to excel.

Aus'zeichnung, (w.) f. 1) a) the marking out, &c.; b) mark; 2) distinction, respect; eminence; 3) Typ. direction-word, catch-word; a-swerth, a-swürdig, adj. worthy of distinction.

Aus'zeideln, (w.) v. tr. see Zeideln.

Aus'zeilen, (w.) v. tr. to plant (vines) in a straight line and at a proper distance from each other.

Aus'zeitigen, (w.) v. tr. to mature fully.

Au'ßen, I. adv. out, without; out of doors; abroad; von — her, from without; from (the) outside; von — gleißen, to make a fine show, to have a fine outside; — bleiben, 1) to stay out; 2) see Ausbleiben; was — ist, outward, exterior; II. in comp. —böschung, f. Fort. counterscarp; —brett, n. Carp. slab; —deich, m. 1) outward dam; outer embankment; 2) or —deichsland, n. alluvial land on the outside of an embankment or dike; —ding, n. any thing that is outside or on the surface, external object; —ende, n. extremity; —fläche, f. surface, (—seite einer Mauer, eines Steines) face, facing; —gegenstand, m. external object; —gestalt, f. outward form; —graben, m. Fort. avant-fosse; —hafen, m. outport; —linie, f. outer line, outline; pl. fig. elements; rudiments; —mauer, f. exterior or outer wall; —mensch, m. outward man; —posten, m. outpost; —rhede, f. outer road; —schein, m. outward appearance; —schlag, m. out-field; —seite, f. outside; superficies, surface; outward appearance; externals; exteriors; face; auf der —seite des Blattes wachsend, Bot. extrafoliaceous; —stand, m. see Ausstand; —stehend, adj. standing out; outstanding; —theil, m. (& n.) external part; pl. exteriors; —thür, f. Archit

profile or section; —räumer, m. sweeper (attached to locomotives): —schienen, f. pl. rails; —schlägel, m. Min. face-hammer; —stollen, m. tunnel; —strecke, f., —stück, n. section; —wärter (provinc. —wart), m. signal-man, flag-man, line-keeper, watchman of the line; —zug, m. (railway) train.

Bah're, (w.) f. barrow, litter; T. strainer, colander; bier, hearse. [Mor.

Bah'ren, (w.) v. tr. to lift, place upon a

Bahr'tuch, (str., pl. Bahr'tücher) n. hearse-cloth. [mittel.

Bäh'ung, (w.) f. fomentation, &c. (Bäh-

Bai, (w.) f. Geogr. &c. bay; die kleine —, cove, creek; —fieber, n. bay fever; —salz, n. see Baysalz. [(w.) f. Bavarian.

Bai'er, (w., sing. gener. str.) m., Bai'erin,

Bai'erisch, **Bai'risch**, adj. Bavarian

Bai'ern, n. Geogr. Bavaria.

Baikalith', (str.) m. Miner. baikalite.

Bail'brechen, (str. & separ.) v. intr. Sport. to cease barking.

Bai'len, (w.) v. intr. Sport. to bark.

* **Baisse** [pr. bäs'se], (w.) f. (Fr.) Comm. auf die (à la) — speculiren, to speculate on a decline (fall) in the funds. — **Baissier** [pr. bässyē'], (str., pl. B-s) m. (Fr.) speculator on the fall or decline; joc. bear.

* **Bajade're**, (w.) f. (Port.) bayadere, Indian dancing girl.

* **Bajaz'zo**, (str., pl. B-s) m. (Ital.) buffoon, clown, merry-andrew (of rope-dancers).

* **Bajonett'**, (str., pl. Bajonet'te) n. (Fr.) Mil. bayonet; das lange —, sword bayonet; das — gefällt! bayonet in charge! — ab! unfix bayonet! das — auf das Gewehr aufsetzen, to fix the bayonet; die Gesetzgebende Versammlung wurde mit gefällten —en aus ihrem Saale vertrieben, the Legislative Body was driven from its hall at the point of the bayonet; —bolt, f. bayonet-stud; —hülse, f. bayonet socket; —träger, m. bayonet-belt. — **Bajonetti'ren**, (w.) v. I. intr. to fight, or (tr.) to stab with a bayonet; II. tr. to furnish with bayonets.

Bak, see Back.

Bake, (w.) f. 1) Mar. beacon, seamark, buoy: — am Ufer, landmark; 2) Engin. slope-stake; B-n errichten, to put up or erect beacons: B-ngeld, n., B-nrecht, n. beaconage: B-ntonne, f. buoy.

* **Ba'kel**, (str.) m. (Lat. baculus) joc. stick, cudgel; ferula, birch-rod; —eisen, n. Tann. scraping- or flesh-knife. — **Ba'keln**, (w.) v. tr. to whip (with a stick or ferule).

Ba'keljau, (str., pl. B-e) m. dried salt cod-fish; —fischer, m. banker.

Ba'ken, **Ba'kern**, (w.) v. tr. to beat (flax).

* **Baket'**, (str.) n. (Fr.) magnetizing tub.

* **Balan'ce** [pr. bäläng'ße], (w.) f. (Fr.) equipoise; das Gewehr in — tragen, Mil. to trail arms.

* **Balancier'** [pr. bälängßiē'], (str., pl. B-e) m. (Fr.) Mech. beam, balancier; —kolben, m. Horol. balance-verge; —dampfmaschine, f. beam (steam) engine; —ringe, f. rings; —vorrichtung, f. balance mechanism.

* **Balanci'ren** [pr. bälängßi'ren], (w.) v. tr. & intr. to poise, balance; Comm. to balance, to strike a balance.

* **Balancir...** [bälängßir], in comp. —klappe, f. Mech. stop-valve; —kolben, m., —flügelchen, n. pl. Entom. balancers; —maschine, f. Watch-m. balance poiser; —stange, f. rope-dancer's pole, poy. [ruby.

Bal'ascrubin, (str.) m. Miner. balas(s)-

Bal'che, (w.) f. provinc. (das Blaufelchen) a species of salmon found in the lake of Constance (Salmo caeruleus or Coregonus Wartmanni).

* **Balcon'** [pr. bälkong'], (str., pl. B-e [pr. bälkong'ē], or Balco'ne) m. (Fr.) balcony; terrace; Archit. corbel-table.

Bald, adv. 1) a) soon, shortly, speedily; ere-long, by-and-by; b) provinc. for (zeitig) früh(zeitig): ich bin heute Morgen — aufgestanden, I rose early this morning; 2) almost: es ist — Nacht, it is almost night; ich wäre — gestorben, I was near dying, coll. I was (had) like to die; easily: er vergibt —, he easily forgives; es ist — gesagt, it is easily said, it is easy talking; ich sterbe! das ist — gesagt | und bälder noch gethan (Göthe, Faust), I'm dying! that is quickly said, | and quicker yet 'tis done (B. Taylor); wie —? how soon? es muß — seine Zeit sein, it must be near his time; komm — zurück, come back soon; es ist — neun Uhr, it is near nine o'clock; er starb — zu Anfange des Gefechts, he died early in the fight; ich werde Ihnen die Zeitung — geben, I'll give you the paper presently; er ist — zufrieden gestellt, he is easily contented; — wirst du deine Thorheit bereuen, ere long you will repent your folly; er wird — hier sein, he will be here ere long; sein Plan wird nicht so — ausgeführt sein, his plan will not be executed for some time; der Gegenstand war noch nicht so — erschöpft, the subject was not nearly exhausted; — ..., — ..., now ..., now ...; sometimes (the one, &c.), sometimes (the other, &c.), one while ..., another while ..., alternately; — hier, — da, now here, now there; — heiter, — traurig, at one time merry, at another sad; es wurde mir — heiß, — kalt, I felt hot and cold by turns; — so, — so, now so, then otherwise.

* **Bal'dachin**, (str.) m. (Mid. Lat.) canopy; dais; cloth of state; Archit. baldachin; mit einem — bedeckt, canopied.

Bäl'de, (w.) f. coll. (only used in): in —, in a short time, soon, shortly. [sooner, &c.

Bäl'der, coll. compar. of Bald (which see):

Bald'greis, (str.) m. Bot. groundsel.

Bal'dig, adj. speedy; early; quick; eine b-e Antwort, a speedy answer: ich wünsche Ihnen glückliche Reise und b-e Rückkehr, I wish you a safe (happy) journey and a speedy return. — **Bal'digst**, I. adj. most speedy; II. adv. as soon as possible; ich bitte — um Antwort, Comm. I beg to be favoured with an answer at your earliest convenience.

Bal'drian, (str.) m. (fr. Lat. valeriana) Bot. valerian, capon's tail (Valeriana L.); der griechische —, Jacob's ladder (Polemonium L.); Chem.-e. —öl, n. valerole; —säure, f. valerianic acid.

Baldthun'lichst, adj. that may be done, instituted, &c. as soon as possible.

Bal'duin, m. Baldwin (P. N.).

Balea'ren, pl. Geogr. the Balearic Isles (P. N.). — **Balea'risch**, adj. Balearic.

* **Balester**, (str.) m. (L.Lat.-Gr.) ballister, cross-bow.

Balg, (str., pl. Bäl'ge) m. 1) a) skin; Vogelbälge, bird's skins; b) (abgelegte Haut einer Schlange) slough: stirbt der Fuchs, so gilt der —, proverb, (Game) cards Jack's alight; 2) Anat. follicle; 3) Bot. glume; husk, pod, shell; aus Bälgen bestehend, glumaceous; 4) body of a doll; 5) coll. (contempt.) brat; 6) (Blase—) bellows; —artig, adj. glumaceous; —blume, —blüte, f. Bot. glumous flower; —gebläse, n. T. leathern bellows; —geschwulst, f. Med. encysted tumour; —kapsel, f. Bot. follicle, conceptacle; —schwengel, m. T. swipe; —zug, m. Org. stop of the bellows.

Bal'ge, (w.) f. see Balje.

Bal'gen, (w.) v. refl. to wrestle, fight, cope together, grapple, scuffle; to romp, to play at romps.

Bäl'gen, (w.) v. refl. to cast the skin.

Bal'gen..., in comp. f-a. —brett, n. upper board of a pair of bellows; —düse, f. nose-pipe; —gestell, n. bellows-support; —klappe, f. valve (of a pair of bellows), clack; —kopf,

[illegible] geht —, the ship goes on ballast; II. *in comp.* —brücke, *f. see* —pforte; (viereckiges) [illegible], *n.* square kentledge.

Ballasti'ren, *(w.) v. tr. Mar.* to ballast.

Ballast'..., *in comp.* —ewer, *m. see* —lichter; —fracht, *f.* dead freight; —fleib, *n.* port [illegible]; —lichter, *m.* ballast-lighter; —pforte, ballast port; *Herol.* looking- (ballast-) wheel; [illegible] *n.,* —schute, *f. see* —lichter.

Ballasti'rung, *(w.) f. Mar.* lastage.

Bällchen, *(str.) n. (dimin. of* Ball) a little ball, &c. [tonic order).

Balle'i, *(w.) f.* commandery (of the Teu-

Ball'eisen, *(str.) n.* 1) *Iron-w.* lump heat-[illegible]; 2) *see* Balleneisen, 1.

Ballen, *(str.) m.* 1) a ball (of earth, &c.); 2) bale (of goods, &c.); pack, bag; ein — Papier, *T.* bundle (ten reams) of paper; ein — Flachs, a kirtle of flax; 3) ball (of the hand, of the foot); *Farr.* sole; 4) *Typ.* ball; 5) *Herald.* ballet; 6) *Join.* handle (of a [illegible]); 7) *Fenc.* button covered with leather on the foil; *Typ.-s.* die — bewegen, to bishop (wet) the balls; — machen, to knock up balls; [illegible], to scrape the balls.

Ballen, *(w.) v.* I. *tr.* to form into balls, [illegible] die Faust —, to clench, double, bend the fist; II. *refl.* to gather into (firm) balls: [illegible], to conglobate: geballt, *adj.* conglobate (of glands or flowers).

Ballen..., *in comp.* —biene, *f. Entom.* species of short-tongued bee *(Halictus);* —binder, *m.* packer; —binderlohn, *n.* package; —bindestock, *m.* packing-stick; —brettchen, *n. Typ.* ball-board; —band, *m. Fire-w.* choking; —eisen, *n.* 1) *T.* ripping-chisel; 2) *see* Balleisen, 1; —fieber, *n.,* —gicht, *f.* the agues, gout in the balls of the hands or feet; —[illegible], *m.,* —holz, *n. Typ.* ball-stock; —haken, *m.* packer's hook; —knechte, *m. pl. Typ.* [illegible]; —kreuz, *n. Herald.* cross bottony, *cf.* [illegible]; —leder, *n. Typ.* leather covering the balls; —meißel, *m. T. see* —eisen, 1; —[illegible], *m. Typ.* ball-maker; —messer, *n.* ball-[illegible]; —nägel, *pl. Typ.* iron tacks, that fasten the leather to the balls; —pflanzung, *f. Hort.* &c. transplantation of plants and young trees with the earth adhering to the roots; —scheren, *f. pl.* bale-scissors, packing-scissors; —schnur, *f.* pack-thread, packing-cord; [illegible] der — schnur verkaufen, to sell under the [illegible]; —stock, *m.* packing-stick; —waare, *f.* bale-goods; —wälzer, *m. Entom.* dor-beetle; [illegible], *adj.* in bales, by the bale; —zinn, *n.* tin in rolls.

[illegible], *(w.) v. intr. coll.* to make a noise, [illegible].

* Ballet', *(str., pl.* die Balle'te) *n. (Ital.)* [illegible] ballet; —meister, *m.* ballet-master; —tänzer, *m.* ballet-dancer; —tänzerin, *f.* [illegible], ballet-dancer.

Ball'..., *in comp.* —fest, *n.* ball; —förmig, [illegible] round, spherical, globular; —gast, *m.* person invited to a ball; —geber, *m.* person that gives a ball; —gesetz, *n.,* —hölle, *m. pl.* [illegible]; —hand, *n.,* —hof, *m.* [illegible]; —holz, *n.* bat, racket; —hut, *m.* [illegible]

[illegible], *(w.) v. tr. bard.* to make [illegible] emendations, or alterations [illegible] worse instead of improving.

[illegible] *(w.) f. (Fr.)* ballistics.

[illegible] *in comp.* —tleid, *n. see* —anzug; [illegible] ball-basket; —meister, *m.* master [illegible] *m.* promise, back-[illegible]; —nagel, *see* Ballennagel; —

[illegible] *(str., pl.* B-e) *m. (Fr.)* [illegible]

[illegible], *pl.* B-e) *m. (Fr.)*

Comm. 1) small bale of goods, package, parcel, bundle; 2) a measure of sheets of glass.

* Ballota'ge [—ā'zhe], *(w.) f. (Fr.)* ballotation, balloting; —kugel, Ballotkugel, *f.* ball.

* Balloti'ren, *(w.) v. intr. (Fr.)* to ballot, to vote by ballot.

Ball'..., *in comp.* —peitsche, *f. see* —holz; —rose, *f. Bot. see* Schneeball; —schlägel, *m.* racket; —schlagen, *n. see* —spiel; —schläger, *m.* tennis- or racket-player; —schnecke, *f.* partridge-shell; —schuhe, *m. pl.* pumps; dress shoes; —spiel, *n.* tennis, game at tennis; hurl, hurling; (mit Stöcken) trap; —spieler, *m.* player at tennis, at rackets; —stock, *m. see* Billardstock; —stoß, *m.* driving, sending of a ball, stroke, hurler; —stoßspiel, *n. see* Billard; —tafel, *f.* billiard-table; —tafelkugel, *f.* billiard-ball; —tafelstock, *m.* billiard-cue.

Bal'sam, *s.* I. *(str.) m.* balm, balsam, *Med.* unguent; II. *in comp. Bot.-s.* —apfel, *m.* balm-apple *(Momordica balsamina* L.); —baum, *m.* 1) *see* Copaivabaum; 2) —tanne, *f. see* Terpentinbaum; 3) ächter —baum, balm-tree *(Amyris gileadensis* L.); —baumholz, *n.* xylobalsamum; —beeren, *f. pl. see* —körner; —birne, *f. see* Muscatellerbirne; —blüte, *f.* blossom of the balm-tree; *fig.* any odoriferous *or* balsamic flower; —büchse, *f.* balm-box; —duft, *m.* balsamic odour; —duftend, *adj.* balmy.

Bal'samen, *(w.) v. tr. see* Balsamiren.

Bal'sam..., *in comp.* —espe, *f. see* —pappel; —frucht, *f. see* —körner; —garbe, *f. Bot.* sweet-maudlin *(Achillea ageratum* L.); —gewächs, *n.* any plant yielding balsam; —holz, *n. see* —baumholz.

Bal'samig, *adj. see* Balsamisch

Balsami'ne, *(w.) f. Bot.* balsamine, balsam, immortal eagle flower *(Impatiens balsamina* L.); wilde —, touch-me-not *(Impatiens noli me tangere* L.). [to perfume.

Balsami'ren, *(w.) v. tr.* to balm, embalm;

Balsa'misch, *adj.* balmy, balsamic.

Bal'sam..., *in comp.* —körner, *pl. Pharm.* fruit-berries of the balsam-tree; *Bot.-s.* —kraut, *n.* balsamic plant; großes —kraut, *see* Frauenmünze; kleines —kraut, *see* Schafgarbe; marvel of Peru *(Mirabilis* L.); —kräutchen, *n.* inglorious *(Adoxa moschatellina* L.); —leiche, *see* Mumie; *Bot.-s.* —münze, *f.* balm-mint *(Mentha arvensis* L.); —pappel, *f.* the tacamahac *(Populus balsamifera* L.); —pflanze, *f.* balm-tree, *see* —baum, 3; —saft, *m. fig.* balsam-juice; —springgurke, *f. see* —apfel; —staude, *f.* balsam-shrub; —tanne, *f. see* Terpentinbaum.

Bal'se, *(w.) f.* 1) *Mar.* balse; 2) *Bot.* odoriferous species of mint.

* Baltimo're, *(w.) f. Ornith.* baltimore bird *(Oriolus baltimore* L.).

Bal'tisch, *adj.* Baltic; b—e Meer, *n.* Baltic sea.

* Balustra'de, *(w.) f. (Fr.-Sp.)* balustrade.

Balze, Balz, *(w.) f.* 1) coupling time of large birds, &c.; 2) *(f. & m.)* place where the coupling is carried on; zur — gehen, *see* Balzen; —zeit, *f. Sport.* coupling-time.

Bal'zen, *(w.) v. intr.* to pair *or* couple (of birds, rabbits, &c.). [(P. N.).

Bal'zer, *contr. from* Balthasar, Balthasar

Bam'bus, *m.* (—rohr, *n.*) bamboo *(Bambusa arundinacea* Schreb.), bamboocane; —sprossen, *f. pl.* achia; —stock, *m.* bamboo-cane *or* walking stick; *pl. Comm.* bamboos; —zucker, *m.* tabasheer.

Bä'mme, *(w.) f. provinc. (N. G.)* a slice of bread (and butter).

Bam'mel, Bam'meln, *see* Bammel &c.

Bams, *(str.) m. Saddl.* saddle-cushion.

Bam'sen, *(w.) v. tr. T.* to beat (skins).

* Ban, Ba'nus, *m. (Slavonic)* Ban, viceroy *or* civil governor (*f. i.* of Croatia and Slavonia). — Banāt', *(str.) n.* 1) the district of a ban; 2) a province of Hungary.

* Banal', *adj. (Fr.)* 1) *see* Zwangsmäßig; 2) *see* Abgedroschen. — Banalität', *(w.) f.* trite *or* common-place sentence.

* Bana'nas, Bana'ne, *(w.) f. Bot.* banana (—feige, fruit of the *Musa paradisiaca* L.).

* Bancal'..., *in comp.* —amt, *n.* (in Austria) bancal office (relating to the customs in general, the stamp-duty, and the imperial monopolies of salt and tobacco).

* Banc'o, *(Ital.) m. & n.* banco, bank-money; in — abschreiben, *Comm.* to reduce (transcribe) in banco; —mark, *f.* mark-banco; —zettel, *m.* bank-billet (formerly a government money-paper in Austria); *cf.* Bank.

Band, *s.* I. *(str., pl.* Bän'der) *n.* 1) riband, ribbon; *Comm.* Wollen—, flannel-galloon; halbwollenes —, twilled tape, union-tape; *Spinn.* sliver; 2) band; 3) *Surg.* fillet, ligature, bandage; 4) *Anat.* ligament; 5) *a) Carp. & Mar.* hoop; *b) Lock-sm.* band, holdfast; (an Thürbeschlägen) strap-hinge; *c) Mech., &c.* brace; *d) Clock-m.* catch, crank; *e) Carp.* key; tie; clamp; truss; *f) Typ.* tie; *g)* Bänder (des Parallelogramms) links; 6) (im Puffspiel, *at backgammon)* two men placed upon a point; ein — machen, to make a point; II. *(str., pl.* Bän'de) *m.* 1) volume, tome; 2) *Bookb.* binding *(cf.* Einband); III. *(str., pl.* Ban'de) *n.* 1) tie, bond; 2) *pl.* fetters, chains, trammels.

* Banda'ge [—ā'zhe], *(w.) f. (Fr.)* bandage; *T.* tire (of a wheel); (Bruch-) truss. — Bandagist' [—zhist'], *(w.) m.* bandage maker, truss-maker, *or* manufacturer.

Band'..., *in comp.* —achat, *m. Miner.* ribbon agate; —ähnlich, *adj.* ribbon-like, striped, streaked; —alabaster, *m.* striped alabaster.

* Banda'na..., *in comp.* —presse, *f. Manuf.* bandana press; —tücher, *n. pl. Comm.* bandana handkerchiefs.

Band'..., *in comp.* —assel, *f. Entom.* streaked centiped; —balken, *m. Herald. see* Gegenbalken; —beinfügung, *f.* synneurosis; —biene, *f. Entom.* Egyptian honeybee *(Apis fasciata);* —blat, *f. Bot.* ligule *(Ligula);* —blume, *f.* 1) artificial flower; 2) *Bot.* streaked *or* striped pink *(Dianthus caryophyllus);* —bohrer, *m. Carp.* small augor.

Bänd'chen, *(str.) n. (dimin. of* Band) 1) bandelet; any small ribbon *or* band; *Archit.* fillet, list; 2) *Anat.* bridle, ligament (of the foreskin), frænulum; 3) a small volume, tomelet.

Band'..., *in comp.* coralle, *f. Zool.* eschar; —draht, *m.* wire of a middle sort.

Ban'de, *(w.) f.* 1) *a)* border, edge; *b)* cushion of a billiard-table; ein Ball dicht an der —, a close ball; *c) Mar.* the side of a ship; auf die — legen, to careen; platte —, plat-band; 2) band, company (of musicians); gang (of thieves, robbers), set; gefährliche —, a dangerous set.

Band'eisen, *(str.) n.* hoop-iron.

* Bandelette' *[Fr.,* bangdlĕt'], *(w.) f. Surg.* small bandage.

* Bandelier', *(str.) n. (Fr.) Mil.* bandoleer, shoulder-belt. [restrained.

Ban'denfrei, *adj.* unfettered; *fig.* un-

Bän'dereich, *adj.* voluminous.

Bän'der..., *in comp.* —haut, *f. Anat.* peridesmium; —jaspis, —kram, *see* Bandjaspis, Bandkram; —latz, *m.* lady's stomacher trimmed with riband; —lehre, *f. Anat.* syndesmology; —reich, *adj.* richly trimmed *or* adorned with ribands; —schuh, *m.* shoe tied with a riband *or* string; —stein, *m. Miner.* riband-stone.

Bän'dern, *(w.) v. tr.* to form into long and broad stripes; 2) to stripe, streak.

* Bandero'le, *(w.) f. (Fr.)* banderol.

Band'..., *in comp.* —fabrik, *f.* ribbon-

manufacture: —käfer, pl. Bot. a genus of hair-wood (Dimidena); —faß, n. a measure of wine in Switzerland (600 Maaße): —fest, adj. see Bandfest; —fisch, see Langenfisch; —förmig, adj. having the form of a ribbon; Bot. ligulate, ligulated: —fries, m. Join. hanging-stile (of a door): —gesims, n. Archit. plain moulding: —gras, n. Bot. riband-grass, ribbon grass, ladies' tresses, painted ladies' grass (Phalaris arundinacea L.): —haken, m. Carp. dog; can- or cant-hook; door-hook: —hammer, m. T. large hammer: —handel, m. ribbon-trade, haberdashery: —händler, m. lace-man, haberdasher: —hobel, m. Coop. spoke-shave: —holz, n. Coop. hoop-wood: Carp. binding, purlin.

Bän'dig, adj. tameable, tame: — machen, to tame.

Bän'digen, (w.) v. tr. to tame (wild beasts), to break (a horse): fig. to restrain, check, subdue, master.

Bän'diger, (str.) m. conqueror, one who tames, breaks in; subduer.

Bän'digung, (w.) f. the act of taming, &c.

Bandi'ren, (w.) v. tr. to form into stripes: to stripe, streak.

* Bandit', (w.) m. bandit (pl. banditti).

Band'..., in comp. —jaspis, m. Miner. ribbon-jasper: —käfer, see Laufkäfer; —kegel, m. see —haken; —kette, f. T. band-chain, pitch-chain; —krämer, m. see —händler; —kraßen, f. pl. T. fillet-cards: —kreuz, n. see Fadenkreuz; —kreuzschnabel, m. Ornith. species of cross-bill (Loxia leucoptera): —laden, m. ribbon-shop: —lauf, m. Gun-sm. twisted barrel or stub: —laus, f. Entom. species of louse (Pediculus fasciatus).

Band'ling, (str.) m. see Bandmotte.

Band'..., in comp. —macher, m. riband-weaver, tape-maker: —makrele, f. streaked or striped mackerel (Scomber sloanitus); —marmor, m. streaked or striped marble: —maß, n. 1) tape measure, measuring-tape: 2) a lineal measure (to ascertain the height of horses); —meißel, m. T. forked chisel; —messer, n. Coop. notcher, hoop-knife: —motte, f. Entom. striped moth (Phalaena geometra fasciata): —mühle, f. ribbon-loom; —muschel, f. see —tute; —nagel, m. Carp. pin, plug, wooden nail: —natter, f. Zool. riband-snake (Coluber lemniscatus): —nudeln, f. pl. ruban vermicelli: —qualle, f. Zool. see Venusgürtel; —reif, m. Coop. hoop; —rohr, n. Gun-sm. twisted barrel: —rose, f. 1) rosette of ribbons; 2) Bot. see Eßigrose; —säge, f. T. belt or strap-saw: —schleife, f. knot or loop of riband, favour: —seil, n. flat (iron-wire) rope; —specht, m. see Baumspecht: —spinne, f. striped spider (Aranea fasciata); —stein, m. striped or streaked mineral: —strauch, m. Bot. see Schlingstrauch; —streif, m. 1) Herald. bend: 2) top-knot: —streifig, adj. Bot. & Zool. banded; —stiel, n. Carp. prick-post, joining-timber: —trappe, f. Ornith. species of bustard (Otis bengalensis): —tresse, f. worsted or livery lace: —tute, f. Moll. listed stamper (Conus): —vereinigungsmaschine, f. T. lapping-machine; —verlängerung, f. Surg. elongation; —waaren, f. pl. small wares: —weber, m. see —macher; —weide, f. Bot. osier, wicker, withy, water willow (Salix viminalis L.): —werk, n. Anat. a connexion of ligaments: —wirker, m. see —macher; —wurm, m. Zool. solitary worm, tape-worm, broad-worm, gourd-worm (Taenia L.): —zieher, m. see —haken; —zwitter, m. Min. tin-ore.

Bang, Bang'e, adj. (compar. & sup. with or without modification of vowel) anxious, uneasy: fearful; timid: es ist (wird) mir — vor (with Dat.), I am afraid or apprehensive of ..., I am dismayed at ...: es ist mir bange um (with Acc.), I am afraid of ... I fear for ...: Einem — machen, to make one afraid of.

Bäng'el, see Bengel.

Bang'en, (w.) v. I. intr. (impers.) & refl. to be afraid; mir bangt vor (with Dat.), I am afraid of ...: II. or Bäng'en, tr. to oppress or constrain with anxiety, &c.: III. refl. sich nach ..., to expect anxiously, to yearn for ....

Bang'(en)kraut, (str.) n. see Schierling.

Bang'igkeit, (w.) f. anxiousness, anxiety, fearfulness, dismay.

Bäng'lich, I. adj. somewhat anxious, uneasy: II. B-keit, (w.) f. apprehension, anxiety. [timid, faint-hearted.

Bang'müthig, adj. anxious, apprehensive;

Bang'sam, adj. anxious, full of anxiety.

Banier', Ban'jer, (str.) n. Mar. half-deck.

Bank, s. I. (str., pl. Bänk'e) f. 1) a) bench, bank: form (Schulbank); seat: unter der — liegen, vulg. to live in an obscure condition: to lie close; b) die geistliche —, the spiritual bench; die weltliche —, the secular bench; c) Mar. aa) (sand-)bank, shelf: (hidden) rocks; bb) Bänke, pl. stern-sheets or seats of a boat; thwarts; d) Gard. bank, parterre: terrace: e) Miner. layer, bed: in Banken, laminated; f) Herald. see Turnierkragen; g) Gam-s. bank, hazard-table; — halten, to keep a hazard-table, to keep bank: — im Bassetspiel halten, to tally at bassel: — an der Presse, Typ. shelf: —(an einer Brustwehr), Mil. banquette; über die — schießen, to fire in barbe: 2) (Verkaufsstand) stall, stand: 3) lathe (of turners, coopers, &c.): — am Horizonte, a cloudy horizon: fig-s. Einen in die — hauen, coll. to cut (one) up; auf die lange — schieben, to delay, put off, to lay on the shelf: durch die —, indiscriminately, at an average, one with another, by (in) the lump, in the gross: II. (w., pl. Bank'en) f. Comm. bank, banking-company or establishment; concessionirte —, chartered bank: städtische —, city bank: Gelder in der — stehen haben, to be a creditor on the bank-books: III. in comp. Comm-s. —abschluß, m. closing of account at the bank, see —ausweis; actie, f. bank-stock: share in bank-stock, bank-bill, bank-share; —agent, m. bank- or exchange-broker: —agio, n. bank-agio, premium.

Bankal', see Bankal.

Bank'..., in comp. —antheilschein, m. see —actie; —anweisung, f. check, banker's note; bankbill, bank-note: —arbeit, f. any kind of work which the artisan performs sitting: T-m. soldering; —arbeiter, m. artisan who sits at his work.

Bank'art, (str.) m. vulg. bantling, bastard.

Bank'..., in comp. —aufgeld, n. bank-agio; —ausweis, m. balance of the bank: —beamte, —bedienter, m. bank-official, clerk of a bank; —berg, m. Min. layer of stone under coal-strata; —bericht, m. bank-report, return (account) of the bank: —bilanz, f. see —ausweis; —billet, n. see —anweisung; —bohrer, m. Carp. large auger: —bruch, m. bankruptcy; —brüchig, adj., —brüchige, m. bankrupt; — brüchig werden, to break, to fail, to become bankrupt: —bürger, m. (in Hamburg) deputy of the bank; —capital, n. stock in (a) bank; —casse, f. (bank-)cashier's office; —commandite, f. branch-bank; —comptoir, n. bank-office: —conto, n. bank-account: ein —conto haben, to be a creditor on the bank-books; —courtage, f. bank-brokerage: —depositum, n. deposit in a bank; —diener, m. see —beamte; —eisen, n. T. iron-band, cramp-iron.

Bänk'el, (provinc. [S. G.] dimin. of Bank, High Germ. Bänk'chen, (str.) n.) in comp. —gesang, m. ballad-singing; ballad; —krämer, m. hawker, pedlar; —sänger, m. 1) ballad-singer, itinerant-singer: 2) a bad poet, small-beer poet: —sängerei, f. balladsinging.

Bänk'eln, (w.) v. intr. to keep a faro-table.

Bank'en, (w.) v. tr. Mar. to lay (a ship) against a bank (for the purpose of careening it).

Ban'nen, *(w.)* v. *tr.* 1) to banish, expel, see **Verbannen**; 2) to enchant: **festgebannt**, spellbound, rooted to the spot: **Geister** —, 1. to raise, conjure (up) spirits; 2. to lay, conjure down spirits, to exorcise.

Ban'ner, *(str.)* n. 1) banner, standard, flag; 2) militia, *see* **Landsturm** & **Landwehr**; —**herr**, m. banneret; —**leute**, *pl.* retainers or vassals belonging to a banneret.

Bann'..., *in comp.* —**fluch**, m. anathema; —**forst**, m. wood fenced in as a (royal) preserve; —**gut**, n. contraband goods; —**kelter**, *f.* common wine-press (belonging to the manor, of which all the vassals are obliged to make use); —**leute**, *pl.* the persons subject to a certain jurisdiction or inhabiting a certain territory.

Bann'ling, *(str.)* m. *(Voss, Sch. 1, 344, cf.* **Bandero***)* *(l. u.)* one under the ban, proscript.

Bann'..., *in comp.* —**meile**, *f.* precinct, boundary of a jurisdiction; —**mühle**, *f.* common mill; —**ofen**, m. common oven; —**richter**, m. criminal judge; —**scheidung**, *f.* landmark noting the boundaries of two jurisdictions; —**schild**, m. the bloody flag; —**schütze**, m. *see* **Flurschütze**; —**spruch**, m. sentence of excommunication or of proscription; exordium; —**stein**, m. landmark; —**strahl**, m. thunder(-bolt) of excommunication, anathematisation; **den —strahl schleudern**, to fulminate excommunication; —**vogt**, m. field-watch (**Flurschütz**); —**waare**, *f. see* —**gut**; —**wald**, m. *see* —**forst**; —**wart**, m. *see* —**vogt**; —**wasser**, n. river or lake forbidden to the vassals; —**wein**, m. wine, the property of the feudal lord, and which was, on certain occasions, to be bought to the entire exclusion of all other wines; —**werk**, n. statute labour.

* **Banquet'** *[pr.* bangket'], *see* **Bankett**.

* **Banquier'** *[pr.* bängkyä'], *(str., pl.* **B-s***)* m. *(Fr.)* banker; exchanger; —**haus**, n. banking-house; —**provision**, *f.* banker's provision (*or* commission).

Ban'se, **Ban'ze**, *(w.) f.* bay (in a barn).

Ban'sen, *(str.)* m. first stomach in ruminating animals, paunch. [a bay.

Ban'sen, *(w.)* v. *tr.* to pile up (sheaves) in

Bar, *adj.* 1) bare, naked; 2) *fig.-a.* destitute, void (of); 3) pure, unmixed: **b-er Unsinn**, sheer, downright nonsense; 4) ready or present (money): —**(es) Geld**, ready money or cash, specie: **hundert Thaler** —, hundred dollars in cash; **b-e Zahlung**, ready or prompt payment; **b-e Entschädigung**, advance (indemnification) in money; —**bezahlen**, to pay ready money, to pay cash in hand, to pay down or in hand; **b-er Ertrag**, proceeds in cash, neat (net) proceeds.

Bär, *(w. & str.)* m. 1) *a)* bear; *b)* bear; **ein junger** —, a cub, whelp; 2) *fig. a)* a rude, rough fellow, a bear: *slang-a.*; *b)* a debt: **einen B-en anbinden**, to contract a debt; **einen B-en abbinden**, to pay a debt; *c)* a fib, flam: **Einem einen B-en aufbinden**, to flam or gammon one; 3) *Astr.-a. a)* **der große** —, the greater bear *(Ursa major)*; *b)* **der kleine** —, the lesser bear *(Ursa minor)*; *T-a.* 4) *(pl.* [illegible] **Bär'e***)* a pile-driver, pile (driving) engine; ram, beetle, punch, monkey; 5) *a)* *Fort.* batardeau; *b)* *Hydr.* (coffer-)dam (batardeau).

* **Bar'aban**, **Bar'akan**, *see* **Berkan**.

* **Baracke**, *(w.) f. (Fr.) Mil.* barrack, hut.

* [illegible], *(w.) f. (Span.) Comm.* Astracan lamb's skins.

Bär..., *in comp.* —**ähnlich**, —**artig**, *adj.* bear-like, bearish, ursine. [truck.

* **Baratti'ren**, *(w.)* v. *intr. Comm.* to barter.

Baratt'artikel, *(str.)* m. cash-article.

* **Baratt'o**, *(str.)* m. barter, truck. —

* **Baratterie'**, **Barratterie'**, *(w.) f.* barratry.

Barba'dos, n. *Geogr.* Barbadoes *(P. N.)*; —**krankheit**, *f. Med.* Barbadoes-leg; —**theer**, m. *see* **Petroleum**.

* **Barbar'**, *(w.)* m. *(Gr.)* 1) barbarian, savage; 2) *see* **Berber**; —**falk**, m. *Ornith.* Barbary falcon *(Falco barbarus)*.

Bar'bara', *f.* Barbara *(P. N.)*.

* **Barbarei'**, *(w.) f. (cf.* **Barber**) 1) *Geogr.* Barbary; 2) barbarity.

* **Barba'ren**..., *in comp.* —**heer**, n. barbarian army; —**joch**, n. barbarian yoke; —**schwärme**, m. *pl.* swarms of barbarians; —**stamm**, m. tribe of barbarians.

Barbares'ken, (—**Staaten**, *m.) pl.* the Barbarian *or* Barbary States in North Africa.

* **Barba'risch**, *adj.* 1) barbarous, barbarian; 2) *see* **Berberisch**. — **Barbaris'mus**, *(pl.* **B-men***)* m. *Gramm.* barbarism

A. **Bar'be**, *(w.) f. Ichth.* barbel, barb *(Cyprinus barbus L.)*.

B. **Bar'be**, *(w.) f.* 1) *see* **Berber**, 2; 2) **Bab**, *dimin. of* **Barbara**.

C. **Bar'be**, *(w.) f. (Fr.)* lace (of a cap), lappet frimle (inside of a lady's bonnet).

Bär'beinig, *adj.* bare-legged.

Bär'beißer, *(str.)* m. bear-dog, bull-dog.

Bär'beißig, *adj.* gruff, quarrelsome; huffy; — **werden**, *coll.* to cut up rough.

Bar'belkraut, **Bar'benkraut**, *(str.)* n. *Bot.* 1) rocket gentle, rocket gallant *(Barbarea vulgaris)*; 2) winter-cress; yellow-rocket *(Barbarea praecox)*.

Bär'betrag, *(str., pl.* **B-träge***)* m. amount in ready money, cash-value.

* **Barbet'te**, *(w.) f. (Fr.)* 1) *see* **Bartmeise**; 2) *Mil.* barbette, parapet without embrasures.

Barbier', *(str.)* m. *(Fr.)* barber, *coll.* shaver.

Barbi'ren, **Barbie'ren**, *(w.)* v. *tr.* 1) to shave; 2) *fig.* to dry-shave, cheat, fleece.

Barbier'..., *in comp.* —**becken**, n. shaving-basin; —**beutel**, m. barber's pouch or case; —**feile**, *f.* raspatory; —**flasche**, *f.* barber's chafer; —**gerechtigkeit**, *f.* barber's licence; —**gesell**, m. barber's-man; —**messer**, n. razor, shaving-knife; —**riemen**, m. razor-strap; —**schere**, *f.* barber's scissors; —**stein**, m. barber's hone; —**stube**, *f.* barber's shop; —**tag**, m. shaving-day; —**toilette**, *f.* shaving-table; —**tuch**, n. shaving-towel; —**zeichen**, n. barber's sign; —**zeug**, n. shaving case.

* **Barcas'se**, *(w.) f. (Span.* barcaza*) Mar.* long boat, launch.

Bar'chent, *(str.)* m. *Comm.* fustian; mouse-skin; **glatter** —, smooth (shiny) fustian; **rauher (gerauhter)** —, napped fustian; **feiner (gestreifter)** —, dimity, twill; — **reißen**, *coll.* to snort aloud, *vulg.* to drive one's hogs; —**macher**, —**weber**, m. fustian-weaver; —**stuhl**, m. fustian-weaver's loom.

Bardauz'! *interj.* smash! dash! bang!

Bar'de, *(w.)* m. bard, poet-musician. — **Bar'denthum**, **Bar'denwesen**, n. bardism.

Bardiet' *[pr.* —dēt], *(str.)* m. & n. *Germ. Lit.* a species of poetry imitating the war songs of the bards, introduced by Klopstock.

Bär'dill, *(str.)* m. *see* **Bärwurz**, **Bärenfenchel**.

Ba're, *(w.) f.* 1) *see* **Barre**, 2; 2) *Mar.* wave, billow; 3) a bushy place, copse.

Bär'eis, *(str.)* n. smooth-ice (ice not covered with snow).

Ba'ren, *(str.)* m. *Org.* a soft flute-stop.

A. **Bä'ren**, *(w.)* v. *intr. provinc.* to bear (fruit, of trees, &c.). [bears).

B. **Bä'ren**, *(w.)* v. *intr. Sport.* to rut (of

Bä'ren..., *in comp.* —**ähnlich**, *adj.* bearish; —**beere**, *f.* fruit of the bearberry; —**beißer**, m. bear-dog, bull-dog; *fig. see* **Bär**, I. 2, *a*; —**beißig**, *see* **Bärbeißig**; —**decke**, *f.* bear-skin (as a mat or foot-cloth); —**dill**, m. *see* **Bärwurz**; —**dreck**, m. 1) bear's dung; 2) liquorice-juice; —**fang**, m. bear-catching; —**fell**, n. bear's skin; —**fett**, n. bear's grease; —**förmig**, *adj.* urviform; —**führer**, m. bear-leader; —**fuß**, m. *Bot.* bear's foot (species of hellebore); —**gerste**, *f.* winter-barley.

Bä'renhaft, *adj.* bearish, bearlike.

Bä'ren..., *in comp.* —**hatz**, —**hetze**, *f.* bear-baiting, bear-hunting; —**haut**, *f.* bear's skin; *fig.-a.* **auf der —haut liegen**, to be idle; —**häuter**, m. 1) idler, lubber, pillowlier; 2) coward; —**häuterei**, *f.* idleness, cowardice; —**hüter**, m. bear-herd; *Astr.* Bootes; —**jagd**, *f. see* —**hatz**; —**klau**, *f. Bot.* 1) (**unächte**) Hercules's all-heal, bear's wort, cow's parsnep *(Heracleum spondylium L.)*; 2) (**ächte**) bear's foot, bear's-breech, bear's paw, set-wort, acanthus *(Acanthus L.)*; —**klee**, m. *Bot.* melilot; —**koth**, m. 1) bear's dung; 2) *Min.* scum, dross; —**kraut**, n. *Bot. see* —**traube**; —**krebs**, m. *Entom.* a species of lobster *(Scyllarus arctus L.)*; —**lauch**, m. *Bot.* wild garlic *(Allium ursinum L.)*; —**moos**, n. *see* **Widerton**, **gülden**; *Bot.-a.* —**öhr**, n. wind seed *(Arctotis L.)*; —**öhrlein**, n. bear's ear, auricula *(Primula auricula L.)*; —**raupe**, *f. Entom.* canker (fly), bear-worm; —**schaum**, m. *Min.* scum, dross; —**schmalz**, m. bear's grease; —**schote**, *f. Bot.* wild liquorice *(Astragalus glycyphyllus L.)*; —**schwanz**, m. bear's tail, *Sport.* wreath; —**tapp**..., *f.* 1) *see* —**tatze**; 2) *see* —**klau**; —**tatze**, *f.* 1) bear's paw; 2) *Bot.* club-top *(Clavaria L.)*; —**traube**, *f. Bot.* strawberry-tree, red-wort, arbute berry, bearberry *(Arbutus uva ursi L.)*; —**vogel**, m. *Entom.* 1) (**brauner**) great tiger moth *(Arctia caja L.)*; 2) (**getigerter**) cream-spot tiger moth *(Arctia villica L.)*; —**wärter**, m. bear-ward, bearherd; —**zahn**, *f. Bot. see* **Löwenzahn**; —**zeit**, *f. Sport.* rutting-season of bears; —**zucker**, m. *Pharm.* liquorice-juice *(cf.* —**schote**); —**zwinger**, m. bear garden.

* **Barett'**, **Baret'**, *(str.)* n. *(Fr.)* bonnet, cap, chaperon; —**kram**, m. haberdashery; —**krämer**, m. haberdasher.

Bär'frost, *(str.)* m. black-frost

Bär'fuß, *adv.* barefoot, unshod.

Bär'füßele, *(str.)* n. *provinc. (S G.; dimin of* **Barfuß***)* a barefooted child.

Bär'füßer, *(str.)* m. *Eccl.* barefooted friar.

Bär'füßig, *adj.* barefooted. [hog.

Barg (**Borg**), *(str.)* m. *provinc.* barrow-

† **Bär'haft(ig)**, *adj. (from* **Bären**, A.) 1) bearing, fecund; 2) *Law*, pregnant.

Bär'haupt, **Bär'häuptig**, *adv. & adj.* bareheaded, uncovered.

* **Baril'la**, *(w.) f. (Span.) Bot. & Comm.* barilla *(Salsola sativa L.)*, *cf.* **Soda**.

Bä'rin, *(w.) f.* she-bear.

* **Bar'iton**, *(str.)* m. *Mus.* barytone. — **Baritonist'**, *(w.)* m. baritonist.

* **Ba'rium**, *(str.)* n. *Chem.* barium (the metallic basis of baryta); —**chlorür**, n. chloride of barium, muriatic baryta.

* **Barkas'se**, *see* **Barcasse**. [chase.

Bär'kauf, *(str., pl.* **Bär'käufe***)* m. cash pur-

Bar'ke, *(w.) f.* bark; **die kleinere** —, barge, craft, lighter; bark-boat; **B-nbauer**, m. barge-builder; **B-nkahn**, m. canoe.

Bar'kenuf, *(str.)* m. *Mar.* snow.

Bark'hölzer, n. *pl. Mar. see* **Berghölzer**.

Bärk'lein, *(str.)* n. *(dimin. of* **Barke**) a little bark *(Voss)*.

Bär'kopf, —**köpfig**, *see* —**haupt**, —**häuptig**.

Bark'schiff, *(str.)* n. bark, barque.

* **Barlu'nen**, *pl. Mar.* yuffers, baulks.

Bär'..., *in comp.* —**lapp**, —**lappen**, m. *Bot.* wolf's claw, club-moss *(Lycopodium L.)*; —**lapp(en)samen**, m. *Pharm.* witch-meal; —**latschen**, m. *pl.* cow-hair slippers; —**lauch**, m. bear's garlic.

Barm, *(str.)* m. *see* **Bärme**.

Bär'maus *(str., pl.* **Bär'mäuse***)* *f. see* **Murmelthier**.

Bar'men, (w.) v. I. tr. & rfl. † for Erbarmen; II. intr. fam. to lament, complain.

Bär'me, (w.) f. barm, yeast: **Bärm'brod**, n. bread with yeast; **Bärm'teig**, m. dough made up with yeast.

Barmher'zig, I. adj. merciful, compassionate, pitiful, charitable; — gegen Einen sein, to shew mercy or have compassion on one, to deal mercifully with one; Eccl. b-e Brüder, brothers of charity, hospitalers; b-e Schwestern, sisters of charity; II. **B-keit**, (w.) f. mercy, compassion, pity, tenderness, charity; Theol. B-keit Gottes, grace.

Bär'..., in comp. —motte, f. Entom. bear-fly; —muff, m., —muffe, f. bear-skin muff.

Bär'mutter, (str.) f. see Gebärmutter; —kraut, n. see Liebstöckel.

Bär'mütze, (w.) f. bearskin cap.

Barn, (str.) m. provinc. 1) crib, manger; 2) barn (Banse); —beißer, m. see Krippenbeißer.

Barn'stein, (str.) m. see Bockstein.

* **Barock'**, (Barock'isch, Wid., l. u.) adj. baroque, quaint; —perlen, pl. rugged pearls.

* **Barome'ter**, (str.) n. & m. (Gr.) Phys. barometer; —stand, m. height or reading of the barometer; —uhr, f. barometrograph. — **Barome'trisch**, adj. barometrical.

* **Baron'**, (str.) m. (Mid. Lat.) baron. — **Baro'nin**, **Barones'se**, (w.) f. baroness. — **Baronie'**, (l. u.) **Baronei'**, (w.) f. barony. — **Baronisi'ren**, (w.) v. tr. to create (one) a baron, to confer the title of baron on (one).

* **Baroskop'**, (str.) n. (Gr.) baroscope, see Barometer.

Bär'pfeife, (w.) f. a very deep-toned pipe of an organ.

Bar're, (w.) f. or **Bar'ren**, (str.) m. 1) a) bar, a wooden rail; b) B-n, pl. Gymn. parallel bars, parallels; c) T. pole (of a piano, &c.); 2) unprepared whale-bone; 3) a long piece of metal, bar, ingot (of gold and silver); 4) bar (bank of sand, &c. at the mouth of a river, &c.); B-eingus, m., B-nform, f. ingot-mould; B-ngold, n. gold in bars, solid gold, gold-ingots; B-nhändler, m. bullion-dealer.

* **Barrica'de**, (w.) f. (Fr.) barricade, barricado; B-nkampf, B-nkrieg, m. street-warfare.

* **Barrie're** [pr. bärjä'ere], (w.) (Fr.) f. barrier; guard; railway-gate; B-nwächter, m. gate-keeper, barrier-waiter.

Bär'sanikel, (str.) m. Bot. bear's ear sanicle (Cortusa L.).

Barsch, **Bärsch**, (str.) m. Ichth. perch (Perca [fluviatilis] L.).

Barsch, I. adj. harsh, bluff, rough, gruff, snappish; II. B-heit, (w.) f. harshness, &c.

Bar'schaft, (w.) f. cash (in hand), ready money; stock; property.

Bar'..., in comp. —schenkelig, adj. bare thighed; —schenkler, m. sansculotte; Comm.-e. —sendung, f. consignment of or in specie; —sendungen machen, to put (send) in cash, to cover.

Bär'schling, m. T. see Bär, 4.

Barsch'ling, (str.) m. see Barsch.

Bart, (str., pl. Bär'te) m. 1) beard; 2) a) whiskers (of a cat); b) wattle (of a cock); c) beard, barb (of a fish); 3) Bot. barb; — an der Artischocke, choke; beard (of corn); 4) chuck, beard of a horse; 5) Lock-sm. beard, ward, (key-)bit; 6) — am Schiff, Mar. foul bottom; 7) Astr. beams, beard, rays (of a comet); 8) Mint. burr, chipped edge, raggedness of the edge; (see Schrötling) Typ. burr, beard of a letter; 9) Found. seam, fash; 10) Archit. Architect. jutty, lap of a rafter; (sich) um des Kaisers — streiten, prov. to dispute about trifles; sich (Dat.) den — abnehmen lassen, to have (get) one's self shaved; in den — brummen, to mumble, speak in a low voice, to grumble between the teeth; Einem etwas in den — sagen or werfen, to tell a thing to a person's face, to throw into one's teeth; coll.-s. frei vom B-e, with frankness, plainly, freely, without reserve; Einem einen — machen, to put a trick upon one, to fob one.

Bart'..., in comp. —adler, m. see —geier; —affe, m. see Brillaffe; —ammer, f. see Rohrammer; —anker, m. T. iron instrument used in loosening the beard or whiskers of a whale.

Bär'tau, (str.) n. T. pile-rope.

Bart'..., in comp. —becken, n. shaving-basin; —beißer, —beißker, m. Ichth. bearded loach (Cobitis barbatula L.); —bürste, f. brush for the beard or whiskers; —dohle, f. Ornith. see —krähe.

Bar'te, (w.) f. 1) beard or barb of a whale; B-n, pl. unprepared whale-bone; 2) broad axe, chip-axe.

Bar'teisen, (str.) n. see —zange.

Bär'teln, (w.) v. tr. Cloth. to give the first cropping or shearing to (the cloth). — **Bär'teltuch**, (str.) n. cloth of the first cropping.

Bart'..., in comp. —eule, see Frühlingsfliege; —faden, m. Ichth. barb; —falke, m. see —geier; —fisch, m. 1) see Barbe; 2) cock-paddle, sea-owl (Cyclopterus gelatinosus); —flaum, m. down (downy beard); —flechte, f. Bot. a genus of lichens (Usnea barbata L.); —fliege, f. Entom. bearded fly (Musca mystacea); —geier, m. Ornith. bearded vulture (Vultur barbatus L.); Bot.-s. —gerste, f. rice-barley, sprat-barley (Hordeum zeocriton L.); —gras, n. beard-grass (Andropogon L.); wohlriechendes —gras, see Kameelheu; —grundel, f. see Schmerle; —hafer, m. wild oats (Avena fatua L.).

Bartholomä'us (**Bar'thel**, abbr.), m. Bartholomew (P. N.): die —nacht, f. Fr. Hist. the massacre of St. Bartholomew.

Bär'tig, adj. bearded; Bot. barbate.

Bart'..., in comp. —kamm, m. comb for the beard or whiskers; —karpfen, m. Ichth. bearded carp; —klappe, f. bit-pincers; —krähe, f. bearded crow (Corvus hottentottus); —kratzer, m. cont. shaver, barber; —kuckuk, m. Ornith. barbet (Bucco L.); —lappen, m. Ornith. gills.

Bärt'ling, (str.) m. a bearded person.

Bart'los, adj. beardless; der B-e, a lack-beard. — **Bart'losigkeit**, (w.) f. beardlessness.

Bart'..., in comp. —männchen, n. 1) Ornith. see —meise; 2) Ichth. see Schlangenfisch, gemeiner; —meise, f. Ornith. the least butcher-bird, bearded titmouse (Parus biarmicus L.); —messer, n. coll. razor; —(moos)moos, m. Bot. bearded moss, barbule (Barbula L.); —neige, f. vulg. the remains of wine, &c. left in a vessel; —nelke, f. Bot. sweet-william (Dianthus barbatus L.); —nuß, f. filbert; —platte, f. Coop. bottom-piece; —putzer, m. shaver, barber; —robbe, f. Zool. bearded seal (Phoca barbata Müll.).

Bär'risch, (str.) m. see Bärenklau.

Bar'sche, (w.) f. sweep, steering-oar (used on board of flat boats or rafts).

Bart'..., in comp. —scherer, m. see —putzer; —schüssel, f. see —becken; —seife, f. shaving-soap; —sittich, m. Ornith. bearded parrot (Psittacus pondicerianus); —sperling, m. see —meise; —spitzen, f. pl. Entom. feelers, palpi; —stern, m. comet; —vogel, m. Ornith. 1) see —kuckuk; 2) grauer —vogel, wattle-bird (Glaucopis cinerea Gmel.); —weizen, m. (red-eared) bearded wheat (Triticum spelta L.); —wildhafer, m. see Fahnenhafer; —zange, m., zängelchen, n. nippers, tweezers.

* **Barut'sche**, (w.) f. (Ital.) coll. barouche.

Bär'..., in comp. —winde, f. Bot.-s. bearbind (Convolvulus sepium L.); —winkel, m. periwinkle, see Wintergrün; —wolf, m. see Währwolf; —wurz, —wurzel, f. see 1) Bärenfenchel; 2) Bärenklau; 3) bear's wort (Bärwurz); 4) candy-carrot (Athamanta Cretensis L.).

(human) skin; 4) *Comm.* name of several Indian stuffs, half bast, half silk.

* Basta! (*Ital.*) I. *interj.* basta! enough! II. *s.* (Baste, [*w.*] *f.* grüner Ober in the Lomber card) *Gam.* basto; (Treff Aß) ace of clubs.

Bas'tard [*sometimes* Bastárd], *s.* I. (*str.*) *m.* 1) bastard; 2) *Zool.* & *Bot.* (—thier, —pflanze) hybrid; II. *in comp.* —adler, *m.* *Ornith.* bold (*Aquila vulturinus* Kl.); —ameise, *f.* *see* Afterameise; —art, *f.* mixed *or* mongrel breed; —artig, *adj.* hybrid, hybridous; —birke, *f.* *see* Geldbirke; —birkhuhn, *n.* a small kind of grouse; —blattlaus, *f.*, —bock, *m.* *see* Afterblattlaus & Afterholzbock; —falke, *m.* *Sport.* coistrel; —feile, *f.* *Mech.* bastard-file; —fenster, *n.* *Archit.* mezzanine; —form, *f.* *Sug-m.* bastard-form *or* mould; —geier, *m.* white-headed vulture (*Vultur fulvus* Gm.); —hieb, *m.* bastard cut (of a file); —jasmin, *m.* white syringa, mock-orange (*Philadelphus coronarius* L.); —jungfer, *f.* *see* Ameisenlöwe; —käfer, *m.* *see* Halbkäfer; —kalmus, *m.* *Bot.* *see* Wasserschwertel; —[illegible], *m.* billiard; —klee, *m.* *Bot.* hybrid clover (*Trifolium hybridum* L.); —kranich, *m.* *see* Schreivogel; —lerche, *f.* *see* Wiesenpieper; —linde, *f.* *see* glatte Sommerlinde; —makrele, *f.* *Ichth.* scad, horse-mackerel (*Caranx trachurus* L.); —nachtigall, *f.* Hungarian nightingale (Sprosser); —natter, *f.* *see* Kurzschwanz; —pflanze, *f.* hybrid (plant); —quitte, *f.* *see* Zwergmispel; —race, *f.* *see* —art; —spindel, —spinnmaschine, *f.* *Spin.* mule; —thier, *n.* hybrid (animal); *Comm-s.* —wechsel, *m.* accommodation bill, *slang*, kite; —wein, *m.* name of *Pedro Ximenes* (a Spanish wine); —wespe, *f.* sand-wasp (Sandwespe); —wolle, *f.* *Comm.* the inferior locks of wool (of a sheep of mixed breed).

* Bastei', Bastion', (*w.*) *f.* (*Fr.-Ital.*) *Mil.* bastion, bulwark; leere (hohle) —, hollow bastion.

Bas'teln, Bäs'teln, (*w.*) *v.* *intr.* *coll.* (*with* an *sich Dat.*) & *tr.* to work minutely (at a petty job), to dawdle (about a thing), to trifle with.

Bas'ten, *adj.* of bast, bark.

Bas'ter, (*str.*, *pl.* *sometimes* (*L. G.*) B-n) *m.* *coll.* *for* Bastard: 1) bastard; 2) *Comm.* bastard sugar, raw sugar.

Bast'..., *in comp.* —hanf, *m.* raw *or* undressed hemp; —hut, *m.* chip-hat, bast-hat; —matte, *f.* bast-cover, bast-matting; —seide, *f.* [illegible] cocoons; —fell, *n.*, —strick, *m.* bast-rope, Indian-cordage; —ulme, *f.* *Bot.* soft-leaved elm (*Ulmus campestris* L.).

Bas'ting, (*str.*) *m.* *see* Bast, 2.

* Bastona'de, (*w.*) *f.* bastinado; Einem die — geben, Bastoni'ren, (*w.*) *v.* *tr.* to bastinado.

* Bataille [*pr.* batal'[je], (*w.*) *f.* (*Fr.*) *Mil-s.* battle; —marsch, *m.* march in battle-array; B-[illegible], *n.* chain *or* strap of a helmet; B-[illegible], *m.* polemoscope.

* Bataillon' [*pr.* batal[jon'], (*str.*) *n.* (*Fr.*) [battalion.

* Bata'te, (*w.*) *f.* 1) batatas, sweet potato; 2) (*or* B-nwinde) *f.* *Bot.* tuberous bind-weed (*Convolvulus batatas* L.).

Bata'vien, *n.* *Anc.* & *Mod.* *Geogr.* Batavia (*the Lat.* name for Holland). — Bata'vier, (*str.*) *m.* Batavian. — Bata'visch, *adj.* Batavian.

[illegible], *v.* *tr.* *provinc.* (*L. G.*) *see* Batten.

[illegible], (*str.*) *n.* knitting-thread.

[illegible], (*str.*) *m.* *Bot.* germander (*Teucrium chamaedrys* L.), common betony (*Betonica officinalis* L.).

[illegible], (*w.*) *f.* *Mar.* (B-sholz) a piece [illegible] to which cables are fastened, *pl.* [illegible] die große —, main bitts; die kleine [illegible] — be- [illegible] of the — [illegible] B-[illegible], *m.* cross-piece

of the bits; B-sbolzen, *m.* *pl.* bolts of the bits; B-sklötzer, *m.* *pl.* bits; B-sknie, *n.* *pl.* spurs of the bits; B-sschlag, *m.* bitter of the cable; B-sspur, *n.* step of the bit-pins; B-sspa(r)ren, B-sstreiten, B-sstützen, *f.* *pl.* bitpins.

* Batist', (*str.*) *m.* (*Fr.*) *Comm.* cambric; —blumen, *pl.* cambric flowers; —tuch, *n.* cambric handkerchief; —weber, *m.* cambric weaver.

* Batock'en, Batog'gen, *pl.* *see* Padoggen.

* Batrach'ier, (*str.*) *m.* *Zool.* (*Gr.*) batrachian (Froschthier).

Bat'ten, (*w.*) *v.* *tr.* *provinc.* (*L. G.* *for* Bessern *&c.*) to boot, avail, profit.

* Batterie', (*w.*) *f.* (*Fr.*) 1) *Mil.* (*also Electr.*) battery; eine — Fußartillerie, a brigade of artillery; eine reitende —, a troop of horse-artillery; eine — aufwerfen, to throw, cast, raise up a battery; 2) *Gunn.* & *Gun-sm.* cover, hammer; 3) *Mar-s.* die untere —, the lower gun-deck; die obere —, the upper battery; die halbe —, tier; —feder, *f.* *Gun-sm.* hammer-spring; —geschütz, *n.* heavy ordnance; —platte, *f.* *Electr.* battery plate; —seite, *f.* broadside; —stein, *m.* striking flint; —stücke, *n.* *pl.* *see* —geschütz; —wurst, *f.* *Gunn.* saucisse.

* Batti'ren, (*w.*) *v.* *intr.* (*Fr.*) 1) *Danc.* to strike the calves together; 2) *Fenc.* to knock the foil out of the antagonist's hand.

Batz'e, (*w.*) *f.* *provinc.* cart-tilt.

Bätz, Bätze, *see* Betz, Betze.

Bat'zen, (*str.*) *m.* 1) *coll.* *a)* a large lump of any soft substance; *b)* a piece of loam, with which the eye of a furnace is closed previous to smelting; *c)* a large quantity; 2) batz (a Swiss coin, four kreutzers); 3) a gold *or* silver ornament for the neck of females.

Bat'zen, (*w.*) *v.* *intr.* to lump (together).

Bat'zig, *adj.* *coll.* snappish, *&c.* *see* Patzig.

Bau, (*str.*) *m.* 1) *a)* the (act of) building, erection, construction; formation; im —(e) begriffen, in course of construction, in progress of erection; sein Haus ist im B-e begriffen, his house is (in) building, *or* is being built; *b)* edifice, structure; 2) *Agr.* culture, cultivation (of lands); 3) *Min.* working (of a mine); 4) *Sport.* (a subterranean structure of animals) hole, den, kennel, cover, earth; aus dem B-e jagen, to uncover, unearth, unkennel; im B-e liegen, to kennel (said of foxes); burrow (of rabbits, *&c.*); in den — schlüpfen, to burrow; 5) *fig.* fabric (of the universe, *&c.*), form, make, manner of organisation, structure; conformation (of the organs); (Körperbau) frame; contexture (of muscles, fibres, *&c.*); auf den — kommen, to be condemned to the public works, *cf.* Festungsbau.

Bau'..., *in comp.* —academie, *f.* architectural academy; —accord, *m.* building-contract; —amt, *n.* board of works; building-court; —anschlag, *m.* builder's estimate; —art, *f.* structure, construction; architecture, style (of building); —aufseher, *m.* superintendent of a building.

Bau'bar, *adj.* cultivable, arable.

Bau'..., *in comp.* —beamte, *m.* member of the board of works; —bedarf, *m.* building-materials; —begnadigung, *f.* building-privilege *or* facility granted by government; —bericht, *m.* report of the board of works, *&c.*

Bauch, (*str.*, *pl.* Bäu'che) *m.* 1) belly; womb; *Anat.* venter, abdomen; zum — gehörig, den — betreffend, abdominal, gastric, ventral; *cont.* (von Menschen) maw, paunch; *Ich.* pouch; seinem B-e dienen, to be given (to pamper) to one's belly; sich (*Dat.*) (vor Lachen) den — halten, to hold one's sides (with laughing); 2) a swelling out, protuberance, *particul.* *a)* *Mar.* bilge; *aa)* the broadest part of a ship's bottom; *bb)* bunt, leech, belly (of a sail); *b)* bulge (of a cask); einen — machen, to bulk out, to bulge.

Bauch'..., *in comp.* —band, *n.* *Coop.* hoop round the middle of a cask; —bedeckung, *f.* *Anat.* abdominal integument; —beschwerden, *f.* *pl.* complaint, disease in the bowels; —bläsig, *adj.* broken-winded (of horses); —blast, *n.* *Vet.* chest-foundering; —bohrer, *m.* *Turn.* broach; —bruch, *m.* hypogastrocele; gastrocele; rupture, hernia; —cirkel, *m.* (outside) callipers; —compresse, *f.* belly-band, truss; —decke, *f.* *see* —bedeckung; —decken(arterie *&c.*), *Anat.* epigastric (artery, *&c.*); —dennungen, —dielen, *pl.* *Mar.* the thick stuff and ceiling placed next to the keel over all the floor-timbers; —diener, *m.* *coll.* glutton, belly-slave; —dienst, *m.* gluttony; *Anat-s.* —drüse, *f.* abdominal gland.

Bäu'che, (*w.*) *f.* buck (Lauge).

Bau'chen, (*w.*) *v.* I. *intr.*, *&c.* *see* Ausbauchen; II. *or* Bäu'chen, *tr.* 1) to form, fashion into a belly; 2) to buck.

Bauch'..., *in comp.* —fell, *n.* peritoneum; —fellentzündung, *f.* *Med.* peritoneal inflammation; —fieber, *n.* gastric fever; *Ichth-s.* —flosse, *f.* ventral fin; —flosser, *m.* *pl.* abdominals; —fluß, *m.* *Med.* looseness, diarrhoea; lientery; dysentery; —flüssig, *adj.* lienteric; —förmig, *adj.* bulgy; —füßler, *m.* *Moll.* gastropod; —gegend, *f.* die obere, untere, mittlere, the epigastric, umbilical, hypogastric region; —geschwulst, *f.* tumor in the belly; —glieder, *pl.* the feet (of birds); the hind-feet (of mammalia); —gordingen, *f.* *pl.* *Mar.* bunt-lines; —grimmen, *n.* *Med.* gripes, colic; belly-ache; —gurt, *m.* belly-band, girt, girth; surcingle; —gürtel, *m.* *see* Leibgürtel; —haken, *m.* *Join.* hook; —haut, *f.* *see* —fell; die fette —haut einer Gans, apron of a goose; —höhle, *f.* *Med.* abdominal cavity.

Bau'chig, Bäu'chig, *adj.* 1) bellied; convex; — sein, to belly; 2) *Bot.* ventricous, ventriculous; — aufgeschwollen, swelling out in knobs.

Bauch'..., *in comp.* —karpfen, *m.* *see* Meerbarbe; —kieme, *f.* *see* Blindaal; —klopfen, *n.* *Med.* abdominal pulsation; —kneipen, *n.* *see* —grimmen; —krampf, *m.* iliac passion; —krankheit, *f.* gastric disease.

Bäuch'lein, (*str.*) *n.* (*dimin.* *of* Bauch) small belly; *iron.* paunch.

Bauch'..., *in comp.* *Anat-s.* —linie, *f.* (*Lat.*) *linea alba*; —mündung, *f.* bottom of the stomach; —naht, *f.* *Surg.* gastroraphy; —nerv, *m.* *Anat.* abdominal nerve; —öffnung, *f.* *Surg.* gastrotomy; —pulsader, *f.* *Anat.* celiac artery; —reden, *n.* ventriloquism; —redner, *m.* ventriloquist; —rednerisch, *adj.* ventriloquous; —rednerkunst, *f.* ventriloquism; —region, *f.* *see* —gegend; —riemen, *m.* *see* —gurt; —ring, *m.* *Anat.* abdominal *or* inguinal ring; —runde, *f.* *see* Bauchung; —säge, *Forest.* felling-saw; —sauger, *m.* *Ichth.* sucker, sucking-fish (*Cyclopterus* L.); —schiene, *f.* *Railw.* fish-bellied- (*or* fish-belly-) rail; —schmerz, *m.* *see* —grimmen; —schnitt, *m.* *Surg.* gastrotomy; —schwimmer, *m.* *Entom.* *see* Wasserwanze; —seisingen, *pl.* *Mar.* bunt-gaskets; —sorge, *f.* belly-care; —speichel, *m.* *Anat.* pancreatic juice; —speicheldrüse, *f.* *Anat.* pancreatic gland, pancreas; —steinschnitt, *m.* *Surg.* lithotomy; —stich, *m.* *Surg.* paracentesis, tapping of the belly; —strippe, *f.* strap of a girt; —stück, *m.* 1) meat from the belly, belly-piece; 2) *Mar-s.* floor-timber; navel-timber; —stücke der Kabspurren, futtock-riders; —stücke der Spanten, flats; —stücke mit einander verbunden, *Ship-b.* cutting down-lines; —thier, *n.* *Zool.* *see* Schleimthier.

Bau'chung, Bäu'chung, (*w.*) *f.* bellying; swelling, protuberance; convexity; bulge.

Bauch'..., *in comp.* —wassersucht, *f.* *Med.* dropsy in the belly, ascites; —weh, *n.* belly-ache; —windsucht, *f.* *Med.* tympanitis, tympany; —wolle, *f.* (von Schafen) *Comm.* under-

dendrite: *Miner. see* —achat; —steinartig, *adj.* dendritic; —stempel, *m. see* Waldhammer; —stock, *m.*, —stubbe, —strunk, *m.* trunk, stem of a tree; —stück, *n.* 1) plot planted with trees; 2) *T.* lower blade of the shears used in cutting coins to their proper weight: —stütze, *f.* stay, prop of a tree: *Mar.-s.* —talje, *f.* main-boom tackle: —tau, *n.* guess-warp, guest rope; —torte, *see* —kuchen; —veilchen, *n. Bot.* tree-violet (*Alsodeia*); —wachs, *n. Gard.* mummy, grafting-wax; —wagen, *m. see* —karre; —wanze, *f. Entom.* knolster, tree-bug: white-bug (on vines); —wärter, *m. see* Förster; —weide, *f. Bot.* white-willow (*Salix alba* L.); —weißling, *m. Entom.* hedge-butterfly (*Pontia crataegi* L.); —werk, *n.* 1) culture and training of trees; 2) *Paint.* foliage; —winde, *f. see* Epheu; —wipfel, *m.* top of a tree.

Baum'wolle, (*w.*) *f.* cotton; gefleckte —, stained cotton; ungereinigte —, cotton in the seed.

Baum'wollen, I. *adj.* (of) cotton; —Futterzeug, cotton lining; b-e Gaze, *f.* tarletane; b-er Casimir, *m.* casimere nankeen; b-es Webegarn, *n.* cotton twist; b-e Tücher, *n. pl.* (cotton) calicoes; II. *in comp.* —abfall, *m.* cotton-waste; —artig, *adj.* cottonous, cottony; —band, *n.* cotton binding *or* tape; —barchent, *m. Comm.* twilled cotton-stuff; —baum, *m.* cotton-tree (*Bombax* L.); —docht, *m.* cotton-wick; —enden, *n. pl.* cotton-waste; —garn, *n.* cotton-yarn *or* twist, spun cotton; —gras, *n. see* Wollgras; —knopf, *m.* twist-button; —kratze, *f.* cotton-card; —manufactur, *f.* cotton-manufacture; —pflanze, *f. Bot.* cotton-tree (*Gossypium* L.); —pflanzer, *m.* cotton-grower; —reinigungsmaschine, *f. Mech.* cotton gin; —same, *m.* cotton-seed; —samenöl, *n.* cotton-seed-oil; —sammt, *m.* cotton-velvet, velveteen; —spinnerei, *f.* 1) cotton-spinning; 2) cotton-mill; —spinnmaschine, *f.* spinning-jenny; —staude, *f. see* —pflanze; —streicher, *m. T.* carder; —streichmaschine, *f.* cotton-machine; —waaren, *f. pl.* cotton-stuffs *or* goods, cottons; —weberei, *f.* cotton-mill, cotton-manufactory; —weide, *f. see* Lorbeerweide; —zeug, *m. & n.* cotton-stuff, cotton fabric, cotton-linen; cottons; —zeugfärberei, *f.* 1) cotton cloth dyeing; 2) cotton cloth dyeing establishment; —zwirn, *m.* cotton thread.

Baum'wollicht, *adj.* cottony, cottonous.

Baum'..., *in comp.* —wurz, *f. see* Engelsüß; —wurzelsauger, *m. see* Fichtenrohrblatt; —zucht, *f.* 1) arboriculture; 2) nursery of trees; —zunder, *m. see* Zunderschwamm; —zweig, *m.* branch of a tree.

Bau'..., *in comp.* —(polizei)ordnung, *f.* (police) regulations for the construction of buildings; —platz, *m.* building-ground, plot (*cf.* —stelle); —polizei, *f.* (government) building-department; —rath, *m.* government surveyor of buildings.

Bäu'risch, *adj. see* Bäuerisch.

Bau'..., *in comp.* —riß, *m.* plan for a building; —sachen, *pl.* building concerns; —sand, *m.* mortar-sand.

Baus'back (Baus'backe), (*str.*) *m.* a person with blowzy cheeks; (*or* B-engesicht), *n. joc.* a blowze, Blowselinda, Blowsabella. — **Baus'bäckig,** *adj.* chub-cheeked, chubfaced, chubby, plump-faced, blob-cheeked, puffed.

Bausch, (*str., pl.* **Bäu'sche**) *m.* pad, bolster; bunch, bundle; (von Federn) tuft; (Wulst) roll, (Masse) lump; *Surg.* pledget, compress; in — und Bogen, in *or* by the lump, in the (at the) great *or* gross, whole sale; in — und Bogen kaufen, to purchase (buy) in the lump; in — und Bogen verkaufen, to sell (goods) by the lump; to sell (nach der Ballenschnur, uneingepackt) under the cords; to sell (a cargo) before the hatches are lifted; —ähnlich, *adj.* resembling a pad *or* bolster; —ärmel, *m.* padded *or* puffed sleeve.

Bau'schäling, (*w.*) *f.* (*L. G.*) wharf for loading and unloading vessels (Bauschalung).

Bäusch'chen, (*str.*) *n.* (*dimin. of* Bausch) 1) little pad; 2) *Typ.* bearer; 3) *Surg.* dossil, pledget, compress.

Bau'sche, (*w.*) *f. see* Bausch.

Bäu'schel, (*str.*) *m. T.* miner's hammer.

Bau'schen, (*w.*) *v. intr.* to swell, to stick, bunch out; to bag; b-de Güter, bulky goods. — **Bau'schig,** *adj.* puffy, swelled, puffed out.

Bausch'..., *in comp.* —hosen, *f. pl.* wide pantaloons, slops; —kauf, *m.* purchase in the lump; —summe, *f.* average sum, sum total.

Bau'..., *in comp.* —schreiber, *m.* clerk of the board of works; —schule, *f.* architectural school.

Bau'se, (*w.*) *f. T.* sketch or design produced by pouncing or tracing.

Bau'sen, (*w.*) *v.* I. *intr. see* Bauschen; II. *tr.* to prick (a design) and rub (it) over with coal dust in order to transfer it on a paper underneath, to pounce, *cf.* Durchzeichnen.

Bau'..., *in comp.* stätte, *see* —stelle; —stein, *m.* stone for building; —stelle, *f.* building-ground, site of a building; *Am.* lot; —stil, *m.* style of building; gothischer —stil, Gothic style; —stoff, *m. see* —materialien; —stück, *n.* block-beam; —sucht, *f.* mania of building; —süchtig, *adj. see* —lustig.

Bau'ten, (*w.*) *f. pl.* buildings, edifices; öffentliche —, public works.

Bau'..., *in comp.* —tischler, *m.* working builder; —unternehmer, *m.* builder; contractor (of a railway, &c.); —verständig, *adj.* skilled in architecture; —verwalter, *m.* steward of building concerns; —werk, *n.* (architectural) structure, building; —wesen, *n.* building matters or concerns, building-department, architecture; —wissenschaft, *f. see* —kunst; —würdig, *adj. Min.* worthy of being worked (*cf.* Abbauwürdig); —wuth, *f.* rage for building (*cf.* —sucht).

Baux, *interj.* bang! bounce! dash! smash!

Bau'zen, (*w.*) *v. intr.* to fall with a banging noise, to bounce, dash, thump.

Bau'..., *in comp.* —zeug, *n. see* —materialien; —zierrat(h), *f.* architectural ornament; —zweck, *m.* building-purpose.

* **Ba'vian,** *see* Pavian.

Ba'xen, (*w.*) *v.* I. *tr. Mar.* to breech (the guns); II. *intr. coll. for* Boxen.

Bay, Bay'er &c., *see* **Bai, Baier** &c.

* **Bayonet',** *see* Bajonet.

* **Bazar',** (*str.*) *m.* (*Turk.*) bazar, bazaar.

* **Bdel'lium,** (*str.*) *n. Pharm.* bdellium.

Beab'schieden, (*w.*) *v. refl. see* Verabschieden.

Beab'sichtigen, (*w.*) *v. tr.* to have in view or contemplation, to contemplate, to aim at; to intend, to purpose, to mean (to do); to propose; beabsichtigt, *p. a.* intentional; der beabsichtigte Zweck, the end in view, the object proposed. — **Beab'sichtigung,** (*w.*) *f.* (*l. u.*) intention (of doing, &c. a thing), premeditation (of a murder, &c).

Beach'ten, (*w.*) *v. tr.* to mind, consider, heed, to give heed to, to pay attention to, to take into consideration; to take notice of, to notice, observe; nicht —, to disregard, overlook, neglect; b-swerth, *adj.* worthy of notice, deserving attention.

Beach'tung, (*w.*) *f.* consideration, notice, remark, attention; b-swerth, b-swürdig, *see* Beachtenswerth.

Beack'ern, (*w.*) *v. tr.* to plough, till, put in tilth (Beackerung).

Beä'dern, (*w.*) *v. tr.* to furnish with veins; to ornament with (something) like veins.

Beam'te (*contr. from* Beam'tete, *which is less usual*), *m.* (*decl. like adj.*) (civil) officer, functionary; official; place-man; B-nherrschaft, *f.* bureaucracy; B-nstand, *m.* class or body of civil officers *or* place-men; B-nstolz, *m.* pride of office.

Beam'ten, (*w.*) *v. tr.* to invest with an office; to commission; beamtet, in office, in place.

Beam'tenthum, (str.) n. functionaryism.

Beäng'stigen, (l. u.:) **Beäng'sten,** (w.) v. tr. to cause anxiety or uneasiness, to make uneasy, to frighten. — **Beäng'stigung,** (w.) f. anxiety, uneasiness, anguish of mind.

Bean'spruchen, (w.) v. tr. to lay claim to, to claim.

Bean'standen, (w.) v. tr. to object to: eine Rechnung —, to demur to (hesitate about) an account.

Bean'tragen, (w.) v. tr. to (make a) motion for, to move for, to propose.

Beant'worten, (w.) v. tr. to answer, to reply to: die Frage beantwortet sich (refl.) leicht, the question is easily answered.

Beant'wortlich, adj. answerable.

Beant'wortung, (w.) f. answering, reply; (eines Räthsels) solution; (witzige) repartee: Law, rejoinder: in — Ihres Geehrten, in reply or answer to your favour.

Bean'wartschaften, (w.) v. tr. Law, to confer a reversion or expectancy on (a person).

Bear'beitbar, adj. what may be worked or treated of, workable: tractable.

Bear'beiten, (w.) v. tr. 1) to work at, to elaborate: a) to produce by labour, prepare, manufacture: b) aa) to dress, till, dig, cultivate (the ground); bb) T. to work, cut, hew (a stone); c) fig. to treat (a subject), to have in hand, execute; to adapt, rearrange: für das Volk —, to popularise; nach einer deutschen Übersetzung bearbeitet, adapted from a German translation; 2) fig. coll. to work or act upon by moral influence, to ply hard, to win round, to make come to; 3) fam. to belabour, thrash, drub, hide: schwer zu —, hard work.

Bear'beitung, (w.) f. the (act of) working at, &c.; composition; rearrangement, adaptation; Metall., &c. manipulation, treatment: elaboration.

Bearg'wöhnen, (w.) v. tr. to suspect.

Beä'ren, (w.) v. tr. to bring into tilth, to till, cultivate.

Beasch'en, (w.) v. tr. to strew with ashes.

Beauf'sichtigen, (w.) v. tr. to inspect, control: to keep one's eye upon. — **Beauf'sichtiger,** (str.) m. inspector, overseer. — **Beauf'sichtigung,** (w.) f. inspection, control.

Beauf'tragen, (w.) v. tr. to commission, to charge, instruct, empower, to request, desire: er wurde mit der Ausführung beauftragt, he was charged with the execution. — **Beauf'träger,** (str.) m. (l. u.) commissioner, constituent. — **Beauf'tragte,** m. (decl. like adj.) he who is commissioned, agent, deputy: der gerichtliche —, commissary.

Beau'genscheinigen, (w.) v. tr. to inspect, to take a view of. — **Beau'genscheinigung,** (w.) f. ocular inspection.

Beäu'geln, (w.) v. tr. to ogle, eye, to leer at.

Beba'ken, (w.) v. tr. Mar. to put out, place, or lay tuns, beacons, buoys: to provide with marks.

Bebän'dern, (w.) v. tr. to decorate, trim, or trick out with ribbons; bebändert, p. a. trimmed, set off with ribbons; hud. be-ribboned: covered with order. [barbed.

Bebär'tet, Bebär'tet, Herald. p. a. bearded,

Bebau'en, (w.) v. tr. 1) to cover with buildings: diese Felder waren bebaut worden, these fields had been built upon: 2) to cultivate, to dress (the ground). [with trees.

Bebäu'men, (w.) v. tr. to cover, plant (over)

Bebau'ung, (w.) f. 1) the (act of) covering with buildings; 2) cultivation (of the soil, &c.).

Be'ben, (w.) v. intr. to quake (vor (with dat.), with), shake, quiver, tremble; to shiver (with cold); to thrill (with joy); b—d, p. a. trembling, &c.; tremulous (voice, &c.).

Be'ber, (str.) m. (or **Be'bezug**) Mus. tremor (of organs): —[illegible], f. Bot. see Zitterpappel.

Be'berig, Be'berlich, adj. coll. inclined or apt to tremble, shiver, shake.

Be'bern (provinc. pr. bew'wern), (w.) v. intr. vulg. to quake, &c. incessantly.

Bebil'dern, (w.) v. tr. to hang or cover with pictures. [cover.

Bebin'den, (str.) v. tr. to bind all over, to

Bebi'samen, (w.) v. tr. to scent with musk.

Bebla'ken, (w.) v. tr. to smoke (the moulds).

Beblät'tern, (w.) v. tr. to cover with leaves: beblättert, p. a. Bot. foliate. [to shoot.

Beblech'en, (w.) v. tr. to cover with tin.

Beblei'en, (w.) v. tr. to cover with lead; to lead: Cloth. to plumb. [trify (Elektrisiren).

Beblitz'en, (w.) v. tr. (Campe, l. u.) to elec-

Beblü'men, (w.) v. tr. to embellish or cover with flowers: wie lieblich beblümt sich die Erde (Hagedorn), how sweetly earth decks herself with flowers. [&c. with blood.

Beblu'ten, (w.) v. tr. to cover, to sully,

Bebo'den, (w.) v. tr. Coop. to bottom (a tub or cask).

Bebol'len, (w.) v. tr. to lay out, line, furnish with thick boards or planks.

Bebom'ben, (w.) v. tr. (Campe, l. u.) to bombard (Bombardiren). [(with lace).

Bebor'den, Bebor'ten, (w.) v. tr. to trim

Bebrä'men, (w.) v. tr. to border, trim, edge.

Bebrä'mung, (w.) f. Herald. imbordering.

Bebril'len, (w.) v. tr. to provide with spectacles: bebrillt, p. a. spectacled, dicht. (Cowper:) spectacle-bestrid.

Bebra'ten, (w.) v. tr. Cook. to bound.

Bebrü'ten, (w.) v. tr. to sit over brooding; to hatch, to brood.

Be'bung, (w.) f. 1) a shaking, palpitation, beating; trembling of (the voice); undulation (as of waves or elastic fluids): Phys. oscillation, vibration: 2) see Beber. [charge.

Bebür'den, (w.) v. tr. to burden, load; to

Bebusch'en, Bebüsch'en, (w.) v. tr. to cover with bushes or bush-like tufts, &c.: bebuscht, bebüscht, p. a. bushy: tufted.

* **Beccafi'ge,** (w.) f. (Ital.) Ornith. 1) fig-pecker epicurean warbler (Motacilla ficedula L.); 2) see Weindrossel.

* **Beccassi'ne,** (w.) f. (Fr.) Ornith. snipe (Scolopax gallinago L.); kleine —, jack-snipe (Scolopax gallinula L.).

Bech'er, a I. (str.) m. 1) a) cup; goblet; bowl: drinking-cup; chalice, beaker; b) zum Würfeln, dice-box: (eines Taschenspielers) juggler's box or cup: 2) Astr. crater: II. in comp. —baum, m. Bot. emetic nut (Trichilia emetica); —blume, f. Bot. salad-burnet (Poterium sanguisorba L.); —druse, f. Miner. crystallised hyalite, transparent quartz; —eisen, n. T. little anvil, beak-(beck- or bick-)iron; —flechte, gemeine, f. Bot. cup-moss (Lichen pyxidatus L.); —förmig, adj. particul. Bot. cup-like, cup-shaped, funnel-shaped, cyathiform; —förmige Galläpfel, cup galls; —glas, n. a cup-shaped glass; —mühle, f. coffee mill with brass hopper (Bail); —schwamm, m. Bot. cup-mushroom: funnel-top (Peziza L.); —spiel, n. a sleight-of-hand trick played with small cups, thimble-rigging; —flappe, f. see —flechte; —stürzer, m. coll. hard drinker, toper; —traube, f. Ent. bat, beetle; —werk, n. T. elevator. [a small cup, goblet, &c.

Bech'erchen, (str.) n. (dimin. of Becher)

Bech'ern, (w.) v. intr. coll. to tipple, tope, bumper.

Bech'ner, (str.) m. provinc. see Faßbinder.

Bech'te(l)n, (w.) v. intr. provinc. to celebrate or keep New Year's tide in a merry way. — **Bech'telistag,** (str.) m. the 2d of January (in Switzerland, the day on which presents are given to children).

Beck'en, (str.) n. 1) a) basin; b) plate: 2) Anat. pelvis: 3) Mus. cymbal: in comp. Anat. &c. —abweichung, f. malformation of the pelvis; —arterie, f. hypogastric artery; —band, n. ligament of the pelvis; —

4) *Herald.* see Beleg; 5) *Mus.* indistinct, not clear (of the voice).

Bedeck'ung, *(w.) f.* 1) the (act of) covering, &c. 2) a covering: *a)* clothes; *b)* cover, tegument; *c)* (*Vim. l. u.*) shelter (vor dem Winde, from the wind); 3) *Astr.* occultation (of a star); 4) *Mil.* escort, convoy, safe-guard; 5) *Comm.* provision; security; 6) *T-s. a)* (eines Windmühlenflügels) clothing; *b)* (der Dampföffnung von den Schiebern) over-lap cover, lap (of the slide), slide-valve lap; *c)* (der Stopfbüchse) packing of the stuffing-box.

Bedeich'en, *(w.) v. tr.* to surround or protect with a dike, to dike.

* **Bedell',** *see* Pedell.

Bedenk'en, *(irr.) v.* I. *tr.* 1) to consider; to think, reflect, ponder, meditate on (upon); to examine, weigh, mind, heed, to bear in mind: bedenke das Ende, consider the end; 2) to care for, to take care of, remember: sich selbst —, to take care of one's own advantage (*coll.* of number one); (Einen) im Testamente —, to remember or put (one) in one's will, to provide for (one), to bequeath something to: Quin hatte den Verfasser der Jahreszeiten mit hundert Pfund bedacht, Quin had set down the author of the Seasons for a hundred pounds: II. *refl.* to advise or reason with one's self, to deliberate, to consider well: 2) to hesitate, pause; sich anders —, to change one's mind: sich eines Bessern —, to bethink one's self (for the better); sich eines Mittels &c. —, *obsolescent*, to devise an expedient, &c.; sich hin und her —, to fluctuate, to waver; Einem zu — geben, to leave to a person's consideration.

Bedenk'en, *n. (str.) n.* 1) *a)* consideration, deliberation, reflection; *b)* † (*Luther, &c.*) opinion, advice (Gutachten); 2) hesitation; doubt (über (*with Acc.*), about), scruple: — tragen, to doubt, hesitate, scruple, to stick at, stagger; ich trage kein —, I entertain no scruple: es ist nicht das mindeste — dabei, there is not the slightest risk to be run in the matter; kein — tragen, not to hesitate, to have no scruple (about), to have no objection (to), not to demur (at); sich (*Dat.*) ein — über (*with Acc.*) machen, to scruple or stumble at ...; ohne —, without any scruple, without hesitation, unhesitatingly.

Bedenk'frist, *(w.) f.* see Bedenkzeit.

Bedenk'lich, I. *adj.* 1) (of persons) hesitating, doubtful; wistful, scrupulous, nice; 2) (of things, &c.) *a)* doubtful, suspicious; hazardous; *b)* critical, serious; er ist — krank, verwundet &c., he is seriously ill, wounded, &c. II. **B-keit,** *(w.) f.* 1) doubtfulness, scrupulousness, scruples, nicety; hesitancy, wavering, irresolution; 2) criticalness, critical state (of affairs, &c.), seriousness (of an illness); [illegible] see Bedenken tragen.

* **Bedenk'zeit,** *(w.) f* time for considering or reflection; respite, delay, leisure.

Bedeuten, I. *(w.) v. tr.* 1) to inform; to give to understand, declare, signify, point out, explain, [illegible]; to set right: lassen Sie sich —! [illegible] sich nicht —, he was [illegible], he would hear no reason, he [illegible] 2) *a)* to enjoin, to [illegible] (with the hand or head); 3) [illegible] auf den Doctern, [illegible] — (*Schiller, An die Freunde*), on [illegible] which represent the world [illegible] sagen Sie mir, was es zu — hat, [illegible] was soll das —? what [illegible] this? how now? 4) to forebode, portend, betoken; 5) to be of [illegible] importance; es hat nichts [illegible], it is of no consequence, [illegible] it matters not, never mind; [illegible] —, it is no great matter. [illegible] II. *n. (str.) n.* intimation; [illegible] intimation (pointing out to [illegible]

Bedeu'tend, *adj.* considerable, important, great: ein b-er Verlust, a great, serious, or heavy loss; er hat ein b-es Farbwaarengeschäft, he is in a large way of business as a colourman or in the colour-line; die Firma gehört unter die minder b-en, the firm ranks among the second-rate ones; significant (Bedeutsam); nichts —, of no consequence.

Bedeut'sam, I. *adj.* significant, significative, full of (*or* fraught with) meaning (looks, &c.); II. **B-keit,** *(w.) f.* significance; importance, consequence.

Bedeu'tung, *(w.) f.* 1) signification, significance, meaning, sense; 2) foreboding, sign, presage; dies ist von guter —, this augurs well; 3) importance, consequence; ein Mann von —, a man of (good) account, of importance, of high standing; es ist von geringer —, it is of little consequence or moment, of slight importance; von keiner —, of no account.

Bedeu'tungs..., *in comp.* **—leer, —los,** *adj.* void of meaning, meaningless, unmeaning, trivial, inconsiderable, insignificant; **—losigkeit,** *f.* insignificance, unmeaningness, triviality: **—reich, —voll,** *adj.* full of meaning, significant; ominous; **—schwer,** *adj.* of great consequence, weighty, momentous.

Bediade'men, *(w.) v. tr.* (*Platen, l. u.*) to adorn with a diadem, to crown.

Bedie'len, *(w.) v. tr.* to board, floor.

Bedie'nen, *(w.) v.* I. *tr.* 1) to serve, attend, to give attendance to, to wait on; 2) (*l. u.*) ein Amt —, to fill an office: eine Kirche —, to do duty in a church, to officiate; was bedient er? what is his employment? 3) (*l. u.*) Einem bedient sein, to be one's counsel; to attend on (as physician); to work for one; sich von Andern — lassen, to make others wait upon us; ich lasse mich nicht gern —, I hate being waited upon; ein Geschütz —, *Gunn.* to work (*w. ü.*: serve) a piece; die Farben (in der Karte) —, *Gam.* to follow suit (at cards); II. *refl.* 1) to help one's self: bitte, — Sie sich! pray, help yourself! 2) sich einer Sache (*Gen.*) —, to make use, or avail one's self of a thing, to turn a thing to (good) advantage or account, to profit by a thing; to apply a thing to; sich einer Gelegenheit —, to avail one's self of, to profit by an opportunity.

Bedienst'en, *(w.) v. tr.* to confer an employment on, to appoint to a situation or office; ein Bediensteter, an official (*cf.* Beamte).

Bedien'te, *m. (decl. like adj.)* 1) servant, serving-man, male servant, servant-man, manservant, lackey, valet; 2) (*l. u.*) official, officer, *see* Beamte.

Bedien'tenhaft, I. *adj. fig.* servile, *slang,* flunkey-like: II. **B-igkeit,** *(w.) f.* servility, *slang,* flunkeyism.

Bedien'ten..., *in comp.* **—kleid,** *n.* servant's livery; square coat; **—lohn,** *m.* wages; **—sitz,** *m.* rumble, dickey (behind a coach); **—zimmer,** *n.* servant's hall.

Bedie'nung, *(w.) f.* 1) (the act of) serving, &c. *cf.* Bedienen; 2) service, waiting, attendance; *Comm.* attention to (execution of) orders; 3) *collect.* servants, domestics; 4) office, employment, place: zu Ihrer —, at your service, for your guide, use, or perusal.

Beding', *(str.) m.* (*now only employed in the higher style*) condition, *see* Bedingung.

Beding'en, *v. tr.* I. (*str.*) to settle terms, to contract, stipulate, to agree for, to condition, to bargain for or about (the price); die Fracht —, to settle the terms of freight; ein Schiff —, to charter a vessel; II. (*w*). to limit, affect; bedingt sein von, to be dependent on, affected by; das ist von Umständen bedingt, that depends on circumstances; **b-d,** *p. a.* conditional.

Beding'niß, *(str.) n.* condition, postulate.

Bedingt', I. *adj.* conditional; hypothetic; b-e Annahme, *Comm.* qualified, partial, enlarged, conditional acceptance; acceptance for part; das B-sein, or II. **B-heit,** *(w.) f.* conditionality, the quality of being conditional, limitation by certain terms.

Beding'ung, *(w.) f.* condition; clause, provision, qualification; terms, stipulation, agreement, proviso: auf gute B-en, on good terms; unter der — (daß), on (the or this) condition, with this understanding, provided (that); auf B-en eingehen, to yield to or accept of conditions; unter billigen B-en, on fair or easy terms; unter jeder —, upon any term; B-en machen, to make terms, to stipulate, to condition; unter keiner —, not upon any terms, on no condition whatever; **B-sweise,** *adv. & adj.* upon condition, on certain conditions; in a qualified sense, conditional, conditionally. [*fig.* to make thorny.

Bedor'nen, *(w.) v. tr.* to cover with thorns;

Bedräng'en, *(w.) v. tr.* to press hard; to oppress, distress, to grieve, afflict, vex, harass; bedrängt, distressed, in distress; necessitous (condition, &c.); *coll.* hard put to, hard up; in bedrängten Verhältnissen, in embarrassed (straitened) circumstances.

Bedräng'niß, *(str.) f.* pressure, grievance, affliction, distress, embarrassment.

Bedräng'ung, *(w.) f.* oppression, pressure, affliction, grievance, vexation: in —, in difficulties. [threaten, menace.

Bedroh'en, *(w.) v. tr.* (Bedräu'en*), to

Bedroh'lich, *adj.* threatening, menacing.

Bedroh'ung, *(w.) f.* (the act of) threatening; *Law,* commination. [to print.

Bedruck'en, *(w.) v. tr.* to cover with print,

Bedrück'en, *(w.) v. tr.* to oppress, distress, vex, torment. — **Bedrück'er,** *(str.) m.* oppressor, exactor, extortioner. — **Bedrück'ung,** *(w.) f.* oppression; persecution; hardship.

Beduf'ten, Bedüf'ten, *(w.) v. tr.* to perfume, scent.

* **Bedui'ne,** *(w.) m.* **Bedui'nisch,** *adj.* (*Arab.*) Bedouin, Bedoween, Bedaween, Badawin: **Beduinenhäuptling,** *m.* Bedouin chief.

Bedüng'en, *(w.) v. tr.* to dung, manure.

Bedün'ken, *(w.) v. impers.* (*with Acc.*) to seem, appear; mich bedünkt, mich will —, methinks, meseems; sich — lassen, to be of opinion: to think; das —, *v. n.* (*str.*) *n.* opinion, estimation; nach meinem — or meines B-s, in my opinion, to my thinking.

Bedunst'en, Bedünst'en, *(w.) v. tr.* to cover with vapour or smoke.

Bedupf'en, *(w.) v. tr. see* Betupfen.

Bedür'fen, *(irr.) v. intr. & tr.* (*with Gen. & Acc.*) to need, to be or stand in need of, to want, lack, to be short of (money, &c.): to require: ich bedarf Geld, I want money, I am in want of money; ich bedarf dringend Geld, I am distressed for money; ich bedarf dringend mein Geld, I am in pressing need of my money; man bedurfte seine Dienste nicht länger, his services were no longer needed: es bedarf keiner Entschuldigung, there needs no excuse; dessen bedurfte es nicht, there was no need or necessity of it. [forderlich.

Bedürf'lich, *adj.* needing, wanting; *see* Er-

Bedürf'niß, *(str.) n.* 1) need, want, necessity; *Comm. see* Bedarf; Ihre B-e (an Waaren), your requirements; sein (natürliches) — verrichten, to do one's want; 2) exigency, occasion; desideratum, requisite; *pl.* necessaries.

Bedürf'tig, I. *adj.* wanting; 1) needy, indigent, poor, necessitous; 2) (*with Gen.*) in want or need of; II. **B-keit,** *(w.) f.* indigence, distress, poverty.

Beduf'(f)eln, *(w.) v. tr. vulg.* to make drunk.

Bedus'en, *(w.) v. tr. coll.* to confound (Verdutzen, Bestürzen).

Beeck'en, *(w.) v. tr.* (*l. u.*) to furnish with corners; to ornament at the corners.

Been'gen, *(w.)* v. *tr.* to harrow.

Beeh'ren, *(w.)* v. *tr.* 1) (mit *or* durch etwas) to honour: — Sie mich bald mit einem Briefe, honour *or* favour me soon with a letter; mit seiner Gegenwart —, to grace with one's presence; 2) *Comm.* see Honoriren.

Beei'digen, Beei'den, *(w.)* v. *tr.* 1) to confirm by (*or* to declare upon an) oath, to take an oath of; 2) to administer an oath to (one); to swear, bind (one) by oath: Hindu-Zeugen werden ebenso darauf (*i. e.* auf das Wasser des Ganges) beeidet, wie die Christen und Muselmänner auf ihre heiligen Bücher, Hindoo witnesses are sworn upon it in the same way as Christians and Mussulmans are sworn upon their sacred books (*Rothwell*); beeidigte Aussage, evidence upon oath; (schriftliche) affidavit; beeidigte Mäkler, sworn brokers.

Beei'digung, *(w.) f.* the act of taking an oath, swearing (in), &c. *cf.* Beeidigen.

Beei'fern, *(w.)* v. *refl.* to endeavour, to exert one's self, to be solicitous *or* zealous (für, um [*with Acc.*], for, of): to take pains, to press eagerly (for), to bestir one's self: sich aufs Äußerste —, to do one's utmost, one's best, to leave no stone unturned: sich für Einen —, to enter warmly into one's interests, to take warm interest in a person's cause, concerns, &c.

Beei'genschaften, *(w.)* v. *tr.* (*l. u.*) to qualify.

Beei'len, *(w.)* v. *tr.* to hasten, hurry, speed: sich —, to bestir one's self, to make haste.

Beein'flussen, *(w.)* v. *tr.* to influence, to bias.

Beein'trächtigen, *(w.)* v. *tr.* to prejudice, injure, wrong, hurt, harm, bias; to invade, infringe, to intrench *or* encroach upon, to interfere with, to weaken, to impair; to endanger, to detract from (one's reputation); der Beeinträchtigte, the injured *or* aggrieved party; b-d, *p. a.* prejudicial, injurious, derogatory (to), infringing, encroaching (upon).

Beein'trächtigung, *(w.) f.* the (act of) prejudicing, &c., prejudice, injury, invasion, infringement, derogation, detraction.

Beei'sen, *(w.)* v. *tr.* 1) to cover with ice, to ice; 2) (*from* Eisen, *n.*) to cover with iron: to shoe (horses).

* **Beel'zebub** [*pr.* bäl' —, *sometimes pr. & spelt* Belzebub], (*str., pl.* B-e) *m.* (*Hebr.*) Beelzebub.

* **Be'en,** *a.* see Behen.

Been'digen, Been'den, *(w.)* v. *tr.* to end, finish, conclude, close; to break up (a party, a ball); to make up, accommodate, settle (a quarrel, dispute); to terminate, put a stop to.

Been'digung, *(w.) f.* termination, close, conclusion.

Been'gen, *(w.)* v. *tr.* to narrow (a road, the bed of a river, *fig.* the mind, &c.); to contract, to confine, to draw closer, to straiten, to cramp: Schuhe welche die Füße —, shoes that pinch (*or* cramp) the feet; *fig.* to limit, trammel, cramp; to oppress; b-d, *p. a.* close, stifling (as air, &c.); beengt, *pp.* confined, close; sich beengt fühlen, *fig.* to feel oppressed.

Been'gung, *(w.) f.* 1) the (act of) narrowing, confining, &c.; 2) *Med. & Surg.* stricture: — der Blase, inversion of the bladder.

Beer'ben, *(w.)* v. *tr.* 1) (Einen) to be one's heir, to inherit from (one), to succeed (one) *or* to (one's estate); 2) beerbt sein (*i. e.* Erben haben), to have issue. — **Beer'ber,** *(str.) m.* inheritor (of), heir (to), successor.

Beer... (*from* Beere), *in comp.* —angelika, *f.* see Beerendolde; —blau, see Beerenblau; —blume, *f.* see Basselle. [issue.

Beer'bung, *(w.) f.* an inheriting, inherit-

Beer'digen, *(w.)* v. *tr.* to inter, bury.

Beer'digung, *(w.) f.* interment, burial, sepulture: B-kasse, *f.* funds of a burial society; B-feier, *f.* funeral solemnities, obsequies; burial; B-feierlichkeit, *f.* funeral rites, obsequies; B-kosten, *pl.* funeral expenses; B-platz, *m.* burial place.

Bee're, *(w.)* v. *f.* berry: persische B-n, *pl. Dy.* French berries, berries of Avignon.

Bee'ren, *(w.)* v. I. *tr.* to furnish with berries; II. *intr.* to pick *or* gather berries.

Bee'ren..., *in comp.* —achat, *m. Miner.* bacciform agate; —ähnlich, —artig, *adj.* berry-like; *Bot.-e.* —baum, *m.* American gooseberry (*Melastoma acinodendron* L.); —blau, *n.* a blue colouring matter in bilberries, elderberries, &c. (used in dyeing); —dolde, *f.* berry-bearing Angelica (*Aralia* L.); —fresser, *m.* see —wanze; —förmig, *adj.* berry-shaped, *Bot.* bacciform; —fressend, *adj.* baccivorous (of birds); —fresser, *m. Ornith.* baccivorous bird; —melde, *f.* strawberry-blite, berry spinnage, blite (*Blitum* L.); —pilz, *m.* see Keulenpilz; —tragend, *adj.* berry-bearing, bacciferous, cocciferous; —wanze, *f. Entom.* garden-bug (*Cimex baccarum* L.).

Beer'..., *in comp.* —esche, *f.* see Eberesche; —gelb, *n.* a yellow colour extracted from the juice of the buck-thorn (in Holland, &c.); —grün, *n.* 1) *Bot.* lesser periwinkle (*Vinca minor* L.); 2) a green colour, see Saftgrün; —heide, *f.* black-berried heath (*Empetrum nigrum* L.).

† **Beer'haft(ig),** *adj.* see Bärhaft.

Bee'rig, *adj.* 1) see Beerenartig; 2) bearing berries, berry-bearing.

Beer'..., *in comp.* —melde, see Beerenmelde; —most, *m.* grape-must, unpressed must; (schwarzer) —strauch, *m.* see Flieder; —wein, *m.* 1) wine obtained from grape-must; 2) wine made stronger by pouring it over fresh grapes to be pressed; —wurz, —zucker, see Bärwurz, Bärenzucker.

Beest, see Biest.

Beet, *(str.) n.* 1) *a) Gard.* bed; das schmale —, platband; parterre; *b)* B-e, *pl. Brew.* couches; 2) see Betwachs.

Bee'te, *(w.) f.* I. see Bete; II. *Bot.* beet, beet-root (*Beta* L.); rothe —, common beet (*Beta vulgaris* L.).

Bee'ten, *(w.)* v. *tr.* to divide into beds.

Beet'ling, *(str.) n. provinc.* dowry, portion (*cf.* Beete, I., Bete).

Befäch'eln, *(w.)* v. *tr.* to fan.

Befä'higen, *(w.)* v. *tr.* to enable, fit, to qualify; geistig befähigt, of intellectual ability.

Befä'higung, *(w.) f.* the act of enabling, &c.; qualification.

Befahr'bar, *adj.* practicable, passable (of roads, &c.), navigable, passable (of rivers).

A. **Befah'ren,** *(str.)* v. *tr.* 1) *a)* to ride on, to travel over *or* on, to frequent, use (a road); *b)* to navigate, to ply on (the sea, a river); die Küsten —, to sail along the coasts, to coast; *Mar.-s.* einen Ort — haben, to be a good pilot for a certain place; b-(es) Volk, veteran sailors; ein b-er Matrose, a weather-beaten sailor; 2) to carry (stones, &c.) in, to cover with (manure, &c.); 3) *Min.* to get, descend into (a mine), *particul.* for purposes of inspection; 4) *Law*, to take possession of (a house, &c.).

B. **Befah'ren,** *(w.)* v. *tr., refl. & intr.* (*obsolescent*) to fear, to be afraid of: sich einer Sache (*Gen.*) —, to anticipate, expect, apprehend.

Befah'rung, *(w.) f.* 1) the act of riding on (a road), &c. *cf.* Befahren; 2) navigation (of a river, &c.); 3) *Min.* *a)* descent into (a mine); *b)* the working of (a mine); B-[illegible]bericht, *m.* report of the inspector as to the state of a mine.

Befal'len, *(str.)* v. *intr. impers.* to befal, attack; — werden, to be attacked (von, with or by); to be taken (by); von einer Krankheit — werden, to be suddenly seized with illness,

Befah'ren, (*str.*) *v. intr.* (*aux.* sein) to be frozen over.

Befrohn'en, (*w.*) *v. tr.* 1) to impose corvée, feudal service, or compulsory labour on ...; 2) *provinc.* to lay an arrest or execution on ..., to seize.

Befruch'ten, (*w.*) *v. tr.* 1) to fructify, fertilise, fecundate; to enrich (as fertile ground); 2) to make prolific, impregnate; *Ichth.* to milt. — **Befruch'tung,** (*w.*) *f.* 1) fructification, fecundation; *Hort.* prolification; 2) *Physiol.* impregnation; *Bot.-e.* verborgene —, cryptogamy; **B-stück,** *m.* perianth of the fructification; **B-röhre,** *f.* pistil.

Befu'gen, (*w.*) *v. tr.* to authorise; to entitle. — **Befug'niß,** (*str.*) *f.* right, competence, privilege, warrant, authority. — **Befugt',** *p. a.* authorised, &c., warranted; legal, legitimate; competent (as a witness, &c.).

Befüh'len, (*w.*) *v. tr.* to feel, touch, handle; to finger, fumble, to examine by feeling.

Befund', (*str.*, *pl.* Befun'de), *m.* 1) state, condition in which a thing is found, *cf.* Befinden, *v. a.*; 2) result; —**bericht,** *m.* report as to the state or condition of the thing or things found; —**buch,** *m.* inventory, store-book; journal; —**zettel,** *m.* bulletin (of a physician).

Befürch'ten, (*w.*) *v. tr.* to fear, apprehend, to be apprehensive of; to suspect. — **Befürch'tung,** (*w.*) *f.* (*l. u.* **Befürcht'niß,** (*str.*) *f.* & *n.*) apprehension, fear. [to second.

Befür'worten, (*w.*) *v. tr.* to recommend,

Bega'ben, (*w.*) *v. tr.* 1) to endow (one with), to bestow (something) upon; *enf-a.* (*l. u.*) 2) sich — *for* to intoxicate one's self (sich betrinken); 3) to deceive, cheat, &c. — **Begabt',** *p. a.* gifted. — **Bega'bung,** (*w.*) *f.* endowment, 1) donation; 2) (*l. u.*: **Begabt'heit,** (*w.*), **Begab'niß,** (*str.*) *f.*) gift; talents.

Begaf'fen, (*w.*) *v. tr.* to gape, stare, gaze at.

Begang', (*str.*, *pl.* Begäng'e) *m.* district of a woodman, forester, or game-keeper.

Begän'geln, (*w.*) *v. refl.* to splash, soil, bespatter.

Begäng'niß, (*str.*) *n.* celebration, solemnisation.

Begat'ten, (*w.*) *v. refl.* to couple, copulate, match; to cohabit. — **Begat'tung,** (*w.*) *f.* copulation, coupling; coition; die verborgene —, *Bot.* cryptogamy; **B-strieb,** *m.* sexual desire; **B-zeit,** *f.* pairing or coupling time; *Sport.* bucking time; *Bot.* time of fecundation.

Begau'keln, (*w.*) *v. tr.* to dazzle by jugglery; to humbug, to hoax.

Bege'ben, (*str.*) *v.* I. *tr. Comm.* to dispose of, negotiate (bills, securities, &c.); zu —, transferable, negotiable; II. *refl.* 1) to repair, betake one's self, resort, adjourn, to go (nach, to); sich hinweg —, to retire; sich zu seinem Regiment —, to join one's regiment; sich auf die Reise or den Weg —, to start upon a journey, to set out; sich auf die hohe See —, to venture on the high sea; sich unter den Schutz des Gerichts —, to put one's self under the protection of the court; sich zu Bett —, to go to bed; sich zur Ruhe —, to compose one's self to rest or sleep; sich in Gefahr —, to venture (one's self) or to run into danger; sich in den Ehestand —, to enter the state of matrimony; sich auf die Flucht —, to betake one's self or to take to flight; sich aus der Stadt —, to leave the town; sich in ein Haus —, to enter a house; sich an (*with Acc.*) —, to set about (a business, &c.); begieb dich an dein Gebet, fall to thy prayers; 2) to happen, come to pass; 3) (*with Gen.*) to renounce, withdraw (one's claim), to resign, forego, waive, to divest one's self of; ich begebe mich jedes Urtheils darüber, I refrain from expressing any opinion upon it.

Bege'benheit, (*w.*) *f.*, **Begeb'niß,** (*str.*) *n.* occurrence; adventure; event.

Bege'bung, (*w.*) *f. Comm.* negotiation (of a bill of exchange, &c.).

Begeg'nen, (*w.*) *v. intr.* (*aux.* sein) with *Dat.* 1) to meet, meet with, encounter, light upon; sich or einander —, to meet; die Briefe haben sich begegnet, the letters crossed each other; ihre Augen begegneten den meinen, her eyes caught mine; unsere Wünsche — sich, our wishes coincide; sich in einem Wunsche —, to coincide in a wish; daß wir uns in der Denkart so — (*Schiller, Piccol.* 4, 6), that we agree so well in our opinions; 2) *fig.* a) to happen, to come to pass; b) to befall; es begegnete ihm ein Unfall, he met with an accident; 3) to meet, prevent, obviate, anticipate (one's doubts, wishes, objections, &c.); 4) to use, to deal with, to treat; to receive (one well or ill); Einem höflich —, to receive one (to come forward) politely; unfreundlich —, to evince unfriendliness towards ....

Begeg'niß, (*str.*) *f.* & *n.* occurrence, event, accident; widrige B-sse, adversities.

Begeg'nung, (*w.*) *f.* 1) a meeting; 2) treatment, usage; reception.

Bege'hen, (*irr.*) *v.* I. *tr.* 1) a) to walk over or through; b) perambulate, to traverse for the purpose of surveying or examining, to visit as an overseer, inspector, &c.; *Sport.* to beat; *fig.-e.* 2) to celebrate, solemnise, keep; 3) to do; to commit, to perpetrate; 4) to cover (of animals); II. *refl.* *see* sich Begatten.

Begehr', (*str.*) *n.* (& *m.*) desire; demand, request, call; was ist Ihr —? what is your wish? what do you want? in —, *see* Begehrt, *p. a.* (in Begehren).

Begeh'ren, (*w.*) *v.* I. *tr.* 1) a) to desire or wish for with eagerness, to desire eagerly, earnestly; b) (*in an ill sense*) to covet, to lust after; 2) to demand, want, crave; 3) *Sport.* to be at heat (of female animals); was — Sie? what do you want? ein Mädchen zur Ehe —, to solicit or sue a maiden in marriage; er begehrt sie zur Frau, he wants (sues) her for his wife; begehrt, *adj. Comm.* in demand, in request, in (great) favour, inquired for; Kaffee ist sehr begehrt, there is a great call for coffee; sought (after); wenig begehrt, flat, languid, dull; II. *intr.* (*with* nach) to long (for), yearn (after).

Begeh'ren, *s.* *v.* (*str.*) *n.* (*cf.* Begehr) 1) desire; longing; craving; 2) a) demand, request; b) pretension; auf Ihr —, at or by your desire; **B-swerth, B-swürdig,** *adj.* desirable.

Begehr'lich, I. *adj.* inordinately desirous, covetous, greedy, craving; sensual, concupiscent; II. **B-keit,** (*w.*) *f.* inordinate desire; covetousness, greediness; concupiscence, sensuality.

Begeh'rung, (*w.*) *f.* desire, longing for, &c. *cf.* Begehren; **B-sklage,** *f. Law,* petitory action; **B-strieb,** *m.* concupiscible appetite; **B-svermögen,** *n.*, **B-skraft,** *f.* the faculty of desiring, appetitive faculty or power.

Bege'hung, (*w.*) *f.* 1) perambulation, &c. *cf.* Begehen; 2) celebration, solemnisation; 3) commission (of a crime, &c.), perpetration; **B-sünde,** *f.* sin of commission (*opp.* Unterlassungssünde).

Begei'fern, (*w.*) *v. tr.* 1) to beslaver, beslabber; 2) *fig.* to calumniate, slander, asperse.

Begei'len, (*w.*) *v. tr.* to manure, to fertilise.

Begeis'terer, (*str.*) *m.* inspirer, &c.

Begeis'tern, (*w.*) *v. tr.* to inspire, to animate, to fill with enthusiasm (ecstasy); to put or throw into raptures or ecstasies; to exalt; begeistert, inspired, &c., in ecstasy, raptures. — **Begeis'terung,** (*w.*) *f.* inspiration; animation; exaltation, enthusiasm, transport, ecstasy; (poetical) rapture; **B-svoll,** *adj.* enthusiastic(al).

Begei'zen, (*w.*) *v. tr.* 1) (*l. u.*) to watch in the manner of a miser; 2) (Einem etwas) to envy, grudge, begrudge.

Begleit'..., *in comp.* —schein, *m.* (*Comm.*) passport, permit, passbill; —schreiben, *n.* accompanying letter; —stimme, *f. Mus.* accompanying voice or part.

Beglei'tung, (*w.*) *f.* 1) the (act of) accompanying, &c., attendance (on); 2) *or* **Beglei'tschaft**, (*w.*) *f.* (*cf.* Geleitschaft): *a)* conduct, escort, convoy; *b)* procession; *c)* suite, retinue, train; 3) *Mus.* accompaniment: Oden wurden unter — von Musik gesungen, odes were sung to music; B-sschiff, *n.* convoy; consort; tender; b-sweise, *adv.* by way of accompaniment; concomitantly.

Beglie'dern, (*w.*) *v. tr.* to provide with limbs, to limb; begliedert, *p. a. Herald.* with legs coloured differently from the main body (of birds). — **Beglie'derung**, (*w.*) *f. Paint.* the manner of joining the several limbs of a figure.

Beglit'ten, *p. a.* (*from an unusual verb* Beglitzen) covered or adorned with glittering ornaments, &c. (on the surface or outside).

Beglot'zen, (*w.*) *v. tr.* to stare, glare, gaze at *or* upon.

Beglü'cken, (*w.*) *v. tr.* to make happy, to bless; beglückt, blessed, prosperous, happy.

Beglück'wünschen, (*w.*) *v. tr.* to congratulate, to felicitate (zu, wegen, on), wish (one) joy (of); aufrichtig —, to offer sincere congratulations to .... — **Beglück'wünschung**, (*w.*) *f.* congratulation, felicitation.

Begna'digen, Begna'den, (*w.*) *v. tr.* 1) to pardon, reprieve; 2) to accept graciously, to favour, grace (one), to grant favours to (one). — **Begna'digung**, (*w.*) *f.* 1) a pardoning, pardon; reprieve; 2) favour, grace; B-srecht, *n.* right of pardoning (a criminal), prerogative of mercy.

Begnü'gen, (*w.*) *v. refl.* to be contented, satisfied, *or* pleased, to content one's self (mit, an (*with Dat.*), with), to acquiesce (in, to).

Begnüg'lich, Begnüg'sam, I. *adj.* easy to be contented, moderate (Genügsam); II. B-keit, (*w.*) *f.* moderation, contentedness.

Begrab'beln, (*w.*) *v. tr. coll.* to tickle, handle.

Begra'ben, (*str.*) *v. tr.* 1) to bury, inter; to sepulchre, inhume; 2) *fig.* to hide, conceal.

Begräb'niß, *n.* I. (*str.*) *n.* 1) burial, funeral, interment, inhumation; obsequies; 2) sepulchre, tomb, grave; 3) *Min.* gobbing; II. *in comp.* —feier, —feierlichkeit, *f.*, —gepränge, *n.* funeral solemnity, rites, or observance, *pl.* obsequies; —gruft, *f.* vault; —grüfte, *f. pl.* catacombs; —kosten, *f. pl.* funeral expenses, burial dues; —lied, *n.* funeral hymn, dirge; —ort, —platz, *m.* burying-place, burial-place, grave-yard, cemetery.

Begrän'zen, *see* Begrenzen.

Begra'sen, (*w.*) *v.* I. *tr.* 1) to cover with grass; begrast, *p. a.* overgrown *or* covered with grass, grassy; 2) to graze (a pasturing ground); II. *refl.* 1) to graze, to feed upon grass; 2) *coll.* to enrich one's self, to feather one's nest.

Begrei'sen, (*w.*) *v. intr.* (*aux.* sein) to grow grey with age.

Begrei'fen, (*str.*) *v.* I. *tr.* 1) to feel, touch, handle, finger; (tastend —) to grope, fumble; 2) [illegible] in sich (*Acc.*) —, to include, comprehend, contain, comprise, *cf.* Begriffen; 3) to understand, to conceive, apprehend; dieser [illegible] begreift den Geist seiner Rolle, [illegible] enters into the spirit of his part; [illegible] —, *coll.* to know one's place; [illegible] to understand, &c.; ich begreife nicht, [illegible] I cannot conceive the reason of [illegible] no longer; schwer —, to be [illegible] of comprehension; schwer *or* langsam —, [illegible] of comprehension, to be slow to [illegible] (with an (*& Dat.*)) [illegible] *or* [illegible] 2) [illegible] one's self (with

= sich Befassen); 3) (*l. u.*) to recover *or* to recollect one's self; 4) to be understood *or* conceived, &c.: es begreift sich leicht, it is easily understood.

Begreif'lich, I. *adj.* conceivable, intelligible, comprehensible: Einem etwas — machen, to make one comprehend, understand, to bring one to comprehend; b-er machen, to make more easy of comprehension; aus b-en Ursachen, for reasons to be easily understood; b-erweise, *adv.* as may easily be conceived, as a matter of course; II. B-keit, (*w.*) *f.* conceivableness, intelligibility, comprehensibleness.

Begrei'fungskraft, (*w.*) *f. see* Begriffsvermögen.

Begrenz'bar, I. *adj.* limitable, confinable; definable; II. B-keit, (*w.*) *f.* limitableness, &c.

Begren'zen, (*w.*) *v. tr.* 1) to border, bound; 2) *a)* to confine, circumscribe, bring within bounds *or* limits, to limit, terminate; *b)* to define. — **Begren'zer**, (*str.*) *m.* limiter, &c. — **Begrenzt'**, I. *p. a.* 1) bounded (gegen Mitternacht von ..., on the north by ...); 2) *fig. a)* limited; *b)* short-sighted; II. B-heit, (*w.*) *f.* limitation.

Begren'zung, (*w.*) *f.* bound, limits; limitation; border.

Begriff', (*str.*) *m.* 1) *a) see* Inbegriff; *b) see* Abriß, 5; 2) the being engaged in ...., act: im —(e) zu ..., in the act of ...; im — sein *or* stehen, to be about, to be on (upon) the point, to be going (to ...); er ist im — abzureisen, he is on the point *or* eve of departure; 3) conception: sich (*Dat.*) einen — machen, to form a conception; perception, conceit; notion, idea: Einem einen — beibringen, to convey to one some notion; verkehrte B-e, crude notions; der falsche —, misconception; das ist über meinen —, that is beyond my comprehension; es geht über seine B-e, that is out of his sphere *or* ken, that is beyond his conception.

Begrif'fen, *p. a.* 1) (mit —, einbegriffen, inbegriffen) included (*cf.* Begreifen, *tr.*, 2), inclusive(ly); die Kosten mit (ein)—, charges included, inclusive of charges; 2) *with* in (*sometimes* auf, über) *& Dat.*, engaged in ...; in (über) einer Sache — sein, to be at *or* about a thing; in der Arbeit —, at work; auf einer Reise —, on a journey; im Bau —, in course of construction (*cf.* Bau).

Begriff'lich, *adj.* notional: — (*adv.*) feststellen, to fix the notion of ....

Begriffs'..., *in comp.* —angabe, —bestimmung, *f.* definition; —fach, *n.* category; —forscher, *m.* speculator; —gesellung, *f.* association of ideas; —vermögen, *n.* apprehensive power *or* faculty; apprehension, comprehension; —verwechselung, *f.* the confounding of ideas; —zergliederung, *f.* analysis of ideas.

Begrin'sen, (*w.*) *v. tr.* (*Göthe*, Tasso 2, 3) to grin in scorn at ....

Begrü'beln, (*w.*) *v. tr. fig.* to ruminate on; to criticise.

Begrün'den, (*w.*) *v. tr.* 1) to found, establish: eine Handlungsgesellschaft —, to form a trading-company; ein Unternehmen —, to start *or* set on foot an undertaking; 2) to base (eine Behauptung, an assertion); to prove, to make good; to confirm; to verify. — **Begrün'der**, (*str.*) *m.* founder, establisher, &c. — **Begrün'dung**, (*w.*) *f.* 1) the act of founding, foundation, establishment; 2) *fig. a)* confirmation, proof; *b)* foundation, reason, rationale.

Begrü'nen, (*w.*) *v.* I. *tr.* to cover with green; II. *refl.* to become green; Bäume, die sich ewig neu — (*Göthe*, Faust I, 4), trees that perpetually clothe themselves with new leaves (*Blackie*: trees which day by day their green repair); begrünt, *p. a.* verdant.

Begrü'ßen, (*w.*) *v. tr.* 1) to greet, salute, hail, welcome; 2) (*with* um (*& Acc.*)) *coll.* to apply to (one), to solicit (for), *cf.* Angehen, I. 2. — **Begrü'ßung**, (*w.*) *f.* greeting, welcome, salutation, hailing; compliments exchanged on meeting.

Begu'cken, (*w.*) *v. tr. fam.* to peep at, to look *or* peer at.

* **Begui'ne**, *see* Begine.

Begün'stigen, (*w.*) *v. tr.* to favour; to keep *or* hold up, to countenance, patronise; to promote, forward; begünstigt von, under favour of; b-d, *p. a.* favourable. — **Begün'stigung**, (*w.*) *f.* the act of favouring, favour shown to ...; encouragement; countenance, patronage; favouritism.

Begür'ten, (*w.*) *v. tr.* to gird, belt.

Beguß', (*str.*, *pl.* Begüsse) *m.* 1) *see* Begießung; 2) *Pott.* a coating with coloured clay.

Begut'achten, (*w.*) *v. tr.* to give one's opinion, to pass one's judgment on; — lassen, to take advice (counsel's opinion, &c.).

Begut'achtung, (*w.*) *f.* opinion of a committee *or* of an expert (on ...).

Begü'tern, (*w.*) *v. tr.* to bestow riches, wealth *or* landed property upon, to enrich.

Begü'tert, *p. a.* wealthy, opulent, rich; possessed of (landed) property; die B-en, the wealthy, &c., landed proprietors.

Begü'tigen (*l. u.* **Begü'ten**), (*w.*) *v. tr.* to appease, assuage, &c. (Besänftigen).

Behaa'ren, (*w.*) *v.* I. *tr.* to cover with hair; II. *refl.* to get hair. — **Behaart'**, I. *p. a.* haired, comate; *Zool.* crinigerous; *Bot.* hirsute, pilose; II. B-heit, (*w.*) *f.* hairiness, &c.

Beha'ben, (*irr.*) *v.* I. *tr.* 1) *Law*, to gain, win (a cause); 2) *provinc.* to maintain; to keep; II. *refl.* to behave.

Behä'big, *adj. coll. see* Wohlhabend.

Behab'niß, (*str.*) *n. Law*, suit gained *or* won.

Behack'en, (*w.*) *v. tr.* to hew (wood for fuel); to prune, (abgipfeln) to lop; (mit der Hacke) to hoe; to dig about the roots of (plants, &c.).

Beha'dern, (*w.*) *v. tr.* 1) to cover with rags; 2) *see* Bestreiten, Bezanken.

Behaf'ten, (*w.*) *v. tr.* 1) *Law*, to take into possession, to keep possession of; 2) *provinc. see* Verhaften; 3) to burden, charge, load (with); to afflict, infect (with); behaftet sein, to be affected (mit, with); to be tinged with; behaftet, *p. a.* burdened, &c.; mit Ohnmachten behaftet, subject to fainting-fits; behaftete Güter, encumbered estates.

Behaf'tung, (*w.*) *f.* a writ by which a person is reinstated in his rights.

Beha'geln, (*w.*) *v. tr.* to cover with hail.

Beha'gen, I. (*w.*) *v. intr. & impers.* (*with Dat.*) to please, to suit, afford, comfort; nur um zu sehen, wie ihnen die Arbeit behagt, just to see how they relish the work; es behagt ihm gar nicht, he does not like it at all; er läßt es sich —, he takes his ease; II. *s.* (*str.*) *n.* delight, comfort, pleasure, complacency, ease; — an etwas (*Dat.*) finden, to delight *or* take pleasure in a thing.

Behag'lich, I. *adj.* easy, comfortable, agreeable, snug, cosy; II. *adv.* at ease, comfortably, &c.; III. B-keit, (*w.*) *f.* comfortableness, ease, snugness, cosiness.

Beha'ken, (*w.*) *v. tr.* to furnish with hooks.

Behalf'tern, (*w.*) *v. tr.* to halter (horses).

Behalmt', *adj. Bot.* stalked, bladed.

† **Behalt'**, (*str.*) *m.* 1) fortified place, fortress; 2) territory; 3) *Comm.* balance of cash; 4) opinion (Dafürhalten, Meinung).

Behalt'bar, *adj.* what may be retained (in the memory).

Behal'ten, (*str.*) *v. tr.* to keep, to retain; das Schlachtfeld —, *see* Behaupten; bei sich, für sich —, to keep to one's self, to keep secret; (im Sinne —, beim Rechnen) to carry over; (im Magen —) to keep in the stomach, to retain; *Mar.-s.* das Land im Gesicht —, to keep the land

abroad: p. a. behalten; der b-e Curs, the true course, the course made good (of a ship): b-e Ankunft, safe arrival; ein b-es Schiff, a ship escaped from danger; b-e Güter, goods well conditioned (cf. Wohlbehalten); das —, v. n. (str.) n. the (act of) keeping, &c.: das — und Erlassen der Sünden, binding and loosing.

Behäl'ter, (str.) m. 1) conservatory; 2) holder, vessel (for liquids); reservoir; fish-pond; 3) pantry; 4) Bot., Anat., &c. receptacle.

Behalt'lich, I. adj. see Behaltbar; II. adv. (with Gen.) Law, with reservation of (Vorbehältlich).

Behält'niß, (str.) n. 1) conservatory; magazine; box, case; 2) room, &c. cf. Behälter; 3) Sport. thicket, copse, bog (as habitation of feathered game): Entom. shroud; (für Eis) ice-preserver, refrigerator.

Behalt'sam, I. adj. 1) retentive, tenacious (memory); 2) lasting, durable; II. B-keit, (w.) f. retentiveness (of memory), &c.

Behal'tung, (w.) f. 1) Law, domicile (cf. Behalt); 2) l. u. for Behältniß.

Behäm'mern, (w.) v. tr. 1) to hammer; 2) instr. to provide with hammers; to arrange the hammers of (a piano, &c.).

Behan'deln, (w.) v. tr. 1) to handle (instruments); to handle, treat (a subject); to manage (a horse, a person), to manipulate, work (iron, clay, marble); 2) a) Med. to attend, to manage, to have under care or under one's hands, to cure; b) to treat, use well or ill, to deal well or ill by or with (one); der Kaiser hat mich übel behandelt (Schiller, Piccol. 2, 5), the Emperor has dealt with me amiss (Coler.); Einen wie einen Fremden —, to make a stranger of one; Jemand redlich, betrügerisch —, to deal honestly, falsely with one; 3) Comm., &c. a) to bargain for; to cheapen, to agree for the price of ...; b) to contract for; 4) Chem. to treat, manipulate.

Behän'digen, (w.) v. tr. to hand (Einhändigen).

Behand'lung (w.) f. 1) the handling, &c. cf. Behandeln; management; manipulation; treatment (also Med.); usage, dealing; in ärztlicher — sein, to be under medical treatment; freundliche —, kindness; 2) Comm. the bargaining for, &c.; B-sart, f. way (of dealing), treatment; usage.

Behang', (str., pl. Behäng'e) m. 1) a) anything suspended for ornament, &c., hanging; b) Archit. label; c) pl. pendants (for lustres); 2) Sport. a) the ears (of a dog); b) the long hair on the fetlocks (of horses).

Behang'en, p. a. 1) hung (with); 2) Sport. gut —, a) having long and broad ears; b) having long hair on the fetlocks.

Behäng'en, (w.) v. I. tr. 1) to hang, cover (with); eine mit Bildern behängte Stube, a room hung with pictures; sich mit etwas —, coll. to deck or trick one's self out with; sich mit schlechten Leuten —, to keep bad company; 2) a) to attack, to stick fast to (the game, used of dogs); b) to tie a hound and lead him; II. refl. coll. sich mit etwas —, to meddle with ..., see Befassen, II.

Behäng'zeit, (w.) f. Sport. season for breaking in dogs.

Behar'ken, (w.) v. tr. to rake.

Behar'nen, (w.) v. tr. to make water upon or bepiss.

Behar'nischen, (w.) v. tr. to clothe with a breast-plate or armour.

Behar'ren, (w.) v. intr. to continue, persevere, persist (bei, in, auf (with Dat.), in), to insist (upon); to hold on or out, to be steadfast (in the faith, &c.), to adhere (to), to stand (by or in), fam. to stick (to an opinion, &c.); auf einer Lüge —, to face out a lie; das —, v. n. (str.) n. the (act of) persevering, &c., perseverance; persistence, Phys. (in Ruhe) permanence.

Beharr'lich, I. adj. persevering, continuous, steady, steadfast; constant; firm, continuing; b-es Stillschweigen, persistent silence; II. B-keit, (w.) f. perseverance, constancy, steadfastness, continuance; persistence.

Behar'rung, (w.) f. perseverance; B-svermögen, n. power of inertness, (Lat.) vis inertiae; B-szustand, m. state of permanence; resistance.

Behär'schen, (w.) v. intr. (aux. sein) to harden, grow hard.

Behar'zen, (w.) v. tr. to cover with resin; to resin.

Behau'ben, (w.) v. tr. to cover with, put on a cap; behaubt, p. a. crested (of birds).

Behau'chen, (w.) v. tr. to breathe upon.

Behau'en, (str.) v. tr. to hew; aus dem Gröbsten —, to rough-hew, to hew roughly; Carp. & Sculp. to chip, cut, square, form by cutting; dress, trim (timber); to poll, to lop (trees); to edge, fresh-cut (a mill-stone); Min. to try, assay (stones); Engr. to chisel.

Behäu'feln, Behäu'fen, (w.) v. tr. to form into or surround with little heaps, to hill, hillock, earth.

Behaup'ten, (w.) v. I. tr. 1) to maintain, defend, support, sustain, hold (an opinion, &c.), to keep or affirm, allege, avouch, avow; make good (one's ground, &c.); 2) to assert; das Schlachtfeld —, to remain master of (to keep) the (battle-) field; II. refl. to stand, hold, or keep one's ground; to hold out, keep or bear up (against); sich gegen den Wind —, to stand (bear up against) the strength of the wind; die Preise — sich, prices maintain themselves, keep their ground, &c.

Behaup'tung, (w.) f. 1) the (act of) maintaining, &c.; 2) assertion, allegation, proposition; statement; B-sbegriff, m., B-swort, n. Log. predicate.

Behau'sen, (w.) v. tr. to lodge; sich —, to settle; behaust, p. a. domiciled, domiciliated.

Behäu'sen, (w.) v. tr. to case.

Behau'sung, (w.) f. lodging, house, housing, domicile, habitation, abode, mansion.

Behäu'ten, (w.) v. tr. to provide or cover with a skin, hide.

Behe'ben, (w.) v. tr. to redress (grievances, &c.), to remove (difficulties, &c.).

Behelf', (str.) m. excuse, pretext; shift, make-shift, device, expedient; der —, the last resource; als —, by way of shift.

Behel'fen, (str.) v. refl. 1) to make shift (with), to make do; 2) to resort to, to fall back upon; sich kümmerlich — müssen, to have but a scanty allowance, to have much ado to make both ends meet, to get through very poorly.

Behelf'lich, adj. serving as an expedient or excuse.

Behel'ligen (l. u. Behel'len), (w.) v. tr. to molest, importune, annoy, trouble.

Behel'ligung, (w.) f. molestation, trouble, importunity, annoyance.

Behel'men, (w.) v. tr. 1) to provide with a helmet; 2) to helve (an axe, &c.); behelmt, p. a. helmeted.

Behemd'et, p. a. (Göthe, Faust II.) provided with a shirt.

* **Be'hemoth(h),** n. (Hebr.) Behemoth.

* **Be'hen,** (str.) m. Bot. behen, ben, bladder-catchfly (Silene inflata); 1) der weiße —, a) white behen, bladder campion (Cucubalus behen L.); b) (or —flockenblume, f.) saw-leaved centaury; white centaury (Centaurea behen L.); 2) der rothe —, red behen, sea lavender (Statice limonium L.); —nuß, f. behen-nut, ben-nut; —(nuß)baum, m. smooth-ben-tree (Moringa pterygosperma); —öl, n. ben-nut oil.

Behend', Behen'de, adj. agile, nimble, active, adroit.

Behen'digkeit, (w.) f. agility, nimbleness, swiftness, adroitness, activity.

Beher'bergen, (w.) v. tr. to harbour, lodge, house; accommodate with lodgings.

Beherr'schen, (w.) v. tr. 1) to rule, govern; to sway; to domineer; 2) to command (also Mil. = to overlook; as, to command the fords of a stream with guns, &c.), to have under one's

Law style) done *or* instituted in behalf of a king, &c.

Behuf't, *p. a.* hoofed.

Behü'geln, *(w.) v. tr.* to cover with hillocks; **behügelt**, *p. a.* hilly.

Behülf'lich, I. *adj.* helpful, serviceable; auxiliary, adjutory, instrumental, adjuvant, favourable, conducible, conducive (to); *(in a bad sense:)* accessory (to); — sein, to assist, further, promote (a plan, &c., bei einem Plan rc.); to assist, help (one), to lend a hand, to be of assistance to (one, Einem); *(in a bad sense:)* to abet (one); II. **B-keit**, *(w.) f.* helpfulness, &c.

Behül'fen, *(w.) v. tr. see* Verhülfen.

Behüp'fen, *(w.) v. tr.* to jump, hop upon.

Behü'ten, *(w.) v. tr.* 1) to guard, watch, to preserve; keep (vor *[with Dat.]*, from): Gott behüte euch! God have you in his keeping! God save you; Gott behüte! God forbid! behüte! no, no! 2) to drive cattle upon (a field *or* meadow) for grazing.

Behü'ter, *(str.) m.* guardian, protector.

Behut'sam, I. *adj.* cautious, heedful, careful, guarded; prudent; wary (Bedachtsam); er drückte sich — aus, he expressed himself guardedly; II. **B-keit**, *(w.) f.* cautiousness, heedfulness, &c.; circumspection, caution, precaution.

Behü'tung, *(w.) f. see* Hutung.

Bei, I. *prep. (with Dat.)* at, near, about, at the house of, with, by, on, upon, to, in; present at, in the presence of: — der Kirche, near the church; Stern — Stern †, star crowding upon star; — offenem Fenster sitzen, to sit at the open window; — offenem Fenster, with the window open; — dem Winde segeln (halten), to sail with a scant wind *or* close to the wind; dicht beim Winde segeln (halten), to sail close hauled; etwas — sich tragen *or* haben, to carry *or* have something about one; behalte das — dir, keep that about you *(cf.* Behalten); diese Papiere wurden — ihm gefunden, these papers were found on his person (on him); Einen — der Hand nehmen, to take one by the hand; — der Hand sein, to be (near) at hand; die Schlacht — Leipzig, the battle of Leipzig; — Seite, aside; ich saß — ihm, I sat next to *(or* close by) him; — Tische sitzen, to be at dinner; sie saßen rauchend und schwatzend — ihrem Biere, they sat smoking and gossiping over their ale; — der Flasche sitzen, to be engaged at the bottle; [illegible] — dem Trinken, [they were stricken by] the plague] as they drank; — Einem wohnen, liegen, stehen rc., to live, lie, stand, &c. with one *or* at one's house; er wohnte — dem Gesandten, he lived at the ambassador's; — Hofe leben, to live at court; Unterricht — Einem nehmen, to have (take) lessons of *or* from one; beim Stabe dienen, to serve on the staff; — solchen Leuten, with *or* among such people; — uns (daheim), with (among) us at home; das Sprachorgan — den Erwachsenen, the organ of speaking in grownups; er genießt keine große Achtung — uns, he enjoys no great esteem among us; beim Homer finden wir ..., we find in Homer ..., [illegible] wir nachher, — dem [illegible], of which we shall speak [illegible] in connection with *(or* when we come [illegible]; — Tage, in the day-time; — Nacht, in the night, by night; — Licht(e), by [illegible]; — Lebzeiten, in life; — seinen [illegible]; — Zeiten, in (good) time, [illegible]; — diesem heißen Wetter, in (ob. mit [illegible]) this hot weather; — dem [illegible], in the presence [illegible] the stroke of the pen in [illegible], being [illegible]; — Gelde sein, to be well [illegible] with money; nicht — [illegible] without money; [illegible]

können Sie — diesem Lärm arbeiten? can you labour with this noise about you? — einem Gewitter ist es gefährlich sich unter einen Baum zu stellen, in a thunderstorm it is dangerous to stand under a tree; — sich denken, to think to one's self; — Ihnen verliere ich die Geduld, you put me beside my patience; das ist — ihm einerlei, that is all one with him; — mir schlagen deine Ausflüchte nicht an, with me your excuses will not take; Einen — Namen nennen, to call one by his name; — Gott schwören, to swear by God; — meiner Seele, upon my soul; — Leibe nicht, by no means; — meiner Ehre, upon my honour; — meiner Seligkeit, as I hope to be saved; — Lebensstrafe, upon (under) pain of death; — deines Königs Zorn *(Schiller*, Don Carlos 2, 2), under pain of your king's displeasure; thue es — deiner Liebe zu mir, do it as you love me; melden Sie sich — ihm, announce, address yourself to him; sich — Jemandem bedanken, to render thanks to one; — Einem anklopfen, to knock at one's door; *fig.* to sound *(fam.* to pump) one; — Einem aushalten, to stand by one; er hat mich — Heller und Pfennig bezahlt, he has paid me to the last farthing; — guter Gesundheit sein, to be in good health; — Jahren sein, to be (advanced) in years; — sich *or* — Sinnen sein, to be in one's right senses; niemand, der — Sinnen ist, denkt daran, no one with his wits about him thinks of ...; — sich bleiben, to keep one's temper; nicht — Verstande sein, to be beside one's self, to be out of one's senses; — alle dem, for all that; — Weitem, by far, by much; — Weitem nicht so viel, not so much by far; — der Sache bleiben, to keep *or* stick to the point; — der Inventur, while taking stock; — diesem Geschäft bleibt kein Nutzen, no profit accrues from this business; — Verkommen (des Wechsels), when presented, on presentation; — Durchlesung Ihres Briefes, on reading your letter; beim ersten Anblick, at first sight; — diesem *(or* auf dieses) Zeichen, at this signal; — dieser Nachricht, at this news; — Gelegenheit, on occasion, &c., *cf.* Gelegenheit; er gewinnt — näherer Bekanntschaft, he improves on acquaintance.

II. *used adverbially (obsolescent)* about, nearly, almost; — hundert Mann, near a hundred men; — tausend, near a thousand.

Beian', *adv. coll.* hard by, close by.

Bei'anker, *(str.) m. Mar.* kedge-anchor; small bow(er) anchor. — **Bei'ankern**, *(w.) v. intr.* to kedge.

Bei'arbeiter, *(str.) m.* assistant-workman; helpmate, assistant.

Bei'behalten, *(str.) v. tr.* to keep (up), keep on, retain (in office, &c.); to continue, preserve. — **Bei'behaltung**, *(w.) f.* the (act of) keeping (on, &c.), retaining, retention.

Bei'biegen, *(str.) v. tr.* to join, subjoin, annex, enclose (a letter, &c.).

Bei'binden, *(str.) v. tr.* to bind *or* tie to; to bind up with.

Bei'blatt, *(str., pl.* **Bei'blätter**), *n.* supplementary sheet; extra(-sheet), supplement (-sheet) (of *or* to a newspaper); *Lit. (Fr.) feuilleton.*

Bei'bote, *(w.) m.* by-messenger; extra-messenger; (in Switzerland, canton of the Grisons) a delegate from a supreme penal court.

Bei'bringen, *(irr.) v. tr.* 1) to bring near *or* forward, to bring in *or* forth, to produce; to show, adduce (proofs, &c.); (Einem etwas:) 2) *a)* to give (one something); *b)* to administer (something to one, gradually *or* without his perceiving it); Einem einen Schlag, Stoß —, to give, deal *or* fetch one a blow, a thrust; Einem eine Wunde —, to inflict a wound upon one; Gift —, to administer poison; 3) *fig. a)* to affect, inspire, *or* influence with (fear, &c.); *b)* to impart, convey, instil (knowledge, &c.); to make understand, teach; man konnte ihm das Reiten nicht —, he could not be taught to ride; *c)* to suggest, hint, insinuate; break (a disagreeable news, &c. to ...): Einem eine schlimme Meinung von einem Anderen —, to injure one in another person's opinion; 4) to bring in *or* have for a marriage-portion; das —, *v. s. (str.) n.* 1) *or* **Beibringung**, *(w.) f.* the (act of) bringing in *or* forward, producing, &c.; adduction; 2) marriage-portion, dowry.

Bei'buch, *(str., pl.* **Bei'bücher**), *n. Comm.* retail-(shop-), counter-book.

Bei'chaise *[pr.* bī'shāse*]*, *(w.) f.* extra-vehicle, extra-coach *(cf.* Beiwagen).

Beich'te, *(w.) f.* (*l. u.* **Beicht**) confession, shrift; zur — gehen, seine — ablegen, to confess, to make confession; Einem — sitzen, — hören, to confess *or* shrive one.

Beich'ten, I. *(w.) v. tr. & intr.* to confess; **B-de**, *p. a. m. & f.* confessant, penitent; II. *v. s. (str.) n.* confession.

Beich'tiger, *(str.) m.* (father-)confessor.

Beicht' ..., *in comp.* **-brief**, *m. Eccl.* letter dimissory; **-buch**, *n.* communion-book, companion to the altar; **-gänger**, *m.*, **-kind**, *n.* penitent, confessant; **-geld**, *n.*, **-pfennig**, *m.* confessor's fees; **-schein**, *m.* certificate of confession; **-siegel**, *n.* seal of confession; **-stuhl**, *m.* confessional, confessionary, confession-chair; **-vater**, *m.* (father-)confessor; **-zeit**, *f.* shrove-tide; **-zettel**, *m. see* **-schein**.

Bei'de, *num.* I. *adj. (& s.) pl.* both, the two, either: — Vettern *or* die b-n Vettern, both the cousins; — für Einen und Einer für —, each for the other; auf *or* zu b-n Seiten, on both sides, on either side; meine b-n Schwestern, both my sisters; wir —, both of us; welche —, *(rel.)* both of whom *(or* which); welcher von b-n? which of the two? jeder von b-n, alle —, either; keiner von b-n, neither of the two; Doctor b-r Rechte, doctor of (both) laws; — Sicilien, *Geogr.* the two Sicilies; II. **B-s**, *s. abs.* both, the one (thing) and the other, either; b-s, ... und ... *(obsolescent)*, both, ... and ..., ... as well as ....

Bei'derlei, *adj.* both, of both, of either (sort, species); — Geschlechts, *Gramm.* common; — Gewand, †, *see* Beiderwand.

Bei'derseitig, *adj.* of *or* on both sides; reciprocal, mutual; b-e Freunde, common friends; b-e Interesse, common interests.

Bei'derseits, *adv.* on both sides; mutually, reciprocally; sie —, both of them.

Bei'derwand, *f. Comm.* linsey-woolsey.

Bei'ding, *(str.) n.* any thing additional *or* supplementary; *provinc. Law*, by-court.

Beid'lebig, *(l. u.)* I. *adj.* amphibious; II. **B-keit**, *(w.) f.* amphibiousness.

Bei'drehen, *(w.) v. Mar.* to bring to; *intr.* to come to, to come up.

Bei'drucken, *(w.) v. tr.* 1) to print to, print with; to annex; 2) *or* **Bei'drücken**, *(w.) v. tr.* to set *or* affix (ein Siegel, a seal) to.

Beid'schattig, *adj.* shaded on both sides; b-e Menschen, *Geogr.* amphiscii, amphiscians.

Bei'eid, *(str.) m.* oath taken by one who is not a citizen *(differ. from* Bürgereid).

Beieinan'der, *adv.* together.

Bei'erbe, *(w.) m.* joint heir, co-heir, coinheritor.

Bei'ern, *(w.) v. intr. provinc.* to toll the church bells slowly, to chime.

Bei'essen, *(str.) n.* intermediate dish; *(Fr.) entremets (pl.).*

Bei'fall, *(str.) m.* applause, approbation, approval, assent; stürmischer —, loud applause, acclamation; Gottes —, the approbation of God; Einem — zollen *(l. u.* geben), to applaud, assent to, approve of; to evince *or* display satisfaction with; — klatschen, to clap applause; Jemandes — haben, sich Jemandes — erwerben, to gain one's applause; er hat meinen

[illegible]; sind Sie so früh auf den B-en? are you [illegible] so early? er ist nicht gut auf den B-en, he is a bad walker; er ist gut auf den B-en, he is a good (stout) walker or pedestrian.

Bein'..., *in comp.* —**ader**, *f. Anat.* crural [illegible]; —**ähnlich**, *adj.* 1) shaped like a leg; 2) resembling bone, *see* —artig.

Beina'he, Beinah', *adv.* almost, nearly, [illegible], well-nigh; within an ace or a little (of), [illegible] to (nothing, &c.), little short (of); all but (unanimous, &c.); es ist — einerlei, *coll.* it is much the same thing; *in comp.* (*T.*, &c.) —**gleich**, sub-equal, nearly equal; —**drei-spaltig**, sub-trifid, nearly trifid; —**ringförmig**, sub-annular, &c.

Bei'name, (*irr.*) *m.* 1) surname, cognomen, [illegible], agnomen; 2) nickname, by-[illegible]; Einem einen B-n geben, to surname; [illegible] *ill names*, to nickname.

Bein'..., *in comp.* **arbeiter**, *m.* worker in bone; —**artig**, *adj.* bony, osseous; —**asche**, *f.* bone ashes; —**blätterung**, *f. Surg.* exfoliation; —**blume**, *f. Bot.* marsh-marigold (*Caltha* L.); —**bohrer**, *m.* 1) *see* Beinbohrer; 2) wimble used by workers in bone: —**brech**, *n.* 1) *Miner.* see Beinwell, 1; 2) —**brechgras**, *n. Bot.* yellow [illegible] (*Anthericum ossifragum* L.); —**brecher**, *m. Ornith.* osprey, bone-breaker, [illegible] buzzard, sea-eagle (*Falco ossifragus* L.); —**bruch**, *m.* fracture or breaking of a leg; —[illegible], *adj.* broken-legged: —**bruchlade**, *f.* see —lade.

Bein'chen, (*str.*) *n.* (*dimin. of* Bein) 1) *a)* [illegible], a small bone; *b) Gam.* cockal, huckle-bone; 2) a little leg.

Bein'..., *in comp.* —**drechsler**, *m.* turner in bone; —**dürr**, *see* Knochendürr.

† **Bei[illegible]**, **Bei(l)[illegible]**, *adv.* near.

Bei[illegible], (*w.*) *v. intr. coll.* to walk with short, quick steps (*cf.* Füßeln).

Bei[illegible], *adj.* made of bone, bony.

Bei[illegible], (*str.*) *m. Anat.* accessory nerve.

Bein'..., *in comp.* —**erzeugung**, *f. Surg.* [illegible]; —**fäule**, —**fäulniß**, *f. Surg.* see [illegible]; —**feile**, *f.* bone file; *Surg.* [illegible], [illegible]; —**fisch**, *m. Ichth.* bone-fish, bottle-fish (*Ostracion* L.); —**fraß**, *m.* see Knochenfraß; —**fügung**, *f.* articulation: *Anat.* symphysis; —**futter**, *n.* lining of the legs of a saddle; —**geige**, *f. Mus.* see Gambe; —[illegible], —**gerüst**, *n.* skeleton; —**geschwulst**, *f. Surg.* exostosis; —**gestell**, *n.* skeleton: —**ge-wächs**, *n.* excrescence of a bone; —**glas**, *n.* [illegible] glass; —**gras**, *n.* see —brech, 2; —[illegible] *m. Ichth.* basking-shark (*Squalus maximus* L.); —[illegible], *m.* cuisses, tasses, greaves [illegible]; —**hart**, *adj.* as hard as bone; —**haus**, *n.* bone-house, charnel-house, ossuary; —**haut**, *f. Anat.* periosteum; —**hebel**, —**heber**, *m. Surg.* [illegible]; —**heil**, *n.* 1) see —well, 1; 2) *Bot.* [illegible], [illegible] (*[illegible]* L.); [illegible], *f. Anat.* cotyle, cotyla; —**holz**, 1) or [illegible], *n.*, —[illegible], *f.* see Hartriegel; 2) see [illegible].

[illegible], *adj.* as hard as bone.

[illegible], *adj.* bony; *in comp.* legged, footed.

[illegible]..., *in comp.* —**kleid**, *n.*, or —**kleider**, [illegible], pantaloons; lange —, breeches, [illegible] [illegible] a man's part given by [illegible] [illegible]

[illegible]

Surg. suture: —**öl**, —**schmalz**, *n.* neat's-foot-oil (Klauenfett); —**ritze**, *f. Surg.* fissure of the bone; —**röhrholz**, *n. see* Heckenkirsche; —**rüstung**, *f. see* —schienen; —**säge**, *f.* bone-saw, surgeon's-saw; —**samen**, *m. Bot.* 1) bone-seed (*Osteospermum*); 2) salfern (*Lithospermum*); —**schellen**, *f. pl.* fetters, shackles; —**schiene**, *f.* 1) *Surg. see* —lade; 2) —**schienen**, *pl. see* —harnisch; —**schwarz**, *n. Chem.* bone-black, ivory-black, velvet-black; —**spalte**, *f. Surg.* longitudinal fissure of the bone; —**spath**, *m. Farr.* bone-spavin; —**stäbe**, *m. pl.* the projecting staves of a cask which serve as stands for it; —**waaren**, *f. pl.* bone-articles, bone-toys; —**well**, *n.* 1) *Miner.* osteocolla, bone-binder, stalochite; 2) *see* —heil; —**wuchs**, *m. see* —erzeugung; —**wurz**, *f. see* —heil, 2.

Bei'ordnen, (*w.*) *v. tr.* to adjoin, coordinate; beigeordnet, *p. a.* coordinate; Beigeordnete, *m.* (*decl. like adj.*) adjunct, assistant. — **Bei'ordnung**, (*w.*) *f.* coordination.

Bei'packen, (*w.*) *v. tr.* to pack up with.

Bei'pferd, (*str.*) *n.* 1) horse in reserve, relay-horse, by-horse; 2) led-horse.

Bei'pflichten, (*w.*) *v. intr.* (Einem) to assent to, to consent, to agree with, to approve; Jemandes Meinung —, to accede to (*or* to be of) one's opinion. — **Bei'pflichtung**, (*w.*) *f.* consent, assent.

Bei'rath, (*str.*, *pl.* Bei'räthe) *m.* 1) advice; 2) auditor of a court of justice. — **Bei'rathen**, (*str.*) *v. intr.* Einem —, to assist a person with one's advice.

Bei'rechnen, (*w.*) *v. intr.* to add to in a reckoning.

Bei'ren, (*w.*) *v. tr.* to mislead, confuse.

Beisam'men, *adv.* together; seine Gedanken — haben, to have one's wits about one; —**liegend**, *adj. Anat.* conglobate (of glands).

Bei'saß, (*w.*) *m.* 1) a small farmer who has not land enough to keep a horse; 2) *see* Beisitzer; 3) *see* Schutzverwandter.

Bei'satz, (*str.*, *pl.* Bei'sätze) *m.* apposition; addition; ohne —, unalloyed; —**wort**, *n. Gramm.* epithet.

Bei'schaffen, (*w.*) *v. tr.* to procure

Bei'schale, (*w.*) *f. Carp.* out-side plank, slab, flitch.

Bei'schießen, (*str.*) *v. tr. see* Beisteuern.

Bei'schiff, (*str.*) *n.* cock-boat; tender: B-sführer, *m.* cock-swain.

Bei'schlaf, (*str.*) *m.* a lying with, cohabitation, copulation; der uneheliche —, concubinage, fornication. — **Bei'schlafen**, (*str.*) *v. intr.* (*with Dat.*) to sleep with ..., *cf.* Beschlafen. — **Bei'schläfer**, (*str.*) *m.* bedfellow: B-in, (*w.*) *f.* concubine; bedfellow.

Bei'schlag, (*str.*) *m.* 1) *Archit.* raised foot-pace (stone-seat) before the door of a house, &c.; perron; 2) *a)* false (base) coin; *b)* bastard (of a person of high rank, &c. *cf.* Beikind).

Bei'schlagen, (*str.*) *v.* I. *intr.* (*aux.* sein) to assent to, to be of one's party; II. *tr.* to enclose (a letter).

Bei'schließen, (*str.*) *v. tr.* 1) to lock up; 2) *fig.* to enclose, add, annex (letters, &c.).

Bei'schluß, (*str.*, *pl.* Bei'schlüsse) *m.* enclosure, enclosed letter; durch —, under cover; im — finden Sie, *Comm.* enclosed you will find.

Bei'schlüssel, (*str.*) *m.* by-key; picklock.

Bei'schmack, (*str.*) *m. see* Beigeschmack.

Bei'schmelzen, (*str.*) *v. tr.* to add to ... in melting.

Bei'schreiben, I. (*str.*) *v. tr.* to write to, note to, add (in writing); to write on the margin; II. *s.* (*str.*) *n.* a writing or letter joined to the principal one; recommendatory or explanatory letter accompanying other writings.

Bei'schreiber, (*str.*) *m.* assistant clerk.

Bei'schrift, (*w.*) *f.* annotation, marginal note; postscript.

Bei'schüssel, (*w.*) *f.* by-dish, side-dish.

Bei'schuß, (*str.*, *pl.* Bei'schüsse) *m.* contribution, share.

Bei'schütten, (*w.*) *v. tr.* 1) to pour to; 2) to loose (the earth) round the vine-roots.

Bei'segel, (*str.*) *n. Mar.* by-sail, drabbler.

Bei'sein, (*str.*) *n.* presence: im — des ..., in the presence of ...; ohne mein —, without my being present.

Beiseit', Beisei'te, Beiseits', I. *adv.* aside, apart; — thun, to remove; — legen, to lay by; to lay aside or apart; etwas — setzen, to lay aside, to set aside; *fig.* to lay or set aside, to forget, make light of; — bringen, 1) to put aside, to remove; 2) to purloin, abstract; II. *s.* (*indecl.*) *n.* (*probably derived from the English*) aside (*Lessing, Schlegel, cf. Sanders & Grimm*).

Bei'setzen, (*w.*) *v. tr.* 1) to put to or set on (the fire); 2) to deposit (in a vault), to bury, entomb; 3) *Mar.* ein Segel —, to heave out, unfurl, unfold a sail; mehr Segel —, to make sail, to unfurl; alle Segel —, to crowd all the sails or canvass, to clap on all the sails; alle Segel beigesetzt haben, to carry a press of sail. — **Bei'setzung**, (*w.*) *f.* 1) the (act of) putting to, &c.; 2) the depositing in a vault, entombment.

Bei'sichtig, *adj. see* Kurzsichtig.

Bei'sitz, (*str.*) *m.* assession, seat or right of sitting (in council, in an assembly, &c.).

Bei'sitzen, (*str.*) *v. intr.* (*aux.* haben) to sit by, to have a seat in: *Law*, to sit in a court of law; das —, *v. s.* (*str.*) *n.* assession.

Bei'sitzer, (*str.*) *m.* 1) assessor, judge lateral, assistant; 2) *see* Schutzverwandter.

Bei'sorge, (*w.*) *f. see* Mitsorge; Vormundschaft. — **Bei'sorger**, (*str.*) *m. see* Vormund.

Bei'spiel, (*str.*) *n.* example, instance; precedent: pattern: zum —, as for example, for instance, such as, such are, viz: nimm dir ihn nicht zum —, don't take an example by or from him: ein — geben, to set an example; sich (*Dat.*) ein — an etwas (*Dat.*) nehmen, to take an example, a lesson from ...; an Einem ein — (Exempel) statuiren (geben, vollziehen), to make an example of one; ein — soll an ihnen vollzogen werden, an example shall be made of them; als — anführen, to instance; durch — (*gener. pl.:* B-e) belegen, to exemplify; böse B-e verderben gute Sitten, *proverb*, bad examples corrupt good manners.

Bei'spiellos, *adj.* unexampled, unprecedented, unparalleled, matchless.

Bei'spiellosigkeit, (*w.*) *f.* unexampled behaviour or state.

Bei'springen, (*str.*) *v. intr.* (*aux.* sein) (Einem) to hasten to one's assistance; to succour, relieve.

Bei'stand, (*str.*, *pl.* Bei'stände) *m.* 1) assistance, succour, support; 2) assistant, helper, supporter; — vor Gericht, counsel; 3) *Mar.* a seconding ship, a ship in a fleet appointed second to the admiral or commanding officer; 4) second (in duels); ohne —, unaided, unassisted; Einem — leisten, to give, afford, or render assistance to, to give (one) help, to succour; B-sgelder, *pl.* subsidies. — **Bei'ständer**, (*str.*) *m.* 1) assistant, bystander; 2) *Mar. see* Beistand, 3. — **Bei'ständig**, *adj.* assisting, assistant; b-es Wort, *Gramm.* adjective.

Bei'stechen, (*str.*) *v. tr. Mar.* to sail close-hauled.

Bei'stecken, (*w.*) *v. tr. coll. see* Einstecken.

Bei'stehen, (*str.*) *v. intr.* 1) to stand by: alle Segel — lassen, *Mar.* to let all sails out; 2) *fig.* (Einem) to assist, help, succour; to support, second; to attend (a sick person, &c.); to relieve (the poor, &c.); to back, countenance, sustain; Gott stehe dir bei, God help you; mit Trost —, to comfort. — **Bei'stehende**, *m.* (*decl. like adj.*) 1) bystander; 2) (legal) adviser, counsel (Beistand). — **Bei'steher**, (str.) m. 1) bystander; 2) backer, &c.; 3) Mar. see Beiboot. — Bei'steherin, (w.) f. 1) female assistant; 2) midwife.

Bei'steuer, (w.) f. contribution, subsidy, supply; collection, alms.

Bei'steuern, (w.) v. tr. to contribute (to a collection).

Bei'stimmen, (w.) v. intr. (Einem) 1) to coincide, agree, or strike in (with one); 2) to join in; to assent (to), consent, accede (to), to concur (in).

Bei'stimmung, (w.) f. assent, consent, concurrence, acquiescence.

Bei'strich, (str.) m. comma.

Bei'strom, (str., pl. Bei'ströme) m. arm of a river.

Bei'stück, (str.) n. additional piece, appendage; dependency.

Beiß'beere, (w.) f. Bot. Indian or Spanish pepper (Pfeffer, spanischer).

Bei'ßen, (str.) v. I. intr. 1) to bite; to bite, snap (nach, at); to bite (on); to bite, nibble (at) (of fish); 2) to cut, smart (of wounds); to itch: Pfeffer beißt auf der Zunge, pepper bites the tongue; [illegible] nicht viel zu — haben, to be poorly off; Hunde, welche bellen, — nicht, barking dogs never bite; in die Angel —, to take the bait, to suffer one's self to be caught; in einen sauern Apfel —, to submit to necessity, to make up one's mind to a disagreeable thing; um sich —, to snap, growl at, to be quarrelsome; ins Gras —, vulg. to die, anal. to bite the dust, to gnaw the ground; II. tr. to bite; to gnaw: der Hund biß mich ins Bein, the dog bit my leg; III. refl. to bite one's self or each other or one another; sich (Dat.) (der Sachen) in (auf) die Zunge, Lippen —, to bite one's lips, to stifle, suppress one's laughter with difficulty; sich um etwas —, to quarrel, fight for.

Bei'ßend, p. a. biting; fig. sharp, smart, keen, pungent; acrid, tart, acrimonious; sarcastical, bitter; b-er Scherz, a biting jest; B-e, n. sharpness, &c., pungency, sarcasticalness, poignancy.

Bei'ßer, (str.) (m.) 1) a biter, biting dog, dog given to biting; 2) quarreller; 3) see Beißker. — Beißerei', (w.) f. 1) (the act or habit of) biting, &c.; 2) fig. quarrelling, noisy dispute.

Beiß'fliege, (w.) f. Entom. stinging fly (Akanthocera pungens).

Bei'ßig, adj. 1) biting, &c., see Beißend; 2) fig. snappish, quarrelsome, doggish, crusty, currish; B-keit, (w.) f. snappishness, tartness.

Beiß'käfer, (str.) m. Entom. stinging-beetle (Carabus).

Beiß'ker, (str.) m. Ichth. mudfish, loach (Cobitis fossilis).

Beiß'..., in comp. -kohl, m. Bot. beet (Beta vulgaris alba L.); -korb (-kober), m. muzzle (which stops biting); -mittel, n. corrosive (Ätzmittel); -mücke, f. see Beißfliege; -rübe, f. see Bete; -wurz, f. root of the Pulsatilla (Wiesen-Küchenschelle); -zahn, m. cutting-tooth, incisor; -zange, f. cutting plyers or nippers.

Beit(e), (w.) f. provinc. biding, respite.

Bei'tel, (str.) m. (from the Dutch) Carp., &c. (Stech—) (Brenner-)chisel.

Bei'ten, (w.) v. intr. (h & s) provinc. to bide, wait.

Bei'thun, (irr.) v. tr. & intr. see Beilegen.

Bei'tisch, (str.) m. side-board.

Bei'trag, (str., pl. Bei'träge) m. contribution; supply, share, contingent, quota; einen — zu ... geben, to contribute to —.

Bei'tragen, (str.) v. I. tr. to contribute, to bear a share; II. intr. to contribute, conduce, be conducive (zu, to), to assist, succour, help: dies wird viel dazu — ihn neu zu kräftigen, this will go far towards giving him new strength.

Bei'träger, (str.) m. contributor.

Bei'treiben, (str.) v. tr. see Eintreiben.

Bei'treten, (str.) v. intr. (aux. sein) 1) a) (Sportsm. speak of deer) to plant the toe of the hind foot near the heel of the fore foot; b) to place one foot near the other; 2) (with Dat.) a) to accede (to), to come over (to some party); to enter into (a league); to take part, to share in; to join in or with, to assent to (an opinion); Einem als Theilnehmer im Geschäft —, to enter or get into partnership with one, to associate one's self with one; Jemandes Partei —, to join one's party, to side with one.

Bei'tritt, (str.) m. 1) a peculiar kind of step, cf. Beitreten, 1; 2) accession, adhesion, concurrence, taking part, &c.

Bei'urtheil, (str.) n. Law, interlocution; injunction.

Bei'vormund, (str., pl. B-münder) m. Law, joint-guardian, co-guardian.

Bei'wache, Bei'wacht, (w.) f. Mil. bivouac. — Bei'wachen, (w.) v. intr. to bivouac.

Bei'wagen, (str.) m. by-coach, by-waggon, extra-coach.

Bei'weg, (str.) m. by-way, by-road.

Bei'weib, (str., pl. B-er) n. concubine.

Bei'werfen, (str.) v. tr. to throw by.

Bei'werk, (str.) n., Bei'wesen, (str.) n. the accessory, non-essential parts of a work, accessories, accompaniments.

Bei'wirkung, (w.) f. Med. midwifery.

Bei'wohnen, (w.) v. intr. (with Dat.) 1) to assist (at), to be present (at), to attend (a meeting, &c.); 2) to lie with, cohabit with; 3) to be inherent; es wohnen ihm gute Eigenschaften bei, he is endowed with good qualities.

Bei'wohnung, (w.) f. 1) presence, attendance; 2) (eheliche) cohabitation.

Bei'wort, (str., pl. Bei'wörter) n. Gramm. adjective; epithet. — Bei'wörtlich, adj. adjectival; epithetic; adv. adjectively.

Bei'zahlen, (w.) v. tr. to contribute.

Bei'zählen, (w.) v. tr. to annumerate, number amongst; er ist den besten beizuzählen, he ranges with the best.

Bei'ze, (w.) f. 1) Sport. a baiting; Falc. hawking, flying; 2) a) Chem., &c. maceration, corrosion; b) Tann. ooze, macerating; tan-liquor; Farr. searing; Dy. mordant, rot-steep; c) (zu Tabak) sauce; den Haaren die — geben, Hatt. to dress the fur; d) (das Beizmittel) corrosive; Engr. aqua fortis; 3) staining-matter, staining, colour.

Bei'zeichen, (str.) n. 1) by-note; countermark; 2) Herald. rebatement.

Bei'zeichnen, (w.) v. tr. to note down.

Beizei'ten, adv. betimes, in (good) time, early, soon.

Bei'zen, (w.) v. tr. 1) Pharm., &c. to macerate, to soak (Tann. skins); Hatt. to dress (the fur); 2) Chem. to corrode; Surg. to cauterise; Dy. to fret, stain; to mordant; to alum; Metall. to fret (gold, silver), to half-scour; to pickle, dip (copper, &c.), to cleanse; Tann. to tan; Join. to stain, colour (wood); schwarz —, to ebonise; Engr. to etch; b-d, p. a. corrosive, corroding, caustic; 3) Sport. a) to bait; b) to make chase on (birds) by means of hawks, intr. to hawk.

Beiz'..., in comp. -falke, m. see Edelfalk; -hund, m. see Spürhund.

Bei'zimmer, (str.) n. see Nebenzimmer.

Beiz'..., in comp. -kraft, f. corrosive power or quality; -kufe, f. tan-vat; -mittel, n. corrosive, mordant.

Bei'zoll, (str., pl. Bei'zölle) m. additional (or extra-)duty.

Beiz'..., in comp. -[illegible], f. see -kufe; -vogel, m. hawk, falcon; -wolle, f. see Sterblingswolle; -wurz, f. see Beißwurz; -zuber, m. see -kufe.

Bei'zügel, (str.) m. left or near rein.

Beja'gen, (w.) v. tr. to chase, hunt, sport in (a certain place or district).

Bejah'en, (w.) v. tr. to affirm, to assert; to answer in the affirmative or affirmatively; alle Fragen —, to say "aye" to every question;

propagandist; B-eifer, m. proselytism; B-s-gesandtschaft, f. mission; B-sgesellschaft, f. missionary society; B-sucht, B-swuth, f. proselytism.

Bekei'fen, (w.) v. tr. to scold, chide.

Bekei'men, (w.) v. intr. & refl. (aux. sein) to get germs, to germ.

Bekennen, (irr.) v. I. tr. 1) to confess, own, acknowledge; 2) Gam. Farbe —, to follow suit; eine Farbe nicht —, to revoke; II. refl. sich zu ... —, to acknowledge, own (a deed, &c.); to advocate, embrace, avow, profess (a religion, an art, &c.); to hold to; (frei, freimüthig) to avow: sich schuldig —, to plead guilty; sich zu einer That —, to confess having done a deed.

Beken'ner, (str.) m. confessor, professor (of a religion), follower.

Bekennt'niß, (str.) n. acknowledgment; avowal; confession; creed: das schriftliche —, recognizance; das eidliche —, affidavit; Theol.-s. —feier, f. sacrament of the Lord's supper; —psalm, m. confessional psalm (Ps. 51); —schriften, f. pl. symbolic books, doctrinal or authorized standards (of a church).

Beker'ben, (w.) v. tr. to notch; bekerbt, p. a. Herald. scaled; embattled.

Beker'zen, (w.) v. tr. to stick, place tapers round.

Beket'ten, (w.) v. tr. to hang, adorn with chains.

Beki'chern, (w.) v. tr. to titter at.

Beki'elen, (w.) v. tr. to quill, see Befiedern.

Beki'esen, (w.) v. tr. to strew over with gravel.

Bekit'zeln, (w.) v. tr. to tickle.

[illegible], (w.) v. intr. Mar. to head the sea.

Bekla'gen, (w.) v. I. tr. 1) a) to deplore, lament, bewail, to bemoan, mourn; es ist zu —, daß ..., it is to be regretted that ...; b) to commiserate, compassionate, pity; 2) †. to mourn, see Anklagen; II. refl. to complain (über [with Acc.], of; bei, to): worüber beklagt er sich? what does he complain of? er beklagt sich über den Mangel an Bequemlichkeit in seinem Wirthshaus, he complains about the bad accommodation of his hotel. — Bekla'genswerth, Bekla'genswürdig, adj. deplorable, &c. — Beklag'te, m. & f. (decl. like adj.) defendant, impeached, accused.

Beklam'mern, (w.) v. tr. T. to provide with cramps.

Beklat'schen, (w.) v. tr. 1) to applaud by clapping hands; 2) vulg. to tell tales of or on, to calumniate, defame.

Beklau'ben, (w.) v. tr. to handle, finger, dabble; to pick with the fingers.

[illegible], p. a. particul. Herald. clawed, furnished with (coloured) talons.

Bekle'ben, (w.) v. I. tr. to paste over, to line (with paper, &c.); mit Etiketten —, to label; to plaster; II. intr. to cleave, stick, adhere.

Beklecken, Beklecksen, (w.) v. tr. to blot, blur, bespot, bespatter; to daub.

Beklei'ben, (str.) v. tr. & intr. see Bekleiben; particul. intr. to cleave, to strike root.

Beklei'den, (w.) v. tr. 1) to clothe, to dress, [illegible], to attire, array; fig. to invest: 2) T.-a. a) to cover over, line, face (also with masonry, wood, or other material), sheath, coat; [illegible] to tub, line (the pit of [illegible] to dress, trim (a bank a) [illegible] to revet (eine Böschung, a slope); f) [illegible] Mar.-s. g) einen Anker [illegible] an anchor; h) die Taue —, to [illegible] ropes: bekleidet, p. a. [illegible] —, to deck an [illegible] & Sculpt. to make [illegible] drape a figure; ein [illegible] to line, coat, clay. [illegible] 3) to invest [illegible] bekleidet, vested [illegible] Stelle, ein Amt) to occupy (a post); to fill, hold (or serve in) an office.

Beklei'dung, (w.) f. 1) clothing, dressing: dress, garment; 2) a) Paint., Sculpt., &c. drapery; hangings, tapestry (of a room); Mar.-s. b) serving (of the ropes); c) (die äußere — an einem Schiffe) bulwark; d) Carp. cage; e) Steam-eng. case, casing, (steam-)jacket (Mantel); f) Join. boxing (of a door); facing, lining (of a pit, &c.); mantle-piece (of a chimney); g) side-planks (of a ship); 3) the (act of) investing; investiture; 4) administration (of an office).

Beklei'dungs..., in comp. —inspector, m. superintendent of the clothing-department; —kissen, n. Mar. (des Stags) pillow; —korb, see Schanzkorb; —mauer, see Futtermauer.

Beklei'stern, (w.) v. tr. 1) to paste or plaster over. Weav. to dress, size; 2) fig. to colour, palliate.

Beklem'men, (w.) v. tr. 1) to pinch, press, confine, straiten; 2) fig. to afflict, oppress: to grieve. — Beklem'mung, (w.) f. pressure; difficulty of breathing, anxiety; anguish: embarrassment.

Beklet'tern, (w.) v. tr. to climb.

Beklin'ken, (w.) v. tr. Carp., &c. to join (by a mortice): to assemble.

Beklom'men, I. p. a. oppressed: breathing with difficulty: uneasy, anxious, sorrowful; II. B-heit, (w.) f. see Beklemmung.

Beklop'fen, (w.) v. tr. to knock, beat repeatedly; Min. to try (the rocks) by beating; Coin. to beat (the blanks).

Beklötz'en, (w.) v. tr. to pave with square pieces of wood.

Beklü'geln, (w.) v. tr. to criticise, censure.

Beknun'kern, (w.) v. tr. & refl. vulg. to bedraggle, drabble, dirty, to clog with dirt.

Beknab'bern (Beknap'pern), (w.) v. tr. to gnaw or to nibble at.

Beknau'peln, (w.) v. tr. to pick ("when I'm sent for a loaf, you should only see how I pick it all round").

Beknau'sern, (w.) v. tr. to cut short or stint from niggardliness (the servants of fees, &c.). [(of cables): bekneift, jammed.

Beknei'fen, (w.) v. refl. Mar. to run foul

Beknur'ren, (w.) v. tr. to snarl at.

Bekö'dern, (w.) v. tr. to bait.

Bekom'men, (str.) v. I. tr. 1) to get, receive, obtain, gain; es ist nicht zu —, it is not to be had or got: er bekam kein Trinkgeld, he had no fee; einen Anfall von ... —, to be taken with a fit of ...: Lust —, to have or get (a) mind: ich konnte ihn nicht zu sehen —, I could not get a sight of him: Land zu Gesicht —, to gain sight of land, to descry land: Blüten —, to begin to blossom: Wurzeln —, to take or strike root: eine Krankheit —, to fall sick, to be taken ill, to take a disease: Zähne —, to cut teeth, to teeth; II. intr. (aux. sein) 1) (obsolescent; Rückert, &c.) to thrive, to prosper (Fortkommen); 2) to agree with the health: diese Speise bekommt mir nicht, this food (meat) does not agree with or disorders me: der gestrige Spaziergang ist mir nicht schlecht —, I am not (or have not been) (any) the worse for (my) yesterday's walk: wie ist Ihnen Ihre Spazierfahrt —? how do you bear your ride? er ist mir gut —, I find myself the better for it: es wird ihm schlecht —, he will come off badly for it, he will be served out for it; seine Speculation ist ihm übel —, his speculation has proved a bad job: wohl bekomme es Ihnen! much good may it do you!

Bekor'ben, (w.) v. tr. to furnish with a basket (cf. einen Korb geben).

Bekor'ken, (w.) v. tr. to cork.

Bekö'pert, p. a. (Hippel, unusual for Beleibt) corpulent.

Beköst'igen (l. u.: Bekö'sten, Beköst'en), (w.) v. tr. to furnish with food; to board, diet; sich —, to find one's own food; coll. to find one's self.

Beköst'iger, (str.) m. nourisher: master of a boarding-house.

Beköst'igung, (w.) f. alimentation, boarding, board, diet, food.

Bekot'zen, (w.) v. tr. vulg. to bespew (Bespeien).

Bekrab'beln, (w.) v. tr. coll. to tickle.

Bekräf'tigen (l. u.: Bekräf'ten), (w.) v. tr. 1) to strengthen, corroborate: 2) to confirm to assert, avouch, aver, sanction.

Bekräf'tigung, (w.) f. 1) corroboration; 2) confirmation, averment, sanction.

Bekrän'zen, (w.) v. tr. to wreath, crown; to garland, festoon.

Bekrat'zen, (w.) v. tr. to scrape on the surface, to cover with scratches, to scratch.

Bekrau'ten, (w.) v. tr. 1) Gard. to weed; 2) see Begrasen.

Bekrei'den, (w.) v. tr. to chalk over.

Bekrei'sen, (w.) v. tr. to encircle, encompass: Sport. ein Gehölz —, to go round a copse.

Bekreu'zen, (w.) v. tr. 1) to cross; (Bekreu'zigen, (w.) v. refl.) to make the sign of the cross upon, cf. Kreuzen; 2) Law, to set a cross under a document; 3) Mil. to command by a cross-fire. — Bekreu'zung, (w.) f. the (act of) crossing, &c.

Bekrie'chen, (str.) v. tr. to creep over.

Bekrie'gen, (w.) v. tr. to make war upon.

Bekrit'teln, (w.) v. tr. to censure, criticise, to find fault with, to carp or cavil at, disparage. — Bekrit'tler, (str.) m. fault-finder, caviller, &c., criticaster.

Bekrit'zeln, (w.) v. tr. to scrawl, scribble over, bescrawl.

Bekrö'nen, (w.) v. tr. to bestow a crown (wreath, &c. cf. Krone) upon (one), to crown.

Bekrö'nung, (w.) f. 1) a crowning: 2) T. (or B-gesims, n.) a) cornice (Kranzgesims); b) Fort., &c. crest; B-gesims einer Brücke, coping.

Bekrü'meln, (w.) v. tr. to strew with crumbs.

Bekrust'en, (w.) v. tr. to crust, incrust. — Bekrust'ung, (w.) f. crustation, incrustation.

Bekül'mern, (w.) v. I. tr. to aggrieve, grieve, afflict, discomfort, trouble; bekümmert, p. a. sorry (um, über [with Acc.], of, at), anxious, solicitous, concerned; um, über or wegen ... bekümmert sein, to be concerned for, affected with, solicitous or careful of ...; II. refl. 1) (über, wegen) to afflict one's self, to be aggrieved by, to be sorrowful, anxious, to grieve (at): 2) to concern or busy one's self with or about, to care for; to attend to, to mind, to take notice of: to meddle with; bekümmere dich um dich, mind your own business or look to your (own) self; 3) Law, to seize, distrain (Verkümmern).

Beküm'merniß, (str.) f. & n. affliction, grief, sorrow, pain, trouble, solicitude, concern.

Beküm'merung, (w.) f. Law, see Verkümmerung.

Bekun'den, (w.) v. tr. 1) Law, to depose, give evidence upon oath: 2) to prove, demonstrate, manifest.

Bekü'ssen, (w.) v. tr. (l. u.) to kiss repeatedly.

Belä'cheln, (w.) v. tr. to smile at.

Bela'chen, (w.) v. tr. 1) to laugh at: 2) see Verlachen.

Belack'en, (w.) v. tr. to cover with varnish, to japan.

Bela'den, (str.) v. tr. 1) to load, charge, freight; 2) to encumber, burden: b-e Kohlenschiffe, laden colliers; ein ganz b-es Schiff, a full ship; alle, die ihr mühselig und — seid (Matth. 11, 28), all ye that labour and are heavy laden.

Belag', (str., pl. Belä'ge) m. 1) a) anything laid over another (cf. Belegen), covering: b) flooring, planking (of a bridge); c) bridge-road, road-way (of a bridge); d) incrustation; 2) voucher, &c., see Beleg.

Bela'gerer, *(str.) m.* besieger.

Bela'gern, *(w.) v. tr.* 1) to besiege, to lay siege to; 2) *fig.* to besiege, beset.

Bela'gerung, *(w.) f.* siege: **B-sgeschütz,** *n.* battering guns *or* pieces, battering train, battering artillery: **B-sheer,** *n.* besieging army: **B-skrone,** *f. Rom. Ant.* obsidional crown: **B-skunst,** *f.* art *or* tactics of besieging: **B-slafette,** *f.* travelling-carriage of a gun; **B-smaschine,** *f.* battering engine (of the ancients): **B-sstück,** *n.* siege-piece; **B-swerke,** *pl.* approaches: **B-szustand,** *m.* state of siege: in (den) B-szustand versetzen, to proclaim (a town).

Belä'mmern, *(w.) v. tr. vulg.* 1) to soil in the dirt, to draggle; 2) to cheat *(cf.* Beschummern); 3) to (en)cumber, impede.

Belä'mmerung, *(w.) f. particul. Mar.* entanglement, lumber, encumbrance, impediment. [import, importance, consequence.

Belang', *(str.) m.* 1) amount; 2) weight,

Belang'bar, *adj. Law,* suable, capable of being summoned before a court.

Belang'en, *(w.) v. tr.* 1) †, to reach (Erlangen); 2) *impers. a)* to concern, belong to, regard: was mich belangt, as far as I am concerned, as for my part, as for me; b-d, concerning, touching: *b)* († &) *provinc.* es belangt mich nach ..., I long *or* yearn for ... *(cf.* Verlangen); 3) *Law,* to go to law with (one), to bring an action against (one), to sue, summon, accuse (one).

Belang'reich, *adj.* important, momentous, of great moment, of consequence.

Belang'ung, *(w.) f. Law,* prosecution.

Belap'pen, *(w.) v. tr.* 1) *Sport.* to hang rags about (a wood) to frighten the game: 2) *provinc.* to patch, botch: belappt, *p. a.* having long hanging upper lips (of hounds).

Belas'sen, *(str.) v. tr.* to leave in the former condition *or* place *(cf.* Bewenden lassen): man bläßt es beim lateinischen Kunstwort *(Grimm),* the Latin technical term is retained; Einen im Commando —, to continue one in command: sie wurden im Amte —, they were continued in their offices. — **Belas'sung,** *(w.) f.* the leaving, &c.; continuation (in office, &c.).

Belas'ten, *(w.) v. tr.* 1) *a)* to burden, load, charge, clog, encumber: *fig-s b)* to confirm a criminal charge against (one, &c.); *c) (l. u.) for* Belästigen; 2) *Comm-s.* to debit, to place to, write down into one's debit, to charge one's account, to enter into: belastet sein *or* stehen, to be charged, to stand debited (mit, for). [to blaspheme.

Beläs'tern, *(w.) v. tr.* to abuse, slander:

Beläs'tigen, *(w.) v. tr.* to molest, trouble, to importune, annoy; *coll.* to pester, pother; b-d, *p. a.* burdensome: vexatious, harassing, oppressive. — **Beläs'tigung,** *(w.) f.* 1) molestation, &c.; vexation, solicitation: 2) *a)* burden; *b)* nuisance.

Belas'tung, *(w.) f.* 1) *a)* the (act of) burdening, &c.; *b)* load, charge; 2) *Law,* confirmation of a criminal charge against ...: **B-szeuge,** *m.* witness for the prosecution.

Belat'ten, *(w.) v. tr.* to lath, fit up with laths.

Belau'ben, *(w.) v. I. tr.* 1) to cover with leaves *or* foliage; to embower; 2) *(l. u.)* to strip of the leaves; II. *refl.* to get leaves; belaubt, *p. a.* leafy, in foliage.

Belau'bung, *(w.) f.* the act *or* the time of getting forth leaves; *Bot.* foliation, frondescence; Wälder in voller —, woods in full foliage; die Farnkräuter sind jetzt in voller —, the ferns are now in full leaf.

Belau'ern, *(w.) v. tr.* 1) to watch, lurk, spy; to lie in wait for, *coll.* to dog: Spione — meine Schritte, spies are dogging my steps; 2) to take (some) in.

Belauf', *(str., pl.* Beläu'fe) *m.* 1) *Mar.* — des Schiffes, rising of the ship's floor afore and abaft; 2) amount; sum: im — von ..., amounting to ...; bis zum — von, to the amount of.

Belau'fen, *(str.) v. I. tr.* 1) *a)* to run, *coll.* to walk over (the ice, &c.); *b)* to perambulate, see Begehen, 1; 2) *Sport.* to line: II. *refl.* 1) *Sport.* to buck, to couple; to copulate; 2) to amount *or* come (auf *[with Acc.],* to, up to): wie hoch beläuft sich meine Rechnung? how much does my bill come to?

Belau'schen, *(w.) v. tr.* to watch, spy, surprise: to listen, to overhear (a conversation).

Beläu'ten, *(w.) v. tr.* to proclaim, celebrate, &c. by the ringing of bells.

Belch, *(str.) m. Ichth.* see Belche.

Bel'che, *(w.) f. Ornith.* see Bläßhuhn.

Bele'ben, *(w.) v. tr.* to animate, enliven: 1) to make alive, to quicken, &c.: die ganze Atmosphäre ist belebt, the whole atmosphere is filled with life: wieder —, to restore to life; 2) *fig.* to vivify, invigorate; to cheer, to elevate; b-d, *p. a.* animating, &c.: ein b-des Mittel, *Med.* restorative, animative.

Belebt', I. *p. a.* 1) having life: 2) *a) fig.* animated, lively, vivacious, sprightly, brisk: die Börse war wenig —, but little spirit was displayed on change: b-e Straßen, crowded streets; *b) Mus. animoso;* II. **B-heit,** *(w.) f.* animation, liveliness, vivacity, &c.

Bele'bung, *(w.) f.* animation.

Belec'ken, *(w.) v. tr.* to lick.

Bele'dern, *(w.) v. tr.* to furnish *or* cover with leather (the hammers of a piano, &c.), to leather.

Beleg', *(str.) m.* 1) *lit. a)* see Belag; *b) Med.* fur (of the tongue of sick persons, &c.): 2) *a)* written *or* authentic proof: B-e beibringen, to furnish *or* to bring forward proofs: einen — liefern zu, to furnish evidence of: zum — dafür, in verification or as a proof of this; *b)* note, receipt: *c) Law, &c.* voucher; deed, document: B-e, authenticated papers (documents).

Bele'ge, *(str.) n. Tail.* border, facing.

Bele'gen, *(w.) v. tr.* 1) to lay over, on, to overlay, cover (with), line: to face (a block of deal, &c. with a different kind of wood, &c.): to garnish, border, lace: mit Dielen —, see Dielen; mit Fliesen —, to flag: mit Marmor &c. —, see Bekleiden; mit Steinen —, to pave; mit Reifen —, to hoop (a cask): to shoe (a wheel); mit Schienen —, *Railw.* to lay down rails on ...; *Mar.* to belay (a rope); mit Rasen —, *Gard.* to cover with turf, to sod; den Huf —, see Beschlagen; einen Spiegel mit Folie —, to silver, tin, or foliate a looking-glass: mit Horn belegt, with horn mounting: *b) aa)* eine Grube mit Arbeitern —, *Min.* to employ workmen in (a mine); *bb)* ein Haus mit Soldaten —, to quarter soldiers upon a house: *c)* einen Platz —, to preoccupy or secure a place or seat (in the theatre, &c.): *fig-s.* 2) mit Abgaben —, to lay duties on ..., to impose taxes; mit Strafe —, to inflict a punishment upon; mit Fluch —, to lay a curse on (one), to execrate, curse; mit einem Namen —, to give a name to; Geld —, see Anlegen, I. 2, *a*; 3) *Law, &c.* to support, shew by documents and vouchers, to verify: 4) (said of the male of animals) to horse (a mare), to cover (of wolves, dogs, &c.), to line: belegt, *p. a.* 1) overlaid, &c.; 2) *Med., &c. a)* coated, furred (of the tongue); *b)* husky, covered (of the voice).

Bele'gen, *p. a.* situated (Gelegen).

Beleg' ..., *in comp.* **-geld,** *n.* see Hengstgeld; **-hölzer,** *n. pl. Mar.* belaying cleats, pins, &c.: **-stelle,** *f.* citation, quotation, (cited) authority. [crew (employed in a mine).

Beleg'schaft, *(w.) f.* (the number of) men,

Bele'gung, *(w.) f.* 1) *a)* the (act of) laying over, covering, &c. *cf.* Belegen; *b)* incumb-

Sie rothen Wein? do you choose red wine? — Sie noch etwas? would you like any thing else? II. intr. (with Dat.) to please; es beliebt ihm, it pleases him, he takes a fancy to, it is his pleasure; diese Speise beliebt mir nicht, I don't like this dish (meat); was beliebt Ihnen? what is your pleasure or will? das beliebt Ihnen zu sagen, you are pleased to say so; es beliebte ihm nicht zu antworten, he did not choose, or deign, or was not pleased to answer; wenn Ihnen dies nicht beliebt, if this is not to your liking; wie beliebt? Sir? ob. Madam? ob. I beg your pardon...; wie (es) Ihnen beliebt, as you like or please; nehmen Sie, was Ihnen beliebt, take your choice.

Belie'ben, (str.) n. will, inclination, pleasure, liking; nach —, at will, Mus. &c. ad libitum; nach Ihrem —, as you please, at your pleasure; Jeder nach —, every one to his taste or at his (own) pleasure; handeln Sie ganz nach Ihrem —, use your own discretion in it; es steht in Ihrem —, it is (left) at your discretion, it rests with you; ich stelle es ganz in Ihr —, I leave that to your own discretion or at your option.

Belie'big, adj. arbitrary, discretionary, to one's liking or pleasure; in b-er Größe, of the size you choose; nehmen Sie einen b-en Maßstab an, take any standard you like; eine b-e Summe, any sum you please; b-e Linie, Zahl, Math. indefinite line, number; in b-er Richtung, in any required direction; zu jeder b-en Zeit, at any time whatever.

Beliebt', I. p. a. liked, beloved; in favour, popular; fashionable (bei, with); sehr —, highly thought of; Comm. in favour (of wares); — machen, to endear; sich — machen, to ingratiate one's self (bei, with); — sein, to be liked, &c., admired; to be a favourite (bei, with); — werden, to grow in or gain favour; II. das B-sein, (str.) n., B-heit, (w.) f. the being liked or in favour, popularity.

Belie'bung, (w.) f. obsolescent, 1) any voluntary contract or agreement (Bdg.); 2) voluntary association, cf. Todten—.

Belie'gen, (str.) v. I. intr. †. to lie; II. tr. to lie on. (adj.) Law, donee.

Beliehe'ne, m. (pp. of Beleihen, decl. like

Belinii'ren, (w.) v. tr. to rule with lines.

Beluch'sen, (w.) v. tr. to deceive, cheat, over-reach, trick, humbug.

* **Belladon'na,** f. Bot. belladonna, deadly night-shade (Atropa belladonna L.).

A. **Bel'le,** (w.) f., or **Bell'baum,** see Abele.

B. **Bel'le,** (w.) f. coll. bark (barking); cough.

Bel'len, (w. & † str.) v. intr. 1) to bark, to yelp; 2) fig. to clamour (against); mein Magen bellt, coll. I am terribly hungry.

Bel'ler, (str.) m. barker, &c.

* **Belletrist',** (w.) m. one versed in the belles-lettres [illegible] belletrist. — B-erei, (w.) f. pretension to polite literature. — B-isch, adj. belonging to belles lettres, [illegible] belletristic(al).

Bell..., in comp. —hammel, m. bell-wether (Leithammel); —hase, m., maus, f. Zool. [illegible] (Lepus pusillus); —horn, n. see [illegible]; —huhn, n. see Bläßhuhn.

Belo'ben, Belo'bigen, (w.) v. tr. to praise, commend, applaud, make honourable mention of. — **Belo'bigung,** (w.) f. praise, commendation; honourable mention; B-s..., in comp. commendatory: B-[illegible], n. [illegible]

Belö'chern, (w.) v. tr. to have holes into [illegible] to make a hole in, to perforate; [illegible]

Belohn'bar, adj. remunerable, requitable; B-keit, (w.) f. remunerability.

Beloh'nen, (w.) v. tr. to reward, to recompense, [illegible] requite (mit Undank — (cf. [illegible]) [illegible] b-de Arbeit, remunerative labour; b-swerth, adj. remunerable, worthy of reward.

Beloh'ner, (str.) m. rewarder, remunerator.

Beloh'nung, (w.) f. reward, recompense, remuneration; gratuity; prize, premium; payment; schlechte —, ill return.

Belt, (str.) m. Geogr. Belt; der große und der kleine —, the greater and the lesser Belt.

Belu'gen, (w.) v. tr. provinc. to view closely.

Belü'gen, (str.) v. tr. to belie, to tell a lie to; to deceive by (a) falsehood; er hat mich belogen, he (has) told me a lie; sich selbst —, to be a liar to one's self.

Belum'sen [pr. —lux'—], (w.) v. tr. coll. to cozen, cheat, trick.

Belus'tigen, (w.) v. I. tr. to amuse, divert, delight; II. refl. to divert, amuse, or enjoy one's self, to make merry; sich lärmend —, to romp. — **Belus'tiger,** (str.) m. diverter, &c., merry-maker, entertainer. — **Belus'tigung,** (w.) f. diversion, delight, sport, entertainment, merry-making.

* **Bel'zebub,** see Beelzebub.

Bel'zen, (w.) v. tr. see Pelzen (Pfropfen).

Belz'..., in comp. —baum, m. see Vellbaum; —meise, f. see Schwanzmeise.

Bema(a)'len, (w.) v. tr. to mask.

Bemach'en, (w.) v. tr. coll. to befoul.

Bemäch'tigen, (w.) v. refl. (with Gen.) 1) to seize (on), to take possession, or make sure, or possess one's self (of), to master; to secure: 2) to usurp. — **Bemäch'tigung,** (w.) f. 1) the (act of) seizing, &c.; 2) usurpation.

Bema'keln, (w.) v. tr. see Bekritteln.

Bema'len, (w.) v. tr. 1) to paint (over), to bepaint; 2) Sport. to mark or foul with excrements. [piece of timber).

Bemal'len, (w.) v. tr. Carp. to mould (a

Bemäng'eln, (w.) v. tr. to object or make objections to, to find fault with.

Beman'nen, (w.) v. tr. to man, equip, fit out (a ship). — **Beman'nung,** (w.) f. the (act of) manning, &c.; equipage, crew.

Bemän'teln, (w.) v. tr. 1) Law, to legitimate (a child); cf. Mantelkind; 2) fig. to cloak, palliate, colour, to set a fine gloss upon, to varnish, to gloss over, to conceal: to extenuate, soften, mince, smooth, cover (a fault, &c.). — **Bemän'telung,** (w.) f. 1) legitimation of a child: 2) cloaking, palliation.

Bemas'ten, (w.) v. tr. to furnish with masts, to mast. — **Bemas'tung,** (w.) f. 1) the act of masting: 2) masts, yards, booms, &c., spars (of a ship). [with a wall.

Bemau'ern, (w.) v. tr. to wall, to enclose

Bemaul'korben, (w.) v. tr. (Wieland, l. u.) to muzzle.

Bemaul'schellen, (w.) v. tr. see Beohrfeigen.

Bemau'sen, (w.) v. tr. vulg. to pilfer or filch from.

Bemei'ßeln, (w.) v. tr. to chisel.

Bemeis'tern, (w.) v. tr. (& refl. with Gen.) to master, to seize on; to vanquish, conquer, overcome; to make one's self master of.

Bemel'den, (w.) v. tr. obsolescent, to mention: bemeldet, p. a. mentioned, aforesaid; bemeldeter Maßen, as aforesaid. [per (mit, with).

Bemen'gen, (w.) v. refl. to meddle, to tam-

Bemerk'bar, I. adj. observable, perceptible, sensible (cf. Bemerklich); II. B-keit, (w.) f. perceptibility.

Bemer'ken, I. v. (w.) tr. 1) to mark, note, remark, notice, observe, perceive; bemerkt wie unten, as noted below; etwas vortheilhaft —, to take a thing in good part (cf. Bemerken); 2) to make an observation, to observe, remark; Comm. to note, state, mention, quote; II. n. s. (str.) n. (the act of) marking, &c.; mit dem —, with the remark, remarking; b-swerth, b-swürdig, adj. worth remarking, deserving notice, noticeable, notable, remarkable, note-worthy; curious.

Bemerk'lich, adj. see Bemerkbar; (Einem etwas) — machen, to hint (something to), make (one) sensible (of); seine Absichten — machen, to mark one's intentions; sich — machen, 1) (of persons) to make one's self (one's presence) noticed; to obtrude one's self; bei..., to push one's self into the notice of ...; 2) (of things) to become apparent.

Bemer'kung, (w.) f. remark; observation; notice; hint; nöthige — nehmen, to take due note; sich (Dat.) (schriftliche) B-en machen, to take notes; über (with Acc.) B-en machen, to make comments on..., to comment upon (on) ..., to observe on...; b-swerth, b-swürdig, see Bemerkenswerth.

Bemes'sen, (str.) v. tr. 1) to subject to measurement, to measure; to ascertain or to adjust by measuring; 2) to mete out, apportion; —, p. a. lit. & fig. measured.

Bemin'nen, (w.) v. tr. provinc. (S. G.) to court, to pay one's addresses to.

Bemis'ten, (w.) v. tr. to manure, dung.

Bemit'leiden, (w.) v. tr. to commiserate, pity, compassionate; b-swürdig, adj. worthy of compassion, pitiable.

Bemit'telt, adj. furnished with means, in easy circumstances, well off, well-to-do, wealthy, substantial; ein b-er Mann, a man of means.

Bem'me, see Bämme.

Bem'mern, (w.) v. intr. (Auerbach, l. u.) see Bimmeln. [= Nachmittagbimmeln].

Bemö'beln, (w.) v. tr. to furnish (rooms

Bemo'dert, p. a. covered with mould, mouldy.

Bemoo'sen, (w.) v. I. tr. to cover with moss; II. intr. to gather moss; bemoost', p. a. mossy, moss-grown; * moss-clad; das bemoos'te Haupt, Acad. slang, old student.

Bemör'teln, (w.) v. tr. to plaster, parget, cover with mortar; to rough-cast.

Bemü'hen, (w.) v. I. tr. to trouble, to inconvenience; darf ich Sie darum —? may I trouble you for it? II. refl. 1) (or Bemüht sein) to take trouble or pains, to trouble one's self, to give one's self trouble; to endeavour, labour, strive, to make efforts, to exert one's self, to contend (for), to struggle, to be anxious; sich umsonst —, to lose one's labour; eifrig um (with Acc.) bemüht, eagerly bent on; er hat sich sehr um sie bemüht, he made great efforts in her behalf; he took great pains to win her; 2) (with zu and other prepositions and adverbs denoting motion to a place) to take the trouble of going to...; es thut mir leid, daß Sie sich haben zu mir — müssen, I am sorry you had the trouble of calling on me; bitte, — Sie sich in den Garten, please to step into the garden; — Sie sich hinauf, be so good as to walk up; wollen Sie sich nicht herein —? won't you please to step in? das —, v. s. (str.) n., **Bemü'hung,** (w.) f. trouble, pains, endeavour, effort, care, exertion. [oblige.

Bemüß'igen, Bemüß'igen, (w.) v. tr. to

Bemut'tern, (w.) v. tr. coll. to supply a mother's place to (one), to provide for (one) in a motherly way; sie bemutterte das junge Mädchen, (at a ball, &c.) she chaperoned the young lady.

Benach'baren, (w.) v. refl. to become neighbours; benachbart, p. a. neighbouring.

Benach'richtigen (l. u.: **Benach'richten**), (w.) v. tr. to inform, advise, apprise, let know, to send word, to notify; to give intelligence, notice, or account (von, of); to warn; ausführlich —, to impart particulars or details, to write in extenso. — **Benach'richtiger,** (str.) m. informer, &c., informant. — **Benach'richtigung,** (w.) f. information; notification; advice; advertisement; B-sschreiben, n. letter of advice; B-swort, n. Mil. cautionary word.

Benach'teln, (w.) v. tr. poet. fig. to benight.

Bequick'en, (w.) v. tr. to silver, foliate (a looking-glass).

Berah'men, (w.) v. tr. 1) to frame: 2) see Beraumen.

Berai'nen, (w.) v. tr. to furnish with boundaries.

† **Beran'men, Beraum'men,** (w.) v. tr. see Anberaumen.

Berän'deln, (w.) v. tr. Mint. to mill, border (coins).

Beran'den (Berän'dern), (w.) v. tr. to furnish with a rim (margin), to rim; to edge.

Berän'dung, (w.) f. engrailed ring.

Berapp', (str.) m. Mas. rough-cast; rough-ashlin. — **Berap'pen,** (w.) v. tr. 1) Mas. to rough-cast; to plaster roughly: 2) Carp. to rough-hew.

Bera'sen, (w.) v. I. tr. to cover with turf, to sod, to turf; bera'set, p. a. turfy: II. refl. & intr. (aux. sein) to get turf, to be grown over with turf.

Beras'peln, (w.) v. tr. to rasp (at).

Bera'then, (str.) v. I. tr. 1) †, see Ausstatten; 2) a) (Einen) to give advice to, to advise, counsel; b) (etwas) aa) to consult (to regard, consider); nur sein eignes Selbst —, to be self-seeking; bb) see Berathschlagen; to concert (a plan); Gott berathe euch! God help you: II. intr. & refl. see Berathschlagen; sich mit sich selbst, mit Gott —, to commune with one's self, with God; b–d, p. a. deliberative (voice, &c.).

Bera'ther, (str.) m. counsellor, adviser.

Berath'schlagen, (w.) v. intr. & refl. to consult, confer, commune, advise (with, &c.); (with über (& Acc.)) to deliberate, to take into deliberation, to debate; to concert (means): es wird über die Sache berathschlagt, the affair is under consideration; b–d, deliberative (body, assembly, &c.).

Berath'schlagung, Bera'thung, (w.) f. consultation, deliberation; conference, council; in — ziehen, to deliberate.

Berau'ben, (w.) v. tr. (Einen eines Dinges) to rob, plunder, spoil, spoliate, strip, divest, bereave, deprive (one of); Einen des Lebens —, to take away a person's life; der Ehre —, to dishonour, &c. (Entehren); der Vorrechte —, to disfranchise (towns).

Berau'bung, (w.) f. the (act of) robbing, &c.; deprivation, privation, spoliation.

Berau'chen, (w.) v. tr. 1) to smoke, fumigate; beraucht, p. a. smoky, blackened by smoke.

Beräu'chern, (w.) v. tr. 1) a) see Berauchen; b) to perfume (with incense, &c.); 2) fig. to flatter excessively, to incense. — **Beräu'cherung,** (w.) f. fumigation, &c.

Berau'fen, (w.) v. tr. see Berupfen.

Berau'men, see Beraumen.

Beräu'men, (w.) v. tr. 1) see Räumen; 2) Sport. to line (of wild boars).

Berau'schen, (w.) v. tr. 1) to intoxicate; see [illegible]; 2) Sport. to line (of wild boars). — **Berau'schung,** (w.) f. intoxication; drunkenness.

Ber'ber, (str.) m. 1) Berber, inhabitant of Barbary; 2) or —roß, n. Barbary horse; —sprache, f. Berber language. — **Berberei',** f. Geogr. Barbary. — **Ber'berisch,** adj. Berber, Barbarian.

Ber'beris..., in comp. —beere, f., —baum, [illegible], m., **Berberit'ze,** (w.) f. Bot. barberry, [illegible] (Berberis vulgaris L.).

[illegible], (w.) v. tr. to rain over.

[illegible], adj. calculable.

[illegible], (w.) v. tr. 1) to calculate, compute, [illegible], to cast up (an amount); 2) [illegible] (with Acc.), etc. 3) (Einem [illegible]) to charge one for ..., to put to one's [illegible] to charge: ich berechne ½ % [illegible] charge ½ per cent commission: [illegible] (über mit-for ...) ..., we charge [illegible] —, to make high charges [illegible] nicht berechnet, on [illegible] sich mit Einem —, [illegible] with one, to set off, to account with one; fremde Münze auf einheimische —, to reduce foreign coin to the home standard; 4) Carp. to lash, switch, strap; berechnet, p. a. calculated, intended: premeditated: made up; wohl berechnet, well-combined; schlecht berechnet, ill-judged.

Berech'nung, (w.) f. 1) calculation, computation; estimation, statement; 2) (Abrechnung) settlement, liquidation, reckoning; settling of accounts; außer aller —, beyond all calculation; Comm.–s. nach vorgängiger —, after previous settlement; ungefähre —, sketch.

Berech'tigen (L. u.: **Berech'ten**), (w.) v. tr. to entitle, to give a right: to authorise, to warrant, empower; zu Hoffnungen —, to bid fair; zu der Hoffnung —, to justify a hope: Sie sind nicht berechtigt zu glauben, you are not justified in believing; berechtigt, p. a. entitled, authorised; competent; legitimate: berechtigte Hoffnung, just hope.

Berech'tigung, (w.) f. authorisation, title, right: — haben, to be legitimate.

Bere'den, (w.) v. I. tr. 1) to persuade; er ließ sich nicht zur Flucht —, he was not to be persuaded to fly; to induce, to prevail with (upon); 2) (Einen einer Sache (Gen.) or von etwas) to make believe; to convince; 3) to speak of a thing; 4) to talk ill of (one), to backbite, abuse, defame (one); to find fault with (a thing): II. refl. to discuss (or discourse on) any thing orally, to confer, concert (cf. Berathschlagen); sie haben sich mit einander beredet, they have agreed how to act in concert.

Bered'sam (pr. bered'sam), more usual, although perhaps less analogical than **Bered't'sam,** I. adj. 1) eloquent; 2) talkative: II. B–keit, (w.) f. eloquence; rhetoric.

Beredt', I. adj. eloquent; talkative, fluent; er hat eine b–e Zunge, he has a fluent utterance: II. B–heit, (w.) f. see Beredsamkeit.

Bere'gen, (w.) v. tr. see Anregen, Erwähnen; der beregte Gegenstand, the matter in question.

Bereg'nen, (w.) v. tr. to rain on, rain over.

Berei'ben, (str.) v. tr. to rub over.

Bereich', (str.) m. 1) reach; range; compass, sphere, line; 2) district, department; position; es liegt außer meinem B–e, it lies beyond my reach, &c.; aus dem — bleiben, to keep out of reach; im —(e) der Stimme sein, to be within call or hearing.

Berei'chern, (w.) v. tr. to enrich; fig. to enlarge; to store (the mind, &c. with ...); sich —, fam. to feather one's nest.

Berei'cherung, (w.) f. the (act of) enriching, enrichment; acquisition of riches.

Berei'fen, (w.) v. I. tr. 1) to cover with hoar-frost; 2) Coop. to hoop; II. intr. to grow hoary: bereift, p. a. hoary; Bot. pruinous.

Berei'men, (w.) v. tr. to make rhymes upon, to berhyme.

Berei'sen, (w.) v. tr. to travel over (a country); to frequent (fairs, &c.); gegenwärtig wird die Riviera wenig bereist, at present the Riviera is little travelled; er bereist Frankreich, 1. he is making a tour in France; 2. Comm. he is travelling France; ich lasse Frankreich —, I have sent a traveller upon a round in France.

Bereit', adj. ready, prompt, prepared; — halten, to have or keep in readiness.

A. **Berei'ten,** (str.) v. tr. 1) to ride over, to visit on horseback; 2) to break in, to manage (a horse).

B. **Berei'ten,** (w.) v. tr. to prepare, to make or get ready (also refl.), to dress; Einem den Untergang —, to work one's ruin, destruction, er wird dir noch einmal Unheil —, he will work you mischief one time or other; diesen Verlust hat er sich (Dat.) selbst bereitet, this loss is of his own making.

A. **Berei'ter,** (str.) m. 1) Man. riding-master, horse-breaker, rough-rider; equestrian (performer); —gesellschaft, f. company of equestrians; —peitsche, f. jockey-whip.

II. **Berei'ter,** (str.) m. preparer, dresser, &c.

Berei'testuhl, (str., pl. B–stühle) m. T. bank or board on which cloth is dressed.

Bereits', adv. already; actually; as early as; — 1788 wurde jedoch eine neue Literatur hier eingeführt, as far back as 1788 a new species of literature [that of Germany] began to be introduced into this country (W. Scott).

Bereit'schaft, (w.) f. readiness, preparation: Geld in — haben, to have money in hand.

Berei'tung, (w.) f. preparation; manufacture, dressing.

Bereit'willig, I. adj. ready, willing; obliging; die b–e Annahme, Comm. due honour or protection; II. B–keit, f. readiness, willingness; obligingness.

Beren'nen, (irr.) v. tr. 1) to run against; 2) Mil. to invest (a fortress), to block up, blockade, to assault, &c.

Beren'nung, (w.) f. investment, assault.

Beren'ten, (w.) v. tr. to furnish with an income.

Bereu'en, (w.) v. tr. to repent (of); to regret, to be sorry for (having offended one, &c.); to rue; du wirst es —, you shall rue it.

Bereu'ung, (w.) f. repentance, regret; b–swerth, b–swürdig, adj. worthy of repentance.

Berg, (str.) m. mountain (Poet. mount); der kleine —, a small mountain, hillock, hill; den — hinan, up (the) hill; zu —(e), (up) on end; goldene B–e versprechen, to make large promises, to promise wonders.

Berg'..., in comp. —ab, adv. down-hill: also fig. es geht —ab mit ihm, he is going down-hill; —abhang, m. slope of a hill; —absprung, m. (Gutsdorf) set-off, ledge (of a mountain); —acker, m. field situated on a hill; —ader, f. metallic vein; —akademie, f. mining-college or mining-academy; —alaun, m. rock-alum.

* **Bergamot'te,** (w.) f. bergamot (pear); B–öl, n. oil or essence of bergamots.

Berg'..., in comp. —ampfer, m. see Alpenampfer; —amsel, f. Ornith. ring-ousel (Turdus torquatus L.); —amt, n. 1) mining-office; 2) court for the decision of mining affairs; —an, adv. up (the) hill, upwards; —anzug, m. miner's dress; —arbeit, f. mining labour, mineworks; —arbeiter, m. mine-worker, miner; —art, f. gang, rock, matrix of the ore; —asche, f. see —blau; —äsche, f. Bot. mountain ash (—esche); —auf, adv. see —an; —auster, f. rock-oyster; —balsam, m. naphtha; —bank, f. mineral bank; —bau, m. mining; —baukunde, —baukunst, f. science of mining; —baukundige, m. one versed in the science of mining; —baumwolle, f. Comm. cotton from the Levant; —beamte(r), m. mining-officer; —begnadigung, f. privilege of working mines; —beschreibung, f. orography; —bewohner, m. mountaineer, highlander, uplander; —blau, n. mountain-blue; lapis lazuli, ultramarine; Olympian or Olympic blue, verditer; —bohrer, m. see Erdbohrer; —braun, n. umber; —butter, f. Miner. rock or stone butter; —compaß, m. miner's compass; —crystall, m. Miner. rock-crystal, sprig-crystal; —dachs, m. see Murmelthier; —dorf, n. mountain-village; mining-village; —drossel, f. Ornith. a species of thrush (Turdus Naumanni Tem.); —eberesche, f. Bot. bastard service; —ei, n. mountain-egg.

Ber'ge..., in comp. (from Bergen) —geld, n., —lohn, m. salvage(-money); —gut, n. salvage (recovered goods).

Berg'..., in comp. —eidechse, m. see Eidechse; —eisen, n. Min. gad.

Ber'gen, (str.) v. tr. 1) to save, shelter,

[illegible]tor, reader (of proof-sheets). — **Berich'tigung,** *(w.) f.* 1) rectification, emendation, correction: adjustment; 2) payment, settlement; **B-Bogen,** *m. Typ.* proof-sheet. [nose

Berie'chen, *(str.) v. tr.* to smell at, *vulg.* to

Berie'fen *(denote* **Berie'feln***)*, *(w.) v. tr. T.* *(Archit.,* &c.*)* to flute, channel, chamfer.

Berie'geln, *(w.) v. tr.* to bolt.

Berie'men, *(w.) v. tr.* to provide with leather straps.

Berie'seln, *(w.) v. tr.* 1) to ripple over: 2) *Agr.* to water (a meadow). [of flannel.

* **Beril',** *(str.) m.* 1) *see* Beryll; 2) a kind

Berin'den, *(w.) v. tr.* to cover with a bark or rinds to crust; berindet, *p. a.* barky.

Berin'gen, *(w.) v. tr.* 1) to furnish with a ring; 2) to ring (mares, pigs).

Berit', *(str.) m.* 1) *Mil.* squad; 2) district under the superintendence of a mounted forest-inspector (Forstbereiter).

Berit'ten, *p. a.* 1) mounted: ein b-es Pferd, a managed horse; 2) — machen, to mount (upon a horse or horses), to horse.

Berit'zen, *(w.) v. tr.* to scrape, scratch (the surface). [can (Beracan).

* **Ber'kan,** *(str.) m. (Arab.) Comm.* barra-

Berlin', *n. Geogr.* (the town of) Berlin. — **Berli'ne,** *(w.) f.* berlin(e) (a coach).

Berli'ner, I. *s. (str.) m.*, **B-in,** *(w.) f.* inhabitant (native) of Berlin, Berliner; II. *or* **Berli'nisch,** *adj.* Berlin: —blau, —roth, *n.* Prussian blue, red: —blausäure, *see* Blausäure; —blausaures Salz, *n.* prussiate.

* **Berloc'ke,** *(w.) f. (Fr.)* metal or ivory trinket, *espec.* watch-trinket.

* **Ber'me,** *(w.) f. (Fr.)* 1) berme; 2) yeast.

Bermu'den, *pl.* Bermudas (*or* Somers' Islands). — **Bermu'disch,** *adj.* Bermudian.

Bern, *n. Geogr.* Bern(e). — **Ber'ner,** I. *m.* (**Ber'nerin,** *(w.) f.)* inhabitant (native) of Bern, Bernese; II. *or* **Ber'nerisch,** *adj.* Bernese.

Bern'hard, *m.* Bernard *(P. N.)*; **B-Kraut,** *n. Bot.* holy *or* blessed thistle *(Centaurea benedicta L.)*; **B-Krebs,** *m. Zool.* (Bernard the) hermit *(Cancer bernhardus L.)*. [(monk).

Bernhardi'ner, *(str.) m.* Bernardine

Bern'stein, *s.* I. *(str.) m.* amber (sea, yellow *or* mineral amber); schwarzer —, jet; II. *in comp.* —alabaster, *m.* succinate of alabaster; —alaun, *m.* aluminous amber; —arbeit, *f.* any thing made of amber; —arbeiter, *m.* worker in amber; —artig, *adj.* resembling amber, amber; —auster, *f. Conch.* small amber oyster *(Anomia electrica L.)*; —corallé, *f.* amber-beads; —dose, *f.* amber box; —drechsler, *m.* turner of amber; —fang, *m.* fishing for (collecting of) amber; —firniß, *m.* amber varnish; —gericht, *n.* court or chamber for the control of amber-fishing; —gruß, *m.* amber-dust; —harz, *m.* [illegible] resin of amber; [illegible] —harz, residuum of distilled amber; [illegible] —harz, [illegible] amber; [illegible] —harz, artificial [illegible]; —[illegible], *f.* [illegible] red and white heart-[illegible]; —[illegible], *f. Chem.* residuum of distilled amber; —lack, *m.* amber-varnish; —[illegible], *f.* [illegible]; —öl, *n.* amber-oil; —[illegible] [illegible], *n.* succinate; —[illegible], *adj.* [illegible]; —säure, *f.* succinic acid, acid of amber; —[illegible], *f. see* —auster; —[illegible], *pl.* [illegible] of amber; —[illegible] amber mouth-piece (of a pipe); —[illegible], *f.* [illegible] of amber.

[illegible], *adj.* made of amber, [illegible] [illegible] [Lebacken.

[illegible] *v. tr.* to graze, to browse; *cf.* [illegible] *v. tr.* to [illegible], line with [illegible] [Iruben.

[illegible] *s.* *m.* [illegible] [illegible] pipes, [illegible] *v. tr.* to [illegible] (a snare). [illegible] [illegible] (sein) to [illegible] [illegible] to [illegible]; II. [illegible]

Berö'theln, *(w.) v. tr.* to ruddle.

Berſch, *(str.) m. see* Barſch.

Berſch'kohl, *provinc. see* Wirſchkohl.

Berſer'ker, *(str.) m. North. Ant.* 1) kind of warriors; 2) savage, violent man: —wuth, *f.* ungovernable fury, rage.

Ber'ſten, *(str.) v. intr. (aux.* sein*)* to burst: to chap; to crack, split, rend: vor Lachen — (wollen), to (be ready to) burst with laughing, to break or split one's sides with laughing: geborſtenes Holz, shaky timber.

Ber'tram, *(str.) m.* 1) Bertram *(P. N.)*; 2) *Bot. a)* sneeze wort, bastard pellitory *(Achillea ptarmica L.)*; *b)* (ſpaniſcher) Spanish camomile, pellitory of Spain *(Anthemis pyrethrum L.)*. [ill-reported, discredited.

Berüch'tigt, *adj.* notorious; ill-spoken of,

Berück'en, *(w.) v. tr.* 1) to entrap, ensnare; 2) *fig.* to take in, to cozen, trick, to impose upon. — **Berück'ung,** *(w.) f.* the (act of) entrapping, &c., cozenage.

Berück'ſichtigen, *(w.) v. tr.* to have or pay regard to, to (bear in) mind, keep in view, attend to, consider. — **Berück'ſichtigung,** *(w.) f.* regard, consideration; aus — ſeiner bedrängten Lage, out of regard for his hard case: unter — aller Formalitäten, with due regard to all formalities.

Beruf', *(str.) m.* 1) call, calling, vocation; 2) duty, office, function, employment, trade, business; profession; province, department; line, sphere; 3) *Law,* appeal; (der innere) —, the inward calling, prompting of nature; es iſt mein — nicht, ich habe keinen — dazu, it is not my office, this is none of my business.

Beru'fen, *(str.) v.* I. *tr.* 1) to call, to call together, to convoke, summon, convene; 2) to appoint (to an office), to nominate; ich ſehe mich — *(pp.)*, *fig.* I find *or* feel myself called upon; 3) to forespeak (a child, &c.), *cf.* Beſchreien, 3; II. *refl.* ſich — auf *(with Acc.)* ..., to appeal to..., to call upon..., to refer to..., to make use of (one's) name. — **Beru'fen,** *p. a. see* Berrufen. — **Beru'fer,** *(str.) m.* 1) caller, &c.; 2) *Law,* appellant.

Beruf'kraut, *(str.) n.* any plant serving as a charm against the forespeaking (Berufen) of a person, such as a species of iron wort *(Sideritis scordioides L.)*, white archangel *(Lamium album L.)*; common groundsel *(Senecio vulgaris L.)*, &c.

Berufs'..., *in comp.* —arbeit, *f.* professional labour (exertion): —eifer, *m.* professional exertion; —fach, *n.*, —geſchäft, *n.* vocation, profession; task, business of one's calling; —genoſſe, *m.* professional gentleman; —mäßig, *adj.* according to one's profession or calling, professional; —recht, *n. see* Berufungsrecht; —reiſe, *f.* official tour; —treue, *f.* faithful discharge of professional duties: —widrig, *adj.* unprofessional.

Beru'fung, *(w.) f.* 1) *a)* the (act of) convening, &c., convocation; *b)* the calling to, appointing, vocation; Matthäi — und Ernennung zum Apoſtel, Matthew's call and appointment as a disciple; 2) appeal (auf *(with Acc.)*, to), appellation; — einlegen, *see* Appelliren; 3) B-en, *pl.* (Beziehungen auf Handelshäuſer) references; 4) *Folk-lore,* the (act of) forespeaking; **B-sgericht,** *n.* court of appeals: **B-srecht,** *n.* right of nomination, patronage.

Beru'hen, *(w.) v. intr.* to rest (auf *(with Dat.* [illegible] — *Leaving,* &c. — *and* I. *w. with Acc.* according to the analogy of ſich auf ... gründen, &c.*)*, on, upon, with), to depend (on); to be founded (on), to be attributable (auf einem Irrthume &c., to an error, &c.): etwas auf ſich — laſſen, to let a thing rest as it is, to let the matter, &c. alone; ich will es dabei *or* darauf — laſſen, I will be satisfied with it, I will let the matter take its course.

Beru'higen, *(w.) v. tr.* to quiet, calm, assuage, soothe, lull, tranquillise, soften, mitigate, pacify, to compose; to console, comfort, to make easy, to ease, to set at ease *or* rest (über *(with Acc.)*, about); beruhige dich, set your heart at rest, compose your mind; die letzten Nachrichten lauten b-d, the latest news are reassuring, encouraging; er kann ſich immer noch nicht über den Verluſt —, he has not yet got over the loss; ſich — bei..., to acquiesce in, to reconcile one's self to...; ein Gericht, bei deſſen Entſcheid ſich alle Parteien vollſtändig — können, a legal tribunal with whose decision all parties might honourably abide.

Beru'higer, *(str.) m.* calmer; quieter, &c.

Beru'higung, *(w.) f.* the (act of) quieting, calming, appeasing, &c., pacification; comfort, tranquillity, quiet, ease of mind: **B-smittel,** *n.* sedative, calmer, quieter, calming remedy, anodyne.

Berüh'men, *(w.) v. refl.* (ſich einer Sache *(Gen.)*) to brag, to boast of.

Berühmt', I. *adj.* famous, famed, renowned, noted, celebrated; eminent, illustrious: ſich — machen, to signalise one's self; II. **B-heit,** *(w.) f.* celebrity, renown, fame: illustriousness, eminence.

Berühr'bar, *adj.* capable of being touched, &c., to be touched, tangible. — **Berühr'barkeit,** *(w.) f.* 1) tangibility; 2) (keen) susceptibility, &c.

Berüh'ren, *(w.) v.* I. *tr.* 1) to touch, to handle; to come in contact with: leiſe —, to dab, to tap; *fig.* &c. 2) to mention slightly, hint at, touch upon; to allude to; 3) to affect (one's interests, &c.): du haſt die wahre (rechte) Seite berührt, you hit it right; Jemandes Gefühle unangenehm —, to jar (upon) one's feelings; noch kein Weib berührt haben, to be unknown to women: berührter Maßen, as mentioned before; II. *refl.* to touch, to be contiguous (to each other).

Berüh'rig, *adj. see* Rührig.

Berüh'rung, *s.* I. *(w.) f.* 1) the (act of) touching, handling, &c.; 2) touch: contact; collision; contiguity, contingence; *Geom.* tangency: osculation (contact of one curve with another); *Bot.* contiguousness: *Astr.* appulse: in — kommen, to come into contact; — mit Einem haben, to have connection with one; II. *in comp.* **B-selectricität,** *f. Elect.* galvanism: **B-s(theil)kreis,** *m. Mech.* pitch-line; **B-slinie,** *f. Geom.* tangent; **B-spunkt,** *m.* point of contact; **B-swinkel,** *m.* angle of contact. [up at.

Berüm'pfen, *(w.) v. tr.* to turn the nose

Berupf'en, *(w.) v. tr.* to injure, tease, deprive, &c. by plucking, to pluck, plume, &c. *see* Rupfen.

Beru'ßen, *(w.) v.* I. *tr.* to begrime, to smear with soot, to besmut, smut, soot, smutch; II. *intr. (aux.* ſein*)* to get sooty: berußt, *adj.* sooty.

* **Beryll',** *(str.) m. (Gr.) Miner.* beryl; blättriger —, disthene; —erde, *f.* glucin; —fluß, *m.* beryl-crystal.

Beſab'bern, *(w.) v. tr. vulg. see* Begeifern.

Beſack'en, *(w.) v.* I. *tr.* to load with sacks or bags; II. *refl. vulg.* to fill one's pockets.

Beſä'en, *(w.) v. tr.* to sow (on, over), to seed; beſäet, *p. a.* studded (as with houses, trees, stars, &c.).

Beſa'ge, I. *s.* †, that which a person says, saying; nach —, *or* II. *as a kind of prep.* (by the omission of nach) *with the Gen.*; according to (the tenor of, &c.).

Beſa'gen, *(w.) v. tr.* 1) †, to accuse, *see* Anklagen; 2) to say, mention, purport, bear (a certain meaning, &c.); was will es —, what is the drift of it? Ihr Brief beſagt, the purport of your letter is, &c.; b-d, to the effect of...; 3) to mean, signify; die Geſchichte in dieſer

Bes

Besprech'en, *(str.) v.* I. *tr.* 1) *a)* to talk (a matter) over, to discuss; *b)* to arrange, settle, agree upon; to notice (a new book in a literary journal); 2) *Folk-lore,* to conjure, charm with words, to spell; das Fieber — können, to have a charm for the ague *or* fever; 3) to defame, &c. *see* Berreden, 4; II. *refl. see* sich Bereden.

Besprech'ung, *(w.) f.* 1) *a)* the (act of) talking over, &c., discussion; *b)* arrangement, &c., agreement; 2) conference, parley; interview; 3) *Folk-lore,* the (act of) conjuring, incantation, spelling; (des Fiebers) ague-spell.

Besprei'ten, Besprei'zen, *(w.) v. tr.* to cover, to spread over.

Bespreng'en, *(w.) v. tr.* (Einen mit etwas) 1) to sprinkle (the earth with water, &c.), to besprinkle; 2) to strew (ashes, &c.) upon. — **Besprengung,** *(w.) f.* the (act of) sprinkling, &c.

Besprenk'eln, *(w.) v. tr.* to speckle, checker.

Bespring'en, *(str.) v. tr.* 1) *a)* to leap or spring upon; *b)* †, to assail; 2) to cover (said of certain animals).

Bespritz'en, *(w.) v. tr.* to squirt at, sprinkle; to bespatter, splash, spatter (with mud).

Besprudeln, *(w.) v. tr.* to bubble against; to sputter over.

Besprüh'en, *(w.) v. tr.* to cover with drizzle, mizzle, sea-dust, or sparks (in a smithy), &c.

Bespuck'en, *(w.) v. tr.* to spit upon; to besputter. [over.

Bespül'en, *(w.) v. tr.* to wash; to ripple

Bessara'bien, *n. Geogr.* Bessarabia.

Bes'ser, I. *adj. & adv.* (*compar. of* Gut) 1) better; preferable: — werden (sich bessern), to grow better; *a) lit.* of things, &c.; *b)* to improve (in morals); *c) coll.* to mend, recover (from illness); immer — werden, to be going from good to better; 2) *coll.* (*cf.* Better, Vol. I.) (a little) more; — bieten, *Gam.* to vie; er nimmt sich — in Acht, he is more cautious; — hin, a little farther; — hinauf, a little more upwards; du mußt — schreien, you must shout louder; II. *s.* (*decl. like adj.*) 1) *m. & f.* better man, woman, &c.; 2) *n.* something better; in Ermangelung eines B-(e)n, for want of anything better; kennen Sie etwas B-es? do you know anything better? das B-e ist des Guten Feind, a good thing is often sacrificed in the vain endeavour to introduce improvements; einen B-en belehren, to teach better. [corrigible.

Bes'serlich, *adj.* capable of improvement,

Bes'sern, *(w.) v.* I. *tr.* 1) to better, improve, reclaim, ameliorate; 2) to amend, to correct; seine Sitten —, to reform one's manners; 3) to mend, repair (Ausbessern); was bin ich dadurch gebessert? what am I the better for it? sie würden sich dadurch um nichts gebessert sehen, their case would not be improved by this; II. *intr.* to make (apparent) amendments, to introduce (would-be) improvements (an [*with Dat.*], in); III. *refl.* 1) to grow (*or* alter for the) better, to correct one's self, to mend, to reform; 2) to improve; to advance; die Preise — sich, the prices are tending (looking) upwards or ruling higher; 3) to recover (from illness); nicht zu —, past mending, incorrigible.

Bes'serung, *(w.) f.* 1) the (act of) bettering, reclaiming, &c., improvement, amelioration; reformation; 2) amendment; 3) recovery (from illness); ich wünsche Ihnen eine gute —, I wish you a speedy recovery; er ist auf dem Wege der —, 1. he is getting better, he is convalescent, *coll.* he is on the mend; 2. he is reforming (morally); B-sanstalt, *f.* 1) *or* B-shaus, *n.* house of correction (of reformation), reformatory; 2) *or* B-sschule, *f.* reformatory school; B-smittel, *n.* corrective.

Bestä'uben, *(w.) v. tr.* to dust.

Bestal'len, *(w.) v. tr.* 1) †, *see* Bestellen; 2) to appoint, confer a place on, to invest with an employment, to install.

Bestal'lung, *(w.) f.* 1) appointment, installation; 2) (B-sbrief, *m.*) warrant, (letter of) commission; 3) emolument, salary; B-srecht, *n.* (right of) investiture.

Bestand', *s.* I. (*str., pl.* Bestän'de) *m.* 1) †, opposition (Widerstand, *cf.* Bestehen, *tr.* 1); Einem — thun, *see* Widerstand leisten; 2) continuance, duration; 3) assurance, certitude, stability, firmness, consistence; 4) *provinc.* lease, hiring; 5) *a)* amount, value, stock; *Forest.* stock of trees in a wood; *b) Comm.* remainder; — der Casse, clear amount, balance in cash; — haben, to continue, last, to be of duration; — geben, to substantiate; in — geben, to farm, let (on lease), to rent (a farm); in — nehmen, to farm; to hire (a house); II. *in comp.* —brief, *m.* lease (of a farm); —buch, *n. Comm.* inventory.

Bestan'den, *p. a.* (*from* Bestehen) 1) of a certain duration, of (long, &c.) standing: b-es Holz, *Forest.* full-grown wood; 2) covered with (dense, &c.) growth (of fields, &c.); stocked (with trees), (well, &c.) wooded; timbered; b-e Jagd, *Sport. see* Bestandjagd.

Bestän'der, *(str.) m.* tenant, farmer, renter.

Bestand'..., *in comp.* —geld, *n.* 1) *see* Cassenbestand; 2) rent (of a farm); —gut, *n.* property which is farmed *or* let; —herr, *m.* owner of a farm which is let.

Bestän'dig, I. *adj.* 1) *a)* constant, stable, firm; durable, lasting; *b)* steadfast, steady, persevering; sure, certain, invariable, standard; 2) continual, continued; permanent; settled (weather); *Bot.* persistent; Johann der B-e, John the Steadfast; b-e Valuta, (regular) standard, certain price; b-e Nachfrage, steady demand; er wiederholte — diese Worte, he continually repeated *or* he kept repeating these words (vgl. To Keep); II. B-keit, *(w.) f.* 1) *a)* constancy, stability, firmness; *b)* steadiness, steadfastness, perseverance; 2) continuance, duration.

Bestand'..., *in comp.* —inhaber, *m. see* Beständer; —jagd, *f.* shooting district, preserves let out on lease.

Bestand'lich, I. *adv. provinc. see* Bestandweise; II. B-keit, *(w.) f.* (*l. u.*) substantiality.

Bestand'liste, *(w.) f. see* Bestandverzeichniß.

Bestand'los, *adj.* unstable, without duration, mutable, infirm. — **Bestand'losigkeit,** *(w.) f.* unstableness, &c.

Bestand'müller, *(str.) m.* mill-tenant.

Bestand'niß, *(str.) f. provinc.* a hiring, letting, lease.

Bestand'..., *in comp.* —stück, *n.,* —theil, *m.* element, constituent part; ingredient; *pl. Chem.* constituents, component parts; —vertrag, *m.* lease; —verzeichniß, *n.* statement of goods in a warehouse, inventory; —weise, *adv.* by lease; —wesen, *n.* substance, essence; —zeit, *f.* term of lease; —zins, *m.* rent (of a farm).

Bestär'ken, *(w.) v. tr.* to corroborate, confirm; to strengthen, fortify (an opinion, &c.); es hat mich in der Überzeugung bestärkt, it has confirmed or deepened my conviction. — **Bestär'kung,** *(w.) f.* corroboration, confirmation.

Bestä'ter, Bestät'ter, *(str.) m. Comm.* conveyer (Gütersbestätter).

Bestä'tigen, *(w.) v.* I. *tr.* 1) to confirm, corroborate, substantiate; to bear out (an assertion, &c.); 2) to ratify, sanction, validate, to lend a sanction to; gerichtlich —, to legalise (by oath, &c.), to verify; to vouch. den Empfang eines Briefes —, to acknowledge the receipt of a letter; die Ausnahme bestätigt die Regel, the exception proves the rule; II. *refl.* to prove (one's self [itself] to be) true, &c., to hold true *or* good; sich nicht —, to prove false.

[illegible]nation; B-system, m. system of corruption; B-versuch, m. attempt at bribery; (auf Geschworenen) embracery.

Besteck', *(str.)* n. 1) case; *Surg.* case of instruments, etui, tweese; 2) set (of knives, [illegible]), knife and fork; 3) *a) Ship-b.* scheme (or plan) which contains the general dimensions) of a ship; *b) Naut.-e.* day's work or the [illegible] of a ship as pricked on a nautical chart; [illegible] — machen, to prick the chart, calculate the day's work; mit dem — voraus sein, to be [illegible] of one's reckoning; mit dem — zurück [illegible], sich im — geirrt haben, to run ahead of [illegible] reckoning; —macher, m. manufacturer of instrument-cases.

Bestecken, *(w.)* v. *tr.* 1) to bestick, stick [illegible] with pins, &c.; 2) to plant; 3) to garnish, [illegible]; 4) *Min.* to helve (the irons).

Bestecker, Beste'der, *(str.)* m. 1) *a)* ship-builder; *b) Comm.* ship's husband, contractor; 2) despatcher, conveyer, forwarder.

Bestedg, *(str.)* n. *Min.* fuscan (Sahlband).

Best'chaupt, *(str.)* n. *Feud. Law*, heriot.

Bestehen, *(w.)* v. I. *intr.* (aux. sein) 1) to [illegible], to coagulate, congeal, curdle; 2) *a)* to last, endure, to be maintained; *b)* to be, [illegible], subsist; to obtain; er kann dabei allenfalls —, he can manage to make both ends meet; *c)* — aus, to consist of, to be composed [illegible] made up of; — in *(with Dat.)*, to consist in; 3) [illegible] (auf *[& Dat.]*) to insist upon, to persist [illegible], to make a point of, to maintain, hold, stand for, urge; — mit, to stand (or to be [illegible]) with; nicht mit ... —, to be inconsistent with ...; nicht neben einander — können, to be inconsistent, incompatible; II. *tr.* 1) *a)* to stand against, resist, oppose; siegreich —, to overcome, conquer; *b)* to encounter (an adventure, &c.), to go or pass through (dangers, &c.), to undergo, suffer, support, sustain, pass (an examination); *also intr.* (aux. haben) to go through or to pass an examination, to [illegible]; nicht —, to be rejected at an examination; die Probe —, to stand the test; wie ein Schiff nach bestandenem Sturme, like a ship after weathering out a storm; 2) *a)* to purchase; *b)* to hire, rent, farm; b-d, *p. a.* [illegible] subsistent, existent; 3) established (laws, &c.); b-de Preise, *Comm.* ruling prices; das —, *s.* *(str.)* n. 1) continuance, duration, standing; 2) subsistence, existence. [mer, lessee.

Besteher, *(str.)* m. purchaser; renter, far-

Bestehlen, *(str.)* v. *tr.* to rob (one) of ...; die Ladung —, to break bulk; die Taschen —, to pick pockets. — **Bestehlung**, *(w.)* f. the (act of) robbing of ..., &c.

Besteigen, *(str.)* v. *tr.* 1) to get up, ascend, [illegible] (a hill, horse, the pulpit, &c.); to step upon (mount); 2) to leap, cover (said of certain animals); ein Schiff —, to go on board a ship; eine Mauer —, to scale a wall; einen Baum —, to climb (up into) a tree; 3) *Min. see* Befahren.

Bestellen, *(w.)* v. *tr. see* Beschottern.

Bestellen, *(w.)* v. *tr.* 1) to place (something) upon ...; etwas mit ... —, to fill a thing with (furniture, pots, &c.); 2) to order, send for, to bespeak, give orders for, to commission [illegible]; Sie sind auf Mittag *(Acc.)* bestellt, they are ordered to come at noon; [illegible] einander auf neun Uhr, they made [illegible] appointment to meet at nine; haben Sie [illegible] an ihn zu —? have you no commission [illegible]; 3) to appoint one to perform something; wir haben Sie zu unserm Agenten bestellt, we have appointed you our agent; er [illegible] diesen Kindern bestellt, he [illegible] appointed (as) guardian of these children [illegible] by the Court; zum Dienst —, to [illegible]; 4) to deliver, forward, [illegible], message, &c.; einen Gruß —, [illegible] one's compliments; 5) *a)* to arrange, put in order; sein Haus or seine Wirthschaft —, to manage one's domestic affairs; *fig.* to set one's house or earthly affairs in order, to prepare for death; ihr habt hier weiter nichts mehr zu — *(Schiller,* Wall. Tod 4, 7), here you have no more business; *b)* to till, sow (a field), to dress (the ground), to plant.

Besteller, *(str.)* m. one who gives orders or a commission for, &c. *cf.* Bestellen.

Bestell'..., *in comp.* —gebühren, *f. pl.*, —geld, n. (letter-)carrier's fees.

Bestellung, *(w.)* f. 1) the (act of) bespeaking, &c.; *Comm.* order; commission; B-en machen, to give orders; auf — gemacht, made to order; 2) appointment, rendezvous; 3) disposition, &c. *see* Verrichtung; management; 4) the (act of) delivering, forwarding, &c.; 5) tillage; B-sbrief, m. letter containing an order; B-sbuch, n. *Comm.* order-book.

Bestell'..., *in comp.* —zeit, f. tilling-season; —zettel, m. *see* Verlangzettel.

Bestempeln, *(w.)* v. *tr.* to stamp.

Bestengelt, *p. a. Bot. see* Bestielt.

Bestens, *adv.* in the best manner, best; *coll.* very much, exceedingly; empfehlen Sie mich ihm —, give him my best compliments.

Besteppen, *(w.)* v. *tr.* to quilt.

Besternen, *(w.)* v. *tr.* 1) to cover, stud with stars; besternt, *p. a.* beset with stars, starred, starry; 2) to mark with an asterisk; 3) *fig.* to decorate with the badge of an order.

Besteuern, *(w.)* v. *tr.* to lay on or impose duties or taxes, to tax, assess.

Besteuerung, *(w.)* f. 1) *Mar.* — eines Schiffes, art of steering a vessel; 2) taxation; assessment; diese Taxe ist eine — der Wissenschaft, this tax is a duty on knowledge.

Besteven, *(w.)* v. *intr. Mar.* (of a ship) to proceed on its course; wo bestevent das Schiff? *(Sanders)*, how is the head? how does the ship wind? [leaves.

Bestgut, *(str.)* n. *Comm.* the best tobacco

* **Bestialisch**, *adj.* *(Lat.)* bestial, beastly. — **Bestialität**, *(w.)* f. bestiality, beastliness.

Bestich, *(str.)* m. 1) *Shoe-m.* bar; 2) *Mas. see* Bewurf.

Besticken, *(w.)* v. *tr.* to embroider.

* **Bestie**, *(w.)* f. *(Lat.)* beast, brute.

Bestieben, *(w.)* v. *tr. see* Bestauben, Bestäuben.

Bestiefeln, *(w.)* v. *tr.* to put boots on, to boot.

Bestielen, *(w.)* v. *tr.* to furnish with a handle, to helve, haft; bestielt, *p. a. Bot.* petiolate, pedunculate.

Bestimmbar, *adj.* determinable, definable; *Phys.*, &c. ascertainable, appreciable.

Bestimmen, *(w.)* v. I. *tr.* 1) *a)* to fix, to determine, define, decide; to set down or out, constitute, stipulate, settle, appoint, state; to regulate; *b)* to ascertain; to determine; astronomisch bestimmte Breiten, astronomically determined latitudes; 2) *a)* to intend (für [eine Person], zu [einer Sache], for), to design, designate; *b)* to allot, appropriate (für, to); (Einem etwas or etwas für ...) to design (something for), to set aside; 3) to induce, lead, influence; II. *refl.* to determine, resolve, make up one's mind; to settle (to something): sich — für, to fix, decide, resolve or pitch upon, to choose, to be for ...; III. *intr.* to decide (über *[with Acc.]*, on); to dispose of.

Bestimmt, I. *p. a.* 1) *a)* fixed, appointed, settled, &c.; determined, determinate; zur b-en Zeit, at the time appointed; *b)* — nach, bound to or for ...; nach Hause —, *Mar.* homewards bound; 2) certain, positive, explicit, precise; 3) distinct, definite; der b-e Artikel, *Gramm.* the definite article; sie glaubten —, they confidently believed; II. B-heit, *(w.)* f. 1) precision; 2) certainty; positiveness; 3) determination; distinctness; mit — versichern, to assert confidently, to assure positively, pointedly.

Bestimmung, *(w.)* f. 1) *a)* the (act of) fixing, determining, &c.; wir erbitten nähere —, wie ..., *Comm.* we request more precise instructions as to how ...; *b)* definition; determination; ein Werk [Dr. Brehm's Papageien], welches uns bei der — unserer Sammlung von Nutzen ist, a work useful to us in the determination of our collection; 2) statement; (die in einem Vertrage festgesetzte —) stipulation, provision, clause; die Unabhängigkeit Krakau's beruhte auf den B-en des Wiener Congresses, the independence of Cracow rested on the provisions of the Congress of Vienna; 3) *a)* destination, end, destiny; vocation (in life), mission; *b) see* B-sort; 4) statement; B-sgrund, m. motive; B-sort, m. place of destination; B-swort, n. *Gramm.* any word determining or modifying the meaning of another word to which it is added.

Bestirnt, *adj. see* Besternt.

Bestmöglich(st), *adj.* as good (well) as possible; in der b-(st)en Laune, in the best humour possible. [ben & Bestauben.

Bestöbern, *(w.)* v. *tr.* & *intr. see* Bestau-

Bestocken, *(w.)* v. *intr.* (aux. sein) or *refl. Bot. & Gard.* to get a stem; bestocktes Holz, *Forest.* full-grown timber.

Bestöpseln, *(w.)* v. *tr.* to cork.

Bestoßen, *(str.)* v. *tr.* 1) to knock against or off; to hurt, injure, damage by knocking about; 2) *a) T.* to break the corner(s) of, to chamfer; *b) Letter-found.* to dress (letters).

Bestoß'..., *in comp.* —feile, f. *T.* planing file; *Letter-found.* justifier; —hobel, *Join.* jack-plane; *Letter-found.* dresser; —zeug, n. *Letter-found.* dressing bench.

Bestrafen, *(w.)* v. *tr.* 1) to punish; to chastise; to correct; to visit (with death, &c.), to resent; 2) *chastisement*, to reprimand, &c. *see* (mit Worten) Strafen; seine Fehler — sich von selbst, his offences carry (or bring about) their own punishment.

Bestrafung, *(w.)* f. 1) punishment, chastisement; 2) *chastisement*, rebuke, &c.

Bestrahlen, *(w.)* v. *tr.* to beam on (upon), to irradiate, to cast rays, to shine on (upon), to cast rays on (upon), illuminate, irradiate. — **Bestrahlung**, *(w.)* f. irradiation.

Bestreben, *(w.)* v. *refl.*, or **Bestrebt sein**, *intr.* (etwas zu thun) to endeavour, strive (einer Sache *[Gen.]*, for a thing); to make efforts, to exert one's self, to be anxious; das —, *v. s.* *(str.)* n., or **Bestrebung**, *(w.)* f. endeavour, effort, exertion; pursuit; tendency.

Bestrebsam, *see* Strebsam.

Bestreichen, *(str.)* v. *tr.* 1) to spread over; to smear, besmear; die Klinge des Dolches war mit Gift bestrichen worden, the blade of the dagger had been smeared with poison; mit Butter —, to butter; mit Fett —, to grease; mit Öl —, to oil, anoint with oil; mit Farben —, to paint; mit Pflaster —, to plaster; mit Wachs —, to wax; mit Magnet —, to polarise; 2) to touch (upon), sweep, stroke, to pass or rub over; eine Küste —, to skim along a coast; 3) *Gunn.-e.* to scour or rake with shot, to sweep (said of a battery), (in gerader Linie —) to enfilade; von der Seite —, to flank.

Bestreifen, *(w.)* v. *tr.* 1) to stripe, streak; 2) to graze, brush.

Bestreitbar, I. *adj.* contestable; debatable, disputable, controvertible; II. B-keit, *(w.)* f. contestableness, &c.

Bestreiten, *(str.)* v. *tr.* 1) to combat, fight; to attack; mit Worten —, to impugn, contest, deny; to dispute, controvert, debate; 2) to bear, afford, to defray (expenses); to provide for, meet, supply (one's wants, &c.); to manage one's business; er kann es nicht —, he cannot

[illegible]gently, to hasten, press, urg[illegible] to pursue, prosecute; to transact; to manage or carry on (a business); eine Sache ernst —, to drive a business home; die Bahn wird noch nicht betrieben, the line is not yet used or open to traffic.

Betrei'bung, (w.) f. 1) the (act of) driving on, &c. upon ..., &c. cf. Betreiben; 2) transaction (of business, &c.), pursuit, management.

Betrit'bar, adj. that may be walked on or (fig.) entered upon.

Betre'ten, (str.) v. tr. 1) to tread, step upon, to set foot upon; poet. to bestride; 2) to feather, tread, compress (as a fowl); 3) a) to fall in with, encounter, find, meet (antreffen, treffen); b) (Betreffen) to catch, surprise (bei, auf, in [with Dat.], in); 4) to enter upon (a career, &c.): ich werde dieses Haus nicht wieder —, I will never set my foot in that house again; die Kanzel —, to mount the pulpit, to preach; die Bühne —, to tread the stage.

Betre'ten, I. p. a. 1) trodden, beaten (path); 2) fig. concerned, abashed, shocked, disconcerted, confused, embarrassed, surprised, puzzled, struck, perplexed (über [with Acc.], at); II. B-heit, (w.) f. (l. u.) see Betroffenheit.

Betre'tung, (w.) f. 1. the (act of) stepping upon, &c.; 2) B-sfall, m. (case of) meeting, encountering, catching, or surprising, &c.

Betrieb', (str.) m. 1) see Betreibung; 2) management, carrying on: operations (of a manufacture); working (of a mine); die Bahn ist im B-e, the line is in operation, or open to traffic; business, trade, profession; 3) desire, instigation.

Betriebs'..., in comp. —capital, n., —fonds, m. stock, fund (employed in business or any undertaking); rolling-stock, floating-capital; trading-capital; —inspector, m. traffic-manager (of a railway-line); —jahr, n. financial year, year of traffic; —kosten, pl. expense of working, working-expenses (of a railway, &c.); —länge, —linie, f. length or line open to traffic, length in operation; —material, n. working-stock; —mittel, n. pl. rolling-stock; —störung, f. break, obstruction to traffic; —telegraph, m. the company's telegraph; government-telegraph; —zeit, f. working-time.

Betrieb'sam, I. adj. busy, active, industrious, stirring, diligent; II. B-keit, (w.) f. industry, activity, diligence.

Betrin'ken, (str. & w.) v. tr. see Betrauern.

Betrie'gen, (str.) v. tr. see Betrügen.

Betrin'ken, (str.) v. tr. refl. to get drunk.

Betrof'fen, I. p. a. struck, alarmed, &c. see Betreten; II. B-heit, (w.) f. perplexedness, perplexity (über [with Acc.], at), confusion.

[illegible] **Betröp'feln,** (w.) v. tr. [illegible]

Betrü'ben, (w.) v. I. tr. to trouble; to afflict, grieve, aggrieve, cast down, deject, distress; II. refl. to be afflicted, to be [illegible], to grieve (über [with Acc.], at).

Betrüb'niß, (str.) f. & n. affliction, grief, [illegible] depression, sadness; desolation; dis[illegible]

Betrübt', I. p. a. afflicted, grieved; sorrowful, [illegible]; melancholy; woeful, woe[illegible] [illegible] [illegible] II. B-heit, (w.) f. [illegible] **Betrü'bung**, [illegible]

[illegible] m. cheat, [illegible] imposition, deception; impos[illegible] [illegible] — [illegible]

[illegible] tr. to cheat, defraud, [illegible] overreach, dupe; [illegible] beguile, deceive, take in, [illegible] [illegible] a servant of his wages; [illegible] adj. to mistake, to be mistaken; to be disappointed: er sand sich in seinen Erwartungen betrogen, he found himself disappointed (in his hopes); der Betrogene, dupe.

Betrü'ger, (str.) m. cheat, defrauder, &c., deceiver; impostor, trickster; swindler, cozener, sharper; waren die Propheten — oder sich selbst täuschende Fanatiker? were the prophets impostors or self-deluded fanatics?

Betrügerei', (w.) f. the (practice of) cheating, deception, imposition, foul-dealing, trickery; deceit (fraudulent trick), imposture, fraud.

Betrü'gerisch, adj. deceitful, cheating, fraudulent, crafty, knavish.

Betrüg'lich, I. adj. deceitful, false, delusory, fraudulent; — handeln, to act deceitfully, to cheat, defraud, vulg. to dodge; der b-e Mensch, false dealer; II. B-keit, (w.) f. deceitfulness, &c., fraudulence.

Betrug'schluß, (str., pl. B-schlüsse) m. Mus. false cadence.

Betrun'ken, I. p. a. drunk, intoxicated, tipsy, in liquor; etwas —, coll. rather fresh in one's cups, cup-shotten, mellow; II. B-heit, (w.) f. (l. u.) drunkenness, see Trunkenheit.

Bet'..., in comp. —saal, m. oratory; —schwester, f. 1) beads-woman; 2) (female) devotee, bigot; —sonntag, m. rogation-day; —stuhl, m. praying-desk; —stunde, f. hour devoted to prayers, prayers (at church), prayer-meeting.

Bett, s. 1. (irr.) n. 1) bed; 2) a) bed, channel (of a river); b) Mill-s. aa) channel, trough; bb) bucket; 3) Geol., &c. layer, bed; 4) Vint. treading trough; 5) Sport. lair, see Lager; der Hirsch ist im —, the stag is harboured; 6) Bot-s. discus; thalamus; torus; das — der Ehre, bed of honour; im —(e), in bed, abed; am —(e), at the bedside; im —(e) liegen, to lie abed; zu —(e) gehen, sich zu —(e) legen, to go to bed; sie kam nicht von seinem —e weg, she never quitted his bedside.

Bet'tag, (str.) m. day devoted to prayers, fast-day.

Bett'..., in comp. —aufhelfer, m. see Aufhelfer, 2; —bank, f. press-bed; settle-bed; —behänge, n. bed-curtains, bed-hangings, valance; —bezug, m. see —überzug.

A. **Bett'chen,** (str.) n. (dimin. of Bett) a small bed; cot; —pflug, see Häufelpflug.

B. **Bett'chen,** (str.) n. (dimin. of Bethi, an abbr. of Elisabeth) Betty, Betsy.

Bett'..., in comp. —damast, m. bed-satin; —decke, f. blanket; coverlet; eine durchnähte —decke, a counterpane, quilt; eine rauhe (grobe, wollene) —decke, a rug; —drell, m. see —zwillich.

Bet'tel, (str.) m. 1) (the act or practice of) begging, mendicancy, mendicity; 2) trumpery, trifle, trash; der ganze —, coll. the whole lot or concern.

Bet'tel... (from Betteln), in comp. —arm, adj. beggarly, mendicant; extremely poor, wholly destitute; —arm werden, to come to the parish; —brief, m. 1) see —schein; 2) begging letter, beggarly supplication; —brot, n. bread of charity; beggar's livelihood; —bruder, m. 1) professed mendicant; 2) see —mönch; —bube, m. beggar-boy. [illegible] abject petition.

Bettelei', (w.) f. 1) see Bettel; 2) importunity.

Bet'telfrau, (w.) f. beggar-woman.

Bet'telhaft, I. adj. beggarly; II. B-igkeit, (w.) f. beggarliness.

Bet'tel..., in comp. —handwerk, n. begging-trade; das —handwerk treiben, to live by begging; —herberge, f. beggar's inn or hut; —hoffart, f. beggarly pride; —junge, m. beggar-boy; —kram, m. see Bettel, 2; —leute, pl. beggars, mendicants; —mann, m. beggar; —mannssuppe, see —suppe; —mönch, m. mendicant friar, mendicant.

Bet'teln, (w.) v. I. intr. to beg, ask alms; — gehen, to go a-begging; sich aufs — legen, to live by begging; II. refl. pomer. in comp. cf. sich durchbetteln, sie bettelten sich weiter ins Land hinein, they begged their way farther into the country.

Bet'tel..., in comp. —orden, m. order of mendicant friars, mendicant order; —pack, —volk, n. vulg. beggarly crew; —pfaffe, m. contempt. mendicant friar, hedge priest; —sack, m. beggar's sack, pouch, or wallet; den —sack umhangen haben, fig. to be reduced to beggary; —sammet, m. plush, shag; —schein, m. begging-licence; —schenke, f. see —herberge; —staat, m. shabby finery, frippery; —stab, m. fig. mendicity, beggary; an den —stab bringen, to reduce to beggary or mendicity; to bring to poverty; an den —stab kommen, to be reduced to beggary; —stolz, m. see —hoffart; —suppe, f. coarse soup made of black bread; —tanz, m. 1) beggar's dance; 2) coll. uprear, dispute, scuffle; —vogt, m. beadle; —volk, n. see —pack; —weib, n. see —frau.

Bet'ten, (w.) v. I. intr. to make the bed or the beds: ward ihm sanft | gebettet unter den Hufen seiner Rosse? (Schiller, Wall. Tod 4, 11), was a soft bed made for him (Coler. had he a soft bed) under the hoofs of his war-horses? II. tr. to bed: a) to place in bed; b) Einen, to make one's bed; Min. to embed; ich bin nicht auf Rosen gebettet, I do not lie on a bed of roses; sich zusammen —, to bed together; sich von einander —, to lie asunder; wie man sich (Dat.) bettet, so schläft man, proverb, as one makes his bed so he must lie in it; da haben wir uns schön gebettet! coll. we have got into a pretty mess!

Bet'tendraht, (str.) m. Bologna wire.

Bett'..., in comp. —feder, f. bed-feather; —flasche, f. warming-pan; —franse, f. bed-fringe, valance; —frau, f. bed-maker; —fuß, m. foot of the bed; —gang, m. bed-side; —gardine, f. bed-curtain; —genoß, m., —genossin, f. bedfellow; —geräth, n. bedding, bed-furniture; —gesell, see —genoß; —gestell, n. bedstead; —gras, n. see Wollgras; —gurt, m. bed-girth; —hängen, f. pl. bed-hangings; —himmel, m. tester; —kasten, m. stump-bedstead; —kranz, m., —krone, f. tester; —lade, f. press-bed; —lägerig, adj. bedridden; (wholly) confined to bed; —lägerig werden, to take to bed; —lägerigkeit, f. the state of being bedridden; —laken, n. sheet; —leinwand, f., —linnen, n. sheeting-linen, sheeting; —leiste, f. bed-staff.

Bett'ler, (str.) m., **Bett'lerin,** (w.) f. beggar, mendicant; der zudringliche —, sturdy beggar.

Bettlerei', see Bettelei.

Bett'lerhaft, Bett'lerisch, adj. beggarly.

Bett'lerin, (w.) f. Entom. grey tiger-moth (Arctia mendica Schrb.)

Bett'ler..., in comp. —kraut, n. Bot. sweet-scented virgin's bower (Clematis flammula L.); —salbe, f. see Räuschsalbe; B-smantel, m. 1) Conch. thorny oyster (Spondylus gaederopus L.); 2) Bot. see Sinau; —sprache, f. beggar's cant.

Bett'..., in comp. —meister, m. master of the bed-chamber; —nagel, m. bed-stud; —pfanne, f. warming-pan; —pfoste, f. bed-post; —quaste, f. bed-tassel (cf. Aufhelfer); —rolle, f. bed-castor; —sack, m. 1) sack used for packing beds in; 2) see Strohsack; —schere, f. bed-staff; —schieber, m. bed-pan; —schirm, m. folding-screen; —schnur, f. bed-lace; suspensory; —schragen, m. truckle-bed; —schrank, m. wardrobe or turn up bedstead, bed-closet; —schraube, f. bed-screw; —schraubenkappe, f. bed-screw-cover; —schraubenschlüssel, m. bed-wrench; —schüssel, f. bed-pan; —sessel, m. sopha-bed; —spinde, f. see —schrank; —stangen, f. pl. rods for the bed-curtains; —statt, —stätte, —stelle, f. bedstead; —stroh, n. bed-straw; unsrer lieben Frauen —stroh, n. Bot. our lady's bed-straw (Galium L.); —stuhl, m. bed-chair, settle-bed; —teppich, m. bedside carpet; —tisch, m. bedside-[illegible] bedstead), table bedstead; —troddel, *f.* bed-tassel; —tuch, *n.* sheet; —überzug, *m.* cover for the bedding, pillow-case.

Bet'tung, *(w.) f.* 1) †, bedding; 2) *a) Build. & Fort.* platform; *b)* bewegliche — mit Drehbolzen, traversing platform; *c) Artill.* carriage for a gun or mortar; *d)* frame of ground-timber (of a sluice); pilework; *e)* (B—material) ballast (gravel, broken stone, &c.) laid in the bed of a railway, &c. to make it firm; B—en, *f. pl. Mar.* bulge-ways.

Bett'..., *in comp.* —vorhang, *m.* bed-curtain; —wanze, *f. Entom.* house-bug (*Cimex lectularius* L.); —wärmer, *m.*, —wärmflasche, *f.* warming-pan; bed-pan; —wärts, *adv.* bedward; —wäsche, *f.* bed-linen; —wand, —zeug, *n.* 1) bedding, bed-linen, bed-clothes; wollenes —zeug, wool-sheeting; 2) *see* —zwillich; —zieche (—züge), *f. see* —überzug; —zopf, *m. see* —aufhelfer.

Betu'chen, *(w.) v. tr.* to cover with cloth.

* **Betu'ches,** *adv. (from the Hebrew) coll. among German Jews,* quietly.

Betün'chen, *(w.) v. tr. see* Tünchen.

Betupfen, Betüpfen *(dimin.* Betüpfeln), *(w.) v. tr.* 1) to dot; 2) to touch gently, to dab, tip, tap, pat.

Betusch'en, *(w.) v. tr. see* Übertuschen.

Betz, *(str.) m.* bear (Betz).

Bet'ze, *(w.) f. see* Petze.

Bet'zimmer, *(str.) n.* oratory, room (in a private house) set apart for prayer.

Beu'che(n) &c., *see* Bäuche &c.

Be-u'fern, *(w.) v. tr.* schön beufert *(Göthe),* having fine shores. — **Be-u'ferung,** *(w.) f.* embankment.

Beug'bar, *see* Biegbar.

Beu'ge, *(w.) f. obsolescent,* 1) bend; bow (Biegung); 2) *Coop.* bender (Reifbeuge); 3) *provinc.* a pile of wood. [tor.

Beu'gemuskel, *(str.) m. Anat.* flexor, flec-

Beu'gen, *(w.) v.* I. *tr.* 1) to bend, bow; *fig.* 2) (das Recht), to warp (justice); 3) *Gramm.* to inflect; 4) to humble, to depress, mortify; to grieve, afflict; gebeugt, *p. a.* worn (with age, cares, &c.); II. *refl.* to bend, bow (one's self down), to stoop; sich vor der Autorität der Bibel —, to bow to the authority of the Bible; III. *intr. (l. u.) see* Biegen, *intr.*

Beu'ger, *(str.) m.* 1) bender, &c. *cf.* Beugen; 2) *see* Beugemuskel.

Beug'sam, I. *adj.* pliant, flexible, tractable (Biegsam); II. B—keit, *(w.) f.* pliancy, &c. (Biegsamkeit).

Beu'gung, *(w.) f.* 1) (the act of) bending, &c. *cf.* Biegen; 2) bend, bow; flexion; diffraction, deflection, inflection (of light); turn, curve (of a river); *Surg.* halbe —, demiflexion; 3) *Gramm. see* Biegung & Biegungsfall; B—spunct, *m. Math.* point of inflexion.

Beu'le, *(w.) f.* 1) boil, bump, swelling; protuberance, tumour; *Vet.* warbles; blains; 2) die — in metallenen Gefäßen, boss; 3) a boss (of wood, &c.); gnarl (*cf.* Buckel, Knorren &c.); B—nklopfer, *m. Pewt.* paring-hammer; B—nsucht, *f. Vet. see* Wilzsucht; B-nperlen, *f. pl.* an inferior kind of pearls. [Beule.

Beu'lig, *adj.* full of boils, bosses, &c. *cf.*

Beu'ling, *(w.) f. Mar.* a sausage-shaped powder-match, train-channel in a fire-ship.

Be-un'fähigung, *(w.) f.* disqualification.

Be-un'ruhigen, *(w.) v. tr.* to disquiet, disturb, trouble, alarm, to discompose, to make uneasy, to annoy, to unsettle; to harass (the enemy); b—d, *p. a.* alarming, distressing.

Be-un'ruhigung, *(w.) f.* 1) the (act of) disquieting, &c., harassing, &c.; 2) inquietude, uneasiness, alarm; disturbance.

Be-ur'baren, *(w.) v. tr.* to cultivate, till.

Be-ur'kunden, *(w.) v. tr.* 1) to attest with records; to authenticate, verify; 2) *fig.* to prove, show, display, substantiate, manifest; beurkundet, recorded, registered, notarial. — **Be-ur'kundung,** *(w.) f.* authentication, verification, &c.

Be-ur'lauben, *(w.) v.* I. *tr.* to give leave (of absence); *Mil.* to furlough; to give a holiday; II. *refl.* to take leave; to withdraw; beurlaubt, *p. a. Mil.* absent with leave; der Beurlaubte, a soldier, &c. on leave of absence (Urlauber).

Be-ur'theilen, *(w.) v. tr.* 1) to judge, criticise (on, upon); falsch —, to misjudge; 2) to estimate; to review (a book, &c.); Andere nach sich —, to judge others by one's self.

Be-ur'theiler, *(str.) m.* judger, &c.; judge, critic; reviewer.

Be-ur'theilung, *(w.) f.* the (act of) judging, judgment, decision; critical examination or opinion; estimate; (literary, &c.) criticism, review; B—skraft, *f.* (power *or* faculty of) judgment, discernment; clearsightedness; estimative faculty; B—skunst, *f.* art of criticising, (art of) criticism; B—slos, *adj.* undiscerning.

Beurt, *see* Bört.

Beu'te, *(w.) f.* I. booty, spoil, prey (to be devoured, &c.); eine — der Geier und Hunde, a prey to the vultures and dogs; eine — der Würmer, a prey to the worms; die — des Siegers, the spoils of the victor; ihr Eigenthum wurde als gute — betrachtet, their property was considered as fair prize; eine — des Kummers, a victim of (to) grief; — machen, to make booty, to plunder; II. 1) *Bak.* a large kneading-trough with a partition in the middle; 2) *Bee,* wooden bee-hive; 3) (Staar—) a wooden box put on a tree for starlings, &c. to breed in.

A. **Beu'tel,** *(str.) m.* 1) *a)* purse; pouch; bag; (Brief—) mail, budget; *b)* a purse of money (in Turkey 500 piastres); *c) fig.* money; 2) *Mill.* bolter, bolt(ing)-bag; 3) *Bill.* pocket; hazard; 4) *T.* beater (Knüttel); 5) *Med.* sac, cyst; 6) *Bot. see* Staubbeutel; aus seinem eigenen — leben, to live at one's own expense; sich nach dem (seinem) — richten, to regulate one's expenses by one's income.

B. **Beu'tel,** *(str.) m. see* Beitel.

Beu'tel... (A), *in comp.* —bisam, *m.* musk in bags, pods, *or* cods; —coralline, *f. Conch.* shepherd's purse coralline (*Cellularia bursaria* Ellis); —dachs, *m.* marsupial badger (*Perameles*); —faß, *n. T.* a cask with a leather covering, that may be drawn together like a purse; —faul, *adj. coll.* unwilling to part with money; —förmig, *adj.* purse-shaped; —gans, *f. see* Kropfgans; —geschwulst, *f. see* Balggeschwulst; —hase, *m.* kangaroo (Känguruh).

Beu'telig, *adj.* baggy, bagged, *Miner.* porous.

Beu'tel..., *in comp.* —kammer, *f.*, —kasten, *m.* bolting-hutch; —koralline, *see* —coralline; —krabbe, *f.*, —krebs, *m. Entom.* purse-crab (*Cancer latro* L.); —maschine, *f.* bolting-mill; —meise, *f. Ornith.* mountain titmouse (*Parus pendulinus* L.); —murmelthier, *n.* wombat.

Beu'teln, *(w.) v.* I. *tr.* 1) to bolt, sift; 2) *Hunt.* to beat (fine); II. *refl.* to bag; to pucker; to wrinkle.

Beu'tel..., *in comp.* —netz, *n.* bag-net, purse-net; —perücke, *f.* bag-wig; —öffnung, *f.* mouth of a purse; —ratte, *f. Zool.* opossum (*Didelphys* L.); —schloß, *n.* purse clasp; lock of a bag; —schneider, *m.* cut-purse, pick-purse, cheat, swindler; —schneiderkraut, *n. Bot.* shepherd's purse (*Thlaspi bursa pastoris* L.); —schnur, *f.* purse-string; —sieb, *n.* bolting-sieve, bolter; —thier, *n.* 1) pouched animal; *pl.* marsupials; 2) *see* —ratte; —thierchen, *n. pl. Zool.* bursaria (*Müll.*); —tischchen, *n.* (für Damen) pouch table; —tuch, *n.* bolting-cloth; —welle, *f.*, —werk, *n.* bolting-mill; —zeug, *n.* common bolter.

Bewir'ken, (w.) v. tr. to effect, to cause, bring about, to work out, do, occasion, produce; die Eintragung der Waarenzeichen ist bewirkt worden, the registration of the trade-marks has been completed.

Bewir'then, (w.) v. tr. to entertain, treat, regale, accommodate; mit einer Flasche Wein &c. —, to treat to a bottle of wine, &c.

Bewirth'schaften, (w.) v. tr. to manage: to conduct (a farm), to husband, till, cultivate; den Acker —, to farm land. — **Bewirth'schaftung,** (w.) f. management, farming, &c.

Bewir'thung, (w.) f. entertainment, reception, treat, cheer, accommodation.

Bewit'thum, see Witthum.

Bewit'thümen, (w.) v. tr. to provide with a jointure.

Bewit'zeln, (w.) v. tr. to treat with light wit, to make sport or game of, to (have one's) joke at, to sneer at.

Bewo'gen, p. a. see Bewegen.

Bewohn'bar, I. adj. habitable, inhabitable; II. B-keit, (w.) f. habitableness.

Bewoh'nen, (w.) v. I. tr. to inhabit, to live in, to occupy. — **Bewoh'ner,** (str.) m., **Bewoh'nerin,** (w.) f. inhabitant; inmate; lodger, occupier (of rooms), tenant of a house, poet. dweller (of the wood, &c.). — **Bewoh'nung,** (w.) f. the (act of) inhabiting.

Bewöl'ken, (w.) v. tr. to cloud, see Umwölken.

Bewol'len, (w.) v. tr. to cover with wool.

Bewuh'len, (w.) v. tr. Mar. to woold.

Bewun'derer, (str.) m. admirer. — **Bewun'dern,** (w.) v. tr. to admire, to wonder at; b-swürdig, b-swerth, adj. admirable, wonderful, marvellous. — **Bewun'derung,** (w.) f. admiration; von — erfüllt, struck with admiration; mit — erfüllend, imposing, striking; b-swürdig, see Bewunderenswürdig.

Bewür'den, (w.) v. tr. (l. u.) to confer a dignity upon (one).

Bewurf', (str., pl. Bewür'fe) m. Mas. the plastering (of a wall); (grober) rough-cast.

Bewur'zeln, (w.) v. ref. & intr. (aux. sein) to get roots, to strike root; bewurzelt, p. a. rooted.

Bewür'zen, (w.) v. tr. see Würzen.

Bewußt', I. adj. 1) known: die b-e Sache, the matter in question; unter den b-en Bedingungen, under the conditions known to you (to him, to them, &c.); 2) (with Gen.) conscious, sensible, aware (of): sich (Dat., rarely Acc.) einer Sache (Gen.) — sein, to be or feel conscious of a thing: to recollect a thing; II. (str.) m. (l. u.) consciousness, knowledge.

Bewußt'los, adj. 1) unconscious; 2) insensible. — **Bewußt'losigkeit,** (w.) f. 1) unconsciousness; 2) insensibility.

Bewußt'sein, (str.) n. 1) consciousness; 2) knowledge, perception: als mir die Wahrheit zum — kam, when the truth came to my perception.

Bewußt'werden, (str.) n. apperception.

Bezacken, (w.) v. tr. to indent, jag, notch.

Bezahl'bar, adj. payable.

Bezah'len, (w.) v. tr. (Einem etwas or Einen) to pay (a sum or [to satisfy] a person); to pay for; to settle, discharge (a debt); nachlässig —, to be negligent in payment, to pay by dribblets; ich bin noch nicht bezahlt, my claims are still unsettled; den Sachwalter —, to give the solicitor his fee, to discharge his bill; (Einem) zu viel —, to overpay; zu wenig —, to underpay; die Kosten —, to defray (the expenses); die und ihres gleichen laßt den Krieg — (Schiller, Piccol. 1, 2), let these, and such as these, support the war; man bezahlt für diesen Artikel ..., this article is sold at (coll. fetches) ...; er kann nicht mehr — (intr.), he is insolvent; sich bezahlt machen, 1. to make one's self paid; das Werk machte sich bezahlt, the work paid its expenses; 2. to take one's due, to pay or reimburse one's self; alte Schulden —, to wipe off old scores; ich habe ihn mit gleicher Münze bezahlt, proverb. I (have) paid him in his own coin; er wird dich schon —, fig. he will pay you off (yet); Comm.-a. bezahlt werden, to meet due honour; to cash (a bill); einen Wechsel, eine Tratte —, to honour a bill of exchange, a draft; (den Betrag) bezahlt erhalten, (amount) settled, contents received; bezahlt und quittirt, paid and acquitted.

Bezah'ler, (str.) m. payer; (ein guter, a sure) paymaster.

Bezah'lung, (w.) f. payment; pay; imbursement, defrayment; (von Wechseln) protection; gegen baare —, for ready money; gegen — von ..., Comm. on payment of, he or they paying ...; B-sschein, m. release, acquitment.

Bezähm'bar, I. adj. tamable; II. B-keit, (w.) f. tamableness.

Bezäh'men, (w.) v. I. tr. to tame; fig. to curb, subdue, keep under, check, bridle, govern, restrain; II. ref. to restrain one's self, to keep one's temper. — **Bezäh'mung,** (w.) f. the (act of) taming, &c.

Bezah'nen, (w.) v. tr. to furnish with teeth; T. to indent, to dovetail; to tooth.

Bezau'bern, (w.) v. tr. to enchant, charm, to bewitch, to fascinate; (durch Zaubersprüche) to cast, set, or lay a spell on; bezaubert, adj. enchanted, &c.; smitten (von, with), under a spell; haunted (house). — **Bezau'berung,** (w.) f. 1) the (act of) charming, &c.; 2) bewitchery, enchantment, spell, fascination.

Bezäu'men, (w.) v. tr. to bridle, see Zäumen.

Bezäu'nen, (w.) v. tr. see Umzäunen.

Bezech'en, (w.) v. tr. to make drunk, see Betrinken.

Bezeich'nen, (w.) v. tr. 1) to mark (out), designate, sign, denote, note, (genau) to point out; to express; 2) to cover or fill with drawings; b-d, p. a. significant, characteristic (für, of). — **Bezeich'nung,** (w.) f. the (act of) marking, designation, notation, &c.; B-szettel, m. signature, ticket.

Bezei'gen, (w.) v. I. tr. (Einem etwas) to show, manifest; to mark, pay (one's respect, &c. to ...); to express (interest, condolence, &c.); II. ref. to behave (one's self) (well or ill); das —, s. s. (l. u.) 1) manifestation; 2) demeanour (Betragen). — **Bezei'gung,** (w.) f. the (act of) showing, demonstration; manifestation; mark, expression.

Bezeih'en, (str.) v. tr. to charge with, accuse of.

Bezep'tern, (w.) v. tr. to sceptre.

Bezet'teln, (w.) v. tr. Comm. to label, to ticket (goods).

* **Bezet'te,** (w.) f. Italian colouring rag (Schminkfleckchen).

* **Bezet'ten,** f. pl. (Fr.) Comm. Italian colouring rags.

Bezeu'gen, (w.) v. tr. (often used for Bezeigen) to attest, bear witness or testimony to, to witness, depose, testify; (schriftlich) to certify, to declare, assure. — **Bezeu'gung,** (w.) f. attestation, testifying, &c.

Bezicht', (str.) m. (& f.) see Bezichtigung.

Bezich'tigen, (w.) v. tr. (Einen einer Sache (Gen.)) to charge or to tax (one) with, to accuse of. — **Bezich'tigung,** (w.) f. charge, accusation, imputation.

Bezie'hen, (str.) v. tr. 1) a) to draw over, to cover (with); mit Saiten —, to string (a violin, &c.); b) see Überziehen; 2) a) to move to, take possession of, enter (a new lodging, &c.); to occupy; die Universität —, to enter college; ein Lager —, to pitch a camp, to encamp; b) to visit, frequent, attend (a fair); 3) to mark out (the boundaries); 4) a) to draw, receive (payment, a salary, &c.); to obtain, order; Comm.-a. b) to draw (a bill) upon; sich gegenseitig —, to counterdraw; c) Waaren —, to obtain, procure, draw (goods); 5) (Etwas auf [with Acc.], occasioned on [with Acc.]) to refer (a thing) to ...; b-d, p. a. Grammar. rela-

[illegible] Bib'bele, (str.) n. provinc. (S. G.) in children's lang.: peeping bird, biddy, dickybird.

Bi'bel..., in comp. –fest, adj. scripture-proof; conversant with the scriptures; –fester, m. textualist, textuary, text-man: –gesellschaft, f. bible-society; –kenner, m. biblical scholar; –kunde, f. biblical knowledge; –mäßig, adj. scriptural: –stelle, f. scriptural passage or text: –werk, n. bible with notes.

Bi'ber, s. I. (str.) m. 1) Zool. beaver, castor (Castor fiber L.); 2) Comm. a) (–zeug) pilot-cloth; b) see Düffel; II. in comp. –bau, m. den, lodgment, or hole of a beaver; –baum, m. Bot. umbrella tree, laurel-leaved tulip-tree, magnolia (Magnolia tripetala L.); –eisen, n. beaver-trap; –ente, f. see –taucher; –falle, f. beaver-trap: –fänger, m. beaver-trapper: –fell, n. beaver skin; –fett, n. beaver's grease; –geil, n. castoreum, beaver's [illegible]: –haar, n. hair of a beaver, beaver's [illegible]: –hut, m. beaver hat: –klee (Fieberklee), see Bitterklee; –kraut, n. see Tausendgüldenkraut.

* Bibernel'le, (w.) f. see Pimpinelle.

Bi'ber..., in comp. –ratte, see Bisamratte; –schwänze, m. pl. Mas. flat tiles, coll. flats; –taucher, –vogel, m. Ornith. dundiver, sparling fowl (Mergus merganser L.); –wammen, f. pl. beaver wombs: –wurz, f. Bot. climbing upright or slender birthwort (Aristolochia [illegible] L.); –zeug, n. see Biber, 2.

* Biblio..., (Gr. biblion, a book) in comp. –graph', (w.) m. bibliographer: –graphie', (w.) f. 1) bibliography: 2) list of books appearing periodically; –ma'ne, (w.) m. bibliomaniac: –thekar', (str.) m. librarian; –thekariat', (str.) n. librarian's office: –theka'risch, adj. relating to a librarian: –thek', (w.) f. library. [illegible]schichte, sacred history.

Bib'lisch, adj. biblical, scriptural; b–e Ge-

* Biblist', (w.) m. scripturist, biblist.

* Biblistik', (w.) f. biblical knowledge.

Bick'beere, Bick'elbeere, (w.) f. provinc. see Heidelbeere.

Bi'cke, (w.) f. pickaxe (Picke).

Bick'eisen, (str.) n. bickhorn, pick (Pickeisen).

Bick'elchen, n. (str.) n. gargane (Knäckente).

Bick'elhäring, Bick'elhaube, Bick'en, see Pickelhäring, Pickelhaube, Picken &c.

Bick'..., in comp. –sand, m. scouring sand; –stein, m. grit-stone.

Bie'der, I. adj. upright, staunch, straightforward, honest, candid, true, righteous, just, honourable; ein b–er Freund, a true-hearted friend; II. in comp. –herz, n. true heart, upright heart: –herzig, adj. true- or good-hearted, plain-hearted.

Bie'derkeit, (w.) f. uprightness, straightforward honesty, true-heartedness, honest dealing, probity, integrity.

Bie'der..., in comp. –leute, pl. honest, plain-hearted people: –mann, (pl. –männer) man of worth, worthy man, plain-dealing [illegible], true-hearted, honest, upright [illegible]; –männisch, adj. thinking and acting [illegible] man of worth, &c., plain-dealing, upright; –[illegible], m. plain-heartedness, true-[illegible], probity of mind, integrity (of [illegible]) (cf. Biederkeit); –sinnig, adj. [illegible]-hearted, true-hearted, upright, honest; [illegible], f. honest manners, uprightness of [illegible] &c. cf. Biederkeit.

[illegible], adj. flexible; pliable, pliant.

[illegible], (w.) f. bend, bow, &c. cf. Beuge, [illegible]

[illegible]..., in comp. F–e. –eisen, n. ply-[illegible] m. andiron snow-check.

[illegible] 2c., see Bügel 2c.

[illegible] see Beugemuskel.

[illegible] (str.) v. I. tr. 1) to bend, curve, [illegible] gebogene Stange, bent rod: 2) [illegible] 3) fig. to bend, warp, &c. (das Recht –, Schiller); II. refl. to bend, warp; to bend, turn (of a road, &c.); sich schmiegen und –, fig. to creep and crouch, to cringe; III. intr. (aux. sein) 1) to bend, be bent; 2) to turn (into a by-way); es muß – oder brechen, proverb, it must bend or break.

Bieg'(e)..., in comp. –scheibe, f. Coop. dog: –schritt, m. Danc. coupee: –walzwerk, n. T. sheet-bending machine; –zange, f. T. (wire-)pliers.

Bieg'sam, I. adj. 1) pliant, flexible, bendable, ductile, pliable, supple, limber; die b–ere animalische Schöpfung (Humboldt, Ansichten &c. 3, 2), the more flexible organisation of animal creation (Sabine); 2) Gramm. declinable; II. B–keit, (w.) f. pliantness, pliability, flexibility, suppleness, ductility.

Bie'gung, (w.) f. 1) bend (of the body, in a road, &c.), bent (of a bow, &c.), curve, curvature, flexion, sinuation; turn; 2) Weav. hook; 3) Gramm. inflection, variation (of nouns and verbs); B–sfall, m. Gramm. case.

Biel, (str.) m. T. scaffolding.

Biel'brief, (str.) m. see Beilbrief.

Bie'ne, (w.) f. 1) Entom. honey-bee, bee (Apis mellifica L.); die wilde –, wild bee; zahme –, hive bee; faule männliche –, drone; 2) Astr. the Fly.

Bie'nen..., in comp. –ameise, f. see Afterbiene; –bär, m. Zool. the common bear (Bär); –bau, m. see –zucht; –behandlung, f. management of bees; –beute, f. wooden hive (made of one solid block of wood); –blume, f. Bot. bee-flower (Ophrys apifera L.); –brot, n. hive dross, bee-bread; –brut, f. the embryos of bees.

Bie'ner, (str.) m. see Bienenmann.

Bie'nen..., in comp. –erde, f. residuum of wax; –erz, &. Miner. alveolar ore: –falk, m. Ornith. honey-buzzard (Falco apivorus L.); –fänger, –feind, see –fresser; –fasser, m. bag to take bees in; –flug, m. quantity of bees kept at any place; –fresser, m. Ornith. bee-eater (Merops apiaster L.); –geier, m. see –falk; –gewächse, n. pl. plants and herbs chiefly frequented by bees; –heide, f. Bot. wild rosemary (Ledum palustre); –harz, n. hive-dross: –haube, f. see –kappe; –haus, n. bee-house, see –stand; –hütte, f. bee-shed, see –haus; –jäger, m. see –fresser; –kappe, f. a cap worn in cutting the honey-combs; –kasten, m. bee-box (hive made of boards); –kitt, m. see –harz; –klee, m. Bot. creeping white trefoil (Trifolium repens L.); –königin, f. queen-bee; –korb, m. 1) bee-hive; 2) or –körbchen, n. Conch. see Waffeleisen; –kraut, n. see –gewächse; –kunde, f. apiarian knowledge; –lager, m. a number of bees; –magen, m. see Honigmagen; –mann, m. bee-master, hiver; –männchen, n. drone; –meise, f. see –fresser; –meister, m. see –mann; –mutter, f. see –königin; –saug, n. (& m.) Bot. 1) white dead nettle (Lamium album L.); 2) woody wound-wort (Stachys alpina L.); –schauer, m. see –stand; –schwarm, m. cluster or swarm of bees; –schwärmer, m. Entom. species of hawk-moth (Sphinx apiformis); –specht, m. see –fresser; –stand, m. hive-stall, bee-house, apiary; –stock, m. bee-hive; –vater, m. see –mann; –wachs, n. (yellow) bees'-wax; –wärter, m. see –mann; –weiser, –weisel, m. see –königin; –wolf, m. 1) see –fresser; 2) Entom. bee-eater (Attelabus apiarium); –zelle, f. cell; –zellig, adj. Bot. favose; –zucht, f. the culture, keeping, or rearing of bees; –züchter, m. bee-keeper, bee-master, hiver, apiarian; –züchterverein, m. apiarian society.

Bien'saug, (str.) n. (& m.) Bienensaug.

Bier, s. I. (str.) n. beer; ungehopftes –, ale; zu B–e gehen, coll. to go to the ale-house; II. in comp. –artig, adj. alish, like ale; –aufschläger, m. see –zwang; –aufseher, m. beer-conner; –bank, f. ale-house bench; –baß, m. see –zwang; –baß, m. coll. coarse voice; –bottich, m. 1) see Maischbottich; 2) beer-vat; –brauen, n. beer-brewing; –brauer, m. brewer; –brauerei, f. brewery; –braugerechtigkeit, f. licence or privilege to brew; –bruder, m. coll. drinker of beer; –eigner, m. (& n.) licensed beer-brewer or retailer of beer.

Bie'rein, (w.) v. intr. coll. 1) to smell of beer; 2) to be addicted to beer-drinking.

Bier'..., in comp. –esel, m. 1) a spectre haunting ale-houses; 2) fig. a drunken fellow; 3) coll. for Pirol; –essig, m. sour ale, a kind of acid made of ale; –faß, n. beer-tub, barrel; –fassen, n. filling up of beer; –fiedler, m. ale-house fiddler; –flasche, f. beer-bottle; –füller, m. pl. beer-fillers; –gischt, m. beer-froth, yeast; –gast, m. ale-house customer; –geld, n. 1) ale-tax; 2) drink-money; 3) money allowed to servants in lieu of beer; –glas, n. beer-glass, tumbler; –hahn, m. see –krahn; –halter, m. can-buck; –haus, n. ale-house, pot-house, tap-house; –hefe, f. barm, yeast, ale-ground; –held, m. 1) beer-drinker (to excess); 2) or –heber, coll. for Pirol; –inspector, m. see –aufseher; –kanne, f. ale-pot, tankard, pint-pot; –karre, f. dray-cart; –kegel, m. see –zeichen; –keller, m. ale-cellar; –kessel, m. boiler or copper for brewing; –kieser, m. see –prober; –kirsche, f. the sour cherry-tree (Cerasus acida Gärt.); –kneipe, f. pot-house; –koster, m. see –prober, 1; –krahn, m. beer-cock; –kranz, m. bush (of a beer-house); –krug, m. 1) pitcher, tankard; 2) coll. ale-house, inn; –kufe, f. beer-back; –meile, f. a certain district, to which a licence to brew and retail beer extends; –molken, f. pl. posset; –prober, m. 1) ale-taster, ale-conner; 2) instrument for testing the quality of beer; –reste, m. pl. broken beer; –sauer, n. see –essig; –schank, m. the act, practice, or place of selling beer; –schaum, m. beer-foam, white froth, nerving; –schenk, m. ale-house keeper; –schenke, f. see –haus; –schröter, m. beer-porter; drayman; –steuer, f. ale-tax, duty upon malt-liquor; –stube, f. tap(-room); –suppe, f. beer-soup; ale-berry; sope; –tanne, f. Bot. Canadian-pine (Pinus Canadensis); –verbrauch, m. consumption of beer; –visirer, m. see –inspector; –wage, f. see –prober, 2; –wirth, m. see –schenk; –wisch, m. see –kranz; –würze, f. wort; –zapfer, m. tapster; –zeichen, n. ale-house sign, ale-stake (ale-post); –zwang, m. the monopoly of selling beer within a certain district.

Bie'sam, see Bisam.

Bie'sen, see Bisen. [see Bremse.

Bies'fliege, (w.) f., Bies'wurm, (str.) m.,

Bie'ster, I. adj. provinc. dark, dismal, gloomy; II. s. (str.) m. Paint. bistre, bister (a dark brown water-colour).

Bie'stern, (w.) v. intr. provinc. to roam, stray about. [see Schnittlauch.

Bies'lauch, Bies'lauch, (str.) m. cut-leek.

Bies'milch, f., Biest, (str.) m. biestings.

Bie'ten, (str.) v. tr. 1) to bid, wish (good morning, &c.); 2) to offer, tender, proffer; weniger als ein Anderer –, to underbid one; mehr als ein Anderer –, to outbid one; (einem Verkäufer) weniger –, to beat (one) down; auf etwas (Acc.) –, to bid for ...; schlecht –, to make bad offers; Einem den Rücken –, to turn one's back on one; ich will mir das nicht von ihm – lassen, I won't stand that from him.

Bie'ter, (str.) m. bidder.

Biet'fenster, (str.) n. Carp. wicket, shutter.

* Bigamie', (w.) f. (Lat.-Gr.) bigamy. – Bigamist', (w.) m. bigamist.

Big'gel, (str.) m. see Bilgen.

* Bignon'ia, (w.) f. Bot. trumpet-flower (Bignonia L.). [f. bigotry.

Bigott', adj. bigoted. – Bigotterie', (w.)

[illegible]-one; Einem etwas auf die Seele —, to lay [illegible] injunctions upon one (to do a thing. [illegible] II. *refl.* to bind one's self (to), make [one]'s self dependent (upon); sich durch Ge[lüb]de —, to tie one's self by vows; III. [illegible] to bind, *particul. Eccl.* (*cf.* Matth. 16, [19]) die Gewalt zu — und zu lösen, the power [given] to St. Peter) of binding and loosing [illegible] the power of the keys [of the kingdom of heaven], *i. e.* of excommunicating and [absolving]; bindend, *p. a. fig.* binding (für, [upon]), obligatory: *Med.* agglutinative, agglutinant.

Bin'denschnalle, (*w.*) *f.* stock-buckle.

Bin'depfennig, (*str.*) *m.* earnest-money.

Bin'der, (*str.*) *m.* 1) binder, tier; 2) *provinc.* cooper; 3) *see* Bindestein; 4) *see* Bindsparren; —barte, *f.* cooper's adze.

Bin'de... (*from* Binden), *in comp.* —riegel, *m. Carp.* tie-beam, rail: —riemen, *m.* strap, [illegible].

Bin'der..., *in comp.* —lohn, *m.* cooperage; —pfahl (einer Spundwand), guide-pile: —schicht, *f. Mas.* bond-course: —sparren, *m. Carp.* binding-rafter.

Bin'de... (*from* Binden), *in comp.* —salat, *m.* summer endive and other kinds of salad the leaves of which are tied up in order to [make] them tender: —scheide, *f.* sheath for a hooping-knife: —schicht, *f. Build.* a course of bond-stones, lockrand: —schlüssel, *m. Eccl.* the key of St. Peter, *cf.* Binden, III.: —seil, *n. Mar.* lashing *or* seizing of a rope; —sohle, *f.* a sole (to be) bound to the foot (by straps), sandal: —sparren, *m. Carp.* tie-beam, rail; —stein, *m. Build.* binding-stone, bond-stone, binder, bonder, stretcher, header; —strich, *m.* (*lit.* binding-, *or* connecting-stroke) *Typ.*, &c. hyphen: —werk, *n. Build.* frame-work, stud-work, lattice-work, lattice-paling, arbour-work: —werkswände, *f. pl.* timber framing, stud-work; —wort, *n.* 1) *Gramm.* conjunction: 2) *Log.* copula, connective; —zeichen, *n.* 1) *see* —strich; 2) *Mus.* tie, bind, legato-mark; —zeug, *n.* surgeon's case; —ziegel, *m. see* —stein.

Bind'... (*cf.* Binde...), *in comp.* —faden, *m.* pack-thread, twine, (shop-)cord, string; —fadenbüchse, *f.* twine-holder; —fadenkapsel, *f.* string-box: —fadenrolle, *f.* pack-thread [reel]; —holz, *n.* 1) twigs, &c. (*cf.* —weide) used in fastening trees to poles, &c.: 2) *see* Bindeholz.
[dense, solid; 2) *see* Bündig.

Bün'dig, *adj.* 1) *lit.* compact, firm, close,

Bind'..., *in comp.* —messer, —pfennig, *see* Bindemesser &c.
[line, seizing.

Bind'sel, (*str.*) *n. Mar.* lashing, furling

Bind'sohle, (*w.*) *f.* 1) [illegible] (Brandsohle) *see* Brandsohle; 2) *see* Bindesohle.

Bin'dung, (*w.*) *f.* 1) the (act of) binding, [illegible]; 2) band, tie, obligation: 3) *Med.* *a*) [agglutination]; *b*) ligature; 4) *Mus.* syncopation; 5) *Math.* point of intersection; 6) *fig.* [illegible]; B-smittel, B-szeichen, *see* Bindemittel &c.

Bind'... (*from* Binden), *in comp.* —wesen, *m.* osier-twigs for binding [illegible]; —weide, *f. Bot.* 1) osier twig (*Salix viminalis* L.); 2) [illegible] (*[illegible]* L.); —wurz, [illegible]; —wurm, *m. Zool. see* Doppelloch.

[illegible], (*str.*) *n. Bot.* mercury (*Mercurialis* L.); das [illegible] —, French mercury [illegible]; englischer —, *see* Heinrich, [illegible] —, dog's mercury (*M.* [illegible] L.)

[illegible], *see* [illegible].

[illegible], I. *prep.* (*with Dat.*) within; — [illegible], within a week; — hier und einem [illegible] the space of a month; — Morgen, [illegible] — [illegible], *Mar.* to sail into a [illegible]; III. *in comp.* internal, inland; [illegible], *m. Mar.* inner-post; —bords, *adv.* in board: —colonie, *f.* back settlement: —deich, *m.* inner dam (dike); —gebiet, *n.* inland; —gericht, *n.* patrimonial court of justice; —gewässer, *n.* waters of the continent, inland-water; —hafen, *m.* basin of a port: —handel, *m.* home trade, inland, *or* inward trade, domestic trade; —land, *n.* inland, interior (country); —länder, *m.* 1) inhabitant of the interior; 2) a small vessel navigating inland rivers; —ländisch, *adj.* internal, *adv.* inwards: —landschaft, *f.* inland province: —lichter, *m. Mar.* lighter: —mauer, *f.* partition-wall: —meer, *n. see* —see; —pfahl, *m.* filling-pile (of a coffer-dam); —see, *f.* inland sea; —schifffahrt, *f.* internal *or* inland navigation; —schote, *f. Mar.* — am Leesegel, inner sheet of a studding-sail: —sohle, *f. see* Brandsohle; —stadt, *f.* inland *or* midland town: —verkehr, *m.* inland communication; —vorsteven, *m. Mar.* apron: —zeit, *f.* interval; —zoll, *m.* inland duty, duty inwards, internal taxes.

* **Binomial'**, **Bino'misch**, *adj.* (*Lat.*) *Math.* binomial: —factoren, *m. pl.* binomial factors.

Bin'se, (*w.*) *f.* rush (*Juncus* L.), club-rush (*Scirpus* L.): sedge (*Carex* L.): bent-grass (*Agrostis* L.); die glatte —, bulrush; die sperrige —, goose corn (*Juncus squarrosus* L.).

Bin'sen..., *in comp.* —ähnlich, *adj.* rush-like, bulrushy; —artig, *adj.* of the nature *or* species of a rush: —blume, *f. Bot.* flowering rush (*Butomus umbellatus* L.): —busch, *m.* rush-bed; —decke, *f.* mat: —gras, *n. Bot.* rush-grass, reed-grass (*Carex* L.): *see* Wollgras.

Bin'senhaft, *adj.* beany, *see* —ähnlich.

Bin'sen..., *in comp.* —korb, *m.* junket: (zu Feigen, Datteln) frail: —lager, *n.* rush couch, * rushy couch; —licht, *n.* rush candle: —matte, *f.* rush-mat: —nachtigall, *f. Ornith.* bog thrush (*Motacilla schoenobaenus* L.): —narcisse, *f. Bot.* jonquille (*Narcissus jonquilla*); —reich, sedgy, juncous: *see* Binsig; —röhre, *f. Bot.* woolly plant (*Corynebium*); —sänger, *m. Ornith.* water-wren (*Sylvia aquatica*); —seide, *f. see* Wollgras; —stuhl, *m.* rush-chair, rout-chair.

Bin'sicht, **Bin'sig**, *adj.* 1) rushy, full of rushes, sedgy: 2) rush-like, like rushes.

* **Biograph'**, (*w.*) *m.* (*Gr.*) biographer. — **Biographie'**, (*w.*) *f.* biography. — **Biogra'phisch**, *adj.* biographical.

* **Bi'quadrat**, (*str.*) *n.* (*Lat.*) *or* —zahl, *f. Math.* biquadrate: B-isch, *adj.* biquadratical.

Bir'ke, (*w.*) *f. Bot.* birch, birch-tree (*Betula* L.); die schwarze virginische —, sweet birch (*Betula nigra* L.); die zähe —, soft birch (*Betula lenta*).

Bir'ken, I. *adj.* birchen; II. (*from* Birke) *in comp.* —baum, *m.* birch-tree: —besen, *m.* birch-broom; —fuchs, *m. Zool.* common fox; —hahn, *m. see* Birkhahn; —hänschen, *n.* (*lit.* little birchen Jack) *burl. for* a birchen rod, *cf.* Dr. Birch; das —hänschen bekommen, to be (well) birched; —heher, *m. see* Birkheher; —kampher, *m. see* Betulin; —kork, *m.* species of fungus (*Boletus suberosus*); —laub, *n.* birch-foliage: —laubsänger, *m. see* Weidensänger; —marder, *m.* pine-martin (Baummarder): —messer, *m. see* —spanner; —pilz, *m. Bot.* birch-agaric (*Agaricus betulinus*); —saft, *m.* birch-juice; birch-wine: —sänger, *m. see* —laubsänger; —schwamm, *m. see* —pilz; —spanner, *m. Entom.* birch-moth (*Phalaena geometra betularia*); —theer, *m.* birch-tar, birch-oil; —wald, *m.* birch-forest; birch-grove; —wasser, *n.*, —wein, *m. see* —saft; —zeisig, *m. Ornith.* linnet (*Fringilla linaria*); —wurz, *f. Bot.* 1) *see* Blutwurz; 2) saltwort (*Chenopodium* L.).

Birk'... (*from* Birke), *in comp.* —fall, *m. Ornith.* Egyptian vulture (*Vultur percnopterus* L.): —fuchs, *m. see* Birkenfuchs; —geflügel, *n. see* —hahn, —henne; *Ornith.* —hahn, *m.* heath-cock (*Tetrao tetrix* L.); —heher, *m.* roller (*Coracias garrula* L.); —henne, *f.*, —huhn, *n.* whiting-pout, heath-pout; —wildjagd, *f. Sport.* grouse- *or* moor-shooting. [*m.* Burmese.

Bir'ma, *n. Geogr.* Birma. — **Birma'ne**, (*w.*)

Birn, (*w.*) *f.* I. *see* Birne; II. *in comp.* —apfel, *m.* pompire; pear-main; —aprikose, *f.* medlar-pear (*Pirus pollveria*); —baum, *m. Bot.* pear-tree (*Pirus* L.): —baumen, *adj.* (made of) pear-tree.

Bir'ne, (*w.*) *f.* 1) *Pom.* pear; 2) *Mus.* that part of a clarionet (and basset horn) into which the mouth-piece is inserted; 3) *Conch.* voluta; 4) choke-pear (instrument of torture).

Bir'nen..., *in comp.* —förmig, *adj.* pear-shaped, pyriform; —pastete, *f. Cook.* pear-pie; —pflaume, *f.* pear-plum: —saft, *m.* juice of pears.

Birn'..., *in comp.* —kraut, *n. Bot.* winter-green (*Pirola* L.); —most, *m. see* —wein; —motte, *f. Entom.* codling-moth (*Tinea pomonella* L.); —mundstück, *n. Man.* pear-bit; —quitte, *f. Bot.* pear-quince (*Pirus cydonia oblonga*); —schnecke, *f. Conch.* round partridge (*Pirula canaliculata*); —stiel, *m.* pear-stalk: —wein, *m.* perry. [*see* Pirol.

Bi'role, (*w.*) *f.*, **Bi'rolf**, **Bi'rolk**, (*str.*) *m.*

Birsch, *or* **Bir'sche**, (*w.*) *f.* 1) the shooting of deer with a rifle, deer-shooting; 2) right of shooting deer: 3) district licensed to shoot on: —meister, *m.* keeper of a preserve; —pferd, *n. Sport.* stalking-horse; —pulver, *n.* fowling powder; —rohr, *n.* rifle; —zeit, *f.* shooting-season (of deer).

Bir'schen, (*w.*) *v. tr.* to shoot deer (with a rifle); das —, *v. s.* (*str.*) *n.* deer stalking.

† **Bis**, *provinc. imper. of* Sein (*for* Sei), be.

Bis, *adv.* till, until; as far as; (— an) up to, to: — jetzt, (— lang) till now, up to the present time, as yet, hitherto: — wohin? how far? — hierher (*provinc.* — daher), thus far; to this place; — dahin, till then; up to that time; by that time: — auf die Letzt, to the last; von London — Paris, from London to Paris; sieben — acht, seven to eight; — an (*with Acc.*), — auf (*with Acc.*), — zu, to, even to, up to, within; — an den Hals im Wasser, up to the chin in water; — an *or* in den Tod, — zum Tode, till death; das Kölner Theater ist — auf den Grund abgebrannt, the theatre of Cologne has been burnt to the ground; den Sorgenbecher — auf die Hefen leeren, to drink off the cup of sorrow even unto the dregs; — zu Thränen bewegt, moved (even) to tears; — aufs Blut, — zum Betrug, *see* Blut, Betrug; — auf ..., except, wanting, save; — auf eine Kleinigkeit, within a trifle *or* an ace; — aufs Haar, to a shade, exactly; — auf einige Fälle, within a few cases: — weit in die nächste Nacht, far into another night; — ins späteste Alter, to the latest period of one's existence; — innerhalb vierzig Fuß, to within forty feet; — nach ..., as far as .... — über die Ohren verliebt, over head and ears in love with ...; — über den Kopf ins Wasser gehen, to go beyond one's depth; er wird roth — an die Ohren, he blushes up to his ears; vom Anfang — zu Ende, from beginning to end; — zum Ekel, to disgust.

II. *conj.* (*orig.* — daß) till: warte — ich komme, wait till I come; Gott wartete nicht, — daß (*obsolescent & coll. for* —) der abgefallene Mensch zu ihm zurückkehrte, God did not wait for apostate man to return to him.

Bi'sam, *s.* I. (*str.*) *m.* musk; II. *in comp.* —affe, *m. Zool.* musk-ape (*Cercopithecus* [illegible] L.); —apfel, *m.* musk-apple; —artig, *adj.* musky; —beutel, *m. Comm.* musk in pods; —biber, *m. see* Zibethmaus; *Bot.* —blume, *f. see* —flockenblume; —eibisch, *m.* abel-musk (Abelmosch).

Bi'samen, (*w.*) *v.* I. *intr.* to smell musk-like; II. *tr.* to scent with musk.

[illegible] flower, floweret; 2) *Sport.* the tail of the [illegible], scut: —kaffee, *m. joc.* (*Saxony*) coffee [illegible] thin that any flower, &c. painted at the [bottom] of a cup, may be discerned easily.

Blu'me, *(w.) f.* 1) *Bot. & Chem.* flower; 2) [a)] *Sport.* single, scut (the tail of deer); *b)* white [spot], star (on horses); *see* Blässe, 2, *a;* 3) the [finest] part of certain substances: *a)* — des [Weines], flavour of wine, *bouquet;* ohne —, [illegible]; *b)* the pink (of society, &c.); die [illegible] Blume aus meinem Leben (*Schiller*, Wall. [illegible]), the bloom is vanished from my life [illegible]; 4) B-n, *pl.* [illegible] blooms, balls; 5) [illegible] bloom, grain; 6) yeast; 7) gloss (on [illegible], silks, &c.); 8) *Rhet.* flourish; trope; die [illegible] —, stamineous *or* sterile flower; [durch] die — reden, to use florid language, to [speak] with covert allusions, &c. (*cf.* Verblümt).

Blü'meln, *(w.) v. intr.* 1) (*lit.* to frequent [the] flowers) to gather honey (said of bees); [2)] to speak *or* write in a flowery style, to use [flourishes]; **Blümelei',** *(w.) f.* 1) (*Göthe, l. u.*) [childish] display of flowers; 2) floridness of style; flourish.

Blü'men, *(w.) v. tr.* to paint *or* adorn with flowers, to figure, diaper, fashion (silks, &c.).

Blu'men..., *in comp.* pertaining to flowers, [floral]: —artig, *adj.* flower-like; flosculous; —[illegible], *m. see* —topf; —ausstellung, *f.* flower-show; —balg, *m. Bot.* glume; —ball, *m. Bot.* [illegible]; —bau, *m.* the cultivation of flowers; [—becher], *m. Bot.* calix, cup; —beet, *n.* bed of flowers, parterre; *Bot-a.* —behältniß, *n.*, —[behälter], *m.* receptacle; —binde, *f.* festoon, [wreath]; —binse, *f.* blooming *or* flowering rush (*Butomus umbellatus* L.); —blatt, *n.* petal; [—blattlos], *adj.* apetalous; —blau, *n. see* Blattblau; —bläte, *f.* flower-bed; —boden, *m. see* [—behältniß]; —brett, *n. see* —gestell; —bringend, [*see*] —tragend; —büschel, *m.* cluster of flowers; *Bot.* corymb; mit —büscheln besetzt, —büschel[tragend], corymbiated, corymbiferous; —cultur, *f.* flori-culture; —decke, *f. see* Blütendecke; [illegible], *f. Ornith.* wild duck; —erde, *f.* garden-mould; —esche, *f.* flowering ash; —feld, *n.* flowery field; a piece of ground destined for *or* laid out with flowers; —flor, *m.* 1) show of flowers; 2) the time of flowering; —flur, *f.* a ground covered with flowers; —förmig, *adj.* [illegible]; —freund, *m. see* —liebhaber; —garten, *m.* flower-garden; —gärtner, *m.* florist, flower-gardener; horticulturist; —gefäß, —ge[schirr], *n.* flower-pot; —gehänge, *n.* festoon, garland, wreath of flowers; —gestell, *n.* flower-[pot]-stand; —gewächs, *n.* flower-plant; —ge[winde], *n. see* —gehänge; —göttin, *f.* the goddess of flowers, Flora; —griffel, *m. Bot.* style.

Blu'menhaft, *adj.* flower-like, flowery.

Blu'men..., *in comp. Bot-a.* —hülle, *f.* in[volucre]; —kelch, *m.* calix, cup, bell of a flower; [illegible]; mit —kelch, calycled; —knospe, *f.* [*see*] —[illegible]; —kohl, *m.* cauliflower (*Brassica* [*oleracea botrytis*] L.); —korb, *m.* flower-basket; *Archit.* [illegible]; —kranz, *m.* garland, wreath of flowers; [chaplet]; —krone, *f. Bot.* corolla; die kleine —[krone], corollet, corollule; —kronenartig, *adj.* [illegible]; —kübel, *m.* tub; —kunst, *f.* the [art] of cultivating flowers, floriculture; —lese, *f.* 1) a gathering of flowers; 2) *fig.* anthology (a selection of poems, &c.); —liebhaber, *m.* [a lover] of flowers, florist; —liebhaberei, [*f.*], fondness for (the culture of) flowers; [—maler], *m.* flower-painter; —malerei, *f.* [flower-painting]; —mehl, *n. Bot.* flower-dust, [pollen]; —monat, *m.* flower-month; —nelke, *f.* [illegible]; —pfad, *m. fig.* primrose way, prim[illegible]; —reich, I. *adj.* bloomy, flowery; II. [illegible] floral kingdom; —rohr, *n.* 1) Indian [illegible] (*Canna* L.); 2) *see* —binse; —same, *m.* [illegible]; —sammlung, *f.* collection of flow[ers]; [illegible]; —schaft, *m. see* —stengel; —scheide, [illegible]; —scheide, *f. Bot.* spatha, sheath; [illegible] eine —scheide habend, spathaceous; —scherbe, *f.*, —scherbel, *m.* flower-pot; —schirm, *m. Bot.* umbel; —schmuck, *m.* 1) ornamental display of flowers; 2) flower work; —schnur, *f. see* —gehänge; —seite, *f. Tann.* hair-side (of a skin); —sonntag, *m. see* Palmensonntag; —[illegible] specht, *m.* humming-bird (Colibri); —speise, *f. see* —balg; —spiele, *n. pl.* floral games; —sprache, *f.* language of flowers; —ständig, *adj. Bot.* floral; —staub, *m. see* —mehl; —stempel, *m. Bookb.* flower-die, form-stamp; —stengel, *m.* flower-stalk, spindle; —stiel, *m.* peduncle; —stielchen, *n. Bot.* pedicle; —stock, *m.* a flower in a pot; —strauß, *m.* nosegay, posy; —stück, *n.* 1) flower-plot (in a garden); platband, parterre; 2) *Paint.* flower-piece (a picture of flowers); —thee, *m.* flower-tea, imperial tea; —topf, *m.* flower-pot; —tragend, *adj. Bot.* floriferous; —vase, *f.* flower-vase, vase; —werk, *n. Archit.* festoons, flower-work; —zeit, *f.* flowering-season; —züchter, *m.* florist; —zierat, *m.* flower-work; —zucht, *f. see* —bau; —zwiebel, *f.* bulb; —zwiebelglas, *n.* root glass.

Blu'mig, Blu'micht, *adj.* 1) *see* Blumenhaft; 2) florid, flowery, bloomy.

Blumist'ne, *(w.) f.* (*Jean Paul, l. u.*) *see* Blumensammlung. — **Blumist',** *(w.) m.* florist. — **Blumist'ik, Blumisterei',** *(w.) f.* floriculture. — **Blumist'isch,** *adj.* floricultural.

Blüm'lein, *(str.) n.* 1) * *for* Blümchen; 2) *pop. for* Vergißmeinnicht.

Blü'se, *(w.) f.* light-house; B-ngeld, *n.* light-money, beaconage.

Blut, *(str.) n.* 1) blood; 2) *fig.* family, race; 3) sap (of blood), juice (of grapes); geronnenes —, coagulated *or* clotted blood, gore; *Med.* cruor; 4) ein junges —, *coll.* a young person (of either sex); (männl.) a youth, a spark; von gutem B-e (Pferde &c.), thorough-bred; — lassen, to let blood, bleed; Fleisch und —, flesh and blood; bis aufs — peinigen, to torment almost to death; bis aufs — schlagen, to beat till blood is drawn; böses — machen, *fig.* to occasion angry feelings, irritation; mit kaltem —, in cold blood.

Blut'..., *in comp.* —abgang, *m.* loss of blood; —achat, *m. Miner.* hemachate, bloody agate; —acker, *m.* field of blood; —ader, *f.* blood-vessel, vein; —aderblut, *n.* venal blood; —adergeschwulst, *f. Med.* varix; —ampfer, *m. Bot.* bloody sorrel, bloodwort (*Rumex sanguineus* L.); —andrang, *m.* congestion of blood; —arm, *adj.* 1) *Med.* anemic, bloodless, destitute of normal blood; 2) *coll.* extremely poor; *Med-a.* —armut, *f.* deficiency of (normal) blood, anemia; —auge, *n.* blood-shot eye; —auswurf, *m.* a spitting of blood, hemoptysis; —bad, *n.* bloodshed, slaughter, massacre, butchery, carnage; —bann, †. *m.* penal judicature; —bedeckt, *adj.* gory; —bereitung, —bildung, *f.* sanguification; —beule, *f.* bloody boil *or* tumour; —blase, *f. Med.* hematocystis; —blume, *f. Bot.* blood-flower (*Hæmanthus coccineus* L.); —braun, *adj.* dark-brown, bloody brown; —brechen, *n.* the vomiting of blood; —buche, *f. Bot.* bloody beech (*Fagus sanguinea*); —bühne, *f.* scaffold (for execution).

Blüt'chen, *(str.) n.* (*dimin. of* Blüte) 1) a little blossom; *Bot.* floscule; 2) pimple.

Blut'..., *in comp.* —coralle, *f.* blood-red coral (*Isis nobilis*); —drossel, *f. Ornith.* red-wing (*Turdus iliacus* L.); —durst, *m.* thirst for blood; —dürstig, *adj.* blood-thirsty.

Blü'te, *(w.) f.* 1) blossom, bloom, flower; *Bot.* florescence; in (der) — stehen, to be in bloom *or* flower; 2) *fig.* bloom, flower, prime of life *or* age; 3) *Med. see* Blutfluß, 3.

Blut'..., *in comp.* —egel, *m.* leech (*Hirudo medicinalis* L.); *fig.* blood-sucker; —eiche, *f.* bloody oak; —eiter, *m.* sanies.

Blu'ten, *(w.) v. intr.* 1) *a)* to bleed; er blutete aus vielen Wunden, he bled from many wounds; aus der Nase —, to bleed at the nose; aus allen Poren —, to bleed at all pores; *b) fig.* to die a violent death, to bleed; *c) Gard.* to lose sap *or* juice, to bleed (as a vine, &c.); 3) *fig.* to suffer, to smart; to pay for; die Nase blutet mir, my nose bleeds. das Herz blutet mir, *fig.* my heart bleeds (within me); mit b-dem Herzen, *and.* broken-hearted; 4) *Miner.* das Erz blutet, the ore is mixed with red silver.

Blü'ten..., *in comp.* —auge, *n.* flower-bud, germ; —büschel, *n.* tuft of flowers; (m. &c.) truss; —decke, *f.* perianth, flower-cup; —fläschen, *n. pl.* (an Weiden &c.) palms; —kelch, *m. see* Blumenkelch; —kranz, *m. Bot.* verticil; —rispe, *f. see* Windhalm; —stand, *m.* inflorescence; —ständig, *adj. Bot.* floral; —staub, *m. see* Blumenstaub; —stengel, *m.* peduncle, foot-stalk.

Blut'entleerung, —entziehung, *(w.) f.* 1) a bleeding; 2) loss of blood.

Blü'ten..., *in comp.* —tragend, *p. a. Bot.* floriferous, producing flowers; —traube, *f.* raceme, bunch; —zeit, *f.* flowering time; florescence, florification; *fig.* flourishing time.

Blut'..., *in comp.* —ergießung, *f.*, —erguß, *m. Med.* effusion of blood; —erz, *n. Min.* 1) red-coloured silver-ore; 2) cinnabar-ore; —erzeugung, *f. Med.* sanguification; —fahne, *f. see* —flagge, 1; —farbe, *f.* blood-colour, dark red, crimson; —farbig, *adj.* blood-coloured; —feige, *f. Bot.* Indian-fig, *Opuntia;* —feind, *m.* mortal enemy; —fennich, *m. Bot.* blood-red panic-grass (*Panicum sanguinale* L.); —feld, *n. see* —acker; —fink, *m.* bull-finch (Gimpel); —flagge, *f. Mar.* 1) flag of defiance, red-flag; 2) sudden squall of wind; —flügel, *m. Ent.* glory of Kent (*Endromis versicolor* L.); —fluß, *m. Med.* 1) bloody flux; 2) hemorrhage; 3) monthly courses, flowers; 4) hemorrhoids (Hämorrhoiden); —flüssig, *adj.* affected with a flux of blood; —fremd, *adj. coll.* entirely strange; ein —fremder Mensch, a perfect stranger; —fülle, *f.* fullness *or* excess of blood, plethora; —gang, *m. see* —fluß; —gefäß, *n.* blood-vessel; —gefäßlehre, *f. Med.* angiology; —geld, *n.* price of blood; —gericht, *n.* 1) tribunal judging of life and death; 2) capital jurisdiction; —gerüst, *n.* scaffold (—bühne); —geschwulst, *f.* bloody swelling, *Med.* thrombus; —geschwür, *n.* bloody abscess *or* tumour, furuncle; —gier, *f.* bloody-mindedness, sanguinary disposition; —gierig, *adj.* bloody-minded, murderous; —gierigkeit, *f.* bloody-mindedness; —glöcke, *f. see* —blume; —gras, *n. Bot.* cock's foot-finger-grass (*Digitaria sanguinalis* L.); —hänfling, *m. Ornith.* red linnet (*Fringilla cannabina* L.); —harnen, *n. Med.* discharge of bloody urine, hæmaturia; *Vet.* red [murrain].

Blü'the, *see* Blüte.

Blut'..., *in comp.* —hirse, *f. see* —gras; —hochzeit, *f.* (*lit.* the bloody nuptials) the massacre of St. Bartholomew; —holz, *n.* blood-wood, Nicaragua-wood, *see* Campecheholz; —hund, *m.* blood-hound; *fig.* blood-hound, blood-shedder; —husten, *m. Med.* anagoge.

Blu'tig, I. *adj.* bloody: 1) gory, covered with blood, 2) cruel, sanguinary; er zeigte mir den — gegeißelten Rücken, he showed me his back scourged to the blood; sich (*Dat.*) die Lippen — beißen, to bite one's lips till blood comes; eine b-e Schlacht, a sanguinary battle; II. B-keit, *(w.) f.* bloodiness, &c.

Blü'tig, *in comp.* ...blooded.

Blut'..., *in comp.* —igel, *see* —egel; —jung, *adj. coll.* very young; —kasten, *m. Sport.* heart of the deer; —klee, *m. Bot.* crimson-clover (*Trifolium incarnatum* L.); —klumpen, *m.* clot of blood; —kohl, *m. Bot.* species of yam (*Dioscorea sativa*); —körperchen, *n.* corpuscle of blood; —krankheit, *f.* 1) *Med.* distemper of the blood, dyscrasy; 2) irregularity of the menstrual discharges; 3) *Vet.* bloody murrain (—harnen); —kraut, *n. Bot.*

2) sanguinary, bloody dock (Rumex sanguineus L.); 3) see Weiderich; Anat.-e. —fasern, m. [illegible]; —kügelchen, n. blood globule; —kupfererz, n. variegated copper; —lassen, n. blood-letting; —lauf, m. 1) bloody flux, dysentery; 2) see —umlauf; —lauge, f. Chem. blood-lye: —laugensalz, n. Chem. prussiate of potash: —leer, see Blutlos; —leere, —leerheit, f. see Blutlosigkeit.

Blut'los, adj. Med. 1) bloodless, exsanguious: 2) destitute of normal blood (blutarm, Anämisch). — Blut'losigkeit, (w.) f. 1) bloodlessness, want of blood: 2) a morbid diminution of the amount of blood in the body, anaemia (Anämie).

Blut..., in comp. —mal, n. a red mole, ecchymosis: —masse, f. mass of blood: —mensch, m. blood-thirsty man, blood-shedder: —napf, m. bleeding-basin; —nieren, n. see —harnen; —nuß, f. red filbert: —pfirsich, m. nectarine: —rache, f. revenge for bloodshed: —rächer, m. avenger of blood, avenger of bloodshed; —reich, adj. abounding with blood: sanguineous; —reinigend, adj. purifying the blood; —reinigungsmittel, n. pl. Med. abluentia; —richter, m. judge in matters of life and death: —rose, f. see —rotlauf; —roth, adj. blood-red, sanguine; n. Chem. hematine: —ruhr, f. bloody flux: —rünstig, adj. running with blood, bloody; Einen —rünstig schlagen, to strike one so as to draw blood: —sack, m. see —beule; —sauer, adj. coll. very toilsome, very hard; es sich (Dat.) —sauer werden lassen, to labour tooth and nail, to toil and moil: —sauger, m. 1) blood-sucker, extortioner; 2) Zool. vampire (Vespertilio spectrum L.); 3) see —egel; —säure, f. Chem. 1) see —lauge; 2) sulphocyanic acid; —schande, f. incest: —schänder, m. incestuous person: —schänderisch, adj. incestuous: —schlag, m. 1) Med. see Schlagfluß; 2) Vet. see Rückenblut; —schlecht, adj. coll. extremely bad; —schuld, f. 1) capital crime, blood-guiltiness; 2) see —schande; —schwamm, m. Bot. trimmed agaric (Boletus sanguinolentus L.): —schwären, m. see —geschwür; —schweiß, m. Med. 1) bloody sweat; 2) diapedesis: —schwelle, f. Vet. see —spath: —seuche, f. Vet. see —harnen; B-sfreund, m. kinsman; B-sfreundin, f. kinswoman; B-sfreundschaft, f. consanguinity, proximity of blood: —fleck, m. Anat. parenchyma: —spath, m. Vet. blood-spavin: —speien, —spucken, n. spitting of blood, hemoptoe: —spur, f. track of blood: —stallen, n., —staupe, f. see —harnen; —stätte, f. the place of bloodshed: —stein, m. Miner. blood-stone, hematite, sanguine stone: manganese: —stillend, p. a. blood-stopping, styptic: —strieme, f. livid mark or weal, suggillation: B-stropfen, m. 1) drop of blood; 2) Bot. see Pimpinelle, Adonis; —sturz, m. hemorrhage: b-sverwandt, adj. kindred or allied by blood, consanguineous: B-sverwandte, m. & f. a person related by blood, kinsman, kinswoman: B-sverwandtschaft, f. consanguinity, blood-relationship; —taufe, f. Ch. Hist. the violent death of such martyrs as had not received Christian baptism; —tausch, m. Surg. transfusion of blood: —that, f. murder; —umlauf, m. circulation of the blood. [rhage.

Blu'tung, (w.) f. Med. a bleeding; hemor-

Blut..., in comp. —unterlaufung, f. extravasation of blood: —urtheil, n. sentence of death: —vergießen, n. bloodshed(ding), slaughter, carnage: ohne —vergießen, bloodless (conquest); —verlust, m. Med. loss or waste of blood; —warm, adj. blood-hot; —wärme, f. blood-heat: Anat.-s. —wasser, n. lymph; [illegible]. serum: serosity; —wassergefäße, n. pl. serous vessels, lymphatic ducts; —wässerig, adj. Med. serous, lymphatic: —wässerigkeit, f. serosity; —wenig, adj. coll. very little, next to nothing: —wolle, f. fell-wool, carrion-wool, skinner's wool; —wurst, f. black-pudding: —wurz, f. 1) set-wort, tormentil (Tormentilla erecta L.); 2) see Schwertel, gelber; —zehnte, m. tithe paid of cattle; —zeuge, m. martyr (cf. —taufe); —zwang, m. Med. tenesmus, bloody flux. [gust.

Bö, (w.) f. Mar. a sudden squall of wind,

* Bo'a, (w.) f. 1) see Abgottsschlange; 2) see Affenbaum; 3) boa (article of ladies' dress).

* Bob'binet, (str.) m. (Engl.) bobbin-net (Spitzengrund).

* Bocci'le, (w.) f. dyer's croton.

Bock, (str., pl. Böcke) m. 1) a) Zool. the male of several animals, f. i. Hirsch—, Reh—, buck; Schaf—, ram; Ziegen—, he-goat; b) Entom. see Bockkäfer; 2) a) T. battering-ram, block, bar, beam; b) jack, horse; (zum Aufhängen der Stiefeln) boot-horse; (zum Kleiderreinigen) beating-horse; (zum Aufhängen der Kleider) clothes-horse; c) (Schemel) stool; cricket, (Gestell im Kamin) dog, andiron; (an der Grube) cradle; (dreibeiniges Gestell) trestle: see Sägebock; Carp. truss; Coach-m. [illegible]; (beim Billardspiel) bridge: d) a machine for lifting or supporting heavy weights: Mar. derrick, sheers (pl.); e) (Folter) stocks; f) the box of a coach: 3) der polnische —, see Sackpfeife; fig.-s. 4) blunder, stumble: 5) a) lewd, debauched fellow; b) cont. for a tailor: snip, knight of the shears or of the thimble: 6) Anat. hircus; 7) Astr. see Steinbock; 8) provinc. see Bockschiff; and-s. Einem den — stehen, Game (at leap-frog) to give one a back; den — zum Gärtner machen or setzen, to set a fox to keep the geese; Einen in den — spannen, to tie one's arms and legs together: einen — machen or schießen, to commit a blunder, to blunder; der — stößt ihn, he blubbers.

Bock..., in comp. —beinig, adj. goat-footed (of horses); —bier, n. a kind of strong Bavarian beer: —blatt, see Bocksblatt.

Böck'chen, (str.) n. (dimin. of Bock) kid.

Bock'decke, (w.) f. hammer-cloth.

Böck'eleisen, (str.) n. Tann. see Abzieheisen.

Bock'en, (w.) v. intr. 1) (of goats) to lust after the he-goat: 2) Mar. to pitch or scend; to heave up and down; 3) (of horses) to bend down the neck and fling out behind; 4) or Böck'eln, Bock'enzen, (w.) to smell like a goat.

Böck'er, (str.) m. small heap of bricks piled up to dry.

Bock..., in comp. —fell, n. goat (buck) skin: —flöte, f. kind of flute with a mouthpiece: —geruch, —gestank, m. a goatish smell; —gestell, n. body of a coach: —hirsch, m. see Antilope; —holz, n. 1) Pernambuco-wood: 2) Guaiacum-wood.

Bock'ig, Bock'icht, adj. 1) (butting, &c.) like a ram; 2) lustful after the he-goat, rutting: 3) a) smelling like a goat: b) or Böck'isch, goatish, rammish; lewd: 4) stubborn, obstinate.

Bock..., in comp. —käfer, m. Entom. capricorn beetle, goat chafer (Cerambyx L.); —kalb, n. buck of the first year; —kissen, m. coach-boot: —kissen, n. box-cushion (of a coach); —leder, n. see —fell; —ledern, adj. buck-skin, kid-skin; —leiter, f. step-ladder; —meisterei, f. fig. useless labour; —messer, n. comb-maker's knife: —mühle, f. a wind-mill built of timber set upon trestles; —pfeife, f. bag-pipe, horn-pipe: —polster, n. see —kissen.

Bocks..., in comp. —bart, m. 1) goat's beard; 2) Bot. a) wilder, gelber, goat's beard, Joseph's flower (Tragopogon pratense L.); b) mit Lauchblättern, goat-marjoram, purple goat's beard (Tragopogon porrifolium L.); —beere, f. dew-berry (Rubus caesius L.); —beutel, m. 1) (S. G.) a roundish pouch-shaped wine-bottle, usually containing a rare Franconian wine, denominated Steinwein; 2) (or —beutelei, f.) coll. quaint old custom, old

[illegible] L.); —schnabelig, *adj.* latirostrous, broad-beaked; —schulterig, *adj.* broad-shouldered, broad-backed; —schwänzig, *adj.* broad-tailed; —seite, *f.* broadside (of a ship); —stahl, *m. T.* turner's paring-chisel; —stirnig, *adj.* broad-faced, broad-fronted; —würfig säen, *Agr.* to sow broadcast; —zahn, *m. see* Brassen; —zange, *f. T.* [illegible]-pincers.

Brei'te, *(w.) f.* 1) breadth; width; depth (of ribbon, lace, &c.); main breadth (of a ship); 2) *Astr. & Geogr.* latitude; 3) a large plain; 4) distention, wideness; 5) *fig.* diffuseness of style; 6) *Agr.* open range of land bearing one sort of corn; — einer Flagge, [illegible] of a flag; in der — fortsegeln, to run down latitude; B-ngrad, *m.* degree of latitude; B-nkreis, *m.* circle of latitude.

Brei'tel, *(str.) m. T.* a number of iron plates taken up by the tongs to be hammered at the same time.

Brei'ten, *(w.) v. tr.* to spread (out), extend; flatten, beat, to hammer flat; die Segel —, *Mar.* to brace the sails in (when the wind veers aft).

Breit'heit, *(w.) f. (l. u.)* broadness, [illegible]; platitude; corpulence.

Breit'ling, *(str.) m.* 1) *Ichth.* sprat (*Clupea sprattus* L.); 2) a kind of agaric (*Agaricus* [illegible]).

Brei'tung, *(w.) f.* expanse.

Brei'..., *in comp.* —umschlag, *m. Med.* cataplasm, poultice; —weich, *adj.* pappy, soft as pap. [Brombeere.

Brem'me, *(w.) f.* 1) *see* Bremse; 2) *see*

Bre'men, *n. Geogr.* Bremen. — **Bre'mer,** I. *adj.* Bremen (Gern, Erde, Blau, Grün, Wolle, [illegible], blue clay, blue, green, ostridge wool); II. *(str.) m.* (B-in, *(w.) f.* female) inhabitant of Bremen.

Brem'mer, *(str.) m. Min.* chamble; —schacht, *m.* shaft with chambles.

Brems, *(str.) m. Railw.* brake, (carriage-) stopper, *cf.* Hemmschuh & Hemmkette; —berg, *m.* self-acting inclined plane.

Brem'se, *(w.) f.* 1) *Entom.* gadfly (*Oestrus* L.); 2) *see* Pferdebremse; 3) (farrier's) brake, barnacle, horse-twitchers; 4) *see* Brems.

Brem'sen, *(w.) v. tr.* 1) ein Pferd —, to apply the barnacle to a horse; 2) *a) Railw.* to put on the brake or carriage-stopper; *b)* ein Rad —, to put the drag to (a wheel).

Brem'ser, *(str.) m. Railw.* brakeman.

Brems'..., *in comp.* —[illegible], —schuh, *m.* block of a brake; —leute, *pl.* brakemen; —schlitten, —[illegible], *m.* brake-sledge, sledge-brake; —schwengel, *m.* brake, stopper; —[illegible], *n.* braking-apparatus, *cf.* Hemmung, 1.

Brenn'... (*from* Brennen), *in comp.* —arbeit, *f. Metall.* assaying by the cupel.

Brenn'bar, I. *adj.* combustible; II. B-keit, *(w.) f.* combustibility.

Brenn'..., *in comp.* —blase, *f.* alembic; —[illegible], *m. Ship-b.* iron claws for bending planks by fire; —bündel, *n. pl. Mar.* breams; —eisen, *n.* 1) *Surg.* brand-iron, cautery, searing-iron; 2) *Hair-dr.* crisping-iron, curling-irons; 3) *Vet.* firing-iron; 4) (für Sträflinge) [illegible]-iron.

Bren'nen, *(irr.) v.* I. *intr.* 1) *a)* to burn, to be on fire, [illegible]; das Haus brennt, the house is on fire; das Licht brennt dunkel (schlecht), the light burns faintly, dim (blue, &c.); *b)* [illegible] the face, &c.); mir — die Augen, [illegible]; 2) *a)* to scorch, parch (of the [illegible]); *b)* to sting (as nettles); *c)* to burn, heat [illegible]; 3) *fig.* to burn (vor Begier, with [illegible] auf (nach &c.) —, to have an [illegible], to be most eagerly bent [illegible] unter den Sohlen (*Göthe.* [illegible]), the floor burns under my feet. [illegible] *Surg.* [illegible] ich brennte, gebrennt) 1) to burn (lime, tiles, &c.); 2) *Pott.* to bake or fire (pots); 3) to roast (coffee; flour, &c.); 4) to distil, still, to draw by distillation; 5) *Surg.* to cauterise, to sear; 6) to brand (sheep, casks, &c.); Kohlen —, to make charcoal, to char wood; Stahl —, to neal, anneal steel; Planken —, *Ship-b.* to bend planks over fire; eine Geschwulst —, *Vet.* to fire a swelling (of a horse); das Haar —, to curl the hair; zu Asche —, to reduce to ashes or cinders; am hellen Tage Licht —, to burn day-light; ein Schiff —, *Mar.* to bream a ship; der Sod brennt mich, I have the heart-burn; sich rein or weiß — wollen, to endeavour or attempt to exculpate one's self.

Bren'nen, *v. s. (str.) n.* 1) (the act of) burning, &c., ignition; 2) distillation; 3) *Surg.* cauterisation, searing; 4) smart (caused by burning); — im Magen, heart-burn.

Bren'nend, *p. a.* 1) burning, &c.; on fire; 2) *Med.* caustic, pungent, smart; 3) glowing (eyes, &c.); ardent, fervid, fervent (desire, &c.); intense (heat); eine b-e Wüste, a scorching desert; b-e Farben, glaring colours; b-e Liebe, *Bot.* scarlet lychnis, catchfly (*Lychnis chalcedonica* L.).

Bren'ner, *(str.) m.* 1) burner, &c.; 2) distiller; 3) brick-maker, burner; 4) burner (in lamps, &c.).

Brenn'erde, *(w.) f.* combustible earth, peat.

Brennerei', *(w.) f.* distillery, still-house.

Brenn'..., *in comp.* —fieber, *n. Med.* inflammatory fever; —glas, *n.* burning-glass; —gras, *n. Bot.* a kind of sedge (*Carex pseudocyperus* L.); —hahn, *m. see* Birkhahn; —haus, *n.* 1) distillery; 2) *Iron-w.* casting-house, forge; —helm, *m.* the top of the still; —herd, *m.* refining-furnace (for silver); —holz, *n.* firewood, fuel; —kaffee, *m. Comm.* shop-keeper's coffee; *Pott.-s., &c.* —kapsel, *f.* seggar, sagger; —kästen, *m. pl. T.* coffins; —knecht, *m.* 1) a workman employed in silver-refining or in calcining ores; 2) a brewer's servant; —kolben, *m.* alembic, still, cucurbit; —kraut, *n. Bot.* 1) mullein, woolblade (*Verbascum thapsus* L.); 2) *see* Sumpfhahnenfuß & Waldrebe, brennende; —linie, *f. Phys. Geom.* caustic curve, diacaustic; —linse, *f. Opt.* burning lens; —luft, *f.* inflammable air; —material, *n. see* —stoff, 1; —messer, *n. Vet.* firing-iron; —mittel, *n. Surg.* caustic, cautery; —nessel, *f. Bot.* stinging nettle (*Urtica urens* L.); —ofen, *m.* burning oven; kiln; refining-furnace; —öl, *n.* lamp-oil; —palme, *f. Bot.* caryota (*Caryota urens*); —pfanne, *f.* crucible, melting-pot; —punct, *m. Opt.* focus, focal point; —punct einer krummen Linie, *Geom.* umbilical point; den —punct betreffend, focal; —raum, *m. Phys.* focal space; —silber, *n.* amalgame; —spiegel, *m.* burning-reflector or mirror; —spiegelhitze, *f. Phys.* heat drawn by the focus of a burning-lens; —spitzen, *pl. Bot.* stings, stimuli; —stahl, *m.* steel of cementation, blistered steel; —stahlofen, *m.* converting-furnace; —stoff, *m.* 1) combustible matter, fuel, combustibles; 2) *Chem.* phlogiston; frei von —stoff, dephlogisticated.

Bren'nung, *(w.) f. (l. u.)* the (act of) burning, &c. *cf.* Brennen.

Brenn'..., *in comp.* —weite, *f. Opt.* focal distance; —wurz, *f. Bot.* 1) *see* Seidelbast; 2) *see* Waldrebe, brennende; —zeug, *n.* distilling-tool; —ziegel, *m.* fire-brick.

Bren'schen, *(w.) v. intr. provinc.* to neigh.

Brent'gans, *f. see* Baumgans.

Bren'zeln, *(w.) v. intr.* to smell or taste of burning.

Brenz'lich, *adj.* 1) having a burnt smell or taste; empyreumatic; 2) *Chem. in comp.* pyro ...; b-e Citronensäure, *f.* pyrocitric acid; b-e Holzsäure, *f.* pyroligneous acid; b-e Schleimsäure, *f.* pyromucous acid; —schleimsaures Salz, *n.* pyromucite; —weinsteinsaures Salz, *n.* pyrotartarite.

* **Bresch'e,** *(w.) f. (Fr.) Mil.* breach, gap. — **Bresch'batterie,** *f.* breaching battery.

† **Brest,** *(str.),* **Bres'te,** *(w.) m.,* **Bres'ten,** *(str.) n.* infirmity, &c. (Gebrechen). — **Brest'haft** (Bresthaft), *adj.* broken (Gebrechlich); maimed; invalid.

Brett [*in N. G.* brêt (*MHG. & OHG.* bret), *& according to this pronunciation, sometimes spelt* Brett], *s.* I. *(str., pl.* B-er) *n.* 1) board, plank; 2) (Regal) shelf; 3) (Zähl—) counting-board; abacus; auf einem — bezahlen, to pay down at once; 4) draught-board, a pair of tables; mit B-ern belegen, to board, to plank; *coll.-s.* ein — vor'm Kopf haben, to be very stupid; ans — kommen, to be raised to a place of distinction; hoch am B-e sitzen, to be high in authority, to have great influence; bei Jemand einen Stein im B-e haben, to be in favour with one; II. *in comp.* —baum, *m.* tree fit for boards and planks; —beute, *f. see* Bienenkasten.

Bret'erdach, *(str., pl.* B-dächer) *n.* board-roof, roof of planks. [mäßig.

Bret'erhaft, *adj. (Göthe) fac. for* Bühnen-

Bret'ermühle, *f.,* **Bret'ernägel,** *m. see* Bretmühle, Bretnagel. [boarded (floor, &c.).

Bret'ern, *adj.* (made) of boards or planks;

Bret'ern, *(w.) v. tr. (l. u.)* to board, plank.

Bret'er..., *in comp.* —planke, *f.* boarding; —verschlag, *m.,* —wand, *f.* partition (of boards).

Bret'..., *in comp.* —geige, *f.* small pocket fiddle; kit; —holz, *n.* plank-timber; —meister, *m. Shoe-m.* cutter-out; —mühle, *f.* saw-mill; —nagel, *m.* board nail, plank nail; —säge, *f.* plank-saw, pit-saw, whip-saw; —schneider, *m.* sawyer; —spiel, *n.* 1) game at tables, as draughts; 2) (das Damen—) draught-board, (a pair of) tables, draughts; —stein, *m.* man (at draughts).

Brett, Bret'tern *rc., (N. G.,* tt *marking the original short pronunc. of the* e; *Luther's* bret, *pl.* bretter) *see* Bret, Bretern *rc.*

Bret'wand, *(w.) f. see* Bretterwand.

Breu'hahn, *see* Breihahn.

* **Bre've,** *(str., pl.* B-s) *n. (Lat.)* 1) *Mus.* breve; 2) apostolical brief. — **Brevier',** *(str.) n.* breviary.

Bre'zel, *(w.) f.* 1) *Bak.* cracknel; clap-bread; 2) *burl.* a pair of handcuffs, darbies.

Bric'ke, *(w.) f.* 1) *Ichth.* river-lamprey, *see* Neunauge; 2) a round mat (for the table); 3) a round wooden plate; B-nkäse, *m.* a small cheese (made in Holland).

Brief, *s.* I. *(str.) m.* 1) letter, epistle; 2) written document, paper; 3) *Comm.* bill of exchange, draught; (im Coursblatt) paper, bills, letter; sellers; offered; von London (*i. e.* Wechseln auf L.) war mehr — als Geld, on L. there were more offers than demands; 4) a paper folded like a letter; ein — Nadeln, a paper of pins; ein — Tabak, a packet of tobacco; unter — und Siegel, under hand and seal; ein eiserner —, *Law,* letter of respite; II. *in comp.* —adel, *m.* patent nobility; —annahme, *f.* 1) reception of letters; 2) (—annahmestelle, —aufgabe, *f.*) collection of letters; receiving house; —ausgabe, *f.* postal delivery; —beschwerer, letter (or note) presser, paper-weight; —beutel, *m.* letter or mail-bag; —bote, *m.* letter-carrier (bearer); —buch, *n.* letter-book. [letter, note, billet.

Brief'chen, *(str.) n. (dimin. of* Brief) little

Brief'..., *in comp.* —cirkel, *m.* close-compasses; —copie, *f.* copy of a letter, (gebrauchte) press copy of a letter; —copierbuch, *n.* letter copy-book; —cours, *m. Comm.* rate of stock offered; —couvert, *n. see* —umschlag; —einwurf, *m.* letter-box; —fach, *n.* pigeon-hole; —felleisen, *n.* mail; budget; —geheimniß, *n.* inviolability of letters conveyed by post; —

Brod, see Brot.

Bro'deln, (w.) v. intr. to bubble.

Bro'del, Bro'dem, Bro'den, (str.) m. steam, vapour, exhalation: Min. foul air.

Bro'deln, (w.) v. intr. Min. for Verdunsten, Verwittern.

Bro'den ..., in comp. -ritze, f. orifice at the top of a bee-hive; -röhre, f. ventilator.

Brod'ling, (str.) m. servant, menial; provincial baker.

Bro'dung, (w.) f. a baking (quantity of bread required).

Brohk, (str.) m. Mar. 1) (rudder-)coat; 2) a large span (used in dock-yards to haul a ship up): 3) — einer Kanone, breeching of a cannon; -stück, n. Ship-carp. lower transom.

Broi'han, see Breihahn.

* Brom, (str.) n. Chem. brome.

Brom'beerbusch, m. see -staude. [berry.

Brom'beere, (w.) f. blackberry, bramble-

Brom'beer ..., in comp. -falter, m. Entom. green butterfly (Papilio rubi L.); -gesträuch, n. brambles, brake; -hecke, f. briery; -staude, f., -strauch, m. Bot. bramble, blackberry-bush, briar (Rubus fruticosus L.).

Brom' ..., in comp. -benzin, n. bromic benzole; -gold, n. bromide of gold; -kalium, n. bromide (of potassium); -säure, f. bromic acid; -wasserstoffsäure, f. hydrobromic acid.

* Bronchial', adj. (Gr.) Med. bronchial (artery, respiration, &c.). — Bron'chien, pl. Anat. bronchia. — Bronchi'tis, f. Med. bronchitis.

* Bron'ze, Bron'ce (pr. brŏng'se), (w.) f. (Fr.) bronze, brass; -farbe, f. brass colour; -metall zu Statuen, n. statue metal, bronze metal. — Bron'zen, adj. of bronze, bronzed. — Bron'ze ..., in comp. -statue, f. bronze-statue; -waaren, f. pl. bronze-articles. — Bronzi'ren, Bronci'ren [brŏngsee'ren], (w.) v. tr. to paint the colour of bronze; to bronze, bronzing; bronzirt, bronzed, bronze-gilt. — Bronzir' ..., in comp. -pulver, n. bronze powder; -vergoldung, f. wash-gilding, water-gilding. — Bronzist' [brŏngsist'], (w.) m. bronzer.

* Bronzit', (str.) m. Miner. bronzite, schiller-spar.

Brook, see Brohk.

Bro'same, (w.) f. crumb.

Brös'chen, (str.) n. sweetbread (of calves and lambs).

* Broschi'ren, (w.) v. tr. 1) to stitch, sew; 2) Manuf. to weave flowers into ..., to figure; broschirt, adj. Bookb. stitched, in boards; wrought; broschirter Flor, flowery or figured gauze; broschirte Zeuge, pl. brocaded stuff.

Broschü're, (w.) f. brochure, pamphlet, stitched book; B-nschreiber, m. pamphleteer.

Brö'selein, (str.) n. (dimin. of Brosame; [illegible]) small crumb or particle (Göthe, Faust, II, 2, Class. Walp.).

Brö'seln, (w.) v. tr. & intr. to crumb, crumble.

Bros'ling, (str.) m. provinc. white straw-berry. [Sprosse.

Brost, (str.) m., Bros'se, (w.) f. see Knospe,

Bros'sen, (w.) v. intr. see Sprossen.

Brot, (str.) n. 1) bread; ein (Laib) —, a loaf (of bread); 2) ein — Zucker, a loaf of sugar; 3) fig. bread, living, livelihood, competency, subsistence, employment; work; das tägliche —, daily bread, staff of life; standing dish; sein — haben, to enjoy a competency; Einen um sein — bringen, to deprive one of his livelihood, to take away one's bread; coll. e. für or um das — arbeiten, to labour for subsistence; [illegible] als — essen, he is a sharp fellow, he knows on which side his bread is buttered; [illegible] wie der Wind, die Kunst geht nach [illegible] must-a-begging; sein eigen — essen, to [illegible] own master.

Brot' ..., in comp. -[illegible], n. bread-bas-[illegible] f. table for bread, bread-stall; -baum, m. Bot. jacca-tree, bread-fruit tree (Artocarpus incisa L.); -beutel, m. haversack, feed-bag; -bohrer, m. Entom. bread-mite (Anobium F.); -dieb, m. depriver of livelihood; -erwerb, m. (act of earning a) livelihood, living; als -erwerb, in a professional way; -fresser, m. see -Bohrer; -frucht, f. 1) bread-corn; 2) bread-fruit, see -baum; -gebäck, n. baked bread; ein -gelehrter, m. one who turns to learning for the sake of gaining his subsistence; -gewinner, m. Mar. spanker (sail); -hange, f. hanging shelf to lay loaves on; -herr, m. nourisher, employer; master of a family; entertainer; -käfer, m. Entom. 1) see -Bohrer; 2) a species of beetle (Tenebrio mauritanicus); -kammer, f. pantry; Mar. bread-room; -korb, m. bread-basket; Einem den -korb höher hängen, coll. 1) to narrow one's means of subsistence; 2) to keep one short; -krume, f. crumb of bread; -kümmel, m. caraway-seed, see Kümmel.

Brot'los, adj. 1) breadless, unemployed; — werden, to be thrown out of employment or work; 2) unprofitable.

Brot' ..., in comp. -masse, f. bread-stuff; -meister, m. pantler; -neid, m. fig. (professional envy or) jealousy; -nußbaum, m. Bot. bread-nut tree (Brosimum alicastrum L.); -pflaster, n. poultice; -raspel, f. bread-rasp; -raspler, m. T. bread-chipper; -reibe, f. bread-grater; -rinde, f. crust of bread; -röster, m. bread-toaster; toasting-fork; -scharren, m. baker's shop; -schätzer, -schauer, m. assiser of baker's bread; -schaufel, f. oven-peel; -scheibe, f. 1) see Schaufel; 2) slice of bread; -schnitte, f. slice of bread; -schnittchen, n. chip of bread; -schragen, m. see -hange; -schrank, m. pantry; bread-cupboard; -spende, f. distribution of bread; -studium, n. see -wissenschaft; -suppe, f. soup made of bread; -taxe, f. assize of bread; -teig, m. bread-stuff; -teller, m. bread-plate; -torte, f. bread-tart; -urtheil, n. Archæol. cornmed, need-bread, bread of necessity; -wandlung, f. Rom. Cath. conversion of the bread (in the eucharist) transubstantiation. -wagen, m. Mil. provision- or close-waggon; -wasser, n. toast and water; bread-water; -wissenschaft, f. professional study or career, a science or learning acquired for the sake of gaining a subsistence; -wurzel, f. yam.

* Brouillon' [brŭlyŏng'], (str., pl. B-s) n. (Fr.) 1) waste-book, memorandum; 2) rough-sketch, first draught. [make a horse stop.

Brr! exclamation of terror, or a sign to

Bruch, (str., pl. Brüch'e) m. 1) breach, rupture (also fig. i. e. infringement), cf. Brechen, v. a.; 2) Math. fraction; 3) Surg. a) fracture, breaking; b) (der Gedärme) hernia, burst, rupture; 4) T-s. crack, flaw; blemish (in metallic casts); crease, fold; Brüche bekommen, T. to rub out in the folds; 5) m. & n. moor, marsh, bog, fen; 6) Sport. a) (abgebrochene Zweige) blemish; b) covert in the snow of a covey of partridges; c) sprig with which a huntsman upon shooting a deer, &c. decorates his hat (Loc.); 7) Min. a) a falling in; b) (muschlicher, conchoidal) fracture; c) rubble, fragments; 8) a) (Glas—) see -glas; b) Comm. broken ware; 9) quarry (Steinbruch, &c.); 10) Herald. rebatement; 11) Anc. Law, a) crime; b) penalty, fine (Geldstrafe); 12) (m., f., & n.) trowsers, gener. pl. Brüche, sailor's slops; 13) (eines Hauses) Comm. bankruptcy, failure; zu B-e gehen, Min. to fall or sink down; in die Brüche fallen, kommen, or gerathen, coll. for Verunglücken or Fehlschlagen; zu offenem B-e kommen, fig. to come to an open rupture.

Bruch' ..., in comp. -artig, adj. boggy, fenny, marshy; -band, n., -bandage, f. Surg. (hernia-)truss; hernial bandage; -bandfedern, f. pl. springs for trusses; -beere, f. see Heidelbeere; -binde, f. bandage for a fracture; sling; -blei, n. used lead broken up for melting; -bohnen, f. pl. Comm. brokens, breakage, triage (of coffee); -dach, n. Archit. curved roof; -dorf, n. a village situated in a boggy country; -drossel, f. Ornith. greater reed-sparrow (Turdus arundinaceus L.).

Brüch'e, † Brüch'te, (w.) f. see Bruch, 11.

Bruch' ..., in comp. -einbringung, f. Surg. reduction of a fracture; -eisen, n. (altes Eisen) broken (scrap or bushel) iron.

† Brüch'(t)en, (w.) v. tr. Law. to fine, amerce.

Bruch' ..., in comp. -fällig, adj. 1) Law. fineable; 2) provinc. decaying, ruinous; -fläche, f. interior of the break; -frei, adj. Comm. free from breakage; -glas, n. Glass-w. cullet, broken glass; -gold, n. broken gold; -hafer, m. wild oats.

Bruch'ig, adj. boggy, marshy, swampy.

Brüch'ig, adj. 1) full of breaks, fissures, holes, &c., decayed; 2) brittle, fragile, apt to break; shivery (stone, &c.); short (iron, &c.); unsound (meat, &c.).

Bruch' ..., in comp. -kraut, n. Bot. 1) rupture-wort, burstwort (Herniaria glabra L.); 2) sanicle (Sanicula europaea L.); 3) see Durchwachs & Hauslaub; -kupfer, n. broken copper; -lade, f. Surg. cradle for a fracture; -land, n. marsh; -mandeln, f. pl. see Krachmandeln; -messing, n. old brass; -ort, m. Min. breach; -pflaster, n. hernia-plaster; -rechnung, f. fractional reckoning; -schiene, -schindel, f. Surg. splint; -schlange, f. see Blindschleiche; -schluß, m. Log. enthymeme; -schneider, m. see -arzt; -schnepfe, f. bog-snipe (Beccasine); -silber, n. broken or battered plate; -stein, m. quarry-stone, rag-stone; -steinmauerwerk, n. rubble work, ashlar stone work; -stück, n. fragment; shred; debris; fig. rhapsody; -stückweise, adv. fragmentarily; -theil, m. small fraction, coll. pl. shred ends, dribblets; -vogel, m. see -schnepfe; -wasser, n. bog-water; -weide, f. Bot. willow growing in marshy ground; crack-willow (Salix fragilis L.); -wurz, f. Bot. 1) bone-set, rupture-wort (Herniaria L.); 2) see Odermennig; -zahl, f. fractional number.

* Brucin', (str.) n. Chem. brucine.

Brück'e, (w.) f. 1) bridge; 2) viaduct; 3) scaffolding, see Gerüst; 4) Typ. till, shelf; 5) Metall. fire-bridge; 6) bridge, joint (of a buckle); die — zu ... bilden, fig. to be the stepping-stone towards ...; Einem die — treten (l. u. vertreten), coll. to take one's part.

Brück'en, (w.) v. tr. to bridge (over); to furnish with a bridge.

Brück'en ..., in comp. -bahn, f. bridge-road, carriage-way; -balken, -baum, m. girder, sleeper, pl. string-pieces; -bau, m. 1) the building or erection of a bridge; 2) construction of bridges; art of building bridges, bridge-building; -belag, m. flooring, road-covering of a bridge; -bock, m. trestle; -bogen, m. arch of a bridge, gullet; -boot, n. pontoon; -decke, f. see -belag; -durchlaß, m. cut, opening for the passage of floating bodies; -feld, n. 1) bay of a bridge; 2) aperture of a bridge; -geländer, n. railing of a bridge, parapet; -geld, n. bridge-toll; -glied, n. floating-pier (of a floating bridge); -joch, n. supports or props (pl.) of a timber-bridge; -kahn, m. pontoon; -klappe, f. leaf or flap of a swipe-bridge; -kopf, m. Mil. tête de pont, head of a bridge; -lehne, f. railing of a bridge; -meister, m. 1) superintendent of bridges; 2) collector of the bridge-toll; -pfahl, m. stilt; -pfeiler, m. pier; -pfennig, m. see -geld; -ruthe, f. see -baum; -schanze, f. see -kopf; -schreiber, m. receiver of the bridge-toll; -schwelle, f. curb-beam; -wage, f. patent weigh-(weighing-)machine, (warranted) scale-beam, platform scales, weigh-bridge; -zoll, *m.* bridge-toll: —zolleinnehmer, *m.* receiver of the bridge-toll.

Brü'ckung, *(w.) f.* wooden floor of a stable.

Bru'del, *(str.) m. see* Brodel.

Bru'deln, *(w.) v. intr.* to bubble, wallop.

Bru'der, *(str., pl.* Brü'der*) m.* 1) brother; 2) friar: der dienende —, lay-brother; so viel ist es unter Brüdern werth, *fam.* that's very cheap, it is a bargain; ein lustiger — (— Lustig), a good fellow, a jovial companion, a jolly blade, jolly dog.

Brü'derchen, *(str.) n. (dimin. of* Bruder*)* little brother; *fig.* (dear) fellow.

Brü'dergemeinde, *(w.) f.* the fraternity of the Moravians; United Brethren.

Bru'der..., *in comp.* —kind, *n.* brother's child; —kuchen, *m. Glas.* bull's eye; —kuß, *m.* fraternal kiss. [*poet. for* Brüderchen.

Brü'derlein, *(str.) n. (provinc. [S. G.] &)*

Brü'derlich, I. *adj.* brotherly, fraternal; fellow-like; II. B-keit, *(w.) f.* brotherly feeling or affection, fraternity.

Bru'der..., *in comp.* —liebe, *f.* brotherly love or affection; —mord, *m.*, —mörder, *m.*, —mörderin, *f.* fratricide.

Brü'dern, *(w.) v. tr.* 1) to treat in a brotherly manner; *refl.* to fraternise; 2) *see* Schmarotzen.

Brü'derschaft, *(w.) f.* brotherhood, fraternity, fellow-ship; — machen or schließen *(or* trinken*),* to fraternise (by means of hob-nobbing), *cf.* Anstoßen, I.

Brü'derthum, *(str.) n. see* Brüderschaft.

Brü'he, *(w.) f.* 1) broth; sauce; gravy; soup; 2) *T.* dye; der Wolle die — geben, to smear the wool; 3) *T.* sauce (for tobacco); eine schöne —, *iron.* a pretty pickle, nice mess, &c.

Brü'hen, *(w.) v. tr.* 1) to scald; to dip in boiling water; 2) *Ship-b.* to caulk (Kalfatern).

Brüh'..., *in comp.* —erz, *n. Min.* yellow copper ore; —faß, *n.* scalding tub; —heiß, *adj.* scalding-hot, boiling-hot, smoking-hot; *fig.* (—warm) brannew; —näpfchen, *n.* sauce-boat, butter-boat, saucer; —pfännchen, *n.* saucepan; —wasser, *n.* (boiling) water used for scalding.

Bruhl, *see* Brol. [grown with bushes.

Brühl, *(str.) m.* a marshy place over-

Brui'ne, *(w.) f. Mar.* the lowest side-plank of a flat-bottomed boat.

Brüll, *(str.) m.* roar, roaring.

Brül'len, *(w.) v. intr.* to roar; to bellow, to low; to howl, to bawl.

Brüll'..., *in comp. Zool.-z.* —affe, *m.* howling monkey (*Mycetes*); —frosch, *m.* bull-frog (*Rana boans* L.); —ochse, *m.* bull (Zuchtochse).

Brumm'..., *in comp.* —bär, —bart, *m. fig.* growler, grumbler; —baß, *m.* 1) *fam. for* Baßgeige & Baß; 2) bombarde-pipe (in an organ); —eisen, *n.* 1) jew's-harp, iron-trump, drone; 2) *see* —bär.

Brum'men, *(w.) v. intr. & tr.* 1) to hum (like a beetle, &c.); to growl (like a bear); to bellow, low (like oxen, &c.); to buzz, drone (like insects, &c.); to drone (litanies, &c.), to mumble (prayers, &c.); 2) *fig.* to grumble growl, quarrel, snub: in den Bart —, *fam.* to grumble to one's self; was brummt er wieder? what is he grumbling again?

Brum'mer, *(str.) m.* 1) bull; 2) *fig.* grumbler, growler.

Brumm'..., *in comp.* —fliege *f. Entom.* bluebottle-fly; —hahn, *m. see* Birkhahn. [crose.

Brum'mig, *adj. coll.* grumbling, snarlish,

Brumm'..., *in comp.* —kater, *m.* gib-cat; —kreisel, *m.* fizgig, humming-top: einen — kreisel brummen lassen, to hum a gig *or* top; —ochse, *m.* bull, parish-bull.

* **Brunel'le,** *f. see* Brunelle.

* **Brünett',** *(Fr.)* I. *adj.* 1) brownish, brown; 2) of a dark complexion; II. B-e, *(w.) f.* brunette (*fig.*), a woman of a dark complexion.

Brunft, *(w.) f. Sport.* rut, rutting (of red-game); brim (of wild boars); der Hirsch tritt in or auf die —, the stag is going to rut; die Stute ist in der —, the mare is horsing; in der — sein, to be in the rut, brim; aus der — treten, to cease rutting or brimming; die — vollbringen, to copulate.

Brunf'ten, *(w.) v. intr.* to rut, to brim.

Brunft'..., *in comp.* —geschrei, *n.* sound or call of rutting animals; (von Hasen, Kaninchen) booting; —hirsch, *m.* rutting stag.

Brunf'tig, *adj.* rutting, brimming.

Brunft'..., *in comp.* —plan, —platz, —stand, *m.* rutting-place; —wildpret, *n.* rutting-game; —zeit, *f.* rutting-season, rutting-time.

* **Bruni'ren,** *(w.) v. tr. (Fr.) Mech.* to burnish, to polish.

* **Brunir'...,** *in comp.* —eisen, *n.* burnishing-stick, burnisher; —glättstein, *m.* burnishing-stone; —gold, *n.* burnished gold; —stahl, *m. see* —eisen; —stein, *m.* burnishing-stone; *Miner.* blood-stone, red iron-ore.

Brün'ne, *(w.) f.* (†, or) *, (coat of) mail.

Brun'nen, *(str.) m.* 1) well, spring; pump, pit, fountain; 2) (Gesund—) watering-place; mineralischer —, mineral water (spring); den — brauchen or trinken, to drink the waters, to be at the wells; einen — graben, to dig, to sink a well; Wasser in den — tragen, *proverb. anal.* to throw water into the Thames, to carry coals to Newcastle.

Brun'nen, *(w.) v. tr. T.* to soak (the skins) in the lime-pit.

Brun'nen..., *in comp.* —ader, *f.* vein of a well; —anstalt, *f.* watering-establishment; —arzt, *m.* physician of a watering-place; —äscher, *m. T.* lime-pit; —bau, *m.* 1) the digging of a well; 2) art of sinking wells; —becken, *n.* basin or vase of a fountain; —beschlag, *m.* pump-gear; —bohrer, *m.* auger, scooping-iron (of the well-diggers); —cur, *f.* cure or use of mineral-waters or a natural spring; eine —cur gebrauchen, to use the mineral waters; —dach, *n.* well-house, well-roof; —deckel, *m.* cover of a well; —eimer, *m.* well-bucket; pail; —einfassung, *f.* curb (*cf.* Einfassung), lining of a well; —feger, *m.* well-cleanser; —gast, *m.* visitor of a watering-place; —gebrauch, *m.* use of mineral waters; —geländer, *n.* rail or balustrade of a well; —gräber, *m.* well-digger; —hafen, *m. see* —stange; —haus, *n.* well-house; —kasten, *m.* 1) wooden case of the basin of a fountain; 2) water-cistern; *Bot.-z.* —kraut, *n.* water-liverwort (*Lichen fontanus* L.); —kresse, Brunnkresse, *f.* water-cresses; balsamite (*Sisymbrium nasturtium* L.); —küster, *m. Ornith. see* Baumhacker; —leberkraut, *n. see* —kraut; —loch, *n.* well-hole, mouth of a well, well-pit; —macher, *m.* pump-maker, well-sinker; —mauer, *f.* curb (of a well); —meister, *m.* 1) inspector of the wells and water-works; 2) master of the pump-room; —moos, *n.* water-moss; —ort, *m.* watering-place; —rand, *m.* brim of a well; —räumer, *m. see* —feger; —röhre, *f.* conduit-pipe; —salz, *n.* brine salt; spring-salt; —schrank, *m.* case, covering of a well; —schwengel, *m.* pump-handle, (well-) sweep, brake, swipe, draw-beam of a well; —seil, *n.* well-rope; —stange, *f.* pole of a draw-well; —steine, *m. pl. T.* compass-bricks; —stube, *f.* building raised over wells or water-works; —sumpf, *m.* discharging-trough; —wasser, *n.* spring-water, pump-water, well-water; —zeit, *f.* season (for using the waters); —ziegel, *m. see* —steine.

Brunn'quell, *(str.) m.,* **Brunn'quelle,** *(w.) f.* spring of a well, fountain-head.

Brunst, *(str., pl.* Brünst'e*) f.* 1) (Feuers—) fire, conflagration; *fig.-s.* 2) heat, ardour, fervency; 3) concupiscence, lust; 4) *see* Brunft & *comp.*

[illegible]anlage, *f.* investment; —ausgebot, *n.* capital offered; —bedarf, *n.* want of money.

* **Capitäl'**, *(str., pl.* C-e, *sometimes* C-er) [illegible], *see* Capital, 1, b.

Capitäl'chen, *(str.) n. (dimin. of* Capital) 1) *Bookb.* head-band; 2) *Typ.* (—schrift, *f.*) small capitals; 3) a small capital *or* sum.

* **Capitäl'conto**, *(str., pl.* C-s, *or* C-conti) [illegible], stock-account. [cus.

* **Capitäl'deckplatte**, *(w.) f. Archit.* aba-

* **Capitalisi'ren**, *(w.) v. tr.* to fund, to convert into capital, to capitalise.

* **Capitalist'**, *(w.) m.* moneyed man, fund- *or* stock-holder, capitalist.

* **Capitäl'...**, *in comp.* —krise, *f.* money crisis; —mangel, *m.* scarcity of money; —markt, *m. see* Geldmarkt; —rechnung, *f. see* [illegible]; —schein, *m.* receipt of capital; C-s[illegible] *or* Capitäl(s)trumpf, *m. Archit.* drum *or* corbel of a capital; —steg, *m. Typ.* head-stick; —verbrechen, *n.* felony, forgery; —vermögen, *n.* funded property; —zinsen, *m. pl.* simple *or* common interest; —zufluß, *m.* influx of money.

* **Capitän'** (Capitain' *[pr.* —tän']), *(str., pl.* C-e, *or* C-s) *m. (Fr.)* captain; —eines Kauffahrers, captain, master.

* **Capi'tel**, *(str.) n. (L. Lat.)* 1) chapter (of a book), head; 2) *Eccl.* chapter (of canons); [illegible] das — lesen, *see* Capiteln, 2; — halten, *to* assemble the canons, to hold a chapter; —haus, *n.* chapter-house.

Capi'teln, *(w.) v. tr.* 1) to divide into chapters; 2) *coll.* to read (one) a lecture.

* **Capito'lium**, **Capitol'**, *(str.) n. (Lat.)* capitol. — **Capitoli'nisch**, *adj.* Capitoline.

* **Capitulation'**, *(w.) f. (Mid. Lat.)* capitulation. — **Capituli'ren**, *(w.) v. intr.* to capitulate.

Cap'laken, *pl. Mar.* primage.

Caplan, *see* Capellan.

Capo *(Ital., pr.* kā'pō*)*, *s.* head, beginning: [illegible] da —, from the beginning; da — rufen, *to* encore; — d'astro, — tasto, nut of the finger-board of a violin, &c.

Capot', *adv. (Hebr.)* — gehen, *v. intr.* to go to the dogs, to be ruined.

* **Capot'**, *(str.) m. (Fr.) Gam.* capot; —machen, *(v. tr.)* to capot.

* **Caprice** *[pr.* kaprī's*]*, *(w.) f. (Fr.)* caprice, whim, freak. — **Capricii'ren** *[pr.* ka-[illegible]*]*, *(w.) v.refl.* to take a fancy (auf *[with acc.]*, to); to be obstinate with respect to a thing, to take into one's head.

* **Capriole**, *(w.) f. (Ital.)* caper; trick; —n machen, to caper, to cut capers; *Man.* to [illegible] [*m. see* Verhaftsbefehl.

[illegible]

* **Carbonade**, *(w.) f. (Fr.)* cutlet; carbonado; rasher done on the coals.

* **Carbun'kel**, *(str.) m. (Lat.) see* Karfunkel.

* **Car'cer**, *(str.) n. (coll. m.) (Lat.)* prison (in schools and universities).

* **Cardamo'me**, *(w.) f. (Gr.)* cardamom; amomum *(Amomum cardamomum* L.).

* **Cardinal'**, I. *adj.* cardinal; II. *s. (str., pl.* Cardinä'le) *m. (Lat.) Eccl., &c.* cardinal; III. *in comp.* C-blume, *f. Bot.* cardinal's flower *(Lobelia* L.); —fink, *m. Ornith.* cardinal *(Loxia cardinalis* L.); C-hut, *m.* cardinal's hat *or* cap; C-würde, *f.*, **Cardinalat'**, *(str.) n.* cardinalate, cardinalship; die (vier) —gegenden, *f.*, —puncte, *m. pl.* the four cardinal points; —tugenden, *f. pl. Eth.* the four cardinal virtues; —zahl, *f.*, —zeichen, *n. Arith.* cardinal number.

* **Cardioi'de**, *(w.) f. (Gr.) Geom.* cardioid.

* **Cardobenedic'tenkraut**, *(str.) n. Bot.* blessed *or* holy thistle *(Cnidus benedicta* L.).

* **Caressi'ren**, *(w.) v. tr. (Fr.) see* Liebkosen, Schmeicheln.

* **Caret'te**, **Carett'schildkröte**, *(w.) f. (Fr.) Zool.* tortoise-shell, hawk's bill-turtle *(Chelonia imbricata* L.).

* **Cargadeur'** *[pr.* —dör'*]*, *(str.) m. Comm. (Span.)* supercargo.

* **Caricatur'**, *(w.) f. (Ital.)* caricature. — **Caricir'ren**, *(w.) v. tr.* to caricature.

* **Cariös'**, *adj. Med. (Lat.)* carious, rotten, decayed (tooth, &c.).

* **Cari'ren**, *(w.) v. intr. (Lat.)* to go without (one's meals: punishment in some schools).

Carl &c., *see* Karl &c.

* **Carmesin'**, *(str.) n. (Fr.)* crimson; —roth färben, to crimson.

* **Carmin'**, *(str.) n.* carmine.

* **Car'neval**, *(str.) m. & n. (Ital.)* carnival, shrove-tide.

* **Carniol'**, **Carneol'**, *(str.) m. Miner.* cornelian (stone), carnelian, carneol.

* **Caro'be**, *(w.) f. Comm.* carob.

* **Caroli'ne**, *(w.) f. (Mod. Lat.)* 1) Caroline, Carolina *(P. N.)*; 2) C-n (Caroli'nische Inseln), *pl. Geogr.* Caroline islands; 3) *Bill.* the red ball; die — machen, to make a red hazard.

* **Caros'se**, *(w.) f. (Fr.) see* Carrosse.

* **Carot'te**, *(w.) f. (Fr.)* 1) *for* Möhre, carrot; 2) *Comm.* carrot, carrot-tobacco.

* **Carpolith'**, *(w. & str.) m. (Gr.) Miner.* carpolite.

* **Carragheen'moos**, *(str.) n.* carrag(h)een, carrigeen, Irish moss (Irländisches [Perl-] Moos, *Fucus Caragahen*, getrocknete Äste des *Chondrus polymorphus*), *see* Isländisches Moos.

Carra'risch, *adj.* (of) Carrara: der c-e Marmor (für Bildhauerarbeiten), Carrara (statuary) marble.

* **Carreau'** *[pr.* karō'*]*, *(str., pl.* C-s) *n. (Fr.)* 1) *Gam.* (in cards) diamond; 2) check (in checked stuff).

* **Carrie're**, *(w.) f. (coll. m.) (Fr.)* 1) *Man.* gallop of two beats: in gestreckter —, at full gallop; 2) *fig. see* Laufbahn.

* **Carrio'le**, *(w.) f. (Fr.)* cabriolet.

* **Carrirt'**, *adj. (Fr.: carré)* checked; grob c-e Zeuge, large checks: *cf.* Würfeln, II.

* **Carrousel'**, *(str., pl.* C-s) *n. (Fr.)* 1) *carrousel*; tilt; 2) a merry-go-round, a roundabout (at fairs, &c.).

* **Cartel'**, *(str., pl.* C-s) *n. (Fr.)* cartel, (letter of) defiance, challenge, provocatory; —schiff, *n.* cartel ship.

Cartesia'ner, *(str.) m.*, **Cartesia'nisch**, **Carte'sisch**, *adj.* Cartesian; cartesianische Wirbel, *m. pl.* vortices of Descartes; das cartesianische Teufelchen (Taucher, Männchen), *Phys.* Cartesian devil.

Cartha'go, **Karthagin'en'ser**, *(str.) m.* (C-in, *[w.] f.*) **Cartha'gisch**, **Carthaginien'sisch**, *adj.* Carthaginian.

* **Carthau'se**, *(w.) f. Eccl.* charter-house. — **Carthäu'ser**, *(str.) m. & adj.* Carthusian friar; —kloster, *n. see* Carthause; —nelke, *f. Bot.* carthusian-pink *(Dianthus carthusianorum* L.); —pulver, *n.* Carthusian powder, kermes mineral (artificial sulphuret of mercury).

* **Carti'ren**, *(w.) v. tr.* 1) to map, to make a draft *or* sketch of; 2) *Post.* to enter on the letter-bill. [lum.

* **Cartisa'ne**, *(w.) f. (Fr.) Comm.* vellum-

* **Carton'** *[pr.* kartong'*]*, *(str., pl.* C-s) *m. (Fr.)* 1) *Bookb.* board; paste-board; 2) *Draw. & Paint.* cartoon; 3) *Typ.* cancel; 4) paper-box; 5) a portfolio for prints and drawings. — **Cartona'ge** *[pr.* —ā'zhe*]*, *(w.) f. (Fr.) Bookb.* boarding. — **Carton(n)i'ren**, *(w.) v. tr.* to put *or* bind in boards: carton(n)irt, *p. a.* in boards *(abbr.* boards, *or* bds*)*.

* **Cartouch'e** *[pr.* kartusch'e*]*, *(w.) f. (Fr.) Gunn.* cartouch *(also T.* roll *or* scroll on the cornice of a column, &c.).

* **Carun'kel**, *(w.) f. (Lat.)* 1) *Med.* caruncle; 2) *Bot. see* Samenbrüse.

* **Caryati'de**, *(w.) f. Archit.* caryatid *(from Gr. karyatis*, she that is from Caryæ, in Laconia), *pl.* caryatides (grch.), caryates, supporters. [w.] (Cäsa'ren) cæsar, emperor.

Cä'sar, *(str.) m.* 1) Cæsar *(P. N.)*; 2) *(pl.*

* **Cascaril'le**, *(w.) f. (Span.) Pharm.* cascarilla (bark).

* **Cas'co**, *m. Comm. & Mar. (Span.)* body, hull, hulk; Versicherung auf —, insurance on body, hull, and appurtenances.

* **Casein'**, *(str.) n. Chem.* casein.

* **Casemat'te**, *(w.) f. Mil. (Ital.)* casemate.

* **Caser'ne**, *(w.) f. (Fr.)* barracks *(pl.)*, (n. d.:) casern.

* **Ca'simir**, *(str.) m.* casimere, casimire; cashmere; gepreßt gestreifter —, embossed casimere; gedruckter —, chintz; baumwollener —, casimire-nankeen. [Caspian sea.

Cas'pisch, *adj. Geogr.* Caspian; das c-e Meer,

* **Cas'sa**, *f. (Ital.) see* Casse; per —, for cash; —conto, *n.* cash-account; —geschäft, *n.* ready-money business; dieser Laden macht ein erhebliches —geschäft, this shop does a large business over the counter; —kauf, *m.* money bargain *or* business (in stocks); *cf.* Bar & Casse.

* **Cassaz'**, *pl. Comm.* cossas.

* **Cassation'**, *(w.) f. (L. Lat.)* cassation; 1) annulment; 2) appeal; 3) reversion (of a judgment); C-sgericht(shof), *m.* court of cassation (highest court of appeal in France); C-sgesuch, *n.* plea in abatement; petition of appeal; C-surtheil, *n.* act of cassation.

* **Cas'se**, *(w.) f. (Ital.)* 1) iron-safe, strong-box; 2) cash-office; pay-office; pay-place; receiver's box (Theatercasse &c.); 3) cash, ready money; die — führen, to act as cashier, to keep the cash, to manage the paying-department; bei — sein, to be in cash *or* funds; *coll.* to be flush of money; nicht (recht) bei — sein, to be short of money; to be out of cash, to be low in cash; gegen —, for cash; per — zahlen, to pay in cash *or* in ready money; — machen, to make up the cash-account; in —, 1. (eingegangen) in cash, cashed; 2. (bar vorräthig) in cash.

Cas'sen..., *in comp.* —abschluß, *m.* closing of cash-account; —anweisung, *f.* treasury-bill, exchequer-bill; —beamte, *m.* revenue-officer; —bestand, *m.* clear amount, balance of (in) cash, money remaining in hand; —betrug, *m. see* —diebstahl; —bilanz, *f.* the balancing of the cash: die —bilanz ziehen, to balance the cash; —billet, *n. see* —anweisung; —brouillon (kleine —buch), *n.* petty cash-book; —buch, *n.* cash-book; —bureau, *n.* cash-office; —conto, *n.* cash-account; —defect, —deficit, *m.* deficiency: einen —defect machen, to embezzle the cash; —dieb, *m.* peculator, embezzler; —diebstahl, *m.* peculation, embezzlement; —

[illegible]-)bild; —rolle, *f. Dram.* character-part; —schwäche, *f.* weakness of character or principle; —stärke, *f.* force or strength of character; —zug, *m.* feature, trait or touch of character.

Char'freitag [kar—], *(str.) m.* Good Friday.

* Char'ge [schar'she], *(w.) f.* 1) office, place, employment, post; 2) *Mil.* charge (Angriff). — Chargirschritt [schärshir'—], *(str.) m. see* Sturmschritt.

* Charivari [scha—], *(Fr.; ? charivari) see* Schariwari.

* Charité [schäritě'], *f. (Fr.)* charité, hospital.

* Char'itin, *(w.) f. Gr. Myth.* Charis (one of the Graces, *Gr.* chär'itäs).

* Charlatan [scharlatan], *(str.) m. (Fr.)* charlatan, quack, mountebank. — Charlatanerie', *(w.) f.* charlatanry.

* Charnier' [schärnir'], *(str.) n. (Fr.) T.* hinge, joint; —band, *n.* joint-frame; hinge; —büchse, *f.* jointed box; —eisen, *n.* joint-tool; —feile, *f.* joint-file; —stift, *m.* joint-pin; —zange, *f.* joint-pliers *(pl.).*

* Charpie' [schär—], *f. (Fr.)* lint (Zupfleinwand).

* Char'tepartie [schär—], *see* Certepartie.

Char'woche [kar—], *(w.) f.* passion-week, week before Easter.

* Chassi'ren [schas—], *(w.) v. tr. (Fr.) Danc.* to chassez, to advance and retire.

* Chatul'le [schat—], *(w.) f. (Fr.) see* Schatulle.

Chau'ken, *m. pl.* Chaucians (ancient tribe in Northern Germany between the rivers Ems and Elbe).

* Chaussee' [schossē'], *(w.) f.* turnpike-road, macadamised road, high-road, high-way; —bau, *m.* turnpike engineering; —geld, *n.* turnpike-money *or* -toll; —geld(er)einnehmer, *f.*, —haus, *n.* toll- *or* gate-house; —(geld)einnehmer, *m.* turnpikeman; —inspector, *m.* road-surveyor; —stein, *m.* broken stone.

* Chaussi'ren [schossi'ren], *(w.) v. tr. (Fr.)* to turnpike, macadamise (a road).

* Chef [schef], *(str.) m. (Fr.)* chief, head; *Comm.* chief (partner), head, principal, senior, elder.

* Chelonit', *(w.) m. (Gr.) Pal.* chelonite.

* Chemie', *(w.) f. (Gr.)* chemistry. — Chemika'lien, (chemische Präparate) *n. pl.* chemicals. — Che'miker, *(str.) m.* chemist. — Che'misch, *adj.* chemical.

* Chenil'le [schenil'je], *(w.) f. (Fr.)* chenille (tufted cord of silk, velvet, &c.).

* Che'rub, *(str., pl.* Ch-s *or [Hebr.]* Cherubim) *m.* cherub. — Che'rubim, *m.* 1) *pl. of* Cherub; 2) *(or* Che'rubin, *(w.)) used by Luther, &c. in the sing. as a str. m. for* Cherub.

Cherus'ker, *(str.) m.* Cheruscan (one of the Cherusci *[Lat. pl.]*, a German tribe on the Weser).

* Chica'ne [schi—], *(w.) f. (Fr.)* chicane, chicanery. — Chicani'ren, *(w.) v. tr.* to persecute with malignity *or* chicanery, to harass with malicious tricks.

* Chif'fre, Chiffre [schifr], *(w.) f. (Fr.)* cipher, figure, character; —schrift, *f.* cipher-writing. — Chiffri'ren, *(w.) v. tr.* 1) to cipher; 2) to [illegible].

* Chiliarch', *(w.) m. (Gr.)* chiliarch (commander of a thousand men, &c.).

* Chiliast', *(w.) m. (Gr.) Eccl.* chiliast, [illegible].

* Chimä're, *(w.) f.* 1) *Gr. Myth. & fig.* chimera; 2) [illegible], sea-ape, king of the herrings ([illegible] L.). — Chimä'risch, *adj.* [illegible].

* China, [illegible], *(str.) n.* [illegible] II. *(pl.* Ch-s) *f. (Peruv.) or* [illegible] china, quinquina, Peruvian bark, [illegible]; 2) *or* —baum, *m.* Peruvian [illegible] (*Cinchona officinalis & lancifolia*) [illegible] —extract, *m.* [illegible], *n.* powder [illegible] —säure, *f.* kinic acid; das —saure Salz, *n.* kinate; —wurz(el), *f.* china-root, Chinese smilax (*Smilax china* L.) — Chine'se, *(w.) m.*, Chine'sin, *(w.) f.*, — Chine'sisch, *adj.* Chinese; das ch-e Gras, China grass, cloth grass; das Ch-e Papier, India paper; die ch-e Tusche, India drawing-ink.

* Chinin', *(str.) n. Chem. & Pharm.* quinia, quinine.

* Chini'ren [*pr.* schi—], *(w.) v. tr. (Fr.) Weav.* to cloud, to tabby.

* Chirographär', *(str.) m. (Gr.) Law,* book-creditor.

* Chiromant', *(w.) m. (Gr.)* chiromancer. — Chiromantie', *(w.) f.* chiromancy, palmistry. — Chiroman'tisch, *adj.* chiromantical.

* Chirurg'(us), *(w.) m. (Lat.-Gr.)* 1) surgeon; 2) *Ornith.* spur-wing (*Parra jacana* L.). — Chirurgie', *(w.) f.* surgery. — Chirur'gisch, *adj.* surgical.

* Chlōr [klōr], *(str.) n.*, Chlori'ne, *(w.) f. (Gr.) Chem.* chlorine; —kali, *n.* chlorate of potash; —kalk, *m.* chloride of lime, bleaching powder; —natrium, *n.* chloride of sodium; —säure, *f.* chloric (hyperoxymuriatic) acid; —saures Salz, *n.* chlorate (hyperoxymuriate); —stickstoff, *m.* bichloride of nitrogen. — Chloral'hydrāt, *(str.) n.* hydrate of chloral. — Chlo'rig, *adj. Chem.* chlorous (acid). — Chlorit'schiefer, *(str.) m. Miner.* chlorite slate. — Chloroform', *(str.) n. (Gr. & Lat.) Chem.* chloroform. — Chloroformi'ren, *(w.) v. tr.* to chloroform.

* Chlorophyll', *(str.) n. (Gr.) Bot.* chlorophyl.

* Chocola'de [schol—], *(w.) f. (Span.)* chocolate (Schokolade); Ch-nbaum, *m.* cacao, cocoa-tree (*Theobrōma cacao* L.); C-nwurzel, *f.* *Arachis hypogaea* L.

* Cho'lera [ko—], *(indecl.) f. (Gr.* cholē, gall) *Med.* cholera (Brechruhr). — Chole'riker [ko—], *(str.) m.* a choleric man. — Choleri'ne, *(w.) f. Med.* cholerine (slight attack of cholera). — Chole'risch, *adj.* choleric.

* Chōr [kōr], *s. (Gr.)* I. *(str., pl.* Chö're) *m. & n.* 1) *Mus.* chorus; 2) choir; Arie und —, air and chorus; —! *Mus.* tutti! 3) *Archit.* choir (of a church); II. *in comp.* —altar, *m.* high *or* great altar; —amt, *n.* cathedral service; altar service; —artig, *adj.* choral; —bischof, *m.* suffragan *or* local bishop; —dienst, *m.* choir-service; —einfassung, *f.* choir-screen; —frau, *f.* canoness; —führer, *m.* leader of the chorus; —gang, *m.* aisle; —gesang, *m.* chorus; choral song; song with chorus; anthem; —gewölbe, *n.* niche-vaulting; —glocke, *f.* mass-bell; —hemd, *n.* surplice, alb; —herr, *m.* canon, prebendary; —nische, *f.* apse, tribunal; —orgel, *f.* choir-organ; —pult, *n.* reading-desk; —rock, *m.* cope, vestment; —sänger, *m.* chorus-singer; member of the choir; (—schüler, *m.*) chorister; —schwester, *f.* female chorister; —stuhl, *m.* stall; —stunden, *f. pl.* canonical hours.

* Choral' [ko—], *m. (Med. Lat.) (str., pl.* Chorä'le) choral song; plain song; psalm-tune. — Choralist', *(w.) m.* choral singer; chorister. — Choral'mäßig, *adj.* in the style of a psalm-tune.

* Chor'de [kor—], *(w.) f. (Gr.)* 1) *Math. & Mus.* chord; 2) *Med.* chordee; Chordotangentenwinkel, *m. Math.* angle of deflection.

* Chorist', *(w.) m.* chorister.

* Chri'sam [kri—], *(str.) m. & n. (Gr.) Eccl.* chrism.

Christ [krist], *s. (Gr.)* I. 1) *(str.) m.* Christ; 2) *(w.) m.* Christian; der heilige —, *coll.* 1. Christmas; 2. *see* —geschenk; II. *in comp.* —abend, *m.* Christmas-eve; —auge, *f.* 1) bearded hawk's-weed (*Thrincia hirta* L.); 2) a species of starwort (*Aster amellus* L.); —ausstellung, *f.* Christmas-show; —baum, *m.* Christmas-tree; —beere, *f. see* Stachelbeere; —birn, *f.* christian pear; —dorn, *m. Bot.* 1) christ-thorn (*Rhamnus paliurus* L.); 2) *see* Stechpalme; 3) *see* Brustbeerbaum; —fest, *n.* Christmas; —geschenk, *n.* Christmas box, gift, *or* present; —kind(lein), *n.* infant Jesus Christ; the child Jesus, the Child-Christ; —messe, —mette, *f.* Christmas-matins; —monat, *m.* December; —nacht, *f.* Christmas-night; —palme, *f. see* Wunderbaum; —palmöl, *n.* castor oil; —rose, *f. see* —wurz, 1; —tag, *m.* Christmas-day; —vogel, *m. see* Kreuzschnabel; —wurz, *f. Bot.* 1) winter aconite, black hellebore, Christmas rose (*Helleborus hiemalis & niger* L.); 2) wolf's bane, aconite (*Aconitum* L.).

Chris'tel, *m. & f. abbr. for* Christian & Christiane.

Chris'teln, *(w.) v. intr.* to affect a Christian bearing.

Chris'ten..., *in comp.* —feind, *m.* antichristian; —heer, *n.* Christian host *or* army.

Chris'tenheit, *(w.) f.* Christendom.

Chris'tenpflicht, *(w.) f.* a Christian's duty.

Chris'tenthum, *(str.) n.* Christianity, Christendom.

Chris'tian, *m.* Christian *(P. N.).* — Christia'na (Christia'ne), *f.* Christiana *(P. N.).*

Chris'tin, *(w.) f.* Christian woman.

Christi'nenkraut, *(str.) n. see* Flöhkraut.

Christ'lich, I. *adj.* Christian; II. Ch-keit, *(w.) f.* Christianity, Christian character, nature, &c.

Christ'oph, *m.* Christopher *(P. N.)*; Ch-skraut, *n. Bot.* 1) herb christopher; baneberry (*Actaea spicata* L.); 2) common vetch (*Vicia sativa* L.); St. —, St. Kits (a Westindian island).

* Chris'tus, *(indecl. or with the Lat. terminations: Gen.* Christi; *Dat.* Christo; *Acc.* Christum; *Voc.* Christe; *pl.* Christi) *m.* Christ; die Wahrheit in Christo, the truth as it is in Jesus; um — *or* Christi willen, *(exclamation)* for Christ's sake; —fisch, *m. Ichth.* common sun-fish, John Dory (*Zeus faber* L.).

* Chrōm [krōm], *(str.) n. (Gr.) Chem.* chrome; —eisenstein, *m.*, —erz, *n.* chrome-iron ore; *Chem.-s.* —säure, *f.* chromic acid; das —saure Salz, chromate; —saures Blei, Kali &c., chromate of lead, of potash, &c. — Chroma'tik, *f.* chromatic, science of colour. — Chroma'tisch, *adj. Mus. & Phys.* chromatic; semitonic.

* Chro'nik [kro—], *(w.) f. (Gr.)* chronicle; Ch-enschreiber, Chronist', *(w.) m.* chronicler; annalist. — Chro'nisch, *adj. Med.* chronic(al). — Chronogramm', *(str.) n. (Gr.)* chronogram. — Chronolog', *(w.) m.* chronologist, chronologer. — Chronologie', *(w.) f.* chronology. — Chronolo'gisch, *adj.* chronological. — Chronome'ter, *(str.) n. & m.* time-keeper, chronometer.

* Chrysoberyll' [kri—], *(str.) m. (Gr.* chrysós, gold) *Miner.* chrysoberyl, cymophane. — Chrysolith', *(str.) m. Miner.* chrysolite. — Chrysoprās, *(str.) m. Miner.* chrysoprasus, prase.

Chūr, *see* Kur.

* Chy'lus, *(indecl.) m. (Gr.) Physiol.* chyle.

† Chymie' &c., *see* Chemie &c.

* Cibe'be, *(w.) f. (Ital.* zibibbo, *from Ar.* cibib) a large kind of raisin.

* Cibo'rium, *(str., pl. (w.)* Cibo'rien) *n. (Lat.) Eccl.* ciborium.

* Cica'de, *(w.) f. Entom.* cicada, grasshopper.

Ci'ceroschrift), *f. Typ.* (die große, grobe) pica; (die kleine) small pica.

* Cic(h)o'rie, *(w.) f. (Lat.) Bot.* succory, chiccory, wild endive (*Cichorium intybus* L.).

* Ci'der, *m. (Fr.) Husb.* cider (Apfelwein).

* Cigar're, *(w.) f. (Span.)* cigar, segar; C-nanzünder, *m.* cigar-light, fusee; C-neinlage, *f.* filler; C-netui, C-nfutteral, *n.*, C-ntasche, *f.* cigar-case; C-nkiste, *f.* cigar-case; C-nkistchen, *n.* cigar-box; C-nmachen, *n.* cigar-twisting; C-nmacher, *m.* cigar-twister; C-nspitze, *f.* 1) (Kopf) cigar-tip; 2) (Mundstück) cigar-tube, cigar-tip; C-numblatt, *f.* first wrapper.

* Cigarret'te, (w.) f. cigarette, paper-cigar.

* Ciliar', adj. (Lat.) Anat. ciliary (process, body, &c.).

Cim'ber, (w.), Cim'brer, (str.) m., Cim'brisch, adj. Cimbrian.

Cimme'risch, adj. Cimmerian.

* Cir'ca, (Lat.) adv. about, nearly.

Circas'sien, (str.) n. Geogr. Circassia.

Circas'sier, (str.) m., Circas'sierin, (w.) f., Circas'sisch, adj. Circassian.

* Circen'sisch, adj. Rom. Ant. Circensian.

* Circular', (str.) n. (Mod. Lat.) circular (Rundschreiben); —schreiben, n. circular letter. — Circulation' (w.) f. circulation, cf. Kreislauf & Umlauf; c-sfähig, adj. valid; C-smittel, n. medium of circulation. — Circuli'ren, (w.) v. intr. to circulate, run; c-der Decimalbruch, m. circulating or recurring decimal; — lassen, to send round.

* Cir'kel, (str.) m. (Lat.) 1) Geom., &c. circle, cf. Kreis; feine —, pl. polite assemblies; 2) (a pair of) compasses; II. in comp. —abschnitt, m. Geom. segment; —ausschnitt, m. Geom. sector; —baum, m. Bot. bitter oak, European nettle tree; —bewegung, f. circular motion; —binde, f. Surg. circular bandage; —bogen, m. Geom. part of a circular line; arc; —brief, m. (l. u. for Circular) circular letter.

* Cir'kelchen, (str.) n. (dimin. of Cirkel) 1) circlet; 2) (a pair of) small compasses.

* Cir'kel..., in comp. —figur, f. circle, orb; —fläche, f. surface surrounded by a circle; —förmig, adj. circular; —gestalt, f. circular form; —instrumente, n. pl. circular instruments; —lauf, m. circular run, circulation (Kreislauf); —linie, f. circular line.

* Cir'keln, (w.) v. tr. & intr. &c. see Zirkeln &c.

* Cir'kel..., in comp. —punct, m. centre (of a circle); —rund, adj. circular; —ründe, f. circularity; —schlüssel, m. a key or instrument to tighten or loosen compasses; —säge, f. compass-saw, see Kreissäge; —schmidt, m. compass-smith; —spitze, f. point of compasses; —tanz, m. circular dance; rotation; —vierung, f. quadrature of the circle; —zahl, f. circular number.

* Cis, n. Mus. C sharp; Cisis, C double sharp; —dur, n. C sharp major; —moll, n. C sharp minor.

* Cisalpi'nisch, adj. Geogr. (Lat.) cisalpine.

* Ciseli'ren, (w.) v. tr. (Fr.) T. to chase (metals), enchase. — Ciselir'arbeit, f. enchased work.

* Cissoi'de, (w.) f. (Gr.) Geom. cissoid.

Cis'ten..., in comp. —röschen, n., —rose, f. Bot. holly rose, sea sun-flower (Helianthemum vulgäre L.); —saft, m. hypocist.

* Cistercien'ser, (str.) m. Eccl. Cistercian monk.

* Cister'ne, (w.) f. (Lat.) cistern; Heißwasser —, f. Mech. hot-well.

* Citadel'le, (w.) f. (Fr.) citadel; strong tower or fortress.

* Citat', (str.) n. (Lat.) citation, quotation, passage quoted. — Citation', (w.) f. (Mod. Lat.) 1) citation, summons; 2) (schriftliche) citatory-letter.

* Cithe'er, (w.) f. (Lat.) cithern.

* Citi'ren, (w.) v. tr. (Lat.) 1) to cite, summon; vor Gericht —, or — lassen, to serve one with a summons, to serve notice or summons upon (one); 2) to call up, conjure up (a ghost); 3) to cite, quote (a passage, &c.). — Citir'zettel, (str.) m. summons.

* Citrat', (str.) n. Chem. citrate. — Citrin', (str.) m. Miner. sprig crystal. — Citrin'chen, (str.) n. (dimin. of Citri'nat), Citronel'le, (w.) f. see Citronensaft. — Citronat', (str.) n. & m. candied citron. — Citro'ne, (w.) f. (Fr.-Gr.) lemon, citron.

* Citro'nen..., in comp. —äther, m. Chem. citric ether; —baum, m. Bot. lemon-tree (Citrus medica L.); —brot, n. lemon-biscuit; —farbig, —gelb, adj. lemon-coloured, citrine; —fink, m. Ornith. tarin, citril-finch (Fringilla citrinella L.); —holz, n. candle-wood; —kraut, n., —melisse, f. Bot. 1) common balm (Melissa officinalis L.); 2) dragon's head (Dracocephalum Canariense L.); 3) see Eberreis; —minze, f. common mint; —myrte, f. lemon leaved pimento; —öl, n. oil of citron; —presse, —quetsche, f. lemon squeezers; —riper, m. lemon-races; —saft, m. lemon-juice; Chem-c. —säure, f. citric or lemon acid; —saures Eisen-Ammonium, n. ammonia-citrate of iron; das —saure Salz, n. citrate; —schale, f. lemon-peel; —schnepfe, f. a species of curlew (Numenius variabilis Bechst.); —sieb, n. lemon-strainer; —speise, f. mould of lemon-juice; —stecher, m. lemon-scoop; —thymian, m. common or garden-thyme; —vogel, m. Entom. brimstone butterfly (Colias rhamni Fabr.); —wasser, n. citron-water, lemonade; —weinstein, m. citrate of potassa; —zeisig, m. see —fink.

* Citrul'le, (w.) f. (Fr.) Bot. water-melon (Wassermelone).

* Civil', I. adj. (Lat.) 1) civil; 2) moderate, reasonable (price); II. (str.) n. see Bürgerstand; III. in comp. —acten, pl. Law, proceedings in a civil case; —anspruch, m. claim founded on civil law; —ehe, f. civil marriage; —etat, m. home-budget (opp. Militäretat); —gericht, n. civil tribunal; —gerichtsbarkeit, f. civil jurisdiction (opp. Militärgerichtsbarkeit); —gerichtshof, m. court of common pleas; —gesetzbuch, n. code of civil procedure; —ingenieur, m. civil engineer.

* Civilisation', (w.) f. (Fr.) civilisation. — Civilisi'ren, (w.) v. tr. to cultivate, civilise.

* Civilist', (w.) m. civilian; citizen (opp. Soldat). — Civilis'tisch, adj. see Staatswissenschaftlich.

* Civil'..., in comp. —klage, f. civil action or suit; —kleidung, f. civilian's dress; in —kleidung (coll. in —), in plain clothes; coll. in mufti; —liste, f. Law. civil list; —obrigkeit, f. civil magistrate; —proceß, m. civil suit; —punct, m. see —anspruch; —recht, n. civil law; —sache, f. see —klage; —stand, m. see Bürgerstand; —standsbeamte, m. registrar; (der höchste) registrar general.

* Clarin', (str.) n. (Ital.) Mus. clarion.

* Clarinet'te, (w.) f. (Ital.) Mus. clarionet; clarinet; C-nblätter, n. pl. clarionet reeds; C-nspieler, Clarinettist', (w.) m. a performer on the clarionet, clarionet-player.

* Clari'ren, (w.) v. tr. Comm. (Lat.) to clear out at the custom-house. — Clari'rer, (str.) m. Comm. see Schiffsmäkler.

* Clari'rung, (w.) f. Comm. clearance; C-sbrief, m., C-smanifest, n., C-sschein, m. clearing-manifest; C-sspesen, f. pl. clearance charges at the custom-house.

* Clas'se, (w.) f. (Lat.) class, rank, order, division; erster —, fig. first-rate; C-nlehrer, m. principal teacher of a school-class. — Classifici'ren, (w.) v. tr. to classify; das — r. s. (str.) n. der Gläubiger, ranking of creditors. — Clas'siker, (str.) m. (Lat.) classic. — Clas'sisch, adj. classic, classical.

Claus, m. abbr. for Nicolaus, Nick (P. N.).

* Clau'sel, (w.) f. (Lat.) 1) clause, condition; stipulation; 2) see Klausel.

* Clausur', (w.) f. (Lat.) 1) the being confined or shut up; 2) T. clasp.

* Claviatur', (w.) f. (Mod. Lat.) Mus. keyboard (the keys of a piano or organ, cf. Manual). — Clavichord', (str.) n. clavichord.

* Clavier', (str.) n. (Fr., from Lat. clavis, key) Mus. 1) see Claviatur; 2) pianoforte (formerly: clavichord; harpsichord); II. in comp. —auszug, m. musical composition arranged for execution on the piano; —brett,

* Coke [pr. [illegible]], vgl. Coak, (str.) m. coke; [illegible]-verei, f., —ofen, m. coking kiln or oven.
* [illegible]optere, Coleop'tera (Gr. koleop'-[illegible]), (str.) n. pl. Entom. coleoptera, beetles.
[illegible], (str.) m. (Lat.) 1) Celestin(e) [illegible]; 2) Miner. celestin(e), native sulphate [illegible]. — Cölesti'ner, (str.) m. Eccl. [illegible](e) (monk).
* [illegible], (str.) m. (& n.) see Cölibat.
* [illegible], (w.) f. (Lat.) collation (of [illegible]scripts, &c.; also a repast between meals). [illegible]ren, (w.) v. tr. to collate, com[pare]; to check; Typ. to prick (the sheets).
* [illegible], (w.) f. (Lat.) collation.
* Collecta'neen (Lat. collectanĕa), (w.) pl. collectaneous notes; —buch, n. common[place]-book.
* Collec'te, (w.) f. (Lat.) 1) (particul. [church]-) collection; 2) collect, chant of the [priest] before the altar or at burials. — Col[lecti]'ren, (w.) v. tr. to collect. — Collectiv', adj. Gramm. collective; —(handels)ge[sellschaft], f. joint-trade, copartnership: —[gesell]schafter, m. copartner; der in der Firma [genannte], ordinary partner; II. (or [Lat.] [Collectiv]um [str., pl. Collecti've], —wort) [(str.)] n. Gramm. collective noun.
* [illegible], (str.) n. (Lat.) coll. for Colle[gium]. — Colle'ge, (w.) f. colleague, associate, [illegible]. — Collegial', adj. collegial, colle[giate]; —kirche, f. collegiate-church. — Colle[gia'lisch], adj. colleague-like, fellow-like. — [Co]llegialität', (w.) f. fellow-feeling of col[leagues]. — Collegiat', (w.) m. collegian, col[legiate]; —kirche, f. see Collegialkirche. — Col[legia]ntur', (w.) f. fellowship. — Colle'gium, [(str.)], pl. [Lat.] Colle'gia, [Germ.] Colle'gien) 1) college; hall, house in a university; 2) [illegible]; 3) board, commission; — lesen, to [give] lectures, to lecture; ein — belegen, to [subscribe] to a course of lectures; ein — hören, [to] attend (a course of) lectures; Colle'gien[illegible], m. fellow-collegian.
* Collet, (str., pl. C-e or C-s) n., Col[le]'tte, (w.) f. (Fr.) collar; (buff-)jerkin; [illegible] —flicken, coll. to lace or trim a [person]'s jacket, to thrash one soundly, &c.
* [Collidi]'ren, (w.) v. intr. (Lat.) to collide.
* Collier [kolyé'], (str., pl. C-s) n. (Fr.) [illegible].
* [Collir]en, (w.) v. tr. (Fr. coller) Bill. to [play] (the ball) close against the cushion; to [gi]ve a close ball.
* [Collision], (w.) f. (Lat.) collision.
[Cöln], n. (Lat. Colonia) Geogr. Cologne. [Cöl']nisch, adj. Cologne; das c-e Wasser, eau [de] Cologne; die c-e Erde, Cologne earth.
* [Collo], (str., pl. [Ital.] Col'li) n. (Ital.) [illegible] bale, package, parcel of goods.
* [illegible], (str.) n. (Lat.-Gr.) Chem. [illegible].
[Colonial'], I. adj. (Lat.) colonial; II. in [comp.] —amt, n. colonial office; —handel, m. [trade] with colonial goods; —minister, m. mi[nister] for the colonial affairs; —waaren, f., [illegible], pl. Comm. colonial produce; [illegible], m. dealer in colonial goods, [illegible]; —zucker, m. colonial sugar.
[illegible], (w.) f. (Lat.) colony; settle[ment] [illegible] m. Comm. plantation trade. [illegible], (w.) v. tr. to colonize. — [illegible], (w.) f. colonization. — Co[illegible] m. colonist, planter, settler. — [illegible] (w.) f. (Fr.) colonnade. — Co[illegible] f. (Fr.) column, line; [illegible] [illegible] freeds.
[illegible] (Gr. [illegible]) [illegible] [illegible] [illegible] to [illegible].

— Colorist', (w.) m. T. colourist. — Colorit', (str.) n. (Ital.) T. colouring.
* Coloß', (str.) m. (Gr.) colossus. — Colossal', coll. Colossa'lisch, adj. colossal, huge.
* Colporta'ge [—tā'zhe], (w.) f. (Fr.) (the act of) hawking, peddling, colportage. — Colporteur' [—tör'], (str.) m. (Fr.) newsman, news-vender; itinerant tradesman, hawker, colporter, canvasser. — Colporti'ren, (w.) v. tr. to hawk about.
Colum'bien, n. Geogr. Columbia. — Colum'bier, (str.) m., Colum'bisch, adj. Columbian.
* Columbit', (str.) m. Miner. columbite.
* Colum'ne, I. (w.) f. (Lat.) Typ. column; page; die gerade —, even page (as, 2, 4, 6, &c.); die ungerade —, odd page (as, 1, 3, 5, &c.); II. in comp. C-nmaß, n. scale, rule; C-nschnur, f. page-cord; C-nsteg, m. reglet; C-ntitel, m. running-title, head-line, heading; C-nträger, m., bearer; c-nweise, adv. in columns.
* Comba'bus, m. Combabus (an Assyrian [Gr. Kombabos], subject of the king Antiochus Soter) who emasculated himself: hence Combab', (w.) m. a castrated man, eunuch.
* Combär', (str., pl. C-s) n. & m. Mar. coverlet. [boose.
* Combü'se, (w.) f. Mar. caboose, cam-
* Combini'ren, (w.) v. tr. (Lat.) to combine. — Combination', (w.) f. combination; C-sschloß, n. Lock-sm. combination-lock.
* Comität', (str.) n. (Lat.) 1) Germ. Archæol. see Gefolgschaft; 2) escort, &c., see Begleitung; 3) a county or district (in Hungary — Gespannschaft). [comitia.
* Comi'tien, (w.) n. pl. (Lat.) Rom. Ant.
* Commandant', (w.) m. (Fr.) commander. — Commandantur', (w.) f. house and office of a commander. — Commandi'ren, (w.) v. tr. (Fr.) to command; commandirt, p. a. Mil. under command.
* Commanditär', (str.) m. (Fr.) Comm. limited partner, limited liability share-holder. — Commandi'te, (w.) f. Comm. (Fr.) 1) commandita, limited liability company; 2) branch (house or establishment); 3) dormant partnership: C-ncapital or C-ngeld, n. capital in commendam; C-ngesellschaft, Commandit'gesellschaft, f. company in commandite, limited partnership.
* Commanditist', (w.) m. see Commanditär.
* Comman'do, (str., pl. C-s) n. (Span.) 1) command, a) order, cf. —wort; b) authority; das — wurde dem General genommen, the general was deprived of his command; 2) a detachment (of soldiers, &c.), command; —pfeife, f. Mar. boatswain's call; —stab, m. baton, truncheon (of command); —wort, n. word (of command). [in) commendam.
* Commen'de, (w.) f. (L. Lat.) (benefice
* Comment [comāng'], (str., pl. C-s) m. (Fr.) Stud. slang, custom and use (among students).
* Commentar', (str.) m. (Lat.) commentary. — Commenta'tor, (str., pl. [w.] Commentato'ren) m. commentator, expositor. — Commenti'ren, (w.) v. tr. to make comments on (upon), to write critical notes upon (an author, &c.), to gloss.
* Commerce [comärs', coll. comä'rsh], (str.) m. (Fr.) 1) Stud. slang, (noisy) drinking-bout; 2) vulg. noise. — Commerci'ren, (w.) v. intr. to hold or attend a drinking-bout.
* Commerz', (str.) m. (Lat.) 1) commerce; 2) coll. see Verkehr; —bank, f. commercial bank; —(ien)collegium, n. college of commerce; —(ien)rath, m. counsellor of commerce. — Commerziell', adj. commercial: — betrachtet, from the commercial (mercantile) point of view.
* Commili'to, (str., pl. Commilito'nen) m. (Lat.) &c. (fellow-)student.

* Commis' [komē'], (str., pl. — [pr. komēs']) m. (Fr.) merchant's clerk.
* Commiß'..., (Fr.-Lat.) in comp. —brot, n. ammunition- or regimental-bread, commissary-bread; —hemden, n., —schuhe, m., —strümpfe, m. pl. ammunition- or regulation-shirts, -shoes, -stockings.
* Commissär' (ius) (Med. Lat.), (Fr.:) Commissār', (str.) m. commissary, commissioner; delegate, deputy. — Commissariat', (str.) n. (military) commissariat.
* Commission', (w.) f. (Fr.) 1) a) commission, order; b) see C-sgebühr; 2) board of commissioners, committee, court of delegates: einer — (Dat.) übertragen, to put in commission (the management of an office, &c.).
* Commissionär', Commissionär', (str.) m. (Fr.) commissioner; commission-merchant; agent, (and) consignee.
* Commissions'..., in comp. —artikel, m. pl. goods in commission, consigned goods; —bericht, m. report of a commission; Comm.-s. —buch, n. order-book; —comptoir, n. agency office; —conto, n. account of commissions; —einkauf, m. purchase by commission (order); —gebühr, f. percentage; commission, factorage; —geschäft, n., —handel, m. agency-(commission-)line; —güter, n. pl. see —artikel; —haus, n. commission-business; —lager, n. store of goods in commission; —note, f. memorandum; —rechnung, f. commission-account; —rimesse, —tratte, f. bill protested upon order and for account of a third person; —verkauf, m. sale by commission; —waaren, f. pl. see —artikel; —waarenbuch, n. book of commission; —wechsel, m. see —rimesse; —weise übernehmen, to undertake in commission; —weise vertreiben, to sell by way of commission.
* Committé, (str., [Fr.] pl. C-s) n. & m., Committee', (w.) f. committee.
* Committent', (w.) m. (Lat.) principal, employer, consignor.
* Committi'ren, (w.) v. tr. (Lat.) to commission (Beauftragen). — Committiv', (str.) n. written power of attorney.
* Commo'de, I. adj. (Fr.-Lat.) coll. commodious, indolent; II. (w.) f. (Fr.) chest or set of drawers, mod. commode; III. in comp. C-nbeschläge, pl. mountings for drawers; C-ngriffe, m. pl. drawer-handles; C-nknopf, m. drawer-knob; C-nschloß, n. drawer-lock.
* Communal', I. adj. (Lat.) communal, relating to a community; II. in comp. —garde, f., —gardist, m. see Bürgergarde &c.; —steuer, f. parochial tax.
* Commu'ne, (w.) f. (Fr.) community.
* Communicant', (w.) m. (Lat.) Ch. receiver or partaker (of the Lord's supper), communicant. — Communication', (w.) f. communication; C-sweg, m. parish (country) cross-cut, road between two villages or estates. — Communici'ren, (w.) v. intr. Ch. to communicate, receive the sacrament. — Communion', (w.) f. Ch. communion, sacrament; C-skelch, m. chalice, communion cup.
* Communis'mus, (indecl.) m. (Fr.-Lat.) communism. — Communist', (w.) m., Communi'stisch, adj. communist.
* Compact', I. adj. (Lat.) compact, dense; II. s. (str.) m. Comm. club contract of insurance.
* Compagnie' [kompanī'], (w.) f. (Fr.) 1) Mil., &c. company; 2) Comm. partnership, association; in — gehen, to enter into (or to contract) a partnership; —geschäft, n., —handlung, f. joint business, co-establishment.
* Compagnon' [pr. kompanyong'], (str., pl. C-s) m. (Fr.) Comm. partner, associate.
* Comparativ', (Lat.) adj. & s. (str.) m. Gramm. comparative. — Comparati'visch, adj. comparative (suffix, &c.).

Comparent', (w.) m. (Lat.) Law, appearer, declarant. — **Comparir'ren**, (w.) v. intr. to appear before court. — **Comparitiön'**, (w.) f. appearance in court.

• **Com'paß**, (str.) m. (Nat.) compass; —bügel, m. gimbals (pl.); —cours, m. course by compass; —häuschen, n. box, binnacle (of a compass); —rose, —scheibe, f. card or face of a sea-compass; —striche, m. pl. rhomb-lines, points; —uhr, f. compass-dial.

• **Compendiös'**, **Compendia'risch**, adj. (Lat.) short, concise. — **Compen'dium**, (str., pl. [Lat.] C-dia, [w.] C-dien) n. compendium, text-book.

• **Compensatiön'**, (w.) f. (Lat.) compensation; C-pendel, m. Horol. (chronometer) compensation balance, gridiron pendulum. — **Compensi'ren**, (w.) v. tr. to compensate, to counter-balance.

• **Competent'**, I. adj. (Lat.) competent, qualified: II. s. (w.) m. competitor. — **Competenz'**, (w.) f. Law, competence; — eines Falliten, bankrupt's allowance; —streit, m. concurrence of jurisdiction.

• **Compilatiön'**, (w.) f. (Lat.) compilation. — **Compila'tor**, (str., pl. [w.] Compilato'ren) m. compiler. — **Compili'ren**, (w.) v. tr. (Lat.) to compile.

• **Complement'**, (str.) n. (Lat.) 1) complement; 2) procuration. — **Complementär'**, I. adj. complementary (colours, &c.); II. s. (str.) m. partner in commendam.

• **Complet'**, adj. (Lat.) complete. — **Comple'te**, (w.) f. Cath. Rel. (Lat.) complin, completory. — **Completi'ren**, (w.) v. tr. to complete.

• **Complex'**, (str.) m. (Lat.) aggregate, congeries. — **Complicirt'**, adj. complicate; intricate.

• **Compliment'**, (str.) n. (Fr.) 1) compliment; 2) bow; keine C-e! no compliments! no ceremony! (Einem) ein — machen, 1. to pay (one) a compliment (on); 2. to bow (to one); er macht nicht viele C-e, he does not use much ceremony, he uses no ceremonies (mit, with); wir machen keine C-e mit Ihnen, we make no stranger of you (cf. Umstände).

• **Complott'**, (str.) n. (Fr.) plot, conspiracy.

• **Componi'ren**, (w.) v. tr. (Lat.) to compose, set (to music). — **Componist'**, (w.) m. (musical) composer. — **Compositiön'**, (w.) f. composition (in the fine arts, music, &c.); mixture of metals, &c. — **Compo'situm**, (str., pl. [Lat.] Compo'sita) n. compound (also Gramm.; Zusammensetzung). — **Compost'**, (str.) m. (contr. from the preceding word) Agr. compost. — **Com'pot(t)**, (str., pl. C-s, C-e) n. (Fr.) Cook. compote: 1) stewed fruit; 2) a stew (of fruit); fruit prepared in sirup, &c.; —schüssel, n. dish for stewed fruit.

• **Compreß'**, adj. condensed, &c. see Gedrängt. — **Compres'se**, (w.) f. (Fr.) Surg. compress, bolster, pledget. — **Compressiön'**, (w.) f. (Lat.) compression; C-smaschine, f. condensing engine, coll. condenser; C-spumpe, f. force-pump; C-verband, m. see Compresse. — **Compresso'rium**, (str. [Mod. Lat.], pl. —'rien) n. Surg. compressor. — **Comprimi'ren**, (w.) v. tr. (Lat.) to compress, condense; comprimirt, p. a. compressed or preserved (vegetables).

• **Compromiß'**, (str.) n. (Lat.) Law, compromise; arbitration; arbitrement; —acte, f. bond of arbitration. — **Compromitti'ren**, (w.) v. tr. 1) Comm. to refer to arbitration, to compromise; 2) fig. to compromise, expose, endanger, commit.

• **Comptant'**, adj. see Baar.

• **Comptoir'** (pr. kongtoahr', coll. kontor'), (str.) n. (Fr.) 1) counting-house, office; 2) see Factorei, 2; in comp. —arbeiten, f. pl. duties of a counting-house, routine of office-work; —bedürfnisse, n. pl. stationery goods or ware; —bücher, n. pl. account books; —diener, **Comptoirist'**, (w.) m. 1) clerk in a counting-house, accountant; 2) porter, messenger; errand-boy; —personal, n. assistants; —stunden, f. pl. office-hours; —stuhl, m. (high-) stool; —wissenschaften, f. pl. mercantile knowledge.

• **Comthür'**, (str.) m. Germ. Hist., &c. commander (of an order). — **Comthurei'**, (w.) f. commandery.

• **Concav'**, adj. (Lat.) concave.

• **Concentratiön'**, **Concentri'rung**, (w.) f. (Lat.) concentration; C-sstein, m. Metall. (in gekörntem Zustande) fine metal; (in Blöcken, Blaustein) blue metal. — **Concentri'ren**, (w.) v. tr. (Lat.) to concentrate. — **Concen'trisch**, adj. concentrical.

• **Concept'**, (str.) n. (Lat.) (rough) draught, sketch, minute; Einem das — verrücken, Einen aus dem — bringen, to put one out (of his bias), to puzzle or confuse one; das — verlieren, to be put out, puzzled, confused; —buch, n. sketch-book; —papier, n. ordinary (copy) paper, draft-paper, common writing-paper.

• **Concert'**, (str.) n. (Fr.) concert; —flügel, m. grand piano; —geber, m. one who gives a concert; —horn, n. concert-horn; —meister, m. conductor of a musical band (in a concert); —musik, f. concerted music; —sänger, m. concert-singer; —spieler, m. solo-player; —stück, n. concerted piece. — **Concertist'**, (w.) m. 1) see Concertgeber; 2) one who performs in a concert.

• **Concessiön'**, (w.) f. (Lat.) 1) licence, grant of permission, sanction (f. i. of a line of railway); 2) concession. — **Concessionirt'**, p. a. licensed, privileged.

• **Conchit'**, (w.) m. (Gr.) Pal. fossil shell.

• **Conchoi'de**, (w.) f. (Gr.) Math. conchoid.

• **Conchy'lien**, (w.) f. pl. (Gr.) shells, testaceous animals.

• **Conci'lium**, (str., pl. [Lat.] C-'lia, or (w.) C-lien), **Concil'**, (str.) n. council.

• **Concipi'ren**, (w.) v. tr. (Lat.) to draw up, pen, sketch. — **Concipist'**, **Concipient'**, (w.) m. draft's man, drawer up. [conclave.

• **Concla've**, (str., pl. C-s) n. (Lat.) Eccl.

• **Conclusiön'**, (w.) f. (Lat.) conclusion (Schluß, Schlußfolgerung &c.)

• **Concordanz'**, (w.) f. (Mod. Lat.) concordance. — **Concordat'**, (str.) n. Law, concordat(e). — **Concor'dienformel**, (w.) f. Eccl. form of concord.

• **Concret'**, adj. (Lat.) concrete.

• **Concubinat'**, (str.) n. (Lat.) concubinage. — **Concubi'ne**, (w.) f. concubine.

• **Concurrent'**, (w.) m. (Lat.) competitor; rival. — **Concurrenz'**, (w.) f. 1) concurrence; 2) competition; Einem — machen, see Concurriren; —linie, f. opposition-line (of steamers, &c.); —system, n. competitive system. — **Concurri'ren**, (w.) v. intr. to compete with, to rival (one).

• **Concurs'**, (str.) m. (Lat.) Law, concourse of creditors; in — gerathen, to become (or declare one's self) insolvent or a bankrupt; — anmelden, to make a declaration of insolvency, to file a petition; zum — treiben, to drive into the court of bankruptcy (into the Gazette); den — abwenden, to avoid a meeting of creditors; —behörde, f. commission (in a statute) of bankruptcy; —erklärung, f. declaration of insolvency; —masse, f. a bankrupt's estate, cf. Masse.

• **Condensatiön'**, (w.) f. (Lat.) condensation; in comp. Mech. C-sapparat, m. condensing apparatus; C-sbehälter, f. condensing cistern. — **Condensa'tor**, (str., pl. Condensato'ren) m. Mech. condenser, condensing-vessel. — **Condensi'ren**, (w.) v. tr. to condense.

* **Connossement'** (Connaissement), (str.) (Fr.) Comm. bill of lading, letter of consignment.

* **Conrector**, (str., pl. [w.] Conrecto'ren) (Lat.) co-rector, subrector (of a grammar-school).

* **Conscribi'ren**, (w.) v. tr. (Lat.) to enlist, levy (soldiers); der Conscribir'te, m. (like adj.) conscript. — Conscription', (w.) f. conscription. [Bestimmung).

* **Consens'**, (str.) m. (Lat.) consent (Zu-

* **Consequent'**, adj. (Lat.) consistent, consequential. — Consequenz', (w.) f. 1) consequence (Folge); 2) (logical) conclusion; 3) consistency (of conduct, character, &c.).

* **Conservation'**, (w.) f. (Lat.) conservation; C-Brille, f. eye-preserving spectacles, preserves. — Conservati(vi)s'mus, m. conservatism. — Conservativ', adj. (Lat.) conservative. — Conserva'tor, (str., pl. [w.] Conservato'ren) m. conservator; taxidermist. — Conservato'rium, (str., pl. [Lat.] C-'ria, & [w.] C-'rien) n. conservatory (musical school).

* **Conser've**, (w.) f. (Fr.) 1) jam, preserve (Eingemachtes); 2) Pharm. conserve. — Conservi'ren, (w.) v. tr. (Lat.) to conserve, preserve.

* **Consignatar'**, (str.) m. (Med. Lat.) 1) Law, consignatary, depositary, fiduciary; 2) Comm. consignee. — Consignateur' [pr. —tör], (str.) (Fr.) Comm. consignor. — Consignation', (w.) f. Comm. consignment, consignation; C-factura, C-berechnung, f. consignment invoice or account; C-Waaren, f. pl. goods in consignment; c-weise, adv. by way of consignment. — Consigni'ren, (w.) v. tr. (Lat.) 1) Comm. to consign; 2) Mil. to confine (soldiers). — Consigni'rung, (w.) f. 1) see Consignation; 2) Mil. confinement (of soldiers).

* **Consi'lium**, (str., pl. [Lat.] C-'lia) n. counsel, advice; warning (to leave a school, university, &c.), notice to quit.

* **Consistent'**, adj. (Med. Lat.) consistent, firm, compact. — Consistenz', (w.) f. consistency, consistence; solidity; compactness.

* **Consistorial'...**, in comp. —gericht, n. consistorial court; —rath, m. counsellor of the consistory. — Consisto'rium, (str., pl. [Lat.] C-'ria, [w.] C-'rien) n. (Lat.) consistory.

* **Conso'le**, (w.) f. (Fr.) 1) Archit. console, bracket (cf. Kragstein); 2) (or Consol'tischchen, Consol'chen, (str.) n). pier-table, console-table.

* **Consolidi'ren**, (w.) v. tr. (Lat.) to consolidate (a public debt); sich —, refl. to consolidate; consolidirte Fonds, Staatspapiere, consolidated stocks, annuities or debts, consols.

* **Consonant'**, (w.) m. (Lat.) Gramm. consonant. — Consonanz', (w.) f. Gramm. & Mus. consonance, concord.

* **Consor'te**, (w.) m. (Lat.) Law, &c. [illegible]. — Consor'tium [pr. —tsium], (str., pl. C-tien [—tsien], [Lat.] C-'tia) n. [illegible].

* **Constabler**, (str.) m. (Mid. Lat.) 1) Mar. gunner; —gat, n. gunner's store-room; —kammer, f. gun-room; 2) mod. constable.

* **Constan'te**, (w.) f. (Lat.) Math., &c. constant, constant quantity, &c.

* **Constantia** [pr. —tsia], f. (Lat.) 1) Constance (P. N.); 2) —wein, m. a racy kind [illegible]

Constantin, m. Constantine (P. N.).

Constanz, n. Geogr. Constance.

Constanze, f. Constance (P. N.).

Constati'ren, (w.) v. tr. (Fr.) to ascertain; [illegible] to state; to [illegible] — Constati'rung, (w.) [illegible] establishing, &c.

[illegible] (w.) v. tr. (Lat.) to constitute [illegible] &c.).

— **Constitution'**, (w.) f. constitution. — Constitutionell', adj. (Fr.) constitutional.

* **Construction'**, (w.) f. (Lat.) construction. — Construi'ren, (w.) v. tr. to construe.

* **Con'sul**, (str., pl. [w.] C-n) m. (Lat.) consul. — Consular', Consula'risch, adj. consular. — Consulat', (str.) n. consulate; consulship; C-Certificat, n. consular certificate. — Consulent', (w.) m. (Lat.) attorney, counsel, advocate. — Consulti'ren, Consulti'ren, (w.) v. tr. (Lat.) to consult, to take counsel of, to ask (medical) advice of (one). — Consultation', (w.) f. consultation.

* **Consum'**, (str.) m. (Ital. [consumo]-Lat.) consumption; —artikel, m. article of consumption. — Consument', (w.) m. (Lat.) consumer. — Consumi'ren, (w.) v. tr. to consume. — Consumtion', (w.) f. consumption. — Consumtibi'lien, pl. victuals, provisions.

* **Contact'**, (str.) m. (Lat.) contact (Berührung).

* **Contagion'**, (w.) f. (Lat.) Med. contagion (Ansteckung). — Contagiös', adj. (Lat.) contagious (ansteckend). — Conta'gium, (str., pl. [Lat.] C-'gia, [w.] C-'gien) n. contagious matter (Ansteckungsstoff).

* **Contant'**, adj. (Ital.) see Baar. — Contan'ten, (w.) f. pl. ready money, specie.

* **Content'**, I. (Lat., sometimes with Fr. pr.: congtäng'] adj. satisfied, content; II. C-en, pl. Comm. contents (of a ship's load). — Contenti'ren, (w.) v. tr. to content, satisfy (Zufriedenstellen). [versed curve.

* **Con'ter...**, see Contre; —curve, f. T. re-

* **Con'terband**, I. adj. obsolescent, contraband; II. (str.) m. or C-e [gener. with half Fr. pronounc.: kong'terbande], (w.) f. contraband (prohibited merchandise or traffic).

* **Con'terfei**, (str., pl. C-s, rarely C-e) n. (Fr.) †, portrait, likeness, picture. — Conterfei'en, (w.) v. tr. 1) to portray, depict; 2) to counterfeit.

* **Context'**, (str.) m. (Lat.) context.

* **Continent'**, (str.) m. (Lat.) continent. — Continental', adj. continental.

* **Contingent'**, (str.) n. (L. Lat.) contingent; share, contributary quota.

* **Con'to**, Comm. I. (str., pl. C-s, or [Ital.] Con'ti) n. (Ital.) account; — a meta, for half or joint account; — mio, nostro, vostro, suo, loro, my, our, your, his, their account; — sospeso, see Zweifelhaft; ein — saldiren, to balance an account; ein — eröffnen, to open an account; — geben, to give credit; — nehmen, to take credit; II. in comp. —buch, n. account-book; —corrent, n. account current; —finto, n. simulated account, colourable or pro forma account; —saldo, n. balance account; à —zahlung, f. payment on account.

* **Contor'**, (str.) n. see Comtoir.

* **Contouche'** [—tusch'e], (w.) f. (Fr.) light, loose, and short gown or coat.

* **Contour'** [kontūr'], (str., pl. [w.] C-en) m. (coll. [w.] f.) (Fr.) outline; trait; —haar, n. Perr. top-hair.

* **Con'tra**, (Lat.) I. adv. counter; per —, Comm. against which, per contra; II. in comp. —baß, m., —baßgeige, f. double-bass, counter-bass; —bassist, m. double-bass singer. — —fagott, n. double-bassoon.

* **Contract'**, (Lat.) I. (str.) m. 1) contract (Vertrag); auf —, see Lieferung; 2) indenture, lease, see Miethcontract; II. adj. lamed, crippled; —fähig, adj. free to contract. — Contraction', (w.) f. contraction (Zusammenziehung). — Contract'lich, adj. & adv. stated or agreed upon by contract, adv. by contract, as contracted.

* **Contractur'**, (w.) f. Med. contractura (Lat.), unnatural contraction of muscles, &c.

Contradic'tor, (Lat.) m. — maunu, Law & Comm. syndic.

* **Contradicto'risch**, adj. contradictory.

* **Con'tra...**, in comp. —fissur, f. Surg. counter-cleft, counter or opposite fissure; — —fuge, f. Mus. counter-fugue.

* **Contrahent'**, (w.) m. (Lat.) stipulator, contractor, conventionist, contracting party. — Contrahi'ren, (w.) v. (Lat.) I. tr. & intr. to contract; to indent; II. intr. Stud. slang, to agree upon fighting a duel.

Con'tra..., in comp. —poni'ren, v. tr. Comm. to transfer (an incorrect charge of an article); —protest, m. counter-protest, cf. Protest; —punct, m. Mus. counter-point; der verzierte —punct, figurate counter-point; —punctist, m. contrapuntist.

* **Conträr'**, adj. (Fr.) contrary; Mar. contrary, foul, dead (wind).

Con'tra..., in comp. —signatur, f. countersign; —signi'ren, v. tr. to countersign.

* **Contrast'**, (str.) m. (Fr.) contrast; set off. — Contrasti'ren, (w.) v. intr. to be contrasted or set off, to contrast.

Con'tra..., in comp. —temps, n. T. counter-time; —töne, m. pl. Mus. the deepest tones of the bass (under the deep C).

* **Contravenient'**, (w.) m. (Lat.) Law, contravener, trespasser. — Contraveni'ren, (w.) v. intr. to contravene, to trespass.

* **Con'trazettel**, (str.) m. counter-check.

* **Con'tre...** [Fr., pr. kong'tr], in comp. counter; —admiral, m. rear-admiral; —approschen, f. pl. Fort. counter-approaches; —band, see Conterband; —baß, see Contrabaß; —mandi'ren, v. tr. to countermand; —marke, f. counter-ticket; counter-mark; —marsch, m. 1) Mil. countermarch; 2) Man. couper (Obertritt); —ordre, f. counter-order; —punze, f. T. counter-punch; —scarpe, f. Fort. counter-scarp; —tanz, m. contra- or counter-dance, quadrille.

* **Contribuent'**, (w.) m. (Lat.) contributor. — Contribution', (w.) f. contribution, tax; in — setzen, to put under contribution.

* **Control'...**, in comp. —amt, n. board of control; —beamte, m. controlling officer; —bohrungen, f. pl. controlling borings.

* **Control'e**, Contro'le, (w.) f. (Fr.) control, check-account. — Controleur' [pr. —lör], (str., pl. C-e, C-s) m. (Fr.) controller, auditor. — Controli'ren, (w.) v. tr. to control, to direct, manage; die Lagerbestände —, to take stock.

* **Controver'se** (provinc. [S. G.]: Controvers'), (w.) f. (Lat.) controversy.

* **Contumaci'ren**, (w.) v. tr. (Lat.) 1) to condemn for contempt of court; er ließ sich —, he suffered judgment to go by default; 2) to indite for contempt of court.

* **Contumaz'**, (w.) f. (Lat.) 1) quarantine; 2) Law, contumacy, contempt of court; in —, in default of appearance; in — erklären, to declare in default; das Urtheil wird in — gefällt, judgment goes by default.

* **Contur'**, see Contour.

* **Contusch'e**, see Contouche.

* **Contusion'**, (w.) f. (Lat.) Surg. contusion, abrasion.

* **Convenienz'**, (w.) f. (Lat.) convenience, suitableness; propriety; —heirat, f. prudent marriage or match. — Conveni'ren, (w.) v. intr. to suit.

* **Convent'**, (str.) m. (Lat.) convention, convent; —bruder, m., —schwester, f. conventual. — Convention', (w.) f. convention, contract, agreement; C-geld, n., C-münze, f. convention-money; C-fuß, m. the (Vienna) convention standard. — Conventionalstrafe, (w.) f. stated fine or penalty. — Conventionell', adj. conventional.

* **Convergenz'**, (w.) f. (L. Lat.) convergence. — Convergi'ren, (w.) v. intr. Math., &c. to converge.

* **Conversation'**, (w.) f. (Lat.) conversation: **C-Lexicon**, n. popular cyclopedia: **C-Sprache**, f. see Umgangssprache; **C-Stück**, n. Dram. comedy of daily and real life. — **Conversi'ren**, (w.) v. intr. (Lat.) to converse.

* **Convertit'**, (w.) m. (Lat.) convert.

* **Convex'**, adj. T. (Lat.) convex.

* **Convoci'ren**, (w.) v. tr. (Lat.) to convoke: die Gläubiger —, to call a meeting of creditors.

* **Convoi'** [pr. longwoa'], (str., pl. C-s) m. (Fr.) convoy: im — segeln, to sail under convoy.

* **Convolut'**, (str.) n. (Lat.) bundle of papers, rolls.

* **Convulsion'**, (w.) f. (Lat.) convulsion. — **Convulsi'visch**, adj. convulsive.

* **Copai'va-Balsam**, (str.) m. Pharm. copaiba-(or copivi-)balsam.

* **Copal'**, (str.) m. Comm. (Mexican) copal; —firniß, —lack, m. copal varnish.

* **Copernica'nisch**, adj. Copernican.

* **Copia'lien**, pl. (Lat.) 1) copying-fee; 2) copies, transcripts. — **Copie'**, (w.) f. copy; duplicate; Paint. imitation; —wechsel, m. pl. Comm. bills in sets, sets of exchange. — **Copi'ren**, (w.) v. tr. 1) to copy, transcribe; 2) Paint. to imitate (a picture). — **Copir'**..., in comp. —buch, n. copy- or letter-book; —maschine, f. copying-machine, copying-press; manifold-writer; —papier, n. copying-paper; —tinte, f. copying-ink. — **Copist'**, (w.) m. copier, copying clerk.

* **Coquet'** [pr. fofet'], adj. (Fr.) coquettish, coquet. — **Coquet'te**, (w.) f. coquette, coquet, jilt, flirt. — **Coquetterie'**, (w.) f. coquetry, flirtation. — **Coquetti'ren**, (w.) v. intr. to coquet; flirt.

* **Coral'le**, (w.) f. (L. u.: **Corall'**, [str.] m. & n.) (Gr.) Zool. coral, sea moss (Isis nobilis L.); runde —, coral bead.

* **Coral'len**, I. adj. coralline, coral; II. in comp. —achat, m. Miner. coral agate; —artig, adj. coralline, coralliaceous, coralloid(al); —ast, m. coral-branch; —bank, f. see —riff; Bot.-s. —baum, m. coral tree (Erythrina L.); —blümchen, n. see —kirsche; —blümchen, n. see Adonis, 2; —blume, —blüte, f. coral flower (young coral coming off the coral reefs); —bohne, f. see —baum; —erbse, f. 1) Jamaica wild liquorice; 2) pl. red coral-beads, seed beads; —erz, n. carbonaceous cinnabar; —fang, m., —fischerei, f. coral-fishing; —fischer, m. coral-fisher, coral-diver; —flechte, f. coral-moss; —förmig, adj. coralliform; —holz, n. coral-wood; —hyacinthe, f. Bot. purple grape hyacinth (Hyacinthus comosus L.); —kalk, —marmor, m. Geol. coral-rag; Bot.-s. —kirsche, f., —nachtschatten, m. winter-cherry, red berry bearing night-shade (Solanum pseudocapsicum L.); —kraut, n. 1) coral-wort (Dentaria bulbifera L.); 2) tooth-wort (Ophrys corallorhiza L.); —moos, n. coralline, coral-moss; —muschel, f. Conch. coral-scallop (Ostrea nodosa L.); —netz, n. coral-net; —riff, n. coral-reef; —rinde, f. Zool. horn wrack (Flustra L.); —roth, adj. coral-red; —schnur, f. string of coral; —schwamm, m. white coral-seed; —stein, m. fossile coral; —thier, —thierchen, n. see —blume; —weizen, m. see Dinkel; —wurz, f. see —kraut; —zinke, f., —zweig, m. see —ast.

* **Coralli'ne**, (w.) f. Bot. coralline.

* **Corallit'**, **Corallinit'**, (w.) m. Pal. corallite.

* **Co'ram**, adv. (Lat.) before; — nehmen, (**Coramisi'ren**, (w.) v. tr.) coll. to take (one) to task. [Lace-m., &c. cord.

* **Cor'de**, (w.) f. (Fr.) 1) see Cordel; 2)

* **Cor'del**, (w.) f. 1) (or **Cor'de**) (Fr.) string, twine; 2) (str.) m. strong sewing thread. — **Cordeli'ren**, (w.) v. tr. 1) see Zwirnen; 2) see Flechten.

* **Cordial'**, adj. cordial. — **Cordialität'**, (w.) f. cordiality.

* **Cordille'ren** [pr. —dilje'—], f. pl. (Span. cordilleras, (mountain-chains) Geogr. the Cordilleras, Andes.

* **Cordon'** [pr. fordong'], (str., pl. C-s) m. (Fr.) Mil. cordon, a line of military posts.

* **Cor'duan**, (str.) m. (Fr.) cordovan, cordwain, Spanish leather; —arbeiter, —macher, m. cordwainer.

* **Corian'der**, (str.) m. (Lat.-Gr.) Bot. coriander (Coriandrum sativum L.).

Corinth', (str.) n. Geogr. Corinth.

Corin'the, (w.) f. Comm. (dried) currant: C-nrebe, f. Bot. Corinthian grape (Vitis vinifera apyrena L.); C-nstaude, f. (tasteless) mountain-currant (Ribes alpinum L.).

Corin'ther, (str.) m. (C-in, [w.] f.), **Corin'thisch**, adj. Corinthian.

* **Corlin'**, (str.) m. Comm. finest gold- and silver-wire.

* **Cor'moran**, (str.) m. (Fr.) Ornith. cormorant (der kleine und große —, see Seeheher & Seerabe).

* **Cornel'**..., (Lat.) in comp. —baum, m. Bot. 1) cornel-tree (Cornus mascula L.); 2) (wilder) see Hartriegel, 2; —(ius)kirsche, **Cornel'le**, (w.) f. cornel(-berry), cornelian cherry.

* **Cornet(t)'**, (str.) I. m. (Fr.-Lat.) Mil. cornet, standard-bearer; II. n. (Ital.) Mus. 1) see Zinken; 2) (—flöte, f., —baß, m.) cornet (name of an organ-stop).

* **Cornet'te**, (w.) f. (Fr.) 1) standard, flag; 2) cornet; mob-cap.

* **Cornut'**, (w.) m. (Lat. cornutus, one that wears horns) cornute.

* **Corporal'**, (str., pl. C-e & Corpora'le) m. (Fr.) Mil. corporal.

* **Corporation'**, (w.) f. (Mid. Lat.) corporation, body, corporate; die — der Kaufmannschaft, the mercantile body, the corporation of merchants. — **Corporativ'**, adj. corporate.

* **Corps** [pr. tor], (str., pl. Corps [pr. fore]) n. (Fr.) Mil., &c. corps; body.

* **Corpulent'**, adj. (Lat.) corpulent, fat, stout. — **Corpulenz'**, (w.) f. corpulency, corpulence, obesity.

* **Cor'pus**, (indecl.) (Lat.) 1) f. Typ. long-primer; 2) n. Instr.-m. case (of a violin).

* **Correct'**, adj. (Lat.) correct, free from error; — verfahren, Comm. to act business-like. — **Correct'heit**, (w.) f. correctness. — **Correction'**, (w.) f. correction; C-shaus, n. penitentiary, house of correction. — **Correc'tor**, (str., pl. Correcto'ren) m. reader, reviser; corrector (of the press), proof-reader. — **Correctur'**, (w.) f. 1) a) correction; b) Comm. rectifications; 2) Typ. or —bogen, m. proof(-sheet); die zweite —, revise; C-en lesen, to correct the (errors of the) press; die — besorgen, to supervise the press; —presse, f. proof-press; —zange, f. pincers; —zeichen, n. (mark of) correction. [&c. cf. Referent.

* **Correferent'**, (w.) m. assistant reporter,

* **Correlat'**, (L. Lat.) I. or **Correlativ'**, adj. correlative; II. (str.) n. correlate. — **Correlation'**, (w.) f. correlation.

Correspondent', (w.) m. 1) (L. Lat.) correspondent; 2) corresponding clerk, correspondent. — **Correspondenz'**, (w.) f. correspondence; epistolar (epistolary) intercourse; —karte, f. postal card, post-card (Postkarte). — **Correspondi'ren**, (w.) v. intr. to correspond. [corridor.

* **Cor'ridor**, (str., pl. C-e & C-s) m. (Fr.)

* **Corrigi'ren**, (w.) v. tr. (Lat.) to correct, revise; eine Feder —, to mend a pen.

* **Corrosiv'**, (Schiller C-lich †) adj. corrosive (Agend). [rupt.

* **Corrumpi'ren**, (w.) v. tr. (Lat.) to corrupt.

* **Corsar'**, (w.) m. (Span.) corsair, pirate.

Cor'se, (w.) m., **Cor'sisch**, adj. Corsican.

* Courti'ne [kūr—], (w.) f. (Fr.) Fort. [illegible].

* Coufin' [kūfäng'], (str., pl. C-s) m. (Fr.) [illegible] (Vetter). — Coufi'ne, (w.) f. (female) [illegible].

[illegible] [kūwĕrt'], (str.) n. (Fr.) 1) cover, [illegible], wrapper; unter —, under (this) cover; cover (plate, knife, fork, and napkin). — [illegible] [kū—], (w.) v. tr. (Fr.) to put [in] an envelop; to wrap (up).

* Co'vent, (str.) m. (Lat.) coll. for Con[vent]; —bier, n. a weak kind of beer, small [beer].

* Craniolog', (w.) m. (Cranium, skull, [Mid.] Lat. from (Gr.) kranion) craniologist. — [Cranio]logie', (w.) f. craniology. — Cranio[lo']gisch, adj. craniological.

* Craß, adj. (Lat.) 1) gross, uncultivated [illegible]; 2) fig. strong, great, unmiti[gated], &c.

* Crawat'te, (w.) f. (Fr.) cravat; stock; [illegible]) neck-tie.

* Crayon' [crayöng'], (str., pl. C-s) m. (Fr.) [crayon]; —papier, n. chalk-paper; —zeichnung, [f.] chalk-drawing. [f. crease, dowlas.

* Cre'as, (indecl.) m. (Span.) —leinwand,

* Creatür, (w.) f. (Lat.) 1) creature; 2) [fig.] creature, tool. — Creatür'chen, (str.) n. [(dim. of Creatur) small creature. — Crea[tür']lich, adj. creatural.

* Creden'zen, (w.) v. tr. (Ital.) to present [illegible] meat or drink); Credenz'teller, m. [illegible]; Credenz'tisch, m. (court) cupboard, [illegible]-board, dresser-board, buffet.

* 1. Cre'dit, (str., pl. C-s) n. (Lat. third pers. [sing.] pres. tense of credere: he entrusts; opp. [illegible], cf. Credent) credit, syn. Haben; (— [sei]te, f.) creditor's side (in a ledger).

* 2. Credit', s. I. (str.) m. (Fr.) 1) cre[dit]; 2) repute; der laufende —, open or run[ning] credit; der offene —, credit in blank, [illegible]-credit; — geben, to grant or give credit, [illegible] credit; auf — geben, see Creditiren; auf — [neh]men, to borrow, to take upon trust or cre[dit]; [illegible], to go upon tick; den — überschreiten, [illegible] or overstrain the credit; einen — [illegible] eröffnen, to lodge a credit with [illegible]; II. in comp. —actien, pl. general credit [illegible]; —anstalt, m. credit-association; — [bank], f. credit-bank; —brief, m. letter of cre[dit]; —fähig, adj. solid, good; —fähigkeit, f. [illegible].

* Crediti'ren, (w.) v. tr. (Fr.) to credit [(an] amount paid, &c.), to give or to sell on [cr]edit, to give upon trust, to trust. — Cre[di]tiv', (str.) n. (L. Lat.) see Beglaubigungs[schreiben]. — Cre'ditor, (str., pl. (w.) Credi[to'ren]) m. (Lat.) creditor (Gläubiger).

[illegible] Credit'..., in comp. —posten, m. item [on] the creditor's side; —seite, f. creditor's [side (in a ledger)]; —versicherung, f. guarantee-[illegible]; —würdig, adj. sound, stable, good; [illegible], f. stability, soundness.

[illegible] (str., pl. C-s) n. (Lat.) Eccl. creed.

[illegible] (Lat., third pers. pl. pres. tense [of credere: they entrust]) Comm. creditors [illegible].

[illegible] (w.) v. tr. (Lat.) 1) to create; [illegible] (a theatre, &c.).

[illegible]

[illegible]

die miserably; 2) (of shells) to be extinguished without exploding.

* Crepon' [krēpöng'], (str., pl. C-s) m. (Fr.) crepon, dress crape.

* Crêpe, m. (Fr.) see Krepp.

Cre'ta, f. Geogr. Crete. — Creten'ser, (str.) m. Cretian, Crete. — Creten'sisch, Cre'tisch, adj. Cretian, Cretan.

* Cre'thi und Ple'thi, see Krethi.

* Cretin', (str. & w.), also with Fr. pr. [krētäng'], (str., pl. C-s) m. cretin. — Cre[ti']nenhaft, adj. cretin-like. — Cretinis'mus, m. cretinism. [schuldner.

* Cridar', (str.) m. (L. Lat.) see Gemein-

* Criminal', I. adj. (Lat.) Law, criminal; II. in comp. —amt, —gericht, n. criminal court; —gesetz, n. criminal law; —gesetzbuch, n. criminal code; —sache, f. criminal case; —verfahren, n. criminal prosecution.

* Criminell', adj. (Fr.) see Criminal.

* Crinoli'ne, (w.) f. (Fr.) crinoline; C-ngestell, n. skeleton of a crinoline.

Critik', rc. see Kritik rc.

* Crocodil(l)', (str. & w.) n. & m. (Gr.) Zool. crocodile; das amerikanische —, cayman, alligator; —schluß, m. Log. crocodile; C(s)-thränen, f. pl. crocodile-tears, sham tears.

* Cro'cus, (indecl.) m. (Gr.) Bot. crocus (Crocus L.). [Conch. see Kreuzmuschel.

* Cru'cifix, (str.) n. (Lat.) 1) crucifix; 2)

* Crustir'en, (w.) v. tr. (Lat.) to crust, incrust.

* Crystall', s. I. (str.) m. (Gr.) crystal; der gelbe —, imitation topaz; der nadelförmige —, spar; C-e ansetzen, Chem. to effloresce; II. in comp. —achat, m. translucent agate (Eisachat); —ähnlich, —artig, adj. crystalline; —drüse, f. cluster of crystals.

* Crystal'len, adj. crystalline, crystal.

* Crystall'..., in comp. —feuchtigkeit, f. Anat. vitreous or crystalline humour; —förmig, adj. see —ähnlich; —glas, n. crystal, crystal-glass; —harz, n. Miner. honey-stone; —hell, adj. crystalline, crystal; —himmel, m. crystalline sky or heaven.

* Crystalli'nisch, adj. crystalline (texture); bright as crystal.

* Crystallisation', (w.) f. Chem. crystallisation; c-sfähig, see Crystallisirbar; C-sgefäß, n. crystallising vessel; C-swasser, n. water of crystallisation.

* Crystallisir'bar, adj. crystallisable. — Crystallisir'ren, (w.) v. tr. & refl. to crystallise. — Crystallisir'rung, (w.) f. crystallisation.

* Crystall'..., in comp. —kapsel, f. Anat. crystalline capsule; —kiesel, m. pebble crystal; —klümpchen, n. see —drüse; —kraut, n. ice-plant (Eiskraut); —körper, m. see —linse; —kunde, —lehre, f. crystallography; Anat. —linse, f. crystalline lens; —linsenkapsel, f. see —kapsel. [wahrsagerei.

* Crystallomantie', (w.) f. see Crystall-

* Crystall'..., in comp. —palast, m. (De la Motte-Fouqué, Undine 63) crystal-palace; —salz, n. sal-gem; —seherei, f. see —wahrsagerei; —spiegel, m. crystalline mirror; —staar, m. Med. membraneous cataract; —stecher, m. engraver on crystal; —stein, m. transparent quartz; —wahrsager, m. crystallomancer; —wahrsagerei, f. crystallomancy; —wasser, n. see Crystallisationswasser; —zinn, n. Miner. grain tin. [Cuba'nisch, adj. Cuban.

Cuba'ner, (str.) m., Cuba'nerin, (w.) f.,

* Cube'be, (w.) f. 1) (Bot. cubebe, from Hind. kababa) (C-npfeffer[baum], m.) Bot. cubeb, cubeb-shrub, Java pepper-shrub, raisin of the sun (Piper cubeba L.); C-nöl, n. essence of cubebs; 2) see Cibebe.

* Cubik', (indecl.) adj. (L. Lat.-Gr.) Math. cubic(al) (adv. cubically); in comp. —fuß, m. cubic foot; —inhalt, m. cubic or solid contents (of a body); substance; capacity; —linie, f. cubic line; —maß, n. cubic measure, measure of capacity; —ruthe, f. cubic perch; —wurzel, f. cube-root; —zahl, f. cube-number, cubic number; auf die —zahl erheben, to cube (a quantity), to raise to the third power by multiplying (a number) twice by itself; —zoll, m. cubic inch.

* Cubi'ren, (w.) v. tr. Math. 1) to cube; 2) to determine the cubic or solid contents of (a body).

* Cu'bisch, adj. Math. cubic(al), see Cubik; der c-e Salpeter, Chem. cubic nitre (nitrate of soda); der c-e Inhalt, see Cubikinhalt.

* Cu'bocubikzahl, (w.) f. cubo-cube.

* Cuboï'disch, adj. cuboid(al).

* Cu'bus, m. (Lat.-Gr.) Math. cube; auf den — bringen, see auf die Cubikzahl erheben.

* Cucu'mer, (w.) f. Bot. cucumis (Lat., pl. cucumeres; a genus of plants, including the cucumber, melon, &c.).

* Cujon', (str.) m. (Fr. couillon, coïon) poltroon, scoundrel. — Cujoni'ren, (w.) v. tr. to treat as a poltroon; to vex, annoy.

* Culis'se, (Fr.) see Coulisse.

* Culmini'ren, (w.) v. intr. (L. Lat.) Astr. to culminate. — Culmination', (w.) f. culmination; C-spunct, m. culminating point.

* Cult, (str.) m. see Cultus.

* Cultivir'bar, adj. cultivable.

Cultivi'ren, (w.) v. tr. (Mid. Lat.) to cultivate, improve, culture; to cultivate, push (an acquaintance).

* Cultur', (w.) f. (Lat.) culture; cultivation, civilisation; civility; —fähig, see Cultivirbar.

* Cul'tus, (indecl., cf. Cult) m. (Lat.) worship; —minister, Minister des — und (des) öffentlichen Unterrichts, m. minister of ecclesiastical affairs (or of public worship) and of public instruction.

* Cum'pan, (str. & w.) m. (for Compan; Mid. Lat.) († &) coll. companion, mate, colleague, fellow; ein lustiger —, joc. a jolly dog

* Cumulation', (w.) f. (Lat.) cumulation; — der Klage (im Wechselproceß), Comm. accumulation of the charges.

* Cupel'le, (w.) f. see Capelle, 2.

* Cupi'do, (str., pl. C-s) m. (Lat.) Cupido, Cupid.

* Cur', (w.) f. (Lat.) cure; in der —, under cure; an einem Badeort zur — sein, to be at a bathing place for the benefit of the waters; in die — nehmen, to treat medicinally; fig. to show what is what; sich bei (or zu) einem Arzt in die — begeben, to place one's self under the treatment of a physician; —kosten, pl. expenses of cure; —liste, f. list of patients or visitors at a watering-place; —ort, m. watering-place; —saal, m. pump-room; —schmidt, m. farrier.

* Cü'raß rc., see Küraß rc.

* Curatel', (w.) f. (L. Lat.) Law, guardianship, trusteeship.

* Cura'tor, (str., pl. (w.) Curato'ren) m. (Lat.) Law, trustee, guardian, administrator, curator, assign, assignee; C-en der Masse, assignees of the estate of a bankrupt, creditors in trust.

* Curbettiren, see Courbettiren.

* Cur'cuma, Cur'cumei, f. (L. Lat.) Pharm. turmeric.

Curd, see Kurd.

* Curia'lien, n. (Mod. Lat.) pl. forms, observances of a court of justice.

* Curial'stil, (str.) m. Law, style of court.

* Curiös', adj. (Lat.) curious. — Curiosität', (w.) f. curiosity, rarity; C-en, pl. articles of virtu; C-enhandel, m. fancy-business; C-enhändler, m. fancy-dealer. [physic.

* Curi'ren, (w.) v. tr. (Lat.) to cure, to

* Curren'de, (w.) f. (Lat.) procession and singing of the pupils of town-schools (Curren-

be'ner, [*str.*]. Currend'schüler, (*str.*) *m.*) through the streets of certain towns for alms.

* Current', *adj.* (*Lat.*) current: —schrift, *f.* 1) current hand-writing, running-hand: 2) *see* Cursivschrift.

* Curs, *f.* Cours.

* Cursi'ren, (*w.*) *v. intr.* (*Lat.*) to circulate.

* Cursiv', *adj.* (*L. Lat.*) *Typ.* italic: — *or* mit (in) —schrift drucken, *v. tr.* to italicise: —schrift, *f.* italic type, italics: cursive characters.

* Cur'sus, (*pl.* [*Lat.*] Cur'sus *or* [*str.*] Curse) *m.* (*Lat.*) course.

* Curu'lisch, *adj.* (*Lat.*) curule.

* Cur've, (*w.*) *f.* (*Lat.*) curve: C-ntafeln, *f. pl.* curve-tables.

* Cus'tos, (*not decl.*, *pl.* [*w.*] Custo'den) *m.* [*Lat.*] 1) *or* Custo'de, (*w.*) *m.* keeper; warder: assistant in a great library: 2) *a*) *Typ.* catch-word, direction-word, direct word; *b*) *Mus.* the direct (*w*).

* Cuvelli'ren, (*w.*) *v. tr.* (*Fr.*) *Min.* to timber (a shaft).

* Cyan', (*str.*) *n.*, Cya'nogen, (*str.*) *n.* (*Gr.*) *Chem.* cyanogen. — Cya'ne, (*w.*) *f.* (*Gr.*) *Bot.* blue bottle (Kornblume). — Cyanome'ter, (*str.*) *n.* & *m.* cyanometer.

* Cycla'den, Cycla'dische Inseln, (*w.*) *f.* (*Gr.*) *pl. Geogr.* the Cyclades.

* Cycloi'de, (*w.*) *f.* (*Gr.*) *Math.* cycloid.

* Cyclop', (*w.*) *m. Gr. Myth.* Cyclops: C-nmauerwerk, *n.* Cyclopean rubble. — Cyclo'pisch, *adj.* cyclopean.

* Cy'clus, Cy'klus (*indecl.*, *pl. sometimes* Cy'clen), Cy'kel, (*str.*) *m.* (*Gr.*) cycle.

* Cylin'der, (*str.*) *m.* (*Gr.*) cylinder; (Lampen—) chimney of a lamp; —ähnlich, *adj.* cylinder-like: —bohrer, *m.* boring-machine: —dampfkessel, *m.* cylindrical boiler; —decke, —bedeckung, *f. Mech.* (steam-)jacket, *see* Mantel, 3, *d*; —deckel, *m.* cylinder cover: —drehbank, *f.* slide-lathe; —förmig (*or* cylindrisch), *adj.* cylindric(al); —gebläse, *n.* (hölzernes) tromp; —bewegung, *f. Naval* cylinder-arrangement: —karten, *f. pl.* cylinder-cards; —lampe, *f.* argand-lamp; —maschine, *f.* 1) *Electr.* cylinder electrical machine: 2) cylinder (steam) engine: —presse, *f. see* Walzenpresse; —scheibe, *f.* sucker, piston: —uhr, *f.* horizontal watch, lever- or cylinder-watch.

* Cylin'dern, (*w.*) *v. tr. Weav.* to calender. — Cylin'drisch, *adj.* cylindric(al). — Cylindroid', (*str.*) *n. Math.* cylindroid.

* Cym'bel, (*w.*) *f.* (*Gr.*) *Mus.* cymbal.

* Cynan'che, (*w.*) *f.* (*Gr.*) *Med. see* Bräune.

* Cy'niker, (*str.*) *m.* (*Gr.*) cynic. — Cy'nisch, *adj.* cynical. — Cynis'mus, (*pl.* C-'men) *m.* cynicism.

Cy'per, *s.* I. 1) (*str.*) *m. Manuf.* cypress (kind of thin stuff); 2) (*w.*) *f.* Cyprus-plum: II. *in comp.* —gras, *n. Bot.* cyperus (*Cyperus* L.); Seat-c. —hund, *m.* the naked *or* Turkish dog (*Canis aegyptius* L.); —katze, *f.* cyperet (*Felis domestica striata* L.); —wein, *m.* Cyprus-wine; —wurz, *f. see* —gras.

Cy'pern, (*str.*) *n. Geogr.* Cyprus: —holz, *n.* prince's-wood: —holzbaum, *m.* Spanish elm.

* Cypres'se, (*w.*) *f.* (*Lat.-Gr.*) cypress (*Cupressus* L.); C-nbaum, *m.* cypress-tree: C-nholz, *n.* cypress-wood: C-nkraut, *n. Bot.* a species of lavender-cotton: C-nnuß, *f.* cypress cone: C-nspäne, *m. pl. Join. & Build.-m.* cypress shingles: C-nstaudenkraut, *f. see* C-nkraut; C-nwald, *m.* cypress wood; C-nwolfsmilch, *f. Bot.* cypress-spurge.

Cyprio't, (*w.*) *m.* Cypriot, inhabitant of Cyprus. — Cy'prisch, *adj.* Cyprian.

* Cy'ste, (*w.*) *f.* (*Gr.*) *Physiol.* 1) cyst, cystis: 2) *see* Balggeschwulst.

* Cythe're, Cythere'a, *f.* (*Lat.-Gr.*) Cytherea (surname of Venus).

* Czakan, Czako, Czapka, *see* Tsch....

* Czar' [*pr.* tsar], (*w.*) *m.* (*Russ.*) czar.

* Czari'na, (*w.*) *f.* (*Russ.*) czarina, czarine, tzarina.

D.

D, d, *n.* 1) *Gramm.* D, d, the fourth letter and third consonant of the Alphabet; 2) *Mus.* D (the second note of the gamut, named re in Italy and France); D-dur, D major; D-moll, D minor.

D., *abbr.* d. *or* dd. *for* dedit (bezahlt), paid; dah. *for* daher, thence; Dän. Bks. *for* Dänische Banko, *Comm.* Danish banks; das. *for* daselbst, there, at that place; D. C. *for* da capo; Deb. *for* Debitor, *Comm.* debtor; dd., ddo., dto. *for* (*Lat.*) de dato, from the date, vom Tage der Ausstellung eines Schreibens; d. E. *for* durch Einschluß, per *or* by enclosure; Dec., Decbr. *for* December, December; Dech. *for* Decher, dicker (of hides); d. Gr. *for* der Große, the great; del. *for* (*Lat.*) deleatur, blot out, erase, man streiche aus; Dep., Dept. *for* Departement, department; (d.) F. f. *for* (die) Fortsetzung folgt, to be continued; d. G. *for* durch Güte, durch Gelegenheit, by the favour *or* politeness of..., favoured by ...; dgl., dergl. *for* dergleichen, the like, such; d. h. *for* das heißt, that is to say; d. i. *for* das ist, that is (*anal. i. e.*); Disc. *for* Disconto, discount; d. J. 1) *for* dieses Jahres, this *or* the present year; 2) *for* der Jüngere, the younger; d. l. M. *for* des letzten Monats, of last month; d. M., ds. Mts., ds. Mts. *for* dieses Monats, of this month; do., dto. *for* ditto, detto, ditto; Dpff. *for* Dampfschiff, steamboat, steamer; ds., dies. *for* dieses, this; Dtz., Dtzd., Dz., Dtzd. *for* Dutzend, dozen; Duc. (Ⅱ) *for* Ducaten, ducat, ducats.

Da, I. *adv.* 1) *a*) there; *b*) †. where (*rel.*); here, present; 2) *a*) then, at that time; *b*) †. when (*rel.*); *coll.-e.* — draußen, out there; — drin(nen), in there, within that place; — oben, — droben, up there; — drüben, (in that place) yonder; — unten, — drunten, below there; — hinten, behind there; — vorn, forward there; — läßt sich nichts weiter thun, there is nothing further to be done in that matter; wo —? where? wo denn —? where then? wer — ba!, he that hear! es waren viele Menschen —, there were many persons present; wie gewöhnlich (ist *or* war) Niemand —, as usual, nobody in the way, *cf.* Dasein; II. *conj.* when, as; since, because; while, whilst, whereas: — ich ihn sah, when I saw him; — doch, — nun, since, since indeed; — hingegen, — sonst, whereas; — wo, where; — nun aber, but now as, now.

Daal, (*str.*) *n.* (*L. G.*) *Mar.* pump-dale.

Dabei' [*sometimes* da'bei, *when opposed to* Hierbei *&c.*], *adv.* 1) thereat, there, near it, by, present; 2) therewith, at the same time, in doing so or thus, withal; 3) thereby, hereby, by it, with it *or* in; 4) so, as it is; 5) besides, withal; nahe —, hard by; — stehen, to stand by; die — Stehenden, the by-standers; — sein, to be present, to assist; ich war eben —, I was just about it; ich bin —! I am with you (him, her, them)! sie ist mit —, she makes one of them; wollen Sie — sein? will you be of the party? ich befinde mich sehr wohl —, I find much good by it; — bleiben, to persist in, to keep *or* stick to it; es bleibt —! done! the thing is settled! — [*pr.* da'bei] blieb es, there the matter rested; es mag — bleiben, let it be so; — ereignete sich ..., it was attended with ...; ich bin — nicht gefährdet, I risk nothing in this affair; — will ich Ihnen noch sagen, besides I will tell you; — müssen Sie bedenken, daß ..., moreover you must consider that ....

Da'bleiben, (*str.*) *v. intr.* (*aux.* sein) to

[illegible]'..., in comp. –falle, f. badger-gin; [illegible], –finder, –hund, –kriecher, –schlie[illegible], m. terrier, turnspit, Spanish pointer; –[illegible], m. badger's-hair pencil; –schwarte, f. [illegible] badger-skin.

[illegible]..., in comp. –span, m. shingle: –[illegible], m. rafter, spar of a roof; –spitze, [illegible] –firste; –stein, m. see –ziegel; –[illegible] n. see –geschoß; –stroh, n. thatch, reed; [illegible], f. garret, attic: –stuhl, m. the frame[illegible] of a roof; –stuhlsäulen, f. pl. the prin[illegible] rafters and uprights of a roof.

[illegible], Dacht, (str.) m. provinc. see Docht.

[illegible], (w.) f. vulg. box on the ear, souse [illegible]. – Dach'teln, (w.) v. tr. to souse.

[illegible]..., in comp. –traufe, f. eaves; –[illegible]ziegel, m. gutter-tile. [Sonnenzelt.

[illegible]ung, (w.) f. 1) roofing, roof; 2) see [illegible]..., in comp. –verbindung, f. roofing; [illegible], n. roof-work, roofing: –wurz, f. see [illegible]; –ziegel, m. roof-tile, roofing-tile; –[illegible]förmig, adj. Bot. & Entom. imbricated, [illegible].

[illegible], n. Anc. Geogr. Dacia. – Da'cier, [illegible]) m., Da'cisch, adj. Dacian.

* [illegible]lisch, adj. Vers. dactylic. – Dac'[illegible], (pl. [w.] Dacty'len) m. (Lat.-Gr.) dac[illegible], dactyl. [dalian.

* [illegible]lisch, adj. Dædal, Dædalian, Dæ-

[illegible], Dadrin'(nen), Dadro'ben, [illegible], Dadrun'ten, coll. see Da.

[illegible]dern, (w.) v. intr. to cackle (Dädern, [illegible], Schnattern).

[illegible], adv. 1) through it, through that [illegible]; 2) by this, by that, by those means, [illegible], thereby.

[illegible]fern', conj. if, in case, provided.

[illegible] [sometimes da'für], adv. 1) for it, [illegible] that, for this; in return; eff' ich mal ein [illegible] | Stück Austern — [pr. da'für] nun — [illegible] Jammer, | ist's Austernzeit (v. Gaudy). [illegible] eat five score | of oysters — well, the [illegible]'s here, | the oyster-season (to be ex[illegible] by a kind of ellipsis: zur Entschuldi[illegible] — kann ich anführen ..., in excuse of [illegible] [extravagance, &c.] I may allege ...); 2) in[illegible] of that, instead of it: was wird mir —? [illegible] I to get (earn) by it? ich bin dir gut [illegible] warrant you, I answer for it; — halten, [illegible] be of opinion, to deem, suppose, imagine; [illegible], opinion, estimation, private judg[illegible]; nach meinem —halten, in my opinion, [illegible] my way of thinking; ganz nach Ihrem [illegible], quite according to your opinion; ich [illegible] nichts —, it is no fault of mine or not [illegible] fault, I cannot help it; — stehen, to war[illegible] it, to be liable for it; — kann ich nicht [illegible], I cannot sell at that figure (price); [illegible], — aber auch besser, dearer, but so [illegible] superior; — sein or stimmen, to be for, [illegible] in favour (on the side) of, to agree to, [illegible] for.

[illegible], Dag'ge, (w.) f. Mar. coll. a rope's end [illegible] punishment; durch die Daggen laufen, to [illegible] the gauntlet.

[illegible] [sometimes da'gegen], I. adv. 1) [illegible] this or it; 2) to it, in comparison; [illegible] it, in return, in exchange; II. conj. on [illegible] hand, on the contrary, whereas, [illegible] ich habe nichts —, ich bin nicht —, I [illegible] no objection to it; — einwenden, to ob[illegible]; — halten, to compare, contrast, con[illegible]; — stimmen, to oppose, vote (declare [illegible]) against it.

[illegible] [pr. [illegible]–], (str.) n. [illegible] – [illegible], [illegible] process. – [illegible], [illegible] v. tr. to daguerreotype. – Da[illegible], adj. Daguerreian, daguerreo[illegible]. – [illegible], (w.) m. [illegible] – [illegible] f. [illegible].

Daheim', adv. at home, in one's native place or country; cf. zu Hause.

Daher, I. adv. [da'hēr] 1) thence, from thence, from that place; 2) from that reason, from that circumstance; hence, out of that; — kommt es, hence it is; bis — gestellt, Comm. delivered here; II. in comp. [dahēr'] —gehen, to walk along, cf. Einher; —kommen, to draw near; —rauschen, to rush on, along; —schleichen, to sneak along; —schreiten, to stalk; —ziehen, to draw on, along; III. conj. therefore.

† Dahe'ro, see Daher.

Da'herum, adv. coll. thereabouts.

Dahier', adv. at this place; cf. Hier.

Dahin, adv. I. [da'hin] thither, there, to that place, to it; along, on; so far; bis —, 1) thus far; 2) till then; — möcht' ich mit dir, o mein Geliebter, ziehn! (Göthe, Mignon), there, with thee, O my beloved one, would that I could flee! (Baskerville); — gehörig, appertaining thereto; sich mit Jemand — vereinigen, to agree with one to the effect; alle seine Sorge ist — gerichtet, all his care is bent that way; — arbeiten, to strive; — bringen, 1) (eine Sache) to carry matters to that point; 2) (Einen) to induce, prevail upon; es — bringen, to get or succeed so far; seine Absicht ging —, his intention was directed to that point; ist es — gekommen? has it come to this? — ist es gekommen?! that it should (ever have) come to this! — ist es mit ihnen gekommen? have matters come so far (to that, to such a pass or pitch) with them? der Brief lautete —, the letter was to this (the) effect.

II. (dahin') away, down; gone; over, past (cf. Hin, also in comp.) —fahren, to go or drive along; to skim along; to pass away, to vanish; —fallen, to fall down; to fade, to droop; —fließen, —gleiten, to flow down or on, to glide along; —geben, fig. to abandon; —gehen, to pass along; —haben, to have got (one's reward, share); —reißen, to carry along or away; fig. to transport, ravish; —rollen, to roll along or on; —scheiden, to die, expire; —sprengen, to dash along or off; —schwinden, I. v. intr. to dwindle or waste away; II. v. s. evanescence; —sein, to be gone, to be lost; —sinken, to sink down; to droop, vanish; es steht (noch) —, fig. it is (as yet) uncertain, it is (as yet) a question, it is precarious, it may not be warranted; —stellen, — gestellt sein lassen, to put in abeyance, to leave uncertain or undecided; to let be as it may; —sterben, to die away, to drop off.

Dahinge'gen, adv. on the contrary, see Dagegen, Hingegen.

Dahin'ten, adv. behind, behind there.

Dahin'ter, adv. behind it (that, this); after it; fig.-a. es ist nichts —, there is nothing in it; er fing an zu glauben, daß etwas — sein könnte, he began to think there might be something in it; — steckt etwas, there is some secret in it; —kommen, to get to the bottom of a thing, to find it out.

Da'..., in comp. —hinum, adv. coll. round there; —hinwärts, adv. thitherward, that way.

Dahl'bord, (str.) m. & n. Mar. border, edging, side-planks all round the deck; gunwale. [dally, play the fool.

Dah'len, (w.) v. intr. provinc. to trifle,

Dak, (str.) m. (L. G.) Mar. thick mist at sea. – Da'ken, (w.) v. intr. to be misty (Nebeln). – Da'kig, adj. misty.

* Daktylisch &c., see Dac...

Dal, (L. G.) I. adj. down; II. (str.) n., see Deal.

Dal'be, (w.) f. (L. G.) Mar. bollard (Duckdalbe). [set, go down (said of the sun).

Da'len, (w.) v. intr. Mar. (cf. Dal) to sink,

A. Dalk, (str.) m. provinc. see 1) Kloß; 2) Klotz; 3) Tölpel.

B. Dalk, (str.) m. a Turkish travelling-carriage.

Dalma'tien [–'tsĭĕn], n. Geogr. Dalmatia. – Dalma'tier, Dalmati'ner, (str.) m., Dalma'tisch, adj. Dalmatian.

* Daltonis'mus, m. see Farbenblindheit.

Da'malig, adj. at, of that time, then; zu d-er Zeit, at that time, then; der d-e König, the then (reigning) king.

Da'mals, adv. then, at that time.

* Dam'ar, see Dammar.

* Damasce'ner, I. adj. Damascene; damask; II. in comp. —erde, f. Miner. adamic earth; —klinge, f. damask-blade; Bot.-a. —pflaume, f. damask-plum, damascene (Prunus domestica damascena L.); —rose, f. damask-rose (Rosa damascena L.); —säbel, m. damaskin; —stahl, m. damask-steel; III. (str.) m. 1) inhabitant of Damascus; 2) see —säbel.

* Damasci'ren, (w.) v. tr. 1) (or Damassi'ren) Weav. to damask; 2) a) Sword-mill. to damaskeen; b) Stahl —, to give a damask-surface to steel. – Damasci'rer, (str.) m. damask-worker. – Damasci'rung, (w.) f. damask-surface (of Damascus-steel).

* Damast', (str.) m. (collat. forms: Dam'mast [Voss], Damask', &c. [cf. Sanders], from Damas'(cus)) Comm. damask; seidener —, damask silk; leinener —, damask linen; wollener —, mock-satin; —artig, adj. like damask; —fabrik, f. damask (linen) factory; —gewebe, n. huckaback; —harnisch, m. Weav. harness; —stuhl, m. loom of a damask-weaver; —weber, —wirker, m. damask-weaver.

* Damast'en, adj. damask; d-es Tafelzeug, damask table-linen.

Dam, (str.) m. see Damhirsch.

Däm'brett, n. see Damenbrett. [lady.

Däm'chen, (str.) n. (dimin. of Dame) little

* Da'me, (w.) f. (Fr.) 1) lady; gentlewoman; meine D-n! ladies! 2) Gam. a) queen (in French playing-cards and at chess); b) king (at draughts); — spielen, die — ziehen, to play at draughts; in die — kommen, to get a crown; einen Stein zur — machen, to crown (to king) a man (at draughts); 3) T. see Handramme (Jungfer); 4) Pom. lange —, kind of pear; 5) Bot. a species of water-flag (Iris Susiana); 6) Entom. a) a species of silk-worm; b) see Fangheuschrecke.

Dä'melack, (str.) m. coll. stupid fellow, dreamer, dolt. – Dämelei', (w.) f. coll. doltishness, blundering stupidity. – Dä'meln, (w.) v. intr. to behave foolishly, to drivel.

Da'men, (w.) v. intr. (h. u.) 1) for Dame spielen; 2) see Aufdamen.

Da'men..., in comp. —brett, n. 1) draught-board, (a pair of) tables; 2) Conch. small dice-casket (Buccinum arcula L.); 3) a kind of butterfly (Hipparchia galathea); —blume, f. Bot. common fritillary, chequered lily (Fritillaria meleagris L.); —gürtel, m. ladies' girdle; —handschuhe, m. pl. ladies' gloves; —hut, m. ladies' bonnet; ein italienischer —hut, Leghorn bonnet; —kaffee, m. beverage made of sweet and bitter almonds, prepared as coffee; —käst-chen, n. see Nähkästchen; —knecht, m. coll. dangler, ladies' man; —kragen, m. a lady's collar; —pflaume, f. see Damascenerpflaume; —putz, m. w. man's attire; —reitanzug, m., —reitkleid, —reithabit, n. ladies' riding habit; joseph; —sattel, m. saddle for ladies, side-saddle; —schneider, m. ladies' tailor (Frauenschneider); —spiel, n. 1) (play at) draughts; 2) see —brett; —(spiel)stein, m. man at draughts; —welt, f. the fair sex.

Dam'..., in comp. —geiß, —hirschkuh, f. doe (the female of the fallow deer); —gemse, f. a species of antelope (Antilope dorcas Licht.); —hirsch, m. fallow deer, buck.

Dä'misch, adj. vulg. dull, stupid, doltish, heavy, drowsy.

Damit', I. *adv.* [da'mit, *sometimes (when not emphasised)* damit'] therewith, with it (this, that): thereby, by it, by that: wozu dienen die Augen? um damit' zu sehen, what are eyes for? to see with: — endete die Sache, there the matter ended: was wollen Sie — sagen? what do you mean by it? — haben wir Alles gesagt, when we have said this we have said all: — ist mir nicht gedient, that will not serve my turn, this will not do for me: — ist es noch nicht vorbei, that is not yet the end of the matter; es ist aus —' [damit'], there is an end of *or* to it: und da'mit gut, and there (is) an end (to it); nur heraus damit'! out with it! II. *conj.* (damit') that: in order to, to: — nicht, lest, for fear (that). [fallow deer).

Dam'lige, *(w.) f.* fawn (the young of the

Däm'lich, *see* Dämisch.

Damm, *(str., pl.* Däm'me) *m.* 1) dam, bank, embankment, dike, water-gage: (Hafen—) mole, jetty, pier: mound: 2) *Fish.* garth, wear; 3) *(or* —weg, *m.)* causeway; 4) *Anat.* perinæum; 5) *T.* pit (of bell-founders); *fig.* e. einem Ding einen — entgegensetzen, to stem the tide of a thing; auf dem — sein, 1. to be stirring, to be on the alert, to be wide awake; 2. to be well off; auf den — bringen, to set up or going, to put in the way of getting on.

* **Dam'mar,** *(str.)* n. (—harz, *n.) Chem.* dammar, dammarine: —fichte, *f. Bot.* dammar-pine (*Dammara orientalis* Lindl.).

Damm'..., *in comp.* —aufseher, *m.* dike-grave, dike-reeve: —bau, *m.* damming, diking: —bruch, *m.* 1) rupture of a dam: 2) *Anat. see* —riß; —distel, *f. see* Brachdistel; —eis, *n.* bag-ice.

Däm'meln, *(w.) v. intr. coll.* to saunter about, to trifle.

Däm'men, *(w.) v.* I. *intr.* 1) to dam; 2) to riot, revel: II. *tr.* 1) to dam (in), embank, to (stop by means of a) dike; 2) *fig.* to curb, restrain, check.

Däm'mer, *(str.) m. & n.* (hazy) down, &c. *see* —licht.

Damm'erde, *(w.) f. Agr.* mould, black-earth, (upper) soil: *Min.* upper-earth.

Däm'merer, *(str.) m.* dreamer.

Däm'merhaft, *adj.* dusky, dim: *fig.* dreamy.

Däm'merig, *adj.* twilight: dusky, dim, gray, cloudy, misty: *fig.* dreamy.

Däm'merlich, *adj.* duskish.

Däm'merlicht, *(str.) n.,* **Däm'merschein,** *(str.) m.* dawn: twilight, glimmer; dusk.

Däm'mern, *(w.) v. intr.* 1) to dawn; to grow *or* be twilight: to grow dusky: to spread a twilight; eine d-de Hoffnung, a faint hope; 2) *fig. a)* to float (of a suspicion, &c.); *b)* to dream.

Däm'merung, *(w.) f.* twilight, crepuscule, gray; dusk, duskiness; Morgen—, *f.* dawn, morning-twilight; Abend—, *f.* dusk, evening-twilight; D-sfalter, D-sschmetterling, D-svogel, *m.* crepuscular butterfly (Abendfalter).

Damm'..., *in comp.* —gegend, *f. Anat.* perinæum: —geld, *n.* 1) pierage; 2) toll; —grund, *m.* upland: —inspector, —meister, *m. see* —aufseher; —riß, *m. Anat.* rupture or laceration of the perinæum: —schüttung, *f.* embankment: —setzer, *m.* pavier: —verwalter, *m. see* —aufseher; —weg, *m.* highway, causeway: —weide, *f. see* Bachweide; —zieher, *m. Gunn.* worm, ladle (for a great gun).

* **Dam'no,** *(str.) n. (Bol.)* loss; — machen, to sell under prime-cost; ein Procent —, one per cent average.

* **Dä'mon,** *(str., pl. [w.]* Dämo'nen) *m.* (*Gr.*) demon. — **Dämo'nisch,** *adj.* demonlike, demoniac, demoniacal.

Dampf, *(str., pl.* Dämpfe) *m.* 1) steam; vapour; smoke; fume, reek; damp, exhalation; 2) *Med.* asthma, pursiness; 3) *Farr.* chest-foundering, broken-wind; das Pferd hat den —, the horse is broken-winded *or* chest-foundered: mit *or* im — kochen, to steam (potatoes, &c.); *vulg. s.* einen — haben, to be flustered, muddled; Einem (Tort und) — anthun, to vex, tease, plague; er ist ein Hans —, he is a giddy-headed *or* heedless fellow.

Dampf'..., *in comp.* —absperrung, *f.* cutting off of steam; —aichmaß ..., *see* —eichmaß; —apparat, *m.* steam-apparatus; —auflösung, *f. Chem.* volatilisation; —auslassungsröhre, *f.* steam-outlet-pipe, eduction-pipe: —bad, *n.* vapour-bath, steam-bath; *Med.* fomentation; —bagger, *m. T.* steam-muddlerer, steam-mud-heaver; —balg, *m.* fumigating-bellows.

Dampf'bar, *adj. Chem.* I. absorbable; II. D-keit, *(w.) f.* absorbableness.

Dämpf'bar, *adj.* capable of being damped, &c. *cf.* Dämpfen.

Dampf'..., *in comp.* —barometer, *n. & m. see* —messer; —beere, *f. see* Aftholder; —behälter, *m.* steam-vessel; —bett, *n.* steam-bed; —blase, *f. see* —kessel; —bleiche, *f.* bleaching by steam; —boot, *n.* steam-boat, *coll.* steamer; —bootfahrt, —bootreise, *f.* steam-voyage; —brennerei, *f.* steam-distillery; —brot, *n.* steam-baked bread; —buchdruckerpresse, *f. see* —presse; —büchse, *f. see* —kammer; —bugsirfahrzeug, *n.* steam-tow-boat, steam-tug; —cur, *f. Med.* fumigation; —cylinder, *m.* steam-cylinder: —dicht, *adj.* steam-tight; —druck, *m.* steam-pressure: —eichmaß(pfeife), *f.* steam-gauge(-whistle): —einlaßventil, *n.* steam-valve.

Dampf'en, *(w.) v.* I. *intr.* to steam; to emit steam, to smoke, to fume; to reek; to exhale, evaporate; II. *tr. coll.* to smoke (tobacco).

Dämpf'en, *(w.) v. tr.* 1) to damp, suffocate; 2) *lit. & fig.* to quench, smother, quell, stifle, suppress, to extinguish, put out, to subdue, repress, to sober down; 3) *Cook.* to stew, to codle; 4) *T.* to steam; 5) *Mus. a)* to deaden (the sound); *b)* to deafen, muffle (a musical instrument); *c)* eine Geige —, to apply a mute to a violin; mit gedämpfter Stimme, in an undertone, under one's breath, with a subdued voice: gedämpfter Ton, muffled sound; gedämpfte Trommeln, muffled drums; den Staub —, to lay the dust.

Dampf'er, *(str.) m. coll.* 1) steam-boat, steam-ship, *usual.* steamer; 2) steam-carriage; 3) *T. see* Windpfeife.

Dämpf'er, *(str.) m.* 1) extinguisher; 2) *T.* damper (of a locomotive, &c.); 3) *Mus.* damper (in a piano-forte), sordine, mute, *or* damper (applied to the bridge of a violin, tenor, &c.); 4) *fig.* damper, moderator; (dem Eifer Jemandes &c.) einen — aufsetzen, to apply a damper (to the ardour of one, &c.), to damp; 5) *see* Dampfer.

Dampf'..., *in comp.* —erzeuger, *m.* steam-generator; —erzeugung, *f.* steam-generation; —esse, *f.* chimney-stalk, smoke-pipe (of a steamer or locomotive engine); stack; —fahrzeug, *n.* steam-vessel; —flinte, *f.* steam-gun; —flotte, *f.* steam-fleet, *cf.* —marine; —fregatte, *f.* steam-frigate: —getriebe, *n. see* —maschine; —geschütz, —gewehr, *n.* steam-gun; —gewichtswage, *f. Mech.* steam-weighing-balance: —gewölbe, *n.* upper part of the boiler; —gitter, *n.* gratings: —gläser, *n. pl. Opt.* glasses blackened with smoke for the observation of eclipses of the sun; —göpel, *m. Min.* machine-winch: —hahn, *m.* steam-cock: —heizung, *f.* heating by steam: —heizungsröhre, *f.* steam-heating pipe: —horn, Dämpf'horn, *n. see* Dämpfer, 1.

Dampf'ig, *adj.* steamy.

Dämpf'ig, *adj. Med.* asthmatical, asthmatic; *Farr.* chest-foundered, broken-winded.

Dampf'..., *in comp.* —kaffee, *m.* coffee roasted by steam: —kammer, *f.,* —kasten, *m.* steam-chamber, steam-room, steam-chest,

[illegible] time, withal: gleich —, dicht —, hard by, [illegible] by; der —stehende, by-stander.

Dä'nemark, (str.) n. Geogr. Denmark.

[illegible]eln, see Dengeln.

Danie'den, adv. († &) *there below, down [illegible] (cf. Hienieden).

Danie'der, adv. on the ground; down, cf. [illegible]; —liegen, I. 1) to lie down, (krank) to lie sick, to be ill (an [with Dat.], of), to [illegible] laid up (with); 2) fig. to lie prostrate, to be subdued (broken, destroyed); to languish; to be at a stand; II. das — liegen, v. s. (str.) stagnation (of trade, &c.).

Da'niel, m. Daniel (P. N.).

Dä'nin, (w.) f. Danish woman, Dane.

Dä'nisch, adj. Danish; das D–e, the Danish language; d–es Leder, Comm. spruce leather.

Dank, (str.) m. 1) thanks; acknowledgment, gratitude; 2) reward; — beim Turnier, prize; (Einem) — abstatten, — sagen, to return or give thanks, to thank, to make one's acknowledgments to ...; wenig — von (einer Sache) haben, to earn but little thanks for ...; Einem etwas — wissen, to take a thing kindly of one; er wird es ihm schlechten — wissen, 1. he will not thank him for it, he will not take it kindly of him; 2. he will not have much to thank him for; das wäre also Ihr — für all meine Mühe! this, then, is your return for all my trouble; das hatte ich zum — dafür, [illegible] I got this for my pains; mit —, gratefully; mit Anerkennung und —, with grateful [illegible]; Gott or dem Himmel sei — ! thank God! God or heaven be praised! es Einem zu [illegible] machen, to give satisfaction, to do to one's liking; man kann es ihm nie zu D–e machen, [illegible] (you) never can make it to please him.

Dank'adresse, (w.) f. vote of thanks.

Dank'bar, I. adj. thankful, grateful (gegen, [illegible]) — verbunden, highly obliged or indebted; [illegible] — würde ich Ihnen sein, I should feel [illegible] grateful to you; II. D–keit, (w.) f. gratitude, thankfulness, acknowledgment; zur — [illegible], bound in gratitude.

Dank'..., in comp. —beflissen, adj. studious [illegible] be grateful; —begier(de), f. desire of manifesting one's gratitude; —begierig, adj. [illegible] to be thankful or grateful.

Dan'ken, (w.) v. tr. & intr. (Einem [für] [illegible]) 1) to return thanks, to thank (for); 2) to return a (or the) bow, to acknowledge a [illegible]; 3) to decline an offer, to refuse: [illegible] Sie noch etwas Suppe? — Ich danke; [illegible] some soup? — No, I thank you (I thank [illegible], ohne zu, würde heißen: Ja, wenn's beliebt [illegible]) see Verdanken.

Dank'enswerth, adj. thankworthy.

Dank'..., in comp. —erfüllt, adj. thankful; [illegible] see Erkenntlichkeit; —gebet, n. prayer [illegible] thanksgiving; —lied, n. thanksgiving-song.

Dank'los, adj. thankless.

Dank'..., in comp. —opfer, n. thank-offering; [illegible] —predigt, f. thanksgiving-sermon; [illegible] speech made to return thanks; —sagung, f. thanksgiving, (rendering or expression of) thanks; [illegible] thanksgiving-day; [illegible] letter of acknowledgment [illegible] —schuldig, adj. see —beflissen; [illegible] —verpflichtet, adj. bound in gratitude; [illegible] adj. ungrateful; —würdig, [illegible]

[illegible] adv. 1) then, at that time; 2) then, [illegible] — und wann, now and then; [illegible]

[illegible] grounded by the grap[illegible] [illegible] times.

[illegible] (sometimes, when emphasised: da'[illegible] [illegible] thereat, about it, [illegible] [illegible] —? do

you doubt of it; er ist Schuld —, it is his fault, he bears the blame; Stäbe mit Bändern —, wands with ribbons attached; — liegend, adjacent, adjoining; nahe —, 1. hard by, close to; 2. fig. about (to fall, &c.), on the point or eve (of); es fehlten 3 Schilling —, there wanted to it 3 shilling; wie sind Sie mit Geld —? how are you off for money? wie sind Sie mit ihm —? how are you situated with him? ich bin — (dran), it is my turn; er thut wohl — [cf. da'ran (emphatically) thut er wohl], he does, acts well in this; Sie würden wohl — thun, zu ..., you would do well to ...; es ist nichts —, coll. there's nothing in it, it is good for nothing; — denken, to think of it; — geben, to yield (up), surrender, renounce, relinquish, abandon; — gehen, to go to it, to go or set about; —gabe, f., —geld, n. see D(a)raufgeld; — kommen, 1. to come to it; 2) to get at it; nun komme or bin ich —, now it is my turn; wir kommen or sind zuerst —, our turn comes first; Gam. we have the innings; Andere — kommen lassen, to give others a turn; — liegen, to signify, to concern, to matter, to import; — [da'ran] liegt mir vor Allem, that is more especially my aim, that is what I am most anxious (solicitous) about; es ist mir — gelegen, it concerns me; es liegt nichts —, es ist nichts — gelegen, it matters (imports) not, it is no matter, it is of no consequence; — machen, to bind or fasten to; sich — machen, see — gehen; — müssen, to be obliged, to be forced to submit or to do; — sein, 1. see — kommen; 2. to be in a certain condition, to be placed in a position; gut — sein, to be well off, to be favourably circumstanced; schlimm or übel — sein, to be ill or badly off, to be in a sad case or plight; er war am schlimmsten or übelsten —, he was the worst off, he had the worst of it; ich weiß nicht, wie ich — bin, I know not what to think of it; wir wissen nicht, wie sie mit ihm — ist, we do not know how she stands with him; Sie sind unrecht —, you are mistaken; es ist etwas —, there is something in it; es ist nichts —, 1. there is nothing (no truth, &c.) in it; 2. it is not good for anything; 3. it matters not, it is of no consequence; er ist eifrig —, he is hard at it; — setzen, to stake, cf. aufs Spiel setzen; Alles — setzen, to do one's utmost, to strain every nerve; — wachsend, Bot. adnascent; — wollen, to intend setting about; nicht — wollen, to decline, refuse, reject; er will nicht gern —, he does not like this business, he is loth to undertake it.

Darauf' [sometimes, when emphasised: da'rauf], adv. 1) thereon; thereupon; upon it, that, on it; at that, to that or it, of that; 2) after (that); afterwards; then; gerade — zu, directly up to or towards it; das Postgeld, welches ich — bezahlte, the postage I paid thereon; es steht der Kopf —, it is a capital offence; es steht der Tod —, it is (no less than) death; — folgend, ensuing; etwas — geben, to give an earnest, to pay earnest-money; — gehen, fig. coll. 1. to be spent, exhausted, wasted; consumed; 2. to die, perish; unser Geld war — gegangen, our money was all gone; viel — gehen lassen, to spend freely; —geld, n. earnest-money, deposit, advance; — hin, on that consideration, on the strength of that; ich arbeite — hin, I strive for that object; — hin reiste er ab, in consequence of this (relying upon this) he departed; — kommen, fig. 1. or — fallen, to hit upon, fall or light on, upon; 2. to call to mind, to remember; wie kommst du —? what should make you think so? es kommt nicht — an, it is of no consequence, cf. Ankommen, I. 3, c; es — wagen, to venture, to hazard it.

Darauf'schlagsteuer, (w.) f. additional tax.

Daraus' [sometimes, when emphasised: da'raus], adv. therefrom, thence; from this, out of this; of it, this; — [da'raus] folgt, hence it follows; — [da'raus] sehe ich, thence I see; ich kann nichts — machen, I can make nothing of it; was ist — geworden? what has become of it? es ist nichts — geworden, it has (is) all come to nothing; es kann nichts — werden, 1. nothing can come of it, coll. that won't do; 2. it cannot be (done, granted, &c.).

† Daraus'sen, see Draußen.

Dar'ben, (w.) v. intr. 1) to suffer want (of food), to suffer extreme hunger, to starve, famish; 2) see Sterben.

Dar'bepfarre, (w.) f. see Hungerpfarre.

Där'bieten, (str.) v. I. tr. to present, offer, tender, hold out or forth, proffer, afford; II. refl. to present, offer; es bietet sich eine Gelegenheit dar, an opportunity offers.

Darb'niß, (w.) f. starvation, famishment.

Där'bringen, (irr.) v. tr. to present, bring in, offer, render; seine Erkenntlichkeit —, to tender one's acknowledgments. — Där'bringung, (w.) f. (the act of) presenting, offering, &c.

Dardanel'len, f. pl. Geogr. the Dardanelles.

Darei'n [da'rein, when emphasised], adv. thereinto, into it or that; — geben, to give into the bargain; sich — geben, fügen, schicken, finden, to reconcile, accommodate one's self, submit to a thing; — willigen, to consent to; sich — legen, to interpose, interfere, mediate; — reden, to interrupt; — schlagen, 1. to strike (at random), to lay about one; 2. refl. or sich — mischen, to meddle in or with a thing, cf. sich — legen.

Darg, (str.) m. provinc. (a layer of) bog-earth under clayey soil.

Dar'ge, (w.) f. provinc. brass-hook for catching pike. — Dar'gen, (w.) v. intr. to fish for pike with such a hook.

Där'geben, (str.) v. tr. to offer up, expose; to give.

Där'halten, (str.) v. tr. to reach forth, hold forth.

Darin' [sometimes, when emphasised: da'rin], adv. therein, in it, that, or this; within; ich habe mich — geirrt, I have been mistaken in this respect; ein guter Mann findet sein größtes Vergnügen —, Anderen Gutes zu thun, a good man finds his greatest enjoyment in doing good to others; — [da'rin] halte ich es mit ..., there I hold with ...; er täuscht sich —, wenn er glaubt..., he deceives himself (is mistaken) in believing ...; mit — begriffen, included (therein).

Darin'nen, adv. within, in the inner parts.

Där'kommen, (str.) n. Law. inherited property.

Där'lage, (w.) f. 1) something laid down; money laid down; deposit; 2) see Darlegung.

Där'legen, (w.) v. tr. 1) to lay down; 2) fig. to show, exhibit, display, lay open, expose; to demonstrate, explain, state; to submit. — Där'legung, (w.) f. 1) (the act of) laying down; 2) fig. exhibition, exposure, exposition, statement; manifestation; nach — der Verhältnisse, after (upon) explaining the circumstances.

Där'lehen, (str.) n., Där'lehe (l. u.), (w.) f. loan, money lent out (on interest). — Där'leihen, (str.) v. tr. to lend (out), advance (money). — Där'leiher, (str.) m. (money-) lender. — Där'leihung, Där'lehnung, (w.) f. (the act of) lending, loan.

Darm, c. I. (str., pl. Där'me) m. gut; Anat. der gerade —, rectum (Mastdarm); der grobe —, colon; der lange —, ileum; pl. intestines, bowels; II. in comp. intestinal; —ausleerung, f. stool, motion; —bad, n., —bähe, f. clyster; —beere, f. see Elsebeerbaum, 2; —bewegung, f. peristaltic motion; —bruch, m. Med. intestinal rupture or hernia, enterocele; —canal, m. intestinal canal; —drehung, f. see —bewegung; —einschiebung, f. introsusception of the intestines; —einschnürung, f. Vet. strangula-

[illegible]'er..., *in comp.* —bier, *n. see* Lager-[illegible]; —blumen, *f. pl.* eternal flowers; —ge-[illegible], *n. pl.*, —pflanzen, *f. pl.* perennials.

Dau'erhaft, (*rarely fig. or of persons*) I. [illegible] durable, lasting, strong; stout; sub-[illegible]; d-e Farben, fast *or* good-wearing [illegible]; d-e Geschäftsverbindung, (*l. u.*) per-[illegible] connection; dergleichen Werkzeuge [illegible] (müßten) — sein, such instruments [illegible] be made to last; II. D-igkeit, (*w.*) *f.* [illegible], durability, &c.; strength.

Dau'erlauf, (*str.*) *m.*, Dau'errennen, (*str.*) [illegible], running race in which duration, not [illegible], determines the victor.

Dau'erlos, *adj.* (*l. u.*) perishable, tran-[illegible], ephemeral.

Dau'ern, (*w.*) *v. intr.* to last, continue, hold [illegible], endure, stand; to keep; es dauerte lange, [illegible] er ... fand, he was long in finding ...; [illegible] dauert lange, ehe er warm wird, *fig.* it [illegible] a great deal to warm him; d-d, *p. a.* [illegible], &c., permanent; *Bot.* perennial; kurz [illegible] short-lived.

Dau'ern, (*w.*) *v. tr. impers.* to make sorry; [illegible] move to pity; to grieve; es (er) dauert [illegible], I am sorry for it (him); sie dauert mich, [illegible] grieved (I feel) for her; du dauerst mich, [illegible] pity you; es hat mich oft gedauert, I have [illegible] regretted it; laß dich die Kosten nicht —, [illegible] grudge the expense.

[illegible]'ling, (*str.*) *m. see* Dell.

[illegible], (*str.*, *pl.* Däu'me *l. u.*) *m.* thumb, [illegible] Daumen; —dreher, *m. vulg. fig.* flatterer, [illegible].

[illegible], *s.* I. (*str.*) *m.* (*dimin.*: Däum'-[illegible] (*str.*) *n.* thumbkin) 1) *a)* thumb; *b)* [illegible], the middle part of the wing of a bird; [illegible] tappet, lift, lifting-cog, wiper; break (a [illegible] piece attached to a break-wheel); [illegible]. Einem den — drehen, to flatter one; [illegible] den — aufdrücken *or* aufs Auge drücken [illegible], halten), to keep a tight hand over one, [illegible] to keep under one's thumb; Einem [illegible] — halten, to support, patronise, counte-[illegible] a person; den — rühren, to pocket out [illegible]; Einem die — schrauben, to put one's [illegible] into a thumb-screw; II. *in comp.* — [illegible], *m. Anat.* flexor of the thumb; — [illegible], *f.* thumb's breadth (an inch); —drücker, [illegible] thumb-latch; —eisen, *n.* 1) *see* — [illegible]; 2) *Wire-dr.* thumb-stall; —feste, *Law,* [illegible]; —klapper, *m.* castanet; — [illegible], *m. Anat.* t(h)enar; —leder, *n.*, —ring, [illegible] thumb-leather, thumb-ring; —schraube, *f.*, [illegible], *m.* thumb-screw; —strecker, *m. Anat.* [illegible] of the thumb; —welle, *f. Mech.* [illegible]-wheel (wheel with tappets or wipers).

[illegible], (*str.*, *pl.* D-[illegible]) *f. Mech.* [illegible], jack.

[illegible], Däu'merling, (*str.*) *m.* 1) [illegible]; 2) *coll.* thumb-stall; 3) [illegible], *see* Daumen, 2; 4) *fig.* Tom thumb.

[illegible], (*str.*, *pl.* D-[illegible]) *n.* thumb [illegible].

[illegible], (*w.*) *f.* down (Flaumfeder).

[illegible], Dau'nig, *adj.* downy.

[illegible] [illegible], (*str.*, *pl.* D-e) *m.* [illegible].

[illegible], (*str.*, *pl.* Dä[illegible]) *n.* [illegible]; [illegible] the [illegible]; the distance;

[illegible] (*sometimes, when emphasised,* be'-[illegible]), *adv.* 1) [illegible], therefrom, of that, of [illegible] that, from it; whereof; by this, by [illegible]; was habe ich —? what do I [illegible] — [illegible] that is [illegible] — [illegible], that comes [illegible] the consequences of) [illegible] —, to keep off or [illegible] alone; — [illegible] [illegible] —fliegen,

to fly off *or* away, to take wing; —gehen, to go off, to take one's self off; —helfen, 1. to help out; 2. to rid of; —kommen, to come off, get off, get clear; —laufen, to run off, run away, to scamper (away, off); es ist zum — laufen, it is past bearing; sich —machen, to get away, make off; to take to one's heels; to slink away, &c.; —tragen, 1) to carry off, away; 2) *fig.* to get, obtain; den Sieg — tragen, to get the victory, to bear away the palm; Schande —tragen, to come off with disgrace; —ziehen, *v. intr.* (*aux.* sein) to draw off, retire, withdraw.

Davor' [*sometimes, when emphasised,* da'-vor], *adv.* 1) before it *or* that; 2) for that, for it; from that, from it; ich habe einen Abscheu —, I have a horror of it; ich fürchte mich nicht —, I am not afraid of it; da'vor fürchte ich mich allerdings, I am sure I am afraid of such things; hüte dich —, take heed of it, beware of it; da'vor behüte uns Gott! God forbid; ich kann nichts —, *see* Dafür.

Dawi'der [*sometimes, when emphasised,* da'wider], *adv.* against it or that (*cf.* Dagegen); nichts — haben, to have no objections to; dafür und —, pro and con, for and against; dafür und — streiten, to dispute the pros and cons; er setzte sich —, he opposed it.

Dazu' (*sometimes, when emphasised,* da'zu), *adv.* 1) thereto; to that, to it; 2) for that, for it; for that purpose, to that end, for the occasion; at it *or* that; 3) (noch —) besides, moreover, in addition to ...; sie aßen Wurzeln —, they ate roots along with it; ich habe meine Ursachen —, I have my reasons for it; da'zu habe ich kein Geld, I have no money for such things; noch — unter der Last, under the additional burden (of, &c.); er spricht auch —, he puts in his word; —geben, to contribute; er gehört auch *or* mit —, he too has a hand (is a sharer) in it; sich —halten, to make haste (sich beeilen); —kommen, 1. to arrive at a certain time *or* moment, to happen to meet *or* find...; ich kam —, als es (dies) stattfand, I chanced to come when it occurred; 2. to be added, to supervene; — kommt, add to this, added to; 3. to come by, obtain a thing; — kommen können, to be able to find time; ich kann nicht — kommen, 1. I cannot get at it; 2. (*coll.* ich kann nicht —) I cannot find time to ...; nichts — können, *provinc. for* nichts dafür können; man muß noch dies —nehmen, it must be added (that, &c.); es ist nichts —, *see* es ist nichts daran, *in* Daran; es hat allen Anschein —, there is every appearance of it; —rechnen, —zählen, to add to the number; wenn Sie noch —rechnen, if you throw in (*or* adding to (it) beside; —thun, 1. to add; ohne etwas — oder davon zu thun, without addition or diminution; 2. *fig.* to make haste, to set about it.

Da'zumal, *adv.* then, at that time.

Dazwisch'en [*sometimes, when emphasised,* da'zwischen], *adv.* between it, between; — befindlich, intermediate; —kommen, to come between, intervene, to interfere, interrupt, hinder, prevent; es ist mir etwas — gekommen, something intervened to prevent me, I was disappointed; —kunft, *f.* 1) intervention, interposition, interference; 2) interruption; —liegend, *adj.* lying between; interjacent; —reden, to interrupt; sich —schlagen, *fig.* to interpose one's authority; —stehen, to stand between *or* betwixt; —treten, I. (*str.*) *v. intr.* to intercede, interfere, interpose; II. *s.* (*str.*) *n.* intercession. [unpack, unbale.

* Dėballi'ren, (*w.*) *v. tr.* (*Fr.*) *Comm.* to

* Debat'te, (*w.*) *f.* (*Fr. débat*) debate (über [*with Acc.*], on, upon), discussion (of). — Debatti'ren, (*w.*) *v. intr.* to debate (über [*with Acc.*], on, upon); über eine Sache —, to discuss a matter.

De'be, (*w.*) *f. provinc.* bitch.

* De'bent, (*Lat. third pers. pl.*, they owe, *cf.* Debet) *Comm.* debtors.

* Debentur', (*w.*) *f.* debenture.

* De'bet, (*orig.* [*Lat.*] *third pers. sing. pres. tense of* debere; he owes, he ought to [soll, *which see*] *i. e.* pay, *opp.* Credit, *A.*) (*str.*, *pl.* D-s, *sometimes* De'bita [*pl. of* De'bitum]) *n. Comm.* debit; — und Credit, debtor and creditor; im — stehen, to be on the debtor-side; —seite, *f.* debit- or debtor-side.

* Debit', (*str.*) *m.* (*Fr.*) *Comm.* sale, market, vent; —commission, *f. see* Concursbehörde; —verfahren, *n. see* Concurs. — Debitant', (*w.*) *m. Comm.* tradesman, dealer. — Debiti'ren, (*w.*) *v. tr. Comm.* 1) to debit; debitirt sein, to be at one's debit; Einen Rechnung —, to place to one's debit, to charge to one's account; 2) to sell, dispose of. [(*Lat.*) *Comm.* debtor.

* De'bitor, (*str.*, *pl.* [*w.*] Debito'ren) *m.*

* Debouchi'ren [—buschi'—], (*w.*) *v. intr.* (*Fr.*) *Mil.* to debouch.

* Deboursi'ren [—bur—], (*w.*) *v. tr.* (*Fr.*) to disburse, *see* Auslegen, 5.

* Debüt' [*pr.* debü'], (*str.*, *pl.* D-s) *m.* (*Fr.*) *début*, a first appearance before the public, as of an actor, &c. — Debütant', (*w.*) *m. débutant.* — Debütan'tin, (*w.*) *f. débutante.* — — Debüti'ren, (*w.*) *v. intr.* to make one's *début*, *coll.* to *début*.

* Deca'de, (*w.*) *f.* (*L. Lat.* decada, *from Gr.* dekás, *acc.*, *number, &c. of ten*) decade. — Deca'disch, *adj.* decadal, pertaining to ten; consisting of, &c. tens.

* Decali'ren, (*w.*) *v. intr. Comm.* to lose in the weight (by exsiccation); *from* Deca'lo, (*str.*, *pl.* D-s) *n.* (*Ital.*) deficiency in weight caused by exsiccation, &c., inlack (of weight *or* measure).

* Decan', (*str.*) (*Lat.*) *m.* dean — Decanat', (*str.*) *n.*, Decanei', (*w.*) *f.* deanship; deanery.

* Decati'ren (*corr.* Decatisi'ren), (*w.*) *v. tr.* (*Fr.*) *Cloth.* to hot-press, lustre *or* steam (cloth), to sponge (woollens).

* De'cem, (*str.*, *pl.* D-s) *m.* (*Lat.* decem, *ten*) 1) tithe; 2) *fig.* a person's due.

Decem'ber, (*str.*) *m.* December.

* Decem'vir, (*str.*, *pl.* [*w.*] D-n) *m. Rom. Ant.* decemvir. — Decemvirat', (*str.*) *n.* decemvirate.

* Decenz', (*w.*) *f.* (*Lat.*) decency.

* Decernent', (*w.*) *m.* (*Lat.*) *Law.* judge.

* Dechant', (*w.*) *m.*, Dechanei', Dechantei', (*w.*) *f. see* Decan, Decanat.

* Dechar'ge [*pr.* deschär'zhe], (*w.*) *f.* (*Fr.*) *Comm.* discharge. — Dechargi'ren [—zhi'ren], (*w.*) *v. tr.* to discharge, release (from an obligation, &c.).

Dech'er, (*str.*) *m.* dicker (a quantity of ten hides, in the leather-trade); timber (forty pieces, of Russian peltry); ein — Häute, a dicker (last) of hides.

* Dechiffri'ren [*pr.* deshiffre'ren], (*w.*) *v. tr.* (*Fr.*) to decipher.

Dech'sel, *see* Dächsel, 1.

* Decimal', *adj.* (*L. Lat.*) *Arith.* decimal; —bruch, *m.* decimal fraction; —fuß, *m.* decimal foot; —maß, *n.* decimal measure; —rechnung, *f.* decimal arithmetic; —stelle, *f.* place of a decimal; —system, *n.* decimal system; —zahl, *f.* decimal (number); —zoll, *m.* decimal inch.

* De'cime, (*w.*) *f.* (*Lat.*) *Mus.* the tenth.

* Decimi'ren, (*w.*) *v. tr.* (*Lat.*) to decimate.

* Decintri'ren, (*w.*) *v. tr.* (*Fr.*) *Build.* to take away the centering by which an arch is supported during its erection.

* Decision', (*w.*) *f.*, Deci'sum, (*str.*, *pl.* [*Lat.*] Deci'sa) *n.* (*Lat.*) decision.

Deck, (*str.*) *n. Mar.* deck, *see* Verdeck; erstes oder unterstes —, lower gun-deck; zweites —, 1) upper deck (of a two-decker); 2) middle-deck (of a three-decker); drittes —, upper deck; glattes —, flush deck; gebrochenes —, deck with a waist or open in the middle; loses —, preventer-deck, loose deck; — von Tauen, netting; mit einem — (versehen), decked.

Deck . . ., in comp. **-balken**, f. pl. Ship-b. beams, the great cross-timbers of a ship; **-bett**, n. feather-covering, coverlet; **-blatt**, n. 1) Bot. bracteal or floral leaf, bract; 2) Tob. wrapper (of a cigar); **-blätterig**, adj. Bot. bracteate; **-brett**, n. chess flooring-plank (of a wooden bridge).

Deck'e, (w.) f. 1) cover, covering; envelope; 2) a) blanket; veil, curtain; b) see Plane; c) (Tisch—) cloth; der Tisch war mit einer hübschen — belegt worden, a nice cloth had been spread over the table; d) see Pferdedecke; e) see Umschlagetuch; f) see Fußdecke; 3) Archit. ceiling; 4) Mus. Instr.-m. sound-board (of a violin, guitar, &c.); 5) case; Herol. cock; 6) T. & Typ. cap; 7) see Thondecke; 8) Mech. crown, roof, fire-place; 9) surface (of felted cloth); 10) a) Bot. integument; b) Anat. coat; c) Sport. skin (of a wolf, bear, &c.); 11) fig. see Deckmantel; die — fiel mir von den Augen, the film fell from my eyes; prov.-s. unter der —, in (a) hugger mugger; unter einer — stecken, to conspire together, to have a secret agreement, to collude; sich nach der — strecken, to accommodate (one's self) to circumstances, coll. to cut the garment according to the cloth.

Deck'el, s. I. (str.) m. (**Deck'elchen**, [str.] n. dimin. a small cover) 1) cover, lid; 2) Print. tympan (of a press); 3) Bot. & Conch. operculum; 4) Archit. cornice; 5) Comm. show-end; 6) Conch. operculum, lid; 7) joc. for hat, coll. tile; kein Topf ist so schief, es paßt ein D-chen darauf, proverb, every Darby finds his Joan; — auf dem Zündloche einer Kanone, apron, cap of a gun; — eines Topfes, pot-lid; II. in comp. **-bänder**, n. pl. Print. (pivot-) joints, hinges; **-becher**, m. covered goblet; **-feder**, f. Gun-sm. hammer-spring; **-förmig**, adj. Bot. operculiform; **-glas**, n. glass with a lid; **-kanne**, f., **-krug**, m. tankard; **-schnecke**, f. Conch. operculate snail; **-sieb**, n. a sieve with a (leather) cover; **-stuhl**, m. Print. gallows. [or lid.

Deck'eln, (w.) v. tr. to provide with a cover

Deck'en, (w.) v. I. tr. 1) a) to cover; b) to screen; to shelter; den Tisch —, to lay or spread the cloth, to set the table; es ist gedeckt, the cloth is laid; 2) Mil. to cover (troops on the retreat, &c.), to bring up (the rear), to convey, escort; 3) to cover (of stallions); 4) Dy. to cover; gut (or weniger gut) —, to have great (or less) covering-power; 5) mit einem Dach —, to roof; mit Ziegeln —, to tile; mit Stroh or Schilf —, to thatch; mit Schiefer —, to slate; mit Schindeln —, to shingle; 6) T. to clay, bottom (sugar); 7) Comm. a) to cover, make provision for, refund (a debt); to reimburse, put in cash (a creditor); b) to answer (a bill); die Hafenkosten —, to settle the freight; sich — gegen ...., to recover against ...; er ist hinlänglich gedeckt, he has sufficient security; ich bin noch nicht gedeckt für ...., I am not yet in cash for ...; einige Gläubiger sind gedeckt, some creditors have had their calls (claims) met; seinen Schaden —, to make good one's loss; die Flagge deckt die Waare, free ships make free goods; so deckt es sich, thus the affair is squared; II. refl. Comm. to reimburse one's self; III. recipr. einander (coll. sich) —, Math. to be in congruity; to cover; sich d-de Figuren, consurring figures.

Deck'en . . ., in comp. **-fechter**, m. malmaker; **-gemälde**, **-stück**, n. Paint. ceiling-piece; die beweglichen —stücke eines Theaters, pl. Theat. soffits, heavens.

Deck . . ., in comp. **-farben**, f. pl. Paint. 1) gener. body-colours; 2) water body-colours; **-federn**, f. pl. Ornith. coverts: (der Ohren) ear-coverts; (der Flügel) wing-coverts; (des Schwanzes) tail-coverts; **-firniß**, m. 1) Paint. cream; 2) Engr. turpentine varnish for covering copper-plates; **-fläche**, f. Mech. over-lap; **-formen**, f. pl. Manuf. ground blocks in calico-printing; **-fuge**, f. Archit. covering-joint; **-garn**, n. Sport. sweep-net, drag-net; **-gesims**, n. cornice; **-gut**, n. tobacco used for wrappers; **-hammer**, m. T. 1) slater's hammer; 2) nail-drawer; **-haut**, f. Anat. integument; **-kniee**, n. pl. Mar. hanging-knees of the decks; **-kraft**, f. covering-power (of a colour); **-leder**, n. Sport. leather covering for the lock of a gun; **-lehm**, m. Found. moulding-clay, luting-loam; **-mantel**, m. fig. cloak, pretence, veil, colour, mask, cover; **-messer**, n. hedging-bill; **-netz**, n. see — garn; **-papp**, m. T. resist-paste, reserve; **-planken**, f. pl. Ship-b. deck-planks; **-platte**, f. 1) Archit. cap, coping-stone (of a column, &c.), abacus; 2) T-s. a) cover-plate; b) top plane-iron, break-iron; 3) flag-stone; **-rasen**, m. T. sod; **-rohr**, n. 1) Bot. see Rohrschilf; 2) thatch; **-schilder**, n. pl. Entom. wing-shells; **-schwabber**, m. Mar. main-stay-sail; **-stein**, m. 1) slab, flag-stone; 2) brim (of a well); **-steine**, m. pl. capping or coping bricks, cf. -platte; **-stroh**, n. thatch; **-stützen**, f. pl. Ship-b. cross-pillars; **-syrup**, m. treacle.

Deck'ung, (w.) f. 1) covering, protection; 2) Geom. congruence; 3) Comm. reimbursement; remittance, provision, the needful; ohne —, without funds in hand; zur (behufs) —, to cover; to meet; wegen Mangel an —, for want of provision being made; schnelle —, quick returns; die — hat Zeit, there is time for the needful; nur halbe — haben, to be only covered for the moiety; zur — beauftragen, to commission to do the needful; — senden, to provide the needful, see Decken, 7; — in Händen haben, to be covered; D-sorder, f. order for reimbursement.

Deck . . ., in comp. **-wachs**, n. Engr. bordering-wax; **-werk**, n. Fort. blind; **-wrangen**, f. pl. Ship-b. deck-transoms; **-zeug**, n. table-linen.

* **Declamatiōn'**, (w.) f. (Lat.) declamation. — **Declama'tor**, (str., pl. [w.] Declamato'ren) m. declaimer, reciter. — **Declamato'risch**, adj. declamatory. — **Declami'ren**, (w.) v. tr. (Lat.) to declaim, recite, deliver rhetorically.

* **Declaratiōn'**, (w.) f. (Lat.) Comm. 1) declaration; 2) see Zollangabe; unter — des Werthes, on declaring the value. — **Declari'ren**, (w.) v. tr. (Lat.) Comm. to enter (goods) at the custom-house; zu wenig —, to enter short; zu viel —, to over-enter; den Werth —, to register the value (at the Post); declarirter Werth, declared value.

* **Declinatiōn'**, (w.) f. (Lat.) 1) a) declination (also Gramm.); b) Gramm. declension; 2) see Abweichung. — **Declinir'bar**, adj. declinable. — **Declini'ren**, (w.) v. tr. & intr. 1) to decline (particul. Gramm.); 2) (intr.) to deviate, swerve, digress. — **Declini'rung**, (w.) f. declination. [coction.

* **Decoct'**, (str.) n. (Lat.) decocture, de-

* **Decoratiōn'**, (w.) f. (Lat.) decoration; Theat. scenery, scene; D-en, traverses; D-smaler, m. ornamental painter; scene- or stage-painter; house-painter; D-smalerei, f. decorative painting; scene- or stage-painting. — **Decori'ren**, (w.) v. tr. (Lat.) to decorate.

* **Decort'**, (str.) n. (Fr.) Comm. deduction, abatement, discount. — **Decorti'ren**, (w.) v. tr. Comm. to deduct, abate, discount.

* **Decoupi'ren** [pr. dekup'—], (w.) v. tr. (Fr.) to cut off; to punch. — **Decoupir'säge**, (w.) f. Join. inlaying saw-machine. — **Decoupoir** [pr. dekupoā'r], (str., pl. D-s) n. T. cut-

[illegible], m. stab of a sword; —stock, m. sword-[illegible], sword-cane.

Degen[illegible], (str.) n. see Birkentheer.

* Degradation', (w.) f. (L. Lat.) degradation. — Degradi'ren, (w.) v. tr. to degrade, [deprive] of office, rank, or title; einen Officier [zum] Gemeinen —, to reduce an officer to the [ranks].

* Degummi'ren, (w.) v. tr. T. to remove [(wash] off, &c.) the gum of ....

Dehn'bar, I. adj. 1) extensible, ductile, [extensible], malleable, dilatable, elastic; 2) fig. [ambiguous] (wording of a contract, &c.); II. [D-keit], (w.) f. 1) extensibility, ductility, malleability, elasticity; 2) ambiguousness, ambiguity.

Deh'nen, (w.) v. I. tr. 1) to extend, stretch; [illegible] to distend; to lengthen; eine Linie [illegible], Geom. to produce a line; 2) fig. to spin [illegible] die Wörter —, to drawl one's words; [gedehnte] Sprache, drawl; II. refl. 1) to extend, [to] stretch; to widen; sich behaglich —, to loll; [2)] fig. to last long.

Dehn'..., in comp. —holz, n. T. stretcher; [—kraft], f. see Ausdehnungskraft; —werkzeug, [n.] stretching tool or instrument, see Streck....

Deh'nung, (w.) f. 1) (the act of) extending, stretching; distension, dilation, extension, widening; 2) Gramm. diastole; D-s-[zeichen], n. sign, mark (circumflex) denoting [a] long syllable.

Deich, s. I. (str.) m. dike, pier of earth, [dam], bank, embankment; II. in comp. —amt, [n.] dike-office; —anker, m. the ground or [foundation] upon which a dike is built; —ar[beiter], m. ditcher; —aufseher, m. see —mei[ster]; —band, n. see —verband; —bau, m. dik[ing]; —bruch, m. 1) breach of a dike; (provincial) goel (in a sea-bank); 2) trespass against [the] dike-regulations; —eidige, m. sworn in[spector] of a dike.

Dei'chel, (str.) m. water-pipe.

Dei'chen, (w.) v. intr. to raise up a dike [illegible]; to mend a dike.

Dei'cher, (str.) m. 1) ditcher (Deicharbei[ter]); 2) (D-in, (w.) f.) one who lives near [a] dike or embankment; —lohn, m. ditcher's [wages].

Deich'..., in comp. —fuß, m. see —anker; —[grube], m. excavation produced by digging up [a] dike; —gräber, m. see —arbeiter; —gräfe, —[illegible], m. dike-grave, dike-reeve; —damm, [illegible] —kappe, f. ridge of a dike; —kolbe, f. Bot. [cat]'s tail, reed-mace (Typha L.); —meister, [m.] dike-master, surveyor of a dike; —pflicht, [illegible], f. charge of keeping a dike in [repair]; —pflichtig, adj. obliged to keep a dike [in] repair; —rath, m. counseller of a dike-[illegible]; —recht, n. dike-laws; —richter, m. [dike]-judge; —[illegible], m. see —[illegible]; —schau, f. [dike]-visitation; —schlacht, f. see —graben; —[schleuse], f. dike-sluice, water-gate in a dike; [illegible], m. dike-contribution; —schulze, m. [illegible].

Deich'sel (pr. deik'sel), (w.) f. 1) Carp., Coop. [illegible] adze, addice; 2) pole (of a carriage), [illegible], thill, shaft; draught-tree (of a horse [illegible] &c.); in comp. —arme, m. pl. shaft-bars; [illegible], n. pole-plate, beam-plate; —eisen, n. [illegible] (of a rail); —gabel, f. see Gabel-[illegible]; —haken, m. pole-hook; —kappe, f. [illegible] [adze.

[illegible], (w.) v. tr. T. to work with the [illegible]

[Deichsel]..., in comp. —nagel, m. pole-pin; [illegible] thill-horse, shaft-horse, wheel-[horse]; —ring, m. pole-ring; —schere, f. cleaves, [illegible]; —schnalle, f. pole-piece buckle; [illegible], f. pl. see —arme; —zapfen, m. pole-[illegible].

[illegible], in comp. —ufer, n. dike-bank; [illegible] dike-union; —vogt, m. see —[illegible]; —weg, m. dike-way, dike-path; —

—wesen, n. diking-matters, any thing relating to dikes; —zwang, m. dike-judicature.

Deil, (str.) m. Iron-w. bloom (Deul).

Dein, († &) * for deiner, Gen. of Du.

Dein, Dei'ne, Dein, pron. poss. 1) thy; 2) for deinige, thine; es ist dein, it is thine or yours. [or you.

Dei'ner, pron. (Gen. sing. of Du) of thee

Dei'net..., in comp. —halben, —wegen, um —willen, adv. for thy (your) sake, in thy (your) behalf, on thy (your) account.

Dei'nige, der, die, das, pron. poss. thine, yours; das —, thy (your) property; thue das — (lit. do what is thine), do thy (your) duty; die D-n, thy (your) family. [ground-swell.

Dei'ning, (w.) f. Mar. swell of the sea.

Dein'sen, Dei'sen, (w.) v. intr. Mar. to go (fall) astern, to have stern-way, to shieve.

Dei'sig, adj. Mar. misty.

Deis'sel, (w.) f. provinc. see Deichsel, 1.

* Deis'mus, (pl. [w.] D-'men) m. (L. Lat.) deism. — Deist', (w.) m. deist. — Deist'isch, adj. deistical. [deuce.

Dei'xel, (str.) m. vulg. for Teufel, the

* Dejuri'ren, (w.) v. intr. (Lat.) Law, 1) to affirm on oath; 2) to take a false oath, to commit perjury.

* Deka'de, (w.) f. see Decade.

* Delcrede're, n. (Ital.) Comm. delcredere, guaranty; — stehen, to stand or warrant delcredere or surety; für die Versicherer — stehen, to insure the solvency of the underwriters; bis zur Hälfte — stehen, to guarantee for the moiety; ohne —, without guarantee (in endorsements).

* Delegat', (w.) m. (Lat.) delegate. — Delegation', (w.) f. 1) delegation; 2) Comm. assignment (of a debt). — Delegi'ren, (w.) v. tr. to delegate. [liberate.

* Deliberi'ren, (w.) v. tr. & intr. to de-

* Delicat', adj. (Lat.) delicate; delicious; nice, dainty. — Delicates'se, (w.) f. (Fr.) 1) delicacy; nicety, daintiness; 2) delicious food, gener. pl. dainties, luxuries; D-nhändler, m. dry-salter, fruiterer; D-nhandlung, f. shop in which delicacies are sold, dry-saltery.

* Delict', (str.) n. (Lat.) Law, crime. — Delinquent', (w.) m. (D-in, (w.) f.) delinquent.

* Delphin', (str.) m. (Gr.) 1) Zool. dolphin; 2) T. dolphin (of a cannon); —blume, f. Bot. branching lark-spur (Rittersporn). — Delphinat', (str.) n. (Dauphiné, f.) Geogr. Dauphiny.

Del'phisch, adj. Delphian, Delphic, relating to Delphi; oracular, oraculous.

* Del'ta, (str., pl. D-s) n. (Gr.) delta (the Greek letter Δ, also an alluvial tract of country between the diverging mouths of a river); in comp. —förmig, adj. trowel-shaped, deltoid; —muskel, m. Anat. deltoid (muscle).

Dem, Dat. sing. of Der.

* Demagog', (w.) m. (Gr.) demagogue, popular leader. — Demago'genthum, (str.) n. demagogism. — Demago'gisch, adj. demagogical; cf. Umtriebe.

* De'mant, (w.) m. († &) * for Diamant; —artig, adj. adamantean. — De'manten, adj. adamantine.

* Demanteli'ren (pr. demang—), (w.) v. tr. (Fr.) to dismantle.

* Demarcation', (w.) f. (Fr.) demarcation; D-slinie, f. 1) Mil. line of demarcation; 2) boundary line. [unmask.

* Demaski'ren, (w.) v. tr. & refl. (Fr.) to

De'mat, Die'mat, (str.) m. provinc. as much land as may be mowed in one day.

* Dementi' (pr. demangti'), (str., pl. D-s) n. (Fr.) a charging with falsehood, denial; contradiction; (einer Person or Sache) ein — geben (Dementi'ren, (w.) v. tr.), to give the lie to ...; to contradict; to deny.

Dem'gemäß, adv. (cf. Gemäß) according to this or that; rarely used as (& decl. like) an adj. being (done, &c.) in accordance with (something stated), conformable.

* Deminutiv', see Diminutiv.

* Demiurg', (w.) m. (Gr.) demiurge.

Dem'nach, conj. 1) according to this, consequently, of course, therefore, then; 2) † see Sintemal.

Dem'nächst', adv. shortly, very soon. — Demnäch'stig, adj. taking or to take place in the next time; die d-e Versammlung, the assembly about to be held.

* Demobilisi'ren, (w.) v. I. tr. (Fr.) to put on (reduce to) the peace-establishment (an army); II. intr. see Abrüsten. — Demobilisi'rung, Demobilisation', (w.) f. the (act of) putting on the peace-establishment, &c.

Dem'ohn'geachtet, Dem'ohn'erachtet, conj. (L. u.) see Dessenungeachtet.

* Demoiselle (pr. demoasell'), (w., pl. sometimes [str.] D-s) demoiselle (Fr.; formerly much in use for Jungfer, Fräulein).

* Democrat' (or —krat'), (w.) m. (Gr.) democrat. — Democratie', (w.) f. democracy. — Democrat'isch, adj. democratical. [lish.

* Demoli'ren, (w.) v. tr. (Lat.) to demo-

* Demonstri'ren, (w.) v. tr. (Lat.) to demonstrate.

Demonstration', (w.) f. demonstration.

* Demonti'ren (pr. dāmongti'ren), (w.) v. tr. (Fr.) Mil. 1) to unhorse; 2) to dismount (a gun); to disable (the guns of a battery).

Demun'geachtet, conj. see Dessenungeachtet.

De'muth, (w.) f. humility, humbleness, lowliness, meekness, submissiveness; —kraut, n., —pflanze, f. Bot. 1) common thyme (Thymian); 2) humble-plant (Mimosa pudica L.); —voll, adj. see Demüthig.

De'müthig, I. adj. humble, submissive, lowly; — bitten, to beg humbly, to supplicate; II. D-keit, (w.) f. humbleness, cf. Demuth.

De'müthigen, (w.) v. I. tr. to humble, humiliate, mortify, to subdue (the enemy); to bring low or down; Einen —, to break one's pride, coll. to fetch, pull, take down; II. refl. to humble one's self, to stoop (down), to submit. — De'müthigung, (w.) f. humiliation, mortification, abasement, prostration.

* Denar', (str.) m. (Lat.) Rom. Num. denarius; Fr. Num. denier.

* Dendrit', (w.) m. (Gr.) Miner. dendrite. — Dendrit'isch, adj. dendritic.

Deng'el, (str.) m. draggled bottom of a dress (Schmutzsaum).

Deng'eln, (w.) v. tr. Husb. 1) to sharpen (a scithe or sickle) by means of a hammer; 2) to emasculate (a bull).

Deng'el..., in comp. —hammer, m. scithe-hammer; —stock, —stock, m. sharpening anvil for scithes; —zeug, n. sharpening tools for scithes.

Denk... (from Denken), in comp. —art, f. mode of thinking; sentiment; mind, disposition; edle —art, noble-mindedness.

Denk'bar, I. adj. conceivable, imaginable (m. b.: thinkable); II. D-keit, f. state of being imaginable, conceivableness.

Denk..., in comp. —bild, n. device; idea; —blatt, n. memorial leaf (for an album, &c.); —brot, n. Jew. Rel. show-bread; —buch, n. memorandum-book, note-book, remembrance-book.

Den'ken, (irr.) v. intr. & tr. 1) to think (an [with Acc.], of); to imagine, conceive, fancy; to suppose; 2) to reflect, meditate; (gener. intr. with auf [& Acc.]), to contemplate, to intend; to contrive; devise, cf. Sinnen; 3) (with an [& Acc.] or with the Gen.) to remember; der Mensch denkt, Gott lenkt, proverb, man proposes, God disposes; wo — Sie hin? how can you think of that? er denkt weggeblieben, he has a mind to stay away: er denkt stark daran, he has a good mind to do so: ich denke nicht im Entferntesten daran, nothing is further from my mind: er dachte nicht mehr (weiter) daran, he dismissed the thought from his mind: ich sagte ihm, was ich von seinem Benehmen dachte, I gave him my opinion (marked my sense) of his conduct: wer hätte das gedacht? who would have thought it? man denkt an andere Maßregeln, other measures are in contemplation: gedacht, gethan, scarce imagined ere it is realised! das Publicum denkt..., the public feeling is ...: das gibt zu —, this is a suggestive subject or a subject fraught with meaning; ich dächte gar! you don't say so! bei sich —, to think to one's self: daran ist gar nicht zu —, that is not to be thought of or quite out of the question: in der Aussprache wird kein Unterschied gehört, wenn der Sprechende nicht daran denkt, einen zu machen, no difference in the pronunciation is heard when the speaker is not on his guard to make one: können Sie sich (Dat.) nicht —, von wem dieser Brief ist? have you no idea from whom this letter comes? — Sie sich (Dat.) das Schlimmste, anticipate the worst: — Sie sich (Dat.) nur! only think! imagine! — Sie sich (Acc.) an meine Stelle, suppose you were in my case, make the case yours or your own: wir vergessen oft, wenn wir mit Anderen reden, uns (Acc.) in ihre Lage zu —, we often forget when we talk to people, to put ourselves in their situation: das habe ich mir gedacht, I thought as much: — Sie sich (Dat.) etwas (aus), think of something: sicherlich würde ich mir keine Eule als Jettchens Lieblingsthier gedacht haben, to be sure I should not soon have thought of an owl for Harriet's pet: so lange ich — kann, since my remembrance: — Sie nicht weiter daran, never mind it: sie sollen an mich —! they shall have cause to remember me! an Bezahlung ist nicht zu —, payment is out of the question: er denkt auf entschiedenere Maßregeln, he meditates (on) more decisive measures: ich muß darauf —, wie ich ihm gefalle, I must consider how I best can please him; d-d, p. a. cogitative, thinking, sensible; ein d-des Wesen, a rational being.

Den'ken, s. n. (str.) n. thinking, thought, cogitation: speculation: tiefes —, deep thoughtfulness.

Den'ker, (str.) m. thinker, reasoner, speculator.

Denk..., in comp. -fähig, adj. capable of thinking or reasoning: -fähigkeit, f. see -kraft; -faul, adj. hating the least effort of thought; -form, f. mode of thinking; -freiheit, f. freedom of thought; -kraft, f. faculty of thinking, cogitative or intellectual power: -lehre, f. logic.

Denk'lich, adj. (l. u.) 1) see Denkbar; 2) possible, presumable.

Denk..., in comp. -mal, n. 1) monument; 2) memorial, memory; zum -mal, in remembrance (see in Andenken); -münze, f. medal; -richtig, adj. logical; -riemen, m. Jew. Rel. phylactery; -ring, m. ring serving as a token of remembrance; -säule, f. monumental column, monument, statue; -schrift, f. 1) (monumental) inscription; 2) memorial; eine -schrift einreichen bei..., to memorialise...; Verfasser einer -schrift, memorialist; 3) memoir; record. -spruch, m. sentence, maxim; motto; apophthegm; -stein, m. monumental stone, monument; -stück, n. memorial; -tafel, f. commemorative or monumental slab or tablet; -übung, f. mental exercise or practice.

Den'kungsart, (w.) f. turn or cast of mind, manner of thinking: unedle —, illiberality; weltliche —, worldly-mindedness.

Denk..., in comp. -vermögen, n. reasoning faculty; -weise, f. see -art; -würdig, adj. memorable, notable, commemorable; -würdigkeit, f. memorableness; memorable occurrence (event, thing); -würdigkeiten, f. pl. memoirs; -zeichen, n. token of remembrance, monument; -zeit, f. epoch; -zettel, m. 1) see -riemen; 2) memorandum-paper; 3) fig. the (act of) reminding a person to do better in future, or actual punishment, chastisement.

Denn, I conj. for; then; so wollen wir — fort, let us then set out; es sei — daß, unless, if, provided: er bezahle mich —, unless he pays what he owes me: was —? but what? what do you mean? to what can you be alluding? verstehst du — keinen Scherz? cannot you (or won't you then) take a jest? weiß er (with emphasis) — nichts, wenn sein Bruder nichts erfahren hat? does he know nothing of the affair, if his brother has not learnt anything? — doch, after all; II. adv. than: but: wer ist reicher — er? who is richer than he? nichts — Gold, nothing but gold (cf. Als).

Den'noch, conj. yet, but yet, notwithstanding, however, nevertheless, all the same.

* Dental', (Lat.) adj. & s. (str.) m. Gramm. dental. — Denta'lien, n. pl. Conch. tooth-shells. — Dentelli'ren, (w.) v. tr. (Fr.) to indent, cf. Auszahnen, Auszacken; dentellirte Arbeit, T. dentelli, modillions. — Dentist', (w.) m. dentist. — Dentür', (w.) f. 1) see Gebiß, 1; 2) condition of teeth.

* Denunciant', (w.) m. (Lat.) Law, accuser; informer. — Denunci'ren, (w.) v. tr. to denounce, inform against (one). — Denunciatio'n', (w.) f. denunciation, information against.

* Departement' [pr. depärtmang'], (str., pl. D-s) n. (Fr.) department: — der inneren (äußeren) Angelegenheiten, home-(foreign) department.

* Depenni'ren, (w.) v. tr. (L. Lat.) Comm. to discharge, strike out (a debt); to cancel (an order).

* Depesch'e, (w.) f. (Fr.) despatch; D-nwechsel, m. interchange of despatches.

* Deploy'i'ren [pr. —ploaji'—], (w.) v. intr. (Fr.) Mil. to deploy.

* Depo'nens, (indecl., pl. [Lat.] Deponen'tia) n. (Lat.) Gramm. deponent (verb).

* Deponent', (w.) m. (Lat.) Law, 1) depositary; 2) deponent, witness. — Deponi'ren, (w.) v. tr. Law, 1) to deposit, depone; 2) to depose, depone, to give evidence.

* Deportatio'n', (w.) f. (Lat.) deportation, transportation. — Deporti'ren, (w.) v. tr. to deport, transport.

* Deposi'tar', (str.) m. (Lat.) Comm. depositary: Comm. & Law, consignatary, fiduciary, trustee; Law, bailee.

* Deposi'ten..., (Lat.) in comp. -bank, f. deposit-bank; -casse, f. trust-funds; -gelder, n. pl. consigned, deposit- or trust-money, trust-funds; -posten, m. amount of deposit; -schein, m. receipt for a deposit.

* Deposita'rin', (w.) f. (Lat.) Law, see Bergemannsfrage.

* Depo'situm, (str., pl. [w.] Deposi'ten, or [Lat.] Depo'sita) n. (Lat.) deposit, funds deposited, trust (money); in — geben, 1. to give in charge; to put in store, cf. Verwahrung; 2. to put in pawn, to give as a pledge; ein — angreifen, to embezzle a deposit.

* Depossedi'ren, (w.) v. tr. to dispossess.

* Depot' (pr. depo'), (str., pl. D-s) n. (Fr.) Mil., &c. depot; Cust. bonding; bonding warehouse.

* Deprimi'ren, (w.) v. tr. (Lat.) 1) to depress; Med. ein deprimirter Puls, a weak pulse; 2) Surg. to couch (a cataract).

* Deputat', (str.) n. (Lat.) a certain allowance in kind, over and above the stipulated salary.

* Deputatio'n', (w.) f. (Lat.) deputation.

* Deputir'te, m. (L. Lat.) (decl. like adj.) deputy; D-nkammer, f. chamber of deputies (as formerly in France).

[illegible] (or d'rer), pron. poss. your, yours; ([illegible] persons of distinction): Seine Majestät haben — Ministern befohlen, his majesty has ordered his ministers: —halben, —wegen, adv. † see Deswegen.

Derselˈbe, Dieselˈbe, Dasselˈbe, pron. dem. the same; he, she, it, that: eben —, ganz —, the very same: mein Leben ist immer ein und dasselbe, my life is the same thing over and over again: — wie ..., the same as or with ....

Derweilˈe, Derweilˈen, adv. († &) coll. in the mean time (Unterdessen).

* Derˈwisch, (str., w. & sometimes without inflexion) m. (Pers.) Mah. Rel. dervis, dervise.

Derˈzeitig, adj. of the time, for the time being. [—moll, D flat minor.

Des, Mus. D flat ($D^{\flat}$); —dur, D flat major;

* Descendent', (w.) m. (Lat.) descendant. — Descendenz', (w.) f. descendants (Nachkommenschaft in absteigender Linie). — Descension', (w.) f. descension (Absteigung); descent.

Des[illegible], (str.) m. see Besemer. — [illegible], v. tr. coll. to weigh on a steel yard.

Deserteur' [pr. —tör'], (str., pl. D-e or D-s) m. (Fr.) deserter, runaway. — Desertion', (w.) f. desertion. — Desertiˈren, (w.) v. intr. (aux. sein) to desert, run away.

* Deserviˈten, n. pl. (Lat.) see Sachwalter[illegible].

Desˈfalls, Desˈfalls, adv. in this or in that case; on that account, therefore. — Desfallsig, adj. on this head; regarding the point.

Desgleiˈchen, Desgleiˈchen, I. adj. see Dergleichen; II. conj. likewise, as also.

Desˈhalb, † Desˈhalben, see Deswegen.

* Desiderat', (str.), Desideraˈtum, (str., pl. [Lat.] Desideraˈta, (w.) D-'ten) n. desideratum. — Desideˈrium, (str., pl. Desideˈrien) n. desire (Wunsch, Verlangen). [(an, for, to).

* Designiˈren, (w.) v. tr. (Lat.) to designate

* Desinfection', (w.) f. (Fr.-Lat.) disinfection: D-smittel, n. disinfectant. — Desinficiˈren, (w.) v. tr. to disinfect.

* Desˈman, (str.) m. (Swed.) Zool. Russian musk-rat (Myogale moschata L.).

* Desolat', adj. (Lat.) distressed, dreary, sad, melancholy (Traurig, Kläglich).

* Desorganisation', (w.) f. (Fr.) disorganisation. — Desorganisiˈren, (w.) v. tr. to disorganise.

* Desoxydation', (w.) f. (Fr.-Gr.) Chem. deoxidation. — Desoxydiˈren, (w.) v. tr. to deoxidate, deoxidise.

* Despectirˈlich, adj. (Lat.) 1) disreputable; 2) disrespectful, contemptuous.

* Desperat', adj. (Lat.) desperate; furious. — Desperation', (w.) f. desperation.

* Despot', (w.) m. (Gr.) despot, tyrant. — Despotie', (w.) f. despotism (despotic or arbitrary power or government). — Despotisiˈren, (w.) v. tr. & intr. to rule in a despotic manner. — Despoˈtisch, adj. despotic(al), arbitrary. — Despotisˈmus, (indecl., pl. [-men]) m. despotism, tyranny.

Dessenunˈgeachtet, Dessenunˈgeachtet, adv. notwithstanding.

Dessent..., in comp. coll. —halben, —wegen, (um) —willen, adv. see Deswegen.

* Dessert', (str., pl. D-s, coll. D-e) n. (Fr.) dessert (Nachtisch): —[illegible], n. doily.

* Dessin' [pr. dessäng'], (str., pl. D-s) n. (Fr.) T. design, pattern, figure: —draht, m. T. figured wire; —maschine, f. T. figuring-machine. — Dessinateur' [—tör'], (str.) m. (Fr.) designer (Musterzeichner).

* Dessiniˈren, (w.) v. tr. (Fr.) T. den Draht —, to draw figured wire. — Dessiniˈrungsmaschine, (w.) f. punching-machine.

* Destillat', (Lat.) (str.) n. produce of a distilling. — Destillateur' [pr. —tör'], (str.) m. distiller. — Destillation', (w.) f. 1) Chem. distillation; 2) distillery. — Destilliˈren, (w.) v. tr. to distil, abstract.

* Destillir'..., in comp. —blase, f., —gefäß (verschiedener Formen), n. still, alembic, glass-still, retort; —helm, —hut, m. helm of a still; —kolben, m. 1) still-head, steam-head, capital of a still; 2) a still; —kunst, f. the art of distilling.

Desto, adv. (before a degree of comparison) the: je mehr — besser, the more the better; — besser, so much the better, (all) the better.

Desˈwegen, Desˈwegen, conj. therefore, for that reason, for that sake, on that account.

Desˈwillen, Desˈwillen, adv. (gener. preceded by um) for that reason.

* Detachement' [pr. detäschmang'], (str., pl. D-s) n. (Fr.) detachment, detached body or party, draught. — Detachiˈren [detäschi'—], (w.) v. tr. (Fr.) Mil., &c. to detach, to draught, to draw out; detachirt', p. a. Paint. detached, (free and) disengaged.

* Detail' [Fr., pr. with l mouillée], (str., pl. D-s) n. 1) particulars, details; 2) retail: im — verkaufen, to (sell by) retail; —bericht, m. detailed statement; —handel, m. retail-business (-trade); —händler, Detaillist', (w.) m. retailer. — Detailliˈren, (w.) v. tr. to particularise, detail. — Detailliˈrung, (w.) f. particularisation.

* Deteniˈren, Detiniˈren, (w.) v. tr. (Lat.) to detain, retain. — Detention', (w.) f. detention; imprisonment.

* Determiniˈren, (w.) v. tr. (Lat.) to determine; determinirt, p. a. determined, resolute. — Determination', (w.) f. determination.

* Detoniˈren, (w.) v. intr. (L. Lat.) 1) to detonate (Verpuffen); 2) Mus. to intonate incorrectly. — Detonation', (w.) f. 1) Chem. detonation (Verpuffung); 2) false or incorrect intonation.

* Detˈto, adv. (Ital.) see Ditto.

Deuˈbe, (w.) f. (S. G.) little theft.

Deuˈker, (str.) m. coll. deuce, cf. Deixel.

Deul, Deuˈling, (str.) m. see Dell.

Deut, (str.) m. 1) Num. doit (a small Dutch copper-coin); 2) fig. a trifle, small farthing, Am. cent.

Deuˈte, (w.) f. provinc. see Dille.

Deuˈtel, (str.) m. Carp. treenail-wedge.

Deutelei', (w.) f. coll. forced or absurd interpretation, malignant exposition.

Deuˈteln, (w.) v. tr. & intr. coll. to explain or interpret malignantly, to tamper with the meaning of ...: er will seine Worte nicht drehen und — lassen, he will not suffer his words to be turned or trifled with, or their meaning explained away.

Deuˈten, (w.) v. I. intr. (with auf [& Acc.]) 1) to point at or to: mit den Augen —, to wink at; 2) to hint at; 3) to indicate, betoken; to prognosticate; II. tr. 1) to explain, expound, interpret; 2) to apply (a meaning) to something, to refer (something) to ...: etwas zum Besten —, to put the best construction upon a thing.

Deuˈter, (str.) m. interpreter, explainer.

Deuterei', (w.) f. see Deutelei.

Deutˈlich, I. adj. clear, plain, distinct, perspicuous, lucid; explicit, intelligible, open; decided (taste, &c.): d-e Handschrift, legible hand; d-e Aussprache, articulate pronunciation; II. D-keit, (w.) f. clearness, distinctness, plainness, perspicuity, lucidity; explicitness, intelligibility.

Deutsch, I. adj. German; der d-e Bund, the German Confederation; der d-e Orden, m. (die d-en Herren, die d-en Ritter, m. pl.) (knights of) the Teutonic Order; das d-e Meer, Geogr. the North-Sea; der d-e Riegel, Lock-sm. sliding catch-bolt; der d-e Safran, see Saflor; der d-e Sandarach, see Wachholdergummi; fig. d. — heraus, in plain terms; — zu sagen, to be candid; II. Deutˈsche, c. (decl. like adj.) 1) m. & f. German: er ist ein alter D-r, coll. he is an honest, plain, straight-forward fellow; 2) n. the German language.

Deutˈschen, (w.) v. I. tr. to make German; II. intr. see Deutschthümeln.

Deutschˈheit, (w.) f. quality of being German; German nature or character.

Deutschˈherrlich, adj. belonging to the Teutonic order.

Deutschˈland, (str.) n. Geogr. Germany.

Deutschˈmeister or Hoch- und Deutschˈmeister, (str.) m. Grand-Master of the Teutonic Order: das Hoch- und Deutschmeisterthum, Grand-Mastership of the Teutonic Order.

Deutschˈthum, (str., pl. D-thümer) n. Germanity. — Deutschthümelei', (w.) f. Teutomania, Germanomania, Germanism. — Deutschˈthümeln, (w.) v. intr. to play the Teutomane, to Germanise. — Deutschˈthümler, (str.) m. Teutomane.

Deuˈtung, (w.) f. interpretation, explanation: einer Sache (Dat.) eine falsche — geben, to put a wrong construction upon a thing: d-svoll, adj. 1) suggestive; 2) ominous.

* Devalvation', (w.) f. (cf. Valviren) depreciation (of coin): D-stabelle, f. table of depreciation. — Devalviˈren, (w.) v. tr. to depreciate (coin), to debase.

Deˈventer, (str.) n. Geogr. (the town of) Daintry.

* Devestiˈren, (w.) v. tr. (Lat.) to divest; Law. to deprive of a fief.

* Deviˈse, (w.) f. (Fr.) 1) device, motto; 2) D-n, pl. Comm. effects, bills, paper.

* Devolution', (w.) f. (L. Lat.) Law, see Heimfall. — Devolviˈren, (w.) v. tr. to devolve.

* Devot', adj. (Lat.) 1) devout; pious; 2) respectful, humble, submissive.

* Dey, (str., pl. Deys) m. (Turk.) Dey.

* Diaboˈlisch, adj. (Lat.-Gr.) diabolical; atrocious.

* Diacon', (str. & [pl. gener.] w.) m. (Gr.) deacon. — Diaconat', (str.) n. deaconry. — Diaconisˈsin, (w.) f. deaconess.

* Diadem', (str.) n. (Gr.) diadem, tiara, crown: —spinne, f. see Kreuzspinne.

* Diagnoˈse, (w.) f. (Gr.) Med. diagnosis, diagnostic.

* Diagonal', I. adj. (Lat.-Gr.) diagonal; —rad, n. Mech. bevelled wheel; II. D-e, a. (w.) f. Geom. diagonal.

* Dialect', (str.) m. (Gr.) dialect. — Dialecˈtik, (w.) f. dialectics. — Dialecˈtiker, (str.) m. dialectician, logician. — Dialecˈtisch, adj. dialectic: 1) relating to dialectics; 2) dialectal, relating to a dialect: d-e Eigenthümlichkeit, f. idiotism.

* Dialog', (str. & w.) m. (Gr.) dialogue. — Dialoˈgisch, adj. dialogistic(al), colloquial.

* Diamant', (w.) m. (Fr., from Lat.-Gr. adamas) 1) diamond, * adamant: roher —, rough diamond, bralt; 2) Glaz. see —spitze; 3) Typ. see —schrift; 4) Fort. see —graben.

Diamanˈten, adj. diamond, of diamonds.

Diamant'..., in comp. D-enbord, D-enbort, n. see D-enpulver; D-engrube, f. diamond-mine; —(en)pulver, n., —(en)staub, m. diamond-powder, diamond-dust; —farbe, f. grey minium; —förmig, adj. diamond-shaped; —gewicht, n. carat; —graben, m. Fort. drop; —mutter, f. diamond-matrix; —schleifer, —schneider, m. diamond-cutter; —schmuck, m. jewel; set of diamonds; —schrift, f. Typ. diamond(-letter); —spath, m. Miner. diamond (adamantine) spar, corundum; —spitze, f. Glaz. diamond(-pencil); —strauß, m. egrette; —werk, n. see —grube.

* Diaˈmeter, (str.) m. (Gr.) see Durch-

messer. — Diame'trisch, Diametral', adj. diametrical.

Dia'na, f. 1) Rom. Myth. Diana; 2) (Span.) Mar. day-watch, reveille; 3) †, Chem. silver; —baum, m. see Silberbaum.

Dia'nen..., in comp. —amsel, f. Ornith. see Ringdrossel; —flügel, m., —ohr, n. Conch. horned broadlip (Strombus auris Dianae L.).

* Dia'rium, (str., pl. [Lat.] Dia'ria & [w.] Dia'rien) n. (Lat.) diary; (traveller's) memorandum.

* Diarrhöe', (w.) f. (Gr.) see Durchfall.

* Diät', I. s. (w.) f. (Gr.) 1) Med. diet, regimen: strenge or knappe —, low, strict diet, regimen; nach der — leben, to be strict in one's diet, to diet (for the removal of disease, &c.); 2) †, Polit. diet (Reichstag, Landtag); 3) D-en, D-engelder, n. pl. extra-pay (Tagegelder); II. adj. coll. strict in one's diet: der Patient musste sich sehr — halten, the patient was obliged to be very careful about his diet. — Diäte'tik, (w.) f. dietetics. — Diäte'tisch, adj. dietary, dietetical; d-e Anordnungen treffen, to prescribe a certain regimen. — Diätist', (w.) m. one who receives extra-pay for occasional or extra-services, supernumerary.

* Diato'nisch, adj. (Gr.) Mus. diatonic (scale, interval, &c.).

* Diatri'be, (w.) f. (Gr.) diatribe.

Dich, pron. (Acc. sing. of Du) thee.

Dicht, I. adj. tight; dense; close; compact, solid, substantial, consistent, thick, massy; ein d-er Wald, a thick forest; — bewaldet, densely wooded; d-e Dünste, impervious vapours; ein d-es Schiff, a tight ship; wo der Kampf am d-esten war, in the very thick of the battle; — an (with Dat.), auf (with Dat.), bei, close by or to, hard or fast by or at; er schnitt die Zweige — am Stamme ab, he cut off the branches close to the trunk; — an einander, close together; coll. sleeve to sleeve; — am Boden hin, close to the ground; — vor meinen Augen, close to my eyes; sich — hinter (with Dat.) anschließen, to close in upon ... (of soldiers, &c.); Mar.-e. — beim Winde, close hauled; — beim Winde segeln, to run close upon a wind; halt ganz — beim Winde, keep her as near as she will lie; — an der Küste hinsegeln, to hug the land; — beim Lande, close in shore; — beim Lande gehalten! keep her in with the land! die Besan — holen, to haul the mizzen sheets close aft; die Schiffe d-er zusammenrücken lassen, to close the line; II. in comp. —anliegend, adj. Bot. compressed; —gewebt, adj. close-webbed.

Dicht'art, (w.) f. style of a poem, species of poetry.

Dich'te, (w.) f. see Dichtheit.

Dicht'eisen, (str.) n. Mar. calking iron.

Dichtelei', (w.) f. coll. versifying; poor poem.

Dich'ten, (w.) v. tr. to make close, tight; to condense; to calk (a ship).

Dich'ten, (w.) v. tr. & intr. 1) to write poetry, to compose (a poem, &c.); 2) a) to meditate, think, muse on; b) to devise, contrive, see Erdichten; das —, v. s. (str.) n. act of meditating, devising, &c.; das — und Trachten, the thoughts; sein — und Trachten geht dahin..., his heart (his every thought) is set upon....

Dich'ter, (str.) m. poet, bard; in comp. poetical, as: —gabe, f. poetical talent, &c.; —epheu, m. common ivy; —taube, f. hooded pigeon, see Nonnentaube.

Dichterei', (w.) f. mock-poetry, bad poetry.

Dich'terin, (w.) f. poetess, poetress.

Dich'terisch, adj. poetic(al).

Dich'terling, (str.) m. poetaster, vile or petty poet.

Dicht'hammer, (str., pl. D-hämmer) m. Mar. calking-mallet.

Dicht'heit, Dich'tigkeit, (w.) f. tightness; density; closeness; compactness, solidity, consistence; thickness; — des Gespels (der Wolle &c.), Comm. cloddiness of the staple; D-smesser, m. Phys. 1) manometer (for elastic fluids); 2) areometer (for liquids).

Dicht'..., in comp. —fibrig, adj. close-grained (wood); —säuliges Gebäude, Archit. pycnostyle.

Dicht'kunst, (w., pl. D-künste) f. poetry, poetic art.

Dich'tung, (w.) f. 1) poesy, poetry; 2) invention, fiction; 3) poetical composition; eine lyrische —, a lyric composition.

Dich'tungs..., in comp. —art, see Dichtart; —gabe, f. poetic talent; —kraft, f., —vermögen, n. imagination.

Dicht'werg, (str.) n. Mar. oakum.

Dick, I. adj. 1) thick; big, large; bulky; — und fett, see Quappig; voluminous; stout, corpulent; 2) swollen; 3) thick, dreggish; d-e Lippen, blubber-lips; das d-e Kinn, a bull-chin; Karl der D-e, Hist. Charles the Fat; die d-e Milch, curdled milk, curds; das d-e Ende, butt-end; coll.-e. — thun, see Prahlen; durch — und Dünn, through thick and thin; sie sind sehr d-e Freunde, they are as thick as thieves together.

Dick..., in comp. —bäckig, adj. blubber-cheeked, plump-faced; —bauch, m. big belly, swag-belly; —bäuchig, adj. big-bellied, gor-bellied, paunch-bellied; —bein, n. thigh; —beinig, adj. thick-legged; —beinige Trappe, f. see —fuß; —cirkel, m. callipers (Bogencirkel); —darm, m. Anat. large intestine.

Dick'e, (w.) f. thickness; bigness, &c. cf. Dick. adj.; consistence; voluminousness.

Dick..., in comp. —farben, f. pl. T. thick colours; —fäustig, adj. club-fisted; —flache Feile, cotter-file; —fuß, m. Ornith. stone-curlew, stone-plover (Oedicnemus crepitans Temm.); —halsig, adj. thick-necked; —häutig, adj. 1) thick-skinned, thick-coated; callous; 2) fig. callous, insensible; —häuter, m. Zool. pachydermatous animal, pl. pachydermata.

Dick'heit, (w.) f. (l. u.) see Dicke.

Dick..., in comp. —horn, n. Zool. American sheep; —hörnig, adj. broad-horned.

Dick'igkeit, (w.) f. thickness, density.

Dick'icht, (str.) n., Dick'ung, (w.) f. thick, thicket; brush; covert.

Dick..., in comp. —kopf, m. 1) a) thick head or scull, an obstinate person; b) see Dummkopf; 2) Ornith. buffle-headed duck (Schellente); 3) Ichth. a) see Alant, A.; b) fuscale; c) pl. —köpfe, see Weitmäuler; 4) Zool. see Caretle; —köpfig, adj. thick- or club-headed; thick-sculled; obstinate, knobby; —köpfigkeit, f. thick-headedness; —leibig, adj. 1) corpulent, thick-bodied, vulg. big-bellied; 2) bookl. bulky; voluminous; —leibigkeit, f. corpulency; bulkiness.

Dick'lich, adj. thickish, somewhat thick.

Dick..., in comp. —lippig, adj. blubber-lipped; —maß, n. Sport. see Gelege, 2; —mäulig, adj. pouch-mouthed; —mühle, f. see Walkmühle; —nasig, adj. bottle-nosed; —nudeln, f. pl. maccaroni; —öhrig, adj. thick of hearing; —rindig, adj. bark bound, thick-coated; —rübe, f. Bot. root of scarcity (Runkelrübe); —schalig, adj. thick-shelled; —schenkelig, adj. big-haunched; —schnabel, m. Ornith. see Kernbeißer; —stein, m. Stone-cutt. big diamond; —tau, n. cable; coll.-e. —thuer, m. braggard, boaster; —thuerei, f. braggardism, bragging.

Dick'ung, (w.) f. see Dickicht.

Dick..., in comp. —wanst, m., —wanstig, adj. vulg. see —bauch, —bäuchig; —zirkel, see —cirkel.

Dictan'do, (Lat.) adv. from or to dictation.

* Dictat', (str.) n. (Lat.) 1) dictate, dictation; 2) rule. — Dicta'tor, (str., pl. Dictato'ren) m. dictator. — Dictato'risch, adj. dictatorial. — Dictatur', (w.) f. dictatorship, dictature.

man; 2) to bargain (um, for); II. tr. to hire, to employ for wages, to engage.

Ding'erchen, (str.) n., pl. coll. (dimin. of the coll. pl. Dinger, cf. Kinderchen 2c.) little things. [see Miethgeld & Handgeld.

Ding'..., in comp. —geld, n., —pfennig, m.

Ding'lich, adj. Law, real, belonging to things. [So und So).

Dings, m. coll. Herr —, Mr. Thingum (cf.

Ding'stelle, see Ding, II.

Ding'zettel, m. see Dingbrief.

Dinkel, (str.) m. (or —weizen) Bot. spelt (-wheat), German wheat, amel-corn (*Triticum spelta* L.); —gerste, f. great barley; —spelze, f. Bot. common rye-grass (*Lolium perenne* L.).

† **Din'sen**, (str.) v. intr. (aux sein) to swell, only used in the pp. gedunsen, swoln, bloated (Aufgedunsen).

Din'stag, see Dienstag.

Din'te 2c., see Tinte 2c.

* **Diöces'**, **Diöce'se**, (w.) f. (Gr.) diocese. — **Diöcesän'**, (str.) m. diocesan.

Dio'genes, or —krebs, m. Entom. hermit-crab (Einsiedlerkrebs).

Dionys', m. Dionysius, Dennis (P. N.).

* **Diop'ter**, (str., pl. [w.] D-n) n. & (w.) f. (Gr.) 1) Phys. (sight-)vane; D-n an einem Astrolabium, pl. pinules; 2) (Diop'tra) Med. see Mutterspiegel; —lineal, n. alidade. — **Diop'trik**, (w.) f. Phys. dioptrics; anaclastics. — **Diop'trisch**, adj. dioptric, dioptrical.

* **Diora'misch**, adj. (Gr.) dioramic.

* **Dioskur'ren**, (w.) m. pl. Gr. Myth. Dioscuri (a name given to Castor & Pollux).

* **Diphtheri'tis**, f. Med. diphtheria.

* **Diphthong'** [pr. —tonch' or —tongch'], (str. & w.) m. (Gr.) diphthong (Doppellaut).

* **Diplom'**, (str.) n. (Gr.) diploma; patent.

* **Diplomat'**, (w.) m. (L. Lat.) diplomatist. — **Diplomatie'**, (w.) f. diplomacy. — **Diplomat'isch**, adj. diplomatic; das d-e Corps, n. body or corps diplomatic. — **Diplomat'ik**, (w.) f. diplomatics. — **Diplomat'iker**, (str.) m. one versed in diplomatics.

* **Dip'tam**, (str.) m. (Gr. diktamnos) Bot. 1) der weiße or gemeine —, white dittany, fraxinella (*Dictamnus* L.); 2) der falsche or wilde —, bastard dittany; 3) der kretische —, dittany of Crete.

Dir, pron. (Dat. of Du) to thee, to you.

* **Direct'**, I. adj. (Lat.) direct: ein d-er (Eisenbahn-)Zug, a through train; sich — einschreiben lassen, to have one's self booked through; II. adv. direct(ly): — nach A., direct (not: directly) to A.; Comm. at first hand; d-er Schaden, positive injury or loss; d-es Interesse, immediate interest; d-e Abgaben, assessed taxes; — wirkende Dampfmaschine, f. Mech. direct acting steam-engine.

* **Direction'**, (w.) f. (Lat.) 1) direction; management; 2) board of direction (Directorium); — der Schwere, Mech. quantity of direction, (power or quantity of) momentum; D-slinie, f. (Direc'trix, (Lat., pl. Directri'ces) Math. directrix.

* **Direc'tor**, (str., pl. Directo'ren) m. (Lat.) 1) director, manager, master; conductor (of a musical performance, &c.); — eines Orchesters, leader of an orchestra; head-master (of a school); governor; chairman; 2) Surg. director, conductor. — **Directo'rium**, (str., pl. [w.] D-rien) n. (Lat.) directory, board of directors or of direction. — **Directri'ce** [pr. —tri'ße], (w.) f. (Fr.) manageress, directress.

* **Dirigent'**, (w.) m. (Lat.) manager, &c. see Director; Comm. head (of a firm), chief-partner. — **Dirigi'ren**, (w.) v. tr. 1) to direct, manage, rule; 2) to send, to forward; d-der Rücken, see Rektor.

Dirk, m. (str.) Mar. peak-halliard (of a gaff).

Dir'ne, (w.) f. (dimin. Dirnchen, Dirnlein, (Austr.) Dirn'del, (str.) n., Italic) maid, maiden, lass, damsel; eine gemeine —, a worthless woman, wench, hussy.

Dis, n. Mus. D sharp; —dur, D sharp major; —moll, D sharp minor.

* **Discant'**, s. I. (str.) m. (M. Lat.) Mus. descant, soprano, (counter-)treble: der hohe —, first or high treble; der tiefe —, second or bass treble; der — durch die Fistel, feigned or faint treble; II. in comp. —bratsche, f. treble viol; —hoboe, f. treble hoboy; —pfeife, f. chanter (of a bag-pipe); —saite, f. treble-string; —sänger, Discantist', (w.) m. treble-singer; —schlüssel, m. soprano or canto clef, the C clef on the first line; —stimme, f. canto.

* **Disciplin'**, (w.) f. (Lat.) 1) discipline; 2) science, profession, system, art. — **Disciplina'risch**, adj. disciplinarian. — **Discipliniren**, (w.) v. tr. to discipline, educate; to regulate; to correct.

* **Disconti'ren**, (w.) v. tr. Comm. to discount. — **Discon'to**, (str., pl. D-s) m. (Ital.) discount, draw-back; der mit 5% —, with 5% discount cash, 5% off for cash; in comp. —bank, f. bank of discount; —casse, f. office of discount; —fuß, m. rate of discount; —geschäfte, n. pl. discounting business; —haus, n. discounting office; —rechnung, f. discount-account; —satz, m. see —fuß; —tage, m. pl. discount-days. [credit.

* **Discrediti'ren**, (w.) v. tr. (Fr.) to dis-

* **Discret'**, adj. (Lat.) 1) discrete; 2) discreet. — **Discretion'**, (w.) f. discretion; sich auf — ergeben, to surrender at discretion; D-stage, m. pl. Comm. days of grace.

* **Discurri'ren**, (w.) v. intr. (Lat.) to discourse, converse. — **Discurs'**, (str.) m. (Fr.) discourse, conversation.

* **Discussion'**, (w.) f. (Lat.) debate, discussion. — **Discuti'ren**, (w.) v. tr. to discuss.

* **Disharmonie'**, (w.) f. (Lat.-Gr.) unharmoniousness, want of concord, discordance. — **Disharmo'nisch**, adj. unharmonious.

* **Dislocation'**, (w.) f. (Lat.) dislocation; Comm. removal (of goods). — **Disloci'ren**, (w.) v. tr. to dislocate; to transpose, remove (goods).

* **Dispa'che** [pr. dispä'she], (w.) f. (Fr.) Comm. statement of general average; — über particuläre Haferei, adjustment of loss. — **Dispacheur'** [—päschör'], (str., pl. D-e or D-s) m. arbitrator, adjuster, or despatcher of averages. — **Dispachi'ren** [—päschi'ren], (w.) v. intr. to adjust, despatch averages.

* **Disparat'**, adj. (Barb. Lat.) disparate.

* **Dispens'**, (str.) m. (Lat.) dispensation.

* **Dispensi'ren**, (w.) v. tr. (Lat.) to dispense. [Rittersartikel.

* **Dispenen'da**, (Lat.) n. pl. see Dispo-

* **Disponent'**, (w.) m. (Lat.) Comm. manager, agent, factor; managing-clerk.

* **Disponi'bel**, adj. (Lat.) disposable, available, free. — **Disponibilität'**, (w.) f. disposableness, &c.; D-sgehalt, m. Mil. half-pay.

* **Disponi'ren**, (w.) v. tr. & intr. (Lat.) to dispose (of); gut or übel disponirt, well- or ill-disposed.

* **Disposition'**, (w.) f. (Lat.) 1) disposition; 2) arrangement; instructions; zur — stellen, 1. to leave or place at one's disposal; 2. to put upon half-pay; seine D-en treffen, to take, adopt one's measures; D-sartikel, m. pl. Book. publications to be disposed of for the account of the owner. — **Dispositions'fähig**, adj. legally qualified to dispose of one's property, of a disposing condition.

* **Disputant'**, (w.) m. (Lat.) disputant, disputer, debater. — **Disputation'**, (w.) f. disputation, controversy, debate. — **Disputi'ren**, (w.) v. tr. & intr. to dispute, debate, argue.

* **Dissertation'**, (w.) f. (Lat.) dissertation, written essay. [non-conformist.

* **Dissident'**, (w.) f. (Lat.) Ch. dissident;

[illegible] ourselves plainly enough! du kommst [illegible] come, though? A. Sie haben — keine [illegible]? B. —! A. you're not in a hurry, I [illegible]? B. I am though! thuen Sie es —! [illegible], do it! do it, though! A. kennst du mich [illegible]? B. —, —! A. don't you know me? B. O yes, yes! — nicht mein Bruder? nay, [illegible] my brother? das ist — nicht (etwa) B.? [illegible] it is never B.! Sie wollen — nicht etwa [illegible] daß ..., you don't say that ...; Sie werden — nicht ein Pfund Fleisch auf einmal essen? [illegible] will surely not eat a pound of meat at [illegible]? Sie werden — nicht dies schwere Packet [illegible] wollen? you surely won't carry this [illegible] parcel? Sie glauben — wohl nicht, daß [illegible] eigener Schuld so lange ausgeblieben [illegible]? you don't think it is my fault that I [illegible] stayed away so long? du wirst — nicht [illegible]? surely, you are not wavering? sie [illegible] dir — nicht den Kopf abreißen, they [illegible] not off your head, you know; wenn's [illegible] wäre? what, if it were true? Sie haben [illegible] Furcht? you are not afraid? are you? [illegible] muß er — wissen, he must know something at all events; sie bewegt sich —, sagte Galilei, it moves for all that, said G.; das verdrießt [illegible] denn —, that does certainly annoy me; [illegible] — so gut! pray, be so good! kommen Sie [illegible] do but come! come, do! setzen Sie sich —! [illegible] sit down! geben Sie sich — in Zukunft mehr [illegible], do take more pains in future; bleib [illegible] — sitzen! just keep your seat! Sie haben [illegible] über nichts zu klagen? you have nothing to complain of, I hope? wären — alle Menschen [illegible] er! oh, that all men were like him! sieht [illegible] die Katze den Kaiser an, anal. why, or well, [illegible] may look at a king; habe ich — nie solchen Unsinn gehört! I am sure I never heard [illegible] nonsense! ist mir's —, als ob ..., I really [illegible] as if ...; ist — die Stadt wie gekehrt! [illegible], H. & D.), well, the town is as if [illegible]! (i. e. quite empty).

[illegible], (str.) m. Chand-s. wick; —bank, — [illegible], f. cutting-board; —garn, n. wick-yarn; —halter, m. wick-holder; —messer, [illegible] chopping-knife, chopper; —nadel, f. wick-[illegible]. [illegible] (ture (on).

* Doctiren, (w.) v. tr. & intr. (Lat.) to lec-[illegible].

[illegible], (str., pl. Docks, i. e. Docke) n. & [illegible] (w.) m. see Docke, 5.

[illegible], (w.) f. 1) rail, baluster, little pil-[illegible]; die — des Kutschergestells, standard; 2) [illegible], peg; 3) Mus. Instr-m. see Anschläger, 3; 4) Turn. mandrel, manderil; puppet; [illegible] Mar. dock, dock-yard; basin of a port; [illegible] — mit Fluththüren, dry-dock, graving-[illegible], repairing-dock; die — ohne Fluththüren, [illegible]-dock; das Schiff ist in die D-e gelegt, [illegible] ship has her berth; 6) Comm. skein [illegible] yarn, &c.), bundle of tobacco-leaves; 7) [illegible] puppet or baby, doll (Puppe); 8) a [illegible] of head-dress; 9) Bot. meadow-saffron [illegible]; 10) see Dogge.

[illegible], Döckeln, (w.) v. I. tr. see Auf-[illegible]; II. intr. to play with dolls.

[illegible], (w.) v. tr. 1) to wind up into a [illegible], to bottom; to roll together; to bind [illegible] (flax, sheaves of corn); 2) Mar. to [illegible] (a ship), lay (her) up in a dock.

[illegible]..., in comp. —bank, f. dock-bank; [illegible], m. dock-official; landing-waiter; [illegible], n. pl. water-dock; —drehstuhl, m. [illegible], balance-tool; —flachs, m. Comm. flax [illegible]; —fluththüre, f. dock-gate; —ge-[illegible], f. —geld, n. dock-charges (-rent); — [illegible], a railing of balusters, a balus-[illegible]; —[illegible], n. closet for a doll; —[illegible], [illegible] (Anethum or Koeleria L.); [illegible] floss-silk; —spiel, n. see Puppen-[illegible], f. mandrel; —[illegible], m. [illegible] —stock, m. wooden bone of a [illegible].

* Doc'ter, (str., pl. D-s) m. vulg. for Doctor. — Doc'tern, vulg. (w.) v. I. tr. to doctor, leech; II. intr. to quack.

* Doc'tor, (str., pl. [w.] Docto'ren) m. (Lat.) doctor; Einen zum — machen, to dub one doctor; — werden, 1) see Doctoriren, 1; 2) to commence doctor; —fisch, m. Ichth. blue thorntail (Stachelschwanz); —hut, m. doctor's cap or hood; coif (of jurists in England); —schmaus, m. a Doctor's-banquet, inauguration feast given on taking a degree. — Doctorat', (str.) n., Doc'torwürde, f. doctorate, doctorship; das Doctorat erhalten, to receive the doctor's degree, to be admitted a doctor. — Doc'torin, (w.) f. 1) doctor's wife (spouse, lady); 2) doctress.

* Doctori'ren, (w.) v. intr. 1) to take the doctoral degree; 2) to practise medicine.

* Doctrin', (w.) f. (Lat.) doctrine, learning, tenet. — Doctrinär', (str.) m. Pol. doctrinaire (Fr.), a theorist, speculatist.

* Document', (str.) n. (Lat.) Law, document, deed, act, writing, record, voucher, legal paper. — Documenti'ren, (w.) v. tr. to prove by documents, authenticate.

* Do'do, (str., pl. D-s) m. (Fr.) see Dronte.

Dog'boot, Dog'gerboot, (str., pl. D-böte) n. Mar. (Dutch) dogger, dogger-boat.

* Do'ge [Ital., pr. dō'dshe], (w.) m. doge (formerly the title of the chief magistrate of Venice and Genoa); D-npalast, m. palace of the doges; D-nwürde, f., Dogat', (str.) n. dogate.

[mastiff.

* Dog'ge, (w.) f. (Dan.) Zool. bull-dog.

Dog'ger, (str.) m. see Dogboot.

Dog'gern, (w.) v. intr. to fish in a dogger-boat.

* Dog'ma, (str., pl. [w.] Dog'men) n. (Gr.) dogma; Dogmengeschichte, f. history of doctrinal theology. — Dogmat'ik, (w.) f. dogmatics, dogmatic or doctrinal theology. — Dogmat'iker, (str.) m. dogmatist. — Dogmat'isch, adj. dogmatical.

Doh'le, (w.) f. 1) a) Ornith. (jack-)daw, chough (Corvus monedula L.); b) slang, a prostitute, anal. jay; 2) provinc. see Abzugsgraben; D-nabressel, f. see Steinrabe; D-nnest, n. rookery.

Doh'ne, (w.) f. (or D-nschlinge) Sport. gin, noose, springe (for catching birds); D-nbeere, f. see Eibischbeere; D-nfang, m. the taking of birds by springes, noosing of black-birds; D-nstrich, m. the line in which the springes are set.

Dolch, (str.) m. 1) dagger, poniard, dirk; der kleine —, stiletto; mit einem — erstechen, to poniard, to stab; 2) Conch. see Hammermuschel.

[dolchen).

Dol'chen, (w.) v. tr. (l. u.) to poniard (Er-

Dolch'..., in comp. —messer, n. dirk; —stab, —stock, m. dart-stick, dart-cane, tuck-stick, Jacob's staff; —stich, —stoß, m. stab (with a poniard); seine Worte sind —stiche (—stöße), he speaks daggers; —stichtaube, f. blood-breasted pigeon.

Döld'chen, (str.) n. (dimin. of Dolde) Bot. umbellet, umbellule.

Dol'de, (w.) f. Bot. umbel; die unechte —, see Afterdolde; d-nähnlich, doldenartig, adj. umbellate(d), umbellar.

Dol'den..., in comp. —blume, f. umbelliferous flower; —förmig, adj. umbellar; —gewächse, n. pl. umbelliferous plants, umbellatae; —rebe, f. see Beerendolde; —ständig, adj. umbellate(d); —tragend, adj. umbelliferous; —traube, f. corymb(us); —traubenförmig, adj. corymbous; —trauben tragend, —traubig, adj. corymbiferous, corymbiated.

Dol'dig, adj. umbellate(d).

Doll'..., in comp. Mar. —baum, m., —bord, n. see Dahlbord.

Dol'le, (w.) f. Mar. thole.

Döl'le, (w.) f. provinc. small deepening on a surface; dent, hollow (Delle).

* Dol'man, Dol'man, (str., pl. D-s) m. (Turk.) 1) dolman, doliman; 2) wheel (used in executions).

Dol'metsch, Dol'metscher, (str.) m. (Slav.) 1) interpreter, (in the East) dragoman; 2) Ornith. see Steinbrecher. — Dol'metschen, (w.) v. tr. to interpret (a foreign language). — Dol'metschung, (w.) f. interpretation.

Dolomit', (str.) m. Miner. dolomite, red lead (or magnesian) lime-stone.

[dral.

Dom, (str.) m. 1) dome; cupola; 2) cathe-

* Domä'ne, (w.) f. (Fr.) domain, demesne; D-nkammer, f. domain-board; D-nverwalter, m. manager of domains.

Dom'..., in comp. —capitel, n. Eccl. chapter; —dechant, m. dean of a cathedral.

[tic.

* Domestik', (w.) m. (Fr.) servant, domes-

Dom'..., in comp. —frau, f. canoness; —freiheit, f. close of a cathedral; —herr, m. canon, prebendary; —herrlich, adj. canonical, capitular; —herrnstelle, f. see Canonicat.

* Domicellar', (str.) m. (Lat.) expectant canon.

* Domicil', (str.) n. (Lat.) 1) domicile; 2) address where a bill is made payable.

* Domiciliat', (w.) m. Comm. payee of an addressed bill. — Domicili'ren, (w.) v. tr. to domiciliate (Comm. einen Wechsel, a bill), to make payable; einen Wechsel nach L. —, to address a bill to L.

Domicil'wechsel, m. 1) removal; 2) Comm. indirect or addressed bill.

* Dominan'te, (w.) f. (Lat.) Mus. dominant (fifth note of the scale); D-naccord, m. dominant chord.

* Dominica'ner, (str.) m. & adj. Eccl. Dominican (monk, nun, &c.), predicant, jacobin.

* Domi'nicus, m. (Lat.) Dominic (P. N.).

* Domini'ren, (w.) v. intr. (Lat.) to domineer, to lord it, see Herrschen & Ueberrichten.

* Do'mino, (str., pl. D-s) m. & n. (Ital.) Eccl., Gam., &c. domino; Gam. dominoes; —spielen, to play at dominoes; —steine, m. pl. dominoes, cards.

Dom'kirche, (w.) f. cathedral.

Dom'mel, (w.) f. see Rohrdommel.

Dom'pen, (w.) v. intr. (L. G.) Mar. to work up and down, to heave and set, to pitch, roll. — Domp'..., in comp. —block, m. upper splitting block; —tane, n. pl. leaders.

Dom'..., in comp. —pfaff, m. 1) cathedral canon; 2) Ornith. see Blutfink; —propst, m. provost of a cathedral; —schule, f. grammar-school founded by a chapter; —stift, n. cathedral, chapter.

* Donatar', (str.) m. (L. Lat.) Law, donee. — Donativ', (str.) n. see Gnadengeschenk.

* Donat', (str.) m. (from Donatus, a Latin grammarian of the fourth cent.) accidence; —schnitzer, m. grammatical blunder, offence against the rules of grammar.

Do'nau, f. Geogr. Danube; die —fürstenthümer, n. pl. the Danubian principalities.

Don'..., in comp. Min-s. —bretter, —hölzer, n. pl., —latten, f. pl. hade-planks; traverses in a hading-shaft; —fach, n. bay of a hading-shaft.

[on the Don river, Don

Do'nisch, adj. pertaining to or situated

Don'..., in comp. Min-s. —lage, —lege, f. hade; —lägig, adj. hading, inclined against the horizon (Tonnlege &c.).

Don'ner, (str.) m. thunder; fig. thunder-peal; vom — gerührt or getroffen, thunderstruck; in comp. —art, f. see —keil, 2; —bart, m., —bohne, f. Bot. orpine, livelong (Sedum Telephium L.); —büchse, f. blunderbuss; —distel, f. Bot. common eryngo (Eryngium campestre L.).

[zergott.

Don'nerer, (str.) m. thunderer, cf. Don-

Don'ner..., in comp. —[illegible], m. see Blitz-

wolk; am Himmel ziehn | des Sturmes —flüge (*Lenau*), o'er Heaven float | the thunder-wings of storm (*Bankers.*); ihre vorgeschriebene Reise | vollendet sie [die Sonne] mit —gang (*Göthe*, Faust 1, 1), the sun with thunder-march sublime moves his pre-destined course along (*Sonnen.*); —gebrüll, —gepolter, —geroll, *n.* rumbling of thunder, thundering noise; —gold, *n. see* Knallgold; —gott, *m.* the Thunderer (Jupiter *in classical*, Thor *in Northern Myth.*); —grün, *n.* house-leek (*Sempervivum L.*); —keil, *m.* 1) thunderbolt; 2) *Miner. see* —stein; —kind, *see* D-Kind; —kraut, *n. see* —bart & —grün; —kröte, *f. see* Seeskorpion; —lehre, *f.* brontology; —messer, *m.* brontometer.

Don'nern, (*w.*) *v. intr.* 1) to thunder; to strike, to peal; 2) *fig.* to fulminate.

Don'ner..., *in comp.* —wolke, *f. see* Kerbhäuserwolke; —rebe, *f. see* Gundermann; —schlag, *m.* thunder-clap *or* crack, burst *or* peal of thunder: D-Kinder, *n. pl.* sons of thunder (Mark 3, 17), boanerges; D-Tag, *m.* Thursday; der grüne (*or* Grün-)D-Tag, Maundy-Thursday, Sheer-Thursday; —stein, *m. Miner.* thunder-stone; *pl.* lyncean-stones, arrow-stones; —stimme, *f.* thundering voice; —strahl, *m.* flash of lightning, thunderbolt; —wetter, *n.* thunder and lightning, (thunder-)storm, tempest; —wetter! *interj. vulg.* (*a curse or vociferation in anger*) zounds! —wolke, *f.* thunder-cloud; —wort, *n.* terrifying word, dreadful sentence.

Don'schacht, (*str.*) *m.* heading-shaft.

Doodshoft, (*str.*) *m.*, *or* —block, *m. Mar.* dead-block; —auge, *n.* eye of a dead-block.

Dop, (*str.*) *m. Mar.* — der Compaßnadel, dob, socket of the needle.

Dop'pe, (*w.*) *f.* 1) *Mar.* round and hollow cleat; 2) case in which the rough diamond is fixed previous to being cut.

Dop'pel..., *in comp.* —adler, *m.* 1) double-eagle (the insignia of Austria and Russia); 2) *Comm.* a species of cotton from the levant: —artig, *adj.* of a double kind; —auge, *n. see* Hochgucker; —axt, *f. Carp.* twibil; — b, *n. Mus.* the double flat (♭♭): —bahn, *f. see* —gleisige Bahn; —band, *n.* double-ribbon; —basisch, *adj. Chem.* with two bases; —becher, *m.* dice-box; —bier, *n.* double or strong beer; —blatt, *n. Bot.* bean-caper (*Zygophyllum L.*); —blech, *n.* double tin-plates; double line of rail; —bogen, *m. Archit.* double-bow; —boot, *m.* twin-boat; —bruch, *m.* 1) *Surg.* compound fracture; 2) *Arith.* compound fraction; —büchse, *f. see* —flinte; —buchstaben, *m. pl. Typ.* ligatures; *Mech.-e.* —cylinder, *m.* twin-cylinder; —cylindermaschine, *f.* double-cylinder engine; —deutig, *adj.* ambiguous, equivocal; —dichte Leinwand, *f.* Constance linen; —diele, *f. see* Bohle; —ehe, *f.* bigamy; —eisen, *n.* double plane-iron; —fagott, *n.* counter-bassoon; —fall, *m.* alternative; —fenster, *n.* double-window; —fernrohr, *n.* binocle, binocular telescope; —flinte, *f.* double-barrelled gun; —fuge, *f. Mus.* counter-fugue, double-fugue; —gänger, *m.* 1) wraith; 2) *fig.* second-self, counter-part, double; —garn, *n.* doubled twist; —geige, *f. Mus.* (*Fr.*) viole d'amour, (*Ital.*) alto-viola; —gesang, *m.* duet; —gewebe, *n.* double-cloth; —glas, *n.* double glass; —gleisig, *n.*, —gleisige (Eisen-)Bahn, *f.* a (railway-)line with two sets of tracks, a double track railway; —gold, *n.* strong gold-leaves; —griffe, *m. pl. Mus.* double stop, double fingering (on the violin); —griffig, *adj.* double-handed; ein —griffiges Ruder, double-handed paddle; —hahn, *m.* a large riffle; bloodee-bean; —herzig, *adj.* double-hearted, false, deceitful; —herzigkeit, *f.* false-heartedness, falsehood; —hobel, *m.* double-ironed plane; —horn, *n. Sm.* bickern, bick-iron, rising anvil; —kinn, *n.* double chin; gill; —köpfig, *adj.* double-headed; —kreuz, *n. Mus.* the double sharp (♯♯ *or* ×); —kümmel, *m. Dist.* caraway cordial; —lauf, *m.* double-barrel; —läufer, *m. see* —schlange; —läufig, *adj.* 1) double-barrelled; 2) *Bot.* amphitropal; —laut, —lauter, *m. Gramm.* diphthong; —lebig, *adj.* amphibious; —loch, *n. Zool.* fluke-worm, gourd-worm (*Fasciola hepatica L.*); —messer, *n.* double-bladed knife; —mittel, *f. Typ.* two-line pica.

Dop'peln, (*w.*) *v. I. tr.* 1) *see* Verdoppeln; 2) *Shoe-m.* a) to sew double; b) to sole; 3) *Tail.* to line with linen; 4) *Mar.* to sheathe; II. *intr. Gam.* 1) to play (at dice or backgammon); 2) to double one's stake.

Dop'pel..., *in comp.* —octave, *f. Mus.* diapason; —ort, *n. Shoe-m.* great awl; —paarig, *adj.* bigeminate; —punkt, *m.* colon; *Math.* double-point; —pyramidenkrystall, *m. Miner.* ditrihedria; —raffinade, *f. Comm.* double-refined sugar; —reihig, *adj.* double-rowed, double-tiered; —ring, *m.* hand-in-hand ring, joint-ring, gemel-ring; —salz, *n. Chem.* double-salt; —satz, *m. Typ.* double; —schattig, *adj.* having two shadows; die —schattigen Völker, amphiscii, amphiscians; —schlag, *m.* 1) *Vers.* spondee; 2) *Mus.* turn; 3) *Cloth.* fine and close-woven woollen cloth; —schlange, *f. Zool.* 1) amphisbæna (a serpent that can go either forward or backward); 2) *or* —schleiche, *f. see* Ringelschlange; —schlitz, *m. Archit.* diglyph; —schluß, *m. Log.* dilemma; —schnepfe, *f. Ornith.* 1) larger wood-cock (Mittelschnepfe); 2) large curlew (großer Brachvogel); —schritt, *m.* quick-march; —sinn, *m.* ambiguity; amphiboly, equivocalness, equivoque, double entendre *or* meaning; —sinnig, *adj.* ambiguous, equivocal; —sinnigkeit, *f.* ambiguity; —sohlig, *adj.* double-soled (of boots); —spath, *m. Miner.* Iceland *or* double-refracting spar; —spatien, *n. pl. Typ.* thick spaces; —spiel, *n.* 1) *Mus.* duet; 2) dice; backgammon; card-playing; —spurige Eisenbahn, double (rail-)way; —stein, *m.* 1) *see* —spath; 2) *Jewel.* doublet; 3) crowned man (at draughts); —stern, *m.* double star; —stöckige Dampfkessel, *m. Mech.* double-storied boiler; —stück, *n.* duplicate.

Dop'pelt, I. *adj.* double, twofold; dies Buch ist — geschickt worden, this work has been sent in two copies *or* in duplicate; II. *adv.* double, doubly, twice; (*in comp.:*) fold; drei—, threefold; — so groß, double the size; — so viel, twice or double as much; mit d-em Verlust, with twice the loss; — verschließen, to double-lock; — für einfach gültig, *Comm.* double (receipt) to pass for one; double receipt, but good only for single, receipt twice for once, signed in duplicate; ich bescheinige hiermit — für einfach gültig ..., I hereby declare, twice for once ...; d-e Buchhaltung, book-keeping by double-entry; d-e Böden, *pl.* double casing.

Dop'peltaffet, (*str.*) *m.* double-taffety.

Dop'pelt..., *in comp.* —dreitheilig, *adj. Bot.* biternate; —gefiedert, *adj. Bot.* doubly winged, bipennated; —gepaart, *adj. Bot.* bigeminate, bijugous; —gewölbt, *adj. Archit.* bivaulted; —gezahnt, *adj. Mech.* double-cogged; —gezähnt, *adj. Bot.* bidentate; —hochrund, *adj.* double convex.

Dop'pelthür, (*w.*) *f.* double-door; folding-door.

Dop'pelt..., *in comp.* —kohlensaures Natrum, *Chem.* bi-carbonate of soda; das —weinsteinsaure Salz, *Chem.* bitartrate; —wirkend, *adj. Mech.* double-acting (steam-engine, air-pump, &c.); —zusammengesetzt, *adj. Bot.* decompound; —zweizählig, *adj. Bot.* twice double, bigeminate.

Dop'pelung, (*w.*) *f. Mar.* sheathing.

Dop'pel..., *in comp.* —wesen, *n. Gramm.* double-essence; —wurz, *m.* dietiah; —weizen, *m. Bot.* Polish wheat (*Triticum polonicum L.*);

Drai'len, *(w.) v. intr. provinc.* & * *for* Drehen.

Drauf, *adv. contr. from* Darauf.

Drauf'bohrer, *(str.) m. T.* drill, wimble.

Draus, *adv. contr.* 1) *from* Daraus; 2) *provinc. for* Draußen.

Drau'schen, *(w.) v. intr.* to shower (down).

Drau'ßen, *adv.* without, out of doors, abroad: er will weder hereinkommen, noch — bleiben, he will neither come in nor stay out: — in der Welt, out in the world.

Drechsel... [*pr.* dreck'sel], *in comp.* —**bank,** *f.* (turning-)lathe, turn-bench: —**mühle,** *f.* turner's mill.

Drech'seln [dreck'—], *(w.) v. tr.* 1) to turn (on a lathe); 2) *fig.* to elaborate over-nicely; gedrechselt, *p. a.* affected, over-wrought.

Drechs'ler [dreck'—], *(str.) m.* 1) turner; 2) *Ornith. see* Neuntödter; *in comp.* —**arbeit,** *f.* turnery; —**bude,** *f.*, —**laden,** *m.* turner's shop; —**waare,** *f.* turnery-ware.

Dreck, *(str.) m. vulg. for* Schmutz: 1) dirt, mire, mud; filth, dung; excrement; 2) *Sm.* pieces of copper as broken up and steeped in water; 3) *fig. vulg.* anything execrably bad: auf dem — sitzen bleiben, to get bogged, to stick in the mire; *in comp.* —**bürste,** *f.* scrubbing brush, scrubber, hard brush: —**feger,** *m. vulg.* scavenger: —**fresser,** *m. vulg.* skinflint; —**hahn,** *m. see* Wiedehopf; —**käfer,** *m. Entom.* muck-worm; dung-beetle, *see* Dungkäfer; —**karren,** *m.* scavenger's cart; —**seele,** *f.* dirty, mean, narrow-minded fellow; —**vogel,** *m. see* Aasgeier.

Dreck'ig, *adj. vulg.* dirty, muddy.

Dreesch, *see* Driesch.

Dreg, Dregg, *(str.) m.* (*or* —**anker**) *Mar.* grapnel; —**haken,** *m.* drag, creeper; —**tau,** *n.* mooring-rope (of a boat); drag-rope.

Dreg'gen, *(w.) v. tr. Mar.* to drag *or* sweep the bottom; to dredge.

Dreh'..., *in comp.* —**bahn,** *f.* 1) a roundabout; 2) *Rope-m.* rope-walk; —**balken,** *m. see* Rollbaum; —**bank,** *f. see* Drechselbank.

Dreh'bar, *adj.* that may be turned round, rotatory.

Dreh'..., *in comp.* —**basse,** *f. Gunn.* swivel- or pivot-gun; —**baum,** *m.* 1) *see* —**kreuz;** 2) crab-bar, handspike (to twist a rope): —**bogen,** *m.* drill-bow; —**brücke,** *f.* turn-bridge, swing-bridge; swivel-bridge; Dampfmaschine mit —**cylindern,** *f.* revolving cylinder engine; —**docke,** *f. T.* puppet; mandril.

Dreh'e, *(w.) f.* 1) whirlpool, gulf; 2) *see* Drehkrankheit; 3) *T.* screw.

Dreh'..., *in comp.* (ein flaches) —**eisen,** *n.* turning chisel; ein hohles —eisen, turning gage; —eisen der Zinngießer, pewterer's iron rod.

Dreh'en, *(w.) v. I. tr.* 1) to turn; to twirl; 2) *see* Drechseln; 3) *Mar.-e.* to ease: das Schiff beim Winde —, to stay the ship; Einem etwas aus der Hand —, to wind, wring, wrest a thing out of one's hand: die Augen —, to goggle, to roll the eyes; die Duchten eines Taues —, *Mar.* to twist the strands of a rope: II. *refl.* 1) to turn (round), *cf.* sich Wenden; to rotate, revolve (um, round); 2) *Mar. a)* to veer *(said of the wind)*; *b)* das Schiff dreht vor dem Anker, the ship winds up; die Frage dreht sich um ..., the (whole) question turns upon ...; dies ist der Punct, um welchen sich Alles dreht, this is the point on which the whole question hinges; er weiß sich zu —, he is never at a loss for a shift; sich — und wenden, *fig.* to wince; der Kopf dreht mir, my brains reel, my head turns.

Dreh'end, *adj.* turning; dizzy, giddy.

Dreh'er, *(str.) m.* 1) *a)* turner; *b)* *Mech. see* Weichensteller; 2) *a)* *see* Drehbaum, 1; *b)* *see* Drehling, 1; 3) *see* Wendehals; 4) *Danc.* a slow waltz; 5) *see* Drehling, 2; 6) *Mar.* lid.

Dreh'..., *in comp.* —**feuer,** *n.* revolving-light, —**haken,** *m. Turn., &c.* heel-tool, hook-tool; —**hals,** *m. Ornith. see* Wendehals; —**häuschen,** *n. see* Drillhäuschen; —**junge,** *m.* a boy turning a crank-wheel; —**käfer,** *m. see* Dreher; —**kloben,** *m. T.* screw-clamp ferrule; —**kolk,** *m.* whirlpool; —**krahn,** *m. T.* wheel-crane; —**krank,** *adv. Vet.* affected with the staggers; —**krankheit,** *f. Vet.* giddiness, sturdy (of sheep); staggers (of horses); —**kraut,** *n.* officinal hartwort *(Tordylium maximum L.)*; —**kreuz,** *n.* turnpike, turnstile; —**lade,** *f. T.* pewterer's turning wheel; turn-bench; founder's lathe.

Dreh'ling, *(str.) m.* 1) *T.* handle of a wheel, winch (Drilling, 2); 2) *Vet.* a dizzy or giddy sheep.

Dreh'..., *in comp.* —**mandel,** —**mangel,** *f.* mangle; —**maschine,** *f.* 1) *see* —**zeug;** 2) sliding-lathe; —**muskel,** *m. Anat.* rotator; —**orgel,** *f.* barrel-organ; —**pfähle,** *m. pl. Rope-m.* laying-poles; —**punct,** *m.* turning-point, pole; —**rad,** *n. Turn.* turning-wheel, lare; *Rope-m.* cord-wheel; twisting-wheel; —**reep,** *n. Mar.* tie; —**ring,** *m.* swivel; —**rolle,** *f.* 1) *Herd.* ferrule; 2) swivel-pulley; 3) *see* —**mangel;** —**schaf,** *n. see* Drehling, 2; —**scheibe,** *f.* 1) *a)* potter's wheel; *b)* diamond-cutter's wheel; 2) *Railw.* turn-table, turning-platform, turn-rail, turn-plate; —**schemel,** *m. coll.* bogie; —**späne,** *m. pl.* turnings; —**spiegel,** *m.* swing-glass, cheval-glass; —**stahl,** *m. see* —**eisen;** —**stichel,** *m.* turning-graver; —**stift,** *m.* arbo(u)r; (der linke) screw-arbor; —stift mit Mutter, screw-arbor with nut; —**stiftstühle,** arbor-stands; —**stock,** *m.* 1) *Fort.* turning-staff; 2) *Surg.* tourniquet; —**stuhl,** *m.* 1) turning- or pivot-chair; 2) *T.* turn-bench; 3) *Bookb.* jaw-chair; —**sucht,** *f. see* —**krankheit;** —**thor,** *n.* 1) *see* Schleuse; 2) *Archit., &c.* balance-(turning-)gate; —**tisch,** *m.* a table turning on a pivot.

Dreh'ung, *(w.) f.* turn, turning; revolution (of a wheel); halbe — der Kurbel, half stroke of the crank: D-swinkel, *see* Drehwinkel.

Dreh'..., *in comp.* —**wage,** *f.* balance of torsion; —**winkel,** *m. pl. Math.* coordinates; —**wirbel,** *m.* totum, whirl-bone; —**zange,** *f. T.* tweezers *(pl.)*; —**zapfen,** *m.* trundle; —**zeug,** *n. T.* twisting apparatus.

Drei, I. *card. numb.* three: *proverbs,* aller guten Dinge sind —, three is lucky; ehe man — zählen konnte, in a trice; ehe ich — zählen konnte, before I could say Jack Robinson; er kann nicht — zählen, he can not say bo to a goose; II. *s. (w.) f.* three; trey (at cards and dice); III. *in comp.* —**achteltact,** *m. Mus.* time or measure of three quavers; —**arten,** *Agr.* 1) *(w.) v. tr.* to three-fallow, trifallow; 2) *s. n. (str.) m.* third-earing; —**band,** *n. Comm.* three-band flax; —**beinig,** three-legged, three-footed; —beiniger Stuhl, trestle; —**blatt,** *n. Bot.* trefoil, three-leaved grass, *see* Klee; —**blattbogen,** *m. Archit.* trefoil bit arch; —**blattkreuz,** *n. Herald.* cross-buttony, cross-patonce; *Bot.-s.* —**blätterig,** *adj.* three-leaved, trifoliate, triphyllous; —(blumen-)blätterig, three-petaled, tripetalous; —**blume,** *f. Bot.* horse-purslane *(Trianthema L.)*: —**blumig,** —**blütig,** *adj.* three-flowered, triflorous; —**brachen,** *see* —**arten;** —**buchstabig,** *adj.* triliteral; —**bund,** *m.*, —**bündniß,** *n.* triple-alliance; —**decker,** *m.* 1) *Mar.* three-decker; 2) *ind.,* three-cornered hat; —**ding,** *n.* village court of justice for petty cases; —**doppelt,** *see* —**fach;** —**draht,** *m.* strong linen, ticking formed of three threads; —**drähtig,** *adj.* three-cord, of three twisted threads; —**eck,** *n.* 1) *Geom.* triangle; 2) *Ichth.* triangular fish; —**eckig,** *adj.* three-cornered; triangular; cocked (hat); *Mar.* lateen (sail); *Surg.* lamdoidal (suture); *Anat.* deltoid (muscle); —eckige Nadel, *Surg.* trocar; —**eckmuschel,** *f. Conch.* wedge-shell *(Donax L.)*; —**eckschen,**

[illegible]

Drü'ber, *adv. contr. from* Darüber.

Druck, *(str.) m.* 1) compression, pressure; squeeze; impulse, impulsion; vor — zu bewahren, *Comm.* to be kept from pressure, to be handled with care; 2) *T.* spring; 3) print, printing; stamp; *Print.* proof; impression; type; heller —, light impression, clear type; kleiner —, small type *or* print; großer —, large print; zweiter —, reimpression; grober, schwarzer —, black-letter; unreiner —, foul copy, slur; 4) *Comm.* depression (of prices); 5) *Archit.* thrust; 6) *fig.* weight, heaviness (of taxes); oppression; pressure; burdensomeness; *Typ.-s.* in (den) — geben, to put in print; im — erscheinen, to appear in print; im — begriffen, in course of printing; im — begriffen sein, to pass through the press; Bismarck erklärte (1867), daß kein — auf die süddeutschen Staaten ausgeübt werden würde, B. declared (in 1867) that no pressure would be put on the South German states.

Druck'bar, *adj.* that may be (*or* fit to be) printed.

Druck...(*from* Drucken & Druck), *in comp.* —berichtiger, *m.*, —berichtigung, *f. see* Corrector & Correctur; —besorger, *m.* editor of a work; —beule, *f.* swelling *or* boil caused by squeezing; —bewilligung, *f. see* —erlaubniß; —buchstabe, *m.* type, (printing-)letter; —drehbank, *f. Mech.* pressing-(chasing-)lathe.

Druck'e, *(w.) f. provinc. (particul. Swiss)* chest; box (Truhe).

Drück'el, *(str.) m. provinc.* lever, bar, &c. (Hebel, Brecheisen, Drücker).

Druck'en, *(w.) v. tr.* to print; to stamp; — lassen, to put in print; er lügt wie gedruckt, *coll.* he lies like (*or* his lies have the appearance of) truth.

Drück'en, *(w.) v.* I. *tr.* 1) to press, squeeze; an einer Feder —, to touch a spring; es drückt mich im Magen, I have pains (feel an oppression) in my stomach; an die Wand —, to jam against the wall; im Gedränge gedrückt werden, to be jammed up in a crowd; den Hut ins Gesicht —, to slouch one's hat; Einen an sich (in die Arme) —, to hug *or* clasp one; er drückte ihn (fest) ans Herz (an die Brust), he clasped (strained) him to his bosom (breast); sie drückte ihm etwas (Geld) in die Hand, she slipped some money in his hand; 2) to pinch (said of shoes); to gall; *fig.-s.* 3) to bear hard upon, to oppress, annoy, vex, afflict, wrong; die Noth drückt ihn, he is pressed with want; er drückt mich sehr, he is very hard upon me; es drückt mich sehr, it weighs (presses) heavily (lies heavy) upon my mind; das drückt mich nicht sehr, that sits lightly upon me; drückt es da? *coll.* is it there the saddle galls? 4) to depress; *Comm.-s.* to be pressing on (the market); Einen im Handel —, to cheat upon one; den Markt —, to overstock the market; die Preise —, to depress prices; das Siegel — auf (*with Acc.*), to put the seal to ..., to impress ... with a seal.

II. *intr.* 1) *Phys.* to gravitate; 2) to draw (of weights); to act by pressure (of a spring); 3) to oppress the stomach (of food).

III. *refl.* 1) to get injured (*or* hurt) by pressure; 2) *vulg.* to cut one's stick, to make one's self scarce, *cf.* Abschieben, II. 2; gedrückt, *p. a. Archit.* depressed (arch); d—d, *adj.* heavy, hard, oppressive; pressing (Noth, want); um der Sache das D—de zu benehmen, to make matters more comfortable, *coll.* to make it sit more lightly.

Druck'er, *(str.) m.* printer; pressman.

Drück'er, *(str.) m.* 1) handle (of a latch), latch, latch-key; *T.* crank-pin; punch; 2) *Gun-sm.* trigger (of a gun); 3) (am Drückerschloß) knob; *Naut.* knob, detent, driver; *Nav.-s.* — unterm Krahnbalken, supporter of the cat-head; — in den Rüsten, knee on the chain-wales; — unter den Rüsten, supporter under the chain-wales.

Druck'er..., *in comp.* —arbeit, *f.* presswork; —ballen, *m. pl. (formerly used)* printing-balls; —baum, *m.* printer's beam.

Druckerei', *(w.) f.* 1) art of printing; 2) printing-house, printing office, printing establishment.

Druck'er..., *in comp.* —farbe, *f.* printing *or* printer's ink (—schwärze); —lohn, *n.* printer's wages; —presse, *f.* printing-press; —saal, *m.*, —zimmer, *n.* printing-office, press-room; —schrift, *n. see* Druckschrift; —schwärze, *f. see* —farbe. [spring stock-lock.

Drück'erschloß, *(str., pl.* D—schlösser) *n.*

Druck'..., *in comp.* —erlaubniß, *f.* license to print (a book), *imprimatur*; —feder, *f. Horol. see* Einfall, 2; —fehler, *m.* typographical error, erratum (*pl.* errata), printer's error, misprint, slip *or* error of the press, error *or* mistake in printing; —fehlerverzeichniß, *n.* (list of) errata; —fertig, *adj.* ready for the press; —festigkeit, *f. Phys.* power of resistance; —form, *f.* 1) *T.* printing-block; 2) *Typ. see* Form, 2; —freiheit, *f. see* Preßfreiheit; —genehmigung, *f. see* —erlaubniß; —hebel, *m. T.* a lever which acts downwards by pressure; downing-lever; —jahr, *n.* the year in which a book is printed; —kattune, *m. pl.* (white) printers; —klappe, *f. Min.* top-clack; —kleister, *m. Bookb.* printing-starch; —kolben, *m. see* —stempel; —kosten, *f. pl.* printing charges; —kraft, *f.* force of pressure; power of gravity; —kugel, *f. Mil.* globe of compression; —läppchen, *n. Surg.* pledget; —leinen, *n.* linen for printing; —linie, *f. Archit.* thrust-line; —maschine, *f. see* Schnellpresse; —messer, *m.* pressure-gauge, manometer; —model, *n.* printing-block; —nagel, *m.* trigger of a cross-bow; —ort, *m.* the place at which a book is *or* was printed, imprint; —papier, *n.* printing-paper; —polsterchen, *n. see* —läppchen; —presse, *f.* printing-press; —probe, *f.* 1) proof, revise; 2) specimen of type; —procente, *n. pl.* printing-expenses expressed in percent; —pumpe, *f. T.* forcing- *or* force-pump; —rad, *n.* (hydraulic) pressure wheel; —richtig, *adj.* correct, without misprint; —sachen, *f. pl.* printed matter; —schrift, *f.* 1) *Typ.* types, type, (printing-)letters, printing-characters; 2) printed book, publication; —schwärze, *see* Druckerschwärze; —schwengel, *m. see* —stange & —hebel.

Druck'sen, *(w.) v. intr. vulg.* to tarry, hesitate, waver. [Duckmäuser.

Druck'ser, *(str.) m.* 1) waverer; 2) *see*

Druck'..., *in comp.* —spiel, *n. see* Beispiel; —stange, *f. T.* forcer, forcing-lever; —stempel, *m.* embolus *or* piston (of a forcing-pump), forcer; —stück, *n.* any thing printed; —tafel, *f.* 1) *or* —tisch, *m. Manuf.* printing-table; 2) *see* Beilkeiltafel); —verband, *m. Surg.* compress; —verbesserung, *f. see* —berichtigung; —verbot, *n.* prohibition to print *or* publish a book; —waaren, *f. pl. Comm.* printed goods; (dargestellt mittelst Ätzbeizen) chemical discharge-works; —wage, *f. Phys.* areometer; —walze, *f.* 1) pressing- *or* pressure-roller, rolling-press; 2) printing-machine, cylinder; —werk, *n.* 1) *see* —pumpe; 2) *Mint.* balancier; 3) printed work (—schrift, 2); —zange, *f. Small.* pincers.

Dru'de, *(w.) m. & f.* 1) wizard; witch; 2) night-mare; D—nbaum, *m.* a tree under which witches are said to meet; D—nbeutel, *m.* pack-ball (Bofist); D—nfuß, *m.* 1) pentacle (a magic sign); 2) *or* D—nkraut, *n. see* Bärlapp; D—nmehl, *n.* (Hexenmehl) *see* Bärlappsamen. [(Gebetchen).

Drud'eln, *(w.) v. intr. provinc.* to thrive

° **Drui'de**, *(w.) m. Archaeol.* Druid, Celtic priest; D—nbaum, *m. see* Steineiche.

° **Drui'disch**, *adj.* druidic.

[illegible]; to crouch; to dive (of ducks); 2) *fig.* to humble or accommodate one's self; to cringe.

Duck'ente, *(w.) f.* diver (kleiner Steißfuß)

Duck'er, *(str.) m.* 1) one who ducks or stoops; 2) *see* Dücker.

Duck'ing, *(w.) f. (L. G.) see* Dücking.

Duck'mäuser, *(str.) m. conl.* a fawning sharper; dissembler, sneaker, hypocritical fellow.

Duck'stein, *(str.) m. Miner.* calcareous tuff.

Du'del..., *in comp.* **—dei,** *(str.) m. & n.* [illegible] 1) empty or idle words, verbiage, empty talk; 2) trifle; **—kasten,** *m.* barrel-organ; **—kastenmann,** *m.* organ-grinder; **—sack,** *m.* bagpipe; **—sackpfeifer,** *m.* bagpiper.

Du'deln, *(w.) v. tr. & intr.* 1) to play on the bagpipe; 2) *conl.* to perform badly on a wind-instrument; to sing badly; to hum. — **Du'dler,** *(str.) m.* bad singer or player. — **Dudelei,** *(w.) f.* (Dudeldei) *conl.* bad musical performance (especially on wind-instruments), bad singing; humming; empty talk.

* **Du'do,** *(str., pl.* D-s*) m. Ornith.* dodo (*Didus* L.).

* **Duell',** *(str.) n. (Lat.)* duel. — **Duellant',** *(w.) m.* duellist, dueller. — **Duellie'ren,** *(w.) v. refl.* to duel, to fight a duel.

* **Duett',** *(str.) n. (Ital.) Mus.* duet, duetto *(Ital.)*.

Duf'fel, *(str.) m. Comm.* duffel, (beaver) [illegible].

Duf'fig, *adj. (N. G.) see* Matt, Schimmlig, Dumpfig.

Duft, *(str., pl.* Düf'te*) m.* I. 1) vapour, exhalement, exhalation; 2) odour, (sweet) scent, fragrancy, perfume; geisterg[l]eiche — gebilde (*Freiligrath*), *n. pl.* spirit-like phantoms of air; **—gewölk,** *n.* haze; **—strauch,** *m. Bot.* diosma (Götterduft); **—wasser,** *n.* moisture on the inner sides of a well stocked bee-hive; II. *(L. G.) Mar. see* Ducht.

Düf'teln (Diefteln, Tüfteln), *(w.) v. intr.* to employ one's self in a minute and trifling way with small matters; to argue or reason about a thing over-nicely, to over-refine, &c.

Duf'ten, Düf'ten, *(w.) v. intr. & tr.* 1) to exhale, vapour, to emit (scent, moisture); to sweat, to be damp (of walls); 2) to perspire gently; 3) to exhale, breathe, give odour or fragrance. — **Duf'tend, Duf'tig,** *adj.* 1) vaporous, misty; 2) scenting, fragrant, odorous.

Dü'ker, *(str.) m. (L. G.)* 1) diver (Taucher); 2) underground sewer constructed under an embankment or canal; 3) *T.* sprig.

Dü'king, *(w.) f. (L. G.) Mar.* dip (der Kimmung, of the horizon).

Duld'bar, *adj.* tolerable, sufferable, allowable.

Dul'den, *(w.) v. tr.* 1) to bear with patience, to abide; to endure; die Sache duldet [illegible], the affair will bear no delay; 2) to tolerate, suffer, *cf.* Leiden; geduldeter [illegible], on sufferance.

Dul'der, *(str.) m.* sufferer.

Duld'sam, I. *adj.* enduring; tolerant; II. D-keit, **Dul'dung,** *(w.) f.* toleration, tolerance, sufferance.

[illegible], *(w.) m. Mar.* thole (Dolle).

[illegible], *(str.) m. provinc. (S. G.)* fair, mar-[illegible].

Dumm, I. *adj.* dull, stupid, blockish, [illegible], doltish, heavy-headed, thick-[illegible], foolish, nonsensical, idiotical; [illegible] — geworden ist, *Prov.* if the [illegible] the sorrow; er ist nicht so — wie [illegible], he is not such a fool as he looks; [illegible], I know better than that; [illegible], an awkward affair; d-es [illegible] — machen, to stultify, stu-[illegible] to sulk, to be sullen; II. [illegible] *see* —kopf; —dreist, [illegible], foolhardy, forward; confident; **—dreistigkeit,** *f.* fool-hardiness; forwardness; confidence.

Dum'merjan, *(str.) m. see* Dümmling.

Dumm'fromm, *adj.* bigoted.

Dumm'heit, *(w.) f.* dullness, stupidity, blockishness; in der — erhalten, to keep in darkness; D-en, *pl.* foolish tricks, foolery.

Dumm'..., *in comp.* **—kopf** (**—sack,** *vulg.*), *m.* blockhead, dullhead, thickhead, numskull, beetle-head, jolt, dunce, lackwit, simpleton; **—köpfig,** *adj.* stupid; **—köpfigkeit,** *f.* stupidity.

Dümm'ling, *(str.),* **Dum'mian, Dumm'rian,** *(str.) m. coll.* stupid fellow, simpleton, dunce, *cf.* Dummkopf.

Dum'pen, Dum'peln, *see* Dompen.

Dumpf, *adj.* 1) dull, flat, hollow, dead, obtuse; gloomy (silence); 2) *see* Dumpfig.

Dumpf, Dumpf'en, *(str.) m. provinc.* asthma, pursiness, cold on the chest.

Dumpf'heit, *(w.) f.* 1) dullness, deadness, obtuseness; 2) *fig.* insensibility, stupor.

Dümpf'el, *(str.) n. provinc.* pool, puddle.

Dumpf'ig, I. *adj.* 1) damp, dank, moist; 2) fusty, musty, mouldy; II. D-keit, *(w.) f.* 1) dampness; 2) mustiness, fustiness.

Du'ne, *provinc. (L. G.)* I. *(w.) f. see* Daune; II. *adj. or* Dün, *coll.* tipsy.

Dü'ne, *(w.) f. gener. pl.* Dünen, downs, sandhills along the coast of the sea; zusammengewehte —, ropes; *in comp. Bot.-z.* D-ngras, *n.* cotton grass (*Eriophorum* L.); D-nhalm, *m.* sea-reed grass (*Calamagrostis* Roth); D-nkäfer, *m.* a species of cockchafer (*Melolontha fullo* L.); D-nrose, *f.* 1) Scotch rose (*Rosa spinosissima* L.); 2) sweet-briar-rose (*Rosa rubiginosa* L.).

Dung, *(str.) m.* 1) *see* Dünger; 2) *see* Fliess; **—artig,** *adj.* stercoraceous.

Dün'gen, *(w.) v. tr. Husb.* to dung, manure, muck; — ohne den Dünger unterzupflügen, to top-dress (pastures, &c.).

Dün'ger, *(str.) m.* dung, manure, muck; künstlicher —, compost; **—erde,** *f.* garden-mould; **—gabel,** *f.* dung-fork; **—haufen,** *m.* dung-hill; **—stätte,** *f.* stercorary, dung-yard; **—streumaschine,** *f.* manure-drill.

Düng'jauche, *(w.) f.* liquid manure.

Dung'..., *in comp.* **—käfer,** *m. Entom.* muck-worm (*Aphodius fimetar* L.; *Scarabaeus stercorarius* F. &c.); **—lage,** *f.* dung-hill.

Dun'gras, *(str.) n. see* Wollgras.

Dün'gung, *(w.) f.* the (act of) dunging, manuring, stercoration; obere —, top-dressing; D-smittel, *n.* dunging-substance; künstliches D-smittel, artificial manure.

Dunk, *(str.) m. provinc. see* Fliess.

Dun'kel, I. *adj.* 1) dark; dusk, dusky, gloomy, murky; dim; cloudy, overcast; als es immer d-er wurde, as the night gathered; ehe es d-er wird (wurde), before dusk; 2) opaque; 3) *fig.* dim; dark, obscure, vague, ambiguous, crabbed, intricate, abstruse; deep; mystic(al), mysterious; die Farben d-er machen, to deepen the colours; d-e Ahnungen, vague forebodings; d-e Begriffe, confused ideas; eine d-e Rückerinnerung, a faint recollection, confused remembrance; es wird mir — vor den Augen, my head swims; II. *s. (str.) n.* (or das D-e *(decl. like adj.) n.*) darkness, *see* Dunkelheit; ins D-e spielend, inclining to a dark colour, darkish; das tiefste — der Nacht, the depth of night; im D-n, *lit. & fig.* in the dark; in obscurity; *fig.* at sea; es ist ein — darüber verbreitet, es liegt im D-n, it is involved in obscurity; ein — über *(with Acc.)* verbreiten, to throw a veil over ....

Dün'kel, *(str.) m.* 1) prejudice; fancy; caprice; whim; 2) or Dünkelhaftigkeit (self-) conceit, conceitedness, presumption; arrogance; — haben, to be presumptuous.

Dun'kel..., *in comp.* **—äugig,** *adj.* dark-eyed; **—blau,** *adj.* dark-blue; **—braun,** *adj.* dun; fuscous; dark (cigar); **—farbig,** *adj.* dark-coloured; **—gelb,** *adj.* tawny; **—haarig,** *adj.* dark-haired.

Dün'kelhaft, I. *adj.* (self-)conceited, arrogant; II. D-igkeit, *(w.) f.* conceitedness, &c. *cf.* Dünkel.

Dun'kelheit, *(w.) f.* 1) darkness; gloom; duskishness; 2) opacity; 3) dimness; obscurity; ambiguity, mysticalness, &c. *cf.* Dunkel, *adj.*; in der — leben, to live in obscurity.

Dun'kelmann, *(str., pl.* D-männer*) m. fig.* one opposed to enlightenment (*opp.* Lichtfreund), *cf.* Obscurant.

Dun'keln, *(w.) v.* I. *intr.* to darken, to grow dusky or dim; II. *tr.* to darken; to cloud.

Dun'kelroth, *adj. & s.* dark-red.

Dün'ken, *(w.) v.* I. *intr. (with the Dat.) & tr.* to seem; appear; sie dünkte mir schön, I thought her beautiful; thue was dir gut dünkt, do what you think proper, do as you like; desto schöner ... dünkt ihn die Gestalt der Sprache (*Grimm*, W.B. III), the more beautiful the form of the language appears to him to be; II. *refl.* 1) (or sich — lassen) to fancy, imagine one's self; sich klug —, to be wise in one's own opinion; er dünkt sich etwas (recht) Großes, he thinks himself a person of great consequence; *vulg.* he does not think small beer of himself; er dünkt sich etwas darauf, he is proud of it; ein sich wichtig d-der Mann, a self-important man; laß dich nicht klug —, don't fancy yourself wise; 2) to presume, to be self-conceited; sich zu viel —, to overween; III. *tr. impers.* es dünkt mich or mich dünkt, methinks, it seems to me; mich dünkt, Sie sollten ..., it strikes me you ought to ....

Dün'kirchen, *n. Geogr.* Dunkirk.

Dün'kling, Dün'kler, *coll.* **Dünk'(e)rich,** *(str.) m.* arrogant or conceited fellow.

Dünn, I. *adj.* 1) thin, slender, slight, small; lank, lean; rare (air); clear, sleazy, flimsy (stuff); dilute, weak (fluids); serous (blood); 2) *coll.* rare, scarce; d-es Bier, small or weak beer; — machen, *see* Verdünnen; das Schwert hing an einem d-en Faden, the sword was suspended by a slender thread; II. *in comp.* **—backig,** *adj.* lantern-jawed; **—bauch,** *m. Ichth. see* Stichling; **—beil,** *n. T.* chip-axe; **—beinig,** *adj.* thin-(spider-)legged; **—bier,** *n.* table or small beer; **—blätterig,** *adj.* thin-leaved; tenuifolious; **—darm,** *m. Anat.* the small intestine; **—eisen,** *n.* sheet-iron for tin-plates.

Dün'ne, *(w.) f.* 1) thinness, slenderness; slightness; rarity, rareness (of the air); 2) die D-n, *pl.,* or **Dün'nung,** *(w.) f. Anat.* the flanks, soft, hypochondria.

Dün'nen, *(w.) v. tr. (l. u.)* to thin (Dünn machen, Verdünnen).

Dünn'..., *in comp.* **—fisch,** *m. see* Aal, chinesischer; **—flache Feile,** *T.* pillar-file; **—gras,** *n. see* Wollgras; **—häutig,** *adj.* thin-skinned; **—köpfig,** *adj. fig.* weak-headed; *Bot.* slender-flowered (thistle); **—leibig,** *adj.* lank-bodied; **—leibigkeit,** *f.* lankness; **—öhrig,** *adj.* quick of hearing; **—schalig,** *adj.* thin-shelled; **—scheibe,** *f. see* Handbret; **—schlagform,** *f. T.* finishing mould (of gold-beaters), second mould of gut; **—schliff,** *m. T.* a section of a (mineral, &c.) substance polished to transparent thinness for (the purpose of) microscopical examination; **—schwanz,** *m. see* Haarschwanz; **—stein,** *m.* 1) light or tabulated diamond; 2) *Metall.* thin matte; **—tuch,** *n.* lawn. [dult.

Duns, *(str.) m. conl.* dunce, thick-scull.

Dun'sen, *(str.) v. intr. l. u. (Schubart, &c.) for †* Dinsen.

Dunst, I. *(str., pl.* Dün'ste*) m.* 1) vapour, damp, steam; fume; 2) dust-shot, small-shot, fowling-shot; 3) *fig. coll.* (blauer —) smoke, anything unreal, false show; Einem (einen) blauen — vormachen, to cast a mist before a

1) *a)* to go, walk, or pass through; d-de Waaren, goods in transit; der d-de Schnellzug, the through train; *b)* to penetrate; 2) to go off, run away: to abscond, *vulg.* to bolt, to cut; 3) to pass, to be approved *or* carried; wird es —? will it take? — lassen, 1. to pass (a road, &c.) through: 2. *Phys.* to allow to pass, to transmit (light, &c.): 3. *fig.* to pass (a bill, &c.); ihre Mutter ließ ihr nichts —, her mother passed her nothing: II. *tr.* 1) to walk through, wear through *or* out by walking: 2) to inspect, to examine (things) one after the other, to peruse, to go through (a book, &c.); Rechnungen —, to go through accounts; III. *refl.* to make sore by walking; sich *(Dat.)* die Füße —, to walk one's foot sore (Aufgehen).

Durchgeh'en, *(irr.) v. tr.* 1) to walk through ...; 2) *see* Durch'gehen, II. 2.

Durch'gehend, I. *p. a.* 1) passing through: pervading, piercing: 2) *Mus.* transient, passing; d-e Geleise, *Railw.* through lines; d-er Accord, *see* Durchgangsaccord; ein D-er, a passenger; II. D-s, *adv.* generally, universally, throughout, every where, in every part.

Durchgeist'en, Durchgeist'igen, *(w.) v. tr.* to render spiritual, to spiritualise; to convert to a spiritual meaning.

Durch'gerben, *(w.) v. tr.* 1) *Tann.* to tan thoroughly: 2) *vulg.* to beat soundly; (Einem das Fell —) to curry one's hide *(or* coat) well.

Durch'gießen, *(str.) v. tr.* to pour through: to filter, percolate, strain. — **Durch'gießung,** *(w.) f.* percolation, filtration, straining through.

Durchgie'ßen, *(str.) v. tr.* to pour through *or* all over; to pervade with fluids, &c. poured on ....

Durch'glänzen, *(w.) v. intr.* to shine through.

Durchglän'zen, *(w.) v. tr.* to illumine, pervade with splendour, &c.

Durch'gleiten, *(w.) v. intr.* to glide through.

Durchglei'ten, *(str.) v. tr.* to glide through ...; kaum daß ein leises Weh | durchgleitet das Gemüth *(Matzner,* Abend), scarce a gentle pain | steals softly through the mind *(Baskerv.)*.

Durch'glühen, *(w.) v.* I. *intr.* to glow through; II. *tr.* to make red hot, *cf.* Ausglühen.

Durchglüh'en, *(w.) v. tr.* 1) to inflame: 2) *fig.* to inspire (with a tender passion, a sense of justice, &c.).

Durch'graben, *(str.) v.* I. *tr.* 1) to dig through: II. *refl.* to dig one's way (through).

Durchgra'ben, *(str.) v. tr.* to pierce, to open by digging, &c.

Durch'greifen, *(str.) v.* I. *intr.* 1) to pass through with the hand grasping: *fig-s.* 2) to act decidedly, to take vigorous *or* decisive measures, to use authority; d-d, *p. a.* effectual, searching: energetic, thorough, radical (reform, &c.), sweeping (measures, &c.); 3) to succeed, prevail; to be efficacious; II. *tr.* to wear through *or* out by frequent handling.

Durchgrü'beln, *(w.) v. tr.* to search through *or* closely, scrutinise, ponder, to examine minutely, to sift thoroughly.

Durch'gucken, *(w.) v. intr.* to peep (look) through.

Durchguck'en, *(w.) v. tr.* to look over, search.

Durch'gucktau, *(str.) n. Mar.* slab-line.

Durch'guß, *(str., pl.* Durch'güsse) *m.* 1) the act of pouring through; 2) percolation; filtration; 3) gutter: sink: 4) strainer, colander, filter.

Durch'haben, *(irr.) v. tr. coll.* to have done with, to have got through *(cf.* Durch, II. *adv.* 1).

Durch'hacken, *(w.) v. tr.* to cut through with an axe, hatchet, &c.

Durch'hallern, *(w.) v. refl. see* Durchhämmern, II.

Durch'hallen, *(w.) v. intr.* to sound through.

Durchhal'len, *(w.) v. tr.* to sound through ..., fill with sound.

Durch'hämmern, *(w.) v.* I. *tr.* 1) *a)* *T.* to work (a thing) thoroughly with the hammer; *b)* to perfect, finish, complete: 2) to wear through (perforate) by hammering: II. *refl. fig.* to work one's way through by hammering.

Durch'hau, *(str.) m. see* Durchhieb.

Durch'hauchen, *(w.) v. intr.* to breathe through.

Durchhau'chen, *(w.) v. tr. see* Durchathmen.

Durch'hauen, *(irr.) v.* I. *tr.* (& *intr.*) 1) *or* Durchhau'en, to hew through, cut through: 2) *coll.* to lick, whip, scourge, to give (one) a thorough licking, &c.; II. *refl.* to cut one's way, to cut through sword in hand.

Durch'haus, *(str., pl.* Durch'häuser) *n.* a house having a thoroughfare.

Durch'hecheln, *(w.) v. tr.* 1) to hatchel thoroughly: 2) *fig.* to censure, criticise severely *or* maliciously, to satirise, to cut (one) up.

Durch'heizen, *(w.) v. tr.* to heat thoroughly.

Durch'helfen, *(str.) v.* I. *intr.* (Einem) to help *or* assist (to get) through; II. *refl.* to contrive to get through (the world), to get along by shifts, to gain a (scanty) livelihood, sich mühsam —, to work hard for a living; *vulg.* to rub through the world, to rub on *(cf.* Durchkommen).

Durchhel'len, *(w.) v. tr. see* Erhellen.

Durchherr'schen, *(w.) v. tr.* to rule over ....

Durch'heulen, *(w.) v. tr.* to pass (a certain time) with howling.

Durchheu'len, *(w.) v. tr.* to pierce with cries, to fill with howling.

Durch'hieb, *(str.) m. Forest.* an opening through a wood, &c., glade (Aushau).

Durch'hin, *adv.* (passing, gliding) through, past (Hindurch).

Durchhin', *adv.* all through, all over, thoroughly.

Durchhit'zen, *(w.) v. tr.* to heat thoroughly.

Durchhöh'len, *(w.) v. tr.* to hollow throughout.

Durch'holen, *(w.) v. tr. coll.* 1) *see* Durchhecheln; 2) *see* Durch'sehen, II. 2; 3) *see* Durch'prügeln.

Durchhor'chen, *(w.) v. tr.* to listen in every part of (the house, &c.).

Durch'hüpfen, *(w.) v. intr. (aux.* sein), **Durchhüpf'en,** *(w.) v. tr.* to hop, skip, jump through.

Durch'huschen, *(w.) v. intr. (aux.* sein) *coll.* 1) to pass quickly and silently through, to glide, pop, flit, *or* slip through: 2) to get through *or* off, to escape, to slip *or* steal away *(cf.* Durchwischen, 2); Einen — lassen, to let one off.

Durchir'ren, *(w.) v. tr.* to wander, ramble, range, rove, err, *or* stray through ....

Durch'jagen, *(w.) v.* I. *tr.* 1) to hunt, pursue through: 2) *fig.* to hurry through *or* over: II. *intr.* 1) to pass through in hunting; 2) *(aux.* sein) to hasten through.

Durchja'gen, *(w.) v. tr.* to hunt through *or* over ...; to gallop over, to pass quickly over, to scour.

Durchjam'mern, *(w.) v. tr.* to pass *or* spend in lamentations.

Durchju'beln, *(w.) v. tr.* 1) *or* Durchjauch'zen, *(w.) v. tr.* to run *or* pass through (the streets, &c.) with joyous cries, to fill (the air, &c.) with shouts (of rejoicing); 2) to pass revelling, rioting, to spend noisily.

Durch'kalen, *(w.) v. tr. Mar.* die Brass —, to change the sheets; ein Giekssegel —, to gybe.

Durchkäl'ten, *(w.) v. tr.* to penetrate with cold, to chill all over.

Durch'kämmen, *(w.) v. tr.* 1) to comb thoroughly; *fig.* & *vulg-s.* 2) *see* Durchhecheln, 2; 3) *see* Durchprügeln.

Durch'kämpfen, *(w.) v. tr.* & *refl. see* Durchfechten.

Durch'käuen, Durch'kauen, *(w.) v. tr.* 1) *or* Durchkäu'en, to chew thoroughly, to masticate sufficiently; 2) *fig.* to repeat again and again, *coll.* to harp (always) on the same string.

[illegible] (in person); Glas läßt die Lichtstrahlen [illegible], glass transmits rays of light; 3) to [illegible] (metals); 4) *Min.* to flatten: to be pervious (to) or permeable (by); durch'lässig, [illegible] pervious (to). — Durch'lassung, *(w.) f.* [illegible]mission (of light), &c.

[illegible], *(str.) n. T.* sluice-wear.

Durchlaucht', *(w.) f.* Highness; Seine —, [illegible] (serene) Highness; Ihre — die Fürstin, [illegible] Highness the princess; Ew. —, your Serenity, your serene Highness.

Durchlauch'tig, I. *adj.* 1) †, renowned, [illegible], illustrious; 2) most high, most [illegible]; august; der d-ste Fürst, his most serene Highness; II. D-keit, *(w.) f. (l. u.) see* Durchlaucht.

Durch'lauf, *(str., pl.* Durch'läufe*) m.* 1) [illegible] (act of) running through; passage; 2) *see* [illegible], 2; 3) *see* Durchlaß, 3.

Durch'laufen, *(str.) v.* I. *intr.* *(aux.* sein*)* [illegible] run through; to strain, filter; — lassen, to [illegible], to pass through; II. *tr.* to wear through [illegible] by running, *cf.* Durch'gehen, II. 1. & III.

Durchlau'fen, *(str.) v. tr.* 1) to run or [illegible] rapidly through ..., to run from one end [illegible] ... to the other; to course, traverse; alle [illegible] —, *coll.* to hunt all the shops or stalls; [illegible] Gerücht durchläuft die Stadt, a rumour [illegible] spread in the town; der Schall durchläuft [illegible] Fuß in einer Minute, sound (at travels [illegible]) 1142 feet in a second; 2) to peruse [illegible], to dip into (a book, &c.), to pass [illegible] over, to hasten or hurry through.

Durch'leben, Durchle'ben, *(w.) v. tr.* to [illegible] over; to pass, to go through; sein Leben [illegible] —, to live one's life out fast; noch einmal durchle'ben, to live over again (one's [illegible], &c.).

Durch'lesen, Durchle'sen, *(str.) v. tr.* to [illegible] through or over, to peruse, go through.

Durchle'sung, *(w.) f.* perusal. [through.

Durch'leuchten, *(w.) v. intr.* to shine

Durchleuch'ten, *(w.) v. tr.* to light through [illegible] fill with light, illumine, * illume.

Durch'liegen, *(str.) v. refl. see* Aufliegen, II.

Durchloch'en, *(w.) v. tr. T.* to punch, to [illegible].

[illegible]'ern, *(w.) v. tr.* to make holes [illegible] ...; to perforate, to pierce or provide [illegible], to punch; to riddle (with bal[illegible]) to honey-comb; *fig.* to transgress, in[illegible]; durchlöchert, *p. a.* worn in holes, [illegible], full of holes, honey-combed; *Bot.* per[illegible], pertuse.

[illegible]'dern, *(w.) v. tr.* 1) to blaze or [illegible] through ...; 2) *fig.* to inflame, enkindle, [illegible] with ardour. [to ventilate.

[illegible], *(w.) v. tr.* to air thoroughly,

[illegible], *(str.) v. refl.* to help one's [illegible] make one's way by lying.

[illegible]machen, *(w.) v. tr. fig.* to go or [illegible] through: 1) to finish, accomplish; 2) to [illegible]; — lassen, to put through.

[illegible], *(str., pl.* Durch'märsche*) m.* [illegible] marching through, passage (of troops); [illegible], the getting all the tricks.

[illegible], *(w.) v. intr.* *(aux.* sein*)* [illegible] through.

[illegible], *(w.) v. tr.* to cut through [illegible] a chisel. [thoroughly.

[illegible], *(w.) v. tr.* to mingle or mix

[illegible], *(w.) v. tr.* to mix up (with).

[illegible], *(str.) v. tr.* to measure [illegible].

[illegible], *(str.) v. tr.* 1) to measure [illegible], every part of ...; 2) *fig.* to pass [illegible] or over ....

[illegible], *(str.) m. Geom.* diameter.

[illegible], *(w.) v. tr. see* Durchmengen.

[illegible], [illegible], *(w.) v. tr.* to [illegible] or thoroughly.

[illegible], [illegible], *(w.) v. tr.*

1) to review all over, to search minutely; to sweep (the heavens with the telescope); 2) *coll.* to scrutinise; to censure, criticise severely or maliciously.

Durchnach'ten, *(w.) v. tr.* * to darken, fill with darkness, to cloud, obscure.

Durch'nagen, Durchna'gen, *(w.) v. tr.* 1) to gnaw or nibble through; 2) *fig.* to gnaw at (one's heart, &c.), to prey upon, corrode.

Durch'nähen, *(w.) v. tr.* 1) to sew through; 2) to make sore by sewing; die durchgenähte Naht, *Nav.* monk's seam.

Durchnäh'en, *(w.) v. tr.* 1) to quilt; 2) *Shoe-m. see* Abdoppeln; 3) durchnähte Arbeit, quilting.

Durch'nässen, Durch'netzen, Durchnäs'sen, Durchnetz'en, *(w.) v. tr.* to wet thoroughly; to moisten, wet through or all over; to drench, soak.

Durch'nehmen, *(str.) v. tr. fig.* 1) to canvass, examine; 2) to censure, criticise.

Durchör'tern, *(w.) v. tr. Min.* to hole; to cut across, intersect. — Durchör'terung, *(w.) f.* (the act of) cutting across, intersection.

Durch'paß, *(str., pl.* Durch'pässe*) m.* a long narrow passage, pass, defile.

Durch'passiren, *(w.) v. tr.* to pass or go through. [or wade through.

Durch'patschen, *(w.) v. tr. coll.* to plash

Durch'pauschen, Durch'pausen, *(w.) v. tr. Paint.* to pounce, to counterdraw.

Durch'peitschen, *(w.) v. tr.* 1) to whip soundly; 2) *coll.* to recapitulate, repeat again and again, to begin the old story.

Durchpfef'fern, *(w.) v. tr.* to pepper thoroughly *(also fig.)*. [the and.

Durch'pfeifen, *(str.) v. tr.* to whistle to

Durchpfei'fen, *(str.) v. tr.* to penetrate or pass through whistling, to pierce (as the wind).

Durch'pflügen, Durchpflü'gen, *(w.) v. tr.* to plough through, to plough all over.

Durch'pilgern, *(w.) v. intr.* to wander through. [..., *cf.* Durchwandern.

Durchpil'gern, *(w.) v. tr.* to wander through

Durch'placken, Durch'plagen, *(w.) v. refl. see* sich Durchquälen, Durchkrüppeln.

Durchplau'dern, *(w.) v. tr.* to spend or pass in (or to beguile [the time] by) talking.

Durch'prassen, *(w.) v. tr.* to spend (one's fortune) in revelry or debauchery.

Durchpras'sen, *(w.) v. tr.* to spend or pass (the time) in revelry or debauchery.

Durch'pressen, *(w.) v. tr.* to press or squeeze through.

Durch'prüfen, *(w.) v. tr.* to examine all over.

Durch'prügeln, *(w.) v. tr.* to beat soundly, to drub, cudgel, *coll.* to belabour, to lick, trounce, wallop, &c. thoroughly.

Durch'quälen, *(w.) v. refl.* to get through with pain or difficulty. [press through.

Durch'quetschen, *(w.) v. tr.* to squeeze or

Durch'rädern, *(w.) v. tr.* to run through a riddle or strainer.

Durchran'ken, *(w.) v. tr.* to intertwine or intertwist with tendrils.

Durchra'sen, *(w.) v. tr.* 1) to run through (the streets, &c.) furiously, frantically; 2) to pass (the night, &c.) in raging or frenzy.

Durchras'seln, *(w.) v. tr.* to rattle through....

Durch'rauchen, *(w.) v. intr.* to fume or smoke through. [fume or smoke.

Durchrau'chen, *(w.) v. tr.* to fill with

Durch'räuchern, Durchräu'chern, *(w.) v. tr.* to smoke thoroughly; to perfume, fumigate all over. [nap (cloth) thoroughly.

Durch'rauhen, *(w.) v. tr. T.* to card or

Durch'rauschen, *(w.) v. intr.* *(aux.* sein*)* to rush, rustle through.

Durchrau'schen, *(w.) v. tr.* to rush through ..., to fill with a rushing or rustling noise.

Durch'rechnen, *(w.) v. tr.* to count, reckon over or through; to examine (an account).

Durch'regnen, *(w.) v. intr. impers.* to rain through. [or to soak with rain.

Durchreg'nen, *(w.) v. tr.* to wet thoroughly

Durch'reiben, *(str.) v. tr.* 1) to rub through: to strain (as through a colander); 2) *a)* to fret and wear by rubbing or friction, to chafe (a cable, &c.); *b)* to make sore by rubbing, to chafe, gall (the skin, &c.).

Durch'reichen, *(w.) v.* I. *tr.* to reach through: II. *intr.* 1) to suffice, to be sufficient; 2) to be sufficiently provided. [passage.

Durch'reise, *(w.) f.* a passing through,

Durch'reisen, *(w.) v. intr.* *(aux.* sein*)* to travel or pass through; der D-de, passenger.

Durchrei'sen, *(w.) v. tr.* to travel over, traverse.

Durch'reißen, *(str.) v.* I. *tr.* (or Durchrei'ßen) to tear (in two), to rend asunder; II. *intr.* *(aux.* sein*)* to break, rend, to be torn asunder.

Durch'reiten, *(str.) v.* I. *intr.* *(aux.* sein*)* to ride through, to go through on horseback; II. *tr.* to gall, hurt by the friction of riding.

Durchrei'ten, *(str.) v. tr.* to ride through or over ..., to traverse, cross on horseback: von den Motten durchritten, worm-eaten.

Durch'rennen, *(irr.) v. intr.* *(aux.* sein*)* to run through.

Durchren'nen, *(irr.) v. tr.* 1) to run through (the streets, &c.), to run all over ...; 2) to run (one) through (with a sword).

Durch'rieseln, *(w.) v. intr.* *(aux.* sein*)*, Durchrie'seln, *(w.) v. tr.* 1) to rill, purl, gurgle through, to glide through with soft murmurs (as a rivulet); 2) to thrill (Durchzittern): von Schrecken durchrieselt, shivering with terror. [2) *see* Durchriffeln.

Durch'riffeln, *(w.) v. tr.* 1) *see* Durchhecheln;

Durch'rinnen, *(str.) v. intr.* *(aux.* sein*)*, Durchrin'nen, *(str.) v. tr.* to run, flow, or leak through.

Durch'riß, *(str.) m.* rent, breach.

Durch'ritt, *(str.) m.* the act of riding through, passage on horseback.

Durch'ritzen, Durchritz'en, *(w.) v. tr.* 1) to scratch through; 2) to scratch all over.

Durch'rollen, *(w.) v. intr.* *(aux.* sein*)*, Durchrol'len, *(w.) v. tr.* to roll through.

Durch'röschen, *(w.) v. tr. Min.* to make stream-works or conduits across (the rock).

Durch'rücken, *(w.) v. intr.* *(aux.* sein*)* *Mil.* to march through. [row through.

Durch'rudern, *(w.) v. intr.* *(aux.* sein*)* to

Durchru'dern, *(w.) v. tr.* to row over, navigate.

Durch'rüffeln, *(w.) v. tr.* to give a severe reprimand, &c. *cf.* Abrüffeln.

Durch'rühren, *(w.) v. tr.* 1) to strain or press through by stirring; 2) to stir up thoroughly. [slide or slip through.

Durch'rutschen, *(w.) v. intr.* *(aux.* sein*)* to

Durch'rütteln, *(w.) v. tr.* to shake through or thoroughly.

Durchs, *contr. from* durch das.

Durch'säbeln, *(w.) v. tr.* to cut through with a sabre. [saw through.

Durch'sägen, Durchsä'gen, *(w.) v. tr.* to

Durch'salzen, Durchsal'zen, *(irr.) v. tr.* to salt thoroughly, sufficiently.

Durch'säuern, Durchsäu'ern, *(w.) v. tr. Bak.* to leaven thoroughly.

Durchsäu'seln, *(w.) v. tr.* to blow or rustle gently through (the leaves, &c. as a breeze).

Durchsau'sen, *(w.) v. tr.* to rush, whistle, bluster through ....

Durch'schaben, *(w.) v. tr.* to scrape through.

Durch'schaffen, *(w.) v. tr.* to carry, convey, or get through.

Durch'schallen, *(w.) v. intr.* to sound through (the air), to penetrate (as sounds).

[illegible] inspection *or* perusal; D-bild, D-ge-mälde, *n.* transparent picture, transparency; D-lehre, *f. Phys.* dioptrics.

Durch'sichtig, I. *adj.* transparent (*different from* Durchscheinend); pellucid, diaphanous; clear, limpid; Glas ist —, glass is pervious to light; halb —, imperfectly transparent, semipellucid; im Wasser —, hydrophanous; II. D-keit, (*w.*) *f.* transparency: 1) pelluciditly, diaphaneity; clearness, limpidness: D-keit des Glases, perviousness of glass to light; 2) *fig.* perspicuity, clearness to the mind; lucidity; D-keitsmesser, *m.* diaphanometer.

Durch'sickern, Durch'sintern, (*w.*) *v. intr.* (*aux.* sein) to trickle *or* ooze through; to percolate.

Durch'sieben, (*w.*) *v. tr.* to sift, riddle, cribble; to bolt (flower): to garble (indigo): *Min.* to screen.

Durch'singen, (*str.*) *v. tr.* to sing through *or* over, to sing to the end. [sink through.

Durch'sinken, (*str.*) *v. intr.* (*aux.* sein) to sink through.

Durchsin'ken, (*str.*) *v. tr. Min.* to sink, to pass through ... (Durchsenken).

Durch'sinnen, (*str.*) *v. tr.* 1) to consider *or* weigh in all parts; to run over in one's mind, *cf.* Durchdenken; 2) to spend musingly *or* in deep thoughts. [upon.

Durch'sitzen, (*str.*) *v. tr.* to wear by sitting

Durchsit'zen, (*str.*) *v. tr.* to pass sitting; ganze Nächte beim Spiele —, to spend whole nights at the gaming-table.

Durchson'nen, (*w.*) *v. tr.* to warm thoroughly by exposing to the sun, to sun, bask.

Durchsor'gen, (*w.*) *v. tr.* to spend *or* pass in care *or* anxiety.

Durchspä'hen, (*w.*) *v. tr.* to spy through, to look into, examine thoroughly.

Durch'spalten, Durchspal'ten, (*w.*) *v. tr.* to cleave through, to split asunder.

Durchspi'cken, (*w.*) *v. tr.* 1) to interlard, lard all over; 2) *fig.* to interlard.

Durch'spielen, (*w.*) *v. tr.* 1) *a)* to play over; *b)* to act over; 2) to play (a musical piece) all through, to practise (thoroughly): eine Rolle —, to support a part throughout *or* to the end.

Durchspie'len, (*w.*) *v. tr.* to pass *or* spend (the night) playing *or* gambling.

Durch'spießen, Durchspie'ßen, (*w.*) *v. tr.* to pierce (with a spear, &c.), to transfix.

Durch'sprechen, (*str.*) *v. tr.* to talk (a matter) over, to discuss.

Durch'sprengen, (*w.*) *v.* I. *intr.* (*aux.* sein) to gallop through, to pass through at full speed: II. *tr.* to make to burst, to burst.

Durchspreng'en, (*w.*) *v. tr.* 1) to gallop through ... *or* over ...; so durchsprengt der [illegible] König [illegible] seines Reiches Grenzen [illegible], thus the king of beasts gallops [illegible] through the expanse of his realm: 2) *a)* to scatter all over; *b)* to intersperse. [illegible] Durchsprü'hen.

Durch'springen, (*str.*) *v. intr.* (*aux.* sein) 1) to leap through *or* across; 2) to crack, to burst through.

Durchsprin'gen, (*str.*) *v. tr.* to leap through [illegible] all corners; er durchsprang den Raum in [illegible] Sätzen, he cleared the space with three [illegible]. [to squirt through.

[illegible], **Durchsprit'zen**, (*w.*) *v. tr.*

[illegible], **Durchspü'ren**, (*w.*) *v. tr.* [illegible] search through; to examine closely [illegible] (alle Winkel) every corner; *Sport.* [illegible], scour (for game).

[illegible], (*w.*) *v. tr.* 1) *or* Durch'-[illegible] to stamp *or* punch through: 2) to [illegible] thoroughly *or* every part of....

[illegible], (*w.*) *v. tr. vulg.* 1) to fill [illegible]; 2) *fig. vulg.* to ferret, rummage, [illegible].

Durch'stäuben, (*w.*) *v. tr.* 1) to drive *or* blow through (as dust): 2) *a)* *see* Durchstäu'-ben, 1; *b)* to sprinkle all over, to powder (one's hair, &c.): *c)* *T.* to pounce.

Durchstäu'ben, (*w.*) *v. tr.* 1) to cover with dust, to dust throughout *or* all over; 2) to hurry through (a place) raising a dust.

Durch'stäupen, (*w.*) *v. tr.* to whip, beat (soundly) with rods.

Durch'stechen, (*str.*) *v. tr.* 1) to run, drive, *or* push (a pointed instrument) through: 2) to dig *or* cut through; 3) *Husb.* to stir *or* turn (corn); 4) *Forest.* to clear (a wood); 5) *Metall.* to melt, smelt; 6) mit Einem etwas —, *provinc.* to concert clandestinely, to contrive jointly.

Durchste'chen, (*str.*) *v. tr.* 1) to pierce, transfix, run through (with a sword, &c.), to stab (with a poniard), to gore (with horns), to cut through: to prick; 2) *Sew.* to quilt; durchstoch'en, *p. a.* 1. quilted; 2. *Bot.* perfoliate, perforated. [piercer.

Durch'stecher, (*str.*) *m.* *T.* small auger,

Durchstecherei', (*w.*) *f. provinc.* intrigue, secret practice, jobbing, joint contrivance.

Durch'stehlen, (*str.*) *v. tr. refl.* to steal through, *or* away, to get through unperceived.

Durch'steigen, (*str.*) *v. intr.* (*aux.* sein) to step through, to get in through....

Durchstei'gen, (*str.*) *v. tr.* to stride, stalk over. [pass (a thicket) with nets.

Durchstel'len, (*w.*) *v. tr. Sport.* to encom-

Durchstep'pen, (*w.*) *v. tr. Sew.* to stitch, to quilt. [*cf.* Durchschiffen.

Durchsteu'ern, (*w.*) *v. tr.* to steer through,

Durch'stich, (*str.*) *m.* 1) act of piercing *or* cutting through: 2) *Railw.* a cutting, cut; *Min.* & *Fort.* cut, intrenchment, aperture.

Durchsti'cken, (*w.*) *v. tr. Sew.* 1) to stitch, to quilt: 2) to cover with embroidery.

Durch'stinken, (*w.*) *v. intr.* to stink through.

Durchstin'ken, (*w.*) *v. tr.* to fill with stink.

Durchstö'bern, (*w.*) *v. tr.* to search (*i. e. a.*), rummage, ferret, to stir about, rake.

Durchsto'chern, (*w.*) *v. tr.* 1) to prick (through); 2) *or* Durchstö'ren, (*w.*) *v. tr.* *see* Durchstöbern.

Durch'stopfen, (*w.*) *v. tr.* to put, stuff, *or* thrust through (a narrow opening).

Durch'stoßen, (*str.*) *v. tr.* 1) to thrust *or* push through; 2) to break by thrusting; 3) to wear out by pushing against; 4) to make sore by pushing against; 5) *Glass-w.* to open, out (the oven).

Durchsto'ßen, (*str.*) *v. tr.* to stab *or* run through, to pierce, transfix. [shine through.

Durch'strahlen, (*w.*) *v. intr.* to radiate *or*

Durchstrah'len, (*w.*) *v. tr.* to penetrate *or* fill with rays, to irradiate.

Durch'streichen, (*str.*) *v.* I. *tr.* to run a line through (a word, &c.), to cross (with a pen, &c.), strike out, blot out, to erase, cancel; er strich das Wort durch, he drew his pen through that word: II. *intr.* (*aux.* sein) to pass through with velocity; d-de Linie, *f. Phys.* trajectory.

Durchstrei'chen, (*str.*) *v. tr.* 1) *see* Durch'-streichen, I.; 2) *or* Durchstrei'fen, (*w.*) *v. tr.* to ramble through, roam (over), to rove through, run over (the country): das Feld —, *Sport.* to beat abroad, to beat the field.

Durch'strich, (*str.*) *m.* 1) stroke *or* line drawn through (a word, line, *or* page), cross; 2) passage (of migratory birds).

Durch'strömen, (*w.*) *v. intr.* (*aux.* sein), **Durchströ'men**, (*w.*) *v. tr.* 1) to stream *or* run through; 2) to crowd, throng, *or* press through.

Durchstür'men, (*w.*) *v. tr.* to storm, rage *or* rush through.

Durch'stürzen, (*w.*) *v.* I. *intr.* (*aux.* sein) to be precipitated *or* to fall through; II. *tr.* to precipitate *or* thrust through with vehemence.

Durchsu'chen, (*w.*) *v. tr.* to search (through *or* all over), to examine closely: Alles —, to search everywhere: *cf.* Durchstöbern; die Zollbeamten durchsuchten unser Gepäck, the custom-house officers searched our baggage. — Durchsu'cher, (*str.*) *m.* searcher, &c. — Durchsu'chung, (*w.*) *f.* a searching (through), &c., close examination, search: D-srecht, *n.* *Pol.* right of search. [through....

Durchsum'men, (*w.*) *v. tr.* to hum *or* buzz

Durchsü'ßen, (*w.*) *v. tr.* to sweeten thoroughly, to edulcorate.

Durchtän'deln, (*w.*) *v. tr.* to trifle away, to spend *or* pass in trifles *or* in toying.

Durch'tanzen, (*w.*) *v.* I. *intr.* (*aux.* sein) to dance through: II. *tr.* 1) to wear out by dancing; 2) to dance through, to dance from beginning to end: to go through (all the dances). [cing.

Durchtan'zen, (*w.*) *v. tr.* to pass in dan-

Durch'toben, (*w.*) *v. intr.* (*aux.* sein) to rage through. [...; 2) to pass raging.

Durchto'ben, (*w.*) *v. tr.* 1) to rage through

Durch'tönen, (*w.*) *v. intr.* to sound through.

Durchtö'nen, (*w.*) *v. tr.* to resound through ..., to fill with sound.

Durch'tönig, *adj. Mus.* diatonic.

Durchto'sen, (*w.*) *v. tr.* to roar through ..., to fill with roaring.

Durch'traben, (*w.*) *v. intr.* (*aux.* sein), **Durchtra'ben**, (*w.*) *v. tr.* to trot through.

Durch'tragen, (*str.*) *v.* I. *tr.* to carry through; II. *refl.* to wear through.

Durchtrau'ern, (*w.*) *v. tr.* to pass mourning, in woe, in grief.

Durchträu'feln, Durch'träufen, (*w.*) *v. intr.* (*aux.* sein) to drop *or* drip through.

Durchträu'men, (*w.*) *v. tr.* to pass dreaming.

Durch'treiben, (*str.*) *v. tr.* 1) to drive through; *Cook.* to strain (peas): 2) *fig.* to carry out, to effect.

Durch'treten, (*str.*) *v.* I. *intr.* (*aux.* sein) to tread through: II. *tr.* 1) *a)* to tread through (as ice, a board, &c.); *b)* to wear out or through by treading (as shoes, &c.); 2) *a)* to trample (on), to tread repeatedly; *b)* *see* Durchtre'ten.

Durchtre'ten, (*str.*) *v. tr.* to work, prepare (clay, turf, &c.) by treading. [a funnel.

Durch'trichtern, (*w.*) *v. tr.* to pour through

Durch'trieb, (*str.*) *m.* the act and the right of driving through; passage of cattle, sheep, &c.

Durchtrie'ben, I. *adj.* cunning, crafty, practised, artful, arrant: II. D-heit, (*w.*) *f.* cunningness, craftiness.

Durchwa'chen, (*w.*) *v. tr.* (*sometimes* Durch'-wachen) to pass waking; die Nacht —, to watch the whole night; seine durchwachten Nächte, his nights of watchfulness; das —, *s. s.* (*str.*) *n.* das — der Nacht, the (act of) watching through the night.

Durch'wachs (*pr.* —wax), (*str.*) *n. Bot.* 1) thorough wax, (round-leaved) hare's ear (*Bupleurum rotundifolium* L.); 2) *see* Geisblatt; 3) *see* Singrün; 4) *see* Zweiblatt.

Durch'wachsen, (*str.*) *v. intr.* (*aux.* sein) to grow through.

Durchwach'sen, I. (*str.*) *v. tr.* to grow through ..., to interpenetrate: — sein, to be streaked (as meat, &c.); II. *p. a.* 1) marbled (of meat): 2) *Bot.* perfoliate, connate.

Durch'wagen, (*w.*) *v. refl.* to venture through. [(things) one after the other.

Durch'wägen, (*w.* & *str.*) *v. tr.* to weigh

Durch'walken, (*w.*) *v. tr.* 1) to full *or* mill thorougly: 2) *vulg.* to give (one) a milling, thrashing, *see* Durchprügeln.

Durchwal'len, (*w.*) *v. tr.* * 1) to wander through: 2) *fig.* to pervade: 3) Freude durchwallte sein Herz, joy thrilled his bosom.

Durchwal'ten, (*w.*) *v. tr.* 1) to rule over ...; 2) *fig.* to prevail throughout, to pervade.

Durch'walzen, (*w.*) *v. intr.*, **Durchwal'zen**, (*w.*) *v. tr.* to pass *or* spend in waltzing, to waltz through.

Durch'wamsen, *(w.) v. tr. vulg.* to lace one's jacket, to hide (Durchprügeln).

Durchwan'deln, *(w.) v. tr.* to walk, go, *or* pass through.

Durch'wandern, *(w.) v. intr. (aux.* sein) to wander through.

Durchwan'dern, *(w.) v. tr.* 1) to wander through ... *or* over in all directions, to traverse: 2) *fig.* to travel through (history, &c.).

Durchwär'men, *(w.) v. tr.* to warm through *or* thoroughly.

Durch'waschen, Durchwasch'en, *(str.) v. tr.* to wash through, to wear (out) by washing: (sich *[Dat.]* die Hände) to make sure by washing (one's fingers *or* hands).

Durchwäs'sern, *(w.) v. tr.* to water *or* soak thoroughly: to irrigate all over.

Durch'waten, *(w.) v. intr. (aux.* sein), **Durchwa'ten,** *(w.) v. tr.* to ford, to wade through: zu — (Durchwat'bar), fordable.

Durchwe'ben, *(w. & str.) v. tr.* 1) to weave through: mit goldenen Fäden durchwoben, woven through with golden threads: 2) *fig.* to interweave, to mix, mingle with, intermix.

Durch'weg, *(str.) m. see* Durchgang.

Durchweg' *[pr. —wech']*, *adv. coll.* throughout (Durchgängig, II.).

Durch'wehen, *(w.) v. intr.* to blow through.

Durchweh'en, *(w.) v. tr.* 1) to blow through ..., to perflate: 2) *fig.* to pervade.

Durch'weichen, *(w.) v. intr. (aux.* sein) to soak, to be soaked: II. *or* **Durchwei'chen,** *(w.) v. tr.* to soak, steep *or* macerate thoroughly, to drench.

Durchwei'nen, *(w.) v. tr.* to pass *or* spend (hours, days, nights) in tears.

Durch'werfen, *(str.) v. tr.* 1) *gener.* to cast *or* throw through ...; 2) to (run through a) riddle, to screen; 3) *Weav.* die Spule —, to cross.

Durchwet'tert, *p. a.* weather-beaten.

Durch'wichsen, *(w.) v. tr.* 1) to blacken, polish (shoes, &c.) thoroughly; 2) *vulg. see* Durchprügeln.

Durchwim'mern, *(w.) v. tr. (sometimes* **Durch'wimmern**) to pass *or* spend in lamentation, moaning, *or* whimpering.

Durch'winden, *(str.) v.* I. *tr.* to wind through: II. *refl.* to wind, toil, *or* struggle through: to get through with difficulty, *cf.* sich Durchschlagen.

Durchwin'den, *(str.) v. tr.* to wind *or* twist through ..., to entwine, intertwine: Lorbeeren mit Epheu —, to twist bays with ivy.

Durchwin'seln, *(w.) v. tr.* to pass in moaning *or* whining (Durchwimmern).

Durch'wintern, *(w.) v.* I. *tr.* to winter, to keep (plants, &c.) through the winter; (of animals) to hibernate: II. *intr. & refl.* to winter.

Durchwin'tern, *(w.) v. intr.* to pass the [winter.

Durchwir'beln, *(w.) v. tr.* 1) to whirl through: 2) *fig.* to resound through.

Durch'wirken, *(w.) v. tr.* 1) *Bak.* to work *or* knead thoroughly.

Durchwir'ken, *(w.) v. tr.* to interweave, tissue; **durchwirkt'**, *p. a.* interwoven: ganz durchwirkte Shawls, *Comm.* Paisley-shawls.

Durch'wischen, *(w.) v. intr. (aux.* sein) *coll.* 1) to slip *or* slide through, *cf.* Durchschlüpfen, 1; 2) to slip away, to escape, to get off.

Durchwit'tern, *(w.) v. tr. Min.* to intermix with minerals dissolved by the action of air.

Durchwöl'ben, *(w.) v. tr.* to vault *or* arch throughout.

Durch'wühlen, *(w.) v. refl.* to make (force) one's way through by rooting *or* grubbing.

Durchwüh'len, *(w.) v. tr.* 1) to root (up) thoroughly, to grub through: 2) to rummage, ferret, rifle up, ransack: 3) *fig.* vom Schmerz durchwühlt, harrowed by pain.

Durch'wurf, *(str., pl.* Durch'würfe) *m.* 1) the (act of) casting through, &c. *cf.* Durchwerfen; 2) screen, riddle, cribble.

Durch'würgen, *(w.) v.* I. *tr.* to swallow down with difficulty; II. *refl. vulg. see* sich Durchwinden, 2.

Durchwür'zen, *(w.) v. tr.* to season all over, to fill with perfume, to perfume, scent.

Durchwü'then, *(w.) v. tr.* to rage through....

Durch'zählen, *(w.) v. tr.* to count (money) over.

Durchzech'en *(sometimes* **Durch'zechen**), *(w.) v. tr.* to pass *or* spend carousing.

Durch'zeichnen, *(w.) v. tr.* to trace the lines of (a drawing) through transparent paper, to trace, counter-draw.

Durch'zeichnung, *(w.) f.* act of tracing: D-spapier, *n.* tracing-paper, transparent paper.

Durch'ziehen, *(str.) v.* I. *tr.* 1) *a)* to draw, pull through; *b)* to run through (of threads); 2) *see* Durchhecheln, 1 & 2; II. *refl.* to run *or* pass through; III. *intr. (aux.* sein) to pass *or* march through.

Durchzieh'en, *(str.) v. tr.* 1) to interweave, intermix: 2) to furrow, &c.: mit Gräben —, to trench (land, for draining, &c.); 3) to penetrate, soak; 4) to march, wander through in all directions, to traverse: (enge Örtlichkeiten) to thread one's way through ...: 5) *fig.* to run *or* pass through ....

Durch'ziehhaken, *(str.) m. T.* ribbon-maker's [tool.

Durch'zischen, *(w.) v. intr.*, **Durchzisch'en,** *(w.) v. tr.* to hiss *or* whiz through.

Durchzit'tern, *(w.) v. tr.* to tremble, shiver through ..., to thrill, pierce: Fieberfrost durchzitterte seinen Körper, a cold shiver ran *or* passed through his frame.

Durch'zoll, *(str., pl.* Durch'zölle) *m.* transit-[duty.

Durchzuck'en, *(w.) v. tr.* to shoot across ..., to give a sudden shock, to convulse, to flash *or* thrill through ...: der Gedanke durchzuckte ihn, the thought flashed across his mind.

Durch'zug, *(str., pl.* Durch'züge) *m.* 1) *a)* the (act of) passing through, passage: *b)* march, procession: der freie — der Luft, the free circulation of air: 2) *(or* —balken, *m.) Archit.* architrave; collar; dorman (dormant-tree), summer: 3) *T.* drawing-machine: 4) *Tail.* back-case; D-srecht, *n.* right of passing (troops) through a country.

Durch'zwängen, *(w.)*, **Durch'zwingen,** *(str.) v. tr.* to force *or* squeeze through.

Dür'fen, *(irr.) v. intr. & aux.* 1) to dare, venture; 2) *a)* to have the power, to be at liberty (to do something): *b)* to have permission, to be permitted, to be allowed: *c)* to have reason, cause, or a right; 3) to have occasion, to need: 4) *in connection with adverbs of motion, f. i.* durch (*cf.* Durch, II. *adv.* 1), hinab, hinauf, hinüber, *elliptically for* durchgehen, hinabgehen *x.* —; ich habe es nicht thun —, I have not been allowed to do it: wenn ich mich so ausdrücken darf, if I may be allowed the expression: darf ich fragen? may I ask? Sie — es wissen, you may know it: ich darf heute nicht ausgehen I am obliged to stay (at) home to-day: Sie — nicht glauben, you must not believe: er darf sich darüber nicht wundern, he must not wonder at it; wir — unsere Pflichten nicht vergessen, we must not (ought not to) forget our duties: wir — uns nicht darauf einlassen, we cannot enter upon that: wir — es schon unseres Rufes wegen nicht thun, regard for our name forbids us: er darf sich dies schon erlauben, he is at liberty to do this: er darf nur befehlen, he has only to command: du darfst es nur sagen, you need but say: du hättest es nur sagen —, you would only have had to say: das dürfte wohl geschehen, (it) will probably happen: I dare say it will happen: it will happen, I dare say; es dürfte ein Leichtes sein, it would (probably) be an easy thing or matter: es dürfte sich wohl so verhalten,

* Duz'en, Du'zen, (w.) v. tr. & refl. to call [illegible] or each other thou (not you), to thou, to [illegible]-and-thou.

Dutzend, (str.) n. a dozen: im —wohlfeiler, [illegible]. per dozen cheaper, lower by the dozen; [illegible], adv. by the dozen: in or by dozens; [illegible], m. price per dozen.

Duwen, (w.) v. tr. Mar. die Ruderpinne [illegible] —, to put the helm a-weather; das Schiff durch den Wind —, to put the helm a-lee. [shavegrass (Ackerschafthalm).

Du'wock, Du'wenwock, (str.) m. (Bot.)

Dwaal, Dwall, Dweil, (str.) m. Mar. swab, mop. [vary (as the wind).

Dwar'reln, (w.) v. intr. Mar. to shift,

Dwars, adv. Mar.-s. athwart; — durch die [illegible] segeln, to sail against the setting of the [illegible] — See liegen, to stand athwart the [illegible]; —balken, m. cross-beam; —fahlingen, [illegible] pl. cross-trees.

Dweil, see Dwaal.

* Dyna'mik, (w.) f. (Gr.) Phys. dynamics. — Dyna'misch, adj. dynamical.

* Dynast', (w.) m. (Gr.) dynast, feudal [illegible]. — Dynastie', (w.) f. dynasty. — Dynas'tisch, adj. dynastic, dynastical.

* Dysenterie', (w.) f. (Gr.) Med. dysentery, bloody flux.

E.

E, e, n. 1) Gramm. E, e, the fifth letter and second vowel of the Alphabet; 2) Mus. E (the third note of the gamut, named mi in Italy and France); E-dur, E major; E-moll, E minor.

E., abbr. 1) for ein, a; one; 2) E. or Ew. for Euer, your; E.-B. for Eisenbahn, railway; [illegible], ebendas. for ebendaselbst, at the same place, ibidem; Ed., Edit. for Edition, edition; E. E. 1) for Euer Edeln, your honour; 2) for Eure Excellenz, your excellency; Ehrw. 1) for Ehrwürden, Reverend Sir; 2) for Ehrwürdig, reverend: e. g. for exempli gratia (Lat., zum Beispiel, for instance, for example); Ei. for Eimer, rundlet, kilderkin; ej. for ejusdem (Lat., desselben [Monats, Tages], of the same month, day]); Ell. for Ellen, ells; engl. for englisch, English; eod. for eodem (Lat., an demselben Tage, on the same day); Erzb. for Erzbischof, archbishop; etc. for et cetera (Lat., und so weiter, und das Übrige, and so on, and so forth); Ew., Ew., see E., 2; exc. for exceptis (Lat., nimm aus, except); excl. for exclusive (Lat., ausschließlich, exclusive, exclusively); ex con. for ex consensu (Lat., in Übereinstimmung, agreeably to); Extr., extr. for Extract, Auszug, extract.

Ebb'anker, (str.) m. Mar. ebb-anchor.

Eb'be, (w.) f. ebb, ebbing, ebbing water, [illegible], reflux; eine —, an ebb-tide; erste [illegible] —, beginning of the ebb; letzte or [illegible] ([illegible] —), end of the ebb; die niedrige [illegible] [illegible] mit Eintritt der —, at ebb. [illegible] mit der —, Mar. down (the) sound; — [illegible], tide, ebb and flow (or tide), high [illegible] low tide, high water and low water, [illegible] and flood-tide, ebbing and flowing, [illegible] and return; — und [illegible]messer, m. thalassometer [illegible] —, see [illegible] ebbe.

[illegible], (w.) v. intr. to ebb, to fluctuate; [illegible] down, run down; es ebbt, the tide ebbs [illegible] in ebbing water, the tide goes out. [illegible] I. adj. [illegible] plain; level, flat, open [illegible] plane (trigonometry, [illegible]) pretty; fair; b) precise, [illegible] suitable; d) honest; II. [illegible] 1) exactly, accurately; [illegible] es — so! coll. there it is, [illegible] very thing; fig. there's the rub;

(so—) just now; ich komme (so)— von ..., I am (or I come) fresh from ...; — erst, but just; — mit der Ausführung Ihres Auftrags beschäftigt, in the very act of executing your commission; darauf war es —abgesehen, that was my (his, &c.) very object; — jetzt, just (or even) now, but just; —derselbe, —dieselbe, —dasselbe, the very same; —da, —daselbst, adv. at or in the same place; an —demselben Tage, the very same day; —deswegen, for that very reason, on that very account; —falls, adv. also, too, likewise; —so, 1) just so; 2) (quite) as (billig &c., cheap, &c.); ich gehe — so gern als ich bleibe, I had as lief go as stay; — so viel, (even) as much; es ist eben so viel, coll. it is all one; — so oft, as many times; das nun — nicht, not exactly that (so).

Eben, (str.) n. (not usual) see Ebenbaum.

Eben..., in comp. —baum, m. Bot. 1) ebony-tree (Diospyros Ebenum L.); 2) laburnum (Cytisus laburnum L.); 3) see Eibenbaum; —bild, n. image, exact likeness, resemblance, picture; sie ist das —bild ihres Vaters, she is the (very) picture of her father; —bürtig, I. adj. 1) of equal birth; 2) enjoying the same privileges, equal (in dignity, &c.); 3) fig. ein —bürtiger Geist, a commensurate spirit; ich bin ihm nicht —bürtig (i. e. gewachsen), I am no match for him; er ist den Helden aller Zeiten —bürtig, he is the compeer of the heroes of all centuries; II. die —bürtigen, s. pl. 1) peers; 2) equals; —bürtigkeit, f. 1) Law, parage, equality of birth (blood) or dignity; 2) fig. equality, &c.; —drähtig, adj. T. even-threaded; —flächig, adj. with a flat surface; —holz, n. ebony (wood); —kreisig, adj. concentric; —maß, n. symmetry, proportion, harmony; —mäßig, adj. symmetrical, proportional, proportionate, equal; —mäßig machen, ins —maß bringen, to symmetrise; —müthig, see Gleichmüthig; —nächte, f. pl. nights of equal length; —nächtig, —nächtlich, adj. equinoctial; —riß, m. see Nachzeichnung; —söhlig, adj. Min. horizontal; —tischler, m. see Ebenist; —wage, f. see Gleichwage; —weitig, adj. parallel; —zeitig, see Gleichzeitig.

E'bene, Eb'ne, (w.) f. plane, plain, level; in gleicher — mit ..., on a level with ..., flush with ....

E'benen, Eb'nen, (w.) v. tr. 1) to even, level, flatten, plane, plain; 2) a) T. to face (stones, &c.); Gold-sm. to straighten; Join., &c. to planish, plane; b) to smooth (up), to finish; fig. to smooth down or away; eine Rechnung —, Comm. to square an account; dadurch ist unser Conto geebnet, that will balance (settle) our account; einen Weg —, to level or pad a road.

E'benfalls, adv. also, too, likewise.

E'benheit, (w.) f. evenness; levelness.

* Ebeni'ren, (w.) v. tr. T. (L. Lat.) 1) to inlay with ebony; 2) to ebonize. — Ebenist', (w.) m. ebonist, worker in ebony; cabinetmaker.

† E'benteuer, (str.) n. see Abenteuer.

E'ber, I. (str.) m. 1) Zool. boar, wild boar; junger —, boar pig; 2) Mar. see Ewer; 3) †, a kind of cannon (Viertelkarthaune); 4) provinc. see Wehrer; II. in comp. —esche, f. Bot. service-tree, mountain-ash; rowan-tree (Vogelbeerbaum — Sorbus aucuparia L.); Chem.-s. —eschensauer, adj. sorbate; —eschensäure, f. sorbic acid; —frischling, n. brawn; —hirsch, m. Zool. Indian-hog, boar-stag (Porcus babirussa L.); —raute, f., —reis, n. Bot. southern-wood, mug-wort (Artemisia abrotanum L.); E-beere, f. service-berry (Eberesche); —schwanz, m. Sport. wreath; —schwein, n. boar; Bot.-s. —wurz, f. carline-thistle (Carlina vulgaris L.).

E'berhard, m. Ever(h)ard; Eberhardi'ne, f. Everardina (P. N.).

Eb'nen, (w.) v. tr. see Ebenen.

Eb'risch, (str.) m., Eb'rittenkraut, (str.) n. see Eberraute. [leiche.

Ebsch'beere, (w.) f. (Eibischbeere) see Eber-

* Echinit', (w. & str.) m. (Gr.) Pal. echinite (petrified echinus).

* Ech'o, (str., pl. E-s) n. (Gr.) echo; ein — geben, to (re-)echo, re-sound; —hall, m. peal of an echo; —zug, m. Mus. echo-key.

Ech'oen [pr. ech'o-en], (w.) v. intr. to (re-) echo.

Ech'se (pr. eg'se), (w.) f. provinc. see Eidechse.

Echt, adj. genuine, pure, unadulterated, sterling; authentic(al); lawful; real; durable, lasting, fast, true; fig. true, staunch; — gefärbt, dyed in grain, grained; e-e Farbe, fast or lasting colours; —farbig, adj. genuine of colour. — Echt'heit, (w.) f. genuineness, real, pure or sterling quality, purity; authenticity; lawfulness, legitimacy.

Echt'maß, (str.) n. see Eichmaß.

Eck, I. (str.) n. 1) Geom. angular body or figure; 2) corner, see Ecke; 3) (S. G.) see Eiter; II. in comp. —ader, f. Farr. cheek-vein; —apfel, m. Pomol. a kind of calville; rather —apfel, see Harlapfel; —balken, m. corner-post; —band, n. Lock-sm. angular iron-band; —beschläge, n. pl. corner-clips; head-plates (of a carriage); —bogen, m. corner-arch; —bücher, n. pl. Paper-m. corded or outside quires.

Eck'chen, (str.) n. (dimin. of Ecke) 1) little corner; 2) coll. a) a little bit (of bread); b) see Ecke, 2.

Eck'e, (w.) f 1) corner, angle, angular point, hook; edge; 2) Archit. coin, ancone (of a wall); ausspringende — (des Gesimses), external angle, arris; geschliffene —, Jewel. facet; 3) a short space, short distance, a little way; von allen E-n (und Enden), from all parts.

Eck'en..., in comp. —bohrer, m. T. corner-drill (Winkelbohrer); —steher, m. porter (waiting in the streets for work).

Eck'er, (w.) f. 1) coll. (for Eichel) acorn; 2) anything small, diminutive; hop o' my thumb; —doppen, f. pl. see Eichelkappen.

Eck'..., in comp. —federn, f. pl. pinions; —feile, f. T. three-square or triangular file; —fenster, n. corner-window; —first, m. Archit. hip; —haus, n. corner-house; —hölzer, pl. squared timber; —horn, n. small rough whelk.

Eck'ig, I. adj. 1) angular; cornered; adv. cornerwise; 2) fig. angular, harsh, knotty; II. E-keit, (w.) f. lit. & fig. angularity.

Eck'..., in comp. —loch, n. corner-hole; Bill. corner-pocket; —meißel, m. T. ridge-mortice; —mund, m. Conch. trochus (Kreiselschnecke); —pelen, f. see —federn; —pfahl, m. (einer Spundwand) corner-pile, guide pile; —pfeiler, m. 1) or —säule, f. corner-pillar; 2) stone-stud; 3) butt-pier; —säulig, adj. prismatical; —schaft, m. Archit. corner-wall; —schildchen, n. Herald. canton; —schrank, m. corner-cupboard; —sparren, m. see Grat-sparren; —stahl, m. Metall. refined steel; —ständer, m. see —pfeiler, 1; —steher, m. see Eckensteher; —stein, m. 1) corner-stone, edge-stone; head-stone; Archit. (stone-)quoin; Pav. curb-stone; 2) Jewel. precious stone, gem; 3) Card-pl. diamond; —steingras, m. Jewel. gem-powder; —stube, f. corner-room; —stück, n. corner-piece; —stücke, n. pl. Archit. hips; —stütze, f. Archit. buttress, spur; —thor, n. corner-gate; —thurm, m. corner-tower, bastion; —verband, m. edge-joint-bands see Quadern, long and short work; —weise, adv. cornerwise; —weise schneiden, Jewel. to cut into facets; —zahn, m. Anat. corner-tooth, canine-tooth; —ziegel, m. Mas. header; —zierat, f. Archit. moulding; —zierathen, pl. Archit. ornaments; —zimmer, n. corner-room.

* Eclecticis'mus, m. (Gr.) Philos. eclecticism. — Eclec'tiker, (str.) m. eclectic. — Eclec'tisch, I. adj. eclectic; II. adv. eclectically.

* **Eklip'se,** *(w.) f. (Gr.) Astr.* eclipse. — **Eklip'senmaschine,** *(w.) f. Spinn.* eclipse-speeder, eclipse roving-frame, strap- *or* belt-speeder. — **Eklip'tik,** *(w.) f. Astr.* ecliptic.

* **Eklo'ge,** *(w.) f. (Gr.) Poet.* a pastoral poem, eclogue.

* **Eksta'se,** *(w.) f. (Gr.)* ecstasy. — **Ekstat'isch,** I. *adj.* ecstatic(al); II. *adv.* ecstatically.

Edel, I. *adj.* 1) noble; 2) generous, noble, magnanimous; 3) precious, excellent; 4) honoured: edles Blut, high blood; ein edler Gang, *Min.* a rich vein; a live lode; edle Metalle, precious or noble metals; die edeln (*or* edleren) Theile des Körpers, the vital *or* noble parts of the body; die edleren Gefühle des Herzens, the finer feelings of the heart; II. *in comp.* —bürger, *m.*, —bürgerlich, *adj.* patrician; —bürtig, *adj.* noble by birth; —camille, *f.* sweet camomile (Camille); —dame, —frau, *f.* nobleman's lady, noble woman, lady; —denkend, —gesinnt, *p.a.* noble-minded; —distel, *f. Bot.* alpine-eryngo (*Eryngium alpinum* L.); —erz, *n. Min.* rich ore; —esche, *f. Bot.* 1) common ash (Esche); 2) service-tree, sorb-tree (*Sorbus domestica* L.); —falke, *m. Ornith.* falcon gentle, passenger-hawk (*Falco gentilis* L.); —falter, *m. Entom.* 1) *gener. pl.* broad-winged butterflies (*Papilionidae*); 2) *see* Perlmutterfalter; —fink, *m. Ornith.* chaffinch (*Fringilla caelebs* L.); —fräulein, *n.* unmarried lady of noble rank; —früchte, *f. pl.* the finer and rarer sorts of fruit; —gestein, *n. collect.* precious stones, jewels; —herzig, *adj. see* —müthig; —hirsch, *m. Sport.* noble hart, common stag (*Cervus elaphus* L.); —hof, *m.* nobleman's mansion in the country, manor-house, baronial hall *or* country-seat.

Edeling, *(str.) m.* (*l. u.*) 1) nobleman; 2) a follower of the aristocracy.

Edel..., *in comp.* —knabe, *m.* page; —knecht, *m.* squire; —kraut, *n. Bot. see* Goldkräutchen; —leberkraut, *n. Bot.* noble-liverwort (*Anemone hepatica* L.); —mann, *m.* nobleman, *pl.* —leute, noblemen, nobles; —männisch, *adj. & adv.* belonging to a nobleman, nobleman-like; —marder, *m. see* Baummarder; —muth, *m.* generosity, noble-mindedness, magnanimity; —müthig, *adj.* noble-minded, generous-spirited, noble, generous.

Edeln, *(w.) v. tr.* to ennoble, improve, *l. u. for* Adeln, Veredeln.

Edel..., *in comp.* —obst, *n. see* —früchte; —pilz, *m.* eatable fungus, mushroom (*Boletus edulis* Bulliard); —reis, *n.* scion (Pfropfreis); —salbei, *f. see* Salbei; —sinn, *m.* generosity, liberality; —sinnig, *adj.* generous, liberal; —stein, *m.* precious stone, jewel, gem; von schwacher Farbe, pale stone; eckig geschliffener, brilliant; —stolz, *adj.* of a noble pride; —that, *f.* noble deed *or* action; —tanne, *f. Bot.* silver(-leaved) fir-tree, pitch-pine (*Abies pectinata* DC.); —weiß, *n. Bot.* lion's foot (*Leontopodium alpinum* Cass., *Gnaphalium Leont.* Scop.); —wild, *n. collect.* deer.

Eden, *(str.) n.* (*Hebr.*) (the garden of) Eden, paradise. — **Ede'nisch,** (*Daumer, Haug; cf. Sanders* — *l. u.*) *adj.* paradisiacal.

* **Edict',** *(str.) n.* (*Lat.*) edict, decree, proclamation. — **Edictal'ladung, Edictal'citation,** *(w.) f.*, **Edicta'lien,** *n. pl.* letter citatory, summons (issued under the order of a court of justice); exigent.

* **Edi'ren,** *(w.) v. tr.* (*Lat.*) to edit; to publish (any literary production), *see* Herausgeben. — **Edition',** *(w.) f.* edition.

Edler, (*decl. like adj.*) *m.* German (particularly Austrian) degree of nobility between the Freiherr (baron) and the common nobleman (*f. i.* Edler von Frank *rc.*)

Eduard, *m.* Edward (*P. N.*).

* **Effect',** *(str.) m.* (*Lat.*) effect (*fig., cf.* Theatereffect); —hascherei, *f.* a straining for effect; —voll, *adj.* full of striking incidents; producing a powerful effect, effective.

* **Effec'ten,** *n. pl.* 1) *a)* effects, movable goods *or* property, movables, personal estate; *b)* luggage, baggage; traps, kit (of a soldier); 2) *Comm.-c.* state-papers, stocks, public securities, funds; bills, effects; —börse, *f.* stock-exchange; —handel, *m.* business in the stock-exchange; —händler, *m.* stock-jobber, stationary; —societät, *f.* partnership-estate, joint-stock in trade.

* **Effectiv',** *adj.* effective; die Blockade war —, the blockade was established; *Comm.-c.* real, in specie; in e-em Preuß. Courant, in Prussian current coin; e-e Waaren, goods for immediate delivery; —ducaten, *m. pl.* ducats in specie; —geschäft, *n.* money-bargain, bargain for money; money-business; —kraft, *f. Mech.* effective force; —preis, *m.* real price; —zahl, *f.* total number.

* **Effectui'ren,** *(w.) v. tr.* (*Lat.*) *Comm.* to effectuate, execute.

* **Egal',** *adj.* (*Fr.*) equal, *see* Gleich, Einerlei.

Egel, *(str.) m.* leech, *see* Blutegel; —baum, *m. see* Eisbeerbaum, 2; —krankheit, —seuche, *f. Vet.* 1) core; 2) *see* Fäule, 2; —kraut, *n. Bot.* 1) the lesser spear-wort (*Ranunculus flammula* L.); 2) *see* Pfennigkraut; —schnecke, *f.*, —wurm, *m.* liver-fluke (*Distoma hepaticum* L.).

Eger, *s.* Eger, Egra: I. *f.* a river in Bohemia; II. *n.* a town in Bohemia (*P. N.*).

Eg'ge, *(w.) f.* 1) *Agr.* harrow; breitzinkige —, drag; schwere —, brake; 2) *provinc. for* Anschrote; E-(n)zähne, E-(n)zinken, *m. pl.* teeth of a harrow.

Eg'gen, *(w.) v. tr.* to harrow.

* **Egi'de, Egyp'ten** *rc., see* Äg....

* **Egois'mus,** *m.* (*L.Lat.*) egotism, egoism, selfishness. — **Egoist',** *(w.) m.* egotist, a selfish person. — **Egoist'isch,** *adj.* egotistical, selfish, self-seeking.

* **Egreni'ren,** *(w.) v. tr.* (*Fr.*) to gin. — **Egrenir'maschine,** *f. Mech.* cotton gin; (mit Walzen) roller gin, (mit Sägeblättern) saw gin.

* **Egret'te,** *(w.) f.* 1) *Ornith.* egret (*Ardea egretta* Gm.); 2) *Zool. see* Eulenaffe.

Eh'e, Eh, I. *adv. obsolescent,* 1) formerly; — denn, — als, *conj.* ere, before; 2) rather, *see* Eher; II. *conj.* ere, before; — ich das thäte, würde ich lieber ..., sooner than do so, I would ....

Eh'e, *(w.) f.* 1) †, law; 2) matrimony, wedlock; marriage; Stand der —, *see* —stand; die — zur linken Hand, *or* morganatische —, morganatic *or* left-handed marriage; die — brechen, to commit adultery; eine — stiften, schließen, to settle, conclude a marriage; (Jemandem) die — versprechen, to promise marriage (to ...); außer der — gezeugt *or* geboren, born out of wedlock, illegitimate; E-n werden im Himmel geschlossen, *proverb.* marriage goes by destiny.

Eh'e..., *in comp.* —band, *n.* conjugal (*or* nuptial) knot, marriage-tie; —beredung, *f. see* —contract; —bett, *n.* marriage-bed; —brecher, *m.* adulterer; —brecherei, *f.* adultery; —brecherin, *f.* adulteress; —brecherisch, *adj.* adulterous; —bruch, *m.* adultery; *Law, &c.* criminal conversation; —bruch begehen, to commit adultery; —brüchig, *adj.* guilty of adultery; —bund, *m.*, —bündniß, *n.* matrimonial engagement, conjugal union, *cf.* —band; —contract, *m. see* —vertrag.

Eh'dem (**Eh'dem,** *Grimm,* W.B. XLI), **Eh'edessen,** *adv.* (*from* Ehe, *adv.*) formerly, before now, ere now, heretofore, of old, in old times; aforetime.

Eh'e..., *in comp.* —feind, *m.* marriage-hater, misogamist; —fesseln, *f. pl. burl.* marriage-chains; —frau, *f. see* —gattin; —freuden, *f. pl.* connubial or conjugal joys, de-

[illegible]

[illegible] egged moulding; gebröckelter —stab, Greek or quirked ovolo; —staude, f. see —pflanze; —stock, m. 1) Anat. ovary; 2) Zool. & Bot. seed bed; —suppe, f. egg-soup; —tanz, m. (with jugglers) a sort of dance through several ranges of eggs performed blindfold; —weiß, n. see Eiweiß.

Ei'fer, (str.) m. zeal, earnestness, ardour, warmth, eagerness, heat, fervour, fervency; passion, wrath; emulation.

Ei'ferer, (str.) m. zealot.

Ei'fer... (from Eifern), in comp. —geist, m. zeal.

Ei'fern, (w.) v. intr. to be zealous (in); to speak or act with zeal; to vie (with); to be jealous or envious (of), to be angry (über [with Acc.], at); gegen or wider etwas —, to declaim against, denounce, to preach down.

Ei'fer... (from Eifern), in comp. —sucht, f. 1) jealousy (gegen, of); rivalry; 2) envy; —süchtelei, f. petty jealousy; —süchteln, v. intr. to indulge in petty jealousy; —süchtig, adj. jealous (auf [with Acc.], of); envious.

Ei'förmig, I. adj. egg-shaped, oval; Bot., &c. ovate, oviform; fast —, subovate; umgekehrt —, obovate; II. E-keit, (w.) f. oval form or shape, oval.

Eif'rig, I. adj. zealous, strenuous, earnest, ardent, warm, eager, keen, fervent, passionate; er wurde bei dem Gegenstand ganz —, he warmed with the subject; ihre e-e Sorge, her anxious care; ihr eifrigster Wunsch, her most anxious wish; — beschäftigt, closely or intently engaged (mit, with, in), intent (on); eifrigst, aufs Eifrigste, adv. most zealously, in right good earnest, with one's best endeavours; II. E-keit, (w.) f. zealousness, &c.

Ei'gelb, (str.) n. see Eidotter.

Ei'gen, adj. 1) own; self, proper, peculiar (with Dat.); diese Gewohnheit ist dem Löwen —, this habit belongs to the lion; 2) singular, particular; 3) peculiar, strange, odd, whimsical, queer; 4) nice, exact, particular; accurate; e-e Leute, bond-men, serfs; er ist sein e-er Herr, he is his own master; sein e-er Herr werden, to set up for one's self; er hat ein e-es Haus, he has a house of his own; er besitzt nichts E-es, he has nothing of his own; sie bildeten eine e-e Kirche, they organised a church of their own; e-er Wille, will of one's own; aus e-em Willen, aus e-er Wahl, of one's own choice; er wußte dies aus e-er Beobachtung, he knew this from personal observation; einen e-en Boten schicken, to send a special messenger (a messenger express); sein e-er Brief, his own letter; a letter in his own hand-writing; das Recht des e-en Urtheils, the right of private judgment; die der Democratie e-en Übel, the specific evils of democracy; Comm. der e-e Verbrauch, home consumption; der e-e Wechsel, bill of exchange drawn upon one's self, promissory note, single-, sole-, or only bill; für e-e Rechnung, for or on one's own account; sich (etwas) zu — machen, to make (a thing) one's own, to appropriate, to acquire; sich (Dat.) eine Sprache zu — machen, to make one's self master of a language.

Ei'gen..., in comp. self; —behörig, adj., —behörigkeit, f. see Leibeigen, Leibeigenschaft; —beliebig, adj. optional, of free choice; —dünkel, m. self-conceit, self-sufficiency, self-[illegible], self-opinion, presumption, conceitedness; —dünkelig, adj. (l. u.) self-conceited.

Ei'genen, see Eignen.

Ei'gen..., in comp. —gehörig, adj. one's [illegible]; [illegible], f. see —macht; —gewicht, n. [illegible] specific weight; —glanz, f. [illegible]; —gut, n. Law, allodium; —handel, m. [illegible] (private or proper) trade, [illegible] one's own account; —händig, [illegible] 1) in, with, or under one's own hand, autograph (letter, &c.); 2) (—händig zu erbrechen, to be opened) privately, to private hands; —händige Unterschrift, one's own (or proper) signature or handwriting, sign manual, manual sign; Einem —händig übergeben, to deliver into one's own hands.

Ei'genheit, (w.) f. 1) property, peculiarity; 2) singularity, oddity, whim; trick (of voice, &c.); — einer Sprache, idiom.

Ei'gen..., in comp. —hörig, see —behörig; —liebe, f. self-love, self-liking; —lob, n. self-praise, self-applause; —macht, f. arbitrary power; despotism; Pol. autocracy; —mächtig, adj. arbitrary, absolute, independent of others, despotical; sich (Dat.) —mächtig Recht verschaffen, to take the law into one's own hand; —mächtig handeln, to act of one's own authority, &c.; —mittel, n. specific (remedy); —name, m. proper name; —nutz, m. self-interest, selfishness; ohne —nutz handeln, to deal disinterestedly; —nützig, adj. (self-)interested, selfish, worldly; —ruhm, m. self-praise.

Ei'gens, adv. expressly, purposely.

Ei'genschaft, (w.) f. 1) property, attribute, mark, nature; 2) capacity, character, quality, point; — Gottes, divine attribute; E-en der Größe, Math. affections of quantity; Gramm. z. — eines Wortes, accident; E-swort, n. adjective; E-szeichen, n. mark of distinction.

Ei'gensinn, (str.) m. 1) waywardness, wilfulness, caprice, perversity; stubbornness, positiveness, obstinacy; 2) fastidiousness (of taste, &c.).

Ei'gensinnig, I. adj. 1) wayward, wilful, headstrong, perverse, froward, capricious; stubborn, positive, unruly, obstinate; peevish, cross; 2) fastidious, over-nice; II. E-keit, (w.) f. waywardness, &c. cf. Eigensinn.

Ei'gensucht, (w.) f. egotism, self-seeking.

Ei'genthum, (str., pl. E-thümer) n. property; propriety; mein —, my own; mein (Ihr) gegenwärtiges — Comm. the property in my (your) hands (of consigned goods); — in Bankactien, bank-stock.

Ei'genthümer, (str.) m. owner, proprietor; ohne —, unowned, unclaimed; E-in, (w.) f. owner, proprietress.

Ei'genthümlich, I. adj. peculiar; 1) own, proper; etwas — an sich bringen, to acquire the property of ...; (Jemandem) — zugehören, to be one's own property; 2) singular, quaint; 3) characteristic; das E-e, the characteristic mark, characteristicalness; 4) Phys. specific; II. E-keit, (w.) f. 1) property; peculiarity, peculiar disposition; 2) singularity, quaintness.

Ei'genthums..., in comp. —herr, m. proprietor, lord of the manor, head landlord; —recht, n. right of possession, ownership, proprietorship; literarisches —recht, copyright; —steuer, f. property-tax; —übertragung, f. Comm. transfer; —vergehen, —verbrechen, n. crime against property, violation of the right of possession, theft.

Ei'gentlich, I. adj. proper; true, precise, exact, real; intrinsic(al); im e-sten Sinne des Wortes, in the very sense of the word; die Andacht ist die e-e Seele der Frömmigkeit, devotion is the very soul of piety; recht — zur Besichtigung ausgestellt, exposed on purpose for inspection; II. adv. properly or strictly (speaking), exactly, &c.; was soll das — bedeuten? what is the real or exact meaning of this? es ist zweifelhaft, was er — mit diesem Verfahren beabsichtigte, it is doubtful what he exactly meant by this proceeding; — sollte ich zürnen, by rights I ought to be angry; er heißt — Franz, he is really named Frank; e-e Reisende, ohne die Soldaten, passengers proper, setting aside soldiers; Friedrich war recht — ein schlimmer Nachbar, Frederick was emphatically a bad neighbour.

Ei'gen..., in comp. —wärme, f. Phys. specific warmth; —wille, f. self-will, wilfulness; —willig, adj. self-willed, wilful; arbitrary; headstrong, obstinate; —willigkeit, f. wilfulness, &c.

Eig'nen, (w.) v. I. intr. 1) to pertain, appertain; 2) to become, fit, behove; II. tr. to devote, consecrate; fig. to surrender, to give over; III. geeignet sein, or refl. sich — (zu), to be qualified, suited, or fit (for), to be adapted (for, to), to do well (for); dies ist geeignet, Aufmerksamkeit zu erwecken, this is calculated to awaken attention; IV. refl. impers. provinc. see Spuken.

Eig'ner, (str.) m. owner, proprietor, holder.

Ei'la Popei'ja, interj. see Eia Popeia.

Ei'land, (str., pl. E-e or Ei'länder) n. island.

Ei'länder, (str.) m., **Ei'länderin,** (w.) f. islander.

Ei'ländisch, adj. insular.

Eil..., in comp. —boot, n. swift boat; —bote, m. courier; estafet(t)e.

Ei'le, (w.) f. haste, speed, despatch; große —, hurry; in (der) —, in haste, in a hurry, hurriedly; mit möglichster —, with all convenient speed, as speedily as possible; in größter —, post-haste; at the top of one's speed; einen Frieden &c. in aller — zu Stande bringen, to clap (patch) up a peace; entschuldigen Sie die —, excuse haste; — haben, to be pressed for time, to be in a hurry; wir hatten keine —, we were in no hurry; es hat ja keine —, there is no hurry, you know; die Sache hat —, the matter requires speed, despatch, or haste, is urgent or pressing; — mit Weile, proverb. the more haste the worse speed, fair and softly goes far (in a day).

Ei'lein, (str.) n. (dimin. of Ei) a little egg.

Ei'len, (w.) v. I. intr. (aux. sein & haben) 1) to hasten, make haste, to hurry, make speed; to hie; mit etwas —, to be quick at something; was — Sie so? what is your hurry? sie — nicht sehr damit, they take their time about it; 2) to pass quickly or rapidly, to fly, hurry; die Sache eilt sehr (hat Eile), see Eile; II. refl. to make haste, to bestir one's self.

Ei'lend, I. adj. speedy, quick; II. or **Ei'lends,** adv. hastily, speedily, in haste, in a hurry.

Eilf, see Elf.

Eil..., in comp. —fertig, adj. hasty, hastening, precipitate, cf. Eilig; —fertigkeit, f. hastiness, speediness; precipitation; —fracht, f. Railw. conveyance of dispatch; —fuhre, f. fast or quick conveyance, fly-waggon; —gut, n. Railw. goods conveyed by the fast or mail-trains, dispatch-goods.

Ei'lig, I. adj. 1) hasty, speedy; expeditious; zu —, over-hasty; adv. hastily, &c., in haste, in a hurry; 2) requiring haste; wo wollen Sie denn so — hin? whither do you go in such a hurry? what's your haste? ich soll eiligst zu ihm kommen, I am summoned to call on him with the utmost haste or without delay; die Sache ist nicht so —, the matter is not so urgent; es — haben, to be pressed for time; sie hatten es nicht so — damit, they did not press it; cf. Eile; II. E-keit, (w.) f. 1) hastiness, hurry, precipitation; 2) urgency.

Ei..., in comp. —linie, f. Geom. ellipsis, oval (line); —linig, adj. elliptic.

Eil..., in comp. —marsch, m. Mil. forced march; —post, f., —wagen, m. diligence, mail-coach, fly, flying or velocity coach, safe, quick-coach; —zug, m. 1) see —marsch; 2) Railw. fast train, express train, post-train.

Ei'mer, (str.) m. 1) pail, bucket; 2) [illegible], kilderkin (a measure of wine, beer, &c.); ein halber —, firkin; [illegible], f. [illegible] chain-pump, noria, [illegible]; —weise, adv. by pailfuls, by the pail; [illegible], n. see Schöpfwerk. [illegible]

Ei'merig, adj. containing a pail(ful) [illegible]

Ein'bugsen, (w.) v. tr. Mar. to steer or tow into a harbour.

Ein'bündeln, (w.) v. tr. 1) to bundle up; 2) to swathe (a child).

Ein'bürgern, (w.) v. I. tr. 1) to admit to the rights of a citizen, to citizenise, to indenizen; to naturalise; to enfranchise; 2) fig. to adopt (as a word from a foreign language, &c.); II. refl. 1) to settle as a citizen; 2) to become generally adopted; eingebürgert, naturalised; current (articles, &c.). — Ein'bürgerung, (w.) f. 1) enfranchisement; naturalisation; 2) adoption.

Ein'buße, (w.) f. loss, damage.

Ein'büßen, (w.) v. I. tr. to lose, to forfeit; II. intr. to be or to come off a loser, to suffer a loss or damage.

Ein'cassiren, (w.) v. tr. to get in, collect (money), to raise (money); Comm. to cash (a bill), to encash, call in, fetch in, recover (debts).

Ein'cassirung, (w.) f. the act of getting in (money, outstanding debts); Comm. encashment, recovery; E-sspesen, pl. recovery-charges. [(at the custom-house).

Ein'clariren, (w.) v. tr. Comm. to clear in

Ein'dämmen, Ein'deichen, (w.) v. tr. 1) to fill in, to use (certain materials, &c.) in making dams or dikes; 2) to confine by dikes, to dam in or up, embank; fig. to restrain, keep within bounds; das eingedämmte or eingedeichte Land, the innings. [bankment.

Ein'dämmung, Ein'deichung, (w.) f. em-

Ein'dämpfen, (w.) v. tr. Cook. to stew.

Ein'decken, (w.) v. tr. to cover up.

Ein'deichen, see Eindämmen.

Ein'deutig, adj. having but one meaning.

Ein'dicken, (w.) v. tr. to inspissate, see Einkochen, I. — Ein'dickung, (w.) f. inspissation.

Ein'dienen, (w.) v. intr. (aux. sein) & refl. to acquire skill in service, to get fitted for a place. [dingen.

Ein'dingen, (str. & w.) v. tr. see Einbe-

Ein'docken, (w.) v. tr. Mar. to lay up in a dock, to dock. [up, to shrink.

Ein'dorren, (w.) v. intr. (aux. sein) to dry

Ein'dörren, (w.) v. tr. to dry, cause to dry.

Ein'drähtig, adj. single-threaded; e-e Seide, f. Comm. single-thread(ed) silk, silk single-twist. [2) the crowding in, &c.

Ein'drang, (str.) m. 1) see Eindrängung;

Ein'drängen, (w.) v. I. tr. to squeeze, force in (into); II. refl. to crowd in; fig. to intrude (one's self) into, to obtrude (one's self) upon. — Ein'drängung, (w.) f. 1) the act of forcing in (into), &c.; 2) intrusion; obtrusion.

Ein'dringen, (str.) v. intr. (aux. sein) 1) to enter by force, to break in; 2) to penetrate, enter (also fig.), to pierce; tief —, fig. to dive or strike into; auf die Feinde —, to fall upon the enemy; das —, s. v. (str.) n. irruption; — der Feuchtigkeit, penetration of the damp; e-d, p. a. penetrative (intellect); searching, impressive (discourse).

Ein'dringlich, I. adj. 1) impressive, piercing, forcible; urgent, fervent; 2) see Eindringend; II. E-keit, (w.) f. impressiveness, forcibleness, &c.

Ein'dringling, (str.) m. an intruder.

Ein'druck, (str., pl. Ein'drücke) m. impression; 1) marks; 2) fig. sensation; influence; einen — machen (auf [with Acc.]), to affect (one), to make an impression (upon one), to strike (one); einen üblen — auf Einen machen, to impress one unfavourably or with an unfavourable opinion. — Ein'druckslos, adj. unimpressive. — Ein'drucksvoll, adj. affecting, affecting; impressive.

Ein'drucken, (w.) v. tr. 1) to print upon, [illegible]; 2) Typ. to ground in, re-enter; 3) to insert (printed illustrations, &c.) into letter-press.

Ein'drücken, (w.) v. tr. 1) to press or squeeze in or into; 2) to turn inwards, flatten; 3) to knock in, crush, break; 4) fig. (with Dat.) to impress (on), cf. Einprägen; eingedrückt, p. a. Bot. retuse.

Ein'duften, (w.) v. intr. auf Einen — (Gutzkow, l. u.) equal. to auf Einen eindringen, &c.), to assail one with perfumes.

Ein'dunsten, (w.) v. I. tr. to cause to penetrate (of liquids or vapours); II. intr. see Verdünsten. [lay flat; to form.

Ein'eb(e)nen, (w.) v. tr. to level (off), to

Ein'eggen, (w.) v. tr. Agr. to harrow in.

Ein'eisen, (w.) v. tr. to surround with ice; eingeeist, p. a. ice-bound.

Ei'nen, (w.) v. tr. & refl. to unite.

Ein'engen, (w.) v. tr. to compress, concentrate; to confine, limit.

Ei'ner, Eine, Eines (Eins), pron. one; — nach dem Andern, one by one, one after another; — oder der Andere, somebody or other; — oder der Andere (von mehreren) muß es Ihnen gesagt haben, some one or other must have been telling you; der — oder der Andere (von zweien) muß es Ihnen gesagt haben, one of the two must have told you; so —, such a one; das ist mir auch so — (Eine), coll. he (she) is no better than he (she) should be; — für Alle und Alle für Einen, one and all; cf. Alle, II.; dieses (or das) eine Mal, this (that) once.

Ei'ner, (str.) m. Arith. unit, digit.

Ei'nerlei [sometimes Einerlei], I. (indecl.) adj. of one kind, of the same kind or description; the same, one and the same; es ist fast —, it is much the same (thing); es ist mir (alles) —, it is all one (or the same) to me; it is indifferent to me; II. s. (indecl.) n. sameness; identity; uniformity; das ewige —, the unvarying monotony, the dull monotonous round (of business, &c.); III. E-heit, (w.) f. identity; uniformity (of belief, &c.).

Ein'ernten, (w.) v. tr. to gather, reap, cf. Einbringen, 1, b; to earn, obtain.

Ei'nerseits, adv. on the one hand.

Ein'exerciren, (w.) v. tr. Mil. to drill, train (Einüben).

Ein'fach, adj. single; plain; simple; individable; Bot. & Math. incomposite; Chem. uncombined, uncompounded; Log. incomplex (syllogism); primitive (colours); frugal (meal, fare); die Sache liegt sehr —, the matter lies in a nut-shell; e-e Speisen, plain food; e-es Bier, n. single beer; der e-e Bruch, Math. simple fraction; eine — wirkende Dampfmaschine, Mech. single acting steam-engine; e-e Haferei, f. Comm. particular or simple average; die e-e Geschwindigkeit, Phys. simple speed; die e-e Größe, Alg. monome, monomial quantity; die e-e Zahl, 1) Gramm. the singular (number); 2) Math. prime number.

Ein'fächerig, adj. Bot. one-celled, unilocular.

Ein'fachheit, (w.) f. 1) simpleness; 2) simplicity, plainness, &c. cf. Einfach.

Ein'fädeln, (w.) v. tr. 1) to thread (a needle); 2) fig. coll. to bring about, manage, contrive artfully, to carry on (private designs) by intrigue, to plan, scheme, set on foot; einen Briefwechsel —, to lead the way to (begin, open) a correspondence.

Ein'fahren, (str.) v. I. tr. 1) to carry in, bring in (corn, &c.), cf. Einbringen, 1, b; Güter — lassen, Comm. to have goods wheeled in; das Korn ist eingefahren, the corn is lodged; 2) to break in, train, or dress (horses) for drawing or to the wheel; 3) to knock in, to upset, to break or run down by driving over or against; II. intr. (aux. sein) 1) to drive in, to enter; 2) Min. to descend a mine, to go under ground; III. refl. to exercise one's self in driving, to practise driving.

Ein'fahrt, (w.) f. 1) the act of driving in, entrance; 2) Min. descent into or entrance to a mine, adit; 3) entrance, entry, inlet; gateway; mouth (of a harbour); E-ssignal, n. Railw. station- or distant-signal, up-signal.

Ein'fall, (str., pl. Ein'fälle) m. 1) (the act of) falling in; falling down; downfall, ruin, fall; 2) Herol. detent; 3) Opt. incidence; 4) Sport. alighting (of birds on the fowling floor); 5) Lock-sm. catch; 6) entry (of light into a room, &c.); fig.-s. 7) invasion; inroad, raid, irruption, descent (in [with Acc.], on, upon); 8) fancy, conceit; idea, thought; freak; der witzige —, flash or sally of wit; ein lustiger —, a merry conceit, a droll idea; ein wunderlicher —, a whim, freak, oddity, crotchet, caprice, maggot; ein glücklicher —, a lucky hit; er faßt or gerieth auf den —, he took it in his head; er hat Einfälle wie ein altes Haus, coll. he has pitiful fancies in his head; einen — haben or bekommen, to take a fancy.

Ein'fallen, (str.) v. I. intr. (aux. sein) 1) to fall in or into; to fall down or to ruin, to decay; to sink; rette dich! das Haus fällt ein! save yourself! the house is falling! der Himmel wird niemals —, the sky will never fall; 2) Mech. to fall upon, to catch (as the stop in a clock, &c.); fig.-s. 3) to waste away; 4) to make inroads, to invade; to make a descent on ... (from the sea, &c.); 5) a) Mus. to fall in with, to join, come in; b) to strike, cut, or come in (in conversation), to interrupt; 6) to come on, to happen, to break or set in (as bad weather, &c.); 7) to perch, to roost; 8) (with Dat.) to fall, come into the mind, to come to remembrance, to occur, strike; wie es ihm gerade einfiel, as the humour seized him; das ist mir nie eingefallen, I never dreamt of it, that never entered my head or mind; was fällt dir ein? what is it has thus come over you? sich (Dat.) — lassen, to think of, to take into one's head; eingefallen, p. a. fallen, sunken (eyes), hollow, hollow-cheeked; e-des Licht, 1. Archit. skylight; 2. Opt. incident light; II. tr. sich (Dat.) den Schädel —, to split one's skull by a fall; das —, s. v. (str.) n. 1) (act of) falling in, &c.; 2) Mar. — der Inhölzer, tumbling home of the top-timbers, housing-in; 3) Opt. incidence; 4) Mus. ripieno.

Ein'faller, (str.) m. pl. T. small slates for the gutters of roofs. [see also Einfall, 7.

Ein'fallhaken, (str.) m. T. catching-hook.

Ein'fällig, adj. about to fall (down), tottering, falling to ruin.

Ein'falls..., in comp. Opt.-s. —loth, n. cathetus of incidence; —punct, m. point of incidence; —rad, n. 1) Horol. escapement-wheel; 2) Mech. hoop-wheel; —winkel, m. angle of incidence.

Ein'falt, (w.) f. 1) simplicity; simpleness; — des Herzens, single-heartedness, innocence; 2) silliness, simplicity (of a child); E-spinsel, m. coll. simpleton, dolt, block-head, wiseacre, booby, noodle, numskull, idiot, oaf.

Ein'falten, Ein'fälteln, (w.) v. tr. to lay into small folds, to fold, plait.

Ein'faltig, adj. having but one plait or fold.

Ein'fältig, I. adj. 1) simple, plain, innocent, inoffensive; 2) unmeaning, silly, dull, soft, doltish, short-witted, half-witted; ein e-er Mensch, see Einfaltspinsel; II. E-keit, (w.) f. 1) simplicity; 2) silliness, &c.

Ein'falzen, (w.) v. tr. see Einfugen, 1; 2) Turn., &c. to set into a groove; 3) Bookb. to fold in; 4) Coop. to bottom; to head.

Ein'fangen, (str.) v. I. tr. 1) to catch, to apprehend, to take and secure; Sport. der eingefangene Fuchs, bag-fox; 2) fig. to shut up, inclose; einen Garten &c. —, to inclose, to

[illegible]vermögen einer Frau) marriage portion or [illegible], dowry; paraphernalia.

Ein'gebung, *(w.) f.* 1) the (act of) giving or administering, &c.; 2) *fig.* incitement, suggestion, prompting, dictate, (*gen. pl.*:) dictates; göttliche —, divine inspiration; er handelt nach augenblicklicher —, he acts from the impulse of the moment.

Ein'gebürgerte, *m. & f. (decl. like adj.)* [illegible], one naturalised.

Ein'geburt, *(w.) f.* the (state of) being a native of a country; **E-srecht**, *n.* right possessed by the natives of a country; naturalisation.

Ein'gedenk, *adj. (with Gen.)* mindful (of), recollecting, remembering, bearing in mind.

Ein'gefleischt, *p. a.* incarnate; *fig.-s.* ein e-er Teufel, a devil incarnate; ein e-er Schurke, a rogue in grain; ein e-er Republikaner, a Republican in grain, *cf.* Ausgemacht, *p. a.*

Ein'gehen, *(irr.) v.* I. *intr.* (*aux.* sein) 1) to enter, go in; walk in; e-d, *Geom. & Fort.* re-entering (angle, *opp.* Ausspringend); 2) to come in: *a)* to arrive; *b)* *Comm.*, &c. to come to hand (of orders); to be imported; e-de Waaren, imported goods; e-de Briefe, in-coming letters; e-de Fracht, homeward freight; e-des Gewicht, *see* Eingangsgewicht; *c)* to be paid; to be taken up (of bills); eingegangen, in cash, cashed, paid; eingegangene Gelder, [illegible]; *d)* to come to hand; 3) to shrink; to be lost (beim Auspacken, in unpacking); 4) *a)* to be discontinued; sein Geschäft ist eingegangen, his business has come to a stop; *b)* to wither, decay, die, perish; *c)* to fall to ruins, to decay; *fig.-s.* 5) (*with* auf [*with Acc.*]) *a)* to agree to or upon, to subscribe, consent, yield, accede to, or accept of, to comply with (conditions); *b)* to enter into, sympathise with (the feelings of, &c.); to enter into, to descend to (particulars); 6) to dive, search (in [*with Acc.*], into); bei Jemand aus- und —, to frequent one's house; das geht ihm schwer ein, he learns that with difficulty; he cannot comprehend that; das will mir nicht —, this will not (go) down with me; da geht dir das Leben so lieblich ein (*Simrock*), there (*i. e.* on the Rhine) thy stream of existence too sweetly flows; — lassen, to leave off, drop, give up; *Comm.-s.* einen Artikel — lassen, to discontinue the selling, manufacturing, or importation of an article; to let go or drop an article; ein Geschäft — lassen, to leave off or give up a business.

II. *tr.* 1) to accede or agree to ..., &c. *see intr.*, 5; einen Handel —, to make or conclude a bargain; einen Contract —, to enter into a contract; eine Ehe —, to contract a marriage; eine Verbindung —, to form an alliance; 2) *Comm. see* I. 2.

Ein'gehen, *v. s. (str.) n.* the (act of) entering in, &c.; das — einer Ehe, contraction of a marriage.

Ein'gehend, *p. a.* 1) entering in, &c.; 2) entering into details, exact, exhaustive, searching, &c. (Genau, Ausführlich); eine e-e Untersuchung, a thorough investigation.

Ein'ge[illegible], *p. a.* affiliated.

Ein'gemacht, *pp. of* Einmachen, *which see*; **E-es**, *n. (decl. like adj.)* preserved fruits, preserves; confect, confection (made from sugar or chocolate).

Ein'genommen, *p. a.* (*cf.* Einnehmen) *fig.* prepossessed, prejudiced, biased, (blindly) attached (für, to), partial (to), engrossed (by), [illegible] (with); von sich selbst —, (self-)conceited; von seinen eigenen Ansichten —, [illegible], opinionative; ganz für etwas — sein, to be hand and hand for a thing; to be [illegible] (a person); gegen etwas — sein, to be set against a thing; er ist dagegen —, he has taken a dislike to it; mir ist der Kopf [illegible] —, my head is quite giddy.

Ein'genommenheit, *(w.) f.* prepossession (für, in favour of), predilection (for), inclination (to), (blind) attachment (to), *coll.* partiality (for); — für eigne Meinungen, opinionativeness.

Ein'gepfarrt, *pp.* joined to a parish; **E-e**, *m. & f. (decl. like adj.)* parishioner.

Ein'gerichte, *(str.) n. Lock-sm.* ward (of a lock).

Ein'geschlechtig, *adj. Bot.* unisexual.

Ein'geschränkt, I. *p. a.* 1) restrained, &c.; 2) *fig.* narrow, narrow-minded, narrow-spirited; — leben, to live sparingly; — halten, to keep tight; II. **E-heit**, *(w.) f.* 1) confinement; 2) *fig.* narrowness.

Ein'gesessen, *p. a.* settled, established, residentiary; **E-e**, *m. (decl. like adj.)* a person settled in a place as a resident, an inhabitant.

Ein'geständniß, *(str.) n.* confession, avowal, admission; plea of guilty.

Ein'gestehen, *(irr.) v. tr.* 1) to confess; 2) to acknowledge, admit, avow, to allow, grant, concede; eingestandener Maßen, avowedly, declaredly, as admitted.

Ein'gestrichen, *p. a. Mus.* (of notes) belonging to the third octave of the entire scale; e-e Octave, *f.* third octave.

Ein'geweide, *(str.) n., gener. pl. Anat.-s.* entrails, intestines, bowels, viscera, guts; zu den E-n gehörig, intestinal, visceral; —lehre, *f.* splanchnology, enterology; —nerv, *m.* splanchnic nerve; —wurm, *m.* intestinal worm.

Ein'gewöhnen, *(w.) v. tr.* to accustom to [a place or thing (*cf.* Gewöhnen).

Ein'gewurzelt, *p. a.* (*cf.* Einwurzeln) (deep-)rooted, inveterate.

Ein'gezogen, I. *p. a.* (*cf.* Einziehen) retired, solitary, recluse, reclusive; — leben, to lead or live a retired life, to live in retirement; II. **E-heit**, *(w.) f.* retirement, retiredness, solitariness, privacy, seclusion, recluseness.

Ein'gießen, *(str.) v. tr.* 1) to pour in or into; to infuse; to cast in; 2) to seal, fasten in by means of lead, &c.; mit Blei —, to lead.

Ein'gittern, *(w.) v. tr.* to enclose with a railing or iron bars, to grate.

Ein'gleisig, *adj.* (of a railway) consisting only of a single track or line, single-railed (*opp.* Doppelgleisig).

Ein'graben, *(str.) v.* I. *tr.* 1) to dig in, to inter, to hide or lay in the ground; 2) *Engr.* to engrave, cut in; 3) to intrench; to dig ditches round ...; to cut, to make channels or furrows in ...; II. *refl.* to burrow.

Ein'greifen, *(str.) v. intr.* 1) to catch, lock, indent, toothe (in [*with Acc.*], in); *Mech.* to gear together; *Build.* to catch-in (of stones); to grasp; 2) *Mar. & Mech.* to bite (as the anchor, the wheels); 3) *Sport.* to follow the track (of dogs); 4) *fig.* to exert power or influence; to interfere (in [*with Acc.*], with), to interpose (in); to trench, intrench, encroach (upon), to invade (a privilege); in einander —, *fig.* to interlock, interpenetrate each other; das —, *v. s. (str.) n.* act of catching, &c.; interference, interposition; thätiges —, agency.

Ein'greifig, *adj. Forest.* measurable with the span of one hand (said of young trees, *opp.* to Klafterig).

Ein'grenzen, *(w.) v. tr.* to enclose in limits, to set bounds to ..., to limit.

Ein'griff, *(str.) m.* 1) a catching upon, seizure; 2) *Mech.* catch; 3) *fig.* encroachment, trespass (in [*with Acc.*], on), inroad; (forcible) interference, intrenchment (on), invasion, usurpation; — thun, to break in upon, to intrude one's self into, *cf.* Eingreifen, 4.

Ein'griff[illegible], *(str.) m. Forest.* depthening tool.

Ein'gründen, *(w.) v. tr. see* Eingraben.

Ein'gürteln, **Ein'gürten**, *(w.) v. tr.* to gird, girth.

Ein'guß, *(str., pl.* Ein'güsse*) m.* 1) infusion, instillation, a pouring in; 2) *Farr.* potion, drench; 3) *Smelt., Found.*, &c. *a)* (ingot-)mould, cast; *b)* (—röhre, *f.*, —trichter, *m.*) funnel, jet, channel; *c)* bell-mouth; *d)* ingot, lingot.

Ein'hacken, *(w.) v.* I. *tr.* 1) to cut down or up; 2) to insert like an axe, to hack into ...; die Zähne —, to fasten the teeth into the flesh, &c.; II. *intr.* to cut in or into.

Ein'häfteln, **Ein'häkeln**, *(w.) v. tr.* to hook in, clasp, to fasten (a clasp) [hail-stones.

Ein'hageln, *(w.) v. tr. impers.* to break by

Ein'hägen, *(w.) v. tr. see* Einhegen.

Ein'haken, *(w.) v. tr. & intr.* to hook in; to fasten with a hook; to hitch; *Mar. (intr.)* to catch (of anchors).

Ein'halt, *(str.) m.* stop, check; arrest; (einer Sache [*Dat.*]) — thun, to stop, check, stay, arrest (a thing), to give a check, to put a stop (to a thing); keinen — thun, to leave unchecked.

Ein'halten, *(str.) v.* I. *tr.* 1) to keep in, detain; to stop, check; 2) *fig.* *a)* to keep within (certain limits), to restrain, keep under curb; *b)* to observe, follow, continue, adhere to, preserve, to act in pursuance of (a line of policy, &c.), to keep, adhere or stick to ..., to fulfil (a promise, &c.) punctually, to be true to (one's word); eine Frist —, to keep time; die Stunde —, to arrive at the appointed time (hour), to be punctual; 3) *Sew.* to gather, take in, pucker; II. *intr.* 1) to discontinue, pause, leave off; stop; mit dem Verkauf —, to stop the sale; halt ein! stay there! desist! mit der Bezahlung —, 1. to withhold payment; 2. (*l. u.*) to stop payment, *see in* Einstellen; 2) to keep an agreement, *cf.* I. 2, *b*; (pünctlich) mit der Zahlung —, to be punctual in paying, to pay at maturity or when (the money is) due; schlecht mit der Zahlung —, (*H.; l. u.*) to be slow of payment, to be a bad paymaster; III. *refl.* to keep in the house or within doors.

Ein'haltung, *(w.) f.* the (act of) keeping in, &c., observance (of), adherence (to).

Ein'hämmern, *(w.) v. tr.* to hammer into; *fig.* to beat into.

Ein'handeln, *(w.) v.* I. *tr.* 1) to purchase, buy, *cf.* Einkaufen; 2) to put, include into (to comprise within) a bargain; II. *intr.* (im Handel zurückkommen, Haus und Hof —) to ruin one's self in trade or by trading; to fail, to shut up shop. [ed.

Ein'händig, *adj.* one-handed, single-hand-

Ein'händigen, *(w.) v. tr.* (Einem etwas) to hand (over) to, to put or deliver into one's hands, to tender, transmit, remit, consign. — **Ein'händigung**, *(w.) f.* delivery, handing over; **E-sschein**, *m.* receipt.

Ein'hänge..., *in comp.* —zirkel, *m. T.* watchmaker's compasses; —maschine, *f. Min.* skid.

Ein'hängen, *(w.) v. tr.* to hang in; to put in, to suspend; eine Thür —, to hang a door on the hinges; die Hemmkette —, to put on the skid (drag-chain); die Dachziegel —, to lay the tiles; das —, *v. s. (str.) n. Build.* case-work.

Ein'hängig, *adj.* hanging down on one side; das e-e Dach, lean-to roof, pentroof.

Ein'hauchen, *(w.) v. tr.* 1) to breathe in or into; to inspire; 2) to inhale; 3) *fig.* to inspire or imbue with, to instil, inculcate.

Ein'hauen, *(irr.) v.* I. *tr.* 1) to hew in, to cut in or into (*also Engr. & Sculpt.*); *F.* to sink (a hole in a stone); 2) to break or burst open by a blow or by blows; 3) Fleisch —, to cut up meat for corning [illegible]; 4) to mow (corn); 5) to backbite; II. *intr.* 1) to cut into the enemy, to charge; 2) *hum.* *small.* to walk into the dishes, to peg away, to fall to.

Ein'häusig, *adj. Agr. see* Einmännig.

Ein'häusig, *adj.* 1) *(from* Ein, *one.) Bot.* monoecian; 2) *(from* Ein, *adv.) coll.* stay-at-home.

Ein'häusler, *(str.)* m. *Bot.* monoecian.

Ein'häutig, *adj. Build.* smoothed on one side only (of walls).

Ein'heben, *(str.)* v. *tr.* 1) to heave, put on hinges, &c.; 2) *Typ.* to put (a form) into the press, to impose (a form).

Ein'heften, *(w.)* v. *tr.* to sew in, to stitch in; to sew together, to stitch; to file (papers).

Ein'hegen, *(w.)* v. *tr.* to fence or hedge in, enclose. — **Ein'hegung**, *(w.)* f. (the act of) fencing in; fence, enclosure; **E-srecht**, n. *Law*, right of enclosing (lands).

Ein'heilen, *(w.)* v. *tr.* to heal up in a wound.

Ein'heimen, *(w.)* v. *refl.* to settle in a place, to make one's self at home.

Ein'heimisch, *adj.* domestic, native; home-made, home (commodities), intestine, *cf.* Inländisch; indigenous (plants); *Med.* endemic, vernacular: ich bin hier —, I am at home here, this is my home: eine im südlichen Europa e-e Pflanze, a plant indigenous to Southern Europe; — machen, to naturalise, to domiciliate, domesticate; — werden, to be made domestic; to become domiciliated.

Ein'heimsen, *(w.)* v. *tr. Agr.* to get in, to house. — **Ein'heimsung**, *(w.)* f. the (act of) putting (a crop) into the barn.

Ein'heirathen, *(w.)* v. *intr.* & *refl.* to marry into, to get into by marriage.

Ein'heit, *(w.)* f. oneness; unity, unit; uniformity (of belief, &c.).

Ein'heitlich, *adj. fig.* united in one hand (administration, &c.); undivided; uniform.

Ein'heits..., *in comp.* **—gebühr**, *f.* single rate; **—gläubig**, *adj.* unitarian; **—lehre**, *f.* monotheism; **—preis**, *m.* a constant price; **—trieb**, *m. Phren.* concentrativeness.

Ein'heizen, *(w.)* v. I. *intr.* 1) to make or light a fire (in a stove); — lassen, to order a fire; es war heute Morgen so kalt, daß ich — ließ, it was so cold this morning, I had a fire; 2) *coll.* to cause (Einem, one) anxiety or fear; II. *tr. provinc.* to heat (*for* Heizen).

Ein'heizer, *(str.)* m. stoker (Heizer).

Ein'helfen, *(str.)* v. *intr.* *(with Dat.)* to prompt, to help, to assist the memory.

Ein'helfer, *(str.)* m. prompter.

Ein'hellig, I. *adj.* unanimous, concurrent; harmonious; in unison; II. *adv.* unanimously, with one accord, by common consent; — verfahren, to act in concert; III. **E-keit**, *(w.)* f. unanimity; harmony; common consent.

Ein'hemmen, *(w.)* v. *tr.* & *intr.* 1) to put the drag-chain on ..., to skid, lock (a wheel); 2) to shackle, hamper in. [ear).

Ein'henkelig, *adj.* having one handle *(or*

Ein'henken, *(w.)* v. *tr.* to hang in, up.

Ein'her, *adv.* along; — gehen, to go on or along; to carry one's self, appear: erbärmlich — gehen, to go miserably clothed, to go ragged; er geht wie ein Bettler —, he makes a beggarly appearance; stolz — schreiten, — stolziren, to (walk with a pompous) strut, to stalk, sweep along; — ziehen, to move along or on.

Ein'herbsten, *(w.)* v. *tr. provinc.* 1) *gener. for* Einbringen, *which see* 1, *b*; 2) *Vint.* to gather (the vintage).

Ein'hetzen, *(w.)* v. *tr.* 1) *Sport.* to dress, train, break in (a dog for hunting); 2) *coll. for* Einüben. [self by hypocrisy.

Ein'heucheln, *(w.)* v. *refl.* to insinuate one's

Ein'heuern, *(w.)* v. *tr. see* Einmiethen.

Ein'hiebig, *adj.* *T.* single-cut (files); e-e Feile, float.

Ein'hödig, *adj.* *Bot.* having but one testicle.

Ein'holen, *(w.)* v. *tr.* 1) *Mar.* *a)* to round in, haul home (a cleat rope); *b)* to reef (the sails), to take in (a reef); die blinden Raaen —, to strike the sprit-sail yards; *c)* to run in (the guns); *d)* to bring to, join, overtake (a ship); ein Schiff — und vorbeisegeln, to take and leave a ship; 2) to go to meet; 3) *a)* to overtake, overmatch, overrun, overhaul, outrun, to come up with, to catch, join; *b)* to retrieve, repair (the time lost, &c.); 4) to fetch, get, obtain; die Stimmen —, to collect the votes; Befehle —, to require orders; weitere Instructionen —, to ask for further instructions; ein schiedsrichterliches Gutachten —, to apply for arbitration; das Urtheil —, to demand sentence; ärztlichen Rath —, to send for medical advice; Nachricht über *(with Acc.)* —, to apply for advice, to inform one's self about ...., to gather information on .... [of the jib).

Ein'holer, *(str.)* m. inhauler (des Klüvers,

Ein'holetalje, *(w.)* f. *Mar.* train-tackle.

Ein'horn, *(str., pl.* Ein'hörner*)* n. 1) unicorn; 2) or **—fisch**, m. *Ichth.* a horned fish (having a horn on the forehead or growing out at the nose *(Naseus fronticornis* C. *or Monoceros monoceros* L.); **—teufel**, m. *Ichth.* sea-bat *(Malthe* [*Lophius*] *vespertilio* L.); **—wall**, m. *Ichth.* horned narwhal, sea unicorn, unicorn-whale *(Monodon monoceros* L.).

Ein'hörnig, *adj.* unicornous.

Ein'hutzeln, *(w.)* v. *intr. see* Einschrumpfen.

Ein'hufer, *(str.)* m. *Nat.* soliped, solidungulate. — **Ein'hufig**, *adj.* whole-hoofed, soliped, solidungulous. [&c. *cf.* Einhelfen.

Ein'hülfe, *(w.)* f. the (act of) prompting,

Ein'hüllen, *(w.)* v. *tr.* to wrap up, enwrap, envelop, infold, involve, to veil; sich —, to wrap (cuddle) one's self up; e-d, *Bot.* involving.

Ei'nig, *adj.* & *adv.* 1) †, one, only, sole, *see* Einzig, Allein; 2) united, agreeing, living in concord, living on friendly terms; — gehen, *Comm.* to be conformable or in conformity; — sein, to be at one (with), to agree, to be friends; — werden, to agree, to come to an agreement (über *(with Acc.)*, on, upon, about, for the price, &c.), to conclude (a bargain, &c.); das Cabinet ist über diese Maßregel —, the cabinet is united on this measure; mit sich — sein über ..., to have made up one's mind on ...; nicht mit sich — sein, to be in two minds (ob ...., whether ...; über *(with Acc.)*, about ...); er konnte nicht mit sich — werden, he could not make up his mind, he could not reconcile himself (to do it, &c.); — machen, to unite, to make (to) agree.

Ei'nigen, *(w.)* v. I. *tr.* to unite, to make (to) agree; II. *refl.* to agree, to come to terms, to an understanding, to arrange.

Ei'niger, Einige, Einiges, *pron.* some, any; einige wenige, some few; zwanzig und einige Jahr alt, twenty (and) odd years old; einigermaßen, in some measure, in some degree, to some extent.

Ei'nigkeit, *(w.)* f. unity; unanimity, union, concord, harmony, agreement.

Ei'niglich, *see* Einig. [Vereinigung.

Ei'nigung, *(w.)* f. union, agreement, *see*

Ein'impfen, *(w.)* v. *tr.* 1) to inoculate; 2) *fig.* to implant; einem Kinde die Pocken —, to inoculate (vaccinate) a child. [nation.

Ein'impfung, *(w.)* f. inoculation; vacci-

Ei'nist, *adv. provinc.* *(Switz.) for* Einest, Einst) once.

Ein'jagen, *(w.)* v. *tr.* 1) to chase in, to drive in; 2) *Sport.* to dress (a dog) for hunting, *cf.* Einhetzen, 1); 3) *fig.* (Einem) Furcht *(or* einen Schrecken) —, to frighten, terrify, intimidate, to strike with a sudden fright, fear or awe, to strike terror into ....

Ein'jährig, *adj.* 1) *a)* of one year, one year old; *b)* *Bot.* deciduous; 2) **E-keit**, *(w.)* f. *Bot.* deciduousness.

Ein'jochen, *(w.)* v. *tr.* to (put to the) yoke.

Ein'jucheln, *(w.)* v. *coll. for* Einheizen.

Ein'kalken, *(w.)* v. *tr.* *T.* to lay in lime;

consistent (mit sich selbst, with one's self); in — bringen, to adapt or accommodate (to), to make (something) harmonise, to make consistent (with), to reconcile (with, to); ich bin damit ganz im —, I quite accord therein; im — bleiben, to conform (to).

Ein'klappen, *(w.) v.* I. *tr.* 1) to fold, shut (up); 2) to join hands on a bargain; II. *intr.* *(aux.* sein) to clap together; to fold (together).

Ein'klappig, *adj. Bot. & Conch.* having one valve *(or* shell), univalve, univalvular.

Ein'klauig, *adj.* having one claw.

Ein'kleben, *(w.) v. tr.* to glue, stick, paste in.

Ein'kleiden, *(w.) v. tr.* 1) to clothe, invest; to put into uniform; 2) *a) Eccl.* (of monks) to give the hood *or* cowl, (of nuns) to give the veil; sich — lassen, to take the hood *or* veil; einen Rekruten —, to put a recruit into uniform; einen Todten —, to lay out a corpse; *b)* to install (in an office), to invest (with an office); 3) *fig.* to give a certain appearance *or* form, to embody, dress; (in Worte) —, to word, to clothe with words.

Ein'kleidung, *(w.) f.* 1) the (act of) clothing; 2) investiture, installation, instalment; 3) *fig.* dress *or* form (of a thing), wording.

Ein'kleistern, *(w.) v. tr.* 1) to paste in (paste); 2) *coll.* to grease (hair).

Ein'klemmen, *(w.) v. tr.* to squeeze in, to pinch in, to cram in *or* into, to jam.

Ein'klingen, *(str.) v. intr.* to accord, to be unisonant, to chime in.

Ein'klinken, *(w.) v.* I. *tr.* to put in *or* fasten the latch; eingeklinkt, *pp.* upon the latch; II. *intr.* to catch (the latch).

Ein'klopfen, *(w.) v. tr.* to beat *or* knock in.

Ein'klotzen, *(w.) v. intr.* to heat (a stove) with logs.

Ein'knebeln, *(w.) v. tr.* 1) *a)* to insert (a gag), to gag; *b)* to fasten with a gag; 2) *Mar.* ein Tau —, to put (a rope) in the beckets, to fasten (it) by a wooden roller.

Ein'kneipen, *(str.) v.* I. *tr.* to pinch in, to mark with the nail; II. *intr.* *(aux.* sein) *Stud. slang,* to stop at, *or* to frequent, an inn, to turn in.

Ein'kneten, *(w.) v. tr. Bak.* to knead in. [to work (the dough) together.

Ein'knicken, *(w.) v.* I. *tr.* 1) to fold in, over, *or* down; 2) to break, crack; II. *intr.* *(aux.* sein) to break down, give way, fail; im Gehen —, to bend the knees in walking.

Ein'knöpfen, *(w.) v. tr.* to button in.

Ein'knoten, *(w.) v. tr.* 1) to make a knot in; 2) *see* Einschürzen.

Ein'knüpfen, *(w.) v. tr.* 1) to tie in with a knot; to tie up; 2) *coll.* to enjoin.

Ein'kochen, *(w.) v.* I. *tr.* to boil down (bis auf ..., to ...); to boil up to a consistence, to inspissate by boiling; II. *intr.* *(aux.* sein) 1) to grow thick (to be inspissated) by boiling; 2) to evaporate by boiling.

Ein'kommen, *(str.) v. intr.* *(aux.* sein) 1) to come, arrive; to come *or* get in (of revenues, &c.); to be paid; *fig.-e.* 2) to apply (bei, to), to present a petition (to), to petition, sue (um, wegen, for); mit einem Bittschreiben —, to supplicate, bei ... to memorialise; mit einer Klage gegen Jemanden —, to bring an action, to prefer a complaint against one; dagegen —, to protest against; 3) *Law & Comm.* to declare one's insolvency, to fail; 4) to come into one's mind *or* head, to occur; wie sollte (es) mir —, how could I think (that, &c.); das laß dir nicht —, do not think of such a thing; don't take that into your head; don't presume to do anything of the kind.

Ein'kommen, *s. (str.) n.* 1) income, revenue, rent, produce, proceeds, profit; 2) *Mar.* *see* Einkehlen, *v. a.,* 2; —liste, *f.* rent-roll; —steuer, *f.* income-tax. [arrived, immigrant.

Ein'kömmling, *(str.) m.* stranger newly

Ein'koppeln, *(w.) v. tr. see* Einfriedigen.

Ein'körben, *(w.) v. tr.* to put into baskets; to hive (bees).

Ein'korn, *(str.) n. Bot.* one-grained wheat (*Triticum monococcum* L.). [embody.

Ein'körpern, *(w.) v. tr.* to incorporate,

Ein'krachen, *(w.) v. intr.* to fall, come, *or* break down with a crash.

Ein'krallen, *(w.) v. intr. & refl.* to fix *or* to strike the claws into.

Ein'kramen, *(w.) v.* I. *tr.* to put *or* pack up (displayed wares); II. *intr. see* Einhandeln, II.

Ein'kratzen, *(w.) v. tr.* to scratch into (on).

Ein'kreisen, *(w.) v. tr.* to encircle, environ, surround.

Ein'kriechen, *(str.) v. intr.* *(aux.* sein) 1) to creep in; 2) to shrink, shrivel up; 3) *Mar.* der Wind kriecht aus und ein, the wind is variable, veers.

Ein'kriegen, *(w.) v. tr. see* Einbekommen.

Ein'krimpen, *(w.) v. intr. see* Einschrumpfen; *Mar.* to slacken (said of the wind); gegen den Wind —, to sail with a scanty wind *or* close to the wind.

Ein'kritzeln, *(w.) v. tr.* to scrawl or scratch in.

Ein'krümmen, *(w.) v. tr. see* Einbiegen.

Ein'künfte, *(w.) f. pl.* income, comings-in, revenues, rents, fruits.

Ein'kürzen, *(w.) v. tr.* to shorten by drawing in, to draw in, reduce; *Draw.* to foreshorten; *Mar.* to warp (a ship).

Ein'kürzung, *(w.) f.* shortening, reduction, &c.; E-sleine, *f. Mar.* warp.

Ein'laden, *(str.) v. tr.* 1) to lade in, load in, to take in cargo; 2) to invite, ask, bid; ein für allemal eingeladen sein, to have a general invitation; e-d, *p. a. fig.* inviting, enticing, attractive; 3) *Law,* to cite, summon.

Ein'lader, *(str.) m.* 1) one who loads goods, &c., a loader; 2) inviter, bidder.

Ein'ladung, *(w.) f.* 1) the lading (in), &c.; shipment; 2) invitation; *Law,* summons.

Ein'ladungs..., *in comp.* —karte, *f.* invitation card, card of invitation; —platz, *m.* place for lading; quay, wharf; —schreiben, *n.* letter of invitation; —schrift, *f.* 1) zu einer Feierlichkeit, program, programme of a public ceremony (at a college, university, &c.); 2) *Law,* summons.

Ein'lage, *(w.) f.* 1) the (act of) laying in, *cf.* Einlegen; 2) *Tob.* filler (of a cigar); 3) anything put within another: *a) coll.* (cravat-) stiffener; *b)* letter, &c. enclosed, enclosure; 4) stake (at play); 5) *Comm. a)* investment (of a capital); *b)* (—Capital) deposit, money deposited; capital advanced *or* invested, share, stock.

Ein'lager, *(str.) n.* 1) lodging; quarters; 2) † (—recht) the right of taking up a lodging *or* quarters; 3) prison for debtors; 4) *Comm.* warehouse, magazine, repository.

Ein'lagerer, *(str.) m.* soldier lying in quarters.

Ein'lagern, *(w.) v. tr.* 1) to quarter, lodge; to billet; *cf.* Einquartieren; 2) to warehouse, store (up, goods); eingelagert, *p. a. Geol.* imbedded, -instratified, stratified between *or* among other bodies.

Ein'ländisch, *adj. see* Inländisch.

Ein'langen, *(w.) v.* I. *tr. see* Einreichen; II. *intr. see* Anlangen.

Ein'lappig, *adj. Bot.* monocotyledonous; e-e Pflanze, monocotyledon.

Ein'laß, *(str., pl.* **Ein'lässe)** *m.* 1) a letting in, inlet; admission; admittance; *Mech.* injection; 2) place of ingress, wicket, small gate, postern.

Ein'laß... *(from* Einlassen), *in comp.* —band, *n. Weav.* feeding-sliver; —geld, *n.* entrance-price, (price of) admittance; —karte, *f.* admission-ticket; —klappe, *f. Mech.* valve (in a machine); —ofen, *m.* furnace for melting copper; —preis, *m. see* —geld; —röhre, *f. Mech.* injection-slide; inlet-pipe; —schloß, *n. Locksm.* flush-lock; —stöpsel, *m. see* —klappe; —thür, *f. see* Einlaß, 2; —tuch, *n. Weav.* feeding-cloth; —ventil, *n.* 1) *Mech.* exhaustion-(suction-)valve; 2) expansion-valve; —walze, *f. Spinn.* feeding-roller (Einziehwalze); —zettel, *m. see* —karte.

Ein'lassen, *(str.) v.* I. *tr.* 1) to let in, admit; 2) *T. a)* to set into a groove, put in, fix; to sink *or* trim in; to mortise; *b) Mech.* to countersink; *c)* to imbed, insert; nicht — wollen, to deny admittance; 3) *Med.* to inmit; II. *refl.* (*with* mit, in, *or* auf (*& Acc.*)) to enter into (an engagement, an explanation, &c.), to engage (one's self), to embark in (metaphysical disquisitions, &c.); to join in ...; to deal *or* meddle with ..., to commit one's self to ...; sich auf die Klage —, *Law,* to answer (to) the plaintiff's declaration; sie hatte sich mit ihm eingelassen, she had got entangled with him; ich lasse mich darauf nicht ein, I will have nothing to do with it; auf solche Fragen lasse ich mich nicht ein, I shall not answer such questions; er kann sich sogar mit einigen Feinden in eine Verschwörung eingelassen haben, he may even have engaged in a plot with some enemies.

Ein'läßlich, *adj.* entering into details, &c. *see* Eingehend, *p. a.* 2.

Ein'lassung, *(w.) f.* 1) the (act of) letting in, admission, immission, &c.; 2) *Law,* the formal answer (of the defendant) to the plaintiff's declaration.

Ein'lauf, *(str., pl.* **Ein'läufe)** *m.* the (act of) coming in, entering, arrival; 2) anything that has come in *or* received; arrival.

Ein'laufen, *(str.) v. intr.* *(aux.* sein) 1) *a)* to come in, enter, arrive; *b) Mar.* in einen Hafen —, to enter *or* make a port, to sail into (*or* to fall in with) a harbour; to put, drop, *or* get into a harbour, to touch *or* call at a port; das Schiff ist wohlbehalten eingelaufen, the ship has reached her port in safety; 2) *Comm.,* &c. to come to hand, to come in, to pour *or* drop in; 3) *Typ.,* &c. to shrink; — lassen, to shrink (flannel, &c.), to sponge (cloth); *Typ.* to keep in (type).

Ein'läuflinge, *(str.) m. pl. see* Drilassen.

Ein'laugen, *(w.) v. tr.* to wash, steep, *or* soak in lye, to buck.

Ein'läuten, *(w.) v. tr.* to proclaim the beginning of (a thing) by ringing the bells.

Ein'leben, *(w.) v. refl.* 1) to accustom one's self to a certain mode of living; 2) *fig.* (*with* in (*& Acc.*)) to adopt thoroughly, to make one's own, appropriate completely; to devote one's self wholly to ...; andere, die sich noch nicht in ihre Überzeugungen eingelebt hatten, others not yet fully established (*or* more recent) in their convictions; wir haben uns in diese Methode eingelebt, daily custom has rendered this method familiar to us; tief eingelebte Zustände, Gesetze &c., a state of things of very old standing and familiarised to the people; laws, &c. that have worked themselves into habits.

Ein'lege..., *in comp.* —brett, *n.* leaf (of a telescope-table); —brettchen, *n.* veneer; —capital, *n. see* Einlagecapital; —deckel, *m. Print.* inner tympan; —gabel, *f.* clasp-fork; —holz, *n. see* Auslegeholz; —messer, *n.* clasp-knife.

Ein'legen, *(w.) v.* I. *tr.* 1) to lay in, put in; to enclose; 2) *T.* to inlay; to checker; to veneer; to imbed; eingelegte Arbeit, inlaid work; marquetry; 3) to tilt *or* couch (the spear); mit eingelegter Lanze, lance in rest; 4) to put *or* fold up, to turn inwards; 5) *Comm.* to lay in, put up, purchase (goods); 6) to preserve (in Zucker, with sugar, &c.), to put up (fruits); to salt, pickle (meat, cucumbers, &c.); 7) to put away (goods), stow, to

...ne; b) receipt, income, revenue; proceeds, receipts; returns; in — stellen, to put down in receipts (incomings); c) (—stube, f.) receiver's office; 2) the taking possession (of a town, &c.), capture; die — Jerusalems, the taking of Jerusalem; — und Ausgabe, receipts and expenditures; —s und Ausgabebuch, book of accounts of receipts and expenditures.

Ein'nehmen, *(str.) v. tr.* 1) to take in; to take, receive; to earn; 2) to capture, occupy; to take possession of; mit Sturm —, *Mil.* to carry by storm; 3) to take (medicine or physic); *fig.* to take, to put up, swallow (insults, &c.); 4) to occupy, take up (a position); to take up, fill (a space); *fig.-s.* 5) to possess, hold, fill (an office); 6) to captivate, charm, engage, win; to interest, attract; *Mar.-s.* die Segel —, to furl the sails; Holz, frisches Wasser, Kohlen, Mundvorrath —, to wood, water, coal, victual; eine Ladung, Güter —, to take in a cargo, to ship (goods), to put on board; Ladung — nach ..., to (take in) freight for ...; Steuern —, to collect the taxes; er nimmt viel ein, he has a large income; das Mittagessen, Abendessen —, to take (one's) dinner (to dine), supper (to sup); diese Sache nimmt einen größeren Raum in großen Büchern ein, als man sich vorstellen kann, this affair takes up a larger space in great books than you can imagine; eines Andern Stelle —, to succeed to another's place; eine öffentliche Stellung —, to hold a public position; eine bedeutende Stelle —, to hold a conspicuous place, to fill an eminent station; den Kopf —, to benumb the head; gegen Jemanden —, to prejudice or set against one; für Jemanden —, to prepossess in one's favour; sich — lassen or von etwas eingenommen sein, 1. to be taken with; to have a partiality for; blind eingenommen, bigoted (für seine Pläne ic., to one's plans, &c.); 2. to be prejudiced by; diese Leidenschaft nahm ihn allmählich ein, that passion grew upon him.

Ein'nehmend, *p. a. fig.* taking, engaging; winning, captivating; interesting; prepossessing.

Ein'nehmer, *(str.) m.* receiver, collector, gatherer (of taxes); —stelle, *f.*, —posten, *m.* collector's post. [of a collector.

Einnehmerei', *(w.) f.* the office or house

Ein'nehmung, *(w.) f.* the act of taking in, &c., *see* Einnehmen & Einnahme.

Ein'netzen, *(w.) v. tr.* to moisten, to wet; to sponge (cloth).

Ein'nicken, *(w.) v. intr. (aux.* sein) to nap, to fall or drop off, or asleep.

Ein'nieten, *(w.) v. tr.* to fix on the inside with rivets, to rivet.

Ein'nisten, Ein'nisteln, *(w.) v. refl.* 1) to nest; 2) *fig.* to nestle; 3) *coll.* to insinuate one's self. [press (one) to take.

Ein'nöthigen, *(w.) v. tr.* (Einem etwas) to

Ein'öde, *(w.) f.* desert, wilderness, waste; solitude, desolate place. [ear.

Ein'öhrig, *adj.* one-eared, having but one

Ein'ölen, *(w.) v. tr.* to oil, to rub over or lubricate with oil.

Ein'paarig, *adj. Bot.* one-paired, unijugate.

Ein'packen, *(w.) v.* I. *tr.* to pack up, put up, do up, bundle up (goods), to embale, bale; II. *intr. coll.* 1) to shut up shop, *cf.* [illegible]; 2) — müssen, to be obliged to yield, give way, to hush or to be silent. — **Ein'packung,** *(w.) f.* the (act of) packing up, &c. [(a rope).

[illegible], *(w.) v. tr. Mar.* to haul in

Ein'papieren, *(w.) v. tr.* 1) to paper, to wrap up in paper; 2) *T.* to paper, to put paper-bands in (the cloth).

Ein'pappen, *(w.) v. tr.* to paste in.

[illegible], *(w.) v. tr.* to smuggle (in), to [illegible] (goods).

Ein'passen, *(w.) v.* I. *tr.* to fit into, adjust, to fix in; *Carp.* to trim in; II. *intr.* to fit (in).

Ein'passiren, *(w.) v. intr. (aux.* sein) to pass in, enter.

Ein'pauken, *(w.) v. tr. coll.* 1) *see* Einschlagen; 2) *Stud. slang,* a) to train in fencing; b) *conal.* to coach, cram. — **Ein'pauker,** *(str.) m.* crammer, grinder, coach.

Ein'peitschen, *(w.) v. tr.* (Einem etwas) to whip (one) into (good manners, &c.), to beat into. [rind or shoulder.

Ein'pelzen, *(w.) v. tr. Hort.* to graft in the

Ein'pfählen, *(w.) v. tr.* to impale, to enclose, fence, or hedge with pales or stakes, to picket, to palisade.

Ein'pfarren, *(w.) v. tr.* to assign to (or unite with) a parish; eingepfarrte Dörfer, villages belonging to a parish; die Eingepfarrten, the parishioners. [pepper.

Ein'pfeffern, *(w.) v. tr.* to (season with)

Ein'pferchen, *(w.) v. tr.* 1) to pen, fold, impen; 2) *coll.* to coop up, to wedge, cram, or huddle together.

Ein'pflanzen, *(w.) v. tr.* 1) to plant; 2) *fig.* to implant, instil, inculcate; eingepflanzt, implanted, innate, inveterate. — **Ein'pflanzung,** *(w.) f.* 1) implantation; 2) inculcation.

Ein'pflastern, *(w.) v. tr.* 1) to inclose with a pavement; 2) to put into or under a pavement.

Ein'pflöcken, *(w.) v. tr.* to fasten with pegs.

Ein'pflügen, *(w.) v. tr. Agr.* to plough in, to plough down.

Ein'pfropfen, *(w.) v. tr.* 1) a) to cork in; b) *Hort.* to ingraft; to inoculate; 2) a) (Einem etwas) to stuff, to cram with; b) to wedge or cram in, to squeeze into ...; 3) *fig.* to implant.

Ein'pfünder, *(str.) m. Gunn.* one-pounder.

Ein'pfündig, *adj.* of one pound; eine e-e Kanone, *see* Einpfünder.

Ein'pfützen, *(w.) v. tr. Min.* to scoop (the water) with a mug and draw (it) up.

Ein'pichen, *(w.) v. tr.* to fasten with pitch, to pitch (in).

Ein'pilgern, *(w.) v. intr. (aux.* sein) to enter or come in as a pilgrim.

Ein'pladen, *(w.) v. tr. Mar.* ein Schiff —, to apply the sheathing-hair to a ship's bottom.

Ein'plaudern, *(w.) v. tr.* 1) (Einem etwas) to talk (one) into (something), *cf.* Einreden, I.; 2) to lull to sleep by talking. [& 2.

Ein'pochen, *(w.) v. tr. see* Einschlagen, 1

Ein'pökeln, *(w.) v. tr.* to pickle, corn, salt; to souse, to brine; eingepökelte Eßwaaren, dry-salteries; souse; *cf.* Einsalzen.

Ein'prägen, *(w.) v. tr.* 1) to impress, imprint, stamp; 2) *fig.* (Einem etwas) to inculcate, fix, enjoin, impress (something on, upon one), to imbue (one with).

Ein'poldern, *(w.) v. tr. see* Eindämmen.

Ein'prasseln, *(w.) v. intr. (aux.* sein) to fall down crashing.

Ein'predigen, *(w.) v.* I. *tr.* to instil by preaching, to inculcate; II. *refl.* sich —, to acquire the routine of preaching. [or cram in.

Ein'pressen, *(w.) v. tr.* to press, squeeze,

Ein'prügeln, *(w.) v. tr.* (Einem etwas) *coll.* to beat into. [roughly.

Ein'pudern, *(w.) v. tr.* to powder tho-

Ein'pumpen, *(w.) v. tr.* to pump in, into.

Ein'puppen, *(w.) v. refl. Entom.* to change into a chrysalis.

Ein'quartieren, *(w.) v. tr.* to quarter, lodge, billet (bei, on); sich —, to take up one's quarters (bei, with, at); Soldaten konnten nicht bei Privatfamilien einquartiert werden, soldiers could not be quartered on private families. — **Ein'quartierung,** *(w.) f.* 1) the (act of) quartering, &c.; 2) soldiers quartered; 3) *Carp.* (from Quartier, 8) step-groove, stepnotches (Stufenwuth).

Ein'quellen, *(w.) v. tr.* to soak, steep.

Ein'quetschen, *(w.) v. tr.* to squeeze in.

Ein'quirlen, *(w.) v. tr.* to twirl, to beat in.

Ein'raffen, *(w.) v. tr.* to take up hastily and irregularly.

Ein'rahmen, *(w.) v. tr.* to frame, put in a frame; to imborder; to tenter or rack (cloth).

Ein'rammen, Ein'rammeln, *(w.) v. tr.* to ram or drive in or down.

Ein'rangiren [—rängshären], *(w.) v. tr.* 1) a) to arrange in a series or row; b) to insert; 2) to enrol (recruits); 4) to sort (letters).

Ein'rathen, *(str.) v. tr.* (Einem etwas) to persuade (one into ...), to suggest (something to).

Ein'rauchen, *(w.) v. tr.* to season (a pipe): ein gehörig eingerauchter Meerschaumkopf, a well-seasoned meerschaum. [to fumigate.

Ein'räuchern, *(w.) v. tr.* to fill with smoke,

Ein'räumen, *(w.) v. tr.* 1) to house, to put or move (furniture) into a house, room, &c.; to put up; to stow away; 2) *fig.* (Einem etwas) a) to cede, yield, give up, consign over to ...; b) to grant, admit, concede; manches —, to make some admissions; to allow, permit; Einem einen Platz —, to make room for one; Einem ein Zimmer —, to accommodate one with a room. — **Ein'räumung,** *(w.) f.* 1) the (act of) housing, &c.; 2) cession; granting, admission, concession; allowance.

Ein'raunen, *(w.) v. tr.* (Einem etwas) to whisper (something) to ...; to give secret intelligence to; laß dir nichts —, don't listen to any suggestions. [gether.

Ein'rechen, *(w.) v. tr.* to rake in or to-

Ein'rechnen, *(w.) v. tr.* 1) to include, take, or comprise in the same account; 2) to allow for, deduct, *see* Abrechnen, 1. — **Ein'rechnung,** *(w.) f.* 1) the (act of) including, &c. in the same account; 2) deduction, allowance, compensation.

Ein'rede, *(w.) f.* objection; remonstrance, reclamation; *Law,* exception, protest, plea; keine —! no reply!

Ein'reden, *(w.) v.* I. *tr.* (Einem etwas) to persuade to, to talk over, to talk one into something, *cf.* Einsprechen; er hatte sich den Glauben eingeredet, he had reasoned himself into the belief (that, &c.); II. *intr.* 1) to interrupt in speaking; 2) to raise objections, contradict, oppose, remonstrate, protest.

Ein'reffen, *(w.) v. tr. Mar.* to clew, brail up, reef (the sails).

Ein'registriren, *(w.) v. tr.* to insert, register, enter, *see* Eintragen, 3.

Ein'reiben, *(str.) v. tr.* 1) to rub into; 2) *Med.* to embrocate, to moisten and rub a diseased or affected part; sein Bein mit Salbe —, to rub salve on one's leg; 3) *coll. see* Einstreichen, 5. — **Ein'reibung,** *(w.) f.* 1) the (act of) rubbing into, &c.; 2) *Med.* embrocation.

Ein'reichen, *(w.) v.* I. *tr.* to give or bring in; to present, deliver, lay before (a court, &c.), *cf.* Eingeben, 3; der Minister reichte seine Entlassung ein, the minister tendered his resignation; II. *intr.* to eat (of horses). — **Ein'reichung,** *(w.) f.* presentation, &c.

Ein'reihen, *(w.) v. tr.* 1) to place in a line or row, to range, rank; 2) *Weav.* to (prepare for the) slaie; 3) to lay into little plaits or folds; 4) to insert; 5) to enrol (recruits).

Ein'reihig, *adj.* 1) *Tail.* single-breasted; 2) *Bot.* one-ranked, pointing one way.

Ein'reihung, *(w.) f.* the (act of) placing in a line, &c., ranging, &c. *cf.* Einreihen.

Ein'reißen, *(str.) v.* I. *tr.* 1) to tear, break down or through, to rend; 2) to pull or take down, demolish; 3) to tumble, discompose; II. *intr. (aux.* sein) 1) to rend, burst, tear, split; 2) *fig.* a) to spread, gain ground, creep in, to be prevailing or prevalent; b) es reißt ins Geld or in den Beutel, it is an expensive affair.

Ein'reiten, *(str.) v.* I. *tr.* 1) to break or

[illegible]'schirren, (w.) v. tr. to (put into) harness.

[illegible] schlachten, (w.) v. tr. to kill for do[illegible] use or provision.

[illegible]'schlafen, (str.) v. intr. (aux. sein) 1) [illegible] fall or drop asleep, to go to sleep, coll. to [illegible] off; ich konnte gestern Abend nicht —, I [illegible] not get asleep last night; eingeschlafen [illegible], to be off or asleep; wieder —, to relapse [illegible] sleep; der Diener hatte ihn gerufen, aber [illegible] wieder eingeschlafen, the servant had [illegible] him, but he had gone to sleep again; [illegible] die away, to die an easy death; 3) to [illegible] asleep or numbed (of limbs); der Fuß ist [illegible] eingeschlafen, my foot is asleep; 4) fig. [illegible] fall into oblivion or disuse, to be dropped [illegible], to be discontinued, &c. cf. Ein[illegible]; — lassen, to leave off, drop, give up, [illegible]; to neglect. [(bed).

[illegible]'schläferig, Ein'schläfrig, adj. single

[illegible]'schläfern, (w.) v. tr. to lull to sleep: to make sleepy or drowsy; 2) fig. to lull [illegible] or into security, to quiet; e-d, p. a. [illegible], narcotic, somniferous, somnific. — [illegible]schläferung, (w.) f. a lulling to sleep; [illegible]mittel, n. soporific, narcotic, opiate.

[illegible]'schlag, (str., pl. Ein'schläge) m. 1) the [illegible] striking or driving in, &c. cf. Einschla[illegible] 2) a) the act of wrapping up; b) cover, [illegible]; 3) letter, &c. enclosed; enclosure; [illegible] a turning in, &c.; tuck, plait, fold; 5) Weav. [illegible], woof, shoot; mule-twist (opp. water-[illegible]); 6) harp; 7) see Handschlag; 8) Comm.-e. [illegible] coopering, cooperage (of casks or barrels); [illegible] cartage, porterage, drayage, haulage; c) a [illegible], housing; 9) see Weineinschlag; den [illegible] den — geben, see Einschlagen, I. 8, b; 10) [illegible] Einschläge, Min. horizontal openings of [illegible]; 11) fig. advice, counsel, suggestion.

[illegible]'schlag(e)..., in comp. —faden, m. [illegible]-thread (opp. Kettenfaden); —garn, n. [illegible] yarn; —messer, n. clasp-knife.

[illegible]'schlagen, (str.) v. I. tr. 1) to strike [illegible], beat in, knock in, drive in (a nail, &c.); [illegible] to break in or open, to burst, open, or [illegible] by a blow or blows; to knock down; [illegible] Fensterscheibe —, to break a pane; Einem [illegible] Schädel —, to knock a person's brain out; [illegible] Fasse den Boden —, to stave a cask; [illegible] Cook. to break or put in (eggs into a soup, &c.); 4) a) to wrap up, fold, envelop, to en[illegible], do or pack up, to cover, to paper; to [illegible]; b) to sack (corn); in Papier —, to [illegible] (bandage, &c.); 5) to turn in, to fold, [illegible] or double down (a leaf, &c.); ein Blatt [illegible] Buche) —, to fold or turn down a leaf; [illegible] Arme —, to cross or fold one's arms; 6) [illegible], to turn or tuck in (the edge of cloth, [illegible]), overcast, to make a tuck, to take in (a [illegible]), cf. [illegible]; 7) Weav. to pass or shoot [illegible] (woof) across the warp; 8) a) to improve [illegible] in colour or strength; b) to brimstone, [illegible]; to prune (wine), cf. Weineinschlag; [illegible], &c. Jagdfreunde bei Jemand —, to put [illegible] to kennel with somebody; Schweine —, [illegible]; Bienen —, to hive bees; Bäume [illegible], to earth the roots of trees; 10) einen Weg, [illegible] Richtung &c. —, a) to take a road; b) fig. [illegible] out a road, to take a course; to [illegible] (a mode of proceeding, a policy, &c.), [illegible] (a manner of life); ich habe alle [illegible] Wege eingeschlagen, I have tried all [illegible] means; auf dem eingeschlagenen Wege [illegible], to hold on one's course.

[illegible] II. intr. (aux. haben) 1) to clasp or shake [illegible] (as a token of agreement); schlag ein! [illegible] your hand upon it! shake hands [illegible]; 2) [illegible] dig in, to break ground; Min. [illegible], to sink a mine; 3) to strike [illegible] — (der Blitz) [illegible] [illegible], [illegible] occasioned by fire from [illegible]; 4) [illegible] Dach [illegible] —, to dig [illegible]; 5) fig. to belong to; to have re-ference to; to concern (with in (& Acc.)); dies schlägt nicht in mein Fach ein, this does not fall under my department, that is not within my province; that does not come in my line of business; III. intr. (aux. sein) 1) Paint. to sink in (of colours), cf. Durchschlagen, III. 1; 2) to be checked (of diseases); 3) to turn out, succeed, take or thrive well; to prosper; Husb. to yield a good crop; das Spiel schlug ihm ein, the play was in his favour; nicht —, to turn out badly; to prove a failure; to miscarry; dies Fabricat schlägt nicht ein, this manufacture does not take. — Ein'schläger, (str.) m. 1) T. ore-digger; 2) working-miner who puts the ore into the bucket; 3) woodman who piles up the wood in heaps.

Ein'schläg(e)..., in comp. —papier, n. wrapping-paper; —seide, f. shoot-silk; —span, m. splinter dipped in sulphur; cf. Einschlagen, I. 8, b; —tuch, n. Tail. dressing cloth.

Ein'schlägig, adj. belonging or having reference to something; competent (authority).

Ein'schleichen, (str.) v. intr. (aux. sein) or refl. 1) to sneak, slide, slip, steal, creep in or into; fig.-e. 2) to creep or steal in; sich bei Jemandem —, to steal (creep) into one's favour; Versehen schleichen sich in Bücher ein, corruptions creep into books; ich weiß nicht, wie sich der Irrthum hat in meine Übersetzung — können, I do not know how the mistake could have crept into my translation; es haben sich einige Irrthümer in Ihre Rechnung eingeschlichen, some errors have found their way (have slipped) into your account; 3) to insinuate one's self, to worm one's self into (one's favour, &c.).

Ein'schleiern, (w.) v. tr. 1) to veil, wrap up in a veil; 2) Eccl. to give the veil to (a novice about to enter a nunnery), cf. Einkleiden; sich — lassen, to take the veil.

Ein'schleifen, v. tr. I. (str.) to grind, cut in or on (a glass, &c.); II. (w.) 1) to bring in upon a sledge; 2) to drag in; 3) to smuggle in.

Ein'schleppen, (w.) v. tr. 1) a) to drag in; Mar. to tow (into port); b) see Einschleifen, 2; 3) to bring in or introduce (a disease into a country, &c.). [throwing (from a sling).

Ein'schleudern, (w.) v. tr. to break by

Ein'schließen, (str.) v. I. tr. 1) to lock (in), lock up, shut in or up; to confine; in ein Zimmer —, to closet; mit Mauern —, to wall (in); in ein Futteral —, to encase; in ein Pult —, to desk; mit einem Geländer —, to enrail; mit einer Hecke —, to hedge in; eingeschlossene Luft, close air; 2) a) to enclose; to encompass, surround; b) Mil. to block up, invest (a town), to surround; c) (in Klammern —) to put, enclose (in brackets), to include (in crotchets, &c.); 3) fig. to embrace, include, comprise; schließt mich in euer Gebet ein, remember me in your prayers; II. intr. to shut close, to fold in, to fit, to catch.

Ein'schließer, (str.) m. one who locks up, &c.; T. upper part of the chamber of a pump.

Ein'schließlich, adv. inclusively, including, inclusive of.

Ein'schließung, (w.) f. 1) the (act of) locking up, &c.; confinement; cf. Einschließen & Einschluß; 2) Mil. investment, blockade; E-s-zeichen, n. Typ. bracket, crotchet; cf. Klammer, 2.

Ein'schlingen, (str.) v. tr. 1) to sling, to put into a sling; 2) to draw in hastily, to swallow up greedily. [to slit.

Ein'schlitzen, (w.) v. tr. to cut lengthwise,

Ein'schlucken, (w.) v. tr. 1) to swallow (up), gulp down; 2) to absorb; 3) see Einstecken, 4.

Ein'schlummern, (w.) v. I. intr. (aux. sein) to drop, fall, or sink into a slumber, &c., see Einschlafen; fig. to die an easy death; eine Sache — lassen, to let a matter drop, to drop a matter; II. tr. see Einschläfern.

Ein'schlüpfen, (w.) v. intr. (aux. sein) to glide, slip, or slide in, cf. Einschleichen.

Ein'schlürfen, (w.) v. tr. to sip in (a fluid).

Ein'schluß, (str., pl. Ein'schlüsse) m. 1) the (act of) including, &c. cf. Einschließen; inclusion; 2) enclosure; 3) any thing enclosed (as a letter); als —, under cover; mit —, inclusive(ly); ... included; von Mittwoch bis mit — Sonnabend, from Wednesday to Saturday inclusive; mit — der Kosten, including (inclusive of) the charges; —klammer, f., —zeichen, n. see Einschließungszeichen. [grease; 2) to oil (wool).

Ein'schmalzen, (w.) v. tr. 1) to (rub with)

Ein'schmalztrog, (str., pl. E-tröge) m. Cloth-m. oiling-trough.

Ein'schmeicheln, (w.) v. refl. (with bei) to insinuate or ingratiate one's self (with); to creep or steal (to worm one's self) into one's favour; to steal on one's affections; e-d, p. a. insinuating, winning. — Ein'schmeichelung, (w.) f. insinuation, ingratiation.

Ein'schmeißen, (str.) v. vulg. for Einwerfen.

Ein'schmelzen, v. I. (str.) intr. (aux. sein) 1) to melt down, to get reduced in melting; 2) fig. to diminish, to become reduced; II. (w. & str.) tr. to melt down (plate, &c.).

Ein'schmettern, (w.) v. I. intr. to fall with a crash; II. tr. to knock down with a crash, to smash (in).

Ein'schmieden, (w.) v. tr. to put into irons, to enchain (an offender, a criminal).

Ein'schmiegen, (w.) v. refl. 1) to bend inwards; to cling to; 2) fig. a) to give in to ...; b) cf. Einschmeicheln.

Ein'schmieren, (w.) v. tr. 1) to smear, grease, anoint, lubricate; mit Öl —, to oil; vulg.-e. 2) to scrawl over; 3) see Einpökeln.

Ein'schmuggeln, (w.) v. tr. see Einschwärzen, 2. [dirty.

Ein'schmu(t)zen, (w.) v. tr. to foul, soil,

Ein'schnallen, (w.) v. tr. to buckle in.

Ein'schnappen, (w.) v. intr. (aux. sein) to snap in, to catch. [bolt.

Ein'schnappfeder, (w.) f. Horol. spring-

Ein'schnarchen, (w.) v. intr. to fall asleep with a snore. [turning-chisel.

Ein'schneide, (w.) f. Turn. a one-edged

Ein'schneide ... (from Einschneiden), in comp. —decke, f. Build. sound-floor, sound-boarding, false ceiling (Einschub); —maschine, f. see —zeug.

Ein'schneiden, (str.) v. I. tr. 1) a) to cut in, into, to notch, indent, carve, incise, cf. Einkerben; b) Surg. to remove restriction in ... by incision; 2) to cut up (bread, &c. in order to put into a soup, &c.); 3) Bookb. ein Buch —, to let the bands into the book; II. intr. 1) to cut in, (auch fig.) to cut; seine Worte schnitten um so tiefer ein, je weniger man sie von ihm erwartet hatte, his words cut the deeper, the less they were expected from him; 2) Typ. to bite; e-d, p. a. incisive; trenchant; telling; eingeschnitten, p. a. Bot. incised, notched, gashed; das Eingeschnittene, Cook. fricassee.

Ein'schneide..., in comp. —säge, f. bookbinder's hand-saw; —zeug, n. T. fuse-engine; screw- or wheel-cutting engine.

Ein'schneidig, adj. one-edged; der e-e Bohrer, single-cutting drill; Degen, back-sword.

Ein'schneidung, (w.) f. the (act of) cutting in or into, &c. cf. Einschneiden; incision.

Ein'schneien, (w.) v. tr. to snow up, to cover all over with snow, to bury in snow; die Reisenden waren auf ihrem Wege zur Stadt eingeschneit worden, the travellers had been snowed up on their way to town; eingeschneit, p. a. snow-bound.

Ein'schnitt, I. (str.) m. 1) incision: a) the (act of) cutting in, &c. cf. Einschneiden; b) cut, track, indentation, notch, cf. Kerbe; [illegible], &c. a cutting (Durchstich, 2); 2) Mil. embrasure, port-hole; 3) Lock-sm. tooth (of a key-bit);

Ein'siedlerin, (w.) f. hermitess.

Ein'siedlerisch, adj. hermitical, anachoretical; solitary, retired.

Ein'siegeln, (w.) v. tr. to seal up. [lable.

Ein'silbler, (str.) m. Gramm. monosyl-

Ein'silbig, I. adj. 1) monosyllabic: 2) fig. sparing of words, taciturn; II. E-keit, (w.) f. monosyllabism, &c.

Ein'singen, (str.) v. I. tr. to sing (lull) asleep; II. refl. to acquire readiness or perfection in singing, to practise singing.

Ein'sinken, (str.) v. intr. (aux. sein) to sink in, give way, fall down: eingesunken, p. p. sunken (eyes, &c.), cf. Eingefallen; das —, (str.) n. the (act of) sinking in, &c.: subsidence (of ground, &c.).

Ein'sintern, (w.) v. intr. see Einsickern.

Ein'sitzen, (str.) v. I. tr. to press down by sitting on (as the seat of a padded chair); II. intr. (aux. haben) 1) to stay at home: 2) to get into a carriage. [seat, for one person.

Ein'sitzig, adj. of one seat only, with one

Einst'malig, adv. once: one day, cf. Einst.

Ein'sohlig, adj. having but one sole; single-soled.

Ein'sommern, (w.) v. intr. (aux. sein) & refl. to get inured, accustomed, acclimated to the heat of summer.

Ein'spänen, (w.) v. tr. see Einpapieren, 2.

Ein'spannen, (w.) v. tr. 1) to enchase, to put into a frame: 2) to put into harness, to harness, put (the horses) to.

Ein'spänner, (str.) m. 1) a person keeping a one-horse-vehicle: 2) one-horse-carriage (-waggon, -vehicle); 3) Min. he that works [illegible] a mine by himself; 4) provinc. load-[illegible].

Ein'spännig, I. adj. 1) drawn by one horse (only); — fahren, to drive with one horse; der e-e Wagen, see 1) Einspänner, 2; 2) (of a bed-[illegible]) see Einschläferig; II. E-r, m. (decl. like adj.) see Einspänner, 3.

Ein'speichern, (w.) v. tr. to put, lay, or stow (goods) in the warehouse, to warehouse, store.

[illegible], adj. Bot. univalve, univalvular.

Ein'sperren, (w.) v. tr. to lock up, shut up, pen or coop up, crib; to confine; to imprison; to cage. — Ein'sperrung, (w.) f. the (act of) locking up, &c.

Ein'spielen, (w.) v. refl. to play frequently (upon a musical instrument); to acquire precision in a musical or dramatical performance; eingespielt sein, to be well practised: ein gut eingespieltes Orchester, a well-drilled band of musical performers.

Ein'spinnen, (str.) v. I. tr. to insert by spinning; to spin in; II. refl. Entom. to spin or wind (the filaments) round itself (as a caterpillar or spider).

Ein'spitze, (w.) f. see Spitzhacke.

Ein'sprache, (w.) f. objection: Law, exception, protest; — thun, to take exception (gegen, at, to, or against), to protest (against), to traverse; cf. Einspruch.

Ein'sprechen, (str.) v. I. tr. (Einem etwas) to instil, insinuate by words, to influence [illegible] Muth —, to encourage, hearten; Trost —, to comfort; II. intr. 1) (bei Einem) to call (in) or speak to give a call; to turn in; [illegible] & Einreden, II. 2.

Ein'sprecher, (str.) m. Law, excepter, one who makes exceptions.

Ein'sprengen, (w.) v. I. tr. 1) a) to besprinkle, sprinkle; b) Bookb. to marble (the edges of a book); 2) to burst open, to break [illegible] &c. [illegible] interspense, intersperse, [illegible] cf. [illegible]; eingesprengt, [illegible] II. intr. (aux. sein) to [illegible] in. — Ein'sprengung, (w.) f. 1) the [illegible], &c. cf. Einsprengen; 2) [illegible]; 3) Geol. [illegible].

Ein'spelzig, adj. Bot. unipaleaceous.

Ein'springen, (str.) v. intr. (aux. sein) 1) to leap in: 2) to catch with the spring (said of locks); 3) Cloth. see Einlaufen, 3; 4) a) to bend or turn in: der e-de Winkel, see der eingehende Winkel, see Eingehen, I. 1; b) Weav., &c. to shrink in with.

Ein'spritzen, (w.) v. tr. to inject, squirt in, immit; to syringe (a wound).

Ein'spritzer, (str.) m. Surg. syringe.

Ein'spritz..., in comp. Mech.-e. —hahn, m. injection-cock: —röhre, f. injection-pipe; —ventil, n. injection-valve.

Ein'spritzung, (w.) f. injection, immission; E-shahn, m., &c. see Einspritzhahn &c.

Ein'spruch, (str., pl. Ein'sprüche) m. Law, exception (cf. Einsprache), protestation, (der gerichtliche —) caveat; — thun, to protest against, to enter a caveat; — thun gegen eine Heirat, to forbid the bans; ohne — hingehen lassen, to suffer (allow) to pass unchallenged: E-srecht, n. veto.

Ein'sprung, (str., pl. Ein'sprünge) m. 1) a) the (act of) entering; b) entrance-place; 2) Archit. return (of a moulding, projection, &c.).

Ein'spunden, Ein'spünden, (w.) v. tr. to close (a cask) with a bung, to bung.

Ein'spurig, adj. see Eingleisig.

Einst, adv. 1) once, one day, one time (though no more), in time past, formerly; 2) some day, one day, some time, i. e. at a future time, hereafter.

Ein'stäben, (w.) v. tr. Tann. to dress (leather) with hot water.

Ein'stallen, (w.) v. tr. to (put into a) stable; to harbour, shelter (as in a stable).

Ein'stämmig, adj. having but one stem; made out of one stem.

Ein'stampfen, (w.) v. tr. 1) to ram, stamp in or down; 2) to break by ramming or stamping.

Ein'stand, (str., pl. Ein'stände) m. Law, 1) a) entrance into office: b) coll. for Einstandsgeld; 2) entrance into the rights or privileges of a purchaser: 3) state of being equal (at play).

Ein'stands..., in comp. —gebühr, f. see Delcredere; —geld, n. 1) entrance-money, money paid on entering an office: coll. footing: —geld geben, to pay footing; 2) see Handgeld, 2; —recht, n., —gerechtigkeit, f. the right (of a person) to enter into a purchase, concluded between two others.

Ein'stänkern, (w.) v. tr. to fill with stench.

Ein'stauben, (w.) v. intr. (aux. sein) to be covered or filled with dust, to gather dust.

Ein'stäuben, (w.) v. tr. to cover with dust. [&c.).

Ein'stauen, (w.) v. tr. to stow in (goods,

Ein'stechbogen, (str.) m. Print. tympan-sheet.

Ein'stechen, (str.) v. I. tr. 1) to stick or thrust in (any sharp instrument); to pierce or prick with ...; 2) Print., &c. to prick; to stitch or sew in; 3) Min. to fill up; 4) T. to paper (pins); 5) Gam. to trump (at cards); II. intr. (aux. sein) Mar. (seewärts) to stand off or out (to sea).

Ein'stecher, (str.) m. Ship-b. false-futtock.

Ein'steckschloß, (str., pl. E-schlösser) n. see das eingestellte Schloß (Einstellen I. 1).

Ein'stecken, (w.) v. tr. 1) to put in; to put by, to put up (the sword, &c.); to pocket (up); to purse up, pouch; 2) T. see Einlochen, 1; das eingesteckte Schloß, see das eingestellte Schloß; 3) to imprison, clap up in prison: 4) coll. to put up with or to pocket, stomach (an affront).

Ein'stehen, (str.) v. intr. 1) (aux. sein) provinc. to enter: in die Miethe —, to take possession of a house: in einen Kauf —, a) to participate in a purchase; b) to enter into the rights of a purchaser: 2) (aux. haben) to answer (für, for), to be answerable (for), to stand or become security (for).

Ein'steher, (str.) m. 1) one who enters, &c. cf. Einstehen; 2) (one who becomes) surety, &c.; 3) Mil. a substitute.

Ein'stehlen, (str.) v. refl. to steal in, to enter stealthily or privately, or by illicit means.

Ein'steigen, (str.) v. intr. (aux. sein) to step or get in, into, to enter (a carriage, a train, &c.); to go or get on board (a vessel); das Zeichen zum — ist schon gegeben, the signal for entering the carriages (Am. cars) has already been given: zum Fenster —, to get in at the window.

Ein'steigeplatz, (str., pl. E-plätze) m. entrance-place; starting-place (of carriages, boats, &c.).

Ein'steinen, (w.) v. tr. to stone, to mark out with stones; to enclose with stones.

Ein'stellen, (w.) v. I. tr. 1) to put in: a) to put up; to put or set into; Güter irgendwo —, to stow goods somewhere or other; b) to insert, &c.; ein eingestelltes Schloß, Lock-sm. a woodstock lock, mortise-lock; 2) fig. a) to leave or put off, discontinue, intermit, stop; to suspend, interrupt: das Feuer —, Mil. to cease one's fire or firing; die Feindseligkeiten —, to suspend hostilities; die Arbeit —, to cease from work; to quit or strike work; to turn out on strike; seine Zahlungen —, to stop payment, to suspend one's payments; b) see Abstellen, b; II. refl. to make one's appearance, to come or drop in (at the time appointed); — bei ..., to wait or call upon ...: der Winter hat sich eingestellt, winter has set in; es stellte sich die Lust ein, a desire sprang up; sich wieder —, to return, come back again (cf. sich Einfinden).

Ein'stellung, (w.) f. 1) the (act of) putting in or up, &c. cf. Einstellen; 2) fig. discontinuance, cessation, suspension (of hostilities, &c.); stopping or suspension (of payment, &c.): — der Arbeit (Gen.), cessation from work; strike

Ein'stemmen, (w.) v. tr. 1) to put, set, or place in or between, to interpose: die Arme —, to set the arms a-kimbo: 2) Carp. ein Zapfenloch —, to (make a) mortise; eine eingestemmte Thür (opp. Leistenthür), a panel door; 3) Min. see Abteufen.

Einst'ens, Einst'en, adv. († &) * for Einst.

Ein'stich, (str.) m. 1) the (act of) pricking with a sharp point, &c. cf. Einstechen; 2) a pricking into, puncture. [upon.

Ein'sticken, (w.) v. tr. to embroider in or

Ein'stieben, (str. & w.) v. tr. see Einstäuben.

Einst'ig, adj. future, that is to be, to come.

Ein'stimmen, (w.) v. intr. 1) Mus. to accord in tune; 2) to chime in; to join in; in das Geschrei (den Ruf) —, to swell the cry; 3) fig. to agree, consent, coincide in opinion; to be unanimous.

Ein'stimmig, I. adj. 1) Mus. a) consonant, unison; b) univocal, of or for one voice; ein e-er Gesang, a solo; 2) fig. unanimous, adv. unanimously, with one accord, as one man, to a man, by or with one consent, without a (or one) dissentient voice; sie behaupten —, they are agreed in affirming: —sein, to agree; II. E-keit, (w.) f. 1) consonance, unison; 2) fig. unanimity, agreement.

Ein'stippen, (w.) v. tr. see Eintunken.

Einst'mals, adv. see Einstmals.

Ein'stöckig, adj. one-storied (house, &c.).

Ein'stopfen, (w.) v. tr. to stuff, cram in, to tuck in. [ring up.

Ein'stören, (w.) v. tr. to destroy by stir-

Ein'stoßen, (str.) v. tr. 1) to thrust in, push in, drive in; to ram in, stamp in; 2) to break, knock in; to stave, unbottom (a cask); to throw or knock down (a wall): die Ladung —, Gunn. to ram down the cartridge.

Ein'verleiben, *(w.)* *v. tr.* to incorporate, embody (etwas einer Sache *[Dat.]*, something with *or* in), to annex (to). — **Ein'verleibung,** *(w.)* *f.* incorporation, annexation (in *[with Acc.]*, mit, to).

Ein'vernehmen, *(str.)* *n.* (mutual) understanding, agreement, *cf.* Vernehmen, 2; in gutem —, on good terms (with).

Ein'verständlich, *adj.* agreeing (with = im Einverständniß).

Ein'verständniß, *(str.)* *n.*, **Ein'verstand,** *(str.)* *m.* intelligence, agreement, understanding, *cf.* Verständniß; im E-e, in concert; im — mit ..., in concert *or* accord with; in gutem E-e mit ihm, on good terms with him; in — bringen (*or* **Ein'verständigen,** *[w.]* *v. tr., l. u.*), to bring to an understanding; das geheime —, collusion; *Law,* (mit der Gegenpartei) prevarication; ein geheimes — haben, to collude (mit, with); *Law,* to prevaricate, to plead by covin.

Ein'verstehen, *(irr.)* *v. refl. or* ein'verstanden sein (*v. intr.*) mit, to agree with ... (über *[with Acc.]*, on, about); to be in a proper understanding; man war vollkommen einverstanden, it was perfectly understood; ich bin mit Ihnen ganz einverstanden, I am quite with you; einverstanden! agreed! Provision mit einverstanden, *Comm.* commission included.

Ein'vettern, *(w.)* *v. refl. coll.* to get connected *or* familiar by intrusion (bei, with), to intrude on (*cf.* Einbrüdern).

Ein'vieren, *(w.)* *v. tr.* to enclose in a square. — **Ein'vierung,** *(w.)* *f.* quadrature.

Ein'wachsen, *(str.)* *v. intr.* (*aux.* sein) to grow in *or* into.

Ein'wage, *(w.)* *f. Comm.* loss in the weight (by weighing out *or* by retail), inleak.

Ein'wägen, *(w. & str.)* *v.* I. *tr.* to weigh and put in; to weigh down; II. *refl.* to diminish, to loose *or* to be lost by being weighed.

Ein'walken, *(w.)* *v.* I. *tr.* 1) *Tann.* to grease, to oil (Stockfisch); 2) *Cloth, &c.* to full (close); II. *intr.* to shrink.

Ein'walzen, *(w.)* *v. tr.* to roll in (seeds, gravel, &c.), to roll into the ground.

Ein'wand, *(str., pl.* **Ein'wände***)* *m.* objection; pretext, plea, *cf.* Ausflucht.

Ein'wanderer, *(str.)* *m.* immigrant. — **Ein'wandern,** *(w.)* *v. intr.* (*aux.* sein) 1) to wander, come, *or* turn in; 2) to enter a country, to immigrate. — **Ein'wanderung,** *(w.)* *f.* a wandering in, immigration.

Ein'wärts, *adv.* inward, inwards; — gebogen, bent inwards, incurved; *Bot.* inflected; — gerollt, *Bot.* involved; — kehren, to turn one's toes in; — gehend, *see* Eingehend in Eingehen I. 1; — stehende Knie, *n.* in-knee; — wenden, to turn in; — gekehrt, *Herald* counter passant; der — ziehende Muskel, — zieher, *m. Anat.* adductor.

Ein'waschen, *(str.)* *v. tr. T.* to wash (ore).

Ein'wässern, *(w.)* *v. tr.* to steep, soak, lay in water.

Ein'weben, *(w. & str.)* *v.* I. *tr.* to weave in *or* into, to inweave; to interweave; II. *refl. Weav.* to shrink.

Ein'wechseln, *(w.)* *v. tr.* to change; Dukaten &c. —, to buy ducats, &c.

Ein'wehen, *(w.)* *v. tr.* to blow in *or* down.

Ein'weiberig, *adj. Bot.* monogynian; die — Pflanze, monogyn.

Ein'weichen, *(w.)* *v. tr.* to soak, steep, macerate, drench; Wäsche —, to steep, wet linen; in Lauge —, to buck; eingeweicht, *p. a.* as drunk as a toast. — **Ein'weichung,** *(w.)* *f.* the (act of) soaking, &c., maceration.

Ein'weihen, *(w.)* *v. tr.* 1) to consecrate; dedicate (a church, &c.); to ordain (a priest): to install, to inaugurate; *coll.* to post up [illegible] *[with Acc.]*, into; 2) *coll.* to use (a thing) for the first time; to handsel; to flesh (one's sword); meine Stiefel sind noch nicht eingeweiht, my boots are yet unbroken; in ein Geheimniß —, to let into a secret; der Eingeweihte, one who is initiated, adept.

Ein'weihung, *(w.)* *f.* 1) consecration, dedication (of a church, &c.); ordination (of a priest); 2) initiation, inauguration; zur — gehörig, initiatory, inauguratory; E-sfest, *n.*, E-sfestlichkeit, *f.* inaugural *fête,* ceremony of inaugurating (a statue, &c.); inaugural solemnity *or* ceremonies; E-srede, *f.* inaugural address; E-sreise, *f.* inaugural tour (first trip on the opening of a [line of] railway).

Ein'weisen, *(str.)* *v. tr.* 1) to show in *or* into; 2) *fig.* to instal, introduce, induct; in Jemandes Güter —, *Law,* to put in possession of an(other's) estate. — **Ein'weisung,** *(w.)* *f.* installation, introduction, induction. [up.

Ein'welken, *(w.)* *v. intr.* to fade, to wither

Ein'wenden, *(w. & irr.)* *v. tr.* 1) to turn in; 2) *fig.* to object, to oppose; to reply, dissent; dagegen läßt sich nichts —, there is nothing to be said against this; there can be no objection to that. — **Ein'wendung,** *(w.)* *f.* objection, exception, remonstrance; plea, reply; argument; E-en machen, to make *or* raise objections, to object (to); to urge, remonstrate (against), to take exception (at, against), to demur (to).

Ein'werfen, *(str.)* *v. tr.* 1) to throw in; to break, smash; to put into the box (a letter); 2) to throw down; 3) *fig.* to object, *cf.* Einwenden, 2. — **Ein'werfung,** *(w.)* *f.* 1) the (act of) throwing in *or* down, breaking, &c.; 2) *Law,* collation (of estates).

Ein'wetzen, *(w.)* *v. tr.* to whet on *or* into.

Ein'wichsen, *(w.)* *v. tr.* to blacken (boots); to rub with wax, to wax.

Ein'wickeln, *(w.)* *v. tr.* 1) to wrap up, inwrap, infold, involve, envelop, *cf.* Einschlagen, 4, *a*; to swathe, swaddle (a child); 2) *cant.* to apprehend, catch, imprison, *coll.* to nab. — **Ein'wickelung,** *(w.)* *f.* the (act of) wrapping in *or* up, involution, envelopment.

Ein'wiegen, *v. tr.* I. *(w.)* to rock (a child) to sleep; to lull; II. *(str.)* *see* Einwägen, I.

Ein'willigen, *(w.)* *v. intr.* to consent, assent (in *[with Acc.]*, to), to comply (with); to approve (of), to sanction, permit, agree, to acquiesce (in), subscribe, accede (to). — **Ein'willigung,** *(w.)* *f.* consent, assent, compliance; permission, approbation, approval; sanction, acquiescence.

Ein'windedraht, *(str., pl.* E-drähte*)* *m. T.* falling wire.

Ein'windeln, *(w.)* *v. tr.* to swathe, swaddle.

Ein'winden, *(str.)* *v. tr.* 1) to wind in; to entwine; 2) to heave (up) (a weight); *Mar.* das Ankertau mit dem Bratspill —, to heave at the windlass; das Ankertau mit der Kabelaring —, to heave upon the cable with the messenger.

Ein'winkeln, *(w.)* *v. tr. Archit.* to square.

Ein'wintern, *(w.)* *v.* I. *tr.* to put up for preserving during winter; II. *intr.* 1) (*aux.* sein) & *refl.* to prepare for winter; to get accustomed to the winter, to get inured to the cold of winter; 2) (*impers.; aux.* haben) es wintert ein, it is getting wintry, the winter sets in.

Ein'wirken, *(w.)* *v.* I. *tr.* to work in, embroider, interweave, interlace; eingewirkt, *p. a.* inwrought; II. *intr.* to act *or* operate (auf *[with Acc.]*, on), to affect, to exert influence (upon), to influence (*cf.* Einfluß haben); — lassen, to bring to bear (upon). — **Ein'wirkung,** *(w.)* *f.* action (upon), &c., influence.

Ein'wirren, *(w.)* *v. tr. see* Verwirren.

Ein'witschen, *(w.)* *v.* I. *tr.* to soil in rubbing; II. *intr.* (*aux.* sein) to slip in.

Ein'wittern, *(w.)* *v. intr.* (*aux.* sein) *Min.* (of minerals) to be introduced *or* engendered by subterranean vapours *or* gases.

Ein'wöchentlich, *adj.* of one week.

Ein'wöchig, *adj.* lasting one week.

Ein'wohnen, *(w.)* *v.* I. *intr.* 1) (*aux.* sein) & *refl.* to settle, make one's self at home; 2) to live in *or* inhabit a place; 3) *fig.* to inhere, *see* Inwohnen; II. *tr.* to deteriorate (lodgings) while living in them.

Ein'wohner, *(str.)* *m.* (E-in, *(w.)* *f.* female) inhabitant; —zählung, *f. see* Volkszählung. — **Ein'wohnerschaft,** *(w.)* *f.* inhabitants collectively, community of a place *or* country.

Ein'wohnung, *(w.)* *f. Theol.* inhabitation, indwelling (of the Holy Spirit, &c.).

Ein'wölben, *(w.)* *v. tr.* to arch *or* vault in.

Ein'wölken, *(w.)* *v. tr.* to involve (as) in a cloud *or* clouds, to cloud; *fig.* to darken.

Ein'wollen, *(irr.)* *v. intr. see* Ein, *adv.;* das will mir nicht ein, I cannot understand that; it will never go down with me.

Ein'wüchsig, *adj. Bot.* having a smooth stem *or* stalk (*i. e.* without knots *or* joints).

Ein'wühlen, *(w.)* *v. tr.* 1) to wallow *or* dig in *or* into; 2) to bury *or* hide in the ground; 3) to disorder, confuse by rummaging.

Ein'wurf, *(str., pl.* **Ein'würfe***)* *m.* 1) (*l. u.*) a place *or* opening where a thing may be thrown in, *cf.* Briefeinwurf; 2) *fig.* objection, exception; answer, plea (in law, &c.), *cf.* Einwendung; einen — abweisen, to repel an argument; sich selbst (*Dat.*) Einwürfe und Einwendungen machen, to reply and rejoin on one's self. [vour greedily, to gorge.

Ein'würgen, *(w.)* *v. tr.* to swallow *or* de-

Ein'wurzeln, *(w.)* *v. intr.* (*aux.* sein) 1) to root (in), to take *or* strike root; 2) *fig.* to become rooted *or* inveterate; eingewurzelt, *p. a.* (deep-)rooted, inveterate; er stand wie —, he stood rooted to the ground. — **Ein'wurzelung,** *(w.)* *f.* the (act of) rooting, taking, *or* striking root, &c.; *fig.* inveteration.

Ein'zacken, *(w.)* *v. tr.* to indent, notch, jag.

Ein'zahl, *(w.)* *f. Gramm.* the singular (number).

Ein'zahlen, *(w.)* *v. tr.* to pay in; voll —, to pay up; eingezahlt (als Rubrik), paid.

Ein'zählen, *(w.)* *v. tr.* 1) to count in; 2) to comprise, include (within a certain number).

Ein'zahlung, *(w.)* *f.* a payment in part made on shares; a call *or* instalment; share; eine — ausschreiben, to make a call for funds; E-ssumme, *f.* instalment.

Ein'zahn, *(str.)* *m. Entom.* a species of shells belonging to the genus of Trochina (*Monodonta modiolus L.*).

Ein'zahnen, Ein'zähnen, *(w.)* *v. tr.* to indent, *Carp.* to dovetail. — **Ein'zahnung, Ein'zähnung,** *(w.)* *f.* indentation, *Carp.* dovetailing.

Ein'zapfen, *(w.)* *v. tr.* 1) to tap in, draw out into; 2) *Carp.* to mortise (in, into).

Ein'zaubern, *(w.)* *v. tr.* to instil by a charm.

Ein'zäunen, *(w.)* *v. tr.* to enclose with a hedge, *or* fence, to fence in, to palisade. — **Ein'zäunung,** *(w.)* *f.* 1) the act of fencing in, &c.; 2) the state of being fenced in, enclosure, hedge, fence. [tylous.

Ein'zehig, *adj. Nat.* one-toed, monodac-

Ein'zehren, *(w.)* *v. intr. & refl.* to diminish by absorption, to waste, to lose in substance; Wein in Fässern zehrt ein, wine in wood loses in quantity.

Ein'zeichnen, *(w.)* *v. tr.* 1) to insert a drawing (in a book, &c.), to draw in *or* upon; 2) (eine Schriftstelle) to mark (a passage, &c.); 3) *a)* to enter, to write *or* note down, inscribe, *cf.* Einschreiben; *b)* sich —, to subscribe. — **Ein'zeichnung,** *(w.)* *f. see* Einschreibung.

Ein'zeilig, *adj. Bot.* secund, unilateral; following one direction.

Ein'zel..., *in comp.* single; —handbuch,

[illegible]mid, n. *Chem.* ferruginous bromide, bromide of iron; —bruch, m. see —bergwerk; —[illegible], m. *T.* iron-cement; —chlorid, n. *Chem.* [illegible]-chloride of iron; —chlorür, n. chloride of iron; —chrom, n. *Miner.* chrome ore, [illegible] of iron, the ferruginous oxide of [illegible]; —chrysolith, m. *Miner.* ferruginous [illegible]; —crystall, m. *Miner.* crystal of [illegible]; —cur, f. iron-cure; *Chem.-s.* —cyanid, n. cyanide of iron; —cyanidkalium, [illegible] sesqui-ferro-cyanate of potash; —cyanidwasserstoff, m. ferro-cyanic acid; —cyanür, [illegible] cyanide of iron; —cyanürammonium, n. [illegible]-cyanate; —cyanürkalium, n. ferro-cyanide of potassa; —cyanürkupfer, n. ferro-cyanate of copper; —cyanürwasserstoff, m. [illegible]-cyanic acid; —cyanverbindung, f. [illegible] of iron; —cylinder, m. iron cylinder; —draht, m. iron-wire; —drahtband, [illegible], n. flat iron-wire rope; —drahtmühle, f. iron-wire drawing-mill; —drahtseil, n. cable [illegible] iron-wire; —drahtzieher, see Drahtzieher; [illegible], f. crystallised iron-ore; —erde, f. ferruginous earth, iron-mould; —erz, n. *Miner.* iron-ore; —extract, m. *Pharm.* extract of [illegible]; —farbe, f. iron-gray; —farbig, adj. iron-coloured; —feilicht, —feilig, n., —feilspäne, pl. iron-filings, swarf; —fest, adj. 1) as hard as iron; 2) *fig.* most resolute; —firniß, m. iron-varnish; —fleck(en), m. iron-stain, iron-mould; —fleckig, adj. iron-mouldered; —fluß, [illegible] crystallisation of iron; —fluorid, n. *Chem.* fluoride of iron; —fresser, m. *coll.* fire-eater; bully, hector; —frischschlacke, f. *Metall.* [illegible]-cinders; —gang, m. iron-lode; —[illegible], f. *Smelt.* iron-pig; —garn, n. wire-[illegible]; —gart, m. see Eisvogel; —gehalt, m. ferruginous parts; —geiß, m. see —lies; —gemisch, [illegible] amalgam of iron; —geräth, —geschirr, n. iron utensils or tools; —gewölbe, n. ironmonger's shop or warehouse; —gießer, m. iron-founder; —gießerei, f. iron-founding, iron-foundery; —gilbe, f. *Miner.* yellow ochre; [illegible], m. iron-glance, iron-glimmer, micaceous iron-ore; —glanzerz, n. see —gilbe; [illegible] n. *Miner.* brittle iron-ore; —glimmer, [illegible] see —glanz; —granat, m. *Miner.* rothoffite; —grau, adj. iron-gray; —graupen, f. pl. *Miner.* granular iron; —grube, f. iron-mine, iron-pit; —guß, m. cast-iron; —gußwaaren, pl. hard iron-castings; (feine) fancy-hardware; —gyps, m. see —blau; —haken, m. book [illegible] (brass-founders); —haltig, adj. ferriferous [illegible]; ferruginous, chalybeate (water); *Chem.* [illegible]; —hammer, m. 1) large hammer; 2) or —hammerwerk, n. forge, iron-mill, iron-works; [illegible]handel, m. iron-trade, iron-mongery; —händler, m. hardware-merchant, iron-monger; —handlung, f. see —gewölbe; —hart, I. adj. as hard as iron; II. s. (str.) m. *Bot.* common vervain (—kraut, 2); —holz, n. iron-wood; —holzbaum, see —baum; —hut, m., —hütchen, —hütlein, n. 1) *Bot.* wolf's bane, [illegible]-flower, aconite (*Aconitum [illegible]* [illegible] L.); 2) *Herald.* vair(e); —hütte, f. forge, iron-works; —hüttenkunde, f. metallurgy of iron; —jaspis, m. *Miner.* ferruginous jasper; *Chem.-s.* —jodid, n. iodide of iron; —kalium, n. ferrate of potassium; [illegible], m. unmixed iron; —kasten, m. [illegible]; —kies, m. martial or iron pyrites; [illegible], m. iron flint, ferruginous quartz; —[illegible], adj. ferro-silicic; —kieselsaures [illegible], ferro-silicate; —kieselsäure, f. ferro-silicic acid; —kitt, m. iron-glue; —klumpen, [illegible], sow or pig of iron; —knecht, m. [illegible]; —kochsalz, n. iron-salt; —[illegible], m. iron-mongery, iron(or nail)-trade; [illegible]; —[illegible], m. see —händler; —[illegible], iron-clad (of a ship); —kraut, [illegible] *Bot.* 1) iron-wort (*Sideritis* L. [illegible]); 2) vervain (*Verbena officinalis* L.);

—krystall, see —crystall; —kuchen, m. wafer (-cake); —kugel, f. see —niere; —kupfer, n. composition of iron and copper; —lack, m. iron-varnish; —laden, m. see —gewölbe; —lage, f. casing; —lahn, m. *T.* flattened iron-wire; —lech, n. iron-dross; —legirung, f. amalgama of iron; —letten, m. iron-clay; —loth, n. iron-solder; —luppen, f. *Smelt.* pl. iron lumps or loops; —ma(a)l, n. see —fleck; —mandelstein, m. *Miner.* clay-stone; —manganerz, n. *Miner.* ferriferous manganese; —mann, m. *Miner.* see —glimmer; —mine, f. 1) see —bergwerk; 2) poor iron-ore not adapted to smelting purposes; —mineral, n. granulated iron-ore (from Elba); —mohr, m. *Pharm.* black deutoxide of iron, *aethiops martialis* (lat.); —mulm, m. efflorescing clayey iron-ore; —niederschlag, m. *Chem.* precipitate of iron; —niere, f. 1) *Miner.* aetites, eagle stone, geode, clay-iron-ore; 2) *Geogn.* pea-ore; —nüsse, f. pl. *Miner.* globular blood-stones or hematites containing ferruginous parts; —ocher, n. iron-ochre, ochre of iron; —ofen, m. foundry, finery; —öl, n. *Chem.* solution of iron in muriatic acid; *Miner.-s.* —oolith, m. see —roggenstein; —opal, m. striped jasper; —oxyd, n. magnetic iron-stone, oxide of iron; *Chem.-s.* —oxydhydrat, n. hydratic oxide of iron; —oxydsalze, f. pl. sesquioxide salts; —oxydul, n. protoxide of iron; —oxydulammonial, m. (blausaurer) ferro-cyanate of ammonia; —oxydulkali, n. (blausaures) ferro-cyanate of potassa; —oxydulkupferoxyd, n. (blausaures) ferro-cyanate of copper; —oxydulsalze, n. magnetic iron-stone; —oxydulsalze, n. pl. iron-salts; —pecherz, n. *Miner.* brown iron-ore; —platin, n. amalgamation of iron with platina; —platte, f. iron-plate; dünne —platten, pl. sheet-iron; —präparate, n. pl. *Chem. & Pharm.* ferruginous medicines, chalybeates; —probe, f. iron-test; —pulver, n. *Pharm.* pulverised iron-filings; —quarz, m. see —kiesel; —quelle, f. see Stahlquelle; —rahm, m. *Miner.* hematite (brown and red); —rahmig, adj. hematitic, covered with iron-froth; —reichkraut, n. *Bot.* common vervain (—kraut, 2); —reif(en), m. iron hoop; *Miner.-s.* —resin, m. oxalate of iron (*Tuh.*); roggenstein, m. ferruginous egg- or roe-stone; —rosen, pl. crystallised groups of iron-ore (found in Switzerland); —rost, m. rust of iron; (aufgelöster) iron-liquor; —rostfarbe, f. ferruginous colour; —rostfarbig, adj. ferruginous; —roth, n. *T.* colcothar, English red; —ruthe, f. (flache) flat iron-bar; —safran, m. *Pharm.* *crocus martis* (lat.); —salmiak, m. *Miner.* native ferruginous sal-ammoniac; *Chem.* (—salmiakblumen, f. pl.) mixture of sal-ammoniac and muriate of iron; —salz, n. *Chem.* sulphate of iron; —salze, pl. *Miner.* sparry iron-stone; *Miner.-s.* —sammeterz, n. scaly brown iron, brown iron-froth; —sand, m. ferruginous or iron-sand; —sanderz, n. conglomerate of quartz with iron ochre; —sandstein, m. a brown or yellow lias-sandstone containing many ferruginous parts; —sau, f. *Smelt.* see —schwüle; *Miner.-s.* —säuerling, —schaum, m. iron-froth, kish; —scheel, n. wolfram; —scheibe, f. miner's compass; —schicht, f. *Smelt.* batch of iron; —schiene, see —bahnschiene; —schimmel, m. iron gray (horse); —schlacke, f. dross of iron, iron-dross; —schlag, m. 1) *a)* slag of iron; *b)* see Hammerschlag; 2) *provinc.* the privilege or monopoly of dealing in iron wares; —schlich, —schlick, m. muddy iron-ore; —schmidt, m. iron-smith, blacksmith; —schmiede, f. iron-forge; —schneidemühle, f. iron-slitting mill; —schneider, m. engraver of stamps; —schneidewerk, n. see —schneidemühle; —schörl, m. *Miner.* ferruginous shorl; —schrot, m. small-shot; —schuß, m. see —fleck; —schüssig, adj. see —haltig; —schwärze, f. 1) *Miner.* see

—glanz; 2) *T.* iron-liquor; —schweif, m. see —glimmer; —schweifig, adj. containing granular iron-glance; —schwerstein, m. *Miner.* tungsten; —schwüle, f. *Smelt.* sow of iron; —seil, n. see —riemen; —silicat, n. *Chem.* silicate of iron; —sinter, m. 1) *Sm.* iron-scale (Hammerschlag); 2) *Miner.* iron-sinter; pitchy iron-ore; —spaltwerk, n. *T.* slitting-rollers, slitters, cutters; *Miner.-s.* —spath, m. sparry iron-ore; —spiegel, m. specular iron-stone; —spinell, m. ceylanite, pleonaste; —sprott, m. arsenical pyrites; —stab, m., —stange, f. iron-bar; —staub, m. iron-dust; —stein, m. iron-stone; siderite; hematite ore; —steinig, adj. containing iron-stone; —stufe, f. lump of iron-ore; —stück, n. ingot, wedge; —sulfür, n. sulphuret of iron; —sulphat, n. sulphate of iron; —sulphuret, n. sulphuret of iron; —sumpf, m. martial bog or clay; —sumpferz, n. *Miner.* bog iron-ore; —syrup, m. *Chem.* iron-syrup.

Eis'ente, (*w.*) *f. Ornith.* long-tailed northern duck, the black-throated diver (*Harelda glacialis* L.).

Ei'sen ..., *in comp.* —theilchen, n. iron(y) or martial particle; kleine —theile des Oberbaus einer Eisenbahn, m. pl. the little iron fittings of the permanent way (*Herbelot*); —thon, m. *Miner.* iron-clay; —thor, n. iron-gate; —tinctur, f. *Pharm.* tincture of iron; —titan, m. *Miner.* iserine; —träger, m. *T.* (einer Brücke) iron girder. *Chem.-s.* —übersulfid, n. bisulphuret; —vitriol, n. green vitriol, sulphate of iron; —vitriolblumen, f. pl. flowers of green vitriol; —vitriolzapfen, m. pl. green copper in the form of stalactites; —vogel, m. see Braunelle; —waare, f. iron-ware; hardware; —wasser, n. chalybeate water; —weinstein, m. *Pharm.* tartrate of iron; —weinsteinsauer, adj. *Chem.* ferro-tartaric; —werk, n. 1) the iron-work (of a ship, &c.); 2) see —hammer; —wurz, —wurzel, f. 1) see Glockenblume; 2) see —kraut, 1; —zeitte, f. *Bot.* iron-wood tree; —zeug, n. iron tools or implements; *Miner.-s.* —zinkblende, f. a variety of zincblende; —zinnerz, n. fibrous tin-ore.

Ei'sern, adj. iron: 1) (made) of iron, irony; *fig.-s.* 2) most persevering, intense, strong, durable; 3) fatal, stern, unbending; 4) unfeeling, hard, insensible; 5) †, *Law-s.* standing, inalienable; ein e-es Boot, an iron-built boat; e-er Brief, letter of respite, protection, or grace; ein e-es Capital, capital invested or sunk, of which only the interest is paid; das e-e Zeitalter, iron age; e-e Stirn, brazen face; e-er Fleiß, unwearied industry or application; e-e Geduld, imperturbable patience; e-e Gesundheit, robust health; e-e Herzen, hearts of steel; e-e Nothwendigkeit, dire necessity; e-er Schlaf, unbroken sleep; e-er Entschluß, e-e Treue, unwavering resolution, fidelity; e-er Pacht, see Erbpacht.

Eis' ..., *in comp.* E-esbande, pl. *fig.* icy-fetters, the being locked up or chained by severe frost; —fahrt, f. see lauf; [die Bächlein] die er in seiner E-esfalle | so streng gefangen hielt (*Lenau*), [the brooklets] which he held closely imprisoned in his icy thrall; —falter, m. riband-butterfly; —feld, n. ice-field; —fisch, m. *Zool.* ice-whale; —fischerei, f. fishing under the ice; —fläche, f. field or sheet of ice, ice-field; —flacke, —flarde, —flösse, f. floe of ice, ice-patch; —frei, adj. clear of ice; —freie See, clear water; —fuchs, m. *Zool.* arctic fox (*Canis lagopus* L.); —gang, m. 1) the driving or floating of ice (in a river); 2) *Mar.* the first lining of the bow of a ship; der —gang der Elbe hielt die Fahrt des Schiffes auf, the floating ice of the Elbe impeded the progress of the vessel; —gebirge, n. ice-mountains; —gegend, f. frozen region; —gestade, n. frozen shore; —glas, n. frosted glass;

[illegible] *brasiliensis* Bl.); —orden, *m.* order of the elephant (a Danish order); —papier, *n.* [illegible] elephant-paper (a sort of very large paper); —reis, *m.* species of rice (white and [illegible]-corned); —robbe, *f. Zool.* sea-elephant, [illegible], bottle-nose (*Macrorhinus proboscideus* F. C. [*Phoca leonina* L.]); —rüssel, *m.* [illegible], trunk of an elephant; —wal, *m.* [illegible] grampus; —zahn, *m.* tooth of an elephant: ivory; *Comm.* —zähne (*pl.*) von frisch [illegible] Thieren, first sort elephant's tusks; [illegible] —zähne, split tusks, fissures; [illegible] —zähne, scrivelloes.

* Elevatiōn', (*w.*) *f.* (*Lat.*) *T.* elevation; [illegible]winkel, *m.* angle of elevation. — Elevi'ren, (*w.*) *v. tr. Comm.* to return (a protested [bill]) to the last endorser.

Elf, *cardinal number*, eleven.

Elf, (*w.*) *m.*, El'fe, Elfin, (*w.*) *f.* elf, fairy, goblin; —bogenspitze, *m. pl.* elf arrow-heads, elf arrows.

Elf'eck, (*str.*) *n. Geom.* hendecagon.

Elfen, *adj. see* Elfenbeinern.

Elfenartig, *adj.* elf-like, elfish, fairy-like.

Elfenbein, *s.* I. (*str.*) *n.* ivory; das gebrannte —, bone- *or* ivory-black; geraspeltes —, ivory-shavings; gegrabenes —, ivory of Muscovy; vegetabilisches —, *see* —nuß; weiß gebranntes —, burnt hartshorn; II. *in comp.* —blätter, *n. pl.* ivory leaves, sheet ivory; —drechsler, *m.* turner in ivory. [ivory.

Elfenbeinern, Elfenbeinen, *adj.* (of)

Elfenbein..., *in comp.* —küste, *f. Geogr.* Ivory Coast (in Africa); —möve, *f. Ornith.* ivory gull (*Larus eburneus* L.); —nuß, *f. Bot.* ivory-nut (*Phytelephas macrocarpa*); —papier, *n.* ivory-paper; —schwarz, *n.* bone- *or* ivory-black.

Elfengras, *n. Bot.* moor-grass.

Elfenhaft, *adj.* fairy-like.

Elfen..., *in comp.* —könig, *m.* king of the elfs; —königin, *f.* fairy queen; —kreise, —ringe, *m. pl.* fairy-rings; —märchen, *n.* fairy-tale.

Elfer, (*str.*) *m.* 1) member of a commission, society, &c. consisting of eleven in number; 2) wine of the vintage of the year (1700, 1800 and) eleven.

Elferlei, *adj.* (of) eleven sorts.

Elffach, *adj.* elevenfold.

Elfjährig, *adj.* of eleven years.

Elflocke, (*w.*) *f.* elf-lock.

Elfmal, *adv.* eleven times. [elf-shot.

Elfschuß, (*str.*; *pl.* E-schüsse) *m.* elf-arrow,

[illegible], [illegible]e, (*w.*) *f. provinc.* fin-scale, rudd (Rotte). [half.

Elfte, *adj.* eleventh; —halb, ten and a

Elftel, (*str.*) *n.* the eleventh part.

Elftens, *adv.* in the eleventh place, eleventhly.

Elger, (*str.*) *m. Mar.* fisgig, fish-gig.

Eli'a, Eli'as, *m.* Elijah, Eliah, Elias (*P. N.*); E-feuer, (*str.*) *n. see* Helenenfeuer.

* Elidi'ren, (*w.*) *v. tr.* (*Lat.*) *Gramm.* to elide.

Eli'sa, *m.* Elisha, Elis (*P. N.*).

Eli'sa, Eli'se, *f.* Eliza, Eliza (*P. N.*).

Eli'sabeth, *f.* Elizabeth (*P. N.*); E-[illegible], (*str.*) *n.* sweet-cicely.

* Elisiōn', (*w.*) *f.* (*Lat.*) *Gramm.* elision.

* Eli'te, (*w.*) *f.* (*Fr.*) the best *or* chosen part, (*Fr.*) élite (*gener.* of an army).

* Elixir', (*str.*) *n.* (*M. Lat.*) *Pharm.* elixir.

Elk, (*str.*) *m. see* Elch.

Ell'bogen, *see* Ellbogen.

Elle, (*w.*) *f.* ell (a measure [*usually*] of [illegible] —, yard; mit der — [illegible], to mete by the yard-measure.

[illegible], *see* Ellbogen.

[illegible]..., *in comp.* —breit, *adj.* one ell [illegible]; —handel, *m.* draper's trade; —lang, [illegible], *adj.* 1) an ell (a yard) [illegible]; —maß, *m.*,

—stock, *m.* ell; yard-measure *or* -stick; —waare, *f. Comm.* dry goods; —waarenhändler, *m.* dry-goods merchant; —waarenhandlung, *f.* dry-goods business; —weise, *adv.* by the ell *or* yard.

El'ler, (*w.*) *f.* alder (Erle).

El'lerling, (*str.*) *m.* minnow (Elritze).

El'lern, *adj.* aldern (Erlen).

* Ellip'se, (*w.*) *f.* (*Gr.*) *Gramm.* & *Geom.* ellipsis. — Ellipsoid', (*str.*) *n.* ellipsoid. — Ellipsoi'disch, *adj.* ellipsoidal. — Ellip'tisch, I. *adj.* elliptic(al); II. *adv.* elliptically.

Elms'feuer, (*str.*) *n. see* Helenenfeuer.

* Elo'ge [*pr.* el'ohe], (*w.*) *f. rarely n.* (*Fr.* éloge, *from Lat.* elogium, *n.*) eulogy, praise, encomium, panegyric; *pl.* compliments.

El'rich, *m.* Alaric (*P. N.*).

El'ritze (Eld'ritze, El'deritze, El'leritze, Eld'rich, El'terse), (*w.*) *f.* 1) *Ichth.* minnow (*Leuciscus phoxinus* L.); 2) (Elritze) *see* Elsebeerbaum.

El'saß, (*str.*) *n. Geogr.* Alsace; Alsatia. — El'sasser, El'sässer, (*str.*) *m.* an inhabitant of Alsace, Alsatian. — El'sassisch, El'sässisch, *adj.* Alsatian.

Els'beere, *see* Elsebeere.

A. Else, Els'beth, *f.* (*dimin.* Els'chen, *n.*) Elspeth, Alison, Alice (*P. N.*).

B. El'se (Elst), (*w.*) *f. provinc.* 1) *for* Erle; 2) *for* Alose; 3) *T.* awl (of sail-makers); —baum, *m.* black alder-tree; —beere, *f.* service-berry; —beerbaum, *m. Bot.* 1) service-(berry)-tree (*Sorbus torminalis* L.); 2) *see* Traubenkirsche.

El'ster, (*w.*) *f. Ornith.* pie, magpie (*Pica caudata* Briss.); —alk, *m. Ornith.* black-billed auk (*Alca torda* L.); —auge, *n.* corn (on the toes, &c.); —baum, *m.* 1) *see* Erle; 2) *see* Traubenkirsche; —entchen, *n. Ornith.* smew (*Mergus albellus* L.); —kirsche, *f. see* Traubenkirsche; —würger, *m. Ornith.* Brazilian king-bird (*Bethylus picatus* Lath.).

El'terlich, *adj.* parental.

El'termutter, (*str.*, *pl.* E-mütter) *f.* great grandmother, grandam.

El'tern, *pl.* parents.

El'ternlos, *adj.* parentless.

El'tern..., *in comp.* —mord, —mörder, *m.* parenticide, parricide.

El'ternschaft, (*w.*) *f.* character *or* social position of parents, parentage.

El'tervater, (*str.*, *pl.* E-väter) *m.* great grandfather; ancestor, forefather.

El'tis, (*str.*) *m. see* Iltis. [Elysian.

* Elysä'isch, Ely'sisch, *adj.* *Gr. Myth.*

* Ely'sium, (*str.*, *pl.* (*w.*) Ely'sien, (*Schiller*, *unusual*: Ely'sen)) *n. Gr. Myth.* Elysium.

* Email' [*pr.* emal[']], (*str.*, *pl.* E-s) *n.* & *m.* (*Fr.*) enamel; —farben, *f. pl.* vitrifiable pigments; —gemälde, *n.* enamelled picture; —maler, *m.* painter in enamel; —malerei, *f.* enamel painting. — Emailleur' [*pr.* emal-[ö]r'], (*str.*) *m.* enameller. — Emailli'ren [emalye'ren], (*w.*) *v. tr.* to enamel; das —, *s. s.* (*str.*) *n.* (art of) enamelling.

* Emancipatiōn', (*w.*) *f.* (*Lat.*) emancipation. — Emancipi'ren, (*w.*) *v. tr.* to emancipate.

* Emballa'ge [*pr.* —â'zhe], (*w.*) *f.* (*Fr.*) envelop(e), *Comm.* packing, mailing; (in Speisewirthschaften) package; die — abnehmen, to strip the bale; —kosten, *f. pl.* charge for packing, package. — Emballi'ren, (*w.*) *v. tr.* to bale *or* pack up, to embale, to mail; emballirt, *p. a.* mailed up.

* Embar'go, (*str.*, *pl.* E-s) *n.* (*Span.*) embargo; unter — legen, mit — belegen, to (put under) embargo; das — aufheben, to raise the embargo.

Em'bergans, *f. see* Imber, 2.

* Emblem', (*str.*) *n.* (*Gr.*) emblem (Sinnbild). — Emblema'tisch, *adj.* emblematic(al).

* Em'bolus, (*pl.* (*Lat.*) Em'boli) *m.* (*Lat.*) *Mech.* piston, forcer, embolus.

* Em'bryo, (*str.*, *pl.* E-s, *or* (*w.*) Embryo'nen) *m.* (*Gr.*) *Physiol.*, &c. embryo. [ment).

Emd, (*str.*) *n.* (*Swiss.*) after-grass (Grum-

* Emeritirt', *p. a.* (*L. Lat.*) emerited, having been allowed to retire from office *or* public service.

* Emigrant', (*w.*) *m.*, Emigran'tin, (*w.*) *f.* (*Lat.*) emigrant. — Emigratiōn', (*w.*) *f.* emigration. — Emigri'ren, (*w.*) *v. intr.* (*aux.* sein) to emigrate.

E'mil, *m.* Æmilius, Emile (*P. N.*).

Emi'lie, *f.* (*dimin.* Emil'chen, (*str.*) *n.* Emmy) Emily, Emilia (*P. N.*).

* Eminent', *adj.* (*Lat.*) eminent.

* Eminenz', (*w.*) *f.* (*Lat.*) *Rom. Cath.* eminence (a title given to cardinals).

E'mir, (*str.*, *pl.* E-e *or* E-s) *m.* (*Arab.*) Emir, Emeer, Ameer, Amir (prince, lord, a title of dignity among the Arabs & Turks).

* Emissär', (*str.*) *m.* (*Fr.*) emissary.

* Emissiōn', (*w.*) *f.* (*Lat.*) issue, emission; E-course, *m.* rate of issue. — Emittir'bar, *adj.* issuable. — Emitti'ren, (*w.*) *v. tr.* to issue (money *or* paper currency). — Emitti'rung, (*w.*) *f.* the (act of) issuing (Emission), issue (of money). [emmet (Ameise).

† Em'meise, (*w.*) *f.* (*Luther*, &c.) ant,

A. Em'mer, (*w.*, *pl.* E-n) *f.* †, embers.

B. Em'mer, (*str.*) *m.* (—korn, *n.*) *see* Dinkel.

Em'merich, *m.* Emory, Merick (*P. N.*).

Em'merling, (*str.*) *m.* 1) *see* Goldammer; 2) *see* Engerling; 3) *see* Amarelle.

Em'merseegel, (*str.*) *n. Mar.* sprit-sail.

Empfah'en, († &) * *see* Empfangen.

Empfang', (*str.*) *m.* receipt; reception; bei —, on receipt *or* delivery; nach —, on (*or* after the) receipt, when received; vor —, previous to receipt; in — nehmen, to receive, accept; to take in possession, to take charge of (goods); den Tag zum — bestimmen, to fix the day for receiving or delivery; indem wir (Ihnen) den besten — wünschen, wishing it (*or* them) safe to hand; guten — bereiten, to provide the needful, due reception *or* acceptance (for a bill); — erklärt (Rentenbriefe), on acknowledgment of delivery or receipt.

Empfang'en, (*str.*) *v.* I. *tr.* to receive, take, get; *Comm.* to be favoured with or in receipt of (a letter); — Sie unsern besten Dank, accept our best thanks; Einen —, to receive, to welcome one; to give one a (kind, &c.) reception; er wurde kalt —, he met with a cold reception; wenn Sie dieses —, when this comes to hand; II. *intr.* to become pregnant, to conceive; —, *pp.* (auf Quittungen) received payment (Rd. Pt.), settled, acquitted, paid, *pr.* acquit; baar und richtig —, payment duly received.

Empfäng'er, (*str.*) *m.*, E-in, (*w.*) *f.* receiver, recipient; *Comm.* consignee (of a cargo).

Empfäng'lich, I. *adj.* susceptible (für, of), sensible (to); sehr *or* lebhaft —, feelingly alive, delicately responsive (to); — machen, to dispose (für, to). II. E-keit, (*w.*) *f.* susceptibility (für, of), sensibility (to).

Empfäng'niß, (*str.*) *f.* conception.

Empfang'..., *in comp.* E-anzeige, *f.* acknowledgment; E-anzeige machen, to give an acknowledgment, to acknowledge; unter E-anzeige, under (with) advice; E-berechtigung, *f.* (Nachweis der —) authority for the receipt; —nahme, *f.* reception, receipt; —schein, *m.* receipt (in writing, &c.), acquittance, quittance; E-zimmer, *m.* reception- (*or* receiving-)room. [[illegible]

Empfeh', *s. s.* (*str.*) *m. coll. for* Empfeh-

Empfeh'lbar, *adj.* recommendable.

Empfeh'len, (*str.*) *v.* I. *tr.* to recommend,

commend (with an [& Acc.], or with the Dat., to); an wen or wem wird er Sie —? to whom will he recommend you? dringend —, to press upon (the attention, &c.); II. refl. 1) to present one's respects (Einem, to one); 2) to take (one's) leave, to bid adieu, to make one's adieux (to one); — Sie mich ..., present my compliments (duty) to ..., remember me (kindly) or (give) my service to ...; er empfiehlt sich Ihnen bestens, he presents his best respects or regards to you; ich empfehle mich Ihnen, farewell, adieu, your servant; das Unglück empfiehlt sich unserm Mitleid, misfortune is a recommendation to our pity; eine Methode, die sich empfiehlt, an eligible method; unser Empfohlener, Comm. the gentleman we address (recommend) to you.

Empfeh'lenswerth, *adj.* see Empfehlungswerth. [person recommending.

Empfeh'ler, *(str.) m.* recommender, the

Empfeh'lung, *(w.) f.* 1) recommendation: *a)* commendation; *b)* introduction; *c) Comm.* reference; 2) expression of regard: compliments, respects: auf die —, at the recommendation: er hat gute E-en, he is well (or respectably) recommended, &c.: machen Sie meine —, see Empfehlen Sie mich.

Empfeh'lungs..., *in comp.* —brief, *m.*, —schreiben, *n.* letter of recommendation (introduction), commendatory (recommendative) letter: *fig.* passport, credential; —karte, *f.* card of introduction: trade (or trading)-card, business-card (of a travelling clerk, &c.); —werth, —würdig, *adj.* recommendable: —würdigkeit, *f.* recommendableness.

Empfind'bar, I. *adj.* sensible, perceptible, perceivable; II. E-keit, *(w.) f.* perceptibility.

Empfindelei', *(w.) f.* sentimentalism, affectation or show of sentiment or sensibility.

Empfin'deln, *(w.) v. intr.* to sentimentalise, to affect sentiment or sensibility.

Empfin'den, *(str.) v. tr.* to feel; to perceive, to be sensible of: to experience; etwas übel —, to take ill or offence at...; tief empfunden, home-felt; er ließ sie sein höchstes Mißfallen —, he visited her with his sternest displeasure: *cf. also* Fühlen.

Empfind'ler, *(str.) m.*, **Empfind'lerin**, *(w.) f. conf.* sentimentalist.

Empfind'lich, I. *adj.* 1) sensible (für or gegen, to); 2) *a)* sensitive, easily affected, fastidious, nice; *b)* irritable, touchy, resenting, resentful, thin-skinned, pettish; 3) causing pain, keen, smart (blow, &c.); sore (affliction), tender (point); grievous (loss); acute (pains); eine e-e Stelle, a raw; — im Maule sein, *Man.* having a fine or good mouth; — kalt, pinching cold; die Beleidigung war ihm sehr —, he felt the offence deeply or keenly; II. E-keit, *(w.) f.* 1) sensibility (gegen, to); 2) sensitiveness, fastidiousness; irritability, touchiness, pettishness; 3) keenness, sharpness, &c.

Empfind'ling, *(str.) m. conf.* sentimentalist.

Empfind'niß, *(str.) f. & n.* sentiment, feeling.

Empfind'sam, I. *adj.* 1) delicate (in feeling or sentiment, also in taste), feeling, sensible, susceptible; 2) (morbidly) sentimental; *coll.* lackadaisical; II. E-keit, *(w.) f.* 1) sensibility, susceptibility; 2) sentimentality.

Empfin'dung, *(w.) f.* sensation, sense, perception; feeling; sentiment.

Empfin'dungs..., *in comp., &c.* —eigenheit, *f.* idiosyncrasy; —fähig, *adj.* sensible; —fähigkeit, —kraft, *f.* sensitive faculty, sensitiveness; —laut, *m. Gramm.* interjection; —leer, —los, *adj.* void of sensation or feeling, insensible, unfeeling, apathetic, dead; —losigkeit, *f.* want of feeling, unfeelingness; insensibility; —sitz, *m.* sensory, sensorium; —vermögen, *n.* sensitive faculty, (power of) perception or sensation, perceptibility; —voll, *adj.* full of feeling; *adv.* feelingly; —wort, *n. Gramm.* interjection.

* **Empha'se**, *(w.) f. (Gr.)* emphasis. — **Empha'tisch**, *adj.* emphatic(al).

* **Empirie'**, **Empi'rik**, *(w.) f. (Gr.)* empiricism. — **Empi'riker**, *(str.) m.* empiric. — **Empi'risch**, *adj.* empirical.

Empor', *adv.* on high, up, upwards, aloft, *cf.* Auf *with its comp., and* in die Höhe; sich —arbeiten, to work one's way (up), to rise; —bringen, to raise; —fahren, *see* Auffahren, *intr.*; —heben, to uplift, heave up, upheave; —hebung, *f. Rom. Cath.* elevation (of the host); —helfen, to help up; —bühne, —kirche, *f.* church-gallery, quire; aisle; — kömmling, *m.* an upstart, parvenu; —kommen, 1) to get up or on (in the world), to raise one's self; 2) to rise, thrive, succeed; come up; to spring up; —läutern, *see* —treiben; —ragen, *see* Hervorragen; sich —ranken (*Plants*, of the ivy), to rise or climb upwards by its tendrils; —schener, *f. see* Balken, 4, *b*; —schnellen, *v.* I. *tr.* to jerk upwards; II. *intr.* to fly upwards; sich —schwingen, to soar aloft; to rise (to distinction); —stehen, to stand upright or on end; —steigen, to rise; —streben, to strive to rise, to strive upwards; to aspire (to); —strebend, *p. a.* aspiring; —treiben, *Chem.* to sublimate.

Empö'ren, *(w.) v.* I. *tr.* 1) to stir up; to agitate; to raise, revolt; 2) *fig.* to revolt, shock (the feelings, &c.); II. *refl.* to rebel, revolt, mutiny, rise against; e-d, *p. a.* shocking, revolting.

Empö'rer, *(str.) m.* mutineer, revolter, rebel, reboller, insurgent, insurrectionist.

Empö'rerisch, *adj.* seditious, mutinous, insurrectionary, rebellious.

* **Empo'rium**, *(str., pl.* Empo'rien*) n. (Lat.) fig.* staple(-town), market-town, mart, emporium.

Empö'rung, *(w.) f.* 1) the (act of) rising against ...; sedition, mutiny, rebellion, revolt, insurrection; 2) *fig.* indignation; E-sgeist, *m.* seditiousness; e-süchtig, *adj. see* Empörerisch.

Em'se, *(w.) f. provinc.* ant (Ameise).

Em'sig, I. *adj.* assiduous, industrious, diligent; active, busy, eager, sedulous, earnest, hard (study, &c.); II. E-keit, *(w.) f.* assiduity, industry, diligence, activity; sedulousness, eagerness. [busily, &c.

Em'siglich, *adv.* († &) *provinc.* assiduously,

* **Emulsion'**, *(w.) f. (L. Lat.) Pharm.* emulsion.

* **Enkau'stik**, *(w.) f. (Gr.) Paint.* encaustic painting. — **Enkau'stisch**, *adj.* encaustic (Platten, tiles).

* **Encla've** [*pr.* angklä'vel, *(w.) f. (Fr.)* a piece of land (country) enclosed within another state or dominion.

* **Enkli'tica**, *(undecl., pl. [Lat.]* E-'icä*) f. (Lat.-Gr.) Gramm.* enclitic noun. — **Enkli'tisch**, *adj.* enclitic.

* **Encyklopädie'**, *(w.) f. (Gr.)* encyclopedia, cyclopedia. — **Encyklopä'disch**, *adj.* encyclopedical, encyclopedian. — **Encyklopädist'**, *(w.) m.* encyclopedist.

End'..., *in comp.* —absicht, *f.* final design, final view, end; —bahnhof, *m.* (railway-) terminus.

End'bar, *adj.* endable, terminable.

End'..., *in comp.* —beschluß, *m.* ultimatum; —brei, *n. see* Schalbrett; —buchstabe, *m.* final letter.

End'chen, *(str.) n.* (*dimin. of* Ende) end, a small remnant, fragment; das — Licht, candle's end.

En'de, *(str.) n.* 1) *a)* end; issue; limit; close, termination, conclusion; expiration (of a term); *b) fig.* death; 2) *Sport. a)* single (of a hart); *b) pl.* antlers, branches, broaches;

Endnis, (*str.*) *n.* (*l. u.*) end, termination.

* **Endossi'ren**, (*w.*) *v. tr. see* Indossiren.

End..., *in comp.* —pfeiler, *m. Archit.* (einer Wendeltreppe) newel: —punkt, *m.* extreme point; terminus (of a railway): —rede, *f.* epilogue; —reim, *m.* rhyme at the end of a line. [— erreichen, to come to an end.

End'schaft, (*w.*) *f.* end, close, issue; seine

End..., *in comp.* —schraube, *f. T.* endless screw; —silbe, *f.* final syllable, termination; —spitze, *f.* extremity; —spruch, *m. see* —urtheil.

* **Endstehend**, *adj. & adv.* 1) *see* Endesgenannt, 2; 2) below, at foot.

Endung, (*w.*) *f.* termination, end; die griechischen Adjective dreier E-en, the Greek adjectives of three endings.

End..., *in comp.* —ursache, *f.* final cause; —urtheil, *n. Law,* ultimate *or* definitive sentence *or* decision, decretory; —vertrag, *m.* definitive treaty; —zeit, *f.* final term; —ziel, *n.* final aim; —zweck, *m.* (ultimate) end, (final) aim, purpose, scope, design, intention.

* **Energie'**, (*w.*) *f.* (*Gr.*) energy. — **Ener'gisch**, *adj.* energetical.

Eng, *adj. see* Enge.

* **Engagement** [*pr.* Anggāhschmāng'], (*str., pl.* E-s), *n.* (*Fr.*) engagement. — **Engagi'ren**, [illegible] (*w.*) *v. tr.* to engage; engagirtes Capital, *Comm.* funds locked up: unsere Geldkräfte sind schon sehr engagirt, our funds are already heavily drawn upon (*Nob. & Gr.*).

Eng..., *in comp.* —brüstig, *adj.* narrow-chested; —befreundet, *adj.* intimately connected *or* acquainted; —brüstig, *adj.* asthmatic(al), short-breathed, short-winded, pursy; *Farr.* short-foundered; —brüstigkeit, *f.* asthma, dyspnoea, shortness of breath, pursiness; *Farr.* short-foundering.

Eng'e, I. *adj.* narrow; close (*also fig.*); tight, strait; contracted, condensed, small; restricted (sense of a word, &c.); es wurde mir zu —, I felt oppressed and stifled; — Fugen, *Mas.* close joints; ein e-r Paß, Weg, narrow pass, defile; e-r Athem, asthma; der e-re Ausschuß, select committee; — zusammenziehen, to straiten, contract tightly *or* closely, to tighten; e-r machen, to tighten; to take in (a dress); II. e. (*w.*) *f.* 1) narrowness; closeness, straitness, tightness; 2) narrow place *or* passage; 3) *fig.* straits, difficulty, embarrassment; in die — treiben, to hem in, to drive *or* reduce to straits, to beset, press hard, embarrass, to drive home, to run down *or* close.

Eng'el, s. I. (*str.*) *m.* 1) angel; 2) *see* —fisch; II. *in comp.* —blümchen, *n. Bot.* mountain everlasting, mountain cudweed, cat's-foot (*Gnaphalium dioicum* L.); —brot, *n.* angelical food, manna.

Eng'elchen, **Eng'elein**, (*str.*) *n.* (*dimin. of* Engel) 1) little angel; 2) *Bot. a)* poetic *or* white narcissus (*Narcissus poeticus* L.); *b)* mistletoe (*Viscum album* L.); 3) *Entom.* a species of dragon-fly (*Libellula puella* (*virgo* L.)); 4) *Ornith. see* Zeisig.

Eng'el..., *in comp.* —fisch, *m. Ichth.* angel-fish, monk, fallow-scale (*Squatina angelus* C.); —gleich, *adj.* angel-like, angelic; —hai, *m. see* —fisch; —köpfchen, *n.* 1) little angel's head; 2) *Bot.* common *or* lesser maple (*Acer campestre* L.); —kraut, *n. Bot.* mountain avens (*Dryas octopetala* L.).

* **Eng'elland**, *n. see* England.

Eng'elram, *m.* Ingram (*P. N.*).

Eng'el..., *in comp.* —rein, *adj.* as pure as an angel; —roche, *m. Ichth.* a species of ray ([illegible] C.); E-[illegible], *m. Fossil.* [illegible]; E-[illegible], *m.* angelic apparition; [illegible]; E-[illegible], *f.* a species of pear; [illegible], E-[illegible], *n.* mountain globe-flower (*Trollius europaeus* L.); E-geduld, *f.* angelic patience; E-gruß, *m.* Ave-Mary; E-kopf, *m. Archit., &c.* seraph, cherub; E-de

köpfchen, *n. see* Engelsköpfchen; —speise, *f. see* —brot; *Bot.-s.* —süß, *n.* polypody, wall-fern (*Polypodium vulgare* L.); —weihe, *f.* Michaelmas; —wurz, *f.* angelica (*Archangelica officinalis* L.); wilde —wurz, *Angelica silvestris* L.

Eng'en, (*w.*) *v.* I. *tr.* to straiten, narrow; to pinch; to press; II. *refl.* to get narrow, small, to contract.

Eng'erling, (*str.*) *m. Entom.* canker-worm, grub; stag-worm; wornil.

Eng'heit, (*w.*) *f. l. u. for* Enge.

Eng'..., *in comp.* —herzig, *adj.* narrow-minded, narrow-hearted (*or* -souled), illiberal; —herzigkeit, *f.* narrow-mindedness, illiberality.

Eng'land, *n.* England.

Eng'länder, (*str.*) *m.* 1) Englishman: die —, *pl.* the English; 2) *a)* an English horse; *b) see* Stutzschwanz; —sucht, **Engländerei'**, (*w.*) *f.* Anglomania. [English lady.

Eng'länderin, (*w.*) *f.* Englishwoman, an

Eng'ländern, (*w.*) *v. tr. see* Anglisiren.

Eng'lisch (**Eng'ländisch**, *l. u.*), I. *adj.* English; Anglican (church, &c.); e-e Bereiter, *m. pl.* equestrians; e-es Blau, queen's blue; e-e Distel, *Bot.* carline-thistle (*Carlina vulgaris* L.); e-e Erde, rotten-stone; e-es Gras, *see* Sandgras; ein e-er Garten, a garden *or* pleasure-grounds in the English style; e-es Gelb, patent yellow; e-es Gewürz, *see* Piment; e-e Haut, goldbeater's skin; e-er Haken, *Horol.* escapement; e-e Krankheit, rickets; mit der e-en Krankheit behaftet, rickety; e-es Leder, castinet; e-es Pflaster, court-plaster; e-es Pulver, algarot; e-es Roth, trip; e-es Salz, Epsom salt; e-er Schweiß, sweating-sickness; e-er Spinat, patience-dock (*Rumex patientia* L.); e-e kurze Waare, Birmingham ware; II. *or* das E-e, *s.* (*w.*) *n.* (die e-e Sprache) English.

Eng'lisch, *adj.* angelic(al), seraphic(al).

Englisi'ren, (*w.*) *v. tr. see* Anglisiren.

Eng'paß, (*str., pl.* Eng'pässe) *m.* a narrow pass *or* passage; strait; *Mil.* defile, defilee.

* **Engros'** [*pr.* Anggrō'] (*Fr. en gros*), in the gross, wholesale; —geschäft, *n.*, —handel, *m.* wholesale-business; —händler, *m. see* —verkäufer; —käufer, *m.* wholesale-purchaser; —preis, *m.* wholesale-price *or* cost; —verkauf, *m.* wholesale; —verkäufer, *m.* wholesale merchant, dealer in (the) gross.

Eng'schalig, *adj. see* Dichtschalig. [monic.

* **Enharmo'nisch**, *adj.* (*Gr.*) *Mus.* enhar-

* **Enkaustik'**, **Enkaus'tisch**, *see* Enc....

Enk'e, (*w.*) *m. provinc.* 1) plough-boy; 2) plough-peg.

Enk'el, (*str.*) *m.* 1) grandchild, grandson; 2) *provinc.* ankle. [ter.

Enk'elin, (*w.*) *f.* grandchild, granddaugh-

Enk'en, (*w.*) *v. tr. provinc.* 1) *see* Impfen; 2) *see* Pfropfen.

* **Enklave**, **Enklitica**, *see* Encl....

* **Enlevage** [*pr.* Anglvä'schä], (*w.*) *f.* (*Fr.*) chemical discharge; —druck, *m.* discharge-style, discolouring-style.

* **Ennuyi'ren** [*pr.* annüi'ren], (*w.*) *v. tr.* (*Fr.*) to tire; to annoy; *coll.* to bore, bother. — **Ennuyant'**, *adj.* annoying, tiresome, tedious, irksome; ein ennuyanter Mensch, a tiresome person (fellow), a bore.

* **Enorm'**, *adj.* (*Lat.*) enormous; huge (in dimension). — **Enormität'**, (*w.*) *f.* enormousness, hugeness; enormity (atrocity).

* **Enquête** [*pr.* angkä'te], (*w.*) *f.* (*Fr.*) *Parl., &c.* inquiry; *cf.* Ermittelung.

Ens'baum, (*str.*) *m. Hydr.* sleeper, stringpiece (Schwellbalken).

Ent..., *inseparable particle, prefixed to verbs, implying usually negation, privation, or separation, and sometimes the proceeding from the beginning, &c.*

Entad'ern, (*w.*) *v. tr.* to relieve *or* free from outlawry. [ty; *fig.* to degrade.

Entadeln, (*w.*) *v. tr.* to deprive of nobili-

Entä'dern, (*w.*) *v. tr.* to take out the veins *or* sinews of.

Entamt'en, (*w.*) *v. tr.* to deprive of office, to dismiss *or* discharge from office, to cashier.

Entar'ten, (*w.*) *v. intr.* (*aux.* sein) to degenerate, deteriorate; entar'tet, *p. a.* degenerate, depraved. — **Entar'tung**, (*w.*) *f.* degeneration, degeneracy, depravation.

Entäst'en, (*w.*) *v. tr.* to lop off the branches of (trees).

Entäu'ßern, (*w.*) *v. refl.* (*with Gen.*) to divest *or* strip one's self of, to deny one's self, to part with, abstain from, dispense with, forbear; to renounce, discard, disown.

Entäu'ßerung, (*w.*) *f.* 1) *see* Veräußerung; 2) privation, disowning, rejection, renunciation, abstinence.

Entbal'len, (*w.*) *v. tr.* to unbale, unpack.

Entbang'en, (*w.*) *v. tr.* to deprive of fear (Beruhigen).

Entbeh'ren, (*w.*) *v. tr.* (*& intr., with the Gen.*) 1) to be in want, destitute *or* void of, to be without, to be deprived of, to want, miss; 2) to do *or* to make shift without, to dispense with, to do without, to spare; ich kann noch etwas —, I have some (some of it *or* them) to spare; Einem etwas — lassen, to withhold a thing from one.

Entbeh'rlich, I. *adj.* dispensable, unnecessary; superfluous; — machen, to render unnecessary, to supersede; II. E-keit, (*w.*) *f.* dispensableness, superfluousness.

Entbeh'rung, (*w.*) *f.* privation; want; deprivation; abstinence.

Entbie'ten, (*str.*) *v. tr.* 1) to send word, to send for, to summon, to bid, order, command; to announce; 2) Einem seinen Gruß —, to send one's greeting *or* compliments to one, to present one's respects *or* regards; er ward zu seinem Regimente entboten, he was ordered to join his regiment.

Entbin'den, (*str.*) *v. tr.* 1) to unbind, untie, loose, loosen; 2) (*with Gen. or* von) to release (of *or* from), to disengage, (set) free, absolve, exonerate (from), rid (of); 3) *Chem.* to evolve (gas); 4) *fig.* to deliver (a woman in labour); entbunden werden, to be delivered *or* brought to bed (von einem Kinde, of a child).

Entbin'dung, (*w.*) *f.* 1) the (act of) releasing, &c., disengagement (*also Chem.*); deliverance; 2) delivery, childbirth, accouchement.

Entbin'dungs..., *in comp.* —anstalt, *f.*, —haus, *n.*, —schule, *f.* lying-in hospital *or* charity; —instrumente, *n. pl.* obstetric instruments; —kunst, *f.* obstetrics, midwifery; —stuhl, *m.* obstetric chair; —urtheil, *n. Law,* (sentence of) absolution, definitive sentence of acquittal; —zange, *f.* midwifery forceps.

Entbit'tern, (*w.*) *v. tr.* to disembitter.

Entblät'tern, (*w.*) *v.* I. *tr.* to unleave, to defoliate, strip (*or* divest) of the leaves; II. *refl.* to lose *or* drop the leaves. — **Entblät'terung**, (*w.*) *f.* defoliation.

Entblei'en, (*w.*) *v. tr. Cust.* to unlead, unplumb, take away the leaden seal from (the bales, &c. of transit-goods).

Entblen'den, (*w.*) *v. tr.* to cause *or* make to see.

Entblö'den, (*w.*) *v. refl.* 1) to divest one's self of shame *or* modesty; to dare; to be so bold (as to ...); 2) to be bashful; er entblödete sich nicht zu sagen, he did not blush to say.

Entblö'ßen, (*w.*) *v. tr.* 1) to bare, denude, denudate; to unclothe, divest, strip; to uncover (the head, &c.); 2) *fig.* to deprive, strip of; den Degen —, to draw, unsheath the sword; 3) *Mil.* to disgarnish; to dismantle (a fortress); entblößt, *p. a.* (*with Gen.*) bare, destitute, devoid (of); von baarem Gelde entblößt, out of cash. — **Entblö'ßung**, (*w.*) *f.* 1) the (act of) baring, &c., denudation; 2) deprivation, want; destitution; 2) disgarnishment; dismantling.

Entblü'hen, (w.) v. intr. (aux. sein) * to spring up (in blossom), to blossom, cf. Erblühen. [blossoms.

Entblät'tern, (w.) v. tr. to deprive of the

Entbrau'sen, (w.) v. intr. * (aux. sein) to roar from, to escape with roaring, rushing.

Entbrech'en, (str.) v. refl. (sich [Acc.] einer Sache (Gen.)) 1) to break loose (from restraint), to renounce, refuse (obedience, &c.); 2) to forbear, abstain, refrain (from).

Entbren'nen, (irr.) v. I. intr. (aux. sein) fig. to inflame, kindle, burn; im Zorn —, to fly into a passion; vor Wuth —, to flash with rage; der Kampf entbrennt immer heftiger, the conflict thickens; II. tr. * to kindle.

Entbür'den, (w.) v. tr. to disburden, unburden. — **Entbür'dung,** (w.) f. the (act of) disburdening, &c. [duck, duckling.

Ent'chen, (str.) n. (dimin. of Ente) a little

Entdach'en, (w.) v. tr. to unroof.

Entdäm'mern, (w.) v. intr. (aux. sein) to break forth from the dawn (like the sun).

Entdampf'en, (w.) v. intr. (aux. sein) to rise in vapour, to proceed from (as steam, vapour, &c.).

Entdeck'bar, adj. discoverable.

Entdeck'eln, (w.) v. tr. to divest of the lid.

Entdeck'en, (w.) v. tr. 1) to discover; to detect; to find out, to descry; 2) to disclose, reveal, (lay) open: sich Jemandem —, to make one's self known to somebody; sich seinen Gläubigern —, to disclose the state of one's affairs to one's creditors; Einem sein Herz —, to open one's heart, to break one's mind, to unbosom one's self to another; Land —, Mar. to descry land.

Entdeck'er, (str.) m. 1) discoverer, &c. cf. Entdecken; 2) Lock-sm. detector.

Entdeck'ung, (w.) f. 1) discovery; detection; 2) a revealing, disclosure; E-Reise, f. voyage of discovery, exploring or exploratory expedition. [thronging against.

Entdräng'en, (w.) v. tr. to remove by

Entdrück'en, (w.) v. tr. (Voss, l. u.) 1) see Entwinden; 2) see Abpressen.

Entduf'ten, (w.) v. intr. (aux. sein) to proceed from, to come forth (said of odour, perfume, &c.).

Entdunst'en, (w.) v. intr. see Entdampfen.

En'te, (w.) f. 1) (the female) duck; junge —, duckling; schwarze —, black diver, scoter (Anas nigra L.); türkische —, Indian or Guinea duck (Anas moschata L.); 2) fig. flam, hoax (Zeitungsente).

Entehr'en, (w.) v. tr. 1) to dishonour, disgrace, to degrade; to prostitute; to profane; 2) to violate, to ravish, to deflower: e-d, p. a. degrading, disgraceful. — **Entehr'er,** (str.) m. dishonourer, disgracer; ravisher. — **Entehr'ung,** (w.) f. 1) the (act of) dishonouring, &c., degradation; defamation; 2) violation, &c.

Enteig'nen, (w.) v. tr. to expropriate. — **Enteig'nung,** (w.) f. expropriation.

Enteil'en, (w.) v. intr. (aux. sein) 1) to hasten or hurry away (from), to pass rapidly; 2) (with Dat.) to escape (from).

Enteis'en, (w.) v. tr. to free from ice.

En'ten..., in comp. —adler, m. Ornith. duck-eagle, bald buzzard, river-eagle; osprey (Pandion haliaëtus L.); —beize, f. duck-shooting; —braten, m. roast duck; —büchse, f. duck-gun; —dunst, m. duck-shot; —fang, m. 1) decoying of ducks; duck-hunting; 2) see —herd; auf den —fang gehen, to duck; —fänger, m. decoy-man; —flinte, f. duck-gun; —fraß, m. Bot. duck-meat, duck's meat (Meerlinse); —fuß, m. Bot. duck's foot (Podophyllum peltatum); —geier, see —adler; —gras, —grün, n., —grütze, f. see Wasserlinsen; —habicht, m. see —adler; —hagel, m. see —dunst; —herd, m. decoy-pond, decoy for ducks; —jagd, f. duck-shooting; —kraut, n. Bot. see —fraß; —muschel, f. Conch. barnacle (Anatifera laevis Lam.); —pfuhl, m. duck-pond; —[illegible], m. duck-hunting; —schnabel, m. Zool. pike-headed whale (Balaenoptera boops L., or B. rostrata Bdt. & Ratz.); Ornith. s. —stößer, m. see —adler; —taucher, m. large loon-diver, black-throated diver (Eistaucher).

En'terbeil, (str.) n. Mar. pole-ax, battle-ax.

Enter'ben, (w.) v. tr. to disinherit, to cut off. — **Enter'ber,** (str.) m. disinheritor. — **Enter'bung,** (w.) f. 1) the (act of) disinheriting, disinheritance; 2) the (state of) being disinherited, disinherison.

En'terdregg, En'terhaken, (str.) m. Mar. grapnel, grapple, grappling-hook or -iron; (der große) sheer-hook. [in ducks.

En'terich, (str.) m. the male of the duck.

En'terkisten, f. pl. Mar. boarding-[illegible].

En'tern, (w.) v. tr. & intr. Mar. to grapple (a ship), to board; das —, v. n. (str.) n., or **En'terung,** (w.) f. the (act of) grappling, boarding. — **En'ter...,** in comp. —netze, n. pl. boarding-nettings; —pieke, f. boarding-pike, half-pike. [to enkindle.

Entfach'en, (w.) v. tr. poet. (Flammen, &c.)

Entfäch'ern, (w.) v. tr. to take out or remove the compartments of.... [needle).

Entfä'deln, (w.) v. tr. to unthread (a

Entfah'ren, (str.) v. intr. (aux. sein) 1) to fly off, slip off; 2) fig. to escape, to slip out; es entfuhr ihm ein Wort, a word escaped him, he blurted out a word, &c.; sich (Dat.) (etwas) — lassen, to let slip (an opportunity, &c.).

Entfal'len, (str.) v. intr. (aux. sein) 1) to drop, slip, fall from or out; 2) fig. to slip or escape one's memory; es entfällt mir, I forget it; es entfiel ihm der Muth, his courage failed him; 3) (with auf [& Acc.]) to fall to (one's) share, to devolve (upon); zu Gunsten der Actionäre — 10%, 10% result in favour of the share-holders.

Entfal'ten, (w.) v. tr. lit. & fig. to unfold: 1) to smooth; to clear up (the countenance), to unbend (the brow); 2) to display, develop, expand, put forth; to discover; 3) Mil. tr. & refl. to deploy; 4) Comm. to receive under cover of a letter. — **Entfal'tung,** (w.) f. the (act of) unfolding, &c., display; development; evolution.

Entfär'ben, (w.) v. I. tr. to deprive of the colour, to discharge the colour from, to discolour: entfärbt, p. a. discoloured, pale; II. refl. to change colour, grow pale: er entfärbt sich, his colour changes. — **Entfär'bung,** (w.) f. 1) discoloration; Paint. decoloration; 2) a) the (act of) growing pale; b) pallidity, lividness.

Entfa'sern, (w.) v. tr. to strip or divest of fibres, to string (beans, &c.); refl. to unravel.

Entfer'nen, (w.) v. I. tr. 1) to remove, put away, turn off; 2) fig. to alienate; II. refl. to withdraw, to absent one's self, to get away; (heimlich) to abscond; sich — von ..., to deviate, turn, withdraw, depart, recede from ..., to leave; sich von seinem Gegenstand —, to discourse widely from the matter; sich von einander —, Math., &c. to diverge.

Entfernt', p. a. I. distant, remote, far; off, aloof; weit —, 1) far off, &c. see Weit; 2) fig. with daß ... following: (so) far from (mit fig. Gerundium); weit —, daß sie sich gegen den gemeinsamen Feind verbunden hätten, spalteten sie sich unter einander mehr als je, so far from uniting against the common enemy, they disputed among themselves more than ever; Sie sind so weit — davon, mein Bittsteller zu werden, daß ich Sie vielmehr bitten muß meine Freundschaft anzunehmen, you are so far from displeasing me, that I must beg you'll accept

[illegible] *or* act in opposition to; to contravene [illegible] infringe (den Gesetzen, laws); das —han[deln], v. n. *(str.)* n. contravention: —kom[men], 1) to come *or* advance to meet; *fig.-s.* [t]o make advances: Jemandes Wünschen —[kom]men, to meet one's wishes; ich rechne auf [ein] freundliches —kommen, I reckon upon a [fr]iendly return *or* upon being met in a friend[ly] spirit; 2) to obviate, prevent; —laufen, [t]o run to meet; to run up to *or* towards; [t]o be counter *or* contrary, to clash with; [—neh]men, *see* Empfangen; —reden, to con[tradict]; —reisen, to travel *or* go to meet; [—sto]ßen, v. I. *tr.* to push towards; II. *intr.* to [[illegible]], advance towards; —sehen, to look for, [to] look forward to, to expect, await; —sehend, [p. a.] expecting, in expectation of; Ihrer Ant[wort] *(Dat.)* —sehend, awaiting your reply; [—set]zen, *(w.)* v. I. *tr.* 1) to oppose, to set a[gainst]; 2) *fig.* to contrast, to put in compa[rison] (Einem, with one); II. *refl.* (*with Dat.*) to [op]pose, confront; —setzung, *f.* 1) the (act of) op[pos]ing, &c.; opposition; 2) *Rhet.* antithesis; —[ste]hen, I. *see* —setzen; II. *refl.* to hinder, to be [[illegible]] in the way of; —treten, (*with Dat.*) [to] advance towards, *fig.* to oppose, to set one's [fa]ce against; —wirken, *see* —arbeiten; —ziehen, [t]o advance towards.

Entgeg'nen, *(w.)* v. *tr.* (Einem etwas) to re[tort], remonstrate, reply, rejoin. — Entgeg'[nung], *(w.)* f. retort, reply, rejoinder, remon[str]ance: in — Ihres Briefes, in answer to your [let]ter.

[Entge]h'en, *(irr.)* v. *intr.* (*aux.* sein, *with* [Dat.]) 1) *a)* to escape, get off, avoid; man kann [de]m Tode nicht —, there is no avoiding death; [b)] to escape the observation *or* notice of; es [ka]nn Ihnen nicht —, you cannot fail to observe; [c)] to fail (as strength, &c.); to leave: dies ent[geh]t mir, *fig.* I (shall) lose that, I am (*or* shall [be]) deprived of it; das entgeht mir nicht, ich [k]ann dem nicht —, *coll.* I am booked for it; sich [(Dat.)] (eine Gelegenheit) — lassen, to let slip [a]n opportunity; sich nicht — lassen, to secure; [ent]gangen, p. a. lost (profit, freight).

Entgei'len, *(w.)* v. *tr.* to castrate; to geld.

Entgeis'ten, *(w.)* v. *tr.* to exanimate; — or [Entgeist]'igen, *(w.)* v. *tr.* to unspiritualise, to [de]prive of spirituality.

[Entgeist]'ern, *(w.)* v. *tr.* * to deprive of spi[rit] *or* sense; entgeistert, *p. a.* exanimate.

[Entg]elt', *(str.)* m. requital &c.; ohne —, without remuneration *or* fee, gratis; gegen —, [f]or an equivalent.

Entgel'ten, *(str.)* v. *tr.* (Einem etwas) to pay [fo]r, atone for, to suffer; Einen etwas — lassen, [t]o make one suffer for, to make one feel a [[illegible]], to visit upon one.

[Entglas]'ten, *(w.)* v. *tr.* *Chem.*, &c. to devi[trify].

[Entglei]'sen, *(w.)* v. I. *intr.* (*aux.* sein) to [ru]n off the rails *or* the track; II. *tr.* to take [off] the rails of (a railway). — Entglei'sung, [(w.)] *f.* the (act of) running off the track, &c.

[Entglei]'ten, *(str.)* v. *intr.* (*aux.* sein, *with* [Dat.]) to slip, slide from; to escape, drop from.

[Entglie]'dern, *(w.)* v. *tr.* 1) to deprive of [[illegible]], to dismember; 2) *fig.* to disorganise.

[[illegible]], *(str.)* v. *intr.* (*aux.* sein) *lit.* [&] *fig.* to kindle, inflame.

[[illegible]], *(w.)* v. *intr.* (*aux.* sein) *lit.* & [fig.] to begin to burn, to kindle, to glow.

[Entgöt]'tern, *(w.)* v. *tr.* to ungod, undeify, [to] [[illegible]] of divinity.

[Entgrä]'ten, *(w.)* v. *tr.* to bone (a fish).

[[illegible]], *(w.)* v. *intr.* (*aux.* sein) to [[illegible]] unprovoked, to sprout forth (*with* [[illegible]]).

[[illegible]], *(w.)* v. *tr.* to invalidate.

[[illegible]], *(w.)* v. *tr.* *see* Degummieren.

[[illegible]]. [Entgür]'ten, *(w.)* v. *tr.* & *refl.* [to] [[illegible]] from a band, girdle, or girt, to un[gird] [[illegible]].

Enthaa'ren, *(w.)* v. *tr.* to deprive of hair, *cf.* Abhaaren; to depilate. — Enthaa'rung, *(w.)* f. depilation: E-smittel, n. *Med.* depilatory.

Enthalf'tern, *(w.)* v. *tr.* to unhalter.

Enthal'len, *(w.)* v. *intr.* (*aux.* sein) * to sound from.

Enthal'ten, *(str.)* v. I. *tr.* to contain, comprise, comprehend, hold, include: *Comm.* to cover; II. *refl.* (*with Gen.*) to abstain (from); to forbear, to refrain: ich kann mich des Lachens nicht —, I cannot help laughing.

Enthalt'sam, I. *adj.* abstemious, abstinent, continent, sober, temperate; II. E-keit, *(w.)* f. abstemiousness, abstinence, continence, soberness; discretion. [ance; restraint.

Enthal'tung, *(w.)* f. abstinence; forbear-

Enthär'ten, *(w.)* v. *tr.* to unharden, soften: Stahl —, to anneal steel. [of its resin.

Enthar'zen, *(w.)* v. *tr.* to deprive (a tree)

Enthasch'en, *(w.)* v. *tr.* to snatch away: [den Jüngling freut es, wie die Wellen] hinlärmen durchs Gefild, | und wie sie scherzend sich *(Dat.)* — | sein aufgeblühtes Bild *(Lenau)*, [It glads the youth to see them] ... prattle through the field, | and from each other snatch away | his image just revealed *(Beskow.)*.

Enthau'ben, *(w.)* v. *tr.* to take one's cap off, to uncoif.

Enthaup'ten, *(w.)* v. *tr.* to behead, decapitate. — Enthaup'tung, *(w.)* f. the (act of) beheading, decapitation.

Enthäu'ten, *(w.)* v. *tr.* to skin, flay, excoriate. — Enthäu'tung, *(w.)* f. the (act of) skinning, &c., excoriation.

Enthe'ben, *(str.)* v. *tr.* 1) to take away, lift from: 2) *fig.* (Einen einer Sache *(Gen.)*) to ease (of a burden, &c.), to exonerate, exempt, deliver, *or* free from: — Sie uns dieser Mühe, spare us this trouble: eines Amtes —, to dismiss from an employment. — Enthe'bung, *(w.)* f. 1) exemption: 2) dismissal.

Enthei'ligen, *(w.)* v. *tr.* to unhallow, profane, desecrate, to violate. — Enthei'ligung, *(w.)* f. profanation, desecration, violation.

Enthel'men, *(w.)* v. *tr.* to unhelmet, deprive of the helmet.

Enther'zen, *(w.)* v. *tr.* to dishearten.

Enthir'nen, *(w.)* v. *tr.* to deprive of the brain: *Cook.* to brain.

Enthol'zen, *(w.)* v. *tr.* to deprive of wood.

Enthu'fen, *(w.)* v. *tr.* to unhoof, deprive of the hoof.

Enthül'len, *(w.)* v. *tr.* to unfold: to unveil, disclose, reveal: to unmask; das Denkmal wird heute enthüllt werden, the monument will be unveiled this day. — Enthül'lung, *(w.)* f. the (act of) unfolding, &c., unveiling (of a statue, &c.); exposure (of political secrets, &c.).

Enthül'sen, *(w.)* v. *tr.* to husk, decorticate, peel, shell; to gin (cotton). — Enthül'sung, *(w.)* f. the (act of) husking, &c.; decortication: E-smaschine, E-smühle, *f.* *Mech.* hulling machine; pulping mill.

Enthüpf'en, *(w.)* v. *intr.* (*aux.* sein) to hop *or* skip (out of *or* away from).

* Enthusiasmi'ren, *(w.)* v. *tr.* (*Gr.*) to fill with enthusiasm *or* rapture, to enrapture. — Enthusias'mus, *(indecl.)* m. enthusiasm. — Enthusiast', *(w.)* m. enthusiast. — Enthusias'tisch, *adj.* enthusiastic(al); *adv.* enthusiastically. [(open); *fig.* to discover.

Entjach'ern, *(w.)* v. *tr.* to unyoke, unbosom

Entjung'fern, *(w.)* v. *tr.* to deflower. — Entjung'ferung, *(w.)* f. defloration.

Entkei'men, *(w.)* v. *intr.* (*aux.* sein) to germinate (from), to spring up (of germs).

Entker'kern, *(w.)* v. *tr.* to release, set free, *or* deliver from prison.

Entker'nen, *(w.)* v. *tr.* to [[illegible]] (fruits, &c.), to stone (fruit), *cf.* Auskernen.

Entket'ten, *(w.)* v. *tr.* to unchain, unfetter.

Entklei'den, *(w.)* v. I. *tr.* to undress, divest, unrobe, disrobe, unclothe, strip; entkleidet sein, to be in undress: II. *refl.* to undress.

Entknöp'fen, *(w.)* v. *tr.* (*H. Voss*, *l. u.*) to unbutton. [break forth from the bud.

Entknos'pen, *(w.)* v. *intr.* (*aux.* sein) to

Entkoh'len, *(w.)* v. *tr.* *Chem.* to decarbonise.

Entkom'men, *(str.)* v. *intr.* (*aux.* sein) to escape, evade, to come *or* get off: mit genauer Noth —, to make *or* have a narrow *or* hair-breadth escape. [&c.).

Entkop'peln, *(w.)* v. *tr.* to uncouple (dogs,

Entkor'ken, *(w.)* v. *tr.* to uncork.

Entkör'pern, *(w.)* v. *tr.* to disembody, divest of flesh *or* the body.

Entkräf'ten, *(w.)* v. *tr.* 1) to debilitate, enervate, enfeeble, exhaust; 2) *fig.* to weaken, unnerve: to disprove, invalidate: ein Grundstück —, to wear land out of heart. — Entkräf'tung, *(w.)* f. debilitation, enervation; exhaustion, fatigue, weariness; invalidation: *Med.* inanition: E-sfieber, n. consumptive fever. [prive of a wreath.

Entkrän'zen, *(w.)* v. *tr.* to divest *or* de-

Entkräu'seln, *(w.)* v. *tr.* & *refl.* to uncurl.

Entkrie'chen, *(str.)* v. *intr.* (*with Dat.*) to creep out of *or* away from. [crown.

Entkrö'nen, *(w.)* v. *tr.* to discrown, un-

Entkup'peln, *(w.)* v. *tr.* *Mech.* to disconnect, to throw out of gear.

Entla'den, *(str.)* v. *tr.* to disburden, unload, exonerate; to discharge; to ease (one's conscience): sich (*with Gen.*) —, to ease one's self (of a burden, &c.): das Pulver entlud sich, the powder exploded *or* blew up: die Wolke entlud sich über mir, the cloud broke over me. — Entla'der, *(str.)* m. *Mech.* discharger, discharging-rod. — Entla'dung, *(w.)* f. 1) exoneration: 2) discharge, eruption.

Entlang', *adv.* (*with Acc. after the subst. & Gen. or Dat. before it*) along; — gehen, laufen, reiten 2c., to skirt (a wood, &c.).

Entlar'ven, *(w.)* v. *tr.* to unmask. — Entlar'vung, *(w.)* f. the (act of) unmasking.

Entlas'sen, *(str.)* v. *tr.* 1) to dismiss, give leave, discharge; *coll.* to give the sack: — werden, to have *or* get the sack; (wegen eines Vergehens) to turn away *or* off, to dissolve (a meeting); to disband (soldiers): 2) (Einen einer Sache *(Gen.)*) (*l. u.*) to discharge (from duty, &c.); to absolve (of an oath, &c.); Einen aus dem Gefängnisse —, to discharge, release a prisoner; to emancipate: *Law-a.* vom Gerichte völlig — sein, to be dismissed without day, to go without day: der Haft — sein, to have a writ of ease.

Entlas'sung, *s.* I. *(w.)* f. leave, dismission, removal (from office, &c.), dismissal, discharge; release; resignation (of a minister, &c.): — der Gefangenen, jail delivery; seine — nehmen, to resign one's office, &c.; II. *in comp.* E-sattest, E-szeugniß, n., E-sschein, m. certificate (in den Strafkolonien, ticket) of leave, discharge-ticket; E-sschreiben, n. (letter) dimissory.

Entlas'ten, *(w.)* v. *tr.* (Einen einer Sache *(Gen.)*) 1) to disburden, discharge, disencumber, unload, exonerate; sein Gewissen —, to unburden one's conscience; 2) *Comm.* (Einen für eine gewisse Summe) to credit, to pass (an amount) to the credit of any one's account. — Entlas'tung, *(w.)* f. discharge, exoneration; zu meiner —, *Comm.* to my credit; — des Grundbesitzes, enfranchisement of landed property; E-sbogen, m. *Archit.* discharging-arch (Ablastebogen); E-szeuge, m. witness in favour of an accused, witness for the defence; friendly witness.

Entlau'ben, *(w.)* v. *tr.* to unleave; to strip of the foliage. — Entlau'bung, *(w.)* f. frondation.

[illegible] Mittelsorte, he settled upon the middling [illegible]; sich für oder gegen —, to decide one way [or] the other.

Entschei'dend, *p. a.* decisive, determinate, [illegible], peremptory, conclusive, final: e-e [illegible], final answer; e-e Stimme, casting [illegible] *or* vote; e-es Beispiel, crucial instance; [illegible] Schritt, decided step.

Entschei'dung, *(w.) f.* the (act of) deciding, &c., decision, determination; decisive sentence; judgment, verdict: die — des Schwertes, the arbitration of the sword; gefälliger — entgegensehend, *Comm.* awaiting your resolution; zu einer endlichen (schließlichen) — bringen, to bring to a final issue.

Entschei'dungs..., *in comp.* —eid, *m.* decisory oath; —grund, *m.* ground of decision; motive; —punct, *m.*, —zeichen, *n.*, —[illegible], *m.* crisis, critical point; —stimme, *f.* casting voice *or* vote; —tage, *m. pl. Med.* [illegible] *or* critical days.

Entschie'den, I. *p. a.* decided: 1) made [illegible], *cf.* Entscheiden; 2) resolute, determined, [illegible]; 3) peremptory, positive, *cf.* Entscheiden; ich bin — der Meinung, I am decidedly of [illegible] opinion, &c.; II. **E-heit**, *(w.) f.* decision, determination, resoluteness, &c.

Entschie'nen, *(w.) v. intr. (aux.* sein) *see* [illegible].

Entschie'ßen, *(str.) v. intr. (aux.* sein) to [illegible] from; to fall, burst, *or* break loose [illegible], to burst forth.

Entschif'fen, *(w.) v.* I. *intr. (aux.* sein) to [illegible] off *or* away (from): to escape in a ship; II. *tr.* to ship off. [gear.

Entschir'ren, *(w.) v. tr.* to unharness, un-

Entschla'fen, *(str.) v. intr. (aux.* sein) 1) to fall asleep; wenn wir sterben, — wir nicht, [illegible] ändern nur den Ort, when we die we do [illegible] fall asleep, we only change our place; [illegible] *fig.* to expire, die, to breathe one's last; der (die) Entschlafene, *(decl. like adj.) m. (f.)*, *pl.* die Entschlafenen, the deceased.

Entschla'gen, *(str.) v. refl. with Gen.* (sich einer Sache *(Gen.)*) to divest one's self *or* to get rid of, to dismiss from one's mind, to put out of one's head, to banish, throw aside, [illegible] away (care), to forget, eines Fallimente — *(pp.)* sein, *Comm.* to be cleared, *coll.* to begin anew, to begin the world again. — **Entschla'gung**, *(w.) f. Comm.* release, discharge.

Entschlei'chen, *(str.) v. intr. (aux.* sein) *(l. u.)* to sneak, creep, *or* steal away (from).

Entschlei'ern, *(w.) v. tr. lit. & fig.* to unveil; reveal.

Entschlei'men, *(w.) v. tr. see* Entschälen, 2.

Entschleu'dern, *(w.) v. tr.* to fling away or forth.

Entschlich'ten, *(w.) v. tr. T.* to steep, un[illegible] (cotton in bleaching, &c.).

Entschlie'ßen, *(str.) v.* I. *tr.* to unlock; to [illegible]; II. *refl.* to resolve, fix, determine, decide (zu, on, upon), to make up one's mind; ich kann mich nicht dazu —, I cannot bring myself to do it; sie war entschlossen, ihres [illegible] Rechte zu vertheidigen, she was determined on asserting her sex's rights.

Entschlie'ßung, *(w.) f.* resolution, determination. [the noose.

[illegible], *(w.) v. tr.* to take out of

Entschlos'sen, I. *p. a.* determined, resolved (*cf.* Entschließen), resolute; firm, prompt; [illegible] e-er Mann, a man of resolution: [illegible] this only sharpened [illegible] determination; II. **E-heit**, *(w.) f.* resoluteness, determination, decision, courage.

[illegible], *(w.) v. intr. (aux.* sein) [illegible] 2) to expire, die [illegible].

[illegible], *(w.) v. intr. (aux.* sein, [illegible]) to slip *or* glide out of, from, to [illegible] —; to [illegible] one, *coll.* to give one the slip; das Wort entschlüpfte mir, the word slipped from my tongue.

Entschluß', *(str., pl.* Entschlüs'se) *m.* resolution, resolve; einen — fassen, to take (come to, *or* fix upon) a resolution, to make a determination, to determine (about), to resolve; zu einem — kommen, to make up one's mind, to fix upon something; zu keinem — kommen können, to be unsettled in one's mind.

Entschmü'cken, *(w.) v. tr. (l. u.)* to divest *or* strip of ornament. [untie.

Entschnü'ren, *(w.) v. tr. (l. u.)* to unlace,

Entschöp'fen, *(w.) v. tr.* to draw (water, &c.) from; *fig.* to exhaust. [of shoes.

Entschu'hen, *(w.) v. tr.* to divest *or* strip

Entschuld'bar, *adv.* excusable, *see* Verzeihlich.

Entschul'digen, *(w.) v. tr.* to excuse, exculpate; to justify, defend; sich —, to apologise (bei, gegen, to, wegen, for); Karl I. entschuldigte sich bei dem Könige von Spanien dafür, daß er dabei betheiligt gewesen sei, Charles I. apologised to the king of Spain for having had any thing to do with it: ich bitte mich zu —, I'd rather be excused; er ist nicht (einigermaßen) zu —, there is nothing (something) to be said for him: sich mit Krankheit, Unwissenheit 2c. —, to plead sickness, ignorance, &c.; — Sie mich, (pray) excuse me, have *or* hold me excused; — Sie mich bei ihm, make my excuses to him; — Sie die Eile, excuse haste; es läßt sich nicht —, it admits of no excuse, there is no excuse for it; — Sie! I beg your pardon! — Sie sich nicht, make no apologies.

Entschul'digung, *s.* I. *(w.) f.* exculpation; excuse, apology; plea; als (zur) —, for one's (my, &c.) excuse; als — für ..., in excuse *or* palliation of ...; keine —! never tell me! um — bitten, to apologise (wegen, for); II. *in comp.* **E-sgrund**, *m.* the reason for an excuse, plea; **E-sschreiben**, *n.* letter of excuse, apology, deprecatory letter.

Entschup'pen, *(w.) v. tr.* to unscale (a fish).

Entschür'zen, *(w.) v. tr.* to divest *or* strip of an apron. [out of.

Entschüt'teln, *(w.) v. tr. (l. u.)* to shake

Entschwär'men, *(w.) v. intr. (aux.* sein) to swarm forth.

Entschwe'ben, *(w.) v. intr. (aux.* sein) * to soar away *or* up (from).

Entschwe'feln, *(w.) v. tr. Chem.* to desulphurate. — **Entschwe'felung**, *(w.) f.* desulphuration.

Entschwei'ßen, *(w.) v. tr. T.* to deprive of sweat *or* impurities, to scour (wool).

Entschwim'men, *(str.) v. intr. (aux.* sein) to swim off, to escape from ... by swimming.

Entschwin'den, *(str.) v. intr. (aux.* sein) to disappear; to vanish (quickly) *(with Dat.*, from). [soar above, aloft

Entschwing'en, *(str.) v. refl.* * to fly away,

Entschwir'ren, *(w.) v. intr. (aux.* sein) to whiz, buz from.

Entsee'len, *(w.) v. intr.* to exanimate; entseelt, *p. a.* deprived of life, lifeless, dead.

Entse'geln, *(w.) v. intr. (aux.* sein) to sail off *or* away (from), *cf.* Entschiffen.

Entseh'en, *(w.) v. refl.* †. to be ashamed *or* afraid of, to be loath (to).

Entsen'den, *(irr.) v. tr.* to send off *or* from, to despatch; to (let) fly (an arrow, &c.).

Entsetz'bar, *adj.* 1) removable; 2) that may be relieved *or* rescued.

Entsetz'en, *(w.) v.* I. *tr.* 1) (Einen einer Sache *(Gen.)*) to displace, depose; to remove, dismiss (one from office); to suspend; *Mil.* to discard, cashier; der [illegible] —, to deprive (a clergyman); des Thrones —, to depose from the throne, to dethrone; 2) *Mil.* to relieve, succour, to raise the siege of (a fortress); to come to the rescue of ...; II. *refl.* to shudder (vor *(with Dat.)*, at), to be shocked, terrified, amazed (at).

Entsetz'en, *s. (str.) n.* 1) *see* Entsetzung & Entsatz; 2) terror, horror, amazement.

Entsetz'lich, I. *adj.* terrible, horrible, horrid, frightful, shocking: atrocious, monstrous, heinous, dire; II. **E-keit**, *(w.) f.* terribleness, &c., atrocity, monstrosity, heinousness.

Entsetz'ung, *(w.) f.* 1) removal, dismissal, dismission, suspension, deprivation, deposition, deposal, degradation, displacement; 2) *see* Entsatz.

Entsie'geln, *(w.) v. tr.* to unseal, open.

Entsin'ken, *(str.) v. intr. (aux.* sein) to drop from; to sink (gradually) down; es entsinkt mir der Muth, my heart sinks (within me), my courage fails me.

Entsin'nen, *(str.) v. refl. (with Gen.)* to remember, recollect, to call to mind.

Entsinn'lichen, *(w.) v. tr.* to free from, to raise above the sensual *or* earthly, to spiritualise.

Entsitt'lichen, *(w.) v. tr.* to demoralise. — **Entsitt'lichung**, *(w.) f.* demoralisation, depravation of morals. [nen.

Entsöh'nen, *(w.) v. tr. (l. u.) see* Entsüh-

Entspan'nen, *(w.) v. tr.* to unbend (a bow, &c.).

Entspin'nen, *(str.) v.* I. *tr. fig.* to contrive, bring about, originate, *cf.* Anspinnen, 3; II. *refl.* to arise, to originate (aus, in); to ensue.

Entsprech'en, *(str.) v. intr. (with Dat.)* to answer, correspond to, to be equal to ...; to suit, meet, to come up to (a demand, &c.); to be in keeping *or* to tally with, to comply with (a request); to come up to (einer Probe, a sample); einer Bitte —, to comply with a request; nicht —, to fall short (of expectation, &c.); es entspricht dem Zweck, it will do; e-d, answering, &c., suitable, just, adequate; schöne Augen und andere e-e Reize, *fac.* fine eyes and other charms to correspond (to match, to answer): Ihrem Verlangen e-d, in accordance with your wish; dem e-d, accordingly.

Entsprie'ßen, *(str.) v. intr. (aux.* sein) 1) to sprout forth *(with Dat.*, from); Blätter — dem Zweige, leaves spring from the twig; 2) *fig. see* Entspringen, 3.

Entspring'en, *(str.) v. intr. (aux.* sein) 1) to spring *or* run away, to escape; 2) to spring, (take) rise (said of rivers, &c.); to burst out; 3) *fig.* *a)* to spring, arise (aus, from); to come from, proceed, *cf.* Entstehen; *b)* to descend, *cf.* Entstammen.

Entspru'deln, *(w.) v. intr. (aux.* sein) to flow *or* burst from.

Entsprüh'en, *(w.) v. intr. (aux.* sein) to fly from, to be cast *or* thrown out (of sparks).

Entstaat'lichen, *(w.) v. tr. mod.* to disestablish (a church). — **Entstaat'lichung**, *(w.) f.* disestablishment.

Entstal'ten, *(w.) v. tr.* to disfigure, deform.

Entstam'men, *(w.) v. intr. (aux.* sein) *(with Dat.)* to descend (einem adligen Geschlechte, from a noble family, &c.); dem Himmel e-d, heaven-descended, heaven-born; der Hölle entstammt, hell-born.

Entstän'kern, *(w.) v. tr. T.* to unsmell.

Entsten'geln, *(w.) v. tr.* to deprive of the stalk. [the dust from ..., to dust.

Entstäu'ben, *(w.) v. tr. (l. u.)* to remove

Entsteh'en, *(irr.) v. intr.* 1) *(aux.* sein) to arise, rise, spring (up), begin (aus, from), originate (in), to be formed (by *or* of); to proceed, take rise (from); to grow (out of); to ensue; was wird daraus —? what will come of (from) it? entstehe was da will (*or* wolle), come what come may, happen what may; 2) *(aux.* haben, *with Dat.)* *(l. u.)* to fail, to be wanting; das —, *s. (str.) n.* the act of arising, &c. *cf.* Entstehung; es ist noch im —

begriffen, it is still forming, it is still in its beginning, in embryo.

Entsprie'ßen, (str.) v. intr. & refl. see Sprießen.

Entste'hung, (w.) f. the (act of) arising, beginning, origin; genesis, formation, original creation; E-sart, E-sweise, f. the nature or manner of the beginning, origin: im E-sfall, Law, in the event, eventually.

Entstei'gen, (str.) v. intr. (aux. sein) to rise (with Dat., from); to come forth (from or out of), to emerge (from).

Entstei'nen, (w.) v. tr. 1) to free from stones; 2) to unkernel (as stone-fruit).

Entstel'len, (w.) v. tr. 1) to disfigure, deform, deface; to distort; 2) fig. to misrepresent, distort, garble (a fact); to falsify (another's speech); to discolour, distort (the truth); entstellte Züge, lit. features out of drawing; lit. & fig. distorted features. — **Entstel'lung,** (w.) f. 1) the (act of) disfiguring, disfigurement, defacement; distortion; 2) misrepresentation, perversion.

Entstie'feln, (w.) v. tr. (do u. or lud.) to unboot.

Entstie'len, (w.) v. tr. to deprive of the stalk.

Entstrah'len, (w.) v. intr. (aux. sein) to radiate (from).

Entstri'cken, (w.) v. tr. to untie, unfasten; to extricate, disengage.

Entströ'men, (w.) v. intr. (aux. sein) to flow rapidly, to stream, rush, gush (from).

Entstür'men, (w.) v. intr. (aux. sein) (l. u.) to rush away from.

Entstür'zen, (w.) v. tr. (aux. sein) to rush, fall, or gush (from), cf. Entströmen.

Entsüh'nen, (w.) v. tr * to clear from guilt or sin, to expiate; er ist entsühnt, he has expiated (or atoned for) his crime.

Entsum'pfen, (w.) v. tr. to drain of swamps.

Entsün'digen, (w.) v. tr. to clear from sin, to purify, absolve, sanctify. — **Entsün'digung,** (w.) f. expiation, purification.

Entta'feln, (w.) v. tr. 1) to take off the panels from; 2) T. to take off the pressing-boards from.

Enttau'chen, (w.) v. intr. (aux. sein) * to emerge from.

Enttäu'schen, (w.) v. tr. to undeceive, disabuse; to disappoint. — **Enttäu'schung,** (w.) f. disappointment.

Entthro'nen, (w.) v. tr. to dethrone, discrown, depose, unthrone, unking. — **Entthro'nung,** (w.) f. dethronement, deposition.

Enttö'nen, (w.) v. intr. (aux. sein) to sound (from), flow (from, of sound).

Entträu'feln, Enttröp'feln, Enttrop'fen, (w.) v. intr. (aux. sein) to trickle out, to drip or drop down (from).

Entü'brigen, (w.) v. tr. & intr. see Erübrigen; einer Sache (Gen.) entübrigt sein, to do without a thing, to dispense with a thing.

Entvöl'kern, (w.) v. tr. to depopulate, unpeople; entvölkert, p. a. destitute of inhabitants. — **Entvöl'kerung,** (w.) f. depopulation.

Entwach'sen, (str.) v. intr. (aux. sein, with Dat.) fig. to outgrow (a thing); to grow too great or too old for ...; er ist seinen Kleidern —, he has grown out of his clothes; der Ruthe — sein, to have outgrown the rod.

Entwaff'nen, (w.) v. tr. to disarm. — **Entwaff'nung,** (w.) f. the (act of) disarming.

Entwäh'ren, (w.) v. tr. Law, to evict, eject, to drive from ... or dispossess by legal process. — **Entwäh'rung,** (w.) f. Law, eviction, ejection.

Entwal'den, (w.) v. tr. (eine Gegend) to cut down the forests of (a country).

Entwal'len, (w.) v. intr. (aux. sein) 1) to flow from; 2) or **Entwan'deln, Entwan'dern,** (w.) v. intr. (aux. sein) * to wander (with Dat., from), to begin a pilgrimage (from).

Entwäs'sern, (w.) v. tr. 1) to drain, make dry; 2) Chem. to distil, to dephlegmate. — **Entwäs'serung,** (w.) f. 1) the (act of) draining, drainage; 2) Chem. dephlegmation.

Ent'weder, conj. either: — ..., oder —, either ..., or ...; das — oder, an alternative.

Entweh'ren, (w.) v. I. tr. for Entwaffnen; II. refl. (with Gen.) see Erwehren.

Entwei'ben, (w.) v. tr. to unwoman, unsex.

Entwei'chen, (str.) v. intr. (aux. sein) 1) to give way, to disappear; (Chem. said of gas, &c.) to escape; 2) to run away, escape, evade; to abscond (from one's creditors); to elope (with a lover); der e-de Dampf, Mech. waste steam; nicht — lassen, Phys. to retain.

Entwei'chung, (w.) f. the (act of) absconding, &c.; escape; elopement: Mech.-s. E-s-röhre, f. eduction-pipe; E-s-klappe, f., E-s-ventil, n. discharging- or delivery-valve.

Entwei'hen, (w.) v. tr. to profane, unhallow, desecrate, pollute; to defile, violate. — **Entwei'her,** (str.) m. polluter; violator. — **Entwei'hung,** (w.) f. profanation, desecration, &c.

Entwelt'lichen, (w.) v. tr. to wean from worldly thoughts.

Entwen'den, (w. & irr.) v. tr. to purloin, pilfer, filch, steal, abstract; to embezzle (public money). — **Entwen'der,** (str.) m. purloiner, pilferer. — **Entwen'dung,** (w.) f. the (act of) purloining, stealing, &c., abstraction; peculation, embezzlement.

Entwer'fen, (str.) v. tr. 1) to trace out; to sketch, delineate, chalk, roughdraw; 2) to strike out, design, project, plan, plot, forecast, scheme, contrive, devise; roh —, to make a rough sketch; Pläne —, to lay down or make plans; Friedensartikel —, to draw up articles of peace. — **Entwer'fer,** (str.) m. designer, projector, planner, contriver. — **Entwer'fung,** (w.) f. (l. u.) see Entwurf; E-s-ebene, f. Math. projection.

Entwer'then, (w.) v. tr. to deprive of value, to reduce (money), depreciate, disprize; schlechtes Geld —, to call in clipped or base money; to deface, cancel, blacken, dab (letter-stamps). — **Entwer'thung,** (w.) f. reduction (in the value), depreciation.

Entwi'ckeln, (w.) v. tr. to unfold: 1) to unrol, unravel, unfurl; to develop: fig.-s. 2) Mil. to deploy; 3) to display; 4) to lay open, evolve, clear, explain, explicate, solve; 5) to give out, emit (gas, &c.): sich —, to evolve (of gas); vollkommen entwickelt, fully formed.

Entwi'ckelung, (w.) f. 1) the (act of) unfolding, development; 2) Math., Mil. &c. evolution; 3) explanation, explication; exposition; 4) Theat., &c. the unravelling or discovery of the plot in a drama, &c., catastrophe, denouement: E-s-gang, m. course of development; E-s-lehre, f. the doctrine or theory of development or of evolution (in the theory of generation); E-s-periode, f. puberty, the period in which the generative faculties begin to be developed; E-s-stufe, f. phase of development.

Entwil'dern, (w.) v. tr. to civilise.

Entwim'meln, (w.) v. intr. (aux. sein) (l. u.) to issue forth (from or in consequence of ...) in crowds or swarms.

Entwin'den, (str.) v. I. tr. (Einem etwas) to wrest from, wrest out of (one's hands); II. refl. (with Dat.) to break (from), to struggle forth.

Entwir'beln, (w.) v. tr. & intr. (aux. sein) to whirl off or away (as the wind the foliage, &c.).

Entwir'ren, (w.) v. tr. to disentangle, unravel, extricate, rescue from confusion. — **Entwir'rung,** (w.) f. unravelment, extrication (from confusion).

Entwi'schen, (w.) v. intr. (aux. sein, with Dat.) to escape, to slip, sneak, or get off, steal away; Einem —, to give one the slip.

Entwöh'nen, (w.) v. intr. (aux. sein) to get out of practice; (with Gen.) to lose the

[illegible] in two; —**fallen**, —**gehen**, *v. intr.* to fall to pieces; to go to pieces; —**schlagen**, *v. tr.* to break or stave to pieces.

Entzwei'en, *(w.) v.* I. *tr.* to disunite, to put at variance *or* at odds; II. *refl.* to fall out with one another; **entzweit**, *p. a.* at variance, at odds. — **Entzwei'ung**, *(w.) f.* division (act of disuniting and state of being at variance); dissension, variance, bad feeling; dies war nun eine verhängnißvolle — zwischen König und Volk, there was a fatal division between the king and the people.

* **Enzian'**, *(str.) m. Bot.* gentian (*Gentiana L.*); gelber *or* rother —, bitter-wort (*G. lutea L., G. purpurea L.*); stengelloser —, dwarf-gentian (*G. acaulis L.*); gemeiner —, marsh-gentian (*G. pneumonanthe L.*).

* **Epac'ten**, *pl. (Gr.) Chron. (Astr.)* epact.

* **Epaulet'te** [*pr.* Epolët'te], *(w.) f. (Fr.) Mil.* epaulet, shoulder-knot.

* **Epheme'r**, **Epheme'risch**, *adj. (Gr.)* ephemeral, temporary; e-e **Waaren**, *f. pl. Comm.* 1) fancy articles, goods subject to varying fashions; 2) perishable goods (such as fruits, &c.). — **Epheme're**, *(w.) f.* 1) *see* Eintagsfliege; 2) *Med.* ephemera. — **Epheme'ri'de**, *(w.) f. Astr., &c.* ephemeris, *pl.* ephemerides. [sian.

Epheser, *(str.) m.*, **Ephe'sisch**, *adj.* Ephe-

Epheu, *(str.) m. Bot.* ivy (*Hedĕra helix L.*); mit — bewachsen, bekleidet, bedeckt, *poet.* ivied, ivy-clad, ivy-mantled; —**ähnlich**, hederaceous; —**harz**, *n.* ivy-resin, ivy-gum; —**ranke**, *f.* ivy-branch. [mare.

* **Ephial'tes**, *(indecl.) m. (Gr.) Med.* night-

* **Ephor'**, *(w.)*, **Epho'rus**, *(str., pl. [w.]* **Epho'ren** [*Lat.* **Epho'ri**]) *m.* 1) *Gr. Archaeol.* ephor; 2) *Eccl.* ecclesiastical superior (*in several Protestant churches*), superintendent. — **Ephorat'**, *(str.) n.*, **Epho'rie**, *(w.) f.* 1) *Gr. Archaeol.* ephoralty; 2) *Eccl.* office *or* district of a superintendent.

* **Epicurä'er**, *(str.) m. (Gr.)* epicure, epicurean. — **Epicurä'isch**, *adj.* epicurean; luxurious. — **Epicurä'is'mus**, *m.* epicurism, epicureanism.

* **Epicycloi'de**, *(w.) f. (Gr.) Geom.* epicycloid. — **Epicycloi'disch**, *adj.* epicycloidal. — **Epicy'kel**, *(str.) m. Astr.* epicycle.

* **Epidemie'**, *(w.) f. (Gr.) Med.* epidemic, epidemic disease. — **Epide'misch**, *adj.* epidemic(al).

* **Epigo'nen**, *(w.) m. pl. Gr. Myth., &c.* epigoni, the sons and descendants of heroes.

* **Epigramm'**, *(str.) n. (Gr.)* epigram: E-endichter, **Epigrammatis'ter**, *(str.) m.* epigrammatist. — **Epigramma'tisch**, *adj.* epigrammatic (style, poem, &c.), pointed.

* **Epigra'phik**, *(w.) f. (Gr.)* epigraphics.

* **E'piker**, *(str.) m. (Gr.)* epic poet.

* **Epilepsie'**, *(w.) f. (Gr.) Med.* epilepsy. — **Epilep'tisch**, *adj.* epileptic(al); ein e-er Anfall, an epileptic fit.

* **Epilog'**, *(str.) m. (Gr.) Poet.* epilogue. — **Epilo'gisch**, *adj.* epilogistic. [Epirus.

* **Epirot'**, *(w.) m. (Gr.)* inhabitant of

* **E'pisch**, *adj. (Gr.)* epic; heroic.

* **Episcopal'**, I. **Episcopa'lisch**, *adj. (Gr.)* episcopal, episcopalian; II. E-e, *(w.) m. Eccl.* episcopalian. — **Episcopat'**, *(str.) n. Eccl.* episcopacy, episcopate.

* **Episo'de**, *(w.) f. (Gr.)* episode. — **Episo'disch**, *adj.* episodic(al), episodal.

* **Epis'tel**, *(w.) f. (Gr.)* epistle; *fig.* reprimand; einem die — (*cf.* Leviten) lesen, *coll.* to lecture *or* reprimand a person. — **Epistolographie'**, *(w.) f.* epistolography.

* [illegible], *(str.)*, **Epithe'ton** (*Lat.; str., pl.* [illegible] *or* [w.] E-then), *n. (Gr.)* epithet, [illegible].

* [illegible], *pl. (Gr.)* [illegible] *m.* [illegible].

* **Epo'che**, *(w.) f. (Gr.)* epoch: epocha; — **machend**, *p. a.* marking an epoch.

* **Epo'de**, *(w.) f. (Gr.) Poet.* epode.

* **Epopö'e**, *(w.) f. (Gr.) Poet.* epopee.

* **E'pos**, *(sing. indecl., pl. [w.]* **E'pen**) *n. (Gr.) Poet.* epos, epic, epic poem.

Ep'pich, *(str.) m. coll. for* Petersilie, Epheu, & Sellerie, *which see*; der wilde —, *Bot.* milk parsley, marsh selinum (*Selinum carvifolium L.*).

* **Equilibrist'**, *(w.) m. (Fr.)* rope-dancer.

* **Equipa'ge** [*pr.* Eki— *or* Equipā'she], *(w.) f. (Fr.)* 1) *Mar. & Mil.* equipage; 2) *a)* equipage, *coll.* turn-out; *b) fam.* outfit, equipment, dress.

* **Equipi'ren**, *(w.) v. tr. (Fr.)* to fit out, equip; to furnish with men; to man (a ship).

Er, I. *pron.* 1) (*third pers. sing.*) he; — ist es, it is he; — selbst, he himself; — würde nicht mehr — sein, he would cease to be himself; 2) you (*a formal mode of addressing inferiors and servants, instead of* Du, *now growing out of use*); — soll gehen! you are to go! II. *(str.) m.* (of birds) he, male.

Erach'ten, *(w.) v. tr.* to think, judge, deem; to conceive, imagine, presume; für nöthig —, to think, deem, *or* find necessary; das —, *v. s. (str.) n.* judgment, opinion; meinem — nach, *or* meines E-s, according to my judgment, in my opinion, for aught I know.

Eral'ten, *(w.) v. intr. (L. u.)* to grow old, *see* Veralten.

Erang'eln, *(w.) v. tr.* 1) to catch with an angle, to fish; 2) *coll.* to obtain *or* gain by perseverance *or* unceasing efforts, *cf.* Ergattern.

Erar'beiten, *(w.) v. tr.* (sich [*Dat.*] etwas) to gain by working, to obtain by labour.

Erar'men, *(w.) v. intr. see* Verarmen.

Erath'men, *(w.) v.* I. *intr.* to draw a long breath (Aufathmen); to pant, to breathe; II. *tr.* to take in by breathing, to breathe.

Erb'..., (*from* Erben), *in comp.* hereditary; —**adel**, *m.* hereditary nobility; —**amt**, *n.* hereditary office; —**anfall**, *m. Law*, hereditary conveyance, heritage; —**antheil**, *m. see* —theil.

Erbang'en, *(w.) v. intr. (aux.* sein) * to grow anxious, apprehensive.

Erbar'men, *(w.) v.* I. *tr.* to excite pity (in one); to move to (to cause, raise) pity *or* commiseration: daß Gott erbarme! God a mercy; II. *refl.* (*with Gen. or* über [*with Acc.*]) to commiserate, pity, compassionate, to take pity *or* compassion (on), to show mercy (to), to have mercy (upon); III. *refl.* (*impers.*) to move to pity (*with Acc. & Gen.*); erbarme dich meiner! have mercy upon me! mich erbarmet dieses Armen, this poor man moves me to pity, *i. e.* I pity, have compassion on this poor man; e-d, *p. a.* compassionate, merciful.

Erbar'men, *s. (str.) n.* pity, commiseration, compassion, mercy; es ist zum —, it is pitiful; it is most miserable: er sieht zum — aus, he looks most wretched; — haben, to take pity (mit, on, upon); er hat kein —, he has no bowels; e-swürdig, e-swerth, *adj.* deserving pity, pitiable, commiserable.

Erbar'mer, *(str.) m.* pitier.

Erbärm'lich, I. *adj.* pitiful, pitiable, miserable, wretched; II. **E-keit**, *(w.) f.* 1) pitiableness, miserable condition, miserableness, wretchedness; 2) *gener. pl.* mean, miserable actions *or* conduct, *coll.* shabby tricks.

Erbar'mung, *(w.) f.* pity, *see* Erbarmen, *a.*; e-slos, *adj.* merciless; e-svoll, *adj.* compassionate; e-swürdig, *see* Erbarmenswürdig; **E-swürdigkeit**, *f.* pitiableness.

Erbau'en, *(w.) v.* I. *tr.* 1) to build, build up, erect, construct; 2) to raise, to grow, cultivate; 3) *fig.* to edify; II. *refl.* to be edified.

Erbau'er, *(str.) m.* builder, founder, creator, &c.

Erbau'lich, I. *adj.* edifying; II. **E-keit**, *(w.) f.* the quality of edifying, edification.

Erbau'ung, *(w.) f.* 1) the (act of) building, erection, foundation; 2) *Agr.* the practice of growing, cultivation, culture; 3) *fig.* edification; im zweiten Jahre nach — Roms, in the second year after the building of Rome.

Erbau'ungs..., *in comp.* —**buch**, *n.* book of devotion, devotional book (Andachtsbuch), religious work; —**rede**, *f.* edifying (religious) discourse; —**schrift**, *f.* edifying publication, religious tract; —**stunde**, *f.* hour of devotion *or* meditation, devotional hour; —**vortrag**, *m. see* —rede.

Erb'bar, *adj.* inheritable.

Erb'..., *in comp.* —**beamtete**, *m.* one in possession of hereditary office; —**begräbniß**, *n.* hereditary sepulchre, family vault; —**besitz**, *m.* hereditary possession; —**bestand**, *m.*, —**bestandniß**, *n. see* —pacht; —**buch**, *n. see* —register; —**contract**, *see* —vertrag.

Er'be, *s.* I. *(w.) m.* heir, inheritor; successor: der muthmaßliche —, heir presumptive; der unstreitige —, heir apparent; — werden, to fall heir; II. *(str.) n.* inheritance, heritage; heirdom; *Law*, hereditament.

Erbe'ben, *(w.) v. intr. (aux.* sein) to shake, quake, tremble, totter, shudder (vor [*with Dat.*], at).

Erb'..., *in comp.* —**eid**, *m.* oath of fealty; —**eigen**, *adj.* possessed by inheritance, allodial; —**einigung**, *f. see* —vereinigung; —**einsetzung**, *f.* bequeathment.

Erbei'ßen, *(str.) v. tr.* 1) *coll.* to bite through; to crush with the teeth, to masticate; to bite open; 2) to bite to death.

Er'ben, *(w.) v.* I. *tr. a)* to inherit, to get by inheritance; ein großes Vermögen —, to succeed to, come into a large fortune; *b)* to be a person's heir, to succeed to any one's estate; II. *intr. (aux.* sein) 1) to inherit (*or* succeed to) an estate; 2) to descend, devolve by inheritance (auf [*with Acc.*], upon); er soll noch —, his fortune is in expectancy (of an inheritance).

Erbe'ten, *(w.) v. tr. & refl.* (sich [*Dat.*] etwas) to (endeavour to) obtain by praying *or* request; to pray (solicit) for ....

Erbet'teln, *(w.) v. tr.* to obtain by begging.

Erbeu'ten, *(w.) v. tr.* 1) to take *or* get as booty, to make booty of ..., to capture; 2) *fig.* to carry off, bear away (the bell, palm, prize).

Erbeu'ter, *(str.) m.* captor.

Erb'..., *in comp.* —**fähig**, *adj. Law*, heritable; —**fähigkeit**, *f.* capability of taking inheritance; —**fall**, *m.* case of succession, fortune in reversion; heritage, succession; —**fällig**, *adj.* hereditary; entailed; —**fälligkeit**, *f.* hereditariness; entail; —**fehler**, *m.* an inherited natural fault *or* defect; —**feind**, *m.* hereditary enemy, sworn enemy; —**feld**, *n.* lot worked for the benefit of the land-owner; —**folge**, *f.* succession: die —folge bestimmen, to entail; —**folgekrieg**, *m.* war of succession; —**folgerecht**, *n.* right of succession; —**fürst**, *m.* hereditary prince; —**fürstenthum**, *n.* hereditary principality; —**fürstin**, *f.* hereditary princess; —**gang**, *m. Law*, *see* —folge; —**gangsgedinge**, *n. see* —vertrag; —**ganggenoß**, *m. see* —genoß; —**ganggenossenschaft**, *f.* coheritage; —**ganggenossin**, *f.* coheiress, joint-heiress; —**gangsrecht**, *n. see* —folgerecht; —**geld**, *n.* money inherited, inheritance; —**genoß**, *m.* coheir, joint-heir; —**gerechtigkeit**, *f.* 1) *see* —recht; 2) hereditary title; —**gericht**, *n.* court-baron; —**gerichtsbarkeit**, *f.* jurisdiction of a court-baron; —**gerichtsherr**, *m.* hereditary justice, lord of the manor; —**gesessen**, *p. a.* 1) settled, *cf.* Eingesessen; 2) possessed of real property; —**gesessener**, *m.* (*decl. like adj.*) owner of an estate, *cf.* Eingesessener; —**graf**, *m.* heir (eldest son)

of a scull; —grind, m. Med. scall, scaldhead; —grund, m. landed property possessed by inheritance, heirloom; —grundherr, m. see —herr; —gut, n. heritage, (estate of) inheritance, patrimonial estate; (freies) allodium, manor, freehold-estate; (das freieigne) domain; —herr, m. owner by succession; lord of the manor; —herrlich, adj. manorial: —herrschaft, f. 1) hereditary possession of a manor; 2) family of a lord of the manor; —hof, m. see —gut; —huldigung, f. homage, oath of fealty.

Erbieten, (str.) I. v. refl. to profess a readiness (zu einer Sache, to a thing), to offer, to promise; freiwillig —, to volunteer; II. v. s. (str.) n., or Erbiet'ung, (w.) f. offer, tender, proffer.

Erbie'tig, adj. see Erbötig. [ritrix.

Er'bin, (w.) f. heiress, inheritress, inhe-

Erbit'ten, (str.) v. tr. 1) to obtain (or to endeavour to obtain) by entreaties or by praying, to solicit; ich erbitte mir eine Antwort &c., I request an answer, &c.; die erbetene Frist, the respite asked for; to bespeak; ich erbitte es mir von Ihnen zurück, I beg you to return it; 2) to move or induce by entreaties: sich leicht — lassen, to be easy to be prevailed upon; er läßt sich nicht —, he is inexorable.

Erbit'tern, (w.) v. tr. to exasperate, irritate, provoke, incense, nettle, exacerbate; erbittert, p.a. exasperate, irritated, &c.; hostile. — Erbit'terung, (w.) f. exasperation, irritation, violent anger (über [with Acc.], at); animosity (gegen, against).

Erbitt'lich, I. adj. exorable, flexible; II. E-keit, (w.) f. exorability, flexibility.

Erb'..., in comp. —kaiser, m. hereditary emperor; —kaiserthum, n. hereditary empire; —kämmerer, m. hereditary chamberlain; — —könig, m. hereditary king; —königreich, n. hereditary kingdom; —krankheit, f. hereditary disease; —land, n. hereditary land; die kaiserlichen —lande, the emperor's patrimonial dominions.

Erbla'sen, (str.) v. refl. (sich [Dat.] etwas) coll. to get or gain by blowing on a wind-instrument.

Erblas'sen, (w.) v. intr. (aux. sein) 1) to grow or turn pale; to fade, to lose the colour; 2) fig. to expire, die.

Erb'..., in comp. —lassenschaft, (w.) f. (l. u.) see Nachlaß; —lasser, m. (str.) testator, bequeather, (of real property) devisor; —lasserin, f. testatrix; —lassungsrecht, n. the right of bequeathing one's property by will. [blue.

Erblau'en, (w.) v. intr. to get or become

Erb'..., in comp. —lehn, n. hereditary fief, absolute fee, fee-simple, fee-tail; —lehnherr, m. proprietor of a fee, lord of the manor; —lehn(s)leute, pl. tenants in fee-simple; —lehre, f. (l. u.) tradition.

Erblei'chen, (str.) v. intr. (aux. sein) 1) to grow or turn pale, * to pale; 2) fig. to expire, die. [poch; 2) see Erbleichen.

Erb'leihe, (w.) f. (l. u.) Law. 1) see Erb-

Erb'lich, I. adj. hereditary, inheritable; II. E-keit, (w.) f. hereditariness.

Erblick'en, (w.) v. tr. to descry, perceive, behold, see, discover, to get a sight of, to catch sight or a glimpse of; das Licht der Welt —, fig. to be born. [blind.

Erblin'den, (w.) v. intr. (aux. sein) to grow

Erblö'den, (w.) v. refl. to be bashful, ashamed, afraid; er erblödete sich nicht, he did not scruple, he was impudent enough (to ...).

Erb'los, adj. 1) heirless, without heir; 2) excluded from succession, disinherited.

Erblü'hen, (w.) v. intr. (aux. sein) to bloom, blossom; to grow up, to be developed; to bud out (into womanhood, &c.).

Erb'..., in comp. —mangel, m. hereditary deficiency or defect; —marschall, m. hereditary marshal; —meier, m. hereditary farmer; —meierei, f., —meiergut, n., —meierstätte, f. hereditary farm; —monarch, m. hereditary monarch; —monarchie, f. hereditary monarchy; —nehmer, m. inheritor, heir.

Erb'niß, (str.) n. (l. u.) see Erbschaft.

Erboh'ren, (w.) v. tr. to light on (certain strata, &c.) in boring or sinking a shaft, &c.

Erb'ordnung, (w.) f. order of succession.

Erbor'gen, (w.) v. tr. to borrow; erborgtes Wissen, second-hand knowledge; erborgte Macht, secondary power.

Erbo'sen, Erbö'ßen, (w.) v. I. tr. to exasperate, provoke; II. refl. to grow angry, to get into a passion, to fret; erbost, p. a. in a rage, angry, incensed (über [with Acc.], at).

Erbot', (str.) n. offer, tender, proffer.

Erbö'tig, adv. ready to perform something; — sein, to be ready, to offer.

Erb'..., in comp. —pacht, f. fee-farm; hereditary tenement, long-lease; —pächter, m. fee-farmer; copy holder, hereditary tenant; —pflicht, f. oath of fealty, homage; —portion, f. see —theil; —prinz, m. hereditary prince (of a duchy); —prinzessin, f. hereditary princess (of a duchy). [surge up (of the sea).

Erbrau'den, (w.) v. intr. (aux. sein) * to

Erbrau'sen, (w.) v. intr. (aux. sein) * to begin or rise roaring (of a storm); to roar or rush along.

Erbrech'bar, adj. easily broken, fragile.

Erbrech'en, (str.) v. I. tr. 1) to break or force open (a door, &c.); 2) to open (a letter); II. refl. to vomit; sich — wollen, to feel sick, to reach, retch, keck.

Erbrech'en, s. (str.) n. 1) or Erbrech'ung, (w.) f. the (act of) breaking open, &c. cf. Erbrechen, v.; 2) the (act of) vomiting, vomition, vomit; das schwarze —, the black vomit; — erregend, vomitory, emetic; — stillend, antemetic.

Erb'..., in comp. —recht, n. right of inheriting or inheritance; right of succession, heirship, or descent, ancestral right; —register, n. register of hereditary estates; —reich, n. hereditary realm, kingdom, empire, or monarchy; —richter, m. hereditary judge; —ritter, m. hereditary knight.

Erbrül'len, (w.) v. intr. (l. u.) to roar (out); to begin to bellow, &c.

Erbrü'ten, (w.) v. tr. (l. u.) see Ergrübeln.

Erb'..., in comp. —saß(e), m. see —gesessener; —satzung, f. will, testament; —schacht, m. deepest pit in a mine; —schaden, m. hereditary defect, disadvantage going down to the heirs.

Erb'schaft, (w.) f. inheritance, heritage; succession, heirdom; eine — thun, to inherit property, cf. Erben; eine reiche — thun, to have a large estate, or sum of money left one; E-smasse, f. the mass of property to be divided among the heirs; E-srichter, m. person appointed to settle the just division of an inheritance among the heirs; E-sverfüger, m. testator; E-sverfügung, f. will, testament.

Erb'schaftlich, adj. relating or pertaining to an inheritance.

Erb'..., in comp. —schicht, —schichtung, f. see —theilung; —schichter, m. see Erbschaftsrichter; —schirm, m. protection given by the heir; —schirmherr, m. one giving such protection, patron; —schleicher, m. legacy-hunter; legacy-sneaker; —schleicherei, f. legacy-hunting; —schoß, m. ground rent; —schuld, f. debt descending to the heir, incumbrance on the inheritance; —schutz, m. see —schirm.

Erb'se, (w.) f. Bot. pea (Pisum L.); die wilde —, see Ackererbse; die große, englische (markreiche) —, marrow-fat (pea).

Erb'sel, (w.) f. Bot. barberry, pipperidge; —dorn, m. Bot. pipperidge-bush (Berberis vulgaris L.).

Erb'sen..., in comp. —baum, m. Bot. Si-

Erd'..., *in comp.* —rübe, *f.* 1) *see* Kohlrübe; 2) *see* —scheibe; —rücken, *m.* elevation of land, *cf.* Bergrücken.

Erdrücken, *(w.) v. tr.* 1) *a)* to press to death, to stifle, choke, suffocate; to overlay, zum — voll, crowded to suffocation; *b) fig.* to crush (a rebellion, &c.), to overwhelm; 2) *provinc. for* Zerdrücken.

Erdrück'ung, *(w.) f.* the (act of) stifling, &c., suffocation. [(Erdball).

Erd'rund, *(str.) m.* terrestrial ball, globe

Erdrusch', *(str., pl.* Erdrüsch'e) *m. (from* Erdreschen) that which is gained by thrashing, yield (Ausdrusch, 2; Ertrag).

Erd'..., *in comp.* —sack, *m. Fort.* earth-bag; —saft, *m.* mineral juice (such as petroleum and asphaltos); —salz, *n.* rock-salt, saltpetre; —sand, *m.* sand found on land *(opp.* Flußsand); —säure, *f. Phys.* terreous acid; —schaf, *n. Zool.* lama *(Auchenia glama* L.); —schatten, *m. see* Mondsfinsterniß; —schatz, *m. Law,* ground-rent; —schau, *f.* inspection of a dike; —scheibe, *f. Bot.* sow-bread *(Cyclamen europaeum* L.); —schicht, *f.* stratum, layer or bed of earth; die untere —schicht, subsoil; —schildkröte, *f. Zool. see* Landschildkröte; —schlacke, *f. Geogn.* earthy slag; —schlägel, *m. Agr.* clod-beater; —schmidt, *m.,* —schmiedlein, *n. see* Kellerwurm; —schnecke, *f. Zool.* slug (-snail) *(Limax agrestis* L.); —schocke, *f. see* Artischocke; —scholle, *f.* clod, *cf.* —kloß; —schollenpflug, *m.* stubble-plough; —schote, *f. Bot. see* —eichel, 1; —schraube, *f. see* Linksschnecke; —schwalbe, *f. see* Uferschwalbe; —schwamm, *m. Bot.* 1) mushroom, champignon *(Agaricus campestris* L.); 2) *see* Trüffel; —schwefel, *m. Pharm.* club-moss seed; —seife, *f. see* Bergseife; —specht, *m. Ornith. see* Wendehals; —spinne, *f. Entom.* field-spider *(Lycosa ruricola* Deg.); —spitze, *f. see* —zunge; —stachelnuß, *f. Bot.* caltrops *(Tribulus terrestris* L.); —stamm, *m. Forest.* young tree grown from seed; —stein, *m. Miner.* aetites; —stern, *m. see* Mondstern; —stoß, *m.* shock of an earthquake: —stöße sind in der Nähe von Calcutta gespürt worden, shocks of earthquake have been felt near C.; —strich, *m.* zone; —stufe, *f.* terrace; brow of a hill; —sturz, *m.* fall of earth, land-slip; —theil, *m. see* Welttheil; —theer, *m.* mineral tar; —toffel, *f. see* Kartoffel.

Erdul'den, *(w.) v. tr.* to suffer, endure, bear, tolerate. — Erdul'dung, *(w.) f.* a state of suffering, &c., endurance. [grow stupid.

Erdumm'men, *(w.) v. intr.* *(aux.* sein) to

Erd'..., *in comp.* —umschiffer, —umsegler, *m.* circumnavigator (of the globe); —umschiffung, —umsegelung, *f.* circumnavigation (of the globe).

Erdurs'ten, *(w.) v. intr.* *(aux.* sein *(l. u.)* 1) to grow thirsty; 2) to die with thirst.

Erd'..., *in comp.* —vielfuß, *m. see* Assel, große; —viertel, *n.* quarter of the globe; —wachs, *n. Miner.* ozokerite; —wall, *m. see* —werk; —wand, *f.* earthen wall, *cf.* —bank; —wärme, *f.* temperature of (the interior of) the earth; —wärts, *adv.* towards the earth, ground, earthward(s); —weichsel, *f. Bot.* 1) *see* —kirschenstrauch; 2) a variety of the broad-leaved speed-well *(Veronica pseudochamaedrys* Jacq.); —weide, *f. Bot.* dwarf willow *(Salix repens* L., *S. ambigua* Ehrh., &c.); —weihrauch, *m., Bot. see* —kiefer; —weihrauchkraut, *n. Bot.* common germander *(Teucrium chamaedrys* L.); —weite, *f. Astr.* medium-distance of the earth from the sun; —weizen, *m. see* Roggenweizen; —werk, *n. Fort., &c.* earth-work, terrace, *cf.* —bank; —winde, *f.* 1) *see* Ackerwinde; 2) *Mech.* crab; —wolf, *m. Zool. see* Wasserratte; —wühler, *m. see* Ameisenscharrer; —wurm, *m.* earth-worm; —zeichnen, —zeichen, *n. Zool. see* Ziefelmaus; —zirkel, *m. see* —cirkel; —zone, *f. see* —strich; —zunge, *f.* neck of land.

Erei'fern, *(w.) v. refl.* to put one's self, fly, or fall into a passion, to fume (über *(with Acc.),* about); to grow warm with passion, to chafe.

Ereig'nen, *(w.) v. refl.* to happen, chance, come to pass, to take place, occur, betide.

Ereig'niß, *(str.) n.* event, occurrence, incident; das zufällige *or* unglückliche —, (the happening of an) accident; —reich, *adj.* eventful.

Ereig'nung, *(w.) f.* the happening of any thing (good or bad), event; E-sfall, *m.* case of emergency.

Erei'len, *(w.) v. tr.* to overtake, to come up with, to fetch up; to befall suddenly: der Tod ereilte ihn mitten unter seinen Arbeiten, death overtook him in the midst of his labours.

* Eremit', *(w.) m. (Gr.)* hermit, anchoret, &c. *(also Ornith. & Crust.) see* Einsiedler.

* Eremita'ge, [—tä'she], *(w.) f. (Fr.)* hermitage (also a Rhone wine so called).

Erer'ben, *(w.) v. tr.* to get by inheritance, to inherit; ererbt, *p. a.* hereditary.

Erfa'beln, *(w.) v. tr. see* Erdichten.

Erfach'en, *(w.) v. tr. (l. u.) see* Anfachen.

Erfah'ren, *(str.) v. tr.* 1) *coll. a)* to acquire; *b)* to overtake by driving (shipping); *c)* to kill by running over with a carriage; 2) *fig. a)* to learn, hear, to (come to) know, to be informed of ...; to understand; *b)* to experience, suffer, go through, undergo; to meet with; *c)* to learn, prove, know, *or* have from experience.

Erfah'ren, I. *p. a.* experienced (in *(with Dat.),* in), having (much) experience, expert, skilled, skilful, able, thorough-bred, versed, practised; im Geschäft — sein, to be well versed in business; wenig — in, but little experienced in ..., not much up to ...; nicht — in ..., ignorant of ...; II. E-heit, *(w.) f.* experience, practice, skill, experience.

Erfah'rung, *(w.) f.* experience, knowledge, practice; in — bringen, to learn, ascertain; durch — gewonnen *or* erlangt, experimental.

Erfah'rungs..., *in comp.* —arzt, *m.* empiric; —begriff, *m.* inductive idea; —beweis, *m.* experimental proof; —kunde, *f.* empiricism.

Erfah'rungslos, *adj.* inexperienced.

Erfah'rungs..., *in comp.* —mäßig, *adj.* empirical; inductive; —satz, *m.* principle derived from experience; —seelenkunde, —seelenlehre, *f.* empirical psychology; —weg, *m.* way of experience; auf dem —wege, experimentally; —welt, *f. Philos.* the world of experience; —wissen, *n.,* —wissenschaft, *f.* empirical knowledge.

Erfaß'bar, *adj. see* Faßbar.

Erfas'sen, *(w.) v. tr.* 1) to lay hold of (suddenly), to grasp, seize (on, upon); 2) *fig.* to comprehend, to grasp, *cf.* Auffassen, 2.

Erfech'ten, *(str.) v. tr.* 1) *(also refl.* sich *(Dat.)* etwas —) to get or obtain by fighting; den Sieg —, to gain the victory, carry the day, bear away the palm (Erkämpfen); 2) *vulg. for* Erbetteln, *cf.* Fechten, 4.

Erfie'deln, *(w.) v. refl.* (sich *(Dat.)* etwas) *vulg.* to get or gain by fiddling, *see* Ergeigen.

Erfind'bar, *adj.* inventible, contrivable, deviseable, *cf.* Erfindlich.

Erfin'den, *(str.) v. tr.* 1) to find out, invent; 2) to contrive, fabricate, devise, strike out, *cf.* Erdichten; 3) to find by experience; Jemanden treu —, to find (prove) one faithful or true.

Erfin'der, *(str.) m.* inventor; contriver, deviser, designer; projector.

Erfin'derin, *(w.) f.* inventress.

Erfin'derisch, *adj. see* Erfinderisch.

Erfind'lich, *adj.* 1) inventible, &c. *cf.* Er-

rejoiced in the name of Martin; erfreut, p. a. glad (über [with Acc.], of, at, about), delighted (at, with), pleased (with, by).

Erfreu'er, (str.) m. comforter, gratifier.

Erfreu'lich, I. adj. delightful, pleasing, cheering, agreeable, gratifying; e-e Nachrichten, satisfactory news: es läßt sich nur wenig E-es über ihn sagen, but little can be said in his favour; II. E-keit, (w.) f. delightfulness, gratifying nature (of an event, &c.).

Erfreu'ung, (w.) f. the act of gladdening, &c. cf. Erfreuen; exhilaration.

Erfrie'ren, (str.) v. I. intr. (aux. sein) to freeze, to freeze to death; to die with (or to perish from the) cold; to chill: du wirst —, you'll be frozen to death; II. refl. sich (Dat.) ein Glied —, to have a limb frozen; erfroren, p. a. dead from or benumbed with cold; chilled; frozen.

Erfri'schen, (w.) v. tr. to cool, refresh, recreate, refrigerate; e-des Mittel, refrigerant.

Erfri'schung, (w.) f. the (act of) refreshing, refreshment, recreation, refrigeration; E-s-hafen, m. Mar. harbour of refreshment.

Erfül'len, (w.) v. I. tr. 1) to fill, fill up, replenish; mit Leben —, to inspire with life: fig.-a. 2) to fill, strike (with fear, &c.); to impress, imbue, absorb, engross, possess; 3) to fulfil, perform, make good, discharge (one's duty, &c.); to comply with, to satisfy (a request); to accomplish, realise; eine Verbindlichkeit —, to acquit, discharge an obligation; Jemandes Erwartungen —, to satisfy (come up to) a person's expectations; seine Bestimmung —, to work out one's destinies; II. refl. 1) Sport. to fill (said of deer); 2) to fulfil itself, to be fulfilled.

Erfül'lung, (w.) f. 1) the (act of) filling, &c.; 2) fulfilling, fulfilment, performance, discharge (of one's duty, &c.); accomplishment, consummation; realisation; die — seiner Bitte ist unmöglich, it is impossible to comply with his request; in — bringen, to bring about, fulfil; in — gehen, to be fulfilled, to be accomplished, realised; to be verified, to come true, to prove correct (of predictions, &c.); to come to pass (of dreams); E-s-eid, m. Law, supplementary oath; E-s-tag, m. Comm. settling-day, name-day.

Erfünf'eln, (w.) v. intr. see Ergänzen.

Ergän'zen, (w.) v. tr. 1) to mend, repair; 2) to supply; to complete; to renew, recruit; to make up, compensate; das Fehlende —, to make up the complement or a deficiency; to supplement; einander (less correctly sich) —, to act as (a) supplement the one to the other: e-d, p. a. supplementary, supplemental, complemental.

Ergän'zung, (w.) f. 1) integration, redintegration; renovation, renewal; the (act of) recruiting, &c. cf. Ergänzen; 2) a) completion; b) supplement, complement; supply.

Ergän'zungs..., in comp. Book-s. —band, m. supplementary volume; —blatt, n. supplementary sheet, rider, supplement; —bogen, m. Typ. imperfect sheet; —bruch, m. Math. complemental fracture; —credit, m. supplementary credit; —eid, m. Law, supplementary oath; —gesetz, n. supplemental law; —heft, n. supplementary number, supplement; —mannschaft, f. a complement (of soldiers); —[illegible], m. Typ. bar, ellipsis [—]; —stück, n. supplement; —theil, m. integral part; —vertrag, m. supplementary or complementary pact or treaty; —verhältniß, m. complement (of [illegible]); —winkel, m. Geom. supplement of an angle. [in a net; 2) fig. to ensnare.

Ergat'tern, (w.) v. tr. (L. u.) 1) to catch

Ergau'nern, (w.) v. tr. coll. to obtain (by [illegible]), to snatch, to fish or pick up.

Ergau'keln, (w.) v. tr. to obtain by [illegible].

Erge'ben, (str.) v. I. tr. 1) †, to deliver up; 2) a) to yield (good or bad results, &c.); Verlust —, to result in loss; b) to prove, show; II. refl. 1) a) to surrender, submit, yield: b) (in etwas [Acc.]) to acquiesce (in), to resign one's self (to); 2) (with Dat.) to devote, apply, or addict one's self to, to give one's self up to; to indulge in (vice, &c.), to abandon one's self or take to (drinking, &c.); sich einem schlechten Wandel —, to give one's self over to evil courses: 3) a) to result, follow, appear (aus, from); b) to occur, take place; sollte sich —, daß die Qualität geringer ist, should the quality prove inferior; hier ergab sich eine Schwierigkeit, here a difficulty occurred or arose; III. intr. for Ergiebig sein.

Erge'ben, p. a. 1) devoted, attached, addicted, given (to); mit Leib und Seele —, wedded (to a cause); 2) resigned; unser E-(st)es, Comm. our respects; e-st, adj. & adv. (at the conclusion of letters) most humble, humbly, &c.: Ihr e-ster Diener, your most humble (or obedient) servant; respectfully or sincerely yours, yours truly; ich beziehe mich auf mein E-(st)es mit letzter Post, I refer to my respects (to you) of last post.

Erge'benheit, (w.) f. 1) submission; 2) devotion; attachment; devotedness, addictedness; fidelity; adherence, loyalty: versichern Sie ihr meine —, present my respects to her: 3) see Ergebung.

Ergeb'niß, (str.) n. result; yield (of a harvest); E-sse haben, to produce (lead to) results: Math. product; E-los, adj. without result, leading to no result, insufficient, vain.

Erge'bung, (w.) f. submission, resignation.

Ergeg'nen, (w.) v. tr. Law, to reply.

Erge'hen, (str.) v. I. tr. 1) †, to overtake reach; 2) to walk to the end of; 3) (sich [Dat.] etwas) coll. to gain, earn by walking (as a messenger); II. refl. 1) to take the exercise of walking, to walk; 2) fig. (with in [& Dat.]) to indulge in, to launch forth into, to pour forth (eulogiums, &c.); III. intr. (aux. sein) 1) to come out, to be published, promulgated or issued; 2) a) (über [with Acc.]) to befall, to happen to (one); b) to come to pass, to fall out; es erging das Urtheil über ihn, sentence was passed upon him; — lassen, a) to issue (out or forth); b) to do (justice), to show (mercy); laß Gnade für Recht —, let right give way to mercy; Mahnungen — lassen, to write (send out) dunning letters; (etwas) über sich (Acc.) — lassen, to take upon one's self, to submit to, to bear, suffer patiently; 3) to go or fare with; es wird ihm schlimm —, he will fare ill; wie würde es dir —? what would become of you? so sollte es allen Verräthern —, all traitors should be served thus; möge es ihm wohl —! may he do well! may he thrive!

Ergei'gen, (w.) v. tr. (sich [Dat.] etwas) coll. to get or gain by playing on the violin.

Ergei'zen, (w.) v. tr. (sich [Dat.] etwas) to get by avarice, coll. to scrape together, cf. Erkargen.

* **Er'gel,** adv. vulg. (corruption of the Lat. ergo) therefore (cf. Schlegel, transl. of Sh.'s Haml. 5, 1 & Argal. Vol. I.). [yellow.

Ergel'ben, (w.) v. intr. (aux. sein) to turn

Ergetzbar, adj. susceptible of amusement.

Erget'zen, (w.) v. I. tr. to delight, please, divert, amuse, regale, entertain; II. refl. to be delighted or pleased (an [with Dat.], mit, bei?, with), to amuse one's self (with), to (take) delight (in), to enjoy.

Ergetz'lich, I. adj. amusing, delightful, delectable, pleasing, pleasant, diverting; II. E-keit, (w.) f. 1) delightfulness, &c., delight; 2) amusement, entertainment, pleasure, pl. revels. [pleasure,

Erget'zung, (w.) f. delectation, delight,

Ergie'big, I. adj. yielding, productive; abundant, copious, plentiful; rich, fertile: dieser Geschäftszweig ist ziemlich —, this branch of business gives a pretty good result; II. E-keit, (w.) f. yieldingness, productiveness; abundance; richness, fertility.

Ergie'ßen, (str.) v. I. tr. to pour forth, out, to effuse; II. refl. 1) to flow or issue out, to discharge, empty, or disembogue itself, to fall (in, into); 2) a) to gush or pour forth or down; b) to overflow, run over: 3) fig. to break out, forth (into tears, &c.), to burst (into); sich — in (with Acc. & [l. u.] Dat.), to run out into, to pour forth, cf. Ergeben, refl. 2.

Ergie'ßung, (w.) f. 1) the (act of) pouring forth, outpouring, effusion; Med. overflowing (of bile); 2) discharge (of water, &c.), flowing out, disemboguement, &c. cf. Ergießen.

Ergil'ben, (w.) v. intr. see Ergelben.

Ergir'ren, (w.) v. tr. (& refl. sich [Dat.] etwas) to obtain by cooing.

Erglän'zen, (w.) v. intr. (aux. haben & sein) to begin to shine, to burst forth in splendour, to emit lustre.

Erglim'men, (w.) v. intr. (aux. sein) to enkindle, begin to glow, to glow up.

Erglü'hen, (w.) v. I. intr. (aux. sein) to glow: II. tr. to kindle, make glowing.

Ergötz'bar, Ergöt'zen &c., see Ergetzbar &c.

Ergra'ben, (str.) v. tr. (sich [Dat.] etwas) to gain by digging.

Ergrä'men, (w.) v. tr. (particul. refl. sich [Dat.] eine Krankheit &c.) to bring on (an illness, &c.) by grieving.

Ergrau'en, (w.) v. intr. (aux. sein) 1) to grow hoary; in Geschäften, im Dienste &c. ergraut, grown gray in business, in service, &c.; veteran; 2) to dawn; 3) or Ergrau'sen, (w.) to shudder, to be dismayed, to feel awe.

Ergrei'fen, (str.) v. tr. 1) a) to seize, to lay (take, catch, seize, or get) hold of, to take (up), to lay hand upon, to gripe, grasp; die Waffen —, to take up arms; b) to catch, apprehend; fig.-a. 2) to resort (have recourse) to, adopt, take (measures, &c.); to take, seize, embrace (eine Gelegenheit &c., an opportunity, &c.); 3) to seize, move, touch, affect, to strike (with admiration, &c.); die Feder —, to take pen in hand; das Wort —, to take (up) the word, cf. Wort; eine Partei —, to take or espouse a party; ein Geschäft —, to follow a business or profession; ein Gewerbe —, to take up a trade; die Flucht —, to make one's escape, to take to flight; die Offensive —, to assume (or act on) the offensive; e-d, p. a. fig. affecting, striking, thrilling (Mährend); ergriffen, p. a. fig. seized (von, with), struck, smitten, touched (with), moved, affected (by); von Ehrfurcht ergriffen, awe-struck; von Grausen ergriffen, horror-struck, aghast with horror.

Ergrei'fung, (w.) f. 1) the (act of) seizing, taking up, &c. cf. Ergreifen; 2) seizure, capture, apprehension; 3) fig. adoption (of measures, &c.).

Ergrim'men, (w.) v. intr. (aux. sein) to chafe, grow furious; ergrimmt, p. a. enraged, angry; fierce, grim. [for Vergrößern.

Ergrö'ßern, (w.) v. tr. & intr. († &) provinc.

Ergrü'beln, (w.) v. tr. to find out by minute and persevering investigation; to search out.

Ergrün'den, (w.) v. tr. 1) to fathom: 1) to explore, sound; 2) fig. to penetrate, sound, sift, search out, dive into.

Ergrün'der, (str.) m. fathomer, explorer.

Ergründ'lich, adj. fathomable, soundable, penetrable. [ploration.

Ergrün'dung, (w.) f. a fathoming, &c., exploration.

Ergrü'nen, (w.) v. intr. (aux. sein) to grow verdant. [ground, cf. Ergießung.

Erguß', (str., pl. Ergüsse) m. effusion,

Erha'ben, I. *adj.* 1) elevated, raised (above the base), high, lofty; 2) *fig.* sublime, exalted, lofty; eminent, illustrious; noble, august, high, grand; raised above (others, &c.), superior (über [*with Acc.*], to); ich bin darüber —, I am above that; über allen Tadel —, beyond blame; e-e Arbeit, *f. T.* (mezzo) relievo, relief, raised work, embossment; halb e-e Arbeit, demi- *or* half-relief; flach e-e Arbeit, bas-relief, low relief; e-e Arbeit machen, to emboss; e-er Winkel, *Geom.* re-entering angle; der e-e Stil, the elevated style (of diction); II. *s.* (*decl. like adj.*) *n.* the sublime; etwas E-eres ist nicht denkbar, anything more sublime is not to be conceived; III. E-heit, (*w.*) *f.* 1) loftiness, elevation; 2) protuberance, prominence; inequality; ridge; 3) *fig.* sublimity; eminence; loftiness; nobleness, grandeur.

Erhacken, (*w.*) *v. tr.* 1) *coll.* to hew *or* cleave through; 2) to get *or* acquire by hoeing *or* hewing.

Erha'dern, (*w.*) *v. tr.* to obtain *or* acquire by contention *or* litigation.

Erhal'len, (*w.*) *v. intr.* (*aux.* sein) to resound. [ä] preservable, conservable.

Erhalt'bar, *adj.* 1) obtainable (Erhältlich);

Erhal'ten, (*str.*) *v.* I. *tr.* 1) *a)* to check, to hold in; *b)* to preserve from falling; 2) to keep, to keep up, support, maintain; in Kleidungsstücken —, to keep *or* find in clothes; ein Feuer —, to keep up a fire; Einen am Leben —, to save any one's life; wenn mich Gott am Leben erhält, if God saves my life, if I am spared; der Vater ist uns noch —, our father is still spared to us; Jemandes Andenken dauernd —, to perpetuate a person's memory; — Sie mir Ihre Freundschaft, retain your friendly feelings towards me; einen höheren Preis —, *Comm.* to fetch a higher price; — Sie mir Ihr Vertrauen, continue your confidence in me; 3) to save, preserve, conserve; 4) to receive, get; to gain, obtain, have, acquire; wenn Sie dieses (*i. e.* Schreiben) —, when this reaches you; ich habe zugesandt —, I have had sent to me; — (*pp.*), received (*cf.* Empfangen); ein nicht e-er Brief, a letter unreceived; II. *refl.* 1) *a)* to keep on one's legs; *b)* to keep; die Früchte haben sich frisch —, the fruits have kept sound; *c)* to maintain one's position, station, &c.; 2) to support one's self; to live, subsist (von, durch, on, by); sich im Preise —, to continue steady in price, to maintain, support, keep up the price; sich fest — auf (*with Dat.*), to remain firm at ... (of prices); sich in Gunst — bei ..., to keep in favour with; sein Andenken erhielt sich bis auf die neueste Zeit, his memory lingered till recent days.

Erhal'ten, *p. a.* preserved; gut —, 1) (of houses, &c.) in a good state of repair; 2) in (a state of) good preservation.

Erhal'ter, (*str.*) *m.*, **Erhal'terin,** (*w.*) *f.* preserver, maintainer, &c.

Erhält'lich, *adj.* obtainable, to be had.

Erhal'tung, (*w.*) *f.* preservation; conservation; maintenance; support; E-brille, *f.* eye-preservers.

Erhäm'mern, (*w.*) *v. tr.* 1) to shape by hammering; 2) to get *or* acquire by hammering.

Erhan'deln, (*w.*) *v. tr.* (sich [*Dat.*] etwas) 1) to purchase, buy, [illegible] bargain for; 2) to acquire by trade.

Erhän'gen, (*w.*) *v. refl.* to hang one's self.

Erhar'ren, (*w.*) *v. tr.* to expect, await (with patience); to obtain by patient waiting.

Erhar'schen, (*w.*) *v. intr.* (*aux.* sein) to become harsh, hard, *or* rough to the touch.

Erhar'ten, (*w.*) *v. intr.* (*aux.* sein) to grow hard, to harden.

Erhär'ten, (*w.*) *v. tr. fig.* to corroborate, prove, confirm, verify, substantiate, *cf.* Eidlich.

Erhär'tung, (*w.*) *f.* corroboration; a proving of ..., confirmation, &c., asseveration.

Erhasch'en, (*w.*) *v. tr.* to catch, overtake, snatch (at), lay hold of, seize; einen Augenblick, einen Kuß &c. —, to snatch a moment, &c.

Erhau'en, (*irr.*) *v. tr. coll.* 1) to hew *or* cut through; 2) to strike *or* cut down; 3) to get *or* acquire by cutting, &c.

Erhe'ben, (*str.*) *v.* I. *tr.* 1) to heave, heave up, to lift (up); to elevate, raise; *fig.-e.* 2) to raise, lift up, exalt; 3) to raise, advance, prefer, promote; 4) to praise, extol; bis an *or* in den Himmel —, to laud, extol *or* exalt (one) to the (very) skies; 5) *a)* to raise *or* levy (money, taxes, &c.), to take up, collect (a sum, bei, with); lassen Sie den Betrag bei uns —, *Comm.* procure the amount from our firm; lassen Sie den Betrag bei der Bank —, get the amount at the bank; die Herren H. & Comp. sind ersucht worden, Ihnen die Kisten kostenfrei zuzustellen und den Betrag von uns zu —, Messrs. H. & Co. have been requested to deliver the cases to you free of expense, collecting the amount from us; *b)* to receive, gather, collect, take (taxes, &c.), to take possession of (an inheritance); 6) *T. & Paint.* to bring out, relieve; 7) to set up, raise (a cry, claims, &c.), to start (objections, &c.), begin; einen Zweifel —, to raise a doubt; 8) *Arith.* to involve: aufs Quadrat —, to square; auf die Cubikzahl —, to raise (a number) to the third power, &c. *cf.* Cubikzahl; die Stimme, die Augen —, to lift up, raise, *or* elevate one's voice, eyes; Protest —, *Comm.* to raise *or* make protest, to order a protest; ein Protocoll —, to note down, record the proceedings; amtlich — lassen, to have a legal enquiry instituted; es darf keine Provision erhoben werden, *Comm.* no commission is recoverable; II. *refl.* 1) to raise one's self, arise, rise; to mount, to soar (of birds and *fig.*); sich plötzlich —, to start up; to spring up (of a breeze); to arise (of a storm); wie sich der Wind erhebt! how the wind is rising! 2) to start, fly up (as dust); *fig.-e.* 3) to rise up (in arms); sich gegen Jemand —, to rise, to rebel against ...; 4) to take rise, spread (as a rumour); sich über Andere —, to elevate one's self above others; to be arrogant; sich stolz —, to be upon the high strain; e-d, *p. a. see* Ergreifend; e-der Muskel des Schulterblattes, *m. Anat.* uplifting muscle of the scapula.

Erheb'lich, I. *adj.* important, weighty, material, cogent, considerable; II. E-keit, (*w.*) *f.* importance, consequence, weightiness, considerableness.

Erhe'bung, (*w.*) *f.* 1) *a)* a raising, &c.; *b)* upheaval, a raising (of part of the surface of the earth, &c.); 2) elevation, rise, rising ground; *fig.-e.* 3) elevation, exaltation; promotion, advancement, preferment; 4) a receiving, levying, gathering (of taxes, &c.); collection; 5) a rising (of a people against its oppressors, &c.); 6) examination, (statistical, &c.) enquiry; audit; 7) *Arith.* involution; 8) *Chem.* sublimation.

Erhe'bungs..., *in comp.* —art, *f.* mode of collecting (taxes); —kosten, *pl. see* Incassospesen; —schein, *m. Comm.* check; —winkel, *m.* angle of elevation; *Mar.* (des Bugspriets) steeving.

Erhei'raten, (*w.*) *v. tr.* (sich [*Dat.*] etwas) to obtain (as a fortune, &c.) by marriage.

Erhei'schen, (*w.*) *v. tr.* to render necessary, to require, demand; ein Mißstand, der sofortige Abstellung erheischt, a grievance which [illegible] for immediate redress. [heitern.

Erhei'terer, (*str.*) *m.* cheerer, &c. *cf.* Er-

Erhei'tern, (*w.*) *v.* I. *tr.* 1) to brighten *or* clear up; to cheer (up), make serene; 2) to gladden, exhilarate; to enliven; II. *refl.* 1) to brighten *or* clear up; 2) *fig.* to become cheerful.

[illegible]; es ist mir —, I remember it; so viel [illegible] — ist, as far as I remember.

Erin'nern, (w.) v. I. tr. 1) a) to put in mind (an [with Acc.], of), to remind (of), put in remembrance; b) to admonish; 2) to observe, state, mention; II. refl. (with Gen. or an [with Acc.]) to remember, recollect, bear in mind, to call to memory or mind; — Sie sich meiner or an mich, remember me.

Erin'nerung, (w.) f. 1) a) the faculty of remembering, a reminding (an [with Acc.], of); mention; b) admonition; 2) remembrance, recollection, memory; meine E-en an Mendelssohn, my recollections of M.; zur — an (with Acc.), in memory (or remembrance) of ...; historische E-en, historical associations; es bedurfte keiner —, it required or needed no reminder; etwas in — bringen, to call to mind, remind (one) of (a thing), to put (one) in mind of (a thing); — thun, to make mention; ohne vorläufige —, without previous notice.

Erin'nerungs ..., in comp. —buch, n. remembrance-book, memorandum-book, agenda; —kraft, f., —vermögen, n. memory, power of recollection; —kunst, f. mnemonics, the art of memory; —schreiben, n. monitory letter; —schrift, f. memorial; —zeichen, n. keepsake, token of remembrance, memento.

* **Eris**, f. Gr. Myth. Eris, (goddess of) dissention; —apfel, m. see Zankapfel.

Erja'gen, (w.) v. tr. to overtake, or to get by hunting or running after; to obtain by ardent endeavours.

Erkal'ten, (w.) v. intr. (aux. sein) 1) to cool (down), grow cold; 2) fig. to cool, relent, abate.

Erkäl'ten, (w.) v. I. tr. to cool, chill; II. refl. to catch (take or get a) cold.

Erkal'tung, (w.) f. 1) the (act of) cooling, see Erkalten; 2) (often fig.) coolness.

Erkäl'tung, (w.) f. 1) (the catching) cold, catarrh; 2) see Erkaltung, 2.

Erkämpf'en, (w.) v. tr. to obtain or gain by fighting, cf. Erfechten, 1.

Erkar'gen, (w.) v. tr. (sich [Dat.] etwas) to acquire, get, or lay up by niggardliness, coll. to scrape together, to rake and scrape (Ergeizen).

Erkau'fen, (w.) v. tr. 1) to purchase, buy; 2) to bribe, corrupt (Bestechen); 3) to ransom (Loskaufen).

Erkäuf'lich, I. adj. venal, see Käuflich; II. E-keit, (w.) f. venality (Käuflichkeit).

Erkauf'ung, (w.) f. 1) purchase; 2) the (act of) bribing, &c. [presume.

Erkeck'en, (w.) v. refl. to dare, make bold,

Erkenn'bar, I. adj. 1) capable of being known, knowable; 2) discernible, distinguishable, perceptible, capable of recognition; II. E-keit, (w.) f. 1) capability of being known; 2) discernibleness; perceptibility.

Erken'nen, (irr.) v. tr. 1) to perceive accurately; identify, to make out; to know, understand, apprehend; to be sensible of; es läßt sich nicht —, ob ..., there is no way of knowing (judging) whether ...; es ist leicht zu —, it is easy to be understood, it is easy to be known; 2) to recognize, to know; 3) to discern, distinguish; 4) a) to acknowledge, own; b) Comm. to credit (für, for); [illegible] für ..., to be or stand credited for ...; 5) Law, to decide, judge, award, pronounce judgment, pass sentence; 6) to allow, admit; etwas für [illegible] —, to admit a thing to be sacred; 7) Bibl. to know, have carnal intercourse with; [illegible] an (with Dat.) ... —, to know one by ...; [illegible] —, I should know him out of a thousand; zu — geben, to give (one) to understand, intimate, signify, to let know, make known, show, evince, exhibit; sich zu — geben, to discover one's self, to make one's self known; Einem

or etwas für etwas —, to own, recognize as; to judge, doom (a thing right, wrong, &c.); sich für schuldig —, to plead guilty.

Erkennt'lich, I. adj. 1) see Erkennbar, 2; 2) a) thankful, grateful; b) acknowledging (services, &c., in a liberal way); II. E-keit, (w.) f. 1) thankfulness, gratitude, sense of obligation; 2) (liberal) acknowledgment (of services rendered), liberality.

Erkennt'niß, n. I. (str.) f. 1) knowledge, (ocular) perception, cognition; 2) acknowledgment; zur — kommen, to repent; zur — einer Sache bringen, to lead one to perceive a thing; II. (str.) n. Law, judgment, sentence; verdict; III. in comp. —grund, m. criterion; —kraft, f., —vermögen, n. faculty of perception or of knowing, intellect, cognitive power; —lehre, f. doctrine or theory which treats of the faculty of perception.

Erken'nung, (w.) f. ocular perception, &c. cf. Erkennen; recognition; E-swort, n. Mil. watch-word; fig. (E-szeichen, n.) shibboleth.

Er'ker, (str.) m. projection, jutty (in a building), projecting story; —fenster, n. bay-window; oriel-window; jut-window; —stube, f. jutty-room.

Erkie'sen, (w.) v. tr. († &)* see Erwählen.

Erklaf'tern, (w.) v. tr. to encompass with extended arms (for the purpose of ascertaining the measure of ...), to fathom.

Erkla'gen, (w.) v. tr. to obtain by a lawsuit, to acquire by litigation.

Erklär'bar, I. adj. explicable, explainable, to be accounted for; II. E-keit, (w.) f. explicableness, capability of being interpreted or explained.

Erklä'ren, (w) v. I. tr. 1) to explain, expound, interpret, elucidate, illustrate; to define; to account for; 2) to declare (Krieg, war), to announce, state, express, set forth; to profess; einen Schriftsteller —, to interpret, explain an author; — für, to declare, pronounce to be, to set down for; für schuldig —, Law, to find guilty; für unschuldig —, to declare, pronounce innocent; Law, to find not guilty; in die Acht —, to outlaw; II. refl. 1) to declare, explain, express one's self; sich für oder gegen ... —, to declare for or against ...; sich für ... —, to be for ..., to advocate; 2) to be explained (aus, durch, by), to grow clear or evident; daraus erklärt sich sein Eifer, that accounts for his zeal; 3) (sich [Dat.] etwas) to account for (a thing, durch, by); ich kann mir das nicht —, I cannot account for it, or make that out; e-d, p. a. explanatory (notes, &c.), illustrative; erklärt, p. a. declared, avowed, professed; ein erklärter Feind, a sworn enemy; Empfang erklärt, Comm. receipt acknowledged.

Erklä'rer, (str.) m. explainer, expounder, interpreter, commentator, scholiast.

Erklär'lich, I. adj. see Erklärbar; aus e-en Gründen, for plain reasons; II. E-keit, see Erklärbarkeit.

Erklä'rung, (w.) f. 1) explanation, explication, exposition, illustration, elucidation, interpretation; definition; es findet seine — in dem Umstande, it is accounted for by the circumstance; 2) declaration; avowal; (öffentliche) public statement; zur — des ..., in explanation or illustration of ...; zur — dienend, illustrative, cf. Erklärend; die letzte —, ultimatum; E-swissenschaft, f. Theol. hermeneutics.

† **Erkle'cken**, (w.) v. intr. to be of use, to yield profit, to benefit; to suffice.

Erkleck'lich, adj. 1) †, profitable, advantageous; 2) sufficient; considerable; e-en Gewinn machen, to gain considerably, (niedr.:) to make a rattling profit.

Erklet'tern, (w.), **Erklim'men**, (str., less usual w.) v. tr. to climb, ascend, coll. to scramble up, to scale (as a mountain).

Erklimm'bar, adj. climbable, ascendable.

Erkling'eln, (w.) v. (I. w.) I. intr. see Erklingen; II. tr. 1) to cause to tinkle, jingle, &c.; 2) see Aufklingeln, Anschellen.

Erkling'en, (str.) v. intr. (aux. sein, rarely haben) to (begin to) sound, to jingle; to resound, to ring out.

Erklir'ren, (w.) v. intr. (aux. sein) to (begin to) rattle, clank, ring.

Erklopf'en, (w.) v. tr. 1) to beat or break to pieces; to crack (as nuts); 2) to awaken (one) by knocking. [tile investigation.

Erklü'geln, (w.) v. tr. to find out by sub-

Erknal'len, (w.) v. intr. (aux. sein) to give a report (as a gun); to crack (with a whip).

Erknar'ren, (w.) v. intr. (aux. sein) to (begin to) creak.

Erknau'sern, **Erknick'ern**, (w.) v. tr. coll. (gener. refl. sich [Dat.] etwas) to acquire or amass by niggardliness (Erkargen). [a bait.

Erkö'dern, (w.) v. tr. to catch, take with

Erko'ren, pp. (of an obsolete verb Erkiesen) chosen, elected; die E-en, the elect.

Erko'sen, (w.) v. tr. to obtain by caressing.

Erkrach'en, (w.) v. intr. (aux. sein & haben) to crash, begin to crash. [claws, to clutch.

Erkral'len, (w.) v. tr. to seize with the

Erkran'ken, (w.) v. intr. (aux. sein) to be taken ill, to fall ill (an [with Dat.], with), to sicken, grow sick.

Erkran'kung, (w.) f. (the incident of) falling sick; the state of being taken ill.

Erkrie'chen, (str.) v. tr. (sich [Dat.] etwas) to get or obtain by crouching or cringing.

Erkrie'gen, (w.) v. tr. to acquire, gain by waging war, to conquer. [by scribbling.

Erkrit'zeln, (w.) v. tr. cont. to get or gain

Erkrüm'men, (w.) v. intr. (aux. sein) to become crooked, to warp.

Erküh'len, (w.) v. I. intr. (aux. sein) to become cool; II. tr. to cool, refrigerate.

Erkühn'en, (w.) v. refl. to dare, presume, to make bold, to have the boldness.

Erkun'den, **Erkund'schaften**, (w.) v. tr. to explore, cf. Auskundschaften.

Erkun'digen, (w.) v. refl. to inquire or ask (nach, after or about; bei, of), to make inquiry, to institute inquiries (as to, about); sich — lassen, to cause inquiry to be made.

Erkun'digung, (w.) f. inquiry, search; — einziehen über (with Acc.) or wegen ..., to gather (or to request) information on ..., to make inquiry after, to inquire into ...; to take cognizance of ...; E-sreise, f. reconnoitering tour; E-sschreiben, n. letter of inquiry.

Erkünst'eln, (w.) v. tr. to feign, affect, counterfeit, simulate, (vulg.:) to sham; erkünstelt, p. a. artificial, feigned, affected, forced, studied, (vulg.:) sham. [ing, affectation.

Erkünst'elung, (w.) f. (the act of) feign-

Erkupp'eln, (w.) v. tr. to get or acquire by pimping or pandering.

Erla'ben, (w.) v. tr. (& refl.) to refresh, regale (one's self). [down (Erlegung).

Erlag', (str., pl. Erlä'ge) m. (act of) paying

Erlah'men, (w.) v. intr. (aux. sein) 1) to become lame; 2) fig. to flag, droop, to become languid.

Erlang'bar, adj. attainable, acquirable.

Erlang'en, (w.) v. tr. 1) to reach, get at by reaching, to reach by extending the arm; 2) to obtain, acquire, attain, get; coll. to come at or by; er erlangte seinen Wunsch, he obtained what he desired; man konnte nicht von ihm —, daß er es that, he could not be induced (got) to do it; schwer (mit Mühe) erlangt, hard-got; schwer zu —, hard to come at or to be had; Kunde, Kenntniß —, to obtain or gain intelligence; cf. Erreichen.

Erlang'ung, (w.) f. 1) the (act of) reaching, &c. cf. Erreichen; 2) attainment, acquisition, acquirement; Law, recovery.

Erlängerung, *(w.) f. Min., &c.* elongation, (act of) lengthening (out), &c. (Verlängerung).

Erlaß', *(str., pl.* Erlasse & Erlässe) *m.* 1) *a)* issue (of an order); *b)* order, decree, ordinance; öffentlicher —, edict, public act; 2) *Comm., &c. a)* (ein theilweiser) deduction, abatement, allowance; (einer Schuld) reduction; *b)* (gänzlicher) remission, release; 3) pardon; indulgence, dispensation.

Erlas'sen, *(str.) v. tr.* 1) to issue (a proclamation, &c.), publish; Gesetze —, to enact or make laws; (Einem etwas or Einen einer Sache *[Gen.]*) 2) to remit; to excuse; 3) to release, free, exempt from, acquit of, to dispense; 4) *Comm., &c.* to deduct, to make or grant an allowance; 5) to dismiss, discharge; *Comm.-s.* zu billigem Preise —, to let have at a cheap price; zum Course von … —, to let go at the rate of …; Einem eine Schuld —, to acquit one of (forgive one) a debt; Einem die Strafe —, to pardon one; Einen des Arrestes —, to set one free; der Leibeigenschaft —, to set free from servitude, emancipate, enfranchise: — Sie mir die Antwort auf diese Frage, dispense me from (or excuse my) answering this question; erlassene Summe, *Comm.* sum abated in composition.

Erlaß' …, *in comp.* —geld, *n.* money paid for dispensation; —jahr, *n. Script. see* Brachjahr.

Erläß'lich, I. *adj.* remissible, dispensable, pardonable, venial; II. **E-keit**, *(w.) f.* remissibility, dispensableness, &c.

Erlas'sung, *(w.) f.* 1) the (act of) issuing, &c. *cf.* Erlassen; issue, publication; 2) remission, release; dispensation; pardon; E-s-sünde, Erlaßsünde, *f.* venial sin.

Erlaß'urtel (—urtheil), *(str.) n. Law*, sentence of absolution.

Erlau'ben, *(w.) v. tr.* (Einem etwas) to permit, allow, to give leave or permission; (obrigkeitlich) to grant, license; es ist ihm erlaubt, he is permitted (licensed); man erlaube mir, may I be allowed, I beg leave; seine Mittel — ihm dies, his means justify this; gesetzlich erlaubt, permitted or warranted by law; legal; lawful; ein erlaubtes Verfahren, an allowable conduct; erlaubte Vergnügungen, innocent amusements; sich *(Dat.)* etwas —, to allow one's self (to do, &c.), to indulge (one's self) in …; sich *(Dat.)* Freiheiten —, to take liberties; er erlaubte sich *(Dat.)* Schritte *(Schiller)*, he ventured on measures which …; darf ich mir — zu fragen, may I presume (or may I be permitted) to ask; ich erlaube mir, Ihnen die Fräulein B. vorzustellen, I beg leave to introduce to you the Misses B.; ich erlaube mir, Ihnen anzuzeigen, I beg (leave) to announce; ich erlaube mir zu gestehen, I am free to own; wenn es zu fragen erlaubt ist, if it is a fair question; — Sie (permit me, sir, to ask), welches ist der Weg zum Hafen? pray, which is the way to the port?

Erlaub'niß, *s.* I. *(str.) f.* permission, leave; *Law*, licence; allowance, concession, grant; *Eccl.* dispensation; (Einen) um — bitten, to request permission, to beg or ask (one's) leave; mit Ihrer —, with your permission; under or by your favour, by your leave; mit höherer — gedruckt, printed by authority; II. *in comp.* —brief, *m.* licence, letters patent; —schein, *m. Comm.* letters patent, permit, licence; bill of sufferance, docket; pass-port, (zur Ausfuhr) licence outward, permit for exportation.

Erlaucht', I. *adj.* illustrious; high, noble, most honourable; II. *s. (w.) f.* lordship (title of a count, earl), *cf.* Durchlaucht.

Erlau'ern, *(w.) v. tr.* 1) *a)* to seize after having lain in wait, to surprise; *b)* to obtain or learn by lying in wait (by lurking, watching, spying); 2) to watch for, to watch (the favourable moment, &c.).

Erlau'fen, *(str.) v. tr.* 1) to overtake by running; 2) (sich *[Dat.]* etwas) to get by running after; 3) *coll.* to (be able to) go (a certain distance), to reach by walking.

Erlau'schen, *(w.) v. tr.* to get at (a secret, &c.) or to learn by watching, listening, to discover by eavesdropping, to overhear.

Erläu'tern, *(w.) v. tr.* to explain, &c. *cf.* Erklären; durch Beispiele —, to exemplify; e-d, *p. a.* explanatory; dem Ganzen sollen e-de Abbildungen beigegeben werden, the whole to be accompanied by appropriate illustrations. — **Erläu'terung**, *(w.) f.* explanation, explication, &c.; es bedarf keiner —, it needs no comment; *cf.* Erklärung.

Er'le, *(w.) f. Bot.* alder, alder-tree *(Alnus Tournef.)*.

Erle'ben, *(w.) v. tr.* 1) to live or survive to see or witness; 2) to experience, pass or go through, undergo, meet with; dieses Werk hat 20 Auflagen erlebt, this work has gone through 20 editions; ich werde nie den Tag —, I shall never see the day; Freude an … —, to live to see or to experience joy or satisfaction from; ich erlebe viel Freude an ihm, he is a source of great joy or comfort to me; ich habe es erlebt, daß sich dergleichen Dinge zutrugen, I have known such things to happen.

Erleb'niß, *(str.) n.* occurrence in a person's life, experience, event; Erlebnisse, adventures; widrige Erlebnisse, adversities.

Erle'digen, *(w.) v.* I. *tr.* 1) to empty, free, release, deliver, set free, to acquit, discharge (einer Sache *[Gen.]*, from …); 2) to vacate (a place); 3) *a)* to execute, finish; to settle, to dispose of (an affair); to despatch, discharge (business); *b) fig.* to set at rest, settle, remove (a doubt, &c.); adjust (a difference), to discharge (a debt); to answer (an enquiry); erledigt werden, (said of an office) to become vacant, to fall in; erledigt, *p. a.* void, vacant; die erledigte Stelle, vacancy; erledigtes Lehn, fief in abeyance; II. *refl.* to be settled (of doubtful questions, &c.), to be set at rest; hiermit erledigt sich Ihre Anfrage, herewith your inquiry is answered.

Erle'digung, *(w.) f.* 1) release; 2) *a)* discharge, despatch (of business); *b)* settlement, adjustment (of differences, &c.); discharge (of a debt); answer (to an enquiry); 3) vacancy, vacation; — des Thrones, vacancy of the throne; demise of the crown; (einer Pfründe) *Law*, ejection from a benefice, voidance; E-s-schein, *m.* (note of) acquittance, receipt.

Erle'gen, *(w.) v. tr.* 1) to pay (down), deposit; wieder —, to repay, refund; 2) to slay, kill. — **Erle'gung**, *(w.) f.* the (act of) paying down; killing, &c.

Erleich'tern, *(w.) v. tr.* to lighten, ease, disburden, relieve; 2) *fig.* to facilitate, alleviate, soften, lessen; warum erleichterst du es dem armen L. nicht? why do you not facilitate poor L.'s labours? der Barbar erleichterte es ihm nicht, the barbarous fellow did not relieve him; II. *refl.* 1) to ease nature; 2) (sich *[Dat.]* etwas) to make (one's life) easy, to disburden one's self (from any thing troublesome).

Erleich'terung, *(w.) f.* the (act of) lightening, &c.; alleviation, facilitation; facility; ease, relief; E-s-mittel, *n. pl.* facilities.

Erlei'den, *(str.) v. tr.* to suffer, sustain, bear, abide, endure, undergo.

Erleid'lich, *adj.* tolerable, *see* leidlich.

Er'len, I. *adj.* made of alder, aldern; II. *in comp.* —aue, *f. see* —wald; —bach, *m. (Mitchinson)*, the alder-margined stream *(Bodmer)*, &c. —baum, *m.* alder-tree *(see* Erle); —fink, *m. see* Zeisig; —holz, *n.* 1) alder-wood; 2) *see* —wald; —wald, *m.* alder-forest; —zeisichen, *n.*

[illegible]rede, *f.* admonitory discourse, hortatory speech, exhortation.

Ermangeln, *(w.) v. intr. (with Gen.)* 1) to be in want *or* devoid of, to be without, to want, *cf.* Mangeln; 2) to fail, want, to be wanting, deficient (in), to fall short (of *or* in); ich werde nicht — zu ..., I shall not fail to ...; nichts — lassen, to spare nothing *or* no pains, to do one's utmost. — **Ermangelung,** *(w.) f.* want, deficiency, default, failure: in — [illegible] Schutzes &c.), in the absence (of legal protection, &c.); in — dessen, in default *or* for want of which; in default whereof; in — eines Bessern, for want of anything better; [illegible]ge, *f. Law*, cessavit.

Ermannen, *(w.) v. I. tr. (l. u.)* to encourage, fortify, inspirit; II. *rfl.* to regain manly strength *or* courage, to take *or* recover courage, to arouse one's self (from inaction).

Ermartern, *(w.) v. tr.* to extort.

Ermäßigen, *(w.) v. tr.* 1) *a)* to moderate, abate, lessen, limit; *b) (Grimm, Wb. XI)* to qualify (Modificiren); 2) †, *Law*, to consider, judge. — **Ermäßigung,** *(w.) f.* 1) abatement, mitigation; reduction (of prices, of postage, &c.); 2) consideration, judgment.

Ermatten, *(w.) v.* I. *tr.* to weary, tire, fatigue; II. *intr. (aux.* sein) to grow tired, faint, fatigued, to flag, *cf.* Erschlaffen. — **Ermattung,** *(w.) f.* lassitude, weariness, exhaustion; *Med.* weakness, faintness; *cf.* Erschlaffung.

Ermaulen, *(w.) v. tr.* to get by pouting [or sulking.

Ermeißeln, *(w.) v. tr. coll.* 1) to chisel through (as a rock in mining); 2) to acquire by chiseling.

Ermel, *(str.) m. see* Ärmel.

Ermelden, *(w.) v. tr. see* Melden.

Ermessen, *(str.) v. tr.* († &) * 1) to measure, fathom; *fig.-a.* 2) to judge, consider, weigh, estimate; to conjecture; 3) to infer, conclude; das —, *(str.) v. n.* judgment, estimation; opinion; discretion; meines E-s *or* nach meinem —, according to my judgment, in my estimation *or* opinion.

Ermeßlich, I. *adj.* 1) measurable, fathomable; 2) conceivable; II. E-keit, *(w.) f.* measurableness.

Ermeucheln, *(w.) v. tr.* to assassinate.

Ermildern, *(w.) v. tr. see* Mildern.

Ermittelbar, *adj.* ascertainable.

Ermitteln, *(w.) v. tr.* to ascertain, find out, make certain, identify; nicht zu —, not ascertainable. — **Ermittelung,** *(w.) f.* the act of ascertaining, &c.

Ermöglichen, *(w.) v. tr.* to make possible, to render feasible, *cf.* Möglich machen.

Ermorden, *(w.) v. tr.* to murder; meuchlings —, to assassinate. — **Ermordung,** *(w.) f.* the (act of) murdering, murder, assassination.

Ermüden, *(w.) v.* I. *tr.* to tire (out), weary, fatigue, become troublesome to, to [illegible], wear out; nicht zu —, incapable of fatigue; e-d, *p. a.* tiresome, wearisome, irksome; II. *intr. (aux.* sein) to grow, get, *or* be tired, to grow weary.

Ermüdlich, *adj.* liable to be weary, easily [wearied.

Ermüdung, *(w.) f.* 1) the (act of) tiring out, &c. *cf.* Ermüden; 2) fatigue, weariness, lassitude.

Ermühen, *(w.) v. tr. (l. u.)* to obtain by [laborious efforts *or* pains.

Ermuntern, *(w.) v. tr.* 1) to rouse, awake; [illegible] 2) to stir up, animate, encourage, [illegible] to enliven; to urge (Anregen); 3) to [illegible], cheer up. — **Ermunterung,** *(w.)* 1) the (act of) rousing, &c.; 2) *fig.* encouragement, incitement, excitation; animation; [illegible] *n.* incentive.

Ermutigen [illegible] *(l. u.)*, *(w.) v.* I. [illegible]; II. *rfl.* to take courage. — [illegible] *(w.) f.* encouragement.

Ernähen, *(w.) v. tr.* (sich *[Dat.]* etwas) to acquire (gain) by sewing, by needle-work.

Ernähren, *(w.) v.* I. *tr.* 1) to nourish, feed, foster; 2) *fig.* to maintain, keep, support; II. *rfl.* 1) to feed, live (von, on); 2) *fig.* to maintain one's self, to gain one's livelihood, to live (durch, by); sich von Jemandem — lassen, to depend upon somebody for one's maintenance; III. *intr.* to nourish, *see* Nähren, *intr.:* Friede ernährt, Unfriede verzehrt, *proverb.* peace promotes prosperity, while discord brings on destruction.

Ernährer, *(str.) m.* nourisher, &c.; maintainer, supporter.

Ernährung, *(w.) f.* 1) the (act of) nourishing, &c., nutrition; 2) maintenance, support, subsistence: E-skunde, *f.* dietetics: E-sorgane, *n. pl.* organs of nutrition: E-strieb, *m.* appetence.

Ernannte, Ernannten, *see* Ernan, Ernannt.

Ernennbar, *adj.* fit to be nominated, &c. *cf.* Ernennen, appointable.

Ernennen, *(irr.) v. tr.* (Einen zu ...) 1) to nominate, appoint, name Einen zum Präsidenten, one president, &c.; zu einem Amte, einer Würde, to *or* for an office *or* dignity); to designate; 2) to create (one a duke, &c.); die Geschworenen —, to impanel a jury, to array a panel.

Ernennung, *(w.) f.* appointment, nomination (zu ..., to the office *or* dignity of ..., for ...), creation; designation; promotion: E-sbrief, *m.*, E-surkunde, *f.* letter of appointment; commission: E-srecht, *n.* right of appointing, of presentation, patronage; advowson.

Erneuen, Erneuern, *(w.) v.* I. *tr.* 1) *lit. & fig.* to renew, renovate, to repair; to refresh (colours); to regenerate (steam); to repeat (an offer); die Societät —, *Comm.* to renew a partnership; 2) *fig.* to revive, recommence; II. *rfl.* to renew itself, to be renewed, &c.; to be revived, recommenced; dieselben Scenen erneuerten sich zu Hause, the same scenes were reacted at home.

Erneuerer, *(str.) m.* renewer, renovator.

Erneuung, Erneuerung, *(w.) f.* renewal; renovation; revival; reparation; prolongation (of a contract).

Erniedrigen (**Erniedern,** *l. u.*), *(w.) v.* I. *tr.* 1) to lower; *fig.-a.* 2) *Mus.* to depress, lower *or* flatten (a note); 3) to humble, degrade, humiliate, debase, abase, bring down *or* low; II. *rfl.* to humble, degrade one's self, to condescend, stoop.

Erniedriger, *(str.) m.* humbler, debaser.

Erniedrigung, *(w.) f.* 1) the (act of) lowering; *fig.-a.* 2) *Mus.* the depression (of a note) by means of a flat; 3) *Comm.* depression (of prices); 4) humiliation, degradation, abasement, debasement; 5) reduction (of a tariff); E-szeichen, *n. Mus.* mark of depression, a flat (marked thus, ♭, depressing the note before which it is placed half a tone).

Ernst, *m.* Ernest, Ernestus *(P. N.).*

Ernst, *(str.) m.* 1) seriousness, gravity, earnest, earnestness; der heilige —, solemnity; mit heiligem —, solemnly; 2) fervour, assiduity; 3) severity, sternness; im E-e, earnestly, seriously; alles E-es, in earnest, in all seriousness; mit —, earnestly, eagerly; — machen, to make (be in) earnest: ist es Ihr —? are you in earnest? are you serious? es ist mein heiliger —, I am quite serious, I really mean so; das ist nicht Ihr —? you do not mean to say so? im allen —, in good earnest, *coll.* for good and all; etwas im — nehmen, to take anything in earnest; aus einem Spaß — machen, to take in earnest what was intended as a joke; es ist ihm — zu ..., he means to ...; es war ihm — damit, he was in earnest about it; es ist ihm nicht — um ..., he is not serious in ...; wenn es Euch — ist, was zu sagen *(Göthe, Faust)*, if you are seriously intent on saying something *(i. e.* worth hearing, in opp. to mere phrases; *Tayl.:* if thou'rt moved to speak in earnest).

Ernst, Ernsthaft, *adj.* earnest, serious, grave; stern; solemn; ernster Wille, Vorsatz, earnestness, sincerity of purpose; ernste Unterhaltung, Musik, serious conversation, music; eine ernste Stunde, a trying hour; es — meinen *or* nehmen, to be in earnest (mit, about), to deal seriously (with).

Ernsthaftigkeit, *(w.) f.* earnestness, seriousness, gravity: sternness; demureness.

Ernsthaftkomisch [illegible], *adj.* serio-comic.

Ernstlich, I. *adv. of* Ernst, earnestly, &c.; er meinte es — damit, he was in earnest about it; II. *adj.* earnest, fervent, ardent, intent, eager; forcible, impressive; Einem etwas — empfehlen, to give one a strict charge; — mahnen, to press heavily; — verbieten, to forbid positively; III. E-keit, *(w.) f.* earnestness, &c.

Ernte, *(w.) f.* 1) *lit. & fig.* harvest, crop; gathering; 2) *see* —zeit; *in comp.* —arbeit, *f.* harvest-work; —bier, *n.* harvest-home beer; —dienst, *m.* service to be rendered to the lord of the manor during harvest-time; —e(dank)fest, —mahl, *n.*, —schmaus, *m.* harvest-feast, harvest-home; —göttin, *f. Myth.* the goddess of corn and of harvests, Ceres; —kranz, *m.* harvest-wreath, harvest-garland; —lied, *n.* harvest-song, harvest-home; —maschine, *f.* reaping-(mowing-)machine; —maus, *f. Zool.* dwarf-mouse *(Mus minutus Pall.)*; —monat, *m.* harvest-month, August; —reif, *adj.* ripe for reaping *or* gathering; —tanz, *m.* harvest-dance, barley-brake; —zeit, *f.* harvest-time, reaping-time, harvest-home.

Ernten, *(w.) v. tr.* to reap, gather, harvest; *fig.* to reap (advantage, ingratitude): wie er säet, wird er —, *proverb.* as he sows he must reap.

Ernüchtern, *(w.) v.* I. *intr. (aux.* sein) & *rfl.* to sober (down); II. *tr. lit. & fig.* to sober.

Eroberer, *(str.) m.* conqueror; captor.

Erobern, *(w.) v. tr.* 1) to conquer (von, from); to overcome; to take (by force of arms); to carry (a rampart, a town, &c.), to reduce (a place); to capture, take, bring up (a ship); 2) *fig.* to gain, win, captivate (one's heart, &c.); (eine Festung) mit Sturm —, to take (a fortress) by storm; nicht zu —, impregnable; wieder —, to reconquer.

Eroberung, *(w.) f.* 1) the (act of) conquering, taking, &c. *cf.* Erobern; capture (of a ship, &c.); 2) conquest, acquisition: sie fing an zu glauben, daß sie eine — gemacht hätte, she began to think that she had made a conquest.

Eroberungs..., *in comp.* —geist, *m.*, —lust, *f.* desire of (or eagerness for) conquest; —krieg, *m.* war of conquest; —plan, *m.* scheme *or* view of conquest; —sucht, *f.* spirit of conquest, thirst after conquest, rage of (*gen.* for) conquest; —süchtig, *adj.* eager for conquest: (of a woman) coquettish; ein —süchtiges Mädchen, a coquette, flirt.

Eröffnen, *(w.) v.* I. *tr.* 1) to open: *fig.-a.* 2) (Einem etwas) to lay open, discover, disclose, make known, communicate, reveal, to give (one) an insight of; to notify; to publish (a judgment); 3) to open (a campaign, the trenches, fire, &c.), to begin; to set on foot; to enter into; to establish (a business); to open (a shop); den Ball —, to open the ball, to lead (off) the dance; ein Parlament —, to open a parliament; die erste Sitzung des norddeutschen Reichstages wurde vom Könige persönlich eröffnet, the first session of the North German Diet was opened by the

King in person; *Comm.-e.* ein Conto —, to open an account; einen Credit —, to lodge a credit (bei, with); II. *refl.* 1) to open, unclose; to present itself; 2) *fig.* to open, reveal, disclose one's mind; e-d, *p. a. Med.* aperient, laxative; ein e-des Mittel, an aperient, a laxative.

Eröff'nung, *(w.) f.* 1) the opening (of the navigation, an account, a diet, will, railway, ball, &c.); inauguration; beginning; die — des norddeutschen Reichstages, (the) opening of the North German Parliament; des Kaisers Rede bei der — der französischen Kammern, the Emperor's speech on the opening of the French chambers; 2) overture; disclosure; intelligence, communication, notification; publication (of a judgment); 3) — des Concurses, *Law,* the first legal steps taken in cases of insolvency; Festlichkeit bei der — der Wasserleitung zu Caracas, opening festival of the new waterworks at C.; E-sgedicht, *n.* introductory poem, prologue; E-smittel, *n. Med.* aperient, laxative; E-srede, *f.* opening speech *or* address; E-sstück, *n. Mus.* overture.

Erör'tern, *(w.) v. tr.* to discuss, examine closely, sift, decide, clear up, settle; eine Frage —, to agitate, canvass, debate, ventilate a question.

Erör'terung, *(w.) f.* discussion, agitation, debate; decision; explanation, a clearing up.

* **Eros,** *m. Gr. Myth.* Love, Cupid. — **Ero'tisch,** *adj.* erotic, erotical.

Erpach'ten, *(w.) v. tr.* to rent, farm.

Erpack'en, *(w.) v. tr.* to seize, take hold of.

Erpas'sen, *(w.) v. tr.* to watch and seize, *cf.* Erlauern.

Er'pel, *(str.) m. provinc.* drake (Enterich).

Erpflü'gen, *(w.) v. tr.* to acquire, get by ploughing.

Erpicht', *adj. coll.* intent (auf *[with Acc.]*, upon), greedy (after), eager (for, at, after), eagerly bent, set (on), keen (at, upon), *coll.* mad (for, of, after, upon); auf seine Meinung —, headstrong. [to get by drudgery.

Erpla'gen, *(w.) v. tr.* (sich *[Dat.]* etwas)

Erplün'dern, *(w.) v. tr.* to get by pillaging.

Erpoch'en, *(w.) v. tr.* to get by force (obstinacy).

Erpras'seln, *(w.) v. intr. (aux.* sein) to begin to crackle; (of fire) to blaze up.

Erpre'digen, *(w.) v. tr.* to accomplish *or* obtain by preaching.

Erpres'sen, *(w.) v. tr.* to exact, extort; to press out of, to force, screw, wring from. — **Erpres'ser,** *(str.) m.* extortioner, extorter, exactor. — **Erpres'sung,** *(w.) f.* extortion, exaction.

Erpro'ben (**Erprü'fen,** *l. u.*), *(w.) v. tr.* to try, prove, test, put to the test, to experience.

Erquick'en, *(w.) v. tr.* to refresh, comfort, revive; to regale, recreate; sie erquickten sich an dem Wein, they regaled themselves with the wine; e-d, *p. a.,* or **Erquick'lich,** *adj.* refreshing, recreative, giving comfort, comforting. — **Erquick'ung,** *(w.) f.* recreation, refreshment, regalement; comfort; repose.

Erraf'fen, *(w.) v. tr.* to snatch (up), gripe, grasp; to seize hastily *or* abruptly; to gain by great exertion. [be guessed.

Errath'bar, *adj.* conjecturable; that may

Erra'then, *(str.) v. tr.* to guess, conjecture, divine (aus, from); to hit upon *or* at, to devise, find out; to solve (a riddle); das —, *(str.) v. s.,* or **Erra'thung,** *(w.) f.* a guessing; divining. — **Erra'ther,** *(str.) m.* diviner. [(Flicker, blocks).

* **Errat'isch,** *adj.* (*Lat.*) *Geol.* erratic

Erraub'en, *(w.) v. tr.* to get by robbing.

Errech'nen, *(w.) v. tr.* to get *or* obtain by computing (*cf.* Ausrechnen).

Errech'ten, *(w.) v. tr.* to get by litigation.

Erreg'bar, I. *adj.* excitable, irritable; II. **E-keit,** *(w.) f.* excitability, irritability.

Erre'gen, *(w.) v. tr.* 1) to stir (up), rouse, raise; 2) to excite, move, agitate, to create, cause; 3) to provoke, irritate; 4) *Min.* to discover; ein e-des Mittel, *Med.* stimulant.

Erre'ger, *(str.) m.* exciter, agitator.

Erreg'lich, *see* Erregbar.

Erre'gung, *(w.) f.* the (act of) stirring up, &c., excitation, commotion, agitation; E-smittel, *n. Med.* stimulant.

Erreich', *(str.) m.* (*l. u.*) *see* Bereich.

Erreich'bar, I. *adj.* attainable; Jedem —, within every man's reach; II. **E-keit,** *(w.) f.* attainableness.

Errei'chen, *(w.) v. tr.* 1) to get at by reaching; *fig.-e.* 2) *a)* to come up to *or* with, *cf.* Einholen; *b)* to equal, match; 3) to reach, attain, obtain, get, acquire, to come at, arrive at; to carry, secure (one's object), to gain, compass (one's end, &c.); seinen Zweck nicht —, to miss one's mark *or* aim, to fail of (in) one's purpose; *coll.* to be baulked; den Hafen —, *Mar.* to make the port; das mannbare Alter —, to come to man's (woman's) estate; ein hohes Alter —, to live to a good old *or* a great age; einen Vortheil —, to secure an advantage; nicht —, to be *or* fall short of; nicht zu —, out of reach; *Comm.-e.* einen Preis —, to fetch a price (of merchandise); to obtain a price; es war unmöglich Ihre Limite zu —, it was impossible to succeed at your limit.

Errei'chung, *(w.) f.* the (act of) coming up to, &c. *cf.* Erreichen; attainment.

Errei'sen, *(w.) v. tr.* (sich *[Dat.]* etwas) to acquire, get by travelling.

Errei'ten, *(str.) v. tr.* 1) *a)* to overtake on horseback; *b) provinc.* to ride over *or* down; 2) (sich *[Dat.]* etwas) to acquire by riding.

Errei'zen, *(w.) v. tr. see* Aufreizen.

Erren'nen, *(irr.) v. tr.* to reach, overtake, *or* acquire by running, *cf.* Erlaufen.

Errett'bar, *adj.* savable, salvable.

Erret'ten, *(w.) v. tr.* to save, rescue, deliver. — **Erret'ter,** *(str.) m.* deliverer, saviour.

Erret'tung, *(w.) f.* the (act of) saving, deliverance, delivery.

Errich'ten, *(w.) v. tr.* 1) *a)* to erect, build up, raise, to set up; einen Altar —, to set up an altar; *b) Coop.* to mount (a cask); eine Perpendiculare —, *Geom.* to raise *or* erect a perpendicular; 2) to establish, found (a business, &c.); ein Geschäft —, to set up in business; to set up, form (an establishment, &c.); einen Bund —, to make a covenant; ein Testament —, to make a will, to draw up a testament; to institute (laws). — **Errich'tung,** *(w.) f.* 1) erection, &c.; 2) the forming (of a commercial, &c. establishment), establishment.

Erring'en, *(str.) v. tr.* 1) to gain by wrestling; 2) *fig.* to obtain by exerting one's self *or* by strenuous efforts; to achieve (a success, victory, fame, fortune, &c.); den Preis —, to carry the prize. — **Erring'bar,** *adj.* that may be gained *or* obtained by exertion, &c. — **Erring'ung,** *(w.) f.* the (act of) gaining *or* obtaining any end by strong efforts.

Errö'then, *(w.) v. intr. (aux.* sein) to redden, blush, colour (über *[with Acc.]*, at); — machen, to put to the blush; das —, *(str.) v. s.,* or **Errö'thung,** *(w.) f.* a reddening, blushing, blush.

Erru'dern, *(w.) v. tr.* to reach by paddling, rowing.

Erruf'bar, *adj.* within call.

Erru'fen, *(str.) v. tr.* to reach by calling; man kann ihn —, he is within call; man kann ihn nicht —, he is out of (my, your, &c.) call.

[illegible]ſ'fen, (w.) v. tr. to get, acquire by [illegible]tion. [sparkle, glisten.

[illegible]im'mern, (w.) v. intr. (aux. ſein) to

[illegible]impf'en, (w.) v. tr. to get or obtain [illegible] abusive language.

[illegible]r'ben, (str.) v. tr. vulg. (ſich [Dat.] [illegible]) to get by extortion, by usury.

[illegible]la'fen, (str.) v. tr. to reach while [illegible]. ſich (Dat.) etwas —, to obtain while [illegible].

[illegible]laf'fen, (w.) v. I. intr. (aux. ſein) to [illegible], relax, flag: to be enervated, to ef[illegible]; — machen & II. tr. to slacken, re[illegible], enervate.

[illegible]laf'fer, (str.) m. slackener, &c.; Anat. membrane of the tympanum.

[illegible]laf'fung, (w.) f. relaxation, unstring[illegible], flagging; Med. dialysis, atony; fig. ef[illegible], enervation. [strike to death.

[illegible]la'gen, (str.) v. tr. to slay, kill, to

[illegible]lei'chen, (str.) v. tr. 1) to steal upon [illegible]: to catch or take by surprise; den Be[illegible] —, Log. to beg the question; 2) (ſich [illegible] etwas) to obtain by sneaking or sur[illegible]titiously; erſchlichen, p. a. surreptitious, [illegible]ulently obtained.

[illegible]lei'chung, (w.) f. 1) the (act of) steal[illegible] upon, subreption, surreption, secret in[illegible]; the (act of) taking by surprise: 2) sur[illegible]titious acquisition or mode of obtaining [illegible]thing; 3) Log. a begging of the question.

[illegible]lep'pen, (w.) v. tr. to move with dif[illegible]lty or labour, to drag along. [ailing.

[illegible]len'dern, (w.) v. tr. to reach with a

[illegible]ließ'bar, adj. capable of being opened,

[illegible]ließ'en, (str.) v. tr. 1) gener. fig. a) [illegible] refl.) to open, disclose: b) to open up, make accessible; 2) to conclude, infer.

[illegible]mei'cheln, (w.) v. tr. (ſich [Dat.] et[illegible]) to obtain by flattery or caresses, to get [illegible]ing; ſich (Dat.) ein Mittagsmahl —, [illegible] to cog a dinner.

[illegible]mol'len, (w.) v. tr. to obtain by sulk[illegible] ([illegible]).

[illegible]nap'pen, (w.) v. tr. 1) to catch (with [illegible] mouth); 2) to catch up, snap up.

[illegible]pf'bar, see Erſchöpflich.

[illegible]pf'en, (w.) v. I. tr. 1) to drain; fig. a) to exhaust, spend, wear out; Je[illegible] Geduld —, to wear out a person's [illegible]; b) to exhaust, to bring out or develop [illegible]: II. refl. 1) to exhaust one's self; [illegible] to exhaust one's subject (in speaking); [illegible] Vermuthungen —, to exhaust (one's [illegible]) conjectures; e-d, p. a. exhaustive; [illegible], exhaustively or amply proved; [illegible] p. a. exhausted, spent; coll. knocked [illegible] erſchöpftes Stück Land, a piece of [illegible] out of heart.

[illegible]pf'lich, adj. exhaustible.

[illegible]heit, (w.) f. the (state of) being [illegible], exhaustion. [dialysis.

[illegible]ung, (w.) f. exhaustion; Med.

[illegible]en, v. I. (str.) intr. (aux. ſein) & [illegible] refl. to be terrified, frightened (über [illegible]); a) to be struck with fear or ter[illegible] be alarmed (über [with Acc.], at); to [illegible]; b) to be startled or confounded [illegible], don't be frightened; II. (w.) [illegible], terrify, strike with terror, to [illegible], appal.

[illegible] (str.) m. affrighter, &c.

[illegible] adj. 1) frightful, dreadful, [illegible]; 2) coll. tremendous.

[illegible] (w.) f. frightfulness, &c.

[illegible] (str.) n. 1) fright, terror, [illegible]

[illegible] (str.) v. tr. (gener. refl. ſich [illegible]) to get or gain by writing.

[illegible] v. tr. to reach by cry[illegible]

Erſchrei'ten, (str.) v. to reach by stepping.

Erſchrock'en, I. p. a. frightened; aghast; II. E-heit, (w.) f. fright, fear, terror.

Erſchür'fen, Erſchür'fen, (w.) v. tr. Min. to reach, open, or discover (einen Gang, a vein) by digging.

Erſchüt'terer, (str.) m. one who shakes, a shaker (of...), agitator.

Erſchüt'tern, (w.) v. I. tr. 1) to shake, toss; 2) fig. to shake or stagger (one's resolution), to agitate violently, to move (the heart); to convulse (the world, &c.); II. intr. (aux. ſein) to quake, tremble, shake; e-d, p. a. awfully affecting, thrilling.

Erſchüt'terung, (w.) f. 1) the (act of) shaking, &c., shake; 2) shock, violent motion, commotion, concussion, percussion; politiſche —, political convulsion; E-streis, m. Phys. sphere of commotion; E-sſchale, f. Med. percussion-shell. [(w.) to grow weak.

Erſchwach'en, (w.) v. intr. (aux. ſein) (l.

Erſchwar'zen, (w.) v. intr. (aux. ſein) to become black, to blacken.

Erſchwatz'en, (w.) v. tr. (gener. refl. ſich [Dat.] etwas) to get by prattling.

Erſchwe'ben, (w.) v. tr. to reach by flying.

Erſchwel'len, (str.) v. intr. (aux. ſein) to begin to swell, cf. Schwellen, I.

Erſchwe'ren, (w.) v. tr. 1) to make heavy or heavier; 2) fig. a) to aggravate (a crime, &c.); b) to render difficult, onerous, laborious or more difficult, &c., to aggravate (the evils of life, &c.); es erſchwert die Laſt, it augments or increases the burden; die Bewegung —, to impede or obstruct motion; e-d, p. a. onerous (conditions); obstructive (measures).

Erſchwer'niß, (str.) n aggravation, impediment, difficulty.

Erſchwe'rung, (w.) f. a making heavy or difficult, &c.; aggravation. [ming.

Erſchwim'men, (str.) v. tr. to reach swim-

Erſchwin'deln, (w.) v. tr. to obtain by swindling tricks.

Erſchwing'en, (str.) v. tr. 1) to soar up to or reach by soaring: 2) fig. a) see Erringen, 2; b) to afford (to buy, &c.), to get, raise, furnish: ich kann die Unkoſten nicht —, I cannot afford the charges.

Erſchwing'lich, adj. that may be afforded or raised, attainable, furnishable.

Erſchwing'ung, (w.) f. an affording, &c. cf. Erſchwingen.

Erſe'geln, (w.) v. tr. to reach sailing.

Erſeh'en, (str.) v. I. tr. 1) to see, perceive: to descry, distinguish; 2) to learn, understand (aus, from, by), to find; 3) (ſich [Dat.] etwas) to choose, elect; 4) to observe, watch, avail one's self of; 5) to choose, elect; aus Ihrem Briefe erſehe ich, by your letter I learn or perceive; Zeit und Gelegenheit —, to bide time and opportunity; Einen nicht — können, not to be able to bear the sight of one; ſie kann ihn nicht —, she cannot abide or bear him; II. refl. (l. u.) to divert or amuse one's self by looking about.

Erſeh'nen, (w.) v. tr. to long, yearn, or wish for, to hanker after, to desire fervently.

Erſeſ'ſen, p. a. see Verſeſſen & Erſitzen.

Erſetz'bar, adj. see Erſetzlich.

Erſetz'en, (w.) v. tr. 1) to supply, replace, retrieve, repair, restore, make up (for), to make good, recover, to make amends for, compensate; einen Verluſt erſetzt erhalten or bekommen, to recover damages; ich habe es noch nicht erſetzt erhalten, it has not yet been restored to me; 2) (Einem etwas) to reimburse; to refund, to indemnify (one for); Einen —, to fill (up) another's place; to supply the loss of a person; Jute kann Baumwolle nicht —, jute cannot supply the place of cotton; du mußt mich ſeinem Vater —, you must replace me to your father; er erſetzt ſeinen Vorgänger nicht, he is not equal or does not come up to (falls short of) his predecessor.

Erſetz'lich, I. adj. 1) that may be supplied, replaced, &c., replaceable, cf. Erſetzen; 2) reparable, retrievable; recoverable; repayable; II. E-keit, (w.) f. capability of being supplied, replaced, retrieved, or compensated, &c.

Erſetz'ung, (w.) f. the (act of) supplying, &c. cf. Erſetzen; reparation, compensation; amends, reimbursement.

Erſeuf'zen, (w.) v. I. intr. to fetch or heave a sigh; II. tr. (ſich [Dat.] etwas) to sigh after, wish for, or obtain by sighing.

Erſicht'lich, I. adj. visible, perceptible; evident, manifest, clear; — ſein, to be visible, &c., to appear; II. E-keit, (w.) f. visibleness, perceptibility, evidence, manifestness.

Erſie'chen, (w.) v. intr. (aux. ſein) see Erkranken.

Erſie'gen, (w.) v. tr. to obtain by victory.

Erſing'en, (str.) v. tr. (gener. refl. ſich [Dat.] etwas) to acquire, get by singing.

Erſink'en, (str.) v. tr. Min. to get at or to obtain by sinking a shaft.

Erſin'nen, (str.) v. tr. to devise, contrive, excogitate, conceive, imagine, project; to invent, fabricate, forge.

Erſinn'lich, adj. conceivable, imaginable; auf alle e-e Weiſe, in every possible manner.

Er'ſiſch, adj. Erse, Irish.

Erſitz'en, (str.) v. tr. 1) (gener. refl. ſich [Dat.] etwas) to draw on, contract (a disease) by leading a sedentary life; 2) Law, to acquire by prescription.

Erſitz'ung, (w.) f. Law, usucaption, acquirement of property by prescription.

Erſor'gen, (w.) v. tr. to obtain by care or anxiety.

Erſpäh'en, (w.) v. tr. to descry, espy.

Erſpan'nen, (w.) v. tr. to span; to reach by the span, or by spanning.

Erſpa'ren, (w.) v. tr. to spare, save, lay up; Einem etwas —, to spare one from ...; erſpare mir dieſe Mühe, spare me (from) this trouble; — Sie ſich (Dat.) das Leugnen, spare your denials; um Mühe und Koſten zu —, to save trouble and charges; das Erſpar'te, n. (decl. like adj.) savings.

Erſpar'niß, (str.) f. savings; der — wegen, to save, for economy's sake; laſſen Sie alle möglichen Erſparniſſe eintreten, be as saving (economical) as possible. [saving.

Erſpa'rung, (w.) f. the (act of) sparing,

Erſpie'len, (w.) v. tr (gener. refl. ſich [Dat.] etwas) to get by playing or gambling.

Erſpie'ßen, (w.) v. tr. to kill with a spear.

Erſpin'nen, (str.) v. tr. (gener. refl. ſich [Dat.] etwas) to get, earn, or obtain by spinning.

Erſprie'ßen, (str.) v. intr. (aux. ſein) 1) to shoot up (as plants): 2) fig. to profit, to be of use. — Erſprieß'lich, I. adj. useful, profitable, advantageous, beneficial; II. E-keit, (w.) f. usefulness, &c.; profit.

Erſpring'en, (str.) v. tr. to reach by leaping: to get or obtain by leaping.

Erſpü'ren, (w.) v. tr. to spy out, find out.

Erſt (or Erſt), I. adj. first; prime, head; der e-e Lehrer, head master: dies iſt das E-e was ich höre, this is the first word I have heard of it; die e-en Anfangsgründe, the rudiments; der e-e Arbeiter (in Fabriken), the foreman; die e-e Kirche, the primitive church; die e-en Geiſter des Jahrhunderts, the master-spirits (-minds) of the age; das E-e, the first thing; Comm.-e. e-er Commis, head or confidential clerk; mit e-er Gelegenheit, by the first opportunity; mit e-er Poſt, by the first (or earliest) mail or post, by return of post; e-e Qualität, first or prime quality; aus der e-en Hand kaufen, to buy (at) first hand; e-es Papier, first-rate paper; Hand e-en Ranges,

[illegible]langer: eine Beleidigung ruhig (geduldig) —, to bear an affront quietly, &c. cf. Einstecken, 4; nicht zu —, not to be borne, insupportable, &c. cf. Unerträglich.

Erträg'lich, I. *adj.* 1) tolerable, supportable, sufferable, bearable, endurable; 2) †, productive (Ertragsfähig); II. E-keit, *(w.) f.* 1) tolerableness, &c.; mediocrity; 2) *obsolescent*, productiveness.

Ertrag'niß, *(str.) n.* the act or capability of yielding, &c., produce, &c. cf. Ertrag.

Ertrag'sam, *adj.* yielding, productive, profitable.

Ertrag'sfähig, I. *adj.* capable of yielding produce, &c. cf. Ertrag; productive; II. E-keit, *(w.) f.* capability of yielding produce: productiveness.

Ertra'gung, *(w.) f.* the (act of) bearing, &c., state of enduring, sufferance, toleration.

Ertränk'en, *(w.) v. tr.* to drown. — **Ertrank'ung**, *(w.) f.* the (act of) drowning.

Erträum'en, *(w.) v. tr.* to dream or to form visionary schemes of ...; erträumt, *p. a.* imaginary, visionary: chimerical.

Ertret'en, *(str.) v. tr.* 1) to tread or trample to death (Zertreten); 2) *fig.* to trample down, to destroy, to bring to utter ruin.

Ertrink'en, *(str.) v.* I. *intr.* (*aux.* sein) to be drowned; II. *tr.* to get by drinking.

Ertröd'eln, *(w.) v. tr.* 1) to purchase; 2) to acquire by dealing in second-hand articles.

Ertrotz'en, *(w.) v. tr.* to get by obstinacy, defiance.

Erüb'en, *(w.) v. tr.* to acquire by practice.

Erüb'rigen (*i. u.* **Erü'bern**), *(w.) v.* I. *intr.* (*aux.* haben) (cf. Übrig sein) 1) to be left or to remain over and above; 2) to remain (still) behind; to remain to be done; to be wanting; II. *tr.* to save, lay by, spare; nichts dabei —, to have nothing over by it (*i. e.* by a business-transaction, &c.). — **Erü'brigung**, *(w.) f.* the (act of) saving, &c.

Eruditio'n, *(w.) f.* (*Lat.*) erudition.

Eruir'en, *(w.) v. tr.* (*Lat.* eruere, to break, root, or dig out) *fig.* to draw or bring out, to elicit (by investigation, &c.), cf. Herausbekommen.

Er've, *(w.) f. Bot.* bitter vetch (*Ervum ervilia* L.); E-würger, *m. Bot.* broom-rape (*Orobanche* L.).

Erwach'en, *(w.) v. intr.* (*aux.* sein) to awake, wake, to be roused; das —, *(str.) v. s.* an awakening.

Erwach'sen, *(str.) v. intr.* (*aux.* sein) 1) to grow; to grow up; zu Männern —, to grow up to be men; 2) *fig.* to arise, spring, proceed (aus, from); to accrue (zu etwas) to somebody, to rise to; —, *p. a.* adult, grown up, grown to maturity, (full-)grown; E-e, *(decl. like adj.)* grown person, adult; die Taufe der E-en, adult baptism.

Erwach'senheit, *(w.) f.* (*i. u.*) 1) adultness, ripe age, puberty; 2) grown up persons collectively.

Erwä'gen, *(str.) v. tr. fig.* to weigh, ponder, consider, reflect upon, canvass, deliberate, discuss; ich will es —, I will think of it.

Erwä'gung, *(w.) f.* a considering of ..., reflection (upon), deliberation, discussion; in — [illegible] in consideration, in regard (of); in — ziehen, to take into (or to under) consideration; [illegible] to give one's consideration to.

Erwähl'en, *(w.) v. tr.* to choose, elect: [illegible], pl. the elect — **Erwäh'lung**, *(w.) f.* the (act of) choosing, election, nomination.

Erwähn'en, *(w.) v. tr.* (& *intr.* [*with Gen.*]) [illegible], make mention of (gegen, to); to [illegible], refer to; noch ist zu —, it remains [illegible] mentioned, it is further to be [illegible]

Erwäh'nung, *(w.) f.* mention; — thun, to mention, to make mention *of* or reference to; einer Sache geschieht —, a matter is mentioned; meines Namens geschah —, my name was introduced; bei —, at a (on the) mention.

Erwahr'en, *(w.) v.* (*particul. Swiss.*) I. *tr.* († **Erwähr'en**) to make true, to prove, confirm by the event; II *refl.* & *intr.* (*aux.* sein) to prove true.

Erwal'len, *(w.) v. intr.* to boil up (Aufwallen).

Erwar'men, *(w.) v. intr.* (*aux.* sein) to grow warm, to be warmed.

Erwär'men, *(w.) v. tr.* 1) to warm; to heat; to foment (durch Umschläge); 2) *fig.* to warm (the heart, &c.), to excite ardour or zeal in (one; für, for), to engage, interest (in behalf of). — **Erwär'mung**, *(w.) f.* the (act of) warming, &c., fomentation; E-skraft, *f. Phys.* caloric power.

Erwar'ten, *(w.) v. tr.* to expect, to stay (wait or look) for; to await; er kann die Zeit nicht —, he cannot bide his time; was wird der Leser nach einem solchen Titel —? what will the reader expect from such a title as this? erwartet, *p. a.* expected, looked for.

Erwar'tung, *(w.) f.* expectation, expectance, anticipation; suspense; in der festen —, in the full (confident) expectation; die getäuschte —, disappointment; voller — or e-svoll, *adj.* full of expectation or hope, eager.

Erwa'ten, *(w.) v. tr.* to reach or to get through by wading.

Erweck'bar, *adj.* capable of being awakened, aroused, or excited, resuscitable.

Erweck'en, *(w.) v. tr.* 1) to waken, awaken, rouse (from sleep), arouse; 2) to resuscitate (from the dead); 3) to animate, excite, stir up; 4) to breed, raise, cause, create, occasion; Verdacht —, to excite suspicion; Vertrauen —, to inspire confidence; e-de Mittel, *n. pl.* incentives.

Erweck'lich, *adj. fig.* arousing, impressive; exciting devotion, edifying.

Erweck'ung, *(w.) f.* 1) the (act of) awakening, &c.; religiöse —, revival; 2) resuscitation; 3) animation, incitation; 4) encouragement, excitation.

Erweh'ren, *(w.) v. refl.* (*with Gen.*) to keep or ward off, to defend one's self from, against; to resist; ich konnte mich des Lachens nicht —, I could not refrain from (or help) laughing; ich kann mich des Schlafes nicht —, I cannot forbear sleeping.

Erweich'bar, *adj.* that may be softened, &c.

Erwei'chen, *(w.) v. tr.* 1) to soften, mollify; *T.* to macerate; to soak; 2) *fig.* to soften, move (bis zu Thränen, to tears), cf. Rühren; sich — lassen, to relent; *Med.* e. e-d, *p. a.* emollient, lenient, demulcent; e-de Mittel, *n. pl.* emollients, lenitives.

Erwei'chung, *(w.) f.* the (act of) softening, &c., *Med.* mollification; *Chem.* maceration; E-smittel, *n.* emollient.

Erweis', *(str.) m.* proof, showing, demonstration; result.

Erwei'sen, *(str.) v.* I. *tr.* 1) to show, do, render (Einem Ehre *&c.*, honour, services, &c. to ...), to confer (a favour upon ...), pay (attentions to ..., &c.); 2) to prove, make good or out, demonstrate; II. *refl.* to prove, prove one's self, to be found, to turn out (to be, &c.).

Erweis'lich, I. *adj.* demonstrable, provable; II. E-keit, *(w.) f.* demonstrableness, &c.

Erwei'sung, *(w.) f.* the (act of) showing, &c., demonstration, cf. Erweisen.

Erwei'terer, *(str.) m.* enlarger, extender.

Erwei'tern, *(w.) v.* I. *tr.* 1) to enlarge, widen, extend, expand, dilate; to let out in the width; 2) *fig.* to enlarge, amplify; to aggrandize; to expand; II. *refl.* to get, grow larger; to expand, enlarge itself; erweitert, *p. a. Med.* dilated; der e-de Muskel, *Anat.* dilator.

Erwei'terung, *(w.) f.* 1) enlargement, extension, expansion; amplification; aggrandisement; *Med.* dilatation, enlargement; — der Adern, aneurism; — der Gefäßenden, anastomosis; — der Herzkammern, diastole; 2) *Found.* bell-mouth (of moulds).

Erwerb', *(str.) m.* acquisition; gain, profit; kleiner —, aber rascher Umsatz, small profits but quick returns; business, pursuit, cf. Gewerbe.

Erwer'ben, *(str.) v. tr.* to acquire, earn, get, gain, obtain, *coll.* to come by; to purchase; erworben, *p. a.* acquired, &c.; mit Unrecht erworben, ill-gotten; theuer erworben, dearly bought; erworbene Vorzüge, Kenntnisse, Fertigkeiten, acquirements, attainments, accomplishments.

Erwer'ber, *(str.) m.*, **Erwer'berin**, *(w.) f.* acquirer, *Law*, cessionary, transferree.

Erwerb'los, *adj.* unprofitable, hard (times).

Erwerb'niß, *(str.) n.* acquisition, earning; perquisite.

Erwerb'sam, I. *adj.* industrious; II. E-keit, *(w.) f.* industriousness.

Erwerbs'..., *in comp.* —fleiß, *m.* industry; —mittel, *n.*, —quelle, *f.* means, source of industry, *i. e.* of making a living; —schule, *f.* school of industry; —sinn, *m. Phren.* acquisitiveness.

Erwerbs'..., *in comp.* —stand, *m.* industrial or working class; E-swissenschaft, *f. see* Brotwissenschaft; E-szweig, *m.* branch of industry, business, trade, profession.

Erwer'bung, *(w.) f.* the (act of) acquiring, &c. cf. Erwerben; acquisition.

Erwi'dern, **Erwie'dern**, *(w.) v. tr.* to return: 1) to requite, render; to reciprocate (favours, sentiments, &c.); ich erwidere seinen Gruß, I beg to be remembered in return; cf. Vergelten; 2) to rejoin, to return answer, reply (auf [*with Acc.*], to); darauf erwidere ich nur, I only say in reply; er hat mir Gutes mit Bösem erwidert, he has returned me evil for good, has ill requited me.

Erwi'derung, **Erwie'derung**, *(w.) f.* 1) return; diese Gefühle fanden keine —, these sentiments were not responded to or reciprocated; 2) answer, reply; ich ließ Ihr Schreiben vorläufig ohne —, I deferred answering your letter, I left your letter unanswered till now; in — (*with* auf [& *Acc.*] *or Gen.*), in reply or answer (to); E-sschrift, *f. Law*, rejoinder.

Erwin'den, *(str.) v.* I. *tr.* † 1) to earn, acquire; 2) to effect; II. *refl.* to dare, venture; to make free; III. *intr.* to desist; to fail (in performing something, &c.).

Erwir'ken, *(w.) v. tr.* to effect, cf. Auswirken.

Erwisch'en, *(w.) v. tr. coll.* to catch, cf. Ertappen.

Erwit'tern, *(w.) v. tr. see* Auswittern, *v. tr.* 2.

Erwuch'ern, *(w.) v. tr.* to get by usury.

Erwünsch'en, *(w.) v. tr.* to wish for, desire; erwünscht, *p. a.* wished for, desired; desirable; erwünscht kommen, to come most opportunely, to be welcome; es wäre mir erwünscht, I should be glad.

Erwür'feln, *(w.) v. tr.* to win by dicing or raffles.

Erwür'gen, *(w.) v.* I. *tr.* 1) to choke, strangle, throttle; 2) to kill, slay, slaughter; II. *intr.* (*aux.* sein) to choke (an [*with Dat.*], of). — **Erwür'gung**, *(w.) f.* strangulation, &c.

A. **Erz**, *s.* I. *(str.) n.* 1) ore; metal; 2) (red) brass, bronze; II. *in comp. Min.-a., &c.* —abgabe, *f.* mining-due, lot; —ader, *f.* vein of ore, metallic or metalliferous vein, a live lode.

B. **Erz...**, *in comp.* [illegible] 1) chief, high, first, great; excellent, capital; very, extremely, exceeding; excessively; 2) [illegible] arrant, confirmed, *cpd.* [illegible]

[illegible] guten Leben (*Grimm*, D. Sagen 1, 84), [illegible] had a jolly life of it: er hat — gut, he [illegible] a nice time of it; — Einem bequem ma[illegible], — Einem leicht machen, to make one [com]fortable, to relieve one; Gott sprach: — [wer]de Licht. Und — ward Licht (Gen. 1, 3), [God] said, Let there be light: and there was [light]; — ist ein Gott, there is a God; — gibt [Leute], there are people: — sind ihrer drei, [there] are three of them: — waren unserer [fünf], there were five of us; — sind unserer [nur] wenige, there are only a few of us; Hur[rah] [illegible] schallte — von Klippe zu Klippe, Hurra! [resoun]ded from cliff to cliff; der Fall mit dem [illegible] — zu thun haben, the case with which [we] have to do; — spiele, wer da will, let play [who] will; — lebe der König! long live the [King]! — wurde gespielt, there was playing: [er] sollte — besser wissen, he should know bet[ter]; [illegible] in dem Glauben, daß er — mit einer [illegible] Wahnsinniger zu thun hätte, believing [he] had to do with a company of madmen; — ist so klar, als — nur sein kann, it is as [clear] as can be; — sei denn, unless, except; provided.

Esai'as, *m.* Esaias (*P. N.*).

Es'bucht, (*w.*) *f.* *Mar.* S-rounding.

* **Escadre** [*pr.* [illegible]], (*w.*) *f.* (*Fr.*) *see* [Ge]schwader. [Schwadron.

* **Escadron'** [*pr.* [illegible]], *f.* (*Fr.*) *see*

* **Esca'le**, (*w.*) *f.* (*Fr.*) *Mar.* harbour of [an]chorage, port; E-n machen, to touch at ports.

* **Escapa'de**, (*w.*) *f.* (*Fr.*) 1) *Man.* false [spring]ing of a trained horse; 2) foolish action, [wanton] trick. [escarp.

* **Escar'pe**, (*w.*) *f.* (*Fr.*) *Fort.* escarp,

Esch'..., *in comp.* —ahorn, *m.* ash-leaved [maple] (*Acer negundo* L.); —baum, *m.* *see* [Esche]; —blau, *n.* *see* Eichel.

A. **Esch'e**, (*w.*) *f.* 1) *Bot.* ash, ash-tree (*Fraxinus excelsior* L.); blühende —, *see* Blu[men]esche; junge —, ground-ash; 2) *Ichth.* *see* [Äsche], 1.

B. **Esch'e**, (*w.*), **Esch**, (*str.*) *m.* *provinc.* a common (tract of arable ground).

Esch'el, (*str.*) *n.* saffre (the third quality of powder-blue).

Esch'en, I. *adj.* ashen, of ash; II. *in comp.* —holz, *n.* ash-wood; —manna, *f.* *see* Manna[esche]; —rine, *f.* *provinc.* *see* Eberesche; —wurz, *f.* *Bot.* white-dittany (*Dictamnus albus* L.).

Esch'..., *in comp.* —lauch, *m.* *see* Scha[lotte]; —röschen, —rösel, *n.* *see* Elsebeere.

* **Escompt'e**, **Escomptiren**, *see* Disconto, Discontiren.

* **Escor'te**, (*w.*) *f.* (*Fr.*) escort (Geleit). — **Escortiren**, (*w.*) *v.* *tr.* to escort (Geleiten).

E'sel, *a.* I. (*str.*) *m.* 1) ass (*Equus asinus* L.), donkey; 2) *T.* *a)* easel, horse; *b)* *Comb-m.* tool for rounding the teeth; *c)* *see* Eis[illegible]; *d)* *Build.* rammer; *e)* *Typ.* horse; *f)* *Paper-m.* dropping-board; der hölzerne —, wooden horse; Einem einen — bohren, *proverb.* to make a fool, a butt of one; II. *in comp.* —füllen *&c.*, *see* E-sfüllen *&c.*

E'selchen, **E'selein**, (*str.*) *n.* (*dimin.* of Esel) 1) little ass; 2) a species of cowry.

Eselei', (*w.*) *f.* *vulg.* 1) stupidity, blockish[ness], doltishness; 2) stupid trick, blunder.

E'selhaft, *adj.* *coll.* like an ass, ass-like.

E'selin, (*w.*) *f.* female ass, she-ass.

E'seln, (*w.*) *v.* I. *intr.* *coll.* 1) to labour [illegible], drudge (Büffeln, Ochsen); 2) to [commit] [illegible] blunders; 3) to grow ass-like [or] stupid, to become an ass; II. *tr.* 1) to [call] (one) an ass, to scold (one); 2) *refl.* *see* [illegible].

E'sels..., *in comp.* —arbeit, *f.* drudgery; —[illegible], *m.* *see* —gurke; —bohne, *f.* [illegible] horse-bean (the small-grained *Vicia* [faba] L.); —brücke, *f.* *fig.* asses' bridge, crib, [illegible]; —brust, *m.* *Anat.* [illegible] worship; *Bot.-s.* —distel, *f.* cotton or woolly thistle (*Onopordon acanthium* L.); —farn, *m.* true maiden hair (*Adiantum capillus Veneris* L., Frauenhaar); —fenchel, *m.* a species of fennel (*Foeniculum piperitum* DC.); —füllen, *n.* colt or foal of an ass; —fuß, *m.* *see* Lazarusklappe; —geschrei, *n.* bray; —grau, *adj.* ass-gray; —gurke, *f.* *Bot.* squirting cucumber (*Momordica elaterium* L.); —haupt, *n.* *Mar.* cap (of the mast-head); ein —haupt ansetzen, to cap; —huf, *m.* *see* Huflattich; —käfer, *m.* *see* Warzenkäfer; —kopf, *m.* 1) *Techn.* upper part of a rammer; 2) *fig.* dunce, ass, blockhead; —kürbis, *m.* *see* —gurke; —kuh, *f.* *Zool.* tapir (*Tapirus* L.); —lattich, *m* *see* Huflattich; —milch, *f.* 1) asses' milk; 2) *Bot.* a species of spurge (*Euphorbia Esula* L.); —möhre, *f.* *Bot.* wild carrot (*Daucus carota* L.); —ohr, *n.* 1) an ass's ear; 2) *Conch.* horned broadlip; 3) *Mar.* strops under the cap of the top-mast; 4) *coll.* a dog's ear (marginal fold in a book); —petersilie, *f.* *Bot.* wood-parsley (*Anthriscus silvestris* Hoffm.); —rücken, *m.* 1) back of an ass; 2) something shelving up on both sides: *a)* *Archit.* ogee-arch; *b)* *Mar.* semicircular covering of the whipstaff-hole; —schreier, *m.* *Ornith.* common pelican (*Pelecanus onocrotalus* L.); —tracht, *f.* ass's load.

E'sel(s)treiber, *m.* ass-driver.

Es'hammer, (*str.*, *pl.* Es'hämmer) *m.* *T.* S-hammer.

* **Esla'le**, *see* Escale.

* **Esote'risch**, *adj.* (*Gr.*) esoteric, secret.

* **Esparset'te**, (*w.*) *f.* (*Fr.*) *Bot.* esparcet (*Onobrychis sativa* L.).

Es'pe, (*w.*) *f.* *Bot.* aspen(-tree), asp, trembling poplar (*Populus tremula* L.); E-nlaub, *n.* foliage of an asp, aspen leaves; er zittert wie ein E-nlaub, *coll.* he trembles like a leaf. — **Es'pen**, *adj.* made of asp, aspen.

* **Esplana'de**, (*w.*) *f.* (*Fr.*) esplanade.

* **Esponton'**, *n.* (*Fr.*) *Mil.* half-pike, spontoon.

Es'quimo, (*str.*, *pl.* E-s) *m.* Esquimeau.

Es'ra, *m.* Ezra (*P. N.*).

Eß'bar, I. *adj.* eatable, edible, esculent; e-e Dinge, eatables; II. E-keit, (*w.*) *f.* eatableness, *&c.*

Eß'begier, (*w.*) *f.* *see* Eßgier.

Es'se, *n.* (*Lat.* *v.* "to be"; *according to others from the Fr.* [à son] aise) *slang*, comfortable state; in seinem — sein, to enjoy one's self, to be in one's proper element.

Es'se, (*w.*) *f.* 1) *T.* forge; 2) chimney; flue; E-nfeger, E-nkehrer, *m.* sweep, chimney-sweeper; E-nkopf, *m.* chimney-head.

Es'sen, (*irr.*) *v.* I. *tr.* to eat, feed; zu Mittage —, to dine; zu Abend —, to sup; wenig —, to eat but little, to be a little *or* poor eater; viel *or* stark —, to be a large feeder, *cf.* Esser; gut —, to live high; man ißt da sehr gut, the fare *or* board is very good there; im Speisehaus —, to take one's meals in an ordinary; ich esse bei ihm, I board with him; was haben Sie zu —? what have you got for dinner (supper)? herrlich — und trinken, to fare sumptuously; er hat kaum das liebe Brot zu —, *coll.* he makes a hard shift to live; II. *refl.* to eat; Suppe ißt sich besser warm als kalt, soup eats better warm than cold.

Es'sen, *s.* (*str.*) *n.* 1) the (act of) eating, *&c.*; dinner; zum — bleiben, to stay dinner; 2) *a)* meal, victuals, provisions; *b)* dish, (*m. &c.*) mess; 3) meal, repast; entertainment; ein gesundes —, a healthy diet; schmeckt Ihnen das —? *a)* do you like this fare? *b)* do you relish your meals? das war ihm ein gefundenes —, *coll.* that was water on his mill: E-szeit, *see* Eßzeit.

* **Essenz'**, (*w.*) *f.* (*L. Lat.*) essence.

Es'ser, (*str.*) *m.* eater; ein starker —, a great eater, strong feeder; ein schlechter —, *coll.* a poor knife and fork.

Esserei', (*w.*) *f.* *cont.* the (act or practice of) eating, *cf.* Schmauserei.

Es'serlich, *adj.* 1) †, *see* Eßbar; 2) es ist mir —, *coll.* I am inclined to eat.

Eß'gier, (*w.*) *f.* eagerness of appetite, greediness; voracity, gluttony.

Es'sig, (*str.*) *m.* vinegar; *in comp.* —älchen, *n.* *Zool.* vinegar-eel (*Anguillula aceti* Goese), *cf.* Kaltbierchen; —äther, *m.* acetic ether; —baum, *m.* *see* Gerberbaum; —beerstrauch, *m.* *Bot.* *see* Berberitze; —bildung, *f.* acidification, acetification; —brauer, *m.* vinegar manufacturer; —brauerei, *f.* vinegar manufactory; —dorn, *m.* *see* Berberitze; —fläschchen, *n.* vinegar-cruet; —gährung, *f.* *Chem.* acetous fermentation; —geist, *m.* spirit of vinegar; (brenzlicher) pyro-acetic spirit; —gurke, *f.* pickled cucumber *or* gherkin; —handel, *m.* vinegar-trade; —händler, *m.* vinegar-seller; —hefen, *f.* *pl.* vinegar dregs; —honig, *m.* *Pharm.* oxymel; —kolben, *m.* *see* Hirschhornbaum; —mutter, *f.* *Chem.* acetous ferment; —rose, *f.* *Bot.* gallican, damask, *or* French rose (*Rosa gallica* L.); —salmiak, *m.* acetate of ammonia; —salz, *n.* acetate of potash; —sauer, *adj.* as sour as vinegar; *Chem.* acetic; —saure Kali, *n.* acetate of potash; —säure, *f.* *Chem.* acetic acid, acid of vinegar; —saure Salz, *n.* acetate; —sieder, *m.* *see* —brauer; —siederei, *f.* *see* —brauerei; —soda, *n.* acetate of soda; —syrup, *m.* *see* —honig; —weinstein, *m.* acetate of tartar; acetate of potash; —zucker, *m.* oxysaccharum.

Eß'..., *in comp.* —korb, *m.* basket for provisions; —löffel, *m.* table-spoon; ein —löffel voll, a table-spoonful; —lust, *f.* appetite; —lustig, *adj.* disposed to eat; —saal, *m.* dining-room, dining-hall; —stunde, *f.* *see* —zeit; —tisch, *m.* dining- (breakfast-, supper-)table; —waare, *f.* victuals, eatables; —wurzel, *f.* *Bot.* willow-herb (*Epilobium* L.); —zeit, *f.* meal-time; dinner-time; supper-time; —zimmer, *n.* dining-room.

* **Estafet'te**, (*w.*) *f.* (*Fr.*) estafet(te), courier, express.

Esth'e, (*w.*) *m.* (**Esth'in**, (*w.*) *f.*) Esthonian. — **Esth'land**, *n.* Esthonia. — **Esth'nisch**, *adj.* Esthonian. [stage.

* **Estra'de**, (*w.*) *f.* (*Fr.*) *Archit.* estrade;

* **Es'tragon**, (*str.*) *m.* (*Fr.* estragon) *Bot.* tarragon (*Artemisia dracunculus* L.).

Es'trich, (*str.*) *m.* & *n.* a floor of a composition of lime, plaster of Paris, *&c.*, lime-floor.

* **Etabliren**, (*w.*) *v.* *tr.* & *refl.* (*Fr.*) to establish (sich, one's self), to settle, to set up a *or* in business; *cf.* Errichten.

* **Etablissement'** [*pr.* —mang'], (*str.*, *pl.* E-s) *n.* (*Fr.*) establishment, settlement, the setting up (of a business); E-sanzeige, *f.* establishment's circular.

* **Eta'ge** [*pr.* [illegible]], (*w.*) *f.* (*Fr.*) story (storey), floor (of a house); E-nkessel, *m.* *T.* doublestoried boiler. [stamin; tammy.

* **Etamin'**, (*str.*, *pl.* E-s) *m.* (*Fr.*) *Comm.*

* **Etap'e**, **Etap'pe**, (*w.*) *f.* (*Fr.*) *Mil.* halting place (for soldiers upon the march); E-nstraße, *f.* regular line of halting-places; military road.

* **Etat'** [*pr.* [illegible]], (*str.*, *pl.* E-s) *m.* (*Fr.*) 1) state, *cf.* Staat; 2) state, condition; 3) *Comm.* state; statement, balance, *cf.* Bestand; den — aufstellen, to make a statement, to balance; 4) account, estimate (of state expenses, *&c.*); über den — hinaus, above the estimate; list (of officers, *&c.*), return; 5) establishment; E-sbuch, *n.* *Comm.* ledger; E-sjahr, *n.* fiscal year; e-(s)mäßig, *adj.* & *adv.* according to the estimate *or* calculation; E-srath, *m.* *see* Staatsrath; E-süberschreitung, *f.*

sum or total (also sum-total) of a statement.

* Etatisi'ren, (w.) v. tr. (Fr.) to state, make a statement of ..., to balance.

* Etce'tera, (Lat.) et cetera, and the rest (gener. contracted: etc., &c., cf. u. s. w.).

* E'thik, (w.) f. (Gr.) ethics, moral philosophy.

* E'thisch, adj. (Gr.) ethic, ethical (adv. ethically).

* Eth'nisch, adj. (Gr.) ethnic, ethnical.

* Eth'no..., in comp. (Gr.) —graph, (w.) m. ethnographer; —graphie', (w.) f. ethnography; —gra'phisch, adj. ethnographic(al); —log', (w.) m. ethnologist; —logie', (w.) f. ethnology: —lo'gisch, adj. ethnologic(al).

* Etiquet'te [pr. ētikĕt'e], (w.) f. (Fr.) 1) etiquette; 2) label: ticket: E-nschutz, m. protection on trade-marks (Markenschutz). — Etiquetti'ren, (w.) v. tr. to label: to ticket.

Et'lich, adj. pron. (gener. used in the pl.) e-e, some, several, sundry; e-e Worte, a few words; er ist achtzig und e-e Jahre alt, he is four score and odd; fünfzig und e-e Jahre alt, (a man, &c.) of fifty odd (years of age).

Et'mal, (str.) n. Mar. day's work, the run of a ship for twenty-four hours.

Etru'rien, n. Geogr. Etruria. — Etru'risch, Etrus'kisch, adj. Etrurian, Etruscan.

Etsch, f. Geogr. Adige (a river taking its rise in the Grisons).

Et'ter, (str.) m. & n. provinc. 1) fence (Zaun); 2) (border-)district.

* Etü'de, (w.) f. (Fr.) Paint. & Mus. study.

* Etui' [pr. ĕt-wē'], (str., pl. E-s) n. (Fr.) a small (portable) case (for instruments, cigars, &c.).

Et'wa, Et'wan, adv. 1) †, somewhere; 2) †, at some time or other; 3) perhaps, perchance, possibly, peradventure; 4) about, nearly; ist Ihnen — um 5 Uhr gefällig? shall we say five o'clock? — um vier, say four o'clock; — 500, something like (or say) 500; was — vorkommen mag, anything that may chance or happen to occur; — auf diese Weise, in some such way as this; Alles was ich — brauche, all things I am likely to want; denke nicht —, (beware you) do not think: betritt diesen Ort nicht — in einem guten Rock, don't think of going there in a good coat: er betrete ihn nicht — &c., let him beware how he enters it, &c.: dies warnt uns, nicht — zu glauben, daß ..., this warns us how to believe that ....

Etwa(n)'ig, adj. eventual, that may happen to be, that may (chance to) occur, &c., contingent; die e-en Kosten, the expenses that may be incurred, contingent expenses.

Et'was, pron. I. adj. & s. something, somewhat; (adj.) some: any; — Neues, something new, some news; — Schönes, a fine thing: es ist — Schreckliches, sich (Dat.) den Ermordeten zu denken, it is an awful thing to think of the murdered man: so —, such a thing; haben Sie je so — gehört? did you ever hear the like of it? wenn ich — sage, if I say a thing: er that — Besseres für ihn, he did better things for him; so — bedarf Zeit, these things require time; wissen Sie — Neues? have you any news? irgend —, any thing: — Anderes, something else; irgend — Anderes, any thing else: das ist — Anderes, that's a different thing; in —, um —, in some respects or measure; in some degree; er gilt — bei ihm, he is in high esteem or favour with him, has much influence; sie bilden sich — ein, they are rather conceited; zeige daß du — bist, show that you are somebody; es spinnt sich — gegen die Vögte (Schiller), there is some plot against the governors; II. adv. a little; er ist — weitschweifig, he is rather prolix; — roth, reddish; — sauer, sourish, &c.; III. s. (indecl.) n. Philos. entity, a real being.

Etwel'cher, e, es, pron. † for Einiger.

* Etymolog', (w.) m. (Gr.) etymologist. — Etymologie', (w.) f. etymology. — Etymolo'gisch, adj. etymological. — Etymologisi'ren, (w.) v. intr. to etymologize.

Euch, pron. pers. & refl. (Acc. & Dat.) you, to you: yourselves, to yourselves.

Eu'er, pron. pers. Gen. of you.

Eu'er, Eu'ere, Eu'er, pron. poss. your, der, die, das Eurer, Eu'erer, Eu'ere, Eu'eres, yours.

Eu'ert (Euret, coll. Eurent), in comp. —halben, —wegen, —willen, adv. for your sake, on your account, in your behalf.

Eu'gen, Euge'nius, m. Eugene, Eugenius (P. N.).

Eu'le, (w.) f. 1) Ornith. e. owl, (die kleine) owlet (Strix L.); die großköpfige —, brown owl (Strix aluco L.); die graue (braunschwarze) —, ivy owl (Strix stridula L.); die große, röthliche, see Uhu; E-n nach Athen bringen, proverb. to carry coals to Newcastle: 2) provinc. a large broom, besom (Kehrbesen); eine — fangen, Mar. to bring to the lee, to broach to, to chapel a ship, to build a chapel.

Eu'len, (w.) v. tr. to dust (cf. Eule, 2).

Eu'len..., in comp. —affe, m. Zool. egret (Simia aygula L., a variety of Inuus cynomolgus L.); —artig, adj. owl-like, owlish; —äugig, adj. owl-eyed; —flucht, f. provinc. dusk of the evening, owl-light; —flug, m. fig. secret flight; —geschrei, n. hooting or screeching of owls; —kopf, m. Ornith. 1) see Schnepfe; 2) see Brachvogel; —spiegel, m. 1) name of a popular German jester of the fifteenth century; 2) merry jester, wag: —spiegelei, f., —spiegelsstreich, m. coll. a merry trick, a waggery; —spiegeln, (w.) v. intr. coll. to play the merry-andrew or merry tricks: —stimme, f. screech-owl voice.

* Eumeni'den, (w.) f. pl. Gr. Myth. Eumenides, the Furies.

* Eunuch', (w.) m. (Gr.) eunuch.

* Euphemis'mus, m. (Gr.) euphemism. — Euphemisti'sch, adj. euphemistic.

* Euphonie', (w.) f. (Gr.) euphony. — Eupho'nisch, adj. euphonic(al), euphonious.

* Euphor'bie, (w.) f. (Gr.) Bot. euphorbia, spurge: E-ngummi, n. Pharm. euphorbium.

Eu'phrat, m. Geogr. Euphrates (a river).

Eu'rige, (der, die, das) pron. poss. absol. yours.

Euro'pa, n. (Gen. E-s or Euro'pens) Europe. — Europä'er, (str.) m., Europä'erin, (w.) f. a European, European woman. — Europä'isch, adj. European. — Europäisi'ren, (w.) v. tr. to Europeanise. — Euro'pia, f. (Clausius, Rheinweinlied), lud. for Europa.

Eustach'isch, adj. Anat. Eustachian (tube, &c.).

Eustach'ius, Eusta'sius, m. Eustace (P. N.).

Eu'ter, (str.) n. udder, bag (of a cow, &c.): mit vollem —, big-uddered; —theil, n. Trom. dugs. — Eu'tern, (w.) v. intr. to have full udders.

E'va, coll. E've, f. (dimin. E'vchen, (str.) n.) Eve (P. N.).

* Evacuation', (w.) f. (Lat.) Med. see Ausleerung.

* Evalvation', (w.) f. (Med. Lat.) Comm. valuation. — Evalvi'ren, (w.) v. tr. to value.

* Evange'lisch, adj. (Gr.) evangelical; e-e Wahrheit, f. gospel-truth. — Evangelist', (w.) f. evangelist. — Evange'lium, (str., pl. (w.) Evange'lien) n. gospel; das heutige — handelt von Paulus, the text of this day treats of St. Paul: auf das — schwören, to take a gospel-oath; was er ihr sagte, war ihr ein —, coll. she received his words like gospel-truth.

* Evection', (w.) f. (Lat.) Astr. evection.

E'vens ... (Gen. of Eva), in comp. —kind, n. Eve's child, mortal; —sohn, m. Eve's son, man; —tochter, f. Eve's daughter, woman.

* Eventuell', adj. see Etwaig. — Eventualität', (w.) f. eventuality, contingency.

* Exceß', (str.) m. (Lat.) excess, extravagance, outrage, disorderly doings.

* Excitato'rium, (str., pl. [Lat.] E-'ria, or [w.] E-'rien) n. Law, citation.

* Excludi'ren, (w.) v. tr. (Lat.) to exclude (ausschließen). — Exclusion', (w.) f. exclusion. — Exclusiv', adj. exclusive. — Exclusi've, adv. exclusively.

* Excommunication', (w.) f. (Lat.) excommunication. — Excommunici'ren, (w.) v. tr. to excommunicate. [ment.

* Excrement', (str.) n. (Lat.) Med. excre-

* Excrescenz', (w.) f. (L. Lat.) excrescence.

* Excretion', (w.) f. (Lat.) excretion, secretion.

* Excurs', (str.) m. (Lat.) Lit. excursus, digression. [jaunt, tour.

* Excursion', (w.) f. (Lat.) excursion, trip,

* Execution', (w.) f. (Lat.) execution; distress; auf — antragen, to seek (apply for) execution; eine — extrahiren, to levy a distress, to put in or take out an execution (gegen, against); eine — vollstrecken, to put in a distress; E-sgericht, n., E-sinstanz, f. court from which execution has passed or issued; E-smandat, n. warrant of distress, (writ of) execution, (E-sverfahren, n.) final process. — Executi'ren, (w.) v. tr. to execute. — Executiv', adj. 1) executive (Gewalt, power); e-e Beamte, ministerial officer; —proceß, m. suit where the proofs in support of a claim are based on authenticated documents. — Execu'tor, (str., pl. [w.] Executo'ren) m. executor. — Executi'visch, Executo'risch, adj. done or effected with judicial aid.

* Exege'se, (w.) f. (Gr.) Theol. & Lit. exegesis, exposition (of the Scriptures, &c.). — Exeget', (w.) m. one versed in exegesis, expounder, interpreter. — Exege'tik, (w.) f. science of literary interpretation, exegesis. — Exege'tisch, adj. exegetic(al); adv. exegetically.

* Exem'pel, (str.) n. (Lat.) 1) example, see Beispiel; 2) arithmetical problem or task; ein — rechnen, to reckon, work (coll. do) a sum; ein Additions— rechnen, to do a sum in addition (coll. addition sum).

* Exemplar', (str.) n. (Lat.) copy (of a book); specimen; Comm.-e. — eines Wechsels, part of a set of bills of exchange; eine Quittung in doppelten E-en, duplicate receipts. — Exempla'risch, adj. exemplary; — leben, to live exemplarily.

* Exem(p)t', adj. (Lat.) Law, exempt (from taxes, &c.). — Exem(p)tion', (w.) f. Law, exemption (from taxes, &c.).

* Exequa'tur, (str., pl. E-s) n. (Lat.) exequatur; das — ertheilen, to grant the exequatur.

* Exe'quien, f. (Lat.) pl. obsequies.

* Exequi'ren, (w.) v. tr. & intr. (Lat.) to enforce (payment), to enforce payment from —, to execute, perform (a legal charge).

* Exerci'ren, (w.) v. tr. (Lat.) to exercise; to drill, train (soldiers); to practise; er ließ sie —, he put them through their manoeuvres; sie sind zum (beim) — (v. n.), they are out for exercise or on drill.

* Exercir' … in comp. —detachement, n. squad; —meister, m. drill-sergeant; trainer; —platz, m. exercise-ground, drilling-ground.

* Exerci'tium, (str., pl. [Lat.] E-tia, or [w.] Exerci'tien) n. (Lat.) exercise: 1) drill; 2) specimen (of scholars or pupils), task.

* [illegible], (str.) m. (Barb. Lat.) Surg. [illegible].

* Exhibi'ren, (w.) v. tr. (Lat.) Law, to exhibit. — Exhibition', (w.) f. exhibition. — Exhi'bitum, (str., pl. [Lat.] Exhi'bita) n. a writing exhibited.

* Exhortation', (w.) f. (Lat.) exhortation.

* Exil', (str.) n. (Lat.) exile, banishment. — Exili'ren, (w.) v. tr. to exile, banish.

* Eximi'ren, (w.) v. tr. (Lat.) to exempt; eximirt', p. a. exempt (from taxes, &c.).

* Existenz', (w.) f. (L. Lat.) 1) existence (Dasein); 2) subsistence, means of support, living, livelihood. — Existi'ren, (w.) v. intr. 1) to exist (Dasein); 2) coll. to subsist, have the means of living.

* Exitär', (w.) m. (Lat.) Comm. Law, bankrupt.

* Exmatriculi'ren, (w.) v. tr. to remove the name of (a student) from the register of a university; to strike out from a list (said of lawyers, citizens, &c.); sich — lassen, to take one's name off the books.

* Exmission', (w.) f. (Lat.) Law, ejectment. — Exmitti'ren, (w.) v. tr. to eject.

* Exorcisi'ren, (w.) v. tr. (L. Lat.) to exorcise. — Exorcis'mus, m. exorcism. — Exorcist', (w.) m. exorciser, exorcist.

* Exote'risch, adj. (Gr.) exoteric, exoterical.

* Exo'tisch, adj. (Gr.) exotic, exotical.

* Expansibilität', (w.) f. (L. Lat.) expansibility.

* Expansion', (w.) f. (L. Lat.) expansion; T-e.: E-s(dampf)maschine, f. expanding or expansive (steam-)engine; E-sschraubenbohrer, m. expanding-tap; E-sventil, n. expansion-valve.

* Expectant', (w.) m. (Lat.) expectant. — Expectanz', (w.) f. expectancy (Anwartschaft).

* Expectori'ren, (w.) v. I. tr. (Lat.) to expectorate; II. refl. to unbosom one's self, to open or pour out one's heart.

* Expedient', (w.) m. clerk, assistant, assistant clerk, despatcher, manager. — Expedi'ren, (w.) v. tr. (Lat.) 1) to despatch, expedite, forward; 2) to dispatch one's business. — Expedition', (w.) f. expedition: 1) a dispatching, dispatch; 2) a military, naval, or similar enterprise; 3) office, bureau; E-slocal, n. office.

* Expen'sen, (w.) f. (Lat.) pl. Comm. expenses, charges.

* Experiment', (str.) n. (Lat.) experiment, cf. Versuch. — Experimental', adj. experimental; —physik, f. experimental philosophy. — Experimenta'tor, (str., pl. [w.] E-tato'ren) m. experimenter, experimentalist. — Experimenti'ren, (w.) v. intr. to experiment (mit, upon). [dig).

* Expert', adj. & s. expert (Sachverstän-

* Explication', (w.) f. (Lat.) explication, explanation. — Explici'ren, (w.) v. tr. 1) to explicate, disclose, explain; 2) to finish.

* Explodi'ren, (w.) v. intr. (Lat.) to explode, Chem. to fulminate, detonate; e-de Kraft, f. explosive force or power. — Explosion', (w.) f. explosion, blowing up; Chem. deton(iz)ation.

* Exponent', (w.) m. (Lat.) 1) declarant; 2) Math. exponent, index (of a power); characteristic (of a logarithm); denominator (of a proportion). — Exponi'ren, (w.) v. tr. to expose: 1) to commit, endanger (one); 2) to expound.

* Exporta'bel, adj. (L. Lat.) exportable.

* Export', m. (Lat.) 1) (str.) Comm. or —handel, m., Exportation', (w.) f. exportation, export-trade; 2) E-en, (w.) pl. export (or exportable) goods or articles, exports; —häuser, n. pl. export-houses; —zoll, m. see Ausfuhrzoll.

* Exporteur' (pr. —tör'), (str.) m. (Fr.) Comm. exporter. — Exporti'ren, (w.) v. tr. (Lat.) to export.

* Exposé, (str., pl. E-s) n. (Fr.) exposition, detailed statement.

* Exposition', (w.) f. (Lat.) exposition.

* Expreß', I. adj. (Lat.) express; positive; II. adv. expressly, purposely, on purpose; III. Expres'se, s. m. (decl. like adj.) or —bote, m. express (messenger); —zug, m. Railw. express or through-train.

* Expromission', (w.) f. (L. Lat.) Law, the taking upon one's self the security for the payment of another's debts, expromission. — Expromis'sor, (str., pl. E-o'ren) m. the person answering for the payment of another's debts, cf. Schuldbürge. — Expromitti'ren, (w.) v. intr. to answer for the payment of another's debts.

* Expropriation', (w.) f. (L. Lat.) Law, appropriation; dispossession. — Exproprii'ren, (w.) v. tr. to appropriate, dispossess, to take possession of the private landed property of (one) for public purposes.

* Expulsiv', adj. (Lat.) expulsive (also Surg.).

* Exsudat', (str.) n. (Lat.) Med. exudation.

* Exta'se, (w.) f. (Gr.) ecstasy, elocation; in — gerathen, to go into extasies.

* Extempora'le, (str., pl. [Lat.] E-ra'lia) n. (Med. Lat.) 1) extempore; 2) Mus. voluntary, an extemporary performance (on the organ). — Extem'pore, adv. (Lat.) extempore, off hand, Mus. unpremeditated, extemporaneous. — Extemporii'ren, (w.) v. intr. to extemporise, to speak extempore.

* Extendi'ren, (w.) v. tr. (Lat.) to extend.

* Exten'sum, (str., pl. [Lat.] Exten'sa) n. Comm. statement of a failure.

* Extern', I. adj. e-er Verkehr, external, outward traffic; foreign correspondence; II. (w.) or Exter'nus, (Lat., pl. Exter'ni) m. see Extraner.

* Ex'tra, adv. (Lat.) extra, besides; into the bargain; in comp. extra-, special, extraordinary: —arbeit, f. extra-work; —ausgaben, f. pl. see —kosten; —beilage, f. extra-supplement (of a newspaper); —bezahlung, f. extra-pay; —blatt, n. extra-gazette; —bote, m. an express; einen —boten senden, to send a messenger express; —bürgschaftsschein, m. Law, special contract; —dampfschiff, n. special steamer; —fahrt, f. Railw. excursion-train; —fein, adj. superfine; —kosten, f. pl. extraordinary expenses, extraordinaries, sundries; —liegetage, m. pl., —liegezeit, f. days of demurrage, extra-laydays; —ordinär, adj. see Außerordentlich; —post, f. (in Germ.) special mail, private posting; mit —post reisen, to travel with post-horses; —spesen, pl. see —kosten; —vergütung, f. Comm. bonus; —zoll (auf fremde Waaren), m. alien's duty; —zug, m. Railw. special train.

* Extract', (str.) n. (Lat.) extract: 1) abstract, statement; 2) essence. — Extraction', (w.) f. extraction. — Extractiv'stoff, (str.) m. Chem. extractive principle; thierischer —, osmazome.

* Extradi'ren, (w.) v. tr. (L. Lat.) to deliver. — Extradition', (w.) f. 1) delivery (Auslieferung); 2) (aus Handlungsbüchern) excerpt; E-sschein, m. Comm. 1) bill of delivery; 2) certificate that the extract is correct.

* Extrahi'ren, (w.) v. tr. (Lat.) to extract; eine Execution —, see Execution. — Extrahi'rung, (w.) f. Math. evolution.

* Extra'ner, Extra'neer, (str.) m. (Lat.) day scholar, extern; oppidan, &c.

* Extravagant', I. adj. (Lat.) extravagant; II. s. (w.) f. pl. Eccl. Hist. extravagants. — Extravaganz', (w.) f. extravagance, eccentricity. — Extravagi'ren, (w.) v. intr. to extravagate.

* Extrem', I. (str.) n. (Lat.) extreme; E-e begegnen sich, extremes meet; II. adj. e-e Lage, extreme case, extremities. — Extremität', (w.) f. Anat., &c. extremity.

* Exulant', (w.) m. (Lat.) exile. — Exuli'ren, (w.) v. intr. to live in exile.

Ey, see Ei.

Eze'chiel, m. Ezekiel, Jehezekel (P. N.).

[illegible] tendes; er ist mein —, he is all and all with me. [fact, matter of fact.

* Fac'tum, (str., pl. [Lat.] Fac'ta) n. (Lat.)

* Factur', (w.), Factu'ra, f. (Lat.) Comm.-s. invoice; laut —, as per invoice; — geben, see facturiren; eine — ausziehen or schreiben, to make out an invoice; Factura- or Facturen-buch, n. invoice book, book of invoices; unter dem —preis verkaufen, to sell at a loss on the invoice; —werth, m. invoice amount, value as per invoice. — Facturi'ren, (w.) v. tr. to invoice.

* Facultät', (w.) f. (Lat.) faculty; die theologische —, the faculty of divinity; die medicinische —, college of physicians; die juristische —, the faculty of law. — Facultativ', adj. optional. — Facultist', (w.) m. member of a faculty.

Fäd'chen, (str.) n. (dimin. of Faden) 1) a small thread; 2) Sport. trail of deer.

Fa'de, adj. 1) stale, flat, dull, insipid, tasteless; 2) unmeaning, blind, lean, lame (excuse, &c.).

Fä'deln, (w.) v. I. tr. to thread (a needle), see Einfädeln; II. intr. & refl. 1) to untwist, unravel, untwine, come out (of threads); 2) to be stringy (of liquids).

Fa'den, s. I. (str., pl. Fä'den or Fa'den) m. 1) lit. & fig. thread; gedrehter —, twine; 2) Weav. see Einschlag, 5; 3) fathom, cord (of wood); 4) Anat. string; 5) Cloth. ground; 6) file (in Ketten); 7) thread, rough edge (of a knife); sein Leben hängt an einem —, his life hangs by a thread; zu — schlagen, 1. Tail., &c. to baste, to whip-stitch; 2. Forest. (Holz) to cord (wood); coll.-s. an einem — weg, uninterruptedly, without stopping; ich habe ihn am —, he follows blindly my directions; II. in comp. —ähnlich, adj. thread-like; —algen, f. pl. hair-algæ; —bruch, m. 1) Weav. slipping, gliding, or running thread(s); 2) see Afilock, 2; —dreieck, n. Astr. reticle, reticule; —förmig, adj. Bot. (of roots, &c.) thread-shaped, filiform; —führer, m. Weav. guide; —garn, n. linen-thread; —gerade, adj. according to the thread, straight; —gold, n. gold-thread; Weav.-s. —glitte, f. (coll. —hülse, —hefel) hiddle; —halter, m. band wise on silk reels; —holz, n. see Klafterholz; —klee, m. Bot. least trefoil (Trifolium filiforme L.); —kraut, n. common cudweed, cotton-rose (Filago L.); —kreuz, n. 1) Weav. lease; 2) Astr. see —dreieck; —leiter, m. see —führer; —nackt, adj. coll. stark naked; —nudeln, f. pl. vermicelli; —probe, f. Sug.-r. string-test; —recht, adj. see —gerade; —rein, adj. clear of threads; —scheinig, adj. threadbare; —schlag, m. Tail. basting; —seide, f. 1) waste-silk; 2) Bot. dodder (Cuscuta L.); —sichtig, adj. see —scheinig; —silber, n. silver-thread; —stein, m. Miner. see Tropfstein; —stempel, m. Bookb. back-tool; —weise, adv. & adv. by threads; by cords; —werg, n. oakum; —wurm, m. 1) Zool. see Drahtwurm; 2) pl. Fish. & Vet. Slanders; —zähler, m. T. thread-counter. [sense; absurdity.

Fad'heit, (w.) f. staleness, insipidity; dull-

Fa'dicht, Fä'dig, Fä'denig, adj. filaceous, thready; in comp. threaded.

* Fagott', (str.) n. (Fr.) Mus. bassoon; —zill, n. serpentine crook of a bassoon. — Fagottist', (w.) m. performer on the bassoon, bassoonist.

Fäh'e, (w.) f. Sport. 1) bitch; 2) the female of quadruped beasts of prey.

Fa'hen, (str.) v. I. tr. († &) * to catch, take, seize; II. intr. to fall, to be of effect.

Fä'hig, adj. capable (of), able, apt, fit (zu, for), susceptible (of); — machen, to enable, fit, [illegible]; sich — machen zu ..., to qualify one's self for (an office, &c.); ein f-er Kopf, a man of parts.

Fä'higkeit, (w.) f. ability; 1) capability, aptness; 2) capacity, aptitude; 3) faculty, talent; F-en, pl. abilities, parts; über seine F-en, out of the reach of his faculties, coll. out of his ken.

Fahl, I. s. (str.) m. see Spießglanz; II. adj. fallow; fawn-coloured; dun-coloured; pale; faded; Einen auf dem f-en Pferde (Rosse, auf einer f-en Ziege) finden (erwischen, ertappen), coll. to catch one tripping or lying; III. in comp. Miner.-s. —bleierz, n. see Bleischweif; —(kupfer)erz, n. gray copper-ore; —farbe, f. fawn-colour; —leder, n. Tann. vamp (an inferior sort of upper-leather); neat's leather, dressing-leather; —stein, m. gray-slate.

Fahl'heit, (w.) f. dimness, paleness, fadedness.

Fähn'chen, (str.) n. (dimin. of Fahne) 1) a small flag (Fähnlein); 2) Bot. banner, banneret; 3) Mar. bandroll.

Fahn'den, (w.) v. intr. — auf (with Acc.), Law, to pursue (a criminal), to endeavour to seize or recover.

Fähn'drich, (str.) m. see Fähnrich.

Fah'ne, (w.) f. 1) Mil. a) colours, ensign, standard; banner; flag; b) †, aa) a company (of soldiers); bb) squadron (of horsemen); 2) Bot. vexil, banner; 3) anything resembling a standard or flag: a) vane (of a weathercock); b) feather, beard (of a quill), feather (of a pen); c) Sport. the tail of a hare or squirrel; d) a net for catching larks; e) coll. reckoning at an alehouse; f) F-n, pl. Print. slips (proofs in loose or flying leaves or stripes); mit fliegenden F-n, with flying colours, with colours displayed; die — verlassen, to desert (one's colours).

Fah'nen..., in comp. —eid, m. oath of fidelity to the colours; —flucht, f. Mil. desertion; —flüchtig, adj. deserting (one's colours); —futter(al), n. case or cover for the colours; —hafer, m. Bot. bearded oats (Avena orientalis Schreb.); —junker, m. see Fähnrich; —marsch, m. Mil. the tune or march which is struck up when the colours are lodged; —peloton, n. Mil. subaltern officers and soldiers appointed to defend the colours; —pflichtig, see Militärpflichtig; —schmidt, m. see Fahnschmidt; —schuh, m. colour-rest; —stange, f., —stock, m. staff or shaft of a standard; —träger, m. colour-(or ensign-, or standard-)bearer, ensign; —wache, —wacht, f. Mil. standard-guard, field-guard; —weihe, f. consecration or inauguration of colours; —weise, adv. & adj. by companies, by squadrons.

Fähn'lein, (str.) n. (dimin. of Fahne) 1) a small flag; 2) Mil. see Fahne, 1, b.

Fähn'rich, (str.) m. ensign; F-sstelle, f. ensigncy. [dron, blacksmith.

Fahn'schmidt, (str.) m. farrier of a squa-

Fahr, (w.) f. († &) *, danger (Gefahr).

Fahr'bahn, (w.) f. 1) main-road; 2) main-stream (of a river), see Fahrwasser.

Fahr'bar, I. adj. 1) fit for passage, practicable; navigable, sailable; 2) transportable; die f-e Küste, clear coast; das f-e Eis, sailing or open ice; II. F-keit, (w.) f. practicableness (of roads); navigableness, &c.

Fahr'..., in comp. —betrieb, m. traffic (on a railway, &c.); —billet, n. (railway-)ticket.

Fähr'boot, (str., pl. F-böte) n. skiff, ferry-boat, ferry, wherry.

Fahr'..., in comp. —brücke, f. flying-bridge; —buch, n. Min. journal of the mines; —büchse, f. Mind. box for assayed money; —damm, m. 1) see Straßendamm; 2) or —deich, m. dike that may be passed in a vehicle.

† Fäh'rde, (w.) f., Fähr'den, (w.) v. tr. see Gefahr, Gefährden.

Fah're, (w.) f. Sport. furrow, track.

Fäh're, (w.) f. 1) ferry; ferry-boat, passage-boat; in einer — übersetzen, to ferry over; 2) Sport. track, trail.

Fah'ren, (str.) v. I. intr. (aux. sein) 1) to move quickly, to run, slip, slide, start, rush, dart, &c.; 2) to move from one place to another, to pass, go; to descend, ascend; to travel, depart; to ride, to go in a carriage, in a boat or ship, to drive; to row, sail, navigate; to ply (as a line of vessels, &c. between two places, &c.); auf der Eisenbahn —, to go by rail; ich fahre mit der dritten &c. Classe, I go or travel third, &c. (class); auf einem Dampfschiffe —, to go by steam, to steam it; 3) fig. to proceed; to do (fare, live, get on, come off) well or ill; der Hase fährt gen Feld, Sport. the hare takes (to) the field; er fuhr dieses Weges, he travelled this road; mit der Hand in ... —, to run, put, or slide one's hand into ...; mit der Hand hin und her —, to move one's hand to and fro; mit der Hand durch den Ärmel &c. —, to pass one's hand through the sleeve, &c.; es fuhr ihm aus der Hand, it slipped from (out of) his hand; einander in die Haare —, fig. to fall together by the ears; aus dem Bette —, to start up from one's bed; gen Himmel —, to ascend to heaven; zur Hölle —, to descend, to go to hell; ich kann (in einem Wagen) nicht rückwärts —, I cannot ride backwards (in a carriage); zu Jemandem —, to drive to one, one's house; irre —, to ride astray; spazieren —, to take an airing (in a coach, &c.); aus dem Wege —, to turn aside (in a carriage), to break the way, to give way (Einem, to one); er fährt mit 4 Pferden, he drives four-in-hand; über einen Fluß —, to go over, pass, or cross a river; über das Meer —, to sail across (or to cross) the ocean; über einen Meerbusen —, to shoot a gulf; ans Land —, to land, to put to shore; auf den Grund —, to run aground, to ground; Mar.-s. aus dem Hafen —, to clear the port; gegen den Wind —, to sail against the wind; mit dem Senkblei —, to run with the lead; es fuhr mir durch alle Glieder, it (terror, transport, &c.) thrilled through my limbs; — lassen, 1. to cause to ride, drive, &c.; to run (a line of packets, railway-trains, &c.); 2. to let go (or quit) one's hold, to run loose, to let fly; 3. fig. a) to let pass or slip; b) to part with, give up; to leave, forsake, forego, relinquish, abandon; to drop, fling or cast away (hopes, &c.), to waive (claims, &c.); to neglect; c) Mar. to pass or let go through a block; einen Wind — lassen, vulg. to break wind downwards; fig.-s. Jemandem durch den Sinn (vulg. über das Maul) —, to snap one up, to contradict one, to give one a smart reply; durch den Kopf —, to shoot or flash across one's mind; er fährt dabei am besten, he has (got) the best of it (coll. of the bargain); er fuhr am übelsten bei diesem Streit, he had the worst of the argument, &c.; fahre wohl! farewell!

II. tr. to drive; to row, &c.; to carry, convey; to run; to steer, navigate; to command (a ship); Einen über einen Fluß —, to ferry one over a river; Steine —, to cart stones; auf die Rhede —, Mar. to put out (a vessel) to the road.

III. refl. to drive one's self or itself; sich müde —, to tire one's self by driving or going in a carriage, &c.; der Wagen fährt sich gut, the carriage goes easily; impers. es fährt sich gut, angenehm &c. in diesem Wagen &c., it is pleasant, agreeable to go (ride) in this carriage, the carriage is well hung.

Fah'rend, p. a. 1) going, riding, &c. see Fahren; 2) vagrant; travelling; f-e Habe, f. movable goods, property, estate, personal property, movables; die f-e Post, stage-coach, mail-coach (opp. horse-mail); ein f-er Ritter, a knight-errant; ein f-er Scholast or Schüler, a travelling scholar.

Fah'rer, (str.) m. driver.

Fahrerei, (w.) f. (act or practice of) driving about.

Fahr'..., in comp. **–gang**, m. see –weg; **–gast**, m. passenger; fare; **–gebühr**, f., **–geld**, n. fare (price of convenience), carriage.

Fähr'geld, (str., pl. F–er) n. fare, ferriage, passage-money.

Fahr'..., in comp. **–geleise**, **–geleis**, n. track of a carriage, (cart) rut, riding-bed; **–genosse**, m. 1) fellow-traveller; 2) neighbour whose land is separated from that of another merely by a furrow.

Fähr'gerechtigkeit, (w.) f. right or privilege of having a ferry.

Fahr'gut, (str., pl. F–güter) n. Law, movable goods or property, movables. [house.

Fähr'haus, (str., pl. F–häuser) n. ferry-

Fah'rig, adj. 1) moving about (impetuously or incautiously), dashing or rushing thoughtlessly at an object; 2) rash, hasty, incautious, giddy, thoughtless.

Fäh'rig, adj. 1) see Fahrig; 2) Law, f–e Habe, see Fahrende Habe.

Fahr'..., in comp. **–kahn**, m. see –boot; **–kappe**, f. miner's cap. [man.

Fähr'knecht, (str.) m. servant of a ferry-

Fahr'kunst, (str., pl. F–künste) f. Min. man-engine.

Fahr'lässig, I. adj. inattentive (to business or duty); negligent, careless; II. F–keit, (w.) f. inattention, disregard, negligence, carelessness.

Fahr'..., in comp. **–leder**, n. Min. miner's breech-leather; **–leise**, see –geleise.

Fähr'lich, adj. († &) * dangerous (Gefährlich). [hole; **–lohn**, m. see –geld.

Fahr'..., in comp. **–loch**, n. Mech. man-

Fahr'los &c., see Gefahrlos &c.

Fähr'mann, (str., pl. F–leute, F–männer) m. ferry man. [Feldmaus.

Fahr'maus, (str., pl. Fahr'mäuse) f. see

Fähr'meister, (str.) m. master of a ferry-boat. [pin.

Fahr'nagel, (str., pl. F–nägel) m. T. thill-

Fahr'niß, (str.) f. (l. u.) movable goods or property, movables (Fahrende Habe); **–zeit**, f. quarter-day.

Fahr'..., in comp. **–plan**, m. time-table, railway-times; **–post**, f. waggon-post; **–preis**, m. price of conveyance, fare; **–schacht**, m. Min. descending and ascending shaft; footway-shaft; **–schatz**, m. ferriage; **–schein**, m. see –billet; **–schiff**, n. see Fähre.

Fähr'schiff, (str.) n. ferry-boat, ferry (with mast and sails).

Fahr'..., in comp. **–schlitten**, m. T. carriage, sliding-frame; **–seil**, n. rein in driving; ferry-rope; **–sessel**, m. rolling chair; **–stange**, f. coach-bit; **–steiger**, m. inspector of a mine; **–stoß**, m. see –schacht; **–straße**, f. high-road; **–stuhl**, m. 1) see –sessel; 2) T. a slide or engine for raising, lowering, or removing heavy objects (in factories, &c.); elevator.

Fahrt, (w.) f. 1) passage, journey, turn; drive; run; ride (in a carriage or boat); trip; excursion; voyage, course, way (of a ship); navigation; eine (Bahn–)– benutzen, Railw. to take a train; 2) load, cart-load; 3) a) way, road; b) see Fährte; 4) Min. miner's or mining ladder; 5) Sport. barrow, hole (of some animals); 6) water-pipe; 7) provinc. ploughing; 8) fig. coll. (foolish) trick, see Streich, 2; 9) see Fahrniß; auf der –, †, on the spot, immediately; auf der – sein, †, to be about or on the point; Mar.-s. wo geht Ihre – hin? which way do you steer your course? keine – (mehr) haben, to have no steerage way, to be out of sailing-trim; das Schiff hat gute –, the ship runs well, is a quick sailer (in fair weather); das Schiff hat harte –, she is not a very quick sailer; es hat feine –, she sails fast (with stormy weather); **–flagge**, f. Mar. flag twisted at the stern as a signal of departure; **–haken**, **–haspe**, **–schenkel**, **–sprosse**, see Fahrtehaken &c.; **–leder**, n. see Fahrleder; **–messer**, m. Mar. log; **–meßkunst**, f. Phys. trochometry. [use of a ferry.

Fahr'tafel, (w.) f. tariff of fares for the

Fähr'te, (w.) f. 1) track, mark, footing; Sport-s. seal (of the otter); ball print (of the fox); pricking (of the hare); strain slot, trail; die kalte –, dry foot; der Hund schwenkt auf der –, the hound beats up and down; von der – abkommen, to be at fault; auf eine falsche – leiten, lit. & fig. to put on a wrong scent; auf falscher – sein, to be on a wrong scent or at fault; fig. also to go on a wrong tack (hinsichtlich, as to); die – wiedersuchen, to try back (of hare-hounds); auf or in der – bleiben, to keep one's game; 2) miner's ladder; Min.-s. **–haken**, m. ladder-hook; **–haspe**, f. ladder-hasp; **–schenkel**, m. ladder-cheek; **–sprosse**, f. ladder-step. [with the tracks of game.

Fährt'gerecht, adj. Sport. well acquainted

Fah'rung, (w.) f. Min. descent into, or ascent from, a pit, footway.

Fahr'..., in comp. **–wasser**, n. navigable water, track, course, (main-)channel, fair way; **–weg**, m. cart-way, carriage-way, carriage-road, coach-road, road-way, waggon-way; **–wetter**, n. Mar. fair weather (for navigation); **–wind**, m. Mar. fair wind; **–zeug**, n. 1) T. pulley-frame, pulley; 2) a) any kind of vehicle; (railway-)carriage, &c.; b) particul. vessel (of any kind or size), bark, boat, craft.

Fähr'zoll, (str., pl. F–zölle) m. 1) toll paid at a ferry, waterage; 2) see –geld.

* **Faience** [pr. fajangß'], (w.) f. (Fr.) T. faience, pottery embellished with painted designs; (printed) crockery-ware; holländische –, delf, delft(-ware), Dutch-ware; **–fabrik**, f. crockery-ware factory; pottery.

Faim, **Fai'men**, see Feim, Feimen.

Faisch, (str.) m. Sport. blood of a deer; **–hund**, m. blood-hound.

Fa'land, (str.) m. †, deuce, devil (Teufel).

Falb, adj. fallow, pale, faded, pale yellow, cream-coloured, sorrel; F–e, m. & f. a cream-coloured horse; den F–en streichen, fig. to flatter, coll. to curry favour († favel).

Fal'bel, (w.) f. furbelow; flounce; fringe; **Fal'beln**, mit F–n besetzen, **Falbli'ren**, (w.) v. tr. to flounce. [into pale yellow, to fade.

Fal'ben, (w.) v. intr. (aux. sein) to turn

Fal'bicht, adj. having a shade of yellow, faded.

* **Falconet'**, (str.) n. (Fr.) Gunn. falconet.

* **Falconier'**, (str.) m. (Fr.) see Falkner.

Faler'nerwein, (str.) m. Falernian wine.

Fal'ge, **Fal'gen**, see Felge, 2, & Felgen, 2.

Falkonet', (w.) f., **Falke**, (w.) m. Gunn. falcon; der kleine Falke, falconet.

Fal'ke, or **Falk**, (w.) m. falcon, hawk (Falco L.); männlicher –, tercel; (den F–n) steigen or fliegen lassen, to cast (the hawk); (den F–n) niederlassen, herabsteigen lassen, an sich ziehen, to rabate, to recover (a hawk) to the fist.

Fal'ken..., in comp. **–auge**, n. the eye of a hawk, keen eye; mit –augen, hawk-eyed; **–beize**, f. hawking-excursion, falconry; **–blick**, m. fig. an eagle's eye or glance; **–eule**, f. Ornith. hawk-owl (Surnia nisoria Wolf); **–futter**, n. gorge; **–geschühe**, n. jesses; **–haube**, f. hood of a hawk; **–hof**, m. a place where falcons, &c. are kept, falconry; **–hosen**, pl. see –geschühe; **–jagd**, f. see –beize; **–jäger**, m. hawker, falconer; **–kappe**, f. see –haube; **–leine**, f. see –riemen; **–meister**, m. master of a falconry, falconer; **–nest**, n. eyrie; **–papagei**, m. Ornith. hawk-parrot (Hypophicus nonce Kellandia Wagl.); **–pille**, f.

[illegible]

to fall to pieces; er ist gefährlich gefallen, he has met with a dangerous fall; der Vorhang fällt, the curtain drops; der Nebel fällt, the mist descends; die Last fiel ihm vom Rücken, the burden fell from off his back; mein Geburtstag fiel auf einen Freitag, my birthday came, fell, or happened on a Friday; der Anfang des Frühlings (1847) fiel auf den 21. März, the beginning of spring (1847) fell on the 21st of March; ins Gewicht —, to be of heavy weight; in ein Land —, to invade a country; in Ohnmacht —, to faint or swoon (away); to fall into a swoon, to sink into a fainting fit; in Krankheit —, to fall sick or ill; Einem zu Füßen —, to throw one's self at one's feet; als or zum Opfer —, to fall a sacrifice; als or zur Beute —, to fall a prey; sein Auge fiel auf folgende Stelle, his eye hit on the following passage; auf den Gedanken —, to hit or light upon an idea; ich fiel auf den Gedanken, the thought struck me; aus dem Himmel gefallen, coll. greatly amazed, thunder-struck; aus der Rolle —, to act out of character; — lassen, 1. a) to let fall, to drop (the curtain); to shed (leaves); b) to let down (eine Masche, a stitch); fig-s. 2. to abate (something of the price); 3. to drop, throw out (hints, &c.); 4. to put or lay aside, to drop, to sink (a scheme, &c.), to dismiss (a thought, &c.); 5. to forsake (a friend, &c.); 6. to lose (one's courage, &c.); Einen — machen, to give one a fall; Einem in die Zügel —, to seize the bridle of another person's horse; Einem in den Arm —, to seize the arm of a person about to strike; Einem in den Kauf —, to interfere with another's bargain; fig. to put a spoke in another's wheel; Einem in die Rede —, to interrupt one; in Strafe —, to incur a penalty; in die Sinne or Augen —, to strike the senses or eyes; Einem in die Augen —, to catch one's eyes; in die Augen f-d, conspicuous; beschwerlich, zur Last —, to be troublesome, burdensome, or chargeable, to inconvenience (durch, by); der Gemeinde zur Last —, to come upon the parish; es fällt mir schwer, leicht &c., it is difficult, easy to me; der Gedanke fällt mir schwer, the thought falls heavy upon me; es fällt ins Rothe, it inclines to red, it has a red cast; es fällt ins Pöbelhafte, it partakes (smacks) of vulgarity; wenn es fällt, as it happens; mit der Thüre ins Haus —, coll. to blunder out; to set about a thing in an awkward way; Mar-s. das Schiff fällt verkehrt, the ship casts the wrong way; in See —, to make leeway, to drive (fall) to leeward; fall! fall ins Boot! man the boat! see Abfallen, I. 4. b.&c. or die f-e Sucht, see Fallsucht; II. tr. er fiel das Kind todt, he killed the child by his fall; er fiel sich (Dat.) einen Arm aus dem Gelenk, he dislocated his arm by a fall: III. rfl. sich todt or wund —, to kill or wound one's self by falling; gefallen, p. a. ruined, seduced, lost (of a girl); ein g-er Engel, a fallen angel.

Fal'len, s. n. (str.) m. 1) falling, fall; 2) Comm. fall (cf. Baisse), decline, reduction, depression, lowering (of prices), depreciation; Neigung zum —, tendency to fall or decline, tendency downwards; eine Neigung zum — haben, to have a downward tendency, to look down; auf das — speculiren, to speculate on a decline (of the funds), to speculate for the fall.

Fäl'len, (w.) v. tr. 1) to fell, to cut, or hew down (wood); to pull down (a wall, &c.); 2) Chem. to precipitate; 3) Mar. to cast (anchor); 4) Min. to sink, deepen (a shaft); fig-s. 5) provinc. a) to cast or shed (teeth: of cattle and horses); b) to gold (a foal); 6) a) to kill; b) to ruin; 7) Law, &c. a) to pass, pronounce (sentence or judgment); to give (one's opinion); b) provinc. to devolve, leave, transmit (an estate); Mil-s. (das) Bajonett gefällt! bayonet in charge! charge bayonet! mit gefälltem Bajonett angreifen, to charge with fixed bayonet; mit gefälltem Bajonett (er)stürmen, to carry at the point of the bayonet; ein Perpendikel —, Geom. to drop a perpendicular.

Fal'lend, p. a. falling; die f-e Sucht, see Fallsucht; die f-e Reihe, Math. descending series.

Fall'endung, (w.) f. Gramm. case termination.

Fal'len..., in comp. —leger, —steller, m. one employed in entrapping animals, trapper; —riegel, m. see Fallriegel.

Fall'..., in comp. —fenster, n. sash-window; —fertig, adj. about to fall; —fleck, m. bruise from a fall; —gatter, n. falling-gate, portcullis; —grube, f. pit-fall; —gut, n. Law, personal fief; —hammer, m. T. falling hammer; —haus, n. flayer's house; —häutchen, n. Anat. valve; —holz, n. windfallen wood; —hut, m. roller (a turban-like pad for small children).

Fäl'lig, adj. due, payable; — werden, to become due; to expire; die Post aus der Levante war gestern —, the Levante mail was due yesterday.

* **Falliment', Fallissement'**, (str.) n. (Ital.) Comm. failure, bankruptcy, insolvency. — **Falli'ren**, (w.) v. intr. to fail, become (or turn) a bankrupt, coll. to break. — **Fallit'**, (w.) m. bankrupt; coll. broken tradesman or merchant; F-enbuchhalter, m. bankruptcy book-keeper; F-engericht, n. court (or commission in a statute) of bankruptcy; F-engesetz, n. bankrupt law; — or F-enmasse, f. (the general mass of) a bankrupt's estate; Director einer F-enmasse, assignee of the estate of a bankrupt, creditor in trust.

Fall'..., in comp. —käfer, m. Entom. a genus of coleopterous insects, gold-beetle (Cryptocephalus sericeus F.); —kessel, m. Min. precipitating kettle; —kind, n. a chance-child; —klappe, f. trap-board; —klinke, f. falling-latch; —kloben, m. knocker; —klotz, m. see —block; —kraut, n. Bot. mountain-arnica (Arnica montana L.); —laden, m. shutter of a sky-light; —latte, f. Mech. copping-rail; —maschine, f. Phys. a mechanical contrivance or instrument for ascertaining experimentally the laws relative to falling bodies, Attwood's machine; —meister, m. provinc. flayer; —mütze, f. see —hut; —netz, n. 1) a net for catching deer, birds, &c. cf. Schlagnetz; 2) Bill. pocket net.

* **Fallo'pisch**, adj. Anat. Fallopian (tubes or ducts).

Fall'..., in comp. —reep, n. Mar. ladder-rope, man-rope, entering-rope; (der Sturmleiter) concluding line; —reepstreppe, f. accommodation-ladder, gang-way; —riegel, m. Lock-sm. latch-bolt; —rohr, n. fall-pipe; Build. gutter-pipe, waste-pipe.

Falls, conj. in case (...), if; provided.

Fall'..., in comp. —schirm, m. parachute; —schloß, n. spring-(chest-)lock; —silber, n. precipitated silver; —strick, m. gin, snare, noose; fig. snare, trap; —sucht, f. epilepsy, falling sickness; —süchtig, adj. epileptic(al); —tau, n. see —reep; —thor, n. see —gatter; —thür, f. trap-door; —thürchen, n. Anat. valve; —tisch, m. folding-table; —ton, m. Mus. cadence; —treppe, f. trap stairs; —tuch, n. Sport. a screen-like net.

Fäl'lung, (w.) f. 1) the (act of) felling, &c. cf. Fällen; 2) Chem. precipitation; F-smittel, n. precipitant.

Fall'..., in comp. —verwechselung, f. Gramm. antiptosis; —werk, n. Mint. stamp; —wild, n. morkin, game that has died a natural death; —wind, m. eddy wind, gust of wind; —winkel, m. gradient; —wunde, f. wound received by a fall.

Falsch, adj. 1) lit. & fig. a) false (also Mus. cf. Quarte, Quinte); sham, wrong; b) erroneous; mistaken; c) Build. false, mock, dead; d) Dy. fugitive (colour); 2) falsified, counterfeit, adulterated, forged; spurious, fictitious; 3) deceitful, perfidious, malicious, vicious, double; ein f-er Mensch, a double-dealer; 4) provinc. angry, cross; — werden, to snap (of dogs); to become tricksy (of horses); — angegebenes Schiff und Gut, masked ship and property; f-e Brut, see Faulbrut; der f-e Discant, Mus. falsetto; f-er Eid, see Meineid; der — eingetragene Posten, Comm. false (or wrong) entry, mischarge, mis-entry, cross-entry; —gebucht, misentered; f-e Flagge führen, to carry false colours; f-es Geld, f-e Münze, base, counterfeit, or adulterated money or coin; die f-en Pocken, Med. chicken pox, water pox; ein f-er Stein, see Unecht; f-e Wechsel, forged or counterfeit bills of exchange; f-e Wechsel machen, to forge or counterfeit bills of exchange; f-er Name, feigned name; Gam-s. das f-e Spiel, foul play; der f-e Stich, odd trick; der f-e Spieler, cogging gamester, sharper, cheat; Anat-s. die f-e Naht, bastard or false suture; die f-en Rippen, short ribs; meine Uhr geht —, my watch goes wrong; das Exempel ist —, the sum is wrong; — schwören, to swear false, to forswear or perjure one's self; — singen, to sing out of tune; — spielen, to cheat at play; Mus. to play out of tune; — anführen, to misquote; in ein f-es Licht setzen or — darstellen, to misrepresent.

Falsch, (str.) m. & n. 1) provinc. malt; 2) n. obsolescent, †. falsehood, guile; ohne —, without guile, deceitless; Script. ohne — wie die Tauben, harmless as doves.

Fäl'schen, (w.) v. tr. to falsify, counterfeit, forge, adulterate, cf. Verfälschen. — **Fäl'scher**, (str.) m. falsifier, adulterer, forger.

Falsch'..., in comp. —freundlich, adj. hypocritically kind; —gläubig, adj. heterodox.

Falsch'heit, (w.) f. 1) falseness, falsity, spuriousness, &c. cf. Falsch; 2) falsehood; deceit, guile; perfidiousness, treachery; duplicity.

Falsch'herzig, adj. false-hearted.

Fälsch'lich, adj. & adv. false, falsely, &c. cf. Falsch; (etwas) — für ... halten, to mistake (something) for ....

Falsch'..., in comp. —münzer, m. counterfeiter of coin, (false) coiner; —münzerei, f. false coining, forging; —namig, adj. of a fictitious name, pseudonymous; —spieler, m. cheat (in playing).

Fäl'schung, (w.) f. falsification, fabrication, adulteration, counterfeiting, forgery, fraud.

Falsch'werber, (str.) m. Law, one who clandestinely enlists persons belonging to a foreign country. — **Falsch'werbung**, (w.) f. clandestine enlistment, &c.

* **Falset'**, (str., pl. F-tte) n. (Ital.) Mus. falsetto.

* **Falsificat'**, (str.) n. (Lat.) falsification; forgery. — **Fal'sum**, (str., pl. [Lat.] Fal'sa) n. 1) falsehood; deceit; 2) fraud, forgery.

Fält'chen, (str.) n. (dimin. of Falte) little plait, fold, &c.

Fal'te, (w.) f. 1) fold, plait; 2) wrinkle, crease, rumple; gather (made in a dress); Cloth. (fehlerhafte) crumple; 3) Anat. duplicature; 4) fig. fold, recess (of the heart, &c.); F-n schlagen or werfen, to cast folds; to make wrinkles, to pucker; keine F-n werfen, to sit close to the body; F-n bekommen, to pucker, crumple; in F-n legen, ziehen, to put, draw in plaits or folds; die Stirn in F-n ziehen, to knit, wrinkle (the brow); die geheimsten F-n der Seele, fig. the inmost recesses of the soul.

Fäl'teln, (w.) v. tr. to frill, ruffle, plait.

Fal'ten, (w.) v. tr. to fold, to fold or gather up; to plait; einen Brief —, to fold or make up a letter; sich —, Anat. to duplicate; die Stirn —, to knit, wrinkle the brow; die Hände —, to fold, join, or clasp one's hands (as in prayer).

Fal'ten..., in comp. —blume, f. see Winde; —brüche, pl. Paint. folds in drapery or dress; —hund, m. Moll. a species of trochus (Trochus ruber L.); —kammer, f. Sug.-r. room where the sugar-loaves are wrapt up in paper; —kleid, n. see —rock.

Fal'tenlos, adj. 1) without folds or wrinkles, wrinkleless, creaseless, smooth; 2) fig. a) unruffled; b) open; blameless.

Fal'ten..., in comp. —magen, m. Zool. see Blättermagen; —morchel, f. Bot. turban-top (Helvella infula Schaeffer); —ohr, n. Bot. umbelliferous plant of the genus ptychotis (Ptychotis heterophylla Koch & Pt. ammoides Koch); —rand, —saum (an einem Himmelbett), m. valance; —reich, adj. full of folds or wrinkles; —rock, m. coat, gown, or dress with many folds; —schlag, m. Sculpt., &c. (cast of) drapery, the plaits and folding of drapery, casting of draperies; —voll, adj. see —reich; —weise, adv. in plaits or folds; —wurf, m. see —schlag. [Blättermagen.

Fal'ter, (str.) m. 1) butterfly; 2) Zool. see

Fal'tig, adj. having folds or plaits, Bot. rugose; fig. wrinkled, furrowed (brow). — Fal'tig, Fäl'tig, adj. in comp. -fold.

Falt'..., in comp. —stock, m. folding-stick, folder; —stuhl, m. folding-chair; —tisch, m. folding-table.

Fal'tung, (w.) f. 1) the (act of) folding, &c.; 2) — der Gebirgsschichten, corrugation of the rocky strata.

Falz, Fal'zen, Sport-s. see Balz, Balzen.

Falz, s. I. (str.) m. (sometimes Fal'ze [w.] f.) 1) fold; 2) T. furrow, hollow incision; (Nuth) gutter; Coop., &c. groove, notch; (am Gesimse) rebate; Bookb. guard; T-s. flute, channel (in a column); chase (of a crossbow); Carp. rebate, butment; II. in comp. —amboß, m. coppersmith's anvil; —bank, f. Carp. wooden leg; —bein, n. folding-bone, (paper-) folder, (bone) paper-knife, folding-knife, cf. Brieffstreicher; —brett, n. Bookb. folding board; —eisen, n. Tann. paring-knife.

Fal'zen, (w.) v. tr. 1) to fold, fold up; Bogen —, to sheet; 2) T. to groove, join, &c. cf. Falz, 2; 3) Tann. to pare (hides).

Falz'..., in comp. —hobel, m. see Einschneide; —hammer, m. coppersmith's soldering-hammer; —hobel, m. notching-plane, fluting or grooving plane, plough.

Fal'zicht, Fal'zig, adj. like grooves, having grooves, grooved.

Falz'..., in comp. —maschine, f. grooving-engine; —messer, n. see —eisen; —schienen, f. pl. Railw. tram-rails; —schienenweg, m. tram-road; —zange, f. T. soldering-pliers; shoemaker's pinchers; —ziegel, m. ridge-tile, hollow tile, gutter tile.

* Fa'ma, f. (Lat.) 1) fame, public report, rumour; 2) Rom. Myth. (the Goddess) Fame.

* Familiär', adj. familiar. — Familiarität', (w.) f. familiarity. — Fami'lie, (w.) f. (Lat.) family; Nat., &c. tribe.

Fami'lien..., in comp. —ähnlichkeit, f. family likeness; —begräbniß, n see —gruft; —brot, n. home-made bread; —fehler, m. family failing; —gemälde, n. 1) family-picture; 2) description of a family-life; —geräth, n. heirloom; —glück, n. domestic happiness; —gruft, f. family-vault; —gut, n family estate; entailed estate.

Fami'lienhaft, Fami'lienmäßig, adj. family-like, domestic.

Fami'lien..., in comp. —haupt, n. head or father of a family; —krankheit, f. family distemper, hereditary disorder; —kreis, m. domestic circle; —leben, n. fire-side or domestic life; —name, m. family-name, surname; —neigung, m. see Eheneigung; —sinn, m. inclination for a family-life, domestic turn; —sitz, m. family-seat; family-mansion; —stolz, m. family pride; —stück, n. 1) see —gemälde; 2) (—erbstück) family-piece, anything kept in a family as a memorial; —tafel, f. family-dinner; —vater, m. family-man; house-father; —vermächtniß, n. entail; —vertrag, m. family-compact; —wappen, n. coat of arms of a family; —zirkel, m. see —kreis; —zwist, m family-discord.

* Famos', adj. (Lat.) Stud. slang, famous, excellent, prime.

* Fa'mulus, (Lat., pl. Fa'muli) m. (Lat.) amanuensis; Med. (visiting) assistant.

* Fanal', (str.) m. (Fr.) 1) ship's lantern; 2) signal-light, beacon.

* Fanat'iker, (str.) m. (Lat.) fanatic. — Fanat'isch, adj. fanatical, fanatic. — Fanatisi'ren, (w.) v. tr. to fanaticise. — Fanatis'mus, m. fanaticism.

* Fanfa're, (w.) f. Mil. fanfare.

Fang, (str., pl. Fäng'e) m. 1) a) the (act of) catching, &c. cf. Fangen; catch; b) place where any thing is taken or caught; pit-fall; 2) capture, draught; 3) gin, snare, trap; Sport-s. 4) thrust, stab; (einem Hirsche &c.) den — geben, to kill (a deer, &c.) with the hanger; 5) a) see —zahn; b) pl. talons, clutches, claws; tooth (of the wolf); 6) the bite of a dog; 7) hole or cave of the lynx; 8) handle, hilt (of a sword).

Fang'..., in comp. —ball, m. play-ball, cricket; —bäume, m. pl. Min. joists; —brief, m. warrant of capture; —bühne, f. Hydr. weer; —damm, m. a temporary coffer-dam to protect the coffer-dam which it surrounds; —eisen, n. 1) Sport. iron spear (for stabbing wild beasts); huntsman's pole; 2) iron-trap.

Fang'en, (str.) v. I. tr. lit. & fig. to catch, take, seize; to capture; to captivate; to entrap; mit der Angel —, to hook; Feuer —, to catch or take fire; leicht Feuer —, fig. to be irascible; Einen in seiner Rede —, to entangle one in his talk; den Rauch —, to confine the smoke; Mar.-s. die Ankerboje —, to hitch the buoy; die Raaen —, to secure the yards; Tann. to soften (the hides); II. refl. to catch one's self, go into a snare or trap; die Buchten — sich (for einander), the fakes catch each other; III. intr. Sport. to bite, to snap, snatch; sich — lassen, to allow or suffer one's self to be caught, to run one's self into a noose. [ter; 2) see Fang, 5.

Fäng'er, (str.) m. 1) catcher, taker, cap-

Fang'..., in comp. —garn, n. Sport. net; —heuschrecke, f. Entom. praying cricket (Mantis religiosa L.); —jagd, f. Sport. catching of wild beasts by driving them into nets; —leine, f. Mar. painter; Sport. leash; —messer, n. hanger, (Fr.) couteau de chasse; —rad, n. see Anschlagrad; —schelle, f. Sport. low bell; —schürzen, f. pl. Min. catches; —stock, m. police-man's or bailiff's staff; —taue, n. pl. Mar. short pieces of rope or railine; —tuch, n. tinder; —vogel, m. Sport. decoy-bird; —wort, n. Typ. catch-word; Theat. cue; —zahn, m. fang, tusk; mit —zähnen, fanged, tusked. [chen.

Fan'ny, Fänn'chen, see Franciska, Frieg-

Fant, (str.) m. (dimin. Fänt'chen, (str.) n.) († &) * a childish vain youth, fop, dandy; coxcomb. [in Zs) ....

* Fantasie', (w.) f., Fantasi'ren &c., see

Far'be, (w.) f. 1) colour, hue, tinge, tint, die, paint, tincture; 2) complexion; 3) printer's or printing ink; 4) coll. see Farbstoff; 5) Cards, suit (in cards); die — machen, to make trumps; 6) livery; 7) Typ. ink; fig.-s. 8) kind, species, description; 9) colour, varnish, pretext; — halten, Paint. to bear a

[illegible]; —theorie, f. theory of colours; —ton, m. tone of coloration; —topf, m. ink-pot; paint-jar; —waaren, f. pl. Comm. dye-stuffs, dyeing drugs or materials, dry-saltery; —waarenhändler, m. see —händler; —wechsler, m. Ichth. cackerel (Maena vulgaris C.).

Fär'ber, (str.) m. dyer: in comp. Bot-s. —baum, m. Venice sumach, Venus's sumach (Rhus cotinus L.); —beere, f. see Färberdorn; —blume, f. see Färberginster; —camille, f. a species of chamomile (Anthemis tinctoria L.); —croton, m. turnsole (Croton tinctorium L.) (Tournesolkraut); —distel, f. 1) see —saflor; 2) see —ginster; —dorn, m. purging buckthorn (Rhamnus catharticus L.); kleiner —dorn, dyer's buckthorn (Rh. infectoria L.).

Färberei', (w.) f. 1) a) (the art or practice of) dyeing; b) dyer's trade; 2) dye-house, dyery.

Fär'ber..., in comp. —eiche, f. Bot. dyer's oak (Quercus infectoria Willdenow); —farbe, f. colouring drugs; —flechte, f. archil, orchilla-weed (Kräuterorseille); dyer's lichen; canary wood, see Orseille, 2 (von [illegible]); —geselle, m. dyer's journeyman; Bot-s. —ginster, m. common dyer's genista, dyer's broom or green-broom, green-wood, wood-wash, wood-waxen, woad (Genista tinctoria L.); —knöterich, m. dyer's knot-grass (Polygonum tinctorium Lour.); —kraut, n. see —waid; —maulbeerbaum, m. dyer's mulberry (Broussonetia tinctoria L.); —meister, m. master-dyer; Bot-s. —ochsenzunge, f. alkanet-plant (Anchusa tinctoria L.); —pfrieme, f. see Färberginster; —rinde, f. Jesuit's bark; —röthe, f. madder-plant (Rubia tinctorum L.); T. madder (see Krapp); —saflor, m. safflower, bastard saffron (gemeiner Saflor; Carthamus tinctorius L.); —scharte, f. see Färberginster; common saw-wort (Serratula tinctoria L.); —trompetenblume, f. dyer's trumpet-flower; —waid, m. common woad (Isatis tinctoria L.); —wau, f. wild woad, dyer's weed (Reseda luteola L.); —wurzel, f. see —röthe.

Far'be..., in comp. —stein, —stoff, —waaren, see Farbenstein &c.

Fär'be..., in comp. —stoff, m. colouring-matter, gener. pl. dyeing stuffs, colouring materials; —zeit, f. moulting-season, the time of changing the hair (said of deer, &c.); —zeug, n. dyeing- or dyer's utensils.

Far'big, adj. coloured; stained (paper, &c.); f-er Druck, coloured impression, illuminated painting; cf. Bunt; F-e, m. & f. (decl. like adj.) a person of (black, copper, &c.) colour, coloured man, coloured woman; F-e, pl. coloured people.

Farb'los, adj. colourless; Opt. achromatic; — machen, to deprive of colour, achromatise.

Farb'losigkeit, (w.) f. 1) colourlessness; 2) fig. neutrality, (gener. political) indifference.

Fär'bung, (w.) f. 1) the (act of) colouring, staining; 2) tinge, shade; complexion; tincture; eine bestimmte — erhalten, fig. to be tempered (of colours).

* Far'ce [pr. far'se], (w.) f. (Fr.) farce: 1) Dram. a short piece or entertainment of a comic character; 2) Mus. a burlesque.

* Farce [pr. farß], (str., pl. F-s) n. (Fr.) Cook. 1) stuffing; 2) force-meat, forced meat.

— Farciren [pr. farß'—], (w.) v. tr. to stuff (chickens, &c.), to farce.

* Fardel [pr. fard'l], (str., pl. F-s) m. (Fr.) Comm. (in the Netherlands & France) a small bale of goods, packet.

* Farin', (str.) m. (Lat.) brown, moist, or raw-sugar; der weiße — or Puder-Zucker, whitish sugar.

[illegible], (str.) m. (provinc. for Ferkel?) [illegible] 1) hog; 2) see Wasserflieger; —[illegible], [illegible]; —[illegible], m. 1) slow sailing ship; 2) workman who stows away the greaves.

Farn, (str.) m. see —kraut; —baum, m. tree-fern; —gebüsch, n. fern-brake; —kraut, n. fern, polypody; —männchen, n. male fern; —samen, m. fern-seed; —weibchen, n. common brake.

* Fa'ro, (str.) n. (coll. for Pharao, Fr. pharaon) faro (game at cards).

Far'öer, —inseln, pl. Geogr. Faroe islands.

Far're, (w.) m. bullock; F-nhäute, pl. bullock's hides. [Farnkraut.

Far'renkraut, (str., pl. F-kräuter) n. see

Fär'se, (w.) f. a young cow, heifer.

Fasan', (w. & str.) m. Ornith. pheasant (Phasianus L.); der junge —, pheasant-poult; —ente, f. Ornith. sea-pheasant, pin-tailed duck (Anas acuta L.); —hahn, m. pheasant-cock; —haus, n. pheasant-house; —henne, f., —huhn, n. hen-pheasant; —nest, n. nide of pheasants.

Fasa'nen..., in comp. —beize, f. Sport. pheasant hawking; —beller, m. pheasant-dog; —fang, m. pheasant taking; —garten, m., —gehege, n., —hof, m. pheasant-walk, pheasant-preserve, pheasantry; —hund, m. see —beller; —jagd, f. pheasant shooting; —kraut, n. Bot. the spring bitter-vetch (Orobus vernus L.); —meister, m. keeper (breeder) of pheasants; —netz, —stoßgarn, —treibzeug, n. Sport. pheasant net; cocking cloth; —wärter, m. see —meister; —zucht, f. breeding of pheasants.

Fasanerie', (w.) f. pheasantry (Fasanenhof).

Fasch, (str.) m. T. a piece of sole-leather.

Fasch'e, Fäsch'e, (w.) f. 1) provinc. bodice, stays; 2) T. stay (of a window-roofing, &c.).

Fasch'enstahl, (str.) m. see Bundstahl.

Fäs'chen, (str.) n. (dimin. of Faser) see Fäserchen.

* Faschi'nen, (w.) f. (Ital.) pl. Fort. & Dik. fascines; Fort. bavins; in comp. —bänder, n. pl. bands of fascines; —bänke, f. pl. tressels for fascines; —bekleidung, f. chandelier; —messer, n. (hedging-)bill, bill hook.

* Fasch'ing, (str., pl. F-e & F-s) m. (S. G.) carnival. [or file of papers.

* Fascikel, (str.) n. (Lat.) fascicle, bundle

A. Fa'se, (w.) f. 1) see Faser; 2) Bot. sneeze-wort (Achillea millefolium L.).

B. Fa'se, see Fase.

Fa'sel, (w.) m. & f. provinc. 1) fry; 2) hatch; 3) propagation (breeding of cattle); 4) Bot. see Heilbohne; 5) vulg. see Gesindel; —hengst, m. see Beschäler; —schwein, n. see Zuchtschwein; —vieh, n. see Zuchtvieh.

Fäselei', (w.) f. foolish, flighty, or indiscreet behaviour or act, levity, giddiness, frivolity, thoughtlessness.

Fa'seler, (str.), coll. Fa'selgänge, (w.), Fa'selhans, (str., pl. F-hänse) m. a silly, inconsiderate, giddy, or blundering person, driveller, dotard.

Fa'selhaft, Fa'selig, adj. foolish, inconsiderate, light-headed, thoughtless, indiscreet, flighty, giddy, silly.

A. Fa'seln, (w.) v. intr. 1) provinc. to bring forth young ones, to breed; 2) to behave or talk foolishly, &c. cf. Faselig; to dote, dream, drivel, cf. Phantasiren; 3) to increase, thrive (of beans); 4) to farrow.

B. Fa'seln, Fa'sen, Fä'seln, (w.) v. I. tr. to separate the fibres or threads of (a textile fabric); II. refl. to be separated (of fibres, &c.), to fuzz.

Fa'selnackt, adj. see Fasernackt.

Fa'sen, (str.) m. see Faser. [naked.

Fa'sernackt, adj. entirely naked, stark-

Fa'ser, s. I. (w.) f. thread, filament, Anat. & Bot. fibre; string; fine; harl; II. in comp. —alaun, m. fibrous alum; —aragonit, m. Miner. coralloidal arragonite, flos ferri; —bündel, n. Anat. bunch of fibres; —geschwulst, f. Surg. fibrous tumour; —gewächse, n. pl. Bot. see Aftermoose; Miner-s. —gyps, m. English talc; —kalk, m. fibrous limestone; —kiesel, m. fibrolite; —kupfer(erz), n. wood-copper. —stoff, m. Chem. fibrine.

Fä'ser, (str.) m. Vint. see Fächser.

Fä'serchen, (str.) n. (dimin. of Faser) fibril.

Fa'sericht, Fa'serig, Fa'sig, adj. like or resembling fibres; fibrous; fibrinous (tumours, &c.), filamentous, stringy; —knorpelig, adj. fibro-cartilaginous; f-es Zinnerz, n. Miner. wood-like tin-ore, wood-tin.

Fa'sern, (w.) v. tr. & refl. see Faseln.

Faß, s. I. (str., pl. Fäs'ser) n. 1) (offenes) vat, tub; (verschlossenes) butt, coop, cask, barrel, firkin, vessel; (für Zucker, Wein, Taback) hogshead; (Wein) pipe, cask; (Rum) puncheon; (Feigen) drum; 2) fig. & Script. vessel, body; 3) vulg. paunch, fat person; nach dem — schmecken, to taste of the cask; in ein — thun or füllen, to barrel or tun (up), incask; auf Fässer gefüllt, in Fässer gepackt, barrelled up.

Faß'band, (str., pl. Faß'bänder) n. hoop.

Faß'bar, adj. 1) tangible; 2) see Faßlich.

Faß..., in comp. —bärme, f. lees of beer; —bier, n. beer in casks; —binder, m. cooper, hooper; —binderlohn, m. &c. Comm. cooperage, coopering (of the casks); —blech, n. small-sized tin-plates; —boden, m. head of a cask; —bodenmittelstück, n. clap-board; —bohrer, m. piercer; —brücke, f. cask-bridge; —butter, f. firkin-butter.

Fäß'chen, (str.) n. (dimin. of Faß) little barrel, firkin, keg, cade, rundlet.

Faß..., in comp. —daube, f. staff, stave; —daubenholz, n. staff-wood.

Fas'sen, (w.) v. I. tr. 1) to seize, grasp, lay hold on, take hold of, hold, catch, take; Wurzel —, to take root; in der Flanke —, Mil. to take in flank; 2) to put in any thing, to barrel, fill up (beer, &c.), to sack (corn, &c.); 3) T. a) to set, enchase, mount; in Gold gefaßt, set in gold, gold-bound, cf. Einfassen, 1, b, &c.; b) Min. see Auszimmern, 2; c) eine Quelle —, to curb a well (cf. Einfassen, 1, a); fig-s. 4) (in sich —) to hold, take in, embody, contain, compass, comprise, include; 5) to conceive, comprehend, understand, reach, penetrate, catch; to form (an idea, &c.), to take (a dislike to ..., &c.); 6) to couch, state (in certain terms), to clothe in a certain form, to put into words, word, turn; in einen Rahmen —, to (put in a) frame; das Schiff faßt den Wind, the ship gripes; fig-s. in die Augen —, to fix one's eyes upon ..., to take a look at ..., to observe; ins Gedächtniß —, to retain, keep in memory; Einen bei seinem Worte —, to take one at his word; eine Meinung —, to form an opinion; einen Entschluß —, to take (or to fix upon) a resolution; Muth or Herz —, to take courage or heart; II. refl. 1) to compose (collect) one's self; fasse dich, compose your mind; sich wieder —, to recover one's self, to recover one's balance or self-possession; 2) sich kurz —, a) to be brief; b) to be quick of resolution; 3) (Grimm, WB. LV) l. u. for sich auf ... gefaßt machen; III. intr. to take, catch, gripe, cf. Greifen; die Pumpe faßt, Mar. the pump is fetched; der Knabe faßt leicht, the boy is quick of comprehension; to bite (said of a screw or an anchor); gefaßt, p. a. composed, firm, collected (in mind), calm, ready, prepared (auf [with Acc.], for); sich gefaßt machen, to prepare one's self (auf [with Acc.], for); machen Sie sich darauf gefaßt, make up your mind to that; sich gefaßt halten, to stand in readiness, to be prepared.

Faf'fer, (str.) m. provinc. 1) or Fäß'ler, see Faßbinder; 2) temporary bee-hive.

Faß..., in comp. —fest, adj. tasting of

the cask; —feigen, f. pl. Comm. Cyprus figs packed in casks; —futter, n. outer cask; —hahn, m. cock; —hefe, f. see —bärme; —holz, n. wood for staves.

Faß'lich, I. adj. conceivable, intelligible, comprehensible, easy of comprehension; leicht or allgemein —, easily understood, popular; II. F–keit, (w.) f. conceivableness, comprehensibility.

Faß'..., in comp. —meßkunst, f. gauging; —pech, n. 1) cooper's pitch; 2) pitch in casks; —stahl, m. steel in barrels.

Fas'sung, s. I. (w.) f. 1) the act of putting in, filling, &c. cf. Fassen, 2; 2) a) the (act of) setting, enchasing, &c.; b) enclosure, mounting, setting (of a diamond, &c.); c) Min. lining (of a shaft); fig. &c. 3) a) version; b) (schriftliche —) (verbal) construction, wording; style, tenor, terms (pl.); 4) a) the taking (eines Entschlusses, a resolution); b) composure, self-command, countenance: aus der or außer — sein, to be out of countenance, to be disconcerted or off one's guard; aus der — kommen, to lose one's self-command, to be put (thrown) off one's guard; aus der — bringen, 1. to put out of countenance, disconcert, unsettle; to discompose, to put or throw off one's guard; (durch Blicke) to look or stare out of countenance; 2. to put beside one's gravity; nicht aus der — kommen, die — behalten, to keep countenance or self-possession; II. in comp. F–sgabe, F–skraft, f., F–svermögen, n. power, faculty of comprehension; apprehensiveness, capacity, conception.

Faß'..., in comp. —waaren, f. pl. goods in barrels or carried in casks; —s or fässerweise, adv. in the cask, by the cask; —zapfen, m. bung, faucet, tap.

Fast, adv. 1) †, very; 2) almost, nearly; (well) nigh, (well) near, all but; — bis zu Thränen, short of tears; — (gar) nicht, hardly (at all); — nichts, next to nothing (or none), hardly any thing; — nie, scarcely (hardly) ever; er geht — nie in die Kirche, he scarcely ever goes to church; — nur, almost only or entirely, little more than; — ohne Ausnahme, with scarcely any exception; almost invariably.

Fasta'ge (pr. —ahe), (w.) f. Comm. cooperage.

Fast'..., in comp. —bäcker, m. baker of brown bread; —brot, n. brown bread.

Fast'en, (w.) f. pl. († & provinc. used also as a sing., besides Fast(e)) fast, fasting; Lent; in comp. —abend, m. Shrove-Tuesday; —s —blume, f. common cow-slip; —brezel, f. a kind of cracknel baked during Lent; —dienstag, m. see —abend; —gebet, n. Lent-prayer; —mäßig, adj. lenten; —mahlzeit, f. lenten fare (or feast); —prediger, m. he who preaches during Lent; —predigt, f. Lent-sermon; —sonntag, m. Sunday in Lent; —speise, f. Lent-provision, lenten-food; —zeit, f. Ch. Lent, the quadragesimal fast, Shrove-tide.

Fast'en, (w.) v. intr. to fast; das —, (str.) v. s. (religious mortification by) fasting, abstinence.

Fast'nacht, s. I. f. coll. F–en, 1) Ch. Shrove-Tuesday, Shrove-tide; 2) Rom. Cath. carnival.

Fast'nachts..., in comp. —feier, f. shroving; —kleid, n. carnival's habit; —lust, —lustbarkeit, f. carnival diversion, amusements; —narr, m. masker in carnival, carnival's buffoon, zany; —schmaus, m. carnival entertainment; —posse, f., —spiel, n. carnival play, farce (taking place before Lent and lasting twelve days); —spuk, m. carnival masquerade.

Fast'tag, (str.) m. fasting-day, fast-day; day of abstinence; F–e, pl. fast- (coll. meager) days.

* **Fa'ta**, I. (Lat.) pl. of Fatum; II. (Ital.) f. fairy (cf. Fee); — Morgana, f. Phys. Fata Morgana, cf. Luftspiegelung.

* **Fatal'**, adj. (Lat.) coll. (differ. from the E. fatal) extremely disagreeable, annoying, odious; f–e Lage, awkward predicament.

* **Fatalis'mus**, m. (L. Lat.) fatalism. — **Fatalist'**, (w.) m. fatalist.

* **Fatalität'**, (w.) f. coll. (differ. from the E. fatality) mischance, awkward incident, unpleasantness.

* **Fa'tum**, (str., pl. [Lat.] Fa'ta) n. (Lat.) 1) fate, destiny, lot; 2) good or ill fortune, chance.

Fatz, (str.) m. († &) provinc. see Einfaltspinsel.

Fau'e, (w.) f. Mar. a small sail under the foot of a top-sail.

Fau'chen, **Fauch'zen**, (w.) v. intr. to mew and spit (as cats do).

Faul, adj. 1) rotten, corrupt, putrid; carious; 2) fig. a) lazy, idle, slothful, sluggish, indolent; slow; f–er Mensch, sluggard, lazy-bones; b) drowsy; sleepy; c) fig. bad, idle, worthless; f–er Wechsel, Comm. queer bill; f–es Fleisch, proud flesh; f–er Fleck, sore point, foul spot; f–er Fels, Min. mouldering stone; Mar. &c. f–e Küste, dangerous coast; f–er Ankergrund, foul bottom; f–e See, calm sea; f–es Schiff, foul ship; das Schiff macht das Wasser —, the ship makes foul water; der f–e Knecht, Arith. ready reckoner; nicht —, coll. not remaining behindhand, directly, immediately; f–e Eier, addled or rotten eggs; die f–e Gährung, Chem. putrid or putrefactive fermentation; f–es Eisen, eager or brittle iron; f–e Bäuche, m. pl. (Luther) lazy bellies.

Faul'..., in comp. —affe, f. Zool. loris; —baum, m. Bot. 1) (alder-)buckthorn (Rhamnus frangula L.); 2) common bird-cherry tree (Prunus padus L.); —beere, f. bird-cherry; —bett, n. 1) bed of ease, couch of idleness; 2) fig. inactivity, apathy; —boden, m. see Fehlboden; —brand, m. see Kornbrand; —brut, f. rotten brood (of bees); —bütte, f. Paper-m. fermenting trough.

Fau'le, s. (decl. like adj.) m. (& f.) sluggard, idler, drone, lazy fellow (a lazy, sluggish girl or woman).

Fäu'le, (w.) f. 1) see Fäulniß; 2) a) Vet. flap (a disease in horses); b) dry rot (in sheep); 3) dry rot (in wood); 4) blight (in corn); 5) Min. brittle stones.

Fau'len, (w.) v. intr. (aux. sein) to rot, corrupt, putrefy; das —, (str.) v. s. Paper-m. rotting, fermentation.

Fau'lenzen, (w.) v. intr. to idle (away the time), to be (lie) idle, to be sluggish or lazy, to lounge.

Fau'lenzer, (str.) m. 1) idler, sluggard, drone, idle or lazy fellow, ind. do-little, lazy-bones; 2) a) stool or support for a sick leg; b) Arith. ready reckoner.

Faulenzerei', (w.) f. the propensity to lounging, sluggishness, idleness, laziness.

Faul'..., in comp. —fieber, n. Med. putrid fever; —fleck, —flecken, m. putrid spot; —fleckig, adj. having putrid spots; —fuß, m. see —thier; —holz, n. see —baum.

Faul'heit, (w.) f. laziness, idleness, slothfulness, sloth; drowsiness, sleepiness.

Fau'licht, **Fau'lig**, **Fäu'lig**, adj. having the appearance of being rotten, tasting rotten, putrid; putrescent, rotten.

Faul'matte, (w.) f. foot- (or rope-)hose or mat.

Fäul'niß, (str.) f. rottenness, corruption, putrefaction, putrification; in — übergehen or gerathen, to putrefy, to rot; der — ausgesetzt, putrescible; — bewirkend, septic; — hindernd, antiseptic.

Faul'..., in comp. —pelz, m. coll. sluggard, ind. lazybones; —pfründe, —stelle, f. coll. sinecure; —pfründner, m. sinecure; —thier, n. Zool. 1) tardigrade; 2) or —fuß, m. a) sloth, ai; b) (amerikanisches) ai; a) (zweifingerige) unau; —weide, f. sweet willow.

the cask; —feigen, f. pl. Comm. Cypress figs packed in casks; —futter, n. outer cask; —hahn, m. cock; —[illegible], f. see —[illegible]; —holz, n. wood for staves.

Faß'lich, I. adj. conceivable, intelligible, comprehensible, easy of comprehension; leicht or allgemein —, easily understood, popular; II. F-keit, (w.) f. conceivableness, comprehensibility.

Faß'..., in comp. —meßkunst, f. gauging; —pech, n. 1) cooper's pitch; 2) pitch in casks; —stahl, n. steel in barrels.

Fas'sung, s. I. (w.) f. 1) the act of putting in, filling, &c. cf. Fassen, 2; 2) a) the (act of) setting, enchasing, &c.; b) enclosure, mounting, setting (of a diamond, &c.); c) Min. lining (of a shaft); fig.-e. 3) a) version; b) (stilistische —) (verbal) construction, wording; style, tenor, terms (pl.); 4) a) the taking (eines Entschlusses, a resolution); b) composure, self-command, countenance; aus der or außer — sein, to be out of countenance, to be disconcerted or off one's guard; aus der — kommen, to lose one's self-command, to be put (thrown) off one's guard; aus der — bringen, 1. to put out of countenance, disconcert, unsettle; to discompose, to put or throw off one's guard; (durch Blicke) to look or stare out of countenance; 2. to put beside one's gravity; nicht aus der — kommen, die — behalten, to keep countenance or self-possession: II. in comp. F-sgabe, F-skraft, f., F-svermögen, n. power, faculty of comprehension; apprehensiveness, capacity, conception.

Faß'..., in comp. —waaren, f. pl. goods in barrels or carried in casks; — or fässerweise, adv. in the cask, by the cask; —zapfen, m. bung, faucet, tap.

Fast, adv. 1) †, very; 2) almost, nearly; (well) nigh, (well) near, all but; — bis zu Thränen, short of tears; — (gar) nicht, hardly (at all); — nichts, next to nothing (or none), hardly any thing; — nie, scarcely (hardly) ever; er geht — nie in die Kirche, he scarcely ever goes to church; — nur, almost only or entirely, little more than; — ohne Ausnahme, with scarcely any exception; almost invariably.

Fasta'ge (pr. —ahe), (w.) f. Comm. cooperage.

Fast'..., in comp. —bäcker, m. baker of brown bread; —brot, n. brown bread.

Fas'ten, (w.) f. pl. († & provinc. used also as a sing., besides Faste) fast, fasting; Lent; in comp. —abend, m. Shrove-Tuesday; — —blume, f. common cow-slip; —brezel, f. a kind of cracknel baked during Lent; —dienstag, m. see —abend; —gebet, n. Lent-prayer; —mäßig, adj. lenten; —mahlzeit, f. lenten fare (or feast); —prediger, m. he who preaches during Lent; —predigt, f. Lent-sermon; —sonntag, m. Sunday in Lent; —speise, f. Lent-provision, lenten-food; —zeit, f. Ch. Lent, the quadragesimal fast, Shrove-tide.

Fas'ten, (w.) v. intr. to fast; das —, (str.) s. n. (religious mortification by) fasting, abstinence.

Fast'nacht, s. I. f. coll. F-en, 1) Ch. Shrove-Tuesday, Shrove-tide; 2) Rom. Cath. carnival.

Fast'nachts..., in comp. —feier, f. shroving; —kleid, n. carnival's habit; —lust, —lustbarkeit, f. carnival diversion, amusements; —narr, m. masker in carnival, carnival's buffoon, zany; —schmaus, m. carnival entertainment; —posse, f., —spiel, n. carnival play, farce (taking place before Lent and lasting twelve days); —spuk, m. carnival masquerade.

Fast'tag, (str.) m. fasting-day, fast-day; day of abstinence; F-e, pl. fast- (coll. meager) days.

* Fa'ta, I. (Lat.) pl. of Fatum; II. (Ital.) f. fairy (cf. Fee); — Morgana, f. Phys. Fata Morgana, cf. Luftspiegelung.

* Fatal', adj. (Lat.) coll. (differ. from the E. fatal) extremely disagreeable, annoying, odious; f-e Lage, awkward predicament.

* Fatalis'mus, m. (L. Lat.) fatalism. — Fatalist', (w.) m. fatalist.

* Fatalität', (w.) f. coll. (differ. from the E. fatality) mischance, awkward incident, unpleasantness.

* Fa'tum, (str., pl. (Lat.) Fa'ta) n. (Lat.) 1) fate, destiny, lot; 2) good or ill fortune, chance. [pinsel.

Fatz, (str.) m. († &) provinc. see Einfalts-

Fau'se, (w.) f. Mar. a small sail under the foot of a top-sail. [and spit (as cats do).

Fau'chen, Fauch'zen, (w.) v. intr. to mew

Faul, adj. 1) rotten, corrupt, putrid; carious; 2) fig. a) lazy, idle, slothful, sluggish, indolent; slow; f-er Mensch, sluggard, lazybones; b) drowsy; sleepy; c) fig. bad, idle, worthless; f-er Wechsel, Comm. queer bill; f-es Fleisch, proud flesh; f-er Fleck, sore point, foul spot; f-er Fels, Min. mouldering stone; Mar.-e. f-e Küste, dangerous coast; f-er Ankergrund, foul bottom; f-e See, calm sea; f-es Schiff, foul ship; das Schiff macht das Wasser —, the ship makes foul water; der f-e Knecht, Arith. ready reckoner; nicht —, coll. not remaining behindhand, directly, immediately; f-e Eier, addled or rotten eggs; die f-e Gährung, Chem. putrid or putrefactive fermentation; f-es Eisen, eager or brittle iron; f-e Bäuche, m. pl. (Luther) lazy bellies.

Faul'..., in comp. —affe, f. Zool. loris; —baum, m. Bot. 1) (alder-)buckthorn (Rhamnus frangula L.); 2) common bird-cherry tree (Prunus padus L.); —beere, f. bird-cherry; —bett, n. 1) bed of ease, couch of idleness; 2) fig. inactivity, apathy; —boden, m. see Fehlboden; —brand, m. see Kornbrand; —brut, f. rotten brood (of bees); —bütte, f. Paper-m. fermenting trough.

Fau'le, s. (decl. like adj.) m. (& f.) sluggard, idler, drone, lazy fellow (a lazy, sluggish girl or woman).

Fäu'le, (w.) f. 1) see Fäulniß; 2) a) Vet. Sap (a disease in horses); b) dry rot (in sheep); 3) dry rot (in wood); 4) blight (in corn); 5) Min. brittle stones.

Fau'len, (w.) v. intr. (aux. sein) to rot, corrupt, putrefy; das —, (str.) s. n. Paper-m. rotting, fermentation.

Fau'lenzen, (w.) v. intr. to idle (away the time), to be (lie) idle, to be sluggish or lazy, to lounge.

Fau'lenzer, (str.) m. 1) idler, sluggard, drone, idle or lazy fellow, lud. do-little, lazybones; 2) a) stool or support for a sick leg; b) Arith. ready reckoner.

Faulenzerei', (w.) f. the propensity to lounging, sluggishness, idleness, laziness.

Faul'..., in comp. —fieber, n. Med. putrid fever; —fleck, —flecken, m. putrid spot; —fleckig, adj. having putrid spots; —fuß, m. see —thier; —holz, n. see —baum.

Faul'heit, (w.) f. laziness, idleness, slothfulness, sloth; drowsiness, sleepiness.

Fau'licht, Fau'lig, Fäu'lig, adj. having the appearance of being rotten, tasting rotten, putrid; putrescent, rotten.

Faul'matte, (w.) f. foot- (or rope-)bass or mat.

Fäul'niß, (str.) f. rottenness, corruption, putrefaction, putrification; in — übergehen or gerathen, to putrefy, to rot; der — ausgesetzt, putrescible; — bewirkend, septic; — hindernd, antiseptic.

Faul'..., in comp. —pelz, m. coll. sluggard, lud. lazybones; —pritsche, —stelle, f. coll. sinecure; —pfründner, m. sinecure; —thier, n. Zool. 1) tardigrade; 2) or —fuß, m. a) sloth, [illegible]; b) (amerikanisches) ai; c) (zweifingeriges) unau; —weide, f. sweet willow.

[illegible]-disclaiming); 4) *coll.* (*or* — gehen) to go [illegible] begging (*cf.* Durchfechten, *refl.* 2).

Fech′ter, *s.* I. (*str.*) *m.* fighter, fencer; [illegible]-player, swordsman; gladiator; pugilist, boxer; II. *in comp.* —kampf, *m.* combat of gladiators; prize-fight; —spiel, *n. see* —[illegible]; —sprung, *m.* leap backwards, fencer's [illegible]; —streich, *m.* sword-player's trick.

Fe′der, *s.* I. (*w.*) *f.* 1) *a)* feather, plume (of a bird, &c.); flue; *b)* (instrument for writing) pen; quill; 2) *Mech.* spring; 3) *Ichth.* fin (of a fish); *Sport-s.* 4) *a)* tail (of a hare, &c.); *b)* F-n, *pl.* bristles (of wild boars); spines *or* [illegible] (of hedgehogs); quills (of porcupines); [illegible] boar-spear; 6) *Carp.* tongue; 7) *Fort.* wall-[illegible]; 8) *Build.* cross-lathe; 9) *Jewel.* blemish [illegible] jewels; die — führen, to use the pen, to [illegible]; eine spitzige — führen, to write with a [illegible] dipped in gall; unter der — haben, to have [illegible] literary composition in hand; to have on [illegible] anvil; eine — schneiden, to make (cut) a [illegible]; eine — corrigieren, to mend a pen; in die [illegible] sagen, to dictate; II. *in comp.* —ähnlich, *adj.* featherlike, *cf.* —artig; —alaun, *m. Miner.* [illegible] alum, stone-alum; —antimonerz, *m. Miner.* [illegible]; —angel, *f.* spring-hinge; —arbeiter, *m.* feather-worker; —artig, *adj.* feathery, downy, plumaceous; —auswischer, *m.* pen-wiper; —ball, *m.* shuttlecock; —besen, *m.* feather-duster, feather-brush; —bett, *n.* feather-bed; —blatt, —blättchen, *n.* 1) *Bot.* the segment of a pinnated leaf; 2) *T.* the leaf [illegible] blade of a lock's spring, spring-plate; —blech, *n.* thin sheet-iron; —bleiche, *f.* bleaching of feathers; —bleicher, *m.* feather-bleacher; —blume, *f.* feather-flower, artificial flower of feathers; —bolzen, *m.* spring-bolt; —brett, *n.* [illegible] spring-board (of an organ); —büchse, *f.* pen-case; —bügel, *m. Mech.* spring-chape; —bürste, *f.* feather-brush; —busch, *m.* tuft *or* bunch of feathers, plume; plumage; *Zool.* tuft, crest, crown; chaplet (bei Pfauen); topping (bei [illegible]); —buschreiher, *m. Ornith.* the white *or* great silver heron (*Ardea egretta* Gm.).

Fe′derchen, (*str.*) *n.* (*dimin. of* Feder) 1) small feather, plumelet; 2) *Bot.* plumule, [illegible].

Fe′der..., *in comp.* —cirkel, *m.* 1) *T.* spring-[illegible]; 2) *see* Bogencirkel; —decke, *f.* feather *or* down coverlet; —deckel, *m. Horol.* spring-[illegible]; —dose, *f.* spring-box; —eisen, *n. T.* watch-maker's anvil; spring-chape; —erz, *n. Miner.* [illegible] silver-ore, salamander's hair; —fechter, *m. coll.* pen-warrior, hero of the quill, [illegible]; a pettifogging writer; —feil-[illegible], *m. T.* pin-vice; —förmig, *adj. Bot.* [illegible]form; —fuchser, *m. see* —fechter; *coll.* scribbler; —fuß, *m. Ornith.* rough-footed pigeon, plumiped; —füßig, *adj.* feet-feathered, rough-footed, plumiped; —gehäuse, *n. Horol.* barrel, spring-box; —gold, *n. T.* spring-gold, [illegible] gold; —gras, *n. Bot.* common feather-grass (*Stipa pennata* L.); —gyps, *m. Miner.* [illegible] Gasergyps; —hahn, *m. Ornith. see* Auer-hahn; —hahn, *m. T.* spring-trigger; —halter, *m.* pen-holder, pen-handle; *Horol.* spring-barrel [illegible]; —handel, *m.* feather-trade; —händler, *m.* dealer in feathers, feather-seller; —hart, *adj.* hard and elastic like a spring, springy; —härte, *f.* elasticity; —harz, *n.* elastic gum, India-rubber; caoutchouc; —harzbaum, *m.* [illegible] caoutchouc-tree, ule-tree (*Siphonia* [illegible] L.); —hatz, *m. Sport.* reel; —haus, [illegible] *see* —gehäuse; —hausberichtigt, *m.* barrel-[illegible]; —hausrad, *n.* barrel-wheel; —heber, *m.* [illegible] spring-lever, spring-tongs; —held, [illegible] hero of the quill; —hut, *m.* hat *or* bonnet with feathers.

Fe′derich, Fe′derig, *adj.* like feathers; [illegible] feathery; plumose, plumy; fine.

Fe′der..., *in comp.* —[illegible], *m. see* —krieg; —[illegible], *f.* a cap with feathers; *Ornith.* mandarin-duck; —kasten, *m.* pen-box; —kegel, *m.* 1) *Horol.* barrel-arbour; 2) *Conch.* a species of conus (*Conus textilis* L.); —kiel, *m.* quill; —kissen, *n.* pillow *or* cushion with feathers; —klappe, *f. T.* steam-trigger; —klinke, *f.* spring-latch; —köcher, *m. see* —büchse; —kohl, *m. Bot.* curled (crisp) cabbage (a variety of *Brassica oleracea* L.); —kork, *m.* a species of sea-cork, *see* Gallertschwamm; —kraft, *f.* elasticity; —kräftig, *adj.* elastic; springy; —kraut, *n. Bot.* spiked water-milfoil (*Myriophyllum spicatum* L.); —krieg, *m.* paper-war, controversy; —krone, *f. Bot.* pappus, down, feather, puff-ball; —lade, *f. Weav.* flyer-lathe; —lanzette, *f.* spring-lancet; —lappen, *m. Sport.* a bunch of feathers tied to a string to frighten the game, scarecrow; —leicht, *adj.* as light as a feather; —leinwand, *f.* a kind of fine linen fustian with a cotton weft; —lesen, *n.* 1) the picking of feathers; 2) *fig.* ceremony, hesitation; viel —lesens machen, to be ceremonious, to insist upon formalities; to stand out on trifles, to pick up straws; nicht viel —lesens machen, to act without any ceremony; to set boldly about a thing.

Fe′derlos, *adj.* featherless, plumeless, implumed, implumous; unfledged, callow.

Fe′der..., *in comp.* —mann, *m. see* —händler; —maß, *n. Horol.* an instrument for testing the power of a watch-spring, watch-spring-test; —meißel, *m. Surg.* pledget; —messer, *n.* pen-knife; —mütze, *f.* a cap made of feathers, feather-cap; feathered cap.

Fe′dern, (*w.*) *v.* I. *intr.* 1) to lose feathers; 2) to spring, to rise with elastic motion; II. *v. tr.* 1) to stuff with feathers, to feather; 2) *Sport.* to feather (a bird by shooting); 3) *T.* (Bohlen) to double-groove and slip (planks) — *Herbald*; III. *refl.* to moult, mew.

Fe′der..., *in comp.* —nelke, *f. Bot.* single *or* feathered pink, sweet William (*Dianthus plumarius* L.); —nervig, *adj. Bot.* penninerved; —pfühl, *m.* bolster; —pose, *f. see* —kiel; —reiniger, *m. see* —fänger; —riegel, *m. T.* spring-bolt; —rohr, *n. see* —büchse; —salz, *n. Miner.* native alum (of fibrous quality); —scheuche, *f. see* —lappen; —schilf, *n. Bot.* the berry-bearing bamboo (*Bambusa baccifera* Roxb.); —schleiße, *f.*, —schleißen, *n. see* —lesen; —schloß, *n.* spring-lock; —schmücker, *m.* feather-maker, plumassier; —schneidemaschine, *f.* pen-nibber; —schraube, *f.*, —spanner, *m. T.* spring-vice; —schütze, *m. see* Feldjäger; —spannschlüssel, *m. T.* key with a screw instead of the bit; —spath, *m. Miner.* radiated (fibrous) spar; —sperrrad, *n. Horol.* spring-ratchet wheel; —spiel, *n.* 1) *see* Falkenbeize; 2) *see* —lappen; 3) lure, falconer's game; 4) spillekins; 5) *provinc.* fowls; —spule, *f.* quill; gezogene F-n, Dutch quills; —stäuber, *m.* 1) *see* —besen; 2) *a)* feather-driver; *b)* *see* —händler; —stahl, *m.* spring-steel; —staub, *m.* down; —stein, *m. see* Pfauenstein; —stellage, *f.* pen-rack; —stieber, *m.* 1) feather-driver; 2) feather-seller; —stift, *m. Horol. see* —kegel; —strauß, *m.* tuft of feathers; —streit, *m. see* —krieg; —strich, *m.* stroke of the pen; —stutz, *m. see* —busch; —stütze, *f. Coach-m.* spring-stay; —thürangeln, *f. pl.* spring-centre and top pivot-hinges.

Fe′derthum, (*str.*) *n.* (*l. u.*) feathers, plumage (Gefieder).

Fe′der..., *in comp.* —tüchtig, *adj.* well versed in writing; —tüchtigkeit, *f.* penmanship; —uhr, *f.* watch *or* clock moved by a spring; —vieh, *n.* poultry, fowls; —viehhändler, *m.* poulterer; —wage, *f.* spring-balance, spring-steel-yard; —wechsel, *m.* moulting of birds; —weiß, *n. Miner.* stone-alum; earth-flax, asbest; —wellbaum, *m. Horol. see* —kegel, 1; —werk, *n.* 1) anything stuffed with feathers; plumage; 2) *T.* the spring *or* ward of a lock; —wild, —wildpret, *n.* feathered game, wild-fowl; —wilhelm, *m.*, —winde, *f. Bot.* scarlet bindweed, cypress-vine (*Quamoclit* Mönch.); —winder, *m. Horol.* spring-tool; —wisch, *m. see* —besen; —wischer, *m.* pen-wiper; —wolke, *f.* cirrus, curled cloud; —zange, *f.* (butler's) pliers; —zeichnung, *f.* drawing in (*or* made with) pen and ink, pen and ink sketch; —zins, *m.* rent paid in poultry; —zirkel, *m. see* —cirkel; —zug, *m. see* —strich.

Fee, (*w.*, *pl.* Fe(e)′en (*pr.* fā′en)) *f.* fairy, * fay.

Fe′en..., *in comp.* —artig, *adj.* fairy-like; —gabe, *f.* fairy-favour; —gestalt, *f.* fairy-form.

Fe′enhaft, *adj.* fairy-like; marvellous, wonderful.

Fe′en..., *in comp.* —könig, *m.* fairy-king; —königin, *f.* fairy-queen; —land, *n.* fairy-land; —märchen, *n.* fairy-tale; —palast, *m.*, —schloß, *n.* fairy-palace; —reich, *n. see* —land; —ringe, *m. pl.* fairy-rings; —vogel, *m. Ornith.* fairy-bird (*Crassalbus puella* Lath.); —welt, *f.* fairy-world (*cf. also* Elf, *comp.*). [lism.

Fee′rei, (*w.*) *f.*, Fe′enthum, (*str.*) *n.* fairy-

Fe′ge, (*w.*) *f.* 1) the (act of) sweeping; 2) tool for sweeping; 3) corn-sift; 4) *see* Fegsel.

Fe′ge..., *in comp.* —beutel, *m. coll.* anybody *or* anything that drains the purse, purse-drainer; —fässer, *n. pl. see* —schober; —feuer, *n. Rom. Cath.* purgatory; —hammer, *m. Salt-w.* salt-boiler's hammer; —kraut, *n. Bot.* shave-grass (Schachtelhalm); —maschine, —mühle, *f.* fan-blowing *or* winnowing machine.

Fe′gen, (*w.*) *v.* I. *tr.* 1) to scour; to sweep, wipe; 2) to clean, cleanse; Einem den Beutel —, to drain a person's purse; 3) to winnow (corn); 4) to furbish (a sword); 5) *vulg.* to hide, thrash; to chastise; to rebuke; to scold, rate; 6) *Sport.* to rub off; die Bienen —, to take part of the honey away from the hives; *fig.* to sweep *or* brush over (of a wind); II. *intr.* to hasten, run, scamper; to sweep over.

Fe′ger, (*str.*) *m.* sweeper, cleanser, scourer.

Fe′ge..., *in comp.* —opfer, *n. see* Reinigungsopfer; —reiter, *f.* slope-riddle; —salpeter, *m.* salpetre on walls; —sand, *m.* scouring *or* fine sand; —schober, *m.* salt-boiler's scum-pan.

Fe′get(e) (*for* Fe′gicht), (*w.*) *f. provinc.* (*Allem.*) 1) the (act *or* time of) sweeping; 2) *see* Fegsel.

Feg′sel, (*str.*) *n.* sweepings (Kehricht).

Fe′gung, (*w.*) *f.* the (act of) sweeping, &c. *see* Fegen.

Feh, (*w.*) *f. Furr.* calabar-skins, Siberian squirrel-skins; —händler, *m. see* Rauchhändler; —pinsel, *m.* squirrel-pencil; —rücken, *m.* the skin taken off the back of the squirrel; —wam, *n.*, —wamme, *f.* the skin taken off the belly of the squirrel, meniver, miniver.

Feh′de, (*w.*) *f.* 1) (knightly) feud, quarrel, war; private warfare; literarische —, literary strife; 2) †. security, compact; —brief, *m.* letter of defiance (Absagebrief), declaration of enmity, challenge, cartel; —handschuh, *m.* gauntlet of battle; (Einem) den —handschuh hinwerfen, to throw down the gauntlet, to challenge (a person); *fig.* to hurl defiance at ...; den —handschuh aufheben, to take up the gauntlet, to accept the challenge; —recht, *n.* right of declaring enmity and making war.

Feh′e, (*w.*) *f. see* Feh.

Fehl, I. (*str.*) *m.* († *&*) * fault, failing, blemish (Fehler); II. *adv. in comp.* mis- (*cf.* Miß-) 1) wrong, amiss; contrary to purpose *or* expectation; 2) in vain, to no purpose.

Fehl′bar, I. *adj.* fallible, uncertain; II. F-keit, (*w.*) *f.* fallibility, uncertainty.

Fehl′..., *in comp.* —bitte, *f.* vain request; eine —bitte thun, to meet with a refusal, to sue in vain; —bitten, to beg in vain; —blatt, *n. Gam.* 1) card wanting in a suit, missing card; 2) card of no value; —blick, *m.* mistaken view; —boden, *m. Build.* false ceiling (Einschnellbedeckt); —bogen, m. Typ. imperfect sheet; —druck, m. 1) misprint, foul impression; 2) a book failing in its object; —drucken, to misprint.

Feh'len, (w.) v. intr. 1) a) to fail, miss; b) fig. to fail, err, commit a fault, mistake, to be mistaken, to be in the wrong, to do amiss; to offend (gegen, against); 2) a) to be absent, to fail, want, to be wanting, missing, or deficient; to be overdue (of a mail); b) impers. (with Dat.) to want, to be or fall short of: es fehlt mir an Geld, I want money; dir fehlt, you want; mir fehlt meine Dose, der erste Band &c., I miss my snuff-box, the first volume, &c.; es soll ihr an nichts —, she shall want for nothing; es fehlte uns an Lebensmitteln, we fell short of provisions; 3) impers. to ail; was fehlt Ihnen? what ails you? what is your complaint? what is the matter with you? ihr fehlt immer etwas, she is ever ailing or on the sick-list; fühle mir an den Puls und sieh ob mir etwas fehlt, feel my pulse, and see whether I be disordered; mir fehlt nichts, I ail nothing: es fehlt noch eine Viertelstunde an 12 Uhr, it wants yet a quarter of an hour to twelve; da fehlt noch ein Schilling, there is a shilling short; es kann ihm nicht —, he is sure of success; es kann nicht —, it cannot fail; es fehlte nur, daß …, all that was wanting was that …; es fehlte wenig, so …, a little more and …; es fehlte nicht viel, so wäre er ertrunken &c., he was very near being drowned, he had a narrow (hair-breadth) escape from being drowned, &c.: weit gefehlt, far from the mark, coll. you are in the wrong box; es — lassen an … (with Dat.), to be wanting in …; an mir soll es nicht —, I shall not be wanting (on my part); it shall be no fault of mine; das fehlte nur (gerade) noch! that would be a pretty piece of business! there only needed that! gefehlt ist gefehlt (ob dicht dabei oder weit davon), a miss is as good as a mile; das F-de, n. deficiency, want, wantage.

Feh'ler, s. I. (str.) m. fault; deficiency, defect; failing; error, mistake; blunder; miss; slip (of the pen, of the memory, &c.); Jeder hat seine —, coll. every bean has its black; II. in comp. —frei, see —los; —grenze, f. T. a (limited) tolerance at the mint, as allowed by the law, for deviation in weight or fineness (of gold- and silver-coins).

Feh'lerhaft, I. adj. faulty, defective, incorrect, exceptionable; damaged; ein f-er Buchstaben, miscastry; II. F-igkeit, (w.) f. faultiness, incorrectness; Med. abnormity.

Feh'lerlos, I. adj. faultless; correct; sound; nicht ganz —, slightly defective; II. F-igkeit, (w.) f. faultlessness; soundness.

Feh'lervoll, adj. full of faults or errors.

Fehl'…, in comp. —fahren, to drive the wrong way; to get into a wrong way; —farbe, f. Gam. (at cards) renounce, act of renouncing; —führen, to lead wrong, mislead; —gang, m. 1) wrong way; 2) walk to no purpose, useless exertion, coll. sleeveless errand; —gebären, to miscarry; —geburt, f. miscarriage, abortion; —gehen, 1) to go wrong, to miss or mistake one's way; to miscarry (also of letters); cf. Um'gehen; 2) fig. see —schießen; —greifen, to mistake; —griff, m. mistake, blunder, cf. Mißgriff; —hauen, to make a false cut, to miss in hewing; —hieb, m. a missing, false cut; —jagen, to miss the game, to be disappointed in chasing; —jahr, n. see Mißjahr; —kauf, m. a bad or losing bargain; —kaufen, to strike a bad or losing bargain; —laufen, to miss in running, cf. —gehen; —leiten, see —führen; —los, see Fehlerlos; —rechnen, to reckon wrong; —reiten, to ride the wrong way; —rippe, f. one of the lower, short ribs of an animal; —ritt, m. 1) ride on the wrong way; 2) ride in vain.

Fehl'sam, I. adj. apt or inclined to err, easily fallible; II. F-keit, (w.) f. proneness to err, fallibility.

Fehl'…, in comp. —schießen, 1) to miss the mark; 2) fig. to be entirely mistaken, to err, coll. to be quite out or wrong; —schlag, m. 1) see —hieb; 2) fig. failure, disappointment; —schlagen, 1) to miss one's blow; 2) fig. to fail, miscarry, to prove a failure, to prove abortive; es schlägt mir fehl, meine Erwartungen schlagen fehl, I am disappointed; —geschlagene Hoffnung, disappointed or frustrated hope, disappointment; das —schlagen, (str.) n. s. failure, disappointment; —schließen, to draw a wrong conclusion, to form a false deduction; —schluß, m. false conclusion, paralogism; Sie haben einen —schluß gemacht, you are quite beside the mark; —schneiden, to cut wrong; —schnitt, m. false or wrong cut; —schreiben, to write wrong; to miswrite; —schritt, m. see —tritt; —schuß, m. a missing of the mark, miss; —sehen, to see wrong; —springen, to leap short of the mark; —stoß, m. missing thrust, miss; —stoßen, to thrust amiss; —tram, m. Carp. ceiling-joist; —treten, to make a false step, to stumble, slide, slip (out), to miss one's footing; —tritt, m. false (or devious) step, stumble, slip, lapse; —werfen, to throw wrong, to miss one's throw or cast, to miss by throwing; —wurf, m. misthrow, miss; —ziehen, to draw, pull amiss; to draw a blank; —zielen, to aim amiss; to miss the aim; to take a wrong or bad aim; —zug, m. 1) false draught; 2) a wrong move (at chess); einen —zug thun, to get or draw a blank (in a lottery).

A. Fehm, (str.) m. provinc. stack of hay or corn; —gerüst, n. stacking-stage.

B. Fehm, (w.) f. beech-mast, Law, pannage; —geld, n., —schilling, m. Law, pannage, agistage(-money); —holz, n. see Fabenholz; —meister, m. agister, agistator.

C. Fehm(e), (w.) f. Germ. Archaeol. (—gericht, —ding, n.) criminal tribunal, vehme, vehmic court, secret court of criminal justice established in the middle ages; —recht, n. vehmic laws; —richter, —schöppe, m. vehmic judge; —statt or —stätte, f. 1) place where the vehmic court assembled, vehmic court or tribunal; place of that tribunal; 2) provinc. place of execution.

A. Feh'men, (str.) m. see Fehm, A.

B. Feh'men, (w.) v. tr. to put (hogs) upon pannage.

C. Feh'men, (w.) v. tr. Germ. Archaeol. to summon before the secret tribunal and to execute.

Fehn, (str.) n., Fehn(e), (w.) f. see Fenn(e).

Feh'rücken, Feh'wamme, see in Feh.

Fei'e, (w.) f. see Fee.

Fei'en, (w.) v. tr. (†&)* to charm; gefeit, p. a. fig. proof (gegen, against).

Fei'er, (w.) f. 1) cessation from labour, rest; holiday; 2) a) celebration, solemnization, observance (of the Lord's day, &c.); b) festival, solemnity, ceremony.

Fei'er…, in comp. —abend, m. provinc. evening-time when work is suspended; (time for) leaving off working; eve, vigil; —abend machen, to leave off working; —abendarbeit, f. overtime-work (done in the hours of rest); —abendglocke, f. evening-bell, curfew-bell; —brauch, m. ceremony; —bursche, m. coll. mechanic out of employment; —gang, m. solemn procession; —gesang, m. solemn hymn, anthem; —gesell, m. see —bursche; —gewand, n. festival raiment or habit; —glocke, f. see —abendglocke; —jahr, n. see Brachjahr; —kleid, n. see —gewand; —stunde, f. 1) leisure-hour, vacation-hour (particularly in the evening); 2) festive or solemn hour; —tag, m. holiday, festival; —tage, m. pl. Law, non-

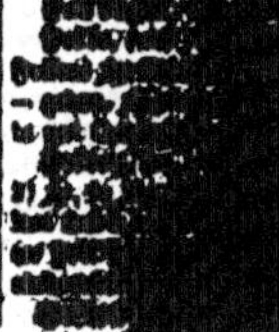

[illegible]-tree, -wood (*Cecropia peltata* L.); —[illegible], m. *Ichth.* a species of Chirus (*Chirus Stel*[illegible]); —griff, m. file-handle; —halter, m. file-[illegible] or -fastener; —hauer, m. file-cutter; —[illegible], m. *see* —griff. [prostitution.

Feil'heit, *(w.) f.* venality, corruptibility,

Feil'holz, *(str.) n. T.* filing-board, filing-block.

[illegible], Feil'sel, *(str.) n. see* Feilspäne.

Feil'..., *in comp.* —kloben, m. *T.* hand-vice, pin-vice, tail-vice; —kluppe, *f.* sloping-clamp; —kolben, m. *see* Senkkolben (*Plover*); —maschine, *f.* filing-engine. [for sale.

Feil'schaft, *(w.) f. provinc.* goods exposed

Feil'schen, *(w.) v. tr.* 1) to expose to sale; 2) (*also intr. with* um [*& Acc.*]) to cheapen, bargain, barter, higgle, haggle (for).

Feil'scher, *(str.) m.* higgler, haggler.

Feil'..., *in comp.* —spänbad, n. medicated bath saturated with filings; —späne, m. *pl.*, —staub, m. file-dust, filings; —stock, m. hand-vice; —strich, m. cut with a file, file-stroke; —tuch, n. 1) *Comm.* (Dutch) barras; 2) *Gold-sm.* dusting.

Feim, Fei'mel, Fei'men, *(str.) m.*, **Feime,** *f.* 1) *see* Fehm, *A.*; 2) (Feim) *see* Schaum.

Fein, I. *adj.* 1) fine, delicate; keen (edge); thin (skin); *fig.-s.* 2) pretty, smart, nice, handsome; 3) polite, courteous; genteel, elegant, fashionable; 4) fine, pure, refined; 5) acute, quick (of the senses, &c.): f-es Ohr, fine, discriminative ear; 6) skilful, cunning, artful, shrewd, subtle, sly; 7) *Comm.-s.* fair (of cotton); fine (of paper grain, workmanship, sorts, &c.); gut —, good-fine; *T.-s.* f-e Stahlarbeiten, steel-jewelry; f-es Steingut, iron-stone ware, [illegible] ware, opaque porcelain, stone-china; [illegible] Vorgespinnst, (fine) roving (Vorgarn); der f-e Regen, drizzling rain; ein f-er Mann, a well-bred gentleman; die f-e Welt, the higher [illegible]; fine folks, people of fashion, (*Fr.*) beau monde; f-es Gefühl, refined sentiment; refinement; er (sie) hat einen f-en Ton, he (she) is quite the gentleman (lady); sich — machen, [illegible] to dress finely; II. *adv.* 1) finely, &c.: —[illegible], in all due modesty; 2) *coll.* very; seid [illegible] lustig! be merry, I pray! mach' es — kurz! pray, be short! —brennen, *v. tr. T.* to refine (metals).

Feind, I. *adj.* (*indecl.*) hostile, inimical, [illegible]; Einem — sein, — werden, to be or [illegible] an enemy to one; II. *(str.) m.* enemy, foe, adversary; der böse —, (the foul) fiend, devil, the evil one; der heimliche —, secret enemy, [illegible]-enemy.

Fein'den, *(w.) v. tr. see* Anfeinden.

Feind'es..., *in comp.* —land, n. hostile country; —liebe, *f.* charitable feelings towards (love of) one's enemy; —mörder, m. hosticide.

Feind'lich, I. *adj.* hostile: 1) inimical; adverse, unfriendly, contrary, opposed (to), not agreeing; 2) belonging to the enemy; II. [illegible], *(w.) f.* hostile character or feeling, hostility, *cf.* Feindschaft.

Feind'schaft, *(w.) f.* 1) enmity, hostility; 2) hate, hatred, dislike, ill-will; animosity, rancour; in — stehen mit ..., to be at enmity with ...; in offener — leben mit ..., to live in open defiance with ....

Feind'schaftlich, *adj.* hostile, inimical.

Feind'selig, I. *adj.* hostile, inimical; malevolent, malignant, rancorous; II. F-keit, *(w.)* *f.* 1) hostility; war; 2) malevolence, malignity.

[illegible], *(w.) f. coll.* fineness, *see* Feinheit.

[illegible]..., *in comp.* —eisen, n. fine metal (refiner's metal); —eisenfeuer, n. *see* Raffinirfeuer.

[illegible], *(w.) v. tr. coll.* to refine in a finikin (finical or affected) manner.

[illegible], *(w.) v. tr.* to fine, refine.

[illegible]..., *in comp.* —fädig, *adj.* fine-threaded; —farbig, *adj.* of fine colour —fein, *adj.* *Comm.* prime; —fühlend, *adj.* of delicate feeling, sensitive; —gefühl, n. nicety of feeling, delicacy, sensitiveness; —gehalt, m. *see* Feinheit, 2; —gekerbt, *adj.* *Bot.* crenulate(d); —gesägt, *adj.* *Bot.* serrulate; —gespitzt, *adj.* *Bot.* cuspidate; —gesponnen, *adj.* *lit.* & *fig.* fine-spun; —gesprenkelt, *adj.* minutely speckled; —gewicht, n. fine-weight; —gezahnt, *adj.* finely toothed; —gold, n. pure or fine gold; —hechel, *f. T.* finishing-hackle.

Fein'heit, *(w.) f.* 1) fineness; 2) *Mint.* fineness, standard (of coins, gold, &c.); 3) rarity, thinness; 4) sharpness, acuteness, quickness; 5) delicacy; 6) politeness, gentility; 7) niceness, elegance; 8) finesse, cunning, art, address, subtleness, subtlety.

Fein'..., *in comp.* —hörend, *adj.* quick of hearing; —korneisen, n. fine-grained iron, steely iron; —körnig, *adj.* fine-grained (said of wood); —krämpel, *f.*, —kratze, *f.* *Mech.* finisher, finishing-card; —kupfer, n. refined copper. [petit-maître; *cf.* Stutzer.

Fein'ling, *(str.) m. cont.* fine-gentleman,

Fein'..., *in comp.* —machen, *v. tr. T.* 1) to refine (metals); 2) to finish (paper); —maler, m. miniature-painter; —malerei, *f.* miniature-painting; —maschine, *f.* shaping-machine; —raspel, *f.* fine-cut rasp; —schlicht, *adj.* dead-smooth; —schmecker, m. epicure; —schnäbler, m. *Ornith.* water-wagtail (*Motacilla* Bchst.); —sichtig, *adj.* quick or acute of sight, sharp- or keen-sighted; —silber, n. pure or fine silver; —sinn, m. *see* —gefühl; —sinnig, *adj.* *see* —fühlend; —spindelbank, —spulmaschine, *f.* *Mech.* jack-frame; —spinnmaschine, *f. T.* spinning-jenny; —spitzer, m. *see* Spitzring; —wäscherin, *f.* clear-starcher; —wollig, *adj.* fine-wooled; —zeugholländer, m. *Paper-m.* beating-engine, beater, finisher; —zinn, n. grain tin; —zinnpfanne, *f. T.* wash-pot.

Feist, I. *adj. gener.* fat (especially of venison), obese; *joc.* round; f-es Bäuchlein, *joc.* paunch; der f-e Sonntag (Feistsonntag), last sunday before lent; II. *s. (str.) n. Sport.* the fat of deer; —jagen, n. hunting at the time when deer are fat; —zeit, *f.* the season or time when deer are fat. [ness.

Feist'e, Feist'heit, Feist'igkeit, *(w.) f.* fat-

Feist'en, *(w.) v. tr. provinc.* to fat, fatten.

Fei'zen, *(w.) v. intr. provinc.* to grin.

Fel'be, *(w.) f. see* Felber.

Fel'bel, Fel'pel, *(str.) m.* (*Ital.*) velveteen; —hut, m. velvet hat.

Fel'ber, Fel'binger, *(str.) m. Bot.* 1) white-willow (*Salix alba* L.); 2) crack-willow (*Salix fragilis* L.).

Felch, *(str.) m.*, **Fel'chen,** *(str.) n. Ichth.* a species of salmon (*Coregonus Wartmanni* [*lavaretus* Nils.]).

Feld, *(str., pl.* **Fel'der***) n.* 1) *lit.* & *fig.* field; 2) plain; 3) *Archit., &c.* pane, pan(n)el; compartition, compartment; 4) *Herald.* shield; sol, compartment; 5) square, house (of a chess-board); 6) *Min.* ground; 7) *Art.* reinforce; 8) middle bridge (of combs); 9) *Mar.* das — der Ehre, deck of honour; 10) *fig.* department, province (of a science); die Sache steht noch im weiten F-e, the matter is far from being settled; das freie —, open field, plain, field, Wild; ins — gehen, or zu F-e ziehen, ins — rücken, to take the field, make war (gegen, against); zu F-e liegen, im F-e stehen, to keep the field; eine Armee ins — stellen, to raise an army and lead it into the field; aus dem F-e schlagen, to beat off (the enemy); to oust, distance (a rival); das — behaupten, behalten, to maintain, keep, or win the field, to carry the day; das — räumen, to quit one's ground, to give way, to yield the victory; *fig.-s.* — der Thätigkeit, field of activity; das ist sein — nicht, that is not his line; *cf.* Fach; *coll.-s.* das ist noch in weitem F-e, that is a long way off; freies — haben, to have a clear stage; das — ist frei, the coast is clear; — gewinnen, to get (or gain) ground.

Feld'..., *in comp.* —acten, *f. pl.* army reports; —ahorn, m. *Bot.* common or lesser maple (*Acer campestre* L.); —ameise, *f.* field-ant (*Formica nigra* Latr.); —ampfer, m. *Bot.* sheep's sorrel (*Rumex acetosella* L.); —anger, m. ridge or border between two fields; —apotheke, *f.* field-dispensary; —apotheker, m. field-apothecary; —arbeit, *f.* labour in the field; agricultural labour; —arbeiter, m. farm-labourer; —arzt, m. field or army physician; —bachstelze, *f. Ornith. see* —lerche, 2; —basilian, m. *see* Sichelkraut; —bäcker, m. field-baker; —bäckerei, *f.* baking establishment for an army; —baldrian, m. *see* —salat, 2; —banner, n. colours in or for a campaign; —bau, m. agriculture; tillage, farming, husbandry; —bauer, m. husbandman; —befestigungen, *f. pl.* field works; —befestigungskunst, *f.* (the art of) temporary or field fortification. —beifuß, m. *Bot.* field-artemisia (*Artemisia campestris* L.); —bett, n. camp-bed (stead), fieldbed, folding or tent-bed, campaign-bed; —biene, *f.* wild bee; —binde, *f.* sash, scarf; —binse, *f. Bot.* (hairy) field rush (*Juncus campestris* L.); —birnbaum, m. *Bot.* wild pear-tree; —blätterschwamm, m. *see* —schwamm; —blume, *f.* field-flower, wild-flower; —bohne, *f. see* Saubohne; —brand, m. bricks burnt in a clamp; —brücke, *f.* bridge over a ditch or rivulet; —brustwehr, *f.* glacis; —camille, *f. Bot.* 1) (echte) field-camomile (*Matricaria chamomilla* L.); 2) (wilde) corn- or unsavoury camomile (*Anthemis arvensis* L.): —casse, *f.* military chest; —chirurgus, m. surgeon of an army, military surgeon; —cirkel, m. surveyor's compasses; —cypresse, *f. Bot.* ground pine, fieldbugle (*Ajuga chamæpitys* L.); —dieb, m. thief that robs the fields; —dieberei, *f.*, —diebstahl, m. the practice of robbing the fields; —dienst, m. *Mil.* active service, service in the field; —dienstübung, *f.* field-day; —distel, *f. Bot.* way-thistle, corn saw-wort (*Serratula arvensis* L.); —ehrenpreis, m. *Bot.* field-speedwell (*Veronica arvensis* L.); (quer) —ein, —einwärts, *adv.* across the fields; —enzian, m. *Bot.* field-gentian, gentianella; —equipage, *f. see* —geräthe, 2.

Fel'der..., *in comp.* —bau, m. *Min.* panel-work in coal-mines; —decke, *f. Archit.* coffered ceiling; soffit.

Feld'..., *in comp.* —erbse, *f.* wild pea (*opp.* Gartenerbse) (*Pisum arvense* L.); —erde, *f.* hazel-mould; —fink, m. *see* —sperling; —flasche, *f.* soldier's flask, canteen; —flucht, *f.* desertion from the army in the open field or in a battle: —flüchtig werden, to desert, to run away from one's colours; —flüchter, m. *provinc. see* —taube; —flüchtige, m. deserter; —frevel, m. *see* —schaden; —frucht, *f.* (*gener. pl.*) produce of the fields; —fuß, m. *see* Kriegsfuß; —garbe, *f. Bot.* milfoil (*Achillea millefolium* L.); —geflügel, n. birds of the field; —gehege, n. *Sport.* warren; —geist, m. sylvan spirit, *cf.* —teufel; —geistliche, m. *see* —prediger; —gepäck, n. baggage (of an army); —geräthe, n. 1) *see* Ackergeräthe; 2) *Mil.* field equipage; —gerecht, *adj. Sport.* trained to sport: —gericht, n. 1) court for trying questions relating to agriculture; 2) military jurisdiction; —geschirr, n. *see* —geräthe; —geschrei, n. 1) war-cry; 2) watch-word; 3) legend (of a party); —geschütz, n. field-guns, field-pieces; —gespenst, n. spectre which haunts the fields; —gestänge, n. *Min.* flats, flat rods; —gott, m. 1) *Myth.* rural god; 2) *Ent.* horned Sajou (a species of ape [illegible] L.); —gottesdienst, m. 1) divine service performed in military camps; 2) religious meeting (of the methodists, &c.) held in the open air, camp-meeting; —grenze, f. see —mark; —grille, f. Entom. field-cricket (*Gryllus campestris* L.); —hase, m. Zool. common or field-hare (*Lepus timidus* L.); —heimchen, n. see —grille; —herr (—hauptmann, †) m. commander-in-chief, general, captain; —herrenkunst, f. strategic art, strategy; —herrenstab, m. baton; —herrenwürde, f. the generalship, dignity of a commander; —heu, n. hay gained from fallow field; —hirse, f. Bot. a species of gromwell (*Lithospermum arvense* L.); —hollunder, m. Bot. common elder (Ackerholder); —hospital, n. field-hospital; —huhn, n. see Rebhuhn; —hut, f. guard, watch of fields; —hüter, m. field-watch, field-guard, field-constable; —hütte, f. Mil. hut, barrack; —jäger, m. 1) sportsman shooting small game; 2) Mil. sharp-shooter, rifleman; 3) king's messenger. [squares.

Fel'dig, adj. in comp. having fields or

Feld'..., in comp. —kamille, see —camille; —katze, f. 1) Bot. wild oat (*Avena fatua* L.); 2) Bot. see —hirse; —keller, m. cellar dug in a field; —kerze, f. see Königskerze; —kerzenkraut, n. Bot. see Wollkraut, gemeines; —kessel, m. field-kettle, camp-kettle; —kirche, f. field-church; —klee, m. Bot. harefoot (trefoil), white clover (Ackerklee); —knoblauch, m. Bot. field-garlic (*Allium scorodoprasum* L.); —koch, m. army-cook; —kohl, m. Bot. 1) field-cabbage, Swedish turnip (*Brassica campestris* [a variety of *Br. Rapa* L.]); 2) wild radish (*Raphanus raphanistrum* L.); —krähe, f. Ornith. rook (*Corvus frugilegus* L.); —kraut, n. 1) any field-herb; 2) Bot. common fumitory, earth-smoke; —küche, f. field-kitchen; —kümmel, m. Bot. 1) wild (or common) caraway (*Carum carvi* L.); 2) creeping, wild (or mother of) thyme (*Thymus serpyllum* L.); —kunst, f. Min. machine for drawing off water from the pits; —laffette, f. Gunn. travelling-carriage; —lager, n. 1) Mil. camp: the ground on which an army pitches its tents; the army encamped; 2) fig. encampment: ein —lager aufschlagen, to pitch a camp, to encamp; —lattich, m. see —salat; —läufer, m. Ornith. golden plover (*Charadrius pluvialis* L.); —lazareth, n. see —hospital; —lerche, f. 1) field-lark, sky-lark (*Alauda arvensis* L.); 2) meadow lark (*Anthus campestris* Bechst.); Bot-s. —lichtblume, f. evening-catchfly (*Lychnis vespertina* L.); —lilie, f. purple martagon-lily (*Lilium martagon* L.); —löwenmaul, n. small snap-dragon (*Antirrhinum orontium* L.); —losung, f. Mil. watch-word; —mannstreue, f. Bot. filled eryngo (*Eryngium campestre* L.); —marder, m. Zool. see Baummarder; —mark, —markung, f. land-mark; —marschall, m. field-marshal; —marschalllieutenant, m. (in Austria) major-general commanding a division, Fr. *chef de division*; —marschallstab, m. baton, (fig.) bâton; —maus, f. field-mouse (*Hypudaeus arvalis* Pall.); —meister, m. see Abdecker; —messen, n. (land) survey, surveying (of land), geodesy; —messer, m. surveyor, geometrician; —meßkunst, f. art of surveying, geometry, geodesy; —mohn, m. Bot. wild (red or corn) poppy, cup rose (*Papaver rhoeas* L.); —mühle, f. camp-mill; —münze, f. see Ackermünze; —musik, f. military music; —nachbar, m. landmate; —nelke, f. Bot. field-pink, Carthusian pink (1. *Dianthus deltoides* & 2. *D. Carthusianorum* L.); (weiße) see —lichtblume; —oberst, m. 1) see Oberst; 2) general of cavalry; —officier, m. field officer; —[illegible]kraut, n. see [illegible]; —ort, m. Min. forehead; prolonged drift, level; —pappel, f. see Gänsepappel; —pfau, m. Ornith. see Kiebitz; —pfeife, f. see Querpfeife; —pieper, m. see —lerche, 2; —post, f. military post(-office); —posten, m. Mil. out-post (of an army), cf. —wache; —prediger, —priester, m. chaplain to a regiment; field-preacher; —propst, m. chaplain general to an army; —quartiermeister, m. field-quartermaster; —quendel, m. see —thymian; —rapunzel, f. see —salat, 2; —ratte, f. Zool. brown or Norway-rat (Wanderratte); —raute, f. Bot. common fumitory (Erdrauch); —regiment, n. field-regiment, regiment of the line; —richter, m. 1) provinc. see Dorfrichter; 2) Mil. see Auditeur; Bot-s. —ringelblume, f. field-marigold (*Calendula arvensis* L.); —rittersporn, m. field-lark-spur (*Delphinium consolida* L.); —rose, f. 1) wild-rose, dog-rose (*Rosa canina* L.); 2) (wohlriechende) sweet briar (*Rosa rubiginosa* L.); —rübe, f. turnip (the bulb of *Brassica oleracea* L., *Br. rapa* L., &c.); —ruf, m. 1) call to the field; 2) see —geschrei; —ruthe, f. surveyor's rod; —safranwurzel, f. Pharm. root of the carline thistle; —salat, m. Bot. 1) prickly lettuce (*Lactuca scariola* L. [Ackerlattich, 3]); 2) lamb's lettuce, corn valerian (*Valerianella olitoria* L. [Rapunzel]); —schaden, m. damage done to the fields; —schanze, f. field-redoubt, field-work; —scharte, f. see —distel; —scheide, —scheidung, f. see —mark; —scherer, m. surgeon in the army; —schlacht, f. (field) battle; —schlange, f. 1) common field-snake; 2) Gunn. culverin; —schmiede, f. forge of an army-blacksmith, travelling-forge; —schnecke, f. Zool. slug(-snail) (Erdschnecke); —schnepfe, f. common snipe (*Scolopax gallinago* L.) (opp. Waldschnepfe, woodcock); —schöppe, m. competent arbitrator in agricultural affairs; —schote, f. see —erbse; —schreiber, m. military clerk, clerk of a regiment; —schütz, m. see —hüter; Bot-s. —schwamm, m. common mushroom, champignon (*Agaricus campestris* L.); —schwarzkümmel, m. Bot. wild fennel-flower (*Nigella arvensis* L.); —senf, m. see Ackersenf; —siech, adj. leprous; —soldat, m. soldier of the line; —spath, m. Miner. fel(d)spar, fel(d)spath, rhombic quartz; (edler) polychromatic or Labrador fel(d)spar; (rhomboëdrischer) rhombohedral f., nepheline; —spathschiefer, m. see Granulit; —sperling, m. Ornith. tree- or mountain sparrow (*Passer montanus* L.); —spiegel, m. camp-glass; —spinat, m. see Heinrich, guter; —spinne, f. Entom. field-spider (*Lycosa ruricola* Deg. [Erdspinne]); —stein, m. 1) a) field-stone; b) Archit. rubble-stone; 2) Min. compact felspar; 3) land-mark; —steinmauer, f. Archit. rubble-wall; —steinmauerwerk, n. rubble-work; —stück, n. 1) Mil. field-piece, light piece of ordnance; 2) Paint. see Landschaft; —stuhl, m. camp-stool, folding-chair; —sucht, f. leprosy; —täschelkraut, n. Bot. see —kresse; —taube, f. Ornith. field pigeon, common pigeon (*Columba domestica arvensis*); —teufel, m. a demon that haunts the fields, sylvan spirit; —thymian, m. Bot. wild thyme (*Thymus serpyllum* L.); —tisch, m. camp-table; —ton, m. Mus. E flat major; —treiben, n. see Treibjagd.

Fel'bung, (w.) f. see Feld, 8.

Feld'..., in comp. —verpflegung, f. commissariat(e); —verschanzung, f. field-fortification; —viertel, n. Mil. quarter; —vogt, m. see —hüter; —wache, or —wacht, f. field-watch, scout-watch, advance-post, picket, out-post; —wächter, m. see —hüter; —wachtmeister, m. major of cavalry; —wärts, adv. towards the fields; —webel, m. sergeant(-major); —weg, m. field-path, field-way, country-road, by-road; —wegs, n. obsolescent, furlong; —wegwart, m. Bot. succory (*Cichorium intybus* L.); —wehre, f. 1) precinct, boundary; 2) Mil. under in-

[illegible]rose, rock-rose (1. *Helianthemum vulgare* L. or 2. *Cistus creticus* L. [Ciſtenröschen]); —[illegible], m., —ſchlucht, f., —ſchlund, m. chasm [illegible] a rock, glen, ravine; —ſchicht, f. lay ridge or ledge of rock; —ſchnecke, f. *Conch.* rock-shell, murex (*Murex saxatilis* L.); —ſchwalbe, f. *Ornith.* mountain-swallow (*Hirundo rupestris* [illegible]); —ſpitze, f. peak, crag; —ſteg, —ſteig, m. path, bridge, way across rocks; rocky-path; —ſtrandläufer, m. *Ornith.* a species of sand-piper (*Calidris arenaria* L.); —ſtrauch, m. *Bot.* azalea (*Azalea procumbens* L.); —ſtück, n. piece of rock; —ſturz, m. falling of a rock; steep declivity of a rock; —taube, f. rock-pigeon; —thal, n. rocky vale; —ufer, n. bluff; —wand, f. wall of rock, precipice, steep side of a rock; —weg, m. see —pfad; —wegdorn, m. *Bot.* a species of buck-thorn (*Rhamnus saxatilis* L.); —werk, n. *Min.* pulverised stones; —ziege, f. the wild she-goat, see Steinziege.

Fel'ſicht, Fel'ſig, *adj.* rock-like, rocky; full of rocks, rocky, cliffy, cragged; formed of rocks.

Felſit', (*str.*) m. *Miner.* felsite (Feldſpath).

Fels'ſtein, (*str.*) m. rock-stone.

* Feluc'e, (*w.*) f. (*Fr.*) *Mar.* felucca (a small vessel in the Mediterranean propelled by oars).

* Feminin'(iſch), *adj.* (*Lat.*) *Gramm.* feminine. — Feminin'num, (*str.*, *pl.* [*Lat.*] Feminin'na) n. *Gramm.* feminine (noun).

Fench, Fen'nich, (*str.*) m. *Bot.* panic, wild millet (*Panicum crus galli* L.).

Fen'chel, s. I. (*str.*) m. *Bot.* fennel (*Foeniculum officinale* L.); II. *in comp.* —apfel, m. fennel-apple; —blättrig, *adj.* fennel-leaved; —blume, f. *Bot.* fennel-flower (a variety of *Nigella* L.); —gurke, f. pickled cucumber; —holz, n. sassafras wood; —öl, n. fennel-oil; —waſſer, n. fennel-water.

Fenn, (*str.*) n., Fen'ne, (*w.*) f. *provinc.* fen, marsh, low and moist ground; —beere, see Moosbeere.

Fen'nich, see Fench.

Fenſter, (*str.*) n. window: Mauer ohne —, dead wall; blindes, rundes —, deadman's eye; zum — hinein, in at the window; *fig.-s.* eye; blank (in writing); aus hohem — ſehen, to carry high; das Geld zum — hinauswerfen, to be prodigal of or throw away one's money.

Fenſter..., *in comp.* —ausſchnitt, m. see —ſchmiege; —austritt, m. balcony; —band, n. 1) window-cramp iron; 2) glass-holder (in carriages); —bank, f. 1) window-bench; 2) see —ſohlbank; —bekleidung, f. see —verkleidung; —beſchläge, n. pl. fastenings and hinges of a window; —blei, n. *Glaz.* came, glazier's lead for windows; —blende, f. window-blind; [illegible] Drahtgaze) wire-blind; —bogen, m. arch of a window; —bret, n. board of a window-sill, elbow-board; —brüſtung, f. elbow-place, parapet; breast-wall of a window, window-sill; —einfaſſung, f. see —verkleidung; —eiſen, n. pl. see —ſtäbe; —fach, —feld, n. pan(n)el, square of a window; —flaſche, f. see Flaſche; —flügel, m. wing of a window, valve, sash, casement; (feſtſtehender) dead sash; —futter, n. sash-frame (of a window); —gardine, f. window-curtain; —geld, n. window-tax; —gewände, n. side-walls of a window; —giebel, m. *Build.* pediment of a window, frontal; —gitter, n. lattice, trellis, grate before a window; [illegible]; —glas, n. window-glass; —glimmer, m. *Miner.* see Frauen-[illegible]; —halter, m. window-stay; —haspe, f. hinge of a window; —hocker, m. gipsy (of [illegible]).

Fenſt(e)rig, *adj.* *in comp.* -windowed; [illegible], four-windowed, &c.

Fenſter..., *in comp.* —inſchrift, f. [illegible]; —jalouſien, f. pl. Venetian blinds; —kiſſen, n. window-cushion; —kitt, m. putty; —korb, m. lattice-work before a window; —krampe, f. casement staple; —kreuz, n. crossbars of a window, mullions; —laden, m. (window-)shutter; —ladenſchrauben, f. pl. shutter screws; —laibung, f. *Build.* flanning, rabbet-wall; —lehne, f. see —brüſtung; —leiſte, m., —loch, n., —öffnung, f. *Build.* bay, opening in a building left for a window.

Fenſt'ern, (*w.*) v. I. *tr.* 1) to window, furnish with windows; 2) *vulg.* to rebuke, reprimand severely; II. *intr.* 1) *Stud. slang.* to break or smash windows; 2) (*provinc.* — gehen) to visit one's sweetheart under the window.

Fenſt'er..., *in comp.* —niſche, f. window-bay; —parade, f. window-parade; —pfeiler, m. pier, wall between two windows; —pfoſten, m. window-post, jamb; —polſter, n. see —kiſſen; —rahmen, m. window-frame; see —futter; —rahmenſchloß, n. sash fastener; —raute, f. see —ſcheibe; —reiber, —riegel, m. sash-bolt; —rollen, f. pl. sash-pulleys; —roſe, f. *Archit.* rose-window; —ſäule, f. see —pfoſten; —ſchaft, m. see —pfeiler; —ſcheibe, f. pane, square, light (of a window); —ſchirm, m. shade; window-blind; —ſchmiege, f. *Build.* embrasure of a window; —ſchwalbe, f. *Ornith.* see Hausſchwalbe; —ſchweiß, m. dew, moisture of windows; —ſchwelle, f. see —ſohlbank; —ſitz, m. settee; —ſohlbank, f. window-sill; —ſpiegel, m. 1) pier-glass, mirror between two windows; 2) a looking-glass in a frame at the outside of a window for the observation of what is going on in the street, &c. (Spion); —ſproſſe, f. wooden window-bar; —ſtäbe, m. pl., —ſtangen, f. pl. window-bars, fences; —ſteuer, f. window-tax; —ſtock, m. see —bret; —ſturz, m. *Build.* lintel, head-piece over a window; —thüre, f. glass-door; —verdachung, f. window-roofing; —verkleidung, f. boxing of a window; —vertiefung, f. see —ſchmiege; —vorhänge, m. pl. window-curtains; —verſetzer, m. see —blende; —wand, f. wall with windows; —werk, n. the windows; —wirbel, m. sash-fastener, turn-buckle, turn-button; —zarge, f. see —futter; —zelt, n. see Marquiſe, 2; —zwickel, m. triangular piece of glass between round panes. (ſant).

† Fen'zig, *adj.* gallant, fashionable (Ge-

A. Ferch, (*str.*) m. 1) *Min.* pernicious exhalation from the bottom of a mine, choke-damp.

B. Ferch, (*str.*) m. *provinc.* see Pferch.

C. † Ferch, (*str.*) n. life, blood.

Fer'chen, (*w.*) v. *tr.* (*S. G.*) to despatch.

Ferch'enbaum, (*str.*, *pl.* F-bäume) m. pine-tree (Ferche).

Fer'den, *adv.* *provinc.* see Fern.

Fer'ge, (*w.*) m. († &) *provinc.* see Fährmann.

* Fe'rien, f. (*Lat.*) *pl.* (—zeit, f.) vacation-time, vacancies, holidays; recess (of the Parliament); die großen —, the long vacations; —reiſe, f. holiday-tour, holiday-trip.

Fer'kel, s. I. (*str.*) n. 1) pig. (Saug—) sucking-pig; 2) *fig.-s.* piggish person, hog; 3) blunder; 4) blot (of ink); 5) *Mar.* see Ferſen; 6) *pl.* *Astr.* Hyades; II. *in comp.* —kaninchen, n. *Zool.* agouti, long-nosed cavy (Meerſchweinchen); —kraut, n. *Bot.* cat's ear (*Hypochaeris* L.); —maus, f. *Zool.* see Meerſchweinchen; —monat, m. January; —ſtall, m. pig-sty.

Ferkelei', (*w.*) f. piggishness, &c. see Sauerei.

Fer'keln, (*w.*) v. *intr.* 1) to farrow, to bring forth pigs, to pig; 2) *fig.* to behave piggishly.

* Ferm, *adj.* (*Fr.*) firm (Firm).

* Ferman', (*str.*, *pl.* F-s & F-e) m. (*Pers.*) firman (government decree, &c.).

* Ferma'te, (*w.*) f. (*Ital.* fermata) *Mus.* pause, hold (a rest, thus indicated 𝄐).

* Ferment', (*str.*) n. (*Lat.*) ferment (Gährungsſtoff). — Fermenti'ren, (*w.*) v. *intr.* to ferment (Gähren).

Fern, *adj.* far, distant, far off, remote; aloof; f-es Ausland, far distant countries; von —, afar, from afar, at a distance; nicht von —, *fig.* by far not; nicht von — ſo ſchlecht, wie..., not nearly (so) as bad as ...; in wie —, how far, to what degree; das ſei —! far be it! *fig.-s.* — bleiben, ſich — halten, to keep clear or out of reach, to keep or stand aloof; ſich — halten von etwas, to give a thing a wide berth; Einen von ſich — halten, to keep one at a distance or at arm's length; einer Sache (*Dat.*) — ſtehen, to be a stranger to ....

Fer'nambukholz, (*str.*) n. *Comm.* Fernambuck-wood, Brazil-wood.

Fern'..., *in comp.* —anſicht, f. distant view, perspective; —darſtellung, f. perspective, perspective representation.

Fer'ne, (*w.*) f. 1) farness, distance, remoteness; 2) *Paint.* see Fernung; aus der —, from afar; in der —, in the distance; at a distance; das liegt in weiter —, see in weitem — Felde, im Feld; ſich in der — halten, see Fern bleiben.

Fer'nen, (*w.*) v. I. *tr.* (*l. u.*) to distance, see Entfernen; II. *intr.* 1) to carry a great distance (said of telescopes); 2) to look fine at a distance.

Fer'ner, *adj.* & *adv.* farther, farther; furthermore, again, moreover; additional(ly); ulterior; f-e Zuſchriften, *Comm.* future letters; — etwas thun, to continue (doing, &c.); — im Amte bleiben, to continue in office; Einen — im Amte laſſen, to continue one in (his) office; und ſo —, and so on, and so forth, and so of the rest, et cetera; —hin, *adv.* for the future, henceforth, henceforward; —weit, —weitig, *adj.* (& *adv.*) additional(ly), further, farther.

Fer'ner, (*str.*) m. *provinc.* glacier (Firner).

Fern'..., *in comp.* —gefühl, n. (morbid, unusual, &c.) perception of distant objects (*cf.* Ahnung; [in animals] Inſtinct); —glas, n. telescope, perspective (glass), *coll.* spy-glass, spying-glass; —hintreffend, *adv.* * (*Voss*) far-shooting; —liegend, *adj.* remote; —malerei, f. scenography; —maleriſch, *adj.* scenographical; —rohr, n. see —glas; —ſäulig, *adj.* *Archit.* areostyle; —ſchreibekunſt, f. telegraphic art; —ſchreiber, m. telegraph; —ſchrift, f. writing seen at a distance, telegraphic signal; —ſicht, f. distant prospect, perspective view; vista; —ſichtig, *adj.* far-sighted, long-sighted; —ſichtigkeit, f. long-sightedness; —ſichtmalerei, f. perspective (or perspective painting).

Fer'nung, (*w.*) f. *Paint.* distance, offskip.

Fern'..., *in comp.* —werk, n. *Mus.* echo-keys (of an organ); —zeichnung, f. (*l. u.*) perspective drawing.

Fer'ſe, (*w.*) f. heel; die F-n, *pl.* hind quarters (of a horse's hoof); Einem auf den F-n folgen, to follow close to one's heels, to be at one's heels; die F-n zeigen, to take to one's heels, to show a clean pair of heels.

Fer'ſen..., *in comp.* *Anat.-s.* —bein, n. heel-bone; —eng, *adj.* narrow-quartered (of horses); —flechſe, f. *tendo Achillis*, tendon of the heel; —flüchtig, *adj.* *Man.* (to be) well upon the heel; —geld (*n.*) geben, *coll.* to take to one's heels; —leder, n. *Shoe-m.* quarter-piece, heel-piece; —punct, m. *Astr.* nadir; —ſchlag, m. kick of one's heels; —ſehne, f. see —flechſe.

Fer'tig, I. *adj.* 1) ready, prepared; f-e Waare, ready-made goods; f-e Kleider, ready-made clothes, slop(-work); 2) done, finished; *fig.-s.* 3) quick, prompt; 4) practised, handy, skilful, dexterous; 5) drunk; II. *adv.* readily, &c., fluently; ich bin bereit es zu thun, aber noch nicht —, I am willing to do it but not yet quite ready (fully prepared) for it; [illegible]

—, *coll.* 1. it is all over or up with him (of a sick person); 2. he is drunk; — sein mit ..., to be or have done with ..., to have finished; ich bin mit dem Essen —, I have done dinner: ich bin mit Schreiben —, I have done writing; etwas — bringen *or* schaffen, to accomplish, effect, *or* do a thing: er ist mit seinem Vermögen —, he has got through (with) his fortune; das bekäme ich nicht —, I should not be able to do it; — machen, 1. to get ready, to perform; 2. *Letter-found.* to adjust: sich — machen, to get ready: — werden, to get ready, to get through, to get on: mag er sehen wie er — wird, let him see how he can manage it: ich würde nicht — werden (wenn ich Ihnen Alles auf einmal erzählen sollte, *Gellert*), I should not come to an end, &c.: wir können ohne ihn nicht — werden, we cannot do without him, we cannot dispense with his services; mit ihm ist kein — werden, there is no dealing with him; — werden mit Einem, to get the better of one, to bring one round, to gain one's point with a person, manage one: ich will schon mit ihm — werden, I shall deal with him well enough; eine f-e Zunge haben, to have a great volubility of tongue, (to be) nimble-tongued, to have the gift of the gab.

Fer'tigen, *(w.) v. tr.* 1) to make ready, to complete: 2) *a)* to make, manufacture: *b)* to perform; 3) *T.* to finish (adjust, &c.); 4) *see* Ab- & Ausfertigen; der Gefertigte (Unterfertigte), *provinc.* *(S. G.) see* Unterzeichnete; eine Pflasterung —, to lay (a pavement), to place close.

Fer'tigkeit, *(w.) f.* readiness, quickness, practice, skill, knack (in, at), dexterity, accomplishment, perfectness, routine, facility.

Fer'tig..., *in comp.* —macheisen, *n. Letter-found.* adjusting-stick; —macher, *m.* 1) *Glass-w.*, &c. finisher (*coll.* gaffer, first); foreman; 2) *(in laminating)* finishing-rollers *(Tolh.)*; *Letter-found.* adjustor; —stuhl, *m. Spinn.* finishing-box, finishing-head.

Fer'tigung, *(w.) f. see* Verfertigung; *Law, see* Gewährleistung.

Fer'tigwalze, *(w.) f.* finishing-roller.

* **Fes,** *(indecl.) n. Mus.* F flat.

Fe'sen, *(str.) m.* 1) husk of corn; 2) *pl.* [fescue.]

Fes'sel, *a.* I. *(w.) f.* 1) *gener. pl.* fetters, chains: shackles; lock, trammel, hamper (for horses), jesses (of falcons); *fig.* trammels; in F-n legen *or* schlagen, to put into chains, to chain down, to fetter, shackle, *cf.* Fesseln; 2) pastern (of a horse's leg); 3) *Script.* die F-n der Sünde, cords of sin; II. *in comp.* —bein, *n. Vet.* pastern; —beingelenk, *n.* pastern-joint; —frei, *adj.* freed from fetters, unfettered, unshackled; —gelenk, *n.* pastern-joint; —haar, *n.* fetlock; —los, *adj. see* —frei; —wund, *adj.* wounded, sore at the pastern.

Fes'seln, *(w.) v. tr.* 1) to fetter, shackle, chain; to hobble (a horse); 2) *fig.* to captivate, engross, rivet; to fascinate, engage.

Fest, I. *adj.* 1) *a)* fast, (strongly) fixed; *b)* stationary (as a steam-engine, &c.); 2) firm, hard, solid; consistent, dense, condense; strong; *Min.* compact, conglobate; *fig.-s.* 3) sound (of sleep); — schlafen, to sleep sound(ly); Knaben schlafen —, boys sleep sound; 4) constant, durable, firm, steadfast, steady, stout, staunch; set (in one's opinions); 5) sure; 6) close, tight; 7) positive, settled, fixed, established; 8) well versed, well up; 9) invulnerable: proof (against); 10) brave; f-e Anstellung, permanent situation; das f-e Bauholz, hearty timber; f-es Brot, sad bread; f-es Eis, fast *or* packed ice (in the arctic regions); f-er Erdboden, very strong ground; f-es Einkommen, settled *or* regular income: f-e Erwartung, confident expectation; f-e Gesundheit, sound state of health; das f-e Land, 1. solid earth, *terra firma*; 2. continent, mainland, *see* —land; ein f-er Ort, stronghold, fortified place; das f-e Papier, paper of good body; f-e Tonne, watertight tun; f-es Tauwerk, *Mar.* standing rigging; *Comm.-s.* f-es Capital, fixed capital: Kauf auf (in) f-e Hand, effective purchase; f-er Handel, fast bargain; f-e Kundschaft, steady customers; f-er (f-es) Gehalt, fixed salary: auf (in) f-e Rechnung, taken (bought) for good; Österr. Papiere (sind) —, Austrian paper steady; die Börse ist —, the money-market is firm; f-e Handschrift, firm hand; f-e Preise, fixed, steady, *or* set prices; f-e Gebote, positive offers; f-e Valuta, (regular) standard, certain price; in f-en Händen sein, (of goods, &c.) to be in firm hands; f-e Überzeugung, thorough conviction; II. *adv.* fast, firmly: — eingeschlafen, fast asleep, fast off; — entschlossen sein, to be fully resolved; — im Sattel sitzen, *lit. & fig.* to sit firm in one's saddle; — umschlossen von Feinden, closely surrounded by enemies.

Fest'..., *(adj.) in comp.* —bannen, *v. tr.* to pin to the spot; —gebannt, *see* Bannen, 3; —binden, *v. tr.* to tie up, fasten, attach firmly (an, to): —bleiben, —stehen, sich —erhalten, *v. intr. Comm.* (of prices) to remain firm (auf, at): —fahren, to run aground (of a ship), to stick fast (in the mud, &c.); sich —fahren auf ..., to run foul of ...; —gesetzt, *adj.* fixed, settled, established; der —gesetzte Tag, stated day, term; —halten, *v.* I. *tr.* to arrest; to tackle; II. *refl.* or *intr.* to hold (fast) (an [*with Acc. & Dat.*], to or on), to stick *or* cling (close) (to); III. *intr. fig.* to adhere (an [*with Dat.*], to); das —halten, *(str.) n. s.* (firm) adherence (an [*with Dat.*], to); —klemmern, *v. tr.* to clamp (an instrument, &c.); —land, *n.* continent, mainland; —ländisch, *adj.* (—lands ...) continental; *Mar.-s.* sich —legen, to berth one's self; —liegen, to be home (of ships); sich —lügen, to be caught in one's own lies; —machen, 1) *a)* to make fast, to fasten, fix; *cf.* —binden; der Frost hat die Wege —gemacht, the frost has hardened the roads; *fig.-s.* to conclude a bargain; to settle (an affair); *Mar.* to belay (a rope); to clinch (a cable); *b) Mar.* to stow, furl, band (the sails); *c)* to house (the guns); 2) to fortify (a town, &c.); 3) to imprison; —nehmen, to apprehend, arrest; —rammen, *see* —stampfen; —schrauben, *v. tr.* to fix with a screw, &c. *cf.* —klammern; —setzen, *v.* I. *tr.* 1) *see* —nehmen; 2) *or* —stellen, to establish, settle, fix, appoint, set down, to decree; to stipulate; to lay down (as a rule, &c.), institute; to assess (taxes); er setzte seine Abreise auf den dritten Tag —, he appointed the third day for his departure; II. *refl.* to settle; to take root, to be confirmed, &c.; *Mil.* to effect a lodgment; —setzung, *f.* establishment, settlement, appointment, statement; (auf dem Sande &c.) —sitzend, *p. a. Mar.* aground, benneaped; (im Eise) ice-bound, beset; —stampfen, *v. tr.* to beat down, to ram (the earth); —stehen, 1) to stand firm, to be stable *or* stationary; 2) *see* —bleiben; 3) to be settled, ascertained, *or* established; so viel steht —, this is evident (manifest) to a certainty; thus much is certain; —stehend, *p. a.* stationary: —stellen, to establish, *see* —setzen; —stellung, *f.* establishment, *see* —setzung; —treten, *v. tr.* to fix, to level, &c. by treading upon; sich —treten, not to be able to get away from the bottle; —walzen, *n. F.* close-fulling.

Fest, *a.* *(str.) n* feast, festival, holiday; fête; *fig.* treat; bewegliches —, movable, variable festival *or* holiday; unbewegliches —, immovable, fixed festival *or* holiday.

Fest'..., *(a.) in comp.* —abend, *m.* eve, vigil of a holiday; —abschnitt, *m. see* —tagsabschnitt; —aufzug, *m.* festive procession; —

[illegible]

fat belly; maw: —bäuchig, *adj. vulg.* having a fat belly; —bruch, *m. Surg.* steatocele; —darm, *m. Cook.* double tripe; —drüsen, *f. pl. Anat.* sebaceous glands.

Fet'te, *(w.) f.* 1) *see* Fettheit & Fettigkeit; 2) *Archit. see* Dachfette.

Fet'ten, *(w.) v. tr.* 1) *provinc.* to make fat, greasy; 2) to grease, oil (wool, &c.); 3) *Cook.* to baste, lard.

Fett'..., *in comp.* —feder, *f.* a small bunch of feathers standing upright on the rump of some birds (*f. i.* geese) and which are always moist; —fleck(en), *m.* 1) *or* —fell, *n.* yellow spot in the white of the eye; 2) spot of grease; —gänge, *pl. Anat.* adipose ducts; —gans, *f. Ornith.* penguin (*Aptenodytes patagonica* L.); —gar, *adj. T.* tanned in fat; —geschwulst, *f.*, —gewächs, *n. Surg.* wen, steatoma; —gewebe, *n. Anat.* adipose membrane; —glanz, *m.* greasy lustre; —hammel, *m.* fattened sheep; —händler, *m. see* —krämer; —haut, *f. Anat.* adipose membrane or tissue. [ture of a thing, richness.

Fett'heit, *(w.) f.* fatness, &c., fat, rich na-

Fett'henne, *(w.) f. Bot.* orpine (*Sedum* L.).

Fet'tig, Fet'ticht, *adj.* greasy, fatty.

Fet'tigkeit, *(w.) f.* 1) fatness, &c. *cf.* Fett; 2) greasiness, richness; oiliness, unctuosity.

Fett'..., *in comp.* —käfer, *m. see* Speckkäfer; —kalk, *m.* fat or white lime; —kelle, *f.* baster, basting-ladle; —kohle, *f. see* Glanzkohle, 2; —kram, *m.* dealing in fat or greasy goods; —krämer, *m.* dealer in fat or greasy goods, chandler; —krankheit, *f.* a puffing up, swelling (of the silk-worms); —kraut, *n. Bot.* the common butter-wort (*Pinguicula vulgaris* L.); —leibig, *adj.* corpulent; —leibigkeit, *f.* corpulence.

Fett'lich, *adj.* fattish.

Fett'..., *in comp.* —magen, *m. see* Labmagen; —markt, *m.* market for butter, oil; fat-cattle-market; —maul, *n. vulg.* greasy chops or chaps; —nabel, *m. Surg.* navel-rupture; —näpfchen, *n. see* Näpfchen; —noppen, *n. T.* second burling (of cloth); —ochs, *m.* a fattened ox; —pflanze, *f. Bot.* succulent plant; *Chem.-s.* —säure, *f.* sebacic acid; das —saure Salz, sebate; —saures Kali, sebate of potash; —schmelzen, *n. Vet.* molten grease (a disease); —schwanz, *m.* fat tail (of African, &c. sheep); —stein, *m. Miner.* elaeolite; —sucht, *f.* excessive fatness, obesity; —taucher, *m. see* —gans; —thon, *m.* fuller's-earth.

Fet'tung, *(w.) f.* the (act of) greasing, &c. *cf.* Fetten.

Fett'..., *in comp.* —viehhandel, *m.* trade in fattened cattle; —waare, *f.* fat or greasy goods (butter, cheese, porkery, pork meats), chandlery; —wachs, *n.* adipocire, adipocere; —wanst, *m. vulg.* fat-guts; —wanstig, *adj. vulg.* gorbellied; —werden des Weines, ropiness, viscidity of wine; —wolle, *f.* wool in the yolk; —zellen, *f. pl. Anat.* adipose ducts.

Fet'zen, *(str.) m.* (*dimin.* Fetz'chen, *[str.] n.*) 1) *coll.* shred, tatter, rag; *gener. pl.* shreds, &c.; 2) *fig.* trash, trifle, bagatelle. [fetzen.

Fet'zen, *(w.) v. tr.* to shred, &c. *see* Zer-

Fet'zer, *(str.) m.* 1) shredder; 2) any instrument for shredding; 3) *fig. & coll. a)* pedant, pokar; *b)* rod, ferrule.

Fet'zig, *adj.* in rags, ragged.

Feucht, I. *adj.* moist, humid, damp; dank; meine Füße sind —, my feet are damp; f-es Gemüt, phlegmatic; f-er Brand, *Med.* gangrene; f-es Grab, *poet.* watery grave; II. *in comp.* —blatt, *n. Sport. see* Feigenblatt; —brett, *n. Print.* paper-board. [nature.

Feuch'te, Feucht'heit, *(w.) f.* moist, damp

Feuch'ten, *(w.) v.* I. *tr.* to moisten, wet, [illegible] gefeuchtet, *p. p. Chem.* washed; II. *intr.* *Sport.* to yield-water (of deer, &c.).

Feuch'tigkeit, *(str.) n.* plain (of things, &c.).

Feuch'tig, I. *adj.* (*l. u.*) dampish, &c. *see* Feucht; II. F-keit, *(w.) f.* moisture, moistness, dampness, humidity, humour(s); fluid; schleimige —, phlegm, mucosity; die crystallene, wässerige — des Auges, *Anat.* aqueous or albugineous humour; *Phys.-s.* (Luft-)F-smesser, *m.* hygrometer; F-szeiger, *m.* hygroscope.

Feucht'..., *in comp.* —kalt, *adj.* moist and cold, damp and raw; —kammer, *f. Typ.* wetting room. [or moist.

Feucht'lich, *adj.* dampish, somewhat damp

Feucht'messer, *(str.) m. see* Feuchtigkeitsmesser.

Feucht'niß, *(str.) f. see* Feuchtigkeit.

Feucht'..., *in comp.* —sack, *m. Sport.* bladder; —tenne, *f. see* Fichtentenne.

Feuch'tung, *(w.) f.* the act of moistening, &c. *cf.* Feuchten.

Feucht'zieher, *(str.) m. Phys.* hygroscope.

* Feudal', *adj.* (*Mid. Lat.*) feudal; —herrschaft, *f.* feudal sovereignty; —recht, *n.* feudal law; —regierung, *f.* feudal government; —system, *n.* feudalism, feudal system; —zeit, *f.* feudal times. — Feudalist', *(w.) m.* feudist.

* Feudalität', *(w.) f.* feudality.

Feu'er, *(str.) n.* 1) fire; 2) *see* F-sbrunst; 3) a distemper of cattle; *fig.-s.* 4) *a) Jewel.* brightness (of diamonds); *b)* cast, warmth (of a colour); 5) body, raciness (of wine); 6) *a)* fire, ardour, spirit; glow; mettle (of a horse); *b)* passion, flame; 7) *Mar. a)* lighthouse; fire of a light-house; *b)* lantern; *c)* drunsy, druzy; 8) *a) Metall.* forge, hearth; *b) Smith.* forge-hearth; *c)* heat (of a blast-furnace); am —, at the fire; das helle (*Chem.* offene) —, light (*Chem.* open or naked) fire; das gelinde —, slow fire; — fangen, to take fire, to ignite; — schlagen, to strike a light; — machen, to light, kindle a fire; — geben, *Mil.*, &c. to (give) fire; können Sie mir — geben? have you got a light (for a cigar, &c.)? in — stehen, to be on fire; der Berg speit —, the mountain burns; der Pfeffer hat —, pepper is hot; das wilde —, *Vet.* anticor (of horses); measles (of swine); das kalte — des Rindviehes, inflammatory affection peculiar to cattle; das heilige —, *Med.* St. Anthony's fire, erysipelas; das erste — aushalten, to abide the first charge, to stand the first brunt; zwischen zwei — bringen, to double (the enemy, a fleet); zum ersten Mal im —, (of soldiers) first under fire; die Truppen schonten ihr —, the troops were sparing of their ammunition; ein gebranntes Kind scheut das —, *proverb*, a burnt child shuns the fire; *coll.-s.* — und Flamme sein (speien), to be in a violent rage; — und Flamme werden, to flare up; er kommt leicht in —, his blood is soon up; sich in — jagen, to work one's self up into a violent passion; ins — gehen für ..., to go into the fire (through fire and water) for ....

Feu'er ..., *in comp.* —ader, *f.* caudal vein of cattle; —amt, *n.* fire-office; —anbeter, *m.* fire-worshipper; —anbetung, *f.* fire-worship, pyrolatry; —anstalt, *f.* 1) *see* —ordnung; 2) *or* —assecuranz, *f. a)* insurance against fire, fire-insurance; *b)* fire-(insurance-)office; —arbeiter, *m.* mechanic using fire, as smiths, &c.; —artig, *adj.* igneous, like fire; —assecuranz, *f. see* —versicherung; —assel, *f. Entom.* a species of centipede (*Scolopendra electrica* L.); —aufseher, *m.* fire-warden; —auge, *n.* 1) inflamed eye; 2) *fig.* eye of fire; —bake, *f. Mar.* beacon, light-house; —ball, *m. Metall.* fire-ball, *see* —kugel; —becken, *n.* fire-pan, coal-pan, chafing-dish; —beckenrichtstaffen, *n. T.* chasing-anvil; —behälter, *m. see* —büchse, 1; —berg, *m.* burning mountain, *see* —speiender Berg; —beständig, *adj.* fire-proof, apyrous; refractory; fixed; flüchtige Körper —beständig machen, to deprive volatiles of their volatility; —beständigkeit, *f.* the (state of) being fire-proof; *Phys.* fixidity; —blase, *f.* blister caused by fire; —blatter, *f. Med.* (a fugacious kind of) nettle-rash, epinyctis, *gener. pl.* epinyctides, vesicles arising during the night and disappearing in the morning; —blume, *f. Bot.* corn-poppy (*Papaver rhoeas* L.); —bock, *m.* andiron, *see* Brandbock; —bohne, *f. Bot.* scarlet-runner, scarlet-bean (*Phaseolus multiflorus* Lam.); —brand, *m.* fire-brand, fire-stick; —büchse, *f.* 1) tinder-box; 2) *Mech.* fire-box, fire-place; —bühne, *f. Min.* pile of burning wood; —busch, *m. see* —dorn; —butzen, *m. pl. Fire-w.* little fire-balls in fire-works; —canal, *m. T.* flue; —casse, *f.* fire-insurance-office; —compagnie, *f.* fire-company; —diener, *m. see* —anbeter; —dienst, *m. see* —anbetung; —dorn, *m. Bot.* pyracanth (*Crataegus pyracantha* L.); —drache, *m. Meteor.* fire-drake, bolis; —ecke, *f.* wire-edge; —eifer, *m.* ardent zeal, ardour; heat of passion, burning wrath, anger; —eimer, *m.* fire-bucket; —eisen, *n.* fire-iron; —esse, *f.* 1) chimney; 2) forge; —eule, *f. Ornith.* barn-owl (*Strix flammea* L.); —fächer, *m.* fan, wing to blow the fire; —fahne, *f.* fire-ensign; —fangend, *adj.* apt to take fire; —farbe, *f.* fire- or flame-colour; —farben, —farbig, *adj.* fire- or flame-coloured; —faß, *n.* 1) fire-tub, quenching tub; 2) *see* —tonnen; —fest, *adj.* fire-proof, *cf.* —beständig; —fester Thon, *Metall.* fire-clay; —feste Ziegel, fire-bricks; —fester Schrank, salamander-safe; —festigkeit, *f.* quality of being fire-proof; fixidity; —fink, *m. Ornith.* flaming finch (Brandfink); —flamme, *f.* fire-flame; —flasche, *f. Mar.* powder-flask; —flecken, *pl. Med. see* Rötheln; —folge, *f.* obligation of the inhabitants to assist in extinguishing a conflagration; —fuchs, *m. Sport.* flaming sorrel; —funke, *m.* spark of fire; —gabel, *f.* fire-fork; —garbe, *f.* 1) *Fire-w.* a kind of fire-work having the form of a sheaf, fire-sheaf; 2) *fig.* sheet of fire or flames; —gatter, *n.* fender; —gefahr, *f.* danger of (from) fire; —gefährlich, *adj.* tending to set on fire; inflammable, combustible; —gefährliche Gegenstände, combustibles; —gefährlichkeit, *f.* tendency to set on fire; inflammability, combustibility; —geist, *m.* 1) *Fab.* spirit of the fire; 2) *fig.* aspiring genius; —geld, *n.* chimney-money; —geräth, *n.* 1) implement(s) used for extinguishing fire, *cf.* —haken, 1; 2) fire-set: fire-irons (andirons), shovel, tongs, and poker; —geschrei, *n.* cry (alarm) of fire; —gewehr, *n.* fire-arm, fire-lock, gun; —gewölbe, *n. T.* fire-vault; —gitter, *n.* fire-guard, chimney-fender; —glocke, *f.* fire-bell, alarm-bell; —gott, *m. Anc. Myth.* god of fire, Vulcan; —gradmesser, *m. Phys.* pyrometer; —gradmessung, *f.* pyrometry; —grube, *f.* ash-pit; —hahn, *m.* fire-cock; —haken, *m.* 1) fire-hook, large hook used in pulling down buildings on fire; 2) pot-hook, pot-hanger; 3) crooked poker; —hemd, *n. Mar.* curtain; —herd, *m.* hearth, fire-side, fire-place; —himmel, *m. Phys.* empyrean, empyreal heaven, the highest heaven; —holz, *n.* fire-wood, fuel; —hund, *m. see* 1) —bock; 2) Brandbock; —hüter, *m. Min.* fire-watch.

Feu'erig, *see* Feurig.

Feu'er ..., *in comp.* —kammer, *f. see* —büchse, 1; —kasse, *see* —casse; —kasten, *m.* fire-box; —katze, *f. Gunn.* chamber, fowler; —kessel, *m.* fire-kettle; —keule, *f. Fire-w.* a kind of wooden slab filled with gunpowder, brimstone, saltpetre, &c.; —kieke, *f. provinc.* foot-stove; —kiesel, *m. Miner.* obsidian; —kiste, *f.* fire-trunk; powder-chest; —kitt, *m. see* Brandkitt; —kleider, *n. pl. Mar.* raw-hides; —kluft, *f. see* —gasse; —knauel, *m. see* Brandkugel; —knecht, *m.* fire-man; —kopf, *m. fig.* fiery head, spit-fire; —kraut, *n. Bot.* 1) cup-moss (*Lichen pyxidatus* L.); 2) small-leaved

willow-herb (*Epilobium angustifolium* L.); —frösche, *f.* *Zool.* glistering toad (*Bombinator igneus* Merr.); —friede, *f.* iron-cake; —fuße, *f.* see —faß; —kugel, *f.* fire-ball: 1) a ball filled with combustibles, a bomb; 2) *Meteor.* a fiery meteor, bolis; —kunst, *f.* pyrotechnics; —land, *n.* *Geogr.* Tierra del Fuego, land of fire; —länder, *m.*, —länderin, *f.* inhabitant of Tierra del Fuego, Patagonian; —ländisch, *adj.* Patagonian; —lanze, *f.* fire-pole; —lärm, *m.* cry *or* alarm of fire; —lehre, *f.* *Phys.* pyrology; —leiter, *f.* fire-ladder; —leitung, *f.* *T.* train, priming of mines; —leute, *pl.* 1) fire-men; 2) furnace-men, engine-men, stokers; —lilie, *f.* *Bot.* bulbiferous lily (*Lilium bulbiferum* L.); —linie, *f.* front-line in battle; —löschanstalt, *f.*, —löschwesen, *n.* see Löschanstalt, Löschwesen.

Feu'erlos, *adj.* 1) fireless; 2) lustreless; *Jewel.* cloudy (diamond).

Feu'er..., *in comp.* —luft, *f.* *Chem.* oxygen; —luken, *f. pl.* *Mar.* fire-scuttles; —mal, *n.* 1) burnt mark; 2) (angeborenes) mole (on the skin); —malerei, *f.* encaustic painting; —mann, *m.* fire-man, *cf.* —leute; —männchen, *n.* *coll.* jack o' lantern, see Irrlicht; —marter, *f.* fiery torture; —masern, *pl.* *Med.* see Rötheln; —material, *n.* fuel; —materie, *f.* fiery substance; —mauer, *f.* 1) party wall; 2) chimney; 3) *Sm.* back; —meer, *n.* * a sea of fire, sheet of fire *or* flames, a broad expanse *or* mass of fire: den Leuchtwurm und der Sonne —meer | schuf eine Vaterhand (*Matthisson*), the glow-worm small, the sun's bright sea of flame | confess a Father's hand (*Hackers.*); —messer, *m.* *Phys.* pyrometer; —meßkunst, *f.* pyrometry; —mörser, *m.* *Gunn.* mortar; howitzer.

Feu'ern, (*w.*) *v.* I. *tr.* 1) to burn; to kindle; 2) to make fiery; 3) to sulphurate (wine); II. *intr.* 1) see Heizen; 2) to fire (auf [with Acc.], at, upon), to give fire (upon); 3) to glow, burn; der Indigo feuert, the indigo is reddish; die Pottasche feuert, the potash is heated.

Feu'er..., *in comp.* —napf, *m.* fire-sheet (in fire-works); —nelke, *f.* *Bot.* scarlet-lychnis (*Lychnis chalcedonica* [brennende Liebe]); —ofen, *m.* stove, furnace; —ordnung, *f.* fire-regulation; —pfanne, *f.* 1) chafing-dish; chafer, fire-pan; 2) censer, perfuming-pan; —pfeil, *m.* fire-arrow, fire-dart; —pfeiler, *m.* fire-column; —pfosten, *pl.* fire-plugs; —platte, *f.* back of a chimney; —platz, *m.* fire-place, *med.* hypocaust (in hot-houses); —probe, *f.* 1) fire-ordeal, fiery trial; 2) fire-proof; probational fire; 3) *fig.* ordeal; —pumpe, *f.* fire-pump; —punct, *m.* 1) *Min.* hearth; 2) *Opt.* focus; —rabe, *m.* *Ornith.* see Schneekrähe; —rad, *n.* 1) fire-wheel; 2) lock of an arquebus; —raben, *m.* see —nelke; —raum, *m.* fire-place; fire-box (of a steam-engine); —regen, *m.* rain of fire; —reinigung, *f.* purification by fire; —religion, *f.* pyrolatry, fire-worship; —rettungsapparat, *m.*, —rettungsmaschine, *f.* fire-escape; —rohr, *n.* 1) fire-arm, rifle; fire-lock; 2) see Donnerbüchse; —röschen, *n.* *Bot.* bird's eye, pheasant's eye, adonis (*Adonis aestivalis* L.); —rose, *f.* *Bot.* wine-rose, eglantine (*Rosa rubiginosa* L.); —rost, *m.* fire-grate; —roth, *adj.* 1) as red as fire, fiery red; vermilion; 2) red-hot; —ruf, *m.* cry *or* alarm of fire; —säule, *f.* pillar of fire, fire-column, fire-spout; —schäre, *f.* see Kohlenschärre; F-sbrunst, *f.* a general fire, conflagration; —schaden, *m.* damage (caused) by fire; —schau, *f.* official inspection of buildings so as to guard from fire; —schaufel, *f.* fire-shovel; —schein, *m.* fire-light; —scheu, I. *adj.* afraid of fire; II. *f.* dread of fire; —schiff, *n.* fire-ship; —schirm, *m.* fire-screen; —schlange, *f.* see —drache; —schloß, *n.* fire-lock; —schlund, *m.* 1) fiery abyss, crater; 2) *fig.* cannon; —schröter, *m.* *Entom.* horn-beetle, stag-beetle, bull(y)-fly (*Lucanus cervus* L.); —schwaden, *m.* *Min.* fire-damp; —schwalbe, *f.* *Ornith.* 1) swift (*Cypselus apus* L.); 2) chimney-swallow (*Hirundo rustica* L.); —schwamm, *m.* spunk, German tinder; —schwärmer, *m.* *Fire-w.* (fire-) cracker, squib; —schwert, *n.* *Fire-w.* a kind of wooden sword filled with little rockets, star-fires, &c.; —segen, *m.* charm, conjuration of the fire; —seite, *f.* chimney corner; F-sgefahr, *f.* danger of fire; —setzen, *n.* *Min.* firing of piles of wood in pits; —sicher, *adj.* see —fest; —sicherheit, *f.* 1) see —festigkeit; 2) see —versicherung; F-snoth, *f.* distress of fire; conflagration; —speiend, *adj.* vomiting *or* spitting fire, ignivomous, volcanic; ein —speiender Berg, a volcano; —spiegel, *m.* see Brennspiegel; —spieß, *m.* see —lanze; —spritze, *f.* fire-engine, extinguishing engine; —sprühend, *adj.* * fire-flashing; —stahl, *m.* fire-steel; steel (pocket) light; —stätte, —stelle, *f.* 1) scene of conflagration; 2) *a)* fire-place, hearth; *b)* *meton.* dwelling-house; —stein, *m.* flint (stone), fire-stone; —steinpapier, *n.* flint-paper; —stoff, *m.* *Phys.* elementary fire; *Chem.* caloric; —strafe, *f.* punishment by fire; —strahl, *m.* flash of fire, fire-spout; —strauch, *m.* see —dorn; —strudel, *m.* stream of fire; —stübchen, *n.* *provinc.* (foot-) stove; —stülper, *m.* fender, fire-guard; —taufe, *f.* baptism with fire; —teufel, *m.* *Fire-w.* serpent; —theilchen, *n. pl.* fiery particles; —thon, *m.* fire-clay; —thür, *f.* *Mech.* fire-box-door; —thurm, *m.* beacon, light-house; —tod, *m.* death by fire; —tonnen, *f. pl.* *Mar.* fire-barrels, thundering-barrels; —topf, *m.* fire-pot.

Feu'erung, (*w.*) *f.* 1) the (act of) making *or* lighting a fire, heating, application of fire *or* heat, fire; 2) (F-smaterial, F-smittel, *n.*) fuel; firing; 3) fire-place (Feuerraum).

Feu'er..., *in comp.* —vergoldung, —versilberung, *f.* hot gilding, hot silvering, gilding *or* silvering on glass *or* porcelain by burning in; —versicherung, *f.*, —versicherungsanstalt, *f.* fire-(insurance)office; —versicherungsgesellschaft, *f.* fire-insurance-company; —vogel, *m.* *Ornith.* Baltimore bird (*Icterus* [*Xanthornus*] *Baltimore* Gm.); —wache, *f.* fire-watch; —wächter, *m.* fire-watcher; —waffen, *f. pl.* fire-arms; —wahrsager, *m.* pyromantic; —wahrsagerei, *f.* pyromancy; —warte, *f.* see —thurm; —wehr, *f.* fire-brigade; —werk, *n.* fire-work; —werker, *m.* 1) (*or* —werkskünstler) (artificial) fire-work maker, pyrotechnist; 2) artillery-man, *Mil.* & *Mar.* gunner, artificer; —werkerkunst, —werkskunst, *f.* pyrotechny, pyrotechnics; —werkerwerkstätte, *f.* laboratory of a fire-worker; —werksbühne, *f.* pyrotechnical theatre; —werkskörper, *m.* a composition of fire-work; —werkskunst, *f.* see —werkerkunst; —werkskünstler, *m.* see —werker, 1; —wolf, *m.* a puff, whiff, blast of fire (that sometimes shoots out of a furnace); —wurm, *m.* see —schröter; —zange, *f.* fire-tongs; —zeichen, *n.* 1) fiery meteor, 2) fire-sign, signal-light; —zeug, *n.* 1) any contrivance to light a fire, tinder-box, steel, flint and tinder, pocket-fire, *cf.* Schnellfeuerzeug, Zündmaschine; 2) *coal.* *Print.* a small printing office, *cant.* hedge-press; —zug, *m.* flue.

Feul, (*w.*) *f.* *Mar.* see Föhl.

Feu'rig, I. *adj.* fiery: 1) hot, burning; igneous; f-er Wagen, chariot of fire; 2) *fig.* ardent, passionate; fervid, fervent; hasty; brisk, generous (wine); mettlesome, high-mettled (of a horse); II. F-keit, *n.* fieriness, &c. ardour; mettle; *cf.* Feuer, 6. [felt.

* **Fez** [fês], *m.* (*n.*) fez, Turkish cap of red

Ff., see abbr. at the beginning of F; auf dem —, *coll.* with a vengeance.

Fi, *adv.* see Pfui.

Flä'chen, *(w.) v. tr.* to flatten, (make) level.

Flä'chen..., *in comp.* —**größe,** *f.* extent of surface; —**inhalt,** *m.* (the) area (of the surface), superficial area *or* contents; —**maß,** *n.* superficial measure, square-measure; —**meile,** *f.* square-mile; —**messung,** —**meßkunst,** *f. Math.* planimetry; —**raum,** *m. see* —inhalt; —**winkel,** *m. Math.* plane-angle; —**zahl,** *f.* square number.

Flach'..., *in comp.* —**fallender Gang,** *Min.* hade, hading-shaft; —**feld,** *n.* open field, plain; —**fisch,** *m.* flat-fish (*Platessa vulgaris* L.); —**gangen,** *m. pl. Mar.* planks of the bottom or floor; —**gängig,** *adj. T.* (of screws) square-threaded (*opp.* Scharfgängig); —**gedrückt,** *adj. Bot.* depressed; —**geschliffen,** *adj. Jewel.* tabulated; —**gipfelständig,** *adj. Bot.* flat-topped; —**glas,** *n. Glass-m.* pane or plate-glass; —**hammer,** *m. T.* flatt(en)ing hammer.

Flach'heit, *(w.) f.* 1) flatness; 2) *fig. a)* shallowness; platitude; insipidity; *b) pl.* flat, insipid things, nonsense.

Flach'..., *in comp.* —**hohleisen,** *n.* sculptor's gouge; —**kettig,** *adj.* having a plain *or* flat warp; —**kopf,** *m.* 1) a flat, low head; 2) *fig.* shallow head, a superficial person; —**köpfig,** *adj.* 1) flat-headed; 2) *fig.* dull-headed, shallow; —**land,** *n.* flat land, level, plain; —**länder,** *m.* level-lander, lowlander.

Flach'lich, *adj.* flattish, approaching to flatness.

Flach'..., *in comp.* —**maler,** *m.* room, chamber, *or* house-painter; painter of lacquered *or* Japan goods; —**meißel,** *m.* flat chisel; —**relief,** *n. see* Basrelief; —**ruthe,** *f.* velvet-maker's wire.

Flachs, *(str.) m.* flax (*Linum usitatissimum* L.); neuseeländischer —, *Bot.* flax-lily, New Zealand flax (*Phormium tenax* Forst.); wilder —, common dodder (Flachsseide); lebendiger —, *Miner.* asbestos; — bauen, riffeln, bläuen, brechen, schwingen, hecheln, spinnen, to raise, peel, beat, break (brake), comb (dress *or* hatchel), spin flax.

Flachs'..., *in comp.* —**acker,** *m.* flax-plat; —**ähnlich,** *adj.* flax-like, flaxy; —**artig,** *adj.* like flax, flaxy; —**bandmaschine,** *f.* drawing-machine; —**bart,** *m.* down; flaxen beard; —**bärtig,** *adj.* flaxen-bearded; —**bau,** *m.* cultivation (raising) of flax; —**bauer,** *m.* flax-raiser; —**baum,** *m. Bot.* Chinese laurel, antidesma (*Antidesma alexiteria* L.); —**baumwolle,** *f.* flax-cotton, flax-wool; —**bereiter,** *m.* flax-dresser; —**bläuel,** *m.* swingle-staff; —**blütfarbe,** *f.* gridelin, gray violet colour; —**breche,** *f.* flax-break *or* -brake; —**brechen,** *n.* flax-dressing.

Flach'..., *in comp.* —**scheibe,** *f. Horol.* flat-plate; —**schicht,** *f. Mas.* brick flat; —**schiene,** *f. Railw.* flat *or* plate rail; —**schnabel,** *m. Ornith.* long-beaked plover (*Eurhinorhynchus angustirostris* Illig.); —**schnäbler,** *m. pl. Ornith.* fly-catchers.

Flachs'..., *in comp.* —**darre,** *f.* flax-kiln; —**dotter,** *m.* 1) *see* Leindotter; 2) *see* —seide.

Flach'seitig, *adj.* flat-sided, flat. [linen.

Fläch'sen [*pr.* flĕk'sn], *adj.* of flax, flaxen,

Flachs'..., *in comp.* —**farbe,** *f.* flaxen colour; —**farben,** —**farbig,** *adj.* flaxen(-coloured); —**fasern,** *f. pl.* harl, herl; —**feld,** *n.* field sown with flax; —**fink,** *m. Ornith.* flax-finch (*Fringilla linaria* L.); —**gelb,** *adj.* flaxen; —**gras,** *n.* wild cotton (*Eriophorum* L.); —**haar,** *n.* flaxen hair; —**haarig,** *adj.* flaxen-haired; —**handel,** *m.* flax-trade; —**händler,** *m.* dealer in flax; —**hänfling,** *m. see* —fink; —**hechel,** *f.* flax-comb, hatchel; —**hede,** *f.* flax-tow, hards.

Flachs'icht, Flach'sig, *adj.* flaxy, like flax.

Flachs'..., *in comp.* —**kopf,** *m.* 1) *see* —haar; 2) —**köpfe,** *pl.* (— im Bauten) flax heads; —**kraut,** *n. Bot.* flax-weed, toad flax (Leinkraut); —**land,** *n.* flax-plat; —**lilie,** *f. Bot.* flax-lily (neuseeländischer Flachs); —**mühle,** *f.* flax-mill; —**raufe,** *f.* 1) the plucking *or* pulling of flax; 2) (*or* —riffel, *f.*) ripple; —**röste,** *f.* 1) the steeping, watering, *or* retting of flax, steep; 2) flax watering time (season); 3) pond *or* pool in which flax is steeped, retting pool; —**samen,** *m.* flax-seed, linseed; —**schäbe,** *f.* shaw *or* shive of flax; —**schwinge,** *f.* scutcher; —**seide,** *f. Bot.* devil's guts, dodder of thyme (*Cuscuta epithymum* Weihe); —**stein,** *m.* asbestos.

Flach'..., *in comp.* —**stab,** *m.* flat bar; —**stichel,** *m. Engr.* flat scalper (scooper); —**tellerförmig,** *adj.* salver-shaped; *Bot.* hypocrateriform; —**vertieft,** *adj.* concave; —**werk,** *n. Build.* flat-tile roofed; —**zange,** *f.* flat-nosed pliers; —**ziegel,** *m.* flat tile.

Flack, *(str.) m.* 1) *see* Flach, II. 1; 2) (—maschine, *f.*) *see* Flechtmaschine.

Flack'en, *(w.) v.* I. *intr.* 1) *see* Flackern; 2) *provinc.* to lie idly; II. *tr. Hatt. see* Fachen, 3.

Flack'er..., *in comp.* —**feuer,** *n.* flaring *or* blazing fire; —**leben,** *n.* *, flickering life.

Flack'erig, *adj coll.* flaring; flickering.

Flack'ern, *(w.) v. intr.* to flare, flicker, flutter.

Flack'maschine, *(w.) f. see* Flechtmaschine.

* **Flacon'** [*pr.* flakŏng'], *(str., pl.* F-s) *m.* (*Fr.*) a small bottle, scent-bottle, *coll.* smelling-bottle. [cake.

Fla'den, *(str.) m.* flat-cake; a kind of curd-

Fla'der, *(w.) f.* 1) *see* Flinglech, 1; 2) spot, speck, streak, vein (in wood *or* stone) (Flaser); —**baum,** *m. Bot.* common maple (*Acer* L.); —**gras,** *n. see* Hirsengras; —**holz,** *n.* veined wood.

Fla'derig, *adj.* veined; grainy (Maserig); spotted, speckled; *Miner.* brittly.

Fla'ge, *(w.) f. provinc.* 1) bog, quagmire; 2) flaw, a sudden gust of wind; 3) *Min.* a vein of solid stone crossing a mine.

* **Flagellant',** *(w.) m.* (*L. Lat.*) *Eccl.* flagellant. — **Flagelli'ren,** *(w.) v. tr. & intr.* to flagellate.

* **Flageolet'** [*pr.* flazholĕt'], *(str., pl.* F-s) *n.* (*Fr.*) *Mus.* flageolet; —**ton,** *m.* flute-like tone, harmonic.

Flag'ge, *s.* I. *(w.) f.* flag, standard, ensign; II. *in comp.* **Flagg'capitän,** *m.* flag-captain; F-**naufseher, Flagg'gast,** *m.* a mariner who has the care of the flags; F-**noffizier** *or* **Flagg'mann,** *m.* flag-officer; F-**nschiff** *or* **Flagg'schiff,** *n.* flag-ship; F-**nstange,** *f.*, F-**nstock,** *m.* ensign- *or* flag-staff; F-**ntuch,** *n.* bunting.

Flag'gen, *(w.) v. Mar.* I. *tr.* to dress (a ship); II. *intr.* 1) to wave (of a flag); 2) to display the flag; auf halber Stange —, to display the flag at halfstaff.

Fla'ke, *(w.) f.* 1) net-work; 2) hurdle-work; 3) large fishing net. [nets.

Fla'ken, *(w.) v. intr.* to fish with large

Flam'länder, *(str.) m.,* **Flam'länderin,** *(w.) f.* Fleming, Flemish man, woman.

Flamant', *(w. & str.),* **Flambert,** *(str.) m. see* Flamingo.

Flam'berg, *(str., Gallic [nonsensical] m. of Flanders) m.* († &) *, broad-sword, brand.

Fla'me, *(w.) f. Vet.* fleam (an instrument for bleeding cattle).

Flaming'o, *(str., pl.* F-s) *m. Ornith.* flamingo (*Phoenicopterus ruber* L.).

Flä'misch, *adj.* 1) Flemish; 2) *coll.* surly, boorish, insolent, *coarse*.

Flam'länder, F-**in,** *see* Flamländer.

Flämm'chen, *(str.) n.* (*dimin. of* Flamme) a small flame, flamelet.

Flam'me, *(w.) f.* 1) flame, blaze; in F-n stehen, to be in flames; in F-n setzen, to set in a flame, inflame; 2) *fig.* ardour of tem-

gourd, calabash (*Cucurbita lagenaria* L.); —n-**kürbisbaum**, *m.* calabash-tree (*Crescentia cujete*); —**maschine**, *f. T.* can-roving frame; can-frame; —**schild**, *n.* (bottle-)label; —**ständer**, —**teller**, —**untersetzer**, *m.* bottle-stand; —**träger**, *m.* bottle-carrier, bottle-tray; —**zug**, *m. Mech.* polyspast, (tackle) pulley, hand-screw, jack (in a *or* the box).

* **Flaschinett'**, (*str.*) *n. see* Flageolet.

Flasch'ner, (*str.*) *m.* tinman, lamp-maker.

Fla'ser, *m.*, **Fla'serig**, *adj. see* Flader, Fladerig.

Flat'ter..., *in comp.* —**espe**, *f. Bot.* aspen (tree); —**binse**, *f. Bot.* common soft-rush (*Juncus effusus* L.); —**eidechse**, *f. Nat.* flying dragon (*Draco volans* L.).

Flat'terer, (*str.*) *m.* 1) *see* Flattergeist, 2; 2) *Bot.* chabropter.

Flat'ter..., *in comp. Nat-s.* —**füßig**, *adj.* wing-footed, aliped; —**füßler**, *m.*, —**füßige Thiere**, *n. pl.* alipeds; —**geist**, *m.* 1) light-mindedness, inconstancy; 2) a person who is light-minded *or* fickle, inconstant person, weather-cock; —**gold**, *n. see* Flittergold.

Flat'terhaft, I. *adj.* fickle, unsteady, inconstant, flighty, giddy, light-minded; (of women) flirting; II. F-**igkeit**, (*w.*) *f.* fickleness, &c., inconstancy. [hund.

Flat'terhund, (*str.*) *m. Zool. see* Fieder-

Flat'terig, *adj.* 1) *see* Flatterhaft; 2) *see* Fladerig.

Flat'terkatze, (*w.*) *f. Zool.* flying cat (Maki, Flugmaki).

Flat'terling, (*str.*) *m. Zool.* butterfly.

Flat'terminе, (*w.*) *f. Fort.* fougade.

Flat'tern, (*w.*) *v. intr.* 1) to flit, flirt, flutter, flicker; to float, stream, wave; to hang loose, to dangle; 2) to run about, rove, roam, ramble; 3) to be unsteady (flighty).

Flat'ter..., *in comp.* —**pappel**, *f. see* —rose; —**rose**, *f. see* Klatschrose; —**rüster**, *f. Bot.* large-leaved elm (*Ulmus effusa* Willd.); —**ruß**, *m.* flocky soot; —**sinn**, *m. see* —geist.

Flau, *adj. coll.* 1) lukewarm; 2) *a)* weak, faint; stale, insipid; *b)* flat, flagging; *c)* dull, dead, inactive; *Comm.* dull *or* heavy of sale, heavy upon hand (of goods), flat, stale, languid, stagnant (of trade); die Börse war —, the exchange was spiritless; der Artikel geht — ab, the article goes off heavily; die Geschäfte gehen —, trade is languishing; Gewürze sind sehr —, spices are extremely flat (*i. e.* heavy of sale); der Wind wird f—er, *Mar.* it grows calm.

Flau'en, (*w.*) *v.* I. *tr. provinc. & Min.* to rinse, to wash in running water; II. *intr.* to be heavy of sale; (of trade, &c.) to be languishing *or* stagnant; *cf.* Flau, 2, c.

Flau'faß, (*str., pl.* F-**fässer**) *n. Min.* buddle.

Flau'heit, **Flau'igkeit**, (*w.*) *f.* flatness; *Comm.* dulness (of sale), deadness, stagnation *or* languination (of trade, &c.).

Flaum, (*str., no pl.*) *m.* 1) down; *pl. Bot.* villi; 2) *provinc.* suet; lard; 3) F-**en**, *pl. Sport.* bristles of the wild boar; *coll.* einem den — [illegible], to coax, flatter; —**bart**, *m.* soft-[illegible]; —**feder**, *f.* down(y-feather), pin-feather.

Flau'mig, *adj.* downy; soft, tender.

Flaus, *coll.* **Flausch**, (*str.*) *m.* 1) tuft; 2) pilot-cloth, flushing; 3) *fig. see* Flausen-macher.

Flau'se, (*w.*) *f. coll.* false pretence, equivocation, shuffle, evasion, shift, fib; F-**n-macher**, *m.* a shuffler, trickster.

Flau'trog, (*str., pl.* F-**tröge**) *m. Min.* washing-trough.

Flaz, (*str.*) *m.* an untrained, coarse, rude [illegible], lubber, *cf.* Flegel.

Flech'se, **Flechs**, (*w.*) *f.* tendon, sinew.

Flech'sen..., *in comp.* —**artig**, —**ähnlich**, *adj.* [illegible]; —**bein**, *n. see* Sehnen-[illegible]; —**[illegible]**, *f.* [illegible].

Flech'sig, **Flech'sicht**, *adj.* like a tendon; tendinous, sinewy.

Flecht'binse, (*w.*) *f. gener. pl.* rush-platting.

Flech'te, (*w.*) *f.* 1) twist, braid, plait, tress (of hair); 2) hurdle, hamper, *cf.* Flechtwerk; 3) *Med.* herpetic eruption, herpes, tetter, *vulg.* ring-worm; 4) *Bot.* lichen.

Flech'ten, (*str.*) *v.* I. *tr.* to braid, plait, twist, entwine; *Gard.* to plash, interweave (branches, &c.); einen Kranz —, to wreath *or* make a garland; durch *or* in einander —, to interlace, entwine; einen Korb —, to make a basket; ein geflochtener Korb, wicker-basket; ein geflochtener Zaun (Flechtzaun), a fence (hedge) made of plashing; aufs Rad —, to fasten on the wheel (a criminal); II. *refl.* 1) to plait; Binsen — sich leicht, rushes plait easily; 2) *fig.* to interfere, to meddle (in, with).

Flech'ten..., *in comp.* —**artig**, *adj.* 1) *Med.* herpetic; 2) partaking of the nature of lichens; —**ausschlag**, *m. Med.* herpetic eruption; *Chem-s.* —**bitter**, *n.* picrolichenine; —**orseille**, *f.* archil (Kräuterorseille); —**säure**, *f.* lichenic acid; —**stärkemehl**, *n.* lichen-starch.

Flecht'ling, (*str., pl. w.*) *m. Mar.* nettings, the shrouds and other rigging at the mast-head.

Flecht'..., *in comp.* —**korb**, *m.* wicker-basket; —**ring**, *m.* gemel-ring; —**rohr**, *n.* cane-platting, bonnet-cane; —**stroh**, *n.* straw-platting; —**weide**, *f.* osier, *see* Korbweide; —**weiden**, *pl.* wickers; —**werk**, *n.* hurdle-work, net-work, wicker-work, wattling; *Archit., &c.* trellis, mat-work; —**zaun**, *m.* plashed quickset-hedge.

Fleck, (*str.*) *m.* 1) spot, place; piece (of land); vom F-e kommen, to get on, to get along, stir; gehe nicht vom —! do not stir! den rechten — treffen, to hit home, to hit the (right) nail on the head; auf dem —(e), on the spot; er hat das Herz auf dem rechten —, his heart is in the right place; 2) speck; *lit. & fig.* spot, stain, blot, blur; flaw, taint, blemish; 3) *a)* patch, piece; botch, tatter; shred; *b) Shoe-m.* heelpiece; *c)* F-e, *pl. Cook.* tripe; 4) *Tail.* patch; 5) *Med.* botch; *Vet.* speck in the eye, haw; F-e ausmachen aus ..., to scour (an article of dress); —**ausmacher**, *m.* cleanser, scourer (of clothes).

Fleck'chen, (*str.*) *n.* (*dimin. of* Fleck) 1) little spot; speckle; 2) little piece; patch (of ground); shred.

Fleck'en, (*str.*) *m.* 1) borough, country-town, market-town; 2) spot, blot, stain; blur, flaw; speck, speckle; mark; mole; macula, spot (of the sun); 3) *fig.* blemish, spot, stain, blur, flaw, taint.

Fleck'en, (*w.*) *v.* I. *tr.* 1) to spot, stain, speck, speckle, bespeckle; gefleckte Zeuge, speckled, spotted, mottled stuffs; 2) to put a patch *or* heel-piece on ...; II. *intr.* 1) to stain, blot; to get stained, spotted; diese Farbe fleckt leicht, this colour soils easily; 2) (*gener. impers.*) *fig. coll.* to get on, to proceed, speed; es fleckt ihm nicht, he does not get on with his work.

Fleck'enlos, I. *adj.* spotless, untainted, pure; II. F-**igkeit**, (*w.*) *f.* spotlessness, &c.

Fleck'enschnepfe, (*w.*) *f. Ornith.* spotted snipe (*Rhynchaea variegata, &c.*).

Fleck'ig, **Fleck'icht**, *adj.* († & *provinc.*: **Fleck'et**) 1) like spots, specks; 2) spotted, stained, blotted, speckled; freckly, freckled; muddy (diamond, &c.); hard (tin).

Fleck'..., *in comp.* —**fieber**, *n. Med.* petechial *or* spotted-fever, purples; —**kugel**, —**seife**, *f.* soap-ball (to take out spots of grease, &c.), scouring-ball; —**leder**, *n.* strong leather for heel-pieces; —**stein**, *m.* scouring-stone; —**wasser**, *n.* scouring-drops, benzine.

* **Fleddu'**, *see* Flöhkraut(?)

Flectí'ren, (*w.*) *v. tr. Gramm.* to inflect.

Fle'der..., *in comp.* —**fisch**, *m. Ichth.* flying fish (fliegender Fisch); —**hund**, *m.* flying dog (*Pteropus vulgaris* Geoffr., *Vespertilio caninus* L.); —**maus**, *f.* bat, rear-mouse, flitter-mouse (*Vespertilio murinus* L.); (die bärtige) whiskered bat (*Vespertilio mystacinus* Leisler); —**mausdachfenster**, *n. Archit.* dormant, dormer; —**mausfisch**, *m. Ichth.* a species of angler (fishing frog) (*Malthe vespertilio* L.); die —**mausflügelförmigen Bänder**, *n. pl. Anat.* bat-wings; —**thier**, *n. Zool.* cheiropter, aliped; —**wisch**, *m.* duster, goosewing for dusting, feather-broom.

Fle'dern, (*w.*) *v.* I. *intr. see* Flattern; II. *tr.* 1) to beat, hide, leather; 2) to clean with a duster.

Fleet, (*str.*) *n.*, **Flee'te**, (*w.*) *f. provinc.* (*N. G.*) I. (*Old Engl.* fleet) 1) a water-course, canal; 2) rill, rivulet; II. foam (Fließe); III. *T.* roll of carded wool; IV. *Mar.* all necessaries for a Greenland whale-boat; V. *Typ.* double.

Fle'gel (*or* **Flö'gel**), (*str.*) *m.* 1) *a)* swiple, swingle (of a thrashing flail); *b)* flail; 2) *only* an insolent, unmannerly, impertinent, *or* saucy fellow, boor, churl; —**jahre**, *n. pl.* the years of saucy boyhood; —**kappen**, *f. pl.* caplins (of a thrashing-flail). — **Flegelei'**, (*w.*) *f.* 1) insolence, impertinence, boorishness, sauciness; 2) piece of insolence, &c. — **Fle'gelhaft**, I. *adj.* insolent, unmannerly, impertinent, saucy, churlish; II. F-**igkeit**, (*w.*) *f.* unmannerliness, &c. (Flegelei). — **Fle'geln**, (*w.*) *v.* I. *tr.* 1) to thrash; 2) to call names, to abuse; II. *intr. & refl.* to behave churlishly, to loll about unmannerly. — **Fle'gelthum**, (*str.*) *n. see* Flegelhaftigkeit, Flegeljahre.

Fle'hen, (*w.*) *v.* I. *intr.* (um eine Sache zu Einem, * Einem) to pray, implore, supplicate, beseech; II. *tr.* (*l. u.*) *see* Anflehen & Erflehen.

Fle'hen, *v. s.* (*str.*) *n.* supplication; prayers.

Fleh'entlich, I. *adv.* suppliantly; — bitten, to entreat, implore, solicit, crave; II. *adj.* (*occurring only in conjunction with verbal nouns*) suppliant.

* **Flei'er**, (*str.*) *m.* (*Engl.*) *Spinn.* flyer, (bobbin and) fly-frame (Spindelbank).

Fleisch, (*str.*) *n.* 1) flesh; 2) (Koch—) meat; 3) *Bot.* pulp; parenchyma; das — einer Apfelsine, the pulp of an orange; 4) *Paint.* carnation; 5) *fig.* animal nature, carnality, flesh (*as opposed to* the spirit); wildes —, *Surg.* fungous, proud, *or* dead flesh; gehacktes —, *Cook.* minced meat; — von leichtem Vieh, *Comm.* cargo beef; das lebendige —, quick; ins — schneiden, to cut to the quick; den Weg alles F-es gehen, to go the way of all flesh.

Fleisch'..., *in comp.* —**abfall**, *m.* offal of meat; —**auswuchs**, *m. Surg.* fleshy excrescence, carnosity, caruncle; —**bank**, *f. gener. pl.* —**bänke**, butcher's stalls *or* row, shambles; —**blume**, *f. Bot.* common lady's-smock, cuckoo flower (*Cardamine pratensis* L.); —**bruch**, *m. Surg.* sarcocele; —**brühe**, *f.* meat-broth; gravy; —**eisen**, *n. Tann.* fleshing-knife.

Flei'schen, (*w.*) *v. tr.* to clear of flesh; to flesh.

Flei'scher, (*str.*) *m.* butcher; —**beil**, *n.* butcher's-axe, cleaver; —**bursch**, *m.* butcher's boy; butcher's (journey)man; —**gang**, *m. coll.* fruitless journey; sleeveless errand; —**gesell**, *m.* butcher's (journey)man; —**gewerbe**, —**handwerk**, *n.* butcher's trade; —**gewicht**, *n.* butcher's weight; —**hund**, *m.* butcher's dog; —**knecht**, *m. see* —gesell; —**messer**, *n.* butcher's knife; —**stand**, *m.* butcher's stall, *see* Fleischbank; —**talg**, *m.* unmelted tallow; —**vogel**, *m. Ornith.* butcher-bird (*Vanga destructor* Temminck). [sual.

Flei'schern, *adj.* 1) of flesh; fleshy; 2) sen-

Fleisch'..., *in comp. Surg-s.* —**erzeugend**,

adj. generating *or* breeding (new) flesh, sarcotic, incarnative, anaplerotic; —erzeugung, *f.* formation of flesh, sarcosis; F-eslust, *f.* lust of the flesh, carnal appetite; —esser, *m.* a person (fond of) eating much meat; F-es-vergehen, *n.* carnal crime; Liebig's —extract, *n.* Liebig's extract of meat; —farbe, *f.* flesh-colour, carnation; —farben, —farbig, *adj.* flesh-coloured, carnation(-coloured), incarnate; —fasern, *f. pl. Anat.* (lat.:) *villi*; —faß, *n.* salting-tub; —fliege, *f.* flesh-fly (*Sarcophaga carnaria* L.); —fressend, *adj.* carnivorous, flesh-devouring, sarcophagous; —fresser, *m.* 1) *or* —fressendes Thier, *n.* carnivorous animal; zoophagan; 2) *vulg.* a devourer of meat (—esser); —gabel, *f.* meat-fork, steak-fork; —gebung, *f. Paint.* carnation; —geschwulst, *f.* swelling in the flesh, wen, *cf.* —bruch; —gewächs, *n. Surg.* fleshy tumour *or* excrescence; sarcoma; —gummi, *m. see* —leim; —hacker, *m. see* Fleischer; —haken, *m.* flesh-hook, hook to hang meat upon; —halle, *f. see* —bänke; —haltung, *f. see* —gebung; —händler, *m.* flesh-monger, one who deals in flesh; —hauer, *m. see* Fleischer; —haut, *f.* 1) *Anat.* a fat sort of membrane which covers the whole body, (*Lat.*) *panniculus carnosus*; 2) *Bot.* sarcocarp; —horn, *n. see* —kamm.

Flei'schig, I. *adj.* 1) *or* Flei'schicht, like flesh, flesh-like; 2) fleshy, mealy (also applied to fruit), pulpous, pulpy; plump, brawny; II. F-keit, (*w.*) *f.* fleshiness; pulpousness; plumpness.

Fleisch'..., *in comp.* —kamm, *m. Ornith.* caruncle (of fowls); —kammer, *f.* larder, lardery; —kegel, *m. Ornith.* caruncle (of the turkey); —kiel, *m. see* Kiel; —kloß, *m.*, —klößchen, *n. Cook.* meat-ball (of minced meat); —klumpen, *m.* lump of flesh *or* meat; —knochengeschwulst, *f. Surg.* osteosarcoma; —korb, *m.* meat-basket; —kost, *f.* 1) *see* —speise; 2) meat-diet, flesh-meat, animal food; —krone, *f.* coronet *or* cornet of a horse; —kuchen, *m.* meat-pie, pasty; —lake, *f.* brine of meat, pickle; —lappen, *m.* fleshy appendage, lappet; —lauch, *m. Bot.* 1) leek (*Allium porrum* L.); 2) welsh onion (*Allium fistulosum* L.); —lehre, *f. Anat.* sarcology; —leim, *m. Pharm.* sarcocol(la).

Fleisch'lich, I. *adj.* fleshly, of the flesh, sensual, carnal; f-e Lüste, *f. pl.* lusts of the flesh, carnal desires; f-e Verbrechen, *n. pl.* carnal crimes; sich — vermischen, to have carnal intercourse; — gesinnt, fleshly- *or* carnal-minded; II. F-keit, (*w.*) *f.* fleshliness, fleshly lust, carnality.

Fleisch'los, *adj.* fleshless.

Fleisch'..., *in comp.* —machend, *p. a. see* —erzeugend; —made, *f.* maggot, the larva of a flesh-fly (*Sarcophaga* M.); —mahlzeit, *f.* flesh-meal; —mäkler, *m. fig.* flesh-monger, pimp; —markt, *m.* meat *or* butcher's market, shambles; —masse, *f. fig.* a great lump of flesh; —messer, *n.* kitchen-knife; —mittel, *n. pl. Med.* sarcotics; —nabelbruch, *m. Med.* umbilical rupture; —nahrung, *f.* animal food, *see* —kost, 2; —pastete, *f.* meat-pie, mince-pie; —räucherer, *m.* smoke-drier; —roth, *adj.* flesh-coloured; —scharren, *m. see* —bank; —schäper, —schauer, *m.* officer who inspects the shambles and regulates the price of meat; —schau, *f.* inspection of shambles; —schnitte, *f.* slice of meat, steak; —seite, *f. Tann.* flesh-side (of hides); —speise, *f.* flesh-meat, animal food (*as opposed to* Mehlspeise &c.); —spieß, *m.* meat-spit; —ständer, *m. see* —faß; —stärke, *f. T.* thickness of metal (*Inst.*); —steuer, *f.* meat-tax; —suppe, *f.* soup made of broth; —tag, *m.* a day on which meat is eaten, flesh-day; —taxe, *f.* assize of meat; —töne, *m. pl. Paint.* carnation *or* flesh-tints; —topf, *m.* flesh-pot, meat-pot; —waare, *f.* dry-saltery; —waarenhändler, *m.* dry-salter; —waage, *f.* balance *or* scales for weighing meat, meat-scales; —warze, *f.* caruncle; —warzenförmig, *adj.* caruncular; —wasserbruch, *m. Surg.* sarcohydrocele; —werdung, *f. fig.* incarnation; —wuchs, *m.* recruiting of flesh; *Surg.* incarnation; —wunde, *f.* flesh-wound; —wurm, *m. see* —made; —wurst, *f.* meat-pudding; —zahn, *m. Anat.* foretooth, projecting tooth, buck-tooth (Fletschor Raffzahn); —zehnte, *m.* a tithe paid of animals which are killed for meat.

Fleiß, (*str.*) *m.* diligence, application, industry, assiduity, carefulness; mit —, 1. industriously, with diligence and care; 2. on purpose, purposely, designedly, intentionally, wilfully.

Flei'ßen, (*w.*) *v. refl. see* Befleißen; Befleißigen.

Flei'ßig, I. *adj.* diligent, assiduous, industrious, sedulous, careful, painstaking, hard working; ein f-er Besucher, a frequent visitor, a close attendant (in parliament, &c.); II. *adv.* 1) diligently, &c.; 2) repeatedly, often, frequently; — gearbeitet, *Comm.* highly worked up *or* wrought; sich — Bewegung machen, to take frequent exercise; — studiren, to study hard (close).

Flei'ßigen, (*w.*) *v. refl. see* Befleißigen.

Flen'nen, (*w.*) *v. intr.* († *h*) *provinc.* 1) to make wry faces; 2) to weep, cry; 3) to grin, laugh.

Flep'pe, (*w.*) *f. Stud. slang. see* Aufschneiderei. — Flep'pen, *see* Aufschneiden, II.

Fle'te, (*w.*) *f. Ichth.* gray skate (*Raja batis* L.).

Fleth(e), *see* Fleet(e).

Flet'schen, (*w.*) *v. tr.* 1) to broaden, expand; *T.* to flatten; 2) die Zähne —, to show one's teeth (in laughing, weeping, *or* in anger); to smirk, to grin.

Fletsch'zahn, (*str.*, *pl.* Fletsch'zähne) *m.* projecting tooth.

Fleu'te, (*w.*) *f.* (*or* Fleut'schiff, *n.*) *Mar.* a Dutch flute *or* flight, pink.

* Flexiōn', (*w.*) *f.* (*Lat.*) *Gramm.* inflection; F-ssystem, *n.* inflectional system.

* Flibust'(i)er, (*str.*) *m.* filibuster, buccaneer.

Flick, (*str.*) *m. see* Flicken, *m.*

Flick'arbeit, (*w.*) *f.* patchwork, botching work.

Flick'en, (*w.*) *v. tr.* to patch (up), to botch, clout; to vamp (up), cobble (shoes, &c.); to darn (stockings, &c. *cf.* Stopfen); to piece out (shirts, &c.); to mend (coarsely), to repair; Einem etwas am Zeuge —, *coll.* to pick up a quarrel with one, to pick a hole in a person's coat. — Flick'en, (*str.*) *m.* patch, botch.

Flick'er, (*str.*) *m.* patcher, botcher; cobbler.

Flickerei', (*w.*) *f.* patchwork (Flickwerk).

Flick'..., *in comp.* —fleck, *m.* patch, botch; —gans, *f. provinc.* smoked goose; —gedicht, *n.* cento; —häring, *m. provinc.* smoked herring; —lappen, *m. see* —fleck; —messer, *n.* glazier's knife; —schneider, *m.* jobbing tailor, botcher; —werk, *n.* patchwork, botching, patchery; cento; —wort, *n.* expletive, waste-word; —zeug, *n.* cloth, &c. to make patches of (for old garments).

Flie'boot, (*str.*, *pl.* F-böte) *n. Mar.* (Dutch) fly-boat.

Flie'de, (*w.*) *f. see* Fliet, III.

Flie'der, *a.* I. (*str.*) *m.* (*or* —baum) *Bot.* elder, bore-tree (*Sambucus nigra* L.); der spanische —, lilac (*Syringa vulgaris* L.); II. *in comp.* —beere, *f.* elder-berry; —blüte, *f.* elder-blossom; —essig, *m.* vinegar of elder; —mus, *n.* elder-jam; —saft, *m.* elder-juice; —thee, *m.* elder-tea; —wein, *m.* elder-wine.

Flie'ge, (*w.*) *f.* 1) *Entom.* fly (*Musca* L.); mit F-n angeln, to fly-fish; zwei F-n mit einem Schlage treffen, *proverb.* to kill two birds with one stone; 2) *T.* sight (of a gun), *see* Korn, 3, b; 3) *Mech.* (*for* Flügel an der

A. Fließ, (str.) n. fleece (of wool); das goldene —, Herald. the golden fleece.

B. Fließ, (str.) n. provinc. flowing water, a small brook.

Fließ... (from Fließen), in comp. —bette, n. see Gerinne; —blattern, —pocken, f. pl. confluent small-pox.

Flie'ßen, (str.) v. intr. (aux. sein) 1) a) to flow, run, stream; to float; b) to drop, trickle down; to run, gutter (of candles); c) to flow, disembogue (in [with Acc.], into; of streams); 2) to blot, sink (of paper); 3) fig. to pass away, to run (of time); to flow, ensue, result (aus, from), arise: sanft dahin —, to glide smoothly along; stark —, to rush, gush, shoot; diese Dinte fließt nicht, this ink does not run; Blut ist geflossen, blood has been shed; dies ist aus seiner Feder geflossen, this has proceeded from his pen.

Flie'ßend, p. a. 1) flowing, running; fluid, liquid; drifting (sand); 2) fig. flowing, fluent, smooth, easy; f-e Handschrift, cursive or running hand; f-e Hitze, Iron-w. welding heat; — machen, to dissolve, liquify, melt; eine Sprache — sprechen, to speak a language fluently or with fluency; das F-e des Stils, fluency of style.

Fließ..., in comp. —feder, f. fountain-pen; —garn, n. a large fishing net; —glätte, f. wet litharge; —gold, n. gold found in running water; —harz, n. turpentine.

Flie'ßig, adj. fleecy.

Fließ..., in comp. —loch, n. Smelt. furnace-door; —papier, n. blotting- or sinking-paper; —wasser, n. 1) running-water; 2) Anat. lymph.

Flie'te, (w.) f., Fliet'messer, (str.) n. Vet. fleam; Surg. lancet; Weav. flute.

Flim'mer, (str.) m. 1) see Glimmer; 2) see Flitter; 3) see Schimmer; —bewegung, f. Physiol. ciliary motion; —epithel, n. Anat. ciliated epithelium (Wimperepithel).

Flim'mern, or Flim'mern, (w.) v. intr. to glitter, glimmer, twinkle, glisten, sparkle, scintillate; das —, (str.) s. a. glittering, scintillation (of the stars).

Flin'der, (str.) m. 1) provinc. see Flitter; 2) flounder (Flunder). [brisk, light, alert.

Flink, adj. nimble, quick, active, dapper,

Flin'ke, (w.) f. bleak. [mern.

Flin'ken, Flin'kern, (w.) v. intr. see Flim-

Flin'ker, (str.) m. see Flitter; —erz, n. glittering lumps of ore.

Flink'messer, (str.) n. latherkin (Strei-[illegible]).

Flin'se, (w.) f. see Fliese.

Flin'te, (w.) f. gun, musket, fire-lock.

Flin'ten..., in comp. —beschlag, m. mounting of a gun; —bohrmühle, f. musket-boring-mill; —dolch, m. bayonet (Bajonett); —[illegible], n. gun-cock; —hammer, m. gun-hammer; —kolben, m. butt-end of a gun; —krätzer, m. gun-worm; —kugel, f. musket-ball; —lauf, m., —rohr, n. gun-barrel; (musket) barrel; —riemen, m. gun-sling; —schaft, m. gun-stock; —schloß, n. gun-lock, fire-lock; —schloßblech, n. lock-plate of a gun; —[illegible], m. musket-case; —schuß, m. gun-shot, musket-shot; —schütze, m. fusileer; —spieß, m. see —dolch; —stein, m. (gun-)flint; —[illegible], m. covering for a gun; —[illegible], n. see Doppelflinte & Buchsflinte.

Flint..., in comp. —glas, n. flint-glass; —sand, m. flint or pebble-sand.

Flinz, (str.) m. Miner. sparry iron-stone ([illegible]).

[illegible], (w.) v. intr. to glitter, flit.

[illegible], (str.) n. Smelt. sheet-iron.

[illegible]..., in comp. —bogen, m. a boy's bow; —[illegible], m. a boy's arrow in his bow; —[illegible], f. see [illegible].

[illegible], (str.) m. & (w.) f. [illegible] Flit-terchen, [str.] n.) 1) spangle, tinsel; 2) Mar. see —segel.

Flit'ter..., in comp. —amboß, m. spangle-maker's anvil; —glanz, m. tinsel, false lustre; —glas, n. T. pounded glass, frost; —gold, n. brass-foil, leaf-brass, leaf-gold; —gras, n. Bot. middle or common quaking grass, shakers, ladies' hair (Briza media L.).

Flit'terhaft, Flit'terig, adj. (of) tinsel; fig. light, showy.

Flit'ter..., in comp. —haube, f. cap with spangles; —jahr, n. first year of marriage; —kram, m. tinsel-finery; —macher, m. spangle-maker; —monat, m. see —wochen. [glisten.

Flit'tern, (w.) v. intr. to glitter, sparkle,

Flit'ter..., in comp. —sand, m. micaceous or sparkling sand; —schein, —schimmer, m. see —glanz; —schmiele, f. Bot. a species of hair-grass (Aira flexuosa Roth.); —segel, n. Mar. spanker-sail; —staat, m., —tand, m., —werk, n. (tawdry) finery, tinsel, gewgaws, foppery; —witz, m. shallow witticism; —wochen, f. pl. honey-moon.

Flit'tich, provinc. for Fittig.

Flitz..., in comp. see Flitsch ....

Flit'zen, (w.) v. intr. to flit.

Flo'cke, (w.) f., Flo'cken, (str.) m. 1) flake, tuft, lock, flock; flue; 2) hards (of hemp or flax); waste-wool; 3) Min. flaky stone.

Flo'cken, (w.) v. I. tr. to beat into flocks; II. intr. to come down in flakes (like snow); to flake.

Flo'cken..., in comp. —artig, adj. see Flockicht; —bett, n. flock-bed, wadded or quilted bed; —binse, f. see Wollgras; —blume, f. Bot. centaury, knap-weed (Centaurea L.); —erz, n. Miner. filamentous arseniate of lead; —gestäube, n. Smelt. mill; —lesen, n. Med. floccillation; —maschine, f. see Flockmaschine; —papier, n. flock-paper; —papiertapete, f. flock-paper hanging; —salpeter, m. efflorescent saltpetre; —seide, f. floss-silk, flock-silk; —tuch, n. coarse cloth; —weise, adv. in flakes; —wolle, f. waste or loose wool.

Flock..., in comp. —feder, f. see Flaumfeder; —feuer, n. flashing fire, flame; —gestäube, n. see Flockengestäube.

Flock'icht, Flock'ig, adj. like flocks or locks; flocky, flaky, flocculent, Miner. filamentous, woolly. [engine.

Flock'maschine, (w.) f. Mech. scutching

Flock'seide, Flock'wolle, see Flockenseide &c.

Floh, (str., pl. Flöh'e) m. Entom. flea; Einem einen — ins Ohr setzen, coll. to send any one away with a flea in his ear; —alant, m. see —kraut, 1; —biß, —stich, m. flea-bite; —braun, adj. see —farben. [from ....

Flöh'en, (w.) v. tr. to catch, pick the fleas

Floh'..., in comp. —fang, m. flea-catching; —farbe, f. flea-colour, puce-colour; —farben, —farbig, adj. puce-coloured; —käfer, m. see Dorler; —kräuterig, m. see —kraut, 3; —kraut (or Flöh'kraut), n. Bot. 1) flea-bane (Pulicaria vulgaris Gärtn.); 2) flea-wort (Plantago psyllium L. & arenaria WK.); 3) willow wood, smart-weed, smart-wort (Polygonum persicaria L. & Hydropiper); —krebs, m. Crust. flea-lobster (Gammarus pulex F.); —same, m. Bot. seed of flea-wort (Plantago arenaria WK.).

* Flor, s. (Lat. flos, Gen. floris) I. (str., pl. Flo're or [w.] Flo'ren) m. 1) bloom, blossom, blooming-time; 2) collection of blooming flowers; 3) fig. flourishing state: ein — von Hyacinthen, a blow of hyacinths; in — sein, to flourish; in — bringen, to render flourishing; II. (str., pl. gener. Flö're) m. 1) crape, gauze; 2) fig. *, veil; Einem den — von den Augen ziehen, fig. to undeceive one.

Flo'ra, f. 1) Rom. Myth. Flora, the goddess of flowers; 2) (pl. (w.) Flo'ren) Nat. flora (the plants peculiar to a country). — Flora'lien, n. pl. floral games.

Flor'..., in comp. —ähnlich, —artig, adj. gauze-like, gauzy; —band, n. gauze-ribbon, love-ribbon; —binde, f. crape-band.

Flo'ren, adj. of gauze or crape, gauzy.

Floren'tia, f. Florence (P. N.).

Florenti'ner, (str.) m., F-in, (w.) f., Florenti'nisch, adj. Florentine; —atlas, m. Comm. florentine.

Floren'tius, m. Florence (P. N.).

Florenz', n. Geogr. Florence (town in Italy).

* Floret(t)', (str., pl. F-e) n. (Fr.) 1) (fencing-)foil; 2) (—seide, f.) (silk) ferret, flirt silk, flock- or floss-silk; floret-silk; —band, n. ferret-ribbon.

Flor'..., in comp. —fliege, f. Entom. golden eye, pearl-fly (Hemerobius [Chrysopa] perla L.); —haube, f. gauze-cap; —hut, m. 1) crape-hat; crape-bonnet; 2) hat with a crape-band.

Flo'rig, adj. see Floren.

* Florin' [pr. flörăng'], (str., pl. F-e) m. (Fr.) florin (a coin of different values, cf. Gulden).

* Flori'ren, (w.) v. intr. (Lat.) lit. & fig. to flourish. — Florist', (w.) m. florist.

Flor'..., in comp. —kappe, f. see —haube; —kleid, n. gauze-dress; —seide, f. a kind of organzine; —stuhl, m. gauze-loom; —tuch, n. gauze or crape kerchief.

* Flos'kel, (w.) f. (Lat.) (rhetorical) flourish; lateinische F-n, scraps of Latin. — Flos'keln, (w.) v. intr. to use (rhetorical) flourishes.

Floß, (str., pl. Flöß'e) n. 1) raft, float, boat; 2) provinc. running water, stream; 3) Iron-w. pig or bloom (of iron); 4) float (on nets and fishing-lines).

Floß'... or Flöß'..., in comp. —amt, n. float-office; —beamter, m. inspector of rafts; —bett, n. 1) scaffolding of a rammer; Smelt. pig-mould; —brücke, f. floating-bridge; Floßbutter, f. clarified butter.

Flos'se, (w.) f. 1) fin; 2) F-n, pl. Fish. floats, buoys on a fishing net.

Flö'ße, (w.) f. 1) the floating of timber down a stream; 2) float, raft; 3) see Floß, 4; 4) see Floßrecht; 5) trough for washing tin-ore.

Flö'ßen, (w.) v. tr. 1) to float; 2) see Einflößen; 3) to skim (milk); 4) to fish with a floating or buoying net; 5) provinc. to rinse (linen-clothes). — Flö'ßer, (str.) m. raftsman.

Floß'... or Flöß'..., in comp. —feder, f. fin; —führer, m. raftsman; —füßig, adj. having fin-like feet; —gallen, pl. see Stringallen; —garn, —netz, n. Fish. a floating (fishing-)net; —haken, m. raftsman's hook; —holz, n. floated wood or timber.

Flos'sig, adj. finny, having fins.

Floß'... or Flöß'..., in comp. —loch, n. water-gate; —meister, m. overseer of a timber-yard; —ofen, m. Smelt. flowing-furnace; —ordnung, f. regulation for the floating of wood; —platz, m. floated-timber-yard, wood yard for floated wood; —recht, n., —gerechtigkeit, f. the right of floating timber on a river; —seide, f. see Flockseide; —wasser, n. water on which timber is floated. [3) see Spule, 1.

Flö'te, (w.) f. 1) Mus. flute; 2) see Fleute;

Flö'ten, (w.) v. tr. & intr. 1) to play on the flute; 2) to sing (of a nightingale); — gehen, coll. 1. to be lost, vulg. to go to the dogs; 2. to lie.

Flö'ten..., in comp. —baß, m. 1) recorder (organ-stop); 2) see Baßflöte; —begleitung, f. flute-accompaniment; —bläser, m. flute-player, flutist; —bohrer, m. 1) flute-maker; 2) T. auger; —futter, n. flute-case; —maul, n. Ichth. Chinese trumpet-fish (Aulostoma chinensis C.); —pfeife, f. open pipe (in an

strauch; –rohr, n. Bot. common lilac (Syringa vulgaris L.); –spieler, m. see –bläser; –stock, m. flute-stick; –zug, m., –register, n. flute-stop (in organs). [(Bertin abbiam Shw.).

Flö'ter, (str.) m. Ornith. piping crow

* **Flotil'le**, (w.) f. (Fr.) squadron, flotilla.

Flötist', (w.) m. flute-player, flutist.

Flotsch'en, (w.) v. intr. provinc. to paddle (about).

Flott, adj. 1) swimming, afloat, floaty; 2) fig. a) abundant, luxurious: da ging es — zu, there were jolly doings; b) merry, jolly, fast; ein f-er Bursche, rollicky chap, gay dog; dashing fellow: — leben, to lead a jolly life, to live high or in clover; Mar-s. nur eben —, water-borne: nicht —, beneaped; — liegend, T. floating, flushing; — machen, to get or set afloat, to haul off; — sein, to float; wieder — werden, to get off again.

Flott, s. provinc. I. (str., pl. (w.) Flot'ten) n. (N. G.) 1) see Floß; 2) pl. a) Ship-carp. punts or floating stages; b) see Flosse, 2; 3) Mar. stove; II. (str.) n. 1) cream, see Rahm; 2) fat or grease swimming on the top.

Flot'te, (w.) f. 1) fleet: navy; 2) Dy. dye, dyeing fluid; F-nabtheilung, f. detachment of a squadron: F-ncapitän, m. captain of the navy; (wirklicher) post-captain; F-nführer, m. admiral: F-noffizier, m. naval officer.

* **Flottir'en**, (w.) v. intr. (Fr.) to float, to waver; to fluctuate, to be uncertain (fluctuiren); f-de Bevölkerung, fluctuating population (population not residing permanently at a place); f-de Schuld, see Schwebende Schuld.

Flott'..., in comp. –milch, f. sheep's milk; –seide, f. Com. untwisted silk; –stahl, m. hard steel.

Flötz, Flöz, (str.) n. Geol. & Miner. (–lage, –schicht, f.) horizontal stratum, flotz; in F-en, in layers, stratified; –asche, f. earthy marl; –bau, m. Min. working of a layer; –erz, n. ore in beds; –formation, f., –gebirge, n. flotz-formation, mountains formed in horizontal layers, sedimentary rocks; –granit, m. secondary granite; –grünstein, m. dolerite; –kalk, m. common compact lime-stone; –kluft, f. fissure in a stratum, fault; –porphyr, m. secondary sandstone (Weil); –riffel, m. sterile lode; –sandstein, m. new red sandstone (Weil); –schicht, see above; –schwarte, f. upper stratum of a slate quarry; –weise, adv. in layers, beds, strata.

Fluch, (str., pl. Flü'che) m. 1) curse, malediction, imprecation, execration; blasphemy; 2) accursed person, curse; — über dich, a curse upon you; damnation on thee! –beladen, adj. laden with a curse, under a curse.

Flu'chen, (w.) v. I. intr. (with Dat. or auf [with Acc.]) 1) to curse, imprecate, execrate; to swear, blaspheme; auf Einen —, to swear at one; 2) coll. for Schwören, to take one's oath (on); II. tr. to wish, affix by imprecation; to swear. [Fluchwürdig.

Flu'chenswerth, Flu'chenswürdig, see

Flu'cher, (str.) m. curser, swearer, blasphemer. [curse or swear.

Flu'chig, adj. (Archit. l. u.) disposed to

Flucht, (w.) f. I. 1) T. play, full play, swing, scope, space, room; 2) a) straight line; range, row; zwei Zimmer in einer —, two rooms on one floor; b) flight of steps, see Treppen-Absatz; 3) Forest. break of a wood; 4) Archit. line of direction; II. 1) flight; rout; escape, run; slip; 2) Sport. a) flight of birds, cf. Flug, 2; b) place of refuge, volery; die — ergreifen or nehmen, sich auf die — begeben, see Flüchten, I.; Mar. to sheer off, to run or scud for it; das Schiff liegt in der —, the ship is in her sailing-trim; in die — schlagen or treiben, to put to flight; to rout (an army); er ist vor ihm stets in der —, coll. he is afraid of his censure, &c., he fears him;

very much; –bau, m. Sport. retreat in a kennel or burrow (of a fox, &c.).

Flüch'ten, (w.) v. I. intr. (aux. sein) & refl. to flee, to take to flight, run away, escape; to fly (to), to make one's escape; II. tr. to save by flight, to secure.

Flüch'tig, adj. 1) flying, fugitive: fig-s. 2) fleeting, transient, transitory, perishable; 3) Chem. volatile; 4) fleet, light, nimble, easy; fig-s. 5) fickle, volatile, inconstant; giddy: 6) slight, passing, cursory, hasty, flighty, superficial, careless; vague; desultory: — werden, sich — machen, to become fugitive, take to flight, to abscond, run away, coll. to bolt; eine f-e Hand, a cursive or short hand: f-e Gewänder, Paint. flowing robes: Fort-s. f-e Befestigungskunst, f. temporary fortification: f-e Sappe, f. flying sap; f-es Gestein, Miner. brittle stone (rock); — ansehen, to pass one's eye over; selbst eine f-e Durchsicht des Werkes, even a cursory examination of the work (will convince the reader, &c.); — durchsehen, to run over, to skim.

† **Flüch'tigen**, (w.) v. refl. see Flüchten.

Flüch'tigkeit, (w.) f. 1) fugacity; 2) Chem. volatility; 3) fleetness, lightness; 4) flightiness, fickleness, giddiness; 5) desultoriness, cursoriness, &c. cf. Flüchtig.

Flücht'ling, (str.) m. 1) fugitive, refugee: deserter; 2) (l. u.) inconstant, giddy person; F-schaft, (w.) f. (l. u.) state or situation of a fugitive.

Flucht'..., in comp. –linie, f. Persp. vanishing line; –recht, adj. worked fair (Mas., &c. of a wall, &c.): –röhre, f. see –bau; –schleuse, f. outlet-sluice; –stäbe, m. pl. (ranging) poles, boning rods.

Fluch'würdig, adj. execrable, (ac)cursed.

Flück, adj. provinc. see Flügge.

Flu'der, (str.) n. T. a course for water, a canal, (mill-)race; –brücke, f. bridge over a channel.

Flü'elerche, (w.) f., **Flü'evögel**, (str., pl. F-vögel) m. Ornith. alpine hedge-sparrow (Accentor alpinus L.).

Flug, s. I. (str., pl. Flü'ge) m. 1) the (act of) flying; flight, soaring; Fals. career; 2) flight, flock, swarm (of birds); Sport-s. flight or brood (of pigeons), cast (of hawks), nye (of pheasants), walk (of snipes), watch (of nightingales), bevy (of quails), covey (of partridges): ein — Bienen, a swarm of bees; 3) Med. lichen; im F-e, 1. flying, on the wing: im F-e schießen, to shoot flying: 2. fig. in a hurry; II. in comp. –bahn, f. Phys. trajectory (of a missile), projectile curve, range; –bett, n. T. hidden bottom of a mill, where the mill-dust is gathered; –beulen, pl. Med. shingles: –beutler, pl. Zool. a genus of marsupials with a kind of wing-membrane (Petaurus Shaw.); –biene, f. working bee; –blatt, n. fugitive piece, cf. –schrift; –brand, m. Agr. rot (in corn) (Uredo segetum Persoon).

Flu'ge, (w.) f. Miner. flaky stone.

Flü'gel, s. I. (str.) m. 1) lit. & fig. wing; pinion; 2) Mus. Instr-m. grand or royal piano; 3) Archit. a) wing (of a building); b) a cross-aisle (of a church), transept; 4) flap, skirt (of a coat); 5) a) leaf valve, fold, (either side or part of a folding door); b) casement (of a window); stehender —, dead sash (of a sash-window); c) sweep (of a wind-mill); d) Mech. back, fly, flyer (of a spindle); e) rest (of a bathing-bench); f) aa) wing (of a bridge); bb) leaf or flap of a draw-bridge; 6) Mar., &c. a) vane, weather-cock; b) palm, fluke (of an anchor); 7) Mil. wing; — einer Haube, flap (of a woman's cap), lappet; — (pl.) der Nase, wings of the nose; mit den F-n schlagen, to flap the wings; die — hängen lassen, fig. to be crestfallen, to despond, flag; II. in comp. –adjutant, m. adjutant-major; –artig, adj. wing-like; Anat.

[illegible]

Flugs [pr. flux; l. u. flugs, i. e. flüchtig], adv. (originally on the wing) in a hurry, quickly, speedily, instantly. [Feldwand.

Fluh, Flüh'e, (w.) f. 1) stratum; 2) see Fluh'vögel, see Flühvogel. [(Lat.) fluid.

* Flu'idum, (str., pl. [Lat.] Flu'ida) n.

Flun'der, Flün'der, (str.) m. Ichth. flounder, shard, but-end (Platessa flesus L.).

Flunk, (str.) m., Flun'ke, (w.) f. hook, fluke, palm (of an anchor).

Flunkerei', (w.) f. 1) (the act or practice of) bragging; shuffling, fibbing; 2) fib, flam.

Flun'kern, (w.) v. intr. provinc. 1) see Funkeln; 2) coll. a) to brag, boast; b) to shuffle, tell fibs.

* Flu'or, Fluorin', (str.) n. (Lat.) Chem.-s. fluor, fluorin; in comp. –bor(on)gas, n. fluoboric-gas; –bor(on)säure, f. fluoboric-acid; –kieselsäure, f. fluosilic-acid; –kieselsaure Salz, –silikat, n. fluosilicate.

Flur, s. I. (w.) f. 1) field, plain, level ground; 2) plot or piece of ground belonging to a village, village-field, pasture, common; 3) (also [str.] m.) a) floor, flooring; b) entrance-hall of a house; corridor; II. in comp. –Begang, m. see –gang; –buch, n. terrier, register of lands; –deck, f. floor-cloth.

Flu'ren, (w.) v. tr. 1) to floor, to pave; 2) to perambulate (cf. Begehen) the boundaries of (a village or township), in order to inspect or to fix them, fam. to run the bounds.

Flur'..., in comp. –gang, m. 1) perambulation (Begehung), inspection of lands (cf. Fluren); 2) see Flur, 3, b; –graben, m. boundary-ditch of fields; –grenze, f. see –scheidung; –hölzer, n. pl. see Bauchstücke; –hüter, m. see –schütz; –recht, n. jurisdiction over the fields of a village or township.

Flur'ren, (w.) v. intr. to buzz.

Flur'..., in comp. –scheidung, f. confines, boundaries, borders of village-fields; –schütz, m. ranger; field-guard, watch; –stein, m. 1) mark, boundary stone; 2) square-tile, flag; –tuch, n. see –decke; –ziegel, m. paving-tile or brick.

Fluß, (str., pl. Flüs'se) m. 1) flow: a) flowing, flux; b) fig. fluency; 2) river; (den) – abwärts, down the river, down stream; (den) – aufwärts, up the river, up stream; 3) Med. fluxion, flux, course, or discharge of (diseased) humours; catarrh, rheum, cold; (im Munde) catch; weißer –, the whites, blenorrhea; 4) fusion, melting; melted metal; Metall., &c. flux; Metalle im F–e, metals in fusion; in – bringen, to put into fusion, to fuse, to render fluid or liquefy (by heat); Miner. fluor; Chem. calcined potash; 5) T. paste; 6) water (of diamonds); 7) Gam. flush (at cards).

Fluß'..., in comp. fluviatic, fluvial; –adler, m. river-eagle (Entenadler); –ammoniak, m. fluorid of ammonia; –arche, f. Moll. river-ark; –artig, adj. 1) river-like; 2) Med. catarrhal, catarrhous; –äther, m. Chem. fluoric ether; –bad, n. river-bath; –bau, m. works carried out on the shore of a river; –bett, n. channel, bed of a river; –bewohner, m. one dwelling near a river; –bundsfisch, –brassen, m. Ichth. bream (Abramis brama L.); –bricke, f. river-lamprey (Petromyzon fluviatilis L.). [river, rivulet.

Flüß'chen, (str.) n. (dimin. of Fluß) small

Fluß'..., in comp. –eisen, n. T. bloom (of [illegible]); –erde, f. Miner. earthy fluor-spar; –fahrt, f. river-trip, sail or run on the river; –fall, m. fall of a river; –fieber, n. rheumatic fever, [illegible] fever, influenza; –fisch, m. river-fish, fresh-water fish; –flachsadler, see –adler; –gebiet, f. bed or formation of a river; –gott, f. [illegible], angel, vengeance; –grundel, f. a species of [illegible] ([illegible]); –gebiet, n. the whole [illegible] watered or drained by a river; –gott, m. river-god; –grundel, m. Ichth. loach (Cobitis barbatula L.); –hafen, m. river-harbour; –harz, n. Pharm. gum-animi.

Flüs'sig, I. adj. 1) fluid, liquid; fusible; melted; 2) Med. affected by rheum, rheumy; 3) Comm. disposable (Disponibel); f–e Capitalien, ready-money-funds, cash-funds; – machen, 1. to render fluid, to liquefy; 2. Comm. to unlock (funds); – werden, 1. to become liquid, to deliquate; 2. Comm. to fall due; II. F–keit, (w.) f. 1) fluidness, fluidity, liquidity; 2) fluid, liquor; 3) Med. humour; F–keitsmaß, n. liquid or wet measure.

Fluß'..., in comp. –insel, f. bank or small island formed in a river by gravel or mud; holm; –karpfen, m. Zool. river-carp (Cyprinus carpio L.); –kieselsauer, adj. Chem. fluosilicate; –kieselsaures Salz, fluosilicate; –krebs, m. Crust. river-crawfish (Astacus fluviatilis F.); –messer, n. tawer's shaving-knife; –mittel, n. Med. & Chem. flux; Med. anti-catarrhal; –moos, n. water-moss; –muschel, f. fresh-water-muscle (clam) (Unio Retz); –nachtigall, f. see Rohrdrossel; –napf, m. Moll. river-limpet; –ochse, m. see –pferd; –ofen, m. blast-furnace; –otter, f. Zool. common otter (Fischotter); –pferd, n. Zool. hippopotamus, river-horse, water-elephant (Hippopotamus amphibius L.); –pflanze, f. fluvial or fluviatic plant; –pflaster, n. rheumatic plaster; –pricke, f. see –bricke; –pulver, n. 1) powder of fusion; 2) Med. rheumatic powder; –reich, adj. abounding in rivers, streamy; –sand, m. river-sand; –säure &c., see –spathsäure; –scheide, f. see –gabelung; –schiff, n. river-ship, (river-)boat; –schiffer, m. captain or master of a (river-)boat, sweet- (or fresh-) water-man, cf. Stromschiffer; –schifffahrt, f. river-navigation or -traffic; –schlamm, m. river-silt; –schwalbe, f. Ornith. (river-)plover (Charadrius minor M. et W. [fluviatilis Bechst.]); –schwein, n. Zool. cabiai, thick-nosed tapir (Hydrochaerus capybara L.); –spath, m. 1) Miner. fluor spar, fluoride of calcium; 2) Farr. blood spavin; Chem.-s. –spathsauer, adj. fluoric, hydrofluoric; –spathsaure Salz, n. hydrofluate, fluate; –spathsäure, f. hydrofluoric acid, fluor(ic) acid; –spathsaure Soda, f. cryolite; –stein, m. 1) river-stone; 2) Miner. compact fluor-spar; –stoff, m. Med. rheumatic matter; –strecke, f. (gerade) reach; –system, n. network of streams and torrents; –taucher, m. see Dachente; –transport, m. conveyance by water; –trische, f. see Kolbutte; –uferläufer, m. Ornith. sand-piper (Totanus hypoleucos L.); –verpfählung, f. Fort., &c. stoccade; –wage, f. Hydr. level with a T-square; –wasser, n. river-water.

Flüs'tern, (w.) v. tr. & intr. to whisper.

Flut, Fluth, s. I. (w.) f. 1) flood; inundation; 2) high-water, (high-)tide; F–en, floods, waves, billows; Ebbe und –, ebb and tide, see Ebbe; die erste –, beginning of the flood; die letzte –, end of the flood; hohe –, full sea, full tide, high-water; die volle –, spring-tide; die niedrige or taube –, neap-tide, dead-neap; die – kommt, the tide flows, comes, makes, sets in or is coming on, it is flowing water; die – geht, the tide goes out, ebbs, or falls, it is ebbing water; mit der – fahren, to (take the) tide; II. in comp. –anker, m. flood-anchor; –berg, m. Min. heap of poor ore; –bett, n. see –gang; –brecher, m. flood- or tide-breaker.

Flöt'te, (w.) f. see Flotte.

Flu'ten, Flu'then, (w.) v. intr. 1) to flow; to swell, rise, tide; 2) fig. to stream, crowd; es flutet, the tide flows (die Flut kommt).

Flut'..., in comp. –gang, m. 1) channel; 2) mill-trough, leat; –gatter, n. see –thor; –gerinne, n. 1) waste-weir; 2) see –gang; –graben, m. see –gang, 2; –hafen, m. dry-harbour; tide-harbour; –höhe, f. water-level.

Flu'tig, Flu'tenhaft, adj. rushing along, &c. like a flood, in floods.

Flut'..., in comp. –karte, f. tide or tidal chart; –messer, m. tide-gage; –mühle, f. tide-mill; –rad, n. hydraulic wheel; –schleuße, f. tide-lock; –thor, n., –thür, f. tide- (or flood-)gate; –wasser, n. 1) water of the mill-race; 2) tidal water; –werk, n. Min. stream-work; –zeichen, n. flood-mark, water-mark; –zeit, f. flood-tide, high-water; es war – zeit, the tide made.

* Fluxion', (w.) f. (Lat.) Math. fluxion; F–sgröße, f. fluency, flowing-quantity.

* Focal', adj. (Lat.) focal, relating to the focus; –distanz, f. focal distance (Brennweite).

Fock, (str.) m. see Focke, 2.

Fock..., in comp. Mar.-s. –brassen, f. pl. fore-braces; –buline, f. fore-bowline; –drehreep, n. fore-tye.

Fock'e, (w.) f. 1) Mar. see Focksegel; 2) the night heron (Nachtreiher).

Fock..., in comp. Mar.-s. –furbeele, pl. fore-jears; –mast, m. fore-mast; –raa, f. fore-yard; –segel, n. fore-sail; –stag, n. fore-stay; –stenge, f. fore-top-mast; –stengenleesegel, n. fore-top-mast steering-sail; –wand, f. fore-shrouds.

* Fo'cus, (pl. [Lat.] Fo'ci) m. (Lat.) Opt. focus, distinct base; –länge, f. focal length.

* Föderal', adj. (Lat.) federal. – Föderalisi'ren, (w.) v. tr. to confederate, join in a league. – Föderalis'mus, m. federalism. – Föderalist', (w.) m. federalist. – Föderalis'tisch, adj. federalist. – Föderativ', adj. federative, federal; –staat, m. federal state. – Föderirt', p. a. confederate.

Fo'dern, (w.) v. tr. (†, * &) provinc. for Fordern.

Föhl, Föl, (w.) f. provinc. (N. G.) a small inlet, creek, cove.

Foh'le, (w.) f. used by Schiller, Æneide 4, 94 for Stutenfüllen, filly.

Foh'len, (w.) v. intr. to foal.

Foh'len, (str.) n. see Füllen.

Föhn, Fön, (str.) m. & f. a humid south wind in the valleys and on the lakes of Switzerland; a storm.

Föhr'de, (w.) f. (N. G.) creek, inlet.

Foh're, (w.) f. I. see Forelle; II. or Föh're, f. fir (Pinus silvestris L. [Kiefer]).

Föh'ren, I. adj. of fir, fir; II. in comp. –baum, m. fir-tree; –eule, see Fichteneule; –klotz, m. fir-block.

Foh'lich, adj. coll. decayed, soft; (of wood, &c.) rotten, unsound, &c. (cf. Boll, 2, Mürbe &c.).

Föl'chen, (str.) n. see Felchen.

Fol'ge, (w.) f. 1) a) succession, sequence, sequel, continuation; b) series, line, train; order; c) set, collection, suit; flush, run (of cards); 2) †, suit, attendance; 3) sequel: a) time to come, futurity, future; b) event; consequence; issue, end, result, effect; 4) (logical) sequence, consecution, conclusion, inference; 5) Sport. the right of following and taking wounded game upon another's property; in der –, subsequently; for the (or in) future, hereafter; in –, zu – (with Gen.), in consequence of, owing to; in pursuance of, conformably or agreeably to, in compliance with ...; dem zu –, in pursuance or consequence of which; zur – haben, to cause, occasion; die – sein von ..., to be owing to ... or the consequence of ..., to result from ...; – leisten or geben (with Dat.), to comply (with), to attend (to ...), to obey, observe; gerichtlicher Vorladung – leisten, Law, to answer a summons, to answer in law.

Fol'ge..., in comp. –alter, n. times to come, aftertimes; –güter, n. pl. Law, second-any goods; —jahr, n. subsequent year; —leistung, f. (ready) obedience.

Fol'gen, (w.) v. intr. (aux. sein) (with Dat.) 1) to follow, attend; 2) to succeed; 3) to follow, ensue, result (aus, from), to be the consequence (of); 4) (aux. haben) to obey; to follow, to be guided by, to listen to; — lassen, see Verabfolgen lassen; seinen Lüsten —, to indulge one's desires; seinem Kopfe —, to follow one's bent or inclination, to persist in (or to adhere pertinaciously to) one's own opinion, to be obstinately bent on one's purpose; dem Strom —, to go, swim with or down the stream; dem Strom der öffentlichen Meinung —, to yield to the current of public opinion; (lautend &c.) wie folgt, as follows; — Sie mir, take or follow my advice, do as I would have you; seinem Glücke —, to take one's fortune; Fortsetzung folgt, to be continued; dem Wunsch folgt der Gedanke, the wish is father to the thought; was folgt daraus? what then? f—d, p. a. following, ensuing, &c., subsequent; auf einander f—d, successive, consecutive; am f—den Tage, the day following or after, the next day; f—de Woche, next week.

Fol'gendergestalt, Fol'gendermaßen, adv. in the following manner, as follows.

Fol'gends, adv. †, afterwards; in future.

Fol'genlos, adj. without any consequences, of no effect.

Fol'genreich, Fol'genschwer, adj. of important consequences, results.

Fol'ger, (str.) m. 1) follower; 2) successor; 3) T. & Horol. a sliding-plate in the balance; Rope-m. leper, leaper.

Fol'gerecht, adj. in due succession, by order of succession; consequent, consequential; consistent, logical.

Folgerei', (w.) f. the (act or practice of) drawing false conclusions or inferences, false or useless reasoning.

Fol'ge..., in comp. —reihe, f. order of succession; series; —richtig, see —recht; —richtigkeit, f. right logical consequence, congruity.

Fol'gern, (w.) v. tr. to infer, conclude (aus, from); to reason; falsch —, to draw a false inference, to misinfer.

Fol'gerung, (w.) f 1) the (act of) inferring, &c.; 2) conclusion, induction, implication; inference, consequence; durch —, by induction, &c., inductively; eine — machen, ziehen, to draw a conclusion, inference, or argument; auf — beruhend, inferential; F-satz, m. deduction, conclusion, corollary; f-sweise, adv. inductively, inferentially.

Fol'ge..., in comp. —satz, m. deduction, conclusion, Math. porism; —stern, m. Astr. satellite; —welt, f. see Nachwelt; —widrig, adj. inconsequent, incoherent; inconsistent; —widrigkeit, f. inconsequence, &c.; —zeiger, m. Typ. catchword (at the bottom of a page); —zeit, f. time to come, futurity, aftertimes, afterdays.

Folg'lich, adv. consequently, by (in) consequence, of course, therefore.

Folg'sam, I. adj. obedient, tractable, complying, pliant, dutiful; II. F-keit, (w.) f. obedience, tractableness, pliancy, complying disposition.

* **Foliant',** (w.) m. (from Folio) folio (-volume), book in folio. — **Fo'lie,** (w.) f. (Lat.) foil; (in Ringen) tent; mit — belegen, to foliate, silver; einer Sache (Dat.) eine — geben, fig. to set a thing off; F-nschläger, m. T. (leaf-)beater. — **Folii'ren,** (w.) v. tr. 1) to page; foliirt, Comm. folioed; 2) to foliate (mit Folie belegen). — **Folii'rung,** (w.) f. 1) the (act of) paging; 2) foliation.

* **Fo'lio,** (str., pl. F-s) n. 1) a) (from the Lat. in folio, of the size of a sheet of paper once folded) folio, large page; b) (or —format) folio; ein Buch in —(format), a folio (-book); 2) (Ital. foglio) leaf, page (in an account-book); ein — in der Bank haben, Comm. to have an account at the bank.

Fol'ter, (w.) f. 1) rack; 2) fig. torture, torment; auf die — spannen or legen, to put to the rack; —bank, f. rack; —geräth, n., —instrument, n. instrument of torture; —kammer, f. torture-chamber; —knecht, m. see Folterer; —pein, —qual, f. racking torture, agony.

Fol'terer, (str.) m. torturer, tormentor.

Fol'tern, (w.) v. tr. to put to the rack; to torture, torment; f—d, p. a. torturing, &c., excruciating.

* **Foment',** (str.) n. fomentation, warm lotion. — **Fomenti'ren,** (w.) v. tr. (Lat.) to foment.

* **Fond** [pr. fong], (str., pl. Fonds) m. (Fr.) 1) funds; a) (capital) stock, capital; b) (public) funds, state papers; — im Handel, stock in trade; 2) fig. fund, ample stock or store. — **Fonds,** m. pl. funds, see Fond; —anweisung, f. appropriation; —besitzer, m. stock-holder, capitalist; —börse, f. stock-exchange; —geschäfte, n. pl. exchange-business; —händler, m. see Actienhändler; —mäkler, m. stock-broker; —markt, m. see —börse; —speculant, m. speculator in the funds.

* **Fontai'ne** [pr. fongtä'ne], (w.) f. (Fr.) (artificial) fountain, jet.

* **Fontanell',** (str.) n., **Fontanel'le,** (w.) f. (L. Lat.) 1) Surg. fontanel, issue, seton; Vet. rowel; ein — anlegen or setzen, to apply a fontanel; 2) Anat. fontanel; —erbse, f., —kügelchen, n. issue-pea; —papier, n. issue-paper; —pflaster, n. issue-plaster.

Fop'pen (dimin. **Föp'peln**), (w.) v. tr. to jeer, banter, rally. — **Fopperei',** (w.) f. banter, jeering, hoax.

* **Force** [pr. för'ße, coll. for'sche], (w.) f. (Fr.) 1) force; 2) Gam. highest card of a suit.

For'che, (w.) f. provinc. for (Föhre).

* **Forciren** [pr. forßi'—], (w.) v. tr. (Fr.) to force; 1) to compel; 2) to take by force or violence; 3) to overdo, over-urge.

† **För'der,** adv. farther, further, see Fürder.

För'der..., in comp. Min-s. —bahn, f. road belonging to a mine; tram-way; —dampfmaschine, f. drawing-engine.

For'derer, (str.) m. demander, &c., dun.

För'derer, (str.) m. furtherer (Beförderer).

För'derfahrt, (w.) f. hurrying-way.

För'dergefäß, (str.) n. skep, gin-tub.

För'derjunge, (w.) m. putter, trammer.

För'derlich, I. adj. 1) (with Dat.) furthering, conducive (to), promoting, useful, serviceable, beneficial; 2) speedy; auf das F-ste, in the speediest manner; II. F-keit, (w.) f. conduciveness, &c.

För'der..., in comp. Min-s. —mann, m. putter, trammer; —maschine, f. machine whim.

For'dern, (w.) v. tr. 1) to demand, ask (von, of), desire, call for; 2) to require; to claim; 3) coll. see Herausfordern; wer an mich zu — hat, whoever has claims on me; die Grafen hatten an freie Männer nichts zu — (J. v. Müller), the Counts had to advance no claims on free men; einen Preis —, to ask a price; zu viel —, to be exacting in the price, to ask out of the way, to overcharge; dringend or heftig —, to crave; zu trinken —, to call for drink; gewaltsam —, to exact; vor Gericht —, to summon before a court; to serve summons upon ..; Rechenschaft von Einem —, or zur Rechenschaft —, to call one to account; — lassen, 1. to send for; to summon; 2. to send a challenge; auf Kugeln —, to challenge with pistols.

För'dern, (w.) v. I. tr. 1) to further, assist, promote, advance; 2) to dispatch; zu Tage —, 1. to bring to day, or light; 2. Min. to draw

board; **—draht**, *m. T.* mould-wire; **—einrichtung**, *f. Typ.* imposing; **—eisen**, *n.* round bodkin for hollowing bullet-moulds.

* **For'mel**, *(w.) f. (Lat.) Math.* rule, (set) form, formula; **—buch**, *n.* formulary.

* **Formell'**, *adj. (Fr.)* formal.

For'men, *(w.) v. tr.* to form; to mould, model, fashion, figure, frame, shape, make; *Hatt.* to put upon the block.

For'men..., *in comp.* **—brett**, *n. see* Formbrett; **—gießer**, *m. see* Formgießer; **—lehre**, *f. T.* that part of grammar which treats of the formation and inflection of words, etymology; **—macher**, *m.* form-cutter, mould-maker; **—mantel**, *m. see* Formbekleidung; **—schneider**, **—stecher**, *m. see* Formschneider; **—trog**, *m. Soap-m.* filling-trough; **—wesen**, *n.* formalism; formalities.

For'mer, *(str.) m.* moulder, &c.

Form'erde, *(w.) f. T.* moulding-clay.

Formerei', *(w.) f.* 1) *or* **Förmerei'**, (act of) moulding; 2) moulding-house.

Form'... *(from* Formen *&* Form*), in comp.* **—erz**, *n.* rich silver-ore; **—fäustel**, *m.* miner's hammer *or* pickaxe; **—fehler**, *m. Law, &c.* informality, flaw; **—futter**, **—futteral**, *n. T.* mantle, coat; **—gebend**, *adj.* formative (power, &c.); **—gebung**, *f.* fashioning; **—gewölbe**, *n. Metall.* twyer-arch; **—gießer**, *m.* moulder in brass, &c.; **—hagel**, *m. see* **—schrot**; **—haken**, *m. T.* tool used in cleaning towels; **—hammer**, *m.* gold-beater's hammer; **—holz**, *n.* frame-board. [shape; fächer—, fan-shaped.

För'mig, *adj. in comp.* having a form *or*

Formir'eisen, *(str.) n.* square-rule.

* **Formi'ren**, *(w.) v. (Lat.) tr. (& refl. Mil., &c.)* to form; die Partien —, (in book-keeping) to post articles of account; sich in Reihen —, *Mil.* to fall in.

Form'... *(from* Formen *&* Form*), in comp.* **—kappe**, *f. T.* shell of a mould; **—kopf**, *m.* wig-maker's block; **—kugel**, *f.* (iron) form-ball; **—kunst**, *f.* art of making moulds for casting; **—lade**, *f.* moulding-table; **—lehm**, *m. see* **—erde**; **—lehre**, *f. see* Formenlehre.

Förm'lich, I. *adj.* 1) formal, ceremonial, stiff; punctilious; proper; 2) plain, express: eine f—e Schlacht, a pitched *or* regular battle; eine f—e Lüge, downright lie; eine f—e Erklärung, declaration in form; II. *adv.* formally, in due form; er hatte es — darauf abgesehen, it was evidently his intention; III. F-keit, *(w.) f.* formality.

Form'los, *adj.* formless, rude, shapeless. — **Form'losigkeit**, *(w.) f.* formlessness, rude state, shapelessness.

Form'... *(from* Formen *&* Form*), in comp.* **—macher**, **—meister**, *m. see* Formenmacher; **—naht**, *f.* seam (of castings); blister (upon clay-pipes, &c.); **—presse**, *f.* gold-beater's press; **—rahmen**, *m. Typ.* chase; *Paper-m.* frame; **—sand**, *m.* moulding sand; **—scheibe**, *f.* upper part of a potter's wheel; **—schneiden**, *n.* form-engraving, print-cutting; **—schneider**, *m.* form-cutter, stamp-cutter; *Paper-m.* framer; **—schrot**, *m.* mould-shot; **—span**, *m. Typ.* reglet; **—spath**, *m. Min.* moulding-spar; **—stechen**, **—stecher**, *see* **—schneiden**, **—schneider**; **—stege**, *m. pl. Typ.* furniture; **—stein**, *m.*, **—stück**, *n. T.* form-piece (in a blast *or* smelting furnace); **—stempel**, *m. Build.* flourishing tool; **—stock**, *m.* glover's forming-stick; **—stößer**, *m.* cleaning iron (for the pipes of the bellows in foundries); **—tisch**, *m. Chandl.* mould-frame.

* **Formular'**, *(str.) n. (Lat.)* (set) form, formulary, specimen; *Law,* precedent; **—buch**, *n.* precedent book.

* **Formuli'ren**, *(w.) v. tr.* to draw up (a contract, &c.); eine Klage —, to set forth a [illegible].

Form'... *(from* Formen *&* Form*), in comp.* **—waaren**, *f. pl. Comm.* figured articles, fancy-articles, fashioned goods; **—wechsel**, *m. Comm.* accommodation-bill.

* **Forsch**, *adj. Stud. slang,* 1) vigorous, sound; hardy, sturdy; powerful, strong; 2) rough, forcible; violent, coarse.

Forsch'... *(from* Forschen*), in comp.* **—begier(de)**, *f.* inquisitiveness, curiosity, thirst of knowledge; **—begierig**, *adj.* inquisitive, curious; **—eisen**, *(l. u.) n. Surg.* probe (Sonde).

For'schen, *(w.) v. intr.* to search (nach, for, after), inquire (after, into), to examine (into); to investigate; *(in an ill sense)* to pry (into); tief —, to scrutinize; Einer der nach Wahrheit forscht, a seeker of truth; bei Einem —, to sound, *coll.* pump a person; f—d, *p. a.* searching, inquisitive (look, &c.); ein forschender Blick, a keen look of scrutiny.

For'scher, *(str.) m.* inquirer, searcher, investigator; **—blick**, *m.* look, eye of an inquirer; searching glance; **—geist**, *m.* spirit of an inquirer, inquiring mind; **—sinn**, *m. see* Forschbegier.

Forsch'kraft, *(str., pl.* F-kräfte*) f.* sagacity.

For'schung, *(w.) f.* inquiry, disquisition, investigation, research; **F-sgeist**, *m.* spirit of inquiry.

A. **Forst**, *(str.) m. (pl.* Förste*) see* Firste.

B. **Forst**, *(str., pl. [l. u.]* Forste *or* Förste, *gener. w.* Forsten*) m.* forest.

Forst..., *in comp.* **—academie**, *f. see* **—schule**; **—amt**, *n.* forest-office, office of woods and forests; **—anschlag**, *m.* taxation, valuation of a forest; **—aufseher**, *m.* agistor, keeper of a forest; **—beamte(te)**, *m.* officer of the forest; **—bediente**, *m.* forester's assistant; **—begang**, **—belauf**, **—beritt**, *m. see* **—revier**; **—bereiter**, *m.* mounted forest-inspector; **—bezirk**, *m.* forest-district; **—buch**, *n.* 1) book about forest-matters; 2) code of forest-laws; **—casse**, *f.* office of the forest-revenues; **—dienst**, *m.* 1) *see* **—frohne**; 2) employment *or* office in the forest; **—direction**, *f.* forest-board. [Försterei.

Forstei', *(w.) f.* 1) *see* Forstrevier; 2) *see*

Forstei'lich, *adj.* relating to a forest-district *or* forest-house.

Forst'en, *(w.) v. tr.* 1) to afforest (Verforsten); 2) *see* Einforsten.

Förs'ter, *(str.) m.* forest-keeper, keeper, under-keeper, forester, warden; ranger.

Försterei', *(w.) f.* 1) ranger's district *or* place; 2) ranger's house, forest-house; 3) woodman's craft (Jägerei).

Forst..., *in comp.* **—frevel**, *m.* trespass *or* infringement of the forest-laws; rape of the forest, assart; **—frohne**, *f.* forest-average *or* day's-work; **—gebühren**, *f. pl.* fees *or* dues to be paid to a forester; **—gefälle**, *n.* revenue arising from forests; **—geräume**, *n.* glade, piece of forest-land cleared; **—gerecht**, *adj.* 1) skilled in forest-matters; 2) properly kept (of a forest); **—gerechtigkeit**, *f. see* **—recht**, 1; **—gericht**, *n.* forest-court, court of attachment, † woodm[illegible]swainmote; **—gerichtsbarkeit**, *f.* jurisdiction of a forest-court; **—gesetz**, *n.* forest-law; **—haus**, *n.* forest-house, house of a forester *or* ranger; **—herr**, *m.* free-holder of a forest; **—hube**, **—hufe**, *f.* forest's district *or* extent; **—hut**, *f.* inspection of a forest; **—hüter**, *m.* keeper of a forest, wood-ward, forester's assistant.

Forst'ig, I. *adj. see* Forstlich; II. F-keit, *(w.) f.* 1) *see* Forstrevier; 2) *see* Forstgerechtigkeit.

Forst..., *in comp.* **—inspector**, *m.* regarder of a forest; **—kasse**, *see* **—casse**; **—knecht**, *m. see* **—hüter**; **—kunde**, *f.* knowledge or science of forestry; **—kundig**, *adj.* having a knowledge of forestry; **—läufer**, *m. see* **—hüter**; **—lehranstalt**, *f. see* **—academie**.

Forst'lich, *adj.* relating or belonging to a forest; f—e Angelegenheiten, forest-matters.

Forst..., *in comp.* **—mann**, *m.* a person experienced in the concerns of a forest; forester; **—mäßig**, *adj.* according to the rules for the management of forests; **—marmor**, *m. Miner.* forest-marble; **—meister**, *m.* ranger, regarder (an officer *or* overseer) of the forests; **—miethe**, *f. see* **—zins**; **—nutzung**, *f.* usufruct and profits of a forest; **—ordnung**, *f.* regulation of forests; **—pfennig**, *m. see* **—zins**; **—rath**, *m.* counsellor to a forest-board; **—recht**, *n.* 1) the proprietorship of a forest; 2) forest laws (collectively), forest-law; **—rechtlich**, *adj.* that relates to the forest-laws; **—regal**, *n.* sovereign right over a forest; **—regel**, *f. see* **—ordnung**; **—revier**, *n.* forest-district; **—richter**, *m.* judge in forest-concerns, regarder; **—röhre**, *f.* ridge-tree (Rainbaum); **—rüge**, *f.* 1) *see* **—gericht**; 2) court-day of the forest-court; 3) presentment certified from the court of attachment against offences in vert and venison; **—sache**, *f.* forest-concern; **—säule**, *f.* boundary-pillar of a forest; **—schreiber**, *m.* forest-clerk; forest-secretary; **—schule**, *f.* an academy for forest-concerns; **—schüler**, *m.* a student of forest-concerns; **—secretär**, *m. see* **—schreiber**; **—stein**, *m. see* **—säule**; **—verbrechen**, **—vergehen**, *n. see* **—frevel**; **—verwalter**, *m.* steward of the forest; ranger; **—verwaltung**, *f.* 1) management *or* stewardship of woods and forests; 2) forest-board; **—wächter**, *m.* wood-ward; **—wesen**, *n.* every thing relating to the cultivation, management, &c. of forests; **—wiese**, *f.* (forest-)glade; **—wirth**, *m. see* **—mann**; **—wirthschaft**, *f.* management of the forests; Wochenblatt für Land- und —wirthschaft, a weekly paper of agriculture and forest-matters; **—wissenschaft**, *f.* science of cultivating and managing forests; **—wissenschaftlich**, *adj.* relating *or* belonging to the science of forests; **—zeichen**, *n.* mark on trees to be felled.

Forst'ziegel, *(str.) m. (from* Forst, *A.) T.* ridge-tile (Firstziegel); Forst- und Gratziegel, *pl.* ridge-and-hip tiles.

Forst'..., *in comp.* **—zins**, *m.* rent paid for the use of a forest *or* part of it; **—zögling**, *m. see* **—schüler**.

Fort, I. *adv.* 1) on, onward(s), forward, along; 2) away, off, gone, *cf.* Weg; 3) continually; er ist schon —, he is already gone; all mein Geld ist —, all my money is spent; — ist —, gone is gone; und so —, and so forth; — und —, on and on, continually, in Einem —, continuously, continually; er lachte in Einem —, he continued *or* kept laughing (all the time); II. *interj.* off! begone! hence! get you gone! — mit dir! away with thee, out with thee! begone!

* **Fort** *[pr. för]*, *(str., pl.* F-s*) n. (Fr.)* fort, small fortress, fortification.

Fort, *in comp. expresses* 1) *onward movement:* on, onward, forward, &c.; 2) *separation:* away, off *(in this case it is equivalent to* Weg, *which may be compared)*; 3) *continuation, when it is rendered by the verb to continue or to keep, f. i.* es regnet —, it continues to rain; **—ackern**, to continue ploughing; **—an'**, *adv.* from this time, hence forth, hence-forward; **—arbeiten**, *v.* I. *intr.* to continue to work, to continue *or* go on working; II. *refl.* to work one's way; **—arten**, to continue in one's species; **—athmen**, to continue to breathe, to continue in breath; **—backen**, **—baden**, **—balgen** rc., to continue baking, bathing, wrestling, &c.; **—bannen**, to banish *or* drive away; to exorcise, lay, expel (evil spirits); **—bau**, *m.* prosecution of building; **—bauen**, to build on; *Min.* to continue working a mine; **—baumen**, *v. intr. Sport.* to leap from tree to tree; **—begeben**, sich, to go away *or* off; to depart, leave; **—[illegible]**, *v.* I. *tr.*

to continue biting; II. *tr.* to drive away by biting; —bellen, —beten *2c.*, to continue barking, praying, &c.; —bestehen, I. *(irr.) v. intr.* to continue; die Firma wird —bestehen, the firm will be continued; II. *s.* *(str.)* *n.*, or —bestand, *(str.)* *m.* continuance, *cf.* —dauer; sich —betteln, to get along by begging; —bewegen, *v. tr. & refl.* 1) to move on; 2) to remove, *see* Wegbewegen; 3) to continue or keep moving; —bewegung, *f.* locomotion; progressive motion, progression; die —bewegung des Sonnensystems, *Astr.* translation of the solar system; —bieten, —bilden, —bitten, to continue to bid, to continue one's education, to continue to beg; —bleiben, to stay away, &c. *see* Wegbleiben; —blasen, —blühen, —bluten, —brauchen *2c.*, to continue blowing, blossoming, bleeding, using, &c.; —brausen, to roar on; to rush away; —breiten, *v. tr. & refl.* to spread; —bringen, *v.* I. *tr.* 1) to carry away, to remove, transport, convey; 2) to rear, to bring up (plants); 3) *fig.* to help on; II. *refl.* to make one's way, to get on; to make one's livelihood; sich ehrlich —bringen, to make an honest living; —bringlich, *adj.* removable, conveyable, transportable; —dampfen, to smoke on; to steam away; to evaporate; —dauer, *f.* continuation, duration, continuance; continued existence; beständige —dauer, perpetuity, permanence; —dauern, to continue, last; —dehnen, *Mus.* to hold out, sustain; —donnern, —drücken *2c.*, to continue thundering, to pinch, &c.; —dürfen, *(ellipt. for* fortgehen dürfen) to be allowed to go away; —duven, *(w.) v. tr. Mar.* to push forward (a boat).

* Forte, *(str., pl.* F-s) *n.* *(Ital.)* *Mus.* forte; —piano, *(str., pl.* F-s) *n.* pianoforte (Pianoforte); —pianospieler, *m.* pianist.

Fort..., *in comp.* —eitern, to matter continually; sich —entwickeln, to continue displaying, unfolding, developing; —erben, *v. intr.* *(& refl.)* to devolve, descend; to communicate (itself) by inheritance; sich —erhalten, to continue in use or custom; to survive; *Comm.* to remain steady in price; —erzählen, —essen, *v.* I. *intr.* to continue explaining, eating; II. *tr.* to explain, eat away; sich —erstrecken, to stretch away, to extend; —fahren, *(str.)* *v.* I. *tr.* to carry or drive off, away (in a vehicle); II. *intr.* 1) *(aux.* sein) to leave, depart in a vehicle, to drive or ride away or off; 2) *(aux.* haben) to continue, go on, *coll.* to keep (on); mit or in ... —fahren, to pursue, continue; unser N. wird —fahren zu zeichnen, *Comm.* our Mr. N. will sign as heretofore; —fallen, *see* —bleiben; —feuern, to keep up the fire; —flackern, —flattern, —fliegen, —fließen *2c.*, to continue to flicker, to flutter, to fly, to flow, &c.; —fluchen, *v.* I. *intr.* to continue cursing; II. *tr.* to drive away with cursing; —führen, 1) *a)* to lead on; *b)* to lead or carry away, off, to convey; 2) to carry on, out; to continue, to keep or go on with; to prosecute; to keep up, maintain (a conversation, &c.); —gang, *m.* 1) progress, advance; —gang haben, to proceed, advance, get on or along; 2) continuation; 3) success; 4) departure (Weggang); —geben, *(str.)* *v.* I. *tr.* to give away; II. *intr.* to continue to give (*Cam.* to deal); —gehen, *(irr.)* *v. intr.* *(aux.* sein) 1) to go or move on, to go along; 2) to go on, continue, to be continued, to proceed; 3) to advance, succeed; 4) to go away, depart, set out, *cf.* Weggehen; Einer nach dem Anderen ging —, one after another dropped off; seinen Gang —gehen, to continue one's course, to pursue the same course; das kann ich nicht so —gehen lassen, I cannot have this going on; es geht —, (*impers.* (man geht —, es wird —gegangen) they go away, depart; —gehend, *see* —laufend; —gießen, *v.* I. *intr.* to continue pouring; II. *tr.* to pour away; —glimmen, —glühen, —graben, to continue, to glimmer (to smoulder), to glow, to dig; —haben, *see* —schaffen; ich möchte ihn gern —haben, I should be glad to see him gone; —häkeln, *Spinn.* to tack or shift (the thread) to the next hook; —hallen, —halten, —handeln, —hauchen, —hauen, to continue to resound, to hold, to act, to breathe, to beat, &c.; Einen —hauen, *coll.* to drive one away by blows; —heben, *v.* I. *tr.* to lift up and carry away; II. *refl.* to take one's self off (*cf.* Wegheben); —helfen, *(str.)* *v.* I. *intr.* (Einem) 1) to help, assist (one) to get away or to escape; 2) *fig.* to help on, assist (one) on; II. *refl.* *see* —bringen, II. & Durchbringen, II.; —herrschen, to continue to reign, to continue ruling; —hin', *adv.* *see* —an; —hinken, —hören, —hungern *2c.*, to continue to limp, to hear, to hunger, &c.

* Fortification', *(w.)* *f.* *(Lat.)* fortification. — Fortificiren, *(w.)* *v. tr.* to fortify.

* Fortis'simo, *(Ital. superl. of* Forte) *adv.* & *s.*, *(str., pl.* F-s) *n.* *Mus.* fortissimo.

Fort..., *in comp.* —jagen, *v.* I. *tr.* to drive or chase away, to turn away, out, or off; II. *intr.* 1) *(aux.* sein) *a)* to gallop, ride on, along; *b)* to gallop, ride off, away; 2) *(aux.* haben) to continue hunting; —jammern, —jubeln, —kämpfen, —klingen *2c.*, to continue or keep on lamenting, triumphing, fighting, ringing, &c.; —kochen, 1) to continue boiling; 2) to evaporate by boiling; —kochen lassen, to keep constantly on the boil; —kollern, 1) to roll on, along; 2) to continue rolling; 3) to roll away; —kommen, *(str.)* *v. intr.* *(aux.* sein) 1) to get on or along, to proceed; 2) *fig.* *a)* (of plants) to get on, thrive, grow; *b)* to come or get on in the world, to prosper, thrive, make one's way; 3) to come or get away, off; to escape, *cf.* Entkommen; damit kommt man nicht —, this will not do; mache, daß du —kommst, get you gone! take yourself off! das —kommen, *(str.)* *n.* the (act of) getting on, advancement, success; sein —kommen finden, to make one's way; —können, *(ellipt. for* —kommen or —gehen können) to be able to proceed, &c.; —kränkeln, to continue to be sickly; —kratzen, *v.* I. *tr.* to scratch away; II. *intr.* *vulg.* *see* Auskratzen, II.; —kreuzen, to continue one's cruise; —kriegen, to continue the war; —lassen, *(ellipt. for* —gehen lassen) 1) to suffer (one, &c.) to go on or to proceed; 2) to suffer to go away, to let off; —lauf, *m.* *see* —gang (1 & *phr.*), Verlauf, Verfolg; —laufen, 1) *a)* to run on or along; *b)* to run away or off, to escape; 2) *fig.* to run on, continue (without interruption); —laufend, *p. a.* continued, uninterrupted; running (accompaniment, commentary); successive (numbers); *Math.*, &c. continuous; current; —leben, to continue to live, to live on, to survive; —läugnen, —lehren, —leiden *2c.*, to continue to deny, to teach, to suffer, &c.; —leiten, 1) *see* —führen, 2; 2) to transmit (electricity, &c.); —lernen, —lesen *2c.*, to continue to learn, to read, &c.; —machen, *coll.* *v.* I. *tr.* to remove; II. *intr.* to make haste, to be quick; III. *refl.* to get or hurry away, off; to make one's escape; —mahlen *2c.*, to continue grinding, &c.; —marschiren, 1) to march on, along; 2) to march away, off; —mögen, —müssen, *v. intr.* *(ellipt. for* —gehen mögen & müssen) to desire to go, to be obliged to go; er muß —, 1) he must go away, he must be off, &c.; 2) *coll.* he must die; —nehmen, —nöthigen, to continue to take, to urge, &c.; —packen, *v.* I. *intr.* to continue packing; II. *tr.* to pack away, out of the way; III. *refl.* *coll.* to be gone, to bundle off; packe dich —! get thee gone! *cf.* Fort, II.; —pflanzen, *v.* I. *tr.* 1) to transplant (flowers, &c.); 2) to pro-

[illegible]schreiten) progressiveness, onward march (of science, &c.); die Theorie des menschlichen Fortschrittes, the theory of human progression; in (math. &c.) —schritte machen, to make progress, to progress, to be a proficient in (mathematics, music, &c.); to improve (in); macht er im Englischen —schritte? does he improve in English? er macht schnelle —schritte, he improves rapidly; —schrittler, m. one belonging to the party of (political) progress; —schrittspartei, f. party of progress, progressive party; —schwatzen, —schwelgen &c., to continue to babble, to riot, &c.; —schwemmen, to wash away, cf. Wegschwemmen; —schwimmen, (str.) v. intr. 1) (aux. sein) a) to swim on, along; b) to swim away; 2) (aux. haben) to continue to swim; —segeln, 1) to sail on, along, to direct (to steer) one's course (at sea); 2) to sail off, set sail, cf. Absegeln, I. 2; sich —sehnen, to wish one's self away; —setzen, 1) to set forward, to put forth, to put forward, on; 2) a) to set or put away; b) see —pflanzen, I. 1; 3) fig. to continue, carry on, prosecute, pursue; to continue, to keep on (a business, &c.); to proceed with (an auction, &c.); eine Reise —setzen, to proceed on, resume a journey; nicht —setzen, to discontinue; wieder —setzen, to resume; —gesetztes Denken, continuous thought; —setzer, m. continuator, continuer; —setzung, f. continuation, prosecution, proceeding in or with, pursuance; —setzung folgt, to be continued; —singen, —sitzen &c., to continue or keep singing, sitting, &c.; —sollen, (ellipt. —gehen, —müssen &c. sollen) to be obliged, bound, or ordered to go (or depart, &c.); —spazieren, 1) to walk on, to pursue one's walk; 2) to walk off; —spielen, —spinnen, to continue to play, to spin; —sprechen, see —reden; —sprengen, to ride away at full speed; —springen, (str.) v. intr. (aux. sein) to leap or jump on or away; —spülen, to wash away, cf. Wegspülen; —stecken, to put away, to fix at a greater distance; —steckungel, m. check-pin (of the plough); —stehlen, (str.) v. I. intr. (aux. haben) to continue to steal; II. tr. to steal, take away secretly; III. refl. to steal, sneak away, cf. sich —machen; —stellen, 1) to put or place farther on; 2) to put or place out of the way, to put away or aside; 3) to go on with, to continue; —stillen, to continue to suckle a child; —stoßen, 1) to push on, forward, to propel; to jog on; 2) to push away, to hustle; to spurn away, repel; to jerk (with one's foot); —strömen, v. I. intr. 1) (aux. sein) to flow on, to be carried on by the stream; 2) (aux. haben) to flow on, continue to stream; II. tr. see —schwemmen; —stürmen, v. intr. 1) or —stürzen, (aux. sein) a) to storm, rush, or dash on, along; b) to storm, rush away or out, to bluster away or off, to depart with a noise or in great haste; 2) (aux. haben) to continue to storm, to roar; —sündigen, to sin on; —tanzen, v. intr. 1) (aux. sein) a) to dance on, along; b) to dance away, to go off (or away) dancing; 2) (aux. haben) to dance on, continue to dance; —tappen, v. intr. (aux. sein) to grope one's way out; —toben, v. intr. 1) (aux. sein) to go away with great noise; 2) (aux. haben) to continue raging, making a noise; —traben, v. intr. (aux. sein) to trot or jog on, along, or away; —tragen, 1) to carry along, &c.; 2) to carry or take away, off; —trauern, —träumen, to continue mourning, dreaming; —treiben, (str.) v. I. tr. 1) to drive onwards, along, on; Mech., &c. to propel; 2) to drive away, off, out; 3) fig. to carry on, pursue, continue; er treibt es noch immer so —, he goes on just at the same rate; II. intr. (aux. sein) Mar. to float on, along; to drift away, [illegible]; —treibung, f. 1) the (act of) driving onwards, propulsion; 2) the (act of) driving away, &c., expulsion; sich —trollen, coll. see sich —scheren.

* Fortu'na, f. Rom. Myth. (the Goddess of) Fortune.

Fort'..., in comp. —wachsen, to continue to grow; to go on increasing; to thrive; —währen, to continue to be, to last; —während, p. a. continual, continuous, continuing; adv. continually, without interruption, constantly, permanently; —wallen, —wandeln, —wandern, v. intr. (aux. sein) 1) to walk or move on, to proceed, to walk forth or forward; 2) to walk or go away, off, to depart, to set out or forth; —weben, to continue weaving; [das] Schicksal, welches unsichtbar sich dem Auge —webt (Klopstock), destiny which invisible to human eye e'er weaves on its thread; —wehen, v. I. intr. to continue to blow (of the wind); II. tr. to blow away, off; —weisen, v. tr. to show the way, to turn or send away; sich —winden, to wind, meander on, onwards; —wischen, v. I. tr. to wipe off; II. intr. 1) to continue wiping; 2) to slip off, &c. (Entwischen); —wollen, (ellipt. for —gehen wollen) to intend to go or to leave; er will durchaus —, he absolutely wants to go; es will mit ihm nicht —, he speeds not, his affairs do not thrive; —wüthen, to continue to rage; —zeigen, see —weisen; —ziehen, (str.) v. I. tr. 1) to drag on, to pull or draw along; 2) to draw away, cf. Wegziehen; II. intr. (aux. sein) 1) to move onwards, to march on; (of clouds) to flit along; 2) to depart, remove, emigrate, (of birds) to migrate; cf. Wegziehen; III. refl. to be protracted (of wars, &c.); —zug, m. see Wegzug.

* Fo'rum, (str., pl. [Lat.] Fo'ra) n. (Lat.) forum: 1) Rom. Ant. a public place in Rome where causes were tried; 2) Law & fig. tribunal, court, pleading-place.

Fösch, Fösch [often pr. fösch], adj. provinc. see Forsch.

* Fossil', I. or Fossil'isch, adj. (Lat.) fossil; II. s. (str., pl. F—e or Fossil'ien) n. fossil.

* Fossi'lien..., in comp. —beschreibung, f. oryctography; —bildung, f. fossilification; —haltig, adj. fossiliferous; —kenner, —kundige, m. fossilist, fossilogist, one versed in the knowledge of fossils; —kunde, —lehre, f. knowledge or science of fossils, fossilogy, oryctology; —sammler, m. collector of fossils, fossilist.

* Fö'tus, (either not declined, or str. [Gen. F—tes, pl. F—tes]) m. (Lat.) Anat. fœtus.

* Foulard' [fülar'], (str.) m. (Fr., orig. Hind.) foulard; silk-handkerchief.

* Foura'ge [füra'zhe], (w.) f. (Fr.) Mil. forage. — Fouragi'ren [fürazhē'ren], Mil. (w.) v. intr. to (make a) forage; das —, (str.) n. s. or Fouragi'rung, (w.) f. (the act of) foraging, forage; Fouragir'zug, m. foraging-expedition, forage; Fouragi'rungs-Commando, n. foraging-party.

* Fourier' [fürēr'], (str.) m. (Fr.) 1) harbinger (of the royal household); 2) Mil. quarter-master; —schütze, m. an officer's servant.

* Fourieris'mus, m. (from Fourier, a French socialist) Fourierism. — Fourierist', (w.) m., Fourierist'isch, adj. Fourierite, Fourierist.

* Fournier' [fürnēr'], (str.) n. (Fr.) (in cabinet-making) veneer, inlay. — Fourni(e)'ren, (w.) v. tr. to veneer, inlay.

* Fournier'..., in comp. —hobel, m. veneering or cabinet-maker's plane; —holz, n., —platten, f. pl. veneer-sheets, veneers; —säge, f. veneer-saw; —schneidemaschine, —(schneide)mühle, —schneiderei, f. veneer-cutting machinery; —späne, m. pl. see —holz.

* Fourni'ren, (w.) f. pl. see Fournierholz.

Fracht, (w.) f. 1) freight, load, loading; cargo; shipment; 2) see —lohn; — des ganzen Schiffes, freight by the great; ein Schiff in — nehmen, to take a ship to freight, to charter a ship; Comm. um die — zu verdienen, to cover the freight; franco (frei) —, free of freight; carriage paid; für — und Auslagen, freight and disbursements; in —, he (or they) paying freight for said goods; in gewöhnlicher —, at (or paying) the usual freight, paying freight as customary; in ganzer —, in the whole freight, full freight; in niedrigster —, at the lowest freight; volle —, full or whole freight; die ganze —, gross freight; in — geben, to freight, to let go on freight; — bedingen, to engage goods or freight.

Fracht'..., in comp. —aufschlag, m. additional freight; —aufseher, m. supercargo.

Fracht'bar, adj. transportable.

Fracht'..., in comp. —bedingungen, f. pl. terms of freight; —besorger, m. despatcher, forwarding agent; —brief, m. bill of lading, carriage, or freight, letter of conveyance; —buch, n. book of cargo; —contract, m. Mar. Law, charter party, (articles of) charter; —empfänger, m. consignee.

Frach'ten, (w.) v. tr. & intr. to freight, load, carry (goods); nach ... —, to take in freight, to be loading for ...; nach ... gefrachtet haben, to be bound to or for; wohin habt Ihr gefrachtet? what place are you bound for?

Frach'ter, (str.) m. 1) freighter; 2) see Frachtfuhrmann.

Fracht'..., in comp. —fahren, n. waggoning; shipping-trade; —fahrer, m. see —fuhrmann, —schiffer; —fahrt betreiben, to carry on freighting- or shipping-business; —frei, adj. freight-(or carriage-)free; —fuhre, f. land-carriage; durch —fuhre, by land-carriage, by land, by van, by waggon; —führer, —fuhrmann, m. carrier, carter, waggoner; cart-man, teamster; —fuhr-Unternehmer, m. see —besorger; —gebühr, f. charge of freight; —geld, n. see —lohn; —geschäft, n. freight-business; —gespann, n. a team of horses; —gewerbe, n. carrying-trade; —gut, n. load, lading, cargo; goods to be shipped or sent by carriage; —handel, m. carrying trade; —liste, f. freight-list; —lohn, m. (terms of or money paid for) freight, freightage; carriage, cartage, waggonage; in —lohn an ..., he (or they) paying freight for the said goods ...; —makler, m. ship-broker, shipping-agent; —nachnahme, f. Comm. the (act of) taking charges forward; unter —nachnahme, collecting expenses; expenses to follow the goods; —post, f. stage-waggon; —preis, —satz, m. term of freight, freightage; —schein, m. see —brief; —schiff, n. merchant-man, trader, trading-ship; —schiffer, m. shipper; (an der Küste) shipper; (auf Flüssen) lighterman; —stück, n. package (of any kind), cf. —gut.

Frach'tung, (w.) f. freighting.

Fracht'..., in comp. —verkehr, m. 1) see —handel; 2) goods-traffic; —vertrag, m. see —contract; —versender, m. consigner; —wagen, m. waggon; —zettel, m. see —brief; —zoll, m. tonnage-fees or rate; —zulage, f. additional-freight.

Frack, (str.) m. dress-coat.

* Fraction', (w.) f. (Lat.) fraction.

* Fractur', (w.) f. (Lat.) 1) Surg. fracture; 2) black letter, Gothic letters; —schrift, f. Typ. German text, capitals.

Fra'ge, (w.) f. 1) question, query, interrogation; 2) Comm. &c. demand (Nachfrage); in —, inquired for, sought after, in demand, cf. Gesucht, 1; stark in — sein, to be much in demand; to be in great request or favour; diese Waare ist ohne —, nobody looks at this article; 3) die peinliche —, Law, torture, rack; die gerichtliche —, interrogatory; 4) Gram. the

[illegible]hasser, misogynist; —fest, n. Lady-day; —feste, pl. festivals of the holy Virgin; —fingerkraut, n. Bot. bird's foot trefoil (*Lotus corniculatus* L.); —fisch, m. Ichth. bleak finscale, rudd (*Leuciscus erythrophthalmus* L.); —flachs, m. Bot. lady's laces, wild flax, toad-flax (*Linaria vulgaris* L.); —fuß, m. female foot; —glas, n. Miner. 1) see —eis; 2) (russisches) Muscovy glass, specular stone; —gut, n. Law, property belonging to a woman, dowry; paraphernalia, paraphernal property; —haar, n. Bot. true maiden-hair, lady's hair, Venus's hair (*Adiantum capillus Veneris* L.); —haarsyrup, m. Pharm. syrup obtained from maiden-hair, (Fr.) capillaire.

Frau'enhaft, I. adj. woman-like, womanly; II. F-igkeit, (w.) f. womanliness.

Frau'en..., in comp. —hand, f. female hand; —handschuh, m. 1) woman's glove; 2) Bot. see Ugiei; —haß, m. misogyny; —hemd, n. chemise (umgangspr. shift); —herrschaft, f. hud. petticoat government; —herz, n. woman's heart; —hut, m. bonnet; —jäger, m. gay Lothario, gallant; vulg. smell-smock; —käfer, m. Entom. Lady-bird (Marienkäfer, [illegible] L.); —kleid, n. woman's gown or dress; —kleider, n. pl. women's clothes; —kloster, n. nunnery; —knecht, m. cont. a man servilely devoted to the female sex; —krankheit, f. disorder or disease of women or females; —kraut, n. see —nabel; —krieg, m. Bot. virgin's bugloss; —lehn, n. Law, see Weiberlehn; —liebe, f. woman's love; love for women; —list, f. woman's tricks; —mantel, m. 1) a lady's cloak or mantle, mantua; 2) Bot. our lady's mantle, alchemilla (*Alchemilla vulgaris* L.); —milch, f. 1) woman's milk; 2) the name of a Rhenish wine; Bot-e. —milchkraut, n. lungwort, our lady's wild-wort (*Pulmonaria* L.); —minze, f. costmary, spear-mint (*Tanacetum balsamita* L.); —nabel, m. lady's cushion, pyramidal saxifrage (*Saxifraga pyramidalis* Lap.); —pflaume, f. Pomol. reine-claude; —putz, m. dress, finery of women; —raub, m. rape of women; —regierung, f., —regiment, n. see [illegible]; —rock, m. see —kleid; —rose, f. Bot. rose campion (*Agrostemma Githago* L.); —sattel, f. see —schuh; —sattel, m. side saddle, pillion; —schmuck, m. Jewel. trinkets for women; —schneider, m. woman's or lady's tailor, mantua-maker; —schneiderin, f. dress-maker; —schuh, m. 1) woman's shoe; 2) Bot. lady's slipper (*Cypripedium calceolus* L.); —schuhmacher, m. ladies' shoemaker; —sinn, m. woman's way of thinking; F-leute, pl. coll. women, females; —sommer, m. gossamer; —spath, m. see —eis; F-sperson, f. woman, female; —spiegel, m. Bot. 1) Venus' looking-glass (*Specularia speculum* A. DC.); 2) saintfoin; —staat, m. 1) community or state composed of women; 2) see —putz; —stand, m. condition or dignity of a wife, state of a (married) woman, Law, coverture; —stift, n. a religious establishment for women; nunnery; —stimme, f. female voice; —stuhl, m. woman's seat or pew (in churches); —sucht, f. immoderate fondness for women; —tag, m. Eccl. Lady-day; —tanz, m. swoop-dance, consoling dance; —taube, f. see Turteltaube; —theil, n. Law, woman's settlement, jointure.

Frauenzimmer, (str.) n. see Frauensperson.

Frau'en..., in comp. —tracht, f. woman's dress, female attire; —treu, m., —veilchen, n. Bot. dame's violet (*Hesperis matronalis* L.); —verein, m. Ladies' association (for a charitable purpose); —volk, n. hud. women, females; —welt, f. women's company, women; —zimmer, n. 1) woman's apartments; 2) a) † collect. the [illegible]; b) female, woman; das [illegible] —zimmer, lady-chamber; —zimmerkrankheit, f. see —krankheit; —zwinger, m. harem, [illegible].

Fräu'lein, (str.) n. 1) †, female: Männlein und —, male and female; 2) a nobleman's daughter or young lady of respectable parents; * damsel; — P. M., Miss P. M.; —stift, n. chapter or endowment for young ladies of rank.

Fräu'lich, Frau'lich, adj. (L. u.) relating to a woman (Weiblich).

Frech, I. adj. (& adv. † Frech'lich) shameless, impudent, audacious, barefaced, saucy, insolent; brazen-faced; mit f-er Stirn, with a brazen face; II. F-heit, (w.) f. shamelessness, licentiousness, effrontery, impudence, audaciousness, sauciness, insolence.

* F[illegible]te, (w.) f. (Fr.) Mar. 1) frigate; 2) ([illegible]reischiff) full-rigged ship; f-n[illegible] [illegible] f-nförmig, I. adj. like a frigate; II. [illegible] f-nartig gebaut, frigate-built; F-nvogel, m. Ornith. frigate-bird, man-of-war bird (*Tachypetes aquila* L.).

Frei, adj. 1) a) free (von, from); at liberty, at large; b) let off, discharged, acquitted; 2) exempt, clear (of), free (from taxes, &c.); 3) unfettered, unshackled, unhindered; 4) safe, secure; 5) unconnected, disengaged, detached; 6) unbiassed, independent; 7) voluntary, spontaneous; 8) (porto—) post-paid (cf. Franco); Comm-e. (bei Sendungen) expenses covered, free from charges; ganz —, all expenses prepaid; paid all; — ins Haus, delivered free of charge; — zur Fuhre, — auf die Fuhre gelegt, free on carriage (on the waggon); — auf die Bahn, delivered free up to the station; — ab Cuxhaven, to be delivered at C.; — [bis zur] Grenze, paid to the frontier; 9) vacant; 10) open, public; 11) free: a) frank, open, candid; b) bold; shameless, wanton, cf. Frech; — heraus, frankly, openly; point-blank, downright (cf. below); — und ungehindert, without let or hinderance; der f-e Tag, holiday, open day; eine f-e Nacht machen, coll. to make a night of it; f-en Tisch haben, to have free board; aus f-er Hand, off hand; aus f-er Wahl, of one's own choice; aus f-en Stücken, of one's own accord or free will, spontaneously, cf. Freiwillig; without cause or provocation; f-e Wärme, Phys. sensible heat; ein f-er Gang, an easy gait; ein f-er Anstand, easy manners; f-er Gang, 1. easy gait; 2. Min. unworked lode; f-e Augenblicke, vacant or leisure moments; f-e Zeit, leisure, off-time; der f-e Bürger, see Freibürger; eine f-e Reichsstadt, an imperial city; f-e Stadt, free town; auf f-er Straße, in the open street; unter f-em Himmel, in the open air; under the open sky; f-es Feld, 1. open country; 2. Min. unclaimed mine; f-es Feld haben, to have full power, to be unlimited, unrestrained; f-er Raum, free, clear space; f-e Concurrenz, open competition; Comm-e. — von Beschädigung, free of damages; (warranted) free from average; f-er Port or Theil, free of charges, damages, &c.; — von Schulden, clear of debt, unembarrassed, unencumbered; — Schiff, — Gut, free ship, free goods; f-er Verkehr, free trade; Einem f-es Spiel lassen, to give one free scope, to give one fair play; Einem in or bei ... f-e Hand geben, to leave ... at one's discretion, cf. Freistellen; f-e Hand haben, to be at liberty, to have free hand or scope; aus f-er Hand verkaufen, to sell off hand or out of hand; etwas aus f-er Hand thun, to do a thing of one's own accord; aus f-er Hand gearbeitet, done off hand, without a model; f-e Handzeichnung, free-hand drawing; f-er Handwerker, artisan belonging to no guild; f-e Birsch or Jagd, frank or free chase; ein f-es Leben, a loose manner of life; die f-en Künste, the liberal (fine, polite, or elegant) arts; die f-e Schreibart, Mus. the free style of composition; auf f-en Fuß stellen, setzen, see Freigeben & Freilassen, 2; einen Tag, zwei Tage &c. — geben, to give a holiday (of one day), of two days, &c. (at school); — haben, 1. to have at one's disposal; haben Sie einige Zimmer —? have you any spare rooms? ich habe zwei Zimmer —, I have two spare rooms; Passagiere haben 30 Pfund (Gepäck) —, passengers are allowed 30 pounds (of luggage), 30 lbs. allowed (to passengers); [Augenblicke] wo er eine Frage — hat an das Schicksal (*Schiller*, Wall. Tod 2, 3), when [man] is allowed to question his destiny; 2. (at school) to have a holiday; ich sehre fest mich von allen Parteien — zu halten (*Prince Albert*), I resolutely hold myself aloof from all parties; — machen, 1. to (set) free, deliver, release, rescue, redeem, enfranchise; 2. to pay the postage of (letters), to frank, prepay; 3. to disencumber, disembarrass, disengage, to clear (an estate, one's conscience, &c.); Güter, ein Schiff — machen, to clear goods, a ship; 4. sich — machen, to break loose (of beasts); — sein, 1. to be at liberty (or leisure); 2. Chem. to be free or disengaged; — werden, Chem. to be liberated or to become disengaged; darf ich so — sein? may I take the liberty? may I presume? — stehen, 1. to stand isolated or insulated; 2. see Freistehen; — heraus sprechen, to speak one's mind freely; sprich — heraus! speak out! — sprechen, reden, 1. to speak freely; 2. to speak without book or off hand; — ausgehen, fig. to come off unharmed, unscathed; Comm-e. to go out free (of duty) (said of goods); — unter Zelt, free at the quay; — vom Schiff, free ex ship; — von Abgaben, exempt from charges; — von Kosten (Spesen), free from expenses; — von Leckage, Verderb, Haverei, free of leakage, rot, average; — umhergehen, to go at large.

Frei'..., in comp. —acker, m. free ground, acre to which no soccage service is attached; —altar, m. 1) altar at which masses may be held at any time; 2) portable altar; —artiger Acker, see —acker; —balken, m. beam on which no girder rests; —bank, f. 1) portable frame of statuaries; 2) common shambles; —bau, m. Min. mine whose products cover the expenses without realising any profit; —bauen, refl. Min. die Zeche baut sich frei, the mine pays its own expenses; —bauer, m. free peasant (exempt from all average or servitude to his landlord); —beuter, m. free-booter, pirate; —beuterei, f. free-booting, piracy, pillage; —beuterisch, adj. like a free-booter; —bier, n. 1) beer exempt from the beer-tax; 2) beer given gratis (to workmen); —billet, n. free-ticket; (für die Eisenbahn) pass(-ticket); —birsche, f. frank or free chase; —brauer, m. brewer exempt from paying the beer-tax; —brief, m. 1) license, charter, patent, privilege; permit; passport; 2) Comm. Law, letter of respite, see Anstands-Brief; —brüstig, adj. (N. G.) see —müthig (Lus.); —bürger, m. freeman; denizen, citizen of a free-town or republic, republican; —bürgerlich, adj. republican; —corps, n. corps of volunteers, free-company; —couvert, n. stamped or postage envelope; —denker, m. freethinker; —denkerei, f. freethinking. [gamesome, wanton.

† Frei'dig, adj. 1) free, courageous; 2)

† Frei'ding, (str.) n. free court of justice.

Frei'e, (decl. like adj.) 1) m. & f. free man, free woman; 2) n. & f. open air, space, field, or country; lawn, glade (in woods); ins — gehen, to take the air, to go abroad, out of doors, or into the open air; im F-en sitzen, to sit in the open air; Bewegung im F-en, outdoor exercise; 3) n. (im Wesen) openness, ingenuousness, candidness.

Frei'eigen, adj. Feud. Law, allodial (Allodial), freehold.

Frei'en, (w.) v. I. intr. (with um ...) to woo, court, to make love, pay one's addresses to

...; II. *tr.* to marry; das —, *(str.)* n. s. the (act of) wooing, courtship. [Befreien.

Frei'en, *(w.)* v. *tr.* to free, privilege, *see*

Frei'er, *(str.)* m. (F-smann, *(str.)* m., *pl.* F-sleute) wooer, suitor; courter; auf F-s Füßen gehen, *fig.* to be a marrying man *(cf.* auf die Freite gehen).

Freierdings', *adv.* *(Lessing, cf. Grimm, WB.; L. u.)* of one's own accord (Freiwillig).

Freierei', *(w.)* f. the (act or practice of) wooing, courtship.

Frei'..., *in comp.* —exemplar, n. presentation-copy; —fechter, m. privileged fencing master; —fleischer, m. butcher not belonging to the butcher-guild; —frau, f. baroness; —fräulein, n. daughter of a baron; —gabe, f. restitution, release; —gänger, m. soldier belonging to a partisan corps, partisan; —geben, *(str.)* v. *tr.* *(cf.* Frei) to release (a prize, &c.), to set free, *cf.* —lassen; gegen Sicherheit — geben, to replevy; —gebig, *adj.* free, liberal, generous, bounteous, bountiful, munificent; —gebigkeit, f. liberality, generosity, bounty, bountifulness, munificence; —gebung, f. release; restitution; mainprise; —geding, n. 1) *see* —gericht; 2) wages of a miner calculated by the quantity of produce; —geist, m. freethinker; —geisterei, f. freethinking; latitudinarianism; —geisterisch, *adj.* freethinking; latitudinarian; infidel; —geistig, *adj.* unprepossessed, unbiassed, unshackled (of the mind); —gelassene, *(decl. like adj.)* m. & f. freed man, freed woman; —gepäck, n. a certain amount of luggage allowed to passengers travelling per post, railway, &c.; *Mar.* adventure; —gericht, n. 1) free (criminal) court of justice; 2) *for* Fehmgericht, *which see;* —gerinne, n. outlet-channel; —gesinnt, *adj.* free-minded, independent; —gewicht, n. weight (of luggage) allowed (to passengers); —glauben, m. free or independent faith; —gläubig, *adj.* independent, unbiassed in faith; —gläubigkeit, f. independence (of belief); —gold, n. *Miner.* apparent native gold; —graf, m. †, judge of the Fehmgericht, *which see;* bailiff, sheriff; —gut, n. 1) freehold (estate), free-tenement, allodium; 2) *Comm.* goods (that are) duty-free; —hafen, m. free-port; —halten, *(str.)* v. *tr.* to defray one's expenses, to entertain without expense; to treat (mit, to); ich habe sie —gehalten, I stood (the) treat (for them); —handel, m., —händlerisch, *adj.* free trade; —händlerische Grundsätze, free-trade principles.

† Frei'hart, *(str.)* m. vagabond (Landstreicher).

Frei'..., *in comp.* —haus, n. a house enjoying certain immunities; —häusler, m. 1) owner of a —haus, *which see;* 2) *see* Ansiedler, 2.

Frei'heit, *(w.)* f. 1) liberty, freedom; 2) privilege, charter; 3) license; latitude; 4) (— von Abgaben *ꝛc.*) exemption, immunity, franchise; die F-en der gallicanischen Kirche, the immunities, liberties of the Gallican church; 5) *a)* privileged place; close *(cf.* Domfreiheit, Schloßfreiheit *ꝛc.*); *b) Archit.* esplanade, parade; in —, at liberty, at large; die — geben, in — setzen, to set (free or) at liberty, to deliver; to emancipate (a slave); Einem volle — lassen, to leave one fully at liberty; sich *(Dat.)* die — nehmen, to take the liberty, to make free or bold; sich zu viel — heraus nehmen, to be too free; poetische —, poetical license; —liebend, *adj.* (warmly) attached to liberty.

Frei'heitler, *(str.)* m. *cont.* a would-be liberal, pretended advocate of liberty.

Frei'heits..., *in comp.* —baum, m. tree of liberty; —brief, m. charter, patent, *cf.* Freibrief, 1; —bund, m. alliance or union for the defence of liberty; —drang, —durst, —eifer, m., —liebe, f., —sinn, m. thirst, zeal, love, spirit of liberty; —freund, m. friend to liberty, lover of liberty; —held, m. hero, champion of liberty; —kampf, —krieg, m. struggle, war for asserting liberty, war of independence; —mütze, f. cap of liberty; —ritter, m. champion of liberty; —schwärmer, m. fanatic for liberty; —schwindel, m., —sucht, —wuth, f. rage, excessive desire for liberty.

Frei'..., *in comp.* —herr, m. baronet, baron; —herrin, Frei'in, *(w.)* f. baroness; —herrlich, *adj.* baronial; —herrschaft, f. barony; —herzig, *adj.* free, open-hearted; —herzigkeit, f. free-heartedness, frankness; —hof, m. free-farm, free manor; —jahr, n. free year, year of immunity; —käufer, m. peasant [illegible] has redeemed himself from servitude [illegible] m. flayer, knacker; —krug, m. privileged [illegible] house (exempt from the beer-tax); —kugel, [illegible] charmed bullet; —kux, m. share in a mine to be worked gratis; —lager, n. *Mil.* bivouac; —lagern, *Mil.* to bivouac; —lassen, *(str.)* v. *tr.* 1) to release, enfranchise, free, to set free, at liberty, or at large, emancipate; 2) *fig. see* —stellen; —lassung, f. the (act of) releasing, setting free, &c., manumission, emancipation; (gegen Bürgschaft) *Law,* mainprise; —lauf, m. *see* —gerinne; —laut sein, *Sport.* to open too soon (of dogs); —ledig, *adj.* unmarried; —lehen, n. freehold, free-tenement, frank-fee, free-simple.

Frei'lich, *adv.* 1) certainly, to be sure, of course; 2) indeed, sure, it is true; ja —, yes, it is true, to be sure.

Frei'..., *in comp.* —machung, f. 1) the (act of) freeing, &c. *cf.* — machen; deliverance; 2) disengagement; 3) *see* Frankirung; —mann, m. 1) free-man; free-holder; 2) († *A) premier, see* Schinder; —marke, f. (postage-)stamp (Briefmarke); —markt, m. free-market, privileged fair; —maurer, m. free-mason; —maurerei, f. *see* —maurerwesen; —maurergesell, m. fellow-craft; —maurergesellschaft, f., —maurerorden, —maurerverein, m. fraternity or company of free-masons; —maurerisch, *adj.* free-masonic; —maurerloge, f. free-mason's or masonic lodge; —maurerwesen, n. free-masonry; —meister, m. free-master; —meisterschaft, f. free-mastership; —messe, f. *see* —markt; —mündig, *adj.* free-spoken; —muth, m. frankness, candour, plain-dealing; —müthig, *adj.* frank, free-hearted; open, upright, candid, ingenuous; free-spoken; —müthigkeit, f. frankness, candour, ingenuousness, openness of heart; —ort, m. *see* —stätte; —partei, f. *see* —schaar; —paß, m. passport; —procente, n. *pl.* exonerating percentages (in assurances); —recht, n. right of a freeman to reside where he likes; —saß, m. free-holder, yeoman; —schaar, f. free-corps (—corps); —schärler, m. *cont.* one belonging to a free-corps; free-companion; —schein, m. license; —schießen, n. public shooting; —schöppe, m. *see* Freischöppe; —schule, f. free-school, charity-school; —schüler, m. 1) pupil of a free-school; 2) pupil who is instructed gratis; —schütz, —schütze, m. 1) *Folklore.* free-archer, one who shoots with charmed bullets; 2) *(also* —schütze, *f.) Hydr.* sash-gate, sliding-gate; —sinn, m. 1) free-unbiassed manner of thinking; 2) sense of liberty; —sinnig, *adj.* free-minded, large-minded, liberal; —sinnigkeit, f. free-mindedness, largeness of mind; liberality of opinion; —sitz, m. freehold; —sitzer, m. freeholder; —sprechen, *(w.)* v. *tr.* to absolve, acquit, dispense, discharge, clear; to bring in not guilty; —sprechendes Urtheil, verdict of not guilty; —sprechung, f. 1) absolution, acquittal, discharge; deliverance (by the verdict of a jury); 2) emancipation, *cf.* —lassung; —staat, m. free state, republic; —staatsbürger, m. republican; —stadt, f. free town; —statt, —stätte, f. asylum, refuge; sanctuary; —stellung,

[illegible] foreign legion; —liste, f. list of arrivals; [illegible]recht, n. rights and privileges of aliens; [illegible]sitte, n. manners and customs of foreigners; —zimmer, n. guest chamber.

† Frem'denzen, (w.) v. intr. to ape the language and manners of foreigners. [ness.

Fremd'heit, (w.) f. strangeness; foreign-

Fremd'lich, adj. see Fremd, Fremdartig.

Fremd'ling, (str.) m. foreigner; stranger; [illegible], alien; F-srecht, n. Law, escheatage, cf. [illegible]recht.

* Frequent', adj. (Lat.) 1) frequented; [illegible] Comm. current (article).

* Frequenti'ren, (w.) v. tr. (Lat.) to frequent, see Besuchen, 1. — Frequenz', (w.) f. frequency, concourse, (full) attendance; traffic (on railways, &c.), cf. Verkehr.

* Fres'co, adj. & (str., pl. F-s, or (w.) [illegible]) n. (Ital.) Paint. fresco; —maler, m. painter in fresco; —malerei, f. 1) (art of) painting in fresco; 2) or —gemälde, n. fresco-painting.

Freß..., in comp. —bauch, m. vulg. glutton; —begierde, f. greediness, gluttony, voracity.

Fres'se, (w.) f. vulg. mouth, anal. chaps.

Fres'sen, (str.) v. I. tr. 1) (only used of animals) to eat; 2) contempt. vulg. to eat greedily, swallow, guttle, devour; 3) fig. & T. to corrode, eat, fret; (of engines) to grind, to [illegible], to wear out; zu — geben, to feed; seinen Ärger in sich —, to devour one's vexation; friß mich nur nicht! don't bite my nose off! [illegible] intr. to eat (into, &c.); friß Vogel oder stirb, proverb, pay or play; um sich —, to spread (of an ulcer, &c.), to diffuse itself; [illegible], p. a. eating, corrosive, stocking, consuming.

Fres'sen, s. (str.) n. 1) food (for animals); 2) vulg. the (act of) eating greedily, &c.; ein gefundenes —, vulg. a thing wished for, anal. windfall, godsend; das ist ein gefundenes — für ihn, that is meat and drink for him.

Fres'ser (l. u.: Freß'ling), (str.) m. 1) eater, great feeder (of animals); 2) contempt. devourer, guttler, glutton, gormandiser; 3) Hort. & Forest. canker, cancerous affection of (fruit-)trees.

Fresserei', (w.) f. 1) contempt. the (act or practice of) eating greedily, &c. cf. Fressen; gluttony; 2) vulg. banquet, treat.

Freß..., in comp. —fieber, n. a diseased, ravenous appetite; Vet. b(o)ulimy; —gier, voracity, gluttony; —gierig, Freß'ig, adj. greedy, voracious, ravenous, gluttonous; —[illegible], f. hungry evil (of horses); see —[illegible]; —lust, f. appetite for food (of beasts); [illegible], m. 1) victual-bag (scrip); 2) contempt. glutton; —säure, f. Manuf. discharging acid; —[illegible], f. pl. Entom. the (maxillary and labial) feelers, palpi; —stein, m. see Höllenstein; —sucht, f. see —begierde; —süchtig, [illegible] see —gierig; —trog, m. trough, manger; [illegible], m. see —bauch; —wurzel, f. see Fleischwurzel; —zange, f., —[illegible], n. pl. [illegible]—feelers.

[illegible], (str.) m. T. screw-auger.

Frett, Frettchen, Frettwiesel, (str.) n. [illegible] ferret (Mustela furo L.); mit Frettchen [illegible], to ferret; —jäger, m. ferreter.

[illegible], (w.) f. T. ferrule, iron-hoop.

[illegible], (w.) v. intr. provinc. to bungle; [illegible]-drudge.

[illegible], (w.) v. intr. to ferret.

[illegible], (w.) v. tr. provinc. 1) to feed, [illegible]; 2) to eat, corrode.

Freude, (w.) f. joy, pleasure; gladness, [illegible], delight, merriment; comfort, satisfaction; [illegible] — sein, to be joyful or over[illegible]; [illegible] — machen, to give (one) joy. [illegible] I: [illegible] — an [illegible] [illegible], to [illegible] [illegible] in Freud' und Leid, for better, for worse; mit F-n, gladly, joyfully; —glänzend, —strahlend, adj. beaming with joy.

Freu'den..., in comp. —becher, m. cup of joy; —bezeigung, f. show or expression of joy; rejoicing; —blick, m. 1) joyous look; 2) fleeting or transient joy; —bote, m. messenger of joy; —botschaft, f. glad tidings, joyful news; —feier, f., —fest, n. public festivity, festival, jubilee; —feuer, n. bonfire; —gesang, m. hymn of rejoicing; —geschrei, n. shouts of joy, &c. cf. —ruf; —haus, n. house of joy; —kelch, m. see —becher; —kleid, n. festival garment; —leben, n. a joyful life, merry life, [illegible]; —leer, —los, adj. void of joy, [illegible] cheerless; —mädchen, n. prostitute; [illegible]meer, n. *, sea of joys; —opfer, n. thank-offering; —pferd, n. prancing-horse (at burials); —post, f. joyful news; —rausch, m. (lit. intoxication) transport of joy; —reich, adj. joyful, rich in joy, most happy; —ruf, m. joyful exclamation, shout, acclamation of joy, cheer, huzza; —schießen, n. firing of the guns (for victory, &c.); —schmuck, m. festive ornaments; —schüsse, m. pl. rejoicing fire; —selig, see Freudetrunken; —störer, m. disturber of joy or pleasure; —tag, m. day devoted to joy, festival day; —taumel, m. transport of joy; —thräne, f. tear of joy; —traum, m. dream of pleasure; —trunk, m. rejoicing cup; —voll, adj. full of joy, joyful; —wein, m. festival wine; —zähre, f. *, see —thräne; —zeit, f. joyful time.

Freu'de..., in comp. —trunken, adj. intoxicated with joy; —trunkenheit, f. transport of joy (Freudenrausch, Freudentaumel).

Freu'dig, I. adj. glad, joyful; joyous, cheerful, gladsome; hearty, ready; etwas — thun, to do a thing with pleasure or readily; II. F-keit, (w.) f. 1) joyfulness; joyousness, gladsomeness, cheerfulness; 2) cheerful alacrity, readiness.

Freud'voll, adj. full of joy (Freudenvoll).

Freu'en, (w.) v. I. refl. 1) (sich über eine Sache or einer Sache [Gen.], l. u. an einer Sache —) to rejoice, be rejoiced (at) to be pleased (with), to delight (in), be glad (of); to enjoy one's self; wir — uns zu erfahren, we are happy to learn; 2) sich auf eine Sache (Acc.) —, to look forward to a thing, &c. with pleasure; to rejoice (in the idea) of a thing; to rejoice at the approach of, to enjoy by anticipation; sie wußte, wie sehr ich mich darauf freute, euch wieder zu sehen, she knew how much I anticipated the pleasure of seeing you again; II. tr. (cf. Erfreuen) & impers. to afford joy, pleasure; es freut mich, I am glad of it, it gives me joy.

Freund, s. 1. (str.) m. 1) a) friend; acquaintance; b) Comm. friend, correspondent; 2) relation, kin, kinsman; einer seiner F-e, a friend of his; Jemandes — sein, to be a friend to one; ein guter — von mir, a friend of mine, an old acquaintance; fig.-e. ein — einer (or von einer) Sache sein, to be a friend to a thing (commerce, poetry, &c.), to be fond of it, to like it; kein — von ... sein, to be averse to ...; ein — der Menschheit, Wahrheit rc., a lover of mankind, truth, &c.; die F-e einer guten Regierung (eines guten Regierungssystems), the lovers of good government; ein — im Glück, a fair-weather friend; II. in comp. —brüderlich, adj. friendly and brotherly; —dienstlich, adj. friendly and obsequious.

Freun'den, (w.) v. intr. *, to gain friends; die Wahrheit lautet wohl, freundet aber nicht, proverb, he who speaks the truth will have no want of enemies.

Freun'din, (w.) f. (female) friend.

Freund'lich, adj. 1) kind, friendly, affable, gentle, mild, sweet(-tempered), benevolent, gracious, courteous; 2) cheerful, pleasing, pleasant, agreeable; fair, favorable, propitious; — grüßend verbleibe rc., with kind regards I am, &c.; f-er Leser, gentle (courteous) reader; f-es Wetter, fair, good weather; smiling; ein f-es Zimmer, a pleasant room.

Freund'lichkeit, (w.) f. 1) kindness, friendliness, affability, &c. cf. Freundlich; pleasing demeanour, civility; graciousness, &c.; 2) cheerfulness, &c.; F-en, pl. civilities, favours, kind services.

Freund'los, adj. friendless; unfriended.

Freundnach'barlich, adj. being (or acting as) a friend and neighbour.

Freund'schaft, (w.) f. 1) friendship, amity; Comm. friendly disposition, countenance; 2) friendly act (F-sdienst); 3) coll. relation, kindred, family; — knüpfen, schließen, to make friendship; eine — erweisen, to do or show a favour; Einem ewige — schwören, to swear eternal friendship with one; — trinken, to plight friendship over the glass.

Freundschaftelei', (w.) f. affected friendship, vain show of friendship.

Freund'schaftlich, I. adj. friendly, amicable; — gesinnt sein, to have a friendly feeling (gegen, towards); II. F-keit, (w.) f. friendly or kind disposition, amicableness.

Freund'schafts'..., in comp. —band, n. bond of friendship; —betheuerung, f. protestation of friendship; —beweis, m., —bezeigung, f. proof, testimony of friendship; —bund, m. friendly alliance, league of amity; —dienst, m. act of friendship, good office, friendly or good turn, service, favour, kindness; —inseln, f. pl. Geogr. Friendly Islands; —sinn, m. friendly disposition; —stück, n. see —dienst; —trieb, m. disposition to friendship; —versicherung, f. see —betheuerung.

Fre'vel, I. (str.) m. 1) outrage, enormity, crime, offence, act of violence, trespass; mischief, wantonness; sacrilege; 2) Law, fine for a violence committed; II. adj. († & *), see Frevelhaft.

Fre'velgericht, (str.) n. Law, criminal court for trying trespasses.

Fre'velhaft, I. adj. outrageous, criminal; cruel; wanton, impious, wicked, insolent, presumptuous; II. F-igkeit, (w.) f. outrageousness, wantonness, wickedness.

Fre'vel..., in comp. —beginnung, f. see —that; —lust, f., —muth, —sinn, m. mischievous mind, malicious disposition, wickedness; insolence; —mord, m. wicked, wanton, or cruel murder.

Fre'veln, (w.) v. intr. to commit a crime or injustice, to be mischievous; with an (& Dat.), to outrage, insult, offend, offer violence to.

Fre'vel..., in comp. —that, f. atrocious action, atrocity; —wort, n. insult; blasphemy; —zunge, f. 1) wicked tongue; 2) backbiter.

Fre'ventlich, adj. see Frevelhaft.

Frev'ler, (str.) m., F-in, (w.) f. 1) a wicked, wanton person; outrager, offender; 2) blasphemer.

Frev'lerisch, see Frevelhaft.

Frey'a, more correct: Frey'ja, f. North. Myth. Frayja (the goddess of love).

* Friandi'se, (w.) f. (Fr.) dainty, nice thing (Delicatesse); —händler, m. Comm. fruiterer; dry-salter.

Friaul', n. Geogr. Friuli.

* Fricassee', (str., pl. F-s) n. (Fr.) Cook. fricassee. — Fricassi'ren, (w.) v. tr. Cook. to fricassee.

* Friction', (w.) f. (Lat.) friction (Reibung); F-sfeuerzeug, n. see Streichfeuerzeug; F-sfidibus, m., F-szündhölzchen, n. lucifer-match, see Reibzündhölzchen; F-smesser, m. Phys. & Mech. tribometer; F-srad, n., F-srolle, f. friction-roller, friction-wheel; F-sscheibe, f. friction plate.

Fried'brüchig, *adj.* breaking the peace, guilty of a violation of the peace.

Fried'chen, *(str.) n.*, **Frie'de**, *m. dimin. & abbr. of* Friedrich *(cf.* Friedel*) &* Gottfried *(engl. Jeff) (P. N-s.).*

Frie'de, Frie'den, *s.* I. *(str.) m.* 1) peace; tranquillity; quiet of mind; 2) *Archit., &c. see* Einfriedigung; — machen, schließen, to make peace: — haben, in — leben, to live in peace, to be at peace (mit, with): — halten, to keep peace: in F-n lassen, to let alone, to let be quiet; II. *in comp.* —gebot, *n.* order *or* injunction to keep peace; —kauf, *m.* purchase in the lump. [Freddy *(P. N.).*

Frie'del, *m. (abbr. of* Friedrich*) coll.* Fred,

Frie'deler, *(str.) m. Bot.* imperial crown.

Frie'delos, *adj.* 1) †, outlawed; 2) unpeaceable, quarrelsome.

Frie'demachend, *adj.* pacifying.

Frie'denbringend, *adj.* paciferous.

Frie'dens..., *in comp.* —absicht, *f.* pacific intention: —antrag, *m.* offer of peace; —artikel, *m.* article of peace: —bedingung, *f.* condition of peace: —bote, *m.* messenger (herald) of peace; —brecher, *m.* peace-breaker; —bruch, *m.* breach (rupture) of peace; —brüchig, *see* Friedbrüchig; —congreß, *m.* congress for making peace; —einleitungen, *f. pl.* preliminaries of peace: —engel, *m.* angel of peace; —fest, *n.*, —feier, *f.* celebration of a peace; —feuer, *n.* bonfire in celebration of a peace: —flagge, *f.* flag of truce (peace); —fürst, *m.* Prince of peace *(i. e.* Jesus Christ): —fuß, *m.* 1) peaceable footing; 2) *Mil.* peace-establishment, peace-footing; —gedanken, *m. pl.* peaceable sentiments *or* thoughts; —gericht, *n.* county-court, court of quarter-sessions; —geschäft, *n.* negotiation of *or* for peace; —gesinnungen, *f. pl. see* —gedanken; —künste, *f. pl.* arts cultivated in time of peace; —kuß, *m.* kiss of peace; —liebe, *f.* love of peace; —münze, *f.* medal struck in commemoration of a peace; —partei, *f.* peace party; —pfeife, *f. (among the Am. Indians)* pipe of peace, calumet; —politik, *f.* pacific policy; —punct, *m. see* —artikel; —richter, *m.* justice of the peace, magistrate; —schluß, *m.* treaty (conclusion) of peace, pacification; —stifter, *m.* pacifier, peace-maker; mediator, conciliator: —stiftung, *f.* pacification; —störer, *m.* disturber of peace; —störung, *f.* disturbance: —tag, *m.* 1) day of peace; anniversary day of peace; 2) day on which the working journeymen (in Germany) hold public meetings: —tractat, *m.* treaty of peace: —unterhandlung, *f.* negotiation of peace; —vermittelung, *f.* interference, mediation of peace; —vorschlag, *m.* proposition (proposal) of peace; —zeit, *f.* time of peace.

Friederi'ke, *f.* Frederica *(P. N.).*

Fried'fertig, I. *adj.* peaceable, pacific, inclined to peace; II. F-keit, *(w.) f.* peaceableness, pacific disposition.

Fried'..., *in comp.* —hag, *m. see* —zaun; —hof, *m. (origin.* an inclosed [eingefriedeter] space round churches, asylum) churchyard.

Frie'digen, *(w.) v. tr. see* Einfriedigen.

Fried'lich, I. *adj.* peaceful, peaceable, pacific; quiet, secure; II. F-keit, *(w.) f.* peacefulness, &c. [able, peaceful.

Fried'liebend, *p. a.* loving peace, peace-

Fried'los, *see* Friedelos.

Fried'rich, *m.* Frederic *(P. N.).* — **Fried'richsd'or**, *(str.) m. Num.* Frederic d'or.

Fried'sam, Fried'selig *&c., see* Friedfertig.

Fried'zaun, *(str., pl.* F-zäune) *m.* fence, hedge.

Frie'ren, *(str.) v. intr. (aux.* haben) to be cold, feel cold *(with* an *& Dat. or Acc.)*; ich friere an den Füßen *(less correctly* an die Füße), my feet are cold; to be chilled; II. *tr. impers.* es friert mich, I am *(or* feel) cold, chilled; es friert mich an die Füße *(or* an den Füßen), my feet are cold; III. *intr.* 1) *(with* sein) to freeze, congeal: 2) *impers. (with* haben) es friert, it freezes (stark, hard): das —, *(str.) v. s.* 1) fre[illegible] congelation; 2) *Med.* ague.

Fr[illegible], *adj. coll.* frosty, shivery; shaking with cold [illegible] ague.

Frier'punct, *(str.) m.* freezing-point (Gefrierpunct).

Fries, *(str.) m.* 1) *a) Archit. & Mar.* frieze; *b) Join.* frame-wood, door-frame: 2) *Gunn.* astragal, the ring *or* moulding near the mouth of a cannon; 3) *Comm.* frieze, baize.

Frie'se, *(w.) m.* (**Frie'sin**, *(w.) f.)* Frieson, Frieslander.

Frie'sel, *(str.) n. & m. Med.* [illegible]; —ähnlich, —artig, *adj.* miliary: —[illegible] miliary fever; —flechte, *f.* miliary herp[illegible] schlange, *f. Zool.* a species of boa *(Boa cenchris* C.).

Frie'sen, *adj.* made of frieze. [floor.

Fries'fußboden, *(str.) m. Archit.* inland

Frie'sisch, *adj.* of Friesland; f-er Reiter, *see* Spanischer Reiter; f-es Grün, Brunswick green. — **Fries'land**, *n. Geogr.* Friesland. — **Fries'länder**, *(str.) m.* (F-in, *(w.) f.)* Frieslander.

Fries'rahmen, *(str.) m.* door-frame.

Fringi'ren, Fring'en, *(w.) v. tr. Dy.* to wring: Fring(ir)eisen, *n.* wringing pole.

Frisch, I. *adj.* 1) fresh, cool; 2) fresh, recent, sweet, new; green, raw; 3) brisk, vigorous, lively, flush, gay; 4) *Min.* compact, solid; eine f-e Gesichtsfarbe, a hale, ruddy complexion; ein f-er Greis, hale old man; — und gesund, healthful and gay, safe *(or* whole) and sound; fresh; f-e Spur, burning scent; f-e Eier, new-laid eggs; f-e Butter, fresh butter; f-er Käse, fresh cheese, new cheese; f-es Brot, new bread; ein f-er (ungesalzener) Hering, white herring; f-e *or* — angekommene Waaren, fresh goods *or* supplies; f-e Truppen, new raised (newly levied) supplies, fresh supplies; f-e Wäsche, clean linen; f-es Wetter, 1. fresh weather: 2. *Min.* good air in the pit; f-e Wunde, green *or* raw wound; f-e Milch, new milk; f-es Gras, new grass; ein f-er Wind, a brisk gale of wind; f-e Zufuhr, fresh supplies; auf f-er That, in the very act, deed, *or* fact, red-handed: II. *adv.* 1) freshly, &c.; 2) briskly, lively, gaily; cheerfully, in high spirits, in high feather: — gelegt, new-laid (eggs); — gemacht, new-made; — gemähtes Gras, new-mown hay: —! — auf! cheer up! — zu! *Mar.* bear a hand! — darauf los! — vorwärts! — voran! — zu! cheerily! on then! go ahead! courage! on them! at them! sie gingen — daran, they went at it with a will; von F-em, afresh, anew: — gewagt ist halb gewonnen, *proverb,* well begun, is half done; a good beginning is half the battle; (a) faint heart never won fair lady.

Frisch'..., *in comp.* —arbeit, *f.* refining of metals, &c.; —backen, *adj.* new (bread); —bäcker, *m.* baker that sells new bread; —balg, *m. Iron-w.* bellows in a finery; —blei, *n.* lead not calcinated; refined lead; —boden, *m.* hearth of a puddling-furnace.

Frisch'e, *(w.) f.* 1) freshness; coolness; newness; brightness; ruddiness; briskness; die — des Geistes, edge of spirit; 2) summer-residence; 3) *Sport.* springy place.

Frisch'eisen, *(str.) n.* refined *or* bloom-iron.

Frisch'en, *(w.) v.* I. *tr.* 1) *a) see* Erfrischen; *b) Sport.* to purge (dogs); *c)* sich —, to drink (of dogs); 2) *Metall.* to remelt, refine; to puddle (iron), to revive (copper); 3) *Gunn.* to new-rifle (the barrel of a gun); II. *intr. Sport.* to pig, farrow. [metals].

Frisch'er, *(str.) m. Min.* finer, refiner (of

Frisch'erdings, *adv. (Lessing, l. n.)* afresh, a-new (von Neuem).

[illegible], *m. (abbr. for* Friedrich) Fred *(P. N.)*.
[illegible]chen, *(str.) n. (dimin. of* Fritz *&* Frie[illegible]) Freddy *(P. N.)*.
* **Frivol'**, *adj. (Lat.)* frivolous, flippant.
Frivolität', *(w.) f.* 1) frivolity; flippancy; [illegible]-en, *pl. Comm.* tattings.
Froh, *adj.* glad, joyful, rejoiced; happy; [illegible] *(with Acc.)* ... — sein, to be glad of, re[illegible] at ...; er mußte — sein sich zurückziehen [illegible], he was fain to withdraw; einer [illegible] *(Gen.)* — werden, to enjoy a thing; —[illegible], *n.* sensation of joy, happiness.
[illegible]heit, *(w.) f. see* Frohsinn.
[illegible]lich, *adj.* joyful, joyous, gladsome, [illegible], cheerful, blithesome, blithe, pleasant, [illegible], jovial, merry, genial; — machen, to glad, [illegible], cheer, exhilarate.
[illegible]lichkeit, *(w.) f.* joyfulness, &c. *cf.* [illegible]; gladness, gladsomeness, joviality, [illegible].
[illegible]locken, *(w. & insep.) v. intr.* to exult, [illegible], triumph, rejoice (über [*with Acc.*], in; [illegible] *with Dat.)* frohlocket dem Herrn! shout [illegible] rejoice in the Lord! das —, *(str.) v. s.* [illegible], shouting, triumph, jubilation.
[illegible]müthig, *adj.* jovial.
[illegible], I. *adj.* † 1) lordly; 2) holy, august; [illegible]; II. *s.* 1) *(str.) m. see* Frohne; 2) [illegible], *(str.) m.* beadle (Gerichtsbote).
[illegible]..., *in comp.* —acker, *m.* land held [illegible] soccage; —altar, *m. provinc.* high or holy [illegible]; —amt, *n.* high mass; —arbeit, *f.* 1) [illegible] service, soccage; 2) *fig.* unprofit[illegible] job; drudgery; —arbeiter, *m.* 1) soc[illegible]; 2) *fig.* drudge. [position.
[illegible]muth, *(w.) f. (Göthe)* happy dis-
[illegible]aufseher, *(str.) m. see* Frohnvogt.
[illegible]bar, *adj.* 1) liable to soccage; 2) [illegible] in soccage.
[illegible]..., *in comp.* —bauer, *m.* soccager, [illegible], villain; —bote, *m. provinc.* beadle, [illegible] Gerichtsbote; —botschaft, *f.* foot-service; [illegible], *n.* †, canopy (Baldachin).
[illegible]de, *(w.) f. see* Frohndienst.
[illegible]de, *(w.) f. Law,* execution.
[illegible]..., *in comp.* —dienst, *m.* service [illegible] in soccage, service due to the lord of [illegible] manor, compulsory or compelled service, [illegible], statute labour; —dienstlich, *adj.* [illegible] to soccage.
[illegible]ne, *(w.) f.* service to be rendered to [illegible] lord of the manor, soccage, compulsory [illegible].
[illegible]nen, *(w.) v. intr.* 1) *(or* Fröh'nen, [illegible]) to do service in soccage; 2) *fig.* [illegible], toil, slave; *(with Dat.)* to serve [illegible] in a slavish manner, to be a slave (to), [illegible] homage; to pander (to the passions of [illegible], &c.); to indulge (in), to be addicted [illegible] Jemandes Launen —, to humour one's [illegible].
[illegible]ner, *(str.) m.* 1) one who is bound [illegible] soccage-service, soccager; 2) *fig.* drudge; [illegible] creditor, who has caused execution.
[illegible], *(w.) f. see* Frohnleiste.
[illegible]..., *in comp.* —fasten, *f. pl.* the [illegible] quarter-fastings; —feste, [illegible]; —frei, *adj.* exempt from com[illegible] services; —fuhre, *f.* a compulsory [illegible] of waggons and horses; —geld, *n.* [illegible] paid in lieu of soccage-service; —ge[illegible], *n.* over-seer; —gut, *n.* tenement liable [illegible]; —herr, *m.* lord or proprietor who [illegible] to exact soccage-service; —hof, *m.* [illegible]; —hufe, *f.* soccage-ground; —[illegible], *m.* 1) vassal obliged to perform soc[illegible]-service, villain, serf; 2) sub-beadle; —[illegible], *n.* over-seer; —[illegible], *n.* soccage-labours, [illegible]; —[illegible], *m.* †, the [illegible] body; —[illegible] [illegible].
[illegible]

Frohn'los, *adj. see* Frohnfrei.
Frohn'..., *in comp.* —pflichtig, *adj.* obliged to soccage-duty; —pflichtigkeit, *f.* obligation to perform soccage-duty; —recht, *n.* 1) right of a —herr, *which see;* 2) municipal [illegible]; —tag, *m.* day on which soccage-d[illegible] performed.
Fröh'nung, *(w.) f.* 1) s[illegible]hne; 2) öffentliche —, *see* Concurs; [illegible] indulgence (des Lasters, in vice).
Frohn'..., *in comp.* —vogt, *m.* task-master, overseer of soccagers; —walm, *m. Eccl. Archit.* sacrament-house, holy roof; —weise, *adv.* by way of soccage, in soccage.
Froh'..., *in comp.* —sinn, *m.* cheerfulness, joyful, happy disposition; —sinnig, *adj.* cheerful, joyful, happy.
Fromm, *adj.* 1) †, *a)* brave, honest, upright; *b)* kind; *c)* brave, valiant, strong; 2) *a)* pious, godly, religious, devout; *b)* superstitiously devout, bigoted; 3) inoffensive, harmless, tame, quiet; artless, simple; 4) *Script.* just, right; ein f-er Betrug, a pious fraud; ein f-es Pferd, a quiet (gentle) horse; ein f-es Schaf, *fig.* an ignorant person, *anal.* a poor innocent; ein f-er Wunsch, an innocent (*i. e.* vain) wish; desideratum; f-e Wuth, religious fanaticism; — werden, *cont.* to turn a saint; — thun, sich — stellen, to play the saint; ein F-er, a pious man; *cont.* saint; eine F-e, a pious woman; die F-en, *pl.* the pious.
Frömmelei', *(w.) f.* affected piety, pietism, hypocrisy, bigotry, canting.
Fröm'meln, *(w.) v. intr.* to affect piety, to act the hypocrite, to cant; f-d, *p. a.* pietistic, pietistical, bigoted, sanctimonious; canting, *vulg.* psalm-smiting.
From'men, *(w.) v. intr.* to avail, profit, be of use; wozu frommt das? what boots it? das —, *(str.) v. s.* benefit, advantage, behalf, behoof; es dient zu deinem —, it is for your good or benefit.
Fröm'migkeit, *(w.) f.* piety, godliness, devoutness, devotion, meekness.
Frömm'ler, Frömmling, *(str.) m.* devotee, pietist, religionist, devotionalist; hypocrite, canting fellow, *anal.* saint.
Frömm'lerisch, *adj. see* Frömmelnd.
Frommthuerei', *(w.) f.* sanctimoniousness of deportment.
* **Fron'te, Front**, *(w.) f. (Fr.)* front: 1) *Archit.* frontispiece (of a building); 2) *a) Mil.* head, foremost rank (of an army, &c.); *b) Fort.* (einer Festung) face of a work; 3) breast (of a hill); eine Flotte in Frontlinie, *Naut.* a fleet formed abreast; — machen, 1. *Mil.* to form front; 2. *fig.* to turn head, to turn round (gegen, upon); der Gleichessinn machte — gegen jene Partei, loyalty arrayed itself against that party; in der —, a front; in — aufgestellt, fronted.
* **Frontal'**, *adj. (Lat.)* frontal; —feuer, *n. Mil.* direct fire. — **Fronta'le**, *(str.) n.* 1) *see* Stirnblatt; 2) *Med. see* Stirnumschlag.
* **Frontispiz'**, *(str.) n. (Lat.) Archit.* frontispiece (Giebelseite).
* **Fronton'** *[pr.* frongtong*]*, *(str., pl.* F-s*) m. (Fr.) Archit.* fronton; pediment.
Frosch, *s.* I. *(str., pl.* Frösch'e*) m.* 1) *a) Zool.* frog *(Rana L.)*; *b) Conch.* tongued whelk; 2) *a) Med.* ranula (an inflammatory or indolent tumour under the tongue); *b) Farr.* carney, lampas (a swelling in the palate (of a horse's mouth); 3) *Mus.* nut (of a bow for the violin, bass, &c.); 4) *Typ.* pan; 5) *Coop.* chine; 6) *Saddl.* cantle, the protuberant part of a saddle behind; 7) *Fire-w.* cracker; 8) *Carp. & Mech.* bracket; 9) *Mech. see* Daumen, 2; 10) *Min.* ladder-peg; 11) *Cloth.* sole-socket; 12) tread (of a stilt); 13) *see* Schwaben; 14) *Acad. slang,* grammar-school-pupil; II. *in comp.* —ader, *f. Anat.* ranular vein; —arten, *pl. Zool.* batrachians; —biß, *m. Bot.* frogbit *(Hydrocharis morsus ranae L.)*; —distel, *f. see* Frauendistel; —eier, *n. pl. see* —laich; —eisen, *n. Vet.* fleam for piercing the carney; —eppich, *m. Bot.* marsh-crowfoot *(Ranunculus sceleratus L.)*; —fisch, *m. Ichth.* toad-fish, sea-devil, fish-frog *(Lophius piscatorius L.,* Fischteufel); —geier, *m. Ornith.* honey-buzzard *(Pernis apivorus L.,* Wespenfalke); —gequake, *n.* the croaking of frogs; —geschwulst, *f. see* Frosch, 2; —hecht, *m. Ichth.* frog-pike (spawning in April, the spawning-time of frogs); —jagd, *f.* frog-catching; —keule, *f.* hind leg of a frog; —laich, —leich, *m. & n.* fry or spawn of frogs; —lattich, *m. Bot.* pond-weed, frog-lettuce *(Potamogeton compressum L.)*; —löffel (-kraut), *m. Bot.* water-plantain *(Alisma plantago L.)*; —maul, *n. Archit.* semi-circular dormer-window; —mäusekrieg, *m. Lit.* Batrachomyomachia; *Bot.* —pfeffer, *m. see* —eppich; —pulsader, *f. Anat. see* —ader; —quappe, *f.* bull-head, tadpole, a young frog; —reich, *adj.* abounding with frogs, froggy; —sattel, *m.* English saddle; —schnecke, *f. Conch.* toad-snail *(Ranella canina Lam.)*; —stein, *m.* toad-stone; —teufel, *m. see* —fisch; —thiere, *pl. Zool.* batrachians; —versteinerung, *f. see* —stein; —wegerich, *m. Bot. see* —löffel; —wurm, *m. see* —quappe.
Fröschel, Frösch'chen, (†, *provinc.,* & *:) **Frösch'lein**, *(str.) n.* 1) a little frog; 2) or **Frösch'elring**, *m. Min.* coin-ring, wedge-ring; **Frösch'leingeschwulst**, *f. see* Frosch, 2.
Frösch'en, Frosch'en, *(w.) v. intr. coll.* to catch frogs.
Frost, *s.* I. *(str., pl.* Fröst'e*) m.* 1) frost; cold, chill, chilling; 2) fever-shivering; 3) chilblains, *pl.;* 4) *fig.* coldness, apathy; frigidity; vom — beschädigt, frost-bitten; II. *in comp.* —beule, *f.* chilblain; aufgebrochene, kibe; —bohrer, *m.* an instrument for boring holes in the frozen ground; —falter, *m.,* —motte, *f. Entom.* a species of Phalaenidae (Geometra) L. *(Acidalia brumata L.)*; —fieber, *n.* ague; —mittel, —pflaster, *n.,* —salbe, *f.* remedy, plaster, salve (ointment) against frozen limbs or chilblains; —monat, *m.* December; —nacht, *f.* frosty night; —punct, *m.* freezing point (Gefrierpunct); —rauch, *m.* frozen vapour in the air, frosty mist, frost smoke; —wetter, *n.* frosty weather.
Fröst'eln, *(w.) v. intr. (impers.)* 1) to shiver (a little); mich fröstelt, I feel rather (or a little) cold, chilly; 2) to begin to freeze, to freeze a little; das —, *(str.) v. s.* slight chill or shiver.
Frost'ig, *adj.* 1) frosty; chilly; 2) *fig. a)* cold, cool; frigid; *b)* insipid, flat, dull; das f-e Wesen, frostiness, coolness, coldness; frigidity.
Fröst'ler, Fröstling, *(str.) m.* a person easily affected by cold, *coll.* a chilly body.
* **Frottı'ren**, *(w.) v. tr. (Fr.)* to rub; das —, *(str.) v. s. Surg.* friction. — **Frottir'bürste**, *(w.) f.* flesh-brush.
Frucht, *(str., pl.* Früch'te*) f.* 1) *a)* fruit; *b) also used for* corn, or any plants the earth produces for nourishment; Früchte, *pl.* harvest; 2) (Leibesfrucht) *Med.* fruit, fœtus; 3) *fig.* fruit, benefit, profit, product, effect; versteinerte Früchte, *see* Fruchtversteinerungen; — bringen, *fig.* to do good, to profit.
Frucht'..., *in comp.* —abgabe, *f.* duty, tax on corn, &c., corn-tax; —acker, *m.* corn-field, corn-land; —ansetzen, *n.* germination; —ast, *m.* fruit-bearing branch; —auge, *n.* bud, blossom of a fruit, germ; —balg, *m. Bot.* follicle, one-valved pericarp or seed-vessel; —band, *n. see* —schnur.
Frucht'bar, I. *adj.* fruitful, fat, fertile, productive; teeming; prolific; *fig.* rich, copious; ein f-es Jahr, a plenteous year; ein f-er Gedanke, suggestive idea; — machen, to

make fertile, fertilise; II. F-keit, (w.) f. fruitfulness, &c., fertility, productiveness, fecundity; plenteousness; fig. richness, copiousness.

Frucht'..., in comp. —bau, m. growing or culture of corn; —baum, m. fruit-tree; —beerpflanzen, f. pl. Bot. berry-bearing trees; —beet, n. hot-bed; —behälter, m., behältniß, n. Bot. receptacle; —beschreibung, f. see —lehre; —bildung, f. fructification; —boden, m. 1) fruit-loft, fruitery; 2) granary, corn-loft; 3) Bot. bottom of flowers, discus; —brand, m. blight in corn, ergot, smut; —branntwein, m. fruit-brandy; —bringend, p. a. 1) fruit-bearing, producing fruit, frugiferous, fructiferous; 2) fig. productive.

Früchtchen, (str.) n. (dimin. of Frucht) 1) little fruit; 2) joc. disorderly young person, ne'er-do-well.

Frucht'..., in comp. —darre, f. kiln for drying grain; —decke, f. Bot. epicarp.

Fruchten, (w.) v. intr. fig. to produce fruit, good effect, to be of use, to avail, to have effect; guter Rath fruchtet nichts, proverb, nobody is better for good advice. [dung.

Frucht'entwickelung, (w.) f. see Fruchtbil-

Fruchter, (str.) m. (l. u.) see Fruchtpflanze.

Frucht'..., in comp. —erde, f. upper stratum of earth, mould, soil (fit for the growth of plants); —essend, adj. frugivorous; —essig, m. fruit-vinegar; —fäule, f. see —brand; —feld, n. 1) corn-field; 2) fertile land; —folge, f. succession of crops (—wechsel); —garten, m. orchard; kitchen garden; —gehänge, n. see —schnur; —gehäuse, n. see —hülle; —geländer, n. railing with fruit-trees, espalier; —genuß, m., —genießung, f. usufruct; —gewinde, n. see —schnur; —göttin, f. goddess of fruit (applied to Pomona or Ceres); —gülte, f. dry-rent, rent-stock; —halter, m. see Gebärmutter; —handel, m. fruit-trade; corn-trade; —händler, m. 1) fruit-seller, fruiterer; 2) corn-merchant; —haus, n. corn-magazine, granary; —häutchen, n. Anat. chorioid; —horn, n. cornucopia; Bot-a. —hülle, f. seed-vessel, pericarp; —hülse, f. pod, cod, husk, shell of grains.

Fruchtig, adj. provinc. see Fruchtbar.

Frucht'..., in comp. —kammer, f. granary; —kapsel, f. see —balg; —kasten, m. 1) bin; 2) tub for trees or shrubs wintered in green-houses; —keim, m. 1) Bot. germ, germen; 2) Physiol. embryo; Bot-a. —kelch, m. see —hülle; —kern, m. kernel; —knospe, f. bud, germ; —knoten, m. germ, seed-bed, ovary; —korb, m. fruit-basket; —korn, n. seed-corn; —kranz, m. Archit., &c. festoon, garland; —kunde, f. see —lehre; —kundige, m. carpologist; —lager, n. Bot. fruit-bed; —land, n. corn-land; —lehre, f. carpology; —lese, f. gathering of fruit.

Fruchtlos, I. adj. fruitless; 1) unproductive, barren; 2) fig. vain, without avail; II. adv. fruitlessly, in vain, unsuccessfully; III. F-igkeit, (w.) f. barrenness; fruitlessness.

Frucht'..., in comp. —magazin, n., —müller, m., —maß, n. &c., see Getreidemüller &c.; —messer, n. fruit-knife; —monat, m. fruit-month; —mus, n. stewed fruit, jam; Law-a. —nießer, m. usufructuary; —nießung, —nutzung, f. usufruct; —pflanze, f. fruit-bearing shrub; —reich, adj. 1) rich or abounding in fruit, fruitful; 2) fig. fruitful, profitable; (die Zeit der) —reife, f. the ripening of fruits; fructescence, fruiting-season; —röhre, f. Bot. pistil; —saft, m. fruit-juice, fruit-jam; —schnur, f. Archit. festoon, garland; —sperre, f. prohibition (stoppage) of corn-exportation; —staude, f. fruit-bearing plant; —stein, m. 1) Fol. a) see Pfennigstein; b) carpolite; 2) Miner. variety of clay-stone; —stiel, m. fruit-stalk, foot-stalk of fruit; —stück, n. Paint. fruit-piece; —teller, m. fruit-plate; —tragend, adj. fruit-bearing, cf. —bringend; —versteinerungen, f. pl. Fol. carpolites; —wasser, n. Med. amniotic liquor; —wechsel, m. Agr. rotation or [illegible] of crops; —wein, m. cider, perry, [illegible]; —wolle, f. Bot. seed-down; —wucher, m. usurious trade in corn; —wucherer, m. usurious [illegible] in corn; —zehnt(e), m. predial tithe, corn-tithe; —zeit, f. 1) fruit-time, autumn; 2) Bot. fructescence; —zins, m. dry-rent, rent-stock.

Früh, Frühe, adj. & adv. 1) early; in the morning; 2) adv. soon, at an early hour, in good time; gar zu —, overseen; 3) premature; untimely; 4) early, hasty (of fruits); — Morgens, early in the morning; am f-en Tage, early in the day; in f-er Jugend, in early life; von — bis in die Nacht, from morning till night; gestern —, yesterday morning; heute —, (early) this morning; morgen —, to-morrow morning; f-er oder später, sooner or later; — nach Hause kommen, 1. to come home at an early hour; 2. to keep good hours.

Früh'..., in comp. 1) morning-, matinal, matutinal, cf. Morgen; 2) early, &c.; —apfel, m. summer-apple; —auf, m. early riser; —beet, n. hot-bed; —birne, f. summer- (or hasting-) pear; —blume, f. early (spring) flower.

Frühe, (w.) f. early time, morning time; earliness; in aller —, early in the morning.

Früher, I. adj. (compar. of Früh) 1) earlier, &c.; 2) former, previous, prior, preceding; die f-e Anlage, predisposition; die f-e Anordnung, previous determination, preordination; der f-e Besitzer, prepossessor; das f-e Datum, antidate; — vorhanden, pre-existent; II. adv. formerly; heretofore, in former times; wie — bemerkt, as already observed; — ansetzen, to advance (a term, &c.).

Früh'..., in comp. —erbsen, f. pl. hastings; —ernte, f. fore-crop, fore-harvest.

Frühestens, adv. at the earliest.

Früh'..., in comp. —geburt, f. premature labour, abortion, cf. Fehlgeburt; —gerste, f. forward barley; —gottesdienst, m. morning service; —jahr, n. spring; —kartoffeln, f. pl. early potatoes; —kirche, f. see —gottesdienst; —klug, adj. forward, precocious, prematurely wise, of forward wit, cf. —reif; —kost, f., —mahl, n. (l. u.) see —stück; —licht, n. (Freiligrath) the light of dawn.

Frühling, (str.) m. 1) spring; zum — gehörig, vernal; 2) (opp. Spätling) a) an animal born early in the year, especially a lamb; b) child born too soon; 3) fig. youth, prime of life. [become spring.

Frühlingen, (w.) v. intr. (impers.) to

Frühlings..., in comp. spring-, vernal; —adonis, m. Bot. spring-adonis, pheasant's eye (Adonis vernalis L.); —anfang, m. commencement of spring (usually the 21st of March); —bedarf, m. Comm. spring-demand; —blume, f. vernal or spring flower; —farbe, f. vernal tint; —feier, f. celebration of spring; —fieber, n. spring-fever; —fliege, f. Entom. spring-fly, water-moth, phryganea (Phryganida L.); —grün, n. vernal green.

Frühlingshaft, adj. spring-like, vernal, spring ....

Frühlings..., in comp. —hauch, m. vernal air or breeze; —himmel, m. spring (i. e. clear) sky; —hungerblümchen, n. Bot. spring-whitlow-grass (Draba verna L.); —jahre, n. pl. years of youth; —knotenblume, f. Bot. spring-snow-flake (Leucoium vernum L.); —kohl, m. see Schnittkohl; —luft, f. spring-time air, vernal air; —monat, m. spring month, March; —morgen, m. morning of a spring-day; —nachtgleiche, f. vernal equinox; —punct, m. Astr. vernal point; —regen, m. vernal rain; —tag, m. spring-day; —trieb, m. generative or productive power or impulse of spring;

Füch'sin, *(w.) f.* bitch-fox, she-fox.

Fuchs'..., *in comp.* —**jagd,** *f.* fox-hunt, fox-chase, fox-hunting; —**jäger,** *m.* fox-hunter.

Füchs'chen, *(str.) n. pl. Var.* foxes.

Fuchs'..., *in comp.* —**kaninchen,** *n.* a species of weasel; —**kopf,** *m. see* Rothkopf; —**kaffe,** *m. Zool.* maki; —**korb,** *m. Sport.* fanzia, scamber.

Füchs'lein, *(str.) n. (provinc. S G. &)* see Füchschen.

Fuchs'..., *in comp.* —**loch,** *n. see* —bau; —**pelz,** *m.* 1) *Comm.* fox-skins; 2) fur (lining) of foxes; den —pelz anziehen, *coll.* to play a trick, to use cunning; —**perücke,** *f.* a kind of periwig; —**prellen,** *n. Sport.* the (act of) tossing a fox in a blanket; —**räude,** *f. Vet.* scurf, fox-evil, alopecy; —**recht,** *n.* fagging system at schools, &c.; —**riedgras,** *n. Bot.* fox reed-grass (*Carex vulpina* L.); —**röhre,** *f. see* —bau; —**roth,** *adj.* fox-coloured, sorrel; —**roth,** *n.* sorrel colour, red bay; —**schlep-pen,** *n. Min. slang,* idling; —**schrot,** *m.* swan-shot; —**schwanz,** *m.* 1) fox-tail, *Sport.* brush; 2) *Carp.,* &c. dove-tail saw, whip-saw; 3) *Bot.* fox-tail, flower gentle; love-lies-bleeding (*Alopecurus* L.); 4) *see* —schwänzer; den —schwanz streichen, —schwänzen, *(w. & insep.) v. intr. coll.* to flatter, fawn, to pick thanks; backslander; —**schwänzer,** *m. coll.* fawner, please-man, tell-tale, pick-thank; slanderer, back-biter; —**schwänzerei,** *f. coll.* (act of) fawning, (abject) adulation; slander, backbiting; —**schwänzerisch,** *adj. coll.* fawning; slandering; —**schwanzgras,** *n. Bot.* fox-tail grass (—schwanz); —**schwanzsäge,** *f. see* —schwanz, 2; —**sucht,** *f. see* —räude; *Bot.-s.* —**traube,** *f.* fox-grape (*Vitis labrusca* W.); —**übel,** *n. see* —räude; —**wein,** *m.* wine made from the fox-grape; —**wild,** *adj. fam.* horn-mad; —**zunge,** *f. Bot. see* Eisenhut, 1.

Fuch'tel, *(w.) f.* 1) broad sword, blade; 2) whip, scourge, rod, ferule; unter der — halten, to keep under the ferule, strict discipline; 3) *vulg.* mien, visage; —**klinge,** *f.* a flexible blade without an edge.

Fuch'teln, *(w.) v.* I. *tr.* strike with a broad sword, &c., to whip, ferule; II. *intr.* to flourish a sword *or* switch.

Fu'der, *(str.) n.* 1) cart-load, waggon-load; 2) *Comm.* a measure for wine containing six ohm; —**weise,** *adv.* by cart-loads.

Fu'derig, *adj.* containing a cart-load.

Fug, *(str.) m.* 1) †. aptness, convenience; 2) right, authority; mit — und Recht, mit gutem —, with full right.

1. **Fu'ge,** *(w.) f.* 1) *Join. & Mas.* joint, groove; *Carp.* mortise, rabbet; *Arch., Anat., Bot., & Zool.* commissure; 2) *Anat.* seam, suture; aus der — bringen, to hold the mortise; aus den F—en bringen, to put out of joint, disjoint; *fig.* to disjoint, disorder, confuse, to unhinge; aus den F—n sein, *fig.* to be unhinged *or* off the hinges *or* hooks.

2. **Fu'ge,** *(w.) f. Mus.* fugue.

Fü'ge..., *in comp.* —**bank,** *f. Carp. & Join.* 1) grooving bench; 2) *or* —**hobel,** *m.* long plane; groove-(fluting *or* grooving-)plane, rabbeting-plane; —**eisen,** —**messer,** *n. Glaz.* grooving-iron.

Fü'gekellen, *(str.) n. Mas.* trowel (Kelle).

Fü'genmeißel, *m. T.* caulking-chisel.

Fü'geln, *(w.) v.* I. *intr.* to fit; to join; II. *tr. T.* to join, groove, rabbet.

Fü'gen, *(w.) v.* I. *tr.* 1) to join, unite, put *or* fit together; 2) *fig.* to ordain, dispose, dispense (said of Divine Providence); 3) *Join.* to [illegible]; II. *refl.* 1) to suit, to be suitable, convenient, proper, fit; 2) to happen, to come to pass; [illegible] sich in [illegible] —, to accommodate, reconcile, [illegible]; to comply with, submit [illegible].

Fü'ge..., *in comp.* —**nagel,** *m. T.* joining-peg; —**wort,** *(str., pl. F-wörter) n. Gramm.* conjunction.

Fu'gen..., *in comp.* —**componist,** *m.* fuguist; —**dicht,** *adj. Join.* joined; —**gelenk,** *n. Med.* articulation.

Fu'genhaft, *adj.* in the manner of a fugue.

Fu'gen..., *in comp.* —**leim,** *m.* hive-dross (the viscous substance of bees, by which they join their cells); —**schnitt,** *m.* the cutting into a conic form (stones, &c.); —**spieler,** *m.* fuguist; —**verstreichung,** *f. Mas.* pointing (*cf.* Ausstreichen, I. 1, *a*).

* **Fugirt',** *adj. (Ital.) Mus.* in style of fugue *or* double counterpoint.

Füg'lich, I. *adj.* convenient, proper, fit, apt, suitable, opportune, seasonable; II. *adv.* 1) conveniently, &c.; easily; seine Börse wurde so leer wie sie — konnte, his purse became as empty as it well could; 2) lawfully, by right *or* reason, reasonably; du kannst es — unerwähnt lassen, you may as well leave it unmentioned; — antworten, to answer to the purpose.

Füg'lichkeit, *(w.) f.* conveniency, propriety, fitness, &c. *cf.* Füglich; congruity, easiness.

Füg'los, I. *adj. (l. u.)* incompetent (Unbefugt); without right *or* reason, unreasonable; II. **F-igkeit,** *(w.) f.* incompetence; unreasonableness.

Füg'sam, I. *adj.* pliant, yielding, ductile; II. **F-keit,** *(w.) f.* pliancy, pliableness, yieldingness, ductility.

Fü'gung, *(w.) f.* 1) the (act of) joining, &c.; *fig.*-s. 2) contingency, juncture; 3) disposition (of Divine Providence), dispensation, decree.

Fühl'bar, I. *adj.* sensible; tangible, palpable; perceptible; II. **F-keit,** *(w.) f.* sensibility; tangibility, palpableness, perceptibility.

Fühl'eisen, *(str.) n. Surg.* sound (Sonde).

Füh'len, *(w.) v.* I. *tr. & intr.* 1) to feel, to touch; to be sensible of; 2) to perceive; Einem (an) den Puls —, *lit. & fig.* to touch *or* feel one's pulse; Einem auf den Zahn —, *fig.* 1) to feel one's mind; to sound one; 2) to try one; fein —, to be of a nice *or* delicate feeling; du sollst es —, you shall smart for it; ich werde es ihn — lassen, it shall fall heavy upon him; I'll make him smart for it; II. *refl.* to be sensible *or* conscious of; to feel (one's self); es fühlt sich weich (an), it feels soft; ich fühle mich ganz wohl, I feel perfectly well; ich fühle mich nicht (ganz) wohl, I do not feel well, *coll.* I do not feel myself; er fühlte sich beleidigt, he felt hurt; f-d, *p. a. fig.* feeling, sensitive, susceptible, tender. (*see* Fühlfäden.

Füh'ler, *(str.) m.* 1) feeler; 2) *gener. pl.*

Fühl'..., *in comp.* —**fäden,** *m. pl. Nat.* feelers (as of molluscs, &c.); —**hebel,** *m. T.* lever of contact; —**hörner,** *n. pl. Entom.* feelers (antennæ), tentacles; —**farn,** *m. Bot.* sensitive fern (*Onoclea sensibilis* L.); —**kraft,** *f.* faculty of feeling *or* of perception; —**kraut,** *n. Bot.* sensitive plant, mimosa (*Mimosa pudica* L.).

Fühl'los, I. *adj.* insensible (gegen, to), unfeeling, void of feeling, cold; II. **F-igkeit,** *(w.) f.* unfeelingness, coldness, apathy.

Fühl'..., *in comp.* —**niveau,** *n. T.* level of contact; —**spitzen,** *f. pl. see* —hörner.

Füh'lung, *(w.) f.* 1) *see* Gefühl; 2) *mil. a)* connexion; *b)* zur —, as a feeler.

Fuh'ne, *(w.) f. provinc.* ditch in peat-land.

Führ'band, *(str., pl. F-bänder) n. gener. pl.* leading-strings (Gängelband).

Führ'bar, *adj.* 1) portable, manageable; 2) capable of being conducted *or* carried on.

Fuhr'brief, *(str.) m. see* Frachtbrief.

Fuh're, Fuhr, *(w.) f.* 1) the (act of) carrying, carriage; 2) carriage, conveyance, cart, waggon; 3) cart-load, waggon-load, load; 4) carriage, fare; 5) *a) T.* groove (of a needle, &c.); *b) provinc.* furrow (Furche); per *or* mit —, *see* mit Fuhrgelegenheit.

Füh'ren, *(w.) v. tr.* 1) to carry, convey, bring; 2) to lead, guide, conduct; to command; 3) to form *or* build in a certain direction, to carry on *or* up, *cf.* Aufführen, I. 2; 4) *Comm.,* &c. *a)* to deal in, to keep (certain articles); *b)* to manage, carry on (a business, &c.); *c)* to keep (the books); 5) to bear, to wear; 6) to wield, manage, handle; 7) to have; to hold, contain; 8) to wage (war, &c.), carry on; das Vieh zur Tränke —, to drive the cattle to water; (das Glas *rc.*) zum Munde —, to raise to one's lips; das Schiff führt 30 Kanonen, the ship mounts thirty guns; den Bogen —, *Mus.* to manage the bow; er weiß den Degen gut zu —, he is a good swordsman; das Schwert, die Feder *rc.* —, to wield *or* handle the sword, the pen, &c.; Geld bei sich —, to have *or* carry money about, by, *or* with one *or* about one's person; falsche Gewichte —, to keep false weights; aus dem Lande —, to export; ins Land —, to import; einen Adler im Wappen —, to bear an eagle in one's coat of arms; er führt den Namen ..., he goes (passes) by the name of ...; einen Titel —, to bear a title; ein Leben —, to lead a life, to live a (miserable, &c.) life; eine glückliche Ehe —, to be happy in wedlock; eine Sache —, to direct, manage, *or* carry on a business; ein Schiff —, to steer, to navigate a ship; die Regierung, das Ruder —, to govern, rule; to sit at the helm; die Haushaltung —, to keep the house; aufs Eis —, *coll.* 1. to bring, draw into danger; 2. to deceive, take in; das Wort —, to be speaker in the name of others; garstige Reden —, to hold foul language; Krieg —, to wage war (mit, gegen, against), to make war (on); einen Proceß —, to carry on a law-suit; to plead a cause; Klage —, to complain (über [*with Acc.*], of); Staat — (*or* machen) to dress sumptuously; einen Beweis —, to hold an argument; den Beweis —, to shew proof; den Befehl —, to have the command; den Tanz —, to lead *or* to open the dance; eine Dame zum Tanze —, to lead a lady to the (*or* out to) dance; eine Dame zu Tische —, to take a lady in to dinner; den Pinsel —, to use, handle the brush, to paint; etwas im Schilde —, *fig.* to have some design in one's head; hinter das Licht —, *coll.* to deceive; in die Höhe —, to raise, erect; zu ... —, *fig.* to conduce to, to be conducive to; wozu soll das —? what is to come of this? what (benefit, &c.) will result from it? es führt zu nichts, it avails nothing, it is to no purpose; zu Gemüthe —, to bring home, &c. *see* Gemüth; in Versuchung —, to lead into temptation; mit sich — (of things), to carry along with it, to cause, to be productive of, *cf.* (mit sich) Bringen.

Füh'rer, *(str.) m.* 1) conductor, leader, guide, governor, director, commander, headman; — eines Schiffes, master; steersman; 2) *Mus.* the subject (of a fugue).

Füh'rerin, *(w.) f.* conductress, manageress, directress, governess.

Füh'rerschaft, *(w.) f.* leadership, guidance.

Fuhr'..., *in comp.* —**frohne,** *f.* soccage-service with waggon and horse; —**gelegenheit,** *f.* (chance-)conveyance; mit —gelegenheit, by land-carriage, by land, by (the) waggon; —**geräth,** *n.* waggon-furniture; —**handel,** *m. see* Frachthandel.

Füh'rig, *adj. Sport.* capable of being led (of hounds).

Fuhr'..., *in comp.* —**knecht,** *m.* carter's man; —**lohn,** *n.* freight, cartage, carriage, waggonage; fare, passage; driver's wages; —**mann,** *m.* (*pl.* —**leute**) 1) carrier, carman, carter, waggoner, charioteer; driver; 2) *Astr.* Waggoner, Auriga; durch —leute F., *Comm.*

per carman &c.; —mannsbinde, *f. Surg.* auriga; —mannshemd, *n.*, —mannskittel, *m.* smock-frock; —mannspeitsche, *f.* waggon (crop or driving) whip, waggoner's whip; —manns-pferd, *m.* cart-horse; —mannssattel, *m.* carrier's saddle: —mannswagen, *m. see* Frachtwagen; —mannswinde, *f. see* Wagenwinde.

Fuhr'straße, *see* Fahrstraße.

Füh'rung, *(w.) f.* 1) the (act of) carrying, &c., conveyance; 2) *Man.* hand; 3) *a) Paint.* the handling (of the brush); *b) Mus.* management (of the bow); *c)* — der Waffen, *Mil.* manual exercise; 4) *a)* the (act of) leading, guidance, conduct; *b)* direction, management; conduct (of a business, &c.); *c)* command; *d)* conduct: sittliche *or* gute —, good conduct; 5) the keeping (of books); 6) *Mar. see* Beilast; F—smannschaft, *f.* the men (sailors, &c.) able to navigate a vessel, crew; F—szeugniß, *n.* character.

Fuhr'..., *in comp.* —weg, *m.* highway, carriage road, *cf.* Fahrweg; —werk, *n.* 1) vehicle, conveyance, carriage, cart, waggon; 2) (wheeled) vehicles (collectively); —wesen, *n.* carrying, conveyance, carriages.

Füll'..., *in comp.* —band, *n. T.* border of a door-panel; —baum, *m. Min.* first frame of a shaft; —bier, *n.* beer with which a cask is filled up; —blatt, *n. Gold-b.* empty book; —brett, *n. Join., &c.* panel; —dachstuhl, *m. Build.* principal rafter (of a roof).

Fül'le, *(w.) f.* 1) *Cook. see* Füllsel; 2) fulness, plenty; abundance; profusion, exuberance; 3) filling, contents of barrel; die —, *coll. sometimes used adverbially:* in (super) abundance.

A. Fül'len, *(w.) v.* I. *tr.* 1) to fill, fill up; auf Flaschen —, to bottle; in Fässer —, to put into casks, to cask, barrel; in Säcke —, to put in sacks; einen Luftballon —, to fill, inflate a balloon; eine Lücke —, to make up for a deficiency (*cf.* Ausfüllen); wieder —, to replenish; 2) *a)* to stuff; *b) Cook.* to farce, force, stuff; 3) to pour, put in; II. *refl.* to stuff, fill, cram.

B. Fül'len, *(str.) n.* foal, filly; —stute, *f.* brood-mare; —zahn, *m.* colt's tooth, nipper; —zucht, *f.* breeding of foals. — Fül'len, *(w.) v. intr.* to foal.

Fül'ler, *(str.) m.*, Fül'lerin, *(w.) f.* 1) filler; 2) fuller.

Füll'..., *in comp.* —erde, *f. T.* fill; —faß, *n.* 1) any smaller vessel used in filling up a larger one; 2) *Min. a)* coal-basket; *b)* coal-measure; —gelte, *f. Brew.* pail, basket, pitcher; —haar, *n.* (hair for) stuffing, wadding; —hals, *m.* 1) a large funnel for filling casks; 2) *Build.* filler; —heckbalken, *m. Ship-b.* filling-transom; —horn, *n.* horn of plenty, cornucopia.

Fül'lingen, *(w.) f. pl. Ship-b.* limber-boards.

Füll'..., *in comp.* —kanne, *f. see* —gelte; —kelle, *f.* (pot-)ladle; *Mas.* filling-trowel; —kord, *m. see* —faß, 2, *a*; —kraut, *n. Cook.* cabbages filled with forced meat; —lager, *n. Brew., &c.* stilling, stand; —löffel, *m.* filling-ladle *or* spoon; —mauer, *m. Build.* backing (filling of a wall, &c.).

Füll'nis, *(str.) n. & f. see* 1) Füllsel; 2) Füllung.

Füll'..., *in comp.* —öffnung, *f. Gunn.* charging-hole; —opfer, *n. Jew. Rel.* sacrifice of consecrations; —ort, *m. Min.* pit-eye; *Build.-s.* —pfosten, *m.* middle-post; —quader, *m.* filler; —röhre, *f. Mech.* feed-pipe.

Füll'sel, *(str.) n. Cook.* stuffing, farcing, forced meat, minced meat.

Füll'..., *in comp.* —span, *m. T.* filling-piece; —spannen, *f. pl. Ship-b.* filling-timbers; —sparren, *m.* principal rafter; —stange, *f.* stirring-pole; —steine, *m. pl. Mas.* explotives; —stift, *m. Typ.* space, quadrate; — Stifte einsetzen, to space; —stimme, *f. Mus.* ripieno (ital.), part introduced to fill up the chorus (Ripienstimme); —stock, *m.* 1) *Fire-w.* driver; 2) *Gunn.* setter; —stück, *n.* a piece of wood, &c. used to fill up a space; —trichter, *m. see* —hals, 1.

Fül'lung, *(w.) f.* 1) the (act of) filling, &c.; 2) filling-ingredients, stuffing; 3) *Bibl.* first fruits as a sacrifice; 4) *Med.* anaplerosis; 5) *a) T.* panel(-square), pane; (blinde) false panel; (bündige) flush panel; *b) Sugar-m.* set of filled moulds; F—splanken, *f. pl. Ship-b.* planks between the wales; F—sröhre, *f. Mech.* supply-pipe (of a steam engine); F—sspannen, *f. pl. Ship-b.* filling-timbers.

Füll'..., *in comp.* —wein, *m.* wine with which a cask is filled up; —werk, *n. Build.* backing, rubble-work (Füllmauer); —wort, *n. Gramm.* expletive.

* Fulminiren, *(w.) v. intr. (Lat.)* to fulminate.

Fum'mel, I. *(str.) m. or* —bein, —holz, *n.*, —knochen, *m. T.* polisher, polishing-stick; II. *(w.) f. vulg.* a low woman, slut.

Fum'meln, *vulg. (w.) v.* I. *intr.* to fumble; II. *tr. T.* to polish, to smooth.

* Function', *(w.) f. gener. & Math. (Lat.)* function. — Functioni'ren, *see* Fungiren.

Fund, *(str., pl.* Fün'de) *m.* 1) the (act of) finding; 2) any thing found, find; 3) *fig.* discovery, invention, contrivance, *cf.* Erfindung; — und Bauer, *Min.* spot where the working of a mine commences; einen — thun, to find something of value.

* Fundament', *(str.) n. (Lat.)* 1) foundation, basis; 2) *Print.* table (of a printing-press) — Fundamental', *adj.* fundamental, *cf.* Grund..., *in comp.* —baß, *m. Mus.* fundamental bass; —bret, *n. T.* cross-bar; —linie, *f. Geom., &c.* ground-line, base-line.

* Fundation', *(w.) f. (Lat.)* foundation, a revenue established, establishment, endowment; F—ssystem, *n.* founding system.

Fund'..., *in comp.* —buch, *n.* inventory; —diebstahl, *m. Law,* fraudulent retention of any thing given in trust *or* embezzlement of an unowned object (*furtum inventionis*); —gebühr, *f.*, —geld, *n.* recompense (for finding and restoring something); —gegenstand, *m.* object found; —grube, *f.* 1) mine, shaft; 2) *fig.* a mine or rich source, (literary *or* scientific) treasure; —gräbner, *m. Min.* proprietor, owner of a mine, miner.

Fün'dig, *adj. Min.* containing *or* yielding ore, metalliferous (*opp.* Taub).

* Fundi'ren, *(w.) v. tr. (Lat.)* to fund, consolidate; die fundirte Schuld, funded *or* consolidated debt, *pl.* consols.

Fund'..., *in comp.* —ort, 1) place where a species of minerals, plants, &c. is found, habitat; 2) *or* —punct, *m. Min.* place where a mine has been discovered; —recht, *n.* right *or* claim from having found a thing; —register, *n. see* —buch; —schacht, *m.* shaft by which a mine has first been discovered; —schein, *m.* 1) certificate of having found a thing; 2) *Law,* certificate of a physician as to the cause of a person's death; —zettel, *m. Law,* inventory.

Fünf, *card. numb.* five; *Gam.* cinque (at dice); — vom Hundert, five in the hundred; — gerade sein lassen, *fam. proverb,* to be not over-nice, to connive at something, to strain a point; to stand not upon niceties; er kann nicht — zählen, *see* Drei, I.

Fünf..., *in comp.* —actig, *adj.* of five acts; —actige Stücke, five-act plays; —blätterig, *adj. Bot.* quinquecapsular; —blatt, *n. see* —fingerkraut; —blätterig, *adj. Bot.* 1) five-leaved, quinquefoliate(d), pentaphyllous; 2) —(blumen-)blätterig, *adj.* five-petaled, pentapetalous; —doppelt, *adj.* five-fold, quintuple.

Fün'fe, *(w.) f.*, Fün'fer, *(str.) m.* 1) five;

[illegible]nke, *(irr.)*, **Funken,** *(str.)* m. 1) spark, [illegible]; 2) *fig.* glimpse, ray; spark, flash [illegible] spark, particle (of virtue, &c.); die [illegible] nachglimmenden F-n der Empörung, [illegible] smouldering embers of rebellion.

Funkeln, Funken, *(w.)* v. *intr.* to emit [illegible], to sparkle, glitter, scintillate, twinkle, [illegible], shine; f-d, *p. a.* sparkling, &c., [illegible], bright; das —, *(str.)* s. s. sparkling, scintillation; coruscation.

Funkelnagelneu, *adj. coll.* bran-new, [spick] and span(-new).

Funken, s. I. *(str.)* m. see Funke; II. *in [com]p.* —fänger, m. spark-catcher, spark-ar[rester] (of a steam-engine); —holz, n. touch[wood]; —sehen, n. twinkling of the eyes; —[sprü]hend, —werfend, emitting sparks, scin[tilla]ting; —wurm, m. fire-fly (Glühwurm).

Für, I. *prep. (with Acc.)* for; instead of; — allemal, once for all; — Bezahlung an[neh]men, to take in payment; — gut *or* recht [halt]en, to think (a thing) right, advisable, *or* [pro]per; es — einen Schimpf achten, to con[side]r it as an affront; ich lebe wöchentlich — [zehn] Thaler, I live at the rate of ten dollars [a wee]k; — einen Pfennig, a pennyworth; — [den] Preis von ..., at the rate (*or* price) of ...; [— da]s *or* das Jahr, per annum; ich — meine [Pers]on, as for (*or* to) me, for my part; I, [for] one; diese Thür ist — dich geschlossen, this [door] is closed to you; er ist todt — mich, he [is dea]d to me; der Knabe war groß — sein [Alte]r, the boy was tall of his age; ein Mitt[ags]mahl — die Pächter, a dinner to the ten[ants]; ein günstiges Vorzeichen — etwas, fa[vour]able omen to something; ehrenvoll — [ihr], aber hart — mich, honourable to her, but [hard] upon me; wichtig — mich, important to [me]; — die Zeit der Noth, against the time of [need]; — dich würde ich es thun, I should do [it fo]r your sake; — sich, per se, separately; [an u]nd — sich, in itself, by itself, apart from [othe]r things *or* persons, abstractedly; — sich [lebe]n, to live by one's self; — sich bleiben, to [rem]ain single; sie nehmen ein Stadtviertel — [sich] ein, they occupy a distinct quarter of the [tow]n; sie hat einiges Vermögen — sich, she has [some] property of her own; — sich sprechen, to [spe]ak to one's self; er sprach dies nur — sich, he [sai]d this for an aside; ich habe es — mein Leben [gern], (*lit.* I like it for my life) I dote upon it: [Man]n — Mann, man by man, one and all, [ever]y one; Tag — Tag, day by day; Schritt [— S]chritt, step by step; — etwas sein, to be [for] *or* in favour of ..., to advocate for ...; [— u]nd wider, for and against, *coll.* pro and con; [die] Argumente — und wider, the arguments [on] both sides; *Comm*-c. — mich an die Order [des] Herrn N., pay to Mr. N. or order; — [Ih]re Rechnung und Gefahr, for your account [and r]isk.

[I]I. *adv.* († &) *, — und —, for ever and [ever], ever and anon. [then, on.

[Für]baß [*or* fürbaß], *adv.* †, forward, fur[ther].

[Für]bieten, *(str.)* v. *tr.* (S. G.) to cite, [summ]on (Vorladen, Herladen).

Fürbitte, *(w.)* f. intercession, mediation; [inter]cessory prayer; — der Heiligen, suffrage [of t]he Saints; — einlegen, to intercede, to [illegible] [mediator.

Fürbitter, *(str.)* m. intercessor, pleader,

Fürbittschreiben, *(str.)* n. letter of in[tercessi]on.

[Furchen]..., *in comp.* [illegible], —[illegible], —[illegible], m. furrow-neighbour.

Furche, *(w.)* f. 1) furrow; 2) *T.* groove; [illegible] *fig.* wrinkle; F-n [illegible] [illegible] furrows.

[Furchen], *(w.)* v. *tr.* & *intr.* to furrow; *fig.* to [illegible]; [illegible] *p. a. Bot.* sulcate(d) [illegible]. [illegible] —egge, f. drill-harrow; —harke, f., —rechen, m. implement for making drains; —rain, m. furrow slice, balk; —sonde, f. *Surg.* see Hohlsonde; —weise, *adv.* furrow-like, in furrows; —zieher, m. *Agr.* drill-plough, drilling-machine.

Fur'chig, *adj.* 1) furrowed; wrinkled; *Bot.* sulcate(d).

Furcht, (*pl.* [*w.*] F-en, *n. u.*) f. fear [illegible] (*with Dat.*), of), fright, terror, dread, awe; die — Gottes, the fear of God; die — vor dem Tode, the fear of death; ich vergaß alle — vor der Zukunft, I forgot all fear of [the] future; aus — vor (*with Dat.*), for (from) fear of ...; außer sich vor —, frightened out of one's wits; ohne —, fearless; vor ... (*with Dat.*) — haben, to be afraid of ...; in — gerathen, to take the alarm, to be frightened; in — setzen, to frighten, terrify, to make afraid, to put in fear.

Furcht'bar, I. *adj.* (F-lich, †, *adv.*) fearful, formidable, dreadful, frightful, terrible, dread, awful, tremendous; II. F-keit, *(w.)* f. formidableness, dreadfulness, terribleness.

Fürch'ten, *(w.)* v. I. *tr.* to fear, be afraid *or* apprehensive of, to apprehend, dread; das ist nicht zu —, there is no fear of that; Sie haben dabei nichts zu —, you run no risk in it; ich fürchte für sein Leben, I am afraid for his life; es wird sehr gefürchtet, daß ..., there is great fear evinced that ...; (zu) — machen, to make afraid, to frighten; II. *ref.* to be in fear, to be afraid *or* apprehensive (vor [*with Dat.*], of), to stand in fear or awe (of).

Fürch'terlich, I. *adj.* frightful, terrible, horrible, horrid, fearful, tremendous; II. F-keit, *(w.)* f. frightfulness, &c.

Furcht'los, I. *adj.* fearless, free from (*or* devoid of) fear; II. F-igkeit, *(w.)* f. fearlessness.

Furcht'sam, I. *adj.* timorous, timid, faint-hearted, apprehensive, pusillanimous, cowardly; nervous; — machen, to make afraid, to dishearten; II. F-keit, *(w.)* f. timorousness, timidity, faint-heartedness.

Für'der, *adv.* († &) *, onwards, farther, further, *cf.* Förder &c.

* **Fu'rie,** *(w.)* f. (*Lat.*) 1) *Anc. Myth.* Fury, goddess of vengeance; 2) fury, rage; 3) *fig.* a raging woman, fury, hag: f-nartig, f-nähnlich, f-nhaft, *adj.* fury-like, furious.

Fürlieb', *adv. only used in the phrase* — nehmen, to be satisfied *or* content with, to make shift with; er nimmt mit Allem —, nothing comes amiss to him.

* **Furnier',** *see* Fournier.

* **Furo're,** (*str.*) *m.* & *n.* (*Heine* [*unusual*]: f. *cf. Sanders*) (*Ital.*) sensation, impression made on others; — machen, to make a sensation.

Für'sehung, *(w.)* f. († &) * see Vorsehung.

Für'sorge, *(w.)* f. care (Vorsorge); f-nd, *adj.* caring for. [provider; guardian.

Für'sorger, *(str.)* m. he who cares for,

Für'sprache, *(w.)* f., **Für'spruch,** *(str.)* m. intercession, recommendation, *cf.* Fürbitte; — einlegen, to make intercession; erst auf meine —, not till I had interceded.

Für'sprecher, *(str.)* m. interceder, intercessor, mediator, advocate.

Fürst, *(w.)* m. prince, sovereign, liege (lord); der weltliche —, lay-prince; —abt, —bischof, m. abbot, bishop bearing the title of prince, sovereign abbot, sovereign bishop.

Fürst'en, *(w.)* v. *tr.* 1) to elevate to the rank *or* to invest with the dignity of a prince; der gefürstete Abt, *see* Fürst-Abt; 2) to raise (a country) to the dignity of a principality.

Für'sten..., *in comp.* —bank, f. (*formerly*) seat of the princes in the German diet; —birne, f. *Pomol.* bergamot-pear; —brief, m. letters patent conferring the dignity of a prince; —bund, m. confederation *or* league of princes; —diener, m. attendant of a prince, courtier; —dienst, m. [illegible] of a prince; —geschlecht, n. race [illegible], dynasty; —größe, f. greatness [illegible]our of a prince, princely grandeur; —gruft, f. tomb or vault of princes; —gunst, f. favour of princes, court-favour; —gut, n. estate, domain of a prince; —haus, n. family (house, court) of a prince; —hut, m. prince's coronet; —mantel, m. robe, ermine of a prince; —mäßig, *adj.* prince-like, princely; —rath, m. college of princes; —recht, n. right *or* prerogative of princes; —ruf, m. *Sport.* horn-signal to advertise the prince where the chase is.

Für'stenschaft, *(w.)* f. see Fürstenstand.

Für'sten..., *in comp.* —schnepfe, f. *Ornith.* common snipe; —schule, f. prince's school: 1) school for young princes; 2) a learned school founded by the sovereign; —sitz, m. seat, residence of a prince; —stamm, m. see —geschlecht; —stand, m. 1) princedom, rank of a prince (—würde); in den —stand erheben, see Fürsten; 2) the body of princes; —stuhl, m. a prince's throne; —tag, m. assembly of princes.

Für'stenthum, (*str.*, *pl.* F-thümer) n. principality, dominion of a prince.

Für'sten..., *in comp.* —verein, m. see —bund; —würde, f. princely dignity, see —stand, 1.

Für'stin, *(w.)* f. princess.

Für'stlich, I. *adj.* & *adv.* princely, prince-like; das f-e Benehmen, princeliness; f-e Durchlaucht, Serene Highness; II. F-keit, *(w.)* f. 1) princeliness; splendour; 2) (as a title) Serene Highness, Serenity.

Fürtreff'lich, *adj.* †, see Vortrefflich.

Furt *or* **Fürth,** *(w.)* f. a shallow part of a river, ford. [certainly, truly, verily.

Fürwahr', *adv.* in truth, indeed, forsooth,

Für'witz, *(str.)* m. see Vorwitz.

Für'wort, (*str.*, *pl.* F-wörter) n. 1) *see* Fürsprache; 2) *Gramm.* pronoun. — **Für'wörtlich,** *adj.* pronominal.

Furz, *(str.)* m. *vulg.* fart (Blähung).

Fur'zen, *(w.)* v. *intr. vulg.* to fart, *see* Wind lassen. [fraudulent dealing.

Fuschelei', *(w.)* f. *provinc.* underhand or

Fusch'eln, *(w.)* v. *intr. provinc.* 1) to bungle; 2) to cheat (at cards). [2) *Chem.* fusel.

Fu'sel, *(str.)* m. 1) common or bad gin;

Fu'selig, *adj.* 1) containing fusel-oil; 2) intoxicated from drinking bad gin.

Fu'seln, *(w.)* v. *intr.* to drink or smell of common gin.

Fu'sel..., *in comp.* —öl, n. fusel-oil; —politiker, m. *cont.* alehouse-politician.

* **Füsilier', Füselier',** (*str.*) m. (*Fr.*) *Mil.* fusileer; —regiment, n. regiment of fusileers.

* **Füsili'ren,** *(w.)* v. *tr.* (*Fr.*) to shoot (as a punishment).

* **Fusion',** *(w.)* f. (*Lat.*) fusion.

Fuß, (*str.*, *pl.* Fü'ße) m. 1) foot; 2) *a)* a measure consisting of twelve inches, *pl.* Fü'ße &c., *in conjunction with numerals*: Fuß; mehrere — hoch, several feet high; fünf — lang und zwei — breit, five feet by two; zehn — und darüber, ten feet and better; *b)* (*pl.* Füße) *Poet.* foot; 3) bottom, lower part of any thing, foot (of the bed, of a column, a mountain, an account, &c.); heel (of a mast); stem (of a glass); *Archit.* pedestal, socle, base; leg (of a wheel-barrow); lower flange (of a rail); 4) foot, sediment (of oil, tar, &c.): *fig.*-s. 5) *a)* standard, plan of establishment; *b)* way of life; footing; *c)* *Mint.* standard; im 30-Thaler-Fuß; at the 30 thaler-standard; 6) *Mus.* higher *or* lower pitch of tones: am F-e eines Berges, at the foot or bottom of a mountain; am F-e dieses, *Comm.* at the foot of the present; here below; keinen — breit weichen, not to yield one foot of ground.

[illegible]-üre, *f. see* –bank; –mauer, *f. Mas., &c.* [illegible]-ing-wall; *Metall.,&c.* lining-wall; –mütze, [illegible] hanging cap.

[illegible] Füttern, *(w.) v. tr.* 1) to case, to cover the inside or outside of ...; to sheath; to line; mit Pelz –, to fur; mit Blei –, to lead: 2) see Füttern, I.

Füttern, *(w.) v. tr.* 1) to feed, give the provender; 2) see Futtern, 1.

Futter..., *in comp.* –netz, *n.* feeding net [illegible]); –papier, *n. Mar.* sheathing-paper; [illegible] *f. pl. see* –kräuter; –raufe, *f.* rack; [illegible], *f. Vet. see* Fressfrankheit; –reich, *adj.* abounding in forage; –rübe, *f.* cattle turnip; [illegible], *m.* 1) fodder-bag, feed-bag; 2) *see* –[illegible]; –schneide, *f. see* –bank; –schneider, *m.* [illegible]-chopper; –schwinge, *f.* van, fan; winnowing basket; –sieb, *n.* oat-sieve; –stätte, *f.* place of feeding; –stroh, *n.* feeding-straw; [illegible], *f.* riser (of a stair); –taffet, *m.* sarsenet; –trosch, *m.*, –trespe, *f. Bot.* tall fescue-grass (*Festuca gigantea* L.); –tuch, *n.* cloth or stuff for lining.

Fütterung, *(w.) f.* 1) the (act of) feeding, &c. *cf.* Füttern; 2) food, forage; pasture, fodder; provender; auf – *(Acc.)* ausgehen, to forage; 3) *a)* the (act of) casing, &c. *cf.* Füttern; *b)* covering, &c., see Futter, I.; – [illegible], *Mar.-s.* back of the rudder; – für [illegible], lining of the bow; – des Brat- und Sangfisches, whelps.

Futter..., *in comp.* –wanne, *f. see* –[illegible]; –wicke, *f. Bot.* common vetch (*Vicia sativa* L.); –zeug, *n. & m.* lining-stuff.

* Futu'rum, *(str., pl. [Lat.]* Futu'ra) *n.* *(Lat.) Gramm.* future, the future tense.

G.

G, g, *n.* 1) *Gramm.* G, g, the seventh letter and fifth consonant of the alphabet; 2) *Mus.* G (the fifth note of the gamut, named *sol* in Italy and France); G dur (the key of) G major; G moll, (the key of) G minor; G-schlüssel, G (or treble) clef [𝄞].

G., *abbr. for* Geld, money (on bills of exchange); G., g., Gl., gl., Gr., gr. *for* Groschen, groschen; Gatt. *for* Gattung, kind, genus; Gb. *for* Gebrüder, brothers; g. D. *for* gehorsamster Diener, most obedient servant; G. D., Ger. Dir. *for* Gerichts-Director, [illegible]; geb. 1) *for* geboren, born; 2) *for* gebunden, bound; geh. *for* geheftet, stitched; gezeichn. *for* gezeichnet, marked; Gen. 1) *for* Genealogie, genealogy; 2) *for* General, general; 3) *for* Genetiv; Gen. Lt. *for* General-Lieutenant, lieutenant general; Geogr. *for* Geographie, geography; Geom. *for* Geometrie, geometry; Ger. *for* Gericht, court of justice; Gesch. *for* Geschichte, history; Geschl. *for* Geschlecht, genus; gest. *for* gestorben, deceased, [illegible], late; Gew. 1) *for* Gewerbe, trade, profession; 2) *for* Gewicht, weight; G. G. *for* Gottes Gnaden, von –, by the grace of God; g. G. *for* gut Geld, good money; Gg., Ggl., [illegible] *for* Gold-Gulden, gold-florin; [illegible] [illegible]

[illegible]

vlm. for Groot-Flämisch, great Flemish; Grt. *for* Groot, groat; Grt. *for* Groß-Tausend (1200), a number of twelve hundred; G. Schrbr. *for* Gerichts-Schreiber, clerk, actuary; G. V., G. Vltr., G. Vwltr. *for* Gerichts-Verwalter, see G. D.; Gymn. *for* Gymnasium, Gymnastik, gymnasium, gymnastics.

* Gä'a, *f. Gr. Myth.* (the goddess) Earth *(P. N.)*.

Gaban'holz, *(str.) n.* camwood.

* Gabar(r)'e, *(w.) f. (Fr.)* gabare (a flat-bottomed lighter, barge).

Ga'be, *(w.) f.* 1) gift, donative, donation, present; 2) alms, charity; 3) *Med.* dose; 4) *for* Abgabe, 1, Übergabe, *which see*; 5) *fig.* gift, endowment, talent; *pl.* parts, qualities; *coll.* turn, knack.

A. Ga'bel, *(w.) f.* 1) fork; 2) shafts, thills (of a vehicle); 3) *Bot.* tendril; fork, crotch (of a tree); clasper (of vines); 4) trigger (of a cross-bow); 5) *pl.* shafts, thills (of a carriage); 6) *Sport.* forked end (of a deer's horn); 7) *Mar.* crotch (for supporting a boom, &c.). 8) sweep (of a pump); 9) forked bone (of a fowl's breast, &c.); 10) *Sew.* gusset; 11) *ellipt. for* Heugabel, Stimmgabel &c.; 12) a forking, furcation (–theilung). [excise.

B. Ga'bel, *(w.) f.* (†&) *provinc.* tax, duty,

Ga'bel..., *in comp.* –anker, *m.* 1) *Mar.* small bow-anchor, bower; den –anker auswerfen, to moor across *or* athwart; 2) *T.* cramp-iron; –antilope, *f. Zool.* a species of antelope (*Antilope furcifer* Smith); –arm, *m.* shaft, thill; –bäume, *m. pl.* shafts, thills; –bespannung, *f.* treble draught; –bock, *m.* see –hirsch; –bürste, *f.* fork-brush.

Gä'belchen, *(str.) n.* (*dimin. of* Gabel) 1) a little fork; 2) *Bot.* tendril.

Ga'bel..., *in comp.* –deichsel, *f.* shafts, thills; –fisch, *m.* a species of gurnard (*Peristedion cataphractum* L.); –förmig, *adj.* forked; –förmig gespalten, *Bot.* bifurcate(d); (sich) –förmig theilen, to fork off, to divide into two; –förmige Röhre, *coll.* breeches-pipe; –förmige Theilung, bifurcation; –förmig getheilt, *Bot.* two-forked, dichotomous; –frühstück, *n.* second breakfast (eaten with knife and fork), lunch, luncheon; *(Fr.) déjeuner à la fourchette*; –gehörn, *n. Sport.* forked attire, forked head; –geier, *m. see* Milan; –gemse, *f. see* –antilope; –hirsch, *m. Sport.* brock, brocket; –holz, *n.* a forked piece of wood, *pl. Ship-b.* futtock, crotch.

Ga'belicht, Ga'belig, *adj.* forky, forked; *Herald.* fourchee. [III. 1 (*cf.* Schnabeliren).

Gabeli'ren, *(w.) v. intr. joc. see* Gabeln

Ga'bel..., *in comp.* –klinge, *f.* fork-blade; –kreuz, *n.* a forked cross, *Herald.* cross pall, cross furchee; –maß, *n.* an instrument for measuring the diameter of a tree; –mast, *m.* *Mar.* forked mast; –mehl, *n. Mill.* superfine flour.

Ga'beln, *(w.) v.* I. *tr.* 1) to fork, to prong (Aufgabeln); 2) to gore (with the horns); II. *rfl. Min., &c.* to run out in a forked shape, to fork off, to diverge; III. *intr. vulg.* 1) to take up with the fork and eat, to prog; 2) (*with* nach) to covet, long for, *mod.* to fish for (Angeln).

Ga'bel..., *in comp.* –nadel, *f. see* Haarnadel; –pferd, *n.* thiller, thill-horse, shaft-horse; –pflug, *m. Agr.* forked plough; –punkt, *m.* point where a road, railway, &c. forks off or diverges; –rad, *n. Mech.* forked wheel; –richter, *m. Cutl.* a piece of iron put in the stock of an anvil, on which the tines of forks are formed; –riegel, *m.* shaft-bar; –röhre, *f. Mech.* bifurcated pipe; –schwanz, *m.* 1) *Ent.* forky tail, double tail, spring-tail (*Podura* L.); 2) *Entom.* puss-moth (*Bombyx vinula* L.); –spaltung, *f. see* –theilung; –spaltig, *adj.* *Bot.* dichotomous; –stange, *f.* a forked pole or rod; –stich, *m.* thrust or prick with a fork; –stiel, *m.* handle of a fork; –stück, *n.* 1) a forky piece of timber, bracket (*cf.* –holz); 2) *Gunn.* a piece of cannon lying on iron forks; –stütze, *f.* thill-prop; –theilung, *f.* a forking, furcation, bifurcation (of a river, &c.), a branching (like the prongs of a fork).

Ga'belung, *(w.) f.* a forking (Gabeltheilung).

Ga'bel..., *in comp.* –wagen, *m.* a waggon with shafts, thill-waggon; –weihe, *f. Ornith.* kite, glede (Milan, *Milvus regalis* Briss.); –zeug, *n. Mill.* shaking-apparatus; –zinken, *f. pl.* tines or teeth of a fork; prongs of a pitch-fork.

Gäb'ler, *(str.) m. coll. see* Gabelhirsch.

Ga'ben, *(w.) v. tr. (l. u.)* to present (Schenken).

Gach, *adj. provinc.* steep (Jäh).

* Gachi'ren [*pr.* gäschē'ren], *(w.) v. tr. (Fr.)* 1) to daub, paint badly; 2) to undersell.

Gäcke (Gacke, Gäke), *(w.) f. provinc. see* Dohle. [ling, grabbling.

Gackelig, *adj. lit. & fig.* cackling, chatter-

Gackeln, Gackern, *(w.) v. intr.* 1) to cackle, gaggle (like fowls); 2) *fig.* to chatter, gabble.

† Ga'den, Ga'dem, *(str.) n. & m.* 1) cottage, house; 2) *a)* chamber, room, apartment; *b)* shed, stall.

Gaffel, *(w.) f. provinc.* I. *(N. G.)* 1) fork; 2) *Mar.* gaff; peak; –fall, *m.* throat-halliard; –segel, *n.* gaff-(top-)sail; II. *(S. G.)* 1) *see* Gabel, *B*; 2) corporation, guild, ward.

Gäffeln, *(w.) v. intr. (l. u.)* to gape with delight, to leer.

Gaffen, *(w.) v. intr.* 1) *coll.* to gape, open, crack, chink, *cf.* Klaffen; 2) to gape, gaze, stare. [*Conch. see* Gienmuschel.

Gaffer, *(str.) m.* 1) gaper, gazer, &c.; 2)

* Gagat, *(str.) m. (Gr.) or* –kohle, *Miner.* *f.* jet, pitch-coal. – Gaga'ten, *adj.* made of jet, jet-, jetty. [salary, pay.

* Ga'ge [*pr.* gä'sche], *(w.) f. (Fr.)* wages;

Gäh, *adj. see* Jäh.

Gähn'affe, *(w.) m. coll.* gaper, gazer.

Gäh'nen, *(w.) v. intr.* to yawn, gape.

Gähn..., *in comp.* –laut, *m. Gramm.* hiatus; –muschel, *f. see* Gienmuschel; –sucht, *f.* oscitancy, yawning fits.

Gähr'bottich, *(str.) m.*, Gähr'stock *(str., pl.* Gähr'stöcke), *m. Brew.* gyle-tun, working-tun; *Mel.* bee.

Geh're, Gäh're, *(w.) f.* 1) ferment, fermentation; 2) yeast, barm, leaven.

Gäh'ren, *(str.) v. intr. lit. & fig.* to ferment, work, effervesce.

Gähr..., *in comp.* –kammer, *f.* room in which beer or mash ferments; –messer, *m.* *T.* zymometer; –mittel, *n.*, –stoff, *m. Chem.* ferment, any thing causing fermentation, leavening; –teig, *m.* leaven.

Gäh'rung, *(w.) f.* fermentation; in – bringen, to put or set in (a) fermentation; *fig.* fermentation, turbulence, tumult (of the passions, &c.).

Gäh'rungs..., *in comp.* –fähig, *adj.* fermentable; –kraft, *f.* fermentative power; –küpe, *f. Dy.* steeping-vat; –messer, *m.* zymosimeter; –mittel, *n.*, –stoff, *m. see* Gährmittel; –proceß, *m.* process of fermentation, fermenting or fermentative process.

* Gaillar'de [*pr.* galiar'de], *(w.) f. (Fr.)* *Typ.* galliard.

Gais, *see* Geis.

Ga'keln, Gak'sen, *(w.) v. intr. see* Gackeln.

* Ga'la, *f. (Span.)* gala, show, pomp, state; in –, in gala, in court-dress; in full dress; *coll.* in full fig; –degen, *m.* dress-sword; –hut, *m.* court-hat; –kleid, *n.* court-dress, full dress, presentation-suit; –tag, *m.* gala-day, court-day; –uniform, *f.* gala-uniform.

[illegible], *Ind.* strut; *b)* motion (of a watch, &c.), rate [illegible]going, course; march, progress; *c)* errand, [illegible]: der — zum Eisenhammer, (*Schiller's Poem:*) the Message to the Foundry; er [illegible] alle Gänge für mich, he runs all my errands; 2) way, passage; corridor; 3) *Anat.* [illegible], canal, duct; (Gehör—) meatus; 4) *a)* *Min.* vein, streak, lode, *corr.* load (of a mine); [illegible] edler —, alive lode; ein tauber —, dead [illegible]; der fallende —, hade; *b)* *T.* groove (of [illegible]); *c)* *Mill.* a run *or* set (of stones); 5) [illegible]. board, track; 6) *a)* *Sport.* haunt; *b)* *fig.* [illegible], place of resort, haunt; visit; course; [illegible] *Fenc.* passade, passado, pass, round; 8) [illegible] (of dishes), remove; 9) *Mus.* *a)* passage; *b)* progression; 10) *Mill.* *a)* run; *b)* [illegible]-work; 11) *Mech.* working; speed, velocity; 12) *fig.* turn, direction; course, way; progress, march (of intellect, &c.); way *or* manner of living; Jeder geht seinen —, each [illegible] his own way of acting; er geht noch seinen alten —, he still follows his own course; er belauert alle meine Gänge, he watches [illegible] narrowly, he watches all my motions; in — bringen *or* setzen, 1. to set going, to set *or* put in motion (trade), to bring into play; [illegible] *fig.* to bring about, to get up (a controversy, &c.), to set on foot, to bring in vogue, [illegible] up (an opinion); *Comm.-s.* so ist der — [illegible] Geschäftes, such is the routine of business; der Artikel ist nicht mehr recht im G-e, the article is not much in favour now; im G-e, at work, in operation; ein Plan ist im G-e, a scheme is on foot; in vollem —, properly at work; in full play, motion, *or* activity; die Maschine ist im vollen G-e, the [illegible] hammer is in full play; im G-e sein, 1. to be in operation, to be going on, to be in progress, to be in training; 2. to be in vogue, to prevail; diese Münze ist nicht mehr im G-e, this coin is no longer current; in — kommen, to come in play; im —(e) erhalten, to keep going, to keep up, continue; die Dinge gehen (gemächlich) ihren gewohnten —, things go on (much) as usual; die Dinge *or* Sachen ihren — gehen lassen, to let things take their own way (*or* course).

Gang'art, (*w.*) *f.* 1) *Man.* pace (of a horse); 2) *see* Ganggestein.

Gang'bar, *adj.* 1) passable, practicable, accessible; in good repair (of water-pipes); 2) frequented; 3) going, current, prevalent, received; *Comm.*, *&c.* saleable, vendible; merchantable; g-e Artikel, current *or* leading articles, staple commodities *or* goods; g-e Münze, current coin; eine g-e Waare, a saleable *or* marketable commodity; die g-ste Sorte, the favourite, most current, easiest sort; dieser Artikel ist —, this article is in season; die g-en Preise kennen, to understand the market.

Gang'barkeit, (*w.*) *f.* 1) passableness, &c.; currency (of coin); 2) frequency; 3) currency, saleableness; merchantableness; — der Waaren, a current *or* ready sale of commodities; [illegible], day; die — dieses Artikels ist längst vorüber, the day for this article is long past.

Gang'..., *in comp.* —bildung, *f.* *Geol.* formation of gangs; —bord, *m.* *Mar.* gang-way.

Gäng'ig, *adj.* 1) current: — und gäbe, in [illegible], current, in vogue; usual, frequent; 2) *Sport.* nimble, [illegible], active (of dogs and [illegible]) (*compare*); 4) practicable (road).

[illegible], (*str.*) *m.* rocker of a cradle: — [illegible] *n.* leading-strings (*pl.*); *see* —band [illegible] *see* Gängeln, I. 2.

[illegible] *f. coll.* (the act *or* process of) keeping in leading-strings.

[illegible], *v. tr.* 1) to lead (a child) [illegible] leading-strings, to keep [illegible]; II. *intr.* to toddle. [illegible] [illegible], *adj.* [illegible] go-cart, standing-

Gän'ger, (*str.*) *m.* goer, walker (*usually in comp.*).

Gang'erz, (*str.*) *n.* ore found in veins.

Gan'ges, *m.* *Geogr.* Ganges (a river in Asia); —hirsch, *m.* *Zool.* axis (*Cervus Axis* L.).

Gang'..., *in comp.* —fisch, *m.* *Ichth.* a kind of salmon found in the lake of Constance (*Coregonus Wartmanni*, *lavaretus* Nils. [Blau-] Felchen, Balche); —formation, *f.* *Geol.* *see* —bildung; —führer, *m.* *Spinn.* jack, heck-box; —gebirge, *n.* *Miner.* mountain *or* mine containing veins of ore (*opp.* Flötzgebirge); —gestein, *n.* *Miner.* matrix of the ore, gang (gangue); —granit, *m.* *Geol.* name given to two kinds of granite found near Heidelberg; —haspel, *f.* *see* —rad; —häuer, *m.* *Min.* lodesman.

Gäng'ig, *adj.* 1) *see* Gänge, 2; 2) *or* Gang'haft, *Min.* containing veins, *adv.* in veins, in streaks.

Gang'..., *in comp.* —kreuz, *n.* 1) *Min.* the point where two gangs *or* veins meet; the union of two veins; 2) *Weav.* crossing of the porters; —lehre, *f.* that part of mineralogy, which treats of gangs and their metallic products.

Gäng'ler, (*str.*) *m.* *fig.* he who leads *or* keeps in leading-strings.

* Gang'lion, (*str.*, *pl.* (*w.*) Gang'lien) *n.* (*Gr.*) *Anat.* ganglion.

Gang'..., *in comp.* —masse, *f.* *see* —gestein; —pfosten, *m.* *Carp.* baluster; —rad, *n.* *Carp.* tread-wheel, double wheel of a crane.

* Gangrä'ne, (*w.*) *f.* (*Gr.*) *Med.* gangrene (Brand). — Gangränös', *adj.* gangrenous.

Gang'säule, (*w.*) *f.* *Archit.* column of a portico.

Gang'spill, (*str.*) *n.*, G-e, (*w.*) *f.* *Mar.* capstan (capstern); das hintere *or* kleine —, after-capstan, gear-capstan; das große —, main capstan; das — klar machen, to rig the capstan.

Gang'..., *in comp.* —stein, *m.* *Geol.* gang- *or* gangue-stone (earthy substance surrounding the ore); —textur, *f.* *Geol.* the succession of minerals in a gang; —vögel, *pl.* *Ornith.* the Ambulatores of Illiger, ravens, swallows, and most singing birds; —weise, *adv.* *Min.* in veins; —werk, *n.* *Horol.*, *&c.* movement; —woche, *f.* *Cath. Relig.* rogation-week.

Gans, (*str.*, *pl.* Gän'se) *f.* 1) *Ornith.* goose (*Anser* L.); die junge —, green goose, gosling; 2) *Iron-w.* sow, pig (a great lump of melted iron); gereinigte —, loop, bloom; 3) *Salt-w.* a lump of prepared salt; 4) *Min.* a hard-stone *or* rock.

Gän'sich, (*str.*) *m.* *vulg.* *for* Gänserich.

Gäns'chen, (*str.*) *n.* (*dimin.* *of* Gans) little goose, gosling, (Kindersprache:) goosey.

Gän'se..., *in comp.* —aar, —adler, *m.* *Ornith.* goshawk; kite; black-crested vulture (*cf.* Fischadler, 2); —apfel, *m.* *Pomol.* a kind of late autumn-apple; —augen, *n.* *pl.* *see* —füßchen; —backe, —bake, *f.* *Cook.* one half of a smoked goose; —baum, *m.* *Bot.* a species of maple; plane-tree; —blume, *f.*, —blümchen, *n.* *Bot.* daisy (*Bellis perennis* L.); große —blume, common ox-eye *or* great daisy (*Chrysanthemum* L.); —braten, *m.* roast(ed) goose; —brust, *f.* (smoked) breast of a goose; —distel, *f.* *Bot.* corn sow-thistle, hare's lettuce (*Sonchus* L.); —dreck, *m.* goose-dung; —feder, *f.* 1) goose-feather; 2) *see* —kiel; —fett, *n.* goose-grease; *Cook.* goose's fat; —fingerkraut, *n.* *Bot.* silver-weed (*Potentilla anserina* L.); —fuß, *m.* *Bot.* goose-foot (*Chenopodium* L.); (Stinkende) stinking blite (*Chenopodium olidum* Lam.); (rother) sowbane, good Henry (*Chenopodium bonus Henricus* L.); —füßchen, *n.* *pl.* *Typ.* inverted commas, signs of quotation („ " „ "); —gang, *m.* goose-step (—marsch); —gasse, *f.* *see* —fingerkraut; —geier, *m.* *see* —aar; —gekröse, —geschneide, *n.* goose-giblets; —grün, *s.* & *adj.* gosling-green; —habicht, *m.* *see* —aar.

Gän'sehaft, *adj.* stupid.

Gän'se..., *in comp.* —haut, *f.* *fam.* goose-skin, corrugated skin, (*Lat.*) *cutis anserina*; ich bekomme (es überläuft mich wie) eine —haut, it makes my flesh creep, my flesh begins to creep; —hirt, *m.* gooseherd; —kiel, *m.* goose-quill; —klein, *n.* *see* —gekröse; —kohl, *m.* *see* —distel; —kopf, *m.* head of a goose; *fig.* ninny, goose-cap; —koth, *m.* goose-dung; —köthiges (Silber-)Erz, *n.* *Min.* goose-dung ore; —kraut, *n.* *Bot.* 1) *see* —blume; 2) *see* —fingerkraut; 3) wall *or* rock cress (Gänsekresse, *Arabis hirsuta* L.); —kresse, *f.* *Bot.* 1) shepherd's purse (*Capsella bursa pastoris* Mönch); 2) a kind of wall-cress (*Arabis hirsuta* L.); —küchlein, *n.* gosling; —leber, *f.* goose's liver; —leberpastete, *f.* goose-liver-pie, Strassburg-pie.

Gän'seln, (*w.*) *v.* I. *tr.* (*L. u.*) to lead by the nose; *cf.* übertölpeln; II. *intr.* (*S. G.*) to chatter, gaggle.

Gän'se..., *in comp.* —löffel, *m.* *Surg.* goose-bill; —mann, *m.* *coll.* goose-seller; —marsch, *m.* *Ind.* goose-step, single-file; *Am* Indian file; —nabel, *f.* an oblong cake of oatmeal (to fatten geese); —pappel, *f.* *Bot.* round-leaved mallow (*Malva rotundifolia* L.); —pfeffer, *m.* *Cook.* giblets dressed in the blood of the goose.

Gän'serich, Gan'sert, (*str.*) *m.* 1) gander, the male of the goose; 2) *see* Gänsefingerkraut.

Gän'se..., *in comp.* —säger, *m.* *Ornith.* goosander (Sägetaucher); —schmalz, *n.* *see* —fett; —schwarz, *n.* *see* —pfeffer; —seuche, *f.* *Vet.* gargil; —spiel, *n.* the game of Mother Goose; —stall, *m.*, —steige, —stiege, *f.* goose-stall; —stückchen, *n.* *see* —blümchen; —tod, *m.* *see* —seuche; —wein, *m.* *fig. joc.* Adam's ale, *i. e.* water; —witz, *m.* *contempt.* false wit; —zehnte, *m.* tithe on *or* of geese; —zucht, *f.* breeding of geese.

Gän'sig, Gän'sicht, *adj.* like a goose.

Gäns'lein, (*str.*) *n.* gosling.

Gant, *s.* I. (*w.*) *f.* *provinc.* 1) auction, public sale; 2) bankruptcy (Bankerott, Concurs); II. *in comp.* —buch, *n.* book of effects; —haus, *n.*, —laden, *m.* auction room *or* office; —mann (—schuldner), *m.* bankrupt (Fallit); —masse, *f.* bankrupt's estate (Concurs-Masse); —meister, —verkäufer, *m.* auctioneer; —proceß, *m.* *see* Concurs; —recht, *n.* auction-law; statute of bankruptcy; —zeit, time of a public sale.

* Ganymed', (*str.*) *m.* *Gr. Myth.* Ganymede.

Ganz, I. *adj.* 1) whole, entire; not broken, not divided, unbroken; all, total; full; 2) perfect, complete, accomplished, finished; 3) *coll.* excellent, capital; 4) *Min.* virgin (pit *or* mine); ein g-es Werk, a complete work; ein g-es Pferd, entire horse (Hengst, *opp.* Wallach); g-er Pfeffer, pepper in grain, pepper-corns; g-er Zimmt, cinnamon in rolls; g-es Geld, large (pieces of) money; nehmen Sie es —, take it all, take the whole; die g-e Summe, the whole sum, gross sum, the (sum) total; die g-e Welt, all the world; über die g-e Welt, all over the world; durch das g-e Land hin, throughout the length and breadth of the country; den g-en Tag (über *or* lang), all day (long); die g-e Nacht (hindurch), all night (long); eine g-e Stunde, a full hour; g-e vierzehn Tage, full fourteen days; mein g-es Leben hindurch, all my life long; in der g-en Stadt, all over the town; *Mus.-a.* der g-e Tact, whole measure; die g-e (Tact-)Note, semibreve, measure-note, time-note; der g-e Ton, a whole tone; keine g-e Stunde, not an hour; er ist ein g-er Mann, he is a man every inch of him; er ist ein g-er Geschäftsmann, he is quite the man of business; von g-em Herzen, with all my heart; es ist mein g-er Ernst,

I am in good *(or* full) earnest: — machen, to complete, mend.

II. *adv.* quite, wholly, entirely, utterly; all, altogether; perfectly, completely; fully; thoroughly; pretty, tolerably; very, very much; — ähnlich, precisely similar; — Freude sein, to be full of joy; ich bin — Ohr, *(lit.* I am quite ear:) I am all attention; — anders, far otherwise; — wohl, — gut, very well; — ebenso gut, every bit as well; — nackt *or* toll, stark naked *or* mad; — naß, wet all over; ich bin hier — fremd, I am an utter stranger here; — recht, all right; just so; ehe der Wagen — still stand, before the carriage had well stopped; — und gar, quite, totally, utterly, altogether; — und gar nicht, not at all, by no means, not a whit; — und gar nichts, nothing at all; nicht — 100, not quite *(or* somewhat less than) 100; nicht — eine Stunde, not an hour; — der Ihrige, entirely yours.

Gan'ze, *n. (decl. like adj.)* 1) entirety, whole, totality; 2) die G-n, *pl. Arith.* integers, whole numbers; im G-n (genommen), upon *(or* in) the whole, collectively, generally, in general; im G-n betrachtet, looking at it broadly; *Comm.* by *(or* at) the great, by the bulk, wholesale, (taken) in the gross; im G-n handeln, to sell by wholesale; im G-n kaufen, to purchase by the lot.

Ganz'fabricāte, *(str.) n. pl. Comm.* made up articles.

Ganz'heit, *(w.) f.* entireness, integrity.

Ganz'..., *in comp.* —holz, *n. T.* unhewed timber; —hufig, *adj.* whole-hoofed, solidungulous; —hüfner, *m.* owner of a hide of land requiring four horses for tilling.

Gänz'lich, I. *adj.* whole, total, entire, complete, absolute, full: g-e Bezahlung, full payment; II. *adv.* wholly, &c., thoroughly, quite, utterly, by all means; — zum Stehen bringen, to bring to a dead stop.

Ganz'..., *in comp.* —lähner, *m. see* —hüfner; —randig, *adj. Bot.* entire (leaves); —wolle, *f. Comm.* whole wool; —zeug, *n. Paper-m.* (paper-)pulp; —zeugkasten, *m.* stuff-chest.

Ga'pen, *(w.) v. intr. provinc. (L. G.)* 1) to gape; 2) to gaze at wonderingly; 3) to long for....

Gap'sen, *(w.) v. intr. coll.* to gasp.

Gär, *(str.) n. (Tans, m. u.)* a kind of fishnomes.

Gar, I. *adj.* 1) *a) Cook.* done, dressed, (sufficiently) boiled, roasted; *b) Tann.* dressed: *Metall.* refined, purified; 2) *Agr.* in a proper stage of tillage; 3) *provinc.* finished, ready: Kupfer — machen, to refine copper; das Leder — machen, to dress leather; g-es Leder, dressed leather; nicht — sein, *Cook.* not done enough, to be underdone.

II. *adv.* fully, quite, entirely, very; at all; ist sie krank oder — todt? is she ill *or* even (I hope not) dead? — oft, very often; ein — herrlicher Bissen, a most delicious morsel; — sehr, very much; ich habe es nicht so — nöthig, I am not so much in want of it; — zu, too: — zu sehr, — zu viel, too much; — zu wenig, too little; — zu wohl, — zu gut, over-well; — zu früh, over-soon; wo nicht — noch, perhaps even; vielleicht gefällt er mir —, perhaps I shall *(or* may) even like him; — selten, mighty rarely; — zu neugierig, overcurious, too curious by half; es ist mit ihm — aus, he is undone; he is a dead man; — so *(or* zu) theuer, so very dear; — nicht, not at all, by no means; und nun —, and now: indeed; wo nicht —, if not indeed; so — schlimm wird es wohl nicht werden, it will not be quite so bad; ich glaube — ! indeed! ich glaube —, er will &c., I trow he means to, &c.; es läßt sich — nicht sagen, there is no saying; — nichts, nothing at all, *coll.* never a whit; ich mache mir — nichts aus ihm, I do not care a bit *(or* not a jot) for him; — nichts haben, to be out of all; — Niemand, nobody at all, never a man; — Keiner, not one; — keine, none whatever, none at all; ich dächte —! warum nicht —! *or coll.* lieber —! why indeed! why truly! you don't say so!

Garaf'fel, *(w.) f.* —margel, *f. Bot.* bennet *(Geum urbanum* L.).

* **Garanci'ne,** *(w.) f. Comm. see* Krapp.

* **Garant',** *(w.) m. (Fr.) Comm., &c.* guarantee, warrantee. — **Garantie',** *(w.) f.* guarantee, warranty, security. — **Garanti'ren,** *(w.) v. tr.* to warrant, guarantee.

Gar'..., *in comp.* —arbeit, *f. Smelt.* refining, refinement (of copper, &c.); —arbeiter, *m.* refiner (of copper, &c.); —aus, *m. & n.* finishing stroke, utter ruin, end, death; Einem *or* einer Sache den *(or* das) —aus machen, to complete one's ruin, to settle *or* kill one, to finish *or* polish one off; to crush, to put down.

Gar'be, *(w.) f.* I. 1) (Getreide—) sheaf; in G-n binden, to sheaf; 2) *Herald.* garb, garbe; 3) *Bot. a) (or* G-nkraut, *n.) see* Schafgarbe; *b) provinc. see* Kümmel; II. *provinc. Butch.* neck of beef.

* **Garbeli'ren,** *(w.) v. tr. (cf.* Gerbuliren) *Min.* to prepare (ores) for melting by sifting, &c. [be plentiful.

Gar'ben, *(w.) v. intr.* to yield sheaves, to

Gar'ben..., *in comp.* —band, *n.* wisp *or* band of straw for tying a sheaf; —binder, *m.*, —binderin, *f.* sheaves-binder; —feuer, *n. Fire-w.* Chinese tree; —friße, *f. see* Mandelfriße; —kraut, *n. see* Garbe, 4; —schichter, *m.* workman who piles up the sheaves; —zehnt, *m.* tithe paid in sheaves.

Gar'..., *in comp.* —brater (—bräter), *m. see* —koch; —brühe, *f. Tann.* alum mordant.

* **Gar'de,** *(w.) f. (Fr.)* guard; — zu Fuß, the foot-guards; — zu Pferde, the horse-guards; unter der —, in the guards; —officier, *m.* officer of *or* in the guards; —regiment, *n.* regiment of guards.

* **Gardero'be,** *(w.) f. (Fr.)* (G-nzimmer, *n.)* wardrobe; cloak-room; (Damen—) shawl-room; G-ngeld, *n.* indemnification to actors and actresses for dress. — **Garderobier'** *(pr.* gärd'robië'], *(str., pl.* G-s) *m.* 1) (G-e, *(w.) f.)* keeper of the wardrobe; 2) *Theat. a)* property-man; *b)* dresser.

Gar'deser-Öl, *(str.) n. Comm.* Verona oil, sweet oil of Garda.

* **Gardi'ne,** *(w.) f. (Fr.)* (window-, bed-, &c.) curtain.

* **Gardi'nen...,** *in comp.* —arm, *m. see* —halter; —behänge, *n.* valance; —franzen, *f. pl.* curtain-fringes; —haken, *m.* curtain-hooks; —halter, *m.* curtain-peg; —predigt, *f. joc.* curtain-lecture; —ring, *m.* curtain-ring; —rolle, *f.* curtain-pulley; —schraube, *f.* curtain-pin; —stange, *f.* curtain-rod; —zug, *m.* curtain-line. [soldier of the guards.

* **Gardist',** *(w.) m. (Fr.)* guards-man,

Ga're, *(w.) f.* 1) *T. gener.* condition of any thing that is dressed *or* quite done; 2) *Tann. a)* condition of dressed leather, dressing; *b)* a number of twenty-four hides.

Gä're, *(w.) f.* bouquet of Rhenish and Moselle wines.

Gar'..., *in comp.* —eisen, *n. T.* 1) iron-rod, probe used in refining copper; 2) refined iron; —erde, *f.* earth mixed with soot; —erz, *n.* roasted *or* burnt ore; —faß, *n. Tann.* dressing tub *or* vat; —feuer, *n.* roasting fire (for copper, &c.); —gekrätz, *n. T.* slags of refined copper.

Gar'heit, *(w.) f. see* Gare, 1.

Gar'..., *in comp.* —herd, *m.* hearth of a refining furnace; —knecht, *m.* refiner's man; —koch, *m.* owner of a cook-shop; —könig, *m. Chem.* regulus of pure-copper; —kräßt, *f. see*

[illegible] gleich wieder von sich —, to bring up [illegible] thing as soon as swallowed; 4. seine [illegible] von sich —, to give utterance to one's [illegible], to utter or speak one's mind; Feuer [illegible] fire (a gun), cf. Feuer; Geld auf Zinsen —, to put out money to interest; [illegible] wie — Sie es? what is your price? [illegible] wissen, wie ich es gebe, you know the price [illegible]; zu diesem Preise wollte er die [illegible] nicht —, he would not part with the [illegible] at this rate; er wird es wohlfeil —, [illegible] let it go cheap: Gott gebe! God grant! [illegible] zu Leipzig, (at the foot of documents, [illegible]) done at Leipzig; seinen Willen dazu —, [illegible] to, yield to; ich gebe es als einen [illegible], I mention it by way of a hint; [illegible] gibt die gesunde Vernunft, common sense [illegible] it; der Zusammenhang gibt es, the [illegible] shows or proves it; die Sache selbst [illegible] es, the thing or matter speaks of or for [illegible] zu bedenken —, to put to one's consideration; ich möchte Ihnen zu bedenken —, I [illegible] have you remember: zu verstehen —, [illegible] to understand, cf. Verstehen; etwas [illegible] wenig rc.) auf eine Sache —, to set (great, [illegible]) value upon, to esteem, value ...; to [illegible] to, to mind, cf. Beachten; nichts worauf [illegible] make no account of a thing: verloren [illegible] give up (as lost).

[illegible] refl. A) sich (Acc.) —, 1) to yield, to [illegible], give in; 2) to resign; 3) to show one's [illegible] to prove one's self to be; 4) to relent, [illegible], subside; es wird sich schon —, it will [illegible] or follow in course; sich gefangen —, see [illegible]; sich zufrieden —, to compose one's [illegible]; to acquiesce (mit, in), cf. Zufrieden; [illegible] in die Hände —, to give one's self [illegible] to surrender one's self into a person's [illegible]; sich an etwas (Acc.) —, to commence [illegible] a thing, to fall to; das Tuch gibt sich, [illegible] cloth stretches; das wird sich schon —, 1. [illegible] things) will settle down in course of time; [illegible] will follow or come in (due) course, or [illegible] matter of course, coll. it will take care [illegible] itself; B) sich (Dat.) etwas —, gener. fig. [illegible] give one's self (ein Ansehen rc., airs, &c.); [illegible] take to one's self; to assume, to adopt; [illegible] (Dat.) Mühe —, to take pains.

III. tr. impers. a) (with Dat.) es ist mir [illegible] gegeben (zu verzeihen rc.), it is not in my [illegible], it is not in me (to forgive, &c.); b) [illegible] Acc.) to be, to exist; es gibt, gab rc., [illegible] is, are, there was, were, &c.: der größte [illegible] den es gibt, the greatest liar in existence; was gibt's? what's the matter? what [illegible] going on? was gibt es Neues? what (is [illegible]) news? es wird Schläge —, there will be [illegible]; sei artig oder es gibt Schläge, be [illegible] or you will be whipped; heute gibt es [illegible] oder [illegible], today we have fish or [illegible]; ich möchte etwas genießen; was [illegible]? I should like to take something; [illegible] have you got? wenn es kein Schöpsen[illegible] gibt, mag er Rindfleisch bringen, if there [illegible] (or if they have) no mutton, let him bring [illegible] kann es nicht früher hier ein Wirths[illegible] gegeben haben? may there not have [illegible] an inn here formerly? gab es nicht zuweilen [illegible] hier Wölfe? were there not [illegible] here now and then last winter? es [illegible] einen Aufruhr geben, there might be a [illegible]; es gab einen Zank, a quarrel [illegible] took place.

[illegible], (str.) m., Ge'berin, (w.) f. giver, [illegible]; dispenser; — des Wortes [illegible], giver of the value, [illegible]; — und Nehmer, pl. tellers and buyers; [illegible] Nehmer, more often than takers.

[illegible], (w.) f. gesture, posture (of the [illegible]), carriage, demeanour; [illegible], play antic tricks.

[illegible] (w.) v. refl. 1) to make ges-tures; 2) to demean, carry, or behave one's self, coll. to take on (as if, &c.); sich ernsthaft —, to put on a serious air; sich närrisch —, to play the fool.

Gebär'den..., in comp. —kunde, —kunst, f. art of posture-making, mimics; —spiel, n. pantomime, coll. dumb show; —spieler, m. mimic, mime; —sprache, f. conversation by gestures, mimicry, pantomime.

Gebär'dung, (w.) f. gesticulation, demeanour, behaviour.

Gebet', s. I. (str.) n. 1) (the act or practice of) praying; 2) prayer; devotion; das — des Herrn, the Lord's Prayer; sein — verrichten, to perform (to be at or to say) one's prayers or devotion; das — sprechen, to offer prayer; einsames —, secret or private prayer, closet-prayer; ins — nehmen, fam. to take to task, to question closely, &c., see ins Verhör nehmen; II. in comp. —buch, n. prayer-book; —formel, f. form of prayer; —glocke, f. prayer-bell; —zeit, f. prayer-time; G-sstimmung, f. prayerful state or disposition.

Gebett', (str.) n. bedding, set of bedding.

Gebet'tel, (str.) n. the practice of (continual or incessant) begging.

Geb'hard, (str.) m. (OHG. Gebahart, one who is strong in giving, a liberal man) Gebhard (P. N.).

Gebiet', (str.) n. 1) †, command (Gebot); government; 2) district, territory; ground; domain; dominion, jurisdiction; 3) fig. province, department, sphere, region, realm, field, range.

Gebie'ten, (str.) v. tr. (Einem etwas) to command, order, bid; to enjoin, impose; to dictate; über Einen or Einem —, to govern (over), to rule; to control, check; zu — haben, to have the command, to be the master; Ehrfurcht —, to command respect; Stillschweigen —, to command (fig. to impose) silence; die Freundschaft gebietet es, friendship requires it; g-d, p. a. imperative (also Gramm. [mood, &c.], &c.). [governor, master, lord.

Gebie'ter, (str.) m. commander, ruler,

Gebie'terin, (w.) f. mistress, lady.

Gebie'terisch, adj. commanding, imperative; imperious, domineering, authoritative, dictatorial, haughty.

Gebil'de, (str.) n. 1) a) any thing formed, Min., &c. formation; structure; creation; b) form, frame; 2) picture in the mind, image, imagery; 3) Manuf. diaper.

Gebil'det, p. a. (liberally) educated, cultivated, refined, polite, see Bilden; die G-en, pl. the educated classes.

Gebin'de, (str.) n. 1) any quantity of threads, &c. tied together: skein, bundle, lea, warp, rap, cut; 2) a large cask for liquids; 3) T-s, a) truss, couple of a roof; b) dragon-beam, bond; c) hoops (pl.) of a cask; d) row, range (of tiles); 4) Mar. raft; Gebind'sparren, m. pl. Carp. tie-beams.

Gebir'ge, (str.) n. (chain of) mountains; mountainous district, highland.

Gebir'ger, (str.) m. see Gebirgsbewohner.

Gebir'gig, adj. mountainous.

Gebir'gisch, adj. relating to mountains; living in the mountains, &c.

Gebirgs'..., in comp. (cf. Berg- & Fels-) —abfall, —abhang, m. decline, slope of mountains; —art, f. species of stone, Geol. pl. rocks; —ast, m. side-branch of a mountain-range; —beschreibung, f. description of mountains, orography; —bewohner, m. mountaineer, highlander; —druck, m. Min. pressure of the ground; —fluß, m. mountain stream; —fuß, m. foot or base of mountains; —gegend, f. mountainous region or country; —höhe, f. height of a range of mountains; —joch, n., —kamm, m. mountain-ridge; —kenner, m. geognost; —kette, f. chain of mountains; —knoten, m. centre of several mountain-ranges; —kunde, —lehre, f. knowledge of mountains, orology; geognosy; —kundige, m. orologist; —land, n. mountainous country; —ort, m. a place situated among mountains; —paß, m. mountain-pass, Mil. defile, defilee; —rücken, m. see —joch; —stadt, f. town situated among mountains; —stock, m. see —knoten; —volk, n. a people inhabiting mountains, mountain-tribe; —wand, f. a wall or steep declivity of rock; —weg, m. mountain road or path; —zug, m. range of mountains; —zweig, m. branch or subordinate range of mountains that shoots out from a larger range, spur.

Gebiß', (str.) n. 1) (set of) teeth; ein gutes — haben, to have good teeth, to be well toothed; 2) bridle-bit, horse-bit, bit-mouth; — mit Stangen, moon-bit, fast-mouth; — ohne Stangen, snaffle or water-bit; Man-e. das — geben, to bit; das — nehmen, to unbit; —kette, f. curb.

Gebla'se, (str.) n. (the act or practice of) blowing, trumpeting, &c. cf. Blasen.

Geblä'se, (str.) n. bellows (of a forge), blast, blast engine, blast apparatus; heißes, kaltes —, hot, cold blast; das — anlassen, to set the bellows a-going; das — arbeitet or spielt, the bellows are in action; —ofen, m. blast-furnace; —röhre, f. blast-pipe.

Geblie'ben, p. a. perished, lost (of ships, &c. cf. Bleiben, b); die Zahl der G-en, the number of killed or slain (in battle).

Geblö'ke, (str.) n. bleating; bellowing, lowing.

Geblüm', (str.) n. 1) collect. flowers, blossoms; 2) honey of flowers collected by bees.

Geblümt', adj. 1) flowered (stuffs, &c.), figured, floriated (in Archit., &c.), sprigged; diapered (linen, towels); speaky (indigo); adorned with flowers, flowery; 2) das G-e, n. coll. flowers which serve as food for bees.

Geblüt', (str.) n. 1) blood, the mass of the blood in the animal body; 2) fig. blood, kindred, consanguinity; line, race, family, house; es steckt im —, it runs in the blood, die Prinzen vom —, the princes of the imperial, royal, &c. family; zu nahe in das — heirathen, to marry too near of kin.

Geblu'te, (str.) n. continued bleeding.

Gebo'gen, p. a. bent, crooked, &c. (cf. Biegen, I. 1); eine g-e Nase, a Roman nose.

Gebohr're, (str.) n. (continued) boring.

Gebo'ren, I. pp. of Gebären, which see; im Katholicismus — und erzogen, born and educated a catholic; ein solcher Kritiker soll noch — werden, such a critic is still in the future; zu ... — sein, to be born to ...; wir sind zum Leiden —, we are made to suffer; man muß dazu — sein, it comes by nature; er ist nicht zum Schriftsteller —, coll. he is not cut out for an author; er ist ein g-er Geschäftsmann, he is a thorough man of business; er war zum Astronomen —, or er war ein g-er Astronom, he was born an astronomer; II. p. a. born; native; ein g-er Böhme, a native of Bohemia, a Bohemian born; der junge König war ein g-er Engländer, the young king was a born Englishman; Newton's Mutter war eine g-e Ayscough, Newton's mother was born Ayscough (Ath.); Mad. B. ist eine g-e C., Mrs. B.'s maiden name is C.; Frau Dr. M., g-e K., Mrs. M., late or née Miss K.; Madame Flahaut, g-e (gener. abbr.: geb.) Friederike Werner, Madame Flahaut (Miss Werner that was).

Gebor'ge, (str.) n. (repeated) borrowing.

Gebor'gen, I. p. a. 1) saved, &c. cf. Bergen, 1; safe, secure, above board; 2) fig. well off, in easy circumstances; II. G-heit, (w.) f. security, safety.

enigmatical language, language of ciphers, cryptology; —thuerei, f. see Geheimnißkrämerei; —verständniß, n. secret understanding or plot; —wirkend, adj. 1) of secret or mystic influence; 2) sympathetic; —zimmer, n. cabinet (of a prince). [direction.

Geheiß, (abr.) n. command, bidding, order,

Geheimt', adj. helmeted; Bot. galeate(d).

Gehen, (irr.) v. I. intr (aux. sein) 1) to go; to pass; 2) to walk; 3) to depart, go away; 4) to extend to; 5) to rise, swell (of the dough); — lassen, to raise (the dough); 6) Comm. a) (of coins) to go, pass, be current; b) (of goods) to be current, to be in (great) favour; to sell well; schlecht —, to be heavy; reißend —, to have a rattling sale; 7) to succeed, to go on well; 8) to continue or be in a certain state; schwanger —, to be pregnant, with child; die Thür geht, the door opens; die Post geht um 6 Uhr, the post sets off or leaves at 6; ein Schiff, das nach America geht, a ship bound for America; der Wind geht, the wind blows; die See geht hoch, the sea runs high; der Hirsch geht hoch, Sport. the stag has his full antlers; meine Absicht geht dahin, my intention is, I purpose; der Fluß geht mit Eis, the river is full of drift-ice; das Eis fängt an zu —, the ice begins to break; dies Dampfboot geht zwischen Hamburg und London, this steamer runs or plies between H. and L.; das Licht geht schneller als der Schall, light travels faster than sound; zu Bett —, to go or come to bed; wir wollen —, let us go or come (Gehen im Engl. oft durch To Come ausgedrückt: vgl. Aufgehen, to come loose, &c.; he found the bridge broken down, but mended it, and came across (Dickens), &c.); zu geschwind —, to go too fast, to advance (of the watch); die Uhr geht falsch, the clock (watch) is wrong; meine Uhr geht nicht richtig or recht, my watch is not right, or is out of order; geht Ihre (Wand-)Uhr richtig? is your clock right? sie kann vielleicht um fünf Minuten zu spät —, it may perhaps be five minutes too slow; wie — die Geschäfte? how is (or goes) business? die Geschäfte — schlecht, business is very low, dull; Handel und Wandel geht nicht, there is no business stirring; das geht von selbst, there is no difficulty in the thing; es geht nicht, it will not do; coll. it is no go, this won't do; die Brücke geht nicht mehr auszubessern, the bridge is incapable of reparation; das geht bei mir nicht so (an), that won't do with me; es wird schon (an)—, it will be sure to do; it will be very possible; I dare say it may be done; it may easily be done; es würde —, wenn ..., it might be done, if ...; es wollte nicht —, [I strove to laugh the thought away, but] it would not be; wir — jetzt conform, Comm. we are in conformity now; die Flöte geht gut, the flute sounds (goes) well; sie versprach [ihrem Lehrer], daß es morgen besser — sollte, she promised better doings to-morrow; geradezu —, to act candidly; — lassen, to let or leave alone; laßt mich —! let me alone! let me be! laßt es —, leave it to take its (own) course, never mind it! sich — lassen, 1. to indulge one's humour, inclinations; 2. to be inobservant of the proper forms and conventions; 3. to launch out; to speak out one's mind freely; sie läßt sich niemals —, she is always on her guard; er ließ die Dinge —, wie sie gingen, he let (the) things take their course; an ein Geschäft —, to go about a business; an den Minister —, to apply to the minister; ungern or schwer entschlossen —, to be loth to do a thing; an den Wind —, Mar. see Anluven; als er fort war, gingen wir an unseren Virgil und die griechische Grammatik, when he was gone, we went to our Virgil and Greek grammar; bis an (with Acc.), or bis zu ..., see Bis) —, to reach to, to come up to; das Wasser ging mir bis an den Hals, the water reached up to my neck; wenn (die) Noth an (den) Mann geht, when necessity urges or requires it, if it comes to the worst; auf die Jagd —, to go (a-)hunting; die Frau ging dann und wann auf Tagelohn, the woman occasionally went out for a day's washing or charing; es geht auf fünf, it turns on or is getting on for five; es geht gegen Morgen, it is getting on towards morning; das Fenster geht auf die Straße, the window looks into or out on, faces (overlooks) the street; auf (with Acc.) —, fig. 1. to amount to, come to, constitute; zwanzig Schillinge — auf ein Pfund, twenty shillings go to or make a pound; 2. to concern; a) to aim at; das geht auf mich, that is aimed or is a hit at me; b) to affect the interest of, to be of importance to; es geht auf Leib und Leben, it is a matter of life and death, life is at stake; aus den Fugen —, to get out of joint; das Stück geht aus E-dur, the piece (of music) is in E major; aus dem Wege —, to step aside; das Mittelhochdeutsche geht (or reicht) vom 12. Jahrhundert bis zur Reformation, Middle High German ranges from the twelfth century to the Reformation; durch's Herz —, to strike to the very heart; der Zug geht durch die ganze Familie, this trait runs through the whole family; durch's Feuer — lassen, to pass through the fire (silver, &c.); in Ähren —, to shoot into ears (of corn); Thüren — in Angeln, doors turn in hinges; der Wagen geht in Federn, the carriage hangs in springs; der Hund geht ins Wasser, the dog takes the water; es geht nicht in die Schachtel, the box cannot hold it; er geht ins zwanzigste Jahr, he is in his twentieth year; es geht jetzt ins vierte Jahr, daß ..., it is now nearly four years since ...; in Seide —, to be dressed in silk, &c.; fig. e. ins Feuer —, to be bold, confident, courageous, forward; in sich —, to descend to, retire into, reflect upon, or examine one's self; to feel remorse, to repent; to mend, reform; nach ... —, 1. to go for or in search of; 2. (of a road, &c.) to lead, go, conduct, take to (a place); der Fisch geht nach dem Köder, the fish follows the bait; nach Brot —, to try to get one's livelihood; über (with Acc.) —, fig. e. 1. to be superior to, to surpass; Tugend geht über Alles, virtue is above all things; es geht nichts über das Reisen, there is nothing like travelling; es geht über alle Beschreibung, it baffles description; 2. to befall; es geht über mich (her), I am attacked, censured; es geht über meinen Verstand, it is above my comprehension; es geht dabei über's Geld, coll. that costs much money; über sich — lassen, see Ertragen; der Ring geht nicht über das Gelenk des Fingers, the ring is too small to pass the joint of the finger; es geht um Geld, 1. it is about or concerns money; 2. Gam. we are playing for money; es geht um Nichts, Gam. we are playing for love; er geht unter dem Namen ..., he goes (passes) by the name of ...; von der Arbeit —, to leave off work; (Einem) von der Hand —, to speed well (with one); es geht ihm von der Hand, he is a quick hand at a thing; he speeds well; von Herzen —, to come from the heart, to be meant sincerely; vor sich —, 1. to go on (well); to proceed; 2. to go on or forward, to take place; vor sich —, to take place, to come off, to proceed; es geht etwas vor sich, something is going on; zu Einem —, see Besuchen, 1; seine Liebe geht bis zur Tollheit, his love borders on madness; es geht mir zu Herzen, I am grieved, afflicted.

II. intr. impers. to be, to fare: wie geht es? how is it? how goes it? es mag — wie es will, go as it may; so geht es in der Welt, so goes the world; wie es geht (for wie es zu — pflegt), as it often happens; wie geht es Ihnen?

how do you do? how are you? how fare you? O, es geht, O. pretty well; es geht mir wohl, I am (doing) well; es geht mir schlecht, things go very hard with me, I am badly off; I fare ill; es geht ihm elend, he makes a hard shift to live; es geht ihm wie mir, it fares with him as with me; wie wird mir's —! what will become of me! wie geht es mit der Sache? how is this affair getting on? how stands the affair? es geht nun an mein Ende (*Uhland*, Volksl. 1, 301), my end is now drawing near; nun ging es an ein Tanzen, Schreien &c., *coll.* then they fell to (*or* a-)dancing, (a-)crying, &c.; jetzt geht es an ein Schädelspalten (*Göthe*, Faust I.), now then for a scull-cracking!

III. *tr.* einen Weg &c. —, to go a certain way; ich gehe gern diese Straße, I like to take this road.

IV. *impers.* & *refl.* es geht sich angenehm, schlecht &c. hier, it is pleasant, bad walking here, &c.

V. *refl.* sich (*Acc.*) müde —, to tire one's self with walking; sich (*Dat.*) etwas —, to contract, get (blisters, &c.) by walking; sich (*Dat.*) die Füße wund —, to gall one's feet with walking; sich (*Dat.*) Blasen —, to blister one's feet by *or* with walking.

Geh'end, *p. a.* 1) going (*opp.* Kommend); 2) *Herald.* passant; g-e Fracht, freight outwards *or* (for the voyage) out; — für Rechnung von ..., being for account of ....

Gehenk', (*str.*) *n.* belt; handle, hook; *Sport.* leather-strap of the bugle-horn.

Geheu'er, *adj.* secure, safe (from ghosts), not haunted; in diesem Hause ist es nicht —, this house is haunted.

Geheul', (*str.*) *n.* a (continual) howling, howl, yelling; roaring (of the wind).

Gehilfe, *see* **Gehülfe**.

Gehirn', *s.* I. (*str.*) *n.* brain, brains; *fig.* understanding, sense; das kleine —, the little brain, cerebellum; ein leeres — haben, to be addle-brained; das kommt nicht aus seinem —, that is no invention of his; im — nicht richtig sein, to be cracked *or* crack-brained; II. *in comp. Anat.*, *Med.*, &c. pertaining to the brain, cerebral (*cf.* Hirn); —balken, *m.* corpus callosum (lat.); —behälter, *m.* brain-pan; —bruch, *m.* rupture of the brain, encephalocele; —brücke, *f.* annular protuberance of the brain, (lat.) *Pons Varolii*; —coralle, *f. Zool.* a coral of the species Meandrina (*Meandrina labyrinthica* L.); —eiterung, *f.* abscess of the (lat.) *dura mater*; —entzündung, *f.* inflammation of the brain, brain fever; —erschütterung, *f.* concussion of the brain; —erweichung, *f.* softening of the brain; —fett, *n.* *Chem.* cerebrine, brain-fat; —haut, *f.* cerebral membrane, membrane of (*or* skin covering) the brain; obere —haut, *dura mater*; untere (weiche, dünne) —haut, *pia mater*; —höhle, —kammer, *f.* ventricle *or* cavity of the brain; —klappe, *f.* valve of the cerebellum; —knoten, *m. see* —brücke; —krank, *adj.*, —krankheit, *f. see* Hirnkrankheit; —lappen, *m. pl.* lobes of the brain; —lehre, *f.* cranology; phrenology; die —lehre betreffend, craniological; phrenological.

Gehirn'los, *adj. lit.* & *fig.* brainless (Hirnlos).

Gehirn'..., *in comp.* —mark, *n.* *Anat.* medullary (white) substance of the brain; —masse, *f.* substance of the brain; —nerven, *m. pl.* cerebral nerves; —quese, *f.* coenure, *see* Hirnblasenwurm; —rinde, *f.* cortical substance of the brain; —sand, *m. see* Hirnsand; —schlag, *m.* apoplexy of the brain; —schwamm, *m.* fungus of the brain (*Fungus cerebri*); —schwindel, *f. see* Hirnschwindel; —spalten, *f. pl.* fissures of the brain; —steine, *see* Hirnsand.

Gehirnt', *p. a.* brained (*in comp.*).

Gehirn'..., *in comp.* —thätigkeit, *f.* cerebral activity; —verhärtung, *f.* induration of the brain; —wassersucht, *f.* dropsy of the head, hydrocephalus; —wuth, *f. see* Hirnwuth.

Gehl, *adj. provinc.* (*L. G.*) yellow.

Gehöf'ter, (*str.*) *m.* tenant of a farm.

Gehöft', (*str.*) *n.* premises of a farm; farm-yard; court(-yard). [jeering.

Gehöhn', (*str.*) *n.* (continual) mocking,

Gehölz', (*str.*) *n.* a close wood, thicket.

Gehör', *s.* I. (*str.*) *n.* 1) hearing; ear; 2) *Sport.* ears; 3) *fig.* hearing, audience; attention; ein scharfes —, a quick *or* a good ear; ein musikalisches —, a musical ear, a correct ear for music; nach dem — spielen, to play by ear; — geben (*with Dat.*), to give ear (*or* audience), to give a hearing; to listen (to); einer Bitte — geben, to grant a request; — finden, to be heard, to obtain *or* find a hearing; to be admitted; er fand ein geneigtes —, he was favourably heard; sich (*Dat.*) — verschaffen, to make one's self heard; das — betreffend, acoustic; auditory.

Gehor'chen, (*w.*) *v. intr.* (*with Dat.*) to obey; nicht —, to disobey.

Gehö'ren, (*w.*) *v. intr.* (*with Dat.*) to belong, appertain to; to be one's own, to be owned by; ein Garten gehört dazu, a garden is attached to it; vor, unter Jemand *or* etwas —, to belong to, be subject(ed) to; *Law* & *fig.* to fall under the cognizance of ...; zu etwas —, 1. to belong to, to be connected with, to form part of; 2. to be requisite *or* necessary for; es gehört viel Arbeit dazu, it requires much labour; wohin gehört das? where does that belong to? (*cf.* Hingehören); wem gehört dieses Haus? who owns this house? Alexander gehört zu den Jünglingen, welche ..., Alexander is one of those young men who ...; das gehört nicht hierher, this is (entirely) out of place, it is alien *or* totally aside from (*or* nothing to) the purpose, that has nothing to do with the question in hand; dies gehört recht sehr dazu, it has much to do with the subject; auf eine solche Frage gehört eine solche Antwort, such a question deserves such an answer; der *gordius* [ist keine Schlange, sondern] gehört unter die Würmer, the gordius ... belongs among the worms; Einen dahin weisen, wo er hin gehört, to send one about his business; II. *refl.* & *impers.* to be fit, becoming, right, suitable, *or* proper; es gehört sich, it is fit, &c., decent, seemly; so gehörte es sich, it ought to be thus; wie sich's gehört, duly, properly, in a proper way.

Gehör'..., *in comp.* —fehler, *m.* defect of the ear; —gang, *m. Anat.* auditory passage, acoustic duct; —höhle, *f. Anat.* alveary.

Gehö'rig, I. *adj.* 1) (*with Dat.*) belonging, appertaining (to); 2) required; requisite, necessary; 3) due (notice, time, &c.), proper, fit, decent, right, just, fair, appropriate; alles hierher G-e, every thing appertaining hereto; für g-e Verpackung sorgen, *Comm.* to see proper care taken in the packing; II. *adv.* duly, &c.; ganz —, *coll.* with a vengeance; in g-er Form (Rechtens), in due form (of law); g-en Schutz finden, *Comm.* to meet due protection; nicht zur Sache —, not pertinent, irrelevant, foreign to the matter; alles G-e veranlassen, to adopt all proper measures.

Gehö'rigkeit, (*w.*) *f.* fitness, propriety.

Gehör'..., *in comp.* —krankheit, *f.* disease of the ear; —kunst, —lehre, *f.* acoustics; —schwächung, *f.* deafness, surdity; —loch, *n.* auditory hole. [deafness.

Gehör'los, *adj.* deaf; G-igkeit, (*w.*) *f.*

Gehör'mangel, (*str.*) *m.* imperfect hearing; deafness.

Gehörn', (*str.*) *n.* horns (especially of deer), *Sport.* & *Herald.* attire; das erste —, revenue (of a stag).

Gehör'nerven, *m. pl.* auditory nerves.

Gehörnt', *adj.* horned; *Bot.* cornute; cuck-

Gei'fer, s. I. *(str.)* m. drivel, spittle, slabber, foam; *fig.* anger, spleen, rancour: seinen (or den) — wider Einen ausschäumen, to vent one's spleen or bitterness upon one; II. *in comp.* —bart, m. *contempt.* driveller, slaverer, slabberer, *vul.* slabberchops: —läppchen, —tüchen, —tuch, —tüchlein, n. slavering-cloth, slabbering-bib, pinafore; —thierchen, n. froth-locust (Schaumcicade); —wurz, f. *Bot.* Spanish camomile or pellitory.

Gei'ferich, **Gei'ferig**, *adj.* drivel-like, slaver-like; slavering, drivelling.

Gei'fern, *(w.)* v. *intr.* to drivel, dribble; to slaver; to foam; to sputter (in speaking); über etwas *(Acc.)* —, *fig.* to be furiously angry about a thing (mit Einem, to quarrel with).

Gei'ge, *(w.)* f. 1) violin, fiddle; 2) *T.* combmaker's polishing blade; 3) *Hust.* see Fiedelbaum, 2; 4) instrument for fastening hands and neck during whipping; der Himmel hängt voller G-n, *iron.* things bear a bright and promising aspect; die erste — spielen, *lit.* & *fig.* to play (the) first fiddle.

Gei'gen, *(w.)* v. *tr.* & *intr.* 1) to play on the violin, *coll.* to fiddle; 2) to whip, scourge; *coll.* e. Einem die Wahrheit —, to tell one (of) his faults; ich werde ihm was —! fiddlesticks!

Gei'gen..., *in comp.* —ampfer, m. *Bot.* fiddle-dock; —artige Instrumente, n. *pl.* see Streichinstrumente; —blatt, n. finger-board of a violin; —bogen, m. see Violinbogen; —bohrer, m. drill, wimble; —bohrer und Bogen, drill-box and bow; —förmig, *adj.* shaped like a violin, *Bot.* guitar-shaped, panduriform; —futter(al), n. case for a violin; —hals, m. neck of a violin; —harz, n. Spanish rosin, hard rosin, colophony; —holz, n. fiddle-wood; —macher, m. violin-maker; —saite, f. string for a violin; —sattel, m. see —steg; —schlüssel, m. treble-clef, see G-schlüssel; —spieler, m. violinist; —steg, m. bridge of a violin; —strich, m. stroke of the fiddle-stick, *coll.* bow; —stück, n. piece of music for the violin; —ton, m. sound of the violin; —werk, n. celestina; —wirbel, m. peg of a violin; —zug, m. violin-stop (of an organ). [*coll.* fiddler.

Gei'ger, *(str.)* m. violin-player, violinist,

Geil, *adj.* 1) rank; fat, rich; well manured; *fig.* 2) wanton, luxuriant; 3) lewd, lecherous, prurient, lascivious, libidinous, lustful, goatish; 4) *Surg.* proud (flesh); — wachsend, growing luxuriantly, rank.

Gei'le, *(w.)* f. 1) (*l. u.*) manure; 2) see Geilheit; 3) *Anat. gener. pl.* G-n, *a)* testicles; *b)* the ovaria in the womb; *c)* *Sport.* [illegible] of a hart or stag.

Gei'len, *(w.)* v. I. *intr.* 1) to be lascivious; *Sport.* to rut; 2) †, to beg hard for, be importunate; II. *tr.* 1) †, to manure; 2) to emasculate, geld, castrate; 3) to prune, lop.

Geil'heit, *(w.)* f. 1) *a)* rankness; *b)* *fig.* luxuriancy; 2) lewdness, lechery, wantonness, pruriency.

Geil'wurz, f. see Knabenkraut.

* **Gein'** [[illegible]], *(str.)* n. *Chem.* geine; —säure, f. humic acid.

Geip, *(str.)* m. *Mar.* main boom of a boat.

Geist, s. I. *(str.*, pl. Gei'ster) m. 1) *a)* ghost, spirit; *b)* soul; mind; *c)* genius; intelligence; *d)* sprightliness, spirits; 2) spectre, ghost; apparition; demon; 4) life; 5) *Chem.* volatile liquid, refined fluid, spirit; ein guter —, a (good) Genius; ein böser —, demon; *fig.* intelligence; ein großer —, a master-spirit, master-mind; die Wissenschaft des G-es im Gegensatz zu der der Natur, moral science as opposed to physical science; der — seiner Sprache, temper of his language; der heilige —, the Holy Ghost, (Holy) Spirit; ein umfassender —, a comprehensive mind; ein freier —, an independent thinker, *cf.* Freigeist; ein schöner —, see Schöngeist; — der Gegenwart, spirit of the time; den — bilden, to cultivate, enlarge, expand, refine, improve the mind; den — aufgeben, to give (or yield) up the ghost, to breathe one's last; den — auf *(with Acc.)* richten, to direct the attention, to attend (to); im G-e betrachten, to consider in one's mind; ich bin im G-e bei dir, I am standing mentally at your side; ich sehe im G-e, I see in my mind's eye; ich weiß, weß G-es Kind er ist, I know him thoroughly; — der Vergangenheit, spirit of the past; II. *in comp.* —arm, *adj.* spiritless; dull, stupid, lifeless; vapid, insipid; weak; —begabt, *adj.* possessed of genius or ingenuity, ingenious, spirited.

Geis'ten, *(w.)* v. *intr.* 1) †, to ferment (Gähren); 2) to wander as a spirit, to haunt.

Geis'ter, *(str.)* m. 1) †, enthusiast (Schwärmer); 2) *provinc.* white-fish, dace (Weißfisch).

Gei'ster..., *in comp.* —ähnlich, *adj.* ghostlike; —banner, —beschwörer, m. one that lays ghosts, exorciser; conjurer; necromancer; —bannung, —beschwörung, f. necromancy; exorcism; —erscheinung, f. apparition; —furcht, f. fear of ghosts, spectres, &c.; —geschichte, f. ghost-story; —glaube, m. belief in the existence of spirits, ghosts, &c.

Geis'terhaft, *adj.* ghastly, ghostlike, *cf.* übernatürlich.

Gei'ster..., *in comp.* —herrschaft, f. domination of spirits; —klopfen, n. spirit-rapping; —kunde, —lehre, f. doctrine of spirits, pneumatology; —mäßig, *adj.* ghostly.

Geist'..., *in comp.* —ermüdend, *adj.* fatiguing the mind; —erquickend, *adj.* refreshing the mind.

Gei'ster..., *in comp.* —reich, I. *adj.* (Göthe, Faust I, 3, end) abounding with spirits, full of spirits; II. n. see —welt; —schar, f. host of spirits; —schatz, m. magic treasure; —seher, m., —seherin, f. visionary; ghost-seer; apparitionist; —seherei, f. visionary fancies; ghost-seeing, second-sight; —stunde, f. hour in which ghosts are said to walk, ghostly hour (midnight); —welt, f. 1) the world of spirits, spirit-world; 2) spiritual world; intelligent creation, intellectual world; invisible world.

Geis'tes..., *in comp.* —abwesend, *adj.* absent in mind; light-headed; —abwesenheit, f. absence of mind; lightness of the head, delirium; —anmuth, f. grace of mind; —arbeit, f. work of thought and consideration; —armuth, f. poverty of mind or of intellect; —bildung, —cultur, f. cultivation of the mind; —drang, m. the ardour, impulse of the mind; —erstarrung, f. torpidity of mind; —fähigkeit, f. see —gabe; —flug, m. flight of the mind; —freude, f. mental enjoyment; —frucht, —geburt, f. work or production of the mind; —funken, m. spark or flash of thought; —gabe, f. mental gift, attainment, talent; —gegenwart, f. presence of mind; —genuß, m. see —freude; —größe, f. magnanimity; —knechtschaft, f. mental slavery; —kraft, f. faculty of the mind; power of the mind, mental power, vigour; —krank, *adj.* weak of mind, disordered; —krankheit, f. disorder of the mind, insanity, *cf.* —schwäche; —leere, f. vacancy of mind; —nahrung, f. nourishment of the mind; —product, n. see —frucht; —richtung, f. turn or tendency of mind; —ruhe, f. tranquillity of mind; —schwach, *adj.* 1) feeble-minded, narrow-spirited; 2) imbecile; —schwäche, f. weakness or impotence of mind, narrow-spiritedness, (mental) imbecility; —schwung, m. elevation of mind; —sclaverei, f. see —knechtschaft; —spannung, f. exertion, stretch of the mind; —stärke, f. mental vigour; fortitude; —stimmung, f. see —verfassung; —störung, f. derangement of the mind; —stumpf, *adj.* torpid, imbecile; —träge, *adj.* heavy, dull, see —stumpf; —trägheit, f. intellectual indolence; torpor, imbecility; —verfassung, f. frame of mind; —verwandt, *adj.* congenial (of mind); —verwandtschaft, f. congeniality (of mind); —verwirrung, f. delirium, alienation of mind; —werk, n. production of the mind; —zerrüttung, f. disorder or derangement of the mind; —zwang, m. spiritual restraint.

Geist'haft, *adj.* see Geisterhaft.

Geis'tig, I. *adj.* 1) *Chem.* spirituous, volatile; 2) spiritual, immaterial; 3) *a)* intellectual, mental; moral; *b)* intelligent, spirited, ingenious; 4) spirituous, racy, generous; g-e Getränke, spirituous liquors, (ardent) spirits; g-e Liebe, platonic love; die g-e Welt, intellectual world; II. G-keit, *(w.)* f. spirituality, immateriality, incorporeity.

Geist'lich, *adj.* spiritual, belonging to the spirits.

Geist'..., *in comp.* —lähmend, *adj.* lamings the spirit; —leer, see —arm.

Geist'lich, *adj.* 1) spiritual; 2) ecclesiastical, clerical; religious (order, book, &c.); ein g-es Amt, ministerial charge; g-e Musik, sacred harmony; g-es Lied, hymn; g-e Herrschaft, spiritual dominion (of the pope, &c.); das g-e Recht, canon law; ein Lehrer des g-en Rechts, canonist; der g-e Stand, 1. clerical state; 2. (body or order of) clergymen, clergy; in den g-en Stand treten, to take orders; zum g-en Stande bestimmt sein, to be destined for the church; die g-en Güter, churchlands.

Geist'liche, m. *(decl. like adj.)* clergyman, ecclesiastic, minister, divine, churchman, priest; der hohe —, dignitary (in the episcopal church).

Geist'lichkeit, *(w.)* f. 1) spirituality, religiousness, sanctity; 2) the clergy (collectively).

Geist'los, *adj.* I. spiritless; dull; stupid, &c. *cf.* Geistarm; II. G-igkeit, *(w.)* f. spiritlessness; deadness; dulness; insipidity, vapidness.

Geist'..., *in comp.* —reich, *adj.* ingenious, genial, clever, witty, quickwitted; —tödtend, *adj.* killing the spirit, soul-killing; —voll, *adj.* full of spirit, intelligent; spirited, witty.

Geiß, s. I. or **Gei'ße**, *(w.)* f. goat; roe; II. *in comp.* —auge, n. *Med.* egilops; *Bot.* s. —bart, m. goat's beard (*Tragopogon pratensis* L.); —baum, m. see Esche, 1; —blatt, n. honey-suckle, woodbine, caprifole (*Lonicera caprifolium* L.); —blume, f. 1) marsh or celery-leaved crow-foot (*Ranunculus sceleratus* L.); 2) (große) great ox-eye daisy, maudlin-wort (*Chrysanthemum leucanthemum* L.); —bock, m. 1) buck-goat, *coll.* he-goat; 2) roebuck; —brassen, m. *Ichth.* a species of bream (*Sargus Rondeletii* C.).

Gei'ßel, I. *(w.)* m. & f. hostage; II. *(w.)* f. 1) whip, scourge; 2) *fig.* severe censure or mockery; die — schwingen über ..., *fig.* to scourge, &c. see Geißeln, 2; III. *in comp.* —brüder, m. *pl.* *Eccl.* flagellants; —gras, n. *Bot.* scleria (*Scleria flagellum*); —mönch, m. flagellant.

Gei'ßeln, *(w.)* v. *tr.* to lash: 1) to whip, scourge, flog, flagellate; 2) *fig.* to lash, to scourge, to criticise severely.

Geißel'ruthe, *(w.)* f. scourge.

Gei'ßelung, *(w.)* f. flagellation, scourging.

Geiß'..., *in comp.* —fuß, 1) *Bot.* goat or goat-weed, goat's foot (*Aegopodium podagraria* L.); 2) *T.* *a)* socket chisel; *b)* see Brecheisen, 1; *c)* *Dent.* punch; —hirt, m. goat-herd; —klee, m. *Bot.* 1) bean-trefoil tree, laburnum (*Cytisus laburnum* L.); 2) see —raute; —laube, f. honeysuckle-bower; —leder, n. goat-skin or -leather.

Geiß'lein, (*dimin. of* Geiß) *(str.)* n. kid.

[illegible]gel, m. Ornith. witwall (Oriolus galbula); —wasser, n. Med. ascites: —weiß, n. yellowish white, cream-coloured white; —wurz, f. see Curcuma.

Geld, n. 1. (str., pl. Gel'der) n. money, coin; (baares —, ready) cash, specie: kleines —, small (or loose) money, change; fremdes —, Comm. borrowed capital; ohne —, see —los; von seinem G-e leben, to live upon the interest of one's capital; es ist kein — unter den Leuten, money is scarce, there is no money stirring; — verdienen or machen, to make money; etwas zu — machen, to turn (convert) into money, to make money of ...; to cash (a bill, &c.); bei G-e sein, to be in cash: nicht bei G-e sein, to be out of cash, or short of money; fac. to want the needful: für — und gute Worte, for love and money: er hat — wie Heu (Mist, Stroh &c.), he rolls in money; es ist verlorenes or weggeworfenes —, it is so much money thrown away or lost; gutes — dem schlechten nachwerfen, to throw good money after bad; Comm. Briefe 101, — 100½, paper (seller, offered) at 101, money (wanted, required after) at 101½; II. in comp. money-; monetary; pecuniary: —adel, m. 1) purchased nobility: 2) moneyed nobility: —angelegenheit, f. money-matter, pl. money-affairs or transactions: —anlage, f. Comm. investment of funds: —anleihe, f. loan (of money): —aristocratie, f. moneyed aristocracy, (Ld. Brougham's) burl. capitalocracy: —arm, adj. moneyless, in want of money: —auflage, f. imposition, tax; —ausgabe, f. expense, disbursement, payment: —ausleiher, m. money-lender; —bedarf, m. 1) want of money; 2) requisite money, cash: —bedürftig, adj. see —arm; —begierde, f., —begierig, adj. see —gier, —gierig; —beitrag, m. contribution in money: —belohnung, f. pecuniary reward, remuneration: —beutel, m. purse; money-bag: —beutelringe, m. pl. purse runners or sliders: —bewilligung, f. (des Parlaments) supply: —brief, m. letter containing money, money-letter: —büchse, f. money-box; till (in a shop): —buße, f. see —strafe; —casse, f. coffer, iron-chest, strong-box: (in einem Gewölbe) till, tiller (money-box or -drawer in a shop), cf. Kasse; —cours, m. 1) course of exchange: 2) (im Gegensatz zu Briefcours) money, wanted, required after: —courszettel, m. bill or note of the course of exchange, quotations or statement of specie; —crisis, f. see —krise; —durst, m. thirst of, for, or after money: —durstig, adj. see —gierig; —einnahme, f. receipt of money; —einnehmer, m. receiver of money, cashier.

Gel'dern, (str.) n. Geogr. Guelders (a town of the Netherlands). — Gel'derland, (str.) n. Guelderland.

Gel'derrose, (w.) f. Bot. guelder-rose.

Geld'..., in comp. —erwerb, m. acquisition of money, money-making: G-eswerth, m. money's-worth: —forderung, f. demand, cf. Forderung: 1) money-demand; pecuniary demand; request for money; dunning; 2) money due to one: —freier, m. fortune-hunter; —fressend, adj. coll. money-consuming, expensive: —geben, n. payment, paying, expense; —gefälle, n. pl. duties paid in money (opp. to duties paid in kind); —gehalt, m. 1) intrinsic value of a coin, standard; 2) see —werth; —geiz, m. avarice: —geizig, adj. avaricious; —geschäfte, n. pl. money-transactions, money-trade, banking (cf. —handel), [illegible] stock-jobbing; —geschenk, n. gratuity [illegible], pecuniary present: —gier, f. covetousness, inordinate desire or greediness for money; —gierig, adj. covetous of, or greedy for money; —gülte, f. see —gefälle; —gürtel, m. [illegible], belt for money; —handel, m. money-dealing, money transaction, money-trade; —händler, m. see —mäkler & —wechsler; —heirat, f. a marriage contracted in consequence of pecuniary speculation, vulg. a Smithfield bargain or match: —hülfe, f. pecuniary assistance; —hunger, m. see —durst; —kasten, m. chest, cash-box, money-box, strong-box, cf. —casse; —katze, f. see —gürtel; —kiste, f. coffer, see —kasten; —klemme, f. necessity of cash, scarcity of money, pecuniary embarrassment, money-difficulties: cf. —mangel, —noth; —kräfte, f. pl. see —mittel; —krise, —krisis, f. monetary or money-crisis; —lade, f. see —kasten; —lehen, n. fief obtained by money: —leistung, f. 1) supply of money: 2) see —gefälle.

Geld'los, I. adj. moneyless, unmoneyed; bare of money, penniless; II. G-igkeit, (w.) f. see —mangel.

Geld'..., in comp. —macher, m. money-maker: 1) see Falschmünzer; 2) one whose only business and aim in life is to make money: —macht, f. financial power; —mäkler, m. money- (or stock-)broker; —mangel, m. want, lack, or scarcity of money, cf. —noth; —mann, m. moneyed man: capitalist: —männchen, n. Bot. mandrake; —markt, m. money-market, stock-exchange: —mensch, m. see —macher; —mittel, n. pl. money-means, (pecuniary) resources; hinlängliche —mittel, the necessary capital; —münze, f. coin: —muschel, f. Conch. cowry; —noth, f. distress or pressure for money, cf. —klemme, —mangel; in —noth sein, see in —verlegenheit sein; —packet, n. see —rolle; —posten, m. (any) sum of money (either received or paid away); —preis, m. cash-price; exchange: —protz, m. coll. purse-proud fellow; —rechnung, f. money-account; —reich, adj. moneyed; —reichthum, m. wealth in money; —rolle, f. roll (pack) of money, money-packet, (Fr.) rouleau: —rücksicht, f. regard for money; pecuniary consideration; —sache, f. money-matter, cf. —angelegenheit; —sack, m. money-bag: —sammlung, f. collection or collecting of money; eine —sammlung durch Subscription veranstalten, to raise money by subscription: —schaden, m. loss of money; —schachtel, f. money-box; —schatz, m. hoard of money; —schneider, m. extortioner; coll. sharper, shark; —schneiderei, f. coll. extortion, imposition; —schrank, m. iron safe; —schuld, f. money-debt; —sendung, f. remittance of money: —sorte, f. sort, species, denomination of coin; —spende, f. contribution or alms in money: —splitterung, f. waste of money: —stand, m. state of money-affairs, condition of the money-market; —steuer, f. tax or contribution in money; —stock, m. 1) money-box, strong-box: 2) stock, see Capital; —stolz, I. s. m. purse-pride; II. adj. purse-proud, stuck-up; —strafe, f. fine, amercement, forfeit, pecuniary penalty, mulct; —stück, n. piece of money, coin: —sucht, f. love of money, cf. —gier; —süchtig, adj. greedy of gain or money; —summe, f. sum of money; —surrogate, n. pl. substitutes of money: —tasche, f. 1) pocket for carrying money in: 2) or —täschchen, n. flat-purse; porte-monnaie; (zum Umhängen) courier's bag; —tisch, m. counter; —umlauf, —umsatz, m. circulation or flux of money; —unterstützung, f. pecuniary aid: —valuta, f. see —werth; —verkehr, m. see —handel; —verlegenheit, f. pecuniary embarrassment, cf. —noth; in —verlegenheit sein, to be straitened for money; fam. to be down upon one's luck; —verleiher, m. money lender; —verlust, m. loss of money: —vorschuß, m. advance of (or in) money, previous payment; disbursement, money disbursed; —wage, f. money-balance or scale; —wechsel, m. exchange of money; banking; —wechsler, m. exchanger, banker, money-changer: —werth, m. 1) value of the money; 2) money's-worth: value in money; —wesen, n. money or monetary affairs, matters, or concerns; —wucher, m. usury, money jobbing; —zins, m. interest of money.

Gel'ben, (w.) v. intr. (L. u. for Leben) to live (with Gen., in hopes of, &c.).

Gele'cke, (str.) n. (the act or repeated action of) licking; cont. continual kissing.

* Gelée' (pr. zhelā'), (str., pl. G-s, or (w.) G-n) n. (sometimes f.) (Fr.) jelly (Gallerte); —form, f. jelly mould.

Gele'ge, (str.) n. any thing that is laid or put down: 1) small heaps of corn; 2) layers of vine: operation of layering (as of vines); 3) quantity of eggs laid by a hen-bird in one year.

Gele'gen, p. a. 1) situated: 2) fig. convenient, fit, apt, commodious, proper, seasonable, opportune, agreeable, pleasing: mir ganz —, just the thing for me: ein g-erer Weg, provinc. nearer way, short cut: — kommen, to come in handy, to be very welcome or acceptable: Sie kommen mir sehr —, you come very opportunely: zur g-en Zeit, in the very nick of time, seasonably, opportunely, in season; es ist mir an einer Sache (viel, wenig, nichts &c.) —, impers. it is of (great, little, no, &c.) consequence to me, see liegen, impers.; an Gottes Segen ist Alles —, proverb. God's blessing is all-important, everything depends on God's blessing.

Gele'genheit, (w.) f. 1) fitness, convenience, aptness, &c.; 2) a) occasion, opportunity; (gute, lucky) chance; b) way, manner, means: 3) conveyance, coll. convenience; 4) coll. a) lodging; b) necessary, privy; gute or günstige G-en, facilities; bei (vorkommender) —, when occasion or opportunity offers or serves: bei dieser —, on this occasion; bei — dieses Vorfalls will ich erwähnen, speaking of this now, I'll mention: — geben, to give an opportunity; so oft sich — bietet, whenever the occasion serves or a chance occurs; mit nächster (Fuhr-) —, by the next conveyance: mit erster —, by or upon the first opportunity; suchen Sie (Fuhr-) —, mein Herr? coll. (do you) want a coach, Sir? pflegen Sie Ihrer —, use your pleasure; make yourself at home or comfortable: — macht Diebe, proverb. temptation makes a thief.

Gele'genheitlich, see Gelegentlich.

Gele'genheits..., in comp. —dichter, m. one who writes poems for certain occasions: —gedicht, n. poem upon some occasion, occasional poem; —gesellschaft, f. Comm. occasional copartnership; —kauf, m. chance-purchase; —macher, m. cont. procurer, setter, pimp, go-between; —macherin, f. cont. procuress, bawd: —predigt, f. sermon held on particular occasion: —rede, f. address: —schrift, f. fugitive tract or writing, pamphlet; —ursache, f. Philos. occasional cause.

Gele'gentlich, I. adj. occasional, opportune; II. adv. 1) occasionally (i. e. as often as occasion offers); incidentally; at times, now and then; er hörte — manche übelwollende Bemerkung über seinen Onkel, he heard incidentally many an ill-natured remark upon his uncle; 2) a) when occasion offers or offered, on (a certain) occasion, incidentally; wie — in einem früheren Capitel angedeutet worden ist, as it has been incidentally implied in a previous chapter; by and by, at leisure, at convenience; conveniently; 3) nur ganz — erfuhr ich, I learned quite accidentally. — dieses Gegenstandes will ich bemerken, à propos of this subject, I will observe.

Gelehr'ig, I. adj. docile, tractable, instructible, teachable, disciplinable; II. G-keit, (w.) f. docility, tractableness.

Gelehr'samkeit, (w.) f. erudition, learning, knowledge, scholarship.

Gelehrt', I. adj. 1) learned, erudite, le-

[illegible] (or so little)? is my credit so trifling? [illegible], to apply to, hold good for; g-d machen, [illegible] the best of, to make good; to bring [illegible], to assert; to urge; to lay stress upon; [illegible]; to vindicate, assert; to bring forward (claims); to bring into prominence or [illegible] (a principle, &c.); sich g-d machen, to [illegible] itself felt (bei, with); to come home [illegible] to tell; to make one's self conspicuous; [illegible], to let pass, admit; not to dispute [illegible] question, to grant, concede; das lasse ich [illegible], that will do; es gilt mir gleich, it is all [illegible] (or the same) to me; es gilt mir wenig, [illegible] light of it, it has no weight with me; [illegible] bei Jemandem —, to be much with one; [illegible] Hofe —, to have credit at court; das gilt [illegible], that is not permitted, this is not fair [illegible]; fam. that's no go; das gilt für nichts, [illegible] goes for nothing, stands for a cypher; [illegible] Spott gilt mir, the ridicule is intended, meant for me, aimed, pointed, levelled at me; [illegible] Münze gilt nicht mehr, the coin does not [illegible] current now; II. impers. 1) (with Acc.) [illegible] concern; es gilt meine Ehre, it concerns my honour; es gilt sein Leben, his life is at stake; es gilt Kampf, combat is the word; [illegible] gilt' es Felsen zu verglasen (Schiller, Frid.), [illegible] the (i. e. their) object were to melt down [illegible] into glass; 2) (with Dat.) to be aimed [illegible]; es galt mir, I was aimed at; gilt es mir? [illegible] intended for me? das gilt Ihnen, it is [illegible] or aimed at you, that is (intended) [illegible] you; es (i. e. das Spiel, die Wette) gilt! [illegible] agreed! jetzt gilt es zu ..., the main or [illegible] point is (there is the time) now to ...; [illegible] es galt, when it came to the test.

[illegible], (w.) v. tr. to geld (hogs).

[illegible], (str.) m. 1) eunuch; 2) gelding; [illegible] one year old calf.

[illegible], (str.) n. gelding, barren cattle.

[illegible], (w.) f. 1) the being worth, valid, current, &c. cf. Gelten; value; authority; [illegible]; currency, acceptance; noch in —, still [illegible], current; 2) Mus. & Gramm. duration; [illegible] Gesetze — verschaffen, to enforce the law; [illegible] — bringen, see Geltend machen (under [illegible]) in — kommen, to come into favour.

[illegible], (str.) n. see Geltthier.

[illegible], (str.) n. vow; solemn promise; [illegible] — thun, to make a vow; —opfer, n. votive [illegible]; —tafel, f. votive table.

[illegible], (str.) m. pluck (of animals).

[illegible], (str.) n. desire, longing; carnal [illegible], concupiscence, cupidity; itch, hankering (nach, after); das — der Schwangern, [illegible] longing, pica.

[illegible], (w.) v. tr. (& intr.) impers. (rarely pers.) (with nach) to desire, covet, to long for, lust after; mich gelüstet danach, I [illegible] after it; es gelüstet mich (less usual mir) [illegible] ..., or with Gen.) I (feel a) desire; sich [illegible] nach &c., to have a longing for or [illegible], to covet, to be tempted.

[illegible], adj. see Lüstern.

[illegible], adj. tempting.

[illegible], (w.) f. spayed or gelded sow.

[illegible], (w.) v. tr. to spay, geld.

[illegible], Gel'zer, (str.) m swine-[illegible], sow-gelder.

[illegible] [illegible]; gemäch'], adv. [illegible] gently; by degrees; (rarely) adj. easy, [illegible] —! —! gently, gently! fair and [illegible] hold there!

[illegible], (str., pl. [illegible]) n. 1) room, [illegible], apartment, closet; 2) see Gemäch-[illegible]; das heimliche —, coll. privy, (water) [illegible], necessary; convenient house.

[illegible], I. or (I. w.) [illegible], adj. [illegible] easy, convenient, commodious, comfortable; [illegible] — [illegible]; — leben, to live comfortably or at ease; II. G-keit, (w.) f. convenienc[y], ease, easiness, comfortableness, comfort; G-keitsgesellschaft, f. Comm. see Handelsgesellschaft, Commanditgesellschaft.

Gemacht', p. a. (cf. Machen) made: 1) lit. cf. Selbstgemacht; fig.-s. 2) got up, fabricated; artificial; affected; 3) fitted (zu, for); born (to; cf. Geboren); cut out (for a mathematician, &c.); 4) raised to good fortune, secured in riches or happiness: g-e (Wechsel-)Briefe, g-es Papier, bills (drafts) ready for further endorsement, endorsed bills; wir sind g-e Leute, we are made men; 5) (auf Courszetteln) business done; 6) ein g-er Handel, a concluded bargain; 7) artificial (gold, &c.).

Gemächt', (str.) n. 1) coll. see Machwerk; 2) genitals, private or privy parts; 3) provinc. a) ingredients; b) see Vermächtniß.

Gemahl', (str.) m. († & * n. applied to both sexes), G-in, (w.) f. consort, spouse, m. husband; Ihre (Frau) G-in, Mrs... (m. fl.: your lady, your wife).

Gemah'nen, (w.) v. I. tr. († &) *, to put in mind, remind (an [with Acc.], of); II. tr. (& intr.) impers. es gemahnt mich (mir), it seems, appears to me, it strikes me.

Gemähnt', p. a. having a mane, maned.

Gemäl'de, s. I. (str.) n. picture: 1) painting, drawing; portrait, likeness; 2) fig. description; II. in comp. —ausstellung, f. exhibition of pictures; —gallerie, f. picture-gallery; —handel, m. picture-trade; —händler, m. picture-dealer; —rahmen, m. picture-frame; —saal, m. picture-room, gallery; —sammlung, f. collection of pictures; —verkauf, m. sale of pictures.

Gemang', (str.) m. mixture, cf. Gemenge; —brot, n. Bak. mixed bread; —korn, n. mixed corn, meslin.

Gemansch', (str.) n. vulg. see Manscherei.

Gemark', (str.) n. mark or stamp (on plate, silver, or gold wares, &c.).

Gemar'kung, (w.) f. 1) march, boundary; 2) territory, see Feldmark.

Gemar'ter, (str.) n. the (act or practice of) tormenting.

Gema'sert, p. a. (cf. Masern & Maserig) curled, speckled (of wood).

Gemäß', (str.) n. measure.

Gemäß', I. adj. conformable, suitable, agreeable; —sein, to agree (einer Sache [Dat.], with ...); II. adv. (with Dat., which always precedes the adv.) conformably (to), in conformity (to or with), agreeably, suitably, according (to), correspondent (with), pursuant (to); III. G-heit, (w.) f. conformity, congruency, accordance, accommodation, suitableness; in G-heit einer Sache (Gen.), in conformity to or with ....

Gemä'ßigt, p. a. temperate; moderate; [mild.

Gemäu'er, (str.) n. connected walls, masonry, walling; ein altes —, old, ruined walls, ruins.

Gemecker, (str.) n. coll. (act, practice, or [mode of) bleating.

Gemein', adj. 1) common; 2) fig. common, ordinary, mean; low, vulgar; base, coarse; menial; 3) public; frequent; general, universal; g-e Töpferwaare, coarse pottery; ein g-er Mensch, a low, mean fellow; mit g-en Menschen umgehen, to keep low company; der g-e Mann, collect. common people; das g-e Leben, common life; im g-en Leben, 1. in common life; 2. generally: usually; das g-e Volk, 1. common people; 2. the vulgar; ein g-er Soldat, a private soldier; pl. privates, rank and file; der g-e Menschenverstand, common sense; das g-e Recht, common law; der g-e Bruch, Arith. vulgar fraction; das g-e Wesen, commonwealth; das g-e Beste, the public or common welfare or weal; die g-e Weide, common; das Recht der g-en Hut, commonage; etwas mit Einem — haben, to have a thing in common with one; to partake with; — machen, 1. to make vulgar; 2. to make popular, to popularise; sich — machen, to make one's self familiar, to degrade one's self; insg or im —, in common; commonly.

Gemein'..., in comp. (cf. Gemeinde) —besitz, m. common possession or property; —brett, n. Carp. inch-plank, board; —capitalien, n. pl. joint stocks.

Gemein'de (Gemei'ne), s. I. (w.) f. 1) commonalty, community; die christliche —, Christian communion, church; 2) congregation, parish, parishioners; 3) common; von der — ausschließen, to excommunicate; II. in comp. (cf. Gemein'..., in comp.) —acker, m. common; —anger, m. common pasture, common; —auflagen, f. pl. local taxes, parish-rates; —beamte, m. municipal or parish-officer; —bezirk, m. municipality; parish; —bier, n. certain quantity of beer allowed by the community to its members at their sittings; —boden, m. common ground; —bulle, m. see —ochs; —einkommen, n. common revenue; —feld, n. common (field); —gesang, m. congregational singing; —gerichtsbarkeit, f. local jurisdiction; —glied, n. member of a community; —grund, m. common (pasture-)ground; —gut, n. common, parish-ground; —haus, n. 1) house belonging to a community; 2) common-hall; —haushalt, m. local administration; —herde, f. common flock (of a village); —hirt, m. herdsman of the parish; —hut, —hutung, f. see —grund; —land, n. Law, common appurtenant; —meister, m. tax-gatherer of the parish; G-zeche, f. Min. mine worked by a community; —ochs, m. parish-bull; —ordnung, f. municipal or parish regulations.

Gemein'der, (str.) m. 1) see Gemeindeglied; 2) see Gemeindevorsteher, 2; 3) provinc. partner, associate.

Gemein'de (Gemei'ne)..., in comp. —rath, m. town or common council; —recht, n. 1) privilege of the parish; 2) right of common; —regierung, f. local self-government; —schenke, f. ale-house of the parish; —schießen, n. shooting-feast of a parish; —schreiber, m. parish-clerk; —schule, f. parish-school; —siegel, n. parish-seal; —stück, n. see —gut; —trift, f. see Gemeintrift; —unterlagen, f. pl. see —auflagen; —verrechner, m. treasurer of a community; —verwaltung, f. see —haushalt; —vorstand, m. town or parish-council; —vorsteher, m. 1) master of a company; 2) magistrate of a parish; —wald, m. parish-wood or -forest; —wappen, n. coat of arms of a community; —weide, f. see —anger.

Gemei'ne, m. (decl. like adj.) 1) commoner, pl. commons; das Haus der G-n, house of commons; 2) Mil. private (soldier).

Gemein'..., in comp. —erz, n. Miner. common ore; —faßlich, adj. apprehensible, intelligible to a common understanding, popular; —faßlich machen, to popularise; —gefährlich, adj. generally dangerous; —gefühl, n. see —sinn; —geist, m. public spirit; —gläubiger, m. pl. Comm. creditors under a commission of bankruptcy; —gültig, adj. generally received or admitted; —gut, n. common good; common or public property; diese Meinung ist noch kein —gut geworden, fig. this opinion has not yet gained possession of the general mind.

Gemein'heit, (w.) f. 1) community; common; 2) fig. commonness, meanness, coarseness, grossness, low familiarity, vulgarity; mean, low, or dirty conduct or trick.

Gemein'..., in comp. —herrschaft, f. common jurisdiction; —hin, adv. commonly.

Gemei'niglich, adv. commonly, ordinarily, usually, generally.

Gemein'..., in comp. —latte, f. Carp. half-(inch-)plank, shelf; —name, m. common noun; —nützig, adj. of public use, of public benefit, popular; die —nützige Gesellschaft, so-

[illegible]sion; assent; sanction; 2) approbation, approval; 3) acceptance; mit —, with (the) consent (of); **G-urkunde**, *f.* deed of composition.

Geneig'ge, *(str.)* *n.* 1) *coll.* (the act and repetition of) bowing, courtesying; 2) *T.* inclination (downwards).

Geneigt', *p. a.* 1) inclined, bent; *fig.-s.* 2) inclined (*zu*, to), bent (on), disposed, willing, ready; noch nicht —, not yet prepared; prone, addicted; 3) *a)* favourable; propitious; *b)* favourably inclined *or* disposed (Einem, towards one); gracious, kind; affectionate; sich [illegible] lassen, to consent, to condescend; [illegible] machen, 1. to dispose (*zu*, to, for), incline ([illegible], for); 2. to propitiate; g-er Leser, *Lit.* gentle (courteous) reader.

Geneigt'heit, *(w.)* *f.* 1) inclination; *fig.-s.* 2) inclination, disposition, willingness; bent, tendency, proneness, propensity; 3) favour, kindness, affection.

* **General'**, I. *adj.* *(Lat.)* general; II. *s.* *(str., pl.* Genera'le, *coll.* Genera'le) *m.* general, commander; III. *in comp.* —accise, *f.* excise-general; —accisedirector, *m.* director general of the excise; —acciseeinnehmer, *m.* receiver general of the excise: —adjutant, *m.* aide-de-camp, adjutant-general; —advocat, [illegible], *m.* advocate-general, attorney-general; —agent, *m.* general agent: —agentur, *f.* general agency; —archivar, *m.* master of the rolls; —arzt, *m.* surgeon of the army.

* **Generalat'**, *(str.)* *(L. Lat.)* 1) generalship; 2) district superintended by a general.

General'..., *in comp.* —auditeur, *m.* judge-advocate general, judge-marshal (of an army); —baß, *m.* *Mus.* thorough-bass *or* -base, continued base; —baßspieler, *m.* thorough-base player; —befahrung, *f.* *Min.* general visit by the superior officers of a mine; —befehl, *m.* general order: —bilanz, *f.* *Comm.* annual balance; —capitän, *m.* captain general; —capitel, *n.* chapter-general; —commandant, *m.* general in command; —commando, *n.* office of the commanding general: —commissar, *m.* commissary general; —consul, *m.* consul general; —consulat, *n.* 1) consulate general; 2) general consulship; —director, *m.* director-general. [neral law.

* **Genera'le**, *(str.)* *n.* *(Lat.)* statute, ge-

* **General'**..., *in comp.* —erlaß, *m.* *Comm.* general release; —feldmarschall, *m.* field-marshal-general, generalissimo; —feldwachtmeister, *m.* major-general; —feldzeugmeister, *m.* master-general of the ordnance; —fiscal, *m.* attorney-general; —gewaltige, *m.* †, *see* —auditeur; —gouverneur, *m.* governor-general; —handel, *m.* trade in general.

* **Genera'lin**, *(w.)* *f.* (a) general's wife [illegible].

* **General'**..., *in comp.* —inspector, *m.* inspector-general; —intendant, *m.* chief *or* superintendent of the commissariat (in [illegible]).

* **Generalisi'ren**, *(w.)* *v. tr.* to generalize.

* **Generalis'simus**, *m.* *(L. Lat.)* generalissimo. [generals, generality.

* **Generalität'**, *(w.)* *f.* *(L. Lat.)* body of

General'..., *in comp.* —karte, *f.* general [illegible]; —kriegscommissär, *m.* commissary-general; —kriegszahlmeister, *m.* paymaster-general; —lieutenant, *m.* lieutenant-general; —major, *m.* major-general; —marsch, *m.* general [illegible] of trumpet; der —marsch with [illegible], the general beat; —[illegible], *m.* [illegible]-general; —pardon, *m.* general pardon, act of oblivion; —plan, *m.* principal plan; —[illegible], *n.* general post-office; —[illegible], [illegible] directory of the general post-office; —[illegible], *m.* postmaster-general; —[illegible], [illegible]; —[illegible], *m.* [illegible]-general; —[illegible], *m.* provost-mar-

shal; —proviantmeister, *m.* chief of the commissariat; —quartiermeister, *m.* quarter- (*or* barrack-)master-general; —quittung, *f.* acquittance in full of all accounts (*or* demands); receipt in full, general release; —schmelzung, *f.* *Min.* smelting of all sorts of poor ore; —staaten, *m. pl.* states general; the States of Holland: —stab, *m.* staff: generality: —stabsarzt, *(str.)* *m.* surgeon general: —stabskarte, *f.* ordinance-map; —schuldverschreibung, *f.* omnium: —statthalter, *m.* Stadtholder general (of the former Austrian Netherlands): —stelle, *f.* generalship; —sturm, *m.* general assault: —superintendent, *m.* superintendent general (in dignity in the Lutheran church): —superintendentur, *f.* office and residence of the superintendent general: G-swürde, *f.* generalship: —versammlung, *f.* general assembly: —verweser, —vicar, *m.* grand-vicar; —vollmacht, *f.* general power of attorney; —waarenconto, *n.* *Comm.* merchandise-account: —wache, *f.* *see* Ehrenwache; —wachtmeister, *m.* master general of the train: —zahlmeister, *m.* 1) paymaster-general; 2) controller of the navy.

* **Generation'**, *(w.)* *f.* *(Lat.)* generation.

* **Generell'**, *adj.* *(Lat.)* general (General *[Lat.]*). [nerical.

* **Gene'risch**, *adj.* *(L. Lat.)* generic, ge-

* **Generös'** *[pr.* zhön—], *adj.* *(Fr.)* generous (Großmüthig).

Gene'sen, *(str.)* *v. intr.* *(aux.* sein) to recover, grow well; eines Kindes — († &) *, to be delivered of a child; der (*or* die) G-e, *m.* (& *f.*) *(decl. like adj.)* convalescent

* **Gene'sis**, *f.* *(Gr.)* genesis *(also Bibl.)*.

Gene'sung, *(w.)* *f.* recovery, convalescence; auf dem Wege der — sein, to be in a fair way of recovery: G-smittel, *n.* remedy, medicine; allgemeines G-smittel, panacea, catholicon.

* **Gene'tisch**, *adj.* *(Gr.)* genetic.

* **Genet'te** *[pr.* zhen—], *(w.)* *f.* *(Fr.)* *Zool.* (Genettkatze) genet *(Viverra genetta* L.).

* **Gen(i)e'ver** [zhe—], *(str.)* *m.* *(Fr.)* Hollands, geneva, gin (Wachholderbranntwein).

Genf, *n.* *Geogr.* Geneva (a town in Switzerland). — **Gen'fer**, *(str.)* *m.* & *adj.* Genevese; —see, *m.* lake of Geneva, lake Leman.

* **Genial'**, **Genia'lisch**, *adj.* *(Lat.)* highly gifted, ingenious, genial; spirited, bold, full of genius; ein g-er Mann, a man of genius *(pl.* geniuses).

* **Genialität'**, *(w.)* *f.* geniality, genius.

Genick', *(str.)* *n.* nape, back of the neck, scruff; zum — gehörig, cervical; das — brechen, to break one's neck. [continued) nodding.

Genick'e, *(str.)* *n.* *coll.* (the act of, *or* a

Genick'en, *(w.)* *v. tr.* 1) to break *or* cut the neck; 2) *Sport.* to stab *or* kill (a deer, &c.) with the hanger.

Genick'..., *in comp.* —fang, *m.* *Hunt.* a stab, thrust with the hanger; —fänger, *m.* *see* Hirschfänger & Fangmesser; —fistel, *f.* *Med.* poll-evil; —krampf, *m.* *Med.* spasmodic contraction of the neck, cerebro-spinal meningitis; —mäuslein, *n.* *Anat.* one of the three muscles of the thorax; —schmerz, *m.* pain in the nape *or* neck; —stoß, *m.* *see* —fang.

* **Genie'** *[pr.* zhenē'], *(str., pl.* G-s) *n.* *(Fr.)* 1) genius *(pl.* geniuses); spirit; talent; 2) *coll.* an original, queer fellow; —corps, *n.* *see* Ingenieurcorps. [nius.

* **Ge'nien**, *(w.)* *pl.* *Myth.* genii, *cf.* Ge-

Genieß', *(str.)* *m.* 1) †, *see* Genuß; 2) *Sport.* intestines and blood of deer, &c. given to the hounds as food.

Genieß'bar, I. *adj.* fit for enjoyment; 1) eatable, drinkable; edible, esculent; palatable; 2) *fig.* palatable, relishing; readable: II. G-keit, *(w.)* *f.* quality of being eatable *or* drinkable; tastefulness, relish.

Genieß'brauch, *(str.)* *m.* *see* Nießbrauch.

Genieß'en, *(str.)* *v. tr.* (& [† &] * *intr* *with Gen.*: als ob es [das Krokodil] der Kühe — will *(Freiligrath)*, as if wanting to enjoy the coolness) 1) to enjoy, make use of: to have the benefit (use) of; wenig Credit —, to have little credit; 2) to take, taste (food *or* drink); etwas —, to take some refreshment; 3) to enjoy, receive; das heilige Abendmahl —, to take (*or* partake of) the Lord's supper; 4) *Sport.* to scent, smell, catch the scent *or* track of ...; Einem etwas für genossen hingehen lassen, *coll.* to let one off with impunity *or* scot-free; die Hunde genossen machen, *Sport.* to give the dogs of the intestines and blood of game.

Genieß'lich, *adj.* 1) *see* Genießbar; 2) comfortable; 3) †, profitable; 4) †, self-seeking, selfish; 5) over-fond of enjoying one's self (Genußsüchtig). — **Genieß'ling**, *(str.)* *m.* a person excessively fond of enjoyments.

* **Genie'**... [zhenē'], *in comp.* —streich, *m.* *coll.* extravagant feat *or* exploit; —wesen, *n.* 1) military engineering; 2) *see* —corps.

* **Geni'ren** *[pr.* zhenē'ren], *(w.)* *v. tr.* *(Fr.)* to incommode, inconvenience, to cause inconvenience, constrain, restrain; to make uneasy, uncomfortable, to embarrass; to trouble, annoy; sich —, to feel embarrassed *or* under restraint; — Sie sich nicht, make free, make yourself at home (*beri.* the ladies do not *gêner* themselves before the old fogy, *Thack.*); genirt, *p. a.* *Comm.* straitened for money, *coll.* pushed.

Genist'(e), *(str.)* *n.* 1) (the act *or* practice of) nesting; 2) *a)* *see* Nest; *b)* old building; 3) brood; 4) brush-wood; small limbs, twigs, shrubs. [ginster.

* **Genist'e**, *(w.)* *f.* *Bot.* genista, *see* Färbe-

* **Genital'**, *adj.* *(Lat.)* *Anat.* genital. — **Genita'lien**, *n. pl.* *(Lat.)* genitals, privy parts. [tive (case).

* **Genitiv'**, *(str.)* *m.* *(Lat.)* *Gramm.* geni-

* **Ge'nius**, *(str., pl.* [*w.*] Ge'nien) *m.* *(Lat.)* genius: 1) *Myth.* a guardian-angel; 2) *see* Genie, 1.

Genoß', **Genos'se**, *(w.)* *m.* 1) consort, companion, comrade, mate, fellow: 2) confederate: associate, accomplice, partner; *Comm.* J. C. F. und G-en, I. C. F. & Company (Co.).

Genos'senschaft, *(w.)* *f.* 1) fellowship, partnership, society, association, company: 2) confederacy; G-sgesellschaft, *f.* co-operative association *or* society; G-swesen, *n.* co-operative system. [sort, mate.

Genos'sin, *(w.)* *f.* female companion, con-

Genö'thige, *(str.)* *n.* (incessant) solicitation, invitation, pressing, urging, importunity.

Genove'fa, *f.* Genevieve *(P. N.)*.

* **Genre** *[pr.* zhängr], *(str., pl.* G-s, *or unaltered)* *n.*, *(Fr.)* *Paint.*, *Sculpt.*, &c. *genre*; —bild, *n.*, —malerei, *f.* genre-painting, painting of incident.

* **Gensdarme'** [zhängdärm'], *(w.)* *m.* *(Fr.)* *gendarme*, an armed policeman.

Gen'sel, *(str.)* *m.* *see* Portulak.

Genst, **Genst'er**, *(str.)* *m.* *see* Ginster.

Gent, *n.* *Geogr.* Ghent (a town in East-Flanders).

* **Gen'tian**, *(str.)* *m.* *see* Enzian.

Ge'nua, *n.* *Geogr.* Genoa.

Genue'se, *(w.)*, **Genue'ser**, *(str.)* *m.*, **Genue'sisch**, *adj.* Genoese.

Genug', I. *adv.* sufficient, enough, sufficiently: Einem — thun, to satisfy one; sich *(Dat.)* — sein lassen, — haben, to be satisfied; übrig — haben, to have more than enough, to have enough and to spare; ich habe schon an seiner Stimme —, *coll.* his very voice is sufficient for (*Gram. for*: edious to) me, or ich

an Einem Unglück —, one misfortune is enough; (Einem) — sein, see Genügen, I.; es ist mir —, it is enough or it will do for me; ich bin mir selbst —, I am satisfied with myself; es kann nicht — empfohlen werden, it cannot be too warmly recommended; — der Thränen! no more tears! — des Streites! a truce to quarrelling!

Genü'ge, *f.* 1) sufficiency; competency; 2) satisfaction; 3) discharge of a duty; zur —, enough, sufficiently; an allem dem habe ich kein —, all that cannot satisfy me; — thun or leisten *(with Dat.)*, 1. to comply with, satisfy, content (one), to acquit one's self (of a thing); 2. to do justice (to); den (meinen &c.) Ansprüchen — leisten, to come up (keep) to the (my, &c.) mark; —leistung, *f.* satisfaction.

Genü'gen, I. *(w.) v. intr.* to suffice, be enough; Einem —, to satisfy, *cf.* Genüge leisten; einem Wechsel —, *Comm.* to answer a bill; sich *(Dat.)* — lassen (an *[with Dat.]*), to be content or satisfied, to content one's self (with); g-d, *p. a.* sufficient, sufficing, enough; satisfactory; das —, *(str.) v. s.* 1) satisfaction, contentment; 2) sufficiency; *cf.* Genüge.

Genüg'lich, I. *adj.* 1) sufficient; satisfactory; 2) frugal, moderate (Genügsam); 3) pleasant, agreeable; II. G-keit, *(w.) f.* 1) sufficiency, &c.; 2) see Genügsamkeit.

Genug'sam, I. *adj.* sufficient; competent; II. *adv.* sufficiently, enough; III. G-keit, *(w.) f.* sufficiency (Genüge).

Genüg'sam, I. *adj.* easy to be contented, modest; moderate, sober, frugal; II. G-keit, *(w.) f.* contentedness; satisfaction; moderation, frugality.

Genug'..., *in comp.* —thuend, *adj.* satisfactory; —thuung, *f.* satisfaction; Einem —thuung leisten, to make amends, give satisfaction to one; sich *(Dat.)* selbst —thuung verschaffen, to do one's self justice, to take the law into one's own hands; es gereicht mir zur —thuung, it is satisfactory to me, it causes me satisfaction.

* **Ge'nus**, *(str., pl. [Lat.]* Gen'era) *n.* *(Lat.) T.* genus; *Gramm.* gender.

Genuß', *s.* I. *(str., pl.* Genüs'se) *m.* 1) enjoyment, pleasure, delight, gratification; 2) taking (food or drink); 3) fruition, usufruct, enjoyment, benefit, profit; die feineren Genüsse des Lebens, the elegant luxuries of life; II. *in comp.* —reich, *adj.* full of enjoyment, pleasurable; luxurious; —sucht, *f.* inordinate longing after enjoyments, love of pleasure; —süchtig, *adj.* eager for enjoyments; —süchtige, *m.* see Genießling.

* **Geo...**, *in comp.* *(Gr.)* —däsie', *(w.) f.* geodesy; —dät', *(w.) m.* land-surveyor; —dä'tisch, *adj.* geodetic(al); —genie', —gonie', *(w.) f.* geogeny; —ge'nisch, —go'nisch, *adj.* geogenic; —gnosie', *(w.) f.* geognosy; —gnost', *(w.) m.* geognost; —gnos'tisch, *adj.* geognostical; —graph', *(w.) m.* geographer; —graphie', *(w.) f.* geography; —gra'phisch, *adj.* geographical; —log', *(w.) m.* geologist; —logie', *(w.) f.* geology; —lo'gisch, *adj.* geological; —mant', *(w.) m.* geomancer; —mantie', *(w.) f.* geomancy; —man'tisch, *adj.* geomantical; —me'ter, *(str.) m.* geometrician, geometer; —metrie', *(w.) f.* geometry; —me'trisch, *adj.* geometric(al); —ponie', *f.* geoponics *(pl.)*.

Geöhrt', *adj.* eared; *Bot., &c.* auriculate.

Georg', *m.* *(Gr.)* George *(P. N.)*.

Geor'gel, *(str.) n.* (act, practice, or mode of) playing on an organ; *contempt.* bad music, strumming.

Geor'gen..., *in comp.* —gestirn, *n.* see —planet; —kraut, *n.*, see Zahnkraut; —planet, *m.* *Astr.* Georgium Sidus, Uranus; —schwamm, *m.* *Bot.* St. George's agaric *(Agaricus Georgii L.)*.

* **Geor'gia Augus'ta**, *f.* the university of Göttingen *(so named after its founder, George the Second).* [of Asia).

Geor'gien, *n.* *Geogr.* Georgia (a country

Geor'gier, *(str.) m.*, G-in, *(w.) f.* Georgian. [(Georgina [Dahlia] variabilis W.).

* **Georgi'ne**, *(w.) f.* *Bot.* dahlia, georgina

Gepäck', *(str.) n.* baggage, luggage; —adresse, *f.* paper of direction, luggage-table; —bewahrzimmer, *n.* see —zimmer; —büreau, *n.*, —expedition, *f.* luggage-office; —schein, —zettel, *m.* baggage- or luggage-check, counterfoil; —stück, *n.* article of luggage; —träger, *m.* porter; —wagen, *m.* baggage-truck; luggage-van; —zimmer, *n.* cloak-room.

Gepard, *(str.) m.* *Zool.* hunting-cat.

Gepfei'fe, *(str.) n.* (continual) whistling.

Gepflo'genheit, *(w.) f.* *(partical. Austr., f. d. Jahrb. der Geol. Reichsanst. 1866, 125, &c.)* usage, custom, use. [see Genieß, 2.

Gepfnäsch', **Gepfnetsch'**, *(str.) n.* *Sport.*

Gepin'sel, **Geplap'per**, **Geplärr'**, **Geplät'scher**, **Geplau'der**, **Gepoch'e**, *(str.) n.* (continual) piping; daubing; babbling (chattling, tittle-tattle, chit-chat); bawling; plashing (splashing); talking (tattling, prattle, small talk); knocking, &c. *cf.* Pinseln, Plappern, Plärren &c.

Gepolst'ert, *p. a.* 1) stuffed (with wadding, &c.), cushioned, stuff-bottomed (chairs, &c.); 2) *Bot.* pulvinated, cushion-shaped.

Gepol'ter, *(str.) n.* 1) a rumbling noise; 2) (the act or practice of) blustering, boisterousness.

Geprä'ge, *(str.) n.* impression, impress, stamp, coinage; *fig.* stamp, cast.

Geprah'le, *(str.) n.* *cont.* (the act of) boasting, bragging.

Gepräng'e, *(str.) n.* pomp, state, magnificence, pageantry, great show, parade; *fig.* ostentation, vanity.

Gepras'se, *(str.) n.* a frequent revelling, carousing. [brustling.

Geprassel, *(str.) n.* a continued crackling,

Gepur'purt, *adj.* empurpled.

Gequa'ke, *(str.) n.* a (continual) croaking (as of frogs).

Gequä'le, *(str.) n.* (the act or practice of) tormenting, vexing, fretting, teasing.

Gequet'sche, *(str.) n.* (the act of) squashing, crushing, crush.

Gequie'ke, *(str.) n.* (repeated) screaking, squeaking, screaming, squealing.

Gerad'bohrer, *(str.) m.* *T.* straight-piercing tool. **Ger**, = **Gehr**.

Gera'de, *gener. contr.* **Gra'de**, **Grad**, I. *adj.* 1) straight, right, direct, even; level; 2) erect, upright, aright; 3) plain, straightforward, honest, upright; eine — Brücke, a bridge on the square; — Columnen, *Typ.* even page; das — Gegentheil, quite the contrary, just the reverse; eine — Linie, straight line; in g-r Linie, as the crow flies; in g-r Linie absteigen von ..., to descend in a straight line from; eine — Zahl, an even number; die — Regel de tri, the rule of three direct; — oder ungerade, even or odd; — und ungerade spielen, to play at even and odd; g-s Weges, straightways, immediately; *Mus.* — Tact, binary measure, common time; — Bewegung, similar or direct motion; — deshalb thue ich es, that's why I do it; das ist — recht, that answers the purpose, that's the very thing; das ist mir — recht, das will ich —, that's the very thing I want; [illegible] — sein lassen, to connive (at), to be not over-rigid; der — Weg ist der beste, honesty is the best policy; II. *adv.* 1) straightly, &c.; 2) precisely, just, exactly; 3) without reserve, plainly, &c.; Augen — aus! *Mil.* eyes front! — das Boot! *Nav.* trim the boat! — [illegible] begegnete ich, whom should I meet but

utensils; 2) moveable goods, furniture; bedding; 3) effects, chattels; cf. Gepäck; linen, apparel; —holz, n. see Nutzholz; —kammer, f. 1) laundry; 2) lumber-room; —kasten, m. box for tools, &c.; chest for linen.

Gera'then, (str.) v. intr. (aux. sein) 1) to come (auf, in, an [with Acc.] etc., into, to, &c.), to fall (into [an ambuscade, &c.], upon, &c.), to get, to be thrown (unter [with Acc.], between, among); to hit, light (auf [with Acc.], upon); to come or fall (on) by chance; to meet, to light upon or find as by accident; 2) to turn out, to prove; 3) (with Dat.) to succeed (well), to prosper, thrive; nicht —, to fail; an einander —, to fall out with ...., Milit.: to engage together in close fight; to fall together by the ears, to come to blows; ich bin auf den Gedanken —, it has occurred to my mind, the thought struck me; auf einen Einfall —, to get a fancy; aus den Schienen —, to get off the rails; außer sich —, to lose temper, to fall into a passion; auf eine Meinung —, to embrace, adopt, or get hold of an opinion; gegen etwas —, to hit or strike against; in Brand —, to take or catch fire; in Gefahr —, to run into danger, to incur the risk (of —); in Ekstase —, to go or fly into ecstasies (über [with Acc.], with); in ein falsches Conto —, Comm. to get upon a wrong account; in Irrthümer —, to fall into errors; in Schulden —, to run in or into debt, to contract or incur debts; in(s) Stocken —, to cease to move, to (begin to) stagnate, to stop; in Streit —, to fall out, to fall quarrelling (mit, with); in Unruhe —, to grow (or become) agitated or alarmed; in (den) Verdacht —, to incur (the) suspicion (of); in Verfall —, to run to waste or ruin, to (begin to) decay; in Vergessenheit —, to fall into oblivion or neglect; in Verwirrung —, to run into confusion; to become or be confused; in Zorn —, to fall into a passion; — nach, fig. to take after; der Wein ist dieses Jahr nicht —, the vines have failed (missed) this year; wohl —, to come to good; wohl- or gutgerathene Kinder, well-bred, well-mannered children; es gerathe oder mißrathe, hit or miss; zum Ärgerniß etc. —, †, see Gereichen & Ausfallen, 6.

Gera'then, p. a. (from Rathen) advisable; useful, advantageous; sich (Dat.) — sein lassen, to be advised, to take (good) counsel; für — halten, to think (it) advisable; damit wäre mir —, that would answer all my wants.

Gerathewohl', (undecl.) n. random, chance, hazard; aufs —, at random, at hap-hazard, at a venture.

Geräth'schaft, (w.) f. or G-en, pl. see Ge-räth.

Geräu'cher, (str.) n. the (act or practice of) fumigating, perfuming, fumigation.

Gerau'fe, (str.) n. the (act or practice of) plucking, pulling one's hair, &c. cf. Raufen; scuffle, fight.

Geraum', adj. 1) see Geräumig; 2) fig. long; eine g-e Zeit, a long time; seit g-er Zeit, this long time.

Geräu'mig (l. u.: Geraum'lich), I. adj. ample, large, wide, spacious, capacious, roomy, broad; II. G-keit, (w.) f. ampleness, spaciousness, &c., room, capacity.

Geräum'te, (str.) n. Forest. clearing (Reubruch).

Geräusch', (str.) n. 1) noise, bustle, rustling; clanking, din, clattering (of arms), murmuring (of rivers, &c.); fig. noise, sensation; mit —, fig. with ostentation, ostentatiously; ohne —, fig. in a quiet way, without noise; 2) Sport. see Geschlinge.

Geräusch'los, I. adj. noiseless; II. G-igkeit, (w.) f. noiselessness.

Geräusch'voll, adj. noisy, boisterous, bustling, obstreperous; fig. also ostentatious.

Geräus'per, (str.) n. the (act or custom of) hawking, spitting, cf. Räuspern.

Gerau'tet, adj. Herald. lozengy.

Gerb'brühe, (w.) f. see Gerberlohe, 2.

Ger'be... (cf. Gerb ...), in comp. T-s. —bank, f. bench for paring hides on; —baum, m. tanner's horse or beam; —eisen, n. paring-knife; —hammer, m. T. tilt-hammer; —hobel, m. cooper's smoothing-plane; —haus, n. see Gerberei, 1; —kammer, f. 1) tanner's workshop; 2) provinc. see Sacristei; —mühle, f. 1) oakbark mill; 2) husking-mill.

Ger'ben, (w.) v. tr. 1) Tann. to tan, curry, dress (hides); 2) T. to tilt (steel); to polish (metals); 3) Mill. a) to decorticate, husk; b) (Swiss.) to winnow (Worfeln); 4) coll. to beat, thrash, vulg. to curry one's hide.

Ger'ber, s. I. (str.) m. 1) tanner, currier, leather-dresser; 2) Entom. saw-beetle (Prionus coriarius L.); II. in comp. —baum, m. Bot. 1) sumach (tree) (Rhus coriaria L.); 2) myrtle-leaved sumach (Coriaria myrtifolia L.); —gang, m. see Gerbemühle, 2; —grube, f. tan-pit; —handwerk, n. tanner's trade; —hof, m. tanning yard; —kalk, m. tanning-lime; —kinne, f. see Gerbekufe; —lohe, f. 1) tan, tanner's bark; 2) ooze, liquor of a tanner's vat (in which the hides are soaked); —messer, n. currier's or tanner's knife; —mühle, f. tanning-mill; —myrte, f. Bot. common-myrtle (Myrtus communis L.); —rinde, f. quercitron-bark; —strauch, —sumach, m. see —baum, 2; —weide, f. Bot. white willow (Salix alba L.); —wolle, f. skinner's wool, mortlings.

Gerberei', (w.) f. 1) tanning-house, tan-yard, tannery; 2) tanner's trade.

Gerb'... (cf. Gerbe ...), in comp. —säure, f. Chem. tannic acid, tannin; —stahl, m. 1) tilted (cast) steel; 2) burnishing steel; —stoff, m. tanning-principle, tan, Chem. tannin; —stube, f. shade or drying room.

* **Gerbuli'ren,** (w.) v. tr. (Span. garbillar, Fr. grabeller, cf. Garbeliren) Comm. to cast out the refuse, to garble. — **Gerbulür',** (w.) f. Comm. 1) refuse (of spices, &c.), brack, garbles, trash, outshot; 2) deduction made for refuse.

Gerecht', adj. 1) fit, suitable; 2) versed, skilled; according to rules; 3) right, merited, legitimate; 4) just, righteous; der, die G-e, 1. the just; ich bin unschuldig am Blute dieses G-en (Math. 27, 24), I am innocent of the blood of this just person; 2. der G-e (i. e. Gott), the Allrighteous; die G-en, pl. the righteous; g-er Gott! good God! coll. good gracious! — werden (with Dat.), to do justice, to give a fair trial; to meet (demands, &c.), to satisfy (creditors); sich (Dat.) selbst — werden, to do one's self justice, to take the law in one's own hands; — sein, to fit, suit (of clothes); allen Sätteln — sein, fig. to be jack at all trades, apt (fit) for anything, to accommodate one's self to anything; —machung, f. justification.

Gerech'tigkeit, (w.) f. 1) justness; 2) justice, law; 3) justice, righteousness, impartiality; 4) right, privilege, immunity, license; Jemandem — widerfahren lassen, to do one justice; die — handhaben, to administer or distribute justice; in comp. G-sliebe, f. love of justice, equity; g-sliebend, adj. equitable; G-spflege, f. (administration of) justice.

Gerecht'sam, I. adj. provinc. lawful, legitimate; II. G-e, (w.) f. (sometimes used as a str. pl.) right, privilege, immunity; prerogative, franchise.

Gereed', Gereeh', adj. Mar. ready, clear, prepared.

Gere'de, (str.) n. (act or way of) talking, talk, sayings; report, rumour, cf. Reden, II.; ein langes — machen, to descant (von, über [with Acc.], on, upon); ins — kommen, to get a bad character or name; sich ins — bringen, to get one's self talked about; Einen ins — bringen, to defame, to slander or asperse a person's reputation, to hitch one into a story.

Gere'den, (w.) v. tr. provinc. to talk; Law, to promise, assure; to confirm.

Gerei'be, (str.) n. (the act of, or a continued) rubbing, friction.

Gerei'chen, (w.) v. intr. (with zu) to tend, redound, turn to, to prove; es gereicht dir zum Ruhme, Lobe, zur Ehre, that redounds to your glory, praise, honour; Einem zur Befriedigung —, to give one (great) satisfaction; Einem zum Verderben —, to prove fatal to one, to prove one's ruin; es würde mir zur Ehre —, I should consider it an honour; zum Vergnügen —, to afford pleasure.

Gerei'me, (str.) n. coll. (the act, practice, or way of) rhyming; doggerel, bad poetry.

Gerei'ße, (str.) n. the (act of) tearing, &c., scramble, cf. Reißen.

Gereizt', I. p. a. irritated, exasperated, angry; II. G-heit, (w.) f. irritation, indignation, resentment.

Geren'ne, (str.) n. a (continual) running.

Gereu'en, (w.) v. impers. to cause regret, to influence with repentance; es gereuet mich, I repent (of) it; sich (Acc.) etwas — lassen, to repent of.

Gereut', (str.) n. 1) Forest. a clearing (Reubruch); 2) provinc. wood belonging to a community; —genossen or Gereu'ter, (w.) m. pl. participators in the advantages of such a wood; —herd, m. Metall. pit before the furnace for the reception of the melted pewter; —lerche, f. Ornith. tit-lark, wood-lark.

Ger'falk, (w.) m. see Geierfalk.

Ger'gel (Gargel), (str.) m. & (w.) f. 1) Carp. chimb (Kreise, Kimme, Zarge); 2) Coop. chimb-notch, crose (Kröse). — **Ger'geln,** (w.) v. tr. to provide with chimbs or notches (Zargen).

Gerg'vogel, (str.) m. Ornith. gray-bunting.

Ger'had, Ger'haber, (str.) m. († &) provinc. guardian, &c. see Vormund.

Ger'hard, m. Gerard (P. N.); G-skraut, n. herb-gerhard, goat-wort, gout-wort (Aegopodium podagraria L.).

Gericht', (str.) n. I. 1) dish, mess; ein — Fische, a dish of fish; 2) Sport. gins, springes; II. 1) judgment; doom; sentence; 2) court; tribunal; court of justice; 3) jurisdiction; 4) place of execution; vor —, at the bar of justice; vor — (Acc.) fordern, to summon; to enter an action or to proceed against; Einen vor — bringen or stellen, to bring one to his trial, to put one on his trial; to summon before a court; sich vor — stellen, vor — erscheinen, to appear in court; to answer the summons; eine Sache vor — bringen, ans or vor — geben, to go or to proceed to law, to follow the law, to enter or to commence an action, to institute proceedings; — halten or im — sitzen, zu — sitzen (über Einen), to sit in judgment (on one), to administer justice, to judge or hear causes; — halten über (with Acc.), to sit upon ...., to try; sich auf ein höheres — berufen, to interpose appeal; das jüngste —, doomsday, day of judgment, last judgment.

Gericht'lich, adj. 1) judicial, judiciary; good or valid in law; legal, notarial; adv. judicially, in a judicial way, before the justice, at law, by law; in due form of law; in legal form; 2) forensic (as f. eloquence, medicine, &c.): — abgefaßt or gemacht, legalised, verified, in due form of law; — bestallt, duly commissioned; — ernennen, to designate, nominate officially; — liquid erkannte Schulden, pl. judgment debts; — verkaufen, to sell by subhastation; — vorladen, to warn, to summon; die g-e Medizin, medical jurisprudence; das g-e Erkenntniß, recognizance; die g-e Hülfe, execution in a civil cause; g-e Hülfe suchen, g-e Schritte thun, to take legal steps, to seek legal redress; eine g-e Urkunde, a legal (legalised, verified) *or* notarial document; ein g-er Verkauf, open sale, sale by order of a court of law, subhastation; g-es Verfahren, judicial *or* legal proceedings: proceedings at law.

Gerichtlichkeit, *(w.) f.* legal qualification.

Gerichts'..., *in comp.*, **—acte,** *f.* record; **—advocat,** *m.* barrister; **—amt,** *n.* court, tribunal; **—amtmann,** *m.* judge; **—anstand,** *m. Law, see* **—ferien**; **—arzt,** *m.* forensic physician; **—bank,** *f. see* **—amt**; **—bann,** *m. see* Bannmeile.

Gerichtsbarkeit, *(w.) f.* jurisdiction, resort; das Recht der —, cognisance.

Gerichts'..., *in comp.* **—beamte(r),** *m.* officer of the law, justiciary; **—befehl,** *m.* warrant; **—behörde,** *f.* court; **—beisitzer,** *m.* judge lateral; **—bescheid,** *m.* decree, sentence; **—bestellung,** *f.* establishment of a court of justice; **—bezirk,** *m.* district of jurisdiction, resort; **—bote,** *m.* messenger, summoner of a court of justice; apparitor (of an ecclesiastical court); **—brauch,** *m.* usage of a tribunal; **—buch,** *n.* record, register, roll; **—diener,** *m.* constable, usher of a court of justice; beadle; *see* **—bote**; **—director,** *m.* president of a court of justice; **—dorf,** *n.* village possessing a jurisdiction; **—eid,** *m.* oath taken in a court of justice; **—fach,** *n.* legal profession; **—ferien,** *f. pl.* non-term, vacations; **—folge,** *f.* help, succour, aid due to a court of justice; **—frohn,** *m.* 1) *see* **—bote**; 2) beadle, jailer; **—frist,** *f.* proper time of appearing in court; **—gang,** *m.* legal procedure; **—gebrauch,** *m. see* **—brauch**; **—gebühren,** *pl.* law charges, fees, &c. *see* **—kosten**; **—gefälle,** *pl.* dues *or* fees of a court *or* judge; **—grenze,** *f.* limits of a jurisdiction; **—halle,** *f.* session-hall, judgment-hall; **—halter,** *m.* magistrate, justiciary, lawyer; **—halterei,** *f.* magistrate's office *or* house; **—haltung,** *f.* jurisdiction; **—handel,** *m.* action, lawsuit; **—haus,** *n.* court of justice, session-house, town-hall; *Am.* court-house; **—herr,** *m.* lord of the manor, who has the right of judicature; **—herrschaft,** *f.* right of judicature; jurisdiction; **—hof,** *m.* court of justice, court, judicature, (judicatory) tribunal; ein oberster —hof, supreme court of judicature; der geistliche —hof, ecclesiastical court; consistory; **—hörigkeit,** *f.* competence of a court; **—instanz,** *f.* competent court; **—kammer,** *f.* chamber of justice, tribunal, session-hall; **—kanzlei,** *f.* record-office, archives; **—kosten,** *pl.* law-charges *or* expenses, (court-) fees, costs (of a suit *or* procedure), mise; **—verlängerung,** *f.* stoppage in the legal proceedings; **—lehen,** *n.* the right of judicature considered as a fief; **—leute,** *pl.* 1) court-officers; 2) inhabitants of a jurisdiction; **—mündigkeit,** *f.* legal majority; **—obrigkeit,** *f.* magistrate; **—ordnung,** *f.* statute regulating the proceedings of a court of justice: rules (statutes) of a court; **—person,** *f.* judge, magistrate; **—pflege,** *f.* (administration of) justice; **—platz,** *m.* 1) session-house; 2) place of execution; **—posaune,** *f. Bibl.* last trumpet; **—rath,** *m.* judge, counsellor; **—saal,** *m.* judgment-hall; **—sache,** *f. see* **—handel**; **—sassen,** *m. pl.* persons under a certain jurisdiction; **—schöppe,** *m.* assistant judge; **—schreiber,** *m.* clerk, actuary, *or* secretary in a court of justice; **—schreiberei,** *f.* office of a —schreiber; **—siegel,** *n.* seal of a court of justice; **—sitzung,** *f.* judicial sitting, session (of a court); **—sporteln,** *pl.* court-fees; **—sprengel,** *m. see* **—bezirk**; **—stab,** *m.* judge's staff; **—stadt,** *f.* town that has a court of justice; **—stand,** *m. see* **—stelle**; **—statt,** **—stätte,** *f.* 1) court; 2) place of execution; **—stelle,** *f.* the being subject to a certain jurisdiction *or* the court to which one is subject; instance, forum; **—stil,** *m.* law-style; **—stube,** *f.* judgment-chamber; office; **—stuhl,** *m.* tribunal, seat of justice; **—tag,** *m.* law-day, court-day; **—unterthanen,** *pl. see* **—sassen**; **—verbesserung,** *f.* law-reform; **—verfahren,** *n.* legal *or* judicial proceedings, judicial acts, proceedings of a court; **—verfassung,** *f.* constitution of courts of justice, law-regulations; **—verhandlung,** *f. see* **—verfahren**; **—verwalter,** *m.* justiciary, deputy-justiciary, lawyer; **—verwaltung,** *f.* 1) the office of a deputy-justiciary; 2) administration of justice; **—verwandte,** *m.* 1) one subject to a certain jurisdiction; 2) member of a tribunal; **—verweisung,** *f.* expulsion from a certain jurisdiction; **—verweser,** *m.* administrator of justice, justiciary; **—vogt,** *m.* judge, justice; **—vogtei,** *f.* magistrate's house; (von) **—wegen,** *adv.* by warrant of the court (of justice); **—zimmer,** *n.* justice-room; **—zwang,** *m.* jurisdiction; **—zwingig,** *adj.* subject to a jurisdiction.

Gerie'ben, *p. a.* (*from* Reiben) *fig.* sharp, knowing.

Gerie'sel, *(str.) n.* the (act of, *or* a continued) purling, rippling.

Geriest', *p. a.* fluted, grooved.

Gering', I. *or* **Gerin'ge,** *adj.* 1) little, trifling, small; scanty; slender; 2) deficient in weight *or* in value; inferior, of poor order, of bad quality (of goods, &c.); cheap; 3) light, slight, insignificant, unimportant, indifferent; trivial, futile; 4) low, mean, base, humble, obscure; mit g-en Ausnahmen, with but a few exceptions; sich nichts G-es einbilden, not to hold one's self in low estimate, *fam.* not to think small beer of one's self; —schätzen, to slight, neglect, disregard, despise, disrespect, to make light *or* nothing of; — geschätzt werden, *coll.* to be at a discount; meine g-e Einsicht, my imperfect knowledge (of); g-e Kost, low *or* meager fare; es fehlt nur ein G-s, there wants but a trifle; um ein G-s, at (a) small expense, for a trifle; die g-en Leute, common people, the inferior class.

Gering'achtung, *(w.) f see* Geringschätzung.

Gering'el, *(str.) n.* 1) the (act of) curling: 2) curls; curves.

Gering'er, *adj.* (*compar. of* Gering) less, inferior; — werden, to decline, fall off (*cf.* Abnehmen); g-e Qualitäten, *Comm.*, &c. inferior qualities: kein G-er als B., no less a man than B.; nichts G-es als ..., nothing short of ...; ich bin nicht — als er, I am not inferior to him.

Gering'..., *in comp.* **—fügig,** *adj.* insignificant, trifling; unimportant, little, petty, slight, of no account, trivial, futile; **—fügigkeit,** *f.* insignificance; littleness, pettiness, trivialness, triviality; trifle, small matter; **—haltig,** *adj.* (of coins, &c.) below the (legal) standard, of a base standard, of base alloy, of little worth, worthless; futile, weak (proof); **—haltigkeit,** *f.* the being below the (legal) standard, worthlessness; futility, weakness; **—haltung,** *f. see* **—schätzung.**

Gering'heit, *(w.) f.* littleness, smallness, &c. *cf.* Gering.

Gering'..., *in comp.* **—schätzig,** *adj.* 1) depreciating, undervaluing; disregardful, neglecting, disrespectful, disdainful; supercilious (remarks); slighting; 2) contemptible, despicable, mean, vile; **—schätzigkeit,** *f.* 1) undervaluation, neglect, irreverence, disrespect, disregard; 2) slightness, despicableness; **—schätzung,** *f.* contempt, neglect, disregard, act of scorn, slight, disdain; mit —schätzung behandeln, to disdain, slight.

Gering'ste, *adj.* (*superl. of* Gering) least, slightest, minutest; nicht das —, not the least, not a whit, not a jot; nothing at all; ich habe darüber nicht das — erfahren, I have not obtained the least information upon it; der — Zweifel, the least doubt, *coll.* a shadow of a

Geröl'le, *(str.) n. Geol.* boulder-stones: rubble-stones, rubble. [&c.).

Geröl'lig, *adj. coll.* rubbly, stony (ground,

Geröll'masse, *(w.) f.* detritus.

Gerös'ne, *(str.) n. Vint.* roots of vines.

Gersch, *(str.) m. Bot. see* Giersch.

Gerst'ammer, *(w.) f.* corn-bunting (Grauammer).

Gers'te, *(w.) f. Bot.* barley (*Hordéum vulgáre* L.); die kleine *or* nackte —, naked barley (*Hordéum nudum* L.); geschälte —, peeled *or* hulled barley: lange, zweizeilige —, long-eared barley (*Hordéum distichum* L.).

Gerst'en, *(str.) m. provinc.* dish of flour, eggs, and milk.

Gerst'en, *adj. (l. u.)* of barley, hordaceous.

Gerst'en..., *in comp.* —**acker,** *m.* field of barley; —**ähre,** *f.* ear of barley; —**ammer,** *f. see* Gerstammer; —**beize,** *f. Tann.* a scouring consisting of water strongly impregnated with a vegetable acid prepared from barley; —**bier,** *n.* beer (brewed of barley); —**boden,** *m.* soil adapted for the cultivation of barley; —**brot,** *n.* barley-bread: barley-loaf; —**brühe,** *f.* barley-water; —**ernte,** *f.* barley-harvest; —**graupen,** *f. pl.* peeled *or* hulled barley; —**grütze,** *f.* barley-groats; —**halm,** *m.* culm, stalk of barley; —**haufen,** *m.* barley-rick; —**kaffee,** *m.* a substitute for coffee consisting of roasted barley; —**kleie,** *f.* barley bran; —**korn,** *n.* 1) barley-corn; 2) *Med.* wisp in the eye, stye, hordeolum; —**kuchen,** *m.* barley-cake; —**mahd,** *f* barley-mow; —**malz,** *n.* barley-malt; —**mehl,** *n.* barley-meal; —**milch,** *f.* orgeat; —**mutter,** *f.* degenerated barley-corn; —**saft,** *m.* barley-broth, worts; *fig.* beer; —**schleim,** —**seim,** *m. see* —trank &c. 1; —**stoff,** *m. Chem.* starchy matter of barley, hordeine; —**stroh,** *n.* barley-straw; —**trank,** *m.* 1) *or* —**wasser,** *n. Med.* barley-water, ptisan, orgeat; *anal.* water-gruel; 2) beer; —**zucker,** *m.* barley-sugar. [Gerstammer.

Gerst'ling, *(str.) m.,* **Gerst'vogel,** *m. see*

Ger'te, *(w.) f.* (*dimin.* **Gert'chen,** *[str.] n.)* switch, whip; **G-nkraut,** *n.,* **G-nwurz,** *f. Bot.* 1) fennel-giant, gigantic fennel; 2) *see* Eberraute.

Ger'traud, Ger'trud, *f.* Gertrude (*P. N.*)

Gert'weide, *(w.) f.* common osier.

Geruch', *(str., pl.* **Gerüch'e)** *m.* 1) smell; *a)* the sense *or* power of smelling; *b)* odour, scent, savour, flavour (nach, of), flavour, bouquet (of wine); Thran—, Theer— &c., smell of train-oil, tar, &c.; 2) *fig.* reputation, character; nicht im besten — stehen, *fig.* not to be in the best odour; im G-e der Heiligkeit, *fig.* in odour of sanctity.

Geruch'los, I. *adj.* 1) scentless, without smell; 2) inodorous; savourless; II. **G-igkeit,** *(w.) f.* 1) the being destitute of smell; 2) inodorousness.

Geruchs'..., *in comp.* —**nerv,** *m.* olfactory nerve; —**sinn,** *m.* sense of smelling; —**vermögen,** *n.* power *or* sense of smelling; —**werkzeug (—organ),** *n.* organ of smell.

Gerücht', *(str.) n.* 1) (flying *or* popular) report, rumour, (*in pl-e.*) story, saying, hearsay; ein bloßes —, a mere hearsay; *cf.* Gerede; 2) name, character, reputation, credit, esteem; in ein böses — bringen, to bring into ill repute; es geht *or* läuft ein —, there is *or* goes a report, a rumour is abroad, the story goes; dem — nach, as the report goes.

Gerücht'lich, *adj. & adv.* according to report. [peated) moving.

Gerück'e, *(str.) n.* (the act of, *or* a re-

Gerü'der, *(str.) n.* 1) (the act, practice, *or* mode of) rowing; 2) *Mar.* oars (collectively).

Geru'fe, *(str.) n.* a (repeated) calling (after a person, &c.).

Geruh'en, *(w.) v. intr.* to be pleased, to deign, condescend; Seine Majestät haben geruht, his majesty has been pleased (to ...); — Euer Majestät, may it please your majesty.

Geruh'ig, Geruh'sam, *adj. provinc.* quiet, &c. *see* Ruhig. [boasting.

Geruh'me, *(str.) n. cont.* a (continual)

Gerüh'rig, *adj. see* Rührig.

Gerül'le, *(str.) n.* 1) loose *or* boulder-stones, &c. *see* Gerölle; das Erz macht ein —, *Min.* the veins intermingle; 2) lumber (Gerümpel). [bling.

Gerum'pel, *(str.) n.* a (continued) rum-

Gerüm'pel, *(str.) n.* lumber, trash, rubbish; —**boden,** *m.,* —**kammer,** *f.* lumber-room; —**markt,** *m.* rag-fair.

* **Gerun'dium,** *(str., pl. [Lat.]* Gerun'dia, *or [w.]* Gerun'dien) *n. (Lat.) Gramm.* gerund. — **Gerundi'visch,** *adj.* gerundial. — **Gerundi'vum,** *(str., pl. [Lat.]* Gerundi'va) *n.* gerundive. [wrinkling.

Gerun'zel, *(str.) n. collect.* wrinkles,

Gerüst', *s.* I. *(str.) n.* scaffold, scaffolding, stage (*Am.* staging), frame, frame-work; trestle; fliegendes, bewegliches, *or* hängendes —, flying, movable, *or* hanging scaffold; II. *in comp. Build-s.* —**band,** *n.* truss; —**bock,** *m.* trestle, horse; —**kammer,** *f.* room for machines, tools, &c.; —**rippe,** *f.* 1) truss; 2) rib of a centre; —**stange,** *f. see* Rüstbaum.

Gerüt'tel, *(str.) n.* a (continued) shaking, jolting (as a carriage on rough ground).

Ger'vas, Gerva'sius, *m.* Gervas(e), Jarvis (*P. N.*).

Ges, *(indecl.) n. Mus.* G flat; — dur, G flat major; — moll, G flat minor.

Gesa'ge, *(str.) n. coll.* (incessant) talk, talking, *cf.* Gerede & Gerücht, 1.

Gesä'ge, *(str.) n.* a (continual) sawing.

Gesägt', *p. a. Bot.* toothed like a saw, serrate.

Gesal'bader, *(str.) n. see* Salbaderei.

Gesä'me, *(str.) n. coll.* seeds, *see* Sämerei.

Gesam'mel, *(str.) n.* (the act *or* practice of) gathering, collecting; collection.

Gesammt', I. *adj.* whole, united, joint, aggregate, collective; total; all the, &c.; das G-e, the total, whole; die g-en Einwohner, all the inhabitants; der g-e Adel, the entire body of nobility; II. *adv.* conjointly, collectively; III. *in comp.* total, joint, &c.; —**amt,** *n.* joint-office; —**ausgabe,** *f.* collected edition (z. B. of the writings of D. Jerrold, &c.); —**belehnung,** *f. Law,* joint investiture; —**betrag,** *m.* sum total, total amount; —**capital,** *n.* joint-stock; —**eindruck,** *m.* total impression; —**einnahme,** *f.* total receipts; —**erbe,** *m.* heir general; —**ertrag,** *m.* total proceeds *or* return; —**gebrauch,** *m.* joint use; —**größe,** *f. Arith.* integer; —**gut,** *n.* joint property.

Gesammt'heit, *(w.) f.* 1) totality; universality; 2) *or* **Gesammt'schaft,** *(w.) f.* (whole, entire) body, corporation, community; in der — genommen, taken collectively.

Gesammt'..., *in comp.* —**herr,** *m.* joint governor *or* lord; —**herrschaft,** *f.* joint command; —**kauf,** *m.* joint purchase *or* wholesale purchase; —**lehen,** *n.* fief held in common; —**macht,** *f.* whole power; —**ministerium,** *n.* body of the ministers of state, joint ministry; —**production,** *f.* total produce; —**quantum,** *n. see* —betrag; —**rath,** *m.* joint *or* full council; —**recht,** *n.* joint privilege; —**regierung,** *f.* joint government.

Gesammt'schaftlich, I. *adj.* relating to a community, common; II. *adv.* in common.

Gesammt'..., *in comp.* —**stimme,** *f.* common *or* joint vote; —**verbürgung,** *f.* joint bail, security; —**werth,** *m.* total *or* aggregate value; —**wille,** *m.* common will, unanimous consent; —**zahl,** *f.* total number.

Gesand'te, *m. (decl. like adj.)* messenger; ambassador, envoy; ein päpstlicher —, nuncio; die auswärtigen G-n, the foreign ministers.

Gesand'tin, *(w.) f,* an ambassador's wife (lady), ambassadress.

Gesandt'schaft, *(w.) f.* embassy, legation; die päpstliche —, nunciature.

Gesandt'schaftlich, *adj.* relating *or* belonging to an embassy, diplomatic.

Gesandt'schafts..., *in comp.* —**kunde,** —**kunst,** *f.* diplomacy; —**personal,** *n.* the persons belonging to an embassy; —**posten,** *m.* post *or* office of an ambassador; —**prediger,** *m.* chaplain to an embassy; —**rath,** *m.* counsellor of the embassy; —**recht,** *n.* rights and privileges of an ambassador; —**schreiber,** —**secretair,** *m.* secretary to an embassy, secretary of legation; —**träger,** *m* *chargé d'affaires;* —**wesen,** *n.* matters relating to diplomacy, diplomatic affairs; —**wissenschaft,** *f.* diplomacy.

Gesang', *s.* I. *(str., pl.* Gesäng'e) *m.* 1) *a)* the (act of) singing; *b)* (G-(s)kunst) art of singing; *c)* vocal music; 2) song, chant, hymn, air, (*Ital.*) aria, lay; warble (of birds); 3) poetry, poem; 4) book, canto; 5) *Sport.* bird-call; II. *in comp.* —**buch,** *n.* book of psalms *or* songs, hymn-book; **G-(s)composition,** *f.* vocal composition; —**drossel,** *f. see* Singdrossel; **G-(s)fest,** *n.* singing-festival, *see* Sängerfest; —**grasmücke,** *f.* slate-coloured warbler; —**lehrer,** *m.* singing master; —**reich,** *adj.* rich in song; skilful in singing; melodious; —**stimme,** *f.* voice *or* vocal part; **G-sweise,** *adv.* in the manner of a song; —**verein,** *m.* glee-club, catch-club; —**vogel,** *m.* singing bird; —**weise,** I. *s. f.* melody, tune; II. *adv. see* G-sweise.

Gesäß', I *s. (str.) n.* 1) seat, sitting-part (of the body), fundament, *pl.* posteriors; 2) seat (as a chair, bench, &c.), *see* Sitz; 3) *Smelt.* stage, floor; II. *in comp.* —**arterien,** *f. pl.* gluteal arteries; —**bein,** *n.,* —**knochen,** *m.* huckle-bone, hip-bone; —**fistel,** *f.* *fistula in ano* (w. ll.: *f. ani* [lat.]); —**muskeln,** *m. pl.* glutaeus; —**nerv,** *m.* gluteal nerve.

Gesätz', *(str.) n.* number of things inserted one into another, set, nest (Satz).

Gesätz', *(str.) n.* nest of brass- *or* copper-goods.

Gesau'fe, *(str.) n. vulg.* hard drinking, carousing, swigging, swilling.

Gesäu'ge, *(str.) n. Sport.,* &c. the dugs of deer, dogs, and other brute females.

Gesäul'(e), *(str.) n. collect.* the columns of a building. [humming.

Gesau'se, *(str.) n.* a rushing, buzzing,

Gesäu'sel, *(str.) n.* gentle breeze, gentle murmuring (of the wind).

Geschacht', *adj. Herald.* checkered, checky.

Geschäft', *(str.) n.* 1) *a)* employment, occupation; *b)* business, transaction, negociation; affair, concern; charge; commission; 2) *a)* mercantile establishment, business; ein — im Großen, a wholesale-business; ein großes Thee—, a large house in the tea-line; *b)* commerce, trade; *c) see* G-szweig; *d)* vocation; 3) *see* G-slocal; 4) †, testament, will; 5) *fig.* business, affair; G-e haben, to have something to do; ich habe G-e mit ihm, I have something to transact with him; *Comm.-s.* in Kaffee &c. kein —, in coffee, &c. no business *or* nothing doing; die G-e in Kaffee &c., the transactions in coffee, &c.; unsere G-e, our transactions; ein — abthun, abmachen, *or* verrichten, to settle *or* adjust a business, to strike a bargain; ein — führen *or* einem G-e vorstehen, to conduct, manage (*or* to have charge of) a business; ein — *or* G-e anfangen *or* anlegen, to commence, establish a business, to [illegible] (*or* set up in) business; sein eigenes — anfangen, to set up for one's self; in G-en stehen mit ..., to be connected in business with ...; G-en vorstehen, to manage affairs; die G-e besorgen, to have the charge of the affairs, to attend to, *or* manage the business. Gmachen, to carry on or do business, to buy and sell, to deal (in); gute G-e machen, to get or go on thrivingly; er hat ein gutes — gemacht, he has made a good (profitable) affair or bargain; er macht große G-e, he carries on a large or great business. in einem G-e sein, Comm. to be employed (or engaged) in a house; er ist im G-e bei ..., he is engaged with ...; sich (Dat.) ein — woraus machen, to make it one's business; es ist nicht mein —, it is no business of mine; it is out of my line or way; dies soll mein erstes — sein, I will make this my first object; der —leitende Ausschuß, managing committee, committee of management.

Geschäf'tet, p. a. Herald., &c. shafted.

Geschäf'tig, I. adj. 1) busy, busied, employed, active, at work; 2) bustling, in a bustle; officious; übermäßig —, fussy, fidgety: — sein, to be full of action, to bustle; den G-en spielen, to play at shop or the busy body; II. G-keit, (w.) f. 1) activity, application in business; 2) bustle, stir (in business); officiousness; übermäßige —, fussiness.

Geschäft'lich, I. adj. relating to business, cf. Geschäfts ...; business-like; g-e Pünctlichkeit, correctness as a man of business; mercantile correctness: der g-e Theil eines Briefes, business-portion of a letter; g-e Nothwendigkeit, necessity of business; — betrachtet, regarded from a business-point of view; g-e Angelegenheiten, business-concerns, business-matters; II. adv. in a business-like manner.

Geschäfts'..., in comp. —besorger, m. see —führer; —betrieb, m. working of the business; —blick, m. business-eye; —buch, n. (kleines) debt book; —drang, m. pressure of business; —eifer, m. zeal or earnestness of business; —eifrig, adj. intent on business; —erfahren, adj. see —kundig; —erfahrung, f. experience, routine in business, versatility; —fach, n. department; —fähig, adj. able for business; —fertig, practised or quick in business; —fertigkeit, f. routine; —fleiß, m. application to business; —frei, free from business, unemployed, idle; —freund, m. Comm. a friend or partner (in business); employer; correspondent; —führer, m. 1) manager of a business; head-clerk; leading hand; factor; (in Fabriken) overseer; 2) functionary, agent; 3) commission merchant, commissioner; —führung, f. managing or management of a business; —gang, m. 1) walk on business, errand; 2) routine, round, or run of business; way of doing (business); —gegend, f. shoppy neighbourhood; —geist, m. mind or turn for business; —genoß, m. partner; —gewandtheit, f. dexterity in business, routine; —jahreszeit, f. (brisk) season; —kenntniß, f. professional skill; cf. —kunde; —klugheit, f. knowledge of business; —kreis, m. department, sphere of business; —kunde, f. skill in business, routine; —kundig, versed, practised in business, experienced (skilled or versed) in trade; —leben, n. trade, business-life; —leitend, adj. managing; —leitung, f. see —führung; —leute, pl. men of business, tradesmen, dealers, traffickers; professional men; —local, n. counting-house, office, shop; (in Amerika) store.

Geschäfts'los, adj. 1) unemployed (clerk, &c.), see —frei; 2) dull, cf. Flau, 2, c; g-e Zeit, dead (slack) period or season; II. G-igkeit, (w.) f. 1) the being unemployed; inactivity, idleness; 2) dulness (of trade), stagnation, slack; cf. Flauheit.

Geschäfts'..., in comp. —mann, m. man of business, cf. —leute; —männisch, adj. belonging to a man of business, business-like; —mäßig, adj. business-like; —ordnung, f. order of business, (im Parlament) standing orders; —periode, f. season; —personal, n. person (men) employed in a business (establishment); coll. business-hands; —regel, f. rule of business; —reise, f. journey on (tour of) business; business-round; —reisende, m. travelling clerk, commercial traveller; —routine, f. experience in business, routine; —sache, f. matter of business, business-transaction; —schwung, m. briskness of trade; —sprache, f. commercial language; —stil, m. business-like (or commercial) style; —stille, —stockung, f. dulness of trade, cf. Flauheit; —stube, f. see —zimmer; —stunden, f. pl. hours of business, office-hours; (der Bank) bank-hours; außer der —zeit, out of office-hours; —träger, m. 1) a) agent, consignee; b) proxy, mandatory; 2) Polit. chargé d'affaires, envoy; —unternehmen, n., —unternehmung, f. Comm. (commercial) undertaking, enterprise, speculation; —unterredung, f. conference; —verbindung, f. (business) connexion, (commercial) relation; correspondence; in —verbindung stehen mit ..., to stand (be in: to be) in correspondence, transact business with ...; in —verbindung (mit ...) treten, 1. to enter into connexion or correspondence (with); 2. to enter into (or to contract) a partnership; —verkehr, m. (commercial) intercourse; dealings; —verwalter, —verweser, m. procurator; proctor; assignee; —verwaltung, —verwesung, f. see —führung; —vorfall, m. transaction; —vorfälle darstellen, to state or record transactions; —zimmer, n. office; bureau; counting-(room or) house; shop; cabinet; —zweig, m. line or branch of business or trade.

Geschä'ker, (str.) n. playfulness; (act or practice of) playing, joking.

Geschä'mig, adj., G-keit, (w.) f. (L. u.) see Schamhaft, Schamhaftigkeit.

Gescharre, Gescharr'e, Gescharrel, (str.) n. a (repeated or incessant) scratching, pawing (the ground, as horses do), looking, swinging, &c. cf. Scharren 2c.

Gescheckt', p. a. pied, see Scheckig.

Gesche'hen, (str.) v. intr. (aux. sein) & impers. to happen; to take place, to occur; to be done; to come to pass, chance, befal; to come about; dein Wille geschehe! thy will be done! es geschehe! let it be done! well, let it be so! als dies — war, this done; es ist bereits —, it is already done; was soll in der Sache —? what shall be done about it? es geschehe, was da wolle, let (may) happen what will, no matter what may happen: es soll ihm kein Leid —, he shall not be hurt, no harm shall befal him; es ist gern —, you are welcome (to it); — lassen, not to hinder, to let pass, endure passively, to connive at ...; etwas nicht — lassen, to keep a thing from being done; es ist ihm recht —, it served him right(ly), he is rightly served; es ist mir, ihm 2c. zu viel —, I have, he has, &c. been wronged or unfairly dealt with; er wußte nicht, wie ihm geschah, he did not know what to make of it; es ist um mich —, I am undone, it is all over (up) with me, my business is done; so — (p. p.) Leipzig den 20. Juli, so done at L. this 20th day of July; g-e Dinge sind nicht zu ändern, proverb, what's done, cannot be undone, it is too late to consult today.

Gescheh'niß, (str.) n. (not usual) event, occurrence, see Ereigniß, Vorgang.

Gescheide, (str.) n. Sport. the entrails of deer, &c., hambles, numbles, umbles.

Gescheidt', Gescheit', I. adj. discreet, prudent, intelligent, judicious, clever, sensible, coll. knowing; nicht (recht) — sein, to be half-witted or out of one's wits, to be a little cracked; aus einer Sache — werden, coll. to understand or comprehend a thing; nichts G-es, coll. nothing worth talking of; II. G-heit, (w.) f. discretion, prudence, intelligence, wit; judiciousness, cleverness.

Geschelle, (str.) n. a (continual or incessant ...

Scheiden; wir sind g-e Leute, *coll.* we have done with each other, there is an end of our friendship; II. G-heit, *(w.) f.* state of separation, separateness; divorcement. [shooting.

Geschie'ße, *(str.) n.* (the act *or* practice of)

Geschilf', *(str.) n.* place (overgrown) with reed, reed-bank, reed-bed, cane-brake.

Geschim'mer, *(str.) n.* a (continued) glittering, &c., *cf.* Schimmern.

Geschimpf'e, *(str.) n.* (the act of, *or* a continued) abusing, (incessant) abuse, abusive language.

Geschin'delt, *adj. Herald. see* Geranirt.

Geschirr', *s.* I. *(str.) n.* 1) vessel; 2) (das irdene —) earthen-ware, crockery; pottery; eisernes —, iron-pots; Silber—, Glas— &c., plate, glass-ware, &c.; 3) *a)* furniture; *b)* tools, implements, utensils; 4) gear, trappings; harness; 5) carriage, waggon, equipage; mit Fuhrmann N.'s —, by carrier N.'s conveyance; *coll.-s.* Einen im — halten, to keep one up to the traces; aus dem — kommen, to lose temper; aus dem — bringen, to put out of countenance; ins — gehen, to launch out; II. *in comp.* —brett, *n.* shelves; cup-board; —bürste, *f.* harness-brush; —holz, *n.* wood fit for tools, &c.; —kamm, *m.* weaver's leaf; —kammer, *f.* room for tools, implements, &c.; saddle-room, harness-room; plate-room, (die königliche) ewry; —leder, *n. T.* harness-leather; —meister, *m. see* Schirrmeister; —schnalle, *f.* harness-buckle; —schreiber, *m.* keeper of the plate (in courts); —tax, *n.* trace-book.

Geschlab'ber(e), *(str.) n. coll.* idle talking, *mod.* tittle-tattle, twaddle, twattling.

Geschlacht', *adj.* († & *provinc.*) 1) *for* Geartet, Geeignet, Artig; 2) meek, mild, soft.

Geschla'ge, *(str.) n.* (the act *or* practice of) beating, (incessant) striking. [hounds).

Geschlam'pe, *(str.) n. Sport.* slop (for

Geschläng'el, *(str.) n.* a meandering, winding.

Geschlank', *adj. obsolescent.* slender (Schlank).

Geschlecht', *s.* I. *(str., pl.* G-er) *n.* 1) genus, kind, species; tribe; race; 2) *a)* family, lineage; house; *b)* descent, origin, stock, extraction, birth; 3) generation; 4) sex; 5) *Gramm.* gender; das menschliche —, mankind, the human species, human race; das schöne —, the fair sex; II. *in comp.* —art, *f.* generic character; G-erkunde, *f. see* G-skunde.

† **Geschlech'ter,** *(str.) m.* patrician.

Geschlecht'lich, *adj.* sexual; generic(al).

Geschlecht'los, I. *adj.* neuter, without sexual distinction; II. G-igkeit, *(w.) f.* absence of the characteristics of genus *or* sex.

Geschlechts'..., *in comp.* —adel, *m. see* Erbadel; —alter, *n.* generation, period of human life; age; —art, *f. see* Geschlecht, 1; —baum, *m.* pedigree; —beugung, *f. Gramm.* termination *or* inflection of gender, as changing a masculine into a feminine termination; —brief, *m. see* —urkunde; —endung, *f.*, —fall, *m. Gramm.* termination of gender; —folge, *f.* succession of generations, lineage; (line of) descent; genealogy; —forscher, *m.* genealogist; —glied, *n.* 1) member of a generation; 2) *Anat.* sexual organs, genitals; —gut, *n.* entailed estate; —krankheit, *f.* sexual disease; —kunde, *f.* genealogy; —kundige, *m.* genealogist; —lehre, *f. see* —kunde; —leiter, —linie, *f. see* —folge; —liebe, *f.* sexual love; —name, *m.* generic(al) name; family-name, surname; —neigung, *f. see* —trieb; —organ, *n.* sexual organ; —register, *m.* genealogy, pedigree; —reife, *f.* maturity of age, puberty; —stamm, *m.* pedigree; —system, *n.* sexual system *or* method; —tafel, *f.* genealogical table, table of descent; —theile, *m. pl.* private (*or* privy) parts, genitals; *Bot.* anthers and pistils; —trieb, *m.* sexual desire, impulse, instinct; *Phren.* amativeness; Befriedigung des —triebes, sexual indulgence; —unterschied, *n.* difference of genus *or* sex; —urkunde, *f.* document of pedigree; —verbindung, *f.* sexual intercourse *or* commerce; —verzeichniß, *n. see* register; —wappen, *n.* family-arms; —wissenschaft, *f.* genealogy; —wort, *n. Gramm.* article; —zeichen, *n. pl. see* —theile.

Geschlei'che, *(str.) n.* (the act *or* habit of) sneaking, creeping.

Geschleif', *(str.) n. Sport.* entrance into the kennel (earth *or* burrow) of foxes, &c.; kennel of a beaver.

Geschlei'fe, Geschlen'ker &c., *(str.) n.* (the act *or* habit of) dragging, flinging, &c. *cf.* Schleifen, Schlenkern &c.

Geschlepp'(e), *(str.) n.* 1) the (act *or* habit of) drawing, dragging, &c. *cf.* Schleppen; 2) train; cumbersome luggage; 3) *Sport.* drag (a bait fastened to a line and dragged along the hunting-ground in a wood); 4) *Min.* sweep, flats.

Geschleu'der, *(str.) n.* the (act *or* practice of) slinging, throwing with a sling.

Geschlif'fen, I. *p. a.* cut (of glass), &c. *see* Schleifen; II. G-heit, *(w.) f.* polish, refinement (of manners), politeness.

Geschling'e, *(str.) n.* 1) *see* Verschlingung, 2; 2) (a hog's) harslets *or* haslets (the liver, heart, and lights), pluck; ropes (the intestines of a bird); *cf.* Gekröse, 1. [slit.

Geschlitz', *(str.) n. T.* a jagging, jag, notch,

Geschlitzt', *p. a. Bot.* wing-cleft, laciniate(d).

Geschlot'ter, *(str.) n. see* Schlotter, *m.* 1 & 2.

Geschluch'ze, *(str.) n.* an incessant (convulsive) sobbing, &c. *cf.* Schluchzen.

Geschlür'fe, *(str.) n.* the (act of) sipping.

Geschmack', *s.* I. *(str., pl. coll. & bad.* Geschmäcke, Geschmäcker) *m.* 1) taste, savour; 2) relish, flavour; raciness; 3) *fig. a)* taste (an *[with Dat.]*, for), appetite (for), relish (for, of), gusto, fancy, liking; *b)* manner, style, way; den — verlieren, to grow unsavoury, tasteless, insipid, to lose taste; *fig.* 1. to grow flat; 2. to lose all inclination (an *[with Dat.]*, for); Einem den — verleiden, to spoil one's pleasure (an *[with Dat.]*, in); — an einer Sache haben *or* finden, to relish a thing, to take a fancy to, to fancy, to have a liking for; nach meinem —, to my liking; Jeder nach seinem —, every one to his taste or fancy; über den — läßt sich nicht streiten, there is no disputing about (accounting for) tastes; einen schlechten — haben, 1. *lit.* to have one's mouth out of taste; 2. *fig.* to have a bad *or* vitiated taste; nach dem neuesten —, after the last fashion, in the first style; in Rubens' —, in Rubens' style *or* manner; II. *in comp.* —frei, *adj.* 1) without taste; 2) *or* —los, tasteless; unsavoury; flat, stale, insipid. [tender to taste.

Geschmäck'ler, *(str.) m.* (*l. u.*) *cont.* pre-

Geschmack'los, I. *adj. see* Geschmackfrei; II. G-igkeit, *(w.) f.* tastelessness; unsavouriness; insipidity, insipidness, flatness.

Geschmack'..., *in comp.* G-skunde, G-slehre, *f.* aesthetics; G-snerv, *m. Anat.* gustatory nerve; G-sorgan, *n.* organ of taste; G-ssache, *f.* matter of taste; G-ssinn, *m.* sense of taste; —voll, *adj. fig.* tasteful, elegant; judicious; —widrig, *adj.* adverse to good taste; tasteless, inelegant; —widrigkeit, *f.* offence against good taste, inelegance; —wissenschaft, *f.* aesthetics.

Geschmad'der, Geschmatz'e, Geschmauch'e, Geschmau'se, Geschmei'chel, *(str.) n. coll.* (the act *or* habit of) scribbling, smacking (kissing), smoking, feasting, flattering, *cf.* Schmaddern, Schmatzen, Schmauchen &c.

Geschmei'de, *s.* I. *(str.) n.* 1) († *&) provinc. a)* things wrought of metal, armour, arms; *b)* fetters, shackles; 2) (a set of) trinkets, jewels, jewelry; II. *in comp.* —handel, *m.* jeweller's trade; —händler, *m.* a dealer in jewelry, jeweller; —kästchen, *n.* casket, jewel-case, jewel-box; —macher, *m.* a maker of jewelry, jeweller.

Geschmei'dig, I. *adj.* malleable, ductile; limber; smooth; soft; pliant, flexible, supple, tractable; II. G-keit, *(w.) f.* malleableness, ductility (of metals); smoothness; softness, pliantness, flexibility, suppleness; G-keit der Zunge, volubility of (the) tongue; G-keit des Geistes, dexterity (flexibility) of mind.

Geschmeiß', *(str.) n.* 1) dung, eggs (of flies, &c.), fly-blow; 2) vermin, flies, and other injurious and troublesome insects; 3) *cont.* dregs of the people, mob, rabble, vermin.

Geschmei'ße, *(str.) n. vulg.* (the act *or* habit of) throwing (Geworfe).

Geschmet'ter, *(str.) n.* 1) an (incessant) battering; 2) the shrill sounds (of a trumpet).

Geschmie'de, *(str.) n.* a (continued) forging.

Geschmie're, *(str.) n.* 1) (the act *or* habit of) greasing; 2) *Typ.* choking, mackling; 3) *cont.* daubing; scribbling, scrawling, scrawl.

Geschmink'e, Geschmol'le, Geschmun'zel, Geschnä'bel, Geschnat'te, Geschnarch'e, Geschnar're, *(str.) n. coll.* (the act *or* habit of) putting on rouge, pouting, smirking, billing, tattling, snoring, rattling, &c. *cf.* Schminken, Schmollen, Schmunzeln &c. [trated.

Geschnä'belt, *adj.* beaked; *Bot., &c.* ros-

Geschnat'ter, *(str.) n.* 1) cackle, gaggling; 2) chatter, gabbling, jabber, jabbering, clatter. [ing of the nose, snorting.

Geschnau'fe, *(str.) n.* an (incessant) blow-

Geschnei'de, *(str.) n.* 1) (the act *or* practice of) cutting; 2) *Sport.* a springe, noose, gin (for catching birds). [*cf.* Schneiden).

Geschnit'ten, *p. a.* cut (*also of salad, &c.*

Geschnit'ze, *(str.) n.* 1) (the act *or* practice of) cutting, carving; 2) carved work (Schnitzwerk).

Geschnör'kel, *(str.) n.* showy, useless, *or* tasteless embellishment; flourish (Schnörkelei).

Geschnüf'fel, *(str.) n.* the (act of) sniffing, &c. *cf.* Schnüffeln. [purring.

Geschnur're, *(str.) n.* a continual rattling,

Geschöpf', *(str.) n.* 1) a created being, creature; 2) *fig. a)* creation, production; *b)* (*in an ill sense*) instrument, tool.

Geschöpf'chen, *(str.) n.* (*dimin. of* Geschöpf) a little creature.

Geschöpft', *adj. Nat.* created.

Geschoß', *s.* I. *(str.) n.* 1) shot, projectile, missile, missive weapon; arrow, dart; firearms; shooting-engine; 2) *Build.* story, floor (of a building); —balken, *m.* joist; II. *(str.) m. provinc. see* Schoß. [paling, hurdle.

Geschrä'ge, *(str.) n. T.* fence of pales,

Geschrau'be, *(str.) n. fig.* the (act of) screwing, jeering, bantering, &c. *cf.* Schrauben.

Geschrei', *(str.) n.* 1) cry, clamour, outcry, exclamation, vociferation, shouting, screaming, squalling, *coll.* bawling; höhnendes —, hooting; — der Hasen, beating; — des Hahnes, *see* Krähen; — der Krähe, cawing; — des Esels, braying; *fig.-s.* 2) *a)* clamour, noise; *coll.* hubbub; *b)* outcry, lamentations, complaints; 3) *a)* flying report, rumour; *b)* discredit, disrepute; ein — machen, to set up or raise a clamour, to make a (great) noise (fuss) (*von*, about); viel — und wenig Wolle, *proverb.* much cry and little wool, a fine show and a small crop.

Geschrei'be, *(str.) n.* 1) (the act *or* practice of) writing; incessant writing; 2) *or* **Geschreib'sel,** *(str.) n. cont.* inelegant writing, scrawl, scribbling. [or song.

Geschrill', *(str.) n.* a chirping, shrill sound

Geschröt', *(str.) n. Anat.* scrotum, cods (of horses and other quadrupeds).

Geschuh', Geschü'he, *vulg.* **Geschüh'ter,** *(str.) n.* shoeing, covering for the feet.

the law; —gebend, *adj.* legislative, lawgiving, constitutive; die —gebende Gewalt, legislature; der —gebende Körper, legislative body, legislature; —geber, *m.* lawgiver, legislator; —geberin, *f.* legislatrix, legislatress; —gebung, *f.* legislation, legislature; —gültig, *adj.* valid in law, legally sanctioned *or* enacted; —kenntniß, *f.* legal knowledge; —kräftig, *adj. see* —gültig; —kunde, *f. see* —kenntniß.

Gesetz'lich, I. *adj.* lawful, legal, legitimate, conformable to the law; statutory; II. *adv.* lawfully, &c., according to law; — erlaubt, allowed *or* warranted by law; III. **G-keit**, *(w.) f.* lawfulness, legality, legitimacy, conformity to law.

Gesetz'los, I. *adj.* lawless; 1) without laws, not acknowledging any laws, anarchical; 2) illegal; II. **G-igkeit**, *(w.) f.* lawlessness; 1) anarchy; 2) illegalness.

Gesetz'..., *in comp.* —mäßig, —mäßigkeit, *see* Gesetzlich, Gesetzlichkeit; —prediger, *m. iron.* moraliser; —predigt, *f. iron.* moral sermon; —rolle, *f.* scroll of laws; —sammlung, *f.* code, body of laws.

Gesetzt', I. *pp. of* Setzen; zur g-en Zeit, at the time stipulated; II. *p. a. fig.* sedate, settled, steady, staid, solid, composed, serious, sober, grave, of mature age; die g-en Jahre, the years of discretion; III. **G-heit**, *(w.) f.* sedateness, steadiness, gravity, &c.

Gesetz'..., *in comp.* —tafel, *f.* table of laws; —übertretung, *f.* transgression, violation of the law; —verletzer, *m.* law-breaker; —vollzieher, —vollstrecker, *m.* executor of the laws; —vorschlag, *m.* bill; —widrig, *adj.* illegal, unlawful, contrary to law; unstatutable; —widrigkeit, *f.* illegality, unlawfulness.

Geseuf'ze, *(str.) n.* a (continual) sighing, groaning, lamentation.

Gesicht', *(str.) n.* 1) sight, eyesight; eye, view; 2) *(pl.* G-er) face; visage; countenance; looks, look, mien; (einer Waare) *Comm. see* Aussehen; 3) *(pl.* G-e) vision, apparition, form; 4) sight, visor (of a rifle, gun, &c.); das — richten auf ..., to cast one's eyes upon ...; von — kennen, to know by sight; das schöne —, *Bot.* thick seed sun-flower; Einem (gerade) ins — sehen, to look one (full) in the face, to look full at one; Einem ins — schlagen, to slap one's face; über's ganze — lachen, to laugh from ear to ear; Einem ins — lachen, to laugh in one's face; ihm ins —, to (before) his face, presence, *or* eyes, *coll.* in(to) his teeth, to his beard; ein scharfes, langes — haben, to be quick-sighted, near-sighted; aus dem G-e, out of sight; im Bereiche des G-es, within eye-sight; zu —(e) kommen, to come in one's sight, appear; zu —(e) bekommen, to get a sight of, to get in sight of; wieder zu —(e) bekommen, to regain sight of; wir haben England im G-e, we are in sight of England; aus dem — verlieren, to lose sight of; *Mar.* to lay *or* settle the land; das — verlieren, to lose the eye-sight; Einem ein freundliches — machen, to look kindly *or* cheerfully at one; Einem G-er schneiden, to make faces, grimaces, mouths, mows at one; ein langes — machen *or* ziehen, to pull a long face; zu G-e stehen, *see* zu Stehen; *Mar.-e.* aus dem — des Landes, land-laid; man hat kein —, there is no sight of land; das Land im — behalten, to keep the land aboard; das Land höher (*or* näher) zu — bekommen, to raise the land; das Land aus dem — verlieren, to lay *or* settle the land; ein anderes Land zu — bekommen, to make a bad landfall; das — betreffend, visual.

Gesicht'chen, *(str.) n.* *(dimin. of* Gesicht, 2; *pl. coll.* Gesichterchen) a small *or* little face.

Gesicht'los, I. *adj.* without sight, blind; II. **G-igkeit**, *(w.) f.* sightlessness, blindness.

Gesicht'maler, *(str.) m. see* Portrait-Maler.

Gesichts'..., *in comp.* —achse, *f.* optic *or* visual axis; —arterie, *f.* facial artery; —ausdruck, *m.* physiognomy, expression of countenance, features, countenance, mien; im — bereiche, within eye-sight; —betrug, *m.* optic illusion; —bild, *n.* portrait; —bildung, *f. see* —ausdruck; —blätterchen, *n.* pimple; —deuter, —forscher, *m.* physiognomist; —deutung, —forschung, *f.* physiognomy; —farbe, *f.* complexion; —feld, *n.* 1) field of view (of a telescope); 2) *see* —kreis; —grind, *m. Med.* milk-scab; —kreis, *m.* 1) field (*or* range) of view (of a telescope, &c.), space within which objects are visible; 2) *Astr.* finitor, horizon, *cf.* Horizont; 3) *fig.* intellectual horizon, sphere, range of vision, observation, *or* contemplation; im —kreise liegen *or* sich befinden, to lie *or* be within the range of vision, within sight *or* ken; —kunde, *f.* physiognomy; —kundige, *m.* physiognomist; —länge, *f.* length of face; —linie, *f.* 1) visual line; level; 2) *Anat.* feature, line; 3) *Fort.* outer line of a fortification; *Anat.-e.* —muskel, *m.* facial muscle; —nerv, *m.* facial nerve; sympathetic (nerve); —pulsader, *f.* facial artery; —punct, *m.* point of view, visual point, aspect; eine Sache aus ihrem richtigen —punct betrachten, to look upon a thing from its true point of view, to view a thing in its true aspect *or* light; wir sehen dies aus verschiedenen —puncten an, we see this differently; —rose, *f. Med.* erysipelas (*or coll.* St. Anthony's fire) in the face; —schmerz, *m. Med.* facial neuralgia, face-ache, *(Fr.)* tic-douloureux; —schwäche, *f.* weakness of sight; —seite, *f.* front, face; —sinn, *m.* sight, eye-sight; —strahl, *m.* visual ray; —täuschung, *f.* optical deception; (zauberische) glamour; —wahrsager, *m.* metoposcopist; —wahrsagung, *f.* metoposcopy; —weite, *f.* eye-shot; —winkel, *m.* facial (*or* visual) angle; —zug, *m.* lineament, line, *pl.* features.

Gesie'bent, *adj.* septenary.

Gesie'de, *(str.) n.* the (act of) boiling, [stewing.

Gesied'fähig, *adj. T.* privileged *or* licensed to boil salt.

Gesims', *(str.) n.* 1) *Archit., Join., &c.* moulding, jutting, cornice; shelf; (Fenster—) plain; moulding; (Kamin—) mantle-piece, chimney-piece; entablature; pediment; 2) *coll.* shelf; —enter, *m. Archit.* peg, dowel; —hobel, *m.* moulding-plane, rabbet-plane; —kachel, *f.* cornice-tile; —klammer, *f.* peg, dowel; —verzierung, *f.* annulet; —werk, *n.* cable-moulding.

Gesin'de, *n.* I. *(str.) n.* domestics, servants, menials, *particul.* farm-servants, labourers; II. *in comp.* —amt, —bureau, *n.* office for servants; —bier, *n.* beer for the servants, small beer; —brot, *n.* household bread, brown bread; —gericht, *n.* statute-sessions.

Gesin'del, *(str.) n.* rabble, mob, tag-rag.

Gesin'de..., *in comp.* —lohn, *m.* wages; —ordnung, *f.* regulations for servants, code of menial service; —posten, *m.* menial office; —stube, *f.*, —zimmer, *n.* servants' hall; —tisch, *m.* 1) table for the servants; 2) servants' board; —zeugniß-Buch, *n.* character-book of servants.

Gesing'e, *(str.) n.* 1) the (act *or* practice of) [singing; 2) bad singing.

Gesinnt', *p. a.* minded, disposed; affected; gleich —, of one mind; anders —, of a different opinion; gegen Jemand feindlich *or* übel — sein, to bear one ill-will, to be ill-affected (ill-disposed) towards one; französisch — sein, to affect the French party, to side with the French.

Gesin'nung, *(w.) f.* mind, view, opinion, idea; sentiment, inclination, disposition, feeling, temper; principles; seine — ändern, to change one's mind; eine wohlwollende —, a friendly feeling.

Gesin'nungslos, I. *adj.* characterless, without character; fickle-minded, unstable, inconstant; II. **G-igkeit**, *(w.) f.* want of character.

Gesin'nungs..., *in comp.* —tüchtig, —voll, *adj.* energetic, gallant, brave; true-hearted, constant, candid; —tüchtigkeit, *f.* energy of character, decision; true-heartedness, constancy.

Gesip'pe, *(str.) n.* kindred, tribe (Sippschaft).

Gesit'tet, I. *adj.* (gut —, well-mannered; orderly; good, moral; civilised; wohl —, well bred *or* behaved; g-es Wesen, good manners, orderliness; — machen, to polish; to civilise; II. **G-heit**, *(w.) f.* morality.

Gesit'tigung, **Gesit'tung**, *(w.) f.* civilisation, humanisation, cultivation.

Gesitz'e, *(str.) n.* the (act, mode, *or* practice of) sitting; sedentary habits.

Gesöff', *(str.) n. vulg.* 1) *see* Gesaufe; 2) bad liquor, bad drink, *anal.* slip slop.

Geson'nen, *p. a.* disposed, inclined, intending; — sein, to be *or* feel inclined, to have an intention, a mind, to intend, purpose, mean; anders — sein, to be of a different opinion.

Gesott', *(str.) n.* mash (food for cattle).

Gespann', *a.* I. *(str.) m.* 1) † & *bad* comrade, mate, fellow; 2) count (in Hungary); II. *(str.) n.* a team, set of (carriage-)horses; team, span (of oxen).

Gespann'schaft, *(w.) f.* a district, county *or* shire (in Hungary).

Gespannt', I. *p. a.* stretched, tight (rope, &c.); *fig.-e.* 1) intense, attentive; g-e Aufmerksamkeit, earnest, serious attention; die Erwartung war im höchsten Grade —, expectation was wound up to the highest pitch; Jemands Aufmerksamkeit — erhalten, to keep a person's attention on the stretch; ängstlich —, anxious, solicitous (auf [*with Acc.*], about); 2) (*coll.* über den Fuß —) on ill, bad, *or* distant terms, at variance (mit, with); II. **G-heit**, *(w.) f.* 1) intensity, attention; 2) variance, disagreement (mit, with).

Gesparr', **Gespär're**, *(str.) n. Carp.* timber-work (of a roof), rafters, couple-close.

Gespa'ße, *(str.) n.* the (act *or* practice of) joking, jesting, *cf.* Spaßen.

Gespei'e, *(str.) n.* the (act of) vomiting, vomit; a (continual) vomiting, spitting, &c.

Gespei'de, *(str.) n. see* Gespilde.

Gespenst', *(str., pl.* G-er) *n.* spectre, ghost, apparition, phantom.

Gespenst'er..., *in comp.* —artig, *adj.* spectral, ghastly; —erscheinung, *f.* apparition of a ghost; —furcht, *f.* fear of ghosts, apparitions; —geschichte, *f.* ghost story; —glaube, *m.* belief in apparitions; —heuschrecke, *f. Entom.* 1) spectre (*Phasma* Fabr.); 2) walking-leaf (*Phyllium siccifolium* L.); —käfer, *m. Entom.* praying cricket, praying mantis (*Mantis religiosa* L.); —reich, *n.* realm *or* world of spirits, ghosts, apparitions; —stunde, *f. see* Geisterstunde; —süchtig, *adj.* spectre-smitten; —thier, *n. see* Maki.

Gespenst'ig, **Gespenst'isch**, *adj.* spectral, ghostlike, phantomlike, ghastly.

Gesperr'..., *in comp.* —baum, *m. Mar.* knee (of a ship); —draht, *m. Horol.* click-wire.

Gesper're, *(str.) n.* 1) *a) Carp. see* Gesparr; *b) Horol.* ratchet with catch (Sperrrad); *c)* — an einem Buche, clasps of a book; *d) Sport.* a nide (of pheasants); *e) Typ.* frisket; *f) see* Wagendecke; *g)* click and ratchet wheel; 2) *a)* the (act of) struggling against, resistance, *cf.* sich Sperren; *b)* encumbrance; viel — machen, to be cumbersome, to take up much room; in dieser Straße ist ein immerwährendes —, this street is continually obstructed, blocked up, *or* choked.

Gesperr'macher, *(str.) m. see* Gürtler.

Gesperrt', *p. a.* (*cf.* Sperren) 1) *Mar.* [...]

a port) shut up; land-locked; 2) *Typ.* spaced out; mit g—er Schrift, printed with italics.

Gespie'le, I. *(str.)* n. the (act, mode, or practice of) playing; fortwährendes —, incessant playing; II. *(w.)* m., **Gespie'lin**, *(w.)* f. (male or female) associate, companion, playfellow, play-mate.

Gespiel'schaft, *(w.)* f. companionship, fellowship, familiar intercourse.

Gespil'de, Gespil'derecht, *(str.)* n. *provinc. Law*, right of preemption.

Gespin'ne, *(str.)* n. the (act, mode, or practice of) spinning; a (continual) spinning, &c.

Gespin(n)st', *(str.)* n. what is spun, spinning, web, textile fabric; den feinem —, fine-spun; —faser, f. textile fibre, filament.

* **Gespons'**, *(str.)* m., n., & *(w.)* f. (*Lat. sponsus, sponsa*, betrothed) († &) *ind.* bridegroom; bride (*coll.* Gespon'sin, Gesponsi).

Gespött'(e), *(str.)* n. 1) (the act or practice of) scoffing, mocking, mockery, ridicule, deriding, derision, jeering, banter, bantering, raillery, jest; 2) laughing-stock; (sich) zum — machen, to expose (one's self) to mockery, ridicule, Andern zum — dienen, werden, to be a laughing-stock or mockery to others; sein — mit etwas treiben, to laugh, scoff, mock, jeer at, to deride, banter.

Gespot'te, *(str.)* n. the (act or practice of) mocking, &c. *cf.* Spotten; mockery. [satire.

Gespöt'tel, *(str.)* n. mockery, ridicule,

Gespräch', *(str.)* n. discourse; talk, conversation, colloquy; dialogue; conference, parley; zum — der Stadt werden, to become the talk of the town; —buch, n. book of dialogues.

Gesprä'chig, Gespräch'sam, I. *adj.* 1) affable, of fair address, easy to be spoken to; 2) communicative, conversable; talkative; II. G-keit, *(w.)* f. 1) affability, easiness of address; 2) communicativeness, talkativeness.

Gesprächs'..., *in comp.* —form, f. form of a dialogue, interlocutory form; —gegenstand, —stoff, m. subject of conversation, topic; —ton, m. tone of conversation; —weise, *adv.* 1) by way of dialogue; in the course of conversation; —zimmer, n. parlour, conversation-room, sitting-room.

Gespre'che, *(str.)* n. *coll.* the (act or practice of) talking, incessant talking, speaking; *contp.* longwinded talking, palaver.

Gespreizt', I. *p. a. fig.* stilted, stilty, pompous; II. G-heit, *(w.)* f. stiltiness, pomposity (of style, &c.).

Gespreng'e, *(str.)* n. 1) the (act of) sprinkling, &c. *cf.* Sprengen; 2) *Min. a)* the (act of) blasting the ores by gunpowder; *b)* fragment separated by blasting; 3) *Archit.* pent-roof, compluvium.

Gesprenk'elt, *p. a.* speckled, sprinkled, spotted (as the edges of a book, &c.), splash (paper).

Gespring'e, *(str.)* n. (the act or practice of) leaping; incessant leaping, jumping.

Gespritz'e, *(str.)* n. a spirting, squirting, splash.

Gesproß', *(str.)* n.*, what sprouts, sprouts.

Gespru'del, *(str.)* n. a (continual) bubbling, rippling, spouting, sputtering.

Gespuc'ke, *(str.)* n. the (act or practice of) spitting, incessant spitting.

Gespu'ke, *(str.)* n. the (act of) haunting, &c. *cf.* Spuken. [(sea) coast.

Gesta'de, *(str.)* n.*, shore, bank, beach,

Gestalt, *(w.)* I. *(w.)* f. 1) figure, form, shape, frame, fashion; 2) stature, size; 3) countenance, mien, look, air, countenance, face; der Ritter von der traurigen —, the knight of the Sorrowful Countenance (*i. e.* Don Quixote); 4) *fig. a)* aspect, face, appearance; *b)* manner, way; gleicher —, in like (the same) manner; folgender —, in the following manner; welcher —, how, by what means, which way; das Abendmahl unter einerlei —, half communion; in or unter beiderlei —, in both kinds; der Mensch zeigt sich in seiner wahren —, man appears as he really is.

Gestal'ten, *(w.)* v. I. *tr.* to shape, form, figure, fashion; II. *refl.* to take or assume a figure, shape, appearance; to be, turn out, to show, prove itself; sich nach Wunsch —, to succeed according to wish; die Sache gestaltete sich ganz anders, the affair took quite a different aspect; die gestaltende Kraft der Natur, the plastic virtue of nature. [or forms.

Gestal'tenreich, *adj.* abounding in figures

Gestal'tet, *contr.* **Gestalt'**, *p. a.* shaped, framed, figured; bei so gestalteten Sachen, matters standing thus, under such circumstances.

Gestal'tig, *adj.* having form, formed.

Gestalt'los, I. *adj.* 1) having no imaginable form or shape, immaterial; 2) shapeless, formless; amorphous; II. G-igkeit, *(w.)* f. 1) immateriality; 2) shapelessness.

Gestalt'niß, *(w.)* f. *provinc.* form, figure.

Gestal'tung, *(w.)* f. 1) *gener.* formation; 2) *Astrol.* configuration; 3) form, figure; shape, appearance; die jetzige — des Handels, present state of trade; G-sfähigkeit, f. 1) plastic faculty or force; 2) figurability.

Gestam'mel, *(str.)* n. (the act or habit of) stammering, stammer, hesitation of speech.

Gestampf'(e), *(str.)* n. the (act of) stamping.

Gestän'de, *(str.)* n. *Sport.* the feet of birds of prey.

Gestän'dert, *adj. Herald.* gyronee.

Geständ'ig, *adv.* confessing, having confessed; — sein (with *Gen.* or Einem etwas), or **Gestän'digen**, *(w.)* v. *tr. Law*, to confess, acknowledge, avow, own; to plead guilty (to an offence, a defect, &c.).

Geständ'niß, *(str.)* n. confession, acknowledgment, avowal.

Gestäng'bewegung, *(w.)* f. *Mech.* see-saw-gear (motion), reciprocating motion.

Gestäng'e, *(str.)* n. 1) poles, rails, enclosure of stakes; 2) *Min.* pit-work; 3) *Sport.* head, horn, branches of a deer, *Herald.* & *Sport.* attire.

Gestank', *(str.)* m. *coll.* stench; stink; 2) *fig.* evil report, ill name.

Gestat'ten, *(w.)* v. *tr.* (Einem etwas) to permit, allow, admit, suffer, grant, consent to, *cf.* Verstatten & Erlauben

Gestatt'bar, Gestatt'lich, *adj.* allowable, admissible; lawful. [consent.

Gestat'tung, *(w.)* f. permission, allowance,

Gestäu'be, *(str.)* n. (the act of spreading) dust.

Gestäu'de, *(str.)* n. 1) *collect.* shrubs, bushes; 2) *Sport.* aerie, nest of a hawk.

Gesteck', *(str.)* n. see Besteck.

Geste'hen, *(irr.)* v. I. *intr.* (*aux.* sein) see Gerinnen; II. *tr.* to confess, own, acknowledge, avow; man muß —, it must be admitted, granted, avowed; das gestehe ich! nun, das muß ich —! well, I declare! is it possible! indeed! you don't say so! well, I never (*i. e.* saw the like)! III. *refl. provinc.* to dare, venture.

Gestein', *(str.)* n. 1) *a)* stone, rock; *b)* *Miner.* *particul.* G-e, *pl.* rock specimens, rocks; 2) precious stones, gems; das taube —, *Min.* dead heaps, deads, attle; —arbeit, *f. Weav.* damboard, checker; —kunde, G-lehre, f. mineralogy; —kundige, m. mineralogist; G-sgang, m. *Min.* vein, streak, lode.

Gestell', *(str.)* n. 1) frame; *a)* trestle; *b)* (booting-)horse; *c)* *Mech.* dog; *d)* foot, basis, pedestal, stand; *Archit.* socle; *Bot.* foot-stalk; *e)* the frame (framework) of a carriage with its wheels upon which the body is placed; frame or timber-work of a windmill; *f)* head-stall (of a bridle); *g)* skeleton, stretchers (of an umbrella); *h)* rims (of spectacles); —

Geströ'm(e), (str.) n. the (act of) streaming, &c.; waters.

Gestru'del, (str.) n. the (act of) boiling, bubbling up, rippling, whirling (of water).

Gestrunkt', adj. Bot. stipitate.

Gestrüpp'(e) (Gestripp), (str.) n. collect. a thicket of shrubs and thorns, bushes, briars; copsewood, underwood, undergrowth, scrub.

Gestü'be, (str.) n. 1) the (act of) spreading dust; 2) (Kohlen—) coal-dust; 3) Smelt. brasque, lute; —kammer, f. room where brasque is prepared. [wild fowl, droppings.

Gestü'ber, (str.) n. Sport. the dung of

Gestück', (str.) n. (l. u.) see Stück, 3.

Gestühl', (str.) n. 1) collect. seats, chairs; (Kirchen—) pews; 2) gener. Gestell, which see.

Gestüm'melt, p. a. see Stümmeln.

Gestüm'per, (str.) n. bungle, a botch, work clumsily (or badly) done.

Gestun'den, (w.) v. tr. Comm., Law, &c. to grant delay (of payment) (Stunden, Fristen).

Gestun'dung, (w.) f. Comm., Law, &c. delay (of payment), respite.

Gestür'me, (str.) n. the (act of) storming: a constant storming, roaring, cf. Stürmen.

Gestüt'(e), s. I. (str.) n. stud; breed of horses; II. in comp. —garten, m. stud; —hengst, m. stallion; —herr, m. owner of a stud; —meister, see —verwalter; —stute, f. brood-mare, stud-mare; —verwalter, m. manager of a stud; equerry; —zeichen, n. a brand on a horse from a stud.

Gesuch', (str.) n. suit, demand, request, solicitation, entreaty, supplication, application (um, for); petition, memorial; (newspaper, &c. advertisements:) (Agentur 2c.) —, (agency, &c.) wanted. [searching.

Gesu'che, (str.) n. a continued seeking,

Gesucht', p. a. 1) Comm. (of goods) inquired or called for, in request, in demand, sought after, in favour; sehr —, in great favour, eagerly sought, much wanted, in very brisk demand; Kaffee ist jetzt sehr —, there is a great call for coffee; nicht —, without inquiry, out of favour, not in request; es ist gar nicht —, nobody looks at it; etwas mehr —, rather more inquired for; es ist wenig —, there is but an indifferent inquiry (call) for it; es ist minder —, there is a falling off in the demand for it; — wird ... (in Zeitungsinseraten), wanted ...; 2) fig. affected, formal, assumed; over-nice, far-fetched.

Gesu'del, (str.) n. conl. a dirty or bungling piece of work, cf. Sudelei.

Gesum'me, Gesum'se, (str.) n. a (continual) humming, buzzing, hum, buzz.

Gesümpf', (str.) n. a marshy tract of country, marshes, bog, fen, quagmire, morass.

Gesund', I. adj. 1) sound: a) healthy; healthful, in health; b) hale; 2) wholesome, salubrious, salutary; 3) fig. sound; — und frisch (or munter), hale (or safe) and sound; der g—e Verstand, common sense; g—e Gesichtsfarbe, hale complexion; wieder — werden, to get well again, to recover (one's health); wieder — machen, to restore to health; das war ihm sehr —, 1. that did him much good; 2. coll. that served him right; II. in comp. —bad, n. watering-place, bath; —brunnen, m. 1) mineral spring, well, mineral (medicated) waters; 2) see —bad.

Gesun'den, (w.) v. intr. (aux. sein) to recover, to be restored to health.

Gesund'heit, (w.) f. 1) health; healthfulness, healthiness; soundness; 2) wholesomeness, salubrity; (zur) —! (beim Niesen), God bless you! (im Engl. u. ü.); auf Jemandes — trinken, Einem eine — bringen, to drink one's health, to toast one; auf Ihre —! (beim Trinken), your health! happy (glad) to see you! here (here's) to you! er stattete seinen Dank für eine ausgebrachte — ab, he returned thanks for some health-drinking; bei guter —, in good (or in a perfect state of) health.

Gesund'heitlich, adj. relating to health, sanatory, cf. Gesundheits....

Gesund'heits..., in comp. —amt, n., — commission, f. board of health, sanitary board, sanatory commission; —attest(at), n. see —paß; —beamte(r), m. officer of health; —brief, m. Mar. see —paß; —chocolade, f. sanative chocolate; —flanell, m. Comm. fleecy hosiery, Welsh flannel; —geschirr(e), n. hygienic pottery or crockery; —kunde, —lehre, f. science of health, dietetics; —paß, m. bill (or certificate) of health; —pflege, f. regimen; —polizei, f. health office; —probe, f. quarantine; —rath, m. council, board, or college of health; —regel, f. rule of diet, regimen; den —regeln gemäß, dietetical; —schein, m. see —paß; —schokolade, see —chocolade; —(wachs-)taffet, m. medicated oil-cloth; —zustand, m. state of health, sanitary condition.

Geta'del, (str.) n. the (act or habit of) blaming, incessant blaming, censuring, &c. cf. Tadeln; malicious criticism.

Getä'fel, (str.) n. a wainscoting, wainscot (aus echtem Eichenholz); panelling.

Getan'ze, Getän'del, Getatsch'(e), Getän'sche, Getan'zel, (str.) n. (the act or practice of) dancing, (continual) dancing, sporting, &c. see Tanzen, Tändeln, Tatschen 2c.

Getheilt', I. p. a. disjoint, disjointed (cf. Theilen); Herald. party; Bot. partite; — handeln, to act disjointedly; II. G—heit, (w.) f. disjointedness, disconnection, disunion, separation; diversity.

Gethu'e, (str.) n. coll. 1) the (way of) doing a thing, proceeding; 2) affectation; dissembling, feigning (cf. Thun).

Getigert, p. a. spotted like a tiger; fleabit, fleabitten (of horses); Comm. shagged, shaggy (of tobacco).

Geto'be, (str.) n. the (act or habit of) raging, an incessant raging, roaring, din.

Getön', (str.) n. a (continual) sounding, sound. [dine) (str.) n. a roaring noise.

Geto'se, Getös', (De la Motte Fouqué, Un-

Getö'se, (str.) n. a violent, complicated noise, din, clashing, crashing, clatter.

Getra'be, (str.) n. the (act of) trotting.

Getra'gen, p. a. Mus. sustained, continuous in regard to tone, sostenuto (Ital.).

Getram'pel, (str.) n. a trampling (clattering noise caused by hard treads), pitapat.

Getränk', (str.) n. drink, beverage, liquor; Med. potion, decoction; abgezogene G—e, distilled waters; geistige G—e, spirituous liquors.

Getrap'pel, (str.) n. see Getrabe & Getrampel. [idle talk (Geschlabber).

Geträtsch', (str.) n. coll. nonsensical or

Getrau'en, (w.) v. refl. 1) sich (Dat.) etwas —, to trust one's self, to dare, venture, to be bold enough to undertake a thing, &c.; ich getraue es mir nicht, I dare not do it; 2) sich (Acc.) wohin —, to dare to go to a place, &c.; er getraute sich nicht dahin, he did not venture thither.

Getrau'er, (str.) n. (the act of) mourning.

Geträu'fel, (str.) n. a (constant) dropping, dripping; drops.

Geträu'me, (str.) n. (incessant) dreaming.

Getrei'be, (str.) n. 1) a (continual) urging, pressing, &c.; 2) activity, &c. cf. Treiben, v. a.

Getrei'de, s. I. (str.) n. corn, grain; das noch stehende —, — auf dem Halme, standing corn, green corn; crop; — schneiden, to cut, reap; II. in comp. —acker, m. plough-land; —art, f. species of corn; —arten, pl. the cereal grasses, cerealia; —bau, m. cultivation of corn (grain), tillage; —bauer, m. grower of corn; —boden, m. 1) see —land, 1; 2) granary, corn-loft, corn-floor; —börse, f. corn-exchange; —brand, m. smut; —fege, f. see —reinigungsmaschine; —feld, n. corn-field; —geschäft, n. corn-business; —gülte, f. see —zins; —halm, m. stalk of corn, corn stalk; —handel, m. corn-trade; —händler, m. corn-merchant; —harfe, f. Husb. fry; —haufen, m. corn heap; —haus, n. corn-magazine; —kasten, m. hutch; —kord, m. skep; —land, n. 1) corn-land; 2) corn-growing country; —magazin, n. granary; —mäkler, m. corn-broker, corn-factor, chandler; —markt, m. corn-market; —maß, n. corn-measure; —messer, m. corn-meter; —motte, f. Entom. corn-moth (Tinea granella L.); —mühle, f. corn-mill; —pacht, f. see —zins; —preis, m. price of corn or grain; —putzer, m., —reinigungsmaschine, f. winnowing machine, smut-mill; —rüsler, m. Entom. red corn-worm (Apion frumentarium L.); —sendung, f. shipment of corn; —sperre, f. prohibition on the exportation of grain; —träger, m. corn-porter; —vorräthe, m. pl. provisions of corn; —wagen, m. corn-waggon; —wucher 2c., see Kornwucher; —wurm, m. Entom. corn-moth (—motte); (schwarzer) corn weevil (Calandra granaria L.); —zehent, m. corn-tithes; —zins, m. rent paid in corn; —zoll, m. corn-duty.

Getrennt', I. p. a. separated (cf. Trennen), separate; distinct; Bot. segregate; II. adv. asunder; III. G—heit, (w.) f. disunion, separation, diversity.

Getreu', I. adj. faithful; true, trusty, honest; loyal; Einem — sein, to be true, constant to one; — und ohne Gefährde, in good faith; cf. Treu; II. or G—lich, adv. faithfully, &c.; III. G—e, s. m. & f. (decl. like adj.) faithful or loyal person or subject; unserem Lieben G—en (ancient epistolary style), to our trusty and well-beloved; G—heit, (w.) f. see Treue.

Getrie'be, (str.) n. 1) motive power, motion, machinery, machine-work; 2) Mech. a) driving-gear; b) pinion, trundle, wallower, cf. Vorgelege; das conische —, bevelled gear; das gerade, cylindrische —, spur gear; 3) Min. a) south- or summer-side of a mountain; b) the underpropping of a ruinous drift; 4) fig. the working (of parliamentary, &c. machinery); —zirkel (—zirkel), m. pinion-gage; —pfahl, m. prop, lath; —scheibe, f. pinion-plate; —stöcke, m. pl. staves of a trundle or wallower.

Getril'ler, Getrip'pel, Getröpf'el, (str.) n. a (repeated or incessant) trilling, tripping, dripping, cf. Trillern, Trippeln, Tröpfeln.

Getrost', I. adj. confident, courageous; of good cheer, hopes; — or g—en Muthes sein, to be of good courage or heart, to take comfort; II. adv. confidently, &c., with assurance, securely, safely; cheerfully; er bildet sich — ein, he fondly imagines; III. interj. cheer up! be of good cheer! take courage!

Getrös'ten, (w.) v. refl. (with Gen.) to expect confidently or patiently, to be assured or confident (of), to rely or depend (on, upon).

Getrüm'mer, (str.) n. ruins, cf. Trümmer.

Getü'che, (str.) n. (l. u.) linen-clothes.

Getum'mel, Getüm'mel, (str.) n. a noisy bustling about, bustle, tumultuary noise, tumult, riot, stir, turmoil, disturbance.

Geübt', I. p. a. practised, exercised, versed, expert, ready; II. G—heit, (w.) f. expertness, skill, practice. [weak) witticism.

Geur'theile, (str.) n. conl. (malicious or

Gevat'ter, s. I. (str.) m. godfather; coll. gossip; Einen, Eine zu — bitten, to desire one to be godfather or godmother; bei ... — stehen, 1. to stand godfather (sponsor) or godmother (bei, to ...); 2. coll. to be laid up in lavender, to be at my uncle's or up the spout (i. e. at pawn); II. in comp. —bitter, m. a person who invites the godfathers and godmothers; —brief, m. invitatory letter to stand godfather or godmother.

Gewe'be, *(str.)* n. 1) (the act *or* art of) [illegible]ving; 2) texture, web, weft: *Nat., Bot., [illegible], &c.* tissue, texture (of the nerves, &c.); [illegible] (of the veins); 3) cells (of bees); 4) [illegible] web (of intrigue, &c.), tissue (of lies, &c.), [illegible] (of sophisms, &c.), fabric; **–ähnlich**, *adj.* [illegible]-like; **–baum**, m. *T.* weaver's beam; **–[illegible]**, *f. Anat.* histology.

Geweckt, I. *p. a.* lively, *see* Aufgeweckt; II. *adj. Herald.* fusilly, covered with fusils.

Gewehr', *s.* I. *(str.)* n. 1) weapon, arm, [illegible]; 2) gun, musket, fire-lock; 3) sword; [illegible] [illegible]'s arms; 5) *Sport. see* Gewäff; zum [illegible] greifen, to take up arms; das — strecken, [illegible] lay down arms; unterm — stehen, to be under arms; ins — treten, to get under arms; [illegible] — rufen, to call to arms; die G–e zusammensetzen, to pile *or* stack arms: *Mil.-s.* ins [illegible] to arms! — hoch! recover arms! (greift's) [illegible] an! handle arms! schultert's —! shoulder [illegible]! — über! *or* über 's —! slope arms! das [illegible] auf die andere Schulter! change! in Arm [illegible] —! support arms! — in die Balance! trail [illegible]! — ab *or* beim Fuß! *or* beim Fuß 's —! [illegible] arms! II. *in comp.* **–fabrik**, *f.* manufactory of arms, muskets; **–feuer**, n. discharge of musketry, firing; **–gallerie**, *f.* armoury; **–gerecht**, *adj.* practised in the use [illegible] fire-arms; **–hammer**, m. gun-hammer; **–[illegible]**, m. armourer, a seller *or* maker of [illegible]; **–handlung**, *f.* armourer's shop; **–[illegible]mer**, *f.* armoury; **–kasten**, m. gun-box, [illegible] case; **–kiste**, *f.* gun-tool-chest; **–kreuz**, n., [illegible], **–lade**, *f.* gun-rack; **–lauf**, m. barrel (of a gun); **–mantel**, m. gun-case (of [illegible]); **–probe**, *f.* trial *or* proof of a gun *or* [illegible]; **–pulver**, n. musket-powder; **–pyramide**, *f.* arms piled together (in form of a pyramid), pile of muskets; **–reff**, n., **–riemen**, [illegible] *Mar. see* **–kreuz**; **–saal**, m. *see* **–kammer**; **–schein**, m. licence to carry a gun, shooting-licence; **–schloß**, n. firelock, gun-lock; **–schmied**, m. gun-smith; **–schmiede**, *f. see* **–[illegible]**; **–schrank**, m. armoury; **–schraube**, *f.* [illegible]-vice; **–stand**, m. *see* **–kreuz**; **–stein**, m. [illegible] Flintenstein; **–strumpf**, m. gun-case.

Gewei'dicht, *(str.)* n. a place overgrown with willows, willow-plot, osier-bed.

Geweih, *(str.)* n. horns, (die Enden am —) branches, antlers, *(also Herald.)* attire (of a stag); *Sport.* head; das erste (zarte) —, tender-[illegible]; mit einem — versehen, antlered.

Gewei'ne, *(str.)* n. the (act *or* habit of) weeping, a continual weeping, crying, whining.

Gewen'de, *(str.)* n. 1) *Agr. a)* the (act of) turning the land (with the plough); *b)* an [illegible]; 2) *a)* a set (of things), suit (of clothes); [illegible] team (of horses).

Gewen'dig, I. *adj.* [illegible] *(Hotmation)* 1) [illegible] turned *or* moved easily; 2) active (Behend); II. **G–keit**, *(w.) f. see* Gewandtheit.

Gewerb'sausstellung *etc., see* Gewerbe....

Gewer'be, *s.* I. *(str.)* n. 1) *a)* trade, profession; craft; *b)* industry: 2) *fig.* business, [illegible], errand; commission; 3) *Anat.* [illegible], vertebra; 4) *Mech.* joint; er ist [illegible] [illegible] ein Tischler, he is a joiner by trade; [illegible] anfangen, to set up (in) a trade *or* business; II. *in comp.* **–ausstellung**, *f.* exhibition of (products of) industry, industrial exhibition; **–bein**, n. *Anat.* vertebra; **–blatt**, [illegible] weekly, &c.) paper of the industrial arts; **–freiheit**, *f.* liberty of trade, liberty of exercising any craft; **–geld**, n. *see* Gewerbsteuer.

Gewerb'... *(cf.* Gewerbe...*), in comp.* **–[illegible]**, industry; Verein zur Beförderung [illegible] [illegible], association for the promotion of industry; **–fleißig**, *adj.* industrious; **–kunde**, technology, technics; **–kundig**, *adj.* having knowledge of a (certain) trade *or* craft; technological; **–kundige**, m. technologist; **–[illegible]**, *adj.* technological.

Gewerb'lich, Gewerbs'sam, *adj.* industrious, professional.

Gewerbs'..., *in comp.* **–recht**, n. privilege *or* right of exercising any trade; **–schein**, m. licence for carrying on a trade, &c.; **–schule**, *f.* polytechnic school; technological *or* mechanics' institution; **G–lehre**, *f. see* **–kunde**; **G–mann**, m. *(pl.* **G–leute***)* tradesman, dealer, artificer; **–steuer**, *f.* tax for carrying on a trade, &c.; **G–wissenschaft**, *f. see* **–kunde**; **G–zweig**, m. branch of industry *or* manufacture; **–thätig**, *adj.* industrial; **–thätigkeit**, *f.* industry; **–treibend**, *adj.* carrying on a trade *or* craft; manufacturing: der **–treibende**, m. craftsman; tradesman; die **–treibenden**, *pl.* tradespeople; **–verein**, m. 1) trades-union; 2) polytechnic society; **–zweig**, m. *see* **G–s**zweig.

Gewerf', *(str.)* n. *Sport. see* Gewäff.

Gewerk', I. *(w.)* m. 1) *a) see* **G–sherr**; *b)* miner; 2) coproprietor (of a mine), partner; owner; II. *(str.)* n. 1) work; 2) manufactory; trade; 3) guild, corporation; trade; **G–endiener**, m. servant *or* clerk to a mining company; **G–antheil**, m. share in a mine; **–haus**, n. manufactory, fabric; **–holz**, n. *Forest. see* Nutzholz; **G–(s)herr, Gewer'ker**, m. 1) master *or* owner of a manufactory; 2) *or* **G–smann**, **G–smeister**, m. manufacturer, maker; **–probirer**, m. assayer to a mine; **G–sgenossenschaft**, *f.* trade-society; **g–smäßig**, *adj.* in the manner of manufactories.

Gewerk'schaft, *(w.) f.* (mining-)company, a company working, a slate-quarry, &c.

Gewe'sen, *pp. of* Sein, *which see;* mein g–er Freund, my friend that was, my former friend; ein g–er Präsident, a past *or* late president; eine g–e Schönheit, a *ci-devant* beauty.

Gewet'te, *(str.)* n. 1) *provinc. (N. G.)* an (inferior) court of justice; 2) the (act *or* practice of) betting.

Gewicht', *s.* I. *(str.)* n. 1) weight; *Phys. & Mech.* gravity: 2) *fig. a)* stress; *b)* weight, importance, consequence, moment; 3) *Sport. see* Geweih; *Comm.-s., &c.* einstehendes —, equality of weight; schweres —, avoirdupois weight; leichtes —, troy weight; nach dem G–e verkaufen, to sell by (the) weight; das — halten, to hold out (sustain) weight; das — nicht haben, to fall short of weight, to be deficient in the weight; am G–e fehlen, to be wanting in weight; am — fehlt ein Pfund, there is a deficiency of one pound in the weight; an — *(Dat.)* ... haben, to weigh; an — *(Dat.)* verlieren, to lose (in the) weight; gutes — geben, to make good weight; falsches — führen, to keep false weights; (einer Sache *[Dat.]*) — geben *or* ein — auf eine Sache legen, 1. to add force to ...; 2. to lay stress upon ..., to attach (great) importance to ...; II. *in comp.* **–eicher**, m. assizer of weights; **–kunst**, **–lehre**, *f.* statics.

Gewich'tig, I. *adj.* weighty: 1) ponderous; 2) of full weight (Vollwichtig); 3) *fig.* important, momentous; forcible; powerful, impressive; influential; II. **G–keit**, *(w.) f.* 1) weight; 2) importance, moment; force, power.

Gewicht'los, *adj.* 1) weightless; 2) *fig.* unimportant.

Gewicht'..., *in comp.* **–macher**, m. a (brass) founder of weights; *Comm.-s.* **G–abgang**, m. *see* **G–smanco**; **G–abnahme**, *f.* loss of weight; **G–abzug**, m. deduction; **G–überschuß**, m. overplus *or* surplus of weight; **G–smanco**, n. underweight, deficiency in the weight; **G–snote**, **G–sspecification**, *f.* bill of weight *or* parcels, specification of weight; **–stange**, *f.* a rope-dancer's pole, poy; **–stein**, m. a stone used for a weight; **G–sverlust**, m. loss in (the) weight; **G–sverzeichniß**, n. *see* **G–snote**; **G–swaaren**, *f. pl.* weighed goods; **G–swissenschaft**, *f. see* **–kunst**; **–voll**, *adj. see* Gewichtig, 2 & 3.

Gewick'el, Gewie'ge, Gewie'her, *(str.)* n. (the act of *[or* repeated]) wrapping, rocking, neighing, &c. *cf.* Wickeln, Wiegen *etc.*

Gewie'rig, *adj. (l. u.)* complying (Gewährend), granting, favourable.

Gewild', *(str.)* n. *collect.* game, deer, beasts.

Gewil'lig, *adj. provinc.* willing (Willig).

Gewillt', *adj.* having an intention, inclined, disposed; ich bin nicht —, I do not intend, have no mind.

Gewim'mel, *(str.)* n. 1) the (act of) crawling about, swarming; 2) swarm, crowd, throng.

Gewim'mer, *(str.)* n. the (act *or* habit of) whimpering, wailing, whining.

Gewim'pert, *adj. Bot.* ciliated.

Gewin'de, *(str.)* n. 1) the (act of) winding, twisting, &c. *cf.* Winden; 2) any twisted thing; winding, coil; twirl; bottom, skein (of thread); whirl (of a snail); maze; *Anat.* labyrinth; 3) twisted *or* plaited ornament; 4) *a)* thread *or* worm (of a screw); *b)* joints, hinges; *c)* bilt; 5) *Mar.* pintles; **–bohrer**, m. 1) (wp. wimble; 2) *Mech.* screw-tap; **–eisen**, n. *T.* iron-cross (in mills); screw-plate; **–fenster**, n. window turning on hinges; **–gang**, m. *T.* thread.

Gewin'dig, *adj. in comp.* with one *or* more windings.

Gewin'ke, *(str.)* n. the ([repeated]) act of) beckoning.

Gewinn', *s.* I. *(str.)* m. 1) the (act of) gaining (a battle, &c.), winning *or* carrying (the day); 2) gain, profit, lucre, produce; winnings; acquisition; *Comm.* advance; return; proceeds; percentage; 3) emolument, advantage; 4) the object (sum) pledged *or* wagered, stake; prize (in a lottery, &c.); der reine —, clear gain, neat-proceeds, net-produce; — abwerfen *or* bringen, to yield (*or* to leave a) profit, to turn to account; — ziehen aus ..., to realise (derive) a profit from, to turn to account; den — davon tragen, to carry the prize; um des G–es willen, for the sake of gain, of interest; *Comm.-s.* — und Verlust-Conto, account of profit and loss; ein sicherer —, a certain percentage; entgangener —, loss of profit; ein unverhoffter —, god-send, wind-fall; mit — verkaufen, to make a good market; to sell to advantage; bei etwas — machen, to make gain of anything.

Gewinn'antheil, *(str.)* m. *Comm.* (super-)dividend, quota.

Gewinn'bar, *adj.* gainable, obtainable, attainable.

Gewinn'..., *in comp.* **–begierde**, *f. see* **–sucht**; **–bringend**, *adj.* profitable, &c. *see* **–reich**.

Gewin'nen, *(str.)* *s.* I. *tr.* 1) to win, to gain, obtain, to carry (the prize, the day, one's cause, &c.); 2) to profit, acquire, get, to earn; 3) to take possession of; to get, take; den Wind *or* die Luv —, *Mar.* to gain the wind; einen Ausgang —, to gain an issue; ein Ende —, to take an end; eine andere Gestalt *or* ein anderes Ansehen —, to assume a different shape *or* aspect; Geschmack an etwas *(Dat.)* —, *see* Abgewinnen; Kenntniß —, to acquire knowledge; Jemands Achtung —, to grow into *or* conciliate (enlist) one's esteem; Kraft —, to gather strength; zu — suchen, *fig.* to court (favour, an alliance, &c.); die Parteien suchen das Bündniß mit dieser Zeitschrift zu —, the parties court the alliance of that journal; damit ist viel gewonnen, that is a great step gained; alle — dabei, all parties are gainers; Jemanden —, to gain, win, persuade one to ...; to prevail upon; für eine Sache —, to win to a cause; für sich —, to enlist (a person) in one's cause, to interest (a person) in one's favour; über sich —, to prevail upon one's self *or* to bring one's self (to do

[illegible]mestication; die — der Thiere und Haus, [do]mestication of animals.

Gewöl'be, (str.) n. 1) Archit. vault, arch, [arch]ed ceiling; vaulted cave, cellar; das — des Himmels, the vault or canopy of heaven; [...] shop, warehouse; 2) — des Gehirns, Anat. [vault] or fornix of the brain; ein — haben, to [keep] a shop.

Gewölb'(e)..., in comp. Archit.-e. —ähn[lich], adj. arch-like; —anfang, m. spring, [spring]ing of a vault; —anfänger, m. springer, [spring]ing-stone (of an arch, &c.); skew-back; —[illegible], m. coat; —bock, m. centering of an [arch]; —bogen, m. arch, vault, arch-work; cope, [cop]ing; —bruch, m. Surg. fracture of the skull; [illegible]; —bedeckung, m. flooded soffits; —fach, [n.] 1) cellular space of a vaulting; 2) [illegible]; —fenster, n. sky-light; —fläche, [f. (äußere)] back of a vault, extrados; (innere) [intr]ados; soffit; —fuge, f. bed, joint; —gurt, [m.] (Praying, Boll & H. 1. 76) girth of columns [sup]porting a vault; —kappe, f. calotte, ogive; [—kr]one, f. top or crown of a vault; —mauer[werk], n. vaulting-masonry, arch-masonry; [—p]feiler, m. flying or arched buttress, (Fr.) [illegible]; —rüstung, f. see —bock; —schenkel, [m.] haunch (hanuch) of an arch; (keilförmige) [...]stein, m. key-stone, arch-stone; —stütze, f. [illegible], flying buttress; —winkel, m. see —[illegible]; —zins, m. shop-rent, storage, house[-rent]; —zwickel, m. spandrel.

Gewölbt, p. a. (cf. Wölben) arched, vaulted-over.

Gewölk', (str.) n. collect. clouds.

Gewölkt, p. a. (cf. Wölken) 1) covered with clouds, cloudy; 2) Herald. nebulee.

Gewöl'le, (str.) n. Zool. hair, feathers, &c.

Gewu'cher, (str.) n. (habitual) usury.

Gewüchs', (str.) n. provinc. for Gewächs.

Gewühl', (str.) n. 1) (the act of) rooting, [burr]owing up (the ground); 2) bustle; crowd, [thr]ong.

Gewun'den, p. a. wound; tortuous (cf. [Winden]); spiral; Herald. torqued; Archit. [tw]isted, serpentine (of columns); g-e Stufen, see Wendeltreppe; Anat. g-er Darm, see Dünndarm.

Gewür'fel, (str.) n. coll. (the act or practice of) playing at dice.

Gewür'felt, p. a. checkered, checked, &c. cf. Würfeln.

Gewür'ge, (str.) n. 1) (the act of) throttling, choking, &c. cf. Würgen; 2) carnage, slaughter, cf. Gemetzel.

Gewürm(e), (str.) n. vermin, reptiles.

Gewürz, s. I. (str.) n. spice, cf. —waare; aromatics; voll —, spicy; II. in comp. —apfel, m. Pomol. brown redstreak; —artig, adj. spicy, aromatic(al); —birne, f. Pomol. aromatic pear; —brühe, f. spiced sauce; —büchse, f. spice-box; —essenz, f. see —tinctur; —essig, m. aromatic vinegar; —fleisch, n. ragout.

Gewürzhaft, Gewürzhaltig, I. adj. spicy, aromatic; II. Gewürzhaftigkeit, (w.) f. spicy quality, aroma.

Gewürz..., in comp. —handel, m. spice-trade, grocery; —händler, m. see —krämer; —handlung, f. grocery, grocer's shop; —inseln, f. pl. Spice-islands; —kammer, f. spicery; —kram, spices (grocery) for retail; —krämer, m. spicer, grocer; —krämerkrätze, f. Med. a kind of psoriasis; —kuchen, m. spiced ginger-bread; —kümmel, m. fennel-flower seed; —laden, m. spicery, grocer's shop; —mühle, f. spice-mill; —myrte, f. Bot. pimento, all-spice, Jamaica-pepper (Myrtus pimenta L.); —nägelein, n., —nelke, f. clove, all-spice; —nelkenbaum, m. all-spice tree, clove-tree (Caryophyllus aromaticus L.); —nelkenöl, n. oil of cloves; —reich, adj. rich in spices; aromatic, spicy; —rindenbaum, m. Bot. drimys (Drimys Winteri L.); —schachtel, f. see —büchse; —staude, f. spice, aromatic plant; —stein, m. Miner. [illegible]; —stoffe, m. pl. aromatic stuffs; —strauch, m. Bot. Carolinian all-spice tree (Calycanthus floridus L.); —tinctur, f. aromatic tincture; —waare, f. spice, spicery; grocery-ware, groceries; —wein, m. spiced or aromatic wine.

Gezä'he, (str.) n. Min. see Gezeug.

Gezäh'nelt, adj. Bot., &c. set with little teeth, denticulate, toothleted, jagged (leaves, &c.).

Gezahnt', Gezähnt', adj. Bot., Mech., &c. toothed; dentate; g-e Räder, cog-wheels.

Gezänk'(e), (str.) n. continual quarrelling; quarrel, dispute, contention, squabble.

Gezap'pel, (str.) n. the (act or practice of) kicking, striving with the feet, fidgeting, &c.

Gezau'der, (str.) n. the (act of) tarrying, lingering, loitering; (habitual) delay.

Gezäum', (str.) n. collect. a bridle and all the straps or ligaments belonging to it.

Gezau'se, (str.) n. the (act of) pulling about, cf. Zausen.

Gezech', (str.) n. hard drinking, drinking bout.

Gezeit', (w.) f. Mar. tide, flood-tide; die — läuft Süd, the sea sets to the south; G-en, pl. Rom. Cath. hours: G-enbuch, n. breviary.

Gezelt', (str.) n. († &) *, pavilion, tabernacle, tent; canopy, cf. Zelt.

Gezerr', (str.) n. a (continual) pulling, dragging &c. cf. Zerren.

Gezé'ter, (str.) n. (anxious or furious) cries, yell of murder, &c. cf. Zeter.

Gezeug', (str.) n. collect. tools, implements; Min. (Kunst—) tools for pit-work; see Zeug, Werkzeug; —kasten, m. tool-chest.

Gezie'fer, (str.) n. (l. u.) collect. insects, vermin, see Ungeziefer.

Gezie'ge, adj. Min., &c. 1) fusible; 2) soft, malleable.

Gezie'he, (str.) n. the ([repeated] act of) drawing (about), &c., (a continued) drawing, pulling, &c. cf. Ziehen.

Gezie'men, (w.) v. intr. impers. (with Dat.) & refl. to become, beseem, to be decent, meet, seemly, or fit, to befit; es geziemt ihm nicht, it does not become him; es geziemt sich nicht, it is unseemly (für, for); wie es sich geziemt, as decency requires it, as it ought to be.

Gezie'mend, p. a. becoming, due, proper, fit, suitable, decent, seemly; sich — aufführen, to behave (one's self) with propriety.

Geziem'lich, adj. see Schicklich & Ziemlich.

Gezie're, (str.) n. affected behaviour, affectation, affectedness, primness, cf. Zierrerei.

Geziert', I. p. a. affected; finical, prim; quaint; dainty; slang, namby-pamby, cf. Zimperlich; — sprechen, to mince one's words, to speak mincingly; II. G-heit, (w.) f. affectedness, &c., affectation, cf. Zimperlichkeit.

Gezim'mer, (str.) n. 1) (the act of) building, framing, the forming of timber-work; 2) frame-work, timber-work, carpenter's work.

Gezirp', Gezisch', Gezisch'el, Gezit'ter, (str.) n. (the [repeated] act of) chirping, hissing, whispering, &c. cf. Zirpen, Zischeln &c.

Gezo'gen, p. a. (cf. Ziehen) eine g-e Büchse, a rifled gun: der g-e Lauf, das g-e Rohr, rifled barrel; ein g-es Licht, dipped candle, dip; (opp. gegossene Licht) see in Giessen; g-e Federn, g-e Kiele, hardened or prepared quills (for writing); g-e Wechselbriefe, drawn bills (opp. Sola-Wechsel); der g-e Galopp, main or full gallop.

Gezücht', (str.) n. (usually of animals, or cont. of persons) breed, offspring, progeny, issue; brood.

Gezüng'elt, adj. Herald. lambent (lion).

Gezüng'el, Gezupf'e, Gezwack'e, Gezwicke &c., (str.) n. a quick motion of the tongue (like that of a snake); the ([repeated] act of) pulling, &c.; a (repeated) pinching, nipping, &c. cf. Züngeln, Zupfen &c.

Gezweig', (str.) n. collect. boughs, branches.

Gezweigt', adj. branched, having branches.

Gezweit', adj. consisting of two parts or unition, double; binary; Bot. bipartite.

Gezwit'scher, (str.) n. (the act of) chirping, cheerful noise of birds, chirp, twitter.

Gezwölft', adj. of or in twelve parts.

Gezwung'en, I. p. a. forced: 1) compelled, &c. (cf. Zwingen); compulsory; 2) constrained, stiff, precise, formal; uneasy; affected, unnatural; — lachen, to force a laugh; II. G-heit, (w.) f. forcedness; 1) state of being compelled, compulsion; 2) a) constraint, stiffness, &c.; b) affected manners, affectation, stiff airs.

G(h)ibelli'ne, (w.) m. Germ. Hist. Ghibelline.

Gibraltär, n. Geogr. Gibraltar.

Gi'bushut, (str., pl. G-hüte) m. crush-hat.

A. Gicht, (w.) f. gout, arthritis; laufende —, flying gout; reißende —, articular disease; — in den Hüften, hip-gout.

B. Gicht, (w.) f. Metall. 1) the quantity of iron-ore and charcoal poured into the furnace at once; charge; 2) mouth, throat, furnace-top; — aufgeben, aufziehen, — laufen, to charge the furnace; —brücke, f. bridge over the furnace; G-gang, m. descent of the charge (Hartmann); —haus, n. top of a furnace; —mantel, m. crown, dome (of a blast furnace); —öffnung, f. tunnel-head (of a smelting-furnace).

C. Gicht, (w.) f. († &) Law, avowal, confession.

Gicht'..., in comp. —anfall, m. attack of the gout; —artig, adj. gouty, arthritic; —balsam, m. arthritic balsam; —beere, f. see Johannisbeere, schwarze, & Traubenkirsche; —blume, f. see Schlüsselblume; —bruch, m. palsy; —brüchig, adj. paralytic, palsied; —brüchige, m. & f. (decl. like adj.) a palsied person, paralytic; —brüchigkeit, f. palsy.

A. Gich'ten, (w.) v. tr. †, to torture into confession.

B. Gich'ten, (w.) v. intr. coll. to suffer from gout.

Gicht'..., in comp. —fieber, n. arthritic fever; —fisch, m. Ichth. a species of scaly-finned fish (Chaetodon Cuv.); —heilend, —lindernd, adj. antarthritic.

Gich'tig, adj. 1) †, see Geständig; 2) see Gichtisch.

Gich'tisch, adj. arthritic, arthritical, gouty; having (or being diseased with) the gout.

Gicht'..., in comp. —knoten, m. Med. tophus; —kolik, f. arthritic gripes, gout in the stomach; —körner, n. pl. grains of peony; —krank, adj. gouty, ill of the gout; —kraut, n. plants (said to be) good for curing the gout, see Darmgichtkraut & Moosbeere; —leiden, n. gouty affection; —materie, f. see —stoff; —mittel, n. antarthritic; —morchel, f. Bot. stinkhorn (Phallus impudicus L.); —papier, n. rheumatic paper, gout paper; —pflaster, n. antarthritic plaster, cf. —papier; —pille, f. goutpill; —pilz, m. see —morchel; —pulver, n. antarthritic powder; —rose, f. Bot. peony (Paeonia officinalis L.); —rübe, f. white bryony (Bryonia alba L.); —schmerzen, m. pl. pains (shoots, twinges) of the gout; —schwamm, m. 1) see —morchel; 2) Miner. see Giftstein; —stoff, m. gouty matter; —taffet, m. see Gesundheitstaffet; —tanne, f. Bot. wild rosemary (Ledum palustre L.); —thran, m. see Lebertran; —wasser, n. antarthritic water; —wurz, f. dittany (Dictamnus albus L.).

Gick'gack, (str.) n. coll. 1) cackle, cackling noise of a goose; 2) a (cackling) goose.

Gie'be, (w.) f. 1) Fin.-m. reel, wheel (for winding off and straightening the wire); 2) Weav. beam of a loom.

Gie'bel, s. I. (str.) m. 1) gable, gable-end; Archit. frontispiece; pediment; fronton; 2) m. (& (w.) f.) Ichth. see Giebel, &c.; II. in comp. —ähre, f. iron gable-ear; —balken, m. top-timber or -beam; —bogen, m. triangular arch; —dach, n. gabled roof; —façade, f. frontispiece-face; —feld, n. tympan, pedi-

[illegible] —stock, m. rubber (of card-makers); —[illegible], n. reduction of litharge to lead; —[illegible], n. sleeking- or smoothing-glass; —haken, hook (of leadmakers); —hammer, m. [illegible] smoothing-hammer.

[illegible]heit, (w.) f. see Glätte.

[illegible]..., in comp. —hobel, m. smoothing-plane; Join. jointer; —holz, n. polishing-[illegible]; —horn, n. polishing-stick; —kalender [illegible]kalender), m. T. friction-calender; —[illegible], f. (glass-)sleeker; —kolben, m. burnisher, Bookb., &c. polishing-iron; —kugel, f. [illegible]-ball for smoothing.

[illegible], adj. half-smooth.

Glättling, (str.) m. see Schmeichler.

[illegible]..., in comp. —linnen, n. sleeked [illegible]; —maschine, —mühle, f. calendering machine; —platte, f. Paper-m. sleeking-stone; [illegible], f. calender, smoothing press; —[illegible], —scheine, f. Shoe-m. sleeking-stone; [illegible], m. polisher; —stahl, m. burnishing-steel, burnisher; —stein, m. sleek-stone, sleeking-stone; —stube, f. sleeking-room; [illegible]-room; —werkzeug, n. sleeking- or [illegible]-tool; —zahn, m. wolf's or dog's [illegible], polishing tooth, burnisher.

[illegible], (w.) f. baldness, calvity, coll. bald [illegible].

[illegible], Glatzköpfig, adj. bald, bald-pated.

[illegible]kopf, (str., pl. G-köpfe) m. coll. bald-[illegible] person.

[illegible], adj. provinc. clear, bright; brisk, [illegible], quick; clear, sharp-sighted; —äugig, [illegible] bright-eyed; sharp-sighted.

Glaub'bar, I. adj. credible, see Glaublich; [illegible] G-keit, (w.) f. see Glaublichkeit.

Glau'be, (irr.), Glau'ben, (str.) m. 1) [illegible]; faith (an [with Acc.], in); 2) credit, [illegible]; 3) religious faith, religion; (G-s-bekenntniß) creed, profession; Treue und —, [illegible] faith; in gutem —, in good faith, bona [illegible]; —, Liebe, Hoffnung, faith, hope, and [illegible]; der christliche —, the Christian faith; [illegible] G-n abfallen, to desert from one's faith, [illegible]; auf (Treue und) G-n, on trust; [illegible] allen G-n verloren, he has lost all credit; [illegible] (einer Sache [Dat.]) G-n beimessen or [illegible], to give credit (or credence) to, to [illegible] credit to, to put faith in ..., to credit; [illegible], dazu gehört ein starker —, that is [illegible] to be believed; der — wird ihm an die [illegible] kommen, experience will teach him; [illegible], adj. firm in one's (religious) belief.

Glau'ben, (w.) v. tr. (& intr.) 1) to believe [illegible] (with Acc.], in); to trust, to credit; 2) to [illegible], suppose; to imagine; Einem (etwas) —, [illegible] believe one; ich kann es ihm nicht —, I cannot believe him; — machen, to make believe, [illegible] to believe; einen Gott —, to believe [illegible] God; an Gott —, to believe in God; ich [illegible] wohl, I am inclined to believe, I dare [illegible]; er glaubt nicht so leicht, he is no easy [illegible]; ich glaube, daß es eine Fabel ist, I [illegible] it to be a fiction; das kann ich nicht —, I [illegible] not believe that; wer — Sie, daß ich bin [illegible] (für wen halten Sie mich)? who do you [illegible] I am? whom do you take me for? Sie [illegible] nicht ...? you do not suppose ...? man [illegible], it is thought; man glaubt von ihm, daß [illegible] he is thought (suspected) to ...; er mußte [illegible] —, coll. 1. he could not escape his fate, [illegible] to die; 2. he had to suffer heavily; [illegible] was obliged to submit or to truckle.

[illegible]bens..., in comp. —abfall, m. apostasy; —artikel, m. article of faith or of the [illegible]; pl. credenda; —bekenner, m. confessor [illegible] religion; —bekenntniß, n. confession of [illegible], profession, symbol; —bote, m. apostle, [illegible]; —bruder, m. brother in faith, cf. [illegible]; —bund, m. Script. covenant, testament; —eifer, m. (religious) zeal; —eiferer, [illegible]; —eifrig, adj. zealous; —einheit, f. unity in faith; —feurig, adj. see —eifrig; —flüchtling, m. refugee on account of his religion; —form, f. form of faith, creed; —formel, f. confession of faith; —freiheit, f. religious liberty; —freudigkeit, f. boldness, confidence (from faith); —frucht, f. fruit of faith, i. e. good works; —genoß, m. co-religionist; cf. —bruder; —genossenschaft, f. conformity of faith; —gericht, n. inquisition; —grund, m. foundation or argument of faith; —held, m. hero or champion of faith; —heuchler, m. religious hypocrite; —irrthum, m. error in matters of faith; —lehre, f. doctrine of faith; 1) system of religion; dogmatics; 2) see —satz; —lehrling, m. catechumen.

Glau'benslos, adj. unbelieving, sceptical.

Glau'bens..., in comp. —meinung, f. opinion in matters of faith; —menger, m. syncretist; —mengerei, f. syncretism; —opfer, n. victim of or for faith; —partei, f. religious sect or party; —pflicht, f. religious duty; —probe, f. religious test; —regel, f. rule of faith; —reich, adj. full of faith; ein —reicher Schwärmer (Schiller), an enthusiastic visionary; —reiniger, m. reformer (of religion); —reinigung, f. reformation (of the church); —richter, m. inquisitor; —sache, f. matter of faith; —satz, m. dogma, established tenet, doctrine; —schwärmer, m. religious enthusiast, fanatic; —schwärmerei, f. religious enthusiasm, fanaticism; —schwärmerisch, adj. fanatical; —scrupel, m. see —zweifel; —streit, m. dispute concerning faith, controversy; —streiter, m. champion of faith; —treue, f. constancy in faith; —verbesserer, m., —verbesserung, f. see —reiniger, —reinigung; —verfassung, f. 1) system of faith; 2) constitution respecting matters of faith; —verläugner, m. renegade, apostate; —verwandte, m. see —genoß; —verwandtschaft, f. see —genossenschaft; —voll, adj. full of faith; —vorschrift, f. see —regel; —warm, adj. see —eifrig; —weise, f. creed; —werber, m. proselyte-maker; missionary; —werberei, f. proselytism; —wissenschaft, f. theology; —wuth, f. excessive religious frenzy, fanaticism; —wüthig, adj. religiously frantic, fanatical; —zeuge, m. martyr; —zunft, f. sect; —zünftelei, f. sectarianism; —zünftler, m. sectarian; —zuversicht, f. confidence of faith; —zwang, m. coercion of faith, intolerance; —zweifel, m. doubts of faith, scepticism; —zweifler, m. sceptic; —zwist, m. see —streit.

Glau'bersalz, (str.) n. Chem. Glauber's salt (sulphate of soda).

Glaub'haft, I. or Glaub'haftig, adj. credible, authentic; ein g-es Zeugniß, an authentic or unquestionable testimony; II. G-igkeit, (w.) f. credibility, authenticity; probability.

Gläu'big, adj. 1) believing (easily), having faith; undoubting; 2) devout, faithful; G-e, m. & f. (decl. like adj.) (faithful) believer; righteous person; die G-en, believing men, the faithful.

Gläu'bigen, Glau'bigen, (w.) v. tr. (Göthe, l. u.) to impress with a strong belief, to confirm.

Gläu'biger, (str.) m. Comm. & Law, creditor; G-in, (w.) f. creditrix.

Glaub'lich, I. adj. credible, creditable; probable, likely; II. G-keit, (w.) f. credibility; probability, likelihood.

Glaub'würdig, I. adj. credible; authentic(al); trustworthy; g-e Nachrichten haben, to be credibly informed; II. G-keit, (w.) f. credibility; authenticity; trustworthiness.

Glauch, adj. Min. 1) greenish, sea-green; 2) dead, containing no metal (cf. Taub); 3) provinc. smart, neat, pretty; —erz, n. Min. sterile ore; —herd, m. 1) T. wash-bench; 2) Sport. little fowling-floor.

Glau'kopf, (str.) m. provinc. see Glatzkopf.

Gle'be, (w.) f. Husb. a handful of corn-stalks (to form the sheaf).

Gleditsch'ie, (w.) f. see Schotendorn.

Gleich, I. adj. (s.) & adv. (with Dat.) 1) like, alike, same; similar; 2) equal; coll-s. 3) even, level, plain; 4) direct, straight, just; 5) adequate, proportional; 6) even (number); der Erde —, even with the ground; — vor dem Gesetze, equal before the law; des g-en Namens, of the same name; fünf weniger vier ist — eins, five less four is equal to one; g-en Antheil haben, to have an equal share, to share alike; auf g-e Weise, in like manner; auf ganz g-e Weise, all alike; zu g-er Zeit, at the same time; auf g-er Höhe sein or stehen, to be upon a level; der g-e Fuß or Werth, Comm. par; auf g-em Fuße, upon the same level; upon the same terms; in g-em Werth, at par; von g-em Umfange, co-extensive; von g-em Werthe, equivalent; wir sind nicht von g-em Stande, we are not equals; g-es Wesens, co-essential, consubstantial; stets sich (Dat.) —, always the same, unvarying; undeviating; sich (Dat.) — bleiben, to remain the same, to suffer no change or alteration; to be consistent with one's self; to go regularly (of clocks, watches); er bleibt sich immer —, he is always like himself; das bleibt sich —, that is the same; sich — bleibend, uniform, consistent; sich nicht — bleiben, to vary, alter, fluctuate; to be inconsistent; — denken, to agree, (g-er Ansicht sein) to be of the same opinion (über [with Acc.], on, about); — gelten, to be equivalent (to), see — sein; — kommen (with Dat.), to equal, match, come up to ... or with ...; to be equivalent (to); nicht — kommen, to be (come or fall) short of; dem nichts — kommt, unparalleled, cf. ohne G-en; — machen, to equal, equalise; to even, level, to make level, to bring to one level; dem Boden — machen, to level with the ground; — sein, 1. (with Dat. or mit) to be equal or equivalent (to), to be on (upon) a par (with ...), cf. — kommen; 2. (impers.) to be indifferent (to one); es ist mir (Alles) —, it is all one (equal, or the same) to me; das ist — viel, that is all the same; — viel, wer es gesagt hat, no matter who said so; es ist ihm Alles —, nothing affects him; he scruples at nothing; — stehen, to stand or be upon a par or level, cf. — sein, 1; — stellen, to place on a par, to put on a level (Einem or einer Sache [Dat.], with ...), to put on a footing of (or upon an) equality; sich Einem — stellen, to put one's self in a parallel with one; es Einem — thun, to equal, match, cf. — kommen; es Einem — thun wollen, to vie with ..., to emulate; meines, deines, seines G-en, my, your, his like or equals; wie mit seines G-en, as equal with equal, on terms of equality; dessen G-en, the like of which; von seines G-en gerichtet werden, to be tried by one's peers; er hat nicht seines G-en, he has not his like; seines G-en suchen (i. e. nicht haben), ohne G-en sein, to be without a parallel, to be matchless, unrivalled, unparalleled, unprecedented, unmatched, unique; ins G-e bringen or setzen, to bring to a level, to equalise; to set (things) right; ich will ein G-es für dich thun, I will do as much for you; (Einem) G-es mit G-em vergelten, or (Einem) mit g-er Münze bezahlen, to render (do or give) like for like, to retaliate in kind; — und — gesellt sich gern, proverb. birds of a feather flock together, like draws to like, every like loves his like.

II. adv. 1) like, alike; 2) equally, &c. cf. I.; — alt, of the same age; — ewig, equally eternal (with ...), co-eternal; — (weit) entfernt, (being) equally distant, equidistant; — schwer or wichtig, of equal weight, (equi-)poised; 3) just; — als ob, — als wenn, [illegible]

[illegible]

(or Als) as if, just as; — wie, as, even as, just as; 4) adv. (for Sogleich; sofort) directly, straightway(s); immediately, presently; ich bin — fertig, I have just done; — bar zahlen, to pay down; to pay ready money (cash); — zu Anfang, — anfangs, at the very beginning, on the outset; — bei der Hand, ready at hand; es ist — zwölf, it is upon the turn of twelve; wie heißt er doch —? what is his name (again)? — zu, see Geradezu.

III. conj. though, although; bin ich — noch jung, though I still am young.

Gleich'..., *in comp.* —abständig, —abstehend, *adj.* equidistant; —abständigkeit, *f.* equidistance; —ähnlich, *adj.* similar; congruent; —alterig, *adj.* of the same age, *cf.* —zeitig; —armig, *adj.* having equal arms; —artig, *adj.* of the same kind, congener, homogeneous; analogous, similar; congenial; *coll.* (all) of a piece; —artigkeit, *f.* sameness of nature, homogeneousness; similarity; congeniality.

Gleich'bar, *adj.* comparable.

Gleich'..., *in comp.* —bedeutend, *adj.* having the same meaning, identical in meaning, synonymous, convertible; —bedeutung, *f.* sameness of meaning; —bein, *n.* *Anat.* see Gelenkbein; —berechtigt, *adj.* equally entitled; enjoying the same privileges *or* rights; —betrag, *m.* equal amount, tantamount, equivalent; —breit, *adj.* of the same breadth; *Bot.* linear; —bürtig, *see* Ebenbürtig; —denkend, *adj.* (a)like-minded, of the same mind *or* opinion, agreeing; congenial; —deutig, *adj.* synonymous; —deutigkeit, *f.* synonymy.

Glei'che, *(w.) f.* 1) equalness; 2) evenness (*cf.* Gleichheit).

Gleich'..., *in comp.* —eck, *n.* *Geom.* isagon; —empfindend, *adj.* sympathetic.

Glei'chen, *v.* I. *(str.) intr.* (*with Dat.*) 1) to equal, be equal to ..., to match, *cf.* Gleich kommen; 2) to resemble, to be like; er gleicht ihm nicht, he is not like him; II. *(w.) tr.* 1) to equalise, to make equal *or* like; 2) to adjust (the weight of coins, &c.); 3) to make even *or* plain, to level, smooth; 4) († &) *, to compare, liken; 5) *T.* see Justiren; Eichen.

Gleich'entfernt, *adj.* equidistant.

Glei'cher, *(str.) m.* 1) *T.*, &c. flattener, smoother; 2) *Astr.* equator, equinoctial line; —höhe, *f.* see Meridianshöhe.

Gleich'..., *in comp.* —ewig, *adj.* co-eternal; —fallend, *adj.* *Comm.* even; —falls, *conj.* likewise, also, too; —farbig, *adj.* of the same colour, isochromatic; —farbigkeit, *f.* sameness of colour; —fassen, *(w.) v. tr.* *Hatt.* to press out (a hat) by the blunt edge of a stamper; —fließend, *adj.* see —lautend, 1; —förmig, *adj.* 1) conformable, having the same form, uniform; *fig.* &c. 2) equable, even, equal and uniform at all times (as motion); —förmig beschleunigt, *Mech.* uniformly accelerated; 3) *a)* equal, uniform, agreeing; *b)* same, *cf.* Einförmig, 2; —förmig machen, to reduce to the same form, manner, *or* character (mit, with), to conform (to); —förmig buchen, vortragen, *or* notiren, *Comm.* to note *or* to pass in conformity; —förmigkeit, *f.* 1) conformity, equiformity, uniformity; congruity; proportion; *fig.* &c. 2) equability, evenness (of motion, temper, &c.); 3) *a)* equality, uniformity, agreement; *b)* consistency; *c)* sameness, *cf.* Einförmigkeit, 2; —fühlend, *adj.* sympathising; —geartet, *adj.* see —artig; —gefühl, *n.* sympathy; —geltend, *adj.* equivalent, tantamount (to); —gesinnt, *adj.* having the same mind, fellow-believer, *cf.* —denkend; —gestaltet, *adj.* equal or similar as to form, *Cryst.* isomorphous; —gestaltigkeit, *f.* sameness *or* equality of form, *Cryst.* isomorphism; —gestimmt, *adj.* 1) equally tuned; 2) congenial, *cf.* —gesinnt; —getheilt, *p. a.* divided into equal parts, equidivided; *Phys.* isomeric; *cf.* —theilig; —gewicht, *n.* 1) *a)* equilibrium, equipoise, (even) balance; *b)* proportion; *c)* *fig.* balance of power; das europäische —gewicht, *Polit.* the balance of power of Europe; *Mar.* &c. trim (of a ship); aus dem —gewicht, out of trim (said of the cargo); ins —gewicht setzen *or* bringen, to equipoise, poise, equilibrate, (*Mar.*) to trim; das —gewicht wieder herstellen, *fig.* to redress the balance; das —gewicht aufheben, to turn the scale; im —gewicht erhalten, to balance equally, to poise; aus dem —gewicht kommen, to lose its balance; (einer Sache [*Dat.*] &c.) das —gewicht halten, to counterpoise (a thing); im —gewicht ruhend, poised; —gewichtslehre, *f.* *Phys.* statics; —gewichtspunkt, *m.* centre of gravity; —gewichtsstange, *f.* balancing-pole, poy; —gewichtsventil, *n.* *Mech.* equilibrium valve; —gradig, *adj.* *T.* having equal degrees, *cf.* —getheilt; —gültig, *adj.* 1) equivalent, equal; 2) *fig.* indifferent (gegen, für, to); insensible (to, of), unconcerned (about); listless, apathetic; careless, regardless (of); unimportant; das ist mir —gültig, that's all the same to me; sie ist mir —gültig, I do not care about her; —gültigkeit, *f.* 1) equalness, equivalence; 2) indifference, &c.

Gleich'heit, *(w.) f.* 1) *a)* equality, equalness; *b)* parity (of numbers, &c.); *c)* sameness; 2) *coll.* evenness, levelness; 3) *a)* conformity; just proportion; *b)* resemblance, likeness; 4) uniformity (in weights and measures); — des Wechselcourses, *Comm.* par of exchange; G-szeichen, *n.* sign of equation [=].

Gleich'..., *in comp.* —hoch, *adj.* of the same height; *Bot.* fastigiate(d); —jährig, *adj.* of the same age; —klang, *m.* conformity of sound, consonance, *cf.* —laut; —klingend, *see* —lautend, 1; —ländisch, *adj.* of the same country; —lang, *adj.* of the same length; —langzeitig, *adj.* of equal time; isochronal; —lastig, *adj.* *Mar.* upon an even keel; —lauf, *m.* parallelism; —laufend, *adj.* 1) *or* —läufig, having the same course, parallel, regular; 2) *fig.* *see* —förmig; —läufigkeit, *f.* *see* —lauf; —laut, *m.* equality *or* sameness of sound, unison; consonance; assonance; *Rhet.* paronomasia; —lautend, I. *adj.* 1) of the same sound or pitch, unisonous; consonant; assonant; 2) of the same tenor (and date) *or* contents, *cf.* —förmig, 3, &c.; —lautend sein, to agree; —lautende Abschrift, duplicate, counterpart; true copy; II. *adv.* *Comm.* conformably, in conformity; —macher, *m.* evener, leveller, equaliser; *Typ.* justifier; —macherei, *f.* and. *fig.* levelling-system; —machung, *f.* equalisation, &c.; assimilation; —maß, *n.* proportion, symmetry; commensuration; —mäßig, *adj.* proportionable, symmetrical, uniform, equal; similar; —mäßige Bewegung, isochronism (of a pendulum); *cf.* —förmig, *fig.*; —mäßigkeit, *f.* proportionableness, equability, symmetry, &c. *cf.* —förmigkeit, *fig.*; —meßbar, *adj.* *Math.* commensurable; —meßbarkeit, *f.* commensurability; —messer, *m.* *see* Gleicher, 2; —muth, *m.*, —müthigkeit, *f.* equanimity, equability *or* evenness of temper, serenity, imperturbation, *cf.* —gültigkeit, 2; —müthig, *adj.* even-tempered; —namig, *adj.* having the same name, homonymous; *Math.* homologous, correspondent; —namigkeit, *f.* sameness of name, homonymy.

Gleich'niß, *(str.) n.* 1) † similitude, likeness; 2) comparison; simile; 3) *or* —rede, *f.* parable, allegory; —weise, *adv.* by way of simile, allegorically, parabolically; —wort, *n.* figurative expression, rhetorical figure.

Gleich'richten, *(str.) n.* *T.* 1) stretching out (of cloth in the breadth); 2) *Hatt.* wrapping up and rolling the felt.

Gleich'sam, *adv.* as it were, (even) so as, like as if, as though (it were) almost.

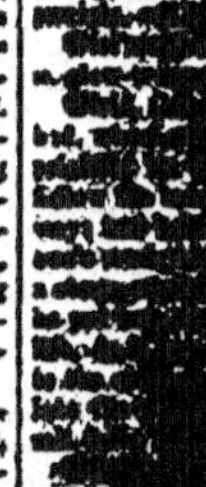

Gleiß'en, *(str. & w.) v. intr.* 1) to shine, glisten, glitter: 2) *fig.* to play the hypocrite; [illegible]; g-d, *p. a. see* Gleißnerisch.

Gleiß'hammer, *(str.) m. see* Gleißhammer.

Gleiß'ling, *(str.) m. see* Gleiße, 1.

Gleiß'ner, *(str.) m.,* **Gleiß'nerin,** *(w.) f.* dissembler, hypocrite, double-dealer, pharisee.

Gleißnerei', *(w.) f.* hypocrisy, dissimulation, double-dealing, pharisaism.

Gleiß'nerisch, *adj.* dissembling, feigned, hypocritical, pharisaical.

Gleit'..., *in comp.* —walze, *f.* road-roller; —wurm, *m. see* Glitschwurm.

Gleit', *(w.) f. T.* slide, shoot.

Gleit'bahn, *(w.) f.* slide (as on the ice), sliding-place: *Mech.* slide-bar.

Glei'ten, *(str. & [l. u.] w.) v. intr. (aux.* sein & haben) to glide, slide; to slip; g-de Reime, rhyming dactyls.

Gleit'stuhl, *(str., pl.* G-stühle) *m. Railw.* [illegible]-chair.

Glet'scher, *(str.) m.* ice-mountain, glacier; —gallerie, *f.* glacier-gallery; —gebläse, *n.* glacier-blast.

Glied, *a.* I. *(str., pl.* G-er) *n.* 1) *Anat. a)* limb, member, joint: *b)* joint, knuckle: *pl.* members, frame, body; 2) *Mil.* rank, file; 3) *Math. & Log.* term; particle: 4) *Archit.* member: 5) *Bot.* article (the part of an articulated stem lying between two knots); 6) ring, link, shank (of a chain); 7) degree, generation; Vettern im dritten G-e, third cousins; 8) member, fellow (of a society, &c.); das männliche —, *penis, membrum virile,* a man's privy member; doppelte G-er, *Med.* rhachitis, rickets; *Mil.-s.* Soldaten in G-er stellen, to rank soldiers; G-er formiren, to fall in: die G-er schließen, to double the file; in G-ern marschiren, to march by files, to file; im G-e bleiben, to keep the ranks; aus dem G-e treten, to quit the ranks; — für —, link by link: die äußeren G-er eines Verhältnisses, *Math.* extremes: II. *in comp.* —bad, *n.* partial bath: —buße, *f. Anc. Law,* indemnification for injury done to any particular member of the body.

Glied'chen, *(str.) n. (dimin. of* Glied, *pl.* *coll.* Glie'derchen) small limb, link, &c.

Glie'der..., *in comp.* —band, *m. Anat.* ligament; —bau, *m.* structure of the limbs, articulation: von starkem —bau, strong-limbed: —[illegible], *f. pl. see* —reißen; —brand, *m.* a disease in the bones of animals; —[illegible], *f. see* —[illegible]; —fluß, *m. see* —reißen; —frucht, *f. see* —hülse; —fuge, *f. T.* joint, juncture: —geist, *m.* antarthritic water; —geschwulst, *f.* swelling of the limbs: —gicht, *f.* articular disease, (joint) gout; —haken, —halter, *m.* *T.* swivel-hook, *cf.* Wurf; —hülse, *f. Bot.* loment, lomentum. [strong-limbed.

Glie'derig, *adj. in comp.* -limbed; stark—,

Glie'der..., *in comp.* —kette, *f.* chain with links; —knöchel, *m. Anat.* knuckle, joint (of the limbs); —krank, *adj.* gouty; —krankheit, *f.* articular disease; —kraut, *n. see* Gliedkraut; —lahm, *adj.* palsied, paralytic; —lähme, —lähmung, *f.* paralysis, palsy; —mann, *m.,* —puppe, *f.* swivel-doll; automaton, dummy; [illegible], lay-figure, lay-man.

Glie'dern, *(w.) v. tr.* 1) to furnish with limbs, to limb; 2) *Mil.* to form into files or ranks; 3) to organize, *cf.* Gegliedert, 3.

Glie'der..., *in comp.* —reißen, *n.,* —[illegible], *m.,* —weh, *n.* violent pain in the joints *or* limbs, (joint) gout, rheumatism; [illegible]. —salbe, *f.* antarthritic salve; —[illegible], *m. see* Gliedschwamm, 1; —schwinden, *n.* atrophy (of the limbs); —spannen, *n.* [illegible], cramp; —stärkend, *adj.* tonic; —[illegible], *n.* [illegible]; —thiere, *n. pl.* articulata (*Articulata* L.).

Glie'derung, *(w.) f.* systematical arrangement, form, *or* construction of parts, organisation.

Glie'der..., *in comp.* —wasser, *n. see* Gliedwasser; —weh, *n. see* —reißen; —wein, *m.* antarthritic wine: —weise, *adv.* 1) by joints, by limbs; 2) by files, by ranks.

Glied'..., *in comp. Bot.-s.* —kraut, *n.* iron wort, bastard hoarhound (*Sideritis* L.); —länge, *f. see* Teufelsabbiß.

Glied'lich, *adj. (unusual)* relating to the member of a society.

Glied'los, *adj.* without members *or* limbs.

Glied'maßen, *(w.) n. (pl. sing. orig. str.; rarely: [w.] f.* Gliedmaße) limbs, members (of the body).

Glied'schaft, *(w.) f.* corporation.

Glied'..., *in comp.* —schwamm, *m.* 1) *Med.* white swelling; 2) *Bot.* stinkhorn (Gichtschwamm); —stein, *m. Miner.* prinapolite; —wasser, *n. Anat.* lymphatic humour: synovia; —wassersucht, *f.* hydropsy, dropsy; —weise, *adv. Mil.* in files, in divisions.

Gli'me, *(w.) f. coll. see* Engerling.

Glimm, *(S. G.)* I. *s. (str.) m.* spark; II. *adj.* sparkling, glowing.

Glim'men, *(str. & w.) v. intr.* to burn or shine faintly, to glimmer, glow, gleam, sparkle: unter der Asche —, to lie hid *or* to be concealed under the ashes; g-de Asche, embers.

Glim'mer, I. *(str.) m.* 1) *provinc.* gleam, glimmer; 2) *Miner.* glimmer, mica; II. *in comp.* —artig, *adj.* micaceous; —blättchen, *n. pl.* scales of mica; —erde, *f.* micaceous earth, mica; —haltig, *adj.* micaceous.

Glim'merig, *adj.* 1) glimmering, glittering; 2) *Miner.* micaceous.

Glim'mer..., *in comp.* —käfer, *m. Entom.* sparkler (Glühwurm); —kalk, *m.* micaceous lime. [glimmern.

Glim'mern, *(w.) v. intr.* to glimmer: *see*

Glim'mer..., *in comp.* —sand, *m.* micaceous sand; —schiefer, *m.* mica-slate, mica-schist; —thon, *m.* micaceous clay.

Glimpf, *(str.) m.* moderation, lenity, mildness, indulgence; mit —, mildly, gently: Fug und —, right and justice.

Glimpf'lich, *adj.* moderate, gentle, kind.

Glin'stern, Glin'zen, Glis'tern, *(w.) v. intr. provinc. see* Glitzern.

Glis, *(str.) m. Miner.* amber.

Glitsch'e, *(w.) f. coll.* slide.

Glitsch'en, *(w.) v. intr. (aux.* sein & haben) *coll.* to glide quickly, *cf.* Gleiten.

Glitsch'er, *(str.) m.* 1) slider; 2) *Bot.* yellow-rattle (*Rhinanthus* L.).

Glitsch'fuß, *(str.) m. Entom.* vine-moth (*Bombyx lubricipeda* L.).

Glitsch'ig, Glitsch'erig, *adj. coll.* slippery; G-keit, *(w.) f.* slipperiness.

Glitz, *adj. provinc.* glistening, sparkling.

Glitz'en, *pl.* lilies, amaryllis. [sparkle.

Glitz'ern, *(w.) v. intr.* to glimmer, glister,

* **Glo'bus,** *(sing. not decl., pl. [w.]* Glo'ben) *m. (Lat.)* globe.

Glöck'chen, *(str.) n. (dimin. of* Glocke) 1) a little bell, small bell, hand-bell, *cf.* Schelle; 2) *Conch.* Neptune's cap; 3) *see* Glocke, 5.

Glock'e, *(w.) f.* 1) bell; 2) *coll.* clock; 3) (bell-shaped) glass-shade (*cf.* Glasglocke); 4) *Phys.* receiver; 5) pendent excrescence on the necks of goats; 6) basket of a foil; 7) *Sport. see* Glockrauch; 8) *provinc. see* Kolleisen; 9) *Herald.* vair: was ist die —? *coll. (for* wie spät ist es?) what o'clock is it? — zehn &c., just (at) ten (o'clock), &c. (zehn Uhr); die — schlägt, the bell strikes; die G-n läuten, to ring *or* toll the bells; *coll.-s.* die große — *or* alle G-n läuten, to make a great noise *or* fuss about a thing (in order to praise it); an die große — hängen, to divulge, to blaze abroad: er weiß nicht, wo die G-n hangen *or* er hat die G-n läuten hören, weiß aber nicht wo, he is at sea about the matter; wissen, wo die G-n hangen *or* was die — geschlagen hat, to see where the land lies, to know what's what: ich will ihm sagen, was die — geschlagen hat, I'll serve him out; die — in einer Uhr, the bell of a clock.

Glock'eisen, *(str.) n.* quilling-iron.

Glöck'el, *(str.) m. see* Glockenklöppel.

Glöck'eln, *(w.) v. intr. provinc.* to ring little bells, to tingle, jingle; *see* Schellen.

Glock'en, *(w.) v. tr.* to ruffle, quill, plait.

Glock'en..., *in comp.* —apfel, *m. Pomol.* bell-apple; —balken, *m.* beam of a bell: —birn, *f. Pomol.* bell-pear; —blume, *f. Bot.* bell-flower, blue-bell, Canterbury bell (*Campanula* L.); (rundblätterige) hare-bell; (breitblätterige) throat-wort; (grasblätterige) violet marian; (rauchblätterige) bearded bell-flower: —blumig, *adj. Bot.* campaniform; —blütler, *m. pl. Bot.* bell-flowers (*Campanulaceae* L.); —bronze, *f.* bell-metal: —bügel, *m.* bell-spring: —coralle, *f.* arborescent coral with bell-shaped cells (*Campanularia syringa* Lam.); —draht, *m.* bell-wire; —erz, *n.* bell-metal; —förmig, *adj.* bell-shaped, bell-fashioned, *Bot.* campaniform, campanulate; —galgen, *m. see* —stuhl; —garn, *n. see* —netz; —gebiß, *n.* bell-bit; —gehäuse, *n. see* —haus; —geläute, *n.* 1) chime *or* ringing of bells; sound of bells in harmony; 2) a set of bells, *see* —spiel, 1; —gelenkwirbel, *f.* bell-crank; —gerüst, *n.* belfry; —getön, *n. see* —klang; —gewicht, *n.* bell-weight; —gießer, *m.* bell-founder; —gießerei, *f.* bell-foundery; —gut, *n. see* —metall; —hammer, *m.* bell-clapper; hammer of a bell; —haus, *n.* belfry, bell-house.

Glockenist', *(w.) m. (l. u.)* 1) *see* Glöckner; 2) one who plays the musical glasses.

Glock'en..., *in comp.* —klang, *m.* sound of bells: —klöppel, *m.* bell-clapper, hammer *or* tongue of a bell; —kolbe, *f. see* —balken; —läuter, *m.* bell-ringer: —leiste, *f. Archit.* rampant ogee: —männchen, *n.* Jack of the bell: —mantel, *m.* the upper part of a bell-mould: —maß, *n.* bell-founder's diapason: —metall, *n.* bell-metal; —netz, *n. Sport.* bell-shaped net, tunnel-net: —pappel, *f. Bot.* holly-hock (*Althaea rosea* L.): —pfeffer, *m.* bell-pepper (*Capsicum annuum* L.): —quast, *m.* 1) tassel of a bell-rope; 2) *Archit.* bell-shaped ornament: —rand, *m.* edge of a bell; —riemen, *m.* bell-strap; —ruf, *m.* a bell's summons; —schieber, *m.* bell-lever; —schlag, *m.* 1) stroke of a clock; 2) *T.* thickness of the rim of a bell: —schwengel, *m.* 1) bell-swipe: 2) bell-clapper: —seil, *n.* bell-rope (rope of a church bell); —speise, *f.* bell-metal: —spiel, *n.* 1) a set of musical bells *or* a chime of bells; 2) an air adapted to such bells: —strang, *m. see* —seil; —stube, *f.,* —stuhl, *m.* belfry: —stunde, *f.* hour by the clock: —tau, *n. see* —seil; —taufe, *f.* baptism of bells; —thiere, *n. pl.* a genus of infusoria (*Vorticellina* L.); —thurm, *m.* bell-tower, bell-turret, belfry: —ton, *m.* 1) sound of a bell; 2) tone of a bell: —tönig, *adj. (Mus. Geibel)* sounding full like a bell: deep-toned: —treter, *m.* treader *or* ringer of the bells; —walze, *f. Mus.* harmonica: —weihe, *f. see* —taufe; —welle, *f.* cannon *or* ear of a bell: —zapfen, *m. see* —welle; —zieher, *m.* 1) *see* —läuter; 2) *or* —zug, bell-pull: —ziehring, *m.* bell-ring: —ziehwirbel, *m.* bell-crank; —zug, *m.* 1) bell-hanging: 2) bell-rope; 3) chimes; 4) bell-stop. [*, *see* Glöckchen.

Glöck'lein, *(str.) n. dimin. (provinc. &)*

Glöck'ner, *(str.) m.* bell-ringer, chimer, sexton. [ringer.

Glöcknerei', *(w.) f.* dwelling of a bell-

Glomm, *(str.) m. provinc.* curds.

Glop, *(str.) m. Mar.* narrow channel.

[Glo]ckenblume, (w.) f. Bot. crow-foot (Ranunculus L.).

Glyceliuit', (str.) m. Miner. hydrolite.

Gnab'beln, Gnab'bern, (w.) v. intr. provincial. (N. G.) see Knabbern.

Gna'de, (w.) f. 1) Theol. (die göttliche —, divine) grace, unmerited favour; 2) benevolence, kindness; 3) mercy, clemency; pardon, quarters; Mil. quarter; freie —, sovereign mercy (of God); Wir ... von Gottes G-n 2c., (of sovereign princes) We ... by the grace of God, &c.; bei Jemand in G-n stehen, to be in favour with one; — finden (vor [with Dat.]), to find mercy or favour (with); sich (Dat.) eine — ausbitten, to beg a favour; von Jemandes — leben, to live upon one's favours; (Einem) — ertheilen, to grant pardon; um — flehen, to sue for mercy; sich auf — und Ungnade ergeben, to surrender at discretion, to make an unconditional surrender; zu G-n halten, to pardon (graciously); zu G-n annehmen, to take into favour; wieder zu G-n angenommen werden, to be restored to favour; — für Recht ergehen lassen, to show favour instead of inflicting deserved punishment; Ew. G-n, your lordship, your worship, your honour.

Gna'den, (w.) v. intr. †, to be gracious; (still used in the following solemn phrase:) gnade uns (Dat.), die 2c. Gott! God be propitious unto us (you, &c.)! God have mercy upon us!

Gna'den..., in comp. —act, m., —acte, f. Law, act of grace; seine Rechnung durch die —acte abgeschlossen haben, (of bankrupts) to be cleared by the act of grace; —anstalt, f. Theol. dispensation of grace; —arie, f. a famous aria occurring in the opera Robert le Diable by Meyerbeer, so called from the principal word (Gnade! mercy!): Theol-s. —belohnung, f. divine reward of righteousness; —beruf, m. divine calling, grace, vocation; —bewilligung, f. 1) Rom. Cath. indult; 2) see —frist; —bezeigung, f. favour; bounty, beneficence, grace; —bild, n. Rom. Cath. a wonder-working (miraculous) image; —blick, m. gracious look; —brief, m. 1) letter of grace, pardon; 2) privilege; —brot, n. livelihood granted as a favour, scanty allowance; das —brot essen, to live on the mercy of others; —brunn(en), m. see —quell; —bund, m. Theol. covenant of grace or mercy; —einfluß, m., —einwirkung, f. see —wirkung; —ertheilung, f. 1) communication of divine grace; 2) see —bezeigung; —frist, f. reprieve, respite; —gabe, f. Theol. gift of grace; —gehalt, m., —geld, n. pension, (yearly) allowance, annuity; —geschenk, n. gratification, donative; —gut, n. blessing; Theol-s. —hand, f. hand of grace; —heimsuchung, f. visitation of grace; —jahr, n. 1) year of grace; 2) year of our Lord; —kasten, m. Rom. Cath. a chest in which to deposit the money for indulgences, &c.; —kraft, f. Theol. power of grace; —kraut, n. Bot. hedge- or water-hyssop (Gratiola officinalis L.); —lehen, n. fief granted as a favour; reversionary benefit, survivorship; —licht, n. light of grace; —lohn, m. pension, gratuity; Theol-s. —mittel, n. means of grace, saving means; —ordnung, f. divine ordinance of grace; —ort, m. Rom. Cath. a place where a wonder-working relic is deposited; —pfennig, m. medal granted as a token of favour; —pforte, f. gate of mercy; —platz, m. see —ort; —quell, m. fountain of grace; —reich, I. adj. gracious, merciful; II. n. kingdom of grace; —ruf, m. see —beruf; —sache, f. matter depending on the will and favour of a superior; —siegel, n. seal of grace, concession; —sold, m. pension; —spende, —spendung, f. distribution of grace; —stand, m. Theol. state of grace; —steuer, f. subsidy, charitable contribution; —stimmt, f. voice of grace; —stoß, m. finishing blow, death-blow, coup de grâce, coll. home-thrust, finisher; —stuhl, m. Bibl. mercy-seat, propitiatory; Theol-s. —tafel, f. see —tisch, 1; —tag, m. day of grace; —tage, pl. Comm. see Respecttage; —termin, m. see —zeit; —thron, m. throne of grace; —thür, f. see —pforte; —tisch, m. 1) communion-table; 2) improp. for Freitisch, which see; —verheißung, f. promise derived from divine mercy; —voll, adj. see —reich, I.; —wahl, f. election by (free) grace, predestination; —wahllehre, f. doctrine of election by grace; —wappen, n. coats of arms granted as a token of favour; eine Strafe im —wege erlassen, to remit a punishment by way of grace; —werk, n. work of grace; —wirkung, f. effect of (divine) grace; —zeichen, n. mark of favour; —zeit, f., —ziel, n. Theol. time of grace.

Gnä'dig, I. adj. 1) gracious, merciful; propitious, favourable; 2) condescending; Gott sei uns (mir 2c.) —! God have mercy on us (me, &c.)! g-er, g-ster Herr! my lord; honoured sir! g-e, g-ste Frau! my lady, madam! g-ster Herr und Fürst! most gracious sovereign! II. or † Gnä'diglich, adv. graciously, &c.

Gnar'ren, (w.) v. intr. provinc. (N. G.) to snarl (cf. to gnarl, Knurren, Knarren).

Gnatz, (str.) m., Gnat'ze (Gnät'ze, Gneist, Gneiß, Gnit'ze), (w.) f. scab; itch.

Gnat'ze, (w.) f. provinc. mosquito, gnat.

Gna'tzig, adj. 1) scabby, scabbed; itchy; 2) provinc. peevish, sullen.

Gneiß, (str.) m. Miner. gneiss; —artig, adj. gneissic; —block, m. Geol. gneiss rock.

Gnei'ßicht, Gnei'ßig, adj. resembling gneiss; containing gneiss.

Gnie'beln, Gnie'ben, (w.) v. tr. provinc. to make smooth, to rub, to polish.

* Gnōm, (w.) m. (Gr.) Superst. gnome, an elemental spirit supposed to inhabit the interior of the earth, fairy of the mine (Erdgeist, Kobold). [dialing.

* Gnomo'nik, f. (Gr.) Dial. gnomonics,

* Gnosti'ker, (str.) m. (Gr.), Gnos'tisch, adj. Eccl. gnostic. [(Catoblepas gnu Gm.).

Gnu, (str., pl. Gnus) n. Zool. gnu, gnoo

Gnub'ber (Gnup'per)krankheit, (w.) f. Vet. disease peculiar to sheep, itch.

Gnub'bern, (w.) v. tr. & intr. provinc. (N. G.) to nibble (Knabbern, Knuppern).

Gnüg, Gnü'ge 2c., see Genug, Genüge 2c.

Gnur'ren, (w.) v. intr. provinc. (N. G.) to snarl (cf. Gnarren, Knurren).

Gob, (str.), Go'be, (w.) m. Ichth. gudgeon (Gobio fluviatilis L.). [iron.

Go'belsalz, (str.) n. Miner. sulphate of

Go'ckelhahn, (str.) m. house-cock.

Go'de, (w.) m. provinc. see Pathe.

Go'deleisen, Gö'deleisen, (str.) n. T. 1) washed iron; 2) forged and marked iron.

Go'der, (str.) m. provinc. throat; double-chin (L. G. Kuder, in Mecklenb.: Kare).

Gold, s. I. (str.) n. 1) gold; 2) Chem. sol; 3) Herald. or; weißes —, see Platin; gemahlenes —, water-gold, painter's gold; gezogenes —, gold-wire; gearbeitetes —, wrought gold; — in Klumpen, gold in lumps or nuggets; geldes —, antique gold; geschlagenes —, beaten gold; es ist nicht Alles —, was glänzt, proverb. all is not gold that glitters; II. in comp. —ader, f. 1) Min. vein of gold ore, lode of gold; 2) Med. a) hemorrhoidal vein; b) hemorrhoids, piles; —adler, m. royal eagle, golden eagle (Aquila chrysaëtos L.); —after (-spinner), m. Entom. yellow tail moth, devil's gold ring (Liparis chrysorrhoea L.); —agio, n. rate for gold; —ammer, f. Ornith. gold-hammer, yellow-hammer, yellow-bunting (Emberiza citrinella L.); —amsel, f. see —drossel; —apfel, m. 1) Pomol. golden pippin; 2) Bot. love-apple, tomato (Solanum lycopersicum L.); —arbeit, f. goldsmith's work; —arbeiter, m. worker in gold; goldsmith; —artig, adj. gold-like; —auflösung, f. tincture of gold; —auge, f., —äuglein, n. Ornith. golden-eye (Anas clangula L.); —bach, m. gold-brook; —bad, n. Chem. gold-bath; —barren, f. pl. ingots or bars of gold; —barsch, m. Ichth. river-perch (Acerina cernua L.); —bergwerk, n. gold mine; —beryll, m. Miner. chrysoberyl; —blatt, —blättchen, n. 1) Gold. & Bookb. gold-leaf, gold-foil; 2) Bot. bully tree, star apple (Chrysophyllum cainito L.); —blatt-Electrometer, n. Phys. gold-leaf electrometer; —blech, n. plate of gold; —blick, m. Metall. glance, shine of gold; —blume, f. Bot. 1) everlasting flower (Strohblume); gold-flower; 2) marigold (Calendula officinalis L.); —blumig, adj. yellow blossomed; —borte, f. gold-lace; —brachsen, —brassen, m. Ichth. gilt-head, gilt-bream (Chrysophrys aurata L.); —brätling, m. a species of eatable mushroom (Agaricus ... L.); —braun, adj. yellow-dun; —braunes Pferd, Sport. gilded bay (horse); —brocat, m. gold-brocade; —bronze, f. gold bronze; (echte) shell-gold; —bruch, m. old gold; —buchstabe, m. gilt-letter; —butt, m. or —butte, f. Ichth. plaise (Pleuronectes platessa L.); —cement, m. & n. royal cement; —decke, f. Ichth. paru (Stromateus paru L.); —distel, f. Bot. yellow (golden) thistle (Scolymus hispanicus L.); —draht, m. gold-wire; —drahtzieher, m. gold-wire drawer; —drossel, f. Ornith. yellow or golden thrush (Pirol); —druck, m. gold-leaf printing; —durchwirkt, adj. interwoven with gold-threads; —durst, m. thirst of gold; —einleger, m. one who inlays in gold; —elixir, n. gold-tincture.

Gol'den, adj. 1) gold, golden; gilt; 2) fig. golden, precious, happy; sich (Dat.) g-e Berge versprechen, coll. to expect to find Tom Tiddler's ground(s); g-e Hochzeit, the celebration of the fiftieth anniversary of one's nuptials; g-e Regel, Arith. golden rule, rule of three; g-e Zahl, Chron. golden number; g-e Zeit, g-e Zeitalter, * the primeval age of innocence and happiness, golden-age; g-e Ader, see Goldader, 2.

Gold'..., in comp. —erde, f. auriferous earth; —erdwurzel, f. Bot. ipecacuanha (Cephaëlis ipecacuanha Rich.); —erz, n. gold ore; —esche, f. Bot. gold-ash, common ash (Fraxinus excelsior L.); —eule, f. see Schleiereule; —fabrik, f. manufactory of gold-vessels; —faden, m. gold-thread, spun gold; —fahl, adj. pale yellow, gold-yellow; —farbe, f. gold-colour; Herald. or; Paint. orpiment; —farben, —farbig, adj. golden, gold-coloured; —fasan, m. Ornith. gold(en) pheasant (Phasianus pictus L.); —feilicht, n. filings of gold; —finger, m. ring-finger; —fink, m. Ornith. see Bergfink & Blutfink; —firniß, m. gold-varnish; —fisch, m. Ichth. 1) goldfish (Cyprinus auratus L.); 2) see —brachsen; —fischer, m. gold-washer; —fliege, f. Entom. a kind of fly (Musca Caesar L.); —flimmer, m., —flitter, m. & f. gold-spangle; —föhre, —forelle, f. Ichth. golding-trout (a variety of the common trout, Forelle); —fuchs, m. a yellow-dun horse; —führend, adj. auriferous; —gang, m. course of gold-ore in a mine; gold-gang(ue); —gänschen, n. see —ammer; —gefäße, n. pl. gold-plate; —gefleckt, adj. speckled with gold; —gehalt, m. intrinsic value of gold; —geier, m. see Lämmergeier; —gelb, I. adj. golden, yellow like gold; II. n. minim colour; —gelockt, adj. having golden curls, ringlets; —geschiebe, n. Geol. river ore; —geschirr, n. see —gefäße; —gespinnst, n. spun gold; —gestickt, adj. embroidered with gold-threads; —gewicht, n. gold-weight, troy weight; —gewinn, m. produce of mines in gold; —gewirkt, see —durchwirkt; —gier, f. immoderate thirst or lust after gold; —glanz, m. splendour or lustre of gold; Miner-s. —glätte, f. gold-litharge; —glimmer, m. yellow mica; —glas, m. 1) idol of gold; 2) mam-

[illegible]e, (w.) f. coll. 1) see Rapuse; 2) [illegible] hand, paw; 3) strange whim.

[illegible]en, (w.) v. intr. coll. to scramble [illegible], fork to grasp, to lay hold of.

Gras [N. G. grôs], n. I. (str., pl. Grä'[illegible]) 1) grass; 2) pl. Bot. gramineous plants, [illegible]; spanisches, englisches, or französisches [illegible]bon-grass, see Bandgras; ins — thun, [illegible] lassen; ins — beißen, vulg. to die, [illegible] to bite the dust or ground; darüber ist [illegible]wachsen, it is forgotten; er hört das — [illegible], fig. he is or fancies himself exceedingly wise or clever; II. in comp. —affe, m. [illegible] a young monkey, cf. —hecht, —hirsch, [illegible]schnabel, a green goose, &c. & Affe) coll. [illegible]young, unripe girl, green Miss; often used [illegible] Göthe, to designate in a good-humoured, only [illegible]-ironical way, a tender young girl or even [illegible]ly married) woman; der —aff! Ist er weg? [illegible] Marthens Garten), the monkey! is she [illegible]? (Meph. of Gretchen); —ähre, f., —ähr[illegible], n. Bot. spikelet, spiket; —anger, m. [illegible], grass-plot, pasture-ground; —art, f. [illegible]-kind; —artig, adj. gramineous, grami[illegible]; —bank, f. grassy bank, seat of grass; [illegible], m. grass-whisk; —bewachsen, adj. [illegible]-grown; —blattfänger, m. Entom. grass[illegible] (Chrysomela graminis L.); —blume, f. 1) [illegible] kinds of flowers growing wild; 2) see [illegible]; —boden, m. grass land; —bringend, adj. herbiferous; —butter, f. May-butter.

—**Gräs'chen, Gräs'lein**, (str.) n. (dimin. of [illegible]) a small blade of grass.

Gras'ebene, f. prairie, savanna (in America). [illegible]

Gras'[illegible], (w.) v. intr. Sport. to tear up the grass with the hoof (said of deer when [illegible]).

Gra'sen, (w.) v. I. intr. 1) to graze; — lassen, to turn (or put) to grass; 2) to cut grass; 3) [illegible] to roll and bound (said of cannon-balls); [illegible] fig. to aim (nach, at), aspire (to); II. tr. [illegible] Getreide) to cut off the grassy part of growing corn).

A. **Gra'sen**, (w.) v. tr. to fatten on grass [(cattle).

B. **Gra'sen**, (w.) v. intr. (impers.) see [illegible].

Gra'ser, (str.) m. 1) grass-cutter; 2) Sport. the tongue of a stag.

Graserei', (w.) f. 1) (the act of) cutting [illegible]; 2) a grass field; 3) collect. grass, her[illegible].

Gras'..., in comp. —eule, f. Entom. grass-moth (Noctua graminis L.); —farbe, f. grass-green colour; —faser, f. herbaceous thread; —fleck, m. 1) grass-plot; 2) grass-stain; —[illegible], f. see —[illegible]; —fressend, adj. graminivorous, herbivorous; —fressende Thiere, n. pl. [illegible] graminivorous quadrupeds, (Lat.) graminivora; —frosch, m. Zool. brown grass-frog (Rana temporaria L.); —frucht, f. caryopsis; —futter, n. grass-fodder, green food; —[illegible], f. feeding on grass; —garten, m. grass-garden, (sometimes) an orchard; —ge[illegible], n. grass-[illegible]; —gesch[illegible], m. grassy [illegible]; —grün, adj. grass-green; —halm, m. blade of grass; culm; —hecht, m. pickerel; —[illegible], m. Sport. lean stag, rascal; —hirse, f. [illegible] floating sweet-grass (Glyceria fluitans [illegible]); —huhn, m. Ornith. crake or landrail [illegible]; —hummel, f. Entom. humble-bee, bumble-bee (Bombus L.); —hüpfer, m. Entom. grass-hopper (Tettix bipunctata L.).

Gras'[illegible], Gras'[illegible], adj. like (similar to) grass; covered with grass, grassy.

Gras'[illegible], n. (str.) n. grass (collect.).

Gras'[illegible], adj. see Gräßlich, Grausig.

Gras'ling, (str.) m. Ichth. see Gründling, 1, b.

Gras'..., in comp. —[illegible], f. grass-[illegible]; —[illegible], m. [illegible]; —[illegible], adj. [illegible] spreading in the stalks instead of in [illegible]; —land, n. grass-land, grazing [illegible], meadow; —lauch, m. Bot. bladed leek, rocambole (Allium scorodoprasum L.); —läufer, m. see —huhn; —leder, n. Bot. river-weed (Conferva rivularis L.).

Gräs'lein, (str.) n. 1) see Gräschen; 2) Sport. grass trod up by deer, serving as a trace; 3) linnet (Hänfling).

Gras'..., in comp. —leinen, n. grass-cloth; —lilie, f. a plant of the order of Asphodeleae (Anthericum Liliago L.).

Gras'ling, (str.) m. 1) Vint. vine-sprig (a year old); 2) Ichth. see Gründling, 1, b.

Gras'..., in comp. —loch, n. Min. hole bored horizontally for blasting; —magd, f. grass-maid; —mäher, m. mower of grass, grass-cutter; —meise, f. see Kohlmeise; —mette, f. Entom. dragon-fly, adder-fly (Libellula L.); —monat, m. April; —mücke, f. Ornith. 1) (die graue) garden-warbler (Sylvia cinerea Briss); 2) (die rostgraue) white throat (Sylvia curruca Lath.); 3) (die braungefleckte) hedge-sparrow (Braunelle); —nelke, f. Bot. maiden-pink, thrift (Statice armeria L.); —pappel, f. round-leaved mallow (Malva rotundifolia L.); —pferd, n. see —hüpfer; —platz, m. grass-plot, green-plot; bowling green; —rätscher, m. Ornith. corn-crake (Wiesenknarrer); —raupe, f. caterpillar of the Graseule; —reich, adj. abounding with grass, grassy; —rost, m. a kind of smut (Puccinia graminis Pers.); —schere, f. Gard. grass-shears; —schnecke, f. Zool. slug (Erdschnecke); —schnepfe, f. see Becassine; —sense, —sichel, f. scythe, sickle for cutting grass.

* **Grassi'ren**, (w.) v. intr. (Lat.) to rage [(of a disease).

Gras'..., in comp. —specht, m. Ornith. green woodpecker (Grünspecht); —sperling, m. see —mücke; —stück, n. grass-plot; —teppich, —tafft, m. aridas (of herbs); —wachs, m., —weide, f. pasture-ground; —wuchs, m. growth of grass; pasture.

Gräß'lich, I. adj. or **Graß**, horrible, terrible, frightful, hideous, dire, grisly, ghastly; II. G-keit, (w.) f. 1) horribleness, &c., hideousness, direness, ghastliness; 2) atrocity, a hideous or horrible deed.

Grât, Grath, (str.) m. 1) edge, ridge; 2) Carp. rabbet (Leiste); 3) Archit. hip (auch von Ziegeln), arris; groin; T. burr; blister; Archit-s. —balken, m. arris-beam; —bogen, m. cross-springer.

Grä'te, (w.) f. 1) fish-bone; 2) Vet. ne[illegible]; 3) provinc. dead wood; 4) Archit. see Grat, 3; 5) pl. slang (ein paar G-n, also Krä[illegible]) money, small. shiners, dust, tin; G-n[illegible]stich, m. Sew. herring-stitch, herring-bone.

Grät(h)'..., in comp. —eisen, n. cooper's knife; —hobel, m. filleting plane.

* **Gra'tia**, f. (Lat.) Grace, Gracy (P. N.).

* **Gra'tias**, (Lat.) s. thanks! — sagen, — beten, to render thanks, to say grace.

* **Gratificatio'n**, (w.) f. (Lat.) gratuity, free gift. [irritated.

Grä'tig, adj. 1) full of fish-bones; 2) fig.

* **Gra'tis**, adv. gratis; —beilage, f. gratis supplement. [rity-scholar.

* **Gratist'**, (w.) m. 1) beneficiary; 2) charity-scholar.

Grät'ling, (str.) m. little bony fish.

Grät(h)'..., in comp. —rippe, f. groin-rib; —säge, f. a (small) saw for cutting grooves.

Grätsch, (str.) m. Gymn., &c. straddle, (the act of) straddling. — **Grät'schen**, coll. **Grät'scheln**, (w.) v. intr. to straddle.

Grät(h)'..., in comp. —sparren, m. Carp. hip-rafter; (eine Spundwand) mit einer — spundung aneinanderfügen, to groove and tongue; —thier, n. provinc. mountain goat, red chamois.

* **Gratulir'en**, (w.) v. intr. (Lat.) to congratulate (Glück wünschen). — **Gratulant'**, (w.) m. congratulator, well-wisher. — **Gratulation'**, (w.) f. congratulation (Glückwünschung).

Grau, I. adj. 1) gray (grey); grizzled, grizzle; 2) fig. gray (with age), hoary; aged, ancient, former: g-e Vorzeit, remote antiquity; in g-er Vorzeit, in times out of mind; die g-e Substanz, Anat. gray substance (external substance or coat of the brain); g-es Geld, silver-money; g-es Brot, mouldy bread; g-er Bruder, gray friar, Cistercian; (englischer) g-er Häkelzwirn, flax-coloured tambour-thread; II. s. (str.) n. gray colour; fig. morning-dawn; — in —, Paint. (to paint) gray in gray (cf. Camaieu); III. in comp. —äugig, adj. gray-eyed; —ammer, f. Ornith. corn-bunting, groundfinch (Emberiza miliaria L.); —artsche, f. Ornith. linnet (Fringilla cannabina L.); —asche, f. ashes of straw and stubble; —bart, m. gray-beard.

Graubünd(t)'en, n. Geogr. (orig. Land der Graubünd(t)ner, Fr. pays des Grisons) the Grisons (largest canton of Switzerland, so called from the Graue Bund, Gray League, the principal of several alliances formed by the oppressed inhabitants in the 15th cent.).

Graubünd(t)'ner, (str.) m., G-in, (w.) f. a Grison. [donkey.

Grau'chen, (str.) n. (dimin. of Grau) joc.

Grau'drossel, (w.) f. Ornith. thrush (Turdus musicus L.). [il.

Grau'el, (str.) m. coll. provinc. see Grauen,

Gräu'el, (str.) m. 1) horror, abomination; abhorrence, detestation; 2) (or —that, f.) horrible or abominable deed, crime, atrocity, enormity, outrage; es ist mir ein —, I abominate or hate.... [Grausig, 2.

Gräu'elhaft, Gräu'elvoll, adj. horrid, see

Grau'eln, (w.) v. refl. & intr. (impers.) see Grauen.

A. **Grau'en**, (w.) v. I. intr. 1) to turn gray (Ergrauen); 2) to pass from darkness into light, to dawn; der Tag grauet, it dawns; das —, (str.) s. n. the (act of) dawning, dawn.

B. **Grau'en** (coll. **Grau'eln**), (w.) v. intr. impers. (with Dat.) to be awed (vor [with Dat.], by), to have a horror, an aversion, to dread, fear: es grauet mir (or mir grauet) vor ..., I dread, fear, I am in dread or horror of ...., I shudder at ...; Heinrich, mir graut vor dir (Göthe, Faust I. end), Henry! I shudder to think of thee; das —, (str.) s. n. 1) horror, abhorrence; 2) dismay, fear, dread (vor [with Dat.], of); in comp. —erregend, —haft, —voll, adj. full of horror, horrid, appalling.

Grau'erlich, adj. see Greulich, II. 1 (l. u.).

Grau'..., in comp. —erz, n. Miner. silver-steel ore; —farben, —farbig, adj. gray-coloured, drab, drab-coloured; —fink, m. Ornith. gray-finch (Fringilla petronia L.); —fuchs, m. gray fox; —golderz, n. Miner. black tellurium-ore; —grün, adj. dull green, sea-green, glaucous; —haarig, adj. gray-haired; —hänfling, m. Ornith. gray-linnet (Graufink).

Grau'heit, (w.) f. grayness, the quality of being gray, &c. cf. Grau; hoariness.

Grau'..., in comp. —kehlchen, n. Ornith. see Braunelle, 1; —kopf, m. 1) a gray-headed person; 2) Ornith. see —specht; —köpfig, adj. gray-headed; —kupfererz, n. Miner. copper-galena; —lachs, m. an inferior species of salmon.

Grau'lich, adj. I. or (occasional:) **Grau'licht** (Schiller, Kran. des Ibykus) grayish, grizzly; II. 1) or **Grau'erlich**, coll. fearful, filled with fear, timorous; 2) see Gräulich.

Gräu'lich, adj. horrible, terrible, horrid, dreadful, shocking, heinous, monstrous, enormous.

Grau'ling, (str.) m. 1) anything gray or grayish; jack-ass; gray coat; 2) Bot. a species of agaric.

Grau'..., in comp. —malerei, f. Paint. (the act of) painting gray in gray, camaieu-painting; —mantel, m. Ornith. a. [illegible]

[illegible] gut; —graben, m. boundary-ditch; —gut, [illegible], n. estate, house on the boundary of [a] district or country; —herr, m. owner of a [—gut], which see; —holz, n. border-wood; —[hüter], m. 1) see —bereiter; 2) see —schütze; [—kette], f. Mil. cordon: —krieg, m. border-[war]; —land, n. border-country, limitary.

[Grenz'lich], adj. bordering, relating to the [borders].

Grenz'..., in comp. —linie, f. boundary-line, line of demarcation: —mal, n. landmark; —mauer, f. boundary-wall: Archit. partition-wall; —messer, m. surveyor of the boundaries; —nachbar, m. confiner, borderer, [bord]er-neighbour; —nachbarschaft, f. confinity; [illegible], —platz, m. limitary, frontier-place; —[pfahl], m. boundary-post; —punct, m. 1) point [of] a boundary-line; 2) fig. extreme, highest point; —receß, m. boundary treaty; —säule, [f.] a column to mark a boundary, boundary-[post]; —scheide, f. see —linie; —scheider, m. [see] —messer & —[illegible]; —scheidung, f. the [act of] determining (or setting of) a boundary; [illegible] boundary; —schloß, n. frontier-castle; —[schütze], m. game-keeper, who keeps the boun[daries] of a manor; —soldat, m. soldier serving on the frontiers, cf. Grenzer, 2; —sperre, [f.] the (act of) closing the barriers (in order to [pro]hibit trade): stop put to trade; —stadt, f. frontier-town; —stein, m. boundary-stone, bounding-stone; land-mark; —streit, m., —[streitig]keit, f. dispute concerning boundaries; [—strom], m. see —fluß; —vergleich, —vertrag, m. treaty, agreement concerning the boun[daries] of two districts; —wache, f. boundary [guard], line of defence; —wächter, m. boundary-guard, cf. —jäger; —wall, m. rampart [illegible] marking the boundary; —weg, m. road [illegible] marking the boundary; —wehr, f. de[fence], turnpike, &c. of a boundary; —zaun, [m.] boundary-hedge; —zeichen, n. landmark; [—zoll], m. duties, customs, toll; —zug, m. in[spection] of the boundaries.

[illegible], (str.) n. T. & Weav. pattern.

[Gret'chen], (str.) n. (dimin. of Grete) 1) Margery, Meg, Madge, Peg, Peggy, Padge [illegible]; 2) Mar. mizzen-top-gallant-sail; —[illegible], Bot. fennel flower (Nigella damascena L.).

[Gre'te], f. (abbr. of Margarethe) Margaret, Margery, &c. cf. Gretchen; faule —, Bot. fool's parsley (Aethusa cynapium L.).

[illegible], see Gretchen.

[Greu'el], (str.) m. see Gräuel.

[illegible], (str.) m. Miner. nugget.

[Grie'be], (w.) f. the fibrous or skinny remains of lard, &c. after its being fried: greaves.

[Griebs], (str.) m. 1) see Griebe; 2) fig. re[illegible], trash.

[Grie'che], (w.) m., Grie'chin, (w.) f. Greek, Grecian; G-nfreund, m. philhellene.

[Grie'chenland], n. Geogr. Greece.

[Grie'chenthum], (str.) n., Griechheit, (w.) [f.] peculiarity or spirit of the Greeks.

[Grie'chisch], I. adj. Greek, Grecian, Hellenic; II. das G-e, n. Greek: eine g-e Stadt, a Grecian city; in der g-en Grammatik, in Greek grammar; das (wilde) g-e Feuer, Greek [or] Grecian fire, wild-fire; das g-e Heu, Bot. fenugreek; g-es Pech, colophon: —Weißenburg, n. (the town of) Belgrade; —aussehend, adj. Greek-looking; —katholisch, adj. belonging to the Greek church, Greek.

[illegible], (w.) f. see Griebe.

[illegible], (str.) m. 1) Zool. fat dormouse ([illegible] L.); 2) Ornith. a species of curlew ([illegible]); 3) provinc. hedge-sparrow [illegible]; —[illegible], f. field-duck (Otis te[trax] L.).

[illegible], (str.) m. see Gries.

[illegible], see Griechen.

[illegible], adj. —käse, m. Gruyère cheese.

Gries, adj. provinc. (N. G.) gray.

Gries, s. I. (str.) m. 1) coarse sand, gravel; grit; 2) see Harngries; 3) fine groats, ground grits; 4) Comm. garblings: 5) Min. (nordd.:) rubbish, (schott.:) drash, (Stafford.:) smucks (Kohlengruß); II. in comp. —asche, f. provinc. coarse sediments in wine-casks, unpurified or crude tartar: —bart, m. see Geißfuß; —birne, f. Pomol. beurré gris; —brei, m. pap of groats; —bade, f. Build. see Stützdiele.

Grie'selig, adj. 1) sandy, gritty, gravelly: 2) containing groats.

Grie'seln, (w.) v. I. intr. to break or fall into little pieces, to crumble; II. tr. to pound, grind; III. intr. coll. see Gruseln.

Gries'..., in comp. —flechte, f. Med. herpes, tetters; —fuchs, m. see Graufuchs.

Gries'gram, coll. I. (str.) m. 1) the spleen; 2) a grumbler; II. or Gries'grämisch, Gries'grämlich, adj. peevish, morose, sullen.

Gries'grämen, (w.) v. intr. coll. to be fretting, morose, peevish.

Gries'..., in comp. —holz, n. Pharm. nephritic wood: —horst, m. gravel-isle: —huhn, n. Ornith. 1) see Strandläufer; 2) see Sandhuhn.

Grie'sicht, Grie'sig, I. adj. resembling gravel or grit: gravelly (of urine, &c.), gritty; calculous; II. s. (str.) m. dirt of bees.

Gries'..., in comp. —kleie, f. bran of groats: —kolik, f. Med. nephritic colic; —kraut, n. Bot. wild tansy, silver weed (Potentilla anserina L.); —kuchen, m. cake made of grits; —mehl, n. 1) meal-groats; 2) the finest sort of wheat-flour: —mittel, n. Med. antinephritic; —säulen, f. pl. Mill. posts between which the flood-gates of water-mills are fixed: —sieb, n. groats sieve, oatmeal sieve; —stein, m. Miner. nephritic stone: —suppe, f. soup made of grits; —trank, m. drink of oatmeal, water-gruel; —wart, —wärtel, m. Archaeol. overseer of the tournaments; —wasser, n. Med. nephritic water: —werk, n. Mill. flood-gate, pen-stock, pentrough; —wurzel, f. Bot. cissampelos, wild vine, velvet leaf (Cissampelos Pareira L.).

Grieß, more correct, but less usual than Gries, s.

Grie'ten, (w.) f. pl. Mar. ledges.

Griff, s. I. (str.) m. 1) gripe, grip, grasp; hold, touch; pinch; snatch; 2) handle, hilt: T. haft, bow, or handle (of scissors, &c.); head (of a cork-screw, &c.); tang (of a file); ear (of a pitcher); toe (of a horse-shoe); fret (of guitars); tiller (of a saw); Typ. rounce, handle of a printing-press; 3) as much as may be grasped, a handful; 4) Sport. claws (of birds of prey); 5) fig. trick, shift, fetch: — zurück! Mil. (in Prussia) as you were! etwas am G-e haben, to have a knack at a thing; coll. to be a dab at a thing; to know a thing by the touch.

Griff'brett, (str.) n. finger-board (of a violin, violoncello, &c.); key-board (of a pianoforte, &c. see Claviatur).

Grif'fel, s. I. (str.) m. 1) style; pin of a table-book, fescue; 2) coll. for Schieferstift; 3) Bot. style, spindle (of a pink, &c.), shaft; II. in comp. —ähnlich, adj. styloid, styloid: —baum, m. Bot. judas tree (Cercis siliquastrum L.); —beere, f. Bot. 1) red whortleberry (Vaccinium vitis idaea L.); 2) African myrsine (Myrsine africana L.); Anat.-e. —förmig, adj. styloid, styliform; —förmiger Fortsatz, styloid apophysis; —loch, n. stylo-mastoid hole.

Grif'fellos, adj. Bot. having neither styles nor pistils.

Grif'fel[zungen]muskel, m. Anat. (der Zunge) styloglossus; (des Zungenbeins) stylo-hyoid muscle.

Grif'feln, (w.) v. tr. to mark, notch, or engrave with a tool.

Grif'fel..., in comp. —schiefer, m. Miner. graphiolite; Anat.-e. —schlundkopfmuskel, m. stylo-pharyngean muscle; —zitzenschlagader, f. stylo-mastoid artery.

Grif'fen, (w.) v. tr. provinc. to rough-shoe (a horse).

Grif'fig, adj. Forest. see Eingreifig.

Griff'..., in comp. —loch, n. key-hole (of wind instruments); Sword-cutl.-e. —treiber, —triebel, m. driver; —winde, f. a small iron reel, to wind the wire about the handle of a sword.

Grill, (str.) m. see Splint.

Gril'le, (w.) f. 1) Entom. cricket (Gryllus domesticus L.); 2) fig. whim, grub, maggot, freak, caprice, humour, crotchet, fancy, vagary: 3) pl. anxious cares, melancholy thoughts, coll. blue-devils: 4) coll. a capricious, sullen, whimsical person: G-n haben, sich (Dat.) G-n machen, G-n fangen to be whimsical, freakish, humoursome, crotchety; to be melancholy, gloomy. [(also refl.) see Grillen haben.

Gril'len, (w.) v. intr. 1) see Grellen: 2)

Gril'len..., in comp. —fang, m. freakishness, fancifulness; —fänger, m. a whimsical person; —fängerei, f. whimsicalness, fancifulness; whims, freaks; —fängerisch, adj. whimsical, &c.

Gril'lenhaft, I. adj. see Grillig; II. G-igkeit, (w.) f. whimsicalness, freakishness, capriciousness.

Gril'len..., in comp. —frank, —süchtig, adj. hypochondriacal; —lerche, f. Ornith. tit-lark (Alauda pratensis L.); —spiel, n. a sort of game to try ingenuity, puzzle, Fr. solitaire; —sucht, f. hypochondria; —vertreiber, m. anything that drives away melancholy thoughts; —werk, n. grotesque work.

Gril'lig, I. adj. whimsical, freakish, fanciful, capricious, crotchety: II. G-keit, (w.) f. see Grillenhaftigkeit.

* Grilli'ren, (w.) v. tr. (Fr.) Cook. to grill.

Grill'vogel, (str.) m. Ornith. golden-plover (Goldregenpfeifer).

* Grimas'se, (w.) f. (Fr.) 1) grimace, wry face; Paint. caricature; 2) Moll. a species of shell (Murex L.).

Grimm, I. adj. († &) *, see Grimmig; II. (str.) m. fury, rage, wrath, cf. Wuth; III. in comp. Anat.-e. —darm, m. the large intestine, colon; —darmband, n. ligament of the colon; —darmgegend, f. epicolic region: —darmgekröse, n. mesocolon: —darmschlagader, f. artery of the colon.

Grim'men, I. (w.) v. intr. †, to rage, chafe, fume; II. tr. 1) fig. to annoy, fret, vex; 2) (impers.) to gripe: es grimmt mir (or mich) im Leibe, I have the gripes: fig. I am annoyed, vexed, I fret: das —, (str.) n. s. the gripes, colic.

Grim'mig, I. adj. 1) grim, ferocious, fierce, fell, furious, enraged, wrathful; 2) coll. excessive, extreme, terrible: II. G-keit, (w.) f. ferocity, wildness, fierceness, cruelty.

Grim'pel, (str.) m. Ichth. minnow (Phoxinus laevis Ag.).

Grind, (str.) m. 1) a) scab, scurf, scald, scall; fig. dirt, filth: b) itch (Krätze); c) mange (Räude); d) Surg. eschar; 2) coll. a) head; b) Sport. head of a stag; 3) Bot. see Flechtseide: 4) Zool. roundheaded dolphin (Delphinus delphis L.); 5) groats.

Grin'del &c., provinc. see Grendel.

Grind..., in comp. —haube, f. cap against the scald; —holz, n. Bot. buckthorn (Rhamnus frangula L.).

Grin'dicht, Grin'dig, adj. like scurf or scab; scabbed, scabby, scurfy, scalled.

Grind'..., in comp. —kopf, m. scabhead; cf. [illegible]; —köpfig, adj. scab-headed, scald-headed; —kraut, n. Bot. 1) scabious (Scabiosa L.); 2) groundsel (Kreuzkraut); 3) a kind of dock (Rumex obtusifolius L.); —mittel, n. Med. scab; —rübe, —schnabel, m. see [illegible]; —stein, m. Miner. granite; —warzen, f. pl. syphilitic warts; —wurz, —wurzel, f. see —kraut.

[illegible]ness; 2) size; pitch; natürliche —, T. natural scale; 3) Math. magnitude; power; quantity; die bekannte —, known quantity; die unbekannte —, unknown quantity; symbol; unendlich kleine —, infinitesimal quantity; veränderliche G-n, variable quantities; fig.-s. [illegible] greatness; nobleness; grandeur; 5) enormity (of a crime), magnitude, amount (of [illegible], &c.); extent (of sale, &c.); amount (of a sum); Sterne erster —, Astr. stars of the first magnitude; parlamentarische G-n, parliamentary notabilities; Gelehrter erster —, first-rate scholar.

Groß…, in comp. —elephant (octav), n. double elephant; —elterlich, adj. concerning (or proceeding from) grand-parents; —eltern, pl. grand-parents; —enke, m. see —[illegible]; —enkel, m. great grandson; —enkelin, f. great grand-daughter.

Größen…, in comp. Math-s. —lehre, f. 1) mathematics; 2) (Raumgrößenlehre) geometry; —reihe, f. series of quantities; —ver[illegible], f. conversion of ratios; —wahnsinn, m. Med. ambitious monomania (Fr. [illegible] ou délire des grandeurs).

[illegible]feile, (w.) f. combmaker's file.

[illegible]ern, (w.) v. tr. to enlarge; T. to widen.

Groß…, in comp. —falconier, —falkenier, m. grand falconer; —feldherr, m. commander in chief; —fürst, m. grand-duke; grand-prince; der —fürst Thronfolger, the hereditary Grand Duke; —fürstenthum, n. grand-duchy; —fürstin, f. grand-duchess; —fürstlich, adj. grand-ducal; —garn, n. fisher's sweep-net; —garten, m. grass-farm; —gemustert, adj. large-patterned; —geschäft, n. mercantile house; wholesale-business; —gewerb, n. fabric, manufacture; —gliederig, adj. strong-limbed, large-limbed; —günstig, adj. most-gracious.

[illegible]haft, (l. w.) I. adj. powerful; II. G-igkeit, (w.) f. power.

Groß'…, in comp. —handel, m. wholesale-business; —handel treiben, to deal (trade) wholesale; to carry on wholesale-business; —händler, m. wholesale-merchant, wholesale-dealer, dealer in the gross, coll. wholesale-man; —handlung, f. wholesale-business or establishment; —[illegible], m. [illegible] bat.

Groß'heit, (w.) f. fig. greatness, cf. Größe, [illegible] 5.

Groß…, in comp. —herr, m. grand-seignior; —herrisch, adj. lordly, haughty; —herrisch thun, to lord it; —herrlich, adj. pertaining to the grand-seignior; —herzig, adj. magnanimous; —herzigkeit, f. magnanimity; —herzog, m. grand-duke; —herzogin, f. grand-duchess; —herzoglich, adj. grand-ducal; —herzogthum, n. grand-dukedom, grand-duchy; —hofmeister, m. lord steward of the king's household; —hornig, adj. large-horned; —hundert, (a number of) one hundred and twenty; —inquisitor, m. grand-inquisitor.

* **Grossier,** (str.) m., **Grossist',** (w.) m. (Fr.) a wholesale-merchant (Großhändler).

Groß…, in comp. —jährig, adj. of age (volljährig); —kammerherr, m. grand-chamberlain; —kanzler, m. great-chancellor, lord high-chancellor; —kind, n. grand-child; —knecht, m. 1) head-servant (of a farm); 2) [illegible]-knight; —knochig, adj. large-boned; —kopf, m. 1) big-head; 2) Ichth. mullet, pollack (Mullus barbatus L.); 3) Entom. a kind of butterfly (Liparis dispar L.); —köpfig, adj. big-headed; —körnig, adj. big- (or large-) [illegible], big-grained; —kreuz, n. Herald. & Pol. grand-cross; —küchenmeister, m. grand master of the kitchen; —lauch, m. rocambole (Grus[illegible]); —lefzig, adj. see —lippig; —leibig, adj. big-bellied.

Groß'lich, adj. somewhat great, rather large, fam. greatish, biggish.

Groß…, in comp. —lippig, adj. blubber-lipped; —mächte, f. pl. Pol. the great powers; —mächtig, adj. high-potent, high and mighty; fam. enormous, huge; —magd, f. first or upper maid-servant on a farm; —marschall, m. lord-marshal, lord-high-steward; —maschig, adj. of large (net-)meshes; —maul, n. vulg. 1) large mouth; 2) braggart, bully, huff; —mäulig, adj. vulg. 1) large- or wide-mouthed; 2) swaggering, bragging, tongue-valiant; —meise, f. see Kohlmeise; T-s. —meister, m. grand-master; —meisterthum, n., —meisterschaft, f. grand-mastership; —mögend, adj. Pol. high and mighty, worshipful; —mogul, m. great mogul; —muhme, f. see —tante; —mundschenk, m. grand-cup-bearer; —muth, f. high spirit; magnanimity; generosity, greatness of mind; munificence; —müthig, adj. magnanimous, generous; munificent; Johann Friedrich der —müthige, John Frederic the Magnanimous; —müthigkeit, f. generousness, magnanimity; —mutter, f. grandmother; —mütterlich, adj. concerning a grandmother, of or by the grandmother; —nase, f. great-nosed person, jos. nosey; —nasig, adj. great-nosed, bottle-nosed, big-nosed; —neffe, m. great-nephew; —nichte, f. great-niece; —octav, n. 1) Typ. large octavo; 2) Mus. full organ.

* **Gros'so-Handel,** (str.) m. (Ital.-Germ.) wholesale-business.

Groß…, in comp. —oheim, —onkel, m. great-uncle; —ohr, n. Zool. serde; —ohrig, adj. having great ears; —pensionär, m. grand pensionary; —prahler, m. (vain) boaster, swaggerer, braggart, braggadocio, hector; —prahlerei, f. vain-glory, boastfulness, boasting, bravado, brag, rodomontade, bluster, swagger; —prahlerisch, adj. vainly ostentatious, vain-glorious, swaggering, vaunting, boastful, braggart; —prior, m. grand-prior; —quart, n. Typ. large quarto; —rath, m. grand council; —richter, m. chief justice, grand-judge; —schatzmeister, m. grand-treasurer; —schlächter, m. wholesale-butcher; —schnäbler, m. Ornith. a genus of birds (Ramphastidae); —schreier, m. see —maul; —schuppig, adj. large-scaled; —seite, f. Geom. hypotenuse; —siegelbewahrer, m. keeper of the great seal; —sinn, m. see —herzigkeit; —sinnig, adj. high- or noble-minded, cf. —herzig; —sohn, m. grandson; —sprecher, m. boaster, see —prahler; —sprecherei, f. (the act or habit of) boasting, cf. —prahlerei; —sprecherisch, adj. boastful, cf. —prahlerisch; —städter, m., —städterin, f. inhabitant of a large town; —städtisch, adj. in the manner of a large town, fashionable; —stallmeister, m. grand-master of the horse; equerry of the king or queen; —sultan, m. grand-seignior, sultan; —tante, f. grand-aunt; —tausend, n. (a number of) twelve hundred.

Größ'tentheils, adv. for the greatest or most part, chiefly, generally.

Groß…, in comp. —that, f. noble achievement, (heroic) feat, exploit, prowess, bravery; —thuer, m. bragger, boaster; —thuerei, f. see —prahlerei; —thuerisch, —thuig, adj. coll. boasting, swaggering, vain, cf. —prahlerisch; —tochter, f. grand-daughter; —traubig, adj. with large grapes; —truchseß, m. grand seneschal; foretaster; —uhrmacher, m. clock-maker; —urenkel, m. great grandson; —urenkelin, f. great grand-daughter; —vater, m. grandfather; grandsire; —väterlich, adj. of or by one's grandfather; —vaterstuhl, m. elbow-chair, arm-chair, easy-chair; —vatertanz, m. grandfather's-dance (usually danced at the close of a wedding-ball); —verkauf, m. wholesale-business, wholesale; —verkehr, m. wholesale-traffic; —vezier, m. grand-vizier; —vicar, m. Rom. Cath. apostolical vicar; —vogt, m. provost-marshal; high sheriff; —weibel, m. chief sergeant of a court of justice (in Switzerland); —wanstig, adj. paunch-bellied; —wesir, m. see —vezier; —würdenträger, m. high dignitary; —ziemer, m. see Krammetsvogel.

Grot, Groot, (str.), **Gro'te,** (w.) m. groat, grot (a German coin of four pfennigs value).

Grot'chen, Gröt'chen, (str.) n., dimin. of Grot.

* **Grotesk',** adj. (Ital.) grotesque, grotesk; G-enmaler, m. grotesque painter; G-entänzer, m. comic dancer.

Grot'te, s. I. (w.) f. grotto; II. in comp. G-narbeit, f., G-nwerk, n. rock-work, shell-work; G-narbeiter, G-nmacher, m. grotto maker.

Grüb'chen, (str.) n. (dimin. of Grube) 1) a small cavity, a little hole; 2) a dimple; 3) or —spiel, n. cherry-pit, chuck-hole, chuck-farthing; — in (with Acc.) machen, to dimple; — bekommen, to dimple.

Gru'be, (w.) f. 1) pit, cavity, hole, ditch; den; 2) Min. pit, mine; (Stein—) quarry; 3) coll. for Abtrittsgrube, which see; 4) fig. (Script.) the grave; 5) scar, mark; 6) Anat. fossa; 7) Shoe-m. patch; 8) Metall. see Gatir, I. 3; 9) Sport. a) see Fallgrube; b) hole (of foxes); kennel, den (of wild animals); fig.-s. er geht auf die —, he is near his grave; Einem eine — graben, to lay a snare for one; wer Andern eine — (or G-n) gräbt, fällt selbst hinein, proverb. harm watch, harm catch.

Grü'bel, (str.) m. see Grübelei.

Grübelei', (w.) f. close and subtile investigation of trifles; the (act or custom of) brooding, pondering, weighing mentally, &c.

Grü'belhaft, adj. indulging in hypercriticism or trifling inquiries, over-nice, subtile; plodding mentally, brooding, pondering.

Grü'bel…, in comp. —kopf, m. see Grübler; —krank, adj. splenetic; —krankheit, f. spleen.

Grü'beln, (w.) v. I. intr. 1) to grub; dig; 2) fig. (with über (gener. followed by the Acc.)) a) to refine, to indulge in subtile inquiries; to be hypercritical (in trifles); to speculate; b) to rack one's brains (about), to pry (into), to ruminate (on, upon, over), to plod (upon); to ponder, muse, brood, ruminate (over misfortunes, &c.); 3) impers. (v. Horn [cf. Sanders], I. w.) Einem —, to fill one with brooding thoughts, to puzzle; II. refl. sich (Acc.) zu Tode —, to kill one's self by constant reflection, meditation.

Grü'belnuß, (str., pl. G-nüsse) f. thick-shelled walnut.

Gru'ben, (w.) v. intr. 1) to lay traps (for wild animals); 2) Vint. to provine.

Gru'ben…, in comp. Min-s. —arbeit, f. the working in a mine; —arbeiter, m. miner, workman in a mine, pit-man; —aufstand, m. report of the state of a mine; —bau, m. mine-digging; —beil, n. miner's axe, pick-axe; —bericht, m. see —aufstand; —blende, f. miner's lantern; —compaß, m. miner's compass; —dünger, m. Husb. manure; —ende, n. Vint. provine; —erz, n. ore gained in a mine; —förderung, f. working of mines; —gebäude, n. mine-pits, shafts; —gericht, n. court of mines; —gezähe, n. miner's tools; —gut, n. fossils; —holz, n. timber used for mines; —hüter, m. guard of a mine; —junge, m. miner's boy; —kittel, m., —kleid, n. miner's dress; —kohle, f. charcoal; —[illegible], m. see —arbeiter; —licht, n. miner's lamp; —loch, n. Shoe-m. patch; —messung, f. see —zug; —mütze, f. miner's cap; —pulver, n. blasting-powder; —reich, adj. abounding in mines; —säge, f. pit-saw; —sand, m. pit-sand; —steiger, m. overseer of miners; —tasche, f. miner's pocket; —tscherper, m. miner's knife; —wasser, n. swallet; —werk, n. pit-work; —wetter, n. choke damp (frequently found in mines and wells); —zeug, n. see —[illegible]; —zug, m. the measuring of a mine.

[illegible] for drawing anything from the bottom of a river, &c.; 2) see Dreghaken; —höse, m. [illegible] of the valley; —hecht, m. pike that keeps [to] the bottom of the water: —hefe, f. lees, [sed]iment; —heil, n. Bot. 1) stone or mountain [pars]ley (Peucedanum oreoselinum Moench): [see] Ehrenpreis; 2) corn-pimpernel: —herr, [m.] lord of the soil; —herrlichkeit, f. lordship, [territorial) dominion, jurisdiction; —herr[schaft], f. 1) see —herrlichkeit; 2) lord or lady of [the] manor; —heuer, f. †, ground rent; —hieb, [m.] F. the first and lowest cuts or strokes on [a t]ree; —hobel, m. Join., &c. grooving plane, [pl]ough; —hold, m. 1) possessor of a ground-[plot]; 2) vassal, villein.

Grun'dig, Grün'dig, adj. 1) having a taste [of the] grounds; 2) in comp. ... bottomed.

Grundir'bällchen, (str.) n. Engr. dabber [to] lay the ground for etching.

Grundi'ren, (w.) v. tr. T. see Gründen, 2; [grundirte] Leinwand, printed linen.

Grundir'rolle, (w.) f. grounding roller.

Grund'..., in comp. —irrthum, m. fun[da]mental error; —joch, n. Build. foundation-[[illegible]]; —kenntniß, f. fundamental knowledge; [—kette], f. Weav. (fundamental) warp, main [warp], ground; —kettenfaden, m. thread of the [gro]und-warp; —köder, m. Angl. ground-bait; [—kraft], f. primitive, primary, essential force, [genuine] or true power; —kugel, f. fire-ball [burning] under water (in fireworks); —lage, f. [fo]undament, groundwork, foundation, basis, [[illegible]] Chem. radical base; —lagerholz, n. Build. [[illegible]]: —lasten, pl. fees and soccage on [landed] property; —laut, —lauter, m. vowel; [—leger], m. founder; —legung, f. the laying a [fo]undation; founding, foundation; establish[ment]; —lehre, f. fundamental doctrine.

Gründ'lich, I. adj. 1) fundamental, well [grounded], solid, thorough, profound; adv. [thor]oughly, to the bottom; 2) radical (as a [reform, &c.); ein g-er Beweis, a clear, evident, or apodictical proof; ein g-er Gelehrter, a [deep] scholar; II. G-keit, (w.) f. fundamen[tal]ness, solidity, profoundness; firmness, [thor]oughness; radicality; ein Buch von großer [G-]keit, a book of deep research.

Gründ'ling, (str.) m. 1) Ichth. a) ground[ling] (Cobitis taenia L.); b) gudgeon (Gobio [fluviatilis] C.); 2) Forest. crooked and knotty [tim]ber; G-sreuse, f. Fish. bow-net. [line.

Grund'linie, (w.) f. T. ground-line, base-

Grund'los, I. adj. groundless: 1) bottom[less]; 2) unfathomable; 3) unfounded, cause[less]; unsupported; II. G-igkeit, (w.) f. 1) [groundlessness]; 2) unfathomableness.

Grund'..., in comp. —mauer, f. founda[tion]-wall, arch-wall; —meißel, m. T chasing-[[illegible]]; —mischung, f. mixture of the ele[ments]; —mörtel, m. Mas., Dik., &c. concrete; [—neigung], f. original propensity.

Grün'donnerstag, (str.) m. Maundy-[Thurs]day.

Grund'..., in comp. —pfahl, m. (founda[tion-])pile, post; —pfeiler, m. 1) ground, [foundation-pillar]; 2) fig. pillar, sheet-[anchor]; —platte, f. bed-plate; —quell, m., —[quelle], f. original fountain; —rabe, f. 1) vine-[[illegible]] that shoots from the dew or water-[[illegible]]; 2) see —ephen; —rechnungsart, f. one [of] the four first rules of arithmetic; —recht, [n.] 1) right or privilege derived from the [possession] of territory; 2) fundamental law, [[illegible]]; —regel, f. fundamental rule, axiom, [[illegible]]; —regiment, n. see —buch; —reich, adj. [[illegible]], very rich; —rente, f. ground-rent; —[richtig], adj. very right, thoroughly right; [—richtung], f. primitive, original, or principal [[illegible]] or tendency (of mind, &c.); —risse, f. [[illegible]] sewer; —riß, m. first sketch; [[illegible]], ground plan (of a building); —satz, m. [principle], axiom, maxim; aus —satz, from principle; upon system; von guten (schlechten) —sätzen, well-(ill-)principled; ohne —sätze, unprincipled; ich habe es mir zum —satze gemacht, I have laid it down as a maxim, it is a firm rule with me; I have made it a rule; allgemeine —sätze, general rules; —sätzlich, I. adj. founded or based on principles; fundamental (cf. Principiell); die —sätzliche Verschiedenheit, difference in principle; II. adv. from principle; —sauer, m. Bak. chief leaven; —säule, f. foot, pedestal, basis; supporter, foundation pillar; —schäfte, m. pl. Weav. ground-leaves; —schelm, m. coll. arch-rogue; Archit.-a. —schicht, f. footings (of a wall): —schlag, m. model; —schnitt, m. projection; —schnur, f. see —angel; —schoß, m. see —steuer; —schreiber, m. terrier-clerk; —schuld, f. mortgage; —schwelle, f. groundsel, groundsil(l), Railw., &c. ground plate, sleeper; —see, f. Mar. roller, shoal; —sicher, adj. 1) of a firm, sure foundation; 2) fig. very sure, secure; —silbe, f. fundamental (radical) syllable; —sprache, f. original language, original: —spruch, m. text; —stein, m. 1) Min. primary rock; 2) Archit. foundation-stone, ground-stone, corner-stone; 3) bedder, bedstter (of a mill); —steinlegung, f. laying of the foundation or first-stone; —steuer, f. land-tax, ground-rent, cess; —stimme, f. 1) bass voice; 2) see —baß; —stoff, m. Chem. element, radical; first principle, coll. stone-laying; —strauch, m. Bot. trailing arbutus (Epigaea repens L.); —strich, m. 1) Paint. knotting; 2) down stroke (in writing, opp. Haarstrich); —stück, n. 1) ground-property, real estate, cf. Grund, 7; premises; 2) essential part of a thing; —stütze, f. fundamental prop or support; —substanz, f. see —stoff; —suppe, f. coll. grounds, dregs, sediment: —sylbe, see —silbe; Mar.-a. —takelage, f. ground-tackle; —talje, f. see yoke, rudder-tackle, relieving tackle (of the rudder): —tau, n. relieving-rope, pl. relieving-tackles; —taube, f. a species of very small pigeon; —text, m. original text; —thatsache, f. fundamental fact; —theil, m. fundamental part: —theilchen, n. atom; —theilung, f. division of a real estate; —ton, m. fundamental or principal tone; key-note, root, tonic, the bass note (—baß); —trieb, m. fundamental or natural impulse, fundamental principle of action: —übel, n. primary, radical evil, fault.

Grün'dung, (w.) f. 1) foundation; establishment; erection; 2) Paint. priming; G-seisen, n. Engr. grounding-tool.

Grund'..., in comp. —ursache, f. principal reason, original (primitive) cause: —verbesserung, f. thorough reform; —verfassung, f. fundamental constitution; —vermögen, n. 1) (—besitz) landed property; 2) Comm. capital, fund; 3) see —kraft; —verpfändung, f. mortgaging of land: —verschieden, adj. radically, totally, or entirely different; —verschiedenheit, f. fundamental or radical difference; —wachs, n. bee-bread, propolis; —wage, f. T. (plumb) level; hydrostatic level; —wägekunst, f. hydrostatics; —wahrheit, f. fundamental, primary, or radical truth; —wasser, n. water found under ground; —weide, f. Bot. dwarf creeping-willow (Salix viminalis L.); —werk, n. ground-work, lower work; —wesen, n. the original, intrinsic, or radical nature, essence; —wissenschaft, f. fundamental science; —wolle, f. Comm. bottom-hair; —wort, n. primitive or primary word; root; —zahl, f. 1) Math. unit; 2) Gramm. cardinal number; —zapfen, m. floodgate (of a pond); —zehnte, m. tithes paid of lands; —zeichnung, f. ichnography; —zins, m. ground-rent; rent-service; —zinsherr, m. lord of the manor; —zinsmann, m. tenant; —zug, m. 1) ground-line or feature of a thing; outline, sketch; 2) fig. a distinguishing mark, characteristic, leading trait or feature; in den —zügen, substantially.

Grü'ne, Grü'nes, n. see Grün, II.

Grün'..., in comp. —eiche, f. a variety of the common British oak; —eisenerde, f. green martial earth; —eisenerz, n., —eisenstein, m. Miner. green iron-ore.

Grü'neln, (w.) v. intr. 1) to begin to get green; 2) to smell of green.

Grü'nen, (w.) v. I. intr. 1) to become green, to strike leaves; 2) fig. to thrive, flourish, prosper; II. tr. Dy. to air (green-dyed stuffs); g-d, p. a. verdant.

Grün'..., in comp. —erde, f. green earth: —fenchbaum, m. Bot. common privet (Ligustrum vulgare L.); —fink, m. Ornith. green-finch, barley-bird (Linota chloris L.): —gelb, adj. greenish-yellow: —hänfling, m. Ornith. see —fink; —harz, n. Chem. chlorophyll.

Grün'heit, (w.) f. greenness.

Grün'..., in comp. —herzholz, n. green heart-wood; —holz, n. Bot. 1) dwarf-pine (Pinus pumilio Hänke); 2) Scotch fir (Pinus sylvestris L.); 3) dyer's green-wood (Färberginster).

Grü'nitz, (str.) m. 1) Ornith. see Grünfink; 2) Bot. green-broom (Färberginster).

Grün'..., in comp. —kohl, m. Bot. green kail or kale, cabbage: Ornith.-a. —kopf, m. a kind of thrush; —krähe, f. roller (Mandelkrähe); —kraut, n. green herbs, see Grün, II. 2, b; —land, n. provinc. meadow-land.

Grün'lich, adj. greenish, greenly.

Grün'ling, (str.) m. 1) one dressed in green; 2) coll. see Grünschnabel, 2; 3) Ornith. grossbeak (Kernbeißer); 4) Bot. green agaric (Agaricus virescens).

Grün'..., in comp. —markt, m. vegetable-market; —ober, see Ober, grüner; —rock, m. fam. 1) (one wearing a) green coat; 2) game-keeper, forester; —rostig, adj. eruginous; —säure, f. Chem. verdic acid; —sand, m. Geol. greensand, galt; (der untere) shanklin-sand, blue-clay; —schnabel, m. 1) Ornith. (or —schnäbler) thick-kneed plover, stone curlew (Dickfuß); 2) coll. young saucy person (gener. Gelbschnabel); —schwanz, m. see —fink; —schwarz, adj. greenish-black; —span, m. 1) verdigris, copper rust; crystallisirter —span, crystals of verdigris; 2) Bot. dyer's green-wood (Färberginster); —spanblumen, f. pl. Chem. acetous salts; —spancerat, n. Pharm. green-wax; —spanessig, m. vinegar of verdigris, acetic vinegar; —spangeist, m. Chem. acetic acid: —spansalbe, f. Egyptian salve; —spath, m. Miner. malacolite; —specht, m. Ornith. green-peak (Picus viridis L.); —stein, m. green stone, diabase; (dichter) green porphyr; (schiefriger) aphanite: —streifig, adj. having green streaks; —sucht, f. Med. green sickness, chlorosis: —vogel, m. see —fink.

Grun'zen, (w.) v. intr. to grunt (as a hog); das —, (str.) v. a grunt (of hogs), grunting.

Grunz'ochs, (w.) m. Zool. the grunting ox, or yak of Tartary (Bos grunniens L.).

* Grup'pe, (w.) f. (Fr. group(p)e, Ital. groppo, gruppo) group; cluster; eine — von Bäumen, a clump or cluster of trees; g-nweise, adv. in or by groups. — Grup'pen, Gruppi'ren, (w.) v. tr. to group. — Gruppi'rung, (w.) f. a grouping.

Grus, (str.) m. I. (orig. Gruß) rubbish, garble; II. (Göthe, cf. Weigand) for Graus.

Gru'sche, (w.) f. provinc. gosling.

Gru'sel, (str.) m. provinc. cold shuddering, fright. [ful shape (Grausel).

Grü'sel, (str.) m. provinc. (Suabia.) fright-

Gru'selig, adj. coll. see Graulig.

Gru'seln, (w.) v. intr. (impers.) (with Dat.) to shudder, shiver; es gruselt mir, I feel a cold shudder. cf. Grausen.

[illegible]ur'ren, (w.) v. intr. to coo, croo, lurr, [illegible].

[illegible]urt, s. I. (str.) m. 1) girdle; girt, girth: [illegible]-girdle (of a cannon); 3) Archit. a) [illegible] Säule) girt, girth; b) groining; archi-[illegible] 4) (or —band) webbing, webe; II. in [illegible], —bett, n. a bedstead with a bottom of [illegible]girt fastened crosswise; —bogen, m. Archit. [illegible] Tech.) 1) (Verstärkungsbogen, Quergurt) [illegible]verse arch; 2) (eines Tonnengewölbes) [illegible] of a cylindrical vault; unten bündiger, [illegible] vortretender —bogen (Obergurt), over-[illegible], head-arch; sichtbarer, unten vortretender [illegible]bogen, archivault; —bogenvorlage, f. see [illegible].

[illegible]ür'tel, s. I. (str.) m. 1) girdle; girt, [illegible]; 2) sash, belt; 3) T. zone; 4) virgin-[illegible], fig. virginity; 5) Astr. fascia, belt; 6) [illegible] shingles, herpes zoster (a variety of her-[illegible], or tetter, in which the vesicles spread [illegible] the body like a girdle); 7) Mar. see Gor-[illegible]; — der Venus, cestus; II. in comp. —bahn, [illegible]circling railway (T. Tech.); —flechte, f. see [illegible], 6; —förmig, adj. belt- or girdle-like: [illegible], f. key-chain; —kraut, n. see Bärlapp.

[illegible]ür'teln, (w.) v. tr. 1) see Gürten; 2) [illegible] to peel off the bark of (a tree).

[illegible]ür'tel..., in comp. —ring, m girdle-ring, [illegible]ring; —rose, f. see Gürtel, 6; —schloß, n. [illegible] of a belt; —schnalle, f. buckle of a belt; [illegible] girth-buckle; —schnecke, f. Conch. zoned [illegible] (Turbo cilicia); —thier, n. Zool. arma-[illegible] (Dasypus L.); —wurm, m. see Riemen-[illegible]. [with girts.

[illegible]ur'ten, (w.) v. tr. to tie, fix, or fasten

[illegible]ür'ten, (w.) v. tr. & refl. to gird, girdle, [illegible]; fig. to make one's self ready, to prepare.

[illegible]urt..., in comp. —gehenk, n. something [illegible]pended by a belt; —gesims, n. see —sims; [illegible], m. girth-clasp.

[illegible]ürt'ler, (str.) m. 1) girdler, girdle-maker, [illegible]maker; 2) brass-founder.

[illegible]urt..., in comp. —pfeiler, m. Archit. [illegible] pier (of a cellar-vault); —riemen, [illegible] girt-leather; —ring, m., —schnalle, f. girt-[illegible]; —schnecke, f. zoned snail; —sims, m., [illegible], n. Archit. plinth (of a pillar, wall, &c.), [illegible].

[illegible]ur'tung, (w.) f. Carp. binding-piece, tie.

[illegible]u'sche, (w.) f. vulg. see Gosche.

[illegible]uß, s. I. (str., pl. Güs'se) m. 1) casting, [illegible]; cast, ingot; aus Einem —, of one [illegible] or cast; Found-s. a) Typ. font, fount; [illegible] —recht; ein — Lettern, a set of letters; [illegible], torrent, shower, peal (of rain); 3) [illegible], drain; sink; 4) lip, spout (of a cream-[illegible], tea-pot, &c.); 5) T. water for one brew-[illegible] mash; II. in comp. (cf. Gieß...) —ab-[illegible], m. Typ. cast; —abdrucksverfertigung, f. [illegible]; —arbeit, f. 1) casting, founding; [illegible] —waare; —eisen, n. cast iron; —eisern, [illegible] (of) cast iron; — und schmiedeeiserne Ka-[illegible] —eiserne haben große Härte ..., cast-[illegible] wrought-iron cannons: cast-iron possess [illegible] hardness (Mech. Mag. 1855); —erz, n. [illegible]copper; —form, f. casting-mould; —loch, [illegible] gate; —messing, n. cast brass; — [illegible], f. T. 1) mouth-piece of a water-[illegible] 2) discharging-hole; —mutter, f. matrix; [illegible], f. see Formsand; —pfeife, f. T. runner; [illegible], m. shower of rain; —röhre, f. pipe, [illegible] of a fountain; —stahl, m. cast steel; [illegible], m. sink; gutter-stone, drain, sewer; [illegible], f. —werk, n. casting work; —waa-[illegible], pl. castings.

[illegible] adj. provinc. sterile, barren. [illegible], m. Gustavus (P. N.). [time.

[illegible]e, (w.) f. provinc. 1) fallow; 2) fallow-[illegible] (str.) m. provinc. 1) sweet willow [illegible] 2) Bot. black, bay (Weide).

[illegible] I. adj. 1) good; adv. well; — unter-[illegible] under-feeding; Comm. in good condition; so — er kann, as he best may; 2) agreeable, pleasant, convenient, easy; good-natured; favourable, well-disposed, friendly, kind; 3) genuine, pure; 4) sound; wholesome; 5) considerable, sufficient; 6) Cook. done, see Gar; 7) Comm. creditable, respectable, good, safe: vorzüglich —, of high standing (of firms); g-es Gold, Silber, fine or pure gold, silver; g-es Wetter, fair weather: ein g-er Wind, a fair wind: g-er Heinrich, see Heinrich; g-en or g-es Muthes, of good comfort; g-es Muthes, g-er Dinge sein, to be of good cheer, to be in good hopes; (Einem) g-e Worte geben, to speak (one) fair, to beg (pardon); g-e Tage haben, to live in ease and prosperity; sich einen g-en Tag machen, to make one's self easy, to make a holiday of it; eine g-e Meile, a good or full mile; in g-en Umständen, well off; es — haben, to be well off; sich — kleiden, to dress well; ein g-es Gedächtniß, a tenacious memory; in g-em Sinne, in a good sense: — dem Dinge, coll. so far, so good; Ende —, Alles —, proverb. all's well that ends well; es ist schon —, 'tis enough, that will do; auch —! good again! es wäre vielleicht — zu..., it may be as well to ...; es ist —, daß ich nicht gegangen bin, it is well or fortunate that I did not go; ich kann ihn nicht — hören, I cannot hear him well; kann seine Schwester so — singen als er? can his sister sing as well as he; sie könnte sich — verheirathen, she might marry well; — verheirathet, married well; eben so — wie, as well as; so — als gethan or geschehen, as well as done, all but done; der Posten (Waare) ist so — als angebracht, the item may be considered as disposed of; sein Sie so — und sagen Sie mir, be so kind as to tell me, I will thank you for telling me; sein Sie so — mir das Salz zu reichen, I will thank you for the salt; und damit —! and there let it end, and there is an end of it; lassen Sie es — sein, let it pass; don't mention it; never mind it; let us have done with it; cf. Lassen, B, 1; — sein, — sagen, — stehen, to answer (für, for), to be security or responsible (for), to pass one's word, to warrant, vouch (for); für g-e Qualität wird eingestanden (in Zeitungsanzeigen), warranted; — thun, coll. 1. (or — sein) to do (one) good, to be of use or service, to benefit; 2. to behave well (of servants, &c.); er fand es nicht für —, es zu thun, he did not see fit or think proper to do so; — heißen, to approve of, agree to, sanction, allow; sich — halten, to keep good (as fruits, &c.); für — halten, ansehen, to think proper; (eine Sache) — aufnehmen, to take (a matter) in good part; — machen, to make good, to prove (an assertion); Bäume — machen, see Pfropfen, Okuliren; einen Verlust — machen, to make up for a loss; wieder — machen, 1. to make amends or reparation for, to redress, repair; 2. to appease (one); — sein zu, to be adapted or fit for; — zu gebrauchen, of good use; dazu ist er — zu gebrauchen, he is good at it; so ist's —, that will do; es war — für uns, it was well for us; (Einem) — sein, to wish (one) well, to love, like; mit Einem — sein, to be on friendly terms with one; sie sind wieder —, they have made it up again; sei wieder —, be friends again; (Einem) — bleiben, to continue to like; Sie haben — reden, ('tis) very easy for you to talk; er hat — lachen, he may well laugh; kurz und —, in short; sich (Dat.) etwas zu g-(e) thun, see sich Gütlich thun; sich (Dat.) etwas mehr zu g-(e) thun, to make a merit of, to take merit (credit) to one's self for, to value one's self upon, to be proud of a thing; (Einem etwas) zu g-e halten, to excuse, pardon, bear with (one); uns (Dat.) zu g-e, for our good, in our behalf; to our advantage; Einem zu g-(e) kommen, to serve or be to one's benefit; to be of use or service to one; das kommt ihm zu g-e, he has the benefit of it; Einem etwas zu g-e kommen lassen, to give or allow one the benefit of ...; zum G-en auslegen, to judge charitably; Comm-s. — abgehen, to go off readily; — und wohlbehalten, in good order and well-conditioned, in a sound state; ein g-es Haus, a house of high standing or of established credit; g-es Papier, good, negociable, or first-rate paper; g-e Waare verkauft sich von selbst, good ware makes quick markets; Einem etwas zu g-e (or —) schreiben or bringen, to place (or carry) to one's credit, to make good to one, to make one creditor for; es soll Ihnen — geschrieben werden, it shall appear in your credit; Ihre Remessen sollen Ihnen — gebracht werden, your remittances shall appear to your credit; — haben, to have a balance in one's favour; es kommen Ihnen noch zwei Thaler zu g-(e) or Sie haben noch zwei Thaler —, there are two dollars due to you; — (i. e. creditfähig) sein, — stehen, to be good, solid, creditable; — für ..., good for ....

II. s. der, die, das G-e, (decl. like adj.) the good man, good woman, a good thing; der G-e fürchtet sich nicht, the good man is not afraid; G-es, good things, good; G-es thun, to do good; viel G-es, many good things; much good; man kann des G-en nicht zu viel haben, one cannot have too much of a good thing; es kann zu nichts G-em führen, it cannot lead to good; ein Vorschlag im G-en (or zur Güte), proposal for amicable settlement, &c.; das G-e, (moral) good; alles G-e und Große, whatever is good and great; es ist manches G-e an ..., there are many good parts in ...; es ist nichts G-es an ihm, there is no good in him; Einem viel G-es thun, to do one many favours and kindnesses; im G-en, in G-em, amicably, friendly; by fair means; im G-en oder im Bösen, by fair or foul means; Einem etwas im G-en sagen, to tell one a thing in a friendly manner; Einem G-es gönnen, wünschen, to wish one well; gern etwas G-es essen, to love tid-bits, dainties; um ein G-es näher, a good deal nearer.

Gūt, (str., pl. Gü'ter) n. 1) good; blessing; 2) valuable possession; gift, endowment; portion; (landed, &c.) property, estate, fortune; wealth; 3) estate; country-seat, country-house, Am. farm; 4) Comm. gener. pl. goods, wares, commodities; Law-s. das erworbene —, acquisition; das heimgefallene —, escheat; bewegliche Güter, movable goods, movables; Güter eines Falliten, assets; — und Blut, life and fortune; das Leben ist der Güter höchstes nicht (Schiller, Braut v. Mess., end), of man's possessions life is not the best.

Gūt'..., adj. in comp. —achten, n. professional opinion (of a committee or of competent judges), decision, award, arbitration, arbitrement, judgment, verdict; advice, thought; approbation; ein —achten über (with Acc.) einholen, sich einem —achten unterwerfen, to leave or submit (a matter) to the opinion or verdict of a select committee (of merchants, &c.), to submit to or apply for (an) arbitration; nach meinem —achten, in my opinion; nach Ihrem —achten, as you think proper; sein —achten geben, to pass one's judgment; —achtlich, adj. & adv. as or by way of an opinion or judgment; discretionary; —artig, adj. 1) good-natured, habitually kind; 2) see Unschädlich; 3) Med. (scarlatina, &c.) of a favourable or mild kind; das —artige Fieber, typical fever; —artigkeit, f. good-naturedness, &c.; good nature; —befinden, n. 1) approbation, liking, pleasure, discretion; nach Ihrem —befinden, 1. according to your judgment; 2. upon your own terms; 2) see —achten; 3) see Wohlbefinden; —belaubt, adj. Sport. well-mouthed (said of hounds); —dünkel, m.

[illegible], *f. provinc. for* Eberraute; —reis, *m.* [illegible] American oat-rice; —rispe, *f. see* Haargras[illegible]; —rohr, *n.* rural *or* oaten-pipe; —rose, [illegible] creeping rose-bush; —saat, *f.* 1) oat-sowing; 2) season for sowing oats; 3) oat-[illegible]; —sack, *m.* a sack for oats; —schlehe, *f.* [illegible]-pflaume; —schleim, *m.* water-gruel; —schrecke, *f. see* Heuschrecke; —schrot, *m. see* —[illegible]; —seim, *m. see* —schleim; —spieß, *m.* [illegible] dogwood; —spreu, *f.* oats-chaff; —stoppel, *f.* oats-stubble; —stroh, *n.* oat-straw; [illegible], *m. see* —acker; —suppe, *f.* oatmeal-soup; [illegible], *m. see* —schleim; —wurz(el), *f. see* [illegible]bart, 2; —ziege, *f. see* —bock; —zins, *m.* [illegible].

Haff, *s.* I. *(str.) n.* († & *) provinc.* sea; bay, [illegible]; II. *in comp.* —deich, *m.* a dike on the sea-shore; —dorn, *m. Bot.* sea-buckthorn *(Hippophaë rhamnoides* L.); —padde, *f. provinc.* lump-fish (Meerhase).

Häf'ner, *(str.) m. provinc. (S. G.)* potter [(Töpfer).

Haft, *(str., pl. sometimes [w.]* H-en) *m.* & [illegible] 1) hold, the quality of clinging, holding, [illegible] fast to ...; 2) clasp, rivet, brace, [illegible]; 3) *see* Eintagsfliege.

Haft, *(w.) f.* prison, arrest, durance, confinement, custody, detention, imprisonment; [illegible] —, in prison, under arrest; in enger — sein, to be a close prisoner.

Haft'bar, I. *adj.* answerable (für, for); II. [illegible], *(w.) f.* liability; beschränkte —, limited liability.

Haft..., *in comp.* —befehl, *m.* warrant *or* writ of arrest, detainder; —beschwerde, *f.* servitude; —brief, *m. see* —befehl; —dolde, *f. Bot.* bur-parsley *(Caucalis daucoides* L.); —dorn, *m. Bot.* sea-buckthorn (Haffdorn).

Haf'ten, *(w.) v. intr.* 1) *lit.* & *fig.* (with [illegible], auf [& *Dat.*], bei *2c.*) to cleave, cling, hold, stick (to), to be attached, to attach (to); 2) to remain, be fixed; 3) (*with* für, *cf.* Bürgen & Stehen für) to answer, warrant, *or* be liable for; persönlich —, to stand *or* be bound personally; für Jemanden —, to bail one; es [illegible] Schulden auf dem Gute, the estate is encumbered; es haftet nichts an *or* bei ihm, nothing affects him *or* remains in (takes any hold [illegible]) his memory; dies haftet mir für seine Verschwiegenheit, this insures me of his secrecy.

Haf'tenstiel, *(str.) n.* glazier's bands *or* [illegible].

Haft'geld, *(str.) n.* 1) prison fee, bar-fee; 2) *provinc.* earnest-money, *cf.* Angeld.

Häft'ling, *(str.) m.* one detained in custody, prisoner. [chisel.

Haft'meißel, *(str.) m.* gunmaker's socket-

Haft'pflichtig, *adj.* answerable (Haftbar).

Haf'tung, *(w.) f.* surety, bond.

Hag, *(str.) m.* I. 1) hedge, fence; 2) bush, coppice; wood; 3) a place fenced *or* hedged in; II. *provinc.* bull; III. *in comp.* —apfel, *m.* crab-apple, wild apple, wildling; —apfelbaum, *m. see* [illegible].

Ha'gen, Ha'gart, *(str.) m. see* Hagerfalk.

Ha'ge..., *in comp.* —buche, *f. Bot.* horn- *or* hard-beam, yoke elm *(Carpinus betulus* L.); —büchen, *adj. only.* 1) beechen; 2) *fig.* coarse; —buchenrüster, *f.* cork-elm; *Bot.-s.* —butte, *f.* hip, haw; —buttenbirne, *f.* medlar-pear; —buttenstrauch, *m.* dog-rose tree; —dorn, *m. Bot.* 1) *see* —rose; 2) hawthorn, white thorn; —drüsen, *f. pl. coll.* king's evil; —gans, *f. provinc.* common goose. [gall-bearing oak.

Ha'geiche, *(w.) f.* holm-oak, scarlet-oak,

Ha'gel, *(str.) m.* I. 1) hail; sleet; 2) small shot, hand-shot, hail-shot; II. trendle; III. *Anat.* stye (Gerstenkorn); IV. Jan—, Hans—, *provinc.* the mob, mobility; V. *in comp.* —dicht, *adj.* as thick as hail; —korn, *m. see* —[illegible]; —drüsen, *f. pl. see* Hagedrüsen; —[illegible], *m. see* Hagel, III.; —gans, *f. Ornith.* wild-goose *(Anser cinereus* M. & W.); —gießerei, *f.* shot-foundery; —korn, *n.* 1) hail-stone; 2) *Med.* sty, stian; —kugel, *f.* grape-shot.

Ha'geln, *(w.) v. intr. (impers.)* to hail; es hagelt, it hails.

Ha'gel..., *in comp.* —schaden, *m.* peal of hail, damage done by hail; —schädenversicherungsgesellschaft, *f.* hail-insurance-company; —schauer, —schlag, *m.* hail-shower, hail-stroke, a shower of hail; —schrot, *m. see* Hagel, 2; —stein, *m.* hail-stone; —sturm, *m.* hail-storm, a tempest with hail; —versicherung, *f.* insurance against damage done by hail; —weiß, *adj.* as white as hail; —wetter, *n.* thunder with hail, sleety storm; drift; —wolke, *f.* hail-cloud.

Ha'gemesser, *(str.) n.* hedging bill.

Ha'gen, *(w.) v.* I. *intr. provinc. see* Behagen; II. *refl.* to be delighted, to enjoy one's self.

Hä'gen, *(w.) v. tr.* 1) to fence, enclose, to bar, stop; 2) to preserve, protect; 3) *see* Hegen; das Unterholz —, to copse; gehägte Waldungen, forests hedged in *or* in fence.

Häg'ente, *(w.) f. Ornith. provinc.* wild-duck.

Hä'genweide, *(w.) f. see* Mandelweide.

Ha'geprunk, *(str.) m. (unusual)* one who delights in outward show, ostentatious man; fop. [slender, lank.

Ha'ger, *adj.* haggard, lean, meager, thin,

Hä'ger, *(str.) m.* 1) *see* Heger, 1; 2) *(or* Sandhäger) a small sandy island; —buhne, *f. see* Fangbuhne.

Hä'gereis *2c., see* Hege..., *in comp.*

Ha'gerfalk, *(w.) m. Ornith.* haggard, harrower *(Circus cyaneus* L.).

Ha'gerkeit, *(w.) f.* leanness, meagerness.

Ha'gern, *(w.) v. intr.* to grow haggard, lean, &c.

Ha'gerose, *(w.) f.* 1) dog-rose, wild-rose, dog-briar, wild-briar, hip-tree *(Rosa canina* L.); 2) die wohlriechende —rose, sweet briar, eglantine *(Rosa rubiginosa* L.).

Ha'gestolz, *(w.) m.* an old bachelor, marriage-hater; den H-en spielen, to behave like a whimsical old bachelor; H-e, Ha'gestolzin, *(w.) f. (Adelung; Lw.)* a whimsical old maid.

Häg'ling, *(str.) m. provinc.* a small kind of whiting (Weißling). [(Elritze).

Häg'ner, *(str.) m. Ichth.* minnow, pink

Häg..., *in comp.* —seilrebe, *f.* common traveller's joy *(Clematis vitalba* L.); —weide, *f.* crack-willow (Bruchweide).

Haha'! *interj.* ha! ha!

Haha', *(str., pl.* H-s) *n. Gard.* ha-ha, haw-haw, sunk-fence.

Hä'he, *(w.) f. Sport.* hen-bird.

Hä'her, *(str.) m. see* Eichelhäher.

Hahl, *adj. provinc.* 1) *see* Geheim, Verborgen; 2) *see* Glatt, Schlüpfrig; —kappe, *f.* flatterer, coaxer; —streichen, to flatter, coax.

A. Hahn, *(str., pl.* Häh'ne, *orig.* & *still provinc. [particul. S. G.]* & *poet. w.; cf.* Schl. Heml. 1, 1: des Hahnen Krähn) *m.* 1) cock; *joc.* chanticleer; indianische —, turkey; 2) *T. a)* cock, stop-cock; *b)* cock (of a gun); den — (am Gewehr) spannen, to cock (a gun), to draw the trigger; den — in Ruhe setzen, to half-cock (a gun); *c)* capsule inclosing the balance of a watch; *d) see* Treibkörner; *e) Mar. pl.* brass-cock in a block-sheave; 3) *fig.* bold, courageous fellow; saucy, impudent fellow; *cant-s.* der rothe —, incendiarism; Einem einen rothen — auf das Dach setzen, to set fire to a person's house; *coll.-s.* — im Korbe sein, to be cock of the walk *(coll.* on the wall, cock-a-hoop, &c.); es kräht weder — noch Huhn *(improp.* Hund) danach, *coll.* nobody cares about it; —kerl, *m. T.* clay and coal-dust paste.

B. Hahn, *m. provinc. for* Hain, Hag; —buche, —butte *2c., see* Hagebuche *2c.*

Häh'nchen, Häh'nlein, *(str.) n. (dimin. of* Hahn) a little cock, cockerel.

Häh'ne..., *in comp., see* Hahnen....

Hahn'eisen, *(str.) n. Gun-sm.* cock-stake.

Hahne'kamm, *see* Hahnenkamm.

Hah'nen, *(w.) v.* I. *tr.* to cuckold; II. *intr.* to bray (Jahnen).

Hah'nen..., *in comp.* —balken, *m.* 1) *Carp.* collar-beam, strut-beam, wind-beam, top-beam (of a roof); 2) *coll.* cock-loft, roost; —bart, *m.* wattles, waddles; —ei, *n.* an unusually small egg; —fuß, *m.* 1) *Bot.* crow-foot, ranunculus *(Ranunculus* L.); 2) *Mar. see* —poot; —fütterer, *m.* cock-master, cock-feeder; —gefecht, *n.* cock-fight, cock-fighting; cock-match; —gehäuse, *n. Min.* box of the cock; —geschrei, *n. see* —ruf; —hode, *f.* 1) stone, testicle of a cock; 2) *a)* Cornelian cherry (Cornelkirsche); *b) see* Hagebutte; *c)* horse-plum; —kamm, *m.* 1) crest, cock's-comb; 2) *Bot. a)* coxcomb *(Celosia cristata* L.); *b)* gelber —kamm, yellow rattle *(Rhinanthus* L.); *c) see* —kopf; *d) Conch.* hog's ear, oyster *(Ostrea Marshii* Sow.); —kampf, *m. see* —gefecht; —kopf(klee), *m. see* Esparsette; —kraut, *n. Bot.* cock-weed *(Lepidium* L.); —pfötchen, *n. Bot.* common spindle-tree *(Evonymus europaeus* L.); *Mar.-s.* —platz, *m.* cock-pit; —poot, *m.* crow-foot; —poot an den Marsen, crow-foot of the tops; in einem —poot vertauen, to moor (a ship) by the head; —ruf, —schrei, *m.* crowing of the cock, cock-crow; —schlag(en), *n. Gam.* cock-throwing; —schritt, *m.* 1) cock-stride; 2) *(or* —spatz) *see* —tritt, 2; —sporn, *m.* 1) cock's spur; 2) *Bot. a)* bulbous ranunculus *(Ranunculus bulbosus* L.); *b)* a species of birth wort *(Aristolochia rotunda* L.); *c)* cockspur-thorn *(Crataegus crus galli* L.); *d)* a species of fumitory *(Fumaria bulbosa* L.); —stein, *m. Miner.* obsidian; —stück, *n. see* —gehäuse; —tritt, *m.* 1) cock's tread, cock's treadle (in an egg); 2) *Farr.* string-halt; 3) *Bot.* red pimpernel *(Anagallis arvensis* L.); —wachtel, —wecker, *m. coll.* early breakfast (after a midnight's debauch); —wahrsagerei, *f.* alectryomancy.

Hahn'..., *in comp.* —maul, *n.* lower jaw (of a gun-cock); —poot, *m. see* Hahnenpoot.

Hahn'rei, *(str.) m. coll.* 1) cuckold, tup; (wissentlicher) wittol; (weiblicher) cotquean, cuckquean; 2) name of a game at cards; zum — machen, to cuckold.—Hahn'reischaft, *(w.) f.* cuckoldom, forked plague.

Hahn'..., *in comp.* —schlüssel, *m.* key *or* plug of a (stop-)cock; —tritt, *m. see* Hahnentritt.

Hai, *(str.* & *w.) m. (or* —fisch) *Ichth.* shark, sea-dog, dog-fish *(Carcharias* Cuv.); der getigerte —, spotted *or* tiger shark *(Scyllium maculatum* Blainv.); der glatte —, smooth hound(-fish) *(Mustelus laevis* Rond.); —roche, *m. Ichth.* a kind of ray *(Raja rhinobatos* C.).

Laibe, *see* Heide, A.

Hain, *(str.) m.* I. *, grove, wood, hurst; *Bot.-s.* —ampfer, *m. provinc.* wood-sorrel; —binse, *f.* wood-rush *(Luzula* DC.); —buche, —butte, *see* Hagebuche, Hagebutte; —götze, *m. Myth.* an idol worshipped in a grove; *Bot.-s.* —rose, *f. see* Hundsrose; —weide, *f. see* Schilfweide; II. Freund —, *, (an epithet of) death.

Häk'chen, *provinc.* Hä'kel, *(str.) n. (dimin. of* Haken, *which see)* 1) a little hook, crotchet, *cf.* Haken; 2) *Typ.* apostrophe [']; —stickerei, *f.* embroidery (made in a frame).

Hä'keleisen, *(str.) n.* iron-rod (of pewterers).

Hä'kelarbeit, *(w.) f.* crochet-work.

Häkelei', *(w.) f.* 1) *a) or* Hä'keln, *(str.) n.* crochet-work (a kind of knitting performed with a small hook); *b)* (a piece of) crochet-work; 2) (the act of) teasing, provocation, cavil.

Hä'kelig, I. *adj.* 1) hooked; 2) *fig.* critical, nice, particular; delicate; eine h-e Sache, a ticklish matter; II. H-keit, *(w.) f.* niceness, ticklishness; captiousness.

[illegible]…, *in comp.* —[illegible]er, *m. see* —bauer; [illegible], *m.* 1) *see* —pachter; 2) eunuch; —[illegible], *f.* beech-mast; —meier, *m. see* —hüfner; [illegible] *adv.* at half mast; —mensch, *m.* 1) demi-man: *Fab.* a fabulous being half man [illegible] brute; 2) *fig.* a barbarian; —messer, *m.* [illegible]messer; —metall, *n.* semi-metal; —[illegible], *m.* half-moon (*also Fort.*): *Herald.*, &c. [illegible]: —mondförmig, *adj.* semi-lunar, crescent[illegible]; *Bot.*, &c. crescent-shaped; *Anat.* semilunar *or* sigmoidal (valves); —meißel, *m. T.* [illegible]; —mondschnecke, *f. Conch.* nerita (*Nerita fluviatilis* L.); —mondwinde, *f.* cooper's [illegible] *or* screw; —mutter, *f.* step-mother; —[illegible], *adj.* half-naked; —oberschlächtiges [illegible], *Mill.* breast-wheel; —officiell, *adj.* [illegible]amtlich; —pacht, *f.* renting of a farm for [illegible] half of the product; —pachter, *m.* a tenant [illegible] his rent from half the proceeds of [illegible] soil; —parquet, *n.* cased (clamped) floor; [illegible], *f.* halves; auf —part einstreichen, *coll.* [illegible] halves; —part! rufen, to cry halves; [illegible], *m. Archit.* pilaster; —pfünder, *m.* [illegible] a half pounder; —pfündig, *adj.* weighing *or* containing half a pound; —pfundpackete, *pl. Comm.* half-pound packages, *coll.* halves; [illegible], *f.* half-pike; —piqué, *m.* mock-quilt[illegible]; —porphyr, *m.* semi-porphyry; —porzellan, *n.* mock-china, Wedgewood ware; *cf.* [illegible]; —recht, *n. see* Raubafer; —reif, I. *adj.* [illegible]; II. *s. m. Mar.* an iron hoop that [illegible] the top-gallant-masts to the main[illegible]; —reinhanf, *m. Comm.* third sort of [illegible] hemp; —ring, *m.* semicircular ring; [illegible] wall-hook; —röhrig, *adj. Bot.* semi-[illegible]; —rund, *adj.* half round, semi-circular, semi-spherical; —säule, *f. Archit.* im[illegible] column; —säulenförmig, *adj. Bot.* [illegible]-columnar; —säure, *f. Chem.* oxyd, oxyde; [illegible]schatten, *m. Opt.*, &c. penumbra, half *or* [illegible] shade; —scheid, —schied, *f. coll.* half, [illegible]; die zarte —scheid, *joc.* the tender (*i. e.* [illegible]) sex; the better half (wife of a man); [illegible], *adj. see* —schlägig; —schlag, *m.* mixed breed, mongrel (breed *or* race); [illegible] hemiplegy; —schlägig, *adj.* mongrel, [illegible], hybrid; —schlägiger Vogel, —schläger, [illegible] mule bird; —schlicht, *f. Fisc.* second cut; [illegible], *f. see* Haarschnepfe; —schrittig, *adj.* [illegible] chromatic, semitonic; —schuh, *m.* slip[illegible]; —schürig, *adj.* 1) (wool) of the second [illegible]; 2) *fig.* inferior, mediocre; —schwer, *adj.* middling (figure); —schwester, *f.* half-sister, step-sister; —sehen, *n. Med.* hemi[illegible]; —sehne, *f. Geom.* half-sine; —[illegible], *f.* silk mixed with cotton, &c.; —seiden, *adj.* half silk half cotton, &c.; —seidene [illegible], *pl. Comm.* half silk stuffs, half-silks; [illegible], *f. Typ.* column; —seitige Lähmung, *Med.* hemi-plegy; —silber, *n. see* Platin; —[illegible], *m.* half-pay; —sopran, *m. Mus.* mezzo-soprano; —spänner, *m. see* —hüfner; —spar[illegible], *m. Build.* half-spar, sleeper; —spann[illegible] *T.* reheating-plates; —stämmig, *adj.* half-grown (of trees); —stiefel, *m. pl.* [illegible], half-boots, *Am.* Upstoons; —stock, *adv.* [illegible]; —stoßig, *adj. Bot.* semi[illegible]; —stoß, *m.* unfinished; —strümpfe, *pl.* half-stockings, socks; —stündig, *adj.* lasting *or* consisting half an hour, of half an [illegible]; eine —stündige Unterhaltung, half an hour's conversation; —stündlich, *adj.* taking [illegible] every half-hour; —tägig, *adj.* lasting [illegible] a day; —täglich, *adj.* taking place every [illegible]; —theil, *m.* half-share; —theilig, *adj.* [illegible]; —tinte, *f. Paint.* demi-tinte; —[illegible] [illegible]

m. hemistich; —vetter, *m. coll.* distant relative; —vocal, *m. see* —laut(er); —voll, *adj.* half-full; —wach, *adj.* half-awake; —wagen, *m.* chaise; —weg, —wege, —wegs, *adv.* 1) half-way; 2) [*vulg. pr.* hal'wegs] tolerably; —weihe, *f. Ornith.* hen-harrier (*Circus cyaneus* L.); —werk, *n.* half a day's work; —wild, *adj.*, der —wilde, *m.* semi-savage; —wisser, *m.* sciolist; —wisserei, *f.* sciolism; —wollene Waare, mixed woollen goods; —wollenes Tuch, cotton-warp cloth; —wüchsig, *adj.* of half its growth; —zeug, *n. Paper-m.* half-stuff, first-stuff; —zimmer, *n.* room in an *entresol*; —zinn, *n.* base tin; —zirkel, *see* —cirkel; —zitz, *m.* half-chintz.

Hal'de, (*w.*) *f.* 1) *provinc.* sloping ground; hill; †, holt; 2) *Min.* barrow, hillock, *or* mound of dead ore and earth; **H-nschlacke,** *f.* castaway slag; **H-nsturz,** *m.* 1) place where slag is heaped up; 2) right of depositing slag; **H-nwäsche,** *f. see* Erzwäsche.

Hal'den, (*w.*) *v. intr. provinc.* to slope.

Häl'der, (*str.*) *m.* auriferous sliver.

Ha'len, (*w.*) *v. tr. Mar.* to haul, *cf.* Anholen.

Hal'fen, (*str.*) *m. provinc.* (*on the Rhine*) *see* Halbauer.

Hälf'te, (*w.*) *f.* half, moiety; middle; um die — kleiner, less by half; (mit Einem) zur — gehen, to go halves (with one); ich will mich zur — betheiligen, I will be concerned for one moiety; wir sind unser die — zu viel, we are too many by half; bis zur —, to the middle; auf der — des Wegs, half way; Rechnung zur —, *Comm. see* für halbe Rechnung *in* Halb; eine gute —, a fair half; die größere —, the greatest *or* better half; die bessere —, *joc.* the better half (*i. e.* the fair sex, or the wife of a husband).

Hälf'tern, (*w.*) *v. tr. coll. see* Halbiren.

Half'ter, *s.* I. (*w.*) *f.* 1) *a*) halter; *b*) *see* Holfter; 2) *Surg.* (—binde) halter-bandage; 3) *fig.* the gallows; 4) *Ornith.* frontlet (the margin of the head behind the bill of birds); II. *in comp.* —geld, *n.* money given by the purchaser of a horse to the groom of the seller; —kette, *f.* halter-chain; —leine, *f.*, —strick, *m.* halter-rope; —riemen, *m.* halter-strap.

Half'tern, (*w.*) *v. tr.* to (tie by the) halter.

Hälf'tig, *adv.* half, to the half, half-way.

A. **Hall,** (*str.*) *m.* sound.

B. **Hall,** (*str.*) *n.* †, salt-works; —bursch, *m.* (*pl.* —leute) *see* Halloren.

Hall'drommete, (*w.*) *f.* * *see* —trompete.

Hal'le, (*w.*) *f.* 1) hall; 2) porch, portico; 3) the buildings of a salt-work; 4) a hall *or* row of stalls, shops for retail dealers; 5) *Geogr. cf.* Halloren.

* **Hallelu'jah,** *n.* (*Hebr.*) 1) hallelujah; 2) *Bot.* cuckoo-sorrel (*Oxalis acetosella* L.).

Hal'len, (*w.*) *v. intr.* to sound, clang.

Hal'lengeld, (*str.*) *n.* rent paid for salt-stalls. [Erde, *Miner.* aluminite.

Hal'lisch, *adj.* of (the town of) Halle; h-e

Hall'jahr, (*str.*) *n. Jew. Ant. see* Jubeljahr.

Hallo'h! *interj.* halloo! holla! hollo! hey! hoay! — rufen, to (give a) halloo.

Hallo'r(e), (*w.*) *m.* a workman in salt-works (especially at the city of Halle near Leipzig). [pet.

Hall'trompete, (*w.*) *f.* a powerful trum-

Hallunk'(e), (*w.*) *m. see* Halunk.

Halm, (*str.*, *pl.* Hal'me & [*w.*] Hal'men) *m.* 1) blade (of grass, straw, &c.), *Bot.* culm; stalk, halm, straw; Getreide auf dem H-e, green corn; die Frucht auf dem H-e verkaufen, to sell the crop standing *or* the growing crop; 2) (*or* Hal'men, Hälm) Helm, *provinc.* common lime-grass.

Hälm'chen, (*str.*, *pl.* —, *coll.* Häl'merchen) *n.* (*dimin. of* Halm) small blade, stalk, &c.; —ziehen, a kind of children's play consisting in drawing lots with long and short stalks.

Hal'men, (*w.*) *v. intr.* to get stalks.

Halm'…, *in comp.* H-endach, *n.*, —hütte, *f. see* Strohdach &c.; —früchte, *f. pl. see* Getreide.

Hal'mig, *adj.* stalky.

Halm'…, *in comp.* —knoten, *m.* knot of a stalk; —lese, *f.* gleaning; —leser, *m.*, —leserin, *f.* gleaner; —pfeife, *f.* rural *or* oaten pipe; —rübe, *f.* late turnip; —tragend, *adj.* culmiferous.

Hals, (*str.*, *pl.* Häl'se) *m.* 1) neck (*also T.* of a spur, a violin, &c.); throat; head (of a lute); *Archit.* neck (of a capital); 2) collar; 3) *Railw.* web (Steg der Schiene); 4) (*pl.* [*w.*] H-en) *Mar.* *a*) tack (of a sail); *b*) — eines Knieholzes, throat; elbow of a knee; *c*) *see* Außerhals; die H-en aufstechen, to ease the tacks; den — zuleien, to haul aboard the tack of a sail; zwischen zwei H-en fahren, to sail with both sheets aft; die H-en umholen, to tack about, to jib; den — brechen, to break one's neck; *fig.* Einem, to be *or* prove the ruin of one, to undo one; es geht ihm an den —, he may be hung for it; einen langen — machen, to stretch out one's neck (from curiosity), to crane; sich Einem an den — werfen, to jump down one's throat (said of a woman); Einem Alles an den — werfen, to lavish everything on a person; Einem etwas Schlimmes an den — wünschen, to wish one some evil; sich (*Dat.*) etwas an den — reden, to bring something upon one's self by saying something; sich (*Dat.*) die Schwindsucht an den — ärgern, to vex one's self into a consumption; Einem einen Proceß an den — werfen, to bring an action against one; bleib mir damit vom H-e, don't bother me with it; das muß er mit dem H-e bezahlen, his life must pay (atone) for it; einen bösen — haben, to have a sore throat; Einem den — abschneiden, to cut a person's throat; einer Flasche den — brechen, to *knock* *or* crack a bottle; das bricht ihm den —, *coll.* that will prove his ruin; (Einem) um den — fallen, to embrace; *adv.-s.* sich (*Dat.*) etwas vom H-e schaffen, to get rid of; auf dem H-e haben, to be troubled, burthened, encumbered, *or* saddled with; Einem auf dem H-e liegen, to be always at one's elbow, to importune one; to lie upon one's hands; aus vollem — schreien, lachen &c., to cry, laugh, &c. with all one's might (lungs), *or* at the top of one's voice; über — und Kopf, headlong, over head and ears, precipitately, in the utmost haste, *fam.* helter skelter; Einem über den — kommen, to come upon one (at) unawares; bis an den —, (up) to the ears; bis an den — in Schulden, over head and ears (up to the arm-pits) in debt; das wächst mir aus dem H-e, *joc.* I am sick of it.

Hals'…, *in comp.* —ader, *f. Anat.* jugular vein *or* artery; —amboß, *m.* brazier's anvil; —band, *n.* collar, necklace; (—geschmeide, *which see*) †, carcanet; mit einem —bande, *Herald.* collared; *Ornith.-s.* —banddrossel, *f.* ring-ousel (Ringdrossel); —bandregenpfeifer, *m.* ringed dotterel (*Charadrius hiaticula* L.); —bein, *n.* collar bone; —binde, *f.* 1) necklace; (neck-)stock, cravat; 2) *see* —tucheinlage; —blutader, *f. Anat.* throat vein; —braten, *m.* the scraggy end of a deer's neck; —bräune, *f. Med.* inflammation of the throat, angina; —breche, *f.* breakneck (enterprise); —brechend, *adj.* neckbreaking; *fig.* dangerous, perilous, ruinous; —brüchig, *adj. Law*, capital (crime); —bund, *m.* neck-band (of a shirt).

Häls'chen, (*str.*) *n.* (*dimin. of* Hals) 1) little neck; 2) *coll.* *a*) kerchief (of ladies); *b*) *see* Läffchen; *c*) *see* Vorhemdchen.

Hals'…, *in comp.* —dreher, *m. Ornith.* wry-neck (Wendehals); —drüse, *f. Anat.* jugular gland.

emphatically denies that the use of this word can be exemplified from any Austrian writter or popular Austrian usage.

Häl'ter, *(str.) m.* 1) reservoir (of water, fish), *see* Behälter; 2) *see* Fruchtboden, 3.

Hal'te..., *in comp. (cf.* Halt...) –statt, –stelle, –stelle, *f. see* Haltеplatz.

Hal'tig, *adj. in comp.* containing, *as:* silberhaltig, containing silver.

Halt'kette, *(w.) f.* pole-chain of a vehicle.

Halt'los, I. *adj.* 1) without support or stay; unsteady; infirm; 2) untenable (Unhaltbar); II. H-igkeit, *(w.) f.* 1) want of support; unsteadiness; infirmity; 2) untenableness.

Halt'nagel, *(str., pl.* H-nägel) *m.* linch-pin.

Halt'sam, *adj. (l. u.) see* Haltbar.

Halt'..., *in comp.* –seil, –tau, *n. Mar.* vang of a mizen-gaff.

Hal'tung, *(w.) f.* 1) the (act of) holding &c. *see* Halten; hold; 2) carriage, attitude, address, bearing, demeanour; 3) *Paint., &c.* the just proportion of light and shade; harmony, unison of grouping; ohne –, not in keeping; *fig-s.* 4) deportment, behaviour; 5) delivery (of an oration); 6) *Comm-s.* tone, state, &c. (of prices, &c.); – der Börse, feeling on 'Change, state of 'Change; matte –, spiritless state, feeling of dullness; eine abwartende –, expectant attitude; ruhige –, quiet tone; eine festere – annehmen, to acquire or assume more steadiness (or a more lively appearance). [of suspension.

Halt'zeichen, *(str.) n. Gramm.* break, mark

Halun'ke(n), *(w.) m. coll.* ragamuffin, rascal, tatterdemalion, ruffian; H-nburg, *f. local.* (in large cities) a place for rogues and prostitutes; a rookery, *anal.* Alsatia.

Hal'wege, *adv. coll. for* Halbweg. [dryad.

* **Hamadrya'de**, *(w.) f. Gr. Myth.* Hama-

* **Hämatin'**, *(str.) n. (Gr.) Chem.* hematine.

Ham'butte, *see* Hainbutte, Hagebutte.

Hamel'(e), **Hamel'de** 2c., *(w.) f.* 1) fence, &c. (Hamme); 2) *see* Gatterthor.

Ha'men, *(str.) m. Fish.* drag-net, draw-net; *Sport.* tunnel-net.

Hä'misch, *adj.* heinous, malicious, ill-natured, rancorous, spiteful. [marsh, bog.

Hamm, *(str.) m.* † 1) forest (Holz); 2)

Ham'me, *(w.) f. (†* & *) provinc.* 1) ham, leg (of an animal), *cf.* Kniebug; 2) lower part of a scythe; 3) fence, &c. *(N. G.) see* Gehäge.

Ham'mel, *s.* I. *(str., pl.* Häm'mel *or* –) *m.* 1) wether; 2) der Cap'sche –, *Ornith.* albatross (*Diomedea exulans* L.; Capschaf); *fig-s.* 3) blockhead; 4) draggle-tail; um wieder auf besagten – zu kommen, *fig.* to return to our muttons; II. *in comp.* –braten, *m.* roast mutton; –brühe, *f.* mutton-broth; –brust, *f.*, –bug, *m.* shoulder of mutton; –fell, *n.* skin of a wether, sheep-skin; –fett, *n.* mutton-fat; –fleisch, *n.* mutton; –jährling, *m.*, –lamm, *n.* a gelded tup-lamb (one year old); –keule, *f.* a leg of mutton; –knecht, *m.* a man that tends the sheep; –korn, *n.* battledoor-barley; –möhre, *f.* common parsnip. [(lambs).

Ham'meln, **Häm'meln**, *(w.) v. tr.* to geld

Ham'mel..., *in comp.* –pelz, *m.* 1) coat or garment of sheep's skin; 2) sheep-skin with the wool on; –rippchen, *n. pl.* mutton chops; –schlegel, *f.* half leg of mutton; –schlägel, *m.* see –keule; –talg, *m.* mutton-suet; –viertel, *n.* a quarter of mutton.

Ham'mer, *s.* I. *(str., pl.* Häm'mer) *m.* 1) hammer; hölzerner –, mallet; 2) chopper, [illegible]; 3) (–werk) forge; 4) the leg (of an animal); 5) *Ichth.* hammer-headed shark, balance-fish (*Squalus zygaena* L.); 6) *see* –muschel; 7) *provinc. Bot.* darnel; 8) *fig.* a) strong, muscular man; b) blustering fellow, bully; daß dich der – (Schlag)! *coll.* the deuce take you! unter den – kommen, *Com.* hammer-dressed; unter den – bringen (versteigern), to put to the hammer; II. *in comp.* –amboß, *m.* coppersmith's anvil; –arbeiter, *m.* workman in a forge; –auge, *n.* eye of a hammer; –axt, *f.* a hammer with a small hatchet on the back, hammer hatchet; –bahn, *f.* face of a hammer. [(w.) *f.* malleability.

Häm'merbär, I. *adj.* malleable; II. H-keit,

Ham'mer..., *in comp.* –beere, *f. provinc.* red-whortleberry; –beil, *n. see* –axt; –block, *m.* anvil-block.

Häm'merer, *(str.) m.* hammerer.

Ham'mer..., *in comp.* –fisch, *m. see* Hammer, 5; –gekrätz, *n.* copper-refuse; –gerüst, –gestell, *n.* tilt-frame; –hai, *m. see* Hammer, 5; –haue, *f.* miner's mattock; –herr, *m.* proprietor of a forge; –hülse, *f.* helve-ring; –hütte, *f.* forge; iron-works; –kalk, *m.* marl.

Häm'merling *(corr.* Hämpferling), *(str.) m. (†* & *) provinc.* 1) Jack pudding, merry Andrew (in a puppet-show); 2) *see* Poltergeist; 3) (Meister –) *a)* Jack Ketch, hangman; *b)* a flayer; 4) *see* Goldhammer.

Ham'mer..., *in comp.* –loch, *n. see* –auge; –meister, *m.* master of a forge; –mühle, *f. see* –hütte; –muschel, *f. Conch.* hammer-oyster (*Malleus vulgaris* Lam.).

Häm'mern, *(w.) v. tr.* to hammer, malleate.

Ham'mer..., *in comp.* –ordnung, *f.* regulations for iron-works; –pfinne, –pinne, *f. see* –bahn; –pochwerk, *n. see* –werk; –rad, *n.* wheel that keeps the forge hammer in motion; –rahmen, *m. Instr-m.* hammer-rail; –recht, *n. see* –streich; –schlacke, *f.* iron-dross; –schlag, *m.* 1) stroke or blow with a hammer; 2) small particles of iron that fall from a forge; iron sparkles or scales, dross of iron, slag; –schmidt, *m.* hammer-smith; –stiel, *m.* tail or handle of a hammer; –strauch, *m. Bot.* poison-berry (*Cestrum* L.); –streich, *m.* space of 18 inches appointed by law between the principal walls of neighbouring houses; –tuch, *n. Instr-m.* hammer-cloth; –walke, *f.* fulling-mill (Walkmühle); –werk, *n.* forge, iron mill, foundery; –zeichen, *n. Forest.* mark on trees made by a wood-hammer.

Häm'merling (**Häm'ling**), *(str.) m.* eunuch.

* **Hämorrhoidal'** *(pr.* hämoridāl), **H-isch**, *(Gr.) adj.* hemorrhoidal; –fluß, *m. see* Hämorrhoiden; –knoten, *m. Surg.* hemorrhoidal tumour. – **Hämorrhoi'den** *(pr.* hämori'den), *(w.) f. pl.* hemorrhoids, (bloody) piles.

Ham'pelmann, *(str., pl.* H-männer) *m.* a little image (puppet) moved by a wire (in a puppet-show), *cf.* Zappelmann.

Ham'peln, *(w.) v. intr. provinc.* 1) to bob, dangle; 2) to limp, hobble *(cf.* Humpeln).

Hamst'er, *(str.) m. Zool.* German marmot (*Cricetus frumentarius* Pall.); –bau, *m.* the den (earth or burrow) of a marmot; –felle, *n. pl. Comm.* German marmots; –gräber, *m.* hamster-catcher; –höhle, –röhre, *f. see* –bau.

Hän'butte, *(w.) f. see* Hainbutte, Hagebutte.

Hand, *(str., pl.* Hän'de) *f.* 1) *a)* hand, *b)* paw, claw (of the bear, wolf, &c.); claw, clutch (of the falcon); *c)* palms or flukes (of the anchor); 2) hand(-writing); von seiner eigenen –, in his own handwriting; 3) *fig.* hand, side, direction; die hohle –, hollow of the hand; die verkehrte –, back of the hand; die flache –, 1) palm; 2) *Sport. see* –gehörn; die obere –, feudal lord; die untere –, vassal; die todte –, *Law.* mortmain; treue –, trust; die – Gottes, the hand of God; um die – eines Mädchens anhalten, to propose for a girl; – über – ! *Mar.* hand over hand; – in –, hand in hand, jointly; Einem die – geben (drücken, schütteln), to shake hands with one; to give one one's hand; Einem die – auf etwas *(Acc.)* geben, to give one the hand upon a thing, to pledge one's word to do something; lange Hände haben, to have extensive power; lange Hände machen, to steal, pilfer; weder – noch Fuß rühren, to stir neither hand nor foot; die Hände sinken lassen, to lose courage; seine milde – aufthun, to be charitable, to give alms; *fac.* to loosen one's purse-strings; sich auf eigene – setzen, to set up for one's self; er sitzt auf eigene –, he makes himself his living; die Arbeit geht ihm flink aus (von) der –, he is a quick hand; von einer – in die andere, from hand to hand; aus einer – in die andere geben, to hand about; *fig-s.* – anlegen, 1. to apprehend, seize on (upon), to lay hands (on, upon somebody); 2. *or* vor (in) die – nehmen, to take up or in hand, to set one's hand to (a thing), to put (the) hand to work, to begin; – an sich *([Acc.]* selbst) legen, to lay (violent) hands upon one's self, to attempt one's (own) life; to commit suicide; die letzte – an etwas *(Acc.)* legen, to give a finishing stroke, to put the finishing stroke to, *cf.* Feile, 2; bei (an) der –, zur –, (near) at hand, handy; ready, in readiness; nicht bei der – sein, to be out of the way; hinter der – sitzen, *Gam.* to be youngest hand; vor der – sitzen, to be eldest hand; Geld hinter der – haben, to have savings; hinter (nach) der –, afterwards, subsequently; ein Sperling in der – ist besser als zwei auf dem Dache, *proverb.* a bird in the hand is worth two in the bush; es liegt in Ihrer –, it depends on you; it is in your power; das Pferd liegt schwer in der –, the horse pulls hard at the bit; in guter – or guten Händen sein, to be in able hands, to be well provided for; du kannst nicht in besseren Händen sein, you cannot be in abler hands; Einem in die Hände arbeiten, to play into one's hands; mit beiden Händen zugreifen, to catch at or seize with avidity, *fam.* to jump at; mit – (Händen) und Fuß (Füßen), with might and main; mit leichter –, with ease, easily; mit stürmender –, by storm; nach der – erziehen, to bring up to one's own liking or according to one's own pleasure; mit Einem über der – sein, to be on ill terms with one; unter der – des Arztes sein, to be in the doctor's hands; unter Händen haben, to have in hand, to have on the stithy; Einem unter die Hände kommen, to get into a person's hands or power; von der – weisen or schlagen, to decline, reject; zur – nehmen, to take up; Einem zu Händen stellen, to deliver into one's hands; etwas schlägt mir zur –, I have success or luck with something; sein Recht aus der – geben, to waive one's right; sich (or einander) bei den Händen fassen (von Mehreren), to take hands; mit vollen Händen ausstreuen, to sow broadcast; die – auf den Mund legen, to be silent, *fam.* to be mum; an die – geben, to suggest, prompt; (Einem) Mittel an die – geben, to afford (one) means; Einem die – bieten, Einem zur (an die) – gehen, to aide, help, lend one a (helping) hand; sich gegenseitig die – bieten, to cooperate, act conjointly; die – zum Frieden, zu einem Vergleiche bieten, to make offers of peace, to offer terms, to be open to some arrangement; ein Unglück bietet dem andern die –, misfortune follows misfortune; alle Hände voll zu thun haben, to have one's hands quite full; Einem die Hände unter die Füße legen or Einen auf den Händen tragen, to treat with great regard or affection; aus den Händen lassen, to let escape, to let slip; to give up possession of; aus der – legen, to put, lay down or away; in (den) Händen haben, to hold, to be in possession of, to have in keeping; *Comm-s.* zu Handen or zu Händen kommen, to come to hand or hands; Ihr Werthes ist in meinen Händen, your favour is to hand; aus freier – or aus der – *(i. e.* ohne Mäkler) verkaufen, to sell by (off, out of) hand or from hand to hand; aus der ersten, zweiten 2c. –, at first, second, &c. hand; aus der ersten – kaufen, to

—fisch, m. dried fish (cod); —garn, n. Sport. draw-net; —gerüst, n. flying scaffold; —griff, m. T. pendent ring; —haken, m. suspension-hook; —holz, n. Butch. cambrel; —kette, f. slung-chain; —kluft, f. Min. sloping lode.

Häng'el, (str.) m. provinc. 1) joint; 2) see Henkel.

Häng'e..., in comp. —lampe, f. hanging-lamp; —leuchter, m. lustre, chandelier, pendant.

Häng'eln, (w.) v. intr. Mar. 1) to convey merchandise from one ship or roadstead to another; 2) to sail from port to port.

Häng'ematte, (w.) f. hammock.

Hang'emörser, (str.) m. Gunn. mortar suspended by its trunnions.

Häng'emuskel, (irr.) m. suspensory muscle.

Hang'en, (str.) v. intr. (obsolescent & almost entirely superseded by Hängen, which was originally only used as a transitive verb) 1) to hang; to be suspended (an [with Dat.], on, by); 2) to dangle, hang loose, droop; 3) to adhere, to be fixed, attached (to), connected (with), dependent (on), to depend (on); to cling, cleave, stick (to), to be given (to); 4) coll. to hitch; stagnate; er weiß, wo es hangt und langt, fig. he knows the whole affair or intrigue.

Häng'en, (w.) v. I. tr. to hang (the pp. in this sense often strong [from Hangen]: gehangen, compare the Engl. hung for hanged); to attach, fasten; sein Herz an (with Acc.) —, to set one's heart upon ...; die Ohren — or — lassen, to hang down the ears; den Kopf — or — lassen, 1. to hang the head, to droop; to be dispirited, desponding, to flag; to be disconcerted; 2. to affect piety, to act the devotee; 3. Man. to carry low.

II. refl. 1) to hang one's self; 2) (with an sich Acc.) to stick, cleave (to); to attach one's self (to), to be attached (to).

III. often used as an intr. instead of Hangen (which see) but with the str. imperf. & pp.: to hang, &c.); das Schwert hing an einem dünnen Faden, the sword was suspended by a slender thread; das Schwert des Damocles hängt über seinem Haupte, the sword of Damocles hangs over his head; das stete Bewußtsein, daß unser Leben an einem Faden hänge, the ever-present consciousness that our lives hang upon a thread; die Wand hängt († hangt), the wall inclines; der Proceß hängt († hangt), the suit is pending; — bleiben (an, in [with Dat.] &c.), 1. to be caught (by, in, &c.); 2. fig. a) to be pending; b) to adhere (to), to cling (to); ihr Kleid blieb an einem Rosenstrauche —, her gown was caught in a rose bush; mein Rock blieb an einem Nagel —, my coat caught a nail; ich blieb an einem Nagel —, a nail caught me; woran hängt die Sache? what stops (on what hitches) the matter? wer('s) lang hat, läßt('s) lang —, coll. he who has fine feathers likes to show them; h—d, p. a. hanging; pendent, pensile (gardens), pendulous (excrescences); h—de Lippen, pouting lips; mit h—den Ohren, dangle-(lap- or loll-)eared; h—de Brücke, see Hängebrücke; h—de Eisenbahn, suspension-railway; h—de Eisenbahnbrücke, suspension-railway-bridge.

Hang'ende, Häng'ende, n. (decl. like adj.) Min. top (hanging surface of a lode), hanging wall.

Häng'enswürdig, adj. deserving to be hanged.

Häng'eohren, n. pl. loose or dangling ears; mit —, lap- or loll-eared.

[illegible], (w.) f. Mar. [illegible].

Häng'eplatte, (w.) f. Build. (beim Gesims) corona; (beim Dachgesims) drip (Karnies).

Häng'er, Hang'er, (str.) m. Mar. pendant; der — am großen Mast, main-tackle pendant; der — am Fockmast, fore-tackle pendant.

Hang'eriemen, (str.) m. see Hängeriemen &c.

Häng'e..., in comp. —riemen, m. pl. leather-braces, main or spring braces (of a coach); —riemfedern, f. pl. brace springs; —säule, f. T. queen post, king post, crown-post, joggle post, truss; —schaufel, f. Mach. scoop; —schloß, n. padlock; —schwert, n. walking sword; —seil, n. Hunt. a leash for drawing or leading the (lime-)hounds; —seilkunst, f. Hydraul. the art of making chain-pumps, paternoster-works; —ständer, m. pl. see —säule; —stock, m. see —holz; —tisch, m. hanging-table; —wage, f. Hydraul. level; —wand, f. Carp. truss-partition; —weide, f. Bot. weeping willow (Salix babylonica L.); —werk, n. Carp. truss(-work), trussing; —zierat, m. Archit. pendant; —zirkel, see —cirkel.

Häng'ig, Häng'lich, adj. see Abhängig, 1.

Häng'ling, (str.) m. a species of the common vine.

Häng'sel, (str.) n. 1) something that hangs, a pendant, bob; 2) hook (to suspend something by).

Hank'e, (w.) f. haunch, hind-quarter (of a horse); h-hoch, adj. Man. high in the hind-quarters; H-knochen, m. haunch-bone (of a horse); h-tief, adj. low in the hind-quarters.

Han'nah, f. Hannah, Ann, Anne (P. N.).

Han'ne, f. (dimin. Hann'chen, n.) Jean, Jane, Jenny, Jennet (P. N.).

Hanno'ver, n. Geogr. Hanover. — Hannovera'ner, (str.) m., Hanno'verisch, adj. Hanoverian.

Hans, (str., pl. Hän'se; sometimes w.) m. (dimin. Häns'chen, [† &] * Häns'lein, provinc. Han'sel, Hän'sel, n.) 1) John (Johnny, Jack, Jackey); — und Grete, Jack and Gill; coll. e. ein dummer —, a dunce; — Achtnicht, — ohne Sorge, Tom Careless, a careless fellow; — Affe, jackanapes; — Allerlei, Jack of all trades; — Dampf, a vapouring fool; — Klecker, slovenly, dirty eater; — Küchenmeister, cotquean; — in allen Gassen, a busy-body, a stirring or bustling person, a man about town, one who lounges about everywhere; — der Träumer, John-a-dreams; — Liederlich, Jack Rake; wie — Liederlich, like old wickedness; — hinter der Mauer, a timid fellow; — Narr, fool; coxcomb, fop; dunce, blockhead; — oben im Dorfe, the great man, first fiddle; — Sachte, idler, lazybones; — Tapps, awkward fellow, blockhead, bumpkin (Tölpel); — und Kunz, Dick, Tom, and Harry; — oder Kunz, Smith or Jones; wenn das wahr ist, dann heiße ich —, if that is true, my name is Jack Robinson; prov. e. — ohne Fleiß wird nimmer weis', of idleness comes no goodness; — bleibt immer —, Jack will never be a gentleman; was Hänschen nicht lernt (lernen will), lernt — nimmermehr, you can't teach an old dog new tricks; Hänschen im Keller, Jack in the low cellar; 2) Bot. a) klingender —, yellow rattle (Rhinanthus L.); b) schöner —, bearded pink (Bartnelke); c) Hänsel am Wege, see Wegetritt.

Han'se, Han'sa, f. 1) †, association, league; 2) Germ. Hist. the Hanseatic union.

Hanseat', (w.) m. a native of one of the Hanse-towns.

Hanseat'isch, adj. Hanseatic; der h-e Bund, the Hanseatic body, union, or league, league of the Hanse-towns.

Han'sel, (str.) m. provinc. (S. G.) dimin. of Hans, Jack.

Hän'sel..., in comp. —becher, m. cup presented to novices upon their initiation; —geld, n. a novice's fees.

Hän'seln, (w.) v. tr. 1) or Han'sen, coll. to initiate with some ridiculous or merry ceremony (especially of sailors on first passing the line), to duck; to receive into any society; 2) to make a fool of or play tricks upon, to vex, tease.

Han'sestadt, (str., pl. H-städte) f. Hanse-town.

Hans'narr, (w.) m. see Hans.

Hanswurst', (str., pl. Hanswürst'e) m. Jackpudding, harlequin, buffoon, merry Andrew, zany, clown, funnyman.

Hanswurstia'de, (w.) f. burl. buffoonery (cf. Harlekinade).

Hanswurst'..., in comp. —mäßig, adj. like a fool, foolish, buffoonish.

Han'tel, (w.) f. dumb bell.

Hantie'ren, Hanti'ren, Hanthie'ren, (w.) v. intr. & tr. 1) to handle, manage, treat; 2) to work (with the hands), to labour; to bustle, stir about; 3) to deal, transact business. — Hantie'rung, (w.) f. occupation, employment, transaction, business, trade; management.

Hä'pel, (str.) m. green husk of nuts.

Ha'perig, adj. coll. uneven, rough; obstructed; difficult; embarrassed.

Ha'pern, (w.) v. intr. (impers.) coll. to stick, stop; to be obstructed or retarded; da hapert's, there lies the difficulty, there's the rub; es hapert mit der Sache, the affair is at a stand-still.

Happ, (str.) m., Hap'pen, (str.) m. only (Häpp'chen, (str.) n. dimin. a little) bit, morsel, a mouthful.

Hap'pen, (w.) v. intr. coll. to snap, bite.

Hap'pig, coll. I. adj. snapping, greedy, eager; II. H-keit, (w.) f. greediness, eagerness. [see Wiste.

Här! († for her) interj. hey! to the left!

Här'chen, (str.) n. (dimin. of Haar) a little hair; mit feinen — besetzt, downy.

Hard, Harde, (str.) m. & (w.) f. (pine-)forest, particul. in mountain-districts (Bergwald).

* Ha'rem, (str., pl. H-s; less usual: die — [Klenger]; die Harem'me [Bodenstedt], cf. Sanders) n. (Arab. haram) harem.

Hä'ren, I. adj. made of hair, hairy; ein h-es Hemd, a hair-shirt; II. (w.) v. refl. see Haaren.

Har'fe, (w.) f. 1) harp; 2) provinc. a) Husb. a screen, riddle; b) an open shed; die (or auf der) — spielen, to play on the harp, to harp.

Har'fen, Har'fenen, (w.) v. I. intr. 1) †, to (play on the) harp; 2) Min. to slide; II. tr. to riddle, screen.

Har'fener, Harf'ner, (str.) m., Harfenist', (w.) m. harper, harpist; Harf'nerin, (w.) f. a female harper.

Harfenett', (str.) n. a little harp.

Har'fen..., in comp. —getöne, n., —klang, m., —klingen, n. sound of the harp; —mädchen, n. (an itinerant) girl playing the harp, harper; —muschel, f. Conch. a clam (Venus meretrix L.); —saite, f. harp-string; —schläger, m. harper; —schnecke, f. Conch. harp-shell (Harpa ventricosa Lam.); —spiel, n. harp-playing; —spielen, n. harping; —spieler, m. harper; —ton, m. tone, sound of the harp.

Hä'ring, (str.) m. herring (Clupea harengus L.); frischer —, fresh or white herring; gesalzener —, pickled herring; geräucherter —, bloated, cured, or red-herring, bloater.

Hä'ringer, (str.) m. provinc. a seller of herrings.

Hä'rings..., in comp. —blick, m. Fish. a glimmering light of the herrings; —[illegible], m. see —speicher; —brühe, f. see —lake; —bude, f. herring-booth; —büse, f. herring-buss, cobble; —fang, m., —fänger, m. see —fischerei, —fischer; —faß, —fäßchen, n. a cade, keg, or barrel for herrings; —fisch, m. Ichth. [illegible] ([illegible] L.); —fischer, m. herring-fisher; —fischerei, f. herring-fishery; —frau, f. herring-woman; —grätenverband, m. Archit. herring-bone-

[illegible]mouthedness; *fig.* unruliness; —**meißel**, *m.* cold-chisel; —**metall**, *n.* a mixture of [illegible] metals; —**näckig**, *adj.* stiff-necked, head-strong, stubborn, inflexible, obstinate, pertinacious, sturdy, unbending; (*said of* diseases, *&c.*) inveterate, persistent; ein —näckiger Winter, a severe winter; —**näckigkeit**, *f.* stubbornness, obstinacy, pertinacity, persistence (of an inflammation), inveteracy; —**nagel**, *m.* clout-nail.

Härt'pulver, *(str.) n.* powder for tempering (files, *&c.*).

Härt'..., *in comp.* —**riegel**, *m. Bot.* 1) (common) privet (*Ligustrum vulgare* L.); 2) dog-wood, dog-berry tree, bloody twig (*Cornus sanguinea* L.); —**rindig**, *adj.* hard-rinded, having a hard shell; —**roth**, *adj.* glaring red; —**schalig**, *adj.* 1) *see* —rindig; 2) testaceous; —schalige Erbsen, *Comm.* non-boilers.

* **Hartschier'**, *(str.) m.* (*Ital.* arciere) imperial horse-guard (in Austria).

Härt'..., *in comp.* —**schlächtig**, *adj. Farr.* pursy, short-breathed; —**schlächtigkeit**, *f.* pursiness; —**schlagen**, *n.* hammer-hardening; —**schlägig**, *adj.* hardened against blows; —**schlagloth**, *n. see* —loth; —**schnaufigkeit**, *f. Vet.* roaring; —**schwingel**, *m. Bot.* red fescue-grass (*Festuca rubra* L.); —**sehnig**, *adj.* hard-sinewed; —**sinnig**, *adj. see* —näckig; —**spath**, *m. Miner.* andalusite; —**stich**, *m.*, —**stück**, *n. T.* copper in bricks *or* pigs; —**traber**, *m.* hard-trotter (of a horse). [*&c.*; tempering.

Här'tung, *(w.) f.* the (act of) hardening,

Härt'..., *in comp.* —**walze**, *f. T.* chilled roll, case-hardened roller; —**waaren**, *f. pl.* hard-ware; —**wasser**, *n. Metall.* chalybeate *or* tempering water.

Härt'wasser, *(str.) n.* chalybeate water.

Härt'..., *in comp.* —**werk**, *n. Smelt.* tutty of tin; —**wurm**, *m.* blind-worm, slow-worm (Blindschleiche).

Härz, *a.* I. *(str.) n.* resin, rosin; gum (of trees); elastisches —, indian rubber; II. *(str.) m.* 1) †. woody mountain; 2) *Geogr.* Hartz *or* Hercynian mountains; III. *in comp.* —**artig**, *adj.* like resin, resinous; —**baum**, *m.* pine-tree; pitch-tree; —**bewohner**, *m. see* Harzer, 3; —**eiche**, *f. Bot.* common oak (Wintereiche); —**electricität**, *f. Phys.* resinous *or* negative electricity.

Här'zen, *(w.) v.* I. *tr.* 1) to clear (trees) from resin; 2) to rub with resin; Bäume —, to cut the bark of trees to make them exude the resin; II. *intr.* to scrape resin (from pines), to stick like resin, *fig. see* Hapern.

Här'zer, *(str.) m.* 1) *see* Harzscharrer; 2) miser, curmudgeon; 3) inhabitant of the Hartz-mountains.

Härz'..., *in comp.* —**fett**, *n. Chem.* metanaphthaline; —**fichte**, *f. see* —baum; —**firniß**, *m.* lac; —**förmig**, *adj.* resiniform; —**galle**, *f.* accumulation of resin in the wood of the pine; —**gallenmotte**, *m. Entom.* pine-moth ([illegible]); —**gebend**, *adj.* resiniferous, yielding resin; —**gebirge**, *n.* Hartz-mountains; —**holz**, *n.* resinous wood.

Här'zicht, **Här'zig**, *adj.* rosiny, resembling resin; resinous, resiniferous.

Härz'..., *in comp.* —**kohle**, *f.* resinous coal; —**kratze**, *f. see* —scharre; —**kuchen**, *m.* cake of resin; —**malerei**, *f.* encaustic painting; —**meise**, *f. Ornith.* coal-titmouse (Tannenmeise); —**messer**, *m. see* —scharre; —**öl**, *n. Chem.* resinous oil; —**pflanze**, *f.* resinous plant; —**reißen**, *n.*, —**riß**, *m.*, —**schaben**, *n.* the cutting of trees to make the resin come out; —**scharre**, *f.* the knife of a resin-scraper; —**scharrer**, *m.* resin-scraper; —**seife**, *f.* resinous soap; —**stein**, *m.* soap-stone, steatite; —**tanne**, *f. Bot.* pine-tree, Norway fir (*Pinus abies* L.); —**theer**, *m.* common tar; —**theeröl**, *n.* distilled resin; —**tragend**, *adj.* resiniferous; —**wald**, *m.* Hercynian forest; —**wasser**, *n.* water in which resin is dissolved.

Häs, *(indecl.) n. provinc.* (*S. G.*) suit (of clothes); Kilbehäs, holiday-suit.

* **Hasard'**, *(str.) m.* (*Fr.*) hap, hazard, chance; —**spiel**, *n.* game of hazard.

Häs'chen, *(str.) n.* (*dimin. of* Hase) young hare, puss; — machen, to make rabbits (a children's play).

Hasch'en, *(w.) v.* I. *tr.* to catch, apprehend, seize; II. *intr.* (*with* nach) *lit. & fig.* to catch *or* snatch (at), to fish (for); to aspire (to), aim (at), to strain *or* strive (after effect, *&c.*); das —, *(str.) s. s.* catching (a children's game), *mod.* touchwood.

Häsch'er, *(str.) m.* (under) bailiff, *vulg.* bumbailiff; —**knechte**, *m. pl.*, —**schaar**, *f.* bailiffs, myrmidons.

* **Haschi'ren**, *(w.) v. tr. Engr.* to hatch.

Ha'se, *(w.) m.* 1) *Zool.* hare (*Lepus timidus* L.); *fig.*-s. 2) coward, poltroon; 3) fop, coxcomb, droll; der veränderliche —, *Zool.* alpine hare (*Lepus alpinus variabilis* Pall.); *proverbs*, da liegt der — im Pfeffer, there is the rub, there it sticks; der — (Fuchs) braut, die H-n kochen, the mist rises (in mountainous regions); mich hat ein — geleckt, I am a lucky fellow.

Ha'sel, *a.* I. *(w.) f.* 1) hazel-nut tree; 2) *Ichth.* a species of dace (*Leuciscus dobula* Cuv.); II. *in comp.* —**busch**, *m.* hazel-bush; —**eiche**, *f. Bot.* common oak(-tree) (Sommereiche). [coxcomb, fop, buffoon.

Hä'selier, *(str.)*, *joc.*: **Haselant'**, *(w.) m.*

Ha'sel..., *in comp.* —**erde**, *f.* hazel-mould; —**gebüsch**, *n.* hazel-wood; —**geflügel**, *n.* hazel-hens, heath-pouts; —**huhn**, *n. Ornith.* hazel-hen; heath-cock, heath-pout (*Tetrao bonasia* L.)

Hä'seling, *(str.) m. see* Hasel, 2.

Haseliren, **Hä'seln**, *(w.) v. coll.* I. *intr.* to play the buffoon, to jest; II. *tr.* to buffoon, tease, make sport of.

Ha'sel..., *in comp.* —**kätzchen**, *n. pl.* catkins of the hazel; —**kraut**, *n. Bot.* wild nard (—wurz); —**maus**, *f. Zool.* garden dormouse, sleeper (*Myoxus avellanarius* L.).

Ha'seln, **Hä'seln**, *adj.* hazel, of hazel.

Ha'sel..., *in comp.* —**nuß**, *f.* hazel-nut; —**nußbraun**, *adj.* hazel; —**nußstrauch**, *m. see* Hasel; —**öl**, *n.* filbert-oil, hazel-oil; —**ratze**, *f.* dormouse; —**ruthe**, *f.* hazel-rod, switch; —**schläfer**, *m. see* —maus; —**staude**, *f. Bot.* hazel-tree, hazel-bush, filbert-tree (*Corylus avellana* L.); —**stock**, *m.* (knotted) hazel-stick; —**wurm**, *m. see* Hartwurm; —**wurz**, —**wurzel**, *f. Bot.* hazel-wort, wild spikenard (*Asarum europaeum* L.); —**zaun**, *m.* filbert-hedge.

Ha'sen..., *in comp.* —**adler**, *m. Ornith.* black eagle (*Falco fulvus* L.); —**ampfer**, *m. see* Sauerklee; —**art**, *f.* nature of a hare; von — art, faint-hearted, cowardly; —**artig**, *adj.* leporine; —**auge**, *n.* 1) hare's eye; 2) *Med.* lagophthalmy; 3) *Bot.* common avens, herb bennet (*Geum urbanum* L.); —**balg**, *m.* hare's skin; —**braten**, *m.* roast-hare; —**bräutigam**, *m. Bot.* common broom (—heide, 1); —**brecher**, *m.* an iron instrument to break the spine, *&c.* of a roasted hare (in order to facilitate carving); —**brot**, *n. Bot.* 1) hare-grass, trembling grass (*Briza media* L.); —**distel**, *f. Bot.* common sow-thistle (Saudistel, 1); —**fährte**, *f.* prick *or* trace of a hare; —**fell**, *n.* hare's skin; —**fett**, *n.* grease of a hare; —**fuß**, *m.* 1) (gelber) *see* —klee, 1; 2) *fig. see* Hase, 2 & 3; 3) *Zool.* arctic fox (*Canis lagopus* L.); 4) *Ornith.* a) ptarmigan (Schneehuhn); b) *provinc.* hare-foot (the name of the partridge, wood-cock, *&c.*); —**fußkraut**, *n. see* —klee, 1; *Sport.*-s. —**garn**, *n.* hare-net, hare-pipe; —**gehege**, *n.* lepery; —**geier**, *m. Ornith.* black-crested *or* Arabic vulture (*Cathartes percnopterus* L.); —**geil**, *geilkraut*, *n.* dyer's weed (Färberginster); —**gras**, *n. see* —brot; —**haare**, *n. pl.* hare-wool, hare-down.

Ha'senhaft, I. *or* **Ha'sig**, *adj.* 1) leporine; *fig.*-s. 2) timid, timorous, cowardly; 3) coxcomical, foppish, buffoonish, droll; **H-igkeit**, *(w.)*, **Haserei'**, *(w.) f.* 1) cowardice; 2) coxcombry.

Ha'sen..., *in comp.* —**hatz**, *f.* hare-hunting; —**heide**, *f. Bot.* 1) common broom (*Spartium scoparium* L.); 2) green-wood (Färberginster); —**herz**, *n. coll.* pusillanimity, cowardice; —**hetze**, *f. see* —hatz; —**hund**, *m.* hare-hound, harrier; —**jagd**, *f.* coursing *or* chase of hares, hare-hunting; —**klee**, *m. Bot.* 1) hare-foot, trinity grass (*Trifolium arvense* L.); 2) kidney vetch (*Anthyllis vulneraria* L.); 3) wood sorrel (Sauerklee); —**klein**, *n.* the liver, head, *&c.* of a hare, *Cook.* hare-ragout; —**kohl**, *m. Bot.* 1) hare-thistle (Saudistel, 1); 2) dock cresses, nipple wort (*Lapsana communis* L.); 3) *see* Sauerklee; —**kopf**, *m.* 1) hare's head; 2) *see* Hase, 2 & 3; 3) *Pomol.* name of a winter-apple; —**koth**, *m.* ordure *or* dung of a hare, *Sport.* crotels; —**kraut**, *n. Bot.* St. John's wort (Johanniskraut); —**lager**, *n.* form of a hare, repair, cover; —**lattich**, *m.* wall-lettuce (*Prenanthes muralis* L.); —**lippe**, *f. see* —scharte; —**lorbeeren**, *pl. see* —koth; —**lest**, *n. see* —lager; —**maul**, *n.* horse-mouth; —**maus**, *f.* rat-hare (*Lagomys* Pall.); —**moor**, *n.* sough-pit, sewer; —**mund**, *m. see* —scharte; —**netz**, *n. see* —garn; —**öhrchen**, *n.* 1) *Bot.* hare's ear (*Bupleurum* L.); 2) *Mar.* latin-sail; 3) *pl. Typ.* inverted commas; —**panier**, *n. fig.* quick flight; das —panier ergreifen, to run away, to take to one's heels; —**pappel**, *f. Bot.* common *or* wild mallow (Malve); —**pastete**, *f.* hare-pie; —**pfeffer**, *m. see* —klein; —**pfötchen**, *n. see* Kugelbäumchen & —klee; —**pfote**, *f.* 1) hare's foot; 2) *Bot. see* —klee; —**rampe**, *f. see* Gliedschaft; —**salat**, *m. see* —lattich; —**scharte**, *f.* harelip; —**scheide**, *f. Bot. see* —geilkraut; —**schlaf**, *m. see* —auge; er schläft den —schlaf, he sleeps with open eyes; —**schrot**, *m.* hare-shot; —**schwarz**, *n. see* —klein; —**sprung**, *m.* 1) hare's leap; 2) hind legs of a hare; 3) *see* —fährte; —**spur**, *f. see* —fährte; —**stößer**, *m. see* —geier; —**strauch**, *m. Bot.* wall-lettuce (—lattich); —**wolle**, *f. see* —haare; —**zwirn**, *m.* thick thread for making hare-nets.

Hä'sin, *(w.) f.* doe- *or* female hare. [chen.

Häs'lein, *(str.) n.* (*provinc.* &) * *for* Häs-

Häs'linger, *(str.) m. joc.* hazel-stick.

Has'pe, **Häs'pe**, *(w.) f.* 1) hasp, clamp; 2) hinge, hook, holdfast (of a door); *Carp.* dog.

Has'pel, *(str.) m.* (*provinc.* [*w.*] *f.*) 1) reel; 2) windlass, winch, windle, crab, draw beam; *Mar.* capstan; 3) hook on which a loop turns, *cf.* Haspe, 2; 4) (*or* —kreuz) *T.* cross (of a copper-plate press); 5) *see* Drehkreuz; 6) *Min.* whim, winding-engine; 7) *Gunn.* horns; handle.

Has'pelbar, *adj.* that may be reeled, *&c.*

Has'pelbaum, *(str., pl.* H-bäume) *m.* tree or beam of a windlass, *&c.*, lever; cheek of a crane.

Has'p(e)ler, *(str.) m. see* Haspelknecht.

Has'pel..., *in comp.* —**gerüst**, —**gestell**, *n.* trestle of a reel, the capstan, the windlass; —**horn**, *n.* winch-handle; —**knecht**, *m.* one that works at a windlass *or* reel, winder, reeler; —**kreuz**, *n.* reel-cross, reel-arms; —**kunst**, —**maschine**, *f. T.* winding-engine.

Has'peln, *(w.) v.* I. *tr. & intr.* to reel, wind on a reel; to draw up by a windlass; II. *intr. coll.* 1) to fidget about; 2) to prattle, to talk quickly.

Has'pel..., *in comp.* —**welle**, —**winde**, *f. see* Windebaum; —**wurzel**, *f.* sea-onion, squill; —**zieher**, *m. see* —knecht.

Haß, *(str.) m.* hate (gegen, to), hatred, ill-will, grudge, spite (against), detestation (of).

…gallant stay-sail; —brett, n. head-board, …-piece (of a bedstead); —buch, n. principal book; Comm. ledger; —buchposten, m. …ger. ledger-item; —buchstabe, m. capital letter; —bund, m. Mus. see Capodasto; —bureau, n. chief or head office; —canal, m. principal …; main channel; —casse, f. treasury; —…ssirer, m. receiver general; —comptoir, n. —bureau; —damm, —deich, m. main dike; —drüse, f. 1) cephalic gland; 2) principal gland; —eid, m. Law, decisory oath; —eigenschaft, f. principal or leading quality; —eingang, m. principal entrance.

Häuptel, (str.) n. provinc. (dimin. of Haupt) 1) little head; 2) Min. (also m.) upper …st stick or slich; in comp. —kohl, m. Bot. headed cabbage; —salat, m. cabbage-lettuce.

Häupteln, (w.) v. refl. provinc. to head, form a head (as a plant).

Haupt'…, in comp. —erbe, m. see —bert; —erbe, m. chief or principal heir; —erbin, f. chief or principal heiress; —erforderniß, n. chief or prime requisite; —facette, f. Jewel. … edition; —fach, n. 1) principal division or …; 2) fig. chief or principal department; —fall, m. 1) chief case, principal case; 2) Law, … of the liege-man or tenant; —farben, pl. primary or principal colours; —feder, f. master-spring, main-spring; —fehler, m. chief fault, principal fault, mistake; principal …; —feind, m. principal or capital enemy; —festung, f. principal fortress; —figur, f. principal figure; Herald. bearing; —flügel, m. … main-wing; —fluß, m. 1) principal river; 2) rheumatism in the head; —frage, f. chief (main or leading) question; —front, f. … front; —gang, m. principal passage; …, main lode; —gasse, f. principal street; —gesims, n. Archit. entablature, entablement; —gebäude, n. principal building; —gedanke, m. principal or chief thought, idea; —gedingehäuer, m. Min. charter master; contracter; …-collier; —gegend, f. principal region; cardinal point; —gegenstand, m. principal or chief object; —geld, n. 1) see —steuer; 2) see …, 3; —gemälde, n. leading picture; —gericht, n. principal dish; —geschäft, n. main principal business; —geschäftigung, m. busy …; —geschoß, n. principal story of a house, first floor; —geschwulst, f. Med. swelling of the head; —gesims, n. Archit. chief frieze, capital; crowning moulding; —gestänge, n. … pump-spears; —gestell, n. principal scaffolding, principal stand (frame); —gewinn, m. capital prize, gain; main profit; —gewölbe, n. Archit. main-vaulting; —gläubiger, m. Comm. principal creditor; —glied, n. principal member; —grind, m. Med. scald; —grund, m. principal reason; —grundsatz, m. fundamental leading principle; —gut, n. capital stock; principal possession (estate); —haar, n. hair of the head; —handlung, f. 1) principal action, chief plot; 2) chief (commercial) establishment; —heer, n. see —armee; —hinderniß, n. principal, chief, or main obstacle; —hirsch, m. … a stag of eight years and upwards, hart …; —holz, n. 1) Archit. cabilcre, raising-…; 2) Min. bearding-plank, traverse; —…, f. sufficient land to constitute a farm; —hüfner, m. a farmer having sufficient … to constitute a farm; —inhalt, m. chief …; abstract, summary; substance; —…, f.; —jagen, n. grand chase; —kirche, f. principal, parish church (as distinguished from district church); —kissen, n. pillow; —…, m. Mus. see —ton, 1, a; —knoten, m. principal plot, intrigue; —krankheit, f. 1) disease in the head; 2) principal disease; [illegible]; —lager, n. main camp …; head-quarters; —land, n. main …; [illegible]; —laster, n. capital …; —leben, n. principal …; —lehre, f.

chief or cardinal doctrine; —lehrer, m. principal or head-master; —leidenschaft, f. master-passion; —leidtragende, m. chief-mourner; —leiter, 1) m. Phys. chief conductor; 2) f. Mus. fundamental scale; —leute, pl. of —mann; —licht, n. principal light.

Häuptling, (str.) m. chief, chieftain; leader.

Häuptlings, adv. over head, head foremost.

Hauptlinie, (w.) f. principal line; Min. principal direction of a lode.

Hauptlos, adj. 1) headless, without a leader; 2) see Kopflos.

Haupt…, in comp. —mangel, m. principal want, main defect; —mann, m. Mil. captain; chieftain, headman; —männin, f. wife of a captain; —mannschaft, f. captainship; —mannsstelle, f. captaincy; —manual, n. T. the set of keys belonging to the great organ; —marssegel, n. Mar. main top-sail; —mast, m. main-mast; —mauer, f. chief or main wall; —merkmal, n. chief (distinctive, main) characteristic, sign, mark; —mittel, n. principal remedy; —narr, m. great fool; —neigung, f. leading propensity; —nenner, m. Math. common denominator; —niederlage, f. 1) a) Comm. principal magazine; ware-house; b) staple town, emporium; 2) general defeat; —note, f. Mus. principal note (of a shake or that over which the mark tr. is placed); —ort, m. chief place; —periode, f. Mus. a capital period; —person, f. principal person, head, chief, leader; —pfeiler, m. main or arch pillar; —pflicht, f. chief duty; —pforte, f. chief gate, front gate; —pfosten, m. Archit. crown-post; —pfühl, m. pillow; —plan, m. main design; —postamt, n. general post-office, head-letter-office; (eines Bezirks) district-office; —posten, pl. Comm. principal items; —prämie, f. capital prize; —priester, m. chief or head priest; —product, n. 1) chief produce; 2) Math. total produce; —pulver, n. cephalic powder; —punct, m. 1) principal or chief point, main point; 2) pl. a) Astr. the equinoctial and solstitial points; b) Geogr. see Cardinalpuncte; —quartier, n. head-quarters; —quelle, f. chief source, head-spring, fountain-head; —querbalken, m. Archit. architrave; —raa, f. Mar. main-yard; —rebell, m. arch-rebel; chief rebel; —rechnung, f. main account, general account; —recht, n. Law, right of heriot; —regel, f. main or leading rule; —regenbogen, m. primary rainbow; —register, n. 1) principal register; general index; 2) main stop (of organs); —reif, m. T. trussing-hoop; —reparatur, f. thorough repair; —rheder, m. Mar. principal owner; —riegel, m. principal bolt; Gunn. cross-bar of a gun-carriage; —riß, m. general plan of a building; —röhren, pl. mains; —rolle, f. principal or prominent part, leading character; die —rolle spielen, to be the principal performer, to act the principal part, coll. to play the first fiddle; —ruder, n. stroke-oar; —rüstung, f. Build. principal scaffolding; —runde, f. Mil. main-rounds; —sache, f. main point, principal thing, main part, chief business; substance, gist; —sachen, f. pl. essentials; —sächlich, adj. chief, principal, main, essential; adv. chiefly, &c., especially; —sächlich, adj. capital (adv. capitally); —sammelplatz (des Handels), m. general rendezvous (of trade); —sänger, m. first or principal singer; —sängerin, f. prima donna; —satz, m. 1) capital proposition, main point; axiom; theme; 2) Gramm. principal clause; principal sentence; 3) Mus. principal subject or theme; —schiff, n. 1) Archit. middle-aisle; 2) Mar. admiral-ship, admiral; —schild, n. Herald. principal escutcheon; —schlacht, f. pitched battle, general fight, main battle; —schluß, m. Mus. final cadence; —schlüssel, m. master-key; pass-key; —schmerz, m. head-ache; —schmuck, m. 1) ornament for the head; 2) principal ornament; —schrift, f. principal writing, composition; —schuldner, m. Comm. principal debtor; —schule, f. principal school; —schwein, n. boar of five years and upwards; —schwierigkeit, f. main difficulty; —segel, n. Mar. main-sail; —sehne, f. master-sinew (of horses); —seite, f. 1) principal side; Archit. front, fore-part (of a building); obverse, face, or head-side (of a coin); —siech, adj. affected in the head (of horses); —sitz, m. principal seat or residence; —sorge, f. principal care; —spann, —spant, m. Mar. midship-frame; —spaß, m. capital joke; cream of a jest; —spieker, m. Mar. doubling nail; —spieler, m. desperate gambler; —sprache, f. principal language; original or mother tongue; —spruch, m. 1) principal sentence or verse; 2) Law, last sentence; —stadt, f. chief city, capital (city), metropolis; —städter, m. inhabitant of a capital; —städtisch, adj. relating or belonging to a capital; —stagsegel, n. mainstay-sail; —stamm, m. 1) main trunk, main root, main stem; 2) chief tribe (of a people); 3) capital stock, principal; —ständer, m. Archit. principal or king-post, king-piece; —stärke, f. 1) chief strength, energy; 2) that in which one excels, one's force; ein —stärkendes Mittel, Med. cephalic; —station, f. principal station, (railway-)terminus; —stein, m. Mas. head-stone, header; —stelle, f. principal passage (in a book); —steuer, f. 1) poll-tax; 2) principal tax; —steueramt, n. receiver general's office (for taxes); custom's office; —stimme, f. Mus., &c. principal voice; principal part; —stock, m. principal story of a house, first floor; —stoff, m. fundamental or material principle or matter; —straße, f. 1) principal or main street; 2) highway; main road; —streich, m. fig. capital trick; —streichen, n., —strich, m. principal direction of a lode; —strom, m. principal current, body of a river; main stream; —stück, n. principal article; head, chapter; body, solid (of a machine); —stuhl, m. see —stamm, 3; —sturm, m. main or general assault or storm; —stütze, f. mainstay, main support, prop; —sucht, f. Vet. distemper in the head (of horses); —süchtig, adj. see —siech; —summe, f. 1) principal sum, sum total; 2) capital sum or stock; —sünde, f. chief sin, cardinal sin; besetting sin; —tänzer, m., —tänzerin, f. first dancer, head-dancer; —tau, n. Mar. main-cable; —thäter, m. chief perpetrator; —theil, m. principal or greatest part; —thor, n. main-gate; —thür, f. principal door; —titel, m. Typ. principal or capital title; —ton, m. 1) Mus. a) fundamental or principal tone, key-note; b) see —note; 2) Gramm. principal accent; —träger, m. T. main support (of a turn-table, &c.); —treffen, n. see —schlacht; —treiben, n. see —jagd; —treppe, f. principal stair-case; —trumpf, m. chief trump, matadore; —tugend, f. cardinal virtue; —übel, n. principal evil; —umstand, m. leading circumstance; —und Staats-Action, Germ. Dram. a dramatised grand historical or other event, generally performed by puppets (usurping the place of the real drama towards the end of the 17th cent.); —ursache, f. principal cause; —verbandstück, n. Carp. main-timber; —verbrechen, n. greatest or capital crime; —verbrecher, m. master criminal; —verhör, n. Law, examination-in-chief; —vermögen, n. principal (capital), property; —wache, f. Mil. 1) main guard; 2) main guard-house; —wall, m. Fort. principal rampart; —wasser, n. main branch of a river; —weg, m. principal way or footpath; —werk, n. 1) main work; 2) standard work; master-piece; 3) chief matter; 4) Mus. the great organ; —wind, m. cardinal wind; —wirbel, m. crown of the head; —wirkung, f. principal or main effect; —wissenschaft, f. fundamental science; —wort, n. Gramm. 1) principal word; subject; 2) noun.

[illegible] plain, simple: sich — niederlassen, to settle, to become domiciliated; h-e Arbeit, domestic labour; h-er Fleiß, diligence at home (out of school hours); II. H-keit, (w.) f. domesticity, domestic life or habits; plainness, simplicity; frugality, thriftiness.

Haus'lilie, (w.) f. see Zaunlilie. [mate.

Häus'ling, (str.) m. 1) see Häusler; 2) in-

Haus'..., in comp. —macht, f. domestic power (of a prince); —mädchen, n. housemaid, chambermaid; —magd, f. servant of all-work; —maier, m. see —meier; —mann, m. 1) door- or gate-keeper, porter; 2) lodger, inmate; 3) master of the house; 4) cottager.

Hausmannit', (str.) m. Miner. hausmannite, black manganese ore.

Haus'..., in comp. —mannskost, f. household, homely or frugal fare, (short) commons; —marder, m. Zool. (house-)martin (Mustela foina L.); —märchen, n. household-story, tale; —mark, n. see Bärwurz; —marschall, m. marshal of the household; —mast, —mästung, f. stall-feeding (of hogs); —maus, f. Zool. domestic or common mouse (Mus musculus L.); —maier, m. Hist. Mayor of the palace, (Lat.) major domus; —meister, m. keeper of a house; —miethe, f. house-rent; —miether, m. householder; —mittel, n. domestic or empiric remedy, household or family medicine; —mühle, f. hand-mill; —münze, f. Bot. curled mint (Krausemünze); —mutter, f. 1) mother of the family; matron; 2) Entom. a species of butterfly (Triphaena pronuba L.); —mütterlich, adj. & adv. maternally, motherly; —mütze, f. study-cap; —natter, f. see —otter; —nummer, f. number of a house; —ordnung, f. regulation or rule of the house(-hold); —otter, f. Zool. ringed snake (Ringelnatter); —pflanze, f. window-plant; green-house plant; —pflichten, f. pl. domestic duties; —plage, f. domestic trouble; —plan, m. plan of a house or housekeeping; —platz, m. 1) lot, ground-plot; 2) see —flur; —postille, f. collection of sermons for family-use; —prediger, m. domestic chaplain; —rath, m. see —geräth; —ratte, f. Zool. common rat (Mus rattus L.); —rechnung, f. household-account; —recht, n. house-right, domestic authority; —regel, f. household-rule; —regiment, n. government of the family, household government; in-door dominion; —riegel, m. bolt of the street-door; —rock, m. coat for wearing in the house, cf. Schlafrock; —sache, f. domestic affair; —sasse, m. see —be-[illegible]; —sässig, adj. possessed of a house, settled; —schabe, f. Entom. house-beetle, black beetle (Blatta L.); —schatz, m. privy purse of a prince; —schlachten, n. the killing of sheep, pigs, or cattle for domestic use; —schlächter, m. domestic butcher; —schlange, f. see —otter; —schloß, n. lock of the street-door; —schlüssel, m. street-door key; —schmätzer, m. Ornith. stone-chat (Saxicola rubicola L.); —schneider, m. tailor to a family; —schoß, m. see —steuer; —schuhe, m. pl. slippers; —schuhmacher, m. family-shoemaker; —schwalbe, f. Ornith. house-swallow, house-martin (Hirundo urbica L.); —schwamm, m. Bot. dry-rot (Merulius lacrymans Schum.); —schwelle, f. threshold of a house.

* Hausse [hōß'ĕ], (w.) f. Comm. rise (of public funds); —bewegung, f. rising tendency.

Haus'segen, (str.) m. domestic blessing; children. [nen; cf. Draußen).

Hau'ßen, adv. coll. out here (opp. Drin-

* Haussier [hōßjē'], (str.) m. Comm. [illegible], stag, bull.

Haus'..., in comp. —sorge, f. domestic care; —spatz, m. see —sperling; —speise, f. see —kost; —sperling, m. Ornith. domestic sparrow (Passer domesticus L.); —spinne, f. Entom. domestic spider (Tegenaria domestica L.); —stand, m. domestic state (condition); household; —steuer, f. tax paid of a house; —streit, m. see —krieg; —stunde, f. usual hour of coming home at night; —suchung, f. domiciliary visitation or visit, search of a man's house; —suchung thun, to search the house; —suchungsbefehl, m. search-warrant; —tafel, f. table (in the catechism) containing the duties of domestic life; —taube, f. Ornith. tame pigeon, house pigeon (Columba livia Briss.); —taufe, f. private christening.

Hau'..., in comp. —stein, m. T. ashlar, free-stone; —steinmauerwerk, n. Archit. free-(stone)-masonry, ashlar-stone-work; —steinmaurer, m. free-mason; —stempel, m. puncheon.

Haus'..., in comp. —tenne, f. floor (of a house); —teufel, m. 1) domestic devil, &c. see —drache, 2; 2) Ornith. ruff (Machetes pugnax L.); —thier, n. domestic, domesticated, or domiciliated animal; —thür, f. street-door; —thürfenster, n. fan-light; —trauer, f. family-mourning; —trauung, f. private wedding; —trunk, m. family-beverage; —truppen, f. pl. household-troops; —tuch, n. home-made cloth; —tugend, f. domestic virtue; —übel, n. family affliction; —uhr, f. house-clock; —unke, f. 1) see Unke, 1; 2) fig. a) a person being always at home, home-sticking person, stay-at-home, fixture, coll. tarry-at-home bird; b) house-servant, cf. Aschenbrödel; —unkosten, pl. household expenses; —unkostenbuch, n. book of household expenses; —unterstützung, f. out-door relief; —vater, m. house-father, householder; housekeeper; —väterlich, adj. & adv. relating to (or in the manner of) a father of a family; —verbrauch, m. house-consumption; —verstand, m. coll. common sense; —vertrag, m. family compact; —verwalter, m. steward; care-taker; —verwaltung, f. stewardship, management of a house; —vieh, n. domestic cattle; —vögel, m. pl. house or domesticated birds; —vogt, m. judge, castle-ward; jailor; overseer of prisoners; steward; —vogtei, f. prison, jail; —wanze, f. house or bed-bug (Acanthia lectularia L.); —wappen, n. family-arms; —wäsche, f. 1) (the act of) washing in the house; 2) house-linen; —wesen, n. domestic concerns, economy, household; ein —wesen anfangen, to commence housekeeping, to set up house; —wiesel, n. Zool. the common weasel, mouser (Mustela vulgaris L.); —wirth, m. husband, householder; master or proprietor of the house; landlord; ein guter —wirth, good manager of a house; —wirthin, f. housekeeper, housewife; mistress of the house; proprietress of a house; landlady; —wirthschaft, f. housekeeping, management of a house; household, economy; —wurz, —wurzel, f. Bot. 1) houseleek (Hauslauch, 1); 2) wall-pepper (Mauerpfeffer); —ziege, f. common goat (Capra hircus L.); —zins, m. house-rent; —zucht, f. domestic discipline.

Haut, s. (str., pl. Häu'te) f. 1) skin; 2) hide, skin, case; skin, film (of liquids); slough, cast skin (of serpents); Anat. membrane; tunic, (in)tegument; Bot. coat; 3) Mar. skin (of a ship, i. e. all the planks of the outer sides); zur — gehörig, cutaneous, dermal, dermoid; bis auf die — durchnäßt, wet to the skin; in der —, cutaneous; unter der —, subcutaneous; die — abstreifen, to cast off the skin or slough; coll. e. mit — und Haaren verschlingen, to devour neck and crop; es gilt — und Haar, it is a matter of life and death; da möchte man (je) aus der — fahren! it is enough to drive one wild; aus der — fahren wollen, to be ready to leap out of one's skin; sich seiner — wehren, to defend one's own life; er ist eine gute, ehrliche —, he is a good, honest fellow; mit heiler — davon kommen, to come off with a whole skin, to save one's self harmless, vulg. to save one's bacon; er ist nichts als — und Knochen, he is brought to skin and bones; das sitzt nur auf der —, that is only skin-deep; er steckt in seiner gesunden —, he has a diseased body; es steckt ihm in der —, it is his nature; sich seiner — (Gen.) wehren (seine — theuer verkaufen), to defend one's self to the utmost; Einem die — über die Ohren ziehen, see Fell; seine — zu Markte tragen, to do a thing at one's own risk, to expose one's self; auf der faulen — liegen, to be idle.

Haut'..., in comp. —absonderung, f. cutaneous secretion; —artig, adj. skinny; —ausdünstung, f. perspiration; —ausschlag, m. cutaneous eruption, see Ausschlag, b; Med.-s. —beschuppung, f. desquamation.

* Hautbois' [pr. hobŏă'], n. (Fr.), Hautboist' [hoboĭßt'], (w.) m. see Hoboe &c.

Haut'..., in comp. —bräune, f. croup; —brennen, n. itching and burning sensation in the skin, uredo.

Häut'chen, (str.) n. (dimin. of Haut) thin skin, membrane, Chem & Bot. pellicle, cuticle.

Haut'..., in comp. —cultur, f. see —pflege; —drüse, f. cutaneous (or miliary) gland; —drüsenkrankheit, f. scrofula.

* Hautelis'se [hō—], (w.) f. (Fr.) tapestry of the highwarp; —stuhl, m. T. upright loom.

Häu'teln, (w.) v. tr. to skin, peel.

Häu'ten, (w.) v. I. tr. to skin, strip of the skin; II. refl. to cast or (Entom.) change the skin, to cast the slough.

Haut'..., in comp. —farbe, f. colour of the skin, complexion; —flügelig, adj. Entom. membrane-winged, hymenopteral; —flügler, m. pl. hymenoptera; —form, f. Gold-b. mould of about a thousand leaves; Med.-s. —geschwulst, f. œdema; —gries, m. chronic eruption of the skin.

Häu'tig, Häu'ticht, adj. skinny, like skin; cuticular, skinned, membranous; h-e Bräune, see Hautbräune.

Haut'..., in comp. —krankheit, f. cutaneous disease, disease of the skin; —lehre, f. Med. dermatology; —männchen, n. see —ausschlag(?); —moos, n. Med lichen; —muskel, m. cutaneous muscle; —pflanzen, f. pl. Bot. see Hülsenpflanzen; —pflege, f. culture of the skin; —planken, f. pl. Ship-b. planks of the outer sides of a ship; —reinigend, adj. cosmetic; —reinigendes Mittel, cosmetic; —reinigung, f. cleaning of the skin.

* Hautrelief' [pr. hōreljĕf'], n. (Fr.) T. alto rilievo, high relief.

Haut'..., in comp. —risse, m. pl. see —schrunden; —röthe, f. Med. red-rash, erythema; —schmiere, f. sebaceous humour; —schrunden, —spalten, f. pl. dry and malignant cutaneous fissures, rhagades.

Häu'tung, (w.) f. 1) (the act of) skinning, &c. cf. Häuten; 2) Entom., &c. casting or change of the skin; Med. desquamation (of the skin).

Haut'..., in comp. Med.-s. —wassersucht, anasarca; —wassersüchtig, adj. anasarcous; —windsucht, f. emphysema; —wurm, m. see Medinawurm. [fit for felling.

Hau'wald, (str., pl. Hau'wälder) m. wood

* Hauyn', (str.) m. Miner. dodecahedral zeolite or lapis lazuli.

Hau'zahn, (str., pl. Hau'zähne) m. tusk, fang.

Havan'nah, f. Geogr. the Havannah.

* Havarie', Haverei', Haverie', (w.) f. (Fr. avaria) Comm.-s. average; damage by sea; große (allgemeine or General-)—, gross (or general) average; einfache or besondere —, particular (or simple) average; kleine (gemeine or ordinäre) —, petty average; — und Kapplaken, average and primage; — leiden or machen, to suffer damage, to become damaged.

Hee'de, see Hede.

Heer, s. I. (str.) m. 1) large number, quantity; 2) host, army; das wilde or wüthende —, [illegible]'s chase; 3) fig. multitude (of passions, [illegible]); II. in comp. —abtheilung, f., —arm, m. see Heeresabtheilung; —bann, m. 1) arrière-ban, militia; 2) the obligation of taking the field; —biene, f. Bee, thieving bee.

Heerd, Hee'rde [hērd, hēr'—], see Herd &c.

Hee'res..., in comp. —abtheilung, f. division or column of an army; —bewegung, f. movement or manœuvre of an army; —flucht, f., —flüchtling, m., &c. see Heerflucht &c.; —folge, f. obligation of following the army of the sovereign; —haufen, m. host, army; —kraft, —macht, f. forces, troops, army; power; —menge, f. host; —zucht, f. discipline.

Heer..., in comp. —fahne, f. banner, standard; —fahrt, f. campaign; —flucht, f. desertion (from an army); —flüchtig, adj. deserting: —flüchtig werden, to desert; ein —flüchtiger, a deserter; —flügel, m. flank (of an army); —führer (+ —fürst), m. chief of the army, commander-in-chief; general, chieftain, captain; —gans, f. Ornith. gray hern or [illegible] (Ardea cinerea L.); —geräth, n. 1) (camp, or field) equipage, furniture of an army; 2) or [illegible], —gewette, n. heriot; —haufe, m. troops, division, squadron; —heuschrecke, f. Entom. migratory cricket (Zugheuschrecke); —holz, m. Ornith. common jay (Garrulus glandarius L., Holzhäher); —horn, n. +, war-trumpet; —kuh, f. bell-cow; —lager, n. camp of an army; —[illegible], army; —liste, f. army-list; —meister, m. grand-master or head of certain knightly orders; —meisterschaft, f. grand-mastership; —pauke, f. kettle-drum, tymbal; —rauch, m. [illegible] thick yellowish fog (Höhenrauch); —[illegible], f. see —wurm; —säule, f. column of the army; —schar, f. army, host; legion; der Herr or Gott der —scharen, Script. Lord of Hosts, God sabaoth; —schatz, m. 1) military [illegible]; 2) Law, fines of alienation; —schau, f. review; —schild, m. 1) buckler, shield; 2) dignity of a knight; —schnepfe, f. Ornith. common snipe (Scolopax gallinago L.); —[illegible], f. manœuvre of an army; —spitze, f. van, vanguard; —steuer, f. war-tax; —straße, f. 1) military road; 2) highway, road; 3) fig. beaten road or track; —strom, m. large (principal or main) river; —theil, n. army, [illegible]; —wagen, m. 1) baggage-waggon; 2) Astr. Charles's wain; —weg, m. see —straße; —wesen, n. anything relating to an army, military concerns; —wurm, m. army-worm, migrating flock of larvæ of the Sciara Thomæ [illegible], moving along in snake-like windings of [illegible] length; —zug, m. march; —zwang, m. see —bann.

He'fe, s. I. (w.) f. 1) H-n, pl. lees, dregs, grounds, sediment, mother, fæcula, fæces; [illegible] barm, yeast, yest; 2) fig. the dregs (of the people), sink (of the mob); (bis) auf die H-n kommen, to come, get to the bottom, to be reduced to extremities; bis auf die H-n leeren, to empty to the (very) dregs; auf der — [illegible], coll. to be aground. [illegible]

[illegible] (w.) f. Wine. middle (Meisn.; Fadern-[illegible]) [illegible]..., in comp. —brot, n., —kuchen, m. [illegible] bread, cake; —prüfer, m. T. zymometer; —säure, f. Chem. lactic acid; —teig, [illegible] leavened dough.

[illegible], He'fig, adj. yeast-like; barmy, [illegible] tasting of yeast; full of lees, dreggy.

Heft, (str.) n. (& m.) 1) haft, handle; hilt [illegible] a sword; hook, pin; 2) of some sheets [illegible] together, stitched (or stitch) book; [illegible], part; 3) fig. power; [illegible] das [illegible], to wrest the staff out of one's [illegible]; das — in der Hand haben, to bear sway. [illegible] (w.) f. (the act of) fastening the [illegible] of a vine.

Heft'eisen, (str.) n. Glass-m. punt.

Hef'tel, (str.) m. clasp, hook, pin; — und Schlinge, hook and eye.

Hef'teln, (w.) v. tr. 1) to clasp, to fasten with hooks and eyes; to pin.

Hef'ten, (w.) v. tr. 1) to fasten, attach, tie; to nail; to hook; to pin; 2) Bookb. & Surg. to stitch, sew; Sew. to baste; 3) fig. to fix (the eyes, &c. upon); eine Wunde —, to sew a wound together.

Heft'..., in comp. —faden, m. basting thread; —haken, m. hook of a binder's press.

Hef'tig, adj. 1) vehement, violent, impetuous; impatient, fierce; hot, ardent, intense, keen; high (wind, quarrel, passions); heavy (rain); sharp (cold, lightnings); 2) earnest, eager; passionate; — hassen, to hate bitterly; — lieben, to be passionately fond of, to dote upon.

Hef'tigkeit, (w.) f. vehemence, violence, impetuosity; intensity; heat, eagerness, ardour; mit —, fig. sharply.

Heft'..., in comp. —lade, f. Bookb. sewing-frame, sewing-board, sewing-press; —macher, m. haftmaker; —nadel, f. stitching-needle; book-binder's needle; —pflaster, n. Surg. adhesive or sticking-plaster; —pulver, n. agglutinative powder; —scharte, f. osier for binding hoops; —schnur, f. band-string; Bookb.-s. —schnüre, pl. bands; —stift, m. pointel; —weise, adv. in numbers (of publications); —zwecken, f. pl. drawing pins or points; —zwirn, m. see —faden. [preserve.

A. He'ge, (w.) f. 1) see Schutz; 2) Sport.

B. He'ge, (w.) f. see Heie.

He'geholz, (str.) n. see Hegewald.

A. He'geling, (str.) m. 1) trunk of a fir-tree used in making fences; 2) provinc. a species of trout.

B. He'geling, (str.) m. coll. a follower of Hegel (a German philosopher, 1770—1831).

* Hegemonie', (w.) f. Gr. Hist. hegemony, headship (Vorherrschaft).

He'gen, (w.) v. tr. 1) see Hägen; 2) to foster, cherish; to entertain, cherish, nurse, harbour, have (suspicion, hopes, doubts); Groll, Haß — gegen..., to bear one a grudge (spite), to bear hatred or malice, to have a spite, ill-will against....

He'ger, (str.) m. 1) cherisher, fosterer, keeper; auf einen — kommt ein Feger, proverb, a spendthrift son consumes the prudent father's savings; 2) possessor of a small socage estate (—gut); 3) forester, keeper; 4) see Häger, 2.

He'ge..., in comp. —reis, n. Forest. tiller, standard, stad(d)le; —reiter, m. gamekeeper, Law, verderer.

He'gerweide, (w.) f. see Wahdelweide.

He'ge..., in comp. —säulen, f. pl. boundary-posts of a post, &c.; —thiere, n. pl. beasts and fowls of the warren; —wald, m. a forest fenced in; —wasser, n. pond or river in which it is not allowed to fish; —weide, f. pasture-ground on which no cattle are allowed to feed; —wiese, f. meadow fenced in; —wisch, m. wisp of hay or straw stuck on a pole, as a sign of an acre, forest, &c. fenced in; —zeit, f. time when no game is killed, Law, fence month.

Heh'er, (str.) m. see Häher.

Hehl, (str.) m. or n. concealment, secrecy, only in: ohne —, without secrecy, openly; kein — haben (with Gen.), kein — machen aus..., to make no secret of..., not to conceal or deny.

Heh'le, (w.) f. Ornith. bullfinch (Gimpel).

Heh'len, (w.) v. tr. to conceal (Verhehlen); Gestohlenes —, to receive stolen goods.

Heh'ler, (str.) m., H-in, (w.) f. concealer; receiver (of stolen goods).

Hehr, adj. *, sublime, high, elevated, august, holy; Hoch-a. —messe, f. high-mass.

† Hehr'thum, (str., pl. H-thümer) n. ornament.

Hei, Hei'da, interj. huzza.

A. Hei'de, (w., Gen. & Dat. sing. (+ &) * H-n) f. 1) heath; 2) provinc. wood, forest; 3) Bot. see —kraut.

B. Hei'de, (w.) m. heathen, pagan, gentile.

Hei'de... (A.), in comp. —besen, m. heath-broom; —biene, f. heath-bee; —bienenkraut, n. Bot. wild rosemary (Ledum palustre L.); —blume, f. heath-flower; —boden, m. see —land, 1; —bückchen, n. heap of buck-wheat; —busch, m. furze, gorse, briars; —drossel, f. Ornith. red-wing (Turdus iliacus L.); —eiche, f. Bot. see Steineiche; —erde, f. Gard. heath mould; —fennig, m. see —korn; —flachs, m. flax-weed; —futter, n. fodder growing on heaths; —gebüsch, n. heath thicket, cf. —busch; —geflügel, n. moor-game; —gewächse, pl. heaths; —gras, n. Bot. 1) heath-grass (Triodia decumbens Beauv.); 2) see —korn; —grütze, f. grit, groats made of buck-wheat; —hahn, m. heath-cock (Tetrao tetrix L.); —honig, m. honey of heath bees; —huhn, n. Ornith. heath-pout, moor-hen (Tetrao cupido Gm.); —hecht, m. see —laufer; Bot.-s. —korn, n. buckwheat, panicle (Buchweizen); —kraut, n. heath, heather, sweet-broom (Erica vulgaris L.); —kresse, f. see Felsenkresse.

Hei'del, s. I. or Hei'den, (str.) m. provinc. buck-wheat; II. in comp. —beere, f. Bot. bilberry (Vaccinium myrtillus L.); (rothe) red whortleberry (Vaccinium vitis idæa L.); —beermyrte, f. Dutch myrtle (Myrica gale L.); —beerstrauch, m. bilberry-bush; —hahn, m. see Heidehahn.

Hei'de... (A.), in comp. —land, n. 1) heathy ground or land; 2) heath country; —läufer, m. keeper of a forest, forester's assistant; —lerche, f. Ornith. 1) pipit (Baumpieper); 2) woodlark (Baumlerche).

Hei'den... (from Heide, B.), in comp. —apostel, m. apostle of the Gentiles; —bekehrer, m. converter of pagans or heathens, missionary; —bild, n. idol.

Hei'de... (A.), in comp. —nelke, f. Bot. pink with white deltoid spots on the petals (Dianthus deltoides L.). [heidekrähe).

Hei'denelster, (w.) f. Ornith. roller (Man-

Hei'den... (from Heide, B.), in comp. —geld, n. slang, enormous sum of money; —glaube, m. pagan belief; —land, n. pagan country; —leben, n. heathenish life; —lehrer, m. see —bekehrer.

Hei'den... (from Heide A.), in comp. —meise, f. Ornith. 1) tit-lark (Heidelerche); 2) tufted lark (Haubenlerche); —pfeifer, m. Ornith. golden plover (Goldregenpfeifer); Bot.-s. —pfrieme, f. 1) common broom (Spartium scoparium L.); 2) dyer's weed (Färberginster); —rettig, m. 1) field-radish (Raphanus raphanistrum L.); 2) penny-cress (Thlaspi L.); —schmuck, m. 1) common rock-rose (Helianthemum vulgare L.); 2) see —pfrieme, 2; 3) common saw-wort (Serratula tinctoria L.).

Hei'den... (from Heide, B.), in comp. —sitte, f. heathenish manner or custom; —tempel, m. pagan temple.

Hei'denthum, (str.) n. (& w. Hei'denschaft, (w.) f.) 1) paganism, heathenism; 2) collect. heathens, pagans.

Hei'den... (from Heide, A.), in comp. —wundkraut, n. 1) golden-rod (Goldruthe); 2) woundwort (Anthyllis vulneraria L.); —wisch, m. see —schmuck, 1.

Hei'de... (A.), in comp. —partie, f. Gard. heathery; —rauch, m. fog on a forest; —reiter, m. +, mounted ranger, forester.

Hei'derling, (str.) m. Bot. a mushroom (Champignon).

Hei'de... (A.), in comp. —rose, f. Bot. sweet-briar; heath-rose, Scottish rose (Rosa rubiginosa L.); —schaf, n. (provinc. —schnucke, —schnucke, f.) heath-mutton, [illegible]

[illegible]gen, *Comm.* see Abandonniren; –selig, [illegible] see Heimlich, 2.

Heim'sen, *(w.) v. tr.* see Einheimsen.

Heim'..., *in comp* –sied, *adj.* longing for [illegible] home, home-sick; –steuer, *f.* dowry, [illegible]tion, dotal property.

Heim'suchen, *(w.) v. tr. fig.* 1) to haunt, [illegible]; 2) *Script.* to visit (Sünden an *[with* [illegible]*]*, sins upon ...), to punish.

Heim'sucht, *(w.) f.* see Heimweh.

Heim'suchung, *(w.) f.* visitation: 1) *Script.* [illegible] visiting: – Mariä, *Rom. Cath.* feast of [illegible]tation of our Lady; 2) punishment, visiting.

Heim'thüm, *(str.) n. provinc.* longing for [illegible] home.

Heim'tücke, *(w.) f.* (secret) malice, ma[illegible], spite; (malicious) trick.

Heim'tückisch, *adj.* malicious, malignant.

Heim'..., *in comp.* –wärts, *adv.* homeward; –weg, *m.* way home; den –weg antreten, to set out homewards; auf dem –wege, [illegible] coming home; –weh, *n.* home-sickness, nostalgia; das –weh haben, to be home-sick; –wesen, *n.* homestead, home; –zahlung, *f.* [illegible]. reimbursement, payment at fall: –[illegible], *m.* return home.

Hein, Freund –, see Hain, II.

Hein'rich, *m.* Henry *(P. N.)*; *Bot.-s.* der gute –, good Henry *(Chenopodium bonus Henricus L.)*; der böse –, greater broom-rape *(Orobanche major L.)*; der stolze (blaue) –, viper's bugloss *(Echium vulgare L.)*; der große –, elecampane *(Inula helenium L.)*; der wilde –, spiked rampion *(Phyteuma spicatum L.)*.

Heint, *adv. provinc.* this night; today.

Heinz, *m. abbr. for* Heinrich, Hal, Harry *(P. N.)*.

Heinz, *(w.) m.* 1) *or* H-enkunst, *f.* a kind of chain-pump *or* bucket-engine; 2) der faule –, *Chem.* athanor.

Hein'ze, *(w.) f. provinc.* bee.

Hein'zel..., *in comp.* –bank, *f. T.* form to [illegible] (carve) upon; *Husb.* straw-cutter; –männchen, *n.* a kind of family spirit, Robin Goodfellow.

Hein'zenseil, *(str.) n. T.* 1) chain of a bucket engine, &c.; 2) chain for moving a pair of bellows.

Hei'rath, *(w.) f.* marriage; match: eine reiche – thun, to marry a fortune.

Hei'rath(h)en, *(w.) v. tr. & intr.* to marry.

Hei'rath(h)s..., *in comp.* –antrag, *m.* offer of marriage, offered alliance, proposal: –brief, *m.* marriage-contract, see Ehevertrag; –bureau, *n. burl.* marriage-monger's office; –contract, *m.* see –brief; –fähig, *adj.* fit for marriage, marriageable; –gebräuche, *m. pl.* marriage-ceremonies; sich mit –gedanken tragen, see –lustig sein; –gut, *n.* dowry, portion, dotal property; –lust, *f.* desire, inclination for marrying; –lustig, *adj.* desirous of marrying; –lustig sein, to think of marrying, to be a marrying man; –macher, *m.*, –macherin, *f.*, –stifter, *m.*, match-maker; –schein, *m.* 1) marriage-licence; 2) certificate of marriage; –stiftung, *f.* 1) match-making; 2) *or* –vertrag, *m.* see –brief; –verwandtschaft, *f.* relation by marriage, affinity.

Hei'sa *or* Hei'ßa! *interj.* huzzah! huzza!

Heisch, *adj. coll. for* Heiser.

Hei'schen, *(w.) v. tr. (provinc. &c.)*°, to desire, require (Begehren, Fordern).

Hei'schesatz, *(str., pl.* H-sätze) *m. Log.* postulatum, postulate.

Hei'ser, I. *adj.* hoarse; II. H-keit, *(w.) f.* hoarseness.

Hei'ster, *(str.) m.* 1) magpie (Elster); 2) *(also (w.) f.)* young oak *or* beech.

Heiß, I. *adj.* 1) hot; *fig.-s.* 2) torrid (zone); 3) hot, ardent, fervent; [illegible]; vehement; [illegible] –, and hot; [illegible]; II. hot pursuit; [illegible] –, I grow hot; was ich nicht weiß,

macht mir (*or* mich) nicht –, *proverb.* what the eye cannot see the heart never grieves; Einem den Kopf – machen, to set a person's head whirling, to bother one; to cause one anxiety *or* fear; II. *in comp.* –blütig, *adj.* warm-blooded; –brüchig, *adj.* hot-short (iron); –durst, *m.* violent thirst.

Hei'ßen, *(str.) v. I. tr.* 1) *(with two Acc.)* to call, name; Einen willkommen –, to bid or make one welcome; gut –, see Gut; 2) *(with Acc. & Inf.)* Einen gehen, (sich) setzen &c. –, to bid one go, take a seat, &c.; Einen sich setzen –, to bid one to a seat; er hieß mich hereinkommen, he bade me come in; 3) (Einem *or* Einen etwas) to bid, desire, tell, enjoin (one to do a thing); thue was ich dir heiße, do my bidding; das habe ich euch nicht geheißen, I did not tell you to do it; er hat es mir geheißen, he made me do it; thue, wie dir geheißen, do as you were bid; 4) *coll. for* Nennen: das heiße ich gut einkaufen, that is what I call making a good bargain: heiß' ich mir das doch eine Messe! *(Göthe, Faust)*, this, with a vengeance, is a fair.

II. *intr.* 1) to be called, to bear a name; wie – Sie? what is your name? ich will ein Schelm –, wenn ..., call me a rogue if ...; wie heißt dies Wort auf Französisch? what is the French for this word? 2) to mean, signify; 3) to be, to be considered; das heißt, that is to say, that is; ich will ihm zeigen, was es heißt, I will show him what it is; was soll das –? what is the meaning of this? what does it signify? was heißt das anders als ..., what is this but saying that ...; das hieße ihn forttreiben, this would be (as much as) to drive him away; lieben heißt leben, to love is to live; er lachte geradezu, was so viel – sollte, als ..., he laughed outright, as much as to say ...; das heißt eine Liebe! this is love! das heißt doch (ge)laufen &c.! this is indeed running! that's what I call running! jetzt heißt es aufpassen! attention is now the word! es heißt die Artigkeit zu weit treiben, it is carrying politeness too far (to ...).

III. *impers.* es heißt, it is said; it is given out, it is reported, the story goes: „Versichern Sie ihm," hieß es in einem Briefe, „daß ...", "assure him," said one letter, "that ..."; wie es im Liede heißt, as the song has it; es heißt in der Bibel &c., it says in the Bible, &c.

Heiß'..., *in comp.* –gebläse, *n. T.* hot blast; –geliebt, *adj.* ardently *or* passionately loved; –grätig, *adj.* 1) *Metall.* difficult of fusion, refractory; 2) sterile (of the soil); –hunger, *m.* 1) canine (*or* dog) appetite, hungry evil; voracious hunger; 2) *fig.* craving greediness, famished voracity; –hungrig, *adj.* affected with the canine appetite; voracious, greedy; (of horses) foul-feeding; –wassercisterne, *f. Mech.* hot water cistern (of a steam engine); –wasserheizung, *f.* calorifiere of water.

Hei'ter, I. *adj.* 1) serene; clear, fair, bright; ein Blitz aus h-m Himmel, a thunderbolt from the blue; 2) cheerful, in (high) spirits, merry; glad, happy, contented; unruffled; – werden, to clear up; II. H-keit, *(w.)*, *poet.* Hei't(e)re, *f.* 1) serenity; clearness, brightness; 2) cheerfulness, hilarity, gladness, mirth, &c.

Hei'tern, *(w.) v. tr. & refl.*°, to exhilarate, cheer (up), see Aufheitern, Erheitern.

Heiz'apparat, *(str.) m. Mech.* apparatus of *or* for heating.

Heiz'bar, I. *adj.* that may be heated; easily heated; h-es Zimmer, room containing a fireplace or stove; II. H-keit, *(w.) f.* capability of being heated.

Hei'zen, *(w.) v. tr. & intr.* to heat, to make *or* light a fire (in a stove, &c.); mit Holz –, to burn wood, to have a wood-fire;

das Zimmer heizt sich gut, the room gets soon warm. [fire-man, furnace-man, fire-boy.

Hei'zer, *(str.) m.* fire-maker, *T.* stoker,

Heiz'..., *in comp.* *Mech.-s.* –kraft, *f.* heating-power; –loch, *n.* stoke-hole; –ort, *m.* fire-place; –röhre, *f.* steam-heating pipe; *pl.* hot-air flues (of a locomotive); –thür, *f.* fire-box-door.

Hei'zung, *(w.) f.* 1) (the act of) heating, warming; – durch Dampf, heating by steam; 2) *(or* H-smaterial, *n.)* fuel.

* Hekatom'be, *(w.) f. (Gr.)* hecatomb.

* Hek'tik, *(w.) f.*, Hek'tisch, *adj. (Gr.)* hectic.

Held, *(w.) m.* 1) hero; champion; 2) *Theat.* actor of (the) heroic parts.

Hel'de, *(w.) f. provinc.* 1) see Fessel; 2) H-en, *pl. Mar.* bulge ways.

Hel'den..., *in comp.* heroic: –alter, *n.* heroic age; –bahn, *f.* heroic career; –brief, *m.* heroic [illegible]; –buch, *n.* book of heroes (a collection of old German heroic poems, dating from the thirteenth century); –dichter, *m.* epic poet; –dichtung, –fabel, *f.* see –sage; –gedicht, *n.* *Poet.* epic or heroic poem, epopee; –geist, –gesang, *m.*, –geschlecht, *n.*, –gestalt, –größe, *f.* heroic spirit, poem, race, form, grandeur.

Hel'denhaft, *adj.* heroic; *adv.* heroically.

Hel'den..., *in comp.* –heer, *n.* army of heroes; –herz, *n.* heroic(al) spirit, heroic courage; –herzig, *adj.* heroic; –jüngling, *m.* heroic youth, youthful hero; –jungfrau, *f.* heroic maid; –kühn *(Schiller)*, *adj.* brave as a hero, *(Bulwer:)* hero-brave; –lied, *n.* heroic song; –mäßig, –müthig, *adj.* heroic, heroical, hero-like; –muth, *m.* heroism, heroicalness, heroic(al) spirit, valour; –reich, *adj.* abounding in heroes; –rolle, *f.* part of the *(or* a) hero; –ruhm, *m.* fame of a hero; –sage, *f.* heroic legend.

Hel'denschaft, *(w.) f. iron.* heroism.

Hel'den..., *in comp.* –schar, *f.* band of heroes, heroic band; –seele, *f.*, –sinn, *m.* &c. heroic soul, heroic feeling, &c.; –that, *f.* deed of heroism; heroic feat, achievement, *or* action.

Hel'denthum, *(str.) n.* heroism; age of heroism.

Hel'denthümlich, *adj.* heroic, heroical.

Hel'den..., *in comp.* –tod, *m.* heroic death; –tugend, *f.* heroic virtue; –weib, *n.* heroine; –zeit, *f.* time of heroes, heroic age.

Hel'din, *(w.) f.* heroine.

Hel'disch, *adj.* heroic.

Hele'ne, Hel'ena, *f.* 1) Helena, Helen *(P. N.)*; 2) *provinc.* common eel; H-nfeuer, *n. Mar.* fire of St. Helme, St. Elmo's *(or* Elmo's) fire, corposant; H-nkraut, *n. Bot.* elecampane *(Inula helenium L.)*.

* Helenit', *(str.) m. Miner.* adularia.

Hel'fe, *(w.) Weav.* hiddle (Fadenhälfte).

Hel'fen, *(str.) v. intr.* 1) *(with Dat.)* to help, aid; to support, succour, assist, relieve (bei, in, in); 2) to avail, profit, to do good; to remedy, cure, remove; to be good (für, gegen, for *or* against...), to be of use *or* efficacious; aus dem Wagen, dem Sattel, einer Verlegenheit &c. –, to assist out of the carriage, from the saddle, out of a scrape, &c.; sich aus etwas –, to extricate one's self from ...; (Einem) aus dem Traume –, *coll.* to help one out of his dream, *i. e.* to undeceive; hinauf, hinunter, hinein, hinaus &c. –, to help up, down, out, in, &c.; über etwas (weg)–, to help over; Einem von ... –, 1. to help *or* bring off; 2. to rid of, deliver from; Einem vom Brote –, *coll.* to ruin *(iron.* to speed) one; Einem zu etwas –, to help one to get; es hilft (zu) nichts, it answers *(or* it is to) no purpose, it is of no use *or* avail; es hilft mir zu nichts, I am not the better for it; dagegen hilft nichts mehr, it is past remedy; Einem wieder zurecht –, to lead one in the right way; so wahr mir Gott helfe!

so help me God! helf (dir) Gott! God bless you! was hilft es? or wozu hilft das? what is the use of it? what boots it? what does it come to? hier ist nicht mehr zu —, this is past help or irremediable; wem nicht zu rathen ist, dem ist nicht zu —, proverb, they that will not be counselled cannot be helped; was wird es mir —? what shall I be the better for it? was wird es Ihnen —? what good will it do you? was hülfe es dem Menschen, wenn er die ganze Welt gewönne &c. (Matth. 16, 26), what is a man profited, if he shall gain the whole world, &c.; es kann nichts —, it cannot be helped; ich kann mir nicht —, I cannot help it; I do not know what to do; sich nicht mehr (or kaum noch) zu — wissen, not to know which way to turn, to be put to one's last shifts; ich weiß mir nicht anders zu —, I know not what else to do, I have no alternative (als, but); sich immer zu — wissen, to be fruitful in expedients; er weiß sich zu —, he knows to shift for himself.

Hel'fenbein, (str.) n. †, see Elfenbein.

Hel'fer, (str.) m., Hel'ferin, (w.) f. helper, aider, assistant, adjutor; —amt, n. office of a helper, &c.; H-shelfer, (str.) m. 1) accomplice, accessory, abettor; 2) fig. tool, pl. myrmidons.

Helf'rede, (w.) f. Law, excuse.

Helf'willig, I. adj. ready to help; II. H-keit, (w.) f. readiness to help.

Hel'ger, (str.) m. Mar. ﬁzgig.

Hel'goland, n. Geogr. Heligoland (an island in the German ocean). — Hel'goländer, Hel'golander, (str.) m. 1) inhabitant of Heligoland; 2) sun-bonnet (for ladies).

He'ling, (str.) m. Mar. carrick-bend, granny's bend. [Sun-god.

* He'lios, m. Gr. Myth. Helios, the sun,

* Helioskop', (str.) n. (Gr.) helioscope.

* Heliotrop', (str.) n. & m. (Gr.), Heliotro'pium, n. heliotrope: 1) Min. blood-stone; 2) Bot. turnsole (Heliotropium peruvianum L.).

Hell, (str.) n. Mar. boatswain's store-room.

Hell, adj. 1) clear, distinct, shrill (of sound); 2) clear, light, bright, luminous, brilliant (of light); 3) fig. clear, plain, evident; h-e Farben, light colours; das h-e Feuer, light fire; am h-n (coll. lichten) Tage, in or at broad daylight: Mordthaten wurden völlig straflos am h-n Tage begangen, murders were committed in the face of day with perfect impunity (Macaulay); es liegt am h-en Tage, it is as clear as day (-light); h-e Flamme, blaze; h-er Mittag, broad noon; es ist —, it is bright; — machen, werden, to brighten; es fängt an — zu werden, the day begins to dawn; von h-er Hautfarbe, fair-skinned; ein h-es Gelächter, a broad or hearty laugh; ein h-er Kopf, a clear-sighted man; h-e Thränen, big tears; h-e Augenblicke, Med. lucid intervals; 4) coll. whole, entire, &c.; in h-en Haufen, in thick crowds, in full force: die h-e Wahrheit, plain truth: der h-e Neid, downright envy.

* Hel'las, n. (Gr.) Geogr. Hellas, Greece.

Hell'..., in comp. —äugig, adj. clear- or bright-eyed, clear-sighted; —blau, adj. light-blue; —bläulich, adj. lightish blue; —braun, adj. light-brown; —brennend, adj. bright burning.

Hell'butte, (w.) f. see Heilbutte.

Hell'..., in comp. —denkend, adj. clear-headed; —dunkel, n. Paint. claro-obscuro: 1) chiaro-oscuro (Ital.), proper distribution of light and shade; 2) twilight.

A. Hel'le, (w.) f. clearness, distinctness, &c. cf. Hell, adj.; brightness, light; 2) Pyrotech. glade; 3) powder for polishing gold.

B. Hel'le, (w.) f. see Hölle, 2.

Hellebar'de, Hellebar'te, (w.) f. halberd; h-nförmig, adj. Bot. auriculate; H-nträger or Hellebardier', (str.) m. halberdier, billman.

Hel'len, (w.) v. tr. 1) see Aufhellen & Erhellen; 2) to polish.

Hel'len, provinc. (w.) v. I. tr. to slope, cut sloping; II. intr. 1) to slope, flow down; 2) Mar. to heel.

* Helle'ne, (w.) m. (Gr.) Greek, Grecian, pl. Hellenes. — Helle'nisch, adj. Hellenic, Greek. — Hellenis'mus, m. Hellenism, Grecism. — Hellenist', (w.) m. Hellenist. — Hellenist'isch, adj. Hellenistic, Hellenistical.

Hel'ler, (str.) m. 1) Num. a small German copper coin two of which make a pfennig; 2) one sixteenth of an ounce; keinen — werth, coll. not worth a rush (straw, button); bei — und Pfennig bezahlen, to pay to the last or utmost farthing, coll. to pay scot and lot; —arm, adj. excessively poor; —kraut, n. Bot. penny-cress (Thlaspi arvense L.). [Hellespont.

* Hellespont', (str.) m. (Gr.) Geogr.

Hell'..., in comp. —farbig, adj. light-coloured, fair; —fuchs, m. light-coloured chestnut horse; —gelb, adj. light-yellow, bright-yellow; —glänzend, adj. bright or clear shining; —grau, —grün, —haarig, adj. light-gray, light-green, light-haired. [weaned.

Hel'lig, adj. († & provinc.) exhausted,

Hel'ligkeit, (w.) f. clearness, cf. Helle, A. 1; — eines Zimmers, lightsomeness of a room.

Hel'ling, I. (str.) m. 1) Mar. ways; 2) provinc. crust of bread, &c.; II. (w.) f. 1) Ship-b. launch, slip; 2) female hemp.

Hell'..., in comp. —roth, adj. light-red; —sehen, n. clair voyance, clear-seeing, lucid vision; —sehend, —sichtig, adj. clear-sighted; —seher, m., —seherin, f. somnambulist, somnambule; —seherei, f. somnambulism; —sichtigkeit, f. clear-sightedness.

Hel'lung, (w.) f. see Erhellung & Helle, A. 1.

Hell'weiß, adj. bright-white.

Hell'weg, (str.) m. sloping way, slope.

Helm, (str.) m. 1) helve, handle; 2) Mar. rudder, helm; steering oar; —stock, m. tiller.

Helm, s. I. (str.) m. 1) (also Herald., Bot., &c.) helm, helmet; 2) Dist., &c. helm, head, cap, capital (of a still or an alembic); 3) Archit. see —dach; 4) Anat. caul: II. in comp. —biene, f. see Drohne; —binde, f. band belonging to a helmet; —busch, m. plume of the helmet, crest; —dach, n. Archit. dome, cupola, round roof; —decke, f. Herald. mantling, mantle (about the helmet); —drehling, m. provinc. tway-blade.

Hel'men, (w.) v. tr. I. to furnish with a helve, handle; II. to furnish with a helmet; gehelmt, helmed; gehelmtes Dach, cupola; gehelmte (l. u. for geharnischte) Verrede, preface in harness.

Hel'menfeuer, (str.) n. see Helenenfeuer.

Hel'merchen, (str.) n. coll. wild chamomile.

Helm'..., in comp. —fenster, n. visor (of a helmet); —förmig, adj. helmet-like; Bot. galeated; die —förmige Blume, hood-flower; —gewölbe, n. spherical vault, vaulted roof; —gitter, n. visor, grate (of a helmet); —gras, n. Bot. 1) common reed (Arundo phragmites L.); 2) lyme-grass (Elymus arenarius L.); —holz, n. see —stock; —kamm, m. crest; —kappe, f. burganet; cask; —kleinod, n. Herald. ornament of a helmet, crest, timbre; —kraut, n. Bot. scull-cap (Scutellaria galericulata L.); —lehen, n. noble fief, manor; —loch, n. eye of an axe; —mantel, m. see —decke; —rolle, m. bar of the visor; —röhre, f. nose, nozzle (of a still); —rost, m. see —gitter; —schieber, m. ventail, visor (of a helmet); —schmidt, m. helmet-maker; —schmuck, m. see —kleinod; —stange, f. Carp. broach-post; —stock, m. Mar. tiller; —strauß, —stutz, m. see —busch; —taube, f. Ornith. crested or helmet pigeon; —tonne, f. Conch. partridge-shell (Dolium maculatum Lam.); —visir, n. visor, beaver; —zeichen, n. Herald. cognizance; —zierat, m., —zierde, f. see —kleinod.

Henkeln, *(w.) v. tr.* to furnish with a handle, &c.; gehenkelt, *p. a.* having handles.

Henkel..., *in comp.* **—stück,** *n.* coin or medal with a ring; **—tasse,** *f.* cup with a handle; **—topf,** *m.* pot with a handle.

Henken, *(w.) v. tr. (l. u.)* to hang; **H-s-würdig,** *adj.* deserving to be hanged.

Henker, *s.* I. *(str.) m.* 1) hangman, executioner; 2) *fig.* torturer, tormentor; der —! the deuce! was zum —! &c. *cf.* Teufel; zum — mit seiner Unverschämtheit! *coll.* hang his impudence! II. *in comp.* **—beil,** *n.* executioner's knife, hatchet; **—block,** *m.* executioner's block.

Henkerei', *(w.) f. provinc. see* Scharfrichterei.

Henker..., *in comp.* **—frist,** *f. see* Galgenfrist; **—geld,** *n. see* —lohn.

Henkerisch, *adj. see* Henkermäßig.

Henker..., *in comp.* **—lohn,** *m.* hangman's wages, executioner's fee; **—mahl,** *n.*, **—mahlzeit,** *f.* 1) last meal of one sentenced to death; 2) *coll.* farewell-dinner; **—mäßig,** *adj.* hangman-like; barbarous.

Henkern, *(w.) v. intr. coll.* to play the torturer, to torture, to torment.

Henkerschaft, *(w.) f.* band of torturers.

Henker..., *in comp.* **—schwert,** *n.* executioner's sword; **H-knecht,** *m.* hangman's servant *or* subordinate; **—strick,** *m.* halter.

Henkerthum, *(str.) n. lit. & fig.* trade of a torturer.

Hen'na, *(w.) f. (Arab.) Bot.* henna-plant ((*Lawsonia alba* Lam.).

Hen'ne, *(w.) f.* hen; junge —, pullet; die [illegible] —, *provinc.* red wild-lettuce; fette —, *Bot.* 1) house leek (Hauslauch); 2) live-ever (*Sedum* L.).

Hen'negat, *(str., pl. w.) n. Mar.* helm-port.

Hen'negau, *n. Geogr.* Hainault (a province in Belgium).

Hen'nen..., *in comp.* **—silber,** *n. Miner. see* Katzensilber; **—vogel,** *m. provinc. see* Hühnergeier.

Hen'ning, *(str.) m. († &) provinc.* (the (domestic) cock.

Henriet'te, *f.* Harriet, Harriot *(P. N.).*

* **Hepatit',** *(str.) m. (Gr.) Miner.* fetid heavy spar, hepatite.

Hep'pig, *adj. provinc.* miserable, poor, lean.

* **Heptarch',** *(w.) m. (Gr.)* heptarchist. — **Heptarchie',** *(w.) f.* heptarchy. — **Heptar'chisch,** *adj.* heptarchic.

Her, *adv.* 1) hither, hitherward (implying motion towards him who speaks, *opp.* Hin); 2) (*with* von, from) von Süden —, from the south; von dort —, (from) thence; 3) *(after an Acc.)* since, ago; komm —, come hither, come near; ein Messer —! *ellipt.* give me a knife (directly)! a knife here! wo ist das —? whence is that from? wo seid Ihr —? from whence are you? what is your country? wo bist du —? where were you born? weit —, from afar; *cf.* Weither; „wer ist draußen?" [illegible] mit Schreckenstone eine Stimme tief — aus der Höhle *(Goethe)*, ... cried a voice deep from the hollow; hinter—, behind, following; um mich —, around me; es ist viele Jahre, lange &c. —, it is many years, long, &c. since; noch keine Viertelstunde —, *coll.* not a quarter of an hour ago; die ganze Zeit —, all this (or that) time, *coll.* all along; (schafft) Bier —! (bring us, &c.) beer! (gebt) Geld —! down (or out) with the money!

Herab', I. *adv. (sometimes with Acc., which precedes the adv.)* down, down here *(i. e. in the direction towards him who speaks, opp.* Hinab), down from, down, downward; den Berg —, down from the mountain; die Wangen —, down the cheeks; von oben —, from on high; vom Himmel —, down from heaven; II. *in comp.* **—bemühen,** *v. tr. & refl.* to give [illegible] of coming down; **—bringen,** to bring down; to spoil (a business); **—bücken,** [illegible]; **—flehen,** *v. tr.* to call down by prayer; den Segen auf seine Feinde —flehen, to invoke blessings upon one's enemies; **—fließend,** *adj. Bot. see* —laufend; **—führen,** to lead *or* bring down; **—gebogen,** *adj. Bot.* deflected; **—gefallen,** *adj. Med.* delapsed; **—gehen,** to go down; noch weiter (mit seinem Preise) —gehen, to come down still lower; *Bot.-s.* **—geknickt,** *adj.* refracted; **—gerissen,** **—geschlagen,** *adj.* retrofracted; pendulous; **—gestimmt,** *adj.* low, dejected; **—helfen,** *v. tr.* to assist in stepping down, alighting, &c. (*cf.* Helfen, *opp.* Hinaufhelfen); **—kommen,** *see* Herunterkommen; **—lassen,** *v.* I. *tr.* to let down; II. *refl.* to descend, condescend; to stoop (to meanness, &c.); **—lassend,** *adj.* condescending; **—lassung,** *f.* condescension; **—laufend,** *adj. Bot.* decurrent; **—purzeln,** to tumble down; **—schießen,** to shoot down; to stoop, swoop (of birds of prey); **—sehen,** *fig.* to look down (auf *[with Acc.]*, upon) (contemptibly); **—setzen,** 1) to lower, degrade, depreciate, underrate; undervalue; 2) *Comm.* to diminish *or* reduce the value of (coins, &c.); to depress; to lower (the discount, &c.); der Preis wurde auf eine Mark —gesetzt, the price was reduced to one mark; —gesetzte Preise, reduced prices; **—setzung,** *f.* (the act of) lowering, degradation, depreciation, undervaluation; reduction (of coin); **—sinken,** *v. intr. see* —steigen, 2; **—steigen,** 1) to descend, dismount; 2) *fig.* to sink down *or* below, to degrade one's self; to fall off (from former greatness, &c.); **—stimmen,** 1) *Mus.* to lower the pitch (of a musical instrument); 2) *fig.* to lower (one's pretensions, &c.); 3) to moderate, check; **—strich,** *m. see* Herstrich; **—wärts,** *adv.* downwards; **—wünschen,** *v. tr. fig.* to call down (curses, &c.); **—würdigen,** to degrade, abase, debase; **—würdigung,** *f.* degradation, abasing, abasement, &c.; **—ziehen,** to draw down; *fig.* zu sich —ziehen, to reduce to one's own level.

* **Heral'dik,** *(w.) f.* heraldry, armory. — **Heral'diker,** *(str.) m.* an heraldic student, one skilled in heraldry, † armorist. — **Heral'disch,** *adj.* heraldic, heraldical.

Heran', I. *adv. (sometimes with Acc., which precedes the adv.; the latter always implies motion towards him who speaks)* 1) on, near; 2) up (here), upwards; (an *with Acc.*) —, up to; er ging an sie —, he went up to them; II. *in comp.* **—bilden,** *fig.* to bring up, educate, fit for; **—blühen,** *fig.* to bloom, grow up; **—drohen,** to approach threateningly; **—kommen,** 1) to come up; 2) to come on, near, *or* nigh; to approach, draw near; **—kunft,** *f.* approach; **—nahen,** *v. intr. (aux.* sein) to draw near, approach; das —nahen, *(str.) v. s.* approach; **—reifen,** *fig.* to grow to maturity; **—rücken,** to advance, draw near; **—steigen,** 1) to ascend; 2) to draw near; **—wachsen,** to grow up; to grow tall; zum Manne *or* zur Frau —wachsen, to grow to be *(or* to grow into) a man *or* woman, to grow to man's *or* woman's estate; er war zum jungen Manne —gewachsen, he had grown to be a young man; die meisten, welche zu großen und guten Menschen —wachsen, most men who grow to be great and good; das —wachsende Geschlecht, the rising generation; **—ziehen,** *v.* I. *tr.* to draw near; II. *intr. (aux.* sein) to approach, draw near, to come on; **—zug,** *m.* approach.

Herauf', *adv. (sometimes with Acc., which precedes the adv.)* up, up here *(i. e. in the direction towards him who speaks)*; upwards; **—bringen,** to bring *or* fetch up; er rief hinunter: bringt das Wasser — und nimmt den Wein hinab, he called down, bring up the water, and take down the wine; **—kommen,** 1) to come up, *cf.* Heraufkommen; 2) to advance; er ist vier Classen —gekommen, he has gone up four removes (at school); **—steigen,** to draw up *or* near, to approach (as a storm); **—wärts,** *adv.* upwards; **—ziehen,** *v.* I. *tr.* to draw up; II. *intr. see* —steigen; zu sich —ziehen, *fig.* to raise to one's level.

Heraus', I. *adv. (sometimes with Acc., which precedes the adv.)* out, out here *(expressing motion towards the speaker)*; die Wahrheit (der Mord &c.) ist —, the truth (murder, &c.) is out; er hat es — *(ellipt. for* —bekommen), he knows what it is; — damit! nur frei —! out with it! speak out! gerade —, downright; frei —, bluntly, plainly, flatly; von innen —, from within; II. *in comp.* **—arbeiten,** *v.* I. *tr.* to work out; II. *refl.* to work one's self clear or out of (extricate one's self from) a thing, to get out with labour; **—bekommen,** 1) *a)* to get back in exchange (in return), to get change; er bekommt noch etwas —, some odds are on his side; das was man —bekommt, the change; nicht die Zinsen —bekommen, *Comm.* not to make the interest; *b)* to elicit (an answer, avowal, &c.); 2) to get out: *a)* to remove; *b)* to find out (the truth, &c.), to elicit, to get at the bottom of, *coll.* to draw *or* fish out; *c)* to make out; to solve, resolve, to work out (a problem, &c.); to decipher; **—bringen,** 1) to bring *or* get out; 2) *fig.* to draw out (secrets, &c.) by artful management, to elicit, &c. *cf.* —bekommen, 1, *b*, 2, *b*; 3) to put out, perplex; **—dringen,** (of fluids, &c.) to rush, come out with violence; **—fahren,** 1) to carry *or* cart out; to drive out; 2) to start out, to rush out; 3) *(with* mit) *see* —platzen; **—finden,** *v.* I. *tr.* to find out, discover (something sought for); II. *refl.* 1) to find one's way out, to extricate one's self; 2) to see one's way clearly, to comprehend; **—forderer,** *m.* challenger, &c.; **—fordern,** 1) to claim back, reclaim (money); 2) to challenge (to the combat), to call, have *or* take out (auf Pistolen *[Acc.]*, with pistols); **—fordernd,** *p. a.* defiant (act, look); 3) *fig.* to provoke, defy; to court (danger, &c.); to invite (criticism); **—forderung,** *f.* challenge, provocation; **—fressen,** *v. refl.* to grow fat by feeding, to fatten; **—fühlen,** to discover *or* select by means of the sense of touch, feeling; **—gabe,** *f.* 1) (the act of) giving up (of a pledge, bond, &c.); 2) the editing *or* edition (of a book, &c.), publication; editorship; **—geben,** 1) to give out; 2) to hand over, to give *or* deliver up; 3) to give the change *or* balance of an account, to give back; geben Sie mir —, give me (the) change; 4) to edit, publish, to put in print, to put forth (a book); to issue; **—geber,** *m.*, **—geberin,** *f.* editor, publisher; **—gehen,** to go *or* come out; to jut, project, to branch out; *fig.-s.* aus sich (selbst) —gehen, to go out of one's self; mit der Wahrheit (frei) —gehen, to speak out; **—greifen,** to take at random (the first the best); **—hauen,** to cut out; *fig.* to rescue (from amidst the enemy); **—heben,** 1) *Typ.* to pick out; 2) *fig.* to make conspicuous, to put in relief; to lay stress on; **—helfen,** (Einem) to get one out (aus, of); to bring off; **—klauben,** to get, draw out (with pains); **—klopfen,** to awaken by knocking, to knock up; **—kommen,** *v. intr. (aux.* sein) 1) to come out *or* forth, to issue; er kam zum Hause —, he came out of the house (*cf.* er ging zum Hause hinaus); *fig.-s.* 2) to be divulged, to become known; das Geheimniß kam —, the secret leaked (oozed) out; 3) to be edited, published, *or* issued, to make its appearance; *cf.* Erscheinen, 1; 4) to get out (of a difficulty); 5) to answer previous expectation, to prove correct; 6) to be of use, to yield profit, advantage; 7) to amount (auf *[with Acc.]*, to); eben —gekommen, just out; was kam (dabei) —? what was the result *or* upshot? dabei kommt nichts —, there is nothing to be gained in (by) it; es wird nichts Gutes dabei —kommen, no good will come of it; mit einem Gewinn —kommen, to get *or* come up a prize (in the lottery), [illegible]

overtake; —gehen, 1) to walk in, enter; 2) to find room; —lassen, to let in, admit; nicht — lassen, to keep out; —nöthigen, to call or ask in; das —ragen einer Geisterwelt in die unsrige, the interdiffusion of a world of spirits in the one we inhabit; —schneien, coll. to arrive unexpectedly, suddenly; —strömen, to flood in; —stürzen, to dart in.

Her'..., in comp. (cf. Her) —erzählen, to relate, rehearse; —erzählung, f. enarration; —fahren, (str.) v. I. intr. (aux. sein) 1) to move along, to come here or hither in a carriage; 2) or —fallen (with über [& Acc.]), to fall or pounce upon, to fall foul upon or of, to rush in upon, to make a dead set at; to come down upon; to fall to; to attack, assail; to rush in (upon); II. tr. to bring here in a carriage or any vehicle; —finden, (str.) v. refl. fig. to find one's way hither (to a place); —fließen, 1) to flow in or on; 2) fig. to originate, take its origin from; —fordern, to summon (hither); —fracht, f. freight home, freight inwards (opp. Hinfracht); —für', adv. † see Hervor; —führen, to lead, conduct, bring, or convey hither, on, in; —gang, m. fig. proceedings, circumstances, (connexion of) events; der —gang der Sache war der, the way it happened was this; the facts of the matter are these; der ganze —gang, coll. the whole story; —geben, 1) to hand over, hand to; to give (in); to deliver; 2) to yield, afford; das giebt's nicht —, I can't afford it, coll. it is no go, it won't do; sich zu ... —geben, to lend one's self to ..., to undertake (willingly); —gebracht, see —bringen; —ge'gen, adv. † see Hingegen; —gehen, 1) to go or walk here, hither (i. e. towards him who speaks, opp. Hingehen); vor (Einem or etwas) —gehen, to go before ...; 2) see Einhergehen; fig-s. 3) (with über [& Acc.]) a) to set about (a thing), to go to work, commence, cf. Hand anlegen, 2; b) to fall upon, set to (drinking, &c.); es soll gleich darüber —gehen, we'll set to presently; 4) (gener. impers.) a) to come to pass, happen; b) to proceed, to go on, to be carried on; so geht es (in der Welt) her, thus it goes, that's the course of the world; wie's in der Welt —geht, as the world goes; es geht lustig —, they are all in full mirth; es geht arg —, things wear a bad face; es geht sehr knapp —, there is very hard shifting; es geht heute schmal —, there is poor fare today; da geht es heiß —, there is hot work; es geht über ihn —, coll. they are down upon him, they take him to pieces, cf. Herfallen; —gehören, to belong to a place, or to the matter; to be to the purpose; nicht —gehören, to be alien from ...; —gehörig, adj. to the purpose, apposite; nicht —gehörig, irrelevant; —haben, coll. to take from; wo haben Sie das —? whence did you get this? —halten, (str.) v. I. tr. to hold forth, tender, offer; halt' deine Hand —! hold out your hand (i. e. to me); II. intr. fig. to submit, to suffer (for); to pay, coll. to come down, lug out; —holen, to fetch hither; weit —holen, fig. to go far for; weit —geholt, far-fetched.

† Her'ichaum, see Herzbaum.

Hering, (str.) m. see Häring.

Her'..., in comp. (cf. Her) —kommen, (str.) v. intr. (aux. sein) 1) to come here, hither, or on; to approach, advance; fig-s. 2) a) to come, proceed, or be derived (von, from); b) to arise (from), originate (with or in), issue (from); to be caused (by), to be owing to, to be the consequence (of), to result (from); c) to be established by custom, to be transmitted, to descend; das —kommen, (str.) 1) origin, see Herkunft, 2; 2) a) custom, use, usage; b) conf. conventionalism; 3) Law, see [illegible]; —kömmlich, adj. established by custom, customary, usual, cf. Hergebracht.

under Herbringen; —können, ellipt. to be able to come or go hither or near.

Her'kules, see Hercules.

Her'..., in comp. (cf. Her) —kunft, f. 1) (the act of) coming hither, arrival; 2) origin, descent, birth, parentage, extraction; 3) Comm. place where (an article, &c. has been) produced, country of growth; —laden, to summon or invite hither; —lallen, to say, recite in a faltering, lisping voice; —langen, to reach or tender forth, to hand to; —lassen, ellipt. to let, allow to come hither, &c.; —laufen, to run hither or on; ein —gelaufener Mensch, a vagabond, adventurer; —legen, 1) to lay down here or hither; Waaren —legen, Comm. to import, ship in (goods); 2) refl. Comm. to stand (zu, in); —leiern, coll. 1) to recite or deliver in a monotonous manner; 2) to drone, drawl (out, &c.); hergeleiert kommen, to come along loitering; —leiten, (w.) v. I. tr. 1) to conduct, lead hither; 2) fig. to derive, deduce (von, from), to refer (to a cause or origin); II. refl. sich —leiten, to date from; —leitung, f. derivation, deduction (cf. also Ableitung, 3); —lesen, to read off or out, to recite.

Her'lich, see Herrlich.

Her'ling, (str.) m. provinc. late grape; unripe, sour grape, cf. Herbling, 2. [lisping.

Her'lispeln, (w.) v. tr. to say or recite

Her'litze, (w.) f. see Cornelkirsche.

Her'..., in comp. (cf. Her) —locken, to allure; —machen, (w.) v. refl. to set (über [with Acc.], about), to fall (upon), cf. Herfahren, 2.

* Hermaphrodit', (w.) m. (Gr.) hermaphrodite. — Hermaphrodit'isch, adj. hermaphroditic(al): h—e Blumen, hermaphrodite (united) flowers.

Her'marsch, (str., pl. Her'märsche) m. march or (the act of) marching hither (opp. Hinmarsch).

Herm'chen, (str.) n. provinc. see Wiesel.

* Her'me, (w.) f. see Hermensäule.

Her'mel, (w.) f., Her'melchen, (str.) n. Bot. wild chamomile, may-weed (Anthemis cotula L.).

Hermelin', (str.) n. (MHG. dimin. [her'melin], with foreign accent, of harm [MHG.], weasel) 1) Zool. ermine, stoat (Mustela erminea L.); 2) Conch. ermine-stamper (Conus capitaneus L.); 3) a cream-coloured horse; —kragen, m. cape of ermine; —mantel, m. cloak lined with ermine; —motte, f. see Stützschuß; —schwänzchen, pl. 1) Comm. ermine tips; 2) Herald. timbers of ermine.

* Hermeneu'tik, (w.) f. (Gr.) hermeneutics, science of interpretation.

* Hermeneu'tisch, adj. hermeneutical.

* Her'mensäule, (w.) f. (Gr.) Hermes, statue of Mercury. [metically.

* Herme'tisch, adj. hermetic(al); adv. her-

Her'..., in comp. (cf. Her) —mögen, ellipt. to like to come hither; —murmeln, to murmur, mutter forth or over; —müssen, ellipt. to be obliged to come; —nach [pr. hērnāch'], adv. (sometimes preceded by an Acc.) afterwards, after, hereafter, after that; —nehmen, 1) to take from, get from; fig. to draw (arguments); 2) Mar. to retake (eine Prise, i. e. Wiedernehmen); 3) fig. to derive, deduce; wo nimmt er die Geduld her? how has he this patience? 4) fig. fam. to take to task; —nehmungsrecht, n. Comm. salvage upon recapture; —nennen, to call over, to name in succession, to recite; —nie'der [pr. hēr—], adv. down, cf. Herab; —nöthigen, to oblige or invite to come hither.

* Hero'en, (w.) pl. of Heros; —alter, —sage, see Heldenalter, Heldensage.

* Heroi'ne, (w.) f. heroine.

* Hero'isch, adj. (Gr.) heroic(al); adv. heroically; —komisch, adj. heroi-comical.

He'rold, (str.) m. 1) herald; 2) fig. proclaimer, harbinger; H-amt, n. herald's office; heraldship; † H-figuren, pl. heraldic delineations; H-kunst, f. heraldic art, heraldry; H-mantel, H-rock, m. tabard; H-stab, m. herald's staff, wand; H-wissenschaft, f. heraldic science, heraldry. [the organ.

Her'orgeln, (w.) v. tr. coll. to play off on

He'ros, (sing. not decl., pl. [w.] Hero'en) Gr. Myth. hero.

Her'..., in comp. —peitschen, to whip up; —plappern, to prattle out, patter out (prayers, &c.), to repeat by rote.

Herr, (w.) m. 1) master; lord; gentleman; (in addressing a person) sir; — M., Mr. M.; meine H-en! gentlemen! 2) principal; employer, master; head: Ihr — Vater, your (worthy) father; Gott der —, God, our Lord; unser —, our Lord (Jesus Christ; the Saviour); das Haus des H-n, the Lord's house; im Jahre des H-n, in the year of the Lord; der Tag des H-n, the Lord's day (Sunday); der Tisch des H-n, the Lord's table (communion-table); — Gott, dich loben wir, we praise thee, O God! (translation of the first words of St. Ambrose's [Latin] hymn: Te Deum laudamus); — von or über etwas sein, to be master of; sein eigener — sein, to be one's own master; — zur See sein, to master the sea, to rule the waves; ein großer —, a lord; den großen H-n spielen, to lord it, to play the fine gentleman; einer Sache (Gen.) — werden, to master a thing; des Feuers — werden, to get a fire under; wie der — so der Knecht, proverb. like master, like man.

Her'rauschen, (w.) v. intr. (aux. sein) to rush hither or in; to rush on, glide along; to pass with noise.

Herr'chen, (str.) n. (dimin. of Herr) little master, gentleman, &c.; lordling; iron. spark, beau, dandy.

Her'..., in comp. —rechnen, coll. to reckon up, see Aufrechnen, 2; —recken, to stretch forth; —reichen, to reach, hand; reichen Sie mir die Zeitung —, hand me the newspaper; —reise, f. travelling, journey hither, home-journey; home-voyage (of a ship, &c.) (opp. Hinreise); —reisen, to travel hither; —reiten, to come hither on horseback.

Her'ren..., in comp. —apfel, m. Pomol. prince's apple; —arbeit, f. compelled service, see Frohnarbeit, 1; —artikel, m. pl. Comm. gentlemen's wearing-apparel; —bank, f. bench of lords; —bier, n. double beer, strong beer; —brett, n. T. half-plank; —brod, n. master's bread; —brot essen, fig. to serve; —diener, m. cont. cringer; —dienst, m. (lord's) service, cf. Frohndienst; —essen, delicious meal; —fastnacht, n. see —sonntag; —garten, m. garden of a lord; —gebot, n. lord's command; —gefälle, n. pl. income of the lord of the manor; —gülte, f. duty or tax on the produce of a tenure paid to the lord of the manor; —gunst, f. favour of a master; —haus, n. 1) lord's house, manor-house, mansion; 2) upper house (in Prussia and Austria); —hof, m. lord's seat, manor-house, country-house; —hut, m. man's hat; —kirsche, f. cornel cherry; —knecht, m. see —diener; —korn, n. rent paid in corn; —krankheit, f. hud. the gout; —leben, n. fig. high life; ein —leben führen, to live like a lord.

Her'renlos, adj. without a master; 1) out of place, out of service or employment; 2) unowned, Law, vacant, unappropriated; —lose Güter, pl. Law, 1. goods relinquished by the owner, derelicts; 2. (or Sachen) goods or things found of which the owner is not known, waifs, strays.

Her'ren..., in comp. —pfründe, f. benefice in the gift of a patron; —pilz, —schwamm, m. Bot. Eatable mushroom, see Champignon;

Heu'ern, (w.) v.tr. 1) to hire, cf. Miethen, Dingen; 2) to charter (a ship).

Heu'ernte, (w.) f. hay-harvest; hay-time.

Heu'erververtrag, (str., pl. H-verträge) m. 1) contract for work; 2) see Heuerbrief.

Heu'et, (str.) n. provinc. see Heuernte.

Heu'..., in comp. –fehm, –feimen, m. hay-stack, hay-cock; –fieber, n. Med. hay-fever; –futter, n. hay-fodder; –gabel, f. hay-fork, pitchfork; –gewinn, m. hay-crop, hay-produce; –haufen, m. hay-cock, hay-rick, cf. –fehm; –hechel, f. see Handhechel; –huppe, f. hay-cock.

Heul'affe, (w.) m. see Brüllaffe.

Heu'..., in comp. –land, n. meadow-land; hay-land; –leine, f. see –seil.

Heu'len, (w.) v. intr. 1) to howl, yell; 2) cont. to cry (aloud), whine, howl, blubber (of men); to roar (of the wind); to scream (in singing).

Heu'ler, (str.) m. 1) howler, &c.; 2) Icon. a) croaker; b) see Meerleuchte.

Heul'kreisel, (str.) m. humming-top.

Heu'..., in comp. –machen, n. (provinc. –mahd, f.) hay-making; –macher, –mäher, m. 1) hay-maker; 2) Ornith. bee-eater (Merops apiaster L.); –meister, m. he who has the care of the hay in a stud; –monat, –mond, m. hay-month, July.

Heun, (str.) m. provinc. see Uhu.

Heu'ne, (w.) f. see Hüne.

Heunt, adv. provinc. tonight.

Heu'pferd, (str.) n. see Grille, 1; Heimchen & Heuschrecke, 1, a.

Heu'rath, (w.) f. see Heirat.

Heu'..., in comp. –raufe (–rede), f. hay-rack, rails for hay; –rechen, m. hay-harrow, rake; –recht, n. 1) right of making hay; 2) see –gebühr. (of the present time or date.

Heu'rig, adj. 1) of this year or season; 2)

Heu'..., in comp. –same, m. hay-seed; –schwad, m. swathe or wisp of hay; –schobe, f. hay-cock; –scheuer, –scheune, f. hay-barn; –schober, m. see –haufen; –schoppen, m. shed for keeping hay; –schrecke, f. 1) Entom. a) locust (Locusta viridissima L.); b) grass-hopper (Gryllus campestris L.); 2) Gymn. grass-hopper jump, cf. Knieflug; –schreckenbaum, m. Bot. locust-tree, three-thorned acacia (Acacia paradoxa L.); –schreckenfedern, f. pl. T. grass-hopper springs; –seil, n. hay-rope (for securing the hay on a waggon); –spriesel, m. see –boden; –stange, m. hay-stall; –stock, m. hay-stack.

Heu'te, Heut, adv. 1) today, this day; 2) fig. (heut zu Tage, heutigen Tages) now-a-days, in this age; in these days; – Abend, – Morgen, this evening (to-night), this morning; – Nacht, tonight; – vor acht Tagen, – über acht Tage, this day sennight or week; – vor vierzehn Tagen, – über vierzehn Tage, this day fortnight; – über ein Jahr, in a year from this; von – an, from this day forward; – heute, this very day; es ist mir noch wie –, it is in my memory as yesterday; was schreiben wir –? what day of the month is this? – oder morgen, one day or other; – mir, morgen dir, prov. today mine, tomorrow yours.

Heu'tig, adj. 1) of this day, of this date; 2) of this age, modern; das h-e Fest, today's festival; mit h-er Post, by this day's mail, by tonight's post; der h-e Tag, this day; Comm. c. unterm h-en, under this day's date; mit dem h-en Tage, this day; Ihr h-es, your letter of this day; da wir vielleicht morgen sterben, laßt uns daher den h-en Tag genießen, ... let us therefore enjoy today; in der h-en Nummer des Athenaeum, ... in the Athenaeum of tod[illegible] ... von h-en Tag[illegible] ... auf den h-en Tag, bis jetzt [illegible]

this day; h-en or h-es Tages, now-a-days; at present; die h-e Welt, the present age.

Heu'..., in comp. –vogel, m. 1) see –mäher, 2; 2) (gelber) provinc. a species of butterfly; –wage, f. balance for weighing hay; –wagen, m. waggon for bringing the hay in; –wiese, f. meadow kept for mowing, hay-field; –zehnte, m. tithes paid in hay; –zeit, f. haying-time.

* **Hexaë'drisch**, adj. (Gr.) hexahedral; h-er Bleiglanz, lead glance, hexahedral galena.

* **Hexaë'dron**, (Gr.), **Hexaë'der**, (str.) n. Geom. hexaedron.

* **Hexa'meter**, (str.) m. (Gr.) Poet. hexameter. – **Hexame'trisch**, adj. hexametrical.

* **Hexan'drisch**, adj. (Gr.) Bot. hexandrous.

Hex'e, (w.) f. 1) witch, hag; 2) Ornith. see Ziegenmelker; 3) Ichth. see Mondfisch.

Hex'en, (w.) v. tr. & intr. to practise witchcraft, to conjure, to produce (a certain effect) by witchcraft.

Hex'en..., in comp. –bann, m. charm, spell of a witch, &c.; –baum, m. Bot. common bird cherry-tree (Vogelkirschbaum); –berg, m. witches' mountain, wizard hill; –buch, n. conjuring book, book containing spells; –butter, f. 1) coll. butter containing still some milk; 2) Bot. a species of yellow fungus; –ei, n. 1) egg without yolk; 2) Bot. stinkhorn (Gichtmorchel); –fahrt, f. expedition of the witches; –gelag, n. night-revelling of witches; –geschichte, f. fairy-tale; story of witches and sorcerers, story of witchcraft; –kraut, n. Bot. 1) enchanter's night-shade (Circaea lutetiana L.); 2) brown club-moss (Lycopodium selago L.); –kreis, m. fairy-ring; –kunst, f. magic art; –männchen, n. see Alraun, 2; –mehl, n. vegetable sulphur, lycopodium, witch meal; –meister, m. 1) sorcerer, wizard; 2) joc. conjurer; –probe, f. witches' ordeal; –proceß, m. trial of witches; –ring, m. see –kreis; –ritt, m. see –fahrt; –sabbath, m. witches' sabbath; –schuß, m. (lit. witch-shot, cf. elf-shot (Scot.), a disease supposed to be produced by the stroke of an elf-arrow) sudden rheumatic, &c. pang (Wind[illegible]); –segen, m. spell; –spiel, n. a kind of game with thirty-six cards; –stich, m. Sew. herring-bone stitch; –strang, m. traveller's joy (Clematis); –tanz, m. dance of witches; –werk, n. witches' work, witchery; –wesen, n. witchcraft, witchery; –zunft, f. meeting of witches.

Hex'er, (str.) m. (l. u.) joc. **Hex'rich**, (str.) m. for Hexenmeister) sorcerer, wizard.

Hexerei', (w.) f. sorcery, witchery, witchcraft; jugglery, tricks.

Hey! Hey'da! &c., see Hei &c.

* **Hia'tus**, (indecl.) m. (Lat.) gap, hiatus.

Hiber'nien, n. Hibernia, Ireland.

Hiber'nier, (str.) m., **Hiber'nisch**, adj. Hibernian.

Hick, (str.) m. provinc. hiccough.

Hick'en, (w.) v. intr. provinc. to hiccough.

† **Hie**, adv. here (Hier); – bevor, heretofore.

Hieb, (str.) m. 1) a) stroke, blow; wipe, lash, cut; slash; b) cut (of a stick); 2) Forest. a) the place in a forest where timber is being or has been felled; b) the right of felling wood (timber) in a forest; 3) mark, scar by a cut; 4) fig. sarcasm, cut, hit (auf (with acc.) at); einen – haben, fam. to be a little tipsy.

Hie'ber, (str.) m. coll. broad-sword.

Hieb'fechten, n. Fenc. cut, (the practice of) cutting, broad-sword exercise (opp. Stoßfechten).

Hie'big, adj. Forest. see Haubar.

Hieb..., in comp. –waffen, pl. arms for cutting; –wunde, f. wound by a cut.

Hief, (str.) m. Sport. (or –Hift, m.) blast upon a bugle-horn, bugle-note, sound given by the hunting horn.

Hief'te, (w.) f. provinc. for Hagebutte.

Hief'..., in comp. –horn, n. hunting-horn, bugle-horn; –riemen, m. bugle-strap.

Hie'für, Hie'her &c., see Hierfür &c.

Hie'fe, (w.) f. Min. single grain of a mineral (in other ores).

Hiel, Hie'ling, (str.) m. Mar. heel.

Hie'len, (w.) v. intr. to heel by the stern.

Hienie'den, adv. *, here below, in this life.

Hien'schen, (w.) v. intr. to howl, whine (of dogs).

Hier (Hie), I. adv. 1) here; Comm., &c. at (or in) this city, in town, present; (– zu Lande) in this (or our) country or quarter, (on) this side of the water; er ist von – abgereist, he has left this; komme ich – nach Fleetstreet? will this lead me to Fleet-street? – ist nicht zu scherzen, there is no joking in this matter; Comm. a. auf – trassiren, to draw on this place; Wechsel auf –, bills on this place; auf – verladen, shipped (laden) for this place; 2) fig. in this world or life; 3) in this; at this point; binnen – und sechs Monaten, within a sixmonth from this; von –, of this city; – nachzemeldet, herein after-mentioned; II. in comp. –ab, adv. here from, from this; –an, adv. hereat, at this, at it; up here; hereon, on this; by this; of this.

* **Hierarch'**, (w.) m. (Gr.) hierarch. – **Hierarchie'**, (w.) f. hierarchy. – **Hierar'chisch**, adj. hierarchical.

Hier (Hie) ..., in comp. –auf, adv. up here; hereupon, upon this, at this, after this; –auf erwidere ich, to this I reply; –aus, adv. out here, hereout; out of this, hence, from hence, from this, hereby, by this; –außen, adv. out here; –bei, adv. herewith, hereat, herein, hereby; with, at, in, or by this; –bevor, adv. heretofore; –durch, adv. 1) through this place; through here; 2) a) by this means, by so doing, thus; b) (–mit) hereby, by this, by the present; enclosed, annexed; –ein, adv. in here, in, hereinto, into this or it; –für, adv. for this, for it; –gegen, adv. hereagainst, against this or it; –her, adv. hither, here, this way; as far as this; bis –her, hitherto, till now, so as thus far; (on bills of exchange) thus far copy; –herüber, see –über; –herum, adv. hereabout(s); –herwärts, adv. hitherward; –hin, adv. hither, this way; to this place; in this direction, along, forward; bald –hin, bald dorthin, now here now there; –hinein, adv. in here, into this place; –in, adv. in here, herewithin; herein, in this, in it; –ländisch, adj. of this country; –mit, adv. here with, with this, with it; by this, by it; in doing, saying this; by the present, enclosed, annexed; –nach, adv. after this, after it; from this; according to this; –nach gemeldet, herein after mentioned; –nächst, adv. next, next to this; next door; –neben, adv. next to this (place), close by; Comm. annexed; besides; –nieden, see Hienieden; –ob, adv. see –über.

* **Hieroglyph'e**, (w.) f. (Gr.) hieroglyph. – **Hieroglyph'ik**, (w.) f. hieroglyphics. – **Hieroglyph'isch**, adj. hieroglyphical.

* **Hieronymi'ter**, (str.) m. pl. Eccl. Hieronymites. [(F. N.)

Hiero'nymus, m. Jerome, Hieronymus

* **Hierophant'**, (w.) m. (Gr.) hierophant.

Hier (Hie) ..., in comp. –ortig, adj. of this place, of this country; –orts, adv. at this place, here; –sein, n. being here, presence; –selbst, adv. here, in this place, present; –über, adj. over here; –über, adv. 1) over this place, over here; beyond this or it; 2) hereat, at this, at it, of this, of it, on this account; on this head, about this or it; –um, adv. about this place, hereabout; about this or it, concerning this; –unten, adv. below here, here below; (in letters, &c.) at foot;

[illegible]), up (to, *cf.* Hinauf); den Berg —, up [illegible] hill; —reichen, to reach up; *fig.* to touch [illegible] *with Acc.*], on); —steigen, to ascend, [illegible].

[illegible]arbeiten, *(w.)* v. I. *intr.* to aim (auf [*with Acc.*], at), to direct one's efforts (to); [illegible] 1) to attain with difficulty; to work [illegible] way to ...; 2) to ruin one's health, &c. [illegible] excessive work.

[Hin]auf', *adv.* up (there, *different:* Herauf, [illegible]); up (to); on high (*often with the Acc., [which] precedes the adv.*); den Berg —, up the [mountain], up (the) hill; die Treppe —, up [stairs]; als ich — ging, kam er herunter, when [I went] up (stairs), he came down; —arbeiten, [v. refl.] to toil (work one's way) up; —bringen, [to] bring up; —drücken, to force up (water); [die] Flamme lodert wie zu Gott —gefodert [illegible]), as if summoned upwards to the [God]'s presence; —gehen, to go *or* walk up; [—sch]rauben, *(w.)* v. *tr. lit.* & *fig.* to screw up; [eine] künstlich —geschraubte Bilanz, *Comm.* a [manipulated] balance; —steigen, to step up, [ascend], mount; sie ist nach mir die Treppe — [gestiegen], she went up stairs after me; —[strich], m. *see* Hinstrich, 1; —treiben, to push, [drive], run, work up (prices); —wärts, *adv.* [upward].

[Hin]aus', *adv.* 1) out (there, *different:* Heraus, *cf.* Hin); 2) beyond; — mit ihm! out [with] him! zum Fenster —, out of the window; [wo] denken Sie —? what are you thinking [of]? (*i. e.* you are entirely out *or* mistaken); [in] *comp.* (*cf.* Aus, *in comp.*) —führen, 1) to [lead] out, to take out, &c.; 2) *fig.* to carry [out] (a design, &c.); —gehen, v. *intr.* (*aux.* [sein]) 1) to go out; *fig.-s.* 2) (*with* über [*& Acc.*]) [to] go *or* step beyond ..., to surpass, tran[scend] (beyond a limit *or* measure); 3) über [(*with* Acc.)] nicht —gehen, to be limited by ...; [4) a)] to look (auf [*with Acc.*], into), to front, [face] (of a room, &c.); *b)* or —kommen, *see* —[laufen]; —jagen, to expel, turn out; —kehren, [to] sweep out; —können, *ellipt.* to be able to [go] or get out; auf Eins *or* dasselbe —laufen, [to] come, amount to the same thing; to be the [same] in the end; seine Rede lief (ging *or* kam) [darauf] —, the drift of his discourse was ...; [sich] zum Fenster —legen, to stretch one's self [out] of the window; Einem —leuchten, to light [one] out; —machen, v. *refl.* to get, go *or* run out; —räumen, to clear *or* take away, *see* Ab[räumen], 1, a; —reichen, to reach *or* stretch beyond; darüber —reichend, *adj.* ulterior (object, &c.); über das Ziel —schießen, to overreach the aim; —setzen, *(w.)* v. I. *tr.* or —rücken, —schieben, to defer, to stave off, postpone; II. *refl.* (*with* über [*& Acc.*]) to disregard, set at nought; über (*with Acc.*) —schweifen, to stray, to aspire beyond ...; —sein, to be above, not to care for; —sollen, to have a certain aim, *cf.* —wollen; —stoßen, to put *or* turn out; in die Welt —stoßen, to cast loose (send adrift, throw) upon the world; —streben, to aspire beyond ...; —stürzen, to rush, bolt, *or* fling out; —treiben, *see* —jagen; —wärts, *adj.* outward; —werfen, to cast, bundle, *or* turn out, eject, expel; —wollen, *ellipt. fig.* to end (in), to aim (at); wo will das —? wo soll das —? where is this to end? ich sah, wo er —wollte, I saw what he was driving at, I saw his drift; hoch —wollen, to aim high, be proud; er will zu hoch —, he is soaring too high.

Hin'..., *in comp.* (*cf.* Hin) —bannen, to banish thither, to remove to (a place); —bescheiden, to order to (a place); —begeben, v. *refl.* to repair, resort to; —bestellen, to appoint to a place; —blick, m. look, regard (auf [*with Acc.*], to); im —blick auf..., with regard to...; *cf.* Hinsicht; —blicken, to look towards (a place), to look forward (to ...); —bringen, to take (away); —brüten, *fig.* to die, give one's life; —bringen, 1) to bring *or* carry to a place, to take along; 2) *fig. a)* to waste, to squander (away), to dissipate (one's fortune); *b)* to pass, spend (the time); sich *or* sein Leben —bringen, to make shift to live; vor sich —brummen, to mutter to one's self; —brüten, to live, pass (the time) in a kind of stupor.

Hind, *(str.)* n., **Hin'de,** *(w.)* f. († &) * *see* Hindin.

Hin'denken, *(irr.)* v. *intr.* to think of *or* turn one's mind to a remote (*fig.* impracticable) object; wo denken Sie hin? what are you thinking of? *cf.* Hinaus.

Hin'derlich, I. *adj.* hindering, impeding, obstructing, troublesome, cumbersome; II. H-keit, *(w.)* f. the quality of hindering; hinderance.

Hin'dern, *(w.)* v. *tr.* to hinder, impede, prevent (an [*with Dat.*], from).

Hin'derniß, *(str.)* n. hinderance; impediment, obstacle; resistance, stop; difficulty; Einem H-sse in den Weg legen, to throw obstacles in one's way; Rennen ohne H-sse, *Sport.* flat race.

Hin'derung, *(w.)* f. the (act of) hindering, &c. *cf.* Hindern; hinderance, impediment, *cf.* Hinderniß; H-sgrund, m. cause of impediment.

Hin'deuten, *(w.)* v. *intr.* (*with* auf [*& Acc.*]) to hint (at); to point at, to aim at, to be a sign of; to forebode.

Hin'deutung, *(w.)* f. intimation, hint.

Hin'din, *(w.)* f. *Sport.* female of the stag, hind.

Hin'..., *in comp.* (*cf.* Hin) —donnern, to thunder down, strike down with thunder; —dorren, to wither gradually, to fade away; —drang, m. (the act of) thronging, pressing to a place; —drängen, v. *tr.* & *refl.* to throng, press, urge to. [India.

Hindo'stan, *n. Geogr.* Hindostan, Hindustan,

Hindosta'ner, *(str.)* m. Hindostanee.

Hindosta'nisch, *adj.* Hindostanee, Hindustani. [Gentoo.

Hin'du, *(str.)* m. (*pl.* Hin'dus) Hindoo,

Hindurch', *adv.* (*sometimes with Acc., which precedes the adv.*) through, (*cf.* Durch & *comp.*) throughout; during; den ganzen Tag —, all day long, the livelong day; mein ganzes Leben —, all my life long; die Nacht —, all night; das ganze Jahr —, all the year round; sich —arbeiten &c., *see* sich Durcharbeiten &c.; —lassen, to let through, to transmit (light).

Hin'dürfen, *(irr.)* v. *intr. ellipt.* to be permitted to go to a place. [hie to.

Hin'eilen, *(w.)* v. *intr.* (*aux.* sein) to hasten,

Hinein', *adv.* in (there), into (in a direction from him who speaks, *opp.* Herein); da —, nicht hier —, into that place, not into this; zum Fenster —, in at the window; ich will —, I'll in; bis in die Stadt —, into the very town; in den Tag —, ins Gelag —, *coll.* at a venture, at random, inconsiderately; —arbeiten, v. *refl.* *see* Einarbeiten; —bringen &c., to get in, &c.; —denken, v. *refl.* to fancy one's self to be in; *fig.* to go deep (into a subject); —gehen, 1) to go in; 2) to find room; —stecken, 1) to put in, &c.; 2) *or* —werfen, *Comm.* to lock up, engage (funds); —ziehen, to draw *or* pull in; *fig.* to entangle, involve.

Hin'..., *in comp.* (*cf.* Hin) —fahren, *(str.)* v. I. *tr.* to carry off *or* to; II. *intr.* (*aux.* sein) 1) to be carried off *or* to; to drive, go in a carriage to; an (*or* längs) der Küste —fahren, to coast, to sail *or* range along the coast; *fig.-s.* 2) *a)* to pass away, depart; *b)* (*coll.* &) *, to die, decease; leicht über ... —fahren, to skim over (the surface, &c.), to slip over, to do (perform) superficially; to pass over (mit der Hand, the hand); fahre hin! go! —fahrt, *f.* 1) the (act of) carrying *or* 2) going to a place; departure; 3) *Sport.* trace of the deer back to the wood; 4) *fig.* decease; —fall, m. 1) falling down; 2) *fig.* decay; —fallen, 1) to fall down; 2) to decay; —fällig, *adj.* 1) disposed to fall, ready to fall; falling; *Bot.* deciduous, caducous, shedding; 2) *fig.* decaying, frail, crazy, weak, transient, perishable; —fälligkeit, *f.* frailty, weakness, perishableness, craziness; decrepitude; —finden, v. *refl.* to find one's way to a place; —fliegen, 1) to fly thither, to ...; 2) to pass away, to fly away, to be gone; —fliehen, to fly to a place, to flee, to escape to; —fließen, to flow to, along; —fort', *adv.* henceforth, for the future, from this time forward *or* forth; —fracht, *f.* freight outwards, outward-freight (*opp.* Herfracht); —fragen, v. *refl.* to enquire one's way, to find out one's way by enquiring; —führen, to conduct, lead, guide, carry, *or* bring there, to a place; —für', —fü'ro, *adv.* henceforth, in future; —gabe, *f.* 1) (the act of) giving away, &c. *cf.* —geben; surrender; 2) devotion; resignation; devotedness; —gang, m. the (act of) going to a place, passage (to ..., there); 2) *fig.* decease (—tritt); —geben, v. I. *tr.* 1) to give to, to reach; to pass round, to give away; 2) to resign, to give up, yield, surrender; to abandon; to devote, sacrifice, lay down (one's life); II. *refl.* to devote, resign, *or* abandon one's self (*with Dat.*, to); sich dem Laster —geben, to indulge vice; —gebung, *f.* 1) (the act of) giving away, &c.; 2) *see* —gabe; gebenken, *see* —denken; —gegen, *adv.* on the contrary; whereas; —gehen, 1) to go *or* pass there; to repair to a place; gehe — und sündige nicht mehr, go and sin no more; gehe — und thue desgleichen, go, and do thou likewise; 2) to pass, elapse; 3) *with* über [*& Acc.*]) to skim, skip, slide, *or* pass over with slight attention; 4) *coll.* to pass (muster), to be tolerable; wo geht die Reise —? whither are you bound? es mag noch so —gehen, it may pass, let it pass; —gehen lassen, to pass over, to suffer *or* allow to pass unnoticed, unchallenged, *or* unpunished, to tolerate, (Einem etwas) not to punish for; —gehören, to belong to; *cf.* Gehören, I.; —gelangen, to attain to, to arrive at, reach a place; —gerathen, to get to a place; to light (on), to fall in (with); wo bin ich —gerathen? where have I got to? —gestreckt, *p. a. Bot.* prostrate; —gießen, 1) to pour out *or* down; 2) *fig.* to do, execute in an easy manner; —gegossen, *p. a.* stretched out, lying in an easy manner, negligently reclining; —gleiten, to skim (along), über (etwas [*Acc.*]), to skim over ...; —grämen, v. *refl.* to pine away; —halten, 1) to hold, keep to a place; to stretch, hold out *or* forth, to present; *fig.-s.* 2) einen Kranken —halten, to keep a sick person in life; 3) *a)* to keep in suspense *or* off and on, to hold *or* keep in play, to put off, amuse (with fair hopes *or* promises), to procrastinate with one; *b)* to defer, put off, delay; Königin Elisabeth hielt diesen französischen Herzog mehrere Jahre lang hin, *coll.* Queen Elizabeth held this French duke off and on through several years; Jemanden mit der Bezahlung —halten, *Comm.* to delay (put off) the payment, to keep one out of his money; —haltung, *f.* 1) (the act of) holding, stretching forth; 2) delaying, putting off; —hängen, to be deferred, protracted, prolonged, *or* put off; —hängen lassen, to defer, &c.; —hauchen, to breathe, to put on lightly (of colours); —helfen, v. I. *intr.* (Einem) 1) to assist one in reaching something; 2) *coll.* to ruin; II. *refl.* (sich kümmerlich) to support one's self with difficulty, to struggle on, to make shift to live; —horchen, to listen to a thing; *fig.* to throw out a feeler; —jagen, v. I. *tr.* to drive, hunt to ..., along; II. *intr.* (*aux.* sein) to hurry, sweep to, along; —[illegible], to [illegible]

time) in lamentation; –kehren, 1) to turn to; 2) to sweep to.

Hinkel, (*str.*) *n. provinc.* little hen (Hühnchen); –taube, *f.* curved-beak pigeon.

Hinken, (*w.*) *v. intr.* (*aux.* haben & sein) 1) to go lame, to halt, limp, hobble; 2) *fig.* *a)* to halt, to be lame, incomplete, imperfect; unfit, unsuitable; *b)* to be in an unfavourable condition, to proceed badly; h–d, *p. a.* hobbling, limping, lame; der h–de Bote, *see* Bote; der h–de Teufel, the devil upon two sticks.

Hin'..., *in comp.* (*cf.* Hin) –knieen, to kneel down; –kommen, to come, get to, at; wird es –kommen? will it get there *or* arrive (safely)? wo ist er –gekommen? where did he get to? what is become of him? laßt mich nur –kommen! *coll.* I'll be among you presently! –können, *ellipt.* to be able to go, get to *or* there; –kränkeln, to pass life, &c. in a sickly state; –kriechen, to creep to a place; –kritzeln, to scribble down; –kunft, *f.* the coming there, arrival; –langen, *see* –reichen; –länglich, I. *adj.* sufficient, competent, adequate; requisite (stock, provisions); ample (reason, authority); nicht –länglich, insufficient; ein –längliches Auskommen, sufficiency, competence; II. *adv.* sufficiently, enough; –länglichkeit, *f.* sufficiency; –lassen, *ellipt.* to suffer to go to a place, to let pass *or* go to, to admit; –lässig, *adj. provinc.* careless, negligent; –lauf, *m.* running *or* course thither; –laufen, to run to, to go thither; to run *or* pass along, round, &c. (as a gallery, &c.); der Bach läuft am Rande des Waldes –, the brook skirts the forest; er mag –laufen, he may be gone, he may go his way; –leben, to pass one's life (carelessly), to live on; still vor sich –leben, to lead a calm secluded life; –legen, *v.* I. *tr.* to lay down, put down; to lay up; II. *refl.* to lie down; –lehnen, to lean against; –leihen, (*I. u.*) to lend out; –leiten, to lead, conduct, convey to ...; –lenken, to turn *or* incline to; –leuchten (Einem nach einem Orte), to light, show on the way to a place; –liefern, *v. tr.* 1) to deliver, expose, reach forth; 2) *see* –helfen, I. 2; –machen, *v. tr.* 1) to apply, fasten, &c. to a place; 2) to make, perform, &c. superficially; 3) (sich) *coll.* to resort, repair to ..., to go to ...; –mähen, to mow down; –marsch, *m.* march to a place *or* there (*opp.* Hermarsch); –marschiren, to march to ... *or* there; –martern, to put to death *or* kill by torments; –metzeln, –morden, to slaughter, to murder recklessly, –müssen, *ellipt.* to be obliged to go thither *or* to ...; –nahme, *f.* the (act of) taking (to), receiving, reception; –nehmen, 1) to take, receive; *fig.-s.* 2) to bear, suffer (insults), to put up with; to submit to, to acquiesce in; 3) to take up, absorb, *see* Einnehmen; –neigen, *v. refl.* & *intr.* to incline to; –neigung, *f.* inclination, leaning.

Hin'nen, *adv.* 1) *coll.* (*provinc.* Hin'ne) in here, in doors, &c. (*opp.* Haußen, *cf.* Drinnen *for* Darinnen); 2) (von –, from) hence; von –scheiden, to die.

Hin'..., *in comp.* (*cf.* Hin) –opfern, to sacrifice, despatch, make away with; –opferung, *f.* sacrifice; –passen, to fit in, to fit for; to be fit to stand *or* be there; –pflanzen, to plant in a place; –quälen, *v.* I. *tr.* to pass in torments; II. *refl.* to drag on a painful existence; –raffen, 1) to take *or* snatch away; 2) *fig.* to sweep away, to kill; –rauschen, to murmur, rustle, *or* gush along; –reichen, *v.* I. *tr.*; *coll.* –recken (Einem etwas), to reach, hand over (to), to hold *or* stretch forth (to); II. *intr.* 1) to reach, extend to; 2) to suffice, be sufficient, *or* adequate (zu, for); to extend far enough; das reicht –, that will suffice, *coll.* do; ein Wort wird –reichen, one word will do; –reichend, *p. a. see* –länglich; –reise, *f.* journey *or* travel (zur See, voyage) thither *or* to a place (*opp.* Herreise), *see* Hin; –reisen, to go, travel, make a journey (zur See, a voyage) thither *or* to ...; –reißen, 1) to tear along, to carry away *or* along with violence; to snatch away; 2) *fig.* to hurry *or* sweep away *or* along; to overcome, carry along, transport, ravish, enrapture; sich – reißen lassen, to give way (von, to); –reiten, to go thither on horseback, to ride to ...; –richten, 1) to direct *or* turn towards; 2) *coll.* to ruin, waste, spoil; 3) to execute, to put to death; –richtung, *f.* execution, capital punishment; –ritt, *m.* a ride to a place; –rücken, to move thither (on *or* to ...), to remove; –schaffen, to bring, transport, *or* convey to ...; –schauen, *see* –sehen; –scheid, *m.* death, decease; –scheiden, *fig.* to die, decease; der, die –geschiedene, the deceased; –scheren, *v. refl.* *coll.* to go off to ..., to pack; –scherzen, to pass in playfulness *or* trifling; –schicken, to send thither *or* to a place; –schieben, to shove *or* push thither *or* to a place, on, along; –schießen, *v.* I. *tr. see* Vorschießen; II. *intr.* (*aux.* sein) to shoot, fly, dart away; to rush, hasten along; –schiffen, *v.* I. *intr.* to sail towards *or* along; II. *tr.* to convey *or* send in a ship; am Ufer –schiffen, to coast along, to keep close to the shore, *Mar.* to hug the land; –schlachten, to kill, murder, butcher recklessly; –schlafen, *v. intr.* 1) (*aux.* haben) to sleep on; 2) (*aux.* sein) *see* –schlummern; –schlagen, *v.* I. *tr.* 1) to beat *or* cast to a place; 2) to knock down; II. *intr.* (*aux.* sein) *coll.* to fall *or* bang down, to get a fall; –schlängeln, *v. refl.* to wind in a serpentine manner, to meander along; –schleichen, *v. intr.* (*aux.* sein) & *refl.* 1) to creep, sneak, *or* steal thither, to a place; 2) to creep on, along; 3) *fig.* to be overlooked *or* forgotten; –schlendern, to saunter, lounge, loiter to a place, on, along; –schleppen, 1) to drag *or* draw to a place; 2) to drag *or* draw on, along; ein elendes Leben –schleppen, sich –schleppen, to drag out a wretched life, a miserable existence; –schleudern, to fling to, fling away; –schlummern, *fig.* to die an easy death; –schlüpfen, to slide along, to pass lightly; –schmachten, to pine *or* waste gradually away, to languish; –schmeißen, *coll. see* –werfen, 1 & 2; –schmelzen, to melt *or* die away gradually; –schmelzend, *adv. Mus.* (*Ital.*) calando, gradually diminishing in tone and quickness, becoming softer and slower by degrees; –schmettern, to dash down; –schmieren, to scrawl down, to scribble; –schreiben, 1) to write to a place, to send word to; 2) to write *or* pen down; –schütten, to pour down; to spill, drop; –schweben, to soar along; –schwinden, to pass away, vanish, to waste *or* die away; –schwindend, *p. a.* evanescent; das langsame –schwinden, insensible decay; –segeln, *see* –schiffen; –sehen, to look to a place, thither, at; fest –sehen, to look fixedly (nach, at); –sehnen, *v. refl.* to long to be there, to long for a place; –senden, *see* –schicken; –setzen, *v.* I. *tr.* 1) to set *or* put to *or* down; to lay down; 2) *coll.* to put in prison, to confine, commit; II. *refl.* to sit down; –setzung, *f.* 1) the (act of) setting down, &c.; 2) confinement.

Hin'sicht, (*w.*) *f.* view, consideration, respect, regard, relation; in – (*with Gen. or* auf [*and Acc.*]), in respect (of), with regard to, in point of, in order to; respecting, regarding ...; Sie haben Recht in dieser –, you are right on this point; in jeder (in aller) –, in every respect, in all respects, to all intents and purposes, every way.

Hin'sichtlich, *adv.* (*with Gen.*) in respect (of), with regard (to), as regards.

Hin'..., *in comp.* (*cf.* Hin) –siechen, to pine away (by sickness), to languish; –sinken, to sink down, to fall to the ground, ...

zumachen), to turn the key (to close the door) upon one; — der Zeit zurück sein, to be behind one's age; er zog die Thür — sich (*Dat.*) zu, he pulled the door to after him; — sich (*Acc.*) fallen, to fall backwards; — sich (*Acc.*) gehen, 1. to go backwards; 2. *fig.* not to thrive or succeed; die Heirat ist — sich gegangen, the match has been broken off; — eine Sache kommen, to find out, get at, discover, detect a thing; — Jemands Streiche (Schliche) kommen, to find one out; ich bin — sein Geheimniß gekommen, I have got behind *or* at his secret; — sich (*Dat.*) lassen, to leave behind, (im Gehen, Laufen rc.) to outstrip, distance (to outgo, outpace, outrun, &c.), to surpass; — sich (*Acc.*) lassen, *ellipt.* to suffer a person to pass behind one; — sich (*Acc.*) sehen, to look back; — sich (*Acc.*) sehend, *Herald.* regardant; — sich (*Acc.*) nehmen, stellen, to take, put behind *or* back; III. *adv.* 1) behind, back; komm —! come back here! 2) *coll.* down.

Hin'ter, *adj. see* Hintere.

Hin'ter..., *in comp.* —**achse**, *f.* hind axle-tree; *Mech.* trailing-axle; —**arche**, *f. Hydr.* hind trough; —**backen**, *f. pl.* buttocks; —**baum**, *m.* 1) *Weav. see* Garnbaum; 2) *see* —gestell, 2; —**bein**, *n.* hind leg; sich auf die —beine setzen *or* stellen, *coll.* 1. to put one's self in a posture of defence; to defend one's self obstinately; 2. to draw back, retract, recant; *coll.* to back out, to slip one's neck out of the collar; —**blei'ben**, (*str.*) *v. intr.* (*aux.* sein) 1) to be left behind *or* alive, to survive; 2) (*i. u.*) to be left undone; —**blie'bene**, (*decl. like adj.*) I. *m.* & *f.* (*pl.* die —bliebenen) he, she (those) left behind, survivor; die —blie'bene, relict; II. *n.* remains, rest; —**boden**, *m.* 1) back-garret; 2) *T.* back (of a watch); —**bracke**, *f.* 1) splinter-bar; 2) *Gunn.* rear trace-bar; —**bring'en**, (*irr.*) *v. tr.* (Einem etwas) to inform of (secretly), to acquaint with, to give notice; diese unschmeichelhaften Ausdrücke schnappten die Hofdamen sogleich auf und —brachten sie der Königin, these uncomplimentary expressions, the ladies of the court immediately snapped up, and carried to the Queen; —**bring'er**, *m.* informer; —**bring'ung**, *f.* (secret) information, intelligence; —**bug**, *m.* ham, leg; —**castell**, —**deck**, *n. Mar.* poop, quarter deck; —**drein**, *see* —her.

Hin'tere, I. *adj.* he (she) who or that which is behind *or* follows, hind, back; II. *m.* (*decl. like adj.*) breech, posterior, bottom, *vulg.* backside.

Hin'ter..., *in comp.* —**ebbe**, *f. Mar.* the lowest (of the) ebb; —**einander**, one after another, successively, consecutively; at a time, together, at a stretch; fünf mal —einander, five times running; —**eisen**, *n. Farr.* hind shoe of a horse; —**faden**, *m. Weav.* hind-thread; —**fährte**, *f. Sport.* 1) track, trace of the hind-foot; 2) *see* Widerfährte; —**flagge**, *f. Mar.* (naval) ensign; —**fleck**, *m.* heel-piece; einen —fleck aufsetzen auf (*with Acc.*), to heel-piece; —**flügel**, *m.* hind- (*or* hinder) wing; —**fries**, *m. Gunn.* first re-inforcement (of a gun); —**führen**, to lead behind, back, or to the rear; —**füßren**, *see* —gehen; —**fuß**, *m.* hind-foot, *cf.* —bein; (der rechte) spear-foot (of a horse); auf die —füße treten, *see* sich auf die —beine setzen; —**gallerie**, *f. Mar.* stern-gallery; —**gang**, *m. Sport.* going out (of a deer into the fields); —**gäßchen**, *n.* back-lane; —**gebäude**, *n.* back-building; back-house; out-house; —**gebirge**, *n.* back part of mountains; —**gedanke**, *m.* mental reservation, mental reserve; secret thought *or* intention; —**gehänge**, *n. Sport.* posterior part of a hare; —**geh'en**, to deceive, delude; to decoy, take in; —**geschirr**, *n.* 1) breechings (of a horse's harness); 2) wheel-harness; —**gestell**, *n.* 1) *Wheel-w.* a) hind-part of a waggon or coach; b) hind carriage (of a plough); 2) *Saddl.* cantle, quarters of a saddle; 3) *Man.* hind quarters (of a horse); —**gewölbe**, *n.* back-shop; —**glied**, *n.* 1) rear-rank; 2) *Log.* predicate; 3) *Math.* consequent; —**grund**, *m. Paint.*, &c. background; flat scene, deepening (of a picture); rear; —**gurt**, *m. Gunn.* vent-astragal; —**haar**, *n.* back hair; —**halb**, *adv.* & *prep.* (*with Gen.*) (*i. u.*) behind; —**halt**, *m.* 1) ambush, ambuscade, wait; 2) rear, reserve (of an army); im —halt liegen, to lie in ambush; sich in —halt legen, to form an ambush; im —halt haben, *fig.* to have in reserve; —**hal'ten**, (*str.*) *v. tr. see* Vorenthalten; —**haltig**, *coll.* —**hältisch**, *adj.* reserved, secret; —**hand**, *f.* 1) back of the hand; 2) *Man.* hind-hand (of a horse); 3) *Gam.* (at cards) youngest hand (*opp.* Vorhand); die —hand haben, to be the youngest hand; —**hang**, *m. provinc.* vessel taken in tow; —**haupt**, *n.* occiput, hind part of the head; —**hauptsbein**, *n. Anat.* occipital bone; —**haus**, *n.* back-house (—gebäude); —**her'**, *adv.* after: 1) behind, following; 2) subsequently, afterwards; —her' ist gut reden, *coll.* good counsel is cheap when the result is known; —her' sein, *coll.* 1. to follow close; 2. to be earnest in the pursuit of ...; to be hard at it, to work away; —**hof**, *m.* back-yard, court-yard; —**indien**, *n. Geogr.* Further India, Indo-China; —**kammer**, *f.* back-chamber; —**kanonen**, *f. pl. Mar.* stern-chases; —**keule**, *f.* leg (of veal, mutton, &c.); —**klauen**, *f. pl.* hind claws (of birds of prey); —**knie**, *n.* hough (of a horse); —**kopf**, *m. see* —haupt; —**laden**, *m.* back-shop; —**lader**, *m.* (*coll. for* —ladungsgewehr, *n.*) breech-loader (breech-loading gun); —**lage**, *f.* deposit, consignment, pledge; —**laß**, *m.* 1) *or* —**lassenschaft**, (*w.*) *f.* inheritance (Nachlaß); 2) *Sport.* trace of a deer; —**las'sen**, (*str.*) *v. tr.* 1) to leave behind; 2) *see* Nachlassen, 1; Nachricht —lassen, to leave word; —**lassen**, *p. a.* posthumous (works, &c.); die trauernden —lassenen, the mourning survivors; —**lastig**, *adj. Mar.* charged (loaded) too much behind; ein —lastiges Schiff, a ship (which is) too much by the stern; —**laterne**, *f. Mar.* poop-lantern; —**lauf**, *m. Sport.* hind leg; —**leder**, *n. Shoe-m.* hind quarter of a shoe; —**legen**, (*w.*) *v. tr.* to place or put behind or back, &c.; —**le'gen**, (*w.*) *v. tr.* to deposit, give in trust, consign; —**le'ger**, (*str.*) *m.* deponent; das —**leg'te**, *n.* deposit; —**le'gung**, (*w.*) *f.* the (act of) depositing, &c.; —**list**, *f.* artifice, cunning, deceit; fraud; —**listig**, *adj.* cunning, deceitful, artful, designing, fraudulent, insidious, fallacious; —**listigkeit**, *f.* cunningness, &c.; —**luke**, *f. Mar.* after-hatchway; —**mann**, *m.* 1) *Mil.* rear-rank man; (*Bulw., transl. of Schiller's* Schlacht:) the hinder-man; 2) *Comm.* subsequent indorser (on bills of exchange); —**mast**, *m. Mar.* mizzen-mast; —**matratze**, *f.* back-quilt (of a carriage); —**naht**, *f. Shoe-m.* seam, stitch on the hind quarter; —**pfanne**, *f. Salt-w.* graduation-pan; —**pferd**, *n. see* Deichselpferd; —**plicht**, *f. Mar.* after-caddy; —**pforte**, *f.* 1) back-gate; 2) —**pforten**, *pl. Mar.* stern-ports; —**pfote**, *f.* hind foot, hind paw; —**quartier**, *n. see* —leder; —**rad**, *n.* hind wheel, *pl.* trailing wheels (*opp.* Vorderräder); —**rast**, *f. Gun-sm.* large sear; —**raum**, *m.* 1) back space; 2) *Mar.* after-hold; —**rücks**, *adv.* backwards, from behind; —**ruß**, *f. see* —**sass**; —**sasse**, —**saß**, *m.* copyholder, vassal; small farmer, low tenant; —**sassengut**, *n.* estate of a copy-holder; —**satz**, *m. Gramm.* apodosis, *cf.* Nachsatz; —**schanze**, *f. Mar.* poop; —**schenkel**, *m.* hind leg; —**schiff**, *n. Mar.* after-body, hind-part; —**schinken**, *m.* hind-quarter of a wild boar; —**schleichen**, (*str.*) *v. tr.* to attack by stealth or surprise, to steal (a march) upon; —**schlingen**, (*str.*), —**schlucken**, (*w.*) *v. tr.* to swallow or gulp down; —**segel**, *n. pl. Mar.* after-sails; —**seite**, *f.* hind part, rear; —**seitentakel**, *n. Mar.* mizzen-tackle; —**siedler**, *m. see* —sasse; —**sitz**, *m.* back seat; —**spitzig**, *adj. T.* unevenly shorn (of cloth); —**spill**, *n. Mar.* main capstan; —**sporn**, *m. Gild.* cramp; —**sprung**, *m. Weav.* lower shed.

Hin'terst, I. *adj.* hindmost, last; *Mar.* sternmost; II. H—e, (*decl. like adj.*) *m. vulg. see* Hintere; III. *adv.* ((ganz) zu —) sternmost, aftmost.

Hin'ter..., *in comp.* —**stab**, *m. Gunn.* muzzle astragal (and fillets); —**ständer**, *m. T.* cleft posts in paper-mills, in which the hind part of the swing is movable by way of a bolt; —**ständig**, *adj. Bot.* backward; —**stapfen**, *m.* hind-foot of a sofa; —**staude**, *f. see* —ständer; —**stellig**, *provinc. adj.* 1) remaining, left; outstanding, owing, due; 2) retrograde; 3) insidious, treacherous; —stellig machen, to frustrate; —**steven**, *m. Mar.* main post, stern post; —**stich**, *m.* backstitch; —**stube**, *f.* back-room; —**stück**, *n.* 1) hind-piece, back-part; 2) —**stücke**, *pl. Mar.* a) pieces of timber by which the planks at the stern of a vessel are fastened; b) stern-chases; —**tatze**, *f.* hind paw; —**tau**, *n.* 1) hind or shaft-trace (of a cart, &c.); 2) *Mar.* stern fast; —**theil**, *n.* hind-part, back-part; —theil eines Schiffes, stern, after *or* hinder part (of a ship); im —theile des Schiffes, astern, aft, abaft; das —theil am Hemde, hind flap, seat of a shirt; —theil eines Pferdes, hind hand (of a horse); —theil am Karren rc., cart-tail, back; —**thor**, *n.* back-gate; —**thür**, *f.* back-door; *fig.* (door of) escape, loop-hole; —**treffen**, *n. Mil.* rear-guard, reserve of an army; —**trei'ben**, (*str.*) *v. tr.* to frustrate, thwart, balk, hinder, prevent; to counteract; to disappoint; to break off (a marriage, &c.); —**trei'bung**, (*w.*) *f.* frustration, thwarting, &c.; —**treppe**, *f.* back-stairs; —**troß**, *m. Mil.* hind-baggage; —**verdeck**, *n. Mar.* quarter-deck; —**viertel**, *n.* hind quarter, loin; *Am-e.* —**wald**, *m.* back-wood; —**wäldler**, *m.* backwoodsman; —**wand**, *f.* 1) back-wall; 2) back (of a chimney); 3) tail-rack of a cart, &c.; —**wärts**, *adv.* backward, backwards, behind; —**zange**, *f.* hind-screw (of a joiner's bench); —**zeug**, *n. see* —geschirr; —**zieh'en**, (*str.*) *v. tr.* to evade by subterfuge, to elude, to omit to comply with the requirements of the law; —**zieh'ung**, (*w.*) *f.* fraudulent evasion, elusion, &c.

Hin'..., *in comp.* (*cf.* Hin) —**thun**, *coll.* to place or put to ..., there; wo soll ich es —thun? where shall I put it? what shall I do with it? —**tippen**, *coll.* to hint at, to throw out a feeler; —**tragen**, to carry to ..., there; —**trauern**, to pass, spend in sorrow, mourning (Vertrauern); —**träumen**, to dream away, to pass dreaming (one's time); —**treffen**, to hit an object; —**treiben**, *v.* I. *tr.* to drive to ..., there; II. *intr.* (*aux.* sein) *Mar.* to drift, go adrift; —**treten**, to step to ..., there; —**tritt**, *m. fig.* decease, demise, death.

Hintsch, (*str.*) *m. provinc.* asthma.

Hinü'ber, *adv.* over (there, *different:* Herüber); across; über die See —, beyond sea; —**bringen**, —**fahren**, —**führen**, —**schaffen**, —**tragen**, to bring, carry over, transport; —**gehen**, to go *or* cross over.

Hinum', *adv.* about (there, *different:* Herum), (da —) that way about; dort um die Ecke —, there about that corner.

Hinun'ter, *adv.* down; down there, that way (*different:* Herunter, *cf.* Hinab); die Treppe —, down stairs; den Berg —, down (the) hill; lassen Sie uns —gehen, let us go down (stairs, &c.); —**stürzen**, *v. tr.* & *intr. see* Hinabstürzen; (ein Glas Wein rc.) to toss off (a glass of wine, &c.); —**wärts**, *adv.* downwards.

Hin'..., *in comp.* (*cf.* Hin) —**wagen**, *v. refl.* to venture (to go) to a place, there,

gerecht, Forstgerechtigkeit; —gericht, n. forest-court, tribunal for forest matters; —gewächs, n. woody plant; —giebel, m. Archit. (carved) timber gable; —glitsche, f. see —riese; —graf, m. intendant of the forests; president of a forest-court; —grafschaft, f. dignity of a Holzgraf; —gräserei, f. pasture in a wood; —graupen, f. pl. Min. ligniform copper-ore; —haare, n. pl. Bot. pointed leaves of the Nadelholz, which see; —hacker, m. 1) wood-cleaver, wood-cutter; 2) Ornith. woodpecker, cf. Baumhacker, 1; —hackerlohn, n. wages of a wood-cutter; —häher, m. Ornith. jay (Garrulus glandarius L.); —handel, m. wood-trading; timber-trade, Am. lumber-trade; —händler, m. wood-trader, dealer in wood, timber merchant, Am. lumberer, lumberman, lumber-trader; —hängen, Min. to let down wood into a shaft; —hase, m. wood-hare; —hau, m. place in a forest where trees are felled; —hauer, m. 1) wood-cutter; feller; 2) see —hacker, 2; —haufen, m. wood-stack, wood-pile; —heher, m. see Nußhäher; —hof, m. wood-yard, timber-yard; —höke, m. wood-monger; —huhn, n. 1) any kind of fowl living in the woods, particularly the Auerhahn, Birkhuhn, Haselhuhn &c., which see; 2) provinc. see Schwarzspecht.

Hol'zicht, adj. woodlike, ligneous; stony (of pears); tough, stringy (of turnips, &c.).

Hol'zig, adj. 1) woody; die h—e Afterkohle, bituminous (or carbonated) wood; 2) Bot. ligneous; 3) see Holzreich; 4) fig. see Hölzern, 2, a.

Holz'..., in comp. —käfer, m. see —bock, 2; —kammer, f. wood-house; —kauf, m. purchase of wood or timber; —kirsche, f. Bot. wild cherry; —knecht, m. servant of a wood-keeper; —knospe, f. Bot. leaf-bud; —kohle, f. charcoal, wood-coal; (mineralische) fibrous coal; (geformte) prepared charcoal; —krähe, f. 1) see Mandelkrähe; 2) see Schwarzspecht; —kupfer, n. Miner. variety of olivenite; —lack, m. stick-lack; —lager, n. 1) wood- or timber-yard; 2) stock of wood or timber; —land, n. wood-land; —laus, f. Entom. 1) wood-louse (Oniscus asellus L.); 2) see —wurm, 1; —leger, m. a person cording wood; —leim, m. see Tischlerleim; —leite, f. woody slope; —lerche, f. Ornith. wood-lark (Anthus arboreus L.); —lese, f. (the act of) wood-gathering; —macher, m. see —hacker, 1; —made, f. see —wurm, 1; —malerei, f. (the act or any specimen of) painting on wood; —mangel, m. want of wood; —männchen, n. Bot. mezereon (Daphne mezereum L.); —markt, m. wood- or timber-market; —maß, n. wood-measure; —masse, f. T. wood-paste; —mast, f. mast of acorn for cattle and hogs; —maus, f. Zool. (garden-) dormouse (Myoxus nitela Schb.); —mehl, n. dust or flour of worm-eaten wood; —meise, f. Ornith. coalmouse (Tannenmeise); —messer, m. wood-measurer; —milbe, f. Entom. wood-mite; —mosaik, f. inlaid (wood-)work; —nagel, m. peg; —nager, m. Entom. wood-worm (Todtenuhr); —nutzung, f. proceeds of a wood; —obst, n. wild fruits; —ofen, m. stove for drying or burning wood; —öl, n. Chem. & Bot. wood-oil; —opal, m. Petr. wood-opal; —ordnung, f. see Forstordnung; —papier, n. wood-paper; —pflanzen (Ofen), f. pl. ligneous plants; —pflaster, n. wood(en) pavement; —pflasterung, f. wood-paving; —platte, f. 1) a flat piece of wood; 2) T. (engraved) wood-block; —platz, m. place for wood, wood-yard, timber-yard; —preis, m. price of wood; —raspel, f. wood-rasp; —raum, m. wood-house; —rechen, m. T. wooden grate to retain floated wood; —rechnung, f. account of wood bought and sold; —recht, n. fire-hole; —reich, adj. wooded; abounding in wood; —reißer, m. instrument for blazing trees; —riese,

—rutsche, f. T. slide (for gliding down wood or timber from precipices); —ring, m. ring in the trunk of trees showing their age; —ruß, m. wood soot; —saat, f. young trees grown from seed; nursery of trees; —säger, m. (timber-)sawyer; —samen, m. wood-seed; Chem. &c. —sauer, adj. pyroligneous; —saures Salz, pyrolignite; —säure, f. ligneous acid; brenzliche —säure, pyroligneous acid; —schaden, m. damage done to a forest; —schicht, f. see —ring; —schieber, m. Bak. oven-rake; —schiene, f. wooden or timber rail; —schiff, n. timber-ship, ship laden with timber; —schlag, m. 1) see —hau; 2) (the act or privilege of) wood-cutting, felling; —schlägel, m. beetle, mallet for driving iron wedges into wood; —schläger, m. wood-cutter, feller, woodman; —schlagung, f. 1) a felling of wood; 2) Build. driving piles into the ground; —schneide-Instrumente, n. pl. carving or wood-engraving tools; —schneidekunst, f. art of carving or cutting in wood, wood-engraving, xylography; —schneider, m. carver or cutter in wood, wood-carver, wood-engraver, xylograph(er); —schnepfe, f. Ornith. wood-cock (Scolopax rusticola L.); —schnitzer, m. carver in wood; —schnitzerei, f., —schnitt, m. wood-engraving, (wood-)cut; —schnitzwerk, n. carving, carved work; —schoppen, m. see —schuppen; —schragen, m. wood-measure; —schrat, m. 1) jay (—häher); 2) see Nußhäher; —schraube, f. wood-screw; —schreiber, m. clerk of the wood-office; —schreier, m. see Eichelhäher; —schuhe, m. pl. wooden shoes, wooden clogs, sabots; —schuppen, m. wood-house, shed; —schwamm, m. Bot. wood-fungus, dry-rot (Merulius destructor L.); —schwarte, f. outside plank; —schwefelsäure, f. Chem. vegetable sulphuric acid; —setzer, m. see —leger; —spalter, m. wood-cleaver; —span, m. chip of wood; —späne, pl. wood-shavings; —sparofen, m. economical wood-stove; —sperling, m. Ornith. tree-sparrow (Passer montanus L., Feldsperling); —spielwaaren, pl. wooden toys; —stall, m. see —schuppen; —stamm, m. baulk (Balken); —stein, m. Petr. wood-stone, petrified wood; —steinkohle, f. bituminous wood; —stengel, m. Bot. ligneous stem; —stich, m. see —schnitt; —stock, —stoß, m. pile or stack of wood; Engr. wood(cut)-block; —tafel, f. see —platte; —tag, m. 1) day on which wood may be gathered in the forest; 2) day on which the felled wood is taken away; —taube, f. Ornith. stock- or wood-pigeon, stock-dove (Columba oenas Gm.); —taxe, f. fixed price of wood; —theer, m. wood-tar; —trage, f. wood-barrow; —träger, m. logman. —thee, —trank, m. wood-drink, a decoction or infusion of medicinal woods; —trift, f. 1) pasture or right of pasturage in a forest; 2) raft; —uhr, f. wooden clock, German clock.

Hol'zung, (w.) f. 1) the (act of) cutting, felling or bringing in of wood; 2) wood, forest.

Holz'..., in comp. —verband, m. T. truss-work; —verbindung, f. joint (mit Nuth und Feder, groove and tongue-joint); —verkauf, m. selling, sale of wood or timber; —verwalter, m. 1) the steward or overseer of a wood; 2) wood-factor; —verwaltung, f. board for superintending the sale of wood or timber; —vogt, m. see Forsthüter; —waare, f. wooden ware; —wand, f. wooden plank wall, board-partition; —wärter, m. wood-ward; —weg, m. 1) wood way, road in a forest, glade; 2) coll. wrong track or direction; auf dem —wege sein, to be mistaken or out, usual. to be planted in queer-street, to be in the wrong box, to be out; —weide, f. wood-pasture, cf. —trift, 1; —werk, n. 1) wood-work, timber-work; 2) Mech. frame, framing; 3) (Täfelwerk) wainscotting; —wesen, n. forest-concerns

[illegible]

gericht, Forstgerechtigkeit; –gericht, n. forest-court, tribunal for forest matters; –gewächs, n. woody plant; –giebel, m. Archit. (carved) timber gable; –gleitsche, f. see –riese; –graf, m. intendant of the forests; president of a forest-court; –grafschaft, f. dignity of a Holzgraf; –gräserei, f. pasture in a wood; –graupen, f. pl. Min. ligniform copper-ore; –haare, n. pl. Bot. pointed leaves of the Nadelholz, which see; –hacker, m. 1) wood-cleaver, wood-cutter; 2) Ornith. woodpecker, cf. Baumhacker, 1; –hackerlohn, n. wages of a wood-cutter; –häher, m. Ornith. jay (Garrulus glandarius L.); –handel, m. wood-trading; timber-trade, Am. lumber-trade; –händler, m. wood-trader, dealer in wood, timber merchant, Am. lumberer, lumberman, lumber-trader; –hängen, Min. to let down wood into a shaft; –hase, m. wood-hare; –hau, m. place in a forest where trees are felled; –hauer, m. 1) wood-cutter; feller; 2) see –hacker, 2; –haufen, m. wood-stack, wood-pile; –heher, m. see Nußhäher; –hof, m. wood-yard, timber-yard; –höke, m. woodmonger; –huhn, n. 1) any kind of fowl living in the woods, particularly the Auerhahn, Birkhuhn, Haselhuhn &c., which see; 2) provinc. see Schwarzspecht.

Hol'zicht, adj. woodlike, ligneous; stony (of pears); flaxy, stringy (of turnips, &c.).

Hol'zig, adj. 1) woody; die h-e Afterkohle, bituminous (or carbonated) wood; 2) Bot. ligneous; 3) see Holzreich; 4) fig. see Hölzern, 2, a.

Holz'..., in comp. –käfer, m. see –bock, 2; –kammer, f. wood-house; –kauf, m. purchase of wood or timber; –kirsche, f. Bot. wild cherry; –knecht, m. servant of a wood-keeper; –knospe, f. Bot. leaf-bud; –kohle, f. charcoal, wood-coal; (mineralische) fibrous coal; (geformte) prepared charcoal; –krähe, f. 1) see Mandelkrähe; 2) see Schwarzspecht; –kupfer, n. Miner. variety of olivenite; –lack, m. stick-lack; –lager, n. 1) wood- or timber-yard; 2) stock of wood or timber; –land, n. wood-land; –laus, f. Entom. 1) wood-louse (Oniscus asellus L.); 2) see –wurm, 1; –leger, m. a person cording wood; –leim, m. see Tischlerleim; –leite, f. woody slope; –lerche, f. Ornith. wood-lark (Anthus arborea L.); –lese, f. (the act of) wood-gathering; –macher, m. see –hacker, 1; –made, f. see –wurm, 1; –malerei, f. (the act or any specimen of) painting on wood; –mangel, m. want of wood; –männchen, n. Bot. mezereon (Daphne mezereum L.); –markt, m. wood- or timber-market; –maß, n. wood-measure; –masse, f. T. wood-paste; –mast, f. mast of acorn for cattle and hogs; –maus, f. Zool. (garden-) dormouse (Myoxus nitela Schb.); –mehl, n. dust or flour of worm-eaten wood; –meise, f. Ornith. coalmouse (Kohlmeise); –messer, m. wood-measurer; –milbe, f. Entom. wood-mite; –mosaik, f. inlaid (wood-)work; –nagel, m. peg; –nager, m. Entom. wood-worm (Todtenuhr); –nutzung, f. proceeds of a wood; –obst, n. wild fruits; –ofen, m. stove for drying or burning wood; –öl, n. Chem. & Bot. wood-oil; –opal, m. Min. wood-opal; –ordnung, f. see Forstordnung; –papier, n. wood-paper; –pflanzen (Olen), f. pl. ligneous plants; –pflaster, n. wood(en) pavement; –pflasterung, f. wood-paving; –platte, f. 1) a flat piece of wood; 2) T. (engraved) wood-block; –platz, m. place for wood, wood-yard, timber-yard; –preis, m. price of wood; –raspel, f. wood-rasp; –raum, m. wood-house; –rechen, m. T. wooden grate to retain floated wood; –rechnung, f. account of wood bought, and sold; –recht, n. fire-bote; –reich, adj. wooded; abounding in wood; –reißer, m. instrument for blazing trees; –riese,

–rutsche, f. T. slide (for gliding down wood or timber from precipices); –ring, m. ring in the trunk of trees showing their age; –ruß, m. wood soot; –saat, f. young trees grown from seed; nursery of trees; –säger, m. (timber-)sawyer; –samen, m. wood-seed; Chem. s. –sauer, adj. pyroligneous; –saures Salz, pyrolignite; –säure, f. ligneous acid; brenzliche –säure, pyroligneous acid; –schaden, m. damage done to a forest; –schicht, f. see –ring; –schieber, m. Bak. oven-rake; –schiene, f. wooden or timber rail; –schiff, n. timber-ship, ship laden with timber; –schlag, m. 1) see –hau; 2) (the act or privilege of) wood-cutting, felling; –schlägel, m. beetle, mallet for driving iron wedges into wood; –schläger, m. wood-cutter, feller, woodman; –schlagung, f. 1) a felling of wood; 2) Build. driving piles into the ground; –schneide-Instrumente, n. pl. carving or wood-engraving tools; –schneidekunst, f. art of carving or cutting in wood, wood-engraving, xylography; –schneider, m. carver or cutter in wood, wood-carver, wood-engraver, xylograph(er); –schnepfe, f. Ornith. wood-cock (Scolopax rusticola L.); –schnitzer, m. carver in wood; –schnitzerei, f., –schnitt, m. wood-engraving, (wood-)cut; –schnitzwerk, n. carving, carved work; –schoppen, m. see –schuppen; –schragen, m. wood-measure; –schrat, m. 1) jay (–häher); 2) see Nußhäher; –schraube, f. wood-screw; –schreiber, m. clerk of the wood-office; –schreier, m. see Eichelhäher; –schuhe, m. pl. wooden shoes, wooden clogs, sabots; –schuppen, m. wood-house, shed; –schwamm, m. Bot. wood-fungus, dry-rot (Merulius destructor L.); –schwarte, f. outside plank; –schwefelsäure, f. Chem. vegetable sulphuric acid; –setzer, m. see –leger; –spalter, m. wood-cleaver; –span, m. chip of wood; –späne, pl. wood-shavings; –sparofen, m. economical wood-stove; –sperling, m. Ornith. tree-sparrow (Passer montanus L., Feldsperling); –spielwaaren, pl. wooden toys; –stall, m. see –schuppen; –stamm, m. baulk (Balken); –stein, m. Min. wood-stone, petrified wood; –steinkohle, f. bituminous wood; –stengel, m. Bot. ligneous stem; –stich, m. see –schnitt; –stock, –stoß, m. pile or stack of wood; Engr. wood(cut)-block; –tafel, f. see –platte; –tag, m. 1) day on which wood may be gathered in the forest; 2) day on which the felled wood is taken away; –taube, f. Ornith. stock- or wood-pigeon, stock-dove (Columba oenas Gm.); –taxe, f. fixed price of wood; –theer, m. wood-tar; –trage, f. wood-barrow; –träger, m. logman; –thee, –trank, m. wood-drink, a decoction or infusion of medicinal woods; –trift, f. 1) pasture or right of pasturage in a forest; 2) raft; –uhr, f. wooden clock, German clock.

Hol'zung, (w.) f. 1) the (act of) cutting, felling or bringing in of wood; 2) wood, forest.

Holz'..., in comp. –verband, m. T. truss-work; –verbindung, f. joint (mit Nuth und Feder, groove and tongue-joint); –verkauf, m. selling, sale of wood or timber; –verwalter, m. 1) the steward or overseer of a wood; 2) wood-factor; –verwaltung, f. board for superintending the sale of wood or timber; –vogt, m. see Forstaufseher; –waare, f. wooden ware; –wand, f. wooden plank wall, board-partition; –wärter, m. wood-ward; –weg, m. 1) wood way, road in a forest, glade; 2) coll. wrong track or direction; auf dem –wege sein, to be mistaken or out, coll. to be planted in queer-street, to be in the wrong box, to be out; –weide, f. wood-pasture, cf. –trift, 1; –werk, n. 1) wood-work, timber-work; 2) Mech. frame, framing; 3) Täfelwerk, wainscotting; –wesen, n. forest-economy

cina L.); —**flee**, m. *Bot.* medic (*Medicago* L.); —**schall**, m. the sound of horns; —**schluß**, m. *Log.* dilemma; —**spitze**, f. horn-tip; —**schube**, —**sporen**, m. pl. cow(horn) knobs; —**toll**, *adj.* horn-mad; —**tragend**, *adj.* cornigerous; —**träger**, m. *fig.* cuckold; der geduldige —träger, wittol.

Hör'nerv, (*str.*) m. *Anat.* auditory nerve.

Horn'..., *in comp.* —**erz**, n. *Miner.* horn (silver) ore, corneous silver-ore; —**eule**, f. *Ornith.* horn owl (*Bubo maximus* Sibb.); —**farbe**, f. 1) horn-colour; 2) colour for dying or staining horn; —**farben**, —**farbig**, *adj.* horn-coloured; —**fäule**, f. *Vet.* (horny) quittor; —**feile**, f. horn-rasp; —**felsstein**, m. *Miner.* horn-stone; —**fisch**, m. *Ichth.* file-fish, old wife (*Balistes vetula* L.); *Miner-s.* —**flint**, m. siliceous shist; —**flötz**, m. stratum (layer) of blackish limestone; —**flügler**, m. pl. *Entom.* beetles (*Coleoptera* L.); —**förmig**, *adj.* horn-shaped, *Bot.* corniform; —**fuß**, m. hoofed foot, hoof; —**füßig**, *adj.* horn-footed; —**geschwür**, n. *Med.* carcinoma; —**geschwulst**, f. *Vet.* swimmer; —**gewebe**, n. *Anat.* corneous tissue; —**gold**, n. gold of $9^1/_2$ to 10 carats: —**griff**, m. horn-handle; —**händler**, m. dealer in horns, horn-merchant; —**hart**, *adj.* hard as horn, horny, callous; —**haspel**, m. windlass with a handle; —**haut**, f. *Anat.* the transparent horny tunicle or membrane of the eye, (*Lat.*) *cornea*; —**hautfleck**, m. *Med.* speck of the cornea, pearl; —**häutig**, *adj.* callous; —**hautschnitt**, m. *Med.* section of the cornea (*Ceratotomia*) to extract a cataract through the opening in the cornea; *Med-s.* —**hautstaphylom**, n. grape-swelling; —**hauttrübung**, f. opacity of the cornea; —**hecht**, m. *Ichth.* gar-pike, gar-fish (*Belone vulgaris* C.).

Hor'nicht, **Hör'nig**, *adj.* & *adv.* hornlike, callous, (horn) hard, hornish, horny.

Horn'igel, (*str.*) m. *see* Igelfisch.

Hor'niß, (*w.*) f. *Entom.* hornet (*Vespa crabro* C.); **H-enbirne**, f. *Pomol.* a species of medlar. [former on the French horn.

Hornist', (*w.*) m. bugleman, bugler, per-

Horn'..., *in comp.* —**jagd**, f. hunting with the bugle; —**käfer**, m. *Entom.* horn-beetle (Nashornkäfer); —**kamm**, m. horn-comb; —**kartoffel**, f. a sort of potatoes; —**kirsche**, f. cornel-cherry; —**klampen**, f. pl. *Mar.* belaying cleats; —**klee**, m. *Bot.* horn-trefoil, bird's foot trefoil (*Lotus corniculatus* L.); —**kluft**, f. cleft, fissure, seam in a hoof; —**klüftig**, *adj.* hoof-cleft; —**knopf**, m. horn-button; —**kraut**, n. *Bot.* mouse-ear; chickweed (*Cerastium* L.); —**kuchen**, m. horn-shaped cake; —**leim**, m. horn-glue; —**mangan**, m. *Miner.* photizite; —**mergel**, m. *Miner.* a variety of roe-stone; —**messer**, n. horn-knife; —**mohn**, m. *Bot.* horned poppy (*Glaucium luteum* L.); —**muschel**, f. horn-muscle; —**ochs**, m. *vulg.* blockhead; —**pergament**, n. horn-parchment; —**platte**, f. horn-plate; —**pomeranze**, f. large orange; —**presse**, f. horn-press; —**quecksilber**, n. *Chem.* corneous mercury, muriate of mercury; —**raspel**, f. horn-rasp; —**richter**, m. *see* —bereiter; —**riß**, m. *see* —spalte; —**rose**, f. *Bot.* wild rose (Hundsrose); —**salbe**, f. hoof-salve, romelade; —**satz**, m. *T.* 1) ornament of a hunter's horn; 2) *Mus.* composition for the horn; —**schiefer**, m. *Miner.* horn-slate; —**schlange**, f. *Zool.* horned serpent, cerastes (*Cerastes aegyptiacus* Dum. Bibr.); —**schlacken**, m. pl. *T.* horn-rings; —**schluß**, m. *Log.* dilemma; —**schnabel**, m. *Ornith.* horn-bill (—vogel); —**schnecke**, f. clubshell (*Cerithium vulgatum* Brug.); —**schrot**, m. *T.* horn-cut; —**schröter**, m. *Entom.* horn-beetle (Hirschkäfer); —**schwein**, n. *see* Eberhirsch; —**schwiele**, f. *see* —fäule; —**signal**, n. signal by bugle; —**silber**, n. *Miner.* horn-silver; —**sohle**, f. sole of the hoof; —**späne**, m. pl. horn-shavings, -scrapings or -clippings; —**spalte**, f. 1) *see* —kluft; 2) *Vet.* false quarter; —**spaltig**, *adj.* *see* —klüftig; —**spitze**, f. horn-tip; —**stein**, m. *Miner.* horn-stone, chert; —**steinartig**, *adj.* cherty; —**strauch**, m. *Bot.* dog-wood (Cornelkirsche); —**thiere**, pl. *Zool.* cavicorns (*Cavicornia*); —**träger**, m. *Ornith.* horned screamer (*Palamedea cornuta* L.).

Hor'nung, (*str.*) m. (the month of) February; **H-blume**, f. *Bot.* snowflake (*Leucojum vernum* L.); **H-hecht**, m. *Ichth.* common pike, spawning in February and March.

Horn'..., *in comp.* —**vieh**, n. 1) horned cattle, black cattle; neat; 2) *vulg.* blockhead; —**viehseuche**, f. *see* Rinderpest; —**vogel**, m. *Ornith.* horn-bill (*Buceros rhinoceros* L.); —**waaren**, f. pl. horn goods; —**wände**, n. pl. quarters of a horse's hoof; —**weide**, f. *Bot.* common sallow (*Salix caprea* L.); —**werk**, n. *Fort.* horn-work.

* **Horoscop'**, (*str.*) n. (*Gr.*) horoscope; das — stellen, to cast the horoscope.

Hör'..., *in comp.* —**rohr**, n. 1) hearing trumpet, hearing or auricular tube; 2) *Med.* stethoscope; —**saal**, m. auditory; lecture-room; —**sage**, f. *see* Hörensagen.

Horsch, (*str.*) m. *Mediaev. Archit.* coping of a wall, &c.

Horst, (*str.*) m. & (*w.*) f. 1) († &) *provinc.* heap, mass; cluster; hurst, thicket; 2) top of a rock; 3) sand-bank; 4) (*Sport.* &) *, eyrie, nest (of birds of prey). [to nest.

Hors'ten, (*w.*) *v. intr.* to build an eyrie,

Hort, (*str.*) m. I. 1) safe retreat; 2) (*Script.* &) *, shield, safety: II. († &) *, treasure.

Hor'te, (*w.*) f. *see* Hürde.

Hor'ten, (*w.*) *v. intr. provinc.* to butt.

Horten'sia, **Horten'sie**, f. 1) Hortensia (*P. N.*); 2) *Bot.* hydrangea hortensis.

Hör'..., *in comp.* —**trichter**, m. ear-cornet; —**weite**, f. reach of the ear or hearing, ear-shot; —**werkzeuge**, n. pl. instruments to facilitate hearing, acoustic instruments; —**zeuge**, m. *see* Ohrenzeuge.

Ho'sche, (*w.*) f. *T.* large wooden funnel, to let something slide down in.

Hös'chen, (*str.*) n. pl. (*dimin.* of Hose) small breeches.

Ho'se, (*w.*) f. 1) pail; tub, firkin; 2) water-spout; 3) *coll.* H-n, pl. trowsers, breeches, small clothes (Beinkleider); lange H-n, pantaloons; *fig-s.* 4) *a*) lower part of a horse's thigh; *b*) rough feathered leg of poultry; *c*) *Bot-s.* cremocarpium; upper leaf-sheath of some species of grasses; tubular fibre round the roots of the flax-plant; *d*) lower part of a pump-chamber; *e*) *Shoe-m.* piece of leather covering the middle of the sole; *vulg-s.* das Herz ist ihm in die H-n gefallen, his heart (head) has gone down to his heels; sie hat die H-n an, she wears the breeches.

Ho'sen, (*w.*) *v. tr.* to furnish with breeches.

Ho'sen..., *in comp.* —**band**, n. knee-band (of breeches); garter: Ritterorden (Ritter) vom blauen —bande or —bandorden, order (knights) of the Garter; —**bund**, —**gurt**, m. waistband; —**butter**, f. firkin-butter; —**flicker**, m. 1) breeches-mender; 2) *Sport.* wild boar four years old; —**gurt**, —**gürtel**, m. *see* —bund; —**gurtschnalle**, f. waistband-buckle; —**hebe**, f. *see* —träger; —**klappe**, f., —**latz**, m. flap of the breeches; —**knopf**, m. button of the breeches.

Ho'senlos, *adj.* without breeches.

Ho'sen..., *in comp.* —**sack**, m. *see* —tasche; —**schlitz**, m. slit of the breeches; —**schnalle**, f. *see* —gurtschnalle; —**stoff**, m. *see* —zeug; —**tasche**, f. breeches'-pocket; —**träger**, m. pl. braces, suspenders; —**zeug**, m. trowsers'-stuff, trowsering.

Hosian'na, (*str.*, pl. H-s) n. hosanna.

...hosig, *adj.* (*in comp.* having... breeches.

* **Hospital'**, (*str.*, pl. **Hospitä'ler**) n. (*Lat.*) hospital, infirmary; die Hospitäler besuchen,

...(gieß zu, add); ingl. *for* ingleichen, likewise, also; ins. *for* insinuirt, eingehändigt, insinuated; Insp. *for* Inspector, inspector; Int. *for* Interesse, interest; it. *for item (Lat.,* desgleichen, moreover); it. *or* ital. *for* italienisch, Italian.

I, Ie, Ih, *interj. coll.* ay, why! ih seht doch, indeed, only look; — was! why!

I'be, *(w.) f.,* **I-nbaum,** *m. see* Eibe.

Ibe'rer, *(str.) m.* Iberian.

Ibe'risch, *adj.* Iberian, Spanish; die i-e Halbinsel, *Geogr.* the Pyrenean peninsula.

I'bis, *(str.) m. Ornith.* ibis.

I'bisch, *(str.) m. see* Eibisch.

[illegible], *(w.) f. Zool.* female of the ibex.

Ich, I. *pron.* I; ich selbst! I myself, my own self; II. *s. (str., pl.* Ichs & Ich'e) *n.* 1) *Philos.* the I or ego, *incorr.* the me; 2) *fig.* self: mein anderes *or* zweites —, my other self; sein liebes —, his own dear self; sein eigenes — suchen, to be selfish; die Menschen sind von ihrem Ich besessen, people are wrapt up in themselves; unser —, our internal selves *(Oxenford).*

Ich'en, Ich'eln, *(w.) v. intr. mod.* to be selfish; always to speak *or* think of self, to egotise.

Ich'heit, *(w.) f. Philos.* I, the quality of being an I *or* ego, egoity; self; selfishness.

Ich'ler, Ich'ling, *(str.) m.* egotist.

* **Ichneu'mon,** *(str., pl.* I-s) *m. & n. (Gr.)* ichneumon: 1) *Zool. Herpestes ichneumon* L.; 2) *Entom. Ichneumon castigator* F.

* **Ichnographie',** *(w.) f. (Gr.)* ichnography. — **Ichnogra'phisch,** *adj.* ichnographical.

Ich'[illegible], *(str.) n. Archit.* corner-nook, nook.

Ich'sprecherei', *(w.) f.* egotism.

Ich'sucht, *(w.) f.* egotism.

Ich'süchtig, *adj.* selfish, egotistical.

Ich'thum, *(str.) n. see* Ichheit.

* **Ich'thyo...,** *in comp. (Gr.)* **—graphie',** *(w.) f.* ichthyography; **—lith',** *(w. & str.) m. Petr.* ichthyolite; **—log',** *(w.) m.* ichthyologist; **—logie',** *(w.) f.* ichthyology; **—lo'gisch,** *adj.* ichthyological; **—phag',** *(w.) m.* ichthyophagist.

Ick'(e)lei, *(str.) m. Ichth.* ablet, ablen (Uklei).

I'da, *f.* Ida, Ied *(P. N.).*

* **Ideal',** I. *or* **I-isch,** *adj.* ideal; imaginary; II. *s. (str.) n. (L. Lat.)* ideal; pattern. — **Idealisi'ren,** *(w.) v. tr.* to idealise. — **Idealis'mus,** *(sing. not decl., pl. (w.)* I-is'men) *m. Philos.* idealism. — **Idealist',** *(w.) m.* idealist.

Idee', *(w., pl.* Ide'en) *f. (Gr.)* idea, notion, thought, conception; image; nach meiner —, in my idea; ich kann mir davon keine rechte (nicht die geringste) — machen, I cannot form anything like an (I cannot form the slightest) idea of it; ohne die geringste — von einem Beweis, without one jot (tittle) of argument; nicht die geringste — von einem Wagen rc., *fig.* not the (slightest) ghost (sb. not a ghost) of a carriage; &c.; **I-nkreis,** *m.* sphere *or* circle of ideas; **I-nlehre,** *f.* ideology; **I-ntausch,** *m.* exchange of ideas; **I-nverbindung,** *f. Philos.* association of ideas; **I-nwelt,** *f.* ideal world. — **Ideell',** *adj.* ideal; imaginary.

* **I'den,** *pl. see* Idus.

* **Identifici'ren,** *(w.) v. tr. (Lat.)* to identify. — **Iden'tisch,** *adj.* identical, selfsame. — **Identität',** *(w.) f.* identity, sameness.

* **Idio-elec'trisch,** *adj. (Gr.)* idio-electric, electric *per se.*

* **Idiogy'nisch,** *adj. (Gr.) Bot.* having two separate sexes.

* **Idiom',** *(str.) n. (Gr.)* idiom. — **Idioma'tisch,** *adj.* idiomatical.

* **Idiopathie',** *(w.) f. (Gr.)* idiopathy.

* **Idiosynkrasie',** *(w.) f. (Gr.)* idiosyncrasy.

* **Idiot',** *(w.) m. (Gr.)* idiot. — **Idiotis'mus,** *(sing. undecl., pl. (w.)* I-is'men) *m.* idiotism.

* **Idokras',** *(str.) m. Miner.* idocrase.

* **Idol',** *(str.) n. (Lat.)* idol. — **Idolatrie',** *(w.) f.* idolatry.

* **I'dus, I'den,** *pl. (Lat.) Chron.* ides.

* **Idyl'le,** *(w.) f. (Gr.)* idyl; **I-ndichter,** *m.* pastoral poet.

* **Idyl'lisch,** *adj.* idyllic; pastoral.

I'gel, *(str.) m.* 1) *Zool.* hedgehog, urchin *(Erinaceus europaeus* L.); 2) *Agr.* drill-harrow; 3) *T.* *a)* porcupine; *b)* urchin; *c) see* Stirnrad; 4) *Cook.* a certain baked dish; *in comp.* **—artig,** *adj.* urchinlike; prickly; echinate; **—fisch,** *m. Ichth.* hedgehog fish, globefish *(Diodon hystrix* L.); **—käfer,** *m. Entom.* prickly beetle *(Hispa* L.); *Bot.-s.* **—klee,** *m.* hedgehog medic *(Medicago intertexta* L.); **—klette,** *f.* prickly parsnip; **—kolbe,** *f.* burr-reed (Igelskolbe); **—kraut,** *n. see* Eselsgurke; **—schnecke,** *f.* sea-urchin, *see* Seeigel; **I-shuf,** *m. Vet.* crown scab; **I-skolbe, I-ssalbe,** *f.,* **I-skopf,** *m. Bot.* bur-reed, reed-grass *(Sparganium* L.); **—stein,** *m. Petr.* echinite; **—weizen,** *m. Bot.* bearded wheat.

Igna'tius, Ig'naz, *m.* Ignatius *(P. N.); Bot.-s.* **—baum,** *m.* St. Ignatius-bean tree *(Strychnos Ignatii);* **—bohne,** *f.* St. Ignatius-bean.

* **Ignorant',** *(w.) m. (Lat.)* ignorant person, *coll.* ignoramus. — **Ignori'ren,** *(w.) v. tr.* to ignore; to take no notice of.

Ihm, *pron. (Dat. sing. of* er & es, *m. & n.)* to him, to it.

Ihn, *pron. (Acc. sing. of* er, *m.)* him.

Ih'nen, *pron. Dat. pl. of* sie, 1) to them; 2) *(in addressing a person)* to you; das gehört —, that belongs to them *or* to you.

Ihr, I. *pron. pers.* 1) *second p. pl.* you, ye; 2) *Dat. sing. of* sie, *f.* to her; II. *pron. possess.* 1) her; hers; 2) *pl.* their; theirs; 3) *(in addressing a person)* your.

Ih'rer, *pron.* I. 1) *Gen. sing. of* sie, of her; 2) *Gen. pl. of* sie: *a)* of them; *b) (in addressing)* of you; erbarmet euch —, take pity on her *or* on them; — sind viele, there are a great many of them; es waren — zu viele für uns, they were too many for us; II. *Gen. & Dat. sing. & Gen. pl. f. of the possess.* ihr, of *or* to her; of their; **—seits,** *adv.* in their turn.

Ih'rethalben, Ih'retwegen, Ih'retwillen, *adv.* for her, their *or* your sake, on her, their *or* your account.

Ih'rige (der, die, das), *pron. possess.* hers; theirs; yours; sie fordert das —, she demands what is hers; Ihre Freunde und die I-n, your friends and theirs; thun Sie nur das —, only do what you can; wenn Sie dabei das — gethan hätten, if you had done your part in it; ich bin der —, die —, I am yours; die I-n leben noch, your friends (family *or* relations) are alive *or* still living; das werthe —, *Comm.* your letter *or* favour, yours.

Ih'ro, *obsolescent (for* Ihrer) *pron.* your, his, her; — Gnaden, your (his) lordship, your (her) ladyship; — Majestät, his *or* her majesty.

Ih'rzen, *(w.) v. tr. coll.* to address with the pronoun Ihr, you, ye.

I'laub, *(str.) n. provinc. Bot.* ivy.

I'len, *(w.) v. tr. T.* to chip *or* scrape off the grosser parts of (horn, ivory, &c.).

I'ler, *(str.) m. T.* scraping-iron, scraper; **—stock,** *m.* polishing-tool of comb-makers.

* **Ilia'de,** *(w.) f. (Gr.)* Iliad.

Ilk, Il'ling, *(str.) m. provinc. for* Iltis.

* **Illa'ta,** *n. pl. (Lat.) see* das Eingebrachte.

* **Illegal',** *adj. (L. Lat.)* illegal. — **Illegalität',** *(w.) f.* illegality.

* **Illiberal',** *adj. (Lat.)* illiberal. — **Illiberalität',** *(w.) f.* illiberality.

* **Illimitirt',** *adj. (L. Lat.)* unlimited.

* **Illiquid',** *adj. (L. Lat.)* unsettled (as claims).

* **Illuminat',** *(w.) m. (Lat.) Hist.* illuminate, one of the illuminati. — **Illumination',** *(w.) f.* illumination; **I-slampe,** *f.* illuminating lamp.

* **Illumini'ren,** *(w.) v. tr. (Lat.)* 1) to illuminate; 2) to colour, illuminate; *Herald.* to blazon; 3) *fig.* to enlighten. — **Illumini'rer,** *(str.) m.* illuminator.

* **Illusion',** *(w.) f. (Lat.)* illusion.

* **Illustration',** *(w.) f. (Lat.)* illustration. — **Illustri'ren,** *(w.) v. tr.* to illustrate; **illustrirt',** *p. a.* illustrated (Zeitung, news).

Illy'rien, *n. Geogr.* Illyria. — **Illy'rier,** *(str.) m.,* **Illy'risch,** *adj.* Illyrian.

Il'me, *f. provinc.* elm (Ulme).

Il'se, *(w.) f.* 1) *or* El'se *(abbr. from* Elisabeth, Elsbeth rc.), Lizzy, Alice, Alce *(P. N.);* 2) *Ichth.* shad *(Alosa* Cuv.).

Il'tis, *(str., Gen.* des Il'tisses *or* Il'tis, *pl.* Il'tisse) *m. & n. Zool.* fitchet, polecat *(Mustela putorius* L.); der gestreifte —, skunk (Stinkthier); der nordamericanische —, minx; **—falle,** *f.* trap for catching fitchets; **—felle,** *n. pl. Comm.* fitchets; **—pinsel,** *m.* fitch-pencil.

Im, *contr. from* in dem, *see* In.

Imaginär', *adj. (Fr.)* imaginary; i-es Capital, floating capital; i-e Rechnung, *proforma-*account. — **Imagination',** *(w.) f. (Lat.)* imagination.

Im'ber, *(str.) m.* 1) *see* Ingwer; 2) *Ornith.* northern diver (Eistaucher).

Im'biß, *(str.) m.* breakfast; small meal, repast.

* **Imitation',** *(w.) f. (Lat.)* imitation (Nachahmung).

Imiti'ren, *(w.) v. tr.* to imitate (Nachahmen).

Im'ker, *(str.) m. provinc.* bee-master (Bienenzüchter). — **Imkerei',** *(w.) f.* keeping of bees (Bienenzucht).

* **Immanent',** *adj. (Lat.)* immanent, inherent.

Imma'nuel, *m. see* Emanuel.

* **Immarini'ren,** *(w.) v. tr. (Fr.)* to pickle.

† **Imma'ßen,** *conj.* 1) so as, according; 2) because, seeing that.

* **Immaterialität',** *(w.) f. (L. Lat.)* immateriality. — **Immateriell',** *adj.* immaterial.

* **Immatriculation',** *(w.) f. Ac.* (im)matriculation.

* **Immatriculi'ren,** *(w.) v. tr. (L. Lat.)* to matriculate, enrol, enter.

Im'me, *(w.) f. (provinc. & P.)**, bee (Biene).

* **Immediat',** *adj. (L. Lat.)* immediate; **—eingabe,** *f.* petition, memorial presented to the sovereign.

Im'mer, *(str.) m.* 1) *Bot. see* Emmer; 2) *Ornith. see* Imber, 2.

Im'mer, *adv.* 1) always, ever; 2) still, yet, nevertheless; 3) *see* **—hin,** 2; auf, für —, for ever, for good (and all); in perpetuity; noch —, — noch, still; er kommt — noch nicht, he is long in coming; — und ewig, for ever and ever, eternally; — mehr, more and more, increasingly; — besser werden, to grow better and better, to go on from good to better; die Menge wurde — größer, the crowd continued to increase; sie gingen — weiter, they kept walking on; er ist schlecht gewesen und ist es — noch, he was bad and continues to be so; — weiter! — fort! nur — zu! further! (go *or* move) on! — und — wieder, again and again, over and over again; ich sagte ihm — wieder, I ever kept telling him; ich habe — wieder gesagt, I have all along said; so reich er auch — sein mag, however rich he may be, let him be ever (never) so rich; *cf.* Auch.

Im'mer..., *in comp.* **—dar,** *adv.* always, ever; **—fort,** *adv.* always, continually; constantly, evermore; for ever and ever; Truppen langten —fort an, troops continued to arrive (kept arriving); **—grün,** *Bot. adj.* evergreen, indeciduous; —grüne Eiche, evergreen oak (Steineiche); *s. (str.) n.* 1) evergreen; 2) ivy (Epheu); 3) periwinkle *(Vinca minor* L.); 4) house-leek (Hauslauch); **—hin,** *adv.* 1) always, constantly; 2) *(expressing consent, no objection)* no matter, never mind; neverthe-

[illegible] *Typ.* register; 5) any directing point or [illegible].

Indian', *(str.)* m. *see* Truthahn.

Indianer, In'dier, *(str.)* m. Indian.

Indianerin, In'dierin, *(w.)* f. Indian woman; *Am.* squaw.

Indianisch, *adj.* Indian: *Bot.-s.* i-e Bohne, [illegible] of the cassia fistula; i-e Feige, Indian fig (*Opuntia ficus indica*); i-e Giftwurzel, Virginian snake-root (*Aristolochia serpentaria* L.); i-e Hyacinthe, tuberose (*Polianthes tuberosa* L.); i-e Hirse, i-es Honiggras, reed-millet (*Sorghum vulgare* L.); i-es Holz, 1. box-wood, [illegible]-wood; 2. *Comm.* Indian dye woods; [illegible]-s. i-e Ente, musk-duck (*Anas moschata* L.); i-es Huhn, *see* Truthahn; i-er Hirsch, [illegible] Indian or axis deer (*Cervus axis* Erxl.); [illegible] Balsam, Peruvian balsam; i-es Brot, cassava bread; i-es Roth, Indian red.

* **Indicativ'**, *(str.)* m. *(Lat.) Gramm.* indicative. [m. *Anat.*, &c. indicator.

* **Indica'tor**, *(str., pl. (w.)* Indicato'ren)

* **Indi'cien**, *pl.* *(Lat., sing.* Indi'cium) [illegible], discriminating marks, *(Lat.) indicia*; -beweis, m. circumstantial proof.

* **Indici'ren**, *(w.)* v. tr. to indicate (also *Med.* = Anzeigen, to point to ... as the proper remedy). [Indies.

In'dien, n. *Geogr.* India; beide —, both the

Indiennes', *pl. Comm.* printed calicoes.

In'dig, In'digo, *(str., pl.* I-s) m. *Comm.* indigo; americanischer Flores—, floral, flores; — von feinem (geschlossenem) Teige, indigo of a fine (close, compact) paste; bröckliger, [illegible], magerer —, crumbling, dull, weak indigo; nicht grauer —, indigo without gray [illegible]; *in comp.* **—bau**, m. culture of indigo; **—bereitung**, f. manufacture of indigo; **—blau**, *adj.* indigo-blue; **—ernte**, f. indigo-crop; **—farbstoff**, m. *Chem.* indigotine; **—haut**, f. indigo-coat; **—küpe**, f. *Dy.* indigo-bath; blue-vat; **—pflanze**, f. *Bot.* indigo, anil, *pl.* indigo-bearing plants, indigofera (*Indigofera tinctoria* L.); *Chem.-s.* **—purpur**, m. phenicine; **—säure**, f. indigotic acid; **—stoff**, m., **Indigotin'**, *(str.)* n. indigogen, indigotine; **—würfel**, m. *pl.* squares of indigo.

* **Indigenat'**, *(str.)* n. *(Lat.)* (I-srecht, n.) rights and privileges of a native, naturalisation.

* **Indigni'ren**, *(w.)* v. tr. to make indignant; indignirt, *p. a.* indignant (über *(with Acc.)*, at, about). [directly.

* **Indirect'**, *adj.* *(Lat.)* indirect; *adv.* in-

* **Indiscret'**, *adj.* indiscreet.

In'disch, *adj.* Indian; i-e Compagnie, East-India-Company; *Comm.* i-e [illegible], corahs: bandannoes; i-e Zeuge, [illegible]; *cf.* Indianisch.

* **Indisponi'bel**, *adj. see* 1) Unverfügbar; 2) Unveräusserlich.

* **Indisponi'ren**, *(w.)* v. tr. to indispose.

* **Individualisi'ren**, *(w.)* v. tr. *(Lat.)* to individuate, individualise. — **Individualisi'rung**, *(w.)* f. individualisation (*Coleridge*, &c.). — **Individualität'**, *(w.)* f individuality.

* **Individuell'**, *adj.* *(L. Lat.)* individual; *adv.* individually.

* **Indivi'duum**, *(str., pl. (w.)* Individu'en) n. *(Lat.)* individual; head.

Indogerma'nisch, *adj.* Indo-Germanic.

* **Indolent'**, *adj.* *(Lat.)* indolent. — **Indolenz'**, *(w.)* f. indolence.

* **Indossa'bel**, *adj. see* Indossirbar.

* **Indossat'**, *(w.)* m. *Comm.* endorsee. — **Indossatär'**, *(str.)* m. indorsee.

* **Indossament'**, *(str., pl.* I-e), *(Ital.)* **Indossement'**, *(str.)* n., **Indossi'rung**, *(w.)* f. *Comm.* endorsement; ein eigentliches (vollständiges) —, full (special) indorsement, indorsement in full; ein uneigentliches —, indorsement under limitation; — ohne Gewährleistung, qualified endorsement. — **Indossent'**, **Indossant'**, *(w.)* m. endorser. — **Indossir'bar**, *adj. Comm.* endorsable. — **Indossi'ren**, *(w.)* v. tr. *Comm.* to endorse.

* **Induction'**, *(w.)* f. *(Lat.) Phys., Philos.*, &c. induction; I-selectricität, f. inductive electricity.

* **Indulgenz'**, *(w.)* f. *(Lat.) Rom. Cath.* indulgence. — **Indulgi'ren**, *(w.)* v. *intr.* (Einem) to indulge (Willfahren, Nachgeben).

* **Indult'**, *(str.)* m. *(L. Lat.)* 1) *Law.* indult, indulto; letter of respite; 2) *Rom. Cath.* indulgence; 3) fair (*orig.* at places where indulgence was granted, and where, in consequence, many people gathered).

* **Industrie'**, *(w.)* f. *(Fr.)* manufacturing industry, manufactures; *in comp.* **—actien**, f. *pl. Comm.* private shares; shares in manufacturing-associations; **—ausstellung**, f. exhibition of (products of) industry (Gewerbe-Ausstellung); **—gesellschaft**, f. manufacturing association; **—papiere**, n. *pl. Comm. slang*, fancy-stocks; **—presse**, f. *Print. see* Schnellpresse; **—ritter**, m. *cant.* industrial; **—schule**, f. *see* Gewerbschule; **—treibende Staaten**, manufacturing states; **—verein**, m. *see* —gesellschaft; **—zweig**, m. branch of industry. — **Industriös'**, *adj.* industrious.

Ineinan'der, *adv.* into one another; *in comp.* **—flechten**, to interlace; **—fließen**, to flow one into another; **—fließend**, *p. a. Bot.* confluent; **—greifen**, to grasp or work one into the other; to cooperate; *cf.* Eingreifen.

* **Infam'**, *adj.* *(Lat.)* infamous. — **Infamie'**, *(w.)* f. infamy. — **Infami'ren**, *(w.)* v. tr. *(Lat.)* to render infamous, to disgrace.

* **Infant'**, *(w.)* m. *(Span.)* (Spain and Portugal) infant, infante, prince royal.

* **Infanterie'**, *(w.)* f. *(Fr.)* infantry, foot-soldiery; **—officier**, m. infantry officer, officer of foot; **—regiment**, n. regiment of infantry; **—wache**, f. (im Lager) quarter guard. — **Infanterist'**, *(w.)* m. foot-soldier, foot-man.

* **Infan'tin**, *(w.)* f. (Spain and Portugal) infanta, princess royal.

* **Infantilisi'ren**, *(w.)* v. tr. (*Göthe, unusual*) to adapt to the mental capacities of an infant or child.

* **In'fel**, *(w.)* f. *see* Inful.

* **Infici'ren**, *(w.)* v. tr. *(Lat.)* to infect.

* **Infinitesimal'rechnung**, *(w.)* f. *(L. Lat.-Germ.) Math.* differential, infinitesimal or fluxional method (*or* calculus). [finitive.

* **Infinitiv'**, *(str.)* m. *(Lat.) Gramm.* in-

* **Inflecti'ren**, *(w.)* v. tr. *(Lat.) Gramm.*, &c. 1) to inflect; 2) to lengthen the pronunciation of (a vowel).

* **Influi'ren**, *(w.)* v. *intr.* *(Lat.)* (*with* auf (*& Acc.*)) to exert influence (on), to influence, *cf.* Einfluß. [nion (Gutachten).

* **Informat'**, *(str.)* n. *(L. Lat.)* legal opi-

* **Information'**, *(w.)* f. 1) information; 2) *Law*, *a)* legal investigation; *b)* report, testimony. [ren) m. tutor (Hauslehrer).

* **Informa'tor**, *(str., pl. (w.)* Informato'-

In'frau, *(w.)* f. *see* Inmann.

* **In'ful**, *(w.)* f. *(Lat.) Eccl.* mitre.

* **Infulirt'**, *adj.* *(L. Lat.)* mitred (Abt, abbot).

* **Infusion'**, *(w.)* f. *(Lat.)* infusion; I-sthierchen, n. infusory animal; *pl.* or Infuso'rien, infusoria; Infuso'rienerde, f. infusorial earth.

Ing'ber, *(str.)* m. *see* Ingwer.

In'gebäude, *(str.)* n. 1) building within a wall or fortification; 2) the interior of a building. [2) springs of a watch.

Ingefie'der, *(str.)* n. 1) feathers of a bed;

Ingeheim', *adv. see* Insgeheim.

[illegible], m. ingrown (*P. N.*).

* **Ingenieur'** [*pr.* inschénjör'], *(str., pl.* I-e, *or* I-s) m. *(Fr.)* engineer; **—corps**, n. *Mil.* body or corps of (military) engineers; **—kunst**, f. engineering; **—verein**, m. association of engineers.

Ing'ermanland, n. *Geogr.* Ingria. [over.

Ingleichen, *conj.* as also, likewise; more-

* **Ingrediens'**, *(irr.)* f. *(Lat.)* ingredient.

In'grimm, *(str.)* m. violent anger, virulence, (inward) rage, resentment, spite.

In'grimmig, *adj.* angry, furious.

* **Ingrossi'ren**, *(w.)* v. tr. *Law*, to enter upon the mortgage register. [mergrün, 2).

In'grün, *(str.)* n. *Bot.* periwinkle (Im-

In'guß, *(str.)* m. *T.* ingot-mould.

In'gut, *(str., pl.* In'güter) n. household furniture.

Ing'wer, *(str.)* m. *Bot.* ginger (*Zingiber officinale* L.); gelber —, turmeric (*Curcuma longa* L.); ganzer —, whole (race) ginger; deutscher —, cuckoo-pint; **—kraut**, n. *Bot.* poor man's pepper (*Lepidium latifolium* L.); **—wurzel** (*coll.* **—klaue**), f. race (of) ginger.

In'haben, *(irr.)* v. tr. (*l. u.*) *see* Innehaben.

In'haber, *(str.)* m. possessor; holder, bearer (of a bill of exchange); commander (of a regiment); occupant; proprietor (of a firm or commercial house); — einer Pfründe, incumbent; — eines Amtes, holder, incumbent; — eines Patents, patentee; — einer Waare, holder, seller; der — dieses, the bearer (owner, holder) of this; auf (an) den — (lautend), to (the) bearer, holder; **—papiere**, *pl. see porteur* papers. [a port, inner harbour.

In'hafen, *(str., pl.* In'häfen) m. basin of

Inhaftat', *(w.)* m. one brought into custody, *see* Verhaften, Verhaftung &c.

Inhafti'ren, *(w.)* v. tr. (*hybrid word*) to imprison, to bring into custody. — **Inhafti'rung**, *(w.)* f. imprisonment.

In'halt, *(str.)* m. contents; tenor, purport (of a letter); substance, sense, meaning; area; capacity (of a cask, &c.); *Log.* comprehension, intension, depth (of a notion); die Abmachung ihrem ganzen — nach, the arrangement in all its details; der übrige — Ihres Briefes, the remainder of your letter; nebst — (auf Frachtbriefen), with enclosure; zum I-e haben, to purport; des I-es, purporting, importing, to the effect (that, &c.), to that effect.

In'haltlich, *adj.* (*& adv.*) concerning the contents (of a document, &c.).

In'haltleer, In'haltlos, *adj.* of no or trifling contents, empty. [full of meaning.

In'haltreich, *adj.* significant; suggestive;

In'halts..., *in comp.* **—angabe**, f. 1) statement of contents; 2) *or* **—anzeige**, f. *see* —verzeichniß.

In'haltschwer, *adj.* momentous.

In'halts..., *in comp.* **—maße**, n. *pl.* cubic measures, measures of capacity; **—theile**, m. *pl.* data; **—verzeichniß**, n. table of contents, index, summary.

In'haltvoll, *adj. see* Inhaltreich.

* **Inhärent'**, *adj.* *(Lat.)* inherent. — **Inhärenz'**, *(w.)* f. inherence, inherency; *Law*, perseverance. — **Inhäri'ren**, *(w.)* v. *intr.* (*with Dat.*) to inhere, to be inherent (in); *Law*, to persevere in, insist upon.

* **Inhibi'ren**, *(w.)* v. tr. *(Lat.) Law*, to stop or stay proceedings (at law), to inhibit; i-d, *p. a.* inhibitory. — **Inhibition'**, *(w.)* f. *Law*, inhibition, supersedeas. — **Inhibito'rium**, *(str., pl. (w.)* Inhibito'rien, *Lat.* Inhibito'ria) n. *(Lat.) Law*, inhibition.

In'hölzer, *(str.)* n. *pl. Mar.* ribs of a ship, timbers.

* **Inhuman'**, *adj.* *(Lat.)* inhuman, barbarous; rude, coarse. — **Inhumanität'**, *(w.)* f. inhumanity; rudeness. [m. initial letter.

* **Initial'**, *adj.* *(Lat.)* initial; **—buchstabe**,

* **Initia'le**, *(w.)* f. *Typ.* initial.

* **Initiati've**, *(w.)* f. *(L. Lat.)* initiative; die — ergreifen, to take the initiative or lead.

Jahr'..., *in comp.* (*cf.* Jahres...) —arbeit, *f.* work by the year; —arbeiter, *m.* workman paid by the year; —begängniß, *n.* anniversary; —buch, *n.* year book, *gener. pl.* —bücher, annals, chronicle, annual register *or* journal; das nautische —buch, the nautical almanac.

Jah'ren, Jäh'ren, (*w.*) *v. rfl.* (*impers.*) to be a year; heute jährt es sich, daß ..., it is this day a twelvemonth since ....

Jah'res..., Jahrs'..., *in comp.* —bericht, *m.* annual report (of a learned society, &c.); —einkommen, *n.*, —einkünfte, *f. pl.* annual income, annual rents; —feier, *f.*, —fest, *n.* anniversary; nach —folge, in chronological order; —frist, *f.* space of twelve months; in (innerhalb) —frist, in (within) the compass of a year; —lohn, *m.* annual wages; —rechnung, *f.* 1) annual account, annual bill; 2) era (Zeitrechnung); —rente, *f.* annuity, *see* —einkommen; —schluß, *m.* close of the year; —tag, *m.* anniversary(-day); —versammlung, *f.* annual meeting; —viertel, *n.* quarter of a year; —vierteltag, *m.* quarter-day; —wechsel, *m.* turn, renewing of the year, new year; —wuchs, *m.* crop; —zahl, *f.* date, year; er geht mit der —zahl, *coll.* he is of the same age with the century; —zeit, *f.* season; —zinsen, *pl.* annual interest.

Jahr'..., *in comp.* (*cf.* Jahres...) —feier, *f.* anniversary; —feld, *n. Agr.* field that is ploughed and sowed every year; —fest, *n. see* —feier; —fünft, *n.* space of five years, lustrum; —funfzig, *n.* space of fifty years; —gang, *m.* 1) annual course; 2) vintage, year's growth (of wine); 3) annual set of any publication, writing *or* lectures; —gebung, *f. Law,* the pronouncing a person of age; —gehalt, *m.* annual stipend, salary; —geld, *n.* pension, yearly allowance, annuity; —gericht, *n.* annual assizes; —gewächs, *n.* year's growth; —hun'dert, *n.* century, age.

Jäh'rig, *adj.* 1) a year old; of a year; lasting a year; 2) a year ago; 3) *see* Jährlich; es ist nun —, it is now a year.

Jäh'rigen, (*w.*) *v.* I. *intr.* (*h. u.*) to attain the age of a year; [dem Wurm] der Mensch heißt, | jähriget, blühet, verblüht und abfällt (*Klopstock*), [the worm called man who] waxeth and bloometh, then, drooping, dieth (*Bunsen*); II. *rfl. see* Jahren.

Jahr'knecht, (*str.*) *m. see* Jahrarbeiter.

Jähr'lich, I. *adj.* yearly, annual; ein j-es Einkommen, *see* Jahreseinkommen; er hat ein j-es Einkommen von 5000 Pfund, he has (is worth) 5000 pound a year; II. *adv.* yearly, annually, every year, a year, per annum.

Jähr'ling, (*str.*) *m.* yearling.

Jahr'..., *in comp.* (*cf.* Jahres...) —lohn, *m.* annual wages; —markt, *m.* 1) fair (*gener.* in small towns); 2) *or* —marktsgeschenk, *n.* fairing; —pacht, *f.* tenure from year to year; —ringe, *m. pl. see* —schuß, 2; —schuß, *m.* 1) *F.* growth of a year; *Bot.* shoots, sprigs, tendrils; 2) *Forest.* annual rings of a tree; —tau'send, *n.* millenium, millenary; —uhr, *f.* clock which is only wound up once in a year; —verbrauch, *m.* annual consumption; —vogel, *m. Ornith.* African hornbill (*Buceros erythrorhynchus*); —weise, *adv.* yearly, annually; —woche, *f. Script.* prophetic week (consisting of seven years); —wuchs, *m.* year's growth; —zahl, *f. see* Jahreszahl; —zehend, *n.* space of ten years, decennium; —zeit, *f.* annual time, anniversary, season.

Jäh'zorn, (*str.*) *m.* sudden anger, propensity to anger, choler, violent passion.

Jäh'zornig, *adj.* given to anger, passionate, choleric, irascible.

* **Ja'kal,** (*str.*, *pl.* J-e) *m.* (*Pers.*) jackal, *see* Goldwolf.

Ja'kob, *see* Jacob.

* **Jalap'e, Jalap'pe,** (*w.*) *f.* (*Span.*) *Bot.* jalap (*Ipomoea jalapa L.*); —harz, *n. Pharm.* jalapine, jalappin, resin jalap.

* **Jalon'** [shalong'], (*str.*, *pl.* J-s) *m.* (*Fr.*) 1) *Engin.* picket, stake, *cf.* Absteckpfahl; 2) *Mil.* field colours. — **Jalonneur'** [shalloneur'], (*str.*, *pl.* J-e, *or* J-s) *m.* (*Fr.*) *Mil.* javelin-man (to mark out a direction); —fähnchen, *n. see* Jalon, 2. — **Jalonni'ren,** (*w.*) *v. tr. Engin.* to lay out (grounds) by pickets *or* stakes, to stake out.

* **Jalousie'** [shalusee'], (*w.*) *f.* (*Fr.*) *gener.* Jalousi'en, *pl.* Venetian blinds, jalousies; —taube, *f. see* Nonnentaube.

Jamai'ca, *n. Geogr.* Jamaica; —holz, *n.* Jamaica logwood, brasilette wood; —pfeffer, *m.* allspice.

* **Jam'be,** (*w.*) *m.* (*Gr.*) *Pros.* iambus, iambic. — **Jam'bisch,** *adj.* iambic.

Jam'mer, *s.* I. (*str.*) *m.* 1) lamentation; 2) misery, calamity, wretchedness; 3) pity; compassion; 4) *provinc.* epilepsy; ein Bild des J-s, an exhibition of misery; der Menschheit ganzer — faßt mich an (*Göthe, Faust,* I. last scene), mankind's collected woe o'erwhelms me, here (*Taylor*); es ist — und Schade *or* —schade, it is a sad pity *or* a thousand pities; II. *in comp.* —bild, *m.* woful look, look of misery; —geschrei, *n.* lamentation, lamentable cry; —gesicht, *n.* pitiable, woful, woebegone face *or* countenance; —gestalt, *f.* miserable figure, object of woe; —haus, *n.* house of distress *or* misery; —leben, *n.* miserable *or* wretched life.

Jäm'merlich, I. *adj.* miserable, lamentable, pitiable, deplorable, woful, wretched, sorry; — durchprügeln, to thrash unmercifully; II. J-keit, (*w.*) *f.* pitiableness, wretchedness.

Jäm'merling, (*str.*) *m.* miserable wretch.

Jam'mermann, (*str.*) *m.* (*Schiller, Räuber*) wretched man, man of woe.

Jam'mern, (*w.*) *v.* I. *intr.* to lament, wail, moan, cry; II. *tr.* & *impers.* to grieve; du jammerst mich, I pity you; es jammert mich, I am moved to pity, it grieves me; († &) * *with Gen.:* mich jammert seiner, I pity *or* deplore him.

Jam'mer..., *in comp.* —ruf, *m. see* —geschrei; —thal, *n.* *, valley *or* vale of tears, abode of calamity; —ton, *m.* doleful accent; —voll, *adj.* most lamentable, miserable, *see* Jämmerlich; —welt, *f.* world of woe and misery; —wort, *n.* word of lamentation; —zustand, *m.* lamentable state, piteous condition.

Jan, *m. abbr. for* Johann, John, Jack; —ha'gel, *m.* rabble, riff-raff, mob, tag-rag and bob-tail.

* **Janitschar',** (*w.*) *m.* janisary; J-(en)musik, *f.* janisary music.

Jan'ken, (*str.*) *m. T.* bung of a furnace.

Jan'ken, (*w.*) *v. intr. provinc.* 1) to whine; 2) to pant.

Jan'ker, (*str.*) *m. provinc.* jacket; bodice.

Jän'ner, Janua'r, *m.* January.

Ja'pan, *n. Geogr.* Japan.

Japa'ner, (*str.*) *m.*, **Japane'se,** (*w.*) *m.*, **Japa'nerin, Japane'sin,** (*w.*) *f.* Japanese.

Ja'panholz, (*str.*) *n.* sapan-wood, sapan.

Japanni'ren, (*w.*) *v. tr. T.* to japan.

Japa'nisch, *adj.* Japanese; j-e Erde, Japan earth, catechu; das j-e Porzellan, Japan china; j-e Waaren, japanned goods.

Jap'pen, Jap'sen, (*w.*) *v. intr.* to gasp (Gapsen, Schnappen).

Ja'se, (*w.*) *f. Bot.* milfoil (Schafgarbe).

Jasmin', (*str.*) *m. Bot.* 1) der echte —, jasmine, jessamine (*Jasminum officinale L.*); 2) der gemeine *or* wilde —, common syringa (*Syringa vulgaris L.*); —baum, *m.* (indischer) Indian jessamine-tree (*Plumeria rubra L.*); —dorn, *m. see* Bocksdorn, 1; —öl, *n.* oil of jessamine.

* **Jaspi'ren,** (*w.*) *v. tr. T.* to marble, give the colour of jasper.

Jas'pis, (*str.*, *Gen.* — *or* Jas'pisses, *pl.*

…fater's bench; —docken, f. pl. graving docks; —eisen, n. calking-iron; —hammer, m. calking mallet; —werg, n. oakum.

* Kalfa'tern, (w.) v. tr. (Fr.) Mar. to calk.

Kalfa'terer, (str.) m. calker.

Kalfo'nium, see Colophonium.

* Ka'li, (str.) n. (Arab.) 1) Bot. glass-wort (Salsola kali L.); 2) Chem.-s. potash, potassa, kali; —alaun, n. Chem. sulphate of alumine; —blausaure, f. see Kalium; —blau, n. prussiate of lime; —cyanid, n. cyanide of potassium; —flüssigkeit, —lauge, f. potash-lye, alkaline liquor, liquor potassæ; —hydrat, n. hydrate of potassa; —metall, n. see Kalium.

* Kalin', (str.) n. see Kalium.

* Kalink'e, (w.) f. (Slav.) guelder-rose.

Ka'lipflanze, (w.) f. berry-bearing glasswort, anabasis (Kali, 1).

* Kalifh', Kalif, (w.) m. (Arab.) Calif. — Kalifat', Kalifat, (str.) n. Califate, Caliphship.

Ka'li…, in comp. —salpeter, m. nitrate of potash; —salz, n. nitrate of potash; —schwefelleber, f. sulphuret of potassium; —solution, f. alkaline solution; —strauch, m. see —pflanze; —turmalin, m. Miner. schorl, shorl.

* Ka'lium, n. Chem.-s. potassium, kalium, metallic base of potassa; —jodid, n. iodide of potassium; —jodüret, n. ioduret of potassium; —peroxyd, n. peroxyde of potassium; —wasserstoffgas, n. hydroguret of potassium.

Kalk, (str.) m. Miner. & Chem. lime; Chem. calx; in — verwandeln, v. tr., zu — werden, v. intr. to calcine; zu — brennen, to calcine, to burn to lime; gebrannter —, quick lime; mit — bewerfen, to rough-cast, parget; eine Wand mit — bestreichen, to whitewash or plaster a wall.

Kalk…, in comp. —ablagerungen, f. pl. Geol. calcareous sediments; —alabaster, m. Miner. calcareous alabaster; —anstrich, m. whitewash; —anwurf, m. parget of lime; —arbeit, f. plaster-work; —artig, adj. calcareous, limy, testaceous (medicines &c.); —artigkeit, f. calcareousness; Tann.-s. —äscher, m. lime-pit; —bad, n. lime-pit (of sugar-refiners); —bad, n. water impregnated with lime, lime-water; —bett, n. Mas., &c. lime-basin; —beule, f. Med. chalky swelling; —boden, m. Agr. calcareous or limy soil; —brei, m. lime-paste; —brennen, n., —brand, m. lime-burning; —brenner, m. lime-burner; —brennerei, f. 1) see —brennen; 2) lime-kiln; —bruch, m. limestone-pit; —brühe, f. Tann. 1) lime-water; 2) lime-pit; —bucht, f. lime-pit; —dunst, m. vapours arising from fresh mortar; —drusen, f. pl. Miner. calcareous spar; —düngung, f. Agr. a manuring with lime; —eisenstein, m. Miner. calcareous or lime-ironstone.

Kal'ken, (w.) v. tr. 1) a) Tann. to soak in lime-water, to lime (hides); b) to sprinkle with lime-water, to lime; 2) to mix with lime; 3) to whitewash (Tünchen).

Kalk…, in comp. —erde, f. calcareous earth; —erdig, adj. calcareous; —estrich, m. lime-floor, cf. Estrich; —faß, n. 1) lime-tub; 2) or —fäßchen, n. mortar-trough, hod; —feldspath, m. Miner. Labrador-felspar; —fels, m. calcareous rock; —flies, m. Miner. turmaline, shorl; —förmig, adj. calciform; —fuge, f. seam of mortar; —gebirge, n. calcareous or lime-stone mountains, chalk-hills; —geff, m. Miner. pharmacolite; —grube, f. lime-pit or basin; —guß, m. thin-mortar; —hafen, m. see —trog; —haltig, adj. limy, calciferous; —hütte, f. a shed in which lime is slackened; —hydrat, n. slaked lime, slack-lime. [limy, calcareous.

Kal'kicht, Kal'kig, adj. limelike; chalky.

Kalki'ren, (w.) v. tr. T. to calk, cover (the back of a design) with chalk.

Kalk…, in comp. —kasten, m. T. 1) lime-pit; 2) mortar-tub; —kelle, f. trowel; —kiesel, m. Miner. calcareous silex, siliceous lime; —kraut, n. Bot. gypsophila (Gypsophila L.); —krücke, f. beater; —kübel, m. mortar-tub or pail; —lauge, f. lime-lye; —leber, f. Chem. sulphurate of lime; —licht, n. Chem. lime light, oxycalcium light, Drummond light (light of incandescent lime); —loch, n. see —grube; —malerei, f. fresco-painting; —mehl, n. powder of lime; —mergel, m. Miner. calcareous marl; —metall, n. Miner. calcium; —milch, f. milk of lime; —mörtel, m. Mas. mortar; —mühle, f. lime-mill; —mulde, f. see —faß, 2; —niederschläge, m. pl. see —ablagerungen; —ofen, m. lime-kiln; —öl, n. lime-oil, chloride of lime; —putz, m. Mas. (feiner) fine stuff; (grober) coarse stuff; —rahm, m. cream of lime; —röste, f. layer of wood and lime-stones to be burnt to lime; —salpeter, m. Miner. calcareous nitre; —salz, n. Chem. salt of lime, wall-salt; —sand, m. 1) calcareous sand; 2) sand to be mixed with lime; —schiefer, m. calcareous slate; —schlotten, pl. hollows in calcareous stones; —schwefelleber, f. Chem. trisulphuret of sulphated calcium; Miner.-s. —sinter, m. calc-sinter; —spath, m. calcareous spar, calc-spar, lime-spar; —staub, m. see —mehl; —stein, m. limestone, calcareous stone; —steinbruch, m. limestone quarry; Miner.-s. —talk, m. calcareous talc; —talkspath, m. dolomite; —thonschiefer, m. calcareous clay-slate; —tuff, m. tufaceous lime-stone, calc- or calcareous tuff; —tünche, f. see —milch.

Kalkuhn', (str.) m., Kalkuhne, (w.) f. turkey-cock, turkey-hen (Truthahn, Truthenne).

Kalk…, in comp. —wad, n. Miner. foliated black manganese; —wand, f. plaster-wall; —wasser, n. Pharm. lime-water; —weiße, f. see —milch; —wolle, f. skinner's wool; —wurf, m. rough-cast; —wurm, m. Zool. serpula.

* Kalligraph', (w.) m. (Gr.) calligrapher. — Kalligraphie', (w.) f. calligraphy. — Kalligra'phisch, adj. calligraphic.

Kalm, Mar.-s. (str.) m. & adj. calm.

* Kalmank', (str.) m. (Fr. calmande) Comm. callimanco; doppelter —, double callimanco, lasting. — Kalmank'en, adj. made of callimanco.

Kalmäu'ser, (str.) m. bud. 1) muser: dotard; anchoret; 2) provinc. miser.

Kalmäu'sern, (w.) v. intr. 1) to muse, to be in a brown study; 2) provinc. to live niggardly. [still.

Kal'men, (w.) v. intr. Mar. to be calm,

Kal'mer, (str.) m. see Dintenfisch.

Kalm'te, (w.) f. see Kalm.

Kalmuk', (str.) m. Comm. bear-skin.

Kalmuck', Kalmück'e, (w.) m., K-in, (w.) f. Calmuc, Calmouck, Kalmuck (a people in Central Asia). [Kalmuck.

Kalmuck'isch, Kalmück'isch, adj. Calmuc,

Kal'mus, Ka'lomel &c., see Cal….

Kalt, adj. 1) cold; frigid, chill; 2) fig. cold, cool; unconcerned, insensible, indifferent, reserved: er blieb bei k-em Blute, he kept his temper, coll. he took it coolly; mir ist or wird —, I am or feel cold; — machen, 1. to chill; 2. coll. to murder; — hämmern, T. to cold-beat; — brechen, Min. to dig out the stone without blasting; — pressen, Cloth. to cold-press; k-e Flecken, damp places (in walls); k-e Pisse, coll. see Harnstrenge; k-e Schlacken, Min. stubborn scoria; ein k-er Schweiß, a cold perspiration, a chilly sweat; ein k-er Schlag, a clap of thunder not attended by ignition; das k-e Fieber, ague; die k-e Fährte, Sport. dry-foot; k-e Küche, cold-meat; k-e Hände, warme Liebe, proverb. a cold hand, a warm heart.

Kalt'…, in comp. —beschlagt, —bereitet, adj. T. cold drawn; —beitel, m. see —meißel; —flüssig, adj. T. hard to be rendered fusible, refractory; —blüter, m. amphibious animal; —blütig, I. adj. 1) having cold blood, cold-blooded; 2) fig. cold, quiet, deliberate, cool-headed; ein —blütiger Mensch, a cool hand; II. adv. coldly, in cold blood; —blütigkeit, f. 1) cold-bloodedness; 2) cold blood, calmness, coolness, equanimity; presence of mind, composedness, deliberateness; stoicism; —bruch, m. brittleness when cold (of iron); —brüchig, adj. brittle when cold (of iron); —brüchiges Eisen, cold-short iron.

Käl'te, (w.) f. lit. & fig. cold, coldness, chill, chilliness, frigidity, frigidness; cold weather; —erzeugend, adj. Phys. frigorific; —grad, m. degree of cold.

Kal'ten, (w.) v. intr. (aux. sein) to grow cold (Erkalten). [to ice.

Käl'ten, (w.) v. tr. to chill; mit Eis —,

Kalt'…, in comp. —gierig, adj. Miner. sulphury; —gründig, adj. cold and damp (of soil); —herzig, adj. cold-hearted; indifferent.

Kält'lich, adj. coldish, chilly.

Kält'ling, (str.) m. (l. u.) cold or indifferent person.

Kalt'…, in comp. —meißel, m. T. cold chisel; —nadel, f. T. dry-point, poitrel; —nagel, m. cold-forged nail; —schale, f. a cold beverage or soup made of beer or wine with grated bread, sugar, lemon, &c., or fruit, such as straw-berries, currants, &c.; —schlächter, m. provinc. see Abdecker; —schlagamboß, m. T. anvil on which copper is beaten without fire; —schmidt, m. brazier; —silber, n. mixture of tartar and calcined silver; —sinn, m., —sinnigkeit, f. coldness, frigidity; indifference; —sinnig, adj. cold, frigid, cool, frosty, indifferent; —wassercur, f. cold-water cure; —wasser-heilanstalt, n. cold water cure, hydropathic establishment.

Kal'ven, pl. Mar. see Kalbe, 2.

* Kamasch'en, f. pl. see Gamaschen.

Kameel', s. I. (str.) n. 1) Zool. camel (Camelus L.); 2) "cable," according to an untenable interpretation of Matth. 19, 24; the word camel is often used in Oriental similes, cf. Matth. 23, 24, &c.; 3) Mech. camel (a machine for raising ships); 4) coll. blockhead; II. in comp. —bad, m. see Kiligen; —bremse, f. Entom. a species of dipterous insects (Tabanus maroccanus); —fliege, f. Entom. a species of neuropterous insects (Raphidia ophiopsis L.); —führer, m. see —treiber; —garn, n. mohair- or angora-yarn; —haar, n. camel's hair; —hären, adj. camel-hair (shawl, &c.); —härner Plüsch, Comm. hair-shag; —hals, m. 1) camel's neck; 2) fig. neck resembling that of a camel; —hengst, m. male camel; —heu, —stroh, n. Bot. camel's hay, beard-grass (Andropogon schænanthus L.); —kuh, —stute, (l. u. Kameelin, (w.)) f. female camel; —parder, m. Zool. camelopard, giraffe (Giraffe); —strauß, m. see Strauß; —treiber, —wärter, m. camel-driver; —zeug, n. see Camelot; —ziege, f. Zool. 1) camel goat, Angora goat (Angoraziege); 2) see Lama; —ziegengarn, n. Angora-(mohair-)yarn; —ziegenhaar, n. Angora goat's hair. [Kameelparder.

* Kameloparb', (str. & w.) m. (Gr.) see

Kä'mel…, in comp. see Kameel, II.

* Kamin', s. (Lat.) I. (str.) m. &c. 1) chimney, fireside, fire place; 2) chimney, funnel (-pipe); II. in comp. —aufsatz, m. chimney ornament; —besen, m. hearth-broom; —brett, n. chimney board; —ecke, f. chimney corner; —einfassung, f. mantelet; —feger, m. chimney-sweeper; —fries, m. chimney-frieze; —geld, n. see —steuer; —geräthe, n. pl. chimney utensils; —gesims, n. see —sims; —gestell, n. cats and dogs (kind of frame); —gitter, n. chimney fender; —haken, m. chimney hook;

Klei'ber, *(str.)* m. 1) mud-waller; 2) *Orn.* common nut-hatch *(Sitta europaea* L.).

Klei'berwerk, *(str.)* n. mudwall-work, mud-walling.

Kleid, *(str., pl.* Klei'der) n. 1) garment, garb, coat, gown, habit, raiment; 2) *T.* cover (of various things), *cf.* Bekleidung; K-e, cloth (of a sail); service (of a pump); *fig.* dress, garb, exterior of a thing; K-er machen Leute, *proverb*, fine feathers make fine birds, the tailor makes the man.

Kleid'chen, *(str.)* n. *(dimin. of* Kleid) small frock (of children); *Bot.* indusium.

Klei'den, *(w.)* v. I. *tr.* 1) to dress, clothe, apparel; 2) to provide with clothing; 3) to deck, *see* Bekleiden; 4) to mount; *see intr.*; II. *intr.* (*with Dat. or Acc.*) to sit well, to become, to be suitable; III. *ref.* to dress, clothe one's self; schwarz gekleidet gehen, to go in black.

Klei'der..., *in comp.* —affe, m. *Zool.* douc (*Simia nemaeus*); —besen, m. whisk(-broom); —brett, m. *see* —rechen; —bürste, *f.* clothes-brush; —gestell, n. *see* —rechen; —haken, m. cloak pin; —händler, m. dealer in clothes, clothes-broker; clothes-man, merchant tailor; —handlung, *f.* clothes-shop; clothier's (d. i. shop); —kammer, *f.* wardrobe; —kämmerer, m. master of the wardrobe; —laus, *f.* *Entom.* large louse infesting clothes (*Pediculus vestimenti* N.); —leiste, *f.* *see* —rechen; —leinwand, *f.* linen for lining; —macher, m. tailor, *see* Frauen-kleidermacher; —macherin, *f.* dress-maker; —markt, m. market for (second hand) clothes; —mode, *f.* fashion *or* mode in clothes; —motte, *f.* *Entom.* woollen moth (*Tinea sarcitella* L.); —nagel, m. *see* —haken; —ordnung, *f.* regulation for wearing clothes, sumptuary laws; —pracht, *f.* gorgeousness, sumptuousness of habit, finery in clothes; —rahm, —rechen, m. clothes-rack, clothes-horse; —schabe, *f.* *see* —motte; —schmuck, m. fine clothes; —schrank, m. clothes-press; —tracht, *f.* manner of clothing, costume, dress, fashion; —trödel, m. frippery; —trödler, m. fripperer, slop-seller; —verleiher, m. one that lends (lets) clothes; —verwahrer, m. keeper of the wardrobe; —vogel, m. *Orn.* honey-sucker (*Melithreptus vestiarius*); —vorrath, m. stock of clothes; —zimmer, n. *see* —kammer.

Kleid'keule, *(w.) f.* *Mar.* serving-mallet.

Kleid'lich, Kleid'sam, *adj.* becoming, effective (of dress). [(in dress).

Kleid'samkeit, *(w.) f.* becomingness, effect

Kleid'span, *(str., pl.* K-späne) m. *Mar.* serving-board.

Klei'dung, *(w.) f.* 1) clothing, dressing, clothes; dress; costume, apparel, attire; vesture; *T.* drapery; 2) *Gunn.* plate-work, mounting; Einem — und Kost geben *or* gewähren, to find one in food and clothing *or* raiment; K-sstück, n. article of dress; K-sstücke, *pl.* clothes.

Klei'e, *(w.) f.* bran, pollard.

Klei'en..., *in comp.* —absud, m. bran-tea; —artig, *adj.* branny; —beize, *f.* Tin-plate-manuf. lye; —bier, n. bran-beer; —brot, n. bread made of bran; —flechte, *f.*, —grind, m., —[illegible], *f.*, *Med.* porrigo; —mehl, n. mixture of bran and meal; —stein, m. *Miner.* variety of [illegible]. [furfuraceous.

Klei'icht, *adj.* 1) clayish; 2) branny; 3) *Med.*

Klei'ig, *adj.* 1) branny; 2) clayey.

Klein, I. *adj.* 1) little; small; minute; diminutive; short; 2) *Mus.* minor in regard to intervals: die k-e Quarte, minor *or* lesser fourth; 3) petty; insignificant, trifling; light (error, sin); 4) mean, contemptible; 5) *adv.* in detail, exactly, circumstantially; ich steckte den Ring an meinen k-en Finger, für den er [illegible] zu groß war, I put the ring on my little finger, for which it was much too large; die Folge davon, daß ich den Ring an einen Finger that, der zu — dafür war, the consequence of my putting the ring on a finger that was too little for it; von ihren Töchtern war die älteste etwas —, die zweite war größer, of her daughters the eldest was rather little, the second was taller; ist Fräulein Helene groß oder —? is Miss Helen tall or short? — kriegen *or* bekommen, *coll.* to master; sich — machen, to humble *or* degrade one's self; der k-e Anker, *Mar.* grapnel; k-e Buchstaben, *Typ.* lean-type; der k-e Finger, little *or* ear-finger; k-es Geld, small *or* loose money, change; —(es) Benholz, sticks of round timber *or* lumbers (*Horti.*); k-es Holz, wood chopped small (for lighting a fire); k-e Meile, short mile; k-e Weine, thin wines; k-er Krieg, small war; k-er Puls, *Med.* small *or* feeble pulse; —geblieben, undergrown, stunted; —(er) werden, to grow less, to diminish, &c., *see* Abnehmen, *intr.*

II. s. 1. *(indecl.)* n. — und Groß, children and grown up persons, old and young, every body; von — an *or* auf, from infancy (von Kindesbeinen an); 2. m., *f.* & n. (*decl. like adj.*) der (die) K-e, the little one; die K-en, the little ones; das K-e, small thing, trifle: wer das K-e nicht ehrt, ist des Großen nicht werth, *proverb*, who will not keep a penny, shall never have many: ins K-e, into a small compass, upon a small scale; ins K-e gehen, to enter into the particulars *or* details: ins K-ste gehend, minute (inquire, interference): um ein K-es wär ich verloren, I had a narrow escape; über ein K-es, after a little while; das ist ihm ein K-es, that's a mere trifle (is easy) to him: im K-en, in a small compass; in (by) retail; in detail; in a minute manner; upon a small scale, in little; eine Welt im K-en, miniature-world; der kleinere Bruder, the younger brother; der kleinste Bruder, the youngest brother.

III. *(str.)* n. 1) giblets; head, liver, &c. of a hare, goose, &c.; 2) *T.* broken-up fragments of all kind.

Klein'..., *in comp.* —achtel, n. small octavo; —ährig, *adj.* with small ears (of corn); —apfelbaum, m. *Bot.* three-grained medlar (*Crataegus azarolus*). [menia.

Klein'armenien, n. *Geogr.* the lesser Ar-

Klein'asien, n. *Geogr.* Asia Minor, the lesser Asia.

Klein'..., *in comp.* —äugig, *adj.* small-eyed: —baß, m., —baßgeige, *f.* *Mus.* violoncello; —bauer, m. a small freeholder *or* farmer; —bild, n. *med.* miniature (picture); —binder, m. *see* Weißbinder; —blätterig, *adj.* small leaved; —bodenrad, n. *T.* third wheel of a watch; —bogenform, *f.* small folio; —bohnig, *adj.* small-berried (coffee); —denkend, *adj.* narrow-souled, little-minded; —drucker, m. job-printer.

Klei'ne, *see* Kleinheit.

Klein'..., *in comp.* —eisen, n. *Miner.* small iron (particles); —elephant, m. *Print.* atlas.

Kleinelei', *(w.) f.* *see* Kleinigkeitskrämerei.

Klei'neln, *(w.)* v. *intr.* to indulge in trifles.

Klei'nen, *(w.)* v. *tr.* *Min.* to make *or* beat small. [kleinern.

Klei'nern, *(w.)* v. *tr.* to lessen, *see* Ver-

Klein'..., *in comp.* —fügig, *adj.* *see* Geringfügig; —geist, m., —geisterei, *f.* trifling disposition, mean spirit; small-mindedness; —geistig, *adj.* small-minded; —gemälde, n. *see* —bild; —gemustert, *adj.* small pattern; —gesägt, *adj.* *Bot.* serrulate; —geschlinge, n. *Sport.* bowels of deer and black-game; —gewehrfeuer, n. discharge of musketry; —gewürfelt, *adj.* small-checked; —gläubig, *adj.* of little faith, faint-hearted, disheartened; —gläubigkeit, *f.* little-faith, faint-heartedness; —grubig, *adj.* *Bot.* favoulated; —gut, n. 1) petty wares; 2) commons of too thin a soil; —handel, m. retail-business, retail-trade; —handel treiben, to retail; —händler, m. retailer, retail-dealer, (retail-)shop-keeper; small-dealer.

Klein'heit, *(w.) f.* littleness, smallness, minuteness, &c. *cf.* Klein, *adj.*

Klein'..., *in comp.* —herzig, *adj.* faint-hearted; narrow-minded; —herzigkeit, *f.* faint-heartedness; narrow-mindedness; —höckerig, *adj.* *Bot.* tuberculated; —hundert, n. *Comm.* a (round) hundred (*opp.* Großhundert).

Klein'igkeit, *(w.) f.* trifle; small *or* minor matter, light *or* trifling matter; große —, mere trifle; über jede — lachen, to laugh at a feather; K-en, *pl.* toys, small trinkets.

Klei'nigkeits..., *in comp.* —geist, m. mind *or* disposition for trifles; —häscher, —jäger, —krämer, m. pedant, piddler; er ist ein —krämer, he stumbles at a straw; —krämerei, *f.* the practice of indulging in *or* giving one's mind to trifles; pedantry; —sinn, m. *see* —geist.

Klein'..., *in comp.* —jährig, *adj.* stunted (of wood); —kinderbewahranstalt, —kinderschule, *f.* asylum, school for little children, public nursery, infant-school; —knecht, m. *see* Unterknecht; —körnig, *adj.* small-grained; —kohle, *f.* small-coal; pit-coal; —laut, *adj. coll.* dejected, disheartened; quiet; —laut werden, to lose courage, to draw in.

Klein'ler, *(str.)* m. mean, paltry fellow.

Klein'lich, I. *adj.* mean, petty, paltry, base; II. K-keit, *(w.) f.* (moral) littleness; meanness, paltriness, narrow-mindedness, pettiness.

Klein'ling, *(str.)* m. 1) *see* Kleinler; 2) *Bot.* bastard pimpernel (*Centunculus minimus* L.).

Klein'..., *in comp.* —maler, m. miniature-painter; —malerei, *f.* art of painting in miniature; —meister, m. (*Fr.*) *petit-maître*, fop, coxcomb; *Paint.* neat master; —meisterei, *f.* coxcombry, &c. *cf.* —meister; —meistern, v. *intr.* *see* Kritteln; —messer, m. *T.* micrometer; —muth, m., —müthigkeit, *f.* pusillanimity, faint-heartedness, despondency, *Theol.* desertion; —müthig, *adj.* pusillanimous, faint-hearted, low-spirited, discouraged, desponding; der —müthige, desponder; die —müthigen, *pl. Bibl.* the feeble-minded; —octav, n. small octavo.

Klein'od, *(str.)* n. 1) jewel, treasure, ornament; 2) (*pl.* Kleino'dien) emblem of royalty; 3) *Herald.* ornament (belonging to the helmet, &c.): K-kästchen, n. casket.

Klein'..., *in comp.* —putzmacherin, *f.* trimming-maker; —quart, n. *Print.* small quarto.

Klein'russe, *(w.)* m. inhabitant of Russia Minor. — **Klein'rußland,** n. *Geogr.* Russia Minor.

Klein'..., *in comp.* —schlächter, m. retail butcher; —schmidt, m. *see* Schlosser (*opp.* Grobschmidt); —schmiedearbeit, *f.* *see* Schlosserarbeit; —schuppig, *adj.* *Bot.* rosulate; —silber, n. *T.* silver-leaf; —sinn, m. narrow-mindedness; —sinnig, *adj.* narrow-minded; —staat, m. minor state (of a confederation, &c.); —stachelig, *adj.* *Bot.* aculeate; —städter, m., —städterin, *f.* inhabitant of a small town; —städterei, *f.* provincial manners, way of acting, &c.; —städtisch, *adj.* like the inhabitants of small (provincial) towns, provincial, countrified; —süchtig, *adj.* *see* Kleinlich; —tausend, n. *Comm.* a (round) thousand (*opp.* Großtausend); —verkauf, m. *see* —handel; —verkaufsbuch, n. retail-sales' book; —verkaufen, *tr.* retail, *see* —handel; —vieh, n. small cattle, tits; —waare, n. petty-ware, small-ware; —warzig, *adj.* *Bot.* verruculose; —wechsel, m. *see* Handwechsel, 2; —ziemer, m. *Ornith.* red-wing (Rothdrossel).

Klei'ster, *(str.)* m. paste, size; —aal, m., —älchen, n. *Zool.* paste eel (*Anguillula glutinis* L.).

[illegible]'..., *in comp. T-s.* —maschine, *f.* graining machine or mill; —(maschinen)haus, *n.* graining-house.

[illegible]'..., *in comp.* —maß, *n.* corn-measure; [illegible], *m.* corn-measurer; corn-meter; —[illegible], *f. see* —wurm; —mohn, *m. see* Feldmohn; —motte, *f. see* —wolf; —mühle, *f.* corn-mill; —mutter, *f.* ergot; —nägelein, *n.*, —nelke, *f. see* —rade; —preis, *m.* price of corn; —pulver, *n.* granulated, grained or corn gunpowder; —rade, *f. see* —rose, 1; —reich, *adj.* productive in grain; —rauter, *m. see* [illegible]; —ringe, *f. see* Fruchtdarre; —rolle, *f. see* —fege; —rose, *f. Bot.* 1) corn-rose campion, corn cockle (*Agrostemma githágo* L.); [illegible] *or* red poppy (Klatschrose); —rüssel[illegible], *m. see* —bohrer; —schabe, *f. see* —wurm; [illegible], *m. see* —frucht; —schneidemaschine, *f. Husb.* reaping-machine; —schnepfe, *f. Orn.* common curlew (*Numenius arquatus* L.); [illegible], *m.* corn-clerk; —schwinge, *f. Husb.* [illegible]-fan; —schwinger, *m.* fanner, winnower; [illegible], *n.* 1) *Husb.* winnowing sieve, cribble; [illegible] *m.* corning sieve (for granulating gunpowder); —speicher, *m.* granary, corn-loft, [illegible]; —sperling, *m.* house-sparrow; —sperre, *f.* prohibition of exporting grain; —stampe, *f.* [illegible]; —steuer, —taxe, *f.* corn-duty; [illegible], *m.* corn-meter or turner.

[illegible]'ung, (*w.*) *f.* the (act of) corning, &c., [illegible], granulation.

[illegible]'..., *in comp.* —vogel, *m.* 1) *Ornith.* [illegible] Goldammer; 2) *see* —weihe; —wage, *f.* balance for weighing corn; —wagen, *m.* corn-[illegible].

[illegible]walze, (*w.*) *f.* granulating roller.

[illegible]'..., *in comp.* —weihe, *f. Ornith.* [illegible]-harrier, ring-tail (*Circus cyaneus* L.); [illegible], *f. Bot.* wild *or* hairy tare (*Vicia hirsuta* L.); —wiebel, *m. see* —wurm; —winde, *f. see* Ackerwinde; —wolf, *m.* (weiße —wurm) [illegible] worm, wolf, grub (*Tinea granella* L.); [illegible], *m.* usurious trade in corn; —wucherer, *m.* usurious dealer *or* speculator in corn; [illegible]wurm, *m. Entom.* calander, mite, weevil (*Calandra granaria* L.); —zange, *f.* 1) assayer's tongs; 2) *see* Kluppstange; —zapfen, *m. see* [illegible]; —zins, *m. see* —steuer; —zuschlag, *m.* [illegible]—sperre.

[illegible]'per, *s.* I. (*str.*) *m. lit. & fig.* body; [illegible] Farbe — geben, *T.* to embody a colour, to thicken a colour; —eines Buchstaben, body of a letter; II. *in comp.* —all, *n. see* —welt; —bau, *m.* structure, frame of body, corporeal frame, contexture; von zartem —bau, delicately framed; von starkem *or* kräftigem —bau, powerful in frame, strong-bodied; —beschaffenheit, *f.* constitution (of body); —bildung, *f. see* —bau.

[illegible]'perchen, (*str.*) *n.* (*dimin. of* Körper) [illegible] corpuscle, little body.

[illegible]'per..., *in comp.* —fülle, *f.* corpulence; —gestalt, *f. see* —bau; —größe, *f.* stature; —kraft, *f.* physical strength *or* power, *pl.* corporeal faculties; —lehre, *f.* somatology.

[illegible]'perlich, I. *adj.* bodily, corporal, corporeal (being, punishment, oath, &c.), material; *Phys.* corpuscular; k-e Winkel, *m.* solid angle; II. K-keit, (*w.*) *f.* corporality, corporeity, substantiality, substantialness, materiality, concreteness.

[illegible]'perlos, I. *adj.* bodiless; II. K-igkeit, *f.* bodiless state, immateriality.

[illegible]'per..., *in comp.* —maß, *n.* cubic(al) measure, measure of capacity; —masse, *f.* mass of a body; bulky body; —messung, *f.* mensuration of solids, stereometry; —reich, [illegible] *see* —welt; II. *adj.* having much body.

[illegible]'perschaft, (*w.*) *f.* corporate body, corporation. [illegible] be a corporation.

[illegible]'perschaftlich, *adj.* [illegible]

[illegible]'perschaftsmitglied, (*str.*) *n.* member of a corporation, corporator.

Kör'per..., *in comp.* —schwäche, *f.* bodily weakness; —stärke, *f. see* —kraft; —stellung, *f.* attitude; —stoff, *m.* matter; —übung, *f.* gymnastic; —welt, *f.* corporeal creation, material world; —winkel, *m.* solid angle; —zahl, *f.* solid *or* cubic number.

Kor'ven, (*w.*) *f. pl. Ship-b.* floor-timbers of a boat.

* Koryphä'e, (*w.*) *m.* (*Gr.*) 1) *Greek Dram.* coryphaeus, leader of the chorus; 2) *fig.* a leader, a chief; master, master-mind *or* spirit.

* Kosak', (*w.*) *m.* (*Russ.*) Cossack. — Kosak'isch, *adj.* Cossack; der bekannte Ausspruch, daß Europa — werden könnte, the well-known saying that Europe might become Cossack.

Kos'beere, (*w.*) *f. provinc.* bog-whortleberry.

Ko'scher, *see* Kauscher.

Ko'seform, (*w.*) *f. Gramm.* a form *or* word of endearment or fondness, fondling term.

Ko'sel, (*w.*) *f. provinc.* sow.

Ko'sen, (*w.*) *v. intr.* to caress; to talk, [prattle.

Ko'sig, *adj.* fondling; cosy (Traut, Traulich).

* Kos'misch, *adj.* (*Gr.*) cosmical. — Kosmo..., *in comp.* —gonie', (*w.*) *f.* cosmogony; —graph', (*w.*) *m.* cosmographer; —graphie', (*w.*) *f.* cosmography; —gra'phisch, *adj.* cosmographic; —log', (*w.*) *m.* cosmologer, cosmologist; —logie', (*w.*) *f.* cosmology; —lo'gisch, *adj.* cosmological; —polit', (*w.*) *m.* cosmopolitan, cosmopolite; —poli'tisch, *adj.* cosmopolitical.

Kossat', (*w.*) *m. provinc.* cottager.

Kost, *f.* food, fare; victuals; board, diet; magere —, slender fare; small diet; nahrhafte, kräftige *or* fette —, rich or high diet; halbe —, half-board; — und Lohn, board (victuals) and wages; in die — geben, to put (out) to board, to board; die — geben, in die — nehmen, in der — sein, in die — gehen, to board; — und Kleidung geben, *see* Kleidung; Einem — und Wohnung geben, to board and lodge one; — und Monatsgeld, *Mar.* wages and provisions.

Kost'bar, I. *adj.* 1) costly, expensive, sumptuous; valuable, rich, splendid; 2) precious; II. K-keit, (*w.*) *f.* 1) costliness, expensiveness, sumptuousness, &c.; 2) jewel, trinket; K-keiten, *pl.* valuables.

Kös'te, (*w.*) *f. provinc.* (marriage-)banquet.

Kost'en, (*w.*) *v. tr.* to taste, try; Kauf auf — (Probe), *Comm.* purchase on tasting.

Kost'en, (*w.*) *v. intr.* (*with Acc. of the price & Dat.* (*& Acc.*) *of pers.*) to cost: 1) to stand in, to bear a price; 2) *fig.* to require; was kostet es Ihnen? what does it stand you in? es koste, was es wolle, at any rate *or* price, cost what it may; es kostet Zeit, it takes time; es kostete ihm drei Stunden, it took him three hours; sich (etwas) viel kosten lassen, 1. to be at great expenses for; es mag — was es wolle, let it cost what it may; at any rate (price); kostender Preis, *see* Kostenpreis; 2. *fig.* to take much pains about, to expend (a great amount of talent, &c.).

Kost'enkraut, (*str.*) *n. Bot.* wall-hawkweed (*Hieracium murórum* L.).

Kosten, *s.* I. *f. pl.* cost(s), charges, expense(s); große —, heavy charges; auf meine, deine &c. —, at my, your, &c. costs, at my expense; es geht auf meine —, I am at the charge of it; auf eines Anderen — leben, zehren, to live at another man's expense, *coll.* to sponge on one; Einen in — setzen, Einem — machen, to cause expenses to, to put one to expense; die — tragen, to bear the charges, to be at the expense (of ...); mit wenig — [illegible], at a moderate charge; in die — [illegible], to assist in the charges; II. *in comp.* —anschlag, *m.* estimate; —aufwand, *m.* expenditure; —buch, *n.* book of charges; —[illegible], *n. see* —[illegible]; —[illegible], *m.* compensation (of the costs); —ersparniß, *f.* saving of expense; der —ersparniß wegen, to save expense. —frei, *adv.* free (clear, quit) of charges *or* expenses, cost-free; —frei an Bord geliefert, *Comm.* free on board; —preis, *m.* cost price, first (prime) cost; unter dem —preis verkaufen (losschlagen), to sell at a sacrifice on the original cost; —rechnung, *f.* account of charges, bill of costs; —reiterei, *f. Comm. slang,* cooking of accounts; —überschlag, *m. see* —anschlag; —verzeichniß, *n.* list of expenses; —vorschuß (*Law,* —vorstand), *m.* advance for expenses to be incurred.

Kost'er, (*str.*) *m.* taster.

Kost'..., *in comp.* —frau, *f. see* —halterin; —frei, *adj.* board-free; —frei halten, to keep in board; —gänger, *m.*, —gängerin, *f.* boarder; —geber, *m. Comm.* reportee; —geld, *n.* board-wages; alimony; —geld bekommen, to be on board wages; —geschäfte, *pl. Comm.* report-(contango-)transactions; —halter, *m.*, —halterin, *f.* keeper (master *or* mistress) of a boarding-house; —haus, *n.* boarding-house; —herr, *m. see* —halter; —kraut, *n. see* Kostenkraut.

Köst'lich, I. *adj.* 1) *see* Kostbar, 2; 2) excellent, charming; delicious; 3) delicate, dainty; das ist —! *coll.* that is capital! II. K-keit, (*w.*) *f.* 1) preciousness; 2) deliciousness, choiceness; 3) delicacy, daintiness; dainty.

Kost'nehmer, (*str.*) *m. Comm.* reporter.

Kost'nitz, *n. Geogr.* (the town of) Constance.

Kost'..., *in comp.* —preis, *m. see* Kaufpreis; —regel, *f. Med.* diet; —schule, *f.* boarding-school; —schüler, *m.* boarder (in a school).

Kost'spielig, I. *adj.* expensive, costly, chargeable; II. K-keit, (*w.*) *f.* costliness, expensiveness.

Kost'..., *in comp.* —verächter, *m.*, —verächterin, *f.* dainty person; —verständig, *adj.* able to appreciate *or* dress (dainty) victuals; —wurzel, *f.* putchock.

Kö'ter, (*str.*) *m. coll.* cur.

Koth, (*str.*) *m.* dirt; mire, filth, mud; turd, excrement; dung, ordure; flüssiger —, sludge, slush; *Sport-s.* spraints (of otters), droppings (of grouse and pheasants); slice (of falcons); lesses (of wild beasts); fiants (of badgers and foxes); fumets (of deer); mute, mewt (of birds in general).

Koth'..., *in comp.* —baum, *m. see* Stinkbaum; —brechen, *n. see* Darmgicht; —bürste, *f.* rubbing-brush.

Ko'the, (*w.*) *f.* 1) cot, cottage; 2) salt-cot.

Kö'the, (*w.*) *f.* 1) *Vet.* (K-ngelenk *n.*) fetlock-joint, pastern joint (of horses); K-nhaar, *n.* fetlock; 2) *provinc. see* Schrank.

Kö'thel, (*str.*) *m.* dirt, excrement of mice, sheep, goats, &c.

Koth'..., *in comp.* —farbig, *adj. Bot.*, &c. lutose; —fink, *m. see* Bergfink; —fliege, *f. Entom.* dung-fly (*Scatophága merdaria* F.); —gang, *m.* passage for filth, sewer, drain; —grube, *f.* puddle, dung-hole, common sewer; —hahn, *m. see* Wiedehopf; —holz, *n. see* Stinkholz.

Ko'thig, *adj.* dirty, miry, filthy; foul.

Koth'..., *in comp.* —käfer, *m. Entom.* dung-beetle, scarab (*Scarabaeus stercorarius* L.); —kärrner, *m.* scavenger; —lache, *f.* mud-puddle; —lerche, *f.*, —mönch, *m. see* Haubenlerche.

Köth'ner, (*str.*) *m. see* Käthner.

Köthnerei', (*w.*) *f.* small farm.

Koth'..., *in comp.* —schieber, *m. provinc.* a species of fungus (Pfefferschwamm); —schuhe, *m. pl.* pattens, clogs; —schwalbe, *f. see* Uferschwalbe.

* Kothurn', (*str.*) *m.* (*Gr.*) *Anc. Dram.* buskin, cothurnus; im —, auf hohem —, *fig.* buskined, in a lofty *or* majestic style.

Koth'vogel, (*str., pl.* K-vögel) *m. see* —hahn.

Koth'..., *in comp.* (*cf.* Kothe) —hof, *m.* small farm; *T-s.* —[illegible], *m.* salt-boiler; —leute, *pl.* workmen employed in a salt-work;

Kram'mets..., *in comp.* **–baum**, *m. Bot.* juniper-tree (*Juniperus communis* L.); **–beere**, *f.* juniper-berry: *Ornith-s.* **–merle**, *f.* ring-ouzel (Ringamsel); **–vogel**, *m.* fieldfare (*Turdus pilaris* L.). [iron; *Lock-sm.* staple.

Kram'pe, *(w.) f.* cramp, crampoon, cramp-

Krem'pe, *(w.) f. Hatt.* cock, flap, brim (of a hat).

Kräm'pel, *(w.) m. (f.)* 1) (**–kamm**, *m.*) card, carding-comb; 2) *coll.* (*cf.* Kram, Trödel) lumber; trash, stuff; lot; **–blatt**, *n.* leather-cover for cards; **–blätter**, *n. pl.* card-leaves; **–brett**, *n.* card-board.

Krämpelei', *(w.) f.* card-factory.

Kräm'peler, *(str.) m. see* Krämpler.

Kräm'pel..., *in comp.* **–garn**, *n.* carded yarn; **–haken**, *m. pl.* the wire-teeth of a card; **–macher**, *m.* card-maker; **–maschine**, *f.* carding *or* combing machine. [(wool).

Kräm'peln, *(w.) v. tr.* to card, comb, tease

Kräm'pel..., *in comp.* **–stube**, *f.* card-room; **–wolle**, *f.* 1) carding wool, wool that is to be carded; 2) carded *or* combed wool.

Kram'pen, *(w.) v. tr.* to cramp.

Krem'pen, *(w.) v. tr.* 1) to bend, turn up, to cock (a hat); 2) *Cloth.* to sponge (cloth).

Krampf, *(str., pl.* Krämpfe*) m.* cramp, spasm; convulsion; *in comp.* **–ader**, *f. Med.* varicose vein, varix; **–aderbruch**, *m. Surg.* varicocele; **–aderig**, *adj.* varicose; **–artig**, *adj.* spasmodic, convulsive; *adv.* spasmodically, convulsively: **–distel**, *f. Bot.* cotton-thistle (*Onopordon acanthium* L.).

Kram'pfen, *(w.) v. tr. & refl.* to cramp, contract convulsively.

Krampf'fisch, *(str.) m. Ichth.* cramp-fish, torpedo (Zitterrochen).

Krampf'haft, I. *adj.* convulsive, spasmodic; k-es Lachen, convulsions of laughter; k-es Lächeln, writhing smile; II. **K-igkeit**, *(w.) f.* convulsiveness. [hooping-cough.

Krampf'husten, *(str.) m.* convulsive cough;

Krampf'ig, *adj. see* Krampfartig.

Krampf..., *in comp.* **–lachen**, *n. Med.* convulsive laugh; **–lindernd**, *adj.* antispasmodic; **–mittel**, *n.* antispasmodic; **–ring**, *m.* ring used as an antispasmodic; **–roche**, *m. see* –fisch; **–stillend**, *see* –lindernd; **–sucht**, *f.* spasm; **–wehen**, *f. pl. Med.* clonic *or* spasmodic travail.

Krem'pig, *adj.* (*in comp.*) brimmed.

Krämp'ler, *(str.) m.*, **Krämp'lerin**, *(w.) f.* wool-carder, comber.

Krams'vogel, *coll. see* Krammetsvogel.

Kram'..., *in comp.* **–stube**, *f. provinc. see* Wochenstube; **–waare**, *f.* articles *or* goods for retail, mercery, groceries; **–wesen**, *n.* retailing business. [beere.

Kran, *m. see* Krahn; **–beere**, *f. see* Preißel-

Kran'ge, *(w.) f. Mar.* hank.

Krang'eln, *(w.) v. tr. & intr. T.* to twist.

Kräng'eln, *(w.) v. intr. & refl.* to twist.

Kräng'en, *(w.) v. intr. Mar.* to heel (said of ships).

Kra'nich, *(str.) m.* 1) *Ornith.* crane (*Grus cinerea* Bech.); 2) *Mech. see* Krahn; *in comp.* **–beere**, *f. Bot.* cranberry ([illegible]); **–hals**, *m.* geranium [illegible] stork's bill, crane's bill [illegible] *Berg.*).

Krank, I. *adj.* ill (an [*with Dat.*], with), sick, infirm, diseased, distempered; afflicted (with); *Mar.* crazy (ship); – werden, to be taken ill, to grow sick, fall sick; sich – stellen, to feign sickness, *coll.* to sham Abram; ein k-es Schiff, *Mar.* crazy ship; – an den Füßen, diseased in one's feet; II. *s. m. & f.* (*decl. like adj.*) sick person, patient.

Kränkelei', *(w.) f.* poorness, sickliness.

Krän'keln, *(w.) v. intr.* to labour under bad health, to be of indifferent health, to be sickly, ill, poorly; er fing an zu –, his health began to decline *or* gave way; k-des Geschäft, flagging business.

Kran'ken, *(w.) v. intr.* 1) to be ill, sick, diseased (an [*with Dat.*], of); *fig.* to suffer (an [*with Dat.*], of).

Krän'ken, *(w.) v.* I. *tr.* to grieve, mortify, afflict, vex, gall: to injure, to detract (an [*with Dat.*], from); gekränkte Eitelkeit, galled vanity; II. *refl. see* sich Grämen.

Kran'ken..., *in comp.* **–anstalt**, *f.* hospital; **–attestat**, *n.* sick certificate; **–bericht**, *m.* report of patients; **–besuch**, *m.* visit to a patient, attendance (of the physician); visit to a sick person: visitation of the sick (of clergymen); **–bett**, *n.* sick-bed; **–casse**, *f.* sick-funds; **–diarium**, *n. see* –journal; **–examen**, *n. Med.* (method of) examination of a sick person; **–gehülfe**, *m.* assistant to a charity: **–haus**, *n.* infirmary, hospital; **–heber**, *m.* any arrangement for a sick person to raise himself in bed; **–hof**, *m. see* –haus; **–journal**, *n.* a physician's journal, visiting-book; **–korb**, *m.* stretcher; **–kost**, *f.* diet, food for patients: auf –kost setzen, to diet; **–lager**, *n. see* –bett; **–liste**, *f.* sick-list *or* report; **–manual**, *n. see* –journal; **–mutter**, *f.* matron attending sick people; **–pflege**, *f.* attendance and care of patients; **–pfleger**, *m.*, **pflegerin**, *f. see* –wärter *xc.*; **–saal**, *m.* sick-room (in hospitals); **–schiff**, *n.* hospital-ship: **–spital**, *n. see* –haus; **–stube**, *f.* sick-room *or* chamber; **–stuhl**, *m.* invalid chair; **–stuhlwagen**, *m.* invalid-wheel-chair; **–verschlag**, *m. Mar.* cock-pit; **–wagen**, *m. Mil.* 1) hospital-waggon; 2) hospital-store-waggon; **–wärter**, *m.*, **–wärterin**, *f.* tender, attendant of sick persons, *f.* nurse; **–zettel**, *m. see* –liste; **–zimmer**, *n. see* –stube.

Krank'haft, I. *adj.* diseased, distempered, morbid; irregular (of the pulse); k-e Reizbarkeit, morbid irritability; II. **K-igkeit**, *(w.) f.* diseased state, morbidity, diseasedness, *see* Kränklichkeit.

Krank'heit, *(w.) f.* disease, sickness, illness, complaint, distemper, malady; derangement; in eine – fallen *or* gerathen, to fall sick.

Krank'heits... *in comp.* **–bericht**, *m.* medical report: **–entscheidung**, *f.* crisis; **–entscheidungslehre**, *f.* pathogeny; **–geschichte**, *f.* history of an illness; **–horoscop**, *n. Astrol.* decumbiture; **–kenner**, **–lehrer**, *m.* pathologist: **–kosten**, *f. pl.* expenses of illness; **–lehre**, *f.* pathology; **–sitz**, *m. Med.* seat of the disease; **–stoff**, *m.* morbid *or* diseased (contagious) matter; **–symptom**, *n.* morbid symptom: **–ursache**, *f.* cause of disease; **–wechsel**, *m.* turn of a malady, crisis; **–zeichen**, *n.* symptom; **–zeichenlehre**, *f.* symptomatology, pathognomonics; **–zufall**, *m.* fit, attack of illness; **–zustand**, *m.* state of disease.

Kränk'ler, *(str.) m.*, **Kränk'lerin**, *(w.) f.* sickly person; valetudinarian.

Kränk'lich, I. *adj.* weak in health, sickly, valetudinarian; *coll.* poorly; decrepit, languishing; II. **K-keit**, *(w.) f.* sickliness, weakness (of health).

Kränk'ling, *(str.) m. see* Kränkler.

Kränk'ung, *(w.) f.* mortification, grief.

Kran'sel, *m. pl. Mar.* puddings, fenders.

Kranz, *s.* I. *(str., pl.* Kränze*) m.* 1) wreath, garland, chaplet (of flowers); 2) *T-s.* *a) Archit.* cornice, crown, festoon; cincture (of a column; also bead, list, moulding-cornice); cordon (of a wall); *b)* (beim Hohofen) curb-plate; *c)* head (of a stake); *d)* rim (of a wheel); *Mech-s.* tire; *e)* brim (of a bell *or* hat); *fig-s.* 3) virginity; 4) circle, society; galaxy (of beauty, &c.); den – schlagen, *Hatt.* to work the brim (of a hat); II. *in comp.* **–ader**, *f.* coronal *or* coronary vein; **–arterie**, *f.* crown-artery, coronary artery; **–band**, *n.* (der Lefzen) coronary ligament; **–beere**, *f. see* Wachholderbeere; **–bein**, *n.* coronal bone, **–blume**, *f.* garland-flower; **–blutader**, *f. see* –ader.

Kränz'chen, *(str.) n.* (*dimin. of* Kranz) 1) a little wreath, garland, &c.; 2) *fig.* society, club, (private) circle.

Kranz'..., *in comp.* **–dicke**, *f. T.* thickness of the brim of a bell; **–eisen**, *n. see* Karnieseisen.

Kränz'eleisen, *(str.) n. T.* engrailing-iron.

Krän'zen, *(w.) v.* I. *tr.* 1) to crown, *see* Bekränzen; 2) to peel off the bark of trees; II. *intr. Sport.* to tear the ground (of stags).

Kranz'..., *in comp.* **–flechter**, *m. see* –winder; **–förmig**, *adj.* in the form of a wreath *or* crown; *Anat.* coronoid: **–gefäß**, *n.* crown-vessel; *Archit-s.* **–gesims**, *n.* belt, corona, cornice; **–holz**, *n. Mar.* dead-eye of a hammock's crow-foot; **–jungfer**, *f. see* Brautjungfer.

Kränz'lein, *(str.) n.* (*provinc. &*) * *for* Kränzchen; **–kraut**, *n. see* Feldquendel; **–tag**, *n. see* Frohnleichnamstag.

Kranz'leiste, *(w.) f. T.* heading-course, cornice; tringle; dripstone; head of the shaft of a chimney. [chen, 2.

Kränz'ler, *(str.) m.* member of a Kränz-

Kranz'..., *in comp.* **–naht**, *f. Anat.* coronal suture; **–pulsader**, **–schlagader**, *f. see* –arterie; **–reif**, *m. Gunn.* cornice-ring; **–rolle**, *f. T.* milling-wheel (Rändeleisen); **–schiene**, *f. Railw.* tram-rail: **–steine**, *m. pl.* place-bricks: **–stück**, *n.* felly (of a hydraulic wheel); **–winder**, *m.* garland-maker: **–ziegel**, *m. pl. see* –steine.

Krapf, *(w.)*, **Krapf'en**, *(str.) m.* (*dimin.* Kräpfchen, Kräpflchen, [*str.*] *n.*) 1) handle (of a pump); 2) cramp, hook; 3) fritter, dough-nut.

Krapp, *(str.) m.* madder; *in comp.* **–brühe**, **–farbe**, *f.* dye made of madder.

Krapp, *adj. T.* too hard twisted (of a rope).

Krap'pe, *(w.) f. T.* staple; *Gun-sm.* catch, tumbler. [Krapf, 3.

Krap'pel, **Kräp'pel(chen)**, *(str.) n. coll. see*

Krap'per, *(str.) m. see* Krapfstaude.

Krapp'..., *in comp.* **–farbendruck**, *m. T.* madder-style; **–farbestoff**, *m. Chem.* alizarine; **–gelb**, *adj. Chem.* xanthine; **–pflanze**, *f. Bot.* dyer's madder (*Rubia tinctorum* L.); **–pulver**, *n.* madder in powder; **–roth**, *n.* madder-red, alizarine; **–see**, *f. Mar.* sugar-loaf sea.

Kraß'selbeere, *(w.) f. see* Kratzbeere.

* **Kra'ter**, *(str.) m.* (*Gr.*) crater; *Arch.* bell, basket, corbel.

Krät'schen, *provinc. see* Grätschen.

Kratz, *(str.) m.* scratch; scar.

Kratz..., *in comp.* **–beere**, *f. provinc.* 1) bramble-berry; 2) *see* Stachelbeere; **–blech**, *n.* brass-plate for polishing buttons; **–brett**, *n. T.* friezing-table; **–bürste**, *f.* 1) scraper, wire-brush; 2) *fig.* a sharp person, a rough brush; **–bürstig**, *adj.* as rough as a brush; **–distel**, *f. Bot.* a species of thistle, Canada thistle (*Cirsium* Tourn.); **–draht**, *m.* card-wire.

Kratz'e, *(w.) f.* scraper, card.

Kratz'eisen, *(str.) n.* scraping-iron, iron rake, scrubber, scraper.

Krat'zen, *(w.) v.* I. *tr. & intr.* to scratch, grate, scrape; to have a bad, harsh taste (of wine); to spit, scratch (of pens); to scrawl, scribble; Wolle –, to card wool; Tuch –, to tease cloth; II. *tr. impers.* es kratzt mich, I feel a scratching.

Kratz'..., *in comp.* **–fuß**, *m.* 1) (*lit.* scrape-foot) an (awkward) reverence, *coll.* leg; *pl.* **–füße**, shuffling of feet; einen –fuß machen, to scrape a leg; 2) *Germ. Fab.* name given to the hen, *coll.* Dame Partlet; **–füßeln**, *v. intr.* to make scrape-legs, to be overpolite; **–füßler**, *m.* scrape-leg, one who bows much;

inwards; —kunst, f. common piloting; —wasser, n. pilot water.

Loots'mann, (str.) m. 1) see Lootse, 1; 2) Ichth. pilot-fish (Naucrates ductor L.).

Lop'pe, (w.) f. T. bundle of hemp.

Lör, (w.) f. & (str.) m. †, leather-strap, thong, brace.

Lor'beer (Lor'ber), s. I. (str.) m. a) bay, laurel; der indische —, royal bay; der wilde —, laurustine; b) Sport. fewmets; II. in comp. —baum, m. Bot. laurel-tree, bay-tree (Laurus nobilis L.); —baumholz, n. sweet-wood; —blatt, n. laurel- or bay-leaf.

Lor'beere, (w.) f. bay-berry, laurel.

Lor'beer..., in comp. —hain, m. grove of laurels; —haupt, n. laurel-crowned head; —kampher, m. Chem. laurine; —kirsche, f. see Kirschlorbeer; —kranz, m., see —krone; —kraut, n. Bot. 1) spurge-laurel (Daphne laureola L.); 2) laurel herb (Seidelbast); —krone, f. laurel-wreath, crown of laurel; —öl, n. laurel-oil, bay-oil; —rose, f. Bot. rose-bay, oleander (Nerium oleander L.); —süchtig, adj. see Ruhmsüchtig; —tragend, adj. lauriferous; —wald, m. wood of laurels; Bot-s. —weide, f. sweet willow, bay-leaved willow (Salix pentandra L.); —winde, f. provinc. lesser periwinkle; —zweig, m. twig of laurel.

Lorch, (str.) m. 1) a) see Kröte; b) see Lerche; 2) fig. rogue; roguish girl; 3) Ornith. crested diver (Steißfuß).

Lorch'e, (w.) f. Bot. 1) or Lorch'baum, m. see Lerchenbaum; 2) or Lorch'el, (w.) f. Bot. 1) morel (Morchel); 2) turban-top (Helvella L.).

Lörch'en, see Lore, A.

Lor'de, (w.) f. 1) or Lor'ding, (str.) m. Mar. four-thread spun yarn; 2) fraud; particul. a false bill of lading (for smuggling purposes).

Lor'den..., in comp. —dreher, m. one who makes out a Lorde; smuggler; —dreherei, f. smuggling. [from Leono're). Lora (P. N.).

A. Lo're, f. (dimin. Lör'chen, n.) (abbr.

B. Lo're, (w.) f. coll. for Lowry.

Lo'renz, m. Laurence (P. N.); —kraut, n. see Schwalbenwurz.

* Lorgnet'te, [pr. lörnyät'tə], (w.) f. (Fr.) opera-glass, (spy-)glass.

* Lorgnon' [pr. lörnyong'], (str., pl. L-s) n. (Fr.) eye-glass; quizzing-glass; quiz.

* Lo'ri, (str. pl. L-s) m. Zool. a kind of ape, loris (Stenops Ill.).

* Lorici'ren, (w.) v. tr. Chem. to loricate.

Lorl, see Lorch. [age; dregs of wine.

Lor'ke, (w.) f. provinc. bad, muddy bever-

Lor'öl, see Lorbeeröl.

Lor'rendreiher, see Lorrendreher.

Lorsch'en, pl. Bot. spurges (Euphorbiaceae).

Lor'tanne, (w.) f. provinc. see Lerchenbaum.

Lös, Lo'sen, see Loos, Losen.

Los, I. adj. & adv. 1) loose, slack, unbent, untied; 2) fig. unconnected, free, loose, independent, disengaged; dishevelled (hair); der Gefangene ist —, the prisoner is free or has escaped; Mar-s. der Anker ist —, the anchor drags; überall —! let go amain! das Wild ist —, Sport. the game is wild; coll-s.: eine Sache — haben, to be up to a thing; — sein, — werden (with Acc. & Gen.), to be or get rid of, to get off one's hands, to be released (of an obligation, &c.); wir konnten sie (or ihrer) nicht — werden, we could not get rid of them; ellipt. for: — sein, to be, come, or go out (of duellists); to fight a duel; der Teufel ist —, coll. (cf. Grimm, Myth. 962) hell is broke loose, the devil is loose; es muß was — sein, there must be something in the wind; something must have happened; er erfuhr allmählich was — wäre, he learned gradually what was toward; es ist nicht viel mit ihm —, he is no great shakes; es ist nicht viel damit —, it is nothing to boast of; was ist hier —? what is the matter? coll. what's up? what's the row?

II. adv. (preceded by auf, darauf) 1) on, up to; 2) coll. away; immer or frisch darauf —! courage! advance; forward! go it or by! auf Einen —fahren, —rennen, —gehen, to make up to one, fly at, rush upon, attack; es geht auf die Ernte —, it grows near harvest; auf Einen —schlagen, see Losprügeln; frisch darauf —hauen, essen &c., to strike, eat away [illegible] darauf — reisen, to travel at a round [illegible] darauf — lügen, to lie impudently; darauf — leben, to live carelessly or at random.

III. interj. Mil. los! stand at ease!

IV. (str.) n. Mar. loose part or bight (of a rope, &c.).

Los, in comp. with subst. ...loss, e.g. gesetzlos &c., lawless, &c.; with verbs, off, away, asunder (cf. Ab-; verbs comp. with Los are separable, the particle having the principal accent); —ackern, v. tr. to make loose by ploughing (the soil); —arbeiten, (w.) v. I. tr. & refl. to work off, get loose, to loosen, to disengage, extricate (with some effort); II. intr. coll. to work away (auf ein Ziel, to attain an aim); —bäcker, m. provinc. white-bread baker.

Lös'bar, Lös'barkeit, see Löslich, Löslichkeit.

Los, in comp. —baum, m. see Losbaum; —bekommen, v. tr. to get off, away, loose; to set free; —binden, v. tr. to untie, unbind, loosen, undo, unfasten, unbrace, uncord; Mar. to unfurl; —bitten, v. tr. to beg a person's release; to effect a release or deliverance by intercession; —blättern, see Abblättern, 2; —brechen, v. tr. & n. (aux. sein) to break off, loose; fig. to break forth or out; to burst out or forth; —brennen, (irr.) v. tr. to burn off; to fire, discharge; to pop off (a pistol, &c.); to let off (fire-works); —bringen, v. tr. see —bekommen; —bröckeln, v. tr. & intr. (aux. sein) to crumble off; —brot, n. provinc. roll; —bruch, m. the (act of) breaking off or loose; —brüchig, adj. crumbling, breaking off (easily); —brüchig machen, Sport. to unearth (a wild boar); —bürgen, v. tr. to bail off.

Lösch, (str.) m. provinc. swarm of bees.

Lösch..., in comp. —anstalt, f. 1) fire-establishment, pl. establishments for extinguishing fires; 2) fire-warden's office; —bank, f. tub for slaking lime. [&c. cf. Löschen.

Lösch'bar, adj. that may be extinguished,

Lösch..., in comp. —blatt, n. a (leaf or sheet of) blotting paper; —blei, n. lead pencil; —bord, m. Mar. fender; skids (pl.); —brand, m. quenched firebrand; —compagnie, f. fire company. [Löschhorn.

Lösch'e, (w.) f. 1) coal-dust; calm; 2) see

Lösch'eimer, (str.) m. fire-bucket.

Lösch'el, (str.) m. T. pump-sucker.

Lösch'en, v. I (str.) intr. to be extinguished, see Erlöschen; II. (w.) tr. 1) to quench, put out; to extinguish; 2) to strike, blot out; to cancel (a debt); Staub —, to lay dust; Kalk —, to slake or kill lime; 3) Comm. to light, unload, unlade, discharge, disembark, land.

Lösch'er, (str.) m. 1) extinguisher, &c., see Löschhorn; 2) Comm. discharger, unlader.

Lösch..., in comp. —faß, n. quenching-tub; —gebühren, pl. fees for lighting, landing-discharges; —geld, n. money for lighting a ship, wharfage; —geräth, n. apparatus for extinguishing fire; —grube, f. [illegible] pit; —haken, m. T. fire-hook; —horn, —[illegible] n. extinguisher; —kalk, m. quick lime; —[illegible] f. quenched charcoal, smith's clinkers; —[illegible] m. see —faß; —mannschaft, f. firemen [illegible] napf, m., —näpfchen, n. see —horn; —[illegible] n. blotting-paper; —platz, m. place [illegible] ships unload; discharging-place, wharf [illegible] of destination or transmission, port [illegible] livery or of discharge; —schaufel, f. [illegible] dust-shovel; —spieß, m. coal-[illegible]

2, *as ill. fig.* ugly person, hag; die — abnehmen, abziehen, *lit. & fig.* to unmask.

Mas'ken..., *in comp.* —anzug, *m. see* —kleid; —ball, *m.*, —fest, *n.*, —gang, *m.* masquerade, masked ball; —gesicht, *n.* mask-house; —kittel, *m.* domino; —blume, *f.* *Bot.* personated flower; —mantel, *m.* domino; —freiheit, *f.* freedom of masquerade or carnival; —kleid, *n.* masquerade dress, mask-dress; —tanz, *m.* dance at a masked ball.

* Maskera'de, *(w.) f.* masquerade; M—kleid, *n.* dress for a masquerade. — Maski'ren, *(w.)* *v.* I. *tr.* to mask, disguise; II. *rgf.* to put on a mask, disguise one's self; maskirt, *p. a.* *Bot.* personate(d).

Mas'kolben, *(str.) m.* *Bot.* reed-mace, cat's-tail (*Typha latifolia* L.).

Mastapel', *(w.) f.* (*Dutch* maatschappy) 1) *provinc.* society or company of merchants, partnership; 2) *obsolescent*, confederacy, fellowship. — Mastapelträger, *(str.) m. pl.* Bremen cornwhippers and heavers who form a sort of guild, and are paid for carrying goods from the ships (*Reb. & Gr.*).

Maß'leidig, *adj. see* Maßleidig.

Maß'liebe, *(w.) f. see* Maßliebe.

Masso'vien, *n.* *Geogr.* Massovia.

* Massacri'ren, *(w.) v. tr.* (*Fr.*) to massacre.

Mas'se, *(w.) f.* 1) mass, bulk, stock, body, quantity; substance; in —, plenty; 2) mallet; 3) *Billiards*: mace, stick (for playing at billiards); 4) *Found.* dry sand; *Pott.* paste, clay-mass; die — des Volks, the bulk or gross of the people, the million; in — verkaufen, to sell by the bulk; *Comm.*: die — eines Fallitens, active property or estate of a bankrupt, mass of bankruptcy; assets; bei der — als Gläubiger einkommen, to claim upon the estate; er vertritt mich bei der Vertheilung der —, he represents me at the adjudication of the bankrupt's estate; die — steht gut, the estate looks well; die — ist geschlossen, the estate is settled; es ist wenig in der —, there are but trifling assets; die — reguliren, to realise, manage, and distribute the estate; die — wird höchstens 40% geben, the assets will give at most 8 shillings in the £.; sind Sie bei der — betheiligt? have you any claim upon the estate? der — sind betrüglicherweise Activa entzogen worden, a part of the estate has been embezzled (*Reb. & Gr.*); die — ausschütten, to distribute a bankrupt's estate; sich zur — melden, to sue for admittance. [ore, pig, sow.

Mas'sel, *(w.) f.* *Iron.* shingled lump of

Mas'sen, *in comp.* —armuth, *f.* pauperism; —anwalt, bankrupt's solicitor; —aufgebot, *n.* posse; —curator, *m.* assignee, syndic; creditor in trust, administrator of the bankrupt's estate; —fence, *n.* general discharge; —gläubiger, *m.* creditor under a commission of bankruptcy; —guß, *m.* dry sand-casting.

Mas'senhaft, I. *adj. see* Massiv; II. *or* Mas'senweise, *adv.* in large quantities, by the mass or bulk: massenhaft auf den Markt werfen, *Comm.* to fling or pitch wholesale (on a large scale) upon the market.

Mas'sen..., *in comp.* —mord, *m.* wholesale murder, butchery; —production, *f.* production on a large scale.

Mas'sig, *adj.* massy, solid, *cf.* Massiv.

* Massi'ren, *(w.) v. tr.* 1) to work up or join into a mass; 2) to shampoo.

* Massiv', *adj.* (*Fr.*) 1) massive, massy, solid; 2) pure, unalloyed (of precious metals); 3) stone-built (house); 4) *coll.* coarse, clumsy, rude.

* Massouri', *(w.) f. see* Mastapel.

1. Mast, (*str.* *sg.* *str.*, *pl.* *w.*) *m.* *Mar.* mast; der große —, main-mast; der vordere —, the fore-mast; der hintere —, mizen-mast; ein zusammengesetzter —, a made mast.

2. Mast, *(w.) f.* 1) (*as* mast), feeding and fattening pigs, poultry, and cattle; [illegible] feeding; 2) food; 3) manner of fattening; in die — thun, to put out to mast; auf der — haben, to fatten.

Mast, *adj. provinc.* (*L. G.*) *see* Mastig.

Mast... (*B.*), *in comp.* —ader, *f.* *Anat.* hemorrhoidal vein; —aderfluß, *m.* bleeding piles; —aderknoten, *f.* blind piles.

* Mastalgie', *(w.) f.* *Med.* pain in the breasts (of women).

Mast'... (*A.*), *in comp.* —band, *n.* —[illegible], *m.* mast-hoop; —baum, *m.* 1) a) mast; [illegible] fit for a mast; 2) silver-leaved fir-tree ([illegible] tanne, Weißtanne).

Mast'bissen (*cf.* Mast *B.*), *m.* *coll.* fat titbit, tidbit. [of the mastbeam, mast's head.

Mast'block, (*str.*, *pl.* M—blöcke) *m.* *Mar.* cap

Mast... (*B.*), *in comp.* —buche, —[illegible], *f.* *Bot.* the common beech, oak (giving mast for pigs); —darm, *m.* *Anat.* rectum, straight gut; —darmbinde, *f. see* Afterbinde; —darmblasen-steinschnitt, *m.* *Surg.* rectovesical lithotomy; —darmfistel, *f.* fistula of the anus; —darmgefäß, *n.* hemorrhoidal vessel; —darmge-kröse, *n.* mesorectum; —darmknoten, *pl.* *Med.* hemorrhoids, piles; —darmkrebs, *m.* *Surg.* cancer in the anus; —darmvorfall, *m.* *Surg.* prolapse of the rectum; —darmwurm, *m. see* —wurm. [illegible]

Mast'ducht (*w.*) *f.* *Mar.* main or middle

Mast'eiche, *see* Mastbuche.

Mast'en, *(w.)* *v. tr.* *Mar.* to furnish with a mast or masts, to mast.

Mäst'en, *(w.)* *v. tr.* to feed, fat, fatten; to cram (poultry); gemästet, *p. a.* stall-fed (of animals); *coll.* fat, well-fed.

Mast'en..., *in comp.* *Mar.* —[illegible], *m. see* Mastband; —cirkel, *m.* callipers; —holz, *n.* trees for masts; mast-timber; —keile, —klötze, *m. pl.* quoins or wedges of a mast; —klampen, *f. pl.* cleats in the shape of a mast; —koker, *m.* mast-trunk, mast-case, *cf.* Koker, 2; —kragen, *m.* coats of a mast; —krahn, *m.* sheers for masting a ship, mast-sheers; —[illegible], —kerer, *m.* mast-maker; —passer, *m.* see —cirkel; —pille, *f.* crab-boom; —reich, *adj.* of many masts or ships; —scheibe, *f.* mast-sheave; —scheien, *f. pl.* fishes of a mast; —spur, see Mastspur; —stützen, *f. pl.* mast-gauges; —zirkel, see —cirkel.

Mäst'er, *(str.)* *m.* feeder, fattener.

Mast... (*B.*), *in comp.* —feder, *f. see* Fettfeder; —fleck, *m.* *Hunt.* rich spot or bed (in fields) where a superabundance of [illegible] has fallen; —freiheit, *f. see* —recht; —futter, *n.* fattening food; —gans, *f.* fatted goose; goose for fattening; —geflügel, *f.*, —[illegible]; —geld, *n.* money paid for driving [illegible] to mast, pannage; —huhn, *n.*, —[illegible] *f.*, —[illegible] *m.*, —schwein, *n.* fattened fowl, sow, [illegible].

Mast'ig, *adj.* 1) (*in comp.*) having [illegible] or masts; 2) fat, well-fed.

* Mas'tix, Mas'tich, (*str.*) *m.* & *n.* ([illegible]) *Pharm.* (gum) mastich, mastic; —baum, *m.* [illegible] mastich tree (*Pistacia lentiscus* L.); —[illegible], *m.* mastich varnish; —holz, *n.* mastich [illegible]; —kraut, *n.* *Bot.* 1) mastic (shrub) [illegible] *mastichina*); 2) cat-thyme (*Teucrium* [illegible] *rum* L.).

Mast... (*A.*), *in comp.* —klampen, *see* Mastenklampen; —[illegible], *m.* [illegible] knopf, *m.* acorn, truck; —korb, *m.* [illegible] scuttle; —korb für Geschütze, [illegible] trestle-trees.

Mast'körner (*from* Mast, *B.*) [illegible] Hämorrhoidalknoten.

Mast'kragen, Mast'kraen, *see* [illegible]

Mast'kraut (*from* Mast, *B.*) [illegible] pearlwort (*Sagina* L.).

Mast'licht, (*str.*) *n.* *Mar.* [illegible] (*signal*) light.

Mäst'ler, (*str.*) *m.* [illegible]

halb schwach, rather soft; —tinto-schaber, *Engrav.* mezzo-tinto-scraper.

* Mias'ma, (*str.*, *pl.* Mias'men) *n.* (*Gr.*) miasm, miasma. — Miasmat'isch, *adj.* miasmatic(al).

Miau'en, (*w.*) *v. intr.* to mew, caterwaul.

Mich, *Accus. of* Ich, me; — selbst, myself.

Mich'ael, *m.* Michael (*P. N.*).

Michae'lis, *n.* (—fest, *n.*) Michaelmas; —tag, *m.* Michaelmas-day.

Mich'aelis..., *in comp.* —birn, *f.* Michael's pear; —blume, *f. see* Herbstzeitlose; —orden, *m.* order of St. Michael; —pflaume, *f. see* Katharinenpflaume.

Mich'el, *m.* 1) (*abbr. of* Michael) Mick; 2) ein —, *contd.* (ein grober, dummer —) a coarse, blunt, stupid fellow; der deutsche —, the German Michael, nickname of the German people (analogous to the English John Bull) representing them as an honest, blunt, unsuspicious fellow, who easily allows himself to be imposed upon, even by those who are greatly his inferiors in point of strength and real worth.

Mick'e (Mick), (*w.*) *f.* 1) *see* Micke, 1; 2) weakly, puny child; 3) *usually pl.* a) *Mar.* crotches, chocks, (an der Gaffel) throat, jaw, horn; b) *Rope-m.* trussels in a rope-yard; stake-heads; — der Pumpe, pump-cheeks; — der Kanone, quoin for the gun.

Mick'en, (*w.*) *v. tr.* to level, point (a gun).

Mick'er, (*str.*) *m. provinc.* fat gut of cattle.

Mick'knopf, (*str.*) *m. Gunn.* sight.

Mick'mack, (*str.*) *m.* tag-rag, riff-raff.

* Microcos'mus, (*pl.* [*w.*] M-'men) *m.* (*Lat. from the Gr.*) microcosm (world in miniature, man).

* Microme'ter, (*str.*) *n.* micrometer; —schraube, *f.* micrometrical screw.

* Microscop', (*str.*) *n. Opt.* microscope.

* Microscop'isch, *adj.* microscopical; m-e Gesellschaft, *f.* microscopical society; m-e Präparate, microscopical slides.

Mie'der, (*str.*) *n.* bodice, jupe, corset.

Mie'gen, (*w.*) *v. intr. provinc. see* Pissen.

Mie'ke, (*w.*) *f.* 1) *Mil.* gun-rack; 2) (*dimin.* Miek'chen, *n.*) *coll. abbr. of* Marie, Pol, Polly, Moll.

Mie'ne, (*w.*) *f.* mien, air, look, countenance; eine kecke *or* dreiste —, an air of assurance; eine sauere —, a frown; ich machte ihm eine finstere —, I gave him a frown; — machen, to make *or* show signs, to show (as if), to offer or prepare to; sich (*Dat.*) die — geben, als ob..., to affect to...; gute — zum bösen Spiele machen, *proverb.* to set (put) a good face on a bad game; — haben, to look.

Mie'nen..., *in comp.* —deuter, —forscher, *m.* physiognomist; —deutung, —forschung, —kunde, *f.* science of physiognomy, physiognomics; —spiel, *n.* play of features; mimics, pantomime; — und Geberdenspiel, by-play (of an actor). [chickweed (*Alsine* L.).

Mie're, (*w.*) *f.* 1) ant (Ameise); 2) *Bot.*

Mies, (*w.*) *f.*, Mies'chen, (*str.*) *n.* (*dimin.*) *see* Mieze, Miezchen.

Mie'sel, (*str.*) *n.* (*probably for* Miezel, Miezchen) *coll.* lass; flirt, sweetheart. — Mie'seln, (*w.*) *v. intr.* to make love, to flirt.

Mies'muschel, (*w.*) *f. Conch.* common (edible or eatable) muscle (*Mytilus edulis* L.).

Mie'te, (*w.*) *f. see* Mithe. [or shocks.

Mie'ten, (*w.*) *v. tr.* to put up into sheaves

Mieth'acker, (*str.*, *pl.* M-äcker) *m.* hired field. — Mieth'bar, *adv.* rentable, tenantable.

Mieth'..., *in comp.* —besitz, *m.* tenancy; —comptoir, *n.* office for hiring servants, registry-office; —contract, *m.* lease, tenure, deed of conveyance; charter-party, contract of affreightment (for a ship); —dienst, *m.* service on hire; hired service.

Mie'the, (*w.*) *f.* 1) the (act of) hiring; 2) hire; 3) (Haus—) (house- or room-)rent; die — für ein Schiff, charter; die — aufkündigen, to give notice, warning; zur — haben, to hold in hire; zur — wohnen, to be a lodger, to have furnished lodgings or rooms.

Mie'then, (*w.*) *v. tr.* to hire; to rent, take (a house); to engage (a house, a coach, &c.); to job (*particul.* a coach, equipage); to charter (a ship).

Mie'ther, (*str.*) *m.*, Mietherin, (*w.*) *f.* a person who hires or rents any thing; lessee; tenant; lodger.

Mieth'..., *in comp.* —frau, *f.* female tenant; lodger; —frei, *adj.* rent-free; —gaul, *m. contd.* hack, job-horse; —geld, *n.* 1) a) hire; b) *see* —zins; 2) *or* —groschen, *m.* earnest, deposit-money; fe(a)sting penny; einem Dienstboten —geld geben, to bind a servant; —gut, *n.* farm, leasehold; —haus, *n.* hired house; —herr, *m.* landlord; master; —hof, *m. see* —gut; —jahr, *n.* year of renting or hiring; —knecht, *m.* servant hired from day to day; —kutsche, *f.* hackney-coach; —kutscher, *m.* hackney-coachman; —lakai, *m.* hired-servant, *valet de place*; —leute, *pl.* lodgers.

Mieth'ling, (*str.*) *m.* hireling, mercenary.

Mieth'..., *in comp.* —lohn, *m.* & *n.* hire, wages; —lustig, *adj.* desirous of hiring or renting; —mann, *m.* lodger, inmate; tenant; lessee; —meister, *m. provinc. see* Miether; —pfennig, *m. see* —geld, 2; —pferd, *n.* hackney-horse, hack-horse, *coll.* hack; job-horse.

Mieths'..., *in comp. see* Mieth....

Mieth'..., *in comp.* —soldat, *m.* mercenary soldier; —stall, *m.* hackney-stable; —stück, *n.* tenement; —truppen, *f. pl.* mercenary troops.

Mie'thung, (*w.*) *f.* the (act of) hiring, &c.

Mieth'..., *in comp.* —vertrag, *m. see* —contract; —vieh, *n.* cattle and sheep taken into pasture for hire; —wagen, *m. see* —kutsche; —weise, *adv.* by way of hire; —wohner, *m.*, —wohnerin, *f.* tenant; lodger; —zeit, *f.* hiring-time; time or duration of lease; —zettel, *m.* bill for letting a house, &c.; —zins, *m.* (house-)rent.

Mie'tig, *adj. provinc.* full of mites.

Mie'ze, (*w.*) *f.* (*dimin.* Miez'chen, [*str.*] *n.*) *coll.* (—katze) cat, puss, pussy.

* Mignon'ne (*pr.* minyŏn'ne), (*w.*) *f.* (*Fr.*) *Typ.* pearl. [bominenzy.

* Migrä'ne, (*w.*) *f.* (*Fr.*) *Med.* megrim.

Mi'guel, *m.* (*Port.*) Miguel, Michael (*P. N.*). — Miguelist', (*w.*) *m.*, Miguelis'tisch, *adj.* Miguelite.

Mikro..., *see* Micro.... [illegible]

* Milan', (*str.*) *m.* (*Fr.*) *Ornith.* kite ([illegible]

Mil'be, (*w.*) *f.* 1) *Entom.* mite; moth; woodlouse; 2) *provinc.* a species of carp (*Cyprinus carpius*).

Mil'big, *adj.* full of mites.

Milch, I. (*w.*) *f.* 1) milk; geronnene —, curds; 2) milt, soft roe (of fishes); in die — geben, to put out to nurse; in erster — *fig.* in infancy; II. *in comp.* —achat, *m.* milk-white agate; —ader, *f. Anat.* lacteal vein; —ähnlich, —artig, *adj.* like (or resembling) milk, lacteal; —ahorn, *m. Bot.* 1) Norway-maple (*Acer platanoides* L.); —asch, *m.* milk-pan; —[illegible], *f. see* —straße; —bart, *m.* 1) downy beard; 2) *coll.* milksop, whey-faced boy; —bärtig, *adj.* 1) having a downy beard; 2) *coll.* whey-faced, boyish, green; —baum, *m. Bot.* milk-tree (*Galactodendron utile* Kth.); —bereitung, *f.* generation or secretion of milk; —[illegible], *see* Kuhpocke; —blume, *f. Bot.* common milkwort (*Polygala* L.); —[illegible], *f. see* —[illegible]; —branntwein, *m.* Tartar brandy; —[illegible] milk-pap; —bretzel, *f.* cracknel made [illegible] and milk; —brod, *n.*, *[illegible]*. —[illegible] French-roll; —bruder, *m.* 1) [illegible] 2) person fond of milk; —[illegible], *f.* [illegible]

n. ministerial edict. — **Ministeriell'**, *adj.* ministerial. — **Ministe'rium**, *(str., pl. (w.)* M-'rien) *n.* ministry; administration; — des Innern, ministry of the interior, home-department.

Mini'ster..., *in comp.* —präsident, *m.* president of the ministry; —rath, *m.* council of ministers; —resident, *m.* minister resident; —verantwortlichkeit, *f.* ministerial responsibility; —wechsel, *m.* change of ministry.

* **Ministrant'**, *(w.) m. see* Meßdiener.

Mink, *m. Zool.* mink, minx (Nörz).

Min'ne, *(w.) f.* († &) *, love: (*cf.* Liebes ...) —barde, —dichter, *m. see* —sänger; —hof, *m. see* Liebeshof; —lohn, —preis, —sold, *m.* swain's reward, crowned love.

Min'nen, *(w.) v. tr. & intr.* († &) *, to love.

Min'nesam, **Min'nig**, **Min'niglich**, *adj.* († &) *, lovely.

Min'ne..., *in comp.* —sänger, —singer, *m.* minnesinger, poet of love (ancient school of German lyric poets from the twelfth to the middle of the thirteenth century).

* **Minorāt'**, *(str.) n. (Lat.)* right of succession of the youngest son.

* **Minorativ**, *adj. Med.* gently purging or weakening.

* **Minorenn'**, *adj.*, **Minorennität'**, *(w.) f. (L. Lat.) see* Minderjährig, Minderjährigkeit.

* **Minorit'**, *(w.) m. (Lat.) Eccl.* Minorite.

* **Minorität'**, *(w.) f. see* Minderheit.

* **Minotaur'**, *(str. & w.) m. Greek Myth.* minotaur.

* **Minuend'**, *(w.) m. (Lat.) see* Abzugszahl.

* **Minus'kel**, *(w.) f. (Lat.) Lit.* minuscule, *pl.* minuscule characters (used in ancient MSS.).

* **Minu'te**, *(w.) f. (Lat.)* minute; auf die —, to a minute; zu jeder — in Bereitschaft, ready at a minute's notice.

* **Minu'ten...**, *in comp.* —glas, *n.* minute-glass; —linie, *n. Mar.* minute-line; —rad, *n.* minute-wheel; —sanduhr, *f.* minute-glass; —uhr, *f.* minute watch; —weiser, —zeiger, *m.* minute-hand.

* **Minutie'ren**, *(w.) v. intr.* to carry on a retail trade (Kleinhandel treiben).

Minüt'lich, **Minüt'lich**, *adj.* occurring every minute; momently.

* **Minz**, *(str.) m. see* Nörz.

Min'ze, *(w.) f. see* Münze, A.

Mir, *pron. (Dat. of* Ich) to me, me: von —, at my hands. [plum; grüne —, green gage.

* **Mirabel'le**, *(w.) f. Pomol.* mirabelle-

* **Miraculös'**, *adj. (L. Lat.)* miraculous, *see* Wunderbar. — **Mira'kel**, *(str.) n.* miracle, prodigy.

* **Mirban-Öl**, *(str.) n.*

* **Misanthrop'**, *(w.) m. (Gr.)* misanthrope, misanthropist. — **Misanthropie'**, *(w.) f.* misanthropy. — **Misanthro'pisch**, *adj.* misanthropical. [nies.

* **Miscella'neen**, **Miscel'len**, *pl.* miscella-

Misch, *(str.) m. see* Mischmasch & Misch-korn; —arznei, *f.* mixture.

Misch'bar, I. *adj.* miscible; II. M-keit, *(w.) f.* miscibility.

Misch'ehe, *(w.) f.* marriage between persons of different creed or rank, mixed marriage.

Misch'el, *(str.) m.*, —korn, *n. see* Mischkorn.

Misch'eln, *(w.) v. tr.* 1) to mix, mingle; 2) to adulterate, drug.

Misch'en, *(w.) v.* I. *tr.* 1) to mix, mingle, blend; die Karten —, to shuffle the cards; (auf betrügerische Weise) to pack the cards; 2) to adulterate, drug; II. *refl.* to mix itself, to be mixed; sich in etwas *(Acc.)* —, *fig.* to interpose, to interfere, to meddle with; sich unter das Volk 2c. —, to mix with the people; *cf.* Mengen.

Misch'er, *(str.) m.* mixer, &c.

Mischerei', *(w.) f. see* Gemisch.

Misch'..., *in comp.* —farbe, *f.* mixed colour; —fleisch, *n. Cook.* salmagundi; —[illegible], *n.* mixed provender; —gefäß, *n.* vessel [illegible] mixing in; —gericht, *n.* medley, olio, ragout; —geschlecht, *n.* half-breed; —[illegible], *m.* [illegible] —korn; —klumpen, *m.* chaos, chaotic [illegible] —korn, *n.* meslin; —krug, *m. see* —gefäß.

Misch'ling, *(str.) m.* 1) *see* [illegible]; 2) a being of a mixed race or breed; hybridous animal; half breed; mongrel.

Misch'..., *in comp.* —masch, *m.* & *(str.)* *m.* medley, hodgepodge, mishmash, olio, balderdash, *fig.* chaos; —maschen, *(w.) v. tr. & intr.* to jumble together, to make a medley of; —metall, *n.* compound metal; —speise, *f. see* —fleisch; —spiel, *n.* tragi-comedy; —theil, *m.* ingredient.

Misch'ung, *(w.) f.* 1) the (act of) mixing, &c.; 2) mixture, *Chem.* composition, alloy, combination; M-sgewicht, *n. Chem.* equivalent, atomic weight; M-srechnung, *f. Arith.* rule of alligation.

Misch'..., *in comp.* —wein, *m.* 1) mixed wine; 2) drugged wine; —wort, *n.* mixed word. [*provinc.* to drizzle.

Mi'seln, **Mis'ern**, *(w.) v. intr.* [illegible]

* **Mise're**, *(w.) f. (Fr.)* 1) wretchedness (Elend, Noth); 2) rabble (Lumpenpack); 3) (*gener.* *(str.) m.*) variety in the game of boston.

* **Misere're**, *(str.) n. (Lat.)* 1) miserere (50th psalm); 2) *Med.* miserere (mei), iliac passion.

Mis'pel, *(w.) f. Bot.* medlar; —baum, *m.* medlar-tree (*Mespilus germanica* L.); —braun, *n. T.* medlar-dye.

* **Mis'pickel**, *(str.) m.* 1) *see* [illegible]; 2) *(J. Paul) fig.* poisonous composition.

* **Missal'**, *n. (L. Lat.)* 1) *Eccl.* missal; 2) *Typ.* French canon.

Mis'sen, *(w.) v. tr.* 1) to miss, to be or do without, to dispense with, to spare; 2) *provinc.* to fail, *see* Verfehlen.

Mis'sethat, *(w.) f.* misdeed, crime, offence.

Mis'sethäter, *(str.) m.*, **Mis'sethäterin**, *(w.) f.* criminal, malefactor, delinquent; convict, felon.

† **Mis'sewende**, *(w.) f.* ill turn, failure.

Mist, *s.* I. *(str.)* 1) dung, manure, muck, soil, dirt; 2) excrements, droppings (of animals); 3) *provinc.* mist, fog; das ist nicht auf seinem — gewachsen, *coll.* that has not grown on his soil; *anal.* he is not father to that child; II. *in comp.* —bad, *n. Dy.* dung-bath; —bauer, *m.* dung-carter; —beet, *n.* hotbed; —beetgabel, *f.* garden-fork; —beetkasten, *m.* garden-frame, glazed box for a hotbed.

Mis'tel, *(w.) f.* mistletoe (*Viscum album* L.); —drossel, *f.*, —fink, *m.*, **Mistler**, *(str.)* *m. Ornith.* mistle-bird, mistle-thrush (*Turdus viscivorus* L.).

Mis'ten, *(w.) v.* I. *intr.* 1) to dung; 2) to mute (of birds of prey); 3) *provinc.* [illegible]; II. *tr.* 1) to dung, muck; 2) *see* [illegible]misten.

Mist'..., *in comp.* —fink, *m.* 1) *a)* [illegible] fink; *b) see* Wiedehopf; 2) *vulg.* a dirty [illegible] nasty person, daggle-tail; —[illegible], dung-fly (*Scatophaga stercoraria* L.); —[illegible] —gabel, *f.* dung-fork; —fuhre, *f.* 1) [illegible] of manure; 2) load of dung; —[illegible] —jauche; —grube, *f.* dung-hole, [illegible] —hammel, *m. see* —fink, 2; —[illegible] midden, hill; —hof, *m.* dung-yard, [illegible] yard.

Mist'ig, *adj.* 1) dungy; [illegible]

Mist'..., *in comp.* —jauche, *f.* dung-[illegible] —käfer, *m. Entom.* muck-worm, [illegible] (*Aphodius fimetarius* L.); —karren, [illegible] *m.* dung-cart; —lache, *f.* puddle.

Mist'ler, *(str.) m. see* [illegible]

Mist'..., *in comp.* —pfütze, *f.* [illegible] —reich, *adj.* dungy; —[illegible], *m.* [illegible]

Miß'wahl, *(w.) f.* wrong choice; bad choice.

Miß'wählen, *(w.) v. tr.* to choose ill.

Miß'weisen, *(str.) v. tr.* to misdirect.

Miß'weisung, *(w.) f. T.* variation, declination (of the needle).

Miß'werfen, *(str.) v. tr.* 1) to cast wrong; to miss the mark; 2) to miscarry (of animals).

Miß'wirken, *(w.) v. intr.* to produce a wrong effect, to effect a bad result.

Miß'wirkung, *(w.) f.* bad effect *or* result.

Miß'wollen, *(irr.) v. intr. (with Dat.)* to be unfavourably disposed towards ..., *see* Übelwollen.

Miß'wort, *(str., pl.* Miß'wörter *&* Miß'worte*) n.* wrongly derived *or* formed word; ill-applied *or* disagreeable word.

Miß'wuchs [wūx], *(str., pl.* M-wüchse*) m.* 1) *see* Mißwachs, 1; 2) *see* Unkraut.

Miß'wurf, *(str., pl.* Miß'würfe*) m.* wrong throw *or* cast.

Miß'zieren, *(w.) v. tr. see* Verunzieren.

Miß'zug, *(str., pl.* Miß'züge*) m.* 1) wrong pull; 2) wrong move; 3) disagreeable feature.

Mit, I. *prep. (with Dat.)* with; by; at; to; kommen Sie — uns, come (along) with us; wir belasten Sie —, *Comm.* we debit you with ...; gebucht — ... Gulden, booked with ... florins; — einander, one with another, *cf.* Einander; — leiser Stimme, in a low *or* soft voice; — goldenen Buchstaben, in golden letters; — Bleistift schreiben, to write in pencil; der Mann — der eisernen Maske, the man in the iron mask; — Namen ..., of the name of ...; Einen — Namen nennen, to call one by his name; ein Topf — Honig, a pot of honey; ein Schiff — Soldaten, a ship full of soldiers; — der dritten &c. Classe fahren, to travel (go) third, &c. class, *coll.* to go third, &c.; — dem Alter, as we get old; — einem Striche, at one blow; — einem Worte, with one word, at (in) a word; — Muße, at leisure, leisurely; — der Post, by the post; — einem (Eisenbahn-)Zuge fahren, to travel by a (railway-)train; der Senat nahm Gen. Schenck's Finanzgesetzvorschlag — 30 gegen 16 Stimmen an, the Senate passed, by thirty votes to sixteen, General Schenck's Finance-Bill; — Gewalt, by force, — Hülfe der Nacht, by (the) favour of the night; — Erlaubniß, under favour; — Protest zurückschicken, to return under protest; bis — dem vierten Juli, to the fourth of July inclusive; — Vorsatz, out of design, on purpose; — der Zeit, in (process of) time; — deinen Possen! get along with your buffoonery! wie geht's — (der Abschrift des) Plutarch? how goes Plutarch?

II. *adv.* together (with), also, too, likewise; jointly, in conjunction, union, *or* company (with others), in common; simultaneously; at the same time; *as an adv. it is often expressed by the verb:* to join; —beten, to join in prayer; —lachen, to join (in) one's laugh; —spaßen, to join (one's) mirth; sie war zu stolz — zu tanzen *(Gellert)*, she was too proud to join (in) the dance; — ansehen, to be an eye-witness of ..., to witness *(cf.* Ansehen, *b)*; — dabei sein, to be of the party; — zu einer Leiche gehen, to accompany a funeral; — daran lag es, it had something to do with it.

III. *in comp. it is often rendered by* con, com, co-, fellow-, joint, &c., *f. i.* —älteste, *m.* fellow-senior, co-elder, &c.

Mit'angeklagte, *m. (decl. like adj.) see* Mitbeklagte.

Mitan'sehen, *see under* Mit.

Mit'anzeige, *(w.) f. Med.* co-indication.

Mit'arbeiten, *(w.) v. intr.* to labour *or* work jointly (an *[with Dat.]*, in); to be fellow-labourer, to assist (in).

Mit'arbeiter, *(str.) m.* fellow-labourer, fellow-worker, work-fellow; assistant; *particul.* contributor (to a literary work, &c.), fellow-writer; die sämmtlichen regelmäßigen — (an einer Zeitschrift &c.), the staff of contributors. [in office, colleague.

Mit'beamte(r), *m. (decl. like adj.)* fellow

Mit'bedachte, *m. (decl. like adj.)* co-legatee.

Mit'bediente, *m. (decl. like adj.)* 1) fellow-servant; 2) person waited upon likewise *or* by the same servant.

Mit'begleitung, *(w.) f.* concomitancy.

Mit'beklagte, *m. (decl. like adj.) Law*, co-defendant. [get, or have for one's portion.

Mit'bekommen, *(str.) v. tr.* to receive,

Mit'belehnen, *(w.) v. tr.* to invest, enfeoff at the same time *or* simultaneously. — **Mit'belehnung**, *(w.) f.* co-investiture.

Mit'bericht, *(str.) m.* report relating to the same subject. [dant.

Mit'beschenkte, *m. (decl. like adj.)* co-

Mit'besitz, *(str.) m. Law*, joint tenancy, possession *or* ownership, parcenary. — **Mit'besitzen**, *(str.) v. tr.* to possess together with or conjointly with another.

Mit'besitzer, *(str.) m.*, M-in, *(w.) f.* joint possessor *or* proprietor, co-proprietor.

Mit'bevollmächtigte, *m. (decl. like adj.)* joint commissary *or* proxy.

Mit'bewerben, *(str.) v. refl.* to be competitor, to compete (um, for).

Mit'bewerber, *(str.) m.* competitor, rival.

Mit'bewerbung, *(w.) f.* competition.

Mit'bewohner, *(str.) m.* joint inhabitant, cohabitant. [share.

Mit'bezahlen, *(w.) v. intr.* to pay one's

Mit'bezeichnen, *(w.) v. tr.* to connotate.

Mit'bieten, *(str.) v. intr.* to bid at the same time.

Mit'bringen, *(irr.) v. tr.* to bring or carry along (with); ich habe einen Stock mitgebracht, I (have) brought a cane; hat er seinen Bruder gestern mitgebracht? did he bring his brother with him yesterday? Einem etwas —, to bring as a present; diese Kenntniß des Alterthums brachte er zur Universität mit, this knowledge of antiquity he carried up to college; diese Ideen brachte er mit zur Beurtheilung des Systems, these notions he carried into his estimates of the system.

Mit'bruder, *(str., pl.* Mit'brüder*) m.* brother; fellow, colleague.

Mit'buhler, *(str.) m.* rival.

Mit'bürge, *(w.) m.* fellow-bail, fellow-guarantee, co-surety. [or joint-bail.

Mit'bürgen, *(w.) v. intr.* to stand fellow

Mit'bürger, *(str.) m.*, M-in, *(w.) f.* fellow-citizen, fellow-townsman (fellow-townswoman).

Mit'bürgschaft, *(w.) f.* joint security.

Mit'cavent, *(w.) m.* co-surety.

Mit'christ, *(w.) m.* fellow-christian.

Mit'contrahent, *(w.) m.* joint contractor.

Mit'dasein, *(str.) n.* coexistence.

Mit'diener, *(str.) m.* fellow-servant.

Mit'dürfen, *(irr.) v. intr. ellipt. for* Mitgehen, Mitfahren &c. dürfen, to be allowed to go along, &c.

Mit'eigenthum, *(str.) n.* joint property; M-srecht, *n.* joint ownership.

Mit'eigenthümer, *(str.) m.* joint proprietor or owner, partner.

Miteinan'der, *adv.* together, jointly.

Mit'einschließen, *(str.) v. tr. fig.* to include with something else, to imply.

Mit'einverstanden, *see* Einverstehen.

Mit'empfinden, *(str.) v. tr.* to feel [illegible] to sympathise; ein Vergnügen —, to [illegible] of a pleasure; das —, *(str.) n. s.* [illegible] dung, *(w.) f.* sympathy, *Med.* consent of [illegible]

* **Mi'ter**, *(w.) f. see* Mitra.

Mit'erbe, *(w.) m.* co-heir, joint heir.

Mit'erben, *(w.) v. intr.* to be [illegible]

Mit'erbin, *(w.) f.* co-heiress, [illegible]

Mit'erbschaft, *(w.) f.* joint [illegible] heritance, *Law:* coparcenary.

—schlößchen, n., —schlummer, m. see —ruhe; —seite, f. south-side: Zimmer auf der —seite, rooms with a southern aspect; —sonne, f. meridian sun; —stunde, f. noon-hour; —tafel, f., —tisch, m. dinner; —uhr, f. dial-plate; —volk, n. southern people; —wind, m. meridional wind, south(ern) wind; —zeche, f. inn-charge for a dinner; —zeit, f. noon-time, noon-tide.

Mit'tagwärts, adv. southward, toward the south.

Mit'tänzer, (str.) m., M-in, (w.) f. partner (at a dance).

Mit'te, (w.) f. 1) middle, midst; centre; waist; 2) mean, medium; aus der —, from amidst; die — des Beines, die — der Fasten, mid-leg, mid-lent &c.; Einer aus unserer —, fig. one of our company, one from among us; die (rechte) — halten, to keep or observe the right medium; das Reich der Mitte, Geogr. the Chinese empire; — dieses Monats, in the middle of this month.

Mit'tel, I. adj. (l. u.) middle; middling; intermediate; mittler Weile, (in the) meanwhile, in the interim.

II. (str.) n. 1) middle, midst, medium; average; 2) means, medium, way, expedient; instrument; falsches —, wrong method; 3) Med. remedy (gegen, for), medicine; ein — gegen das Ausfallen der Haare, a remedy for the falling off of hair; 4) pl. means, property, fortune, funds; mit ungeschwächten M-n, with capital intact; sich ins — schlagen or ins — treten, to interpose, intercede, interfere, intervene, mediate; aus seinen eigenen M-n, at his own expense, out of his own means; aus eigenen M-n sich erhaltend, self-supporting; bei M-n (reich) sein, to be wealthy; — und Wege, ways and means; — und Wege wissen or finden, to find means, to contrive.

III. in comp. —aal, m. middle-sized eel; —ader, f. Med. median vein; —africa, n. central Africa; —alter, n. 1) middling age; 2) Chron. middle ages; —alterlich, adj. middle-age, mediaeval; —america, n. central America, —antiqua, f. Typ. English letter; —armnerv, m. Anat. median nerve; —art, f. middling sort; hybridous breed; —artig, adj. middling; hybridous; —asien, n. central Asia; —balken, m. Ship-b. midshipbeam; —band, n. Gunn. astragal girdle of a cannon.

Mit'telbar, I. adj. mediate, indirect; II. M-keit, (w.) f. mediateness, indirectness.

Mit'tel..., in comp. Mus-s. —baß, m. mean bass; —baßgeige, f. violoncello; —bauchbruch, m. Surg. ventral hernia; —bauchgegend, f. Anat. umbilical or mesogastric region; —begriff, m. Log. middle term; —bogen, m. Archit. centre-arcade; —bohrer, m. middle-tap; —bolzen, m. Coach-m. splinter; —bret, n. T. inch-plank; —brot, n. whity-brown bread; —bruch, m. T. ward (of a lock); —buchstabe, m. Typ. medial letter; —bürger, m. citizen of the middling class; —canon, f. Typ. double-great primer; —cicero, f. Typ. middle pica; —cours, m. median rate of exchange; —darm, m. Anat. great gut; —deck, n. Mar. middle(-)deck; —ding, n. a thing intermediate between two others; —druck, m. Med. middle pressure; —england, n. middle England; mid-England; —ente, f. Ornith. gadwall, gray widgeon (Tafelente); —ernte, f. average harvest; —europa, n. Geogr. middle or central Europe; —fall, m. see Gleitfall; —farbe, f. middle tint, intermediate colour, mezzo-tinto; —fein, adj. middling fine; —feld, n. 1) Herald. centre-field, nombril; 2) Bot. disk; —fell, n. Anat. mediastine; —finger, m. middle-finger; —fläche, f. see —feld, 2; —fleisch, n. Anat. perinaeum; —frei, adj. Law, mediately free; —fuß, m. 1) Anat. metatarsus; 2) foot of middling size; 3) foot in the middle; —fußknochen, m. Anat. metatarsal bone; —[illegible], m. center; —gang, m. 1) Man. [illegible] (of a horse); 2) Archit. middle walk or gallery; —garn, n. middle twist; —gattung, f. 1) middling sort; intermediate species or sort; 2) Gramm. neuter gender; —gebäude, n. centre building; —gebirge, n. central or secondary chain of mountains, intermediate mountains; —geige, f. Mus. violoncello; —geschirr, n. body-harness, ridge-band; —glied, n. middle limber member; Log. middle term; —größe, f. middling size; von —größe, middle-sized; —grund, m. centre ground; —gurt, m. 1) middle girdle (of a saddle), surcingle; 2) see —band; —gut, n. middling goods, goods of second quality; —gute Qualität, second quality, middling; —gute Wechsel, m. Comm. second rate paper, trade-paper; —haar, n. T. crown of a periwig; —hand, f. 1) Anat. metacarpus; zur —hand gehörig, metacarpal; 2) Gam. second hand (at cards); —handknochen, m. metacarpal bone; —handsäge, f. Surg. metacarpal saw; —haut, f. Bot. mesocarp; —holz, n. middle-sized wood of trees; —jagd, f. Sport. the hunting of roes, boars, grouse, &c.; —kalkstein, m. transition limestone; —kasten, m. Carp. middle [illegible]; —klüver, m. Mar. middle jib; —kreis, m. Astr. equator; —land, n. 1) intermediate land; 2) inland; —ländisch, adj. inland; mediterranean; das —ländische Meer, Geogr. Mediterranean (Sea); —latein, n. low Latin; —laut, m. Mus. mediant; —leinwand, f. linen of middling quality; —linie, f. middle line; Med. mesial line; equator; —loch, n. Bill. middle-pocket; —loge, f. Theat. balcony box; Theat. (die große —loge) front box.

Mit'tellos, I. adj. without means, poor; II. M-igkeit, (w.) f. the being without means, poverty.

Mit'tel..., in comp. —mann, m. 1) middle-man, 2) man of the middle class; —maß, n. middle rate, average, medium; mediocrity; —mäßig, adj. middling, indifferent, moderate, mediocre; average; adv. indifferently, tolerably; —mäßig groß, middling-sized, moderate-sized; —mäßigkeit, f. mediocrity, moderateness, tolerableness; —mast, m. Mar. main-mast; —mauer, f. party-wall; partition wall; —meer, n. see das —ländische Meer; —mehl, n. middling or second flour; —nerv, m. an—[illegible]; —papier, n. mean-paper; —pfeiler, m. 1) central pillar; 2) window-pier; —pferd, n. 1) middle-sized horse; 2) centre [illegible]; —preis, m. mean or medium price, average price; —punct, m. centre, central point; —punctständig, adj. Bot. central; —[illegible], m. middle-rail; —rad, n. Watch-m. centre wheel; —radsgetriebe, n. spring of the central wheel; —raß, —rate, f. [illegible]; —raum, m. interval, intermediate or intermediate space; —reifen, m. middle [illegible]; —riegel, m. 1) middle-bolt; 2) [illegible] middle cross-piece; 3) Coach-b. middle [illegible]; —rippe, f. mid-rib; —röhrchen, n. [illegible] small pipe (of a gun).

Mit'tels, adv. (with Gen.) by means of, by the help of, through.

Mit'tel..., in comp. —satz, m. [illegible] pound, secondary, or [illegible] [illegible] Gramm. intermediate sentence; Log. [illegible] —säule, f. central column; —schaft, [illegible] Gewehres) Gun-sm. middling of the [illegible] a musket; —schicht, f. Bot. [illegible] —schiff, n. Archit. middle [illegible] adj. Mill middle-shot; die —[illegible] centre-float mill; das —[illegible] n. breast (water-) wheel; —[illegible] —schrot; 2) middle kind of [illegible] middling, cf. —sorte; —[illegible] larger bog-snipe ([illegible] n. see —gang, 1; —schwert, [illegible]

Modemann, (str., pl. M-männer, M-leute) m. man of fashion, beau, dandy.

Mo'dena, n. Geogr. Modena.

Mo'de..., in comp. –narr, M-aufseher, a fashion-monger, [illegible] fop, dandy; –narrheit, f. see –[illegible]; –[illegible], f. woman ridiculously observant of fashion; –[illegible], adj. foppish. [Modemann.

Modena'ser, (str.) m., Modena'[illegible], adj.

Mo'der, (str.) m. 1) mud; mould; rottenness, putridity; 2) mouldering, decay; zu – werden, to turn to mould, to moulder, decay.

Mo'derartig, adj. see Moderhaft.

* Moderamen' [–tie'], (str.) m. T. moderator; –lampe, f. moderator-lamp.

* Modera'tor, (str. pl. [–en] Moderato'ren) m. 1) moderator; 2) Mech. governor, conical pendulum.

Mo'der..., in comp. –[illegible], –[illegible], –geruch, m. fusty or musty smell; –[illegible], f. Ornith. swamp-duck (Anas marila L.); –erde, f. rotten earth; –erz, n. see Sumpferz; –fisch, m. Ich. mud-fish, amia (Amia calva L.); –flecken, m. mildew-mould; –fleckig, adj. mildewed; –grund, m. 1) muddy soil; 2) muddy bottom. [decaying.

Mo'derhaft, Mo'dericht, adj. mouldering.

Mo'derhamen, (str.) m. dredging-net.

Mo'derig, adj. mouldy, muddy, earthy; mildewed.

Mo'der..., in comp. –käfer, m. Entom. carrion-beetle (Aaskäfer); –kahn, m. see –prahm; –[illegible], m. see [illegible]; –maschine, f. dredging-machine.

Mo'dern, (w.) v. I. intr. to moulder, decay; II. tr. 1) to cause to moulder; 2) to cleanse of mud; 3) to manure with mud.

* Modern', adj. (Fr.) modern, fashionable.

* Modernisi'ren, (w.) v. tr. to modernize.

Mo'derock, (str., pl. M-röcke) m. fashionable coat.

Mo'der..., in comp. –pilz, m. Bot. hypnum (Hypnum Hedw.), –prahm, m. mud-barge, ballast-lighter; –stoff, m. Chem. ulmine.

Mo'de..., in comp. –schneider, m. fashionable tailor; –schneidergeschäft, n. fashionable tailoring establishment; –schriftsteller, m. fashionable author.

* Modesti'en, pl. fam. inexpressibles, unmentionables.

Mo'de..., in comp. –stoffe, m. pl. fancy-stuffs; –sucht, f. mania for fashions; –süchtig, adj. foppish, following fashion eagerly; –tand, m. see –kram; –thor, m. see –narr; –thorheit, f. 1) see –sucht; 2) fashionable folly; –tuch, m. Comm. fancy-cloth; –waaren, f. pl. fancy-articles, fancy-goods; Holz zu –waaren, fancy-wood; –waarenhandel, m. fancy trade; –waarenhändler m., see –händler; –waarenhandlung, see –handlung, 2; haberdashery; –welt, f. world of fashion; –zeitung, f. gazette of fashion; –zeuge, m. pl. fancy cloths.

* Modification', (w.) f. (Lat.) modification. – Modifici'ren, (w.) v. tr. to modify, qualify.

Mo'disch, adj. fashionable, stylish.

* Modist', (w.) m. man-milliner. – Modist'in, (w.) f. milliner, (Fr.) modiste.

Mo'dul, (str., pl. M-e) m. see Model. 1.

* Modulation', (w.) f. (Lat.) Mus. modulation, intonation. – Moduli'ren, (w.) v. tr. to modulate. [mood.

* Mo'dus, (Lat., pl. Mo'di) m. Gramm.

Möff, (str.) m. provinc. (Dutch.) (low) fellow. – Möffeln, (w.) v. intr. provinc. to speak indistinctly, to mumble.

Mö'gen, (irr.) v. intr. 1) †, to be able, can; 2) may; sometimes ellipt. with an Acc. (provinc. & * with a Gen.) to like; to wish, desire; to have a mind to; to choose; daraus möchte nicht[s] werden, that is likely enough to fail or not to be done (to come to nothing), may likely nothing will come of [illegible] ... [illegible] ... it is enough to drive one mad; [illegible] they may do it, but those do it; [illegible] ... it may be, but [illegible] ... [illegible] ... he might (would) then be twenty; [illegible] ... tell him to convey [illegible] ... that might or would be a difficult [illegible], I presume; [illegible] ... would be welcome to know; ich möchte wissen, I should like to know, I am curious to know, I wonder ...; [illegible] ... to dislike; gern –, 1. to like, to be desirous to ...; 2. to like, to be fond of, to be partial to; ich mag ihn sehr gern, I like him very much; [illegible] ... sympathies and antipathies; lieber –, to prefer, to choose rather or in preference; ich möchte gern, I would fain; lieber –, to choose rather; ich möchte lieber, I had rather; [illegible] möchte ich glauben, I am inclined to think; [illegible] möchte ich weinen, I could almost (am almost ready to) weep; ich hätte es ihm nicht sagen –, I should not have liked to tell it him; ich hätte es nicht sehen –, I would not have seen it; ich möchte nicht, daß er es wüßte, I would not have him know it; [illegible] ... [illegible] ... he cares not to confess; nun – sie [illegible] now for them!

Mög'lich, adj. possible, feasible, practicable; so gut als es mir – ist, to the best of my power; es war mir nicht –, it was out of my power; alles M-e, every thing possible (or within one's power); er versprach alles M-e, he promised any thing in life or any thing and every thing; alles M-e versuchen, to try every (possible) means, to strain every nerve; er verspricht alles M-e, coll. he [illegible] all sorts of things; alle nur m-en [illegible], every variety of cases; so gut wie –, to the best advantage; das einzige mir m-e Mittel, the only means within my command; –machen, to make possible, to render feasible, to contrive; to bring about, achieve, [illegible]; suchen Sie es – zu machen, try your best to effect it; er machte es mir – zu ..., he [illegible] in the way to ...; dadurch wurde es [illegible] gemacht, by this I was enabled [illegible] ... Gebrauch des Zuckers sollte den [illegible] Klassen – gemacht werden, the use of sugar ought to be brought within the reach of the labouring classes; Mög'lichst, (superl.) [illegible] as much as possible, to the utmost [illegible] bald, as soon as possible; sein M-es [illegible] to do one's best or utmost; [illegible] Kräften, to the best or utmost of [illegible] die m-ste Vorsicht, the utmost [illegible] ... Ueberfalls, Mög'licherweise, adv. [illegible] in case of possibility; possibly, [illegible] possible, by possibility.

Mög'lichkeit, (w.) f. possibility, [illegible] feasibility, practicability; [illegible] – ist da or vorhanden, coll. it is [illegible] – or M-sfall, m. contingency.

Mo'hammed, m. Mohammed [illegible].

Mohammeda'ner, (str.) m. [illegible] Mahometan; vgl. [illegible].

Mohn, (str.) m. Bot. poppy [illegible] wilder –, see Klatschmohn; [illegible] adj. papaverous; [illegible] garden-poppy; –blume, m. see [illegible]

m. sleep-walker, somnambulist; –tafeln, f. pl. lunar tables; –uhr, f. Astr. moon-dial; –umlauf, m. revolution of the moon; –veilchen, n. –viole, f. see –kraut, 2.; –viertel, n. Astr. quadrature, quarter (of the moon).

Mondswandelung, (w.) f. see Mondwechsel.

Mond'..., in comp. –wechsel, m. periodic change of the moon: lunation; wir haben –wechsel, the moon changes; –wind, m. see –kalb; –zahl, f. epacts (of the moon); –zirkel, see –cirkel.

* **Mone'ten**, f. pl. jock money.

Mongo'le, (w.) m., **Mongo'lisch**, adj. Mongolian, Mongol. Mongul. — **Mongolei'**, f. Geogr. Mongolia.

* **Moni'ren**, (w.) v. tr. 1) see Mahnen, 2; 2) Rügen; ich monire die folgenden Irrthümer, I point out the following errors.

Mon'kalb, (str., pl. Mon'kälber) n. mole, moon-calf, false conception.

* **Monochord'**, (str.) n. (Gr.) monochord.

* **Monodie'**, (w.) f. (Gr.) monody.

* **Monogamie'**, (w.) f. (Gr.) monogamy.

* **Monogamist'**, (w.) m. monogamist.

* **Monogramm'**, (str.) n. (Gr.) monogram.

* **Monographie'**, (w.) f. (Gr.) monography.

* **Monolith'**, (w.) m. (Gr.) monolith.

* **Monolog'**, (str. & (l. u.) w.) m. (Gr.) soliloquy, (l. u.) monologue. — **Monolo'gisch**, adj. & adv. having the form of a soliloquy; soliloquizing. — **Monologisi'ren**, (w.) v. intr. to soliloquize.

* **Monopol'**, (str.) n. (Gr.) monopoly, exclusive privilege; M–e auf Lebensbedürfnisse, monopolies on necessaries of life; — treiben, to monopolise. — **Monopolist'**, (w.) m. monopolist, monopoliser.

* **Monoton'**, adj. (Gr.) monotonous.

* **Monstranz'**, (w.) f. (M. Lat.) Rom. Cath. monstrance, pix (vessel in which the host is placed).

Mon'tag, (str.) m. Monday: eines M–s, on a Monday; (des) M–s, on Mondays; der blaue –, idle Monday, St. Monday, holiday.

Mon'tägig, **Mon'täglich**, adj. & adv. every Monday; on Mondays.

Montenegri'ner, (str.) m., **Montenegri'nisch**, Montenegrine.

* **Monti'ren**, (w.) v. tr. (Fr.) 1) see Fassen, 3, a.; 2) see Bemannen; 3) to mount and equip (horse-soldiers); 4) to clothe in regimentals; 5) to mount (a gun). — **Monti'rung**, (w.) f. soldier's dress; regimentals; accoutrements; uniform: M–kammer, f. magazine of army-clothing; M–slieferung, f. 1) government-contract for clothing; 2) issue of clothing; M–sstücke, n. pl. regimentals, mountings.

* **Montur'**, (w.) f. 1) see Montirung; 2) T. frame of a periwig; –band, n. hair-fillet; –kopf, m. head of a periwig.

* **Monument'**, (str.) n. (Lat.) monument.

Moor, (str.) n. & m. moor, fen, bog; in comp. –artig, adj. swampy, see Moorig; –bad, n. mud-bath; –beere, f. Bot. great or marsh bilberry, bogberry (Vaccinium uliginosum L.); –boden, m. bog, marshy soil; –brandkohle, f. see –kohle; –brennen, n. Agr. burning of heath, peat, &c. for manure; –damm, –deich, m. dike, dam, carried across a marsh; –eiche, f. Bot. bog-oak; –ente, f. fen-duck (Fuligula Leach.); –erde, f. bog-earth, peat-soil; –eule, f. fen- or moor-owl (Strix brachyotus L.); –gegend, f. marshy land, marshy country; –gras, n. Bot. moor-grass, sedge (Carex caespitosa L.); –grund, m. see Moor; –grundel, m. Ichth. mud-fish (Schlammpeitzger); –hahn, m. Ornith. gor-cock, see Wasserhahn; –heide, f. 1) heath on or of moor-land; 2) Bot. marsh-andromeda (Andromeda polifolia L.); –hirse, m. Bot. guinea corn, durra (Mohrenhirse); –huhn, n. Ornith. gor-hen, see Wasserhuhn.

Moo'rig, **Moo'richt**, adj. moory, fenny, marshy, boggy.

worm; —pulver, *n.* gnat poison; —schimmel, *m.* flea-bitten grey-horse; —schmalz, *n. see* —fett; —schnäpper, *m. see* —fänger, 1; —schwamm, *m. see* Fliegenschwamm; —sehen, *n.* a disease of the eyes, in which a person sees black spots resembling flies, &c., myodesopsy; —seiger, *m. fig.* one who strains at a gnat; —stecher, *m. see* —fänger, 1; —stein, *m. see* Fliegenstein; —stich, *m.* sting of a gnat, gnatbite; —vogel, *m. Ornith.* a species of humming-bird (*Trochilus minimus* L.); —wedel, *m.* fly-flap; —würger, *m. Bot.* dog's bane (*Apocynum androsæmifolium* L.).

Mucker, (*str.*) *m.* sulky person; impostor, double-dealer; saint (nickname for religious hypocrites, *cf.* Frömmler). [*n.* hypocrisy.

Muckerei', (*w.*) *f.*, **Muckerthum**, (*str.*)

Muckerhaft, **Muckerisch**, *adj.* canting, hypocritical. [peevish; silent.

Mucksch, *adj. coll.* sullen, saturnine;

Mucksen, *see* Mucken.

Mudder, (*str.*) *m.* 1) *see* Moder; 2) slime, ooze, mud; —mühle, *f.*, —prahm, *m.*, —schute, *f. see* Bagger, 2. — **Mudd'ern**, (*w.*) *v. intr. Mar.* to make foul water.

Müde, *adj.* weary, tired; ich werde nicht — zu versuchen, I don't relax my exertions in trying. [Ermüden.

Müden, (*w.*) *v. tr.* (*L. u.*) to weary *see*

Müdigkeit, (*w.*) *f.* weariness, lassitude, fatigue.

Muff, (*str.*, *pl.* Muffe & Müffe) *m.* 1) muff; 2) *T.* cap; socket, socket-end (of a pipe); (Kuppelungsmuff) *Mech.* coupling-box; 3) a bark, barking; 4) a large, loud barking dog; 5) *fig.* grumbler, snarler; 6) fusty, mouldering smell. [mitten; muffetee.

Müffchen, (*str.*) *n.* (*dimin. of* Muff)

Muffe, (*w.*) *f. T. see* Muff, 2.

Muffel, (*str.*) *m. coll.* 1) dog (*or* other animal) with large hanging lips; 2) hypocrite, canting fellow; 3) (—gesicht, *n.*) *a)* a bloated or blubberly face; *b) Archit.* lion's mouth (as a fountain-spout); 4) *provinc.* musty smell; 5) *Chem.* muffle; —gesicht, *n. see* Muffel 3.

Muffelig, *adj. coll.* ugly-faced; sullen.

Muffelkäfer, (*str.*) *m. Entom.* seed-beetle (Samenkäfer)

Muffeln, (*w.*) *v. intr. coll.* 1) to mumble, mutter; 2) to muffle up; 3) *coll.* to mumble, chew; 4) *see* Müffeln.

Muffel..., *in comp.* —ofen, *m.* muffle furnace; —thier, *n. Zool.* the wild sheep, musmon, muflon (*Ovis Musimon* Pall.).

A. **Muffen**, (*w.*) *v. intr.* to bark; *coll.* to be sulky. [fusty, musty, mouldy, or rank.

B. **Muffen**, **Müffen**, (*w.*) *v. intr.* to smell

Muffenverbindung, (*w.*) *f. T.* (der Röhren) joint with socket and muzzle.

Muffer, (*str.*) *m. coll.* sullen or sulky fellow.

Muffig, *adj. coll.* 1) sullen, pouting; 2) *or* **Müffig**, *adj.* fusty, musty, mouldy; frowzy.

Muffknaster, (*str.*) *m. Comm.* a sort of very good canister-tobacco.

Mufflen, (*w.*) *v. intr.* 1) *see* Mucksen; 2) *see* Müffen, *B.* [*see* Muffelthier.

* **Muflon'** [mŭflŏng'], (*str.*, *pl.* M—s) *m.*

Muh, *interj.* sound of a lowing cow.

Muhamedaner, (*str.*) *m.*, **M—in**, (*w.*) *f.*, **Muhamedanisch**, *adj.* Mahometan. — **Muhamedanis'mus**, *m.* Mahometanism.

Mühe, (*w.*) *f.* pains, trouble, toil, labour, pains-taking, exertion: sich (*Dat.*) — geben (mit, um), to take pains (with); sich (*Dat.*) die — nicht verdrießen lassen, not to shrink from *or* not to mind any pains *or* trouble; Einem — machen, to put one to trouble; — und Kosten haben, to be at pains and charges; die — umsonst haben, to lose one's labour; es kostete mir — es ihm zu sagen, it pained me to tell it him; wir ließen es uns große — kosten, wir gaben uns alle —, we did our best, we made every endeavour, we were at great (much) pains; nur mit vieler —, not without considerable pains; viele — und kein Gewinn, much pains little gains, hard work and no pay; es nimmt sich Niemand die — zu ..., nobody cares to ....

Mühelos (**Müh'los**), I. *adj.* without pains, without trouble, causing no trouble, labourless; II **M—igkeit**, (*w.*) *f.* the being without pains, *or* causing no trouble.

Muhen, (*w.*) *v. intr.* to low (of cows).

Mühen, (*w.*) *v.* I. *tr.* to trouble; II. *rcfl.* to trouble one's self, to endeavour; III. *impers.* to vex.

Mühe..., *in comp.* —voll (**Müh'voll**), *adj.* painful, troublesome, laborious; —waltung, *f.* pains-taking, care, assiduity, activity, efforts; trouble.

Mühl..., *in comp.* (*cf.* Mühlen ...) —arbeiter, *m. Min.* buddler; —arzt, *m. see* —zeugarbeiter; —bach, *m.* mill-brook; —bereiter, *m. Farr.* hand-workman; —berg, *m.* hill with a wind-mill; —beutel, *m.* bolter; —bottich, *m.* drum; —bursch, *m.* miller's man, miller's assistant.

Mühle, (*w.*) *f.* 1) mill; 2) *Gam.* a game at draughts; die — im Spiel, see-saw; das ist Wasser auf seine —, *fig.* that's grist to his mill.

Mühl'eisen, (*str.*) *n.* 1) *Mill.* mill-crank; 2) *Herald.* (*or* **Mühl'eisenkreuz**, *n.*) millrine

Mühlen..., *in comp.* (*cf.* Mühl ...) —amtmann, *m.* overseer of mills; —anker, *m.* mill-anchor; —bau, *m.* construction of a mill; —bauer, *m.* mill-wright; —baukunst, *f.* art of building mills; —bremse, *f.* stop of a windmill; —fachbaum, *m.* axle-tree of a water-mill; —flügel, *m. see* Windmühlenflügel; —gerechtigkeit, *f.* privilege of having a mill; —gerüst, —gestell, *n.* foundation-work of a mill; —getriebe, *n. Mech.* mill-work, mill-gear; —haus, *n.* windmill-cage; —meister, *m. see* —steiger; —ordnung, *f.* government regulations relating to mills; —pferd, *n.* mill-horse, gin-horse; —röhre, *f.* miller's scuttle; —ruder, *n.* mill-rod, mill-rudder; —sandstein, *m. Miner.* mill-stone grit; —schau, *f.* inspection of mills; —spiel, *n. see* Mühle, 2; —steiger, *m.* head man or inspector in mill-works; —stuhl, *m. T.* ribbonmaker's loom.

Mühl..., *in comp.* (*cf.* Mühlen ...) —gang, *m. see* Mahlgang; —gast, *m.* customer to a mill; —gebiet, *n. see* Mühlengerecht; —gerinne, *n.* mill-race, flume, —graben, *m.* mill-stream, water-gang; —klapper, *f.* mill-clack, mill-clapper; —knappe, *m. see* —bursch; —kram, *m.* mull (refuse and peelings of madder); —kunst, *f. see* —werk; —kasten, *m.* box, [illegible] —meister, *m.* 1) master of a mill, miller; 2) *see* —steiger; —metze, *f. see* Mahlmetze.

Mühlos *rc.*, *see* Mühelos.

Mühl'..., *in comp.* (*cf.* Mühlen ...) —[illegible] *m.* mill lever; —pfanne, *f.* [illegible] the iron cross; —rad, *n.* mill-wheel; —[illegible] schaufel, *f.* felly of a mill-wheel; —[illegible] *f.* cylinder of a mill-wheel; —[illegible] mill-grate; —rumpf, *m.* mill-hopper; —[illegible] *f.* mill-saw; —spiel, *n. see* Mühle, 2; —[illegible] der, *m.* sails of a windmill; —[illegible] —eisen, 1; —staub, *m.* mill-dust; —[illegible] bill; —steiger, *m.* Mühlensteiger; —[illegible] mill-stone, grind-stone; [illegible] burrstone; (oberer) runner; [illegible] —steinkiesel, *m. see* Kieselschiefer; —[illegible] *m. Miner* hornstone-quartz; —[illegible] Bandweben) *Weav.* bar-loom; [illegible] —teich, *m.* mill-pond; —trichter, [illegible] hopper, funnel; —zeugschuh, *m.* [illegible] hopper; —wagen *m.* mill-cart; [illegible] mill-water; —wehr, *n.* mill-dam, [illegible] —welle, *f.* main shaft of mill; [illegible] mill-work; mill; —zapfen, *m.* [illegible]

Münz'..., *in comp.* **–fälscher,** *m.* false coiner (Falschmünzer); **–fälschung,** *f.* forgery, adulteration of money; **–feile,** *f.* planchet-file; **–freiheit,** *f.* privilege of coining; **–fuß,** *m.* standard (of coinage); **–gebühr,** *f.*, **–gefälle,** *n.* mintage; **–gegenrechner,** *m.* deputy warden of the mint; **–gehalt,** *m.* standard of fineness, alloy; **–gekrätz,** *n. T.* sissel; **–gepräge,** *n.* stamp, impression of coins; **–geräth,** *n.* minting-tools; **–gerechtigkeit,** *f. see* –freiheit; **–geschichte,** *f.* medallic history; **–gewicht,** *n. T.* standard-weight; **–gleicher,** *m. see* –justirer; **–gold,** *n.* standard-gold; **–güte,** *f. see* –gehalt; **–hammer,** *m.* coiner's hammer; **–haus,** *n.* mint; **–herr,** *m.* 1) †. master of the mint; 2) a lord having the privilege of coining money; **–justirer,** *m.* adjuster, filer, weigher of the mint; **–kenner,** *m.* numismatician, numismatologist; **–knecht,** *m.* servant employed in the mint; **–kosten,** *f. pl.* (costs of) coinage, mintage; **–krätze,** *f. see* –gekrätz; **–kraut,** *n. Bot.* money-wort (Pfennigkraut); **–kunde,** *f.* numismatics; numismatology; **–kundig,** *adj.* skilled in the knowledge of coins; **–kundige,** *m. see* –kenner; **–kunst,** *f.* science of coining *or* coinage; **–liebhaber,** *m.* medallist; **–mahl,** *n.* †. stamp; **–meister,** *m.* mintmaster, warden of the mint; **–metall,** *n.* Muntz's metal; **–muschel,** *f. Conch.* cowry-shell (*Cypræa moneta* L.); **–ordnung,** *f.* regulations of a mint; **–ort,** *m. see* –statt; **–platte,** *f.* planchet; **–presse,** *f.* coining press; **–probe,** *f.* assay of a coin; **–rand,** *m.* edge, brink, rim of a coin; **–recht,** **–regal,** *n.* right of coinage, privilege of coining; **–reduction,** *f.* deterioration of coinage; **–richter,** *m.* provost of the mint; **–sammlung,** *f.* collection of coins, numismatic collection; **–schere,** *f.* cutter, coupoir; **–schiene,** *f.* pressing iron planchet (Tölk.); **–schlag,** *m.* coinage; **–schläger,** *m.* minter, coiner; **–schreiber,** *m.* clerk to the mint; **–schrift,** *f.* inscription of a coin; **–schrötling,** *m.* planchet; **–silber,** *n.* standard-silver; **–sorte,** *f.* species of money; **–stadt,** *f.* city which has the right of coinage, *or* where there is a mint; **–statt,** **–stätte,** *f.* 1) mint; 2) coinage-place; **–stein,** *m. Petr.* nummulite; **–stempel,** *m.* stamp, die; **–streckwerk,** *n.* flatter; **–stück,** *n.* 1) coin; 2) planchet; **–tarif,** *m.* standard of coin; **–verfälscher,** *m. see* –fälscher; **–vertrag,** *m. see* –convention; **–wage,** *f.* mint-scales; coin-weighing machine; **–wäger,** *m.* adjuster of the blanks; **–wardein,** **–wart,** *m.* mint-warden, assay-master, assayer *or* keeper of the mint; **–werk,** *n.* 1) mint-work; 2) number of one sort of coins worked off at one coinage; **–werth,** *m.* intrinsic value of coin; der gesetzlich bestimmte –, mint-price, mint-rate; **–wesen,** *n.* coinage; **–wissenschaft,** *f. see* –kunde; **–würdigung,** *f.* assay of coins; **–zeichen,** *n.* coiner's mark; mark on a coin; money-token; **–zeug,** *n.* coiner's instruments; **–zusatz,** *m.* alloy.

Mür'aal, (*str.*) *m. Ichth.* 1) miegura; 2) (*or* **Murä'ne,** (*w.*) *f.*) murena (*Muræna helena* L.).

Mür'be, *adj.* 1) mellow, tender, soft, (of cake, &c.) short, crisp; 2) *fig. a*) pliable; *b*) exhausted, weary; – machen, to curb, bend, lower, humble; to bring down; to wear out; m–s Eis, unsound ice.

Mür'be, Mür'bigkeit, (*w.*) *f.* mellowness, tenderness, softness, &c.

Mür'ben, (*w.*) *v.* I. *intr.* (*aux.* sein) to get mellow, &c. *see* Mürbe; to rot (as wood); II. *tr. see* Mürbe machen.

Mürb'weide, (*w.*) *f.* common white willow.

Mur'chel, (*w.*) *f. see* Trüffel.

Mür(e), (*w.*) *f. see* Mure.

Murks, (*str.*) *m. coll.* 1) contemptible fellow; 2) grunt of a pig.

Murk'sen, (*w.*) *v. coll.* I. *intr.* 1) to [illegible] 2) to be sulky; II. *tr.* to kill [illegible] despatch. [illegible]

Murl'stein, (*str.*) *m. Miner.* a kind of [illegible]

Mur'mel, (*str.*) *m.* 1) *see* –thier; 2) [illegible] –fisch; 3) marble (Märmel, Schusser[illegible]).

Mur'mel..., *in comp.* –bach, *m.* murmuring brook, babbling brook; –fisch, *m. Ichth.* a species of malacopterygious fish (*Normyrus anguilloides* Cuv.); –thier, *n.*, –maus, *f. Zool.* (alpine) marmot, mountain-rat (*Arctomys marmota* L.); [illegible] wood-chuck (*Arctomys monax* [illegible]).

Mur'meln, (*w.*) *v. intr. & tr.* 1) to murmur; to whisper, hum; 2) to grumble, mutter; der m–de Bach, humming, gurgling, *or* babbling brook.

Mur'ner, (*str.*) *m.* *, male-cat.

Murr'bart, (*str.*, *pl.* Murr'bärte) *m.* [illegible]

Mur're, (*w.*) *f. see* Mure. [illegible]

Mur'ren, (*w.*) *v. intr.* to murmur (über (*with Acc.*), gegen, at, against), mutter, grumble, growl, snarl; to complain.

* **Murrhi'nisch,** *adj.* myrrhine.

Mur'rig, Mür'risch, *adj.* surly, sulky, sullen, morose, cross, peevish, gruff, [illegible]; m–es Wesen, surliness, sullenness, &c.

Murr'..., *in comp.* –kopf, –katze, *m. coll.* a grumbling, peevish person, grumbler; –köpfig, *adj.* peevish, morose; –sinn, *m.* moroseness; –sinnig, *adj.* morose.

Mus, (*str.*) *n.* pap; any thick preparation of fruit, *as:* apple-sauce, &c.; –artig, *adj.* pappy, thick.

* **Musaget',** (*w.*) *m. Gr. Myth.* Musagetes, leader of the Muses (an epithet of Apollo and Hercules).

Muscat', (*str.*) *m. see* Muscatnuß; –blume, –blüte, *f.* mace (the arill of the nutmeg).

* **Musca'te,** (*w.*) *f.* (*Fr.*) nutmeg.

Muscatel'ler, (*str.*) *m.* muscadel, muscadine; *in comp. Pomol.* &c. –apfel, *m.* musk-apple; –birn, *f.* muscadel *or* muscadine pear; –beutel, *m.* musk-pouch; *Bot.* &c. –kirsche, *f.* musk-cherry; –kraut, *n.* moschatel (*Adoxa moschatellina* L., Bisamkraut); –salbei, *f.* clary, sage (*Salvia sclarea* L.); –traube, *f. Vit.* muscadine, grape muscat; –wein, *m. see* Muscateller.

Muscat'en..., *in comp.* –baum, *m. Bot.* nutmeg-tree (*Myristica moschata* Thb.); –birn, *f. see* Muscatellerbirn; –blume, *f.* 1) [illegible] *see* Muscatblume; 2) *Bot.* (falsche) [illegible]; –bohne, *f. Pharm.* pichurim-bean; –butter, *f.* essential oil of nutmegs; –hyacinthe, *f. see* Muscathyacinthe; –kraut, *n. Bot.* [illegible] good Henry; –nuß, *f.* nutmeg; –nußbalsam, *m. see* –butter; –öl, *n.* [illegible]; –rose, *f. see* Moschusrose; –[illegible] mottled gray (horse); –traube, *f. see* Muscatellertraube; –wachs, *n.* nutmeg- [illegible] soap.

Muscat'... *in comp.* (*cf.* Muscaten... &c.) –hyacinthe, *f. Bot.* grape-hyacinth, musk [illegible] (*Muscari moschatum* L.); –[illegible], *m.* [illegible] risticine; –kirsche, *f. see* Muscatellerkirsche; –nuß, *see* M–nuß; –seide, *f.* [illegible]; –rose, *f.* damask-rose; –wein, *m.* [illegible] muscadine (wine). [illegible]

† **Musche,** (*w.*) *f.* (*Fr.*) [illegible]

Mu'schel, (*w.*) *f.* 1) *a*) shell [illegible] *b*) shell-fish, muscle-fish; 2) [illegible] outward part of the ear; 3) [illegible] *muris* (lat.), the turbinated [illegible] moid bone; 5) *Mech.* [illegible] sledge (in the form of a [illegible]) pudenda; 6) basket-hilt of [illegible] 7) *Herald.* whelk; 8) [illegible] [illegible] –, *see* Miesmuschel; [illegible] shell-agate; –[illegible] –blume, *f. Bot.* great [illegible]

Nach'sterben, *(str.)* v. *intr.* *(aux.* sein) to die after, *(with Dat.)* to follow a deceased person.

Nach'steuer, *(w.)* *f.* 1) subsequent, second, or additional tax, duty, or contribution; 2) *see* Abzugsgeld.

Nach'steuern, *(w.)* v. I. *intr.* *(aux.* sein) *Mar.* to steer after; II. *tr.* 1) to pay the arrears of a duty; 2) to contribute again.

Nach'stich, *(str.)* *m.* 1) after-print; 2) Handel auf —, *see* Nachstechen, 3.

Nach'stoppeln, *(w.)* v. *tr.* to glean (the stubbles).

Nach'stoß, *(str.,* *pl.* Nach'stöße) *m.* *Fenc.* after-thrust when the counter-thrust is made.

Nach'stoßen, *(str.)* v. *tr.* & *intr.* 1) to push or thrust after; to push on; 2) to push or thrust again; 3) to stamp or pound again.

Nach'streben, *(w.)* v. *intr.* *(with Dat.)* 1) to strive for or after; to pursue; 2) to emulate zealously; to endeavour to reach or imitate.

Nach'strömen, *(w.)* v. *intr.* *(aux.* sein) to stream after, to follow.

Nach'stück, *(str.)* *n.* after-piece.

Nach'stürmen, *(w.)* v. *intr.* *(aux.* sein; *gener. with Dat.)* to follow with impetuosity.

Nach'sturz, *(str.,* *pl.* N-stürze) *m.* *Comm.* complemental (second) verification (of the cash).

Nach'stürzen, *(w.)* v. I. *intr.* *(aux.* sein) to rush after; II. *tr.* to precipitate after.

Nach'suchebüchse, *(w.)* *f.* *Electr. Tel.* verification-box.

Nach'suchen, *(w.)* v. *intr.* & *tr.* 1) to search, seek or look after; to seek for; 2) *fig.* *(with* um, *or with Acc.)* to apply, sue, or solicit for. — **Nach'sucher,** *(str.)* *m.* 1) searcher, &c.; 2) suitor, applicant. — **Nach'suchung,** *(w.)* *f.* 1) search, research; 2) request, suit, application.

Nach'sündfluthlich, *adj.* post-diluvian.

Nach'sylbe, *see* Nachsilbe.

Nacht, *(str.,* *pl.* Näch'te) *f.* night; die heilige —, Christmas-night; über —, during night; über — kommen, *fig.* to come suddenly, unawares; die ganze — (über), all (the) night long; in der —, bei —, des N-s, at or by night, in the night-time; in tiefer —, in the depth of night; zu — essen, to sup; bei — und Nebel davon gehen, to escape in the night or under the favour of darkness; in geistiger — lebend, benighted; tausend und eine —, *Lit.* the Arabian nights.

Nacht'aar, *(str.)* *m.* *provinc.* owl.

Nach'tag, *(str.)* *m.* day afterwards, next or following day, *Comm.* respite day, day of grace.

Nacht'..., *in comp.* night-, nocturnal; —angel, *f.* *Fish.* night-line, trimmer-hook, night-angle; —angeln, *n.* night-angling; —angelruthe, *f.* clearing-hoop, clearing-rod; —anker, *m.* *Mar.* reserve-anchor.

Nach'tanzen, *(w.)* v. *intr.* *(with Dat.)* 1) *(aux.* sein) to dance after, to follow in dancing; 2) *(aux.* haben) *a)* to dance like ...; *b)* *fig.* to follow another's example.

Nacht'..., *in comp.* —arbeit, *f.* night-work; lucubration; —arbeiter, *m.* 1) worker by candle-light; 2) nightman; —becken, *n.* chamber-utensil; —bild, *n.* night-piece; —blatter, *f.* *Med.* epinyctis, night-pimple; —blau, *adj.* *see* Dunkelblau; —blick, *m.* *fig.* dark, angry look; —blinde, *m.* hemeralops; —blindheit, *f.* night-blindness, hemeralopia; —blume, *f.* *Bot.* Indian jasmine; nyctanthes *(Nyctanthes)*; —bogen, *m.* *Astr.* nocturnal arch; —druck, *m.* night-mare.

Näch'telang, *adv.* whole nights through, for nights together, for many a night.

Nach'ten, *(w.)* v. *intr.* *impers.* to grow or be night: wenn das Leben uns *(Dat.)* nachtet *(Lenau)*, when life darkens around us.

Näch'ten, *adv.* *provinc.* last night; lately.

Nacht'..., *in comp.* —erscheinung, *f.* nocturnal vision, apparition; —essen, *n.* supper; —eule, *f.* *Ornith.* screech-owl *(Strix flammea* L.); —fahrt, *f.* *see* —reise; —falter, *m.* *Entom.* nocturnal butterfly or moth *(Nocturna)*; —feier, *f.* vigil; —fernrohr, *n.* night-glass, night telescope; —fisch, *m.* *see* Häsling; —frau, *f.* night-witch; —gänger, *m.* night-walker, somnambulist; —garn, *n.* *Sport.* nets for catching larks at night; —geist, *m.*, —gespenst, *n.* nocturnal vision, ghost, spectre; —geschirr, *n.* *see* —becken; —gesicht, *n.* nocturnal vision, dream; —gestirn, *n.* star of the night, moon; —gleiche, *f.* *Astr.* equinox; —gleichenpunkt, *m.* equinoctial point; —glas, *n.* *see* —fernrohr; —haube, *f.* (Lady's) night-cap; —haus, —häuschen, *n.* *Mar.* binnacle; —hauskugel, *pl.* gimbals; —hauslampe, *f.* binacle-lamp.

Nach'theil, *(str.)* *m.* disadvantage, prejudice, detriment, injury, loss; drawback; *Law,* damage; ohne — für ..., without derogating from ...; — bringen, to disadvantage, injure; im N-e sein, sich im — befinden, to have the worst; to be at a disadvantage; mit — verkaufen, to sell at a loss; in — bringen, to cause a loss; to prejudice.

Nach'theilig, I. *adj.* disadvantageous, prejudicial, detrimental, injurious; derogatory; — sein *(with Dat.)*, to injure, prejudice, to derogate from; — sprechen von ..., to speak in dispraise of ...; II. N-keit, *(w.)* *f.* disadvantageousness, &c.

Nacht'..., *in comp.* —herberge, *f.* night's lodging, inn; —horn, *n.* *Mus.* register of an organ producing a horn- and flute-like sound.

Nach'thun, *(irr.)* v. *tr.* (Einem etwas) 1) to do after, to do as another does, to imitate; 2) to come up with one.

Näch'tig, Nächt'lich, I. *adj.* 1) nightly, nocturnal; *adv.* at night; 2) *fig.* dark, dismal, awful; bei n-er Weile, in the night-time; II. N-keit, *(w.)* *f.* darkness; dismalness, awfulness.

Nach'tigall, *(w.)* *f.* *Ornith.* nightingale ((*Sylvia luscinia* L.).

Nacht'imbiß, *(str.)* *m.* supper.

Nach'tisch, *(str.)* *m.* the last course, dessert.

Nacht'..., *in comp.* —jagd, *f.* chase in the night (by torch-light); —kauz, *m.* *see* Baumeule; —kerze, *f.* 1) night-candle; 2) *Bot.* evening primrose *(Oenothera biennis* L.); —kleid, *n.* night-dress, night-gown; —lager, *n.* night's lodging; night-quarters; —lampe, *f.* night-lamp; —leimkraut, *n.* *Bot.* night-flowering catchfly *(Silene noctiflora* L.); —leuchter, *m.* flat candlestick; flat or bedroom-candle; —licht, *n.* 1) night-light, night-candle, bedroom-candle; 2) rushlight; floating-wick.

Nächt'ling, *(str.)* *m.* *Zool.* a species of bat *(Nyctophilus)*.

Nacht'..., *in comp.* —mahl, *n.* supper, *cf.* Abendmahl; —mahr, *m.*, —mähre, *f.* nightmare; —mantel, *m.* *see* Frauenmantel, 2; —meister, *m.* overseer of the night-workers; —mette, *f.* *Rom. Cath.* nocturn; —mücke, *f.* *see* Johanniswürmchen; —mütze, *f.* *see* Schlafmütze; —nebel, *m.* *Med.* *see* —blindheit; —netz, *n.* *see* —garn.

Nach'toben, *(w.)* v. *intr.* *(with Dat.)* to roar or rush after.

Nach'tönen, *(w.)* v. *tr.* & *intr.* to resound, echo; repeat.

Nacht'..., *in comp.* —pelz, *m.* fur night-gown; —pfau, *m.* or —pfauenauge, *n.* *Entom.* 1) emperor moth *(Saturnia carpini* Hübn.); 2) eyed hawkmoth *(Sphinx ocellata* L.); —pforte, *f.* outlet; —pille, *f.* *Med.* suppository; —posten, *m.* night-post, night-guard; —quartier, *n.* *see* —lager.

Nach'trab, *(str.)* *m.* *Mil.* arrear, rear.

Nacht'rabe, *(str.)* *m.* 1) night-crow, night-raven; (grüne) night-heron (—reiher); 2) *fig.* *a)* night-reveller; *b)* nightman.

nocturnal; —wind, m. nightly or cool wind, air; —zeit, f. night-time; zur —zeit, at night; —zeug, n. night-dress; —zug, m. 1) see —stellen; 2) Railw. night-train.

Nach'urtheil, (str.) n. after-judgment, sentence; Log. opinion (judgment) formed upon logical conclusions.

Nach'vasall, (w.) m. rear vassal.

Nach'verklären, (w.) v. intr. Comm. to extend the (first) protest. [insure.

Nach'versichern, (w.) v. tr. Comm. to re-

Nach'versicherung, (w.) f. reinsurance.

Nach'verwandte, m. (decl. like adj.) descendant. [supplementary grant.

Nach'verwilligung, (w.) f. subsequent or

Nach'verzollung, (w.) f. Comm. post-entry.

Nach'wachs [—'wax], (str.) m. after-growth.

Nach'wachsen, (str.) v. intr. (aux. sein) to grow after, (with Dat.) to grow up to; to grow in the place of something; n—d, p. a. successive. [after, to try.

Nach'wägen, (w. & str.) v. tr. to weigh

Nach'waise, (w.) f. posthumous child.

Nach'wandeln, (w.) v. intr. (aux. sein) (with Dat.) to wander or walk after; fig. to walk in one's steps, to follow the example of.

Nach'wärts, adv. see Nachher, Nachmals.

Nach'wehen, (w.) n. pl. Med. after-pains, throes; fig. painful, calamitous consequences.

Nach'wein, (str.) m. see Lauer, 2.

Nach'weinen, (w.) v. intr. (aux. sein) (with Dat.) to cry after, lament one's loss.

Nach'weis, (str.) m. 1) intelligence, information; citation, reference; authentication; 2) proof; den — führen, see Nachweisen, 2.

Nach'weisbar, adj. demonstrable, assignable.

Nach'weise..., in comp. —amt, n. see Nachweisungsanstalt; —buch, n. directory, book of address.

Nach'weisen, (str.) v. tr. 1) (Einem etwas) to show, point out, direct, to refer; 2) to authenticate, prove, establish (a right, &c.); to demonstrate. [&c.; index.

Nach'weiser, (str.). m. director, referrer,

Nach'weisezahl, (w.) f. folio-number (in a ledger).

Nach'weislich, adj. see Nachweisbar.

Nach'weisung, (w.) f. 1) direction, reference; 2) authentication, proving, &c. see Nachweis.

Nach'weisungs..., in comp. —anstalt, f., —bureau, n., —stube, f. office of reference or address, register-office; —kalender, m. directory; —zeichen, n. Typ. sign of reference.

Nach'welt, (w.) f. after-days, after-times, after-ages, ensuing or future ages, posterity.

Nach'wille, (irr.) m. codicil.

Nach'wind, (str.) m. wind in one's back, favourable wind. [pressing of the must.

Nach'winder, (str.) m. provinc. Vitic. last

Nach'winkeln, (w.) v. tr. & intr. to examine the squaring. [of winter.

Nach'winter, (str.) m. second winter; rear

Nach'wirken, (w.) v. intr. to operate or work after. — Nach'wirkung, (w.) f. secondary or after-effect, or operation; lingering influence.

Nach'wolle, (w.) f. second wool.

Nach'wollen, (irr.) v. intr. ellipt. for Nachgehen &c. wollen. [address.

Nach'wort, (str.) n. concluding word or

Nach'wuchs [—wuks], (str., pl. Nach'wüchse) m. 1) after-growth; T. new wood; 2) fig. youth; fresh men, recruits.

Nach'wünschen, (w.) v. tr. to follow with one's wishes, to wish. — Nach'wünschung, (w.) f. kind wishes for an absent friend, &c., (good) wish.

Nach'zahlen, (w.) v. tr. & intr. to pay after or later, to supply or pay the remainder of (a sum), to make a subsequent payment.

Nach'zählen, (w.) v. tr. to count or number again, to check; to count or tell over (a second time); to count; durch die Hand —, to shoot (money). — Nach'zähler, (str.) m. Min. teller, counter, controller.

Nach'zahlung, (w.) f. supplementary or after-payment, supply. [over again, &c.

Nach'zählung, (w.) f. the (act of) counting

Nach'zaubern, (w.) v. tr. 1) to imitate, as if by magic; 2) to cause to follow by magic.

Nach'zeichen, (str.) n. Num. counter-mark.

Nach'zeichnen, (w.) v. tr. T. to draw after, from; to copy; to counter-draw. — Nach'zeichner, (str.) m. copyist, copyer. — Nach'zeichnung, (w.) f. copy, drawing from a picture.

Nach'zeit, (w.) f. after-time, the future.

Nach'ziehen, (str.) v. I. tr. 1) to draw after; 2) fig. see (nach sich) Ziehen; II. intr. (aux. sein) (with. Dat.) to follow, to go or travel after; Handel auf —, Comm. bargain on drawing samples.

Nach'zins, (str.) m. quit-rent.

Nach'zirkeln, (w.) v. tr. to imitate or copy minutely.

Nach'zucht, (w.) f. last brood (of chickens, &c.), last swarm (of bees) before winter.

Nach'zug, (str., pl. Nachzüge) m. rear, see Nachtrab. — Nach'zügler, (str.) m. straggler.

Nacken, (str.) m. nape, neck, crag, scrag; coll.-e. (cf. Hals) einen eisernen, harten, störrigen — haben, to be stiff-necked, see Hartnäckig; den — hoch or steif tragen, to carry a high head; Einem auf dem — sein, liegen, to be at one's back; to persecute; to be troublesome, to bore one; den Schelm im — haben, to bear secret malice; in comp. cervical (artery, vein, ligament, &c.); —fistel, f. Vet. poll-evil; —grube, f. hollow of the neck; —haar, n. back-hair; —nerven, m. pl. cervical nerves; —schlag, m. 1) a blow from behind; 2) fig. slander, back-biting; —stück, n. neck, neck-piece; —wolle, f. neck-wool; —wulst, m. long back-hair of females

Nackt, I. or Nackend (coll. Nackicht), adj. naked, nude; bare (cf. also Kahl); in comp. —aal, m. see Blindaal; —armig, —beinig &c., adj. with naked arms, legs, &c.; —brust, f. Ichth. a species of eel (Muraena [Gymnothorax] meleagris Shaw); —früchtig, adj. Bot. gymnocarpous; —rücken, m. Ichth. electric eel (Gymnotus L.); —samig, adj. Bot. gymnospermous; —schnecke, f. Zool. naked snail, slug (Limax L.); II. N—heit, (w.) f. nakedness, nudity; bareness, baldness; bare place.

Na'del, s. I. (w.) f. 1) needle; pin; 2) see Zeiger, 4; 3) trigger (of a gun); 4) quill (of a porcupine, hedgehog); 5) needle (of a crystal); 6) Bot. acerose, needle-leaf (of conifers); eine eingefädelte —, needleful; sich auf die — verstehen, to understand needle-work; wie auf N—n sitzen, fig. to sit on needles; II. in comp. —bahre, f. see —blei; —baum, m. a tree of the fir kind, cf. —holz; —bereit, adj. (of cloth and similar stuffs) finished, ready to be worked with the needle; —blatt, n. Bot. acicular or acerose leaf; —blei, n. tin or leaden foot into which the needles (of a stocking-frame) are stuck; —blende, f. Miner. red antimony ore; —brief, m., —buch, n. needle-book; —büchse, f. needle-case; pin-case; —crystalle, m. pl. Miner. & Bot. rhaphides; —draht, m. needle-wire; pin-wire; —erz, n. Miner. needle-ore; —fabrik, f. needle-mill; —feder, f. T. steel-spring (in the lock of a gun); —feile, f. needle-file; —fertig, see —bereit; —fisch, m. Ichth. 1) horn-back, garfish (Esox belone L.); 2) needle-fish (Syngnathus acus L.); —förmig, adj. in the form of a pin, needle-like, needle-shaped, acicular, aciculated, Bot. acerose, acerous; —geld, n. pin-money; —(schnabel)gras, m., —halter, m. Bot. feather-grass (Stipa pennata L.); —grund, m. bottom of the sea covered with pointed shells; —halter, m. needle-bearer; Surg. acutenaculum, (Fr.) porte-aiguille; —hecht, m. see —fisch, 1; —holz, n. 1) trees of the pine or fir kind, coniferous trees, having pointed and needle-like leaves (opp. Laubholz); 2) pine forest; —kerbel, m. Bot. (samenfrüchtiger) needle-weed, shepherd's needle, Venus's comb (Scandix pecten L.); —kissen, n. pin-cushion; —knopf, —kopf, m. head of a pin; —kohle, f. Miner. acicular lignite; —kopfstahl, m. Turn. nail-head tool; —kram, m. pin- or needle-trade; —kraut, n., —kräuter, f. see —kerbel; —loch, n. pin-hole; —macher, m. see Nadler; —manufaktur, f. see —fabrik; —mühle, f. see —fabrik.

Na'deln, (w.) v. I. tr. (l. u.) to fasten with pins or needles; to sew; II. intr. to lose or shed its leaves (said of coniferous trees).

Na'del..., in comp. —öhr, n. eye of a needle; —papier, n. a kind of (cartridge) paper adapted for packing up needles, and fine steel goods; —poliren, n. needle-grinding; —puncturing, f. see —stechen; —schaft, m. shank or shaft of a pin; —schieben, n. push-pin (a children's play); —sonde, f. see —halter; —spath, m. Miner. needle-spar, aragonite; splicular carbonate spar; —spitze, f. point of a needle or pin; —staub, m. pin-dust; —stechen, n. Surg. acupuncture; —steckerin, f. pin-sticker; —stein, m. 1) *, loadstone, magnet; 2) Min. needlestone; —stich, m. 1) a) pin-prick or stitch; b) see —stechen; 2) pin hole; —streu, f. litter for cattle consisting of the pointed leaves of firs or pines; —träger, m. see —halter; —wurm, m. see Fadenwurm; —zange, f. see —halter; Miner.-e. —zeolith, m. needle zeolite, natrolite, mesotype; —zinnerz, n. needle-tin.

* Na'dir (Arab.; in Germ. poetry &c. gener. with the accent on the last syllable: Nadir'), (str., pl. N—s) m. (Astr. &) *, nadir.

Nad'ler, (str.) m. needle-maker, needler, pin-maker, pinner; in comp. —handwerk, n. needler's trade, pin-making; —kunst, f. art of needle- or pin-making; —waare, f. pins, needles, and other small goods in metal.

Na'gel, (str., pl. Nä'gel) m. 1) nail; 2) pin (a horny induration of the membranes of the eye); der — ohne Kopf, brad; kleine —, tack; der lange —, spike; der hölzerne —, (wooden) peg, pin, plug; trenail; Mar. tree-nail, trennel; 3) see Nägelein, 2 & 3; 4) hysterische —, Med. head-ache confined to a particular part of the head; mit Nägeln versehen, Zool. unguiculate(d); fig.-e. keinen — breit nachgeben, not to yield an inch; etwas auf den — können, to know a thing thoroughly; nicht eher, als bis ihm das Feuer auf die Nägel brennt, not till need drives him, not till hard pressed; es war ein — zu seinem Sarge, it was a nail in his coffin; den — auf den Kopf treffen, to hit the nail on the head; einen hohen or gewaltigen — haben, to be self-conceited or proud, cf. (eine hohe) Meinung (von sich haben); an den — hängen, fig. to lay aside, give up, abandon, leave.

Na'gel..., in comp. —bank, f. Mar. the cross-piece of the windlass, ranges in the shrouds in which belaying-pins are fixed; —bein, n. see Thränenbein; —blüte, f. nail-spot; —bohrer, m. gimlet; —bürste, f. nail-brush.

Nä'gelchen, (str.) n. (dimin. of Nagel) little nail, tack.

Na'gelbohr, (w.) f. see Nagelform.

Nä'gelein, s. I. (str.) n. (dimin. of Nagel) 1) (provinc. &) * for Nägelchen; 2) pink (Nelke); 3) clove (Gewürznägelein); gelbes —, see Goldlack, 1; II. in comp. —baum, m. see Nelkenbaum; —holz, n. see Nelkenrinde; —kopf, m. 1) clove; 2) form of a clove; 3) see Pfeffer;

[illegible]

Obligatorisch, *adj.* (*Lat.*) [illegible]

* **Obligo**, *n.* (*Ital.*) *Comm.* warrant.

* **Oblique**, *adj.* (*Lat.*) [illegible] *Math.* [illegible]

* **Oblongum**, (*str.*, *pl.* [illegible]) (*Lat.*) [illegible]

Obmacht, *f.* [illegible] power, authority.

Obmann, (*str.*, *pl.* [illegible]) *m.* 1) [illegible] *Law* umpire; [illegible] *fig.* [illegible] for man of a jury.

Ob'mannschaft, (*w.*) *f.* [illegible] arbitration award.

Obmaus, *see* [illegible]

* **Obo'e**, (*w.*) *f.* (*Fr.*) *Mus.* hautboy, oboe. [illegible] **röhren**, *f. pl.* [illegible]

Obrigkeit, (*w.*) *f.* magistrate [illegible] authority, [illegible]

Obrigkeitlich, I. *adj.* magisterial, [illegible] magistrate, [illegible] magistracy. II. *adv.* from or by the authority. [illegible] licence, permit by a legal grant.

Obrist, *for* [illegible]

Obschon', *conj.* (*sometimes sep.* ob [illegible] *schon*) [illegible] though, although, albeit.

Ob'schweben, (*w.*) *v. intr.* 1) to be [illegible] moment, at hand, pending; 2) *fig.* to be above or superior, to exceed.

* **Obscön'**, *adj.* (*Lat.*) obscene. — **Obscönität'**, (*w.*) *f.* obscenity.

* **Obscur'**, *adj.* (*Lat.*) obscure.

* **Obscurant'**, (*w.*) *m.* (*Lat.*) obscurant.

[illegible] —**jude**, *f.* [illegible] [illegible]

Obwachen, [illegible]

Obwalten, [illegible]

[illegible]

Obwaltung, (*w.*) *f.* [illegible]

Obwohl', **Obzwar'**, *conj.* [illegible] though, although, albeit.

* **Occident'**, (*str.*) *m.* (*Lat.*) *Geogr.* Occident, West. — **Occidental'**, **Occidentalisch**, *adj.* occidental. [illegible] *Jewel.* white diamond.

* **Ocean'**, (*str.*) *m.* (*Lat.*) ocean. [illegible] — [illegible] **Ocea'nisch**, *adj.* ocean, oceanic.

* **Ocelot'**, (*str.*, *pl.* O-e) *m.* *Zool.* ocelot (*Felis pardalis* L.).

Och'er, **Ock'er**, **O'ker**, (*str.*) *m.* ochre. *In comp.* —**ader**, *f.* *Min.* ochreous vein. —**farbe**, *f.* ochre colour. —**farben**, —**gelb**, *adj.* of the colour of ochre. —**gelb**, *n.* yellow ochre; —**gelblichweiß**, *adj.* ochroleucous. —**haltig**, *adj.* ochreous.

* **Ochlocratie'**, (*w.*) *f.* (*Gr.*) ochlocracy.

Ochs, **Ochse**, [*pr.* oks(e)] (*w.*) *m.* 1) ox: ein junger —, bullock; 2) *vulg.* blockhead, [illegible], da stehen die Ochsen am Berge, *proverb*, there is the rub. — **Ochsen**, (*w.*) *v. intr.* 1) to bull (of cows); 2) *Stud. slang*, to work hard,

[illegible]

Octav', [illegible]

* **Octans**, [illegible]

* **Octav**, [illegible] small) octavo [illegible] *comp.* —**band**, [illegible] *Mus.* flageolet [illegible] — **Octa've**, [illegible]

Octo'ber, [illegible]

* **Octodez**, [illegible] octodecimo.

die erste Thüre —, the first door to the right; —schreiben, Comm. to enter on the creditor's side; —her, adv. from the right side, hither; —hin, adv. towards (or on) the right hand; —stricken, n. plain knitting; —um, adv. to the right about; —um kehrt euch! Mil. to the right about! right about, face!

Rechts'..., in comp. —abtretung, f. cession, transfer of a (the) right; —alterthümer, n. pl. legal antiquities.

Recht'sam, I. adj. (Voss, unusual) just; II. R—e, (w.) f. privilege, see Gerechtsame.

Rechts'..., in comp. —amt, n. judicial office, court of judicature; —anhängig, adj. pending at law or before a court of law; —anspruch, m. legitimate claim; —anwalt, m. see Anwalt; —ausdruck, m. legal or law-term; —ausspruch, m. see —spruch; —beauftragte, f. see —beistand; —beflissen, adj. studying (the) law; ein —beflissener, m. student at law; lawyer; —befugniß, n. competence; —behelf, m. benefice of the law; —behörde, f. court of justice; —beistand, m. 1) legal assistance; 2) legal assistant, advocate; —belehrung, f. consultation, information with respect to legal matters; —berather, m. legal adviser, counsel; —bestand, m. authenticity; —beständig, adj. valid, legal, in due form, authentic, judicial; —beständigkeit, f. validity, legality; authenticity; —betraute, m. (decl. like adj.) see —beistand, 2; —beweis, m. Law. deduction.

Recht'schaffen, I. adj. righteous, just; honest, upright; right; II. R—heit, f. righteousness; honesty, probity, uprightness; integrity.

Recht'schreibung, (w.) f. orthography.

Rechts'..., in comp. —consulent, m. see —anwalt; —drecher, m. coll. pettifogger, caviller, chicaner, prevaricator; —dreherei, f. pettifogging, chicanery; —einwand, m. Law. traverse; plea; einen —einwand gegen ... vorbringen, to traverse.

Recht'seitig, adj. see Rechtlinig.

Rechts'..., in comp. —erfahren, adj. versed, skilled, learned in law or jurisprudence; —erkenntniß, f. see —spruch; —erweis, m. see —beweis; —fähig, adj. competent; —fähigkeit, f. competence; —fall, m. case in law; —fällig werden, to lose one's case, suit, action; —forderung, f. legal claim, lawful demand, legitimate pretension; —form, f. legal form; —förmig, adj. & adv. according to the form of law, in legal terms; nicht —förmig, injudicial; —frage, f. law- or legal question; moot-point; —gang, m. proceeding at law, legal procedure, course of law, operation of the law; —gebäude, n. fig. body of laws; —gelahrtheit, —gelehrsamkeit, —gelehrtheit, f. jurisprudence, law; —gelehrt, adj. learned in law, versed in jurisprudence; —gelehrte, —kundige, m. jurist, lawyer; —gemäß, adv. according to law; —gesuch, n. suit at law; —grund, m. legal ground, argument, or title; —grundsatz, m. principle of jurisprudence; —gültig, adj. valid or good in law; legal (debt); —gültigkeit, f. validity, legal force, sufficiency in law; zur —gültigkeit fehlt noch daß ..., to make it valid it is still required that ...; —gutachten, n. opinion (of counsel); ein —gutachten einholen, to take the opinion of counsel; —handel, m. action, cause, lawsuit, process; —hängig, see —anhängig; —hülfe, f. Law. legal aid, relief; —hülfe suchen, to seek legal redress; —klage, f. accusatory libel; —kniff, m. (legal) artifice, chicane, quirk; —kosten, pl. costs of a lawsuit; —kraft, f. force, might of law; die —kraft verlieren, to fall into abeyance; —kräftig, adj. valid in law, legal; —kräftig werden, to become final; —kräftigen, (w. & insep.) v. tr. to render valid in law, to validate, legalise; —kräftigkeit, f. validity; legality; —kunde, f. 1) science of the law, jurisprudence; 2) legal doctrine; —kundige, m. see —gelehrte; —lage, f. legal situation; —lehre, f. see —kunde; —lehrer, m. teacher of the law, professor of laws; —mittel, n. remedy at law, legal means of redress, legal remedy; —mündel, m. client; —nachtheil, m. prejudice; —pflege, f. administration of justice.

Recht'sprechung, (w.) f. I. (from Recht, adj.) right, correct pronunciation, orthoepy; II. (from Recht, n.) see Rechtsprechung.

Rechts'..., in comp. —regel, f. rule of law; nach der —regel daß ..., according to the law maxim that ...; —sache, f. see —handel; —satz, m. 1) thesis in law; 2) legal axiom; —schließung, f. recess (of the courts of justice); —schlinge, f. snare spread by the law, chicane; —schluß, m. judgment or decree of a court of law; —schrift, f. 1) pl. acts; 2) justificative memoir; 3) any legal writing or work; —sprache, f. language of lawyers, law terms or language, legal terminology; —sprecher, m. judge, magistrate; —sprechung, f. 1) administration of justice; 2) or —spruch, m. legal decision, sentence, verdict, adjudication; —stand, m., —statt, f. jurisdiction; cognizance; —ständig, adj. subject to a certain judicature; —streit, m. 1) lawsuit; 2) controversy on a point of law; —stuhl, m. court of law, tribunal; —titel, m. legal title; ein scheinbarer —titel, title, colourable title.

Recht'sucher, (str.) m. plaintiff.

Rechts'..., in comp. —unfähigkeit, f. disability; —ungleichheit, f. disability; —ungültig, adj. unavailable (in law), insufficient (at law), invalid, illegal, nugatory; —ungültigkeit, f. insufficiency (at law), illegality, informality; —verdreher &c., see —dreher &c.; —verfahren, n. legal procedure, judicial proceeding; ein peinliches —verfahren, a criminal prosecution; —verfassung, f. judicature; —verhandlung, f. suit, proceeding; —verständig, adj. versed in the law or in jurisprudence; —vertreter, m. advocate, solicitor; —verwalter, m. administrator of justice; —vormund, m. legal adviser, counsel; —weg, m. see —gang; den —weg betreten or einschlagen, to have recourse to law; von —wegen, in justice, by rights; so geschehen von —wegen, Law. done in due form of law; —widrig, adj. unlawful, illegal, against the law; —wissenschaft, f. science of the law; jurisprudence; —wohlthat, f. benefit of the law; —wort, n. term in law, law-term; —zug, m. [illegible]; —zwang, m. compulsion by way of law, jurisdiction.

Recht'... (adj.), in comp. —thun, n. acting righteously or honestly; —winkelig, adj. rectangular, right-angled; —winkeligkeit, f. rectangularity; —zeitig, adj. seasonable, in the right or in due time; in due course; —zeitige Kündigung, due warning; —zeitigkeit, f. the being or happening at the right time.

* **Recipient'**, (w.) m. (Lat.) Chem. &c. recipient, receiving vessel, receiver.

* **Reciprocität'**, (w.) f. (L. Lat.) reciprocity. — **Reciprok'**, adj. reciprocal.

* **Recitir'en**, (w.) v. tr. (Lat.) to recite, &c., see Hersagen. — **Recitation'**, (w.) f. recitation. — **Recitativ'**, (str.) n. Mus. recitative.

Reck, (str.) n. 1) Gymn. horizontal pole; 2) provinc. scaffold, wooden beam.

Reck'bank, (str., pl. R—bänke) f. 1) R bench on which metals are stretched or [illegible] 2) rack. [R—eisen, adj. [illegible]

Reck'e, (w.) m. († & [illegible]) [illegible]

Reck'e, (w.) f. 1) the (act of) [illegible] racking, &c.; 2) stretcher; [illegible] stretching; rack; 3) Mar. [illegible] rails; —eisen, m. provinc. [illegible]

Reck'en, (w.) v. tr. 1) to stretch, strain; 2) [illegible] to [illegible] [illegible]

normal; —widrigkeit, (w.) f. the being contrary to rule, abnormity, anomaly; —zwang, m. constraint of rules.

Re'gen, (w.) v. I. tr. to stir, move; das Wild —, Sport. to rouse the game; II. ref. to be stirring, active, moving, alive; to stir, move; to be roused.

Re'gen, (str.) m. rain; shower; feiner —, drizzling rain; aus dem — in die Traufe kommen, proverb. to fall out of the frying pan into the fire, to come from bad to worse; goldener —, see Goldregen, 1.

Re'gen..., in comp. —bach, m. torrent; —bad, n. shower-bath; —bogen, m. Met. rainbow; —bogenartig, adj. iridescent; —bogenfarben, f. pl. colours of the rainbow, prismatic colours; —bogenfarbig, adj. having the colours of the rainbow, iridescent; —bogenflechte, f. see Ringelflechte; —bogenhaut, f. Anat. iris; —bogenmetall, n. iridium; —bogenstein, m. iris-chalcedony; —bogenstrahl, m. Phys. iris beam, prismatic ray or beam; —brachvogel, m. see —vogel, 1; —dach, n. eaves, shed; —deckel, m. leather gun-case; —dicht, adj. rain-proof, rain-tight, waterproof; —fang, m cistern; —fall, m. rainfall; —feuer, n. Pyro-w. fiery rain; —flage, f. see Bö; —galle, f. water-gall, see Wassergalle; —gestirn, n. Astr. the Hyades, —guß, m. sudden and violent shower (flow) of rain.

Re'genhaft, adj see Regnerisch.

Re'gen..., in comp. —hut, m. broad-brimmed or flapping hat, umbrella-hat; —kappe, f. 1) rain-cap, capuchin; 2) hood of a chimney; —kleid, n. dress against rain; —loch, n. 1) spout of a gutter; 2) fig. see —winkel; —luft, f. rainy air; —mantel, m. rain-cloak, waterproof; —menge, f. amount of rain; —maß, m., —messer, m. raingauge, pluviometer; —monat, m. rainy month; —nacht, f. rainy night; —pfeifer, m. Orn. plover (Charadrius L.); (buntschnäbliger) sealark (Charadrius hiaticula L.); —pfuhl, m. rain-puddle; —puppen, m. pl. see —feuer; —rinne, f. gutter.

Re'gensburg, n. Geogr. Ratisbon(e).

Re'gen..., in comp. —schauer, m. shower, cf. —guß; —schirm, m. umbrella; —schirmförmig, adj. Bot. umbellate, umbelliferous; —schirmgestell, n. umbrella-frame; —schirmkappe, f. top-cap; —schnepfe, f. Ornith. greenshank, great plover (Totanus glottis L.); —sterne, f. pl. see —gestirn; —strich, m. region of rains (between the fourth and tenth degrees of N. L.); —strom, m. torrent; —sturm, m. storm, high wind with heavy rain.

* Regent', (w.) m. 1) regent; 2) reigning prince, ruler; 3) principal of a seminary; administrator.

Re'gentag, (str.) m. rainy day. [ess.

Regen'tin, (w.) f. (female) regent, regent-

Re'gentropfen, (str.) m. drop of rain.

Regent'schaft, (w.) f. 1) regency, regentship; 2) board of regents, regency.

Re'gen..., in comp. —vogel, m. Ornith. 1) whimbrel (Numenius phaeopus L.), 2) butcher-bird (Würger); —wasser, n. rain water; —wetter, n. rainy weather; —wind, m. wind bringing rain; —winkel, m. quarter from which rain generally comes; —wolke, f. showery or rain-cloud, nimbus; —wurm, m. Anat. earth-worm (Lumbricus terrestris L.), cf. Erdwurm; —zeichen, n. sign of rain; —zeit, f. rainy season.

* Regie' [pr. reshie'], (w.) f. (Fr.) management, (public) administration; in der — bauen, to build in daywork (Mietlohn); unter —verschluß, in bond; nicht mehr unter —verschluß, out of bond.

* Regie'ren, (w.) v. tr. & intr. (Lat.) to reign, rule, sway, govern; to guide, wield, control, manage, regulate, to preside over; to work, steer (a ship); ein Pferd —, to manage a horse; die r-de Königin, queen regnant; der r-de Bürgermeister, acting or officiating burgomaster (or mayor), mayor in office.

Regie'rer, (str.) m. ruler, swayer, governor.

Regiererei', (w.) f. bad government, misgovernment. [&c. see Herrschsucht.

Regier'sucht, f. overbearing disposition,

Regie'rung, (w.) f. 1) a) the act of reigning, &c. (cf. Regieren); b) reign, government; sway; c) regency; d) administration, management, guidance; Mar. steerage; 2) office of the government; schlechte —, misgovernment, misrule; wieder zur — kommen, to return to power.

Regie'rungs..., in comp. —advocat, m. advocate or counsel to government; —antritt, m. accession to the government; —art, f. mode of government; —assessor, m. assessor to the government or administration; —beamte(r), m. officer of the government; —befehl, m. government-order, order in council; —form, f. form of government; —gebäude, n. government building, office; —gewalt, f. supreme power; —kanzlei, f. chancery of the regency; —kanzel(l)ist, m. clerk of the chancery of government; —kunst, f. art of government.

Regie'rungslos, adj. anarchical; R-losigkeit, f. anarchy.

Regie'rungs..., in comp. —präsident, m. president of the government; —rath, m. counseller of the government (regency); —recht, n. right of supremacy; —sache, f. matter of government, of state, of regency; —secretär, m. government-secretary; —sitz, m. seat of government; —system, n. system of government; —verfassung, f. constitution or mode of government.

* Regiment', (str., pl. R-er) n. (L. Lat.) 1) Mil. regiment; 2) government, power, command; das — haben, to rule; zum — gehörig, regimental; r-erweise, adv. in regiments.

* Regimentirt', p. a. incorporated in a regiment, belonging to a regiment.

* Regiments'..., in comp. regimental; —arzt, m. surgeon-major; —auditeur, m. justice of a regiment, cf. Auditeur; —casse, f. regimental chest; —chirurg, —feldscherer, m. surgeon-major; —commandeur, m. commander of a regiment; —gericht, n. regimental court of justice; —inhaber, m. owner, colonel of a regiment; auf —kosten (pl.) leben, coll. to live at others' costs, to live upon the common; —musik, f. musical band of a regiment; —quartiermeister, m. quarter-master-major; —stab, m. the field-officers of a regiment; —tambour, m. drum-major; —tisch, m. mess; —uniform, f. regimentals; —unkosten, pl. see —kosten.

* Regi'na, f. (Lat.) Regina, Reine (P. N.).

* Region', (w.) f. (Lat.) region.

* Regi'ren, see Regieren &c.

* Regisseur' [pr. reshisö'r], (str., pl. [illegible] or R-e) m. (Fr.) (particul. stage-manager).

* Regis'ter, a. I. (str.) n. (L. Lat.) 1) register, record; 2) table (of contents), index; 3) Mus. organ-stop, draw-stop, register (of an organ); 4) register (of a stove) [illegible] — halten, Typ. to make register; [illegible] schwarzen — stehen, to be in the black books; [illegible] alte —, 1. the superannuated [illegible] 2. [illegible] old person, esp. old woman; [illegible] alte — gehören, to be out of fashion, obsolete, [illegible] old; II. in comp. —auszug, m. [illegible] terly report of the inspector of [illegible] —hafen, m. registered port; [illegible] —papier, n. large and strong [illegible] paper; —schiff, n. Mar. (Spanish) [illegible] ship; —stimme, f., —zug, m. [illegible]

* Registran'de, (w.) f. 1) the [illegible] gistering, &c.; registry, entry; [illegible] gistry. — Registra'tor, (str., [illegible] gistrato'ren) m. registrar, [illegible]

treiben, *Gam.* to play at hoop, to trundle or drive hoops.

Reif..., *in comp.* –bahn, *f.* rope-walk; –bengel, *f. Coop.* hoop-bender; –binder, *m.* hoop-maker.

Rei'fe, *(w.) f.* ripeness, maturity, mellowness; *fig.* fitness; zur – kommen, *fig.* to come to (a state of) maturity.

Reif'eisen, *(str.) n.* hoop-iron, band-iron.

Rei'feln, *(w.) v.* I. *intr.* to play at hoop; II. *tr. Archit., &c.* to chamfer, rifle, flute; **Rei'feleisen, Rei'felholz,** *n.* tool to indent leather, &c.

Rei'fen, *(str.) m.* see Reif, *B.*

A. **Rei'fen,** *(w.) v.* I. *intr. (aux.* sein) to grow ripe, to ripen; to mellow; II. *tr.* to bring to maturity; to ripen, mature; gereift, *p. a.* mature.

B. **Rei'fen,** *(w.) v. intr. (impers.)* to rime *(cf.* Reif, *A.).*

C. **Rei'fen** *(from* Reif, *B.), (w.) v. tr.* 1) *Join., Archit., &c.* to groove, channel; 2) to furnish with a rim or edge; 3) *Coop.* to hoop (a cask).

Rei'fen..., *in comp.* –bahre, *f. Surg.* a contrivance for keeping the bed-clothes from lying on a ruptured limb (lat: *fulcrum lagmilinde*); –spiel, *n.* a game with hoops thrown by means of a stick from one player to another who catches the hoop and throws it back in his turn to his partner similar to the Engl. game, called "the graces".

Reif'..., *in comp.* –glas, *n.* see Paßglas; –haken, *m. T.* tire-hook.

Reif'heit, *(w.) f.* see Reife. [sticks.

Reif'holz, *(str.) n.* wood for hoops, hoop-

Rei'fig, *adj.* channelled, grooved.

Reif'..., *in comp.* –kloben, *m. T.* chamfer-clamp; –kupfer, *n.* hooped copper.

Reif'lich, *adj.* mature.

Reif'messer, *(str.) n. Coop.* hoop-knife.

Reif'monat, *(str.) m. (from* Reif, *A.)* the month of November.

Reif'..., *in comp.* –rock, *m.* hoop-petticoat; –schlagen, –spiel, *n.* playing at hoop, *cf.* Reifenspiel; –schläger, *m.* see Reepschläger; –stäbe, *m.,* –stangen, *f.,* –stecken, *m. pl.* see –holz; –tanz, *m.* see Ringeltanz; –treiber, *m. T.* hoop-cramp; –unterrock, *m.* see –rock; –zange, *f.,* –zieher, *m.* see –bengel; –zwinge, *f. Coop.* hoop-cramp or vice-pin.

Rei'gen, Rei'ger, *m.* see Reihen, Reiher.

Reih, *(str.) n. Mar.* ribband.

Reih'draht, *m.* see Reihfaden.

Rei'he, *(w.) f.* 1) row; string; rank, file; line; 2) range; ridge; tier; 3) order; series; course; 4) suite; train (of thoughts, &c.); suit, set; 5) line, succession; turn; 6) line, see Zeile; die hinterften or letzten R-n, rear; – und Glied, rank and file; in – und Glied, in array; die – ist an mir, ich bin an der –, it is my turn; an wem ist die –? whose turn is it? ich verrichtete es in meiner –, I took (it in) my turn; wenn ich an die – komme, when it comes to my turn; nach der – or der – nach, 1. by ranks, by files; 2. by or in rotation, in order, in turn, by turns, in succession, successively; *coll.* (turn and) turn-about; außer der –, out of turn; ein Jeder nach der –, every one in his turn or course; nach der – stellen, to place in a line or row, to rank, range.

Rei'he..., *in comp.* see Reih....

Rei'hen, *(str.) m.* 1) processional row; row of singing dancers; 2) circular dance accompanied by song and music; 3) song.

A. **Rei'hen,** *(w.) v.* I. *tr.* 1) to put or set in a row; to file, to rank, range; 2) *Sew.* to baste, stitch loosely; 3) to string (together), to connect; 4) to stitch, baste; 5) ... to hollow by hammering; II. *intr.* to dance and sing in chorus.

B. **Rei'hen,** *(w.) v. intr. Sport.* 1) to cry, bark; 2) to be in rut; to tread (of water fowls).

Rei'hen... *(from* Reihe, *f.), in comp.* –fahrt, *f.* passage by turn; –folge, *f.,* –gang, *m.* rotation, succession; –haken, see Reihehaken; –hammer, *m. T.* hollowing-hammer; –marsch, *m. Mil.* file-marching, marching in file; –ordnung, *f.* see –folge; –saat, *f.* Husb. a row of grain sowed by a drill-plough; –säemaschine, *f. Agric.* ridge-drill; –schiff, *n.* see Rangschiff.

Rei'henweise, *adv.* 1) in rows; 2) by turns.

Rei'hentanz, *(str., pl.* R-tänze) *m. (from* Reihen, *m.)* circular dance.

Rei'her, *(str.) m.* 1) *Sport.* wild gander or drake; 2) *Ornith.* heron *(Ardea cinerea* L.); 3) *Mar.* lashing, lasher; *in comp.* –beize, –jagd, *f.* heron-hawking; –busch, –strauß, –stutz, *m.* plume of heron-feathers; *Ornith.* –ente, *f.* tufted pochard *(Fuligula cristata* Ray.); –falk, *m.* see Geierfalke; –feder, *f.* heron's feather; –gehege, *n.,* –hütte, *f.,* –stand, *m.* heronry (†: heronshaw); –gras, *n. Bot.* feather-grass *(Stipa pennata* L.); –meister, *m.* head-falconer; –schnabel, *m. Bot.* heron's-bill *(Erodium cicutarium* L.).

Reih'(e)... *(from* Reihen, *v.), in comp.* –faden, *f.,* –draht, *m. Sew.* basting-thread; –haken, *m. Weav.* heddle-hook; warp-crook; –nadel, *f.* 1) basting-needle; 2) see –haken; –nagel, *m.* pole-bolt (of a carriage); –schank, *m.* the privilege and practice of selling beer and other liquids passing in regular succession from one inhabitant of a (smaller) place to another; –schule, *f.* school held at the different houses of several families in regular succession; –tau, *n. Mar.* lasher, preventer-shoot; –um, I. *adv.* by turns; see (nach der) Reihe; II. *n. (indecl.) n.* rotation, turn.

Rei'ling, see Regeling.

Reil'topp, *(str.) m. Mar.* royal mast.

Reim, *(str.) m.* rhyme; poem, copy of verses; ein – auf *(with Acc.),* a rhyme to ....

Reim'art, *(w.) f.* kind, form of rhyme.

Reim'bar, *adj.* 1) that may be rhymed; 2) *fig.* consonant to reason, reasonable.

Reim'bold, *(str.) m.* see Reimerling.

Rei'meln, *(w.) v. tr. & intr. coll.* to rhyme, to make doggerel verse.

Rei'men, *(w.) v.* I. *intr. & refl.* 1) to rhyme; 2) *fig.* to agree, square, tally; II. *tr.* to make rhyme. – **Rei'mer,** *(str.) m.* rhymer, rhymester. – **Reimerei',** *(w.) f.* (the practice of) rhyming; *coll.* making bad verses. – **Rei'merling,** *(str.) m. coll.* poetaster.

Reim'..., *in comp.* –fall, *m.* cadence, caesural or final pause; –form, *f.* see –art; –frei, –los, *adj.* rhymeless, blank; –flicken, *m.* expletive; –gedicht, *n.* poem in rhymes.

Reim'haft, *adj.* rhymed, in rhyme.

Reim'kunst, *(str., pl.* R-künste) *f.* art of rhyming.

Reim'ler, Reim'ling, *(str.) m.* see Reimerling.

Reim'..., *in comp.* –satz, –strophe, *f.* ... strophe, stanza; –schmied, *m.* rhymer, rhymester; –silbe, *f.* syllable which contains the rhyme; –spruch, *m.* maxim, apophthegm [illegible]; –weise, *adv.* in rhymes; –wort, *n.* the word which rhymes.

Rein, I. *adj.* 1) clean; pure; clear; [illegible] ...cent; 2) correct, pure; 3) clean, [illegible] r-es Vermögen, unincumbered property [illegible] Vieh, see Reinvieh; r-e Lehre, &c. [illegible] doctrine; r-es Gewissen, clear conscience [illegible] that es aus r-em Vergnügen, he did it [illegible] pleasure of doing so; das r-e [illegible] reasoning; r-er Wein, fair [illegible] heit, the plain truth; eine [illegible] right lie; *Comm.* r-e [illegible] neat balance; r-er [illegible] ... ein r-es Gewissen, a [illegible]

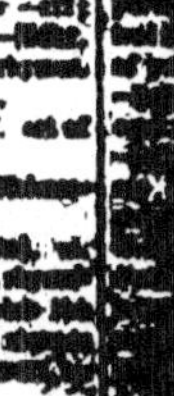

to be buried in the sea; auf dem Hals —, to ride exceedingly hard; II. *tr.* 1) to ride; Gallop —, to gallop; lahm *or* stumpf —, to founder (a horse); die Elle —, *joc.* to sell by retail; ein Princip —, to stick blindly to a principle; 2) *coll.* to ride or pirate (an author); r-d, *p. a.* riding, mounted; die r-de Artillerie, horse-artillery; r-de Polizei, horse-police; ein r-des Blatt, *Bot.* equitant leaf.

A. **Rei'ter**, *s.* I. *(str.) m.* 1) rider, horseman; trooper; 2) *Entom.* see Kornwurm; 3) *Conch.* swift running crab (*Ocypōde cursor* L.); 4) *Ornith.* spur-wing (Chirurg); der rothe —, redshank (*Tringa gambetta* L.); 5) ram, tup, 6) *T.* cross-beam; 7) *Fort.* cavalier; *Mil.* s. ein Regiment —, a regiment of horse; die spanischen —, *chevaux-de-frise.*

B. **Rei'ter**, *(str.) m.* & *(w.) f. provinc.* a large sieve, riddle (*Dorset, &c.:* rudder, *cf.* Ratter, Räder &c.).

Rei'ter..., *in comp.* —aufzug, *m.* cavalcade; —brigade, *f.* horse-brigade; —büchse, *f.* carabine, carbine; —degen, *m.* cavalry-sword; —dienst, *m.* service *or* duty of a horse-soldier.

Reiterei', *(w.) f.* 1) *coll.* (mode *or* custom of) riding; 2) cavalry, horsemen, horse.

Rei'ter... (*from* Reiten), *in comp.* —fahne, *f.* (*dimin.* —fähnlein, *n.*) (*l. u.*) 1) standard; 2) a body of cavalry, squadron; —fähnrich, *m.* cornet; —flinte, *f.* carabine; —gar, *adj. coll.* half done (of meat); —geld, *n. Mar.* salvage.

Rei'terhaft, Rei'terisch, *adj.* horseman-like, trooper-like.

Rei'terin, *(w.) f.* rider, horse-woman.

Rei'ter..., *in comp.* —koller, *n.* see Koller, I; —kraut, *n. Bot.* water-aloe (Wasseraloë); —künste, *f. pl.* equestrian performances, feats of horsemanship.

Rei'tern, *(w.) v. tr. provinc.* for Sieben (*cf.* Rättern &c.).

Rei'ter..., *in comp.* —pferd, *n.* trooper's horse; —pistole, *f.* horse-pistol; —salbe, *f. vulg.* salve against lice *or* the itch, blue ointment.

Rei'terschaft, *(w.) f.* horsemanship.

Rei'ter..., *in comp.* —schar, *f.* cavalcade; —schlacht, *f.* battle, combat of horsemen.

Rei'tersmann, *m. coll. for* Reiter, *A.* 1.

Rei'ter..., *in comp.* —statue, *f.* equestrian statue; —stiefel, *m. pl.* jack-boots; —wache, *f.* 1) horse-guard; 2) sentinel on horse-back, vedette; —zug, *m.* cavalcade.

Reit'... (*from* Reiten), *in comp.* —fertig, *adj.* ready to mount; ready to be mounted; —gamaschen, *f. pl.* stirrup-stockings; —geld, *n. Mar.* see Reitergeld; —gerte, *f.* riding-cane, horse-whip, *cf.* —peitsche.

Reit(h)'gras, *(str.) n. Bot.* bog-reed, water-reed (*Calamagrostis* Roth.).

Reit'... (*from* Reiten), *in comp.* —gurt, *m.* broad girdle; —habit, *n.* see —kleid; —haken, *m.* hook or clasp for fastening up the skirt of a coat when riding; —halde, *f. Min.* heap of ore-dross after washing, heap of slag or rubbish; —hammel, *m.* tup, ram; —handschuh, *m.* habit-glove; —haus, *n.* riding-house; —hengst, *m.* stone-horse, stallion; —hosen, *f. pl.* riding-trowsers; —kissen, *n.* pillion, pad; —kleid, *n.* riding habit (of a lady), joseph; —knecht, *m.* groom; —knie, *n. Mar.* knee of the sternpost; —koller, *n.* doublet; —kröte, *f.* see Reitwurm; —kunst, *f.* horsemanship, equestrian art; —künste, *f. pl.* performances of horsemanship; —laus, —linse, *f.* see Krätzmilbe; —lehrer, *m.* riding-master.

Reit'lings, *adv.* a-straddle (Rittlings).

Reit'... (*from* Reiten), *in comp.* —mantel, *m.* riding-cloak; —maschine, *f. Sport.* foul mash or net; —maus, *f.* see Reutmaus; —meister, *m.* see —lehrer; —milbe, *f.* see —laus; —ochs, *m.* bull; —peitsche, *f.* riding-whip, horse-whip; —pferd, *n.* riding-horse, saddle-horse; —pistole, *f.* horse-pistol; —platz, *m.* riding-place, riding-ground; —post, *f.* mail; —rock, *m.* riding-coat; —sack, *m.* see Mantelsack; —sattel, *m.* riding-saddle; —schimmel, *m.* carriage *or* cart in saw-saddle; —schleife, *f.* knee-strap (of carriage-horses); —scheit, *m.* see Reibescheit; —schmidt, *m.* farrier; —schule, *f.* 1) manege, riding-school; 2) round-about; —sessel, *m.* riding-chair *or* stool; —stall, *m.* stable for riding-horses; —stange, *f.* bridle bit, branch of a bridle; —stiefeln, *m. pl.* riding-boots, jack-boots; —stock, *m.* Turn. riding-puppet, head-stock with centre; —strümpfe, *m. pl.* stirrup-stockings; —stuhl, *m.* 1) *see* —sessel; 2) *see* —stock; —stunde, *f.* riding-lesson; —tasche, *f.* budget; —tenne, *f.* floor on which the corn is trodden out by horses or oxen; —vortheil, *m.* jousting-block; —wechsel, *m. Comm.* slang, accommodation-bill, kite; —weg, *m.* spur-way, horse-way, bridle-path, bridle-road, bridle-track; —wurm, *m.* see Reutwurm; —zeug, *n.* riding-equipage; —zug, *m.* cavalcade.

Reiz, *s. (str.) m.* 1) irritation; tickling; 2) *a)* provocation, provocative, sting; *b)* enticement, allurement, incentive, attractive; stimulus; 3) attraction, charm, grace, gracefulness.

Reiz'bar, I. *adj.* 1) *Med., &c.* inflammable; 2) irritable, susceptible, sensible, nervous, sensitive; II. R-keit, *(w.) f.* irritability, susceptibility, sensibility.

Rei'zen, *(w.) v. tr.* 1) to stimulate, tickle, excite, stir up; to incite, instigate (to evil); 2) to irritate, provoke; 3) *a)* to entice, allure; *b)* to charm, attract; r-d, *p. a.* 1) *Med.* stimulant; 2) charming, graceful.

Reiz'..., *in comp.* —fähig, *adj. Phys.* irritable; —fieber, *n. Med.* irritable ephemeral fever.

Reiz'los, *adj.* charmless, unattractive; R-igkeit, *f.* charmlessness, unattractiveness.

Reiz'mittel, *(str.) n.* incentive, provocative, *Med.* stimulating remedy, *pl.* stimulants; 2) *fig.* inducement, incitement, stimulus.

Rei'zung, *(w.) f.* 1) stimulation, irritation; prompting; 2) provocation; 3) enticement, allurement, inducement; 4) charm.

* **Rejo'len**, *(Fr.)* see Rajolen.

Re'kel, &c. see Räkel, Flegel, 2 &c.

* **Relais'** (*pr.* relä'), *(str., pl.* (*pr.* relä's)) *n.* (*Fr.*) relay.

* **Relatiōn'**, *(w.) f.* (*Lat.*) relation, report.

* **Relativ'**, I. *adj.* (*L. Lat.*) relative, respective; r-er Schaden, comparative damage; II. *s. (str.) n. Gramm.* relative.

* **Relegatiōn'**, *(w.) f. Univ.* (*Lat.*) exclusion, expulsion. — **Relegi'ren**, *(w.) v. tr. Univ.* to expel.

* **Relief'**, *(str., pl.* R-s) *n.* (*Fr.*) 1) *T.* relief, relievo; 2) *fig.* foil; —email, *n.* embossed enamel; —karte, *f.* map in relief-manner; —(metgeschnitt)maschine, *f.* Calico-print. surface-printing-machine.

* **Religiōn'**, *(w.) f.* (*Lat.*) 1) religion, faith, persuasion; form of worship; ein Mensch ohne —, a man of no religion; Gegenstände der —, religious subjects; [illegible] each, blunt, [illegible].

* **Religions'...**, *in comp.* relating to religion, religious; —[illegible] —art, *f.* mode of religion [illegible] religious work; —bildung, *f.* [illegible] —edict, *n.* edict concerning [illegible] *m.* oath to profess a certain [illegible] —eifer, *m.* religious zeal; —[illegible] exercise of a religion [illegible] —friede, *m.* peace by which [illegible] sects are settled [illegible] —gebräuche, *f.* [illegible] —[illegible], *f.* [illegible]

* **Ressour'ce** [*pr.* reßur'ße], (*w.*) *f.* (*Fr.*) 1) resources; 2) club; club-house.

Rest, (*str.*) *m.* rest, remains, remainder; residue; remnant; arrears; balance; im — bleiben, to remain in arrear; heilige R-e eines theuren Mannes (*Schiller*), holy relics of the best of men; *coll.* Einem den — geben, to do one's business, to finish (one), to do for one; seinen — haben, to be done for.

* **Restant',** (*w.*) *m.* (*L. Lat.*) one in arrears, defaulter, reliquator, *coll.* straggler, laggard; R-en, *pl.* arrears.

* **Restaurateur'** [*pr.* —tör'], (*str.*, *pl.* R-e, *or* R-s) *m.* (*Fr.*) eating-house keeper, master of a chop-house, tavern keeper.

* **Restauration',** (*w.*) *f.* (*L. Lat.*) 1) restoration; 2) *restaurant* (*Fr.*), tavern, eating-house; (im Bahnhof) refreshment-room, dining room.

* **Restauri'ren,** (*w.*) *v. tr.* (*Lat.*) to restore; sich —, *fam.* to refresh one's self.

Rest'chen, (*str.*) *n.* (*dimin. of* Rest) small remnant.

Rest'en, Resti'ren, (*w.*) *v. intr.* to be in arrears, to rest; to remain; noch — zwei Posten, two items are still owing.

* **Restitui'ren,** (*w.*) *v. tr.* (*Lat.*) to restore, restitute, retrieve; to return.

* **Restringi'ren,** (*w.*) *v. tr.* (*Lat.*) to restrict.

Rest'zettel, (*str.*) *m.* list of wages due to miners.

* **Resultat',** (*str.*) *n.* (*L. Lat.*) result; inference (Ergebniß). — **Resulti'ren,** (*w.*) *v. intr.* to result. — **Resultan'te,** (*w.*) *f. Phys.* resultant.

* **Resümé,** (*str.*, *pl.* R-s) *n.* (*Fr.*) *résumé*; recapitulation; a summing up; summary; (of judges) charge. [to sum up, &c.

* **Resumi'ren,** (*w.*) *v. tr.* (*Lat.*) to resume;

Reß'baum, (*str.*, *pl.* Reß'bäume) *m. Carp.* beam, rafter, sleeper.

* **Retardir'werk,** (*str.*) *n. Watchm.* stop, check of the regulator.

* **Retension',** (*w.*) *f.* retention; R-srecht, *n.* lien, legal claim.

* **Retira'de,** (*w.*) *f.* (*Fr.*) 1) retreat; 2) privy, *cf.* Abtritt, 2, *b*, b.

* **Retiri'ren,** (*w.*) *v. refl.* & *intr.* (*Fr.*) to retire, make one's retreat.

* **Retor'te,** (*w.*) *f. Chem.* (*Fr.*) retort.

* **Retouchi'ren** [*pr.* retusch—], (*w.*) *v. tr* (*Fr.*) to retouch; nicht retouchirt, untouched.

* **Retour'** [*pr.* retur'], *adv.* (*Fr.*) back; *in comp.* (*cf.* Rück...) —**billet,** *n.* return-ticket, double; —**brief,** *m.* returned letter; dead letter; —**fracht,** *f.* return-freight, home-freight; —**kutsche,** *f.* return-chaise; —**rechnung,** *f.* account of re-exchanges; —**waaren,** *or* **Retou'ren,** *pl.* returns; —**wechsel,** *m.* redraft.

* **Retrai'te** [*pr.* reträ'te], (*w.*) *f.* (*Fr.*) retreat; —**schuß,** *m.* evening-gun. [redraw.

* **Retrassi'ren,** (*w.*) *v. intr. Comm.* to

* **Retrat'te,** (*w.*) *f. Comm.* redraft.

Retsch'e, *see* Rätsche.

Rett'bar, *adj.* savable.

Ret'te, (*w.*) *f. provinc.* male dog.

Ret'ten, (*w.*) *v. tr.* to save, rescue, deliver; seine Ehre —, to vindicate one's honour; Güter aus einem Schiffbruch —, to recover goods from a shipwreck; vor den Dieben wurde wenig gerettet, little was preserved from the thieves; sie retteten sich vor dem Platzregen in eine Capelle, they sought protection from the shower in a chapel.

Ret'ter, (*str.*) *m.*, **Ret'terin,** (*w.*) *f.* saver, deliverer; redeemer.

Rett'gebühr, (*w.*) *f. Comm.* salvage.

Ret'tig, (*str.*) *m. Bot.* radish (*Raphanus* L.).

Rett'los, *adj.* 1) *see* Rettungslos; 2) *Mar.* disabled (Wrack...).

Ret'tung, (*w.*) *f.* the (act of) saving, &c. deliverance, delivery, rescue; recovery; preservation; escape; ohne —, past help, *cf.* Rettungslos.

Ret'tungs..., *in comp.* —**anstalt,** *f.* safety company, safety establishment; life-preserving-establishment; —**boje,** *f.* safety-buoy, life-buoy; —**boot,** *n.* safety boat, life boat; —**gebühren,** *pl.* salvage.

Ret'tungslos, *adj.* irretrievable, irrecoverable; *adv.* irretrievably, beyond recovery, past help; R-igkeit, *f.* irretrievableness, state of being past help.

Ret'tungs..., *in comp.* —**maschine,** *f.* life-preserver; —**mittel,** *n.* resource, remedy, expedient, shift; —**versuch,** *m.* attempt at saving, preserving, or rescue.

Reu'buße, (*w.*) *f. see* Reugeld. [Reu).

Reu'e, (*w.*) *f.* repentance (Reu[illegible]).

Reu'eid, Reu'eoll, *see* Reulos, Reuvoll.

Reu'en, (*w.*) *v. tr.* (*impers.*) to repent, rue, regret; es reu(e)t mich, I repent of it, I repent it; sich (*Acc.*) eines — lassen, to repent of, to repine at a thing.

Reu'geld, (*str.*, *pl.* R-er) *n.* forfeit, forfeiture (upon nonperformance), fine, *coll.* smart-money (Reukauf, *m.*).

Reu'ig, *adj.* repentant, repenting.

Reu'los, *adj.* without (*or* feeling no) repentance, remorseless.

Reu'..., *in comp.* —**muth,** *m.*, —**müthigkeit,** *f.* repentant disposition of mind; —**müthig,** *see* Reuig. [Dachs).

Reu'se, (*w.*) *f. Fish.* weel, bow-net, wicker

Reu'sel, (*str.*) *n.* (*Dutch*) *Mar.* stuff, tallow (for greasing cordage).

Reu'ße, (*w.*) *m.* Russian.

Reu'ßen, *n. Geogr.* Russia. [treasured.

* **Reussi'ren** [*pr.* reüss—], (*w.*) *v. intr.* to

Reu'te, (*w.*) *f.* 1) *a*) the (act of) rooting out, &c.; *b*) *or* **Reut,** (*str.*) *n.* **Reut'bruch,** *m.* ground newly broken (Neubruch); 2) *a*) hoe, mattock; *b*) *Husb.* plough raker; *c*) *Lock-sm.* handle of a key; *d*) *see* Reitel, 2.

Reu'ten, (*w.*) *v. tr.* to root out; to clear (a tract of land) for cultivation.

Reu'ter, (*str.*) *m.* 1) large sieve, *see* [illegible]; 2) *see* Reiter.

Reut'..., *in comp.* —**feld,** —**land,** *n. see* Reute, 1, *b*; —**gabel,** *f.* fork for stirring up the melting soap; —**hacke,** —**haue,** *f.* grubbing-hoe, grubbing-axe, mattock; —**heide,** *see* Reitheide; —**maus,** *f. Zool.* a species of campmouse (*Hypudaeus terrestris* L.); —**spaten,** *m.* grubbing-spade; spud; —**wurm,** *m. Entom.* mole-cricket (Maulwurfsgrille).

Reu'voll, *adj.* full of repentance, repenting.

* **Revan'che** [*pr.* revang'sche], (*w.*) *f.* (*Fr.*) revenge; satisfaction; —**partie,** *f.* return-match. — **Revanchi'ren,** (*w.*) *v. refl.* to take one's revenge.

* **Reveille'** [*pr.* revell'ye], (*w.*) *f.* (*Fr. ré-veil*) *Mil. reveille*; —**schuß,** *m.* morning-gun.

* **Reverbè're,** (*w.*) *f.* (*Fr.*) 1) [illegible] 2) lamp with reflector.

* **Reverberi'ren,** (*w.*) *v. tr.* & *intr.* [illegible] *Chem.*, &c. to reverberate.

* **Reverberir'...,** *in comp. Chem.* [illegible] *n.* reverberated (*or* reverberating) fire, [illegible] ratory; —**lampe,** *f.* lamp with [illegible] —**ofen,** *m.* reverberatory (furnace [illegible] —**schirm,** *m.* reflector. [illegible]

* **Reveren'de,** (*w.*) *f.* (*L. Lat.*) [illegible]

* **Revers',** (*str.*) *m.* (*L. Lat.*) 1) [illegible] reverse (of coins); 2) [illegible] or agreement, reversion; [illegible] versi'ren, (*w.*) *v. refl.* to bind [illegible] declaration.

* **Revidi'ren,** (*w.*) *v. tr.* [illegible]

Revier'bögen, (*str.*) *m.* [illegible]

* **Revidi'ren,** (*w.*) *v. tr.* [illegible] (also *Typ.*), to examine, revise [illegible]

* **Revier',** (*str.*) *m.* [illegible] ter; ward; manor; [illegible]

Riech'... (*from* Riechen), *in comp.* **–essig**, *m.* volatile spirit of vinegar; **–fläschchen**, *n.* smelling bottle; **–kissen**, *n.* perfumed bag, sweet bag; **–nerv**, *m.* *Anat.* olfactory nerve; **–rose**, *f.* *see* –dorn; **–salz**, *n.* smelling-salt; **–stoffe**, *m. pl.* perfumes, scents; **–topf**, *m.* smelling-jar, scented jar; **–waaren**, *f. pl.* perfumes; **–wasser**, *n.* smelling water, sweet water; **–werkzeuge**, *n. pl.* *Anat.* olfactory organs.

Riec'ke, *see* Ricke.

Ried, (*str.*) *n.* 1) reed; 2) boggy country; *in comp.* **–binder**, *m.* reed-cutter; **–blatt**, *n.* *Weav.* slay, reed; **–bock**, *m.* *Zool.* reed-buck; **–dorf**, *n.* village situated near a bog.

Rie'derstein, *see* Tropfstein.

Ried'..., *in comp. Bot.-s.* **–ginster**, *m.* Spanish broom; **–gras**, *n.* 1) reed-grass, bur-grass (*Sparganium* L.); 2) sedge (*Carex* L.); **–graswurzel**, *f.* *Pharm.* German sarsaparilla; **–hahn**, *m.* *see* Auerhahn; **–kamm**, *m.* 1) separator, reval; 2) *see* –blatt; **–kolben**, *m.* *Bot.* reed-mace (*Typha latifolia* L.); **–meise**, *f.* *Ornith.* 1) reed-bunting, reed-sparrow (*Emberiza schoeniclus* L.); 2) fen-titmouse (*Parus palustris* L.); **–pastete**, *f.* *Weav.* slate-book; **–rohr**, *n.* *see* Schilfrohr; **–schnepfe**, *f.* *Ornith.* pewit (*Tringa vanellus* L.); **–sperling**, *m.* *see* Rohrsperling; **–wurm**, *m.* *Entom.* molecricket (Maulwurfsgrille).

Rie'fe, (*w.*) *f.* furrow, groove; *Archit.* chamfer, channel; flute.

Rie'feln, Rie'fen, (*w.*) *v. tr.* to furrow, groove; to chamfer, channel, flute; *Gun-sm.* to rifle; gerieft, *p. a.* *Bot.* angular, angulous.

Rie'fenlos, *adj.* *Bot.* ejugate, uncoupled.

Rie'fig, *adj.* *Bot.* jugated, coupled.

Rie'ge, (*w.*) *f.* *provinc.* 1) row, line; 2) division, class; 3) building for drying grain; 4) cavity made by the encroaching waves of the sea; 5) short oar.

Rie'gel, (*str.*) *m.* 1) *a)* rail, bar; door-bar; cross-beam; cross-bar; transom; intertie; *b)* summers, plates (of a windmill); 2) *Lock-sm.* bolt; 3) *Anat.* coracoid process; 4) *Sew.* loop, eye, eyelet of a button-hole, stay of a shirt bosom; 5) ein — Seife, a bar or square of soap; *Lock-sm.-s.* der stehende —, dead bolt; der deutsche —, sliding catch-bolt; Einem einen — vorschieben, to check, debar one from.

Rie'gel..., *in comp.* **–balken**, *m.* staple; **–band**, *n.* 1) *Carp.* nogging piece; 2) *Saddl.* stirrup-bar; **–bohrer**, *m.* *Coop.* wimble or gimlet for cross-bars.

Rie'gelchen, (*str.*) *n.* (*dimin.* of Riegel) *Archit.* fluting (the three bars) of a Doric capital.

Rie'gel..., *in comp.* **–fest**, *adj.* fastened with bolts, bolted, barred; **–gebäude**, *n.* frame-building; **–haken**, *m.*, **–loch**, *n.* staple; **–haube**, *f.* a kind of ornamental cap of Bavarian women; **–holz**, *n.* bar; **–mauer**, **–wand**, *f.* nogging, brick nogged partition.

Rie'geln, (*w.*) *v. tr.* to bolt (Verriegeln).

Rie'gel..., *in comp.* **–schaufel**, *f.* scoop (of a water-wheel); **–schloß**, *n.* dead lock, stock-lock; **–wand**, *f.* *see* Fachwand; **–werk**, *n.* *see* Fachwerk; **–zaun**, *m.* *Railw.* posts with rails; **–zieher**, *m.* *Coop.* dog.

Rie'gen, (*w.*) *v. tr.* *provinc.* (*L. G.*) 1) *see* Reihen; 2) to plait, to lay in folds.

Rie'ger, (*str.*) *m.* *Mar.* hank.

Rieh'en, (*w.*) *v. tr.* *provinc.* to row (Rudern).

Rieh'mand, (*str.*, *pl.* R-männer) *f.* *provinc.* *Entom.* molecricket (Maulwurfsgrille).

Riek'wurm, *m.* *see* Rielwurm.

Rie'ke, *see* Ricke.

Riel'wurm, (*str.*, *pl.* R-würmer) *m.* *Entom.* larva of the bee-eater (*Trichodes apiarius* L.).

Riem'chen, (*str.*) *n.* (*dimin.* of Riem) 1) little strap; 2) *see* Schmerle; 3) *see* Riemen, 3.

Rie'men, (*w.*) *v. tr.* *Mar.* to row, scull.

Rie'men, *coll.* **Riem**, (*str.*) *m.* 1) strap of leather, thong, brace; latchet; 2) *Mar.* *for* Ruder; 3) *Archit.* (*or* Riem'chen) [illegible]; 4) *Butch.* long strips of meat; 5) ream (of paper); 6) *Typ.* girth; die — ziehen, *coll.* to draw the purse-strings.

Rie'men..., *in comp.* **–bein**, *n.* *Ornith.* stilt-bird (Strandreiter); **–blume**, *f.* *Bot.* loranthus (*Loranthus Europaeus* L.); **–bügel**, *m.* swivel of a gun; **–fisch**, *m.* *Ichth.* 1) sword-fish (Schwertfisch); 2) band-fish (*Cepola rubescens* L.); **–förmige Halsmuskeln**, **–muskeln des Halses**, *m. pl.* *Anat.* splenii muscles; **–klampen**, *pl.* *Mar.* row-locks, crutches, or pegs; **–loch**, *n.* 1) hole in a stirrup-leather, &c.; 2) **–löcher am Stocke**, *pl.* cane-eyes; **–pferd**, *n.* fore-horse, *pl.* leaders; **–seil**, *n.* long reins; **–schneider**, *m.* *see* Riemer; **–stechen**, *n.* fast and loose (a game); **–werk**, **–zeug**, *n.* leather straps, harness, &c., *see* Lederzeug; **–wurm**, *m.* strap-worm; **–scheibe**, sheave-drum, pulley.

Rie'mer, (*str.*) *m.* leather-cutter; harness-maker; belt-maker; saddler; **–messer**, *n.* leather-cutter's knife.

Riem'fisch, *see* Riemenfisch.

Ries, *n.* *see* Rieß; **–bord**, *n.* *Mar.* wash-board.

Riesch, I. *adj.* brickle (said of cotton); II. (*str.*) *n.* *Bot.* spider-wort (*Tradescantia*).

A. **Rie'se**, (*w.*) *m.* giant.

B. **Rie'se**, (*w.*) *f.* slide, *see* Holzriese.

Rie'sel, (*str.*) *m.* 1) the (act of) purling, rippling; 2) drizzling snow or hail; 3) *see* Holzriese; 4) *see* Halde, 2; 5) freckle.

Rie'selig, *adj.* 1) rippling, purling; 2) freckled.

Rie'selleder, (*str.*) *n.* embossed leather (Chagrin).

Rie'seln, (*w.*) *v.* I. *intr.* 1) to thrill; 2) to purl, ripple; to gush; to drizzle; es rieselte mir durch Mark und Bein, a cold shudder ran through my veins; II. *tr.* 1) to water, irrigate; 2) *, to produce, to call forth.

Rie'selregen, (*str.*) *m.* drizzling rain.

Rie'sen, (*w.*) *v. tr.* to slide down (wood), *cf.* Holzriese.

Rie'sen..., *in comp.* relating to a giant, gigantic; **–alk**, *m.* *Ornith.* the large auk, the northern penguin (*Alca impennis* L.); **–ameise**, *f.* *see* Roßameise; **–arbeit**, *f.* gigantic, Herculean work; **–barbe**, *f.* *Ichth.* grey mullet (*Mullus barbatus* L.); **–bau**, *m.* gigantic structure; **–bild**, *n.* gigantic image, gigantic or colossal figure; **–bovist**, *m.* *Bot.* bullfist (*Bovista gigantea* L.); **–büffel**, *m.* *Zool.* West-Indian buffalo (*Bos arni* L.); **–damm**, *m.* *Geogr.* giant's causeway; **–erdbeere**, *f.* *Bot.* Chili strawberry; **–flechte**, *f.* *Med.* [illegible] tetter; **–förmig**, *adj.* *see* –haft; **–gebirge**, *n.* *Geogr.* a chain of mountains between Silesia and Bohemia; **–geier**, *m.* *Ornith.* the largest kind of vulture, condor (Condor); **–geist**, *m.* gigantic intellect; **–gestalt**, *f.* gigantic stature, colossal figure.

Rie'senhaft, I. *or* **Rie'sig**, **Rie'sisch**, *adj.* gigantic, immense, prodigious; II. **Rie'senhaftigkeit**, *f.* giganticalness.

Rie'sen..., *in comp.* **–hai**, *m.* [illegible] basking shark (*Selachus maximus* L.); [illegible] hirsch, *m.* *Palaeont.* giant-deer [illegible] (*...* L.); **–käfer**, *m.* *Entom.* giant [illegible] cules beetle (Herkuleskäfer); [illegible] cabbage; **–kräftig**, *adj.* of gigantic [illegible]; **–kranich**, *m.* *Ornith.* a species of [illegible] marabu (*Ciconia argala* Temm.); [illegible] giant-like, gigantic; [illegible] beloved sloop, bear's paw [illegible] Lam.); *Zool.-s.* **–schildkröte**, *f.* [illegible] turtle (*Chelonia Midas* L.); [illegible] conda; the great boa, boa [illegible] *m.* gigantic step, giant's stride [illegible] **–baum**; **–werk**, *n.* gigantic [illegible] (*in Archaeology*) gigantic cell.

Ries'geld, *adj.* *see* [illegible]

Rit'ter, *(str.) m.* 1) knight; zum — schlagen, to (dub a) knight; ein irrender *or* fahrender —, a knight-errant; arme —, *Cook.* fritters; — von der traurigen Gestalt, knight of the woeful countenance; an Einem zum — werden, *iron.* to win honour by showing one's superiority over another; 2) *fig. a)* champion; *b) joc.* gallant; 3) *Chess.* knight; 4) *Ichth. a)* a species of salmon trout *(Salmo umbla)*; *b) eques (Lat.)*, a species of *Sciænoidei (Eques americanus* Bl.); 6) *see* Breitfeller.

Rit'ter..., *in comp.* knight's, knightly; —academie, *f.* (military) academy for young noblemen; —bank, *f.* bench *or* seat of the knights; —blume, *f. see* —sporn; —buch, *n.* book of chivalry; —burg, *f.* knight's castle; —bürtig, *adj.* of noble descent; —bürtigkeit, *f.* noble descent; —dienst, *m.* 1) knight-service; 2) *fig.* gallant service; —fahrt, *f.* knightly expedition; —gebrauch, *m.* custom of knights; —gedicht, *n.*, —geschichte, *f.* poem, story of chivalry; —geschlecht, *n.* race of knights, noble race; —gut, *n.* knight's fee; manor; —haus, *n.* house of knights *or* nobles; knightly house, noble house; —hof, *m.* manor-house, seat of a knight; —kreuz, *n.* 1) knight's cross; 2) *Bot. see* Scharlachkraut; —lehen, *n. Law*, a tenure of land by knight's service, chivalry.

Rit'terlich, I. *or* **Rit'terhaft,** *adj.* 1) chivalrous, chivalric, knightly; gallant, brave, valiant; 2) equestrian; r-es Thier, *Sport.* epithet of the wild boar; II. R-keit, *(w.) f.* chivalrousness, chivalry; valour, gallantry.

Rit'terling, *(str.) m. cont.* petty knight, would-be knight.

Rit'ter..., *in comp.* —mäßig, *adj. & adv.* knight-like, chivalrous; —orden, *m.* the Teutonic order; —pferd, *n.* 1) horse of a knight; 2) *Entom. see* Wasserjungfer, 1; —pflicht, *f.* knightly duty; —roman, *m.* romance of chivalry; —saal, *m.* hall of the knights.

Rit'terschaft, *(w.) f.* 1) knighthood, chivalry; 2) knights (collectively), equestrian order, nobility; irrende —, knight-errantry.

Rit'terschaftlich, *adj.* belonging to knighthood *or* the equestrian order, knightly, noble.

Rit'ter..., *in comp.* —schlag, *m.* dub; act of knighting; den —schlag empfangen, to be knighted; Einem den —schlag ertheilen, to knight, to (dub a) knight; —schloß, *n.* knight's castle; —schule, *f. see* —academie; —sinn, *m. see* Ritterlichkeit; —sitte, *f.* manner of a knight, courtesy; —sitz, *m. see* —hof; R-smann, *m.* knight; —spiel, *n.* tilt, tournament; —sporn, *m. Bot.* larkspur *(Delphinium consolida* L.); —stand, *m.* 1) *Rom. Ant.* equestrian order; 2) knighthood, body of noblemen, nobility; —statue, *f.* equestrian statue; —steuer, *f.* tax imposed upon the knights in lieu of their services; —stutz, *m.* plume of a knight's helmet; —tafel, *f.* knights' table, nobleman's table; —tag, *m.* day of meeting of knights; —that, *f.* feat of chivalry.

Rit'terthum, *(str.) n.* 1) knighthood; 2) chivalry. — **Rit'terthümlich,** *adj.* pertaining to chivalry.

Rit'ter..., *in comp.* —tracht, *f.* knight's costume; —treue, *f.* fidelity, allegiance of a knight; —weide, *f. see a)* Ritterlist; *b)* Gabelweihe; —wesen, *n.* chivalry; —wort, *n.* word of a knight, knightly word; —würde, *f.* knighthood, dignity of a knight; —zehrung, *f.* († & *)* *fac.* alms; charity given to a noble beggar. —zeit, *f.* age of chivalry, chivalric time(s); —zug, *m.* expedition of knights; crusade. [horses).

Rit'tig, *adj.* (l. *u.*) broken in, trained (of

Rit'lings, *adv.* straddling, astraddle, astride.

Ritt'meister, *(str.) m.* cap'tain of horse.

* **Ritual',** *(str.) n. (Lat.)* ritual; —bücher, *pl. Rom. Ant.* sacred books. — **Rituell',** *adj.* ritual. — **Ri'tus** *(sing. not decl., pl. [Lat.]* — *[w.]* Ri'ten] *or* [l. *u.] str.:* Ri'tusse), *m.* rite.

Ritz! *interj. see* Ritsch.

Ritz, *(str.) m.*, **Ritz'e,** *(w.) f.* slit, rift, cranny, cleft, crevice, crack, flaw, chap; scratch; —eisen, *n.*, —feder, *f.* marking iron; tracing knife *(Tech.)*.

Ritz'en, *(w.) v. tr.* to scratch; to score; *Build., &c.* to trace (the ground).

Ritz'er, *(str.) m. Weav.* uneven weft.

Ritz'ig, *adj.* having rifts *or* slits; cracked, crannied, flawed.

Ritz'messer, *(str.) n.* lancet.

Ritz'ung, *(w.) f.* the (act of) scratching, &c.; scratch.

Ritz'werkzeug, *(str.) n.* picking instrument of miners *(Tech.)*, pick.

* **Rival',** *(str. & w.) m. (Fr.)* rival. — **Rivalisi'ren,** *(w.) v. intr.* to rival. — **Rivalität',** *(w.) f.* rivalry, rivalship.

* **Rivalli'ren,** *(w.) v. tr. (Ital.) Comm.* to reimburse one's self (sich Erholen). — **Rival'so,** *(str.) m. see* Remboursement, Erstattung, 1.

* **Robat(h)',** **Robot(h)',** *(w.) f. (Slav.) see* Robot.

Rob'be, *(w.) m. & f. Zool.* sea-dog, seal, dog-fish *(Phoca* L.).

Rob'ben..., *in comp.* —fang, *m.*, —jagd, *f.* seal-fishing, seal-hunting, sealing; —fänger, *m.* sealer; —fell, *n.* seal-skin, *pl.* seal-fur; —klepper, —klopfer, *m.*, —schiff, *n.* boat of seal-hunters; —knüppel, *m.* club, staff for seal-hunting; —schlag, *m. see* —fang; —schläger, *m.* seal-hunter, seal-killer; —speck, *m.* seal-blubber; —thran, *m.* seal-oil.

* **Rob'ber,** *(str.) m. (Engl.) Gam.* rubber (at whist).

* **Robe,** *(w.) f.* robe.

Ro'bennägel, *m. T.* middle-sized nail.

Ro'bert, *m.* Robert *(P. N.)*; R-skraut, *n. Bot.* herb Robert *(Geranium robertianum* L.).

* **Robi'nie,** *(w.) f. Bot.* locust-tree, bastard-acacia *(Robinia pseudacacia* L.).

* **Robot',** *(w.) f. (Slav.) see* Frohne, Frohndienst. — **Roboten,** *(w.) v. intr. see* frohnen.

* **Rocel'le,** *(w.) f. (Ital.) see* Orseille.

* **Rocha'de,** *(w.) f. Chess.* (act of) castling.

A. **Roch'e,** *(w.) m. & f. Ichth.* roach, thornback, ray *(Raja clavata* L.); der electrische —, torpedo, cramp-fish *(Raja torpedo* L.).

B. **Roch'e,** *(w.) m. (Fr.-Pers.) Gam. (Chess)* rook, castle.

Röch'eln, *(w.) v. intr.* to rattle (in the throat); r-d, *p. a.* rattling, stertorous.

Roch'en, *(str.) m. see* Roche, 1.

Roch'en, **Rochi'ren,** *(w.) v. intr. Gam.* to castle. [—band, *n.* coat-binding.

Rock, *(str., pl.* Röck'e*) m.* coat; gown; robe;

Rock'en, *a.* I. *(str.) m.* 1) a bunch of flax, tow, &c. from which the thread is drawn (in spinning); 2) *see* —stock; 3) *see* Roggen; II. *in comp.* —band, —blatt, *n.*, —brief, *m.* ribbon, leaf, paper wrapped round the distaff; —gespinnst, *n.* spun yarn; cont.-c. —[illegible]; —weisheit, *f.* (old) woman's philosophy; —philosopherin, *f.* states-woman; —stock, *m.* distaff; —stube, *f.* spinning-room.

Rock'..., *in comp.* —falte, *f.* fold of a coat, gown, or petticoat; —halter, *m.* coat-[illegible]

...röckig, *adj. in comp.* ... coated.

Rock'..., *in comp.* —knopf, *m.* coat-button; —schoß, *m.* coat-tail, coat-lap, skirt; —tasche, *f.* coat pocket.

Ro'de, *(w.) f. see* Runke, 1.

Ro'del, *(str.) m.* 1) *see* Rodel, [illegible] 2) *or* Ro'del, *Bot.* yellow rattle; —[illegible] *pl.* packing-boards; —[illegible]

— **Rö'deln,** *(w.) v. tr. see* [illegible]

Ro'den, *(w.) v. tr.* to root up, [illegible] Reuten.

Rod, *(str.) m. Mar.* 1) [illegible]

Ro'gen, *(str.) m.* roe, spawn [illegible]

2) Vet. glanders; —glanz, m. see Glanzstein; —bart, —bube, —löffel, m., —maul, n., —nase, f. vulg. 1) snotty fellow; 2) snivelling brat, chit.

Rotz'en, (w.) v. intr. 1) vulg. to snivel, to snuff up; 2) Vet. to be affected with the glanders.

Rotz'fisch, (str.) m. see Schleimfisch.

Rotz'ig, adj. 1) vulg. snotty; mucous; 2) Vet. glandered.

Rotz'schwefel, (str.) m. common brimstone.

* Rouleau' [pr. rûlō'], (str., pl. R-x [pr. rûlō's']) n. (of Fr. origin, although never used in the same sense in French) blind-roller (Fr. store), (window-)blind or shade (Fensterrolle).

* Rouli'ren [rûlī'ren], (w.) v. intr. (Fr.) to circulate; to turn (upon), &c.

* Routi'ne [rû—], (w.) f. (Fr.) routine. — Routini'ren, (w.) v. refl. to get into the routine of something; routinirt', p. a. versed.

Rü'be, (w.) f. Bot. rape; root, turnip, &c.; weiße (Kohl-) —, turnip; gelbe —, see Möhre, 1; rothe —, see Runkel(rübe); faule —, white bryony (Zaunrübe).

* Ru'bel, (str.) m. Num. rouble.

Rubel'le, (w.) f. Metall. rubber, rubbing-plate.

Rü'ben..., in comp. —acker, m., —feld, n. field of turnips; Bot. e. —hahnenfuß, m. bulbous crowfoot (Ranunculus bulbosus L.); —kerbel, m. cicely, great chervil (Myrrhis ... L.); —kohl, m. rape (Brassica rapa L.); —rettig, m. large black radish; —samen, m., —saat, f. turnip-seed; rape-seed; —stecher, m. turnip-scoop; —zucker, m. beet-root sugar.

Rü'bezahl, (str.) m. Germ. Fab. Number-Nip, name of a mountain demon in the Riesengebirge (Silesia).

* Rubin', (str.) m. (Ital.) Miner. ruby; in comp. —balles, m. Miner. balas-ruby, spinelle; —farben, —farbig, —roth, adj. ruby coloured, ruby-red; —fluß, m. artificial ruby; ruby-fluor; —glas, n. ruby-coloured glas; —glimmer, m. Miner. pyrosiderite; —granate, f. rock-ruby; —röthling, —spinell, m. spinelle-ruby; —schwefel, m. realgar.

Rüb'öl, (str.) n. rape-seed oil.

* Rubricir'ren, (w.) v. tr. (Lat.) to head, to put into a column. — Rubrik', (w.) f. rubric, title, article, head, heading, column (of a page).

Rüb'samen, Rüb'sen, (str.) m. 1) rape-seed; 2) Bot. wild navew, wild navette or colewood (Brassica rapa var. oleifera DC.).

Ruch, (str., pl. Rüche) m. († &) poet. smell (Geruch).

Ruch'bar, I. adj. notorious, rumoured, known; — machen, to rumour, divulge; — werden, to become known, &c., to be noised about, to take wind; II. R-keit, (w.) f. notoriousness.

* Ruch'e [pr. rü'sche], (w.) f. (Fr.) trimming (of ladies' dresses).

Ruch'gras, (str.) n. Bot. spring-grass (Anthoxanthum odoratum L.).

Ruch'los, I. adj. profligate, flagitious, abandoned, vicious, wicked, foul, reprobate, ruffian; impious, sacrilegious; II. R-igkeit, (w.) f. profligacy, flagitiousness, &c.; criminality; nefariousness, wickedness, depravity.

Ruck'sen [pr. ruk'sen], (w.) v. intr. to coo [(as a dove).

Rucht'bar, see Ruchbar.

Ruck, (str.) m. jerk, start, jolt, move; tug, wrench; einen — thun, to give a jerk, pull; to move a short way; mit Einem —, at one jerk.

Rück, adv. †, for Zurück, back.

Rück... (from Rück, adv., Rücken, s. &c.), in comp. —abtretung, f. retrocession; act of receding; —anspruch, m. counter-claim; —antwort, f. Law, reply; —anzeige, f. counter-advertisement, counter-information; —assecuranz, f. re-insurance; —auflanger, m. Mar. top timbers; —äußerung, f. reply; —baum, f. Sport. (from Rücken, v.) net-frame.

Rück'bar, adj. movable.

Rück... (from Rück, adv., Rücken, v. &c.), in comp. —batterie, f. Fort. reverse or [illegible] battery; —befagen, v. tr. [illegible] to postdate; —beitel, m. [illegible] ridge-back chisel, square-chisel; —bettung, f. platform for a gun; —bewegung, f. backward or retrograde movement; —bleibsel, n. remnant, residue; —blick, m. (lit. look thrown back) retrospect, retrospective view (auf (with Acc.), of); ein —blick auf ihren Besuch [illegible], a retrospect of her visit to London; —boot, n. Rope-m. peg-block; —bürge, m. counter-surety; —bürgschaft, f. counter or collateral security, counter-bond; —deuten, v. intr. to reflect, to have a reflective meaning; —deutend, adj. reciprocal, reflective; —discontiren, v. tr. to rediscount.

Rück'e, (w.) f. Sport. bird-net.

Rück'einfuhr, (w.) f. re-importation.

Ruck'en, (w.) v. intr. to jerk; to jolt.

Rück'en, (w.) v. I. tr. to move with a jerk, to remove, move; to push, pull; näher —, to bring closer; eine Uhr —, to set a watch; die Mütze —, to lift the cap; sich —, to edge (one's self); II. intr. (aux. haben & sein) to move, proceed; to remove, edge; to march; der Feind rückte auf uns los, the enemy advanced upon us; näher —, to draw near, advance, approach; in ein Land —, to march into (or to enter) a country; aus dem Lager —, to leave the camp.

Rück'en, s. (str.) m. 1) a) back; b) see —[illegible]; 2) the hinder part of a thing, back (of a violin, &c.); 3) ridge (of the nose, a mountain, &c.); 4) Mil. rear (of an enemy, &c.); 5) Agr. long swath of hay; das Schiff [illegible] einen —, Mar. the ship becomes broken-backed or cambered; mit hohem —, [illegible]-backed; seinen — beugen, 1. to bow; 2. fig. to submit; Einem den — halten, to back, countenance one; Einem den — kehren, to turn one's back on one, to forsake; sich (Dat.) den — frei halten, to secure one's retreat; einen breiten — haben, to have broad shoulders; einen krummen — machen, to stoop, cringe; auf dem — liegen, to be done up; einem hinter Jemandes — thun, to do a thing behind a person's back or without a person's knowledge; es läuft mir kalt über den —, I shudder, my flesh creeps; einen — haben an ... (Acc.), to be backed by ....

Rück'en..., (s.) in comp. Anat. & Med. dorsal; —ader, f. dorsal vein; —batterie, f. see Rückbatterie; —bein, n. see [illegible]; —blatt, n. reredos (of an altar-piece); back-plate (of a fireplace); —blut, n. Vet. [illegible] of cattle (in the milk); —darre, f. spinal complaint in which the marrow dries up (Med. tabes dorsalis); —eisen, n. Bookb. back-tool; —fläche, f. flat surface of the back; [illegible]; —flosse, f. dorsal-fin, back-fin; —[illegible], m. fish with dorsal fins; —füßer, pl. [illegible] poda (Notopōda); —gefäß, n. dorsal [illegible]; —gurt, m. see —riemen; —halt, m. see [illegible] halt, 2; —haum, m. Nat. dorsal [illegible]; —[illegible] men, f. pl. Entom. dorsibranchiata (Dorsibranchia Cuv.); —korb, m. see [illegible]; —krampf, m. Med. opisthotonus; —[illegible], scratch-back, back-scraper; —[illegible] of a chair; —mark, n. Anat. spinal [illegible]; —markarterien, f. pl. spinal arteries; [illegible] darre, —markentzündung, f. see —[illegible]; —markentzündung, f. [illegible]; [illegible] weichung, f. [illegible]; —[illegible], f. paralysis of the spinal [illegible]; [illegible] nerv, m. Anat. spinal nerve; —[illegible] tung, f. [illegible]; —[illegible]

Rüg'bar, I. *adj.* blamable, censurable; II. R-keit, *(w.) f.* blamableness.

Rü'ge, *(w.) f.* 1) †, denunciation, accusation; 2) reproof, censure, blame.

Rü'gen, *(w.) v. tr.* 1) †, to denounce; 2) *a)* to resent; to fine; *b)* to reprove, reprehend, censure, blame, animadvert upon.

Rü'gen..., *in comp.* —amt, —gericht, *n.* inferior court of justice adjudicating claims for, and fining injuries or affronts; —meister, —richter, *m.* judge of such a court; —sache, *f.*, —proceß, *m.* lawsuit concerning an injury or affront.

† Rü'getag, *(str.) m.* court-day.

Rü'gung, *(w.) f. see* Rüge.

Ru'he, *(w.) f.* 1) rest, repose, quiet; *fig.* calm, tranquillity, peace; sleep; mit —, calmly, quietly; tiefe —, halcyon-days; 2) place, state of rest; —! hush! peace! in (der) —, at rest; das Gewehr steht in —, the lock is at half-cock; die Maschine ist in —, the machine is at a stop or still-stand; in — lassen, to let or leave alone; zur — bringen, to calm, quiet, hush; to settle; ein Gewehr in — setzen, to half-cock a gun; sich zur — begeben, to go to rest; sich in — begeben, zur — setzen, to retire from active life or from the world; to retire from (or give up) business; einen Beamte(te)n mit Pension zur — setzen, to superannuate, or pension off an official.

Ru'he..., *in comp.* —bank, *f.* couch, seat of repose; —bett, *n.* bed of ease, couch(-bed); sofa; —brett, *n. Gunn.* sole of a gun-carriage; —bühne, *f. Min.* resting-place, landing-place; —feld, *n.* fallow-field (Brachacker); —fuge, *f. Build.* bed-built joint; —gehalt, *n.* pension; —jahr, *n. see* Brachjahr; —kammer, *f.* sleeping-room; —kämmerlein, *n.* °, narrow cell, grave; —kissen, *n.* pillow; dies Amt ist kein —kissen, *fig.* this place is no sinecure.

Ru'helos, I. *adj.* restless; II. R-igkeit, *(w.) f.* restlessness.

Ru'hen, *(w.) v. intr.* to rest, repose, take rest; to sleep; ich wünsche Ihnen wohl zu —, I wish you a good night's rest; hier ruht ..., here lies ... (on gravestones); unser Briefwechsel ruht jetzt, our correspondence lies dormant now; die Sache ruht jetzt, the matter now rests; die Macht ruht in seinen Händen, the power is lodged in his hands; r-des Vermögen or Capital, dead stock, unapplied funds, dormant capital; auf Waaren r-de Ansprüche, claims existing upon goods; nach gethaner Arbeit ist gut —, after the work is done, repose is sweet.

Ru'he..., *in comp.* —platz, *m.* 1) (or —ort) resting-place; place of rest; 2) landing-place (of a stair-case); —punct, *m.* 1) pause, point of rest, resting-place, rest; 2) *Mus.* point of repose in melody; cadence; 3) *Phys.* centre of gravity; fulcrum; —saat, *f.* corn grown on land that has lain fallow.

Ru'hesam, *adj. see* Ruhsam.

Ru'he..., *in comp.* —sessel, *m.* (lit. chair of rest, of ease, or repose) easy-chair, arm-chair; —sitz, *m.* seat of repose; retirement; —stab, *m. Paint.* maul-stick; —stand, *m.* state of repose, rest, or tranquillity; in —stand versetzen, to superannuate; to invalid; sich in —stand begeben, *see* sich in Ruhe begeben; —statt, —stätte, —stelle, *f. see* —platz, 1; —störer, *m.* disturber of peace or tranquillity; —störung, *f.* breach of peace, perturbation; —stunde, *f.* hour of rest; —tag, *m.* day of rest; —voll, *adj.* very quiet, calm; —winkel, *m. T.* natural slope (of an embankment, &c.); —zeichen, *n.* sign of rest, pause; —zeit, *f.* resting time, pause. [—holz, *n. Mar.* cushion.

Ruh'..., *in comp.* —feld, *n. see* Ruhefeld;

Ru'hig, I. *adj.* quiet, peaceable, calm, sober, tranquil, easy, at rest, at ease; — machen, to appease, pacify; — werden, *Mar.* to fall calm, subside (of the wind); — lassen, to let or leave in peace; Sie können das — thun, you may safely do that; II. R-keit, *(w.) f.* (l. u.) quietness, &c.

Ruh'..., *in comp.* —kraft, *f. Phys.* inertia; —küpe, *f. Dy.* repose-vat. [(Ruhrkraut).

Ruh'kraut, *(str.) m. Bot.* yellow [illegible]

Ruhm, *(str.) m.* glory, renown, fame, reputation; praise; honour; den — muß man ihm lassen, this must be said in his praise.

Ruhm'..., *in comp.* —begier, —begierde, *f.*, —durst, *m.*, —gier, *f. see* —sucht; —begierig, —durstig, —gierig, *see* —süchtig; —bekränzt, —gekrönt, *adj.* °, crowned with fame.

Rüh'men, *(w.) v.* I. *tr.* to commend, praise, glorify, extol, celebrate; to speak highly of; ich darf mich —, I may make it my boast; II. *refl.* to glory (mit, in), boast (of), pride one's self (on, upon); ich rühme mich ein Deutscher zu sein, I am proud of being a German; viel R-s machen von ..., *deon.* to make a great fuss about ..., to extol. [position.

Ruhm'gier(igkeit), *(w.) f.* ambitious dis-

Rühm'lich, I. *adj.* 1) (or Rühm'misch, Rühmig) †, vainglorious, boastful; 2) glorious, laudable, commendable, honourable; — bekannt, highly reputed or respectable; II. R-keit, *(w.) f.* gloriousness, laudableness, &c.

Ruhm'liebe, *(w.) f.* love of glory.

† Rüh'mling, *(str.) m.* boaster (Prahler).

Ruhm'los, I. *adj.* inglorious; II. R-igkeit, *(w.) f.* ingloriousness.

Ruhm'..., *in comp.* —redig, *adj.* vainglorious, boasting; —redigkeit, *f.* vainglory, boasting; —reich, *adj.* glorious; —sucht, *f.* thirst or passion for glory, (inordinate) desire of glory; —süchtig, *adj.* most ambitious; thirsty, greedy, or vehemently desirous of glory; —voll, *adj.* glorious, famous; —würdig, *adj.* praiseworthy; deserving fame; —würdigkeit, *(w.) f.* praiseworthiness; gloriousness.

Ruhr, *s.* I. *(w.) f.* 1) *Vint.* the turning up of the ground of a vineyard; 2) *Med.-a.* (die weiße) diarrhœa; (die rothe) dysentery, bloody flux; 3) *Mar.* the running aground; 4) *Sport.* *a)* decoy-bird; *b)* lure; II. *in comp.* —alant, *m. Bot.* fleabane (*Pulicaria dysenterica*, L.); —artig, *adj.* diarrhetic.

Rühr'bar, I. *adj.* movable, susceptible (of being touched); II. R-keit, *(w.) f.* susceptibility.

Rühr'... (*from* Rühren), *in comp.* —bottich, *m. Dy.* second vat; —ei, *n. Cook.* poached eggs; —eisen, *n.* poker.

Rüh'ren, *(w.) v.* I. *tr.* 1) to stir, move; 2) *Husb.* *a)* to plough the second or third time; *b)* to rake into heaps, to cock (hay); 3) *fig.* to move, affect, touch, strike; die Laute —, to touch the lute; die Trommel —, to beat the drum; Eier —, to poach eggs; Sahne —, to whip cream; Mörtel —, to pug mortar; der Schlag hat ihn gerührt, he has had an apoplectic fit; he has been struck by apoplexy; er war wie vom Donner gerührt, he was thunderstruck; II. *intr.* to touch (at), (with Acc., less frequently with Dat.), [illegible] thing); III. *refl.* to stir, to bustle one's self, to be up and doing. [illegible]

Rüh'rend, *p. a.* touching, &c., [illegible]

Rühr'faß, *(str., pl.* R-fässer) *n.* churn.

Rühr'haft, *adj.* 1) *see* Rührend; 2) [illegible] touched. [illegible]

Ruhr'haken, *(str.) m. Agr.* [illegible]

Rühr'... (*from* Rühren), *in comp.* [illegible] *m.* 1) *Iron-w.* rake, holling [illegible] Heringsfang; —holz, *n.* paddle.

Rüh'rig, Rühr'sam, I. *adj.* [illegible] nimble, active, alert, busy, [illegible] R-keit, *(w.) f.* agility, nimbleness, [illegible] disposition, activity; [illegible]

Rühr'kelle, *(w.) f. Paint.* [illegible]

Ruhr'..., *in comp.* —kraut [illegible]

in surveying; 3) a) *Sport.* brush, drag; b) *Anat.* yard; 4) *see* Labmagen; 5) *Mar.* a) mizen-yard; b) *see* Ankerruthe; 6) sail of a wind-mill; 7) *fig.* chastisement, punishment; einem Kinde die — geben, to whip a child; er hat sich (*Dat.*) selbst eine — gebunden, *meal.* he has made a halter to hang himself.

Ru'theln, (*w.*) *v. tr.* & *intr.* to birch.

Ru'then..., *in comp.* —**bündel,** *n.* bundle of switches, fagot; —**fischer,** *m.* angler; —**förmig,** *adj.* rod-shaped; *Bot.* virgate(d); —**gänger,** —**mann,** *m. Min.* one searching lodes with the divinatory wand; —**hieb,** *m. see* —**schlag**; —**kappe,** *f.* flail-thong; —**kraut,** *n. Bot.* Macedonian parsley (*Bubon galbanum* L.); —**meßkunst,** *f.* baculometry; —**muskel,** *m. Anat.* muscle of the penis; —**schlag,** *m.* stroke with the rod or wand; —**schläger,** *m. see* —**gänger**; —**segel,** *n. Mar.* yard sail; —**streich,** *m. see* —**schlag.** [in a trice.

Rutsch, (*str.*) *m. coll.* slide, push; im —,

Rutsch'bahn, *f.*, **Rutsch'berg,** *m.* gliding hill, slope on which chariots glide down in rails, &c.

Rutsch'e, (*w.*) *f.* slide; *cf.* Holzriese.

Rutsch'en, (*w.*) *v. intr.* (*aux.* sein) to slide, glide, slip.

Rutsch'er, (*str.*) *m. Danc.* gallopade; —**zins,** *m.* †, interest upon interest.

Rut'te, (*w.*) *f. see* Aalquappe.

Rüt'tel..., *in comp.* —**falk,** —**geier,** *m.* kestrel (Thurmfalk); —**holz,** *n.* glover's smoothing-tool. — **Rüt'teln,** (*w.*) *v.* I. *tr.* to shake, rattle, wag, jog, jolt, toss; II. *intr.* an (*with Dat.*) —, to shake. — **Rüt'tel...,** *in comp.* —**stange,** *f.* (or —**stock,** *m.*) *Mill. see* Rührstock; 2) *Paper-m. see* Rührstange, 1; —**weihe,** *f. see* —**falk.** [stroh.

Rütt'stroh, *n.* loose straw, litter, *cf.* Wirr-

Ry'ssel, *n. Geogr.* Lille.

S, s, *n.* S, s, the nineteenth letter and fifteenth consonant of the Alphabet; S bugt, *f. Ship-b.* a piece of timber in the form of an S.

S., *abbr. for* Seite, page, folio; S., s. *for* siehe, see; S. 1) *for* Sou, sou; 2) *for* Solo, Solo (*Mus.*); s., *for* sive (*Lat.* oder, or); SA., Sch.A., Schpf. *for* Schiffs-Pfund, ship-pound; S., Sct., S. *for* Sanct, Saint; Sbgr. *see* Sgr.; s. Br. *for* südliche Breite, southern latitude; S/C. *for* suo Conto (*Ital.*, sein Conto, his [or Mr.[illegible]'s] account); sc., scil. *for* scilicet (*Lat.*, nämlich, namely, to wit, viz.); Schff., Schffl., Schl. *for* Scheffel, bushel; Schiffb., Schifff. *for* Schiffbau, Schifffahrt, ship-building, navigation; schl. G. *for* schlecht Geld, base coin; Schck., Sc. *for* Schock, number of sixty, three score; Schr. *for* Schiffer, skipper, captain, master; Sck., Sc. *for* Sack, Säcke, bag, bags, sack, sacks; s. d. *for* siehe, siehe diesen Artikel, see or compare (that article); Sec. Sa., Sda., Seconda-(Wechsel), second (of exchange); Sect. *for* sectio (*Lat.*, Abschnitt, section); S. E. (et) C. *for* salvo errore (et) calculo, S. E. et O. *for* salvo errore et omissione (*Lat.*, Irrthum vorbehalten, errors [and omissions] excepted); sel. *for* selig, late, deceased; (Steins &c.) sel. Wwe. *for* des seligen (Stein &c.) Wittwe, widow of late (Stein, &c.); Sept., Septbr. *for* September; s. g. *for* sogenannt, (properly) so called; Sgr. *for* Silber-Groschen, silver-groschen; sign. *for* signatum (*Lat.*, signirt, signed); s. L. *for* südliche Länge, southern longitude; Sl. *for* Soldi, soldi (Italian coin); Sld., Sldo. *for* Saldo, balance; s. l. e. a. *for* sine loco et anno (*Lat.*, ohne Ort und Jahr [des Druckes], without place and year); s. m. *for* siehe meine see; S. M. *see* Se. M.; S. O. *for* salvo omissione, *see* S. E., &c.; solv. *for* solve (*Lat.*, löse auf, solve); Sp., Span. *for* spanisch, Spanish; Spec. *for* sporco (*Ital.*, brutto, gross weight). Spec. Rthlr. *for* Species-Thaler, specie dollar; Spcs. *for* Species, [illegible]; spf., spfl. *for* superfein, superfine; Spr. *for* sprich, pronounce; Sps. *for* Species, specie dollars; Spt.K., Spth.K. *for* Super-Kamp, superiare; Se. M. (Maj.) *for* Seiner Majestät, His Majesty; Ss. *for* semis (*Lat.*, halb, half); ß. *for* Schilling, shilling; ßl. *for* Schilling lübisch, shilling lubs; ßSterl. *for* Schilling Sterling, shilling sterling; ßvl. *for* Schilling flämisch, shilling Flemish; S. T. *for* salvo titulo, *see* P. P.; St. 1. *for* Stück, Stück; 2. *for* statt, for, instead of; St. 1. or Sct. *for* Sanct, Saint (St.); 2. *for* Stadt, Sterling, Stück, town (city), sterling, piece; Sta. *for* Santa, (z. B. Sta. Fé); Stb., Stbr. *for* Stüver, stiver; Stbg. *for* Stübchen (Stübgen), measure (of one gallon); Stck., St. *for* Stück, piece; Std. *for* Stunde, hour; Sterl. *for* Sterling, sterling; Stg. *for* Stiege, a number of twenty; a score; st. n. *for* stilo novo (*Lat.*, neuen Stils, [of the] new style); Stpp. *for* Stempel-Papier, stamped paper; Str., Stüb., Stv. *for* Stüber, *see* Stb.; st. v. *for* stilo vetere (*Lat.* alten Stils, old style); s. v. a. *for* so viel als, as much as; Syst. *for* System, system; s. Z. *for* seiner Zeit, in due time. [gaily! merrily!

Sa, *interj.* oh! ho! courage! cheer up!

Saab'holz, *n. see* Rothschwarz.

Saal, (*str.*, *pl.* Sä'le) *m.* hall, (large) room; drawing room, assembly-room; saloon.

Saalbaderei', (*w.*) *f. see* Salbaderei.

Saal'band, Saal'leiste, &c., *see under* Sahl.

Saal'..., *in comp.* —**geselle,** *m. Paper-m.* the journeyman that presses the reams before they are wrapped up; —**kellner,** *m.* head-waiter in large hotels.

Saal'weide, *see* Sal'weide.

Saa'me, Saa'men, *m. see* Same.

Saa're, (*w.*) *f.* (*also* Saar'bache, *f.*, —baum, *m.*, —weide, *f.*) [illegible] (black) poplar.

Saat, *s.* I. (*w.*) *f.* 1) seed; 2) (act and time of) sowing; 3) green corn (lately sprung up); standing corn, grain; II. *in comp.* —**buch,** *n.* † land-book; —**egge,** seed-harrow; Scotch harrow; S-euland, *n.* * (*Am.* [illegible]), cultivated land, corn-fields; —**erbse,** *f.* common pea; —**eule,** *f. see* —motte; —**fahre,** *f. see* —[illegible]; —**feld,** *n.* field sown with corn; corn-field; —**fink,** *m. see* Hänfling, 1; —**furche,** *f. Agr.* third ploughing; —**furchen,** *v. tr.* & *intr.* to give the third ploughing to a field; —**gans,** *f. Ornith.* bean-goose (*Anser segetum* L.); —**grill,** *m. Agr.* a species of cultivator; —**gurke,** *f.* common cucumber; —**hanf,** *m.* [illegible] hemp; —**huhn,** *n. Ornith.* golden or green plover (Goldregenpfeifer); —**käfer,** *m.* [illegible] spring beetle, leaping beetle, [illegible] *segetis* Gyl.); —**kartoffel,** *f. see* [illegible]; —**kasten,** *m.* drill-box (of a sowing-machine); —**kampf,** *m. see* Rothschwarz; —**korn,** *n.* [illegible] corn, seed-grain; —**krähe,** *f. Ornith.* rook (*Corvus frugilegus* L.); —**lerche,** *f.* [illegible] field-lark, sky lark. [illegible]

Saat'ling, (*str.*) *m.* 1) [illegible]

Saat'..., *in comp.* —**motte,** *f.* [illegible] moth (*Segetia frumentalis* L.) [illegible] Saamperle; —**pflug,** *m.* field-[illegible] gen, *n.* fourth ploughing; —[illegible] —**scheibe**; —**rosen,** *f. pl.* [illegible] holly hock (Stockrosenpappel); —[illegible] —**tiefer**; —**vogel,** *m. see* —[illegible] common vetch; —**zeit,** *f.* [illegible] time.

wohl —, &c. to bid (one) good night, farewell, &c.: wird er es Ihnen —? will he tell it you? ich will Ihnen —, was ich von ihnen denke, I will tell you what I think of them; die Wahrheit —, to speak the truth; Lügen —, to tell untruths (coll. fibs); man hat mir gesagt, ich habe mir — lassen, I am told or informed; Einem — lassen, to send one word; mein Vater läßt Ihnen —, I am desired by my father to tell you; mein Meister läßt Ihnen —, my master bids me tell you; das läßt sich von ihm nicht —, that does not apply to him; sich (Dat.) — lassen müssen, to be obliged to put up with (hard words, &c.); sich (Dat.) gesagt sein lassen, to take the hint, to take warning; laß es dir gesagt sein, bear that in mind, let this be a warning to you; sie wollen sich (Dat.) nichts mehr — lassen, they are impatient of control; er sagte nichts dazu, he said nothing to it; er hat von Glück zu —, he may think (call) himself fortunate; wie gesagt, as I said (before); as already before; so zu —, so to speak, as I may say; in einer so zu — unbewußten Weise thut Hrn. Jerrold's Buch dar, in a so to speak unconscious manner, Mr. Jerrold's book makes clear ... (Gentl. Mag. July '74, 126); as it were; (wie) gesagt, (so) gethan, no sooner said than done; so said, so done; was ich — wollte, by the bye! was Sie (nicht) —! you don't say so! was will das —? what is the meaning of this? aber was will das —? but what then? er weiß nicht was das — will, he does not know what that means; das ist viel gesagt, das will viel —, that is saying a great deal, coll. it is a bold word; das will nicht viel —, there is not much in that; das will nichts —, that is of no moment; viel zu — haben, to have much power, authority, interest, or influence; er hat viel zu —, he is a man of great account; es hat wenig zu —, it is of little consequence; es hat nichts zu —, it does not signify, it does not matter, no matter; als wenn er — wollte, as much as to say; man sagt wohl nicht zu viel, wenn man sagt, daß ..., it is not too much to say that ...; was wollen Sie damit —? what do you mean (by that)? what do you aim (or drive) at? es sollte damit so viel gesagt sein, it was intended to say, that ...; aus dem Gesagten erhellt, it appears by (from) what you say or has been said; sage Einhundert Thaler, say one hundred thalers.

Sä'gen, (w.) v. tr. & intr. to saw; to cut.

Sä'gen..., in comp. (—artig, —förmig, &c.) see Sä'ge..., in comp.

Sä'gensch, (str.) n. Fish. saine(-net).

Sa'gen..., in comp. —forschung, f. inquiry into the tales of ancient times, into legends; —geschichte, f. 1) mythical or legendary history; 2) history of traditions, legends.

Sa'genhaft, adj. traditionary, fabulous, legendary.

Sa'gen..., in comp. —kunde, —lehre, f. legendary lore; —reich, adj. rich in traditions, &c., storied; —zeit, f. time of legends, ante-historical time, fabulous or mythical age.

Sä'ger, (str.) m. 1) sawer, sawyer; 2) Ornith. see Sägetaucher.

Sä'ge..., in comp. —rahmen, m. frame of a saw; —richter, m. saw-wrest, saw-set.

Sä'gerstiefe, f. saw-pit (Sägegrube).

Sä'geschiefer, (str.) m. see Griffelschiefer.

Sä'ge..., in comp. —schlitten, m. carriage, sledge of a saw-mill; —schmied, m. smith who makes saws; —schnabel, m. momot (Prionites brasiliensis Latr.); —schnäbler, m. Ornith. see —taucher; —schnitt, m. saw-notch, saw-cut; —schraube, f. saw-screw; —setzer, m. see —richter; —späne, m. pl. saw-dust; —sprung, m. see Wildschwein; —taucher, m. Ornith. (großer) merganser (Mergus merganser L.).

* **Sagett'e,** see Sahett.

Sä'ge..., in comp. —wagen, m. see —schlitten; —werk, n. Fort. redant; —zähnig, adj. Bot. toothed like a saw, serrate.

* **Sa'go,** (str.) m. & m. (Malay.) sago; unechter — (in America) Dutch sago, (in England) pearl or German sago; sago of potatoes; —grütze, f., —mehl, n. sago-porridge; —palme, f. sago-tree.

Säg'weihe, (w.) f. see Holzweihe.

Sahl..., in comp. (cf. Sal...) —band, n., —leiste, f. band, list (of cloth), salvage; edge, border; —bank, f. Archit. window-sill or bench; —buch, n. 1) † register of donations made to church, &c.; 2) see Grundbuch; —gut, n. † estate exempt from taxes.

Sah'lingen, (str.) f. pl. Mar. cross-trees and trestle-trees.

Sahl'weide, see Salweide.

Sah'ne, (w.) f. provinc. cream (Rahm); S-ngießer, m. cream-jug.

Sah'nen, (w.) v. tr. to skim (milk; Abrahmen).

Sai'ger, see Seiger.

* **Sai'son** [sezong'], f. (pl. S-s) season.

Sai'te, (w.) f. string (of a musical instrument); chord; catgut; fig-s. die S-n zu hoch spannen, to strain the strings too high; to claim too much; gelindere S-n aufziehen, to come a peg or two lower, to draw in one's horns, to give in, to sing smaller; andere S-n aufziehen, to turn over a new leaf.

Sai'ten..., in comp. —bezug, m. set of strings; —brett, n. see —halter; —draht, m. music-wire; —fell, n. snare-head (of a drum); —halter, m., —sessel, f. tail-piece (of a violin, &c.); —instrument, n. string-instrument; —klang, m. 1) sound of a string; 2) see —spiel, 2; —spiel, n. 1) string-instrument; 2) music of a string-instrument; —kunst, f. art of playing on stringed instruments; —spieler, m., —spielerin, f. player on a string-instrument; —werkzeug, n. see —instrument; —wurm, m. see Drahtwurm.

...sai'tig, adj. in comp. ... stringed.

Sait'ling, (str.) m. hank of catgut or wire for strings.

Sa'ker, (str.) m. (—falk, m.) Ornith. saker, [sakeret.

* **Salaman'der,** (str.) m. (Lat.-Gr.) Zool. 1) salamander (Salamandra Laur.); 2) Stud. slang. Einem einen — reiben, a mode of drinking in honour of a person, &c. on festive occasions, when all persons present, at certain commands given, have to rub their beer-glasses on the table, repeating the word —! (probably a mere ludicrous corruption of „all zu'sammen!" i. e. (rubbt) alle [Gläser] an einander!) then to drink off a certain quantity, and lastly to put down the glasses simultaneously with a smart rap; —haar, n. Miner. 1) salamander's hair or wool; 2) feathered antimony; 3) a sort of filamentous native silver.

* **Sala'me,** (str., pl. [Ital.] S-'mi) m. (Ital.) a kind of Italian (brain-)sausage.

* **Salär',** (str.) n. (Fr.) salary, annual payment, stated payment, allowance.

* **Salari'ren,** (w.) v. tr. (L. Lat.) to pay wages, give a salary.

Salat', (str.) m. 1) Cook. salad; 2) Bot. lettuce (Lactuca L.); wilder —, prickly lettuce (Lactuca scariola L.); in comp. [illegible] m. Bot. Judas-tree (Judasbaum); [illegible] lettuce leaf; —bohne, f. white bean; [illegible] f. salad-fork; —kopf, m. head of lettuce; —schüssel, f. salad-bowl; —löffel, m. salad-spoon; —napf, m. salad-bowl; —öl, n. salad-oil; —pflanze, f. lettuce plant; [illegible] salad-dish.

Sal'..., in comp. [illegible] idle prattler, twaddler; [illegible] talk, twaddle; [illegible] see Gesalbader; —badern, (w.) [illegible] foolishly and tediously, to [illegible]

stalk; —stiel, m. Bot. funicle (Knospenträger); Anat.-a. —strang, m. seminal string, spermatic cord; —strangnerve, m. spermatic external nerve; —teich, m. Fish. nurse-pond, nursing pond; —thierchen, n. spermatic animalcule; —tragend, adj. seed-bearing, Bot. seminiferous; —träger, m. see —boden; —werkzeug, n. Anat. spermatic organ; —zapfen, m. Bot. cone (of a fir); catkin (of hazel-bushes, &c.); —zerstörer, m. see —läfer; —züchter, m. nursery-man. [(Säen).

Sä'men, (w.) v. tr. († &) provinc. to sow

Sämerei', (w.) f. seeds of different kind, pl. articles of seed, seeds; in comp. —handel, m. trade in seeds; S-enhändler, m. seedsman; —verzeichniß, n. seed-list, seed-catalogue.

Sa'mig, adj. containing seed.

Sa'misch, adj. Samian, relating to the island of Samos.

Sä'misch, adj. soft; s-es or — Leder, chamois, wash-leather; —gerber, m. chamois-dresser; —gerberei', f. trade or house of business of a chamois-dresser. [kraut).

Säm'kraut, (str.) n. Bot. pond-weed (Laich-

Säm'ling, (str.) m. Hort. seedling.

Sam'mel... (from Sam'meln), in comp. —behälter, m. see —kasten; —buch, n. book of extracts; common-place-book.

Sammelei', (w.) f cont. the (act or practice of) gathering, &c.; compilation.

Sam'mel... (from Sam'meln), in comp. —fleiß, m. industry of collecting; —glas, n. Opt. collective glass; —kasten, m. reservoir; —linse, f. Opt. collective lens.

Sam'meln, (w.) v. I. tr. to collect, gather; to rally; to heap, lay, or treasure up, accumulate, amass; für die Armen —, to raise a collection for the poor; Subscribenten —, to procure subscribers; II. refl. 1) to gather, collect; to rally; to increase, accumulate; 2) fig. sich —, to collect one's self, one's thoughts; to settle (down), to be one's self again, to summon one's soul.

Sam'mel... (from Sam'meln), in comp. —namen, m. collective noun; —orden, m. order of mendicant friars; —platz, —punct, m. place of appointment, meeting-place (*: trysting-place), rallying-point, rendezvous (and Mil. = alarm post); —scheibe, f. Phys. collector; —schrift, f. compilation; —schule, f. select school: school established by collecting scholars privately.

Sammelsu'rium, (str., pl. [w.] S-'rien) n. cont. medley (Gemengsel, Mischmasch).

Sam'mel... (from Sam'meln), in comp. —werk, n. compilation; —wort, n. collective word or noun.

Sam'met, Sammt, (str.) m. velvet; glatter —, plain or smooth velvet; geblümter —, branched v.; geschorener —, shorn v.; ungeschorener —, terry v.; unächter or baumwollener —, cotton velvet, Manchester, velveteen; wollener —, plush, worsted shag; in comp. —apfel, m. red summer apple; —artig, adj. velvet-like, velvety; —artiger Stoff, velveret, fustian; —band, n. velvet ribbon; —blende, f. see Braunseisenstein; Bot.-a. —blümchen, n. common daisy (Gänseblümchen); —blume, f. 1) velvet flower, French marigold (Tagetes patula L.); 2) flower gentle (Amaranthus spinosus L.); 3) Comm. artificial flower made of velvet; —borte, f. velvet-galloon, velvet-lace.

Sam'meten, see Sammten.

Sam'met..., in comp. —ente, f. Ornith. velvet-scoter (Oidemia fusca L.); —erde, f. Miner. earthy chlorite; —erz, n. see Federerz; —gleich, see —artig; —gras, n. Bot. hare's tail grass (Lagurus L.). [metartig.

Sam'methaft, Sam'metig, adj. see Sam-

Sam'met..., in comp. —hafen, m. see —weber; —haut, f. das —hautgleiche Darmhäutchen, Anat. velvet membrane; —hühnchen, n. Ornith. water-rail, velvet-[illegible] (Wasserralle); —hut, m. velvet-hat; —kette, f. pile-warp; —kröte, f. Crust. the velvet-puddler, common puddling crab (Portunus puber L.); —macher, m. see —weber; —manchester, m. Comm. velveret, velveteen; —messer, n. velvet-knife, travet ([illegible]); —milbe, f. Entom. taint (Trombidium [illegible]); —mütze, f. velvet-cap; Bot.-a. —nelke, f. common or red rose-campion (Lychnis coronaria L.); —pappel, f. marsh-mallow (Althaea officinalis L.); —rasen, m. close cut-grass; —röschen, n. see —nelke; —rose, f. velvet rose, french, gallicea rose (Essigrose); —schuh, m. velvet-shoe; —schwarz, n. velvet-black, ivory-black; —spitzen, f. pl. velvet-lace; —tüpfchen, n. see —blümchen; —vogel, m. [illegible] velvet-winged butterfly; —weber, m. velvet-maker; —weich, adj. as soft as velvet; —weizen, m. a variety of the common English wheat. [compiler.

Samm'ler, (str.) m. gatherer, collector;

Samm'lung, (w.) f. 1) collection; gathering; compilation; 2) fig. collectedness (of mind); S-spunct, m. see Sammelpunct.

Sammt, I. prep. with Dat. together with; II. adv. — und sonders, all and every one of them (of us, of you, &c.), all together, each and all; III. s. see Sammet.

Samm'ten, adj. velvet.

Sämmt'lich, I. adj. all together; all, whole; collective; der s-e Adel, the body of nobility; die s-en Einwohner, Truppen, all the inhabitants, troops; Shakspeare's s-e Werke, S.'s complete works; II. adv. jointly, in a body; collectively.

Sämmt'ling, (str.) m. coll. velvet-coat.

Samogi'tien, n. Geogr. Samogitia.

Samoje'de, (w.) m. Samoyede.

Sams'tag, (str.) m. provinc. (S. G.) for Sonnabend; der hohe —, Saturday before Easter.

Sa'muel, m. Samuel (P. N.).

* Samum', (str.) m. (Arab.) Phys. simoom.

* Sanct, adj. (Lat.) saint; — Barbara, Mar. slang, powder-room; — Paulus, St. Paul.

Sand, s. I. (str., pl. provinc. Sän'de) m. sand; grober —, gravel, s. Gries, 1; auf den — gerathen, stoßen, laufen, to run aground, ground; Einem — in die Augen streuen, fig. to throw dust in one's eyes; II. in comp. —aal, m. Ichth. 1) sand-eel, grig (Ammodytes tobianus L.); 2) launce, sand-launce (Ammodytes lancea L.); —afterwespe, f. see —wespe.

* Sanda'le, (w.) f. (Gr.) sandal.

Sand'allee, (w.) f. gravel-walk, sand-walk.

San'dart (San'dat, San'nat), (str.) m. see Sander.

Sand'..., in comp. —artig, adj. sand-like; —bad, n. sand-bath, sand-heat; Med. arenation; —bank, f. shelf, bank in the sea, pl. sands, shoals; bar; auf eine —bank gerathen, to run aground; —barren, m. small sandy island; —bars, m. see Sander; —beere, f. 1) see Bärentraube; 2) see [illegible]; —berg, m. sand-hill; —bläser, m. pl. see —[illegible]; —boden, m. sandy soil or ground; —büchse, f. sand-box; —büchsenbaum, m. Bot. sand-box tree (Hura crepitans L.); —capelle, f. [illegible] sand-cupel; —distel, f. Bot. common [illegible] (thistle) (Eberwurz); —dorn, m. Bot. sea-buckthorn (Hippophaë rhamnoides L.); —[illegible], pl. see Dünen; —ebene, f. see —[illegible].

San'del, (str.) m. (—holz, n.) [illegible] ders, sandal (wood); das rothe —holz, [illegible] wood; das blaue —holz, [illegible] echte —holz, der weiße —, green [illegible] holzbaum, m. Bot. sandal tree ([illegible]).

San'deln, (w.) v. intr. & tr. to [illegible] sand or pounce, to pounce [illegible].

San'den, (w.) v. tr. to cover [illegible] (gravel).

[illegible]; —[illegible], *f. see* —[illegible]; —zeug, *n.* saddle and harness.

Satt'heit, *(w.) f.* 1) satiety; fulness; 2) *fig.* weariness (as [with *Dat.*], of).

Sät'tigen, *(w.) v. tr.* 1) *a)* to appease (one's appetite, &c.); to satisfy; *b)* to glut, cloy; 2) *Chem.* to saturate; to impregnate; gesättigt, *p. a.* 1) *see* Satt. 1; 2) *Paint., Dy.* full-bodied, deep, rich (colour). [glut.

Sät'tigkeit, *(w.) f.* Ill. satiety, fulness,

Sät'tigung, *(w.) f.* 1) the (act of) appeasing one's appetite, &c., *cf.* Sättigen; satisfaction; 2) *a) see* Sattheit; *b) Chem., &c.,* saturation.

Satt'ler, *(str.) m.* saddler, saddle-maker; harness-maker; *in comp.* —ahle, *f.,* —arbeit, *f.,* —bursche, *m.,* —hammer, *m.,* —handwerk, *n.,* &c. saddler's awl, work, apprentice, hammer, trade, &c. [saddler's workshop.

Sattlerei', *(w.) f.* 1) saddler's trade; 2)

Sattler..., *in comp.* —meister, *m.* master harness-maker; —messer, *n.* saddler's knife.

Satt'lern, *(w.) v. intr. coll.* to do saddler's work.

Sattlerrolle, *(w.) f.* saddler's rowel.

Satt'sam, I. *adj.* sufficient; *adv.* sufficiently, enough; II. S-keit, *(w.) f.* sufficiency.

* **Sat'urei,** *(w.) f. (Lat.)* savory (*Satureja hortensis* L.).

* **Saturn',** *(str.) m.* 1) *Rom. Myth., Astr., &c.* Saturn; 2) † *Chem.* lead. — Saturna'lien, *pl.* Saturnalia.

* **Sa'tyr,** *(str. [sometimes pr.* Satür', *pl.* Saty'ren) & *w., pl.* Sa'tyr(e)n) *m. (Gr.)* satyr.

* **Saty're** &c., *see* Satire &c.

Satz, *(str., pl.* Sät'ze) *m.* 1) leap, jump; 2) *Mus., Typ., &c.* composition (*also T. for military fireworks and other combustibles*); *Mus.-s.* (langsamer, schneller, slow, quick) movement; set; (musical) sentence; 3) dregs, grounds (of coffee, &c.), *Chem., &c.* deposit, sediment, settling; 4) *T.-s. a)* composition, mixture; *b) Brew.* layer (of barley); *c) Glass-m.* metal; *d)* tanning; 5) *Sport. a)* young fry (of fishes); *b)* drey (of squirrels), nest (of rabbits); *c)* litter (of fox-cubs); 6) *T. a)* set (of weights, vines, &c.); *b)* set or nest (of boxes); 7) *a) Gam.* stake; pool; *b) Comm.* rate, price; 8) *a) Log.* position, proposition; *b) Gramm.* sentence, period; *c) Theol.* tenet; 9) fixed measure; 10) *Stud. slang,* treat, entertainment (einen — geben, to give a jollification, *anal.* to stand treat, to stand Sam); seinen — behaupten, *fig.* to maintain one's point; die (streitige) Frage zum — machen, to beg the question. [—bord, *m. see* Setzbord.

Satz..., *in comp.* —baum, *m. see* —stock;

Sätz'chen, *(str.) n.* (dimin. of Satz) short sentence, &c.

Satz..., *in comp.* —fisch, *m.* young fish; —gezähe, *n. Min.* coin with its furniture; —hase, *m.* she-hare, doe-hare; —holz, *n. see* —stock; —karpfen, *m.* carp (as fry); —lehre, *f. Gramm.* syntax; —löffel, *m. T.* iron spoon; —maß, *n. see* Lotmaß; —mehl, *n.* amylum; starch(-flour); *Pharm.* fecula; —meißel, *m. T.* clincher; —möhre, *f.* seed-carrot; —schachteln, *f. pl.* nest-boxes; —stock, *m.* (willow-) twig planted for growth; —teich, *m.* stock- or store-pond.

Sat'zung, *(w.) f.* statute, law; institution; ordinance; maxim; dogma; S-srecht, *n.* statute-law.

Satz..., *in comp.* —wage, *f.* mason's level; —weide, *f. see* —stock; —weise, *adv. & adj.* 1) by leaps; 2) by sets, by heaps; 3) *fig.* sentence by sentence; —welle, *f. T.* turning-tree, axle-tree (of a mill); —zäpfchen, *n. Med.* suppository; —zeit, *f.* breeding time of hares; —zwiebel, *f.* bulb for transplanting.

A. Sau, *(pl. gener. w., sometimes str.:* Säu'e) *f.* 1) sow, hog; 2) *T.-s. a) Metall.* sow, pig; *b) Hawk.* madder drying kiln; *c) Found.* sow (large trough); *d) see* [illegible]; 3) *vulg.* slut, dirty trollop; 4) *slang, a)* a blot (of ink); *b)* blunder; *c)* a piece of undeserved good luck (Schwein), *particul. at Bill., cf.* Fuchs, 7. [the Austrian [illegible].

B. Sau, Sa've, *f. Geogr.* Save (a river of

Sau'..., *in comp.* —apfel, —birne, *see* Holzapfel, Holzbirne(e); —bohne, *m.* boar-hound.

Sau'ber, Säu'berlich, I. *adj.* 1) *a)* clean, neat; tidy, pretty; *b) fig.* terse (of style, &c.), accurate, neat; gentle; 2) *iron.* dirty; fine, pretty; eine s-e Wirtschaft, pretty work, pretty goings on; II. S-keit, *(w.) f.* 1) cleanliness, neatness; 2) *fig. a)* terseness (of style), accuracy; *b)* fineness; prettiness.

Säu'berkasten, *m. Mill.* bolting-chest.

Säu'bern, *(w.) v. tr.* to clean, cleanse, clear, purge (von, of), *cf.* Reinigen.

Säu'bersieb, *(str.) m. Mill.* meal-bolter.

Säu'berung, *(w.) f.* the (act of) cleansing, clearing, &c.

Sau'..., *in comp.* —bohne, *f. Bot.* 1) broad bean, garden-bean (*Vicia faba* L.); 2) or —erdapfel, *m.* Jerusalem artichoke (*Helianthus tuberosus* L.); —borg, *m.* gelded hog; —brot, *n. Bot.* hog's-bread, sow-bread (*Cyclamen europaeum* L.); —bruch, *m. Sport. see* Gebreche, 3, *a & b.*

* **Sau'ce** *[pr.* so'se], *(w.) f. (Fr.)* sauce (Brühe). — Sauciè're, *(w.) f. (Fr.)* sauce-boat or tureen. (für geschmolzene Butter) butter-boat. — Saucie'ren, *(w.) v. tr. T.* to sauce (tobacco). [*[illegible]* L.).

Sau'distel, *(w.) f. Bot.* sow-thistle (*Sonchus*

Sau'en, *(w.) v. vulg.* I. *intr.* 1) to go about a thing swinishly; 2) to talk bawdy; II. *tr.* voll—, *see* Besauen.

Sau'er, *adj.* 1) sour, acid (*Chem.*), *aggrav.* crabbed, tart, harsh; 2) *fig. a)* troublesome, hard (labour, &c.); *b)* sour, morose, peevish; saure Kirschen, agriots; saure Gurken, pickled cucumbers; ein saures Gesicht, sour look, frown; Einem ein saures Gesicht machen, to look crabbed or surly, to frown at; —machen, 1. to sour, to change (milk); 2. *fig.* to embitter, aggravate, to make (life) a burden (to one); — werden, 1. to sour, to become sour, to turn acid; 2. *fig.* to grow troublesome, to cause difficulty, *cf.* Schwer; es kommt mir sehr — an zu ..., it goes against my grain to ...; es sich (*Dat.*) — werden lassen, to toil or work hard, to plod.

Sau'er..., *in comp. Bot.-s.* —ampfer, *m.* (common) sorrel (*Rumex* L.); —ampferbeere, *f.* common cranberry (*Oxycoccus palustris* L.); —äther, *n. see* —kleeäther; —bad, *n. T.* acid bath.

Säu'erbar, *adj.* acidifiable.

Sau'er..., *in comp.* —biffen, *m.* cow-cup (*Andina [illegible]* L.); —blei, *n. Chem.* chromate of lead; —braten, *m.* beef steeped in vinegar and roasted; —brunnen, *m.* medicinal spring charged with acids, acidulae; chalybeate spring; —brunnensalz, *n. see* [illegible]; —dattel, *f. see* Tamarinde; —dorn, *m.* [illegible] rach.

Sauerei', *(w.) f. vulg.* 1) hoggishness, nastiness; beastliness; 2) [illegible] (Schweinerei); 3) obscenity; obscene [illegible].

Sau'er..., *in comp.* —eisen, *m.* [illegible], oxide of iron (Eisenrost); —honig, *m.* [illegible]mel; —käse, *m.* soft curd cheese; —kirsche, [illegible] agriot, sour cherry; —klee, *m. Bot.* wood-sorrel, three-leaved sorrel (*Oxalis* L.); [illegible] —kleeäther, *m.* oxalic ether; —[illegible] super-oxalate of potash, salt of [illegible]rel; —kleesäure, *f.* oxalic acid; —[illegible] Salz, oxalate; —kobalt, *m. Min.* [illegible] balt containing iron; —kraut, *n.* [illegible] salted or pickled cabbage, [illegible].

Säu'erlich, I. *adj.* sourish, [illegible] lous, acescent; — machen, to [illegible] S-keit, *(w.) f.* acidulity.

per, raker, *cf.* Schabeisen; 2) *cont.* shabby fellow; miser.

Schäberei', *(w.) f.* 1) the (act of) scraping, &c.; 2) *cont.* miserly conduct; shabbiness.

Scha'bernack, *(str.) m. & f. coll.* roguish trick, vexation; mir zum —, to vex me. — **Scha'bernacken**, *(w.) v. tr.* to play (one) a trick, to vex. — **Scha'bernackisch** (**Scha'bernäckisch**), *adj.* fond of playing tricks.

Scha'bewolle, *(w.) f.* skinner's wool.

Schä'big, *coll.* I. *adj.* shabby; scabby, scabbed; II. **S-keit**, *(w.) f.* shabbiness; scabbedness; shabby behaviour, trick, &c.

Schabin', *(str.) n.* Dutch metal parings, gold-beater's waste; —papier, *n.* Dutch metal paper.

* **Schablo'ne**, *(w.) f. (Fr.: ? sablonnier)* 1) model, form, *particul. Carp., Mas.*, &c. pattern; (eines Simses) templet; 2) *Railw. a)* (für geneigte Schienen) gauge (of inclination); *b)* (Richtscheit für Schienenerhöhung) ruler (for elevation of rails); 3) *Cast.* loam-board; modelling-board; 4) *a)* mould (for bricks, &c.); *b) Pott.* (Lehre, Drehbrett) templet, pattern; 5) (Sch-nbrett, *n.*) *Gun-sm.* cutting-out pattern (for musket-stocks); 6) design in full size (for architects); 7) stencil (thin plate of metal, used in painting, marking, &c.). — **Schablo'nenartig**, **Schablo'nenhaft**, *adj. (& adv.* nach der Schablone) *fig.* according to a set or fixed pattern.

Schablo'n(en)eisen, *(str.) n.* strong-wrought iron bars for gun-barrels.

Schablo'nenpapier, *(str.) n. T.* pattern-paper (primed with oil).

* **Schabloni'ren**, *(w.) v. tr.* to stencil.

* **Schabrak'e**, *(w.) f. (Turk.)* caparison, housing.

Schab'sel, *(str.) n.* (*from* Schaben) scrapings, shavings, abrasion.

Schab'zieger, *(str.) m.* chapsegar, green-cheese; —klee, *m.*, —kraut, *n. Bot.* a species of melilot (*Melilotus caeruleus* L.).

Schach, *(str., pl.* Sch-s *or* Sch-e) 1) *m.* king, *see* Schah; 2) *(str.) n.* (*for* —spiel, *n.* the king's play) *Gam.* chess; — spielen, to play at chess; — dem Könige! *(at chess)* check to the king! (dem Könige) — bieten, to check (the king); in — halten, to keep a check upon, to keep in check.

Schach'..., *in comp.* —blume, *f.* checkered lily (*Fritillaria meleagris* L.); —brett, *n.* chess-board; —brettartig, *adj. Bot.* tessellated, checkered; —brettverzierung, *f. Archit.* checker-work. — **Schach'en**, *(w.) v. tr.* to divide into squares, to checker, to check.

Schach'er, *coll.-s. (str.) m.* Jew's traffic or bargain, usury. — **Schacherei'**, *(w.) f.* low trafficking. — **Schach'erer** *or* **Schach'erjude**, *(str.) m.* low trafficker, old-clothes-jew. — **Schach'ermäßig**, *adj.* low trafficking. — **Schach'ern**, *(w.) v. intr.* to traffic, chaffer, barter.

Schäch'er, *(str.) m.* 1) († *&*) *coll.* robber, murderer; *Script.* malefactor, thief; 2) *cont.* ein armer —, a poor fellow; —kreuz, *n. see* Gabelkreuz.

Schach'..., *in comp.* —feld, *n.* square (of a chess-board); —figur, *f.* chess-man; —förmig, *adj.* checkered; —kraut, *n. Bot.* common broom (*Spartium scoparium* L.); —matt, *adj.* 1) check-mate; 2) *fig.* weary, tired out, spent, exhausted; —matt machen, *lit. & fig.* to check-mate; —spiel, *n.* 1) play at chess; 2) the chess-men and board collectively; —spieler, *m.* chess-player; —stein, *m. see* —figur.

Schacht, *(str., pl.* Schäch'te & Schach'te, *provinc. w.) m.* 1) *Min.* shaft, pit; 2) *Metall.* fire-room (of a blast furnace); 3) way (of a quarry); 4) logging (of a book); 5) *Weav.* leaf; 6) *Needle-m.* length; 7) *Mar.* fore-foot; 8) gang (of labourers) (Schicht); 9) pit (Kluft, Schlucht).

Schach'tafel, *(w.) f.* chess-board.

Schacht'..., *in comp.* —arbeiter, *m. pl.* shaft-men; —bühne, *f.* landing in a shaft.

Schach'tel, *(w.) f.* box; chip-box; hand-box; eine alte —, *fac.* an old woman; *in comp.* —borsten, *f. pl.* bristles in boxes; —deckel, *m.* cover or lid of a box; —feigen, *pl.* Comm. drum-figs; —gut, *n. see* —borsten; —halm, *m. Bot.* shave-grass, horse-tail, pewter-grass (*Equisetum* L.); —käse, *m.* cheese in boxes or cases; —macher, *m.* box-maker; —männchen, *n.* jack in a box.

Schach'teln, *(w.) v. tr.* 1) to put into a box; 2) to shave, rub, or polish with shave-grass.

Schach'telsaft, *(str.) m.* marmalade kept in small boxes.

Schäch'ten, *(w.) v. tr.* (*Hebr.* schāchat', to slaughter) *Jew.* to kill (cattle) according to certain rites. — **Schäch'ter**, *(str.) m.* (Jewish) butcher.

Schacht'..., *in comp.* —erz, *n. Miner.* ore detached from the parent mass; —förderung, *f. see* Förderung, 1; —fuß, *m.* measure of a square foot that is an inch thick (*Build.*); —gestänge, *n. Min.* water-engine rods, pump-spears; —grube, *f.* trench, excavation; —halm, *m. see* Schachtelhalm; —haus, —häuschen, *n.* roof (house) over a shaft; —holz, *n.* timber with which a shaft is lined; —[illegible], *m.*, —mütze, *f.* miner's cap; —kraut, *n. Bot.* 1) bladder-catchfly (*Silene inflata* L.); 2) a species of saw-wort (*Serratula* [illegible] L.); 3) dyer's broom (Färberginster); —latte, *f.* [illegible]-plank; —linie, *f.* square measure of a line to the tenth of a line in thickness (*Build.*); —mauerung, *f.* shaft walling, ginging; —meister, *m. see* Schichtmeister; —modell, *n. Needle-m.* length-gauge; —nagel, *m.* lath-nail for shaft-miners; —ofen, *m. Metall.* shaft-furnace, blast-furnace; *Min.-s.* —richt, *m.* gallery (in salt-mines); —ruthe, *f.* measure of a square rod to a foot thickness (*Build.* a volume of 144 Pruss. cubic feet); —scheider, *m.* partition-wall (from top to bottom) of a climbing-shaft; —schuh, *m. see* —fuß; —stange, *f. see* —latte; —stempel, *m.* cross-timber of a pit; —tonne, *f.* tubbing; —trumm, *n.* division of a shaft made by a brattice (*T. Vonsch.*); —winde, *f.* crab(-capstan), crane (of a shaft); —zimmerung, *f.* timbering of a shaft.

Schach'..., *in comp.* —weise, *adv. Herald.* chequered; —ziegel, *m.* shingle (for roofing); —zug, *m.* move (in chess-playing).

Schack'ern, *(w.) v.* I. *intr.* 1) to imitate the cry of the fieldfare (Schack'er, *(str.) m.*); 2) to jog, jolt (in riding on horseback); II. *tr. see* Abschachern.

Schad'bar, *adj. see* Schadhaft.

A. **Scha'de**, *(w.) f. Ich.* shad.

B. **Scha'de**, *(str.)* **Scha'den**, *(str., pl.* Schä'den) *m.* 1) damage, harm, detriment, loss, disadvantage, prejudice; 2) hurt, wound, sore; rother —, *see* Ruhr; innerer —, internal complaint; S-n thun, S-n bringen (zufügen), to damage, hurt, prejudice, injure, disadvantage, *cf.* Zufügen, 1; zu S-n kommen, 1. to be hurt; 2. to miscarry; S-n nehmen *or* leiden, to receive a hurt; to sustain a loss; to suffer damage, to come off or be a loser; to be spoiled; er hat mit S-n verkauft, he has sold under prime cost or at a loss; es soll Ihr — nicht sein, you shall be no loser by it; ich befinde S-n nicht, I do not suffer [illegible]; ich habe den S-n davon, the loss [illegible] me; *Comm.-s.* totaler S-n, total [illegible]; theilweiser S-n, partial damages [illegible] den der See versichert, insured [illegible] dangers of the sea; *fig.* [illegible] den, to learn or buy wit [illegible] darf für den Spott nicht sorgen [illegible] the result, bears the damage [illegible] is a pity; es ist ewig —, [illegible]

skin, bark, scale; to blanch (almonds); II. refl. to shell (off), cast the shell; to peel off, scale (off); to exfoliate; to blister; geschälter Hafer, shelling; geschälter Reis, polished rice.

Scha'len..., *in comp.* –ähnlich, *adj.* shell-like; –blende, *f. Miner.* fibrous blende; –eisen, *n. Iron-w.* (aus Puddelöfen &c.) bottom-iron; (aus dem Masselgraben) sow-iron; –erz, *n. see* Schachterz; –förmig, *adj.* in the shape of shells *or* scales; –guß, *m. Found.* chill-casting; –hart, testaceous; –kalk, *m. Miner.* pea-stone; –mehl, *n.* flour that is yet in the bran; –muschel, *f. see* Schalmuschel; –obst, *n. see* Schalobst; –schnecke, *f. see* Schalschnecke; –schneider, –schröter, *m. T.* hafter; –stein, *m. Miner.* green porphyry *or* serpentine, ophite.

Schäl'..., *in comp.* –ente, *f. Ornith.* shoveller (*Anas clypeata* L.); –erz, *n. see* Schachterz; –fisch, *m.* 1) trunk-fish (Panzerfisch); 2) *see* –thier, 1; –frucht, *f. see* –fern.

Schäl'gang, (*str., pl.* Sch-gänge) *m. Mill.* husking- *or* peeling-mill.

Schäl'gebirge, (*str.*) *n.* rocks formed of thin strata.

Schäl'haken, (*str.*) *m.* peeling-hoe, turf-spud.

Schal'heit, (*w.*) *f.* 1) staleness; 2) *fig.* flatness; insipidity.

Schäl'hengst, (*str.*) *m.* stallion, stone-horse.

Schäl'holz, (*str., pl.* Sch-hölzer) *n.* 1) staff, lath, pannel-stake; 2) *see* Schalbret.

Schäl'holz, (*str., pl.* Sch-hölzer) *n.* barked wood.

Scha'lig, *adj.* shelly, shelled; scaly; *Bot.* tunicate(d).

Schä'lig, (*str.*) *m. Carp.* slab, *cf.* Schale, 9.

Schä'ling, (*w.*) *f. T.* quay, mole, wharf.

Schalk, (*str., pl.* Schäl'ke) *m.* 1) †, servant; 2) rogue, knave; cheat; 3) wag, *cf.* Schelm; ein durchtriebener –, an artful dog; den – hinter den Ohren (im Nacken) haben, *fig.* to be a rogue in disguise; je ärger der –, desto besser das Glück, *proverb*, the more knave the better luck.

Schälkelei', **Schalkerei'**, (*w.*) *f.* waggery, &c., *cf.* Schalkheit.

Schal'ken, (*w.*) *v.* I. *tr. Mar.* to nail (Schalmen); II. *intr.* to play the wag; to deceive.

Schäl'kern, (*str.*) *m. Bot.* caryopsis.

Schalk'haft, I. *adj.* waggish, wanton, disposed to tricks, cunning, subtle, roguish; II. Sch-igkeit, (*w.*) *f.* waggishness, &c.

Schalk'heit, (*w.*) *f.* waggishness, roguery; roguish, wanton trick.

Schal'kisch, *adj. see* Schalkhaft.

Schalk'kohl, (*str.*) *m. provinc.* cabbage without a heart.

Schalk'leisten, (*w.*) *f. pl. Mar.* battens of the tarpaulin(g).

Schäl'knötchen, (*str.*) *n. Med. gener. pl.* a papulous eruption peculiar to infants, (*Lat.*) *strophulus*.

Schalks'..., *in comp.* –auge, *n.* roguish eye; –deckel, *m. fam.* hat; –ernst, *m.* irony; –freude, *f. see* Schadenfreude; –freund, *m.* deceitful friend; –knecht, *m. coll.* wicked *or* deceitful fellow, rogue; –lob, *n.* ironical praise; –narr, *m.* a rogue playing the fool *or* buffoon; –ohr, *n.* cunning ear; –rath, *m.* cunning and deceitful counsel; jester; –sinn, *m.* roguishness; –sinnig, *adj.* roguish.

Schall, (*str. pl.* Schäl'le) *m.* sound; ringing (of bells).

Schall'... (*from* Schall & Schallen), *in comp.* –becher, *m. see* –stück; –becken, *n.* cymbal; –boden, *see* –bret; –brechend, *adj.* phonocamptic; –brechung, *f.* refraction of sound; –brechungslehre, *f.* diacoustics; –bret, *n. Mus.* sounding-board, sound-board.

Schal'len, (*str. & w.*) *v. intr. & (poet.) tr.* to sound, echo, resound; to ring; das sch-de Gelächter, peal of laughter.

Schall'..., *in comp.* –ente, *f. see* Schalente; –gelächter, *n.* peal of laughter; –gewölbe, *n. Archit.* acoustic vault; –horn, *n.* †, horn, trombone, trumpet; –lehre, *f. Phys.* acoustics; –loch, *n.* 1) *Mus.* sound-hole (of guitars, &c.); 2) hole, aperture of a belfry; –maß, *n.*, –messer, *m. Phys.* echometer; –rohr, *n.* speaking trumpet; –strahl, *m. Phys.* ray of sound; –stück, *n.*, –trichter, *m.* bell mouth, the lower funnel- *or* bell-shaped part of a trumpet, &c.; –wort, *n.* word imitative of sound.

Schalm, (*str., provinc. w.*) *m.* 1) part of a forest divided off (for pasturage, &c.); 2) *Mar.-s.* a) link (of a chain); b) timber to stop up; shackle (of a jib-traveller); c) *pl.* die S–e der Luken, the battens of the hatches.

Schalmei'(e), (*w.*) *f. Mus.* chalm.

Schalmei'en, (*w.*) *v. intr.* to play the chalm.

Schalm'eisen, (*str.*) *n.* forester's hammer.

Schal'men, (*w.*) *v. tr.* 1) *Forest.* a) to mark, blaze (trees); b) to cut (a lane); 2) *Mar.* to nail the battens of the hatches along the edges of tarpaulin(g)s.

Schäl'..., *in comp.* –muschel, *f. Conch.* limpet-shell, patella (Napfschnecke); –obst, *n.* fruit with shells, dry fruit; –ohr, *n.* large wide ear of a horse.

* **Schalong'**, (*str., pl.* Sch-e) *m. Comm.* shalloon.

* **Schalot'te**, (*w.*) *f.* (*Fr.*) *Bot.* scallion, shalot.

Schäl'pflug, (*str., pl.* Sch-pflüge) *m. Husb.* paring-plough, stubble-plough.

Schäl'..., *in comp.* –schnecke, *f. Zool.* snail; –stein, *m. Miner.* scale-stone, tabular-spar; –stück, *n.* slab (Schalbret).

Schalt'buchstabe, (*w.*) *m.* intercalary letter.

Schal'te, (*w.*) *f.* 1) *provinc.* batten, lath; 2) *see* Ruderstange.

Schal'ten, (*w.*) *v. intr.* to rule, command; to dispose (mit, of), to deal (with); man ließ ihn frei – und walten, he was allowed his full swing.

Schal'ter, (*str.*) *m.* 1) ruler; 2) *see* Ruderstange; 3) slide, shutter, window; wicket, pigeon-hole; letter-box; 4) *provinc.* [illegible]

Schal'thier, (*str.*) *n.* 1) *Nat.* testaceous *or* crustaceous animal, shell-fish; 2) *Herald.* whelk(s); –kenner, *m.* conchologist, conchyliologist; –kunde, –lehre, *f.* testaceology, conchology.

Schalt'... (*from* Schalten), *in comp.* –jahr, *n.* leap-year; –monat, *m.* intercalary month; –satz, *m.* clause *or* sentence in parenthesis; –tag, *m.* intercalary day; –wort, *n.* interpolated word; –zeile, *f.* interpolated line.

Scha'lung, (*w.*) *f.* lining, boarding, &c., *see* Schalwerk, Verschalung, 2; – über einen Schwibbogen (*Hartstein*), lagging above the centering.

Schä'lung, (*w.*) *f.* 1) the (act of) peeling, &c., *cf.* Schälen; 2) *see* Schilling.

Schalup'pe, (*w.*) *f. Mar.* 1) sloop; 2) (kleines Schiffs-) jolly-boat, yawl.

Schäl'..., *in comp.* –wage, *f.* balance with scales; –wand, *f.* board- *or* plank-partition.

Schäl'weide, (*w.*) *f. Bot.* almond-leaved willow (*Salix amygdalina* L.).

Schäl'werk, (*str.*) *n.* lining of planks.

Schäl'zahn, *m.* decaying tooth.

Schäm, *f.* 1) shame; 2) privy parts, [illegible] pudenda.

* **Schama'de**, (*w.*) *f. see* Chamade.

Schäm'..., *in comp. Anat.* –[illegible] pudic artery; –band, *n.* ligament of the [illegible]; –bein, *n.* share-bone (*os pubis*); –[illegible] *m.* tuber of the pubis; –[illegible] tinated muscle; –[illegible] physis of the pubis; –[illegible] blutader, *f.* pudic vein; –[illegible] drüse, *f.* gland of the pudenda.

Scha'mel, *see* Schemel.

Schä'men, (*w.*) *v. refl.* to be [illegible] med (with über (*& Acc.*), wegen [illegible] ich schäme mich deiner vor [illegible] ashamed of you in respect to my [illegible] schämte mich vor meinem Vater, [illegible] countenance for my father.

Schäm'..., *in comp.* –[illegible]

n. Mus. serpent (a bass wind instrument); –klugheit, *f. see* –list; –knoblauch, *m. Bot.* 1) rocambole (*Allium scorodoprasum*); 2) *or* –kraut, *see* Allermannsharnisch, 1; –kopf, *m.* serpent's head; (*comm.* der blaue –kopf, cowry-shell (*Cypraea caput serpentis* L.); –köpfchen, *n.* cowry (*Cypraea moneta* L.); –köpfig, *adj.* snaky-headed; –kraut, *n. Bot.* 1) snake's wood (*Polygonum bistorta* L.); 2) (gemeines) tarragon (*Artemisia dracunculus* L.); 3) dragon's-water (*Calla palustris* L.); –kreuz, *n. Herald.* cross vivree, snake-headed cross; –krümme, –krümmung, *f. see* –windung; –kunde, *f. Nat.* ophiology; –lauf, *m.* serpentine course; –linie, *f.* serpentine line; –list, *f.* subtlety of a serpent; –moos, *n. Bot.* common club-moss (*Lycopodium clavatum* L.); –mord, *m. Bot.* dwarf viper's-grass (*Scorzonera* L.); –pfad, *m.* winding path; –pulver, *n.* serpentine powder; –rohr, *n.*, –röhre, *f.* winding tube or pipe; *Dist.* worm (of a still); –säule, *f.* serpentine column; –spritze, *f. see* Schlauchspritze; –stab, *m.* wand or sceptre of Mercury, caduceus; –stein, *m.* serpentine-stone, ophite; –stich, *m.* 1) *see* –biß; 2) *Sew.* serpentine stitch; –tanz, *m.* winding dance; –träger, *m. Astr.* the Serpent-bearer, ophiuchus; –verehrer, *m.* snake-worshipper; –verehrung, *f.* ophiolatry, worship of serpents; –vogel, *m. see* –halsvogel; –wahrsagerei, *f.* ophiomancy; –weg, *m.* serpentine road or course; –weise, *adv.* windingly, crookedly; –weise gezogen, *Herald.* tortile, twisted; –windung, *f.* serpentine turning or curve; *Red.-a.* –wurz, –wurzel, *f.* 1) snake's root (*Actaea racemosa* L.); 2) *see* Natterwurz; 3) Virginia snake-root (*Aristolochia serpentaria* L.); –zunge, *f.* 1) adder's-tongue, serpent's-tongue (*Ophioglossum* L.); 2) *fig.* deceitful tongue; –zungen, *pl. Archit.* anchors, tongues; –züngig, *adj. fig.* having a deceitful tongue; –zwang, *m.* wart-cress (*Senebiera coronopus* L.).

Schlank, I. *adj.* slender, slim; tall; lank, thin; II. **Sch-heit**, (*w.*) *f.* slenderness, &c.

Schlapp, I. *interj.* & *s.* (*str.*) *m.* slap, dash; II. *adj.*, *see* Schlaff, 1; –brüstig, swag-breasted.

Schlap'pe, (*w.*) *f.* 1) slap; 2) defeat, discomfiture; loss; 3) slipper, slipshoe; in Sch-en gehen, to go slipshod; 4) *vulg.* mouth, chops.

Schlap'pen, **Schlap'pern**, (*w.*) *v.* I. *intr.* 1) to lap, slap, hang down loosely; 2) to slap; 3) to shuffle along in slippers; II. *tr.* to lap, sip.

Schlap'permilch, *f.* curdled milk.

Schlapp'hut, (*str.*, *pl.* Sch-hüte) *m.* slouching, broad-brimmed-hat.

Schlap'pig, *adj. coll. provinc.* 1) *see* Schlaff, 1; 2) *see* Schlumpig.

Schlapp'..., *in comp. vulg.* –maul, *n.* blubber-lipped mouth; –mäulig, *adj.* flap-mouthed; –ohr, *n.* flaggy or flagging ear; –ohrig, *adj.* lap-eared.

Schlapps, *see* Flapps.

Schlaraf'fe, (*w.*) *m.* 1) sluggard, truant, *coll.* lazy-bones; 2) Utopian.

Schlaraf'fen..., *in comp.* –gesicht, *n.* 1) monkey's or apish face; 2) *Archit.* gutter-spout; –land, *n.* Utopia, fool's paradise; –leben, *n.* Utopian or idle life. – **Schlaraf'fenthum**, (*str.*) *n.* Utopianism.

Schlar'fe, (*w.*) *f.*, **Schlarf'schuh**, (*str.*) *m. coll.* slipper, slip shoe.

Schlar'fen, **Schlär'fen**, (*w.*) *v. intr. coll.* to shuffle, slip, to walk slipshod or shuffling.

Schlau, *adj.* sly, crafty, cunning, sharp.

Schlau'de, (*w.*) *f.*, **Schlau'den**, (*w.*) *v. tr.*, **Schlau'dig**, *pr. see* Hülse, Hülsen, Hülsig.

Schlauch, (*str.*, *pl.* Schläu'che) *m.* 1) *a)* skin; leather bag or bottle; *b)* (leathern) hose; leather-pipe; water-conduit; wooden-pipe; funnel or pipe of a privet; 2) *Bot. a)* aeci-dium; *b)* utriculus; *c)* ampulla; 3) *Mech.* bag-net; 4) *Vet.* sheath (of a horse's pizzle); 5) *F.* spindle-full of yarn; 6) *fig.* drunkard, glutton; *in comp.* –artig, –ähnlich, *adj.* like a leather-pipe; –bohrer, –eisen, *m.* wimble for water-pipes; auger for drawing wine out of a cask. [illegible]

Schlau'chicht, **Schlau'chig**, *adj. see* Schlauch[illegible]

Schlauch'..., *in comp.* –meister, –rohrführer, *m.* conductor of the hose of a fire-engine; –spritze, *f.* fire engine furnished with a (leather-)hose; –thier, –thierchen, *n. see* Kolbthierchen.

Schlau'der, (*w.*) *f.* 1) *provinc. for* Schleuder; 2) *Build.* gable-anchor (of a building), cramp-iron (Schließanker). – **Schlau'dern**, (*w.*) *v. tr.* & *intr.* 1) *see* Schleudern; 2) *Build.* to fasten (a wall) with gable-anchors.

Schlau'..., *in comp.* –fuchs, –kopf, *m.* sly, cunning fellow; *burl.* sly-boots, deep fellow, a knowing one; –köpfig, *adj.* cunning, crafty; –sinn, *m. or* **Schlau'heit**, **Schlau'igkeit**, (*w.*) *f.* slyness, cunningness; craftiness, artifice, policy.

Schlecht, I. *adj.* 1) *obsolescent*, *a)* straight; *b)* (– und recht) plain, upright; 2) bad; 3) evil, ill; wicked; 4) vile, wretched; 5) base, vile, mean, low, dishonest; II. *adv.* badly, &c.; ill; sch-er Tact, *Mus.* common time; sch-es Geld, bad or base coin or money; Einem sch-en Dank wissen, to owe one no thanks; es bei Einem – haben, to be ill (badly) off with one; – sein, 1. to be bad; 2. to be in a very bad state of health or way; *Comm.-a.* sch-e Papiere, bad or dubious debts; sch-er Absatz, heavy sale; der Verkauf geht –, the sale goes off badly; dieses Wort wird gewöhnlich in sch-em Sinne gebraucht, this word is generally used in an ill sense; Zelluloid ist ein sch-er Wärme- und Electricitätsleiter, celluloid is a poor conductor of heat and electricity; sch-er Trost, poor consolation, cold comfort; sch-e Zeiten, hard times; Einen – machen, to abuse one, to decry, *cf.* Heruntermachen; sich – behelfen, to live poorly, to make hard shifts.

Schlecht'..., *in comp.* ill: –beschaffen, –bestellt &c., ill-conditioned, ill-grounded, &c.

Schlech'te, *f. see* Schlechtheit.

Schlechterdings', *adv.* by all means, absolutely, positively, utterly; – nicht, by no means.

Schlecht'..., *in comp.* –färber, *m.* dyer in black; –falk(e), *m. see* Schlechtfalke.

Schlecht'heit, (*w.*) *f.* badness, inferior quality.

Schlechthin', *adv.* 1) unceremoniously, merely, plainly; simply; 2) *provinc.* by all means. – **Schlechthin'nig**, *adj. mod.* absolute.

Schlech'tig, *adj. Min.* cleft, having gaps.

Schlech'tigkeit, (*w.*) *f.* badness, [illegible], baseness; vile behaviour, bad trick, base action.

Schlecht'lüstig, *adj. Min.* [illegible].

Schlechtweg', *adv. see* Schlechthin.

Schleck, (*str.*) *m.* 1) *see* Leckerbissen; [illegible] Leckerhaftigkeit. – **Schleck'en**, [illegible] (*w.*) *v. tr.* & *intr. coll.* to lick, [illegible] smackingly, *cf.* Lecken, B. II, &c.

Schlee, **Schleep**, (*str.*) *m. Mar.* a sort of sledge or cradle under a ship's hull to [illegible] her ashore.

Schleet, (*str.*) *n. Mar.* wrain[illegible]

Schle'he, (*w.*) *f. Bot.* 1) sloe, [illegible] 2) *or* **Schleh'dorn**, (*str.*, *pl.* [illegible]) *see* Schlehendorn.

Schle'hen..., *in comp.* –[illegible] tree (*Prunus spinosa* L.); –[illegible] tree blossom; –dorn, *m.* [illegible] tree, German acacia; –[illegible] wild plums; –roth, *adj.* [illegible]

—rost, m. grate-work of the sluice-bottom; —schütze, f. lock-shutter, sliding shutter of a sluice or flood-gate; —thor, n., —thür, f. flood-gate, (canal-)lock, lock-gate; —ventil, n. sluice-valve; —vorboden, m. see —boden; —wasser, n. water held in the chamber of a sluice; —wehr, n. lock-weir; —zoll, m. sluice dues, cf. —geld.

Schlich, (str.) m. I. 1) secret course, by-way; 2) fig. trick, artifice: er kennt die Sch—e, coll. he is up to snuff; II. Min. pounded ore prepared for further working, slich, slick.

Schlicht, adj. 1) sleek, even, smooth; — feilen, to file smooth; sch—es Haar, flat, sleek, or lank hair; 2) plain; homely; der sch—e Menschenverstand, common sense.

Schlicht'... (from Schlichten), in comp. —axt, f., —beil, n. chip-axe; —bier, n. Mas. beer given to the workmen after plastering a wall.

Schlicht'butte, (w.) f. Ichth. turbot (Steinbutte).

Schlicht'eisen, (str.) n. scraping iron, scraper.

Schlich'te, (w.) f. 1) weaver's glue, weaver's dressing; 2) Found. cinder-paste.

Schlich'ten, (w. Ja. tr. 1) a) to make straight, plain, level; b) to pile up, dispose into layers; c) to smooth, sleek; d) T. to chip, plane, file, scrape smooth; 2) fig. to adjust, settle, compose, to make up; die Kette — Weav. to dress the warp. — **Schlich'ter**, (str.) m. 1) plier, &c.; 2) mediator, arbiter, umpire.

Schlicht'... (from Schlichten), in comp. —feile, f. smooth-file; —hammer, m. T. planing-hammer.

Schlicht'haarig, adj. sleek-haired.

Schlicht'heit, f. plainness, simplicity.

Schlichthin', adv. see Schlechthin.

Schlicht'hobel, (str.) m. smoothing-plane.

Schlich'tig, see Schlicht, adj.

Schlicht'... (from Schlichten), in comp. —klinge, f. 1) smoothing-plane iron; 2) see —messer; —maschine, f. Weav. dressing-machine; —meißel, m. see —stahl; —messer, n. double-edged shaving-knife, slicking knife; —mond, m. perching knife; —pinsel, m. Paint. brush for softening and mellowing the tints; —rahmen, m. Tann. perching stick.

Schlicht'schwein, (str.) n. sty- or domestic pig.

Schlicht'... (from Schlichten), in comp. —stahl, m. Turn. flat tool; —stein, m. sleek-stone.

Schlich'tung, (w.) f. fig. composition, accommodation, settling (of a dispute).

Schlicht'zange, (w.) f. perching pincers, caliber for stretching hides.

Schlick, (str.) m. provinc. slime, mud; —balken, m. Hydr. traverse, sleeper; —boden, m. fat and clammy soil.

Schlick'en, (w.) v. tr. & intr. 1) to fill with mud, &c.; 2) see Schlecken.

Schlick'er, (str.) m. T. a kind of paste or glue; —milch, f. see Schlippermilch.

Schlick'ern, (w.) v. intr. provinc. to curdle; to run or soak through.

Schlick'... in comp. —fänger, m. Hydr. 1) secondary dike; 2) hurdle to catch mud; —grund, m. Mar. oozy ground or bottom; —zaun, see —fänger, 2. **Schlieck**, see Schlich, II.

Schlief, (str.) m. see Schliff.

Schlie'fen, (str.) v. intr. (l. m.) see Schlüpfen.

Schlie'fer, (str.) m. Sport. terrier, see Dachshund.

Schlie'fig, see Schliffig.

Schlier, (str.) m. provinc. loam.

Schlie'ren, (w.) v. tr. Mar. to jam (Zuschieren).

Schließ'anker, (str.) m. Build. gable-anchor, cramp-iron.

Schließ'bar, adj. 1) that may be locked, closed; 2) fig. deducible, inferrible.

Schließ'... (from Schließen), in comp. —baum, m. bar, lock of a harbour; —blech, n. 1) Mason. striking-plate, randle; 2) Lock-sm. escutcheon; —bolzen, m. spring-bolt.

Schlie'ße, (w.) f. 1) fastening-plug, [illegible] Schließhaken; 3) book-clasp; 4) Hydr. shutter, hatch.

Schließ'eisen, (str.) n. clamp.

A. **Schlie'ßen**, (str.) v. I. tr. 1) to shut, lock, close; 2) to finish, end, conclude, close; 3) to conclude, make (a bargain, a treaty, &c.), to contract (friendship, a marriage, &c.); 4) to conclude, reason, [illegible], argue, gather, infer (aus, from); einen Verbrecher —, to fetter a criminal; den Nachtrab —, to close or to bring up the rear; einen Vergleich —, to come to an agreement or to [illegible]; eine Wette —, to lay a wager; eine Form —, Typ. to lock up; einen Kreis —, to form a circle; in seine Arme —, to embrace, clasp; in sich —, to comprehend, include; [illegible] eine Rechnung —, to settle, make up, close, or balance an account; das Hauptbuch —, to balance the ledger; II. intr. 1) to shut, [illegible] 2) a) to suit the lock (of a key); das Schloß schließt nicht, the lock goes wrong; b) to join well; to lock; to sit close, to fit; Fenster, welche nicht —, windows that do not close; 3) to close, finish; eine Geschichte, welche nicht mit der Heirat schließt, a story which does not end in marriage; III. refl. 1) to shut, close; to lock; to get a heart (of cabbages); 2) to end; sch—de Achsen, bolting axes; die sch—de Falle, Lock-sm. draw-back bolt; geschlossen reiten, 1. to sit firm or fast on horseback; 2. Mil. to ride in serried ranks; ein geschlossenes Ganzes, a whole complete in itself; ein dicht- or enggeschlossenes Ganzes, a compact whole; die geschlossene Gesellschaft, private society; die geschlossene Kette, Mech. endless chain; eine geschlossene Körperschaft, a corporate body; ein geschlossenes Pferd, a well barelled horse; das geschlossene Viereck, Mil. solid square.

B. **Schlie'ßen**, (str.) v. tr. [illegible] for Schleißen, I.

Schlie'ßer, (str.) m. 1) a) door-keeper; b) jailer, turnkey; 2) captain of a [illegible]; 3) store-keeper, caterer; 4) see [illegible]

Schlie'ßerin, (w.) f. 1) door-keeper; 2) cateress.

Schließ'... (from Schließen), in comp. —feder, f. 1) locking-spring; 2) [illegible] spring-bolt; —frucht, f. Bot. achenium; —gat, n. see Schloßgat; —geld, n. jailer's fee; —gräbchen, n. see —quadrätchen; —hahn, m. Mech. stop-cock; —holm, m., —holz, n. Carp. under-rafter; —kappe, f. Lock-sm. staple (of a bolt), box-staple; —keil, m. wedge, quoin, [illegible]; —kette, f. barring-chain; —klammer, f. [illegible] iron-dog, holdfast; —kloben, m. see —haken; —knie, n. pl. des Galions, Mar. cheeks of the head; —korb, m. basket with a lid, [illegible] basket; —krampe, f. catch.

Schließ'lich, I. adj. ultimate (object), final; II. adv. lastly, finally, in conclusion, to conclude, in fine, ultimately.

Schließ'... (from Schließen), in comp. —muskel, m., —schließmuskel, m. Anat. sphincter, constrictor; —nagel, m. 1) [illegible] bolt; 2) Typ. shooting-stick; [illegible] n. Typ. M quadrat; —riegel, m. [illegible] bolt, dead bolt; —säge, f. [illegible] m. Print. imposing stone.

Schlie'ßung, (w.) f. the (act of) [illegible] &c.; conclusion; closure; — [illegible] balance of an account.

Schliff, (str.) m. 1) a) the [illegible] of) grinding, &c. cf. [illegible] 2) see Schleifsel; 3) [illegible] of bread, &c.; [illegible] cake is dough.

Schlif'fel, (str.) m. [illegible]

Schlif'fig, adj. doughy, [illegible] slack-baked; (of potatoes) [illegible]

Schlimm, I. adj. 1) [illegible] sorry; 2) sad, [illegible]

ader, subclavian artery; 2) or —beinvenenader, subclavian vein; —balken, m. Carp. trimmer; —bart, m. T. key-bit, web of the key; —bein, n. Anat. collar-bone, clavicle; —beinader, f. see —ader; —blech, n. key-plate; —blume, f. Bot. primrose, cowslip (Primula L.); —büchse, f. shooting-key, pistol made of a key (for boys); —bund, m. bunch of keys; —dorn, m. Lock-sm. stem of a lock; —haken, m. key-hook or ring; key-swivel; —klappe, f. Lock-sm. gag to tie up the key-bit; —krahn, m. lock-cock; —loch, n. key-hole; —lochbüchse, f. key-box; —reif, m. 1) outermost hoop of a cask; 2) Lock-sm. ward; —ring, m. key-ring, key-chain; Herald-s. —ringförmig, adj. cléché; —ringkreuz, n. cléché; —rohr, n. 1) key-shank, key-pipe; 2) see —büchse; —schild, m. escutcheon; —schraube, f. barber's vice; —topf, m. humming-top.

Schluß'..., in comp. —erkenntniß, n. see —urtheil; —fall, m. Mus. cadence; —folge, f. conclusion, syllogism; —folgerung, f. inference, conclusion; —gebäude, n. system of reasoning; —gedanke, m. concluding idea (sentiment); —gerecht, adj. see —recht; —gesang, m. Mus concluding song; —kette, f. chain or train of reasoning, argument; —kunst, f. art of reasoning, logic.

Schlüs'sig, adj. resolved, determined; — werden, to resolve.

Schluß'..., in comp. —mäßig, adj. see —recht; —nagel, m. 1) head-pin; 2) see Schloßnagel, 1; —nahme, f. resolution; —note, f. see —zettel; —notirungen, f., —preise, m. pl. Comm. rates last paid; —punct, m. full stop, period; —rechnung, f. Comm. account of settlement, final or annual balance; —recht, —richtig, adj. logically correct; conclusive; —rede, f. 1) conclusive speech; 2) syllogism; —reif, m. chimb-hoop of a cask; —reihe, f. see —kette; —reim, m. burden; —richtigkeit, f. logical correctness, conclusiveness; —satz, m. 1) concluding sentence, conclusion; 2) conclusive argument; 3) Mus. finale; —schein, m. see —zettel; —seide, f. shoot-silk, trame; —stein, m. Archit. & fig. key-stone; crowning-stone; —stück, n. concluding piece (of music); —urtheil, n. Law, final sentence or judgment; —vergleich, m. final agreement; —vertrag, m. final treaty, ultimate agreement; —vignette, f. Print. tail-piece; —widrig, adj. inconclusive, inconsistent, inconsequential; —wort, n. concluding or closing word; —zeichen, n. sign of conclusion: 1) Mus. double bar; 2) Gramm. full stop; —zeit, f. closing-time; —zettel, m. Comm. broker's note or memorandum, see Abschlußzettel; —zierrat, m. crowning ornament.

Schmach, f. ignominy, disgrace, dishonour; outrage, abuse, offence; in comp. —bedeckt, —beladen, —voll, adj. disgraceful, ignominious; —sache, f. Law, action for libel or assault; —säule, f. pillory; —schrift, f. libel.

Schmach'ten, (w.) v. intr. 1) to languish, pine; 2) to long, yearn (nach, for).

Schmäch'tig, I. adj. slim, slender, slight-made; weak; II. Sch-keit, (w.) f. slimness, &c.

Schmacht'..., in comp —hals, —hans, —lappen, m. coll. 1) starved person, needy wretch; 2) niggard; —korn, n. small and imperfect grain of corn; —locke, f. lovelock, ear-lock, curl; —riemen, m. belt, girth; den —riemen umschnallen, fig. to starve.

A. † Schmack, (str.) m. taste, &c. see Geschmack, 1 & 2.

B. Schmack, (str.) m. Bot. & T. sumach.

Schmack'e, (w.) f. Mar. smack (a vessel).

Schmack'gar, adj. T. boiled or dressed in sumach (of leather: Schmack'leder, n.).

Schmack'haft, I. adj. savoury, tasteful, palatable, relishable; — machen, to season; II. Sch-igkeit, (w.) f. savouriness, &c.

Schmacki'ren, (w.) v. tr. Dy. to boil or dress in sumach (leather).

Schmack'segel, (str.) n. Mar. smack-sail.

Schmad'der, (str.) m. coll. any foul matter, soil, candle-snuff, &c. — Schmad'derschild, Schmad'dern, v., &c. see Schmierfink, Schmieren, 3. [or papers.

Schmäh'artikel, (str.) m. slanderous article

Schmäh'en, (w.) v. tr & intr. 1) to abuse, revile, to inveigh (auf (with Acc.), against), rail (at); 2) to slander, calumniate, insult.

Schmäh'er, (str.) m. abuser, &c.

Schmäh'lich, I. adj. ignominious, disgraceful, outrageous, injurious, scandalous, vile; II. Sch-keit, (w.) f. ignominiousness, &c.

Schmäh'... (from Schmähen), in comp. —rede, f. abuse, libel; —schrift, f. libel, lampoon, pl. abusive writings; —schriftler, m. libeller; —sucht, f. slanderous disposition; —süchtig, adj. slanderous, libellous.

Schmäh'ung, (w.) f. 1) the (act of) abusing, &c.; 2) injury, invective, abuse.

Schmäh'wort, (str.) n. injurious word, abusive expression, invective.

Schmak, see Schmack, B.

Schmal, I. adj. 1) narrow, small; die sch-e Seite, the narrow side, edge (of a board, a brick, &c.); auf der sch-en Seite, edgeways, on edge, on the narrow side; 2) fig. slim, slender, thin; scanty, poor; II. in comp. —backig, adj. coll. lank-cheeked, thin-faced, sharp-visaged; starved; —beet, n. border in a garden, flower-border; —bier, n. small beer; —bock, m. Sport. roe-buck in the first year; —bock(käfer), m. Entom. wasp-beetle, leptura (Leptura lurida F.); —bodig, adj. narrow-bottomed; —brüstig, adj. narrow-breasted.

Schmä'le, (w.) f. 1) (l. u.) see Schmalheit; 2) see Schmiele, 1.

Schmäl'eisen, (str.) n. 1) Mar. calking-iron; 2) Found. iron remaining in the furnace after the fire.

Schmä'len, (w.) v. intr. 1) to chide, scold (auf (with Acc.), at); 2) Sport. to bray, bell (of deer).

Schmal'ente, (w.) f. small white duck.

Schma'ler, (str.) m. T. basket-maker's cleaving tool. [ber.

Schmä'lerer, (str.) m. diminisher, detracter.

Schmä'lern, (w.) v. I. tr. to narrow, lessen, abridge, diminish, shorten, reduce, curtail; to derogate, detract from; II. refl. to grow narrow, to be lessened, to diminish.

Schmä'lerung, (w.) f. the (act of) lessening, &c., diminution, derogation, abridgment.

Schmal'..., in comp. —flügel, —flügler, m. Entom. insect with small wings; —hans, m. joc. niggard; heute ist —hans Küchenmeister, jos. there is but poor fare or short commons today; —hefe, f. Bot. common wall-barrow (Heubeckel). [&c. of Schmal.

Schmal'heit, (w.) f. narrowness, smallness,

Schmal'..., in comp. —heig, n. small-arms; —leder, n. leather of young cattle; —leibig, adj. slender-bodied, slight-made; —reh, n. one year old roe; —saat, f. 1) small seed (of peas, &c.); 2) see Kleefaat; —spießig, see —bock(käfer).

* Schmal'te, (w.) f. (Ital., from the G. Schmalz) 1) †, any (coloured) glass, pulverised and used in enamel-painting, &c.; 2) ... T. smalt, (Smaltsium, n.) smalt-blue, powder-blue.

Schmal'..., in comp. —thier, n. ... hind in her second year, ... narrow cloth; —vieh, n. small cattle, goats, &c.; —zehnt, m. tithe of small ...

Schmalz, (str.) n. & m. 1) fat ... or grease, suet, lard (Fett, 1); 2) ... Butter, II.; Salz und —, ... coll. to be well off or ... —birne, f. Pomol. ... butter-pear; ...

for Salbe, 1; *c)* dirt; 2) *coll.* a thrashing, flogging. [containing grease.

Schmier'eimer, *m.*, Schmier'faß, *n.* vessel

Schmie'ren, *(w.) v. tr.* 1) *a)* to smear; to grease, *see* Einschmieren; *b)* to spread (butter on bread, &c.), to butter; 2) to oil; to salve; to lubricate; 3) *fig.* to scrawl; to scribble; to daub; *coll.-s.* 4) to bribe; 5) to drub, thrash; den Wein —, to adulterate wine; *vulg.-s.* Einem etwas ins Maul —, to make a thing plain to one; Einem Brei ins *or* ums Maul —, to amuse one with idle hopes *or* vain promises; wer gut schmiert, der gut fährt, grease (pay) well and you will go fast; es geht wie geschmiert, things go on swimmingly. [&c. *cf.* Schmieren.

Schmie'rer, *(str.) m.* scrawler; scribbler.

Schmiererei', *(w.) f.* the (act of) smearing, &c. *cf.* Schmieren; (a piece of) scrawling, scribbling, scrawl, daub.

Schmier'... *(from* Schmieren*)*, *in comp.* —[illegible], *m. see* —bemmel; —gording, *f. Mar.* preventer leech-line (of the top-sail); —hahn, *m. Mech.* grease-cock; —hammel, —maz, *m. coll.* dirty fellow; —bühlen, *f. pl. see* Talgdrüsen; —hölzer, *n. pl. see* —bäume.

Schmie'rig, I. *adj.* greasy, smeary, sloppy, slabby; *Bot.* viscous, glutinous; II. Sch-keit, *(w.) f.* greasiness.

Schmier'... *(from* Schmieren*)*, *in comp.* —käse, *m.* soft cheese; whey-cheese; —leder, *n.* leather dressed in train oil; —mittel, *n.* unguent; —ofen, *m.* pitch-furnace; —pfannen, *f. pl. Ship-b.* sliding-planks; —pfropfen, *m.* shot-plug; —quast, *m. Mar.* mop; —rack, *n. Mar.* truss-parrel; —öl, *n.* lubricating oil.

Schmier'öl, *(str.) n. cant.* salve, ointment.

Schmier'... *(from* Schmieren*)*, *in comp.* —salbe, *f.* (soft) salve; —schaf, *n.* scabby sheep; —seife, *f.* barrel-soap, soft soap; —vieh, *n. see* —schaf; —wolle, *f.* dirty wool.

Schmie'te, *see* Schmeite.

Schmink'..., *in comp.* —apfel, *m. Pomol.* a kind of autumn-apple; —beere, *f. Bot.* strawberry spinach, blite *(Blitum capitatum* L.); —bohne, *f. Bot.* common kidney-bean, French bean *(Phaseolus vulgaris* L.); —büchse, —dose, *f.* paint-box.

Schmin'ke, *(w.) f.* 1) paint (for the face, body), rouge; 2) *T.* red colouring stuff *or* matter; 3) *fig.* fine outside, gloss, varnish.

Schmin'ken, *(w.) v. tr. & rfl.* to (paint with) rouge; to patch.

Schmink'..., *in comp.* —fleckchen, —pflästerchen, *n.* 1) patch, beauty-spot; 2) *or* —läppchen, *n.* Spanish clouds, Italian colouring rags (Bezetten); —mittel, *n.* cosmetic; —roth, *n.* rouge; —stein, *m. Miner.* Muscovy-talc; —topf, *m.* rouge-pot, paint-pot; —wasser, *n.* beauty-water, wash; —weiß, *n.* flake-white; —wurz, —wurzel, *f.* 1) stone-weed (Steinsame); 2) alkanet *(Anchusa tinctoria* L.); 3) Solomon's-seal (Salomonssiegel).

Schmir'gel, *(str.) m.* 1) soil in tobacco pipes; 2) *(or* Schmergel*) Miner. & T.* emery; —asche, *f.* —staub, *m.* putty; —cattun, *m.* —leinwand, *f.* emery-cloth; —feile, *f.*, —holz, *n.* emery-stock; —kolben, *m. Gun-sm.* leading-rod (for polishing the inside of rifles).

Schmir'geln, *(w.) v. tr. & intr. coll.* 1) to soil; 2) to smoke (tobacco); 3) *T.* to rub *or* polish with emery; *Cutl.*, &c. to glaze; das — der Büchsenrohre, *Gun-sm.* draw-boring of barrels.

Schmir'gel..., *in comp.* —papier, *n.* emery-paper; —scheibe, *f.* glazer (for edge-tools).

Schmiß, *(str.) m.* 1) dash, stroke, bang, blow; kick; 2) *Stud. slang,* cut, wound (in duelling).

Schmiß'ler, *(str.) m.* kicker (of horses).

Schmit'te, *(w.) f. see* Schichte.

Schmitz, *(str.) m.* 1) lash, cut (with a whip); 2) stain.

Schmit'ze, *(w.) f.* whip-lash, cracker.

Schmit'zen, *(w.) v. tr. & intr.* 1) to lash, whip; 2) to soil, dirty; 3) *T.* to blacken; 4) *Typ.* to mackle. [[illegible]

Schmit'zer, *(str.) m. T.* scourer (of cloths).

Schmitz'erlein, *(str.) n. Pharm.* jujube lozenge.

Schmö'ker, Schmö'ker, *(str.) m. coll.* an old smoky-looking volume; Schmö'kern, *(w.) v. intr.* to pore over such books.

Schmoll'brüder, *m.* pouter.

Schmol'len, *(w.) v. intr.* to pout; to sulk, to be sulky.

Schmol'lig, *adj.* sulky.

Schmolli'ren, *(w.) v. intr. or* Schmol'lis trinken, *Stud. slang, see* Brüderschaft trinken.

Schmoll'..., *in comp.* —winkel, *m.* pouting-place; retired *or* solitary corner; —kämmerchen, *n.* private closet, boudoir.

Schmor'braten, *(str.) m.* stewed meat.

Schmo'ren, *(w.) v. tr. & intr.* 1) to stew (plums, apples), to fry; 2) to swelter; geschmorter Hase, *Cook.* jugged hare.

Schmor'... *(from* Schmoren*)*, *in comp.* —fleisch, *n. see* —braten; —kartoffeln, *f. pl.* potatoes baked in butter; —pfanne, *f.*, —tiegel, *m.* stewing *or* frying pan; —stück, *n.* piece of stewed meat; —topf, *m.* stewing-pot.

Schmot'terig, *adj. see* Schmierig. [profit.

Schmu, *(indecl.) m. Jew. Germ.* (unfair)

Schmuck, I. *adj.* trim, tidy, neat, smart, pretty; sch-es Dirn *(Schiller)*, sleek cattle; II. *s. (str.) m.* 1) ornament, adornment, set-off, trinket, finery; attire, dress; 2) (set of) jewels; rednerischer° —, *fig.* flowers of rhetoric or speech.

Schmuck'..., *in comp.* —arbeit, *f.* fancy-work; jewelry; —bohne, *f. see* Schminkbohne.

Schmuck'chodeh, *(str.) m. I. u. for* Stümper.

Schmück'en, *(w.) v. tr.* to adorn, decorate; to grace; to attire, dress, trim.

Schmuck'..., *in comp.* —federn, *f. pl.* fancy or ornamental feathers; —geräth, *n. see* Schmuck, I; —hand, *f. see* Kaufhand; —händler, *m.* jeweller; —kästchen, *n.*, —kasten, *m.* casket, jewel-box; —laden, *m.* jeweller's shop; —lilie, *f. Bot.* African lily *(Agapanthus* L'Her.).

Schmuck'los, I. *adj.* unadorned, devoid of ornament, simple; II. S-igkeit, *f.* the being without ornament.

Schmuck'..., *in comp.* —nadel, *f.* breast-pin; —redenart, *f.* flowery speaking, declamation; —sachen, *pl.* jewels, ornaments, trinkets.

Schmück'ung, *(w.) f.* adornment, decoration.

Schmuck'..., *in comp.* —vogel, *m. Ornith.* American wax wing *(Ampelis Americana* Wils.); —voll, *adj.* much adorned; —waare, *f.* jewelry, trinkets.

Schmud'del, *(str.) m. coll. see* Schlampe, [illegible]

Schmud'delig, *adj. see* Schlampig.

Schmug'gel, *(str.) m.*, Schmuggelei', [illegible] *f.* smuggling; Schmug'geln, *(w.) v. tr.* [illegible] smuggle; Schmugg'ler, *(str.) m.* smuggler.

Schmu(e)l, *(str.) m. Jew. Germ.* [illegible] *the Hebr.* name Sch'muel, Samuel; [illegible] designation of a Jew, *cf.* Mauschel; [illegible] (profitable) bargain.

Schmun'zeln, *(w.) v. intr.* to simper [illegible]

Schmu'sen, Schmu'sen, *(w.) v.* [illegible] *Germ.* 1) to talk loud and lively [illegible] Jews who want to make a bargain [illegible] such to make bargains or [illegible]

Schmu'sen, *(w.) v. tr. T.* [illegible] pipes'.

Schmutz *(pronounce.* [illegible]*)* [illegible] *m.* dirt, filth, soil, smut, [illegible]

Schmutz'..., *in comp.* [illegible] -ial; —bartel, —buch, *m.* [illegible]

—tropfen, m.; —veilchen, n. see —glöckchen, 2; —verwehung, —verschüttung, f. snow drift, accumulation of snow; —vogel, m. 1) see —ammer; 2) waxwing (Seidenschwanz); —wand, f. snow-shelter; —wasser, n. snow-water; —wehe, f. snow-drift, snow-wreath; —weiß, adj. snow-white; —wetter, n. snowy weather; —wiesel, n. Zool. white weasel (Mustela nivalis L.); —wind, m. wind bringing snow; —wolke, f. snowy cloud; —wurz, f. Bot. butterwort (Fettkraut).

Schneid'..., in comp. see Schnei'de....

Schnei'de, (w.) f. 1) edge; bit (of a bore); 2) Sport. gin, springe; 3) fig. a) keen edge (of intellect); keenness, sharpness; b) (particul. S. G.) full power, energy; c) coll. keen edge of appetite; inclination (Lust, 2).

Schnei'de... (from Schneiden), in comp. —bank, f. see Schnitzbank; —bohne, f. Bot. kidney-bean (Schminkbohne); —bohrer, m. cutting-gimlet; —brett, n. cutting board; —cirkel, m. Bookb. cutting-compasses; —demant, m. Glaz. diamond; —eisen, n. 1) edge-tool; cutting or chopping knife; T-s. 2) saw-file; 3) screw-plate, screw-tap; 4) slit iron; —eisenwalzwerk, n. slitting-rollers; —feile, f. cutting file, enameller's file; —holz, n. timber for sawing; —instrument, n. edge-tool, cutter; —lade, m. rafter, couple (in saw-mills; Tech.); —kluppe, f. 1) screw-stock; 2) see —eisen, 3; —lade, f. chopping bench; —leder, n. leather for cutting or topping; sole-leather.

Schnei'dein, see Schneitein.

Schnei'de... (from Schneiden), in comp. —lohn, m. choppage; sawing-wages; —maschine, f. cutting-machine or engine; —messer, n. cutting-knife, cutter, chopping blade; —model, m. Join. cutting-gauge; —mühle, f. saw-mill, sawing mill.

Schnei'den, (str.) v. I. tr. & intr. 1) a) to cut; to carve; to prune, lop (trees, &c.); to chop (straw); klein —, to mince; to cut up (wood); b) fig. to bite, pinch; 2) to castrate, geld; ein geschnittenes Schwein, a barrow hog; 3) Geom. to bisect; Korn —, to mow or cut corn; eine Feder —, to make or mend a pen; Breter —, to saw boards; Schrauben —, T. to cut screws; Wein —, to adulterate wine; die Cour —, see Cour (machen); viel Geld bei etwas —, to make a great deal of money by ...; es schneidet in die Ohren, it grates (on) the ear; in den Beutel — (intr.), coll. to tell heavily on one's purse; es schneidet mich im Leibe, I have the gripes (cf. Leibschneiden); Gesichter —, to make faces or grimaces; II. refl. coll. to be mistaken, to be disappointed; sch-der Sarcasmus &c., cutting, keen, withering sarcasm, &c.; geschnittenes Eisen, slit iron.

Schnei'de... (from Schneiden), in comp. —nadel, f. T. three-edged needle; —pflug, m. Husb. scarifier, scarificator.

Schnei'der, (str.) m. 1) tailor; 2) see —fisch; 3) see Fregattenvogel; einen zum — machen, coll. to make one lose the game (at draughts, without crowning a man, &c.).

Schnei'de... (from Schneiden), in comp. —rad, n. Horol. wheel-cutting machine; —rädlein, n. Bak. dough-cutter, jagging-iron.

Schnei'derarbeit, (w.) f. tailor's work.

Schneiderei', (w.) f. coll. (the practice of) tailoring, business or work of a tailor.

Schnei'der..., in comp. —eisen, n. tailor's goose; —fisch, m. Ichth. bleak (Ukelei); —friesel, n. joc. ague; —gesell, m. tailor's journeyman; —haft, adj. tailor-like.

Schnei'derin, (w.) f. 1) tailor's wife; 2) dress-maker, woman tailor, tailoress.

Schnei'derkrankheit, (w.) f. coll. itch.

Schnei'derling, (str.) m. cont. (insignificant) tailor.

Schnei'der..., in comp. —lohn, m. tailor's wages; —mamsell, f. see Schneiderin, 2; —mäßig, adj. see —haft; —muskel, m. Anat. tailor's muscle.

Schnei'dern, (w.) v. intr. coll. to make clothes, to tailor; to dressmake. [illegible]

Schnei'der-Stock, (str.) m. Carp. [illegible]

Schnei'der..., in comp. —ring, m. tailor's thimble; —schere, f. tailor's shears; —tisch, m. tailor's stall, tailoring-board; —vogel, m. Ornith. tailor-bird (Sylvia sutoria Lath.).

Schnei'de... (from Schneiden), in comp. —stein, m. see —demant; —stichel, m. sharp-graver; —waaren, f. pl. edge-tools; —walze, f. T. slitting roller; —werkzeug, —zeug, n. edge-tool; cutting-engine; —zahn, m. Anat. cutter, incisor (fore-tooth).

Schnei'dig, adj. 1) soft, easy to be cut; 2) a) in comp. edged; b) particul. N. G. keen; sharp; energetic.

Schnei'en, (w.) v. impers. intr. & tr. to snow; es schneit, it snows; es schneit Blüthen, it showers blossoms.

Schnei'se, (w.) f. lane cut through a forest.

Schnei'ße, (w.) f. snare, springe, noose; Sch-nbeere, f. see Eberesche.

Schnei'teln, (w.) v. tr. (not directly derived from Schneiden, but from MHG. sneiten [Swiss., Schneiten]) to lop, prune, cut.

Schnell, adj. 1) Nerud. see Windschiefes, 2) quick, swift, fast, fleet; speedy, prompt; rapid; sudden; sch-er Umsatz, quick return; sch-er Verlauf, brisk or ready sale; es wird sch-en Absatz finden, it will soon be taken off our, your, &c. hands; er reiste sehr —, he travelled very fast; die, welche einen sch-en Blick haben, werden sich — entschließen und — handeln, those who see quickly, will resolve quickly, and act quickly; zu — urtheilen, to judge too hastily or rashly.

Schnell'... (from Schnell, adj.), in comp. —bleiche, f. whitening of linen, &c. with bleaching liquid or powder; —bote, m. courier.

Schnell'... (from Schnellen), in comp. —brett, n. spring-board (of a mousetrap); —brunnen, m. pump.

Schnel'le, (w.) f. see Schnelligkeit.

Schnel'len, (w.) v. I. intr. (aux. sein & haben) to spring, snap, to fly with an elastic impulse; II. tr. 1) to (send away with a) jerk, to let fly, fillip; to toss; in die Luft —, to kick (the beam); 2) coll. to cheat.

Schnel'ler, (str.) m. 1) Weav. driver, pecker, picker; 2) Gun-sm., &c. spring, tricker, trigger; 3) jerk, fillip; 4) hank (of yarn).

Schnell'... (from Schnell, adj.), in comp. —essigbereitung, f. artificial production of vinegar; pyroligneous acid distillation; —fahrer, m. quick vehicle or boat.

Schnell'... (from Schnellen), in comp. —falle, f. spring-trap; —feder, f. spring.

Schnell'... (from Schnell, adj.), in comp. —feuerzeug, n. tinder-box, pocket-fire, [illegible] —zünder; —fingerig, adj. quick working.

Schnell'fliege, (w.) f. see [illegible]

Schnell'füßig, adj. swift-footed, quick of foot. [illegible]

Schnell'geigen, (str.) m. [illegible]

Schnell'... (from Schnell, adj.), in comp. —gerberei, f. quick tanning; [illegible] hasty in believing.

Schnell'... (from Schnellen), in comp. [illegible] gurke, f. squirting cucumber [illegible] —harz, n. elastic resin.

Schnell'igkeit (L. m.) [illegible] quickness, swiftness, &c. cf. [illegible] velocity, speed, rapidity.

Schnell'... (from Schnellen), [illegible] —käfer, m. Entom. elater, [illegible] (Elater L.); —käulchen, n. [illegible] chen, n. taw, marble [illegible] elasticity; —kräftig, adj. [illegible]

* Schef'fen, see Schöffen.

Sche'lich, adj. l. & Sche'lig, adj. [illegible], wretched, paltry, scurvy, trashy: II. s. [illegible] m. (—mannt, f., —zeug, n.) paltry stuff, [illegible]. [illegible] see Schelle.

Schel'le, see Schelper; Schelf'[illegible], adj.

* Schebaie'de, (Fr.) f. see [illegible].

* Scholar', (a.) m. (Lat.) scholar, disciple.

* Scholarch', (r.) m. (Lat.-Gr.) inspector of a school.

* Scholast', (a.) m. (E. Lat.) scholar; Scholastik, f. school-divinity, scholastic divinity; Scholas'tiker, (str.) m. school-divine, scholastic; Scholas'tisch, adj. scholastical.

* Scholiast', (r.) m. (Gr.) scholiast, commentator. — Scho'lie, (a.) f. scholion, comment.

Schol'len, (w.) v. intr. Mar. to go high, to run against the ship (of the waves).

Schol'le, (w.) f. 1) clod; 2) [illegible] (of land); 3) Ichth. plaice, sole (Platessa vulgaris Cuv.).

Schol'len, (w.) v. tr. & intr. to root up the earth (said of the mole).

Schol'len..., in comp. —brecher, m. Agr. clod-crusher; —[illegible], m. Ornith. stone-chat (Schwarzkehlchen); —pflug, m. stubble-plough; —[illegible], m. clod-beetle.

Schol'lern, (w.) v. intr. to fall (like [illegible]); to roll down.

Schol'licht, adj. like a clod, cloddy.

Schol'lig, adj. consisting of clods, cloddy.

Schöll'..., in comp. —kraut, n. Bot. celandine (Chelidonium L.); —wurz, f. 1) see —kraut; 2) herb Robert (Geranium [illegible]).

Schöl[illegible], (w.) m. see Schellfisch.

Scho'merling, (str.) m. [illegible] ([illegible]).

Schon, adv. 1) already; before; so (as) early as ...; 2) (wenn —, ob —) even, although; 3) indeed; surely, no doubt; — früher (vor jetzt geschehen), before this or now; ist der Tag — bestimmt? is the day yet fixed? er ist — lange abgereist, he left long ago; er ist — lange hier, he has been here for a long time past; wie lange sind Sie — hier? how long have you been here? wir stehen — seit Jahren mit ihm in Rechnung, we have had an account with him for years; — nähert sich die Zeit wo ..., times are coming when ...; es ist — lange her, daß ich ihn sah, it is a long time since I saw him; sind Sie — in Sicilien gewesen? have you ever been in Sicily? es wird sich — finden, we shall see in due (or in good) time; er wollte — gehen, he was ready to go; ich will es — machen, I'll take care to do it; ich werde Sie — bezahlen, I shall (be sure to) pay you; ich werde es Ihnen — zu wissen thun, I shall let you know in due time (without your urging me, &c.); Sie werden mich — verstehen, I dare say you will understand me; ich helfe mir — selbst, I hope I shall help myself; ich könnte hier — wohnen, I could be contented to live here; er kann diese Ausgaben — machen, he can afford (to make) these expenses; ich werde ihn — finden, I warrant you, I'll manage to find him; ich kenne den Schurken und werde ihn — noch kriegen, I know the rogue, and will catch him yet; sie ist ohne Zweifel — todt, by this time she must be dead; darüber können wir — lachen, we can (well) afford to laugh at it; er wird sein Unrecht — einsehen, I doubt not but that he will see his wrong; er mußte — bekennen, he could not help confessing; muß ich es — thun, though I must do it; dieses neue Unrecht regte seinen — von Natur rachsüchtigen Sinn bis zum höchsten Grade auf, this fresh injury worked up his temper, naturally vindictive, to the highest point; — der Anblick, the mere sight, the sight alone; — der Gedanke, the very idea; — das menschliche Gefühl, common humanity; — den folgenden Morgen, the very next morning; — ganz wohl, [illegible] — [illegible] to well.

Schön, adj. beautiful, handsome, [illegible] fair, handsome; nice; fig. noble, [illegible] fine, favourable, convenient; [illegible] die [illegible] Gelegenheit zu ..., you now have a fair chance to ...; [illegible] gold; [illegible] Waare, marketable [illegible] [illegible] Geschlecht, the fair sex; die [illegible] Wissenschaften, the liberal arts, [illegible] lite literature, belles-lettres; [illegible] Perle! a pretty price! ein [illegible] Anfang! a nice (precious, &c.) beginning? [illegible] —, life is sweet; es ist nicht — von [illegible] not nice in him; — thun, to play the gallant, to flirt, coquet; — machen, Mar. to clean [illegible] deck, a ship; sich — machen, to adorn (make) nice one's self; Sie haben — (or gut) reden, sol. it is very easy for you to talk.

Schön'..., in comp. —äugig, —[illegible] —haarig, —häutig, —gefärbt &c., adj. having beautiful eyes, brown, hair, [illegible] &c. Bot. 1) [illegible] 2) a beautiful tree, a native of the Cape of Good Hope (Calodendron capense L.); —blatt, n. Bot. [illegible] (Calophyllum [illegible] L.); —druck, m. Typ. prime, first form.

Schö'ne, a. (decl. like adj.) I. n. the beautiful; II. f. 1) a) fair, fair one (also m. the beautiful one); b) mistress; 2) *, beauty; 3) f. [illegible] (parterre) [illegible].

Schön'thal, (str.) m. see Stendel.

Scho'nen, (w.) v. tr. & intr. (with Gen.) to spare, to save; to forbear; to [illegible] or take care (of); to use tenderly, to treat with indulgence; [illegible] —, to be [illegible] of; to be regardless of.

Schö'nen, (w.) v. tr. 1) see [illegible]; 2) to fine (with isinglass, &c.), refine; [illegible] 3) fig. see Beschönigen.

Scho'ner, (str.) m. 1) a) table-mat; [illegible] mannner; 2) Mar. schooner (a vessel).

Schön'..., in comp. —färberei, n. [illegible]; —färber, m. dyer in fine colours; —färberei, f. 1) art of dyeing in colours; [illegible] see Beschönigung; —fleckchen, —[illegible], n. beauty spot, patch; —geist, m. (fine) wit, polite scholar, bel esprit (of a lady) [illegible] ing; —geisterei, f. coll. witticism, [illegible] at wit or knowledge of literature; —geist, m. see Perigord; —haarig, see —äugig &c.

Schön'heit, (w.) f. beauty; fairness, handsomeness, &c., cf. Schön.

Schön'heits..., in comp. —gefühl, n. —[illegible], n. feeling, sense for (of) beauty, for what is beautiful, taste; —[illegible], f. [illegible] beauty; —mittel, —wasser, n. cosmetic; —[illegible] [illegible] —pflästerchen, n. beauty-spot, patch.

Schön'..., in comp. —[illegible], —[illegible] see Schilfkraut; —[illegible], f. Archit. [illegible] [illegible].

Schön'ling, (str.) m. [illegible]

Schön'..., in comp. —[illegible] speaker; —[illegible], f. declamation.

Schön'[illegible], adj. careful, [illegible] things); sparing.

Schön'..., in comp. —[illegible] —schreibekunst, f. —[illegible] —schreibung, f. calligraphy; —[illegible] fair-writer, calligrapher, —[illegible] attempt at fine writing; —[illegible] one who makes [illegible] or favourable side; —[illegible], f. [illegible]

Schön'[illegible], adv. [illegible]

Schön'..., in comp. —[illegible] f. person who flirts, [illegible] —thuerei, f. flirtation, [illegible]

Scho'nung, (w.) f. 1) [illegible] grace, forbearance, [illegible] forest. nursery of young [illegible]

Scho'nungslos, adj. [illegible]

ker; —**glas**, *n.*, —**kopf**, *m.* cup, cupping-glass; —**zeug**, *n.* cupping instruments.

Schrap'pen, *see* Schrubben.

Schrapp'hobel, *see* Schrobhobel.

Schrot, *(str.) m. (provinc. n.)* 1) *a)* cut, piece; *b)* block, log of wood; 2) *see* Schrote, 1 & 2; 3) *Mint.* due *or* full weight *or* size of a coin; 4) small-shot, hail-shot; *Mar.* langrel; — Nr. 1., swanshot; 5) *Mill.* groats; bruised grain, cribble; 6) *fig.* stamp, cut; von altem *or* gutem — und Korn, sterling, sound.

Schrot'..., *in comp.* —**axt**, *f.* wood-cleaver's axe; —**baum**, *m.* drayman's beam; —**beutel**, *m.* 1) shot-pouch, shot-bag; 2) *Mill.* groats-bolter; —**bock**, *m.* trestle for unloading weights; —**bohrer**, *m.* auger, piercer to bore wooden pipes with; —**breite**, *f.* breadth of cloth between the selvages; —**büchse**, *f.* rifle for small-shot; —**bunzen**, *m.* *Gold-sm.* scalper, chisel.

Schro'te, *(w.) f.* 1) *T.* chisel, cutting knife; 2) list, selvage.

Schrot'eisen, *(str.) n.* 1) *Smith.*, *&c.* great chisel, priming-iron; 2) *Carp.*, *&c.* former, ripping chisel; 3) *Turn.* *see* Schrotstahl; 4) *Gard.* pruning-hook; 5) *a)* *Shoe-m.* cutting-knife; *b)* *Tann.* *see* Schrotmesser; 6) *Surg.* rugine.

Schro'tel, *(str.) m.* shreds, parings, clippings.

Schro'teln, *(w.) v. intr.* to steer clear of the ruts, to keep the ruts between the wheels.

Schro'ten, *(irr.) v. tr.* 1) to bruise, rough-grind, kibble (corn); 2) to cut, saw; to rough-hew; *Turn.* to take off with the gouge; 3) *Mint.* to size (the blanks) for coining; die Münzstücke —, to prune the edges of the coins; 4) to size, assize (boards); 5) Draht zu Nadeln —, to clip the pin-wire into shanks; 6) *Min.* to hollow; 7) to nibble, gnaw (of mice, &c.); 8) to shoot *or* let down into a cellar; am Tau —, to parbuckle (casks).

Schrö'ter, *(str.) m.* 1) cutter; 2) *see* Schrotmeißel; 3) *Entom.* *see* Hirschkäfer; 4) shooter, loader, drayman; cellarman; beer-porter, wine-porter; —**lohn**, *m.* cellarage, shootage.

Schrot'..., *in comp.* —**fabrik**, *f.* shot-factory, shot-manufactory; —**fäustel**, *m.* *Min.* hack iron; —**feile**, *f.* *Mint.* planchet-file; —**form**, *f.* shot-mould; —**förmig**, *adj.* & *adv.* in the shape of small-shot; —**gang**, *m.* *Mill.* pair of mill-stones that rough-grinds corn, barley, &c.; —**gießerei'**, *f.* shot-manufactory; —**güttel**, *m.* shot-belt; —**hammer**, *m.* cutting-chisel in form of a hammer; —**hobel**, *m.* jack-plane; —**kasten**, *m.* *Mill.* bran-chest; —**kleie**, *f.* coarse bran of the groats; —**köker**, —**köcher**, *m.* *Mar.* canister for case-shot, for langrage; —**korn**, *n.* 1) grated, rough-ground, *or* bruised corn; 2) grain of shot; —**kupfer**, *n.* *Miner.* copper clippings; —**leiter**, *f.* drayman's ladder; pulling ladder; *Mar.* range of skids.

Schröt'ling, *(str.) m.* 1) piece cut off, shredding; 2) *Mint.* blank (for coining), planchet.

Schrot'..., *in comp.* —**maß**, *n.* shot-charger; —**mehl**, *n.* coarse meal, coarse flour, groats; —**meißel**, *m.* cutting *or* cold chisel; —**messer**, *n.* cutting or paring knife; —**messing**, *n.* latten clippings; —**model**, *m.* *see* —form; —**mühle**, *f.* bruising- *or* cribbling-mill; —**sack**, *m.* bag filled with shot; —**säge**, *f.* great saw, cross-cut-saw; —**sägeförmig**, *adj.* & *adv.* *Bot.* runcinate (leaf); —**schere**, *f.* plate-shears; —**schwein**, *n.* hog of a small size and not very fat, porker; —**seil**, *n.* rope to let casks down into the cellar; —**sieb**, *n.* sieve through which shot is sized; —**silber**, *n.* *Chem.* silver-ashes, grains of silver; —**speck**, *m.* small lean bacon; —**stahl**, *m.* (turner's) round-tool (Rundstahl); —**stück**, *n.* 1) *see* Schrötling; 2) *Gunn.* heavy gun; —**tau**, *n.* *Mar.* parbuckle; —**thurm**, *m.* *T.* shot-tower; —**waage**, *f.* level, plumb-rule, plummet; —**werk**, *n.* 1) *Min.* lining of a shaft; 2) *see* —**schrot**; —**winde**, *f.* windlass; [illegible] —**wurm**, *m.* *see* Maulwurfsgrille; —**zeug**, *n.* *Mint.* paring-tools.

Schrub'belmaschine, *(w.) f.* *Spinn.* scribbling-machine, scribbler.

Schrub'beln, *(w.) v. tr.* *see* Schrubbeln.

Schrub'ben, *(w.) v. tr.* 1) to scrub; *Mar.* to hog (a vessel); 2) *T.* to rough-work, rough-plane, rough-turn.

Schrub'ber, *(str.) m.* 1) scrubber; 2) *see* Schrubbürste; 3) *Mar.* scrubbing broom, hog.

Schrubb'..., *in comp.* —**bürste**, *f.* scrubbing-brush, scrubber; —**hobel**, *m.* jack-plane; —**säge**, *f.* hand-saw.

Schruf'fen, *(w.) v. tr.* *Turn.* *see* Schrubben, [illegible]

Schrull, *(str.) m.* *Cloth.* prop, stay.

Schrul'le, *(w.) f.* *coll.* whim, odd fancy (Grille, 2).

Schrum'pel, **Schrum'pelig**, *see* Runzel, Runzelig.

Schrum'peln, *(w.) v. intr.* (aux. sein) to wrinkle, shrivel.

Schrumpf, *(str.) m.* waste *or* loss in the weight of (warehoused) corn.

Schrumpf'en, *(w.) v.* I. *intr.* (aux. sein) & *refl.* to shrivel, *cf.* Ein- und Zusammenschrumpfen; II. *intr.* (aux. haben) to rumple (Rumpeln, I, 1); III. *tr.* to cause to shrivel *or* shrink; sch—d, *p. a.* (of the effect of acids, &c.) astringent.

Schrumpf'ig, *adj.* *see* Runzelig.

Schrund, *(str., pl.* Schrün'de*) m.*, **Schrun'de**, *(w.) f.* cleft, chink, crevice, gap, chap.

Schrun'den, *(w.) v. intr.* (aux. sein) & *refl.* to chap, gape, chink, crack, split.

Schrun'dig, *adj.* chappy, chinky; chapped.

Schrupf'en, **Schrup'pen**, *(w.) v. tr.* *see* Schrubben.

Schub [*coll.* schup], *(str., pl.* Schü'be*) m.* 1) shove, push, thrust; throw, turn; 2) *Bak.* batch (of bread); 3) *provinc.* compulsory conveyance *Law*, auf den — bringen, to convey vagabonds to their home; 4) shooting (of the young branches); 5) *see* —fach; 6) *fig.* [illegible] 7) *Gam.* bowl, tip, throw (at ninepins); ein — Kegel, a set of ninepins.

Schu'ben, **Schub'sen**, *(w.) v. tr.* *see* Schieben, &c.

Schub'..., *in comp.* —**blech**, *n.* *Bak.* oven-door-plate; —**fach**, *n.* sliding-box (in a case *or* table), drawer; —**fenster**, *n.* sash, sash-window.

Schub'jack, *(str.) m.* *see* Schuft.

Schub'..., *in comp.* —**karren**, *m.* wheel-barrow; —**kärrner**, *m.* wheel-barrow-man; —**kasten**, *m.* 1) chest of drawers; 2) *or* —**lade**, *f.* drawer; —**ladenschrank**, *m.* *Join.* [illegible]

Schüb'ling, *(str.) m.* 1) young tree; 2) vagabond conveyed to his home by compulsion, *see* Schub, 3; 3) *see* Schubkegel.

Schub'..., *in comp.* —**loch**, *n.* mouth of an oven *or* furnace; —**ochs**, *m.* ox yoked by the head; —**paß**, *m.* *provinc.* compulsory passport, *see* Zwangspaß; —**riegel**, *m.* sliding-bolt, push-bolt; —**sack**, *m.* *coll.* fob, pocket; —**schiff**, *n.* *Mar.* brigantine; —**spiegel**, *m.* looking-glass with a drawer; —**tisch**, *m.* drawer-table; —**transport**, *m.* *see* Schub, 3; —**wand**, *f.* *Min.* bowlders; —**weise**, *adv.* 1) by pushes, thrusts; 2) in turns; 3) [illegible]

Schüch'tern, I. *adj.* shy, coy, [illegible] timid, hesitating, diffident; II. **Sch**[illegible] *f.* shyness, &c., timidity, hesitation, [illegible]

Schuf'teln, *(w.) v. tr.* *for* [illegible]

Schuft, *(str.) m.* scamp, [illegible] muffin, shabby fellow. — **Schuf**[illegible] shabby, rascally behaviour, [illegible] **Schuf'tig**, *adj.* shabby, rascally, [illegible]

Schuh, *(str.) m.* 1) shoe; [illegible] horse's hoof; 2) foot (as a measure) [illegible] shoeing, (pile-shoe, ferrule) [illegible] a mill-hopper); 5) *Mar.* *a)* [illegible] *b)* Sch—e unter einer Stütze, [illegible] unter den Schiffsnadeln, [illegible]

Schumm'perlich, *n.* see Gassenhauer.

Schund, *(str.)* *m.* 1) *orig.* tanner's parings; 2) *a)* filth, offal, refuse; rubbish, trash, lumber; *b) coll.* turd, excrement; *in comp.* —**feger**, —**Gaul**, *m. coll.* scavenger, nightman; —**fett**, *n.* birch-tar; birch-oil; —**grube**, *f.*, —**loch**, *n.* sink. [Schuppen.

Schupf, **Schupfen**, *(S. G.)* see Schupp,

Schupp, *(str.)* *m.* 1) shove, push; 2) *coll.* deceit; 3) see Waschbär.

Schup'pe, *(w.)* *f.* 1) scale; und alsobald fiel es von seinen Augen wie Sch-en (Acts 9, 18), and immediately there fell from his eyes as it had been scales; 2) *pl.* scurf, tetters.

Schüp'pe, *(w.)* *f. provinc.* 1) shovel, scoop; 2) see Spaten, 1.

A. **Schup'pen**, *(w.)* *v. tr.* 1) to furnish with scales; geschuppt, *p. a.* scaly; 2) to scale, unscale.

B. **Schup'pen**, *(w.)* *v. I. tr.* to push, to shove, to elbow; II. *refl.* to scratch, rub one's self. [house; shed, covert.

Schup'pen, *(str.)* *m.* cart-house, coach-

Schüp'pen, *provinc.* see Schäufeln.

Schup'pen..., *in comp.* —**apfel**, *m. Pomol.* custard-apple; —**artig**, *adj.* resembling scales, scaly; —**aussatz**, *m.* leprosy; —**baum**, *m. Petr.* lepidodendron; —**bein**, *n. Anat.* squamous or squamose bone; —**decke**, *f. Bot.* scaly cover; —**eidechse**, *f. Zool.* scaly lizard (a reptile of the genus of *Squamata*); —**fisch**, *m.* scaly fish; —**flechte**, *f.* 1) *Bot. a)* tree-moss, wall-lichen (*Parmelia parietina* L.); *b)* a species of rock-moss (*Lecanora candelaria* L.); 2) *Med.* scaly tetter; —**flosser**, *pl.* squamipens; —**förmig**, *adj.* squamiform, in the form of scales; —**kohle**, *f. Miner.* a kind of pitch-coal; —**kraut**, *n. Bot.* toothwort (*Lathraea squammaria* L.).

Schup'penlos, *adj. Nat.* soft-coated.

Schup'pen..., *in comp.* —**muschel**, *f.* see Riesenmuschel; —**naht**, *f.* the squamous suture or *Anat.* seam of the scull; —**panzer**, *m.* scaly coat of mail; —**pelz**, *m.* raccoon fur-coat, travelling-fur; —**schlange**, *f.* see Kalischlange; —**schnitt**, *m. Herald.* engrailing; —**schwanz**, *m.* scaly tail; —**stein**, *m. Miner.* lepidolite; —**tanne**, *f. Bot.* araucaria (*Araucaria* Juss.); —**thier**, *n. Zool.* manis, pangolin (*Manis* L.); —**wurz**, *f.* see —kraut.

Schup'pig, **Schup'picht**, *adj.* like scales; scaly; scaled; *Bot.* imbricated; ein sch-er Fisch, a rough-coated fish. [fish.

Schupp'messer, *(str.)* *n.* knife for scaling

Schupp'sen, *(w.)* *v. tr.* see Schuppen, *B*, I.

Schur, *(w.)* *f.* 1) the (act of) shearing; clipping (of sheep); shearing-time; 2) fleece, clip; 3) *Cloth.* shearings; 4) crop; 5) fur-skin; 6) *coll.* (*provinc. m.*) spite, vexation; trick.

Schür, *(w.)* *f. T.* mouth of a furnace.

Schür... (*from* Schüren), *in comp.* —**baum**, *m. T.* pole for stirring the fire, poking-pole; —**blech**, *n. T.* wire-frame of a safety-lamp; —**eisen**, *n.* poker, oven-fork.

Schü'ren, *(w.)* *v. tr.* 1) to stir, poke, rake, stoke; 2) *fig.* to stir up, incite; die Flamme —, to add fuel to the flame.

Schü'rer, *(str.)* *m.* 1) poker, raker, stoker; 2) stirrer-up, firebrand.

Schurf, *(str., pl.* Schür'fe) *m.* 1) *T.* scratch, cut; 2) *Min.* opening; einen — werfen, to uncover, open a mine.

Schur'fe, *(w.)* *f.* see Schürfschacht.

Schürf'eisen, *(str.)* *n. Gard.* paddle-staff.

Schür'fen, *(w.)* *v. tr.* 1) to scratch, cut, scrape; 2) *Min.* to open, dig up, uncover (a mine); to trace (veins of metal) by shoads; to trench (the ground) and seek after veins of ore, to burrow.

Schürf... (*from* Schürfen), *in comp.* —**geld**, *n.* reward for the discovery of a vein of ore; —**hobel**, *m.* jack-plane; —**schacht**, *m.* shaft sunk for finding a live lode; —[illegible] —**zettel**, *m.* written permission for a miner to trench the ground and search after veins of ore.

Schür... (*from* Schüren), *in comp.* —**haken**, *m.* fire-hook, poker (—[illegible]); —**herd**, *m.* hearth of a (brick-)kiln; —**holz**, *n.* [illegible] wood for fuel. [illegible]

Schü'rig, *adj.* (*in comp.*) that may be shorn

Schu'rigeln, *(w.)* *v. tr. coll.* to vex, plague, harass.

Schur'ke, *(w.)* *m.* wretch, villain, rascal, knave, scoundrel; Sch-nstreich, *m.*, **Schurkerei'**, *(w.)* *f.* knavery, knavish trick, villany.

Schur'kisch, *adj.* rascally.

Schürf'erz, *(str.)* *n. Miner.* zinc-ore.

Schür'ling, *(str.)* *m.* 1) *cont.* [illegible], shorn priest; 2) sheep with half the wool on it.

Schür'... (*from* Schüren), *in comp.* —**loch**, *n.* 1) stoke-hole, fire-door; 2) flame-or fire-hole, bocca; —**ofen**, *m.* furnace of a kiln.

Schur're, *(w.)* *f.* slide.

Schur'ren, *(w.)* *v. intr.* 1) (*aux.* haben) to scrape, scratch; 2) (*aux.* sein) to slide, fall, rush down.

Schür'... (*from* Schüren), *in comp.* —**schaufel**, *f.* fire-shovel; —**stab**, *m.* poker, *cf.* —**stange**; —**stachel**, *m. Found.* handled poker; —**stange**, *f. Fort.* lance, pole. [wool.

Schur'wolle, *(w.)* *f.* fleece (-wool), shorn

Schurz, *(str., pl.* Schür'ze & Schur'ze) *m.* 1) apron; 2) *T-s. a) Salt-w.* the lower part of a thatched roof or the gutter of a salt-house-roof; *b) Archit.* mantle (of a chimney); *c) Hunt.* hind-part of a deer, wing, &c.; *d) Cook.* apron (of geese); *Min.* chain (round a coal, &c.).

Schür'zange, *(w.)* *f.* chimney-tongs.

Schurz'band, **Schürz'band**, *(str., Sch-bänder)* *n.* scarf; belt.

Schür'ze, *(w.)* *f.* apron.

Schür'zen, *(w.)* *v. tr.* 1) to tie, to tuck, pin, or truss up; 2) to put on apron; den Knoten —, *Dram.* to tie or fasten the knot; der Knoten schürzt sich (enger), the plot thickens.

Schür'zen..., *in comp.* —**band**, *n.* apron-string; *burl-s.* —**stipendiat**, *m.* petticoat-pensioner; —**stipendium**, *n.* petticoat-pension.

Schurz'..., *in comp.* —**fell**, —**leder**, *n.* leather-apron; *Min.* miner's breech-leather; —**fleck**, *m.* small apron; —**holz**, *n. Archit.* mantle-tree. [framing, &c.

Schür'zung, *(w.)* *f.* the (act of) tying,

Schurz'werk, *(str.)* *n. Carp.* [illegible] key-piece (Tüll.).

Schu'sel, *(w.)* *f.* 1) *coll.* a hasty, bustling person, busybody, fidget; *provinc.* [illegible]

Schüs'sel, *(w.)* *f.* dish; bowl; [illegible] (wooden) platter, charger.

Schüs'sel..., *in comp.* —[illegible], *m.* [illegible] plume-alum; —**brett**, *n.* shelf for plates, [illegible] &c., waiter; rack; —[illegible], *m.* [illegible]

Schüs'selchen, *(str.)* *n.* (*dimin.* of Schüssel) small dish; *Bot.* saucer.

Schüs'seler, *(str.)* *m. coll.* see [illegible]

Schüs'sel..., *in comp.* —[illegible], *f.* [illegible] tree-lichen, wall-lichen ([illegible] L.); —**förmig**, *adj.* dish-formed, [illegible] *Nat.* patelliform, scutellated; —[illegible] see Schmarotzer, 1; —[illegible], *f.* [illegible] glass); —[illegible], *m.* see —[illegible] concave or shell-button; —[illegible] basket; —**kranz**, *m.* dish-cover; —[illegible] Schmarotzer, 1; —[illegible], *f.* [illegible] (Napfschnecke); —[illegible], *m.* [illegible] —**ring**, *m.* dish-ring, stand; —[illegible] bicular; —**schrank**, *m.* [illegible] schwamm, *m.* a genus of fungi [illegible] *m. Min.* alveole; —[illegible] *m.* dish-heater; —[illegible], *f.* [illegible] cullion.

Schu'ster, *(str.)* *m.* [illegible]

[illegible], (w.) v. intr. ([illegible]) to [illegible] weakly, or poorly.

[illegible], (w.) v. tr. 1) to weaken, [illegible], [illegible], [illegible]; to impair, [illegible]; 2) to [illegible].

[illegible], I. adj. compar. of Schwach; II. s. (str.) m. 1) weaker, &c.; 2) [illegible].

Schwach'..., in comp. –gläubig, adj. weak in faith, of little faith; –gläubigkeit, f. weakness of faith.

Schwach'heit, (w.) f. weakness, &c. see Schwache; frailty; Sch-sünde, f. venial sin.

Schwach'..., in comp. –herzig, –mütig, adj. faint-hearted; –kopf, m. dunce; –köpfig, adj. silly.

[illegible], I. adj. infirm, feeble, weakly, [illegible], sickly; II. Sch-keit, (w.) f. feebleness, sickliness. [illegible]

[illegible], (str.) m. weakling; weakly

[illegible], m. (from Schwach, with Lat. (ir) termination) [illegible] (cf. [illegible]) person weak in body and mind.

Schwach'..., in comp. –sinn, m., –sinnigkeit, f. weakness of mind; –sinnig, adj. weak in mind.

Schwäch'ung, (w.) f. 1) the (act of) weakening, &c. see Schwächen; debilitation; 2) [illegible]; Sch-mittel, n. Med. lowering medicine; [illegible], f. [illegible] of [illegible].

Schwade, (str.) n. (m.), Schwa'de, (w.) f. swath, row, or line of mowed corn, grass, &c.

Schwa'den, (str.) m. 1) see Schwade; 2) a) Min. damp, exhalation, vapour: [illegible] –, fire-damp; b) [illegible]; 3) [illegible] short tail of a hunt; 4. Bot. or –gras, n. –grütze, f. –[illegible], m. grass [illegible], floating hairgrass, floating fescue-grass ([illegible] L.); –grütze, f. see [illegible]

[illegible], see [illegible]. [illegible]

[illegible], (str.) n. (dimin. = "little babbler") [illegible] for [illegible].

[illegible], (w.) v. intr. to prate, to prattle, babble, &c., cf. [illegible].

[illegible], (w.) f. Mil. squadron, company of horse. [illegible], swaggerer.

[illegible] (pr. –[illegible]), (str.) m. great

[illegible], (w.) v. intr. to swagger; to talk much, to talk big.

[illegible], (w.) v. see [illegible], II.

Schwa'ger, (str., pl. Schwä'ger) m. 1) brother-in-law; 2) fam. postilion.

Schwä'gerin, (w.) f. I sister-in-law; II. coll. for [illegible]. [in-law.

Schwä'gerlich, adj. & adv. like a brother-

Schwä'gerschaft, (w.) f. affinity (by marriage of sisters or brothers), brother-in-lawship.

[illegible], (str.) m., [illegible], (w.) f. [illegible] 1) for [illegible]; 2) for persons whose children have married; 3) for one related by marriage ([illegible]).

[illegible], see [illegible].

[illegible], (w.) f. province. 1) cattle-herd; 2) a) pasture (in the Alps, &c.); b) dairy ([illegible]). — [illegible], (str.) m., [illegible], (w.) f. see [illegible], [illegible].

[illegible], [illegible], (str.) m. or –eisen, (str.) n. Found. [illegible]-slag; –arbeit, f. Metall. slag-bottom process; –boden, m. slag-bed, slag-bottom.

Schwal'be, (w.) f. (dimin. Schwälb'chen, (str.) n. little swallow) 1) swallow (Hirundo L.); 2) see [illegible]; 3) [illegible] on the oar.

Schwal'ben, (w.) v. tr. Carp. to scarf with a swallow-tail, to dovetail.

Schwal'ben..., in comp. –adler, m. [illegible] or white-tailed eagle ([illegible] L.); –beerbaum, m. Bot. [illegible] ([illegible]); –eisen, n. T. dovetailing-iron; –falk, m. sparrow-hawk ([illegible]);

–[illegible], m. [illegible] [illegible]; –fliege, f. [illegible]; –flug, m. flight of swallows; [illegible] –fuß; 2) [illegible]; [illegible] –, [illegible] –kraut, n. Bot. [illegible] wort, [illegible] or great celandine ([illegible] L.); –nelke, f. [illegible]; –nest, n. swallow's [illegible]

Schwal'benschwanz, &c. [illegible] m. 1) swallow-tail; 2) Entom. swallow-tail butterfly ([illegible] L.); 3) [illegible], kite ([illegible]); 4) [illegible] tail, dove-tail; b) Mar. swallow-tail, [illegible] 5) T-a. swallow-tail (a kind of [illegible]), a roof-tail, a window, &c., so called [illegible] their form, cf. [illegible]; [illegible] [illegible], to dovetail ([illegible]) [illegible] –[illegible], m. Carp. dovetail-[illegible] –[illegible], f. swallow-tailed [illegible], dove-tail-hinge; –[illegible], m. Min. [illegible] a swallow-tailed or notched [illegible]; –[illegible], m. T. dovetail-screw; –[illegible], f. dovetail-[illegible] –[illegible], [illegible] man's eyes; –säge, f. dovetail saw; –[illegible], f. dovetailing; –zapfen, m. dovetailed tenon.

Schwal'ben..., in comp. –[illegible], m. [illegible], [illegible]; –[illegible], m. [illegible] ([illegible], 2); –[illegible], m. [illegible] a species of [illegible]-bird ([illegible] L.); –[illegible], f. 1) see –[illegible]; 2) [illegible] ([illegible]).

[illegible], [illegible], (str.) m. T. opening in the partition-wall of a [illegible] furnace, by which the flame goes in upon the melting metal.

[illegible], (w.) f. [illegible]

[illegible], (str.) m. Mar. [illegible]

[illegible], (w.) v. [illegible]. I. intr. [illegible] to [illegible]; II. tr. see [illegible].

[illegible], (str.) m. [illegible]

[illegible], (str.) m. any large mass of agitated things, such as [illegible], rushing and roaring waters, [illegible]; tumult; throng, multitude, [illegible] — [illegible], a host of questions. —

[illegible], (w.) v. intr. to [illegible]

[illegible], (str.) m. [illegible]

[illegible], (w.) f. [illegible] fishes and side-[illegible] of a [illegible].

[illegible], s. I. (str., pl. [illegible]) 1) sponge; 2) Bot. a) fungus; b) for [illegible]; 3) German tinder; 4) [illegible] fungus, [illegible] thrush, [illegible]; b) Surv. [illegible] some; [illegible]; [illegible] affair, &c. the whole [illegible] comp. –artig, adj. fungous, [illegible] form; –baum, m. a [illegible] –[illegible], f. 1) sponge-[illegible] –[illegible], m. sponge-[illegible].

[illegible], (str.) m. [illegible] ([illegible]) 1) little sponge; 2) [illegible] 6, c.

[illegible]..., in comp. [illegible] red [illegible]; –[illegible], adj. [illegible] [illegible], f. Med. [illegible] fungous [illegible]; –[illegible]

[illegible], adj. [illegible]

[illegible], I. adj. [illegible] proud, fungous, [illegible] f. spongious; [illegible].

[illegible]..., in comp. [illegible] wort ([illegible]); –[illegible] acid; –[illegible], f. [illegible] fungine, sponge-[illegible] [illegible]; –[illegible], m. [illegible]

[illegible], (str., [illegible]) [illegible] ([illegible])

[illegible], (str.) [illegible]

Bombyliden, two genera of dipterous insects: *a) Syrphus* F.; *b) Bombylius* L.

Schwe'beln, *(w.) v. intr.* to soar, hover lightly, to float hither and thither; — und nebeln, *coll.* to vapour, brag.

Schwe'ben, *(w.) v. intr.* 1) to wave, soar, hover, plane, hang; to glide, sail, flit, float; 2) to be suspended; to be pending *or* undecided; in Ungewißheit —, to float, to be (kept) in suspense; in Gefahr —, to be in danger; auf der Zunge —, to be at one's tongue's end; sch-d, *p. a.* suspended; pending; sch-de Eisenbahn, suspension railway; sch-de Eisenbahnbrücke, railway suspension bridge; sch-des Gerüst, flying scaffold; sch-de Insel, floating island; sch-de Schuld, floating *or* pending debt.

Schwe'ber, *(str.) m.* 1) *see* Schwebfliege; 2) *Horol.* a) balance; b) balance-wheel, *see* Unruhe, 4.

Schwe'b(e)..., *in comp.* —riemen, *m.* (eines Geschirrs) *Saddl.* bearing-strap, hip-strap *(T. Tusch.)*; —schritt, *m. Danc.* balance; —stange, *f.* balancing pole, poy; —strich, *m. Build.* rubble-floor, wash-floor upon laths *(T. Tusch.)*.

Schwe'bung, *(w.) f.* 1) the (act of) swinging, &c.; vibration; 2) tremor (an organ-stop).

Schwe'de, *(w.) m.* 1) Swede; alter —, *fam.* honest fellow; 2) *coll. for* a Swedish horse, coin, &c.; Sch-kopf, *m.* a closely cropped head of hair, a (Swedish) roundhead. — **Schwe'den**, *n. Geogr.* Sweden. — **Schwe'din**, *(w.) f.* Swedish woman. — **Schwe'disch**, *adj.* Swedish.

Schwe'der, *(str.) m. provinc.* sweetbread.

Schwe'derich, *(str.) m. T.* 1) channel produced by a mill-race; 2) a long fishing-net with a sack-like bottom.

Schwe'fel, *(str.) m. Miner.* brimstone, sulphur; — in Stangen, brimstone in rolls, roll sulphur.

Schwe'fel..., *in comp.* —abdruck, *m.* print in brimstone, sulphur impression; —alkohol, *m. Chem.* sulphuret of carbon, carburet *or* percarburet of sulphur; —ammonium, *n. Chem.* sulphuret of ammonia; —artig, *adj.* sulphurous; —äther, *m. Chem.* sulphuric ether; —bad, *n. Med.* 1) sulphurated bath; 2) sulphurous spring; —balsam, *m. Pharm.* sulphurated oil, balsam of sulphur; —blausäure, *f.* sulpho-cyanic acid; —blausaures Salz, sulphocyanide; —blei, *n.* sulphuret *or* sulphide of lead (Bleiglanz); —blumen, —blüten, *f. pl. Pharm.* flowers of sulphur, sublimed sulphur; —brennofen, *m. see* —treibofen; —brunnen, *m. see* —quelle; —cyan, *n. Chem.* sulpho-cyanogen, bisulphuret of cyanogen; —dampf, *m.* steam of brimstone, sulphurous exhalation; —dampfbad, *n.* sulphur-fume-bath, sulphurous steam-bath; —einschlag, *m.* (act of) sulphuring (wine-casks); —eisen, *n.* sulphuret of iron; —erde, *f.* sulphurous earth; —faden, *m.* brimstone-match; —fang, *m.* hole for roasted sulphur; —farbe, *f.* yellow, brimstone colour; —farben, —farbig, —gelb, *adj.* of the colour of sulphur, sulphurate; —geruch, *m.* smell of sulphur, sulphureous smell. —gold, *n.* protosulphuret of gold; —grube, *f.* brimstone-pit; —haltig, *adj.* sulphurous; —hölzchen, *n.* lucifer(-match); —hütte, *f.* brimstone-house.

Schwe'felicht, *adj.* like sulphur; sulphurous; *Chem.-s.* sch-e Säure, sulphurous acid; —saures Kali, sulphite of potash.

Schwe'felig, *adj.* sulphureous; —saures Salz, sulphite.

Schwe'fel..., *in comp.* —kammer, *f.* sulphuring-room; —kies, *m. Miner.* pyrites; —kobalt, *m.* sulphuret of cobalt; —kohle, *f.* coal containing sulphur; —kohlenstoff, *m. see* —alkohol; —kolben, *m.* retort for purifying brimstone; —kuchen, *m.* plate of sulphur; —kupfer, *n.* sulphuret of copper; —läuterofen, *m. see* —treibofen; —leber, *f.* [illegible] sulphuret of potash (*or* of potassium); [illegible] sulphur; —luft, *f.* sulphureous gas; —[illegible] chen, *n. Min.* sulphur wick; —meister, *m.* foreman of a sulphur-kiln; —milch, *f. Pharm.* precipitated sulphur, milk of sulphur.

Schwe'feln, *(w.) v. tr.* to anoint with sulphur, to sulphurate; to dip in brimstone; ein Faß —, to match a cask; Hüte —, to bleach hats with brimstone.

Schwe'fel..., *in comp.* —öl, *n.* sulphuric acid (Vitriolöl); —quelle, *f.* sulphureous spring; —regen, *m.* shower of rain intermixed with the yellow dust of the blossoms of the red fir; —rose, *f. Gard.* yellow rose; —röste, *f.* roasting of sulphur; *Chem.-s.* —salze, *n. pl.* sulphur salts; —sauer, *adj.* sulphuric; —saures Salz, sulphate; —saures Natron, Kali, *n.*, Kalk, *m.*, Chinin, *n.*, Bittererde, Thonerde, *f.* sulphate of soda, potash, lime, quinine, magnesia, alumina; —saure Strontian, *n. see* Cölestin, 2; —säure, *f.* sulphuric acid; —silber, *n.* sulphuret of silver; —stangen, *pl. see* Schwefel in Stangen; —theil, *m.*, —theilchen, *n.* sulphureous particles; —treibofen, *m.* fixed and capped furnace for refining *or* extracting sulphur.

Schwe'felung, *(w.) f.* sulphuration, washing *or* bleaching with brimstone.

Schwe'fel..., *in comp.* —verbindung, *f.* sulphuret; —wasser, *n.* sulphurated water, sulphureous water; —wasserstoff, *m.* sulphuretted hydrogen, hydro-sulphuric acid; —wasserstoffammonium, *n.* hydrosulphuret of ammonia; —wasserstoffsäure, *f.* hydrosulphuric *or* hydrothionic acid (—wasserstoff); das —wasserstoffsaure Salz, hydrosulphate, hydrothionate; —werk, *n.* brimstone house, place where sulphur is made; —wurz, *f. Bot.* sulphur-wort *(Peucedanum* L.); —zink, [illegible] *n.* sulphuret of zinc, tin. [illegible]

Schwe'rze, *(w.) f. Sport.* [illegible]

Schwe'gel, *(w.) f. provinc.* 1) pipe, flute; 2) flute-register (of an organ).

Schwe'len, *see* Schwelen.

Schwe'ken, *(w.) v. intr. Mar.* to swing, tend. — **Schwe'kenhalse**, *(w.) f.* stopper with lanyards.

Schweif, *(str.) m.* 1) (a large, full) tail; train; 2) end; *cf.* Schwanz; — der Auster, beard of the oyster; *in comp. (cf.* Schwanz) —bratler, *m. Zool.* dasyure (Raubschwanz); —brett, *n.* board across a loommaker's loom for bearing the spools; —bügel, *m.* a kind of stirrup.

Schwei'fen, *(w.) v.* I. *intr.* (*aux.* fein) to rove, stray, ramble, range; II. *tr.* 1) to give a tail to ...; 2) to put into a waving [illegible] sweep; 3) *T.* to put into a curve or [illegible] form, to curve; 4) to winnow [illegible] to warp; 5) to rinse.

Schweif... *(cf.* Schwanz) [illegible] *n. pl.* hairs of the tail; [illegible] (Leierschwanz); —[illegible], *m.* tail-[illegible] men, *m. see* Schwanzriemen; —[illegible] ribbing-saw; —spiegelnd, *adj.* [illegible] spread tail (said of the peacock) [illegible] *see* Sonnenreiher; —stern, *m.* hairy [illegible] —träger, *m.* tail-carrier, train-bearer [illegible]

Schwei'fung, *(w.) f.* curve, [illegible] einer Glocke, body or barrel of a bell [illegible]

Schwei'fwedeln, *(w. insep.)* [illegible] to wag the tail) to fawn.

Schwei'gegeld, *(str., pl.* [illegible]

Schwei'gen, *(str.) v.* I. *intr.* 1) [illegible] to keep silence, to forbear [illegible] shut up; 3) to stop, cease [illegible] or reply nothing; to take no [illegible] 1) *, not to mention, to [illegible] ing; 2) to (put to) silence, [illegible] to nonplus; tasi —, to [illegible]

Schwei'gen, *n. (str.)* [illegible]

Schwie'ger..., *in comp.* –kinder, *n. pl.* children-in-law; –sohn, *m.* son-in-law; –tochter, *f.* daughter-in-law.

Schwie'le, *(w.) f.* callosity, preternatural hardness of the skin; hard swelling; marks of a stripe, weal; *Med.* ecchymosis; sch-nervig, *adj. Bot.* callose; Sch-nsohler, *m. pl. Zool.* the family *Tylopida* [Ill.], *or Camelidæ.*

Schwie'lig, *adj.* callous; marked with weals.

Schwie'mel, *(str.) m. coll.* 1) giddiness; 2) *or* **Schwiem'ler,** *m.* loose, dissolute person, rake. – **Schwiem'lig,** *adj.* 1) giddy; 2) *see* Benebelt; 3) loose, dissolute, rakish. – **Schwie'meln,** *(w.) v. intr.* 1) to reel, stagger; 2) to lead a loose, rakish life.

Schwiem'schlag, *(str., pl.* Sch-schläge) *m. Mar.* das Schiff liegt im Sch–e, the ship stays.

Schwie'ping, *(w.) f. Mar.-s.* point; –stopper, *m.* pointed stopper.

Schwie'rig, I. *adj.* 1) hard, difficult, *cf.* Schwer, 2; sch-e Verhältnisse, trying circumstances; das Volk bleibt –, the people continue refractory *or* mutinous; *fig.-s.* 2) nice, difficult to please, fastidious, scrupulous; 3) unruly, refractory; die Gläubiger zeigen sich etwas –, the creditors prove rather unyielding; II. Sch-keit, *(w.) f.* 1) hardness, difficulty, *&c.*; 2) objection; Sch-en machen, to raise difficulties, to start objections; alles geht ohne –, all goes on swimmingly.

Schwig'ten, *(w.) v. tr. & intr. Mar.* to snake (two ropes) together.

Schwig'ting, *(w.) f. Mar. partic. pl.* (Schwigt'linen) lines to snake two ropes together; Sch-en der Puttingtaue, catharpings; –sorring, *(w.) f.* mainsail's spinning-line.

Schwimm'... *(from* Schwimmen), *in comp.* –angel, *f. Angl.* angling-line with a float; –anstalt, *f.* swimming institution *or* school; –blase, *f.* swimming bladder, air-bladder.

Schwim'men, *(str.) v. intr. (aux.* haben & sein) to swim; to float; es schwimmt mir vor den Augen, my brain swims; – lassen, 1) to set swimming; 2) *fig.* to let pass, to give up without any effort to bring back what seems to be lost, *&c.*; sch-d, *p. a.* floating; sch-des Gebirg, *Min.* boggy rock; in seinem Blute sch-d, bathed in his blood, ° weltering in his gore; in Blut sch-de Straßen, streets deluged in blood; es schwimmt das Herz in Seligkeit, the heart is bathed in bliss.

Schwim'mer, *(str.) m.* 1) swimmer; 2) *Entom. see* Schwimmkäfer; 3) *see* Schwimmfuß, 2; 4) *Mech.* float, water-gage (of a steam-engine boiler); 5) a thin Danish coin: bracteate.

Schwimm'... *(from* Schwimmen), *in comp.* –feder, *n.* fin; –fuß, *m.* 1) palmated *or* webbed foot, swimming paw; 2) *or* –füßler, *m.* web-footed animal, *pl.* palmipeds *(Palmipedia)*; –füßig, *adj.* web-footed; –gürtel, *m.* life-belt *or* buoy; –haut, *f. Ornith.* web; –hemd, *n.* cork-jacket; –hosen, *f. pl.* drawers, bathing trowsers; –jacke, *f.* swimming *or* air-jacket; –käfer, *m. Entom.* water-beetle *(Dytiscus* L.); –kiesel, –stein, *m. Min.* spongiform quartz, float-stone; –krabbe, *f. Crust.* the paddling crab, the paddler *(Portunus* F.); –kraft, *f.* buoyancy; –kugel, *f. see* Schwimmer, 4; –kunst, *f.* art of swimming; –maus, *f.* the South-American water-rat *(Myopotamus coypus* Geoffr.); –netz, *n.* drag-net; –plätter, *m. see* –fuß, 2; –schnecke, *f. Mollusc.* a genus of molluscs *(Neritina* Lam.); –schule, *f.* swimming school; –vogel, *m.* swimming-bird, web-footed bird; –wanze, *f. Entom.* water-bug *(Naucoris cimicoides* L.); –zeug, *n.* no[illegible] for swimming.

Schw[illegible] *f.* latter, *see* Flechte.

Schwin'del, [illegible] *Alfaliness*, giddiness, swimming of the head, turning of the brain; vertigo; *Vet.* staggers; den – bekom-men, to turn giddy; 2) *fig.* extravagant[illegible] *cf.* Schwindel, 1; –[illegible], *m.* [illegible]rifel.

Schwin'delei, *(w.) f.* 1) extravag[illegible] gambling project, bubble, giddy [illegible] thoughtless action; 2) cheat, fraud, [illegible] swindling, dodge, do; bubble.

Schwin'del..., *in comp.* –geist, *m.* 1) [illegible] rit of giddiness, giddy mind; 2) *fig.* [illegible] headed, thoughtless person, *coll.* [illegible] brained fellow; 3) swindler; –geschäft, [illegible] bubbles, gambling projects; –gesellschaft [illegible] bubble-company; –hafer, *m. Bot.* [illegible] tare (Taumellolch).

Schwin'delhaft, *adj.* 1) extravagant [illegible] cheating, fraudulent. [illegible]

Schwin'delhoch, *adj.* so high as to [illegible]

Schwin'delig, *see* Schwindlig.

Schwin'del..., *in comp.* –[illegible], *m.* [illegible] –geist, 2; –korn, *n.* 1) *or* –lolch, *m.* [illegible] hafer; 2) –körner, *n. pl.* coriander seed [illegible] kraut, *n. see* –kern; –mittel, *n.* [illegible] against giddiness.

Schwin'deln, *(w.) v. intr. impers.* ([illegible] *Dat.* es schwindelt mir) 1) to be dizzy, gi[illegible] to reel, to be seized with vertigo; to [illegible] swim; 2) *fig.* a) to act in a thoughtless [illegible] ner; b) to swindle, to cheat; mir schwin[illegible] my brain reels, my head swims, I am gi[illegible] sch-d, *p. a.* dizzy, giddy, *see* Schwindelig.

Schwin'del..., *in comp.* –sucht, *f.* [illegible] vertigo; –süchtig, *adj.* harebrained; –[illegible] *n.* cephalic water; –wurz, *f.* great langu[illegible] bane *(Doronicum* L.).

Schwin'den, I. *(str.) v. intr. (aux.* [illegible] 1) to disappear, vanish; 2) to dwindle [illegible] fail; to wear off; to die away, to decay, [illegible] waste, fade, wane, fall; to shrink, to lo[illegible] weight *or* measure; – lassen, to [illegible] abandon, forego, give up, let go; II. [illegible] *(str.) n. T.* shrinkage.

Schwind'..., *in comp.* –fieber, *m.* h[illegible] fever; –flechte, *f.* tetter; –grube, *f. see* [illegible]grube.

Schwind'ler, *(str.) m.* 1) extravagant [illegible] jector; 2) swindler, dodger, diddler.

Schwind'lig, *adj.* giddy, dizzy; [illegible] giddy.

Schwind'maß, *(str.) n. T.* 1) (gauge [illegible] of) shrinkage; 2) (–stab, *m.*) contraction[illegible]

Schwind'sucht, *(w.) f. Med.* consump[illegible] phthisis. – **Schwind'süchtig,** I. *adj.* [illegible] sumptive, hectic, phthisical; II. Sch-[illegible] *(w.) f.* consumptiveness.

Schwind'wurz, *f. see* Schöllkraut.

Schwing'e, *(w.) f.* 1) winnow; fan; [illegible] swingle, swingle-knife; 2) *pl.* [illegible] waggon-rack); 3) °, wing, pinion.

Schwing'(e)brett, *(str., pl.* Sch-er) [illegible] brake; swingle-board. [illegible]

Schwing'el, *(str.) m. Bot.* fescue, [illegible]

Schwing'en, *(str.) v.* I. *intr.* to swing, [illegible] cillate, vibrate; II. *tr.* 1) to brandish, [illegible] wave, shake; 2) to winnow, fan; 3) [illegible] (flax, *&c.*); 4) to wing; [illegible] schwingt, winged; 5) *see* [illegible] to swing one's self (up, into, *&c.*) [illegible] leap, vault; to soar, to rise, [illegible] Pferd –, to throw one's self on [illegible]

Schwing'... *(from* Schwingen) [illegible] –feder, *f. see* Schwungfeder, 2; –[illegible] *Entom.* balancer, poiser [illegible] gräß.) halteres; –holz, *n.* [illegible] *f. see* Schwungkraft; –[illegible] *or* scutching-machine; –[illegible] er, firstlings; –messer, –[illegible] knife; –pflug, *m. Agric.* [illegible] *n. see* Schwungseil; –[illegible] sieve; –stock, *m.* [illegible] –uhr, *f.* pendulum-clock.

Schwing'ung, *(w.) f.* [illegible] ing, *&c.*, swing; vibration [illegible]

See [illegible] —**aal**, m. [illegible]

[illegible] —**baromèter**, m. marine barometer. —**bericht**, m. [illegible] —**beruf**, m. see [illegible]; —**beruhigung**, [illegible] —**befehls-haber**, m. [illegible] —**berichte**, pl. ship-news; —**beschreibung**, f. hydrography. —**beute**, f. prize. —**beutel**, m. [illegible] —**bieber**, m. see —otter; —**binse**, f. Bot. see [illegible] —**blase**, f. see —beutel; —**blume**, f. 1) Bot. a) water-lily (Seerose); b) [illegible] 2) Polyp. sea-anemone. —**bock**, m. see [illegible]; —**bohne**, f. see [illegible]; —**boot**, n. sea-boat. —**bote**, m. see [illegible]; —**brassen**, m. Ichth. sea-bream [illegible] —**brauch**, m. see [illegible]; —**brause**, f. Mar. [illegible] —**brief**, m. Mar. passport for shipping, sea-letter, sea-brief [illegible] ship's papers. —**buch**, n. log-book. —**bühne**, f. [illegible] —**bulle**, f. Ichth. [illegible] —**cadett**, m. midshipman. —**carte**, f. see —karte; —**compaß**, m. sea- or mariner's compass; —**consulat**, n. maritime court in France, Spain and Italy. —**contract**, m. charter-party. —**dampfboot**, n. ocean-steamer. —**dampfboot-kessel**, m. Mech. marine boiler. —**dieb**, [illegible] naval thief. —**dienst**, m. sea- or maritime service [illegible] —**dorf**, n. Archæol. lacustrine habitation (Pfahlbau, z.); —**drache**, m. Ichth. 1) sea-dragon, [illegible] pegasus (Pe- [illegible]

[illegible] variety of the [illegible] —**fahrer**, m. [illegible] —**fahrt**, f. [illegible] —**fisch**, m. [illegible] —**flagge**, f. [illegible] —**friede**, [illegible] —**gebrauch**, m. custom at sea. —**gefecht**, n. sea-fight, naval combat, engagement at sea. —**gefahr**, —**gefilde**, —**gegend**, [illegible] —**gericht**, n. court of admiralty. —**gericht**, m. [illegible] —**geschäft**, n. shipping business. —**gesicht**, n. see Meeresgesicht. —**gesetz**, n. [illegible] —**gespenst**, m. [illegible] —**gewächs**, n. sea-plant, marine plant. —**gewohnt**, adj. 1) accustomed to a sea-faring life; 2) acquainted with the art of navigation. —**gras**, n. Bot. sea-grass, sea-wrack, grass-wrack (Zostera marina L.). —**grasblatt**, f. [illegible] —**grün**, n. sea-green. —**grund**, m. bottom or ground of the sea. —**gründel**, m. Ichth. smooth blenny (Blennius pholis L.). —**gurke**, f. Echin. sea-cucumber (Holothuria L.). —**gut**, n. Comm. goods for foreign export. —**hafen**, m. sea-port. —**hafer**, m. Bot. Canadian wild rice, Indian rice, water-oat (Zizania aquatica L.); —**hahn**, m. [illegible] (Trigla L.). —**haltend**, adj. seaworthy. —**hand**, f. sea-hand, see —hund; —**handel**, m. maritime commerce, sea-commerce, sea-trade; —**handlungsgesellschaft**, f. society of maritime commerce. —**hanf**, m. a kind of coarse thick hemp. —**hase**, m. 1) Ichth. lump-fish, sea-owl (Lump [illegible]); 2) Molluc. sea-hare (Aplysia depilans L.). —**held**, m. naval hero. —**herrschaft**, f. sovereignty of the ocean. —**heuschrecke**, f. Crust. common lobster (Hummer). —**höhe**, f. Mar. offing. —**holderstrauch**, [illegible] Bot. water-knotgrass (Wasserknöterich); —**hose**, f. water-spout. —**huhn**, n. Ornith. [illegible]

[illegible] **See'fra**[illegible] **See'ra**[illegible] **See'len**[illegible] **See'le**, [illegible] **Seelen**. [illegible] **See**[illegible] **See'len**.. [illegible] —**sub**[illegible] **tigam**, m. [illegible] soul. —**fr**[illegible] chology. [illegible] **bru**, m. [illegible] extremely [illegible] greatness. —**gut** [illegible] tion for any or heart. **See'lenhe**[illegible] **See'len**.. welfare of [illegible]

to manage sails; —kunst, *f.* art of sailing or navigation. [poles.

Se'gellos, *adj.* sailless; *Mar.* under bare

Se'gel..., *in comp.* —macher, *m.* sail-maker; —macherwerkstatt, *f.* sail-(maker's) loft; —meister, *m.* mariner who has the care of the sails.

Se'geln, *(w.) v.* I. *intr.* (aux. haben & sein) to sail; mit vollem Winde —, to sail whole wind; mit halbem Winde —, to go with a tack-wind; hart —, to press sail, to carry a press of sail; ein schlecht beim Winde [—des Schiff, bad plyer; bad sailing vessel upon a wind; vessel that makes much lee-way; II. *tr.* ein Schiff todt —, to beat a ship (in sailing); in den Grund —, to sink (a vessel).

Se'gel..., *in comp.* —nadel, *f.* sail-(maker's) needle; —ordn[illegible] order of sailing; —palme, *f.* sailor's palm; —[illegible]lle, *f.* *Aool.* a genus of Acalepha (*Velella* Lam.); —ring, *m.* ring of a sail; —schiff, *n.* sailing vessel (*opp.* Dampfschiff); —schneider, *m.* sail-maker; —schnelligkeit, *f.* rate of sailing, run (of a ship); —soll, *n.* tack; —spiel, *n.* set or suit of sails; —spinne, *f.* cross-spider, hazel-spider (Kreuzspinne); —spur, *f.* track of a ship; —stange, *f.* sail-yard; —steifes Schiff, stiff ship, a ship which carries her sail very stiff; —stricke, *m. pl.* see Brasse; —tafel, *f.* *Naut.* tables for sailing; —tuch, *n.* sail-cloth, canvass; (leichtes) duck; —vogel, *m.* see —falter; —wagen, *m.* sailing-chariot; —werk, *n.* sails; —wetter, *n.* weather favourable for sailing; (schlechtes) foul weather; —wind, *m.* fair wind *or* breeze; —zunge, *f.* gore of a sail.

Se'gen, *(str.) m.* 1) sign of the cross made with the hand; 2) blessing, benediction: grace; 3) conjuration, see Zaubersegen; 4) *fig.* *a)* bliss, blessing; *b)* rich gift; — des Bergbaues, proceeds of mining (considered as a blessing bestowed by God); viel — bringen, *fig.* to impart a great blessing; den — sprechen, to give the benediction; to say grace; an Gottes — ist alles gelegen, *proverb.* God's blessing gained, is all obtained; das Andenken der Gerechten bleibet im — (*Prov.* 10, 7), the memory of the just is blessed.

Se'gen(s)baum, *m.* see Sadebaum.

Se'gen(s)los, *adj.* unblessed. [ful.

Se'gen(s)reich, *adj.* rich in blessing, bliss-

Se'gens... (*cf.* Segen...), *in comp.* —ernte, *f.* blessed, or abundant harvest; —fülle, *f.* fulness or abundance of blessings; —hand, *f.* blessing hand; —kraft, *f.* power of blessings; —kräftig, *adj.* efficacious in blessing; —land, *n.* land of blessings.

Se'gen... (*cf.* Segens...), *in comp.* —sprecher, *m.* conjurer, enchanter, charmer, sorcerer, spell-writer; —sprecherei', *f.* spelling, conjuration, magical words; —spruch, *m.* benediction, blessing.

Se'gens... (*cf.* Segen...), *in comp.* —quelle, *f.* source of a blessing; —wunsch, *m.* wish for a blessing.

Se'gensvoll, *adj.* blessed.

Seg'ge, *(w.) f.* *Bot.* sag, sedge (Riedgras, 2).

Seg'ler, *(str.) m.* 1) sailor; 2) ship, sailer; ein guter —, a fast-sailing vessel; ein schlechter —, a bad, dull, or heavy sailer or plyer; ein vorzüglicher —, clipper-ship; — der Lüfte, *fig.* aerial travellers (*Schiller*, of the clouds); 3) see [illegible]; 4) *Num.* see Drehling, 1; 5) see Segelfalter; 6) *Ornith.* swift (Thurmschwalbe).

* **Segment',** *(str.) n.* (*Lat.*) *Geom.* segment; —bogen, *m.* segmental arch.

Seg'nen, *(w.) v. tr.* (*cf.* Beiegnen) 1) to bless; to utter a benediction; 2) to make the sign of the cross on, to *[illegible]*; 3) *Bibl.* to [illegible]: gesegneten Leibes, with child, pregnant.

Seg'nung, *(w.) f.* blessing; benediction.

Seh'axe, *(w.) f.* *Opt.* axis of vision. [illegible]

Seh'bar, *adj.* visible. [illegible]

Seh'e, *(w.) f.* *coll.* 1) pupil of the [illegible] 2) eye-sight.

Seh'e... (*from* Sehen), *in comp.* see Seh...

Se'hen (*pr. also* se'gn), *(str.) v. tr. & [illegible]* 1) to see; perceive; 2) to look; 3) to [illegible] view; 4) to be sensible of; 5) to [illegible] *for* Aussehen. 2. to look, *i. e.* have a particular appearance; er sieht gut. *coll.* (*for* er sieht gut aus), he looks well (*cf.* *Mrs.* [illegible], 1, 247: State Street never saw better [illegible] looked, ...) hatte sie besser [illegible] —, to have a good eye-sight; nicht [illegible] sehen, to be short-sighted, [illegible]; [illegible] to be seen on view; ich [illegible] I saw him lying there; die [illegible] welche sie [illegible], the cruelties which she saw committed; — lassen, see in [illegible] b, dd; du darfst dich nicht — lassen, you must not be seen; you are unfit to be seen; die Waare läßt sich —, the article takes the eye; siehe da! sehet! behold, look there! lo! auf etwas or darauf —, 1. to look to ..., to see, consider, observe; 2. to mind, care for; Sie müssen besonders darauf — daß ..., you must be particularly careful in seeing that ...; seine Lust an etwas (*Dat.*) —, to have a pleasure in a thing; gern gesehen sein, to be a welcome guest; hast du nicht gesehen! *coll.* helter-skelter, neck or nought; mehr auf freundliche Behandlung als auf hohe Belohnung —, to make high wages less a consideration than good treatment; Einen selten (oft genug) —, to see but little (enough) of one; wir haben uns schon so lange nicht gesehen, we have not met for so long.

Seh'enswürdig, I. *or* **Seh'enswerth,** *adj.* worth seeing; curious, remarkable; II. S-keit, *(w.) f.* remarkable object, curiosity, *pl.* sights, shows.

Se'her, *s.* I. *(str.) m.* 1) seer, prophet (poet); 2) *Sport.* eye of birds of prey; II. *in comp.* prophetic (office, sight, &c.).

Seh'erin, *(w.) f.* prophetess, seer.

Seh'... (*from* Sehen), *in comp.* —[illegible], *m.* see Gesichtskreis, 1; —hügel, *m.* *Anat.* [illegible] of the optic nerve (*Thalamus opticus*); —[illegible]gel, *m.* visive cone; —kraft, *f.* faculty of seeing; —kreis, *m.* see Gesichtskreis; —[illegible], *f.* optics; —linie, *f.* line of collimation; —loch, *n.* see Sehe, 1.

Seh'ne (*pr. also* se'ne), *(w.) f.* 1) [illegible] tendon, nerve; 2) string (of a bow); [illegible] chord.

Seh'nen (*pr. also* se'nen), I. *(w.) v. intr.* to long, grieve, yearn, hanker (nach, for, after); sich nach Hause —, to long to return home; II. *s.* *(str.) n.* longing, desire, yearning.

Seh'nen..., *in comp.* —haut, *f.* *Anat.* aponeurosis; —hüpfen, —springen, *n.* [illegible] sudden and irregular [illegible] dons; *Anat.-c.* —[illegible] bone; —streifen, *m.* tendinous [illegible] —verrenkung, *f.* *Farr.* upper-attaint.

Seh'... (*from* Sehen), *in comp.* [illegible] —nerv, *m.* visual nerve, optic nerve; [illegible] venhügel, *m.* see —hügel.

Seh'nicht (*pr. also* se'—), *adj.* [illegible] or string, stringy.

Seh'nig (*pr. also* se'—), *adj.* [illegible]

Seh'nlich (*pr. also* se'—), *adj.* [illegible] heartfelt, anxious, ardent, [illegible] wertes, to long, to look [illegible]

Seh'nsucht (*pr. also* se'—), [illegible] ardent desire (nach, for) [illegible] — der Liebe, love-[illegible] [illegible]süchtig, *adj.* see Sehnlich.

Seh'... (*from* Sehen), [illegible] *n.* see —werkzeug; —[illegible]

Sehr (*pr.* se'r), *adv.* [illegible] greatly; — wohl, very [illegible]

one's head; die Augen —, to cast down one's eyes; 2) Gard. to lay (plants); 3) Min. to dig downwards, to delve; II. rgl. to sink, settle, subside; to droop.

Senker, (str.) m. 1) one who sinks, &c.; Min. sinker; 2) Lock-sm., &c. counter-sink; conischer —, cone-countersink; 3) Gard. layer; 4) see Senkgarn.

Senk... (from Senken), in comp. —faschine, f. F. water-fascine; —garn, n. fishing-net sunk into the water; —grube, f. 1) Min., &c. cesspool; 2) Archit. draining-well, waste-well, bog; Railw. sink-hole, sink-trap (T. Teach.); —hamen, m. see —garn; —haue, f. Min. sinker's pick, mattock; —holz, n. sunk raft-wood.

Senkig, adj. (l. u.) subsiding, sloping.

Senk... (from Senken), in comp. —kasten, m. Hydr. caisson, stone-coffin; —kastengründung, f. foundation on sunken stone-coffins; —knecht, m. little peg provided with a hook to fasten a layer; —kolben, m. Lock-sm., &c. (pointed) counter-sink; —korb, m. Min. 1) wire-trellis, wire-sieve at the foot of a pump-barrel; 2) see Saugkorb.

Senkler, (str.) m. tag-maker; —blech, see Senkelblech.

Senk... (from Senken), in comp. —linie, f. vertical or perpendicular line; —loch, n. see —grube, 2; —nadel, f. Surg. probe; —pfahl, m. prop for a young vine; —pumpe, f. Min. sinking-set; —rebe, f. layer of vine; —recht, adj. vertical, perpendicular; Mar. a-peak; Math. right (cone); nicht —recht stehen, Archit. to carry false (of columns); nicht mehr —recht stehen, to be out of the perpendicular; —reuse, f. see —garn; —rippe, f. Hydr. side of a flood-dike; —rücken, m. Vet. swaying in the back of horses; —satz, m. see —pumpe; —schacht, m. a sunk shaft or pit; —(schacht)mauerung, f. sinking-shaft or sinking-pit masonry; —schlacht, f. Hydr. fascine-dike; —schnur, f. plumb-line; —schuh, m. Min. shoe of a sinking-shaft walling; —schuß, m. Mil. depression-shot, plunging fire; —stift, m. see —nadel; —stock, m. 1) Gard. stock from which layers are made; 2) Sword-cutl. grooved anvil; —strich, m. Geom. cathetus; —stück, n. Hydr. wattle-work.

Senkung, (w.) f. 1) a) the (act or state of) sinking, cf. Senken; depression; b) subsiding, settling (of a building, of masses of earth, &c.); c) Phys., &c. inclination, subsidence; d) pitching (of a locomotive); e) lowering (of the component parts of a machine); 2) Gramm. & Mus. thesis.

Senk... (from Senken), in comp. —wage, f. areometer; —werk, n. hurdles or fagots for damming water; —zeit, f. Gard. time of making layers.

Senne, I. see Sehne, 2 & [illegible]; II. (w.) f. herd of cattle (in S[illegible]and); in comp. S-nalpe, f. alp, mountain where there are cattle; S-nhütte or Senn'hütte, f. herdsman's or cow-keeper's cottage; III. (w.) m. 1) or Sen'ner, (str.), Senn'bauer, m. cow-keeper; 2) horse from a good stud.

Sennerei, (w.) f. 1) cheese-dairy; 2) breeding of cattle; 3) herd of cattle.

Sen'nerin, (w.) f. dairy-woman, dairy-maid.

* Sensal', (str.) m. (Ital. sensa'le, Fr. censal, Fr. Lat. censualis, tax-collector) Comm. broker (Mäkler). — Sensa'lie, Sensarie, (w.) f. (Fr. censerie) brokerage (Mäklergebühr).

* Sensation', (w.) f. (Fr.-Lat.) sensation.

Sen'se, (w.) f. scythe.

Sen'sen..., in comp. —baum, m. pole or handle of a scythe; —eisen, n. iron destined for scythes; —gerüst, n. mowing-cradle; —mann, —träger, m. 1) scythe-bearer, scytheman; 2) fig. death; —schmied, m. scythe-smith; —wurf, m. see —baum.

Sen'te, (w.) f. Mar. ribbon; die — des Breits, breadth-ribbon; die S-n der Bergschlunung, topside-lines.

* Sentenz', (w.) f. (Lat.) sentence.

* Sentimental', adj. sentimental. — Sentimentalität', (w.) f. sentimentalism.

* Separat', adj. (Lat.) separate; —conto, n. Comm. separate account; —[illegible], f. [illegible]; —vertrag, m. special contract. — Separi'ren, (w.) v. I. tr. to separate; II. rgl. Comm. to separate, dissolve partnership.

* Se'pie, (w.) f. (Gr.) Zool. sepia (Tintenfisch).

Septem'ber, (str.) m. September.

* Septett', (str.) n. Mus. septet, (Ital.) septetto.

* Sep'time, (w.) f. (Lat.) 1) seventh class of a school; 2) Mus. seventh; die kleine —, the minor or ordinary seventh; die verminderte —, the diminished seventh; die große —, the major or sharp seventh; S-n-accord, m. chord of the seventh.

* Sequester, (str.) m. (Lat.) sequestrator; mit — belegen, see Sequestriren; den — aufheben, to recall the sequestration. — Sequestration', (w.) f. 1) sequestration; 2) attachment, seizin. — Sequestri'ren, (w.) v. tr. to sequester, sequestrate; — lassen, to award sequestration.

* Serail (pr. serailj'), (str., pl. S-s) n. (Fr.) seraglio.

* Se'raph, (str., pl. S-e, S-s, [Rabb.] Seraphim' (unusual: S-phi'me, Wieland: S-phin)) m. seraph. — Sera'phisch, adj. seraphic(al). — Seraphi'ne, f. Seraphine (P. W.).

Ser'be, (w.) m., Ser'bier, (str.) m., Ser'bisch, adj. Serb, Serbian, Servian. — Ser'bien, n. Geogr. Serbia, Servia.

Ser'ben, (w.) v. intr. provinc. to fade, decay. — Serb'ling, (str.) m. weakling, weak, puny plant or creature.

* Serena'de, (w.) f. (Fr.) serenade.

* Ser'ge (pr. sär'zhe), (w.) f. (Fr.) Comm. serge.

* Sergeant (pr. sergeänt'), (w.) m. (Fr.) [Mil. sergeant.

Ser'geantfrau, see Gatzmel.

* Sericin', (str.) n. (Lat.) Chem. oil or butter of nutmegs.

* Se'rie, (w.) f. (Lat.) Comm. series, emission; die zweite — ist ausgegeben, the second emission has taken place.

* Serō'ne, (w.) f. (Span. seron, Fr. séron, suron) Comm. seron, seroon.

* Serös', adj. (Lat.) Med. serous; —blutig, adj. sero-sanguineous.

Ser'pe, (w.) f. see Zwergfalke.

* Serpent (pr. sšrpäng'), (str.) m. (Fr.) Mus. serpent. [Schlange.

* Serpentin', (str.) m. Miner. serpentine

* Ser'sche, see Serge.

* Servelatwurst, (str., pl. S-würste) f. cervelas, Bologna sausage.

* Service' (pr. sšrwiß'), (collect.) n. (Fr.) 1) service; particul. a set of plates, &c.; 2) gratuity for servants at hotels; —geld, n. money paid in lieu of a soldier's quartering; —zettel, m. quartering-billet.

Ser'vier, Ser'vis &c., see Service.

* Serviet'te, (w.) f. (Fr.) [illegible] — zum Rasiren, shaving-cloth; [illegible] plum-pudding.

* Ser'ving, (w.) f. (Engl.) [illegible]

* Servi'ren, (w.) v. tr. & intr. [illegible] to serve; wait upon; 2) to lay [illegible] set or serve (the dishes).

* Servitut', (w.) f. (Lat.) [illegible] pulsory service; obligation; 2) [illegible] an estate for the benefit of [illegible]

Se'sam, m. (or —[illegible]) [illegible] oily grain, oil-plant, [illegible]

his roof; *in comp.* —**feld**, *n. Archit.* square; —**förmig**, *adj. Herald* chevroned; —**holz**, *n.* timber for rafters; —**kopf**, *m. Archit.* end of a rafter, mutule; —**loch**, *n. Mar.* pigeon-hole; —**sohle**, *f. Carp.* hole-plate; —**weise**, *adv.* rafterwise; —**werk**, *or* **Sparr'werk**, *n. collect.* rafters. [*adj.* dentato-squarrose.

Spar'rig, *adj. Bot.* squarrose; — gezähnt,

Sparr'werk, *(str.) n. see* Sparrenwerk.

Spär'sam, I. *adj.* sparing (mit, of, in), saving, thrifty, frugal (of); scanty, parsimonious; — mit... umgehen, to be sparing of..., to husband; II. **S-keit**, *(w.) f.* savingness, &c., economy, parsimony. [thread.

Spär'seide, *(w.) f.* a kind of fine, glossy

* **Sparset'te**, *(w.) f. see* Esparsette.

Spär'... *(from* Sparen*), in comp.* —sucht, *f.* parsimony; —süchtig, *adj.* parsimonious.

A. * **Spart**, *(str.) n. Bot.* matweed (*Lygeum*

B. * **Spart**, *see* Sparte. [*spartum* L.).

Sparta'ner, *(str.) m.*, **Spartia'te**, *(w.) m.*, **Sparta'nerin**, *(w.) f.*, **Sparta'nisch**, *adj* Spartan.

Spärt'chen, *(str.) n.* a little piece, chip (of wood).

* **Spar'te**, *(w.) f. (perhaps from Ital.* spart, spartita, *musical part)* 1) *Mus.* score (Partitur); 2) *fig.* special province.

* **Sparterie'**, *(w.) f. (Fr.) Comm.* mats.

* **Spart'(o)gras**, *(str.) n. Bot.* 1) Spanish broom (*Spartium junceum* L.); 2) esparto (*Stipa tenacissima* L.). [büchse.

Spär'topf, *(str., pl.* S-'töpfe*) m. see* Spar-

Spaß, *(str., pl.* Spä'ße*) m.* jest, sport, joke, pastime, *cf.* Scherz; im —, in jest; zum —, for fun, for a joke; — machen, to make fun *or* sport, *cf.* Spaßen; aus Allem — machen, to turn everything into fun.

Spaß'becher, *(str.) m.* magical cup (with a c[illegible]aled siphon in the handle).

Spa'ßen, *(w.) v. intr.* to joke, sport, jest, play; mit sich — lassen, to understand *or* take a joke; er läßt nicht mit sich —, he is not to be joked *or* trifled with, he does not bear to be joked about; — Sie oder ist es Ihr Ernst? are you in fun or in earnest?

Spa'ßer, *(str.) m.* jester; wag.

Spaßerei', *(w.) f.* the (act *or* habit of) jesting, &c.; joke, jest. [elastic glass.

Spaß'glas, *(str., pl.* S-gläser*) n.* ana-

Spaß'haft, I. *adj.* jocular, facetious, merry, jesting, joking, droll, sportive, ludicrous; II. **S-igkeit**, *(w.) f.* jocularity, facetiousness, drollness, sportiveness.

Spa'ßig, *adj. see* Spaßhaft.

Spaß'ling (*Switz.* **Spaß'ler**), *(str.) m.*

—frost, *m.*, —gerste, *f.*, &c., late ap[...]
vest, frost, barley, &c.; —eiche, *f. se*[...]
eiche; —fährte, *f. Hunt.* dry foot;
m., —licht, —roth, *n.*, —schein, *m.*
of the setting sun; —heu, *n.* afte[...]
after-math; —jahr, *n.* late season, [...]
fall; —kommen, *n.* lateness; —mahl,
per; —obst, *n.* late ripe fruits; —re[...]
rain in the harvest time; —sommer, *m*[...]
part of summer; —sonne, *f. see* Aben[...]
—stern, *m.* evening-star; —zahn, *m.*
nal tooth, wisdom-tooth.

Spa'te, *(w.) f. see* Spaten.

Spä'te, *f.* lateness.

Spa'tel, *(str.) m.* spatula (*coll.* [...]
rake; *Sug-w.* spoon, stirrer; *in comp.*—
Ornith. 1) gray-headed duck (*Anas* [...]
L.); 2) shoveller (Löffelente); 3) gol[...]
(Schellente); —förmig, *adj.* spatulate;
f., —reiher, *m. see* Löffelgans.

Spa'ten, *(str.) m.* 1) spade; 2) *Gam.*
(at cards); —cultur, *f.* spade-hus[...]
spade-work; —gut, *n.* land appointed
preservation of dikes; —recht, *n.* juri[...]
over a dike; —stich, *m.* cut with a spa[...]
ersten —stich thun, *Railw.*, &c. to tu[...]
first sod; to cut the first turf.

Spä'testens, *adv.* at farthest, lates[...]

Spath, *(str.) m.* 1) *Farr.* spavin (a
of horses); 2) *Min.* spar; *in comp.*
adj. see Spathig, 2; —druse, *f.* group [...]
—eisenstein, *m.* 1) sparry iron-ore, s[...]
iron; 2) (strahliger) spherosiderite;
m. fluor spar; —haltig, *adj.* sparry;
m. sparry aetites; —krystall, *m.*, —[...]
crystallised carbonate of lime; —salz
lenitous salt; —sand, *m* arenaceou[...]
—säure, *f. Chem.* fluoric acid; —stein,
cular spar.

Spa'thig, *adv.* 1) *Vet.* spavined; [...]
sparry, spathose.

* **Spa'tium**, *(str., pl. [Lat.]* Spa[...]
Spa'tien*) n. (Lat.)* space; *Typ.* spa[...]

Spät'ling, *(str.) m.* 1) backwar[...]
calf, *or* colt, &c. (*opp.* Frühling, 2);
fruit; 3) *see* Nachzügler; 4) *provinc.* [...]
jahr.

Spatz, *(w.) m.* 1) *for* Sperling; 2)[...]
a kind of dumpling; S-enstrauch, *m*[...]
sparrow-tree (*Struthiola* L.); S-enk[...]
soapwort (Seifenkraut).

Spazie'ren, **Spatzie'ren**, *(w.) v. int*[...]
sein) *or* — gehen, to take a turn, to [...]
walk; — fahren, 1) *tr.* to drive about;
to take a drive, to take the air *or* a[...]
in a coach, in a boat; — reiten, to [...]

ſel, *m.* sulphur of antimony; **—ſilber**, *n. Miner.* antimonial silver(-ore); **—vitriol**, *m. Chem.* vitriol of antimony; **—wein**, *m. see* —auszug; *Miner-s.* **—weiß**, *n.* white oxide of antimony by precipitation; **—zinnober**, *m.* cinnabar of antimony.

Spieß'..., *in comp.* **—glas**, *n. see* —glanz; **—gras**, *n. Bot.* foxtail (*Alopecurus* L.); **—haar**, *n.* stiff, projecting, spiky hair; **—hecht**, *m. Ichth.* a genus of pike (*Sphyræna* Cuv.); **—hirſch**, *m. see* Spießer.

Spie'ßig, *adj.* 1) pointed; consisting of points; 2) *provinc., &c. a)* keen, acrimonious, piercing, sharp; *b)* thin, meagre.

Spieß'..., *in comp.* **—knecht**, *m. see* Lanzknecht; **—kobalt**, *m. Miner.* gray-cobalt ore; **—kuchen**, *m. see* Baumkuchen; **—lerche**, *f. Ornith.* 1) pipit (Baumpieper); 2) meadow-pipit (Wieſenpieper); **—nagel**, *m.* a long nail; **—raubmöve**, *f. Ornith.* arctic gull (*Lestris parasitica* L.); **—ruthe**, *f.* 1) switch; 2) S-n, *pl. Mil.* gauntlet; —ruthen laufen, to run the gauntlet; —ruthen laufen laſſen, to flog through the line; **—ſchaft**, *m.*, **—ſtange**, *f.* spear-staff; **—träger**, *m.* 1) spear-man, pike-man, lancer; 2) *see* Spießer; **—wender (—treiber)**, *m.* turnspit (Bratenwender); **—werfer**, *m.* one who throws a spear; harpooneer; **—wurzel**, *f. see* Pfahlwurzel; **—zahn**, *m. see* Spitzzahn.

Spi'ke, (*w.*) *f. Bot.* spike, spikenard, lavender (*Lavandula spica* L.)

Spi'ker, (*str.*) *m. Mar.* timber-nail, spike; *in comp.* **—bohrer**, *m.* spike-gimlet; **—eiſen**, *n.* spike-iron; **—haut**, *f.* sheathing; **—pinne**, *f. Carp.* spile, spill.

Spi'kern, (*w.*) *v. tr. Mar.* to nail; to spike.

Spik'..., *in comp.* **—öl**, *n. Comm.* spikenard-oil, oil of lavender; **—waſſer**, *n.* lavender-water.

Spill, (*str.*) *n. see* Gangſpill.

Spilla'ge [*pr.* —ä'zhe], (*w.*) *f. coll.* (*N. G.*) *Comm.* outcome of goods, dross and dust, sweepings; waste, spillage.

Spill'..., *in comp.* **—baum**, *m. see* Spindelbaum & Faulbaum, 1; **—bäume**, *m. pl.* bars of the capstan; **—bett**, *n. see* —ſpur; **—blech**, *n.* socket of the capstan.

Spil'le, (*w.*) *f.* 1) *see* Spill; 2) *see* Spindel; 3) peg, pin; rolling-pin; cylinder; 4) *see* Speiche, 2; 5) *see* Spilling; 6) teetotum.

Spil'len, (*w.*) *v. tr.* (*L. G.*) to spill, waste, squander.

5) worm (of a screw); 6) nut (of a pr 7) (des Stückbohrers und der Nadel) sh 8) *see* Speiche, 2; 9) *see* —ſchnecke.

Spin'del..., *in comp.* **—bank**, *f.* Sp flyer, fly-frame, bobbin- (and fly-)fra spindle-roving-frame; —bank mit Preßfl presser-frame; **—baum**, *m.* 1) *Bot.* spin tree, prick-wood, burning-bush (*Euony europæus* L.); 2) *Mech.* beam of a spin *coll-s.* **—bein**, *n.* spindle-shanks; **—beinig**, spindle-shanked; **—birn**, *f.* spindle-like p **—bohrer**, *m.* bung-bore; **—buche**, *f. see* H buche; **—draht**, *m. Watch-m.* fusee-wire; **dünn**, **—dürr**, *adj.* very thin; **—flöte**, *f. see* S lenflöte; **—förmig**, *adj.* spindle-like; *Bot.* f form; **—gewölbe**, *n.* cylindrical vault; —he *m. see* Auerhahn; **—hemmung**, *f. Watch* crown-escapement; fusee-escapement; —h *n.* 1) *see* —baum; 2) *see* Spillenholz; —kaſ *m. T.* mandrel-stock; **—leiter**, *f. see* —pre **—klöbchen**, *n. Watch-m.* balance-vice; —kr *n. Bot.* distaff-thistle (*Atractylis* L.); **—lapp** *m. pl. Watch-m.* pallets, nuts; **—macher**, spindle-maker; **—muskel**, *m. Anat. see* S chenmuskel; **—nieter**, *m. Watch-m.* verge-ri ing-tool; **—pflaume**, *f. see* Spilling; —pre *f.* screw-press; **—rolle**, *f.* spindle-roll; —säu *f. Archit.* spindle-shaped column; **—ſchneck** *Conch.* whelk; **—ſchnecken**, *pl.* various sn (shells) of a spiral form; **—ſeite**, *f. see* S ſeite; **—theil**, *m.* †, spinster's part; **—trep** *f.* winding or cylindrical staircase; **—wir** *m. T.* whirl of a spindle; **—zapfen**, *m.* pi pin of a spindle.

Spin'delig, **Spin'delicht**, *adj.* spin shaped.

* **Spinell'**, (*str.*) *m.* (*Fr.*) *Miner.* spinel(

* **Spinett'**, (*str.*) *n.* (*Ital.*) *Mus.* spi virginals (an old keyed instrument).

Spinn'affe, (*w.*) *m. see* Spinnenaffe.

Spinn'bahn, *see* Seilerbahn.

Spinn'bär, *adj.* that may be spun, tex

Spinn'blume, (*w.*) *f. Bot.* meadow-saf (Herbſtzeitloſe).

Spin'ne, (*w.*) *f.* 1) *Arach.* spider (ani of the family *Araneæ*); 2) spiteful, venom person; 3) whim (Grille, 4); 4) *provinc.* ev ing-meeting of country-girls for spinn (*cf.* Spinnſtube, 2); 5) *Sport.* dug (Geſäu

Spin'nen, (*str.*) *v.* I. *tr.* 1) to spin; T —, to spin, roll tobacco; 2) *fig.* to plot; Ränl to intrigue; II. *intr.* 1) to spin; 2) to thicl

—kuchen; —gurke, *f. see* Spritzgurke; —kanne, *f.* watering-pot; —kuchen, *m.* spouted cake, fritter; —leder, *n.* splashing *or* splash-leather (of a coach); —loch, *n. see* Blaseloch; —mittel, *n.* injection; clyster; —nudel, *f.* vermicelli; —röhrchen, *n.* pipe of a clyster; —röhre, *f.* 1) syringe; 2) *Nat.* nostril (of dolphins, &c.); —wal, *m. see* Finnfisch; —wedel, sprinkling-brush; —wurf, *m. see* —bewurf; —wurm, *m. Echin.* tube-worm, tubular holothure (*Holothuria tubulosa* L.).

Sprock, (*str.*) *m. Entom.* cade-worm; —aas, *n. Entom.* may-fly (Köcherfliege); —(el)weide, Sprö'ckel- *or* Sprö'delweide, *f. see* Springweide.

Sprö'de, I. *adj.* 1) brittle; hard, insensible; dry; chapped (skin, lips); 2) *fig.* cold, reserved; shy, coy, demure; stubborn; II. *f.* 1) (*decl. like adj.*) coy, demure person; prude; 2) (*w.*) *for* Sprödigkeit.

Sprö'derz, (*str.*) *n. Miner.* striated sulphureous lead.

Sprö'digkeit (*l. u.:* Sprö'dheit), (*w.*) *f.* 1) brittleness; *fig.*-s. 2) disobliging behaviour, reserve; 3) coyness, demureness, prudery.

A. Sproß, (*str.*) *m.*, Spro'sse, (*w.*) *m.* & *f.* 1) *Bot.* sprig, shoot, sprout; 2) *fig.* scion, offspring, descendant; 3) *Sport.* antler, *see* Ende, 2. *b.*

B. Spro'sse, (*w.*) *f.* 1) *a)* step, spar, round (of a ladder), rundle; *b)* peg (of a peg-ladder); *c)* bar, rung (of the beam of a windmill); *d)* rundle (of a cart-rack); 2) *Join., &c.* small cross-bar (of a window-frame) between the panes, *cf.* Fenstersprosse, Fensterkreuz; 3) freckle (Sommersprosse).

Spro'ssen, (*w.*) *v. intr.* (*aux.* sein) 1) to sprout, shoot, spring, bud, germinate, burgeon; 2) *fig.* to spring, descend from.

Spro'ssen..., *in comp.* —bier, *n. Brew.* spruce-beer; —bildung, *f. Physiol., Bot., or Zool.* gemmiparous reproduction; —essenz, *f.* spruce-wine; *Bot.-s.* —fichte, *f.* hemlock-spruce (*Abies Canadensis* L.); —kohl, *m.* sprouts; —nelke, *f.* proliferous pink (*Dianthus prolifer* L.); —tanne, *f. see* —fichte.

Spro'sser, (*str.*) *m.* 1) *Ornith.* (Sprossvogel, *m.*) Hungarian nightingale, great nightingale, bastard-nightingale, philomel (*Luscinia philomela* Bechst.); 2) *Sport.* stag with antlers; 3) *Bot.* stolon.

Spro'ßform, (*w.*) *f. Gramm.* derivative form.

Spro'ßling, (*str.*) *m.* 1) sprout, shoot; 2) *fig.* descendant, scion.

Sprott, (*str.*) *m. see* Sprock.

Spro'tte, (*w.*) *f. Ichth.* sprat (*Clupea sprattus* Cuv.).

Sprott'erz, (*str.*) *n. Miner.* black shining lead-ore; sulphurated lead.

Spruch, (*str.*, *pl.* Sprü'che) *m.* 1) sentence, decree, judgment (of a judge), award, *cf.* Urtheil; 2) (short, pithy, and instructive) saying, sententious maxim, apophthegm; adage, motto; passage (from the Bible, &c.); einen — thun, to give, pass, *or* pronounce sentence; zum S-e stehen, to be at issue.

Spruch'..., *in comp.* —behörde, *f. see* —collegium; —buch, *n.* book of sentences; —collegium, *n.* court of arbitration; —dichter, *m.* gnomic poet.

Sprü'chelchen, (*str.*) *n.* (*dimin. of* Spruch; *cf.* Sprüchlein [Sprüchel]) short sentence, short (moral) saying, precept, maxim; aphorism.

Spruch'..., *in comp.* —fähig, *adj.* competent; —fertig, *adj. Law,* ready for judgment to be passed; —geld, *n.* fee for passing an award; —gesang, *m.* anthem.

Sprüch'lein, *provinc.* Sprüch'el (*Schiller,* Wall. Lager, 8), (*str.*) *n.* * *for* Sprüchelchen.

Sprüch'lich, *adj.* sententious, aphoristic, *see* Spruchmäßig.

Spruch'..., *in comp.* —mann, *m.* †, umpire, arbiter; —mäßig, *adj.* sententious, apophthegmatical; —reich, *adj.* sententious; —weise, *adv.* in the manner of sentences; —weiser, *m.* concordance to the bible.

Sprüch'wort, *n. see* Sprichwort.

Spru'del, (*str.*) *m.* 1) fountain, well; 2) one of the hot wells of Carlsbad; —bad, *n. Med.* showerbath. —Spru'delig, *adj.* bubbling, spouting. — Spru'delkopf, (*str.*, *pl.* S-köpfe) *m.* hotheaded person. — Spru'deln, (*w.*) *v. intr.* 1) to bubble, spout; 2) *fig.* to flow, gush; im Sprechen —, (*intr.* & *tr.*) to sputter.

Spru'del..., *in comp.* —quelle, *f.* bubbling fountain; —stein, *m. Miner.* thermal tuff, aragonite.

Sprü'hler, (*str.*) *m.* sputterer, splutterer.

Sprü'gel, *m. see* Spriegel.

Sprüh'auge, (*str.*) *n.* sparkling eye.

Sprü'he, (*w.*) *f. see* Sprühregen.

Sprü'hen, (*w.*) *v.* I. *intr.* to fly out in small particles, to fly out in sparks; to sparkle, beam; to drizzle (of rain); II. *tr.* 1) to sprinkle *or* scatter in small drops, to sputter; 2) *fig.* to beam, dart, sparkle; Tod —, to scatter death, to shower destruction.

Sprüh'feuer, (*str.*) *n.*, Sprüh'teufel, (*str.*) *m. Fire-w.* corruscating fire, devil.

Sprüh'regen, (*str.*) *m.* drizzling rain.

Sprung, (*str.*, *pl.* Sprü'nge) *m.* 1) spring, leap, jump, skip, bound; vault; 2) flaw, chink, crack; chap; einen — haben, to be flawed (of a bottle, &c.); 3) the *(act of)* coupling (said of certain animals); zum — lassen, to let cover; 4) *Sport.* hind-legs of a hare; ein — Rehe, a bevy of roes; 5) *Mar.* bent (of a sail); 6) *Min.* bar, fault, *see* Verwerfung; — ins Hangende, upcast (dyke, slip, fault), upthrow, rise-dyke, rises; — ins Liegende, downcast (dyke, slip, fault), downthrow; Sprünge machen, 1. to leap, gambol; 2. *fig. see* Sperren, II.; nicht viel Sprünge machen können, *fig. coll.* to be forced to keep within bounds; einen — thun, to take a leap; *coll.-s.* auf dem S-e stehen, to be ready, to be on the point; in vollem S-e, at full speed; hinter Einem (*or* Einem auf die) Sprünge kommen, to discover one's tricks *or* pranks; auf seine alten Sprünge kommen, to return to one's former courses; Einem auf die Sprünge helfen, to assist one (*positively,* one's memory); die Preise haben einen großen — gemacht, prices have taken a sudden rise.

Sprung'..., *in comp.* —bein, *n. Anat.* sling-bone, first bone of the foot, ankle-bone, astragalus; —fischerei, *f.* a kind of trout-fishing; —flut, *f. see* Springflut; —gelenk, *n.* hock (of horses); —riemen, *m.* martingale; —röhre, *f. see* Springröhre; —weise, *adv.* by bounds, leaps; *fig.* abruptly.

Sprü'tzel, Sprü'tzen, *see* Sprützel, Sprützen.

Spuck'e, *f. coll.* spittle (Speichel).

Spuck'en, (*w.*) *v. tr.* & *intr. coll.* to spit; Spuck'kästen, Spuck'napf, *m.* spittoon, spitting-box.

Spu'den, *see* Sputen.

Spuhr, (*w.*) *f. Mar. see* Spur.

Spuk, (*str.*) *m.* 1) apparition, hobgoblin, ghost, spectre; 2) *coll. a)* noise, confusion, hubbub, bustle, uproar; *b)* difficulty, [illegible] *c)* trick.

Spu'ken, (*w.*) *v. intr. (impers.* 1) to [illegible] to be haunted; 2) to create a disturbance [illegible] make a noise; es spukt im Hause, the house is haunted; es spukt in seinem Kopfe, he is not quite right in his head. —[illegible] *f.* 1) apparition of hobgoblins; 2) [illegible]

Spuk'haft, *adj.* ghost-like.

Spuk'..., *in comp.* —geschichte, *f.* ghost-story, story of apparitions; —[illegible] of witchery (*Shksp.* witching time) [illegible] hour, ghost-hour.

Spul'..., *in comp.* —[illegible] *f.* [illegible] —baum, *m.* spindle-tree; —[illegible] wire.

finances of a state; — und landwirthschaftliche Academie, academy of political and rural economy; —wissenschaft, f. science of states, politics; municipal philosophy; —wissenschaftlich, adj. politic(al), adv. politically; —wohl, n. —wohlfahrt, f. public or common weal or welfare; —zeitung, f. state gazette; —zimmer, n. room of state.

Stab, (str., pl. Stä'be) m. 1) staff, stick; rod, wand, verge; cf. Commandostab; 2) bar (of metal); eiserne Stäbe, stanchions, cross-bars (of a window-grate); 3) (pl. Stab, indecl.) (a measure of length, varying in different parts of Germany, for manufactured, silk, &c. stuffs:) in Berlin 1¾ Ellen; in Frankfurt a./M. 2⅙ Ellen; on the Rhine, &c. aune; in the Tyrolese misure 1 Elle & 3 Querfinger (395 Paris lines); also a cubic measure for wood; 4) Archit. a) (am Säulenfuße) torus; b) (Rund—) astragal; 5) Mil. staff, staff-officers; 6) Typ. templet; der gebrochene —, a) Weav. broken staff-work; b) Archit. fret; aufgebender —, Glass. dead mullion; Stäbe eines Schirms, sticks or ribs of an umbrella, &c.; seinen — weiter setzen, fig. to proceed on one's way; den — (über Einen, orig. über Einem [& still so construed], referring to the ancient custom of the judge breaking a wand over the head of the condemned criminal; sometimes with the Dat., see below) brechen, 1. to pronounce sentence of death (on); 2. fig. to judge harshly (of), condemn; sich selbst den — brechen, to pronounce one's own sentence; da mir (for, über mich) der — gebrochen ist (Göthe, Tasso 5, 5), since my doom is sealed (Sonnew.).

Stab'..., in comp. —alge, f. Bot. bacillaria (Bacillaria Gmel.); —amsel, f. see Ringamsel; —biel, n. see Kernbeil; —block, m. Mar. stem (of a lighter); —bohne, f. see Stangelbohne.

Stäb'chen, 1) (province. & °: Stäb'lein) (str.) n. (dimin. of Stab) little staff, rod, wand; 2) Archit. astragal, (cock-)bead; **Stäb'chenbacterie**, (w.) f. Bot. microbacterium, bacterium (the cells having an elliptical or cylindrical form, opp. the round cells of the sphærobacterium or micrococcus).

Stab'degen, m. see Stockdegen.

Sta'bel, **Stä'bel**, (str.) m. stick, prop (for climbing plants); —erbsen, f. pl. peas requiring sticking (Stangelerbsen).

Sta'beln, **Stä'beln**, (w.) v. tr. to stick (peas, &c.).

Stab'..., in comp. —eingust, m. T. mould, ingot-mould, wedge-mould; —eisen, n. 1) iron in bars, bar-iron, rod-iron; 2) Comm. merchant-iron; —eisenwalzwerk, n. bar-iron rollers; —feuer, n. forge in which raw iron is formed into bars; —gold, n. gold in bars; —hammer, m. tilt, tilt-hammer; —hobel, m. rabbet-plane, moulding plane; —holz, n. staves; headings.

° **Stabil'**, adj. (Lat.) stationary (fest). — **Stabilist'**, (w.) m. stationary or anti-progressman.

Stab'..., in comp. —kraut, n. see —wurz; —leben, n. episcopal fief; —messung, f. Math. baculometry; —rechenkunst, f., —rechnen, n. rhabdology; —reim, m. alliterative rhyme; —treiber, m. see —schläger; —schimmel, m. Bot. bactridian (Bactridium Kze.); —schläger, m. Forest. he that fells wood for staves; —silber, n. silver in bars; —thierchen, n. pl. Bot. bacillaria (Ehrb.), diatomaceæ (Harv.); —träger, m. verger, mace-bearer; —wurz, f. Bot. 1) southern-wood (Eberraute); 2) (wilde) field mugwort (Artemisia campestris L.); —zange, f. tongs for iron-bars; —zehnte, m. tithe of vetches, &c.

Stabs'..., in comp. —arzt, m. physician of a brigade; —capitän, —hauptmann, —rittmeister, m. second-captain; —offizier, m. staff-officer, field-officer; —quartier, n. head-quarters; —quartiermeister, m. quarter-master-general.

Stach'el, (orr. sing. str., pl. w.) m. 1) sting, piercer; prick, prickle; spine, thorn; quill (of the porcupine); 2) goad; 3) point, prong; tongue (of a buckle).

Stach'el..., in comp. —aloë, f. agave, American aloe (Agave americana L.); —ameise, f. Entom. 1) stinging ant (Ponera Latr.); 2) visiting ant (Atta cephalotes L.); —barsch, m. Ichth. see —bauch; —bauch, m. Ichth. globe-fish (Tetrodon hispidus Lacep.); —beerbusch, m. Bot. gooseberry-bush (Ribes grossularia L.); —beere, f. 1) gooseberry; 2) fig. biting speech, pungent remark, cf. —rede; —beerstrauch, m. Bot. Arabian encounter (Onobrychis prophetarum L.); —beerspanner, m. Entom. a species of span-worm (Abraxas grossulariata L.); —beerstrauch, m. see —beerbusch; —biene, f. common or working bee; —flosser, m. Ichth. 1) diacope, a genus of Percidæ (Diacope Cuv.); 2) a genus of Triglidæ (Platycephalus Cuv.); —distel, f. Bot. thorny milk-thistle (Carduus acanthoides L.); —dolde, f. Bot. prickly samphire (Echinophora spinosa L.); —eiche, f. Bot. Orcadian, valonia-oak (with eatable fruits) (Quercus aegilops L.); —feige, f. Bot. prickly pear (Opuntia vulgaris Mill.); —fisch, m. Ichth. stickleback (Gasterosteus L.); —flosse, f. hard, bony, and prickly fin; —flosser, m. pl. Ichth. acanthopterygious fishes, acanthopterygians; —förmig, see Stachelförmig; —frucht, f. prickly, thorny fruit; —gewächs, n. spiny or prickly plant; —glatze, see —gorgonie; —gorgonie, f. Polyp. a species of sea-fan or gorgonia (Muricea Lam.); —hahnenfuß, m. Bot. corncrowfoot (Ackerhahnenfuß); —haut, f. prickly skin; —häuter, m. pl. Zool. echinoderms; —herz, n. Conch. thorny cockle (Cardium aculeatum L.); —hirse, m. Bot. prickly, bearded millet (Panicum [Echinochloa] crus galli L.).

Stach'elig, **Stach'elicht**, adj. 1) resembling prickles; prickly, spiny; thorny; bristly (beard, &c.); Bot. aculeated, aculeate, [illegible]; 2) fig. pungent; biting, sarcastic.

Stach'el..., in comp. —käfer, m. Entom. nibbler, mordella (Mordella F.); —kraut, m. Bot. thorny rest-harrow (Ononis spinosa L.); —krebs, m. Crust. a species of shrimp (Stenopus F.); —kugel, f. Ichth. tiger-spotted globe-fish (Diodon tigrinus Cuv.); —loch, n. [illegible] spinous foramen. [illegible]

Stach'ellos, adj. without prickles, &c.

Stach'el..., in comp. —makrele, f. Ichth. horse-mackerel (Caranx trachurus L.); —maus, f. Zool. a species of African [illegible] (Acomys Geoffroy); Bot. —mohn, m. [illegible] Mexican prickly poppy (Argemone Mexicana L.).

Stach'eln, (w.) v. tr. 1) a) to sting, prick, goad; b) fig. to spur, stimulate, [illegible], [illegible] on; 2) to provide with a sting or prickles.

Stach'el..., in comp. —nuß, f. Bot. 1) water-nut, water-caltrop [illegible]; 2) thorn-apple (Stechapfel, 1); 3) Conch. [illegible] purple-shell (Purpura hippocastanum [illegible]) [illegible] pilz, m. see —schwamm; —rede, f. [illegible] speech, pl. stinging, poignant, or [illegible] words; —reim, m. satirical verse; [illegible] Ichth. thornback (Raja clavata L.); [illegible] m. Ichth. a genus of fishes belonging to [illegible] Scomberidæ (Notacanthus [illegible]) [illegible] sarcastic jest; —schnabel, m. see [illegible] ler; —schnecke, f. Conch. [illegible] —schrift, f. satirical writing, [illegible] schwalbe, f. Ornith. [illegible] schwalbe); —schwamm, m. [illegible] [illegible] L.); —schwein, n. [illegible] —schwein, n. Zool. porcupine [illegible] L.); —schweinmagen, m. [illegible] ichthyosis; —seel, m. Zool. [illegible]

Stäm'mig(t), strong, bulky, robust, stout; II. St-keit, f. see Stammhaftigkeit.

Stamm'..., in comp. —käfer, m. Entom. a species of stag-beetle (Passalus Fabr.); —karte, f. Gam. stock-card; —land, n. mother-country, primitive country; —lehen, n. fee-simple.

Stamm'ler, (str.) m. stammerer, stutterer.

Stämm'ling, (str.) m. 1) stem of a young tree; 2) derivative.

Stamm'..., in comp. —linie, f. 1) T. trunk-line; main line (of a railway); 2) lineage; —lode, f. Forest. shoot, sprig that comes from the root or trunk of a tree, turio.

Stamm'los, adj. without a trunk or stem, stemless; acaulous.

Stamm'..., in comp. —motte, f. Entom. gipsy moth (—wollenspinner); —mutter, f. ancestress; —nadel, f. Shoe-m. closing-needle; —ochs, m. Husb. bull (kept for breeding); —paar, n. ancestral couple; —pfahl, m. T. guide-pile (of a cofferdam); —raupe, f. Entom. caterpillar of the gipsy-moth; —register, n. genealogical table, pedigree, genealogy; —reihe, f. genealogical series; —schaft, m. Archit. shaft of the column; —schwarm, m. Bee, stock of bees for increase; —schwein, n. breeding-pig; —sitz, m. ancestral seat, residence; —sprache, f. primitive tongue; —silbe, f. primitive syllable, root; —tafel, f. genealogical table, table of descent; —tonleiter, f. Mus. the C-major scale; —tugend, f. cardinal virtue; —vater, m. head of a family, ancestor; —vermächtniß, n. estate the entail of which cannot be cut off; —vermögen, n. Comm. stock, fund; —verwandt, adj. congeneric, of the same origin or descent; der —verwandte, congener; —verwandtschaft, f. sameness of origin; —vieh, n. stock of cattle (which descends with an estate); —volk, n. primitive people, (pl.) aborigines; —wappen, n. arms of a family; —wolle, f. thick coarse wool; —wollenspinner, m. a species of butterfly, gipsy-moth (Liparis dispar L.); Gramm-s. —wort, n. primitive word, principal, root; —zeit, f. radical tense; —zeitwort, n. primitive verb, verb as theme.

Stam'pel &c., see Stempel &c.

Stam'pen, (w.) v. tr. provinc. to stamp, strike, punch.

Stampf'..., in comp. —bau, m. Build. coffer-work of earth, beaten cob-work; —büchse, f. wooden mortar.

Stampf'e, (w.) f. 1) the (act of) stamping, stamp; 2) a) stamper, pestle, pounder; b) beetle, rammer. [Iron pestle.

Stampf'eisen, (str.) n. T. stamp-iron;

Stampf'en, (w.) v. I. tr. to stamp, pound, bray, beat; to ram; II. intr. Mar. to pitch; vor Anker —, to heave and set; das — der Locomotive, T. pitching (overbalancing) of a locomotive. [mer.

Stampf'er, (str.) m. stamper, beater, ram-

Stampf'..., in comp. —erde, f. stamped earth; —gang, m. Mill. crushing-mill; —hammer, m. stamp-hammer; —haufen, m. Paper-m. batch of rags; —klotz, m. T. rammer; —loch, n. see —trog; —maschine, f. stamping-machine; —mühle, f. stamping-mill, knocking-mill; —perle, f. seed-pearl; Mar-s. —reiten, n. intr. to pitch at anchor; —see, f. heavy sea a-head; —stag, m. second preventer-stay; —stevens, m. stem right down upon the keel; —stock, m. martingale; —trog, m. stamping-trough, beating-trough, chopping-trough; —werk, n. see —mühle; —zucker, m. pounded sugar.

Stand, (str., pl. Stän'de) m. 1) stand; standing; standing-place, position; height, level (of water, &c.); 2) stand, jack, horse, &c.; 3) Sport. legs of birds; 4) stall, pew; stall, stand (of a dealer), stall, box, crib (in

a stable); stand (of cabs); fig-s. 5) stat[illegible]
dition, station, situation, case; stage [illegible]
gociations, &c.); 6) rank, profession[illegible];
order, quality, standing; trade, cal[illegible]
steadiness, firmness; 7) a) order or c[illegible]
men (in society or government), est[illegible]
dritte —, the third estate; b) (gener. pl.
(of the realm), deputy; — des Baro[illegible]
reading of the barometer; — des C[illegible]
Comm. 1. rate; 2. statement of the cas[illegible]
— halten, to keep (one's) ground, to h[illegible]
or one's own; einen harten — haben, t[illegible]
great trouble or a hard battle to figh[illegible]
a tough job; außer — setzen, to disable,
prive of the means (of); ich bin nicht[illegible]
bin außer St-e, I cannot afford (to ...),
not able, it is out of my power; im St[illegible]
to be able, to be in a position (to ...);
im St-e sein, 1. to be enable; 2. to [illegible]
of order or repair; im St-e halten, t[illegible]
in repair; in — setzen, 1. to put in ord[illegible]
up, adjust, regulate, arrange; to refit [illegible]
&c.); 2. to enable; to put in a con[illegible]
(to ...), to put in the way; wieder in —
or bringen, to (put in) repair; in bes[illegible]
setzen, to improve; mit etwas zu St-e k[illegible]
or etwas zu St-e bringen, to bring abo[illegible]
compass, accomplish, achieve, to bri[illegible]
pass, contrive, effect, coll. to get up; [illegible]
through (a task), to finish; zu St-e ko[illegible]
to be achieved, accomplished, brought [illegible]
ein Mann von St-e, a man of rank, a [illegible]
quality; unter seinem St-e heiraten, to [illegible]
beneath one('s self); Heirat unter Sta[illegible]
St-e, ill-assorted marriage; die gel[illegible]
Stände, the learned professions.

Standar'te, (w.) f. 1) standard, b[illegible]
2) see Fahne, 2; in comp. St-einhorn[illegible],
träger, m. standard-bearer; St-schu[illegible]
see; St-stange, f. shaft of the standa[illegible]

Stand'..., in comp. —barometer, n.
stationary barometer; —baum, m. see [illegible]
baum; —bild, n. statue; (zu Pferde) e[illegible]
trian statue; (zu Fuß) pedestrian stat[illegible]
block, m. Mar. knight-head; —büchse, f
(-gun) for target-shooting.

Ständ'chen, (str.) n. Mus. serenade; [illegible]
ing-music; (Einem) ein — bringen, to [illegible]
nade (one); ein — erhalten, to be sere[illegible]

Stand'decke, (w.) f. Mar. shaft [illegible]
rudder (in lighters).

Stan'de, (w.) f. see Ständer, 2, a.

Stän'de..., in comp. —eröffnung, f.
ing of the states; —haus, n. house of [illegible]
bly of the states.

Stan'der, (str.) m. Mar-s. 1) broad
[illegible]; 2) traverse horse; 3) — eines [illegible]
tee(?), runner, down-haul of a tie.

Stän'der, (str.) m. 1) Carp-s. a) [illegible]
post (in a stable, &c.); corner-post; [illegible]
standard; stud, upright; b) cross-tie(?)
partition; c) sluice-board, lock-hatch[illegible]
stay (of a pond); small dock for ships[illegible]
2) a) water-tub; b) Mech. crank; 3) Anat[illegible]
destal; 4) Sport. feet of large birds; [illegible]
pillar; 6) axis (of a wind-mill); 7) [illegible]
right waste-pipe; 8) capital lent on [illegible]
gage; 9) or —stock, m. stock of bees (St[illegible]
schwarm); —gerüst, n. T. housing, sta[illegible]
housing frame (of a rolling-mill); —[illegible]
Carp. scantling-work, stud-work.

Stän'desaal, (str., pl. St-säle) m. [illegible]
assembly room of the states (of a [illegible]

Stan'desherr(?), (str.) m. nobility(?) [illegible]

Stan'des..., in comp. —amt, n. [illegible]
office for the solemnization of marriag[illegible]
registration of births, marriages, and [illegible]
registrar's office; —beamte(r) [illegible]
for solemnizing marriages [illegible]
births, marriages, and deaths; [illegible]
erhöhung(?), f. elevation of rank; [illegible]
is due to rank; nach — [illegible]

permitted, allowed; eine Bitte — finden lassen, to grant a petition; an meiner —, in my stead, in my room; an Kindes — annehmen, to adopt; an Zahlungs—, by way of (as) payment.

Statt, *prep. (with Gen.)* instead, in lieu (of); — baaren Geldes, for current payment.

Stät'te, *(w.) f.* place, stead, room; ground; abode; —geld, *n. see* Standgeld.

Stät'telos, *adj.* without a (fixed) place of abode.

Stat'ten, *(Dat. pl. of an obsolete form* Statte *[MHG.* state]:) von — gehen, to proceed, go on (well), to succeed, speed, prosper; zu — kommen, to be useful, to be of use; to serve one's turn, to be favourable, to come in handy; es kommt ihm zu — daß ..., it is to his advantage that ...; die Erfahrung kommt ihm zu —, he has the benefit of experience.

Statt'haft, I. *adj.* 1) admissible, allowable; 2) lawful, legal; II. St-igkeit, *(w.) f.* 1) admissibility; 2) lawfulness.

Statt'halter, *(str.) m.* 1) governor, vicegerent, Lord lieutenant; 2) Stadtholder (in Holland). — **Statthalterei',** *(w.) f.* 1) *see* Statthalterschaft, 1; 2) habitation of a governor. — **Statt'halterin,** *(w.) f.* governess. — **Statt'haltern,** *(w.) v. intr.* to be *or* play governor *or* vicegerent. — **Statt'halterschaft,** *(w.) f.* 1) government, vicegerency, lieutenancy; 2) dignity of a governor.

Statt'lich, I. *adj.* 1) stately, magnificent, splendid; 2) distinguished, excellent, specious; 3) large; portly; respectable (profit); II. St-keit, *(w.) f. (Lat.)* stateliness, &c.

* **Sta'tue** *[pr.* stă'tŭe], *(w.) f. (Lat.)* statue.

* **Statui'ren,** *(w.) v. tr. (Lat.)* 1) to maintain; 2) to lay down, set (an example); an Einem ein Beispiel *or* Exempel —, to make an example of one, to set one forth as an example.

* **Statur',** *(w.) f. (Lat.)* stature, size.

* **Sta'tus,** *(indecl.) m. (Lat.)* state, statement, inventory; balance(-sheet).

* **Statut',** *(irr.: sing. str., pl. w.) n.* statute, rules, articles, regulations; St-enrecht, *n.* statute-law.

Stau, *(str.) m. & (w.) f.* 1) embankment (Damm); 2) stagnant, still *or* standing water.

Staub, *(str.) m.* 1) dust; powder; 2) *fig.* obscurity, low condition; zu — machen, to reduce to powder, to pulverise; sich aus dem St-e machen, *fam.* to be off; to run away, to abscond; to decamp, levant, to cut (sticks); *fig.-s.* am St-e kleben, to grovel; im St-e liegen *or* kriechen, to grovel, crouch; in den — treten, to tread under foot.

Staub'..., *in comp.* —arbeit, *f. T.* 1) dust-work, shearing-work; 2) embossed paper-hangings; —artig, *adj.* dust-like; *Bot.* pulveraceous, pulverulent; —bach, *m.* torrent tumbling down from a great height; —bad, *n.* shower-bath; —balg, *m.*, —behältniß, *n.*, —beutel, *m. Bot.* anther; —besen, *m.* duster; —blüte, *f. Bot.* male flower; —boden, *m. see* Zugboden; —brand, *m. Bot.* a kind of mildew *(Ustilago carbo* Tul.); —brille, *f.* (gauze-) goggles; —bürste, *f.* dust-brush.

Stäub'chen, *(str.) n. (dimin. of* Staub) mote, atom.

Staub'deckel, *(str.) m. T.* false case (of a [watch].

Stäu'be, *(w.) f. see* Staubbach.

Stau'ben, *(w.) v. intr. impers.* es staubt, it is dusty.

Stäu'ben, *(w.) v.* I. *intr.* 1) *a)* to raise dust; *b) see* Stauben, 2) to rise in *or* scatter spray; II. *tr.* 1) to sprinkle, as with dust, to powder; 2) to dust, to sweep away the dust; 3) to pounce (a design); 4) to winnow (corn).

Stäu'ber, *(str.) m.* 1) duster; 2) puff-ball (Stäubling, 2); 3) *(or* —hund) starter, foot-hound, terrier, harrier, wending dog, beagle.

Staub'erde, *(w.) f.* mould, dust (rothe) adamic *or* bole earth.

Stäu'bern, *(w.) v.* I. *tr.* 1) to dus start, raise, chase, beat up; to tur out *or* away; II. *intr. impers.* to s drift (of snow); to drizzle; III. *intr.* t or to smell, about, to rummage.

Staub'..., *in comp.* —fach, *m.* an —faden, *m. Bot.* stamen; —fege, *f.* winnowing-machine; 2) dust-sieve; *f. Bot.* farinaceous lichen (Pulverari —flügel, *m. Entom.* powdered wing; — *adj.* having powdered wings; —flü *pl. Entom.* butterflies; —geboren, a mortal; 2) base-born; —gefäß, *n. Bot.* zum —gefäß gehörig, *adj.* stamineous fäßförmig, *adj.* staminiform; —gefä *adj.* staminiferous; —geschlecht, *n.* kind; —haar, *n.* down; —harz, *m.* mu —häutchen, *n. Bot.* coredium; —haut brane of the anther; —hemd, *n.* —holz, *n.* bed-plates; —hügel, *m.* dust; —hülle, *f.* *, human body; — *see* —behältniß.

Stau'big, I. *adj.* dusty; *Bot.* pulv II. St-keit, *(w.) f.* dustiness.

Staub'..., *in comp.* —käfer, *m. Entom.* of meal-worm (Opatrum F.); —kalk, slacked in the open air; —kamm, *m.* comb; —kapsel, *f. see* —beutel & —be kohlen, *f. pl.* culm; —kolben, *m.* —lappen, *m.* duster.

Stäub'ling, *(str.) m.* 1) earth-fi born man (der Staubgeborene); 2) (Bofist, *Lycoperdon* Tourn.).

Staub'..., *in comp.* —mantel, *m.* —mehl, *n.* flour-dust; —perle, *f.* —regen, *m.* drizzling *or* misling rai *m.* smock-frock, (travelling-)blouse chen, *n. Paint.* pounce; —säge, *f. T.* cutter; —samen, *m.* seedpowder (of —sand, *m.* very fine sand; —schwamm Stäubling, 2; —sieb, *n.* dust-sieve; *m. see* —faden; —vogel, *m. see* — wedel, *m.* dusting whisk, dusting-b weg, *m. Bot.* the style, the cylindric pering-portion of the pistil between t and the stigma; —wirbel, *m.* whirl of dust; —wolke, *f.* dust-cloud.

Stauch, *(str.) m.* 1) toss; jolt; († 2) *provinc. a)* veil; *b)* sleeve; Stau; 4) truss (of flax).

Stau'chen, *(w.) v. tr.* 1) *(also* toss, jog, to jolt; to scuffle; to shak dam, stem; 3) *Smi.* to shorten *or* t by forging, to upset, jump; 4) to pu up (flax) in bundles, to expose (fla the sun; 5) *see* Verstauchen; 6) to cocoons).

Stau'chentäscher, *n. pl.* Appenzell

Stau'chung, *(w.) f.* the (act of) jolting, &c.

Stauch'..., *in comp.* —wagen, calling about the flour-beader; — large longs.

Stau'de, *(w.) f.* 1) shrub, with a stalk; 2) perennial, herbaceous 3) a head (of lettuce). — Stäudche *n. (dimin. of* Staude) little shrub.

Stau'deich, *(str.) m.* (from Stau dike, flood-bank, dam.

Stau'den, *(w.) v. intr.* to grow like plants, to shoot into stalk, to a head.

Stau'den..., *in comp.* —apfel, john-apple; —artig, *adj.* —cerealie, *f.* Pall.); —gewächs, *n.* dwarf-trees; —gewächs, growing like a bush; *m.* a variety of rye, 20 culms out of one grain,

not exceed that sum (or price); er kam auf die Füße zu —, he lighted on his feet; mit or bei Jemandem gut —, to be on good terms with somebody; to be a favourite with one, to stand high in one's favour; zu Jemand —, to stand with ...; es steht zum Verkauf, it is up for sale.

II. *ref.* 1) sich müde —, to be tired with standing; 2) sich (gut, schlecht, &c.) —, to be (well or badly) off; to be in (easy, bad, &c.) circumstances; sie — sich gut dabei, it answers their purpose very well; er steht sich auf 1000 Thaler (*Acc.*) jährlich, his income (altogether) is (or: he gets) 1000 dollars a year.

III. *intr. impers.* 1) (*with. Dat.*) to become, fit, to be suited; 2) to be in a certain condition, to fare, &c.; to be; es steht gut, schlecht, it goes (is) well, ill; es steht schlecht mit ihm, things go badly with him, his affairs are in a bad way; es steht besser mit ihm, things have mended with him; es steht nicht ganz so schlimm mit ..., it is not quite (or matters are not) so bad with ...; wie steht es mit ...? what of ...? wie steht's um euch? how is it with you? wie steht's? how go matters? how does your business go on? wie steht es mit der Sache? how stands the matter? wie steht es mit der Gesundheit, mit Ihnen? how goes your health? how is it with you? es steht bei Ihnen, it rests or lies with you, it depends on you; es steht Ihnen frei, it is at your option, you are free, it is free for you; st-d, *p. a.* standing (army, &c.); stationary; steady; st-des or st-den Fußes, upon the spot, immediately; st-de Maschine, *T.* stationary engine; *Mar.-s.* st-des Tauwerk, standing rigging, dead ropes; st-der Wind, settled wind; st-de Kniee, hanging knees; *Com.-s.* st-de Preise, fixed prices; st-de Schuld, consolidated debt, console; st-de Valuta, certain price; st-de Redensart, standing phrase; stock phrase; st-des Citat, stock quotation; st-der Gegenstand, staple subject; die st-den Gegenstände der Unterhaltung, the ordinary staple of conversation.

Steh'kragen, (*str.*) *m.* straight or stand-up-collar. [step-ladder.

Steh'leiter, (*w.*) *f.* pair or set of steps;

Stehl'bar, *adj.* that may be stolen.

Steh'len, (*str.*) *v. tr.* to steal; to pilfer; rob; die Segel — einander den Wind, *Mar.* the sails overlap (becalm) each other; sich in Jemandes Gunst —, to wind one's self or skulk into one's graces.

Steh'ler, (*str.*) *m.* stealer, thief. [bisch).

Steh'lerisch, *adj.* given to stealing (die-

Steh'..., *in comp.* —männchen, *n.* (cork-) tumbler; —platz, *m.* standing room; —pult, *m.* high desk, standing-desk; —stippe, *f. see* Steg, 8.

Stei'ermark, *f. Geogr.* Styria; **Stei'ermärker**, (*str.*) *m.*, **Stei'ermärkerin**, (*w.*) *f.*, **Stei'ermärkisch**, **Stei'erisch**, *adj.* Styrian.

Steif, *adj.* 1) stiff; firm, rigid; stubby (bristles); 2) hard, fixed, unmoved, inflexible; obstinate; 3) *fig.* stiff, formal; starch; strait-laced; *Paint.* hard (figures); *Mar.* stiff (breeze); — ansehen, to look hard or to stare at or upon, to fix with one's eyes upon; — und fest, strongly, firmly, obstinately.

Steif'bettler, (*str.*) *m.* (*l. u.*) sturdy beggar.

Stei'fe, (*w.*) *f.* 1) stiffness; 2) starch, glazing, stiffening; 3) *Carp.* buttress, prop, stay, supporter.

Stei'fen, (*w.*) *v. tr.* 1) to stiffen; to starch, stiffen with starch; 2) *Carp.* to prop; sich auf etwas (*Acc.*) —, *fig.* 1. to rely or depend upon; 2. to persevere or persist obstinately in ..., to set one's heart on, to urge a thing.

Stei'fer, (*str.*) *m.* stiffener; —blech, *n.* *Mat.* [illegible].

Steif'..., *in comp.* —haarig, *adj.* stiff-haired; bristly; —hals, *m.* stiff-necked person or animal; —halsig, *adj. fig.* stiff-necked, stubborn. [illegible]

Steif'heit, (*w.*) *f.* 1) stiffness; 2) *fig.* [illegible]

Steif'igkeit, (*w.*) *f.* stiffness.

Steif'..., *in comp.* —kette, *f.* *Weav.* stiff warp; —köpfigkeit, *f.* stubbornness, obstinacy; [illegible]leinwand, *f.*, —linnen, *n.*, —[illegible], *m.* [illegible] stiff linen, buckram. [illegible]

Steif'ling, (*str.*) *m.* (*l. u.*) stiff, starched

Steif'..., *in comp.* —[illegible], *m.* [illegible] pot-cheese; —ofen, *m.* *T.* hat-dressing stove; —sinn, *m.* stubbornness; —sinnig, *adj.* stubborn; —stiefel, *m. pl.* jack-boots; —sucht, *f. see* Starrsucht; —wurzel, *f.* *Pharm.* root of blunt-leaved sorrel. [illegible]

Stei'fung, (*w.*) *f.* the (act of) stiffening.

Steig, (*str.*) *m.* path, foot-path, steep-road.

Steig'... (*from* Steigen), *in comp.* —bäume, *m. pl. see* Treppenbalken; —bohne, *f.* *Bot.* kidney-bean, French bean; —bügel, *m.* stirrup (*also Anat.* stapes); —bügelmuskel, *m.* *Anat.* stapedian muscle (of the ear); —bügelriemen, *see* —riemen.

Stei'ge, (*w.*) *f.* 1) stair, stile, set of steps, ladder, staircase; 2) hen-roost, chicken-coop; 3) *see* Stiege, 2; 4) steep path.

Steig'eisen, (*str.*) *n.* climbing spur.

Stei'gen, (*str.*) *v. intr.* (*aux.* sein) 1) to rise; to mount, ascend, to step, climb, or get up; 2) *see* Bäumen, 1, 2; 3) to soar; 4) to come (of noses, &c.); to descend; to march, step, to stalk; 5) to increase; to advance (in prices); to be getting up, to improve; to progress; die Preise werden wohl noch mehr —, the prices will most likely experience a further rise; der Preis ist wieder um 1 % gestiegen, the price has recovered or improved 1 %, is better by a further percent.; der Teig steigt, *Bak.* the dough is beginning to rise or swell; in den (aus dem) Wagen —, to get, step into (out of) the carriage; auf das Pferd —, to mount the horse; vom Pferde —, to alight from one's horse; aus dem Schiffe —, ans Land —, to disembark; to land; (aus einem Stromschiff) to step or get on shore; in den Kopf —, *fig.* to fly up or get into one's head; Wein, der in den Kopf steigt, heady wine; es ist [illegible] Höchste gestiegen, it is strained or screwed up to the highest pitch; das —, (*str.*) *n. s.* the (act of) rising, &c., rise; advance; improvement, enhancement; die Preise [illegible] —, the prices (rates) have an upward tendency, tend upwards; im —, on the rise; im — sein, *Comm.* to be getting (*coll.* to be looking) up, to rise (in price). [*in comp.*

Stei'geleiter, **Steig'gerät** &c., *see* Steig...

Stei'ger, (*str.*) *m.* 1) climber, ascender; 2) *Min.* leader, master miner, deggle, overseer; —bock, *f.* badge worn by master-miners.

Stei'gern, (*w.*) *v. tr.* 1) to raise, enhance, increase, to drive or run up; to [illegible], heighten; to work up (to a high pitch of excitement), to carry out (into cruelty, &c.); 2) *Gramm.* to compare, to form (an adjective) in the degrees of comparison; die [illegible] gesteigerten Ansprüche, the full-blown pretensions.

Stei'gerung, (*w.*) *f.* 1) the (act of) raising, &c., enhancement; 2) auction; 3) gradation, climax; 4) *Gramm.* (the [illegible]) of an adjective in its degrees of comparison; St-sgrad, *m.*, St-sstufe, *f.* degree of comparison.

Steig'... (*from* Steigen), *in comp.* [illegible] *f.* *T.* rising-box, drop-box (of a [illegible] loom); —leiter, *f.* steps (in a [illegible]) *Naval-a.* —rad, *n.* balance-wheel; [illegible] *m.* potence, pot(t)ence; [illegible] balance-wheel engine; —riemen, [illegible] leather, stirrup-strap; [illegible] menträger, *pl.* head of the [illegible]

Stoff'los, I. *adj.* 1) immaterial, incorporeal; 2) *fig.* void; worthless; II. **St-losigkeit**, *(w.) f.* immateriality, incorporality.

Stoff..., *in comp.* **–name**, *m.*, **–wort**, *n. Gramm.* concrete noun; **–theilchen**, *n.* particle of matter; **–verwandtschaft**, *f. Chem.* affinity of matter, material affinity; **–wechsel**, *m. Physiol.* change of matter, metabolic change, metabolic process, metabolism constituting organic bodies.

Stöh'nen, *(w.) v.* I. *intr.* to groan; II. *tr.* to utter with a groan.

* **Stoicis'mus**, *m.* stoicism. — **Sto'iker**, *(str.) m.* stoic; **Sto'isch**, *adj.* stoic(al); *adv.* stoically.

* **Sto'la**, *f. (pl.* **Sto'len***) Rom. Cath.* stole, surplice; **Stol'gebühren**, *f. pl.* surplice-fees.

Stoll'baum, *(str., pl.* **St-bäume***) m. Min.* tubbing-beam.

Stol'len, *(str.) m., provinc.* **Stol'le**, *(w.) f.* 1) prop; post, foot (of the bedstead); baluster; iron-hooks; 2) *a) provinc. (N. G.)* slice of bread; *b) Bak.* cake, butter-cake; wig; 3) *Min.* stulm, adit, level; gallery (of a quarry, &c.); 4) *Farr.* calk, calkin (pointed iron on a horse-shoe); 5) *among the Master-Singers*, strophe and antistrophe considered as a whole.

Stol'len, *(w.) v. tr.* 1) *T.* to furnish with posts, props, *or* hooks; 2) *Farr.* to provide (a horse-shoe) with calkins, to rough-shoe; 3) *Tann.* **Häute –**, to soften hides.

Stol'len..., *in comp. Min.-s.* **–arbeit**, *f.* stulm-work; **–befahrung**, *f.* visiting of a stulm; **–beule**, *f. Vet.* swelling on the fore-foot of a horse; **–firste**, *f.* head, top of a stulm; **–gebäude**, *n.* woodwork of a stulm; **–ort**, *m.* end of a stulm; **–rösche**, *f.* ditch at the entrance of a gallery; **–schacht**, *m.* shaft of a gallery; **–trieb**, *m. see* **–arbeit**; **–wasser**, *n.* water flowing in the drains of a gallery; **–weise**, *adv.* from gallery to gallery; by the gangways; **–zimmerung**, *f.* timber-work of a stulm *or* gallery.

Stöll'ner, *(str.) m.* proprietor of a mine.

Stoll'..., *in comp.* **–ort**, *m. see* **Stollenort**; **–schwamm**, *m. see* **Stollenbeule**.

Stolp, *(str.) m.* 1) block; 2) *see* **Stolp(e)**.

Stol'per, *(str.) m.* 1) stumble, stumbling; 2) *fig.* blunder; **–fuchs**, *m. fam.* 1) stumbler; 2) *fig.* blunderer; **–gang**, *m.* stumbling gait. — **Stol'perer**, *(str.) m.* stumbler, &c. — **Stol'perig**, *adj.* 1) stumbling; 2) rough, so as to occasion stumbling. — **Stol'pern**, *(w.) v. intr. (aux.* **sein***)* 1) to stumble, trip; **über seine eignen Füße –**, (of an awkward person) to fall over one's own legs; 2) *fig.* to stumble, blunder.

Stolp'rian, *(str.) m. see* **Stolperfuchs**.

Stolz, I. *adj.* 1) proud (**auf** *[with Acc.]*, of); haughty, arrogant; **er ist – auf seinen Sohn**, he is proud of his son; **er ist – darauf, mehr trinken zu können, als irgend ein Anderer**, he is proud of being able to drink more than any one else; 2) *(† A)* *, splendid, magnificent, noble, lofty; II. *s. (str.) m.*, pride (**auf** *[with Acc.]*, in); boast; haughtiness, arrogance; **der – auf unsere eigne Sprache** *(Grimm, WB.* XXVIII), the pride in our own language.

Stol'zen, **Stolzi'ren**, *(w.) v. intr.* to be proud, to flaunt, strut, prance.

Stopf'... *(from* **Stopfen***)*, *in comp.* **–anker**, *m. see* **Pflichtanker**; **–arzenei**, *f. Med.* astringent medicine, styptic; **–büchse**, *f. Mech.* stuffing-box; **–farbe**, *f.* 1) *Paint.* colours for repairing pictures; 2) *T.* a kind of putty for filling out chinks, &c.; **–garn**, *n.* darning-yarn, darning-cotton; **–haar**, *n.* stuffing-hair; **–lappen**, **–lappen**, *m.* rags to stop holes up; **–holz**, *n.* 1) *Found.* plug, stopple, pin; 2) *Saddl.* stuffing-stick; **–meißel**, *m.* iron wedge *or* chisel for stopping; **–muskel**, *m. Anat.* obturator(-muscle); **–nadel**, *f.* [illegible] needle; **–naht**, *f.* darn; **–nudel**, *f.* [illegible] nudel; **–kegel**, *n.* drift-sail; **–[illegible]** stopper, stopple; *Mar.-s.* **–[illegible]**, *n.* [illegible] between two butts; **–tafel**, *m.* [illegible] of the mast of a lighter; **–ventil**, *n. Mech.* [illegible] per-valve; **–mus[illegible]**, *n.* [illegible], [illegible] **–wasser**, *n. Mar.* stop-water; **–[illegible]** oakum for caulking.

Stöpf'el, *(str.) m. see* **Stöpsel**.

Stopf'en, *(w.) v. tr.* 1) to fill, stuff [illegible] tresses, birds, &c.); to stop (up), [illegible] cork; 2) to quilt; to wad; 3) to darn, [illegible] stop (a hole); to fine-draw; 4) *Med.* [illegible] struct, constipate, to bind; **eine Pfeife** [illegible] fill a pipe; **ein Leck –**, to stop *or* plug a [illegible] **Einem das Maul –**, *fig.* to stop one's m[illegible] to shut one up, to muzzle one; **sich –**, [illegible] **sich** *(Dat.)* **den Magen voll –**, to cram [illegible] self; *Mar.-s.* **ein Tau –**, to stopper a [illegible] **die Zeit** *or* **Gezeit –**, to stem the tide; [illegible] **voll**, crammed; **unser Markt ist gestopft** [illegible] **davon**, our market is overstocked *or* g[illegible] with it; **st-d**, *p. a. Med.* stopping, [illegible] styptic.

Stopf'er, *(str.) m.* stopper, &c., [illegible]

Stopferei', *(w.) f.* the (act of) st[illegible] up, &c., darning.

Stopf'erin, *(w.) f.* darner.

Stop'pel, *(w.) f.* 1) *Agr.* stubble; 2) [illegible] feathers, pin-feathers; *in comp.* **–[illegible]** **–feld**, *n.* stubble-field; **–bart**, *m.* [illegible] beard; **–butter**, *f.* August-butter; **–[illegible]** thatch-roof.

Stoppelei', *(w.) f. coll.* the (act, [illegible] *or* a piece of) patching, compilation, [illegible] work.

Stop'pel..., *in comp.* **–feder**, *f.* 1) [illegible] feather; 2) *pl.* quill-stumps on the skin [illegible] plucked bird; **–gans**, *f.* stubble-goose; [illegible] **dicht**, *n.* a composition *or* patch-work [illegible] up of scraps from other compositions, [illegible] poem, rhapsody, cento; **–gras**, *n.* [illegible] grass; **–hafer**, *n. provinc.* field-[illegible]

Stop'pelig, *adj.* full of stubble, [illegible]

Stop'pel..., *in comp.* **–korn**, *n.* [illegible] sown in a stubble-field; **–lerche**, *f.* field[illegible] (**Feldlerche**, 2); **–mast**, *f.* stubble [illegible]

Stop'peln, *(w.) v. tr. (& intr.)* 1) to g[illegible] 2) to take the pin-feathers out of (duck[illegible] 3) to patch (**zusammenstoppeln**); 4) [illegible] gen, 2.

Stop'pel..., *in comp.* **–obst**, *n.* [illegible] fruit, gleaning; **–pflug**, *m. Agr.* stubble-[illegible] **–pilz**, **–schwamm**, *m. Bot.* species of [illegible] room *(Hydnum repandum L.)*; **–[illegible]** late turnip *(Brassica rapa [illegible])*; **–[illegible]** *f.* stubble-scythe; **–verse**, *m. pl.* [illegible] (different) poems, *cf.* **–gedicht**; **–[illegible]** gleaning; **–werk**, *n.* patch-work.

Stop'pen, *(w.) v. tr. Mar.* 1) to [illegible] (a cable); 2) to stem (the tide).

Stop'per, *(str.) m. Mar.* stopper.

* **Stoppi'ne**, *(w.) f. T.* [illegible]

Stopp'ler, *(str.) m.* 1) [illegible] (bungling) compiler.

Stopp'wasser, *n. (N. G.) see* [illegible]

Stöp'sel, *(str.) m.* stopper, [illegible] nach dem – schmecken, to taste of [illegible] be corked.

Stöp'seln, *(w.) v. tr.* to stopper, [illegible]

Stör, *(str.) m. Ichth.* sturgeon [illegible] *sturio L.*); **–fang**, *m.* sturgeon-fishing [illegible] *m. Comm.* sturgeon's sperm, [illegible]

* **Sto'rax**, *m. Bot.* storax, [illegible] obtained from a tree, the [illegible]

Storch, *s.* I. *(str., pl.* [illegible] *m.)* *m. Ornith.* stork [illegible] II. *in comp.* **–bein**, *n.* [illegible] leg; *coll.* person with long [illegible] legs *or* shanks; **–beinig**, *adj.* [illegible] **–blume**, *f. Bot.* [illegible]

[illegible]

1) hour-hand; 2) dial; horoscope; —zirkel, see —circkel. [more hours.

...stündig, adj. (in comp.) lasting one or

Stünd'lein, (str.) n. (provinc.: [S. G.] Stünd'le, (Alemann.:) Stünd'li) (dimin. of Stunde) *, little or short hour (cf. Stündchen); sein — ist gekommen, his hour is come.

Stünd'lich, adj. & adv. hourly, (occurring) every hour; T. horary.

Stun'dung, see Gestundung.

Stun'ge, (w.) f. see Gelte.

Stupf, (str.) m. provinc. (S. U.) push. — Stupf'eisen, (str.) n. goad. — Stupf'el, (str.) m. 1) goad; 2) see Ähre, B.; 3) see Stoppel, 1. — Stupf'en, (w.) v. tr. to push; to goad.

Stupp'wachs, (str.) n. hive-dross.

Sturm, (str., pl. Stür'me) m. 1) storm, tempest; Mar. gale; hurricane; 2) violent noise, alarm, tumult; 3) Mil. violent attack, assault, storm; 4) Cook. flummery; 5) fig. turbulence, violence, fury, passion; — blasen, to blow the signal for storming; — läuten, to ring the alarm-bell; — laufen, Mil. to make an assault (auf [with Acc.], upon), to charge with the bayonet; die Einnahme Sebastopols durch —, the capture of S. by assault; den — aushalten, fig. to bear the brunt; die — und Drang-Periode, Germ. Lit. Hist. storm-and-stress-period (period of great intellectual convulsion, during the last quarter of the last century).

Sturm'..., in comp. —anlauf, m. onset; —balken, —block, m. herisson; —band, n. 1) Fort. prick-post, brace; 2) stay (of a military cap, &c.); —bock, m. battering-ram; —bonnet, n. Mar. first bonnet laced on a sail; —brett, n. hersillon; —colonne, f., —commando, n. Mil. scaling- or escalading party; —dach, n. (ancient warfare) tortoise, testudo, a contrivance for screening troops; —deich, m. breakwater; —egge, f. see —balken; —eile (Sturmeseile), f. great haste.

Stür'men, (w.) v. I. intr. 1) to storm; 2) to rush; to roar; 3) to rage, fume; 4) to ring the alarm-bell; es stürmt, it storms, it blows a tempest; es stürmt heftig, (coll.:) it blows great guns; mit stürmender Hand erobern, to take by storm; II. tr. Mil. 1) to assault; 2) to storm, take or carry by storm; ein Thor —, to force a gate

Stür'mer, (str.) m. 1) blusterer; 2) assaulter; 3) coll. a large (cocked) hat, cf. Sturmhut, 1.

Sturm'..., in comp. —fahne, f. war-standard; —faß, n. water-tub used in conflagrations; —fest, adj. tempest-proof, firm; —flasche, f., —hafen, —krug, m. clay powder-flask; —flut, f. high tide raised by a storm, bore; —gatter, n. portcullis; —gepeitscht, p. a. tempest-beaten; —geräth, n. implements for storming; —glocke, f. alarm-bell; —haken, m. see Brechhaken, 1; —haspel, m. Fort. cheval de frise; —haube, f. 1) morion, steel-cap, casque; 2) Conch. helmet- or casque-shell (Cassis Lam.); —hut, m. 1) morion; 2) Bot. (wolfstödter) wolf's-bane, monk's hood, aconite (Aconitum lycoctonum L.); —igel, m. Fort. spiked beam, herisson.

Stür'misch, (S. G.: Stür'mig) adj. 1) stormy, tempestuous, boisterous, blustering; Mar. dirty (weather); 2) impetuous, dashing; fierce; furious; uproarious, tumultuous; die Börse war — bewegt, the Exchange was in an uproar.

Sturm'..., in comp. —kappe, f. see —hut; —klüver, m. Mar. storm-jib; —kolben, m. club; —kranz, m. carcass, fire-circle; —kreuz, n. fiery-cross; —laufen, n. assault; —läufer, m. assailant; —leiter, f. 1) scaling-ladder; 2) fire-ladder; 3) Mar. gallery-ladder, quarter-ladder; —lücke, f. breach in a wall; —mensch, m. see —läufer; —möve, f. Ornith. 1) see —vogel; 2) a kind of gull (Larus canus L.); —partei, f. see —commando; —[illegible] see Sturm; —pfahl, m. palisade; —[illegible] Mar. dead-lights; —pumpe, f. see [illegible] —riemen, m. see —band, 2; —sack, m. sack with fusees; —schritt, m. [illegible] march, quickest time: double quick; —schuß, m. shot with ball; —[illegible] Ornith. storm-finch, storm-petrel (P[illegible] pelagica L.); —see, f. heavy sea; —[illegible] ing-sail; —stange, f. couch-joint; —[illegible] brace (of a window); —taucher, m. shearwater petrel, Manx puffin (Puffinus [illegible] Temm.); —teufel, m. see —[illegible] verkündiger, —vogel, m. Ornith. [illegible] stormy petrel (Procellaria pelagica L.) [illegible] f. see —balken; —wetter, n. stormy or [illegible]tuous weather; —wind, m. storm, hurricane, heavy gale; —wolke, cloud; —zeug, n. see —geräth.

Sturz, (str., pl. Stür'ze) m. 1) a[illegible] and violent fall; tumble; plunge, ru[illegible] waves, &c.), a hurling down; shock[illegible] overthrow, ruin; 2) precipice; fall [illegible] cataract; 3) something projecting; [illegible] 4) Min. place where earth (rubbish) [illegible] 5) plough-tail; 6) Archit. cap-plate [illegible] 7) Sport. single, scut (of a deer); 8) [illegible] iron-plate; 9) apron of the priest [illegible] at the mass; 10) mourning-veil.

Sturz... (cf. Stürz...), in comp[illegible] m. acre ploughed or tilled for the [illegible] after having lain fallow; —bad, n. [illegible] bath; —baum, see Schlagbaum; —ble[illegible] sheet-iron, plate-iron; 2) slab-plate; [illegible] f. Min. stand for the tun or skip.

Stür'ze, (w.) f. 1) cover, (pot-lid[illegible] bell(-mouth) (Schallstück); — aufwärts, mouth upwards; — vorwärts, horizontal mouth; 3) see Sturz, 5; —becher, [illegible] Deckelbecher; 2) tippler.

Stur'zel, Stür'zel, (str.) m. stum[illegible]

Stür'zen, (w.) v. I. intr. (aux. s[illegible] precipitated, to tumble, fall; to ru[illegible] to gush, pour; II. tr. 1) to hurl, plunge, precipitate; 2) a) to overthr[illegible] turn, upset; b) to undo, ruin; 3) to tu[illegible] tilt, shoot (a cart); to turn out, [illegible] to stir (corn); 4) a) to cover with [illegible] lid; b) to put (the cover, &c.) on, [illegible] to plunge, involve (into debts, &c.) [illegible] to poach eggs; den Acker —, Agr. to [illegible] field for the first time; das Getr[illegible] stir the corn with a shovel; vom T[illegible] to dethrone; sich —, fig. to cast one'[illegible] rush, plunge; sich auf (with Acc.) — [illegible] upon ...; gestürzt, p. a. Bot. resupinate, reversed.

Stürz'[illegible], (str.) n. foal, [illegible]

Stür'zer, (str.) m. Min. wheeler[illegible]

Stürz'..., in comp. —[illegible] güter, n. pl. loose, weighable, [illegible] articles which are thrown loose int[illegible] of a ship without being previously [illegible] mit —gütern beladen, laden in bulk; [illegible] m. tumbrel, whip-cart, camp-cart; [illegible] platz, m. see —acker; —[illegible] f. [illegible] versed agree; —schaufel, f. shovel fo[illegible] corn; —statt, f. Sport. place where a deer falls.

Stürz'ling, (str.) m. precipitat[illegible]

Sturz'... (cf. Stürz...) [illegible] m. precipice; —klinge, f. [illegible] on both sides; —[illegible] Min. wheel for emptying [illegible] rann, —rinne, m. see [illegible] Min. tilting-chair; —[illegible] pooping sea; —[illegible] ship seas; —[illegible] f. [illegible] —trog, m. Min. tun, skip [illegible] T. casing of the lintel; —[illegible] steep side of a rock; —[illegible] welle, f. see —see.

Ta'dler, *(str.) m.* fault-finder, blamer, censurer, reprehender, critic, carper.

Ta'fel, *(w.) f.* 1) plate, tablet; table; slab; sheet; *Archit.* table, pane; — mit Kranzleisten, crowned table; erhabene —, projecting table; (*cf.* Glas-, Schiefer- rc. Tafel); 2) cake (of chocolate, &c.); 3) register, roll, index; 4) *see* Tabentisch; in T-n bringen, to tabulate; to register; bei —, at table *or* dinner; — halten, to dine; offene — halten, to dine publicly, to keep open table; to be exceedingly hospitable.

Ta'fel..., *in comp.* **—artig**, *adj. Min.* tabular, lamellar, laminar; **—aufsatz**, *m.* (*fr.*) *epergne*; **—berg**, *m. Geogr.* Table Mountain (above Capetown); **—besteck**, *n.* knife, fork, and spoon; **—bier**, *n.* table-beer, small-beer; **—birne**, *f.* dessert-pear; the prince's pear; **—blei**, *m.* sheet-lead; **—bouillon**, *f.* portable soup (Bouillontafel); **—brot**, *n.* household-bread; **—brett**, *n.* 1) *Mech.* (pulley-)box, case; 2) *Carp.* half(-inch) plank, case (Schalbrett); **—butter**, *f. Comm.* best fresh (butter).

Tä'felchen, *(str.) n.* (*dimin. of* Tafel) small *or* little table, tablet.

Ta'fel..., *in comp.* **—consistenz**, *f. Pharm.* proof (of sugar); **—decker**, *m.* officer who takes care of the linen of a prince's table, lays the cloth, &c., butler; **—druck**, *m. Calico-print.* block-printing. [feasting, *cf.* Tafeln.

Tafelei', *(w.) f.* the (act *or* habit of) dining,

Täfelei', *(w.) f. Archit.* boarded work, (wooden) panelling, flooring, wainscoting.

Ta'fel..., *in comp.* **—ente**, *f. Ornith.* common sea-duck (*Fuligula ferina* L.); **—fähig**, *adj.* entitled to a seat at a prince's table; **—farbe**, *f. Calico-print.* chemical *or* topical colour; **—fisch**, *m. Ichth.* large-scaled chaetodon (*Heniochus macrolepidotus* L.); **—förmig**, *adj.* tabular; **—förmiges Pianoforte**, *Mus.* square-pianoforte; **—freuden**, *f. pl.* pleasures of the table, (free) indulgence at the table; **—gedeck**, *n.* suit of table-linen; **—geld**, *n. gen. pl.* **—gelder**, income, allowance of a prince or nobleman; **—geschirr**, *n.* table-plate; **—glas**, *n.* plate-glass; **—grund**, *m.* ground-line in painting; **—gut**, *n.* domain kept by a lord, &c. for the maintenance of his board *or* table, †: bordland; **—holz**, **Tä'felholz**, *n. T.* timbering; wainscoting(-wood); **—indigo**, *m. Comm.* Dutch indigo; **—knecht**, *m.* dumb-waiter; **—kranz**, *m. see* Schüsselring; **—lack**, *m. Comm.* shell-lac; **—laken**, *n. see* **—tuch**; **—land**, *n.* table-land; **—linnen**, *n.* table-linen, table-cloth; **—meister**, *m. see* **—schneider**; **—messing**, *n.* sheet-brass, latten brass; **—musik**, *f.* table-music.

Ta'feln, *(w.) v. intr.* 1) *Dy.* to drip; 2) to sit at table, to dine, sup, feast.

Tä'feln, *(w.) v. tr. T.* 1) to floor with boards; 2) to wainscot.

Ta'fel..., *in comp.* **—obst**, *n.* table-fruit; **—öl**, *n.* sweet oil; **—rechnen**, *n.* the (act *or* practice of) reckoning on a board *or* slate (*opp.* Kopfrechnen); **—ring**, *m. see* Schüsselring; **—roth**, *n. T.* topical red; **—rubin**, *m. Min.* table-ruby; **—runde**, *f. Celtic Myth.* round table; **—schere**, *f.* shears; **—schiefer**, *m. Min.* table-slate; **—schneider**, *m.* manager of a tailor's business; cutter-out; slab-cutter; **—schörl**, *m. Min.* tabular schorl; **—schwamm**, *m.* edible mushroom; **—seide**, *f. Manuf.* sort of organzine; **—service**, **—silber**, *n.* service of plate for a table; **—spath**, *m. Min.* tabular-spar; **—stein**, *m. Jew.* table-diamond; **—stift**, *m.* slate-pencil; **—stuhl**, *m.* dinner-chair; **—tuch**, *n.* table-cloth.

Tä'felwerk, **Ta'felwerk**, *(str.) n.* 1) *or* **Tä'felung**, *(w.) f. Archit.* wainscot, panelling; checker-work; 2) *Mar.* fluting of a ship.

Ta'fel..., *in comp.* **—waage**, *f. see* Brückenwaage; **—wein**, *m.* table-wine; **—zeug**, *n.* table-cloth and napkins, table-linen; **—zimmer**, *n.* dining-room, dining-hall.

Taf'fet, **Taft** (*coll.* **Taf'fent**), *(str.) m. Comm.* taffeta, taffety; **—band**, *n.* taffeta ribband; **—blumen**, *f. pl.* artificial silk-flowers; **—kleid**, *n.* taffeta dress; **—leder**, *n.* [illegible] leather; **—spiegel**, *m.*, **—streifen**, *pl.* [illegible] of taffeta; **—weber**, *m.* taffeta-weaver.

Taf'feten, *adj.* taffety.

Tag, *(str.) m.* 1) day; 2) light of day, open air; es wird —, the day breaks *or* appears, it dawns; eines T-es, 1. (von der Vergangenheit) once (on a day); 2. (von der Zukunft) some day; zweimal des T-es, twice a day; alle T-e, every day; den ganzen —, all the day, all day long; den ganzen geschlagenen (den lieben langen) —, the whole livelong day; meine T-e sind abgekürzet (Job 17, 1), my days are extinct; mein — (*for* meine Tage, *cf.* Lebtage), my days, *i. e.* all my life long; [illegible] mein — nicht müde [illegible] (*W. Müller*, Wanderschaft), [they] weary not the livelong day (*Bowring*); nächster T-e, in einigen T-en, in a day or two, in a few days, shortly; dieser T-e, 1. these days, the other day, lately; 2. within these days *or* the next few days, very shortly, soon; gute *or* schöne T-e haben, 1. to live at ease; 2. to have a delightful time of it; sich (*Dat.*) einen guten — machen, to make a holiday of it; sich (*Dat.*) gute T-e machen, to make one's self easy and comfortable; bestimmen Sie einen —, name your day; Jahr und —, 1. *Law*, a year and a day; 2. *fam.* a long while; ja, guten —! *iron.* by no means; *vulg.* over the left! man muß den — nicht vor dem Abend loben, don't praise the day till it is over; *cf.* Abend; am T-e vor..., on the eve of ...; am T-e nach ..., on the morrow of; an den — bringen, to bring to light, to disclose, to show; an den — kommen, to come to light; an den — legen, to evince, manifest, set forth, exhibit; es liegt am T-e, it is clear, it is evident; bei T-e, in the day-time; by day-light; heller, hoher, lichter —, broad day, broad day-light; den hellen — [illegible], to outface the sun at mid-day; bei hellerlichtem T-e, in the broad day-light; binnen 8 T-en, within a week, in a week's time; bis zum hellerlichten T-e schlafen, to sleep the day out of countenance; bis auf den heutigen —, to this (very) day; — für —, 1. day by day; 2 *or* einen — nach dem andern, day after day; einen — um den andern, every other day; in seinen besten T-en, in the flower of his age; wir sahen, daß ihre T-e gezählt waren, we saw that her days were numbered; in den — hinein, at a venture, at random; unconcernedly, thoughtlessly, carelessly; in den — hinein reden, to talk at random or at large; 14 T-e nach heute, fourteen days or a fortnight after date, this day fortnight; heute über acht T-e, this day week (sennight); heute vor acht T-en, this day week (ago); heut zu T-e, in these days, now-a-days; zu T-e ausgehen, *Min.* to crop out; zu T-e fördern, to bring up from a mine, (*fig.*) to bring to light.

Tag'... (*cf.* Tage...), *in comp.* [illegible] *m. see* Kalender; **—arbeit**, *f.* 1) [illegible] day-labour; char; 2) *see* [illegible] **—arbeiter**, *m.* 1) day-labourer, daily [illegible] one working by day; [illegible] **—blind**, *adj.* blind in the day, only [illegible] one in the dusk of the evening [illegible] nyctalops; **—blindheit**, *f.* [illegible] *f. Bot.* day-lily (*Hemerocallis* L.) [illegible] *Astr.* diurnal arc.

Ta'ge... (*cf.* Tag...), *in comp.* [illegible] *see* Tag...; **—bau**, *m. Min.* [illegible] ing; **—bedarf**, *m.* daily demand [illegible] *or* portion; allowance [illegible] *m.* daily account, bulletin [illegible]

Sti

—jungfer, *f.* nun; —kanzler, *m.* chancellor of the jurisdiction of a cathedral church; —kirche, *f.* collegiate church; cathedral; —mäßig, *adj.* capable of being chosen a canon; —mitglied, *m.* member of a chapter; —pfarre, *f.* living, cure of a collegiate church; —pfarrer, *m.* parson of a collegiate church; —pfennig, *m.* monastical rents; —pfründe, *f.* prebend; —prediger, *m.* chaplain of a collegiate church; —propst, *m.* provost of a collegiate church; —schule, *f.* foundation school; school attached to a chapter; —stadt, *f.* town belonging to a chapter; —stelle, *f.* canonicate; —tag, *m.* day of the assembly of canons; —versammlung, *f.* meeting of a chapter; —wohnung, *f. see* —gebäude.

Stif'tung, *(w.) f.* 1) the (act of) founding, &c. *cf.* Stiften; 2) foundation; establishment; (charitable) institution; milde St—en, charities.

Stif'tungs . . ., *in comp.* —brief, *m. see* Stiftsbrief; —capital, *n.* capital *or* stock of a foundation; —feier, *f.*, —fest, *n.* commemoration *or* celebration of the foundation (of . . .); —jahr, *n.* year of foundation; —tag, *m.* anniversary; —urkunde, *f. see* Stiftsbrief; —verwalter, *m.* steward of any college; —worte, *n. pl.* (words of) consecration.

* **Stil,** *(str.) m.* (*Lat.* stilus [*this full form* — Stilus — *used in German as late as* 1711, *cf.* Weigand], stylus, *from Gr.* stylos, *a style, writing instrument; Ital.* stilo) style; der strenge *or* gebundene —, *Mus.* style of counterpoint.

* **Stilett',** *(str.) n.* (*Ital.*) stiletto (*dimin. of* stilo), pocket-dagger.

* **Stilist',** *(w.) m.* writer, penman, (*metaphorically:*) pen. — **Stilistik',** *(w.) f.* theory of style or writing.

Still, I. *or* **Stil'le,** *adj.* 1) still, silent, hushed; 2) quiet, calm; peaceable; 3) dull, inanimate, stagnant, flat, heavy, dormant, quiet, calm (said of trade); 4) mental (reservation, prayer); ein st—es Glas trinken *or* leeren, to drink to the memory of a deceased person; eine st—e Messe, low mass; bei st—er Nacht, in the dead of night; — davon! stow that! — liegen, *Mar.* to lie to; — schweigen, to be silent; zu etwas — schweigen, to take no notice of; — halten, 1. to keep still; 2. to stop, pause; im St—en, secretly, privately, by one's self; *Comm.-s.* st—e Zeit, dead, dull season; mit dem Verkauf geht es —, sales slow; es ist darin st—er geworden, there is less doing in it; im St—en verkaufen, to sell underhand; der st—e Compagnon, dormant *or* sleeping partner; das st—e Meer, *Geogr.* the Pacific (Ocean); der st—e Freitag, good Friday; die st—e Woche, the holy week; ein st—er Liebhaber, an unavowed lover; — bleiben, to remain still, to be quiet; attention! — stehen, to stand still, to stop, to pull up; to be at a stand; *fig.* to remain stationary; to stand still; vollkommen — stehen, to be at a perfect stand-still; der Verstand steht mir —, I am perfectly at my wits' end; er kann keinen Augenblick — bleiben *or* stehen, his shoes are made of running leather; — gestanden! *Mil.* stand at attention; — werden, (of a storm, &c.) to lull; st—e Wasser sind tief, *proverb*, the silent stream runs the deepest (*Bulwer*).

II. *or* **Stille!** *(adv.)*, silence! peace! hush!

Still'amme, *(w.) f.* wet-nurse.

Still'bar, *adj.* that may be stilled, &c., *cf.* Stillen; appeasable, quenchable, &c.

Still'beglückt, *adj.* enjoying a quiet bliss.

Stil'le, *(w.) f.* 1) stillness, silence, quietness, calm, calmness; 2) tranquillity; 3) (modest) retirement; 4) dulness, inanimation (of trade); die tiefe — der Nacht, the dead of night; in der *or* aller —, quietly, tacitly, silently, without noise; secretly, underhand; privately; er denkt in der — wie ich, he, in his heart, thinks as I do; in der — leben, to live in retirement.

Stil'len, *(w.) v. tr.* 1) to still; to calm, appease, allay, compose; to assuage, quench (the thirst), to stay, appease (hunger, &c.), mitigate; 2) to stop, stay, staunch; 3) to nurse or suckle (a child); to give suck (to); 4) to silence; st—d, *p. a. Med.* sedative, lenitive; allaying.

Still' . . . (*from* Still & Stillen), *in comp.* —flöte, *f. Mus.* soft flute-stop, [illegible]; —gedackt, *n.* stop of four feet, fourth-stop (of an organ); —heiter, *adj.* quiet and serene; —lager, *n.* cantonment; —leben, *n.* 1) quiet, retired, or lowly life; 2) *Paint.* still-life; —messe, *f.* low mass; —mittel, *n. Med.* sedative; —salz, *n. Med.* sedative salt; —schweigen, *n.* silence, *see* Schweigen; mit —schweigen übergehen, to omit silently, to pass over (in silence); (im [illegible]) to blink (a question, &c.); —schweigend, *p. a.* silent, tacit; eine —schweigende Bedingung, an implied condition, condition in law; —schweigender Vorbehalt, mental reservation; —schweigendes Unterpfand, secret mortgage; —schweigend verpflichtet sein, to be under a tacit obligation; —stand, *m.* stand-still, stagnation, stand, stop, cessation, pause; sich in einem —stand befinden, to be at a standstill; —standsalter, *n.* age of consistence, of full growth; —standsflagge, *f.* flag of truce; —standsmann, *m.* stationary man; —standspolitik, *f.* stationary policy.

Stil'lung, *(w.) f.* the (act of) stilling, &c., *cf.* Stillen; S—smittel, *n. Med.* sedative.

Still' . . . (*from* Still & Stillen), *in comp.* —vergnügt, *adj. see* —heiter; —wasserseide, *f. Bot.* crow-silk (*Conferva rivularis* L.).

Stimm' . . . (*from* Stimmen & Stimme), *in comp.* —bar, *adj.* that may be tuned or brought to accord; —berechtigung, *f. see* —recht; —block, *m. see* —stock; —brett, *m. Org.* sound-board; —draht, *m. Org.* stop-wire.

Stim'me, *(w.) f.* 1) voice; *fig.* sound, tune; 2) *Mus. a)* part (in vocal or instrumental music); *b)* stop of an organ; *c) see* Stimmstock; 3) *a)* voice, vote, suffrage; *b)* right of voting; gut bei —, in good voice; nicht bei —, out of voice, not in voice; sie war [illegible] nur Eine — über (*with Acc.*) . . ., they were agreed as to . . . .

Stim'men, *(w.) v.* I. *intr.* 1) *a)* to be in tune, accord; *b)* to agree in pitch, to be tuned to the same pitch; *c) fig.* to agree, accord, congrue, tally, to be in accordance or keeping (zu, mit, with); die Bilanz stimmt, the balance squares; 2) to vote; II. *tr.* 1) to tune, attune; 2) *fig.* to dispose, move, determine (für, to [*with* folg. Subst.], in favour of), to induce (to); traurig —, to make sad; ich stimme für den Frieden, I vote or am for peace; gut gestimmt sein, to be in a good humour; zu etwas gestimmt sein, to be inclined, disposed for; ich bin nicht zum Schreiben gestimmt, I am not in a writing mood, I do not feel like writing.

Stim'men . . ., *in comp.* [illegible] 1) [illegible] score; 2) poll-book; —führer, *m.* [illegible] director of the song; —[illegible] gleichheit, *f.* tie; —mehrheit, *f.* majority of votes; —minderheit, *f.* minority [illegible]; —prüfung, —sicht, *f.* scrutiny; —[illegible] collecting of the votes; —[illegible] of votes; —zähler, *m.* teller of votes; —[illegible]lung, *f.* counting of votes.

Stim'mer, *(str.) m.* 1) tuner, [illegible] Stimmhammer.

Stimm' . . . (*from* [illegible] *in comp.* —fähig, *adj.* 1) *or* [illegible] titled to vote; 2) *see* —[illegible] pfeife; —freiheit, *f.* liberty of [illegible] voting, *cf.* —recht; —[illegible]

Ta'dler, *(str.) m.* fault-finder, blamer, censurer, reprehender, critic, carper.

Ta'fel, *(w.) f.* 1) plate, tablet; table; slab; sheet; *Archit.* table, pane; — mit Kranzleisten, crowned table; erhabene —, projecting table; (*cf.* Glas-, Schiefer- &c. Tafel); 2) cake (of chocolate, &c.); 3) register, roll, index; 4) *see* Ladentisch; in T-n bringen, to tabulate; to register; bei —, at table *or* dinner; — halten, to dine; offene — halten, to dine publicly, to keep open table; to be exceedingly hospitable.

Ta'fel..., *in comp.* —artig, *adj. Min.* tabular, lamellar, laminar; —aufsatz, *m.* (frz.) *epergne;* —berg, *m. Geogr.* Table Mountain (above Capetown); —besteck, *n.* knife, fork, and spoon; —bier, *n.* table-beer, small-beer; —birne, *f.* dessert-pear; the prince's pear; —blei, *n.* sheet-lead; —bouillon, *f.* portable soup (Bouillontafel); —brot, *n.* household-bread; —brett, *n.* 1) *Mech.* (pulley-)box, case; 2) *Carp.* half(-inch) plank, case (Schalbrett); —butter, *f. Comm.* best fresh (butter).

Tä'felchen, *(str.) n.* (*dimin. of* Tafel) small *or* little table, tablet.

Ta'fel..., *in comp.* —consistenz, *f. Pharm.* proof (of sugar); —decker, *m.* officer who takes care of the linen of a prince's table, lays the cloth, &c., butler; —druck, *m. Calico-print.* block-printing. [feasting, *cf.* Tafeln.

Tafelei', *(w.) f.* the (act *or* habit of) dining,

Täfelei', *(w.) f. Archit.* boarded work, (wooden) panelling, flooring, wainscotting.

Ta'fel..., *in comp.* —ente, *f. Ornith.* common sea-duck (*Fuligula ferina* L.); —fähig, *adj.* entitled to a seat at a prince's table; —farbe, *f. Calico-print.* chemical *or* topical colour; —fisch, *m. Ichth.* large-scaled chaetodon (*Henicchus macrolepidotus* L.); —förmig, *adj.* tabular; —förmiges Pianoforte, *Mus.* square-pianoforte; —freuden, *f. pl.* pleasures of the table, (free) indulgence at the table; —gedeck, *n.* suit of table-linen; —geld, *n. gen. pl.* —gelder, income, allowance of a prince *or* nobleman; —geschirr, *n.* table-plate; —glas, *n.* plate-glass; —grund, *m.* ground-line in painting; —gut, *n.* domain kept by a lord, &c. for the maintenance of his board *or* table, †: bordland; —holz, Tä'felholz, *n. T.* timbering; wainscoting(-wood); —indigo, *m. Comm.* Dutch indigo; —knecht, *m.* dumb-waiter; —kranz, *m. see* Schüsselring; —lack, *m. Comm.* shell-lac; —laken, *n. see* —tuch; —land, *n.* table-land; —linnen, *n.* table-linen, table-cloth; —meister, *m. see* —schneider; —messing, *n.* sheet-brass, latten brass; —musik, *f.* table-music.

Ta'feln, *(w.) v. intr.* 1) *Dy.* to drip; 2) to sit at table, to dine, *esp.* feast.

Tä'feln, *(w.) v. tr. T.* 1) to floor with boards; 2) to wainscot.

Ta'fel..., *in comp.* —obst, *n.* table-fruit; —öl, *n.* sweet oil; —rechnen, *n.* the (act *or* practice of) reckoning on a board *or* slate (*opp.* Kopfrechnen); —ring, *m. see* Schüsselring; —roth, *n. T.* topical red; —rubin, *m. Min.* table-ruby; —runde, *f. Celtic Myth.* round table; —schere, *f.* shears; —schiefer, *m. Min.* table-slate; —schneider, *m.* manager of a tailor's business; cutter-out; slab-cutter; —schörl, *m. Min.* tabular shorl; —schwamm, *m.* edible mushroom; —seide, *f. Manuf.* sort of organzine; —service, —silber, *n.* service of plate for a table; —spath, *m. Min.* tabular-spar; —stein, *m. Jew.* table-diamond; —stift, *m.* slate-pencil; —stuhl, *m.* dinner-chair; —tuch, *n.* table-cloth.

Tä'felwerk, Ta'felwerk, *(str.) n.* 1) *or* **Tä'felung,** *(w.) f. Archit.* wainscot, panelling; checker-work; 2) *Mar.* lining of a ship.

Ta'fel..., *in comp.* —waage, *f. see* Brückenwaage; —wein, *m.* table-wine; —zeug, *n.* table-cloth and napkins, table-linen; —[illegible] *n.* dining-room, dining-hall.

Taf'fet, Taft (*coll.* **Taf'fent**), *(str.) m. Comm.* taffeta, taffety; —band, *n.* [illegible] riband; —blumen, *f. pl.* artificial silk-flowers; —kleid, *n.* taffeta dress; —leder, *n.* [illegible] leather; —spiegel, *m.*, —streifen, *pl.* [illegible] taffeta; —weber, *m.* taffeta-weaver.

Taf'feten, *adj.* taffety.

Tag, *(str.) m.* 1) day; 2) light of day, open air; es wird —, the day breaks *or* appears, it dawns; eines T-es, 1. (von der Vergangenheit) once (on a day); 2. (von der Zukunft) some day; zweimal des T-es, twice a day; alle T-e, every day; den ganzen —, all the day, all day long; den ganzen geschlagenen (den lieben langen) —, the whole livelong day; meine T-e sind abgekürzet (Job 17, 1), my days are extinct; mein — (*for* meine Tage, *cf.* Lebtage), my days, *i. e.* all my life long; [illegible] die sich mein — nicht müde drehn (*W. Müller, Wanderschaft*), [they] weary not the livelong day (*Baskerv.*); nächster T-e, in einigen T-en, in a day or two, in a few days, shortly; dieser T-e, 1. these days, the other day, lately; 2. within these days *or* the next few days, very shortly, soon; gute *or* schöne T-e haben, 1. to live at ease; 2. to have a delightful time of it; sich (*Dat.*) einen guten — machen, to make a holiday of it; sich (*Dat.*) gute T-e machen, to make one's self easy and comfortable; bestimmen Sie einen —, name your day; Jahr und —, 1. *Law.* a year and a day; 2. *fam.* a long while; ja, guten —! *iron.* by no means; *vul.* over the left! man muß den — nicht vor dem Abend loben, don't praise the day till it is over; *cf.* Abend; am T-e vor ..., on the eve of ...; am T-e nach ..., on the morrow of; an den — bringen, to bring to light, to disclose, to show; an den — kommen, to come to light; an den — legen, to evince, manifest, set forth, exhibit; es liegt am T-e, it is clear, it is evident; bei T-e, in the day-time; by day-light; heller, hoher, lichter —, broad day, broad day-light; den hellen — überscheinen, to outface the sun at mid-day; bei hellerlichtem T-e, in the broad day-light; binnen 8 T-en, within a week, in a week's time; bis zum hellerlichten T-e schlafen, to sleep the day out of countenance; bis auf den heutigen —, to this (very) day; — für —, 1. day by day; 2 *or* einen — nach dem andern, day after day; einen — um den andern, every other day; in seinen besten T-en, in the flower of his age; wir sahen, daß ihre T-e gezählt waren, we saw that her days were numbered; in den — hinein, at a venture, at random; unconcernedly, thoughtlessly, recklessly; in den — hinein reden, to talk at random *or* at large; 14 T-e nach heute, fourteen days *or* a fortnight after date, this day fortnight; heute über acht T-e, this day week (sennight); heute vor acht T-en, this day week (ago); heut zu T-e, in these days, nowadays; zu T-e ausgehen, *Min.* to crop out; zu T-e fördern, to bring up from a mine, [illegible] bring to light.

Tag'... (*cf.* Tage ...), *in comp.* —[illegible] *m. see* Tagedieb; —arbeit, *f.* 1) [illegible] day-labour; char; 2) *see* Tagewerk; —arbeiter, *m.* 1) day-labourer, daily workman; [illegible] one working by day; —[illegible] *adj.* [illegible] —blind, *adj.* blind in the day, [illegible] see in the dusk of the evening; [illegible] nyctalops; —blindheit, *f.* nyctalopy; [illegible] *f. Bot.* day-lily (*Hemerocallis* L.); [illegible] *Astr.* diurnal arc.

Ta'ge... (*cf.* Tag ...), *in comp.* [illegible] *see* Tag ...; —bau, *m. Min.* [illegible] ing; —bedarf, *m.* daily consumption [illegible] *or* portion; allowance [illegible] *m.* daily account, bulletin; [illegible]

Taxus, *(indecl.)* m. *Bot.* see Taxbaum.

* **Tazet'te**, *(w.) f. (Ital.) Bot.* pale daffodil, yellow narcissus, tazetta *(Narcissus tazetta L.)*.

* **Tech'nik**, *f. (Gr.)* science of technical terms, technics. — **Tech'nisch**, *adj.* technical. — **Tech'niker**, *(str.)*, **Technolog'(e)**, *(w.) m.* technologist. — **Technologie'**, *(w.) f.* technology. — **Technolo'gisch**, *adj.* technological.

Teck'el, *(str.) m.* see Dachshund.

* **Teckholz**, *n. Comm.* teak-wood, teakwood (Thekaholz). [wafer-seal, &c.).

* **Tectur'**, *(w.) f. (Lat.)* paper-cover (of a

* **Tede'um**, *(str., pl. T-s) n.* Te-deum *(a Latin hymn of thanksgiving, beginning with the words:* Te deum laudamus, *thee, God, we praise)*.

Teerd, **Teerd'je**, *(w.) f. Mar.* toggle.

Te'gel, *(str.) m. Geol.* a species of bluish green marl. [Klüverbaum.

Te'genstock, *(str., pl. T-stöcke) m. Mar.* see

Tel'enter, see Teilenter.

Teich, *(str.) m.* pond; pool; **-binse**, *f.* bulrush *(Scirpus lacustris L.)*. [pipe.

Tei'chel, *(str.) m.* water-conduit, conduit-

Tei'cheln, *(w.) v. tr. Gard.* to inoculate, bud.

Teich'..., *in comp.* **-faden**, *m. Bot.* triple headed pond-weed *(Zannichellia palustris L.)*; **-fenchel**, *m.* water-milfoil *(Myriophyllum L.)*; **-fenster**, *n.* opening in a pond to let off the water; **-fisch**, *m.* pond-fish; **-fischerei'**, *f.* pond-fishing; **-gitter**, *n.* grate of a pond; **-karpfen**, *m.* pond-carp; *Bot.-s.* **-kolbe**, *f.* cat's tail, reed-mace *(Typha L.)*; **-lilie**, *f.* water-lily, water-flag (Wasserschwertlilie); **-linse**, **-nuß**, *f.* see Wasserlinsen, Wassernuß; **-meister**, *m.* pond-master; dike-master; *Conch.-s.* **-muschel**, *f.* fresh-water muscle, anodon *(Anodonta Lam.)*; **-napfschnecke**, *f.* pond-limpet *(Ancylus lacustris L.)*; **-pumpe**, *f.* see **-kolben**; **-rohr**, *n. Bot.* common reed *(Phragmites communis L.)*; **-rohrsänger**, *m. Ornith.* a species of sedge-warbler, willow-lark *(Salicaria arundinacea Bechst.)*; **-rose**, *f. Bot.* pond-lily *(Nuphar luteum L.)*; **-schwamm**, *m. Zooph.* pond-sponge *(Spongilla lacustris Esp.)*; **-ständer**, *m.* pond-sluice; **-wasserläufer**, *m. Ornith.* pond-redshank, poolsnipe *(Totanus stagnatilis Bechst.)*; **-vogt**, **-wärter**, *m.* see **-meister**; **-zapfen**, *m.* lock, tap (of a pond).

Teig, *(str.) m.* dough, paste; *in comp.* **-kasten**, *m.* paper-maker's mellowing box; **-krape**, **-scharre**, *f.* scraper; **-mal**, *n.* morphew, **-rädchen**, *n.* jagging-iron.

Tei'gig *(provinc.* Teig), **Tei'gicht**, *adj.* doughlike; doughy; mellow, rotten from being too ripe, over-ripe.

* **Teint** *(pr.* täng), *(str., pl. T-s) m. (Fr.)* complexion.

* **Teikbaum**, *m. Bot.* teak-tree, Indian oak *(Tectonia grandis L.)*.

* **Telegramm'**, *(str.) n. (Gr.)* telegram. — **Telegrammatik'**, *(w.) f.* telegraphic style. — **Telegraph'**, *(w.) m. (Gr.)* telegraph; durch den T-en or auf telegraphischem Wege, see Telegraphisch, *adv.* — **Telegra'phen...**, *in comp.* **-beamte(te)**, *m.* telegraph clerk; **-draht**, *m.* telegraph-wire; **-leitung**, *f.* telegraph communication; **-linie**, *f.* 1) telegraph line; 2) line of telegraphs; **-stange**, *f.* telegraph-pole; **-strang**, *m.* telegraph-wire; **-verein**, *m.* telegraph-association; **-zone**, *f.* telegraph-zone or district. — **Telegraphie'**, *(w.) f.* art of telegraphing. — **Telegraphi'ren**, *(w.) v. tr. & intr.* to telegraph, to convey intelligence by a telegraph. — **Telegra'phisch**, *adj.* telegraphic; *adv.* by (per) telegraph, per wire.

* **Telephon'**, *(str.) n. (Gr.)* telephone.

* **Teleskop'**, *(str.) n. (Gr.)* telescope. — **Telesko'pisch**, *adj.* telescopic, telescopical.

Tel'le, *(w.) f. provinc.* see Delle.

Tel'ler, *s.* I. *(str.) m.* 1) plate; [illegible] —, trencher; — einer Luftpumpe, plate [illegible] *Bot.* disk; II. *in comp.* **-brett**, *n.* plate-drainer; **-eisen**, *n.* a kind of trap with an iron plate (for catching foxes); **-förmig**, *adj. Bot., &c.* plate-shaped; [illegible]; **-hammer**, *m. T.* flattening-hammer; **-haube**, **-mütze**, *f.* flat cap; **-held**, *m.* trencher-man; **-huf**, *m.* flat hoof; **-knecht**, *m.* dumb-waiter; **-korb**, *m.* plate-basket; **-lecker**, *m. coll.* [illegible] lick-trencher, sponger; **-lecken**, *v. intr.* to sponge; **-muschel**, *f. Conch.* tellina *(Tellina L.)*; **-nase**, *f.* flat nose; **-rechen**, *m.* rails or rack for plates; **-ring**, *m.* wicker-stand for plates; **-roth**, *n. Paint.* carthamine; **-rübe**, *f. Bot.* round-rooted, yellow turnip *(Brassica vulgaris* [illegible]*)*; **-schnecke**, *f. Conch.* a genus of fresh-water snail *(Planorbis Müll.)*; **-schrank**, *m.* china cupboard; **-tuch**, *n.* napkin; **-wärmer**, *m.* plate-warmer.

Tell'muschel, *(w.) f.* see Tellermuschel.

* **Tellur'**, **Tellu'rium**, *(str.) n. (Lat.* tellus *(Gen.* telluris*), earth) Miner.* tellurium; **-säure**, *f.* telluric acid; das **-saure** Salz, tellurate.

Tem'pel, *s.* I. *(str.) m.* 1) temple; church; synagogue; 2) *Weav.* see Spannstange; II. *in comp.* **-balken**, *m. Hydr.* dike-beam; **-diener**, *m.* priest; **-herr**, **-ritter**, *m.* knight-templar, knight of the Temple; **-orden**, *m.* order of the Temple; **-raub**, *m.* sacrilege; **-schänder**, *m.* one guilty of sacrilege; **-zinne**, *f.* pinnacle. [illegible]

* **Tem'peramalerei**, *(w.) f. (Ital.)* [illegible]

* **Temperament'**, *(str.) n. (Lat.)* temper, temperament; **T-sfehler**, *m.* constitutional fault. — **Temperatur'**, *(w.) f.* 1) temperature; 2) *Mus.* temperament; **-wasser**, *n. Still.* [illegible] water. — **Temperi'ren**, *(w.) v. tr.* to temper. — **Temperir'messer**, *n. Paint.* pallet-knife. — **Temperir'pulver**, *n. Med.* sedative powder.

* **Tem'pern**, *(w.) v.* I. *intr. coll.* see [illegible]; II. *tr.* to temper.

* **Tem'perofen**, *(str., pl. T-öfen)* [illegible] annealing-furnace.

Temp'ler, *(str.) m.* knight-templar.

Tempelfür'st, *(str.) m.* see [illegible]

* **Tem'po**, *(str., pl. T-s, or (Ital.)* **Tem'pi)** *n. (Ital.) Mus.* time, measure; *Mil.* [illegible] ment; das — beobachten, 1. to keep time; 2. *fig.* to watch one's time.

* **Temporär'**, *adj.* temporary.

* **Tem'pus**, *(Lat., pl.* **Tem'pora** [illegible]*)* n. *Gramm.* time, tense.

* **Tena'kel**, *(str.) n. (Lat.)* 1) *Typ.* visorium, retinaculum; 2) *Surg.* tenaculum.

* **Tendenz'**, *(w.) f. (Lat.)* tendency.

* **Ten'der**, *(str.) m. (Engl.)* tender (of a locomotive).

Ten'ne, *(w.) f.* floor; threshing-floor, barn-floor; *in comp.* **T-[illegible]**, *m.* [illegible] used in making floors; **T-[illegible]**, *m.* [illegible] ing of the barn-floor.

* **Tenor'**, *(str., pl. T-e, usual.* [illegible] *(Ital.) Mus.* 1) tenor; 2) see [illegible] hohe —, upper tenor; der tiefe —, [illegible] tenor; **-geige**, *f.* see Bratsche; [illegible] **-zeichen**, *n.* tenor-clef. — [illegible] tenor-singer.

Tep'pich, *(str.) m.* [illegible] *cf.* Tapete) carpet; tapestry; [illegible] mit einem — or mit T-en [illegible] to spread with carpets; *in comp.* [illegible] tapestry; **-band**, *n.* [illegible] ing; **-decke**, *m.* carpet [illegible] carpet-cover; **-händler**, *m.* [illegible] and covers; **-macher**, [illegible] carpet-weaver, carpet-[illegible] *m.* tack, little nail; [illegible] **-sticker**, *m.* tapestry-worker [illegible] *(cf.* Bett u. Kabel) [illegible]

party-man; —perspectiv, n. opera-glass; —principal, m. see —director; —routine, f. stage-practice; —saal, m. Archit. spectatory, cavea: —schriftsteller, m. dramatic author; —schwank, —streich, m. stage trick; —stück, n. play, stage piece, entertainment; —wesen, n. theatricals; the theatre; —zettel, m. play-bill; —zimmermann, m. stage-wright.

Theati'ner, (str.) m. Eccl. Theatine (monk).

* Theatra'lisch, adj. theatrical, scenic(al); stage-like; th-e Stellungen annehmen, to attitudinise.

The'ben, n. Geogr. Thebes. — Theba'ner, (str.) m., Theba'nisch, adj. Theban.

Thee, (str., Gen. pr. tā or tā'es, &c.) m. 1) tea; grüner —, green tea; schwarzer —, black tea; 2) see Theegesellschaft.

Thee'..., in comp. —baum, m. see —strauch; —blatt, n. tea-leaf; —blumen, pl. imperial tea; —bret, n. tea-board, tea-tray, waiter; —büchse, f. tea-canister; tea-caddy; — Boy (coll. —bub), m. Bohea (tea), black tea: —geschirr, n. see —zeug; —gesellschaft, f. tea-party; —kanne, f. tea-pot; —kästchen, n. tea-caddy; tea-chest; —kessel, m. 1) tea-kettle; 2) coll. simpleton; —klatsch, m. coll. tea-party of ladies, anal. tattle-broth; —kraut, n. Pharm. simples for tea; —kuchen, m. tea-cake; —löffel, m. tea-spoon; —maschine, f. tea-kitchen; —schale, f. tea-dish; —schäufelchen, n. caddy-spoon, caddy-shell; —sieb, n. tea-strainer; —sorten, pl. teas; —staude, f., strauch, m. Bot. tea-tree, tea-shrub, tea-plant (Thea chinensis Sims.); —stechpalme, f. Bot. Paraguay-tea-plant (Ilex paraguaiensis St. Hil.); —tasse, f. tea-cup and saucer; —tisch, m. tea-board, tea-table; —topf, m. tea-pot; —urne, f. tea-urn; —zeug, n. tea-things, tea-furniture.

Thèr (pr. tār), see Ther.

† Thei'ding, (str.) n. (& f.) 1) a) term; b) agreement; 2) a) speech in defence of ..., pleading; b) talking, idle talk; Th-sleute, pl. Script. judges.

Theil, (str.) m. (& n.) 1) part; division; deal; share, portion; lot; 2) part, tome, volume; 3) party: beide T-e, both parties or sides; 4) Min. the thirty-second part of a mine; 5) Archit. member; — einer Rede, Predigt &c., part or division of a discourse, &c.; großen T-s, in a great measure; größten T-s, for the greatest or most part; zum —, in part, partly, partially; zu gleichen T-en, in equal shares, share and share alike; zu gleichen T-en gehen, to go share and share (alike), S. to go snacks; — an etwas (Dat.) haben, to have a share, to be a sharer in, to participate in, to be (a) party to ..., to be or have art and part in ..., to share; — an etwas (Dat.) nehmen, 1. to take part or share in, to go shares, partake, participate, join in; 2. fig. to take an interest in a thing, to feel sympathy for; zu — werden, to fall to one's lot or share, to be one's lot; (Einem etwas) zu — werden lassen, to grant, bestow (something upon); ich meines T-s, I for my part, as for me.

Theil'bar, I. adj. divisible, partible; II. T-keit, (w.) f. divisibility, divisibleness.

Theil'..., in comp. —begriff, m. partial notion or idea; —betrag, m. equal amount; —bruch, m. Arith. simple fraction.

Theil'chen, (str.) n. (dimin. of Theil) a small part, particle.

Theil'..., in comp. —cirkel, see Theilungscirkel; —eisen, n. T. cutting-iron.

Thei'len, (w.) v. I. tr. 1) to divide, part, share; to partition; in gleiche Theile —, Law, to apportion; wir wollen es or die Differenz —, let us split the difference; 2) fig. to share, join, to participate in, sympathise with ...; II. refl. 1) to split, to separate; 2) to divide (itself), to be divided; to fork (of roads); 3) with in (& Acc.), to share among each other; getheilt, p. a. see this word.

Thei'ler, (str.) m. 1) divider; 2) [illegible]

Theil'haber (str.) m. (Theil'genoss [illegible]) sharer, partaker, participator, partner; [illegible] eintreten, to become (be received or admitted as) a partner; alle — an dem Geschäfte, all parties concerned in this transaction; [illegible] or joint owner.

Theil'haft, I. or Theil'haftig, adj. (with Gen.) partaking (of), sharing, participant (in); Einen einer Sache — machen, to make one share or participate in a thing; sich einer Sache — machen, to participate in; einer Sache — werden, to partake or participate in, to obtain a thing; II. T-igkeit, (w.) f. the (act of) partaking, sharing, participation.

Theil'hafen, (str.) m. iron- or bloom-hook.

...theilig, adj. (in comp.) (consisting) of (a certain number of) parts.

Theil'..., in comp. —kreis, m. T. (—kreis eines Zahnrades) pitch-line, pitch-circle; —maschine, f. T. dividing-engine, cf. —[illegible]; —messer, m. 1) see —eisen; 2) [illegible]; —nahme, —nehmung, f. participation, share; fig. interest, sympathy; —nahmlos, adj. apathetic, listless, passive, uninterested, indifferent, unfeeling; —nehmend, adj. participating; fig. sympathising, affectionate; —nehmer, m. 1) see —haber; 2) one that sympathises; —nehmer eines Verbrechens, partner in a crime, accomplice, accessary, art and part; —rechnung, f. account in participation; —riß, m. Mech. pitch-line.

Theils, adv. partly, in part.

Theil'..., in comp. —scheibe, f. T. dividing-plate (cf. Räderschneidezeug), divider; —[illegible] ling, m. Law, inheritance-fee; —[illegible], m. pl. partial obligations or bonds; —summe, f. see —betrag.

Thei'lung, (w.) f. 1) division, parting, partition, sharing; separation; 2) T. a) (Ab-theilung) graduation (of mathematical instruments), regular division into (equal) parts or degrees; b) pitch (of a cog-wheel).

Thei'lungs..., in comp. —cirkel, m. T. dividers (a kind of compasses); —glied, n. divisional member; [illegible] —grenze, f. [illegible] wall of an aqueduct; —[illegible], m. [illegible]; —kraft, f. capability of division (of [illegible]); —linie, f. dividing-line; —recht, n. right of division; —regel, f. Math. rule of division; —riß, m. see Theilriß; —vertrag, m. treaty of partition; —zahl, f. Math. dividend; —zeichen, n. mark of division; —zirkel, see —cirkel.

Theil'..., in comp. —[illegible], f. [illegible] freight; —wehr, n. Hydr. discharge-[illegible]; —weise, I. adj. partial; II. adv. partially, [illegible] partly; —zahl, f., —zähler, m. Math. [illegible]; —zahlung, f. payment in part; —[illegible] Theilungscirkel.

* Thein', (str.) n. Chem. theine.

* Theis'mus, (indecl.) m. (Gr. [illegible]) theism, belief in the existence of [illegible] Atheismus). — Theist', (w.) m. theist.

The'la..., in comp. —baum, m. [illegible] (-tree) (Teebaum); —holz, m. [illegible]

* The'ke, (w.) f. [illegible]

The'kla, f. Thecla (P. N.).

* The'ma, (str., pl. The'mata or [illegible] mata, or (w.) The'men) n. ([illegible]) subject (also Mus.).

Them'se, f. (the river) Thames.

The'obald, m. Theobald (P. N.).

* Theo..., in comp. [illegible] lite', (w.) f. theodolite; [illegible] theodolite; —gonie', (w.) f. [illegible]; —[illegible] tie', (w.) f. theocracy, —[illegible] cratic(al); —[illegible]; —logie', (w.) f. theology; [illegible] adj. theological; [illegible] tical divinity; —[illegible]

—, to affect astonishment; unwillig —, to pretend indignation; vertraut —, to affect familiarity, to claim familiar acquaintance (with); geschäftig —, to pretend, to be busy, to play the busy-body; stolz —, to be proud (auf *[with Acc.]*, mit, of); — als ob man sich widersetzen wollte, to make a show of resistance; ich that als ob ich schliefe, I pretended to sleep; nur so — (als ob *rc.*), merely to make believe.

II. *tr.* 1) to do, to make, to perform; 2) to put; to pour; sich — lassen, to be practicable *or* feasible; 3) (Einem etwas) to do (something) to (one), to commit violence upon (*cf.* Anthun, 2); er fürchtete, daß sie ihm etwas — könnte, he feared that she might do something to him; 4) to effect, &c.; es —, to do, to suffice, *cf. below*; du mußt etwas (das Deinige) dazu —, you must do something (the best you can) in the matter; was soll ich nun weiter —? how am I to proceed? — Sie was Sie wollen, take your course; eine Bitte —, to make a request; to address a petition (to); ein Gebet —, to offer up a prayer; einen Blick —, to cast *or* give a glance; einen Eid (Schwur) —, to take an oath, to swear; einer Sache (*Gen.*) Erwähnung *or* Meldung —, to make mention (of); einen Fall —, to get a fall; einen Fehltritt —, to make *or* take a false step, to slide, slip; eine Frage —, to ask or put a question; einen Gang —, to take a walk; to execute a commission; einen Griff —, *see* Greifen; einen Knall —, to give a report *or* crack; eine Reise —, to set out on a journey, *cf.* auf Reisen gehen; einen Schlag —, to strike a blow or a stroke; einen Schrei —, to (give a) shriek; er that einen lauten Schrei, he gave a loud cry; ich denke einen langen Schlaf zu — (*Schiller*, Wall. Tod), I mean to take a long sleep; einen Schuß —, to have a shot; to fire a gun, *see* Schießen I, 1; einen Sprung —, to take a leap; der Löwe that einen Sprung, the lion made a spring; einen Trunk, Schluck, Zug —, to take a draught; Wirkung —, to produce or take effect; Einem Gutes —, to confer favours *or* benefits upon one; in diesem Artikel wird nichts gethan, *Comm.* nothing is (being) done *or* is doing in this article; zu — haben, 1. to have business *or* work (on hand); 2. to have to do *or* to deal (with), to have dealings, to be connected (with); er hat andere Dinge zu —, he has other business to attend to, *fam.* he has other fish to fry; er hat mit ihr zu — gehabt, he has had communication with her; nichts mit ... zu — haben, to have no business, dealing(s), *or* concern with ...; to have no reference to ...: ich will nichts mehr mit ihm zu — haben, I will not be concerned with him any more, *coll.* I'll have nothing to say to him; nichts mehr mit ... zu — haben, to have done with ...; nichts zu — haben wollen mit ..., to refuse to meddle with ..., to disclaim all interference with ...; viel zu — haben, to have much work upon one's hands, *coll.* to have a good run of work; zu — bekommen, to get work *or* business, to come into business; (Einem etwas) zu — geben, to give *or* set (one) to do, to give *or* find (one) work, to employ one, *coll.* to cut out work for one; das wird ihnen viel zu — geben, it will give them much trouble, they will have a busy time of it; sich (*Dat.*) zu — machen, to undertake any work, to take to acting; sich (*Dat.*) zu — machen mit ..., to interfere or meddle with, to touch (an intricate question, &c.); sich (*Dat.*) etwas zu — machen, to pretend to have to do something, to find out something to do; zu wissen —, to inform, to give notice, to send word; Einem etwas —, to hurt, damage, offend one; Einem etwas zum Possen (*coll.* zum Schur) —, to do anything to vex, to spite, *or* to offend one; Predigen thut es nicht allein, preaching [illegible] not avail; damit ist es nicht gethan, [illegible] not suffice, that won't do; wenn es [illegible] Freigebigkeit gethan ist, if liberality [illegible] Noth —, to be necessary *or* urgent.

III. *tr. impers.* to matter, to be; was thut es? what does it matter? was thut es [illegible] auch ..., what though ...; es thut nichts, it does not matter *or* signify; never mind; der Name thut nichts zur Sache, the name is nothing to the purpose *or* point; es thut nicht viel zur Sache, it matters not much to the question.

Thun, *v. s.* (*str.*) *n.* the doing, performing, &c.; action; practices, conduct; dein — und Wesen, your ways, your way of acting; — und Treiben, — und Lassen, (ways and) doings, actions, proceedings, course of proceeding); das ist meines T-s nicht, that is none of my business.

Thun′fisch, (*str.*) *m.* *Ichth.* tunny-fish (*Thynnus vulgaris* Cuv.).

Thun′lich, I. *adj.* feasible, achievable, practicable; II. T-keit, (*w.*) *f.* feasibility, practicableness.

Thür, *or* **Thü′re**, (*w.*) *f.* door; vor der —, 1. before *or* outside the door; 2. *fig.* at hand, near; einem Dinge — und Thor öffnen, to make room *or* way; unleugbar wäre der Willkür Thür und Thor eröffnet (*Grimm*, Wb. XXVI), it would undoubtedly pave the way for arbitrariness; hinter der — Abschied nehmen, to take French leave; nach der — sehen, to attend to the door, to answer the bell; mit der — ins Haus fallen, to blunder, blab, *or* bluster out; to be overhasty; (den Leuten mir nichts dir nichts) mit der Thür ins Haus fallen, to tumble in (upon people) without let *or* leave; zwischen — und Angel stecken, to be in a pinch, in a dilemma.

Thür′..., *in comp.* —angel, *f.* door-hinge; —bänder, *n. pl.* iron *or* brass ligaments *or* iron work (loops) of a door; —bekleidung, *f.* door-case, dressing, wooden architrave; —beschlag, *m.*, —beschläge, *n.* door-furniture, plate, handle, &c., of a door; —bogenfeld, *n. Archit.* tympan.

Thür′chen, (*str.*) *n.* (*dimin. of* Thür) 1) little door; wicket; 2) *or* Thür′vel, *Mech.* lower valve (of a suction-pump), suction-valve; —säge, *f.* cooper's small saw.

Thür′..., *in comp.* —einfassung, *f. see* —bekleidung; —feld, *n.* 1) panel, pane, square of a door; 2) *see* —feld; —flügel, *m.* fold *or* leaf of a folding door; —fries, *m. Arch.* frieze-piece; —futter, *n.* boxing of a door, jamb.

Thür′gau, *n. Geogr.* Turgovia. [illegible]

Thür′..., *in comp.* —gerüst, *n.* [illegible] —gerüst, —gestell, —gewände, *n.* door-frame; —gesims, *n.* cornice of a door; —giebel, *m.* gable of a door, pediment; —giebelfeld, *n.* *see* —bogenfeld; —griff, *m.* door-handle; —haken, *m.*, —hänge, *f. see* —angel; —[illegible] *m.* wicket; —haspe, *f. see* —angel; —hüter, *m.* 1) porter, door-keeper; 2) *see* [illegible] pförtner.

Thü′ringen, *n. Geogr.* Thuringia. —[illegible] ringer, (*str.*) *m.*, Th-in, (*w.*) *f.* [illegible] gisch, *adj.* Thuringian.

Thür′..., *in comp.* —[illegible], *f.* [illegible] —klinke, *f.* door-latch; —[illegible], *n. see* —[illegible]

Thurm, (*str.*, *pl.* Thür′me) *m.* 1) [illegible] 2) (Kirch—) steeple, spire; 3) prison, [illegible] 4) *Fam.* (at chess) rook, castle.

Thurm′bau, (*str.*) *m.* building [illegible]

Thürm′chen, (*str.*) *n.* (*dimin.* [illegible]) a little tower, turret.

Thurm′decker, (*str.*) *m.* slater [illegible]

Thür′men, (*w.*) *v.* I. *tr.* 1) [illegible] towers *or* steeples; [illegible] 2) to pile up; II. *refl.* & *intr.* [illegible] rise high.

Thür′mer, (*str.*) *m.* warden [illegible]

stäven, barrel-staves; —stein, m. a species of amber; —waare, f. barrelled goods; —weise, adv. by tuns, by barrels.

Tonn'lägē, Tonn'läge, Tonn'lēgig, Tonn'-lägig, adj. Min., &c. hading, (of a plain, &c.) inclined against the horizon.

Tōn'..., in comp. —papier, n. tinted paper; —platte, f. sound-board; —reihe, f. see —folge & —leiter; —satz, m. see —setzung; —schluß, m. cadence, see —fall; —schlüssel, m. clef, key; —schrift, f. musical notes; —setzer, m. composer; —setzkunst, f. art of composition; —setzung, f. composition; —silbe, f. accented syllable; —sinn, m. talent for music; —spähne, m. pl. see —stäbe; —spiel, n. music, concert; —spieler, m. musician, player; —sprechung, f. see —messung, 2; —stäbe, m. pl. Mus. abstracts; —stück, n. musical piece or composition; —stufe, f. pitch of a note; degree on the stave.

* **Tonsūr',** (w.) f. (Lat.) tonsure, shaven crown. — **Tonsurī'ren,** (w.) v. tr. to shave the crown of ....

Tōn'system, (str.) n. 1) musical system; 2) the whole range of appreciable sounds within the compass of the human voice or instruments.

* **Tontī'ne,** (w.) f. tontine.

Tōn'..., in comp. —umfang, m. compass of tone, sound, or voice; —veränderung, f. change of tone or accent; —verhalt, m., —verhältniß, n. rhythm; —versetzung, f. transposition of accent; —wallung, f. modulation; —werk, n. musical composition; —werkzeug, n. musical instrument; —wissenschaft, f. science of music; —zeichen, n. 1) accent; mit —zeichen versehen, to accentuate; 2) note; 3) see —schlüssel; —zierat, m. musical ornament.

Topās', (str.) m. Miner. topaz; —bruch, n. T. pulverised topaz; —colibri, —fliegenvogel, m. Ornith. a species of humming-bird (Trochilus pella L.); —crystalle, m. pl. Bohemian crystals; —fluß, m. artificial topaz.

Topf, (str., pl. Töpf'e) m. 1) pot; saucepan; 2) provinc. top, whirligig; alles in Einen — werfen, coll. to treat all alike.

Topf'..., in comp. —asche, f. pot-ashes; —baum, m. or —fruchtbaum, m. Bot. pot-plant (Lecythis ollaria L.); —binder, m. mender of broken pots; —blume, f. Gard. flower growing in a pot; —brett, n. pot-shelf, kitchen-rack; —butter, f. crock-butter, pot-butter.

Töpf'chen, (str.) n. (dimin. of Topf) 1) small pot, pipkin; 2) ein — Bier, a pot or glass of beer.

Topf'deckel, (str.) m. pot-lid; saucepan-lid.

Töpf'er, (str.) m. potter; in comp. —arbeit, f., —geschirr, —gut, n. potter's work, see —waare; —blei, n. an inferior sort of black-lead; —erde, f. potter's earth; —scheibe, f. potter's wheel; —thon, m. potter's clay; —vogel, m. Ornith. South-American creeper (Furnarius figulus); —waare, f., —zeug, n. potter's ware, crockery, pottery, earthenware.

Töpferei', (w.) f. pottery.

Töpf'ern, adj. earthen, clayey.

Töpf'ern, (w.) v. intr. to make potter's work.

Topf'..., in comp. —gewächs, n. plant growing in a pot; —gewölbe, n. Archit. tubular vaulting; —glasur, f. glaze; —gucker, m. cont. one who pries into, and meddles with, the details of the kitchen, cotquean; —käse, m. a sort of cheese kept in pots; —kuchen, m. see Aschkuchen; —lecker, —näscher, m. cont. lick-pot; —markt, m. pot-market, pot-fair; —nelke, f. Gard. pink growing in a pot; —pflanze, f. see —gewächs; —rosine, f. jar-raisin; —scherbe, f. potsherd; —stein, m. pot-stone; —stürze, f. lid, cover; —zeug, n. pottery (Töpferzeug).

Topf'stein, m. see Tuffstein.

* **Topograph',** (w.) m. (Gr.) topographer. — **Topographie',** (w.) f. topography. — **Topogra'phisch,** adj. topographic, topographical.

Topp, interj. coll. done! agreed! [illegible]

Topp, (str.) m. Mar. top, head, or upper end; auf halbem —, (to display a flag) at half-mast; mit Mars[segeln] in dem — [illegible], to [illegible] with the top-sails atrip; vor — [illegible] treiben, to scud under bare poles; in comp. —auflanger, m. pl. top-timbers; —[illegible], —feuer, n. St. Elmo's fire.

Top'pen, (w.) v. tr. Mar. to top or to [illegible] up (a yard).

Top'penant, (str.) m. Mar. lift; [illegible] T-e, standing lifts of the sprit-sail-yards.

Top'pen..., in comp. —[illegible], f. —taue, n. Mar. back-stays.

Topp'..., in comp. —[illegible], n. guy, [illegible]-mast-tackle; —[illegible], m. [illegible] —schlitten, m. ropemaker's sledge; —segel, n. top-sail; —[illegible], f. 1) top-timber line; 2) drift-rail; —ständer, m. broad pennant. [illegible]

Tord'alk, m. Ornith. razor-bill (Alca torda).

Torf, (str.) m. peat, (dry) turf; — [illegible], to cut peat; in comp. —artig, adj. like turf or peat; —bauer, m. peasant who cuts and sells turf; —beere, f. Bot. 1) cloud-berry (Rubus chamaemorus L.); 2) cranberry (Moosbeere); —boden, m. 1) turf-ground; peat bog; 2) turf-loft; —feuer, n. peat fire; —feuerung, f. heating with peat; peat-fuel; —gräber, m. peat-cutter, turf-cutter; —[illegible], f. turf-pit; —grund, m. see —boden, 1; —haltend, adj. turfy, peaty; —[illegible], m. turf-man; —kohle, f. turf-coal, peat-coal; —[illegible], n. see —boden, 1; —moor, n. & m. peat-bog, peat-moss; —moos, n. bog-moss (Sphagnum Ehrh.); —mull, m. turf-dust; —[illegible], —[illegible], f., —steine, —ziegel, m. pl. peat and turf bricks; —stecher, m. 1) turf-cutter; 2) (or —spaten) turf- or turfing spade; —stich, m. 1) turf-pit; 2) turf-digging. [illegible]

Tor'fen, (w.) v. tr. Agr. to [illegible]

Tor'fig, adj. peaty, turfy.

Tor'kel, (str.) m. 1) see Kelter; 2) see Taumel 1 & 2.

Tor'keln, (w.) v. intr. see Taumeln.

Torn'kolk, (str., pl. Torn'[illegible]) m. Mar. raft. [illegible]

* **Tornis'ter,** (str.) m. (Hung.?) [illegible]

* **Torquī'ren,** (w.) v. tr. (Fr.-Lat.) [illegible] to spin into rolls (tobacco).

* **Tort,** (str.) m. (Fr.) coll. wrong, vexation, injury: dir zum —, to spite you.

Tört'chen, (str.) n. (dimin. of Torte) [illegible]

Tor'te, (w.) f. Conf. a kind of cake or tart; T-nbäcker, m. pastry-cook, tart-[illegible]; T-nteig, m. fine paste for [illegible] tarts.

* **Tortur',** (w.) f. (Lat.) torture, rack.

Tōs, (str.) m. (l. u.) roaring, [illegible]

Toscā'na, n. Geogr. Tuscany. — [illegible]ner, (str.) m., Toscan'isch, adj. Tuscan.

To'sen, (w.) v. intr. to roar, to [illegible]

Toß, (str.) m. tuft ([illegible], [illegible], [illegible]busch).

* **Total',** adj. (Lat.) total, complete, entire; —eindruck, m. general [illegible]; —summe, f. (sum) total. — [illegible] totality, wholeness.

* **Toupet',** [illegible] (pr. [illegible] T-s) n. (Fr.) Hair-dr. toupet [illegible] eisen, n. see —zange; —kamm, m. [illegible] comb; —nadel, Toupet'nadel, f. [illegible] —zange, f. crisping iron. — [illegible] v. intr. to toupee.

* **Tour** (pr. tūr), (w.) f. (Fr.) [illegible] figure; 2) tour, [illegible] 3) see Haartour; —[illegible] for a certain distance; [illegible] tourbillon). — [illegible]

* **Tournü're** (pr. [illegible]) [illegible] dress, training

intr. coll. to trample, patter, to tread noisily, to stamp.

Trapp'(B.)..., *in comp.* **—gebirge**, *n. pl.* trap-rocks; **—porphyr**, *m.* trachyte; **—sand**, *m.* coarse gravel; **—sandstein**, *m.* trap-sandstone; **—tuff**, *m.* basaltic tuff, trap-tuff; **—wacke**, *f.* stratiform rock.

* **Trassant'**, **Trassent'**, *(w.) m.* *(Ital.)* *Comm.* drawer (*or* giver) of a bill. — **Trassat'**, *(w.) m.* drawee. — **Trassi'ren**, *(w.) v. intr.* to draw *or* pass a bill (of exchange, auf *(with Acc.)*, upon), to value (on); per Saldo —, to draw per appoint; in Blanco —, to draw in blank; viel auf sich — lassen, to be drawn upon heavily; trassirter Wechsel, *see* Tratte.

Trass, *(str.) m.* *Geol.* trass, tarrass.

Trät'schen, *(w.) v. intr. see* Schwatzen.

* **Trat'te**, *(w.) f.* *(Ital.)* *Comm.* draft, draught, drawn bill; assignment; **T-nbuch**, *n.* bill payable book.

Trau'altar, *(str., pl.* T-täre) *m.* marriage altar. — **Trau(e)**, *(w.) f.* 1) *see* Trauung; 2) permission to marry; 3) marriage-present.

Trau'be, *(w.) f.* *(dimin.* **Träub'chen**, *(str.) n.* small cluster, *&c.*) 1) *a)* cluster, bunch of grapes; grape; *b) Bot.* raceme; 2) *Gunn.* cascabel.

Träu'bel..., *in comp.* **—erbse**, *f.* cluster-pea; **—gehörn**, *n.* *Sport.* troachings.

Trau'ben..., *in comp.* **—achat**, *m.* botryoid agate; **—ähnlich**, **—artig**, *see* **—förmig**; **—auge**, *n.* *Med.* staphyloma; **—balg**, *m. see* **—hülse**; **—beere**, *f.* 1) grape; 2) *see* Thauberre; **—blei**, *n. see* Bleiblüte & Flockenerz; **—blut**, *n.**, juice of grapes, (red) wine; **—bohrer**, *m.* wimble; **—bütte**, *f.* vinedresser's dorser; **—cur**, *f.* *Med.* grape-cure; **—eiche**, *f.* stone-oak, winter-oak (*Quercus sessiliflora Sm.*); **—erz**, *n.* *Miner.* arsenicated lead; **—farn**, *m.* *Bot.* flowering fern (*Osmunda L.*); **—fäule**, *f.* grape-disease; **—feuer**, *n. see* **—schuß**; **—form**, *f.* botryoidal form; **—förmig**, *adj.* grape-like; clustery; in clusters; botryoidal; **—gamander**, *m.* *Bot.* botryoidal germander (*Teucrium botrys L.*); **—gebirge**, *n.* vine-hills; **—geländer**, *n.* vine-arbour; **—geschwulst**, *f.* *Med.* grape-swelling; **—gott**, *m.* *Myth.* the god of grapes, Bacchus; *Gunn.-s.* **—hagel**, *m.* grape-shot; **—hals**, *m.* neck of a cascabel; **—haut**, *f.* *Anat.* uvea, uveous coat, third tunic of the eye; **—holunder**, *m.* *Bot.* red-berried elder, racemous, cluster-flowered elder (*Sambucus racemosa L.*); **—hügel**, *m.* vine-clad hill; **—hülse**, *f.* grape-skin; **—hyacinthe**, *f.* cluster-flowered hyacinth, grape-hyacinth (*Muscari racemosum L.*); **—käfer**, *m.* *Entom.* grape-beetle, rove-beetle (*Staphylinus L.*); **—kamm**, *m.* grape-stalk; **—kern**, *m.* stone or seed of grapes, grape-stone; *Bot.-s.* **—kirschbaum**, *m.* (common) bird-cherry tree (*Prunus padus L.*); **—kohl**, *m. see* Blumenkohl; **—krankheit**, *f.* grape-disease; **—kraut**, *n.* butt-leaved goose-foot, oak of Jerusalem (*Chenopodium botrys L.*); **—lese**, *f.* (lit. grape-gathering) vintage; **—leser**, *m.*, **—leserin**, *f.* grape-gatherer, vintager; **—most**, *m.* must; **—mühle**, *f.* grape-press; **—mus**, *n.* confection of grapes; **—nachleser**, *m.* grape-gleaner; **—presse**, *f. see* Kelter; **—reich**, *adj.* abounding in grapes; **—rüster**, *f.* *Bot.* cluster-flowered elm (*Ulmus effusa L.*); **—saft**, *m.* juice of grapes, wine; **—säure**, *f.* *Chem.* racemic acid, paratartaric acid; **—schuß**, *m.* *Gunn.* grape-shot; *Miner.-s.* **—spath**, *m.* grape-spar; **—stein**, *m.* grape-stone, botryolite; **—stengel**, **—stiel**, *m.* grape stalk; **—stock**, *m.* *Bot.* vine (Weinstock); **—syrup**, *m.* sirup of grapes; **—zeit**, *f.* vintage; **—zucker**, *m.* *Chem.* grape-sugar, starch-sugar, glucose.

Trau'big, *adj.* clustered, clustery.

Träub'lich, *adj.* cluster-like.

Trau'brief, *(str.) m.* 1) †. (letter of) credentials; 2) *see* Trauschein.

Trau'en, *(w.)* v. I. *tr.* to marry, [illegible] in wedlock *or* matrimony; sich — lassen, to be (*coll.* to get) married; II. *intr.* to trust, [illegible] fide, to have confidence ([illegible], *Dat.*; [illegible] (upon); auf etwas *(Acc.)* —, to trust in *or* to a thing; trau, schau, wem, *proverb.* if you trust before you try, you may repent before you die; III. *refl. see* Getrauen.

Trau'er, *f.* 1) mourning; 2) sorrow, grief, affliction; die tiefe —, first *or* deep mourning; die halbe —, second *or* half-mourning; [illegible] gehen, to be in mourning.

Trau'er... (*from* Trauern & [illegible]) *in comp.* **—anfänger**, *m. see* Leichenbitter; **—aufzug**, *m. see* **—kleidung**; **—baum**, *m.* *Bot.* sad *or* sorrowful tree (*Nyctanthes arbor tristis L.*); **—begängniß**, *n.* funeral, *see* Leichenbegängniß; **—bild**, *n.* emblem of mourning *or* sadness; **—binde**, *f.* mourning-band; **—birke**, *f.* drooping *or* weeping birch (*Betula alba var. pendula Ehrh.*); **—blick**, *m.* mournful look; **—boi**, *m.* mourning-baize; **—botschaft**, *f.* sad news, mournful tidings *or* intelligence; **—brief**, *m.* letter announcing a person's death; **—bühne**, *f. fig.* 1) tragic stage; earth; 2) stage of execution, scaffold; **—degen**, *m.* mourning-sword; **—druck**, *m.* [illegible] **—ente**, *f.* *Ornith.* black-duck (*[illegible]* L.); **—esche**, *f.* *Bot.* weeping ash (*Fraxinus excelsior pendula L.*); **—essen**, *n. see* [illegible]; **—fackel**, *f.* funeral torch; **—fahne**, *f.* black flag (at a funeral); **—fall**, *m.* mournful case *or* accident; sad event; death, decease; **—farben**, *f. pl.* mourning-colours; **—fest**, *n.* funeral solemnity; **—fliege**, *f.* *Entom.* [illegible] (*Anthrax Scop.*); **—flor**, *m.* mourning-crape; **—geberde**, *f.* mournful *or* sad gesture; **—gedicht**, *n.* mourning-poem; funeral poem, elegy; **—gefolge**, *n. see* **—geleit**; **—gefühl**, *n.* mournful *or* sad feeling; **—geist**, *m.* [illegible] spirit, melancholy mind; **—geläut**, *n.* tolling of the church-bells on the death of a person; **—geleit**, *n.* attendants *or* followers of a funeral, *cf.* **—zug**; **—gepränge**, *n.* funeral pomp; **—gerüst**, *n.* catafalco; **—gesang**, *m.* mourning-song, (funeral) dirge; **—geschichte**, *f.* mournful tale; **—geschrei**, *n.* mournful *or* doleful cries, lamentations; **—gesicht**, *n.* mournful countenance; **—gewand**, *n. see* **—kleid**; **—glocke**, *f.* death-bell, passing-bell; **—gottesdienst**, *m.* church service on the death of a distinguished person, *&c.*; **—gurte**, *f.* mourning-[illegible]; **—haus**, *n.* house of mourning; **—jahr**, *n.* year of mourning, mourning-year; **—klage**, *f.* lamentation; **—kleid**, *n.*, **—kleidung**, *f.* mourning-dress, mourning-suit; **—kutsche**, *f.* mourning-coach; **—laut**, *m.* mournful, sad, lugubrious sound *or* accent, funeral note; [illegible] *see* **—geläut**; **—lettern**, *f. pl.* *Typ.* black-letters; **—leute**, *pl.* mourners, funeral attendants; [illegible] lich, *n. see* **—gesang**.

Trau'erlos, *adj.* devoid of [illegible]

Trau'er... (*from* Trauern & [illegible]) *comp.* **—mahl**, *n.* mourning-feast; [illegible] *see* **—geschichte**; **—mantel**, *m.* 1) [illegible] cloak; 2) *Entom.* a species of butterfly [illegible] *Antiopa L.*); **—marsch**, *m.* funeral [illegible] **—monument**, *n. see* **—denkmal**; [illegible] *Entom.* a species of gnat ([illegible]) [illegible] *f.* the tragic Muse; **—musik**, *f.* [illegible] music; **—mütig**, *adj.* melancholy [illegible] richt, *f. see* **—botschaft**.

Trau'ern, *(w.) v. intr.* 1) to [illegible] lament, to be afflicted; 2) to [illegible] (um, for); **T-de**, *m. & f.* [illegible] mourner.

Trau'er... (*from* [illegible]) *comp.* **—nabel**, *f.* [illegible] **—ordnung**, *f.* mourning-[illegible] pier, *n.* black-edged [illegible] mourning horse (which [illegible]) **—post**, *f. see* **—botschaft**; [illegible]

Tü'der, (str.) m. provinc. tether. — **Tü'dern**, (w.) v. tr. to tether.

Tuff, **Tuf**, (str.) m. (or –wacke, f.) Miner. tuff, tufa; –kalk, –stein, m. tufaceous limestone, calcareous tufa.

Tüf'tel, (str.) m. see Düffel.

Tüf'tein, see Düftein.

Tu'gend, (w.) f. virtue; in comp. –adel, m. nobility acquired by virtue; –arm, adj. poor in virtues; –bahn, f. see –pfad; –bund, m. 1) Germ. Mod. Hist. Association of Virtue; 2) virtuous society (gen. used as a nickname); –eifer, m. zeal for virtue; –feind, m. enemy to virtue; –freund, m. friend to (or lover of) virtue; –gefühl, n. sense of virtue; –gesetz, n. moral law.

Tu'gendhaft, I. (or Tu'gendlich. Tu'gendsam) adj. virtuous; II. T–igkeit, f. virtuousness.

Tu'gend..., in comp. –held, m. hero in virtue; –heuchler, m. sanctified hypocrite; –krämer, m. one who makes a display of virtue; –lehre, f. morals, ethics; –lehrer, m. moralist; –los, adj. without virtue; –pfad, m. path of virtue; –pflichten, f. pl. moral duties; –prediger, m. moralizer; –reich, adj. very virtuous; –reiz, m. charm of virtue, motive to virtue; –ruf, m. reputation for virtue; –schein, m. appearance of virtue; –schwätzer, m. fine virtue-prattler; –spiegel, m. conf. paragon or pattern of virtue; –staat, m. empire of virtue; –stolz, m. pride of conscious virtue; –übung, f. exercise of virtue; –verein, m. society for the promotion of virtue. [metal.

Tu'ladose, (w.) f. snuff-box made of Tula-

* **Tul'ban(d)**, (str.) m. (Turk. tulband, dulband, from Pers. dulband) turban (Turban).

Tullfanz', (str.) m. (dimin. Tullfäntchen, (str.) n.) (cf. Tulban & O Engl. tullbant) a woolly, soft kind of dress for infants.

Tul(i)pa'ne, (w.) f. obsolescent for Tulpe.

Tull, **Tüll**, (str.) m. Comm. net, net-work, net-lace; –spitzen, f. pl. point net.

Tül'le, (w.) f. T. see Dille.

Tul'lius, m. Tully (Rom. P. N.).

Tul'pe, (w.) f. Bot. tulip (Tulipa L.).

Tul'pen..., in comp. –artig, adj. like tulips; –baum, m. tulip-tree, white-wood (Liriodendron tulipifera L.); –baumbitter, n. Chem. liriodendrine; –beet, n. Gard. bed of tulips; –drossel, f. Ornith. hang-bird (Baltimore); –flor, f. blooming or field of tulips; –liebhaber, m. amateur of tulips; –sucht, f. passion for tulips, (–wuth, f.) tulip-mania; –zwiebel, f. bulb of a tulip.

Tum'meln, (w.) v. I. tr. to bustle, to (give much) exercise; ein Pferd –, to tumble, manage a horse; to ride hastily; II. refl. 1) to wrestle, scuffle (with); 2) to bustle, gambol, revel, to hurry, make haste.

Tum'mel, (str.) m. (l. w.) tumult; –baum, m. 1) Min. axle-tree of the windlass; 2) Mar. beam of the capstan; –becher, m. or Tüm'melchen, n. small cup or tumbler; –platz, m. 1) riding-place; 2) wrestling-place; scene of action; place of exercise; 3) Mil. alarm post; –taube, f. Ornith. tumbler (Columba Livia gyratrix L.).

Tumm'ler, (str.) m. 1) tumbler, dancer; 2) see Becher; 3) tumbler (for drinking); 4) T. warp-staff; 5) or Tümmler, a) Mammal. dolphin; porpoise (Delphinus delphis L.); b) Ornith. see Tummeltaube.

Tüm'pel, (str.) m. 1) pool; 2) see Strudel, 1; 3) T. hearth; –stein, m. hearth-pit-stone; –stück, n. hearth-pit.

* **Tumult'**, (str.) m. (Lat.) tumult; uproar. — **Tumultuant'**, (w.) m. rioter. — **Tumultua'risch**, adj. tumultuary, tumultuous, riotous. — **Tumultui'ren**, (w.) v. intr. to (raise a) tumult, riot.

Tün'che, (w.) f. [illegible] Mas. white-wash; lime-[illegible] casting, perget, plaster.

Tün'chen, (w.) v. tr. to [illegible] wash; to plaster, perget; [illegible] m. whitewasher; pargeter, plasterer; [illegible] fel, m. whitewash brush; [illegible] washer's pallet. [2) see [illegible]

Tüncherei', (w.) f. 1) a [illegible]

Tünch'..., in comp. –arbeit, f. [illegible] washer's work; –farbe, f. plastering [illegible] –werk, n. 1) see –arbeit; 2) daubing, bad painting. [illegible]

Tune'ser, (str.) m., **Tune'sisch**, adj. [illegible]

Tüng'el, (str.) m. Bot. goose-grass ([illegible] lium aparine L.).

Tung'stein, (str.) m. Miner. tungsten; –sauer, adj. tungstic; –saures Salz, tungstate; –säure, f. tungstic acid.

Tungu'se, (w.) m. Tungusian.

* **Tu'nica**, (pl. Tu'nicen) f. (Lat.) tunic.

Tu'nis, n. Geogr. Tunis; –blume, f. Bot. velvet-flower, French-marigold ([illegible] blume). [illegible]

Tunk, (str.) m. provinc. room underground,

Tun'ke, (w.) f. sauce.

Tun'ken, (w.) v. tr. to dip, steep. [illegible]

Tunkcommunion, (w.) f. Church. see [illegible]

Tunk..., in comp. –form, f. dipping mould or frame; –napf, m., –schale, f., –schüsselchen, n. sauce-dish.

* **Tun'nel**, (str.) m. (Engl.) tunnel; in comp. –arbeit, f. tunnelling [illegible] –gang, m. interior or bore of a tunnel.

* **Tunnelli'ren**, (w.) v. tr. & intr. to tunnel.

Tupf, (str.) m. see Tüpfelchen.

Tupf'ballen, (str.) m. Print. beater, [illegible]

Tüp'fel, (str.) m. (dimin. [illegible] (str.) n.) point, tittle, dot, spot; –[illegible] Bot. polypody ([illegible]) [illegible] maler, m. fam. miniature-painter.

Tüp'felig, adj. spotted, full of points.

Tüp'feln, (w.) v. tr. to make points, to dot, spot. — **Tüp'fel** (or [illegible]) [illegible] n. Weav. design-paper.

Tupf'en, (str.) m. see Tüpfel.

Tüpfen, **Tupfen**, (w.) v. I. tr. [illegible] to tip, dab, dip; to touch; II. tr. [illegible] shoot, hit; 2) provinc. to [illegible] pfen, 2).

Turf, see Torf. [illegible]

* **Tur'ban**, (str.) m. (Turk. [illegible]

Turcoma'nn, (w.) m. [illegible]

— **Turcomanien**, n. Geogr. [illegible]

Tür'ke, (w.) m. Turk. –[illegible] Turkey.

Tür'kel, **Tür'ken**, (str.) m. [illegible]

Tür'ken..., in comp. –[illegible] dark blue; –bund, m. 1) turban, [illegible] a) purple martagon, Turk's cap ([illegible] lium L.); b) a species of [illegible] (Cucurbita melopepo L.) [illegible] against the Turks; –[illegible] –kopf, m. Saracen's head; [illegible] with the Turks; –[illegible] –sattel, m. Turkish saddle [illegible] steuer, f. (formerly) tax [illegible] war against the Turks.

Tür'kenblut, (str.) [illegible]

Tür'kenzug, (str.) [illegible] tion against the Turks.

Tür'kin, (w.) f. [illegible]

Türkis', (str.) [illegible]

Tür'kisch, adj. [illegible] beans, kidney-beans [illegible] spun cotton dyed [illegible] ber, common-[illegible] Korn, t–er Weizen, [illegible] (Waid) [illegible] pfeffer [illegible] leather; [illegible] (stein), Turkey [illegible]

left on hand; remaining; (von Schulden) surviving; sollte noch Raum — bleiben, should there be any spare-room; dabei bleibt uns nur wenig —, but little is left (over for) us by it; es blieb ihm nichts Anderes —, als ..., there was nothing else left for him but ...; nun war er blieb denn nichts (anderes) —, als nach Schottland vorzugehen, there was nothing left for it then, but to go on to Scotland; es blieb ihm nichts (anderes) —, als sein Jahrgeld aufzugeben, he had nothing for it but to renounce his pension; es blieb nichts —, als den Günstling zu tödten, there was nothing for it but to put the favorite to death; — lassen, to leave a remainder; to leave behind, to let remain; es läßt nichts zu wünschen —, it leaves nothing to be wished for or desired; der, die, das Ü-e, die Ü-en, the rest; die Ü-e Welt, the rest of the world; im Ü-en, as for the rest; es ist noch etwas Geld —, there is some odd money; ein Ü-es thun, to do more than one's due, to stretch or strain a point; auf den Ü-en Inhalt als erledigt nicht zurückkommend, not recurring to what is passed and done with.

Ü'brigens, *adv.* as for the rest, what remains, otherwise; moreover; besides.

Ü'bung, *(w.) f.* 1) exercise; exercising; 2) *Mil.* discipline, drilling, training (up); 3) practice, use; routine, dexterity; 4) exercise or study (for a musical instrument); 5) *Man.* hand; in — bringen, to put in practice; in — bleiben, sich in — erhalten, to keep in practice, *coll.* to keep one's hand in; aus der — kommen, to get out of or to lose practice; aus der — sein, to be out of practice; aus der (durch die) — lernen, to learn by rote.

Ü'bungs..., *in comp.* —haus, *n.* any school where military exercises are taught; —kunst, *f.* gymnastics; —lager, *n.* encampment for the purpose of exercising troops; —lehre, *f.* practical doctrine; gymnastic science; —platz, *m.* place for exercising soldiers (Exercirplatz); —spiel, *n.* gymnastic exercise; —stück, *n.* piece for practising or for study (Übung, 4); —zeit, *f.* time for practising or exercising.

U'fer, *(str.) n.* shore; beach; coast; bank (of a river); am —, an's —, on shore, a-shore.

U'fer..., *in comp.* —aas, *n.* the larva of the may-fly (Eintagsfliege); —abbruch, *m.* damage caused to a bank by the irruption of water; —bau, *m.* dike-building, embankment; —bewohner, *m.* inhabitant on the banks of a river or of the coast; —damm, *m.* dam of stones along a river, &c., embankment, quay; —eigenthümer, *m.* proprietor of land along a river or of coast-land; —feste, *f.* wharf of masonry *(T. Tusch.)*; —gebühr, *f.*, —geld, *n.* shorage, pierage, wharfage; —grille, *f. Entom.* field-cricket (Feldgrille); —lerche, *f.* the lesser plover *(Charadrius minor* M. et W.).

U'ferlos, *adj.* shoreless, *fig.* boundless.

U'fern, *(w.) v. intr.* *(Herder; l. u.)* to shore, to have or exhibit a certain outline of shore.

U'fer..., *in comp.* —pascher, *m. see* Strandreiter, 1 *a*; —pfeiler, *m.* (einer Brücke) *T.* abutment; —recht, *n. see* Strandrecht; —schlick, *m.* alluvial deposit; —schnecke, *f. Conch.* 1) periwinkle *(Litorina litorea* L.); 2) a genus of snail *(Litorina* Fer.); —schwalbe, *f. Ornith.* sand-martin, bank-swallow, shore-bird *(Hirundo riparia* L.); —spinne, *f. Arach.* a genus of spider *(Tetragnatha extensa* L.); —wanze, *f. Entom.* water-bug *(Salda littoralis* L.), —weide, *f. see* Korbweide.

U-förmig, *adj.* shaped like a U; die U-förmige Röhre, *Chem., &c.* U-tube.

Hu! *interj.* hu! (exclamation of awe or terror).

* Uhlan', *(w.) m. see* Ulane.

Uhr, *(w.) f.* 1) clock; (Taschen—) watch; 2) hour; wie viel — ist es? what o'clock is it? fünf —, five o'clock; um sechs —, at six o'clock; ich muß mit dem Zuge fort, [illegible] zwei — (zwei — zwanzig) [illegible], I [illegible] by the two o'clock (two-twenty) [illegible] or über vier —, past four o'clock; nach meiner —, by my watch.

Uhr'..., *in comp.* —band, *n.* watch-string, watch-ribbon; —behänge, *pl.* [illegible] runners; —bord, *m.* [illegible] U-einsteller, *m.* clock-setter; —feder, *f.* watch-spring; —fournituren, *pl.* watch-furnitures; —gehänge, *n.* trinkets of a watch; —gehäuse, *n.* 1) watch-case; 2) or —gestell, *n.* watch-stand, watch-frame; —getriebe, *n.* pinion of a watch; —gewicht, *n.* clock-weight; —glas, *n.* watch-glass; —glocke, *f.* watch-bell, bell of a clock; —hammer, *m.* watch-hammer; —kapsel, *f.* watch-case, étui; —kasten, *m.* clock-case; —kette, *f.* watch-chain, guard (-chain); —lampe, *f.* moderator-lamp; —macher, *m.* clock-maker, watch-maker; —macherarbeiten, *f. pl.* clockmaker's goods; —macherbohrer, *m.* watch-key-drill; —macherei, —macherkunst, *f.* watch-making, clock-making; —macherkloben, *m.* pin-vise; —platte, *f.* dial-plate; —rad, *n.* watch-wheel; —richter, *m.* clock-setter; —röhre, *f.* bore of a watch-key; —sand, *m.* hourglass-sand; —schlüssel, *m.* watch-key; —schrank, *m.* clock-case; —schwengel, *m.* pendulum; —tafel, *f.* dial-[illegible]; —tasche, *f.* watch-pocket, fob; —trommel, *f.* cylinder of a watch; —walze, —zeiger, *m.* hand of a watch or clock; pin of a dial, style; —werk, *n.* works of a clock or watch, clock-work, watch-work; —zeit, *f.* clock-time.

U'hu, *(str., pl.* U'hus, *or not decl.) m.* eagle owl *(Strix bubo* L.).

Uhz, *(str.) m.,* Uhz'en, *(w.) v. tr.* [illegible], *see* Foppen, Foppen.

* Uistiti, *(str., pl.* U-s*) m. Zool.* the [illegible] ted monkey, ouistiti, wistiti, marmoset *(Hapale Jacchus* L.).

U'k(e)lei, Ü'kelei, *(str. [pl.* U-en*] or not decl.) m. Ichth.* bleak, ablet *(Leuciscus alburnus* L.).

Uk'ermark, *f. Geogr.* March Ukraine.

* Ula'ne, *(w.) f. Mil.* ulan, lancer.

Ulk, *(str.) m.* 1) *see* Iltis; 2) [illegible] spree; row, rumpus. [illegible]

Ulm, *(str.) m.* 1) mould, rot [illegible]

Ul'me, *(w.) f.* 1) *Bot.* elm; 2) [illegible] side-wall.

Ul'men, *adj.* of elm; elm-tree ...,

Ul'men, *(w.) v. intr.* to moulder, rot.

Ul'men..., *in comp.* —baum, *m.* elm-tree *(Ulmus* L.); —gallapfel, *m.* elm-gall, elm-[illegible]

Ul'mer, *(str.) m.* (U-in, *[w.] f.*) inhabitant of Ulm (a town of Würtemberg); *adj.* (of) Ulm; — [illegible]

* Ulmin', *(str.) n. Chem.* ulmin, *in comp.* —säure, *f.* ulmic acid; —[illegible] *n.* ulmate, humate.

Ul'rich, *m.* Ulric *(P. N.).*

Ulri'ke, *f.* Ulrica *(P. N.).*

* Ul'timo, *(str., pl.* U-s*)* [illegible] the last, *viz.* day of the month; [illegible] day of the month; — [illegible] auf — gestellt, put for the [illegible] *(or ultimo mense (Lat.)* [illegible] rent, last day of the [illegible] lirung, *f.* last settling-day; —[illegible] time-bill.

* Ultramarin', [illegible]

* Ultramonta'n' [illegible] ta'nisch), *adj.* *(Lat.)* ultramontane [illegible] *pl.* ultramontanists.

Ul'ward, *m.* promise [illegible]

Um, I. *prep.* (with *Acc.*) [illegible] 3) for; 4) near, towards [illegible] to; — ... herum, round [illegible] Ostern, about midday, [illegible] — Jemand sein, to be [illegible] ich bin — meine Uhr, I [illegible]

Um'gegend, *(w.) f.* see Umgebung, 1.

Umgeh'bar, *adj.* 1) that may be gone round; 2) that may be evaded.

Um'gehen, *(irr.) v. intr. (aux.* sein) 1) *a)* to go round *or* about; to make a circuit *or* procession; der Wind geht um, *Mar.* the wind changes *or* shifts; *b)* to go by turns, to alternate; *c)* to walk (of spirits); an einem Orte —, to haunt a place; *(also impers.) see* Spuken, 1; es geht ein Gespenst im Hause um, the house is haunted by a spectre; 2) *a)* to turn round; to revolve, circulate; es geht Alles mit mir um, I am giddy, I turn sick, my head spins round *or* swims; *b)* im Gange sein; in Kaffee geht wenig um, *Comm.* little is doing in coffee; im Geschäft geht wenig um, there is not much stir in business; es ging wenig um, but few transactions were effected, very little changed hands; 3) to go a roundabout way; ich bin eine Meile umgegangen, I went a mile out of my way; I came a mile round; *fig.-e.* with mit: 1) *a)* to be occupied with, to have to do with; to manage: mit der Nadel —, to handle the needle; der Knabe kann mit Garteninstrumenten —, the boy is capable of handling garden tools; er weiß mit diesem Instrumente sehr gut umzugehen, he is most expert in the use of this instrument; mit Zauberei —, to deal in sorcery; mit Lügen —, to deal in falsehoods; mit Betrug —, to practise fraud; to work deceit; *b)* to design, intend, purpose, meditate (murder, &c.); to entertain (a scheme, project); 5) *a)* to have intercourse with, to associate, consort, *or* escort with; *b)* to deal with, to treat (well *or* ill); mit der Zeit sparsam —, to husband one's time; mit ... sparsam —, to be sparing of ...; mit ... verschwenderisch —, to be lavish of *or* with ... .

Umgeh'en, *(irr.) v. tr.* 1) *a)* to go round about ...; *Mil.* to turn (the enemy); *b)* die Grenzen —, to perambulate, survey, *coll.* to tread the boundaries (Hintern, 2); 2) to avoid, to evade, elude; ein Gesetz —, to trespass upon, *or* evade a law; Sie — uns mit Ihren Aufträgen, you overlook us in giving your orders.

Um'gehend, *p. a.* 1) going about, &c.; 2) prevalent, epidemic; mit u-er Post, by return of post, by the returning mail; wir erbitten uns —, we request by return; u-e Antwort, answer by return.

Umgeh'ung, *(w.) f.* 1) *a)* a going round, &c.; *b) Mil.* a turning the enemy's flank, &c.; 2) evasion, elusion; omission.

Um'gekehrt, *p. a.* inverted *(also Mus., &c.) cf.* Umkehren, II. 2; inverse *(Math.* ratio, proportion, &c.); converse, reverse, opposite; *adv.* contrariwise; u-er Köper, turned *or* reversed twill; die u-e Regel de tri, *Math.* the rule of three inverse; der Fall ist gerade —, the case is entirely the reverse *or* the other way; die Schnelligkeit der Verbreitung steht im u-en Verhältnisse zu der Quadratwurzel der specifischen Schwere des ausströmenden Gases, the velocity of diffusion is inversely proportional to the square root of the specific gravity of the effluent gas; — herzförmig, *adj. Bot.* obcordate.

Um'geld, *(str., pl.* U-er) *n.* retail-duty. — **Um'gelder**, *(str.) m.* receiver of retail-duties.

Um'gestalten, *(w.) v. tr. see* Umbilden.

Um'gießen, *(str.) v. tr.* 1) to refound, new-cast; 2) to transfuse.

Umgleis'ßen, *(str.) v. tr.* to circumfuse.

Umgit'tern, *(w.) v. tr.* to surround with a grating or lattice.

Umglän'zen, *(w.) v. tr.* to shine round, surround with splendour.

Umglüh'en, *(w.) v. tr.* to surround with a glow *or* heat.

Um'graben, *(str.) v. tr.* to dig, delve, break, or turn up.

Umgra'ben, *(str.) v. tr.* to dig [illegible] about. [illegible]

Umgren'zen, *(w.) v. tr.* to [illegible]

Um'griff, *(str.) m.* (*l. u.* für das [illegible] greifen) spread, extent, progress (of an epidemic, &c.). [illegible]

Um'gucken, *(w.) v. refl. coll.* to look [illegible]

Um'gürten, *(w.) v. tr.* (sometimes Umgür'ten) to gird round *or* about.

Umgür'ten, *(w.) v. tr.* 1) to surround with a girdle or something similar; 2) *Mar.* to frap (a ship).

Umgür'tung, *(w.) f.* the (act of) surrounding, &c.; U-stauwerk, *n. Mar.* frapping.

Um'guß, *(str., pl.* Um'güsse) *m.* 1) recasting; 2) transfusion.

Um'haben, *(irr.) v. tr.* to have on.

Um'hacken, *(w.) v. tr.* 1) to turn up (break up) with the hoe; 2) to hew, cut down.

Umhaf'ten, *(w.) v. tr.* to take about (a thing).

Umhal'sen, *(w.) v. tr. coll.* to hug, embrace. — **Umhal'sung**, *(w.) f.* embrace, hug.

Um'hang, *(str., pl.* Um'hänge) *m.* [illegible], vail. — **Um'hängen**, *(w.) v. tr.* 1) to hang round or about; to put on; 2) to hang at another place; to hang anew.

Umhang'en, *(str.)*, **Umhän'gen**, *(w.) v. tr.* to hang round, *or* to surround on all sides.

Umhär'tet, *adj.* [illegible] case-hardened.

Um'hauchen, *(w.) v. tr.* to breathe [illegible]

Umhau'chen, *(w.) v. tr.* to surround with breath, *or* fragrance. [illegible] cut down.

Um'hauen, *(str.) v. tr.* to fell, hew down,

Um'heften, *(w.) v. tr.* 1) to fasten round; 2) to stitch anew.

Umhe'gen, *(w.) v. tr.* to fence, palisade.

Umher', *adv.* around, about, round about; *cf.* Herum; — führen, to lead about; to show (in *[with Dat.]*, over); — liegen, to lie about; — sehen, to look about; — laufen, — [illegible], — streifen, — schweifen, — ziehen, to rove, ramble, roam, range, stroll, wander about; — rasen, to rave about; — [illegible], to stand about; sich — treiben, *refl.* to rove, [illegible] or idle about, to go *or* rove idling about.

Umhin', *adv.* only used in — Können; ich kann nicht —, I cannot forbear *or* help, I cannot (choose) but, I cannot, refrain from; wenn Sie nicht — können, if you cannot do otherwise.

Um'holz, *(str., pl.* [illegible]) *n.* [illegible] wood (the staves of which a cask, &c. is formed). [illegible] inquisition, to listen about.

Um'horchen, *(w.) v. intr. coll.* to make [illegible]

Umhül'len, *(w.) v. tr.* to veil, [illegible] wrap round. — **Umhül'lung**, *(w.) f.* anything that envelops, &c.; wrapper; [illegible] casing, case.

Umhüpf'en, *(w.) v. tr.* to frisk, skip [illegible]

Umjauch'zen, **Umjubeln**, *(w.) v.* [illegible] surround with shouts, *or* acclamations.

Umir'ren, *(w.) v.* [illegible]

Um'kalfatern, *(w.) v. tr.* [illegible]

Um'kanten, *(w.) v. tr.* to [illegible] tilt, *Mar.* to cant. [illegible]

Um'kegeln, *(w.) v. tr.* to [illegible]

Um'kehr, *(w.) f.* 1) a turning [illegible] 2) *fig.* conversion.

Um'kehren, *(w.) v.* I. [illegible] to turn round; to turn back [illegible] to mend, reform, to [illegible] 1) *(also refl.* sich —) to [illegible] 2) to turn inside out, [illegible] to turn over *or* up; [illegible] mit umgekehrter Hand, [illegible] hand; ein Schlag mit [illegible] back-handed blow, *coll.* [illegible] gekehrte Seite, 1. [illegible] wrong side (of cloth) [illegible] put in confusion, [illegible] way; to make back [illegible]

Um'ſchrift, (w.) f. inscription (round a coin), legend.

Um'ſchrot, (str.) n. wooden fence, paling.

Um'ſchüren, (w.) v. tr. to stir, rake up.

Um'ſchütteln, (w.) v. tr. to shake about, to stir up, mix.

Um'ſchütten, (w.) v. tr. 1) to spill; overturn; 2) to pour or about into another vessel.

Umſchüt'ten, (w.) v. tr. to throw round about, to heap up round about.

Umſchwär'men, (w.) v. tr. to swarm, buzz round. [round or about.

Umſchwe'ben, (w.) v. tr. to hover, float

Um'ſchwojen, (w.) v. intr. Mar. to turn or swing a ship round, to tend.

Um'ſchweif, (str.) m. 1) Lock-sm. checks (of a lock); 2) round about way; digression; ohne —, without circumlocution, bluntly; durch —, circuitously; 3) T. rim; 4) sieve-frame.

Um'ſchweifen, (w.) v. intr. (aux. haben & ſein) 1) to make a round-about way, cf. Umherſchweifen; 2) to make digressions, to use circumlocution. [round ....

Umſchwei'fen, (w.) v. tr. to flit or flutter

Um'ſchweifig, adj. see Weitſchweifig.

Um'ſchwenken, (w.) v. tr. & intr. to turn or wheel round. [round.

Umſchwim'men, (str.) v. tr. to swim, float

Um'ſchwingen, (str.) v. tr. & refl. to swing, move round, to revolve or turn round.

Umſchwir'ren, (w.) v. tr. to buzz or flit round.

Um'ſchwung, (str., pl. Um'ſchwünge) m. 1) a swinging round, see Umdrehung; 2) rapid and total change, revolution.

Um'ſegeln, (w.) v. I. intr. see Um'ſchiffen I.; II. tr. to sail aground, run foul of, sink (another ship).

Umſe'geln, see Umſchif'fen I.

Um'ſehen, (str.) v. refl. 1) to look round, about, or back; ſich — nach, to look (out) for; ehe man ſich umſieht, in a trice; 2) to have or take a view; hier kann man ſich recht —, here is an extended prospect of view; ſich in der Welt —, to see the world; ſich in Büchern —, to peruse or turn over many books.

Um'ſein, (irr.) v. intr. to be over, past, expired (of a certain term), &c., cf. Um, adv.

Um'ſetzbar, I. adj. (l. u.) vendible, convertible; II. U-keit, f. convertibility (of notes into sovereigns, &c.).

Um'ſetzen, (w.) v. I. tr. 1) a) to put, set otherwise, shift places, transpose; b) to transplant; 2) Typ. to compose again; 3) Mus. to transpose; 4) to sell; to exchange, barter; in baar Geld —, to turn or convert into cash; es wurden anſehnliche Poſten umgeſetzt, considerable parcels changed hands; in Wolle wurde viel umgeſetzt, there was a good business done in wool; II. refl. to change, veer round (of the wind). [about; to surround.

Umſet'zen, (w.) v. tr. to set or plant round

Um'ſetzung, (w.) f. 1) transposition, transposing, &c.; 2) see Umſatz. [sickle.

Um'ſicheln, (w.) v. tr. to cut down with a

Um'ſicht, (w.) f. 1) the (act of) looking about; 2) fig. circumspection, precaution, wariness. — **Um'ſichtig**, adj. (Um'ſichtsvoll) circumspect, wary; U-keit, f. circumspection, circumspectness. [down, to faint away.

Um'ſinken, (str.) v. intr. (aux. ſein) to sink

Umſonſt', adv. 1) gratis, for nothing; halb — verkaufen, to sell next akin to nothing; 2) in vain, vainly; to no purpose, to no profit; alle ihre Bemühungen waren —, all their labours proved abortive; 3) without design, without cause, gratuitously; nicht —, not without reason; not without a purpose; — iſt der Tod, prov. nothing for nothing; no pipe, no dance.

Um'ſpann, (str.) m. relay (of horses).

Um'ſpannen, (w.) v. tr. die Pferde —, to change horses.

Umſpan'nen, (w.) v. tr. to span, embrace; encompass; er umſpannt alle Gebiete des Geiſtes, his grasp of soul partakes of universality; dieſe Anſicht umſpannt die ganze Welt, this view has world-wide circulation.

Umſpie'len, (w.) v. tr. to play round.

Umſpin'nen, (str.) v. tr. to spin all round, to surround with a tissue.

Um'ſpringen, (str.) v. intr. (aux. ſein) 1) to turn round, to shift, see Umſchlagen, I. 2, a; 2) fig. (with mit) to treat, deal with, manage, handle. [round ....

Umſprin'gen, (str.) v. tr. to leap, jump

Um'ſtand, (str., pl. Um'ſtände) m. 1) (& Um'ſtände, pl.) provinc. by-standers; 2) circumstance; Um'ſtände, pl. 3) state, condition, situation; 4) ceremonies, formalities, circumstance; die näheren or einzelnen Umſtände, particulars, details; mit allen Umſtänden erzählen, see Umſtändlich erzählen; unter Umſtänden, under circumstances; unter dieſen Umſtänden, in these circumstances; unter den jetzigen Umſtänden (aber), as it is; unter allen Umſtänden, by all means; in guten Umſtänden ſein, to be in easy circumstances; to be well off; in üblen Umſtänden ſein, to be in low circumstances, to be badly off; in andern Umſtänden ſein, coll. to be in the family-way; (viel) Umſtände machen, 1. to use circumlocution; 2. to hesitate, to raise difficulties; wenn es Ihnen nicht zu viele Umſtände macht, if it does not cause or give you too much difficulty or trouble; machen Sie keine Umſtände, do not use ceremonies; do not put yourself out of your way; keine or nicht viel Umſtände machen mit ..., not to make much ceremony with ...; to be at home with ...; er befindet ſich wohl den Umſtänden nach, he is well, considering circumstances; hier waren wir, den Umſtänden nach, ſicher, here we were, comparatively speaking, safe; Cook-r. Sauerkraut mit Umſtänden, pickled cabbage with meat boiled in it; Kaffee mit Umſtänden, coffee with cakes, &c.; U-swort, n. Gramm. adverb.

Um'ſtändlich, I. adj. 1) circumstantial; particular; minute; detailed; 2) ceremonious, particular, formal; 3) see Schwierig. 3) das wäre zu —, that would cause too much trouble, coll. that would be too great a bother; II. adv. circumstantially, &c.; — erzählen, to particularise, detail; III. U-keit, (w.) f. 1) circumstantiality, particularity; minuteness; 2) ceremoniousness, formality; coll. priggishness.

Um'ſtauen, (w.) v. tr. Mar. to rummage (the hold), to alter or shift (the stowage) in the hold, to restow.

Um'ſtechen, (str.) v. tr. 1) to turn up, stir (corn, &c.) with a fork; 2) to stab, cut [illegible] derſtechen; 3) to engrave (a plate) anew; [illegible] rack (off) (liquour, wine, &c.). [illegible]

Um'ſtecken, (w.) v. tr. to pin, or fasten [illegible]

Umſtec'ken, (w.) v. tr. to fasten around (with pins, &c.).

Um'ſtehen, (irr.) v. intr. (aux. ſein) 1) to stand round, see Umherſtehen; 2) [illegible] grow vapid, &c., see Abſtehen, I. 2, b & Umſchlagen, I. 2, b; 3) (of animals) to die [illegible] Crepiren, 1 & Abſterben, 2, b).

Umſte'hen, (irr.) v. tr. to stand round [illegible]

Um'ſtehend, p. a. 1) standing about [illegible] or by, surrounding; die U-en, pl. by-standers [illegible] 2) on the other side or page [illegible] noted; auf der u-en Seite zu quittiren [illegible] receipted on the opposite page [illegible]

Um'ſtellen, (w.) v. tr. to [illegible]

Umſtel'len, (w.) v. tr. to [illegible] compass (with), to surround, [illegible]

Um'ſtellung, (w.) f. transpo[illegible] sion.

Um'ſtempeln, (w.) v. tr. to [illegible]

Un'antastbar, *adj.* 1) that may not be touched, unapproachable; 2) unimpeachable.

Un'anwendbar, I. *adj.* inapplicable; II. **U-keit**, *(w.) f.* inapplicability.

Un'appetitlich, *adj.* unpleasant, loathsome (Widerlich).

Un'art, *(w.) f.* 1) bad *or* improper behaviour, rudeness, impertinence, want of good manners; 2) unmannered *or* naughty trick, ill habit; naughtiness (of children).

Un'artig, I. *adj.* 1) ill-behaved, rude, improper, disobliging; ill-bred, froward, naughty; 2) unruly (of a horse, &c.), vicious; II. **U-keit**, *(w.) f.* 1) ill-breeding, rudeness, &c. *cf.* Unart, 1; 2) naughty, improper, *or* rude trick, expression, &c.

Un'articulirt, *adj.* inarticulate.

* **U'nau**, *(str., pl.* **U-s**) *m.* *Zool.* anau: 1) the ai (from Ceylon); 2) the two-toed sloth (from the Amazon).

Un'aufgeblüht, *adj.* unblown.

Un'aufgefordert, *p. a.* uncalled for; without being called upon, without having received any application, of one's own accord.

Un'aufgehalten, *p. a.* unchecked, uncontrolled.

Un'aufgeräumt, *p. a.* disordered, untidy (room, &c.). 2) shorn (velvet).

Un'aufgerissen, *p. a.* 1) not torn open;

Un(')aufhalt'bar, **Un(')aufhalt'sam**, I. *adj.* not to be stopped, uncontrollable; incessant, continual; II. **U-keit**, *(w.) f.* the not admitting of being stopped.

Un(')aufhör'lich, I. *adj.* incessant, continual, perpetual, everlasting; ein u-er Canon, *Mus.* a perpetual fugue, an infinite canon; II. **U-keit**, *(w.) f.* incessantness, continuity.

Un'aufkündbar, *adj.* unredeemable, not to be recalled.

Un(')auflös'bar, **Un(')auflös'lich**, I. *adj.* 1) irresolvable (of nebulae, &c.); indissolvable, indissoluble, inseparable; 2) inextricable; incapable of solution (problem); II. **U-keit**, *(w.) f.* 1) irresolvability; indissolubility; 2) inextricability.

Un'aufmerksam, I. *adj.* inattentive, inadvertent; II. **U-keit**, *(w.) f.* inattention, inattentiveness, inadvertence.

Un'aufrichtig, I. *adj.* insincere, disingenuous; II. **U-keit**, *(w.) f.* insincerity, &c.

Un'aufschiebbar, **Un'aufschieblich**, *adj.* not to be delayed, urgent, pressing.

Un'ausbleiblich, I. *adj.* infallible, certain, sure, inevitable; II. **U-keit**, *(w.) f.* infallibility, certainty of occurring.

Un'ausforschlich, *see* Unerforschlich.

Un'ausführbar, I. *adj.* impracticable, unfeasible; that cannot be carried out *or* completed; II. **U-keit**, *(w.) f.* impracticableness.

Un'ausführlich, I. *adj.* incomplete, not detailed; II. **U-keit**, *(w.) f.* incompleteness, want of detail. *[or* supplied.

Un'ausfüllbar, *adj.* not to be filled (up)

Un'ausgebacken, *p. a.* underdone.

Un'ausgebaut, *p. a.* unfinished (house, &c.).

Un'ausgebrannt, *p. a.* not thoroughly burnt through. [cant; 2) left in blank.

Un'ausgefüllt, *p. a.* 1) not filled up; 2) va-

Un'ausgeglichen, *p. a.* not yet settled *or* adjusted.

Un'ausgemacht, *p. a.* undecided, open, still under controversy (question, &c.); es ist noch —, it is still an open question.

Un'ausgepackt, *p. a.* not yet unpacked; — verkaufen, to sell under the cords.

Un'ausgesetzt, I. *adj.* uninterrupted, continual; undelayed; II. *adv.* uninterruptedly, &c., without interruption.

Un'ausgesprochen, *p. a.* unpronounced; unuttered, unconfessed (feelings, &c.).

Un'ausgewachsen *(pr.* —waksn), *p. a.* not fully grown *or* developed

Un'ausgleichbar, *adj.* irreconcilable (contradiction).

Un'auslösch(')bar, **Un'auslösch'lich**, I. *adj.* indelible, inextinguishable, [illegible]; II. **U-keit**, *(w.) f.* indelibleness, &c.

Un'auslösbar, *adj.* unredeemable, past redemption. [illegible]

Un'ausmeßbar, *adj.* *Math.* [illegible]

Un'ausrott(')bar, *adj.* *see* Unausrottbar.

Un'aussprechbar, *adj.* unpronounceable.

Un(')aussprech'lich, I. *adj.* ineffable, unspeakable, inexpressible, unutterable; II. **U-keit**, *(w.) f.* ineffableness, &c.

Un(')aussteh'lich, I. *adj.* insupportable, insufferable, intolerable; II. **U-keit**, *(w.) f.* insupportableness, &c.

Un'austilg(')bar, *adj.* ineradicable, interminable, inextirpable; ineffaceable.

Un(')ausweich'lich, *adj.* unavoidable.

Un'band, *(str., pl.* **U-e** *[Bengel])* *m.* *coll.* unruly child *or* person.

Un'bändig, I. *adj.* unmanageable, ungovernable, untractable, unruly; II. *adv.* 1) unmanageably, &c.; 2) *coll.* very, immoderately; III. **U-keit**, *(w.) f.* unmanageableness, &c.

Un'barmherzig, I. *adj.* unmerciful, merciless, remorseless; II. **U-keit**, *(w.) f.* unmercifulness, &c. [(w.) f. beardlessness.

Un'bärtig, I. *adj.* beardless; II. **U-keit**,

Un'baulich, *adj.* 1) uncultivated, untilled; 2) out of repair.

Un'beabsichtigt, *p. a.* undesigned.

Un'beachtet, *p. a.* unnoticed, disregarded, unheeded; — lassen, to leave unnoticed, to pass (over) without notice, to overpass, to disregard, *mod.* to ignore; — bleiben, to fall dead (of observations, &c.).

Un'beamtet, *p. a.* having no office, private.

Un'beantwortet, *p. a.* unanswered.

Un'beantwort'lich, *adj.* unanswerable.

Un'bearbeitet, *p. a.* unworked, not (yet) worked, unwrought; raw; (of hides) untanned, green, raw. [2) not built upon.

Un'bebaut, *p. a.* 1) uncultivated, untilled;

Un'bedacht, I. *or* **Un'bedächtig**, **Un'bedachtsam**, *adj.* inconsiderate, indiscreet, unwary, rash; II. *s.* *(str.)* *m.* *or* **Un'bedachtsamkeit**, *(w.) f.* inconsiderateness, indiscretion.

Un'bedeckt, *p. a.* uncovered; mit u-em Haupte, bare-headed; u-er Credit, *Comm.* blank credit.

Un'bedenklich, I. *adj.* 1) that requires no thought *or* hesitation; 2) unhesitating, unscrupulous; II. *adv.* without (much) thought or hesitation, unhesitatingly.

Un'bedeutend, *adj.* insignificant, unimportant, trifling, inconsiderable, [illegible]

Un'bedeuten(d)heit, *(w.) f.* insignificance, [illegible]

Un'bedeutsam, I. *adj.* 1) insignificant, unmeaning; 2) unmanageable; II. **U-keit**, *(w.) f.* insignificance, unmeaningness.

Un'bedingt, I. *adj.* unqualified, unconditional, implicit; unlimited; unqualified, absolute; u-e Annahme, absolute or full acceptance (of a bill of exchange); II. *adv.* unconditionally, &c., at all events, [illegible] *cf.* Durchaus; III. **U-heit**, *(w.)* [illegible] tionalness, &c. [illegible]

Un'beeidigt, *p. a.* not sworn, [illegible]

Un'beerbt *(pr.* un'beerbt), [illegible] of a legitimate heir, childless, [illegible]

Un'befahren, *adj.* 1) [illegible] not navigated before; 2) [illegible] experienced sailors.

Un'befangen, I. *adj.* 1) [illegible] biassed, impartial, dispassionate, [illegible] strained, unembarrassed, [illegible] free, candid, ingenuous, [illegible] II. **U-heit**, *(w.) f.* 1) want of [illegible] partialness; 2) unconstraint, [illegible] ness, candour, frankness, [illegible]

&c., pervious to air, &c. (*opp.* dicht); u-e Gasröhren, leaky gas-pipes.

Un'dienlich, I. *adj.* 1) unserviceable, unfit, amiss, improper, inconvenient; 2) unwholesome, unhealthy; II. U-keit, (*w.*) *f.* unserviceableness, &c.

Un'dienst, (*str.*) *m.* disservice.

Un'dienstbar, *adj. see* Dienstunfähig.

Un'dienstfertig, *adj.* inofficious, disobliging.

* Undi'ne, (*w.*) *f.* (*Lat.* unda, *wave, water*) [Undine, water-spirit.

Un'ding, (*str.*) *n.* 1) nonentity, nothing; 2) chimera; monster; nonsense; chaos.

* Undulation', (*w.*) *f.* (*Lat.*) undulation; U-stheorie, *f.* undulatory theory.

Un'duldsam, I. *adj.* intolerant; II. U-keit, (*w.*) *f.* intolerance.

Un'durchdacht, *p. a.* not well thought of, [crude.

Un'durchdringlich, I. *adj.* impenetrable: 1) impermeable, impervious (für, to); 2) *fig.* inscrutable; II. U-keit, (*w.*) *f.* impenetrability, &c.

Un'durchführbar, *adj.* 1) not to be carried through (Unausführbar); 2) untenable.

Un'durchlöchert, *p. a. Bot.* imperforated.

Un'durchsichtig, I. *adj.* untransparent, not pellucid, opaque, impervious to light; II. U-keit, (*w.*) *f.* opacity, opaqueness, imperviousness to light.

Un'durchwachsen, *p. a. Bot.* imperfoliate.

Un'eben, I. *adj.* 1) uneven, unequal, not level, rugged, rough; 2) *fig.* irregular; gar nicht —, not at all amiss, not bad; II. U-heit, (*w.*) *f.* unevenness, &c., inequality.

Un'ebenbürtig, I. *adj.* 1) of unequal birth; 2) *fig.* unequal; II. U-keit, (*w.*) *f.* 1) unequal birth; 2) *fig.* inequality, disparity.

Un'ebenmaß, (*str.*) *m.* asymmetry, disproportion. — Un'ebenmäßig, *adj.* asymmetrical, disproportionable.

Un'echt, I. *adj.* 1) not genuine, counterfeit, sham, artificial, false, spurious; adulterated; 2) illegitimate; u-e Perlen, mock-pearls; u-er Diamant, Rubin &c., mock *or* imitation diamond, ruby, &c.; u-e Steine, false stones; sham jewels, paste, strass; u-e Farbe, fugitive *or* not fast colour, colour that won't wash; u-es Färbeholz, bastard-dyewood; u-er Bruch, *Arith.* improper fraction; II. U-heit, (*w.*) *f.* spuriousness, &c.

Un'edel, *adj.* ignoble, illiberal; mean, low; base (metal).

Un'ehe, (*w.*) *f.* illicit cohabitation, con- [cubinage.

Un'ehelich, I. *adj.* illegitimate, natural; illicit (cohabitation, &c.); u-e Kinder, children born out of wedlock, base-born children; II. *adv.* illegitimately, &c., in adultery.

Un'ehrbar, I. *adj.* 1) unbecoming, immodest, indecent; 2) dishonourable, disgraceful; II. U-keit, (*w.*) *f.* unbecomingness, &c.; indecency.

Un'ehre, (*w.*) *f.* dishonour, disgrace, discredit; Einem — machen, to disgrace one; mit U-n, discreditably, disreputably.

Un'ehrenhaft, *adj.* discreditable, disreputable.

Un'ehrerbietig, I. *adj.* irreverent, disrespectful, undutiful; II. U-keit, (*w.*) *f.* irreverence, undutifulness.

Un'ehrlich, I. *adj.* 1) dishonest; dishonourable; ignominious, infamous; 2) (unaufrichtig) uncandid; II. U-keit, (*w.*) *f.* dishonesty; dishonourableness, disgrace, infamy, ignominy.

Un'eigennützig, I. *adj.* disinterested, unselfish; II. U-keit, (*w.*) *f.* disinterestedness.

Un'eigentlich, I. *adj.* not literal; figurative (sense, &c.); improper (fraction, &c.); II. U-keit, (*w.*) *f.* figurative sense, figurativeness.

Un'eindämmbar, *adj.* irrepleviable.

Un'einbringlich, *adj.* barren (debt).

Un'eingebunden, *p. a.* unbound, in sheets.

Un'eingedenk, (*indecl.*) *adj.* (*with Gen.*) unmindful, regardless; forgetful (of).

Un'eingelöst, *p. a. see* Ungelöst.

Un'eingemacht, *p. a.* not preserved *or* pickled, fresh. [registered, &c.

Un'eingeschrieben, *p. a.* not entered, un-

Un'einig, I. *adj.* disunited; discordant, disagreeing, at difference *or* variance; — sein, to differ, disagree; — machen, to set at variance *or* at odds; to divide; mit Einem — werden, to fall out with one, to quarrel; II. U-keit, (*w.*) *f.* disharmony, dissension, discord, disagreement, variance, disunion.

Un'einnehmbar, *adj.* impregnable.

Un'eins, *adv.* at difference *or* variance, *cf.* Uneinig.

Un'einverstanden, *adj.* not (quite) agreed.

Un'elastisch, *adj.* inelastic, non-elastic.

Un'empfänglich, I. *adj.* not susceptible (für, of), insusceptible; dull; II. U-keit, *f.* insusceptibility, dulness.

Un'empfindbar, I. *adj.* imperceptible; II. U-keit, (*w.*) *f.* imperceptibility.

Un'empfindlich, I. *adj.* insensible, indifferent, unfeeling; cold, callous (gegen, to); *Med.* numb; II. U-keit, (*w.*) *f.* insensibility, indifference; *Med.* numbness.

Un'empfindsam, *adj.* not sensitive; not sentimental.

Un'empfunden, *p. a.* unfelt.

Unend'lich, I. *adj.* infinite, endless; eternal; in's U-e, to infinity, *ad infinitum*; das geht in's U-e, there is no end of (to) it; eine — lange Zeit, *coll.* an age; diese Thatsache sagt — viel, this fact speaks volumes; u-er Canon, *Mus.* infinite canon, perpetual fugue; die Analyse des U-en, infinitesimal calculus; II. U-keit, (*w.*) *f.* infinity; endlessness; eternity.

Un'entbehr(')lich, I. *adj.* indispensable; eine Feder ist zum Schreiben —, a pen is indispensable for writing; II. U-keit, (*w.*) *f.* indispensableness.

Un'entflieh(')bar, *adj.* inevitable.

Un'entgelt(')lich, I. *adj.* gratuitous; II. *adv.* gratuitously; gratis, for nothing, without charge, free of charge.

Un'enthaltsam, I. *adj.* incontinent, intemperate; II. U-keit, (*w.*) *f.* incontinence.

Un'entrinn'bar, *adj.* inevitable.

Un'entscheid'bar, *adj.* undecidable.

Un'entschält, *p. a. T.* unscoured, unboiled (silk).

Un'entschieden, I. *adj.* undecided, undetermined; drawn (game, battle); II. U-heit, (*w.*) *f.* indecision; suspense.

Un'entschlossen, I. *adj.* irresolute; undecided, wavering, doubtful; — sein, to be irresolute, &c., to waver, hesitate, [illegible]; II. U-heit, (*w.*) *f.* irresolution; indecision.

Un'entschuld(')bar, *adj.* inexcusable.

Un'entwegt, *p. a.* unswerving, steadfast.

Un'entwickelt, *p. a.* undeveloped, [illegible] matured; u-er Zustand, embryo-state.

Un'entwirr(')bar, *adj.* inextricable.

Un'entzieh(')bar, *adj.* not to be [illegible] &c., *cf.* Entziehen I.

Un'erachtet, *see* Ungeachtet.

Un'erbaulich, *adj.* not edifying [illegible]

Un'erbeten, *adj.* not asked for, [illegible]

Un'erbittlich, I. *adj.* inexorable, [illegible] unrelenting; II. U-keit, (*w.*) *f.* [illegible] ness.

Un'erfahren, I. *adj.* inexperienced [illegible] *or* unused to; raw; II. U-[illegible] perience.

Un'erforschlich, I. *adj.* [illegible] searchable, impenetrable [illegible] scrutableness, &c.

Un'erfreulich, *adj.* [illegible]

Un'erfüllbar, I. *adj.* [illegible]

opposite, impertinent, irrelevant, out of place, alien; II. U-heit, (w.) f. andueness; impropriety.

Un'gehorsam, I. adj. disobedient; II. s. (str.) m. disobedience; *Law*, default; in die Strafe des U-s verfallen, to incur a default.

Un'gehüllt, adj. *Bot.* naked.

Un'geist, (str., pl. U-er) m. (l. u.) perverse or false spirit; evil-mindedness. [coarse.

Un'geistig, adj. spiritless; weak; material,

Un'geistlich, I. adj. 1) not spiritual, secular; 2) *fig.* unholy, profane; II. U-keit, (w.) f. secularity; profaneness. [affected.

Un'gekünstelt, p. a. artless, natural, un-

Un'gelähmt, p. a. see Ungeschwächt, 1.

Un'geläufig, adj. 1) not fluent, not easy; 2) not generally or commonly used, rare (word, &c.). [unracked.

Un'geläutert, p. a. unclarified, unrefined,

Un'geld, (str., pl. U-er) n. *provinc.* casual expense, additional cost, &c., *Mar.* small average, hat-money and other expenses.

Un'gelegen, I. adj. inconvenient, unseasonable, inopportune, incommodious; es kam mir —, it came upon me inopportunely; II. U-heit, (w.) f. 1) inconvenience (—cy), incommodity, unseasonableness; 2) trouble, vexation; Einem U-en machen, to incommode, inconvenience, molest one, to cause or give one trouble.

Un'gelegt, adj. unlaid, not (yet) laid; sich um u-e Eier bekümmern, *proverb*, to fight with the sword that is yet at the cutler's.

Un'gelehrig, I. adj. indocile, indocible, unteachable; II. U-keit, (w.) f. indocility, indocibleness.

Un'gelehrt, I. adj. unlearned, illiterate, unlettered; II. U-heit, (w.) f. illiterateness, ignorance.

Un'gelenk, Un'gelenksam, I. adj. inflexible, not supple; stiff, awkward, clumsy; II. Un'gelenkigkeit, Un'gelenksamkeit, (w.) f. inflexibility, stiffness, &c.

Un'gelöscht, p. a. unquenched, &c.; u-er Kalk, unslaked lime, quicklime.

Un'gelungen, p. a. (Grimm, WB. Vorrede, XXVII; l. u.) unaccomplished, &c., cf. Gelingen; es ist ihnen —, they have not succeeded.

Un'gemach, (str.) n. toil, hardship, fatigue; trouble, vexation, affliction.

Un'gemächlich, I. adj. inconvenient, incommodious, uncomfortable; toilsome; II. U-keit, (w.) f. inconvenience (—cy), incommodity, incommodiousness, &c., trouble, hardship.

Un'gemalzt, p. a. prepared without malt.

Un'gemäß, I. adj. disproportionate, &c., cf. Unangemessen; II. U-heit, (w.) f. disproportionateness, &c.

Un'gemein (often: ungemein'), adj. uncommon; rare, extraordinary; adv. exceedingly.

Un'gemessen, p. a. 1) unmeasured; 2) *fig.* a) unbounded, unlimited; b) immeasurable; c) unseemly, unbecoming.

Un'gemünzt, p. a. uncoined; u-es edles Metall, bullion. [*Anat.* innominate.

Un'genannt, p. a. unnamed, anonymous;

Un'genau, I. adj. inexact; inaccurate, uncertain, vague; II. U-igkeit, (w.) f. inexactness, inaccuracy, &c.

Un'geneigt, I. adj. 1) disinclined, indisposed, unwilling; 2) averse, disaffected, disaffectionate, unfriendly; II. U-heit, (w.) f. 1) disinclination, unwillingness, reluctance; 2) averseness, &c., ill-will.

Un'genieß(')bar, I. adj. unfit for enjoyment; not eatable or drinkable; not relishable; II. U-keit, f. unfitness for enjoyment, disrelish.

Ungeniert' (pr. ŭnsheneert'), I. adj. unrestrained, untrammelled, unchecked, unfettered, easy-going, unceremonious, without any ceremony, hesitation, embarrassment, or constraint, free and easy; II. U-heit, (w.) f. unconstraint, ease; homeliness (of manners, &c.).

Un'genossen, p. a. 1) unenjoyed, &c.; 2) *coll.* unnoticed, unpunished, see Ungestraft.

Un'genügend, adj. insufficient, inadequate; — frankirt, *Post.* insufficiently (pre)paid.

Un'genügsam, I. adj. unsatisfied, insatiable, greedy, intemperate; hard to be contented or satisfied; II. U-keit, (w.) f. insatiableness, &c.

Un'genutzt, p. a. unused, unemployed, not turned to profit; cf. Unbenutzt.

Un'geöhrt, adj. earless.

Un'geordnet, p. a. *Chem.* uncombined.

Un'geprägt, p. a. see Ungemünzt.

Un'gerade, adj. 1) not straight; uneven; 2) odd (number, &c.); gerade oder — spielen, to play at even and odd; die — Taktart, *Mus.* triple time.

Un'geradflächig, adj. *Cryst.* impair.

Un'gerändert, p. a. unrimmed; *Bot.* immarginate.

Un'geraten, p. a. 1) failed, misgrown, spoiled; 2) ill-bred, spoiled, abandoned, degenerated.

Un'gerechnet, p. a. not counted, &c., cf. Rechnen; *particul.* with an *Acc.* (which gener. precedes): not taken into account, not including ..., not included, exclusive of ..., besides ...; viele und große Mühe —, not to speak of a large amount of trouble.

Un'gerecht, I. adj. unjust; II. U-igkeit, (w.) f. (act of) injustice.

Un'gerechtfertigt, p. a. unwarranted.

Un'geregelt, p. a. not regulated, unregulated; irregular; inordinate.

Un'gereimt, I. adj. 1) unrhymed; 2) *fig.* inconsistent; absurd; preposterous, incongruous, extravagant; u-e Verse, blank verse; u-es Zeug, nonsense; u-e Antworten geben, to be at cross-purposes; II. U-heit, (w.) f. inconsistency; absurdity, incongruity, extravagance.

Un'gerippt, p. a. *Bot.* without nerves.

Un'gerissen, p. a. untorn; u-er Sammet, *Manuf.* uncut velvet, terry velvet.

Un'gern, adv. unwillingly, reluctantly, with displeasure; ich thue es —, I do not like or I am loath to do it; ich sehe es —, I am sorry to see it; ich erfahre —, I hear with regret. [revenged.

Un'gerochen, p. a. 1) unsmelled; 2) un-

Un'gerollt, p. a. 1) unrolled; 2) unprepared (barley). [b) *fig.* insipid.

Un'gesalzen, p. a. 1) unsalted, unseasoned;

Un'gesäuert, p. a. unleavened, unyeasted.

Un'gesäumt, I. adj. 1) unhemmed, &c.; 2) immediate; prompt; II. adv. immediately, &c.

Un'geschäftet, p. a. without a [illegible].

Un'geschäftlich, adj. not businesslike.

Un'geschält, p. a. unpeeled, unhusked; u-er Reis, paddy. [illegible]

Un'geschehen, adj. undone; — [illegible]

Un'gescheit, adj. injudicious, [illegible] silly. [illegible]

Un'ge[illegible], p. a. [illegible], &c. [illegible]

Un'gescheut, I. adj. 1) not [illegible] 2) fearless, unflinching; II. adv. [illegible] boldly; without fear or shame, [illegible]

Un'geschick, (str.) n. 1) [illegible] adverse fate. — Un'geschickt, I. adj. [illegible] lich, adj. awkward, ungainly, [illegible] incapable; II. U-heit, or [illegible] (w.) f. (piece of) awkwardness [illegible] terity.

Un'geschlacht, I. p. a. [illegible] rough, rude, gross; II. [illegible] coarseness, &c.

Un'geschliffen, I. adj. [illegible]

* Unī'ren, (w.) v. tr. (Lat.) to unite. — Unión', (w.) f. union.

* Uni'sono, n. (Ital.) Mus. in unison.

* Unitā'rier, (str.) m., Unitā'risch, adj. Eccl. unitarian.

* Unität', (w.) f. (Lat.) unity.

* Universāl', adj. (Lat.) universal: —erbe, m. heir general: exclusive heir; Mech.-s. —centrumbohrer, m. expanding centre-bit; —futter, n. chuck (of a turning-lathe); —gelenk, n. universal joint, swivel-link; —mittel, n. universal or sovereign remedy, catholicon, panacea; —recept, n. sovereign prescription. — Universalität', f. universality.

* Universität', (w.) f. university, academy; college; U-sfreund, m. college friend, fellow-collegian; U-sgericht, n. court of justice in some German universities, nearly analogous to the Chancellor's (Consistory) Court of English universities; U-sjahr, n. year passed at the university. [n. universe.

* Univer'sum, (str., pl. [Lat.] Univer'sa)

Un'jagdbār, adj. Sport. unfit for the chase.

Un'jährig, adj. under age.

Un'kaiserlich, adj. unlike an emperor.

Un'kaufmännisch, adj. unmercantile, unbusinesslike.

Unke, (w.) f. 1) Zool. a) orange-speckled toad (Bombinātor igneus Merr.); b) common or ringed snake (Ringelnatter); 2) see Stubenhocker. [salt).

Unkelstein, (str.) m. provinc. basalt (Ba-

Unken, (w.) v. intr. (l. u.) to croak.

Un'kennt(')lich Un(')kenn'bār, I. adj. incapable of being known or recognised, unknowable, indiscernible; — machen, to disguise; to deface; II. U-keit, (w.) f. indiscernibleness.

Un'kenntniß, (str.) f. ignorance.

Un'keusch, I. adj. unchaste, lascivious, lewd, impure, unclean; II. U-heit, (w.) f. unchastity, lewdness, &c., impurity.

Un'kindlich, I. adj. 1) unfilial, undutiful; 2) unchildlike; II. U-keit, (w.) f. unfilialness, undutifulness.

Un'kirchlich, I. adj. secular; fig. worldly; II. U-keit, (w.) f. worldliness.

Un'klār, I. adj. 1) unclear, not clear, &c., cf. Klar; troubled; 2) Mar. (— laufend) foul; 3) fig. indistinct; confused; obscure; im U-en sein, to be uncertain; to be in the dark (über [with Acc.], about, as to); cf. Dunkel; II. U-heit, (w.) f. unclearness, &c.

Un'klug, I. adj. imprudent; foolish; II. U-heit, (w.) f. imprudence; (piece of) folly.

Un'körperlich, I. adj. incorporeal, bodiless, immaterial; II. U-keit, (w.) f. incorporeality, immateriality; U-keitslehre, f. immaterialism.

Un'kosten, pl. see Kosten.

Un'kräftig, I. adj. inefficacious, ineffectual; feeble, weak, infirm, invalid, powerless; II. U-keit, (w.) f. inefficaciousness, &c.

Un'kraut, (str., pl. Un'kräuter) n. 1) weed; tare; 2) fig. a) bad, evil thing; b) bad or obnoxious person; — säen, to sow tares; — verdirbt nicht, provinc. (lit. evil weeds never wither) ill weeds grow apace, naught never comes to harm.

Un'kriegerisch, adj. unwarlike.

Un'kündbār, adj. see Unaufkündbar.

Un'kunde, f. want of knowledge, ignorance, unacquaintance.

Un'kundig, adj. (with Gen.) not knowing, ignorant (of), unacquainted (with).

Un'kunst, f. false or bad art.

Un'längst [sometimes unlängst'], adv. of late, lately, recently, not long since, not long ago.

Un'lateinisch, adj. not in conformity with the rules or idiom of the Latin grammar.

Un'läugbār [often unläug'bār], I. adj. undeniable; II. U-keit, (w.) f. undeniableness.

Un'laune, (w.) f. ill humour. — Un'launig, adj. ill-humoured.

Un'lauter, I. adj. impure; unclean; sordid; sinister (motives, &c.); II. U-keit, (w.) f. impurity, &c. [lible.

Un'leben, (str.) n. disagreeable, [illegible]

Un'leid, adj. es ist mir —, I am not sorry.

Un'leidlich, I. adj. 1) or Un'leidig, insufferable, intolerable, insupportable; 2) impatient, intolerant; II. U-keit, (w.) f. intolerableness, &c.

Un'lenksam, I. or Un'lenkbār, adj. unmanageable, ungovernable; II. U-keit, (w.) f. ungovernableness, want of docility.

Un'lesbār, Un'leserlich, I. adj. illegible; gewohnt, u-e Schrift zu entziffern, accustomed to deciphering indistinct writing; II. U-keit, (w.) f. illegibility.

Un'leugbār, see Unläugbar.

Un'lieb, adj. not dear; disagreeable; es ist mir —, I do not like it, I am sorry (for it).

Un'lieblich, I. adj. unpleasant; unsavoury; II. U-keit, (w.) f. unpleasantness.

Un'liebsam, adj. invidious, see Mißfällig.

Un'löblich, adj. not praiseworthy, illaudable, not laudable, blamable.

Un'logisch, adj. illogical. [bar &c.

Un'lösbār, Un'löslich, adj. see Unauflös-

Un'löschbār, I. adj. unquenchable; II. U-keit, (w.) f. unquenchableness. [disinclination.

Un'lust, f. displeasure, dislike; disgust;

Un'lustig, adj. 1) disliking, disinclined; disgustful; 2) dull, heavy, sad.

Un'macht, f. 1) powerlessness, weakness, impotence; 2) *, see Ohnmacht, 2. [tent.

Un'mächtig, adj. powerless, weak, impo-

Un'manierlich, I. adj. unmannerly; rude; II. U-keit, (w.) f. unmannerliness, rudeness.

Un'mann, (str., pl. Un'männer) m. 1) eunuch; 2) fig. a) coward; b) dandy.

Un'mannbār, I. adj. not arrived at manhood; under age; unmarriageable; II. U-keit, (w.) f. the not having attained to manhood or puberty; unmarriageableness.

Un'männlich, I. or Un'mannhaft, adj. unmanly, unmanlike; II. U-keit, (w.) f. unman- [liness.

Un'maß, (str.) n. excess.

Un'maßgeb(')lich, I. adj. without prescribing (any conditions or limits), open to correction, unpresuming, humble; II. adv. under favour, with deference or submission.

Un'mäßig, I. adj. immoderate, intemperate, excessive; II. U-keit, (w.) f. immoderateness, immoderation, intemperance; excess; extravagance.

Un'mensch, (w.) m. inhuman or cruel man, tyrant, barbarian, monster.

Un'menschlich, I. adj. 1) inhuman, cruel, barbarous; pitiless; 2) coll. vast, mighty; II. U-keit, (w.) f. inhumanity, cruelty, barbarity, tyranny; inhuman or cruel deed.

Un'merklich, I. or Un'merkbār, adj. imperceptible, inappreciable; insensible; II. U-keit, (w.) f. imperceptibleness, &c.

Un'meßbār, I. adj. incommensurable; u-e Zahl, surd number; II. U-keit, (w.) f. incommensurability. [(w.) f. [illegible]

Un'mild, I. adj. not mild, harsh; [illegible]

Un'mildthätig, adj. uncompassionate, pitiless.

Un'mittelbār, I. adj. immediate, direct; ein — gefreiter Vasall, Germ. Hist. [illegible] II. U-keit, (w.) f. immediateness, [illegible]

Un'mittheilsam, adj. [illegible]

Un'möblirt, adj. unfurnished [illegible]

Un'möglich [often unmög'lich], I. adj. impossible; out of the question; [illegible] Math. imaginary quantity; [illegible] sterben, coll. to cry for the moon [illegible] (w.) f. impossibility; [illegible] possibility; Einem in die U-keit [illegible] to put it out of one's power [illegible]

mould; weiche —lage, pad; —lager, n. stand, prop, support, base, foot; —lag(s)scheibe, f. Mach., &c. collar, washer; —lag(s)platte, f. Railw. bed-plate (of a rail); —land, n. lowland, nether-land; —länder, m. low-lander; —ländisch, —ländlich, adj. from a low country, peculiar to a low country; —länge, f. Typ. descending part of a letter.

Un'terlaß, (str., pl. U-lässe) m. intermission, ceasing; ohne —, without intermission, unremittingly, incessantly.

Unterlas'sen, (str.) v. tr. to intermit, to leave off, to cease from, to discontinue, fail, forbear, omit, neglect; to abstain (from); wegen u-er Eintragung, Comm. owing to not booking. [tinued, omitted, &c.

Unterläß'lich, adj. that may be discon-

Unterlas'sung, (w.) f. intermission, leaving off, discontinuance, omission, cessation; neglect; Law, default; U-ssünde, f. sin of omission.

Un'ter..., in comp. Mar.-s. —last, f. ballast; —lauf, (str., pl. U-läufe) m. over-deck; des Kiels zum Vorsteven, fore-foot.

Un'terlaufen, (str.) v. intr. (aux. sein) to run under, run in among, slip in; mit —, to run among, slip in; to occur (accidentally); mit — lassen, to slip in (a word, &c.).

Unterlau'fen, (str.) v. tr. 1) to slip under; 2) to spread under the surface of ...; 3) Fenc. to avoid the thrust of; das Wild —, Sport. to steal in on the game; mit Blut — (p. a.), filled or swollen with blood (under the skin), injected; u-es Blut, extravasated blood.

Un'terläufer, (str.) m. 1) intruder, meddler; 2) interloper; smuggler.

Un'ter..., in comp. —leder, n. under-leather; —leesegel, n. Mar. lower studding-sail; —lefze, f. under-lip, nether-lip; —legdecke, f. saddle-cloth.

Un'terlegen, (w.) v. tr. 1) to lay under, put under; 2) (with Dat.) to put to ..., to attach (importance, &c. to a thing), to impute: einem Worte einen andern Sinn —, to put a different meaning or another construction upon a word; frische Pferde —, to change horses, to relay; untergelegte Pferde, relay-horses.

Unterle'gen, (w.) v. tr. to underlay; ein unterlegter Handel, a concerted matter.

Un'terleger, (str.) m. piece or log of wood laid under something; Carp. templet; Mar. pontoon.

Un'terleg..., in comp. —pferd, n. relay-horse, spare horse; —scheibe, f. washer; —trense, f. bridoon; —tuch, n. clout, napkin; —walze, f. (manuf. of mirrors) flattening-cylinder. [putting under, &c.

Un'terlegung, (w.) f. the (act of) laying,

Un'terlehen, (str.) n. fief conditional, under-fief; U-sfall, m. change of vassal.

Un'terlehrer, (str.) m. under-teacher, usher.

Un'terleib, (str., pl. U-er) m. lower part of the belly, abdomen; bowels; zum — gehörig, abdominal, hypogastric; den — betreffend, gastric; in comp. U-sbeschwerde, U-skrankheit, f., U-sleiden, n. disorder in the bowels, abdominal complaint; U-smuskel, m. abdominal muscle.

Un'terleik, (str.) n. Mar. foot-rope.

Un'terliegen, (str.) v. intr. (aux. haben) 1) to lie under; 2) fig. to be (or to serve as) a basis (for); to be at the bottom (of).

Unterlie'gen, (str.) v. intr. (aux. sein; with Dat.) fig. 1) to succumb, to sink (under); to be overthrown, defeated, or overcome, to be worsted, to yield; 2) to be subjected or liable to; es unterliegt einer Abänderung, it undergoes an alteration; es unterliegt keinem Zweifel, there is no doubt of it.

Un'ter..., in comp. —lieutenant, m. second lieutenant; —lippe, f. 1) lower or under-lip; Entom. labium; 2) [illegible] lower part or lip of the cock; 3) Organ. under-labium, under-lip; —litze, f. Weav. hanger.

Un'term, contr. from Unter dem.

Un'ter..., in comp. —maulbarte, f. (Lam.) underwhiskers (of a whale); —magd, f. under-maid, under-servant.

Unterma'len, (w.) v. tr. Paint. to lay the first or ground-colour on (Grundieren). — Unterma'lung, (w.) f. dead-colouring.

Un'ter..., in comp. —mann, m. 1) Mil. left-hand-man; 2) Cards. knave; 3)*, vassal; —masse, f. Min. mass found under a trench; —mast, f. Mar. lower part of the mast; —maß, n. loss in the amount of grain, &c., see Bodenriß; —mäßig, adj. Mil., &c. below the standard (measure of) height.

Untermau'ern, (w.) v. tr. 1) to support by forming a foundation of masonry-work, to underpin; 2) see [illegible]. — Untermau'erung, (w.) f. underpinning (the forming a foundation, and the supporting stone-work).

Un'ter..., in comp. —maul, n. lower mouth (of an animal); —mediante, f. Mus. submediant. [intermingle.

Un'termengen, (w.) v. tr. to intermingle.

Untermeng'en, (w.) v. tr. to mix up (with).

Un'ter[illegible], m. [illegible]

Untermini'ren, (w.) v. tr. to undermine, sap. [menge.

Un'termischen, Untermisch'en, see Unter-

Untermisch'ung, (w.) f. intermixture; sprinkling.

Un'ter..., in comp. —mühle, f. lower mill, mill lower down; —mühlstein, m. bedstone.

Unternäh'en, (w.) v. tr. to sew or stitch underneath or below.

Unterneh'men, (str.) v. tr. to undertake, take in hand, charge one's self with, to enterprise, attempt to venture upon; das —, (str.) n. s. see the next word.

Unterneh'mung, (w.) f. an undertaking; enterprise; U-sgeist, m., U-slust, f. (spirit of) enterprise; speculation.

Unterneh'mer, (str.) m. one who undertakes, undertaker; contractor.

Un'ter..., in comp. —obrigkeit, f. inferior jurisdiction, inferior magistracy; —octave, f. Mus. sub-octave; —[illegible], m. [illegible] copper-slag (Kupferschlacke); —offizier, m. under-officer, subaltern officer, subaltern, non-commissioned officer; corporal; —ordnen, v. tr. to subordinate; —ordnung, f. subordination; —pacht, f. under-lease; —pächter, m. under-tenant; —parlament, n. subordinate parliament; —pfalz, f. Geogr. Lower Palatinate. [strengthen with piles.

Unterpfäh'len, (w.) v. tr. to support or

Un'terpfand, (str., pl. Un'terpfänder) n. (deposited) pledge, deposit, see Pfand.

Un'terpfändlich, adj. (serving) as a pledge or pawn, &c., cf. Pfändlich.

Un'ter..., in comp. —pfarre, —[illegible] f. vicarage; —pfarrer, m. inferior [illegible] vicar, curate; Chem.-s. —[illegible] adj. hypophosphorous; das [illegible] Salz, hypophosphite; —[illegible] f. hypophosphorous acid; —[illegible] f. hypophosphoric acid; —[illegible] president; —prediger, m. [illegible] —prior, m. subprior; —[illegible] under-caterer, under-[illegible] Mar. studding sail-yard; —[illegible] rector.

Unterre'den, (w.) v. [illegible] verse, discourse, commune [illegible]

Unterre'dung, (w.) f. [illegible] sation, discourse; Mil. [illegible] or haben, see [illegible]

Un'ter..., in comp. [illegible]

Verzwick'en, (w.) v. tr. 1) to pinch away, clip; 2) Naut. to lay off the ends of (strands); 3) to clinch, rivet; to bend (nails, &c.); 4) Mas. to fill up (joints, a wall) with garrettings; 5) fig. see Verwirren, 1, Verwickeln, Verwirren, 1; verzwickt', coll. odd, strange, queer.

Verzwie'fachen, (w.) v. tr. to double.

Verzwir'ren, (w.) v. tr. to entangle in quarrels, &c., see Entzweien.

* Ves'per, (w.) f. 1) (–zeit, f.) afternoon; evening; 2) Eccl. vespers, evening prayers or service; die sicilianische –, Hist. Sicilian Vespers; in comp. –brot, –mahl, n., –kost, f. afternoon's luncheon; –gesang, m. evening- or vesper-hymn; –glocke, f. evening(-)bell; –predigt, f. afternoon-sermon; –schnitte, f. slice of bread for one's evening meal. – Ves'pern, (w.) v. intr. coll. to eat one's afternoon's luncheon or collation.

† Vest, Veste &c., see Fest, Feste &c.

* Vesta'lin, (w.) f. 1) Rom. Archaeol. Vestal; 2) jes. a) courtesan; b) cock.

Vesuv', (str.) m. Geogr. (mount) Vesuvius. – Vesuvian', (str.) m. Miner. Vesuvian, idocrase.

* Veteran', (sing. str. & sometimes w., pl. w.) m. (Lat.) veteran (soldier, sailor, officer).

* Veterinär', I. adj. veterinary; II. s. (str.) m. veterinary surgeon (Thierarzt); veterinarian; –kunde, f. see Thierarzneikunde.

* Ve'to, (str., pl. V-s, or not decl.) n. (Lat.) veto.

Vet'tel, (w.) f. coll. doxy, slut, quean.

Vet'ter, (str., sing. str., pl. w.) m. 1) cousin; relation; 2) uncle; V-gunst, f. favour shown to relations, nepotism. – Vet'terlich, adj. & adv. cousinlike. – Vet'tern, (w.) v. refl. coll. to call each other cousin. – Vet'terschaft, (w.) f. state of being related, relationship.

* Vexato'risch, adj. (Lat.) vexatious.

* Vexir'..., in comp. –bessel, m., –börse, f. puzzle-purse; –büchse, f. puzzle-box; –ei, n. mock-egg.

* Vexi'ren, (w.) v. tr. to vex, trouble, tease; to tantalise, deceive. – Vexirerei', (w.) f. vexation, &c. – Vexi'rerisch, adj. coll. vexatious, teasing.

* Vexir'..., in comp. –glas, n. anaclastic glass, vexing glass, singing glass; –garbe, f. see Gleichgarbe; –laterne, f. see Nachtlaterne; –nelke, f. see Gauchheil; –ring, m. puzzle-ring; –schloss, n. puzzle(-bag)-lock, combination-lock; –spiel, n. puzzle(-play); –uhr, f. Naut. clock-puzzle.

* Vezier', (str.) m. vizier. – Vezierat', (str.) n. viziership.

* Via, adv., via, by (way of).

* Viaduct', Viaduct', (str.) m. (Med. Lat.) viaduct.

* Vie'la, (w.) f. Archit. piazzale.

* Via'ticum, (str., pl. (Lat.) Via'tica) n. (Lat.) viaticum: 1) provision for a journey (Reiseproviant, Zehrpfennig); 2) Rom. Cath. extreme unction (letzte Ölung).

* Vibri'ren, (w.) v. intr. (Lat.) to vibrate; vibrirend, p. a. vibratory.

* Vicar', (str.) m. (Lat.) vicar; vicegerent; deputy, substitute. – Vicariat', (str.) n. office or dignity of a deputy or vicegerent; vicarship, vicegerency. – Vicari'ren, (w.) v. intr. to act the part of a deputy, &c.; v-d, p. a. vicarious.

* Vi'ce... (pr. vī'tse), in comp. vice; –admiral, m. vice-admiral; –bürgermeister, m. deputy burgomaster; –consul, m. vice-consul; –director, m. deputy-manager.

* Vi'cedom, (str.) m. see Vizthum.

* Vi'ce... (pr. vī'tse), in comp. –gevatter, m. proxy for a sponsor; –gouverneur, –statthalter, m. deputy-governor; –kanzler, m. vice-chancellor; –könig, m. viceroy; –präsident, m. vice-president; deputy-chairman.

— sagen, to foretell, predict. —sagung, *f.* prediction, prophecy; — schicken, — senden, to send in advance; to premise; —geschickte Bemerkungen, preliminary remarks; dies alles — gesandt (*Grimm*, WB. Vorrede IX), all this premised; — sehen, to foresee, anticipate; —sehend, *p. a.* prescient; — setzen, to suppose, presuppose; to presume; — gesetzt, supposed; provided; ich setze es als gewiß —, I take it for granted; es setzt eine böse Absicht —, it implies a malicious intention; —setzung, *f.* supposition, pre-supposition, presumption, hypothesis; *pl.* premises; in der —setzung, on the supposition; in der angenehmen —setzung, in the pleasing anticipation; in der festen —setzung, in the full persuasion, fully persuaded; —sicht, *f.* foresight; forethought; in der —sicht, anticipating; —sichtlich, *adj.* that may be foreseen *or* anticipated, presumable, probable, prospective; es wird —sichtlich stattfinden, it is anticipated to take place; — verkündigen, to announce beforehand, to foretel; — wissen, I. *v. tr.* to know beforehand, to foreknow, II. *v. s. n.* foreknowledge, prescience.

Vōr'bände, *(str.) m. pl. Comm.* articles of merchandise tied on the outside of packages, to show the contents within, outsides.

Vor'bank, *(str., pl.* V-bänke*) f.* 1) movable bench; 2) card-maker's working-bench.

Vōr'bau, *(str.) m. Archit.* 1) any building in front of another, *cf.* Vorgebäude; 2) screen.

Vōr'bauen, *(w.) v.* I. *tr.* 1) to build before a thing; 2) to build out; II. *intr. (with Dat.)* to prevent, obviate; to take precaution (against). — **Vōr'bauung,** *(w.) f.* prevention, obviation; V-smittel, *n.* preventive, preservative (*cf.* Vorsichtsmaßregel).

Vōr'bedacht, *(str.) m.* forethought, premeditation; mit —, on purpose, purposely, deliberately; on consideration; ohne —, unpremeditatedly, unintentionally.

Vōr'bedächtig, *adj.* considerate, cautious.

Vōr'bedenken, *(irr.) v. tr.* to consider beforehand, to premeditate.

Vōr'bedeuten, *(w.) v. tr.* to forebode, presage, portend. — **Vōr'bedeutsam,** *adj.* (*Grimm*, WB. *s. v.* Angang, &c.) betokening, foreboding, portending. — **Vōr'bedeutung,** *(w.) f.* foreboding, omen, prognostic, portent.

Vōr'beding, *(str.) m.*, **Vōr'bedingung,** *(w.) f.* preliminary condition.

Vōr'begriff, *(str.) m.* preliminary notion,

bygones; — gehen, to go, pa
to blow over; es ist wieder e
gangen, another year has pa
Dat.) —, to pass by (a thing);
to let pass by, to let slip, neg
tunity); Einem — gehen, to p
ticed, to pass over, neglect;
passer-by; im —gehen, in p
(you, they, &c.) pass; —lasse
lassen; —marsch, *m.* the (ac
by, march past (in parades)
intr. fig. to rush *or* tear past.

Vōr'berathen, *(str.) v. tr.*
deliberate beforehand *or* preli

Vōr'bereiten, *(w.) v.* I. *tr.*
auf *(with Acc.)*, for); to disp
prepare, to make ready (auf *(*
sich (zu einem Examen) —, to
fertig vorbereitet, cut and drie
v-d, *adj.* preparative; **Vōr'ber**
preparer.

Vōr'bereitung, *(w.) f.* pr
Mus. a term used in harmony
ohne —, off hand.

Vōr'bereitungs . . ., *in com*
—anstalt, *f.* training-school
—arbeit, *f.* preparatory work;
mentary class; —handlung,
action; —maschine, *f. T.* dre
—mittel, *n. Med.* preparative;
preparatory proposition; —sch
tory school; —stunde, *f.* prep
—unterricht, *m.* preparatory le
tary instruction.

Vōr'berg, *(str.) m.* ante
projecting mountain, spur of

Vōr'bericht, *(str.) m.* preli
or advertisement, preface, pre

Vōr'berührt, Vōr'besagt,

Vōr'bescheid, Vōr'beschieb
citation, summons, 2) prelimina

Vōr'bescheiden, *(str.) v.*
mon. — **Vōr'bescheidung,** *(w*
summoning.

Vōr'beschließen, *(str.) v.*
mine. — **Vōr'beschluß,** *(str.,*
m. preliminary decree.

Vōr'besitz, *(str.) m.* prepo
possession. — **Vōr'besitzer,** *(s*
sessor.

Vōr'besprechung, *(w.) f.* p
cussion, &c. [predeterm

Vōr'bestimmen, *(w.) v. tr.*

Vor'schläglich, *adj.* 1) proposable; 2) in the manner of a proposition.

Vor'schlaggeiger, *(str.)* m. see Vorgeiger.

Vor'schleppen, *(w.)* v. *tr.* to drag forth or before. [ing or glazing of the yarn.

Vor'schlichte, *(w.)* f. *Weav.* the first dress-

Vor'schlingen, *(str.)* v. *tr.* einen Knoten —, to tie a knot before or in front of.

Vor'schlummer, *(str.)* m. first nap.

Vor'schmack, *(str., pl.* Vor'schmäcke) m. 1) prevailing taste or flavour; 2) foretaste.

Vor'schmecken, *(w.)* v. I. *tr.* to foretaste; II. *intr.* to prevail (of a taste or flavour).

Vor'schmidt, *(str., Gen.* V-schmiedes, *pl.* V-schmiede) m. blacksmith's principal aid.

Vor'schneidemesser, *(str.)* n. carving knife.

Vor'schneidezahn, *(str., pl.* V-zähne) m. *T.* nicker (of a centre-bit).

Vor'schneiden, *(str.)* v. I. *tr.* 1) to carve, cut; 2) Einem Gesichter —, to make faces at one; II. *intr.* *(aux.* haben) to cut before a person, to cut out. [carver.

Vor'schneider *(str.)* m. 1) cutter out; 2)

Vor'schnell, *adj.* forward, rash, hasty, precipitate, premature.

Vor'schnellen, *(w.)* v. *tr.* to drive forward with a jerking motion, to jerk forwards.

Vor'schnitt, *(str.)* m. first cut.

Vor'schnitter, *(str.)* m. first cutter or mower.

Vor'schnür, *(w.)* f. see Schmitze.

Vor'schoß, *(str.)* m. *provinc.* property-tax, *cf.* Vermögens-Steuer.

Vor'schreiben, *(str.)* v. *tr.* 1) to write (one's name, &c.) before a thing, to write in front of a thing; 2) to set before (one) in writing, to set a writing-copy; 3) *fig.* to prescribe, dictate, direct, order, command; to appoint; Einem als Regel —, to lay down (as a rule) for one; vorgeschrieben, *p. a.* 1. prescribed, appointed; 2. see Vorschriftsmäßig.

Vor'schreien, *(str.)* v. I. *tr.* 1) to cry before a person; 2) to cry or bawl (to a person), to cry in the ears of a person; II. *intr.* to surpass in crying.

Vor'schreiten, *(str.)* v. *intr.* *(aux.* sein) 1) to step or stride forth; 2) to advance, march on, to step before a person; 3) (Einem) to get the start (of); 4) *fig.* to proceed, go on, *cf.* Vorgehen, 1, 6.

Vor'schrift, *(w.)* f. 1) copy to write after, copy-slip, (writing-)copy; 2) *fig.* prescription, directions, precept, requisition; instructions; dictation; nach —, as directed or prescribed; das Muster ist nicht nach —, the pattern is not according to wish; *Med.* recipe; order, command; (streng) nach der — handeln, to act in (strict) accordance with (the) instructions.

Vor'schriftsmäßig, **Vor'schriftlich**, *adj.* & *adv.* according to prescription, precept, or direction; appointed; regulation —, *e. g.* V-e Mütze, regulation cap.

Vor'schritt, *(str.)* m. step forwards, advance; *fig.* proceeding (Vorgehen, *s. s.*); progress.

Vor'schub, *(str., pl.* Vor'schübe) m. 1) the (act of) pushing or shoving forward, &c. *cf.* Vorschieben, 1; 2) advance; 3) *Game.* first throw (at ninepins), first stroke, lead (at billiards); 4) *fig.* aid, help, supply, assistance; (Einem or einer Sache *(Dat.)*) — leisten, to promote, back (one's view, &c.), to further; to assist; *(in an ill sense)* to abet.

Vor'schuh, *(str.)* m. 1) *Shoe-m.* upper leather, vamp, foot-part of a boot; 2) *Nav.* slip, well. — **Vor'schuhen**, *(w.)* v. *tr.* *Shoe-m.* to put new feet to (boots), to new-vamp, new-foot, refoot. — **Vor'schuhleder**, *(str.)* n. *Shoe-m.* (shoe-)vamps.

Vor'schule, *(w.)* f. preparatory school; — zur Geschichte der Kirchenbaukunst, preparatory introduction to a history of church-architecture.

Vor'schuppen, *(w.)* v. *tr.* to make a [illegible]

Vor'schuß, *(str., pl.* Vor'schüsse) m. 1) [illegible] shot; 2) see Vorschub, 2; 3) [illegible] 4) *Bill.* [illegible]; *fig.* advanced money, advance, previous payment; im V-e haben, to be in advance; im — [illegible], to [illegible] advance; wir sind schon im — gewesen, we have had heavy disbursements; als — auf *(with Acc.)*, as an or in advance on ..., in anticipation of ...; Vorschüsse gegen Unterpfand, advances on deposits; auf — *(Acc.)* drucken, *Print.* to print by subscription; —bank, —verein, f. association for cash-advances; —schein, m. receipt for the subscription money; —weise, *adj.* as an (or in) advance, by way of advance.

Vor'schütt, *(str.)* m. *Sport.* food for game in winter, winter-food.

Vor'schütten, *(w.)* v. *tr.* (Einem etwas) to pour out or throw down before ...; Futter —, to give provender (to).

Vor'schützen, *(w.)* v. *tr.* 1) to hold, put before, to use as a defence; to make a bulwark or defence; to make a dam, weir, or floodgate before or to; 2) *fig.* to pretend, to use a pretence or pretext, to give out, allege, plead, feign. — **Vor'schützung**, *(w.)* f. 1) the (act of) holding before, &c.; 2) defence, fence; protection; 3) the (act of) alleging, pretending, &c., pretence, pretext, plea.

Vor'schwarm, *(str., pl.* Vor'schwärme) m. *Bee.* 1) first swarm of an old hive; 2) singing-swarm.

Vor'schwatzen, *(w.)* v. *tr.* see [illegible], 2, 3.

Vor'schweben, *(w.)* v. *intr.* to float, hover before; Einem —, to be in one's eye, to float before the mind. [swim before.

Vor'schwimmen, *(str.)* v. *intr.* *(aux.* sein) to

Vor'schwingen, n. s. *(str.)* n. *T.* scutching, ruffling (of flax).

Vor'schwören, *(str.)* v. *tr.* to swear in one's presence; to pronounce (an oath) before one. [sail.

Vor'segel, *(str.)* n. *Mar.* fore-sail, head-

Vor'segeln, *(w.)* v. *intr.* *(aux.* sein) 1) to sail before; 2) *(with Dat.)* to out-sail.

Vor'sehen, *(str.)* v. I. *intr.* 1) to look before; 2) to provide *(with Dat.,* for ...); II. *tr.* 1) to foresee; 2) to reflect on, consider; 3) to provide for; III. *refl.* to keep a good look-out, to be on one's guard, to take care, to take heed; to beware (daß nicht ..., how ...); to make preparations (auf *(with Acc.)*, against); to lay in a store (mit, of); sich besser —, to exercise more forethought; to take better aim; vorgesehen! look out! take heed! have a care!

Vor'sehung, *(w.)* f. providence.

Vor'sein, *(irr.)* v. *intr.* *(aux.* sein) 1) to be before; to be foremost; to have the first chance; in Jahren weit —, to be advanced in years; 2) to stand out; 3) to be under examination, to be tried or under [illegible]; 4) *provinc.* etwas ist mir vor, I have a presentiment of or misgiving about [illegible] Gott vor! God forbid!

Vor'seite, *(w.)* f. fore-side, front [illegible] —teil, n. *Mar.* fore-tackle, winding-[illegible] the foremast.

Vor'senden, *(w.)* v. *tr.* see [illegible]

Vor'setzbar, *adj.* that may be put [illegible] before.

Vor'setz..., in comp. —blatt, n. fly-leaf; —blech, n. *T.* [illegible] iron plate put before [illegible] ...ness; —[illegible], m. [illegible] refining sulphur.

Vor'setzen, *(w.)* v. I. *tr.* [illegible] or put before; to put [illegible] fasten to; *Gramm.*, &c. to [illegible]

2) to put or place before a person; fig. 3) to represent, expose; 4) to propose, propound; to submit, [illegible] he submitted his doubts to [illegible] of his own [illegible]; 5) to state, report, make a report on; 6) to deliver; eine Bitte —, to bring in a petition;

[illegible], foregoing, [illegible].

Vor'wachsen (p. —wuchs), (aux.) v. intr. (aux. sein) to out-grow; to gain ground.

Vor'winken, (w.) v. tr. to wave before a person.

* Vor'wahl, (w.) f. preliminary election, nomination. [illegible]

[illegible] watchfulness.

Wach[illegible], *m.* [illegible]

Wach[illegible] [illegible]

Wacher [illegible]

Wach ..., *in comp.* [illegible] —**frei**, *adj.* exempt from [illegible] —**geld**, *n.* watch-money [illegible] —**habend**, *adj.* being on duty, on guard [illegible] —**haus**, *n.* watch-house, guard-house [illegible] —**häuschen**, *n.* watch-box, sentry-box [illegible]

Wachholder, [illegible] *Bot.* juniper (*Juniperus communis*) [illegible] —**baum**, *m.* juniper-tree. —**beere**, *f.* juniper-berry; —**branntwein**, *m.* geneva, hollands, and gin [illegible] —**harz**, *n.* gum-juniper, sandarach; —**latwerge**, *f.* [illegible] *n.* electuary or rob of juniper-berries [illegible] —**öl**, *n.* juniper oil [illegible] juniper-berries [illegible] —**vogel**, *m.* see [illegible] see [illegible]

Wach ..., *in comp.* —**lohn**, *m.* fee for watching, see [illegible] —**meister**, *m.* (cavalry) sergeant; —**ordnung**, *f.* regulations respecting the watch. —**parade**, *f.* *Mil.* see [illegible] —**posten**, *m.* duty, watch, post. —**rolle**, *f.* *Mar.* watch-bill. —**ruf**, *m.* note of alarm.

1. **Wachs** (*pr.* [illegible]) (*str.*, *n.* wax: [illegible] —, see [illegible]; [illegible] —, myrtle-wax [illegible] —, cancerate, mit — [illegible] or [illegible], to coat with wax, to cere.

2. **Wachs** (*pr.* [illegible], *str.*) *m.* (from [illegible]) growth (Wachsthum, 1).

Wachs (*pr.* wax) ..., *in comp.* —**abdruck**, *m.* impression or print on wax, cast in wax; —**achat**, *m.* *Miner.* yellow agate-wax; —**ähnlich**, see —**artig**.

Wachsam, I. *adj.* watchful, vigilant, ein [illegible] Auge auf etwas (*Acc.*) haben, to have a watchful eye over. II. **W**[illegible]**keit**, (*w.*) *f.* watchfulness, vigilance. die nöthige — vergessen, to be off one's guard.

Wachs' (*pr.* wax) ..., *in comp.* —**artig**, *adj.* [illegible]

[illegible] in the increase [illegible] [illegible] increase [illegible] [illegible]

Wachs[illegible] (*pr.* [illegible]

Wachs[illegible] (*pr.* [illegible] wax

Wachs (*pr.* wax) ... [illegible] wax-chandlery; —**bild**, [illegible] *f.* wax-colour; —**farbig** [illegible] —**figur**, *f.* wax-figure. [illegible] *m.* wax-works [illegible] —**form**, *f.* [illegible] —**former**, *m.* see [illegible] —[illegible], *n.* see [illegible] yellow as wax [illegible] —**gießer**, —**händler** [illegible] chandler; —[illegible] *f.* *Orn.* [illegible] —[illegible], *n.* glazed hat.

Wachslicht, **Wachslich**[illegible]

Wachs (*pr.* wax) ... room for provisions, sets [illegible] of crystallisation; —[illegible] —[illegible], *m.* preserve [illegible] *Pomol.* a species of [illegible] *n.* see [illegible] —[illegible], *m.* see [illegible] lamp; —**lappen**, *m.* wa[illegible] —[illegible]; —**leder**, *n.* wa[illegible] cere-cloth, cerate. [illegible] **licht**, *n.* wax-candle, w[illegible] wax-chandler. —[illegible] by means of [illegible] painting. —**malle**, *f.* [illegible] *Bee*, wax-meal, bee's [illegible] wax-tiny [illegible] *f.* *Bot.* wax-myrtle [illegible] distilled from wax; —[illegible] (*Ceroxylon andicola*) [illegible] waxed paper; —**perle**, *f.* [illegible] wax-plaster, cerate, *f.* wax-pomatum; —[illegible] **puppe**, *f.* wax-doll, bougie, catheter; —[illegible] —**salbe**, *f.* cerate, wax-[illegible] honey-moth (*Gall*[illegible]

[illegible]

Be prunk. [illegible]

Be pr [illegible]

Sequen [illegible]

Seq ien. [illegible]

Sig'im. [illegible] **Sig'nett** [illegible]

Sig'ling. [illegible]

Sig'ner [illegible] wheelwright [illegible]

Sig'nis. [illegible] **Sig'mair.** [illegible]

Sig'em. [illegible] perilous.

Sig'diele. [illegible] scale, balance [illegible] to put in the scale or balance [illegible] to be weighty in the scale.

Sig'ten. [illegible]

Sig'tuch. [illegible] see **Bauertuch.**

1\. **Sent.** [illegible] election [illegible] parliament [illegible] candidate for [illegible]

3\. **Saal.** [illegible]

Sinl. [illegible]

Saal [illegible] elective [illegible]

[illegible] at [illegible] to turn [illegible] society.

Sähler, [illegible] elector, constituent. —**ausschuß,** m. [illegible] electoral committee.

Sent erbe, [illegible] heir by will.

Sählerisch, adj. and [illegible]. **Sählig** [illegible] particular in one's choice, nice, fastidious, dainty, proud stomach; 2) feeling [illegible] wanton, playful.

Sähl erklärung, [illegible] call.

Sählerschaft, [illegible]. **Sählertum,** [illegible] of electors, electoral body, constituency; 2) state or quality of an elector.

Sent'... in comp. —**fähig,** adj. 1) eligible; 2) [illegible] —**fähigkeit,** f. 1) eligibility, eligibleness; 2) qualification to vote; property qualification, &c. [illegible] —**fall,** m. case of election. —**feld,** n. 1) field where an election was carried on, especially the election of the former kings of Poland; 2) see [illegible] —**folge,** f. succession to an elective dignity. —**freiheit,** f. freedom of election, suffrage. —**fürst,** m. prince elector [illegible] monarch. —**gesetz,** n. electoral law. —**gesetze,** pl. electoral regulations. —**handlung,** f. the act of electing, [illegible] —**herr,** m. elector.

Sählig, [illegible]

Sent'... in comp. —**intrigen,** f. pl. see [illegible]: —**kaiser,** m. elective emperor; —**kaisertum,** n. elective empire; —**kampf,** [illegible] contest. —**kasten,** m. ballot-box. —**kind,** n. adoptive child. —**könig,** m. elective king. —**königreich,** n. elective kingdom; —[illegible] —**körperschaft,** [illegible] electoral or [illegible] —**krone,** f. elective crown. —**kugel,** f. voting-ball, ballot. —**liste,** f. electoral list; register of the electors. —**mann,** m. delegate for an election; —**mutter,** f. adoptive mother. —**ort,** m. place of election. —**pfründe,** f. elective benefice or living. —**platz,** m. 1) place where an election is carried on, polling-place; 2) field of battle. —**protokoll,** n. register of an election, polling-register, poll-book; —**prüfung,** f. verification of an election; —**rath,** m. 1) elective council; 2) member of an elective council; 3) meeting of electors; einen —rath halten, to meet for an election; —**recht,** n. right of election, electoral or elective franchise; [illegible] —**rechts berauben,** to disfranchise [illegible] —recht, universal or man-

crushing-mill, shot-roller; (laminating) rollers; Gold-sm., &c. flatting-mill, flatting-roller; –zapfen, m. Lock-sm. round spike; –zinn, n. laminated tin.

Wa'men, (w.) v. intr. provinc. to make foul water, to become muddy (of rivers).

Wam'me, (w.) f. 1) († & provinc.) a) womb; b) belly; paunch, cf. Wanst; 2) a) dewlap; b) flank side (esp. Sport. of wild sows); c) Furr. the skin taken off the belly, cf. Schwamme.

Wam'mer, (str.) m. provinc. knot in a tree [or in wood (Wimmer).

Wam'mig, adj. dewlapped.

Wamms, (str., pl. Wämm'ser) n. doublet, waistcoat, jerkin; ledernes –, buff-jerkin; Einem das – ausklopfen, or aufs – greifen, fig. to dust one's jacket; –schneider, m. doublet-maker.

Wam'pe, (w.) f. see Wamme.

Wam'se, Wäm'se, (w.) f. vulg. a beating (Prügel, 2). – **Wam'sen,** (w.) v. tr. to jerk, bang, curry.

Wand, (str., pl. Wän'de) f. 1) a) wall; b) screen; partition; side (of a shaft, vessel, gun-carriage); back (of a chimney); panel (of a coach); cheek (of a press); coat (of the stomach, &c.); 2) Sport. a) pane of nets; b) side of a hart; 3) Furr. quarter of a horse-hoof; 4) Mar. shroud; fig-s. in meinen vier Wänden, in my own house, on my ground; den Wänden vorerzählen, to talk to the wind; mit dem Kopf gegen die – rennen, to knock one's head against the wall; mit dem Kopf durch die – wollen, to run full tilt at everything; den leeren Wänden predigen, to read or deliver wall-lectures.

Wand'..., in comp. –abreißend, adj. Bot. see –lösend; –balken, m. wall-timber; –bank, f. bench fixed to a wall; –beine, n. pl. Anat. parietal bones; –bekleidung, f. wainscoting; –besen, m. hair-broom with a long handle; –bewohnend, p.a. Bot. growing on walls; –bewurf, see Putz, B. 2; –brett, n. hanging shelf; –brüchig, adj. Bot. see –lösend; –calender, m. sheet-almanach; –decke, f. cover for a wall, tapestry.

Wan'del, (str.) m. 1) †, the (act of) walking; walk; 2) Mus. see Wirbelsaiten; fig-s. 3) behaviour, conduct, (course of) life; 4) barter, traffic, commerce, trade; 5) change, mutation; 6) blemish, stain, spot; Handel und –, trade and traffic, business.

Wan'del, adj. provinc. ruinous, out of repair.

Wan'delbahn, (w.) f. (pleasure-)walk.

Wan'delbar, I. adj. 1) versatile; 2) mutable, changeable, variable, inconstant, versatile; fickle; 3) provinc. passable, current; 4) perishable, infirm; 5) out of order; out of repair; 6) †, faulty, blemished; II. W-keit, f. 1) (l. u.) versatility; 2) mutability, changeableness, inconstancy.

Wan'del..., in comp. –baum, m. Bot. red-berried mountain-alder; –bild, n. see Trugbild; –gang, m. see –bahn; –geist, m. ghost that walks; –glück, n. inconstant fortune; –klee, m. Bot. the moving plant; –kragen, m. Mar. wooden mast-coat; –kraut, n. Bot. bladder-campion.

Wan'dellos, I. adj. unalterable, immutable; II. W-igkeit, (w.) f. unalterableness, &c.

Wan'delmonat, (str.) m. (l. u.) April.

Wan'deln, (w.) v. I. intr. (aux. sein & haben) to go, walk; to wander, travel; handeln und –, to trade, traffic; unsträflich –, to lead an irreproachable life; II. tr. († & p) *, to change; to exchange; to transform; das w-de Blatt, see Fangheuschrecke.

Wan'del..., in comp. –scala, f. sliding-scale; –stern, m. erratic star, planet; –thurm, m. movable tower.

Wan'delung, (w.) f. 1) transformation, [illegible] change; 2) Theol. transubstantiation; Rom. Cath. elevation.

Wan'del..., in comp. –modus, f. [illegible] mood of a verb; –wetter, n. changeable weather; –zeit, f. time considered as subject to constant changes.

Wan'der..., in comp. –ameise, f. Ent. visiting ant (Atta cephalotes Fabr.); –block, m. Geol. erratic block; –buch, n. a) kind of passport for travelling journeymen; b) [illegible] of a book; road-book; –bursch, m. [illegible] fell; –drossel, f. Ornith. migratory thrush (Turdus migratorius L.).

Wan'derer, (str.) m. wanderer, traveller (on foot).

Wan'der..., in comp. –falk, m. Ornith. passenger falcon (Falco peregrinus L.); –geräth, n. furniture for travelling, travelling luggage; –gesell, m. travelling journeyman; –hai, m. Ichth. a basking-shark ([illegible] Cuv.); –heuschrecke, f. Entom. the migratory locust (Acridium migratorium L.).

Wan'deringen, (w.) f. pl. Mar. gangways.

Wan'der..., in comp. –jahr, n. travelling year (of journeymen); –leben, n. vagrant life; –lust, f. see Reiselust; –maus, –ratte, f. Zool. 1) brown or Norway rat (Mus decumanus Pall.); 2) see Lemming.

Wan'dern, (w.) intr. (aux. sein & haben) to wander, migrate, to travel (on foot), to walk, go, ramble; aus diesem Leben –, to depart (from) this life; seine Straße –, to go (or wend) one's way; w-d, p. a. wandering, itinerant; strolling (actors, &c.).

Wan'derpaß, (str., pl. W-pässe) m. see Wanderbuch.

Wan'derschaft, (w.) f. travelling, peregrination, travels; auf der – sein, to be travelling; auf die – gehen, to go on one's travels (said of journeymen); W-en durch London, wanderings about London.

Wan'dersmann, (str., pl. Wandersleute) m. traveller (on foot), passer.

Wan'der..., in comp. –[illegible], pl. Mar. rough-trees; [illegible]; –stab, m. walking-staff; den –stab ergreifen, to go on [illegible]; –taube, f. see Zugtaube.

Wan'derung, (w.) f. the (act of) travelling, walking; migration, travel, ramble; W-instinct, m. migratory instinct.

Wan'der..., in comp. –versammlung, f. an association holding regular meetings in different places; –volk, n. nomadic people; –zeit, f. travelling time (of journeymen).

Wand'..., in comp. –fest, adj. fixed to the wall; –flechte, f. (common yellow) wall lichen (Parmelia parietina L.); –[illegible] n. mural painting; [illegible] lever; –haken, m. wall-hook, [illegible] –holz, n. see –balken; [illegible] –calender; [illegible] –karte, f. wall-map [illegible] f. T. flashing; [illegible] pilaster; Mar-s. [illegible] –[illegible], f. pl. shroud-trucks; [illegible] ten, m. double wall-knot, [illegible] –kraut, n. Bot. pellitory of the wall [illegible] litory (Parietaria officinalis [illegible]) [illegible] house-bug; wall-louse [illegible] skirting-board [illegible] candlestick fixed in the wall [illegible] –[illegible], adj. septifragal [illegible]

Wand'lung, (w.) f. [illegible]

Wand'..., in comp. [illegible] painter, see Decorationsmaler [illegible] wall-painting, mural [illegible] wall-moss; [illegible], f. [illegible] m. fallow-lodger; [illegible] pfeiler, m. pillar [illegible] –pianoforte, n. [illegible] upright [illegible] cottage-pianoforte; –[illegible], f. [illegible]

things); — für (ein, eine), what kind of, what; — für ein Mensch ist das? what man is this? — ist das für ein Buch? what book is this? Alles, was, all that; Nichts, —, nothing that; das, —, that which, what; Alles — ich weiß, all (that) I know; — auch (immer), — nur, whatever, whatsoever; — für Leute auch (immer), whatever people; — er nur laufen konnte, as fast as he could run; weißt du — Neues? 1. what is the news? 2. shall I tell you some news? — ich Ihnen sage; es ist so, I assure you, it is so; — Sie (nicht) sagen! *fam.* you don't say so!

Wasch'... (*from* Waschen), *in comp.* —echt, *see* Waschecht; —amber, *m.* common yellow amber; —anstalt, *f.* washing establishment, laundry.

Wasch'bar, *adj.* that may be washed; *particul.* that bears washing, fast (colours).

Wasch'... (*from* Waschen), *in comp.* —bär, *m. Zool.* raccoon (*Procyon lotor* L.); —bank, *f.* washing-bench; —becken, *n.* (wash-hand-) basin, wash-bowl; —besen, *m. Mar.* launder-besom; —blau, *n. Comm.* queen's blue, indigo-blue; —bläuel, *m.* washing-beetle, bucking-beetle; —bock, *m.* washing-stool, washing-horse; —brett, *n. Typ.* washing-board; —bühne, *f. Min.* buddle; —bütte, — butte, *f.* vat for washing (—faß).

Wasch'e, (*w.*) *f. provinc.* 1) *see* Wäsche; 2) gossip, tell-tale.

Wäsch'e, (*w.*) *f.* 1) *a)* a washing, wash; (von kleinen Stücken Weißzeug) dab-wash; große —, washing-day; das Kleid ist in der —, the dress is in the wash; die — der Wolle wurde als gut befunden, the washing of the wool was found good; *b) Min.* buddling; 2) linen; 3) *a)* washhouse; *b) Min.* place where ore is washed; buddle; stream-work; schmutzige *or* schwarze —, foul linen; in die — kommen, *coll.* to get a severe reprimand, to get into a mess (*cf.* Patsche, 2; Tinte, 3).

Wasch'echt, *adj.* fast (Waschbar).

Wasch'eisen, (*str.*) *n. Metall.* buddled iron.

Wasch'el, (*str.*) *m. provinc.* 1) washerman, washer; 2) scrubbing-brush; 3) *fac.* (one who washes his throat) tippler; 4) a (loose and broad) ear (Schlappohr).

Wasch'en, (*str.*) *v. tr. & intr.* 1) to wash; Erze —, *Min.* to wash ores, to buddle; 2) *fig.* to chat, chatter, prattle, babble, gossip; für Jemand —, to take in one's washing; sich — lassen, to wash (to bear washing, of linen, &c.); ich wasche meine Hände in Unschuld, *fig.* I wash my hands of it; *coll.-e.* Einem den Kopf —, to chide *or* reprimand one; sich gewaschen haben, to be as it ought to be, to be of the first water (first-rate), *or comme il faut.*

Wäsch'er, (*str.*) *m.* 1) washer; 2) *fig.* (male) gossip; idle prattler; —lohn, *m.* pay for washing.

Wasch'erde, (*w.*) *f.* fuller's earth.

Wäscherei', (*w.*) *f.* 1) *cont.* bad washing; 2) *a)* washhouse (on a large scale); *b) Min.* buddling-place; 3) *fig.* the practice of gossiping, idle talk.

Wäsch'erin, (*w.*) *f.* 1) washerwoman, laundress; 2) *coll.* gossip, tell-tale.

Wasch'... (*from* Waschen), *in comp.* —erz, *n. Min.* washed ore; —farben, *f. pl.* artificial colours in which (after being dissolved) stuffs are dyed cold; *Paint.* gouache-colours; —faß, *n.* washing-tub, washing-coop; —fest, *n. anal.* washing-day; —frau, *f.* washerwoman, laundress; —geld, *n.* pay for washing; —gelte, *f.* wash pail; —geräth, *n.* 1) articles used in getting up linen; 2) linen; —geschworene, *m. Min.* inspector of the buddlers; —gold, *n.* wash-gold, gold obtained from sand *or* slime by washing; —graben, *m.*, —grube, *f. Min.* trough.

Wasch'haft, I. *adj.* gossiping, loquacious, talkative; II. W-igkeit, *f.* loquacity, [illegible] tiveness.

Wasch'... (*from* Waschen), *in comp.* —[illegible] mer, *m. Cloth-m.* wash(ing)-[illegible]; —[illegible] schuh, *m.* (wash *or* fan-) leather-glove, washing-glove; —haus, *n.* washhouse, washing-house, laundry; —[illegible], *m. see* —[illegible] 2; —holz, *n. see* —bläuel; —[illegible], *m. Min.* boy at the buddle; —kanne, *f.* ewer.

Wäsch'kasten, (*str.*) *m.* wardrobe, closet or press for linen. [illegible]

Wasch'kessel, (*str.*) *m.* wash-kettle, wash-[illegible]

Wäsch'kiste, (*w.*) *f.* linen-chest.

Wasch'... (*from* Waschen), *in comp.* —klammer, Wäschklammer, *f.* clothes-peg; — klöpfel, *m. see* —bläuel; —korb, Wäschkorb, *m.* basket for linen, clothes-basket; —kraut, *n. Bot.* soap-wort (*Saponaria officinalis* L.); —krücke, *f. Min.* rake used in buddling; — küche, *f.* scullery; —kufe, *f.* washing-tub; —kugel, *f.* wash-ball; —kupfer, *n. Metr.* copper from buddled ore; —lappen, *m.* 1) dish-clout, washing-clout; 2) *fig. coll.* weak person; —leder, *n.* oil-leather, chamois; (Wasch-[illegible]) wash-leather; —lederne Handschuhe, *see* —handschuhe; —leine, *f.* line for drying linen, clothes-line; —lohn, *m. see* —geld; —[illegible] *n.*, —magd, *f.* washer-maid, laundry-maid; —manier, *f. Paint.* washing; —markt, *m. fig.* gossiping place; —maschine, *f.* washing-machine; —meister, *m.* master of the laundry (at courts); —pinsel, *m. Paint.* brush for washing or laying designs; —platz, *m. see* —werk, 1; —probe, *f. Min.* assay of buddled ore; —räder, *n. pl. Manuf.* dash-wheels, wash-wheels.

Wäsch'rolle, (*w.*) *f.* mangle, calender.

Wasch'... (*from* Waschen), *in comp.* — scheidebank, *f. Min.* launder; —schwamm, *m.* sponge; —seide, *f.* washing-silk; —seife, *f.* yellow soap, brown soap; Windsor-soap; — silber, *n.* silver-amalgam. [illegible]

Wäsch'stange, Wäsch'stütze, (*w.*) *f.* clothes-[illegible]

Wasch'... (*from* Waschen), *in comp.* —[illegible] ger, *m. see* —geschworene; —stein, *m.* 1) [illegible] stone-slab; 2) *Typ.* washing-tub; 3) *see* Rasenreisenerz; —thon, *m.* fuller's earth; — tisch, *m.* washing-stand, washhand-stand; —trog, *m.* washing-trough; *Min.* [illegible] jor. [illegible] lotion.

Wasch'ung, (*w.*) *f.* the (act of) washing.

Wasch'... (*from* Waschen), *in comp.* — wanne, *f.* washing-tub, scrubbing-tub; —wasser, *n.* 1) water for washing (the hands and face); 2) *Med.* lotion; 3) *Chem.* [illegible] —weib, *n. see* Wäscherin, 1; —werk, *n. Min.* 1) place where ore is washed; 2) ore that is (*or* is to be) washed; —weste, *f.* washing-waistcoat; —wolle, *f.* washed wool; —zettel, *m.* washing-bill, wash-bill, [illegible]; —zeug, *n. see* —geräth; —zinn, *n.* stream-tin; —zuber, *m.* washing-tub, bucking-tub.

Wa'se, (*w.*) *f.* 1) († *&*) *provinc.* [illegible] (female) cousin (Base, A.); 2) faggot.

Wa'sen, (*str.*) *m. provinc.* 1) [illegible] (Rasen); 2) faggot; 3) [illegible]; 4) [illegible] —amt, *n.* office of a public [illegible] (—meister, *m.*); —[illegible]

Was'gau, (*str.*) *n. Geogr.* [illegible]

† **Wasgestalt',** *adv.* as how, in [illegible]

Was'heit, (*w.*) *f.* (*L. u.*) Whatness, [illegible]

Wa'sig, *adj. see* Rasig.

† **Wasma'ßen,** *adv. see* [illegible]

Was'ser, (*str.*) *n.* 1) water [illegible] *Chem.* aqua; gut — [illegible] aquatic; über dem — [illegible] afloat; großes —, *a)* a large [illegible] *b)* high water, flood; 2) [illegible] tion (Schweiß, 1); *b)* [illegible] ihm voll —, his eyes were [illegible] (vgl. To Water); 3) *a)* lustre [illegible] &c.); ein Diamant vom [illegible]

Wie'derdienen, (*w.*) *v. intr.* to render a service in return, to serve in return.

Wie'derdruck, (*str.*) *m.* reimpression; *Typ.* reiteration.

Wiederein'bringen, (*irr.*) *v. tr.* to make up (for deficiencies, &c.); to repair, retrieve; 2) *Surg.* to set, reduce (a broken member).

Wiederein'fuhr, (*w.*) *f.* re-importation; —artikel, *m. pl.* re-imports. — **Wiederein'führen,** (*w.*) *v. tr.* 1) to re-import; 2) to re-introduce.

Wiederein'gang, (*str.*, *pl.* W-gänge) *m.* return; rascher —, early return (of money).

Wiederein'händigung, (*w.*) *f.* redelivery.

Wiederein'kerkerung, (*w.*) *f.* re-imprisonment.

Wiederein'lassen, (*str.*) *v. tr.* to re-admit. — **Wiederein'lassung,** (*w.*) *f.* re-admission.

Wiederein'lösen, (*w.*) *v. tr.* to redeem. — **Wiederein'lösung,** (*w.*) *f.* redemption; W-s-recht, *n. Law*, right of redeeming or re-entering.

Wiederein'nahme, (*w.*) *f.* recapture.

Wiederein'nehmen, (*str.*) *v. tr.* 1) to retake, recapture; 2) to resume one's seat.

Wiederein'richten, (*w.*) *v. tr.* 1) to re-arrange; to reorganise; 2) *see* Wiedereinbringen, 2. — **Wiederein'richtung,** (*w.*) *f.* 1) re-arrangement; reorganisation; 2) *Surg.* reposition (of a bone). [absorb.

Wiederein'saugen, (*w. & str.*) *v. tr.* to re-

Wiederein'schiffen, (*w.*) *v. tr. & refl.* to re-embark. — **Wiederein'schiffung,** (*w.*) *f.* re-embarkation.

Wiederein'setzen, (*w.*) *v. tr.* to replace, re-establish, to re-instate, restore. — **Wiederein'setzung,** (*w.*) *f.* re-installation, restoration, rehabilitation; replevin.

Wie'derergreifung, (*w.*) *f.* re-seizure.

Wie'dererhalten, (*str.*) *v. tr.* to recover; to retrieve. — **Wie'dererhaltung,** (*w.*) *f.* recovery.

Wiederein'nern, (*w.*) *v.* I. *tr.* to remind; II. *refl.* to recall, recollect. — **Wiederein'nerung,** (*w.*) *f.* recollection.

Wie'dererkennen, (*irr.*) *v. tr.* to recognise. — **Wie'dererkennung,** (*w.*) *f.* recognition.

Wie'dererlangen, (*w.*) *v. tr.* to regain, recover; er erlangte das Kind wieder, the child was restored to him. — **Wie'dererlangung,** (*w.*) *f.* recovery.

Wie'derernennen, (*irr.*) *v. tr.* to re-appoint.

Wie'dererobern, (*w.*) *v. tr.* to reconquer, to conquer back. — **Wie'dereroberung,** (*w.*) *f.* recapture; recovery.

Wie'dererschaffen, (*str.*) *v. tr.* to recreate.

Wie'dererscheinen, (*str.*) *v. intr.* (*aux.* sein) to re-appear; ein Werk — lassen, to republish a work.

Wie'derersetzen, Wie'dererstatten, (*w.*) *v. tr.* to return, restore (what has been lost or taken); to refund, reimburse. — **Wie'derersetzung, Wie'dererstattung,** (*w.*) *f.* return, restitution, reddition, reimbursement, repayment. [repurchase (at public sales).

Wie'dererstehen, (*irr.*) *v. tr.* to buy in,

Wie'dererwachen, (*w.*) *v. intr.* (*aux.* sein) to re-awaken, resuscitate.

Wie'dererwählbar, *adj.* re-eligible. — **Wie'dererwählen,** (*w.*) *v. tr.* to re-elect. — **Wie'dererwählung,** (*w.*) *f.* re-election.

Wie'dererwecken, (*w.*) *v. tr.* to resuscitate. — **Wie'dererweckung,** (*w.*) *f.* resuscitation.

Wie'dererzeugen, (*w.*) *v. tr.* to reproduce. — **Wie'dererzeugung,** (*w.*) *f.* reproduction; W-skraft, *f.* power of reproduction, reproductive power. [the same track.

Wie'derfährte, (*w.*) *f. Sport.* return by

Wie'derfangen, (*str.*) *v. tr.* to recapture, retake.

Wie'derfinden, (*str.*) *v. tr.* to find again, to recover; er hat sich wiedergefunden, *fig.* he is himself again. — **Wie'derfindung,** (*w.*) *f.* recovery. [return (of birds of passage).

Wie'derflug, (*str.*, *pl.* W-flüge) *m. Sport.*

Wie'dergabe, (*w.*) *f.* 1) restitution, redelivery; return, restitution; 2) a rendering, translation. [bringen.

Wie'dergang, (*str.*, *pl.* W-gänge) *m.* [illegible]

Wie'dergänger, (*str.*) *m.* (*lit.* one who walks again) ghost, spectre.

Wie'dergebären, (*str.*) *v. tr.* to regenerate; to renew, revive.

Wie'dergeben, (*str.*) *v. tr.* 1) to give or render back, to return, restore; 2) to render (a word, &c. into a different language), to translate. [[illegible]

Wie'dergeboren, *p. a.* born again; [illegible]

Wie'dergeburt, (*w.*) *f.* regeneration, [illegible] new birth.

Wie'dergelangen, (*w.*) *v. intr.* (*aux.* sein) 1) to get back (*sach.* to); 2) to be restored (*zu*, to).

Wie'dergeld, *see* Wehrgeld.

Wie'dergenesen, (*str.*) *v. intr.* (*aux.* sein) to recover from illness; w-d, *pp. a.* convalescent. — **Wie'dergenesung,** (*w.*) *f.* recovery, convalescence.

Wie'dergewinnen, (*str.*) *v. tr.* to regain; to retrieve; to reclaim. [[illegible]

Wie'derglanz, (*str.*) *m.* resplendency, [illegible]

Wie'dergrüßen, (*w.*) *v. tr.* to return a salute, to bow in return.

Wiedergut'machen, (*w.*) *v. tr.* 1) to repair; to retrieve; to make amends for; 2) *fam.* to reconcile.

Wiedergut'werden, (*irr.*) *v. intr.* (*aux.* sein) *fam.* 1) to heal; 2) to become good friends again.

Wie'derhaben, *v. n.* (*str.*) *n.* the having or obtaining again, repossession; [illegible] des W-s, rejoiced at being again re-united.

Wie'derhall, (*str.*) *m.* echo, re-echoing; re-percussion or reverberation of sound; resonance. — **Wie'derhallen,** (*w.*) *v. intr. & tr.* to resound, re-echo, reverberate. [[illegible]

Wiederheraus'bekommen, (*str.*) *v. tr.* to

Wiederheraus'gabe, (*w.*) *f.* redelivery, return.

Wiederherstell'bar, *adj.* restorable. — **Wiederherstell'en,** (*w.*) *v. tr.* to restore (one's health, &c.); to re-establish; [illegible] Gesundheit wird bald wieder [illegible], his health will soon come round; die [illegible] — to save the battle; **Wiederherstell'er,** (*str.*) *m.* restorer. — **Wiederherstell'ung,** (*w.*) *f.* restoration, restitution; re-establishment; reproduction; *in comp.* W-skraft, *f.*, W-svermögen, *n.* power of reproduction; W-[illegible], *n.* restorative; W-szeichen, *n.* 1) [illegible] restores an expunged word; 2) *Mus.* [illegible] *see* B(-quadrat). [[illegible]

Wiederherum'bekommen, (*irr.*) *v. tr.* [illegible]

Wie'derholen, (*w.*) *v. tr.* to bring, [illegible] or fetch back.

Wiederho'len, (*w.*) *v.* I. *tr.* to repeat, reiterate; II. *refl.* 1) (*of persons*) a) to [illegible] of repetition; b) to repeat what has [illegible] already; 2) (*of things*) to be repeated [illegible] cur; diese Worte — sich häufig, [illegible] are of continual recurrence. — [illegible] lich, Wiederholt, *adv.* repeatedly [illegible] over again. — **Wiederho'ler,** (*str.*) [illegible] peater.

Wiederhol'ung, (*w.*) *f.* an [illegible]

Wiederho'lung, (*w.*) *f.* [illegible] duplicate; W-szeichen, *n.* mark [illegible] repetition; *Mus.* repeat.

Wiederhol'wort, (*str.*) *n.* [illegible]

Wie'derkäuen, I. (*w.*) *v. tr.* [illegible] ruminate, to chew the cud [illegible] peat over and over, to [illegible] theme; II. *v. n.* (*str.*) *n.* [illegible] Thier, *n.*, **Wie'derkäuer,** (*str.*) [illegible]

* [illegible], (str.) n. Bot. tooth-ache-tree ([illegible]).
* [illegible], m. (Arab.) Xavier (P. N.).
* [illegible], (w.) f. (Span.) Mar. xebeck, chebeck.
* [illegible], (w.) f. (Gr. xénion, gift to a guest or stranger, Gastgabe) mod. Germ. Poet. xenium (epigram in Martial's style), pl. xenia; X-dichter, m. epigrammatist.
* Xenographie', (w.) f. (Gr.) knowledge of foreign alphabets. — Xenomanie', (w.) f. love for what is foreign; xenomania.
* Xe'nophon, m. Xenophon (Greek P. N.).
* Xerasie', (w.) f. (Gr.) Med. xerasia, dryness of hair. [sherry(-wine).
* Xe'res(wein), (str.) m. (Span.) Comm.
* Xerotribie, (w.) f. (Gr.) Med. dry rubbing of a diseased part of the body.
* Xylit', (str.) n. (Gr. xylon, wood) Chem. xylite. — Xylograph', (w.) m. xylographer, wood-cutter. — Xylographie', f. xylography, wood-engraving, art of wood-cutting. — Xylographi'ren, (w.) v. intr. to engrave on wood. — Xylogra'phisch, adj. xylographic. — Xylolatrie', (w.) f. a worshipping of wooden images.

Y.

Y, y, n. Y, y, the twenty-fifth letter (vowel and consonant) of the Alphabet.
Y'A, hee-haw (cry of an ass). — Y'aen, (w.) v. see [illegible]. [yinsmen.
* Yacht [pr. jacht], (w.) f. Mar. yacht,
* [illegible] [pr. [illegible]], (str.) m. see [illegible].
* Yam'wurzel [pr. jam'—], (w.) f. Bot. yam. [(said of asses).
Ya'nen, (w.) v. intr. to bray, to hee-haw
[illegible], m. see [illegible].
* Y'perbaum, (str., pl. Y-bäume) m. Bot. elm-tree, Dutch-elm (Ulme, 1).
Y'pern, n. Geogr. Ypres, Yperen.
* Ypsiloi'de, (w.) f. Anat. ypsiloid suture.
* Y'sop, (str.) m. Bot. hyssop.
Y'ssel, f. Geogr. Yssel
* Yt'tererde, (w.) f. Chem.-s. yttria; die phosphorsaure —, phosphate of yttria. — Yt'terspath, (str.) m. Miner. phosphate of yttria. — Yt'terstein, (str.) m. Miner. ytterbite. — Yt'tertantal, (str.), Yttrotantalit', (str. & w.) m. Miner. yttro-columbite, yttro-tantalite. — Yttrocer(er)it', (str. & w.) m. Miner. yttrocerite.
* Yuc'ca [pr. juk'a], f. Bot. Adam's needle, beargrass, Spanish-bayonet (Yucca gloriosa L.).

Z.

Words not to be found in Z, may be looked for in C.

Z, z, n. Z, z, the twenty-sixth letter and twentieth consonant of the Alphabet.
Z. abbr. Z. for Zoll, Zeile, Zeit, inch, line, time; z. for zu, zum, zur, by, per; z. B. for zum Beispiel, for instance; z. d. St. for zu dieser Stelle or Stunde, instantly, this hour; z. E. for zum Exempel, for (per) example; Z. F. for Zins-Fuß, rate of interest; Ztg. for Zeitung, gazette, newspaper; zw. for zwischen, between.
Zaar, (w.) m., Za'rin, (w.) f. see Czar.
† Za'bel, (str.) n. (Weigand; m. Sanders) (Lat. tabula) chess (-board). [gl.]).
Za'bern, n. Geogr. Saverne (Lat. Taberna

Zach, adj. coll. tough, [illegible]
Zachariä, m. Zacharias [illegible]
f. see [illegible].
Zä'ckchen, (str.) n. [illegible]
Comm. outlet-lace, purl; [illegible]
Zäcke, (w.) f. [illegible]
Za'cke, (w.) f., Za'cken, [illegible]
tel, jag, tooth, tine, prong; [illegible]
pl. tooling; 2) twig; [illegible]
edging of lace, &c. see [illegible]
Metall. plate; [illegible]
die Z-n am Hirschgeweih, Sport. [illegible]
Z-nbogen, m. Archit. [illegible]
Zack'eisen, (str.) n. [illegible]
Zack'el, (str.) n. [illegible]
or Greek sheep; —wolle, see [illegible].
Zack'eln, (w.) v. intr. [illegible]
Zack'en, (w.) v. tr. to jag, to [illegible] cut out in points or teeth, to tooth, [illegible] gezackt, p. a. see Zackig.
Zack'en ..., in comp. —blatt, n. [illegible] leaf; —felsen, m. jagged rock, [illegible] —kamm, m. tooth comb; —[illegible] nuts, oil-seed (the fruit of [illegible]) [illegible] —linie; —[illegible] (✠); —linie, f. notched line; —[illegible] Sculp. notched [illegible]; —rad, n. [illegible] wheel; —schote, f. Bot. [illegible] podded [illegible] (Bunias [illegible]) [illegible] —leiste, f. dented [illegible] —werk, n. 1) [illegible] or notched work; 2) Fort. [illegible] —wolle, f. refuse-wool, [illegible]
Zack'ern, (w.) v. intr. [illegible]
2) see Zackeln.
Zack'ig, adj. jagged, jaggy, [illegible] toothed, indented; Bot. [illegible]
* Zaf'fer, Zaf'flor, m. [illegible], zaffre, zaffre.
Zäg, adj. († &) *, see Zaghaft; [illegible] (decl. like adj.) m. coward.
Za'gel, (str.) m. († &) [illegible] (also Zahl, Zagel; cf. [illegible]) top (of a tree); —[illegible] —weide, (w.) f. [illegible] (Pavia [illegible] L.).
Za'genhaft, (str.) m. [illegible] see [illegible]
Za'gen, (w.) v. intr. to tremble, [illegible] with fear, to be dismayed or afraid, [illegible] diffident, to despair, to quail. —[illegible] m. timid person. — Zagheit', (w.) f. [illegible] or practice of trembling, timidity, [illegible]
Zag'haft, I. adj. faint-hearted [illegible], timorous, timid, fearful, [illegible] bashful, afraid; — machen, to [illegible] II. Z-igkeit, († &) *, Zag'heit, (w.) [illegible] weit, (str.) f. faint-heartedness, [illegible] timidity, fear, fearfulness, [illegible]
Zäh, Zähe, adj. 1) tough, [illegible] gluey, viscous, clammy; [illegible] ropy; 2) fig. a) obstinate, [illegible] born (habits, &c.); b) tough, [illegible] Metall. tenacious, ductile, [illegible] Glockenspeise, the tough, [illegible] ein z-es Leben, tenacity of life; [illegible] haben, to have a tough life [illegible] of life; —[illegible], f. see [illegible]; —[illegible] Strengflüssig; Bot.-s. —[illegible] —[illegible], n. Metall. tough-[illegible] Bot. 1) white willow; 2) [illegible]
Zähe, Zäh'heit, [illegible] toughness; tenacity; 2) [illegible] clamminess, glutinousness, [illegible]
1. Zahl, (w.) f. 1) number, [illegible] numeral; die [illegible] die gerade —, small number [illegible] gebrochene —, a broken or [illegible] benannte or concrete —, [illegible] benannte or abstracte —, [illegible] ungerade —, multiplying [illegible] the golden number, [illegible] eine —, numbering, [illegible] verstehen, to number; [illegible]

Zerpflück'en, *(w.)* v. *tr.* to pick in pieces.

Zerpflü'gen, *(w.)* v. *tr.* to spoil by ploughing. [asunder.

Zerpick'en, *(w.)* v. *tr.* to peck or pick

Zerplacken, *(w.)* v. *tr.* to vex, plague, excruciate, harass extremely.

Zerplatz'en, *(w.)* v. *intr.* (aux. sein) to burst asunder or to pieces, to split.

Zerplätz'en, *(w.)* v. *tr.* to cause to burst.

Zerpoch'en, *(w.)* v. *tr.* to break, bruise.

Zerprass'eln, *(w.)* v. *intr.* (aux. sein) to crumble, split asunder.

Zerpreß'sen, *(w.)* v. *tr.* to crush by pressing; to press too much.

Zerprü'geln, *(w.)* v. *tr.* to beat (one) soundly, to give (one) a sound drubbing.

Zerpül'vern, *(w.)* v. *tr.* to reduce to powder, to pulverise; to bruise (to powder); zerpülverter Zucker, crushed sugar. — **Zerpül'verung**, *(w.)* *f.* pulverisation.

Zerquä'len, *(w.)* v. *tr.* see Zerplagen.

Zerquetsch'en, *(w.)* v. *tr.* to crush (sich *[Dat.]* den Finger, one's finger), to quash, squash, bruise.

Zerquir'len, *(w.)* v. *tr.* to break, stir up, or mix with a twirling-stick.

Zerrä'dern, *(w.)* v. *tr.* to break or crush with a wheel.

Zerrammeln, *(w.)* v. *tr.* 1) to destroy or break by ramming; 2) to tumble, disorder.

Zerrau'fen, *(w.)* v. *tr.* to tear off (sich *[Dat.]* die Haare, one's hair).

Zerr'bild, *(str., pl.* Z-er) *n.* caricature.

Zerr'bildner, *(str.)* *m.* caricaturist.

Zerrei'ben, *(str.)* v. *tr.* to grind, rub, triturate; to chafe (a rope, &c.); zu Pulver —, to grind to powder, pulverise; to levigate. — **Zerreib'lich**, I. *adj.* friable; II. Z-keit, *(w.)* *f.* friability. — **Zerrei'bung**, *(w.)* *f.* the (act of) grinding, &c., trituration.

Zerr'eiche, *(w.)* *f.* see Zirneiche. [der, &c.).

Zerreiß'bar, *adj.* that may be torn (asun-

Zerrei'ßen, *(str.)* v. I. *tr.* 1) to rend (asunder), to tear to pieces, asunder, in shreds, &c., to tear off, to break (a thread, string, &c.), to snap (a rope, &c.); to break up or off; 2) *Surg.* to dilacerate; 3) *lit.* & *fig.* to dismember; 4) to wear out (clothes); 5) *fig.* a) to dissever (the bonds of friendship, &c.), to break (a tie, &c.), to break up (connections, &c.), to break through (promises, treaties, &c.); b) to lacerate, wring (one's heart, &c.); to distract, harass; c) to grate, jar upon (the ear); die zerrissenen Spitzen seiner Handschuhe, the broken tops of his gloves; Deutschland ist nicht mehr in viele größere und kleinere Staaten zerrissen, Germany is not any longer broken up into a multitude of larger or petty states; die Bande der Disciplin sind zerrissen, the bonds of discipline are snapped; meine zerrissene Seele, my distracted soul; II. *intr.* (aux. sein) to break; to rend; to burst asunder, to rupture, snap; to wear out.

Zerrei'ßung, *(w.)* *f.* 1) the (act of) rending, tearing, &c.; dismemberment; 2) disseverance, disruption; 3) laceration.

Zer'ren, *(w.)* v. I. *tr.* & *intr.* (with an *[& Dat.]*, &c.) to pull (at), tug, towze, lug, drag, haul, tear; *coll.* to worry, tease, vex; das Maul —, to make wry faces; II. *tr. Iron-w.* to melt a second time, to remelt (fagoted iron), to refine.

Zerr'..., *in comp.* —feuer, *n.*, —hammer, —herd, *m.* see Frischfeuer &c.; —geburt, *f.* monster; —gemälde, *n.* caricature; —gesicht, *n.* wry face.

Zerrenk'en, *(w.)* v. *tr.* to wrest asunder.

Zerrön'nen, *(str.)* v. *tr.* see Zerren, II.

Zerrerei', *(w.)* *f.* the act of (repeated, &c.) pulling, *cf.* Gezerr.

Zerrin'gen, *(str.)* v. *tr.* to wring to pieces, to spoil or hurt by wringing.

Zerrin'nen, *(str.)* v. *intr.* (aux. [illegible]) melt, dissolve, liquefy; *fig.* to [illegible] in nichts —, to vanish into thin air [illegible] rinnt unter den Händen, [illegible] fingers, it perishes in the using [illegible] nen, to persevere, proceed, [illegible] lightly go.

Zerris'sen, I. *p. a.* rent, torn, &c. [illegible] reißen; dismembered; *Bot.* [illegible] Z-heit, *(w.)* *f.* torn or dismembered [illegible] distraction. [illegible]

Zerrit'zen, *(w.)* v. *tr.* to [illegible]

Zerrüh'ren, *(w.)* v. *tr.* to mix by [illegible] or stirring up; Eier —, to whip eggs.

Zerrupf'en, *(w.)* v. *tr.* to tear or pull [illegible] little pieces, to pluck in pieces. [illegible]

Zerrüt'teln, *(w.)* v. *tr.* to [illegible]

Zerrüt'ten, *(w.)* v. *tr.* to unsettle, dis[illegible] order, break up, damage, disarrange, dis[illegible] tract, distemper, disturb; to destroy, [illegible] in zerrütteten Umständen, in decayed or de[illegible] ranged circumstances; (geistig) zerrüttet [illegible] deranged; zerrüttete Gesundheit, [illegible] broken, or shattered health, a shattered [illegible] worn-out constitution. — **Zerrüt'tung**, *(w.)* *f.* derangement, disorder, disarrangement, dis[illegible] traction, confusion, trouble; distress [illegible] struction, ruin. [illegible]

Zersä'gen, *(w.)* v. *tr.* to saw to pieces, [illegible]

Zerschab'en, *(w.)* v. *tr.* to fret, to [illegible] or injure by rubbing or fretting. — [illegible] schabt, *p. a.* fretted, &c. *cf.* [illegible] threadbare (said of clothes).

Zerschar'ren, *(w.)* v. *tr.* to destroy or spoil by scraping.

Zerschel'lern, *(w.)* v. *intr.* (aux. sein) [illegible] *tr.* to split, cleave, break; to crack.

Zerschel'len, *(w.)* v. I. *tr.* to dash to pieces, to shatter, shiver (in fragments), to crash; II. *intr.* (aux. sein) to be dashed in pieces; to split (on a rock, &c.).

Zerscher'beln, *(w.)* v. *tr.* to smash [illegible] shards. [illegible]

Zerscheu'ern, *(w.)* v. *tr.* to rub or [illegible]

Zerschie'ßen, *(str.)* v. *tr.* & *intr.* (aux. sein) to shoot to pieces. [illegible]

Zerschin'den, *(str.)* v. *tr.* to rub [illegible]

Zerschla'gen, *(str.)* v. I. *tr.* 1) to [illegible] pieces, to break, to dash (in pieces) [illegible] to bruise; 2) to wear out with beating [illegible] Korn —, to lodge the corn (said of hail, [illegible] das Land —, to batter the [illegible] II. [illegible] 1) *Min.* to divide into smaller [illegible] be broken off, to fall to the ground, [illegible] to nothing; zerschlagen, *p. a.* 1) [illegible] worn out, bruised; 2) *fig.* [illegible] sein, to be bruised all over, to be [illegible] knocked up.

Zerschlei'fen, v. *tr.* 1) *(str.)* [illegible] whetting; 2) *(w.)* to wear out [illegible] by sliding. [illegible] off, to [illegible]

Zerschlei'ßen, *(str.)* v. *intr.* (aux. [illegible])

Zerschlitz'en, *(w.)* v. *tr.* to slit [illegible]

Zerschmei'ßen, *(str.)* v. *tr.* [illegible] schlagen, I. 1, *cf.* [illegible]

Zerschmel'zen, *(str.* & *w.)* v. [illegible] sein) & *tr.* to melt (away), [illegible] — **Zerschmel'zung**, *(w.)* *f.* the [illegible] of) melting, dissolving, &c., [illegible] solution, reduction.

Zerschmet'tern, *(w.)* v. *tr.* [illegible] ter, dash to pieces or into [illegible] schmet'terung, *(w.)* *f.* the [illegible] &c.

Zerschnei'den, *(str.)* v. *tr.* [illegible] ces, to cut up, to carve; [illegible] &c. see Zersägen.

Zerschnip'peln, [illegible] to cut into little pieces, [illegible]

Zerschrei'en, *(str.)* v. [illegible] crying.

Zerschro'ten, *(w.)* v. *tr.* 1) [illegible]

[illegible] and machines; —[illegible], m. see —[illegible]; —[illegible], f. Brew. mash-tub; —leder, m. [illegible]-leather; —macher, m. stuff-weaver; —mantel, m. cloak of stuff; —manufactur, f. stuff-manufactory; —meister, m. keeper of the arsenal; master of the ordnance; —mod-ler, m. [illegible]; —müller, m. millwright.

Zeug'niß, (str.) n. 1) witness, testimony, evidence; deposition (of a witness); zum — dessen, Law, in witness or testimony whereof; 2) testimonial; ein — geben, ablegen, abstatten, to give or bear testimony or evidence, to bear witness, to depose witness; to testify (für, to); to speak (über (with Acc.), to); ein schriftliches —, certificate, voucher, attestation, testimonial; character; haben Sie (Führungs-)Zeugnisse? have you any character? nur solche mögen sich melden, die wenigstens sechs gute Zeugnisse beibringen können; buchhändlerische Zeugnisse sind nicht zulässig, no one need apply unless he can have at least six respectable characters; booksellers' certificates not admissible; er gab ihm das — eines musterhaften jungen Mannes, he gave him the testimony of an exemplary young man.

Zeug'..., in comp. —presse, f. clothes-press, calender; —pritsche, f. Paper-m. beater; —rad, n. see Kunstrad; —rasch, m. a kind of light serge, rash; —regulator, m. Paper-m. pulp-meter; —rock, m. stuff-dress or petticoat; —rolle, f. Manuf. calender for stuffs; —schacht, m. Min. engine-shaft; —schmidt, m. tool-smith; artillery-smith; —schmiede, f. tool-smith's forge; —schneider, m. tailor that makes hunting-toils; —schnur, f. Hall. bow string; —schreiber, m. clerk at an arsenal, clerk of the ordnance; —sichter, m. Paper-m. pulp-strainer; —spanner, m. Weav. self-acting temple; —stadel, m. 1) † see —haus; 2) Hunt. store-house for hunting-toils; — steuer, f. Min. money for drawing off the water of a mine; —stopfer, m. fuse-drawer.

Zeu'gung, (w.) f. 1) the (act of) engendering, breeding, &c. cf. Zeugen, I.; procreation, generation; 2) production (Erzeugung).

Zeu'gungs..., in comp. —artig, adj. analogous or similar to propagation; —fähig, adj. able to beget, procreative, generative, virile, prolific; —fähigkeit, f. procreativeness, virility; —fall, see Zeugefall; —geschäft, n. coition; —glied, n. genital member, pl. genitals; —kraft, f. generative or procreative power or faculty; —organe, n. pl. generative organs; —ort, m. place of birth; —theile, n. pl. genitals; —trieb, m. procreative impulse; —unfähig, adj. impotent, effete; —unfähigkeit, f. impotence; —vermögen, n. see —kraft.

Zeug'..., in comp. —waaren, f. pl. tissues; —wagen, m. cart for transporting implements; —wart, —wärter, m. inspector of arms or an arsenal, see —meister; —warte, f. Sport. see —haus, 1; —weber, —wirker, m. stuff-weaver; —winde, f. crane for mounting the guns on the frames.

Zeus, m. Gr. Myth. Zeus (supreme monarch of gods and men, Lat. name: Jupiter).

Zeven'brief, (str.) m. see Gehnbrief.

Zib'be, (w.) f. province. ewe.

* **Zibe'be,** (w.) f. 1) province. (for Rosine) raisin, grape; 2) see Cubebe.

Zi'bel, see Zwiebel.

* **Zibeth',** (str.) m. Pharm. civet; in comp. —baum, m. Bot. civet-durio (Durio zibethinus L.); —katze, f., —thier, n. Zool. (asiatische) Zibet (Viverra zibetha L.); (afrikanische) civet-cat, civet (Viverra civetta Ruff.); —maus, —ratte, f. musk-rat (Fiber zibethicus L.).

Zibol'le, (w.) f. see Zwiebel.

* **Zibo'rie,** (w.) f. see Cibo(r)erie.

† **Zicht,** (w.) f. Law, accusation, impeachment.

Zick, province. I. adj. (of beer, wine, &c.) turned (sour); II. n. (str.) zig-zag [illegible] [illegible].

Zick'e, (w.) f. province. [illegible], goat.

Zick'chen, Zick'lein, [illegible] (str.) n. (dimin. of Zicke) kid.

Zick'eln, (w.) v. intr. province. to kid.

Zick'en, (w.) v. intr. province. to [illegible] bei dem zickt's, coll. he is slightly [illegible] (somewhat crazy, in love, &c.).

Zick'zack, adv. & (str.) m. zig-zag [illegible] fegeln, to tack; to [illegible] [illegible] in comp. —reiher, m. Zool. [illegible] bittern (Ardea [illegible] [illegible]).

Zick'zackig, adj. zig-zag.

Zi'der, see Cider.

Zie'che, (w.) f. province. tick, cover of a pillow or feather-bed, cf. Überzug, [illegible] nuts), pocket (for boys).

Ziech'ner, (str.) m. province. [illegible]

Zie'fer, (str.) n. 1) insect; 2) [illegible] poultry; —artig, adj. insect-like, [illegible] —kenner, —kundige, m. entomologist; —[illegible] —lehre, f. entomology, insectology.

Zie'ge, I. (w.) f. 1) Zool. goat, she-goat (Capra L.); 2) Ichth. see Ziege; II. [illegible] plus.

Zie'gel, I. (str.) m. brick; tile; [illegible] [illegible] —, stock-bricks; mit Z-n decken, to [illegible] mit Z-n belegen, to lay with bricks, to [illegible] — streichen, to form or mould tiles or bricks [illegible]

Zie'gel..., in comp. —arbeit, f. tile-[illegible] brick-making; —artig, adj. brick-like, [illegible] —brennen, n. burning of tiles or bricks; [illegible] brenner, m. tile-maker, brick-burner; —[illegible] nerei, f. 1) see —brennen; 2) (or —[illegible] ofen, m.) brick-kiln, tile-kiln; —[illegible] broken bricks, brickbats; —dach, n. a [illegible] covered with tiles; —dachförmig, adj. [illegible] imbricated, tiled; —decker, m. [illegible] tiler; —drescher, m. see —schläger.

Ziegelei', (w.) f. brick-kiln; tile-kiln.

Zie'gel..., in comp. —erde, f. brick-[illegible] tile-clay, brick-earth; —erz, n. Min. tile-[illegible] ferruginous red oxide of copper; —[illegible] tile-colour; —farben, —farbig, adj. [illegible] coloured; tile-coloured; —fels, m. [illegible] —flachstein, f. brick-flat; —form, f. [illegible] mould, brick-mould; —gut, n. clay [illegible] with other materials for making bricks [illegible] tiles; —häufung, m. see [illegible] —[illegible] haus, f. brickmaker's [illegible]; —haus, n. [illegible] tile house; —herz, n. Conch. [illegible] (in [illegible] [illegible]); —hütte, f. brick-kiln, tile-[illegible]

Zie'gelig, adj. bricky, formed of bricks [illegible]

Zie'gel..., in comp. —kalk, f. tile-[illegible] —lehm, m. see —erde; —macher, m. [illegible] brickmaker; —maschine, f. see —[illegible] maschine; —mauer, f. brick-wall; —[illegible] rung, f., —mauerwerk, n. brick-work, [illegible] masonry; —mehl, n. brick-dust, tile-[illegible] —meister, m. master-tiler.

Zie'geln, adj. to tiley (Ziegelig).

Zie'geln, (w.) v. intr. (h. u.) to [illegible] bricks or tiles.

Zie'gel..., in comp. —ofen, m. brick-[illegible] tile-kiln; —öl, n. Pharm. brick-oil; —[illegible] f. square brick; —roth, I. adj. brick-red [illegible] brick-coloured; II. n. see —farbe; —[illegible] f. see —hütte & —scheuern; —[illegible] course; —schläger, m. hewer of [illegible] brickmaking; —scheuer, —schuppen, [illegible] for tiles or bricks; —schutt, m. see —[illegible] —sparren, m. tile-rafter; —stein, m. [illegible] brickbat; [illegible] —stein, [illegible] —streichen, n. the moulding of bricks [illegible] making; —streicher, m. brickmaker [illegible] maschine, f. brickmaking machine [illegible] m. brickbat, tile-shard; —[illegible] —torf, m. yellow peat; —[illegible] —werk, n. brick-work.

Zie'gen..., in comp. —[illegible] buck-antelope (Antilope [illegible]

which do not express action, but being *or* a state of being, so called from their not requiring the addition of an *object* (Zielwort) to complete the sense; otherwise called neutral, intransitiv, *or* subjectiv *(opp.* Zielend, 2, *b);* II. Z-**losigkeit,** *(w.) f.* aimlessness, &c.

Ziel'..., *in comp.* —**punct,** *m.* aim; prick, mark; —**scheibe,** *f.* mark, target; —**scheibe des Witzes, Spottes,** butt, laughing-stock; —**stange,** *f.* pole on which the mark or target is fastened; —**station,** *f.* terminal station; —**statt,** *f.* †. shooting-house; —**tag,** *m.* term-day, quarter-day; —**wort,** *n.* any word influenced by another (as a noun governed by a verb), object, accusative.

Zie'men, *(w.) v. intr. impers. (with Dat.)* to become, to be suitable (to), to be fit (for), to befit, to suit (one). [*see* Geziemend.

Zie'mentlich, *adj. (L. u.)* befitting, fit, &c.

Zie'mer, *(str.) m.* 1) *a) Butch.* buttock-piece; *b) Sport.* back-piece (of a hart, &c.); back; 2) yard (of a stag, &c.), pizzle; 3) *a) see* Krammetsvogel; *b) see* Misteldrossel.

Zie'mern, *(w.) v. tr.* to flog with a pizzle.

Ziem'lich, I. *adj.* 1) befitting, seemly, &c. *see* Geziemend; 2) pretty, tolerable, passable, middling; II. *adv.* pretty, tolerably, rather; near: eine z-e Menge, a pretty considerable quantity; eine z-e Strecke davon, a pretty way off; — bei Jahren, well in years, well stepped *or* stricken in years; — gesucht, in tolerable demand; ich bin über die Thatsache — gewiß, I am pretty sure of the fact; es ist schon — lange her, it is a pretty while ago; es ist so — fertig, it is pretty nearly *or* almost ready; er fühlt sich — getäuscht, he feels rather disappointed; der Wind ist — günstig, the wind is pretty fair; in den nächsten zwei Tagen war es — dasselbe, it was pretty much the same for the next two days; die Erziehung ist bei ihnen — so wie bei uns, their education is much as with us.

Ziep'..., *in comp.* —**ammer,** *f. Ornith.* foolish bunting (Zippammer); —**drossel, Zie'pe,** *(w.) f. see* Zippe; —**lerche,** *f. see* Zipplerche.

Zie'pen, *(w.) v.* I. *intr.* to chirp; II. *tr.* to pull (softly) by the hair, &c.

Zier, *(w.) f.* ornament; grace; honour.

Zier'..., *in comp.* —**affe,** *m. cont.* affected man *or* woman, fop, coxcomb; —**äffchen,** *n. cont.* little affected creature.

Zie'rat(h), *(irr., sing. str., pl. w.) m.* ornament, set-off, finery, embellishment, decoration, adornment; flourish; *Bookb.* fillet; Steinzieraten, ornamental stonework, tracery (-work). — Z-**endrechbank,** *f.* lathe for carving.

Zie'rig, *adj. see* Zierrei...
Zie'rling, *(str.) m. see* ...
Zier'..., *in comp. Bo...*
hydrangea; —**kunst,** *f.* ca...
art of adorning *or* orname...
Found. moulding-clay, luti...
n. ornamental trappings ...
carriage-horses.

Zier'lich, I. *adj.* elegant...
smart; II. Z-**keit,** *(w.) f.*
neatness. — **Zier'ling,** *(str...*
spark, coxcomb. — **Zier'lo...**
without ornament, simple.

Zier'..., *in comp.* —...
chisel; —**nase,** *f. Zool.* a sp...
nose *(Megaderma lyra* ...
(fruit of the) Siberian st...
pflanzen, *f. pl.* decorative ...
1) doll; 2) *see* —äffchen; ...
m. ornamental edge; —**rip...**
—**schriften,** *pl. Typ.* ornam...
n. Archit. front-gate, porta...
Ornith. honey-sucker (Klei...

Zie'se, *(w.) f. provinc.* ...
Zie'sel, *(str.) m.* (—maus...
s(o)uslik, zisel, earless mar...
citillus L.).
Zie'ser, *(w.) f. see* Kich...
Ziest, *(str.) m. Bot.* hed...
Zif'fer, I. *(w.) f.* cipher...
mit *or* in Z-n schreiben, to ...
II. *in comp.* —**baß,** *m.* ...
thorough-bass; —**blatt,** *n* ...
—**blattriß,** *m.* a sort of ...
—**brief,** *m.* letter written i...
m. fraction, broken numb...
of writing in ciphers, steg...
Zif'fern, *(w.) v. intr.* t...
Zif'fer..., *in comp.* ...
meral arithmetic; —**schrift,** ...
Zigar're, *f. see* Cigarre.
Zigeu'ner, *(str.) m.* (Z-...
gipsy, gypsy (a wanderi...
found in many countries ...
grant; a fortune-teller. — ...
f. gipsyism; gipsy-trick, ...
Zigeu'ner..., *in comp...*
f. gang of gipsies; —**fran...**
Zigeu'nerhaft, Zigeu'n...
ing to *or* resembling gipsies...
Zigeu'ner..., *in comp.*
Bot. 1) water-horehound ...
Bilsenkraut; —**kunst,** *f.* a...
tunes; —**lauch,** *n. Bot.* bear...
(Allium ursinum L.); —**le...**
gipsyism; —**mädchen,** *n.* g...

-erbse; —schrapsel, n. sugar-scrapings; —schwefelsäure, f. Chem. 1) sulpho-oxalic acid; 2) saccharo-sulphuric acid; —sieden, n. boiling or refining of sugar; —sieder, m. 1) boiler or refiner of sugar; 2) sugar-baker; —siederei, f. sugar-work, sugar-house, boiling-house; —stängel, m. Conf. sugar-stick; —stein, m. Miner. fine-grained albite; —stoff, m. Chem. saccharine matter; sugar; —streuer, m. sugar-sifter; —süß, adj. sweet as sugar, sugary; —süße Reden, sugared speeches; —syrup, m. molasses, treacle; —täfelchen, n. lozenge, bonbon; —tang, m. Bot. sweet fucus (—riementang); —teig, m. comfit-paste; —thierchen, n. see —gast; —tinctur, f. saccharine tincture; —tonne, f. see —faß; —topf, m. see —form; —trommel, f. tin canister for sugar; —vogel, m. 1) see Canarienvogel; 2) the sun-bird (Cinnyris Cuv.); —waare, f. see —werk; —wasser, n. water mixed with sugar, sugar-water; —wein, m. sweet wine, see Sect; —werk, n. sweetmeats, comfit, comfiture, confectionery, fam. goodies, lollipops, sweeties; —worte, n. pl. fig. sweet-words, flatteries; —wurzel, f. Bot. wild parsnep, skirret (Sium sisarum L.); —zahn, m. fam. sweet-tooth; —zange, f. sugar-tongs; —zwieback, m. sweet biscuit.

Zuck'isch, adj. (l. u.) spasmodic, convulsive.

Zuck'ler, (str.) m. provinc. 1) slow walker; 2) irresolute person.

Zuck'ung, (w.) f. Med. convulsion, convulsive fit; Z-en haben, to be seized with convulsions, to have fits; Z-en verursachen (with Dat.), to convulse; Z-en verursachend, convulsive.

Zu'dämmen, (w.) v. tr. to dam up.

Zu'decke, (w.) f. provinc. for Deckbett.

Zu'decken, (w.) v. tr. 1) to cover; 2) coll. a) to bang, belabour (one), to load (one) with blows; b) to drink under the table.

Zu'deichen, (w.) v. tr. to enclose with a dike.

Zudem', adv. besides, moreover, in addition.

Zu'denken, (irr.) v. tr. to destine, intend for.

Zu'donnern, (w.) v. I. tr. 1) to send (greetings, &c.), to salute with the roar of cannon; 2) to cry to one with a thundering voice; II. intr. (preceded by immer) 1) fig. to continue cursing; 2) impers. coll. to thunder on.

Zu'drang, (str.) m. the (act of) crowding or thronging to a place, rush; throng, crowd.

Zu'drängen, (w.) v. I. intr. to push on,

rogate. — **Zu'eigner**, (str.) m. appropriator, &c.; 2) dedicator.—Z (w.) f. 1) appropriation; 2) 3) attribution, (in an ill sense) 4) dedication; Z-Schrift, f. dedi (epistle). [t

Zu'eilen, (w.) v. intr. (aux. sein)

Zu'eisen, (w.) v. intr. (aux. sei up.

Zu'erben, (w.) v. tr. to obtain

Zu'erkennen, (irr.) v. tr. (Ei 1) to adjudge, adjudicate, to award to award a punishment (to ...), t to a punishment; 2) fig. to acknowl right to do a thing, &c.); to allow Vorzug —, to give the preference erkenntniß, (str.) n., **Zu'erkenn** adjudication, award.

Zuerst' [sometimes zu'erst], adv. place, first, firstly, at first, for the most; er sprach —, he was first to die Aufmerksamkeit sich — darauf l attention began to be attracte it; sprechen was Einem — in den S to speak what comes uppermo mind; wer — kommt, mahlt —, f come, first served or first in.

Zu'ertheilen, (w.) v. tr. (Einem allot, assign, apportion, award (to), to bestow, confer (somethin **Zu'ertheilung**, (w.) f. allotment, a &c., award, bestowal.

Zu'essen, (irr.) v. intr. coll. to ing, anal. to peg away; das —, (a Zukost.

Zu'fächeln, (w.) v. tr. to fan to

Zu'fahren, (str.) v. I. intr. (1) a) to go on with a carriage, t b) to drive faster; to drive at a 2) to approach, advance; 3) (auf (w a) to ride or drive (up) to or tow rush upon, to make a dash at; gleich to run upon rashly or blindly; 4) shut of itself rapidly (said of d fahre zu, Kutscher! drive on, coach to convey or carry to.

Zu'fall, (str., pl. Zu'fälle) m. accident, hap; incident, casualty, venture; occurrence; hap-hazard 2) Med. fit (of sudden illness); See, accidents, casualties on the (einen) —, by chance or accident licher —, a lucky hit, a piece of g

[illegible]
drag-net; —geschirr, n. draw-gear; —graben, m. draining ditch; —haken, m. 1) Wagg. &c. trace-hook; pole-hook; draw-hook; 2) Carp. [illegible] —haspel, f. windlass, pulley; [illegible] draw-beam. —heuschrecke, f. Entom. passage-locust, migratory locust (Acridium migratorium L.).

Zu'gießen, (str.) v. I. tr. to pour to; to add or fill up by pouring in; II. intr. (gener. preceded by immer) to go on pouring, to pour [on.

† Zu'gift, (w.) f. see Zugabe.

Zü'gig, adj. exposed to a draught or current of air, draughty.

Zu'gittern, (w.) v. tr. see Zugattern.

Zug'..., in comp. (cf. Zieh...) —kanal, see —canal; —kette, f. chain-trace; Railw. draw-chain, coupling-chain; —klinge, f. see Ziehklinge; —kopf, m. Mus. Instr. slide-head (of flutes); —kraft, f. Mech. tractive force or power, haulage; —leder, n. elastic leather.

Zugleich', adv. 1) at the same time; at once; 2) jointly, together, withal, along with ...; sie standen Alle — auf, they all rose in a body; es dient als Thüre und als Fenster —, it serves both as door and as window.

Zu'gleichen, (w., sometimes str.) v. tr. to make even or smooth; to assimilate, adjust.

Zugleich'sein, (str.) n. co-existence.

Zug'..., in comp. (cf. Zieh...) —leine, f. towing rope; small rope (of a ram); —linie, f. 1) line for dragging or drawing, towing-line; 2) Geom. tractory, tractrix; 3) Mil. line of march, column; —loch, n. vent-hole, air-hole, draught-hole; —luft, f. draught of air; —maus, f. Zool. migratory mouse (Hypudaeus migratorius L.); —meister, m. see —führer, 3; —messer, n. drawing-knife, drawing-shave; —mittel, n. remedy for drawing or blistering, application that raises blisters; —nagel, m. tug-pin; —netz, n. see —garn; —ochs, m. draught-ox; —oper, f. fig. favourite opera, cf. —stück; —ordnung, f. order of a procession or march; —panster, m. see Ziehpanster; —papier, n. blotting paper; —pferd, n. draught-horse; —pflaster, n. Med. vesicatory, blister, cerate.

Zu'graben, (str.) v. I. tr. to cover with earth, to inter, to bury, hide in the ground; II. intr. to continue digging, to dig on.

[illegible]

[illegible]
boots; —stränge, m. pl. harness-ropes, traces; —stück, n. Theat. favourite piece (filling the house), piece or play that has the run, that is in vogue or fashion; —stuhl, m. see Zeugschmied; —tau, n. towing cable; Railw. tail-rope; —taube, f. Ornith. migratory or passenger pigeon, pigeon of passage (Columba migratoria L.); —thier, n. beast of draught, draught cattle; —thor, n. draw-gate; —thür, f. door to produce draught; —trompete, f. slide-trumpet.

Zu'gucken, (w.) v. intr. fam. see Zusehen, 2.

Zu'gürten, (w.) v. tr. to gird, buckle.

Zu'guß, (str., pl. Zu'güsse) m. infusion, [addition.

Zugu'tekommen, see Gut

Zug'..., in comp. (cf. Zieh...) —vieh, n. cattle for draught, draught-cattle; —vogel, m. bird of passage, migratory bird; —volk, n. wandering tribe; —(s)wagen, m. pl. Railw. train-carriages, carriages attached to a locomotive engine; —walze, f. drawing (off) roller; —weise, adv. & adj. by troops; —werk, n. see Ziehwerk; —wind, m. draught of air, periodical wind; —winde, f. pulley, draw-beam; —zeit, f. time of flight of birds of passage.

Zu'haben, (irr.) v. tr. 1) to receive into the bargain; 2) to have or keep shut or locked up; den Rock —, to have one's coat buttoned up.

Zu'hacken, (w.) v. tr. to prepare by hacking.

Zu'haken, Zu'häkeln, (w.) v. tr. to fasten with hooks or little hooks, to clasp.

Zu'halten, (str.) v. I. tr. to keep closed, shut, or locked up; to close, stop, shut; die Hand —, to clinch the fist; sich (Dat.) die Ohren —, to stop one's ears; sie hielt sich die Augen zu, she clapped her hands before her eyes; II. intr. 1) a) to have an understanding, to side (mit, with); b) vulg. to have illicit intercourse (mit, with); 2) provinc. to keep one's word or engagement. — Zu'hälter, (str.) m. fancy-man, pouncey (of a prostitute). — Zu'hälterin, (w.) f. concubine. — Zu'haltung, (w.) f. 1) the (act of) keeping closed, &c. cf. Zuhalten; 2) Lock-sm. tumbler; Z—s-schloß, n. French lock.

Zu'hämmern, (w.) v. tr. to close by hammering.

Zu'hängen, (w., sometimes str.) v. tr. to hang up, to hang with curtains, to cover or close by hanging something over.

[illegible]

CPSIA information can be obtained
at www.ICGtesting.com
Printed in the USA
BVOW06*0926020118
504192BV00008B/94/P

9 780331 943368